Street by Street

GREATER LONDON

4th edition May 2007
© Automobile Association Developments Limited 2007

Original edition printed May 2001

Enabled by [Ordnance Survey] This product includes map data licensed from Ordnance Survey® with the permission of the Controller of Her Majesty's Stationery Office. © Crown copyright 2007. All rights reserved. Licence number: 100021153.

The copyright in all PAF is owned by Royal Mail Group plc.

Published by AA Publishing (a trading name of Automobile Association Developments Limited, whose registered office is Fanum House, Basing View, Basingstoke, Hampshire RG21 4EA. Registered number 1878835).

Produced by the Mapping Services Department of The Automobile Association. (A03278)

A CIP Catalogue record for this book is available from the British Library.

Printed by Oriental Press in Dubai

Key to map pages	ii–iii
Key to map symbols	iv–1
Enlarged map pages	2-19
Main map pages	20-285
Index – towns & villages	286-288
Index – streets	288-375
Index – featured places	375-394
Acknowledgements	394

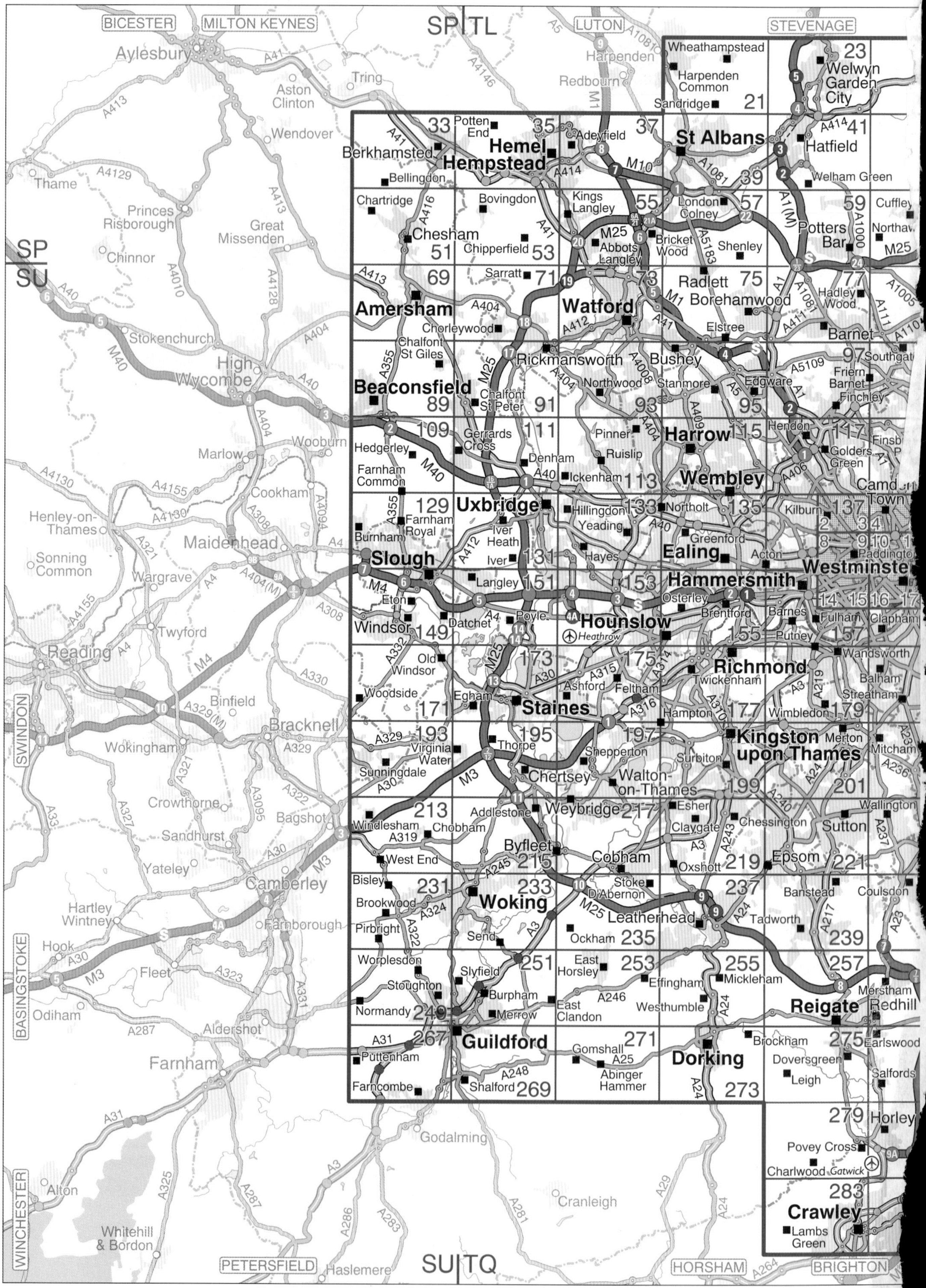

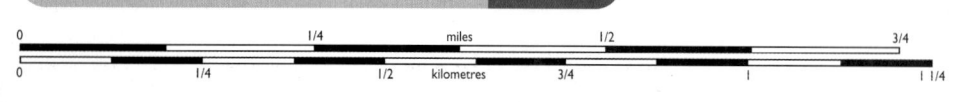

Scale of enlarged map pages 1:10,000 6.3 inches to 1 mile

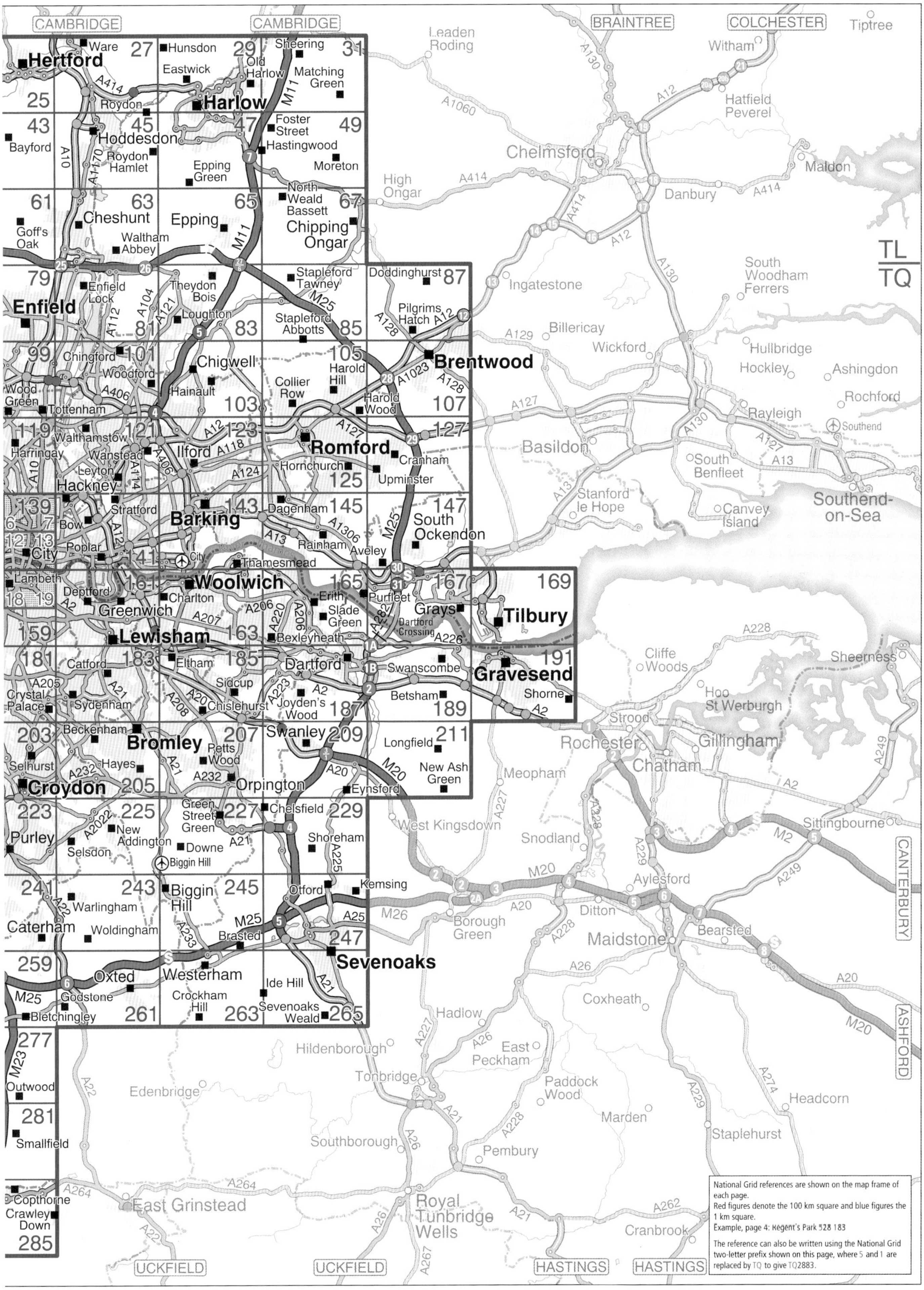

CAMBRIDGE CAMBRIDGE BRAINTREE COLCHESTER Tiptree

Ware 27 Hunsdon 29 Sheering 31 Leaden Roding Witham Hatfield Peverel

Hertford Eastwick Old Harlow Matching Green A130 A12

25 Roydon **Harlow** 47 Foster Street 49 A1060 Chelmsford Maldon

43 Hoddesdon Hastingwood Moreton A414 Danbury A414

Bayford Roydon Hamlet Epping Green North Weald Bassett 67 High Ongar A12

61 Cheshunt 63 Epping 65 Chipping Ongar A414 South Woodham Ferrers

Goff's Oak Waltham Abbey Stapleford Tawney Doddinghurst 87 Ingatestone TL / TQ

79 Enfield Lock Theydon Bois Stapleford Abbotts 85 Pilgrims Hatch A129 Billericay Hullbridge Ashingdon

Enfield 81 Loughton 83 A128 **Brentwood** Wickford Hockley Rochford

99 Chingford 101 Chigwell Harold Hill 105 A1023 A128 Rayleigh Southend

Wood Green Woodford Hainault Collier Row Harold Wood 107 A127 South Benfleet A127 A13

119 121 Ilford 123 A127 **Romford** 127 Basildon Stanford le Hope Canvey Island Southend-on-Sea

Harringay Wanstead A118 Hornchurch Cranham A13 A13

Leyton A124 125 Upminster 147

Hackney **Barking** 143 Dagenham 145 South Ockendon A13

139 Stratford A1306 Rainham Aveley Cliffe Woods Sheerness

Bow Poplar A13 Thamesmead **Tilbury** A228 Hoo St Werburgh

City 141 City 165 Erith 167 169 Strood

Lambeth **Woolwich** Charlton Slade Green Grays Rochester Gillingham

18 19 Deptford Greenwich A206 Bexleyheath Dartford Crossing A226 **Gravesend** 191 Chatham A249

159 **Lewisham** 163 Dartford Swanscombe Shorne A2

181 Catford 183 Eltham 185 A2 Betsham 189 A2 Strood

Crystal Palace Sidcup Chislehurst Joyden's Wood 187 Longfield 211 Meopham Snodland Sittingbourne

203 Beckenham 207 Swanley 209 New Ash Green West Kingsdown A227 A229 A2

Selhurst **Bromley** Petts Wood Longfield Aylesford A249

Croydon 205 Orpington A20 M20 Snodland Ditton

223 225 227 Chelsfield 229 Shoreham Borough Green M20 Maidstone Bearsted

Purley New Addington A21 Eynsford A20 Aylesford A20

241 243 Biggin Hill 245 Otford Kemsing A20 Ditton A20

Warlingham Woldingham M25 A25 A26 M26 Coxheath M20

Caterham Brasted 247 **Sevenoaks** Borough Green A26 ASHFORD

259 Oxted Westerham Ide Hill A21 Hadlow Hildenborough

M25 Godstone Crockham Hill 263 Sevenoaks Weald 265 East Peckham A229

277 Bletchingley 261 Hildenborough Tonbridge Paddock Wood Staplehurst

Outwood Edenbridge Southborough Marden

281 Smallfield A22 A26 Pembury A229

Copthorne Crawley Down A264 **East Grinstead** Royal Tunbridge Wells A262 Cranbrook

285 UCKFIELD UCKFIELD HASTINGS HASTINGS

National Grid references are shown on the map frame of each page.
Red figures denote the 100 km square and blue figures the 1 km square.
Example, page 4: Regent's Park 528 183

The reference can also be written using the National Grid two-letter prefix shown on this page, where 5 and 1 are replaced by TQ to give TQ2883.

3.2 inches to 1 mile **Scale of main map pages 1:20,000**

0 1/2 miles 1

0 1/2 1 kilometres 1 1/2 2

Junction 9	Motorway & junction	*LC*	Level crossing
Services	Motorway service area	•—•—•—•—•	Tramway
J58	Primary road single/dual carriageway & junction		Ferry route
Services	Primary road service area		Airport runway
	A road single/dual carriageway		County, administrative boundary
	B road single/dual carriageway		Congestion Charging Zone *
	Other road single/dual carriageway		Charge-free route through the Charging Zone
	Minor/private road, access may be restricted	**151**	Page continuation 1:20,000
← ←	One-way street	**17**	Page continuation to enlarged scale 1:10,000
	Pedestrian area		River/canal, lake, pier
===========	Track or footpath		Aqueduct, lock, weir
▯▯▯▯▯▯▯▯	Road under construction		Beach
[- - - - -]	Road tunnel		Woodland
P	Parking		Park
P+🚌	Park & Ride		Cemetery
🚌	Bus/coach station		Built-up area
▮ ⇄	Railway & main railway station	🏭	Industrial / business building
▬ ■ ⇄	Railway & minor railway station	🏭	Leisure building
⊖	Underground station	🏭	Retail building
⊖	Docklands Light Railway (DLR) station	🏭	Other building
—⊖—	Light railway & station	**IKEA**	IKEA store

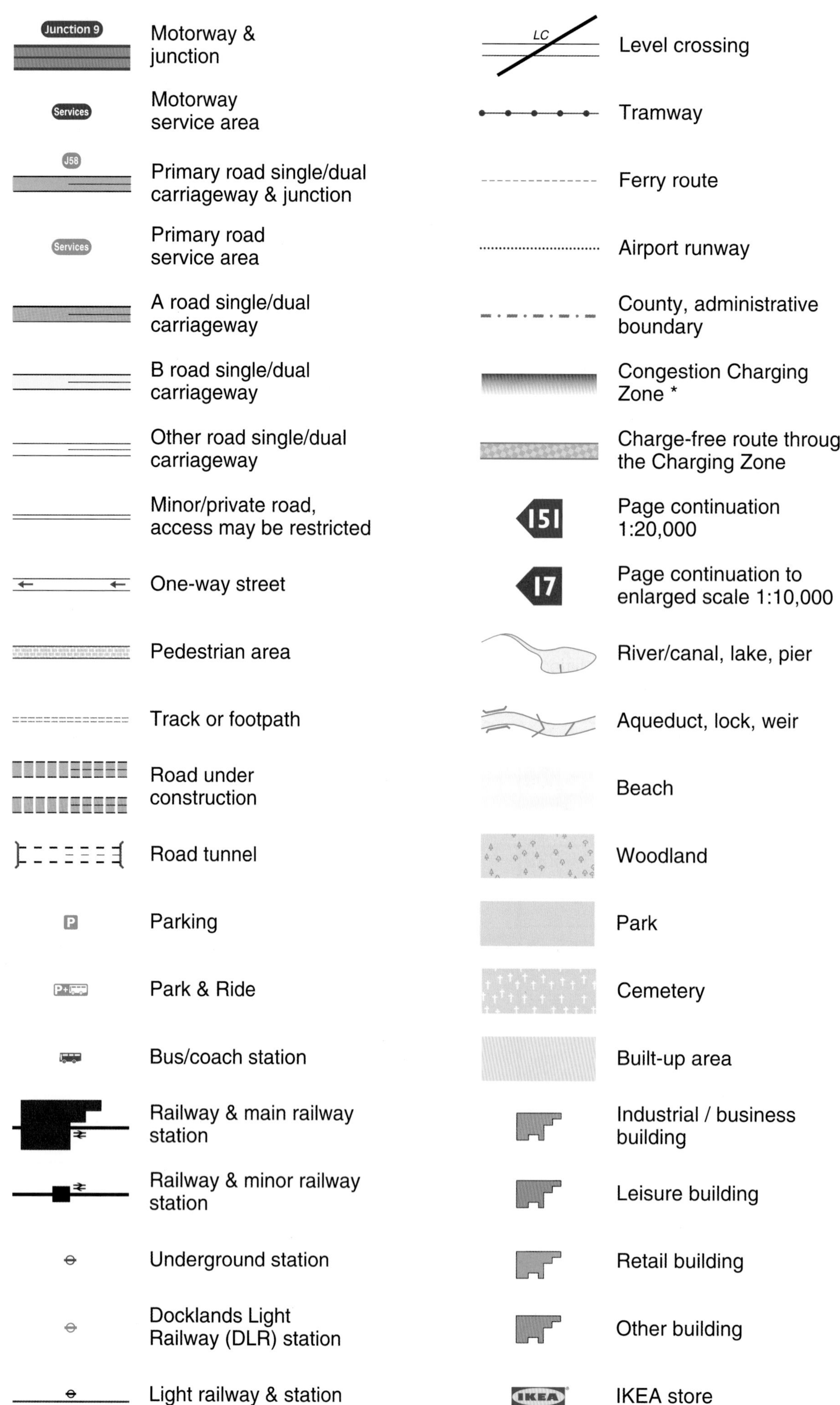

* The AA central London congestion charging map is also available

City wall		Castle	
A&E	Hospital with 24-hour A&E department		Historic house or building
PO	Post Office	Wakehurst Place NT	National Trust property
	Public library	M	Museum or art gallery
ℓ	Tourist Information Centre		Roman antiquity
ℓ	Seasonal Tourist Information Centre		Ancient site, battlefield or monument
	Petrol station, 24 hour Major suppliers only		Industrial interest
†	Church/chapel		Garden
	Public toilets		Garden Centre Garden Centre Association Member
	Toilet with disabled facilities		Garden Centre Wyevale Garden Centre
PH	Public house AA recommended		Arboretum
	Restaurant AA inspected		Farm or animal centre
Madeira Hotel	Hotel AA inspected		Zoological or wildlife collection
	Theatre or performing arts centre		Bird collection
	Cinema		Nature reserve
	Golf course		Aquarium
	Camping AA inspected	V	Visitor or heritage centre
	Caravan site AA inspected		Country park
	Camping & caravan site AA inspected		Cave
	Theme park		Distillery, brewery or vineyard
	Abbey, cathedral or priory		Windmill

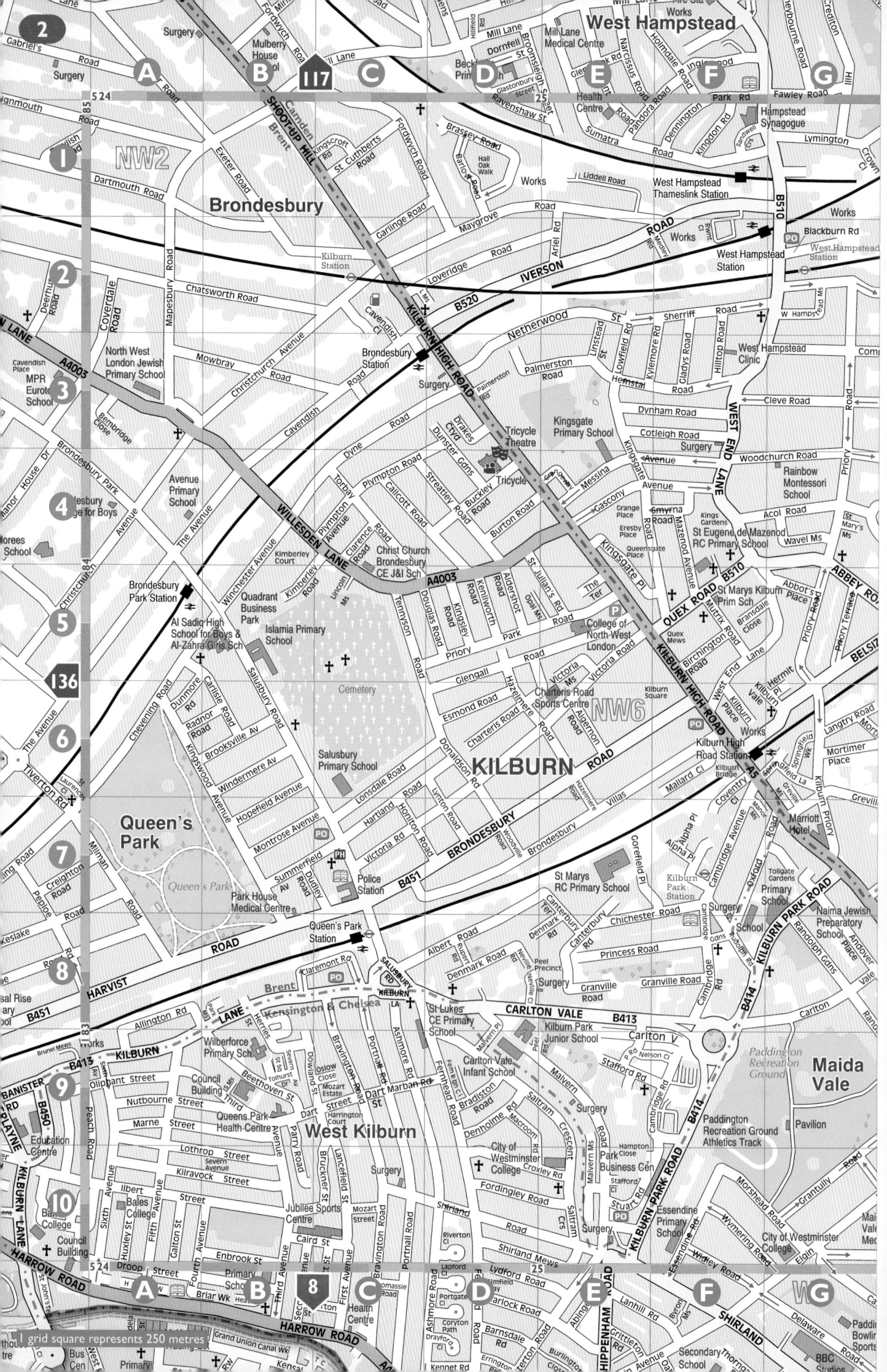

2
117
136
8
A
B
C
D
E
F
G
1
2
3
4
5
6
7
8
9
10
524
525
85
84
83
NW2
NW6
West Hampstead
Brondesbury
KILBURN
Queen's Park
West Kilburn
Maida Vale
Camden
Brent
Kensington & Chelsea
SHOOT-UP HILL
KILBURN HIGH ROAD
WILLESDEN LANE
A4003
B520
B510
IVERSON ROAD
WEST END LANE
QUEX ROAD
ABBEY ROAD
BRONDESBURY ROAD
B451
HARVIST ROAD
CARLTON VALE
B413
KILBURN LANE
HARROW ROAD
KILBURN PARK ROAD
B414
SHIRLAND
A5
West Hampstead Thameslink Station
West Hampstead Station
Kilburn Station
Brondesbury Station
Brondesbury Park Station
Kilburn High Road Station
Queen's Park Station
Kilburn Park Station
Tricycle Theatre
Kingsgate Primary School
Cemetery
Islamia Primary School
Salusbury Primary School
Quadrant Business Park
College of North-West London
Charteris Road Sports Centre
Police Station
Park House Medical Centre
St Marys RC Primary School
Hampstead Synagogue
West Hampstead Clinic
Rainbow Montessori School
St Eugene de Mazenod RC Primary School
St Marys Kilburn Prim Sch
Christ Church Brondesbury CE J&I Sch
North West London Jewish Primary School
Avenue Primary School
Al Sadiq High School for Boys & Al-Zahra Girls Sch
Marriott Hotel
Naima Jewish Preparatory School
Kilburn Park Junior School
Carlton Vale Infant School
St Lukes CE Primary School
Wilberforce Primary Sch
Queens Park Health Centre
City of Westminster College
Paddington Recreation Ground
Paddington Recreation Ground Athletics Track
Pavilion
Park Business Cen
Essendine Primary School
Jubilee Sports Centre
Council Building
Mill Lane Medical Centre
Health Centre
Works
Surgery
1 grid square represents 250 metres

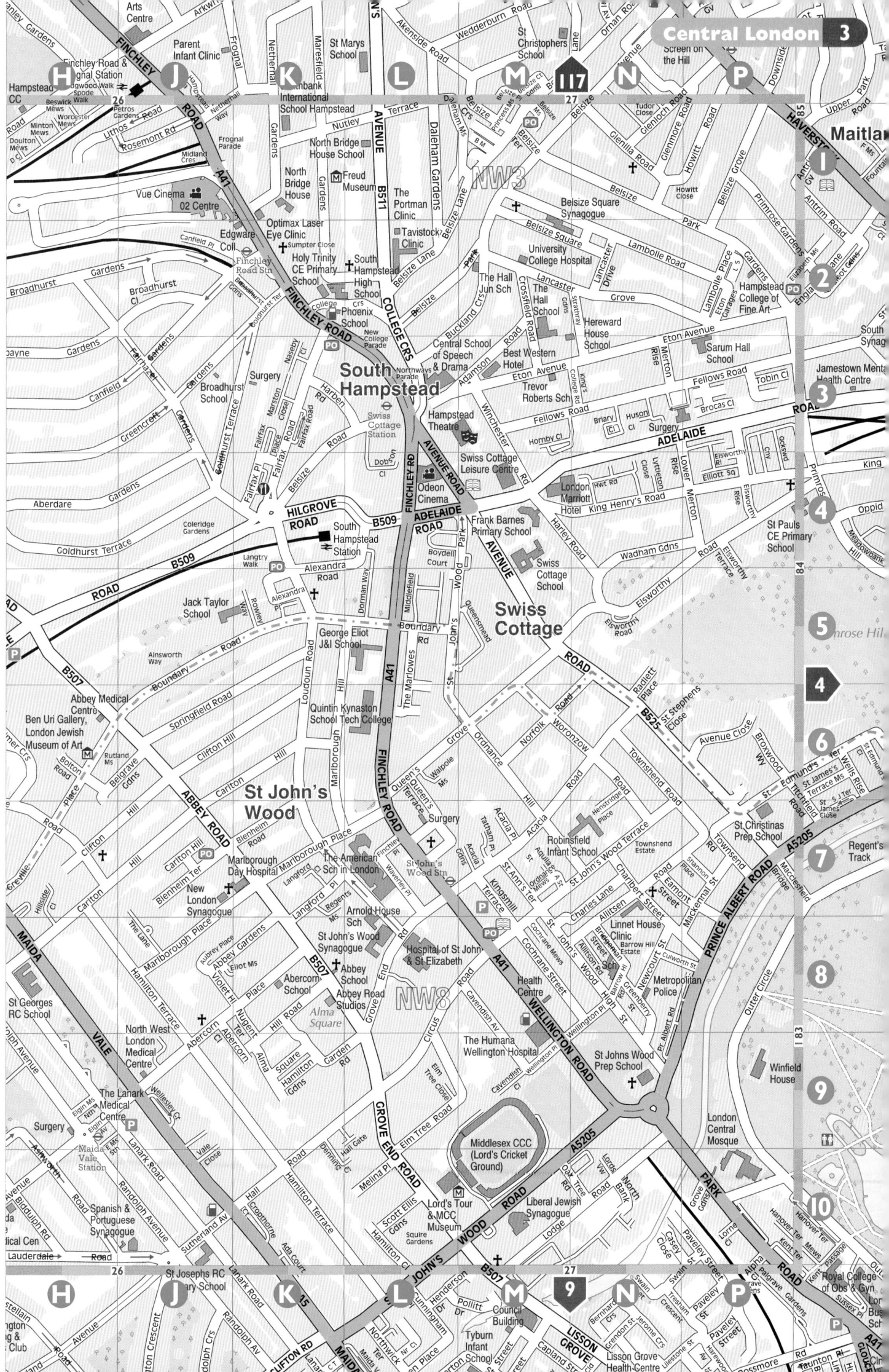
South Hampstead
Swiss Cottage
St John's Wood
NW3
NW8
Finchley Road
Adelaide Road
Abbey Road
Wellington Road
Prince Albert Road
Maida Vale
Middlesex CCC (Lord's Cricket Ground)
London Central Mosque
Freud Museum
Hampstead Theatre
Odeon Cinema
Swiss Cottage Station
South Hampstead Station
St John's Wood Stn
Finchley Road Stn
Maida Vale Station

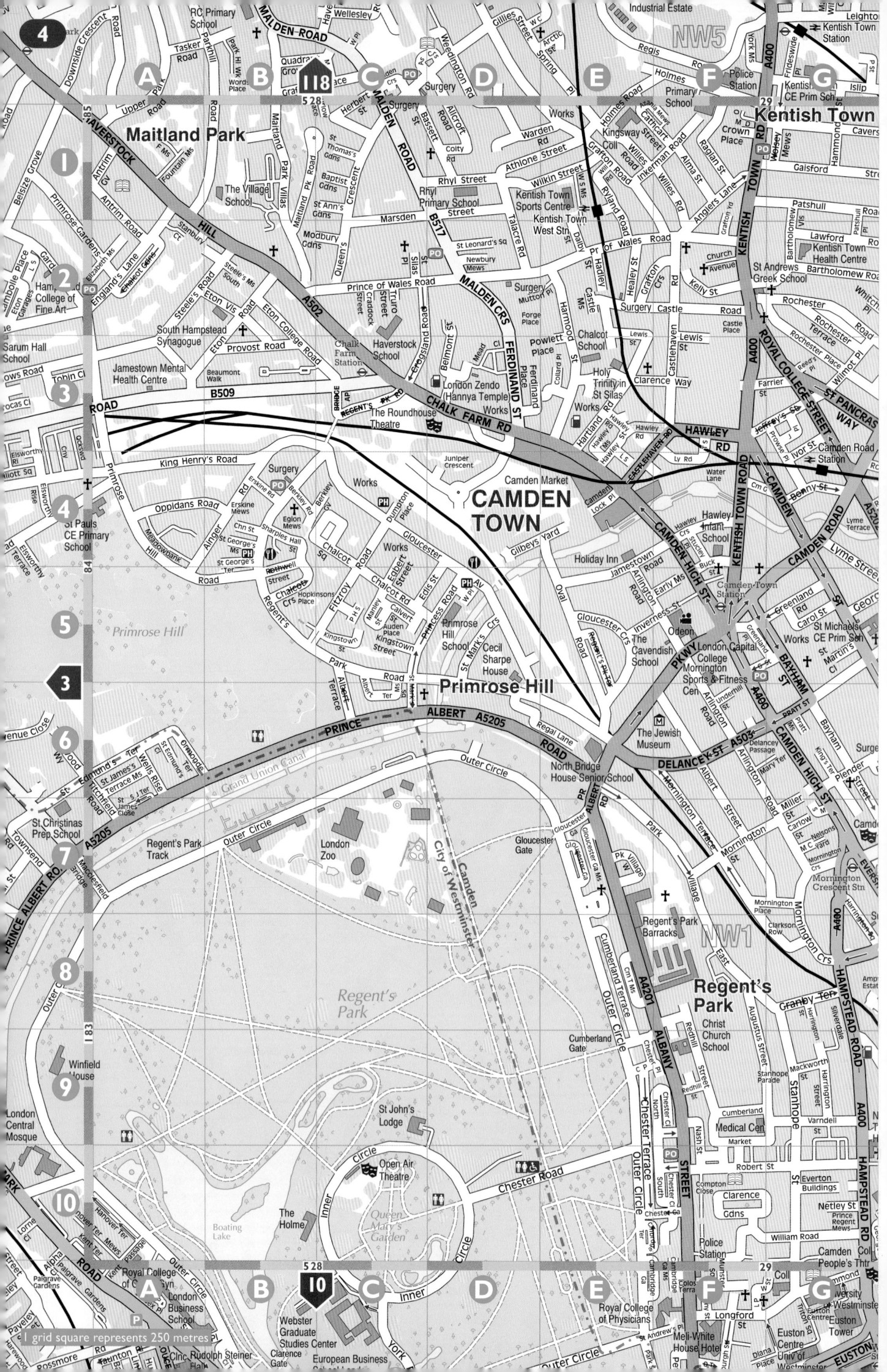
4
118
528
NW5
Kentish Town
Kentish Town Station
Maitland Park
Haverstock Hill
Malden Road
Malden Crs
Ferdinand St
Chalk Farm Rd
Camden Town
Primrose Hill
Prince Albert Road
A5205
A502
A400
A4201
B509
B517
Regent's Park Rd
Gloucester Ave
King Henry's Road
Prince of Wales Road
Haverstock School
Chalk Farm Station
The Roundhouse Theatre
London Zendo (Hannya Temple)
Camden Market
Camden Lock Pl
Camden High St
Kentish Town Road
Camden Road
Camden Road Station
Camden Town Station
Hawley Rd
Royal College Street
St Pancras Way
Delancey St
Parkway
Albany Street
Hampstead Road
Mornington Crescent Stn
Mornington Crs
The Jewish Museum
Odeon
Holiday Inn
North Bridge House Senior School
Cecil Sharpe House
Primrose Hill School
St Pauls CE Primary School
South Hampstead Synagogue
Jamestown Mental Health Centre
Hampstead College of Fine Art
The Village School
Rhyl Primary School
Kentish Town Sports Centre
Kentish Town West Stn
Kentish Town Health Centre
St Andrews Greek School
Chalcot School
Holy Trinity in St Silas
Hawley Infant School
The Cavendish School
London Capital College
Mornington Sports & Fitness Cen
St Christinas Prep School
Regent's Park Track
Grand Union Canal
London Zoo
Outer Circle
Inner Circle
Gloucester Gate
Cumberland Gate
Cumberland Terrace
Chester Terrace
Chester Road
Regent's Park
Regent's Park Barracks
Christ Church School
NW1
City of Westminster
Camden
Winfield House
London Central Mosque
Boating Lake
The Holme
Open Air Theatre
Queen Mary's Garden
St John's Lodge
Royal College of Gyn
London Business School
Webster Graduate Studies Center
European Business School
Rudolph Steiner
Royal College of Physicians
Meli-White House Hotel
Euston Tower
Univ of Westminster
Camden People's Thtr
Cumberland Medical Cen
Police Station
Clarence Gdns
Robert St
William Road
Netley St
Varndell
Everton Buildings
Stanhope
Augustus Street
Granby Ter
Mackworth St
Harrington
Longford St
Euston
1 grid square represents 250 metres

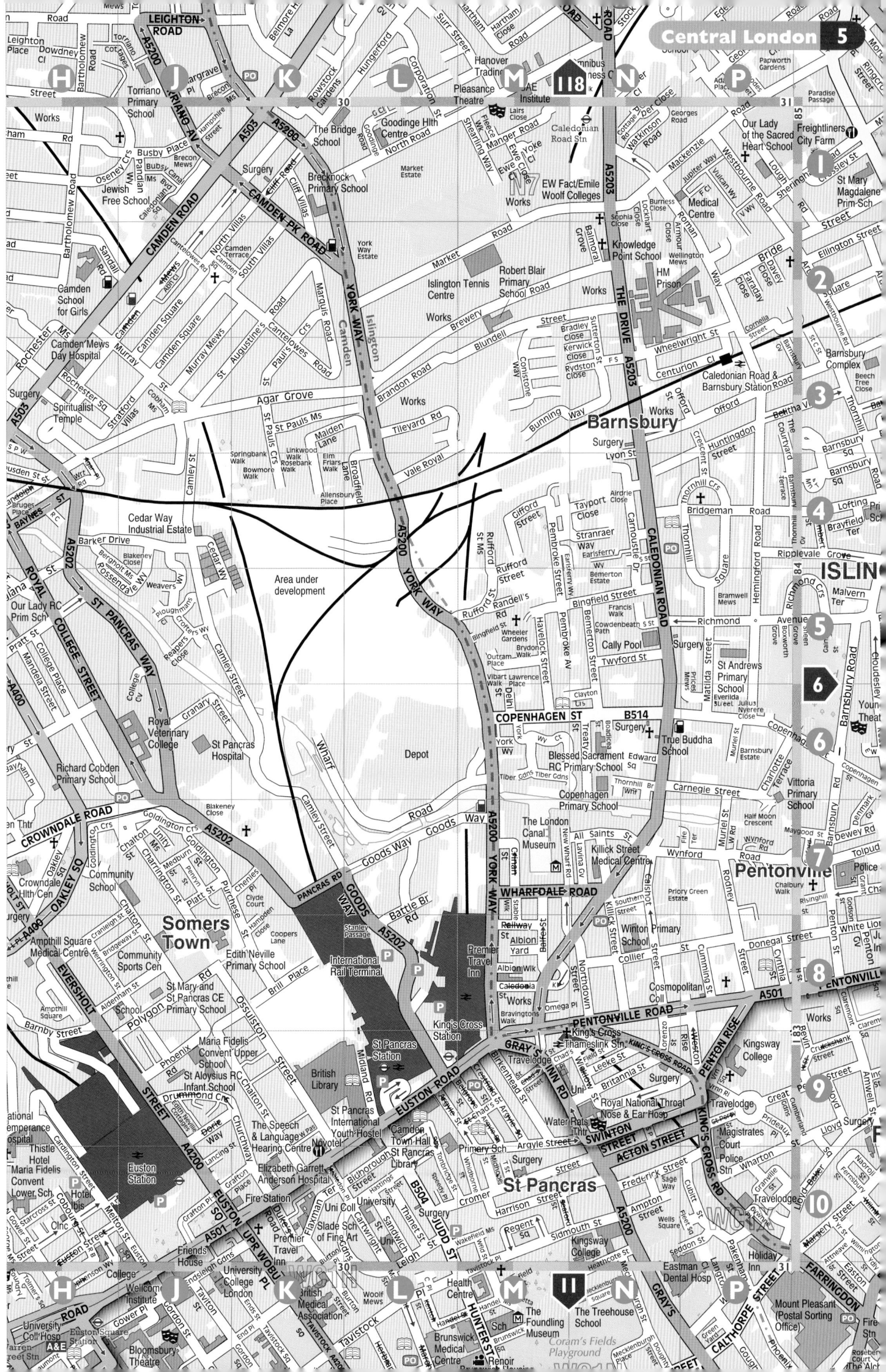
LEIGHTON ROAD
Torriano Primary School
Jewish Free School
CAMDEN ROAD
CAMDEN PK ROAD
Camden School for Girls
Camden Mews Day Hospital
Camden Square
Brecknock Primary School
The Bridge School
Goodinge Hlth Centre
North Road
Pleasance Theatre
Hanover Trading
Caledonian Road Stn
EW Fact/Emile Woolf Colleges
Our Lady of the Sacred Heart School
Freightliners City Farm
St Mary Magdalene Prim Sch
Medical Centre
Knowledge Point School
HM Prison
Robert Blair Primary School
Islington Tennis Centre
YORK WAY
Market Road
Brewery Road
Blundell Street
Agar Grove
Brandon Road
Tileyard Rd
Vale Royal
Barnsbury
Caledonian Road & Barnsbury Station
Spiritualist Temple
Cedar Way Industrial Estate
Area under development
Depot
CALEDONIAN ROAD
THE DRIVE
Bridgeman Road
Ripplevale Grove
ISLIN
Our Lady RC Prim Sch
ROYAL COLLEGE STREET
ST PANCRAS WAY
Royal Veterinary College
St Pancras Hospital
Richard Cobden Primary School
Cally Pool
St Andrews Primary School
COPENHAGEN ST
Blessed Sacrament RC Primary School
True Buddha School
Copenhagen Primary School
Vittoria Primary School
The London Canal Museum
Killick Street Medical Centre
Pentonville
CROWNDALE ROAD
Crowndale Hlth Cen
Community School
Somers Town
WHARFDALE ROAD
Goods Way
PANCRAS RD
International Rail Terminal
Premier Travel Inn
Winton Primary School
Cosmopolitan Coll
PENTONVILLE ROAD
Ampthill Square Medical Centre
Community Sports Cen
Edith Neville Primary School
St Mary and St Pancras CE Primary School
Maria Fidelis Convent Upper School
St Aloysius RC Infant School
King's Cross Station
St Pancras Station
British Library
St Pancras International Youth Hostel
EUSTON ROAD
King's Cross Thameslink Stn
KING'S CROSS ROAD
Kingsway College
Royal National Throat Nose & Ear Hosp
Travelodge
Euston Station
Thistle Hotel
Maria Fidelis Convent Lower Sch
The Speech & Language Hearing Centre
Elizabeth Garrett Anderson Hospital
Camden Town Hall & St Pancras Library
St Pancras
Magistrates Court
Police Stn
Uni Coll
Slade Sch of Fine Art
Premier Travel Inn
Friends House
University College London
British Medical Association
Health Centre
The Foundling Museum
The Treehouse School
Coram's Fields Playground
Eastman Dental Hosp
Holiday Inn
Mount Pleasant (Postal Sorting Office)
FARRINGDON
University Coll Hosp
Wellcome Institute
Bloomsbury Theatre
Euston Square Station
Brunswick Medical Centre
H J K L M N P
1 2 3 4 5 6 7 8 9 10
118
11
6

6
119
12
5
A
B
C
D
E
F
G
1
2
3
4
5
6
7
8
9
10
531
532
84
83
85
Holloway Medical Centre
Highbury Grove School
Highbury Crescent
Highbury New Park
Beresford Road
Grosvenor Avenue
Canonbury Station
Heaven Tree Close
Northampton Park
Freightliners City Farm
Our Lady of the Sacred Heart School
Papworth Gardens
City & Islington College Council Building
Highbury Pool
London Metr Uni
St Mary Magdalene Prim Sch
LIVERPOOL ROAD
Highbury Corner Magistrates Court
Highbury & Islington Station
HIGHBURY CORNER
ST PAUL'S ROAD
A1199
St Pauls Road Medical Cen
St Pauls Steiner Sch
Canonbury Primary School
Laycock Street
Laycock Primary School
Highbury Station Rd
Barnsbury Complex
Barnsbury School for Girls
Caledonian Road & Barnsbury Station
UPPER STREET
A1
A1200
CANONBURY ROAD
ESSEX ROAD
A104
Canonbury
Islington Town Hall
William Tyndale Primary School
River Place Health Cen
Essex Road Station
New North Community School
ISLINGTON
Maples Bus Centre
Almeida Theatre
Cncl Bldg
N1
Kings Head Theatre
Rotherfield Primary School
Canonbury Business Centre
Islington Business Centre
College
St Andrews Primary School
Barnard Park
Samuel Rhodes School
Young Actors Theatre
Screen on the Green Cinema
Islington Green Medical Cen
ISLINGTON GREEN
Islington Green School
The Business Design Centre
Museum of London (Archaeological Research Centre)
Vittoria Primary School
NEW NORTH ROAD
Pentonville
Police Stn
Consulate of Eritrea
N1 Shopping Centre
Angel Station
Clerkenwell Co Court
Colebrooke Works
Primary School
Thomas Fairchild Prim Sch
EAGLE WHF ROAD B144
Hanover Primary School
Faircharm Trading Estate
City Road Basin
Brewery Industrial Estate
Crafts Council
Jurys Inn
PENTONVILLE ROAD
A501
City & Islington Sixth Form College
CITY ROAD
Pop Up Theatre
Kingsway College
City University
London Open College
Crusoe House Sch
Police Station
Travelodge
Lilian Baylis Thr
Sadler's Wells Theatre
FINSBURY
Clerkenwell Parochial CE Prim Sch
Magistrates Court
Police Stn
Moreland Primary School
EC1V
SHEPHERDESS WALK
B144
Thistle Hotel
LEVER STREET
BATH STREET
Moorfields Eye Hospital
City & Islington College
Ironmonger Row Baths
Finsbury Leisure Centre
B502
Town Hall Family Rec Cen
City Business Coll
Holiday Inn
WC1X
Mount Pleasant (Postal Sorting Office)
Finsbury Health Cen
Records Office
University of London
The Bridge School
St Peter & St Pauls Primary School
Dallington School
City University
St Luke's
Clerkenwell
OLD STREET
GOSWELL ROAD
ROSEBERY AVENUE
PERCIVAL ST
1 grid square represents 250 metres

HACKNEY
Dalston
Kingsland
De Beauvoir Town
Haggerston
Hoxton
SHOREDITCH
BETHNAL GREEN
KINGSLAND ROAD
KINGSLAND HIGH ST
BALLS POND ROAD
DALSTON LANE
GRAHAM ROAD
QUEENSBRIDGE ROAD
SOUTHGATE ROAD
HACKNEY ROAD
COLUMBIA ROAD
OLD STREET
CURTAIN ROAD
SHOREDITCH HIGH ST
GREAT EASTERN STREET
BETHNAL GREEN ROAD
OLD BETHNAL GN RD
GOSSET STREET
SQUIRRIES ST
VALLANCE ROAD
CHESHIRE STREET
SCLATER STREET
DUNBRIDGE STREET
WARNER PLACE
PITFIELD STREET
NEW N ROAD
EAST ROAD
ARNOLD CIRCUS
CALVERT AV
CLUB ROW
Dalston Kingsland Station
Kingsland Shopping Centre
Council Buildings
Kingsland Health Cen
Metropolitan Business Cen
Queensbridge Sports Centre
Queensbridge Primary School
Holy Trinity Primary School
Gayhurst Primary School
London Fields
London Fields Primary School
The London Fields Medical Cen
St Paul's with St Michael's CE Prim School
Haggerston Swimming Pool
Haggerston Park
Sebright Primary School
Haggerston School
Hackney City Farm
Ion Square Gardens
Columbia Primary School
Bethnal Green Technology College
Tower Hamlets College
Virginia Prim Sch
Midway Mission Hosp
Geffrye Mus
Trans Atlantic College
St Leonards Hospital
Burbage School
Hoxton Hall Community Thtr
Comprehensive School
Hackney Community College
St John the Baptist CE Prim Sch
St Monica's RC Prim Sch
Britannia Leisure Centre
Whitmore Primary School
Shoreditch Park
City College of Higher Ed
Fire Station
Brick Lane Music Hall
London Coll of Fashion
Shoreditch County Court
Boys School
St Matthias CE Primary School
Bethnal Green Station
Weavers Fields
St Matthew's Gdns
Our Lady & St Joseph Primary School
St Judes & St Pauls CE Primary School
Southgate Road Medical Centre
Colvestone Primary School
Regent's Row
Canal Walk
H J K L M N P
1 2 3 4 5 6 7 8 9 10
119
140
13
E8
E2
A10 A104 A1208 A1209 A5201 B101 B102 B108 B118 B122 B135

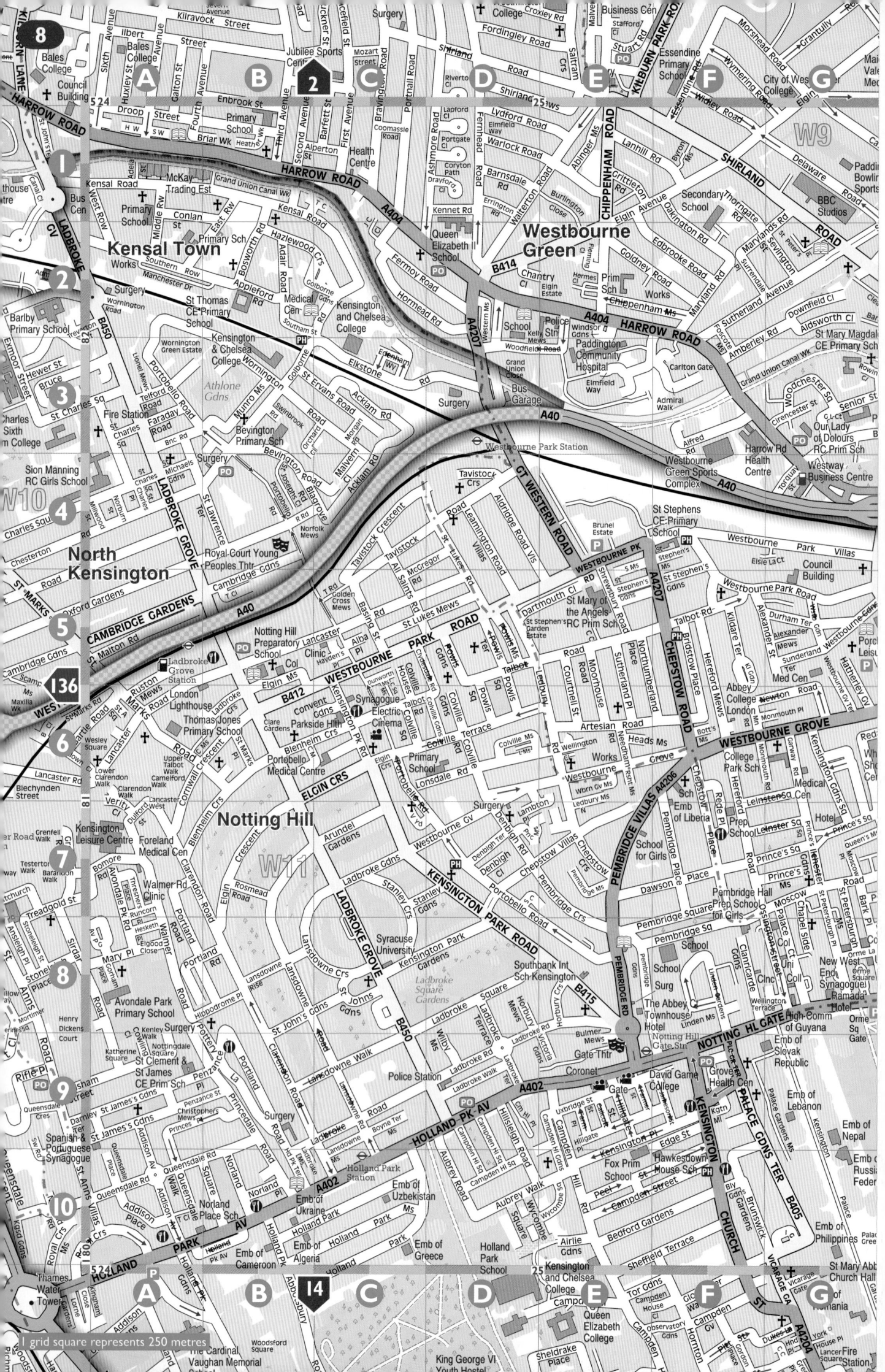

8
2
136
14
A
B
C
D
E
F
G
1
2
3
4
5
6
7
8
9
10
W9
W10
W11
Kensal Town
Westbourne Green
North Kensington
Notting Hill
HARROW ROAD
A404
LADBROKE GROVE
A40
WESTBOURNE PARK ROAD
B412
ELGIN CRS
KENSINGTON PARK ROAD
CHEPSTOW ROAD
A4207
WESTBOURNE GROVE
PEMBROKE VILLAS A4206
NOTTING HL GATE
A402
HOLLAND PK AV
HOLLAND PARK AV
KENSINGTON CHURCH ST
PALACE GDNS TER
B405
CAMBRIDGE GARDENS
GT WESTERN ROAD
SHIRLAND ROAD
KILBURN PARK ROAD
CHIPPENHAM ROAD
B414
B450
B415
A4204
Westbourne Park Station
Ladbroke Grove Station
Notting Hill Gate Stn
Holland Park Station
Kensington & Chelsea College
Paddington Community Hospital
Westbourne Green Sports Complex
Harrow Rd Health Centre
Westway Business Centre
BBC Studios
Queen Elizabeth II School
Kensington Leisure Centre
Avondale Park Primary School
Syracuse University
Southbank Int Sch Kensington
Gate Thtr
Coronet
Police Station
Holland Park School
Royal Court Young Peoples Thtr
Sion Manning RC Girls School
Electric Cinema
Portobello Medical Centre
Ladbroke Square Gardens
Spanish & Portuguese Synagogue
Thames Water Tower
1 grid square represents 250 metres

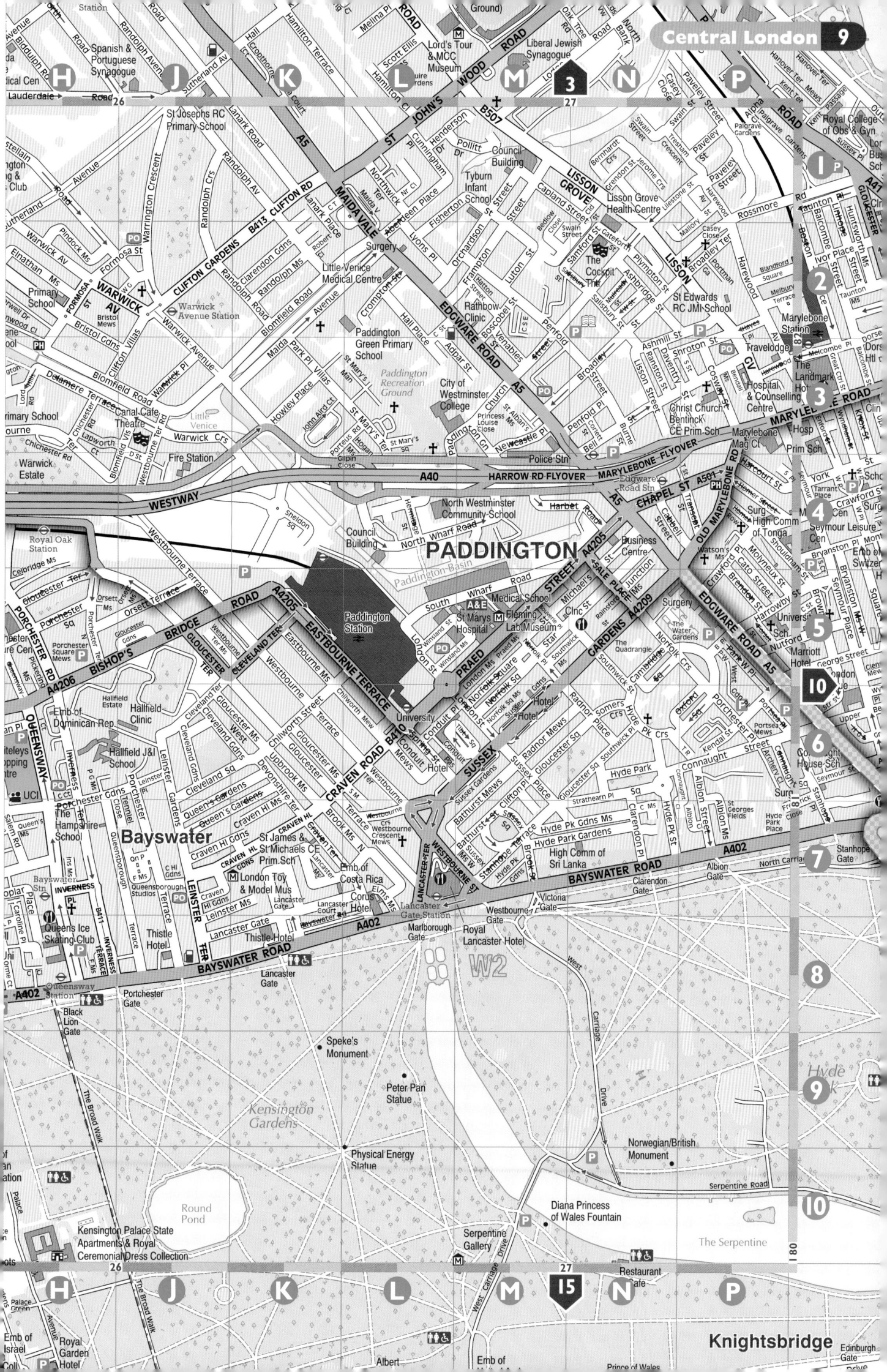
PADDINGTON
Bayswater
Kensington Gardens
Knightsbridge
W2
Paddington Station
Paddington Basin
St Marys Hospital
Fleming Lab Museum
Medical School
Lord's Tour & MCC Museum
Liberal Jewish Synagogue
Spanish & Portuguese Synagogue
St Josephs RC Primary School
Little Venice Medical Centre
Paddington Green Primary School
Paddington Recreation Ground
City of Westminster College
Warwick Avenue Station
Canal Cafe Theatre
Little Venice
Fire Station
Police Stn
Edgware Road Stn
Marylebone Station
Royal Oak Station
North Westminster Community School
Council Building
Business Centre
The Water Gardens
The Quadrangle
Tyburn Infant School
Lisson Grove Health Centre
The Cockpit Thtr
St Edwards RC JMI School
Christ Church Bentinck CE Prim Sch
Hospital & Counselling Centre
Royal College of Obs & Gyn
Hallfield Clinic
Hallfield J&I School
Emb of Dominican Rep
The Hampshire School
St James & St Michaels CE Prim Sch
London Toy & Model Mus
Emb of Costa Rica
Corus Hotel
Thistle Hotel
Queens Ice Skating Club
Queensway Station
Bayswater Stn
Lancaster Gate Station
Royal Lancaster Hotel
High Comm of Sri Lanka
Marriott Hotel
Speke's Monument
Peter Pan Statue
Physical Energy Statue
Round Pond
Kensington Palace State Apartments & Royal Ceremonial Dress Collection
Norwegian/British Monument
Diana Princess of Wales Fountain
Serpentine Gallery
The Serpentine
Restaurant
Royal Garden Hotel
Emb of Israel
EDGWARE ROAD
MAIDA VALE
ST JOHN'S WOOD ROAD
WESTWAY
HARROW RD FLYOVER
MARYLEBONE FLYOVER
PRAED STREET
SUSSEX GARDENS
BAYSWATER ROAD
BISHOP'S BRIDGE ROAD
EASTBOURNE TERRACE
CRAVEN ROAD
WESTBOURNE TERRACE
QUEENSWAY
PORCHESTER RD
LISSON GROVE
CLIFTON GARDENS
MARYLEBONE ROAD
OLD MARYLEBONE RD
CHAPEL ST
North Carriage Drive
West Carriage Drive
Serpentine Road
The Broad Walk
A5
A40
A402
A4205
A4209
A4206
B413
B507
26
27
180
H J K L M N P
1 2 3 4 5 6 7 8 9 10
3
10
15

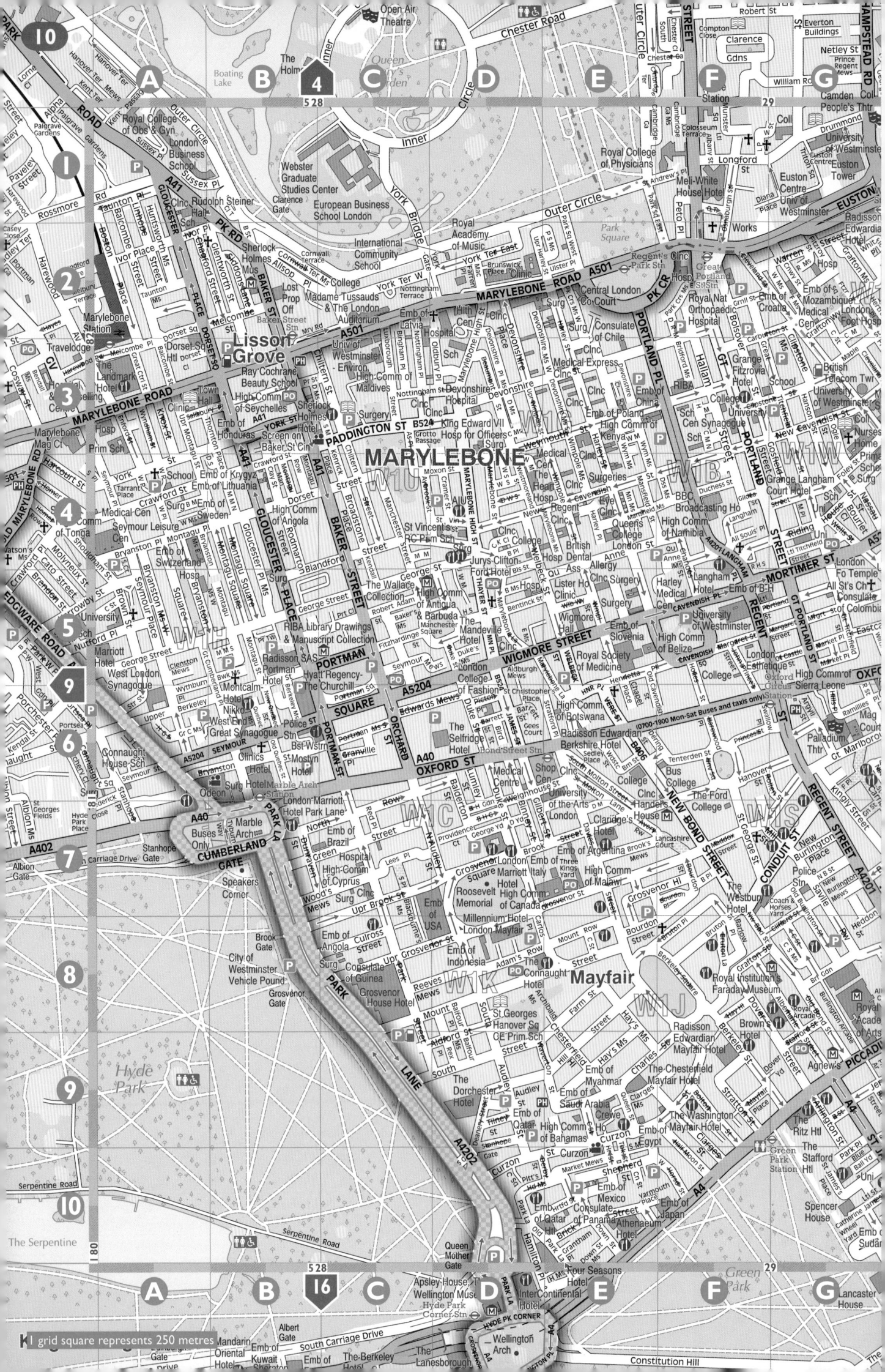

10
4
528
29
A
B
C
D
E
F
G
1
2
3
4
5
6
7
8
9
10
MARYLEBONE
Lisson Grove
Mayfair
Hyde Park
The Serpentine
Green Park
MARYLEBONE ROAD
EDGWARE ROAD
OXFORD ST
WIGMORE STREET
BAKER STREET
GLOUCESTER PLACE
PORTLAND PL
REGENT STREET
NEW BOND STREET
PARK LANE
PARK LA
PADDINGTON ST
PORTMAN SQUARE
CAVENDISH PL
MORTIMER ST
CONDUIT ST
CUMBERLAND GATE
HYDE PK CORNER
Constitution Hill
Serpentine Road
South Carriage Drive
Chester Road
Outer Circle
Inner Circle
York Bridge
Open Air Theatre
Boating Lake
Regent's Park Stn
Great Portland St Stn
Baker Street Stn
Marylebone Station
Bond Street Stn
Oxford Circus Station
Marble Arch Station
Green Park Station
Hyde Park Corner Stn
Madame Tussauds & The London Auditorium
Sherlock Holmes Mus
Royal Academy of Music
Royal College of Physicians
Royal Institution's Faraday Museum
The Wallace Collection
RIBA Library Drawings & Manuscript Collection
BBC Broadcasting Ho
The Selfridge Hotel
The Dorchester Hotel
The Ritz Htl
The Connaught Hotel
Claridge's Hotel
Wellington Arch
Apsley House, The Wellington Museum
Speakers Corner
Marble Arch
Buses Only
Spencer House
Lancaster House
1 grid square represents 250 metres

St Pancras
Euston Station
Bloomsbury
Holborn
St Giles
Soho
China Town
Strand
St James's
WC1H
WC1N
WC1E
WC1B
WC1R
WC1A
WC1V
WC2A
WC2H
WC2B
WC2E
WC2R
WC2N
W1F
SW1Y
SW1A
Maria Fidelis Convent Lower Sch
Elizabeth Garrett Anderson Hospital
Fire Station
Uni Coll
Slade Sch of Fine Art
University
Surgery
Friends House
University College
Wellcome Institute
University College London
British Medical Association
Woolf Mews
Health Centre
The Foundling Museum
The Treehouse School
Coram's Fields Playground
Mount Pleasant (Postal Office)
Eastman Dental Hosp
Holiday Inn
University Coll Hosp
Euston Square Station
Bloomsbury Theatre
University College London
Percival David Fndtn
University of London
Brunswick Medical Centre
Renoir
Brunswick Housing & Shopping Cen
British Cartoon Centre
The Charles Dickens Mus
Uni Church
Institute of Education SOAS
Brunei Gallery
Inst of Education Univ of London
Russell Square Station
The Hotel Russell
National Hosp for Neurology & Neurosurgery
National Hosp for Sick Children (Great Ormond St)
Union of Liberal & Prog Synagogues
Obstetrics Hosp
Birkbeck Coll
London School of Hygiene & Tropical Medicine
RADA
Eckerd College
Royal London Homeopathic Hosp
London Weather Centre
Police Station
Conway Hall
Inns of Court Law School
Goodge St Station
Drill Hall
Uni of London
Huron Univ
Bedford Hotel
Royal College of Anaesthetists
Grange Blooms Hotel
The Montague on the Gardens
Bonnington Hotel
Cavendish Coll
Sch of Physiotherapy
The College of Law
Birkbeck College
Grange Whitehall Hotel
British Museum
Grange Holborn Hotel
Council of Mosques
Sch of Arch
Radisson Edwardian Kenilworth Hotel
Radisson Edwardian Marlborough Hotel
Emb of Turkmenistan
High Comm of Barbados
YMCA
Jurys Hotel
TUC
BPP Law School
London Silver Vaults
Berlitz Sch
Sir John Soane's Mus
Lincoln's Inn
PO Sorting Office
Oxford Ho Coll
Dominion Thtr
Tottenham Court Road Stn
Centre Point
Eye Clnc
Embassy of Cuba
Holborn Tn Hall
City Literary College
Royal College of Surgeons
The Alan D School of Hairdressing
Medical Cen
Oasis Sports Cen
Travelodge
Marlan Coll
New London Thtr
Kings Coll
New Connaught Rooms
Old Curiosity Shop
Hunterian Museum
Hse of St Barnabus
Phoenix Thtr
Warwick Dubbing
Hosp
Medical Cen
The Urdang Academy
The Peacock Thtr
Royal Courts of Justice
Marshall St Leisure Centre
Odeon
Prince Edward Theatre
Donmar Warehouse
SEVEN DIALS
London Int Film Sch
Royal Ballet Sch
Royal Opera House
Fortune Thtr
London School of Economics
Aldwych
Bush Ho (BBC)
Australia House
St Clement Danes
CAMBRIDGE CIRCUS
Palace
Curzon
Covent Garden Station
Thtr Royal
Thtr Mus
Lib & Arc
Duchess
Novello
India House
Roman Bath
Swissotel The Howard
Gielgud
Apollo
Queens
St Martins
Arts Thtr
Africa Cen
The Mkt
Covent Garden Piazza
Jubilee Mkt
St Paul's
St Peter's Hosp
One Aldwych
Courtauld Institute Gal
Somerset House
Gilbert Collection
Temple Stn
Lyric
Piccadilly
Trocadero
UGC
Odeon
Leicester Square Stn
Noel Coward
Wyn
Strand Palace Hotel
Savoy Thtr
Lyceum
Courtauld Institute of Art
Thames Police Station
St Katherine
HQS Wellington (Master Mariners)
Radisson Edwardian Hampshire Htl
Capital Radio
Coliseum
Police Stn
Royal Society of Arts
TS Queen Mary
Entrance to Strand Underpass (northbound only)
PICCADILLY CIRCUS
Piccadilly Circus Stn
Criterion
Eros
Prince of Wales
Odeon
Jermyn St
St James's Church
High Comm of Malta
Hotel
Comedy
Royal
Her Majesty's
Visitor Centre
High Comm of New Zealand
Duke of York St
National Gallery
National Portrait Gal
Garrick
Notre Dame University
St Martin-in-the-Fields
High Comm of Zimbabwe
Proud Gal
Thistle Hotel
Players Thtr
York Water Gate
Savoy Pier
Victoria Embankment Gardens
Cleopatra's Needle
Embankment Pier
Waterloo Bridge
The London Television Cen (LWT)
Trafalgar Square
Nelson's Column
Canada House
High Comm of South Africa
Charing Cross Stn
High Comm of Nigeria
Embankment Station
Festival Pier
National Film Theatre
Cavendish Hotel
High Comm of Papua New Guinea
International School of Havana
High Com of Uganda
KING CHARLES I ISLAND
Gov Offices Gt Scot Yd
The Playhouse
Queen Elizabeth Hall
Golden Jubilee Bridge
Sofitel St James Hotel
ICA
Mall Galleries
Admiralty Arch
Whitehall
DEFRA
Hayward Gallery
Kings College London
The Royal College of Pathology
Carlton House
Duke of York Column
Old Admiralty
The Royal Horseguards Hotel
Hispaniola
Royal Festival Hall
London City Coll & Schiller Int Uni
Kings College London
Schomberg House
Horse Guards Parade
Old War Office
PS Tattershall Castle
BFI London IMAX Cinema
Marlborough House
Privy Council
Ministry of Defence
Banqueting House Whitehall
Jubilee Gardens
Shell Centre
St James's Palace
Clarence Ho
Privy Council Office
Old Treas
Foreign & Commonwealth Office
Cenotaph
Department of Hlth
Norman Shaw Building (MP's Offices)
London Marriott Hotel
Premier Travel Inn
Dali Universe
County Hall
Waterloo Station
Churchill Museum & Cabinet War Rooms
EUSTON ROAD
TOTTENHAM COURT RD
GOWER ST
BLOOMSBURY ST
WOBURN PLACE
SOUTHAMPTON ROW
THEOBALD'S ROAD
GRAY'S INN ROAD
HIGH HOLBORN
KINGSWAY
ALDWYCH
STRAND
SHAFTESBURY AV
CHARING CROSS RD
REGENT ST
HAYMARKET
PALL MALL
NORTHUMBERLAND AV
WHITEHALL
VICTORIA EMBANKMENT
WATERLOO BRIDGE
FLEET ST
CHANCERY LA
NEW OXFORD ST
GUILFORD STREET
FARRINGDON
ROSEBERY AVENUE
H
J
K
L
M
N
P
1
2
3
4
5
6
7
8
9
10
12
17
30
31

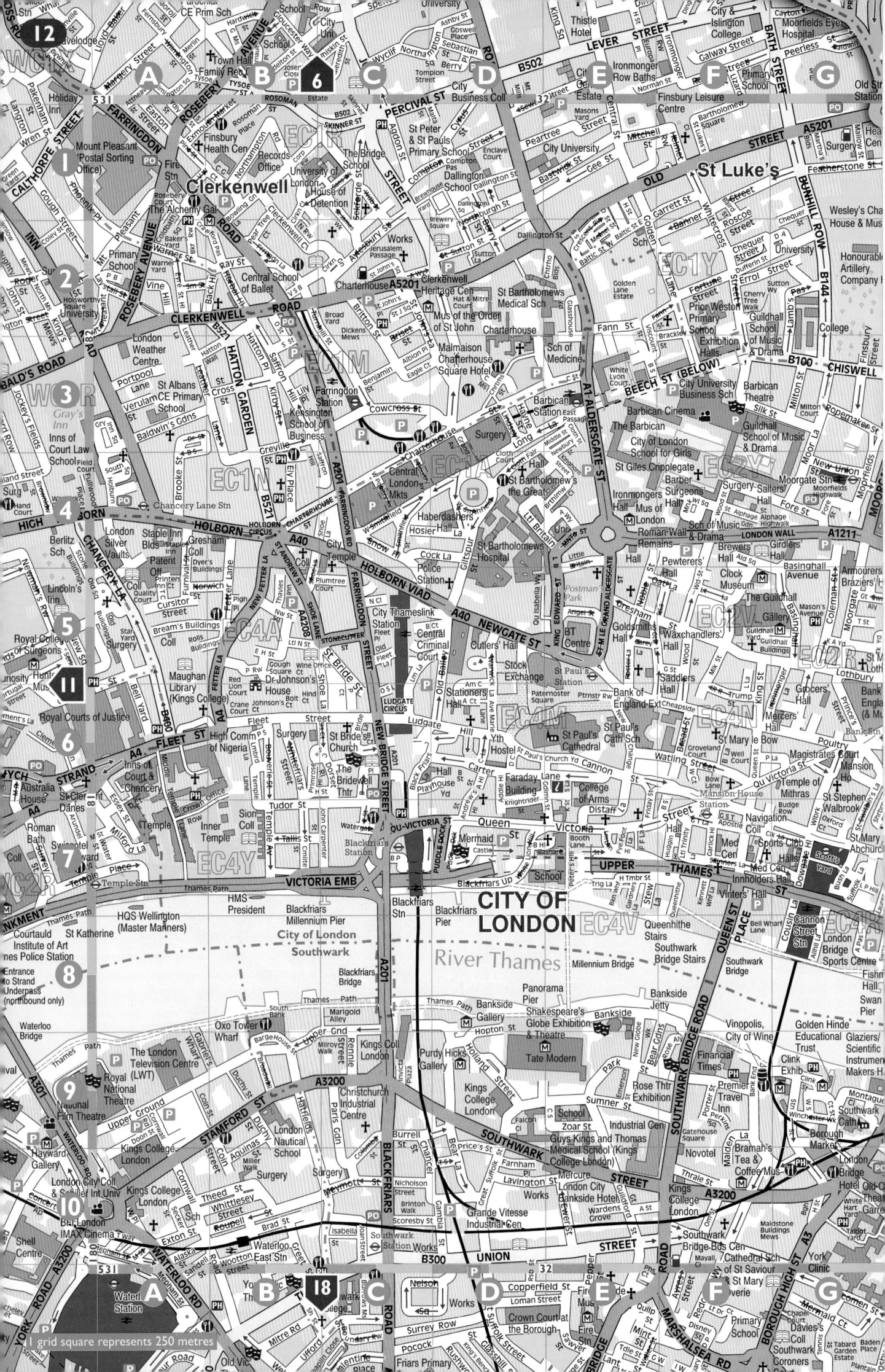
12
6
11
18
A
B
C
D
E
F
G
1
2
3
4
5
6
7
8
9
10
531
32
Clerkenwell
St Luke's
CITY OF LONDON
River Thames
City of London
Southwark
EC1R
EC1M
EC1N
EC1A
EC1Y
EC2Y
EC2V
EC2R
EC4A
EC4M
EC4N
EC4Y
EC4V
EC4R
WC1X
WC1R
WC2R
FARRINGDON
ROSEBERY AVENUE
ROSEBERY AVENUE
CALTHORPE STREET
PERCIVAL ST
LEVER STREET
BATH STREET
OLD STREET
BUNHILL ROW
GOSWELL ROAD
CLERKENWELL ROAD
A1 ALDERSGATE ST
BEECH ST (BELOW)
CHISWELL
HOLBORN
HIGH HOLBORN
CHARTERHOUSE
HOLBORN VIAD
NEWGATE ST
LONDON WALL
FARRINGDON ROAD
FARRINGDON STREET
NEW BRIDGE STREET
HATTON GARDEN
CHANCERY LA
FETTER LANE
NEW FETTER LA
SHOE LANE
STONECUTTER
FLEET ST
STRAND
VICTORIA EMB
QU VICTORIA ST
UPPER THAMES ST
QUEEN ST PLACE
SOUTHWARK BRIDGE ROAD
SOUTHWARK STREET
STAMFORD ST
BLACKFRIARS ROAD
UNION STREET
WATERLOO RD
YORK ROAD
BOROUGH HIGH ST
MARSHALSEA RD
Mount Pleasant (Postal Sorting Office)
Finsbury Health Cen
Clerkenwell Heritage Cen
Mus of the Order of St John
Charterhouse
Farringdon Station
Barbican Station
Barbican Cinema
The Barbican
Barbican Theatre
Guildhall School of Music & Drama
City of London School for Girls
St Giles Cripplegate
Museum of London
St Bartholomew's Hospital
St Bartholomew's the Great
Central London Mkts
Smithfield
City Thameslink Station
Central Criminal Court
St Paul's Cathedral
St Paul's Station
Paternoster Square
Stock Exchange
Bank of England Ext
St Mary le Bow
Mansion House Station
Temple of Mithras
Cannon Street Stn
Blackfriars Station
Blackfriars Stn
Blackfriars Pier
Blackfriars Bridge
Blackfriars Millennium Pier
Millennium Bridge
Southwark Bridge
Bankside Jetty
Bankside Gallery
Panorama Pier
Shakespeare's Globe Exhibition & Theatre
Tate Modern
Oxo Tower Wharf
Royal National Theatre
National Film Theatre
Hayward Gallery
BFI London IMAX Cinema
London Television Centre (LWT)
Waterloo Bridge
Waterloo Station
Waterloo East Stn
Southwark Station
Southwark Cathedral
Borough Market
London Bridge Hospital
Golden Hinde Educational Trust
Vinopolis, City of Wine
Clink Exhib
Financial Times
Rose Thr Exhibition
Royal Courts of Justice
Lincoln's Inn
Gray's Inn
Inns of Court Law School
Royal College of Surgeons
Maughan Library (Kings College)
Dr Johnson's House
St Bride's Church
The Bridewell Thtr
Inns of Court & Chancery
Temple
Inner Temple
Temple Stn
HMS President
HQS Wellington (Master Mariners)
Courtauld Institute of Art
Chancery Lane Stn
Holborn Circus
Ludgate Circus
Moorgate Stn
Guildhall
Clock Museum
Moorfields Eye Hospital
City & Islington College
Old St Station
City University
City University Business Sch
Finsbury Leisure Centre
Ironmonger Row Baths
Sch of Medicine
Malmaison Charterhouse Square Hotel
Honourable Artillery Company HQ
Wesley's Chapel House & Museum
Sion Coll
High Comm of Nigeria
Kings College London
London Nautical School
Christchurch Industrial Centre
Guys Kings and Thomas Medical School (Kings College London)
Mercure London City Bankside Hotel
Grande Vitesse Industrial Cen
Cathedral Sch of St Saviour & St Mary Overie
1 grid square represents 250 metres

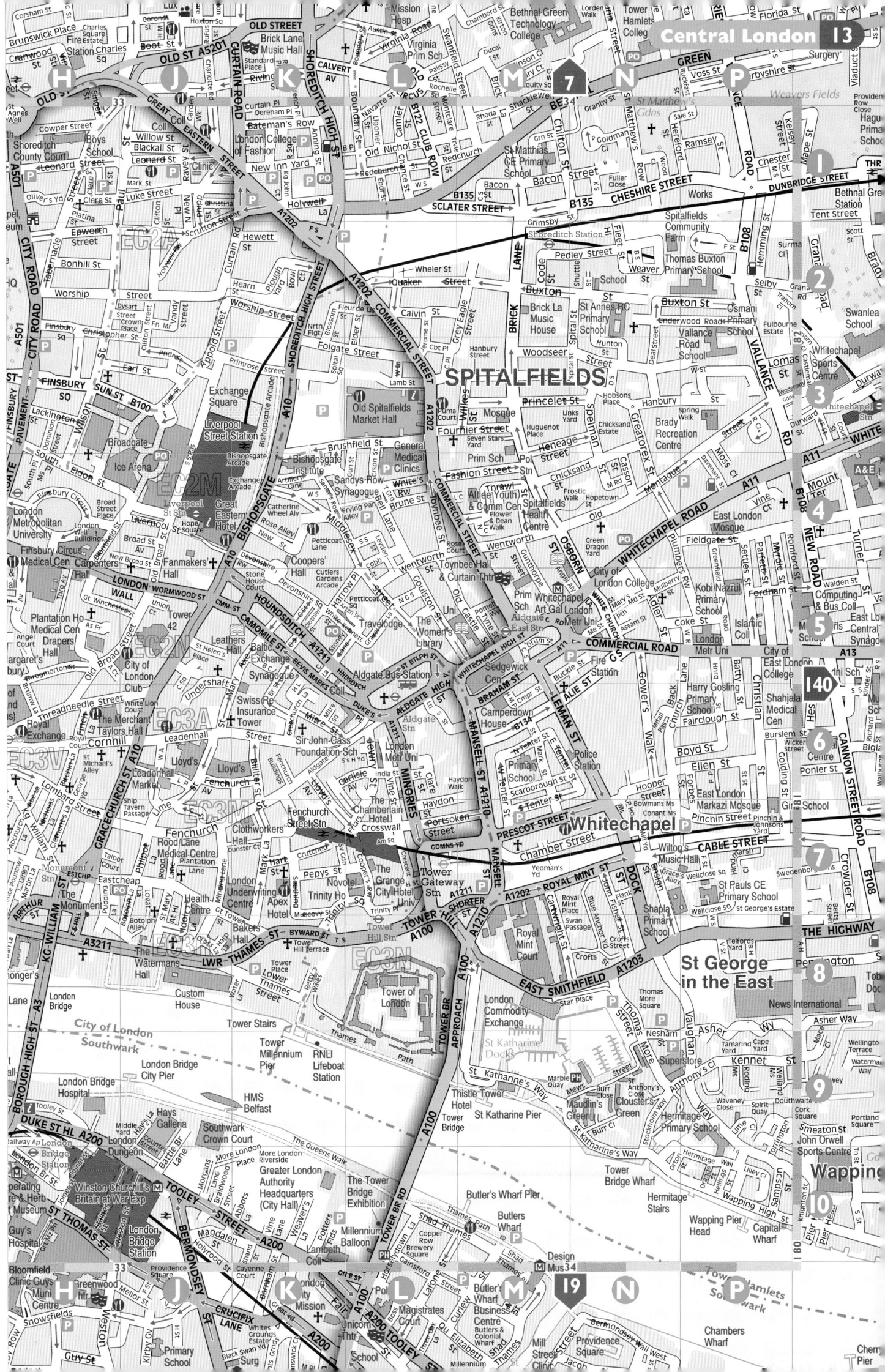
SPITALFIELDS
Whitechapel
St George in the East
Wapping
City of London
Southwark
OLD STREET
CURTAIN ROAD
SHOREDITCH HIGH ST
GREAT EASTERN STREET
COMMERCIAL STREET
BISHOPSGATE
CITY ROAD
BRICK LANE
CHESHIRE STREET
SCLATER STREET
WHITECHAPEL ROAD
COMMERCIAL ROAD
NEW ROAD
VALLANCE RD
CANNON STREET ROAD
CABLE STREET
THE HIGHWAY
EAST SMITHFIELD
ROYAL MINT ST
LEMAN ST
MANSELL ST
MINORIES
HOUNDSDITCH
TOWER HILL
LWR THAMES ST
GRACECHURCH ST
KG WILLIAM ST
BOROUGH HIGH ST
TOOLEY STREET
TOWER BR APPROACH
TOWER BR RD
BERMONDSEY ST
Liverpool Street Station
Old Spitalfields Market Hall
Aldgate Bus Station
Tower of London
Tower Gateway Stn
Fenchurch Street Stn
London Bridge Station
St Katharine Docks
HMS Belfast
Shoreditch Station
Brick Lane Music Hall
EC2A
EC2M
EC2N
EC3A
EC3V
EC3M
EC3N
7
19
140
H
J
K
L
M
N
P
1
2
3
4
5
6
7
8
9
10
33
34

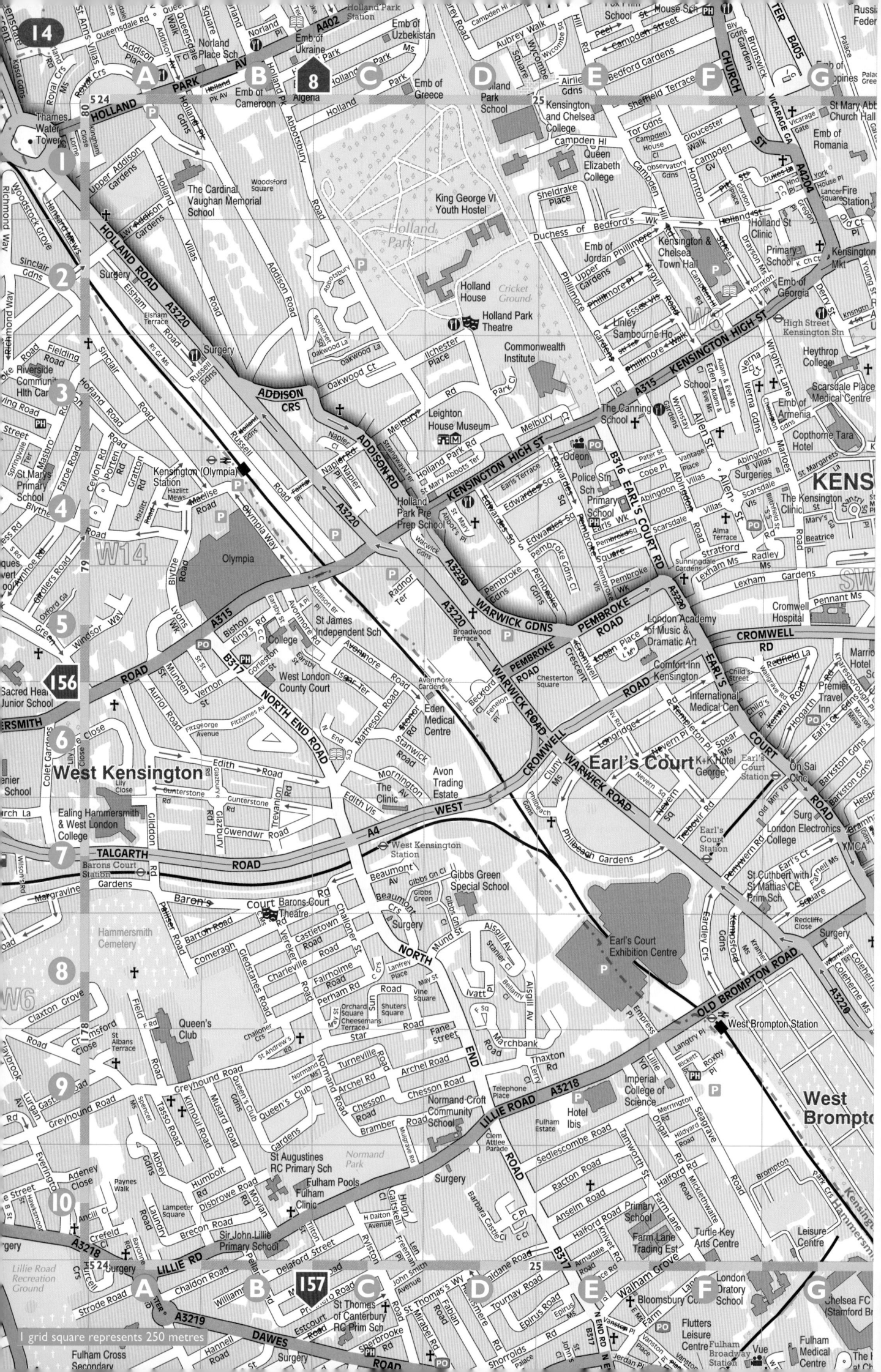

14
A
B
C
D
E
F
G
1
2
3
4
5
6
7
8
9
10
8
156
157
524
25
HOLLAND PARK AV
A402
Holland Park Station
Emb of Ukraine
Emb of Uzbekistan
Emb of Cameroon
Emb of Greece
Algeria
Norland Place Sch
Queensdale Rd
St Anns Villas
Royal Crs
Addison Place
Thames Water Tower
Upper Addison Gardens
The Cardinal Vaughan Memorial School
Woodsford Square
HOLLAND ROAD
A3220
Holland Villas Road
Addison Road
Abbotsbury Road
Holland Park School
Kensington and Chelsea College
Queen Elizabeth College
Campden Hl
Sheffield Terrace
Bedford Gardens
Aubrey Walk
Airlie Gdns
Campden Street
CHURCH ST
B405
VICARAGE GA
A4204
St Mary Abbots Church Hall
Emb of Romania
Fire Station
Holland St Clinic
Primary School
Kensington Mkt
King George VI Youth Hostel
Holland Park
Holland House
Cricket Ground
Holland Park Theatre
Sheldrake Place
Duchess of Bedford's Wk
Emb of Jordan
Upper Phillimore Gardens
Kensington & Chelsea Town Hall
Linley Sambourne Ho
Emb of Georgia
High Street Kensington Stn
Heythrop College
Scarsdale Place Medical Centre
Emb of Armenia
Copthorne Tara Hotel
KENS
Commonwealth Institute
Ilchester Place
Oakwood Ct
Melbury Rd
Leighton House Museum
Holland Park Rd
KENSINGTON HIGH ST
A315
The Canning School
Odeon
Police Stn
Sch
Primary School
Earls Terrace
Edwardes Sq
B316
EARL'S COURT RD
Abingdon Villas
Allen St
Surgeries
The Kensington Clinic
Wright's Lane
Marloes Rd
Stratford Rd
Lexham Gardens
Cromwell Hospital
Pennant Ms
Sinclair Gdns
Richmond Way
Woodstock Grove
Riverside Community Hlth Cen
Surgery
Elsham Road
Russell Gdns
ADDISON CRS
ADDISON RD
Kensington (Olympia) Station
Olympia Way
Olympia
W14
Blythe Road
Hofland Road
St Marys Primary School
Faroe Road
Ceylon Rd
Holland Park Pre Prep School
Warwick Gdns
WARWICK GDNS
PEMBROKE ROAD
Pembroke Gdns
Broadwood Terrace
London Academy of Music & Dramatic Art
Logan Place
Comfort Inn Kensington
International Medical Cen
CROMWELL RD
Marriott Hotel
Premier Travel Inn
Hogarth Road
Kenway Road
Earl's Ct Gdns
Barkston Gdns
HAMMERSMITH ROAD
A315
Sacred Heart Junior School
Bishop King's Rd
College
St James Independent Sch
West London County Court
NORTH END ROAD
B317
Avonmore Rd
Lisgar Ter
Eden Medical Centre
Matheson Road
Stanwick Road
Avon Trading Estate
Mornington Av
The Clinic
Edith Vls
West Kensington
Edith Road
Gunterstone Rd
Trevanion Rd
Gwendwr Road
Glazbury Rd
Ealing Hammersmith & West London College
Gliddon Rd
Colet Gardens
Baron's Court Station
TALGARTH ROAD
A4
WEST CROMWELL RD
West Kensington Station
Beaumont Av
Gibbs Green Special School
Surgery
Barons Court Theatre
Hammersmith Cemetery
Margravine Gardens
Barton Road
Comeragh Road
Gledstanes Road
Castletown Road
Challoner St
Charleville Road
Fairholme Road
Perham Rd
NORTH END RD
Mund St
Aisgill Av
Ivatt Pl
Marchbank Road
Thaxton Rd
Earl's Court Exhibition Centre
Earl's Court
WARWICK ROAD
Philbeach Gardens
Nevern Sq
Trebovir Rd
Earl's Court Station
K+K Hotel George
On Sai Clinic
London Electronics College
YMCA
Penywern Rd
St Cuthbert with St Mattias CE Prim Sch
Redcliffe Close
Surgery
Eardley Crs
Kempsford Gdns
OLD BROMPTON ROAD
West Brompton Station
Coleherne Rd
A3220
W6
Queen's Club
Claxton Grove
Field Rd
Greyhound Road
Star Road
Turneville Road
Archel Road
Chesson Road
Normand Croft Community School
Normand Park
Queen's Club Gardens
Tasso Road
Kinnoul Road
Musard Road
Telephone Place
LILLIE ROAD
A3218
Hotel Ibis
Imperial College of Science
Seagrave Road
West Brompton
Sedlescombe Road
Racton Road
Anselm Road
Halford Road
Primary School
Farm Lane Trading Est
Turtle Key Arts Centre
Leisure Centre
Tamworth St
Surgery
St Augustines RC Primary Sch
Fulham Pools
Fulham Clinic
Sir John Lillie Primary School
Humbolt Rd
Disbrowe Road
Moylan Rd
Brecon Road
Lampeter Square
Laundry Road
Paynes Walk
Adeney Close
Everington St
Crefeld Cl
Lillie Road Recreation Ground
LILLIE RD
A3218
Delaford Street
Chaldon Road
Strode Road
A3219
DAWES ROAD
St Thomas of Canterbury RC Prim Sch
Estcourt Road
Sherbrooke Road
Fulham Cross Secondary
Hannell Road
Tournay Road
Epirus Road
Shorrolds Rd
Walham Grove
Bloomsbury Cl
London Oratory School
Flutters Leisure Centre
Fulham Broadway Station
Vue
Fulham Medical Centre
Chelsea FC (Stamford Br
Brompton Park Crs
1 grid square represents 250 metres

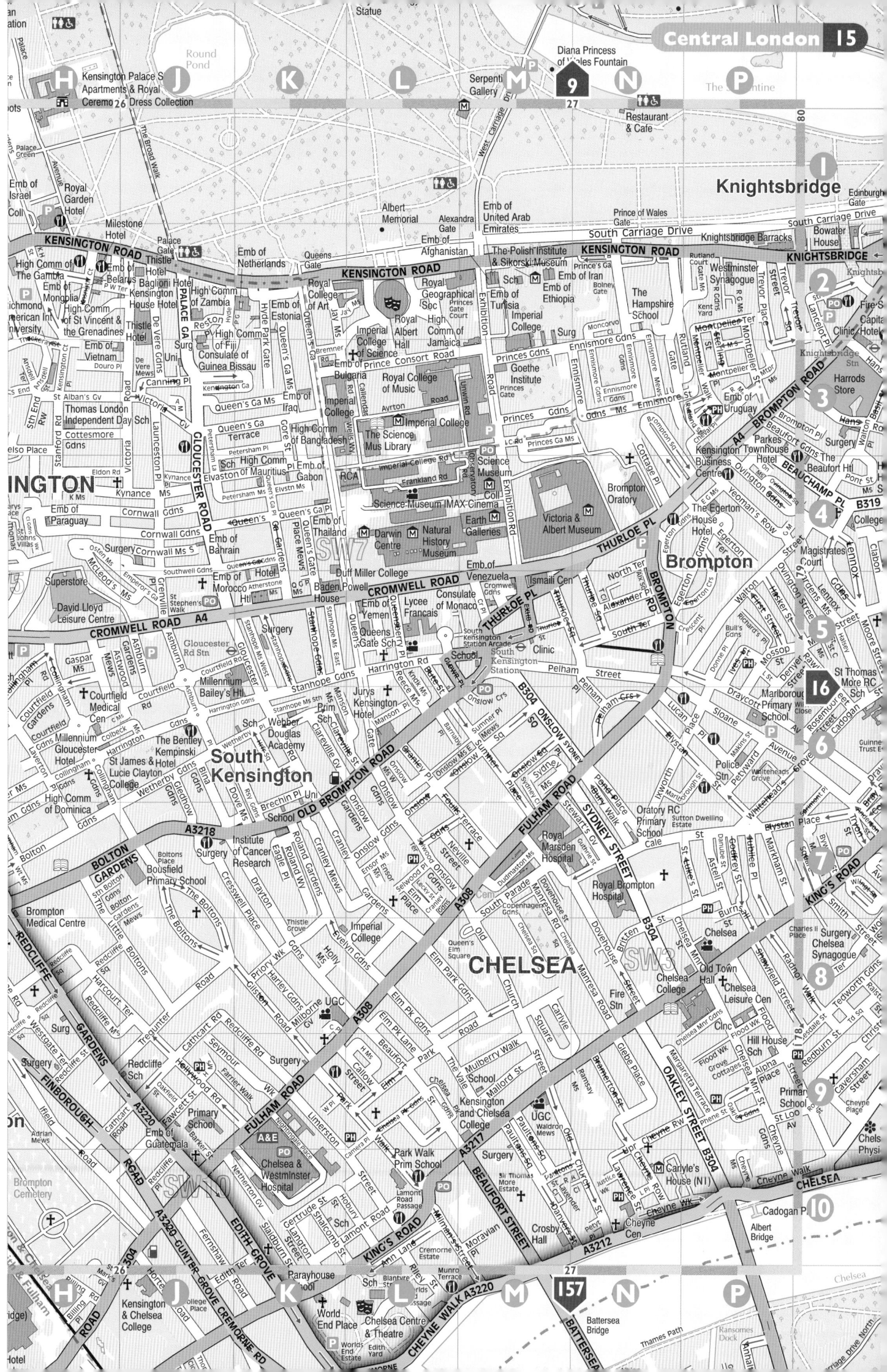
Round Pond
Statue
Diana Princess of Wales Fountain
Kensington Palace State Apartments & Royal Ceremonial Dress Collection
Serpentine Gallery
The Serpentine
Restaurant & Cafe
West Carriage Dr
The Broad Walk
Palace Green
Emb of Israel
Royal Garden Hotel
Milestone Hotel
Palace Gate
Albert Memorial
Alexandra Gate
Emb of United Arab Emirates
Prince of Wales Gate
South Carriage Drive
Knightsbridge
Edinburgh Gate
Knightsbridge Barracks
Bowater House
KNIGHTSBRIDGE
KENSINGTON ROAD
Emb of Netherlands
Queens Gate
Emb of Afghanistan
The Polish Institute & Sikorski Museum
High Comm of The Gambia
Emb of Belarus
Thistle Hotel
Baglioni Hotel
Emb of Mongolia
Kensington House Hotel
High Comm of Zambia
High Comm of St Vincent & the Grenadines
Thistle Hotel
Richmond American Int University
Emb of Estonia
Royal College of Art
Royal Geographical Soc
Royal Albert Hall
High Comm of Jamaica
Emb of Tunisia
Emb of Iran
Emb of Ethiopia
Imperial College
The Hampshire School
Westminster Synagogue
Emb of Vietnam
High Comm of Fiji
Consulate of Guinea Bissau
Imperial College of Science
Emb of Bulgaria
Prince Consort Road
Royal College of Music
Princes Gdns
Goethe Institute
Ennismore Gdns
Harrods Store
Knightsbridge Stn
Thomas London Independent Day Sch
Cottesmore Gdns
Emb of Iraq
Imperial College
The Science Mus Library
Imperial College
High Comm of Bangladesh
High Comm of Mauritius
Emb of Gabon
GLOUCESTER ROAD
Emb of Uruguay
Kensington Business Centre
Parkes Townhouse Hotel
The Beaufort Htl
BEAUCHAMP PL
KENSINGTON
Emb of Paraguay
Queen's Gate
Cornwall Gdns
RCA
Science Museum
Science Museum IMAX Cinema
Earth Galleries
Victoria & Albert Museum
Brompton Oratory
The Egerton House Hotel
THURLOE PL
Brompton
Magistrates Court
Emb of Thailand
Darwin Centre
Natural History Museum
SW7
Emb of Bahrain
Emb of Morocco
Atherstone Htl
Duff Miller College
Emb of Venezuela
Ismaili Cen
Superstore
David Lloyd Leisure Centre
CROMWELL ROAD A4
Baden Powell House
Emb of Yemen
Lycee Francais
Consulate of Monaco
Queens Gate Sch
South Kensington Station Arcade
South Kensington Station
Clinic
Gloucester Rd Stn
Millennium Bailey's Htl
Courtfield Medical Cen
Harrington Rd
Jurys Kensington Hotel
Pelham Street
St Thomas More RC Sch
Marlborough Primary School
Millennium Gloucester Hotel
The Bentley Kempinski Hotel
St James & Lucie Clayton College
Webber Douglas Academy
South Kensington
OLD BROMPTON ROAD
ONSLOW SQ
SYDNEY STREET
Police Stn
High Comm of Dominica
School
Institute of Cancer Research
Royal Marsden Hospital
Oratory RC Primary School
Sutton Dwelling Estate
KING'S ROAD
BOLTON GARDENS
Boltons Place
Bousfield Primary School
Surgery
A3218
Royal Brompton Hospital
Brompton Medical Centre
The Boltons
Imperial College
CHELSEA
SW3
Chelsea College
Old Town Hall
Chelsea Leisure Cen
Surgery
Chelsea Synagogue
REDCLIFFE GARDENS
Fire Stn
UGC
Hill House Sch
Redcliffe Sch
FULHAM ROAD
A308
Kensington and Chelsea College
OAKLEY STREET B304
FINBOROUGH ROAD
Emb of Guatemala
Primary School
A&E
Chelsea & Westminster Hospital
Park Walk Prim School
Carlyle's House (NT)
Primary School
Brompton Cemetery
SW10
A3217
BEAUFORT STREET
Crosby Hall
Cheyne Cen
A3212
Cadogan Pier
Albert Bridge
CHELSEA
Kensington & Chelsea College
Parayhouse School
World End Place
Chelsea Centre & Theatre
CHEYNE WALK A3220
Battersea Bridge
Thames Path
Ransomes Dock
Worlds End Estate
Edith Yard
CREMORNE RD
A3220 GUNTER GROVE
EDITH GROVE
Munro Terrace
Cremorne Estate
H
J
K
L
M
N
P
1
2
3
4
5
6
7
8
9
10
9
16
157
26
27
80
178
179

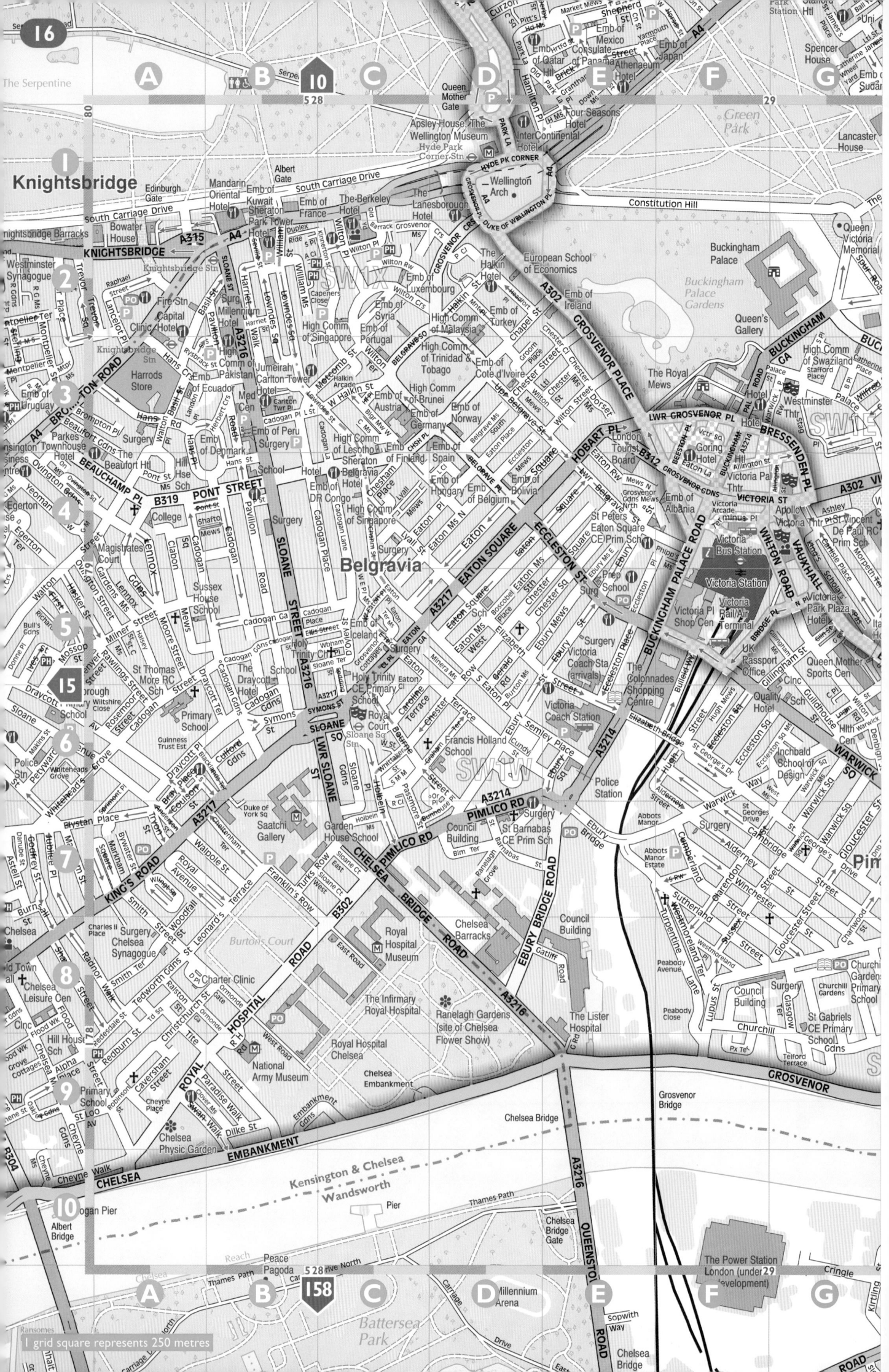
16
The Serpentine
10
A
B
C
D
E
F
G
528
29
Knightsbridge
Queen Mother Gate
Apsley House, The Wellington Museum
Hyde Park Corner Stn
HYDE PK CORNER
Wellington Arch
InterContinental Hotel
Four Seasons Hotel
Emb of Qatar
Emb of Mexico
Consulate of Panama
Emb of Japan
Athenaeum Hotel
Green Park
Lancaster House
Spencer House
Constitution Hill
Albert Gate
South Carriage Drive
Edinburgh Gate
Mandarin Oriental Hotel
Emb of Kuwait
Sheraton Park Tower Hotel
Emb of France
The Berkeley Hotel
The Lanesborough Hotel
Knightsbridge Barracks
Bowater House
KNIGHTSBRIDGE
Knightsbridge Stn
Westminster Synagogue
Fire Stn
Capital Hotel
Clinic
Surg Millennium Hotel
Harrods Store
Jumeirah Carlton Tower Hotel
High Comm of Pakistan
Emb of Ecuador
High Comm of Singapore
Emb of Syria
Emb of Portugal
Emb of Luxembourg
The Halkin Hotel
Emb of Turkey
High Comm of Malaysia
High Comm of Trinidad & Tobago
Emb of Cote d'Ivoire
European School of Economics
Emb of Ireland
GROSVENOR PLACE
Buckingham Palace
Buckingham Palace Gardens
Queen's Gallery
Queen Victoria Memorial
The Royal Mews
High Comm of Swaziland
Westminster Thtr
High Comm of Brunei
Emb of Austria
Emb of Germany
Emb of Norway
Emb of Peru
Emb of Denmark
High Comm of Lesotho
Emb of Finland
Emb of Spain
Sheraton Belgravia Hotel
Emb of DR Congo
High Comm of Singapore
Emb of Hungary
Emb of Belgium
Emb of Bolivia
London Tourist Board
Goring Hotel
Victoria Pal Thtr
Emb of Albania
Apollo Victoria Thtr
BRESSENDEN PL
VICTORIA ST
St Peters Eaton Square CE Prim Sch
Victoria Bus Station
Victoria Station
Victoria Pl Shop Cen
Victoria Rail/Air Terminal
Victoria Park Plaza Hotel
UK Passport Office
Queen Mother Sports Cen
St Vincent De Paul RC Prim Sch
Belgravia
BROMPTON ROAD
PONT STREET
SLOANE STREET
EATON SQUARE
ECCLESTON ST
BUCKINGHAM PALACE ROAD
WILTON ROAD
VAUXHALL BRIDGE RD
Beaufort Htl
Parkes Townhouse Hotel
College
Magistrates Court
Sussex House School
St Thomas More RC Sch
The Draycott Hotel
Primary School
Holy Trinity Ch
Holy Trinity CE Primary School
Royal Court
Sloane Sq Stn
Emb of Iceland
Francis Holland School
Eaton Square Sch
Prep School
Victoria Coach Sta (arrivals)
Victoria Coach Station
The Colonnades Shopping Centre
Police Station
Inchbald School of Design
Quality Hotel
Saatchi Gallery
Duke of York Sq
Garden House School
Council Building
St Barnabas CE Prim Sch
PIMLICO RD
KING'S ROAD
Surgery Chelsea Synagogue
Charter Clinic
Burtons Court
Royal Hospital Museum
The Infirmary Royal Hospital
Ranelagh Gardens (site of Chelsea Flower Show)
Chelsea Barracks
CHELSEA BRIDGE ROAD
EBURY BRIDGE ROAD
The Lister Hospital
Royal Hospital Chelsea
National Army Museum
Chelsea Embankment
Chelsea Physic Garden
Chelsea Leisure Cen
Hill House Sch
Primary School
CHELSEA EMBANKMENT
Cheyne Walk
Kensington & Chelsea
Wandsworth
Chelsea Bridge
Grosvenor Bridge
GROSVENOR
Thames Path
Pier
Chelsea Bridge Gate
QUEENSTOWN ROAD
Albert Bridge
Peace Pagoda
Battersea Park
Millennium Arena
The Power Station London (under development)
Churchill Gardens Primary School
St Gabriels CE Primary School
SW1X
SW1W
SW1E
158
15
1 grid square represents 250 metres

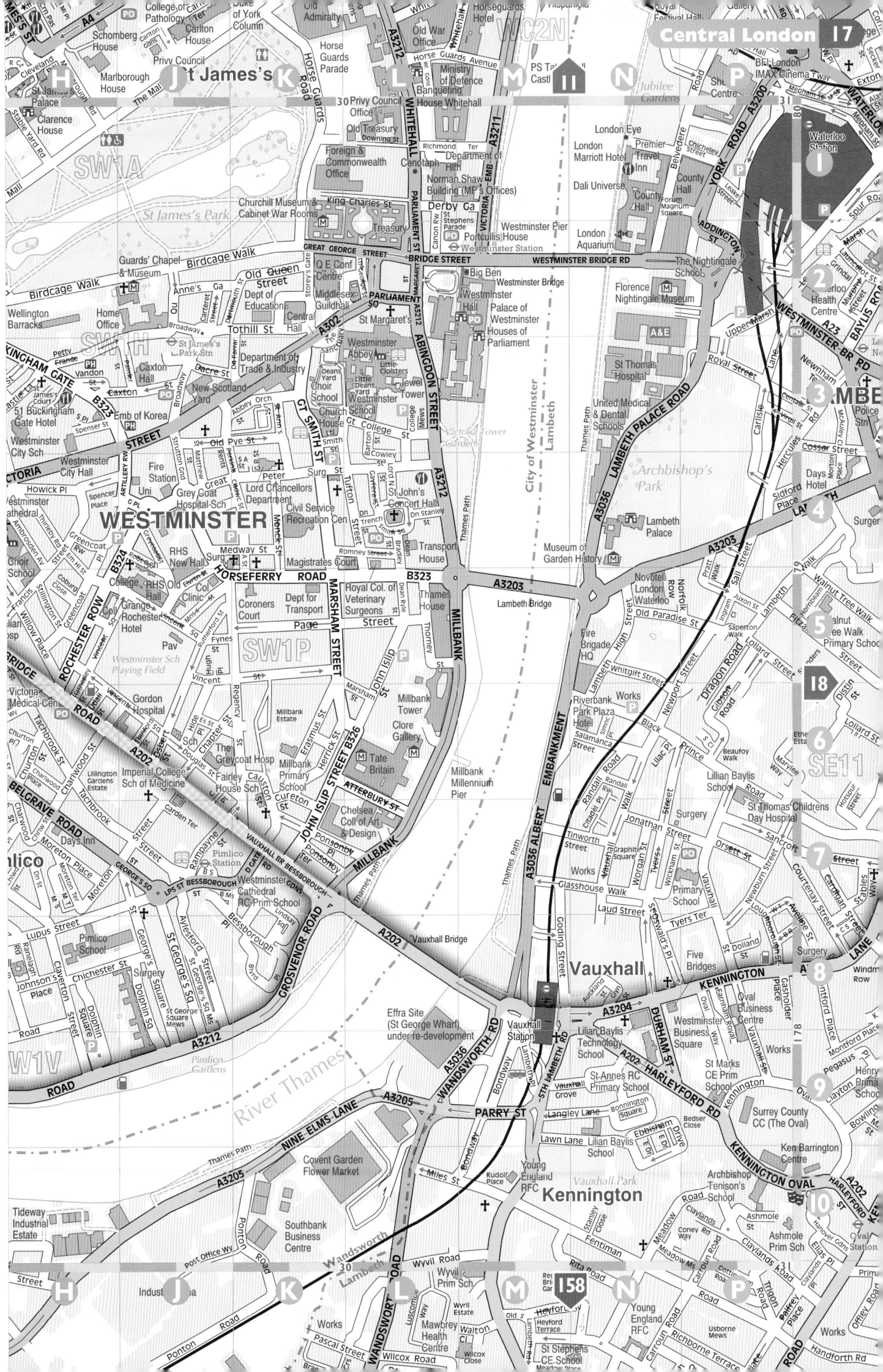
St James's
WESTMINSTER
Vauxhall
Kennington
SW1A
SW1H
SW1P
SE11
WC2N
Marlborough House
Clarence House
St James's Palace
Schomberg House
Carlton House
Privy Council
Horse Guards Parade
Old Admiralty
Old War Office
Horseguards Hotel
Ministry of Defence
Banqueting House Whitehall
Privy Council Office
Old Treasury
Foreign & Commonwealth Office
Cenotaph
Department of Hlth
Norman Shaw Building (MP's Offices)
Churchill Museum & Cabinet War Rooms
Treasury
Derby Ga
Portcullis House
Westminster Station
Westminster Pier
London Eye
London Marriott Hotel
Dali Universe
London Aquarium
Premier Travel Inn
County Hall
Jubilee Gardens
Waterloo Station
BFI London IMAX Cinema
St James's Park
Birdcage Walk
Guards' Chapel & Museum
Wellington Barracks
Home Office
Old Queen Street
Dept of Education
Q E Conf Centre
Middlesex Guildhall
Central Hall
Big Ben
Westminster Bridge
Westminster Hall
Palace of Westminster Houses of Parliament
Parliament Sq
St Margaret's
Westminster Abbey
Jewel Tower
Westminster School
Department of Trade & Industry
New Scotland Yard
Caxton Hall
St James's Park Stn
Tothill St
Broadway
Buckingham Gate
51 Buckingham Gate Hotel
Emb of Korea
Westminster City Sch
Westminster City Hall
Victoria Street
Fire Station
Grey Coat Hospital Sch
Lord Chancellors Department
Civil Service Recreation Cen
St John's Concert Hall
Smith Sq
Transport House
Victoria Tower Gardens
Abingdon Street
Millbank
Great George Street
Bridge Street
Westminster Bridge Rd
Florence Nightingale Museum
The Nightingale School
St Thomas' Hospital
A&E
United Medical & Dental Schools
Lambeth Palace Road
Archbishop's Park
Lambeth Palace
Museum of Garden History
City of Westminster
Lambeth
Thames Path
Horseferry Road
Magistrates Court
Royal Col. of Veterinary Surgeons
Thames House
Lambeth Bridge
Coroners Court
Dept for Transport
Marsham Street
Page Street
John Islip St
Millbank Tower
Clore Gallery
Tate Britain
Millbank Estate
Millbank Primary School
Chelsea Coll of Art & Design
Atterbury St
Millbank Millennium Pier
Rochester Row
Grange Rochester Hotel
Westminster Sch Playing Field
Gordon Hospital
Vauxhall Bridge Road
Victoria Medical Cen
Imperial College Sch of Medicine
The Greycoat Hosp
Fairley House Sch
Lillington Gardens Estate
Belgrave Road
Days Inn
Pimlico
Pimlico Station
Westminster Cathedral RC Prim School
Bessborough Gdns
Grosvenor Road
Vauxhall Bridge
Pimlico School
Lupus Street
St George's Square
Pimlico Gardens
River Thames
Effra Site (St George Wharf) under re-development
Vauxhall Station
Wandsworth Rd
Nine Elms Lane
Parry St
Covent Garden Flower Market
Tideway Industrial Estate
Southbank Business Centre
Ponton Road
Post Office Wy
Albert Embankment
Novotel London Waterloo
Fire Brigade HQ
Old Paradise St
Lambeth High Street
Riverbank Park Plaza Hotel
Black Prince Rd
Lillian Baylis School
St Thomas' Childrens Day Hospital
Glasshouse Walk
Kennington Lane
Lilian Baylis Technology School
St Annes RC Primary School
Harleyford Rd
Durham St
Westminster Business Square
Oval Business Centre
St Marks CE Prim School
Surrey County CC (The Oval)
Ken Barrington Centre
Kennington Oval
Oval Station
Archbishop Tenison's School
Ashmole Prim Sch
Young England RFC
Vauxhall Park
Wyvil Road
Wyvil Prim Sch
Mawbrey Health Centre
St Stephens CE School
Fentiman
Kennington Road
Cosser Street
Days Hotel
Lambeth Police Stn
A3212
A3211
A302
A3203
A3036
A202
A3205
A3204
A23
A4
B323
B324
B326
B s
158
18

18
12
17
159
A
B
C
D
E
F
G
1
2
3
4
5
6
7
8
9
10
LAMBETH
Newington
The Borough
Walworth
SE1
SE11
SE17
Waterloo Station
Imperial War Museum
Elephant and Castle Stn
Lambeth North Stn
Kennington Station
Oval Station
Borough Stn
Surrey County CC (The Oval)
Kennington Park
WATERLOO RD
WESTMINSTER BR RD
BOROUGH ROAD
NEW KENT ROAD
KENNINGTON ROAD
KENNINGTON LANE
KENNINGTON PARK ROAD
WALWORTH ROAD
CAMBERWELL NEW ROAD
BOROUGH HIGH ST
UNION
1 grid square represents 250 metres

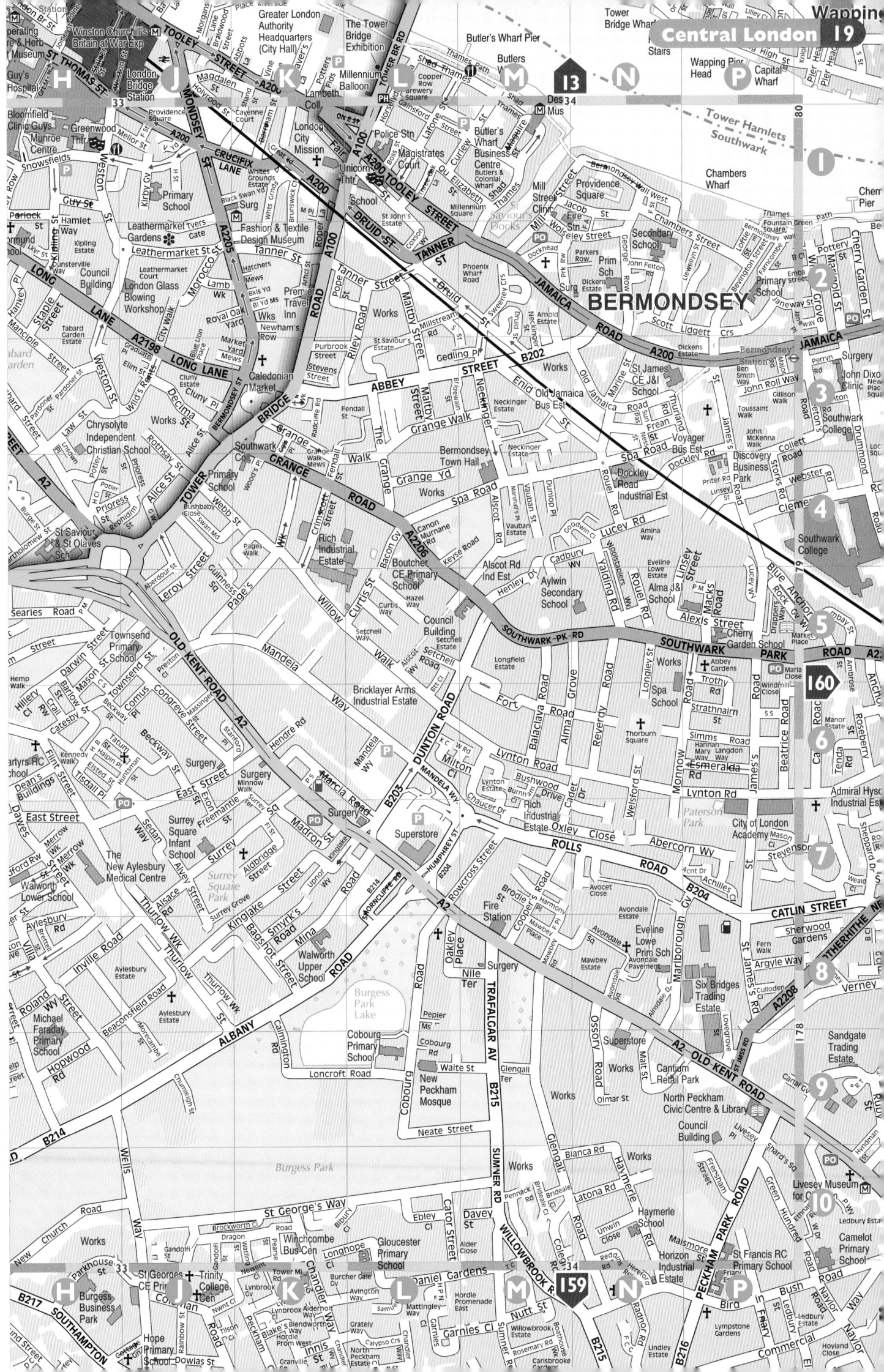

Central London 19
Wapping
Tower Bridge Wharf
Butler's Wharf Pier
Wapping Pier Head
Capital Wharf
Greater London Authority Headquarters (City Hall)
The Tower Bridge Exhibition
Winston Churchill's Britain at War Exp
London Bridge Station
Guy's Hospital
TOOLEY STREET
Millennium Balloon
Lambeth Coll
Copper Row Brewery Square
Butlers Wharf
Des Mus
Tower Hamlets
Southwark
Chambers Wharf
Cherry Pier
Bloomfield Clinic
Guys Munroe Centre
Greenwood Thtr
Providence Square
London City Mission
Police Stn
Magistrates Court
Unicorn Thtr
Butler's Wharf Business Centre
Mill Street Clinic
Jacob Fire Stn
Secondary School
Snowsfields
CRUCIFIX LANE
Primary School
Leathermarket Gardens
Fashion & Textile Design Museum
Tanner St
DRUID ST
TANNER ST
JAMAICA ROAD
BERMONDSEY
Council Building
London Glass Blowing Workshop
LONG LANE
A2198
Premier Travel Inn
Phoenix Wharf Road
Prim Sch
Surg
Primary School
Caledonian Market
ABBEY STREET
Works
St James CE J&I School
Old Jamaica Bus Est
Bermondsey Station
Surgery
John Dixon Clinic
Southwark College
Chrysolyte Independent Christian School
Southwark Coll
GRANGE ROAD
Bermondsey Town Hall
Grange Walk
Voyager Bus Est
Discovery Business Park
Dockley Road Industrial Est
Rich Industrial Estate
Boutcher CE Primary School
Alscot Rd Ind Est
Aylwin Secondary School
Alma J&I School
Alexis Street
Cherry Garden School
St Saviour & St Olaves Sch
OLD KENT ROAD
A2
Townsend Primary School
Council Building
SOUTHWARK PK RD
SOUTHWARK PARK ROAD
160
Bricklayer Arms Industrial Estate
Spa School
DUNTON ROAD
Mandela Way
Surgery
Surrey Square Infant School
Superstore
Rich Industrial Estate
City of London Academy
Paterson Park
Admiral Hyson Industrial Est
The New Aylesbury Medical Centre
Walworth Lower School
Surrey Square Park
ROLLS ROAD
Fire Station
Eveline Lowe Prim Sch
CATLIN STREET
Walworth Upper School
Burgess Park Lake
Six Bridges Trading Estate
Sandgate Trading Estate
Michael Faraday Primary School
ALBANY ROAD
Cobourg Primary School
Superstore
Cantium Retail Park
New Peckham Mosque
TRAFALGAR AV
North Peckham Civic Centre & Library
Council Building
Burgess Park
SUMNER RD
Livesey Museum
St George's Way
Haymerle School
Winchcombe Bus Cen
Gloucester Primary School
Horizon Industrial Estate
St Francis RC Primary School
Camelot Primary School
PECKHAM PARK ROAD
St Georges CE Pri
Trinity College Cen
Burgess Business Park
159
Hope Primary School
SOUTHAMPTON

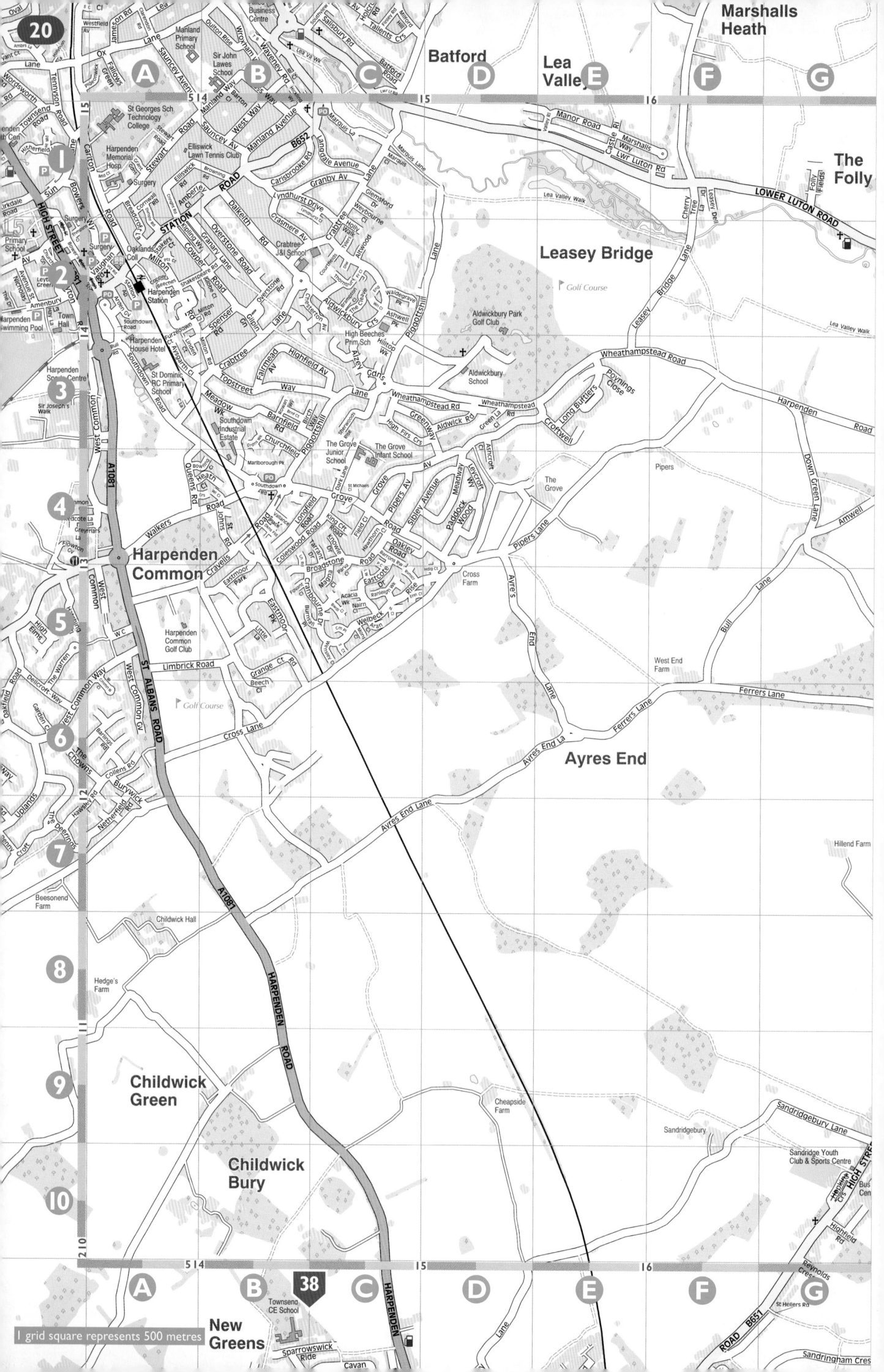
Marshalls Heath
Batford
Lea Valley
The Folly
LOWER LUTON ROAD
Leasey Bridge
Golf Course
Aldwickbury Park Golf Club
Aldwickbury School
Wheathampstead Road
Harpenden Road
Pipers
The Grove
Cross Farm
Harpenden Common
Harpenden Common Golf Club
Golf Course
Ayres End
Ayres End Lane
Ferrers Lane
West End Farm
Hillend Farm
Childwick Hall
Hedge's Farm
Childwick Green
Childwick Bury
Cheapside Farm
Sandridgebury
Sandridgebury Lane
Sandridge Youth Club & Sports Centre
HIGH STREET
ROAD B651
New Greens
Townsend CE School
Sparrowswick Ride
HARPENDEN ROAD
ST ALBANS ROAD
A1081
HIGH STREET
STATION ROAD
Harpenden Station
St Georges Sch Technology College
Harpenden Memorial Hosp
Oaklands Coll
Harpenden House Hotel
St Dominic RC Primary School
Southdown Industrial Estate
The Grove Junior School
The Grove Infant School
High Beeches Prim Sch
Crabtree J&I School
Sir John Lawes School
Manland Primary School
Harpenden Sports Centre
Harpenden Swimming Pool
Town Hall
Beesonend Farm
A B C D E F G
1 2 3 4 5 6 7 8 9 10
38
1 grid square represents 500 metres

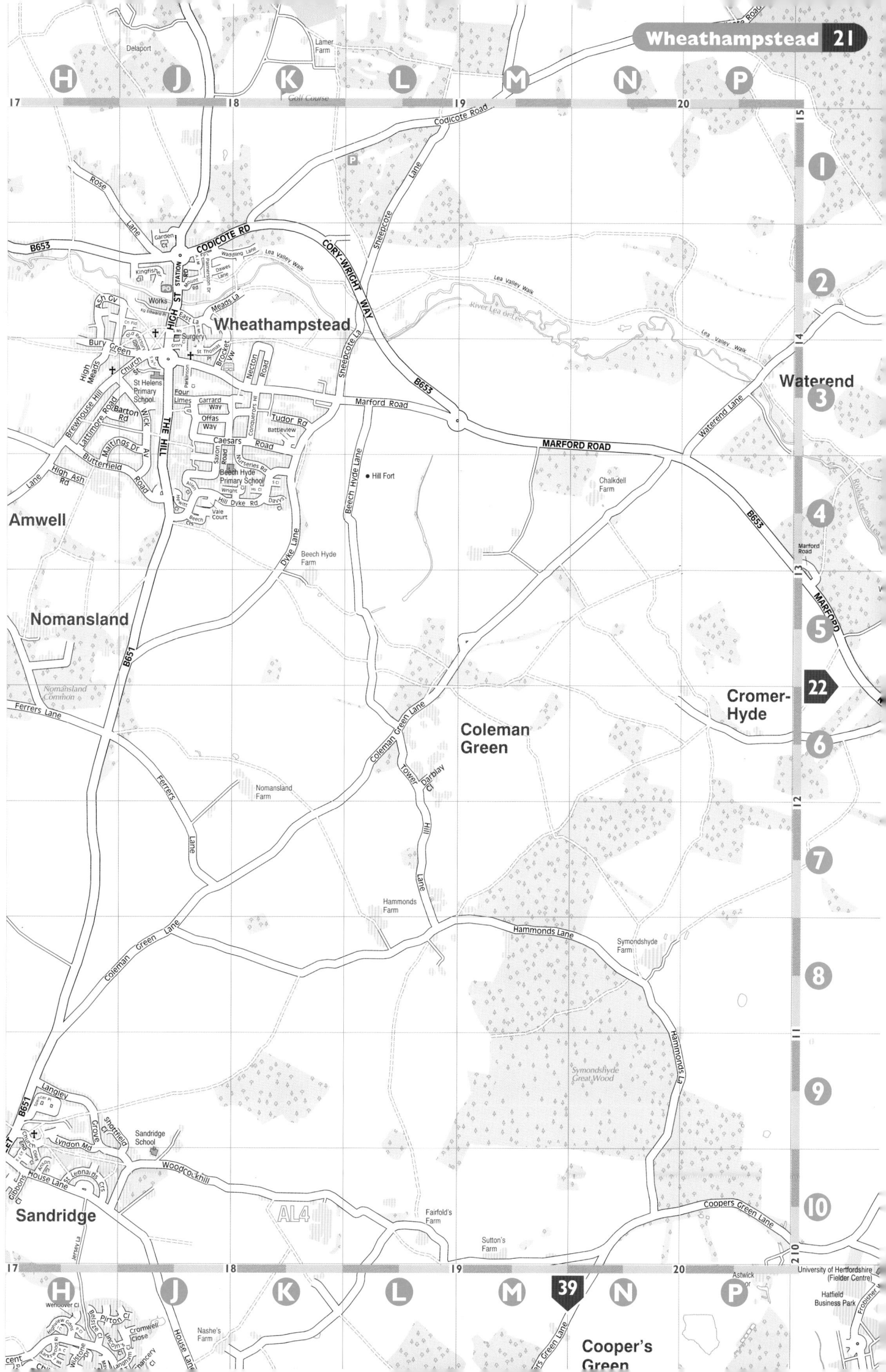
Wheathampstead
Waterend
Amwell
Nomansland
Cromer-Hyde
Coleman Green
Sandridge
Cooper's Green
Delaport
Lamer Farm
Golf Course
Codicote Road
Sheepcote Lane
CODICOTE RD
B653
CORY-WRIGHT WAY
Lea Valley Walk
River Lea or Lee
Marford Road
MARFORD ROAD
Waterend Lane
Beech Hyde Lane
Hill Fort
Chalkdell Farm
Beech Hyde Farm
Dyke Lane
B651
Nomansland Common
Ferrers Lane
Coleman Green Lane
Tower Hill Lane
Darblay Cl
Nomansland Farm
Hammonds Farm
Hammonds Lane
Symondshyde Farm
Symondshyde Great Wood
Hammonds La
Coopers Green Lane
Fairfold's Farm
Sutton's Farm
Sandridge School
Woodcock Hill
House Lane
Langley Grove
Lyndon Md
Shottfield
Jersey La
AL4
Nashe's Farm
University of Hertfordshire (Fielder Centre)
Hatfield Business Park
Marford Road
St Helens Primary School
Beech Hyde Primary School
High Ash Rd
Butterfield Road
Brewhouse Hill
Lattimore Road
Barton Rd
Maltings Dr
Wick Av
THE HILL
HIGH ST
STATION RD
Church St
Bury Green
High Meads
Ash Gv
Works
Surgery
Meads La
East La
Brocket Vw
Necton Road
Garrard Way
Offas Way
Caesars Road
Tudor Rd
Battleview
Conquerors Hl
Saxon Road
Nurseries Rd
Four Limes
Hill Dyke Rd
Davys Cl
Vale Court
Beech Crs
Garden Ct
Kingfisher Cl
Dawes Lane
Waddling Lane
Lea Valley Walk
39
22

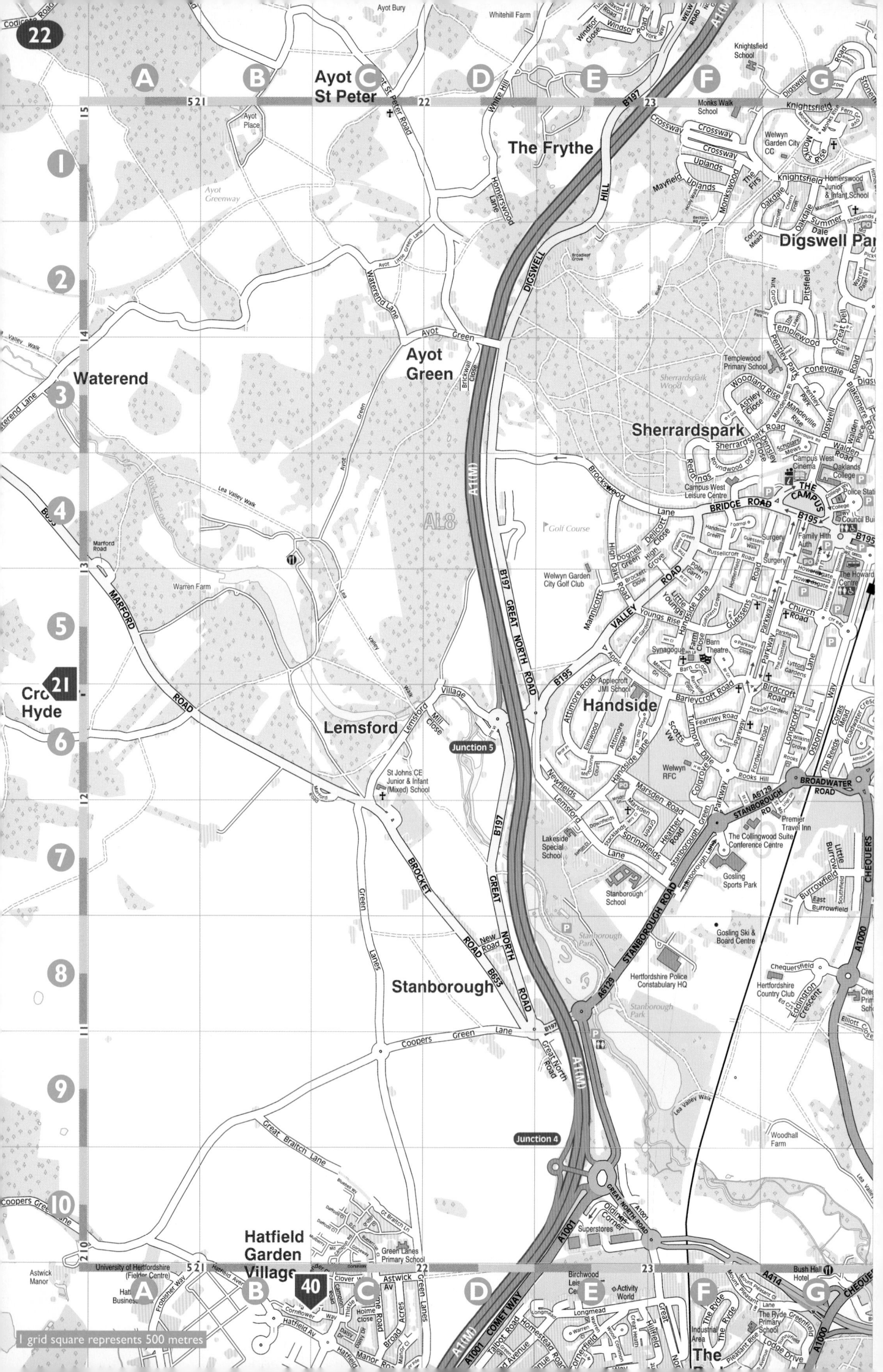
Ayot St Peter
The Frythe
Ayot Green
Waterend
Sherrardspark
Digswell Park
Handside
Lemsford
Stanborough
Hatfield Garden Village
Junction 5
Junction 4
A1(M)
GREAT NORTH ROAD
DIGSWELL HILL
BROCKET ROAD
MARFORD ROAD
VALLEY ROAD
STANBOROUGH ROAD
BRIDGE ROAD
Lea Valley Walk
Welwyn Garden City Golf Club
Golf Course
Sherrardspark Wood
Stanborough Park
Hertfordshire Police Constabulary HQ
Gosling Sports Park
Gosling Ski & Board Centre
Hertfordshire Country Club
Campus West Leisure Centre
Campus West Cinema
Oaklands College
Welwyn RFC
Stanborough School
Lakeside Special School
Applecroft JMI School
St Johns CE Junior & Infant (Mixed) School
Templewood Primary School
Knightsfield School
Monks Walk School
Homerswood Junior & Infant School
Welwyn Garden City CC
The Collingwood Suite Conference Centre
Premier Travel Inn
Green Lanes Primary School
Woodhall Farm
Warren Farm
Ayot Bury
Whitehill Farm
Ayot Place
Ayot Greenway
Coopers Green Lane
Great Braitch Lane
Green Lanes
Superstores
Oldings Corner
University of Hertfordshire (Fielder Centre)
Astwick Manor
Bush Hall Hotel
Activity World
AL8
21
40
1 grid square represents 500 metres

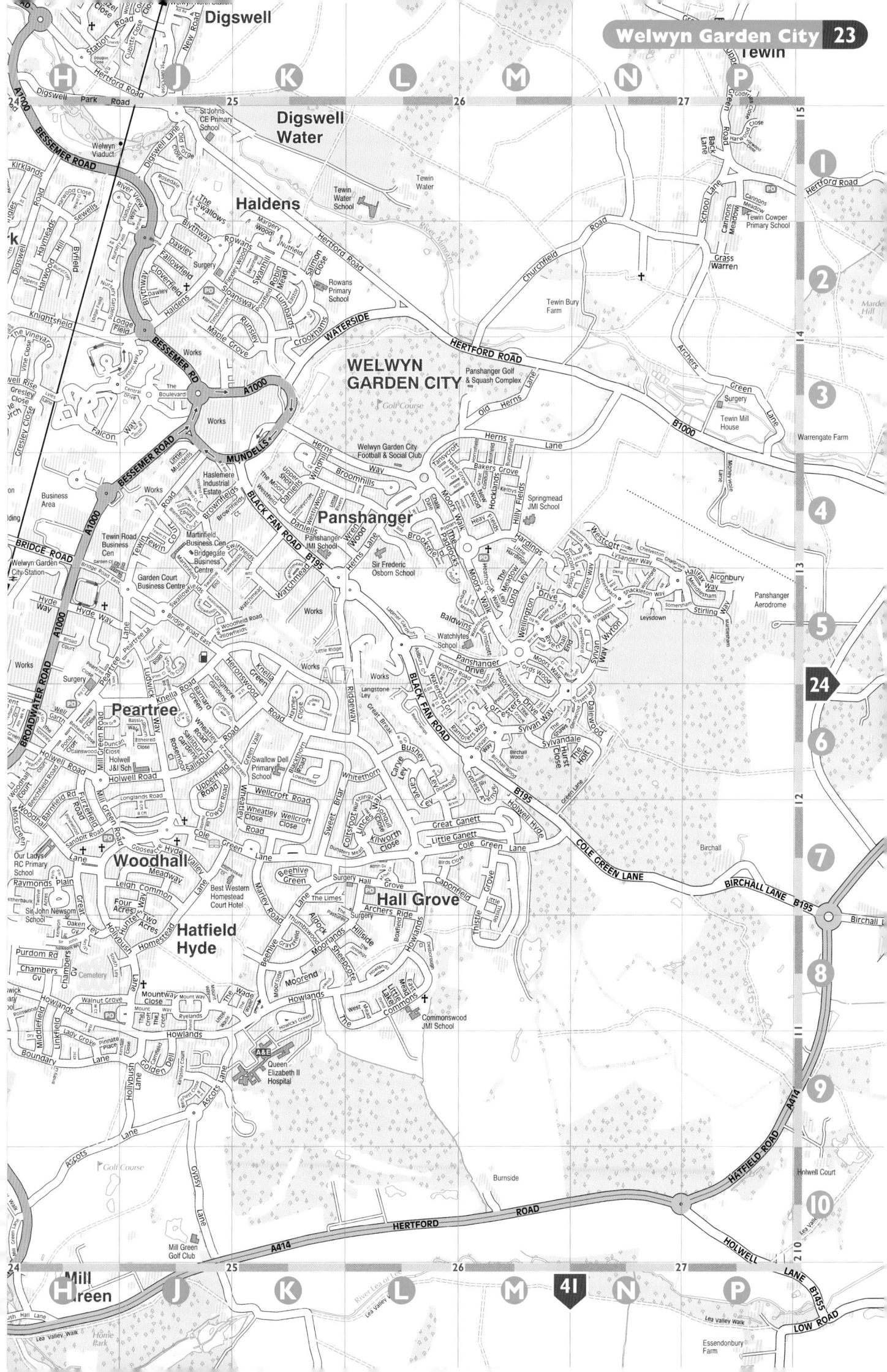
Digswell
Tewin
Digswell Water
Haldens
Tewin Water
Tewin Water School
River Mimram
St Johns CE Primary School
Welwyn Viaduct
Rowans Primary School
Tewin Bury Farm
Tewin Cowper Primary School
Grass Warren
WELWYN GARDEN CITY
Panshanger Golf & Squash Complex
Golf Course
Welwyn Garden City Football & Social Club
Tewin Mill House
Warrengate Farm
Panshanger
Panshanger JMI School
Sir Frederic Osborn School
Springmead JMI School
Panshanger Aerodrome
Haslemere Industrial Estate
Business Area
Tewin Road Business Cen
Martinfield Business Cen
Bridgegate Business Centre
Garden Court Business Centre
Welwyn Garden City Station
Watchlytes School
Leysdown
Peartree
Holwell J&I Sch
Swallow Dell Primary School
Woodhall
Our Ladys RC Primary School
Sir John Newsom School
Best Western Homestead Court Hotel
Hatfield Hyde
Hall Grove
Commonswood JMI School
Queen Elizabeth II Hospital
Cemetery
Birchall
Burnside
Holwell Court
Mill Green Golf Club
Mill Green
Home Park
Essendonbury Farm
River Lea or Lee
A1000
BESSEMER ROAD
BROADWATER ROAD
BRIDGE ROAD
HERTFORD ROAD
B1000
BLACK FAN ROAD
B195
COLE GREEN LANE
BIRCHALL LANE B195
HATFIELD ROAD
A414
HERTFORD ROAD
HOLWELL LANE B1455
LOW ROAD
AL7
24
41

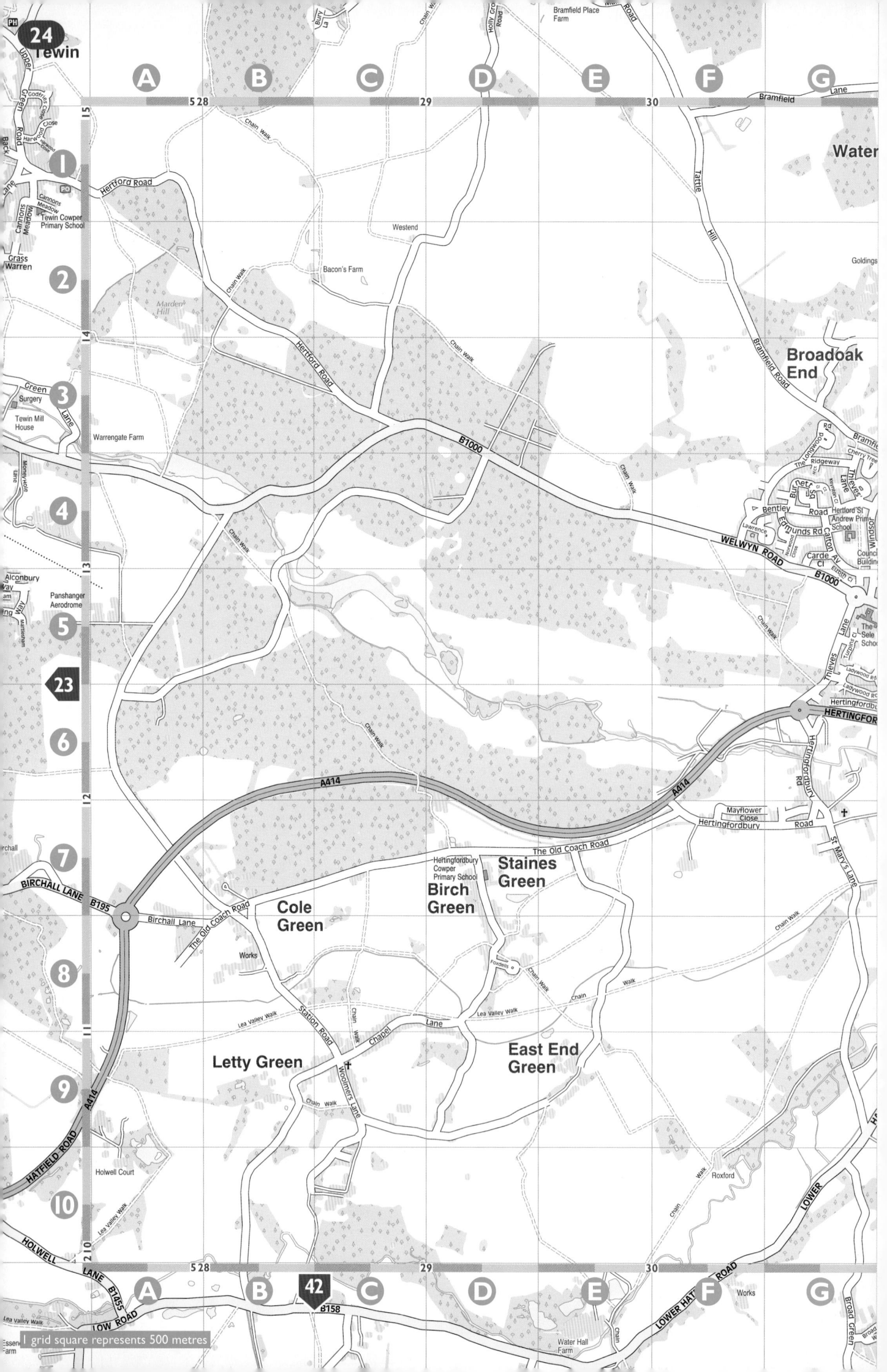

24
Tewin
A
B
C
D
E
F
G
528
29
30
Bramfield Place Farm
Bramfield Lane
Water
Hertford Road
Tewin Cowper Primary School
Grass Warren
Westend
Bacon's Farm
Marden Hill
Chain Walk
Tattle Hill
Bramfield Road
Broadoak End
Goldings
Surgery
Tewin Mill House
Warrengate Farm
B1000
Welwyn Road
Panshanger Aerodrome
Alconbury Way
23
A414
Hertingfordbury Road
Mayflower Close
St Mary's Lane
The Old Coach Road
Hertingfordbury Cowper Primary School
Staines Green
Birch Green
Cole Green
Birchall Lane
B195
Works
Foxdells
Lea Valley Walk
Station Road
Chapel Lane
Letty Green
East End Green
Woolmers Lane
Hatfield Road
Holwell Court
Roxford
Holwell Lane
B1455
Low Road
B158
42
Lower Hatfield Road
Water Hall Farm
Broad Green
1 grid square represents 500 metres

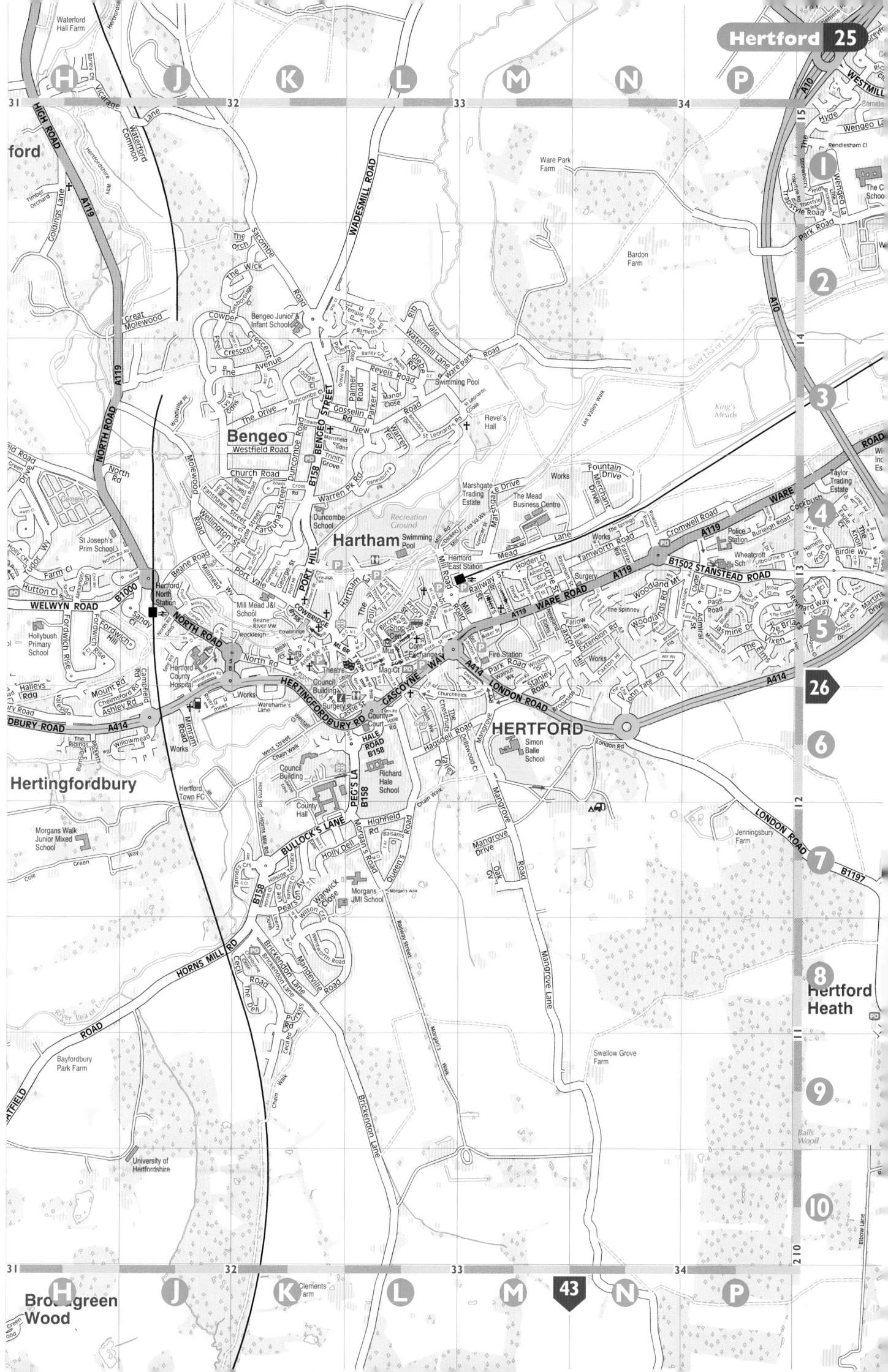

H
J
K
L
M
N
P
31
32
33
34
Waterford Hall Farm
HIGH ROAD
Vicarage
Waterford Common
Lane
Timber Orchard
Goldings Lane
A119
WADESMILL ROAD
Sacombe
Road
The Wick
Ware Park Farm
Bardon Farm
Great Molewood
Bengeo Junior & Infant School
Temple Flds
Bartletts Md
Rib Vale
Watermill Lane
Glebe Rd
Ware Park Road
Swimming Pool
Cowper
Crescent
Peel Crescent
The Avenue
Lodge Cl
Palmer Road
Parker Av
Revels Road
Manor Close
Duncombe Cl
The Drive
Gosselin Rd
New Road
Warren Ter
St Leonard's Rd
Revel's Hall
Lea Valley Walk
River Lea or Lee
King's Meads
NORTH ROAD
Bengeo
Westfield Road
BENGEO STREET
Church Road
Trinity Grove
Warren Pk Rd
Molewood
Duncombe Road
Farquhar Street
Fanshawe Street
Wellington St
Byde Street
Duncombe School
Recreation Ground
Hartham
Swimming Pool
PORT HILL
Marshgate Trading Estate
Marshgate Drive
The Mead Business Centre
Works
Fountain Drive
Merchant Drive
Mead Lane
Tamworth Road
Cromwell Road
Police Station
Burleigh Road
Cockbush
Taylor Trading Estate
North Rd
Cemetery
Tudor Wy
St Joseph's Prim School
Farm Cl
Hutton Cl
WELWYN ROAD
B1000
Hertford North Station
Beane Road
Port Vale
Mill Mead J&I School
Beane River Vw
Rockleigh
Hertford East Station
Railway St
Holden Cl
Surgery
A119
WARE ROAD
B1502 STANSTEAD ROAD
Woodland Mt
Wheatcroft Sch
Birdie Wy
Hollybush Primary School
Fordwich Rise
Fordwich Hill
NORTH ROAD
North Rd
COWBRIDGE
The Folly
Theatre
Council Building
Surgery
Castle St
Mus
Corn Exchange
Fire Station
Park Road
Fallow Rd
Caxton Hill
Extension Rd
Woodlands Rd
Jasmine Dr
Admiral St
Page Road
The Spinney
Hertford County Hospital
Campfield Rd
Mount Rd
Chelmsford Rd
Ashley Rd
Halleys Rdg
Valeside
A414
BURY ROAD
Works
Wareham's Lane
HERTINGFORDBURY RD
GASCOYNE WAY
LONDON ROAD
Stanley Road
Brookside
John Tate Rd
A414
The Ridings
Willowmead
Mimram Road
Works
West Street
Chain Walk
County Court
HALE ROAD
B158
Hagsdell Road
The Chestnuts
Dellswood Cl
Mangrove
HERTFORD
Simon Balle School
London Rd
Hertingfordbury
Hertford Town FC
Council Building
County Hall
PEG'S LA
B158
Richard Hale School
Chain Walk
Highfield Rd
Balsams Cl
Queen's Road
Mangrove Drive
Mangrove Road
Oak Gv
Jenningsbury Farm
LONDON ROAD
B1197
Morgans Walk Junior Mixed School
Green Way
Cole
BULLOCK'S LANE
Holly Dell
Morgan's Road
Hillside Terrace
Pearson Av
Warwick Close
Morgans JMI School
B158
Railway Street
Wilton Crs
Wentworth Road
HORNS MILL RD
Cecil Road
The Dell
Brickendon Lane
Mandeville Road
Purkiss Rd
Cecil Rd
River Lea or Lee
ROAD
Morgan's Walk
Mangrove Lane
Hertford Heath
Swallow Grove Farm
Bayfordbury Park Farm
HERTFIELD
Chain Walk
Brickendon Lane
University of Hertfordshire
Balls Wood
Elbow Lane
Hyde
Wengeo La
Rendlesham Cl
Trapstyle Road
Park Road
WESTMILL
A10
Clements Farm
Broadgreen Wood
1
2
3
4
5
6
7
8
9
10
15
14
13
12
11
210

26
43

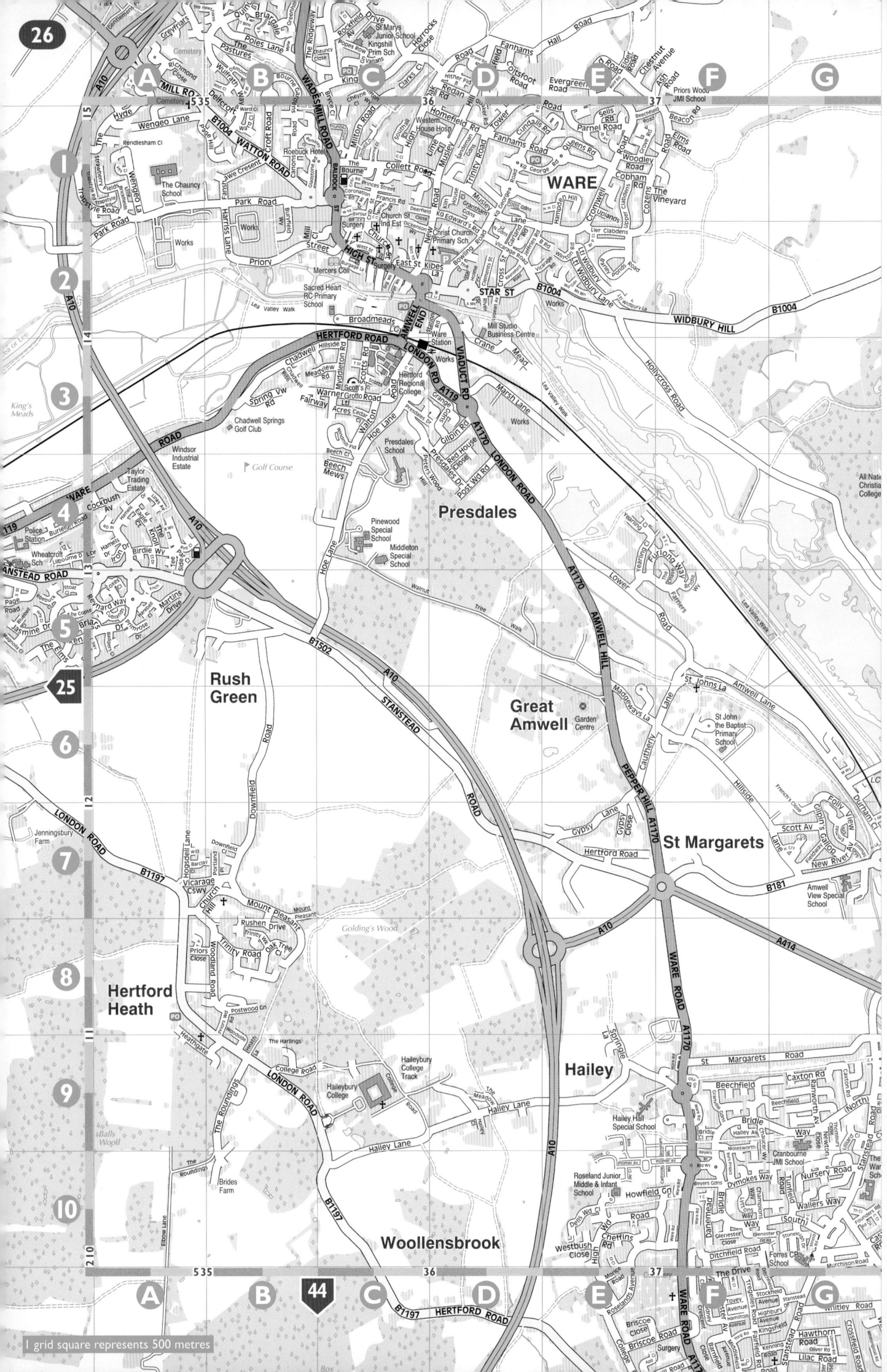
WARE
Presdales
Rush Green
Great Amwell
St Margarets
Hertford Heath
Hailey
Woollensbrook
King's Meads
MILL ROAD
Cemetery
Wengeo Lane
B1004 WATTON ROAD
WADESMILL ROAD
BALDOCK ST
The Chauncy School
Park Road
Priory
Works
HIGH ST
East St
Kibes La
STAR ST
B1004
WIDBURY HILL
Widbury Lane
Hollycross Road
Lea Valley Walk
Broadmeads
AMWELL END
Ware Station
HERTFORD ROAD
LONDON RD A119
VIADUCT RD
Crane Mead
Mill Studio Business Centre
Sacred Heart RC Primary School
Mercers Coll
Hertford Regional College
Chadwell Springs Golf Club
Golf Course
Windsor Industrial Estate
Taylor Trading Estate
Police Station
Wheatcroft Sch
STANSTEAD ROAD
Marsh Lane
Presdales School
Pinewood Special School
Middleton Special School
Hoe Lane
Walnut Tree Walk
A1170 LONDON ROAD
A1170 AMWELL HILL
PEPPER HILL A1170
Lower Road
Amwell Lane
St Johns La
Madgeways La
St John the Baptist Primary School
Garden Centre
Cautherly Lane
Hillside
Gypsy Lane
Hertford Road
New River
B181
Amwell View Special School
A414
A10
B1502
STANSTEAD ROAD
Downfield Road
LONDON ROAD
B1197
Jenningsbury Farm
Mount Pleasant
Golding's Wood
Rushen Drive
Trinity Road
Woodland Road
Priors Close
Postwood Gn
Heathgate
College Road
Haileybury College
Haileybury College Track
Hailey Lane
The Roundings
Brides Farm
Balls Wood
Elbow Lane
WARE ROAD A1170
St Margarets Road
Hailey Hall Special School
Roseland Junior Middle & Infant School
Howfield Gn
Cranbourne JMI School
Nursery Road
Wallers Way
Ditchfield Road
Forres CP School
The Drive
B1197 HERTFORD ROAD
Briscoe Road
Surgery
Priors Wood JMI School
All Nations Christian College
A B C D E F G
1 2 3 4 5 6 7 8 9 10
535 36 37
15 14 13 12 11 210
25
44
1 grid square represents 500 metres

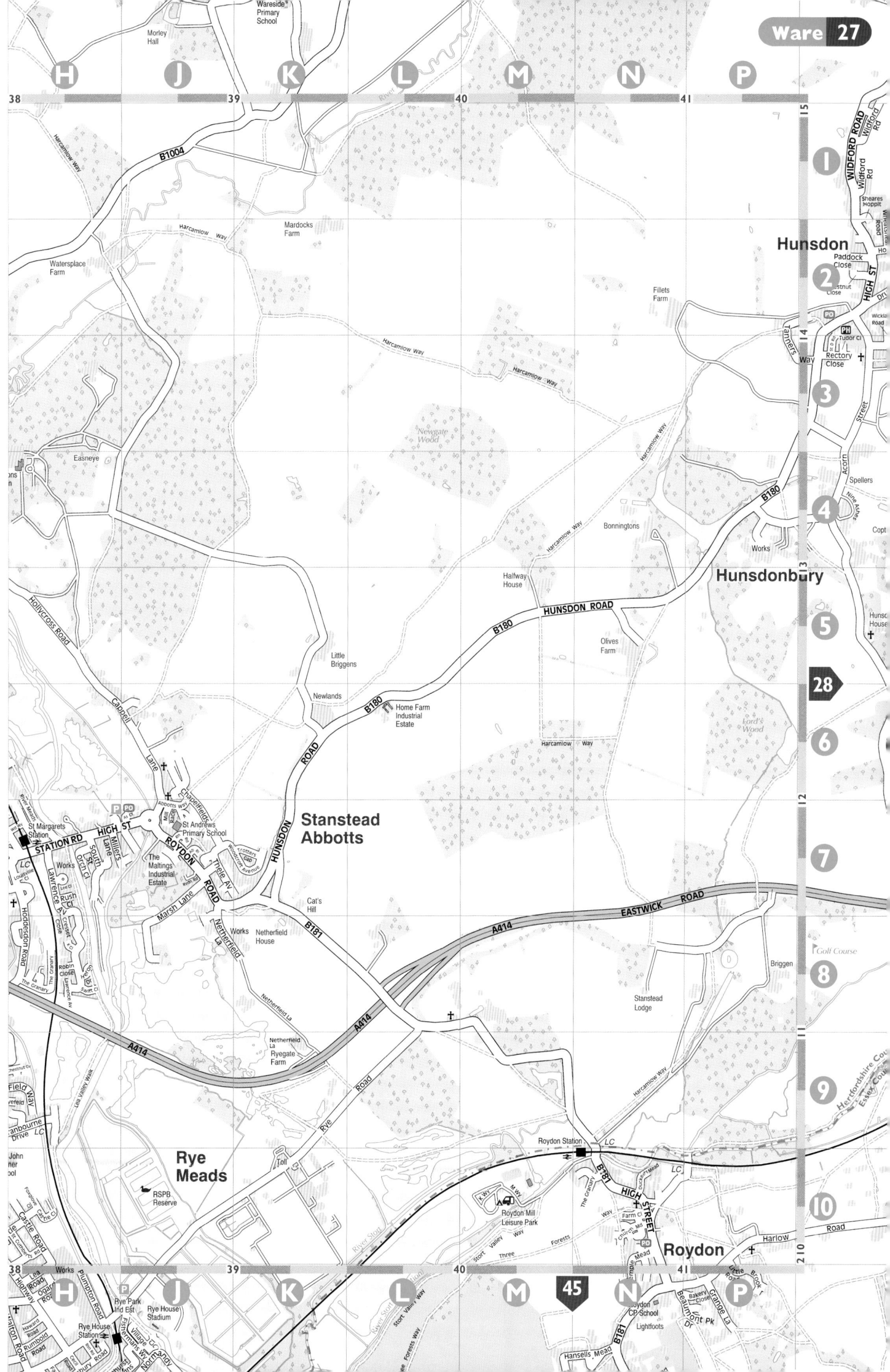
Wareside Primary School
Morley Hall
B1004
Harcamlow Way
Mardocks Farm
Watersplace Farm
Hunsdon
Paddock Close
Fillets Farm
Newgate Wood
Easneye
B180
Bonningtons
Hunsdonbury
Halfway House
HUNSDON ROAD
Olives Farm
Hollycross Road
Little Briggens
Newlands
Home Farm Industrial Estate
Lord's Wood
Stanstead Abbotts
St Margarets Station
STATION RD
HIGH ST
St Andrews Primary School
ROYDON ROAD
The Maltings Industrial Estate
HUNSDON ROAD
Cat's Hill
B181
EASTWICK ROAD
A414
Works
Netherfield House
Stanstead Lodge
Briggen
Golf Course
Netherfield La
Ryegate Farm
Rye Road
Rye Meads
RSPB Reserve
Roydon Station
Roydon Mill Leisure Park
HIGH STREET
Roydon
Harlow Road
Rye Park Ind Est
Rye House Stadium
Rye House Station
Roydon CP School
Lightfoots
Hertfordshire County
Essex County

28
45

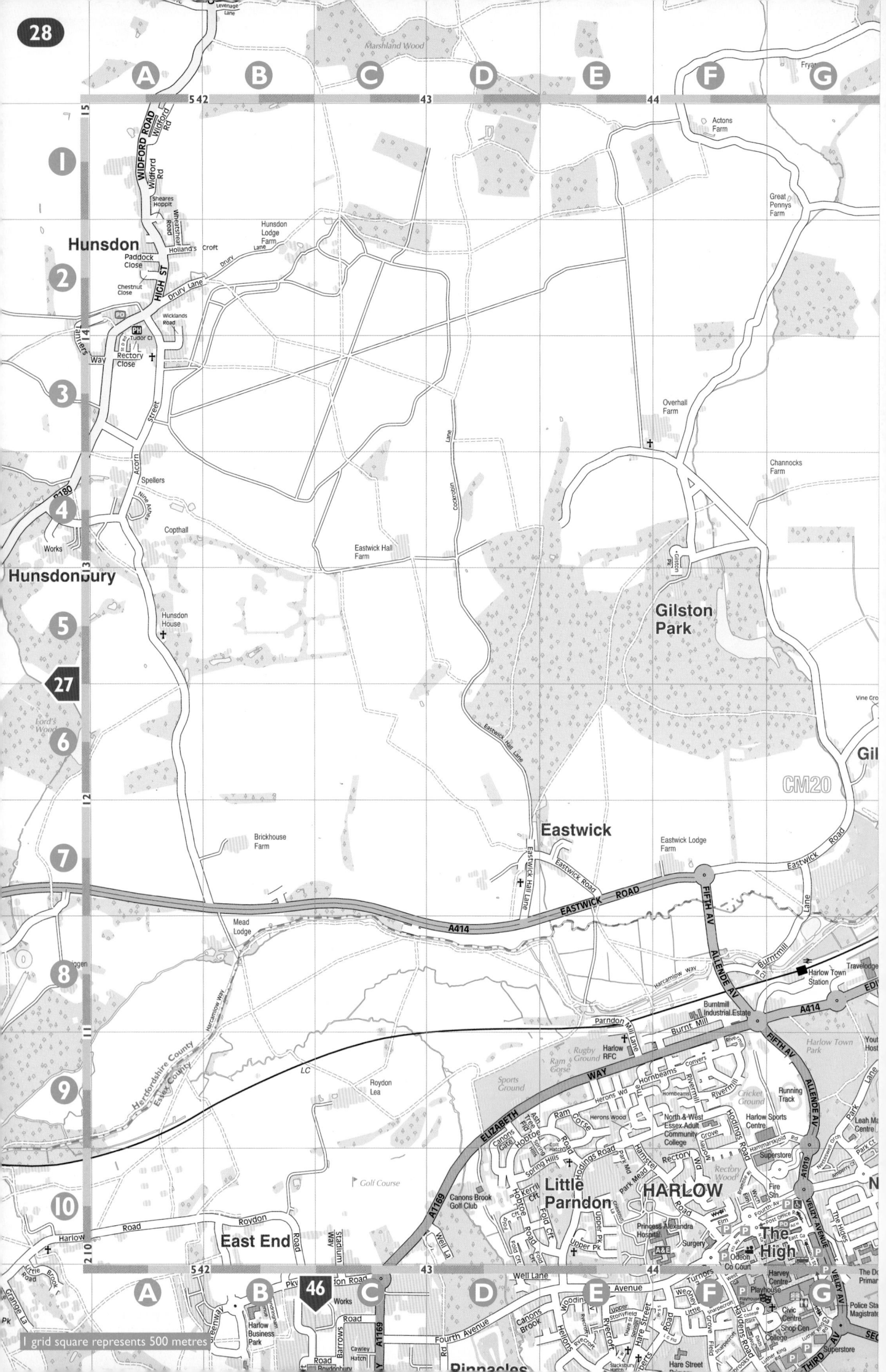
Hunsdon
Hunsdonbury
Hunsdon Lodge Farm
Eastwick Hall Farm
Actons Farm
Great Pennys Farm
Overhall Farm
Channocks Farm
Gilston Park
Eastwick
Eastwick Lodge Farm
Brickhouse Farm
Mead Lodge
Roydon Lea
East End
Little Parndon
HARLOW
The High
CM20
Harlow Town Station
Burntmill Industrial Estate
Canons Brook Golf Club
Princess Alexandra Hospital
Hertfordshire County
Essex County
Marshland Wood
Lord's Wood
Hunsdon House
Copthall
Spellers
Works
Golf Course
Rugby Ground
Harlow RFC
Sports Ground
Cricket Ground
Running Track
Harlow Sports Centre
Superstore
North & West Essex Adult Community College
Rectory Wood
Harlow Town Park
Harlow Business Park
Playhouse
Civic Centre
Police Station
Harvey Centre
Surgery
Odeon
Travelodge
EASTWICK ROAD
A414
FIFTH AV
ALLENDE AV
ELIZABETH WAY
A1169
A1019
VELIZY AVENUE
THIRD AV
Fourth Avenue
WIDFORD ROAD
HIGH ST
Drury Lane
Acorn Street
Cockrobin Lane
Eastwick Hall Lane
Eastwick Road
Parndon Mill Lane
Burnt Mill
Harcamlow Way
Roydon Road
Harlow Road
Well Lane
B180
27
46
A B C D E F G
1 2 3 4 5 6 7 8 9 10
542 43 44
15 14 13 12 11 210
1 grid square represents 500 metres

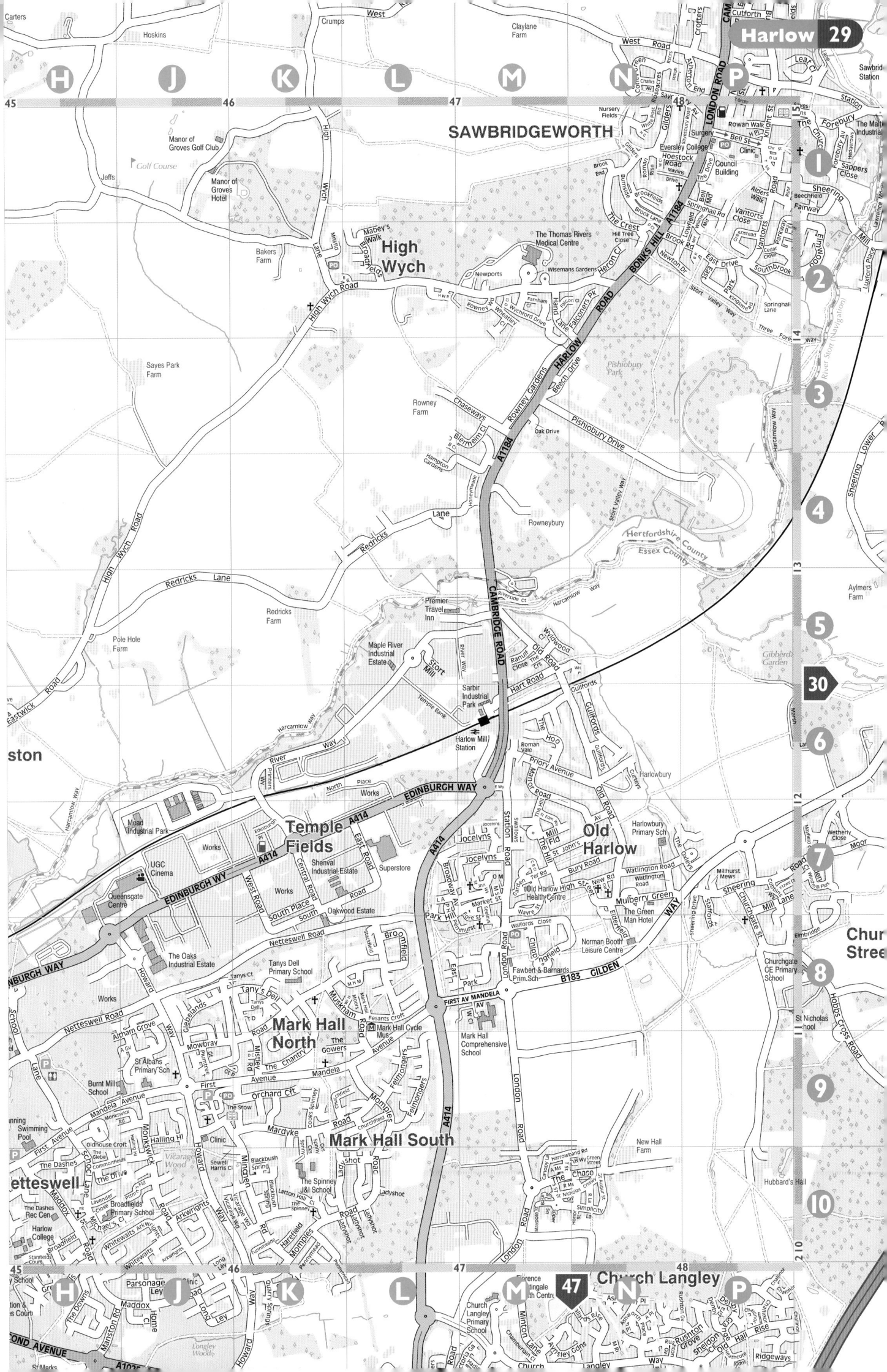
SAWBRIDGEWORTH
High Wych
Manor of Groves Golf Club
Manor of Groves Hotel
Golf Course
The Thomas Rivers Medical Centre
Pishiobury Park
Rowneybury
Hertfordshire County
Essex County
Premier Travel Inn
Maple River Industrial Estate
Sarbir Industrial Park
Harlow Mill Station
Harlowbury
Temple Fields
Old Harlow
Mead Industrial Park
UGC Cinema
Queensgate Centre
Shenval Industrial Estate
Superstore
Oakwood Estate
The Oaks Industrial Estate
Tanys Dell Primary School
Mark Hall North
Mark Hall South
Mark Hall Comprehensive School
Harlowbury Primary Sch
Norman Booth Leisure Centre
Fawbert & Barnards Prim.Sch
Churchgate CE Primary School
St Albans Primary Sch
Burnt Mill School
The Spinney J&I School
Harlow College
Netteswell
Church Langley
Church Langley Primary School
Sawbridgeworth Station
Gibberd's Garden
Redricks Farm
Pole Hole Farm
Sayes Park Farm
Rowney Farm
Bakers Farm
Claylane Farm
New Hall Farm
Aylmers Farm
A1184
A414
B183
EDINBURGH WAY
CAMBRIDGE ROAD
LONDON ROAD
HARLOW ROAD
BONKS HILL
30
47

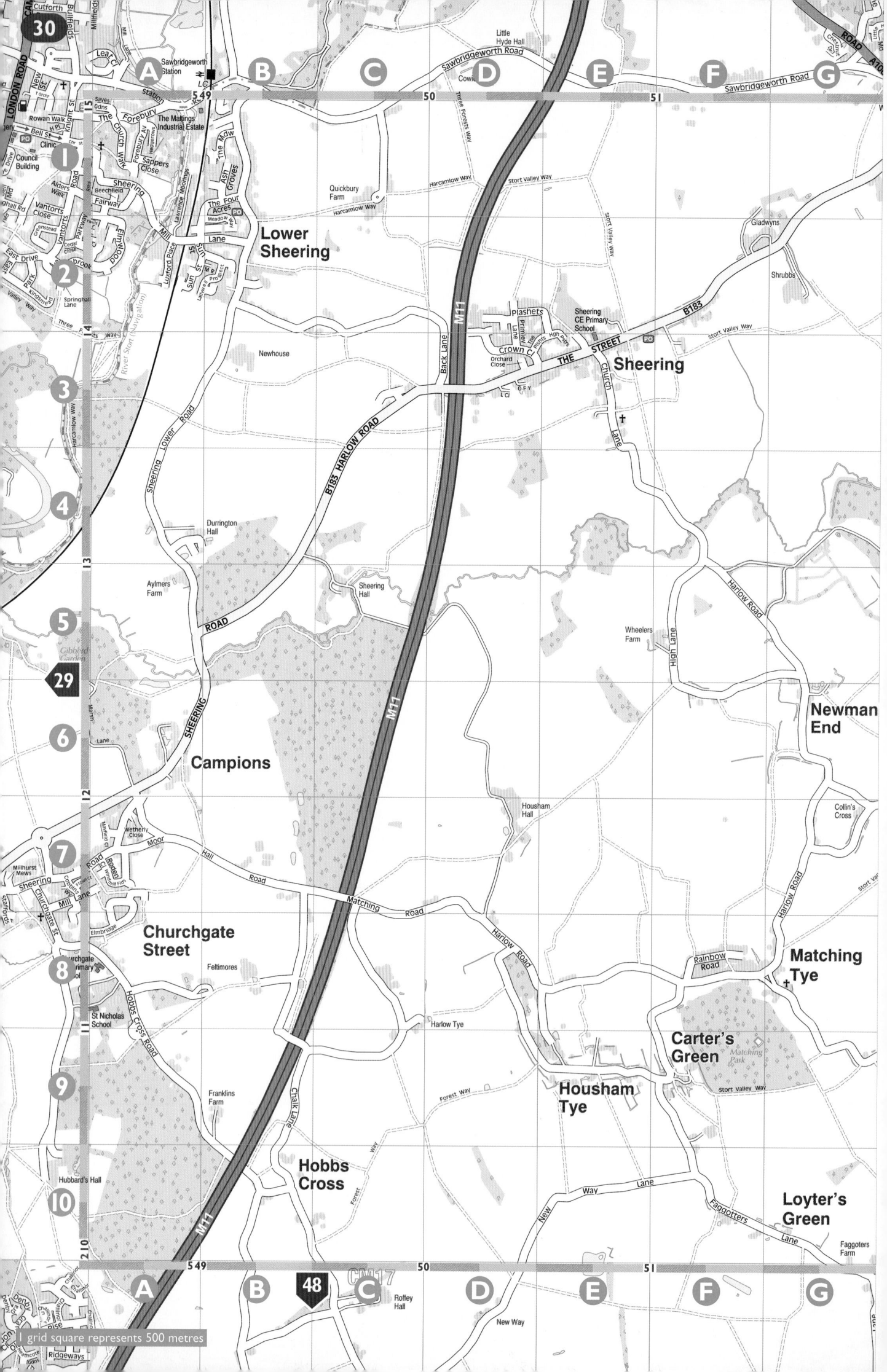
30
Sawbridgeworth Station
The Maltings Industrial Estate
Council Building
Lower Sheering
Quickbury Farm
Little Hyde Hall
Sawbridgeworth Road
Harcamlow Way
Stort Valley Way
Three Forests Way
Gladwyns
Shrubbs
Sheering CE Primary School
THE STREET
Sheering
Church Lane
Back Lane
Newhouse
B183 HARLOW ROAD
Sheering Lower Road
Durrington Hall
Aylmers Farm
Sheering Hall
M11
Wheelers Farm
High Lane
Harlow Road
Newman End
29
Campions
Housham Hall
Collin's Cross
Moor Hall Road
Matching Road
Churchgate Street
Feltimores
Hobbs Cross Road
St Nicholas School
Harlow Tye
Matching Tye
Rainbow Road
Carter's Green
Matching Park
Housham Tye
Franklins Farm
Chalk Lane
Forest Way
Hobbs Cross
Hubbard's Hall
New Way Lane
Faggotters Lane
Loyter's Green
Faggoters Farm
48
Roffey Hall
New Way
Ridgeways
1 grid square represents 500 metres

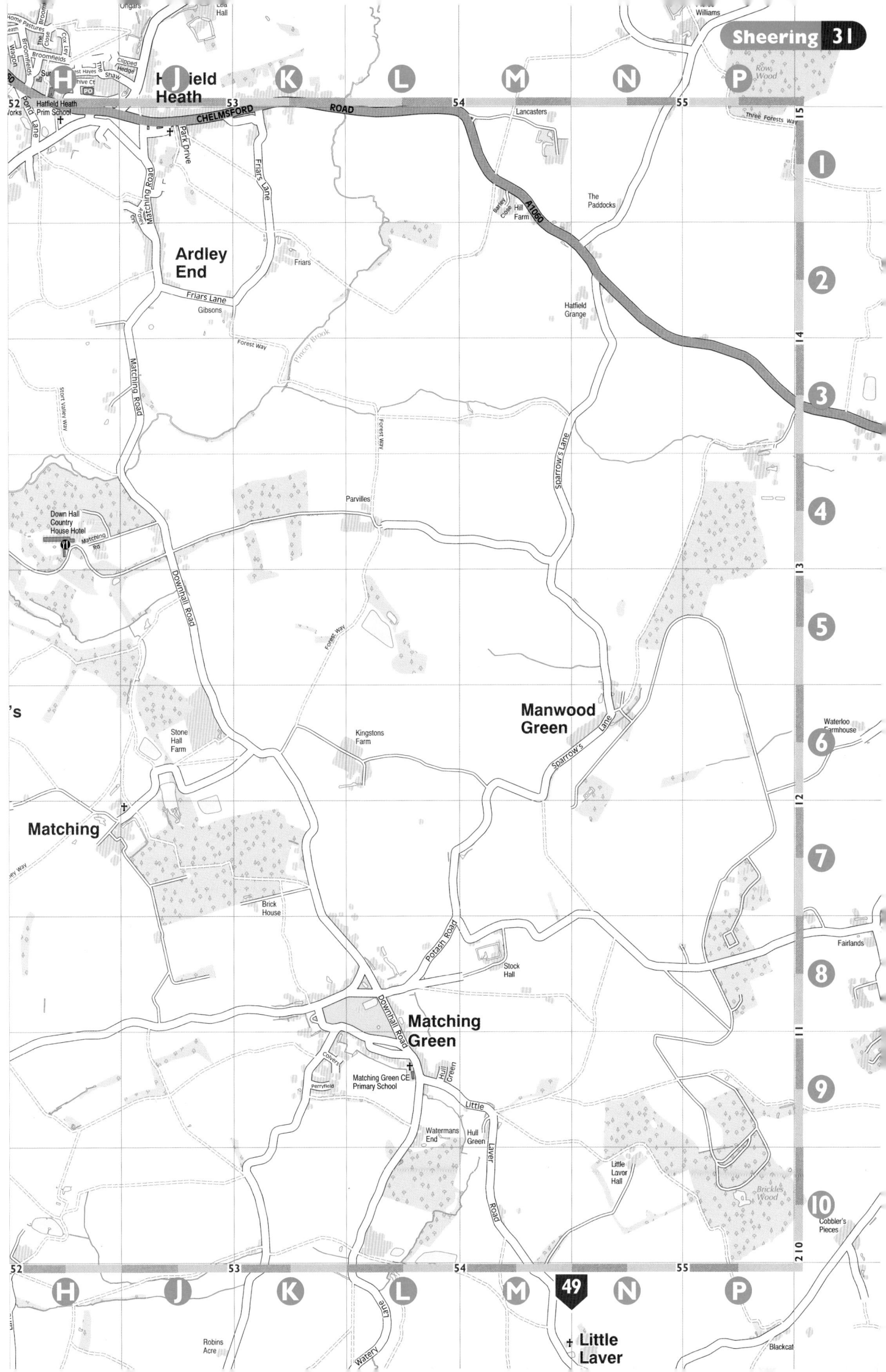
Hatfield Heath
Ardley End
Manwood Green
Matching
Matching Green
Little Laver
CHELMSFORD ROAD
A1060
Matching Road
Friars Lane
Park Drive
Pond Lane
Forest Way
Pincey Brook
Stort Valley Way
Sparrow's Lane
Downhall Road
Potash Road
Little Laver Road
Hull Green
Matching Rd
Watery Lane
Hatfield Heath Prim School
Down Hall Country House Hotel
Lancasters
The Paddocks
Hill Farm
Barley Close
Hatfield Grange
Friars
Gibsons
Parvilles
Kingstons Farm
Stone Hall Farm
Brick House
Stock Hall
Matching Green CE Primary School
Colvers
Perryfield
Watermans End
Little Lavor Hall
Brickles Wood
Row Wood
Three Forests Way
Waterloo Farmhouse
Fairlands
Cobbler's Pieces
Robins Acre
Blackcat
Broomfields
Home Pastures
Cox Ley
The Close
The Shaw
Clipped Hedge
Lea Hall
Ongars
Williams
H J K L M N P
52 53 54 55
1 2 3 4 5 6 7 8 9 10
15 14 13 12 11 210
49

A B C D E F G

493 94 95

Cow Roast

Martin Hill

Ickneild Way

Mary Cross Cl

Vicarage Road

Highfield Rd

St Barts CE Sch

Common Field

Ridgeway

Osborne Way

The Firs

The Bit

Fields End Cl

Hemp Lane

Hemp Lane

Hill Green Farm

A4251

I

Hastoe

Wick Road

Wick Farm

Ridgeway

Wigginton Bottom

Chesham Road

Wigginton Bottom

Crawley's Lane

Crawley's Lane

Rossway

A41

Lane

Hamberlins

2

06

Lane

Kiln Farm

Wood Row

Tinkers Lane

Shootersw

3

05

High Scrubs

Champneys

4

04

Cholesbury Road

The Flats

Chesham Road

Lodge Farm

Shirelane Farm

Hertfordshire County

Buckinghamshire County

Shire Lane

Cholesbury Road

Tring Grange Farm

Chesham Road

Cock Grove

Rossway Home Farm

5

03

Parrott's Farm

6

02

Parrott's Lane

Parrott's Lane

Cholesbury Lane

Cholesbury Road

Buckland Commor

Lane

Cholesbury

Cholesbury Rd

Cholesbury Lane

PH

Cholesbury

Hawridge Common

Cock Grove

Heath End

07

7

Braziers End House

Ray's Hill

Hawridge & Cholesbury CE School

Oak Lane

Braziers End

Hawridge Vale

Cholesbury Lane

Hill Farm

8

Gyles Croft

Chesham Road

Cherry Tree

Peppet's Green

00

Hawridge Lane

9

Wood Farm

Bank Green

Braziers End

Cedar Grove

Hawridge Lane

Bellingdon Farm

Hawridge Lane

Bank Farm

Asheridge Farm

10

205

Two Gates Lane

Chesham Road

Bellingdon

Bloomfield Farm

Ramscote Lane

Vale Road

Ramscote Lane

A B C D E F G

493 94 95

Savecroft Farm

1 grid square represents 500 metres

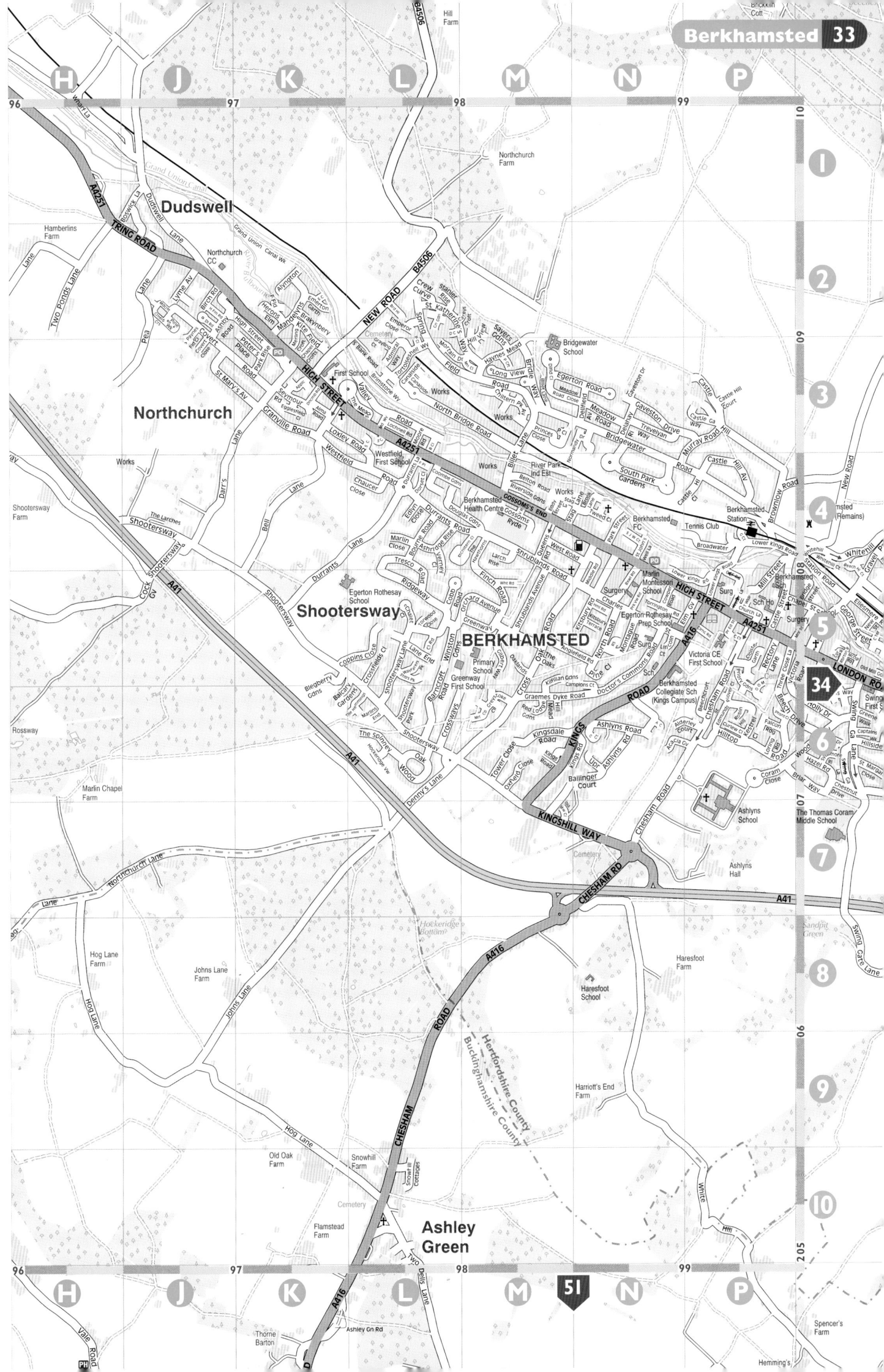
Dudswell
Northchurch
Shootersway
BERKHAMSTED
Ashley Green
HIGH STREET
A4251
TRING ROAD
NEW ROAD
B4506
A41
A416
CHESHAM ROAD
KINGS ROAD
KINGSHILL WAY
LONDON ROAD
Berkhamsted Station
Northchurch Farm
Bridgewater School
Egerton Rothesay School
Berkhamsted Collegiate Sch (Kings Campus)
Ashlyns School
Haresfoot School
The Thomas Coram Middle School
Hertfordshire County
Buckinghamshire County
34
51

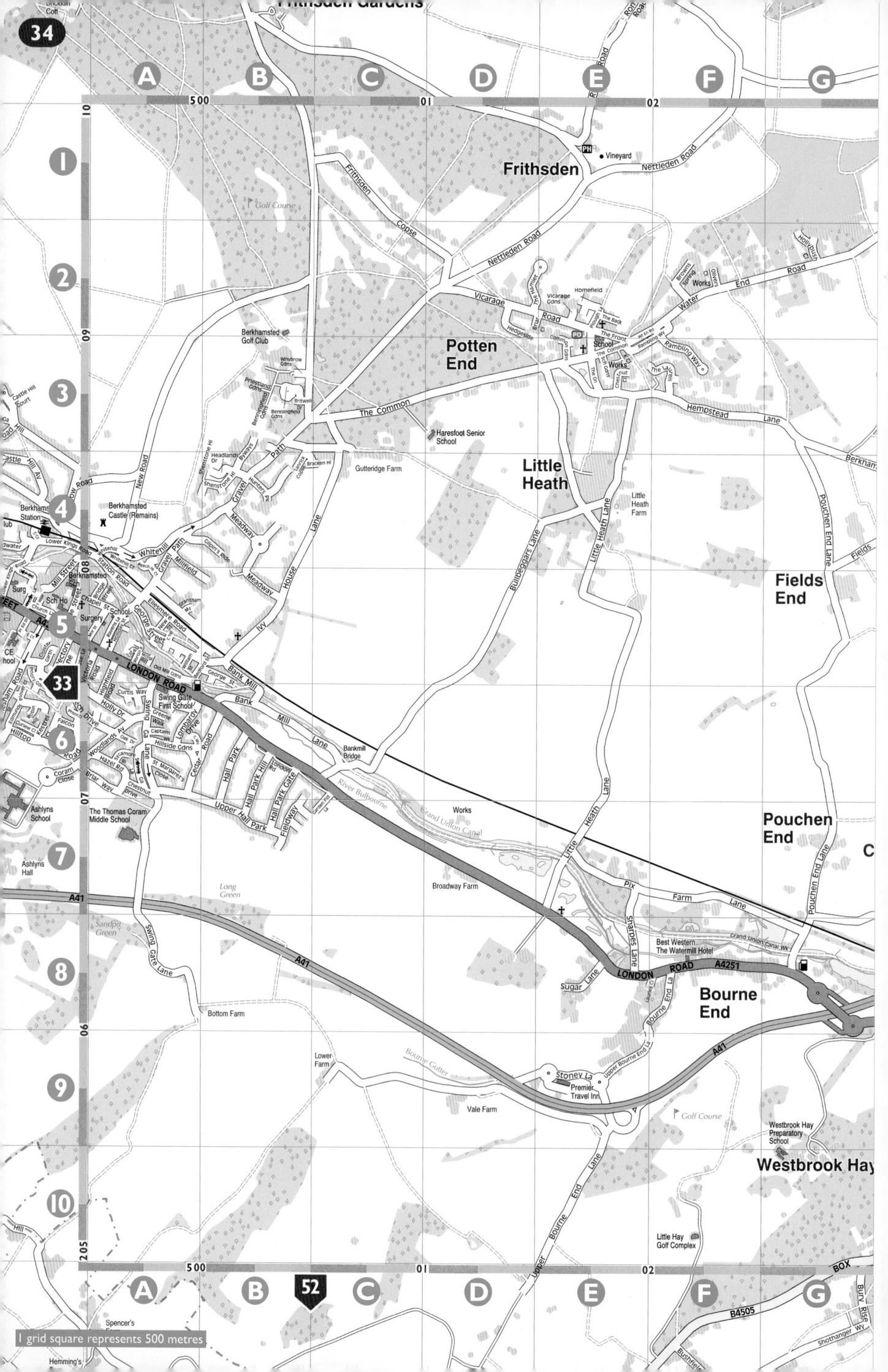
Frithsden Gardens
A
B
C
D
E
F
G
500
01
02
1
2
3
4
5
6
7
8
9
10
Frithsden
Vineyard
Nettleden Road
Frithsden Copse
Golf Course
Nettleden Road
Vicarage Road
The Hamlet
Vicarage Gdns
Homefield
Hedgeside
Briar
Common Gdns
Plough La
The Back
The Front
School
The Common
Works
Water End Road
Browns Spring
Works
Olivers
Hollybush Cl
Rambling Wy
Rambling Way
The Laurels
Potten End
Berkhamsted Golf Club
Whybrow Gdns
Priestland Gdns
Benningfield Gdns
Britwell Dr
The Common
Hempstead Lane
Haresfoot Senior School
Castle Hill Court
Castle Hill Av
Headlands Dr
Byways
Shenstone Hl
Shenstone Hl
Gravel Path
Hunters Pk
Larrick Copse
Bracken Hl
Gutteridge Farm
Little Heath
Little Heath Farm
Berkhamsted
Pouchen End Lane
Berkhamsted Station
Berkhamsted Castle (Remains)
New Road
Lower Kings Road
Whitehill
Gravel Path
Millfield
Gilpin's Ride
Meadway
Meadway
House Lane
Ivy
Bullbeggars Lane
Little Heath Lane
Fields End
Mill Street
Berkhamsted Sch
Chapel
Bridge Street
Station Road
St School
Surgery
Sch Ho
Surg
Ellesmere Road
George Street
New Road
Grantham Ms
Rectory Lane
CE School
Victoria Road
Highfield Road
Old Mill Gdns
George St
Bank Mill
LONDON ROAD
Curtis Way
Holly Dr
Swing Gate First School
Swing Gate Lane
Greene Walk
Captains Wk
Lombardy Drive
Bank Mill Lane
Bankmill Bridge
Hillside Gdns
Cedar Road
Hall Park
Hall Park Hill
Hall Park Gate
London Road
Woodlands Av
Oak Dr
Sycamore
Hazel Rd
Chestnut Drive
St Margaret's Close
Briar Way
Coram Close
Hilltop Road
Upper Hall Park
Fieldway
Garden Fld La
River Bulbourne
Grand Union Canal
Works
Ashlyns School
The Thomas Coram Middle School
Ashlyns Hall
Pouchen End
Pouchen End Lane
Broadway Farm
A41
Long Green
Sandpit Green
Little Heath Lane
Pix Farm Lane
Sharpes Lane
Grand Union Canal Wk
Best Western The Watermill Hotel
A41
Swing Gate Lane
Sugar Lane
LONDON ROAD
A4251
Bourne End
Bourne End La
Laurels Cl
Bottom Farm
Lower Farm
Bourne Gutter
Upper Bourne End La
Stoney La
Premier Travel Inn
A41
Vale Farm
Golf Course
Westbrook Hay Preparatory School
Westbrook Hay
Upper Bourne End Lane
Little Hay Golf Complex
205
06
07
08
09
10
Hill
500
01
02
52
BOX
B4505
Bury Rise
Shothanger Wy
Bushfield
Spencer's
Hemming's
1 grid square represents 500 metres

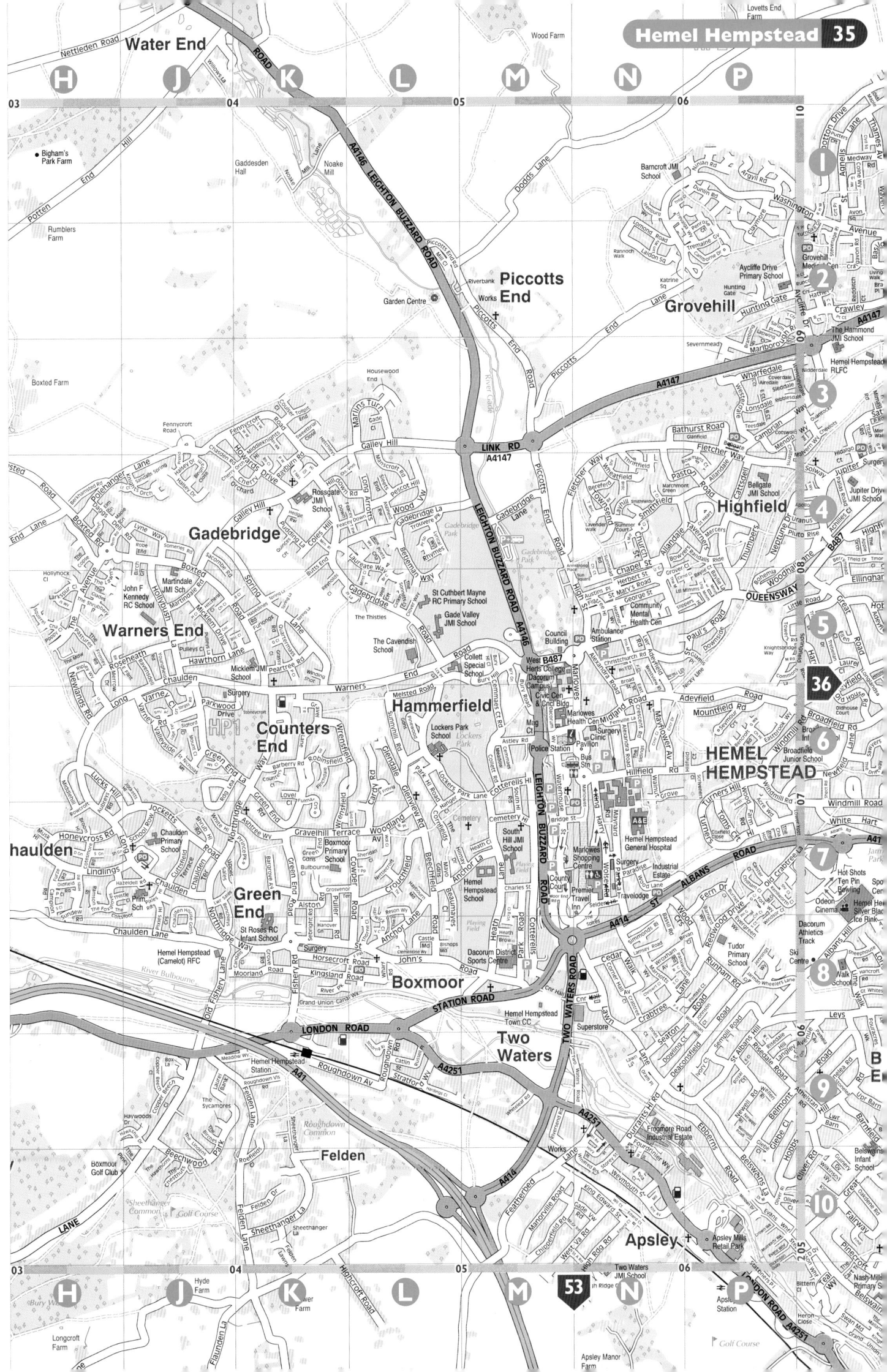

Hemel Hempstead 35
Water End
Nettleden Road
Lovetts End Farm
Wood Farm
Bigham's Park Farm
Potten End Hill
Rumblers Farm
Gaddesden Hall
Noake Mill
A4146 LEIGHTON BUZZARD ROAD
Dodds Lane
Barncroft JMI School
Grovehill
Ayliffe Drive Primary School
Piccotts End
Garden Centre
Boxted Farm
Housewood End
Fennycroft Road
LINK RD
A4147
Gadebridge
Rossgate JMI School
Bellgate JMI School
Highfield
Jupiter Drive JMI School
Hemel Hempstead RLFC
The Hammond JMI School
Gadebridge Park
St Cuthbert Mayne RC Primary School
Gade Valley JMI School
The Thistles
The Cavendish School
John F Kennedy RC School
Martindale JMI Sch
Warners End
Micklem JMI School
Collett Special School
QUEENSWAY
Council Building
Ambulance Station
West Herts College (Dacorum Campus)
Civic Cen & Cncl Bldg
Marlowes Health Cen
Police Station
Hammerfield
Counters End
Lockers Park School
Chaulden
Chaulden Primary School
Boxmoor Primary School
South Hill JMI School
Hemel Hempstead School
Marlowes Shopping Centre
Hemel Hempstead General Hospital
Industrial Estate
HEMEL HEMPSTEAD
Broadfield Junior School
Green End
St Roses RC Infant School
Dacorum District Sports Centre
Hemel Hempstead (Camelot) RFC
River Bulbourne
Boxmoor
STATION ROAD
LONDON ROAD
Hemel Hempstead Station
Hemel Hempstead Town CC
Superstore
Two Waters
TWO WATERS ROAD
ST ALBANS ROAD
A414
A41
A4251
Tudor Primary School
Hot Shots Ten Pin Bowling
Odeon Cinema
Dacorum Athletics Track
Ski Centre
Roughdown Common
Felden
Boxmoor Golf Club
Sheethanger Common
Golf Course
Frogmore Road Industrial Estate
Belswains Infant School
Apsley
Apsley Mills Retail Park
Two Waters JMI School
Apsley Station
Hyde Farm
Longcroft Farm
Apsley Manor Farm
Highcroft Road
LONDON ROAD
H J K L M N P
1 2 3 4 5 6 7 8 9 10
36
53

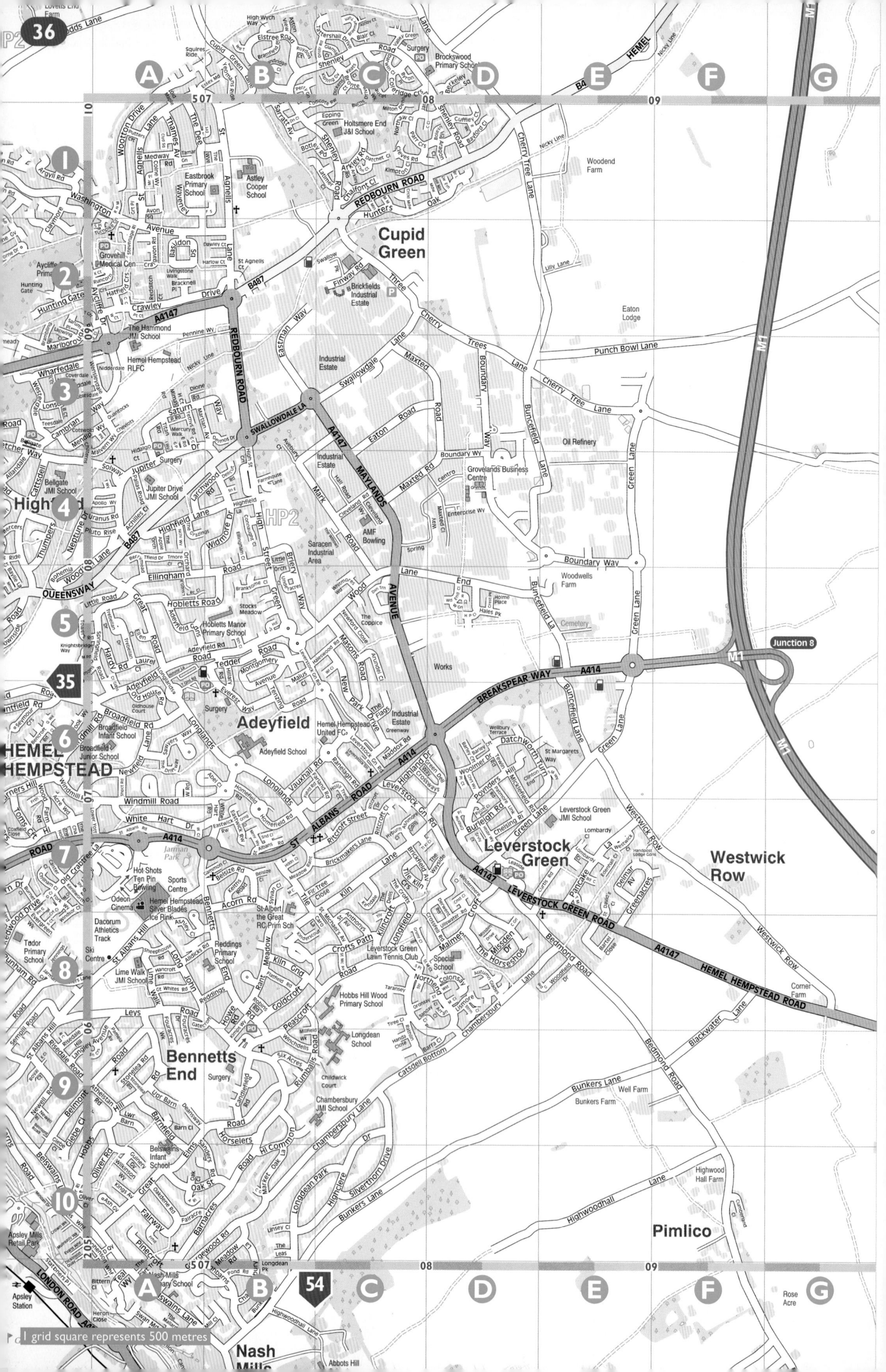

36
35
54
A
B
C
D
E
F
G
1
2
3
4
5
6
7
8
9
10
507
08
09
HP2
Cupid Green
Adeyfield
Leverstock Green
Bennetts End
HEMEL HEMPSTEAD
Highfield
Westwick Row
Pimlico
Nash Mills
M1
Junction 8
A4147
A414
B487
REDBOURN ROAD
SWALLOWDALE LANE
MAYLANDS AVENUE
BREAKSPEAR WAY
LEVERSTOCK GREEN ROAD
HEMEL HEMPSTEAD ROAD
ST ALBANS ROAD
QUEENSWAY
LONDON ROAD
Punch Bowl Lane
Cherry Tree Lane
Buncefield Lane
Green Lane
Boundary Way
Bedmond Road
Westwick Row
Bunkers Lane
Highwoodhall Lane
Blackwater Lane
Chambersbury Lane
Catsdell Bottom
Three Cherry Trees Lane
Eastman Way
Maxted Road
Eaton Road
Wood Lane End
Longlands
Windmill Road
White Hart Dr
Washington Avenue
Crawley Drive
Jupiter Drive
Highfield Lane
High Street Green
Hobletts Road
Broadfield Rd
Belswains Lane
Ritcroft Street
Brickmakers Lane
Shenley Road
Holtsmere End J&I School
Brockswood Primary School
Eastbrook Primary School
Astley Cooper School
Grovehill Medical Cen
Brickfields Industrial Estate
Industrial Estate
Oil Refinery
Grovelands Business Centre
AMF Bowling
Saracen Industrial Area
Woodend Farm
Eaton Lodge
Woodwells Farm
Cemetery
Works
The Hammond JMI School
Hemel Hempstead RLFC
Jupiter Drive JMI School
Bellgate JMI School
Hobletts Manor Primary School
Adeyfield School
Hemel Hempstead United FC
Broadfield Infant School
Broadfield Junior School
Leverstock Green JMI School
Hot Shots Ten Pin Bowling
Odeon Cinema
Sports Centre
Hemel Hempstead Silver Blades Ice Rink
Dacorum Athletics Track
Ski Centre
Tudor Primary School
Lime Walk JMI School
Reddings Primary School
St Albert the Great RC Prim Sch
Leverstock Green Lawn Tennis Club
Special School
Hobbs Hill Wood Primary School
Longdean School
Childwick Court
Chambersbury JMI School
Belswains Infant School
Nash Mills Primary School
Apsley Mills Retail Park
Apsley Station
Well Farm
Bunkers Farm
Highwood Hall Farm
Corner Farm
Rose Acre
Surgery
1 grid square represents 500 metres

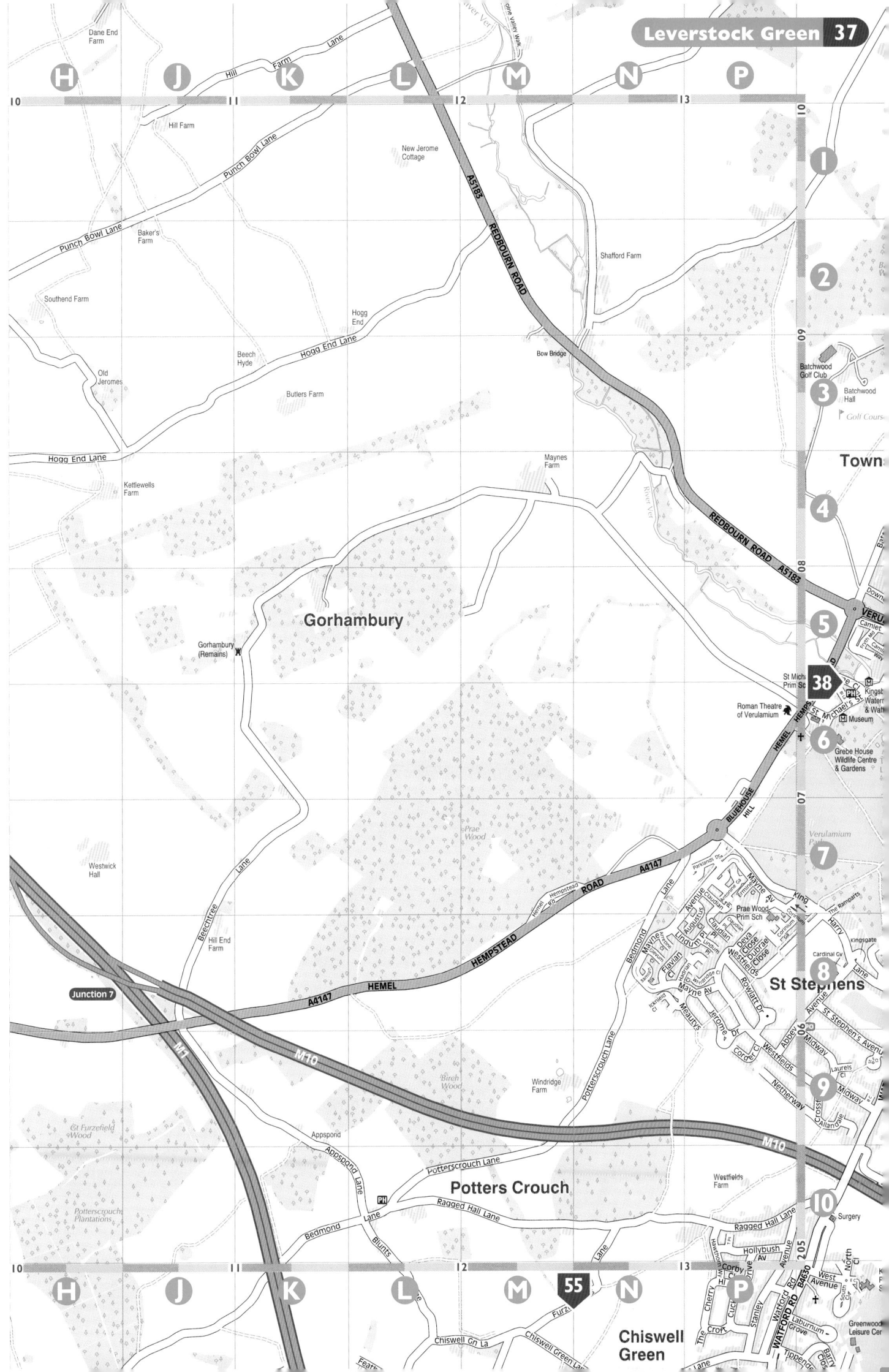

H J K L M N P

Dane End Farm

Hill Farm

Punch Bowl Lane

New Jerome Cottage

A5183 REDBOURN ROAD

Shafford Farm

Batchwood Golf Club

Batchwood Hall

Golf Course

Town

Baker's Farm

Southend Farm

Hogg End

Hogg End Lane

Beech Hyde

Old Jeromes

Butlers Farm

Bow Bridge

Maynes Farm

REDBOURN ROAD A5183

Hogg End Lane

River Ver

VERU

Kettlewells Farm

Camlet

Gorhambury

Gorhambury (Remains)

St Micha Prim Sc

38 PH

Kingsb Water & Wate

Roman Theatre of Verulamium

St Michael's

Museum

Grebe House Wildlife Centre & Gardens

HEMPS

BLUEHOUSE HILL

Verulamium P

Westwick Hall

Prae Wood

Parklands Dr

Mayne

Ermine

King

The Ramparts

HEMPSTEAD ROAD A4147

Avenue Claudian

Prae Wood Prim Sch

Lindum

Harry

Kingsgate

Beechtree Lane

Bedmond

Flavian

Clavian

Deva Close

Westfields

Dubmor Close

Rowlatt Dr

Cardinal Gv

Hill End Farm

Mayne Av

St Stephens

Junction 7

A4147 HEMEL

Abney

Jerome Dr

St Stephen's Avenue

M1

M10

Meautys

Westfields

Netherway

Midway

Laurels Cl

Midway

Birch Wood

Windridge Farm

Crosse

Callande

Gt Furzefield Wood

M10

Appspond

Appspond Lane

Potterscrouch Lane

Westfields Farm

Surgery

Potterscrouch Plantations

PH

Potterscrouch Lane

Potters Crouch

Ragged Hall Lane

Ragged Hall Lane

B4630

Bedmond Lane

Blunts Lane

Lane

Hollybush Av

Corby

North

West Avenue

WATFORD RD

Greenwood Leisure Cen

H J K L M 55 N P

Chiswell Gn La

Chiswell green Lane

Chiswell Green

Feat

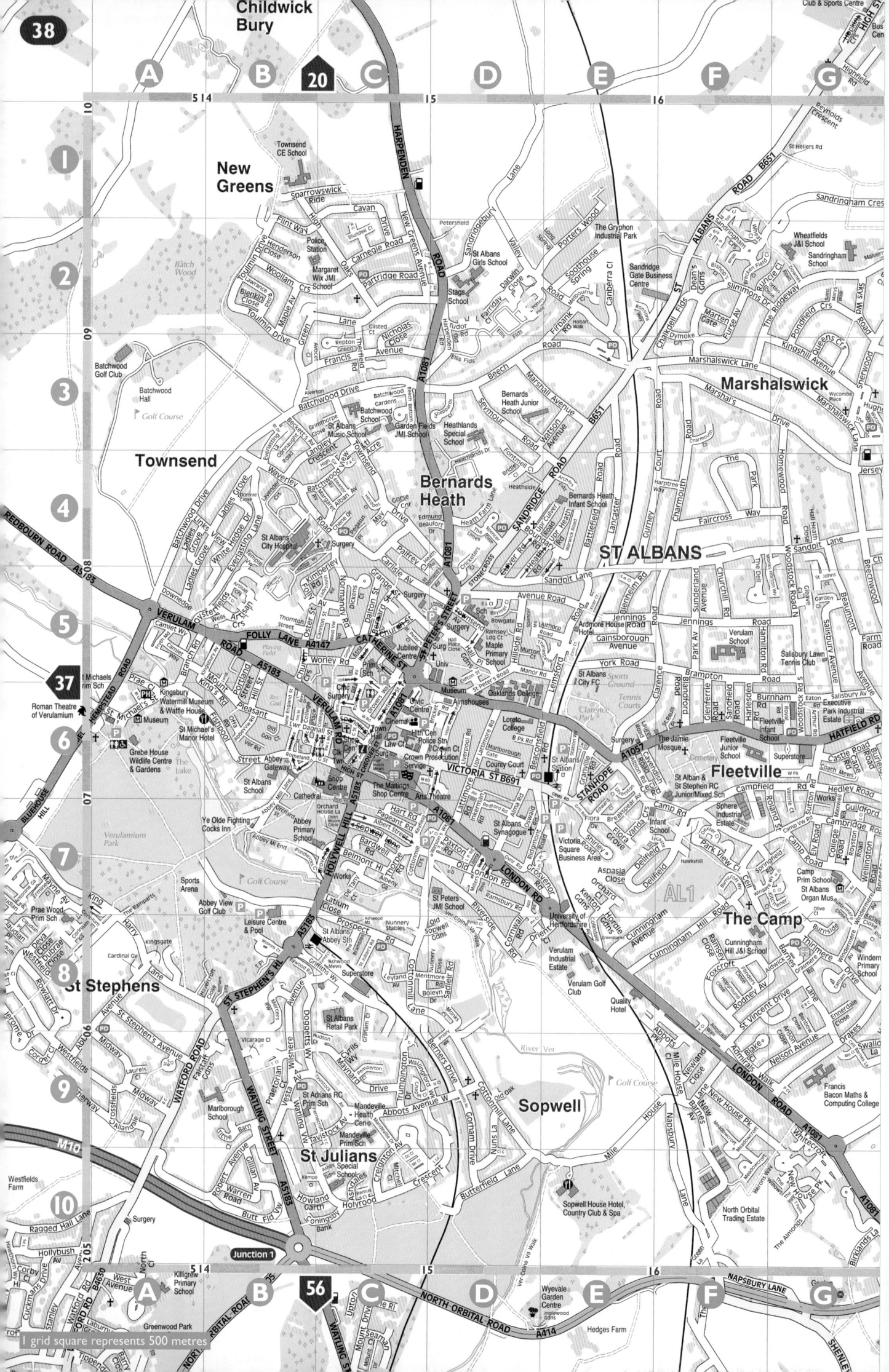
Childwick Bury
20
37
56
A
B
C
D
E
F
G
1
2
3
4
5
6
7
8
9
10
New Greens
Townsend
Bernards Heath
ST ALBANS
Marshalswick
Fleetville
The Camp
St Stephens
Sopwell
St Julians
Townsend CE School
Police Station
Margaret Wix JMI School
Batch Wood
Batchwood Golf Club
Batchwood Hall
Golf Course
St Albans Girls School
Stags School
The Gryphon Industrial Park
Sandridge Gate Business Centre
Wheatfields J&I School
Sandringham School
Bernards Heath Junior School
Heathlands Special School
Bernards Heath Infant School
St Albans Music School
Garden Fields JMI School
St Albans City Hospital
Surgery
Verulam School
Salisbury Lawn Tennis Club
St Albans City FC
Sports Ground
Tennis Courts
Clarence Park
The Jamie Mosque
Fleetville Junior School
Fleetville Infant School
Executive Park Industrial Estate
Superstore
St Alban & St Stephen RC Junior/Mixed Sch
Sphere Industrial Estate
Kingsbury Watermill Museum & Waffle House
Roman Theatre of Verulamium
Museum
St Michael's Manor Hotel
Grebe House Wildlife Centre & Gardens
St Albans School
Cathedral
Ye Olde Fighting Cocks Inn
Verulamium Park
Abbey Primary School
Jubilee Centre
Oaklands College
Loreto College
County Court
Crown Prosecution Service
The Maltings Shop Centre
Arts Theatre
St Albans Synagogue
Victoria Square Business Area
St Albans Station
Sports Arena
Abbey View Golf Club
Leisure Centre & Pool
St Albans Abbey Stn
St Peters JMI School
University of Hertfordshire
Verulam Industrial Estate
Verulam Golf Club
Quality Hotel
Cunningham Hill J&I School
Camp Prim School
St Albans Organ Mus
Francis Bacon Maths & Computing College
St Albans Retail Park
St Adrians RC Prim Sch
Mandeville Health Cen
Mandeville Prim Sch
Special School
Marlborough School
Sopwell House Hotel, Country Club & Spa
North Orbital Trading Estate
Westfields Farm
Killigrew Primary School
Greenwood Park
Wyevale Garden Centre
Hedges Farm
Junction 1
River Ver
HARPENDEN ROAD
VERULAM ROAD A5183
REDBOURN ROAD A5183
FOLLY LANE A4147
CATHERINE ST
ST PETER'S STREET
SANDRIDGE ROAD
HATFIELD RD
VICTORIA ST B697
LONDON RD
HOLYWELL HILL
ST STEPHEN'S HL
WATLING STREET
WATFORD ROAD
ST ALBANS ROAD B651
NORTH ORBITAL ROAD A414
NAPSBURY LANE
M10
A1081
A5183
A1057
AL1
1 grid square represents 500 metres

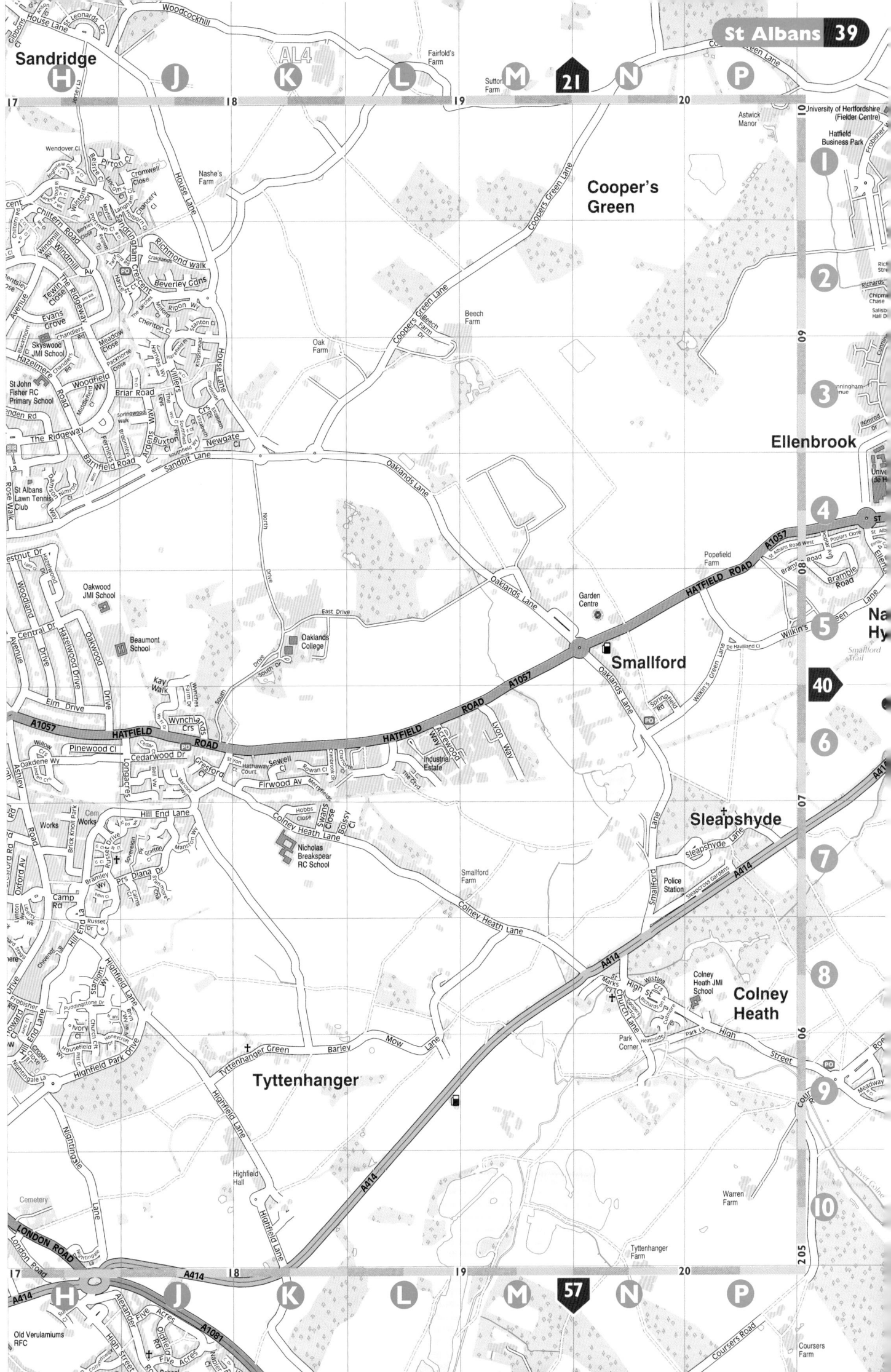

Sandridge
Cooper's Green
Ellenbrook
Smallford
Sleapshyde
Colney Heath
Tyttenhanger
AL4
H
J
K
L
M
N
P
21
40
57
17
18
19
20
10
09
08
07
06
205
1
2
3
4
5
6
7
8
9
10
Woodcockhill
House Lane
St Leonards Crs
Fairfold's Farm
Sutton Farm
Astwick Manor
University of Hertfordshire (Fielder Centre)
Hatfield Business Park
Nashe's Farm
Coopers Green Lane
Beech Farm
Oak Farm
Wendover Cl
Pirton Cl
Cromwell Close
Chiltern Road
Windmill Av
Richmond Walk
Beverley Gdns
Sandringham Crescent
The Ridgeway
Tewin Close
Evans Grove
Ripon Wy
Cheriton Cl
Stanton Cl
Meadow Close
Skyswood JMI School
St John Fisher RC Primary School
Hazelmere Road
Woodfield Wy
Briar Road
Villiers Crs
Newgate Cl
Buxton Cl
Ardens Way
Barnfield Road
Sandpit Lane
St Albans Lawn Tennis Club
Rose Walk
Oaklands Lane
North Drive
East Drive
South Drive
Oaklands College
Oakwood JMI School
Beaumont School
Woodland Drive
Hazelwood Drive
Oakwood Drive
Central Dr
Elm Drive
Kay Walk
Wynchlands Crs
A1057
HATFIELD ROAD
Popefield Farm
Garden Centre
St Albans Road West
Bramble Road
Wilkin's Green Lane
De Havilland Cl
Springfield Rd
Smallford Trail
Pinewood Cl
Cedarwood Dr
Oakdene Wy
Longacres
Gresford Cl
Sewell Cl
Hathaway Court
Firwood Av
Rowan Cl
Acrewood Way
Lyon Way
Industrial Estate
Hill End Lane
Colney Heath Lane
Hobbs Close
Swans Close
Boissy Cl
Nicholas Breakspear RC School
Works
Smallford Farm
Smallford Lane
Police Station
Sleapshyde Lane
Sleapcross Gardens
A414
Highfield Lane
St Marks Cl
High St
Church Lane
Wistlea Crs
Colney Heath JMI School
Park Corner
Park La
High Street
Camp Rd
Hill End La
Starlight Wy
Highfield Park Drive
Tyttenhanger Green
Barley Mow Lane
Nightingale Lane
Highfield Hall
Cemetery
LONDON ROAD
London Road
Warren Farm
River Colne
Tyttenhanger Farm
Alexander
Five Acres
Oldfield Rd
A1081
High Street
Old Verulamiums RFC
Coursers Road
Coursers Farm

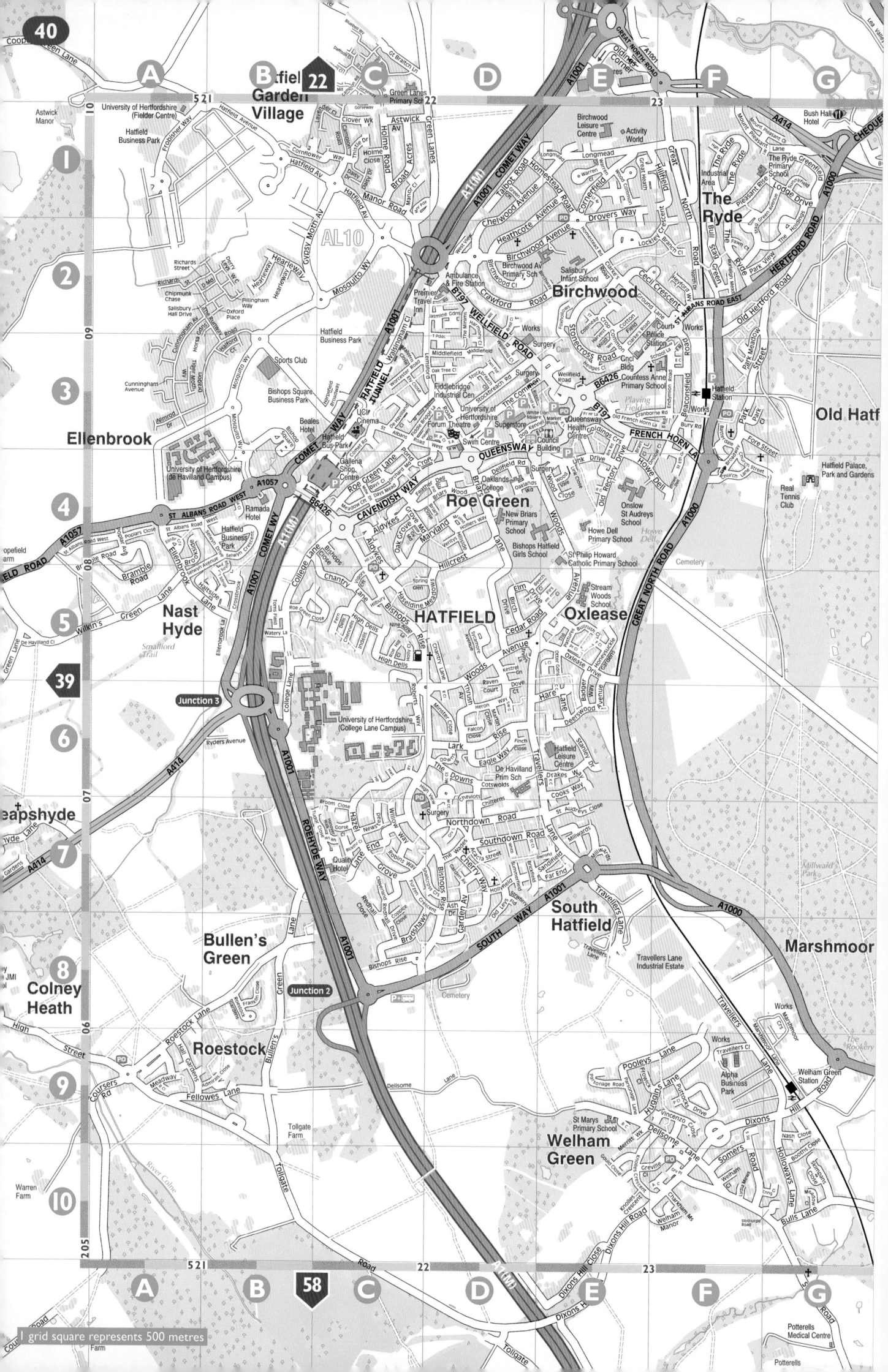
A
B
C
D
E
F
G
1
2
3
4
5
6
7
8
9
10
22
39
58
Hatfield Garden Village
Astwick Manor
University of Hertfordshire (Fielder Centre)
Hatfield Business Park
Green Lanes Primary Sch
Birchwood Leisure Centre
Activity World
Bush Hall Hotel
The Ryde
The Ryde Primary School
Industrial Area
AL10
Ambulance & Fire Station
Premier Travel Inn
Birchwood Av Primary Sch
Salisbury Infant School
Birchwood
Hatfield Business Park
Sports Club
Bishops Square Business Park
Beales Hotel
Hatfield Bus Park
Galleria Shop Centre
UCI Cinema
Fiddlebridge Industrial Cen
University of Hertfordshire
Forum Theatre
Swim Centre
Superstore
Council Building
Queensway Health Centre
Countess Anne Primary School
Cncl Bldg
Police Station
Hatfield Station
Old Hatf
Hatfield Palace, Park and Gardens
Real Tennis Club
Ellenbrook
University of Hertfordshire (de Havilland Campus)
Ramada Hotel
Hatfield Business Park
Oaklands College
Roe Green
New Briars Primary School
Bishops Hatfield Girls School
Howe Dell Primary School
Onslow St Audreys School
St Philip Howard Catholic Primary School
Cemetery
Stream Woods School
Oxlease
HATFIELD
Nast Hyde
Smallford Trail
Junction 3
University of Hertfordshire (College Lane Campus)
Hatfield Leisure Centre
De Havilland Prim Sch
Surgery
Quality Hotel
South Hatfield
Bullen's Green
Colney Heath
Junction 2
Cemetery
Travellers Lane Industrial Estate
Marshmoor
Roestock
Works
Alpha Business Park
Welham Green Station
St Marys Primary School
Welham Green
Welham Manor
Tollgate Farm
River Colne
Warren Farm
Potterells Medical Centre
Potterells
COMET WAY
ROEHYDE WAY
SOUTH WAY
GREAT NORTH ROAD
HERTFORD ROAD
QUEENSWAY
CAVENDISH WAY
WELLFIELD ROAD
ST ALBANS ROAD WEST
ST ALBANS ROAD EAST
FRENCH HORN LA
HATFIELD TUNNEL
A1(M)
A1001
A1000
A1057
A414
B6426
B197
521
22
23
10
09
08
07
06
205
1 grid square represents 500 metres

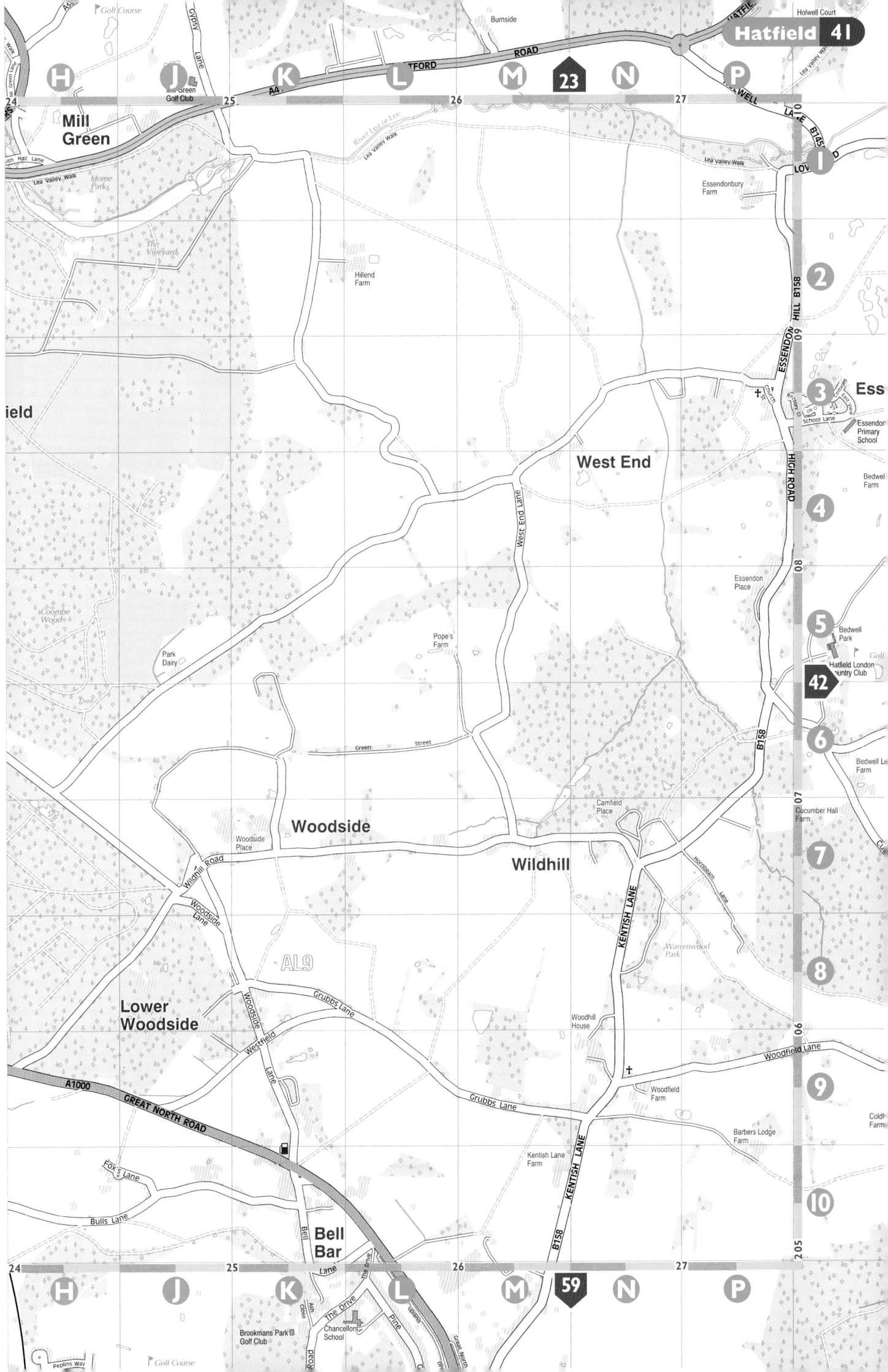
Mill Green
Mill Green Golf Club
Golf Course
Gypsy Lane
Burnside
Holwell Court
A414
TFORD ROAD
Hatfield
B145
Lea Valley Walk
River Lea or Lee
Home Park
The Vineyard
Essendonbury Farm
Hillend Farm
ESSENDON HILL B158
HIGH ROAD
Church St
School Lane
Essendon Primary School
West End
Bedwell Farm
West End Lane
Essendon Place
Coombe Wood
Park Dairy
Pope's Farm
Bedwell Park
Hatfield London Country Club
Golf
Green Street
B158
Bedwell Farm
Woodside
Woodside Place
Camfield Place
Cucumber Hall Farm
Wildhill
Wildhill Road
Woodside Lane
Hornbeam Lane
KENTISH LANE
Warrenwood Park
AL9
Lower Woodside
Woodside Lane
Grubbs Lane
Westfield
Woodhill House
Woodfield Lane
Woodfield Farm
A1000
GREAT NORTH ROAD
Grubbs Lane
Barbers Lodge Farm
Kentish Lane Farm
Fox's Lane
Bulls Lane
Bell Bar
Bell Lane
B158
The Drive
Ash Close
Brookmans Park Golf Club
Chancellors School
Pine
Peplins Way
Golf Course
H J K L M N P
23 42 59
24 25 26 27
09 08 07 06 205
2 3 4 5 6 7 8 9 10

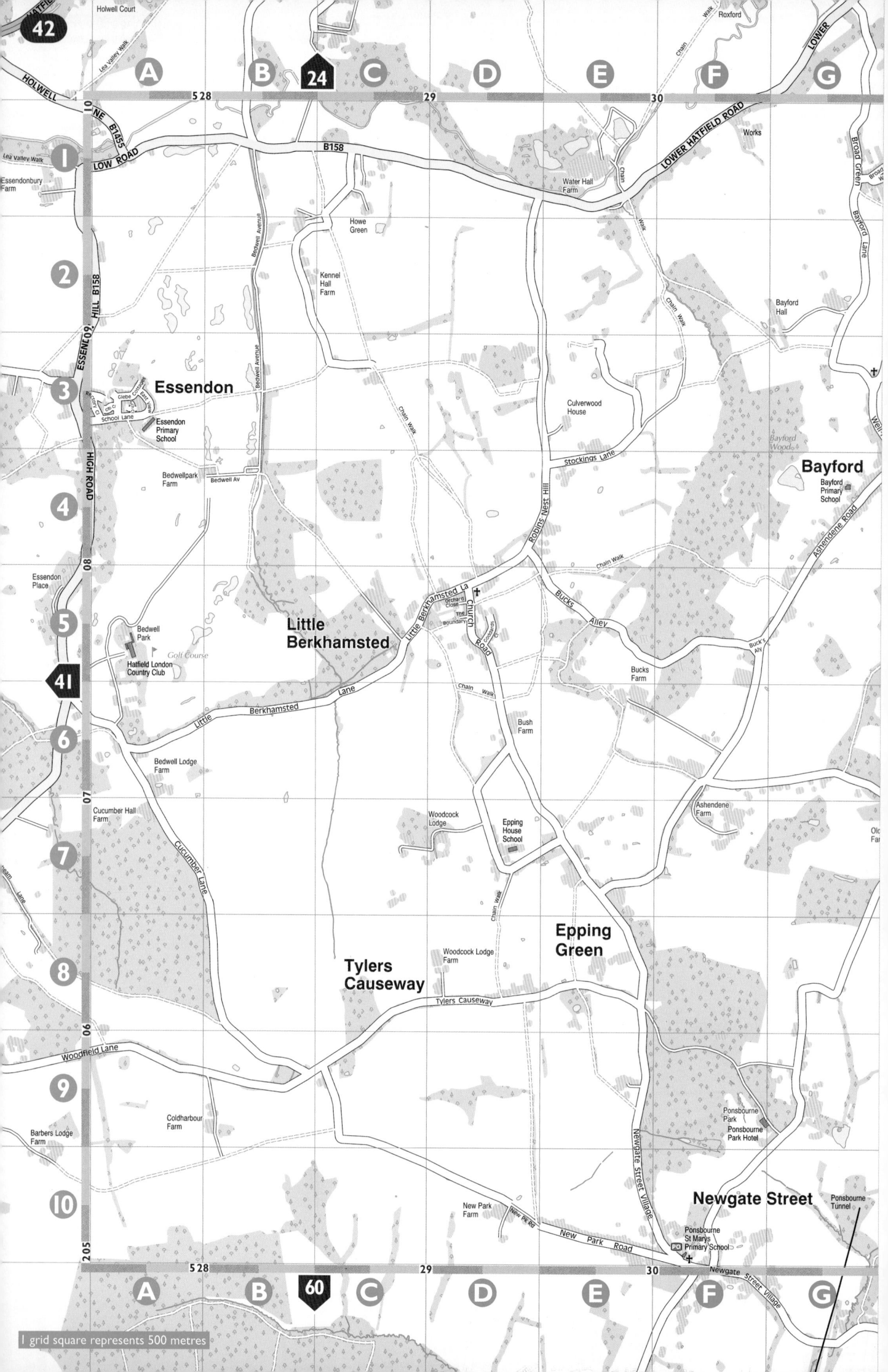

42
24
41
60
Essendon
Little Berkhamsted
Bayford
Epping Green
Tylers Causeway
Newgate Street
Holwell Court
Lea Valley Walk
Roxford
Works
Water Hall Farm
Howe Green
Kennel Hall Farm
Essendonbury Farm
Bedwell Avenue
Chain Walk
Culverwood House
Stockings Lane
Robins Nest Hill
Bayford Hall
Bayford Wood
Bayford Primary School
Broad Green
Bayford Lane
Ashendene Road
LOWER HATFIELD ROAD
HOLWELL
LOW ROAD
B158
B1455
ESSENDON HILL B158
HIGH ROAD
Essendon Primary School
School Lane
Glebe Cottages
Rectory Cl
Bedwellpark Farm
Bedwell Av
Essendon Place
Bedwell Park
Golf Course
Hatfield London Country Club
Little Berkhamsted Lane
Little Berkhamsted La
Orchard Close
The Boundary
Church Road
Goddards
Bucks Alley
Buck's Aly
Bucks Farm
Bush Farm
Bedwell Lodge Farm
Cucumber Hall Farm
Cucumber Lane
Woodcock Lodge
Epping House School
Ashendene Farm
Woodcock Lodge Farm
Tylers Causeway
Woodfield Lane
Coldharbour Farm
Barbers Lodge Farm
Ponsbourne Park
Ponsbourne Park Hotel
Newgate Street Village
New Park Farm
New Pk Rd
New Park Road
Ponsbourne St Marys Primary School
PO
Ponsbourne Tunnel
1 grid square represents 500 metres

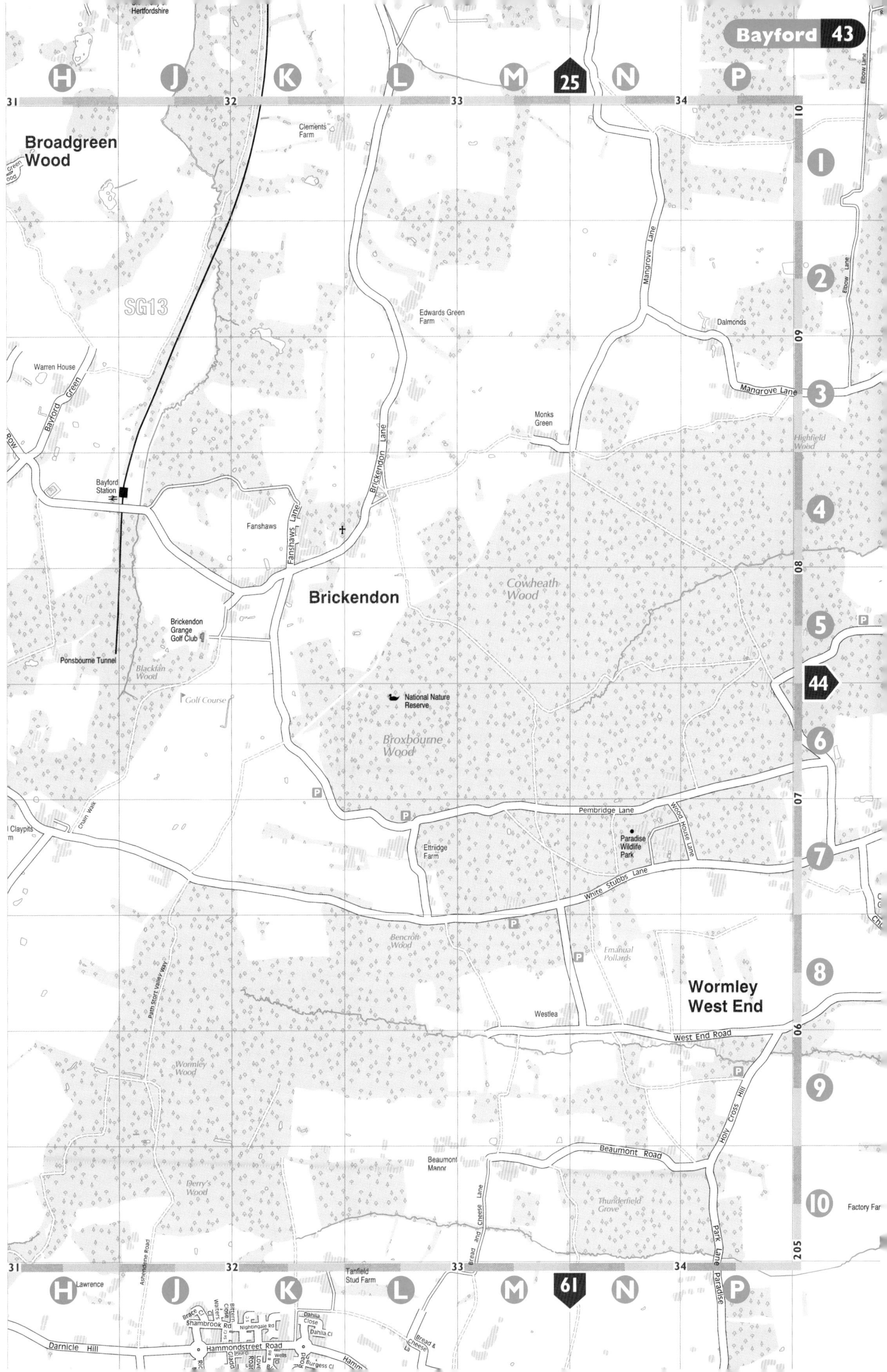

H J K L M **25** N P

31 **32** **33** **34** 10

I

Broadgreen Wood

Green Wood

Hertfordshire

Clements Farm

2

SG13

Edwards Green Farm

Dalmonds

Mangrove Lane

Warren House

Mangrove Lane

3

Bayford Green

Monks Green

Highfield Wood

ROW

Bayford Station

Fanshaws

Brickendon Lane

†

4

Fanshaws Lane

Brickendon

Cowheath Wood

08

Brickendon Grange Golf Club

5

P

Ponsbourne Tunnel

Blackfan Wood

44

National Nature Reserve

Golf Course

6

Chain Walk

Broxbourne Wood

07

Pembridge Lane

Wood House Lane

Claypits m

P

P

Paradise Wildlife Park

7

Ettridge Farm

White Stubbs Lane

Path Start Valley Way

Bencroft Wood

P

Emanual Pollards

8

P

Wormley West End

Westlea

West End Road

06

Wormley Wood

P

Holy Cross Hill

9

Beaumont Road

Park Lane

Derry's Wood

Beaumont Manor

Paradise

205

Thunderfield Grove

10

Factory Far

Bread and Cheese Lane

31 **32** **33** **34**

Lawrence

Darnicle Hill

Atherdone Road

Brace Cl

Betteridge Close

Waters Cl

Shambrook Rd

Nightingale Rd

Dahlia Close

Dahlia Cl

Tanfield Stud Farm

Bread & Cheese La

Hammondstreet Road

RIC

ROAD

LOVE

wells

Burgess Cl

Hamm

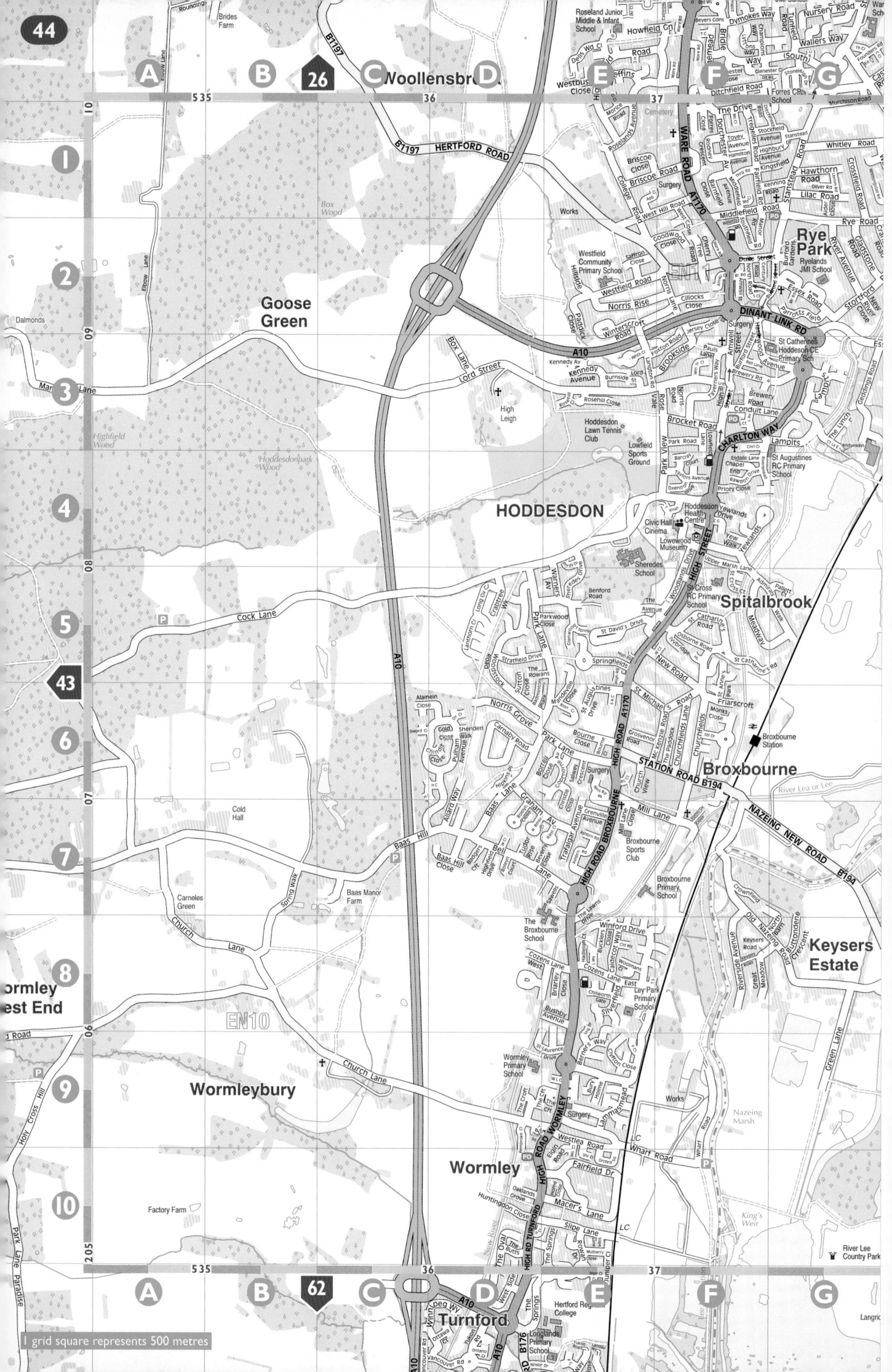
Woollensbrook
Goose Green
HODDESDON
Rye Park
Spitalbrook
Broxbourne
Keysers Estate
Wormleybury
Wormley
Turnford
Wormley West End
EN10
EN11
A10
A1170
B194
B1197
B176
HERTFORD ROAD
DINANT LINK RD
CHARLTON WAY
HIGH STREET
WARE ROAD
HIGH ROAD BROXBOURNE
HIGH ROAD WORMLEY
HIGH RD TURNFORD
STATION ROAD
NAZEING NEW ROAD
Cock Lane
Lord Street
Baas Hill
Church Lane
Broxbourne Station
River Lea or Lee
Nazeing Marsh
King's Weir
River Lee Country Park
Hertford Regional College
Sheredes School
Broxbourne Sports Club
The Broxbourne School
Carneles Green
Baas Manor Farm
Cold Hall
Factory Farm
High Leigh
Box Wood
Highfield Wood
Hoddesdonpark Wood
Dalmonds
Brides Farm
26
43
62
1 grid square represents 500 metres

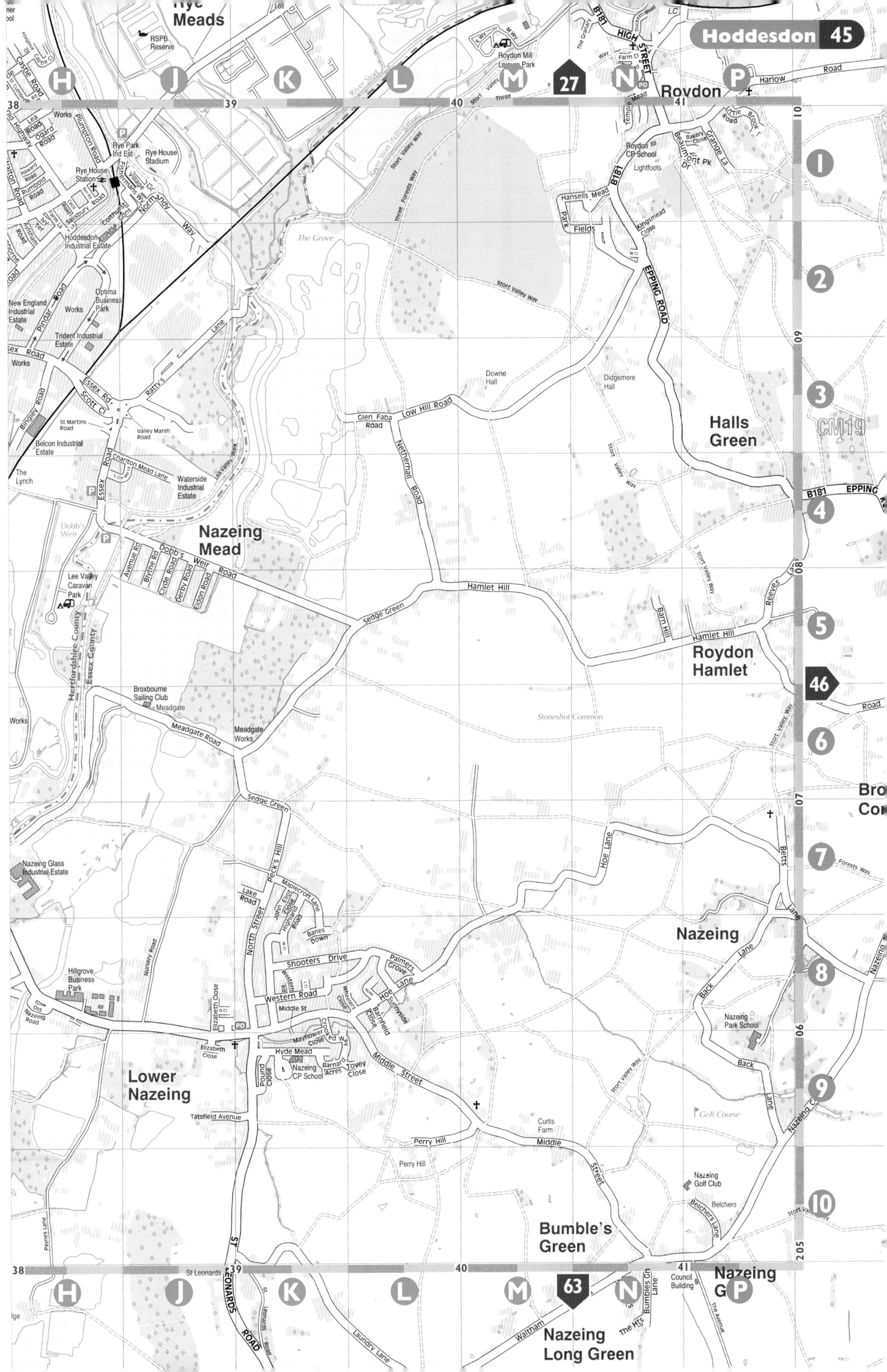
Rye Meads
RSPB Reserve
Roydon Mill Leisure Park
27
Roydon
Harlow Road
High Street
B181
Rye Park Ind Est
Rye House Stadium
Rye House Station
Hoddesdon Industrial Estate
Optima Business Park
New England Industrial Estate
Trident Industrial Estate
Works
The Grove
Stort Valley Way
Three Forests Way
River Stort (Navigation)
Roydon CP School
Lightfoots
Hansells Mead
Kingsmead Close
Epping Road
Downe Hall
Digdemere Hall
Halls Green
CM19
Low Hill Road
Glen Faba Road
Netherhall Road
Belcon Industrial Estate
The Lynch
Waterside Industrial Estate
Charlton Mead Lane
Dobb's Weir
Nazeing Mead
Dobb's Weir Road
Lee Valley Caravan Park
Hertfordshire County
Essex County
Hamlet Hill
Sedge Green
Roydon Hamlet
Reeves Lane
Barn Hill
46
Broxbourne Sailing Club
Meadgate
Meadgate Road
Meadgate Works
Stoneshot Common
Hoe Lane
Betts Lane
Nazeing Glass Industrial Estate
Peck's Hill
Lake Road
North Street
Maplecroft Lane
Shooters Drive
Palmers Grove
Western Road
Middle St
Nazeing
Back Lane
Nazeing Park School
Hillgrove Business Park
Old Nazeing Road
Nursery Road
Elizabeth Close
Lower Nazeing
Hyde Mead
Nazeing CP School
Barnard Acres
Tovey Close
Middle Street
Perry Hill
Curtis Farm
Tatsfield Avenue
Golf Course
Nazeing Golf Club
Belchers
Belchers Lane
Nazeing Common
Bumble's Green
St Leonards Road
Paynes Lane
63
Council Building
Nazeing Long Green
Waltham Road
Laundry Lane
Bumbles Green Lane
The Avenue

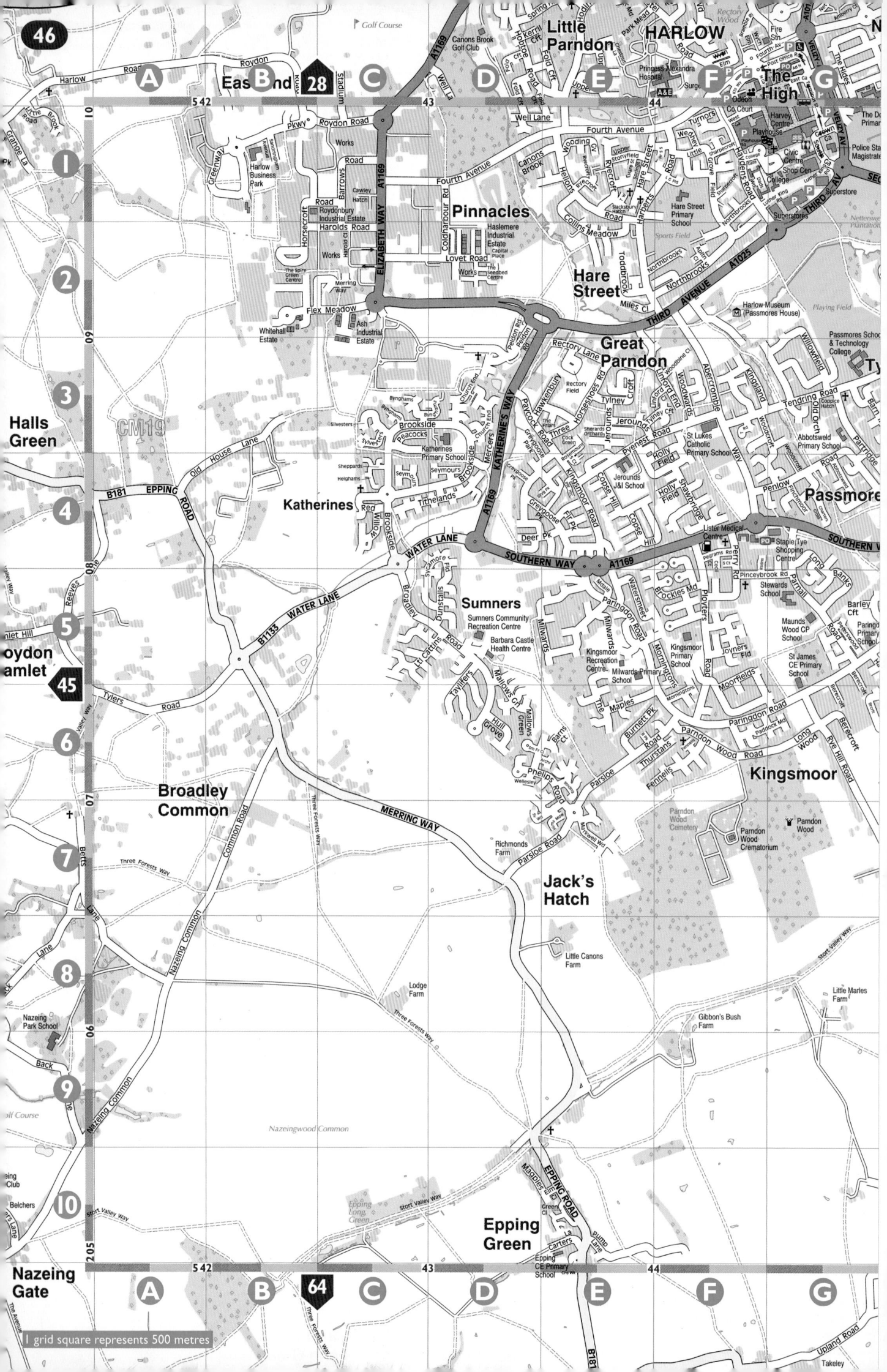

Harlow Road
Roydon Road
East End
28
Golf Course
Canons Brook Golf Club
Little Parndon
HARLOW
Princess Alexandra Hospital
The High
Harvey Centre
Playhouse
Civic Centre
College
Superstore
Harlow Business Park
Roydonbury Industrial Estate
Harolds Road
Works
ELIZABETH WAY
A1169
Fourth Avenue
Pinnacles
Haslemere Industrial Estate
Lovet Road
Hare Street
Hare Street Primary School
Third Avenue
A1025
Flex Meadow
Ash Industrial Estate
Whitehall Estate
Great Parndon
Harlow Museum (Passmores House)
Passmores School & Technology College
Halls Green
CM19
Old House Lane
B181 EPPING ROAD
Katherines
Katherines Primary School
KATHERINE'S WAY
Rectory Field
Tylney
Jerounds J&I School
St Lukes Catholic Primary School
Abbotsweld Primary School
Passmores
Tendring Road
Southern Way
Water Lane
B1133
Sumners
Sumners Community Recreation Centre
Barbara Castle Health Centre
Lister Medical Centre
Staple Tye Shopping Centre
Stewards School
Maunds Wood CP School
St James CE Primary School
Kingsmoor Recreation Centre
Milwards Primary School
Kingsmoor Primary School
Paringdon Road
Parndon Wood Road
Kingsmoor
Roydon Hamlet
45
Tylers Road
Broadley Common
Common Road
Merring Way
Three Forests Way
Parsloe Road
Richmonds Farm
Jack's Hatch
Parndon Wood Cemetery
Parndon Wood Crematorium
Parndon Wood
Little Canons Farm
Lodge Farm
Nazeing Park School
Nazeing Common
Nazeingwood Common
Gibbon's Bush Farm
Little Marles Farm
Stort Valley Way
Epping Long Green
Epping Green
EPPING ROAD
Epping CE Primary School
Nazeing Gate
64
Upland Road
Takeley
B181
1 grid square represents 500 metres

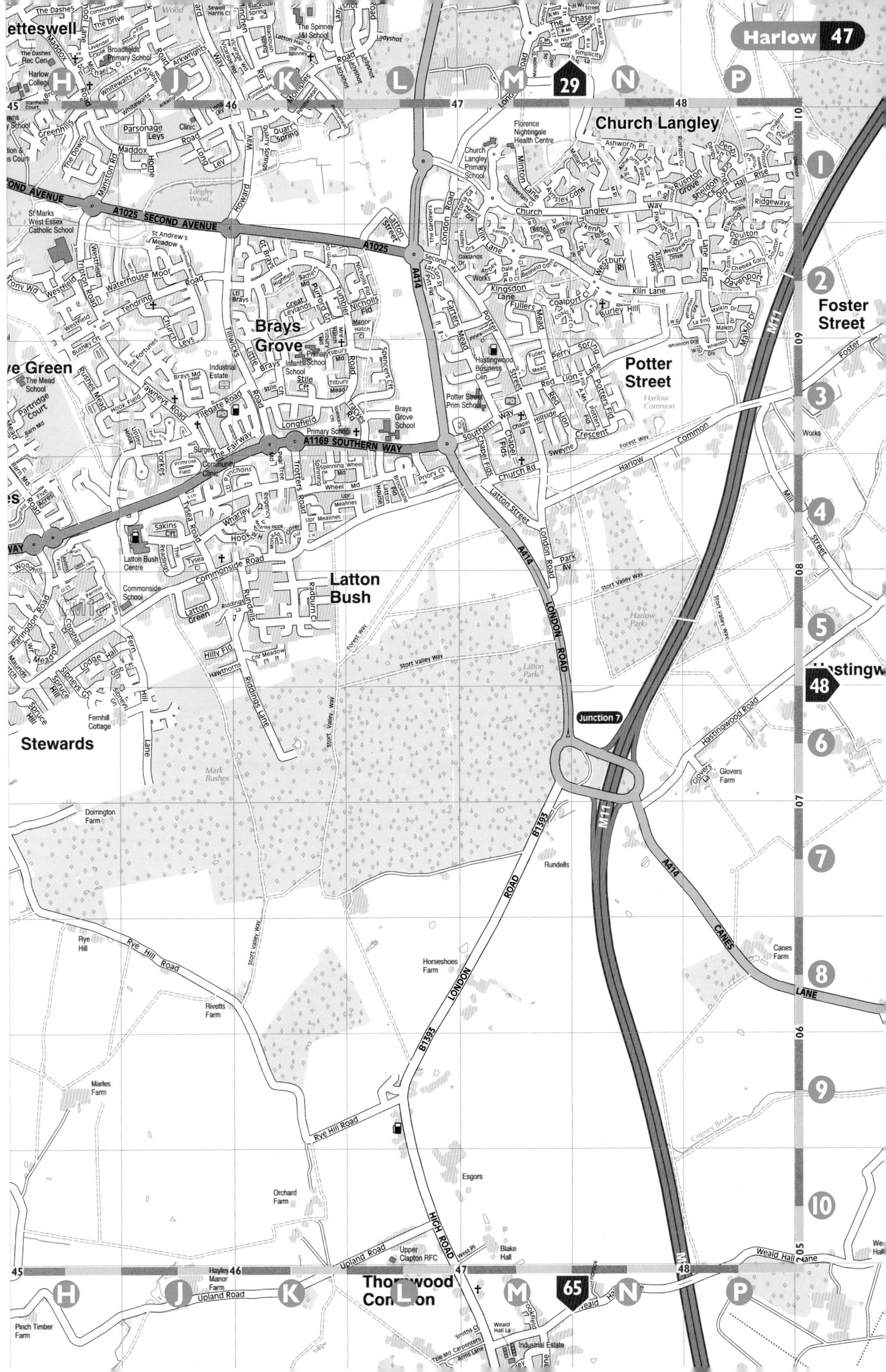
Netteswell
Church Langley
Brays Grove
Potter Street
Foster Street
Latton Bush
Stewards
Thornwood Common
Hastingwood
A1025 SECOND AVENUE
A1169 SOUTHERN WAY
A414
LONDON ROAD
B1393
M11
CANES LANE
HIGH ROAD
Junction 7
Harlow Common
Harlow Park
Latton Park
Mark Bushes
Longley Wood
St Marks West Essex Catholic School
Florence Nightingale Health Centre
Church Langley Primary School
Hastingwood Business Cen
Potter Street Prim School
Brays Grove School
Latton Bush Centre
Commonside School
Industrial Estate
Kiln Lane
Church Langley Way
Tilegate Road
Commonside Road
Rye Hill Road
Upland Road
Stort Valley Way
Forest Way
Hastingwood Road
Mill Street
Weald Hall Lane
Riddings Lane
Dorrington Farm
Rye Hill
Rivetts Farm
Marles Farm
Orchard Farm
Horseshoes Farm
Rundells
Esgors
Canes Farm
Glovers Farm
Fernhill Cottage
Upper Clapton RFC
Blake Hall
Hayley Manor Farm
Pinch Timber Farm
H
J
K
L
M
N
P
45
46
47
48
29
48
65
1
2
3
4
5
6
7
8
9
10

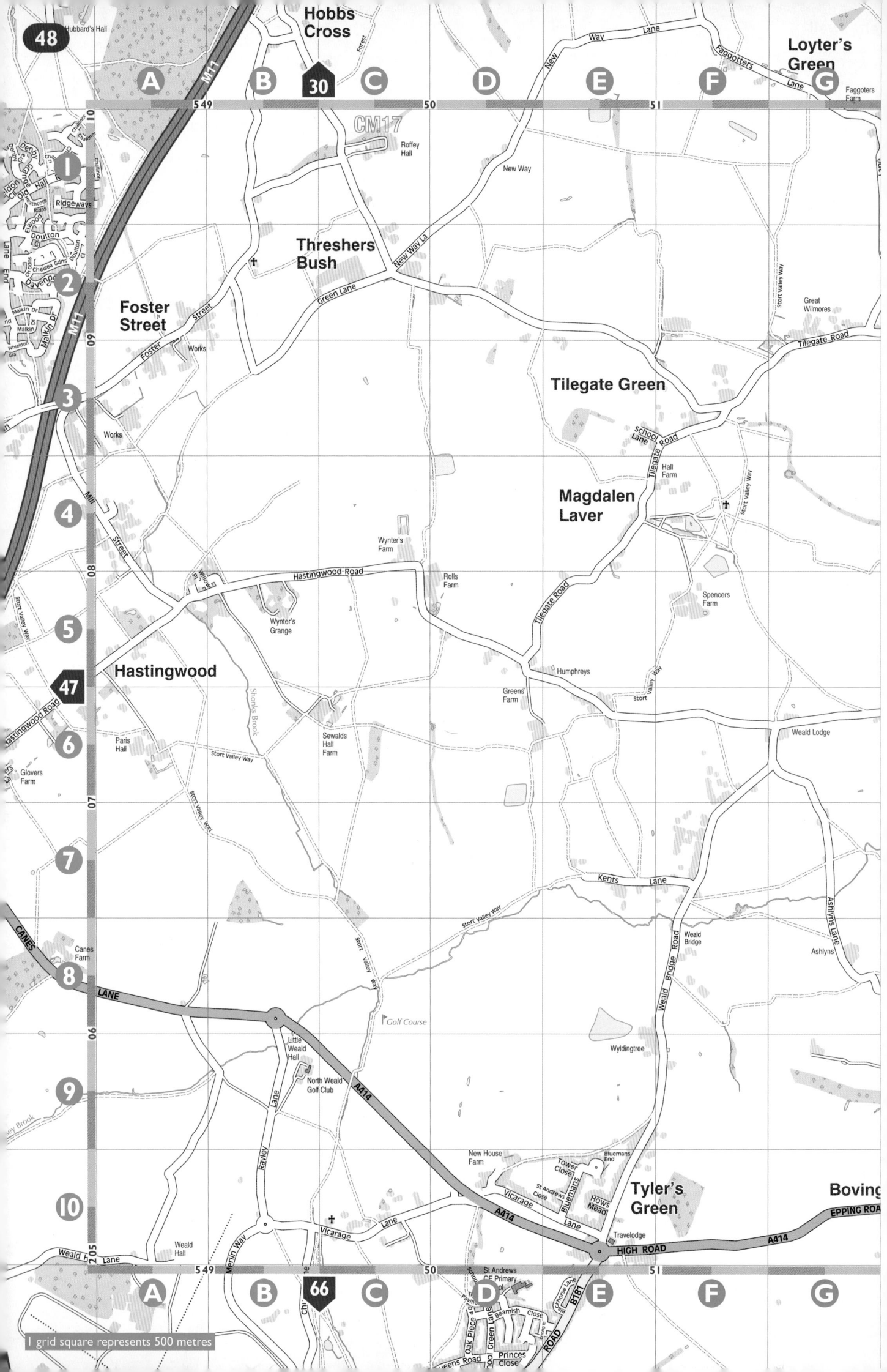
Hubbard's Hall
Hobbs
Cross
30
Forest
Way
Lane
New
Faggotters
Lane
Loyter's
Green
Faggoters
Farm
A
B
C
D
E
F
G
549
50
51
CM17
Roffey
Hall
New Way
M11
Ridgeways
Doulton
Chelsea Gdns
Malkin Dr
Threshers
Bush
New Way La
Green Lane
Foster
Street
Foster
Street
Works
Stort Valley Way
Great
Wilmores
Tilegate Road
Tilegate Green
School
Lane
Tilegate
Road
Hall
Farm
Magdalen
Laver
Works
Mill
Street
Stort Valley Way
Wynter's
Farm
Willow
Pl
Hastingwood Road
Rolls
Farm
Tilegate Road
Spencers
Farm
Wynter's
Grange
Hastingwood
47
Hastingwood Road
Humphreys
Greens
Farm
Stort
Valley
Way
Shonks Brook
Paris
Hall
Sewalds
Hall
Farm
Stort Valley Way
Weald Lodge
Glovers
Farm
Stort
Valley
Way
Kents
Lane
Stort Valley Way
Stort
Valley
Way
Weald
Bridge
Weald
Bridge
Road
Ashlyns
Lane
Ashlyns
Canes
Farm
CANES
LANE
Golf Course
Little
Weald
Hall
North Weald
Golf Club
A414
Wyldingtree
Lane
Rayley
New House
Farm
Bluemans
End
Tower
Close
St Andrews
Close
Bluemans
Hows
Mead
Tyler's
Green
Boving
EPPING ROA
Vicarage
Lane
A414
Vicarage
Lane
Travelodge
HIGH ROAD
A414
Weald
Hall
Weald Hall
Lane
Merlin Way
66
St Andrews
CE Primary
School
B181
ROAD
Beamish
Close
Oak Piece
Green Lane
Princes
Close
1
2
3
4
5
6
7
8
9
10
10
09
08
07
06
205

1 grid square represents 500 metres

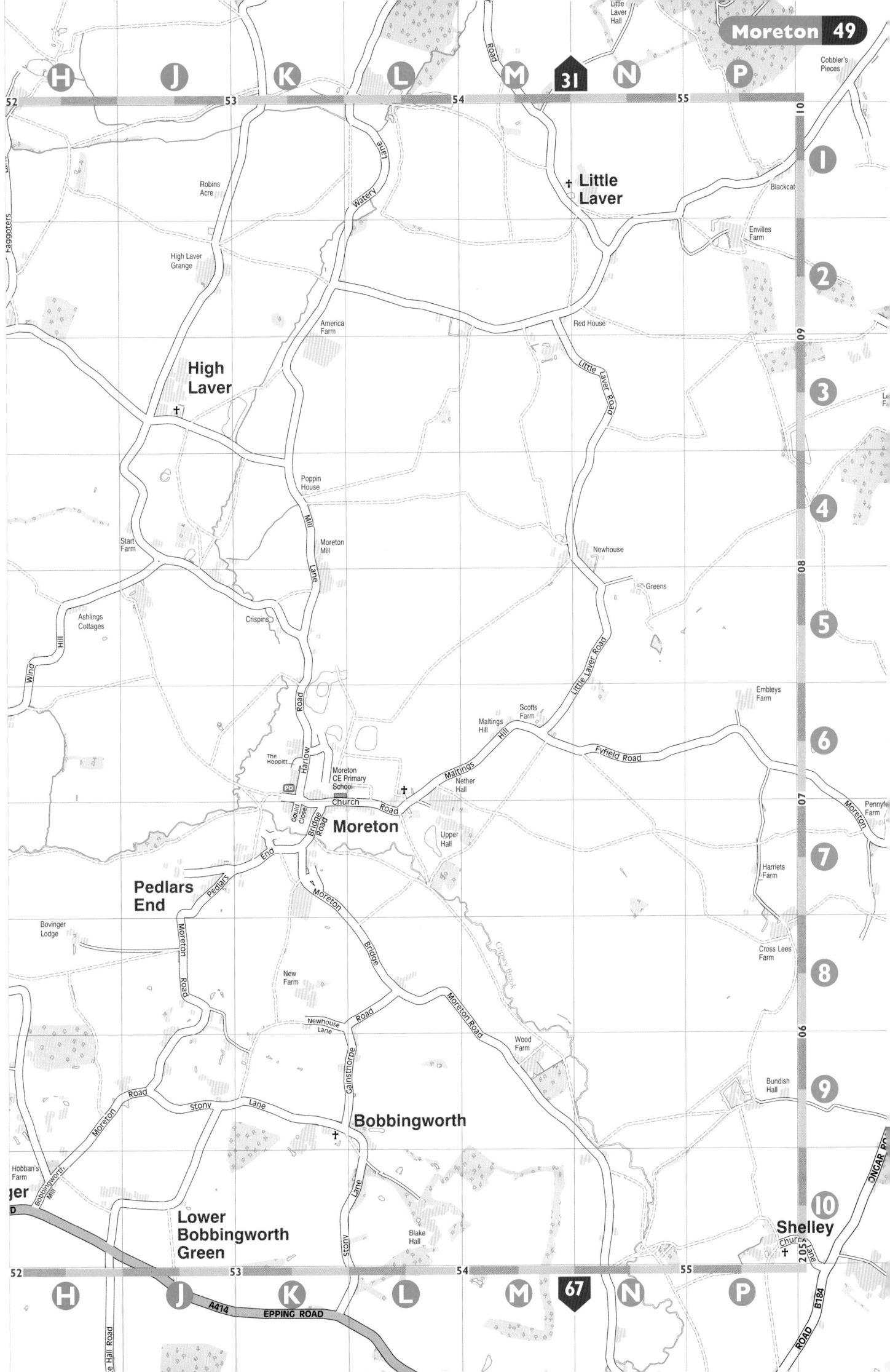

H **J** **K** **L** **M** **31** **N** **P**

52   53   54   55   10

1

Little Laver Hall

Cobbler's Pieces

Blackcat

Envilles Farm

† Little Laver

2

Robins Acre

Watery Lane

High Laver Grange

Red House

Little Laver Road

Le F

3

America Farm

09

High Laver

†

Poppin House

Newhouse

4

Greens

Mill Lane

Moreton Mill

08

Start Farm

Crispins

5

Ashlings Cottages

Embleys Farm

Wind Hill

Scotts Farm

Little Laver Road

6

Maltings Hill

Hill

Fyfield Road

Road

Harlow

The Hoppitt

Moreton CE Primary School

PO

Nether Hall

Maltings Road

†

Moreton Road

Pennyf Farm

07

7

Gould Close

Bridge Road

Church Road

Moreton

Upper Hall

Harriets Farm

Pedlars End

End

Pedlars

Moreton

Cripsey Brook

8

Bovinger Lodge

Moreton Road

Cross Lees Farm

06

New Farm

Bridge Road

Moreton Road

Wood Farm

Bundish Hall

9

Newhouse Lane

Gainsthorpe

Road

Moreton Road

Stony Lane

Bobbingworth

†

10

Hobban's Farm

Bobbingworth Mill

Lower Bobbingworth Green

Stony Lane

Blake Hall

Shelley

Church Lane

†

ONGAR R

ROAD B184

52   53   54   55

H **J** **K** **L** **M** **67** **N** **P**

A414   EPPING ROAD

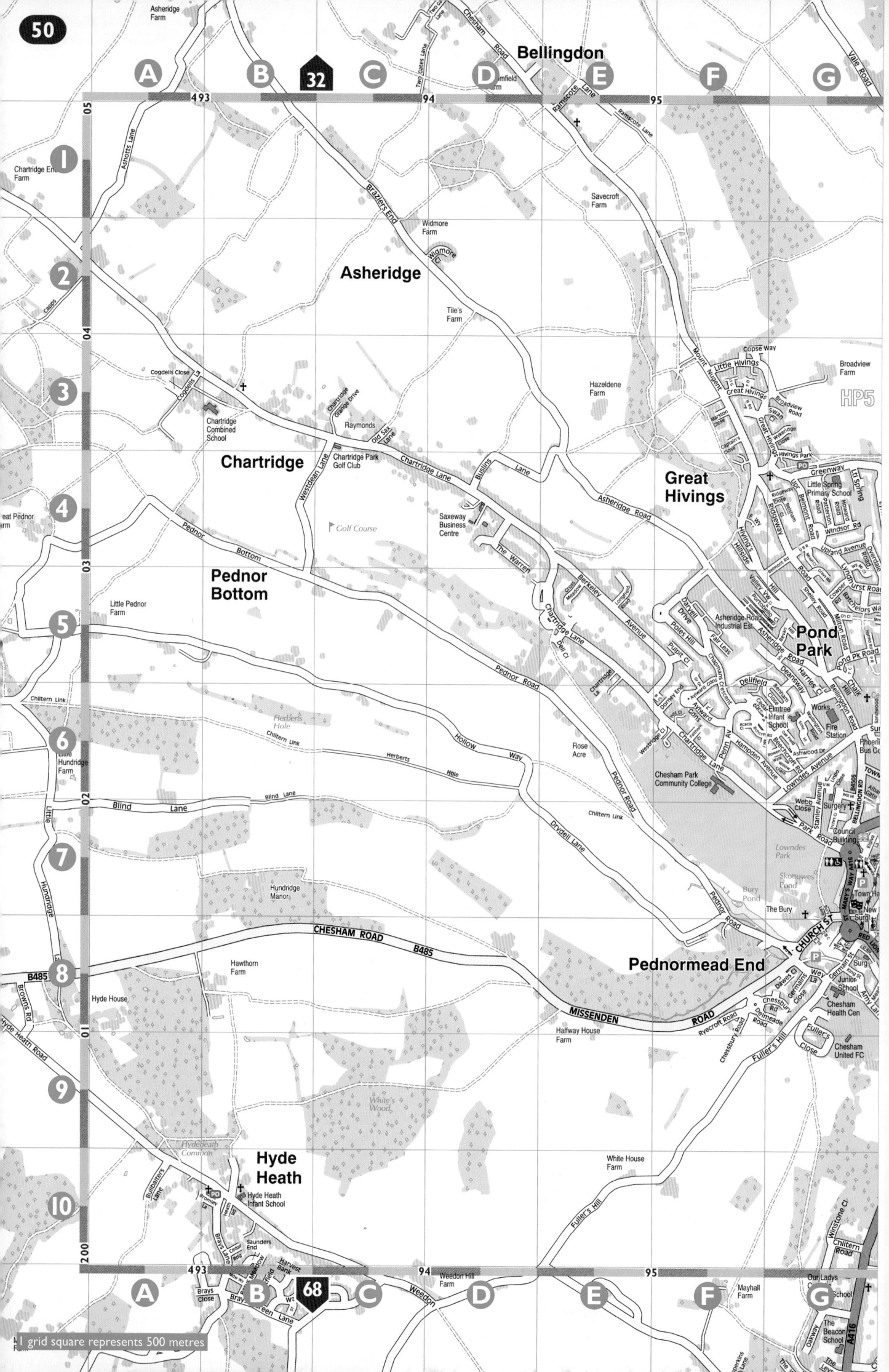

50

A   B   **32**   C   D   E   F   G

05   493   94   **Bellingdon**   95

Two Gates Lane
Chesham Road
Dimfield Farm
Ramscote Lane
Ramscote Lane

I
Chartridge End Farm
Ashotts Lane

Savecroft Farm

2
Capos
Brazlers End
Widmore Farm
Widmore Cl
Asheridge
Tile's Farm
Hazeldene Farm

04

3
Cogdells Close
Cogdells
Chartridge Combined School
Chartridge Grange Drive
Raymonds
Old Sax Lane
Little Hivings
Great Hivings
Broadview Road
Copse Way
Broadview Farm
Marston Close
Captain's Close
PO
Greenway
HP5

03

Chartridge
Westdean Lane
Chartridge Park Golf Club
Chartridge Lane
Buslins Lane
Asheridge Road
Great Hivings
Little Spring Primary School
Windsor Rd
Upland Avenue
Overdale

4
Pednor
Bottom
Golf Course
Saxeway Business Centre
The Warren
Chartridge Lane
Berkeley Avenue
Hillside
Danren Drive
Poles Hill
Tail Leas
Asheridge Road Industrial Est
Deansway
Pond Park
Milton Road
Bachelors Way

Pednor Bottom
Little Pednor Farm

5
Great Pednor Farm
Pednor Bottom
Dell Cl
Fuller Cl
Dorney End
Chartridge La
Aylesbury Gdns
Chesham Avenue Crescent
Cross Gate
Delifield
Elmtree Infant School
Works
Chalk

02

Chiltern Link

6
Little Hundridge Farm
Herberts Hole
Chiltern Link
Herberts Hole
Hollow Way
Rose Acre
Pednor Road
Westridge
Penn Av
Hampden Avenue
Fire Station
Phoenix Bus Cen

7
Little Hundridge
Blind Lane
Blind Lane
Drydell Lane
Chiltern Link
Chesham Park Community College
Lowndes Avenue
Webb Close
Stanley Avenue
BB505
BELLINGDON RD
Surgery
Council Building
New Town

01

8
B485
Hyde House
Hydeheath Road
Hawthorn Farm
CHESHAM ROAD   B485
Lowndes Park
Bury Pond
Skottowes Pond
The Bury
St Mary's Way A416
Town Hall
P
New
Surg
Pednormead End
CHURCH ST
RED LION
P

9
Browns Rd
MISSENDEN   **ROAD**
Halfway House Farm
Ryecroft Road
Chessbury Road
Dermeade Road
Fuller's Hill
Chessbury Rd
Dawes Cl
Germains Close
Chesham Health Cen
Junior School
Amy La
Fuller's Close
Chesham United FC

00

10
Hydeheath Common
Bullbaiters Lane
Bromley
Heath End
PO
Hyde Heath Infant School
Hyde Heath
Saunders End
White House Farm
Chiltern Road

200   493   94   Weedon   95   A416

A   B   **68**   C   D   E   F   G
Brays Close
Brays Green Lane
Cedar Rd
Meadow
Field
Harvest Bank
Weedon Hill Farm
Mayhall Farm
Our Ladys School
The Beacon School
Oakway

1 grid square represents 500 metres

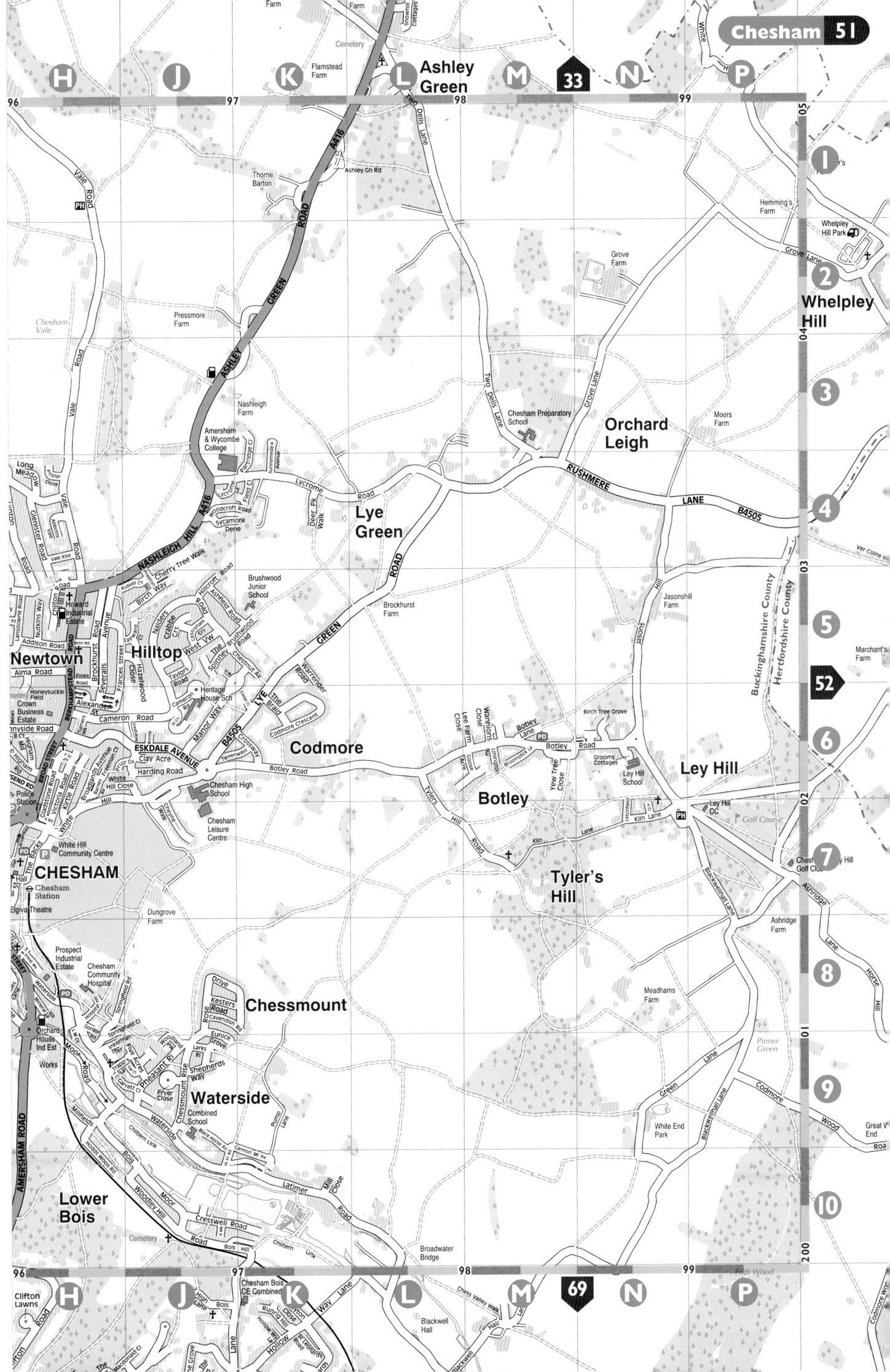
Ashley Green
Cemetery
Flamstead Farm
33
Thorne Barton
Ashley Gn Rd
Two Dells Lane
ASHLEY GREEN ROAD
A416
Vale Road
Chesham Vale
Pressmore Farm
Nashleigh Farm
Amersham & Wycombe College
Grove Farm
Hemming's Farm
Whelpley Hill Park
Grove Lane
Whelpley Hill
Chesham Preparatory School
Grove Lane
Orchard Leigh
Moors Farm
RUSHMERE LANE
B4505
Lycrome Road
Lye Green
Deer Pk Walk
Woodcroft Road
Sycamore Dene
NASHLEIGH HILL
Cherry Tree Walk
Ver Colne Valley
Brushwood Junior School
Brockhurst Farm
Jasonshill Farm
Jasons Hill
Buckinghamshire County
Hertfordshire County
Marchant's Farm
52
Long Meadow
Glenister Road
Howard Industrial Estate
Newtown
Hilltop
Alma Road
Addison Road
BERKHAMPSTEAD ROAD
Crown Business Estate
Cameron Road
Heritage House Sch
LYE GREEN ROAD
Warrender Road
Codmore Crescent
Codmore
ESKDALE AVENUE
Manor Way
B4505
Clay Acre
Harding Road
Botley Road
Chesham High School
Chesham Leisure Centre
White Hill
White Hill Community Centre
CHESHAM
Chesham Station
Elgiva Theatre
Police Station
BROAD STREET
Botley Lane
Birch Tree Grove
Ley Hill School
Ley Hill
Botley
Tylers Hill Road
Kiln Lane
Ley Hill CC
Golf Course
Chesham & Ley Hill Golf Club
Tyler's Hill
Blackwell Hall Lane
Ashridge Lane
Ashridge Farm
Horse Hill
Dungrove Farm
Prospect Industrial Estate
Chesham Community Hospital
Chessmount
Meadhams Farm
Pinner Green
Orchard House Ind Est
Works
Moor Road
Pheasant Ri
Shepherds Way
Waterside
Waterside Combined School
Pump Lane
Green Lane
White End Park
Codmore Wood Road
Great Wood End
AMERSHAM ROAD
Lower Bois
Latimer Road
Mill Close
Cresswell Road
Cemetery
Bois Hill
Broadwater Bridge
Chiltern Link
Frith Wood
69
Clifton Lawns
Chesham Bois CE Combined
Chess Valley Walk
Blackwell Hall
H J K L M N P
96 97 98 99
05 04 03 02 01 200
1 2 3 4 5 6 7 8 9 10

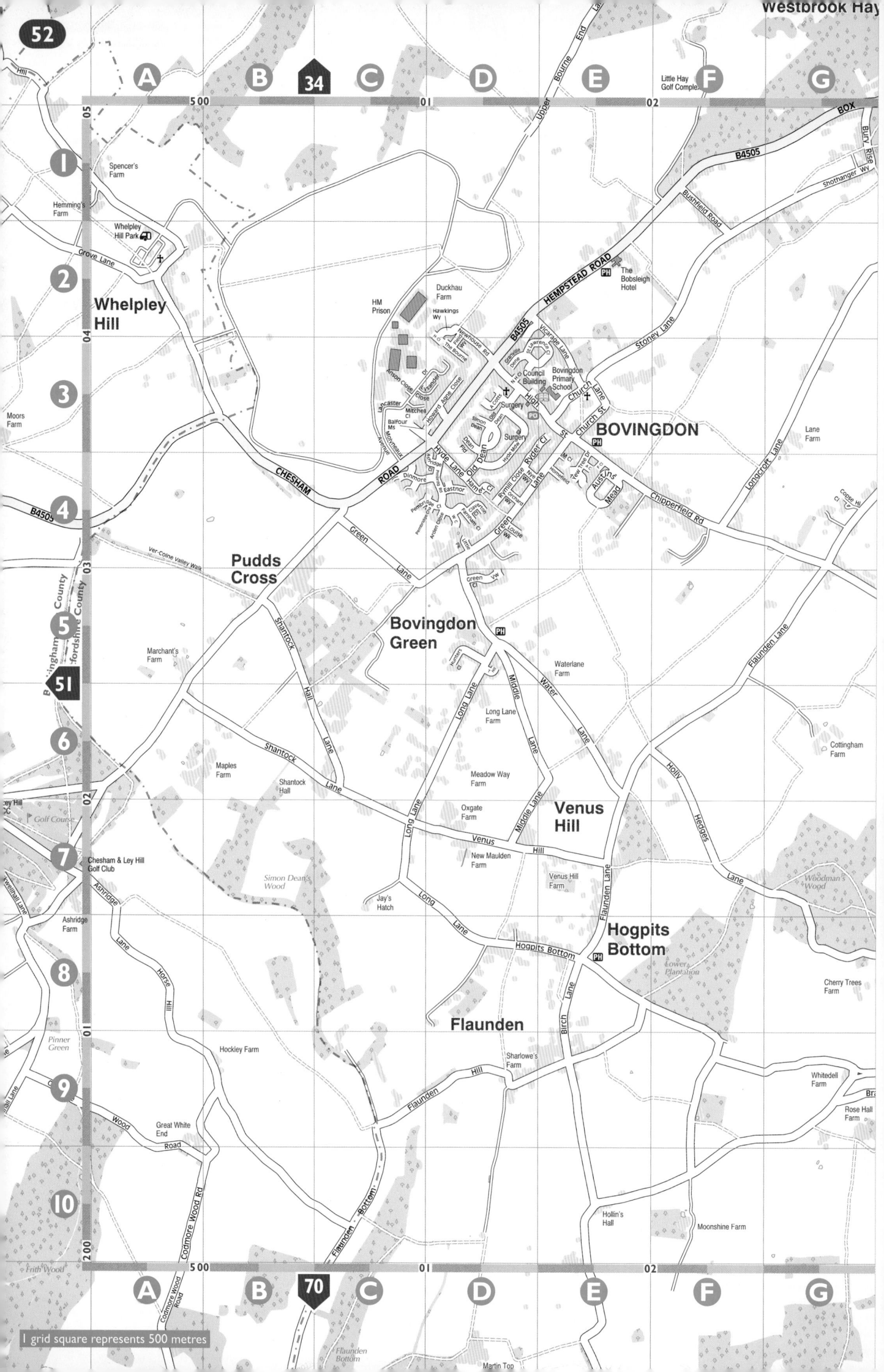
52
Westbrook Hay
34
70
51
500
01
02
05
04
03
02
01
200
Little Hay Golf Complex
Spencer's Farm
Hemming's Farm
Whelpley Hill Park
Grove Lane
Whelpley Hill
Moors Farm
HM Prison
Duckhau Farm
Hawkings Wy
Newhouse Rd
The Bourne
Anson Close
Lancaster
Balfour Ms
Mitchell Cl
Howard Agne Close
Avenue
Molyneaux
HEMPSTEAD ROAD
B4505
The Bobsleigh Hotel
Bushfield Road
Stoney Lane
Shothanger Wy
Bury Rise
BOX
Vicarage Lane
Granville Dene
St Lawrence Cl
Council Building
Bovingdon Primary School
Church Lane
Church St
High St
Surgery
BOVINGDON
Simon Dean
Old Dean
Dean Fld
Hyde Lane
Hyde Mdw
Ryder Cl
Rymill Close
Nye Wy
Orchard Wy
Homefield
Yew Tree Dr
Austins Mead
Chipperfield Rd
Longcroft Lane
Lane Farm
Coppse Hl
Ashridge Cl
Dinmore
Eastnor
Hamer Cl
Pembridge Cl
Pembridge Chase
Clavering Cl
Farnham Cl
Arden Close
Little Green
Green Lane
Louise Wk
CHESHAM ROAD
B4505
Ver-Colne Valley Walk
Pudds Cross
Green Cl
Green Vw
Bovingdon Green
Buckinghamshire County
Hertfordshire County
Marchant's Farm
Shantock Hall Lane
Hunters
Waterlane Farm
Water Lane
Middle Lane
Long Lane
Long Lane Farm
Flaunden Lane
Cottingham Farm
Maples Farm
Shantock Hall
Shantock Lane
Meadow Way Farm
Oxgate Farm
Venus Hill
Holly Hedges Lane
Ley Hill GC
Golf Course
Chesham & Ley Hill Golf Club
Ashridge Lane
New Maulden Farm
Venus Hill Farm
Woodman's Wood
Simon Dean's Wood
Jay's Hatch
Ashridge Farm
Hogpits Bottom
Hogpits Bottom
Lower Plantation
Cherry Trees Farm
Horse Hill
Birch Lane
Flaunden
Pinner Green
Hockley Farm
Sharlowe's Farm
Flaunden Hill
Whitedell Farm
Rose Hall Farm
Wood Road
Great White End
Codmore Wood Rd
Flaunden Bottom
Hollin's Hall
Moonshine Farm
Frith Wood
Codmore Wood Road
Flaunden Bottom
Martin Top
1 grid square represents 500 metres

Bulstrode
Tower Hill
Chipperfield
Whippendell Bottom
Rucklers Lane
Belsize
Commonwood
Bucks Hill
Sarratt
Apsley
HP3
WD4
Scatterdells Wood
Praisels Wood
Chipperfield Common
Rockery Wood
Rosehall Wood
Pepman's Green
Bury Wood
Sheethanger Common
Boxmoor Golf Club
Shendish Manor Golf Club
Apsley Station
Hyde Farm
Tower Farm
Longcroft Farm
Valley Farm
Nuffield Farm
Apsley Manor Farm
Barnes Farm
Balls Pond Farm
Whippendell Farm
Meggacres Farm
Tenements Farm
Tuffs Farm
Chipperfield House
Braziers Farm
Pale Farm
The Two Brewers Hotel
Chipperfield J&I School
Rose Farm
Woodmans Farm
Hollow Hedge
Belsize Farm
Hillmeads Farm
Callipers Hall
Jeffery's Farm
Baytree Farm
Great Sarratt Hall
Langley Lodge Farm
Rudolf Steiner School
Wyevale Garden Centre
Great Westwood
Rucklers Lane
Barnes Lane
Chipperfield Road
Langley Road
Flaunden Lane
Bulstrode Lane
Tower Hill
Scatterdells Lane
Dunny Lane
The Common
Windmill Hill
Bucks Hill
Quickmoor Lane
Plough Lane
Poles Hill
Langley Lodge Lane
A41
A414
London Road A4251
35
54
71

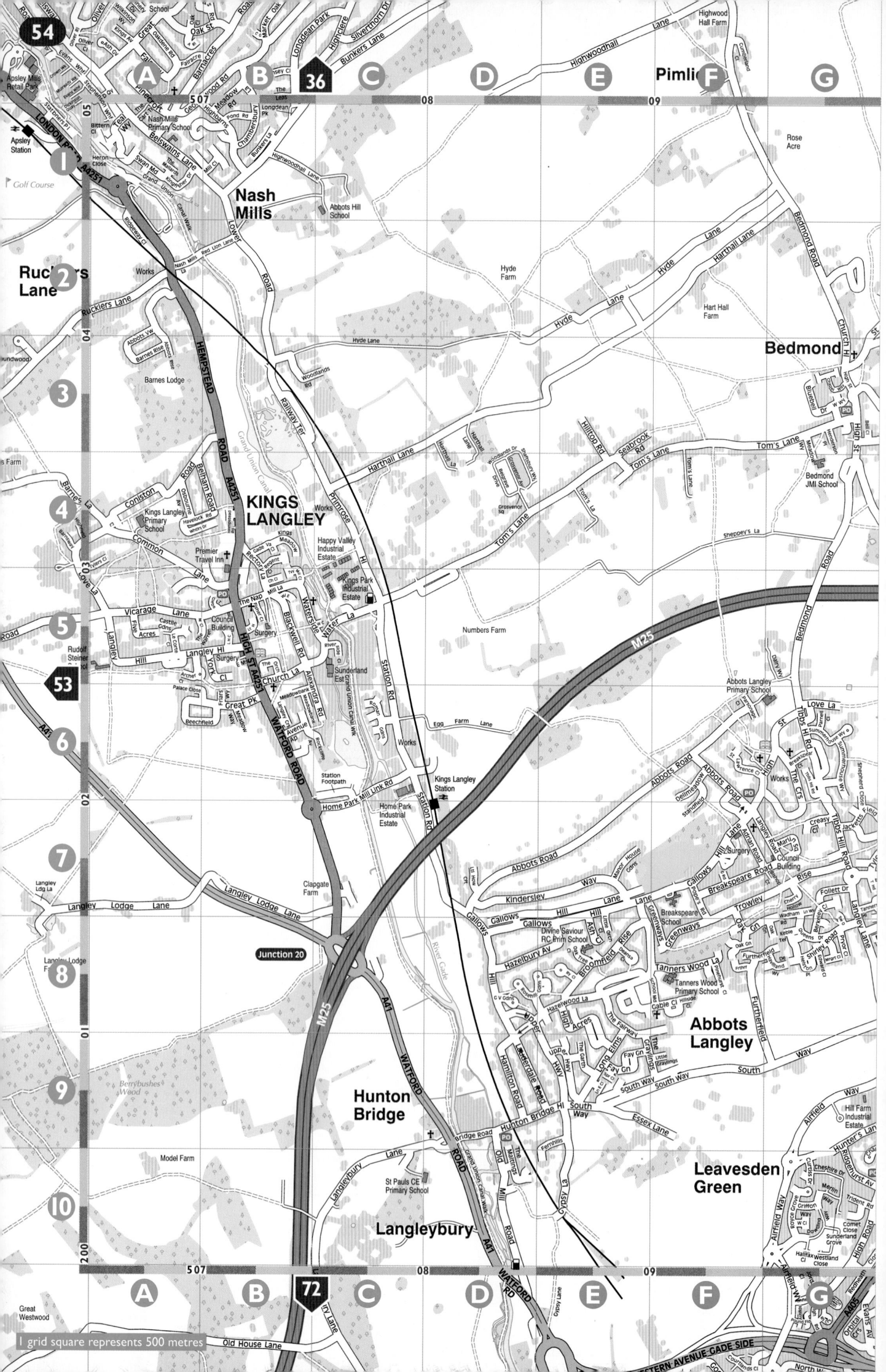
54
36
53
72
A
B
C
D
E
F
G
1
2
3
4
5
6
7
8
9
10
507
08
09
05
04
03
02
01
200
Apsley Mills Retail Park
Apsley Station
LONDON ROAD
A4251
Golf Course
Nash Mills Primary School
Nash Mills
Abbots Hill School
Highwood Hall Farm
Highwoodhall Lane
Bunkers Lane
Longdean Park
Pimlico
Rose Acre
Bedmond Road
Ruckle rs Lane
Ruckle rs Lane
Works
Hyde Farm
Hyde Lane
Harthall Lane
Hart Hall Farm
Bedmond
Church Hl
Barnes Lodge
HEMPSTEAD ROAD
A4251
Grand Union Canal
Railway Ter
Woodlands Rd
Hyde Lane
KINGS LANGLEY
Kings Langley Primary School
Premier Travel Inn
Happy Valley Industrial Estate
Kings Park Industrial Estate
Primrose Hl
Harthall Lane
Tom's Lane
Seabrook Rd
Bedmond JMI School
Sheppey's La
Common Lane
Vicarage Lane
Council Building
Langley Hill
Rudolf Steiner
Surgery
Sunderland Est
Station Rd
Numbers Farm
M25
Bedmond Road
HIGH ST A4251
WATFORD ROAD
Great Pk
Egg Farm Lane
Works
Kings Langley Station
Home Park Mill Link Rd
Home Park Industrial Estate
Station Footpath
Abbots Langley Primary School
Abbots Road
Love La
Tibbs Hl Rd
Langley Ldg La
Langley Lodge Lane
Clapgate Farm
Abbots Road
Kindersley Way
Gallows Hill Lane
Breakspeare Road
Breakspeare School
Divine Saviour RC Prim School
Junction 20
A41
River Gade
Hazelbury Av
Tanners Wood Primary School
Abbots Langley
Furtherfield
Langley Lodge Farm
Berrybushes Wood
WATFORD ROAD
Hunton Bridge
Hamilton Road
South Way
Essex Lane
Hunton Bridge Hl
Bridge Road
Model Farm
Langleybury Lane
St Pauls CE Primary School
Langleybury
Leavesden Green
Airfield Way
Hill Farm Industrial Estate
Mill Road
Gypsy Lane
Old House Lane
1 grid square represents 500 metres

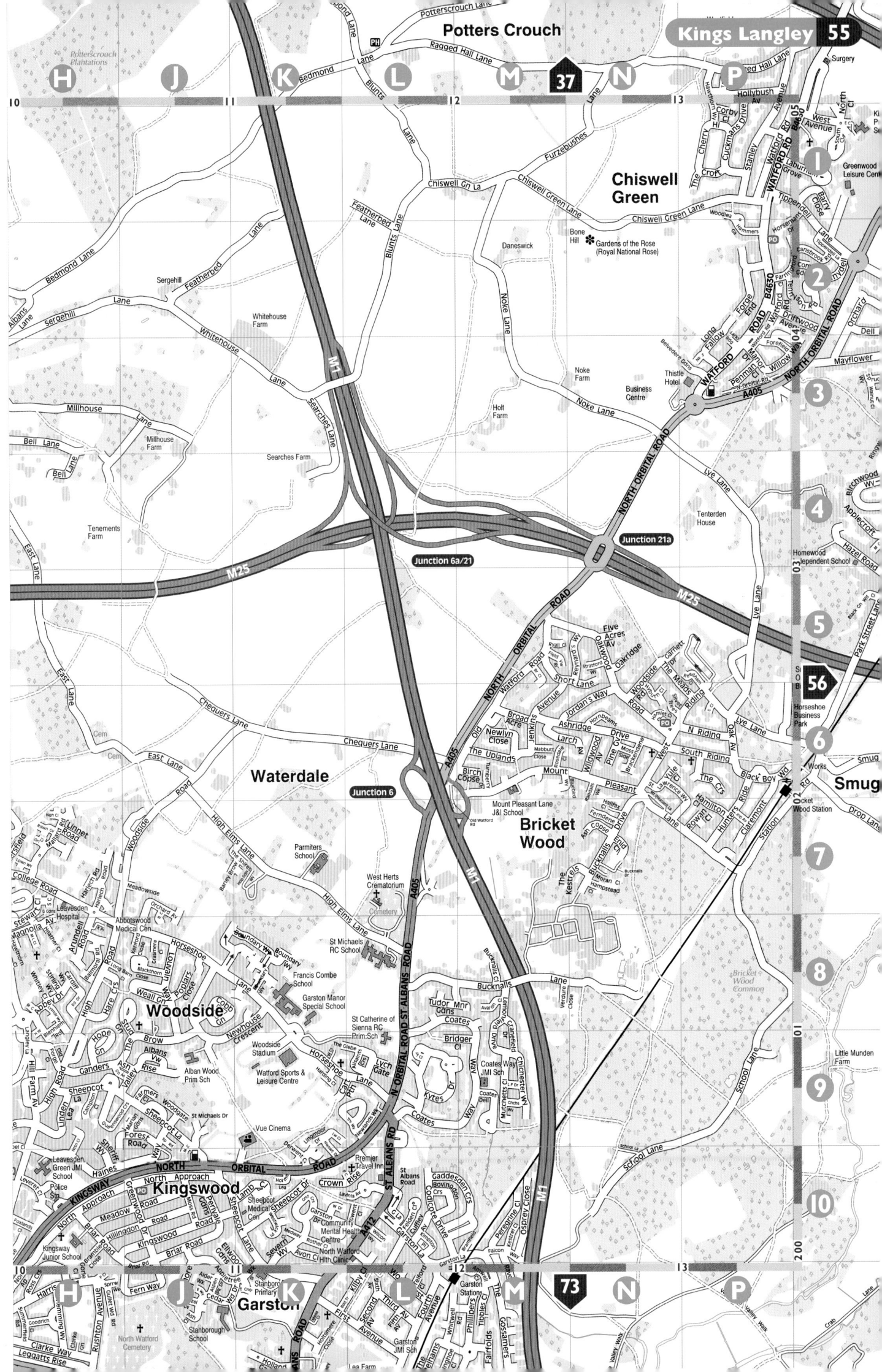
Potters Crouch
Potterscrouch Lane
Ragged Hall Lane
Bedmond Lane
Bluntts Lane
Potterscrouch Plantations
37
Chiswell Green
Chiswell Green Lane
Chiswell Gn La
Furzebushes
Hollybush Av
Watford Rd
Watford Road
B4630
Tippendell Lane
Greenwood Leisure Cen
Bone Hill
Gardens of the Rose (Royal National Rose)
Daneswick
Featherbed Lane
Blunts Lane
Sergehill
Sergehill Lane
Whitehouse Farm
Whitehouse Lane
Noke Lane
Noke Farm
Holt Farm
Business Centre
Thistle Hotel
North Orbital Road
A405
Millhouse Lane
Millhouse Farm
Bell Lane
Searches Lane
Searches Farm
Lye Lane
Tenterden House
Tenements Farm
Junction 21a
Junction 6a/21
M25
M1
East Lane
Homewood Independent School
56
Horseshoe Business Park
Chequers Lane
Waterdale
Junction 6
Bricket Wood
Smug
Bricket Wood Station
Mount Pleasant Lane J&I School
Parmiters School
West Herts Crematorium
Cemetery
High Elms Lane
Leavesden Hospital
Abbotswood Medical Cen
St Michaels RC School
Francis Combe School
Garston Manor Special School
St Catherine of Sienna RC Prim Sch
Woodside
Woodside Stadium
Watford Sports & Leisure Centre
Alban Wood Prim Sch
Coates Way JMI Sch
Bucknalls Lane
Bricket Wood Common
Little Munden Farm
School Lane
Vue Cinema
Premier Travel Inn
North Orbital Road
St Albans Road
A412
Kingswood
Kingsway
Leavesden Green JMI School
Police Stn
Sheepcot Medical Cen
Garston Community Mental Health Centre
North Watford Hlth Clinic
Kingsway Junior School
Garston
Garston Station
Stanborough Primary
Stanborough School
North Watford Cemetery
Garston JMI Sch
73

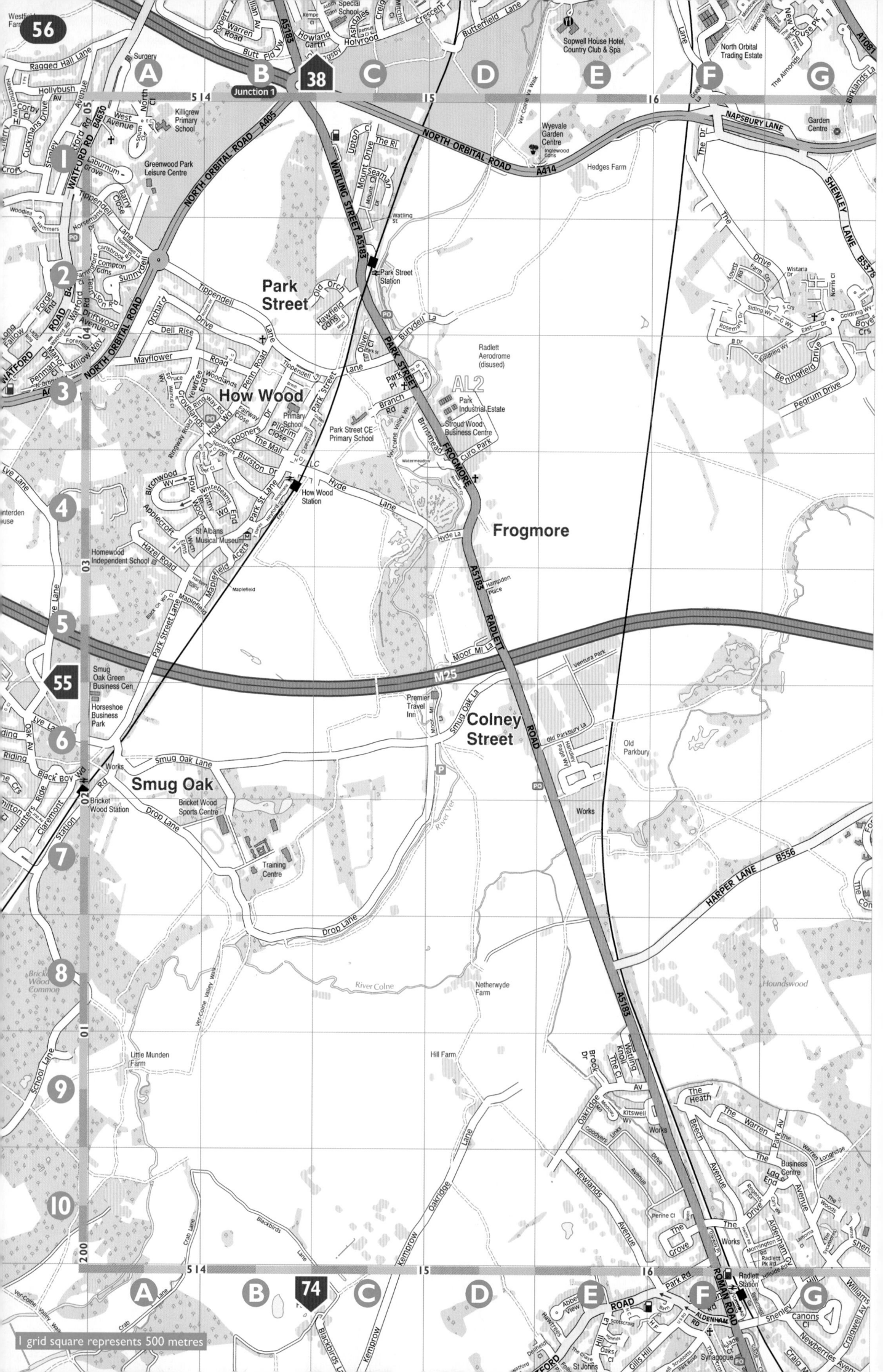

Park Street
How Wood
Frogmore
Colney Street
Smug Oak
AL2
Junction 1
38
55
74
A
B
C
D
E
F
G
1
2
3
4
5
6
7
8
9
10
NORTH ORBITAL ROAD
A405
A414
WATLING STREET A5183
PARK STREET
FROGMORE
RADLETT ROAD
A5183
M25
WATFORD ROAD
B4630
NAPSBURY LANE
SHENLEY LANE B5378
HARPER LANE B556
ROMAN ROAD
ALDENHAM RD
A1081
Sopwell House Hotel, Country Club & Spa
North Orbital Trading Estate
Killigrew Primary School
Greenwood Park Leisure Centre
Wyevale Garden Centre
Garden Centre
Hedges Farm
Park Street Station
Radlett Aerodrome (disused)
Park Industrial Estate
Stroud Wood Business Centre
Park Street CE Primary School
Primary School
How Wood Station
St Albans Musical Museum
Homewood Independent School
Smug Oak Green Business Cen
Horseshoe Business Park
Premier Travel Inn
Old Parkbury
Bricket Wood Station
Bricket Wood Sports Centre
Training Centre
Works
River Ver
River Colne
Netherwyde Farm
Little Munden Farm
Hill Farm
Houndswood
Bricket Wood Common
Radlett Station
Synagogue
Tippendell Lane
Hyde Lane
Burydell La
Mayflower Road
Dell Rise
Orchard Drive
Penn Road
Ringway Road
Spooners Dr
The Mall
Burston Dr
Birchwood Wy
Applecroft
Hazel Road
Maplefield
Park Street Lane
Drop Lane
Smug Oak Lane
Smug Oak La
Old Parkbury La
Moor Mill La
Blackbirds Lane
Crab Lane
Kemprow
Oakridge Lane
School Lane
Lye Lane
Black Boy Wd
Station Rd
Hunters Ride
Claremont
Oak Av
Newlands Avenue
Oakridge Av
Kitswell Wy
Links Avenue
Watling Knoll
Brook Dr
Beech Avenue
The Warren
The Heath
Aldenham Avenue
Regents Drive
Park Av
Longridge
The Business Centre
Pegrum Drive
Beningfield Drive
Butterfield Lane
Holyrood Crescent
Howland Garth
Butt Fld Vw
Warren Road
Ragged Hall Lane
Hollybush Av
Cuckmans Drive
Laburnum Grove
Tippendell La
Sunnydell
Driftwood Avenue
Willow Way
Ver-Colne Valley Walk
Upton Cl
Mount Drive
Old Orch
Hawfield Gdns
Oliver Cl
Branch Rd
Brinsmead
Curo Park
Hampden Place
Park Pl
Surgery
Westfield Farm
Watermeadow
The Almonds
New House Pk
Birklands La
The Drive
Park Rd
St Johns
Scotscraig
1 grid square represents 500 metres

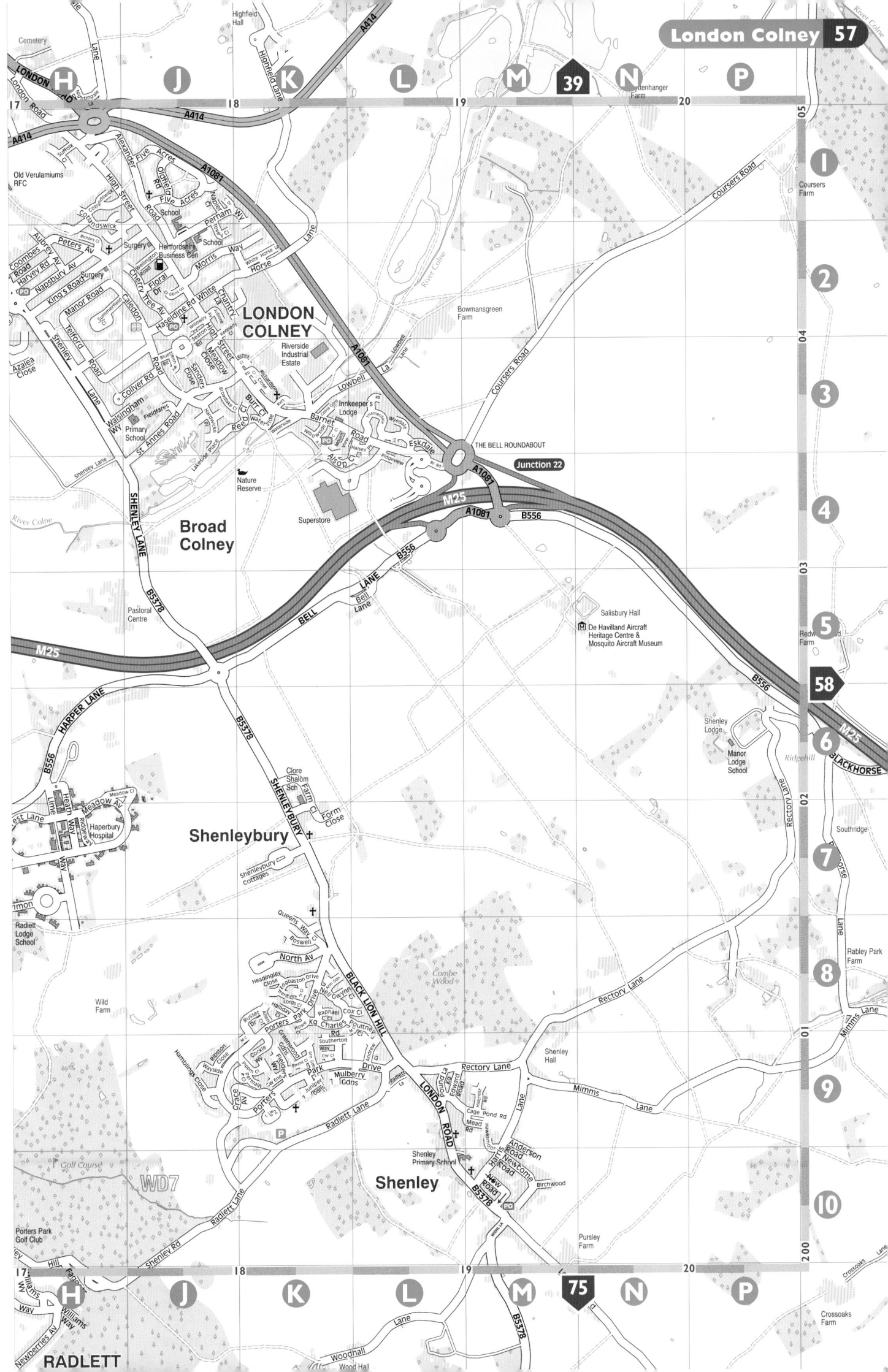
H
J
K
L
M
39
N
P
17
18
19
20
05
04
03
02
01
200
1
2
3
4
5
6
7
8
9
10
58
75
Cemetery
Highfield Hall
Highfield Lane
LONDON ROAD
London Road
A414
Tittenhanger Farm
Old Verulamiums RFC
Alexander Road
Five Acres
High Street
A1081
School
Surgery
Hertfordshire Business Cen
Peters Av
Coombes Road
Harvey Rd
Aubrey Av
Napsbury Av
King's Road
Manor Road
Telford Road
Caledon Road
Cherry Tree Av
Floral Dr
Haseldine Rd
White Horse Lane
Morris Way
Chantry La
LONDON COLNEY
Riverside Industrial Estate
Lowbell Lane
Lowbell La
Innkeeper's Lodge
Barnet Road
Alsop Cl
Eskdale
Meadow Close
Sanders Close
Burr Cl
Reed Cl
Waterside
Colliver Rd
Walsingham Wy
Primary School
St. Annes Road
Fieldfares
Azalea Close
Shenley Lane
SHENLEY LANE
Nature Reserve
Superstore
Broad Colney
River Colne
Bowmansgreen Farm
Coursers Road
Coursers Farm
THE BELL ROUNDABOUT
Junction 22
M25
B556
BELL LANE
Bell Lane
B5378
Pastoral Centre
Salisbury Hall
De Havilland Aircraft Heritage Centre & Mosquito Aircraft Museum
Redwell Wood Farm
HARPER LANE
Shenley Lodge
Manor Lodge School
Ridgehill
BLACKHORSE
Rectory Lane
Southridge
Clore Shalom Sch
SHENLEYBURY
Farm Cl
Farm Close
Shenleybury
Shenleybury Cottages
Haperbury Hospital
Heath Way
Meadow Av
Radlett Lodge School
Queens Way
Boswell Cl
North Av
BLACK LION HILL
Headingley Close
Edgbaston Drive
Porters Park Drive
Kg Charles Rd
Poultney Cl
Combe Wood
Wild Farm
Rabley Park Farm
Mimms Lane
Hamblings Close
Ribston Close
Wayside
Grace Av
Mulberry Gdns
Radlett Lane
Rectory Lane
Shenley Hall
Pound La
Edward Road
Cage Pond Rd
Mead Rd
Anderson Road
Newcome Road
Birchwood
Shenley Primary School
LONDON ROAD
Shenley
Pursley Farm
Golf Course
WD7
Porters Park Golf Club
Shenley Rd
Williams Way
Newberries Av
RADLETT
Woodhall Lane
Wood Hall
Crossoaks Farm
Crossoaks Lane

A
B
40
C
D
E
F
G
521
22
23
05
04
03
02
01
200
1
2
3
4
5
6
7
8
9
10
River Colne
Tollgate Road
Road
A1(M)
Dixons Hill Close
Dixons Hill Road
Welham Manor
Bulls Lane
Station Road
Coursers Road
Coursers Farm
Potterells Medical Centre
Potterells
North Mymms CC
Water End
Bradmore Lane
Walsingham Wood
Brookmans Station
Abdale Lane
Swanland Road
Warrengate Road
Royal Veterinary College
Cobs Ash
Potwells
Mymmshall Wood
Mymmshall Brook
Redwell Wood Farm
Redwell Wood
Hawkshead Wood
57
Manor Lodge School
Ridgehill
M25
BLACKHORSE LANE B556
Blackhorse Lane
The Grange
Warrengate Farm
Rectory Lane
Southridge
Packhorse Lane
Warrengate Lane
Mymms Hall
B556
ST ALBANS ROAD
Deepdene
Windmore Avenue
Wroxham Gardens
Wroxham School
Ormesby Drive
Mimms Hall Road
Oulton Crescent
Catharine Bourne
Brookside
CECIL ROAD
South Mimms
Rabley Park Farm
Mimms Lane
Blanche Lane
Frowycke Crs
St Giles Primary School
St Giles' Avenue
St Albans Road
Deeves Hall
Deeves Hall Lane
Earls Lane
Earl's Farm
Greyhound Lane
Hamilton Close
Bridgefoot
Kimptons Close
Kimptons Mead
Bignell's Corner
Crossoaks Lane
Ridge
Blanche Farm
Days Inn
South Mimms Service Area
Junction 1/23
Bignells Corner
76
Crossoaks Farm
Summerswood Lane
Summerswood Farm
ST ALBANS ROAD A1081
Dancers Hill
1 grid square represents 500 metres

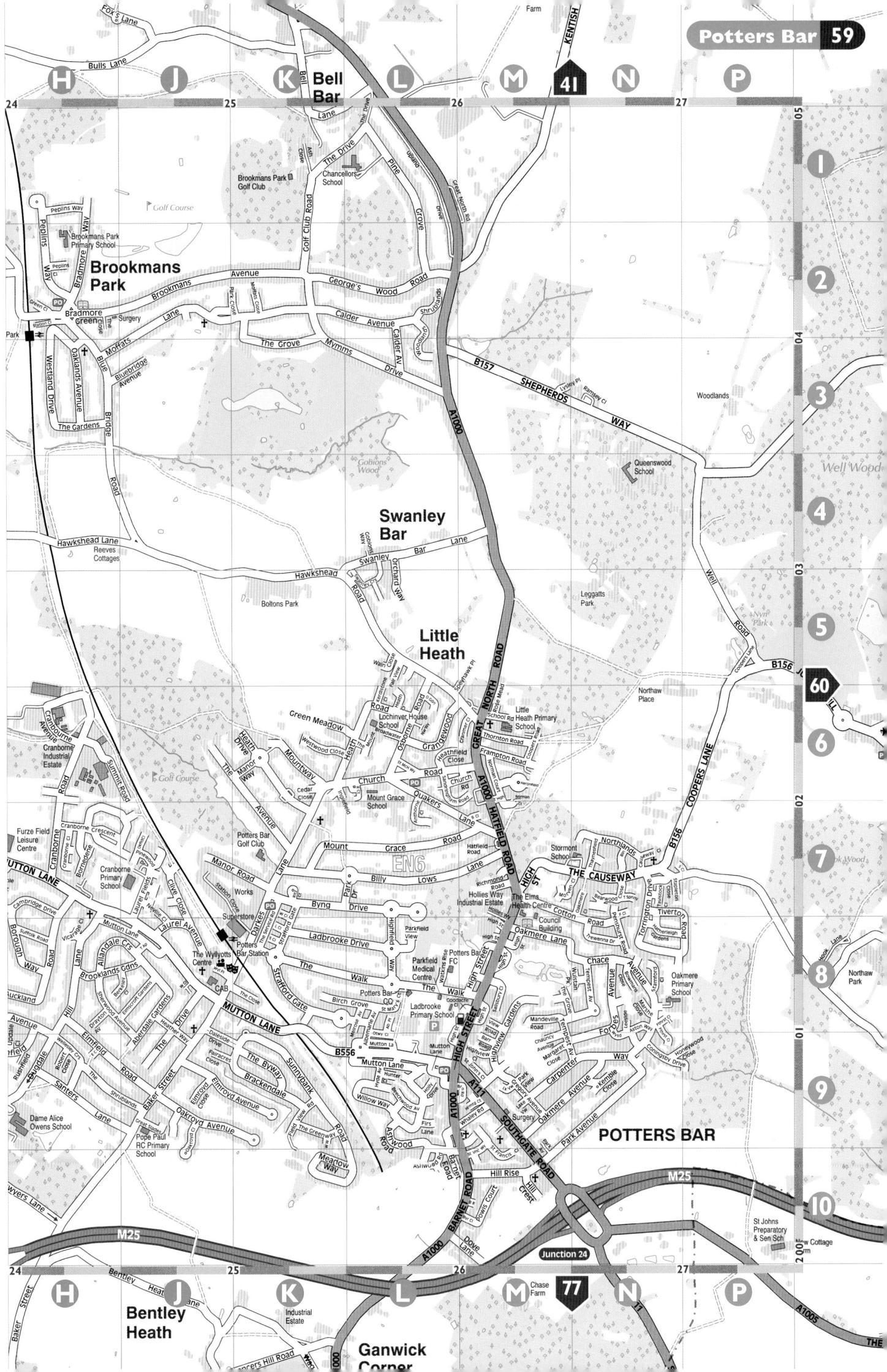
Bell Bar
Brookmans Park
Brookmans Park Golf Club
Chancellors School
Brookmans Park Primary School
Golf Course
Brookmans Avenue
George's Wood Road
Calder Avenue
The Grove
Mymms Drive
Golf Club Road
The Drive
Pine Grove
Great North Rd
Westland Drive
Oaklands Avenue
Bluebridge Avenue
The Gardens
Bridge Road
Moffats Lane
Peplins Way
Bradmore Way
Bradmore Green
Surgery
B157
SHEPHERDS WAY
Woodlands
Queenswood School
Well Wood
Gobions Wood
Swanley Bar
Swanley Bar Lane
Hawkshead Lane
Hawkshead Road
Reeves Cottages
Boltons Park
Orchard Way
Leggatts Park
Well Road
Nyn Park
Little Heath
GREAT NORTH ROAD
Little Heath Primary School
Lochinver House School
Green Meadow
Northaw Place
COOPERS LANE
B156
Cranborne Industrial Estate
Cranborne Road
Summit Road
Golf Course
Potters Bar Golf Club
Mount Grace School
Church Road
Mount Grace Road
Billy Lows Lane
Manor Road
Works
Superstore
Furze Field Leisure Centre
Cranborne Primary School
MUTTON LANE
Byng Drive
Ladbrooke Drive
The Walk
Potters Bar Station
The Wyllyotts Centre
CAB
Parkfield Medical Centre
Potters Bar FC
Ladbrooke Primary School
HATFIELD ROAD
HIGH STREET
The Elms Health Centre
Council Building
Stormont School
THE CAUSEWAY
Northlands
Oakmere Lane
Chace Avenue
Oakmere Primary School
Tiverton Road
Northaw Park
Darkes Lane
Stratford Gate
Baker Street
Oakroyd Avenue
Elmroyd Avenue
Sunnybank
Dame Alice Owens School
Pope Paul RC Primary School
Santers Lane
Elmfield Road
Meadow Way
B556
Mutton Lane
Willow Way
Ashwood Road
BARNET ROAD
SOUTHGATE ROAD
A111
A1000
Hill Rise
Park Avenue
Oakmere Avenue
Surgery
POTTERS BAR
M25
Junction 24
St Johns Preparatory & Sen Sch
New Cottage Fm
Dove Lane
Powis Court
Bentley Heath
Industrial Estate
Chase Farm
Ganwick Corner
A1005
EN6
H J K L M N P
24 25 26 27
41 60 77
1 2 3 4 5 6 7 8 9 10

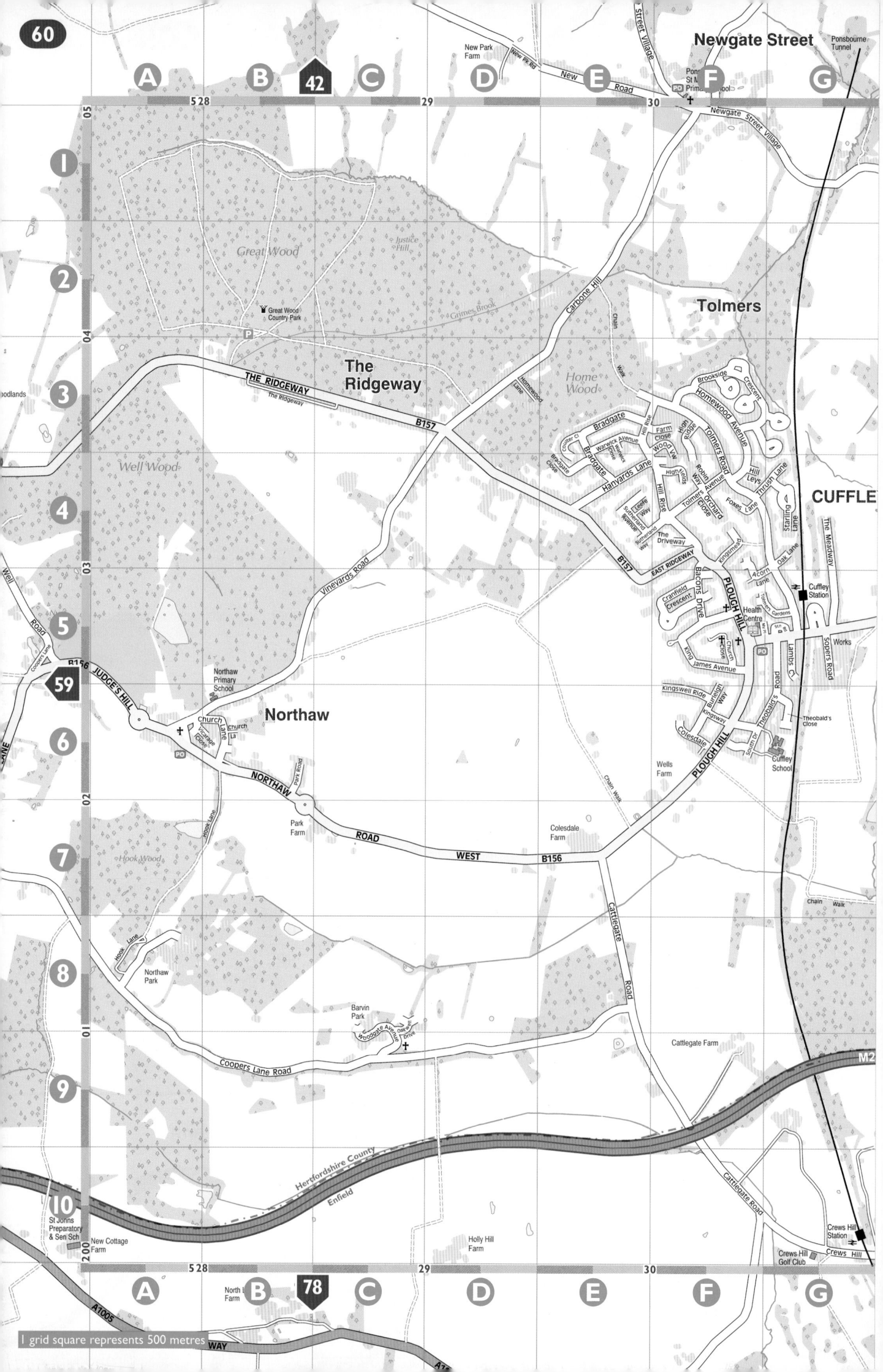
42
59
78
Newgate Street
Ponsbourne Tunnel
New Park Farm
New Pk Rd
New Road
Street Village
Newgate Street Village
Great Wood
Justice Hill
Great Wood Country Park
Grimes Brook
Carbone Hill
Tolmers
The Ridgeway
THE RIDGEWAY
The Ridgeway
B157
Home Wood
Homewood Lane
Chain Walk
Brookside
Crescent
Homewood Avenue
Tolmers Road
Bradgate
Bradgate Close
Coulter Cl
Warwick Avenue
Warwick Close
Hill Rise
Farm Close
Wood Vw
High Ridge
Robin Way
High Fields
Hanyards Lane
Tolmers Avenue
Orchard Close
Hill Leys
Thrush Lane
Foxes Lane
Starling Lane
CUFFLEY
The Meadway
Leefe Way
Sutherland Avenue
Sutherland Way
The Driveway
Kingsmead
Oak Lane
Acorn Lane
Tolmers Gardens
Well Wood
B157
EAST RIDGEWAY
Vineyards Road
Cranfield Crescent
Bacons Drive
PLOUGH HILL
Health Centre
Cuffley Station
Works
Sopers Road
Lambs
Church Close
King James Avenue
Kingswell Ride
Burleigh Way
Kingsway
Theobald's Road
Theobald's Close
Colesdale
PLOUGH HILL
South Dr
Cuffley School
Wells Farm
Well Road
Coopers Lane
B156
JUDGE'S HILL
Northaw Primary School
Northaw
Church Lane
Church La
Vicarage Close
NORTHAW
ROAD
WEST
B156
Park Road
Park Farm
Chain Walk
Colesdale Farm
Hook Wood
Hook Lane
Cattlegate Road
Chain Walk
Northaw Park
Barvin Park
Woodgate Avenue
Oakwell Drive
Coopers Lane Road
Cattlegate Farm
M25
Hertfordshire County
Enfield
Cattlegate Road
St Johns Preparatory & Sen Sch
New Cottage Farm
Holly Hill Farm
Crews Hill Station
Crews Hill
Crews Hill Golf Club
North Farm
A1005
WAY
A B C D E F G
1 2 3 4 5 6 7 8 9 10
528 29 30
05 04 03 02 01 200
1 grid square represents 500 metres

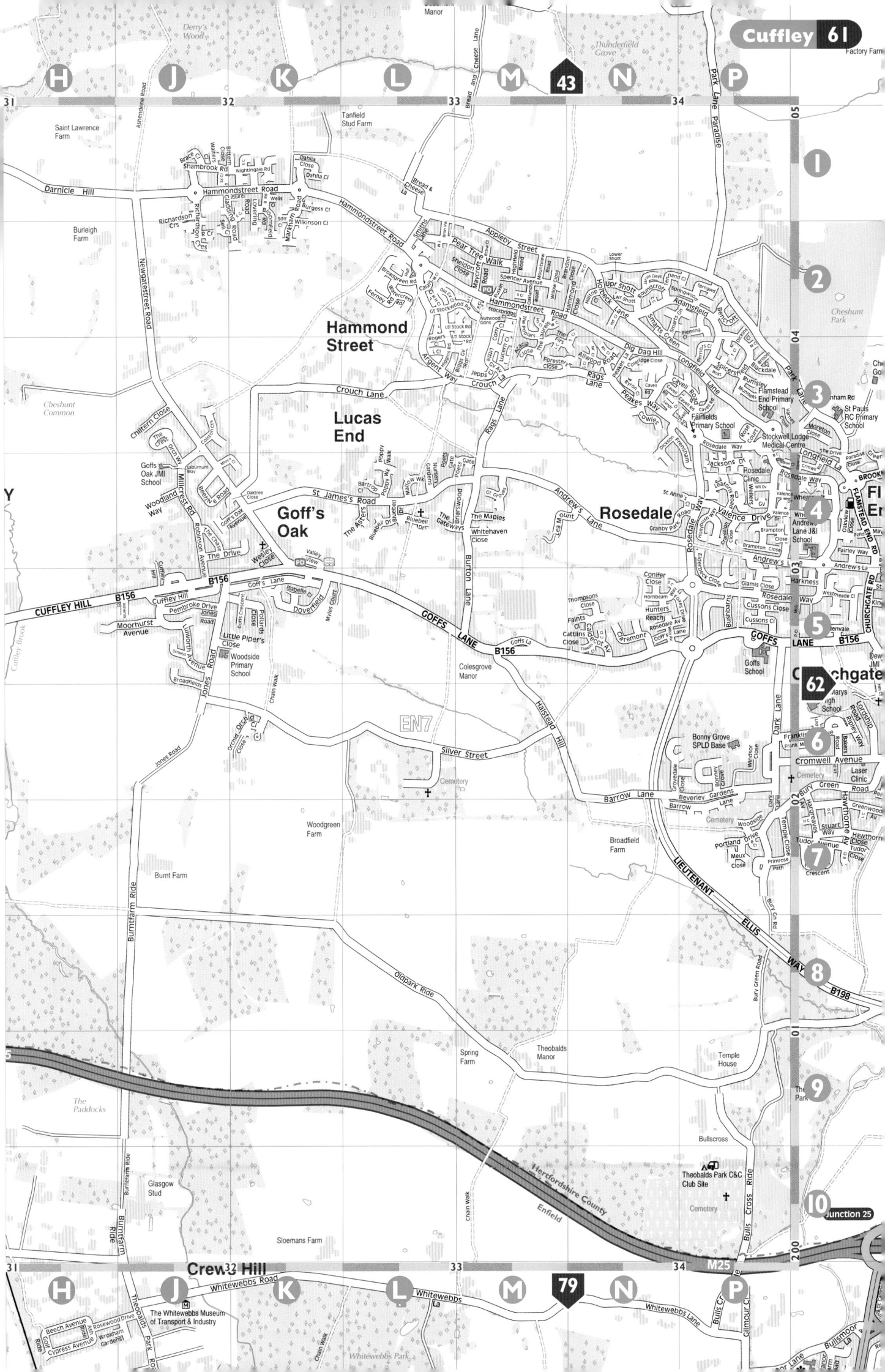
Hammond Street
Lucas End
Goff's Oak
Rosedale
Crews Hill
Cheshunt Common
Derry's Wood
Thunderfield Grove
Saint Lawrence Farm
Burleigh Farm
Tanfield Stud Farm
Darnicle Hill
Hammondstreet Road
Newgatestreet Road
Bread and Cheese Lane
Appleby Street
Park Lane Paradise
Crouch Lane
Rags Lane
St James's Road
Andrew's Lane
Cuffley Hill
B156
Goffs Lane
Burton Lane
Colesgrove Manor
Halstead Hill
Silver Street
EN7
Cemetery
Barrow Lane
Woodgreen Farm
Broadfield Farm
Burnt Farm
Burntfarm Ride
Lieutenant Ellis Way
B198
Oldpark Ride
Spring Farm
Theobalds Manor
Temple House
Bullscross
Theobalds Park C&C Club Site
Bulls Cross Ride
The Paddocks
Glasgow Stud
Sloemans Farm
Hertfordshire County
Enfield
M25
Junction 25
Whitewebbs Road
Whitewebbs Lane
The Whitewebbs Museum of Transport & Industry
Whitewebbs Park
Goffs Oak JMI School
Woodside Primary School
Fairfields Primary School
Flamstead End Primary School
St Pauls RC Primary School
Stockwell Lodge Medical Centre
Goffs School
Bonny Grove SPLD Base
Cheshunt Park
Churchgate
43
62
79
H
J
K
L
M
N
P
1
2
3
4
5
6
7
8
9
10

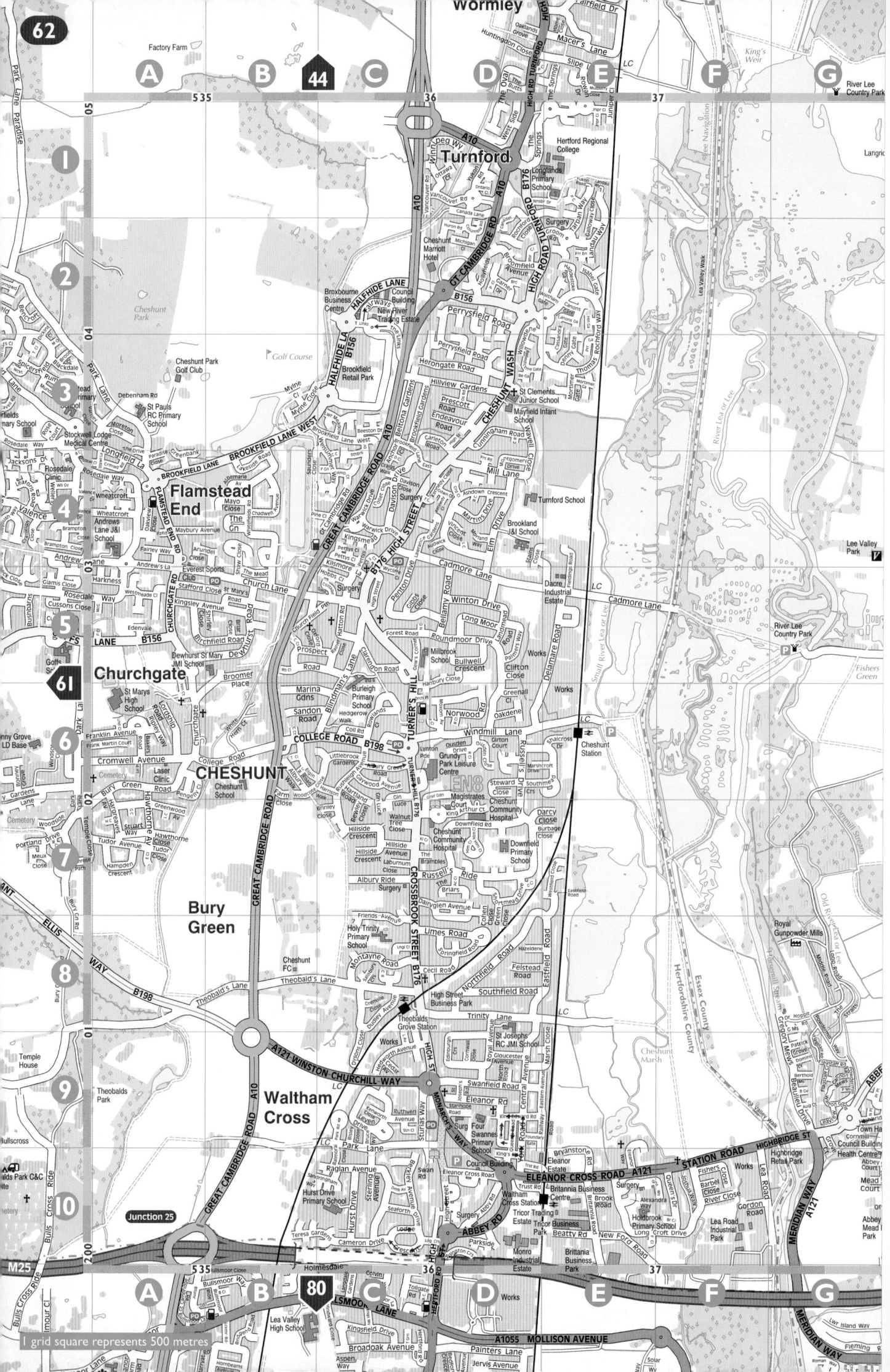
62
Wormley
Factory Farm
44
A
B
C
D
E
F
G
535
36
37
King's Weir
River Lee Country Park
Turnford
Hertford Regional College
Longlands Primary School
Cheshunt Marriott Hotel
GT CAMBRIDGE RD
HIGH ROAD TURNFORD
A10
B156
B176
HALFHIDE LANE
Broxbourne Business Centre
Council Building
New River Trading Estate
Cheshunt Park
Golf Course
Cheshunt Park Golf Club
Brookfield Retail Park
St Pauls RC Primary School
Stockwell Lodge Medical Centre
BROOKFIELD LANE WEST
BROOKFIELD LANE
Flamstead End
Rosedale Clinic
Wheatcroft
Andrews Lane J&I School
Everest Sports Club
Church Lane
Cadmore Lane
GREAT CAMBRIDGE ROAD
CHESHUNT WASH
St Clements Junior School
Mayfield Infant School
Turnford School
Brookland J&I School
Dacre Industrial Estate
Lee Valley Park
Lee Navigation
Lea Valley Walk
River Lea or Lee
Small River Lea or Lee
CHURCHGATE RD
Dewhurst St Mary JMI School
Churchgate
St Marys High School
Millbrook School
Burleigh Primary School
TURNER'S HILL
COLLEGE ROAD
B198
Grundy Park Leisure Centre
Cheshunt Station
Fishers Green
CHESHUNT
Cheshunt School
Laser Clinic
Cemetery
EN8
Magistrates Court
Cheshunt Community Hospital
Downfield Primary School
CROSSBROOK STREET
Holy Trinity Primary School
Cheshunt FC
Bury Green
ELLIS WAY
Theobald's Lane
Theobalds Grove Station
High Street Business Park
St Josephs RC JMI School
Hertfordshire County
Essex County
Cheshunt Marsh
Royal Gunpowder Mills
Cornmill Stream
Old River Lea or Lee
A121 WINSTON CHURCHILL WAY
Waltham Cross
Theobalds Park
Temple House
Four Swannes Primary School
Council Building
MONARCH'S WAY
ELEANOR CROSS ROAD
STATION ROAD
HIGHBRIDGE ST
Highbridge Retail Park
Town Hall
Cornmill
Council Building
Health Centre
Waltham Cross Station
Britannia Business Centre
Tricor Trading Estate
Tricor Business Park
Brittania Business Park
Monro Industrial Estate
Holdbrook Primary School
Lea Road Industrial Park
Abbey Mead Park
MERIDIAN WAY
A121
Hurst Drive Primary School
ABBEY RD
Junction 25
M25
80
Bullsmoor Lane
Lea Valley High School
A1055 MOLLISON AVENUE
Works
61
1 grid square represents 500 metres

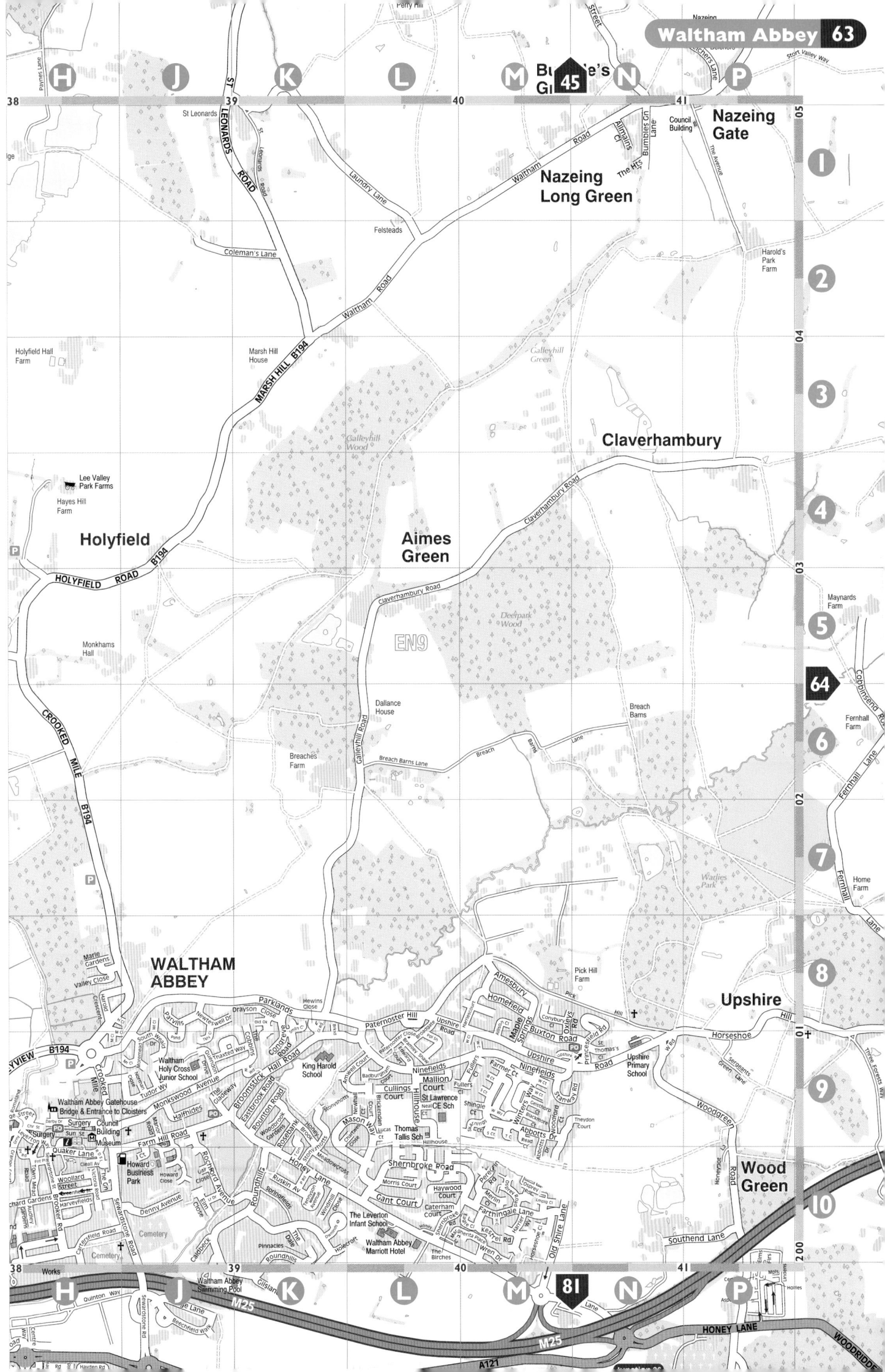
Nazeing Gate
Nazeing Long Green
Council Building
Harold's Park Farm
St Leonards
ST LEONARDS ROAD
Coleman's Lane
Laundry Lane
Felsteads
Waltham Road
Holyfield Hall Farm
Marsh Hill House
MARSH HILL B194
Galleyhill Green
Galleyhill Wood
Claverhambury
Claverhambury Road
Lee Valley Park Farms
Hayes Hill Farm
Holyfield
Aimes Green
HOLYFIELD ROAD B194
Maynards Farm
Deerpark Wood
EN9
Monkhams Hall
CROOKED MILE B194
Dallance House
Breach Barns
Fernhall Farm
Breaches Farm
Breach Barns Lane
Galleyhill Road
Fernhall Lane
Home Farm
Warlies Park
WALTHAM ABBEY
Pick Hill Farm
Upshire
Parklands
Paternoster Hill
Horseshoe Hill
King Harold School
Upshire Primary School
Waltham Holy Cross Junior School
Ninefields
Mallion Court
St Lawrence CE Sch
Thomas Tallis Sch
Waltham Abbey Gatehouse Bridge & Entrance to Cloisters
Council Building
Museum
Howard Business Park
Monkswood Avenue
Farm Hill Road
Honey Lane
Woodgreen
Wood Green
Shernbroke Road
Gant Court
The Leverton Infant School
Waltham Abbey Marriott Hotel
Southend Lane
Cemetery
Denny Avenue
Sewardstone Road
Old Shire Lane
Waltham Abbey Swimming Pool
M25
HONEY LANE
A121
45
64
81

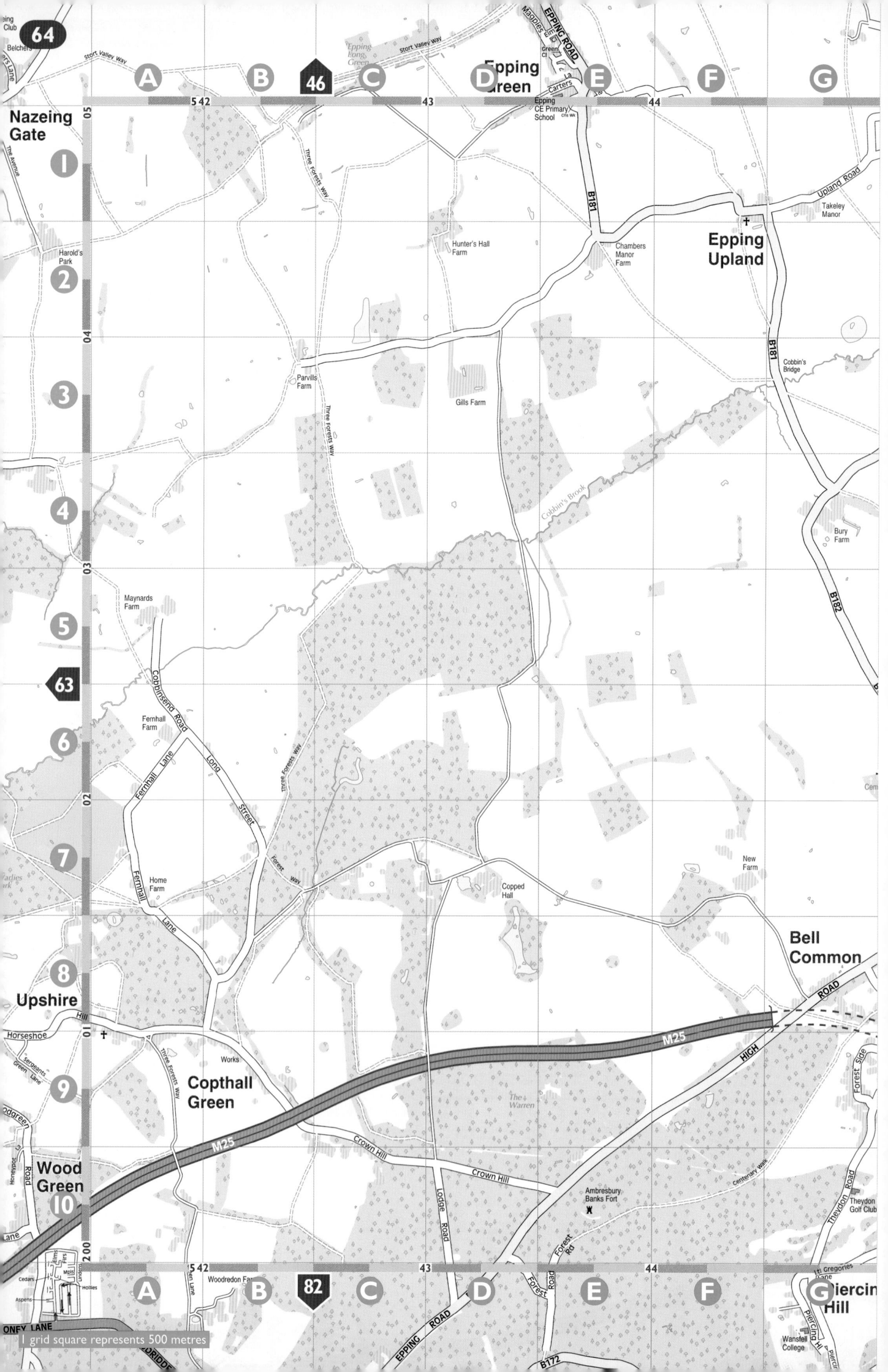
64
Nazeing Gate
Epping Green
Epping Upland
Harold's Park
Hunter's Hall Farm
Chambers Manor Farm
Takeley Manor
Upland Road
Parvills Farm
Gills Farm
Cobbin's Bridge
Cobbin's Brook
Bury Farm
Maynards Farm
Fernhall Farm
Cobbinsend Road
Fernhall Lane
Long Street
Three Forests Way
Forest Way
Home Farm
Copped Hall
New Farm
Bell Common
Upshire
Horseshoe Hill
Sergeants Green Lane
Works
Copthall Green
The Warren
Crown Hill
Lodge Road
Wood Green
Ambresbury Banks Fort
Centenary Walk
Forest Side
Theydon Road
Theydon Golf Club
Forest Rd
Forest Road
Epping Road
High Road
Woodredon Farm
Wansfell College
Piercing Hill
Stort Valley Way
Epping Road
Epping CE Primary School
Carters
B181
B182
B172
M25
46
63
82
1 grid square represents 500 metres

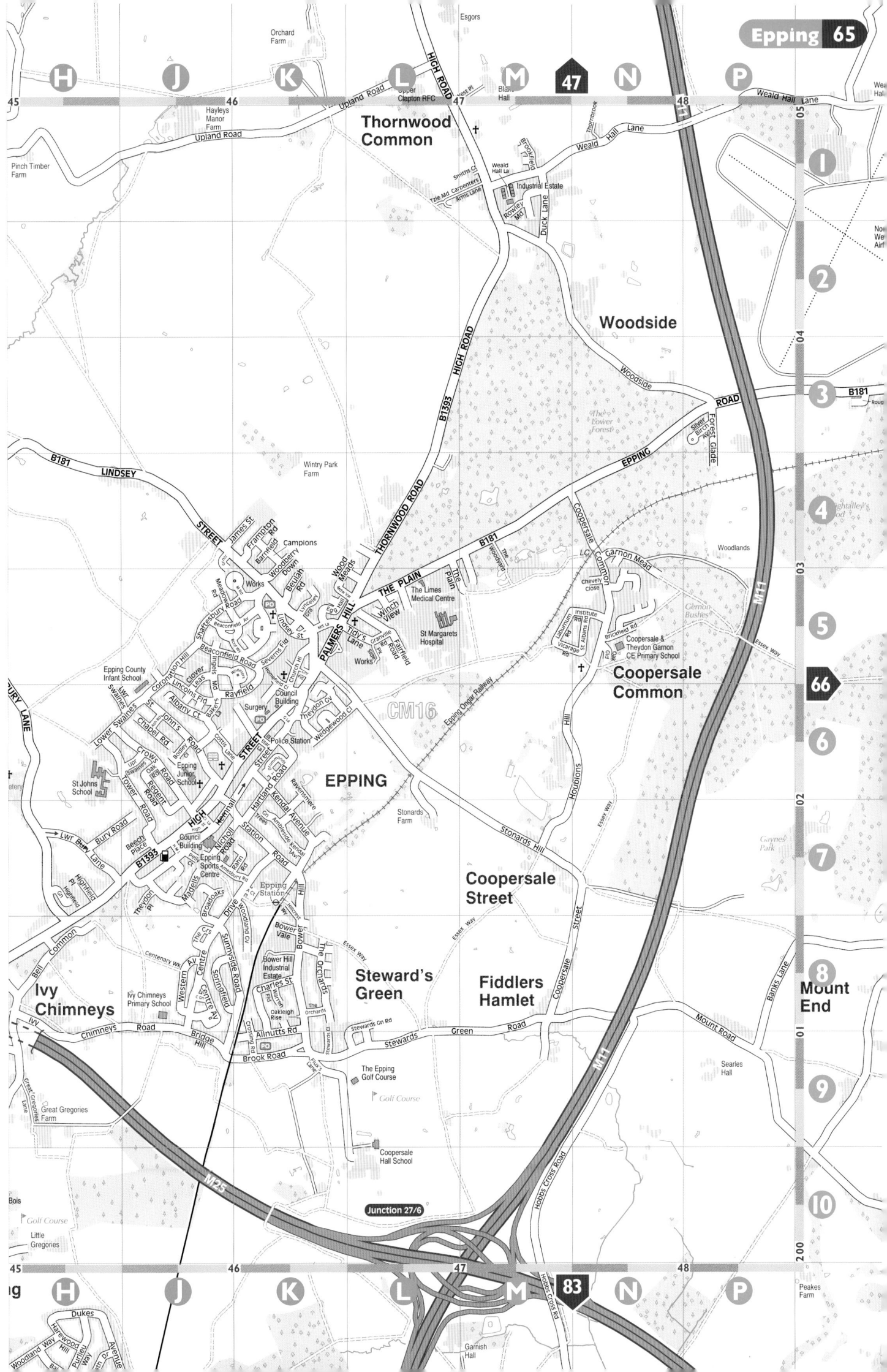
Thornwood Common
Woodside
EPPING
Coopersale Common
Coopersale Street
Steward's Green
Fiddlers Hamlet
Ivy Chimneys
Mount End
HIGH ROAD
B1393
THORNWOOD ROAD
EPPING ROAD
B181
LINDSEY STREET
THE PLAIN
PALMERS HILL
HIGH STREET
Upland Road
Weald Hall Lane
Stonards Hill
Stewards Green Road
Mount Road
Hobbs Cross Road
Brook Road
Bell Common
Epping Station
St Margarets Hospital
The Limes Medical Centre
Epping Ongar Railway
M11
M25
Junction 27/6
The Epping Golf Course
Coopersale Hall School
CM16

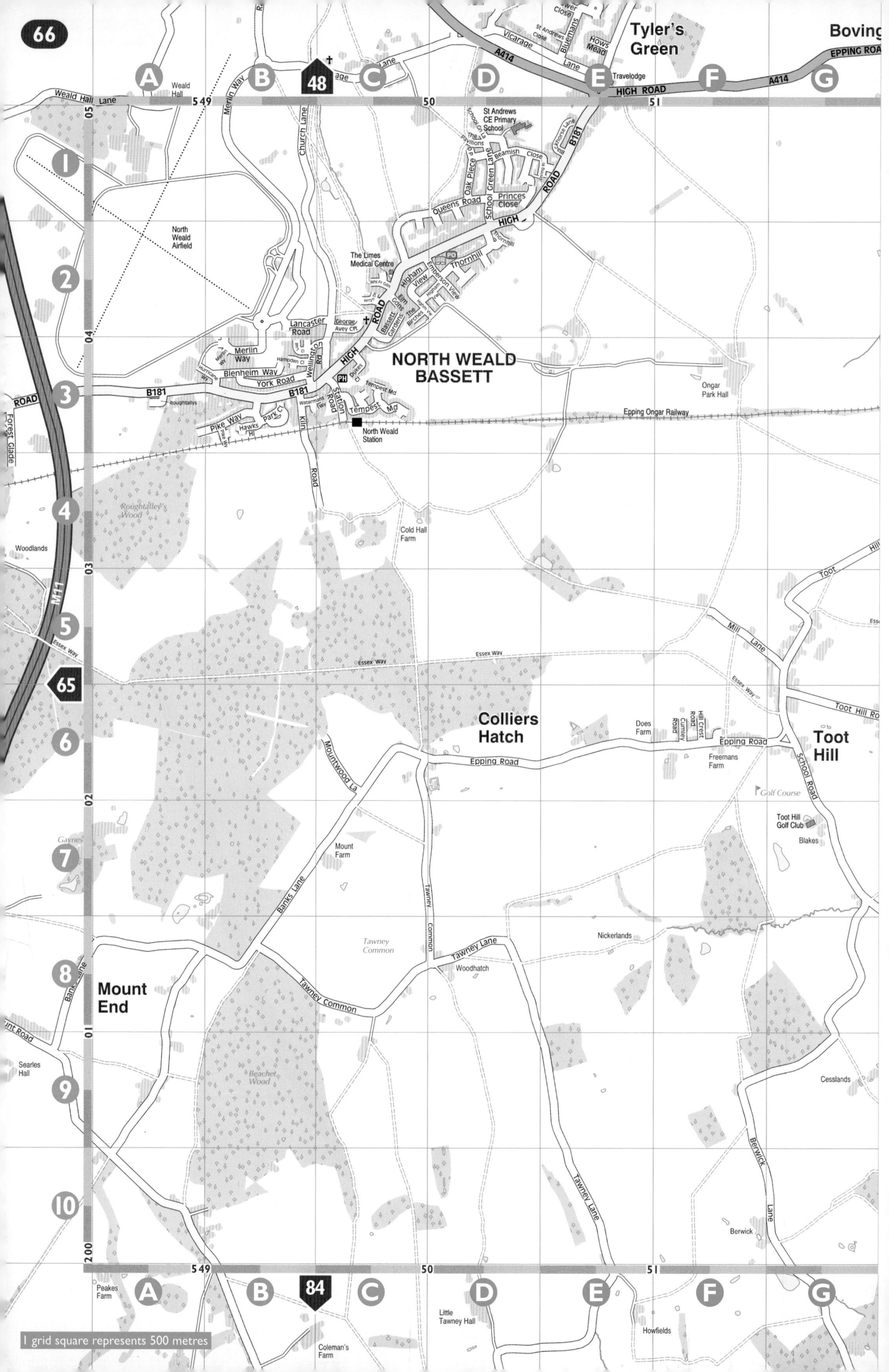

Tyler's Green
Boving
NORTH WEALD BASSETT
North Weald Airfield
Colliers Hatch
Toot Hill
Mount End
Weald Hall
Weald Hall Lane
Merlin Way
Church Lane
Vicarage Lane
St Andrews Close
Bluemans
Hows Mead
Travelodge
HIGH ROAD
A414
EPPING ROAD
St Andrews CE Primary School
School Green Lane
Oak Piece
Beamish Close
Queens Road
Princes Close
B181
Thornhill
The Limes Medical Centre
Higham View
Emberson View
Lancaster Road
George Avey Cft
Merlin Way
Blenheim Way
York Road
Hurricane Way
Wellington Rd
Hampden Cl
Station Road
Tempest Md
Dukes
Kiln Road
Pike Way
Hawks Hl
Park Cl
Roughtallys
Watermans Wy
North Weald Station
Epping Ongar Railway
Ongar Park Hall
Forest Glade
Roughtalley's Wood
Woodlands
Cold Hall Farm
M11
Essex Way
Mill Lane
Toot Hill Road
Does Farm
Cunliey Road
Hill Crest Road
Epping Road
Freemans Farm
School Road
Golf Course
Toot Hill Golf Club
Blakes
Mountwood La
Mount Farm
Banks Lane
Tawney Common
Tawney Lane
Woodhatch
Nickerlands
Gaynes
Searles Hall
Beachet Wood
Cesslands
Berwick Lane
Berwick
Peakes Farm
Little Tawney Hall
Howfields
Coleman's Farm
1 grid square represents 500 metres

48
65
84

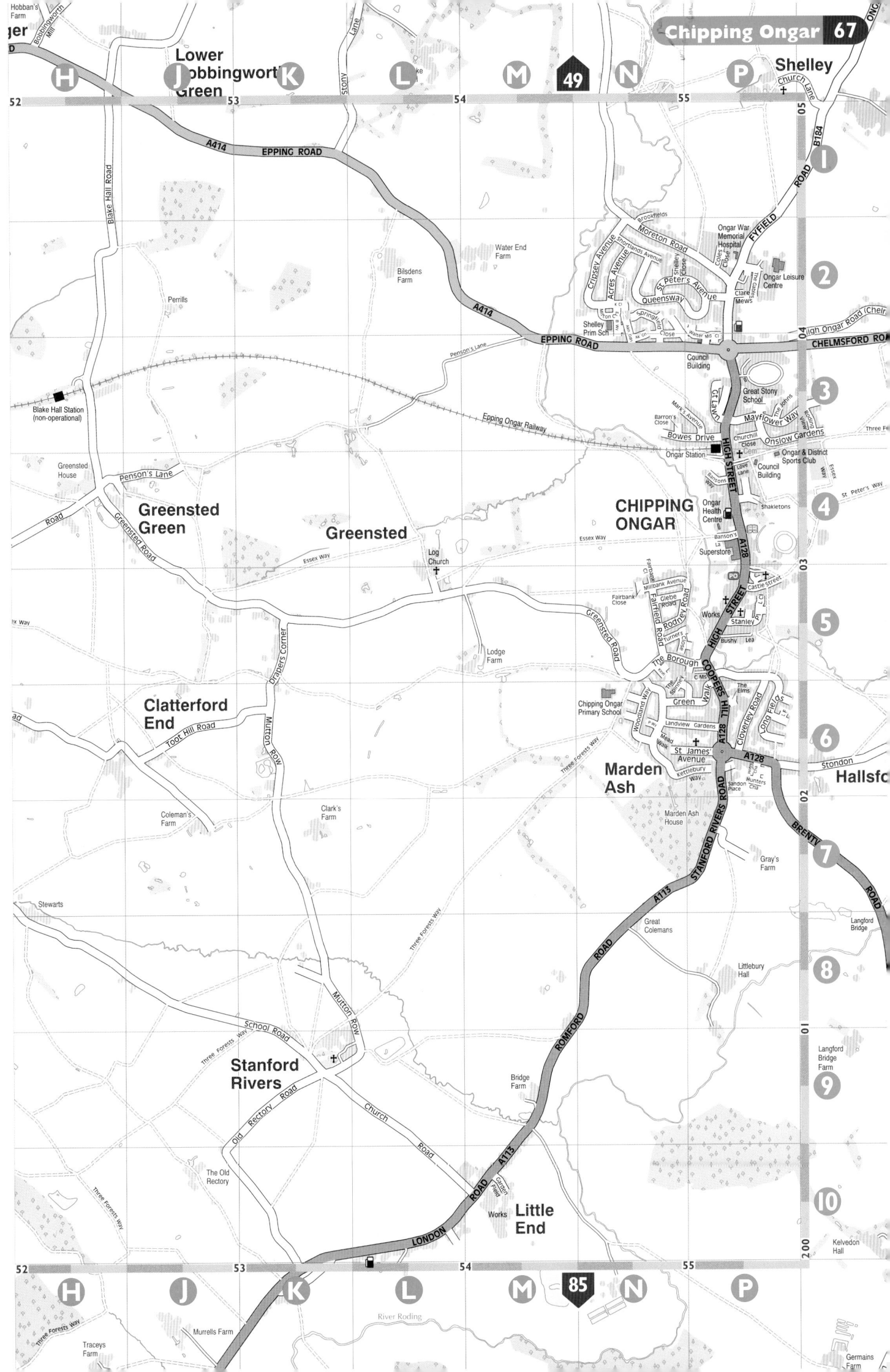

Hobban's Farm
Bobbingworth Mill
Lower Bobbingworth Green
Stony Lane
Shelley
Church Lane
49
A414
EPPING ROAD
B184
FYFIELD ROAD
Blake Hall Road
Water End Farm
Bilsdens Farm
Perrills
Brookfields
Moreton Road
Crispey Avenue
Acres Avenue
Shortlands Avenue
Shelley Close
St Peter's Avenue
Queensway
Ongar War Memorial Hospital
Coles Close
Ongar Leisure Centre
The Gables Mews
Clare Mews
Springfield
Shelley Prim Sch
Walter Mead Cl
Close
High Ongar Road (Chelmsford)
CHELMSFORD ROAD
Penson's Lane
Council Building
Great Stony School
Gt Lawn
Mark's Avenue
Barron's Close
Mayflower Way
The Johns
Bowes Drive
Onslow Gardens
Churchill Close
Three Forests Way
Epping Ongar Railway
Blake Hall Station (non-operational)
Ongar Station
Ongar & District Sports Club
Love Lane
Council Building
Bansons Way
Essex Way
St Peter's Way
HIGH STREET
Greensted House
Penson's Lane
Road
Greensted Green
Greensted Road
Greensted
Essex Way
CHIPPING ONGAR
Ongar Health Centre
Shakletons
Banson's La
Superstore
A128
Log Church
Fairbank Cl
Millbank Avenue
Glebe Road
Castle Street
Fairbank Close
Fairfield Road
Rodney Road
Works
Stanley
Turners Close
Bushy Lea
Lodge Farm
The Borough
Drapers Corner
The Spinney
C Ms
Clatterford End
Toot Hill Road
Mutton Row
Woodland Way
Green Walk
COOPERS HILL
The Elms
Cloverley Road
Long Fields
Chipping Ongar Primary School
Landview Gardens
Mead Walk
St James' Avenue
Kettlebury Way
Stondon
Marden Ash
Hallsford
Sandon Place
Hunters Chase
Coleman's Farm
Clark's Farm
Marden Ash House
STANFORD RIVERS ROAD
BRENTWOOD ROAD
Gray's Farm
A113
Stewarts
Three Forests Way
Great Colemans
Langford Bridge
ROAD
Littlebury Hall
Mutton Row
School Road
ROMFORD
Three Forests Way
Stanford Rivers
Langford Bridge Farm
Bridge Farm
Old Rectory Road
Church Road
The Old Rectory
Three Forests Way
Garden Field
Works
Little End
LONDON ROAD
Kelvedon Hall
85
River Roding
Murrells Farm
Traceys Farm
Germains Farm
Three Forests Way

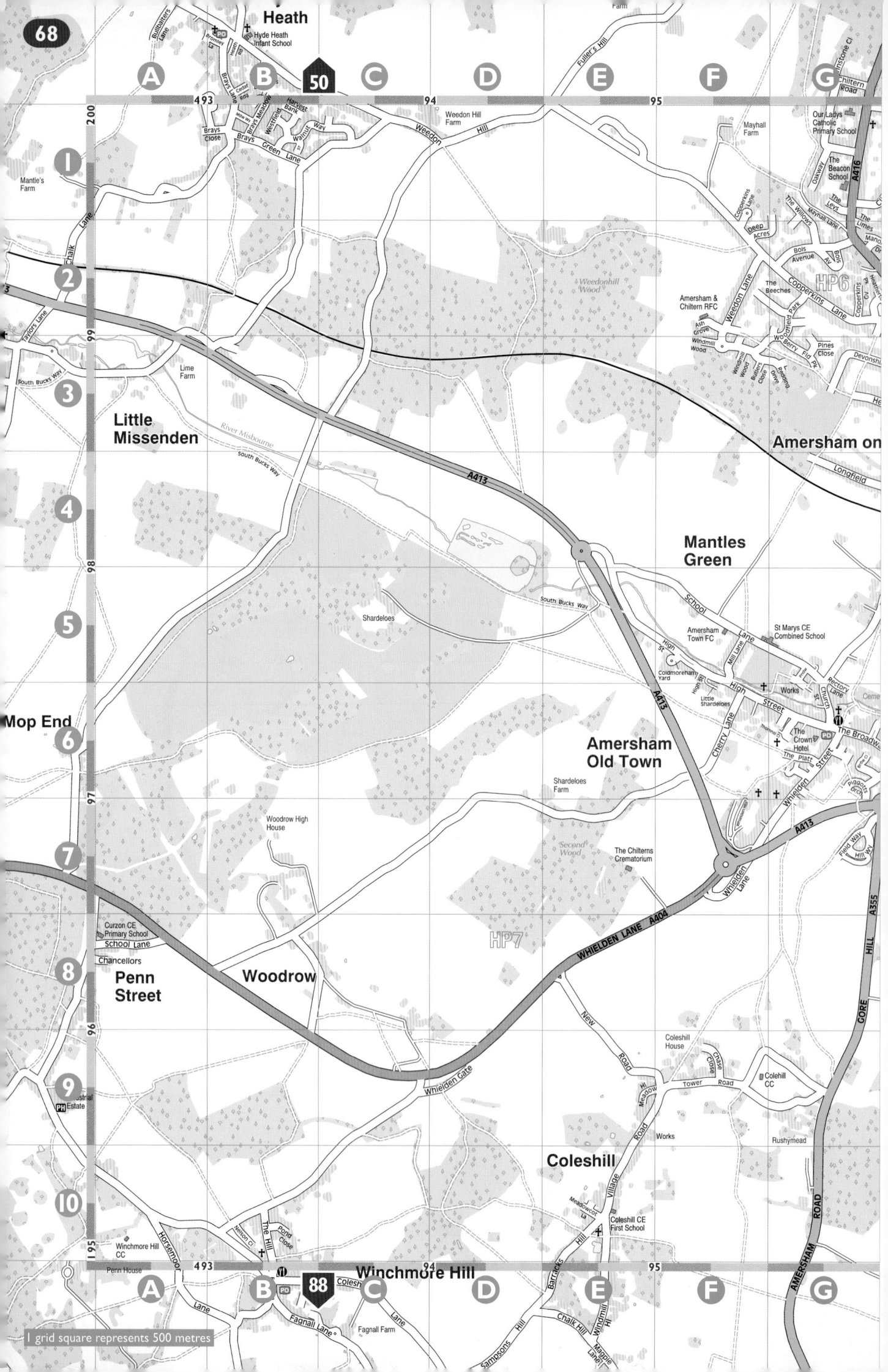

Heath

A   B   **50**   C   D   E   F   G

I
2
3
4
5
6
7
8
9
10

Mantle's Farm

Bullbaiters Lane
Chalk Lane
Taylors Lane

South Bucks Way

Little Missenden

River Misbourne

South Bucks Way

Bromley La
Hyde Heath Infant School

Brays Close
Brays Lane
Westfield
Walnut Way
Brays Green Lane

Cedar Rd

Harvest Bank

493

Lime Farm

200

99

98

97

96

195

Mop End

Penn Street

Curzon CE Primary School
School Lane
Chancellors

Industrial Estate
PH

Winchmore Hill CC

Penn House

Horsemoor Lane

Nelson Cl
The Hill
Pond Close

493

A   B   **88**   C   D   E   F   G

PO

Fagnall Lane

Fagnall Farm

Coleshill La

Samsons Hill

Barracks Hill

Chalk Hill

Windmill H

Magpie Lane

Winchmore Hill

94

Weedon Hill Farm

Weedon Hill

Weedonhill Wood

95

Mayhall Farm

A413

Shardeloes

South Bucks Way

Woodrow High House

Woodrow

Second Wood

The Chilterns Crematorium

Shardeloes Farm

Amersham Old Town

HP7

WHIELDEN LANE A404

Whielden Gate

New Road

Coleshill House

Coleshill

Meadow Road
Village Road
Works

Coleshill CE First School

Meadwcot La

Tower Road
Chase Close
Colehill CC

Rushymead

Mantles Green

Amersham on

Longfield

School Lane

Amersham Town FC

High St
St
Coldmorehan Yard

A413

Little Shardeloes

Mill Lane

High Street

St Marys CE Combined School

Works

Cherry Lane

Whielden Lane

A413

Whielden Lane

GORE HILL

A355

AMERSHAM ROAD

Field Way
Hill Wy

Amersham & Chiltern RFC
Ash Grove
Windmill Wood

Weedon Lane
Coppertons Lane

HP6

Our Ladys Catholic Primary School
A416
The Beacon School
The Leys
The Limes

Chiltern Road
Gunstone Cl

Oakway

The Willows
Deep Acres

Bois Avenue
Bois Av
Bois Dr

Copperkins Lane
Copperkins Cv

The Beeches
Bedding Drive
Woberry Fld Pk
Pines Close
Windmill Wood

Devonshire

Rectory Lane
Church St
Ceme

The Crown Hotel
The Platt
Piggotts Orch

The Broadway
PO

1 grid square represents 500 metres

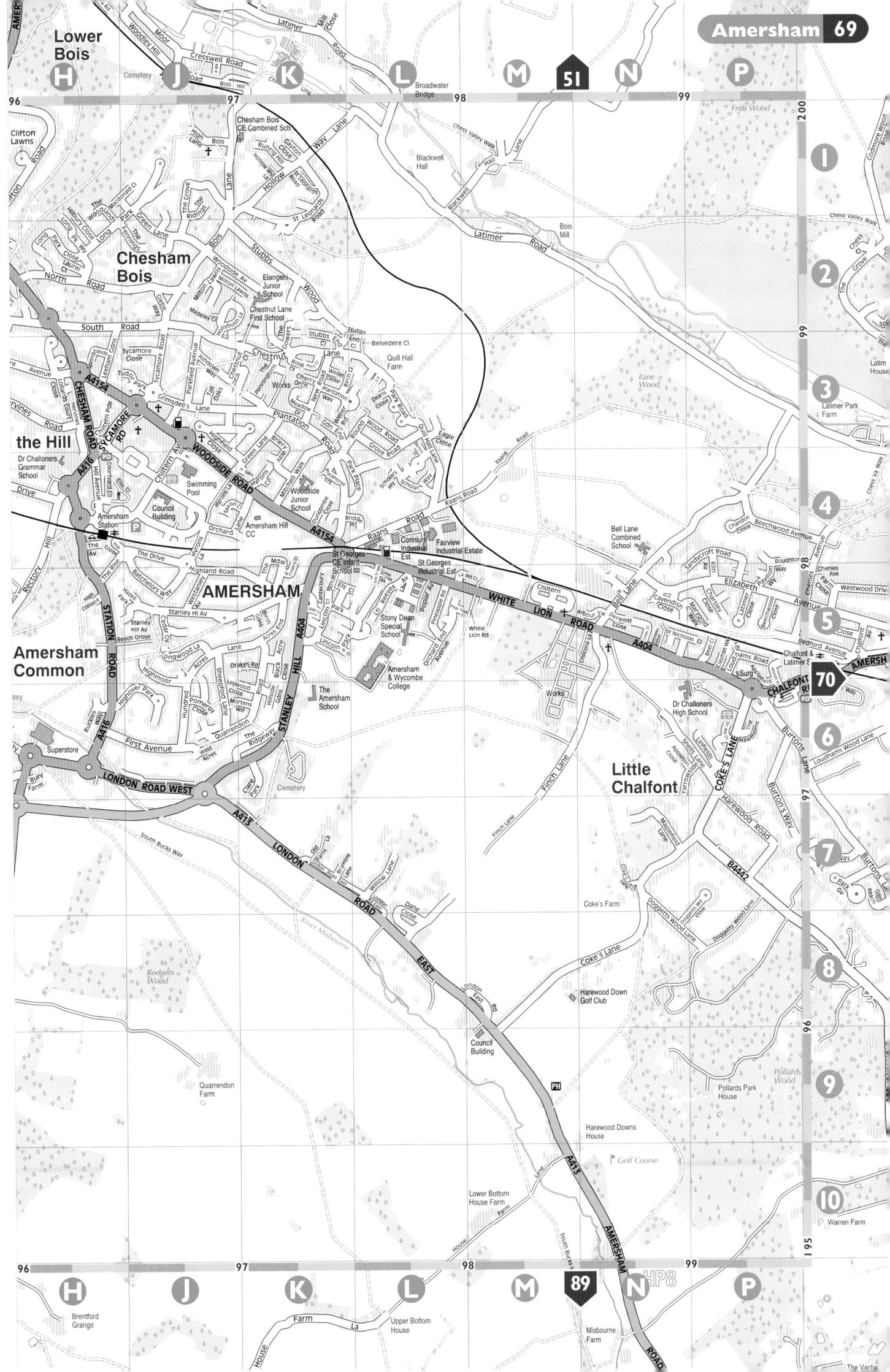
Lower Bois
Chesham Bois
Clifton Lawns
the Hill
AMERSHAM
Amersham Common
Little Chalfont
Amersham Station
Dr Challoners Grammar School
Chesham Bois CE Combined Sch
Elangeni Junior School
Chestnut Lane First School
Woodside Junior School
Swimming Pool
Council Building
Amersham Hill CC
St Georges CE Infant School
Corinium Industrial Est
Fairview Industrial Estate
St Georges Industrial Est
Stony Dean Special School
Amersham & Wycombe College
The Amersham School
Bell Lane Combined School
Dr Challoners High School
Superstore
Bury Farm
Cemetery
Blackwell Hall
Bois Mill
Broadwater Bridge
Quill Hall Farm
Lane Wood
Latimer Park Farm
Frith Wood
Coke's Farm
Harewood Down Golf Club
Harewood Downs House
Golf Course
Pollards Park House
Pollards Wood
Quarrendon Farm
Rodgers Wood
River Misbourne
Lower Bottom House Farm
Upper Bottom House
Brentford Grange
Misbourne Farm
Warren Farm
The Vache
A4154
A416
A404
A413
B4442
CHESHAM ROAD
STATION ROAD
WOODSIDE ROAD
WHITE LION ROAD
STANLEY HILL
LONDON ROAD WEST
LONDON ROAD EAST
AMERSHAM ROAD
COKE'S LANE
CHALFONT RD
Latimer Road
Chess Valley Walk
Raans Road
Bell Lane
Finch Lane
Coke's Lane
Harewood Road
Burtons Lane
Doggetts Wood Lane
South Bucks Way
Highover Park
First Avenue
Quarrendon
Plantation Road
Chestnut Lane
South Road
North Road
Stubbs Wood
Chalfont & Latimer Station
HP8
51
70
89

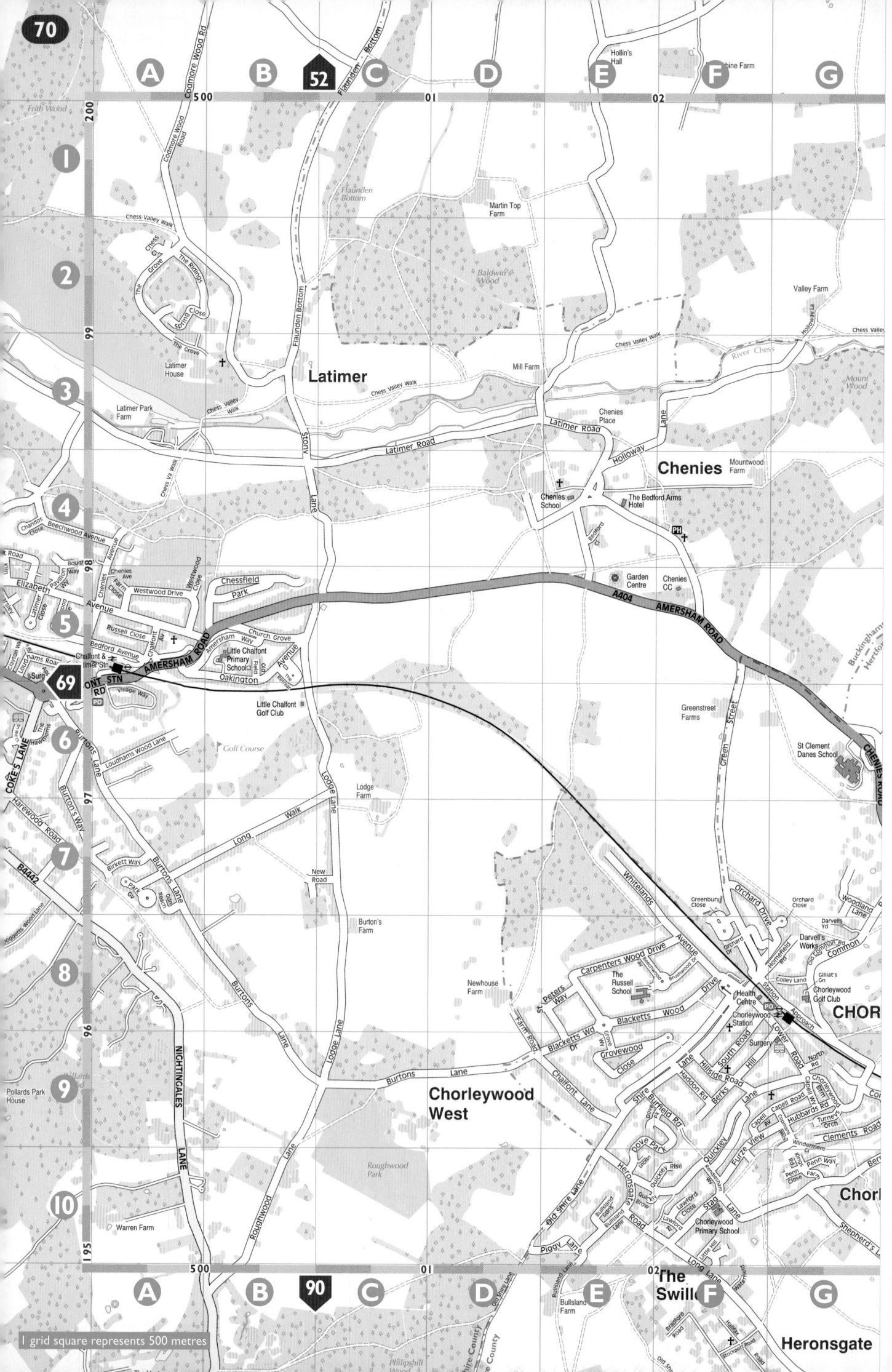

Latimer
Chenies
Chorleywood West
Heronsgate
Hollin's Hall
Flaunden Bottom
Martin Top Farm
Baldwin's Wood
Valley Farm
Latimer House
Latimer Park Farm
Mill Farm
Chenies Place
Mountwood Farm
The Bedford Arms Hotel
Chenies School
Garden Centre
Chenies CC
Little Chalfont Primary School
Chalfont & Latimer Stn
Little Chalfont Golf Club
Golf Course
Greenstreet Farms
St Clement Danes School
Lodge Farm
New Road
Burton's Farm
Newhouse Farm
The Russell School
Health Centre
Chorleywood Station
Chorleywood Golf Club
Chorleywood Primary School
Pollards Park House
Warren Farm
Roughwood Park
Bullsland Farm
Frith Wood
River Chess
Chess Valley Walk
A404 AMERSHAM ROAD
Latimer Road
Burtons Lane
Lodge Lane
Nightingales Lane
Green Street
Chalfont Lane
Old Shire Lane
Long Walk
Long Lane
1 grid square represents 500 metres

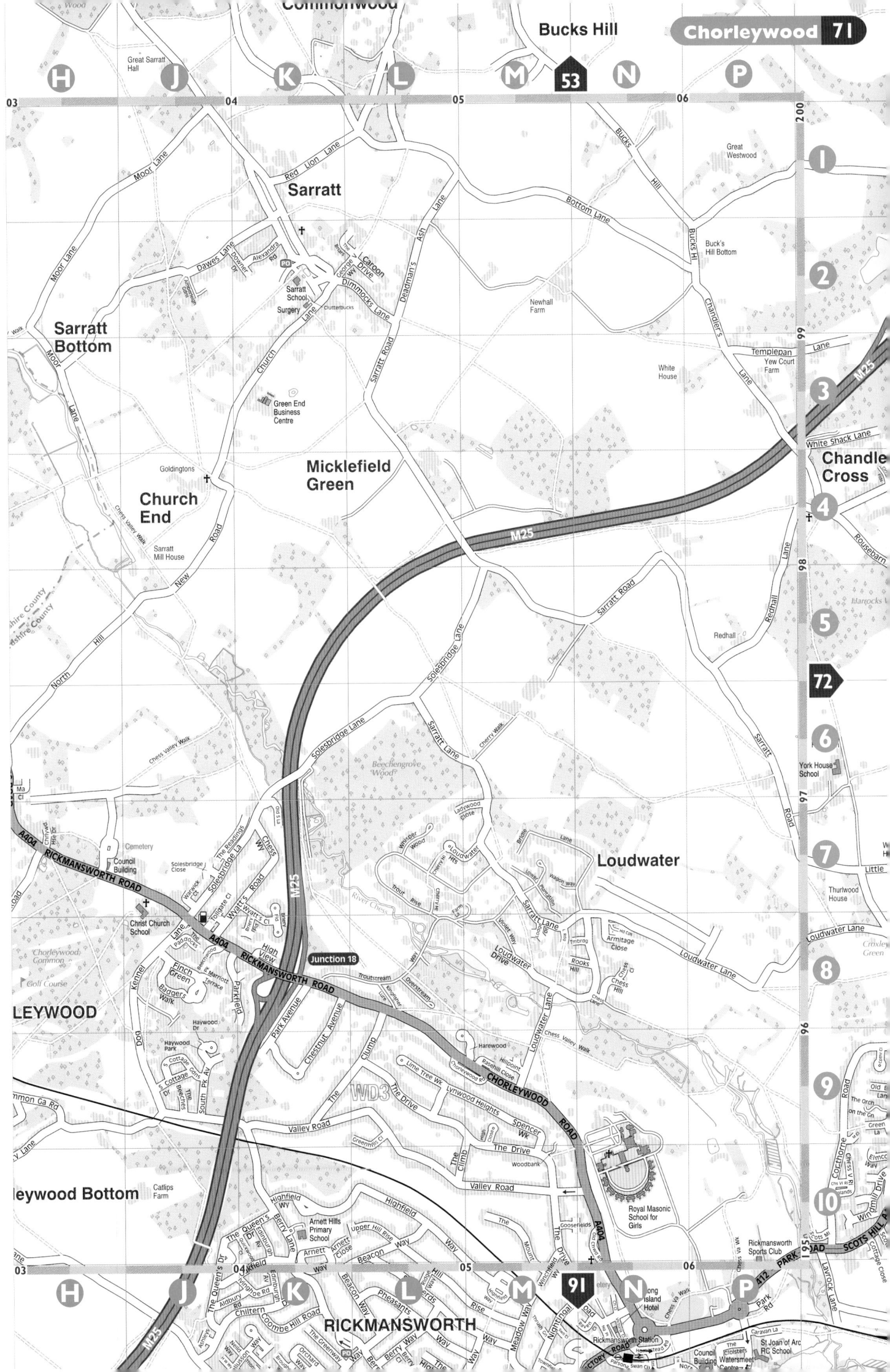

Bucks Hill
Great Sarratt Hall
53
Sarratt
Red Lion Lane
Moor Lane
Bottom Lane
Bucks Hill
Great Westwood
Buck's Hill Bottom
Dawes Lane
Dowler Dr
Alexandra Rd
Sarratt School
Surgery
Clutterbucks
Dimmocks Lane
Caroon Drive
Deadman's Ash Lane
Newhall Farm
Chandler's Lane
Sarratt Bottom
Church Lane
Green End Business Centre
Sarratt Road
Templepan Lane
Yew Court Farm
White House
M25
White Shack Lane
Chandler's Cross
Micklefield Green
Goldingtons
Church End
Chess Valley Walk
Sarratt Mill House
New Road
North Hill
Solesbridge Lane
Sarratt Road
Redhall Lane
Redhall
72
Sarratt Lane
Cherry Walk
Beechengrove Wood
Sarratt Road
York House School
Ladywood Close
Loudwater
Little
Thurlwood House
Loudwater Lane
Croxley Green
A404 Rickmansworth Road
Cemetery
Council Building
Solesbridge Close
Christ Church School
Solesbridge La
Wyatt's Road
The Readings
Chess Way
High View
Junction 18
Troutstream
Overstream
Kingfisher Lure
Loudwater Drive
Violet Way
Armitage Close
Rooks Hill
Chess Hill
Chorleywood Common
Golf Course
Chorleywood
Finch Green
Badgers Walk
Kennel Lane
Parkfield
Park Avenue
Chestnut Avenue
Clump
Harewood
Hillpoint
Rasehill Close
Chess Valley Walk
Chorleywood Road
Dog Kennel Lane
Haywood Dr
Haywood Park
Cottage Gdns
South Pk Av
Beeches
Lime Tree Wk
The Drive
Lynwood Heights
Spencer Wk
WD3
Valley Road
Greenhills Cl
The Drive
Woodbank
The Climb
Royal Masonic School for Girls
Chorleywood Bottom
Catlips Farm
Valley Road
Highfield Wy
Highfield Way
Arnett Hills Primary School
Berry Lane
Upper Hill Rise
The Queen's Dr
Arnett Way
Beacon Way
Goosefields
The Drive
The Mount
Rickmansworth Sports Club
A412 Park Road
Scots Hill
Lavrock Lane
Cottage Close
Windmill Drive
Corthone Road
91
Long Island Hotel
Chess Va Walk
Park Rd
Caravan La
St Joan of Arc RC School
Rickmansworth Station
Council Building
The Cloisters
Watersmeet Centre
Rickmansworth
Chiltern
Coombe Hill Road
The Greenway
Pheasants Way
Meadow Way
Nightingale Road
Aldbury

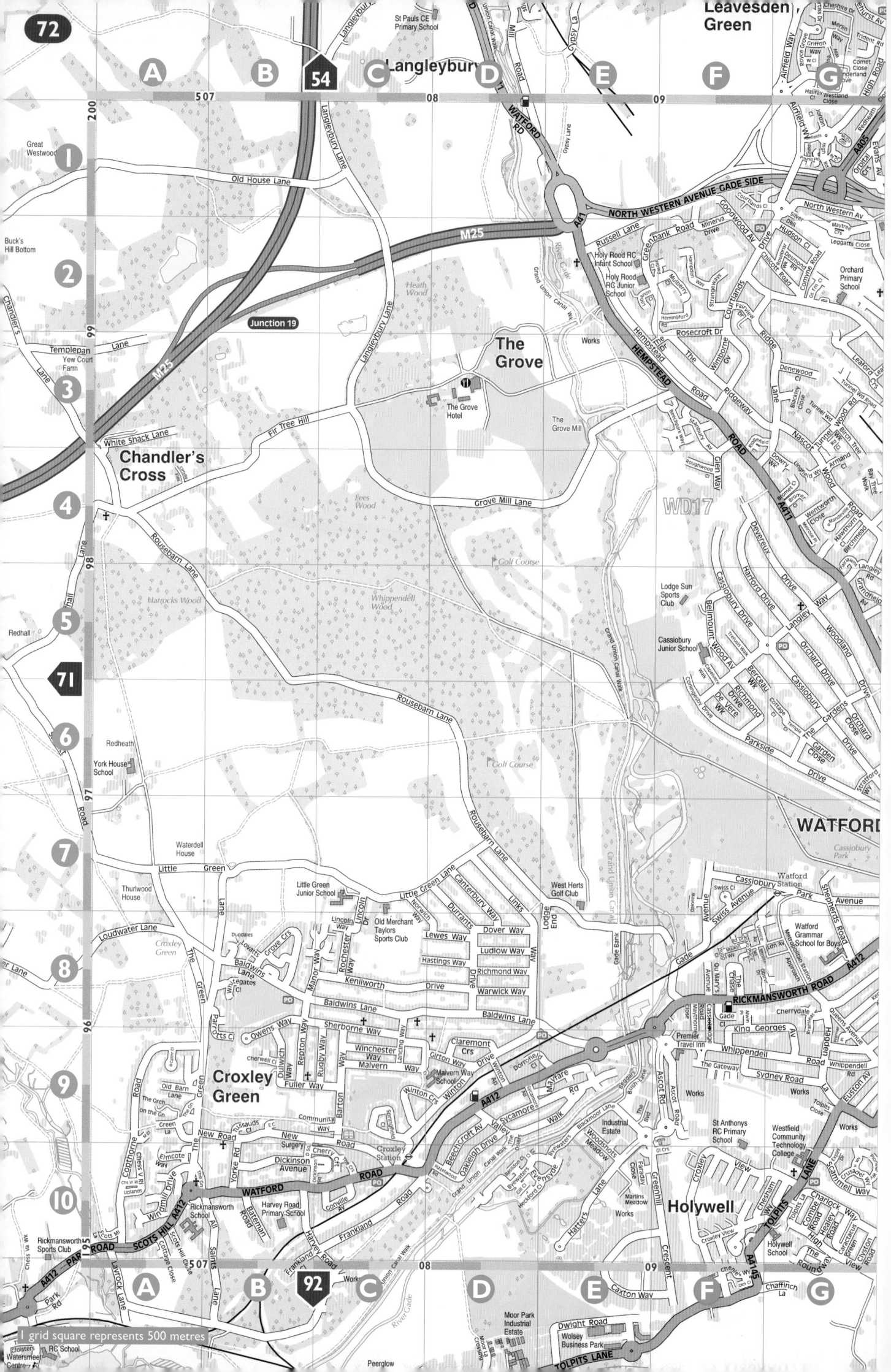
Langleybury
Leavesden Green
The Grove
The Grove Hotel
Chandler's Cross
Junction 19
M25
WD17
WATFORD
Croxley Green
Holywell
Watford Station
Croxley Station
Cassiobury Park
Watford Grammar School for Boys
West Herts Golf Club
Golf Course
Whippendell Wood
Harrocks Wood
Lees Wood
Heath Wood
Redheath
York House School
Little Green Junior School
Old Merchant Taylors Sports Club
Rickmansworth School
Harvey Road Primary School
Malvern Way School
Cassiobury Junior School
Lodge Sun Sports Club
Holy Rood RC Infant School
Holy Rood RC Junior School
St Pauls CE Primary School
Orchard Primary School
St Anthonys RC Primary School
Westfield Community Technology College
Holywell School
Moor Park Industrial Estate
Wolsey Business Park
Premier Travel Inn
Rickmansworth Sports Club
Grand Union Canal
River Gade
NORTH WESTERN AVENUE GADE SIDE
HEMPSTEAD ROAD
RICKMANSWORTH ROAD
WATFORD ROAD
TOLPITS LANE
Rousebarn Lane
Grove Mill Lane
Old House Lane
Fir Tree Hill
Langleybury Lane
Little Green Lane
Baldwins Lane
Cassiobury Drive
Whippendell Road
54
71
92
1 grid square represents 500 metres

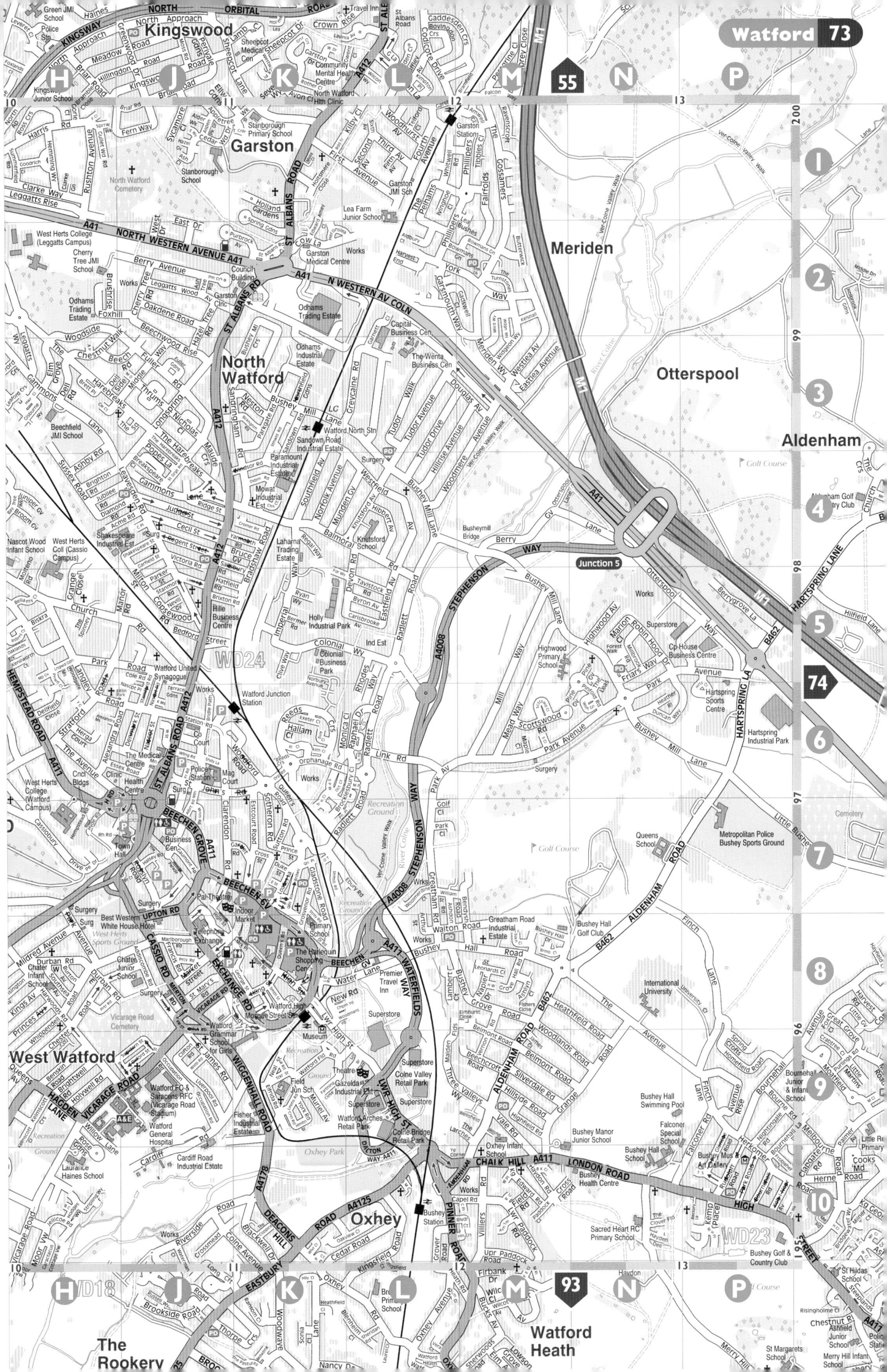
Kingswood
Garston
North Watford
Meriden
Otterspool
Aldenham
West Watford
Oxhey
Watford Heath
The Rookery
NORTH ORBITAL ROAD
KINGSWAY
ST ALBANS ROAD
A412
A41 NORTH WESTERN AVENUE A41
N WESTERN AV COLN
M1
Junction 5
STEPHENSON WAY
A4008
HARTSPRING LANE
HARTSPRING LA
B462
ALDENHAM ROAD
HEMPSTEAD ROAD
A411
BEECHEN GROVE
EXCHANGE RD
VICARAGE ROAD
HAGDEN LANE
WIGGENHALL ROAD
A4178
DEACONS HILL
A4125
EASTBURY
CHALK HILL
LONDON ROAD
HIGH STREET
PINNER ROAD
WATERFIELDS WAY
LWR HIGH ST
UPTON RD
CASSIO RD
Watford Junction Station
Watford North Stn
Watford High Street Stn
Garston Station
Bushey Station
Watford General Hospital
Watford FC & Saracens RFC (Vicarage Road Stadium)
West Herts College (Leggatts Campus)
West Herts College (Watford Campus)
International University
Bushey Hall Golf Club
Metropolitan Police Bushey Sports Ground
Hartspring Industrial Park
Hartspring Sports Centre
Colne Valley Retail Park
The Harlequin Shopping Cen
Watford Grammar School for Girls
North Watford Cemetery
Vicarage Road Cemetery
Oxhey Park
Recreation Ground
Golf Course
Bushey Golf & Country Club
WD24
WD23
WD18
55
93
74
H
J
K
L
M
N
P
1
2
3
4
5
6
7
8
9
10
10
11
12
13
200
99
98
97
96
195

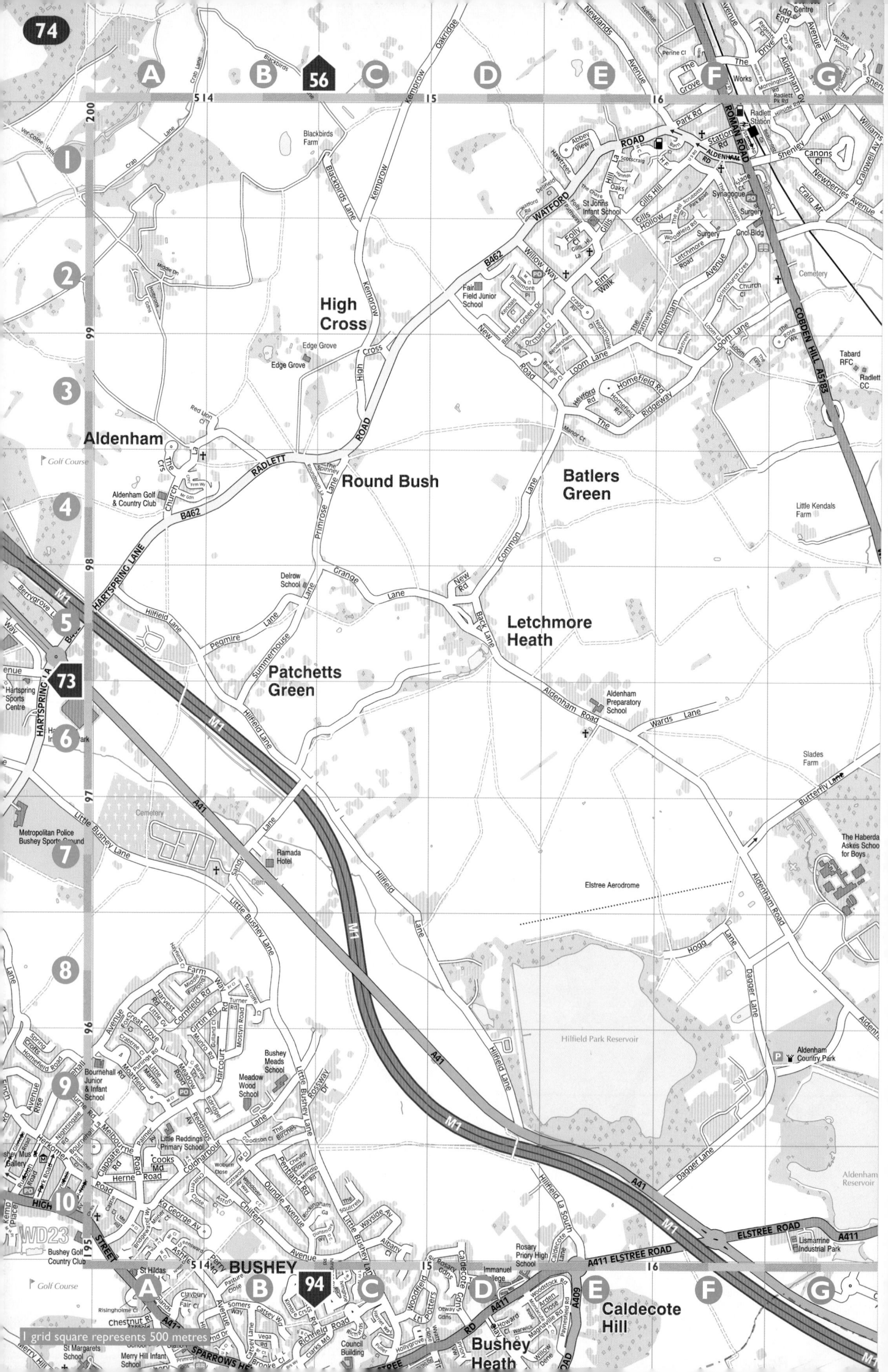
56
73
94
A
B
C
D
E
F
G
1
2
3
4
5
6
7
8
9
10
High Cross
Aldenham
Round Bush
Batlers Green
Letchmore Heath
Patchetts Green
BUSHEY
Caldecote Hill
Bushey Heath
Blackbirds Farm
Edge Grove
Delrow School
Aldenham Golf & Country Club
Golf Course
Fair Field Junior School
St Johns Infant School
Radlett Station
Synagogue
Surgery
Cncl Bldg
Cemetery
Tabard RFC
Radlett CC
Little Kendals Farm
Aldenham Preparatory School
Slades Farm
The Haberdashers' Askes School for Boys
Elstree Aerodrome
Hilfield Park Reservoir
Aldenham Country Park
Aldenham Reservoir
Lismarrine Industrial Park
Ramada Hotel
Metropolitan Police Bushey Sports Ground
Hartspring Sports Centre
Bushey Meads School
Meadow Wood School
Bournehall Junior & Infant School
Little Reddings Primary School
Bushey Golf Country Club
Rosary Priory High School
Immanuel College
St Margarets School
Merry Hill Infant School
Council Building
WATFORD ROAD
RADLETT ROAD
HARTSPRING LANE
ROMAN ROAD
COBDEN HILL A5183
ELSTREE ROAD
A411 ELSTREE ROAD
Aldenham Road
Hilfield Lane
Little Bushey Lane
Common Lane
Kemprow
Grange Lane
Wards Lane
Dagger Lane
Butterfly Lane
M1
A41
B462
WD23
1 grid square represents 500 metres

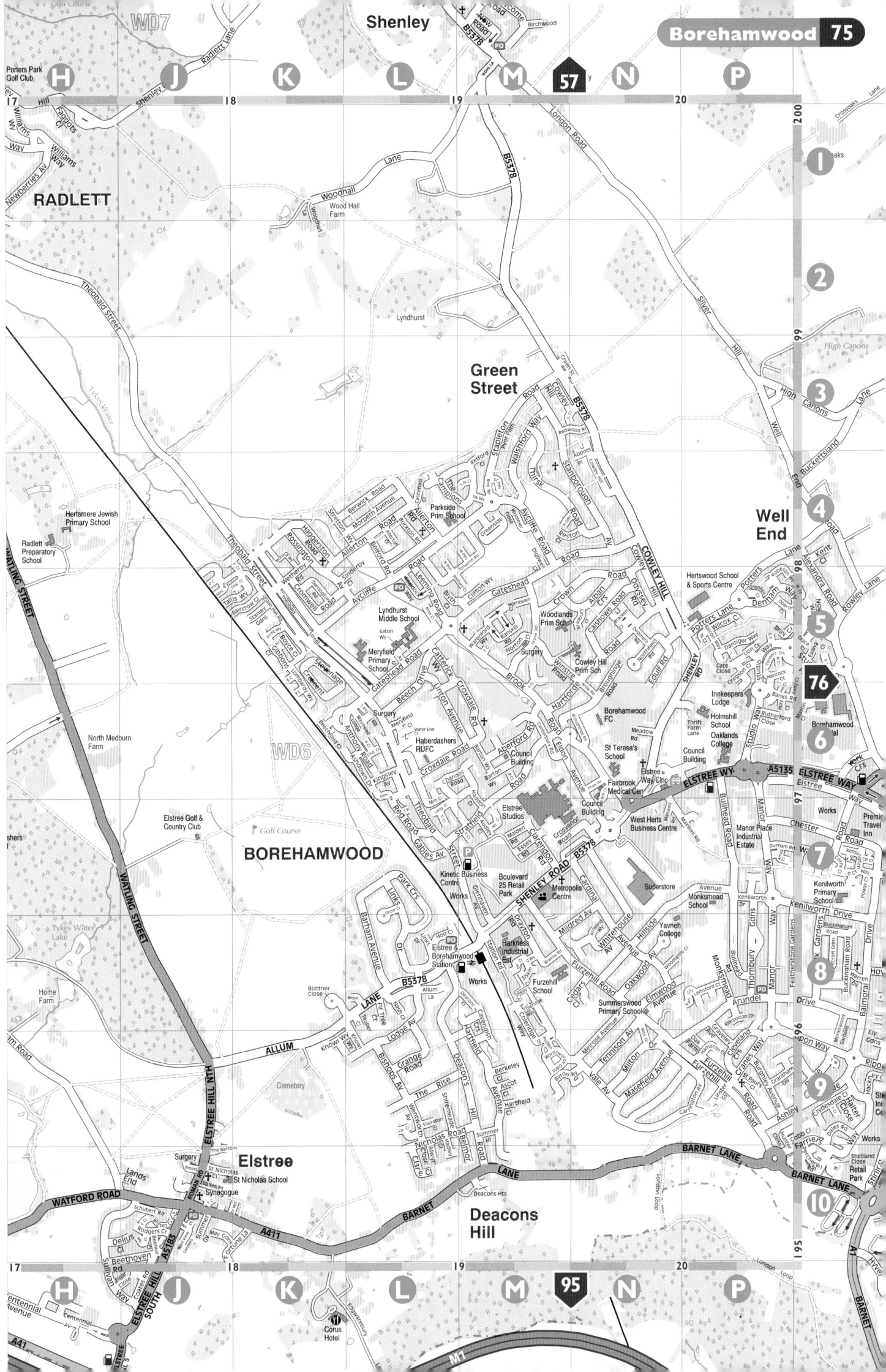
Shenley
RADLETT
Green Street
Well End
BOREHAMWOOD
Elstree
Deacons Hill
WD7
WD6
57
76
95
Theobald Street
Watling Street
Woodhall Lane
Wood Hall Farm
London Road
Silver Hill
High Canons
Cowley Hill
Shenley Road
Elstree Way
Allum Lane
Barnet Lane
Watford Road
Elstree Hill Nth
Elstree Hill South
Hertsmere Jewish Primary School
Radlett Preparatory School
North Medburn Farm
Elstree Golf & Country Club
Golf Course
Tykes Water Lake
Home Farm
Cemetery
Parkside Prim School
Lyndhurst Middle School
Meryfield Primary School
Haberdashers RUFC
Woodlands Prim Sch
Cowley Hill Prim Sch
Borehamwood FC
St Teresa's School
Council Building
Elstree Studios
Kinetic Business Centre
Boulevard 25 Retail Park
Metropolis Centre
Elstree & Borehamwood Station
Harkness Industrial Est
Furzehill School
Summerswood Primary School
Yavneh College
Superstore
West Herts Business Centre
Fairbrook Medical Cen
Hertswood School & Sports Centre
Innkeepers Lodge
Holmshill School
Oaklands College
Manor Place Industrial Estate
Monksmead School
Kenilworth Primary School
St Nicholas School
Synagogue
Deacons Hts
Corus Hotel
Porters Park Golf Club
Lyndhurst
Wood Hall Farm

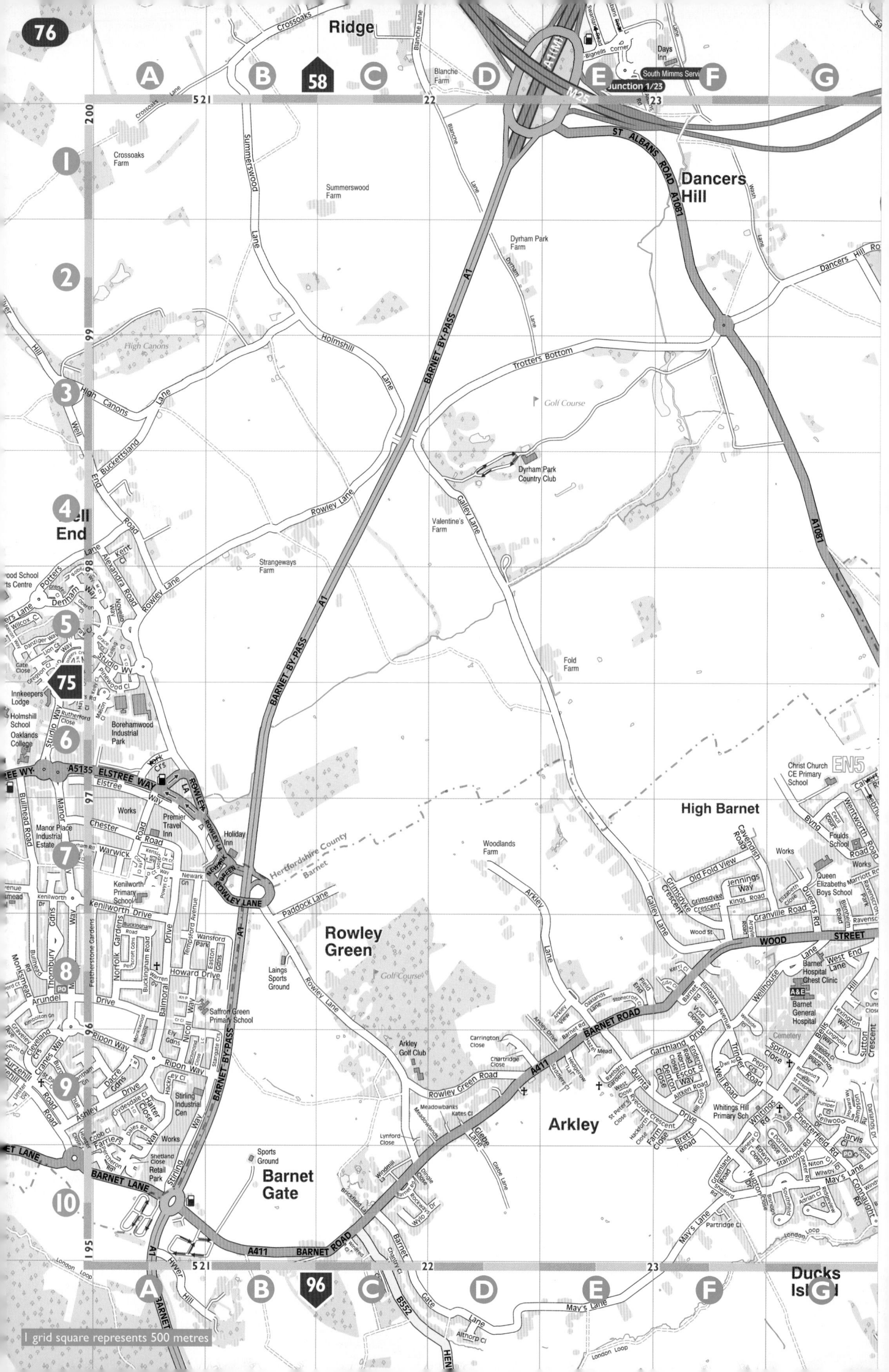
Ridge
Crossoaks Lane
Blanche Lane
Blanche Farm
A1(M)
M25
Junction 1/23
South Mimms Services
Days Inn
Bignells Corner
58
Crossoaks Farm
Summerswood Lane
Summerswood Farm
St Albans Road
A1081
Dancers Hill
Dancers Hill Road
Dyrham Park Farm
Dyrham Lane
Barnet By-Pass
A1
Holmshill Lane
High Canons
High Canons
Buckettsland Lane
Trotters Bottom
Golf Course
Dyrham Park Country Club
Galley Lane
Valentine's Farm
Rowley Lane
Strangeways Farm
Well End
Well End Road
Potters Lane
Alexandra Road
Kent Cl
Denham Way
Studio Way
75
Innkeepers Lodge
Holmshill School
Oaklands College
Borehamwood Industrial Park
Fold Farm
A5135
Elstree Way
Rowley La
Premier Travel Inn
Holiday Inn
Works
Chester Road
Warwick Road
Manor Place Industrial Estate
Bullhead Road
Manor Way
Hertfordshire County
Barnet
Newark Green
Rowley Lane
Paddock Lane
Woodlands Farm
Arkley Lane
Christ Church CE Primary School
EN5
High Barnet
Cavendish Road
Old Fold View
Jennings Way
Grimsdyke Crescent
Kings Road
Granville Road
Queens Road
Queen Elizabeths Boys School
Foulds School
Wentworth Road
Byng Road
Wood Street
Kenilworth Primary School
Kenilworth Drive
Kenilworth Gdns
Thornbury Gdns
Featherstone Gardens
Norfolk Gardens
Buckingham Road
Tempsford Avenue
Wansford Park
Howard Drive
Balmoral
Rowley Green
Laings Sports Ground
Golf Course
Barnet Hospital Chest Clinic
Barnet General Hospital
A&E
West End Lane
Wellhouse Lane
Arundel Drive
Saffron Green Primary School
Ripon Way
Cranes Way
Ashley Drive
Dacre Gdns
Stirling Industrial Cen
Stirling Way
Barnet Road
A411
Arkley Golf Club
Rowley Green Road
Carrington Close
Chartridge Close
Garthland Drive
Quinta Drive
Denton Close
Escot Way
Aitken Road
Trinder Road
Pepys Crescent
Spring Close
Cemetery
Whitings Hill Primary Sch
Chesterfield Rd
Arkley
Ryecroft Crescent
Brett Road
Farriers
Works
Shetland Close
Retail Park
Barnet Lane
Elstree Lane
Sports Ground
Barnet Gate
Meadowbanks
Kates Cl
Glebe Lane
Lynford Close
Windmill
Dingle Close
Wylo Dr
Mays Lane
Partridge Cl
Greenland Road
Nupton Drive
Stanhope Rd
Mays Lane
Connaught Rd
London Loop
Ducks Island
Hyver Hill
Barnet Lane
96
B552
Barnet Gate Lane
Althorp Cl
521
22
23
200
99
98
97
96
195
A B C D E F G
1 2 3 4 5 6 7 8 9 10
1 grid square represents 500 metres

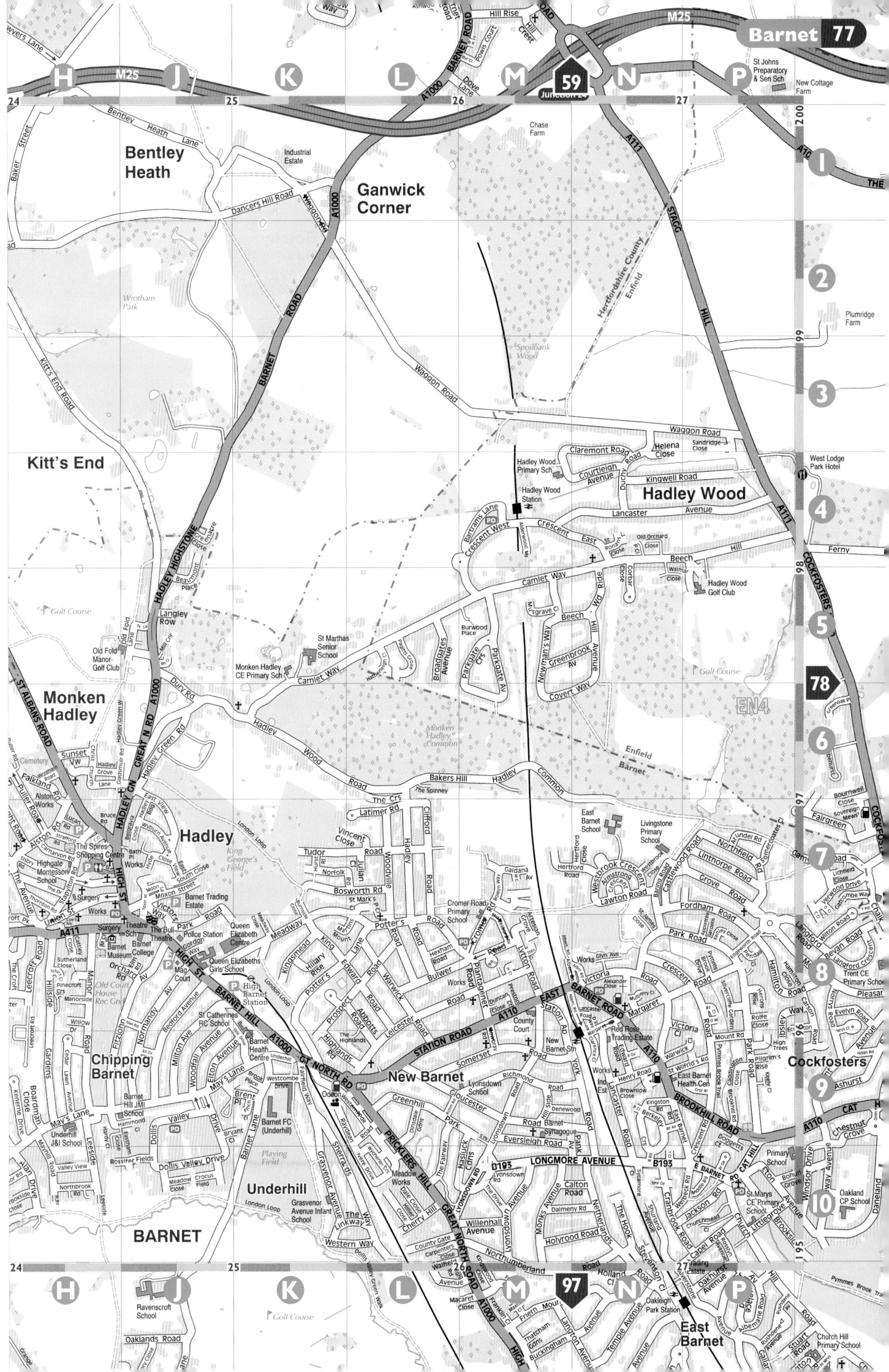

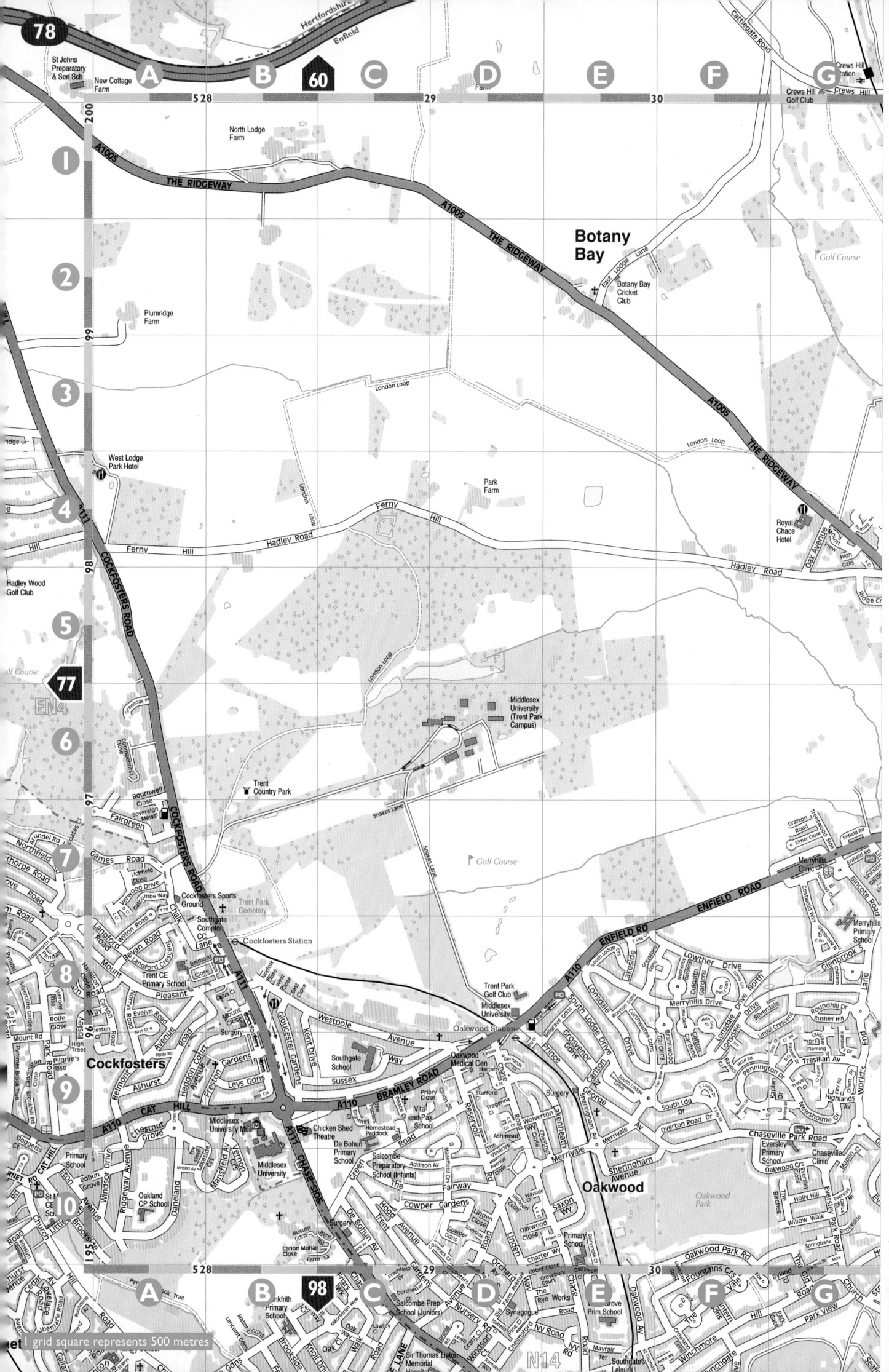

78
Hertfordshire
Enfield
St Johns Preparatory & Sen Sch
New Cottage Farm
A
B
60
C
D
E
F
G
Cattlegate Road
Crews Hill Station
Crews Hill
Crews Hill Golf Club
528
29
30
200
North Lodge Farm
1
A1005
THE RIDGEWAY
Botany Bay
East Lodge Lane
Botany Bay Cricket Club
Golf Course
2
Plumridge Farm
99
3
London Loop
West Lodge Park Hotel
Park Farm
Ferny Hill
Hadley Road
Royal Chace Hotel
Oak Avenue
Mount View
High Oaks
Ridge Cr
4
A111
Hill
98
Hadley Wood Golf Club
COCKFOSTERS ROAD
5
77
EN4
6
Middlesex University (Trent Park Campus)
Trent Country Park
Snakes Lane
Bournwell Close
Sovereign Mews
Fairgreen
97
Coombehurst Close
Games Road
Northfield Rd
7
Golf Course
Grafton Road
Elmer Close
Enfield Rd
Merryhills Clinic
Bincote Road
ENFIELD ROAD
Cockfosters Sports Ground
Trent Park Cemetery
Southgate Compton CC
Cockfosters Station
Verwood Drive
Lichfield Close
Wilton Road
Bevan Road
Langford Crescent
Chalk Lane
Belmont Close
Merryhills Primary School
Glenbrook S
8
Trent CE Primary School
Mount Pleasant
A111
Norfolk Close
West Close
East Close
Trent Park Golf Club
Middlesex University
A110
ENFIELD RD
Lakeside
Lowther Drive
Merryhills Drive
Lonsdale Drive North
Silverdale
Roundhill Dr
Lane
Evelyn Road
Gloucester Gardens
Kent Drive
Westpole Avenue
Way
Oakwood Station
South Lodge Drive
Lonsdale Drive
Culgaith Gardens
Brattwood Gardens
Clifton Gardens
Lindal Crescent
Rushey Hill
96
Mount Rd
Park Road
Pilgrim's Rise
High Trees
Cockfosters
Ashurst
Heddon Court Avenue
Freston Gardens
Leys Gdns
Southgate School
Sussex Way
Oakwood Medical Cen
Prince George Av
Trent Gardens
Tresilian Av
9
CAT HILL
A110
BRAMLEY ROAD
Priory Close
Chase Road
Reservoir Rd
Surgery
Carlton
Sheringham Av
Overton Road Dr
South Lodge Dr
Kaplan Dr
Highlands Av
Newsholme Dr
Middlesex University Mus
Chicken Shed Theatre
A111 CHASE SIDE
Vita et Pax School
Homestead Paddock
Wolverton Wy
Chestnut Close
Lakenheath
Merrivale
Chaseville Park Road
Eversley Primary School
Chaseville Clinic
Chestnut Grove
Primary School
Windsor Drive
Ridgeway Avenue
Daneland
Mansfield Av
Vernon Crs
Middlesex University
De Bohun Primary School
Salcombe Preparatory School (Infants)
Addison Av
The Fairway
Cowper Gardens
Sheringham Avenue
Oakwood
Oakwood Park
Oakwood Crs
Holly Hill
Eversley Park Road
Willow Walk
10
Bohun Grove
Oakland CP School
Brookside
De Bohun Av
Hood Avenue
Linden Close
Saxon Wy
Oakwood Close
Primary School
Surgery
Ruston Gdns
Canon Mohan Close
Charter Wy
Oakwood Park Rd
195
528
29
30
98
A
B
C
D
E
F
G
Pymmes Brook Trail
Monkfrith Primary School
Salcombe Prep School (Juniors)
Nursery Rd
Synagogue
The Rye Works
Ivy Road
Fountains Crs
Park View
Hill
Winchmore
N14
Southgate Leisure
Mayfair Ter
Sir Thomas Lipton Memorial Hospital
1 grid square represents 500 metres

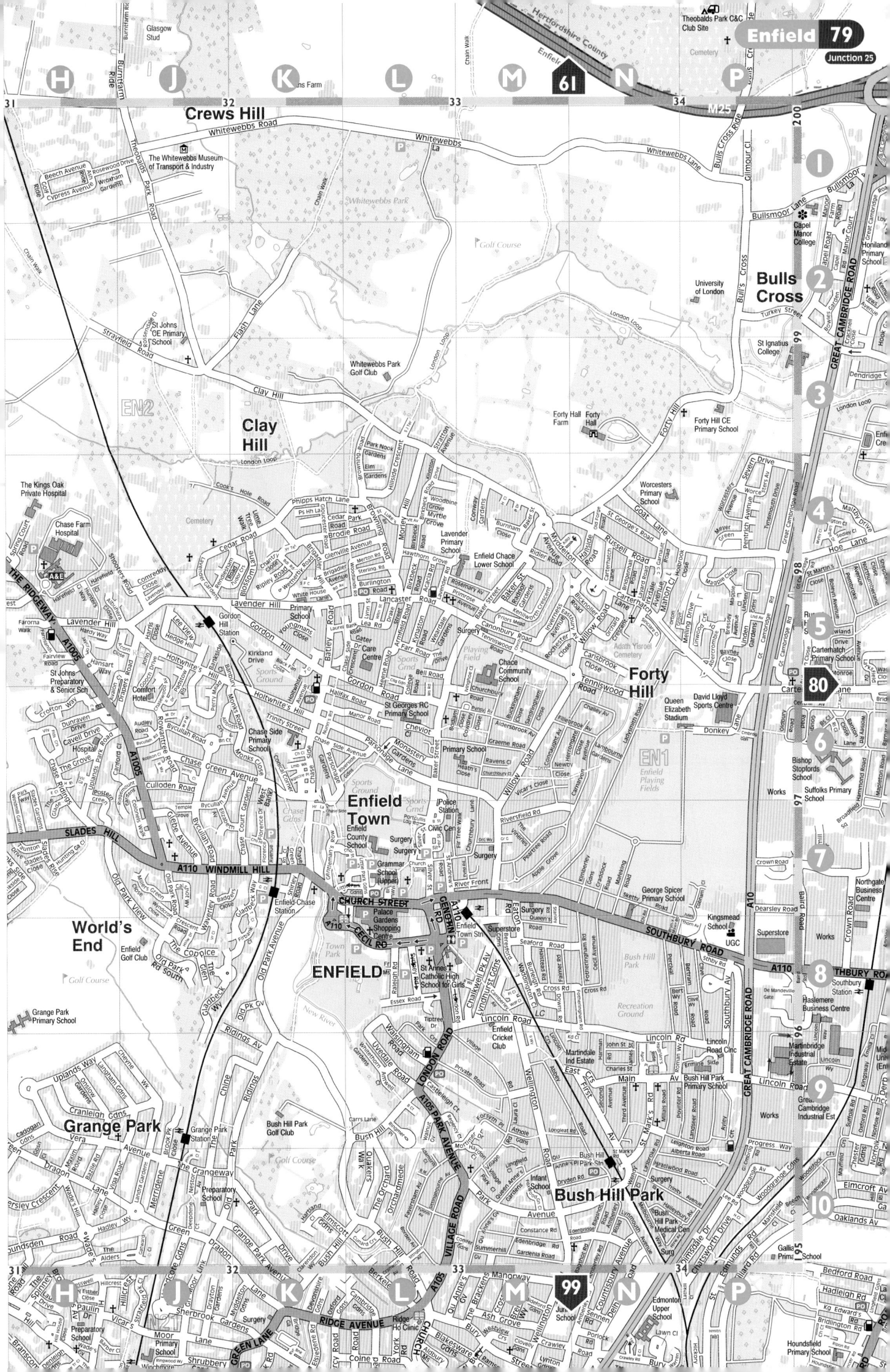
Junction 25
Hertfordshire County
M25
Crews Hill
Whitewebbs Road
Whitewebbs Lane
The Whitewebbs Museum of Transport & Industry
Whitewebbs Park
Golf Course
Whitewebbs Park Golf Club
Theobalds Park C&C Club Site
Cemetery
Bulls Cross Ride
Bullsmoor Lane
Capel Manor College
Bulls Cross
University of London
Turkey Street
St Ignatius College
Great Cambridge Road
Forty Hall Farm
Forty Hall
Forty Hill CE Primary School
Forty Hill
St Johns CE Primary School
Strayfield Road
Flash Lane
Clay Hill
EN2
London Loop
The Kings Oak Private Hospital
Chase Farm Hospital
A&E
The Ridgeway A1005
Lavender Hill
Gordon Hill Station
Gordon Hill
Worcesters Primary School
Goat Lane
Hoe Lane
Lavender Primary School
Enfield Chace Lower School
Chace Community School
St Georges RC Primary School
Chase Side Primary School
Queen Elizabeth Stadium
David Lloyd Sports Centre
Donkey Lane
EN1
Enfield Playing Fields
Carterhatch Primary School
Bishop Stopfords School
Suffolks Primary School
Works
Enfield Town
Enfield County School
Grammar School (Upper)
Police Station
Civic Centre
Slades Hill
A110 Windmill Hill
Enfield Chase Station
Church Street
Palace Gardens Shopping Centre
Cecil Rd
Enfield Town Stn
Southbury Road
George Spicer Primary School
Kingsmead School
Superstore
UGC
Northgate Business Centre
World's End
Enfield Golf Club
ENFIELD
St Anne's Catholic High School for Girls
New River
Recreation Ground
Bush Hill Park
Lincoln Road
Enfield Cricket Club
Martindale Ind Estate
Bush Hill Park Primary School
Southbury Station
Haslemere Business Centre
Martinbridge Industrial Estate
Great Cambridge Industrial Est
Grange Park Primary School
Grange Park
Grange Park Station
The Grangeway
Preparatory School
Bush Hill Park Golf Club
A105 Park Avenue
London Road
Village Road
Bush Hill Park Station
Bush Hill Park Medical Cen
Ridge Avenue
Green Lane
Ridge Ho Clinic
Edmonton Upper School
Houndsfield Primary School
Bedford Road
Hadleigh Rd
Moor Primary School
Oaklands Av
Elmcroft Av
61
80
99

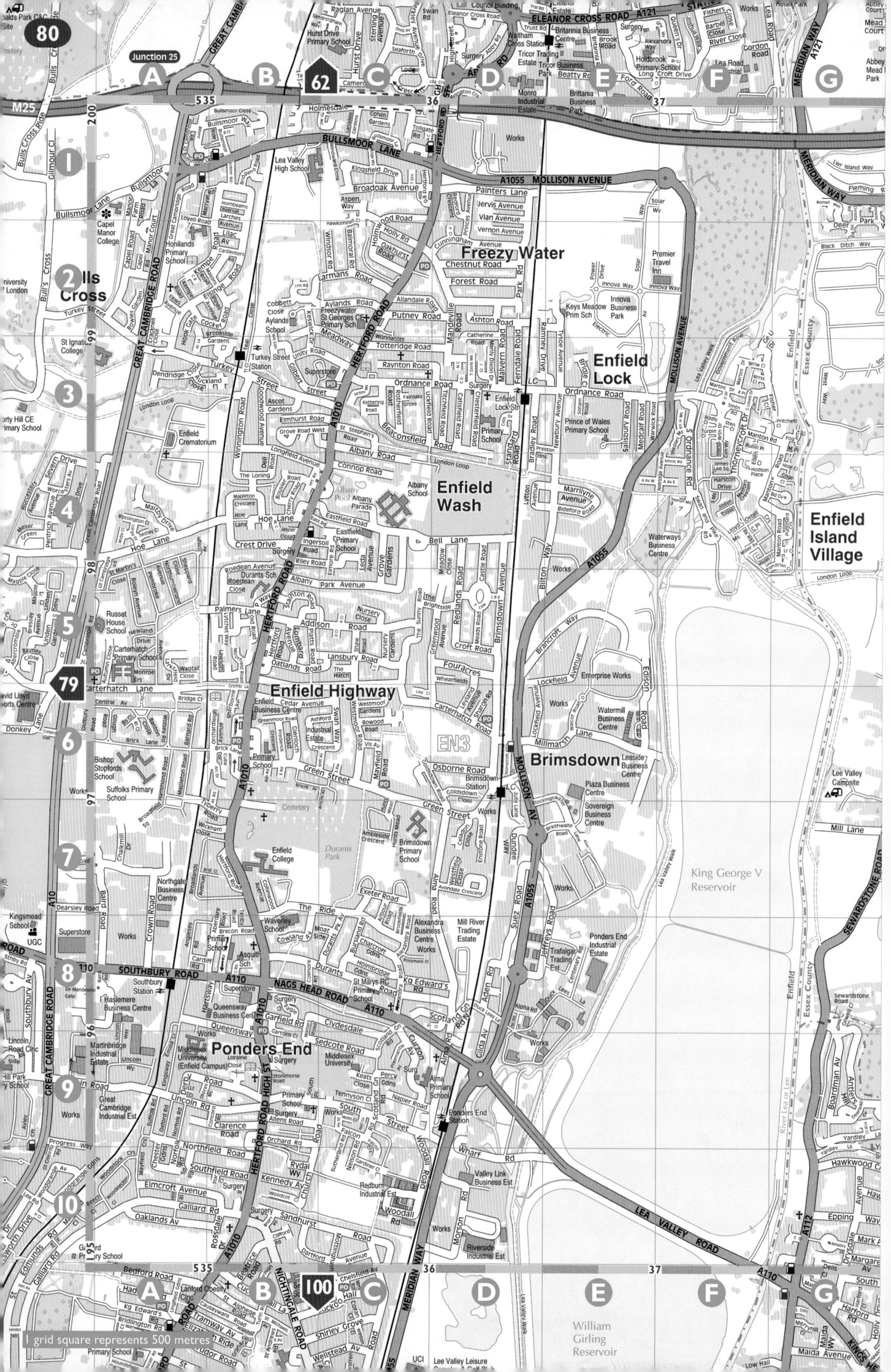

80
Junction 25
M25
62
A
B
C
D
E
F
G
535
36
37
200
99
98
97
96
195
1
2
3
4
5
6
7
8
9
10
Bulls Cross
Freezy Water
Enfield Lock
Enfield Wash
Enfield Island Village
Enfield Highway
EN3
Brimsdown
Ponders End
King George V Reservoir
William Girling Reservoir
ELEANOR CROSS ROAD A121
MERIDIAN WAY A121
BULLSMOOR LANE
A1055 MOLLISON AVENUE
GREAT CAMBRIDGE ROAD
HERTFORD ROAD
A1010
MOLLISON AVENUE
A1055
SOUTHBURY ROAD
A110
NAGS HEAD ROAD
LEA VALLEY ROAD
SEWARDSTONE ROAD
HERTFORD ROAD HIGH ST
NIGHTINGALE ROAD
MERIDIAN WAY
A10
A112
Ordnance Road
Bell Lane
Hoe Lane
Carterhatch Lane
Green Street
Turkey Street
Lea Valley Walk
London Loop
Capel Manor College
Turkey Street Station
Enfield Lock Stn
Brimsdown Station
Southbury Station
Ponders End Station
Enfield Crematorium
Lee Valley Campsite
Middlesex University (Enfield Campus)
79
100
1 grid square represents 500 metres

M25
A121 MERIDIAN WAY
Junction 26
HONEY LANE
SEWARDSTONE ROAD
A112
A104
EPPING NEW ROAD
Sewardstone
Gilwell Park
Lippitts Hill
High Beach
Sewardstonebury
Avey Lane
Mott Street
Lippitts Hill
Church Road
Bury Road
Daws Hill
Gilwell Lane
Hawes Lane
Butlers Drive
Godwin Close
Premier Travel Inn
Manor Road
Church La
Cross Roads
Fairmead Road
Wellington Hill
Pynest Green Lane
Beach Hill Park
Golf Course
High Beech Golf Club
High Beech CE Primary School
Manor House
Wallsgrove House
Epping Forest Conservation Centre
West Essex Golf Club
Essex County
Waltham Forest
London Loop
Green Ride
Centenary Walk
Hornbeam Lane
Woodman Lane
Farm End
Warren Hill
Oaklands School
Surgery
HIGH ROAD
RANGERS ROAD
Royal Epping Forest Golf Club
Queen Elizabeth Museum
Chingford Station
Cemetery
Waltham Abbey Swimming Pool
Waltham Marriott Hotel
The Leverton Infant School
Howard Business Park
Quinton Way
Lodge Lane
Beechfield Walk
Greenwich Way
South Way
Southend Lane
Honey Lane
Woodridden
Eastbrook End Cemetery
63
101
82

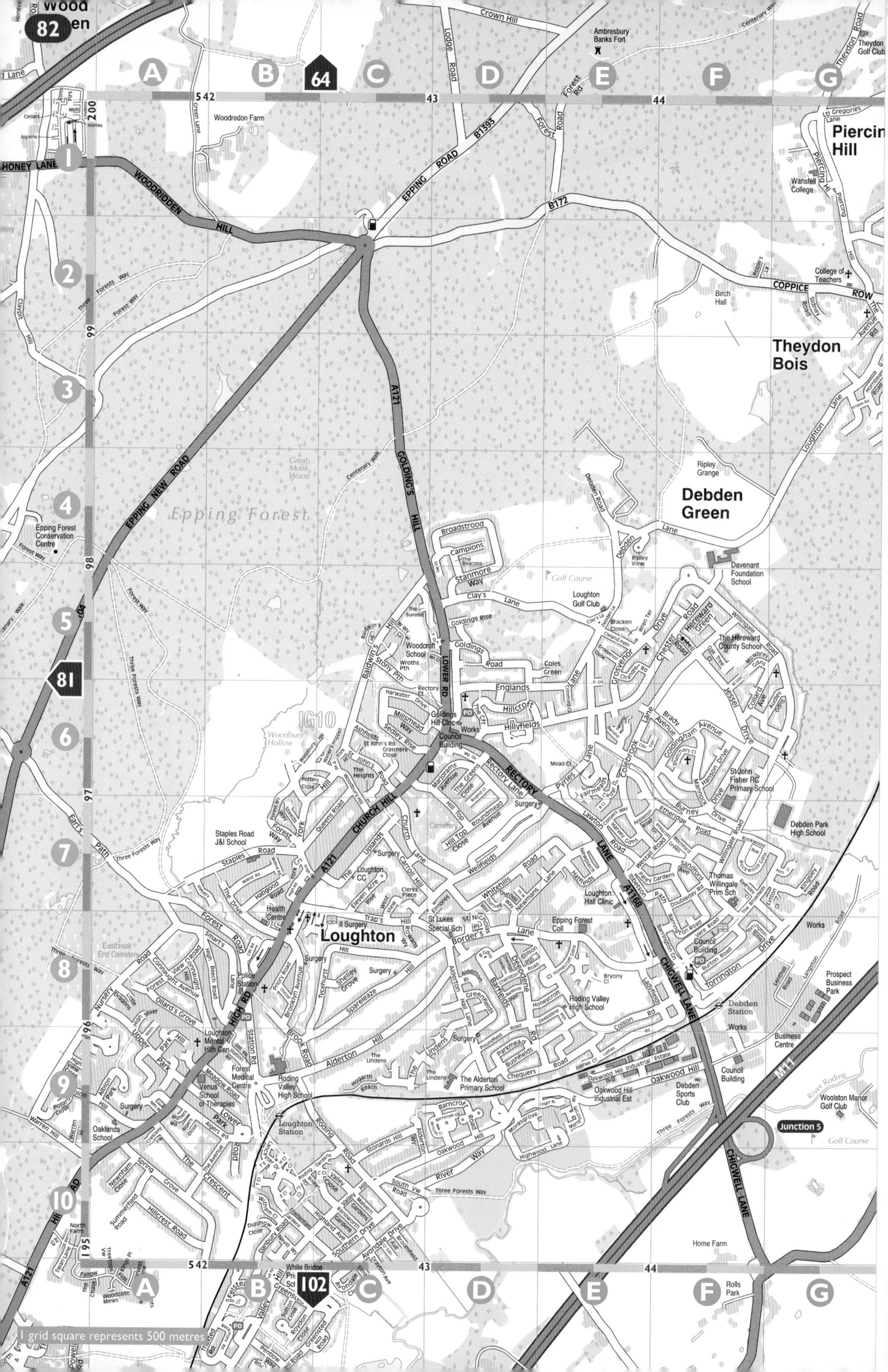

82
64
81
102
A
B
C
D
E
F
G
1
2
3
4
5
6
7
8
9
10
542
43
44
200
99
98
97
96
195
Crown Hill
Ambresbury Banks Fort
Theydon Golf Club
Woodredon Farm
Green Lane
Lodge Road
Forest Rd
Forest Road
Honey Lane
Woodridden Hill
Epping Road B1393
B172
Piercing Hill
Wansfell College
College of Teachers
Coppice Row
Birch Hall
Theydon Bois
Three Forests Way
Forest Way
Claypit Hill
A121
Golding's Hill
Centenary Walk
Great Monk Wood
Epping New Road
Epping Forest
Epping Forest Conservation Centre
Ripley Grange
Debden Green
Debden Road
Debden Lane
Loughton Lane
Ripley View
Davenant Foundation School
Broadstrood
Campions
Stanmore Way
Clay's Lane
Golf Course
Loughton Golf Club
Goldings Rise
Woodcroft School
Baldwin's Hill
Lower Rd
Goldings Road
Coles Green
Englands
Hillcroft
Hillyfields
Grosvenor Drive
Chester Road
Hereward Green
The Hereward County School
Willingale Road
Jessel Drive
Collard Ave
Stony Path
Rectory Ct
Harwater Drive
Millsmead Way
Goldings Hill Clnc
Council Building
Works
IG10
Woodbury Hollow
Ashfields
Church Hill
Rectory Lane
Rectory Lane
Brady Avenue
Goldingham Avenue
Colebrook Lane
St John Fisher RC Primary School
Debden Park High School
Burney Drive
Etheridge Road
Fairmeads
Pyrles Lane
Mead Cl
Surgery
Queens Road
York Hill
Forest Way
Staples Road J&I School
Staples Road
Cemetery
Hill Top Close
Roundmead Avenue
Wellfields
The Loughton CC
Uplands
Carroll Hill
Eleven Acre Rise
Whitehills Road
Newmans Lane
Lawton Road
Loughton Hall Clinic
A1168
Westall Road
Thomas Willingale Prim Sch
Sandford Ave
Rookwood Ave
Kingsley Road
Works
The Drive
Habgood Road
Health Centre
Trap's Hill
Loughton
St Lukes Special Sch
Border's Lane
Epping Forest Coll
Chigwell Lane
Torrington Drive
Council Building
Prospect Business Park
Debden Station
Business Centre
Eastbrook End Cemetery
Forest Road
Smart's Lane
Connaught Avenue
Ollard's Grove
High Beech Road
Police Station
High Rd
Station Rd
Brooklyn Avenue
Shelley Grove
Spareleaze Hill
Deepdene Road
Barfields
Honeycroft
Roding Valley High School
Bryony Cl
Colson Rd
Alderton Hall Lane
Greenfields
Loughton Mental Hlth Cen
Upper Park
Forest Medical Centre
Venus School of Therapies
Meadow Road
Lower Park Road
Alderton Hill
The Lindens
Roding Valley High School
Parkmead
Bushfields
Chequers Road
The Alderton Primary School
Oakwood Hill Industrial Est
Oakwood Hill
Debden Sports Club
Council Building
M11
River Roding
Woolston Manor Golf Club
Junction 5
Golf Course
Oaklands School
Warren Hill
Albion Hill
Surgery
Loughton Station
Roding Road
Stonards Hill
Alderton Way
Oakwood Hill
River Way
Monksgrove
Highwood Lane
Three Forests Way
Newnham Close
Spring Grove
The Crescent
Summerfield Road
Hillcrest Road
South Vw Road
Valley Hill
Southern Drive
Avondale Drive
Highland Ave
Home Farm
North Farm
Swan Lane
Woodcote Mews
White Bridge
Rolls Park
Chigwell Lane
Wood Green
I grid square represents 500 metres

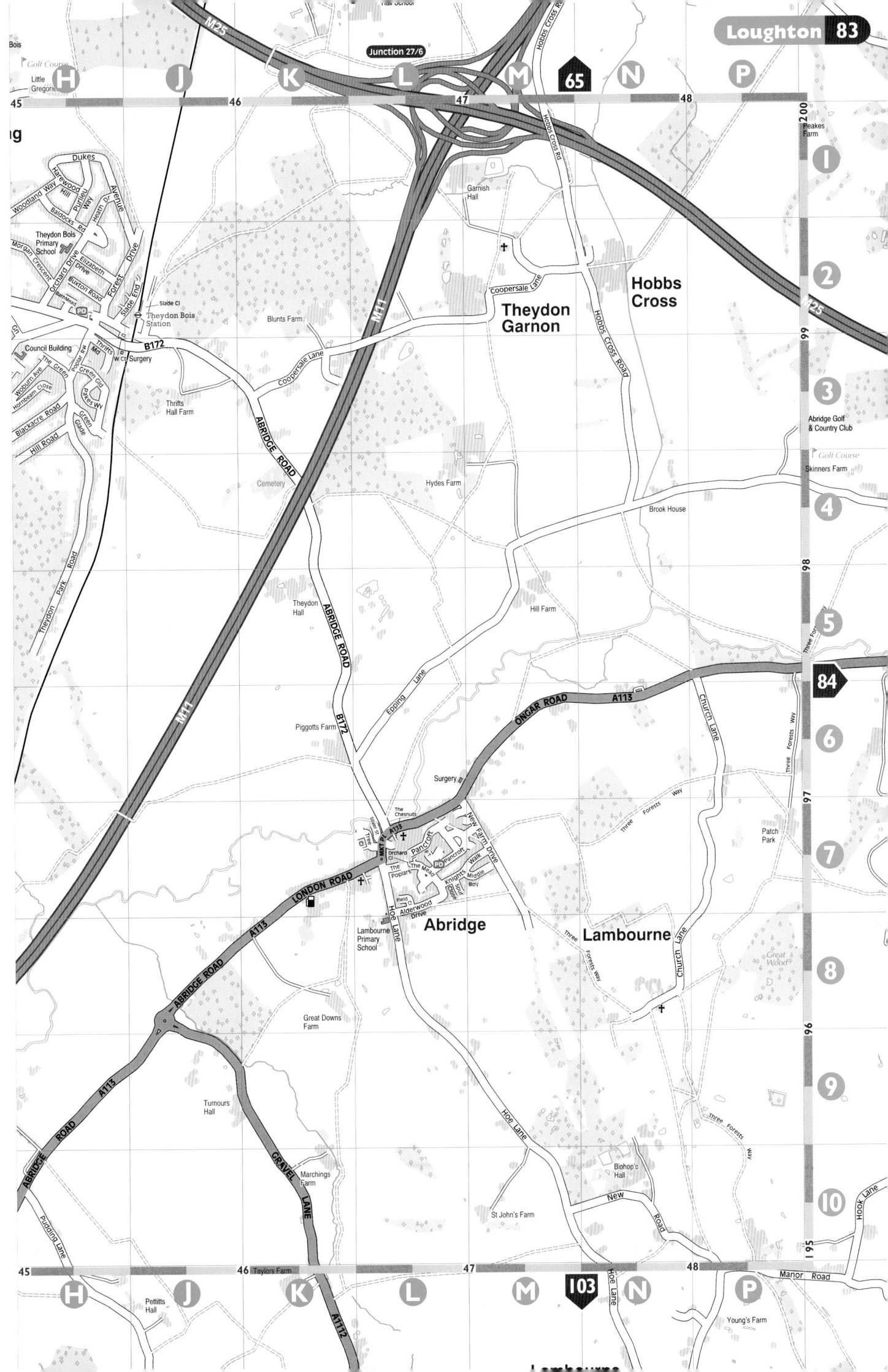

M25

Junction 27/6

Hobbs Cross Rd

65

H J K L M N P

45 46 47 48 200 1

Little Gregorie

Golf Course

Peakes Farm

25 99

Garnish Hall

Coopersale Lane

Theydon Garnon

Hobbs Cross

2

Dukes

Harewood Hill

Purlieu Way

Avenue

Forest Drive

Woodland Way

Baldocks

Heath Dr

Orchard Drive

Elizabeth Drive

Theydon Bois Primary School

Morgan Crescent

Buxton Road

Blunts Farm

Abridge Golf & Country Club

3

PO

Barn Mead

Slade Cl

Theydon Bois Station

B172

Skinners Farm

Golf Course

4

Council Building

Thrifts Mkt

Green Cl

w cts Surgery

Coopersale Lane

Hydes Farm

Brook House

98

The Green

Poplar Pw

Pakes Wy

Thrifts Hall Farm

Woburn Ave

Hornbeam Close

Green Glade

ABRIDGE ROAD

Blackacre Road

Hill Road

Cemetery

Hill Farm

5

Theydon Park Road

Theydon Hall

Three For

84

Epping Lane

ONGAR ROAD

A113

Church Lane

6

ABRIDGE ROAD

B172

Piggotts Farm

Surgery

Three Forests Way

M11

The Chesnuts

New Farm Drive

Patch Park

97

7

Silver Tree

A113

Orchard Cl

Pancroft

PO Pancroft

Knights Walk

Middle Boy

MKT PI

The Poplars

The Mead

Field

South Close

8

LONDON ROAD

Alderwood Drive

Abridge

Lambourne

A113

Hoe Lane

Lambourne Primary School

Three Forests Way

Church Lane

Great Wood

ABRIDGE ROAD

Great Downs Farm

9

A113

Turnours Hall

Hoe Lane

Three Forests Way

10

ABRIDGE ROAD

GRAVEL LANE

Marchings Farm

Bishop's Hall

New Road

Hook Lane

Pudding Lane

St John's Farm

195

H J K L M N P

45 46 Taylors Farm 47 48 Manor Road

103

Pettitts Hall

A112

Hoe Lane

Young's Farm

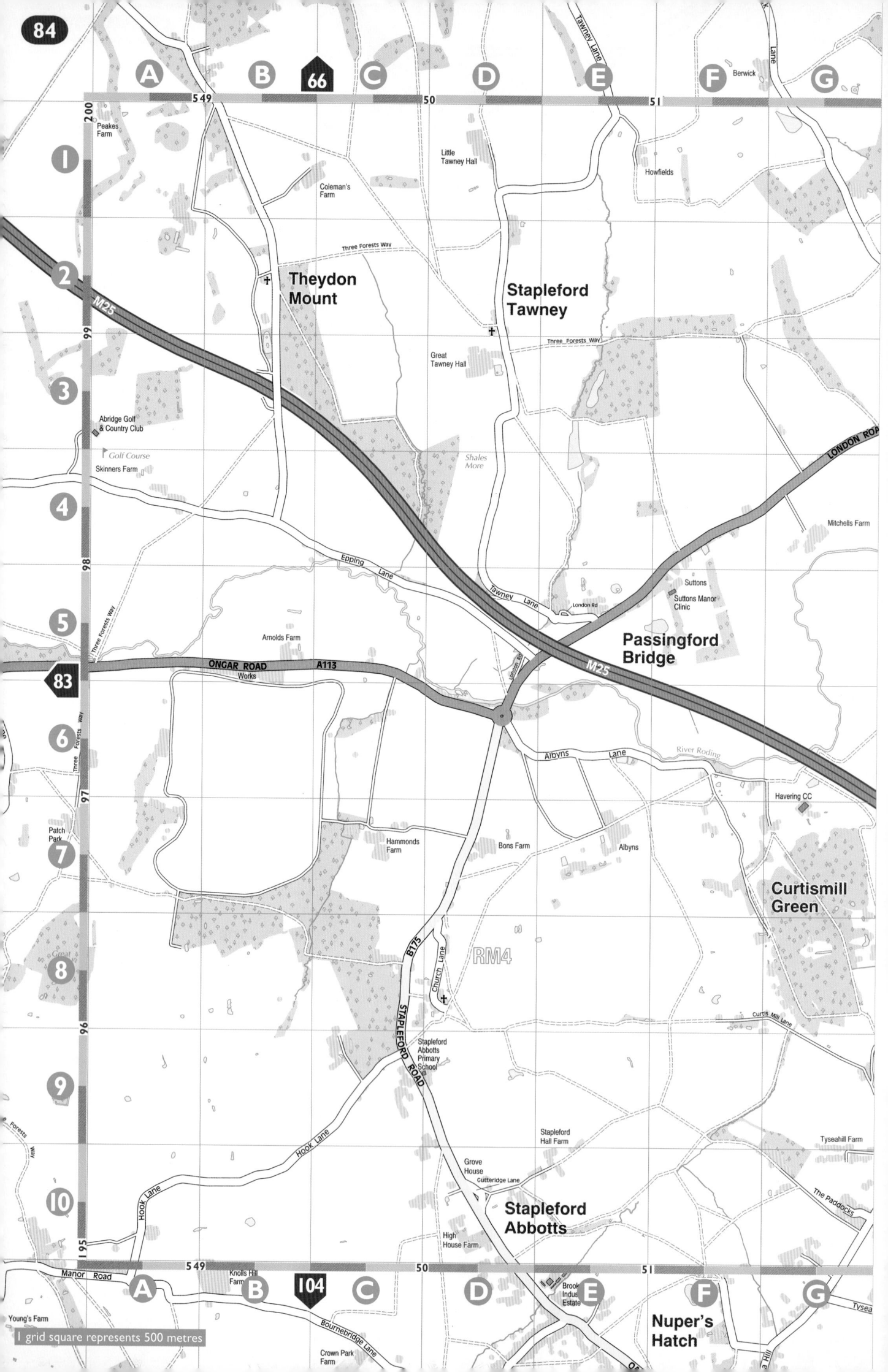

66
104
83
Theydon Mount
Stapleford Tawney
Passingford Bridge
Curtismill Green
Stapleford Abbotts
Nuper's Hatch
Peakes Farm
Coleman's Farm
Little Tawney Hall
Howfields
Berwick
Three Forests Way
Great Tawney Hall
Abridge Golf & Country Club
Golf Course
Skinners Farm
Shales More
Mitchells Farm
Epping Lane
Tawney Lane
London Rd
Suttons
Suttons Manor Clinic
London Road
M25
Arnolds Farm
ONGAR ROAD
A113
Works
River Roding
Albyns Lane
Havering CC
Patch Park
Hammonds Farm
Bons Farm
Albyns
B175
Church Lane
RM4
Curtis Mill Lane
Stapleford Abbotts Primary School
STAPLEFORD ROAD
Hook Lane
Stapleford Hall Farm
Tyseahill Farm
Grove House
Cutteridge Lane
The Paddocks
High House Farm
Manor Road
Knolls Hill Farm
Young's Farm
Bournebridge Lane
Crown Park Farm
Tawney Lane
Lane
1 grid square represents 500 metres

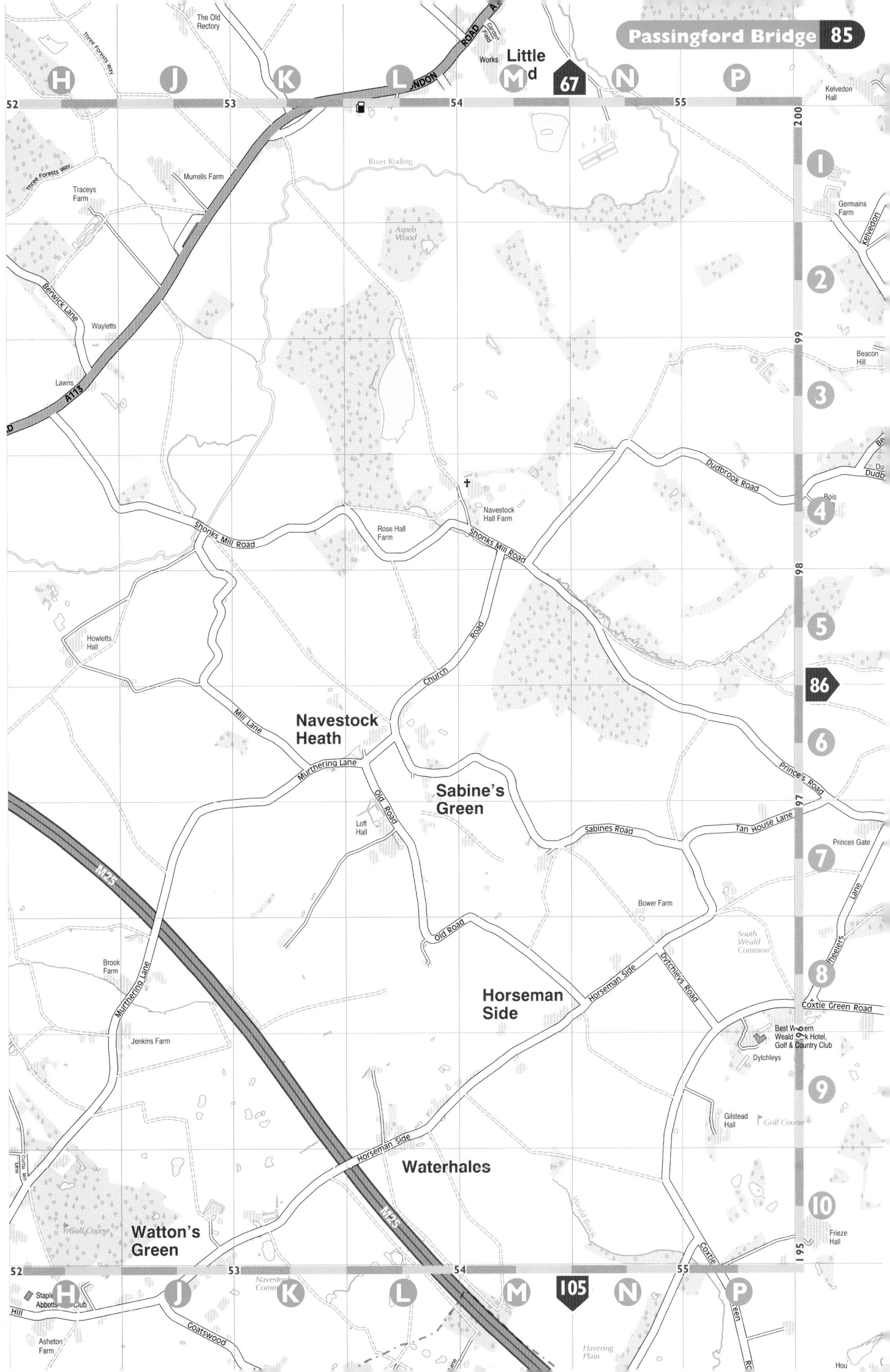
Little
67
86
105
The Old Rectory
Three Forests Way
Murrells Farm
Traceys Farm
Berwick Lane
Wayletts
Lawns
A113
River Roding
Aspen Wood
Kelvedon Hall
Germains Farm
Beacon Hill
Dudbrook Road
Navestock Hall Farm
Rose Hall Farm
Shonks Mill Road
Howletts Hall
Church Road
Mill Lane
Navestock Heath
Murthering Lane
Sabine's Green
Old Road
Loft Hall
Sabines Road
Tan House Lane
Prince's Road
Princes Gate
Bower Farm
South Weald Common
M25
Brook Farm
Horseman Side
Dytchleys Road
Coxtie Green Road
Dytchleys
Gilstead Hall
Golf Course
Jenkins Farm
Waterhales
Weald Brook
Watton's Green
Frieze Hall
Goatswood
Asheton Farm
Havering Plain
Curtis Mill Lane

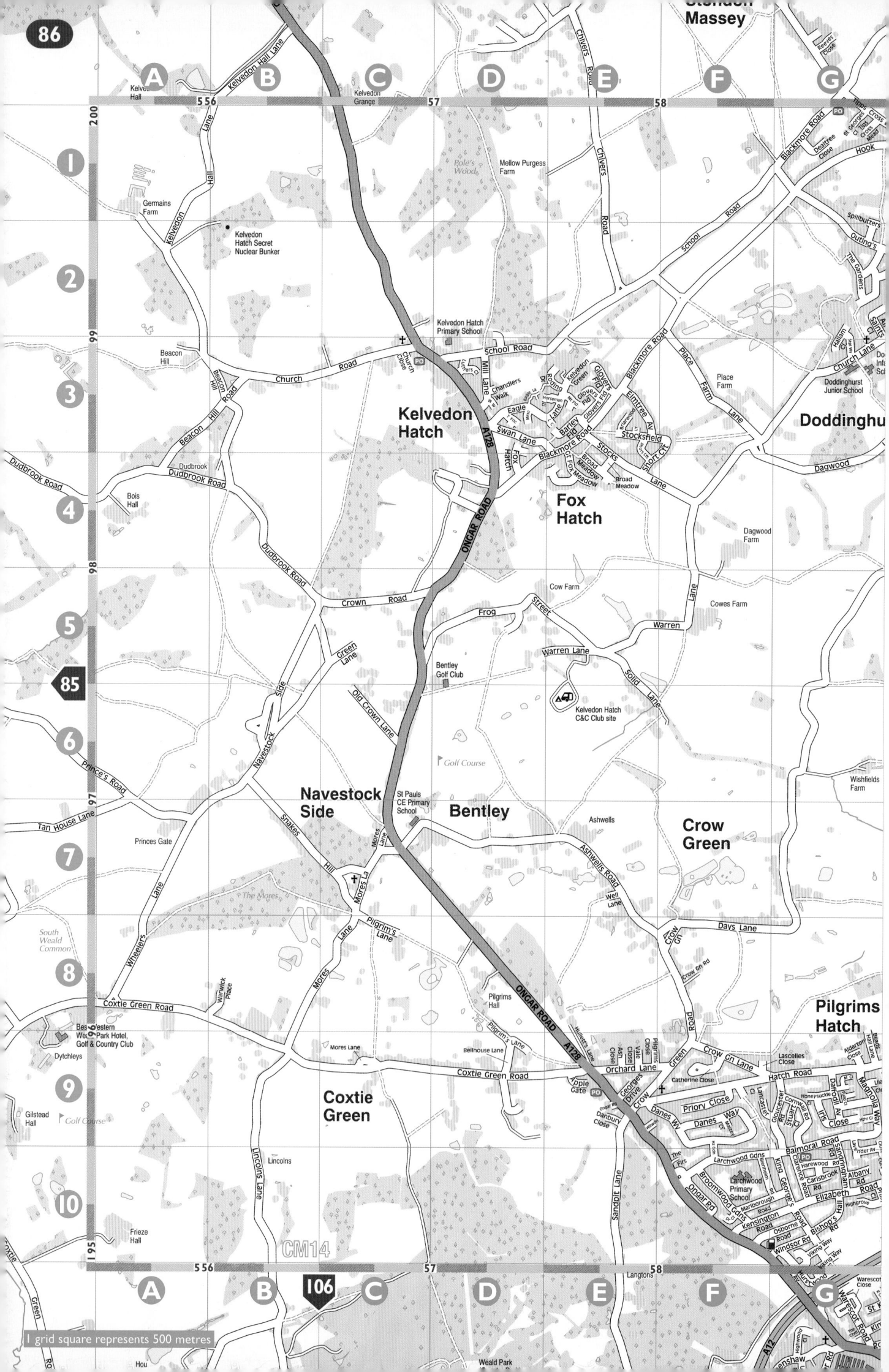
Massey
A
B
C
D
E
F
G
556
57
58
Kelvedon Hall Lane
Kelvedon Grange
Chivers Road
Reeves Close
Blackmore Road
Tipps Cross
Dealtree Close
Hook
1
2
3
4
5
6
7
8
9
10
200
99
98
97
196
195
Germains Farm
Kelvedon Hall Lane
Kelvedon Hatch Secret Nuclear Bunker
Pole's Wood
Mellow Purgess Farm
School Road
Spillbutters
The Gardens
Kelvedon Hatch Primary School
Beacon Hill
Church Road
Church Close
School Road
Mill Lane
Chandlers Walk
Eagle Lane
Swan Lane
Fox Hatch
Kelvedon Green
Glovers Fld
Barley Fld
Blackmore Road
Elmtree Av
Stocksfield
Short Cft
Stocks Lane
Broad Meadow
Place Farm Lane
Place Farm
Church Lane
Doddinghurst Junior School
Doddinghu
Dagwood
Kelvedon Hatch
A128
Dudbrook Road
Dudbrook
Beacon Hill Road
Bois Hall
Fox Hatch
ONGAR ROAD
Dagwood Farm
Dudbrook Road
Crown Road
Cow Farm
Frog Street
Lane
Cowes Farm
Warren
Warren Lane
Green Lane
Bentley Golf Club
Solid Lane
85
Old Crown Lane
Kelvedon Hatch C&C Club site
Navestock Side
Golf Course
Prince's Road
Wishfields Farm
Tan House Lane
Navestock Side
St Pauls CE Primary School
Bentley
Ashwells
Crow Green
Princes Gate
Snakes Hill
Mores Lane
Ashwells Road
Mores La
The Mores
Well Lane
Wheelers Lane
Pilgrim's Lane
South Weald Common
Days Lane
Crow Gn
Crow Gn Rd
Mores Lane
Warwick Place
Pilgrims Hall
Coxtie Green Road
ONGAR ROAD
A128
Pilgrims Hatch
Best Western Weald Park Hotel, Golf & Country Club
Dytchleys
Mores Lane
Bellhouse Lane
Pilgrim's Lane
Coxtie Green Road
Orchard Lane
Crow Green Road
Crow Gn Lane
Lascelles Close
Hatch Road
Apple Gate
Georges Drive
Catherine Close
Coxtie Green
Gilstead Hall
Golf Course
Danbury Close
Danes Wy
Priory Close
Danes Way
Balmoral Road
Lincolns Lane
Lincolns
Sandpit Lane
The Firs
Larchwood Gdns
Larchwood Primary School
King George's Road
Broomwood Gdns
Ongar Rd
Kensington Road
Osborne Road
Windsor Rd
Elizabeth Road
Bishop's Hall Rd
Viking Way
Frieze Hall
CM14
Langtons
106
Warescot Close
Warescot Road
A12
Weald Park
1 grid square represents 500 metres

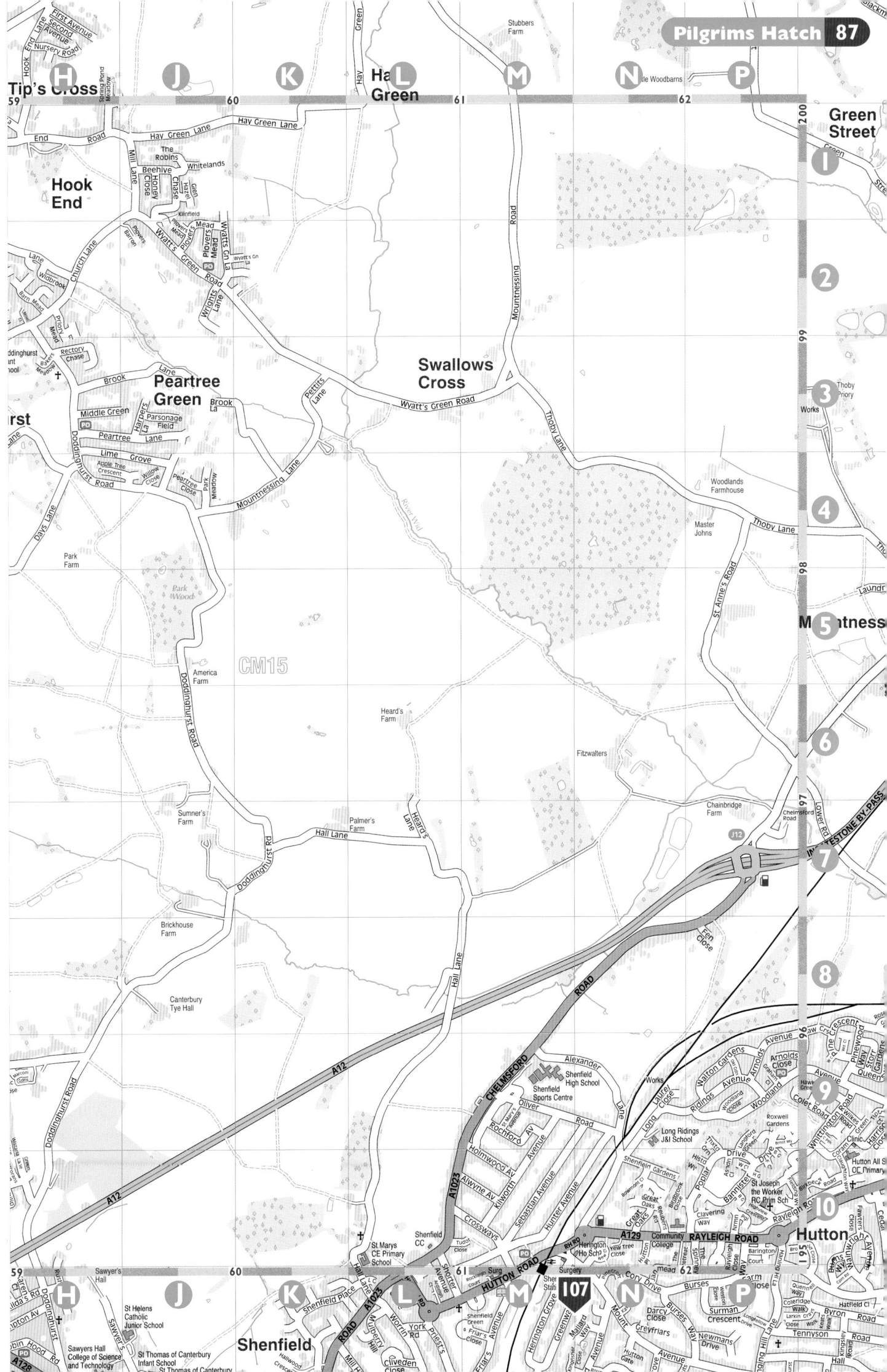

Green
Street

Hal
Green

Tip's Cross

Hook
End

Peartree
Green

Swallows
Cross

Thoby
Priory

Works

Woodlands
Farmhouse

Master
Johns

Mountness

CM15

America
Farm

Heard's
Farm

Fitzwalters

Chainbridge
Farm

Chelmsford
Road

J12

Park
Farm

Park
Wood

Sumner's
Farm

Palmer's
Farm

Hall Lane

Brickhouse
Farm

Canterbury
Tye Hall

Shenfield
High School

Shenfield
Sports Centre

Long Ridings
J&I School

Works

Chelmsford

St Joseph
the Worker
RC Prim Sch

Hutton

RAYLEIGH ROAD

A129

Community
College

St Marys
CE Primary
School

Shenfield
CC

107

Shenfield

St Helens
Catholic
Junior School

St Thomas of Canterbury
Infant School

Sawyers Hall
College of Science
and Technology

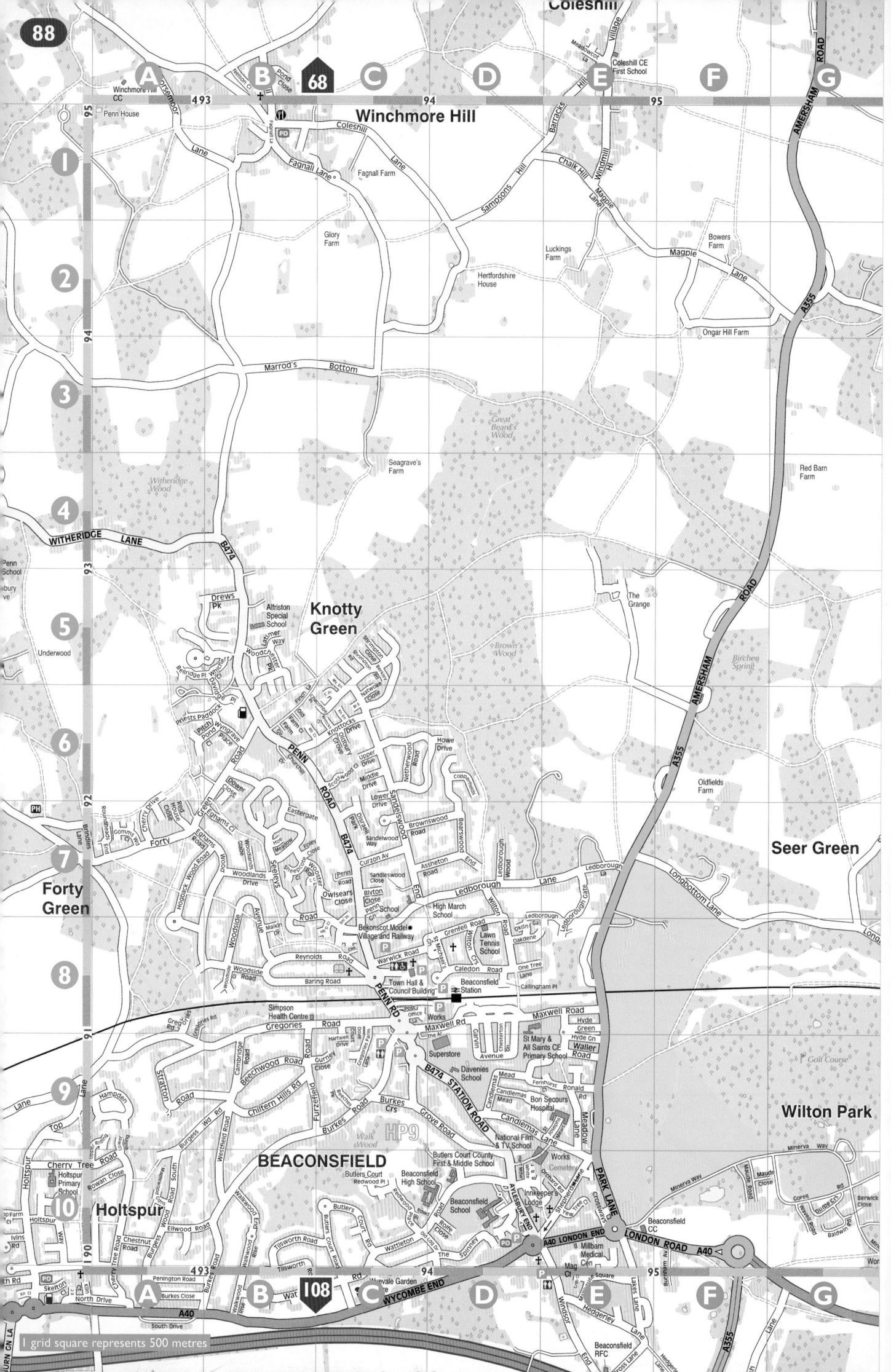

Coleshill
68
Winchmore Hill
Winchmore Hill CC
Penn House
Coleshill CE First School
Fagnall Farm
Glory Farm
Luckings Farm
Bowers Farm
Hertfordshire House
Ongar Hill Farm
Marrod's Bottom
Great Beard's Wood
Seagrave's Farm
Red Barn Farm
Witheridge Wood
WITHERIDGE LANE
Penn School
The Grange
Alfriston Special School
Knotty Green
Underwood
Brown's Wood
Birchen Spring
AMERSHAM ROAD
A355
Oldfields Farm
Seer Green
Forty Green
PENN ROAD
B474
Ledborough Lane
Longbottom Lane
High March School
Bekonscot Model Village and Railway
Lawn Tennis School
Town Hall & Council Building
Beaconsfield Station
Simpson Health Centre
Superstore
St Mary & All Saints CE Primary School
Davenies School
Bon Secours Hospital
Golf Course
Wilton Park
B474 STATION ROAD
National Film & TV School
Butlers Court County First & Middle School
Beaconsfield High School
Beaconsfield School
BEACONSFIELD
HP9
Walk Wood
Holtspur
Holtspur Primary School
Cemetery
Innkeeper's Lodge
Beaconsfield CC
PARK LANE
A40 LONDON END
LONDON ROAD
Millbarn Medical Cen
Minerva Way
WYCOMBE END
108
Beaconsfield RFC
1 grid square represents 500 metres

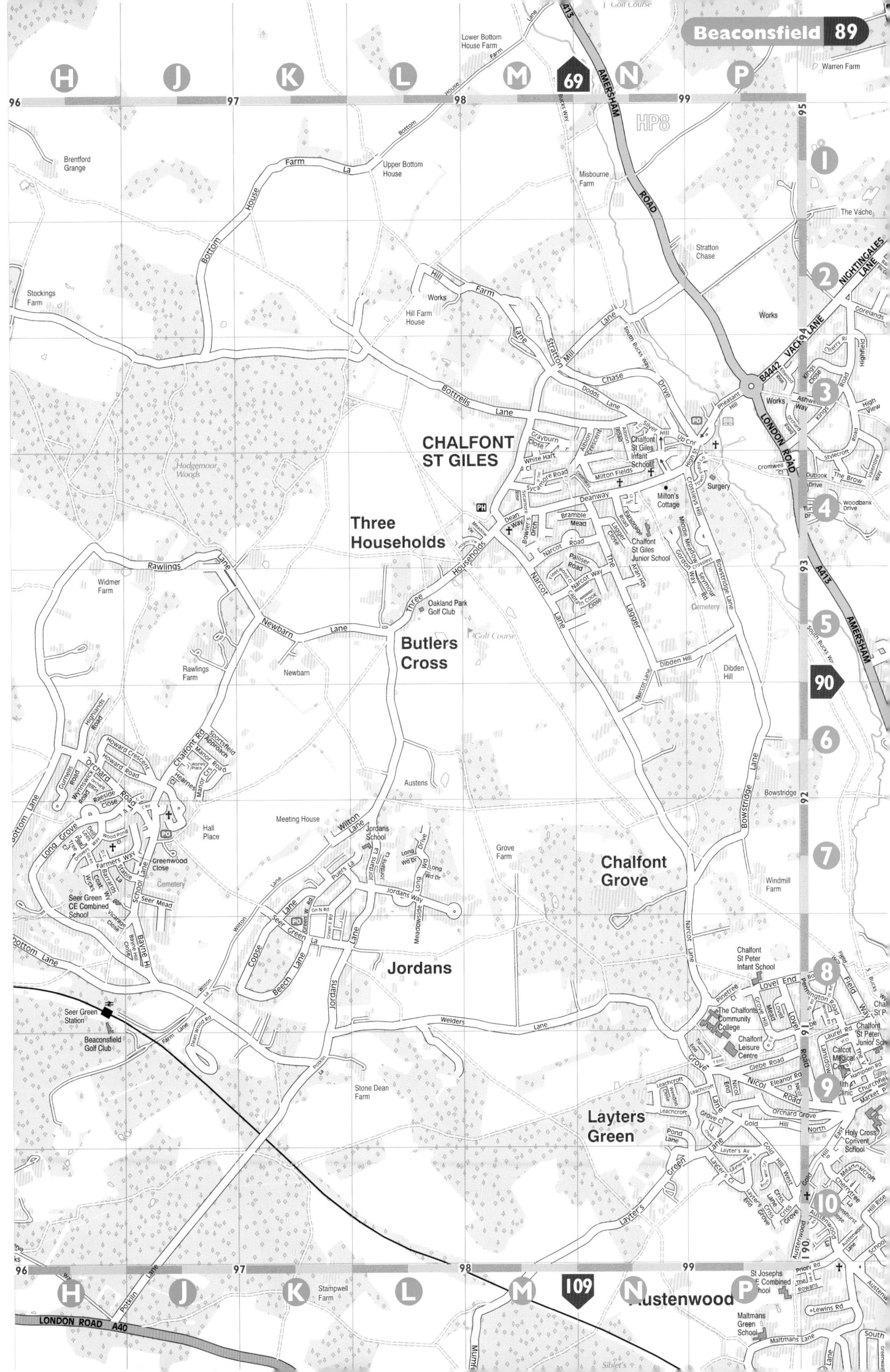

CHALFONT ST GILES
Three Households
Butlers Cross
Jordans
Chalfont Grove
Layters Green
Austenwood
AMERSHAM ROAD
LONDON ROAD
A413
B4442
LONDON ROAD A40
HP8
Brentford Grange
Stockings Farm
Upper Bottom House
Lower Bottom House Farm
Hill Farm House
Works
Misbourne Farm
Stratton Chase
Warren Farm
The Vache
Hodgemoor Woods
Widmer Farm
Rawlings Farm
Newbarn
Oakland Park Golf Club
Golf Course
Milton's Cottage
Surgery
Chalfont St Giles Infant School
Chalfont St Giles Junior School
Cemetery
Dibden Hill
Bowstridge
Windmill Farm
Grove Farm
Austens
Meeting House
Jordans School
Hall Place
Seer Green CE Combined School
Seer Green Station
Beaconsfield Golf Club
Stone Dean Farm
Stampwell Farm
Chalfont St Peter Infant School
The Chalfonts Community College
Chalfont Leisure Centre
Holy Cross Convent School
St Josephs CE Combined School
Maltmans Green School
Bottrells Lane
Farm La
Bottom House Farm La
Rawlings Lane
Newbarn Lane
Three Households
Narcot Lane
Lagger
Bowstridge Lane
Welders Lane
Potkiln Lane
Seer Green La
Long Grove
Layter's Green
Gold Hill West
Chase
Dodds Lane
Silver Hill
Deanway
Milton Fields
Dibden Hill
69
90
109

Roughwood Park
Chorleywood
70
The Swillett
Heronsgate
Bullsland Farm
Old Shire Lane
Piggy Lane
Long Lane
Shepherd's Lane
Philipshill Wood
Buckinghamshire County
Hertfordshire County
The Vache
Nightingales Lane
Vache Lane
B4442
Deanhearn Lane
Gorelands Lane
Gorelands
Works
London Road
Chiltern Open Air Museum
Shrubs Wood
Buckinghamshire Chilterns University College
Old Shire La Circular Walk
Bottom Wood
Chalfont Road
Newland Park
Ashwell's Farm
Chesham Lane
Shire Horse Centre
Brawlings Farm
Brawlings Lane
Shire Lane
A413
Amersham Road
M25
Maple Cross
Horn Hill Court
Horn Hill
Chalfont Common
Micholls Avenue
Rickmansworth Lane
Hornhill Road
Dibden Hill
89
Bowstridge Lane
South Bucks Way
Monument Lane
Cedars Close
Nortoft Road
Roberts Lane
Robert's Farm
Maple Cross JMI School
Windmill Farm
Gravel Hill
Denham Lane
Robertswood Combined School
West Hyde Lane
Chalfont Lane
Copthall Lane
Cemetery
Chalfont St Peter Infant School
The Chalfonts Community College
Chalfont Leisure Centre
Chalfont St Peter FC
Chalfont St Peter Junior School
CHALFONT ST PETER
Warren Farm
Joiners Lane
Holy Cross Convent School
Hogtrough Wood
Mopes Farm
Denham Lane
Old Shire Lane Circular Walk
St Josephs CE Combined School
Maltmans Green
SL9
110
Gerrards Cross Golf Club
Golf Course
Chalfont Park
Kingscote
1 grid square represents 500 metres

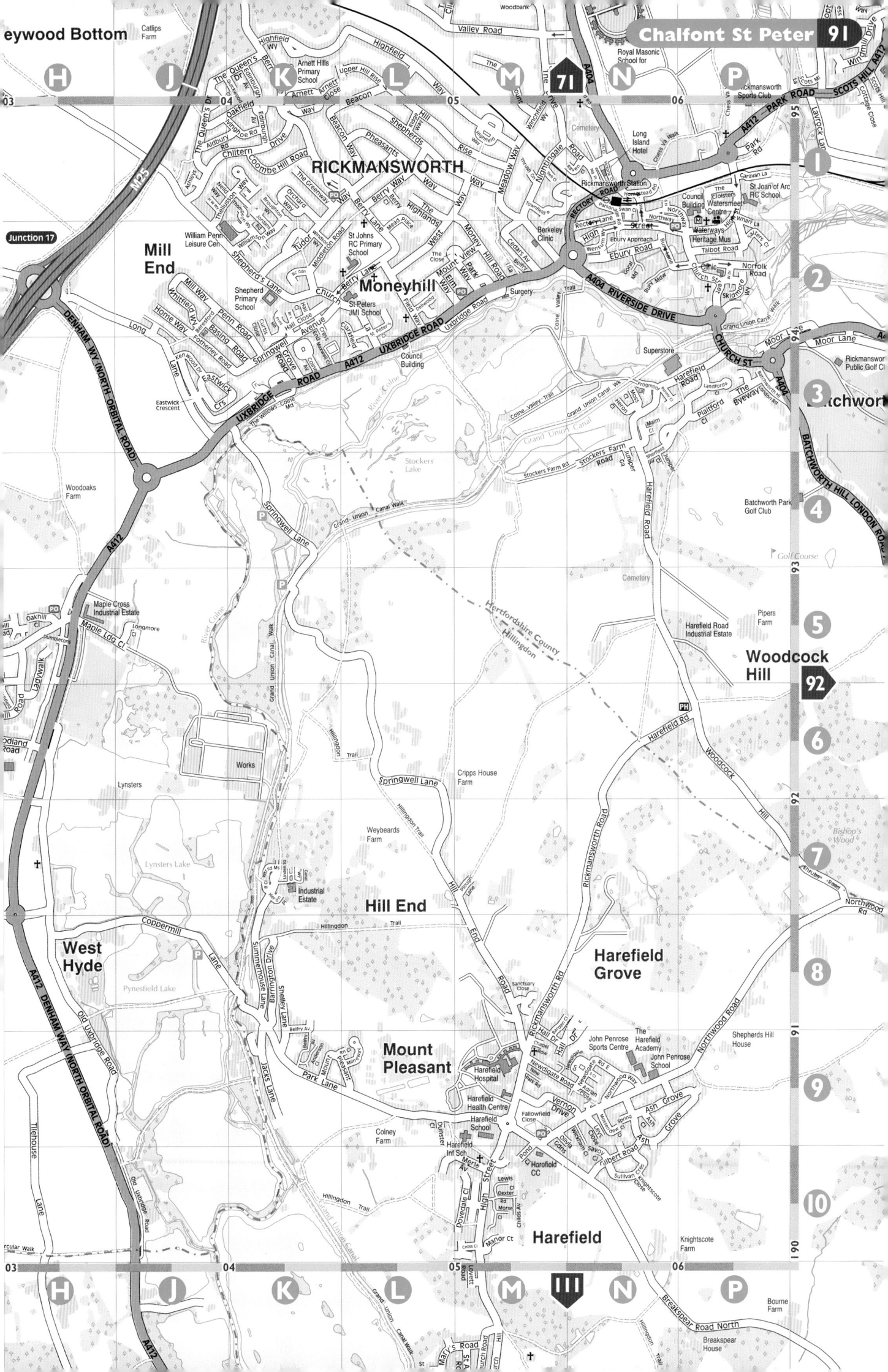

eywood Bottom
Catlips Farm
Valley Road
Woodbank
Royal Masonic School for
Highfield Wy
Highfield Way
Arnett Hills Primary School
Upper Hill Rise
The Queen's Dr
Arnett Way
Arnett Close
Beacon Way
Oakfield Av
Edinburgh Av
Aldbury Rd
Chiltern Drive
Coombe Hill Road
Shepherds Way
Pheasants Way
Rise
Meadow Way
Nightingale Road
Long Island Hotel
Cemetery
Chess Va Walk
Rickmansworth Sports Club
A412 PARK ROAD
SCOTS HILL A412
Lavrock Lane
Cottage Close
Windmill Drive
RICKMANSWORTH
Rickmansworth Station
Homestead Rd
Caravan La
St Joan of Arc RC School
Council Building
The Cloisters
Watersmeet Centre
Waterways Heritage Mus
Talbot Road
Berkeley Clinic
Rectory Lane
High Street
Northway
Ebury Approach
Ebury Road
RECTORY ROAD
Norfolk Road
Church St
Skidmore Wy
A404 RIVERSIDE DRIVE
Grand Union Canal Walk
Moor Lane
Rickmansworth Public Golf Cl
Batchworth
Junction 17
M25
Mill End
William Penn Leisure Cen
St Johns RC Primary School
The Close
Moneyhill
Mount View
Park Way
Money Hill Road
Uxbridge Road
Surgery
Shepherd Primary School
Shepherd's Lane
Mill Way
Whitfield Wy
Home Way
Penn Road
Basing Road
Fotherley Road
Long Lane
Eastwick Crs
Eastwick Crescent
Springwell Avenue
Grove Road
St Peters JMI School
Council Building
A412 UXBRIDGE ROAD
The Willows
Colne Md
Superstore
Harefield Road
Colne Valley Trail
Grand Union Canal
Stockers Farm Road
Stockers Farm Rd
Stockers Lake
Juniper Ga
Plaitford Cl
The Byeway
BATCHWORTH HILL LONDON ROAD
Batchworth Park Golf Club
Golf Course
DENHAM WY (NORTH ORBITAL ROAD)
Woodoaks Farm
A412
Springwell Lane
Grand Union Canal Walk
Cemetery
Hertfordshire County
Hillingdon
Maple Cross Industrial Estate
Oakhill Cl
Maple Lodg Cl
Longmore Cl
Dumbletons
Ladywalk
River Colne
Pipers Farm
Harefield Road Industrial Estate
Woodcock Hill
92
Hillingdon Trail
Harefield Rd
Works
Lynsters
Cripps House Farm
Springwell Lane
Woodcock Hill
Weybeards Farm
Bishop's Wood
Lynsters Lake
Industrial Estate
Hill End
Hill End Road
Rickmansworth Road
Northwood Rd
Shrubs Road
Coppermill Lane
West Hyde
Pynesfield Lake
Summerhouse Lane
Barrington Drive
Shelley Lane
Sanctuary Close
Harefield Grove
Old Uxbridge Road
Belfry Av
Mount Pleasant
Park Lane
Jacks Lane
Harefield Hospital
Hall Dr
John Penrose Sports Centre
The Harefield Academy
John Penrose School
Northwood Road
Shepherds Hill House
Newdigate Road
Vernon Drive
Ash Grove
Harefield Health Centre
Harefield School
Fallowfield Close
Dunster Cl
Colney Farm
Harefield Inf Sch
Merle Av
Pond Cl
Harefield CC
Olivia Gdns
Savoy Cl
Filbert Road
Sullivan Cres
Knightscote Close
Lewis Cl
Dexter Cl
Morse Cl
Childs Av
High Street
Dovedale Cl
Tilehouse Lane
Hillingdon Trail
Old Uxbridge Road
Harefield
Manor Ct
Knightscote Farm
Circular Walk
Lovett Road
Grand Union Canal Walk
Breakspear Road North
Breakspear House
Bourne Farm
Mary's Road
A412
111
71
H J K L M N P
03 04 05 06
1 2 3 4 5 6 7 8 9 10
95 94 93 92 91 190

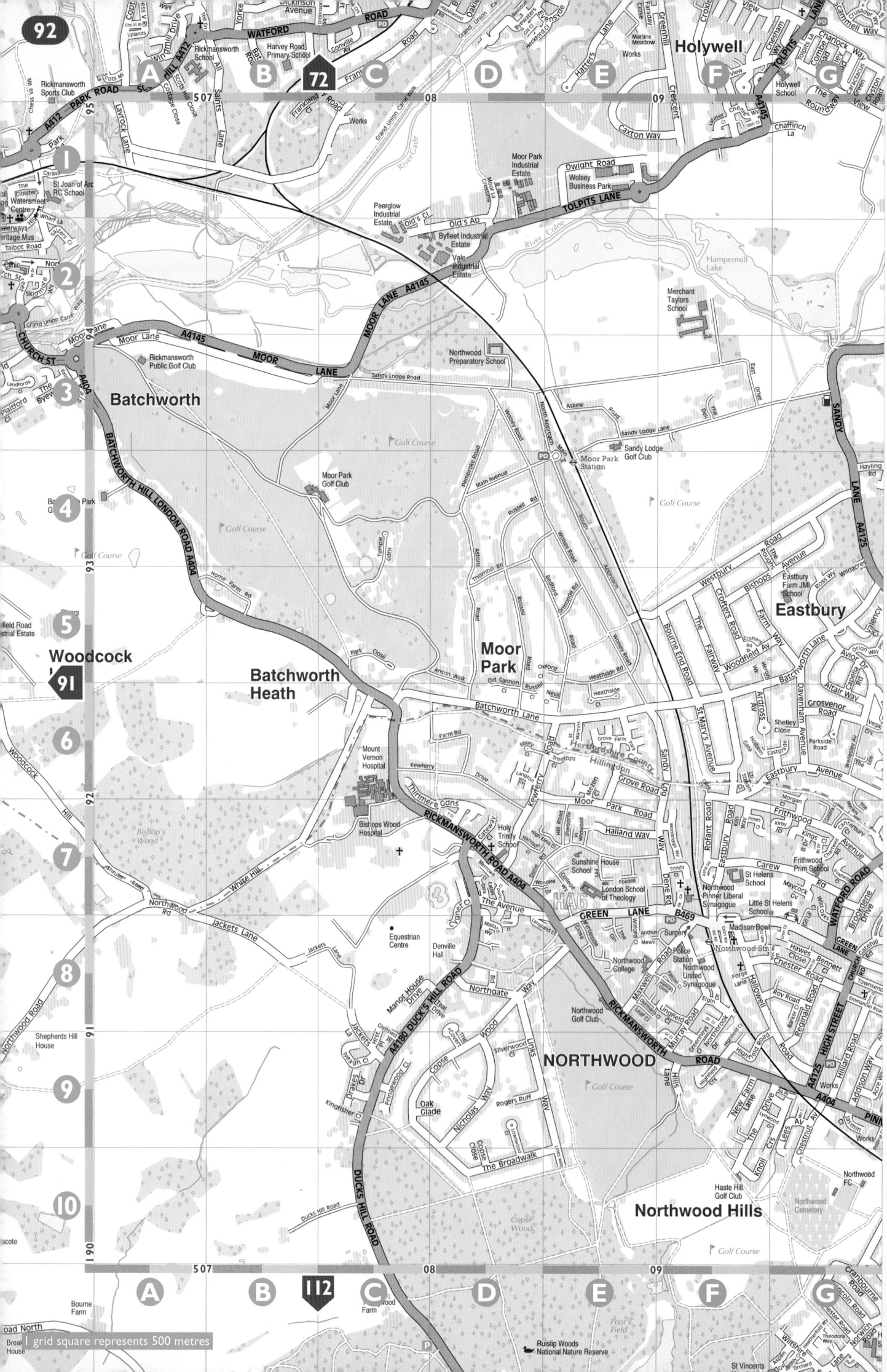

92
Holywell
Batchworth
Woodcock Hill
91
Batchworth Heath
Moor Park
Eastbury
NORTHWOOD
Northwood Hills
72
112
1 grid square represents 500 metres
A412 PARK ROAD
WATFORD ROAD
Rickmansworth Sports Club
Rickmansworth School
Harvey Road Primary School
St Joan of Arc RC School
Moor Park Industrial Estate
Wolsey Business Park
TOLPITS LANE
Peerglow Industrial Estate
Byfleet Industrial Estate
Vale Industrial Estate
Hampermill Lake
Merchant Taylors School
MOOR LANE A4145
Rickmansworth Public Golf Club
Northwood Preparatory School
Sandy Lodge Road
Sandy Lodge Golf Club
Moor Park Station
Moor Park Golf Club
Golf Course
BATCHWORTH HILL LONDON ROAD A404
Batchworth Lane
Mount Vernon Hospital
Bishops Wood Hospital
Bishop's Wood
Holy Trinity School
Sunshine House School
London School of Theology
RICKMANSWORTH ROAD A404
GREEN LANE B469
Northwood Pinner Liberal Synagogue
Northwood College
Northwood United Synagogue
Northwood Stn
Police Station
Equestrian Centre
Denville Hall
Northwood Golf Club
Eastbury Farm JMI School
Frithwood Prim School
St Helens School
Little St Helens School
Madison Bowl
A4125 HIGH STREET
A4180 DUCK'S HILL ROAD
DUCKS HILL ROAD
Shepherds Hill House
Copse Wood
Haste Hill Golf Club
Northwood FC
Northwood Cemetery
Ruislip Woods National Nature Reserve
Bourne Farm
St Vincents
Jackets Lane
White Hill
Northwood Rd
Northgate
The Broadwalk
Hertfordshire County
Hillingdon
HA6

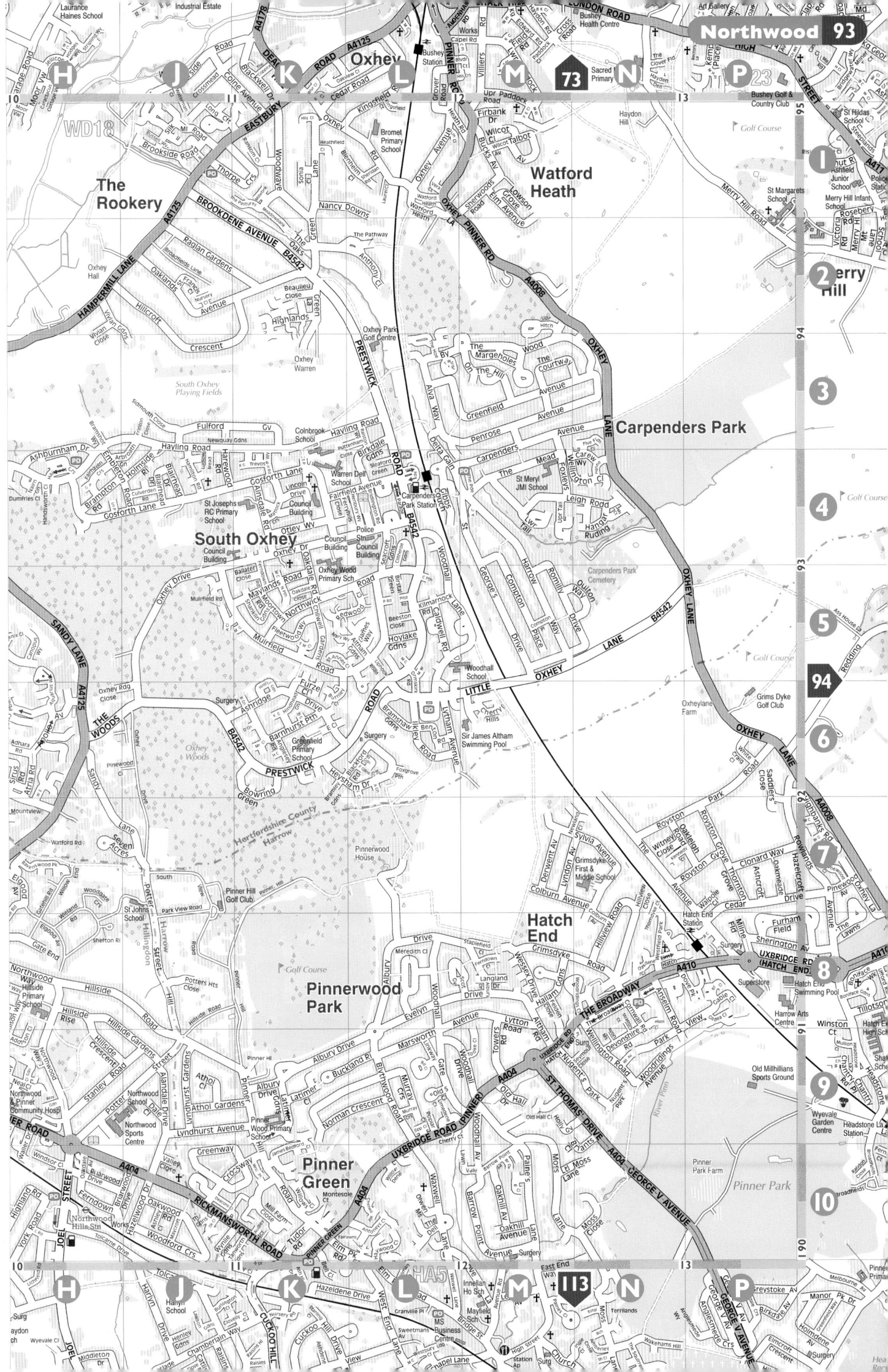
Oxhey
Watford Heath
The Rookery
Carpenders Park
South Oxhey
Hatch End
Pinnerwood Park
Pinner Green
Merry Hill
WD18
HA5
Hertfordshire County
Harrow
Bushey Station
Carpenders Park Station
Hatch End Station
Northwood Hills Stn
Headstone La. Station
Bushey Golf & Country Club
Grims Dyke Golf Club
Pinner Hill Golf Club
Oxhey Park Golf Centre
South Oxhey Playing Fields
Oxhey Woods
Oxhey Warren
Carpenders Park Cemetery
Pinner Park
Pinner Park Farm
Old Millhillians Sports Ground
Wyevale Garden Centre
Harrow Arts Centre
Hatch End Swimming Pool
Sir James Altham Swimming Pool
Northwood & Pinner Community Hosp
Northwood Sports Centre
Superstore
Oxheylane Farm
Pinnerwood House
Oxhey Hall
Golf Course
River Pinn
HAMPERMILL LANE
EASTBURY ROAD
BROOKDENE AVENUE
PRESTWICK ROAD
OXHEY LANE
LITTLE OXHEY LANE
OXHEY PINNER RD
SANDY LANE
THE WOODS
UXBRIDGE ROAD (PINNER)
UXBRIDGE RD (HATCH END)
THE BROADWAY
ST THOMAS' DRIVE
GEORGE V AVENUE
RICKMANSWORTH ROAD
JOEL STREET
CUCKOO HILL
PINNER GREEN
LONDON ROAD
HIGH STREET
A4125
A4008
A404
A410
B4542
A4178
73
94
113
93

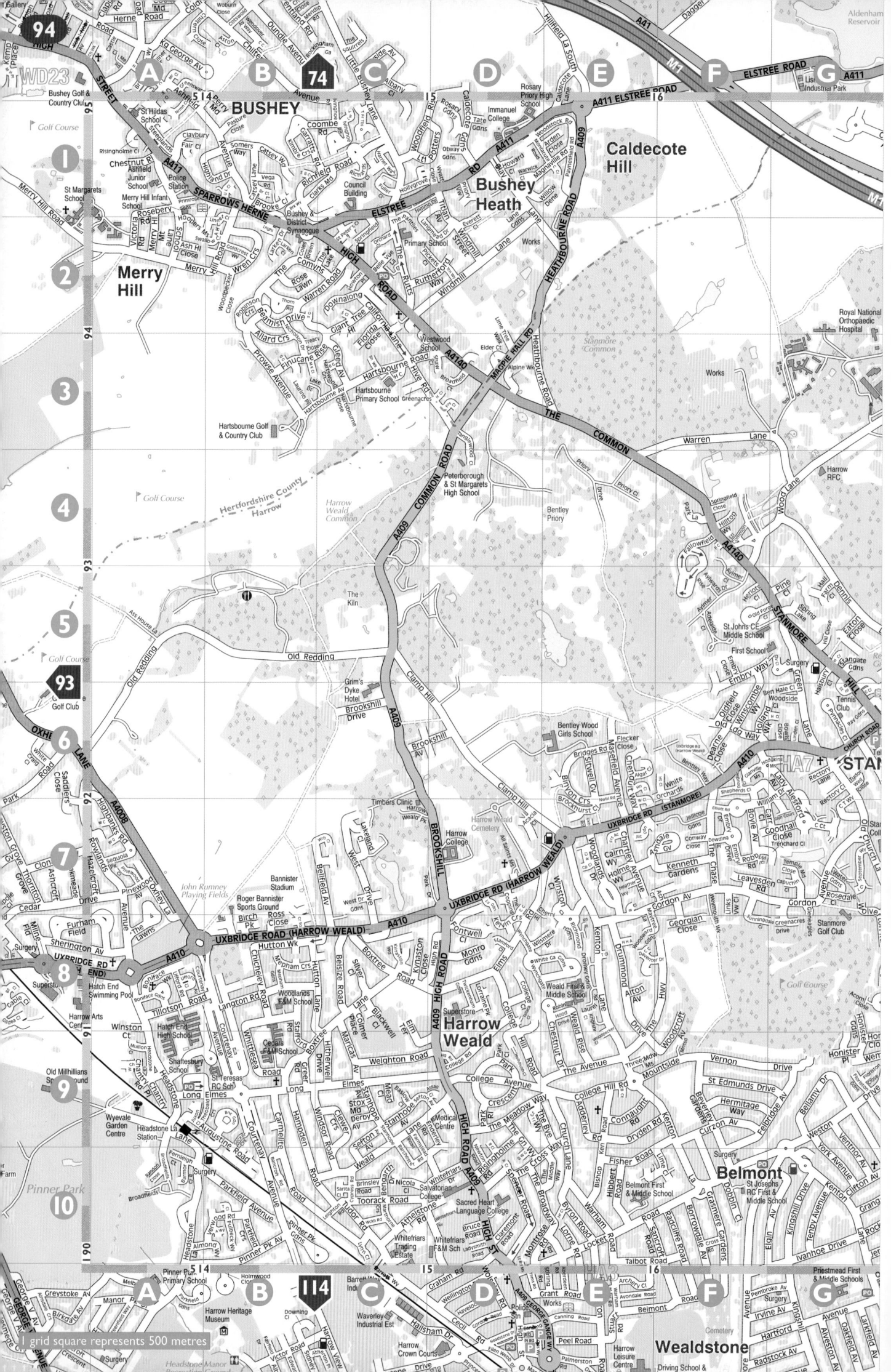
94
74
93
114
BUSHEY
Bushey Heath
Caldecote Hill
Merry Hill
Harrow Weald
Belmont
Wealdstone
Aldenham Reservoir
WD23
HA7
HA3
A41
M1
A411 ELSTREE ROAD
A411 SPARROWS HERNE
HIGH ROAD
A4140
A409 COMMON ROAD
MAGPIE HALL RD
HEATHBOURNE ROAD
THE COMMON
STANMORE HILL
UXBRIDGE RD (STANMORE)
UXBRIDGE ROAD (HARROW WEALD)
A410
A4008
OXHEY LANE
BROOKSHILL
A409 HIGH ROAD
Stanmore Common
Harrow Weald Common
Hertfordshire County
Harrow
Bushey Golf & Country Club
Hartsbourne Golf & Country Club
Royal National Orthopaedic Hospital
Peterborough & St Margarets High School
Bentley Priory
Grim's Dyke Hotel
Old Redding
Warren Lane
Harrow Weald Cemetery
Harrow College
Bannister Stadium
John Rumney Playing Fields
Hatch End Swimming Pool
Headstone Lane Station
Pinner Park
Harrow Heritage Museum
Stanmore Golf Club
Harrow RFC
1 grid square represents 500 metres

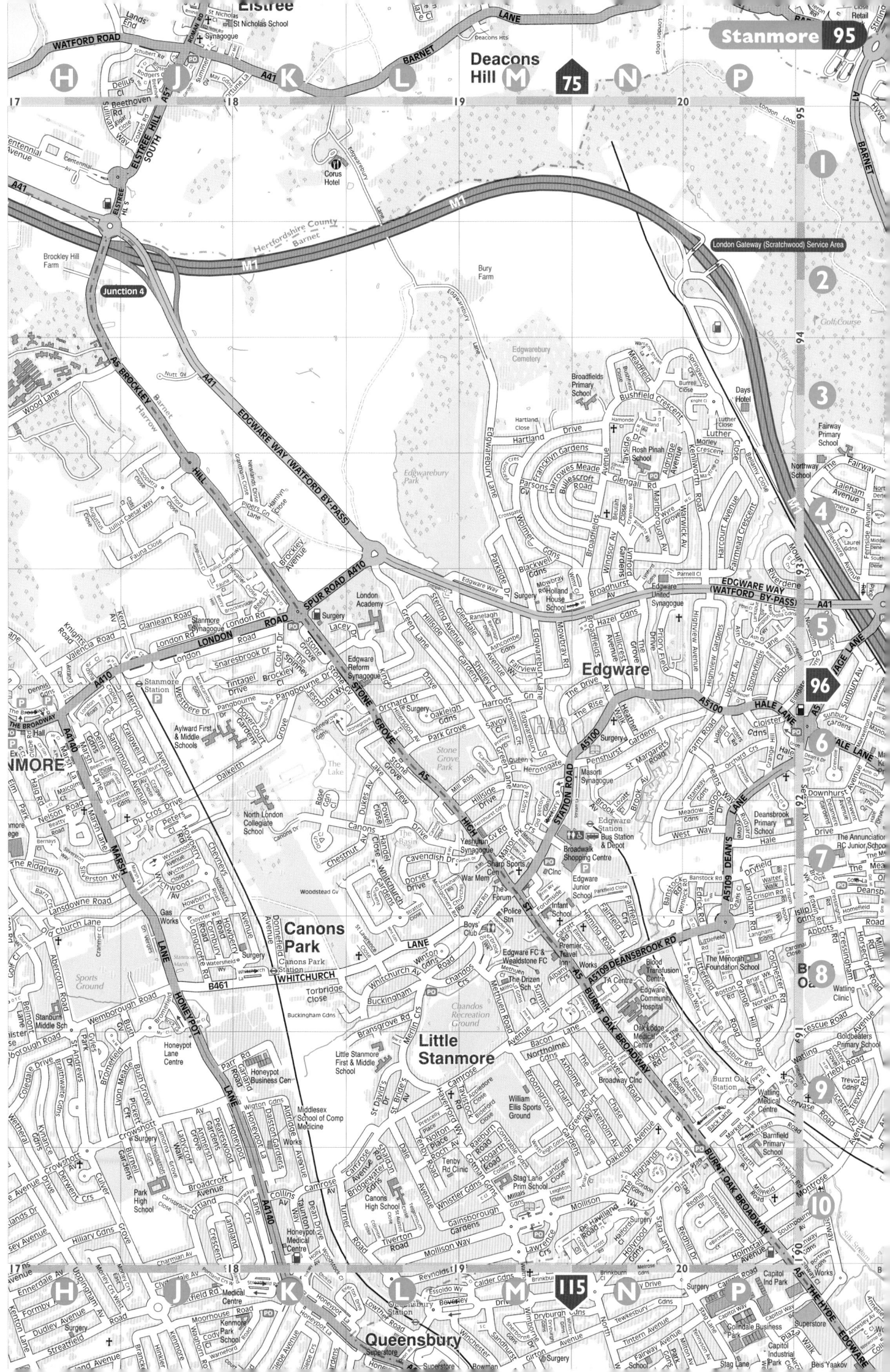

Elstree
Deacons Hill
75
96
115
WATFORD ROAD
BARNET LANE
ELSTREE HILL SOUTH
M1
Hertfordshire County
Barnet
Junction 4
London Gateway (Scratchwood) Service Area
Corus Hotel
Brockley Hill Farm
Bury Farm
Edgwarebury Cemetery
Edgwarebury Park
A5 BROCKLEY HILL
EDGWARE WAY (WATFORD BY-PASS)
SPUR ROAD A410
LONDON ROAD
STONE GROVE
HIGH ST
STATION ROAD
HALE LANE
DEAN'S LANE
DEANSBROOK RD
BURNT OAK BROADWAY
A5 THE HYDE EDGWARE
HONEYPOT LANE
MARSH LANE
WHITCHURCH LANE
Edgware
Canons Park
Little Stanmore
Queensbury
Stanmore Station
Canons Park Station
Edgware Station
Burnt Oak Station
Queensbury Station
Stone Grove Park
Chandos Recreation Ground
North London Collegiate School
London Academy
Edgware Community Hospital
Broadwalk Shopping Centre
Bus Station & Depot
Deansbrook Primary School
Fairway Primary School
Rosh Pinah School
Broadfields Primary School
Days Hotel
Honeypot Lane Centre
Park High School
Canons High School
Stag Lane Prim School
Colindale Business Park
Capitol Industrial Park
HA8

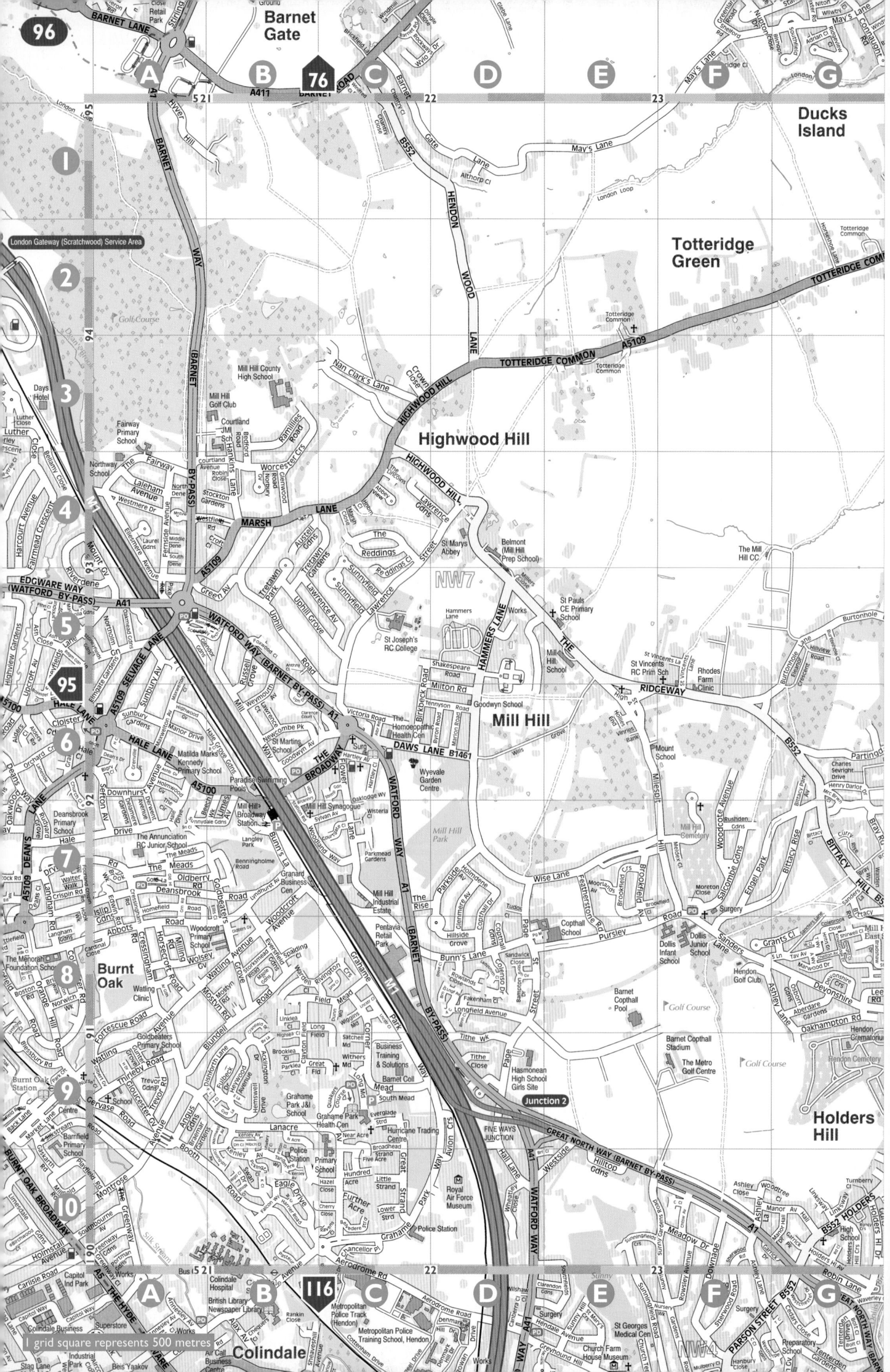

76
95
116
A
B
C
D
E
F
G
1
2
3
4
5
6
7
8
9
10
Barnet Gate
Ducks Island
Totteridge Green
Totteridge Common
Highwood Hill
Mill Hill
NW7
Burnt Oak
Holders Hill
Colindale
NW4
BARNET LANE
BARNET WAY
BARNET WAY (BARNET BY-PASS)
HENDON WOOD LANE
Barnet Gate Lane
May's Lane
TOTTERIDGE COMMON
TOTTERIDGE COMMON A5109
HIGHWOOD HILL
MARSH LANE
EDGWARE WAY (WATFORD BY-PASS) A41
WATFORD WAY (BARNET BY-PASS) A1
SELVAGE LANE A5109
HALE LANE A5100
DEAN'S LANE A5109
THE BROADWAY
DAWS LANE B1461
WATFORD WAY A1 (BARNET BY-PASS)
THE RIDGEWAY
BITTACY HILL B552
GREAT NORTH WAY (BARNET BY-PASS)
BURNT OAK BROADWAY
A5 THE HYDE
Aerodrome Rd
PARSON STREET B552
B552 HOLDERS HILL
M1
London Loop
London Gateway (Scratchwood) Service Area
Golf Course
Days Hotel
Mill Hill County High School
Mill Hill Golf Club
Fairway Primary School
Northway School
St Marys Abbey
Belmont (Mill Hill Prep School)
St Pauls CE Primary School
St Joseph's RC College
Mill Hill School
St Vincents RC Prim Sch
Rhodes Farm Clinic
The Mill Hill CC
Goodwyn School
The Homoeopathic Health Cen
Wyevale Garden Centre
Mill Hill Park
Mount School
Mill Hill Cemetery
Paradise Swimming Pools
Mill Hill Broadway Station
Matilda Marks Kennedy Primary School
Deansbrook Primary School
The Annunciation RC Junior School
Mill Hill Synagogue
Granard Business Cen
Mill Hill Industrial Estate
Pentavia Retail Park
Copthall School
Dollis Infant School
Dollis Junior School
Hendon Golf Club
Barnet Copthall Pool
Barnet Copthall Stadium
The Metro Golf Centre
Hendon Crematorium
Hendon Cemetery
Hasmonean High School Girls Site
Junction 2
FIVE WAYS JUNCTION
Royal Air Force Museum
Police Station
Grahame Park J&I School
Grahame Park Health Cen
Barnet Coll
Hurricane Trading Centre
Business Training & Solutions
Woodcroft Primary School
Goldbeaters Primary School
Watling Clinic
The Menorah Foundation School
Burnt Oak Station
Barnfield Primary School
Colindale Hospital
British Library Newspaper Library
Metropolitan Police Track (Hendon)
Metropolitan Police Training School, Hendon
St Georges Medical Cen
Church Farm House Museum
Capitol Ind Park
Colindale Business Centre
Superstore
Industrial Park
Air Call Business Centre
High School
Preparatory School
Surgery
1 grid square represents 500 metres

Underhill
Totteridge
Whetstone
Oakleigh Park
East Barnet
Woodside Park
FRIERN BARNET
North Finchley
Colney Hatch
FINCHLEY
Church End
East Finchley
N20
N12
N3
77
98
117

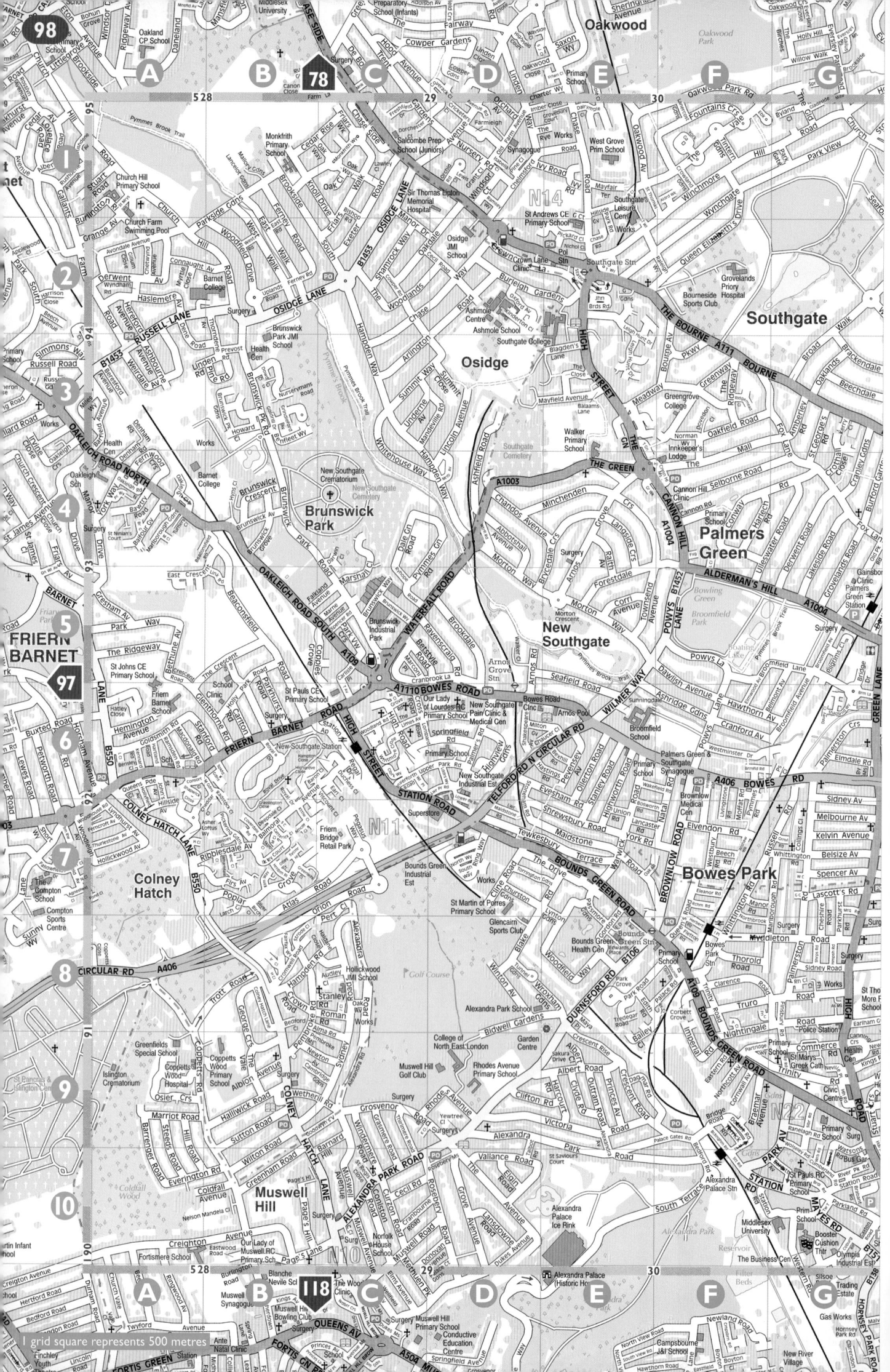
98
78
97
118
Oakwood
Oakwood Park
Southgate
Osidge
Brunswick Park
New Southgate
Palmers Green
Bowes Park
Friern Barnet
Colney Hatch
Muswell Hill
N14
N11
N22
N10
Middlesex University
Oakland CP School
Monkfrith Primary School
Church Hill Primary School
Church Farm Swimming Pool
Salcombe Prep School (Juniors)
Sir Thomas Lipton Memorial Hospital
St Andrews CE Primary School
West Grove Prim School
Southgate Leisure Cen
Southgate Stn
Grovelands Priory Hospital
Bourneside Sports Club
Barnet College
Brunswick Park JMI School
Ashmole Centre
Ashmole School
Southgate College
Greengrove College
Walker Primary School
Innkeeper's Lodge
New Southgate Crematorium
New Southgate Cemetery
Southgate Cemetery
Brunswick Industrial Park
Bowling Green
Broomfield Park
Boating Lake
St Johns CE Primary School
Friern Barnet School
St Pauls CE Primary School
Our Lady of Lourdes RC Primary School
New Southgate Pain Clinic & Medical Cen
New Southgate Station
Broomfield School
Palmers Green & Southgate Synagogue
Brownlow Medical Cen
New Southgate Industrial Est
Superstore
Friern Bridge Retail Park
Bounds Green Industrial Est
St Martin of Porres Primary School
Glencairn Sports Club
Bounds Green Health Cen
Bounds Green Stn
Bowes Park Stn
The Compton School
Compton Sports Centre
Hollickwood JMI School
Golf Course
Alexandra Park School
College of North East London
Muswell Hill Golf Club
Rhodes Avenue Primary School
Greenfields Special School
Coppetts Wood Primary School
Coppetts Wood Hospital
Islington Crematorium
St Pancras & Islington Cem
Coldfall Wood
Alexandra Palace Ice Rink
Alexandra Palace Stn
Alexandra Park
Reservoir
The Business Cen
Booster Cushion Thtr
Olympia Industrial Est
Alexandra Palace (Historic House)
Muswell Hill Primary School
Conductive Education Centre
Campsbourne J&I School
New River Village
Gas Works
OAKLEIGH ROAD NORTH
OAKLEIGH ROAD SOUTH
FRIERN BARNET ROAD
COLNEY HATCH LANE
BOWES ROAD
BOUNDS GREEN ROAD
HIGH STREET
ALDERMAN'S HILL
THE BOURNE
OSIDGE LANE
RUSSELL LANE
WATERFALL ROAD
TELFORD RD N CIRCULAR RD
WILMER WAY
STATION ROAD
CANNON HILL
ALEXANDRA PARK ROAD
QUEENS AV
FORTIS GN RD
GREEN LANES
1 grid square represents 500 metres

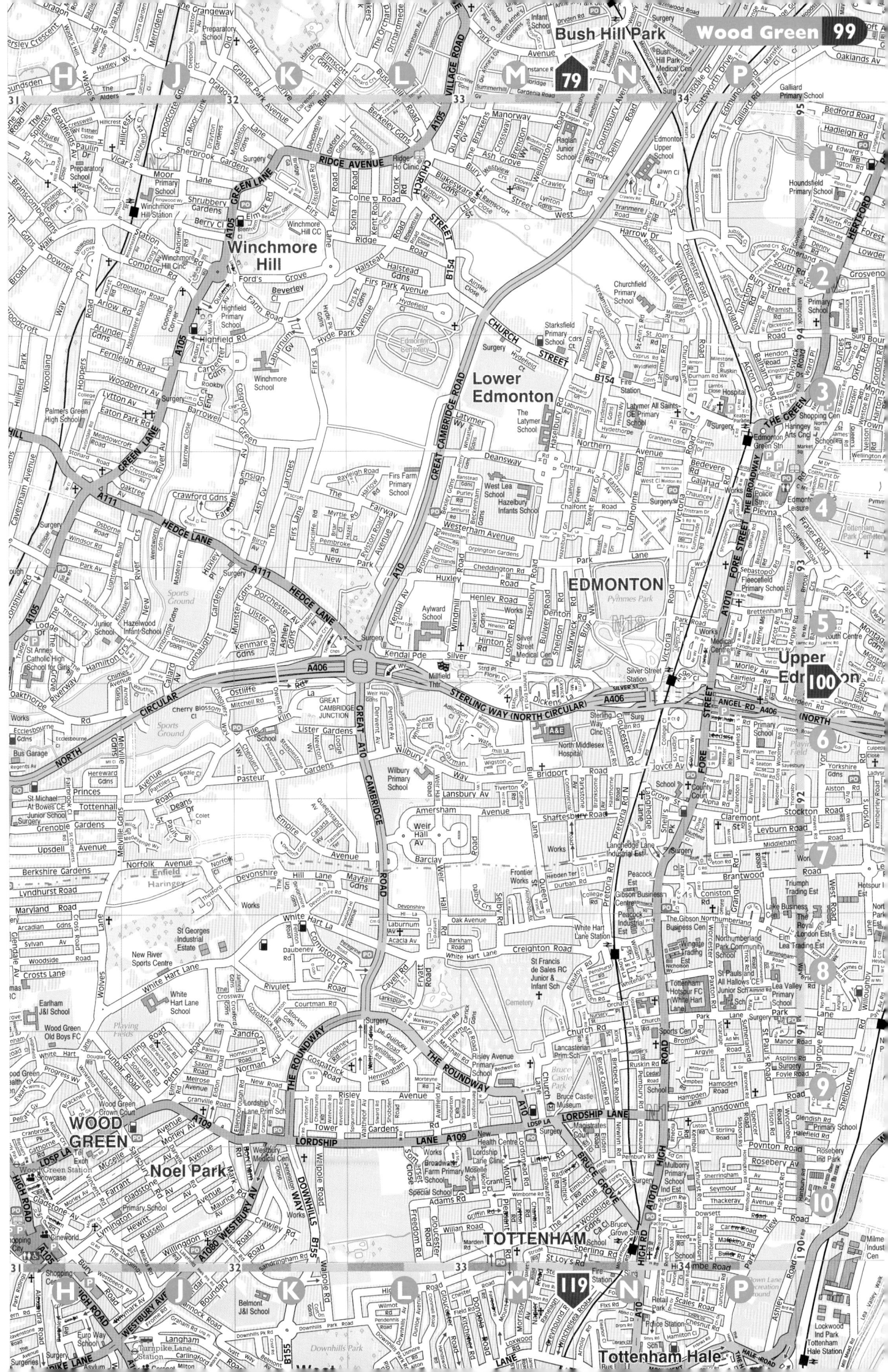
Bush Hill Park
79
Winchmore Hill
Lower Edmonton
EDMONTON
Upper Edmonton
100
WOOD GREEN
Noel Park
TOTTENHAM
Tottenham Hale
119
H
J
K
L
M
N
P
1
2
3
4
5
6
7
8
9
10
31
32
33
34
GREEN LANE
RIDGE AVENUE
VILLAGE ROAD
CHURCH STREET
GREAT CAMBRIDGE ROAD
HEDGE LANE
NORTH CIRCULAR
STERLING WAY (NORTH CIRCULAR)
ANGEL RD
FORE STREET
THE BROADWAY
HERTFORD
THE GREEN
THE ROUNDWAY
LORDSHIP LANE
BRUCE GROVE
HIGH ROAD
HIGH RD
WESTBURY AV
DOWNHILLS WAY
A10
A105
A111
A406
A109
A1010
A1080
B154
B155
Winchmore Hill Station
Edmonton Green Stn
Silver Street Station
White Hart Lane Station
Bruce Grove Stn
Wood Green Station
Turnpike Lane Station
Tottenham Hale Station
Edmonton Cemetery
Pymmes Park
North Middlesex Hospital
Tottenham Hotspur FC (White Hart Lane)
Bruce Castle Museum
Bruce Castle Park
Cemetery
Sports Ground
Playing Fields
Millfield Thtr
Downhills Park
Tottenham Park Cemetery
Lockwood Ind Park
Milmead Indust Cen

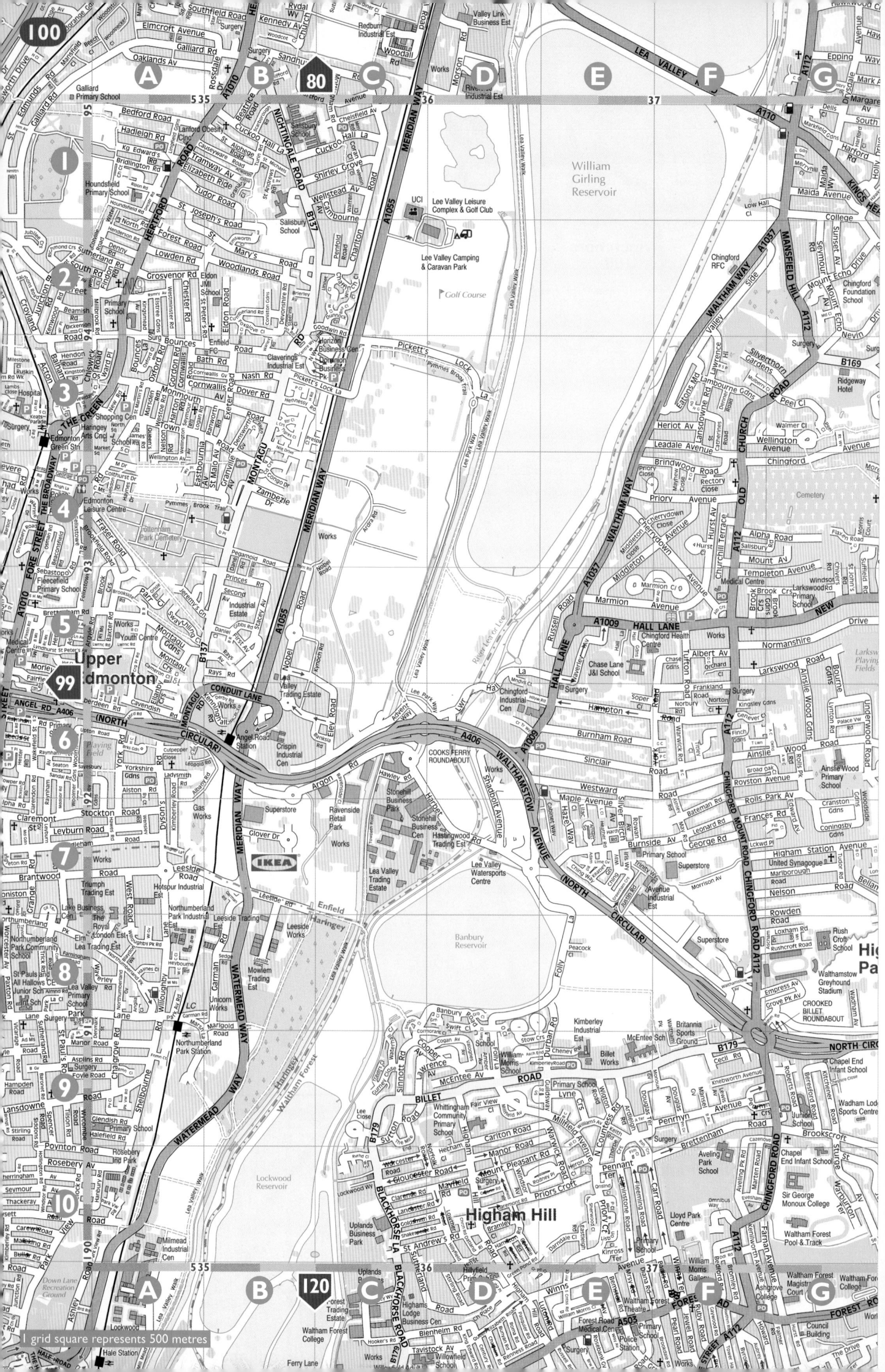

100
80
99
120
A
B
C
D
E
F
G
1
2
3
4
5
6
7
8
9
10
535
36
37
95
94
93
92
91
190
Upper Edmonton
Higham Hill
William Girling Reservoir
Banbury Reservoir
Lockwood Reservoir
Lee Valley Leisure Complex & Golf Club
Lee Valley Camping & Caravan Park
Golf Course
Lee Valley Watersports Centre
LEA VALLEY
MERIDIAN WAY
NIGHTINGALE ROAD
HERTFORD ROAD
FORE STREET
THE GREEN
THE BROADWAY
ANGEL RD
(NORTH CIRCULAR)
CONDUIT LANE
MONTAGU
WALTHAMSTOW AVENUE
WALTHAM WAY
HALL LANE
NEW
CHINGFORD MOUNT ROAD
CHINGFORD ROAD
OLD CHURCH ROAD
MANSFIELD HILL
KINGS HEAD
BILLET ROAD
BLACKHORSE LA
WATERMEAD WAY
FOREST ROAD
A1010
A1055
B137
A406
A1009
A1037
A112
A110
B169
B179
A503
Angel Road Station
Northumberland Park Station
Edmonton Green Stn
Hale Station
Salisbury School
Edmonton Leisure Centre
Tottenham Park Cemetery
Chase Lane J&I School
Chingford Health Centre
Walthamstow Greyhound Stadium
CROOKED BILLET ROUNDABOUT
COOKS FERRY ROUNDABOUT
Sir George Monoux College
Waltham Forest Pool & Track
Waltham Forest College
Haringey
Enfield
Waltham Forest
IKEA
1 grid square represents 500 metres

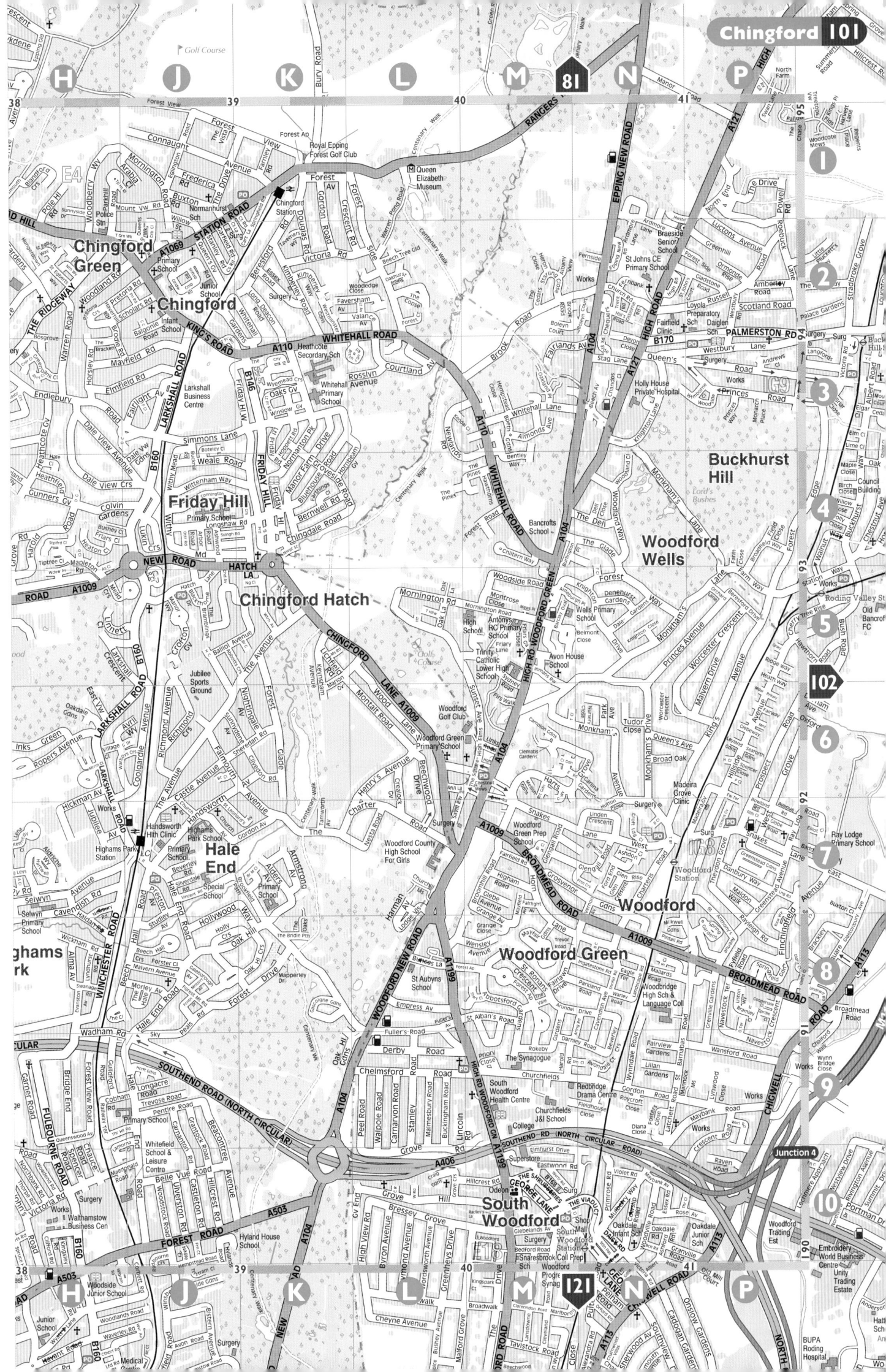
H
J
K
L
M
N
P
81
121
102
38
39
40
41
95
94
93
92
91
90
1
2
3
4
5
6
7
8
9
10
Chingford Green
Chingford
Friday Hill
Chingford Hatch
Hale End
Buckhurst Hill
Woodford Wells
Woodford
Woodford Green
South Woodford
Highams Park
Golf Course
Royal Epping Forest Golf Club
Queen Elizabeth Museum
Chingford Station
Larkshall Business Centre
Jubilee Sports Ground
Woodford Golf Club
Woodford County High School For Girls
Highams Park Station
Woodford Station
South Woodford Station
Walthamstow Business Cen
Woodford Trading Est
Embroidery World Business Centre
Unity Trading Estate
BUPA Roding Hospital
Roding Valley Station
Junction 4
EPPING NEW ROAD
HIGH ROAD
RANGERS ROAD
STATION ROAD
KING'S ROAD
WHITEHALL ROAD
LARKSHALL ROAD
NEW ROAD
HATCH LANE
CHINGFORD LANE
HIGH RD WOODFORD GREEN
WOODFORD NEW ROAD
BROADMEAD ROAD
SOUTHEND ROAD (NORTH CIRCULAR)
FOREST ROAD
WINCHESTER ROAD
FULBOURNE ROAD
CHIGWELL ROAD
GEORGE LANE
THE RIDGEWAY
A104
A110
A121
A1009
A1069
A199
A406
A503
A113
B160
B170
B146

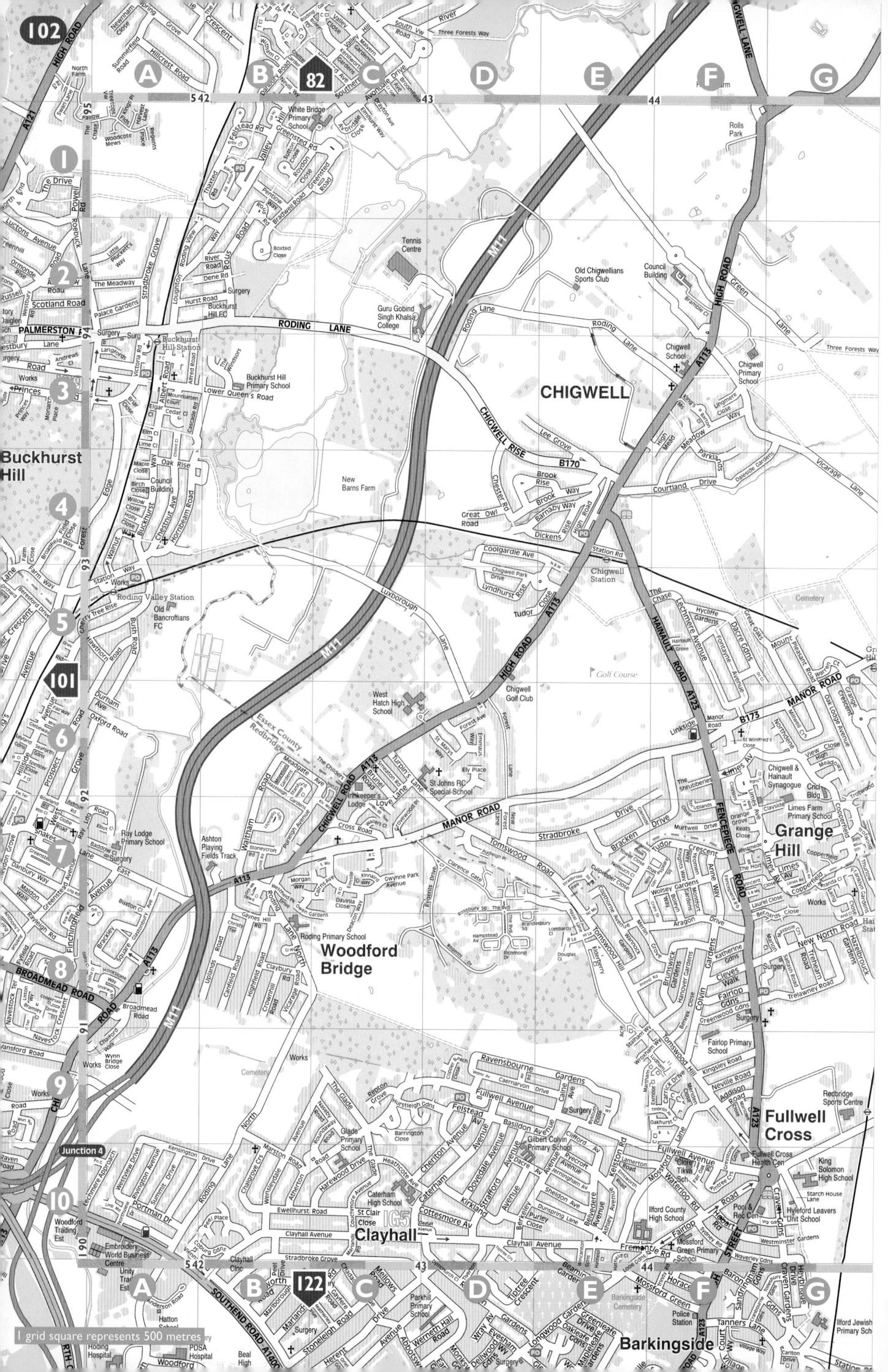
102
82
101
122
A
B
C
D
E
F
G
A
B
C
D
E
F
G
1
2
3
4
5
6
7
8
9
10
542
43
44
95
94
93
92
91
190
CHIGWELL
Buckhurst Hill
Grange Hill
Woodford Bridge
Clayhall
Fullwell Cross
Barkingside
IG5
Junction 4
M11
A113
A123
A121
B170
B173
A1400
HIGH ROAD
RODING LANE
CHIGWELL RISE
CHIGWELL ROAD
MANOR ROAD
HAINAULT ROAD
FENCEPIECE ROAD
HIGH STREET
BROADMEAD ROAD
SOUTHEND ROAD
PALMERSTON ROAD
Luxborough Lane
Three Forests Way
River Roding
Roding Valley Station
Buckhurst Hill Station
Chigwell Station
Golf Course
Chigwell Golf Club
Tennis Centre
Guru Gobind Singh Khalsa College
Old Chigwellians Sports Club
Council Building
Chigwell School
Chigwell Primary School
West Hatch High School
St Johns RC Special School
Ray Lodge Primary School
Roding Primary School
Buckhurst Hill Primary School
Old Bancroftians FC
Ashton Playing Fields Track
New Barns Farm
Rolls Park
Essex County
Redbridge
Chigwell & Hainault Synagogue
Limes Farm Primary School
Fairlop Primary School
Redbridge Sports Centre
Fullwell Cross Health Centre
King Solomon High School
Hyleford Leavers Unit School
Pool & Rec Cen
Ilford County High School
Mossford Green Primary School
Gilbert Colvin Primary School
Caterham High School
Glade Primary School
Parkhill Primary School
Barkingside Cemetery
Police Station
Ilford Jewish Primary School
Woodford Trading Est
Embroidery World Business Centre
Unity Trading Est
Clayhall Clinic
Hatton School
Roding Hospital
PDSA Hospital
Cemetery
Works
Surgery
Innkeeper's Lodge
White Bridge Primary School
Buckhurst Hill FC
Council Building
Tomswood Road
Stradbroke Drive
Fullwell Avenue
Clayhall Avenue
Ravensbourne Gardens
Courtland Drive
Vicarage Lane
Manor Road
1 grid square represents 500 metres

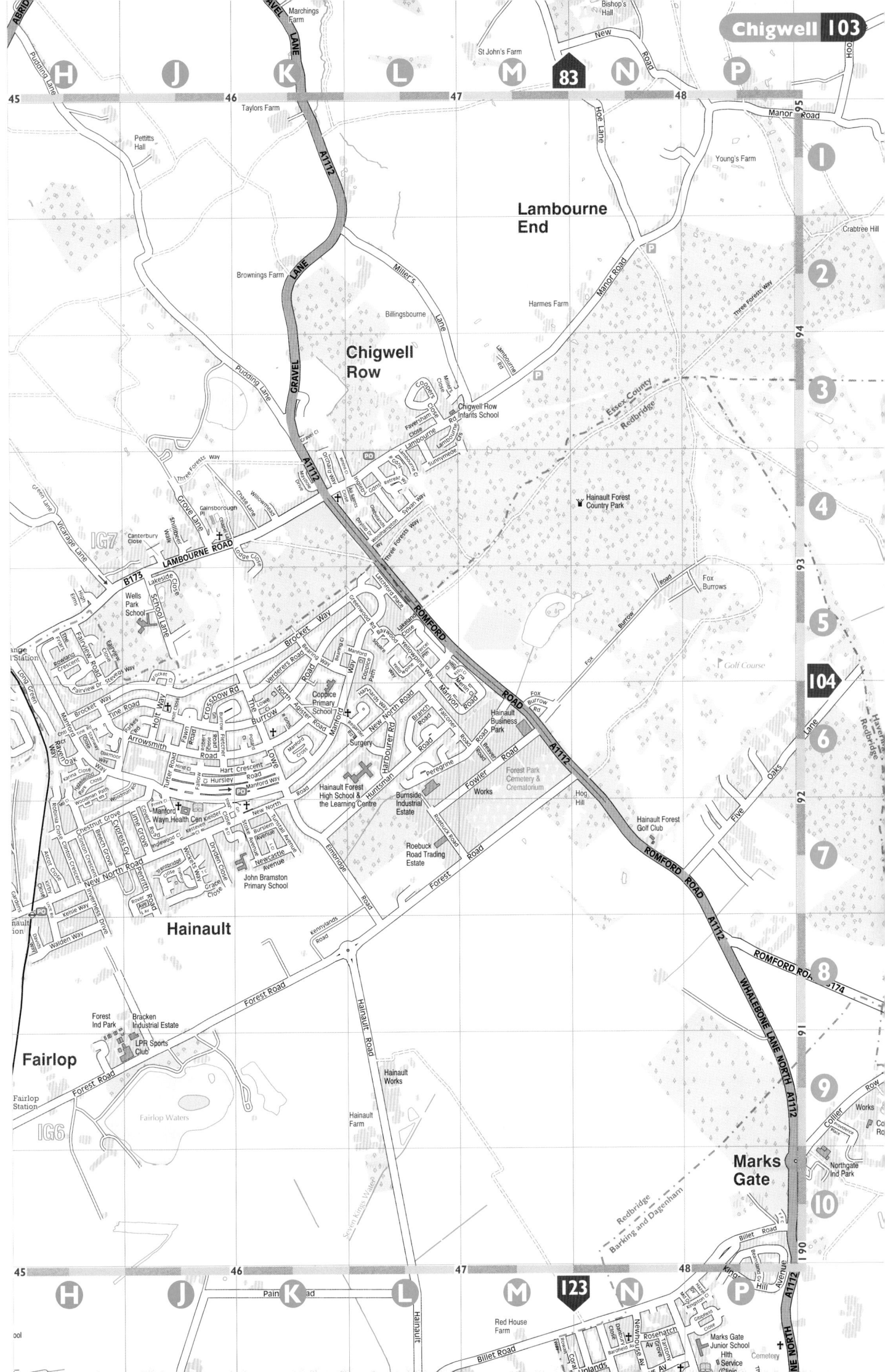
Lambourne End
Chigwell Row
Hainault
Fairlop
Marks Gate
Marchings Farm
Bishop's Hall
St John's Farm
Taylors Farm
Pettitts Hall
Young's Farm
Crabtree Hill
Brownings Farm
Billingsbourne
Harmes Farm
Chigwell Row Infants School
Hainault Forest Country Park
Fox Burrows
Golf Course
Wells Park School
Coppice Primary School
Surgery
Hainault Business Park
Hainault Forest High School & the Learning Centre
Burnside Industrial Estate
Forest Park Cemetery & Crematorium
Works
Hog Hill
Hainault Forest Golf Club
Roebuck Road Trading Estate
John Bramston Primary School
Manford Way Health Cen
Forest Ind Park
Bracken Industrial Estate
LPR Sports Club
Fairlop Station
Fairlop Waters
Hainault Works
Hainault Farm
Northgate Ind Park
Red House Farm
Marks Gate Junior School
Cemetery
GRAVEL LANE
A1112
ROMFORD ROAD
WHALEBONE LANE NORTH
LAMBOURNE ROAD
B173
A1174
Forest Road
Hainault Road
Manor Road
Miller's Lane
Pudding Lane
Vicarage Lane
Billet Road
Essex County
Redbridge
Barking and Dagenham
IG7
IG6
83
104
123

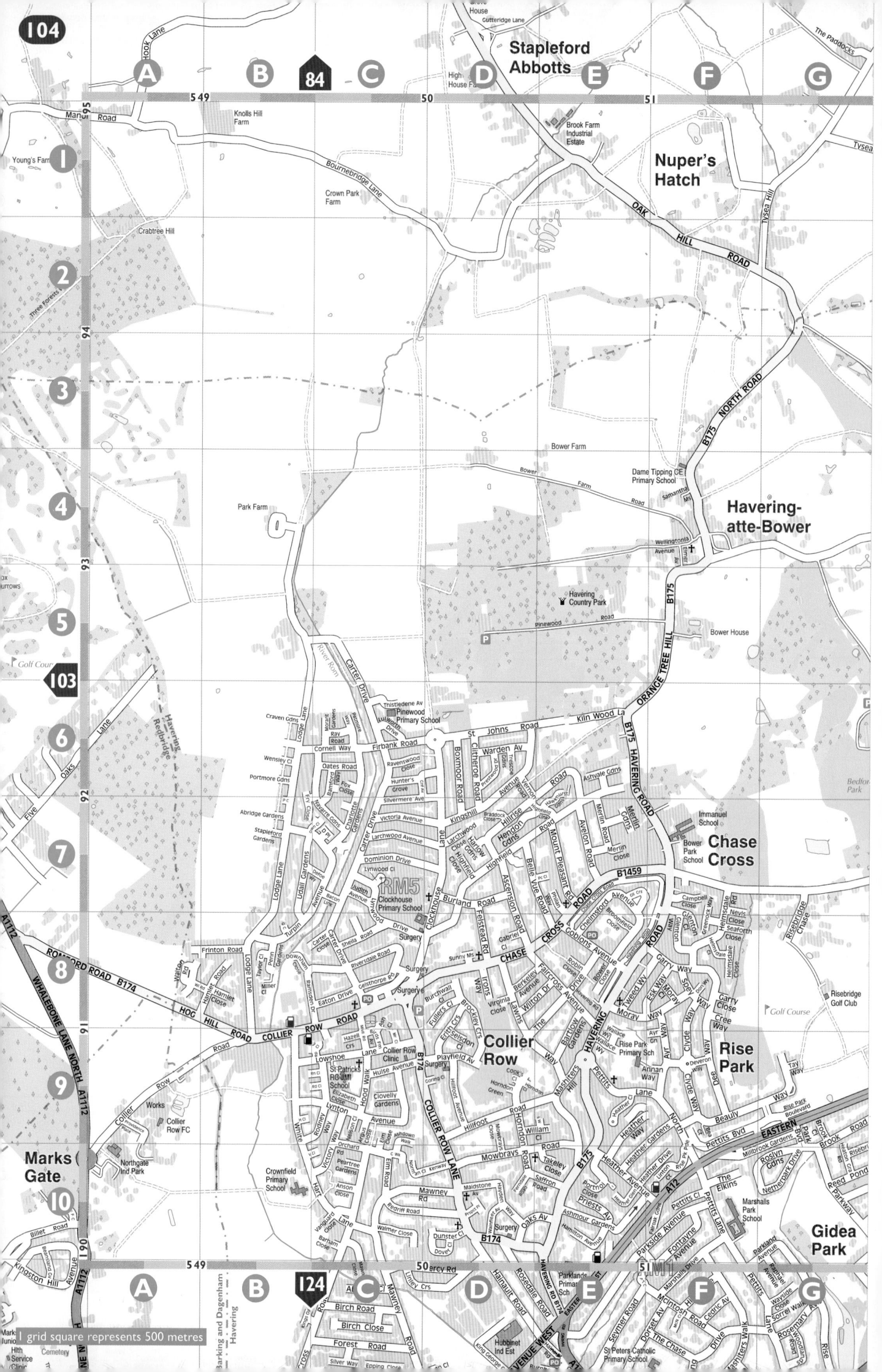

A   B   84   C   D   Stapleford Abbotts   E   F   G

5 49   50   51

Manor Road

Young's Farm   I

Knolls Hill Farm

Bournebridge Lane

Crown Park Farm

Crabtree Hill

Nuper's Hatch

OAK HILL ROAD

Brook Farm Industrial Estate

High House F

Tysea

2

Three Forests

94

3

93

Bower Farm

Bower Road   Samantha

Dame Tipping CE Primary School

Park Farm   4

Havering-atte-Bower

Wellingtonia Avenue

Bower House

B175

B175 NORTH ROAD

103   5

Golf Cour

River Rom

Havering Country Park

Pinewood Road

ORANGE TREE HILL

Carter Drive

B175 HAVERING ROAD

Bower House

P

Lane   6

92

Oaks

Five

Redbridge

Craven Gdns   Lodge Lane   Ray Road   Thistledene Av   Pinewood Primary School

St Johns Road   Klin Wood La

Chase Park School

Immanuel School

Cornell Way   Firbank Road   Warden Av   Clitheroe Road

Wensley Cl   Oates Road   Ravenswood Close   Boxmoor Road   Ashvale Gdns

Portmore Gdns   Hunter's Grove   Silvermere Av   Kingshill

Merlin Gdns

Chase Cross

Abridge Gardens   Bamford   Fox Close   Victoria Avenue   Larchwood   Hendon Gdns   Avelon Road   Merlin Close

Stapleford Gardens   Carter Drive   Larchwood Avenue   Highfield   Mount Pleasant Rd   Merlin Road

7

Lodge Lane   Dominion Drive   Lynwood Cl   Burland Road   Belle Vue Road   B1459

Udall Gardens   Judith Avenue   RM5 Clockhouse Primary School   Ascension Road   Gabriel Road   CROSS   ROAD   Coblins Avenue

Turpin   Bacon Link   Clockhouse Drive   Surgery   Felstead Rd   Chelmsford Avenue   Campbell Close   Nevis Close   Risebridge Chase

Frinton Road   Carter Cl   Sheila Road   Surgery   Sunny Ms   CHASE   Robin   PO   Seaforth Close

ROMFORD ROAD B174   Walta Rd   Downham   Gelsthorpe Dr   Riversdale Road   Surgery   Burchwall   Irons Way   Berkeley Avenue   Bower Close   Glencorn   Helmsdale Chase

8   Taylor Cl   Miller Cl   Eaton Drive   PO   Fullers Cl   Virginia Close   Farrcross Avenue   Tweed Way   Garry Way

16   HOG HILL ROAD   P   Brockley Crs   Wilton Drcs   Moray   Flora   Garry Close

Hamlet Close   Enton Crs   The Lawns   Way   Elk Way   Cree Way

Lowshoe   Hazell Crs   Collier Row Clinic   Playfield Av   Wallace Rise Park Primary Sch   Clyde Way

St Patricks RC JMI School   Hulse Avenue   Surgery   Corling   Wilton Drcs   Wallace Way   Annan Way   Deveron   Tay Way

9   Rodney Way   Clovelly Gardens   Hornhall Road   Mashters Hill   Heather Way   Beauly

Collier Row FC   Works   Elizabeth Gardens   Hilfoot Avenue   Hornton Green   William Cl   Heather Avenue   B175   Pettits Boulevard

Lynton   Victory Way   Orchard   Peartree Gardens   Elm Road   Mowbrays Road   Takeley Close   Heather Drive   EASTERN

Marks Gate   White   Hart   Anson Close   Hilfoot   Portnor Close   The Elkins   Roslyn Gdns   Riseb

Northgate Ind Park   Crownfield Primary School   Mawney Rd   Saffron Close   Priests Av   A12   Millbrook Gardens   Netherpark Drive

10   Vanguard Lane   Redriff Road   Surgery   Ashmour Gardens   Marshalls Park School

Billet Road   Barham Close   COLLIER ROW LANE   Oaks Av   Hamilton Avenue   Marshalls Park

90   Walmer Close   Dunster Cl   Parkside Avenue   Gidea Park

Kingston Hill   Dover   B174   Parklands Primar   McIntosh Road   Cedric Av

5 49   50   Percy Rd   HAVERING RD B174   Rosedale Road   51 M1   Fontayne Avenue   Wayside

A   B   124   C   Linley Crs   D   Hainault Road   E   Parkside   F   Dorset Av   G

Birch Road   St Peters Catholic   Seymer Road   The Chase   Sorrel Walk

Barking and Dagenham   Birch Close   Primary School   King George   McIntosh   Rosewoodland Cl

1 grid square represents 500 metres   Havering   Forest Road   Hubbinet Ind Est   Rosemary   Fairfield Avenue

Kingston Hill   Silver Way   Epping Close   Drive

Hlth Service Clinic   Cemetery   CROSS   AVENUE WEST

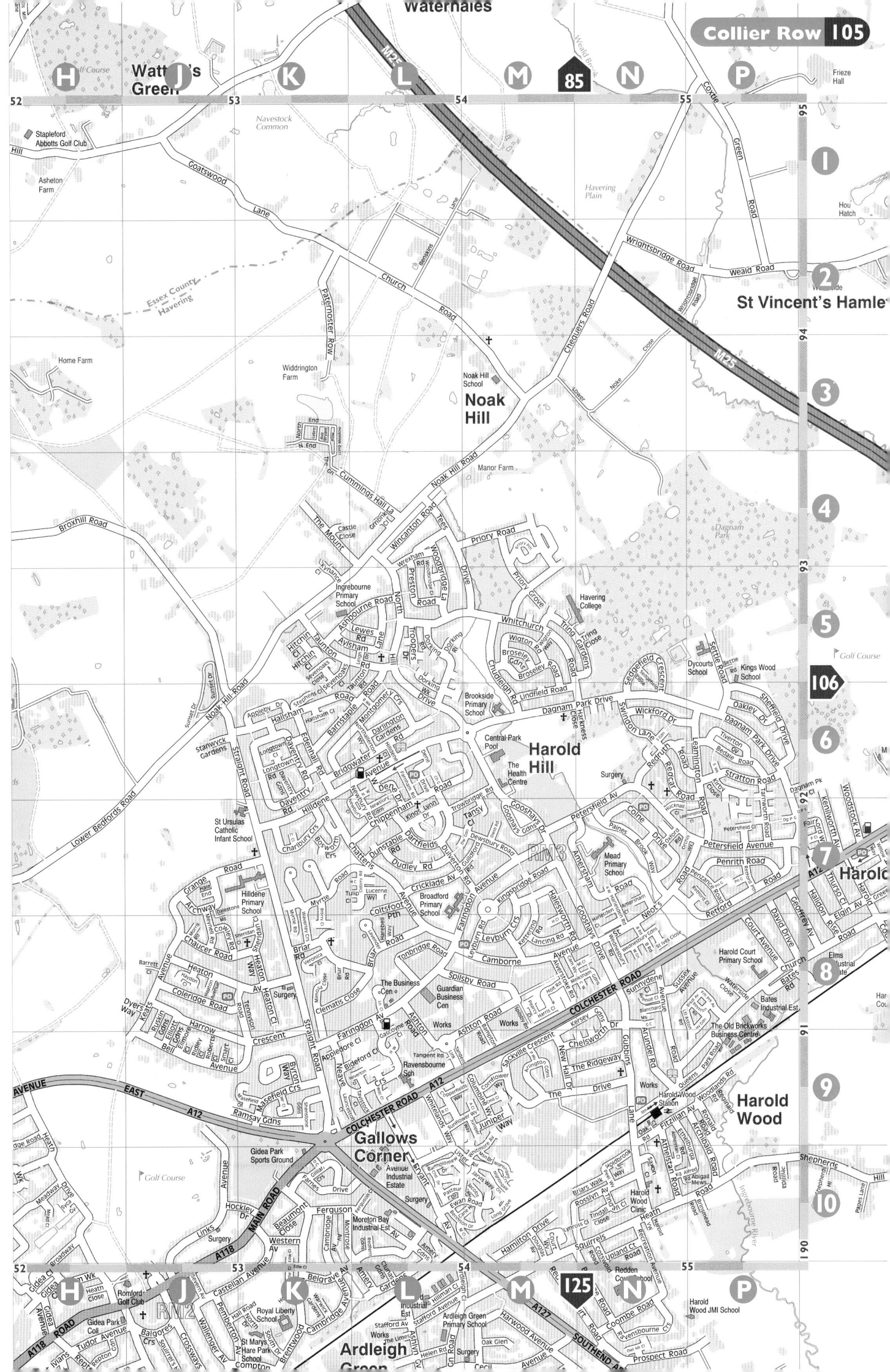
Waterhales
Watton's Green
Stapleford Abbotts Golf Club
Asheton Farm
Navestock Common
Goatswood Lane
Church Road
Paternoster Row
Essex County
Havering
Home Farm
Widdrington Farm
Havering Plain
Wrightsbridge Road
Weald Road
St Vincent's Hamlet
Chequers Road
Noak Hill School
Noak Hill
Noak Hill Road
Manor Farm
Cummings Hall La
Broxhill Road
The Mount
Castle Close
Wincanton Road
Priory Road
Dagnam Park
Ingrebourne Primary School
Havering College
Whitchurch Road
Dycourts School
Kings Wood School
Brookside Primary School
Dagnam Park Drive
Central Park Pool
Harold Hill
The Health Centre
Surgery
Straight Road
Lower Bedfords Road
St Ursulas Catholic Infant School
Hilldene Primary School
Petersfield Av
Petersfield Avenue
Mead Primary School
Broadford Primary School
Chaucer Road
Heaton Av
Coleridge Road
Harrow Crescent
Faringdon Avenue
Tonbridge Road
Spilsby Road
Guardian Business Cen
The Business Cen
Ashton Road
Works
Colchester Road
A12
Harold Court Primary School
Bates Industrial Est
The Old Brickworks Business Centre
Ravensbourne Sch
Gallows Corner
Harold Wood Station
Harold Wood
Harold Wood Clinic
Gidea Park Sports Ground
Golf Course
Avenue Industrial Estate
Moreton Bay Industrial Est
Romford Golf Club
Royal Liberty School
Gidea Park Coll
St Marys Hare Park School
Ardleigh Green Primary School
Ardleigh Green
Harold Wood JMI School
Redden Court School
Shepherds Hill
Ingrebourne River
A118
A127
Southend Arterial Road
RM2
RM3
85
106
125

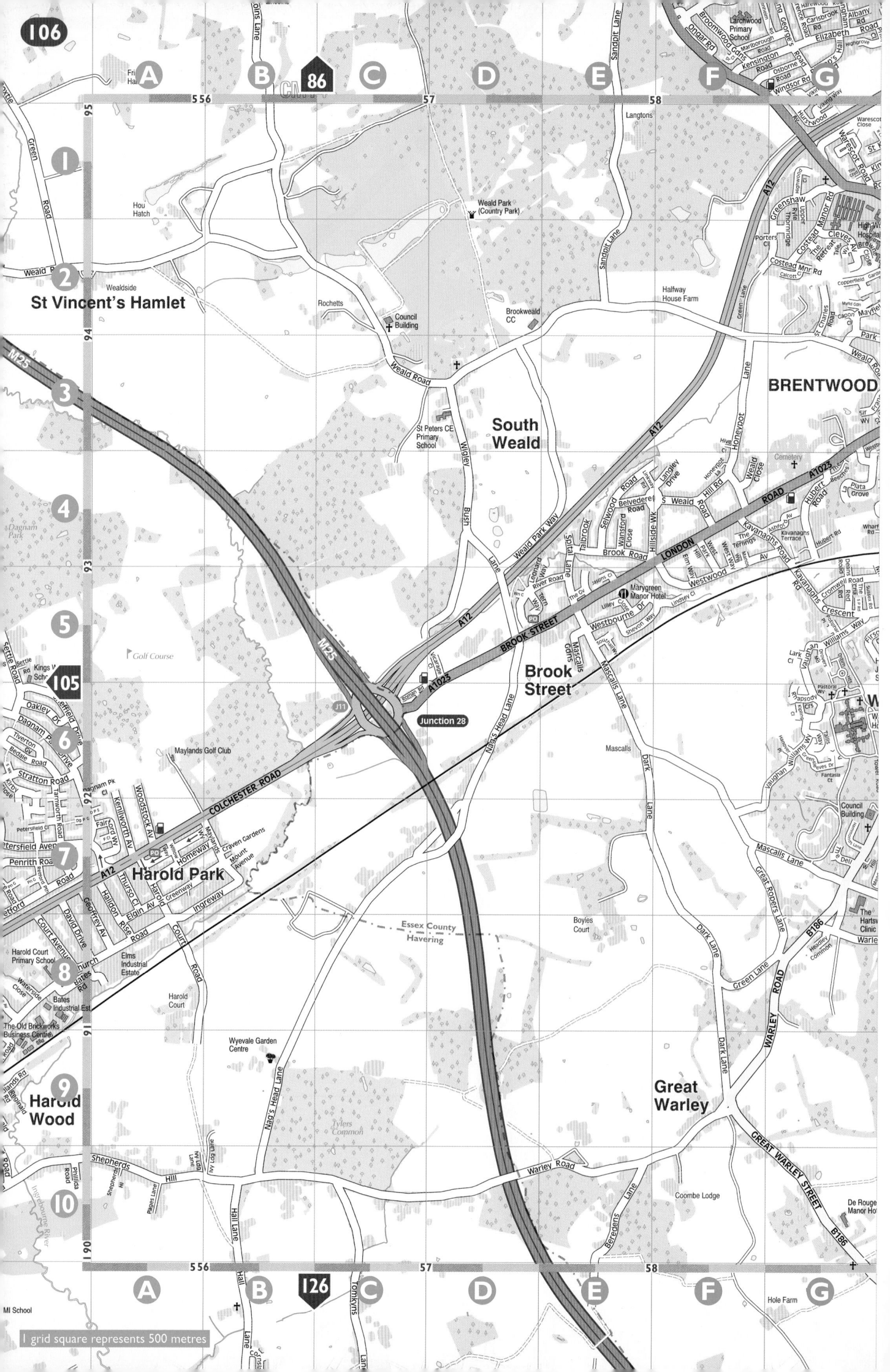
86
105
126
A
B
C
D
E
F
G
556
57
58
95
94
93
92
91
190
1
2
3
4
5
6
7
8
9
10
St Vincent's Hamlet
Wealdside
Hou Hatch
Weald Road
Rochetts
Council Building
Weald Park (Country Park)
Brookweald CC
Langtons
Sandpit Lane
Halfway House Farm
Larchwood Primary School
BRENTWOOD
South Weald
St Peters CE Primary School
Wigley Bush Lane
Weald Park Way
A12
M25
A1023
BROOK STREET
LONDON ROAD
Brook Street
Marygreen Manor Hotel
Junction 28
J11
Golf Course
Dagnam Park
Maylands Golf Club
COLCHESTER ROAD
Harold Park
Nag's Head Lane
Mascalls
Mascalls Lane
Dark Lane
Essex County
Havering
Boyles Court
Harold Court
Harold Court Primary School
Elms Industrial Estate
Bates Industrial Est
The Old Brickworks Business Centre
Wyevale Garden Centre
Tylers Common
Great Warley
WARLEY ROAD
GREAT WARLEY STREET
B186
Warley Road
Shepherds Hill
Hall Lane
Beredens Lane
Coombe Lodge
De Rougemont Manor Hotel
Hole Farm
Harold Wood
Ingrebourne River
Great Ropers Lane
Green Lane
The Hartswood Clinic
Council Building
Cemetery
Green Lane
Honeypot Lane
MI School
1 grid square represents 500 metres

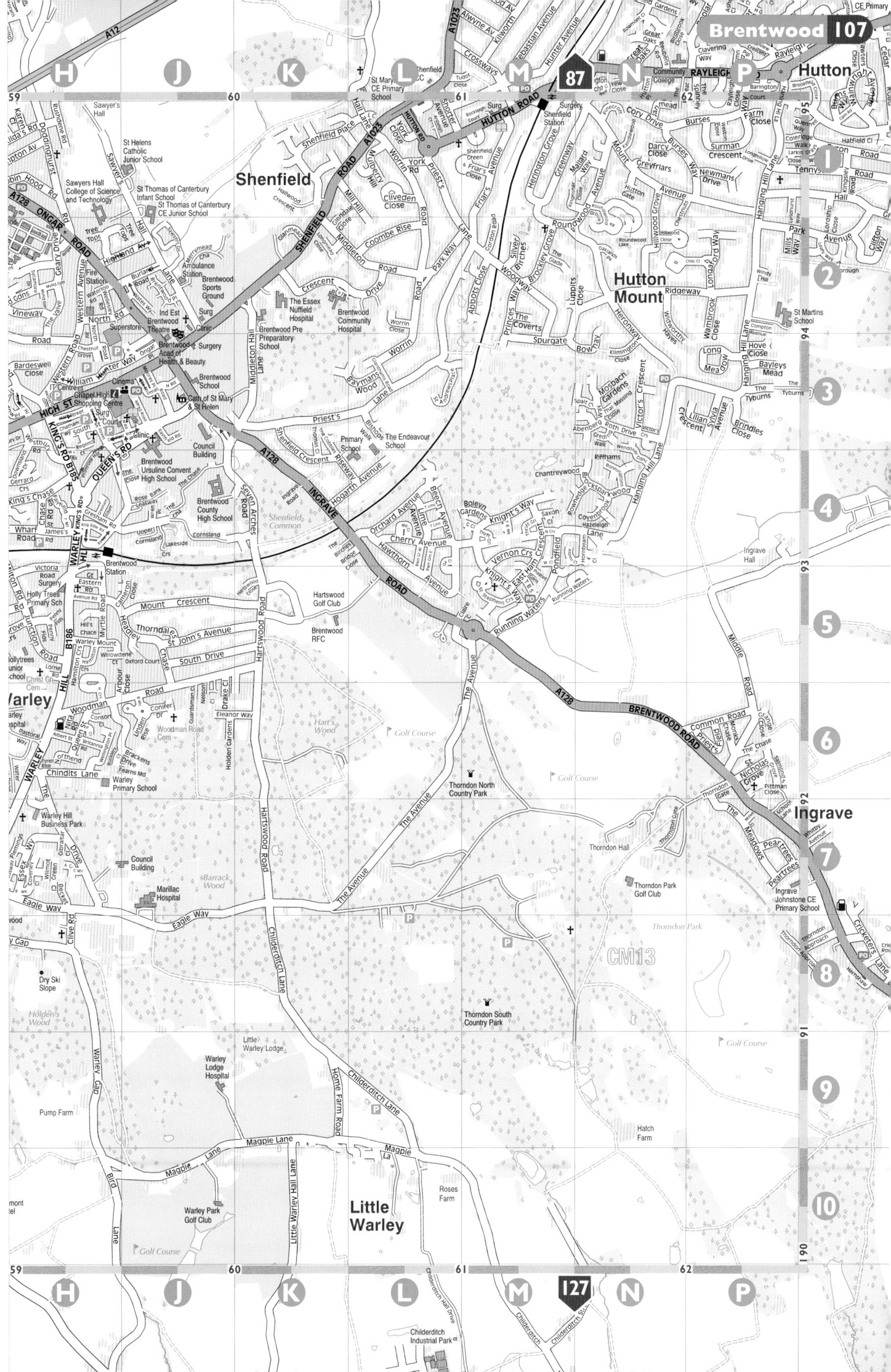

Brentwood
107
87
127
Shenfield
Hutton
Hutton Mount
Ingrave
Warley
Little Warley
CM13
A12
A1023
A128
B185
B186
HIGH ST
ONGAR ROAD
SHENFIELD ROAD
HUTTON ROAD
INGRAVE ROAD
BRENTWOOD ROAD
KING'S RD
QUEEN'S RD
WARLEY HILL
RAYLEIGH
Shenfield Station
Brentwood Station
Hartswood Golf Club
Brentwood RFC
Thorndon North Country Park
Thorndon South Country Park
Thorndon Hall
Thorndon Park Golf Club
Thorndon Park
Golf Course
Ingrave Hall
Hatch Farm
Roses Farm
Pump Farm
Warley Park Golf Club
Warley Lodge Hospital
Little Warley Lodge
Marillac Hospital
Council Building
Dry Ski Slope
Holden's Wood
Barrack Wood
Hart's Wood
Shenfield Common
Childerditch Industrial Park
Warley Hill Business Park
Warley Primary School
Woodman Road Cem
The Essex Nuffield Hospital
Brentwood Community Hospital
Brentwood Pre Preparatory School
Brentwood School
Brentwood County High School
Brentwood Ursuline Convent High School
Cath of St Mary & St Helen
Sawyers Hall College of Science and Technology
St Helens Catholic Junior School
St Thomas of Canterbury Infant School
St Thomas of Canterbury CE Junior School
Brentwood Sports Ground
Ambulance Station
Fire Station
Brentwood Theatre
Brentwood Acad of Health & Beauty
Chapel High Shopping Centre
Cinema
St Martins School
Ingrave Johnstone CE Primary School
Hutton Gate
Riffhams
Chantreywood
Hanging Hill Lane
Middle Road
Hartswood Road
Childerditch Lane
Magpie Lane
Eagle Way
Warley Gap
Bird Lane
Little Warley Hall Lane
Home Farm Road
The Avenue
Running Waters
Priest's Lane
Seven Arches Road
Ridgeway
Spurgate
Heronway
Woodway

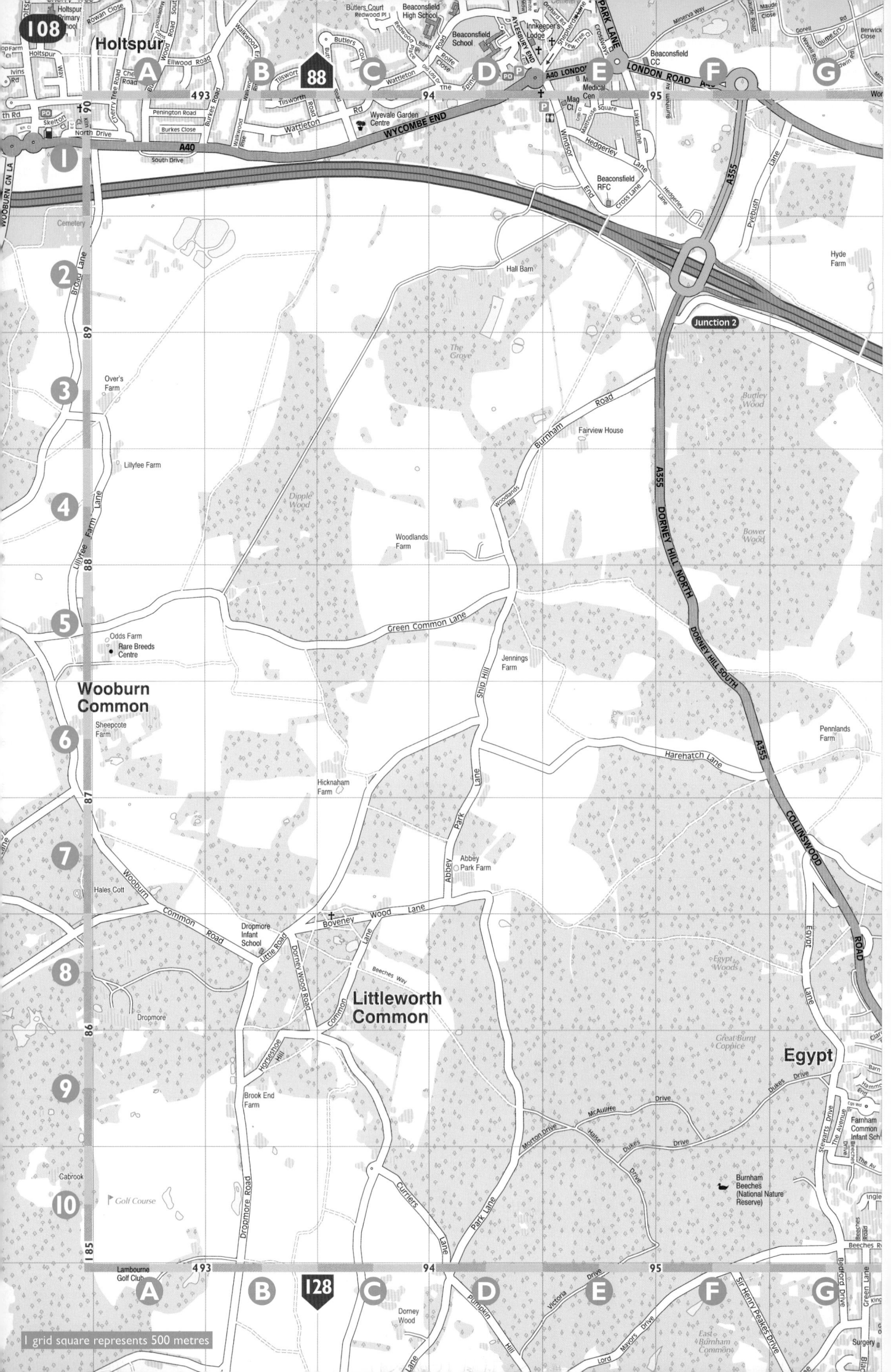

Holtspur
Beaconsfield High School
Beaconsfield School
Beaconsfield CC
Beaconsfield RFC
WYCOMBE END
LONDON ROAD
A40
A355
Junction 2
Hall Barn
The Grove
Over's Farm
Lillyfee Farm
Dipple Wood
Woodlands Farm
Fairview House
Buttley Wood
Bower Wood
Hyde Farm
Odds Farm
Rare Breeds Centre
Wooburn Common
Sheepcote Farm
Green Common Lane
Jennings Farm
Ship Hill
DORNEY HILL NORTH
DORNEY HILL SOUTH
Pennlands Farm
Harehatch Lane
Hicknaham Farm
Abbey Park Lane
Abbey Park Farm
COLLINSWOOD ROAD
Hales Cott
Wooburn Common Road
Dropmore Infant School
Boveney Wood Lane
Littleworth Common
Dorney Wood Road
Dropmore
Egypt Woods
Egypt Lane
Great Burnt Coppice
Egypt
Horseshoe Hill
Brook End Farm
McAuliffe Drive
Dukes Drive
Morton Drive
Halse Drive
Burnham Beeches (National Nature Reserve)
Farnham Common Infant Sch
Cabrook
Golf Course
Dropmore Road
Curriers Lane
Park Lane
Lambourne Golf Club
Pumpkin Hill
Victoria Drive
Dorney Wood
Lord Mayors Drive
Sir Henry Peakes Drive
East Burnham Common
Bedford Drive
Green Lane
Surgery
88
128
1 grid square represents 500 metres

H J K L M **89** N P

96 97 98 99

London Road A40

Austenwood

St Josephs CE Combined School

Maltmans Green School

Stampwell Farm

Mumfords Lane

Gayhurst School

1

Maltmans Lane

South Acrefield Road

Oxford Road A40

Mumfords Farm

The Manor House

Siblet's Wood

South View Road

Layters Way

2

Bull 168

Bentinck Close

Bulstrode

3

Chiltern Hundreds

Main Drive

Top

Park

Bulstrode Park

Valley Way

Woodhill Avenue

4

Hedgerley Lane

Moat Farm

Slade Farm

Wapseys Lane

GERRARDS CROSS

Camp Road

B416

5

Hedgerley Green

Village Lane

Hedgerley Lane

Stoneyfield

Windsor Road

Gerrard Sports C

110

Hillmott's Farm

Beaconsfield Common

PH

Church Wood RSPB Reserve

Hedgerley

Klin Lane

Andrew Hill

Dukes Wood Drive

Howards Thicket

Dukes Wood

The Sommers

High

Birchdale

Beeches

6

Stevenson Road

Hedgerley Hill

Jones Way

Elkins Road

Hedgerley Park

Mount Hill Lane

Dukes Valley

7

Old Nursery Court

Gregory Rd

Cottage Park Road

PO

Longfield

Parish Lane

Collum Green Road

Timberwood

Tara

Cemetery

Low Farm

8

Wood End Close

Colley Hill Lane

Gypsy Lane

Stoke Wood

Woodland Glade

Romsey Drive

Ashenden Walk

Stoke Wd

Fulmer Chase

The Pickeridge

Christmas Lane

Pin

One

Mount Close

Farnham Common Junior School

Crispin Way

Farnham Common Middle School

Sherbourne Walk

Stoke Common Road

Fulmer

9

Oakridge Pl

Common Wood

Scott Close

Marlower

Templewood Lane

Bracken Cl

Larchmoot Park

Stoke Common

B416

Kay Lane

Windmill Road

10

The Highlands

Glen

Templewood Drive

Foxholow Drive

Rowanhurst

Orchard Way

Temple

Dell Cl

Rosewood Way

PO

Fresnam Wk

Brockhurst Wood

Durnford

Gerrards Cross Road

Beeches Way

Frame Wood

96 97 98 99

Farnham Com Jn

H J K L M **129** N P

Beeches Way

Rickmans Lane

Vine Road

Neville Close

Hazel

Cleverhurst Close

Eiderfield Road

185 186 187 188 90

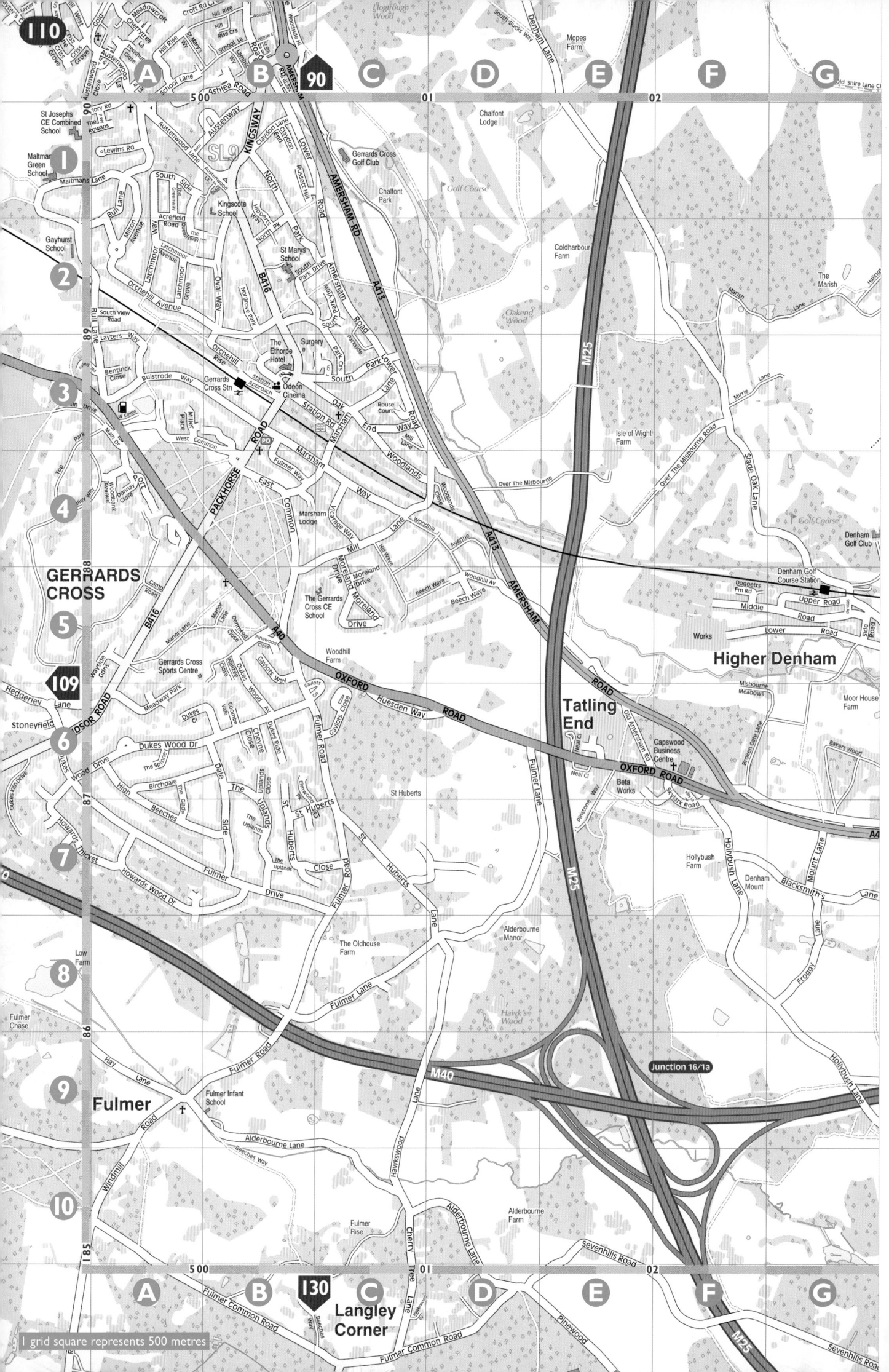
110
90
109
130
A
B
C
D
E
F
G
1
2
3
4
5
6
7
8
9
10
500
01
02
90
89
88
87
86
185
GERRARDS CROSS
SL9
Higher Denham
Tatling End
Fulmer
Langley Corner
Flogtrough Wood
Mopes Farm
Chalfont Lodge
Gerrards Cross Golf Club
Golf Course
Chalfont Park
Coldharbour Farm
Oakend Wood
The Marish
Isle of Wight Farm
Over The Misbourne
Denham Golf Club
Denham Golf Course Station
Works
Moor House Farm
Misbourne Meadows
Capswood Business Centre
Beta Works
Hollybush Farm
Denham Mount
Alderbourne Manor
Hawk's Wood
Junction 16/1a
Alderbourne Farm
The Oldhouse Farm
St Huberts
Woodhill Farm
The Gerrards Cross CE School
Marsham Lodge
Gerrards Cross Sports Centre
Gerrards Cross Stn
Odeon Cinema
The Ethorpe Hotel
Surgery
Rouse Court
St Marys School
Kingscote School
St Josephs CE Combined School
Maltman Green School
Gayhurst School
Stoneyfield
Low Farm
Fulmer Chase
Fulmer Infant School
Fulmer Rise
M25
M40
A40
A413
B416
AMERSHAM RD
AMERSHAM ROAD
OXFORD ROAD
PACKHORSE ROAD
KINGSWAY
Denham Lane
South Bucks Way
Old Shire Lane
Marish Lane
Mirrie Lane
Over The Misbourne Road
Slade Oak Lane
Doggetts Fm Rd
Upper Road
Middle Road
Lower Road
Broken Gate Lane
Bakers Wood
Old Amersham Rd
Neal Cl
Pinstone Way
Skylark Road
Hollybush Lane
Mount Lane
Blacksmith's Lane
Froggy Lane
Fulmer Lane
Huesden Way
Hawkswood Lane
Cherry Tree Lane
Alderbourne Lane
Sevenhills Road
Pinewood Road
Fulmer Common Road
Beeches Way
Windmill Road
Hay Lane
Fulmer Road
Fulmer Drive
Howards Wood Dr
Howards Thicket
Dukes Wood Drive
Dukes Kiln Drive
High Beeches
Birchdale
The Glade
The Spinney
Dale Side
The Uplands
Uplands Close
St Huberts Close
St Huberts Lane
St Huberts Cl
Elmwood Pk
Dukes Ride
Cheyne Close
Coombe Vale
Dukes Cl
Dukes Wood Av
Nalinee Close
Gaviots Way
Gaviots Close
Gaviots Cl
Pinewood Close
Denhead Close
Manor Lane
Meadway Park
Wayside Gdns
Hedgerley Lane
Camp Road
Moreland Drive
Beech Waye
Woodhill Av
Woodhill Avenue
Mill Lane
Hill Waye
Vicarage Way
East Common
Marsham Way
Marsham Lane
Woodlands Close
Woodlands
Oak End Way
Mill Lane
Station Rd
Station Approach
Fulmer Way
West Common
Miller Place
Bulstrode Way
Bentinck Close
Layters Way
South View Road
Orchehill Rise
Orchehill Avenue
Bull Lane
Main Drive
Main Dr
Park
Woodbank Avenue
Donnay Close
Port
Latchmoor Way
Latchmoor Avenue
Latchmoor Grove
Oval Way
Norgrove Park
Acrefield Road
Milton Avenue
Maltmans Lane
Lewins Rd
South Side
The Greenway
Austenwood Lane
Austenway
Austenwood Close
Ashlea Road
School Lane
Hill Rise
Rise Crs
Croft Rd
Meadowcroft
Cherrytree La
Claydon Lane
Claydon End
Lower Road
Russell Hill
North Park
North Pk
Hayes Way
South Park Drive
South Park
South Park Crs
Amersham Road
Lower Road
Lower Lane
Parkside
Malvern Rd
Woodside Hill
1 grid square represents 500 metres

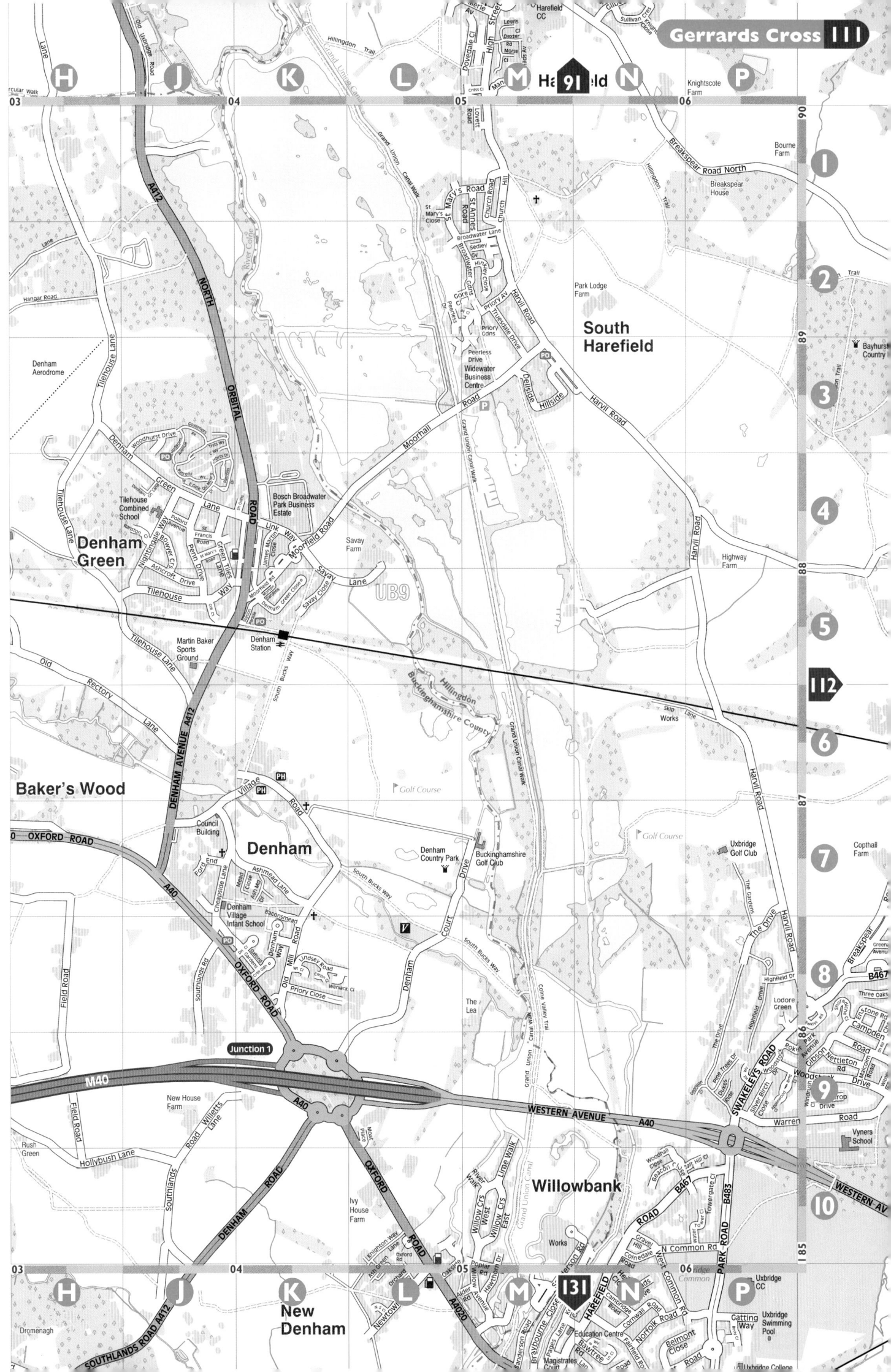
South Harefield
Denham Green
Denham
Baker's Wood
Willowbank
New Denham
Denham Aerodrome
Bosch Broadwater Park Business Estate
Widewater Business Centre
Denham Station
Martin Baker Sports Ground
Denham Country Park
Buckinghamshire Golf Club
Uxbridge Golf Club
Tilehouse Combined School
Denham Village Infant School
Council Building
Savay Farm
Park Lodge Farm
Highway Farm
Bourne Farm
Breakspear House
Knightscote Farm
New House Farm
Ivy House Farm
Rush Green
Dromenagh
Copthall Farm
Lodore Green
Vyners School
Uxbridge CC
Uxbridge Swimming Pool
Education Centre
Magistrates Court
Skip Works
Works
The Lea
Golf Course
NORTH ORBITAL ROAD A412
DENHAM AVENUE A412
OXFORD ROAD A40
WESTERN AVENUE A40
M40
Junction 1
DENHAM ROAD
OXFORD ROAD A4020
SOUTHLANDS ROAD A412
SWAKELEYS ROAD
PARK ROAD B483
B467
Harvil Road
Moorhall Road
Breakspear Road North
Tilehouse Lane
Denham Green Lane
Old Rectory Lane
Village Road
Denham Court Drive
Grand Union Canal
Grand Union Canal Walk
Hillingdon Trail
South Bucks Way
Colne Valley Trail
River Colne
Hillingdon
Buckinghamshire County
UB9
Hangar Road
Field Road
Hollybush Lane
Southlands Rd
Willetts Lane
Savay Lane
Moorfield Road
Link Way
Tilehouse Way
Ashcroft Drive
Nightingale Way
Penn Drive
Green Tiles Way
Cheapside Lane
Ashmead Lane
Priory Close
Lindsey Road
Old Mill Road
Denham Way
Ford End
Mead Close
Baconsmead
St Mary's Road
St Annes Road
Church Road
Church Hill
Broadwater Lane
Priory Av
Truesdale Drive
Peerless Drive
Hillside
Dellside
Common Rd
West Common Rd
Warren Road
Highfield Dr
The Drive
Harefield
Harefield CC
H J K L M N P
03 04 05 06
1 2 3 4 5 6 7 8 9 10
90 89 88 87 86 85
91
112
131

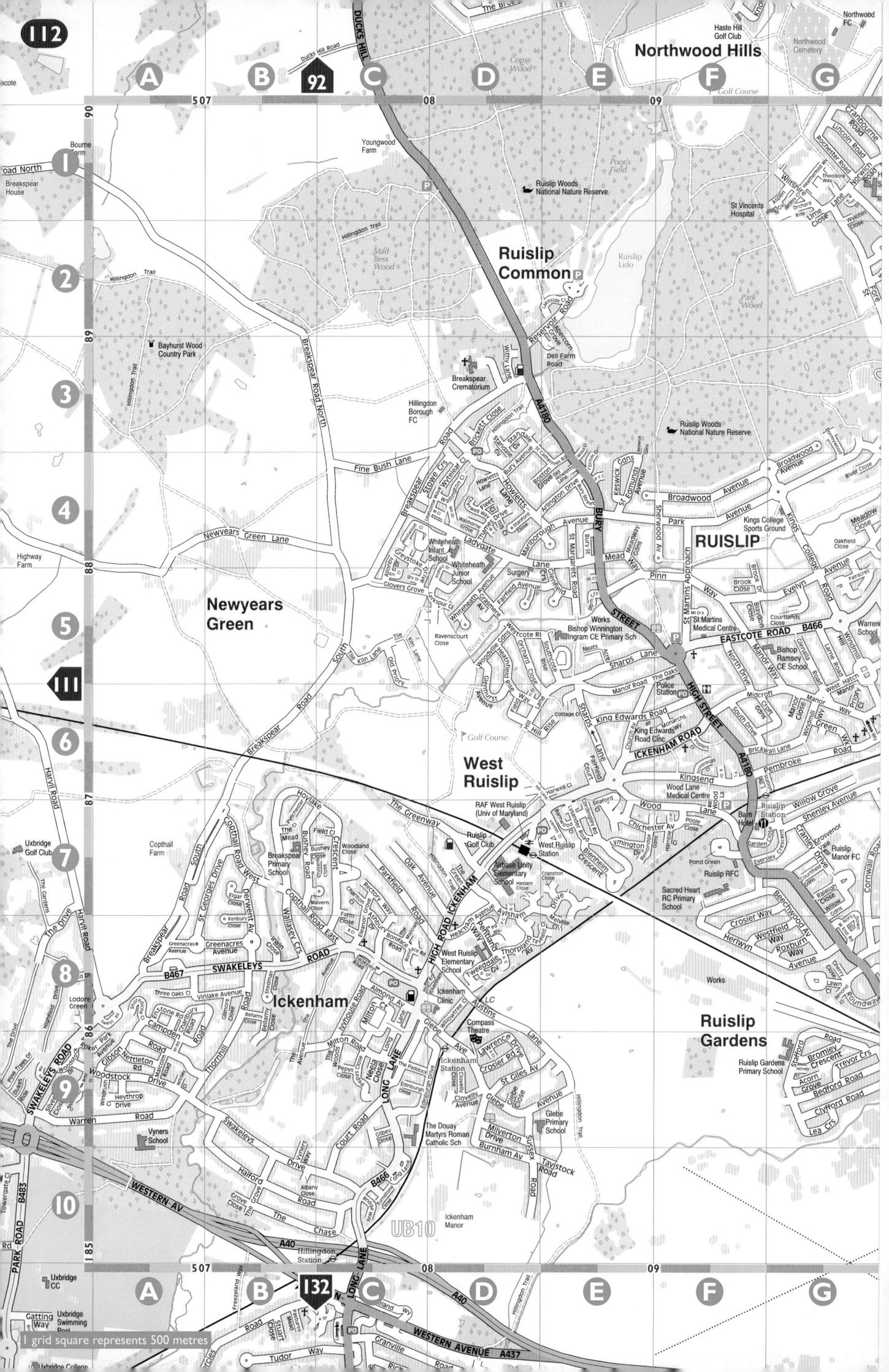

Northwood Hills
Haste Hill Golf Club
Northwood Cemetery
Northwood FC
Golf Course
Ducks Hill Road
DUCKS HILL
92
Copse Wood
Youngwood Farm
Bourne Farm
Breakspear House
Poors Field
Ruislip Woods National Nature Reserve
St Vincents Hospital
Hillingdon Trail
Mad Bess Wood
Ruislip Common
Ruislip Lido
Park Wood
Reservoir Road
Dell Farm Road
Bayhurst Wood Country Park
Breakspear Road North
Breakspear Crematorium
Hillingdon Borough FC
A4180
Ruislip Woods National Nature Reserve
Fine Bush Lane
Newyears Green Lane
Highway Farm
Broadwood Avenue
Park Avenue
Kings College Sports Ground
RUISLIP
Whiteheath Infant School
Whiteheath Junior School
Ladygate Lane
Pinn Way
Newyears Green
Bury Street
St Margarets Road
Surgery
Glovers Grove
Ravenscourt Close
Bishop Winnington Ingram CE Primary Sch
St Martins Medical Centre
EASTCOTE ROAD
B466
Bishop Ramsey CE School
Tile Kiln Lane
Sharps Lane
Manor Road
Police Station
HIGH STREET
111
King Edwards Road
King Edwards Road Clinic
Golf Course
West Ruislip
ICKENHAM ROAD
Kingsend
Wood Lane Medical Centre
Pembroke Road
Harvil Road
Breakspear Road South
The Greenway
RAF West Ruislip (Univ of Maryland)
Ruislip Golf Club
West Ruislip Station
Airbase Unity Elementary School
Ruislip Station
Barn Hotel
Willow Grove
Shenley Avenue
Ruislip Manor FC
Pond Green
Ruislip RFC
Sacred Heart RC Primary School
Uxbridge Golf Club
Copthall Farm
Breakspear Primary School
Copthall Road West
Copthall Road East
Oak Avenue
Parkfield Road
HIGH ROAD ICKENHAM
Crosier Way
Beechwood Av
Works
SWAKELEYS ROAD
B467
Greenacres Avenue
West Ruislip Elementary School
Ickenham
Ickenham Clinic
Compass Theatre
Ruislip Gardens
Ruislip Gardens Primary School
Bedford Road
Clyfford Road
Lea Crs
SWAKELEYS ROAD
Ickenham Station
Glebe Avenue
Glebe Primary School
The Douay Martyrs Roman Catholic Sch
LONG LANE
Warren Road
Vyners School
Swakeleys Drive
Halford Road
The Chase
WESTERN AV
Ickenham Manor
UB10
A40
Hillingdon Station
PARK ROAD
B483
132
Uxbridge CC
Uxbridge Swimming Pool
WESTERN AVENUE A437
Tudor Way
Granville Road
Uxbridge College
1 grid square represents 500 metres

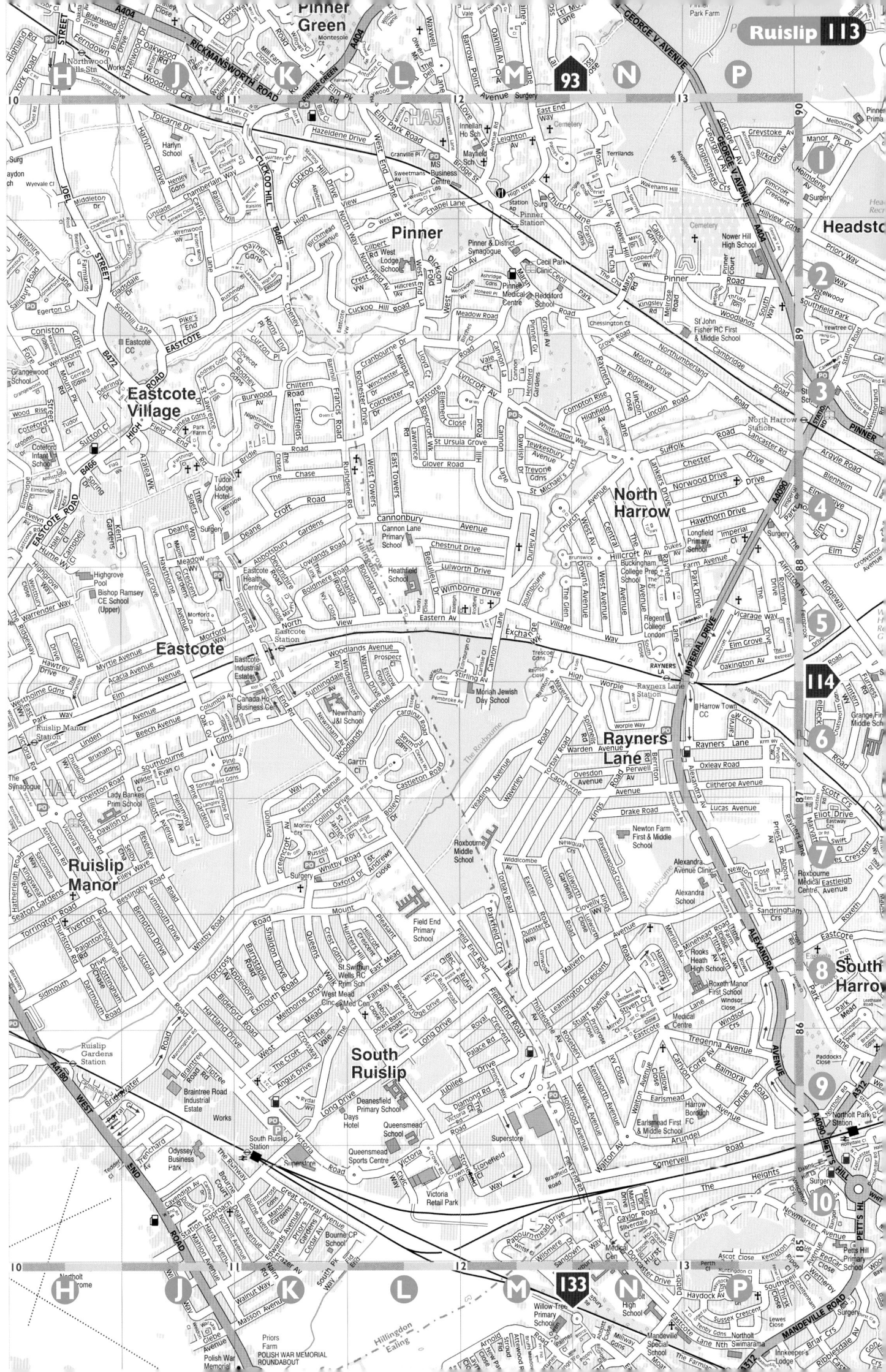
Pinner Green
Northwood Hills Stn
RICKMANSWORTH ROAD
PINNER GREEN
GEORGE V AVENUE
Pinner Park Farm
93
HA5
Pinner
Pinner Station
Headstone
Harlyn School
CUCKOO HILL
JOEL STREET
Eastcote Village
EASTCOTE ROAD
HIGH ROAD
Eastcote CC
West Lodge School
Cannon Lane Primary School
Heathfield School
Reddiford School
Nower Hill High School
St John Fisher RC First & Middle School
North Harrow
North Harrow Station
PINNER ROAD
Longfield Primary School
Buckingham College Prep School
Regent College London
IMPERIAL DRIVE
Eastcote
Eastcote Station
Highgrove Pool
Bishop Ramsey CE School (Upper)
Newnham J&I School
Moriah Jewish Day School
Rayners Lane
Rayners Lane Station
Harrow Town CC
114
Ruislip Manor
Ruislip Manor Station
HA4
Lady Bankes Prim School
Roxbourne Middle School
Newton Farm First & Middle School
Alexandra School
Field End Primary School
St Swithun Wells RC Prim Sch
Rooks Heath High School
Roxeth Manor First School
South Harrow
ALEXANDRA AVENUE
South Ruislip
Ruislip Gardens Station
Braintree Road Industrial Estate
Deanesfield Primary School
Queensmead School
Queensmead Sports Centre
Victoria Retail Park
Odyssey Business Park
South Ruislip Station
Earlsmead First & Middle School
Harrow Borough FC
Northolt Park Station
WEST END ROAD
A4180
Bourne CP School
Northolt Aerodrome
133
Willow Tree Primary School
Mandeville Special School
Northolt Swimarama
Petts Hill Primary School
MANDEVILLE ROAD
Priors Farm
POLISH WAR MEMORIAL ROUNDABOUT
Hillingdon
Ealing
Harrow

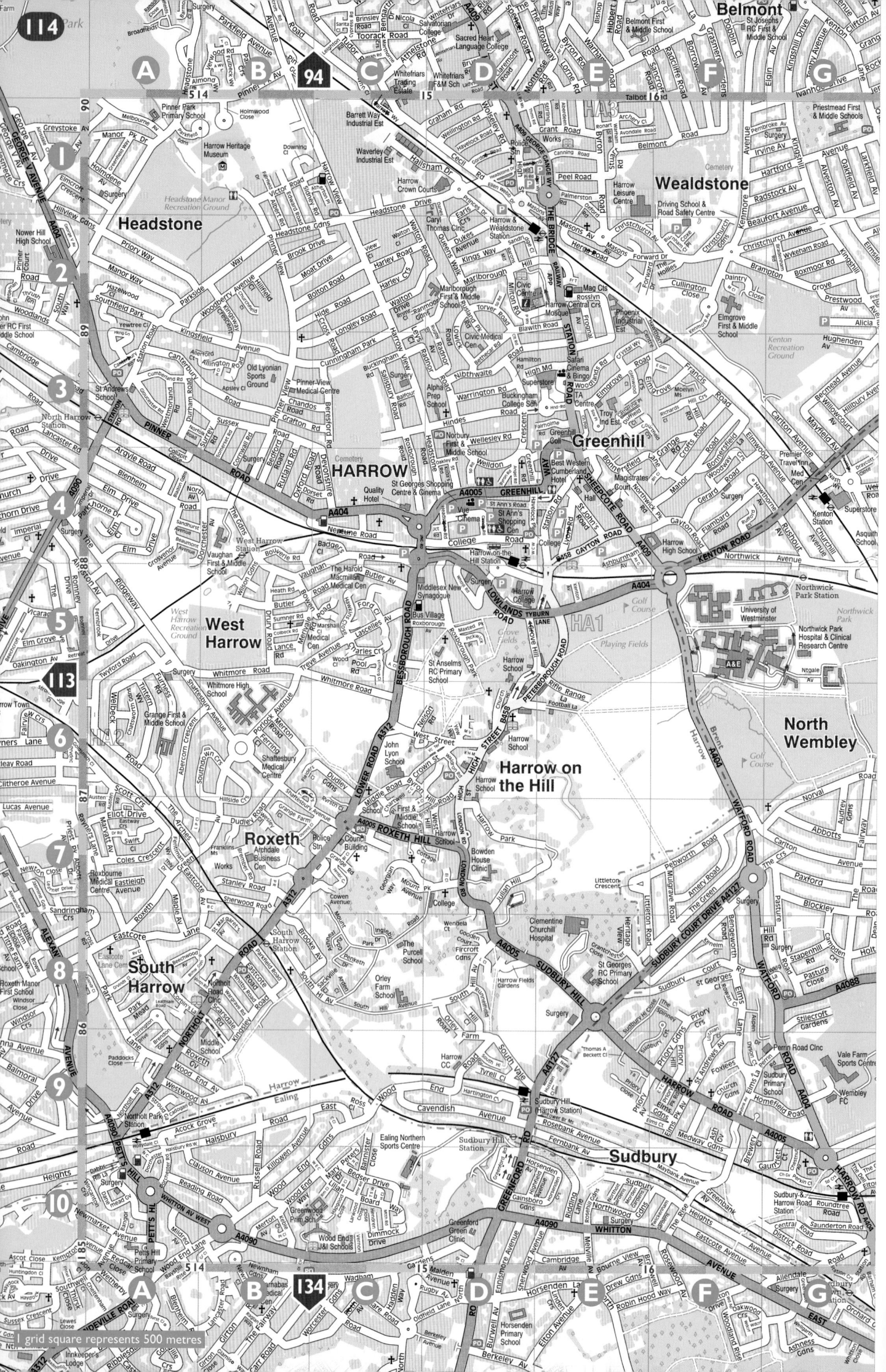

114
94
113
134
A
B
C
D
E
F
G
1
2
3
4
5
6
7
8
9
10
Belmont
Headstone
Wealdstone
HARROW
Greenhill
West Harrow
North Wembley
Harrow on the Hill
Roxeth
South Harrow
Sudbury
HA3
HA1
HA2
Harrow Heritage Museum
Headstone Manor Recreation Ground
Harrow & Wealdstone Station
North Harrow Station
West Harrow Station
Harrow-on-the-Hill Station
Northwick Park Station
Kenton Station
South Harrow Station
Sudbury Hill (Harrow Station)
Sudbury Hill Station
Northolt Park Station
Sudbury & Harrow Road Station
University of Westminster
Northwick Park Hospital & Clinical Research Centre
Harrow School
Clementine Churchill Hospital
Kenton Recreation Ground
West Harrow Recreation Ground
Playing Fields
Golf Course
Cemetery
PINNER ROAD
KENTON ROAD
WATFORD ROAD
HARROW ROAD
LOWER ROAD
GEORGE V AVENUE
SUDBURY HILL
SUDBURY COURT DRIVE A4127
GREENFORD RD
WHITTON AV WEST
A404
A4005
A409
A312
A4090
A4088
A4127
1 grid square represents 500 metres

Queensbury
Kenton
Kingsbury
Preston
Wembley Park
WEMBLEY
Tokyngton
Welsh
Neasden
95
116
135
H
J
K
L
M
N
P
17
18
19
20
2
3
4
5
6
7
8
9
10
KENTON ROAD
HONEYPOT LA
FRYENT WAY
A4140
A4006
A4088
A4089
A479
A404
A406
B454
B4557
FORTY LANE
FORTY AVENUE
SALMON ST
TUDOR GARDENS
CHURCH LANE
BLACKBIRD HILL
KINGSBURY RD
EDGWARE RD
HARROW ROAD
HIGH ROAD
EAST LANE
WEMBLEY PARK DRIVE
EMPIRE WAY
PARK LANE
WEMBLEY HILL ROAD
BRIDGE ROAD
GREAT CENTRAL WAY
SOUTH WAY
EALING ROAD
Queensbury Station
Kenton Station
Kingsbury Station
Preston Road Station
Wembley Park Station
Wembley Stadium Station
Wembley Central Station
North Wembley Station
South Kenton Station
Fryent Country Park
Roe Green Park
King Edward VII Park
Barham Park
Wembley Stadium
Wembley Arena
Exhibition Halls
Conference Centre
Wembley Stadium Ind Estate
Olympic Retail Park
Olympic Trading Estate
Cannon Trading Est
Metro Trading Cen
Towers Business Park
Hallmark Trading Estate
Wembley Stadium Industrial Estate
Drury Way Industrial Estate
IKEA
Kingsbury Hospital
Wembley Hospital
Colindale Business Park
Capitol Ind Park
Kenton Cricket Club
Sudbury Court Sports Club
Wembley Commercial Centre
Copland Specialist Science College
St Raphaels Way Medical Cen
Sri Saddhatissa International Buddhist Temple
Kingsbury Synagogue
Kenton Synagogue
Wembley Synagogue

116
96
115
136
A
B
C
D
E
F
G
1
2
3
4
5
6
7
8
9
10
521
22
23
Colindale
The Hyde
HENDON
West Hendon
Welsh Harp
Dollis Hill
Neasden
Dudden Hill
WILLESDEN
NW9
NW4
NW2
Royal Air Force Museum
Police Station
Aerodrome Rd
Aerodrome Road
Metropolitan Police Track (Hendon)
Metropolitan Police Training School, Hendon
Colindale Hospital
Colindale Station
British Library Newspaper Library
Bus Cen
Capitol Ind Park
Capitol Industrial Park
Superstore
Air Call Business Centre
COLINDEEP LANE
A5150
EDGWARE ROAD
THE HYDE
A5
Beis Yaakov Primary School
Grove Park Ind Est
Stag Lane Medical Cen
Grove Park School
Colindale Primary School
Sheaveshill Avenue
Hay Lane
KINGSBURY ROAD
A4006
Kingsbury Synagogue
Kingsbury Trading Est
Oliver Goldsmith Primary School
St Johns CE School
The Hyde School
The Hyde Industrial Estate
Garrick Industrial Centre
Connaught Business Centre
Hendon Station
Northgate Clinic
Burgess Avenue
Fryent Medical Centre
Sunnymead Road
Meadowbank Rd
West Hendon Playing Fields
Cool Oak Bridge
Cool Oak Lane
Brent Reservoir
JVC Business Park
Aquarius Business Park
London Group Business Park
Woodfield School
CHURCH LANE
B454
THE BROADWAY
Marsh Drive
West Hendon Clinic
M1
WATFORD WAY
A41
Sunny Hill Park
St Georges Medical Cen
Church Farm House Museum
Middlesex University
Central Hendon Clinic
THE BURROUGHS
CHURCH ROAD
FINCHLEY LANE
A504
PARSON STREET B552
GREAT NORTH WAY
HOLDERS HILL
Preparatory School
Agency of Jewish Education
Beth Jacob Grammar School
Hendon School
Independent Jewish Sch
Hendon Reform Synagogue
BRENT STREET
The British Hernia Centre
Little Hands Grove
Brampton Theatre
Brampton College
St Marys & St Johns CE Primary School
Hendon Secretarial College
Hendon Central Station
QUEEN'S ROAD
B551
The Albany College
North London Tutorial College
Hendon Park
STATION ROAD
Barnet College
Parkfield JMI School
Brent Cross Shopping Centre
BRENT CROSS FLYOVER
Brent Cross Station
A406
Brunel Univ
NORTH CIRCULAR ROAD
Junction 1
Staples Corner Business Park
UCG Cinemas
Atlas Business Centre
Edge Business Centre
Humber Trading Estate
Claremont Way Industrial Estate
Recreation Ground
Hendon FC
Clitterhouse Primary School
Mapledown School
Hendon Youth Sports Centre
Whitefield School
Harp Business Centre
Braincroft Primary School
John Kelly Boys & Girls Technology College
Evans Bus Cen
Dollis Hill Lane
Gladstone Park
Brent Arts Council
The Stables Gallery & Art Centre
Synagogue & Torah Temimah Primary School
Junior School
EDGWARE ROAD
CRICKLEWOOD BROADWAY
Cricklewood Station
Broadway Retail Park
Britannia Bus Cen
Crown Moran Hotel
The Mosque & Islamic Centre of Brent
CHICHELE ROAD
WALM LANE
Cricklewood Synagogue
Anson Primary School
Walm Lane Clinic
Willesden Green Station
BLACKBIRD HILL
NEASDEN LANE
OLD CHURCH LANE
A4088
A4140
St Margarets Clitherow RC Prim Sch
Wykeham Primary School
Wembley Stadium Industrial Estate
The Grange Mus
Gladstone Medical Centre
DUDDEN HILL LANE
NEASDEN LANE
B453
Neasden Station
Primary School
Falcon Park Industrial Est
Brent Child & Family Clinic
Coll of North West London
Dollis Hill Station
Gladstone Park Prim Sch
Hallmark Trading Estate
GREAT CENTRAL WAY B4557
Drury Way Industrial Estate
Vernon House Special School
IKEA
Brent Trading Estate
St Raphaels Medical Cen
River Brent
Chapman Park Industrial Est
HIGH ROAD
A407
Church End Medical Centre
Mitchell Brook Primary School
St Andrew & St Francis CE JMI Sch
Convent of Jesus & Mary Inf Sch
Bus Depot
Trojan Business Centre
1 grid square represents 500 metres

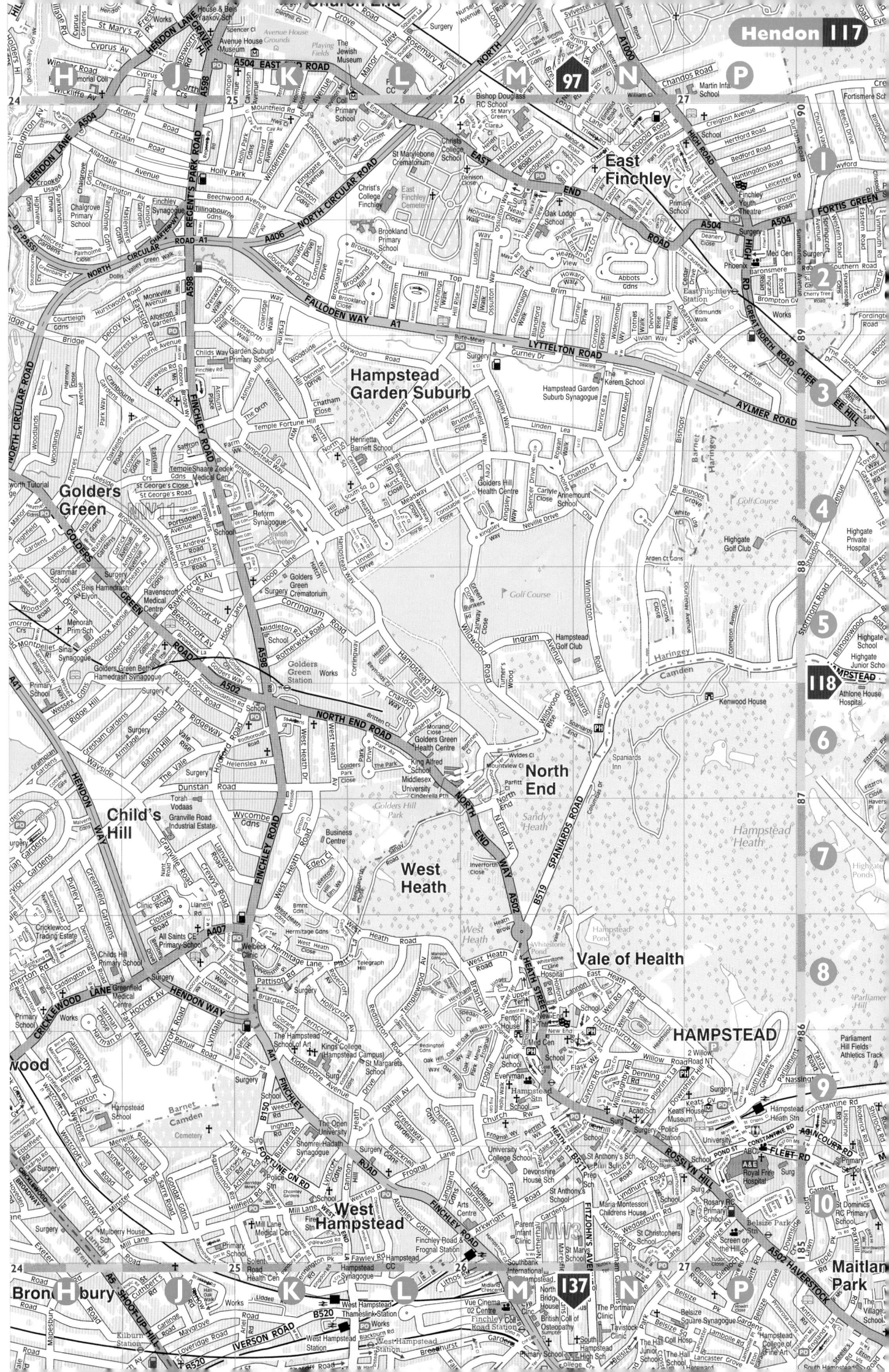

East Finchley
Hampstead Garden Suburb
Golders Green
Child's Hill
North End
West Heath
Vale of Health
HAMPSTEAD
West Hampstead
Brondesbury
Maitland Park
Hampstead Heath
Sandy Heath
Golders Hill Park
NORTH CIRCULAR ROAD
FALLODEN WAY A1
LYTTELTON ROAD
AYLMER ROAD
FINCHLEY ROAD
REGENT'S PARK ROAD
EAST END ROAD
HENDON LANE
HENDON WAY
GOLDERS GREEN ROAD
NORTH END ROAD
NORTH END WAY
SPANIARDS ROAD
HEATH STREET
FITZJOHN'S AV
ROSSLYN HILL
HAVERSTOCK HILL
CRICKLEWOOD LANE
CRICKLEWOOD BROADWAY
SHOOT-UP HILL
IVERSON ROAD
FORTUNE GN RD
GREAT NORTH ROAD
HIGH RD
FORTIS GREEN
HAMPSTEAD LANE
Golders Green Station
Hampstead Stn
Hampstead Heath Stn
Finchley Road & Frognal Station
West Hampstead Station
Finchley Road Station
East Finchley Station
Royal Free Hospital
Kenwood House
Spaniards Inn
Hampstead Golf Club
Highgate Golf Club
97
118
137

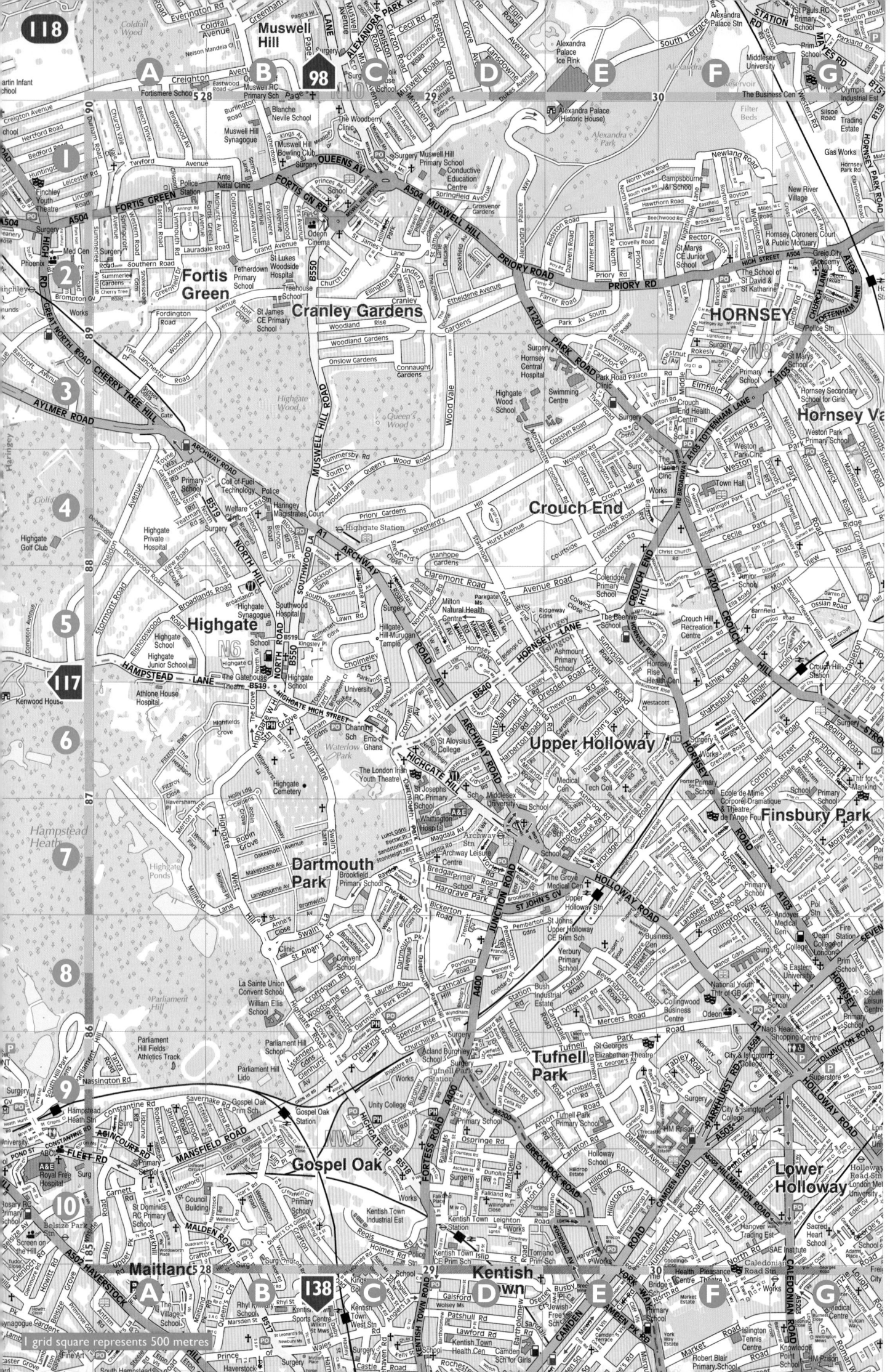

118
98
117
138
Muswell Hill
Fortis Green
Cranley Gardens
Alexandra Palace Ice Rink
Alexandra Palace (Historic House)
Alexandra Park
HORNSEY
Hornsey Vale
Crouch End
Highgate
Highgate Wood
Queen's Wood
Highgate Cemetery
Waterlow Park
Highgate Ponds
Hampstead Heath
Parliament Hill
Parliament Hill Fields Athletics Track
Parliament Hill Lido
Dartmouth Park
Upper Holloway
Finsbury Park
Tufnell Park
Gospel Oak
Kentish Town
Lower Holloway
Maitland Park
Kenwood House
Royal Free Hospital
Whittington Hospital
HM Prison
FORTIS GREEN
MUSWELL HILL
PRIORY ROAD
PARK ROAD
ARCHWAY ROAD
GREAT NORTH ROAD
AYLMER ROAD
CHERRY TREE HILL
NORTH HILL
HAMPSTEAD LANE
HIGHGATE HIGH STREET
HIGHGATE HILL
ARCHWAY ROAD
JUNCTION ROAD
HOLLOWAY ROAD
HORNSEY ROAD
CROUCH HILL
CROUCH END HILL
HORNSEY LANE
TOTTENHAM LANE
FORTESS ROAD
KENTISH TOWN ROAD
CAMDEN ROAD
CALEDONIAN ROAD
BRECKNOCK ROAD
HAVERSTOCK HILL
MANSFIELD ROAD
AGINCOURT RD
FLEET RD
MALDEN ROAD
MUSWELL HILL ROAD
SOUTHWOOD LA
QUEENS AV
1 grid square represents 500 metres

Noel Park
West Green
Tottenham Hale
South Tottenham
Harringay
Stroud Green
Stamford Hill
Upper Clapton
STOKE NEWINGTON
Shacklewell
Highbury
Canonbury
99
120
139
H
J
K
L
M
N
P
1
2
3
4
5
6
7
8
9
10
N4
N5
N15
N16
Finsbury Park
Clissold Park
Downhills Park
Abney Park Cemetery
Hackney Downs
Highbury Fields
Arsenal FC (Emirates Stadium)
Finsbury Park Track
Seven Sisters Station
Finsbury Park Station
Harringay Green Lanes Stn
Harringay Station
Stamford Hill Stn
South Tottenham Stn
Stoke Newington Station
Rectory Road Station
Manor House Station
Turnpike Lane Station
Tottenham Hale Station
Arsenal Station
Drayton Park Station
Canonbury Stn
Highbury & Islington Stn
GREEN LANES
SEVEN SISTERS ROAD
HIGH ROAD
STAMFORD HILL
STOKE NEWINGTON HIGH ST
WEST GREEN ROAD
ST ANN'S ROAD
AMHURST PARK
CLAPTON COMMON
MANOR ROAD
LORDSHIP PARK
BROWNSWOOD ROAD
BLACKSTOCK ROAD
HOLLOWAY ROAD
HIGHBURY PARK
HIGHBURY GROVE
BALLS POND ROAD
DALSTON LANE
GRAHAM ROAD
NORTHWOLD ROAD
TURNPIKE LANE
WESTBURY AVENUE
BROAD LANE
PHILIP LANE
ALBION ROAD

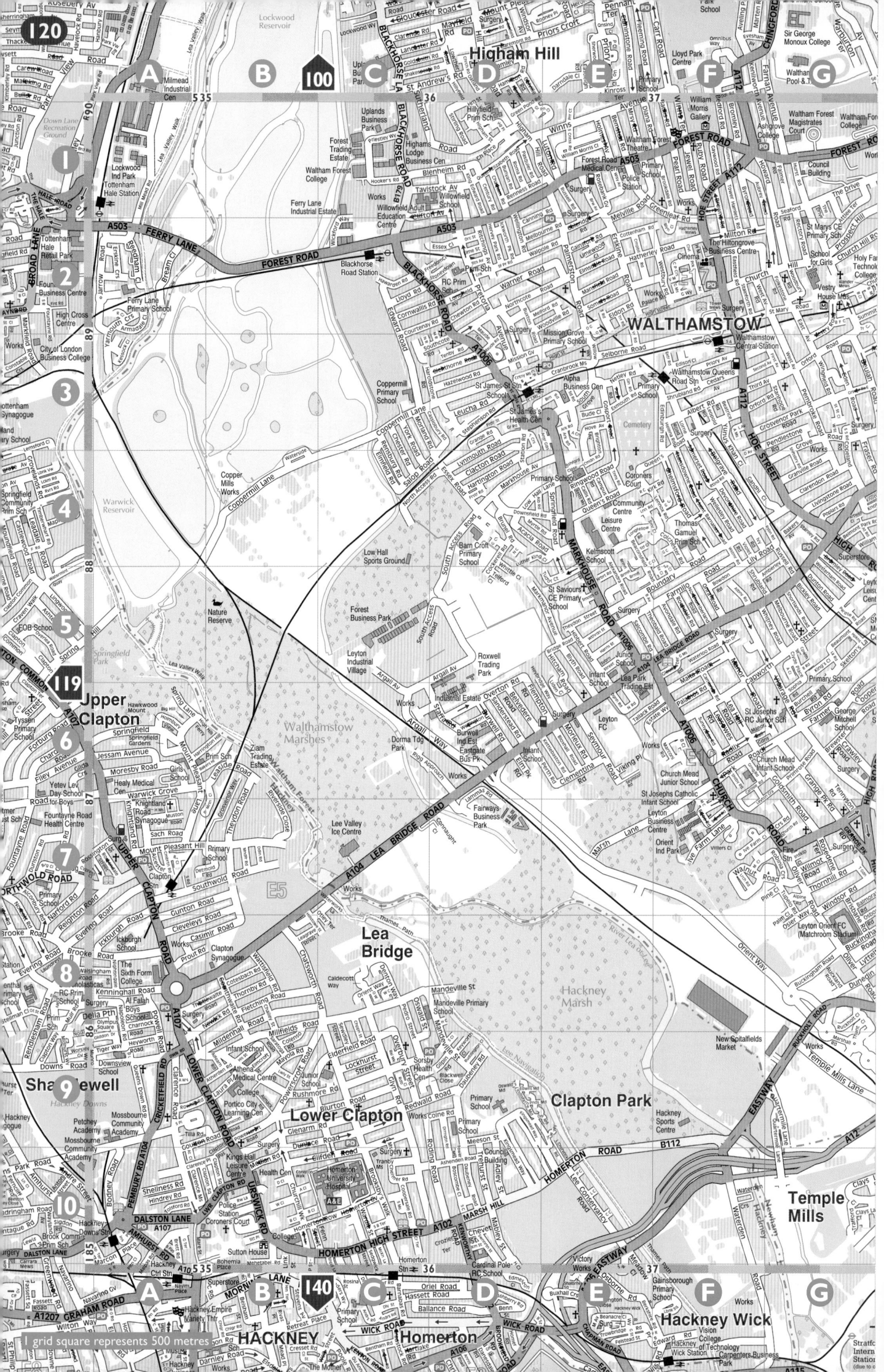

120
100
119
140
A
B
C
D
E
F
G
1
2
3
4
5
6
7
8
9
10
Higham Hill
WALTHAMSTOW
Upper Clapton
Lea Bridge
Lower Clapton
Clapton Park
Hackney Marsh
Walthamstow Marshes
Shacklewell
Temple Mills
HACKNEY
Homerton
Hackney Wick
Lockwood Reservoir
Warwick Reservoir
Sir George Monoux College
Waltham Forest College
Waltham Forest Magistrates Court
Lloyd Park Centre
William Morris Gallery
Forest Road Medical Cen
Willowfield School
Ferry Lane Industrial Estate
Tottenham Hale Station
Tottenham Hale Retail Park
Blackhorse Road Station
Walthamstow Central Station
Walthamstow Queens Road Stn
St James St Stn
Ferry Lane Primary School
City of London Business College
Coppermill Primary School
Copper Mills Works
Nature Reserve
Low Hall Sports Ground
Forest Business Park
Leyton Industrial Village
Roxwell Trading Park
Lee Valley Ice Centre
Fairways Business Park
Leyton FC
Leyton Orient FC (Matchroom Stadium)
New Spitalfields Market
Hackney Sports Centre
Homerton University Hospital
Kings Hall Leisure Centre
The Sixth Form College
Clapton Synagogue
Mossbourne Community Academy
Hackney Downs
Hackney Downs Stn
Hackney Empire Variety Thtr
Sutton House
Gainsborough Primary School
Vision College of Technology
Hackney Wick Station
FOREST ROAD
FERRY LANE
BLACKHORSE ROAD
HOE STREET
MARKHOUSE ROAD
LEA BRIDGE ROAD
CHURCH ROAD
UPPER CLAPTON ROAD
LOWER CLAPTON ROAD
HOMERTON HIGH STREET
HOMERTON ROAD
EASTWAY
RUCKHOLT ROAD
WICK ROAD
GRAHAM ROAD
DALSTON LANE
A503
A1006
A104
A107
A112
A102
A12
B112
E5
E10
E17
535
36
37
1 grid square represents 500 metres

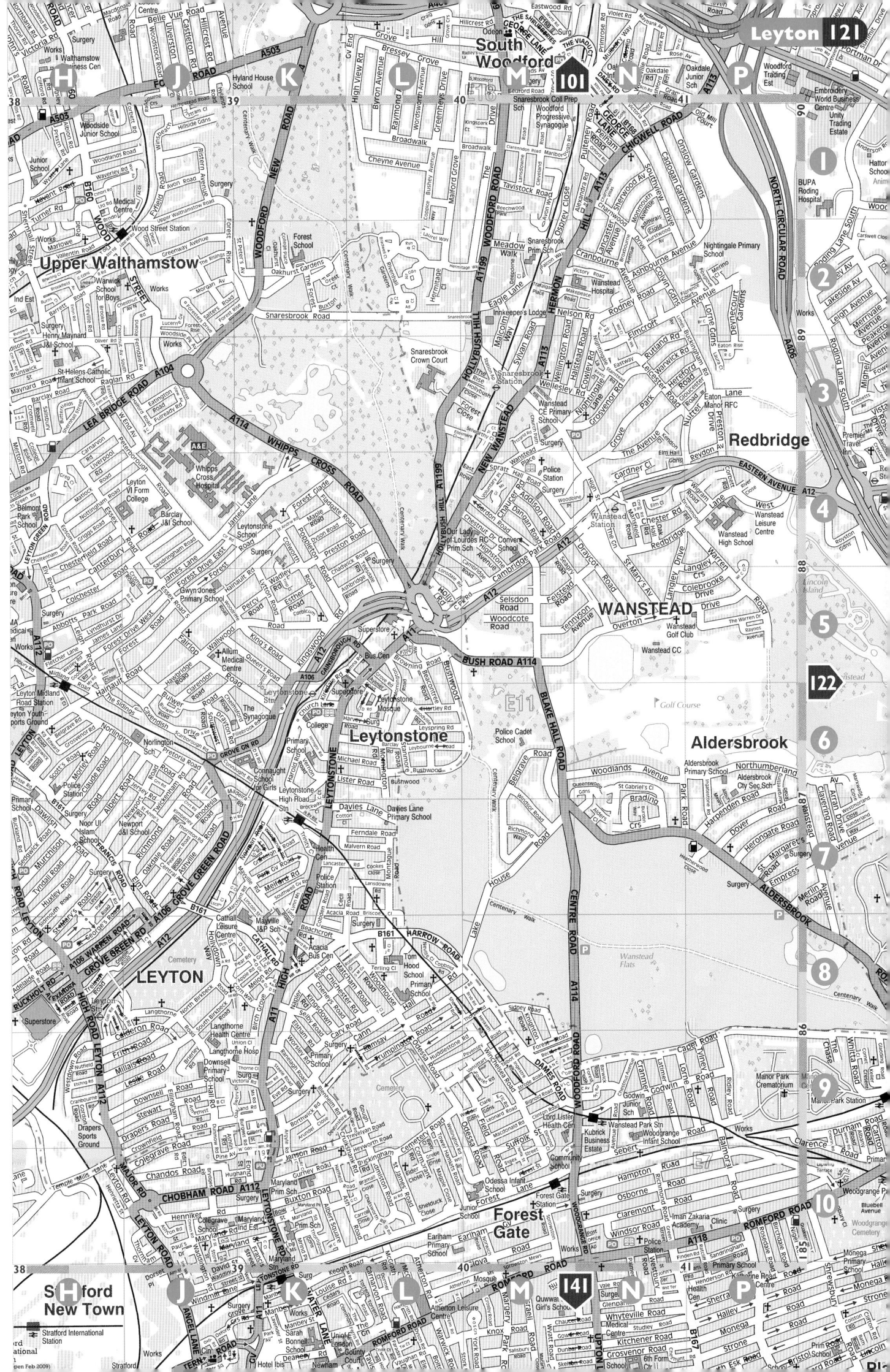
South Woodford
101
Upper Walthamstow
Redbridge
WANSTEAD
Leytonstone
Aldersbrook
LEYTON
Forest Gate
Stratford New Town
122
141
H
J
K
L
M
N
P
1
2
3
4
5
6
7
8
9
10
WOODFORD NEW ROAD
WHIPPS CROSS ROAD
LEA BRIDGE ROAD
HOLLYBUSH HILL
WOODFORD ROAD
NEW WANSTEAD
HERMON HILL
CHIGWELL ROAD
NORTH CIRCULAR ROAD
EASTERN AVENUE
CAMBRIDGE PARK ROAD
BUSH ROAD A114
BLAKE HALL ROAD
CENTRE ROAD
ALDERSBROOK ROAD
GROVE GREEN ROAD
HIGH ROAD LEYTON
LEYTONSTONE RD
CHOBHAM ROAD A112
ROMFORD ROAD
HARROW ROAD
DAMES ROAD
WOODGRANGE RD
Snaresbrook Road
Snaresbrook Crown Court
Snaresbrook Station
Whipps Cross Hospital
Wanstead Station
Wanstead Golf Club
Golf Course
Wanstead Flats
Wood Street Station
Leyton Midland Road Station
Leytonstone High Road Stn
Wanstead Park Stn
Forest Gate Station
Manor Park Station
Stratford International Station
Manor Park Crematorium
Cemetery
E11
E18
E7

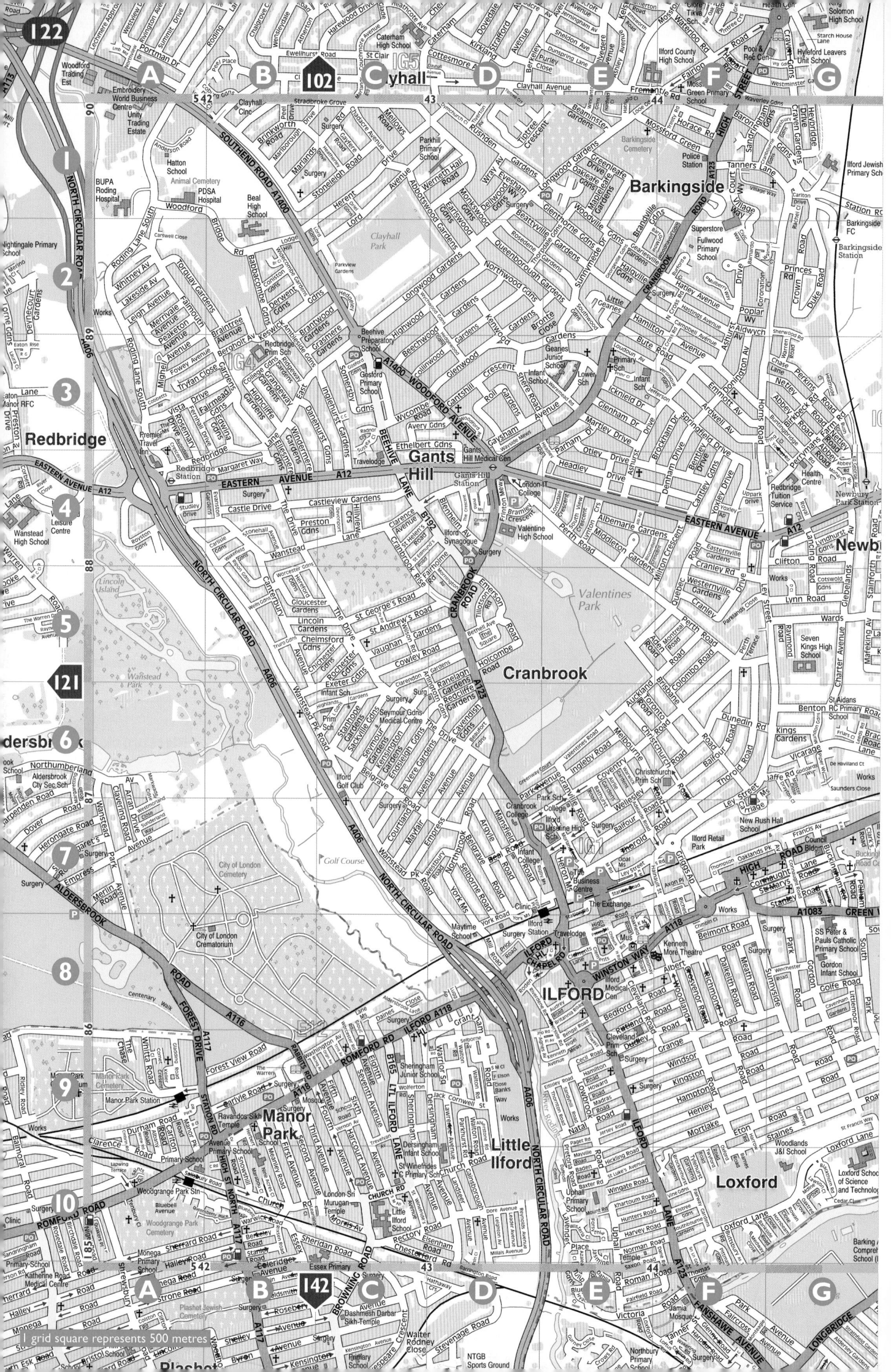

122
102
121
142
A
B
C
D
E
F
G
1
2
3
4
5
6
7
8
9
10
Redbridge
Gants Hill
Barkingside
Clayhall
Cranbrook
Valentines Park
ILFORD
Manor Park
Little Ilford
Loxford
City of London Cemetery
City of London Crematorium
Wanstead Park
NORTH CIRCULAR ROAD
EASTERN AVENUE
SOUTHEND ROAD A1400
A1400 WOODFORD AVENUE
CRANBROOK ROAD
ROMFORD ROAD
ALDERSBROOK ROAD
FOREST DRIVE
HIGH STREET
ILFORD LANE
1 grid square represents 500 metres

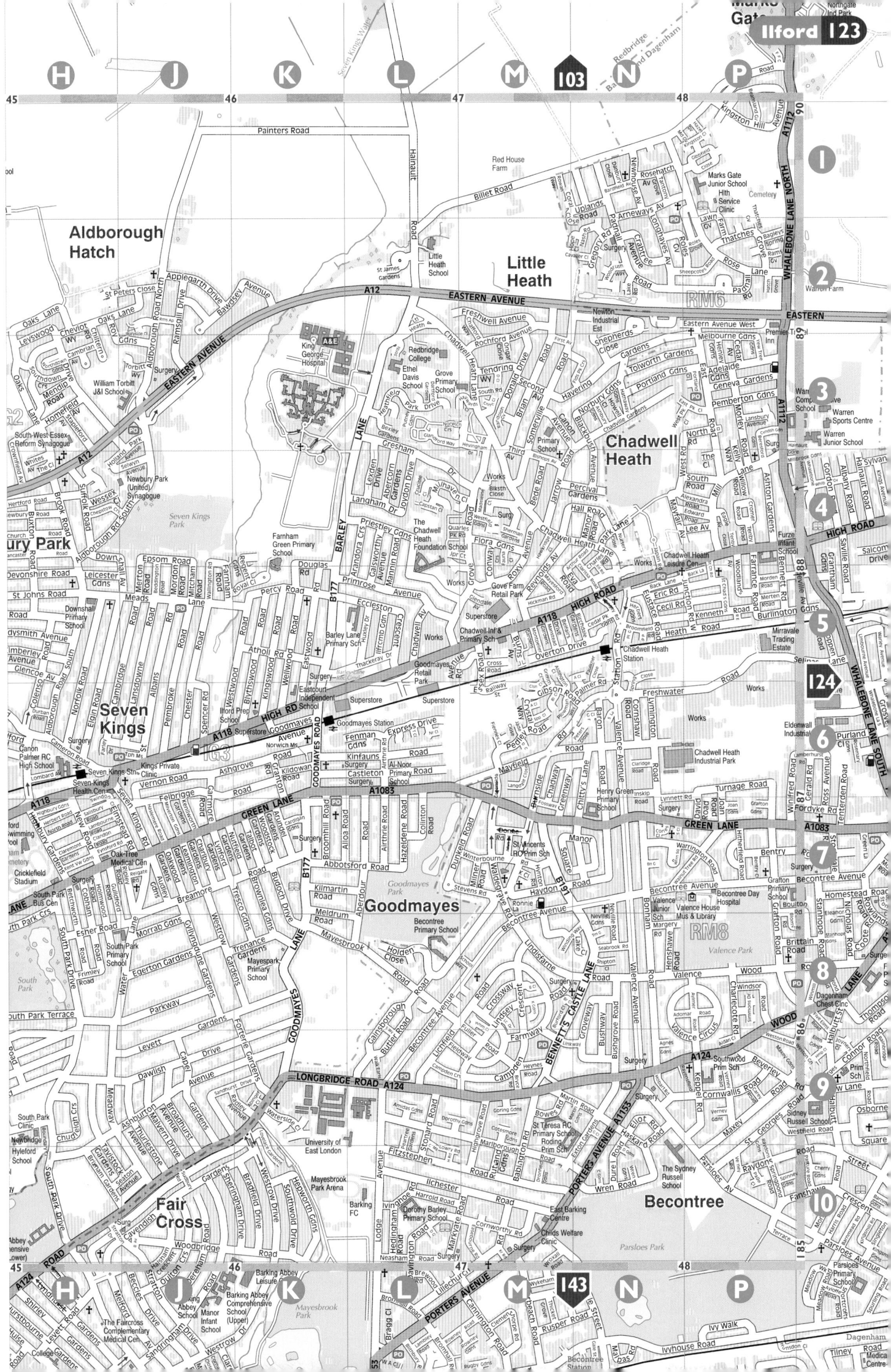
H
J
K
L
M
103
N
P
45
46
47
48
Aldborough Hatch
Little Heath
Chadwell Heath
Seven Kings
Goodmayes
Fair Cross
Becontree
Marks Gate
EASTERN AVENUE
A12
HIGH ROAD
A118
GREEN LANE
A1083
LONGBRIDGE ROAD
A124
WHALEBONE LANE NORTH
WHALEBONE LANE SOUTH
A1112
PORTERS AVENUE
A1153
GOODMAYES LANE
BARLEY LANE
B177
BENNETT'S CASTLE LANE
B191
King George Hospital
Goodmayes Station
Chadwell Heath Station
Seven Kings Stn
Seven Kings Park
South Park
Goodmayes Park
Valence Park
Parsloes Park
Mayesbrook Park
University of East London
RM6
RM8
IG3
124
143
1
2
3
4
5
6
7
8
9
10

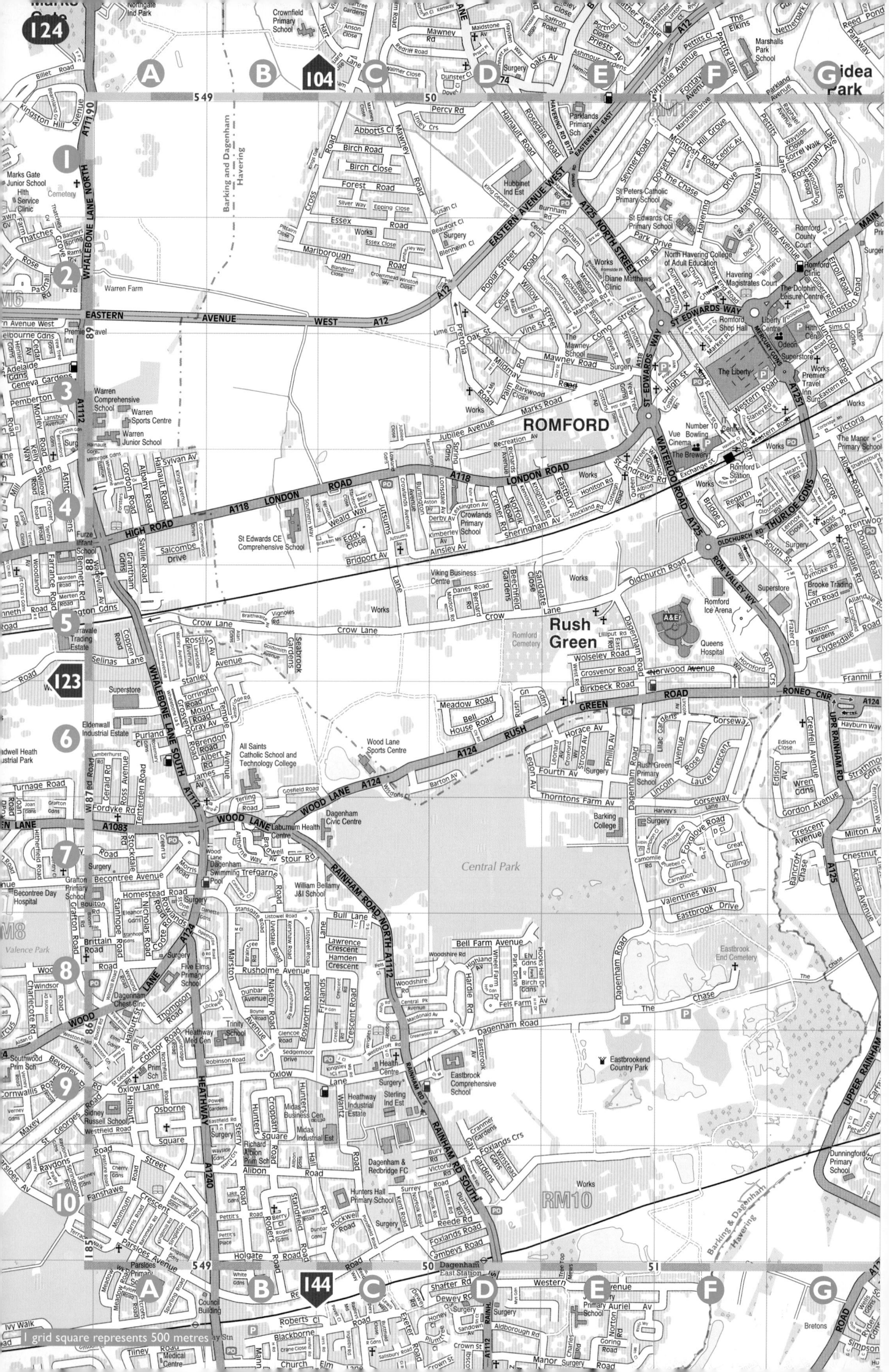
124
104
123
144
A
B
C
D
E
F
G
1
2
3
4
5
6
7
8
9
10
49
50
51
Gidea Park
ROMFORD
Rush Green
Central Park
Eastbrookend Country Park
RM1
RM7
RM10
RM6
RM8
Barking and Dagenham
Havering
WHALEBONE LANE NORTH
WHALEBONE LANE SOUTH
EASTERN AVENUE WEST
EASTERN AV - EAST
A12
A118
A124
A125
A1112
A1240
A1083
A1251
HIGH ROAD
LONDON ROAD
NORTH STREET
ST EDWARDS WAY
WATERLOO ROAD
OLDCHURCH RD
THURLOE GDNS
ROM VALLEY WY
RONEO CNR
UPR RAINHAM RD
UPPER RAINHAM ROAD
RUSH GREEN ROAD
WOOD LANE
RAINHAM ROAD NORTH
RAINHAM RD SOUTH
HEATHWAY
Crow Lane
Dagenham Road
Marks Gate Junior School
Warren Comprehensive School
Warren Junior School
Warren Farm
St Edwards CE Comprehensive School
Crowlands Primary School
Hubbinet Ind Est
Parklands Primary Sch
St Peters Catholic Primary School
St Edwards CE Primary School
North Havering College of Adult Education
Havering Magistrates Court
Romford County Court
The Dolphin Leisure Centre
The Liberty
Romford Shop Hall
Romford Station
Vue Cinema
The Brewery
Romford Ice Arena
Queens Hospital
Romford Cemetery
Viking Business Centre
Rush Green Primary School
Barking College
All Saints Catholic School and Technology College
Wood Lane Sports Centre
Dagenham Civic Centre
Laburnum Health Centre
William Bellamy J&I School
Dagenham Swimming Pool
Five Elms School
Dagenham Chest Clinic
Heathway Med Cen
Trinity School
Sidney Russell School
Richard Alibon Prim Sch
Midas Business Cen
Midas Industrial Est
Heathway Industrial Estate
Sterling Ind Est
Eastbrook Comprehensive School
Dagenham & Redbridge FC
Hunters Hall Primary School
Eastbrook End Cemetery
Dunningford Primary School
Eldenwall Industrial Estate
Furze Infant School
Grafton Primary School
Becontree Day Hospital
Valence Park
Dagenham East Station
Marshalls Park School
Superstore
Works
Surgery
1 grid square represents 500 metres

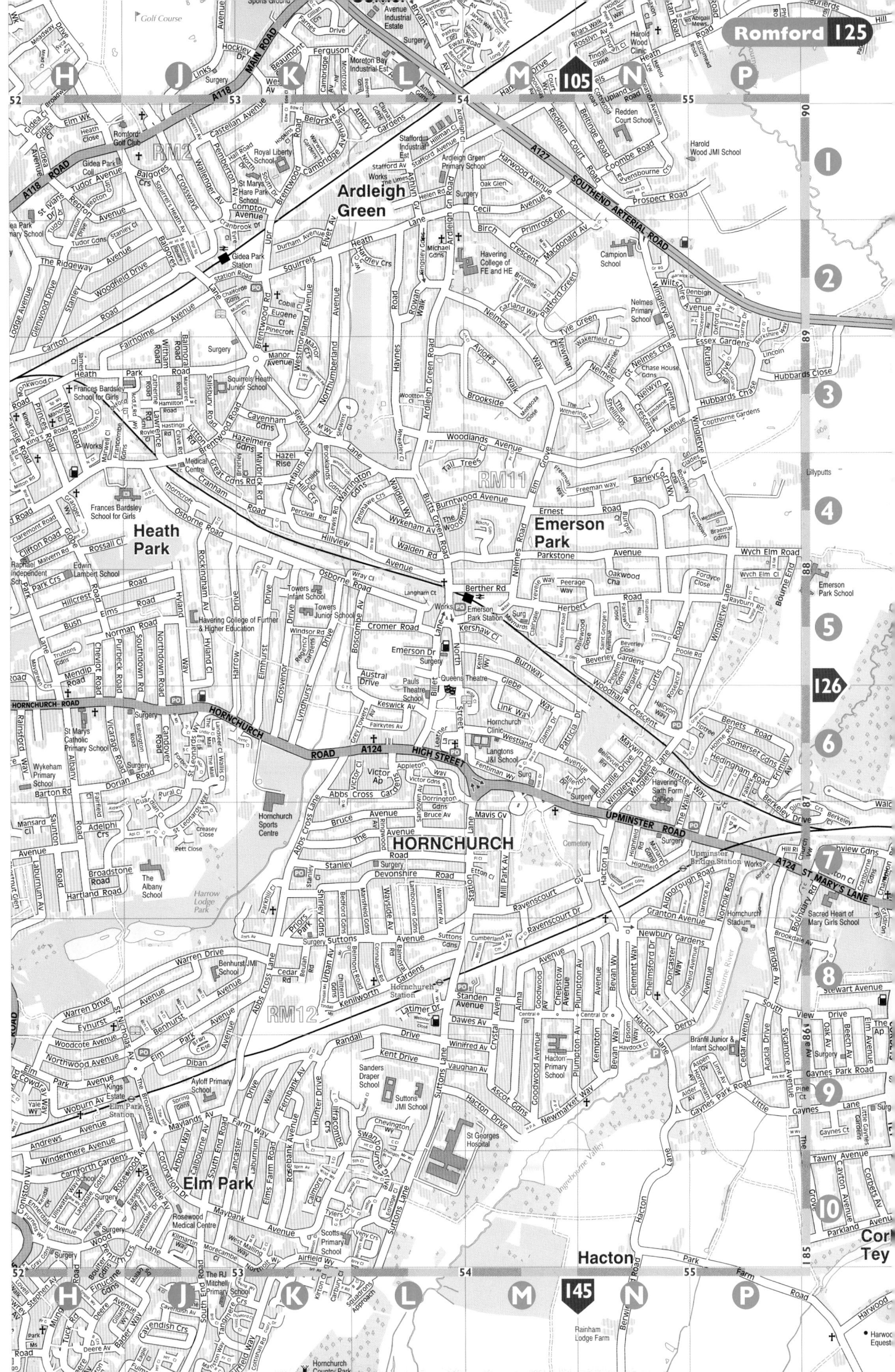
Romford 125
Golf Course
Ardleigh Green
Emerson Park
Heath Park
HORNCHURCH
Elm Park
Hacton
RM2
RM11
RM12
Gidea Park Station
Emerson Park Station
Upminster Bridge Station
Hornchurch Station
Elm Park Station
MAIN ROAD
A118
A127
SOUTHEND ARTERIAL ROAD
HORNCHURCH ROAD
A124
HIGH STREET
UPMINSTER ROAD
ST MARY'S LANE
Romford Golf Club
Royal Liberty School
Ardleigh Green Primary School
Havering College of FE and HE
Campion School
Redden Court School
Harold Wood JMI School
Nelmes Primary School
Squirrels Heath Junior School
Frances Bardsley School for Girls
Emerson Park School
Towers Infant School
Towers Junior School
Havering College of Further & Higher Education
Queens Theatre
Hornchurch Clinic
Langtons J&I School
Havering Sixth Form College
Hornchurch Sports Centre
The Albany School
Harrow Lodge Park
Cemetery
Hornchurch Stadium
Sacred Heart of Mary Girls School
Benhurst JMI School
Ayloff Primary School
Sanders Draper School
Suttons JMI School
St Georges Hospital
Hacton Primary School
Branfil Junior & Infant School
Scotts Primary School
Rosewood Medical Centre
Wykeham Primary School
St Marys Catholic Primary School
Rainham Lodge Farm
Ingrebourne Valley
Ingrebourne River
Lillyputts
105
126
145
H J K L M N P
52 53 54 55
1 2 3 4 5 6 7 8 9 10
90 89 88 87 86 185

126
106
125
146
A
B
C
D
E
F
G
1
2
3
4
5
6
7
8
9
10
UPMINSTER
Cranham
Corbets Tey
A127
SOUTHEND ARTERIAL ROAD
M25
Junction 29
B187
ST MARY'S LANE
B1421
OCKENDON ROAD
Upminster Station
Tithe Barn Museum
Upminster Golf Club
Hall Mead School
Engayne Primary School
Cranham Health Cen
Emerson Park School
Sacred Heart of Mary Girls School
St Josephs School
Upminster Primary School
Coopers Company & Coburn School
James Oglethorpe Primary School
Gaynes School
Upminster Cemetery
South Essex Crematorium
Chapmans Farm
Folkes Farm
Westbury Farm
Franks Farm
Broadfields Farm
Cranham Hall
Codham Hall
Hole Farm
Coombe Lodge
Cranham Place
Lillyputts
Hobbs Hole
Stubbers (Outdoor Pursuits Centre)
Homchurch Stadium
Golf Course
Works
Hall Lane
Bird Lane
Front Lane
Folkes Lane
Moor Lane
Pike Lane
Tomkyns Lane
Warley Road
Station Road
Corbets Tey Road
1 grid square represents 500 metres

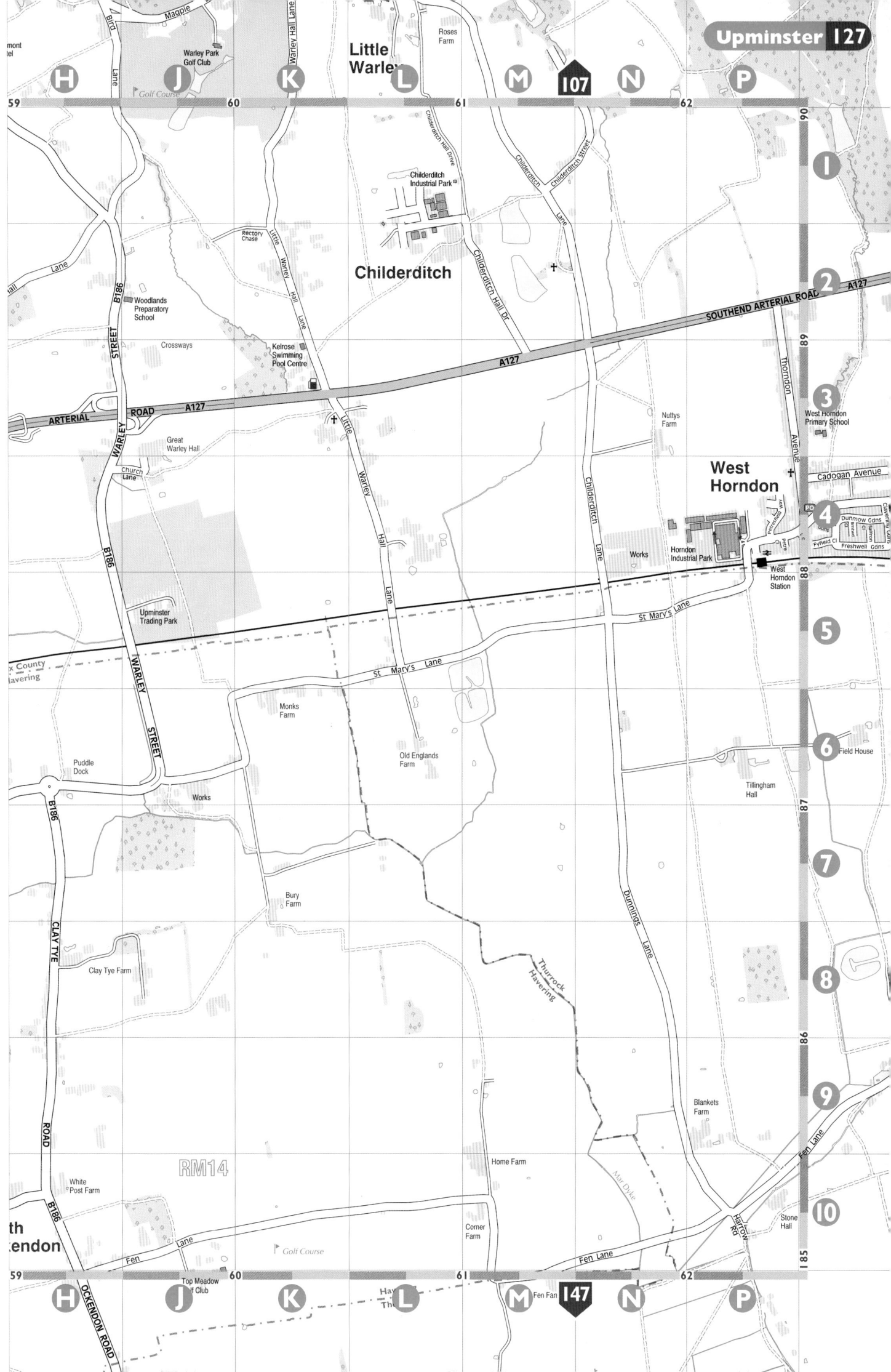

Little Warley
Roses Farm
Warley Park Golf Club
Magpie
Bird Lane
Warley Hall Lane
Golf Course
Childerditch Hall Drive
Childerditch Industrial Park
Childerditch Street
Childerditch Lane
Rectory Chase
Little Warley Hall Lane
Childerditch
Childerditch Hall Dr
SOUTHEND ARTERIAL ROAD
A127
Woodlands Preparatory School
B186
STREET
Crossways
Kelrose Swimming Pool Centre
Thorndon Avenue
ARTERIAL ROAD
WARLEY
Great Warley Hall
Nuttys Farm
West Horndon Primary School
Church Lane
West Horndon
Cadogan Avenue
Dunmow Gdns
Fyfield Cl
Freshwell Gdns
Works
Horndon Industrial Park
West Horndon Station
Upminster Trading Park
St Mary's Lane
Havering
Monks Farm
Old Englands Farm
Field House
Puddle Dock
Works
Tillingham Hall
Bury Farm
Dunnings Lane
CLAY TYE
Clay Tye Farm
Thurrock
Havering
Blankets Farm
ROAD
Fen Lane
RM14
Home Farm
White Post Farm
Mar Dyke
Harrow Rd
Stone Hall
Corner Farm
Fen Lane
Golf Course
Top Meadow Golf Club
OCKENDON ROAD
Fen Farm
107
147
H
J
K
L
M
N
P
1
2
3
4
5
6
7
8
9
10
59
60
61
62
85
86
87
88
89
90

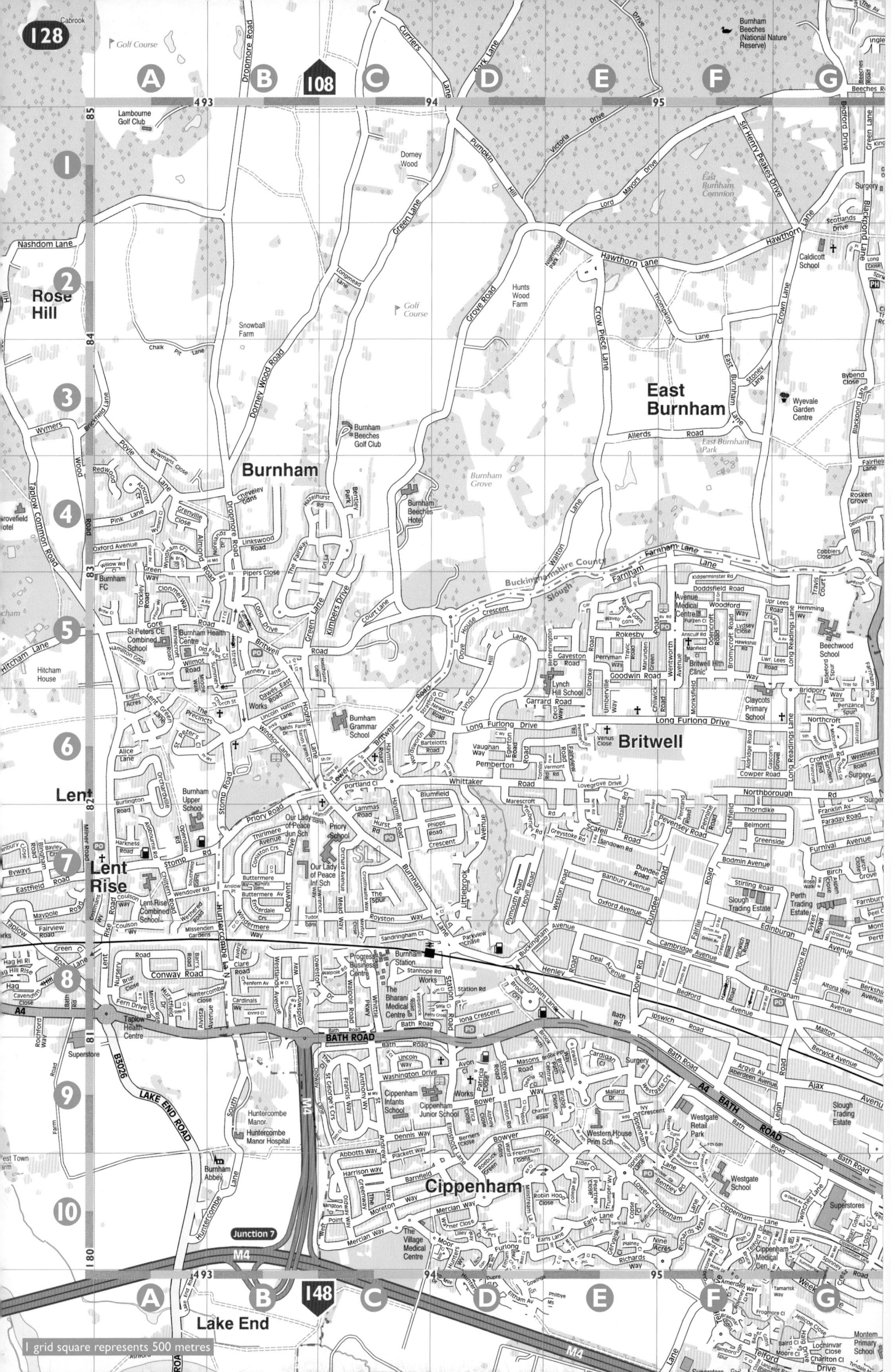

108
148
A
B
C
D
E
F
G
1
2
3
4
5
6
7
8
9
10
493
94
95
85
84
83
82
81
80
Cabrook
Golf Course
Lambourne Golf Club
Dropmore Road
Curriers Lane
Park Lane
Burnham Beeches (National Nature Reserve)
Beeches Road
Pumpkin Hill
Victoria Drive
Sir Henry Peakes Drive
Bedford Drive
Green Lane
Dorney Wood
East Burnham Common
Lord Mayors Drive
Nashdom Lane
Rose Hill
Hawthorn Lane
Caldicott School
Scotlands Drive
Blackpond Lane
Surgery
Longmead Lane
Golf Course
Hunts Wood Farm
Grove Road
Crow Piece Lane
Thompkins Lane
Crown Lane
Snowball Farm
Chalk Pit Lane
Dorney Wood Road
East Burnham
Stoney Lane
East Burnham Lane
Wyevale Garden Centre
Bybend Close
Wymers
Bricksfield Lane
Burnham Beeches Golf Club
Allerds Road
East Burnham Park
Taplow Common Road
Burnham
Burnham Grove
Fairfield Lane
Bowmans Close
Redwood
Hazelhurst Rd
Bentley Park
Burnham Beeches Hotel
Rosken Grove
Pink Lane
Grenville Close
Cheveley Gdns
Linkswood Road
Oxford Avenue
Almond Road
Walton Lane
Cobblers Close
Buckinghamshire County
Slough
Farnham Lane
Burnham FC
Tockley Road
Clonmel Way
Pipers Close
The Fairway
Kimbers Drive
Court Lane
Dove House Crescent
Kidderminster Rd
Doddsfield Road
Avenue Medical Centre
Woodford Way
Hemming Way
Travis Court
Gore Road
St Peters CE Combined School
Burnham Health Centre
Long Drive
Britwell Road
Hill Lane
Rokesby
Hitcham Lane
Hitcham House
Wilmot Road
Jenning Lane
Gaveston Road
Perryman Way
Hawkshill Rd
Beechwood School
Goodwin Road
Britwell Hlth Clinic
Long Readings Lane
Eight Acres
Lent Green Lane
The Precincts
Works
Lincoln Hatch Lane
Hogfair Lane
Burnham Grammar School
Lynch Hill School
Garrard Road
Claycots Primary School
Bridport Way
Long Furlong Drive
Northcroft
Alice Lane
Windsor Lane
Newport Road
Vaughan Way
Venus Close
Britwell
Pemberton
Westfield
Crofthill Rd
Cowper Road
Lent
Burnham Upper School
Orchardville
Stomp Road
Priory Road
Portland Cl
Whittaker Road
Blumfield
Lovegrove Drive
Northborough Road
Burlington Road
Lammas Road
Hurst Rd
Haymill Road
Marescroft Rd
Thorndike
Franklin Av
Faraday Road
Our Lady of Peace Jun Sch
Priory School
Phipps Road
Crescent
Scafell Road
Pevensey Road
Belmont
Greenside
Harkness Road
Aldborough Rd
Opendale Rd
Thirlmere Avenue
Coniston Crs
Greystoke Rd
Sandown Rd
Furnival Avenue
Lent Rise
Stomp Rd
SL1
Littlebrook Avenue
Dundee Road
Bodmin Avenue
Birch Grove
Eastfield Road
Lent Rise Combined School
Chiltern Road
Wendover Rd
Buttermere Av
Derwent Drive
Our Lady of Peace Inf Sch
Orchard Avenue
Burnham Lane
Banbury Avenue
Stirling Road
Perth Trading Estate
Byways
Maypole Road
Fairview Road
Coulson Way
Wethered Road
Missenden Gardens
Huntercombe Lane N
Windermere Way
Royston Way
The Spur
Plymouth Road
Yeovil Road
Weston Road
Oxford Avenue
Slough Trading Estate
Edinburgh Avenue
Taplow Road
Sandringham Ct
Parkview Chase
Buckingham Avenue
Cambridge Avenue
Green Lane
Conway Road
Clare Road
Westlands Avenue
Progress Business Centre
Burnham Station
Stannope Rd
Works
Station Road
Henley Road
Deal Avenue
Dover Rd
Bedford Avenue
Liverpool Rd
Altona Way
Berkshire Avenue
Nursery
Briar Close
Fern Drive
Huntercombe Close
Cardinals Wk
Walpole Road
Whittle Pkwy
The Bharani Medical Centre
Station Rd
Iona Crescent
Ipswich Road
Buckingham Avenue
A4
Taplow Health Centre
Bath Road
BATH ROAD
Bath Rd
Malton Avenue
Superstore
B3026
LAKE END ROAD
Lincoln Way
Washington Drive
Avon Cl
Masons Road
Cardigan Cl
Surgery
Argyll Av
Aberdeen Avenue
Ajax Avenue
Berwick Avenue
Westgate Crs
A4 BATH ROAD
M4
Cippenham Infants School
Cippenham Junior School
Works
Ivy Crescent
Westgate Retail Park
Slough Trading Estate
Huntercombe Manor
Huntercombe Manor Hospital
Dennis Way
Berners Close
Bowyer Drive
Western House Prim Sch
Abbotts Way
Plackett Way
Frenchum Gdns
Bath Road
Burnham Abbey
Harrison Way
Barnfield
Cippenham
Robin Hood Close
Alder Cl
Westgate School
Twinches Lane
Superstores
Mercian Way
Lower Cippenham Lane
Cippenham Lane
Earls Lane
Nine Acres
Richards Way
Cippenham Medical Cen.
Junction 7
The Village Medical Centre
Moor
Furlong
Huntercombe Lane
Amerden Way
Tamarisk Way
Frogmore Cl
Eltham Av
Philbye Ms
Lake End
Telford Drive
Montem Primary School
Lochinvar Close
Charlton Cl
1 grid square represents 500 metres

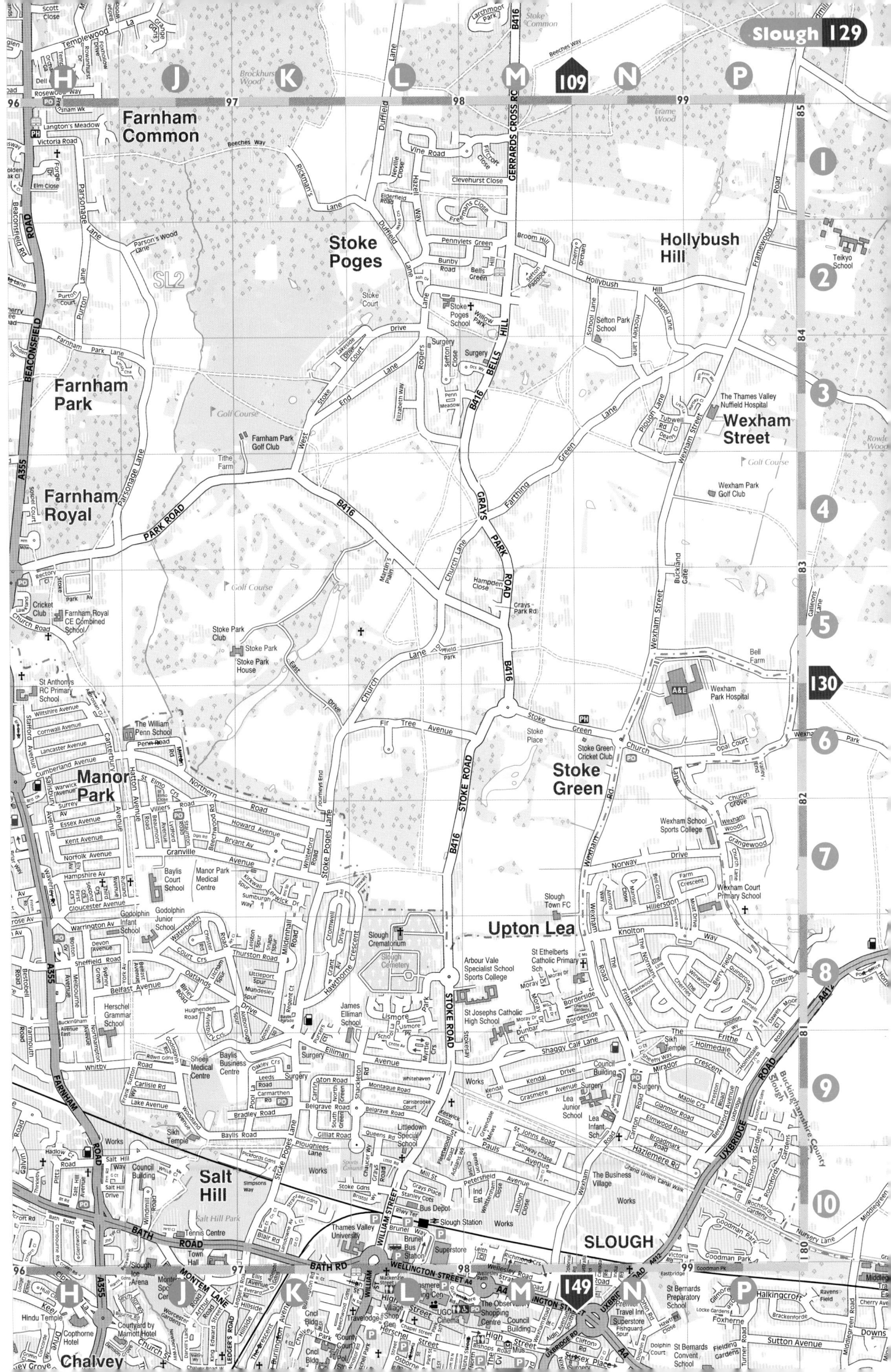

Slough 129
109
130
149
Farnham Common
Farnham Park
Farnham Royal
Stoke Poges
Hollybush Hill
Wexham Street
Stoke Green
Manor Park
Upton Lea
Salt Hill
SLOUGH
Chalvey
SL2
Stoke Common
Brockhurst Wood
Frame Wood
Beeches Way
Templewood La
Rosewood Way
Victoria Road
Langton's Meadow
Parsonage Lane
Parson's Wood Lane
Purton Lane
Farnham Park Lane
BEACONSFIELD ROAD
A355
FARNHAM ROAD
PARK ROAD
B416
GERRARDS CROSS RD
BELLS HILL
GRAYS PARK ROAD
STOKE ROAD
Duffield Lane
Rickman's Lane
Vine Road
Clevehurst Close
Pennylets Green
Bunby Road
Bells Green
Stoke Court
Stoke Poges School
Stoke Court Drive
Stoke End Lane
Rogers Lane
Surgery
Hollybush Hill
Sefton Park School
School Lane
Hockley Lane
Chapel Lane
Framewood Road
Teikyo School
The Thames Valley Nuffield Hospital
Plough Lane
Wexham Street
Golf Course
Wexham Park Golf Club
Farnham Park Golf Club
Tithe Farm
West End Lane
Farthing Green Lane
Church Lane
Hampden Close
Grays Park Rd
Martin's Plain
Stoke Park Club
Stoke Park
Stoke Park House
East Drive
Church Lane
Duffield Park
Fir Tree Avenue
Stoke Green
Stoke Place
Stoke Green Cricket Club
Bell Farm
Wexham Park Hospital
A&E
Wexham Park Lane
Opal Court
Church Lane
Wexham School Sports College
Wexham Court Primary School
Norway Drive
Hillersdon
Knolton Way
Slough Town FC
Rectory Cl
Cricket Club
Farnham Royal CE Combined School
Church Road
St Anthonys RC Primary School
The William Penn School
Penn Road
Northern Road
Canterbury Avenue
Stafford Avenue
Wiltshire Avenue
Cornwall Avenue
Lancaster Avenue
Cumberland Avenue
Salisbury Avenue
Hatton Avenue
Essex Avenue
Kent Avenue
Norfolk Avenue
Hampshire Av
Gloucester Avenue
Warrington Av
Godolphin Infant School
Godolphin Junior School
Baylis Court School
Manor Park Medical Centre
Howard Avenue
Bryant Av
Granville Avenue
Beechwood Rd
Whiteford Road
Stoke Poges Lane
Journeys End
Cromwell Drive
Hawthorne Crescent
Slough Crematorium
Slough Cemetery
Arbour Vale Specialist School Sports College
St Ethelberts Catholic Primary Sch
St Josephs Catholic High School
Moray Dr
Borderside
Shaggy Calf Lane
Kendal Drive
Grasmere Avenue
Council Building
Lea Junior School
Lea Infant Sch
The Sikh Temple
Holmedale
Mirador Crescent
Frithe
Glanmor Road
Elmwood Road
Broadmark Road
Hazlemere Rd
Maple Crs
Beresford Avenue
UXBRIDGE ROAD
A412
Buckinghamshire County
Rochfords Gardens
Goodman Park
Nursery Lane
Middlegreen Road
Sheffield Road
Belfast Avenue
Herschel Grammar School
Thurston Road
Oatlands Dr
Mildenhall Road
James Elliman School
Elliman Avenue
Lismore Park
Sheeji Medical Centre
Baylis Business Centre
Whitby Road
Carlisle Rd
Lake Avenue
Woodland Avenue
Bradley Road
Baylis Road
Sikh Temple
Montague Road
Belgrave Road
Shackleton Rd
Littledown Special School
Queens Rd
Gilliat Road
Ploughlees Lane
Pickfords Gdns
Works
Sports Ground
Mill St
Petersfield Avenue
Ind Est
Albion Close
St Johns Road
Galloway Chase
Grand Union Canal Walk
The Business Village
Keswick Court
Salt Hill Way
Salt Hill Drive
Salt Hill Park
Tennis Centre
Simpsons Way
Stoke Gdns
Bristol Wy
Grays Place
Stanley Cots
Bus Depot
Thames Valley University
WILLIAM STREET
Brunel Way
Brunel Bus Station
Slough Station
Superstore
BATH ROAD
BATH RD
Town Hall
Slough Ice Arena
MONTEM LANE
WELLINGTON STREET A4
Wellesley Road
A4
The Observatory Shopping Centre
Council Building
UGC Cinema
High Street
Herschel Street
Travelodge
Mackenzie Street
Hindu Temple
Copthorne Hotel
Courtyard by Marriott Hotel
Church St
LEDGER'S ROAD
Burlington Avenue
Chalvey Park
Cncl Bldg
County Court
Chapel Street
Osborne
Bishops Road
Mus
UXBRIDGE RD
Sussex Place
Clifton Rd
St Bernards Preparatory School
Premier Travel Inn
Superstore
Fishguard Spur
Halkingcroft
Locke Gardens
Foxherne
Brackenforde
Ravens Field
Cherry Av
Sutton Avenue
Downs
Fielding Gardens
St Bernards Convent School
Dolphin Court
Hadlow Ct
Council Building
Windmill Rd
96
97
98
99
85
84
83
82
81
80
H
J
K
L
M
N
P
1
2
3
4
5
6
7
8
9
10

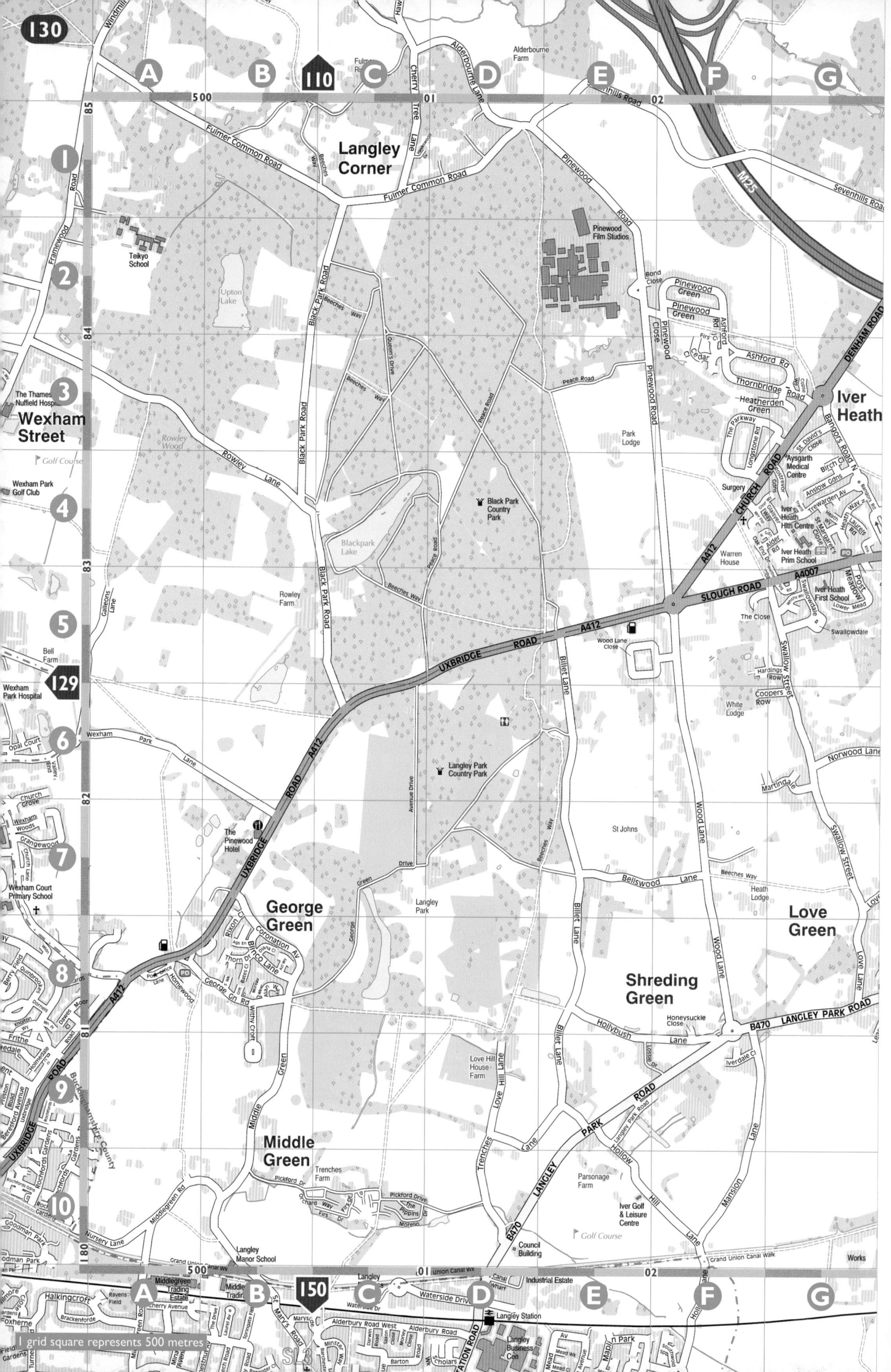

130
110
129
150
A
B
C
D
E
F
G
1
2
3
4
5
6
7
8
9
10
500
01
02
85
84
83
82
81
180
Langley Corner
Wexham Street
George Green
Middle Green
Shreding Green
Love Green
Iver Heath
Fulmer Common Road
Alderbourne Lane
Alderbourne Farm
Sevenhills Road
Pinewood Road
Pinewood Film Studios
Pinewood Green
Ashford Rd
Thornbridge Road
Heatherden Green
DENHAM ROAD
CHURCH ROAD
Bangors Road N
Aysgarth Medical Centre
Surgery
Iver Heath Hlth Centre
Iver Heath Prim School
Iver Heath First School
Warren House
SLOUGH ROAD
A4007
A412
UXBRIDGE ROAD
Wood Lane Close
Park Lodge
Peace Road
Black Park Road
Beeches Way
Queen's Drive
Black Park Country Park
Blackpark Lake
Teikyo School
Upton Lake
Rowley Wood
Rowley Lane
Rowley Farm
The Thames Nuffield Hospital
Golf Course
Wexham Park Golf Club
Galleons Lane
Bell Farm
Wexham Park Hospital
Wexham Park Lane
Opal Court
Church Grove
Wexham Woods
Grangewood
Wexham Court Primary School
The Pinewood Hotel
Langley Park Country Park
Avenue Drive
Langley Park
George Green
Coronation Av
Billet Lane
Bellswood Lane
St Johns
Beeches Way
Heath Lodge
Wood Lane
Swallow Street
Swallowdale
Norwood Lane
Martindale
Hardings Row
Coopers Row
White Lodge
The Close
Love Lane
Hollybush Lane
Honeysuckle Close
B470 LANGLEY PARK ROAD
Iverdale Cl
LANGLEY PARK ROAD
Hollow Hill Lane
Mansion Lane
Love Hill Lane
Love Hill House Farm
Trenches Lane
Trenches Farm
Pickford Dr
Orchard Way
Parsonage Farm
Iver Golf & Leisure Centre
Council Building
Grand Union Canal Walk
Works
Middlegreen Rd
Nursery Lane
Langley Manor School
Middlegreen Trading Estate
Industrial Estate
Waterside Drive
Langley Station
Langley Business Cen
Alderbury Road West
Alderbury Road
STATION ROAD
Halkingcroft
Brackenforde
Cherry Avenue
St Mary's Road
Buckinghamshire County
Goodman Park
M25
1 grid square represents 500 metres
SL3

Willowbank
New Denham
Dromenagh
Round Coppice Farm
Ivy House Farm
SOUTHLANDS ROAD A412
DENHAM ROAD
A412
OXFORD ROAD
A4020
Highbridge Industrial Estate
Union Business Park
Pavilions Shopping Cen
Uxbridge Station
The Chimes Shopping Cen
Civic Centre
Bus Depot
Magistrates Court
County Court
Police Station
Education Centre
Belmont Medical Centre
Hermitage Primary School
Uxbridge College
Uxbridge Common
Uxbridge CC
Uxbridge Swimming Pool
Gatting Way
PARK ROAD
B483
B467
HAREFIELD ROAD
Honeycroft Hill
RAF Uxbridge
HILLINGDON ROAD
HILLINGDON HILL
ROCKINGHAM ROAD
CROSS ST
HIGH ST
Uxbridge Moor
UXBRIDGE
Rockingham Recreation Ground
St Andrews CE Junior & Infant Sch
Whitehall Primary Sch
Uxbridge High School
Golf Course
Hillingdon Golf Club
Hillingdon Cemetery
Mansfield Farm
Brook Business Cen
Cowley Mill Industrial Est
Midas Industrial Est
Chiltern Business Village
Uxbridge Ind Est
Ind Health Clinic
Mill Swan Road Wharf Business Centre
Gas Works
Cowley Business Park
SLOUGH ROAD
ST JOHN'S ROAD
A4007
M25
COWLEY ROAD
UB8
Brunel University
Uxbridge Works
Works
Moorwards
Wyevale Garden Centre
Pield Heath School
Hillingdon Hospital
A&E
Station Road
HIGH STREET
Cowley
Palmer's Moor Lane
IVER LANE
B470
Coppins Lane
SL0
Huntsmoor Park
Cowley St Laurence CE Primary Sch
Meadow High School
A408
HIGH ROAD
Cowley Peachy
Iver
Iver Village Junior School
Iver Village Infant School
HIGH ST
Tong Industrial Estate
Lyons Industrial Estate
Lyons Ind Estate
Packet Boat Lane
Cowley Business Park
Rabbsfarm Primary School
Chantry School
FALLING LANE A408
Yiewsley
Trading Estate
Ridge Way
Grand Union Canal
Grand Union Canal Walk
Court Lane
Tapling Trading Estate
Rainbow Industrial Estate
St Matthews CE Primary School
Providence School
Yiewsley Health Centre
Independent Industrial Est
West Drayton Station
Warwick Rd
Fairway Avenue
Iver Station
Thorney
Thorney Lane South
West Drayton Prim Sch
London Air Control Cen
132
151
H J K L M N P
03 04 05 06
85 84 83 82 81 80

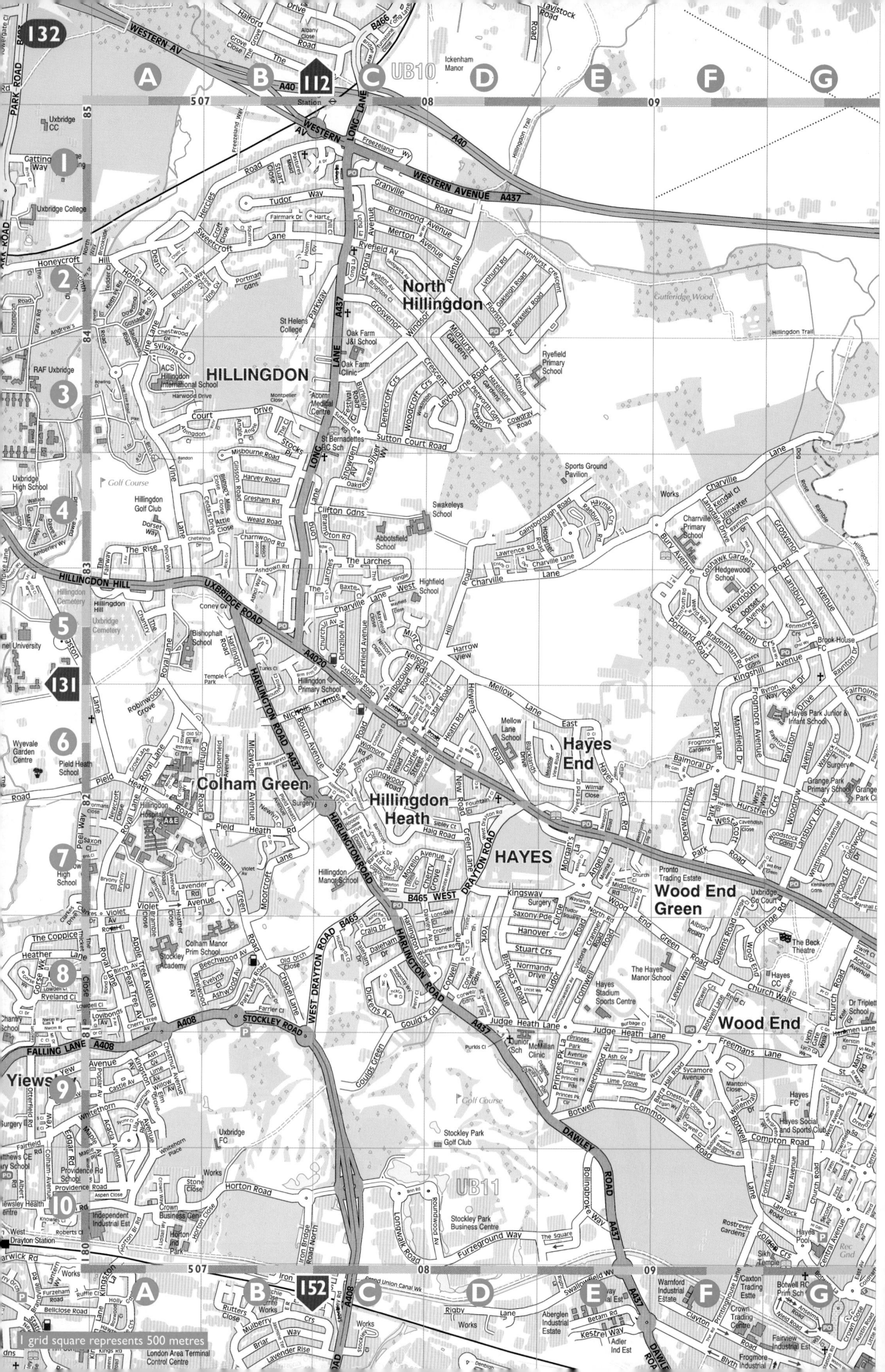

132
112
131
152
A
B
C
D
E
F
G
507
08
09
85
84
83
82
81
80
1
2
3
4
5
6
7
8
9
10
UB10
UB11
WESTERN AV
WESTERN AVENUE
A40
A437
A4020
A408
B465
B466
Station
Ickenham Manor
Hillingdon Trail
Freezeland Wy
Granville Road
Richmond Avenue
Merton Avenue
Ryefield Av
Victoria Avenue
Grosvenor
Windsor Avenue
Lynhurst Crescent
Oakleigh Road
Berkeley Road
Floriston Av
North Hillingdon
HILLINGDON
Gutteridge Wood
Uxbridge CC
Uxbridge College
RAF Uxbridge
ACS Hillingdon International School
Harwood Drive
St Helens College
Oak Farm J&I School
Oak Farm Clinic
Acorn Medical Centre
St Bernadettes RC Sch
Ryefield Primary School
Hercies Road
Tudor Way
Sweetcroft Lane
Honeycroft Hill
Honey Hill
Vine Lane
Court Drive
Sutton Court Road
Leybourne Road
Denecroft Crs
Woodcroft Crs
Midhurst Gardens
Cowdray Road
Misbourne Road
Harvey Road
Gresham Rd
Weald Road
Charnwood Rd
Clifton Gdns
Brampton Rd
Abbotsfield School
Swakeleys School
Sports Ground Pavilion
Works
Charville Lane
Charville Primary School
Hedgewood School
Gainsborough Road
Hayman Crs
Raeburn Rd
Lawrence Rd
Uxbridge High School
Golf Course
Hillingdon Golf Club
The Rise
HILLINGDON HILL
UXBRIDGE ROAD
Hillingdon Cemetery
Uxbridge Cemetery
Bishophalt School
Temple Park
Hillingdon Primary School
Highfield School
Harrow View
Mellow Lane
Mellow Lane School
Hayes End
HAYES
Kingsway
Wood End Green
Wood End
Pronto Trading Estate
Uxbridge Co Court
The Beck Theatre
Hayes Park Junior & Infant School
Grange Park Primary School
Kingshill Avenue
Lansbury Drive
Weymouth
Portland Road
Bury Avenue
Brook House FC
Wyevale Garden Centre
Pield Heath School
Pield Heath Rd
Colham Green
Hillingdon Heath
Hillingdon Hospital
A&E
HARLINGTON ROAD
Hillingdon Manor School
Colham Manor Prim School
Stockley Academy
WEST DRAYTON ROAD
STOCKLEY ROAD
FALLING LANE
Yiewsley
Uxbridge FC
Stockley Park Golf Club
Stockley Park Business Centre
Furzeground Way
Horton Road
Crown Business Cen
Independent Industrial Est
West Drayton Station
Hayes Stadium Sports Centre
The Hayes Manor School
Judge Heath Lane
McMillan Clinic
DAWLEY ROAD
Botwell Common Road
Freemans Lane
Church Walk
Hayes FC
Hayes Social and Sports Club
Compton Road
Hayes Pool
Sikh Temple
Grand Union Canal Wk
Warnford Industrial Estate
Caxton Trading Estate
Crown Trading Centre
Fairview Industrial Est
Botwell RC Prim Sch
Aberglen Industrial Estate
London Area Terminal Control Centre
1 grid square represents 500 metres

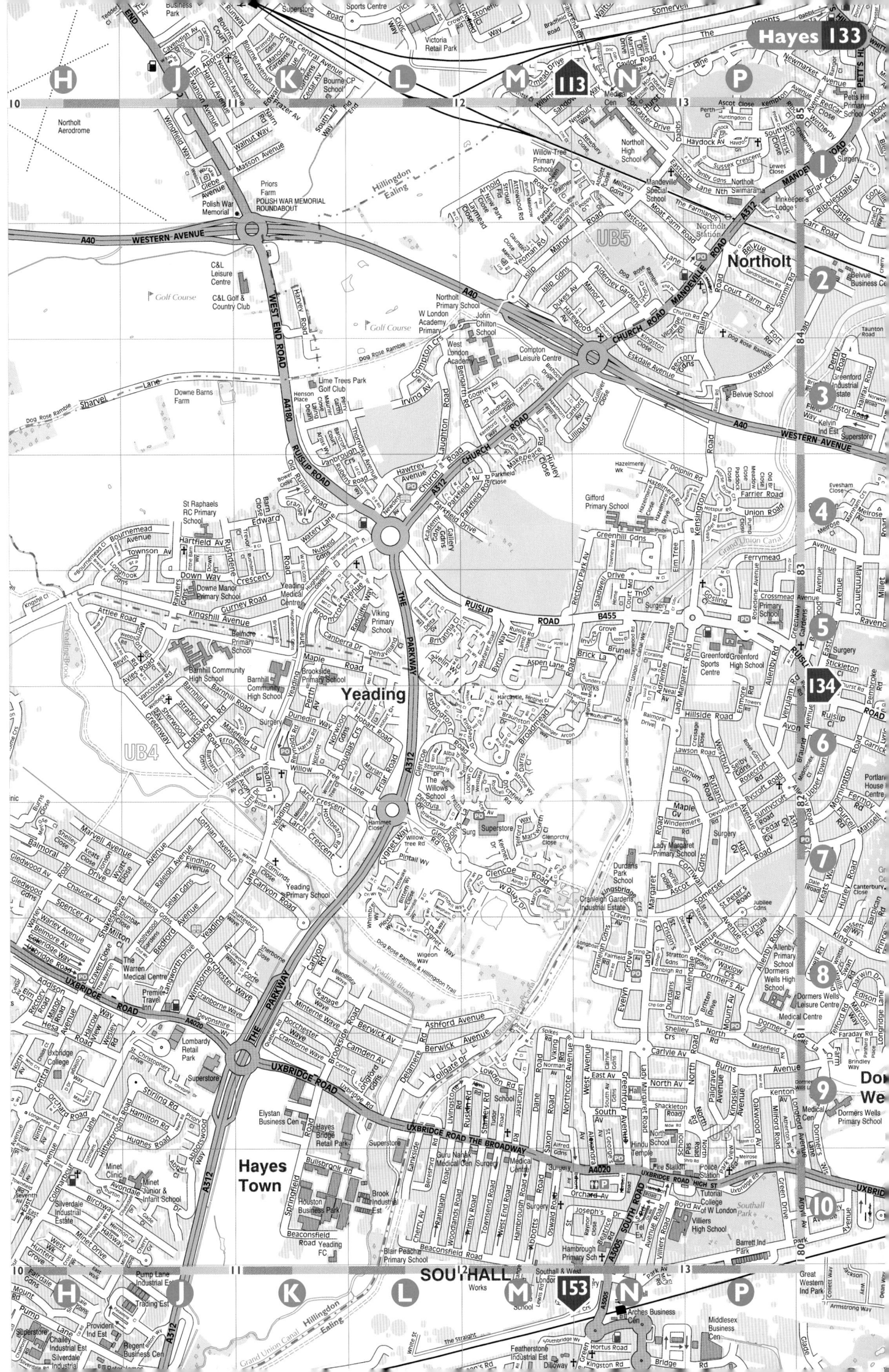
Northolt Aerodrome
Priors Farm
POLISH WAR MEMORIAL ROUNDABOUT
Polish War Memorial
A40 WESTERN AVENUE
Hillingdon
Ealing
C&L Leisure Centre
C&L Golf & Country Club
Golf Course
WEST END ROAD
A4180
Downe Barns Farm
Dog Rose Ramble
Lime Trees Park Golf Club
Northolt Primary School
W London Academy Primary
John Chilton School
West London Academy
Compton Leisure Centre
Northolt
UB5
Northolt Station
Northolt High School
Mandeville Special School
Northolt Swimarama
Innkeeper's Lodge
Belvue School
Belvue Business Cen
Greenford Industrial Estate
Kelvin Ind Est
WESTERN AVENUE
MANDEVILLE ROAD
CHURCH ROAD
A312
RUISLIP ROAD
THE PARKWAY
B455
Yeading
UB4
St Raphaels RC Primary School
Downe Manor Primary School
Belmore Primary School
Barnhill Community High School
Brookside Primary School
Viking Primary School
Gifford Primary School
Greenford Sports Centre
Greenford High School
Grand Union Canal
Yeading Brook
The Willows School
Durdans Park School
Lady Margaret Primary School
Cranleigh Gardens Industrial Estate
Allenby Primary School
Dormers Wells High School
Dormers Wells Leisure Centre
Dormers Wells Primary School
Yeading Primary School
Dog Rose Ramble & Hillingdon Trail
The Warren Medical Centre
Premier Travel Inn
Lombardy Retail Park
Superstore
Uxbridge College
UXBRIDGE ROAD
A4020
Elystan Business Cen
Hayes Bridge Retail Park
Hayes Town
Minet Clinic
Minet Junior & Infant School
Silverdale Industrial Estate
Houston Business Park
Brook Industrial Est
Yeading FC
Blair Peach Primary School
UXBRIDGE ROAD THE BROADWAY
Guru Nanak Medical Cen
Hindu Temple
Fire Station
Police Station
Tutorial College of W London
Villiers High School
Southall Park
Barrett Ind Park
UB1
SOUTHALL
Southall & West London
Hambrough Primary Sch
A3005
SOUTH ROAD
Pump Lane Industrial Est
Trading Est
Provident Ind Est
Chailey Industrial Est
Silverdale Industrial
Regent Business Cen
Featherstone Industrial Est
Arches Business Cen
Middlesex Business Cen
Great Western Ind Park
Hortus Road
Kingston Rd
Bridge
The Straight
113
134
153
H J K L M N P
10 11 12 13
1 2 3 4 5 6 7 8 9 10
85 84 83 82 81 80

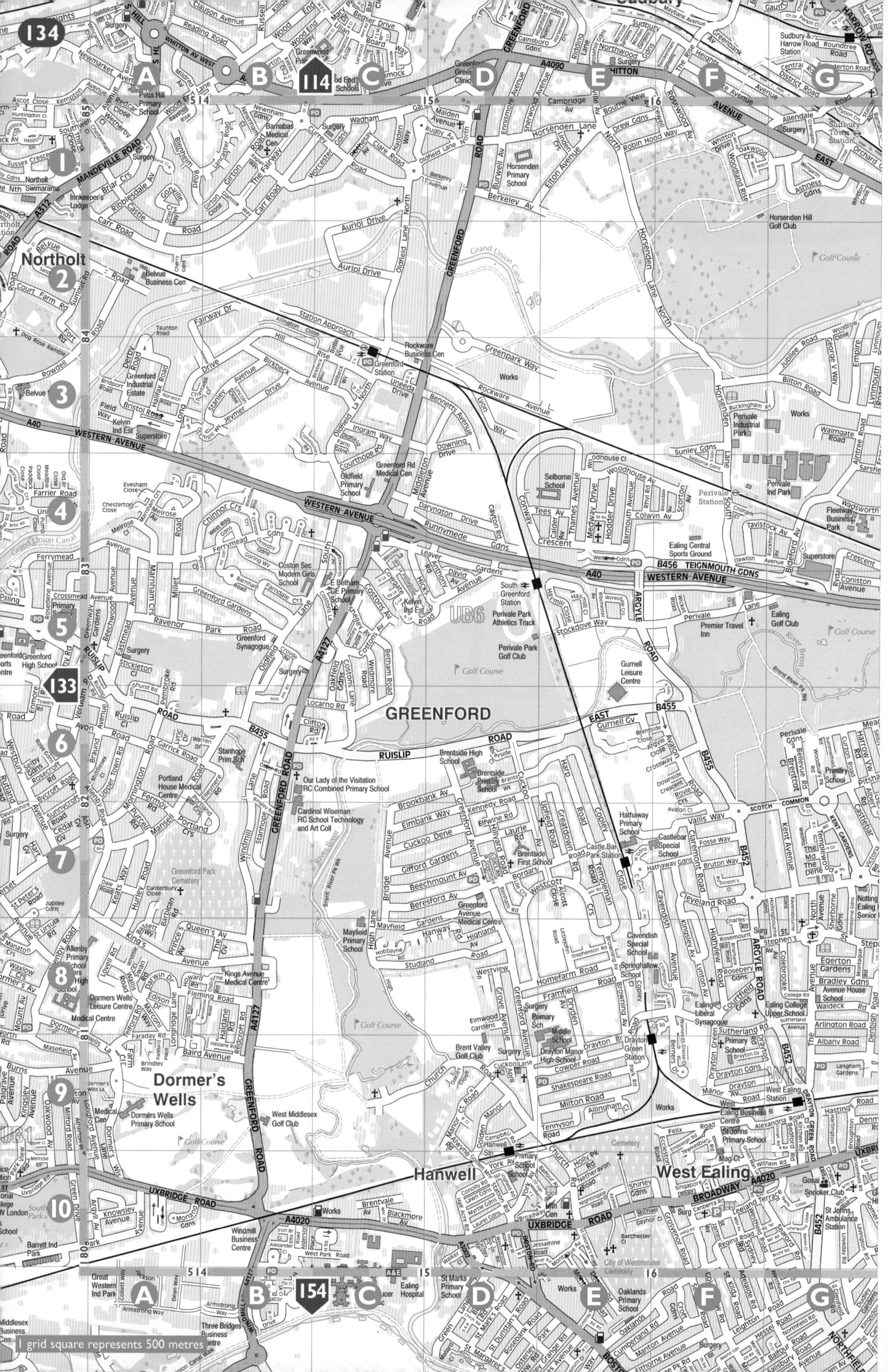
134
114
133
154
A
B
C
D
E
F
G
1
2
3
4
5
6
7
8
9
10
514
15
16
85
84
83
82
81
80
Northolt
GREENFORD
Dormer's Wells
Hanwell
West Ealing
Sudbury
UB6
UB1
W13
MANDEVILLE ROAD
A312
WHITTON AV WEST
WHITTON AVENUE
A4090
GREENFORD ROAD
A4127
WESTERN AVENUE
A40
B456 TEIGNMOUTH GDNS
ARGYLE ROAD
RUISLIP ROAD
B455
UXBRIDGE ROAD
A4020
BROADWAY
DRAYTON GREEN ROAD
B452
HARROW RD A404
Greenford Station
South Greenford Station
Perivale Station
Castle Bar Park Station
Drayton Green Station
West Ealing Station
Hanwell Stn
Sudbury & Harrow Road Station
Sudbury Town Station
Grand Union Canal
River Brent
Golf Course
Horsenden Hill Golf Club
Perivale Park Athletics Track
Perivale Park Golf Club
Ealing Golf Club
Brent Valley Golf Club
West Middlesex Golf Club
Gurnell Leisure Centre
Ealing Central Sports Ground
Greenford Park Cemetery
City of Westminster Cemetery
Ealing Hospital
Rockware Business Cen
Perivale Industrial Park
Perivale Ind Park
Fleetway Business Park
Kelvin Ind Est
Greenford Industrial Estate
Belvue Business Cen
Windmill Business Centre
Great Western Ind Park
Three Bridges Business Centre
Middlesex Business Cen
Barrett Ind Park
Works
Superstore
1 grid square represents 500 metres

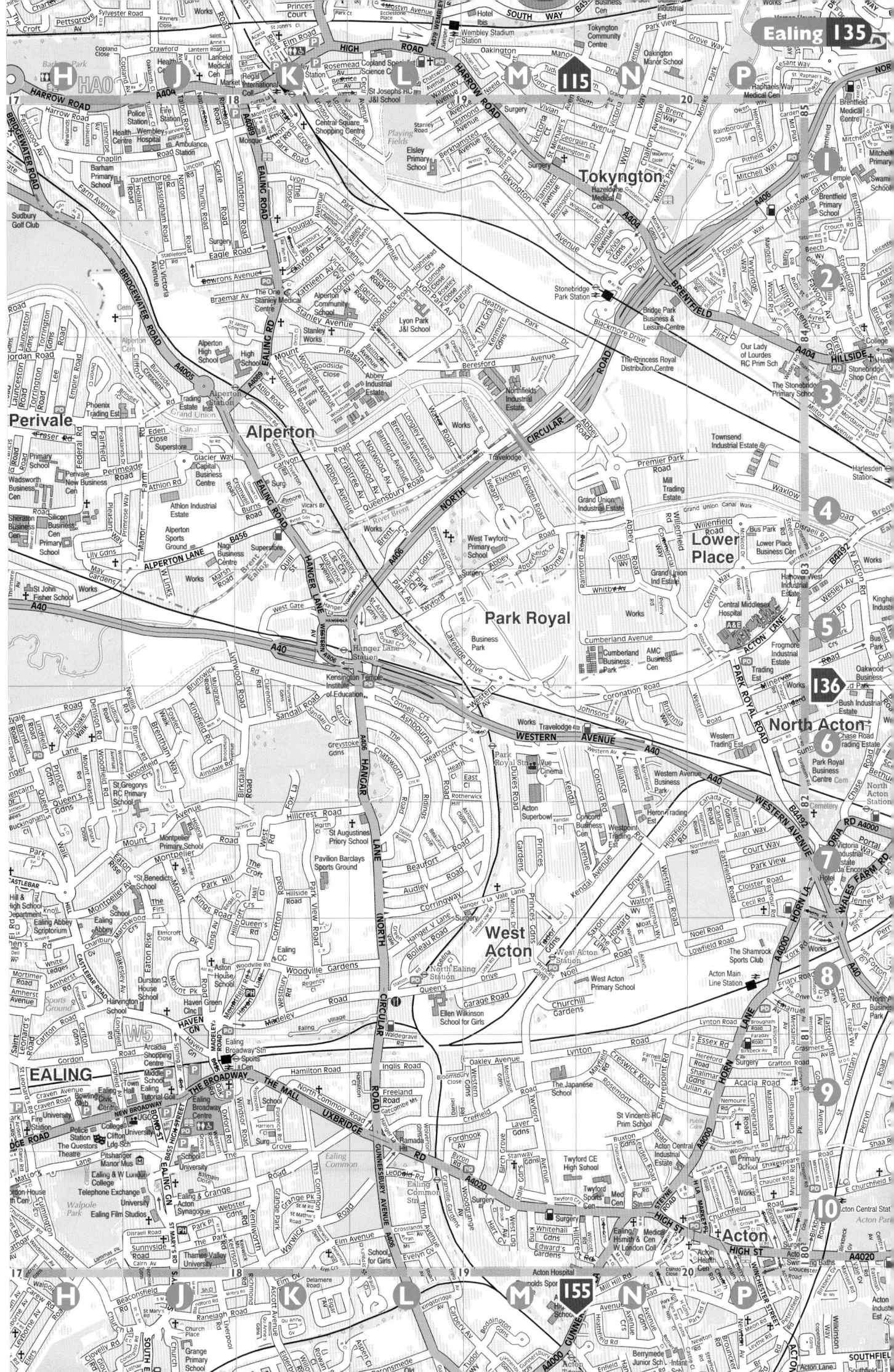
Tokyngton
Perivale
Alperton
Park Royal
Lower Place
North Acton
West Acton
EALING
Acton
HARROW ROAD
HIGH ROAD
EALING ROAD
BRIDGEWATER ROAD
HANGER LANE
NORTH CIRCULAR ROAD
WESTERN AVENUE
ALPERTON LANE
UXBRIDGE RD
THE MALL
THE BROADWAY
NEW BROADWAY
HORN LANE
HIGH ST
GUNNERSBURY AVENUE
BRENTFIELD
HILLSIDE
ACTON LANE
PARK ROYAL ROAD
Hanger Lane Station
Alperton Station
Stonebridge Park Station
Wembley Stadium Station
North Ealing Station
West Acton Station
Acton Main Line Station
Ealing Broadway Stn
Ealing Common Stn
Grand Union Canal
HA0
W5
W3
115
136
155

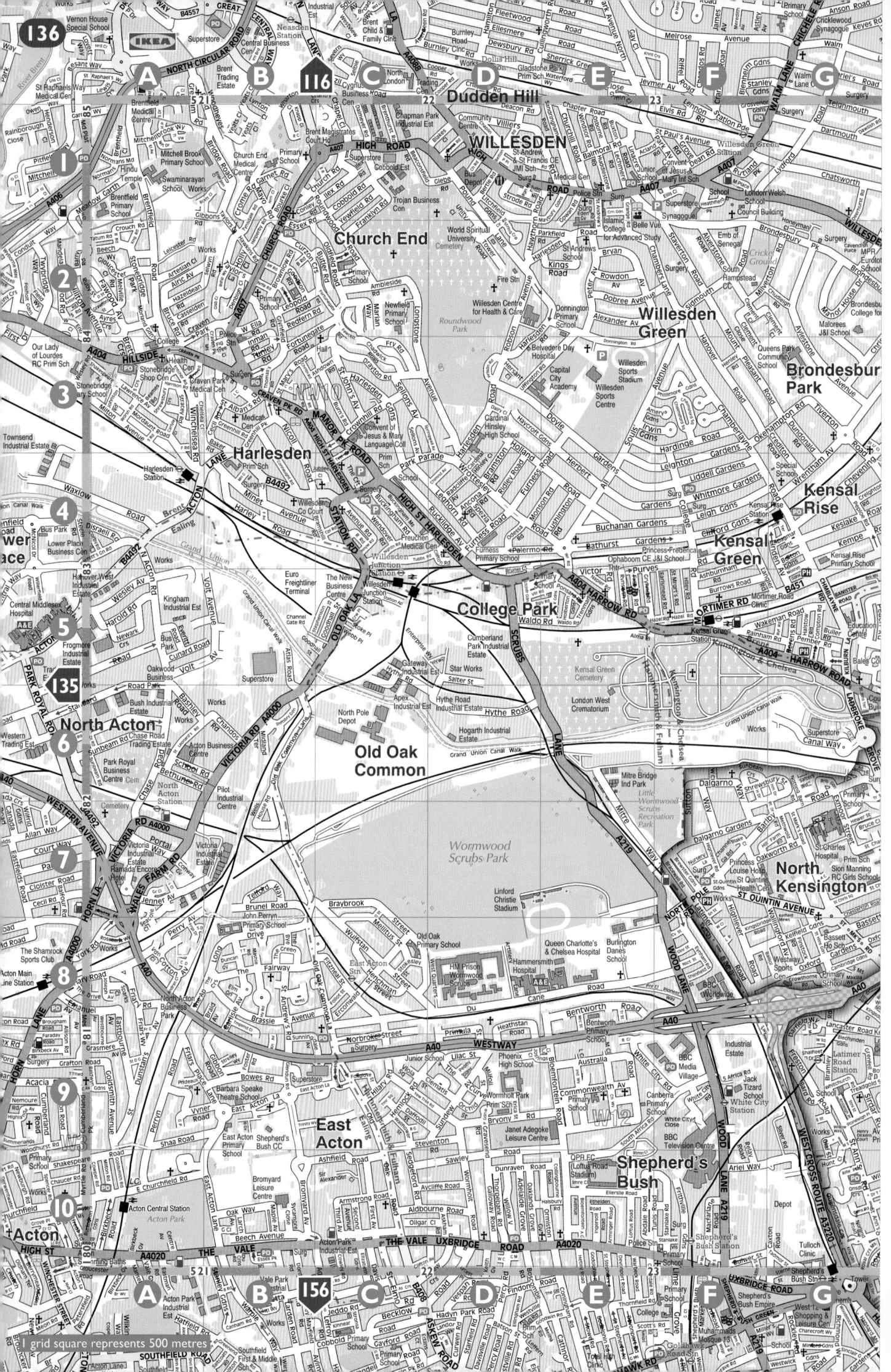

136
116
135
156
A
B
C
D
E
F
G
1
2
3
4
5
6
7
8
9
10
521
22
23
Dudden Hill
WILLESDEN
Church End
Willesden Green
Brondesbury Park
Harlesden
Kensal Rise
Kensal Green
College Park
North Acton
Old Oak Common
Wormwood Scrubs Park
North Kensington
East Acton
Shepherd's Bush
Acton
NORTH CIRCULAR ROAD
HIGH ROAD
CHURCH ROAD
HILLSIDE
CRAVEN PK RD
MANOR PK ROAD
HIGH ST HARLESDEN
STATION RD
ACTON LANE
OLD OAK LA
VICTORIA RD
A404 HARROW RD
HARROW ROAD
SCRUBS LANE
WOOD LANE
WESTERN AVENUE
WESTWAY
HORN LANE
THE VALE
UXBRIDGE ROAD
WEST CROSS ROUTE A3220
WALM LANE
CHICHELE RD
MORTIMER RD
ST QUINTIN AVENUE
NORTH POLE RD
Grand Union Canal
Grand Union Canal Walk
Neasden Station
Harlesden Station
Willesden Junction Station
Kensal Green Station
Kensal Rise Station
Willesden Green Station
North Acton Station
Acton Central Station
East Acton Stn
White City Station
Shepherd's Bush Station
Kensal Green Cemetery
London West Crematorium
Roundwood Park
HM Prison Wormwood Scrubs
Hammersmith Hospital
Queen Charlotte's & Chelsea Hospital
Linford Christie Stadium
Willesden Sports Stadium
Willesden Sports Centre
Central Middlesex Hospital
BBC Media Village
BBC Television Centre
QPR FC (Loftus Road Stadium)
Acton Park
IKEA
1 grid square represents 500 metres

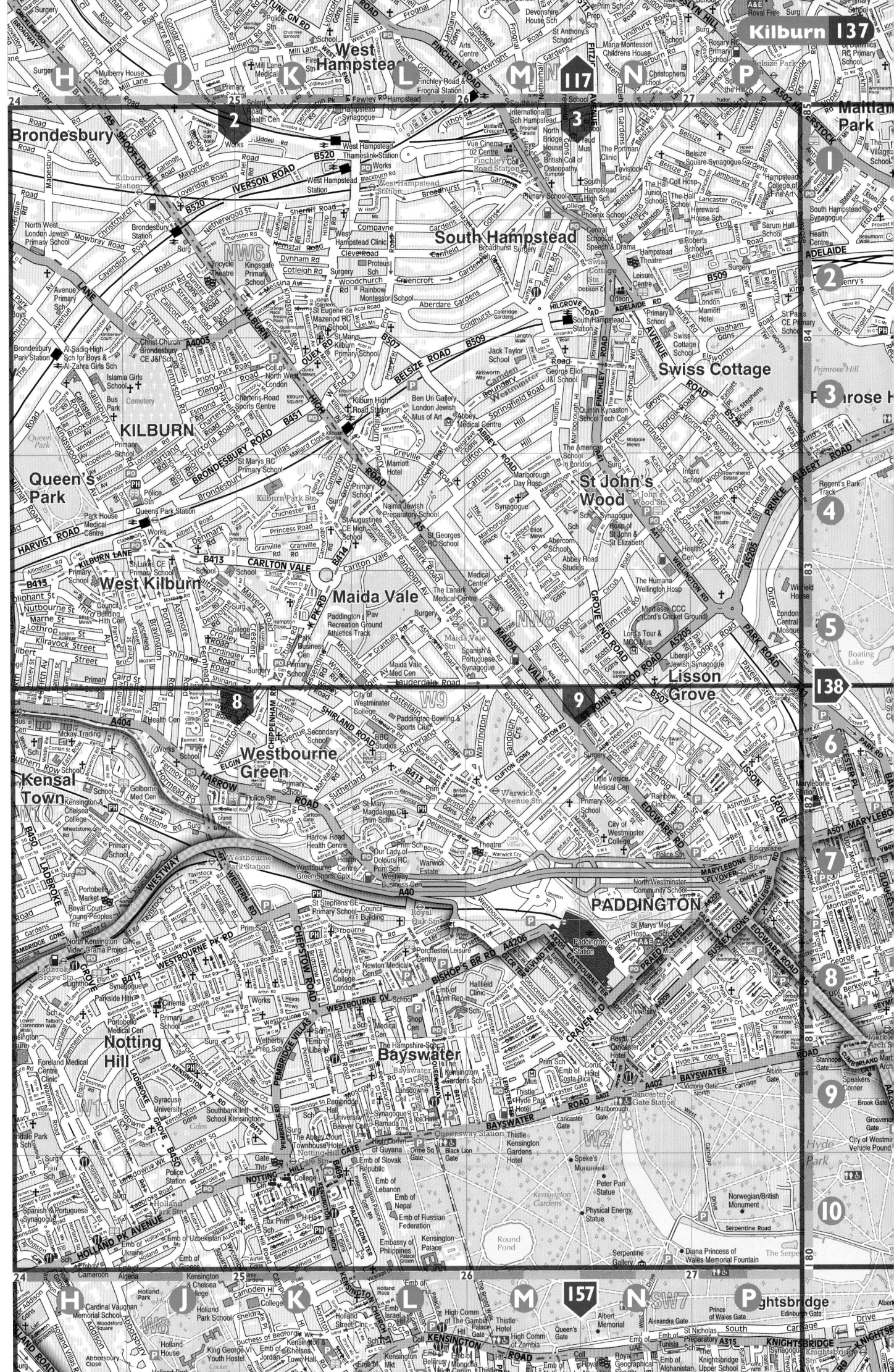
West Hampstead
Brondesbury
South Hampstead
Swiss Cottage
KILBURN
Queen's Park
St John's Wood
West Kilburn
Maida Vale
Lisson Grove
Westbourne Green
Kensal Town
PADDINGTON
Notting Hill
Bayswater
Maitland Park
Primrose Hill
NW6
NW8
W9
W10
W11
W2
W8
SW7
117
138
157
H
J
K
L
M
N
P
1
2
3
4
5
6
7
8
9
10
24
25
26
27
80
81
82
83
84
85
Kensington Gardens
Hyde Park
Round Pond
Paddington Station
Regent's Park

138
Gospel Oak
118
Kentish Town
Lower Holloway
Maitland Park
4
5
Kentish Town Road
Camden Road
York Way
Caledonian Road
Barnsbury
Camden Town
Adelaide Road
Chalk Farm Road
Primrose Hill
Prince Albert Road
London Zoo
Regent's Park
Delancey St
Camden High Street
Somers Town
St Pancras
Euston Road
King's Cross Station
St Pancras Station
International Rail Terminal
British Library
Euston Station
Pentonville Rd
137
10
11
Marylebone Road
Marylebone
Baker Street
Bloomsbury
British Museum
Gower Street
Tottenham Court Road
Oxford Street
Wigmore Street
St Giles
Soho
Regent Street
Mayfair
Piccadilly
Park Lane
Hyde Park
Shaftesbury Av
Charing Cross Road
Strand
Kingsway
Aldwych
Embankment
National Gallery
Trafalgar Sq
Pall Mall
St James's
Buckingham Palace
Constitution Hill
Knightsbridge
London Eye
Waterloo Bridge
Royal Festival Hall
Queen Elizabeth Hall
Golden Jubilee Bridge
158
A
B
C
D
E
F
G
1
2
3
4
5
6
7
8
9
10
1 grid square represents 500 metres

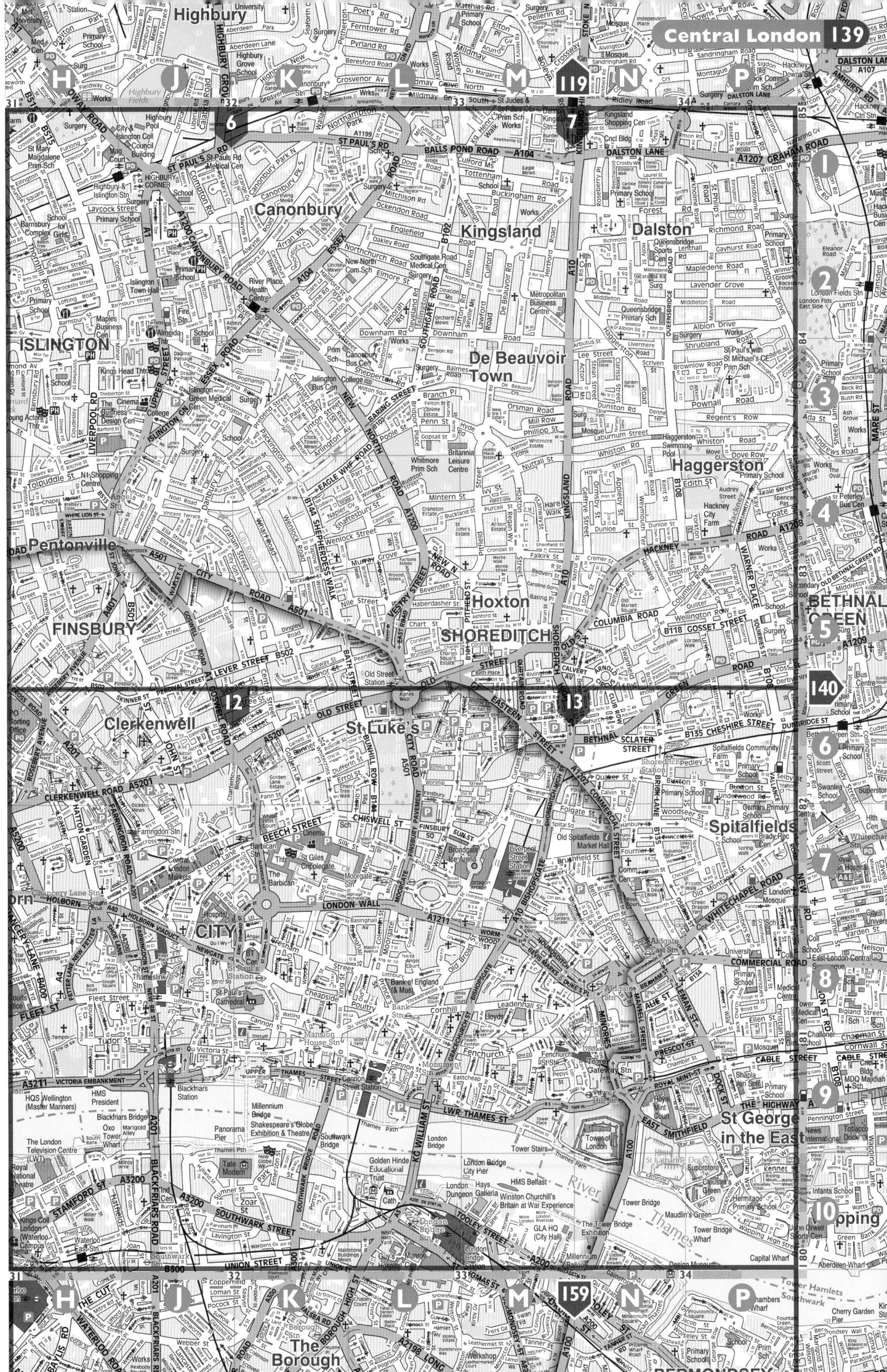
Highbury
Canonbury
Kingsland
Dalston
ISLINGTON
De Beauvoir Town
Haggerston
Pentonville
FINSBURY
Hoxton
SHOREDITCH
BETHNAL GREEN
Clerkenwell
St Luke's
Spitalfields
CITY
St George in the East
Wapping
The Borough
BERMONDSEY
River Thames

140
120
139
160
A
B
C
D
E
F
G
1
2
3
4
5
6
7
8
9
10
Temple Mills
Hackney Wick
HACKNEY
Homerton
Old Ford
South Hackney
Victoria Park
BETHNAL GREEN
Globe Town
BOW
Bromley
Mile End
Spitalfields
STEPNEY
Bow Common
Limehouse
POPLAR
St George in the East
Shadwell
Wapping
Canary Wharf
DALSTON LANE
MARE STREET
CAMBRIDGE HEATH ROAD
VICTORIA PARK ROAD
GROVE ROAD
OLD FORD ROAD
ROMAN ROAD
MILE END ROAD
COMMERCIAL ROAD
EAST INDIA DOCK ROAD
WHITECHAPEL ROAD
THE HIGHWAY
BURDETT ROAD
BLACKWALL TNL NORTHERN AP
EAST CROSS ROUTE
WHITE POST LANE
CARPENTERS
BOW ROAD
LIMEHOUSE LINK
Mile End Stadium
Queen Mary College Uni of London
Tower Hamlets Cemetery
1 grid square represents 500 metres

Stratford New Town
Stratford International Station
STRATFORD
Stratford Station
Forest Gate
Upton
Upton Park
Plaistow
Mill Meads
Canning Town
South Bromley
Blackwall
Silvertown
E13
E16
River Thames
West Ham Park
East London Cemetery
East London Crematorium
Memorial Recreation Ground
Royal Victoria Dock
ExCeL Exhibition Centre
The O2
ROMFORD ROAD
PORTWAY
PLASHET ROAD
BARKING ROAD
NEWHAM WAY A13
LOWER LEA CROSSING
NORTH WOOLWICH ROAD
MANOR ROAD
PRINCE REGENT LANE
SILVERTOWN WAY
EAST INDIA DOCK ROAD
NORTHERN APPROACH
HIGH STREET
West Ham Station
Plaistow Station
Upton Park Station
Canning Town Station
Royal Victoria Station
Custom House for ExCeL Station
Prince Regent Station
West Silvertown Station
Pontoon Dock Station
East India Station
Blackwall Station
Newham General Hospital
Kingsford Community School
Newham Leisure Centre
West Ham United FC (Upton Park)
East London RUFC
Abbey Road Station (due to open Feb 2009)
Stratford High Street Station (due to open Feb 2009)
121
142
161
H
J
K
L
M
N
P
1
2
3
4
5
6
7
8
9
10

142
122
141
162
A
B
C
D
E
F
G
1
2
3
4
5
6
7
8
9
10
Loxford
Plashet
Upton Park
EAST HAM
Wallend
Beckton
Custom House
Silvertown
North Woolwich
E6
ROMFORD ROAD
BARKING ROAD
A124
HIGH STREET NORTH
HIGH STREET SOUTH
A117
NORTH CIRCULAR ROAD
A406
HIGHBRIDGE ROAD
NEWHAM WAY
A13
ROYAL DOCKS ROAD
A1020
WOOLWICH MANOR WAY
ROYAL ALBERT WAY
CONNAUGHT RD
ALBERT RD
PIER ROAD
NORTHERN RELIEF ROAD
FANSHAWE AVENUE
LONGBRIDGE
CENTRAL PK ROAD
RANCLIFFE RD B167
VICTORIA DOCK RD
Woodgrange Park Stn
East Ham Stn
Upton Park Station
Barking Station
Royal Albert Station
Beckton Park Station
Cyprus Station
Gallions Reach Station
King George V Station
London City Airport
Royal Albert Dock
King George V Dock
River Thames
Newham Greenwich
Barking Park
Central Park
East Ham Jewish Cemetery
Plashet Jewish Cemetery
Beckton District Park
New Beckton Park
King George V Park
Thames Barrier Park
Newham General Hospital
West Ham United FC (Upton Park)
Gallions Reach Shopping Park
Beckton Triangle Retail Park
Gateway Retail Park
Showcase Newham Cinema
University of East London
Woolwich Foot Tunnel
WOOLWICH FERRY
Old Station Museum
542
43
44
180
181
182
183
184
185
1 grid square represents 500 metres

Fair Cross
Becontree
ARKING
Castle Green
Creekmouth
Thamesmead
River Thames
Barking Reach
Barking and Dagenham
Bexley
Newham
Greenwich
Cross Ness
Margaret or Tripcock Ness
Mayesbrook Park
Mayesbrook Park Arena
Barking FC
Parsloes Park
Barking Abbey Leisure Centre
Barking Hospital
Upney Station
Becontree Station
East Barking Centre
Cemetery
Barking Ind Park
Alfreds Way Industrial Est
Renwick Industrial Estate
Lyon Business Park
Thames View Clinic
Thames View J&I School
Skillion Business Park
Riverside Industrial Est
River Road Business Park
Bankside Park Industrial Est
Buzzard Creek Industrial Est
Creekmouth Industrial Park
Trafalgar Business Centre
Anglian Industrial Estate
Balmoral Trading Estate
Buzzard Creek Industrial Estate
Goresbrook Leisure Centre
Goresbrook Sports Centre
Barking RUFC
Vue Cinema
Power Station
Industrial Estate
Riverside Golf Club
Thamesmead Leisure Centre
Thamesmead Shopping Centre
Tripcock Point Development Site
Woolwich Polytechnic School
Bishop John Robinson CE Prim School
Castilion Primary School
Jubilee Primary School
St Margaret Clitherow RC Primary School
Hawksmoor Primary School
Police Station
Birchmere Bus Park
Magistrates Court
Southlake Primary School
The Business Academy Bexley
Erith Marshes
RIPPLE ROAD
A13
A123
A124
A1153
A2041
A2016
LODGE AVENUE
PORTERS AVENUE
(EAST HAM AND BARKING BY-PASS)
River Road
Renwick Road
Thames Road
Choats Road
CENTRAL WAY
CARLYLE ROAD
EASTERN WAY
WESTERN WAY
Belvedere Road
IG11
SE28
DA18
123
144
163
H J K L M N P
1 2 3 4 5 6 7 8 9 10
45 46 47 48
80 81 82 83 84 85

144
124
143
164
A
B
C
D
E
F
G
1
2
3
4
5
6
7
8
9
10
5 49
50
51
85
84
83
82
81
180
DAGENHAM
South Hornchurch
RM10
RM9
Dagenham & Redbridge FC
Hunters Hall Primary School
Parsloes Primary School
Parsloes Avenue
Holgate Road
Council Building
Dagenham Heathway Stn
Dagenham East Station
Roberts Cl
Blackborne
Church Elm Lane
Western Avenue
John Perry Primary School
Auriel Av
Surgery
Medical Centre
Rainham Rd S
Rainham Rd South
Aldborough Rd
Manor Road
Beamway
Wellington Drive
The Leys Primary School
Canberra Crs
Godwin Primary School
William Ford CE Junior School
Village Infant School
Dagenham Park Community Sch & Performing Arts Coll
Ballards Road
School Road
Orchard Road
Oval Road North
Oval Rd North
Beam Avenue
Third Avenue
Second
First
Dagenham Superbowl
Marsh Green School
Beam Primary School
Heathway
A1240
A1112
A1306
B178
A13
A2016
Goresbrook Road
Treswell Road
Vue Cinema
St Peters RC Primary School
Ripple Road
Merrielands Retail Park
Merrielands Crs
New Road
Sierra Drive
Dagenham Dock Station
Works
Power Station
Choats Manor Way
Choats Road
Hindmans Way
Chequers Lane
Breach Lane
Industrial Estate
Ford Industrial Park
Kent Avenue
Lake Road
Thames Avenue
Fiesta Drive
Consul Av
Consul Avenue
Courier Road
Hornchurch Marshes
Marsh Way
Manor Way Business Cen
Star Business Centre
Thamesview Business Centre
Lorimar Business Cen
Fairview Industrial Centre
Blackwater Cl
Barlow Way
Creek Way
Salamons Wy
Denver Industrial Estate
Ferry Lane
Industrial Estate Annexe
KP Estate
Frog Island
Albright Industrial Estate
Lamson Rd
Rainham Trading Estate
Mudlands Estate
Dovers Corner Industrial Estate
Suttons Business Park
Fordview Industrial Estate
Newtons Primary School
Mardyke Cl
Lower Mardyke Av
South Street
Walden Av
Askwith Rd
Spencer Road
Manser Road
Betterton
Philip
Frederick Road
Maytree Cl
Edmund Road
Stanley Road
Nelson Road
Rainham Road
Brittons School Technology College
Bretons
Dagenham Rd
Whybridge Junior School
Dunedin
New Zealand Way
Thames
Halfway Reach
Riverside Golf Club
Golf Course
Jenningtree Point
Norman Road
Capital Industrial Est
Crabtree Manorway North
Fisher's Way
Belvedere Industrial Estate
Fordgate Business Park
Mulberry Way
Hailey Rd
Hailey Road Business Park
The Business Ac
1 grid square represents 500 metres

Rainham 145
Elm Park
Hacton
Corbets Tey
Rainham Lodge Farm
Hornchurch Country Park
Albyns Farm
Berwick Ponds Farm
Berwick Manor
The Manor Hotel
Marsh View Industrial Estate
Cemetery
Harwood Equestria
RAINHAM
Parsonage Farm Primary School
Rainham Cem
Police Station
Imperial Trading Est
Deans Trading Est
Chafford School
Chafford Sports Complex
Brady Primary School
RM13
South Hall Farm
Rainham Village Primary School
Rainham Hall (NT)
Ferry Lane Industrial Est
La Salette RC Primary School
Whybridge Infant School
Health & Welfare Clinic
Rosewood Medical Centre
The RJ Mitchell Primary School
Scotts Primary School
St Albans RC JMI School
Wennington Hall Farm Business Centre
Premier Travel Inn
Wennington
Rainham Marshes
RSPB site
Wennington Marshes
Aveley Marshes
Sandy Lane Farm
Moor Hall
Purfleet Ind Park
Ingrebourne River
A1306 NEW ROAD
WENNINGTON ROAD B1335
SANDY LANE B1335
A13
LONDON RD
RAINHAM ROAD A125
BROADWAY
Berwick Pond Road
Gerpins Lane
Warwick Lane
Upminster Rd N
Launder's Lane
East Hall Lane
Church Lane
Coldharbour Lane
Farm Road
Aveley Road
Havering
Thurrock
125
146
165

Corbets Tey
Harwood Hall
Harwood Equestrian Centre
Upminster Cemetery
OCKENDON ROAD
Manor Farm
Stubbers (Outdoor Pursuits Centre)
Sunnings Lane
Stubbers Lane
Gerpins Lane
Aveley Road
Dennises Lane
Havering
Thurrock
Bramble Farm
Bramble Lane
Warwick Lane
Kemps Farm
Baldwins Farm
Dennis Road
M25
North Ockendon
Ockendon Station
Belhus Woods Country Park
Romford Road
Bretts Farm
Kenningtons
Moor Hall
Ockendon School
Woodacre Special School
Dilkes Primary School
Shaw Primary School
Holy Cross RC Primary School
Somers Heath Primary School
RM15
Belhus Park
Golf Course
Belhus Golf Club & Leisure Centre
Kenningtons Primary School
The Aveley School
AVELEY
Aveley FC
Sandy Lane Farm
AVELEY BY-PASS
B1335 STIFFORD ROAD
STIFFORD ROAD
Junction 30
Aveley School (School House)
Aveley Primary School
A13
Arena Essex
Thurrock Service Area
1 grid square represents 500 metres

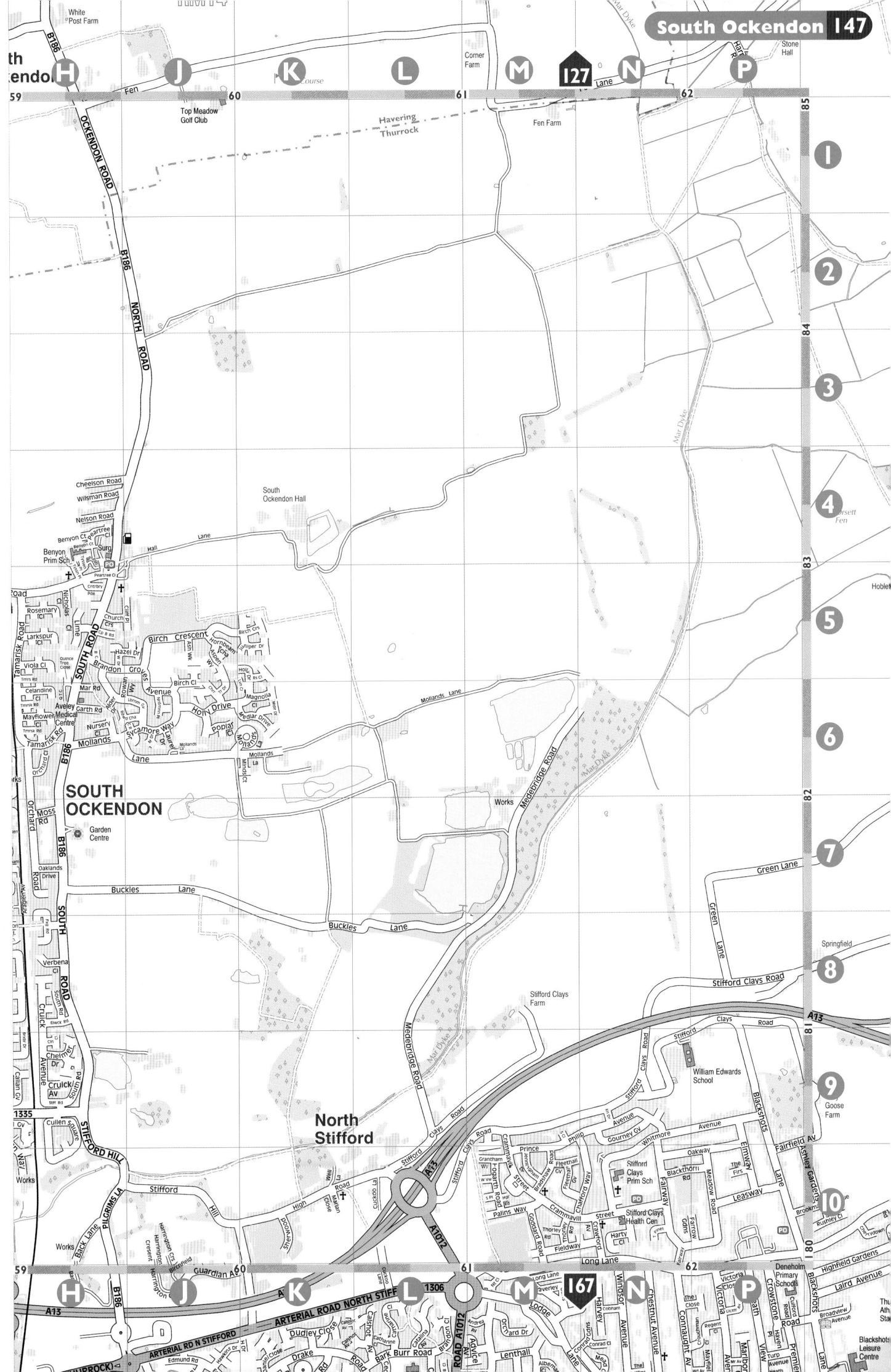
SOUTH OCKENDON
North Stifford
South Ockendon Hall
Mollands Lane
Buckles Lane
Medebridge Road
Stifford Clays Road
Green Lane
Stifford Clays Farm
William Edwards School
Havering
Thurrock
Top Meadow Golf Club
Fen Farm
Corner Farm
White Post Farm
Stone Hall
Mar Dyke
Works
Garden Centre
Aveley Medical Centre
Benyon Prim Sch
Stifford Clays Prim Sch
Stifford Clays Health Cen
Deneholm Primary School
Blackshots Leisure Centre
Goose Farm
Springfield
OCKENDON ROAD
NORTH ROAD
SOUTH ROAD
STIFFORD HILL
ARTERIAL ROAD NORTH STIFFORD
A13
A1012
B186
127
167

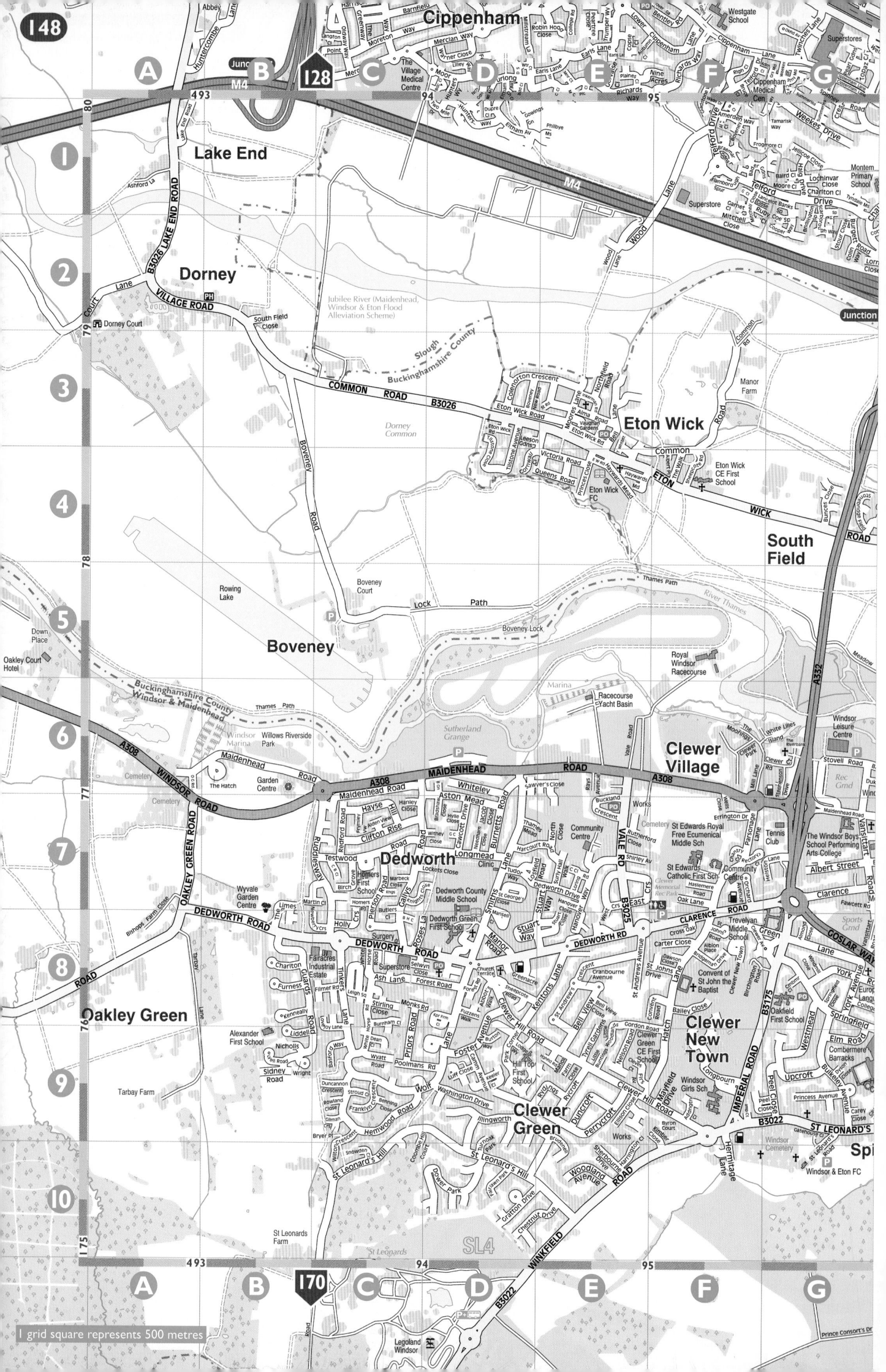

128
Cippenham
Lake End
Dorney
Eton Wick
South Field
Boveney
Rowing Lake
Jubilee River (Maidenhead, Windsor & Eton Flood Alleviation Scheme)
Dorney Common
Dorney Court
Boveney Court
Boveney Lock
River Thames
Thames Path
Royal Windsor Racecourse
Clewer Village
Dedworth
Oakley Green
Clewer Green
Clewer New Town
Windsor Marina
Willows Riverside Park
Racecourse Yacht Basin
Sutherland Grange
Tarbay Farm
St Leonards Farm
Legoland Windsor
Windsor & Eton FC
Windsor Leisure Centre
Manor Farm
COMMON ROAD B3026
DEDWORTH ROAD
MAIDENHEAD ROAD A308
WINDSOR ROAD A308
OAKLEY GREEN ROAD
B3026 LAKE END ROAD
VILLAGE ROAD
CLARENCE ROAD
VALE RD B3025
IMPERIAL ROAD B3175
ST LEONARD'S ROAD B3022
WINKFIELD ROAD B3022
A332
M4
Slough
Buckinghamshire County
Windsor & Maidenhead
SL4
170
1 grid square represents 500 metres

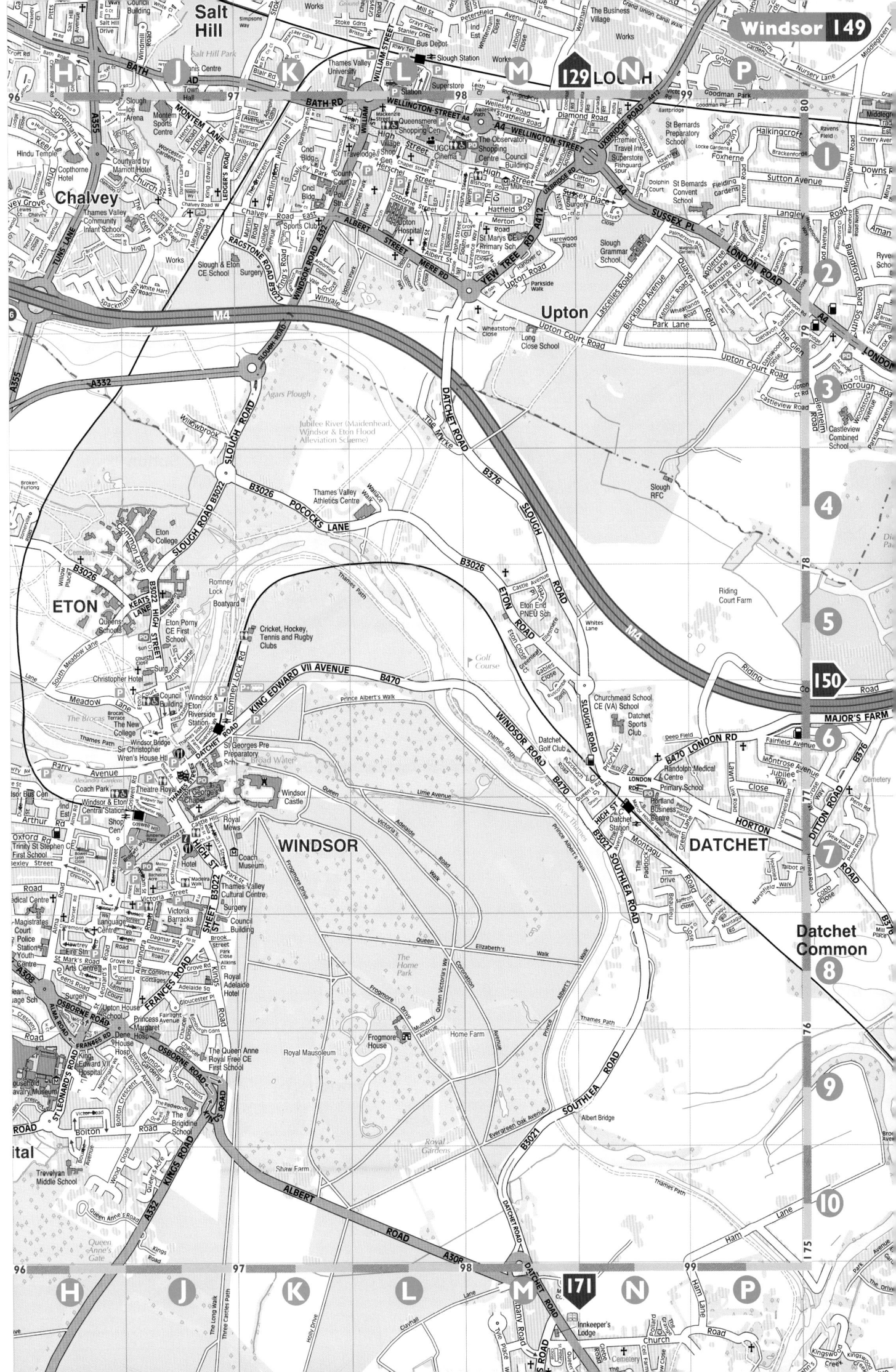

Windsor 149
Salt Hill
Salt Hill Park
Chalvey
Upton
ETON
WINDSOR
DATCHET
Datchet Common
Slough Station
Thames Valley University
Superstore
Bus Depot
Queensmere Shopping Cen
The Observatory Shopping Centre
Council Building
Town Hall
Slough Ice Arena
Montem Sports Centre
Hindu Temple
Copthorne Hotel
Courtyard by Marriott Hotel
Thames Valley Community Infant School
Slough & Eton CE School
Upton Hospital
St Marys CE Primary Sch
Slough Grammar School
St Bernards Preparatory School
St Bernards Convent School
Premier Travel Inn
Superstore
Long Close School
Castleview Combined School
Slough RFC
Riding Court Farm
Thames Valley Athletics Centre
Jubilee River (Maidenhead, Windsor & Eton Flood Alleviation Scheme)
Agars Plough
Eton College
Romney Lock
Boatyard
Cricket, Hockey, Tennis and Rugby Clubs
Eton End PNEU Sch
Eton Porny CE First School
Christopher Hotel
The Brocas
Windsor & Eton Riverside Station
Windsor Bridge
Sir Christopher Wren's House Htl
St Georges Pre Preparatory Sch
Broad Water
Windsor Castle
Royal Mews
Theatre Royal
St George's Chapel
Windsor & Eton Central Station
Coach Park
Coach Museum
Thames Valley Cultural Centre
Victoria Barracks
Royal Adelaide Hotel
The Queen Anne Royal Free CE First School
King Edward VII Hospital
Household Cavalry Museum
Trevelyan Middle School
The Brigidine School
Frogmore House
Royal Mausoleum
Home Farm
The Home Park
Royal Gardens
Shaw Farm
Albert Bridge
Churchmead School CE (VA) School
Datchet Sports Club
Datchet Golf Club
Golf Course
Randolph Medical Centre
Primary School
Portland Business Centre
Datchet Station
Innkeeper's Lodge
Cemetery
M4
A4
A332
A355
A412
A308
B3026
B3022
B470
B376
B3021
A308
BATH RD
WELLINGTON STREET
UXBRIDGE ROAD
SUSSEX PL
LONDON ROAD
YEW TREE RD
MERE RD
ALBERT STREET
WINDSOR ROAD
SLOUGH ROAD
DATCHET ROAD
POCOCKS LANE
ETON ROAD
KING EDWARD VII AVENUE
WINDSOR ROAD
SOUTHLEA ROAD
HIGH STREET
THAMES STREET
SHEET ST
FRANCES ROAD
OSBORNE ROAD
KINGS ROAD
ALBERT ROAD
ST LEONARD'S ROAD
LONDON RD
HORTON ROAD
DITTON ROAD
MAJOR'S FARM
Upton Court Road
Ham Lane
H
J
K
L
M
N
P
96
97
98
99
129
150
171
1
2
3
4
5
6
7
8
9
10
80
79
78
77
76
175

150
130
149
172
A
B
C
D
E
F
G
1
2
3
4
5
6
7
8
9
10
500
01
02
80
79
78
77
76
175
Trenches Farm
Parsonage Farm
Iver Golf & Leisure Centre
Langley Manor School
Council Building
Grand Union Canal Walk
Middlegreen Trading Estate
Middlegreen Trading Est
Langley Business Park
Waterside Drive
Industrial Estate
Langley Station
Langley Business Cen
Works
Halkingcroft
Sutton Avenue
Downs Road
Alderbury Road West
Alderbury Road
STATION ROAD
B470
Meadfield
East Berkshire College (Langley Campus)
Langley Road
Langley
Ryvers School
Langleywood School
Parlaunt Park Combined School
Trelawney Avenue
Ives Road
Marish Inf Sch
HIGH STREET
North Park
LONDON RD
A4
Upton Court Road
Marlborough Road
Castleview Combined School
Langley Grammar School
Slough Community Mental Health Cen
Humber Way
Parlaunt Road
Richings Park Golf Club
Sutton
Golf Course
Holy Family Catholic Sch
Langley Health Cen
Innkeeper's Lodge
LONDON ROAD
Marriott Hotel
Grampian Way
Buckinghamshire County
Slough
M4
Ditton Park
Riding Court Farm
Riding Court Road
Junction 5
Quality Hotel
COLNBROOK BY-PASS
MAJOR'S FARM ROAD
MAJOR'S FARM RD
Court Road
Brands Hill
Mildridge Farm
Horton Road
Colnbrook
Colnbrook CE Primary School
Windsor and Maidenhead
The Queen Mother Reservoir
Cemetery
DITTON ROAD
B376
Datchet Common
HORTON ROAD
Horton Lodge
Colne Valley Way
Datchet Road
Stanwell Road
Horton
Horton Trading Estate
Manor Farm
Sunnymeads Station
WELLEY ROAD
Sunnymeads
Coppermill Road
Wraysbury Reservoir
Surrey County
1 grid square represents 500 metres

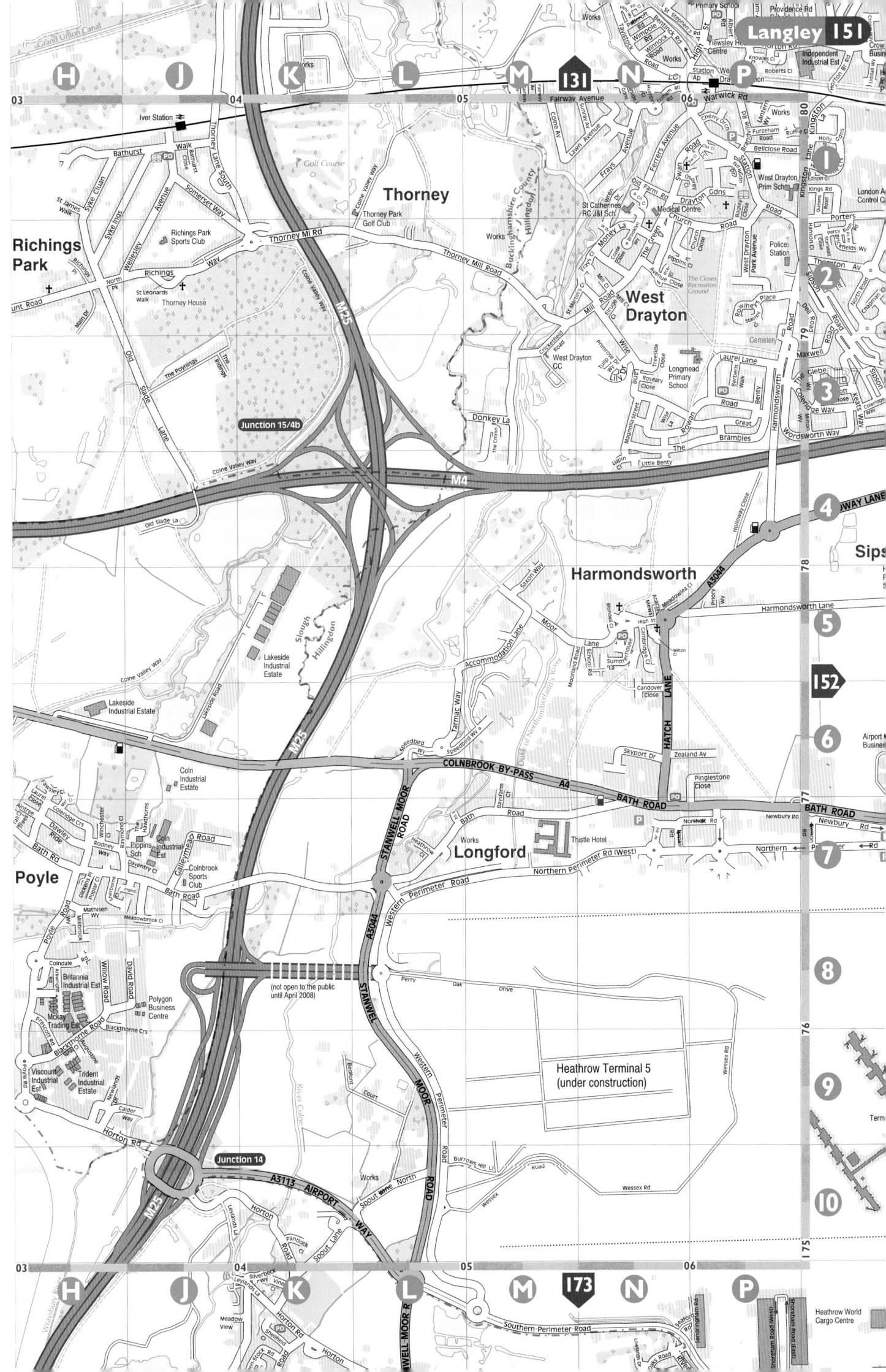

Langley 151
131
152
173
Grand Union Canal
Iver Station
Richings Park
Richings Park Sports Club
Thorney House
Thorney
Thorney Park Golf Club
Golf Course
Thorney Mill Road
Thorney Ml Rd
Somerset Way
Wellesley Avenue
Syke Ings
Syke Cluan
St James Walk
Bathurst Walk
Thorney Lane South
Old Slade Lane
The Poynings
The Ridings
Main Dr
Colne Valley Way
Junction 15/4b
M25
M4
Buckinghamshire County
Hillingdon
Slough
Works
West Drayton
West Drayton CC
Longmead Primary School
St Catherines RC J&I Sch
Medical Centre
Police Station
West Drayton Prim Sch
The Closes Recreation Ground
Cemetery
Harmondsworth
Harmondsworth Lane
Harmondsworth Road
Moor Lane
Accommodation Lane
Saxon Way
Hatch Lane
Candover Close
Skyport Dr
Zealand Av
Pinglestone Close
A3044
Lakeside Industrial Estate
Lakeside Road
Colnbrook By-Pass
A4
Bath Road
Coln Industrial Estate
Colnbrook Sports Club
Poyle
Longford
Thistle Hotel
Northern Perimeter Rd (West)
Western Perimeter Road
Stanwell Moor Road
Tarmac Way
Speedbird Way
Duke of Northumberlands River
River Colne
Britannia Industrial Est
Mckay Trading Est
Polygon Business Centre
Trident Industrial Estate
Viscount Industrial Est
Blackthorne Road
Willow Road
David Road
Horton Rd
Perry Oak Drive
(not open to the public until April 2008)
Heathrow Terminal 5 (under construction)
Wessex Rd
Burrows Hill La
Junction 14
A3113 Airport Way
Spout Lane
Southern Perimeter Road
Heathrow World Cargo Centre
Sipson
Airport Business
London Air Control Centre
Independent Industrial Est
Providence Rd
Warwick Rd
Fairway Avenue
H
J
K
L
M
N
P
03
04
05
06
1
2
3
4
5
6
7
8
9
10
175
76
77
78
79
80

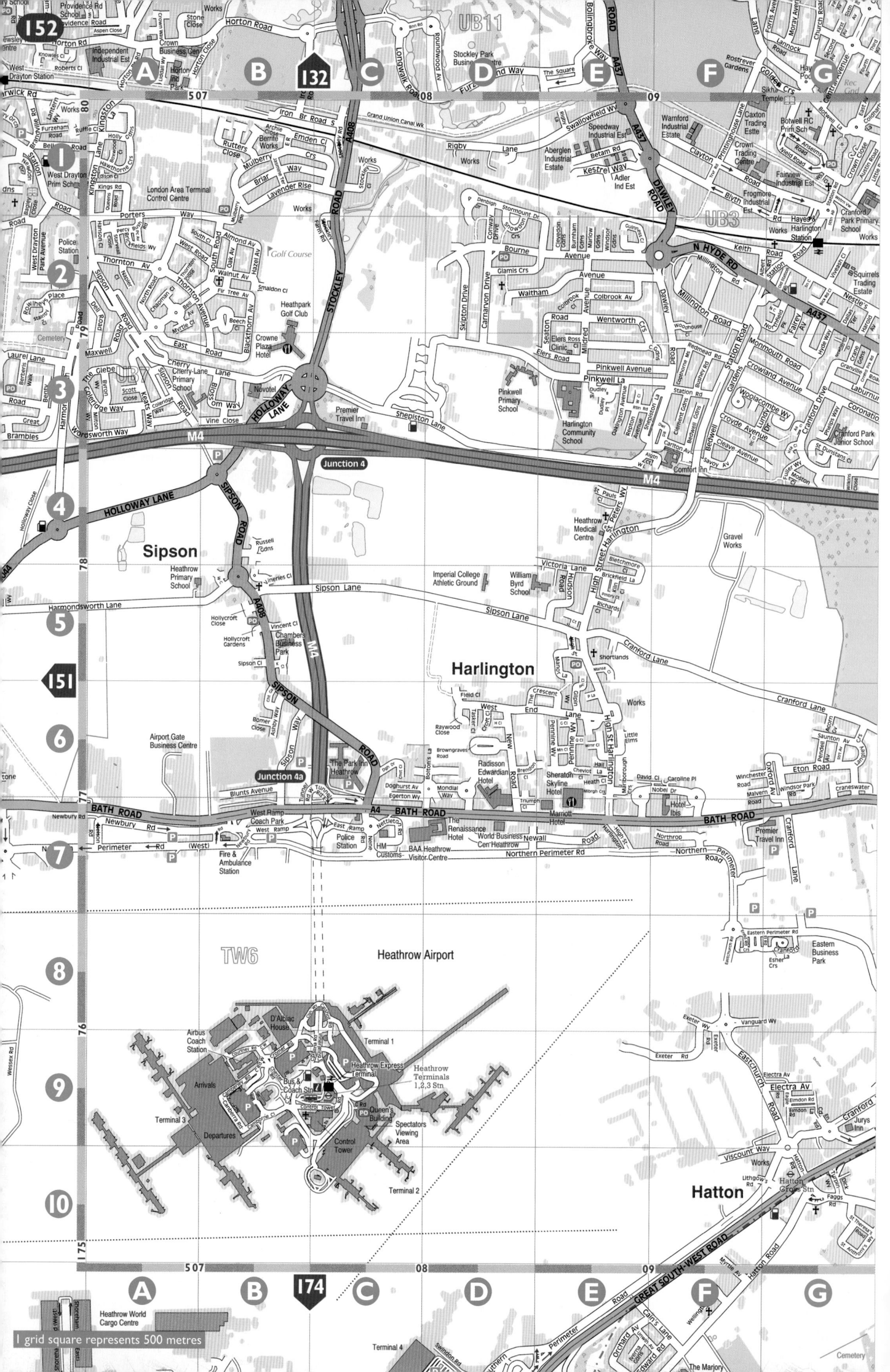

132
UB11
A
B
C
D
E
F
G
1
2
3
4
5
6
7
8
9
10
507
08
09
80
79
78
77
76
175
151
174
Providence Rd
Horton Road
Independent Industrial Est
Crown Business Cen
Horton Ind Park
West Drayton Station
Stockley Park Business Centre
Furzeground Way
The Square
Bolingbroke Way
A437
Rostrever Gardens
Golden Crs
Sikh Temple
Iron Br Road S
Grand Union Canal Wk
Swallowfield Wy
Speedway Industrial Est
Warnford Industrial Estate
Caxton Trading Estate
Botwell RC Prim Sch
Crown Trading Centre
Fairview Industrial Est
Frogmore Industrial Est
Hayes & Harlington Station
Cranford Park Primary School
Works
West Drayton Prim Sch
Emden Cl
Mulberry Crs
Lavender Rise
Rigby Lane
Aberglen Industrial Estate
Betam Rd
Kestrel Way
Adler Ind Est
Dawley Road
Blyth Road
London Area Terminal Control Centre
Porters Way
Golf Course
Stockley Road
A408
Bourne Avenue
Glamis Crs
Waltham Avenue
Colbrook Av
Wentworth Crs
N Hyde Rd
Keith Road
Millington Road
Squirrels Trading Estate
Police Station
West Drayton Park Avenue
Thornton Av
Heathpark Golf Club
Crowne Plaza Hotel
Skipton Drive
Carnarvon Drive
Seaton Road
Elers Road
Pinkwell Avenue
Pinkwell La
Pinkwell Primary School
Harlington Community School
Station Road
Monmouth Road
Crowland Avenue
Laburnum
Cemetery
Laurel Lane
Cherry Lane Primary School
Holloway Lane
Novotel
Premier Travel Inn
Shepiston Lane
Cleave Avenue
Cranford Park Junior School
Coleridge Way
Wordsworth Way
Vine Close
Great
Brambles
M4
Junction 4
Comfort Inn
Heathrow Medical Centre
High Street Harlington
Gravel Works
Sipson
Sipson Road
Heathrow Primary School
Imperial College Athletic Ground
William Byrd School
Victoria Lane
Sipson Lane
Harmondsworth Lane
Hollycroft Close
Chambers Business Park
Cranford Lane
Harlington
Shortlands
West End Lane
Airport Gate Business Centre
Junction 4a
The Park Inn Heathrow
Radisson Edwardian Hotel
Sheraton Skyline Hotel
Marriott Hotel
Hotel Ibis
Eton Road
Premier Travel Inn
Bath Road
A4
Newbury Rd
Perimeter Rd
West Ramp
Coach Park
Fire & Ambulance Station
Police Station
HM Customs
The Renaissance Hotel
World Business Cen Heathrow
BAA Heathrow Visitor Centre
Northern Perimeter Rd
TW6
Heathrow Airport
Eastern Perimeter Rd
Eastern Business Park
D'Albiac House
Airbus Coach Station
Terminal 1
Heathrow Express Terminal
Heathrow Terminals 1,2,3 Stn
Arrivals
Departures
Terminal 3
Bus & Coach Stn
Control Tower
Queen's Building
Spectators Viewing Area
Terminal 2
Exeter Rd
Vanguard Wy
Eastchurch Road
Electra Av
Jurys Inn
Viscount Way
Hatton
Hatton Cross Stn
Great South-West Road
Hatton Road
Heathrow World Cargo Centre
1 grid square represents 500 metres
Terminal 4
Cain's Lane
Cemetery

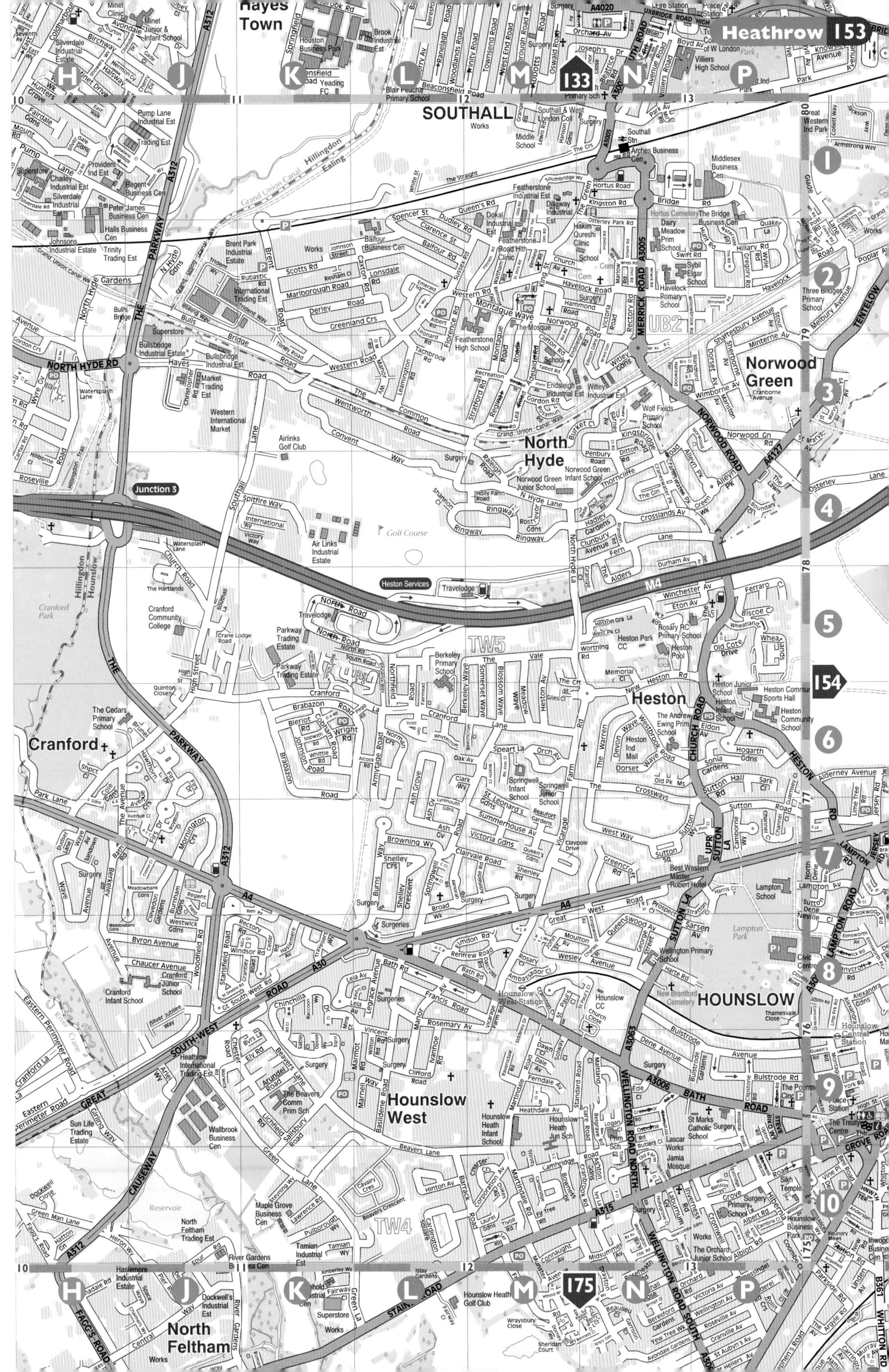
Hayes Town
SOUTHALL
Southall Stn
Norwood Green
North Hyde
Heston
Cranford
HOUNSLOW
Hounslow West
North Feltham
Hounslow Central Station
Hounslow West Station
Heston Services
Travelodge
Junction 3
M4
A4
A30
A312
A3005
A3006
A3063
A4020
A4127
A315
A300
B361
THE PARKWAY
GREAT SOUTH-WEST ROAD
CAUSEWAY
WELLINGTON ROAD NORTH
WELLINGTON ROAD SOUTH
MERRICK ROAD
NORWOOD ROAD
HESTON RD
CHURCH ROAD
SUTTON LA
UPR SUTTON LA
LAMPTON ROAD
BATH ROAD
NORTH HYDE RD
UXBRIDGE ROAD
TENTELOW
Grand Union Canal
Hillingdon
Ealing
Hounslow
Golf Course
Airlinks Golf Club
Lampton Park
Cranford Park
Reservoir
River Crane
New Brentford Cemetery
TW5
TW4
UB2
Heston Pool
Lampton School
Featherstone High School
Cranford Community College
Heathrow International Trading Est
Middlesex Business Cen
H
J
K
L
M
N
P
133
154
175
1
2
3
4
5
6
7
8
9
10
10
11
12
13
75
76
77
78
79
80

154
134
153
152
176
Hanwell
West Ealing
Uxbridge Road
A4020
Broadway
Norwood Green
Osterley
Osterley Park
Osterley Park & House (NT)
Spring Grove
Lampton
Hounslow
Brentford End
Isleworth
Woodlands
Ealing Hospital
Chaucer Clinic
Great Western Ind Park
Three Bridges Business Centre
Three Bridges Primary School
Osterley RFC
The Aviary
Windmill Lane
B454
Tentelow Lane
A4127
Boston Road
A3002
Boston Manor Station
M4
Golf Course
Wyevale Garden Centre
Wyke Green Golf Club
Grasshoppers RFC
Centaurs RFC
Centaurs Business Centre
Syon Lane
Syon Lane Station
Great West Road
A4
Great West Trading Estate
Brunel University (Osterley Campus) Track
Isleworth & Syon School for Boys
The Green School for Girls
Osterley Station
Campion House College
Crown Court
West Thames College
Metro Industrial Centre
London Road
A315
Isleworth Station
B363
Isleworth Town Primary School
West Middlesex University Hosp
Twickenham Road
A310
Spur Road
Syon Park School
Butterfly House
Smallberry Green Primary School
Hounslow East Stn
Hounslow Central Station
Bus Depot
Hounslow Manor School
High Street
Hanworth Road
Grove Road
Inwood Park
Chatsworth J&I School
Heath Business Cen
Worton Hall Industrial Est
Victory Business Cen
Isleworth Recreation Centre
Richmond Road
St Margaret's Rd
A3004
Waterside Business Cen
Oaklands Primary School
Elthorne Park High School
Elthorne Sports Centre
The Waterside Trading Cen
Boston Business Park
River Brent Business Park
River Brent
Fielding Primary School
St Marks Primary School
City of Westminster Cemetery
Lampton Park
Lampton School
Civic Centre
Alexandra Junior School
Farnell Hse Medical Centre
Heston Junior School
Heston Community School
Lampton Road
A3005
Mogden Lane
Ivybridge Retail Park
Superstore
TW7
TW3
A B C D E F G
1 2 3 4 5 6 7 8 9 10
514 15 16
80 79 78 77 76 75
1 grid square represents 500 metres

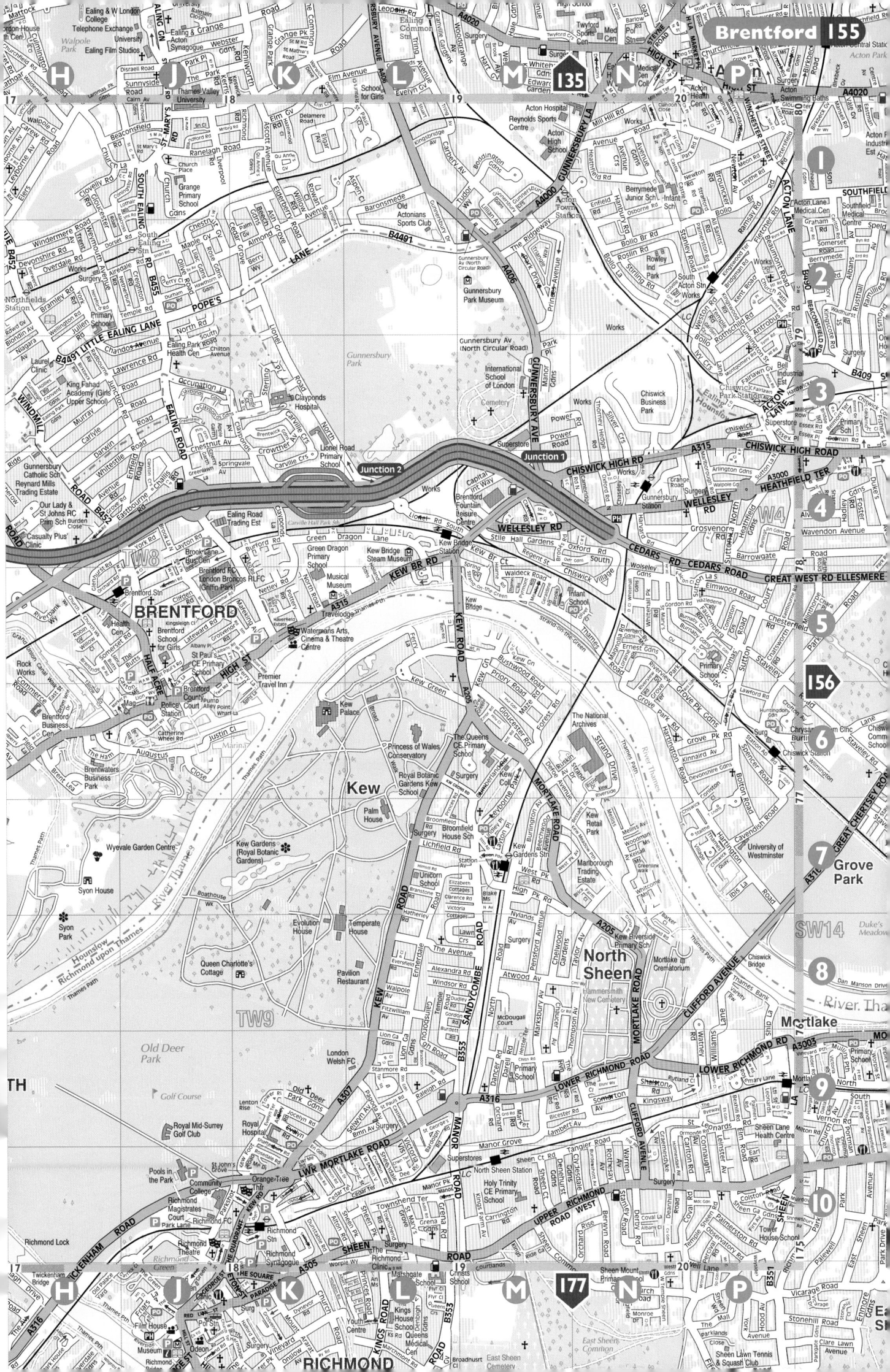
BRENTFORD
Kew
North Sheen
Mortlake
RICHMOND
Grove Park
Gunnersbury Park
Kew Gardens (Royal Botanic Gardens)
Old Deer Park
Syon Park
Syon House
Kew Palace
Palm House
Princess of Wales Conservatory
Temperate House
Evolution House
Pavilion Restaurant
Queen Charlotte's Cottage
Wyevale Garden Centre
Royal Mid-Surrey Golf Club
Golf Course
London Welsh FC
Richmond Lock
Twickenham Bridge
Chiswick Bridge
The National Archives
Mortlake Crematorium
Hammersmith New Cemetery
Gunnersbury Park Museum
Chiswick Business Park
Kew Bridge Steam Museum
Musical Museum
Watermans Arts, Cinema & Theatre Centre
Brentford FC London Broncos RLFC (Griffin Park)
Brentwaters Business Park
Kew Retail Park
Marlborough Trading Estate
University of Westminster
Thames Valley University
Ealing Film Studios
Walpole Park
Junction 1
Junction 2
River Thames
Thames Path
Hounslow
Richmond upon Thames
TW8
TW9
W4
SW14
KEW ROAD
MORTLAKE ROAD
CHISWICK HIGH RD
GREAT WEST RD
LOWER RICHMOND ROAD
UPPER RICHMOND ROAD WEST
SHEEN ROAD
LWR MORTLAKE ROAD
CLIFFORD AVENUE
GUNNERSBURY AVE
SOUTH EALING RD
LITTLE EALING LANE
EALING ROAD
KEW BR RD
HIGH ST
ACTON LANE
SANDYCOMBE ROAD
MANOR ROAD
TWICKENHAM ROAD
A315
A205
A316
A307
A406
A4000
B4491
B452
B353
Kew Bridge Station
Kew Gardens Stn
North Sheen Station
Richmond Stn
Mortlake Stn
Brentford Stn
Gunnersbury Station
Chiswick Station
Chiswick Park Station
Acton Town Station
South Acton Stn
South Ealing Stn
H J K L M N P
17 18 19 20
1 2 3 4 5 6 7 8 9 10
135
156
177

156
136
155
178
A
B
C
D
E
F
G
1
2
3
4
5
6
7
8
9
10
521
22
23
Acton
Shepherd's Bush
Bedford Park
Acton Green
HAMMERSMITH
Brook Green
CHISWICK
BARNES
FULHAM
Mortlake
Grove Park
East Sheen
Roehampton
PUTNEY
W6
SW13
SW14
River Thames
THE VALE
UXBRIDGE ROAD
GOLDHAWK RD
CHISWICK HIGH ROAD
KING STREET
GREAT WEST RD
HAMMERSMITH FLYOVER
HAMMERSMITH BR RD
CASTELNAU
BURLINGTON LANE
GREAT CHERTSEY ROAD
ACTON LANE
SHEPHERD'S BUSH RD
FULHAM PALACE RD
CHURCH ROAD
BARNES HIGH ST
STATION ROAD
MORTLAKE HIGH STREET
LOWER RICHMOND RD
UPPER RICHMOND ROAD
LWR RICHMOND ROAD
QUEEN'S RIDE
ROCKS LANE
MILL HILL ROAD
LONSDALE
SHEEN LANE
ROEHAMPTON LANE
Acton Central Station
Chiswick Station
Barnes Bridge Station
Barnes Station
Mortlake Stn
Hammersmith Bridge
Chiswick House
London Wetland Centre
Fulham FC (Craven Cottage)
Charing Cross Hospital
Barn Elms Athletics Track
The Roehampton Priory Hospital
Roehampton University (Southlands College)
Roehampton University (Digby Stuart College)
Rosslyn Park RFC
Duke's Meadows
Barnes Common
Old Barnes Cemetery
Hounslow
Richmond upon Thames
Hammersmith & Fulham
Wandsworth
1 grid square represents 500 metres

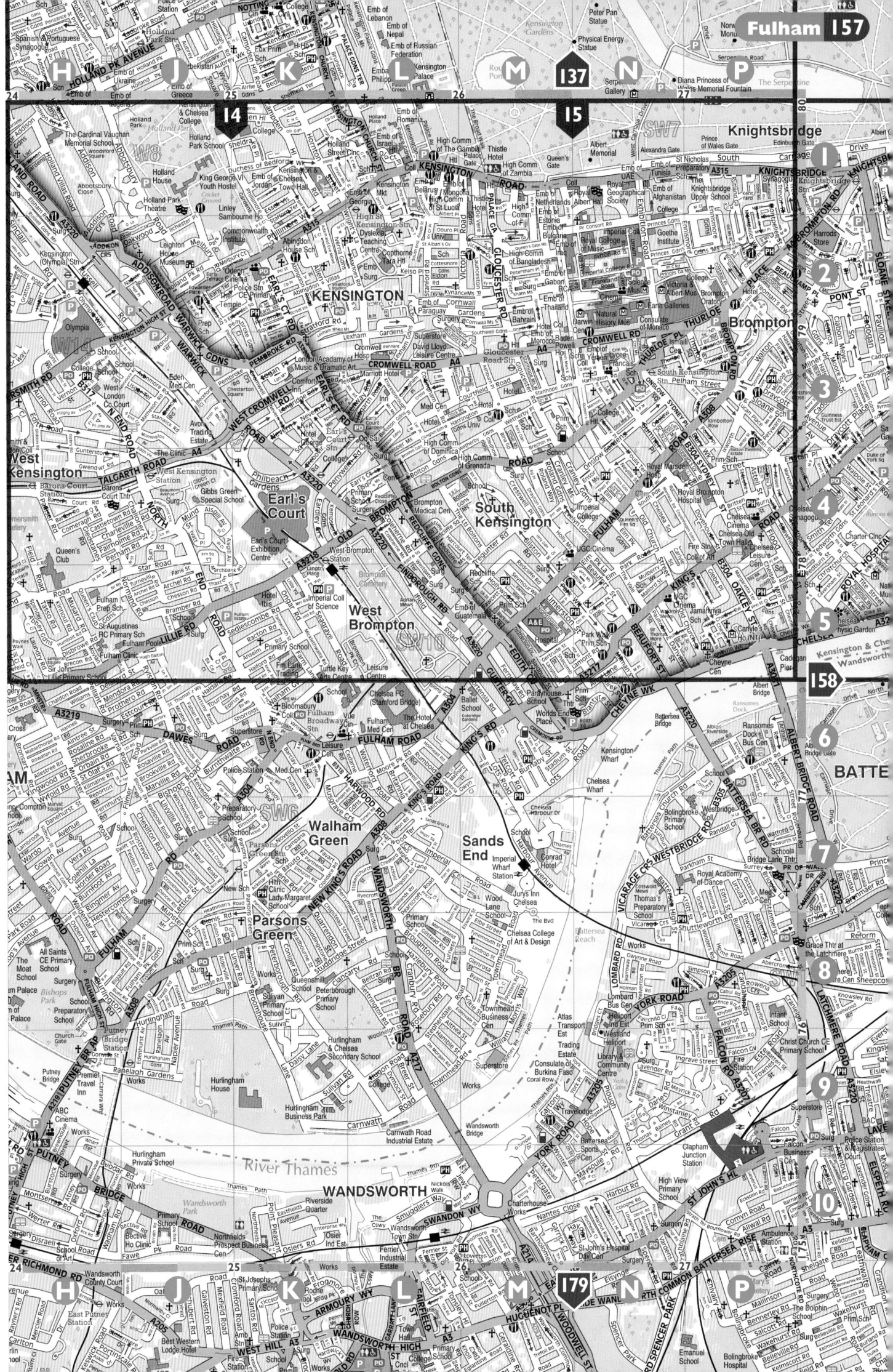
137
14
15
158
179
Knightsbridge
KENSINGTON
Brompton
West Kensington
Earl's Court
South Kensington
West Brompton
Walham Green
Sands End
Parsons Green
WANDSWORTH
River Thames
Kensington Gardens
The Serpentine
Holland Park
Olympia
Brompton Cemetery
Chelsea FC (Stamford Bridge)
Hurlingham House
Clapham Junction Station
KENSINGTON ROAD
CROMWELL ROAD
FULHAM ROAD
KING'S ROAD
NEW KING'S ROAD
CHEYNE WK
HOLLAND PK AVENUE
TALGARTH ROAD
LILLIE RD
YORK ROAD
WANDSWORTH BR ROAD
ALBERT BRIDGE ROAD
BATTERSEA BR RD
PUTNEY BR AP
BATTE

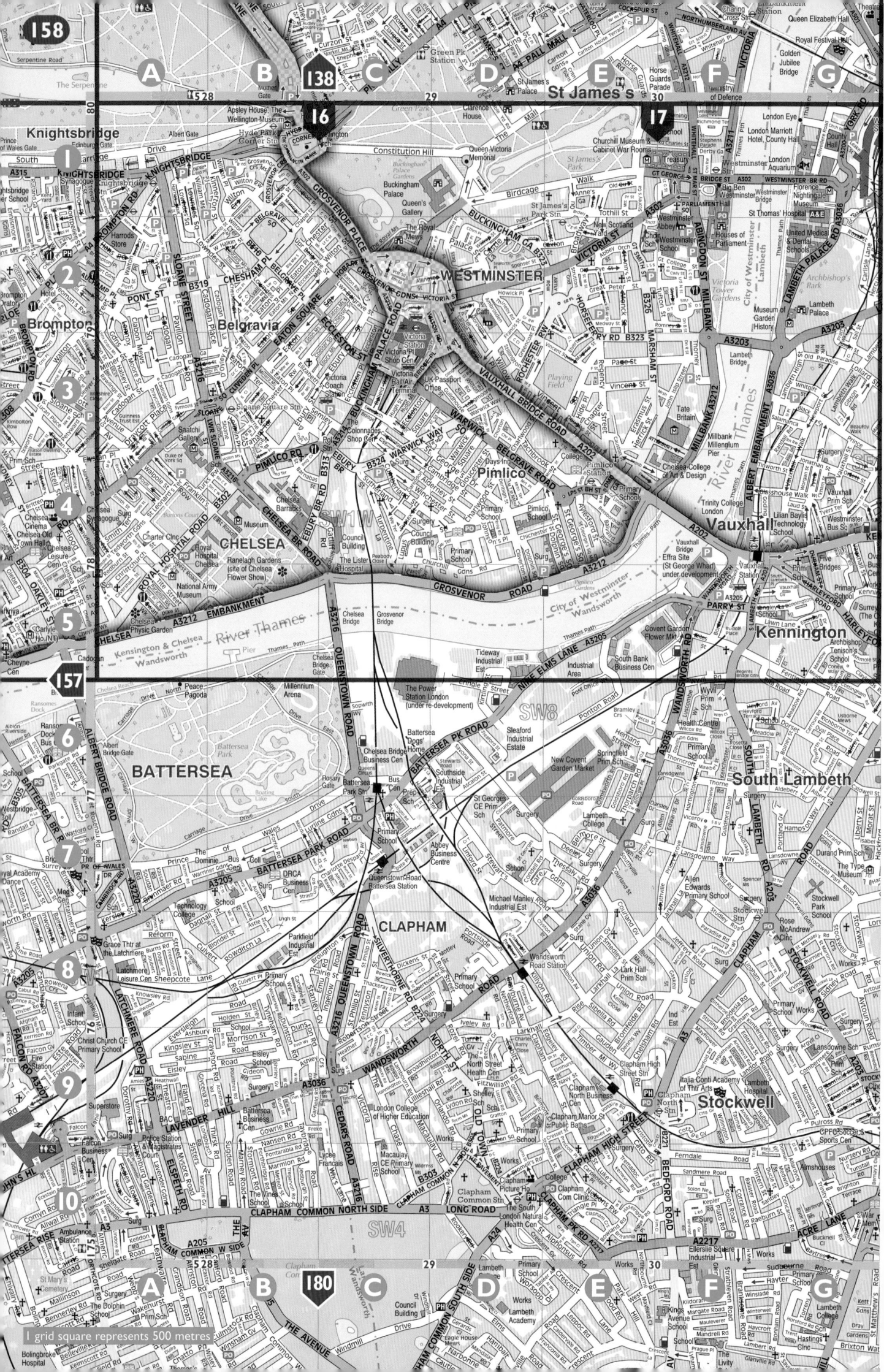

158
138
16
17
157
180
A
B
C
D
E
F
G
1
2
3
4
5
6
7
8
9
10
St James's
Knightsbridge
Brompton
Belgravia
WESTMINSTER
Pimlico
CHELSEA
Vauxhall
Kennington
BATTERSEA
South Lambeth
CLAPHAM
Stockwell
River Thames
SW1W
SW8
SW4
Buckingham Palace
Victoria Station
Houses of Parliament
Battersea Park
Clapham Common
The Power Station London (under re-development)
New Covent Garden Market
1 grid square represents 500 metres

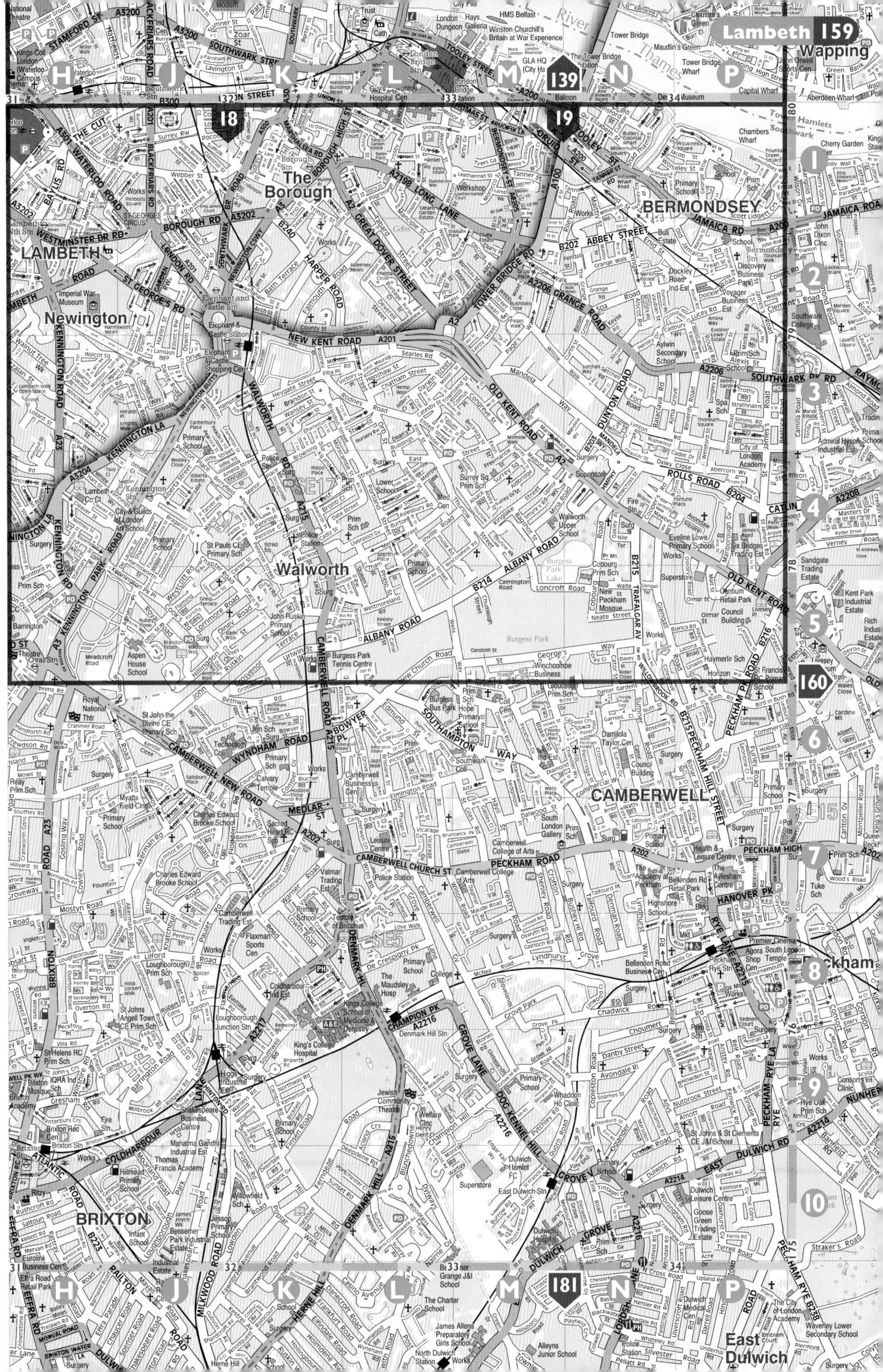

Lambeth 159
H
J
K
L
M
N
P
139
18
19
160
181
1
2
3
4
5
6
7
8
9
10
Wapping
The Borough
BERMONDSEY
LAMBETH
Newington
Walworth
CAMBERWELL
Peckham
BRIXTON
East Dulwich
SE17
SE5
SE15
SW9
River Thames
Tower Bridge
HMS Belfast
London Bridge Stn
Elephant and Castle Stn
Imperial War Museum
Burgess Park
King's College Hospital
Denmark Hill Stn
Peckham Rye Stn
East Dulwich Stn
Brixton Stn
Loughborough Junction Stn
North Dulwich Station
NEW KENT ROAD
OLD KENT ROAD
TOWER BRIDGE RD
WALWORTH RD
CAMBERWELL ROAD
CAMBERWELL NEW ROAD
CAMBERWELL CHURCH ST
PECKHAM ROAD
KENNINGTON PARK ROAD
KENNINGTON RD
BOROUGH HIGH ST
GREAT DOVER STREET
LONG LANE
JAMAICA RD
ALBANY ROAD
DENMARK HILL
GROVE LANE
DOG KENNEL HILL
COLDHARBOUR
BRIXTON ROAD
RYE LANE
EAST DULWICH RD
PECKHAM RYE

160
140
159
182
A
B
C
D
E
F
G
1
2
3
4
5
6
7
8
9
10
535
36
37
80
79
78
77
76
75
Wapping
Rotherhithe
Canary Wharf
Millwall
DEPTFORD
New Cross Gate
New Cross
St Johns
Peckham
Nunhead
Ladywell
Brockley
Dulwich
SE16
SE8
SE14
SE15
SE4
E14
JAMAICA ROAD
LOWER ROAD
SALTER ROAD
REDRIFF RD
PLOUGH WAY
EVELYN ST
CREEK ROAD
DEPTFORD CHURCH STREET
RAYMOUTH ROAD
ROTHERHITHE NEW RD
SOUTHWARK PK RD
OLD KENT ROAD
NEW CROSS RD
QUEEN'S ROAD
LEWISHAM WAY
LOAMPIT HILL
BROCKLEY ROAD
DRAKEFELL ROAD
EVELINA ROAD
NUNHEAD LANE
EAST DULWICH RD
RYE LANE
PECKHAM HILL STREET
WESTFERRY ROAD
GREENWICH HIGH ROAD
BLACKHEATH RD
River Thames
Surrey Quays
Canada Water
Greenland Dock
Southwark Park
Peckham Rye Park
Millwall FC (The New Den)
Goldsmiths College (Univ of London)
Tower Hamlets
Southwark
Lewisham
1 grid square represents 500 metres

The O2
River Thames
Blackwall Reach
Newham
Greenwich
North Greenwich Station
Tunnel Avenue Trading Est
Delta Wharf
Bugsby's Reach
The David Beckham Academy
Millennium Way
Gas Works
Silvertown
Thames Barrier
Thames Barrier Information & Learning Centre
Anchorage Point Industrial Estate
Riverside
BUGSBY'S WAY
UCI Filmworks Cinema
Brocklebank Industrial Estate
Lombard Trading Estate
Meridian Trading Estate
VIP Trading Estate
Ropery Business Park
Stone Lake Retail Park
Angerstein Business Park
Maritime Industrial Estate
Greenwich Industrial Estate
WOOLWICH ROAD
Westcombe Park Station
Charlton Stn
Charlton Athletic FC (The Valley)
Millennium Wharf
Cubitt Town
ISLE OF DOGS
Community Centre (Island History Trust)
Island Gardens Station
MANCHESTER ROAD
George Greens School
Lovell's Wharf
Trinity Hospital
GREENWICH
University of Greenwich
Old Royal Naval College
Trinity College of Music
Cutty Sark Clipper Ship
Cutty Sark Station
Greenwich Pier
TRAFALGAR ROAD
ROMNEY ROAD
National Maritime Museum
The Queens House
Maze Hill Station
SE10
Greenwich Park
Flamsteed House Museum
Old Royal Observatory Greenwich
Conduit House
St Ursulas Convent School
The Wernher Collection at Ranger's House
Greenwich Theatre & Art Gallery
CHARLTON WAY
SHOOTERS HILL RD A2
BLACKHEATH HILL
Blackheath Business Estate
John Roan School
Blackheath High Senior School
Blackheath Preparatory School
SE7
SE3
Blackheath
All Saints CE Primary Sch
Blackheath Stn
Blackheath Park
Blackheath High School GDST
Blackheath Hosp
Brooklands Primary School
SUN IN SANDS ROUNDABOUT
OLD DOVER ROAD
SHOOTERS HILL ROAD
CHARLTON ROAD
Manor Brook Medical Centre
Morden College Homes
Thomas Tallis School
Kidbrooke Station
Kidbrooke
Long Lane AFC
Huntsman Sports Club
Meadowside Leisure Centre
Sutcliffe Park Athletics Track
Old Colfeian Sports Club
ELTHAM ROAD
LEWISHAM
Lewisham Centre
Goldsmiths College
LEE TERRACE
BELMONT HILL
HIGH ROAD
BURNT ASH ROAD
Our Lady of Lourdes RC Primary School
Christ the King Sixth Form College
Camden Ho Clinic
The Blackheath Clinic
Sports Ground
141
162
183

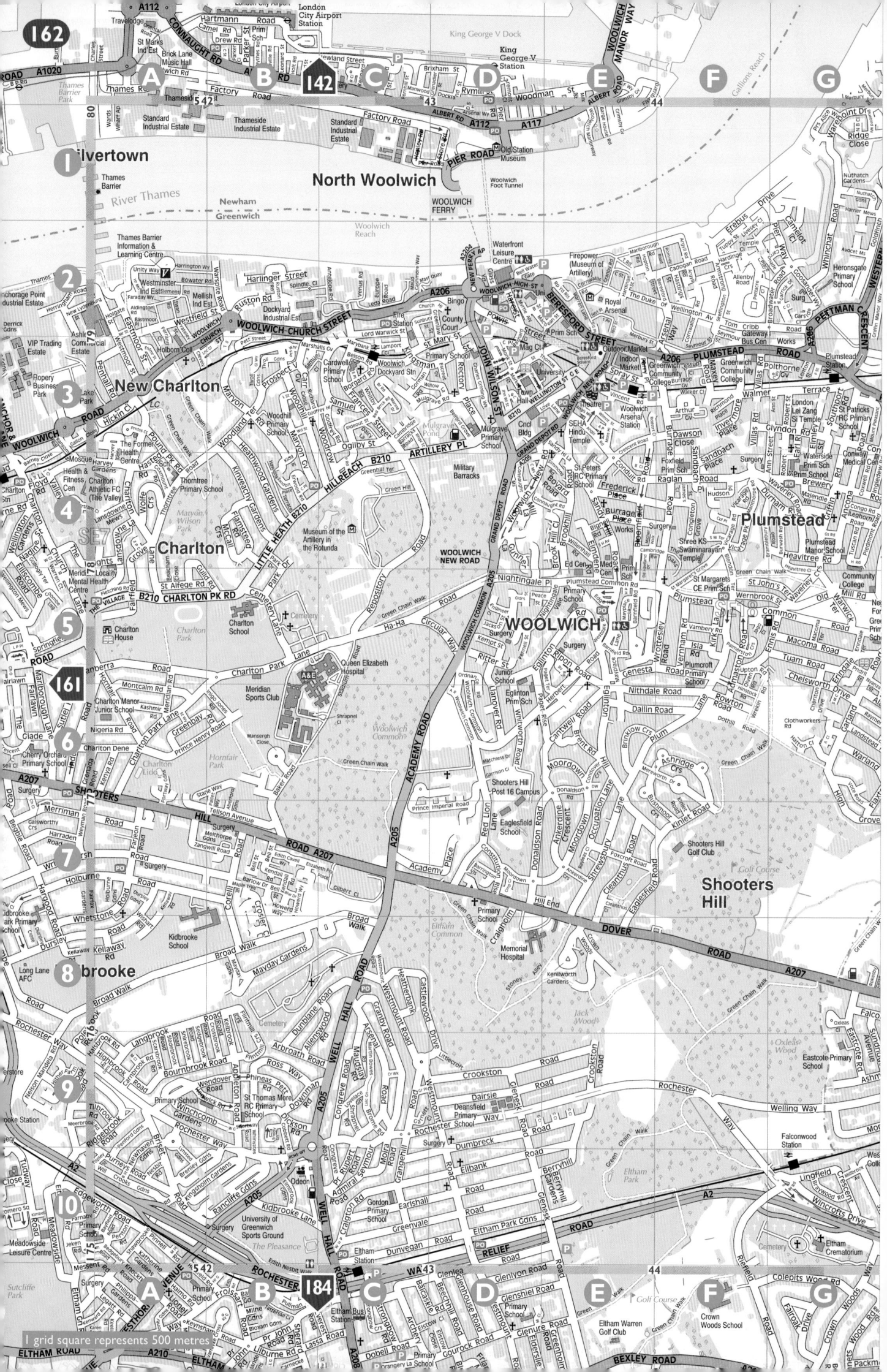

142
161
184
A
B
C
D
E
F
G
1
2
3
4
5
6
7
8
9
10
London City Airport Station
King George V Dock
King George V Station
Silvertown
Thames Barrier
River Thames
Newham
Greenwich
North Woolwich
Old Station Museum
Woolwich Foot Tunnel
WOOLWICH FERRY
Woolwich Reach
Gallions Reach
Thames Barrier Information & Learning Centre
Waterfront Leisure Centre
Firepower (Museum of Artillery)
Royal Arsenal
New Charlton
Charlton
WOOLWICH
Plumstead
Shooters Hill
Charlton House
Charlton Park
Charlton School
Museum of the Artillery in the Rotunda
Military Barracks
Queen Elizabeth Hospital
Meridian Sports Club
Woolwich Common
Woolwich Arsenal Station
Woolwich Dockyard Stn
Plumstead Station
Shooters Hill Golf Club
Golf Course
Eltham Common
Memorial Hospital
Jack Wood
Oxleas Wood
Eltham Park
Falconwood Station
Eltham Crematorium
Eltham Warren Golf Club
Crown Woods School
Eltham Station
Kidbrooke School
Kidbrooke
Long Lane AFC
University of Greenwich Sports Ground
The Pleasance
Sutcliffe Park
Meadowside Leisure Centre
Shooters Hill Post 16 Campus
Eaglesfield School
Cemetery
Woolwich Church Street
Woolwich High St
Beresford Street
Plumstead Road
Woolwich New Road
John Wilson St
Grand Depot Road
Woolwich Common
Academy Road
Well Hall Road
Shooters Hill Road A207
Dover Road
Rochester Way
Rochester Way Relief Road
Kidbrooke Lane
Charlton Park Lane
Charlton Pk Rd
Little Heath
Hillreach
Artillery Pl
Nightingale Pl
Plumstead Common Rd
Welling Way
Bexley Road
Eltham Road
Pier Road
Albert Rd
Woodman St
Factory Road
Connaught Rd
A205
A206
A207
A2
A112
A117
A210
B210
1 grid square represents 500 metres

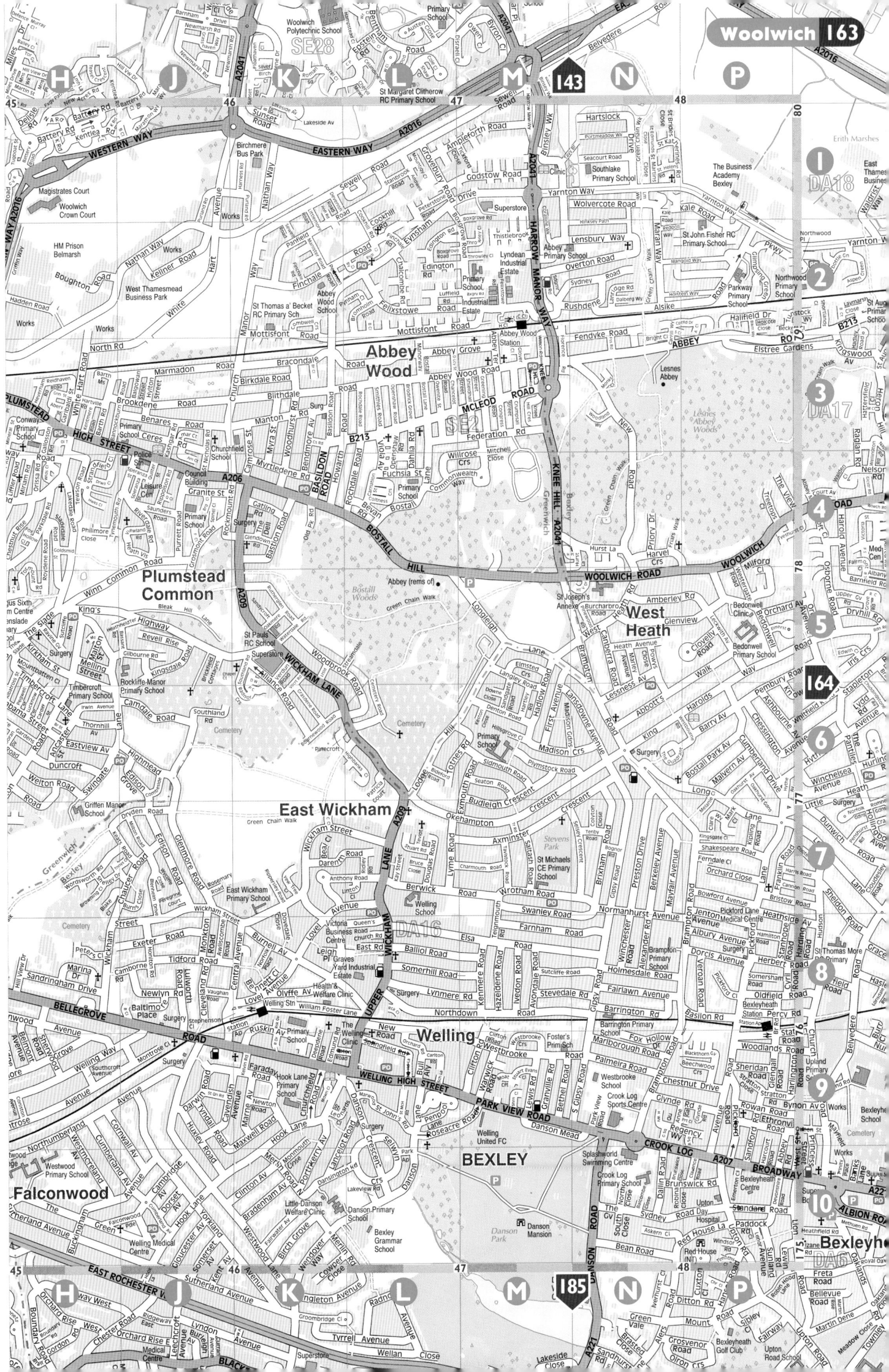
Abbey Wood
SE2
Plumstead Common
West Heath
East Wickham
Welling
BEXLEY
Falconwood
DA16
DA17
DA18
DA6
SE28
143
164
185
H
J
K
L
M
N
P
1
2
3
4
5
6
7
8
9
10
WESTERN WAY
EASTERN WAY
A2016
A2041
A206
A209
A207
A221
B213
HARROW MANOR WAY
KNEE HILL
WOOLWICH ROAD
BOSTALL HILL
WICKHAM LANE
PLUMSTEAD HIGH STREET
BELLEGROVE ROAD
WELLING HIGH STREET
PARK VIEW ROAD
CROOK LOG
BROADWAY
EAST ROCHESTER WAY
DANSON ROAD
MCLEOD ROAD
BASILDON ROAD
Woolwich Polytechnic School
Magistrates Court
Woolwich Crown Court
HM Prison Belmarsh
West Thamesmead Business Park
Birchmere Bus Park
Abbey Wood Station
Lesnes Abbey
Lesnes Abbey Woods
Bostall Woods
Abbey (rems of)
Welling Stn
Bexleyheath Station
Danson Park
Danson Mansion
Welling United FC
Splashworld Swimming Centre
Crook Log Sports Centre
Erith Marshes
Cemetery
Green Chain Walk

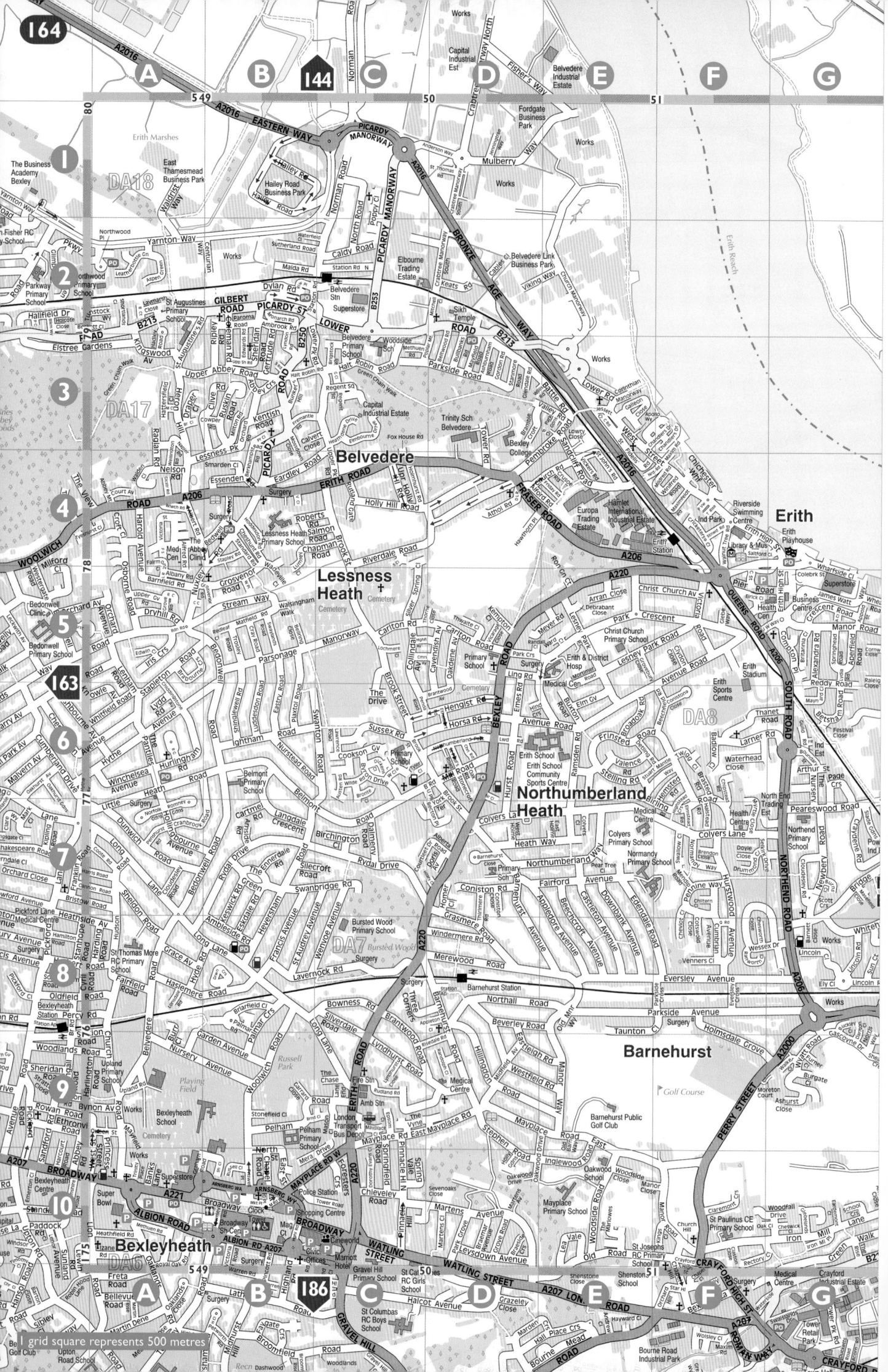
164
144
163
186
A
B
C
D
E
F
G
1
2
3
4
5
6
7
8
9
10
549
50
51
80
79
78
77
76
75
DA18
DA17
DA8
DA7
DA6
Belvedere
Lessness Heath
Erith
Northumberland Heath
Barnehurst
Bexleyheath
Erith Marshes
East Thamesmead Business Park
Hailey Road Business Park
Capital Industrial Est
Belvedere Industrial Estate
Fordgate Business Park
Belvedere Link Business Park
Elbourne Trading Estate
Capital Industrial Estate
Europa Trading Estate
Hamlet International Industrial Estate
Erith Reach
Belvedere Stn
Erith Station
Barnehurst Station
Bexleyheath Station
A2016
EASTERN WAY
PICARDY MANORWAY
BRONZE AGE WAY
A206
ERITH ROAD
FRASER ROAD
WOOLWICH ROAD
A220
BEXLEY ROAD
QUEENS ROAD
SOUTH ROAD
NORTHEND ROAD
A2000
PERRY STREET
A207
BROADWAY
WATLING STREET
CRAYFORD HIGH ST
ROMAN WAY
GRAVEL HILL
MAYPLACE RD W
ALBION ROAD
B213
B250
B253
LOWER ROAD
GILBERT ROAD
PICARDY ST
Erith Playhouse
Riverside Swimming Centre
Erith Sports Centre
Erith Stadium
Erith School
Erith School Community Sports Centre
Erith & District Hosp
Trinity Sch Belvedere
Bexley College
Bexleyheath School
Barnehurst Public Golf Club
Golf Course
Russell Park
Playing Field
Cemetery
London Transport Bus Depot
Broadway Sh Cen
Civic Offices
Cineworld
Marriott Hotel
Police Station
Shopping Centre
Bedonwell Clinic
Bedonwell Primary School
Belmont Primary School
Bursted Wood Primary School
Normandy Primary School
Colyers Primary School
Mayplace Primary School
North End Trading Est
Northend Primary School
Crayford Industrial Estate
Tower Retail Park
Bourne Road Industrial Park
1 grid square represents 500 metres

Coldharbour
Purfleet
Slade Green
North End
Barnes Cray
Crayford
Temple Hill
Dartford Marshes
Crayford Marshes
Aveley Marshes
Wennington Marshes
Crayford Ness
River Thames
Erith Rands
Long Reach
Havering
Bexley
Thurrock
Kent County
145
166
187
Coldharbour Lane
LONDON ROAD
ARTERIAL ROAD PURFLEET
NEW TANK HL RD
TANK HILL RD
Purfleet Ind Park
Milehams Industrial Estate
Purfleet Industrial Access Rd
Fanns Farm
Council Building
Purfleet Primary School
Premier Travel Inn
Purfleet Station
Beacon Hill Industrial Estate
Darent Industrial Park
Landau Way
Dayton Drive
Maypole Crescent
Burnett Road
Ness Road
Manford Industrial Estate
Ray Lamb Way
Wallhouse Road
Bilton Road
Frobisher Rd
Slade Green Primary School
Howbury Centre
Church Trading Estate
Slade Green Road
Hollywood Way
Brompton Dr
Hilden Dr
Forest Road
Elm Road
Hazel Road
Cedar Rd
Moat Lane
Slade Green FC
Slade Green Station
Oak Rd
Dale View
Howbury Lane
Crayside Industrial Estate
Kennet Road
A206 THAMES ROAD
Thames Road
Maiden Lane
Stour Rd
Medway Road
Barnes Cray Primary School
Iron Mill Lane
Beech Walk
Mill Place
Geoffrey Whitworth Theatre
CRAYFORD WAY
Cray Cl
Barnes Cray Rd
Acorn Industrial Park
Whitehill Rd
Joyce Green Lane
Darent Valley Path
UNIVERSITY WAY
A206
Marsh Street
Henderson Drive
Wellcome Av
Central Road
Temple Hill
Swan Business Park
Millside Industrial Estate
Burnham Trading Estate
Sandpit Road
A2026 BURNHAM ROAD
Lawson Rd
Priory Rd
Mayfair Rd
Savoy Road
Holy Trinity CE Prim Sch
Victoria Industrial Park
Riverside Industrial Estate
Business Centre
Bus Garage
Hythe St
St. Anselms RC Prim Sch
Temple Hill Prim Sch
Littlebrook Manor Way
Kingsley Av
Lansbury Crs
Cemetery
Wodehouse Road
Wordsworth Way
Farnol Rd
Cavell Crescent
VICTORIA ROAD
A282
DA1
CRAYFORD
52
53
54
55
H
J
K
L
M
N
P
1
2
3
4
5
6
7
8
9
10
75
76
77
78
79
80

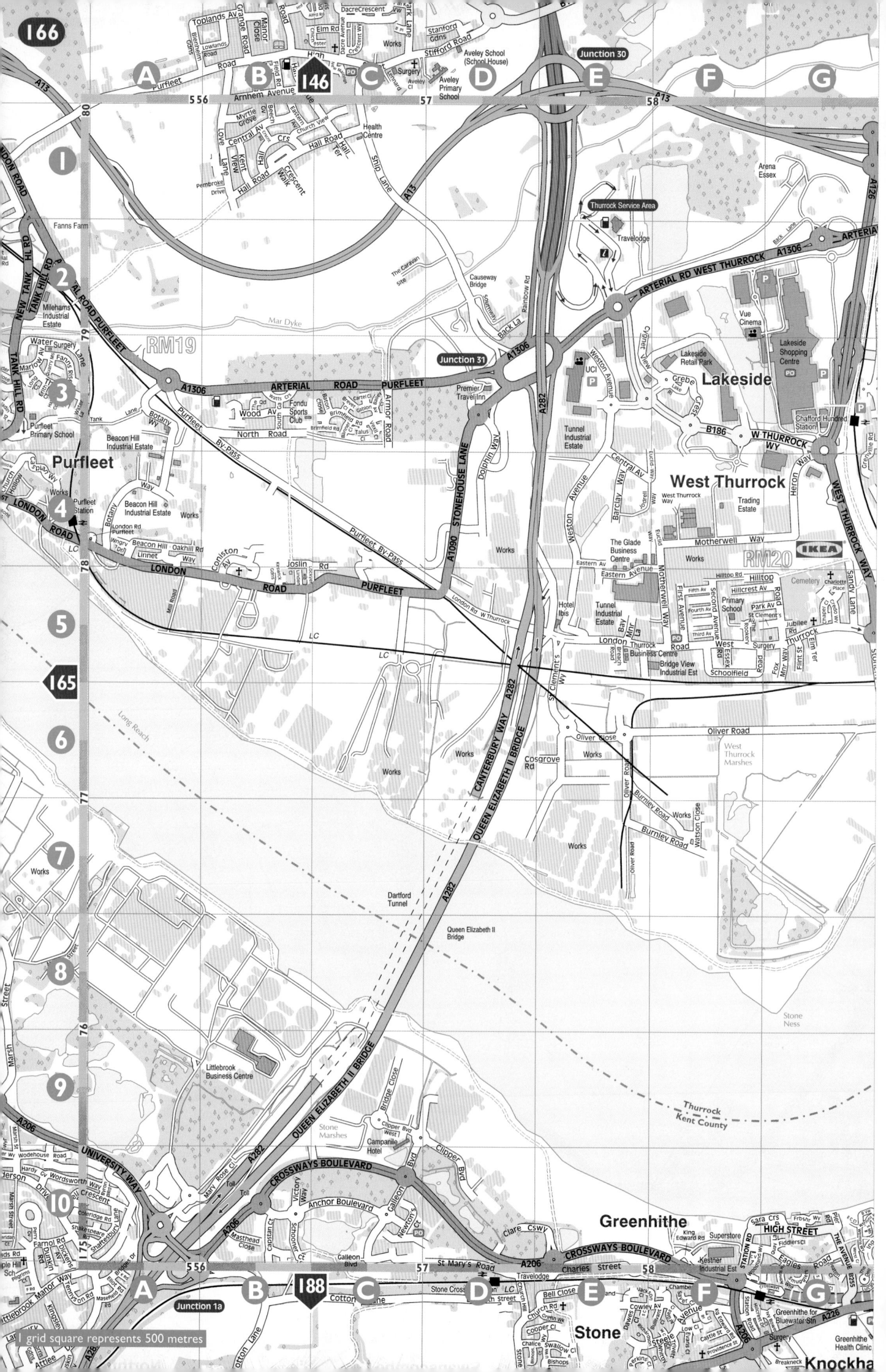
Junction 30
Junction 31
Thurrock Service Area
Travelodge
Arena Essex
Lakeside
Lakeside Shopping Centre
Lakeside Retail Park
Vue Cinema
Chafford Hundred Station
West Thurrock
Trading Estate
IKEA
RM20
RM19
Purfleet
Purfleet Station
Purfleet Primary School
Milehams Industrial Estate
Fanns Farm
Beacon Hill Industrial Estate
Fondu Sports Club
Premier Travel Inn
UCI
Tunnel Industrial Estate
The Glade Business Centre
Hotel Ibis
Bridge View Industrial Est
West Thurrock Marshes
Stone Ness
Dartford Tunnel
Queen Elizabeth II Bridge
Littlebrook Business Centre
Stone Marshes
Campanile Hotel
Greenhithe
Stone
Knockha
Greenhithe for Bluewater Stn
Greenhithe Health Clinic
Junction 1a
Aveley School (School House)
Aveley Primary School
Health Centre
Causeway Bridge
Mar Dyke
Long Reach
Thurrock
Kent County
ARTERIAL ROAD PURFLEET
ARTERIAL RD WEST THURROCK
LONDON ROAD PURFLEET
Purfleet By-Pass
STONEHOUSE LANE
CANTERBURY WAY
QUEEN ELIZABETH II BRIDGE
WEST THURROCK WAY
CROSSWAYS BOULEVARD
UNIVERSITY WAY
Oliver Road
Burnley Road
London Road West Thurrock
A13
A1306
A1090
A282
A126
A206
B186
1 grid square represents 500 metres

146
165
188

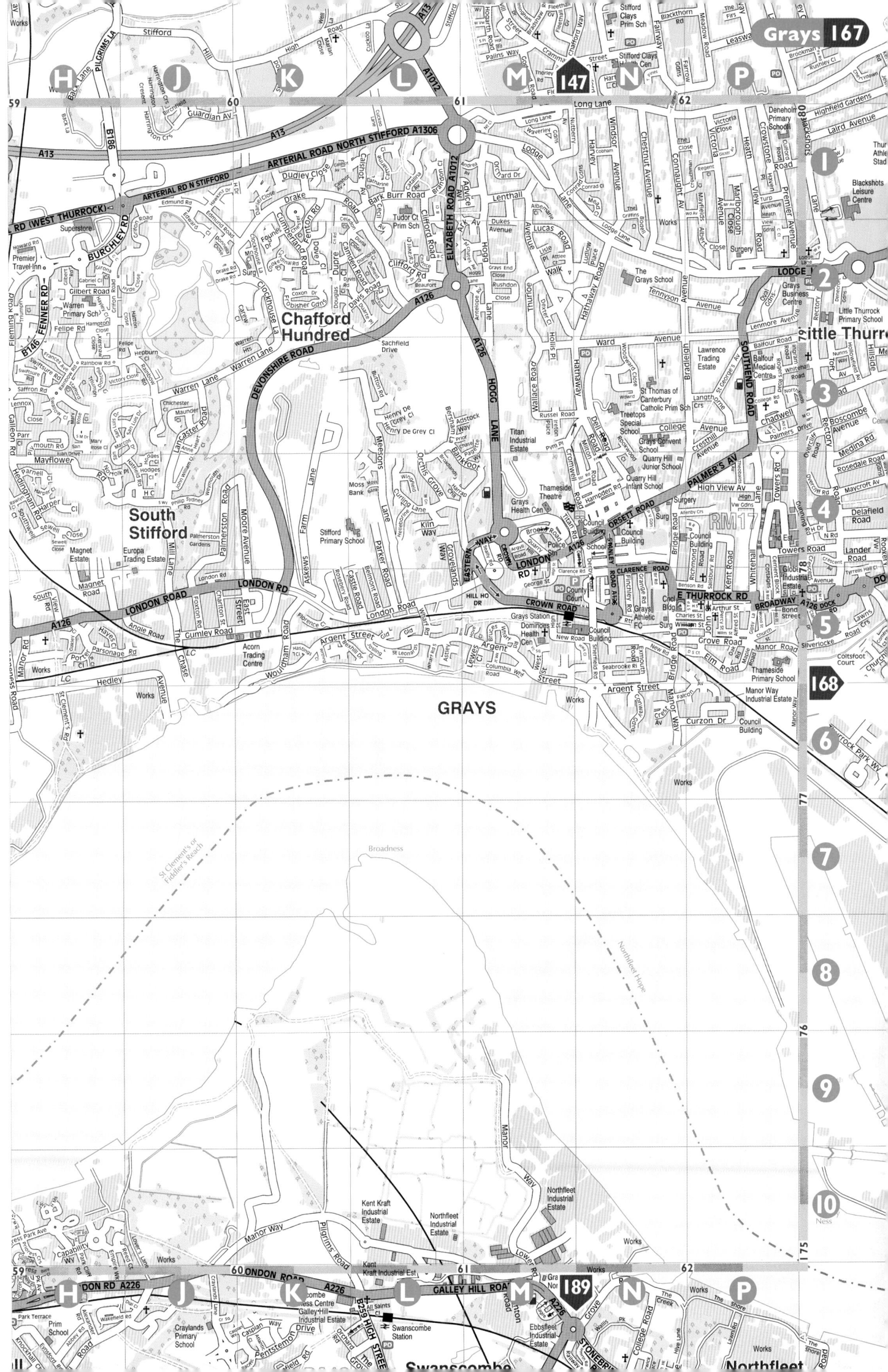
GRAYS
Chafford Hundred
South Stifford
Little Thurrock
Broadness
Northfleet Hope
St Clement's or Fiddler's Reach
Swanscombe
Northfleet
147
168
189

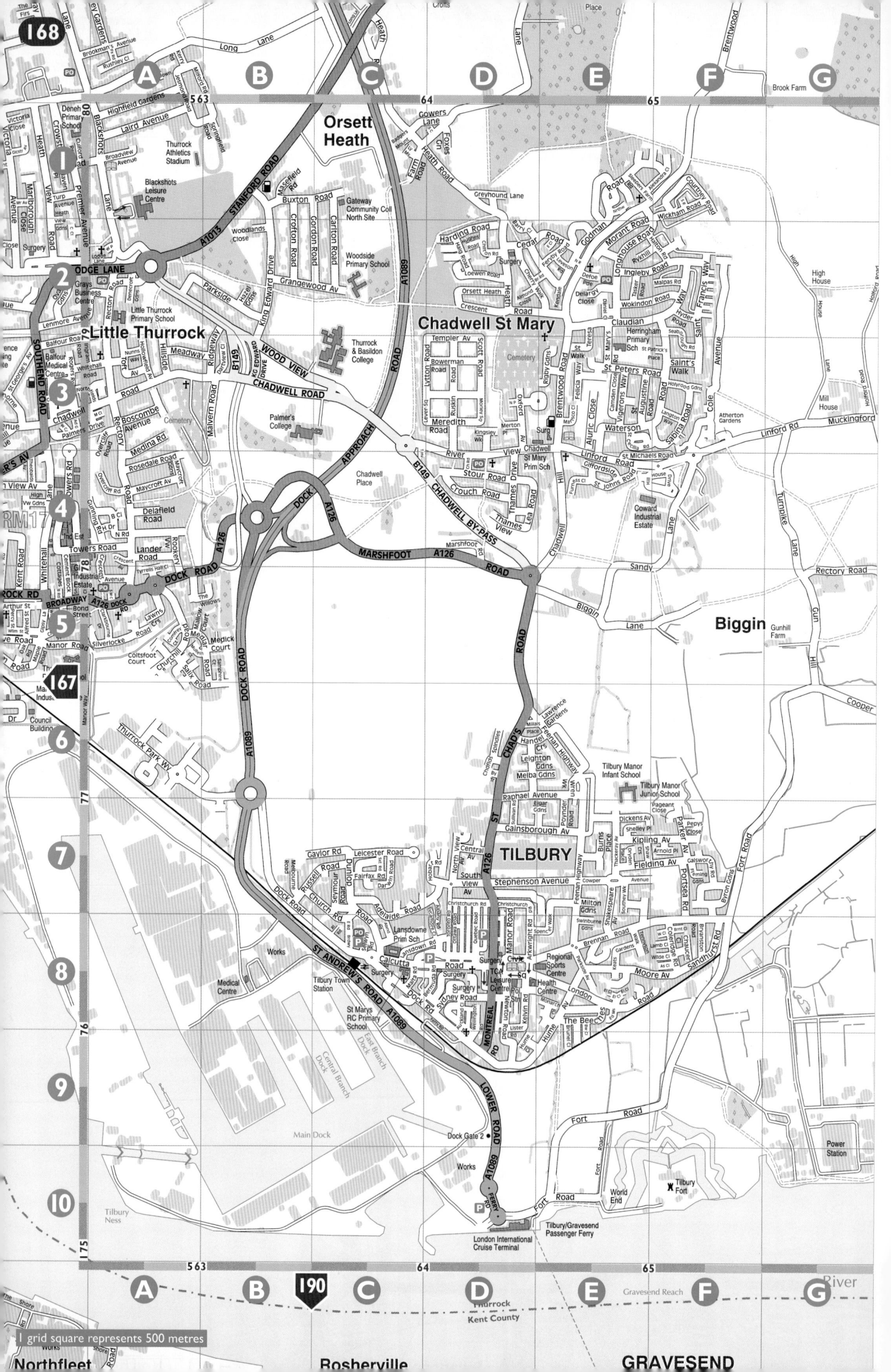
Orsett Heath
Chadwell St Mary
Little Thurrock
TILBURY
Biggin
GRAVESEND
Northfleet
Rosherville
Long Lane
Highfield Gardens
Laird Avenue
Deneh Primary School
Thurrock Athletics Stadium
Blackshots Leisure Centre
A1013 STANFORD ROAD
Gateway Community Coll North Site
Woodside Primary School
Grangewood Av
Woodlands Close
King Edward Drive
Wood View
Chadwell Road
Thurrock & Basildon College
Palmer's College
Little Thurrock Primary School
Grays Business Centre
Southend Road
Dock Approach Road
A1089
Chadwell By-Pass
Marshfoot Road
A126
Dock Road
Chadwell Place
Greyhound Lane
Heath Road
Gowers Lane
Brentwood Road
Linford Road
Herringham Primary Sch
St Mary Prim Sch
Coward Industrial Estate
Sandy Lane
Biggin Lane
Gunhill Farm
Turnpike Lane
Rectory Road
Muckingford Road
Mill House
High House
Brook Farm
St Chad's Road
Tilbury Manor Infant School
Tilbury Manor Junior School
Tilbury Town Station
St Andrew's Road
Lansdowne Prim Sch
St Marys RC Primary School
Regional Sports Centre
Health Centre
Lower Road
Main Dock
Central Branch Dock
East Branch Dock
Dock Gate 2
Works
Fort Road
Tilbury Fort
World End
Power Station
Tilbury/Gravesend Passenger Ferry
London International Cruise Terminal
Tilbury Ness
Medical Centre
Thurrock Park Wy
Gravesend Reach
River
Thurrock
Kent County
190
167
1 grid square represents 500 metres

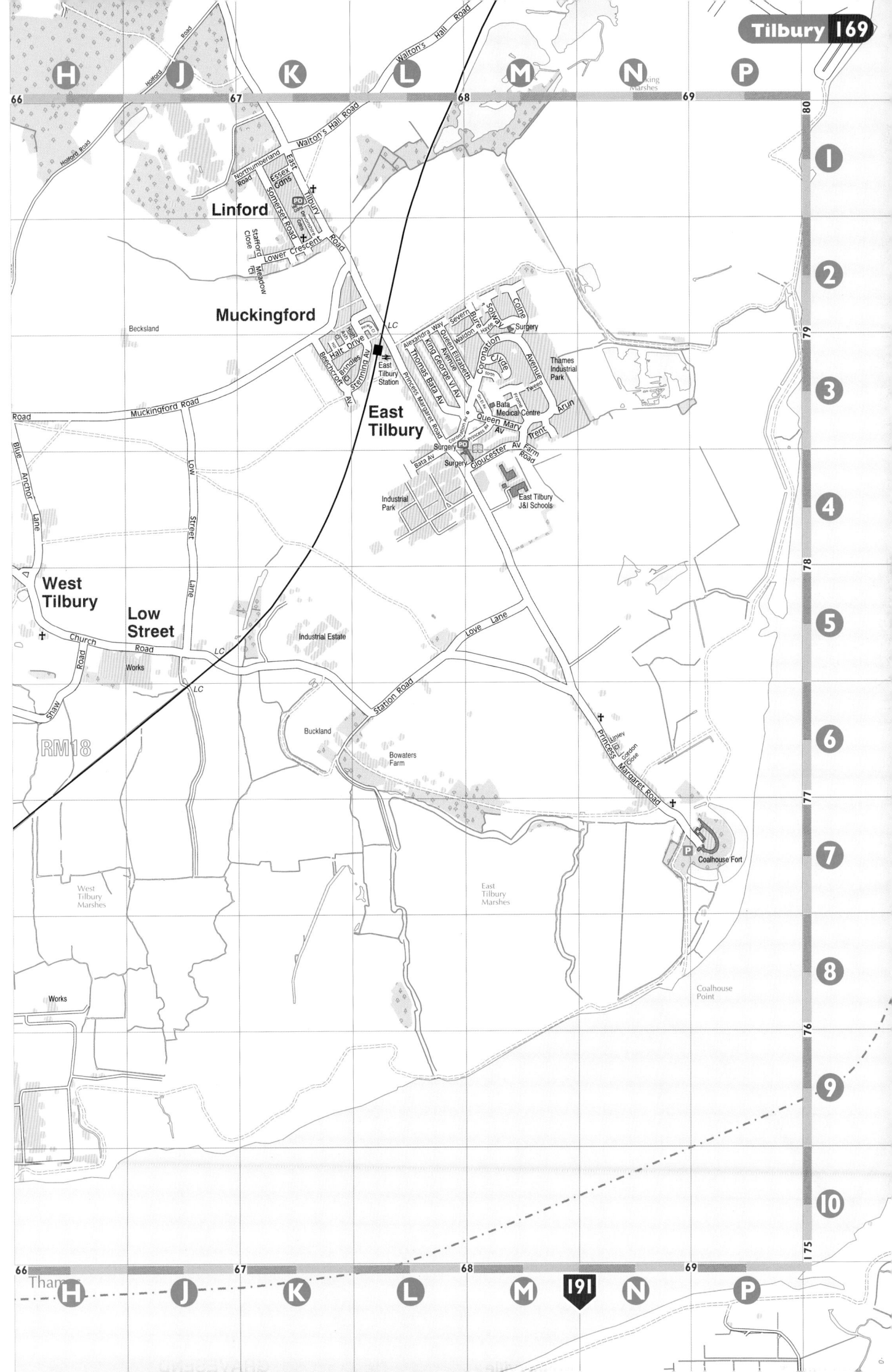
H
J
K
L
M
N
P
66
67
68
69
80
79
78
77
76
175
1
2
3
4
5
6
7
8
9
10
Linford
Muckingford
East Tilbury
West Tilbury
Low Street
Beckslands
Muckingford Road
Walton's Hall Road
Northumberland Road
Somerset Road
Lower Crescent
East Tilbury Road
Stafford Close
Meadow Cl
Essex Gdns
Halt Drive
Stenning Av
Beechcroft Av
Brindles
East Tilbury Station
LC
Princess Margaret Road
Thomas Bata Av
King George VI Av
Queen Elizabeth Avenue
Alexandra Way
Coronation Av
Severn
Waldon
Bure
Solway
Hayle
Colne
Clyde
Surgery
Thames Industrial Park
Avenue
Tweed
Frome
Arun
Bata Medical Centre
Queen Mary Av
Trent
Gloucester Av
Farm Road
Bata Av
East Tilbury J&I Schools
Industrial Park
Blue Anchor Lane
Low Street Lane
Church Road
Shaw Road
Works
Industrial Estate
Love Lane
Station Road
Buckland
Bowaters Farm
RM18
Linley Cl
Gordon Close
Coalhouse Fort
West Tilbury Marshes
East Tilbury Marshes
Coalhouse Point
Holford Road
191

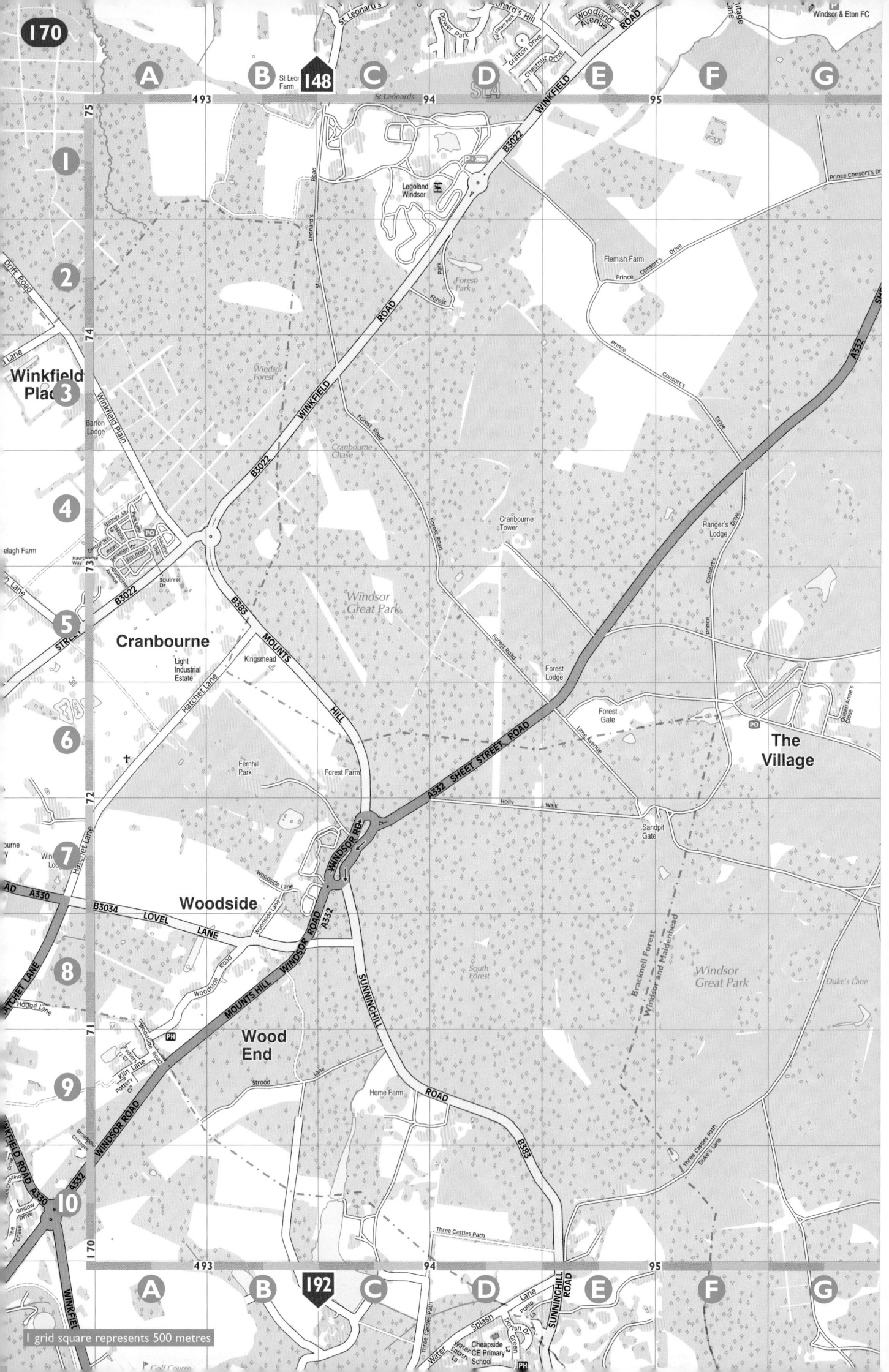

148

A B C D E F G

493   94   95

St Leonard's
St Leonard's Hill
Windsor & Eton FC
Dower Park
Crafton Drive
Woodland Avenue
ROAD
Chestnut Drive
WINKFIELD
Village Lane
Prince Consort's Dr

I

St Leonards
St Leon
Farm
SL4

B3022

Legoland
Windsor

Flemish Farm
Prince Consort's Drive

2

74

Forest
Park
Prince
Consort's

Winkfield
Place
3

WINKFIELD
ROAD
Windsor
Forest
Forest Road

Drive

Winkfield Plain
Barton
Lodge

B3022

Cranbourne
Chase

4

73

Somner La
PO

Cranbourne
Tower

Ranger's
Lodge

Hawthorne
Way

Squirrel
Dr

A332

SUPER

elagh Farm

5

Light
Industrial
Estate

B3022

B383

MOUNTS

Kingsmead

Windsor
Great Park

Forest Road

Forest Lodge

STREET

Cranbourne

Hatchet Lane

Consort's
Drive

Prince

Forest
Gate

The
Village

6

72

Fernhill
Park

HILL

Forest Farm

A332 SHEET STREET ROAD

Lime Avenue

PO

Queen Anne's
Close

Bourne

+

Forest
Gate

Windsor
Lodge

Holly

Walk

7

Hatchet Lane

WINDSOR RD

Sandpit
Gate

Woodside Lane

Woodside

8

B3034

LOVEL

LANE

A330

AD

A330

Hatchet Lane

Hodge Lane

Woodside
Road

WINDSOR ROAD

A332

South
Forest

Bracknell Forest
Windsor and Maidenhead

Windsor
Great Park

Duke's Lane

71

MOUNTS HILL

Kiln Lane

PH

SUNNINGHILL

9

Wood
End

Potters
Cl

strood

Lane

Home Farm

ROAD

B383

WINDSOR ROAD

KFIELD ROAD

A332

Three Castles Path

Duke's Lane

A330

The Chase

Onslow
Drive

10

170

WINKFIELD

Three Castles Path

493   94   95

A B C D E F G

192

Splash

Water

Pump
La

Doran Dr

SUNNINGHILL
ROAD

Three Castles Path

Cheapside
CE Primary
School

Water
Splash La

PH

Golf Course

OLD WINDSOR
Beaumont
Bishopsgate
Englefield Green
Egham Wick
Windsor Great Park
Cooper's Hill
149
172
193
Trevelyan Middle School
St Peters CE Middle School
Kings Court First School
St Johns Beaumont School
Bishopsgate School
Brunel University (Runnymede Campus)
Royal Holloway University of London
The Royal First School (Crown Aided)
Cumberland Lodge
Royal Lodge
Great Meadow Pond
Savill Garden (Windsor Great Park)
Obelisk Pond
Smith's Lawn
Norfolk Farm
Guards Polo Club
Englefield Green Infant School
St Judes CE Junior School
St Cuthberts CE Primary School
ACS Egham International School
Woodside
Bear's Rails
Cemetery
Parkside House
Albert Road
Datchet Road
Straight Road
St Luke's Road
Crimp Hill
Burfield Road
B3021 Road
Priest Hill
St Jude's Road
A328
A308
A30
London Road
Bishopsgate Road
Ridgemead Road
Wick Lane
Prospect Lane
Kings Lane
Wick Road
Ham Lane
Church Road
Ham Lane
Wharf Road
Friary Road
Coopers Hill Lane
Barley Mow Road
Tite Hill
Harvest Hill
Three Castles Path
The Long Walk
Queen Anne's Ride
Queen Anne's Gate
Sheet Street Road
Holly Drive
Rhododendron Ride
Windsor & Maidenhead
Surrey County
96
97
98
99
75
74
73
72
71
70
H
J
K
L
M
N
P
1
2
3
4
5
6
7
8
9
10

150
Wraysbury Reservoir
Wraysbury
Wraysbury Medical Centre
Wraysbury Primary School
Wraysbury Station
WINDSOR ROAD
STAINES ROAD
Magna Carta Lane
Windsor and Maidenhead
Surrey County
Junction 13
WRAYSBURY RD
Hythe End
Runnymede (NT)
Runnymede Hotel & Spa
171
Cooper's Hill
Brunel University (Runnymede Campus)
Royal Holloway University of London (Hall of Residence)
Runnymede Park
Strodes College
EGHAM BY-PASS
A30
A308
M25
THE GLANTY
THE CAUSEWAY
Green Business Centre
Industrial Estate
Superstore
EGHAM HILL
Royal Holloway University of London
Manorcroft Primary School
Egham Stn
EGHAM
Egham Sports Centre
Egham CC
Egham Town FC
Thorpe Lea
Hythe First & Middle School
The Magna Carta School
Egham Hythe
Thorpe Lea Primary School
THORPE LEA ROAD
Lammas Recreation Ground
PRIEST HILL
ST JUDE'S ROAD
St Judes CE Junior School
TW20
LONDON ROAD
Prune Hill
Milton Park
194
Thorpe Industrial Park
Royal Holloway University of London
1 grid square represents 500 metres

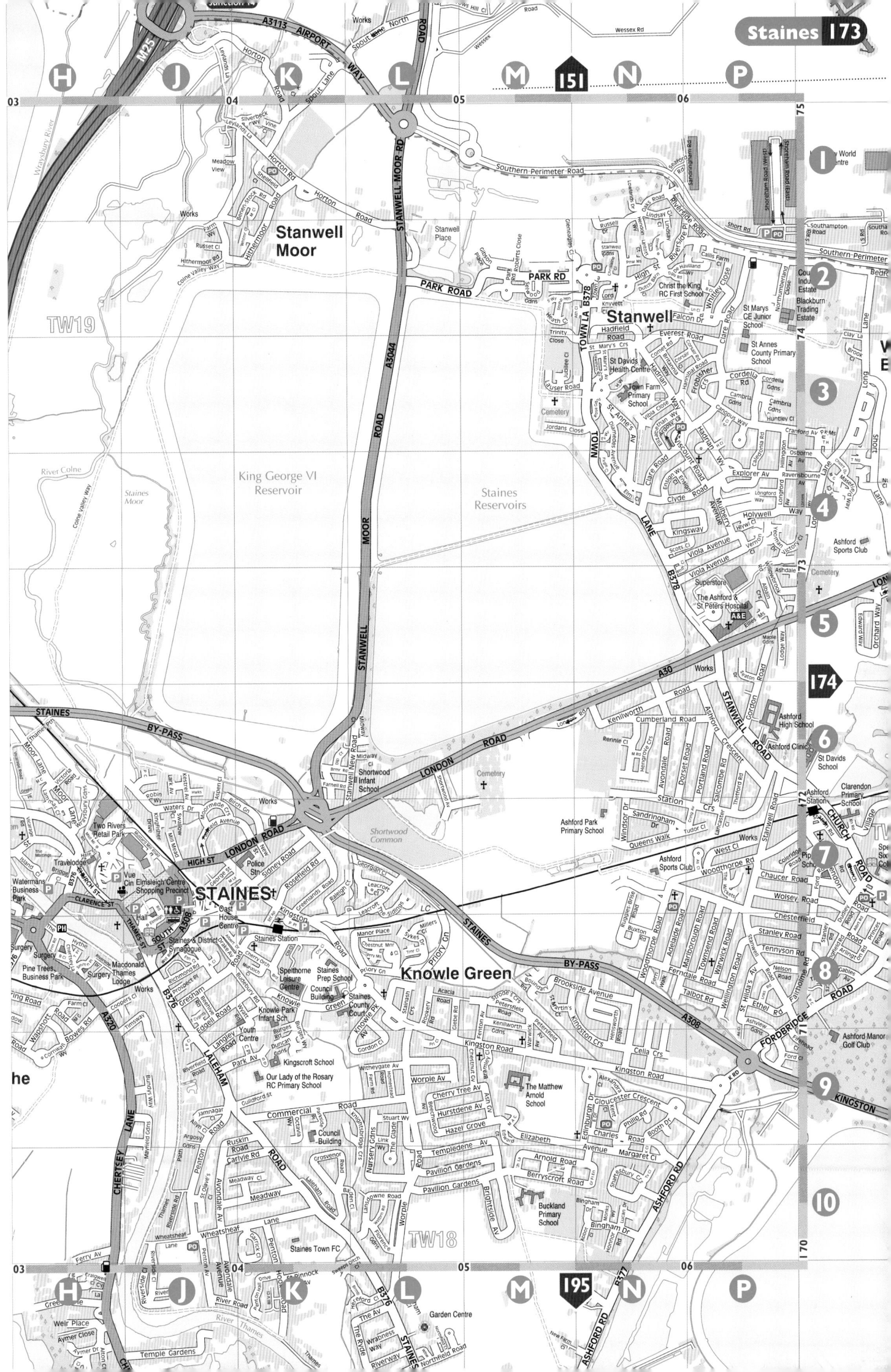

151
H
J
K
L
M
N
P
03
04
05
06
75
74
73
72
71
70
1
2
3
4
5
6
7
8
9
10
174
195
A3113 AIRPORT WAY
M25
Junction 14
STANWELL MOOR RD
Southern Perimeter Road
Horton Road
Stanwell Moor
Stanwell
Stanwell Place
PARK ROAD
PARK RD
TOWN LA
B378
TW19
Wraysbury River
River Colne
Colne Valley Way
Staines Moor
King George VI Reservoir
Staines Reservoirs
STANWELL MOOR ROAD
A3044
St Davids Health Centre
Town Farm Primary School
Christ the King RC First School
St Marys CE Junior School
St Annes County Primary School
Blackburn Trading Estate
Cemetery
Everest Road
Hadfield Road
Viola Avenue
Kingsway
Superstore
The Ashford & St Peters Hospital
A&E
Ashford Sports Club
STAINES BY-PASS
LONDON ROAD
A30
Works
Cumberland Road
Ashford High School
Ashford Clinic
St Davids School
Ashford Station
Clarendon Primary School
Ashford Park Primary School
Shortwood Infant School
Shortwood Common
STAINES
HIGH ST
Two Rivers Retail Park
Travelodge
Elmsleigh Centre Shopping Precinct
Vue Cin
Police Stn
Staines Station
Staines & District Synagogue
Watermans Business Park
Pine Trees Business Park
CLARENCE ST
THAMES ST
Knowle Green
Spelthorne Leisure Centre
Staines Prep School
Council Building
Staines County Court
Knowle Park Infant Sch
Youth Centre
Kingscroft School
Our Lady of the Rosary RC Primary School
Kingston Road
The Matthew Arnold School
Buckland Primary School
Staines Town FC
TW18
A308
A320
B376
B377
CHERTSEY LANE
LALEHAM ROAD
Commercial Road
ASHFORD RD
FORDBRIDGE
Ashford Manor Golf Club
River Thames
Garden Centre
Temple Gardens
Weir Place
Aymer Close

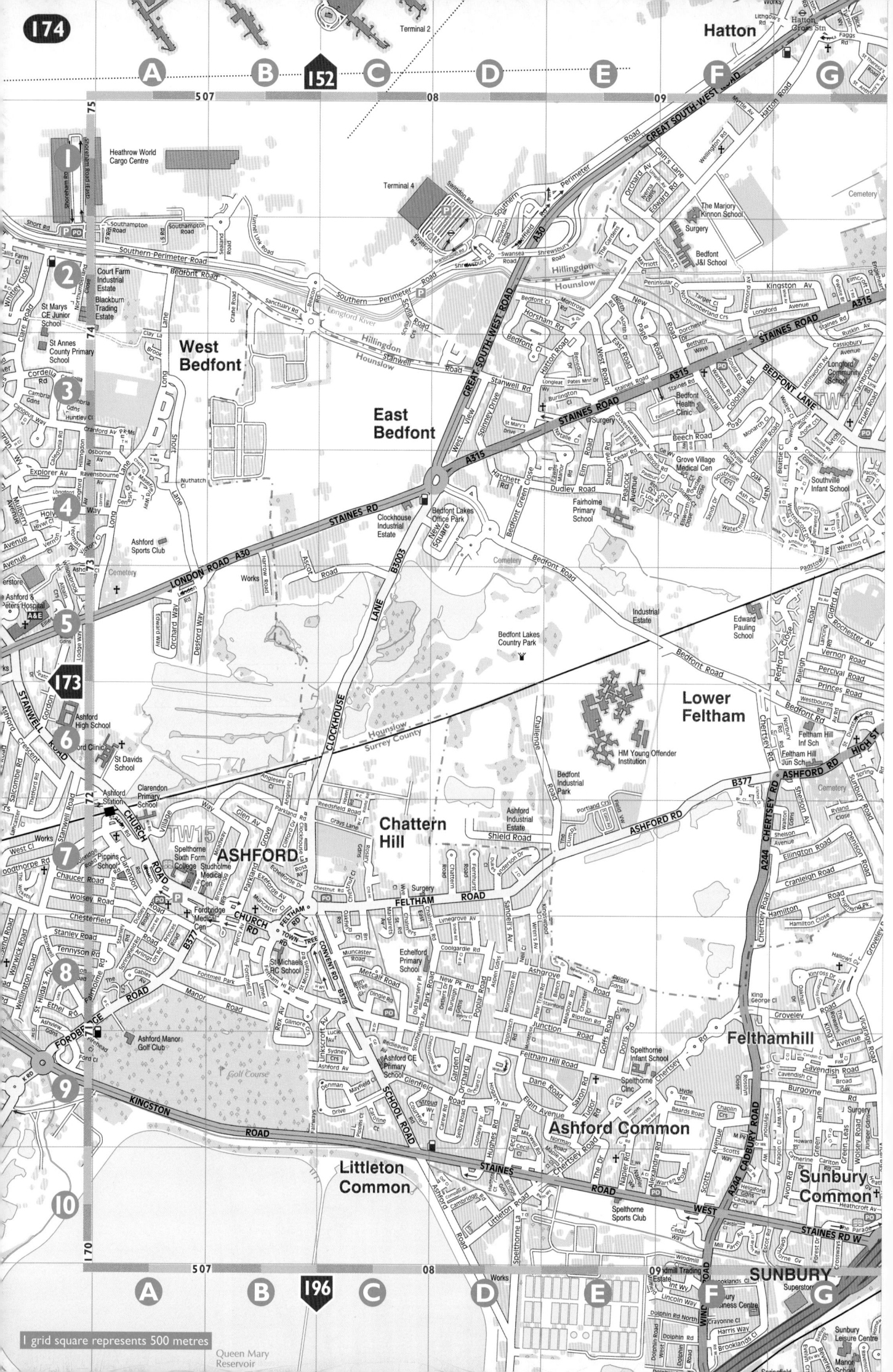
Hatton
Heathrow World Cargo Centre
Terminal 4
Terminal 2
West Bedfont
East Bedfont
Lower Feltham
Chattern Hill
ASHFORD
TW15
TW14
Felthamhill
Ashford Common
Littleton Common
Sunbury Common
SUNBURY
Bedfont Lakes Country Park
HM Young Offender Institution
Ashford Manor Golf Club
GREAT SOUTH-WEST ROAD
STAINES ROAD
LONDON ROAD A30
CLOCKHOUSE LANE
KINGSTON ROAD
STAINES ROAD
FELTHAM ROAD
ASHFORD RD
CHERTSEY RD
CADBURY ROAD
Southern Perimeter Road
Bedfont Road
Hounslow
Surrey County
1 grid square represents 500 metres
Queen Mary Reservoir

152
173
196

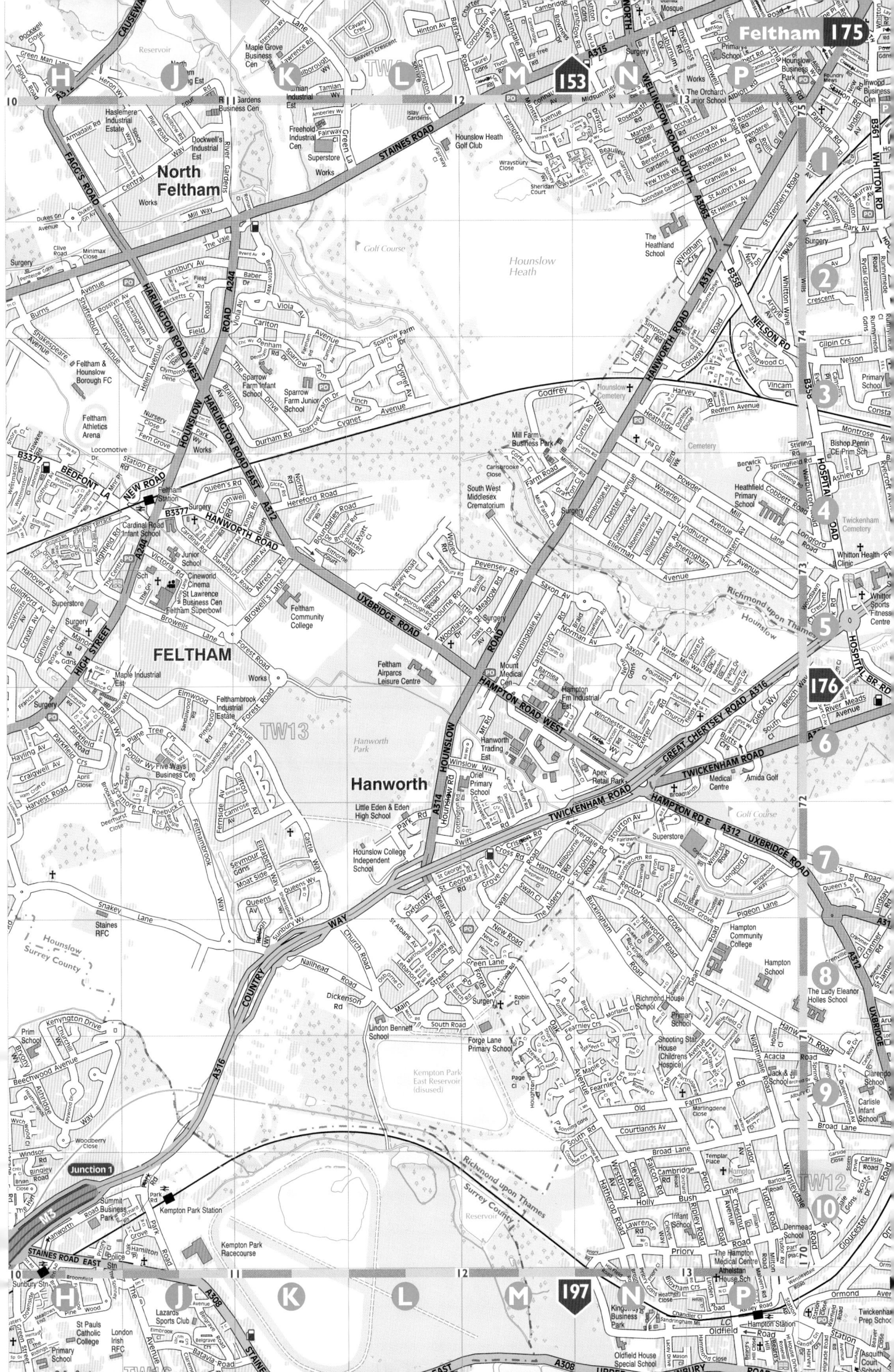
North Feltham
Feltham
Hanworth
Hounslow Heath
Kempton Park Station
Kempton Park Racecourse
Hampton Station
Feltham Station
Junction 1
TW13
TW12

176
154
175
198
A
B
C
D
E
F
G
1
2
3
4
5
6
7
8
9
10
514
15
16
75
74
73
72
71
170
TW1
TW2
TW3
TW11
TW12
Whitton
TWICKENHAM
Cole Park
Strawberry Hill
Hampton Hill
TEDDINGTON
Hampton
Bushy Park
Twickenham Stadium
Museum of Rugby & Twickenham Stadium Tours
Kneller Hall Royal Military School of Music
Whitton Station
Twickenham Stn
Strawberry Hill Station
Fulwell Station
Teddington Station
Hampton Station
Richmond upon Thames College
NEC Harlequins RFC (Twickenham Stoop Stadium)
Twickenham Cemetery
Teddington Cemetery
Strawberry Hill Golf Club
Fulwell Golf Club
St Mary's University College Twickenham
St James Independent School for Senior Boys
Waldegrave Girls School
National Physical Laboratory
Teddington Memorial Hospital
Teddington Lock
Eel Pie Island
River Crane
Thames Path
Hampton Open Air Pool
Bartons Cottage
Worton Hall Industrial Est
Ivybridge Retail Park
Twickenham Trading Est
Victory Business Cen
Mary Wallace Theatre
Orleans House G
Teddington Pool & Fitness Centre
Teddington Business Park
St Clare Business Park
Hampton Community College
The Lady Eleanor Holles School
Twickenham Prep School
WHITTON RD
HOSPITAL BR ROAD
CHERTSEY ROAD
STAINES ROAD
HAMPTON ROAD
WELLINGTON ROAD
UXBRIDGE ROAD
PARK ROAD
HIGH STREET
BROAD ST
WALDEGRAVE ROAD
CROSS DEEP
STRAWBERRY VALE
TWICKENHAM RD
KINGSTON RD
LONDON RD
HEATH ROAD
THE GREEN
SIXTH CROSS ROAD
SOUTH ROAD
QUEEN'S ROAD
SANDY LANE
CHURCH ROAD
ST MARGARET'S RD
THE AVENUE
KNELLER
NELSON RD
1 grid square represents 500 metres

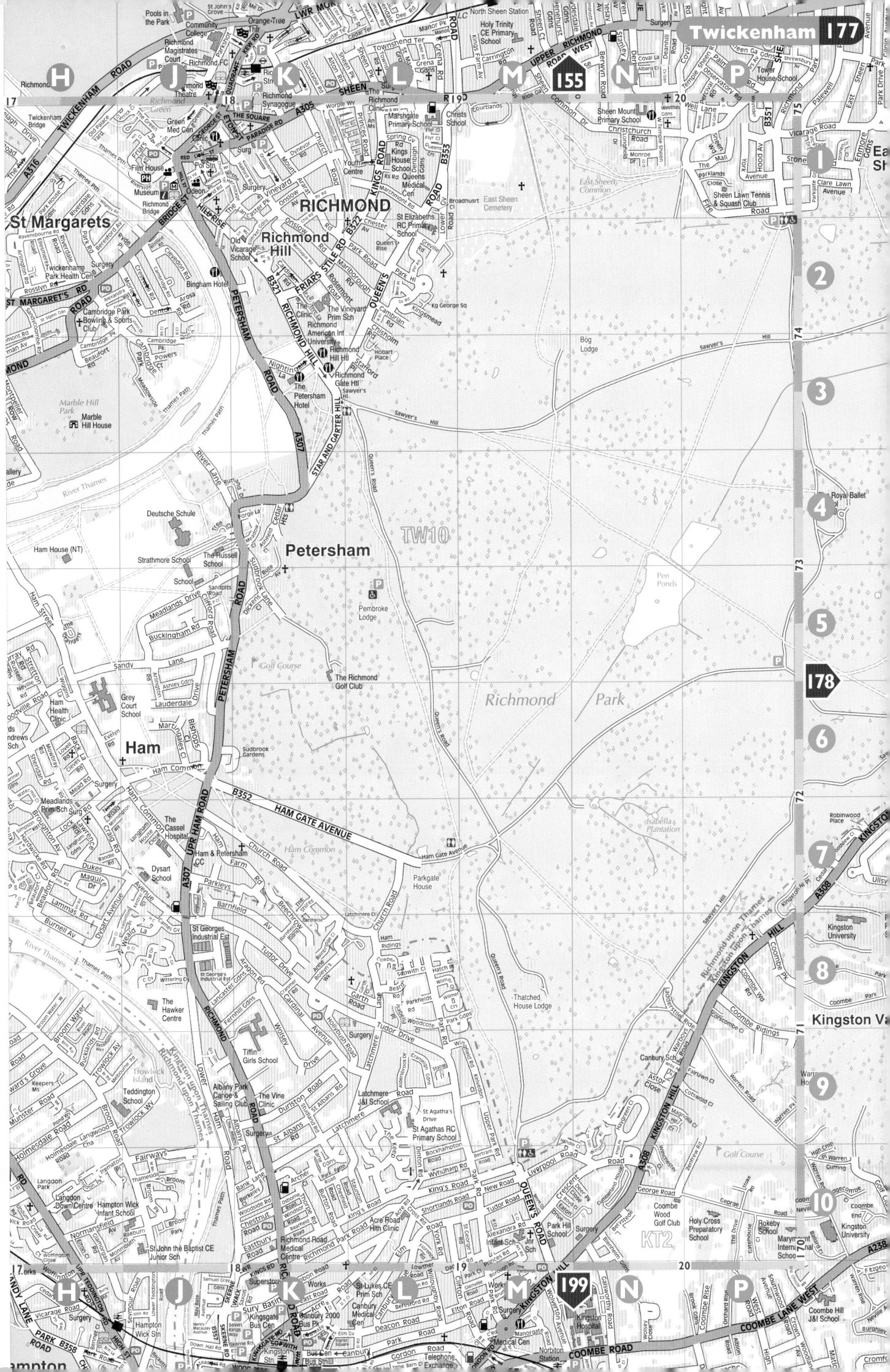
RICHMOND
Richmond Hill
St Margarets
Petersham
Ham
Richmond Park
East Sheen Common
East Sheen Cemetery
Pen Ponds
Isabella Plantation
Ham Common
Marble Hill Park
Marble Hill House
Ham House (NT)
Deutsche Schule
River Thames
TWICKENHAM ROAD
PETERSHAM ROAD
UPR HAM ROAD
RICHMOND ROAD
HAM GATE AVENUE
KINGSTON HILL
COOMBE LANE WEST
COOMBE ROAD
UPPER RICHMOND ROAD WEST
SHEEN ROAD
QUEEN'S ROAD
STAR AND GARTER HILL
Sawyer's Hill
Kingston Hospital
Kingston University
Kingston Va
Pembroke Lodge
The Richmond Golf Club
Thatched House Lodge
Coombe Wood Golf Club
Tiffin Girls School
Teddington School
TW10
KT2
155
178
199
H
J
K
L
M
N
P
1
2
3
4
5
6
7
8
9
10
17
18
19
20
70
71
72
73
74
75

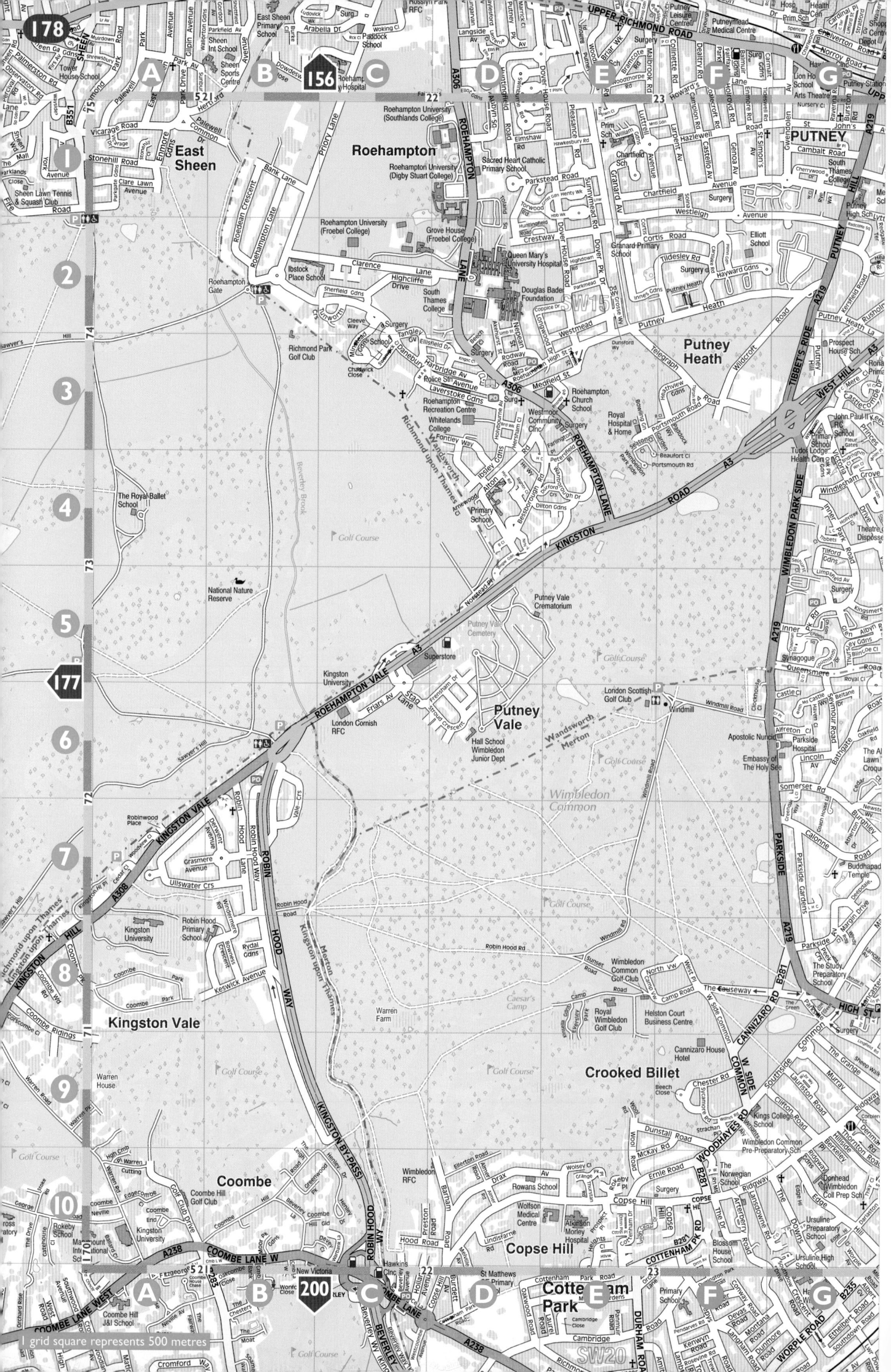
178
156
177
200
A
B
C
D
E
F
G
1
2
3
4
5
6
7
8
9
10
East Sheen
Roehampton
PUTNEY
Putney Heath
Putney Vale
Wimbledon Common
Kingston Vale
Crooked Billet
Coombe
Copse Hill
Cottenham Park
SW15
SW20
UPPER RICHMOND ROAD
ROEHAMPTON LANE
KINGSTON ROAD
A3
A306
A308
A219
A238
A205
B351
B281
B235
PUTNEY HILL
TIBBET'S RIDE
WEST HILL
WIMBLEDON PARK SIDE
PARKSIDE
HIGH ST
CANNIZARO RD
W SIDE COMMON
WOODHAYES RD
ROEHAMPTON VALE
KINGSTON VALE
KINGSTON HILL
ROBIN HOOD WAY
(KINGSTON BY-PASS)
COOMBE LANE W
COOMBE LANE WEST
COTTENHAM PK RD
DURHAM RD
WORPLE ROAD
BEVERLEY WAY
Richmond upon Thames
Wandsworth
Merton
Kingston upon Thames
Roehampton University (Southlands College)
Roehampton University (Digby Stuart College)
Roehampton University (Froebel College)
Grove House (Froebel College)
Queen Mary's University Hospital
Douglas Bader Foundation
South Thames College
Richmond Park Golf Club
Roehampton Gate
Ibstock Place School
Roehampton Recreation Centre
Whitelands College
Roehampton Church School
Royal Hospital & Home
The Royal Ballet School
National Nature Reserve
Putney Vale Crematorium
Putney Vale Cemetery
Superstore
Kingston University
London Cornish RFC
Hall School Wimbledon Junior Dept
London Scottish Golf Club
Windmill
Apostolic Nuncio
Parkside Hospital
Embassy of The Holy See
Buddhapadipa Temple
The Study Preparatory School
Wimbledon Common Golf Club
Royal Wimbledon Golf Club
Helston Court Business Centre
Cannizaro House Hotel
Caesar's Camp
Warren Farm
Warren House
Robin Hood Primary School
Coombe Hill Golf Club
Kings College School
Wimbledon Common Pre-Preparatory Sch
The Norwegian School
Rowans School
Wolfson Medical Centre
Atkinson Morley Hospital
Wimbledon RFC
Blossom House School
Ursuline Preparatory School
Ursuline High School
Donhead (Wimbledon Coll Prep Sch)
Coombe Hill J&I School
Sheen Lawn Tennis & Squash Club
Tower House School
Sheen Int School
Sheen Sports Centre
East Sheen Primary School
Paddock School
Putney Leisure Centre
Putneymead Medical Centre
Lion House School
Arts Theatre
Putney Station
South Thames College
Putney High Sch
Elliott School
Granard Primary School
Sacred Heart Catholic Primary School
Chartfield Sch
Prospect House Sch
John Paul II RC School
Tudor Lodge Health Cen
Synagogue
Golf Course
1 grid square represents 500 metres

H
J
K
L
M
N
P
157
180
201
1
2
3
4
5
6
7
8
9
10
24
25
26
27
74
73
72
71
70
River Thames
WANDSWORTH
West Hill
Southfields
Earlsfield
Summerstown
Upper Tooting
WIMBLEDON
South Wimbledon
Tooting Graveney
Collier's Wood
MERTON
SW18
SW17
SW19
WEST HILL
MERTON ROAD
DURNSFORD ROAD
GARRATT LANE
TRINITY ROAD
BURNTWOOD LANE
EARLSFIELD ROAD
WANDSWORTH HIGH ST
ARMOURY WY
SWANDON WY
HUGUENOT PL
N SIDE WANDSWORTH COMMON
WINDMILL RD
SPENCER PARK
PLOUGH LANE
GAP ROAD
HAYDON'S RD
WIMBLEDON HL ROAD
THE BROADWAY
HARTFIELD RD
KINGSTON ROAD
MERTON HIGH STREET
HIGH ST COLLIER'S WOOD
TOOTING HIGH STREET
UPPER TOOTING ROAD
BOLINGBROKE GROVE
BELLEVUE RD
WORPLE ROAD
ALEXANDRA RD
RICHMOND RD
Wimbledon Park
Boating Lake
Wimbledon Park Golf Club
Wimbledon Lawn Tennis Museum
Wimbledon Stadium
Wandsworth Common
HM Prison
Wandsworth Cemetery
Streatham Cemetery
Lambeth Cemetery
Lambeth Crematorium
St Georges Hospital
Springfield Hospital
Bolingbroke Hospital
King George's Park
Wimbledon Park Station
Southfields Station
Earlsfield Station
Haydons Road Station
Wimbledon Station
Wandsworth Common Station
Southside Shopping Centre
Centre Court Shopping Centre
Wimbledon Theatre
Royal Hospital for Neuro-Disability

180
158
179
202
A
B
C
D
E
F
G
1
2
3
4
5
6
7
8
9
10
Balham
Clapham Park
Streatham Hill
Streatham Park
Furzedown
TOOTING
STREATHAM
Streatham Vale
Clapham Common
Wandsworth Common
Tooting Bec Common
Streatham Common
SW4
SW12
SW16
SW17
CLAPHAM COMMON NORTH SIDE
CLAPHAM COMMON SOUTH SIDE
BALHAM HIGH RD
TOOTING BEC ROAD
STREATHAM HIGH RD
MITCHAM LANE
UPPER TOOTING ROAD
A205 POYNDERS ROAD
BEDFORD HILL
1 grid square represents 500 metres

Streatham 181
159
182
203
BRIXTON
Herne Hill
Knight's Hill
Tulse Hill
West Dulwich
Dulwich Village
East Dulwich
Dulwich
West Norwood
Norwood New Town
Upper Norwood
Upper Sydenham
Crystal Palace
SE24
SE22
SW2
SE21
SE27
SE19
Brockwell Park
Belair Park
Dulwich Park
Crystal Palace Park
Golf Course
Dulwich & Sydenham Hill Golf Club
Southwark Sports Ground
Marlborough CC
Lloyds Register CC
Dulwich Picture Gallery
Dulwich College
Dulwich College Track
Dulwich College Preparatory School
Herne Hill Stadium (Cycle Centre)
West Norwood Crematorium
Cemetery
South London Theatre
Crystal Palace Museum
National Sports Centre
Crystal Palace Station
Crystal Palace Station Road
Herne Hill Station
North Dulwich Station
East Dulwich Stn
Tulse Hill Station
West Dulwich Station
Sydenham Hill Station
Gipsy Hill Station
West Norwood Stn
Penge W Station
Anerley Stn
Brockwell Lido
Ritzy
Eurolink Business Cen
Effra Road Retail Park
Goose Green Trading Estate
Park Hall Trading Est
Hamilton Road Ind Estate
Bath Factory Est
Park Mews Small Business Cen
Bessemer Grange J&I School
The Charter School
James Allens Preparatory Girls School
Alleyns Junior School
Kings College Sch of Medicine & Dentistry
Dulwich Hamlet Junior School
Dulwich Village CE Infant School
Dulwich Medical Cen
Police Station
St Anthonys RC Primary School
Goodrich J&I School
The City of London Academy
Turney School
Rosendale Primary School
St Martin in the Fields High School
Fenstanton J&I School
Medical Centre
Rosemead Preparatory School
Grove House Prim Sch for Deaf Children
Elm Court School
West Norwood Clinic
Hitherfield Primary School
Kingsdale School
Langbourne Primary School
Ducks Infants School
Crown Lane Prim School
Kingswood Primary School
St Josephs RC Infant School
St Josephs RC Junior School
Virgo Fidelis Convent Sch
Rockmount Primary School
St Josephs College
Norwood School
Julians Primary School
Downsview Primary School
Westwood Language College for Girls
The Woodlands
Norbury Manor Secondary Girls School
Kensington Av Primary
David Livingstone Primary School
All Saints CE Primary School
Harris City Academy
James Dixon Primary School
Sydenham High Junior School
Sydenham High Senior School
The Horniman Museum & Gardens
Norbury Park
A204
A205
A215
A2199
A2214
A2216
A212
A214
A234
B219
B223
B232
B273
DULWICH COMMON
HALF MOON LANE
VILLAGE WAY
CROXTED ROAD
SOUTH CROXTED ROAD
THURLOW PARK ROAD
NORWOOD ROAD
NORWOOD HIGH ST
KNIGHTS HILL
ELDER ROAD
TULSE HILL
DULWICH ROAD
RAILTON ROAD
MILKWOOD ROAD
DENMARK HILL
HERNE HILL
LORDSHIP LANE
EAST DULWICH GROVE
GROVE VALE
BARRY ROAD
DULWICH WOOD PARK
COLLEGE ROAD
CRYSTAL PALACE PARADE
WESTOW HILL
CHURCH ROAD
ANERLEY HILL
ANERLEY ROAD
CRYSTAL PALACE PARK ROAD
WESTWOOD HILL
BEULAH HILL
CROWN DALE
CENTRAL HILL
NORTH CROWN LANE
GREEN LANE
BEULAH HILL
31
32
33
34
70
71
72
73
74
H
J
K
L
M
N
P
2
3
4
5
6
7
8
9
10

182
160
181
204
A
B
C
D
E
F
G
1
2
3
4
5
6
7
8
9
10
535
36
37
75
74
73
72
71
170
East Dulwich
SE22
Honor Oak
Brockley
Ladywell
Honor Oak Park
SE23
Forest Hill
Lower Sydenham
Upper Sydenham
SE26
Sydenham
Bell Green
Bellingham
Crystal Palace
New Beckenham
PENGE
Peckham Rye Park
Camberwell New Cemetery
Honor Oak Crematorium
The Horniman Museum & Gardens
Forest Hill Station
Sydenham Station
Lower Sydenham Stn
New Beckenham Station
Catford Station
Catford Bridge Station
Crofton Park Station
Honor Oak Park Station
Ladywell Stn
Bellingham Stn
Penge East Station
Penge West Station
Crystal Palace Station
Anerley Stn
Kent House Station
Beckenham Junction Station
University Hospital
Ladywell Arena
Hilly Fields Medical Centre
Crofton Leisure Centre
Catford Cricket & Sports Club
London Living Theatre
The Bridge Leisure Centre
HSBC Sports Club
Cator Park School for Girls
Blenheim Shopping Cen
LORDSHIP LANE A205
LONDON ROAD
STANSTEAD ROAD
CATFORD ROAD
A212 CATFORD HILL
BROMLEY ROAD
RUSHEY GN
PERRY VALE
PERRY RISE
PERRY HILL
DARTMOUTH ROAD
KIRKDALE A2216
SYDENHAM
WESTWOOD HILL A212
CRYSTAL PALACE PARK ROAD
SOUTHEND LANE
STANTON WY
SOUTHEND ROAD A2015
BECKENHAM HILL ROAD
HONOR OAK PARK
STONDON PK
BROCKLEY RISE
BROCKLEY ROAD
FOREST HILL ROAD
PECKHAM RYE B238
LADYWELL ROAD
ADELAIDE AV
NEWLANDS PARK
PARISH LANE A213
GREEN LANE
HIGH ST
BECKENHAM ROAD
1 grid square represents 500 metres

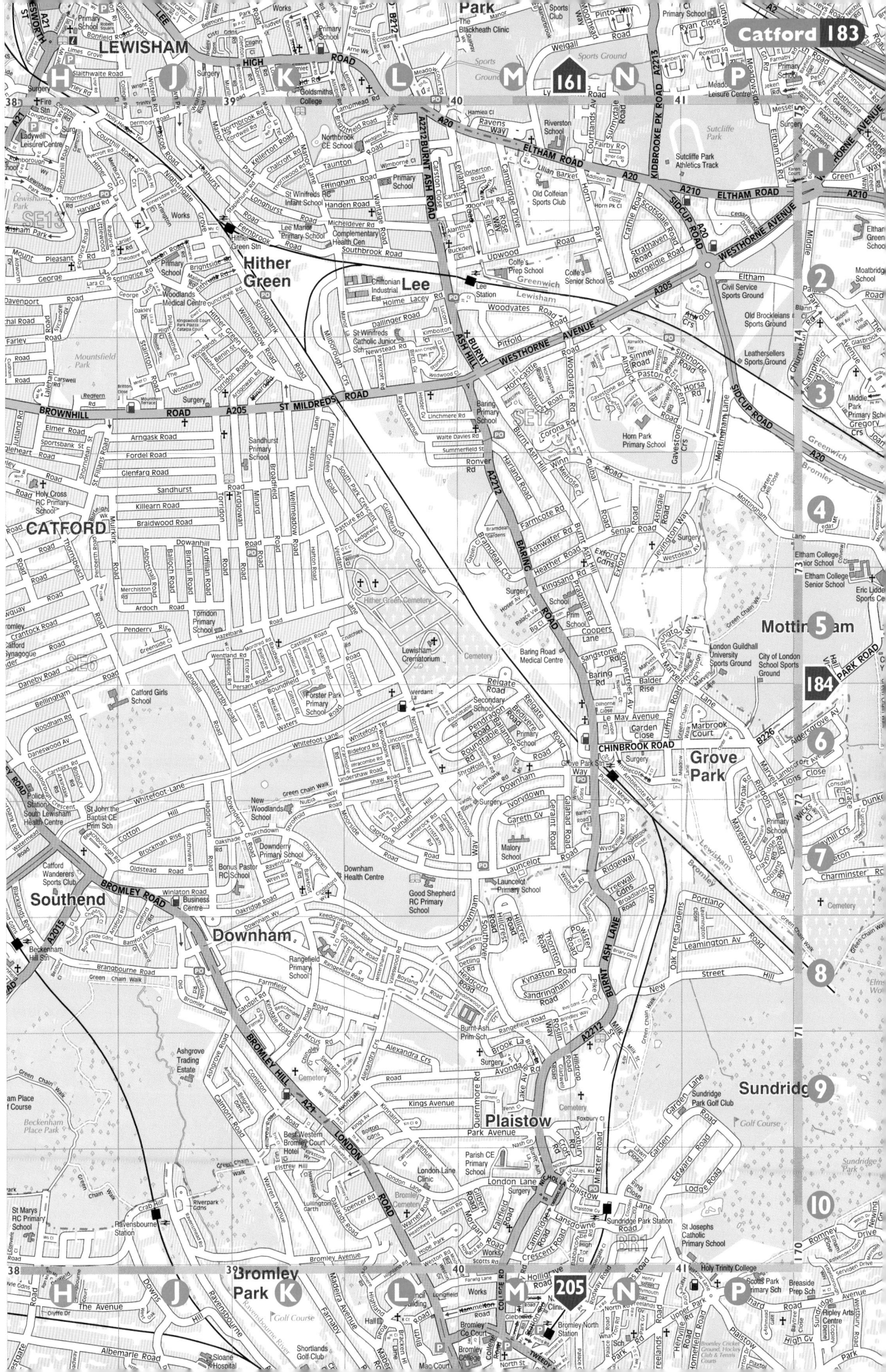
LEWISHAM
HIGH ROAD
Goldsmiths College
Hither Green
Hither Green Stn
Lee
Lee Station
ELTHAM ROAD
A20
A210
KIDBROOKE PK ROAD
A2213
SIDCUP ROAD
WESTHORNE AVENUE
BURNT ASH ROAD
A2212
Sutcliffe Park
Sutcliffe Park Athletics Track
Old Colfeian Sports Club
Colfe's Prep School
Colfe's Senior School
Civil Service Sports Ground
Old Brockleians Sports Ground
Leathersellers Sports Ground
Mountsfield Park
BROWNHILL ROAD
ST MILDREDS ROAD
A205
SE13
SE12
SE6
CATFORD
Holy Cross RC Primary School
Sandhurst Primary School
Horn Park Primary School
Baring Primary School
BARING ROAD
Hither Green Cemetery
Lewisham Crematorium
Cemetery
Torridon Primary School
Catford Girls School
Forster Park Primary School
Catford Synagogue
Mottingham
Eltham College Junior School
Eltham College Senior School
London Guildhall University Sports Ground
City of London School Sports Ground
CHINBROOK ROAD
Grove Park
Grove Park Stn
B226
Whitefoot Lane
Green Chain Walk
New Woodlands School
Downderry Primary School
Bonus Pastor RC School
Downham Health Centre
Good Shepherd RC Primary School
Malory School
Launcelot Primary School
Catford Wanderers Sports Club
Southend
BROMLEY ROAD
A2015
Beckenham Hill Stn
Downham
Rangefield Primary School
Burnt Ash Prim Sch
BURNT ASH LANE
Ashgrove Trading Estate
BROMLEY HILL
A21
LONDON ROAD
Beckenham Place Park
Sundridge
Sundridge Park Golf Club
Golf Course
Plaistow
Parish CE Primary School
London Lane Clinic
Best Western Bromley Court Hotel
Bromley Cemetery
Sundridge Park Station
St Josephs Catholic Primary School
Ravensbourne Station
St Marys RC Primary School
BR1
Bromley Park
Bromley North Station
Holy Trinity College
Scotts Park Primary Sch
Breaside Prep Sch
Ripley Arts Centre
Shortlands Golf Club
Sloane Hospital
161
184
205
38
39
40
41
70
71
72
73
74
75
H
J
K
L
M
N
P
1
2
3
4
5
6
7
8
9
10

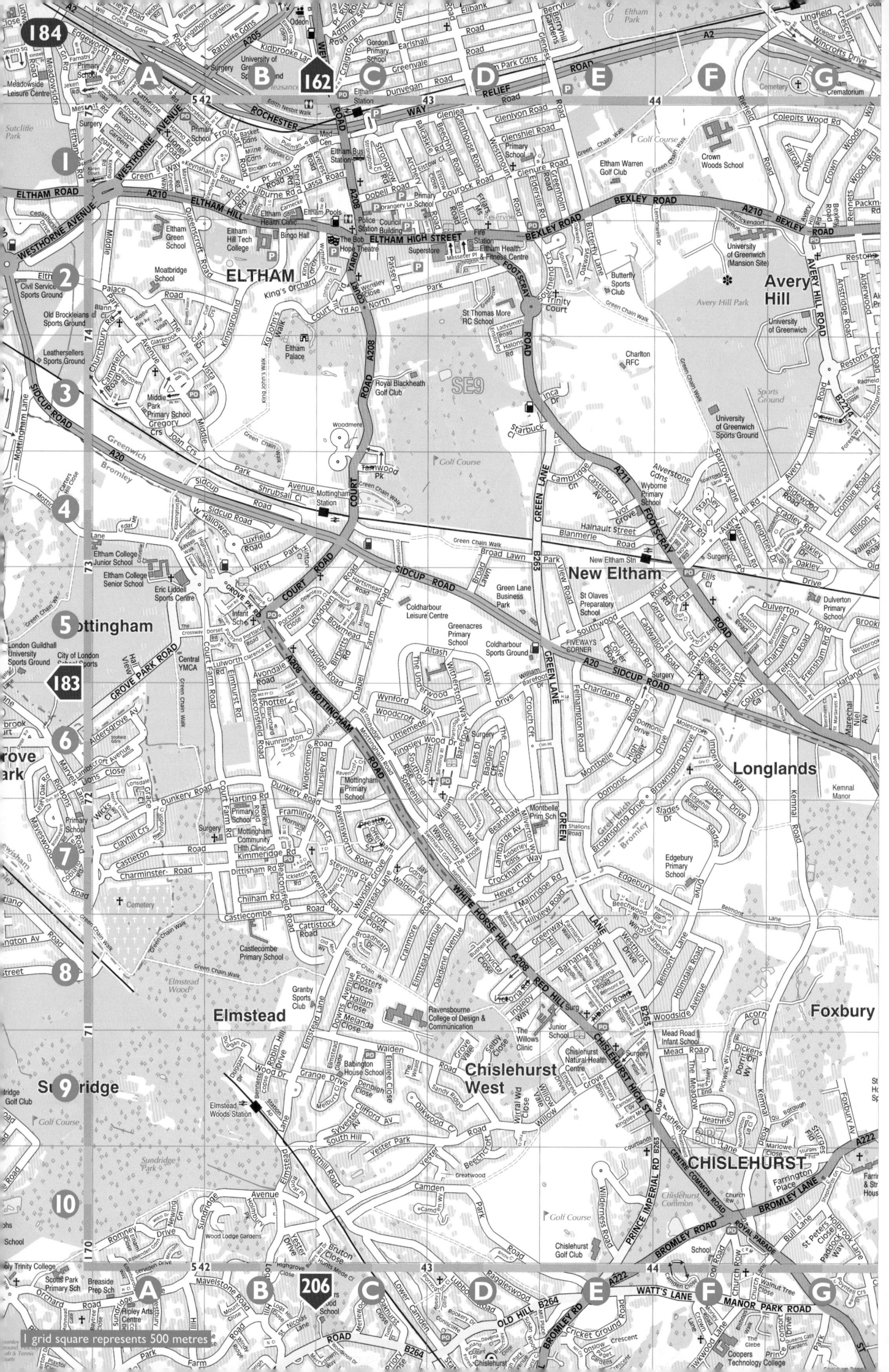
184
162
183
206
A
B
C
D
E
F
G
1
2
3
4
5
6
7
8
9
10
542
43
44
74
73
72
71
170
ELTHAM
Avery Hill
New Eltham
Mottingham
Longlands
Elmstead
Chislehurst West
CHISLEHURST
Foxbury
Sundridge
SE9
BR7
ROCHESTER WAY
RELIEF ROAD
ELTHAM ROAD
ELTHAM HILL
ELTHAM HIGH STREET
BEXLEY ROAD
WESTHORNE AVENUE
SIDCUP ROAD
COURT ROAD
COURT YARD
FOOTSCRAY ROAD
GREEN LANE
MOTTINGHAM ROAD
WHITE HORSE HILL
RED HILL
CHISLEHURST HIGH ST
PRINCE IMPERIAL RD
BROMLEY ROAD
BROMLEY LANE
ROYAL PARADE
GROVE PARK ROAD
AVERY HILL ROAD
WATT'S LANE
MANOR PARK ROAD
OLD HILL
BROMLEY RD
CENTRE COMMON ROAD
A2
A20
A205
A208
A210
A211
A222
A2214
B263
B264
Eltham Palace
Royal Blackheath Golf Club
Eltham Warren Golf Club
Crown Woods School
University of Greenwich (Mansion Site)
Avery Hill Park
Eltham Station
Mottingham Station
New Eltham Stn
Elmstead Woods Station
Eltham Green School
Eltham Hill Tech College
Eltham College Junior School
Eltham College Senior School
Eric Liddell Sports Centre
Coldharbour Leisure Centre
Coldharbour Sports Ground
Green Lane Business Park
St Olaves Preparatory School
Wyborne Primary School
Charlton RFC
Butterfly Sports Club
St Thomas More RC School
Castlecombe Primary School
Granby Sports Club
Ravensbourne College of Design & Communication
Babington House School
Edgebury Primary School
Mead Road Infant School
Chislehurst Golf Club
Chislehurst Common
Kemnal Manor
Elmstead Wood
Sundridge Park
Cemetery
Golf Course
Green Chain Walk
Greenwich
Bromley
Lewisham
1 grid square represents 500 metres

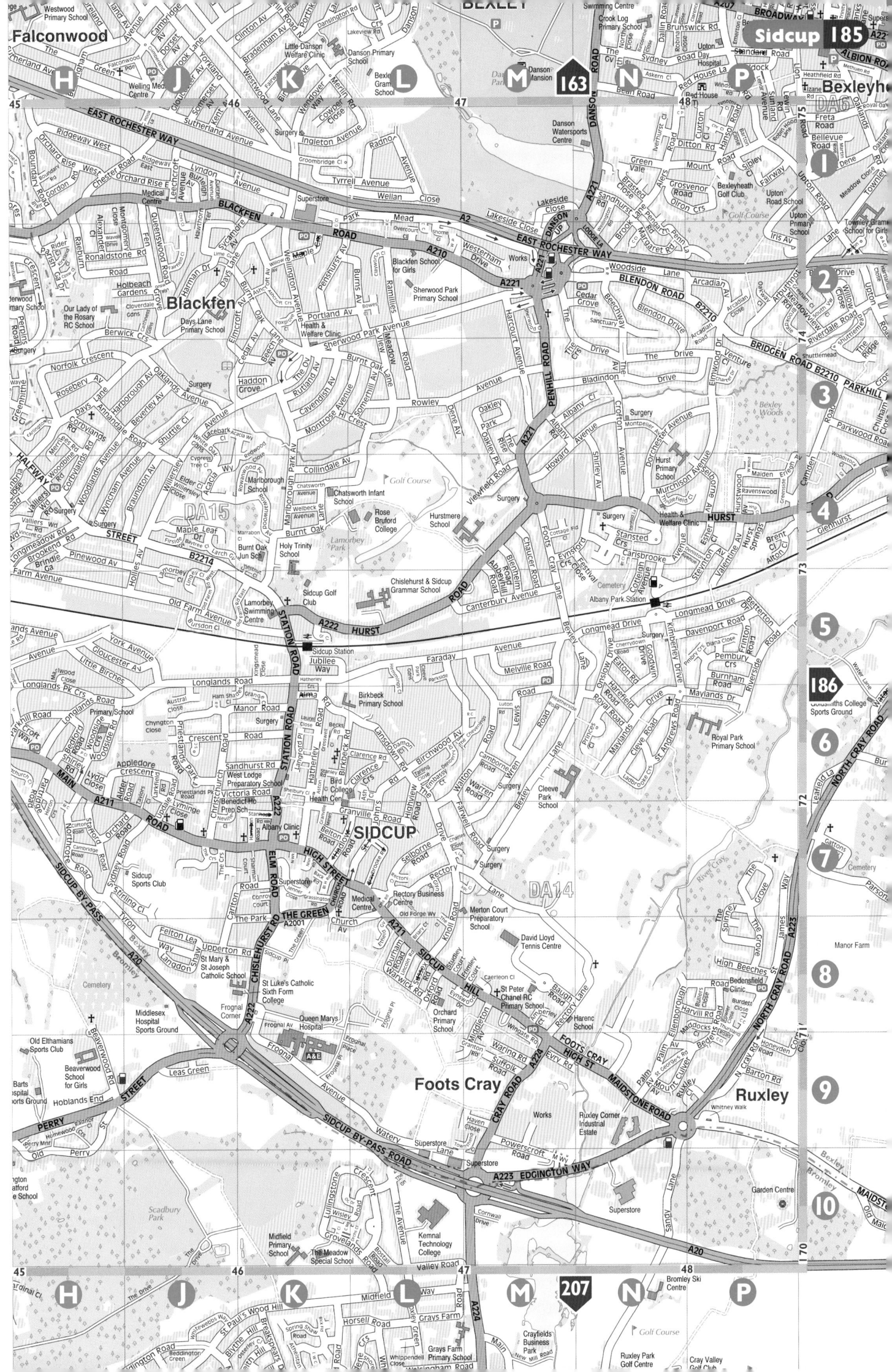
Falconwood
Bexleyheath
Blackfen
SIDCUP
Foots Cray
Ruxley
DA15
DA14
DA6
EAST ROCHESTER WAY
BLACKFEN ROAD
A210
A2
A221
DANSON ROAD
PENHILL ROAD
BLENDON ROAD
B2210
BRIDGEN ROAD B2210
PARKHILL
HURST
A222 HURST ROAD
STATION ROAD
HALFWAY STREET
B2214
MAIN ROAD
A211
HIGH STREET
ELM ROAD
CHISLEHURST RD
THE GREEN
A2001
SIDCUP HILL
SIDCUP BY-PASS
SIDCUP BY-PASS ROAD
A20
PERRY STREET
CRAY ROAD
A224
FOOTS CRAY HIGH ST
MAIDSTONE ROAD
NORTH CRAY ROAD
A223
A223 EDGINGTON WAY
Sidcup Station
Albany Park Station
Danson Mansion
Danson Watersports Centre
Golf Course
Cemetery
Bexley Woods
Scadbury Park
Queen Marys Hospital
A&E
Chislehurst & Sidcup Grammar School
Rose Bruford College
Holy Trinity School
Sidcup Golf Club
Lamorbey Park
Lamorbey Swimming Centre
Hurstmere School
Cleeve Park School
David Lloyd Tennis Centre
Kemnal Technology College
Ruxley Corner Industrial Estate
Bromley Ski Centre
Crayfields Business Park
Garden Centre
Manor Farm
Goldsmiths College Sports Ground
163
186
207
H
J
K
L
M
N
P
1
2
3
4
5
6
7
8
9
10
45
46
47
48
70
71
72
73
74
75

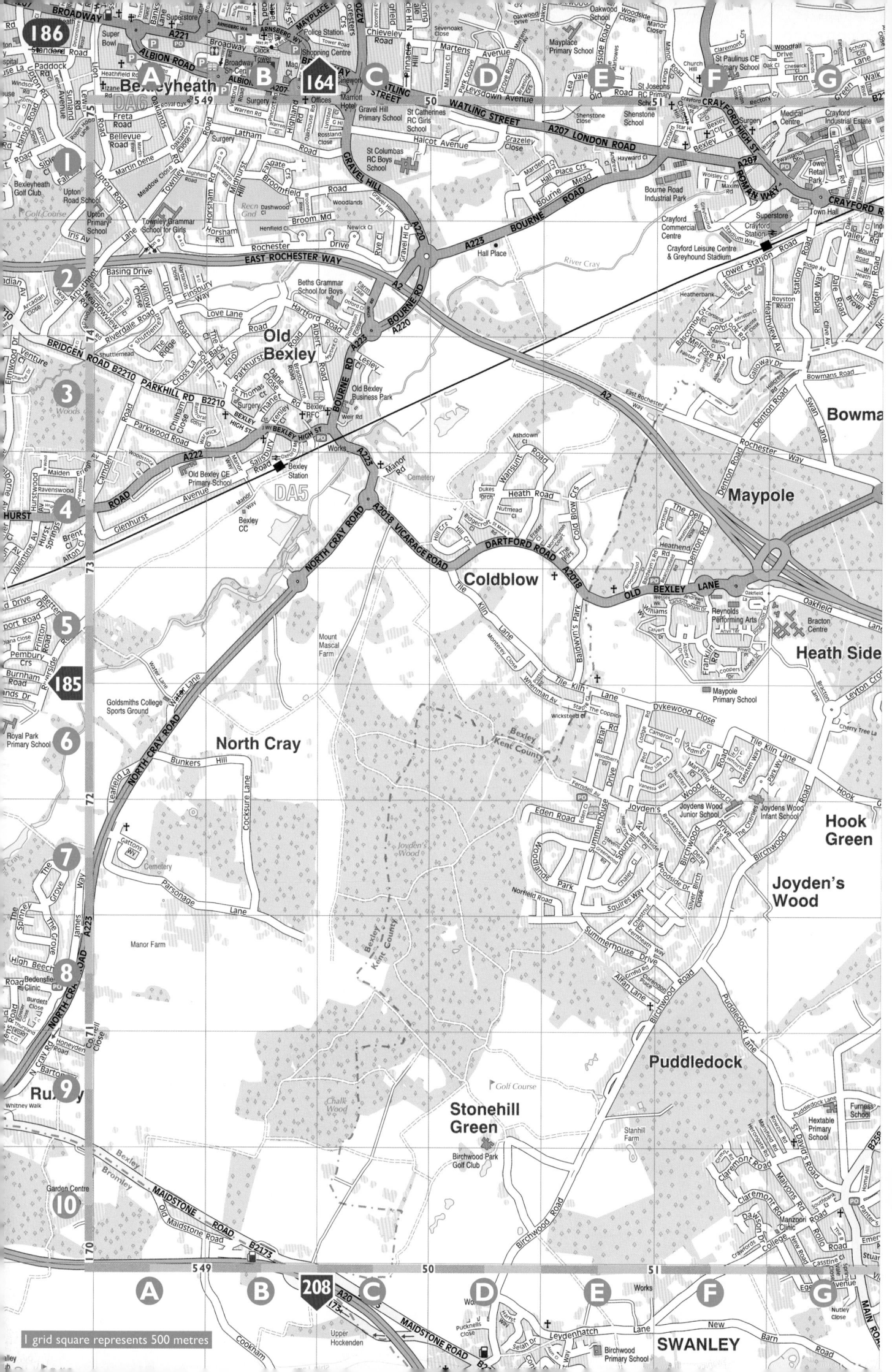
186
164
185
208
A
B
C
D
E
F
G
1
2
3
4
5
6
7
8
9
10
549
50
51
175
74
73
72
71
170
DA6
DA5
BROADWAY
ALBION ROAD
Bexleyheath
MAYPLACE
ARNSBERG WAY
Broadway Sh Cen
Shopping Centre
Police Station
Clock Tower
Super Bowl
Superstore
Standard Road
Paddock Rd
Upton Road
Sunland Avenue
Freta Road
Bellevue Road
Martin Dene
Oaklands
Townley Road
Meadow Close
Latham Road
Halcot Avenue
Chieveley Road
Martens Avenue
Leysdown Avenue
WATLING STREET
A207 LONDON ROAD
Gravel Hill Primary School
St Catherines RC Girls School
St Columbas RC Boys School
GRAVEL HILL
Marriott Hotel
Offices
Cineworld
Pinnacle Hill
Oakwood School
Mayplace Primary School
Oakwood Drive
Woodside Close
Manor Close
St Josephs RC Primary School
Shenstone School
St Paulinus CE Primary School
CRAYFORD HIGH ST
Crayford Industrial Estate
Medical Centre
Tower Retail Park
Town Hall
CRAYFORD RD
ROMAN WAY
A207
Bourne Road Industrial Park
Crayford Commercial Centre
Crayford Station
Superstore
Crayford Leisure Centre & Greyhound Stadium
Stadium Way
Station Road
Lower Station Rd
Hall Place
River Cray
A223 BOURNE ROAD
Bourne Mead
Hall Place Crs
Marden Crs
Grazeley Close
Broomfield Road
Broom Mead
Woodlands
Rochester Drive
Horsham Rd
Midhurst Hill
Recn Gnd
Dashwood Cl
Henfield Cl
Newick Cl
Rye Cl
Gravel Hill Cl
A220
EAST ROCHESTER WAY
A2
Townley Grammar School for Girls
Upton Primary School
Upton Road School
Bexleyheath Golf Club
Golf Course
Iris Av
Basing Drive
Finsbury Way
Willow Close
Arbuthnot La
Meadowview
Riverdale Road
Shuttlemead
Love Lane
Beths Grammar School for Boys
Hartford Road
Albert Road
Old Bexley
BRIDGEN ROAD B2210
PARKHILL RD B2210
Cross La
Parkhurst Rd
Dane Close
Thanet Dr
Bradbourne Road
Bexley RFC
Old Bexley Business Park
Weir Rd
Lesney Pk
BOURNE RD
Woods
Chilham Close
Parkwood Road
BEXLEY HIGH ST
A222
Camden Rd
Maiden Erlegh Av
Ravenswood
Old Bexley CE Primary School
Salisbury Road
Bexley Station
Manor Rd
Cemetery
Works
Glenhurst Avenue
Manor Way
Bexley CC
Hurst Springs
Brent Cl
Alton Cl
Valentine Av
A2018 VICARAGE ROAD
NORTH CRAY ROAD
Ashdown Cl
Wansunt Road
Heath Road
Dukes Orch
Nutmead Cl
Ridgecroft Cl
Hill Crs
Cold Blow Crs
DARTFORD ROAD
A2018
Coldblow
OLD BEXLEY LANE
Maypole
Denton Road
Rochester Way
East Rochester Way
Bowmans Road
Swan Lane
Bowma
Heatherbank
Bascombe Gr
Woodbrook Rd
Melrose Av
Galloway Dr
Heathview Av
Royston Road
Ridge Way
Dale Road
Hill Brow
Valley Rd
The Dell
Heathend Rd
Oakfield
Reynolds Performing Arts
Bracton Centre
Heath Side
Franklin Rd
Maypole Primary School
Tile Kiln Lane
Monterey Close
Baldwyn's Park
Whenman Av
The Coppice
Dykewood Close
Mount Mascal Farm
Goldsmiths College Sports Ground
Water Lane
North Cray
Bunkers Hill
Cocksure Lane
Leafield La
Bexley
Kent County
Cameron Cl
Red Lodge Crs
Maryfield Cl
Eastern Way
Park Way
Hook Lane
Hook Green
Ferndell Av
Eden Road
Joyden's Wood
Joydens Wood Junior School
Joydens Wood Infant School
Birchwood Drive
Summerhouse Drive
Woodlands Park
Norfield Road
Squires Way
Chaucer Cl
Silver Birch Close
Woodside Dr
Joyden's Wood
Cemetery
Parsonage Lane
Manor Farm
The Grove
The Spinney
James Way
A223
High Beech
Bedensfield Clinic
Burdett Close
NORTH CRAY ROAD
Honeyden Road
Court Close
Ruxley
Whitney Walk
Puddledock
Puddledock Lane
Birchwood Road
Alfan Lane
Golf Course
Chalk Wood
Stonehill Green
Birchwood Park Golf Club
Stanhill Farm
Hextable Primary School
Furness School
St David's Road
Claremont Road
Malyons Rd
Dawson Dr
College Road
Manzoori Clinic
Rollo Road
B258
Main Road
Bexley
Bromley
MAIDSTONE ROAD
Old Maidstone Road
B2173
Garden Centre
Cookham
A20
Upper Hockenden
MAIDSTONE ROAD
Pucknells Close
Leydenhatch Lane
Birchwood Primary School
SWANLEY
New Barn Road
Works
Nutley Close
1 grid square represents 500 metres

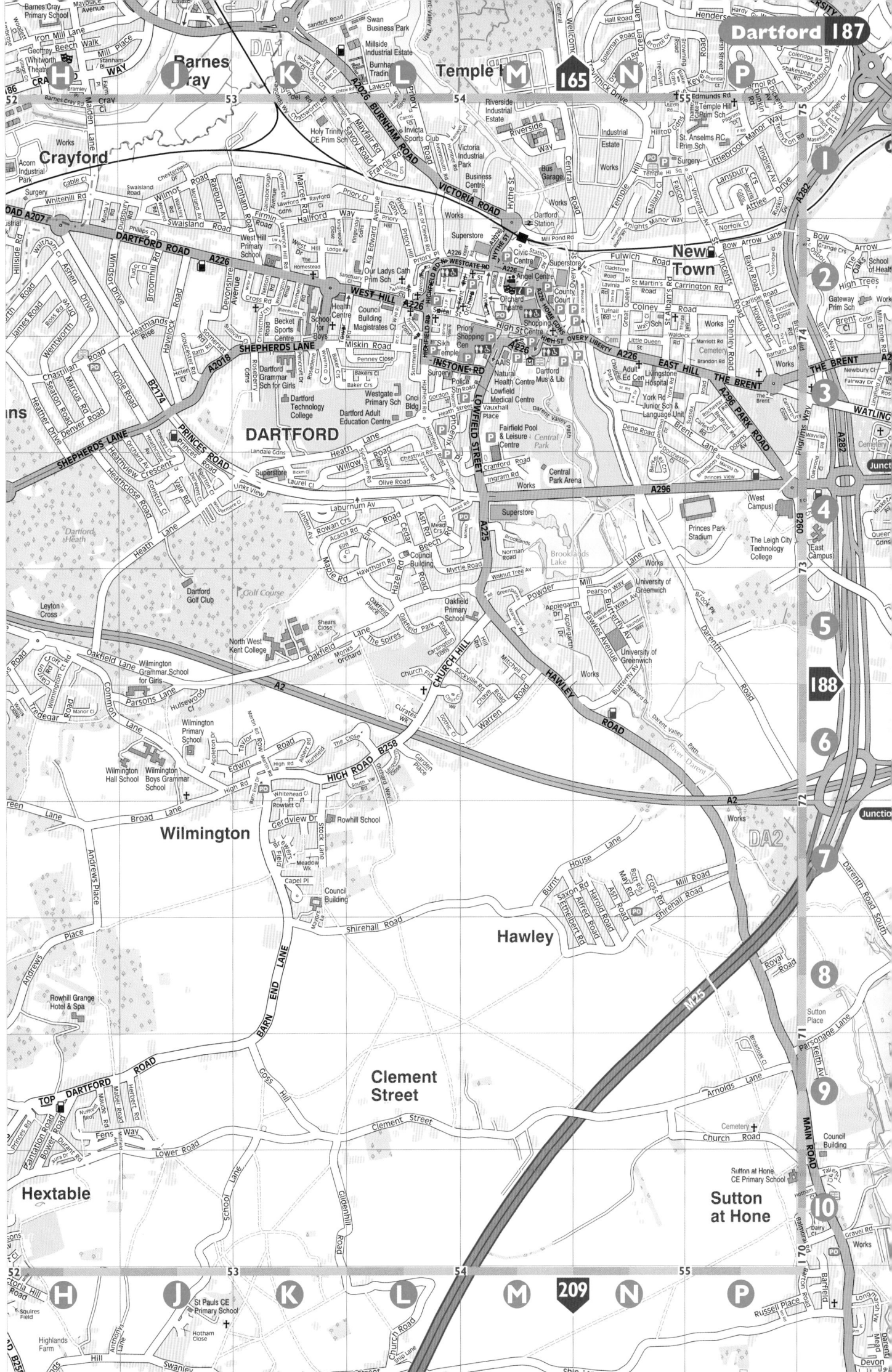
Barnes Cray
Crayford
Temple Hill
New Town
DARTFORD
Dartford Heath
Wilmington
Hawley
Clement Street
Hextable
Sutton at Hone
DA1
DA2
165
188
209
A2
A2026 BURNHAM ROAD
VICTORIA ROAD
DARTFORD ROAD A226
WEST HILL
SHEPHERDS LANE
PRINCES ROAD
LOWFIELD STREET
HAWLEY ROAD
CHURCH HILL
HIGH ROAD B258
BARN END LANE
TOP DARTFORD ROAD
EAST HILL
THE BRENT
A296 PARK ROAD
A296
A225
A282
M25
MAIN ROAD
Darenth Road
Shirehall Road
Broad Lane
Lower Road
Clement Street
Church Road
Arnolds Lane
Parsonage Lane
Dartford Station
Dartford Golf Club
North West Kent College
Wilmington Grammar School for Girls
Wilmington Boys Grammar School
Wilmington Hall School
Wilmington Primary School
Rowhill School
Rowhill Grange Hotel & Spa
Dartford Grammar Sch for Girls
Dartford Technology College
Dartford Adult Education Centre
Fairfield Pool & Leisure Centre
Central Park Arena
Princes Park Stadium
The Leigh City Technology College
University of Greenwich
Brooklands Lake
Sutton at Hone CE Primary School
St Pauls CE Primary School
Highlands Farm
Leyton Cross
Sutton Place

188
166
187
210
Greenhithe
Stone
Horns Cross
Knockhall
Bluewater Shopping Centre
Showcase Bluewater
Fleet Downs
Lane End
Darenth
Bean
Green Street Green
South Darenth
Grubb Street
Sutton at Hone
DA9
DA2
Crossways Boulevard
Anchor Boulevard
London Road
Watling Street
B2500
A206
A226
A282
A296
A2
B255
B260
B262
A225
The Brent
Bow Arrow Lane
Cotton Lane
St Mary's Road
Charles Street
Stone Crossing Station
Elizabeth Street
Hedge Place Road
Bluewater Parkway
St James Lane
Darenth Wood Road
Trolling Down Hill B260
Green Street Green Road
Wood Lane
Roman Villa Road
Darenth Road South
Darenth Hill
Main Road
Parsonage Lane
Shellbank Lane
Bean Lane
Mounts Road
High Street
Princes Road
Fleet Road
Princes Avenue
Louvain Road
Kirby Road
Hayes Road
Pilgrims Way
Junction 1a
Junction 1b
Junction 2
Darent Valley Hospital
A&E
Stone House Hospital
The Brent Primary School
The Leigh City Technology College
Fleetdown J&I School
Darenth Primary School
Sutton at Hone CE Primary School
Parker Industrial Centre
Kestner Industrial Est
Darenth Wood
Lords Wood
Farm Park
Stone Castle
Cemetery
Council Building
Greenhithe Health Clinic
Gill's Road
Gill's Farm
St Margaret's
Sutton Place
1 grid square represents 500 metres

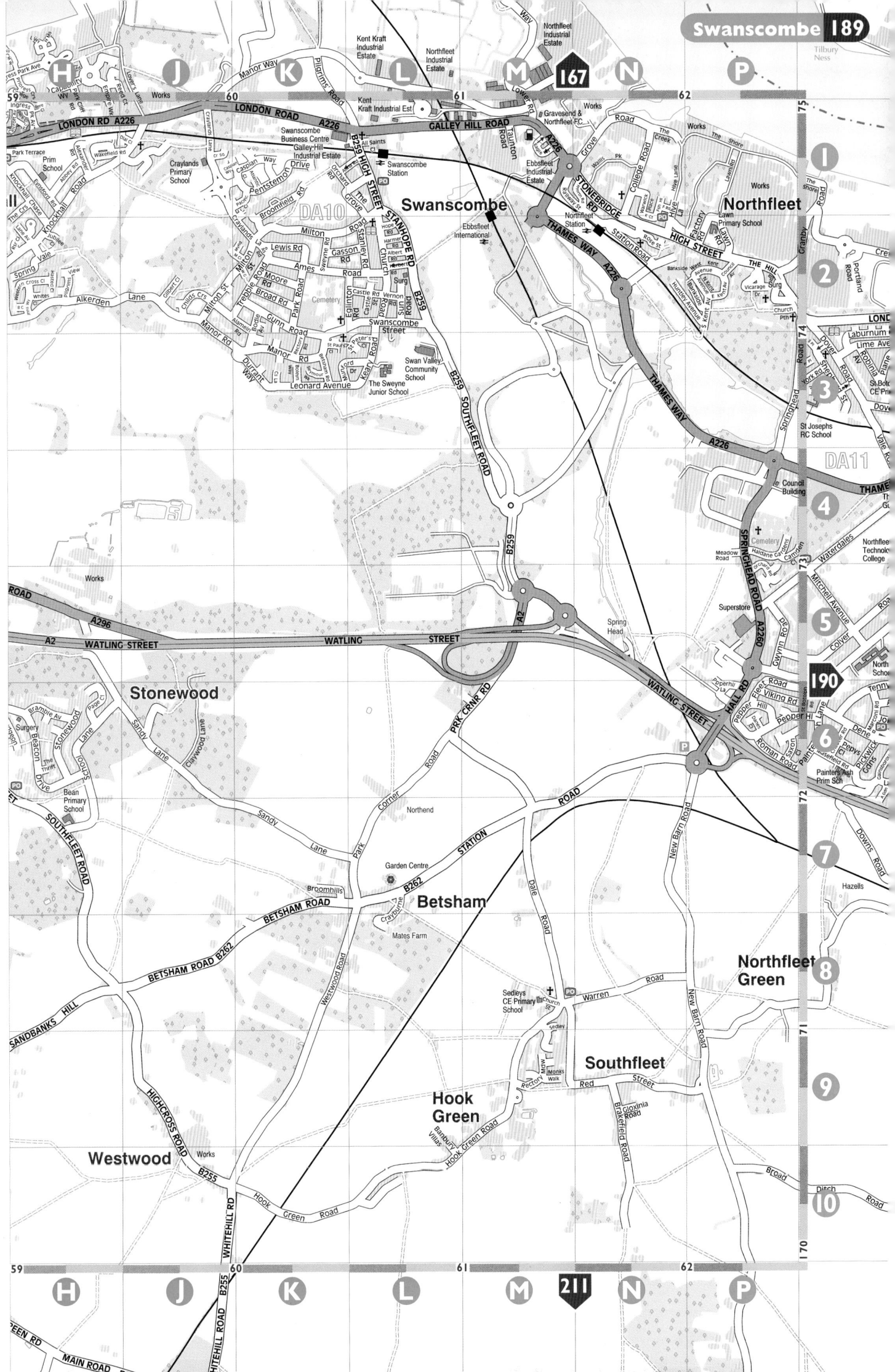

Swanscombe
Northfleet
Stonewood
Betsham
Southfleet
Hook Green
Westwood
Northfleet Green
Northend
Spring Head
DA10
DA11
LONDON ROAD A226
GALLEY HILL ROAD
B259 HIGH STREET
STANHOPE RD
B259 SOUTHFLEET ROAD
THAMES WAY
A226
STONEBRIDGE RD
HIGH STREET
THE HILL
SPRINGHEAD ROAD A2260
A2 WATLING STREET
A296
WATLING STREET
HALL RD
PRK CRNR RD
Park Corner Road
STATION ROAD
B262
BETSHAM ROAD
BETSHAM ROAD B262
SANDBANKS HILL
HIGHCROSS ROAD
B255
WHITEHILL RD
Hook Green Road
Dale Road
Warren Road
Red Street
New Barn Road
Westwood Road
Sandy Lane
Swanscombe Station
Ebbsfleet International
Northfleet Station
Kent Kraft Industrial Estate
Northfleet Industrial Estate
Swanscombe Business Centre
Galley Hill Industrial Estate
Ebbsfleet Industrial Estate
Gravesend & Northfleet FC
Craylands Primary School
Park Terrace Prim School
Swan Valley Community School
The Sweyne Junior School
Lawn Primary School
St Josephs RC School
Council Building
Superstore
Garden Centre
Mates Farm
Sedleys CE Primary School
Bean Primary School
Painters Ash Prim Sch
Northfleet Technology College
Tilbury Ness
Works
Cemetery
167
190
211
H J K L M N P
59 60 61 62
75 74 73 72 71 170
1 2 3 4 5 6 7 8 9 10

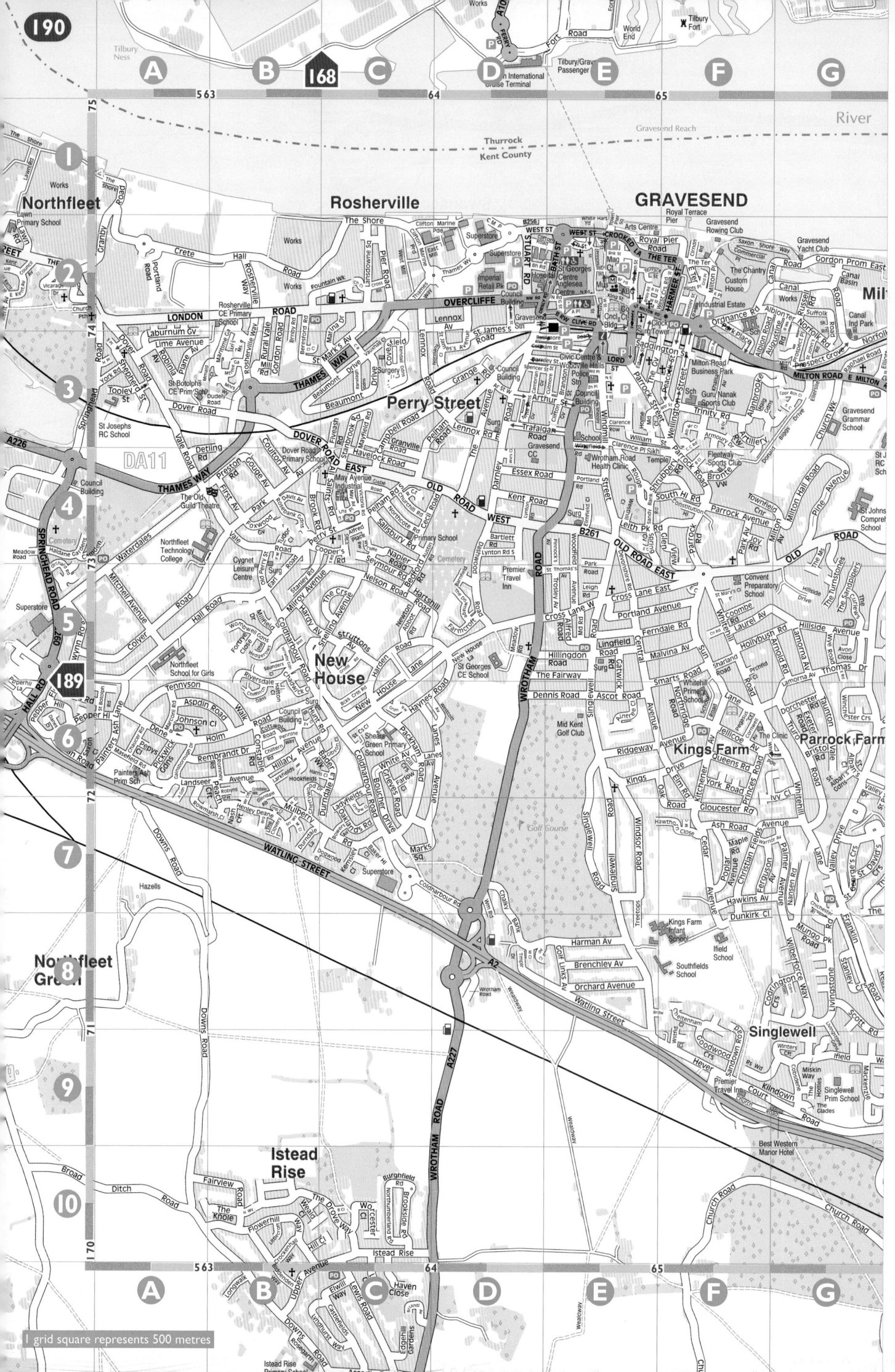
168
189
A
B
C
D
E
F
G
1
2
3
4
5
6
7
8
9
10
563
64
65
75
74
73
72
71
170
River
Gravesend Reach
Thurrock
Kent County
Tilbury Ness
Tilbury Fort
World End
Northfleet
Lawn Primary School
Works
Rosherville
The Shore
GRAVESEND
Royal Terrace Pier
Gravesend Rowing Club
Gravesend Yacht Club
Arts Centre
Royal Pier Road
Crooked La
The Ter
Harmer St
West St
Stuart Rd
Bath St
St Georges Centre
Anglesea Centre
Imperial Retail Pk
Superstore
Overcliffe
London Road
Rosherville CE Primary School
Laburnum Gv
Lime Avenue
Thames Way
Beaumont Drive
Perry Street
Dover Road
Dover Road East
Old Road West
Old Road East
St Joseph's RC School
A226
DA11
The Old Guild Theatre
Council Building
Cemetery
Springhead Road
Northfleet Technology College
Cygnet Leisure Centre
Waterdales
Mitchell Avenue
Hall Road
Colyer
Northfleet School for Girls
Hall Rd
Pepper Hill
Tennyson
Aspdin Road
Johnson Cl
Painters Ash Prim Sch
Watling Street
New House
Shears Green Primary School
Coldharbour Road
Packham Road
Marks Sq
Superstore
Premier Travel Inn
St Georges CE School
Wrotham Road
Mid Kent Golf Club
Golf Course
Singlewell Road
Windsor Road
Kings Farm
Whitehill Primary School
Parrock Farm
Milton Road
Gravesend Grammar School
Guru Nanak Sports Club
Milton Road Business Park
Fleetway Sports Club
Convent Preparatory School
Kings Farm Infant School
Ifield School
Southfields School
Singlewell
Singlewell Prim School
Best Western Manor Hotel
Church Road
Hazells
Northfleet Green
Downs Road
Istead Rise
Broad Ditch Road
Fairview Road
Istead Rise
Wrotham Road
A227
A2
Harman Av
Brenchley Av
Orchard Avenue
Wealdway
1 grid square represents 500 metres

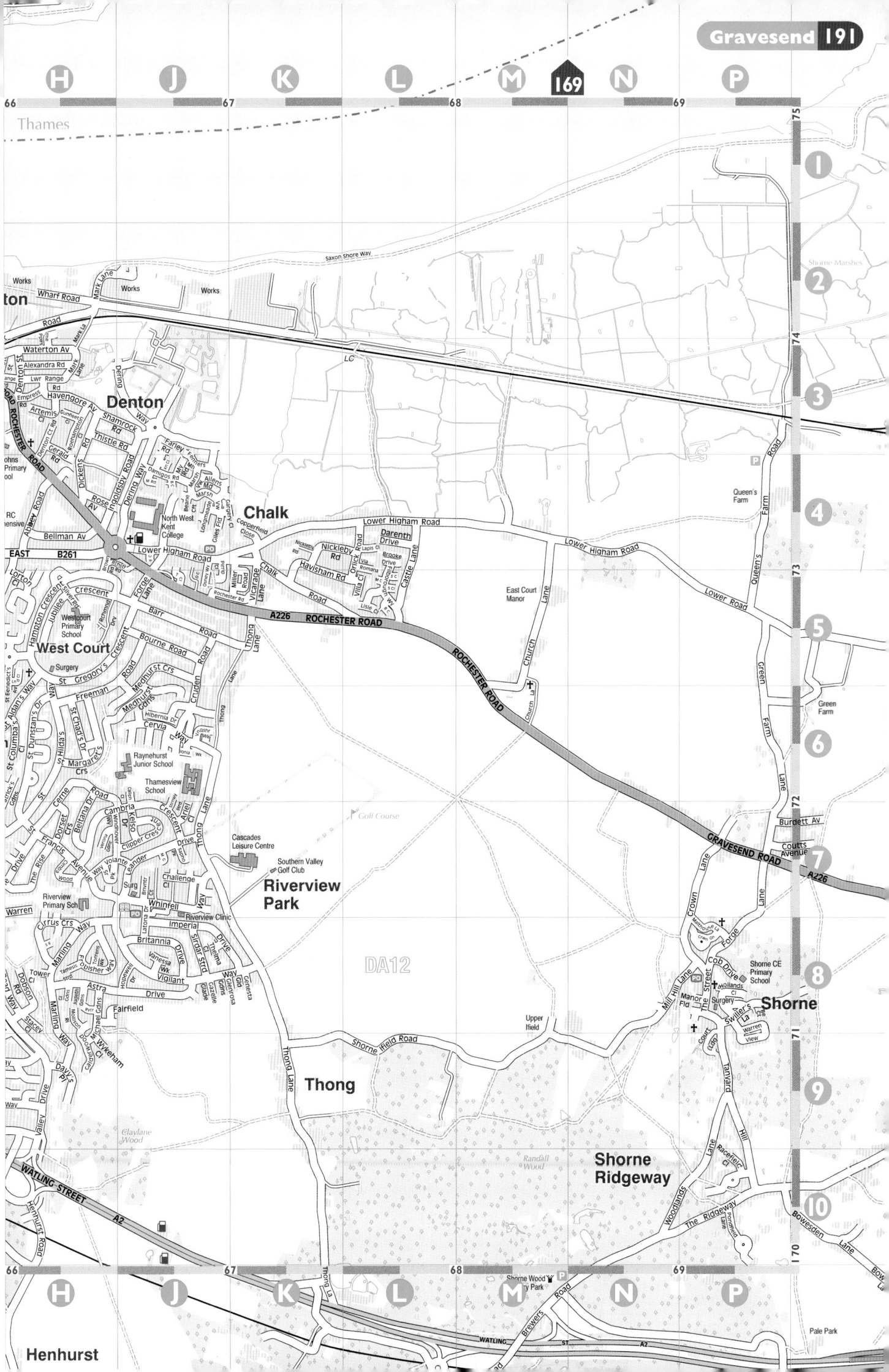

169
Thames
Saxon Shore Way
Shorne Marshes
Works
Wharf Road
Denton
Chalk
North West Kent College
Lower Higham Road
Lower Road
Queen's Farm Road
East Court Manor
Church Lane
ROCHESTER ROAD
A226
West Court
Westcourt Primary School
Raynehurst Junior School
Thamesview School
Cascades Leisure Centre
Southern Valley Golf Club
Golf Course
Riverview Park
Riverview Primary Sch
Riverview Clinic
DA12
GRAVESEND ROAD
Green Farm
Burdett Av
Coutts Avenue
Crown Lane
Forge Lane
Shorne CE Primary School
Shorne
Mill Hill Lane
Upper Ifield
Shorne Ifield Road
Thong Lane
Thong
Claylane Wood
Randall Wood
Shorne Ridgeway
The Ridgeway
Woodlands Lane
Tanyard Hill
WATLING STREET
A2
Henhurst Road
Henhurst
Shorne Wood Country Park
Brewers Road
Bowesden Lane
Pale Park

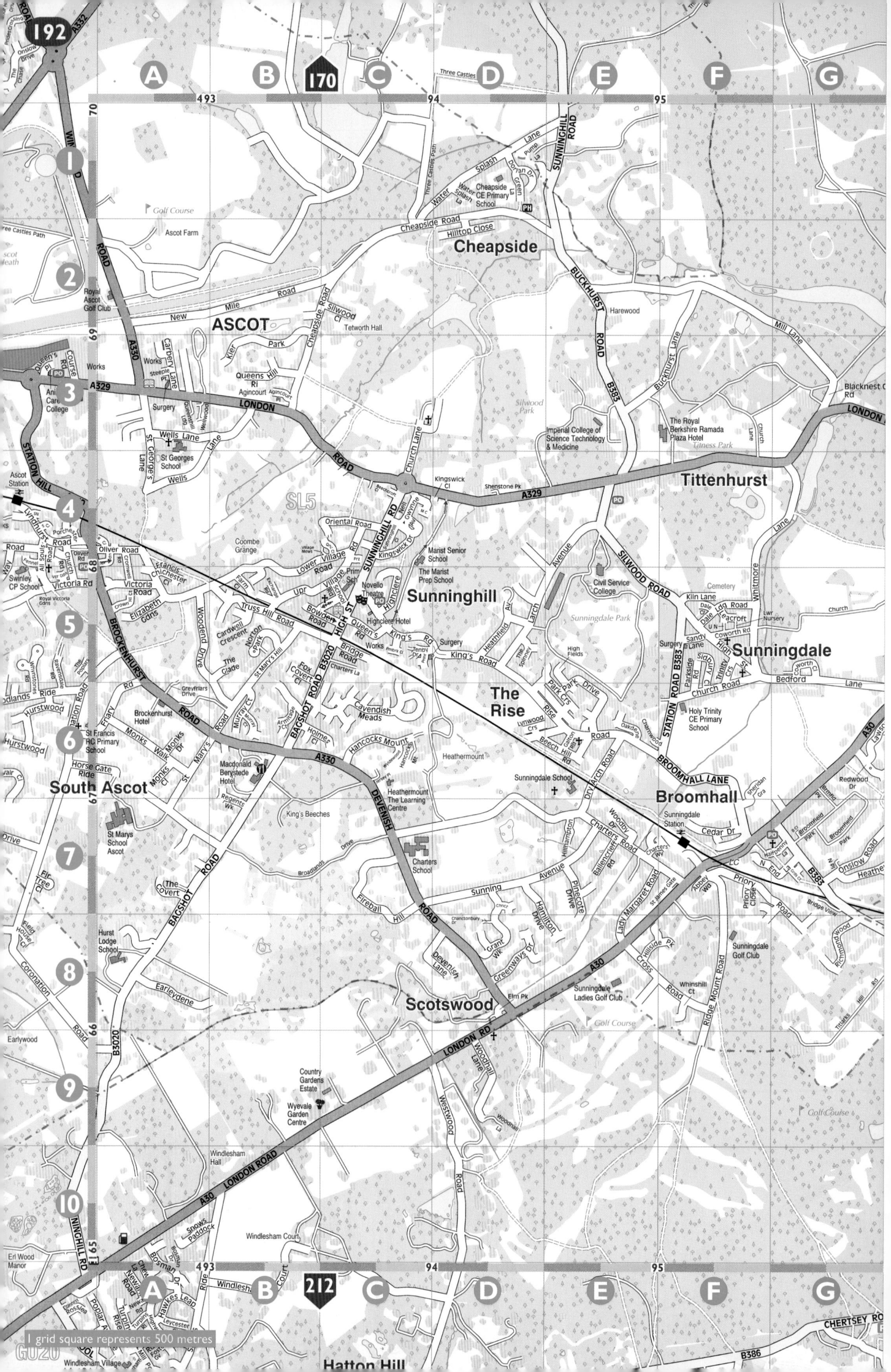

192
170
212
A
B
C
D
E
F
G
493
94
95
1
2
3
4
5
6
7
8
9
10
70
69
68
67
66
65
ASCOT
Cheapside
Sunninghill
Tittenhurst
Sunningdale
The Rise
Broomhall
South Ascot
Scotswood
Hatton Hill
SL5
Golf Course
Ascot Farm
Royal Ascot Golf Club
New Mile Road
Cheapside Road
Hilltop Close
Cheapside CE Primary School
Water Splash Lane
Three Castles Path
Sunninghill Road
Buckhurst Road
B383
Harewood
Mill Lane
Silwood Park
Imperial College of Science Technology & Medicine
The Royal Berkshire Ramada Plaza Hotel
Fitness Park
Blacknest Rd
London Road
A329
A330
A332
Winkfield Road
Kier Park
Queens Hill Ri
Agincourt
Tetworth Hall
Silwood Cl
Works
Surgery
Wells Lane
St Georges School
St George's Lane
Station Hill
Ascot Station
Church Lane
Kingswick Cl
Shenstone Pk
Oriental Road
Coombe Grange
Lower Village Road
Marist Senior School
The Marist Prep School
Novello Theatre
Highclere Hotel
High St
Bagshot Road
B3020
Silwood Road
Civil Service College
Sunningdale Park
Kiln Lane
Cemetery
Whitmore Lane
Station Road
Church Road
Bedford Lane
Holy Trinity CE Primary School
Broomhall Lane
Sunningdale Station
Cedar Dr
Swinley CP School
Victoria Rd
Oliver Road
Elizabeth Gdns
Brockenhurst Road
Woodend Drive
Truss Hill Road
Cardwell Crescent
The Glade
St Mary's Hill
Fox Covert Cl
Cavendish Meads
Hancocks Mount
Heathermount
Heathermount The Learning Centre
King's Road
Sunningdale School
Dry Arch Road
Brockenhurst Hotel
Macdonald Berystede Hotel
St Francis RC Primary School
Monks Walk
Horse Gate Ride
St Marys School Ascot
King's Beeches
Devenish Road
Charters School
Charters Road
Sunning Avenue
Broadlands Drive
Fireball Hill
The Covert
Hurst Lodge School
Earleydene
Coronation Road
Devenish Lane
Greenways Dr
Elm Pk
A30
London Rd
Sunningdale Ladies Golf Club
Sunningdale Golf Club
Ridge Mount Road
Whinshill Ct
Earlywood
Country Gardens Estate
Wyevale Garden Centre
Westwood Road
Woodhall Lane
Windlesham Hall
Windlesham Court
Snows Paddock
Erl Wood Manor
Ninghill Rd
Chertsey Ro
B386
Windlesham Village
1 grid square represents 500 metres

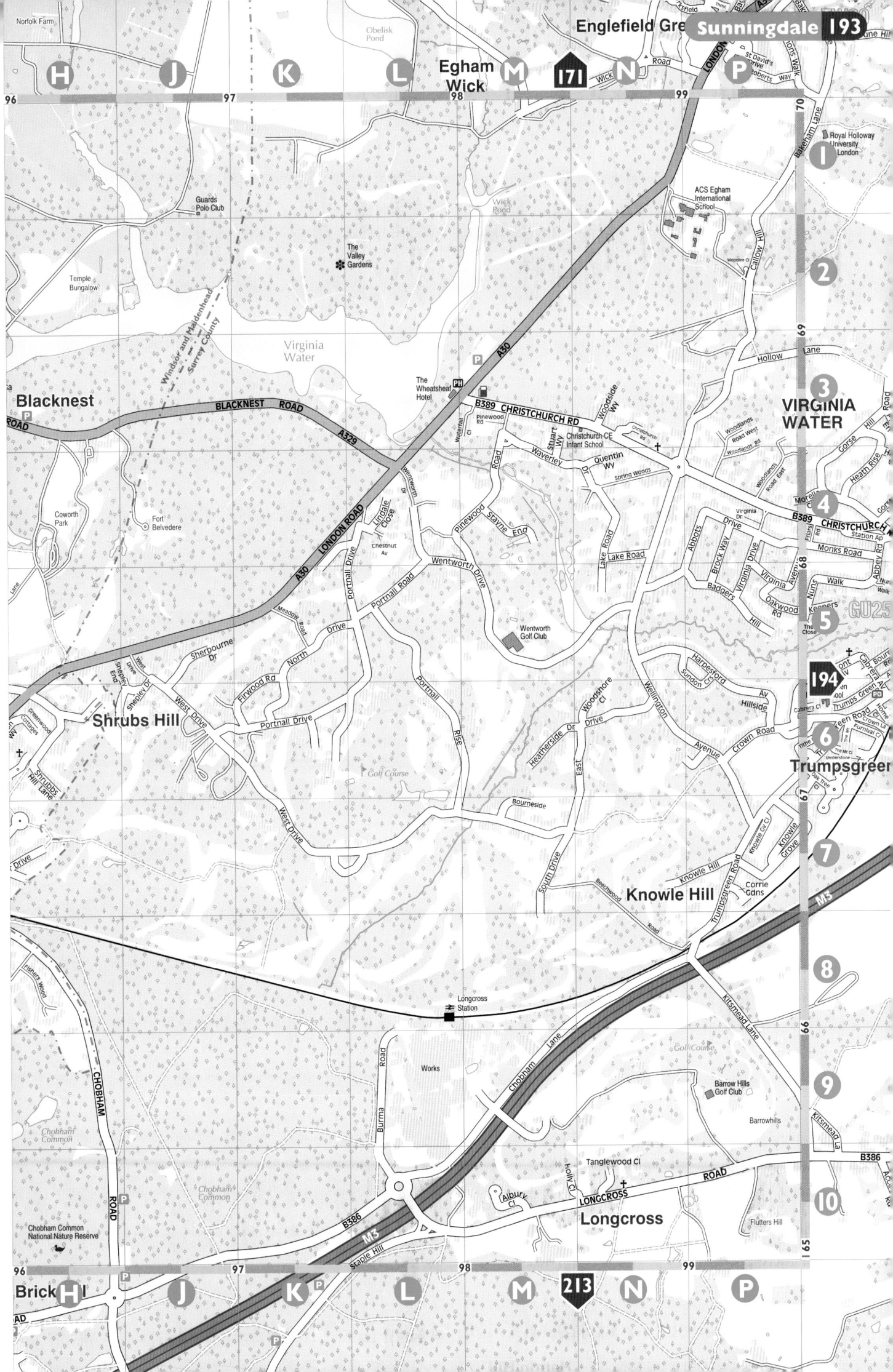
Norfolk Farm
Obelisk Pond
Englefield Green
Egham Wick
171
Guards Polo Club
Royal Holloway University London
ACS Egham International School
Wick Pond
The Valley Gardens
Temple Bungalow
Windsor and Maidenhead
Surrey County
Virginia Water
Blacknest
BLACKNEST ROAD
A329
A30
LONDON ROAD
The Wheatsheaf Hotel
B389 CHRISTCHURCH RD
Christchurch CE Infant School
VIRGINIA WATER
Hollow Lane
Callow Hill
Bakeham Lane
Coworth Park
Fort Belvedere
Wentworth Drive
Portnall Road
Portnall Drive
Wentworth Golf Club
Lake Road
Monks Road
Station Ap
Abbots Drive
Brock Way
Virginia Drive
Badgers Hill
Oakwood Rd
Nuns Walk
Keepers
GU25
194
Trumpsgreen
Trumps Green Road
Crown Road
Harpesford Av
Hillside
Wellington Avenue
Shrubs Hill
Shrubbs Hill Lane
West Drive
Sherbourne Dr
North Drive
Firwood Rd
Heatherside Dr
Woodshore Cl
East Drive
South Drive
Bourneside
Golf Course
Portnall Rise
Knowle Hill
Knowle Grove
Trumpsgreen Road
Corrie Gdns
Beechwood Road
M3
Kitsmead Lane
Longcross Station
Works
Burma Road
Chobham Lane
Barrow Hills Golf Club
Barrowhills
CHOBHAM ROAD
Chobham Common
Chobham Common National Nature Reserve
Tanglewood Cl
Albury Cl
LONGCROSS ROAD
B386
Longcross
Flutters Hill
Staple Hill
Brick Hill
213
H
J
K
L
M
N
P
96
97
98
99
70
69
68
67
66
65
1
2
3
4
5
6
7
8
9
10

194
172
193
214
VIRGINIA WATER
Stroude
Thorpe Green
Thorpe
Lea
Trumpsgreen
Royal Holloway University of London
Milton Park
Thorpe Industrial Park
Egham Business Village
Sky Business Park
Cemetery
Longside Lake
St Ann's Heath
Thorpe CC
Thorpe CE Infant School
Tasis The American School in England
Virginia Water Station
PO Sorting Office
St Anns Heath Junior School
Trumps Green Infant School
Junction 2/12
Trumps Farm
Lyne Place Manor
Alm'ners Barn Farm
Lyne
Hersham Farm
Lyne & Longcross CE Infant School
Silverlands
France Farm
Barrow Hills Golf Club
Barrowhills
Flutters Hill
Golf Course
Foxhills Club Resort
Fox Hills
St Peters Hospital
White Lodge Centre
Runnymede Hospital
A&E
M25
M3
B388
B389
B386
CHRISTCHURCH RD
CHRISTCHURCH ROAD
SANDHILLS LANE
GREEN ROAD
MILL HOUSE LANE
THORPE BY-PASS
LONGCROSS ROAD
TRYS HILL
HOLLOWAY HILL
GUILDFORD ROAD
Stroude Road
Whitehall Lane
Hurst Lane
Lyne Lane
Lyne Crossing Road
Almners Road
Hardwick Lane
Ruxbury Road
St Ann's Hill Road
Coldharbour Lane
Crabtree Road
Bakeham Lane
Prune Hill
Callow Hill
Hollow Lane
Kitsmead Lane
Accommodation Rd
Stonehill Road
Bridge Lane
Trumps Green Road
Trumpsgreen Road
Lyne Road
Harrow Bottom Rd
Monks Road
Nuns Walk
Heath Rise
Gorse Hill
Trotsworth Av
Hillswood Drive
TW20
GU25
KT16
1 grid square represents 500 metres

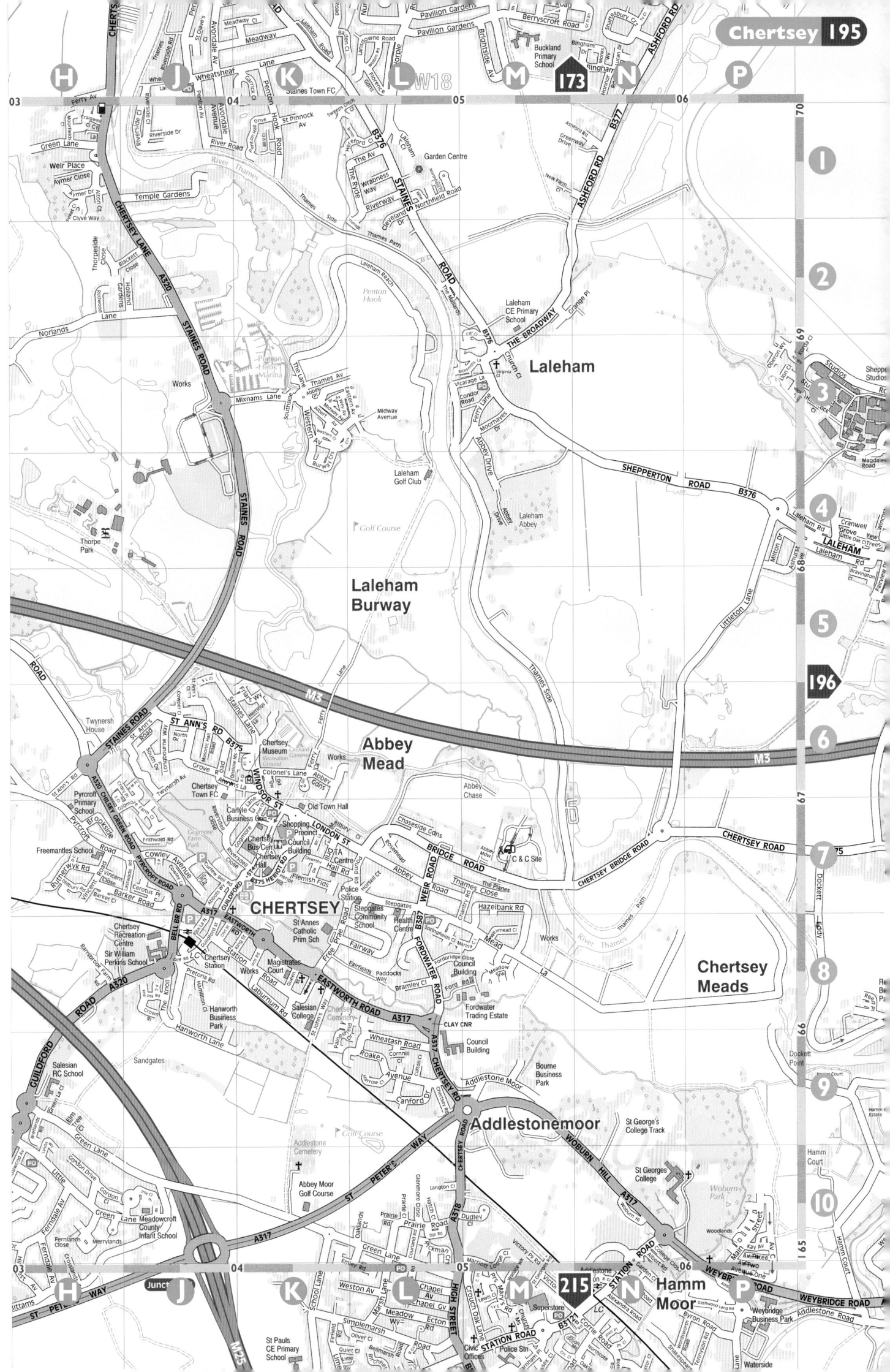

Laleham
Laleham Burway
Abbey Mead
CHERTSEY
Chertsey Meads
Addlestonemoor
Hamm Moor
Penton Hook
Thorpe Park
Laleham Abbey
St Georges College
Woburn Park
M3
M25
Staines Road
Chertsey Lane
Shepperton Road
Chertsey Bridge Road
Chertsey Road
Guildford Road
Eastworth Road
Bridge Road
Woburn Hill
Weybridge Road
St Peter's Way
Staines Town FC
Chertsey Town FC
Chertsey Museum
Chertsey Station
Laleham Golf Club
Abbey Moor Golf Course
Addlestone Cemetery
173
196
215

196
Littleton Common
174
Sunbury Common
STAINES ROAD
Spelthorne Sports Club
WEST
SUNBURY
Sunbury Business Centre
Windmill Trading Estate
Superstore
Queen Mary Reservoir
Works
Sunbury Leisure Centre
Manor School
Springfield Primary School
Upper Halliford Station
Charlton
Bishop Wand CE Secondary School
Hawkedale GM School
Shepperton Studios
Littleton
Littleton CE Infant School
UPR HALLIFORD ROAD
Sunbury Golf Centre
TW17
Upper Halliford
Health Clinic
Garden Centre
Shepperton Green
LALEHAM RD
Saxon CP School
Rodd Estate
Longwood Business Park
195
Shepperton Business Park
Shepperton Station
GREEN LANE
Shepperton
St Nicholas CE Primary School
Thamesmead School
GASTON BR ROAD
Holiday Inn
Shepperton Marina
RENFREE WAY
HIGH STREET
CHERTSEY RD
Halliford School
RUSSELL RD
Lower Halliford
Bishop Duppas Park
University Vandals RFC
WALTON BRIDGE ROAD
River Thames
NEW ZEALAND AV
Reed Place Business Park
Walton Lane
Walton-on-Thames CC
Dockett Point
Hamm Court Estate
Thames Path
Ridgemount
Weybridge CC
Hamm Court
Broad Water
Oatlands Park Hotel
St James CE Primary School
Innkeeper's Lodge
St Charles Borromeo RCP Sch
OATLANDS
ASHLEY ROAD
Weybridge Hospital
Council Building
216
WEYBRIDGE ROAD
Weybridge Business Park
Elmbridge Museum
OATLANDS DRIVE
Oatlands Park
Oatlands School
WEYBRIDGE
1 grid square represents 500 metres

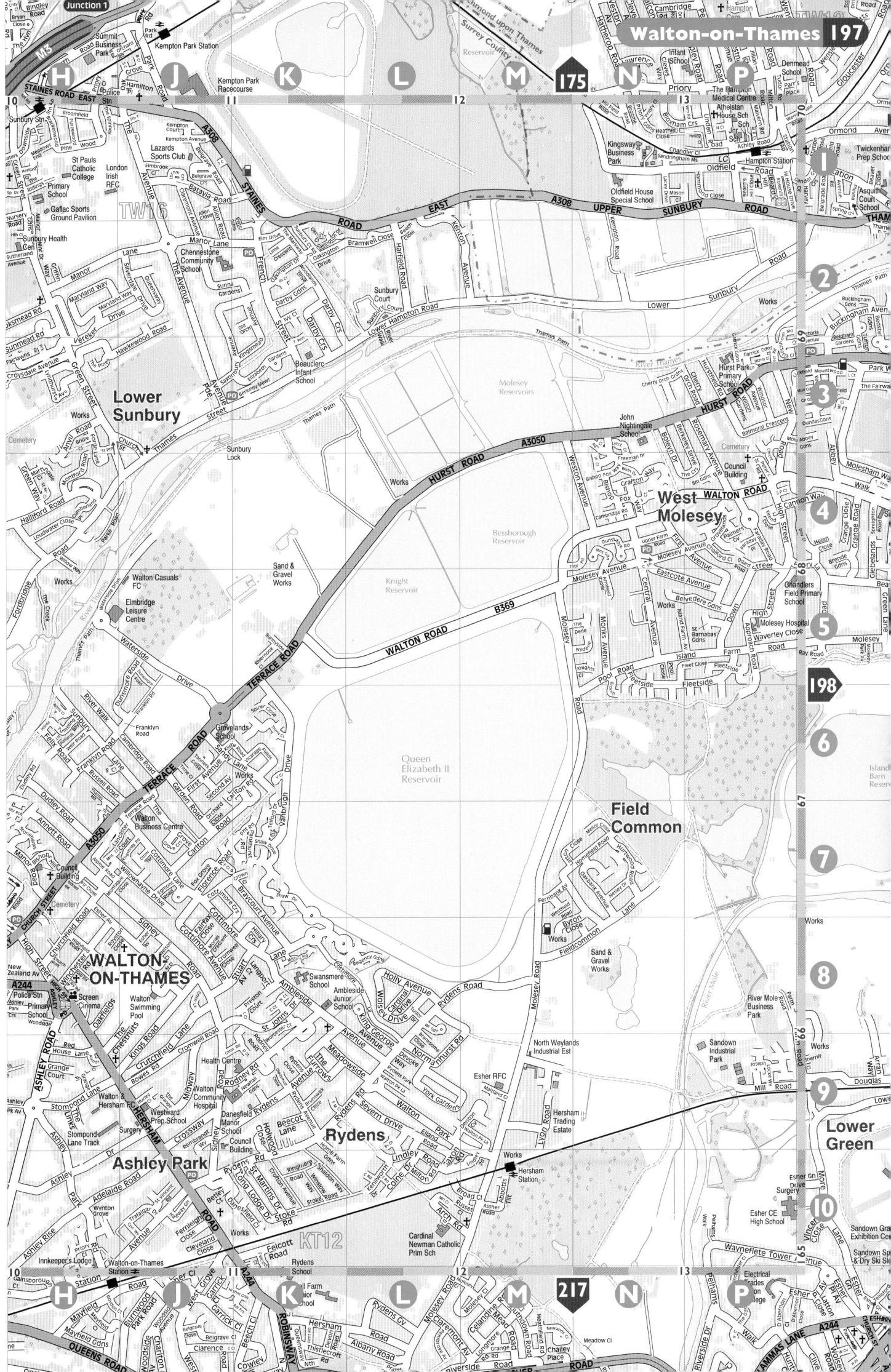
Kempton Park Station
Kempton Park Racecourse
Lower Sunbury
West Molesey
Field Common
WALTON-ON-THAMES
Ashley Park
Rydens
Lower Green
Hampton Station
Hersham Station
Walton-on-Thames Station
Molesey Reservoirs
Bessborough Reservoir
Knight Reservoir
Queen Elizabeth II Reservoir
HURST ROAD
WALTON ROAD
TERRACE ROAD
UPPER SUNBURY ROAD
STAINES ROAD EAST
River Thames
River Mole
TW16
KT12

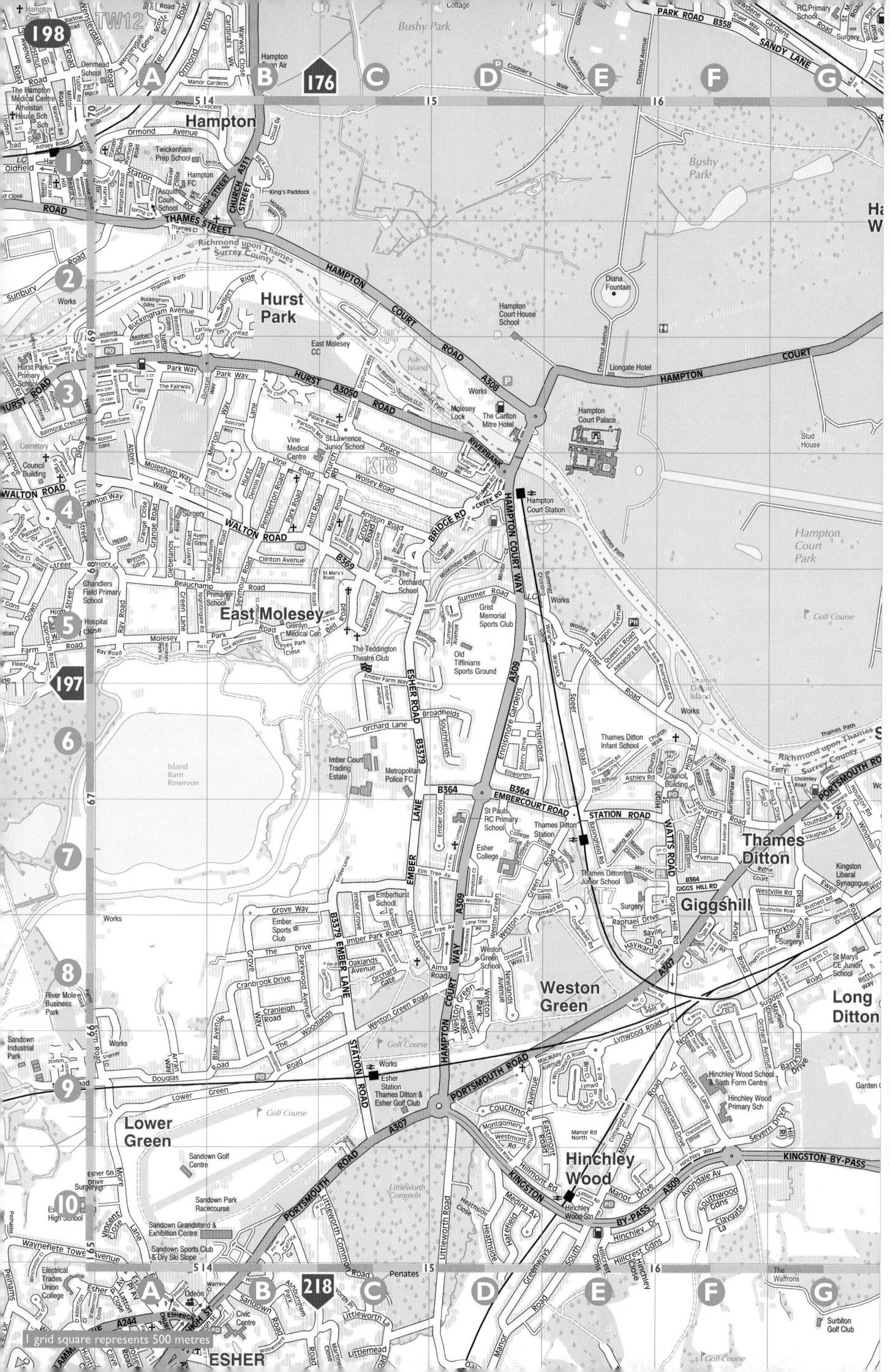
198
176
197
218
A
B
C
D
E
F
G
1
2
3
4
5
6
7
8
9
10
514
15
16
TW12
KT8
KT7
Hampton
Hurst Park
East Molesey
Thames Ditton
Giggshill
Weston Green
Long Ditton
Lower Green
Hinchley Wood
ESHER
Bushy Park
Hampton Court Park
Hampton Court Palace
Hampton Court Station
Hampton Court House School
Diana Fountain
Liongate Hotel
Stud House
Golf Course
Island Barn Reservoir
Imber Court Trading Estate
Metropolitan Police FC
Old Tiffinians Sports Ground
Grist Memorial Sports Club
The Teddington Theatre Club
The Orchard School
Chandlers Field Primary School
Hospital
Glenlyn Medical Cen
St Lawrence Junior School
Vine Medical Centre
East Molesey CC
Tagg's Island
Ash Island
Molesey Lock
The Carlton Mitre Hotel
Thames Ditton Island
Thames Ditton Infant School
Thames Ditton Junior School
Thames Ditton Station
St Pauls RC Primary School
Esher College
Emberhurst School
Ember Sports Club
Weston Green School
Esher Station
Thames Ditton & Esher Golf Club
Sandown Golf Centre
Sandown Park Racecourse
Sandown Grandstand & Exhibition Centre
Sandown Sports Club & Dry Ski Slope
Littleworth Common
River Mole Business Park
Sandown Industrial Park
Esher High School
Electrical Trades Union College
Odeon
Civic Centre
Hinchley Wood Stn
Hinchley Wood School & Sixth Form Centre
Hinchley Wood Primary Sch
Manor Rd North
Kingston Liberal Synagogue
St Marys CE Junior School
Surbiton Golf Club
The Waffrons
Twickenham Prep School
Hampton FC
Asquith Court School
King's Paddock
The Hampton Medical Centre
Denmead School
Cemetery
Council Building
Hurst Park Primary School
Richmond upon Thames
Surrey County
River Thames
River Ember
River Mole
HAMPTON COURT ROAD
HAMPTON COURT WAY
THAMES STREET
HIGH STREET
CHURCH STREET
HURST ROAD
WALTON ROAD
BRIDGE RD
ESHER ROAD
EMBER LANE
EMBERCOURT ROAD
STATION ROAD
WATTS ROAD
GIGGS HILL RD
PORTSMOUTH ROAD
KINGSTON BY-PASS
PARK ROAD
SANDY LANE
A308
A309
A3050
A307
A311
A244
B358
B364
B369
B3379
Works
Surgery
1 grid square represents 500 metres

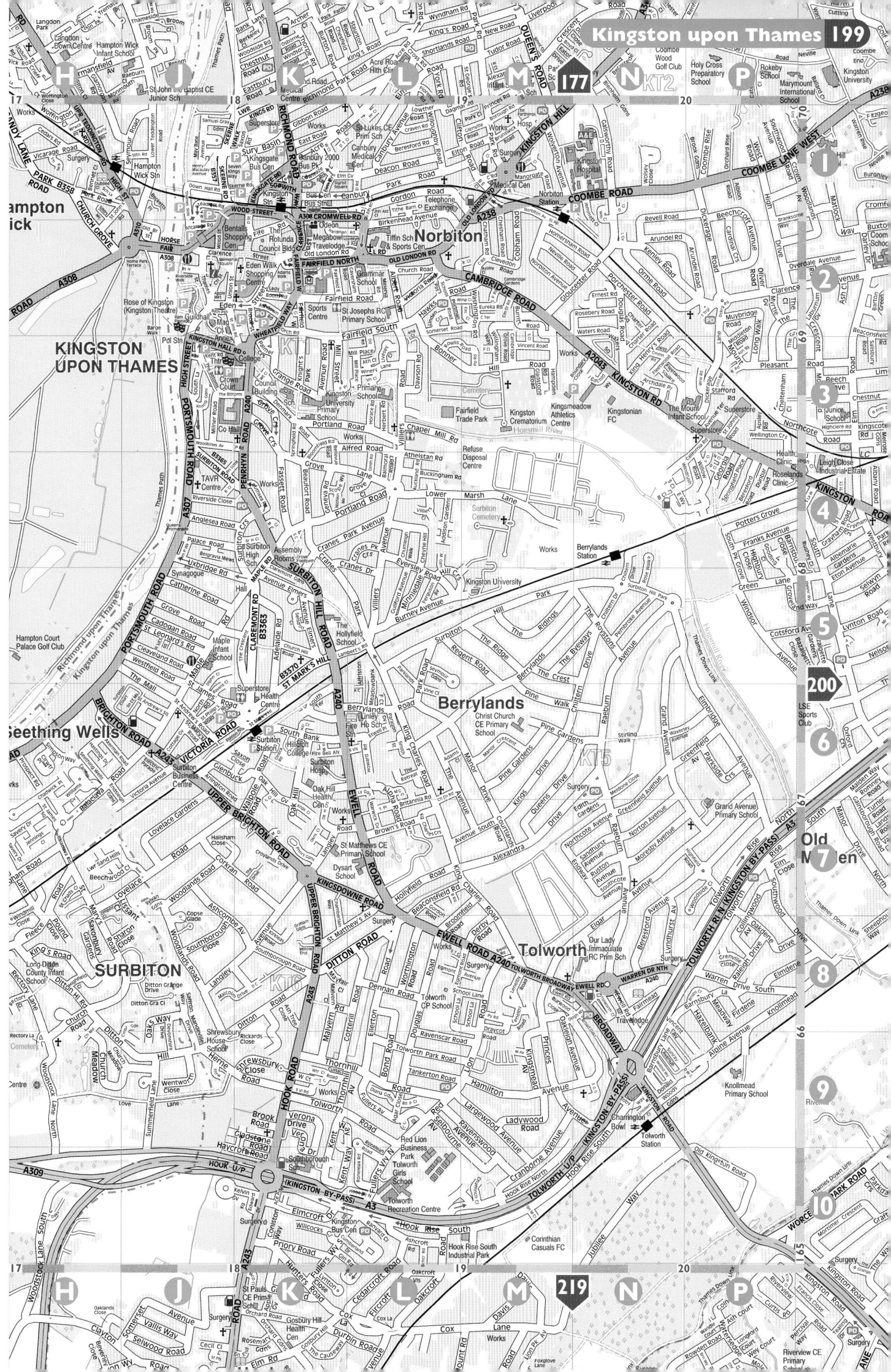

KINGSTON UPON THAMES
Norbiton
Berrylands
Tolworth
SURBITON
Seething Wells
Old Malden
Kingston Hospital
Kingston Stn
Norbiton Station
Berrylands Station
Surbiton Station
Tolworth Station
Hampton Wick Stn
Kingston University
Hampton Court Palace Golf Club
Coombe Wood Golf Club
Kingsmeadow Athletics Centre
Kingstonian FC
Hogsmill River
Thames Down Link
177
200
219
KT1
KT2
KT5
KT6

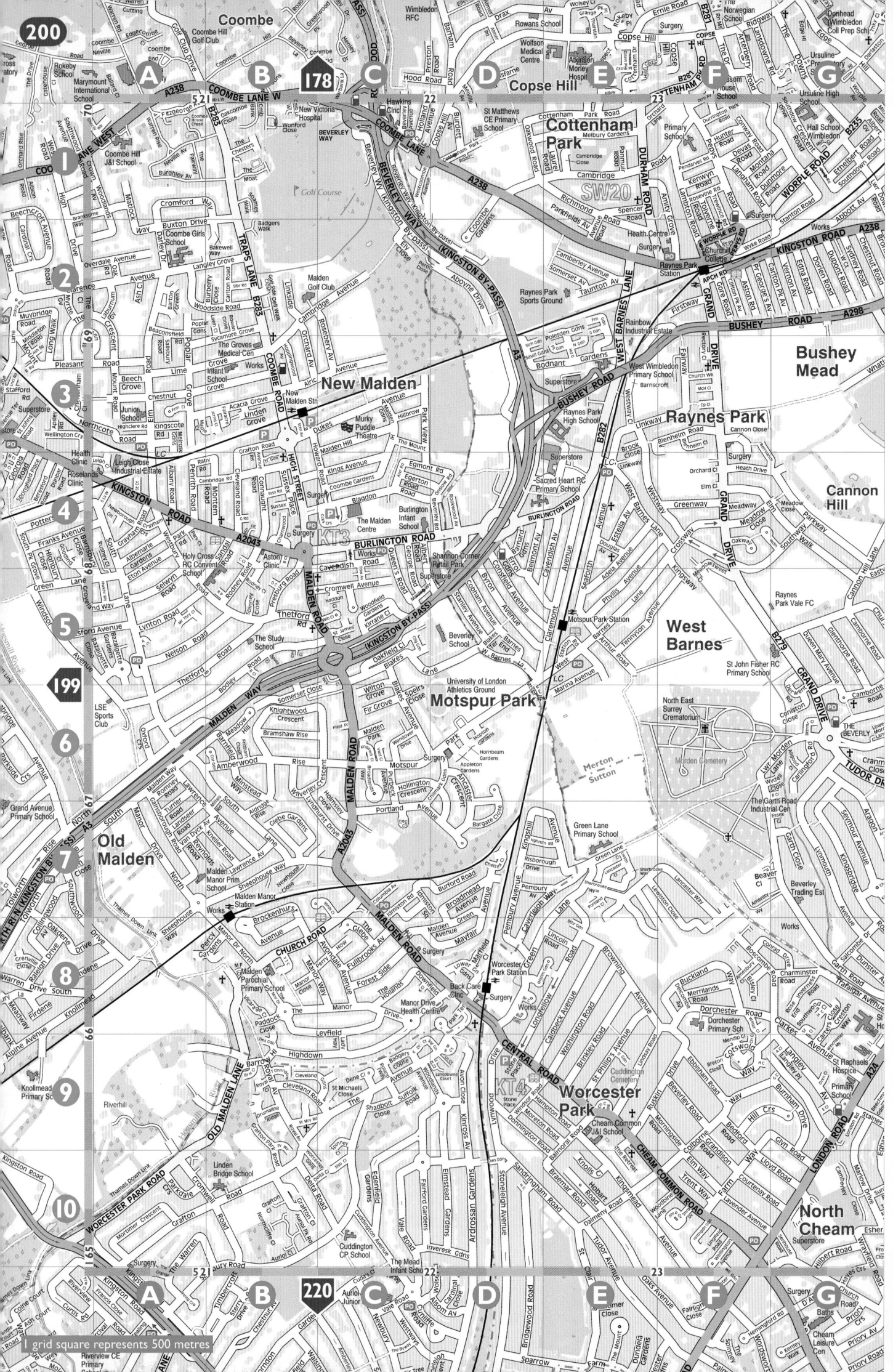

200
178
199
220
A
B
C
D
E
F
G
1
2
3
4
5
6
7
8
9
10
Coombe
Copse Hill
Cottenham Park
SW20
New Malden
KT3
Raynes Park
Bushey Mead
Cannon Hill
West Barnes
Motspur Park
Old Malden
Worcester Park
KT4
North Cheam
COOMBE LANE W
COOMBE LANE WEST
COOMBE LANE
BEVERLEY WAY
KINGSTON BY-PASS
KINGSTON ROAD
BURLINGTON ROAD
MALDEN ROAD
MALDEN WAY
COOMBE ROAD
HIGH STREET
TRAPS LANE
WEST BARNES LANE
BUSHEY ROAD
GRAND DRIVE
DURHAM ROAD
WORPLE ROAD
CENTRAL ROAD
CHURCH ROAD
OLD MALDEN LANE
WORCESTER PARK ROAD
CHEAM COMMON ROAD
LONDON ROAD
A238
A3
A2043
A298
A24
B282
B283
B279
B281
B235
Wimbledon RFC
Coombe Hill Golf Club
Malden Golf Club
Golf Course
Raynes Park Sports Ground
University of London Athletics Ground
North East Surrey Crematorium
Morden Cemetery
Cuddington Cemetery
New Malden Stn
Raynes Park Station
Motspur Park Station
Malden Manor Station
Worcester Park Station
Merton
Sutton
1 grid square represents 500 metres

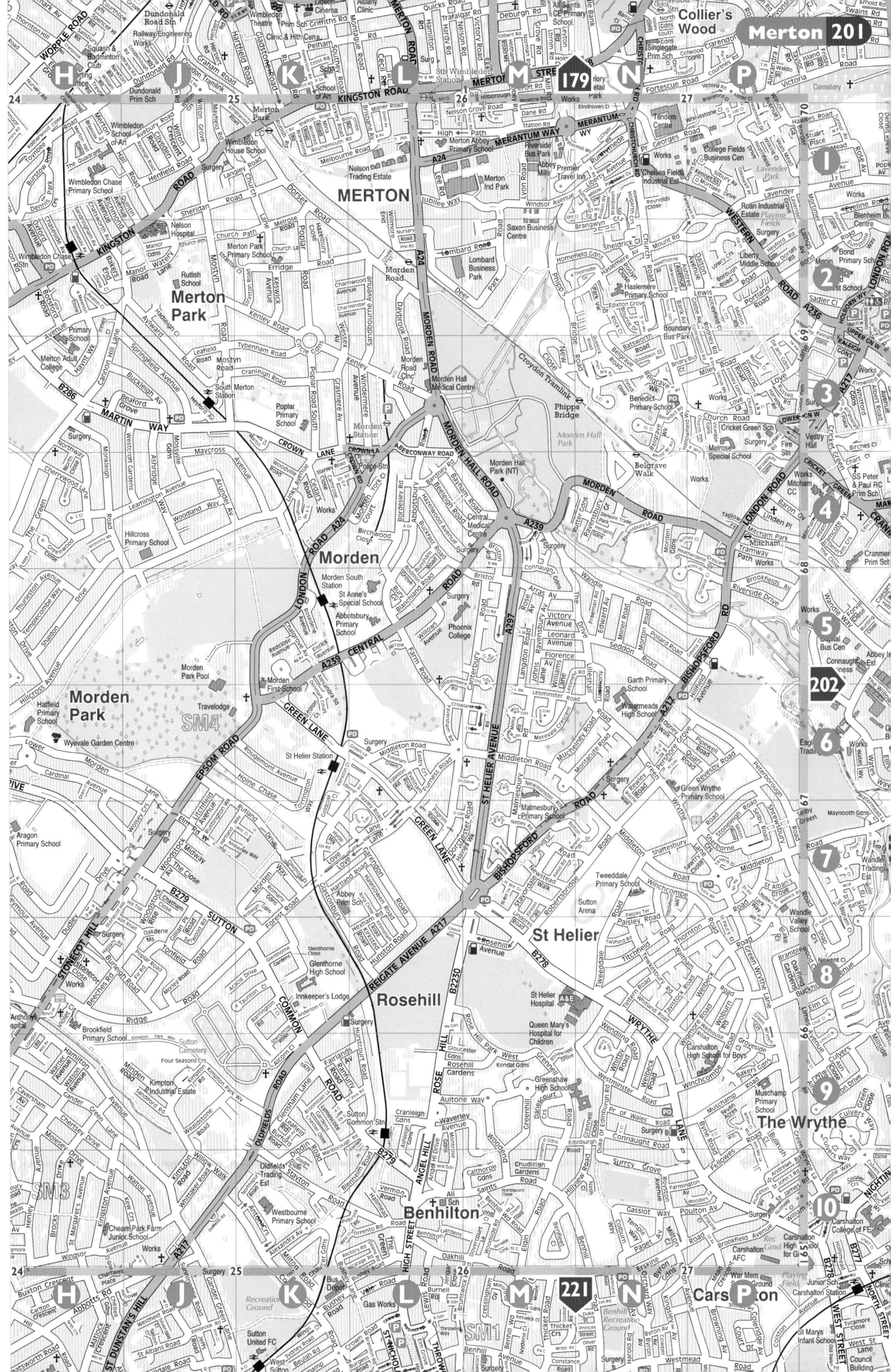

Merton 201
Collier's Wood
MERTON
Merton Park
Morden
Morden Park
SM4
St Helier
Rosehill
Benhilton
The Wrythe
Carshalton
SM3
SM1
179
202
221
H
J
K
L
M
N
P
1
2
3
4
5
6
7
8
9
10
24
25
26
27
KINGSTON ROAD
MERTON ROAD
MORDEN ROAD
MORDEN HALL ROAD
LONDON ROAD
EPSOM ROAD
ST HELIER AVENUE
BISHOPSFORD ROAD
REIGATE AVENUE
STONECOT HILL
WORPLE ROAD
MERANTUM WAY
CHRISTCHURCH RD
WESTERN ROAD
CENTRAL ROAD
GREEN LANE
MARTIN WAY
OLDFIELDS ROAD
ROSE HILL
ANGEL HILL
HIGH STREET
ST DUNSTAN'S HILL
WRYTHE LANE
NORTH STREET
WEST STREET
Morden Hall Park (NT)
St Helier Hospital
Queen Mary's Hospital for Children
Croydon Tramlink
Phipps Bridge
Morden South Station
St Helier Station
South Merton Station
Wimbledon Chase
Sutton Common Stn
Carshalton Station

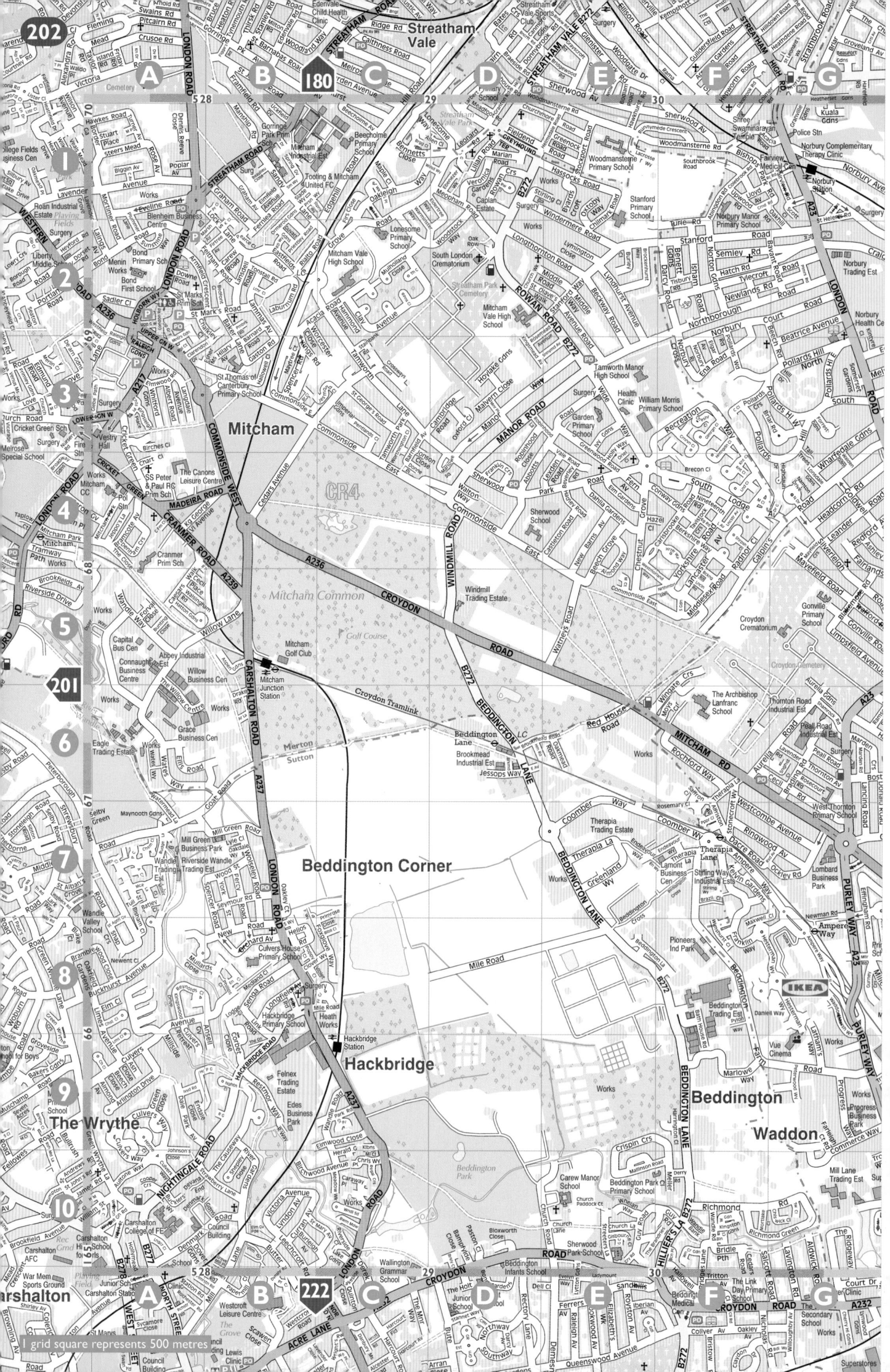

202
180
201
222
A
B
C
D
E
F
G
1
2
3
4
5
6
7
8
9
10
528
29
30
70
69
68
67
66
65
Streatham Vale
Mitcham
Beddington Corner
Hackbridge
Beddington
Waddon
The Wrythe
Carshalton
Mitcham Common
Golf Course
CR4
Merton
Sutton
LONDON ROAD
STREATHAM ROAD
COMMONSIDE WEST
CROYDON ROAD
A236
CARSHALTON ROAD
A237
CRANMER ROAD
A239
WINDMILL ROAD
BEDDINGTON LANE
B272
MITCHAM RD
PURLEY WAY
A23
STREATHAM HIGH RD
ROWAN ROAD
MANOR ROAD
WESTERN ROAD
NIGHTINGALE ROAD
HACKBRIDGE ROAD
Croydon Tramlink
Mitcham Junction Station
Hackbridge Station
Norbury Station
Mitcham Golf Club
Windmill Trading Estate
Croydon Crematorium
Croydon Cemetery
Streatham Park Cemetery
South London Crematorium
Tamworth Manor High School
Mitcham Vale High School
Lonesome Primary School
William Morris Primary School
Sherwood School
The Archbishop Lanfranc School
Beddington Trading Est
Vue Cinema
IKEA
Beddington Park
Carew Manor School
Beddington Park Primary School
Wallington Grammar School
Westcroft Leisure Centre
Carshalton College of FE
Felnex Trading Estate
Edes Business Park
Mile Road
Therapia Trading Estate
Pioneers Ind Park
Mitcham Industrial Est
Tooting & Mitcham United FC
The Canons Leisure Centre
Woodmansterne Primary School
Stanford Primary School
Norbury Manor Primary School
Police Stn
Norbury Trading Est
Thornton Road Industrial Est
Lombard Business Park
Mill Lane Trading Est
1 grid square represents 500 metres

H
J
K
L
M
N
P
181
SE19
Upper Norwood
Norbury
Anerley
SE20
South Norwood
SE25
CR7
Thornton Heath
Selhurst
Woodside
204
Broad Green
Addiscombe
Wandle Park
CR0
CROYDON
223
Norbury Park
Norbury Manor Secondary Girls School
Kensington Av Primary School
David Livingstone Primary School
St Cyprians Greek Orth Prim Sch
Westwood Language College for Girls
Downsview Primary School
All Saints CE Primary School
Harris City Technology College
James Dixon Primary School
Cypress Infant School
Cypress Junior School
Spurgeon's College
Stanley Technical High School
South Norwood Hill Medical Centre
Thornton Heath Station
Thornton Heath Pools & Fitness Cen
Thornton Heath Health Centre
Crystal Palace FC (Selhurst Park)
South Norwood Medical Cen
Priory Special School
Norwood Junction Stn
South Norwood Primary School
South Norwood Pools & Fitness Cen
St Chads RC Primary School
Heavers Farm Primary School
Selhurst Station
Follys End Christian High School
The Selhurst Medical Centre
Selhurst High School for Boys
BRIT School for Performing Arts
St Thomas Becket RC Prim School
Ecclesbourne Primary School
Bensham Manor School
Brigstock Medical Centre
Streatham & Croydon RFC
Winterbourne Infant School
Croydon Mosque & Islamic Cen
Mayday University Hospital
London Road Medical Centre
Eversley Medical Cen
Queen's Rd Cemetery
Council Building
Broadmead Junior & Infant School
Tait Road Ind Est
Davidson Primary School
Woodside Inf Sch
Blackhorse Lane
Roman Industrial Estate
St James Medical Cen
St Marys High School
West Croydon Stn
St Marys RC J&I School
Whitgift Shopping Centre
Wellesley Road
Whitgift Almshouses
East Croydon Station
Jurys Inn
Centrale Shop Cen
Croydon Coll
Fairfield Halls
The Law Courts
Park Hill Junior Sch
Archbishop Tenisons CE School
Addiscombe CC
Old Palace School
Town Hall
Police Stn
Parish Church CE Prim Sch
Fire Station
Occupational Health Centre
Waddon Marsh
Waddon Station
Croydon Tramlink
Superstore
St Andr School
Lloyd Park
South Park Hotel
Sandilands
Addiscombe
A212
A213
A215
A222
A232
A235
A236
B243
B266
B273
GREEN LANE
BEULAH HL
CHURCH ROAD
NORWOOD HILL
HIGH STREET
PORTLAND ROAD
LONDON ROAD
THORNTON ROAD
BRIGSTOCK ROAD
WHITEHORSE ROAD
GRANGE ROAD
NORTHCOTE ROAD
WINDMILL ROAD
ST JAMES'S RD
LWR ADDISCOMBE RD
LOWER ADDISCOMBE
ADDISCOMBE ROAD
WELLESLEY ROAD
PARK LA
FAIRFIELD RD
BARCLAY RD
CHEPSTOW ROAD
MITCHAM ROAD
SUMNER ROAD
ROMAN WAY
OLD TOWN
THE CROYDON FLYOVER A232
DUPPAS HILL ROAD
PURLEY WAY
COOMBE ROAD
SPRING LANE
WOODSIDE GREEN
MORLAND ROAD
SHIRLEY

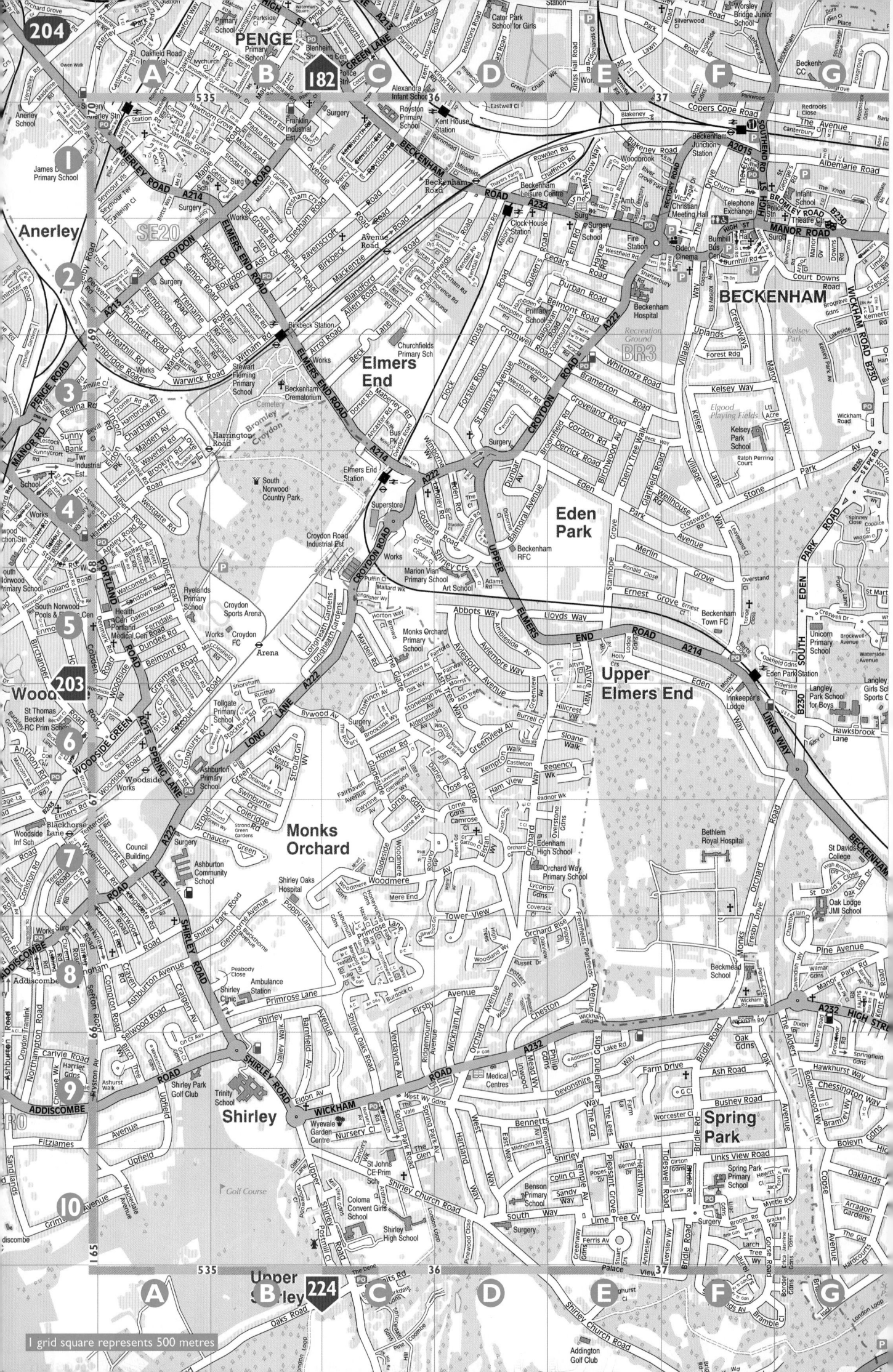

204
182
203
224
A
B
C
D
E
F
G
1
2
3
4
5
6
7
8
9
10
535
36
37
70
69
68
67
66
165
PENGE
Anerley
SE20
BECKENHAM
Elmers End
Eden Park
Upper Elmers End
Monks Orchard
Shirley
Spring Park
Upper Shirley
BR3
Woodside
Addiscombe
Anerley Stn
Anerley Station
Birkbeck Station
Clock House Station
Kent House Station
Beckenham Junction Station
Beckenham Road
Elmers End Station
Eden Park Station
Blackhorse Lane
Woodside
Arena
ANERLEY ROAD
CROYDON ROAD
ELMERS END ROAD
BECKENHAM ROAD
UPPER ELMERS END ROAD
LONG LANE
SPRING LANE
PORTLAND ROAD
WOODSIDE GREEN
SHIRLEY ROAD
WICKHAM ROAD
ADDISCOMBE ROAD
PENGE ROAD
MANOR RD
SOUTH EDEN PARK ROAD
WICKHAM ROAD
LINKS WAY
HIGH ST
RECTORY ROAD
SOUTHEND RD
BROMLEY ROAD
MANOR ROAD
HIGH STREET
GREEN LANE
A213
A214
A222
A215
A232
A234
A2015
A252
B230
B243
Beckenham Crematorium
Cemetery
South Norwood Country Park
Croydon Sports Arena
Croydon FC
Croydon Road Industrial Est
Beckenham Hospital
Bethlem Royal Hospital
Shirley Oaks Hospital
Beckenham RFC
Beckenham Town FC
Recreation Ground
Elgood Playing Fields
Kelsey Park
Kelsey Park School
Shirley Park Golf Club
Golf Course
Addington Golf Club
Trinity School
Ashburton Community School
Monks Orchard Primary School
Edenham High School
Orchard Way Primary School
Spring Park Primary School
Benson Primary School
Coloma Convent Girls School
Shirley High School
St Johns CE Prim Sch
Wyevale Garden Centre
Ambulance Station
Shirley Clinic
Medical Centres
Council Building
Beckmead School
St Davids College
Oak Lodge JMI School
Langley Park School for Boys
Unicorn Primary School
Cator Park School for Girls
Royston Primary School
Alexandra Infant School
Penge Primary School
James Dixon Primary School
Anerley School
Harris Academy
Stewart Fleming Primary School
Churchfields Primary Sch
Marion Vian Primary School
Ryelands Primary School
Tollgate Primary School
Ashburton Primary School
Woodside Inf Sch
St Thomas Becket RC Prim School
South Norwood Pools & Fitness Cen
Health Cen
Portland Medical Cen
Beckenham Leisure Centre
Christian Meeting Hall
Odeon Cinema
Fire Station
Telephone Exchange
Theatre Cen
Burnhill Bus Cen
Worsley Bridge Junior School
Beckenham CC
Langley Girls School
I grid square represents 500 metres

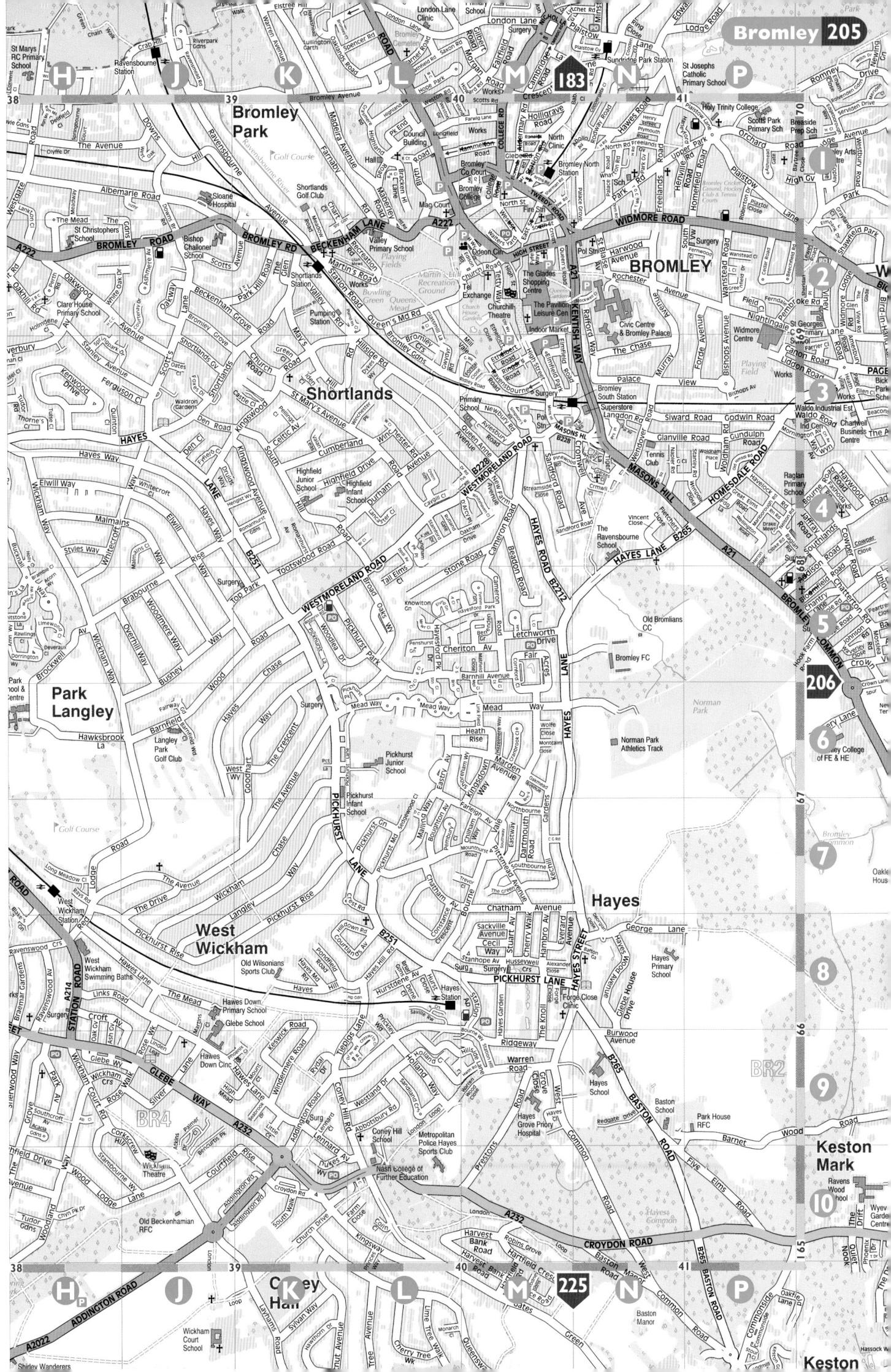
Bromley Park
Shortlands
BROMLEY
Park Langley
West Wickham
Hayes
Keston Mark
Keston
Coney Hall
183
206
225
H
J
K
L
M
N
P
38
39
40
41
1
2
3
4
5
6
7
8
9
10
BR2
BR4
A222
A21
A232
A214
A2022
B228
B251
B265
B2212
BROMLEY ROAD
BECKENHAM LANE
WIDMORE ROAD
MASONS HILL
HAYES LANE
HAYES ROAD
WESTMORELAND ROAD
PICKHURST LANE
HAYES STREET
GLEBE WAY
CROYDON ROAD
BASTON ROAD
ADDINGTON ROAD
STATION ROAD
KENTISH WAY
HOMESDALE ROAD
TWEEDY ROAD
COLLEGE ROAD
HIGH STREET
Ravensbourne Station
Shortlands Station
Bromley North Station
Bromley South Station
Sundridge Park Station
West Wickham Station
Hayes Station
Sloane Hospital
Shortlands Golf Club
Langley Park Golf Club
Civic Centre & Bromley Palace
The Glades Shopping Centre
The Pavilion Leisure Cen
Churchill Theatre
Indoor Market
Bromley FC
Norman Park Athletics Track
Norman Park
Old Bromlians CC
Hayes Primary School
Hayes School
Baston School
Park House RFC
Hayes Grove Priory Hospital
Metropolitan Police Hayes Sports Club
Nash College of Further Education
Coney Hill School
Old Beckenhamian RFC
Wickham Theatre
West Wickham Swimming Baths
Old Wilsonians Sports Club
Hawes Down Primary School
Glebe School
Pickhurst Junior School
Pickhurst Infant School
Highfield Junior School
Highfield Infant School
The Ravensbourne School
Valley Primary School
Bishop Challoner School
Clare House Primary School
St Christophers School
St Marys RC Primary School
St Josephs Catholic Primary School
Holy Trinity College
Widmore Centre
Raglan Primary School
Ravens Wood School
Wickham Court School
Hayes Common
Bromley Common
Golf Course
Shirley Wanderers

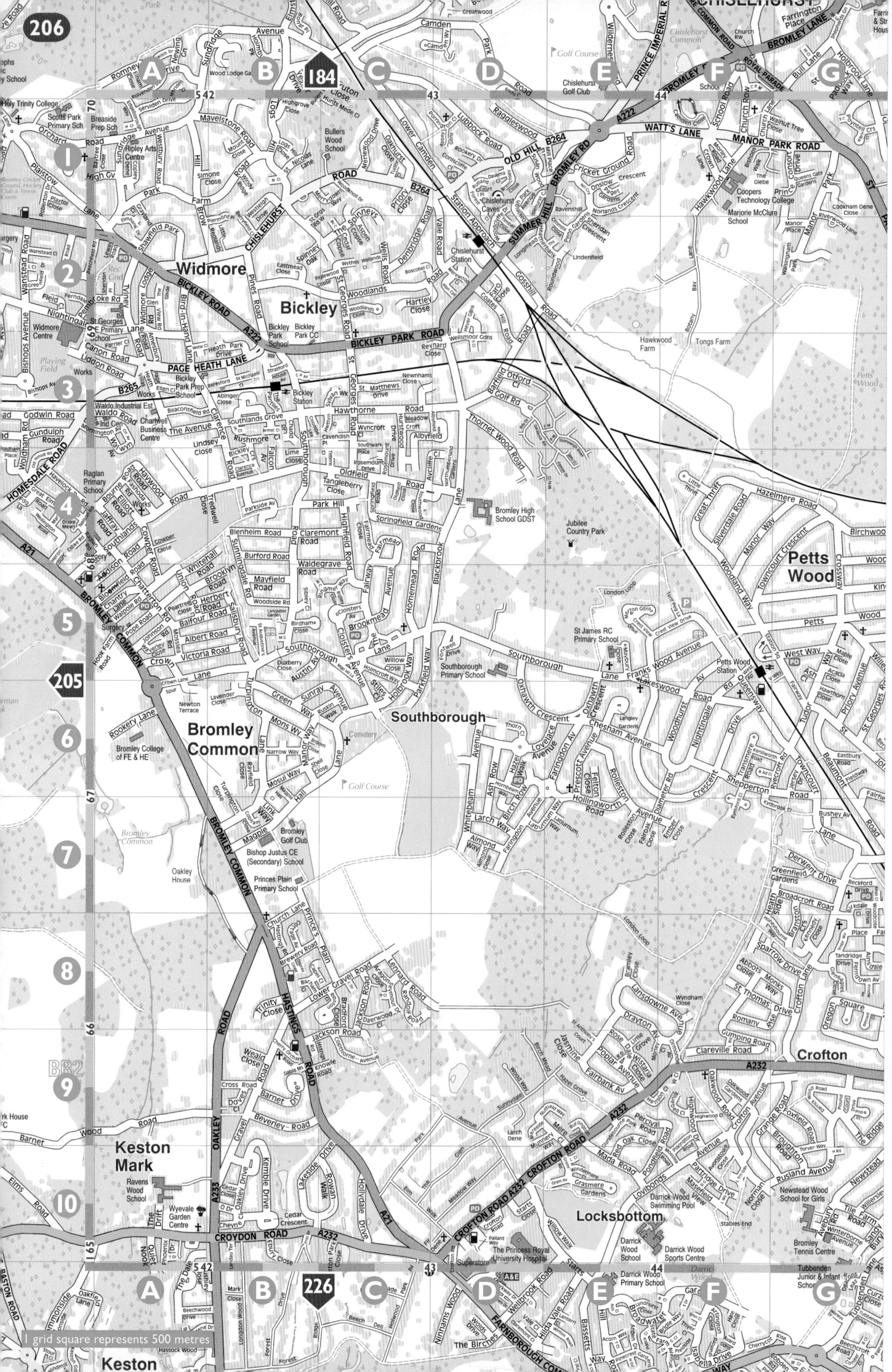

A
B
C
D
E
F
G
1
2
3
4
5
6
7
8
9
10
184
205
226
Widmore
Bickley
Bromley Common
Southborough
Petts Wood
Crofton
Keston Mark
Keston
Locksbottom
Chislehurst Common
Golf Course
Chislehurst Golf Club
PRINCE IMPERIAL RD
BROMLEY LANE
ROYAL PARADE
WATT'S LANE
MANOR PARK ROAD
OLD HILL
SUMMER HILL
BROMLEY RD
BICKLEY ROAD
BICKLEY PARK ROAD
CHISLEHURST ROAD
PAGE HEATH LANE
HOMESDALE ROAD
BROMLEY COMMON
HASTINGS ROAD
OAKLEY ROAD
CROYDON ROAD
CROFTON ROAD
FARNBOROUGH COMMON
Chislehurst Station
Chislehurst Caves
Bickley Station
Petts Wood Station
Jubilee Country Park
Bromley High School GDST
Coopers Technology College
Marjorie McClure School
Hawkwood Farm
Tongs Farm
St James RC Primary School
Southborough Primary School
Bromley College of FE & HE
Bromley Golf Club
Bishop Justus CE (Secondary) School
Princes Plain Primary School
Oakley House
Ravens Wood School
Wyevale Garden Centre
Darrick Wood Swimming Pool
Darrick Wood School
Darrick Wood Sports Centre
Darrick Wood Primary School
The Princess Royal University Hospital
Newstead Wood School for Girls
Bromley Tennis Centre
Tubbenden Junior & Infant School
Raglan Primary School
Widmore Centre
Bickley Park School
Bickley Park Prep School
Holy Trinity College
Scotts Park Primary Sch
Breaside Prep Sch
Ripley Arts Centre
Bullers Wood School
Waldo Industrial Est
Chartwell Business Centre
1 grid square represents 500 metres

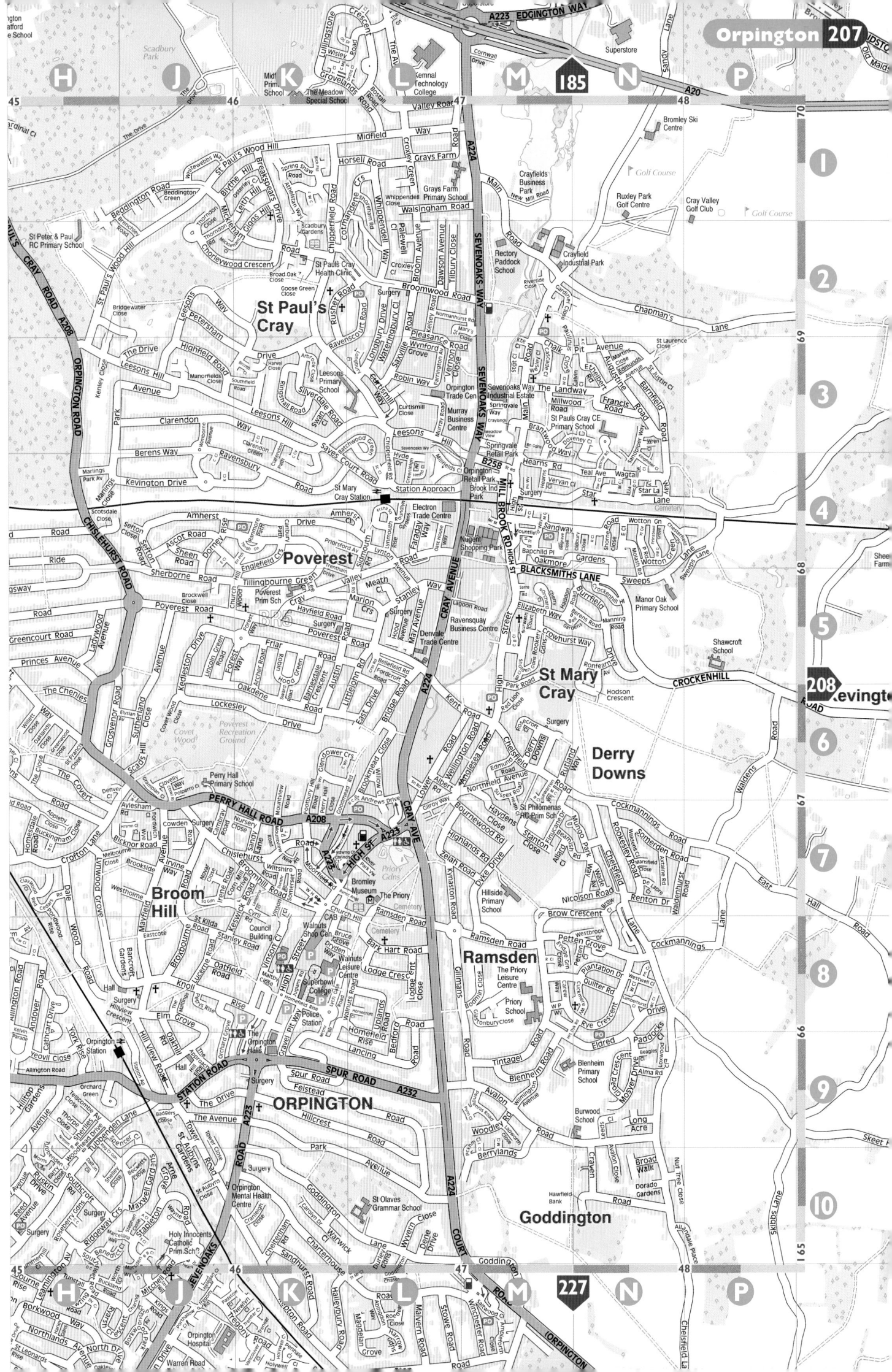
St Paul's Cray
Poverest
St Mary Cray
Derry Downs
Broom Hill
Ramsden
ORPINGTON
Goddington
SEVENOAKS WAY
CRAY AVENUE
ORPINGTON ROAD
CHISLEHURST ROAD
PERRY HALL ROAD
SPUR ROAD
STATION ROAD
HIGH ST
BLACKSMITHS LANE
CROCKENHILL ROAD
A223 EDGINGTON WAY
A20
A208
A224
A223
A232
B258
COURT ROAD
SEVENOAKS ROAD
Scadbury Park
Kemnal Technology College
The Meadow Special School
Bromley Ski Centre
Golf Course
Crayfields Business Park
Ruxley Park Golf Centre
Cray Valley Golf Club
Crayfield Industrial Park
Rectory Paddock School
St Peter & Paul RC Primary School
Grays Farm Primary School
St Pauls Cray Health Clinic
Leesons Primary School
Orpington Trade Cen
Murray Business Centre
Sevenoaks Way Industrial Estate
St Pauls Cray CE Primary School
Springvale Retail Park
Orpington Retail Park
Brook Ind Park
St Mary Cray Station
Electron Trade Centre
Nugent Shopping Park
Poverest Prim Sch
Manor Oak Primary School
Ravensquay Business Centre
Denvale Trade Centre
Shawcroft School
Poverest Recreation Ground
Covet Wood
Perry Hall Primary School
St Philomenas RC Prim Sch
Priory Gdns
Bromley Museum
The Priory
Hillside Primary School
Council Building
Walnuts Shop Cen
Walnuts Leisure Centre
Superbowl College
Police Station
The Orpington Halls
The Priory Leisure Centre
Priory School
Blenheim Primary School
Burwood School
Orpington Station
Orpington Mental Health Centre
St Olaves Grammar School
Holy Innocents Catholic Prim Sch
Orpington Hospital
Superstore
185
208
227

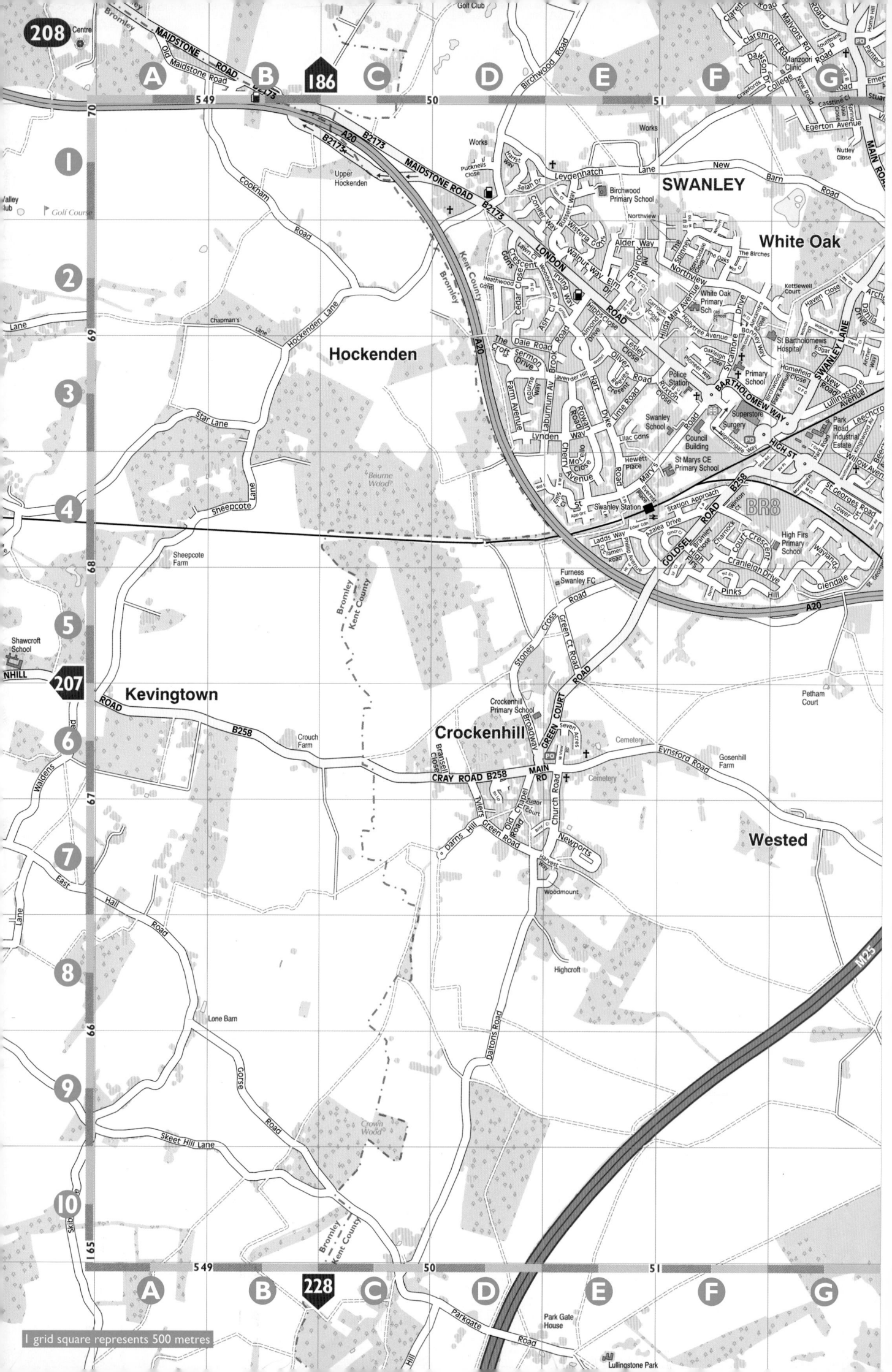

208
186
207
228
A
B
C
D
E
F
G
1
2
3
4
5
6
7
8
9
10
549
50
51
70
69
68
67
66
165
Golf Club
Centre
Bromley
MAIDSTONE ROAD
Old Maidstone Road
B2173
A20
MAIDSTONE ROAD
Upper Hockenden
Works
Pucknells Close
Harfst Way
Selah Dr
Leydenhatch Lane
New Barn Road
Birchwood Road
SWANLEY
White Oak
Birchwood Primary School
LONDON ROAD
Claremont Rd
Dawson Dr
Manzoori Clinic
College
New Road
Crawfords
Southbank
PO
Road
Malyons Rd
Cassine Cl
Spring Vale Close
Egerton Avenue
Nutley Close
MAIN ROAD
Conifer Way
Wisteria Gdns
Walnut Way
Elm Dr
Alder Way
Shurlock Av
Northview
The Spinney
Sprucedale Close
The Oaks
The Birches
Lawn Cl
Crescent Gdns
Heathwood Gdns
Cedar Close
Irving Way
Hibbs Close
Almond Drive
Lesley Close
Garrolds Close
Hilda May Avenue
White Oak Primary Sch
Hollytree Avenue
Bonney Way
Alexandra Close
Drive
Kettlewell Court
Haven Close
Dahlia Drive
St Bartholomews Hospital
Edgar Rd
SWANLEY LANE
The Croft
Dale Road
Sermon Drive
Ash Cl
Brook Road
Lavender Hill
Farm Avenue
Bourne Way
Laburnum Av
Hart Dyke
Oliver Road
Reeves Cresent
Lime Road
Ruxton Close
Police Station
Oakleigh Close
Pioneer Way
Sycamore
Primary School
Homefield Close
Birchwood Park Avenue
New Road
Lullingstone Avenue
BARTHOLOMEW WAY
Superstore
Surgery
PO
Nightingale Way
HIGH ST
Park Road Industrial Estate
Leechcroft
Willow Avenue
Rowan Road
Lynden Way
Cherry Avenue
Morello Close
Lilac Gdns
Swanley School
Council Building
Hewett Place
St Marys CE Primary School
Marys Road
Everest Place
Swanley Station
Station Approach
B258
BR8
St Georges Road
Lower Ct
Ladds Way
Azalea Drive
Phillip Avenue
Goldsel Road
Bramley Close
Charnock
Court Crescent
High Firs
High Firs Primary School
Waylands
Cranleigh Drive
Pinks Hill
Glendale
A20
Hockenden
Cookham Road
Chapman's Lane
Hockenden Lane
Kent County
Bromley
Star Lane
Bourne Wood
Sheepcote Lane
Sheepcote Farm
Furness Swanley FC
Cross Road
Green Ct Road
Stones Cross
GREEN COURT ROAD
Shawcroft School
NHILL
Kevingtown
ROAD
B258
Crouch Farm
Crockenhill Primary School
Crockenhill
Broadway
Seven Acres
Cemetery
Eynsford Road
Gosenhill Farm
Petham Court
Bransell Close
CRAY ROAD B258
MAIN RD
Church Road
Tylers Green Road
Old Chapel Road
Tudor Court
Darns Hill
Newports
Harvest Way
Woodmount
Wested
Waldens
East Hall Road
Lane
Highcroft
M25
Lone Barn
Daltons Road
Gorse Road
Crown Wood
Skeet Hill Lane
Skibbs Lane
Parkgate Road
Park Gate House
Lullingstone Park
Hill
Valley Club
Golf Course
Lane
1 grid square represents 500 metres

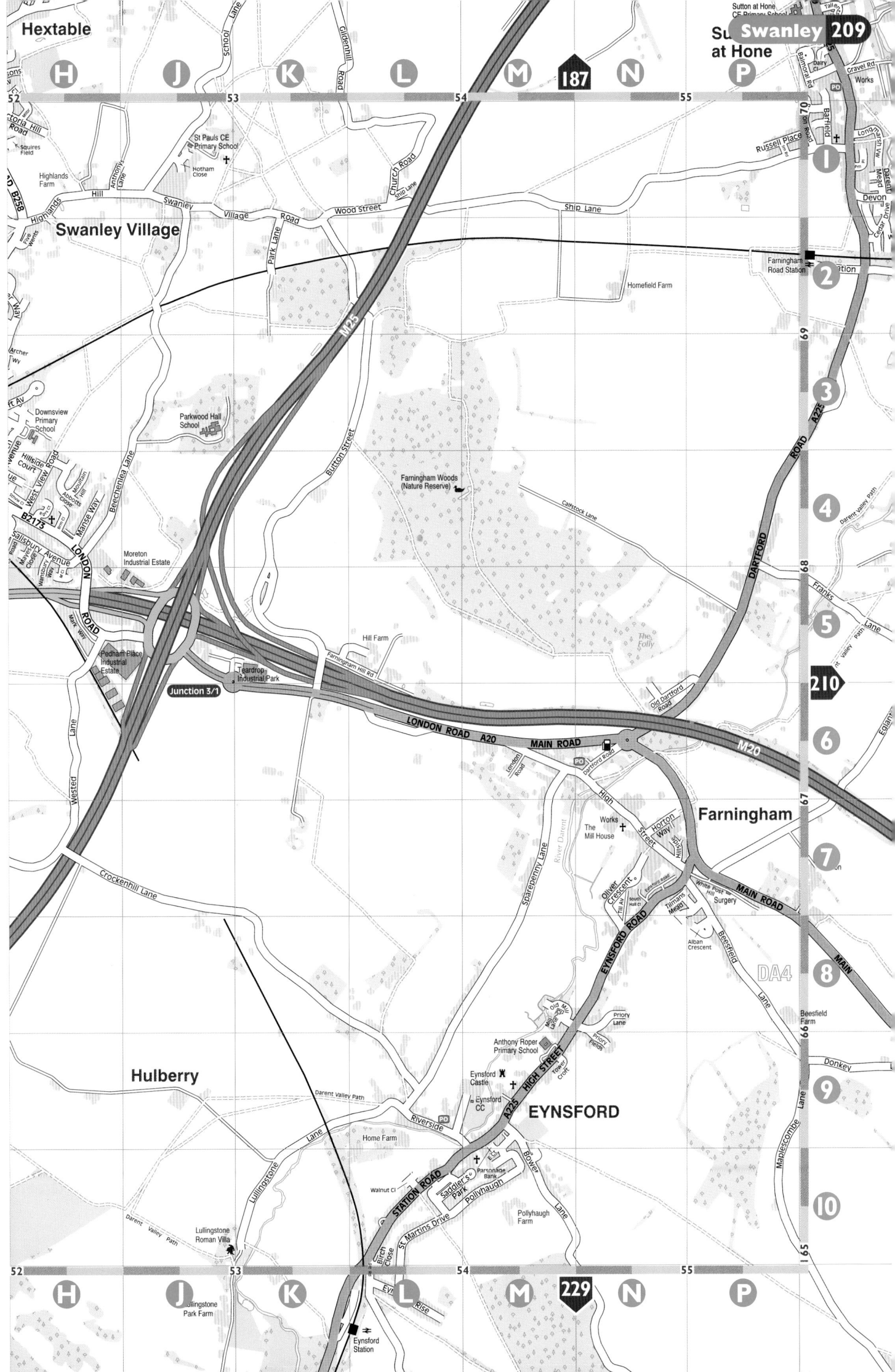

Swanley 209
Hextable
Sutton at Hone
Swanley Village
Highlands Farm
St Pauls CE Primary School
Hotham Close
Swanley Village Road
Wood Street
Church Road
Ship Lane
Park Lane
Russell Place
Farningham Road Station
Homefield Farm
M25
Parkwood Hall School
Downsview Primary School
Beechenlea Lane
Button Street
Farningham Woods (Nature Reserve)
Calfstock Lane
Dartford Road
A225
Moreton Industrial Estate
London Road
B2173
Salisbury Avenue
Hill Farm
Farningham Hill Rd
The Folly
Old Dartford Road
Franks Lane
Pedham Place Industrial Estate
Teardrop Industrial Park
Junction 3/1
London Road A20
Main Road
M20
Wested Lane
Farningham
High Street
The Mill House
Horton Way
Crockenhill Lane
Sparepenny Lane
River Darent
Oliver Crescent
Eynsford Road
White Post Hill
Surgery
Alban Crescent
Beesfield Lane
DA4
Beesfield Farm
Priory Lane
Priory Fields
Anthony Roper Primary School
Hulberry
Eynsford Castle
Eynsford CC
High Street
Tower Croft
EYNSFORD
Darent Valley Path
Donkey Lane
Maplescombe Lane
Riverside
Home Farm
Lullingstone Lane
Station Road
Walnut Cl
Saddler's Park
Pollyhaugh
Parsonage Bank
Bower Lane
Pollyhaugh Farm
St Martins Drive
Birch Close
Lullingstone Roman Villa
Lullingstone Park Farm
Eynsford Station
Eynsford Rise
187
210
229
H J K L M N P
52 53 54 55
65 66 67 68 69 70
1 2 3 4 5 6 7 8 9 10

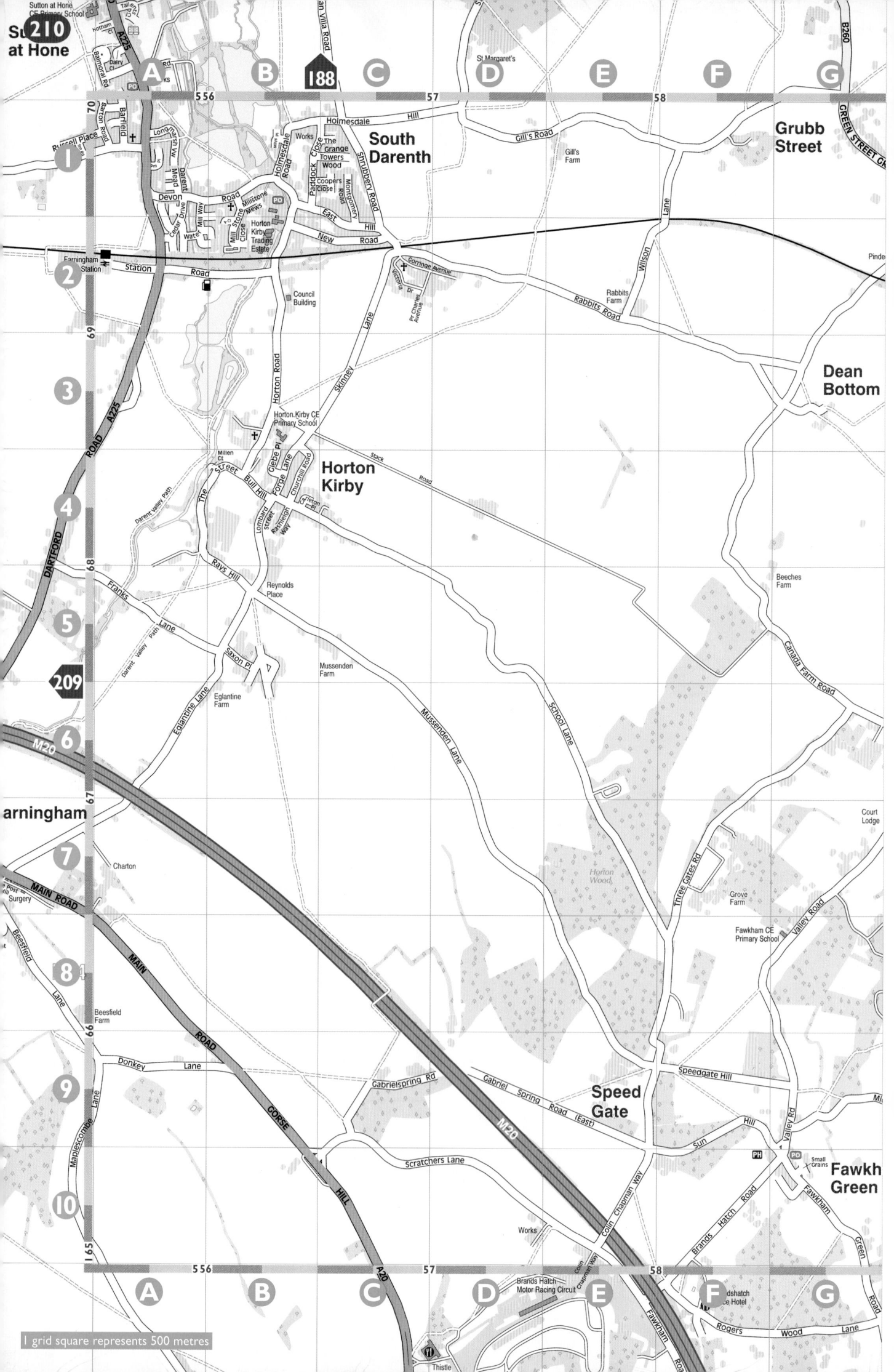
210
188
209
Sutton at Hone
South Darenth
Grubb Street
Horton Kirby
Dean Bottom
Speed Gate
Fawkham Green
Farningham
Holmesdale Hill
Gill's Road
Gill's Farm
Station Road
New Road
East Hill
Shrubbery Road
Horton Road
Skinney Lane
Rabbits Road
Rabbits Farm
Wilson Lane
Stack Road
Franks Lane
Rays Hill
Reynolds Place
Mussenden Farm
Mussenden Lane
Eglantine Lane
Eglantine Farm
School Lane
Beeches Farm
Canada Farm Road
Court Lodge
Three Gates Rd
Horton Wood
Grove Farm
Fawkham CE Primary School
Valley Road
Speedgate Hill
Gabriel Spring Road (East)
Gabrielspring Rd
Sun Hill
Scratchers Lane
Colin Chapman Way
Brands Hatch Road
Fawkham Green Road
Donkey Lane
Maplescombe Lane
Beesfield Lane
Beesfield Farm
Charton
MAIN ROAD
MAIN ROAD
GORSE HILL
DARTFORD ROAD
A225
A20
M20
Works
Brands Hatch Motor Racing Circuit
Rogers Wood Lane
Council Building
Horton Kirby CE Primary School
Darent Valley Path
1 grid square represents 500 metres

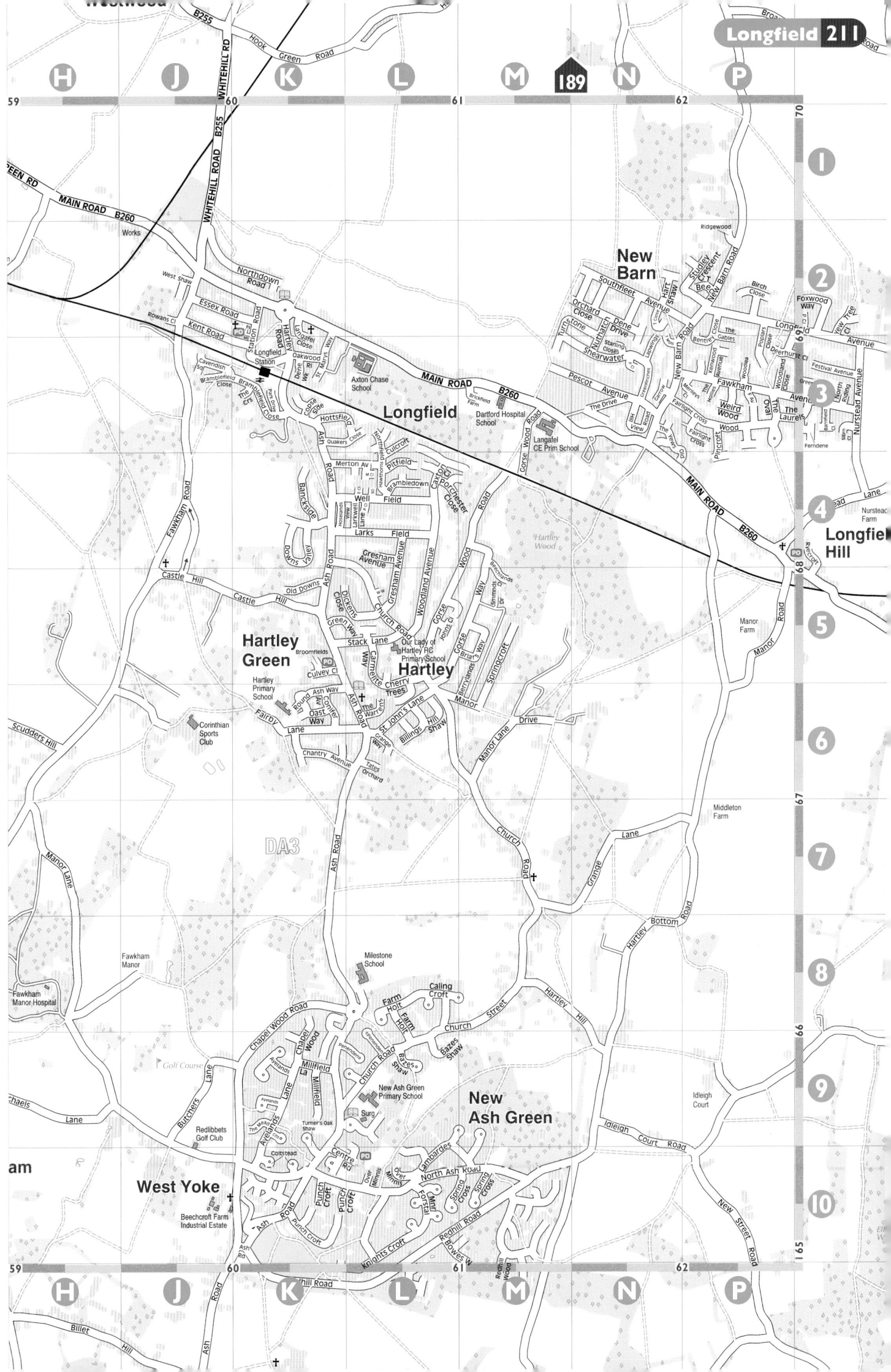
Longfield
New Barn
Longfield Hill
Hartley Green
Hartley
New Ash Green
West Yoke
DA3
189
Main Road
B260
Whitehill Road
B255
Hook Green Road
Northdown Road
Essex Road
Kent Road
Station Road
Hartley Road
Longfield Station
Axton Chase School
Dartford Hospital School
Langafel CE Prim School
Gorse Wood Road
Fawkham Road
Castle Hill
Ash Road
Church Road
Woodland Avenue
Gresham Avenue
Larks Field
Well Field
Stack Lane
Fairby Lane
Chantry Avenue
Manor Lane
Manor Drive
Manor Road
Manor Farm
Middleton Farm
Grange Lane
Hartley Bottom Road
Hartley Hill
Church Street
Idleigh Court Road
Idleigh Court
New Street Road
North Ash Road
Redhill Road
Knights Croft
Chapel Wood Road
Butchers Lane
Redlibbets Golf Club
Beechcroft Farm Industrial Estate
Milestone School
New Ash Green Primary School
Hartley Primary School
Our Lady of Hartley RC Primary School
Corinthian Sports Club
Fawkham Manor
Fawkham Manor Hospital
Scudders Hill
Hartley Wood
Southfleet Avenue
New Barn Road
Pescot Avenue
Nurstead Avenue
Nurstead Farm
Weird Wood
Golf Course
Billet Hill

212
192
230
A
B
C
D
E
F
G
1
2
3
4
5
6
7
8
9
10
493
94
95
GU20
GU18
Hatton Hill
WINDLESHAM
Valley End
LIGHTWATER
Donkey Town
West End
Lucas Green
Junction 3
M3
A30
LONDON RD
A322
A319
B386
B311
SUNNINGHILL RD
SCHOOL ROAD
CHERTSEY ROAD
KENNEL LANE
UPDOWN HILL
GUILDFORD ROAD
RED ROAD
Erl Wood Manor
Windlesham Village Infant School
Woodcote House School
Westwood Road
Windlesham Court
Snows Ride
Snows Paddock
Hatton Hill
Church Road
Birch Hall
Rectory Lane
Hatch End
Pound Lane
Thorndown Lane
Broadley Green
Hutton Cl
Orchard Hl
Ashleigh Farm
Old House Lane
Pine Grove
Oakwood Road
Heathpark Drive
Kings Lane
Valley End CE Infant School
Valley End Cricket Club
Windlesham Park
Twelve Oaks
Woodlands Lane
Windlesham Road
Valley End Road
Highams Lane
Shepherds Lane
Sparrow Row
Woodcock Lane
Westcroft Park
Rye Grove
Broadway Road
Industrial Estate
Windlebrook Farm
Hook Mill Lane
Oldhouse Lane
Windle Brook
Halebourne House
Halebourne Lane
Halebourne Farm
Hookstone Lane
Brook Place
BAGS
Works
South Farm La
Farm La
The Avenue
Lightwater Village School
Guildford Road
Christie Cl
Coniston Ct
Grasmere Road
Macdonald Road
Ridgeway Cl
Junction Road
Ambleside Road
All Saints Rd
Police Station
Blackstroud Lane
Burnt Pollard La
East
Windlesham Road
Golf Course
Windlemere Golf Club
Lightwater Meadow
Keswick Dr
Heronscourt
Red Road
Broom Fld
Coldharbour La
Streets Heath
Fairfield Lane
Malthouse Farm
Holy Trinity CE Primary School
Gordons School
Church Road
New England
Birch Lane
Tanglewood Ride
Broad Street
Cuckoo La
Brentmoor Road
Hook Lane
Revesby Cl
Rounce Lane
Birch Platt
Fenns Lane
Commonfields
Beldam Bridge Road
The Oaks
Pennypot La
Oldhouse Lane
Westend Common
Ford Rd
Lucas Green Road
Cedar Grove
Works
1 grid square represents 500 metres

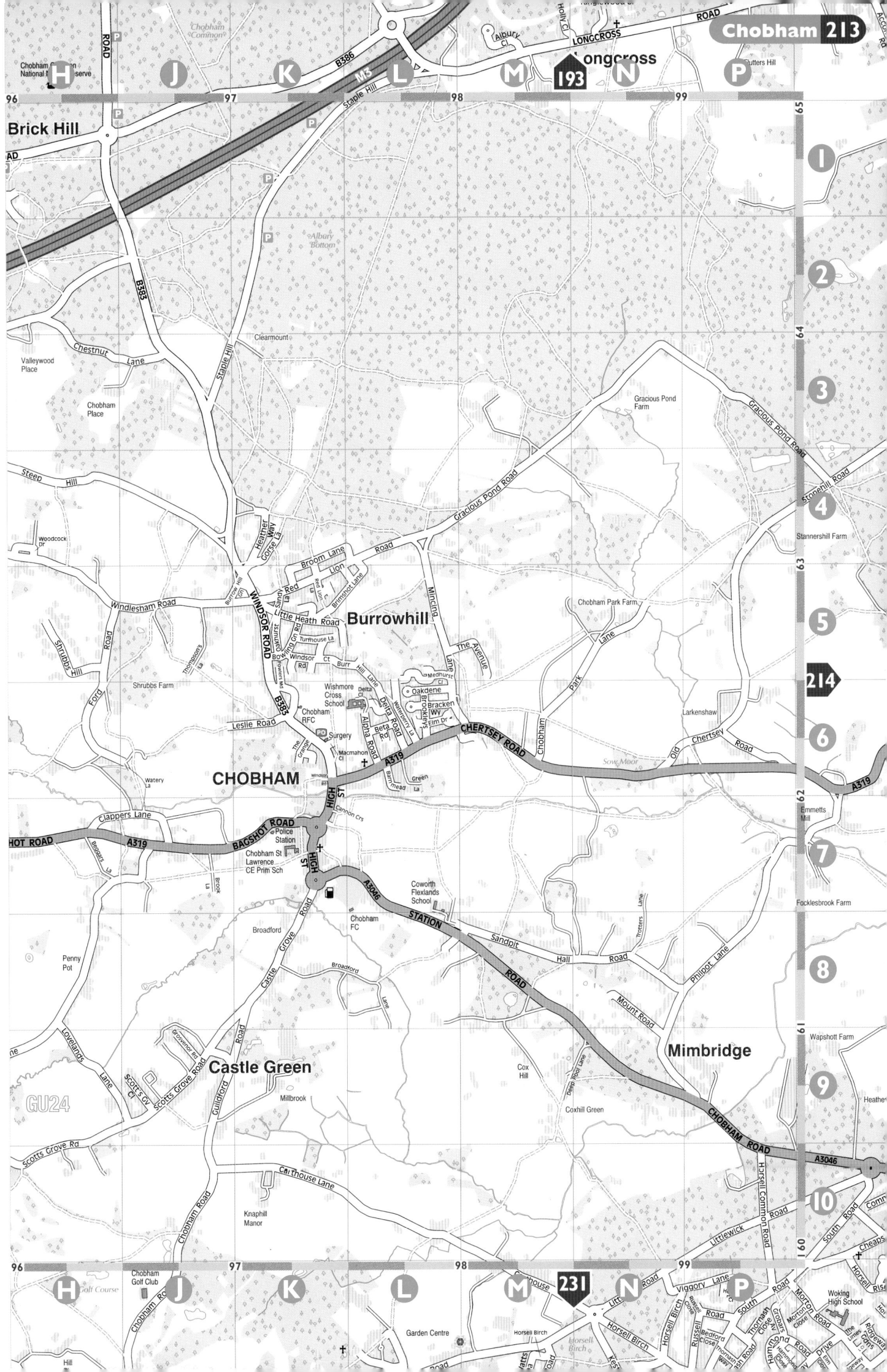
Longcross
Brick Hill
Burrowhill
CHOBHAM
Castle Green
Mimbridge
Chobham Common
Albury Bottom
Clearmount
Valleywood Place
Chobham Place
Gracious Pond Farm
Stannershill Farm
Chobham Park Farm
Larkenshaw
Shrubbs Farm
Wishmore Cross School
Chobham RFC
Surgery
Police Station
Chobham St Lawrence CE Prim Sch
Coworth Flexlands School
Chobham FC
Broadford
Penny Pot
Millbrook
Cox Hill
Coxhill Green
Knaphill Manor
Emmetts Mill
Focklesbrook Farm
Wapshott Farm
Sow Moor
Chobham Golf Club
Golf Course
Garden Centre
Horsell Birch
Woking High School
Flutters Hill
Windsor Road
Bagshot Road
Chertsey Road
Station Road
Chobham Road
Gracious Pond Road
Windlesham Road
Steep Hill
Chestnut Lane
Staple Hill
Sandpit Hall Road
Guildford Road
Castle Grove Road
Scotts Grove Road
Carthouse Lane
Philpot Lane
Mount Road
Littlewick Road
Horsell Common Road
Stonehill Road
Mincing Lane
Park Lane
Clappers Lane
Leslie Road
Broom Lane
Little Heath Road
High St
A319
A3046
B383
B386
M3
GU24
193
214
231
96
97
98
99
65
64
63
62
61
60
H
J
K
L
M
N
P
1
2
3
4
5
6
7
8
9
10

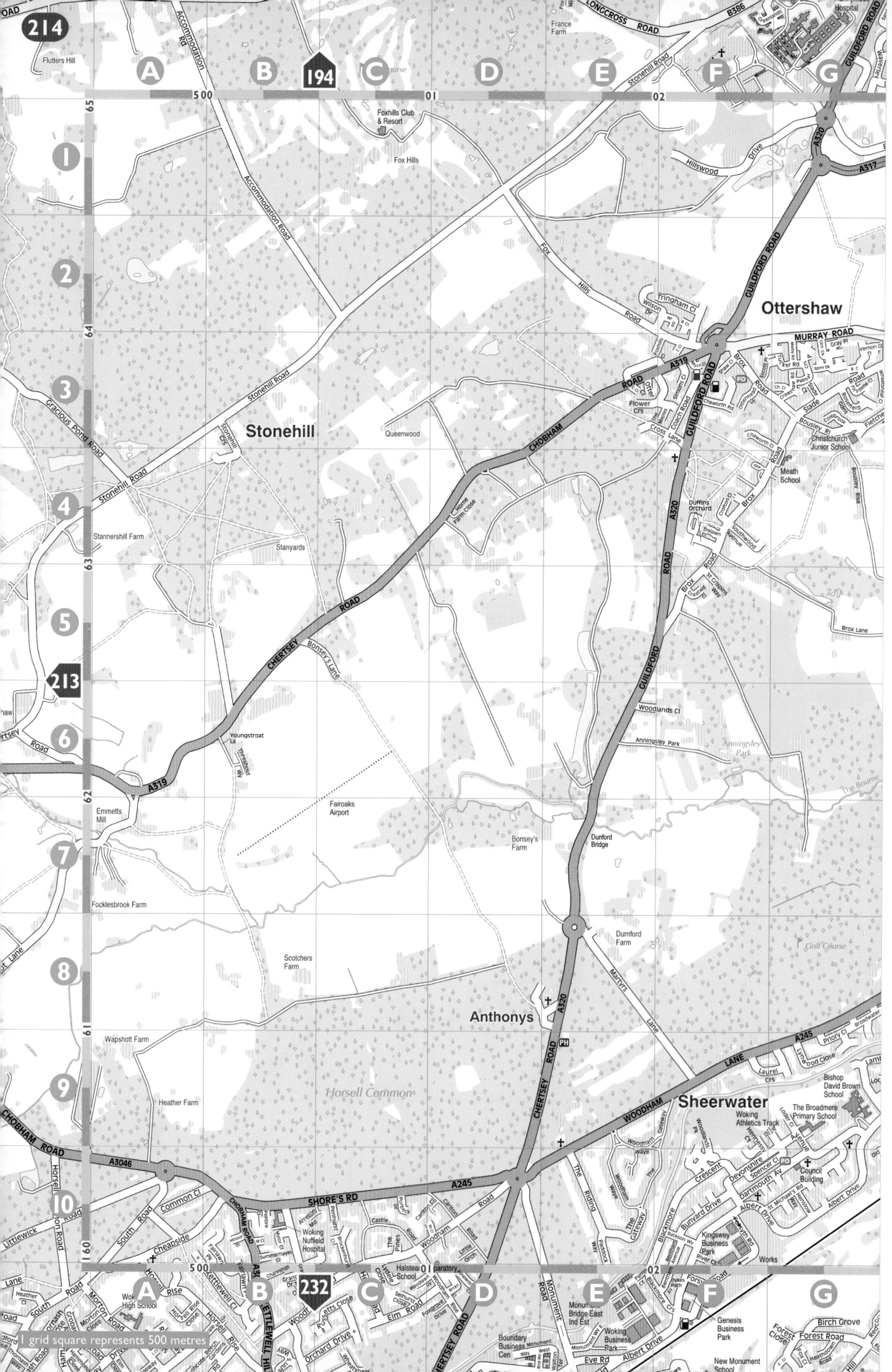
Ottershaw
Stonehill
Anthonys
Sheerwater
Fairoaks Airport
Horsell Common
Foxhills Club & Resort
Fox Hills
France Farm
Flutters Hill
Queenwood
Stannershill Farm
Stanyards
Emmetts Mill
Focklesbrook Farm
Scotchers Farm
Wapshott Farm
Heather Farm
Bonsey's Farm
Dunford Bridge
Durnford Farm
Woodlands Cl
Anningsley Park
Brox Lane
Christchurch Junior School
Meath School
Duffins Orchard
Woking Athletics Track
Bishop David Brown School
The Broadmere Primary School
Council Building
Woking Nuffield Hospital
Woking High School
Monument Bridge East Ind Est
Woking Business Park
Boundary Business Cen
Genesis Business Park
New Monument School
Works
Hospital
CHERTSEY ROAD
CHOBHAM ROAD
GUILDFORD ROAD
MURRAY ROAD
LONGCROSS ROAD
WOODHAM LANE
SHORE'S RD
Stonehill Road
Accommodation Road
Gracious Pond Road
Fox Hills Road
Hillswood Drive
Bonsey's Lane
Martyrs Lane
Youngstroat La
A319
A320
A317
A245
A3046
B386
500
01
02
65
64
63
62
61
160
1 grid square represents 500 metres

194
213
232

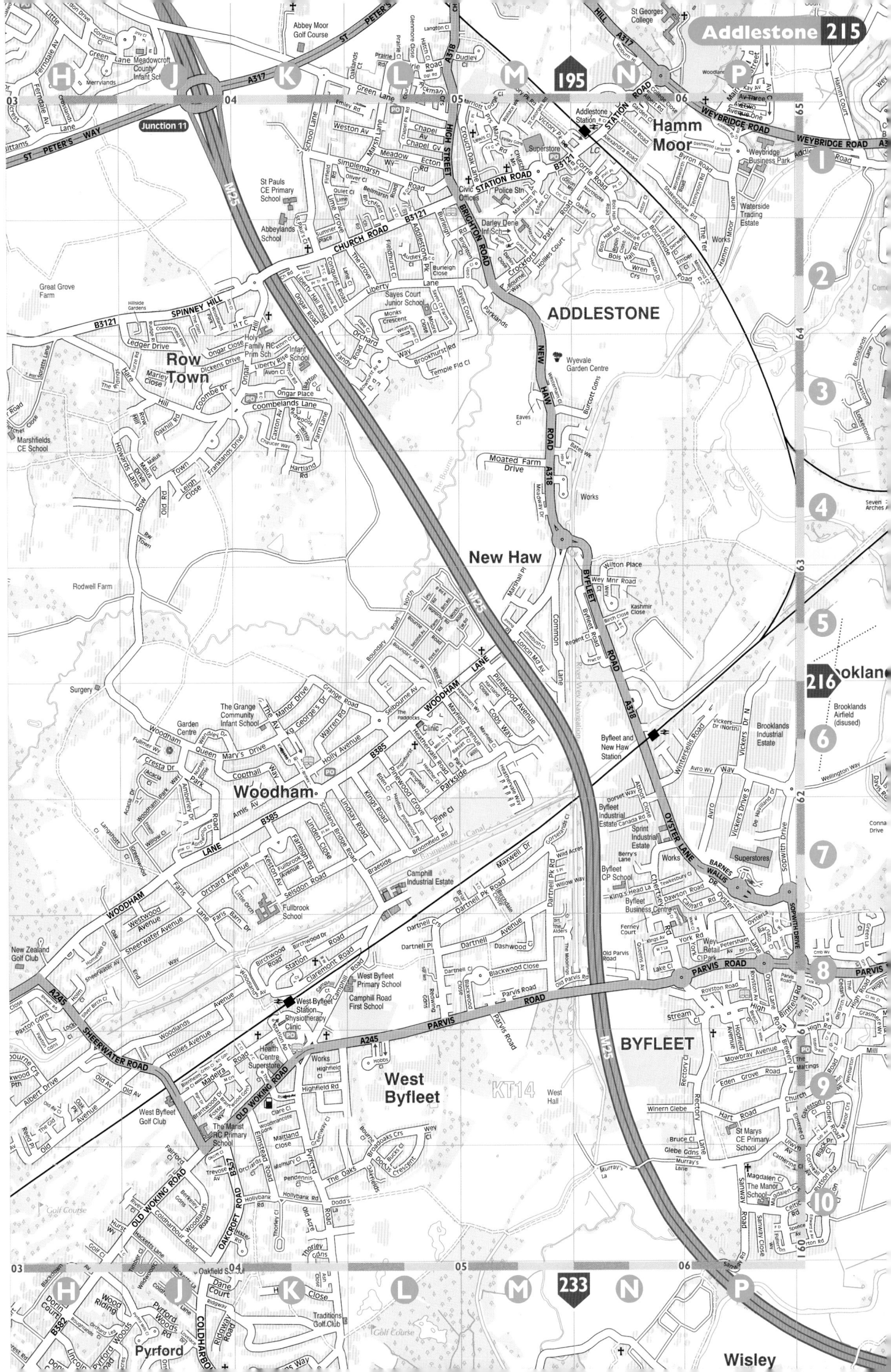

Addlestone 215
195
216
233
ADDLESTONE
Hamm Moor
Row Town
New Haw
Woodham
BYFLEET
West Byfleet
Pyrford
Wisley
M25
Junction 11
ST PETER'S WAY
A317
CHURCH ROAD
B3121
SPINNEY HILL
HIGH STREET
BRIGHTON ROAD
STATION ROAD
WEYBRIDGE ROAD
NEW HAW ROAD
A318
BYFLEET ROAD
OYSTER LANE
BARNES WALLIS DR
SOPWITH DRIVE
PARVIS ROAD
A245
WOODHAM LANE
B385
SHEERWATER ROAD
OLD WOKING ROAD
OAKCROFT ROAD
B337
COLDHARBOUR
Addlestone Station
West Byfleet Station
Byfleet and New Haw Station
Abbey Moor Golf Course
St Georges College
St Pauls CE Primary School
Abbeylands School
Sayes Court Junior School
Holy Family RC Prim Sch
Infant School
Marshfields CE School
Great Grove Farm
Rodwell Farm
Wyevale Garden Centre
Waterside Trading Estate
Weybridge Business Park
Brooklands Industrial Estate
Brooklands Airfield (disused)
The Grange Community Infant School
Fullbrook School
Camphill Industrial Estate
West Byfleet Primary School
Camphill Road First School
West Byfleet Golf Club
The Marist RC Primary School
New Zealand Golf Club
Byfleet CP School
Byfleet Business Centre
Sprint Industrial Estate
Byfleet Industrial Estate
St Marys CE Primary School
The Manor School
Traditions Golf Club
KT14
Basingstoke Canal
River Wey Navigation

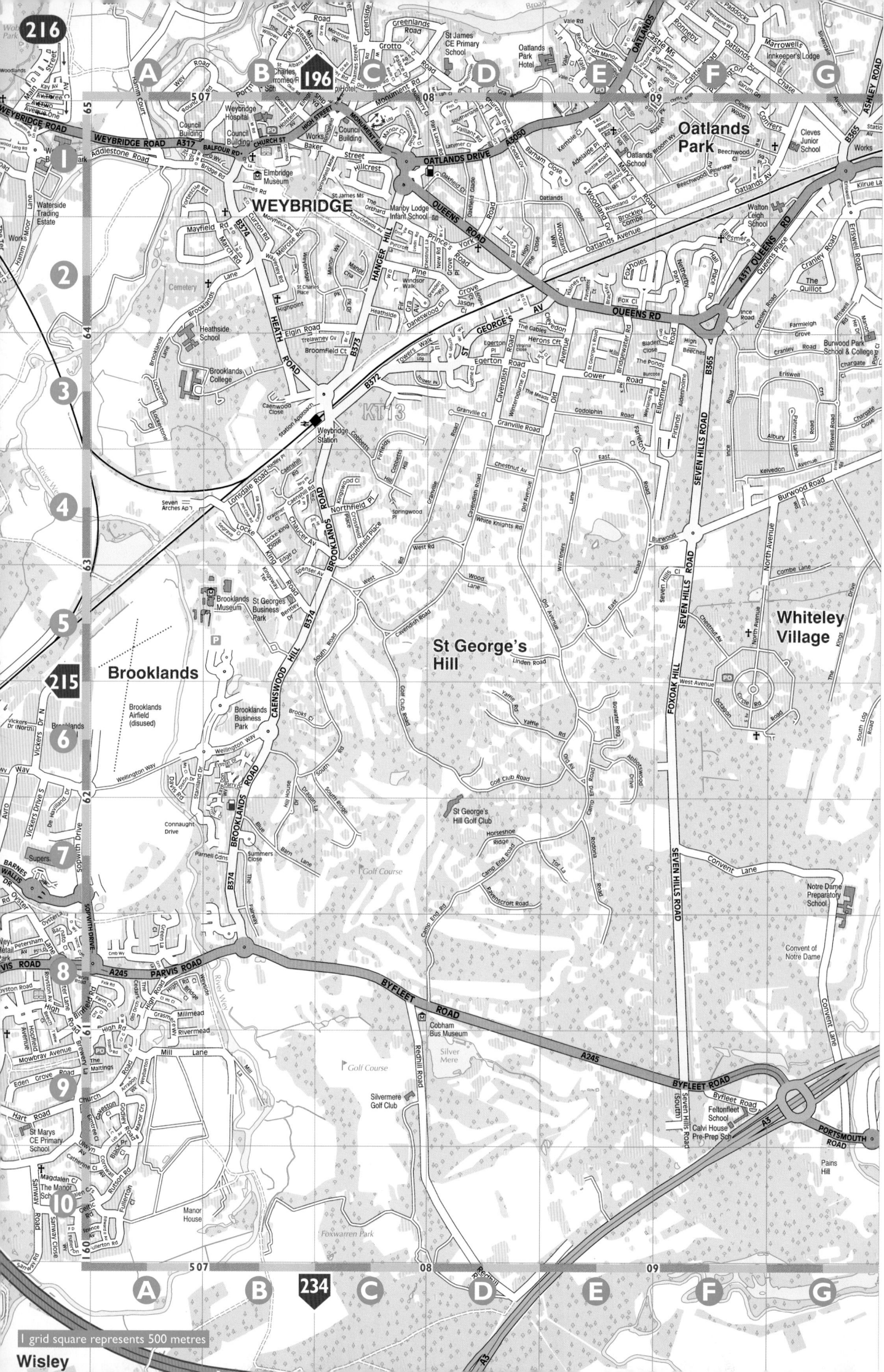

216
196
215
234
WEYBRIDGE
Oatlands Park
St George's Hill
Whiteley Village
Brooklands
Wisley
WEYBRIDGE ROAD
OATLANDS DRIVE
QUEENS ROAD
QUEENS RD
ST GEORGE'S AV
SEVEN HILLS ROAD
FOXOAK HILL
BROOKLANDS ROAD
CAENSWOOD HILL
BYFLEET ROAD
PARVIS ROAD
PORTSMOUTH ROAD
HEATH ROAD
HANGER HILL
ASHLEY ROAD
Weybridge Station
Brooklands Museum
Brooklands College
Heathside School
St George's Hill Golf Club
Cobham Bus Museum
Silvermere Golf Club
Notre Dame Preparatory School
Convent of Notre Dame
Burwood Park School & College
Cleves Junior School
Oatlands Park Hotel
Elmbridge Museum
Weybridge Hospital
Brooklands Airfield (disused)
Brooklands Business Park
St Georges Business Park
Feltonfleet School
Calvi House Pre-Prep Sch
St Marys CE Primary School
Manor House
Foxwarren Park
Golf Course
Silver Mere
Pains Hill
KT13
A3
A245
A317
A3050
B365
B372
B373
B374
1 grid square represents 500 metres

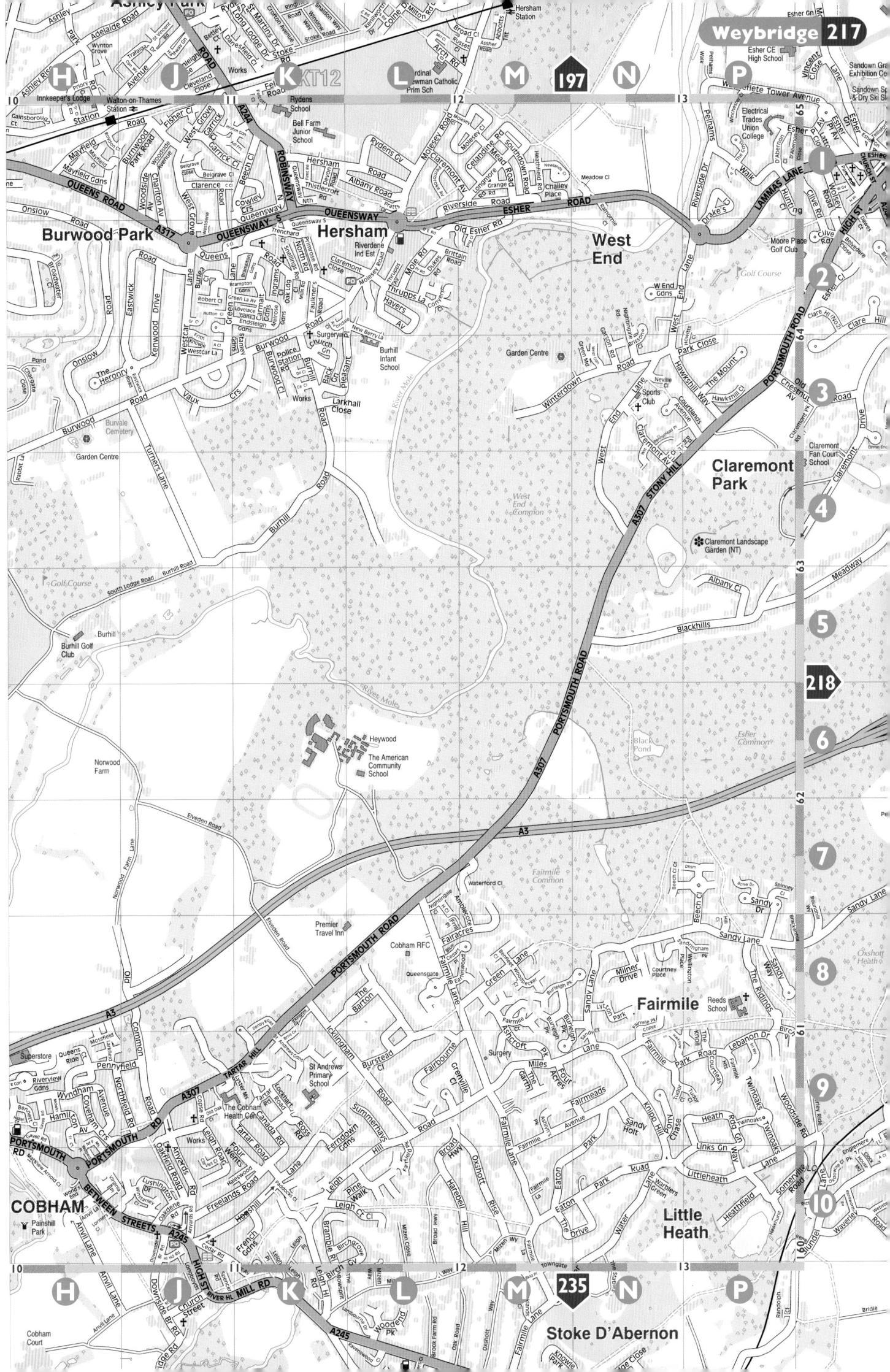

Burwood Park
Hersham
West End
Claremont Park
Fairmile
Little Heath
COBHAM
Stoke D'Abernon
Walton-on-Thames Station
Hersham Station
Innkeeper's Lodge
Rydens School
Bell Farm Junior School
Cardinal Newman Catholic Prim Sch
Esher CE High School
Electrical Trades Union College
Riverdene Ind Est
Burhill Infant School
Police Station
Surgery
Works
Burvale Cemetery
Garden Centre
Golf Course
Burhill Golf Club
Burhill
Norwood Farm
Heywood
The American Community School
Premier Travel Inn
Cobham RFC
Queensgate
St Andrews Primary School
The Cobham Health Centre
Superstore
Painshill Park
Cobham Court
Sports Club
Moore Place Golf Club
Claremont Fan Court School
Claremont Landscape Garden (NT)
West End Common
Black Pond
Esher Common
Fairmile Common
Reeds School
Oxshott Heath
River Mole
QUEENS ROAD
QUEENSWAY
ESHER ROAD
PORTSMOUTH ROAD
STONY HILL
LAMMAS LANE
HIGH ST
TARTAR HILL
BETWEEN STREETS
MILL RD
A3
A307
A244
A245
A317
KT12
197
218
235

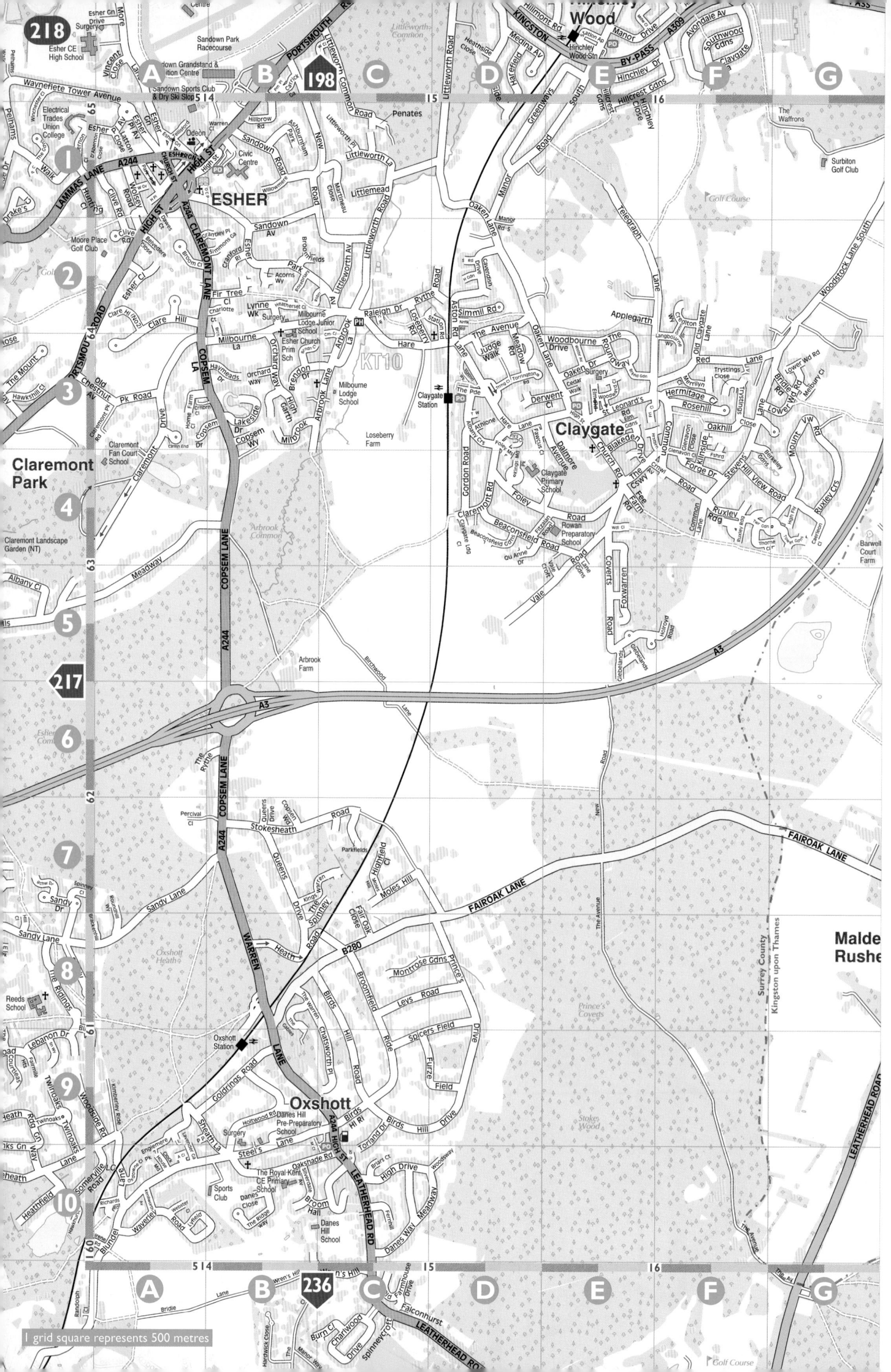

218
198
217
236
A
B
C
D
E
F
G
1
2
3
4
5
6
7
8
9
10
ESHER
Claygate
Oxshott
Claremont Park
Wood
KT10
Esher CE High School
Sandown Park Racecourse
Sandown Sports Club & Dry Ski Slope
Electrical Trades Union College
Moore Place Golf Club
Claremont Fan Court School
Claremont Landscape Garden (NT)
Esher Church Prim Sch
Milbourne Lodge Junior School
Milbourne Lodge School
Loseberry Farm
Claygate Station
Claygate Primary School
Rowan Preparatory School
Arbrook Common
Arbrook Farm
Littleworth Common
Penates
The Waffrons
Surbiton Golf Club
Golf Course
Barwell Court Farm
Hinchley Wood Stn
Oxshott Heath
Oxshott Station
Reeds School
Danes Hill Pre-Preparatory School
The Royal Kent CE Primary School
Danes Hill School
Sports Club
Prince's Coverts
Stoke Wood
Surrey County
Kingston upon Thames
Malde
Rushe
PORTSMOUTH ROAD
A244
A3
A309
B280
KINGSTON BY-PASS
LAMMAS LANE
HIGH ST
CLAREMONT LANE
COPSEM LANE
WARREN LANE
FAIROAK LANE
LEATHERHEAD RD
LEATHERHEAD ROAD
Wayneflete Tower Avenue
Littleworth Road
Littleworth Common Road
Manor Road South
Hinchley Dr
Hillcrest Gdns
Telegraph Lane
Woodstock Lane South
Red Lane
Oaken Lane
Hare Lane
Claremont Rd
Foley Road
Coverts Road
Foxwarren
Stokesheath Road
Sandy Lane
Birds Hill Road
Broomfield Ride
Spicers Field
Furze Field
Steel's Lane
Goldrings Road
Meadway
Milbourne La
Clare Hill
Raleigh Dr
Rythe Road
Hermitage Cl
Rosehill
Oakhill
Ruxley Rdg
Ruxley Crs
Hill View Road
Mount Vw Rd
Gordon Road
Beaconsfield Road
Applegarth
Woodbourne Drive
Derwent Cl
Dalmore Avenue
Church Rd
Common Road
Birchwood Lane
New Road
The Avenue
Queens Drive
Copsem Way
Moles Hill
Montrose Gdns
Leys Road
Princes Drive
1 grid square represents 500 metres

Hook
Chessington
Barwell
The Wells
EPSOM
West
Chessington World of Adventures
Horton Country Park
Epsom Common
Leatherhead Road
Christ Church Road
Rushett Lane
Hook Road
Chessington Road
Ruxley Lane
West Hill
199
220
237

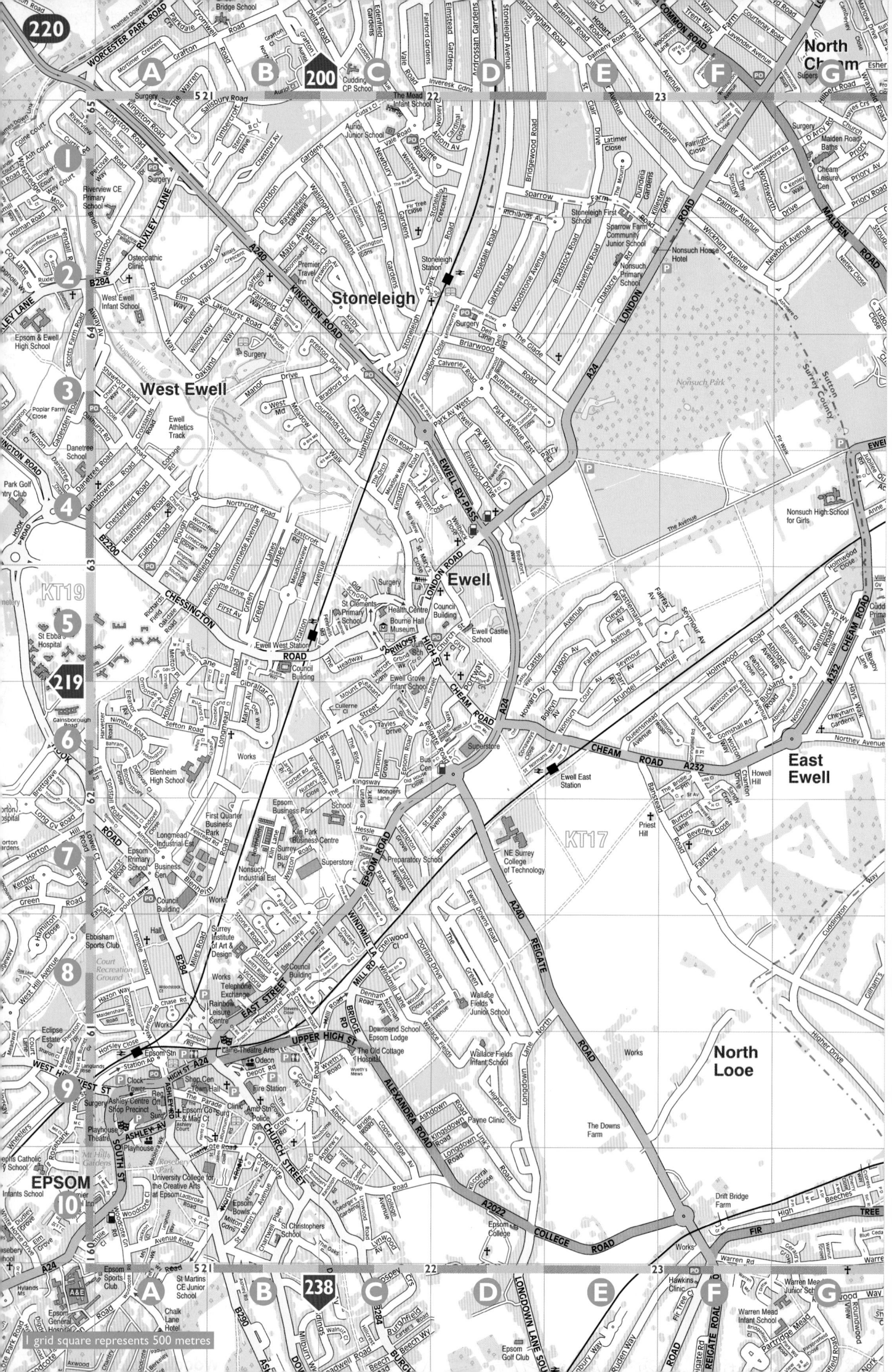

220
200
219
238
A
B
C
D
E
F
G
1
2
3
4
5
6
7
8
9
10
21
22
23
65
64
63
62
61
60
North Cheam
Stoneleigh
West Ewell
Ewell
East Ewell
North Looe
EPSOM
KT19
KT17
Nonsuch Park
WORCESTER PARK ROAD
KINGSTON ROAD
A240
RUXLEY LANE
B284
CHESSINGTON ROAD
B2200
EWELL BY-PASS
A24
LONDON ROAD
CHEAM ROAD
A232
REIGATE ROAD
EPSOM ROAD
EAST STREET
UPPER HIGH ST
ALEXANDRA ROAD
COLLEGE ROAD
A2022
CHURCH STREET
SOUTH ST
WEST ST
HIGH ST
ASHLEY RD
MALDEN ROAD
COMMON ROAD
Stoneleigh Station
Ewell West Station
Ewell East Station
Epsom Stn
Bridge School
Cuddington CP School
The Mead Infant School
Auriol Junior School
Riverview CE Primary School
West Ewell Infant School
Epsom & Ewell High School
Danetree School
Ewell Athletics Track
Stoneleigh First School
Sparrow Farm Community Junior School
Nonsuch Primary School
Nonsuch House Hotel
Nonsuch High School for Girls
Ewell Castle School
St Clements Primary School
Bourne Hall Museum
Health Centre
Council Building
Ewell Grove Infant School
Superstore
Blenheim High School
Epsom Primary School
NE Surrey College of Technology
Wallace Fields Junior School
Wallace Fields Infant School
Downsend School Epsom Lodge
The Old Cottage Hospital
Laine Theatre Arts
Odeon
Rainbow Leisure Centre
Ebbisham Sports Club
Surrey Institute of Art & Design
Ashley Centre Shop Precinct
Playhouse Theatre
Fire Station
Epsom College
St Christophers School
Epsom Sports Club
St Martins CE Junior School
Epsom General Hospital
Hawkins Clinic
Warren Mead Infant School
Epsom Golf Club
The Downs Farm
Drift Bridge Farm
Priest Hill
Howell Hill
St Ebba's Hospital
Cheam Leisure Cen
Malden Road Baths
Payne Clinic
1 grid square represents 500 metres

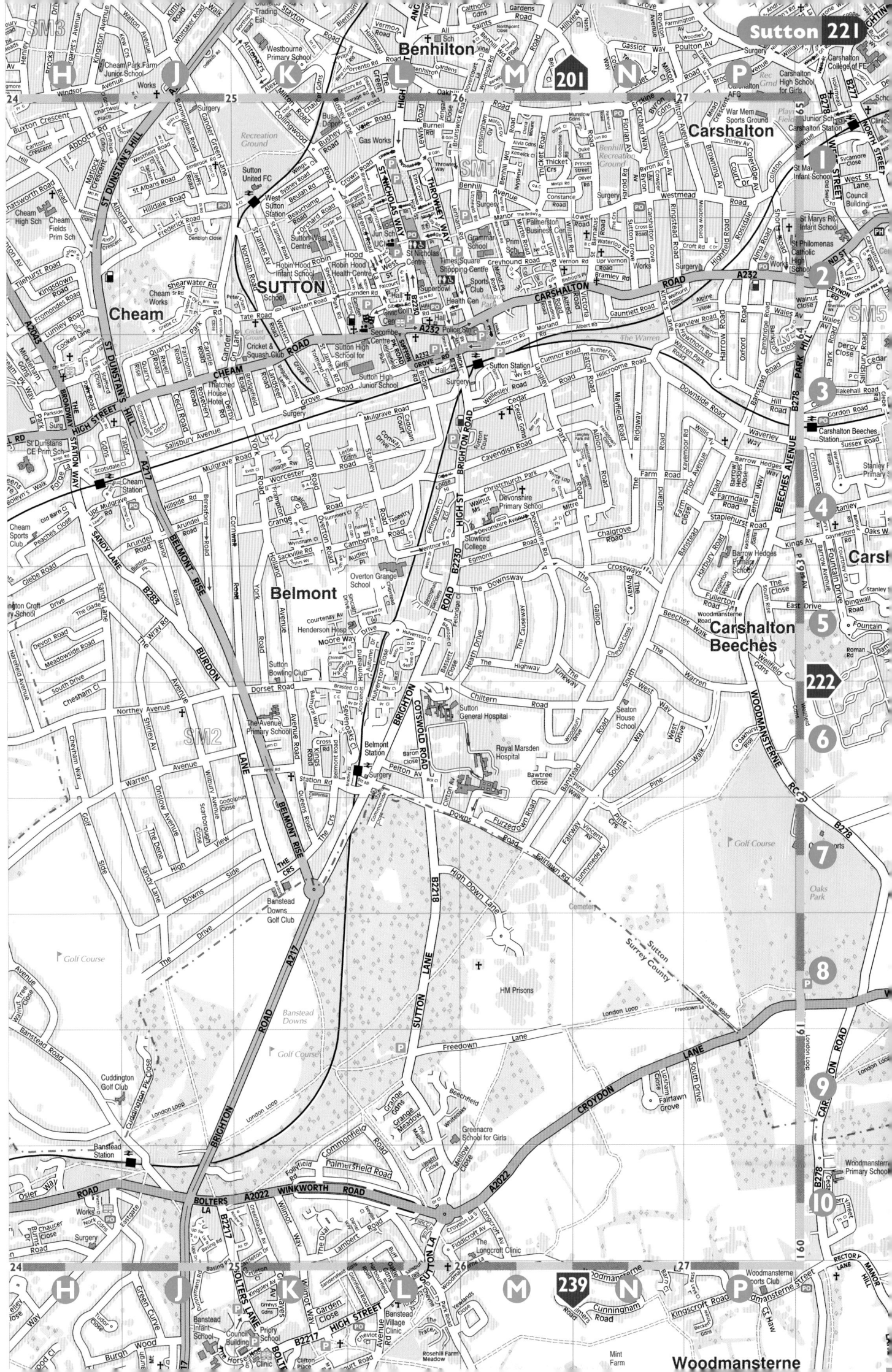

Benhilton
Carshalton
SUTTON
Cheam
Belmont
Carshalton Beeches
Woodmansterne
SM1
SM2
SM3
SM5
201
222
239
H
J
K
L
M
N
P
1
2
3
4
5
6
7
8
9
10
24
25
26
27
64
65
61
60
ST DUNSTAN'S HILL
CHEAM ROAD
CARSHALTON ROAD
BRIGHTON ROAD
BELMONT RISE
BURDON LANE
SUTTON LANE
CROYDON LANE
WINKWORTH ROAD
BOLTERS LA
HIGH STREET
BEECHES AVENUE
WOODMANSTERNE RD
PARK HILL
COTSWOLD ROAD
A232
A217
A2043
A2022
B2230
B2218
B2217
B283
B278
B277
West Sutton Station
Sutton Station
Cheam Station
Belmont Station
Carshalton Beeches Station
Banstead Station
Sutton United FC
Sutton General Hospital
Royal Marsden Hospital
HM Prisons
Banstead Downs Golf Club
Cuddington Golf Club
Banstead Downs
Golf Course
Oaks Park
Sutton High School for Girls
Sutton High Junior School
Overton Grange School
Stowford College
Devonshire Primary School
Seaton House School
Greenacre School for Girls
The Avenue Primary School
Barrow Hedges Primary School
St Philomenas Catholic High School
Cheam High Sch
Cheam Fields Prim Sch
St Dunstans CE Prim Sch
Westbourne Primary School
Cheam Park Farm Junior School
Carshalton High School for Girls
Carshalton College of FE
Woodmansterne Primary School
Banstead Infant School
Priory School
Banstead Village Clinic
The Longcroft Clinic
Times Square Shopping Centre
St Nicholas Centre
Secombe Centre
Civic Centre
Cricket & Squash Club
Thatched House Hotel
Cheam Sports Club
Sutton Bowling Club
Henderson Hosp
Recreation Ground
Gas Works
Bus Depot
Sutton Surrey County
London Loop
Rosehill Farm Meadow
Mint Farm
Woodmansterne Sports Club

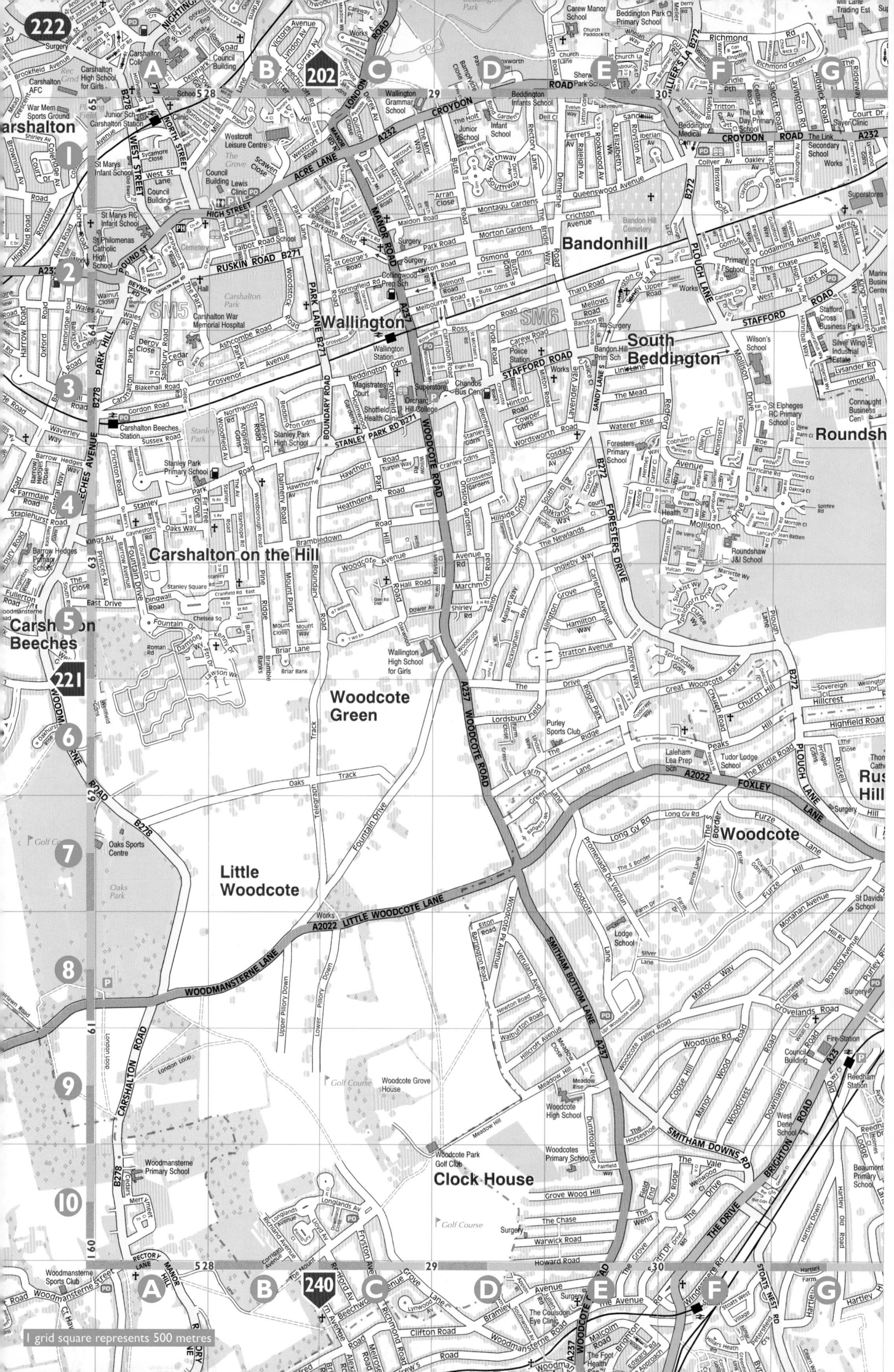
222
202
221
240
Carshalton
Carshalton Beeches
Carshalton on the Hill
Wallington
Bandonhill
South Beddington
Roundshaw
Woodcote Green
Little Woodcote
Woodcote
Clock House
SM5
SM6
A
B
C
D
E
F
G
1
2
3
4
5
6
7
8
9
10
528
29
30
65
64
63
62
61
60
CROYDON ROAD
A232
ACRE LANE
HIGH STREET
RUSKIN ROAD B271
POUND ST
NORTH STREET
WEST STREET
MANOR ROAD
A237
WOODCOTE ROAD
PARK LANE B271
BOUNDARY ROAD
STANLEY PARK RD B271
STAFFORD ROAD
PLOUGH LANE
B272
FORESTERS DRIVE
SANDY LANE S
BEECHES AVENUE
B278
PARK HILL
WOODMANSTERNE ROAD
CARSHALTON ROAD
WOODMANSTERNE LANE
A2022 LITTLE WOODCOTE LANE
A2022 FOXLEY LANE
SMITHAM BOTTOM LANE
SMITHAM DOWNS RD
BRIGHTON ROAD
A23
THE DRIVE
STOATS NEST RD
Carshalton Station
Carshalton Beeches Station
Wallington Station
Reedham Station
Wallington Grammar School
Westcroft Leisure Centre
Carshalton War Memorial Hospital
Stanley Park High School
Stanley Park Primary School
Wallington High School for Girls
Purley Sports Club
Oaks Sports Centre
Oaks Park
Woodcote Grove House
Woodcote Park Golf Club
Woodcote High School
Woodmansterne Primary School
Lodge School
Golf Course
1 grid square represents 500 metres

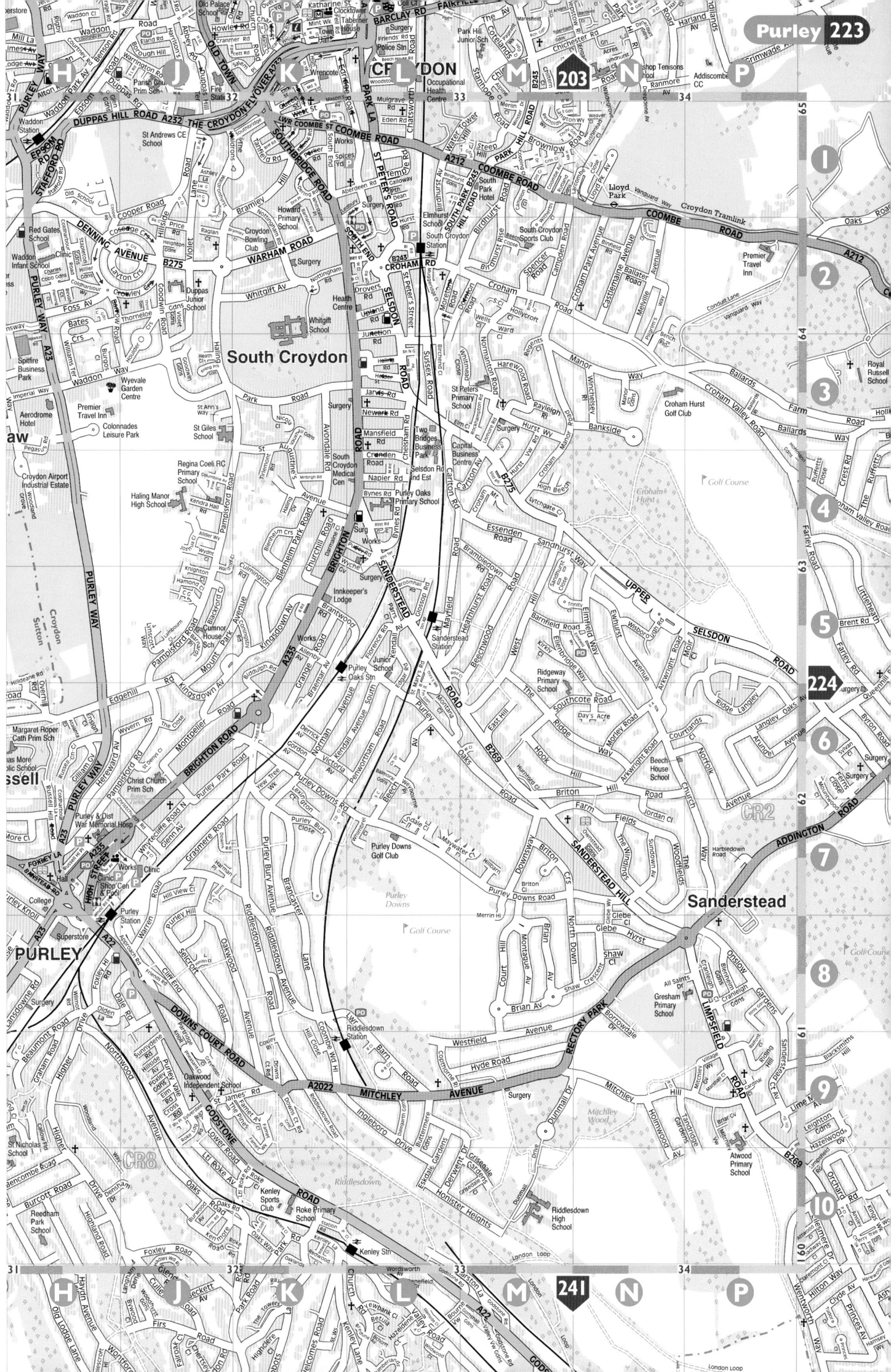
CROYDON
South Croydon
Sanderstead
PURLEY
Purley Downs
Golf Course
Purley Downs Golf Club
Croham Hurst Golf Club
Riddlesdown
Mitchley Wood
CR2
CR8
203
224
241

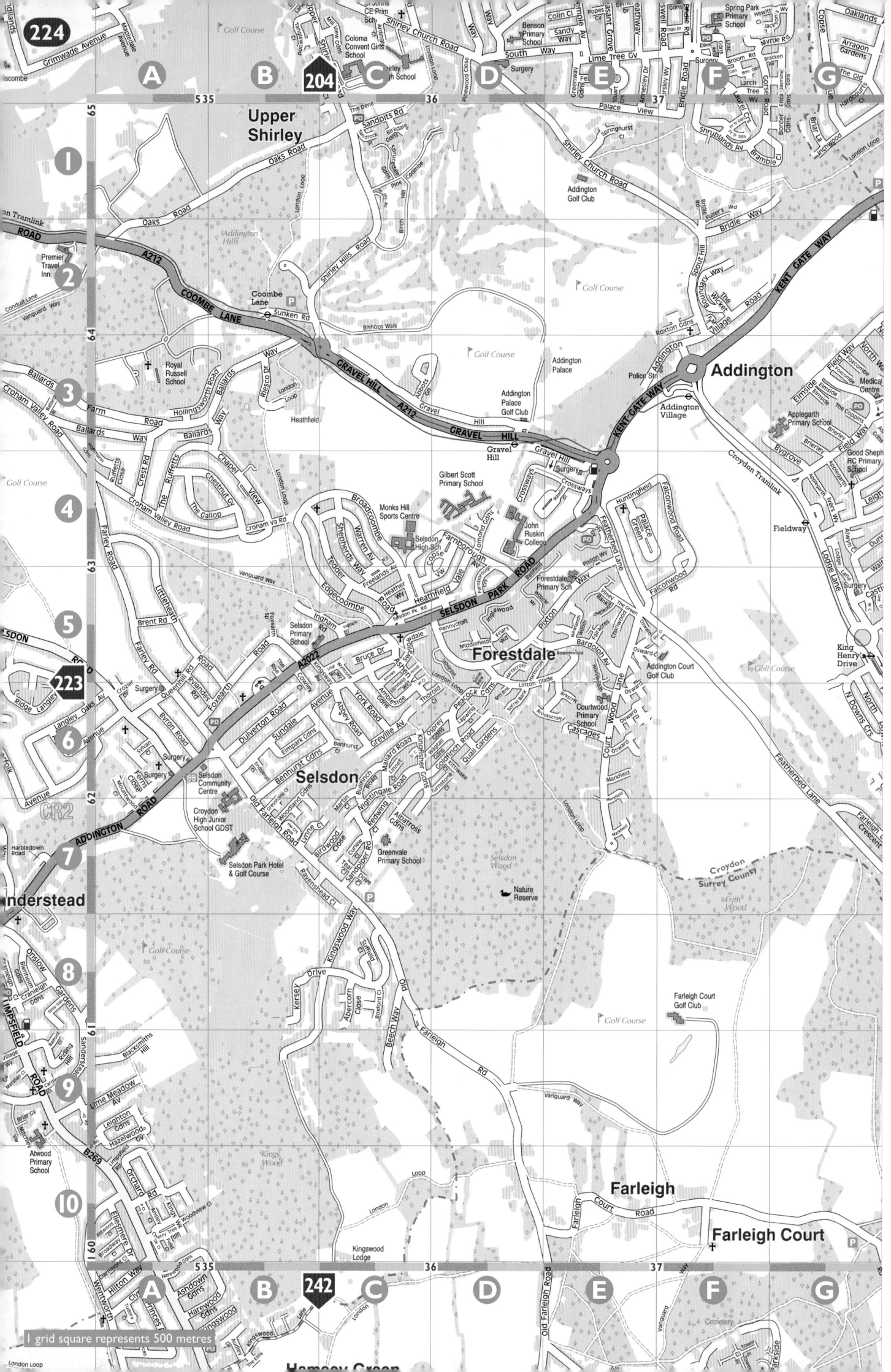

224
204
223
242
A
B
C
D
E
F
G
535
36
37
65
64
63
62
61
60
1
2
3
4
5
6
7
8
9
10
Upper Shirley
Addington
Forestdale
Selsdon
Farleigh
Farleigh Court
Sanderstead
Hamsey Green
CR2
Golf Course
Oaks Road
Shirley Church Road
Shirley Hills Road
Coombe Lane
COOMBE LANE
A212
GRAVEL HILL
Gravel Hill
KENT GATE WAY
SELDSON PARK ROAD
A2022
ADDINGTON ROAD
B269
LIMPSFIELD ROAD
Croham Valley Road
Ballards Way
Farley Road
Featherbed Lane
Old Farleigh Road
Farleigh Rd
Croydon Tramlink
Vanguard Way
London Loop
Addington Hills
Heathfield
Addington Golf Club
Addington Palace
Addington Palace Golf Club
Addington Village
Police Stn
Addington Court Golf Club
Farleigh Court Golf Club
Royal Russell School
Coloma Convent Girls School
Benson Primary School
Spring Park Primary School
Gilbert Scott Primary School
Monks Hill Sports Centre
Selsdon High Sch
John Ruskin College
Forestdale Primary Sch
Selsdon Primary School
Selsdon Community Centre
Croydon High Junior School GDST
Selsdon Park Hotel & Golf Course
Greenvale Primary School
Courtwood Primary School
Applegarth Primary School
Atwood Primary School
Premier Travel Inn
Selsdon Wood
Nature Reserve
Frith Wood
Kings Wood
Kingswood Lodge
Croydon
Surrey County
Fieldway
King Henry's Drive
Cemetery
1 grid square represents 500 metres

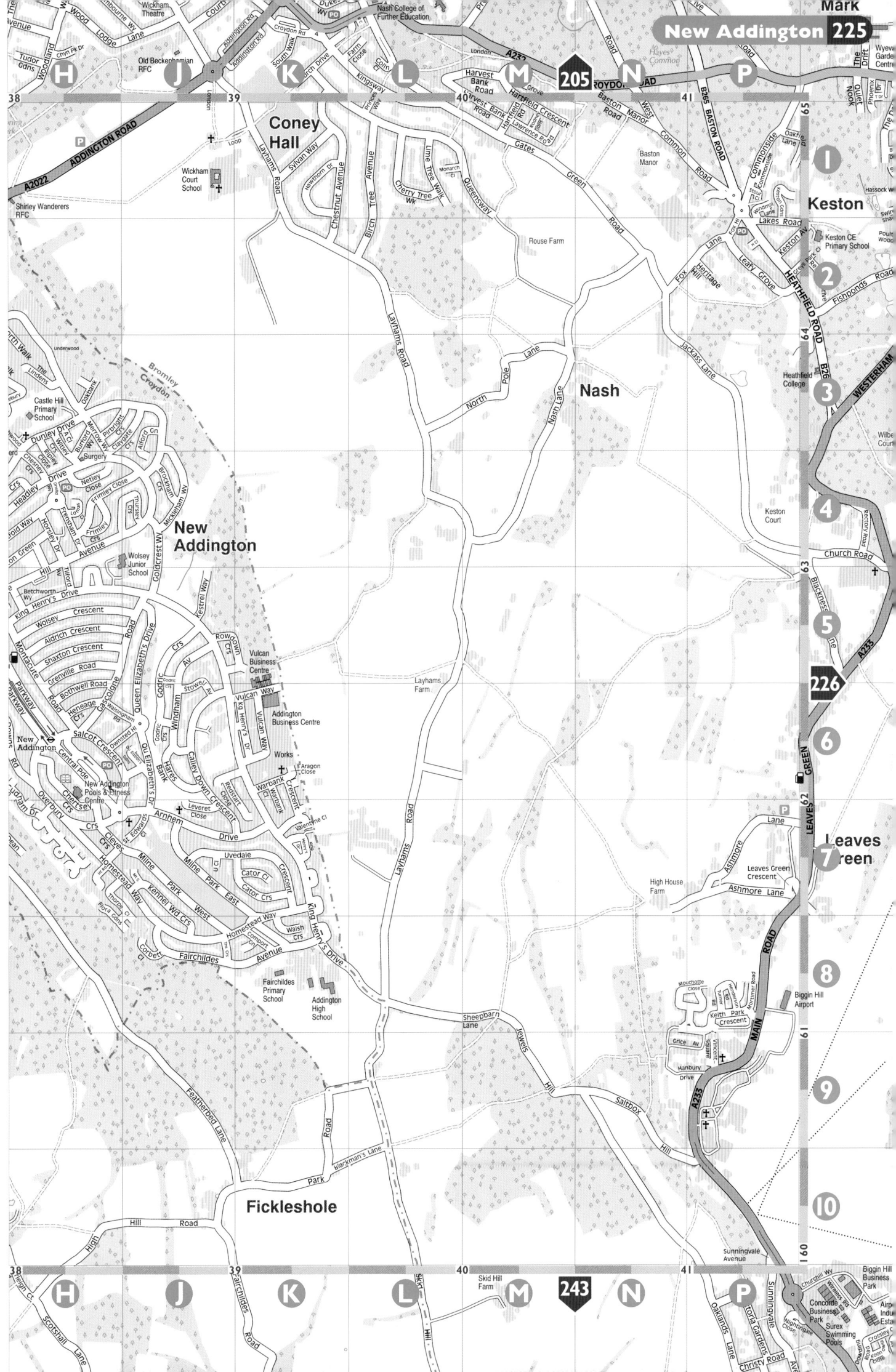

Coney Hall
Keston
Nash
New Addington
Leaves Green
Fickleshole
Wickham Court School
Shirley Wanderers RFC
Old Beckenhamian RFC
Nash College of Further Education
Baston Manor
Rouse Farm
Keston CE Primary School
Heathfield College
Keston Court
Layhams Farm
High House Farm
Biggin Hill Airport
Castle Hill Primary School
Wolsey Junior School
Vulcan Business Centre
Addington Business Centre
New Addington Pools & Fitness Centre
Fairchildes Primary School
Addington High School
Skid Hill Farm
Biggin Hill Business Park
Concorde Business Park
Surex Swimming Pools
ADDINGTON ROAD
HEATHFIELD ROAD
BASTON ROAD
LEAVES GREEN
MAIN ROAD
Layhams Road
Featherbed Lane
Sheepbarn Lane
Jewels Hill
Saltbox Hill
Blackman's Lane
Hill Road
King Henry's Drive
Church Road
Fishponds Road
Ashmore Lane
Nash Lane
North Pole Lane
Gates Green Road
Jackass Lane

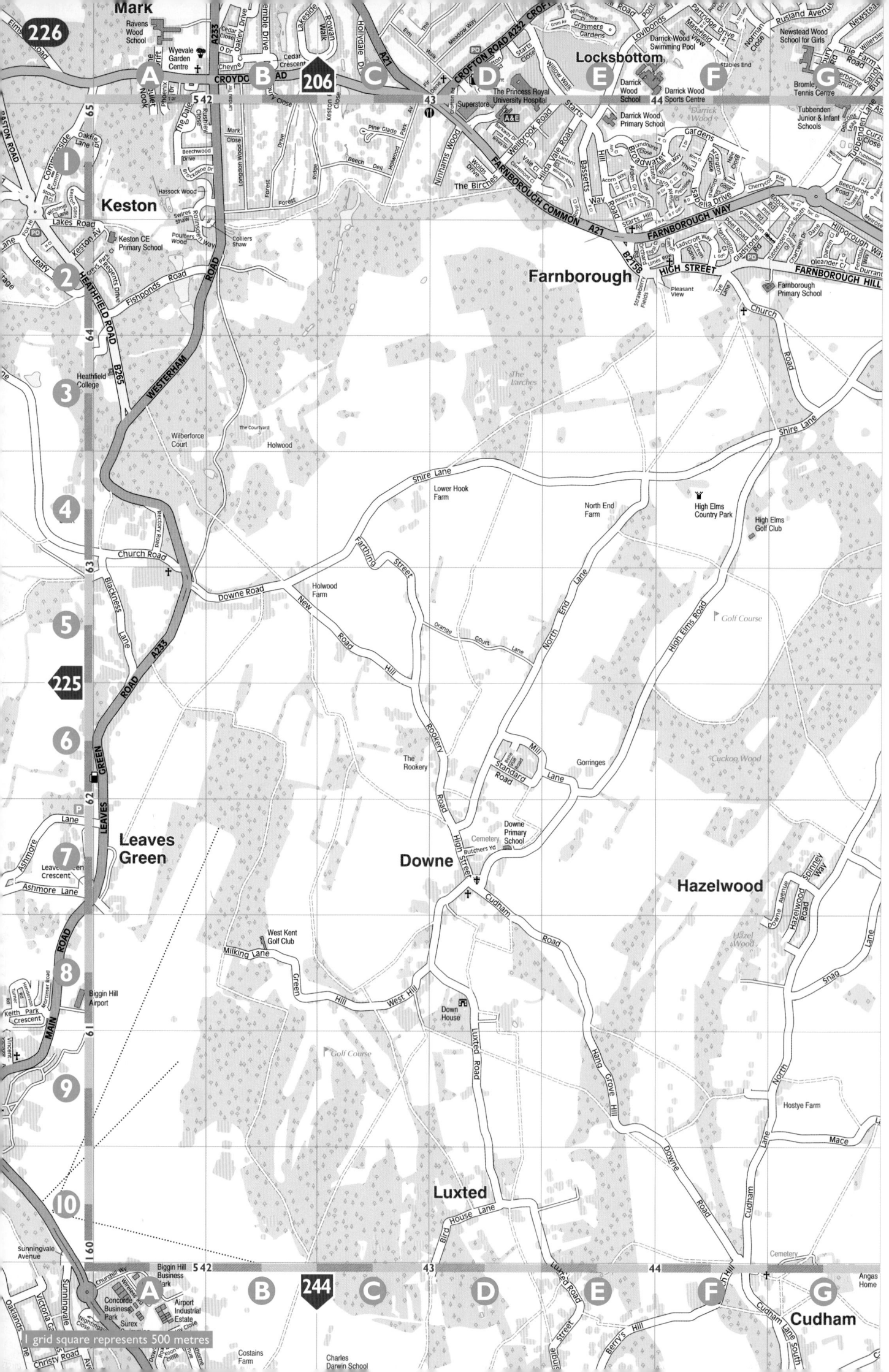
226
206
225
244
Mark
Ravens Wood School
Wyevale Garden Centre
Croydon Road
Keston
Keston CE Primary School
Lakes Road
Keston Av
Fishponds Road
Heathfield Road
B265
Heathfield College
Westerham Road
A233
Hassock Wood
Colliers Shaw
Wilberforce Court
The Courtyard
Holwood
Church Road
Rectory Road
Downe Road
Blackness Lane
Leaves Green Road
Leaves Green
Ashmore Lane
Leaves Green Crescent
Main Road
Biggin Hill Airport
Keith Park Crescent
Sunningvale Avenue
Biggin Hill Business Park
Concorde Business Park
Airport Industrial Estate
Costains Farm
Charles Darwin School
Christy Road
Locksbottom
Princess Royal University Hospital
Superstore
Crofton Road A232
Darrick Wood School
Darrick Wood Primary School
Darrick Wood Sports Centre
Darrick Wood Swimming Pool
Newstead Wood School for Girls
Bromley Tennis Centre
Tubbenden Junior & Infant Schools
Farnborough Common A21
Farnborough Way
Farnborough
High Street
Farnborough Hill
Farnborough Primary School
Pleasant View
Church Road
Shire Lane
Lower Hook Farm
Farthing Street
Holwood Farm
New Road Hill
Orange Court Lane
North End Lane
North End Farm
High Elms Country Park
High Elms Golf Club
High Elms Road
Golf Course
Cuckoo Wood
The Larches
The Rookery
Rookery Road
Mill Lane
Standard Road
Gorringes
Downe Primary School
Cemetery
Butchers Yd
High Street
Downe
Cudham Road
Hazelwood
Hazel Wood
Spinney Way
Snag Lane
West Kent Golf Club
Milking Lane
Green Hill
West Hill
Down House
Luxted Road
Hang Grove Hill
Downe Road
North Lane
Hostye Farm
Mace Lane
Cudham Lane
Luxted
Bird House Lane
Berry's Hill
Cudham
Cudham Lane South
Angas Home
1 grid square represents 500 metres

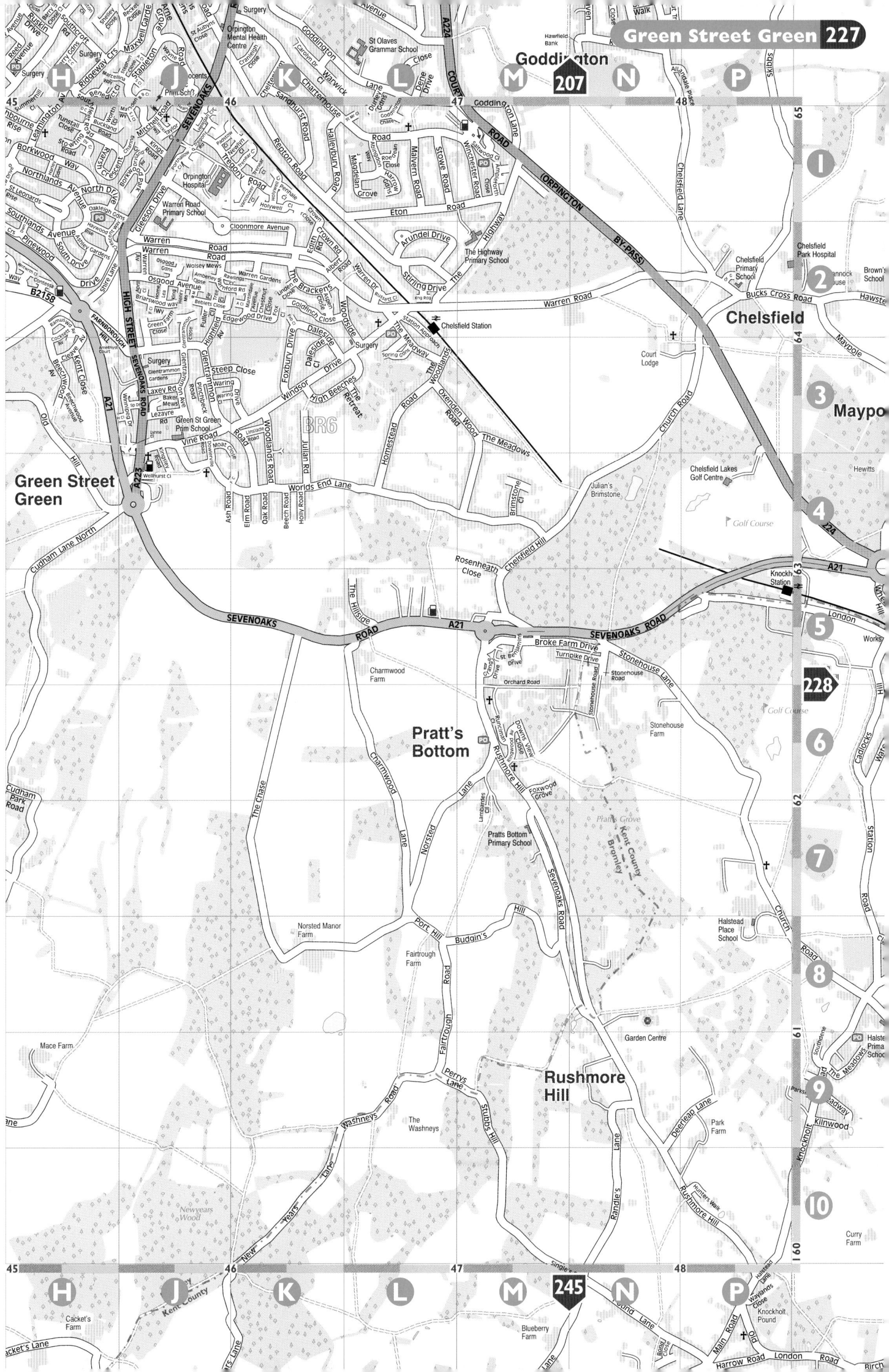
Green Street Green
Chelsfield
Pratt's Bottom
Rushmore Hill
Goddington
Chelsfield Station
Knockholt Station
Sevenoaks Road
A21
A224
A223
High Street
Warren Road
Worlds End Lane
Church Road
Chelsfield Lakes Golf Centre
Orpington Hospital
Pratts Bottom Primary School
Green St Green Prim School
Warren Road Primary School
The Highway Primary School
St Olaves Grammar School
Chelsfield Primary School
Halstead Place School
Norsted Manor Farm
Fairtrough Farm
Stonehouse Farm
Charmwood Farm
Garden Centre
BR6
207
228
245

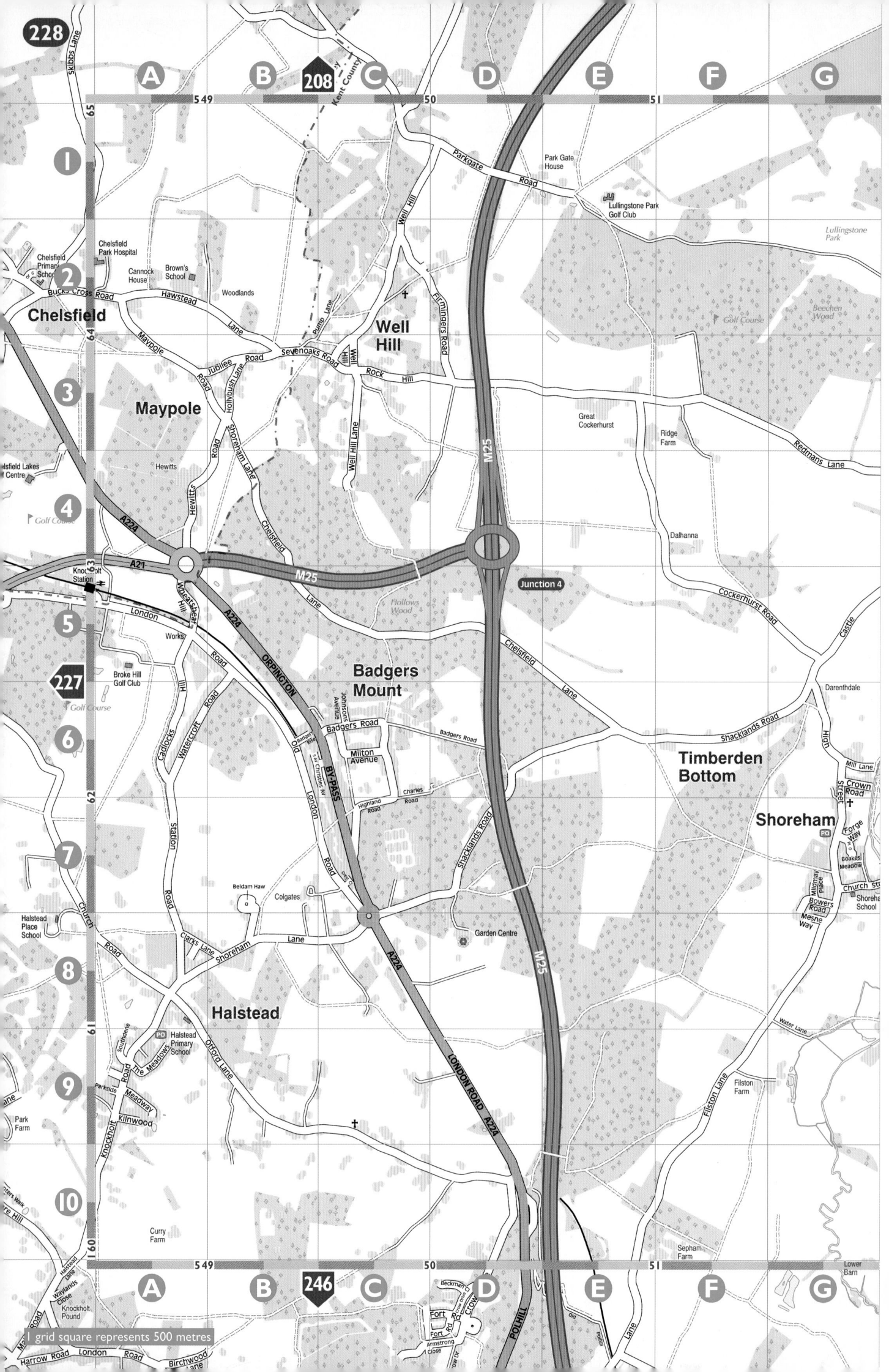
Chelsfield
Maypole
Well Hill
Badgers Mount
Timberden Bottom
Shoreham
Halstead
Chelsfield Park Hospital
Chelsfield Primary School
Cannock House
Brown's School
Woodlands
Park Gate House
Lullingstone Park Golf Club
Lullingstone Park
Beechen Wood
Golf Course
Great Cockerhurst
Ridge Farm
Dalhanna
Junction 4
Hollows Wood
Darenthdale
Hewitts
Knockholt Station
Works
Broke Hill Golf Club
Beldam Haw
Colgates
Garden Centre
Halstead Place School
Halstead Primary School
Park Farm
Curry Farm
Filston Farm
Sepham Farm
Lower Barn
Knockholt Pound
Shoreham School
Parkgate Road
Well Hill
Firmingers Road
Rock Hill
Sevenoaks Road
Jubilee Road
Maypole Road
Hollybush Lane
Shoreham Lane
Hewitts Road
Chelsfield Lane
Bucks Cross Road
Hawstead Lane
Pump Lane
Well Hill Lane
Redmans Lane
Cockerhurst Road
Castle
Shacklands Road
Badgers Road
Johnsons Avenue
Milton Avenue
Highland Road
Charles Road
Christies Av
London Road
Orpington By-Pass
Wheatsheaf Hill
Cadlocks Hill
Watercroft Road
Station Road
Clarks Lane
Shoreham Lane
Otford Lane
Church Road
Southdene
The Meadows
Parkside
Meadway
Kilnwood
Knockholt Road
Waylands Close
Halstead Lane
Harrow Road
Birchwood Lane
Filston Lane
Water Lane
High Street
Mill Lane
Crown Road
Forge Way
Boakes Meadow
Mildmay Place
Church Street
Bowers Road
Mesne Way
Beckman Cl
Fort Rd
Armstrong Close
Polhill
Kent County
A21
A224
M25
London Road A224
549
50
51
65
64
63
62
61
60
208
227
246
1 grid square represents 500 metres

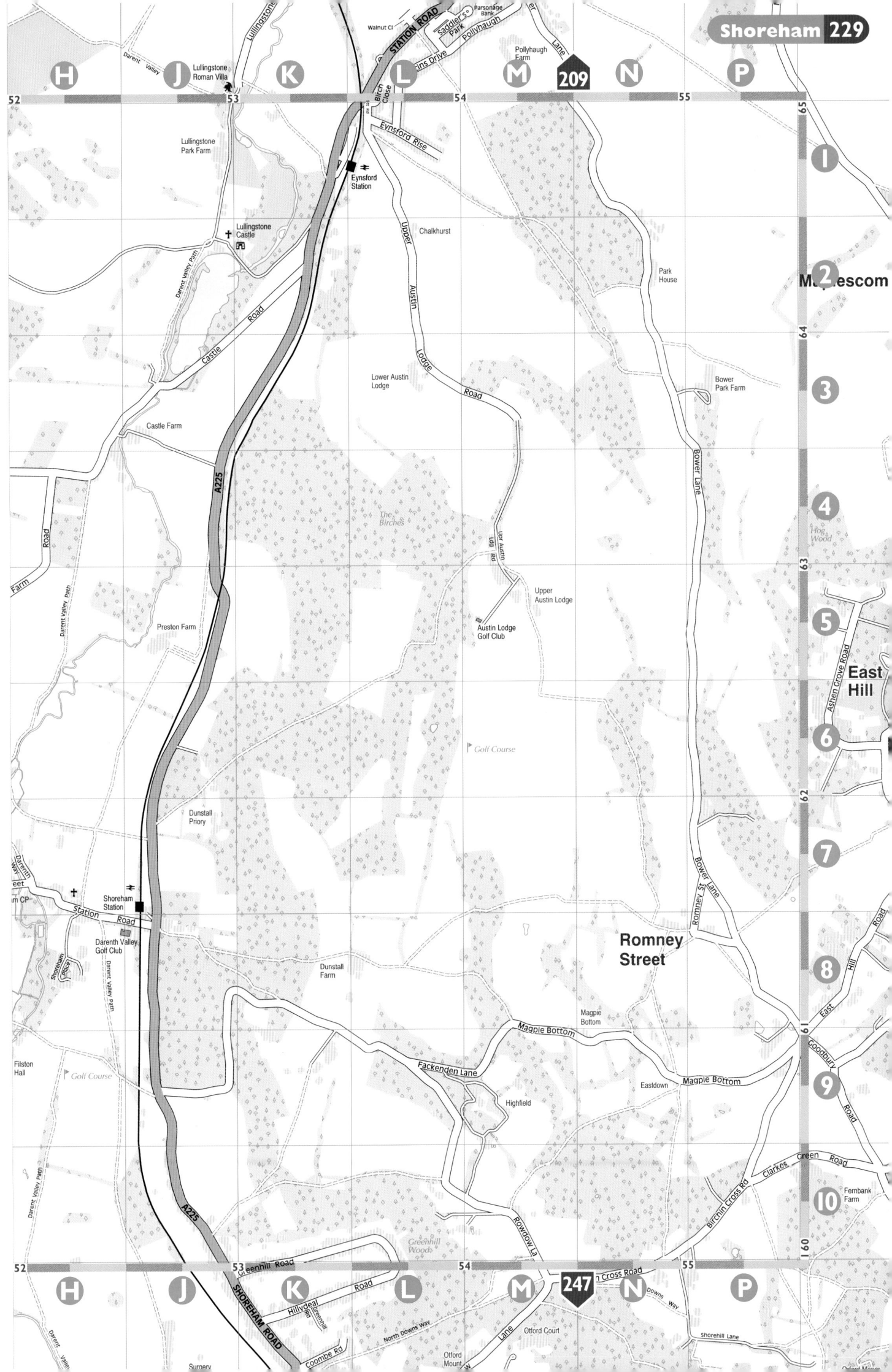

Walnut Cl
STATION ROAD
Saddler's
Park
Pollynaugh
Pollyhaugh
Farm
ins Drive
Lullingstone
Lullingstone
Roman Villa

H **J** **K** **L** **M** **209** **N** **P**

52 53 54 55 65

1

Darent Valley

Eynsford Rise

Birch Close

Lullingstone
Park Farm

Eynsford
Station

2 Ma lescom

Upper

Chalkhurst

Lullingstone
Castle

64

Austin

Park
House

3

Lower Austin
Lodge

Lodge

Bower
Park Farm

Castle

Road

Castle Farm

Road

Bower Lane

4

Hog
Wood

63

The
Birches

A225

Upr Austin
Rd

Darent Valley Path

5

Upper
Austin Lodge

Road

Farm

Austin Lodge
Golf Club

East
Hill

Ashen Grove Road

Preston Farm

6

Farm

Golf Course

62

7

Dunstall
Priory

Bower Lane

Romney St Lane

Romney
Street

Darent
eet
Street
m CP

Shoreham Station

Darenth Valley
Golf Club

8

Road

East Hill Road

Shoreham
Place

Dunstall
Farm

Magpie
Bottom

Goodbury

61

Darent Valley Path

9

Filston
Hall

Golf Course

Magpie Bottom

Fackenden Lane

Magpie Bottom

Eastdown

Highfield

Clarkes Green Road

Birchin Cross Rd

Fernbank
Farm

10

60

A225

Greenhill
Wood

Rowdow La

H **J** **K** **L** **M** **247** **N** **P**

52 53 Greenhill Road 54 n Cross Road 55

SHOREHAM ROAD

Hillygeal

Greenhill

Road

Coombe Rd

North Downs Way

Lane

Otford Court

Downs Way

Shorehill Lane

Surgery

Otford
Mount

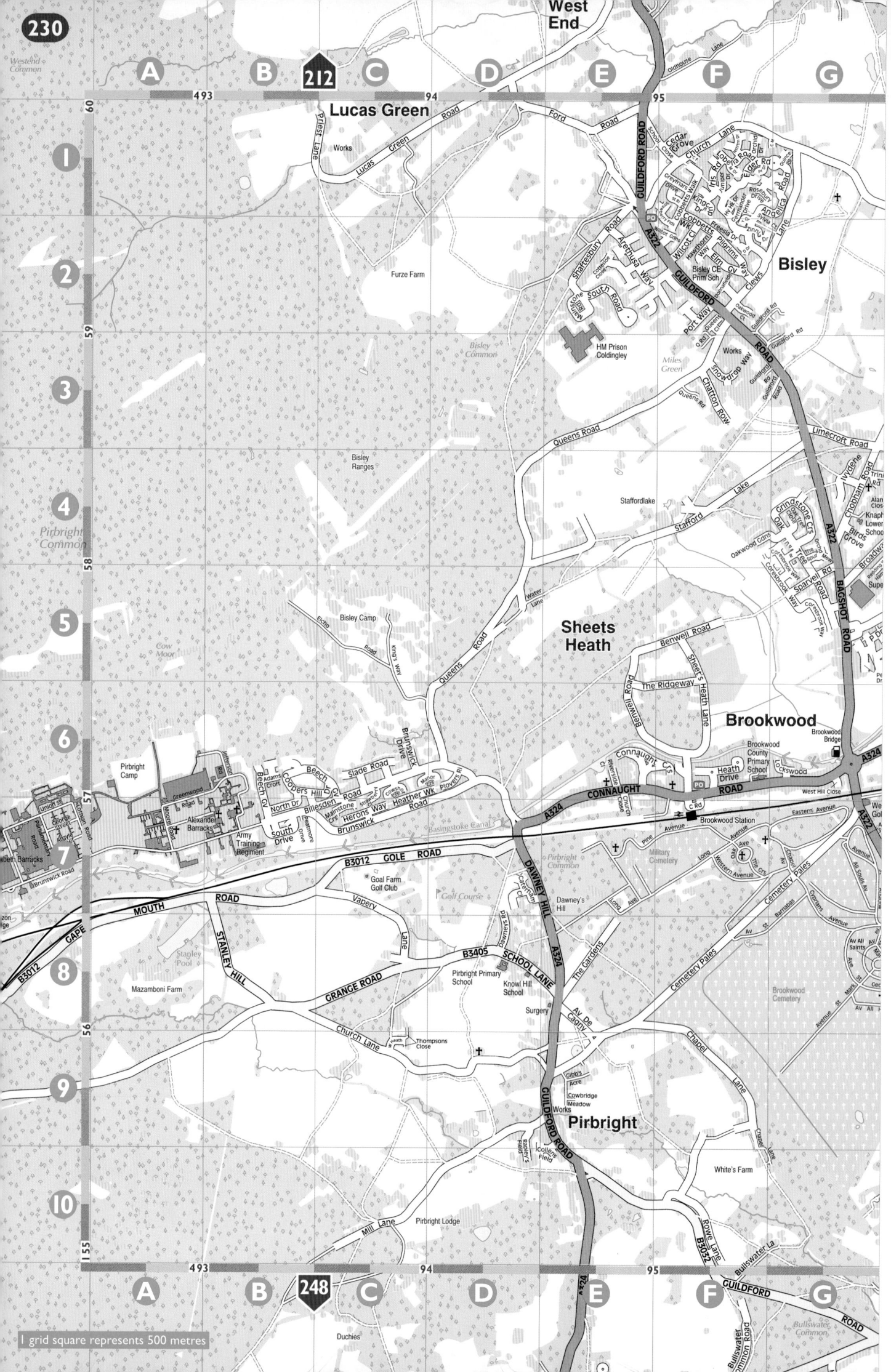

212
248
West End
Lucas Green
Bisley
Sheets Heath
Brookwood
Pirbright
Westend Common
Bisley Common
Pirbright Common
Bisley Ranges
Bisley Camp
Cow Moor
Pirbright Camp
Alexander Barracks
Army Training Regiment
HM Prison Coldingley
Furze Farm
Staffordlake
Miles Green
Brookwood Station
Brookwood Bridge
Military Cemetery
Brookwood Cemetery
Goal Farm Golf Club
Golf Course
Dawney's Hill
Stanley Pool
Mazamboni Farm
Pirbright Primary School
Knowl Hill School
Bisley CE Prim Sch
Brookwood County Primary School
White's Farm
Pirbright Lodge
Duchies
Bullswater Common
GUILDFORD ROAD
BAGSHOT ROAD
CONNAUGHT ROAD
GOLE ROAD
MOUTH ROAD
GAPE
GRANGE ROAD
SCHOOL LANE
DAWNEY HILL
STANLEY HILL
Queens Road
Lucas Green Road
Ford Road
Church Lane
Chapel Lane
Cemetery Pales
Mill Lane
Rowe Lane
Bullswater La
Stafford Lake
Limecroft Road
A322
A324
B3012
B3405
B3032
493
94
95
60
59
58
57
56
155
1 grid square represents 500 metres

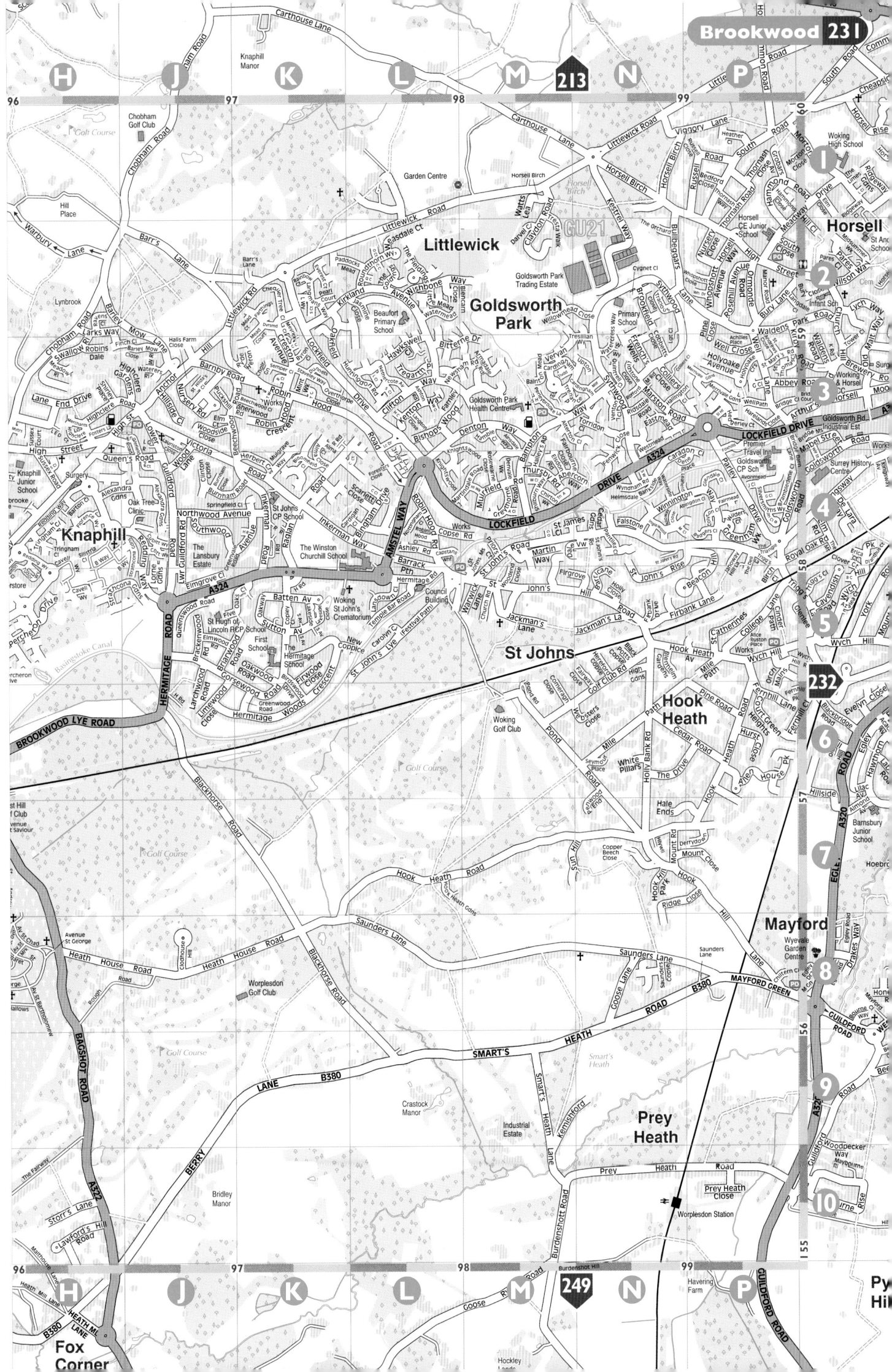
H
J
K
L
M
213
N
P
96
97
98
99
Carthouse Lane
Knaphill Manor
Chobham Golf Club
Golf Course
Chobham Road
Hill Place
Warbury Lane
Barr's Lane
Littlewick Road
Garden Centre
Horsell Birch
Littlewick
GU21
Goldsworth Park Trading Estate
Goldsworth Park
Horsell
Woking High School
Horsell CE Junior School
Lynbrook
Knaphill
Knaphill Junior School
High Street
Barnby Road
Robin Hood Crescent
Lockfield Drive
Lockfield
Amstel Way
A324
Goldsworth Park Health Centre
Beaufort Primary School
Primary School
Premier Travel Inn
Goldsworth CP Sch
Surrey History Centre
Goldsworth Rd Industrial Est
St Johns CP School
The Winston Churchill School
The Lansbury Estate
Northwood Avenue
Inkerman Way
Woking St John's Crematorium
Council Building
St Hugh of Lincoln RCP School
First School
The Hermitage School
Hermitage Road
Brookwood Lye Road
St Johns
Jackman's Lane
Hook Heath
Woking Golf Club
Golf Course
Basingstoke Canal
Blackhorse Road
Hook Heath Road
Saunders Lane
Heath House Road
Worplesdon Golf Club
Mayford
Wyevale Garden Centre
Mayford Green
B380
Smart's Heath Road
Smart's Heath
Crastock Manor
Industrial Estate
Prey Heath
Prey Heath Road
Prey Heath Close
Worplesdon Station
Burdenshott Road
Berry Lane
Bridley Manor
Bagshot Road
A322
A320
Egley Road
Guildford Road
Barnsbury Junior School
232
1
2
3
4
5
6
7
8
9
10
55
56
57
58
59
60
249
Havering Farm
Fox Corner
Heath Mill Lane
Hockley

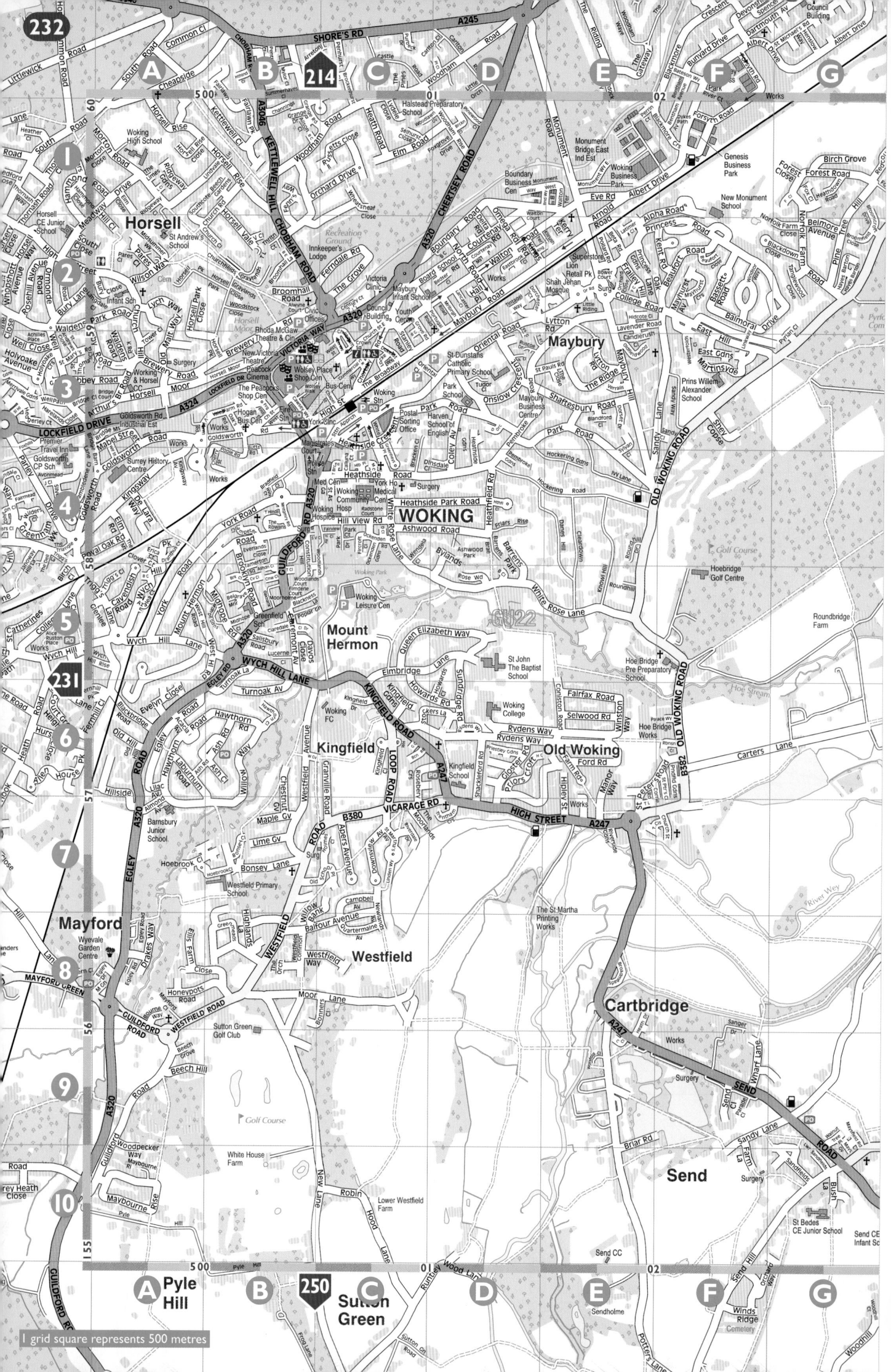
232
214
231
250
Horsell
Maybury
WOKING
Mount Hermon
Kingfield
Old Woking
Mayford
Westfield
Cartbridge
Send
Pyle Hill
Sutton Green
Sendholme
SHORE'S RD
CHOBHAM ROAD
KETTLEWELL HILL
CHERTSEY ROAD
VICTORIA WAY
LOCKFIELD DRIVE
GUILDFORD RD
WYCH HILL LANE
KINGFIELD ROAD
LOOP ROAD
HIGH STREET
OLD WOKING ROAD
EGLEY ROAD
WESTFIELD ROAD
GUILDFORD ROAD
MAYFORD GREEN
SEND ROAD
White Rose Lane
Heathside Park Road
Ashwood Road
Woking Park
Woking Leisure Cen
Golf Course
Hoebridge Golf Centre
Sutton Green Golf Club
Wyevale Garden Centre
Woking High School
Horsell CE Junior School
Woking Community Hosp
St John The Baptist School
Woking College
Kingfield School
Barnsbury Junior School
Westfield Primary School
Hoe Bridge Pre Preparatory School
Prins Willem Alexander School
New Monument School
St Bedes CE Junior School
Genesis Business Park
Monument Bridge East Ind Est
Woking Business Park
The St Martha Printing Works
White House Farm
Lower Westfield Farm
Roundbridge Farm
River Wey
Hoe Stream
1 grid square represents 500 metres

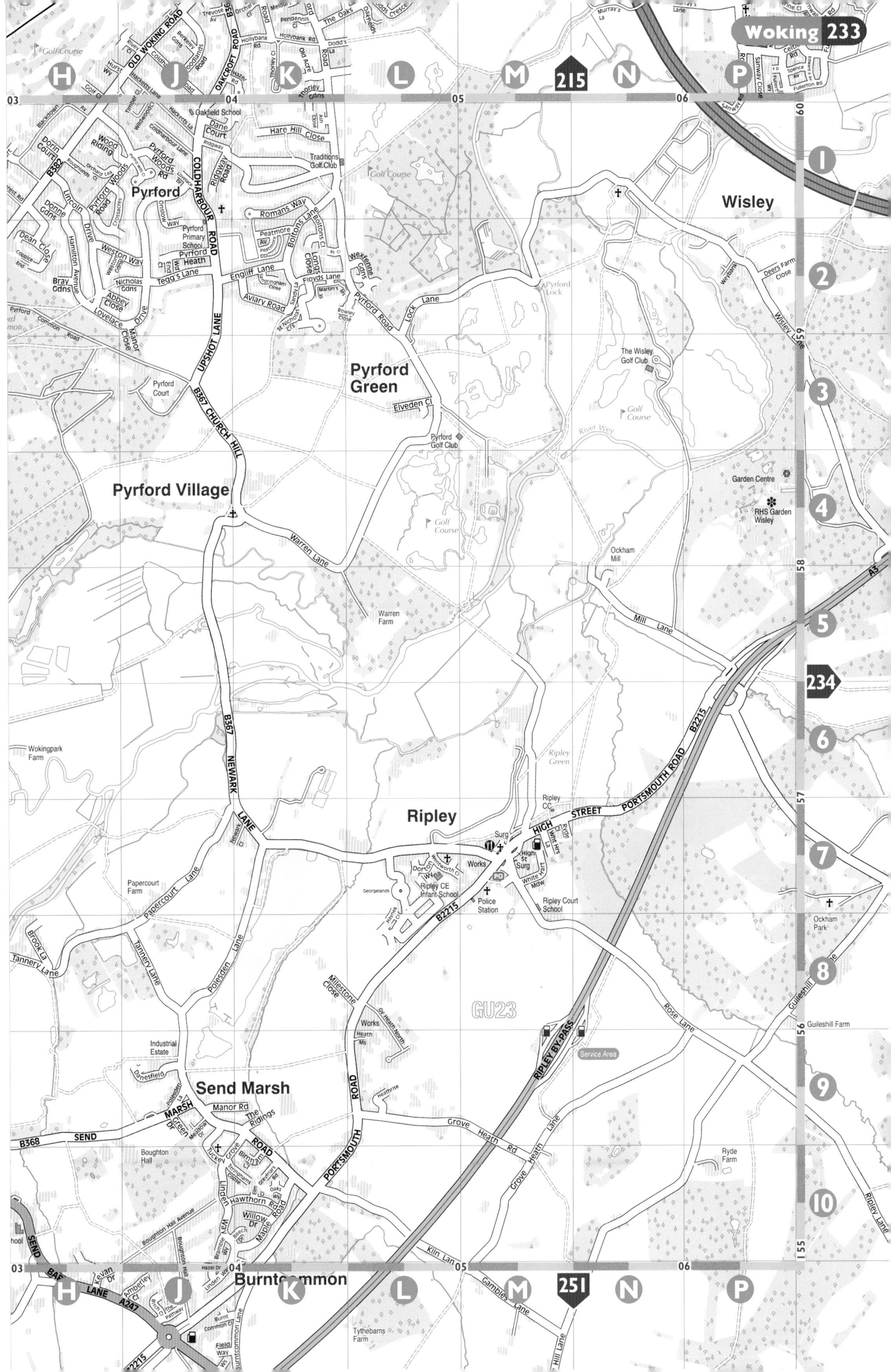
Pyrford
Pyrford Green
Pyrford Village
Wisley
Ripley
Send Marsh
Burntcommon
RHS Garden Wisley
Garden Centre
The Wisley Golf Club
Pyrford Golf Club
Traditions Golf Club
Ockham Mill
Warren Farm
Wokingpark Farm
Papercourt Farm
Ockham Park
Guileshill Farm
Ryde Farm
Boughton Hall
Tythebarns Farm
Ripley Court School
Police Station
Ripley CE Infant School
Pyrford Primary School
Oakfield School
Service Area
GU23
UPSHOT LANE
B367 CHURCH HILL
B367 NEWARK LANE
PORTSMOUTH ROAD
HIGH STREET
RIPLEY BY-PASS
B368 SEND MARSH ROAD
COLDHARBOUR ROAD
OLD WOKING ROAD
OAKCROFT ROAD
A3
B2215
215
234
251

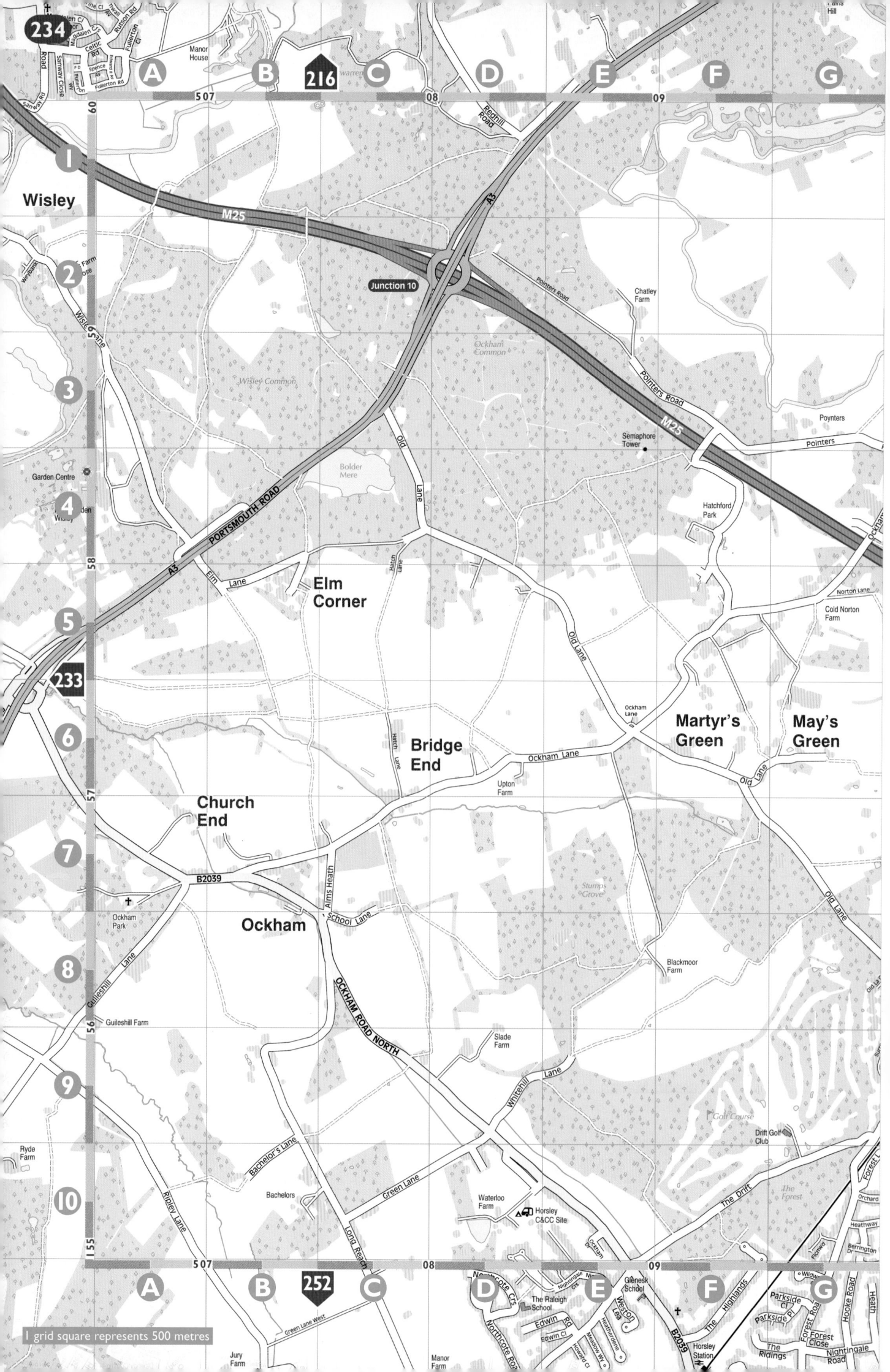
234
216
233
252
A
B
C
D
E
F
G
1
2
3
4
5
6
7
8
9
10
507
08
09
60
59
58
57
56
155
Wisley
Manor House
Redhill Road
M25
A3
Junction 10
Pointers Road
Chatley Farm
Ockham Common
Wisley Common
Wisley Lane
Poynters
Pointers
Semaphore Tower
Garden Centre
Bolder Mere
Old Lane
PORTSMOUTH ROAD
Hatchford Park
Elm Lane
Elm Corner
Hatch Lane
Norton Lane
Cold Norton Farm
Ockham Lane
Martyr's Green
May's Green
Bridge End
Upton Farm
Church End
B2039
Alms Heath
Stumps Grove
Ockham Park
Ockham
School Lane
Blackmoor Farm
Guileshill Lane
OCKHAM ROAD NORTH
Guileshill Farm
Slade Farm
Whitehill Lane
Golf Course
Drift Golf Club
Ryde Farm
Bachelor's Lane
Ripley Lane
Bachelors
Green Lane
Waterloo Farm
Horsley C&CC Site
The Drift
The Forest
Orchard
Heathway
Berrington Rd
Long Reach
Northcote Crs
The Raleigh School
Edwin Rd
Edwin Cl
Glenesk School
Weston Lea
The Highlands
Parkside Cl
Parkside Pl
Forest Road
Hooke Road
The Ridings
Forest Close
Nightingale Road
Horsley Station
Green Lane West
Jury Farm
Manor Farm
Northcote Rd
Meadow Wy
Howard Cl
1 grid square represents 500 metres

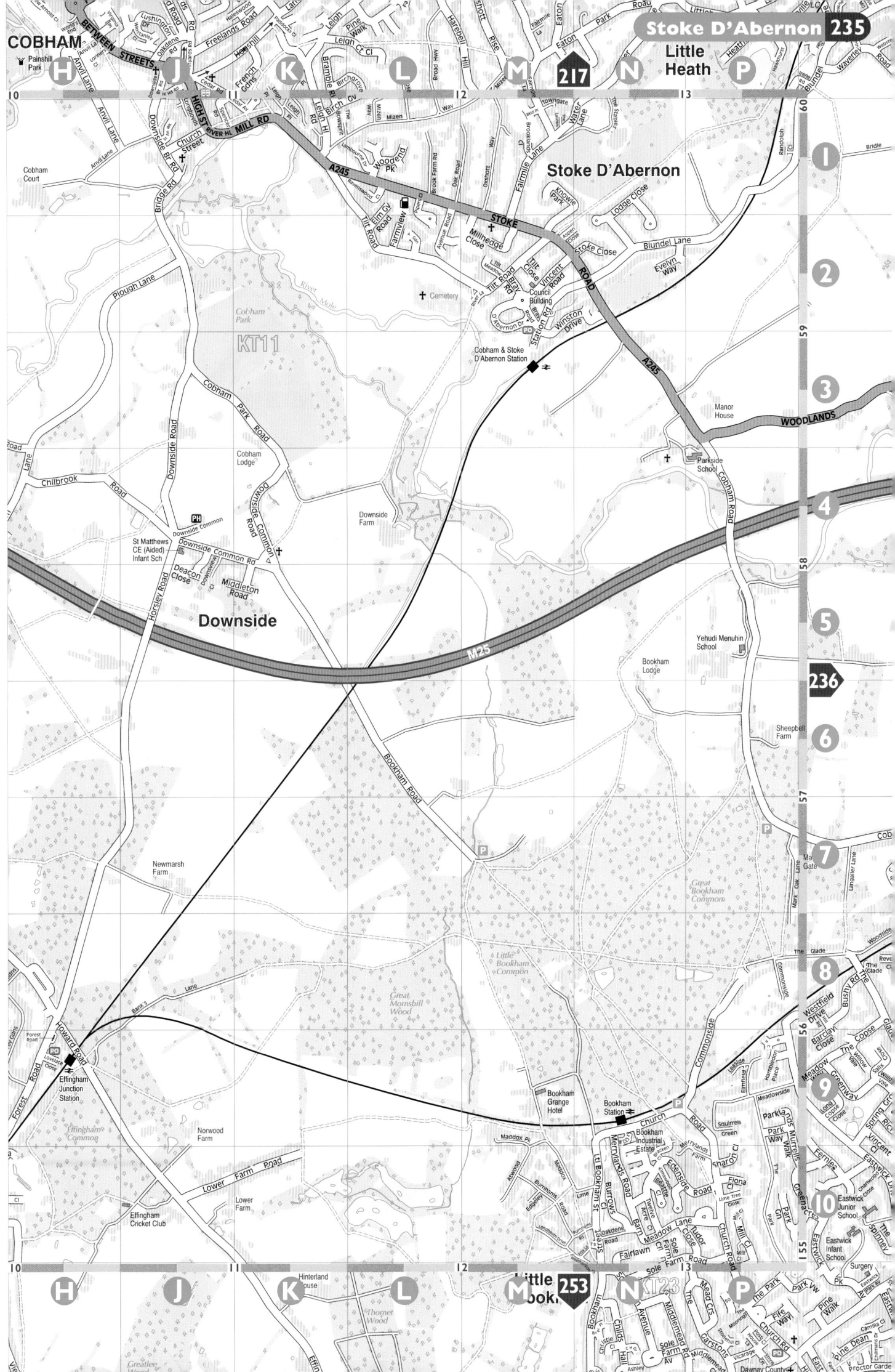
COBHAM
Little Heath
Stoke D'Abernon
Downside
KT11
A245
M25
STOKE ROAD
WOODLANDS
Cobham Park
Cobham Court
Cobham Lodge
Cobham & Stoke D'Abernon Station
Council Building
Cemetery
River Mole
Manor House
Parkside School
Downside Farm
Yehudi Menuhin School
Bookham Lodge
Sheepbell Farm
Newmarsh Farm
Great Bookham Common
Little Bookham Common
Great Mornshill Wood
Effingham Junction Station
Effingham Common
Norwood Farm
Lower Farm
Effingham Cricket Club
Bookham Grange Hotel
Bookham Station
Bookham Industrial Estate
Eastwick Junior School
Eastwick Infant School
Hinterland House
Thornet Wood
St Matthews CE (Aided) Infant Sch
Downside Common
Cobham Park Road
Downside Road
Horsley Road
Bookham Road
Cobham Road
Plough Lane
Chilbrook Road
Anvil Lane
Bridge Rd
Lower Farm Road
Howard Road
Forest Road
Church Road
Commonside
Downside Common Rd
Middleton Road
Deacon Close
Blundel Lane
Stoke Close
Lodge Close
Knowle Park
Evelyn Way
Tilt Road
Elm Gv Road
Farmview
Millhedge Close
Avenue Road
Fairmile Lane
Woodend Pk
Winston Drive
Station Rd
Vincent Road
Mill Rd
High St
Between Streets
Freelands Road
Leigh Hl
Mizen Way
Oak Road
Brook Farm Rd
Merrylands Road
Lime Tree Close
Sharon Cl
Eastwick Rd
Greenacres
217
236
253
KT23
H J K L M N P
1 2 3 4 5 6 7 8 9 10
10 11 12 13
55 56 57 58 59 60

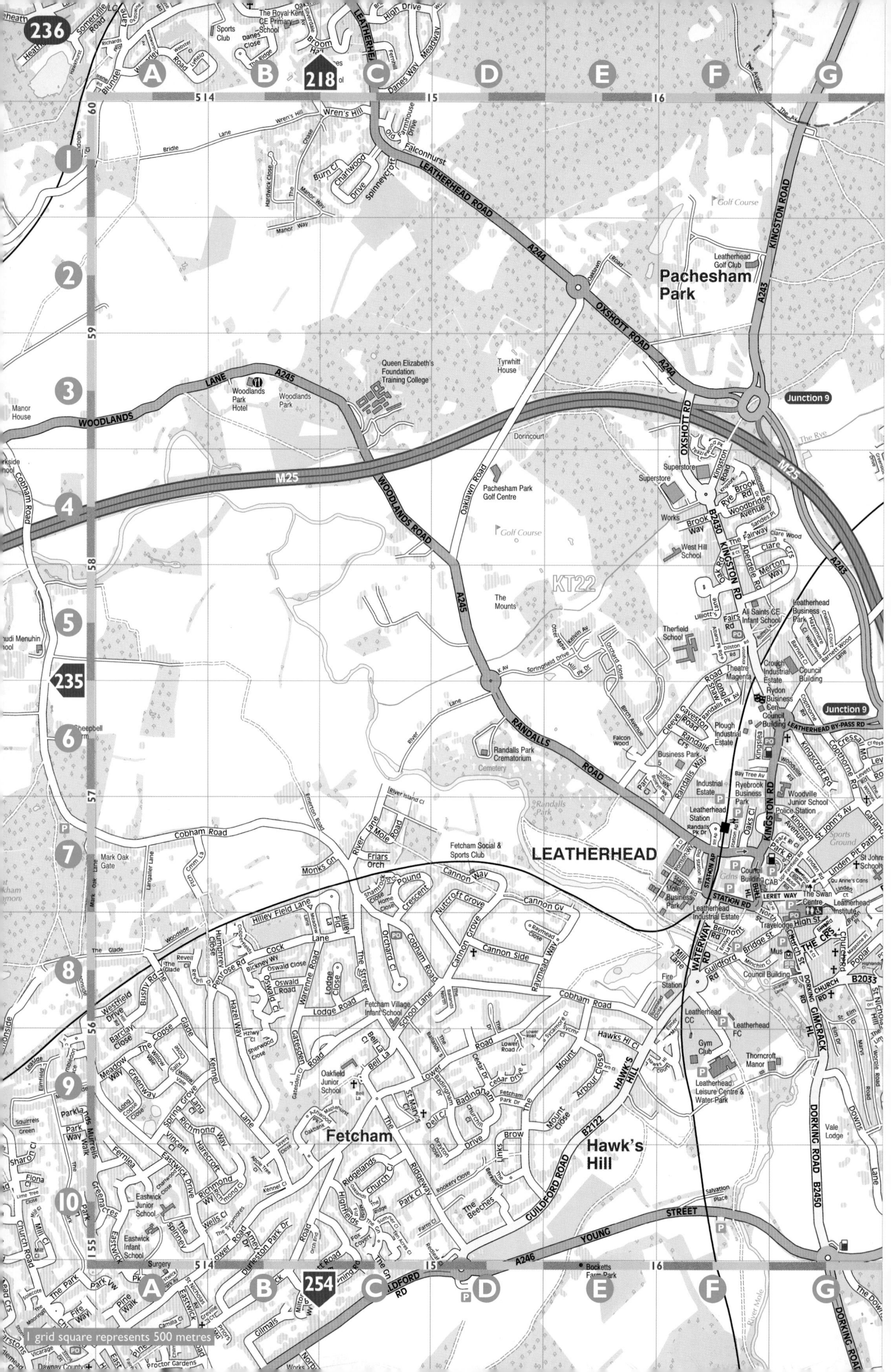
236
218
235
254
A
B
C
D
E
F
G
1
2
3
4
5
6
7
8
9
10
514
15
16
60
59
58
57
56
55
Leatherhead Road
A244
Oxshott Road
Kingston Road
A243
M25
Junction 9
Woodlands Lane
A245
Woodlands Road
Randalls Road
Oaklawn Road
Cobham Road
Bridle Lane
Wren's Hill
Manor Way
Falconhurst
Spinneycroft
Charlwood Drive
Burn Cl
Hardwick Close
The Manor Way
Danes Way
High Drive
Meadway
Fernhill
Sports Club
Danes Close
The Ridge
The Royal Kent CE Primary School
Pachesham Park
Leatherhead Golf Club
Golf Course
Tyrwhitt House
Queen Elizabeth's Foundation Training College
Woodlands Park Hotel
Woodlands Park
Manor House
Dorincourt
Pachesham Park Golf Centre
KT22
The Mounts
Superstore
Works
West Hill School
Brook Way
Woodbridge Avenue
The Fairway
Clare Crs
Merton Way
Aperdele Rd
Oak Rd
B2430
Kingston Rd
Fairs Rd
Therfield School
All Saints CE Infant School
Leatherhead Business Park
Crouch Industrial Estate
Council Building
Theatre Magenta
Rydon Business Cen
Leatherhead By-Pass Rd
Copthorne Rd
Kingscroft Rd
Cressall Md
Springfield Drive
Orchard Close
Birch Avenue
Falcon Wood
Cleeve Road
Gaveston Road
Randalls Crs
Randalls Way
Plough Industrial Estate
Business Park 5
Industrial Estate
Ryebrook Business Park
Woodville Junior School
Police Station
St John's Av
Sports Ground
Linden Pit Path
Randalls Park Crematorium
Cemetery
Randalls Park
River Lane
Mole Road
River Island Cl
Emerton Road
Monks Gn
Friars Orch
Fetcham Social & Sports Club
Cannon Way
Nutcroft Grove
Cannon Gv
Cannon Grove
Cannon Side
Raymead Way
Raymead Close
Cobham Road
Pound Crescent
Orchard Cl
The Street
Hilley Field Lane
Cock Lane
Oswald Close
Oswald Road
Warenne Road
Lodge Close
Lodge Road
Fetcham Village Infant School
School Lane
LEATHERHEAD
Leatherhead Station
Station Ap
Station Rd
Waterway Rd
Mole Business Park
Leatherhead Industrial Estate
Council Building
CAB
Leret Way
The Swan Centre
Leatherhead Institute
High St
Bridge St
Church St
The Crs
Guildford Rd
Belmont Rd
Minchin Cl
Mus
Council Building
Church Rd
B2033
Dorking Road
Gimcrack Hl
Fire Station
Mill Lane
Leatherhead CC
Leatherhead FC
Gym Club
Leatherhead Leisure Centre & Water Park
Thorncroft Manor
Vale Lodge
Downs Lane
B2450
Hawks Hill
Hawk's Hill
B2122
Guildford Road
Hawks Hl Cl
Arbour Close
Mount Close
The Mount
Lower Road
Cedar Drive
Badingham Drive
Churchill Ct
Links Brow
The Beeches
Rookery Close
Ridgeway
Fetcham
Oakfield Junior School
Bell La
St Mary's Cl
Ridgelands
Highfields
Church Cl
Park Cl
Mark Oak Gate
Mark Oak Lane
Langaller Lane
Woodside
The Glade
Bushy Rd
Westfield Drive
Barclay Close
Meadow Way
Greenway
The Copse
Penrose Rd
Humphrey Close
Hazel Way
Sherwood Close
Kennel Lane
Gatesden Road
Spring Grove
Richmond Way
Harecroft
Eastwick Drive
Eastwick Junior School
Eastwick Infant School
The Spinney
Greenacres
Parklands
Murreils Walk
Church Road
Mill Cl
Young Street
A246
Salvation Place
Bocketts Farm Park
Guildford Rd
Surgery
The Park
Park Vw
Cobham Road
Sheepbell Farm
Manor House
Cemetery
River Mole
1 grid square represents 500 metres

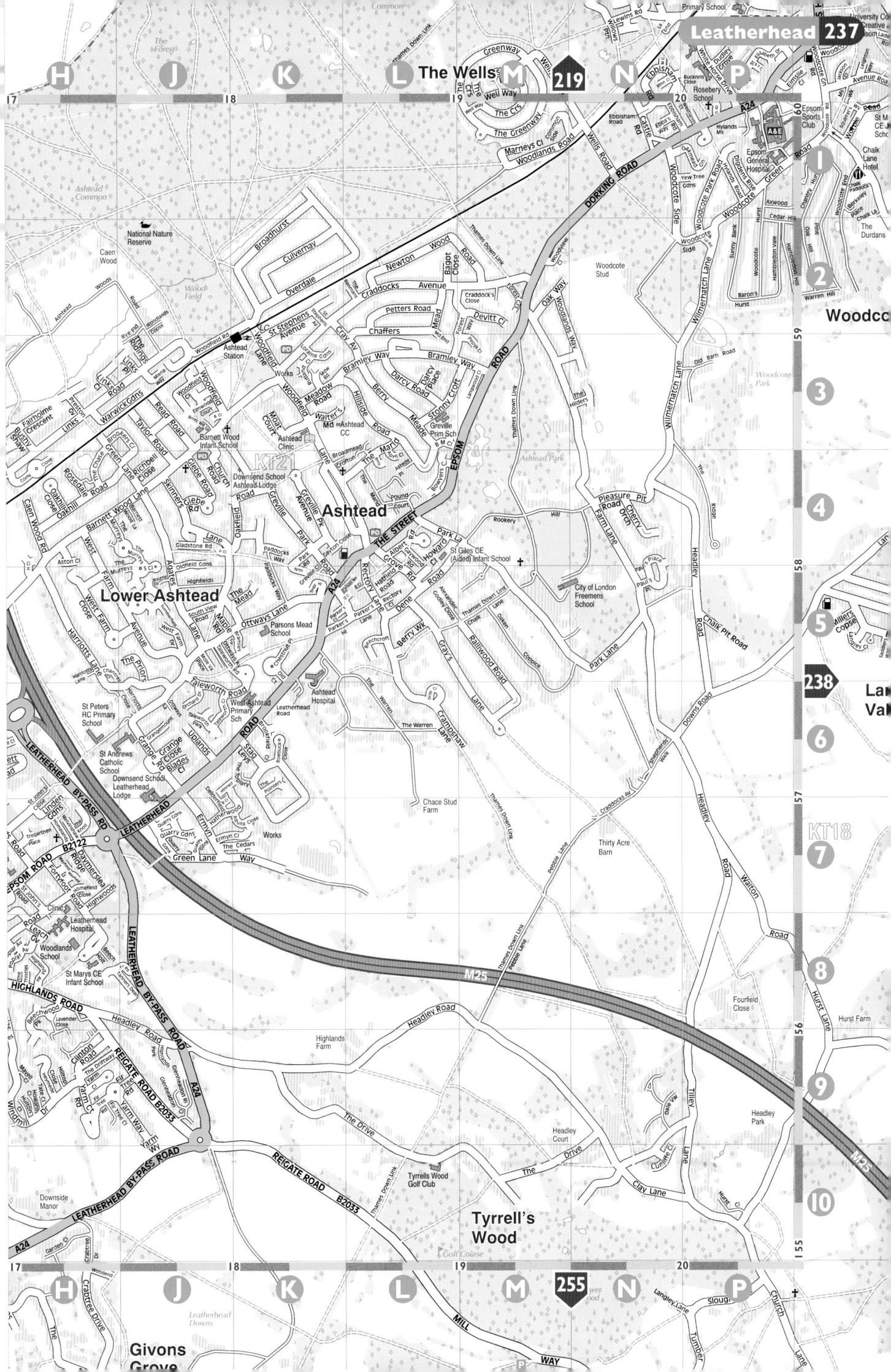

The Wells
219
238
255
Ashtead
Lower Ashtead
Ashtead Common
National Nature Reserve
Caen Wood
Wood Field
Ashtead Station
Ashtead Park
KT21
KT18
Woodcote Park
Woodcote Stud
Woodcote
City of London Freemens School
Epsom General Hospital
Epsom Sports Club
Rosebery School
Chalk Lane Hotel
The Durdans
Greville Prim Sch
Barnett Wood Infant School
Downsend School Ashtead Lodge
Parsons Mead School
St Giles CE (Aided) Infant School
Ashtead Hospital
West Ashtead Primary Sch
St Peters RC Primary School
St Andrews Catholic School
Downsend School Leatherhead Lodge
Leatherhead Hospital
Woodlands School
St Marys CE Infant School
Chace Stud Farm
Thirty Acre Barn
Highlands Farm
Headley Court
Headley Park
Hurst Farm
Fourfield Close
Tyrrells Wood Golf Club
Tyrrell's Wood
Downside Manor
Leatherhead Downs
Givons Grove
DORKING ROAD
EPSOM ROAD
THE STREET
A24
M25
LEATHERHEAD BY-PASS ROAD
REIGATE ROAD B2033
HIGHLANDS ROAD
B2122
Headley Road
The Drive
Clay Lane
Thames Down Link
Pebble Lane
Crampshaw Lane
Park Lane
Chalk Pit Road
Walton Road
Hurst Lane
Tilley Lane
Wilmerhatch Lane
Woodcote Side
Woodlands Road
Wells Road
Craddocks Avenue
Barnett Wood Lane
Ottways Lane
Green Lane
Harriotts Lane
Rookery Hill
Pleasure Pit Road
Railwood Road
Grays Lane
The Warren
Mill Way

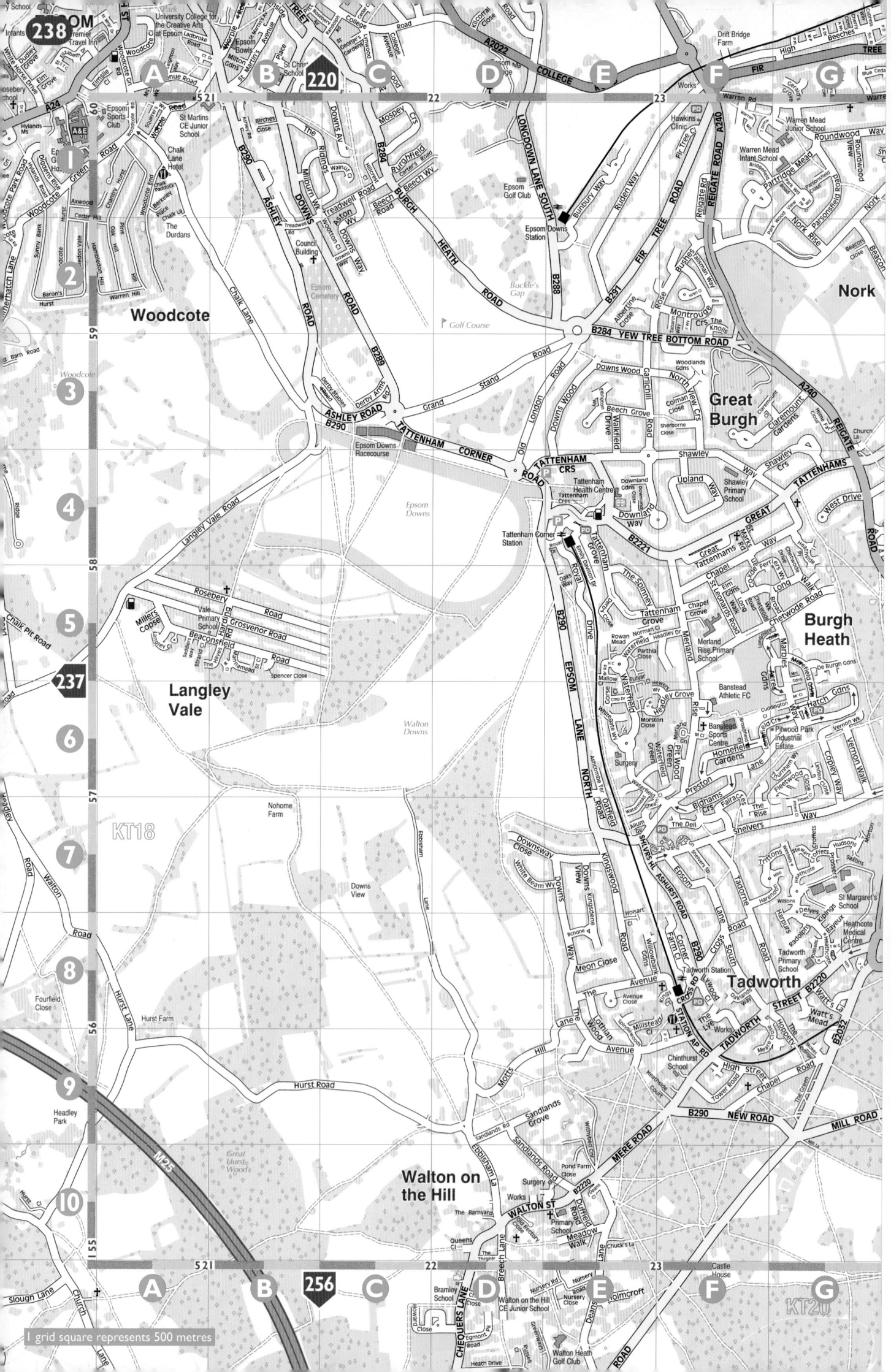

238
220
237
256
Woodcote
Langley Vale
Great Burgh
Nork
Burgh Heath
Tadworth
Walton on the Hill
KT18
KT20
Epsom Downs Racecourse
Epsom Downs
Walton Downs
Epsom Golf Club
Epsom Downs Station
Tattenham Corner Station
Tadworth Station
Golf Course
Buckle's Gap
Epsom Cemetery
Council Building
The Durdans
Chalk Lane Hotel
St Martins CE Junior School
Epsom Sports Club
University College for the Creative Arts at Epsom
Premier Travel Inn
Epsom Bowls
St Christ School
Drift Bridge Farm
Hawkins Clinic
Warren Mead Junior School
Warren Mead Infant School
Shawley Primary School
Tattenham Health Centre
Merland Rise Primary School
Banstead Athletic FC
Banstead Sports Centre
Pitwood Park Industrial Estate
St Margaret's School
Heathcote Medical Centre
Tadworth Primary School
Chinthurst School
Vale Primary School
Nohome Farm
Downs View
Hurst Farm
Fourfield Close
Headley Park
Great Hurst Wood
Walton on the Hill CE Junior School
Walton Heath Golf Club
Primary School
Castle House
A24
A2022 COLLEGE ROAD
A240 REIGATE ROAD
B290 ASHLEY ROAD
B289 DOWNS ROAD
B284 BURCH HEATH ROAD
B284 YEW TREE BOTTOM ROAD
B288 LONGDOWN LANE SOUTH
B291 FIR TREE ROAD
B2221 GREAT TATTENHAMS
B290 EPSOM LANE NORTH
B290 ASHURST ROAD
B2220 TADWORTH STREET
B2032
B290 NEW ROAD
MILL ROAD
MERE ROAD
B2220 WALTON ST
TATTENHAM CORNER ROAD
Grand Stand Road
Langley Vale Road
Chalk Lane
Rosebery Road
Grosvenor Road
Beaconsfield Road
Hurst Road
Hurst Lane
Walton Road
Ebbisham Lane
Sandlands Road
Chequers Lane
Breech Lane
Motts Hill Lane
Kingswood Road
Shelvers Way
Preston Lane
Chetwode Road
Chalk Pit Road
Slough Lane
M25
A B C D E F G
1 2 3 4 5 6 7 8 9 10
521 22 23
60 59 58 57 56 55
1 grid square represents 500 metres

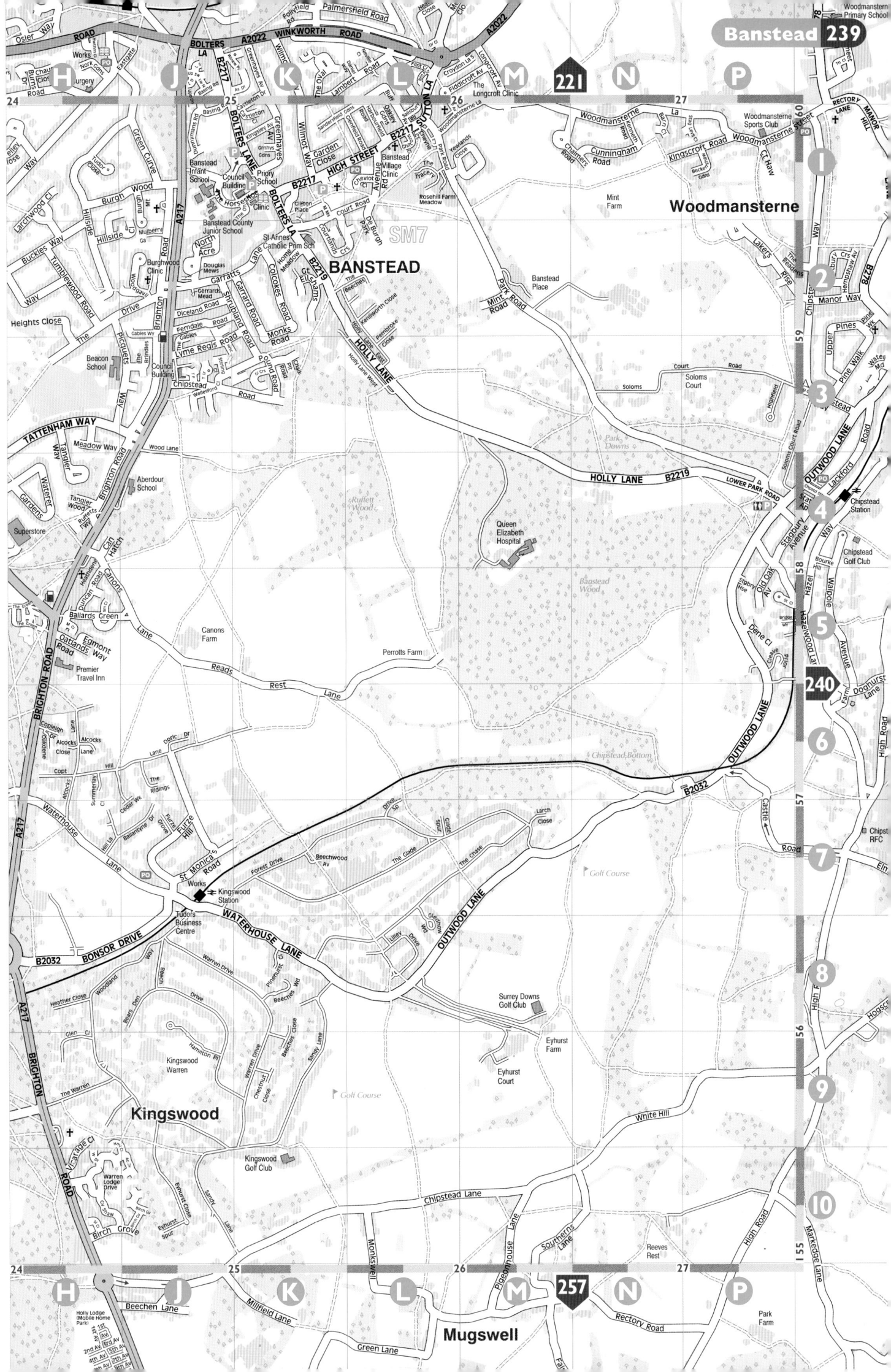

BANSTEAD
Woodmansterne
Kingswood
Mugswell
SM7
221
240
257
WINKWORTH ROAD
A2022
BOLTERS LANE
B2217
HIGH STREET
SUTTON LA
HOLLY LANE
B2219
OUTWOOD LANE
B2032
WATERHOUSE LANE
BONSOR DRIVE
BRIGHTON ROAD
A217
TATTENHAM WAY
LOWER PARK ROAD
Woodmansterne Street
Woodmansterne La
Cunningham Road
Kingscroft Road
Chipstead Lane
White Hill
Reads Rest Lane
Canons Lane
Park Road
Mint Road
Solom's Court Road
Rectory Road
Millfield Lane
Green Lane
Beechen Lane
High Road
Markedge Lane
Queen Elizabeth Hospital
Banstead Wood
Canons Farm
Perrotts Farm
Mint Farm
Banstead Place
Solom's Court
Chipstead Station
Chipstead Golf Club
Kingswood Station
Kingswood Golf Club
Surrey Downs Golf Club
Eyhurst Farm
Eyhurst Court
Kingswood Warren
Golf Course
Beacon School
Aberdour School
Premier Travel Inn
Superstore
Banstead Infant School
Banstead County Junior School
Priory School
Banstead Village Clinic
Woodmansterne Sports Club
The Longcroft Clinic
Reeves Rest
Park Farm
Tudors Business Centre
Works
Council Building
Burghwood Clinic
Rosehill Farm Meadow
Chipstead Bottom
Ruffett Wood
Park Downs
Holly Lodge (Mobile Home Park)

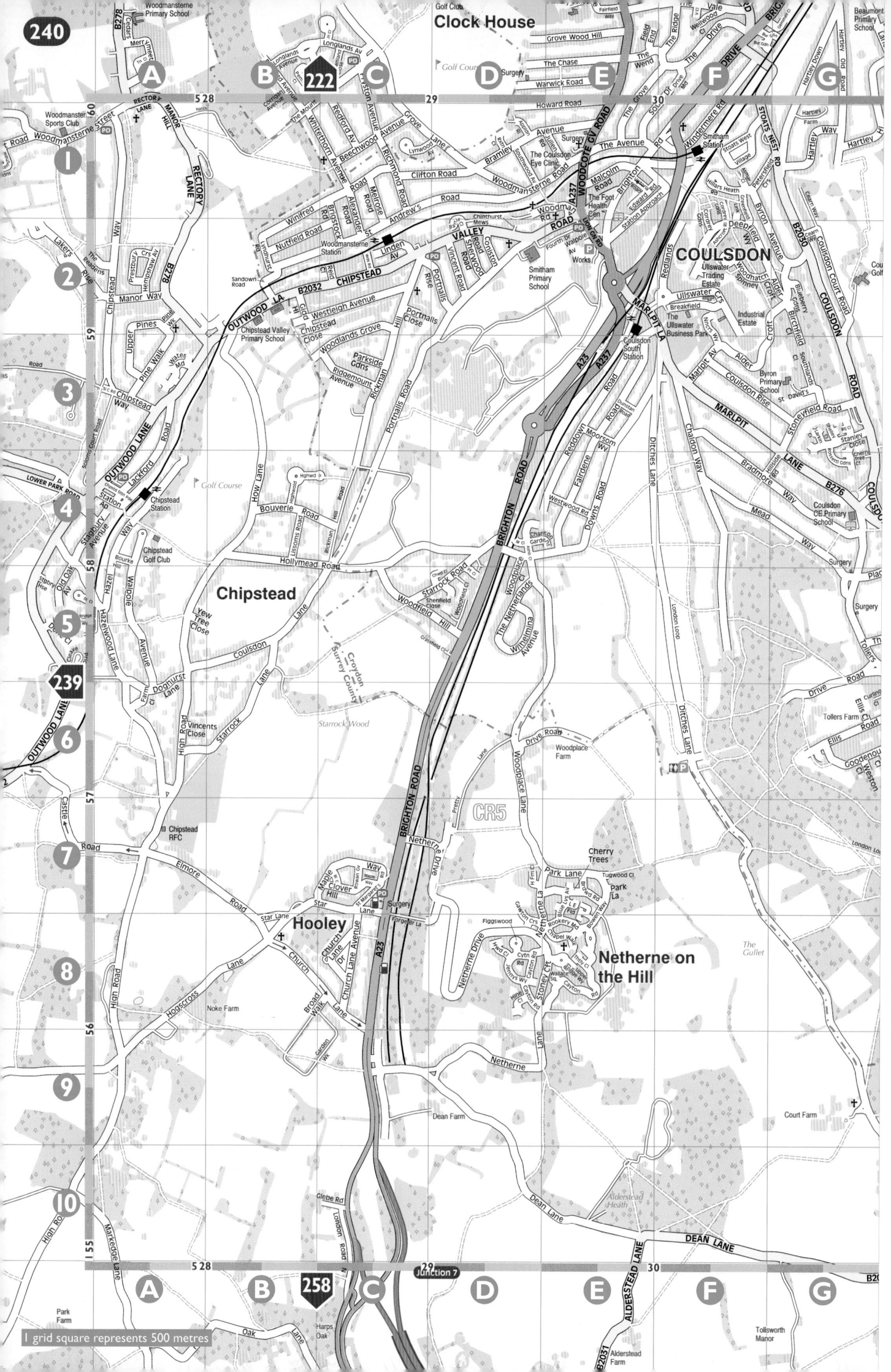
Clock House
Golf Club
Golf Course
222
Woodmansterne Primary School
Woodmansterne Sports Club
Woodmansterne Street
Rectory Lane
Manor Hill
Longlands Avenue
Longlands Av
Fyston Avenue
Redford Av
Whitethorn Avenue
Beechwood Avenue
Richmond Road
Lynwood Av
Grove Lane
Clifton Road
Grove Wood Hill
The Chase
Warwick Road
Howard Road
Woodcote Gv Road
Field End
The Ridge
The Wend
The Grove
The Drive
Brighton Road
Windermere Rd
Smitham Station
Stoats Nest Rd
Hartley Down
Hartley Old Road
Hartley Farm
Hartley Way
Beaumont Primary School
The Avenue
Bramley Avenue
Surgery
The Coulsdon Eye Clinic
Woodmansterne Road
Malcolm Road
The Foot Health Cen
Edward Rd
Station Approach
Winifred Rd
Nutfield Road
Brigstock Rd
Alexander Road
Melrose Road
St Andrew's Road
Woodmansterne Station
Linden Av
Chinthurst Mews
Valley Road
Vincent Road
Sherwood Road
Coniston Road
Fourth Dr
Walpole Av
Works
Smitham Primary School
COULSDON
Ullswater Trading Estate
Ullswater Crs
Breakfield
The Ullswater Business Park
Industrial Estate
Byron Avenue
Deepfield Wy
Woodhatch Spinney
Alder Croft
Hillars Heath Rd
Coulsdon Court Road
B2030
Bluebury Gdns
Birchfield Cl
Southlands
Byron Primary School
Coulsdon Rise
St David's
Stoneyfield Road
Marlpit Lane
Marlpit La
Marlpit Av
Coulsdon South Station
Chaldon Way
Bradmore Way
Mead Way
B276
Coulsdon CE Primary School
Stanley Close
Cherry Tree Ct
Lakers Rise
The Readens
Chipstead Way
Prestbury Crs
Hempshaw Av
B278
Manor Way
Upper Pines
Pine Walk
Pine Wk
Water Md
Sandown Road
Outwood La
B2032 Chipstead Valley Road
Chipstead Valley Primary School
Westleigh Avenue
Chipstead Close
Woodlands Grove
Parkside Gdns
Ridgemount Avenue
Rickman Hill
Portnalls Rise
Portnalls Close
Portnalls Road
A23
A237
Redlands
Ditches Lane
Dunstan Road
Moorsom Wy
Reddown Road
Fairdene Road
Downs Road
Westwood Rd
Chanton Gardens
Outwood Lane
Lackford Road
Chipstead Station
Lower Park Road
Stagbury Avenue
Chipstead Golf Club
Bourke Hill
Hazel Way
Walpole Avenue
Bouverie Road
Lissoms Road
Highwold
Hollymead Road
Chipstead
Starrock Road
Woodfield Hill
Woodfield Cl
Shenfield Close
Grassfield Cl
Woodplace Cl
The Netherlands
Whitelmina Avenue
London Loop
Yew Tree Close
How Lane
Coulsdon Lane
Hazelwood Lane
239
Outwood Lane
Doghurst Lane
Vincents Close
Starrock Lane
High Road
Starrock Wood
Croydon
Surrey County
Woodplace Lane
Drive Road
Woodplace Farm
Pretty Lane
CR5
Tollers Farm
Ellis Rd
Goodenough Cl
Weston
Drive Road
Surgery
Castle Road
Chipstead RFC
Elmore Road
Star Lane
Netherne Drive
Maple Way
Clover Hill
Rowan Gv
St Margaret's
Forge Br La
Hooley
Church Lane Avenue
Church Lane Dr
Church Lane
Cherry Trees
Park Lane
Tugwood Cl
Park La
Figgswood
Gawton Crs
Netherne La
Rookery Md
Bowen Way
Chapel Way
Netherne on the Hill
Cayton Rd
Stoney Cft
Hine Cl
The Gullet
Noke Farm
Hogscross Lane
Broad Walk
Garden Wk
Netherne Lane
Dean Farm
Court Farm
Glebe Rd
London Road
Alderstead Heath
Dean Lane
DEAN LANE
Markedge Lane
High Road
258
Junction 7
Alderstead Lane
B2031
Alderstead Farm
Park Farm
Oak Lane
Harps Oak
Tollsworth Manor
1 grid square represents 500 metres
A B C D E F G
1 2 3 4 5 6 7 8 9 10
528 29 30
60 59 58 57 56 155

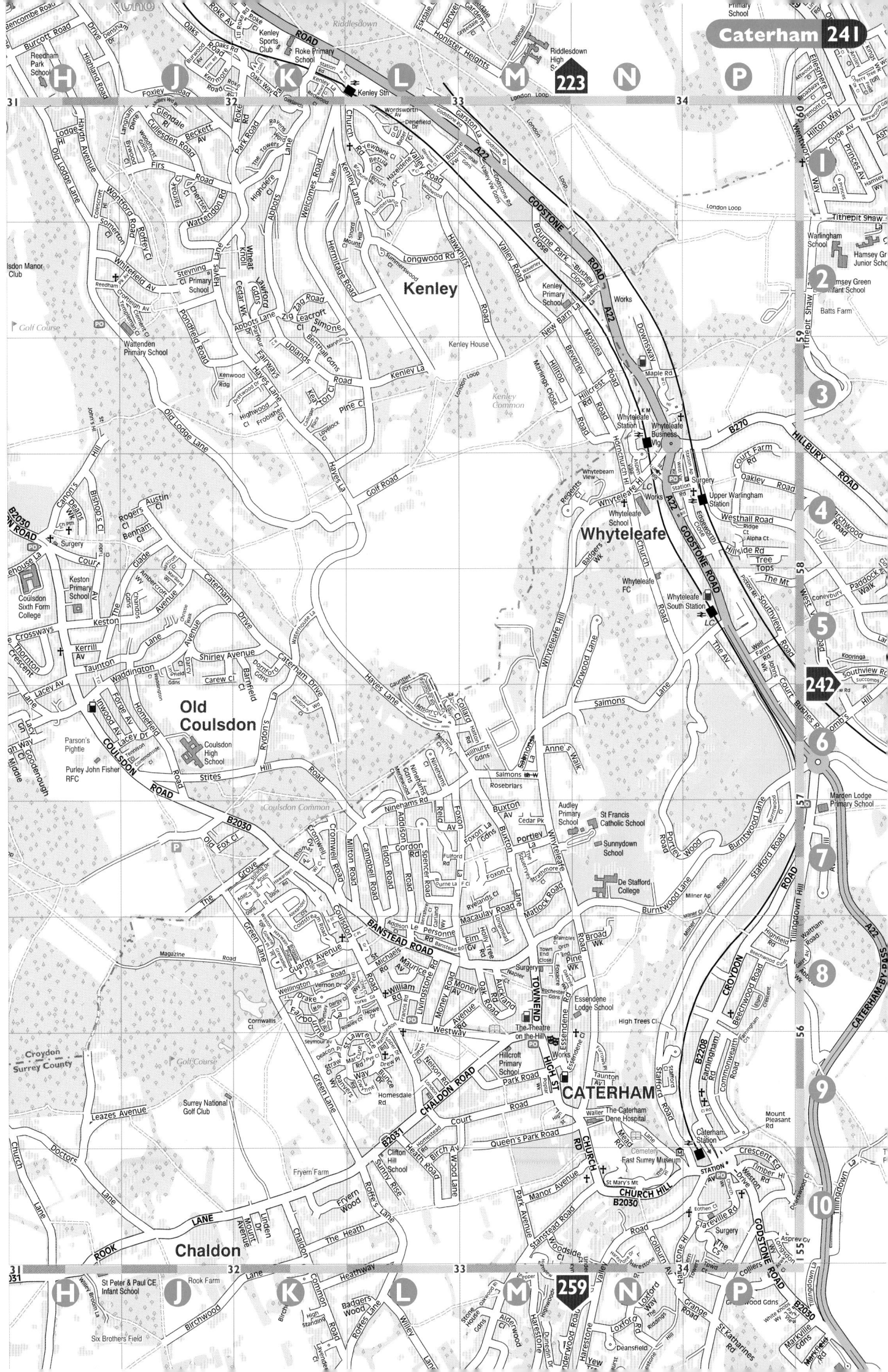
H
J
K
L
M
N
P
223
242
259
31
32
33
34
1
2
3
4
5
6
7
8
9
10
55
56
57
58
59
60
Kenley
Whyteleafe
Old Coulsdon
CATERHAM
Chaldon
Riddlesdown
GODSTONE ROAD
A22
CATERHAM-BY-PASS
CROYDON ROAD
COULSDON ROAD
B2030
B2031
B270
B2208
HILLBURY ROAD
BANSTEAD ROAD
CHALDON ROAD
CHURCH HILL
HIGH ST
TOWNEND
ROOK LANE
Kenley Stn
Kenley Sports Club
Roke Primary School
Riddlesdown High Sch
Reedham Park School
Warlingham School
Hamsey Green Junior School
Hamsey Green Infant School
Batts Farm
Kenley Primary School
Kenley House
Kenley Common
Whyteleafe Station
Whyteleafe Business Vlg
Upper Warlingham Station
Whyteleafe School
Whyteleafe FC
Whyteleafe South Station
Wattenden Primary School
Steyning Cl Primary School
Keston Primary School
Coulsdon Sixth Form College
Coulsdon High School
Parson's Pightle
Purley John Fisher RFC
Coulsdon Common
Audley Primary School
St Francis Catholic School
Sunnydown School
De Stafford College
Marden Lodge Primary School
Essendene Lodge School
The Theatre on the Hill
Hillcroft Primary School
Clifton Hill School
The Caterham Dene Hospital
East Surrey Museum
Caterham Station
Surrey National Golf Club
Fryern Farm
Rook Farm
St Peter & Paul CE Infant School
Six Brothers Field
Croydon
Surrey County
Golf Course
London Loop
Works
Surgery
Cemetery

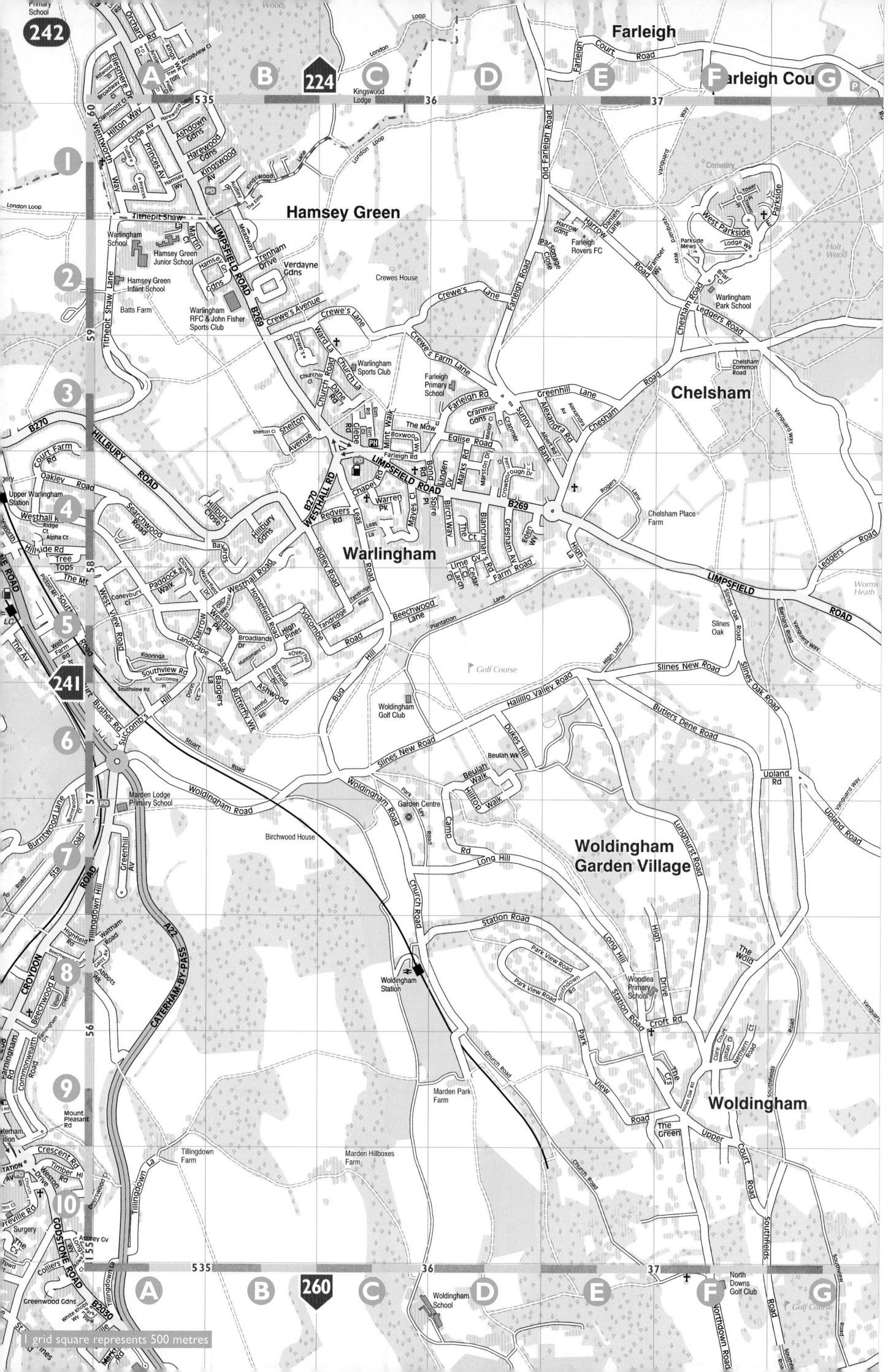
242
224
260
241
Farleigh
Farleigh Court Road
Hamsey Green
Warlingham
Chelsham
Woldingham Garden Village
Woldingham
Limpsfield Road
B269
B270
Westhall Rd
Hillbury Road
Croydon Road
Godstone Road
B2030
A22
Caterham-By-Pass
Old Farleigh Road
Farleigh Road
Crewe's Lane
Crewe's Avenue
Crewe's Farm Lane
Crewes House
Chelsham Road
Ledgers Road
Greenhill Lane
Slines New Road
Slines Oak Road
Halliloo Valley Road
Butlers Dene Road
Woldingham Road
Church Road
Station Road
Long Hill
Lunghurst Road
Upland Rd
Upper Court Road
Southfields Road
Northdown Road
Vanguard Way
London Loop
Tithepit Shaw Lane
Warlingham School
Hamsey Green Junior School
Hamsey Green Infant School
Warlingham RFC & John Fisher Sports Club
Warlingham Sports Club
Farleigh Primary School
Farleigh Rovers FC
Warlingham Park School
Chelsham Common Road
Chelsham Place Farm
Slines Oak
Worms Heath
Holt Wood
Golf Course
Woldingham Golf Club
Garden Centre
Marden Lodge Primary School
Birchwood House
Woldingham Station
Woodlea Primary School
Marden Park Farm
Marden Hillboxes Farm
Tillingdown Farm
Woldingham School
North Downs Golf Club
Upper Warlingham Station
Batts Farm
Kingswood Lodge
1 grid square represents 500 metres

Fickleshole
Titsey
Ledgers Farm
Chelsham Court Farm
Beech Farm
Beddlestead Farm
Cheverells Farm
Skid Hill Farm
Clarks Lane Farm
Titsey Place
Pilgrims Farm
Lusted Hall Farm
Oaklands Junior School
Oaklands Infant Sch
Biggin Hill Business Park
Church Lane
Hesiers Road
Hesiers Hill
Chelsham Court Road
Beddlestead Lane
Beech Farm Road
B269 CROYDON ROAD
B2024 CLARKS LANE
TITSEY HILL
Approach Road
White Lane
North Downs Way
Pilgrims Lane
Lusted Hall Lane
Skid Hill Lane
Fairchildes Road
Scotshall Lane
High
Hill Road
Washpond Lane
The Ridge
Pitchfont Lane
Vanguard Way
A233 MAIN ROAD
Surrey
Bromley
Flint House
Park Farm

225
244
261

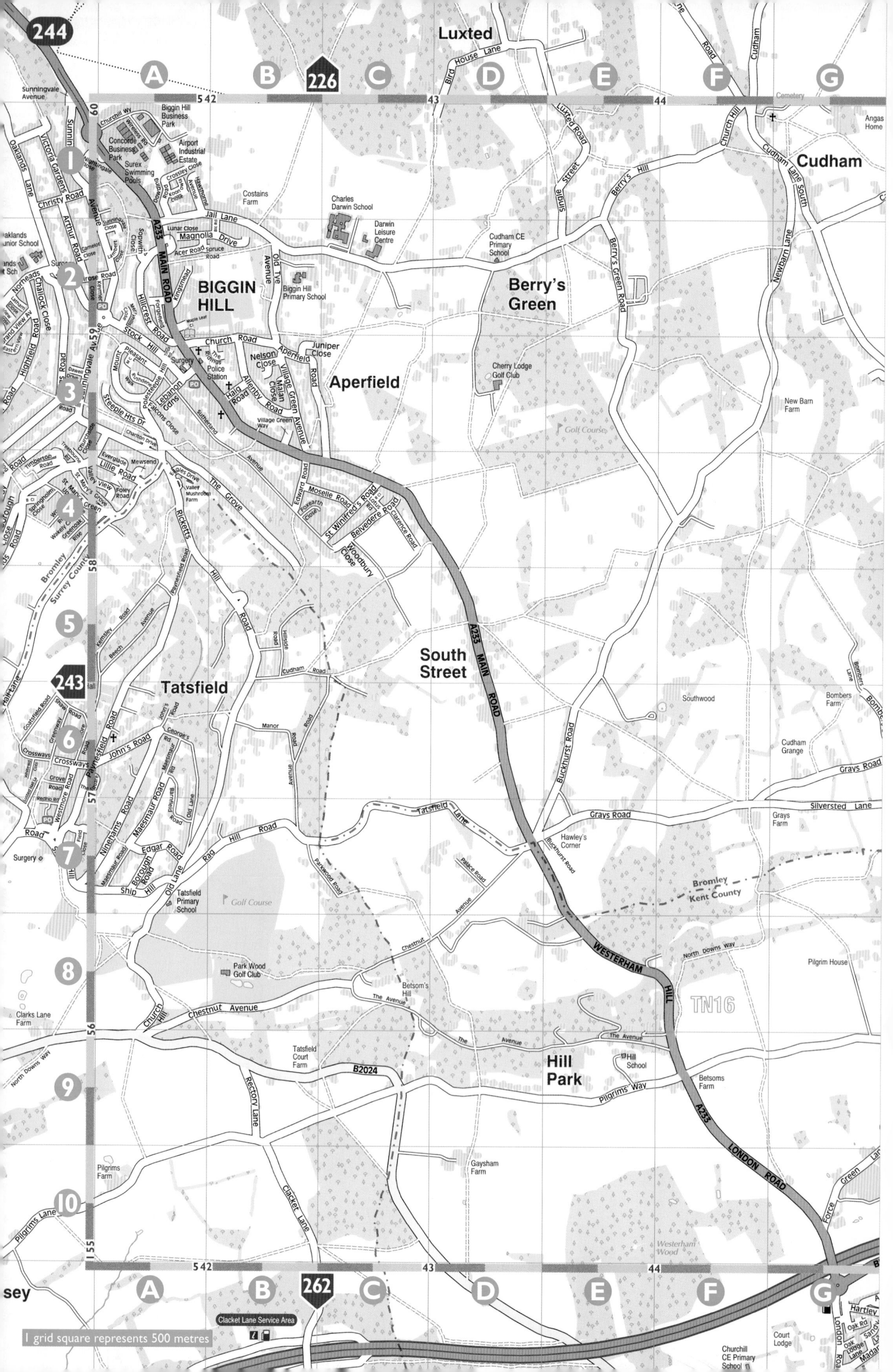

244

A   B   226   C   D   E   F   G

Luxted

Sunningvale
Avenue

5 42   43   44   Cemetery

Oaklands
Junior School   Biggin Hill
Business Park

Christy Road   Concorde
Business
Park   Airport Industrial
Estate   Angas
Home

Surex Swimming
Pools   Cudham

1

Costains
Farm

Cudham CE
Primary
School

Jail Lane

2   Magnolia   Charles
Darwin School   Berry's
Green

Acer Road Spruce
Road   Darwin Leisure
Centre

BIGGIN
HILL   Biggin Hill
Primary School   Cherry Lodge
Golf Club

Church Road   Juniper
Close

Surgery   Aperfield   Village Green

3   Police Station   Aperfield

Village Green
Way   New Barn
Farm

4   Moselle Road
St Winifred's Road   Golf Course

Valley Mushroom
Farm   Belvedere Road

Bromley
Surrey County   Woodbury
Close

5   South
Street   Southwood

243   Bombers
Farm

Tatsfield   Cudham   Road   Cudham
Grange

6   Crossways   Grays Road

Silversted Lane

Manor   Grays
Farm

7   Surgery   Tatsfield
Primary
School   Hawley's
Corner   Bromley
Kent County

Hill   Road   Westerham

8   Park Wood
Golf Club   North Downs Way   Pilgrim House

Clarks Lane
Farm   Betsom's
Hill   TN16

Chestnut Avenue   The Avenue   Hill
School

9   North Downs Way   Tatsfield
Court
Farm   B2024   Hill
Park   Betsoms
Farm

Rectory Lane   Pilgrims Way   LONDON ROAD

10   Pilgrims Lane   Pilgrims
Farm   Gaysham
Farm   Force Green Lane

Westerham
Wood

sey   A   B   262   C   D   E   F   G

5 42   43   44

Clacket Lane Service Area

1 grid square represents 500 metres   Churchill
CE Primary
School   Court
Lodge

Hartley
Oak Rd

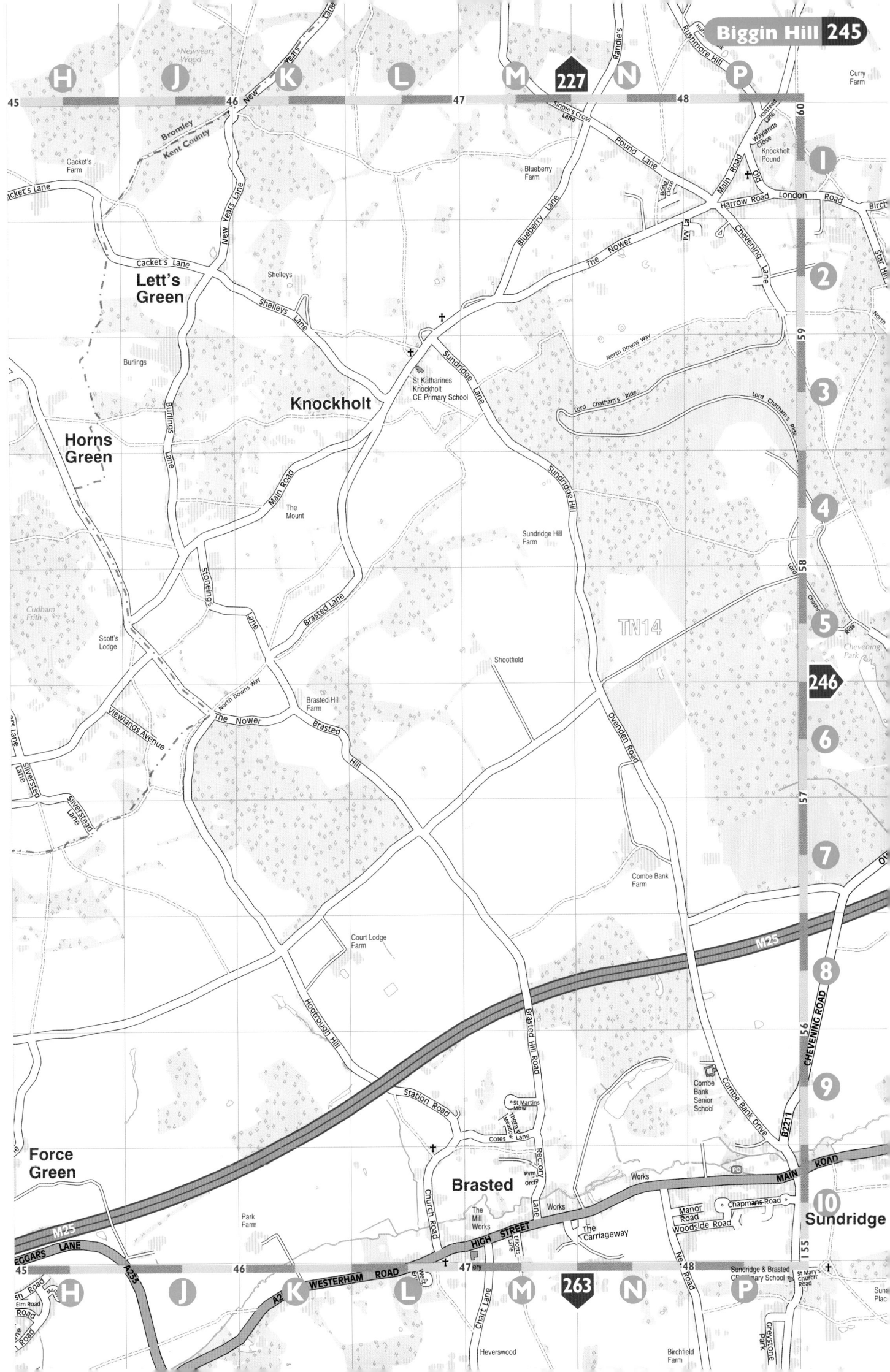
Lett's Green
Knockholt
Horns Green
Force Green
Brasted
Sundridge
TN14
227
246
263
Cacket's Lane
New Years Lane
Burlings Lane
Shelleys Lane
Main Road
Stonelings Lane
Brasted Lane
The Nower
North Downs Way
Viewlands Avenue
Silverstead Lane
Sundridge Lane
Sundridge Hill
Blueberry Lane
Pound Lane
Harrow Road
London Road
Chevening Lane
Lord Chatham's Ride
Ovenden Road
Brasted Hill
Hogtrough Hill
Brasted Hill Road
Station Road
Church Road
Coles Lane
Rectory Lane
High Street
Westerham Road
Beggars Lane
Combe Bank Drive
Chevening Road
Main Road
Chapmans Road
Woodside Road
Manor Road
The Carriageway
Chart Lane
M25
A25
A233
B2211
Cacket's Farm
Burlings
Shelleys
The Mount
Scott's Lodge
Cudham Frith
Brasted Hill Farm
Blueberry Farm
Sundridge Hill Farm
Shootfield
Combe Bank Farm
Court Lodge Farm
Park Farm
Combe Bank Senior School
St Katharines Knockholt CE Primary School
Knockholt Pound
Chevening Park
Curry Farm
Heverswood
Birchfield Farm
Newyears Wood
Bromley
Kent County
The Mill Works
Works
Sundridge & Brasted CE Primary School
Greystone Park
H J K L M N P
1 2 3 4 5 6 7 8 9 10
45 46 47 48
55 56 57 58 59 60

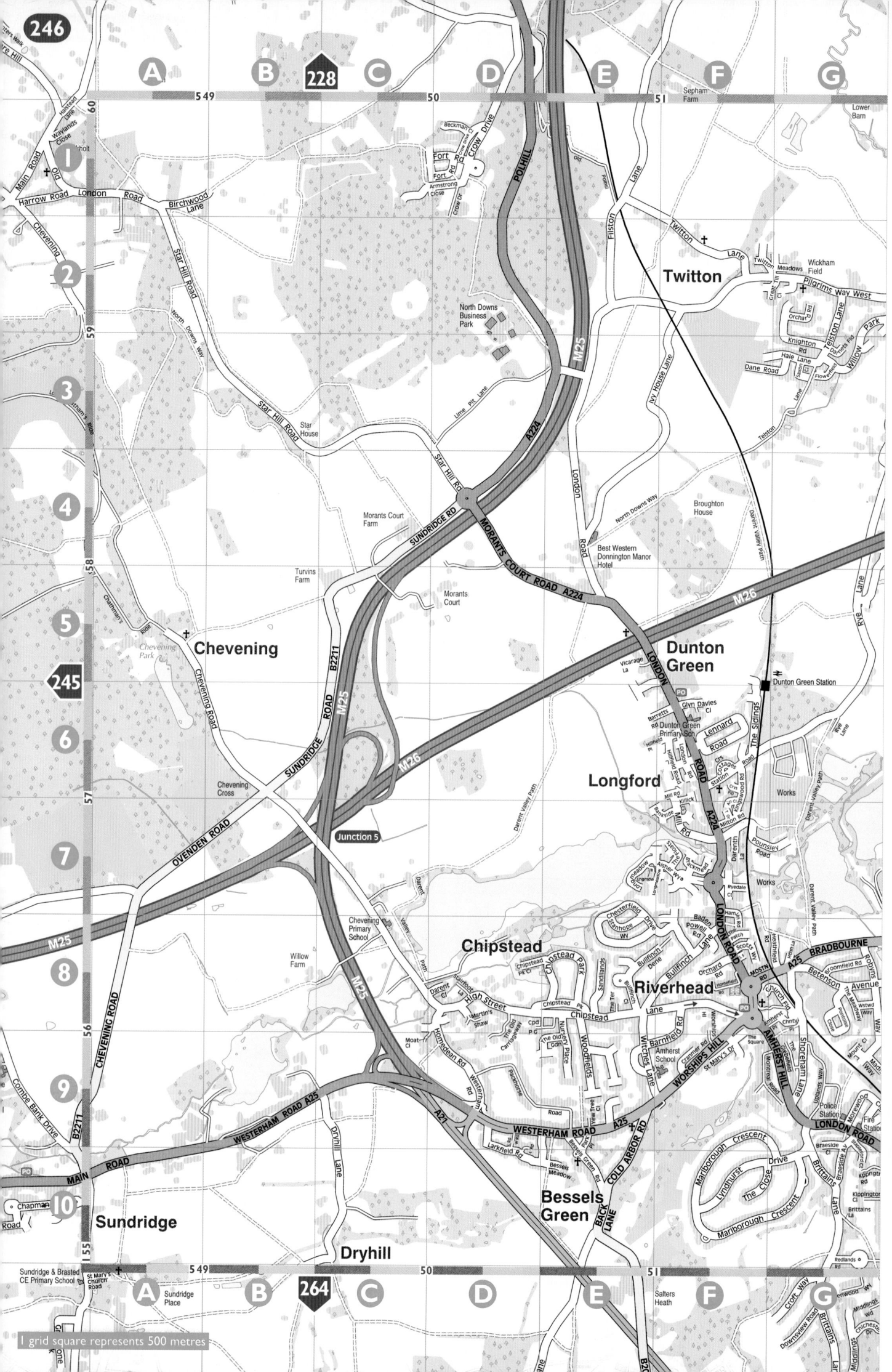
228
245
264
Twitton
Chevening
Dunton Green
Longford
Chipstead
Riverhead
Bessels Green
Sundridge
Dryhill
M25
M26
A224
A25
A21
B2211
Junction 5
North Downs Business Park
Star House
Morants Court Farm
Turvins Farm
Morants Court
Best Western Donnington Manor Hotel
Broughton House
Dunton Green Station
Dunton Green Primary Sch
Chevening Primary School
Willow Farm
Chevening Cross
Chevening Park
Sepham Farm
Lower Barn
Wickham Field
Amherst School
Police Station
Sundridge & Brasted CE Primary School
Sundridge Place
Salters Heath
1 grid square represents 500 metres

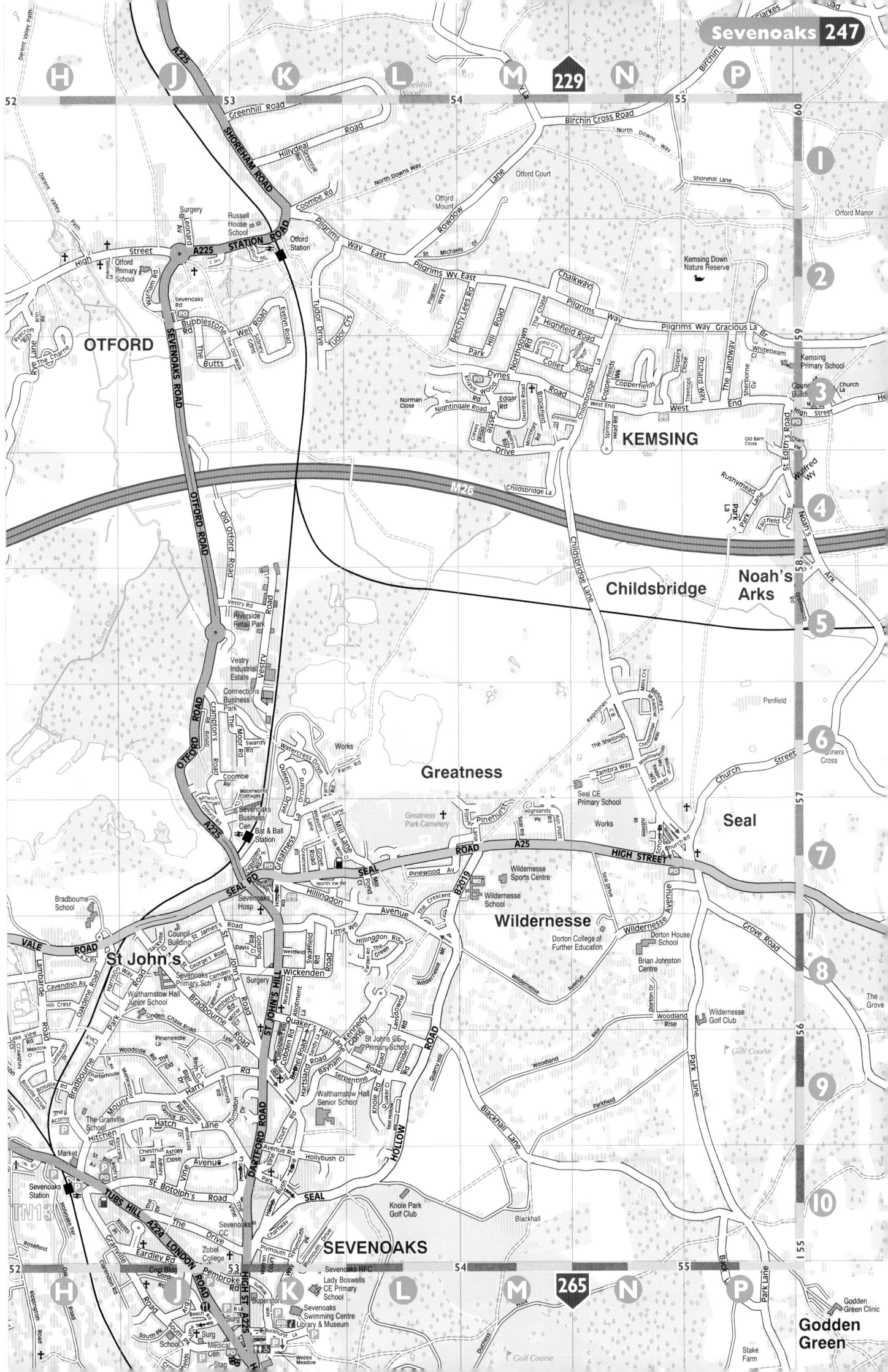
229
265
OTFORD
KEMSING
Childsbridge
Noah's Arks
Greatness
Seal
Wilderness
St John's
SEVENOAKS
Godden Green
TN13
M26
A225
A25
A224
B2019
Shoreham Road
Station Road
Sevenoaks Road
Otford Road
Seal Road
Vale Road
Tubs Hill
London Road
High St
St John's Hill
Dartford Road
Hollow Road
High Street
Pilgrims Way East
Pilgrims Way
Birchin Cross Road
North Downs Way
Rowdow Lane
Greenhill Road
Hillydeal Rd
Coombe Rd
Childsbridge Lane
Church Street
Grove Road
Park Lane
Blackhall Lane
Wildernesse Avenue
Woodland Rise
Otford Station
Bat & Ball Station
Sevenoaks Station
Otford Primary School
Russell House School
Kemsing Primary School
Kemsing Down Nature Reserve
Seal CE Primary School
Wildernesse Sports Centre
Wildernesse School
Dorton House School
Dorton College of Further Education
Brian Johnston Centre
Wildernesse Golf Club
Knole Park Golf Club
Greatness Park Cemetery
Riverside Retail Park
Vestry Industrial Estate
Connections Business Park
Sevenoaks Business Cen
Sevenoaks Hosp
Bradbourne School
Sevenoaks Primary Sch
Walthamstow Hall Junior School
Walthamstow Hall Senior School
St John's CE Primary School
The Granville School
Sevenoaks RFC
Lady Boswells CE Primary School
Sevenoaks Swimming Centre
Library & Museum
Otford Court
Otford Mount
Otford Manor
Penfield
Blackhall
Stake Farm
Godden Green Clinic
Works
Golf Course
River Darent
Darent Valley Path

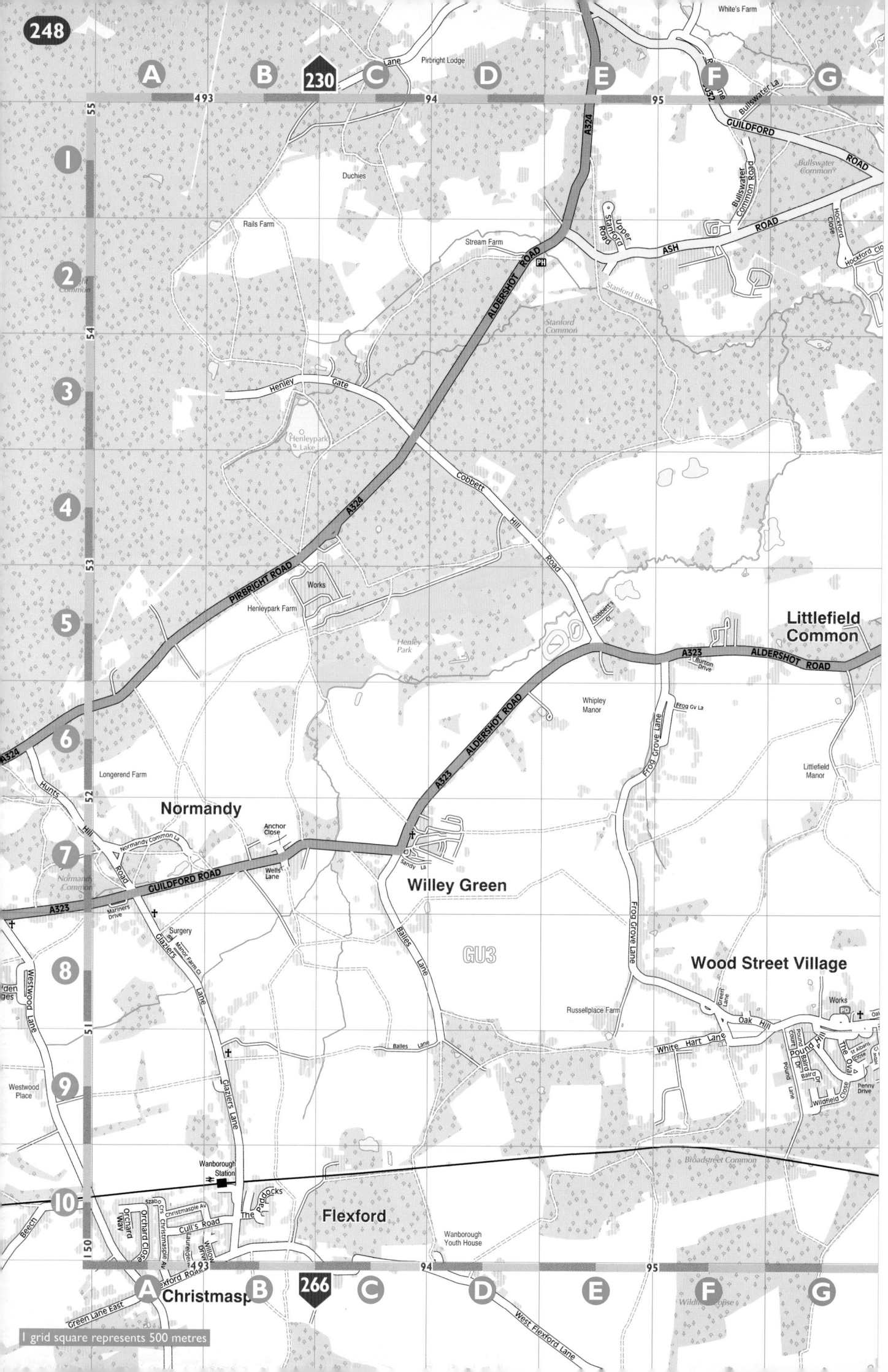

230
266
Pirbright Lodge
White's Farm
Duchies
Rails Farm
Stream Farm
Bullswater Common
Stanford Common
Stanford Brook
Henleypark Lake
Henley Gate
Cobbett Hill Road
ALDERSHOT ROAD
PIRBRIGHT ROAD
A324
GUILDFORD ROAD
ASH ROAD
Upper Stanford Road
Bullswater Common Road
Hockford Close
Works
Henleypark Farm
Henley Park
Littlefield Common
A323
ALDERSHOT ROAD
Burton Drive
Frog Gv La
Frog Grove Lane
Whipley Manor
Littlefield Manor
Longerend Farm
Normandy
Anchor Close
Normandy Common La
Hunts Hill Road
Wells Lane
Normandy Common
Mariners Drive
Surgery
Glaziers Lane
Manor Farm Cl
Willey Green
Sandy La
Balles Lane
GU3
Wood Street Village
Russellplace Farm
Green Lane
Oak Hill
White Hart Lane
Pound Court
Pound Hill
Baird Dr
Pound Lane
The Oval
St Albans Close
Penny Drive
Wildfield Close
Works
Westwood Lane
Westwood Place
Wanborough Station
The Paddocks
Broadstreet Common
Flexford
Wanborough Youth House
Orchard Way
Orchard Close
Christmaspie Av
Cull's Road
Willow Drive
Flexford Road
Christmaspie
Green Lane East
Beech
West Flexford Lane
Wilding Copse
1 grid square represents 500 metres

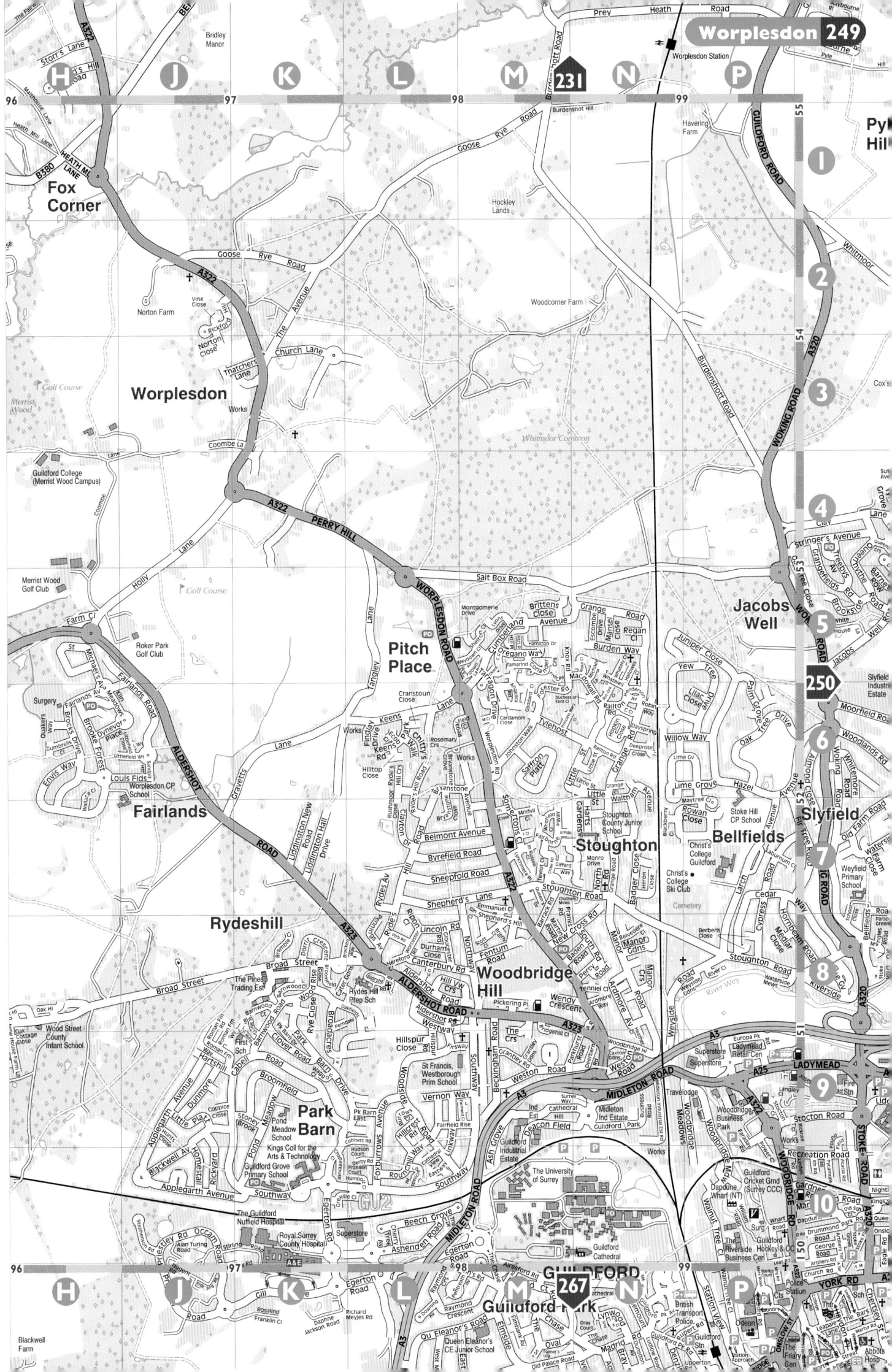
Fox Corner
Worplesdon
Pitch Place
Jacobs Well
Fairlands
Stoughton
Bellfields
Slyfield
Rydeshill
Woodbridge Hill
Park Barn
GUILDFORD
Guildford Park
Worplesdon Station
Hockley Lands
Woodcorner Farm
Whitmoor Common
Norton Farm
Bridley Manor
Havering Farm
Guildford College (Merrist Wood Campus)
Merrist Wood Golf Club
Roker Park Golf Club
Golf Course
Worplesdon CP School
Stoughton County Junior School
Christ's College Guildford
Christ's College Ski Club
Stoke Hill CP School
Weyfield Primary School
Wood Street County Infant School
St Francis, Westborough Prim School
Pond Meadow School
Kings Coll for the Arts & Technology
Guildford Grove Primary School
The Guildford Nuffield Hospital
Royal Surrey County Hospital
The University of Surrey
Guildford Cathedral
Guildford Industrial Estate
Midleton Ind Estate
Guildford Cricket Grnd (Surrey CCC)
Dapdune Wharf (NT)
The Riverside Business Cen
Woodbridge Business Park
Ladymead Retail Cen
Queen Eleanor's CE Junior School
British Transport Police
Guildford Stn
Odeon
Police Station
Abbots Hosp
River Wey
Cemetery
A322
A323
A320
A3
A25
B380
GUILDFORD ROAD
WOKING ROAD
PERRY HILL
WORPLESDON ROAD
ALDERSHOT ROAD
MIDLETON ROAD
WOODBRIDGE RD
STOKE ROAD
YORK RD
LADYMEAD
Goose Rye Road
Salt Box Road
Burdenshott Road
Prey Heath Road
Holly Lane
Broad Street
Stoughton Road
Southway
Applegarth Avenue
Egerton Road
GU2
231
250
267

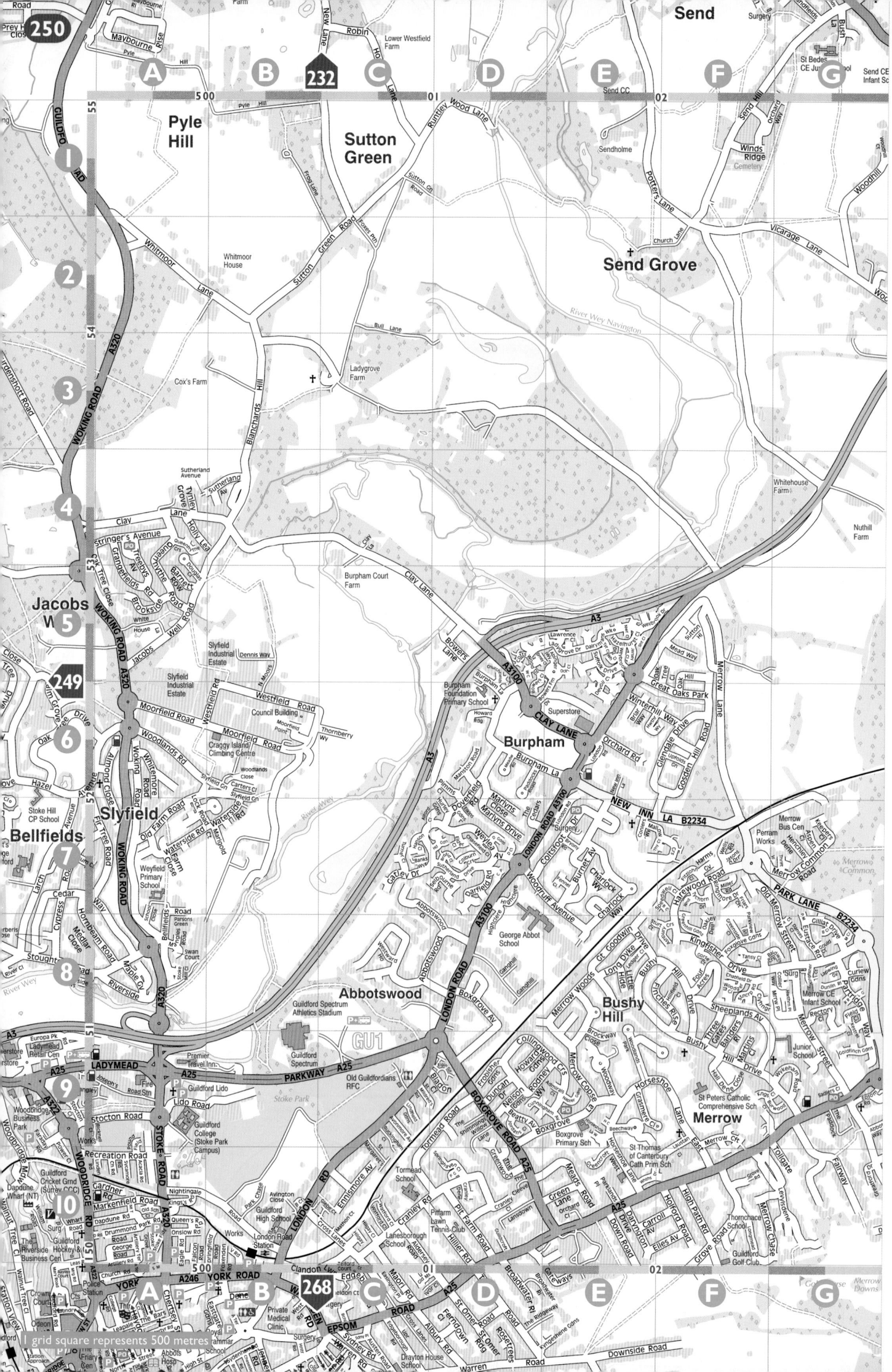
250
232
249
268
A
B
C
D
E
F
G
1
2
3
4
5
6
7
8
9
10
500
01
02
55
54
53
52
51
150
Send
Surgery
Maybourne Rise
Pyle Hill
Robin Hood Lane
New Lane
Lower Westfield Farm
St Bedes CE Junior School
Send CE Infant School
Send CC
Bush La
Pyle Hill
Sutton Green
Runtley Wood Lane
Sendholme
Send Hill
Orchard Way
Winds Ridge
Cemetery
Woodhill
Guildford Road
Frog Lane
Sutton Gn Road
Potter's Lane
Church Lane
Vicarage Lane
Whitmoor Lane
Whitmoor House
Sutton Green Road
Foxes Pth
Send Grove
River Wey Navigation
Bull Lane
Ladygrove Farm
Cox's Farm
Blanchards Hill
Woking Road
A320
Sutherland Avenue
Sutherland Av
Tynley Grove
Clay Lane
Holly Lea
Whitehouse Farm
Nuthill Farm
Stringer's Avenue
Treebys Av
Grangefields Rd
Barnett Row
Brookside
Well Road
Burpham Court Farm
Clay Lane
Jacobs Well
Jacobs Well Road
Oak Tree Close
A3
Bowers Lane
Lawrence
Slyfield Industrial Estate
Dennis Way
Mead Way
Sutton Hl
Burpham Foundation Primary School
Great Oaks Park
Westfield Road
Council Building
Moorfield Road
Moorfield Point
Thornberry Wy
Westfield Rd
Woodlands Rd
Craggy Island Climbing Centre
Superstore
Clay Lane
Orchard Rd
Winterhill Way
Merrow Lane
Glendale Drive
Gosden Hill Road
Burpham
Burpham La
Slyfield Gn
Carters Cl
Woodlands Close
Almond Close
Whitemore Road
Hazel Avenue
Stoke Hill CP School
Slyfield
Bellfields
Old Farm Road
Lock Road
Waterside Rd
Waterside Cl
Marigold
River Wey
Manston Road
Doverfield Rd
Marlyns Close
Marlyns Drive
The Cedars
London Road A3100
New Inn La B2234
Surgery
Coltsfoot Dr
Burnet Av
Charlock Way
Merrow Bus Cen
Perram Works
Merrow Common Road
Merrow Common
Keepers
Weyfield Primary School
Farm Close
Fir Tree Road
Larch
Cedar
Cypress Road
Medlar Close
Hornbeam Road
Gateley Dr
Sutherland Drive
Garfield Rd
Weylea Av
Highclere
Woodruff Avenue
Charlock Way
Harewood Road
Old Merrow Street
Park Lane B2234
Gilliat Drive
Abbotswood
Abbotswood Cl
Westward Ho
George Abbot School
Ganghill
Gt Goodwin Drive
Long Dyke
Little Hide
Bushy Hill Drive
Kingfisher Drive
Foxglove Gdns
Bellfields Road
Parsons Green
Swan Court
Maple Gv
Riverside
Stoughton Road
River Wey
Abbotswood
London Road
Boxgrove Av
Merrow Woods
Bushy Hill
Four Acres
Sheeplands Av
Merrow CE Infant School
Curlew Gdns
Partridge Way
Guildford Spectrum Athletics Stadium
Guildford Spectrum
GU1
Collingwood Crs
Howard Gdns
Merrow Copse
Three Gates
Bushy Hill Drive
Martins Cl
Merrow Street
Rectory Cl
Junior School
Europa Pk
Ladymead Retail Cen
Ladymead
Premier Travel Inn
Parkway A25
Old Guildfordians RFC
Bladon Cl
Froxfield Gdns
Duncan Dr
Nelson Cl
Rodney Wy
Woodway
Horseshoe Lane
Wykeham Road
A25
Joseph's Road
Fire Stn
Guildford Lido
Lido Road
Stoke Park
Boxgrove Road A25
Boxgrove
Boxgrove Primary Sch
Beechway
Grasmere Cl
St Peters Catholic Comprehensive Sch
Merrow
A322
Stocton Road
Stoke Road
Guildford College (Stoke Park Campus)
Tormead Road
St Thomas of Canterbury Cath Prim Sch
Horseshoe Lane West
East Merrow Cft
Tollgate
Fairway
Woodbridge Business Park
Works
Recreation Road
Woodbridge Road
Ennismore Av
Tormead School
Greenwood
Cranley Cleeve
Green Lane
Meads Road
Guildford Cricket Grnd (Surrey CCC)
Dapdune Wharf (NT)
Gardner Road
Markenfield Road
Nightingale Road
Park Chase
Avington Close
Guildford High School
Cranley Rd
Pitfarm Lawn Tennis Club
Pit Farm Road
Lansdown
Orchard Cl
Drive
Down Road
Carroll Av
Hofford Road
High Path Rd
Elles Av
Grove Road
Thornchace School
Merrow Chase
Guildford Golf Club
Dapdune Rd
Surg
Guildford Hockey & Lawn Tennis Club
Drummond Road
Park Rd
Queen's Rd
Onslow Rd
George Road
Artillery Rd
Eagle Rd
Works
London Road Station
Lanesborough School
Cross Lanes
Hillier Rd
The Riverside Business Cen
Walnut Tree Cl
Police Station
York Road A246
Dene
Private Medical Clinic
Epsom Road
Clandon Rd
Maori Rd
Albury Rd
Ferndown Cl
St Omer Road
St Omer Rdg
Broadwater Rl
Gateways
The Ridgeway
Rosetrees
Road
Golf Course
Merrow Downs
Crown Court
Odeon
Station View
Station Approach
Surgery
Sydney Rd
Warren Rd
Drayton House School
Warren Road
Downside Road
Abbots Hosp
High St
Royal Grammar School
1 grid square represents 500 metres

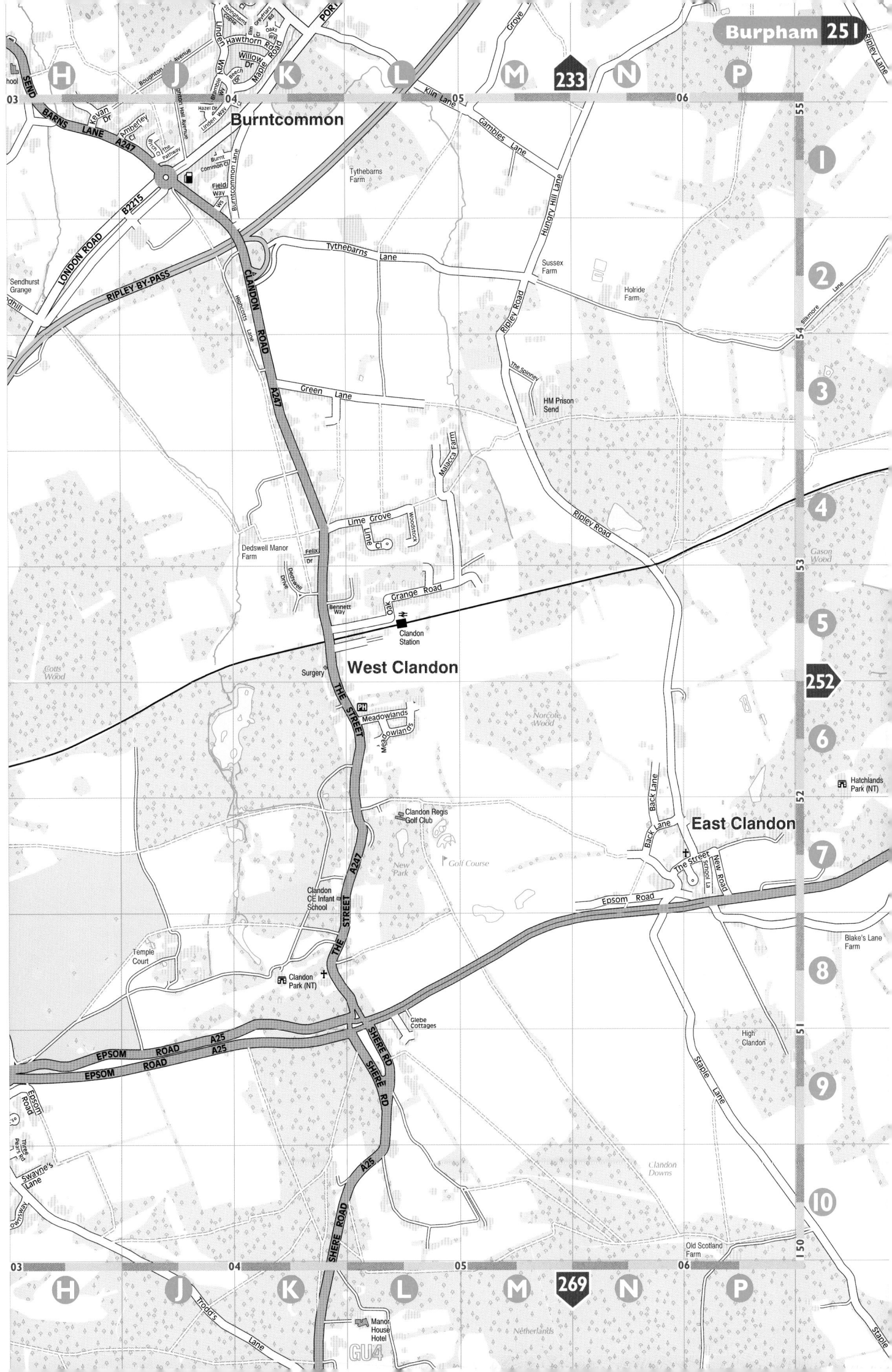

Burntcommon
West Clandon
East Clandon
Clandon Station
Tythebarns Farm
Sussex Farm
Holride Farm
HM Prison Send
Dedswell Manor Farm
Sendhurst Grange
Cotts Wood
Norcote Wood
Gason Wood
Clandon Regis Golf Club
Golf Course
New Park
Clandon CE Infant School
Temple Court
Clandon Park (NT)
Glebe Cottages
Hatchlands Park (NT)
Blake's Lane Farm
High Clandon
Clandon Downs
Old Scotland Farm
Manor House Hotel
Netherlands
Surgery
Tythebarns Lane
Green Lane
Hungry Hill Lane
Ripley Road
Gambles Lane
Kiln Lane
Grange Road
Lime Grove
Lime Cl
Woodstock
Malacca Farm
The Spinney
Highcotts Lane
Dedswell Drive
Felix Dr
Bennett Way
Oak
Meadowlands
CLANDON ROAD
A247
THE STREET
RIPLEY BY-PASS
LONDON ROAD
B2215
SEND BARNS LANE
Kevan Dr
Amberley Cl
Birch Cl
The Pathway
Burnt Common Cl
Field Way
Burntcommon Lane
Boughton Hall Avenue
Hawthorn Road
Willow Dr
Maple Road
Linden Way
Brambie Wy
Hazel Dr
Linden Way
EPSOM ROAD
A25
Epsom Road
SHERE RD
SHERE ROAD
Back Lane
The Street
School La
New Road
Staple Lane
Slikmore Lane
Ripley Lane
Swayne's Lane
Trodd's Lane
Grove
GU4
233
252
269
H J K L M N P
03 04 05 06
55 54 53 52 51 50
1 2 3 4 5 6 7 8 9 10

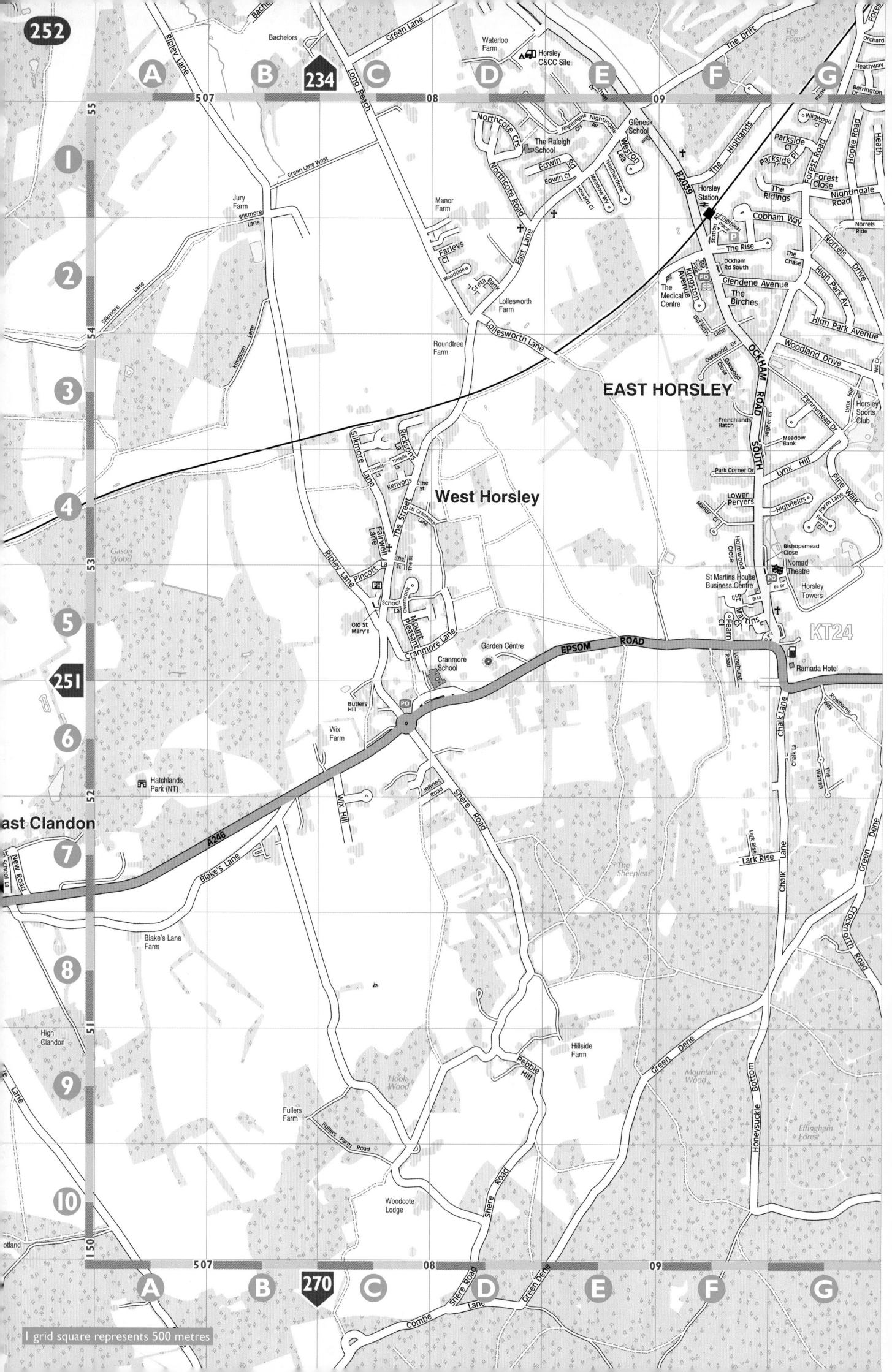

EAST HORSLEY
West Horsley
East Clandon
KT24
Horsley Station
Horsley C&CC Site
Waterloo Farm
Bachelors
Green Lane
Long Reach
Ripley Lane
Jury Farm
Silkmore Lane
Kingston Lane
Green Lane West
Manor Farm
Farleys Cl
Northcote Crs
Northcote Road
The Raleigh School
Edwin Rd
East Lane
Glenesk School
Weston Lea
The Highlands
B2039
The Drift
Lollesworth Farm
Lollesworth Lane
Roundtree Farm
Cobham Way
Station Parade
The Rise
Ockham Rd South
Kingston Avenue
The Medical Centre
Glendene Avenue
The Birches
High Park Avenue
Woodland Drive
Forest Road
Nightingale Road
Norrels Drive
OCKHAM ROAD SOUTH
Pennymead Dr
Lynx Hill
Horsley Sports Club
Frenchlands Hatch
Meadow Bank
Park Corner Dr
Lower Peryers
Highfields
Pine Walk
Farm Lane
Bishopsmead Close
Nomad Theatre
Horsley Towers
St Martins House Business Centre
Ramada Hotel
EPSOM ROAD
Garden Centre
Cranmore School
Cranmore Lane
Mount Pleasant
The Street
Ricksons La
Kenyons
Fairwell Lane
Pincott La
Old St Mary's
Gason Wood
Butlers Hill
Wix Farm
Wix Hill
Jeffries Road
Shere Road
Hatchlands Park (NT)
A246
Blake's Lane
Blake's Lane Farm
Chalk Lane
Lark Rise
The Sheepleas
Green Dene
Crocknorth Road
High Clandon
Hillside Farm
Pebble Hill
Hook Wood
Fullers Farm
Fullers Farm Road
Mountain Wood
Honeysuckle Bottom
Effingham Forest
Woodcote Lodge
Combe Lane
1 grid square represents 500 metres

234
251
270

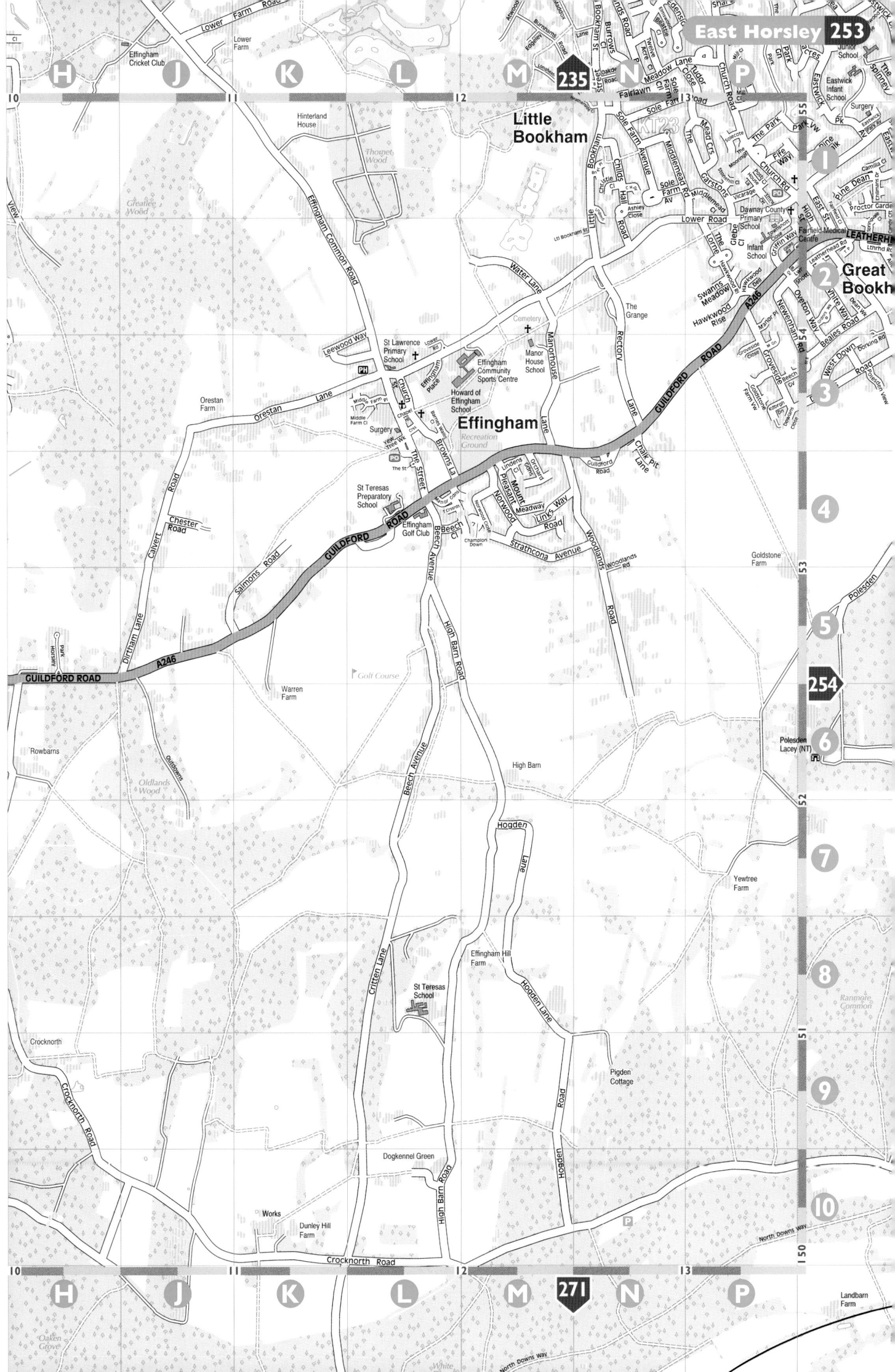

East Horsley 253
235
254
271
H
J
K
L
M
N
P
1
2
3
4
5
6
7
8
9
10
Little Bookham
Effingham
Great Bookham
Lower Farm Road
Lower Farm
Effingham Cricket Club
Hinterland House
Thornet Wood
Greatlee Wood
Effingham Common Road
Orestan Farm
Orestan Lane
Leewood Way
St Lawrence Primary School
Effingham Place
Effingham Community Sports Centre
Howard of Effingham School
Manor House School
Manorhouse Lane
Cemetery
Water Lane
Little Bookham St
Lower Road
Rectory Lane
The Grange
Chalk Pit Lane
Recreation Ground
Church St
Chapel Cl
Middle Farm Cl
Middle Farm Pl
Surgery
Yew Tree Wk
PO
PH
The St
The Street
Browns La
Barnes Wallis Cl
St Teresas Preparatory School
Effingham Golf Club
GUILDFORD ROAD
A246
Beech Cl
Beech Avenue
Champion Down
Norwood
Pleasant
Mount
Meadway
Links Way
Road
Undens Cl
Orchard Gdns
Strathcona Avenue
Woodlands Road
Woodlands Rd
Guildford Road
Calvert Road
Chester Road
Salmons Road
Dirtham Lane
Park Horsley
Warren Farm
Golf Course
High Barn Road
High Barn
Rowbarns
Outdowns
Oldlands Wood
Beech Avenue
Hogden Lane
Hogden Road
Effingham Hill Farm
Critten Lane
St Teresas School
Yewtree Farm
Goldstone Farm
Polesden Lacey (NT)
Polesden
Ranmore Common
Crocknorth
Crocknorth Road
Pigden Cottage
Dogkennel Green
Works
Dunley Hill Farm
North Downs Way
Landbarn Farm
Oaken Grove
White
Sole Farm Avenue
Sole Farm Rd
Childs Hall Road
Christie Cl
Ashley Close
Middlemead Rd
Middlemead Cl
The Garstons
Mead Crs
Church Road
Church Rd
Fife Way
Vicarage
Dawnay County Primary School
Infant School
Glebe Cl
The Lorne
Hawkwood Rise
Hawkwood Dell
Swanns Meadow
Manor Gn
Groveside
Goldstone Farm Vw
Newenham Rd
Dowlans Close
Overton Way
Beales Road
West Down
Dorking Rd
Polesden View
White Way
Dean Wk
High St
East St
Fairfield Medical Centre
LEATHERHEAD
Leatherhead Rd
Lthrhd Rd
Pine Dean
Proctor Gardens
Camilla Cl
Eastwick Infant School
Junior School
Surgery
The Spinney
Eastwick
Fairlawn
Meadow Lane
Tudor Close
Burrows Cl
Bookham St
Beattie Cl
Merelands
Wells Cl
Acre Cl
Oakdene Road
Burnhams Rd
Lane
KT23
Calvert
View

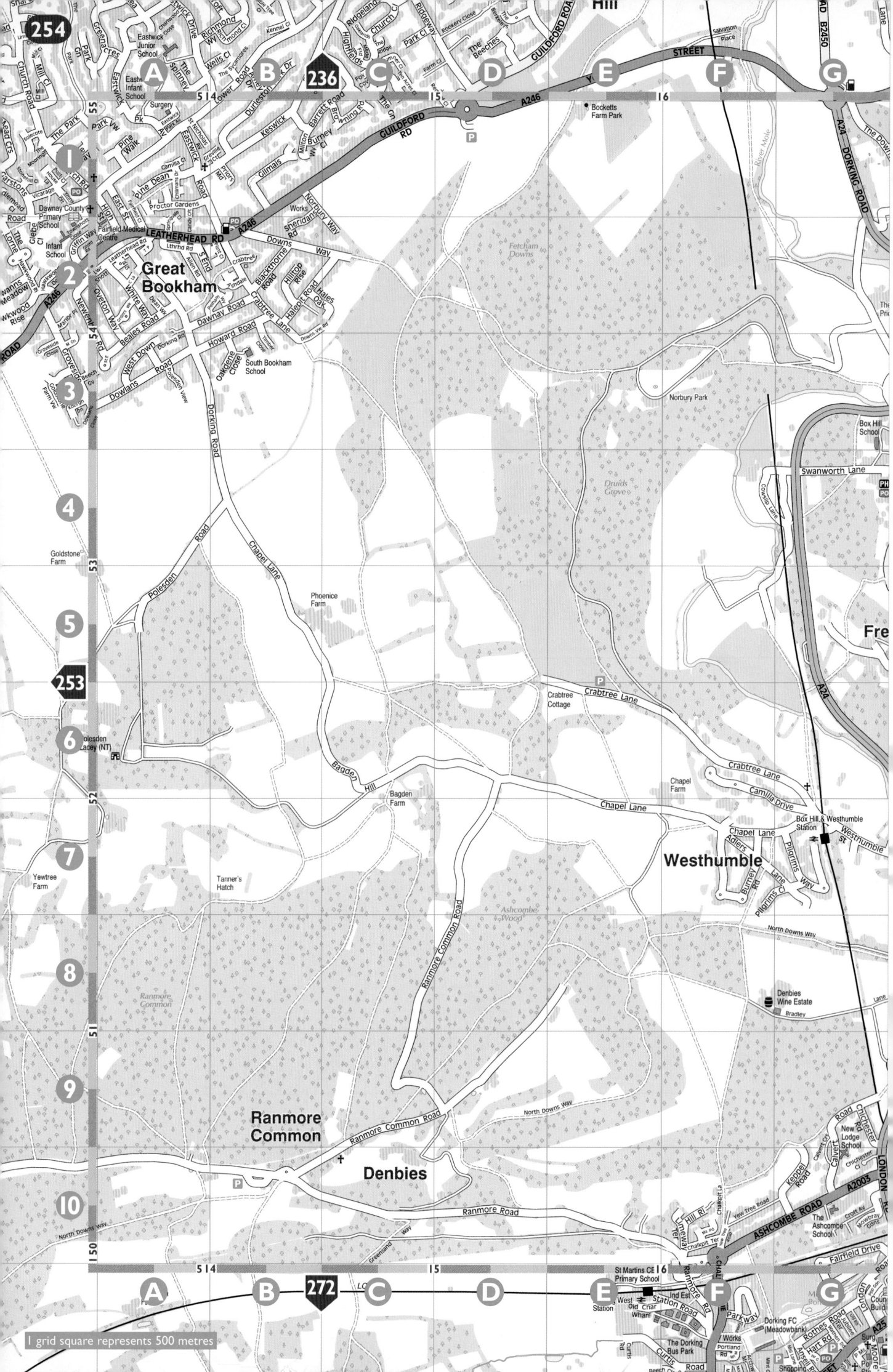

254
236
253
272
Great Bookham
Westhumble
Ranmore Common
Denbies
Fetcham Downs
Druids Grove
Norbury Park
Ashcombe Wood
Polesden Lacey (NT)
Goldstone Farm
Yewtree Farm
Tanner's Hatch
Phoenice Farm
Bagden Farm
Bagden Hill
Crabtree Cottage
Chapel Farm
Box Hill & Westhumble Station
Denbies Wine Estate
Bocketts Farm Park
South Bookham School
Eastwick Junior School
Eastwick Infant School
Dawnay County Primary School
Fairfield Medical Centre
Box Hill School
New Lodge School
The Ashcombe School
St Martins CE Primary School
Dorking FC (Meadowbank)
The Dorking Bus Park
LEATHERHEAD RD
GUILDFORD RD
DORKING ROAD
ASHCOMBE ROAD
Chapel Lane
Crabtree Lane
Dorking Road
Polesden Road
Ranmore Common Road
Ranmore Road
North Downs Way
River Mole
A246
A24
A2003
B2450
A25
1 grid square represents 500 metres

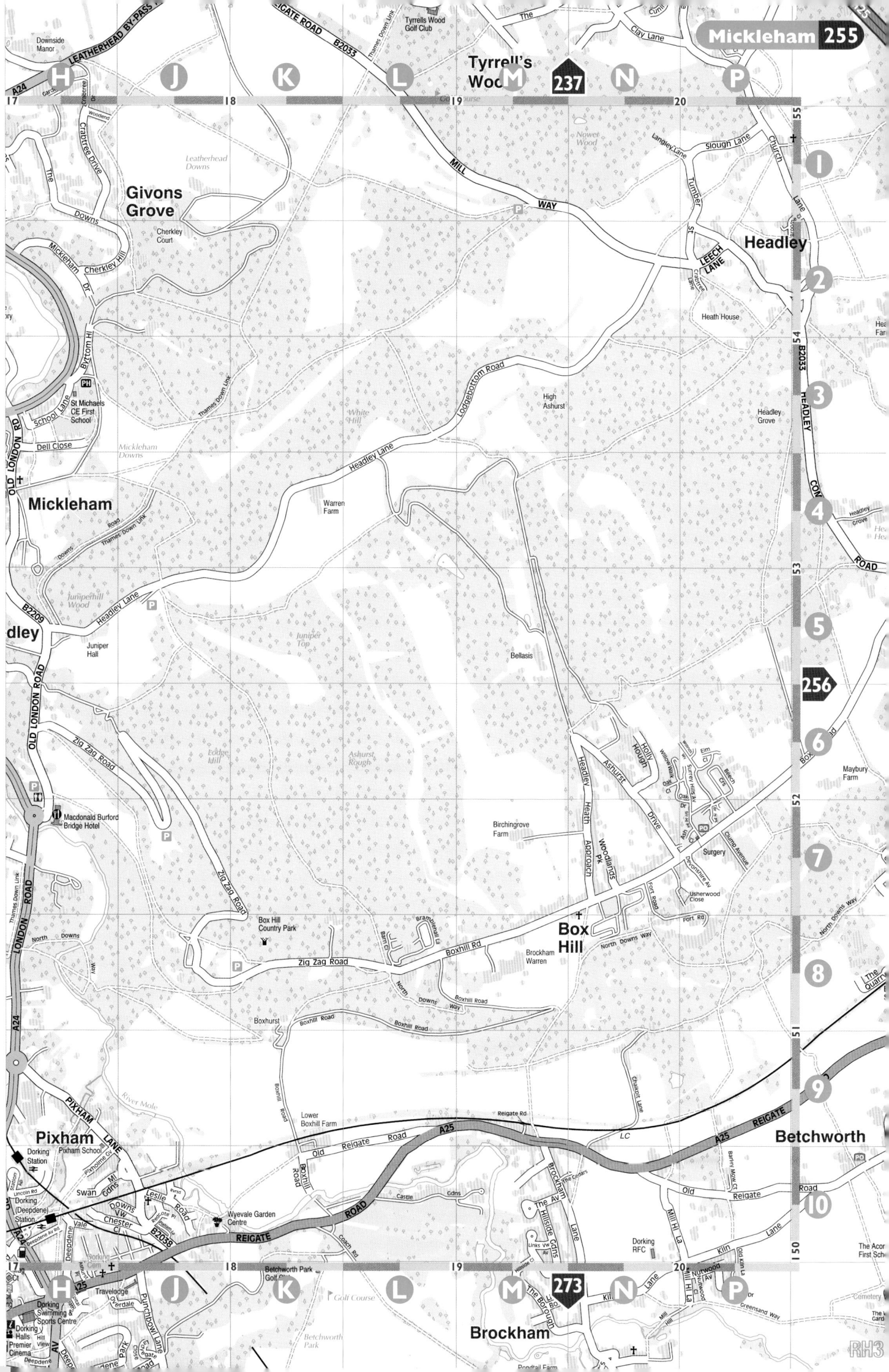
Tyrrell's Wood
Tyrrells Wood Golf Club
237
Givons Grove
Cherkley Court
Leatherhead Downs
Headley
Heath House
High Ashurst
Headley Grove
White Hill
Warren Farm
Mickleham
Mickleham Downs
St Michaels CE First School
Juniperhill Wood
Juniper Hall
Juniper Top
Bellasis
256
Maybury Farm
Lodge Hill
Ashurst Rough
Macdonald Burford Bridge Hotel
Birchingrove Farm
Surgery
Usherwood Close
Box Hill Country Park
Box Hill
Brockham Warren
Boxhurst
Lower Boxhill Farm
River Mole
Pixham
Pixham School
Dorking Station
Dorking (Deepdene) Station
Wyevale Garden Centre
Betchworth
Dorking RFC
Betchworth Park Golf Course
273
Brockham
Travelodge
Dorking Swimming & Sports Centre
Dorking Halls
Premier Cinema
Betchworth Park
Pondtail Farm
Downside Manor
LEATHERHEAD BY-PASS
REIGATE ROAD
B2033
MILL WAY
Thames Down Link
Slough Lane
Langley Lane
Tumber St
LEECH LANE
Crabtree Lane
Church Lane
HEADLEY ROAD
Crabtree Drive
Woodend
The Downs
Mickleham Dr
Cherkley Hill
Byttom Hl
School Lane
Dell Close
OLD LONDON RD
Lodgebottom Road
Headley Lane
Downs Road
B2209
Zig Zag Road
Headley Heath Approach
Ashurst Drive
Holly Hough
Woodlands Pk
Willow Walk
Elm Cl
Oak Cl
Surrey Hills Av
Beech Crs
Clump Avenue
Devonshire Av
Fort Road
Fort Rd
North Downs Way
Boxhill Rd
Boxhill Road
Bramblehall La
Barn Cl
Chalkpit Lane
Reigate Rd
A25
REIGATE ROAD
Old Reigate Road
Brockham Lane
The Cedars
Hillside Gdns
Links Vw Av
Castle Gdns
Coach Rd
Kiln Lane
Old Kiln La
Barley Mow Ct
Mill Hl La
Nutwood Av
Greensand Way
PIXHAM LANE
LONDON ROAD
A24
Leslie Road
Chester Cl
Downs Vw
Swan Mill Gdns
Pixholme Gv
Deepdene Vale
B2038
Punchbowl Lane
Station Ap
Lincoln Rd
Dorking Cem
The Borough
H J K L M N P
17 18 19 20
55 54 53 52 51 150
1 2 3 4 5 6 7 8 9 10
RH3

256
238
255
274
Walton on the Hill
Headley
Mogador
Buckland
Betchworth
A
B
C
D
E
F
G
1
2
3
4
5
6
7
8
9
10
521
22
23
55
54
53
52
51
150
KT20
RH3
M25
A25
B2220
B2032
B2033
DORKING ROAD
HEADLEY COMMON ROAD
PEBBLEHILL ROAD
STATION RD
REIGATE ROAD
CHEQUERS LANE
WALTON ST
LEECH LANE
Slough Lane
Church Lane
Boxhill Road
Clump Avenue
Station Road
The Street
Old Road
Sandy Lane
Rectory Lane
Buckland Lane
Lawrence Lane
Dungates Lane
Kiln Lane
Reigate Road
Breech Lane
Deans Lane
Heath Drive
Hurst Drive
Love Lane
Sturt's Lane
Holmcroft
Nursery Rd
Nursery Road
Chequers Close
Howard Close
Egmont Pk Road
Greenways
Russell Cl
Wonford Cl
Nyefield Park
Queens Cl
The Barnyard
Mead Walk
Chuck's La
Duffield Road
Old Rectory Close
Pond Farm Close
Surgery
Works
Primary School
Bramley School
Walton on the Hill CE Junior School
Walton Heath Golf Club
Sturt Priory Hospital
Castle House
Golf Course
Walton Heath
Banstead Heath
Heath Farm
Heath House
Frith Park
Headley Grove
Headley Heath
The Hermitage
Pebble Coombe
Pebble Cl
North Downs Way
Buckland Hills
Maybury Farm
Underhill Farm
Kemp's Farm
Wildecroft
Dowde's Farm
The Coombe
The Quarry
Betchworth Station
LC
Tranquil Dale
Slough Lane
Clifton's Lane
Colley Mnr Dr
BUCKLAND
Merrywood
Garden Centre
Broome Park
PO
PH
Surgery
Elm Cl
Beech Crs
Barley Mow Ct
Greensand Way
Dungate's Farm
Reigate Heath
Reigate Heath Golf Club
Flanchford
Bonny's Rd
The Acorns First School
Cemetery
The Walled Garden
Betchworth House
Wonham Manor
Wonham Lane
Trumpetshill
Sandy Lane
Heathfield
Old Kiln La
Alberta Dr
Hurst Wood
1 grid square represents 500 metres

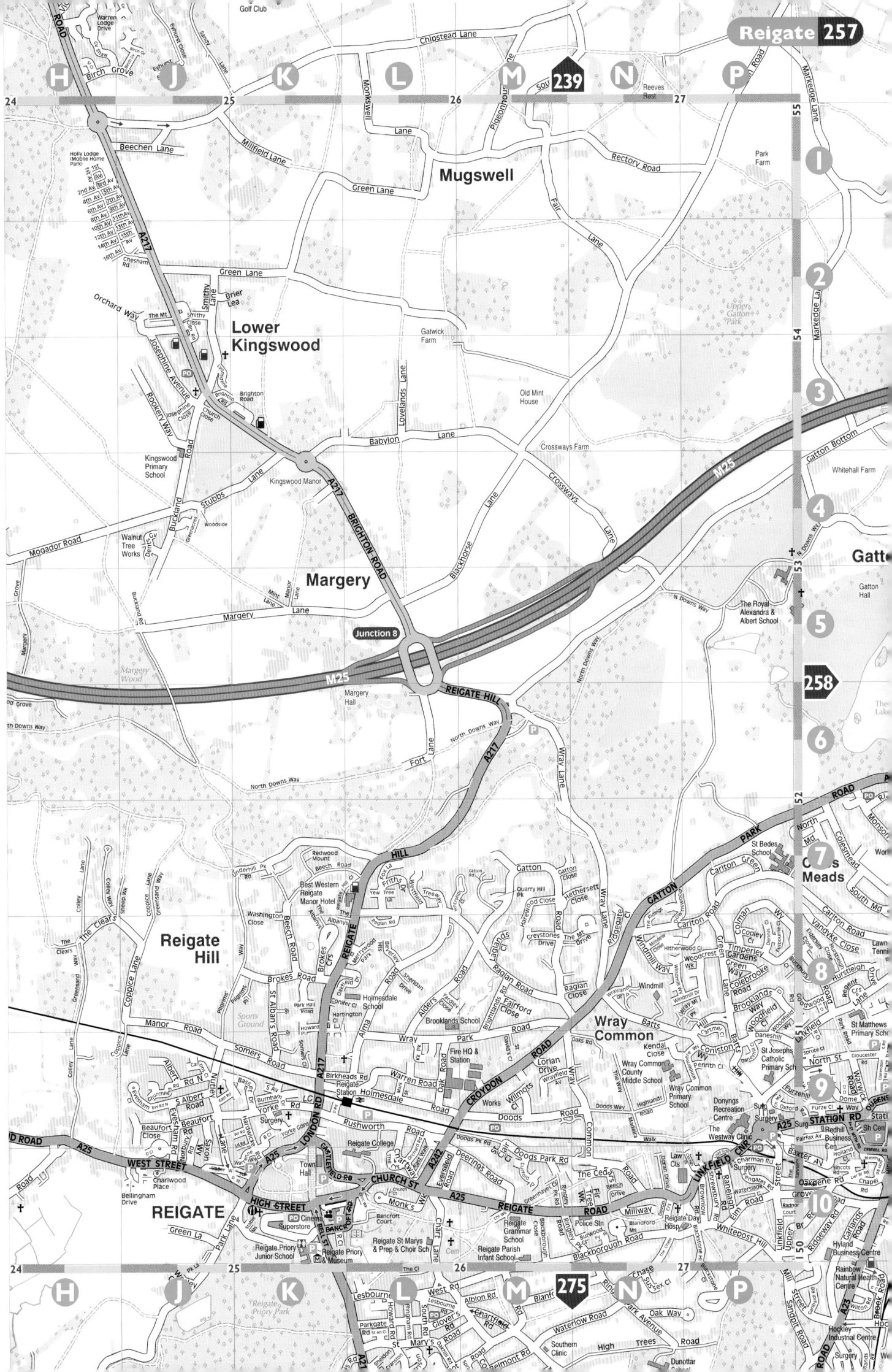
239
258
275
Mugswell
Lower Kingswood
Margery
Reigate Hill
Wray Common
REIGATE
Gatton
Meads
Golf Club
Chipstead Lane
Reeves Rest
Beechen Lane
Millfield Lane
Rectory Road
Park Farm
Green Lane
Fair Lane
Holly Lodge (Mobile Home Park)
Orchard Way
Brier Lea
Smithy Lane
Gatwick Farm
Upper Gatton Park
Markedge Lane
Josephine Avenue
Brighton Road
Old Mint House
Lovelands Lane
Babylon Lane
Crossways Farm
Gatton Bottom
Whitehall Farm
Rookery Way
Kingswood Primary School
Kingswood Manor
Stubbs Lane
Buckland Road
Mogador Road
Walnut Tree Works
Woodside
Crossways Lane
Blackhorse Lane
BRIGHTON ROAD
M25
A217
Margery Lane
Mint Lane
Manor Lane
N Downs Way
The Royal Alexandra & Albert School
Gatton Hall
Junction 8
Margery Wood
Margery Hall
REIGATE HILL
North Downs Way
Fort Lane
Wray Lane
GATTON PARK ROAD
St Bedes School
Colesmead
South Md
Carlton Road
Vandyke Close
Redwood Mount
Beech Road
Underhill Pk Rd
Best Western Reigate Manor Hotel
Gatton Close
Quarry Hill Pk
Hethersett Close
Harewood Close
Greystones Drive
The Mt Drive
Ridgegate Cl
Windmill Way
Colman Wy
Copley Cl
Timperley Gardens
Washington Close
Beech Road
Brokes Road
Brokes Crs
Holmesdale School
Laglands Cl
Raglan Road
Raglan Close
Fairford Close
Brooklands School
Alders Road
Alma Road
Wray Park Road
Fire HQ & Station
Lorian Drive
Kendal Close
Wray Common County Middle School
Wray Common Primary School
Coniston Cl
Penrith Cl
St Josephs Catholic Primary Sch
St Matthews Primary Sch
North St
The Clears
Coppice Lane
Colley Lane
Colley Way
Greensand Way
Sports Ground
Manor Road
Somers Road
St Alban's Road
Birkheads Rd
Reigate Station
Holmesdale Road
Warren Road
Oak Road
CROYDON ROAD
Doods Road
Doods Way
Works
Albert Rd N
S Albert Road
Evesham Road
Beaufort Close
Yorke Rd
LONDON RD
Rushworth Road
Reigate College
Doods Pk Rd
Deerings Road
Doods Park Road
Common Road
Law Cls
Donyngs Recreation Centre
The Westway Clinic
Surgery
STATION RD
Redhill Business Cen
WEST STREET
A25
Charlwood Place
Bellingham Drive
Town Hall
CHURCH ST
A242
Eversfield Road
HIGH STREET
REIGATE ROAD
Millway
Police Stn
Reigate Day Hosp
LINKFIELD CNR
Charman Rd
Ranelagh Rd
Elm Road
Whitepost Hill
Brownlow Rd
Blackborough Road
Cinema
Superstore
Bancroft Court
Reigate St Marys & Prep & Choir Sch
Reigate Grammar School
Reigate Parish Infant School
Reigate Priory Junior School
Reigate Priory & Museum
Park Lane
Green La
Chart Lane
Linkfield
Ridgeway Rd
Hyland Business Centre
Rainbow Natural Health Centre
Hockley Industrial Centre
Reigate Priory Park
Lesbourne Rd
West Rd
South Rd
Albion Rd
Chartfield Rd
Waterlow Road
Oak Way
Park Avenue
High Trees Road
Southern Clinic
Belmont Rd
Sandpit Road
Mill Street
Dunottar School

258
240
257
276
A
B
C
D
E
F
G
1
2
3
4
5
6
7
8
9
10
528
29
30
55
54
53
52
51
50
Junction 7
Junction 7/8
Glebe Rd
London Road N
High Road
Markedge Lane
Dean Lane
Alderstead Heath
Dean Lane
Aldersted Lane
B2031
Harps Oak Lane
Harps Oak
Boars Green Farm
Tollsworth Manor
Alderstead Farm
Beech Road
Shepherd's Hill
Pilgrims' Lane
North Downs Way
Upper Gatton Park
A23 London Road North
M23
M25
Church Hill
Jolliffe Road
Gatton Bottom
Rockshaw Road
Heronswood Mere
Golf Course
North Downs Way
Whitehall Farm
Merstham Stn
Quality St
Station Road North
High St
Merstham
Reigate Hill Golf Club
Gatton
Gatton Hall
The Royal Alexandra & Albert
Grange Close
Grange Dr
School Hill
Hanover Close
Primary School
Brook Road
Wood Street
Mainstone Road
Radstock Way
Laxton Gardens
Furzefield Primary School
Delabole Road
Chesterton Dr
Dundrey Crs
Radstock Way
Bolsover Gv
Nailsworth Crs
Portland Dr
Purbeck Cl
Bletchingley Road
Regent Close
Worsted Green
Drive
Sutton Gdns
Weldon Wy
Taunton
St Nicholas School
Woodfield School
Bletchingley Road
Manor Road
Albert Rd
Endsleigh Rd
Albury Road
Works
Rocky Lane
London Road South
Bramblewood
Bushetts Grove
Wells Place
The Crossways
Gatton Park Business Centre
Battlebridge Lane
New Battlebridge Lane
The Lake
Southcote Road
Deans Road
Nutfield Rd
Devon Road
Melton Road
Orpin Road
Bourne Road
Wyecliffe Gdns
Ash Cl
Chilberton Dr
Tilers
Nutfield Road
Mill Lane
South Merstham
Quarryside Business Park
A23
A242
Park Road
Fairhaven Road
East Surrey College
Elmwood Road
Holcon Court
Ringwood Av
North Md
Colesmead
Monson Road
Lyndale Rd
Claremont Road
Ranmore Close
Westway Gardens
Holmethorpe Industrial Estate
Ormside Way
Trowers Way
Holmethorpe Avenue
Holmethorpe Av
Works
Mercers Farm
Coles Meads
Carlton Green
Alpine Road
East Surrey College
Alpine Road
Frenches Road
Nutfield Marsh Road
Nutfield Marsh
Nutfield Marsh Road
South Md
Colman Wy
Copley Cl
Timperley Gardens
Green Way
Colebrook Road
Brooklands Way
Woodfield Cl
Carlton Road
Vandyke Close
Lawn Tennis Club
Holmethorpe
Chilmead Farm
Chilmead Lane
Hurstleigh Drive
Park Road
Regent Crs
Nash Gdns
Lynwood Road
Ladbroke Rd
Wiggie Lane
Keats
Cormongers Lane
REDHILL
Warwick Quadrant & Harlequin Theatre Cinema & Library
St Matthews CE Primary School
St Josephs Catholic Primary Sch
Daneshill
North St
Gloucester Rd
Warwick Road
The Warwick School
Church Hill
A23 London Rd
Queensway
Princess Way
Donyngs Recreation Centre
Surgery
Station Rd
A25
The Westway Clinic
Redhill Business Cen
Sh Cen
Station Rd
Redhill Stn
Noke Dr
Caxton Rise
Blacklands Meadow
Park Works
Doods Brow School
Shortacres
Hunters Gate
Nutfield Cemetery
Nutfield Road
High Street
Nutfield
Cavendish Rd
Fairfax Av
Baxter Av
Holland
Charman Rd
Surgery
Fengates Rd
Waterslade Rd
Oakdene Rd
Grovehill Road
Chapel Rd
High St
Marketfield Way
Fenton Close
Fenton Road
Redstone Hill
Hillfield Road
Redstone Park
Oakwood Close
Nutfield Road
A25
Nutfield Priory Hotel
Fullers Wood Lane
Sandy Lane
Mid Street
Whitepost Hill
Linkfield
Ridgeway Rd
Garlands Road
Hyland Business Centre
Works
Rural Way
Kingsfield Business Cen
Redstone Hollow
Rainbow
Health
Brook Road
Mill Street
Sandpit
Philanthropic Road
Redstone Cemetery
Redhill College
Hogtrough Lane
Sandy Lane
Greensand Way
Kentwyns Rise
Nutfield Church CE
Hooley Lane
Surgery
Works
Earlswood Infant School
1 grid square represents 500 metres

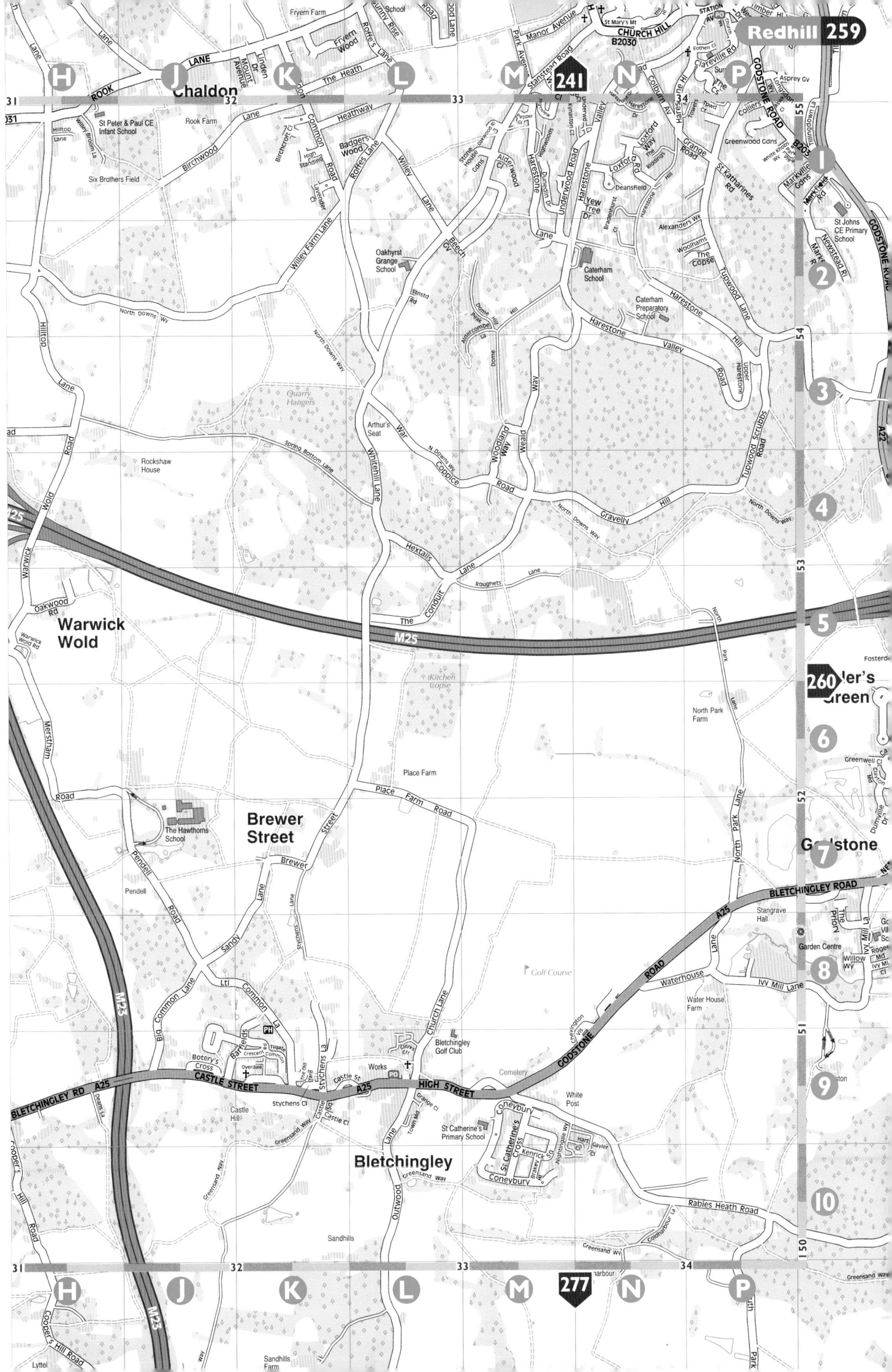
Chaldon
Warwick Wold
Brewer Street
Bletchingley
M25
M23
A25
Redhill 259
241
260
277
H
J
K
L
M
N
P
31
32
33
34
55
54
53
52
51
50
1
2
3
4
5
6
7
8
9
10
Rook Lane
Rook Farm
St Peter & Paul CE Infant School
Six Brothers Field
Birchwood
Heathway
Common Road
Badgers Wood
Roffes Lane
Willey Lane
Willey Farm Lane
Oakhyrst Grange School
Caterham School
Caterham Preparatory School
Harestone Valley Road
Harestone Hill
Tupwood Lane
Tupwood Scrubbs Road
St Katharines Rd
Godstone Road
St Johns CE Primary School
Church Hill
B2030
Manor Avenue
Park Avenue
Stanstead Road
North Downs Way
Hilltop Lane
Quarry Hangers
Arthur's Seat
Whitehill Lane
War Coppice Road
Gravelly Hill
Rockshaw House
Spring Bottom Lane
Wold Road
Warwick
Hextalls Lane
Roughets Lane
The Conduit
Oakwood Rd
Kitchen Copse
North Park Farm
North Park Lane
Mersham Road
Place Farm
Place Farm Road
The Hawthorns School
Pendell
Pendell Road
Brewer Street
Sandy Lane
Big Common Lane
Ltl Common La
Church Lane
Bletchingley Golf Club
Golf Course
Bletchingley Road
Stangrave Hall
Garden Centre
Godstone
Waterhouse Lane
Water House Farm
Ivy Mill Lane
Godstone Road
Castle Street
High Street
Bletchingley Rd
Castle Hill
Stychens Cl
Stychens La
Works
Cemetery
White Post
St Catherine's Primary School
Coneybury
Greensand Way
Outwood Lane
Rabies Heath Road
Sandhills
Sandhills Farm
Cooper's Hill Road
Fryern Farm
Fryern Wood
The Heath
Greenwood Gdns
Deansfield
Alexanders Wk
Woolhams
The Copse
Weald Way
Woodland Way
Dome Hill

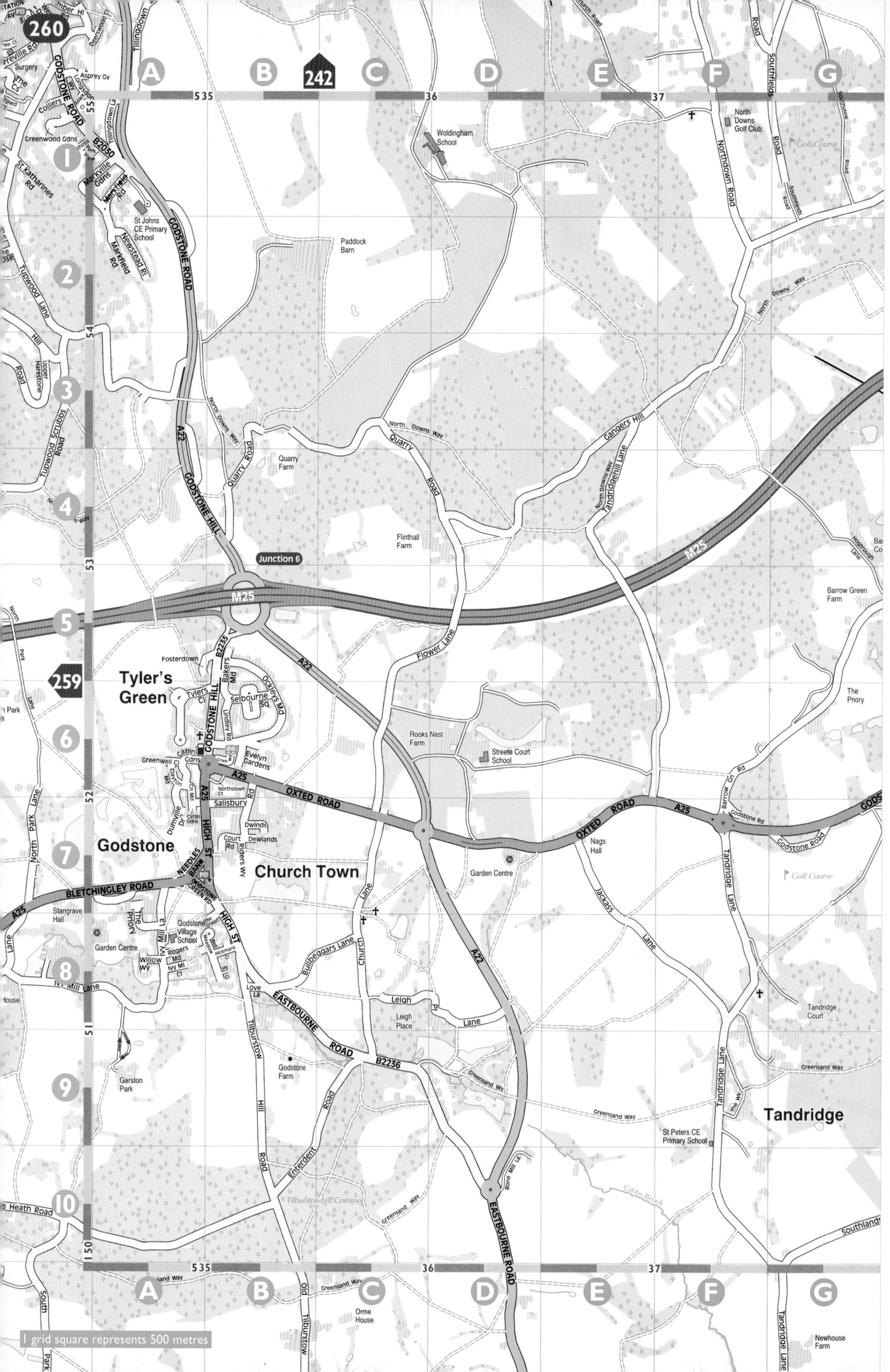
260
242
259
A
B
C
D
E
F
G
1
2
3
4
5
6
7
8
9
10
535
36
37
55
54
53
52
51
50
GODSTONE ROAD
Surgery
Colliers
Greenwood Gdns
B2030
St Katharines Rd
Markville Gdns
Markfield Rd
St Johns CE Primary School
Newstead Ri
Tupwood Lane
Hill Road
Upper Harestone
Tupwood Scrubbs Road
Tillingdown La
Woldingham School
Paddock Barn
North Downs Golf Club
Golf Course
Northdown Road
Southfields Road
North Downs Way
Quarry Road
Quarry Farm
Flinthall Farm
Gangers Hill
Tandridgehill Lane
Junction 6
M25
A22
GODSTONE HILL
Hogtrough Lane
Barrow Green Farm
The Priory
Fosterdown
Tyler's Green
Tylers Cl
B2235
Bakers Md
Selbourne Sq
Ockleys Md
Lindley Rd
Evelyn Gardens
Catlin Gdns
Greenwell Cl
A25
OXTED ROAD
Northdown Ct
Salisbury Rd
Dwlnds
Dewlands
Court Rd
Riders Wy
Flower Lane
Rooks Nest Farm
Streete Court School
Barrow Gn Rd
Godstone Rd
Godstone Road
Nags Hall
Garden Centre
Godstone
HIGH ST
NEEDLES BANK
Church Town
BLETCHINGLEY ROAD
GODSTONE GREEN RD
Stangrave Hall
The Priory
Godstone Village School
Ivy Mill La
Rogers Md
Willow Wy
Ivy Mill Cl
Ivy Mill Lane
Bullbeggars Lane
Church Lane
Jackass Lane
Tandridge Lane
Tandridge Court
Leigh Pl
Leigh Place
Love La
EASTBOURNE ROAD
B2236
Godstone Farm
Tilburstow Hill Road
Garston Park
Greensand Way
Enterdent Road
Tilburstowhill Common
Bone Mill La
Gibbs Brook
St Peters CE Primary School
Tandridge
The Wk
Southlands
North Park Lane
Heath Road
South Park
Old Tilburstow
Orme House
Newhouse Farm
1 grid square represents 500 metres

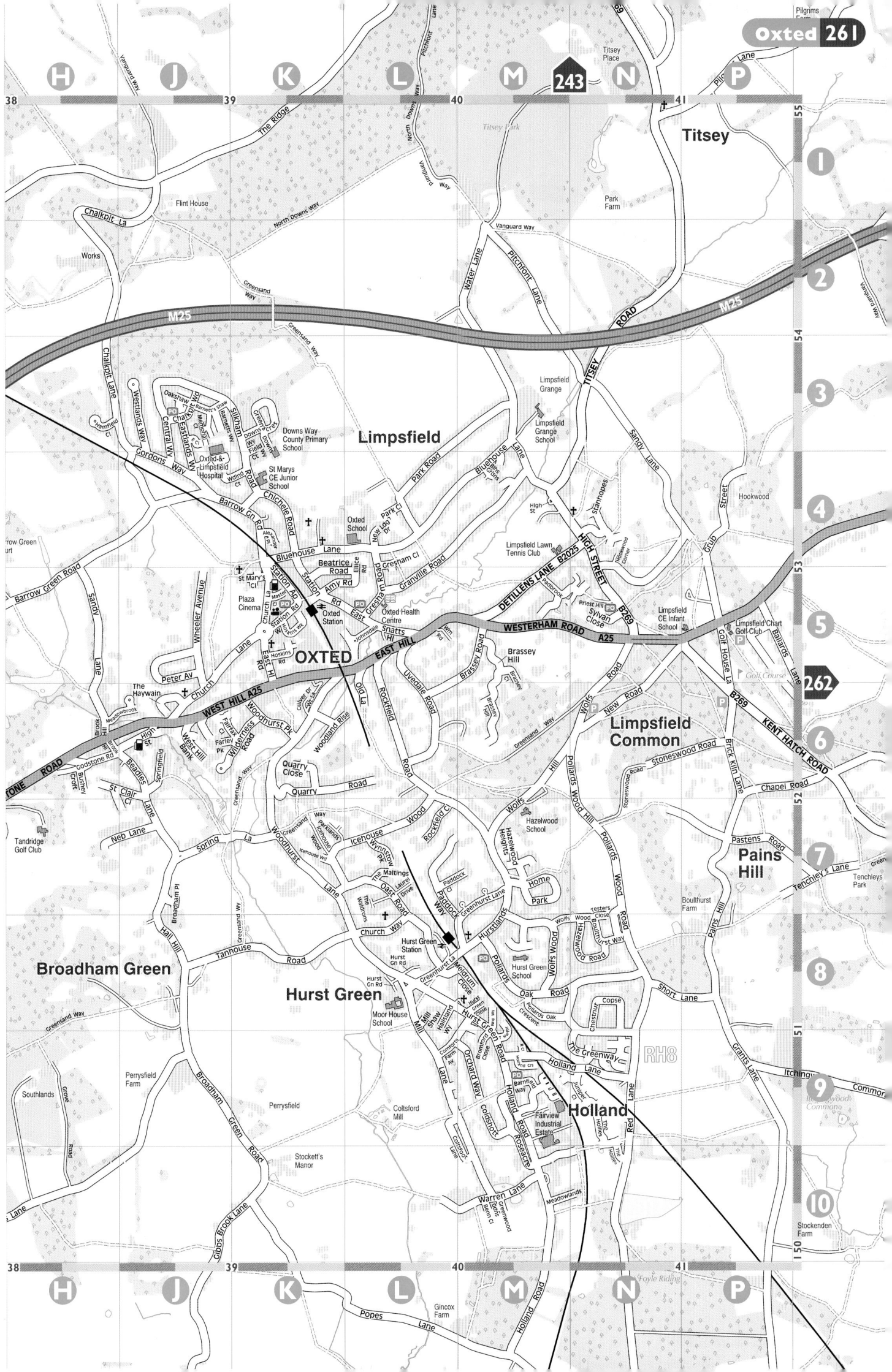

OXTED
Limpsfield
Titsey
Limpsfield Common
Pains Hill
Hurst Green
Broadham Green
Holland
M25
WEST HILL A25
EAST HILL
WESTERHAM ROAD A25
DETILLENS LANE B2025
HIGH STREET
TITSEY ROAD
KENT HATCH ROAD
B269
Oxted Station
Hurst Green Station
Plaza Cinema
Oxted School
Oxted Health Centre
Oxted-&-Limpsfield Hospital
Downs Way County Primary School
St Marys CE Junior School
Limpsfield Grange School
Limpsfield Lawn Tennis Club
Limpsfield CE Infant School
Limpsfield Chart Golf Club
Hazelwood School
Hurst Green School
Moor House School
Tandridge Golf Club
Fairview Industrial Estate
Titsey Park
Titsey Place
Park Farm
Flint House
Works
Hookwood
Boulthurst Farm
Tenchleys Park
Perrysfield Farm
Perrysfield
Southlands
Coltsford Mill
Stockett's Manor
Gincox Farm
Stockenden Farm
Foyle Riding
Pilgrims Farm
RH8
243
262

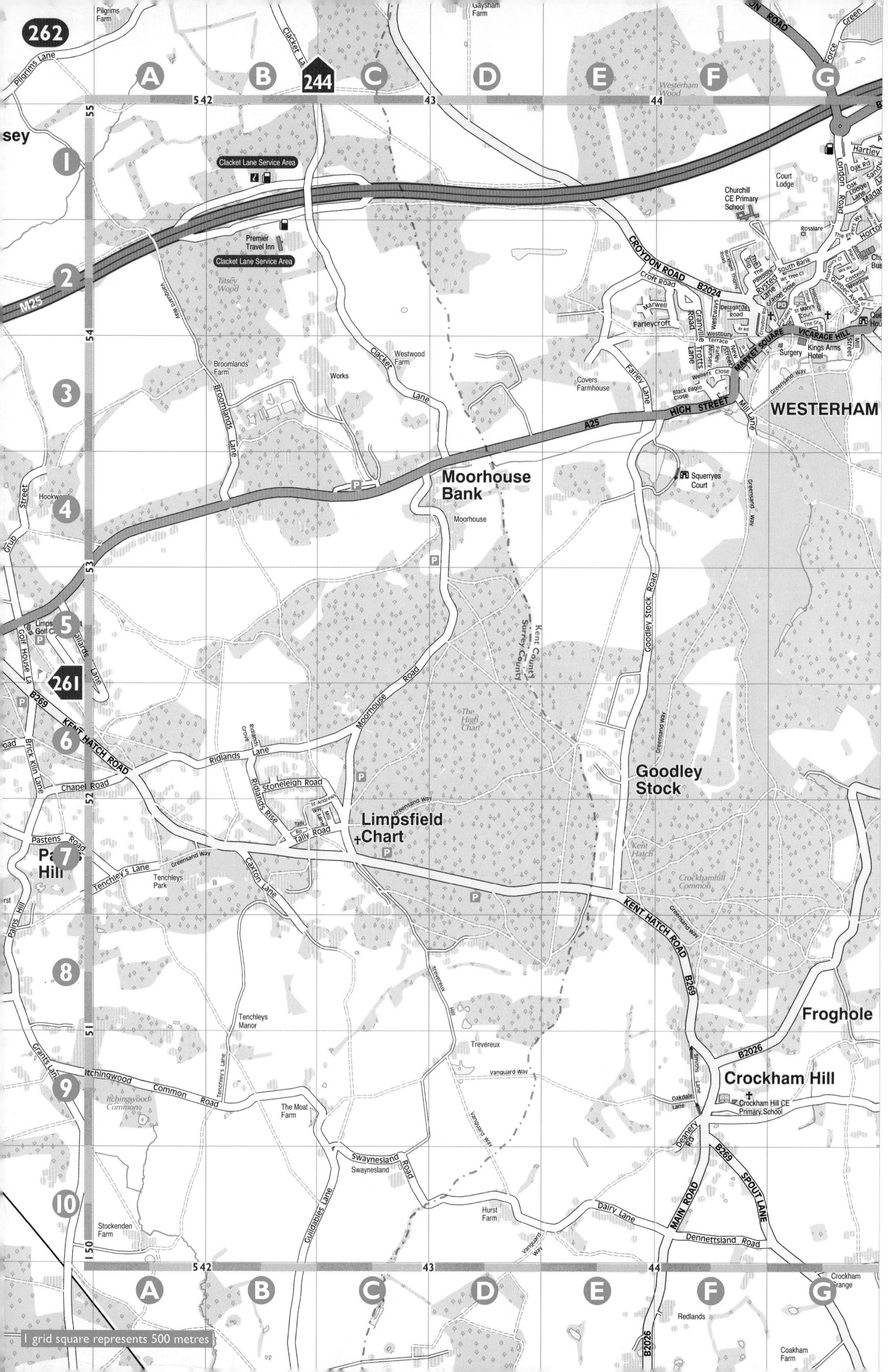

244

261

WESTERHAM

Clacket Lane Service Area

Premier Travel Inn

Clacket Lane Service Area

Pilgrims Farm

Pilgrims Lane

Clacket La

Gaysham Farm

Force Green

Westerham Wood

Court Lodge

Churchill CE Primary School

Croydon Road B2024

Croft Road

Marwell

Farleycroft

Westbury Terrace

Granville Road

Trotts Lane

Farley Lane

Mill Lane

High Street

A25

Squerryes Court

Moorhouse Bank

Moorhouse

Titsey Wood

Broomlands Farm

Broomlands Lane

Vanguard Way

Clacket Lane

Westwood Farm

Works

Covers Farmhouse

Kent County Surrey County

Goodley Stock Road

Greensand Way

Grub Street

Hookwood

Golf House La

Limpsfield Golf Cl

Ballards Lane

B269

Kent Hatch Road

Brick Kiln Lane

Chapel Road

Ridlands Grove

Ridlands Lane

Ridlands Rise

Stoneleigh Road

St Andrews

Tally Rd

Mill Lane

Caxton Lane

Moorhouse Road

The High Chart

Kent Hatch

Goodley Stock

Greensand Way

Limpsfield +Chart

Greensand Way

Kent Hatch Road

B269

Crockhamhill Common

Froghole

Park Hill

Pastens Road

Tenchley's Lane

Tenchleys Park

Greensand Way

Tenchley's Lane

Tenchleys Manor

Trevereux Hill

Trevereux

Vanguard Way

B2026

Crockham Hill

Crockham Hill CE Primary School

Oakdale Lane

Smiths Lane

Pains Hill

Grants Lane

Itchingwood Common Road

Itchingwood Common

The Moat Farm

Guildables Lane

Swaynesland Road

Swaynesland

Hurst Farm

Vanguard Way

Deaney Rd

Main Road

Dairy Lane

Dennettsland Road

B269

Spout Lane

Stockenden Farm

Crockham Grange

Redlands

Coakham Farm

B2026

M25

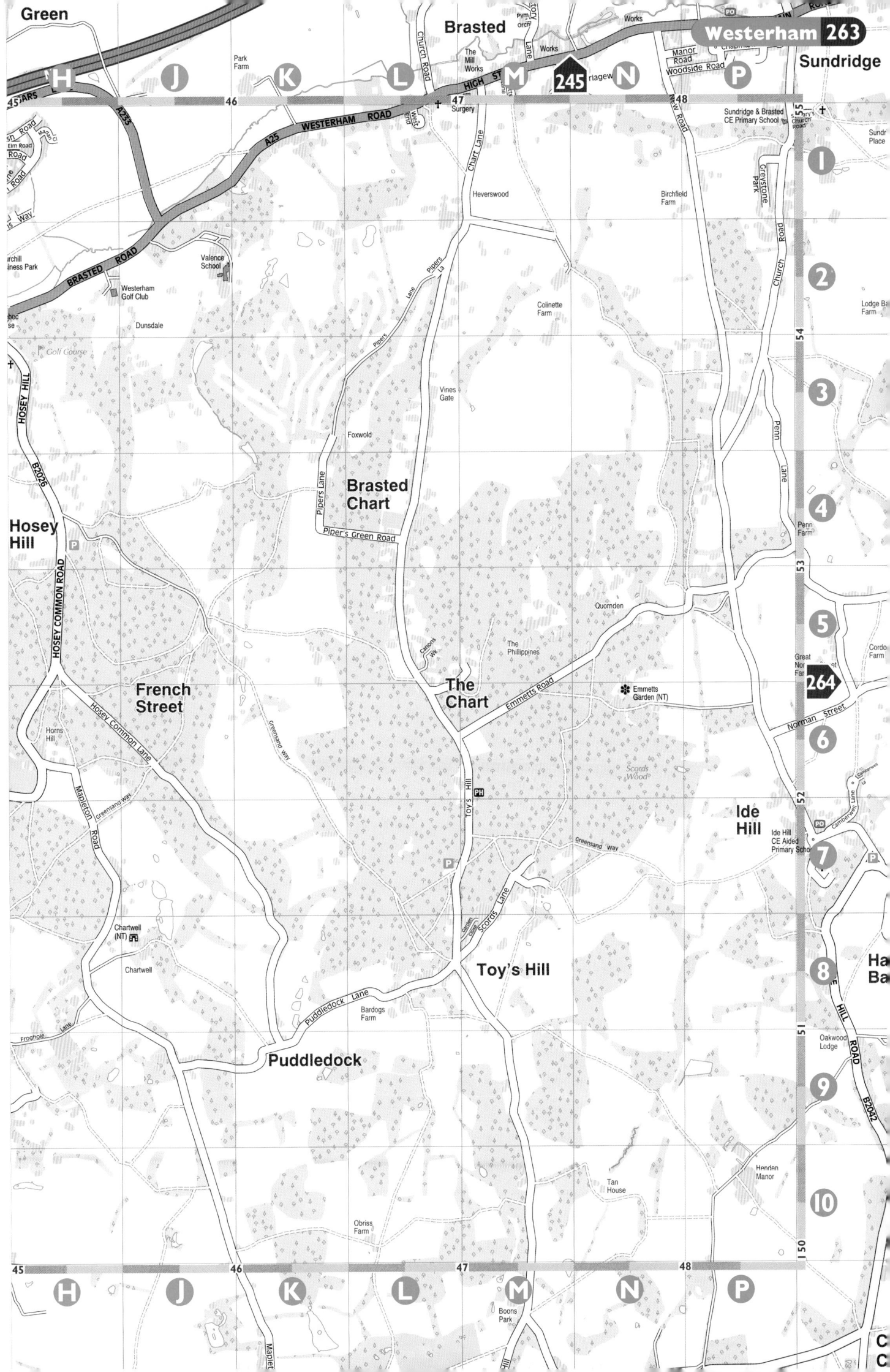
Green
Brasted
Sundridge
Park Farm
The Mill Works
Works
Church Road
High St
Westerham Road
A25
A233
Brasted Road
Manor Road
Woodside Road
New Road
Surgery
Sundridge & Brasted CE Primary School
Chart Lane
Heverswood
Birchfield Farm
Greystone Park
Church Road
Valence School
Westerham Golf Club
Dunsdale
Golf Course
Pipers Lane
Colinette Farm
Lodge Barn Farm
Vines Gate
Foxwold
Penn Lane
Brasted Chart
Pipers Lane
Piper's Green Road
Penn Farm
Hosey Hill
B2026
Hosey Common Road
Quornden
The Phillippines
Canons Wk
Great Norman Farm
Cordon Farm
French Street
The Chart
Emmetts Road
Emmetts Garden (NT)
Norman Street
Horns Hill
Hosey Common Lane
Greensand Way
Scords Wood
Mapleton Road
Toy's Hill
Ide Hill
Ide Hill CE Aided Primary School
Camberwell Lane
Scords Lane
Chartwell (NT)
Chartwell
Toy's Hill
Puddledock Lane
Bardogs Farm
Froghole Lane
Puddledock
Hill Road
B2042
Oakwood Lodge
Henden Manor
Tan House
Obriss Farm
Boons Park
H J K L M N P
1 2 3 4 5 6 7 8 9 10
45 46 47 48
50 51 52 53 54 55
245
264

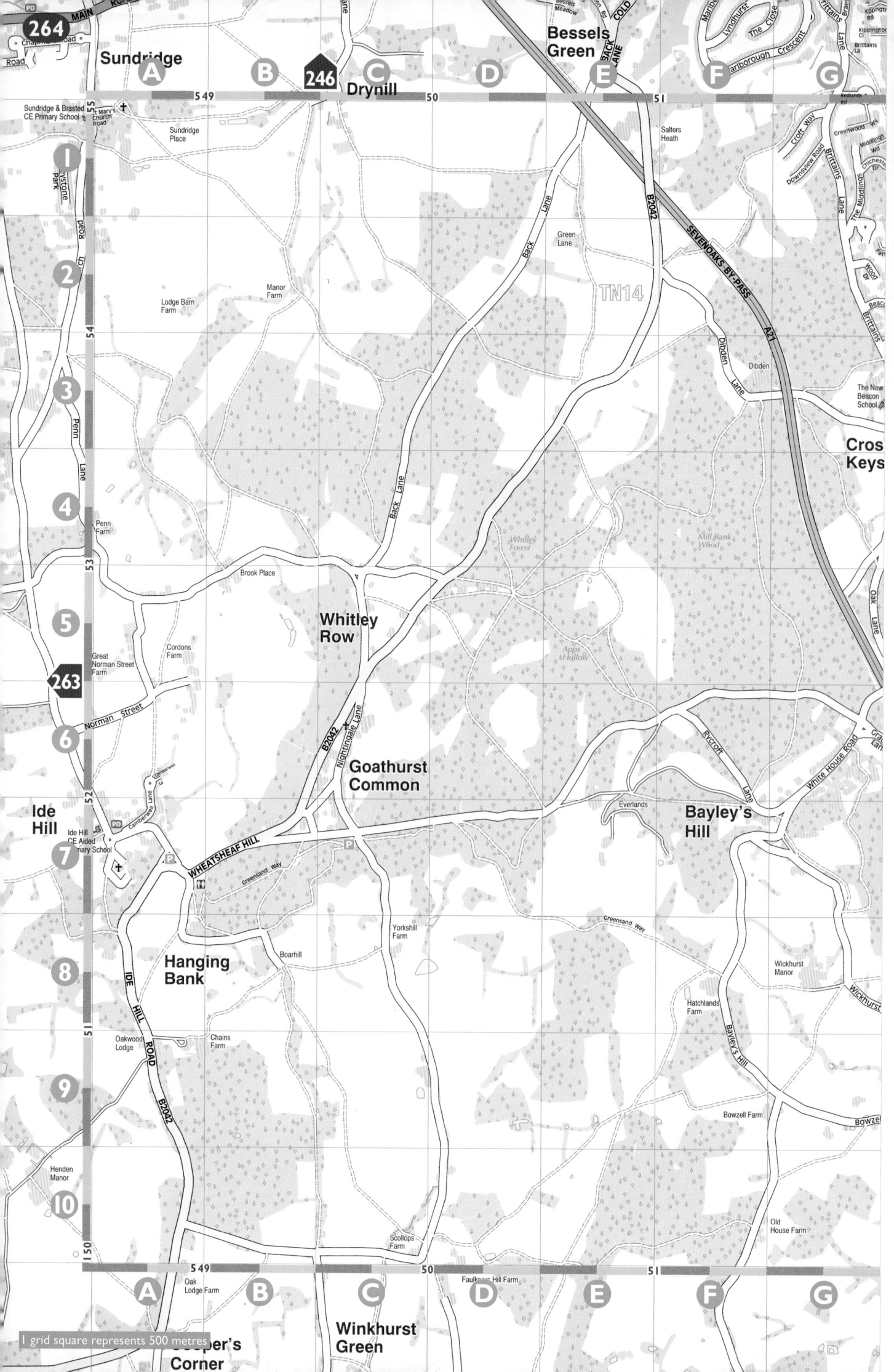

264
Sundridge
246
Drynill
Bessels Green
Sundridge & Brasted CE Primary School
St Mary's Church Road
Sundridge Place
Salters Heath
Green Lane
Back Lane
B2042
SEVENOAKS-BY-PASS
A21
TN14
Manor Farm
Lodge Barn Farm
Dibden Lane
Dibden
The New Beacon School
Brittains Lane
Croft Way
Downsview Road
The Middlings
Penn Lane
Penn Farm
Brook Place
Whitley Forest
Mill Bank Wood
Whitley Row
Cordons Farm
Great Norman Street Farm
263
Norman Street
Apps Hollow
Oak Lane
Nightingale Lane
Goathurst Common
Rycroft Lane
White House Road
Ide Hill
Ide Hill CE Aided Primary School
Camberwell Lane
WHEATSHEAF HILL
Everlands
Bayley's Hill
Greensand Way
Hanging Bank
Yorkshill Farm
Boarhill
Wickhurst Manor
Hatchlands Farm
IDE HILL ROAD
Oakwood Lodge
Chains Farm
Bowzell Farm
Henden Manor
Old House Farm
Scollops Farm
Oak Lodge Farm
Faulkners Hill Farm
Winkhurst Green
Cooper's Corner
1 grid square represents 500 metres

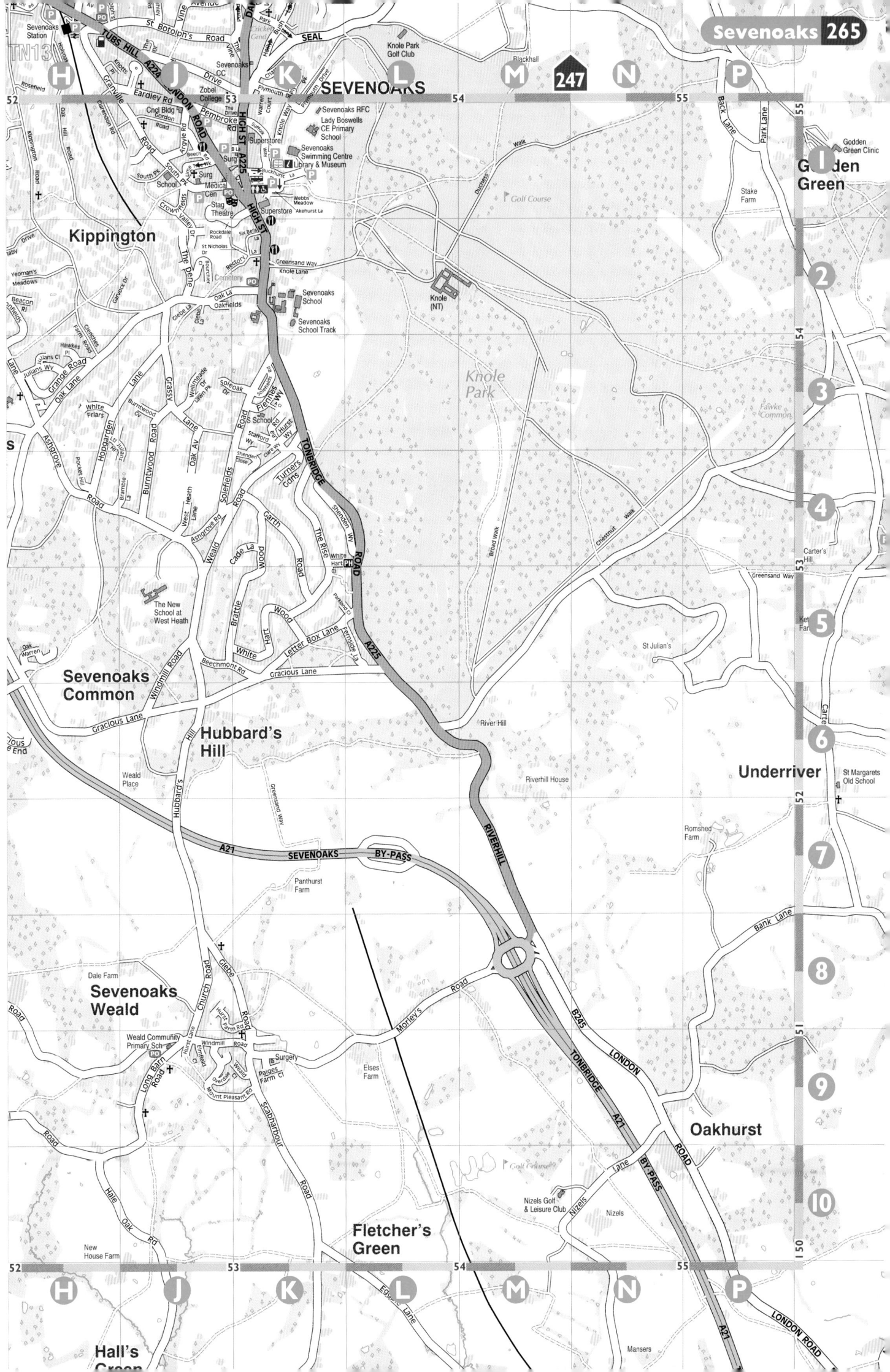
SEVENOAKS
Kippington
Sevenoaks Common
Hubbard's Hill
Sevenoaks Weald
Fletcher's Green
Hall's Green
Knole Park
Knole (NT)
Godden Green
Underriver
Oakhurst
247
A21 SEVENOAKS BY-PASS
TONBRIDGE ROAD
RIVERHILL
B245 LONDON ROAD
Sevenoaks Station
Knole Park Golf Club
Sevenoaks RFC
Lady Boswells CE Primary School
Sevenoaks Swimming Centre
Library & Museum
Stag Theatre
Sevenoaks School
Sevenoaks School Track
The New School at West Heath
Weald Community Primary Sch
Nizels Golf & Leisure Club
Godden Green Clinic
St Margarets Old School
Gracious Lane
Morley's Road
Scabharbour Road
Hubbard's Hill
Church Road
Greensand Way
Chestnut Walk
Broad Walk
Letter Box Lane
Beechmont Rd
Windmill Road
Hale Oak Rd
Long Barn Road
Bank Lane
Nizels Lane
St Julian's
River Hill
Riverhill House
Panthurst Farm
Romshed Farm
Elses Farm
Dale Farm
New House Farm
Stake Farm
Weald Place
Nizels
Mansers
Golf Course

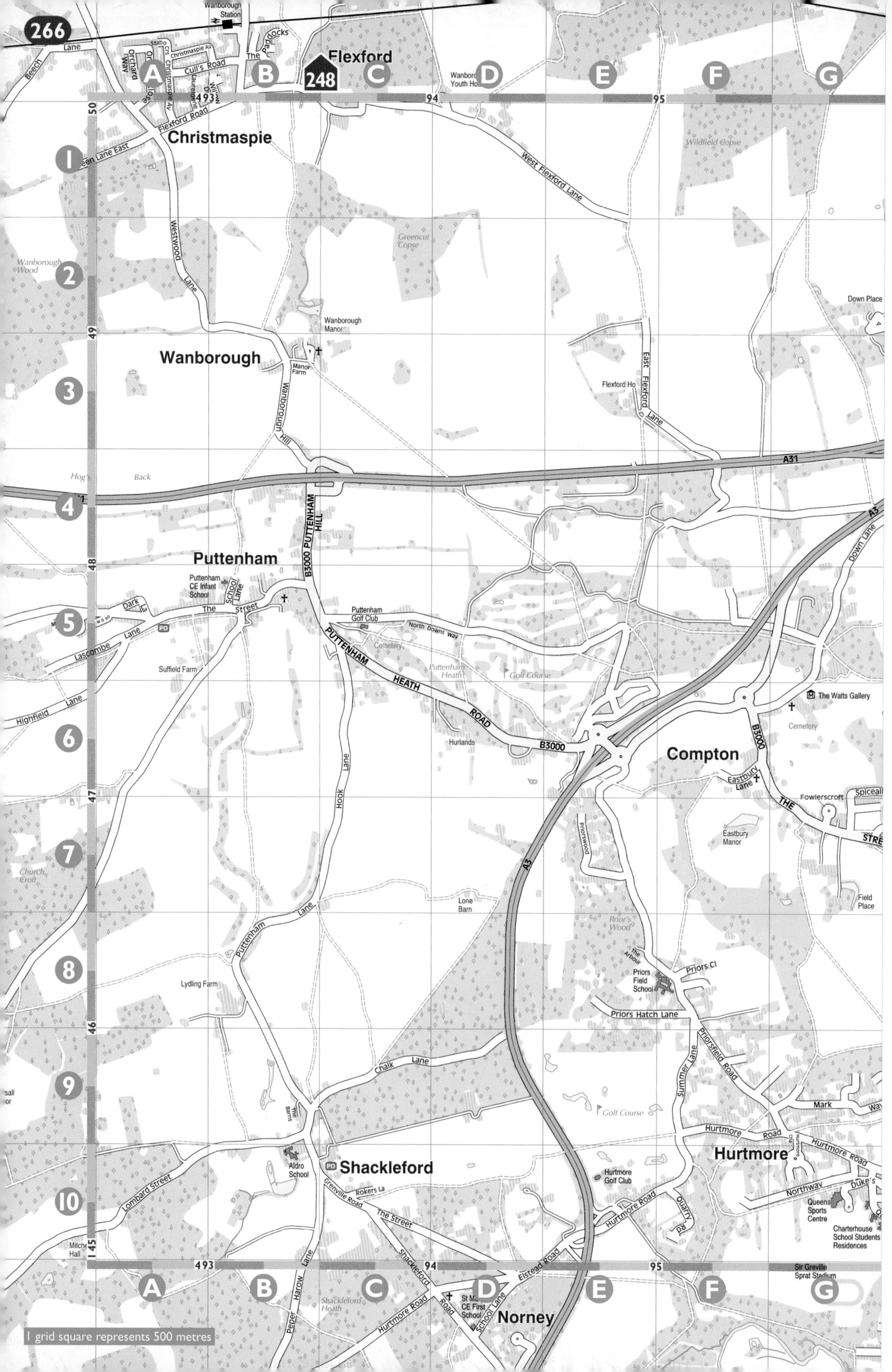

Wanborough Station
Beech
Lane
Orchard Way
Christmaspie Av
Cull's Road
The Paddocks
Flexford
248
Wanborough Youth Hostel
A
B
C
D
E
F
G
493
94
95
50
Flexford Road
Christmaspie
Green Lane East
West Flexford Lane
Wildfield Copse
1
Westwood Lane
Greencut Copse
Wanborough Wood
2
Down Place
49
Wanborough Manor
Wanborough
Manor Farm
3
Wanborough Hill
East Flexford Lane
Flexford Ho
A31
Hog's Back
4
A3
B3000 PUTTENHAM HILL
48
Puttenham
Puttenham CE Infant School
School Lane
Dark La
The Street
5
Lascombe Lane
Puttenham Golf Club
North Downs Way
Cemetery
PUTTENHAM HEATH ROAD
Puttenham Heath
Golf Course
Suffield Farm
The Watts Gallery
Highfield Lane
6
Hook Lane
Hurlands
B3000
Compton
Eastbury Lane
47
Fowlerscroft
Spiceall
THE STREET
Priorswood
Eastbury Manor
7
Church Croft
Field Place
Lone Barn
Puttenham Lane
Prior's Wood
The Arbour
8
Priors Field School
Priors Cl
Lydling Farm
Priors Hatch Lane
46
Priorsfield Road
Chalk Lane
Summer Lane
9
The Barns
Golf Course
Mark Way
Hurtmore Road
Hurtmore
Lombard Street
Aldro School
Shackleford
Hurtmore Golf Club
Rokers La
Northway
Duke's
10
Grenville Road
The Street
Hurtmore Road
Quarry Rd
Queens Sports Centre
Charterhouse School Students Residences
Mitchell Hall
45
Shackleford
Elstead Road
Sir Greville Sprat Stadium
Peper Harow Lane
Shackleford Heath
Hurtmore Road
Road
St Mary's CE First School
School Lane
Norney
1 grid square represents 500 metres

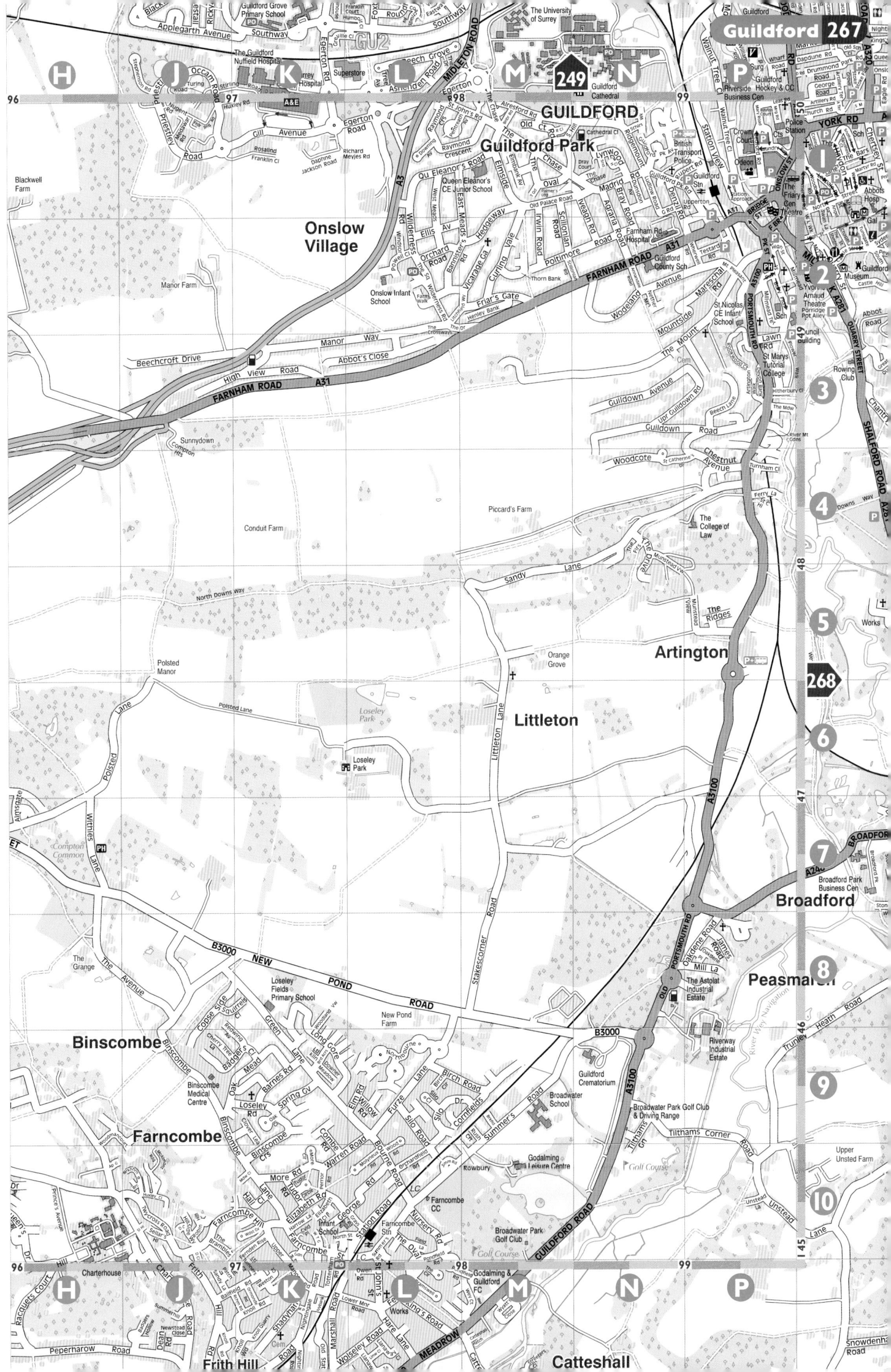
GUILDFORD
Guildford Park
Onslow Village
Artington
Littleton
Broadford
Peasmarsh
Binscombe
Farncombe
Frith Hill
Catteshall
The University of Surrey
The Guildford Nuffield Hospital
Surrey Hospital
Guildford Cathedral
Queen Eleanor's CE Junior School
Onslow Infant School
Farnham Rd Hospital
Guildford County Sch
St Nicolas CE Infant School
St Marys Tutorial College
The College of Law
Loseley Park
Loseley Fields Primary School
Guildford Crematorium
Broadwater School
Godalming Leisure Centre
Broadwater Park Golf Club & Driving Range
Riverway Industrial Estate
The Astolat Industrial Estate
Broadford Park Business Cen
Farncombe Stn
Farncombe CC
Godalming & Guildford FC
Binscombe Medical Centre
Blackwell Farm
Manor Farm
Conduit Farm
Piccard's Farm
Polsted Manor
Orange Grove
New Pond Farm
Upper Unsted Farm
FARNHAM ROAD A31
MIDLETON ROAD
B3000 NEW POND ROAD
A3100
PORTSMOUTH RD
GUILDFORD ROAD
SHALFORD ROAD
QUARRY STREET
North Downs Way
Sandy Lane
Littleton Lane
Stakescorner Road
Polsted Lane
Guildown Avenue
Guildown Road
Chestnut Avenue
Woodcote
The Mount
Mountside
Manor Way
Abbot's Close
Beechcroft Drive
High View Road
Gill Avenue
Applegarth Avenue
Egerton Road
Tilthams Corner Road
Peperharow Road
Meadrow
249
268
96
97
98
99
45
46
47
48
49
50

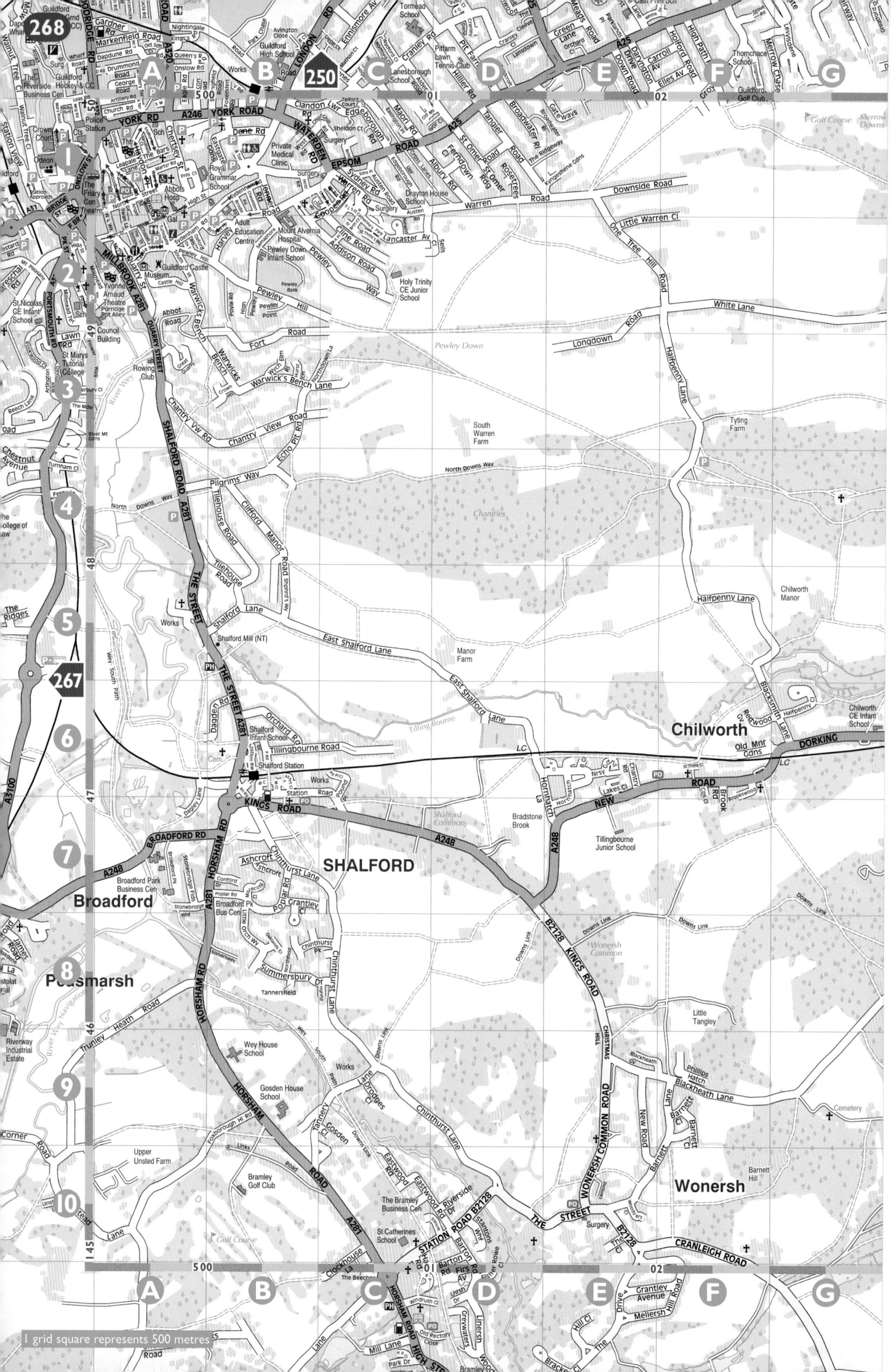

268
250
267
Guildford
Tormead School
Guildford High School
Lanesborough School
Pittfarn Lawn Tennis Club
Thornchace School
Guildford Golf Club
Merrow Downs
Golf Course
YORK RD
YORK ROAD
A246
EPSOM ROAD
WATERDEN RD
LONDON RD
A25
Police Station
Royal Grammar School
Private Medical Clinic
Surgery
Odeon
The Friary Cen
Theatre
Abbots Hosp
Adult Education Centre
Mount Alvernia Hospital
Pewley Down Infant School
Drayton House School
Holy Trinity CE Junior School
Guildford Castle
Museum
Yvonne Arnaud Theatre
St Nicolas CE Infant School
Council Building
St Marys Tutorial College
Rowing Club
The Riverside Business Cen
Guildford Hockey & CC
Warren Road
Downside Road
Little Warren Cl
One Tree Hill Road
White Lane
Longdown Road
Halfpenny Lane
Pewley Down
Pewley Hill
Fort Road
Warwick's Bench Lane
Chantry View Road
Echo Pit Rd
Pilgrims' Way
North Downs Way
Chantries
South Warren Farm
Tyting Farm
Chilworth Manor
Manor Farm
MILLBROOK A281
QUARRY STREET
SHALFORD ROAD A281
THE STREET
THE STREET A281
Tilehouse Road
Clifford Manor Road
Shalford Lane
East Shalford Lane
Shalford Mill (NT)
Tillingbourne
Tilling Bourne
Chilworth
Chilworth CE Infant School
Blacksmith Lane
DORKING
NEW ROAD
A248
Shalford Infant School
Tillingbourne Road
Shalford Station
Station Road
KINGS ROAD
SHALFORD
Shalford Common
Bradstone Brook
Tillingbourne Junior School
BROADFORD RD
Broadford
Broadford Park Business Cen
Broadford Pk Bus Cen
Peasmarsh
River Wey Navigation
Riverway Industrial Estate
Trunley Heath Road
HORSHAM RD
A281 HORSHAM RD
HORSHAM ROAD
Chinthurst Lane
Summersbury Dr
Tannersfield
Wey House School
Gosden House School
Works
Wey South Path
Downs Link
Wonersh Common
B2128 KINGS ROAD
CHRISTMAS HILL
WONERSH COMMON ROAD
Little Tangley
Blackheath Lane
New Road
Barnett Lane
Wonersh
Barnett Hill
Cemetery
THE STREET
CRANLEIGH ROAD
B2128
Surgery
Upper Unsted Farm
Bramley Golf Club
Golf Course
The Bramley Business Cen
St Catherines School
STATION ROAD B2128
Eastwood Rd
Riverside Dr
Clockhouse La
HORSHAM ROAD
HIGH ST
Mill Lane
Park Dr
Grantley Avenue
Mellersh Hill Road
A3100
Corner Road
A B C D E F G
1 2 3 4 5 6 7 8 9 10
500 01 02
49 48 47 46 45
1 grid square represents 500 metres

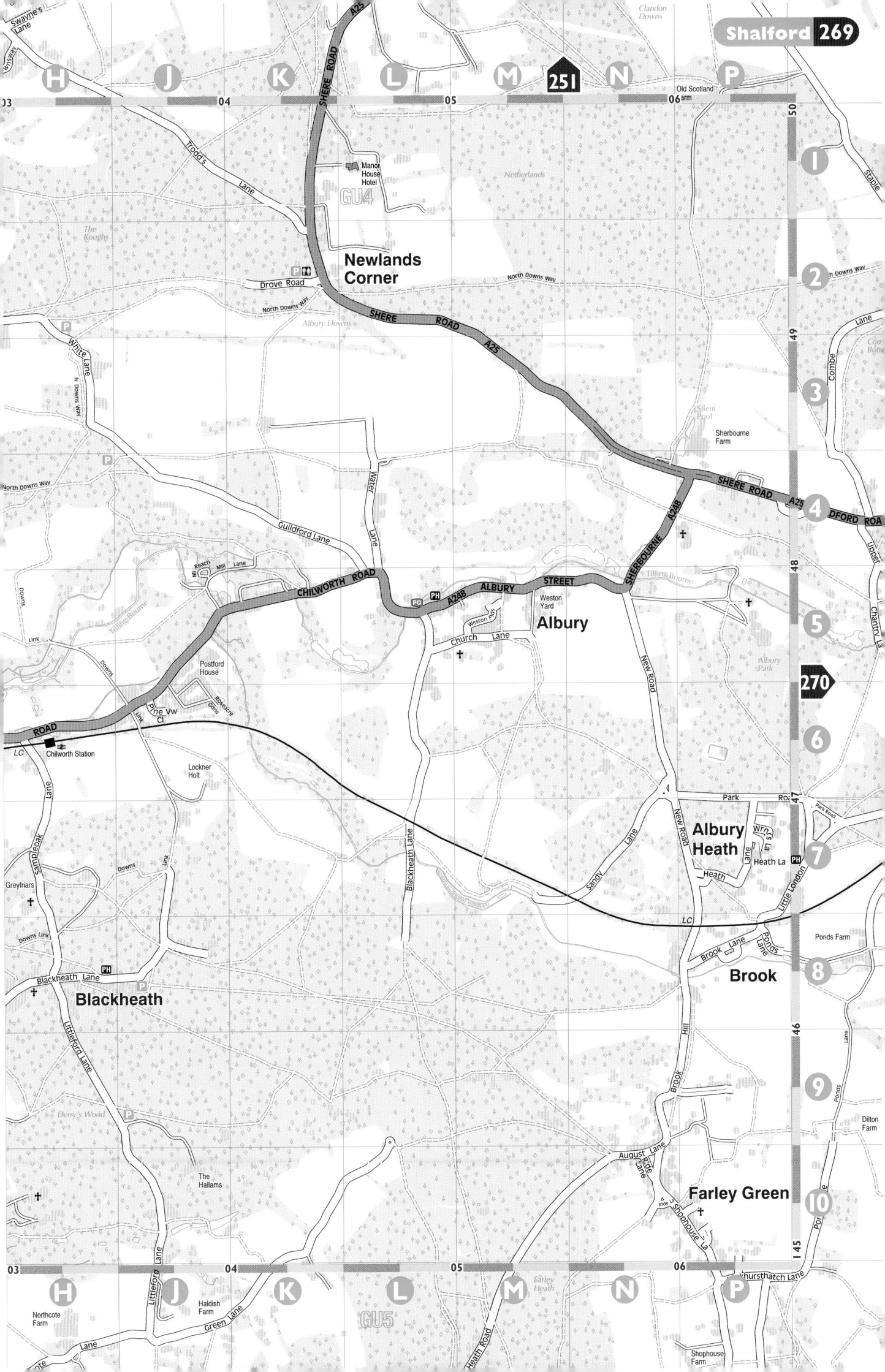
Newlands Corner
Albury
Albury Heath
Brook
Blackheath
Farley Green
Chilworth Station
SHERE ROAD
A25
CHILWORTH ROAD
A248
ALBURY STREET
SHERBOURNE
Drove Road
Trodd's Lane
White Lane
Guildford Lane
Water Lane
Mill Lane
Church Lane
Weston Yard
New Road
Sandy Lane
Blackheath Lane
Sampleoak Lane
Littleford Lane
Brook Lane
Ponds Lane
Brook Hill
August Lane
Shophouse La
Park Road
Heath La
Little London
North Downs Way
Manor House Hotel
GU4
GU5
Netherlands
The Roughs
Albury Downs
Silent Pool
Sherbourne Farm
Tilling Bourne
Albury Park
Postford House
Lockner Holt
Greyfriars
Derry's Wood
The Hallams
Haldish Farm
Northcote Farm
Farley Heath
Shophouse Farm
Ponds Farm
Dilton Farm
Old Scotland Farm
Clandon Downs
Hurtsthatch Lane
Green Lane
Heath Road
251
270

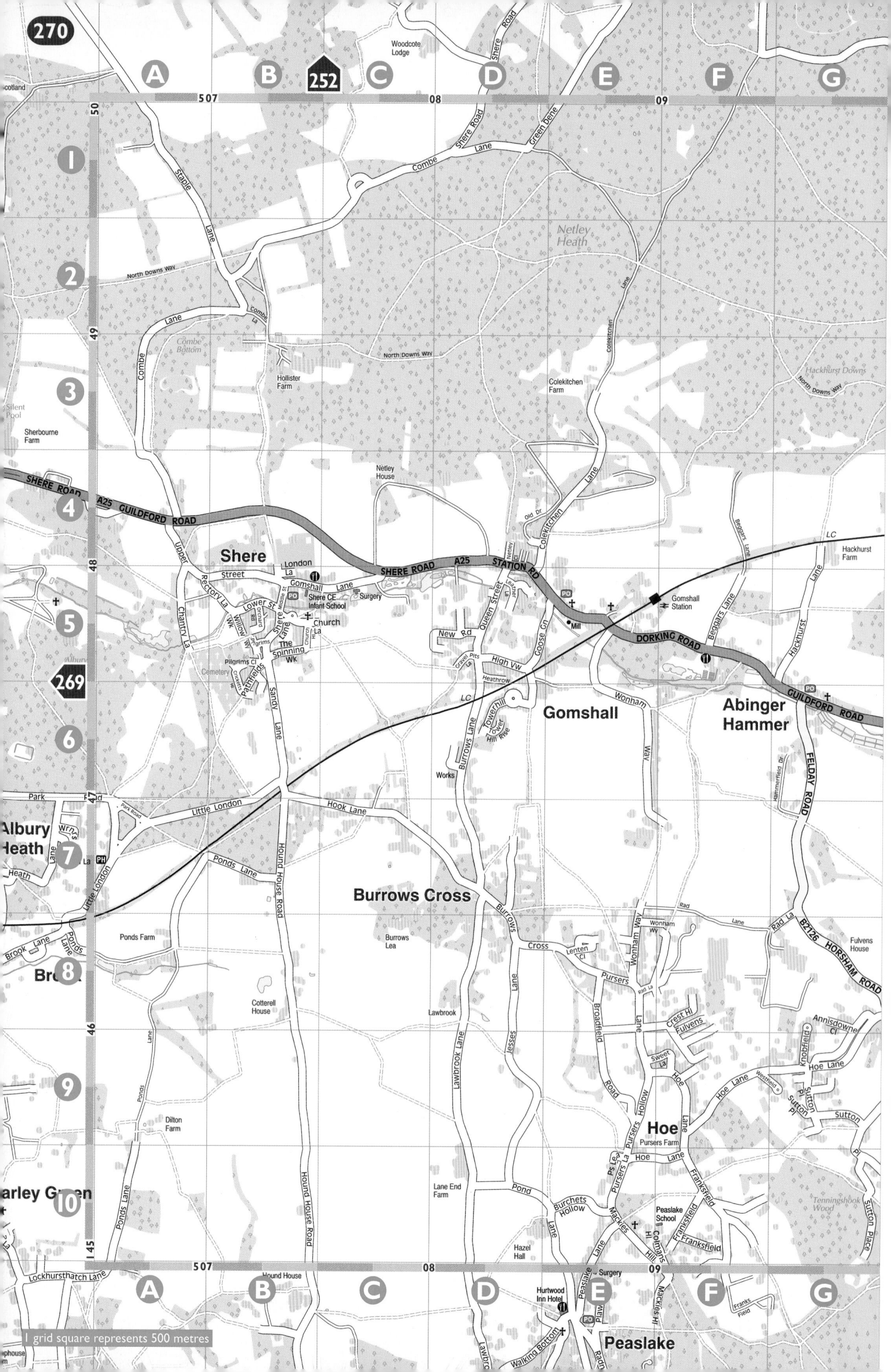
252
269
A
B
C
D
E
F
G
1
2
3
4
5
6
7
8
9
10
507
08
09
50
49
48
47
46
45
Woodcote Lodge
Shere Road
Combe Lane
Green Dene
Staple Lane
Netley Heath
North Downs Way
Combe Bottom
Hollister Farm
Colekitchen Lane
Colekitchen Farm
Hackhurst Downs
Silent Pool
Sherbourne Farm
Netley House
SHERE ROAD
A25 GUILDFORD ROAD
Shere
Upper
Chantry La
Rectory La
Street
London La
Gomshall Lane
Shere CE Infant School
Surgery
Lower St
Middle St
Orchard Rd
Willow Wk
Pilgrims Wy
Shere Lane
Church La
Church Hl
The Spinning Wk
Pilgrims Cl
Pathfields
Crossers Hl
Cemetery
SHERE ROAD
A25
STATION RD
Netley St
Queen Street
Leather La
Old Dr
Colekitchen Lane
New Rd
Gravel Pits La
High Vw
Heathrow
Towerhill
Tower Hill Rise
Goose Gn
Mill
Gomshall Station
DORKING ROAD
Beggars Lane
Hackhurst Farm
Hackhurst Lane
LC
Gomshall
Wonham Way
Abinger Hammer
GUILDFORD ROAD
FELDAY ROAD
Hammerfield Dr
Sandy Lane
Burrows Lane
Works
Park Rd
Park Road
Little London
Hook Lane
Albury Heath
Heath La
Ponds Lane
Hound House Road
Burrows Cross
Ponds Farm
Burrows Lea
Brook Lane
Ponds Lane
Burrows Cross
Lenten Cl
Rad Lane
Wonham Wy
Rad La
B2126 HORSHAM ROAD
Fulvens House
Pursers Lane
Rad La
Broadfield Road
Crest Hl
Fulvens
Annisdowne Cl
Knobfield
Cotterell House
Lawbrook
Lawbrook Lane
Jesses Lane
Sweet La
Hoe Lane
Westfield
Sutton Pl
Hoe Lane
Ponds Lane
Dilton Farm
Pursers Hollow
Hoe
Pursers Farm
Sutton
Hound House Road
Ps La
Pursers La
Hoe Lane
Franksfield
Lane End Farm
Pond Lane
Burchets Hollow
Mackies Hill
Peaslake School
Colmans Hill
Franksfield
Tenningshook Wood
Sutton Place
Farley Green
Hazel Hall
Peaslake Lane
Surgery
Lockhurst Hatch Lane
Hound House
Hurtwood Inn Hotel
Mackies Hl
Franks Field
Walking Bottom
Plaw
Peaslake
1 grid square represents 500 metres

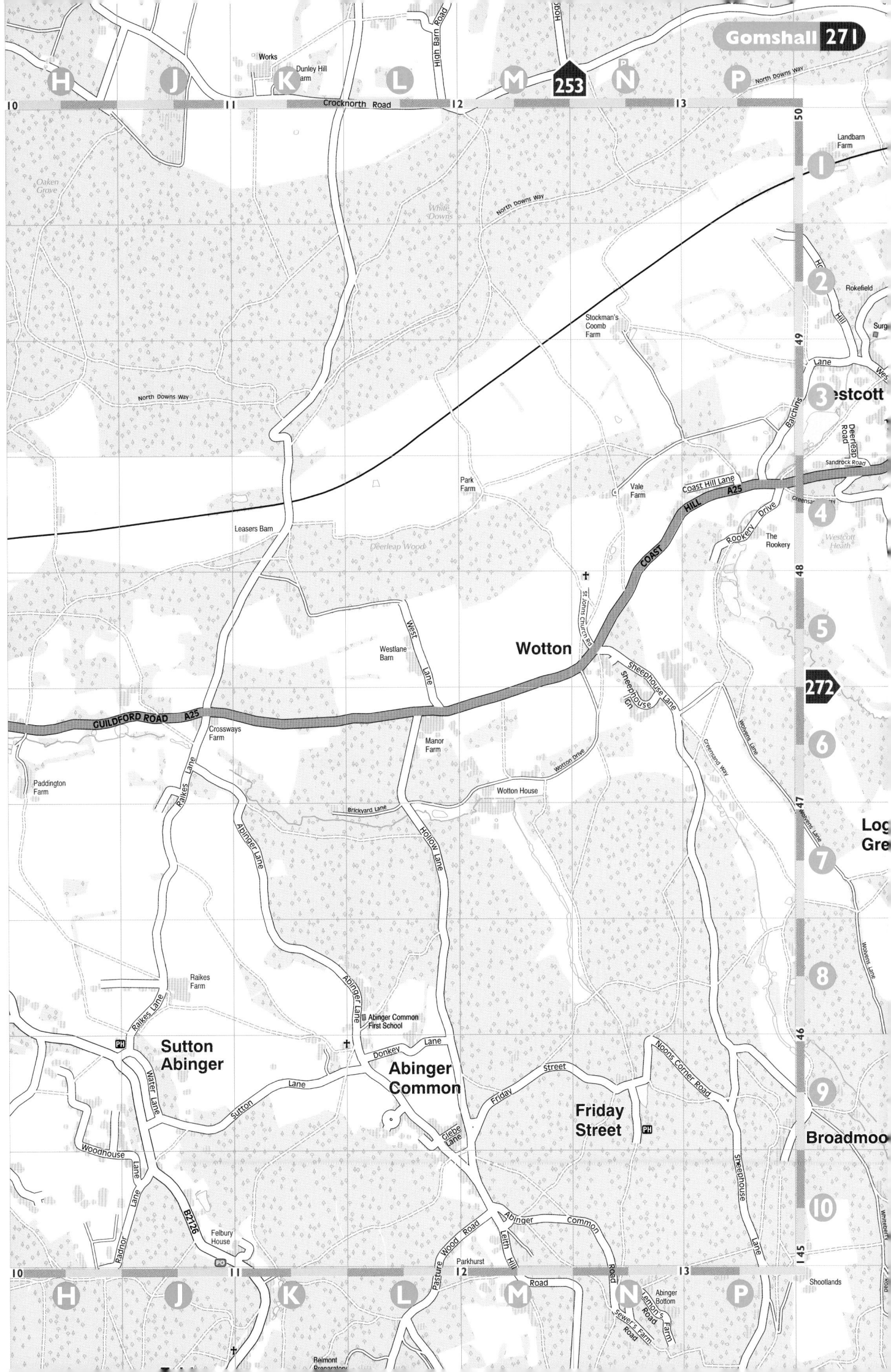
Works
Dunley Hill Farm
High Barn Road
Crocknorth Road
253
North Downs Way
Landbarn Farm
Oaken Grove
White Downs
Rokefield
Stockman's Coomb Farm
North Downs Way
Lane
Westcott
Balchins
Deerleap Road
Sandrock Road
Park Farm
Vale Farm
Coast Hill Lane
A25
Greensand Way
Rookery Drive
The Rookery
Westcott Heath
Leasers Barn
Deerleap Wood
COAST HILL
St Johns Church Rd
West Lane
Westlane Barn
Wotton
Sheephouse Lane
Sheephouse Gn
272
GUILDFORD ROAD A25
Crossways Farm
Manor Farm
Wolvens Lane
Greensand Way
Paddington Farm
Raikes Lane
Wotton Drive
Wotton House
Brickyard Lane
Abinger Lane
Hollow Lane
Logmore Green
Raikes Farm
Abinger Lane
Abinger Common First School
Raikes Lane
Sutton Abinger
Donkey Lane
Abinger Common
Water Lane
Sutton Lane
Friday Street
Noons Corner Road
Friday Street
Broadmoor
Woodhouse Lane
Glebe Lane
Sheephouse Lane
Radnor Lane
B2126
Felbury House
Pasture Wood Road
Abinger Common Road
Leith Hill Road
Parkhurst
Shootlands
Abinger Bottom
Lemon's Farm Road
Sewer's Farm Road
Belmont Preparatory
Wolvens Lane
Whiteberry Road

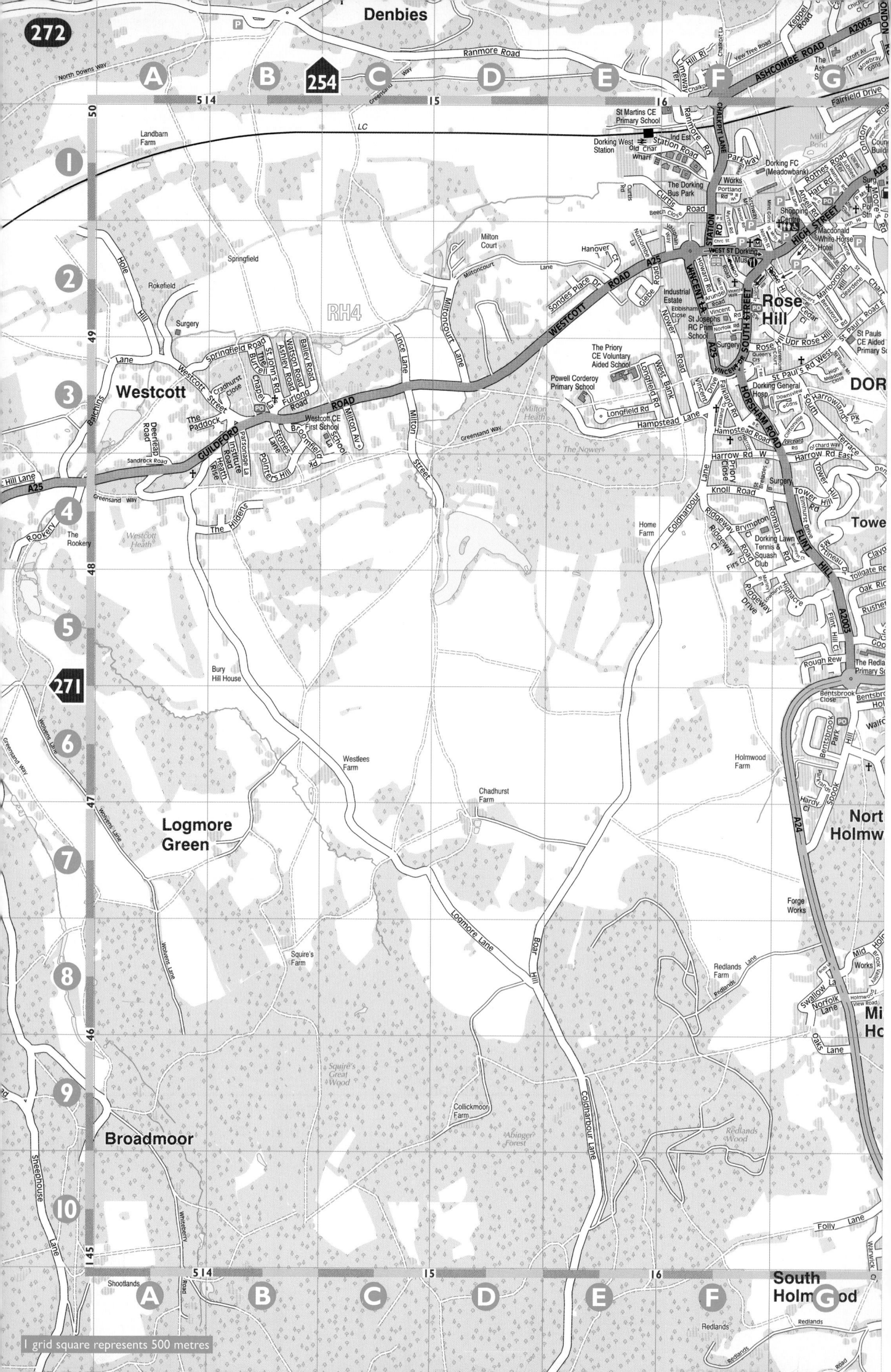

Denbies
254
Ranmore Road
North Downs Way
Greensand Way
ASHCOMBE ROAD
A2003
Fairfield Drive
A B C D E F G
514
15
16
50
49
48
47
46
45
1 2 3 4 5 6 7 8 9 10
271
Landbarn Farm
LC
St Martins CE Primary School
Dorking West Station
Station Road
Ind Est
Ranmore Rd
CHALKPIT LANE
Parkway
Dorking FC (Meadowbank)
Mill Pond
The Dorking Bus Park
Curtis Road
Works
Portland Rd
Rothes Road
Hart Rd
Shopping Centre
Macdonald White Horse Hotel
HIGH STREET
A25
Milton Court
Miltoncourt Lane
Hanover Ct
WEST ST
Mus
Springfield
Rokefield
Hole Hill
Surgery
RH4
Westcott
Springfield Road
Watson Road
Bailey Road
Ashley Road
Lince Lane
WESTCOTT ROAD
Sondes Place Dr
Glebe Rd
Industrial Estate
Ebbisham Close
St Josephs RC Prim School
VINCENT LA
STATION RD
SOUTH STREET
Rose Hill
Upr Rose Hill
St Paul's Rd West
St Pauls CE Aided Primary Sc
DOR
Batchins
Westcott Street
Cradhurst Close
The Paddock
Deerleap Road
Sandrock Road
GUILDFORD ROAD
Parsonage La
Institute Road
Heath Rise
Furlong Road
Westcott CE First School
Stones Lane
Milton Av
Broomfield Pk
Pointers Hill
Milton Street
Greensand Way
The Priory CE Voluntary Aided School
Powell Corderoy Primary School
Longfield Rd
West Bank
Nower Road
Hampstead Lane
Milton Heath
The Nower
Falkland Rd
HORSHAM ROAD
Dorking General Hosp
Harrowlands Pk
Hampstead Road
Harrow Rd W
Harrow Rd East
Priory Close
Knoll Road
Surgery
Tower Hill
Towe
Hill Lane
A25
Greensand Way
The Hildens
Rookery
The Rookery
Westcott Heath
Home Farm
Coldharbour Lane
Ridgeway
Brympton Cl
Roman Rd
Dorking Lawn Tennis & Squash Club
Ridgeway Road
Firs Cl
Ridgeway Drive
FLINT HILL
A2003
Flint Hill Cl
Rough Rew
The Redla Primary Sc
Bentsbrook Close
Bentsbrook Park
Bury Hill House
Wolvens Lane
Greensand Way
Westlees Farm
Holmwood Farm
A24
Chadhurst Farm
Logmore Green
Nort Holmw
Logmore Lane
Boar Hill
Forge Works
Squire's Farm
Redlands Farm
Redlands Lane
Mid Holm
Works
Swallow La
Norfolk Lane
Oaks Lane
Mi Ho
Squire's Great Wood
Collickmoor Farm
Abinger Forest
Redlands Wood
Broadmoor
Sheephouse Lane
Whiteberry Road
Folly Lane
Warwick
Shootlands
South Holmwood
Redlands
1 grid square represents 500 metres

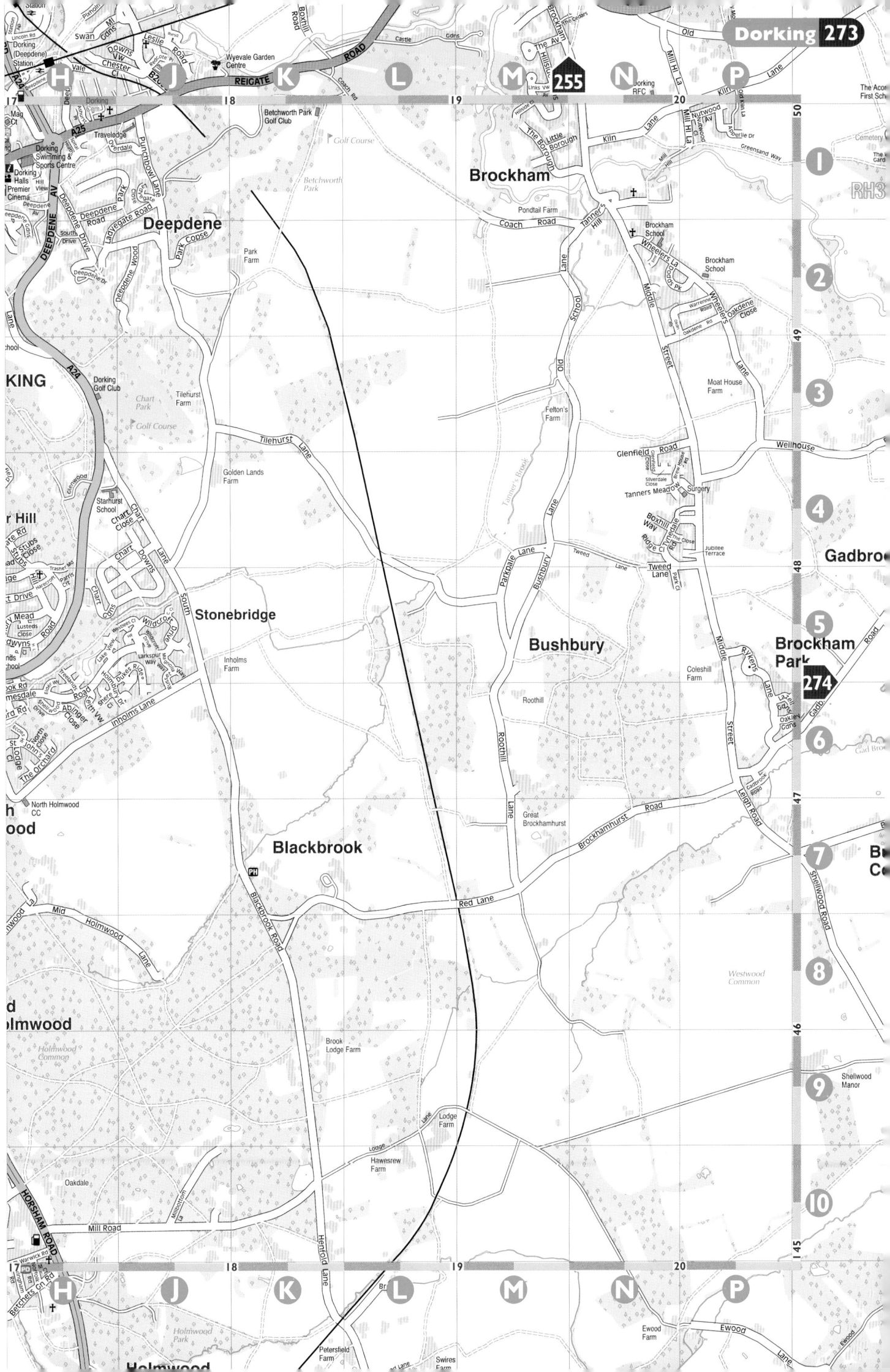
Brockham
Deepdene
Stonebridge
Bushbury
Blackbrook
Brockham Park
Betchworth Park Golf Club
Dorking Golf Club
Tilehurst Lane
Red Lane
Brockhamhurst Road
Middle Street
Wellhouse Lane
Westwood Common
Holmwood Common
Mill Road
Horsham Road
Reigate Road
Coach Road
Inholms Lane
Mid Holmwood Lane
Blackbrook Road
Henfold Lane
Roothill Lane
Parkpale Lane
Tweed Lane
Old School Lane
Shellwood Road
Ewood Lane
255
274

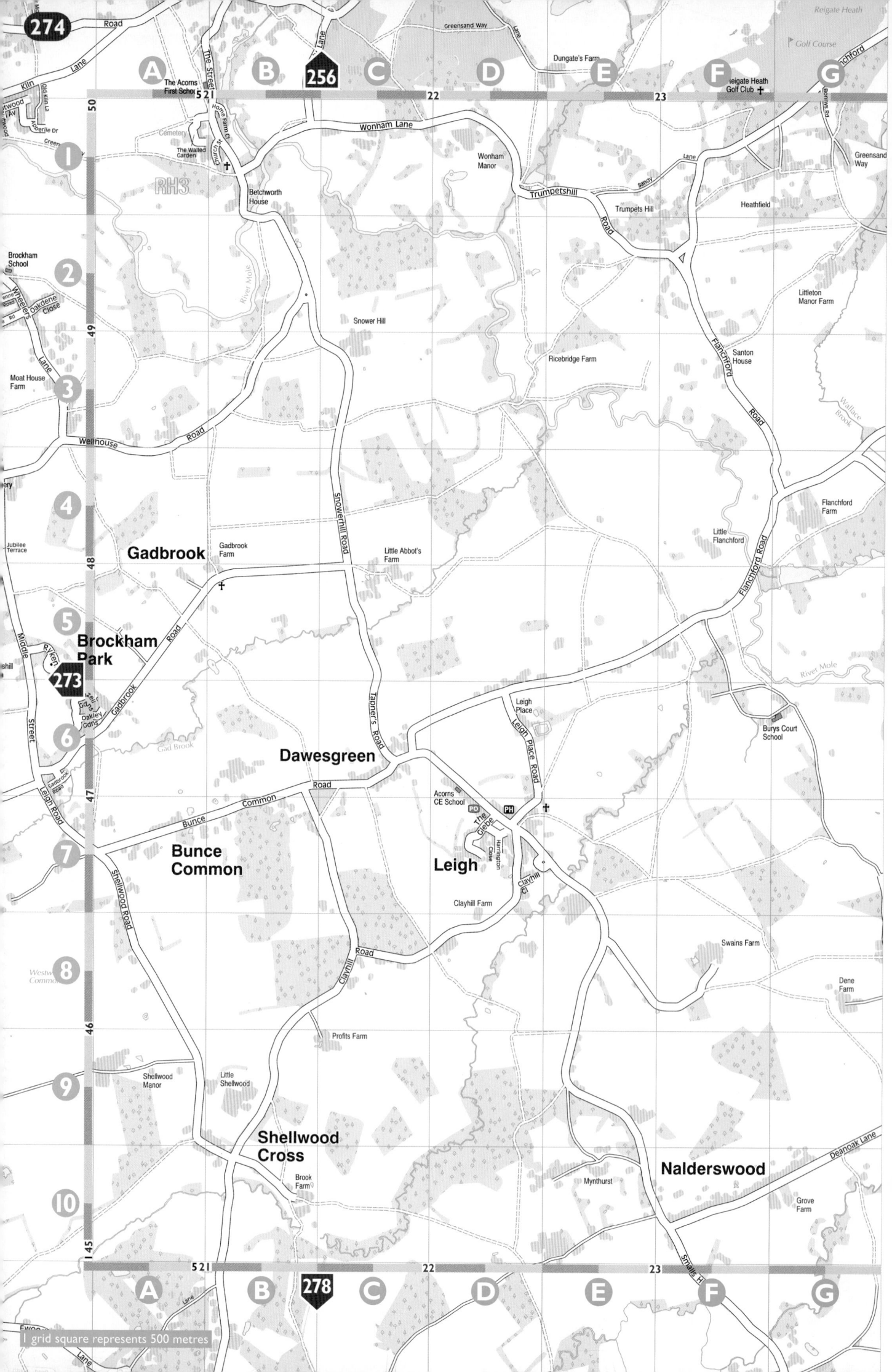
274
256
273
278
Gadbrook
Brockham Park
Dawesgreen
Bunce Common
Leigh
Shellwood Cross
Nalderswood
Wonham Lane
Trumpetshill
Snowerhill Road
Tapner's Road
Flanchford Road
Wellhouse Road
Gadbrook Road
Shellwood Road
Clayhill Road
Leigh Place Road
Bunce Common Road
Wonham Manor
Betchworth House
Snower Hill
Ricebridge Farm
Little Abbot's Farm
Gadbrook Farm
Acorns CE School
Clayhill Farm
Profits Farm
Shellwood Manor
Little Shellwood
Brook Farm
Mynthurst
Swains Farm
Dene Farm
Grove Farm
Burys Court School
Flanchford Farm
Little Flanchford
Santon House
Littleton Manor Farm
Heathfield
Trumpets Hill
Dungate's Farm
Reigate Heath Golf Club
Reigate Heath
Golf Course
River Mole
Brockham School
Moat House Farm
Leigh Place
1 grid square represents 500 metres

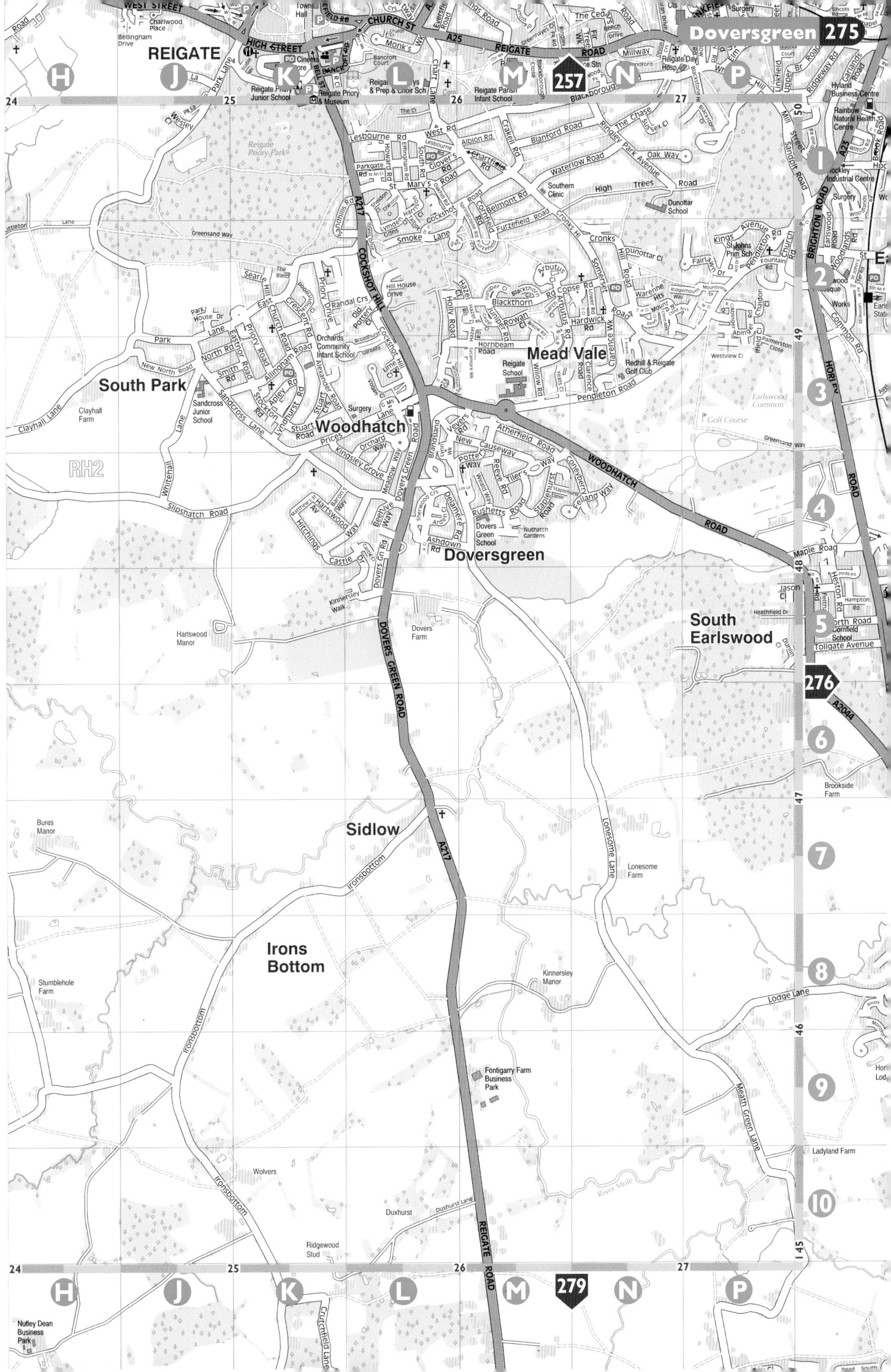
REIGATE
South Park
Woodhatch
Mead Vale
Doversgreen
South Earlswood
Sidlow
Irons Bottom
RH2
257
276
279

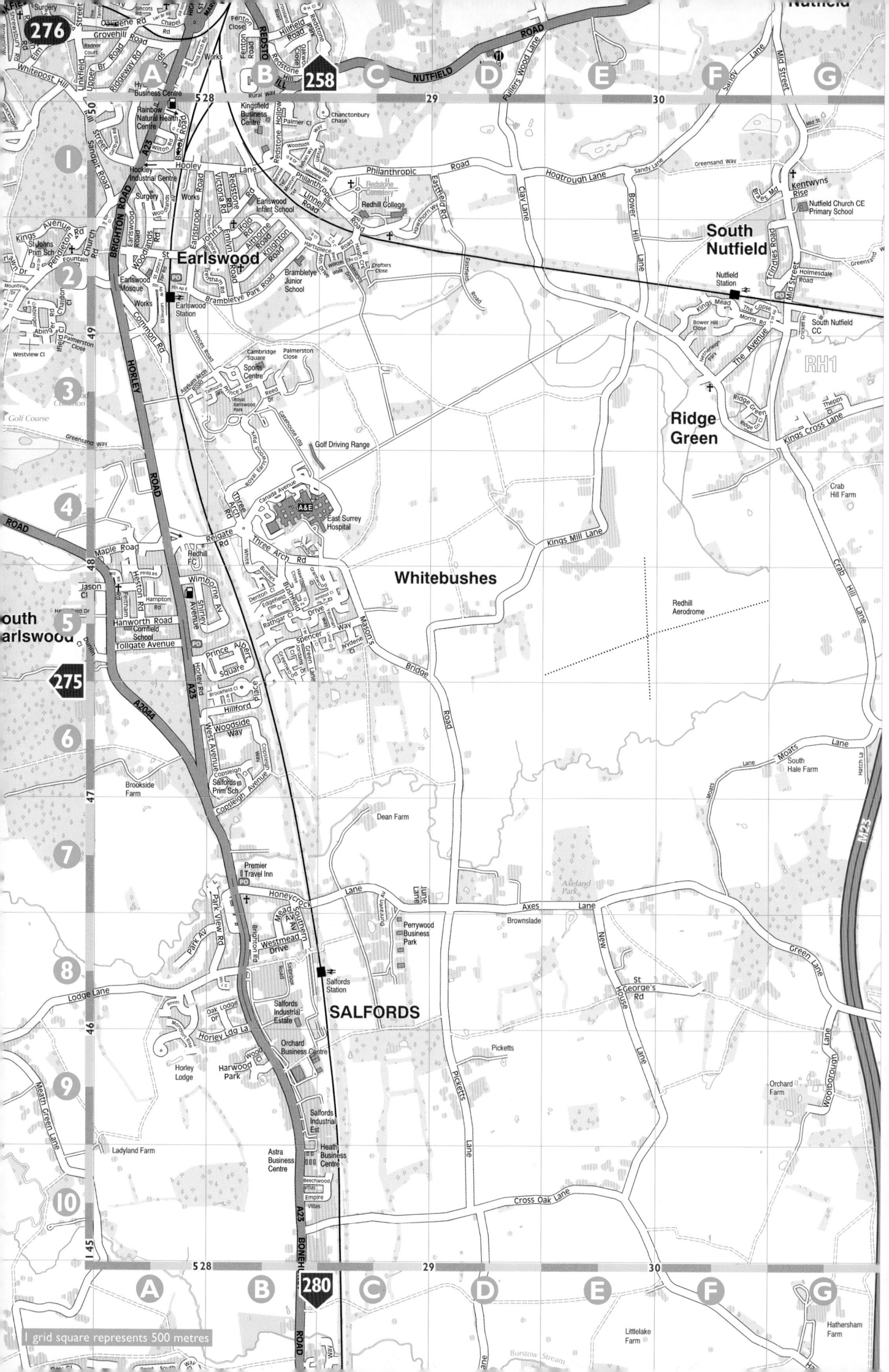

276
258
275
280
A
B
C
D
E
F
G
1
2
3
4
5
6
7
8
9
10
528
29
30
50
49
48
47
46
45
Earlswood
South Nutfield
Ridge Green
Whitebushes
SALFORDS
South Earlswood
Redhill Aerodrome
East Surrey Hospital
Earlswood Station
Nutfield Station
Salfords Station
Redhill College
Redstone Cemetery
Earlswood Infant School
Brambletye Junior School
Nutfield Church CE Primary School
Salfords Prim Sch
Cornfield School
St Johns Prim Sch
Earlswood Mosque
Golf Driving Range
Sports Centre
Redhill FC
Kingsfield Business Centre
Hockley Industrial Centre
Rainbow Natural Health Centre
Perrywood Business Park
Salfords Industrial Estate
Orchard Business Centre
Heath Business Centre
Astra Business Centre
Premier Travel Inn
Crab Hill Farm
South Hale Farm
Brookside Farm
Dean Farm
Horley Lodge
Ladyland Farm
Orchard Farm
Littlelake Farm
Hathersham Farm
Brownslade
Picketts
Axeland Park
South Nutfield CC
RH1
NUTFIELD ROAD
BRIGHTON ROAD
HORLEY ROAD
A23
A2044
M23
Philanthropic Road
Hogtrough Lane
Clay Lane
Bower Hill Lane
Kings Mill Lane
Three Arch Rd
Masons Bridge Road
Honeycrock Lane
Axes Lane
New House Lane
Picketts Lane
Cross Oak Lane
Lodge Lane
Meath Green Lane
Crab Hill Lane
Moats Lane
Green Lane
Woolborough Lane
Kings Cross Lane
Mid Street
Sandy Lane
Fullers Wood Lane
Common Rd
Brambletye Park Road
Hooley Lane
Sandpit Road
Maple Road
Hanworth Road
Tollgate Avenue
Copsleigh Avenue
West Avenue
Woodside Way
Westmead Drive
Horley Ldg La
St George's Rd
Burstow Stream
Golf Course
Greensand Way
1 grid square represents 500 metres

Bletchingley
Greensand Way
Coneybury
Outwood
Rabies Heath Road
Coldharbour La
259
H
J
K
L
M
N
P
Sandhills
31
32
33
34
50
Coldharbour Farm
South Park Lane
M23
Cooper's Hill Road
Lyttel Hall
Sandhills Farm
Wychroft House
49
Cuckseys Farm
South Park Farm
Nutfield Pk
Kennels Farm
Cooper's Hl Rd
Henshaw Farm
Outwood Lane
Lamb Busin Park
48
Burstow Park Farm
Lower South Park
47
Lodge Farm
Carlton Road
Brown's Hill Lane
Prince of Wales Road
Harewood House
Shepheard's Hurst
Outwood Common
46
Tile Barn
Brickfield Road
Wasp Green Lane
Bellwether Lane
Outwood
Outwood Windmill
Gayhouse Lane
Dayseys Hill
Millers Copse
Miller's Lane
Scott's Hill
Wasp Green
Miller's La
Hornecourt Hill
Whitewood
Jarves Farm
Whitewood La
Hornecourt Manor Farm
45
Rookery Farm
Wilmot's Lane
281
Old Hall Farm
Rookery
Whitewood House Farm
1
2
3
4
5
6
7
8
9
10

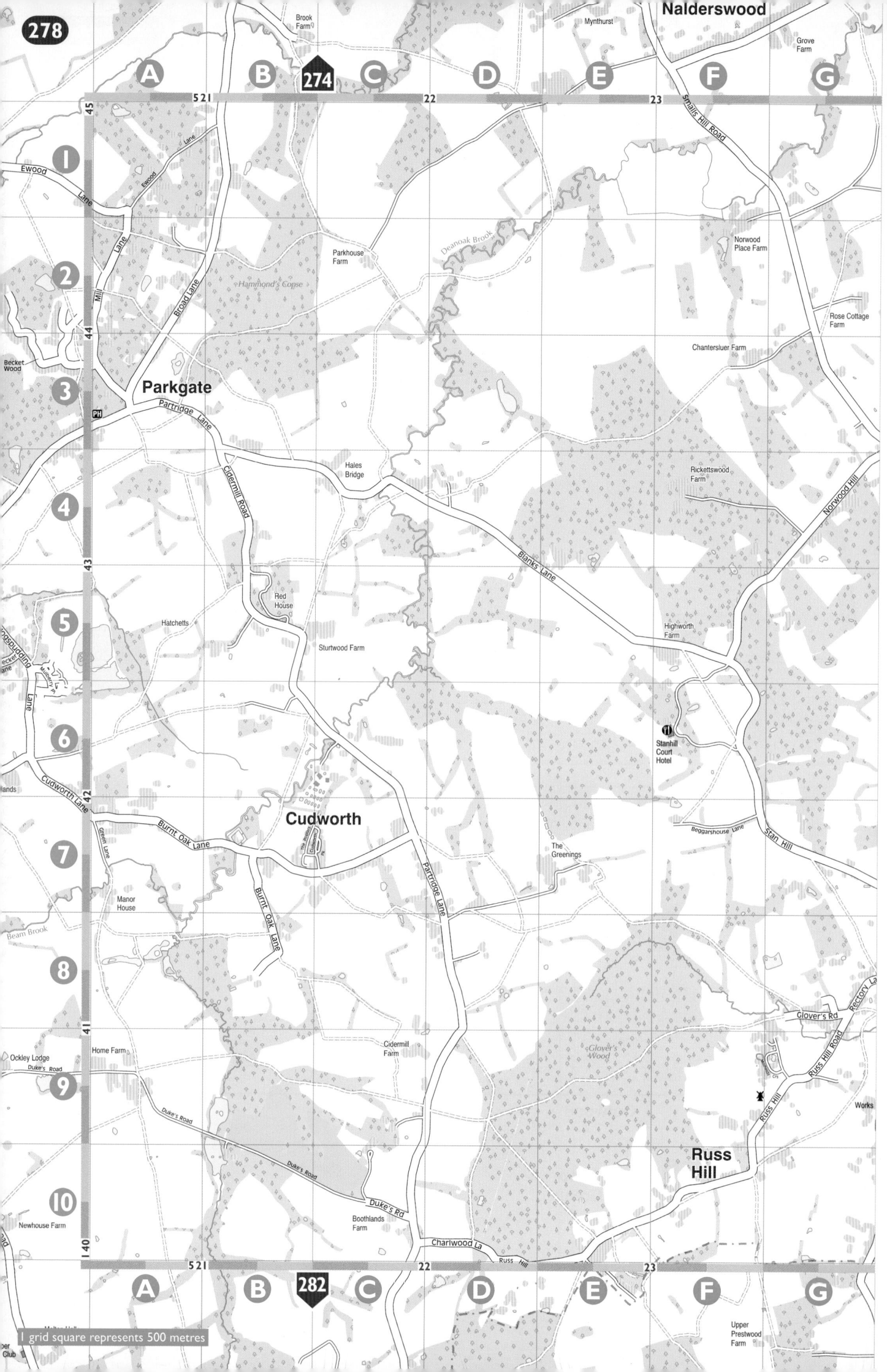

Nalderswood
Brook Farm
Mynthurst
Grove Farm
274
Smalls Hill Road
Ewood Lane
Ewood Lane
Mill Lane
Broad Lane
Hammond's Copse
Parkhouse Farm
Deanoak Brook
Norwood Place Farm
Rose Cottage Farm
Chantersluer Farm
Becket Wood
Parkgate
PH
Partridge Lane
Hales Bridge
Rickettswood Farm
Norwood Hill
Cidermill Road
Blanks Lane
Red House
Hatchetts
Sturtwood Farm
Highworth Farm
Stanhill Court Hotel
Cudworth Lane
Cudworth
Burnt Oak Lane
Green Lane
Beggarshouse Lane
Stan Hill
The Greenings
Manor House
Burnt Oak Lane
Partridge Lane
Beam Brook
Glover's Rd
Rectory La
Russ Hill Road
Ockley Lodge
Duke's Road
Home Farm
Cidermill Farm
Glover's Wood
Russ Hill
Works
Duke's Road
Duke's Road
Russ Hill
Duke's Rd
Newhouse Farm
Boothlands Farm
Charlwood La
Russ Hill
282
Upper Prestwood Farm
1 grid square represents 500 metres

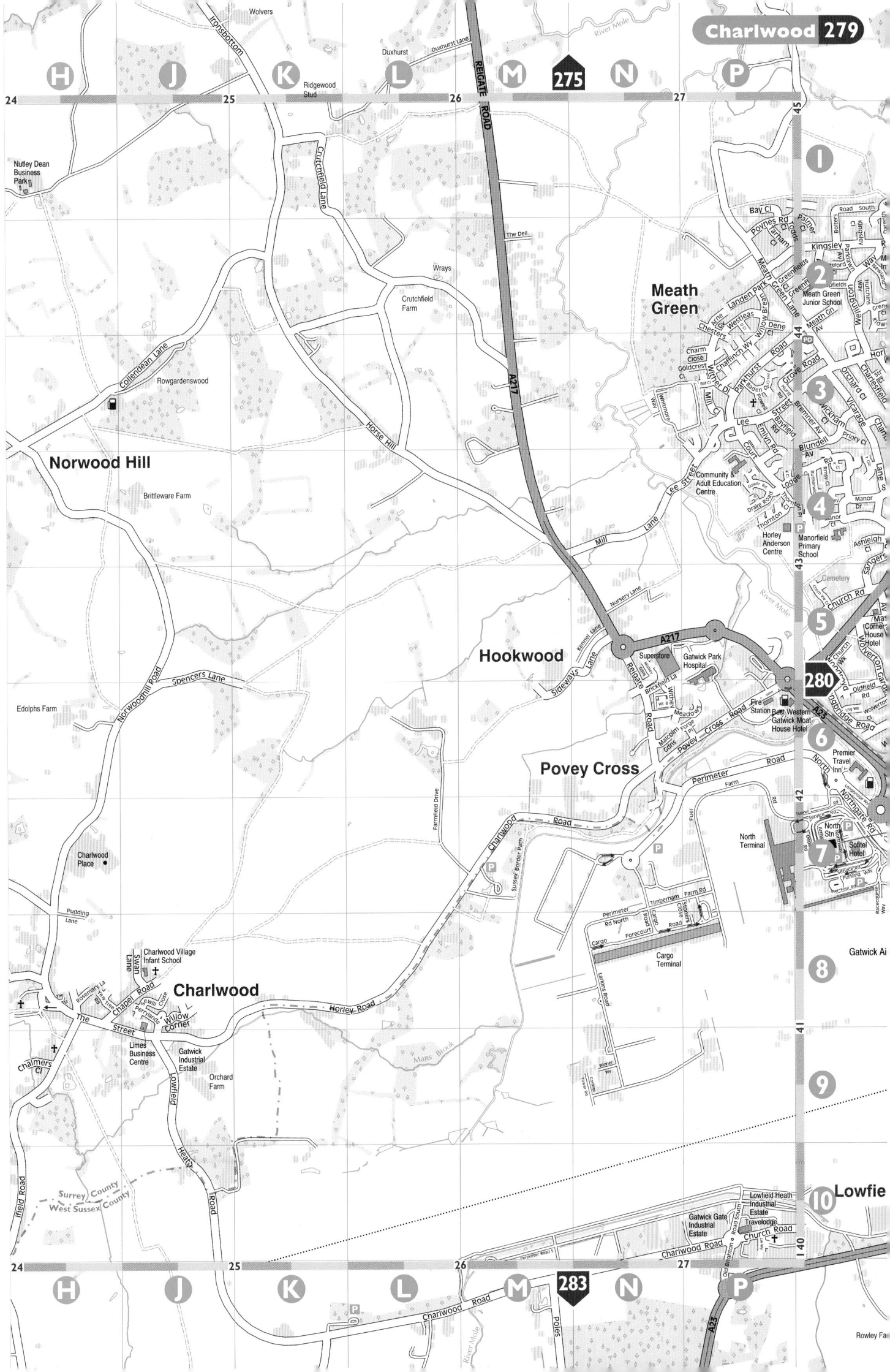

Norwood Hill
Meath Green
Hookwood
Povey Cross
Charlwood
Lowfield Heath
Gatwick Airport
North Terminal
Cargo Terminal
Reigate Road
A217
A23
Horley Road
Charlwood Road
Mill Lane
Lee Street
Perimeter Road
Norwoodhill Road
Spencers Lane
Collendean Lane
Crutchfield Lane
Horse Hill
Ironsbottom
Wolvers
Duxhurst
Ridgewood Stud
Crutchfield Farm
Wrays
Rowgardenswood
Brittleware Farm
Edolphs Farm
Nutley Dean Business Park
Charlwood Place
Pudding Lane
Charlwood Village Infant School
The Street
Chapel Road
Swan Lane
Limes Business Centre
Gatwick Industrial Estate
Orchard Farm
Lowfield Heath
Chalmers Cl
Surrey County
West Sussex County
River Mole
Mans Brook
Superstore
Gatwick Park Hospital
Fire Station
Best Western Gatwick Moat House Hotel
Premier Travel Inn
Sofitel Hotel
Community & Adult Education Centre
Horley Anderson Centre
Manorfield Primary School
Meath Green Junior School
Cemetery
Lowfield Heath Industrial Estate
Gatwick Gate Industrial Estate
Travelodge
Church Road
Farmfield Drive
Sussex Border Path
Rowley Farm
275
280
283

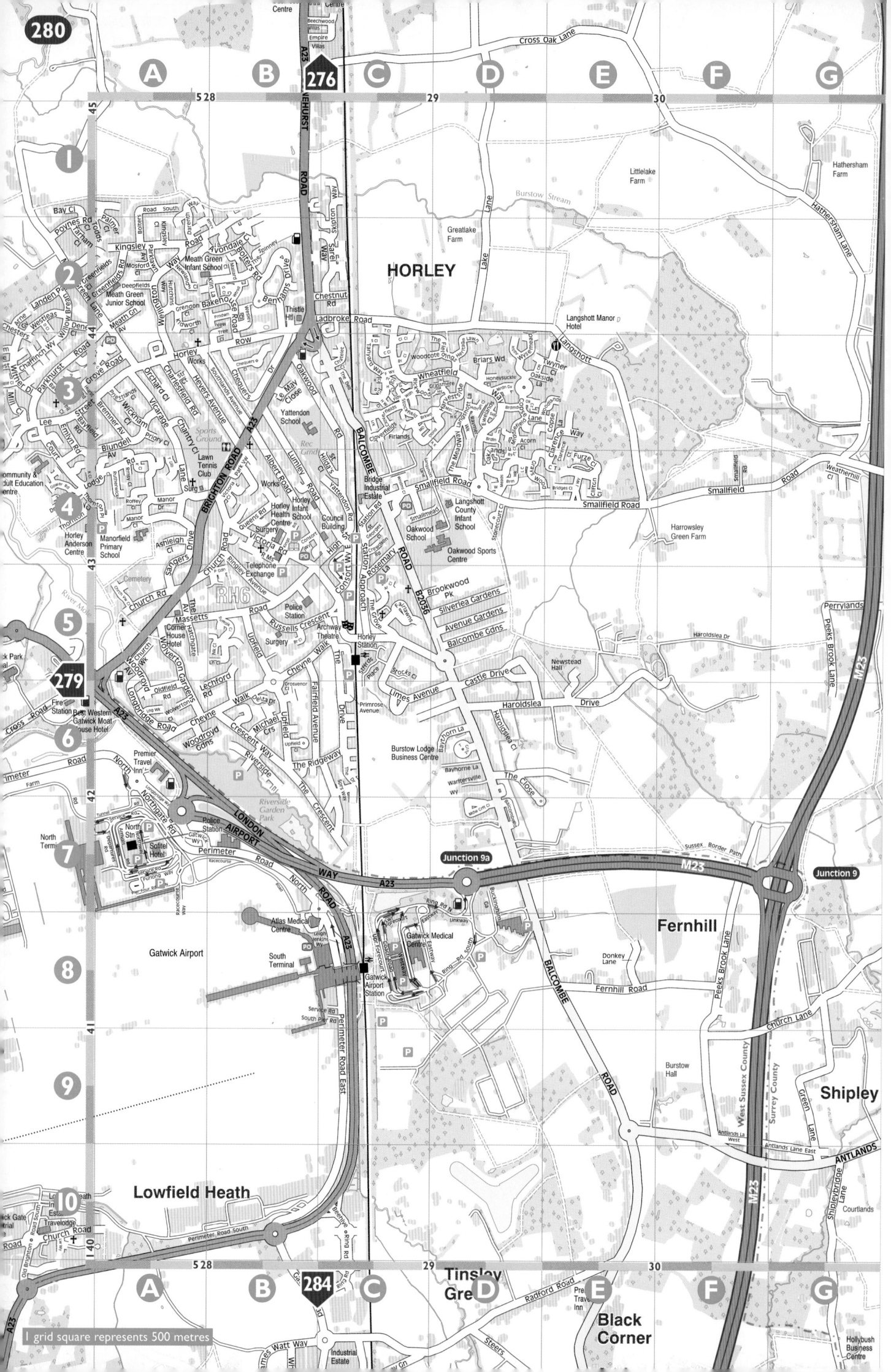

280
276
279
284
A
B
C
D
E
F
G
1
2
3
4
5
6
7
8
9
10
5 28
29
30
45
44
43
42
41
1 40
Cross Oak Lane
Beechwood Villas
Empire Villas
Littlelake Farm
Hathersham Farm
Hathersham Lane
Burstow Stream
Greatlake Farm
Lake Lane
HORLEY
Bay Cl
Poynes Rd
Yarnham Cl
Kingsley
Bolters Road South
Avondale Cl
Meath Green Infant School
Meath Green Junior School
Meath Green Lane
Greenfields Rd
Deepfields
Bakehouse Road
Bennetts Drive
Chestnut Rd
Thistle Htl
Ladbroke Road
Langshott Manor Hotel
Langshott
Skipton Way
Horley Row
Landen Park
Westleas
Chaffinch Wy
Parkhurst Road
Grove Road
Lee Street
Court Lodge Rd
Ashleigh Cl
Blundell Av
Bremner Av
Wickham Cl
Vicarage Lane
Orchard Cl
Charlesfield Rd
Chantry Cl
Hevers Avenue
Southlands Avenue
Albert Road
Lumley Road
Yattendon School
Yattendon Rd
Oakwood Road
Le May Close
Rec Grnd
St Hilda's Cl
Sports Ground
Lawn Tennis Club
Works
Horley Infant School
Horley Health Centre
Surgery
Council Building
Station Rd
High St
Victoria Rd
Queens Rd
Telephone Exchange
Consort Wy
Station Approach
Rosemary La
Bridge Industrial Estate
Balcombe Road B2036
Smallfield Road
Smallfield
Weatherhill Cl
Langshott County Infant School
Oakwood School
Oakwood Sports Centre
Woodcote
Wheatfield Way
Briars Wd
Twyner Cl
Oakside La
Copse Lane
Clarence Way
Furze Cl
Acorn Cl
Firlands
The Meadway
Cloverfields
Harrowsley Green Farm
Brookwood Pk
Silverlea Gardens
Avenue Gardens
Balcombe Gdns
Perrylands
Peeks Brook Lane
Haroldslea Dr
Haroldslea Drive
Newstead Hall
Castle Drive
Limes Avenue
Horley Station
Archway Theatre
Russells Crescent
Police Station
Massetts Road
Corner House Hotel
Church Rd
Cemetery
RH6
River Mole
Manorfield Primary School
Horley Anderson Centre
Community & Adult Education Centre
Thornton
Sangers Drive
Brighton Road A23
Woodroyd Av
Longbridge Road
Wolverton Gardens
Lechford Rd
Oldfield Rd
Cheyne Walk
Crescent Way
Michael Crs
Fairfield Avenue
The Drive
Primrose Avenue
The Ridgeway
The Crescent
Riverside
Riverside Garden Park
Woodroyd Gdns
Fire Station
Best Western Gatwick Moat House Hotel
Cross Road
Perimeter Road
Premier Travel Inn
North Terminal
North Stn
Sofitel Hotel
Northgate Rd
Police Station
London Airport Way A23
Burstow Lodge Business Centre
Haroldslea Cl
The Close
Junction 9a
Junction 9
M23
Sussex Border Path
Fernhill
Atlas Medical Centre
Gatwick Airport
South Terminal
Gatwick Airport Station
Gatwick Medical Centre
Ring Rd North
Ring Rd South
Buckingham Ga
Donkey Lane
Fernhill Road
Church Lane
Burstow Hall
West Sussex County
Surrey County
Green Lane
Shipley
Antlands La West
Antlands Lane East
ANTLANDS
Shipleybridge Lane
Courtlands
Perimeter Road East
Service Rd
South Pier Rd
Lowfield Heath
Travelodge
Church Road
Perimeter Road South
Beehive Ring Rd
Tinsley Green
Radford Road
Premier Travel Inn
Black Corner
Hollybush Business Centre
James Watt Way
Industrial Estate
Steers
1 grid square represents 500 metres

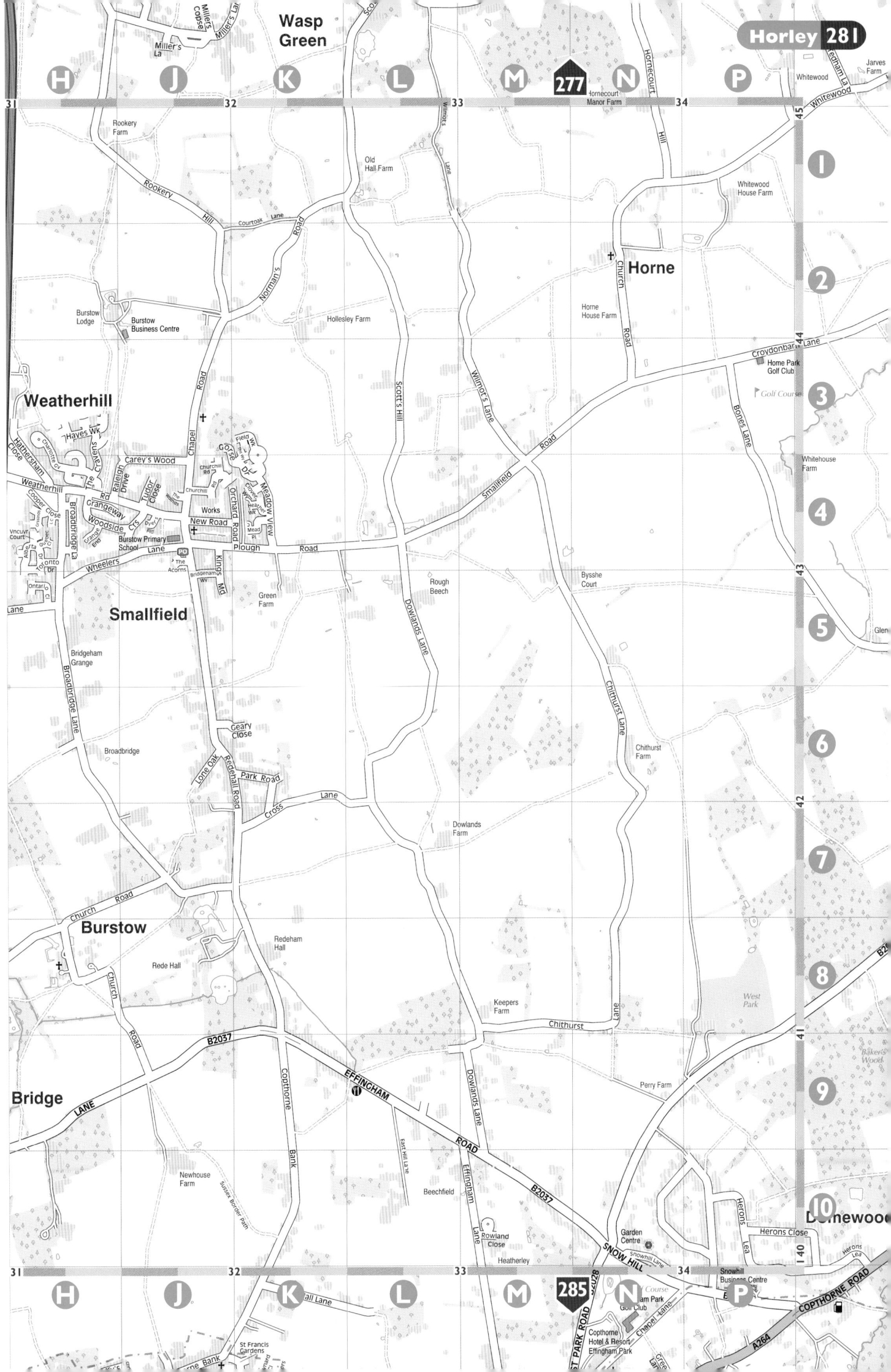

Horley 281
Wasp Green
Miller's Copse
Miller's La
Rookery Farm
Rookery Hill
Courtoak Lane
Norman's Road
Old Hall Farm
Wilmot's Lane
Hornecourt Manor Farm
Hornecourt Hill
Whitewood
Whitewood House Farm
Jarves Farm
Horne
Church Road
Horne House Farm
Hollesley Farm
Burstow Lodge
Burstow Business Centre
Croydonbarn Lane
Home Park Golf Club
Golf Course
Bones Lane
Whitehouse Farm
Weatherhill
Chapel Road
Scott's Hill
Smallfield Road
Haves Wk
Carey's Wood
Raleigh Drive
Tudor Close
Gorse Dr
Meadow View
Orchard Road
New Road
Works
Weatherhill Rd
Cooper Close
Broadbridge La
Grangeway
Woodside Cls
Burstow Primary School
Wheelers Lane
Plough Road
Kings Md
Green Farm
Rough Beech
Bysshe Court
Toronto Dr
Ontario Cl
Smallfield
Dowlands Lane
Chithurst Lane
Bridgeham Grange
Broadbridge Lane
Broadbridge
Geary Close
Lone Oak
Redehall Road
Park Road
Cross Lane
Chithurst Farm
Dowlands Farm
Church Road
Burstow
Redeham Hall
Rede Hall
Keepers Farm
Chithurst Lane
West Park
Bakers Wood
B2037
Bridge
LANE
EFFINGHAM ROAD
Copthorne Bank
Dowlands Lane
Perry Farm
East Hill Lane
Effingham Lane
Newhouse Farm
Sussex Border Path
Beechfield
Rowland Close
Heatherley
Garden Centre
SNOW HILL
Snowhill Lane
Herons Lea
Herons Close
Snowhill Business Centre
COPTHORNE ROAD
A264
Copthorne Hotel & Resort Effingham Park
Chapel Lane
St Francis Gardens
277
285
H J K L M N P
31 32 33 34
1 2 3 4 5 6 7 8 9 10
45 44 43 42 41 40

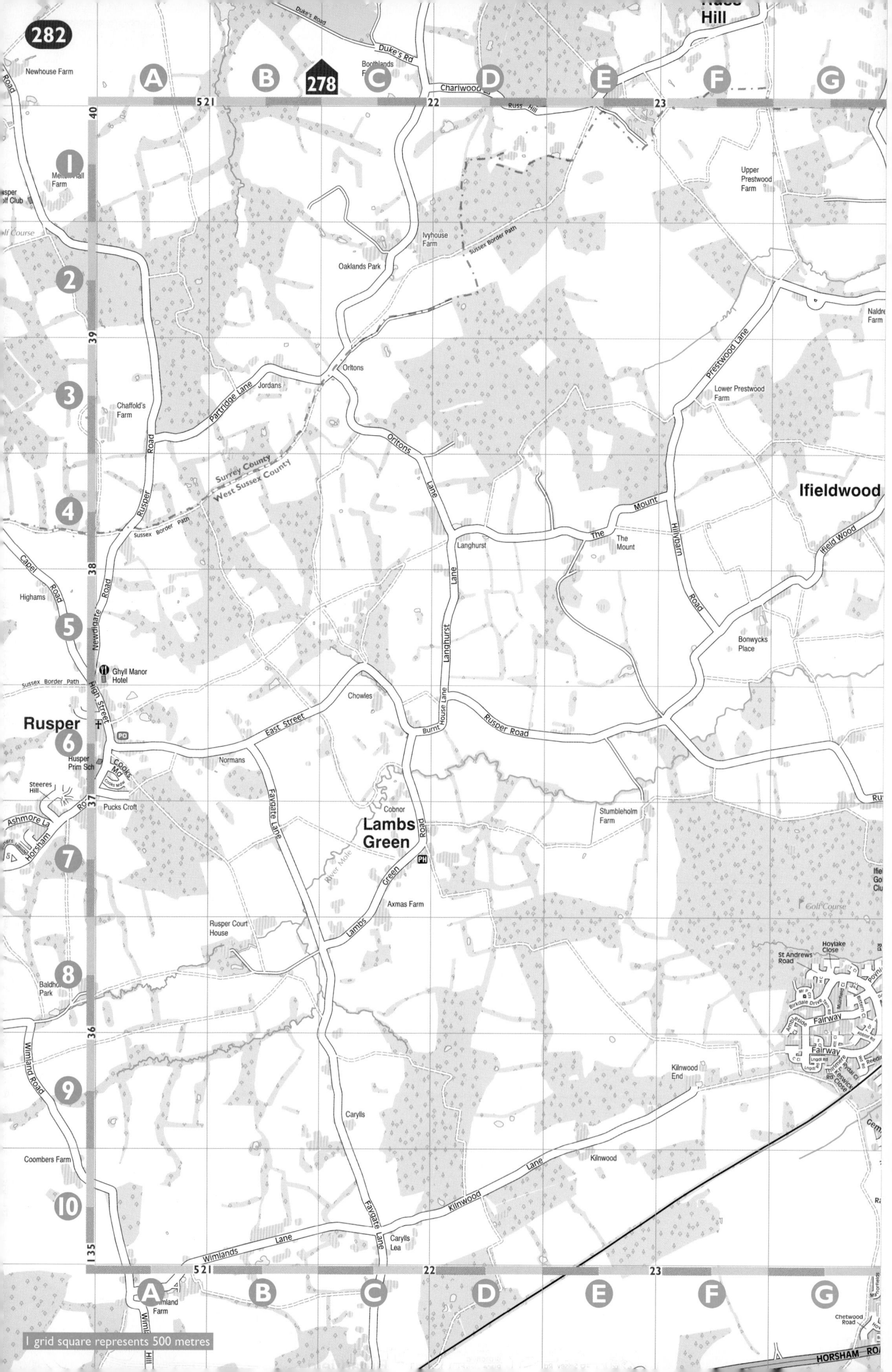
278
Newhouse Farm
Duke's Road
Duke's Rd
Boothlands
Charlwood
Russ Hill
Upper Prestwood Farm
Ivyhouse Farm
Sussex Border Path
Oaklands Park
Naldre Farm
Orltons
Jordans
Partridge Lane
Chaffold's Farm
Prestwood Lane
Lower Prestwood Farm
Orltons Lane
Rusper Road
Surrey County
West Sussex County
Ifieldwood
The Mount
Langhurst
Langhurst Lane
Hillybarn Road
Ifield Wood
Capel Road
Highams
Newdigate Road
Bonwycks Place
Ghyll Manor Hotel
High Street
Chowles
Burnt House Lane
Rusper
East Street
Rusper Road
Rusper Prim Sch
Cooks Mdw
Normans
Steeres Hill
Pucks Croft
Faygate Lane
Cobnor
Stumbleholm Farm
Ashmore La
Horsham Rd
Lambs Green
Lambs Green Road
River Mole
Axmas Farm
Golf Course
Rusper Court House
Hoylake Close
St Andrews Road
Baldhorn Park
Birkdale Drive
Fairway
Wimland Road
Kilnwood End
Carylls
Coombers Farm
Kilnwood
Kilnwood Lane
Faygate Lane
Carylls Lea
Wimlands Lane
Wimland Farm
Chetwood Road
HORSHAM ROAD
A B C D E F G
1 2 3 4 5 6 7 8 9 10
521 22 23
40 39 38 37 36 35
1 grid square represents 500 metres

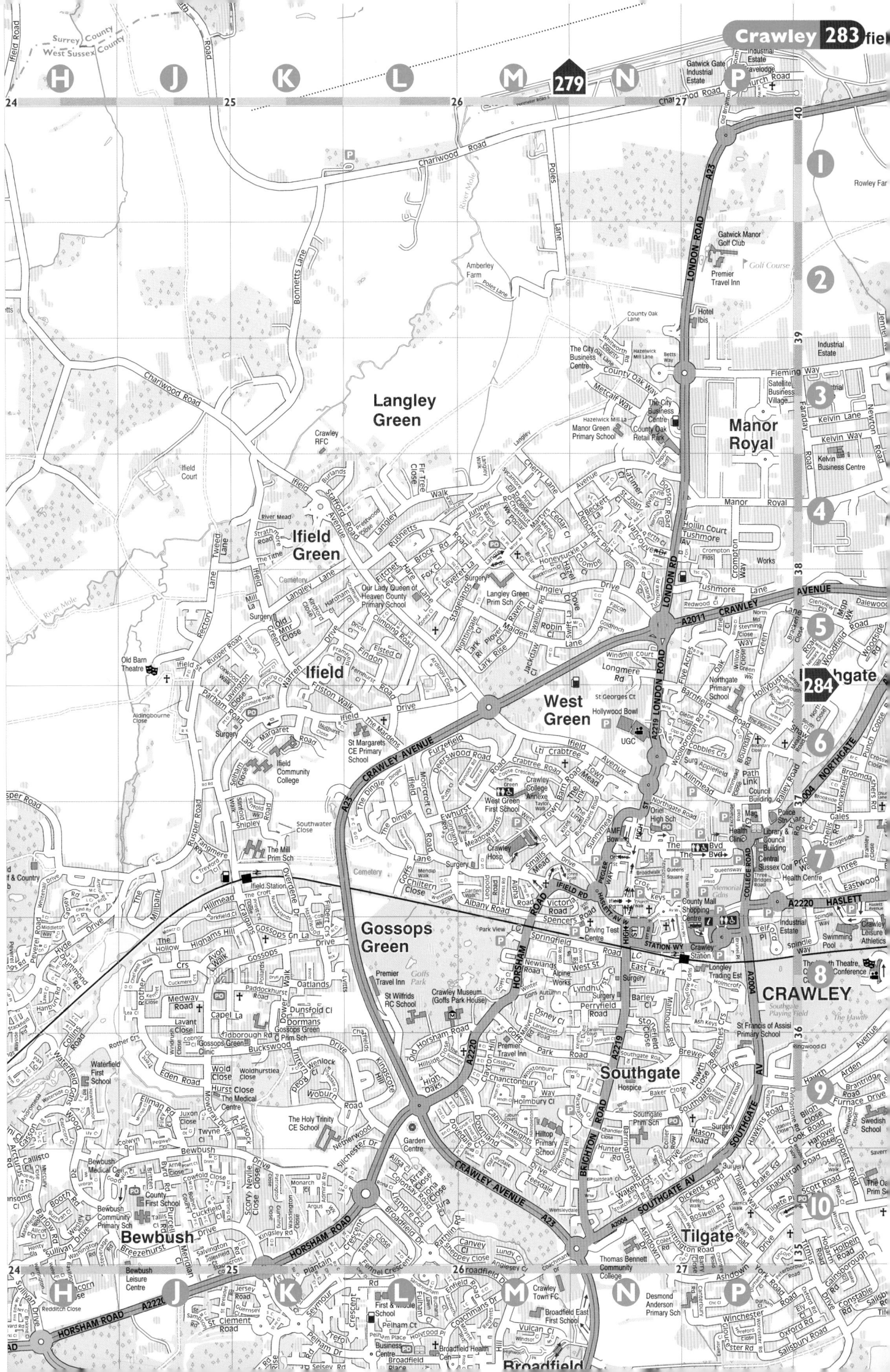

Crawley 283
279
284
Surrey County
West Sussex County
Charlwood Road
Bonnetts Lane
Poles Lane
River Mole
Amberley Farm
Langley Green
Crawley RFC
Ifield Court
Ifield Green
Ifield
Rusper Road
Old Barn Theatre
Gatwick Manor Golf Club
Premier Travel Inn
Hotel Ibis
Golf Course
Industrial Estate
Gatwick Gate Industrial Estate
The City Business Centre
Manor Royal
Manor Green Primary School
County Oak Retail Park
Kelvin Business Centre
Satellite Business Village
Fleming Way
Kelvin Lane
Kelvin Way
Faraday Road
Newton Road
London Road
A23
Crawley Avenue
A2011
Langley Green Prim Sch
Our Lady Queen of Heaven County Primary School
St Margarets CE Primary School
Ifield Community College
The Mill Prim Sch
Ifield Station
West Green
Hollywood Bowl
UGC
Northgate
Northgate Primary School
West Green First School
Crawley College Annexe
Crawley Hosp
Oriel High Sch
Police Stn
Library & Council Building
Central Sussex Coll
Health Centre
Council Building
County Mall Shopping Centre
Crawley Station
Station Wy
Haslett Av
A2220
Longley Trading Est
Industrial Estate
Swimming Pool
Crawley Leisure Athletics
CRAWLEY
Southgate Playing Field
Gossops Green
Premier Travel Inn
Goffs Park
St Wilfrids RC School
Crawley Museum (Goffs Park House)
Gossops Green Prim Sch
Horsham Road
Brighton Road
A2219
A2004
Southgate
Southgate Prim Sch
Hilltop Primary School
Hospice
St Francis of Assisi Primary School
Swedish School
Garden Centre
The Holy Trinity CE School
Waterfield First School
The Medical Centre
Bewbush Medical Cen
County First School
Bewbush Community Primary Sch
Bewbush
Bewbush Leisure Centre
Tilgate
Southgate Av
Thomas Bennett Community College
Desmond Anderson Primary Sch
Crawley Town FC
Broadfield East First School
Broadfield Health Cen
Broadfield

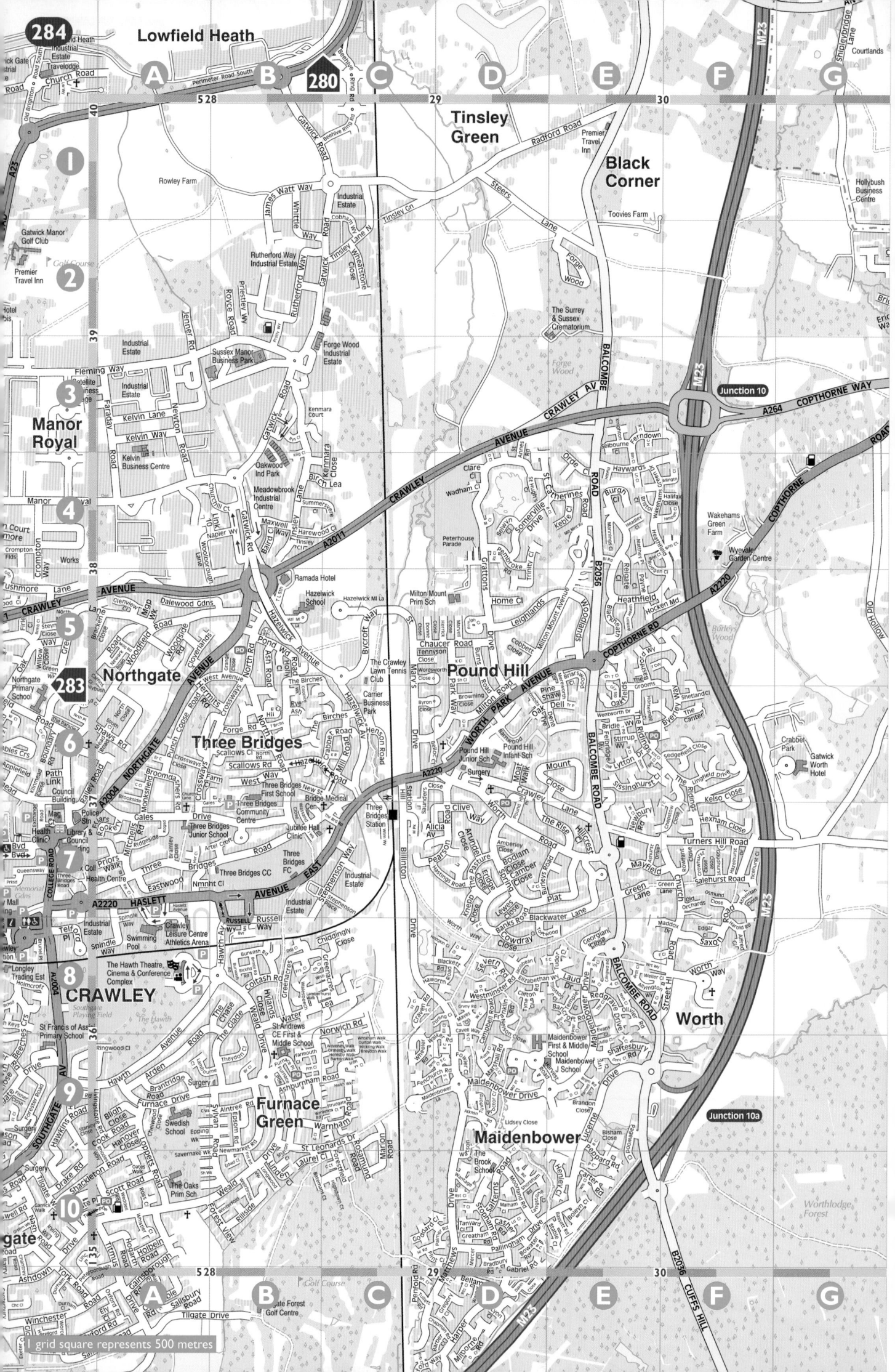

284
280
283
Lowfield Heath
Tinsley Green
Black Corner
Manor Royal
Northgate
Three Bridges
Pound Hill
CRAWLEY
Furnace Green
Maidenbower
Worth
Courtlands
Hollybush Business Centre
Rowley Farm
Gatwick Manor Golf Club
Premier Travel Inn
Rutherford Way Industrial Estate
Sussex Manor Business Park
Forge Wood Industrial Estate
The Surrey & Sussex Crematorium
Toovies Farm
Kelvin Business Centre
Oakwood Ind Park
Meadowbrook Industrial Centre
Ramada Hotel
Hazelwick School
Milton Mount Prim Sch
Peterhouse Parade
Wakehams Green Farm
Wyevale Garden Centre
Crabbet Park
Gatwick Worth Hotel
The Crawley Lawn Tennis Club
Carrier Business Park
Three Bridges Station
Three Bridges FC
Three Bridges CC
Three Bridges Community Centre
Three Bridges Junior School
Pound Hill Junior Sch
Pound Hill Infant Sch
Crawley Leisure Centre Athletics Arena
Swimming Pool
The Hawth Theatre, Cinema & Conference Complex
Longley Trading Est
St Francis of Assisi Primary School
St Andrews CE First & Middle School
Maidenbower First & Middle School
Maidenbower School
Swedish School
The Oaks Prim Sch
The Brook School
Tilgate Forest Golf Centre
Worthlodge Forest
Junction 10
Junction 10a
M23
A23
A2011
A2220
A2004
A264
B2036
CRAWLEY AVENUE
COPTHORNE WAY
COPTHORNE RD
BALCOMBE ROAD
WORTH PARK AVENUE
HASLETT AVENUE EAST
NORTHGATE AVENUE
SOUTHGATE AV
CUFFS HILL
Turners Hill Road
Radford Road
1 grid square represents 500 metres

Domewood
281
COPTHORNE
Down Park
Turners Hill
Copthorne Common Road
Copthorne Bank
Turners Hill Road
Snow Hill
Copthorne Road
West Park Road
Wallage Lane
Worth Way
Church Road
North Street
Selsfield Road
Paddockhurst Road
Standinghall Lane
Major's Hill
Sandy Lane
Grange Road
Vicarage Road
Station Road
Heatherley
Newhouse Farm
Beechfield
Herons Close
Snowhill Business Centre
Effingham Park Golf Club
Copthorne Hotel & Resort Effingham Park
Borers Business Park
Copthorne Preparatory School
Copthorne Golf Club
Copthorne CE Junior School
Copthorne Junior School
Copthorne Fairway Inf Sch
Copthorne Squash Club
Copthorne Hotel
Pot Common
Copthorne Common
Great Frenches Park
Shepherd's Farm
Old Rowfant
Ley House
Home Farm
Rowfant
Huntsland
Hayheath
Compasses Corner
Rowfant Business Centre
Hundred Acres
Worth Hall
Miswells House
Tulleys Farm
Standinghall Farm
The Grove
South Hill
Withypitts Farm
Rashes Farm
Turners Hill CE Primary School
Crawley Down Health Centre
Crawley Down CE Sch
The Grange
RH10

Abbey Mead 195 L6
Abbey Wood 163 L3
Abbots Langley 54 F8
Abbotswood 250 C8
Abinger Common 271 L9
Abinger Hammer 270 F6
Abridge 83 L8
Acton 135 P10
Acton Green 156 A3
Addington 224 F3
Addiscombe 203 N7
Addlestone 215 M2
Addlestonemoor 195 M9
Adeyfield 36 B6
Aimes Green 63 L4
Albury 269 M5
Albury Heath 269 P7
Aldborough Hatch 123 H2
Aldenham 73 P3
Aldersbrook 121 P6
Alperton 135 K3
Amersham 69 J5
Amersham Common 69 H5
Amersham Old Town 68 E6
Amersham on the Hill 68 G3
Amwell 21 H4
Anerley 203 P2
Anthonys 214 D8
Aperfield 244 C3
Apsley 35 N10
Ardleigh Green 125 K1
Ardley End 31 J2
Arkley 76 E9
Artington 267 N5
Ascot 192 B2
Asheridge 50 C2
Ashford 174 B7
Ashford Common 174 E9
Ashley Green 33 L10
Ashley Park 197 H10
Ashtead 237 K4
Austenwood 109 N1
Aveley 146 C9
Avery Hill 184 F2
Ayot Green 22 C3
Ayres End 20 E6
Badgers Mount 228 C5
Baker's Wood 111 H6
Balham 180 A3
Bandonhill 222 E2
Banstead 239 K2
Barking 142 G2
Barkingside 122 E1
Barnehurst 164 E9
Barnes 156 E7
Barnes Cray 165 J10
Barnet 77 J10
Barnet Gate 76 B10
Barnsbury 5 N3
Barwell 219 H4
Batchworth 92 A3
Batchworth Heath 92 B5
Batlers Green 74 E4
Battersea 158 A6
Bayford 42 G4
Bayley's Hill 264 F7
Bayswater 9 J7
Beaconsfield 88 B10
Bean 188 G6
Beaumont 171 N4
Beckenham 204 F2
Beckton 142 C8
Becontree 123 N10
Beddington 202 F9
Beddington Corner 202 B7
Bedford Park 156 C2
Bedmond 54 F3
Belgravia 16 C5
Belgravia 158 B2
Bell Bar 41 K10
Bell Common 64 G8
Bellfields 249 P7
Bell Green 182 E6
Bellingdon 32 D10
Bellingham 182 F7
Belmont 94 F10
Belmont 221 K5
Belsize 53 H8
Belvedere 164 C4
Bengeo 25 J3
Benhilton 201 L10
Bennetts End 36 A9
Bentley 86 D7
Bentley Heath 77 J1
Berkhamsted 33 M5
Bermondsey 19 N2
Bernards Heath 38 C4
Berrylands 199 L6
Berry's Green 244 D2
Bessels Green 246 E10
Betchworth 255 P9
Bethnal Green 140 A5
Betsham 189 L7
Bewbush 283 J10
Bexley 163 M10
Bexleyheath 164 A10
Bickley 206 B2
Biggin 168 F5
Biggin Hill 244 A2
Binscombe 267 H9
Birch Green 24 D7
Birchwood 40 E2
Bishopsgate 171 L7
Bisley 230 G2
Blackbrook 273 K7
Black Corner 284 E1
Blackfen 185 J2
Blackheath 161 L8
Blackheath 269 H8
Blackheath Park 161 M10
Blacknest 193 H3
Blackwall 141 J9
Bletchingley 259 L10
Bloomsbury 11 K3
Bobbingworth 49 L9
Borehamwood 75 K7
The Borough 18 F2
Botany Bay 78 E2
Botley 51 M7
Bourne End 34 F8
Boveney 148 B5
Bovingdon 52 E3
Bovingdon Green 52 C5
Bovinger 48 G10
Bow 140 F4
Bow Common 140 F7
Bowes Park 98 F7
Bowmans 186 G3
Box Hill 255 M8
Boxmoor 35 L8
Brands Hill 150 E6
Brasted 245 L10
Brasted Chart 263 L4
Brays Grove 47 K2
Brentford 155 J5
Brentford End 154 G5
Brentwood 106 G3
Brewer Street 259 K7
Brickendon 43 K5
Bricket Wood 55 M7
Brick Hill 213 H1
Bridge End 234 C6
Brimsdown 80 D6
Britwell 128 E6
Brixton 159 H10
Broad Colney 57 J4
Broadford 267 P7
Broad Green 203 J7
Broadgreen Wood 43 H1
Broadham Green 261 H8
Broadley Common 46 A6
Broadmoor 272 A9
Broadoak End 24 G3
Brockham 273 M1
Brockham Park 273 P5
Brockley 182 E1
Bromley 140 G5
Bromley 205 N2
Bromley Common 206 A6
Bromley Park 205 K1
Brompton 15 N4
Brondesbury 2 B1
Brondesbury Park 136 G3
Brook 269 P8
Brook Green 156 F2
Brooklands 216 A5
Brookmans Park 59 H2
Brook Street 106 D5
Brookwood 230 F6
Broomhall 192 E7
Broom Hill 207 J7
Broxbourne 44 F6
Brunswick Park 98 B4
Buckhurst Hill 101 P4
Buckland 256 D9
Bucks Hill 53 M10
Bullen's Green 40 B8
Bulls Cross 79 P2
Bulstrode 53 H4
Bumble's Green 45 M10
Bunce Common 274 A7
Burgh Heath 238 G5
Burnham 128 B4
Burntcommon 251 J1
Burnt Oak 96 A8
Burpham 250 D6
Burrowhill 213 L5
Burrows Cross 270 C7
Burstow 281 H8
Burwood Park 217 H2
Bury Green 62 A7
Bushbury 273 M5
Bushey 94 B1
Bushey Heath 94 D1
Bushey Mead 200 G3
Bush Hill Park 79 M10
Bushy Hill 250 E8
Butlers Cross 89 L5
Byfleet 215 N9
Caldecote Hill 94 E1
Camberwell 159 N7
Camden Town 4 D4
Campions 30 A6
The Camp 38 F8
Canary Wharf 140 F10
Canning Town 141 N7
Cannon Hill 200 G4
Canonbury 6 E3
Canons Park 95 K8
Carpenders Park 93 N3
Carshalton 221 P1
Carshalton Beeches 221 P5
Carshalton on the Hill 222 A4
Cartbridge 232 E8
Carter's Green 30 F9
Castle Green 143 M3
Castle Green 213 J9
Caterham 241 M9
Catford 183 H4
Chadwell Heath 123 N3
Chadwell St Mary 168 C2
Chafford Hundred 167 K2
Chaldon 241 J10
Chalfont Common 90 C5
Chalfont Grove 89 N7
Chalfont St Giles 89 L3
Chalfont St Peter 90 D8
Chalk 191 K4
Chalvey 149 H1
Chandler's Cross 72 A4
Charlton 162 A4
Charlton 196 D2
Charlwood 279 J8
Chartridge 50 B4
The Chart 263 L6
Chase Cross 104 F7
Chattern Hill 174 C7
Chaulden 34 G7
Cheam 221 H2
Cheapside 192 D2
Chelsea 15 M8
Chelsfield 227 P2
Chelsham 242 F3
Chenies 70 F4
Chertsey 195 K7
Chertsey Meads 195 P8
Chesham 51 H7
Chesham Bois 69 H2
Cheshunt 62 A6
Chessington 219 K3
Chessmount 51 K8
Chevening 246 A5
Chigwell 102 E3
Chigwell Row 103 L3
Childerditch 127 L2
Childsbridge 247 N5
Child's Hill 117 H7
Childwick Bury 20 B10
Childwick Green 20 A9
Chilworth 268 F6
China Town 11 K7
Chingford 101 J2
Chingford Green 101 H2
Chingford Hatch 101 K5
Chipperfield 53 L7
Chipping Barnet 77 H9
Chipping Ongar 67 N4
Chipstead 240 B5
Chipstead 246 D8
Chislehurst 184 F10
Chislehurst West 184 D9
Chiswell Green 55 N1
Chiswick 156 C3
Chobham 213 J6
Cholesbury 32 B7
Chorleywood 70 G8
Chorleywood Bottom 70 G10
Chorleywood West 70 D9
Christmaspie 266 A1
Church End 71 J4
Church End 97 K10
Church End 136 C2
Church End 234 A7
Churchgate 62 A5
Churchgate Street 30 A8
Church Langley 47 N1
Church Town 260 B7
Cippenham 128 C10
City of London 12 D7
Clapham 158 C8
Clapham Park 180 E2
Clapton Park 120 E9
Claremont Park 217 P4
Clatterford End 67 J6
Claverhambury 63 N3
Claygate 218 E3
Clayhall 102 C10
Clay Hill 79 K3
Clement Street 187 L9
Clerkenwell 12 A1
Clerkenwell 139 H6
Clewer Green 148 D9
Clewer New Town 148 F8
Clewer Village 148 F6
Clock House 222 D10
Cobham 217 H10
Cockfosters 77 P9
Codmore 51 K6
Coldblow 186 D5
Coldharbour 165 H3
Cole Green 24 B7
Coleman Green 21 M6
Cole Park 176 F2
Coleshill 68 E10
Coles Meads 258 A7
Colham Green 132 A6
Colindale 116 B1
College Park 136 D5
Collier Row 104 D9
Colliers Hatch 66 D6
Collier's Wood 179 N10
Colnbrook 150 F7
Colney Hatch 98 A7
Colney Heath 39 P8
Colney Street 56 D6
Commonwood 53 K10
Compton 266 F6
Coney Hall 225 K1
Coombe 178 B10
Coopersale Common 65 N5
Coopersale Street 65 M7
Cooper's Green 39 N1
Cooper's Hill 172 A6
Copse Hill 178 D10
Copthall Green 64 A9
Copthorne 285 J2
Corbets Tey 126 A10
Cottenham Park 200 E1
Coulsdon 240 F2
Counters End 35 K6
Cowley 131 M6
Cowley Peachy 131 M8
Coxtie Green 86 C9
Cranbourne 170 A5
Cranbrook 122 D5
Cranford 153 H6
Cranham 126 D5
Cranley Gardens 118 B2
Crawley 283 P8
Crayford 187 H1
Creekmouth 143 H7
Crews Hill 79 J1
Cricklewood 116 G9
Crockenhill 208 D6
Crockham Hill 262 F9
Crofton 206 G9
Cromer-Hyde 21 P6
Crooked Billet 178 E9
Cross Keys 264 G3
Crouch End 118 D4
Crow Green 86 F7
Croxley Green 72 B9
Croydon 203 L10
Crystal Palace 181 P9
Cubitt Town 161 H3
Cudham 244 G1
Cudworth 278 B7
Cuffley 60 G4
Cupid Green 36 C2
Curtismill Green 84 G7
Custom House 142 B9
Dagenham 144 C2
Dalston 7 M2
Dancers Hill 76 F1
Darenth 188 B8
Dartford 187 K3
Dartmouth Park 118 B7
Datchet 149 N7
Datchet Common 149 P8
Dawesgreen 274 B6
Deacons Hill 75 M10
Dean Bottom 210 G3
Debden Green 82 F4
De Beauvoir Town 7 J5
Dedworth 148 C7
Deepdene 273 J2
Denbies 254 C10
Denham 111 K7
Denham Green 111 H4
Denton 191 H3
Deptford 160 E5
Derry Downs 207 N6
Digswell Park 22 G2
Digswell Water 23 K1
Doddinghurst 86 G3
Dollis Hill 116 E8
Donkey Town 212 C9
Dorking 272 G3
Dormer's Wells 134 A9
Dorney 148 A2
Doversgreen 275 L4
Downe 226 C7
Downham 183 J8
Down Park 285 P4
Downside 235 J5
Dryhill 246 C10
Ducks Island 96 G1
Dudden Hill 116 D10
Dudswell 33 J1
Dulwich 181 N5
Dulwich Village 181 M3
Dunton Green 246 F5
Ealing 135 H9
Earl's Court 14 E6
Earlsfield 179 M4
Earlswood 276 A2
East Acton 136 C9
East Barnet 97 N1
East Bedfont 174 C3
East Burnham 128 E3
Eastbury 92 G5
East Clandon 251 P7
Eastcote 113 J5
Eastcote Village 113 J3
East Dulwich 181 P1
East End 28 B10
East End Green 24 D9
East Ewell 220 G6
East Finchley 117 N1
East Ham 142 B4
East Horsley 252 E3
East Molesey 198 B5
East Sheen 178 A1
East Tilbury 169 L3
Eastwick 28 E7
East Wickham 163 K7
Eden Park 204 E4
Edgware 95 N5
Edmonton 99 M5
Effingham 253 L3
Egham 172 D9
Egham Hythe 172 G9
Egham Wick 171 L10
Egypt 108 G9
Ellenbrook 39 P3
Elm Corner 234 B5
Elmers End 204 C3
Elm Park 125 J10
Elmstead 184 B8
Elstree 75 K10
Eltham 184 B2
Emerson Park 125 M4
Enfield 79 K8
Enfield Highway 80 B6
Enfield Island Village 80 G4
Enfield Lock 80 E3
Enfield Town 79 L7
Enfield Wash 80 D4
Englefield Green 171 N10
Epping 65 K6
Epping Green 42 E8
Epping Green 46 D10
Epping Upland 64 F2
Epsom 219 P10
Erith 164 G4
Esher 218 B1
Essendon 42 A3
Eton 149 H5
Eton Wick 148 E3
Ewell 220 D5
Eynsford 209 M9
Fair Cross 123 J10
Fairlands 249 J7
Fairlop 103 H9
Fairmile 217 N8
Falconwood 163 H10
Farleigh 224 E10
Farleigh Court 224 F10
Farley Green 269 P10
Farnborough 226 D2
Farncombe 267 J9
Farnham Common 129 J1
Farnham Park 129 H3
Farnham Royal 129 H4
Farningham 209 P7
Fawkham Green 210 G10
Felden 35 K10
Feltham 175 J5
Felthamhill 174 F9
Fernhill 280 F8
Fetcham 236 C9
Fickleshole 225 K10
Fiddlers Hamlet 65 M8
Field Common 197 N7
Fields End 34 G5
Finchley 97 K9
Finsbury 6 A9
Finsbury Park 118 F7
Flamstead End 62 A4
Flaunden 52 D8
Fleet Downs 188 A5
Fleetville 38 F6
Fletcher's Green 265 L10
Flexford 248 C10
The Folly 20 G1
Foots Cray 185 L9
Force Green 245 H10
Forestdale 224 D5
Forest Gate 121 M10
Forest Hill 182 C4
Fortis Green 118 A2
Forty Hill 79 N5
Foster Street 48 A2
Foxbury 184 G8
Fox Corner 249 H1
Fox Hatch 86 E4
Fredley 254 G5
Freezy Water 80 D2
French Street 263 J6
Friday Hill 101 J4
Friday Street 271 N9
Friern Barnet 97 P5
Frithsden 34 D1
Froghole 262 G8
Frogmore 56 D4
The Frythe 22 D1
Fulham 156 G6
Fullwell Cross 102 G9
Fulmer 110 A9
Furnace Green 284 B9
Furzedown 180 C7
Gadbrook 274 A4
Gadebridge 35 J4
Gallows Corner 105 L9
Gants Hill 122 C4
Ganwick Corner 77 L1
Garston 73 K1
Gatton 258 A4
George Green 130 B7
Gerrards Cross 109 P5
Gidea Park 104 G10
Giggshill 198 F7
Gilston 28 G6
Gilston Park 28 F5
Gilwell Park 81 H7
Givons Grove 255 J1
Globe Town 140 C5
Goathurst Common 264 C6
Goddington 207 M10
Godstone 260 A7
Goff's Oak 61 K4
Golders Green 117 H4
Goldsworth Park 231 M2
Gomshall 270 D6
Goodley Stock 262 E6
Goodmayes 123 L7
Goose Green 44 B2
Gorhambury 37 K5
Gospel Oak 118 B10
Gossops Green 283 L8
Grange Hill 102 G7
Grange Park 79 H9
Gravel Hill 90 C7
Gravesend 190 E1
Grays 167 L6
Great Amwell 26 D6
Great Bookham 254 A2
Great Burgh 238 F3
Great Hivings 50 F4
Greatness 247 L6
Great Parndon 46 E3
Great Warley 106 F9
Green End 35 J7
Greenford 134 C6
Greenhill 114 E3
Greenhithe 166 E10
Greensted 67 K4
Greensted Green 67 J4
Green Street 75 M3
Green Street Green 188 F9
Green Street Green 227 H4
Greenwich 161 J4
Grovehill 35 N2
Grove Park 156 A7
Grove Park 183 P6
The Grove 72 D3
Grubb Street 210 G1
Guildford 267 M1
Guildford Park 267 M1
Hackbridge 202 C9
Hackney 7 P1
Hackney Wick 140 F1
Hacton 125 M10
Hadley 77 J7
Hadley Wood 77 N4
Haggerston 7 N7
Hailey 26 E9
Hainault 103 J8
Haldens 23 K1
Hale End 101 J7
Hall Grove 23 L7
Halls Green 45 P3
Halstead 228 B8
Ham 177 J6
Hammerfield 35 L6
Hammersmith 156 E3
Hamm Moor 215 N1
Hammond Street 61 K2
Hampstead 117 N9
Hampstead Garden Suburb 117 L3
Hampton 198 A1
Hampton Hill 176 B7
Hampton Wick 198 G1
Hamsey Green 242 B1
Handside 22 E6
Hanging Bank 264 A8
Hanwell 134 C10
Hanworth 175 L6
Harefield 91 M10
Harefield Grove 91 N8
Hare Street 46 E2
Harlesden 136 B4
Harlington 152 D5
Harlow 28 E10
Harmondsworth 151 M5
Harold Hill 105 M6
Harold Park 106 A7
Harold Wood 105 P9
Harpenden Common 20 A4
Harringay 119 H3
Harrow 114 C4
Harrow on the Hill 114 D6
Harrow Weald 94 D8
Hartham 25 K4
Hartley 211 L5
Hartley Green 211 K5
Hastingwood 48 A5
Hatch End 93 M8
Hatfield 40 C5
Hatfield Garden Village 22 B10
Hatfield Hyde 23 J8
Hatton 152 F10
Hatton Hill 212 C1
Havering-atte-Bower 104 F4
Hawk's Hill 236 E10
Hawley 187 M8
Hayes 132 D7
Hayes 205 N7
Hayes End 132 E6
Hayes Town 133 K10
Hazelwood 226 F7
Headley 255 P2
Headstone 114 A2
Heath End 32 F7
Heath Park 125 J4
Heath Side 186 G5
Hedgerley 109 J6
Hedgerley Green 109 L5
Hedgerley Hill 109 K7
Hemel Hempstead 35 P6
Hendon 116 E3
Herne Hill 181 K2
Heronsgate 90 G1
Hersham 217 K2
Hertford 25 M6
Hertford Heath 26 A8
Hertingfordbury 25 H6
Heston 153 N6
Hextable 187 H10
Higham Hill 100 D10
Highams Park 100 G8
High Barnet 76 F7
High Beach 81 N5
Highbury 119 J10
High Cross 74 C2
Higher Denham 110 F5
Highfield 35 P4
Highgate 118 A5
High Laver 49 J3
The High 28 F10
Highwood Hill 96 C3
High Wych 29 L2
Hill End 91 L7
Hillingdon 132 B3
Hillingdon Heath 132 C7
Hill Park 244 E9
Hilltop 51 J5
Hinchley Wood 198 E10
Hither Green 183 K2
Hobbs Cross 30 B10
Hobbs Cross 83 N2
Hockenden 208 C3
Hoddesdon 44 D4
Hoe 270 E9
Hogpits Bottom 52 E8
Holborn 11 N4
Holders Hill 96 G9
Holland 261 M9
Hollybush Hill 129 N2
Holmethorpe 258 C8
Holtspur 88 A10
Holyfield 63 H4
Holywell 72 F10
Homerton 140 C1
Honor Oak 182 C2
Honor Oak Park 182 D2
Hook 219 K2
Hook End 87 H1
Hook Green 186 G7
Hook Green 189 L9
Hook Heath 231 N6
Hookwood 279 M5
Hooley 240 B8
Horley 280 C2
Hornchurch 125 L7
Horne 281 N2
Horn Hill 90 E5
Horns Cross 188 E2
Hornsey 118 F2
Hornsey Vale 118 G3
Horns Green 245 H3
Horsell 232 A2
Horseman Side 85 M8
Horton 150 D9
Horton Kirby 210 C4
Hosey Hill 263 H4
Hounslow 153 P8
Hounslow West 153 L9
Housham Tye 30 E9
How Wood 56 B3
Hoxton 7 J8
Hubbard's Hill 265 J6
Hulberry 209 J9
Hunsdon 27 P2
Hunsdonbury 27 P5
Hunton Bridge 54 C9
Hurst Green 261 K8
Hurst Park 198 B2
Hurtmore 266 F10
Hutton 87 P10
Hutton Mount 107 N2
Hyde Heath 50 B10
The Hyde 116 C3
Hythe End 172 E6
Ickenham 112 B8
Ide Hill 263 P7
Ifield 283 K5
Ifield Green 283 K4
Ifieldwood 282 G4
Ilford 122 E8
Ingrave 107 P7
Irons Bottom 275 K8
Isle of Dogs 161 H3
Isleworth 154 G9
Islington 6 A5
Istead Rise 190 B10
Iver 131 J8
Iver Heath 130 G3
Ivy Chimneys 65 H8
Jack's Hatch 46 E7
Jacobs Well 249 P5
Jordans 89 L8
Joyden's Wood 186 G7
Katherines 46 B4
Kelvedon Hatch 86 C3
Kemsing 247 N3
Kenley 241 L2
Kennington 17 M10
Kensal Green 136 F4
Kensal Rise 136 G4
Kensal Town 8 A2
Kensington 14 G4
Kentish Town 4 F1
Kenton 115 H3
Keston 226 A1
Keston Mark 206 A10
Kevingtown 208 A6
Kew 155 L6
Keysers Estate 44 G8
Kidbrooke 161 P8
Kilburn 2 D6
Kingfield 232 B6
Kingsbury 115 N4
Kings Farm 190 F6
Kingsland 7 J3
Kings Langley 54 B4
Kingsmoor 46 F6
Kingston upon Thames 199 H3
Kingston Vale 178 A8
Kingswood 55 J10
Kingswood 239 J9
Kippington 265 H2
Kitt's End 77 H4
Knaphill 231 H4
Knightsbridge 15 P1
Knight's Hill 181 K4
Knockhall 188 G1
Knockholt 245 K3
Knotty Green 88 B5
Knowle Green 173 L8
Knowle Hill 193 N7
Ladywell 160 F10
Lake End 148 A1
Lakeside 166 F3
Laleham 195 M3
Laleham Burway 195 L5
Lambeth 18 A3
Lambourne 83 N8
Lambourne End 103 M1
Lambs Green 282 C7
Lampton 154 A7
Lane End 188 C8
Langley 150 C2
Langleybury 54 C10
Langley Corner 130 C1
Langley Green 283 L3
Langley Vale 238 A6
Latimer 70 B3
Latton Bush 47 K5
Layters Green 89 N9
Lea Bridge 120 C8
Leasey Bridge 20 E2
Leatherhead 236 D7
Leavesden Green 54 F10
Leaves Green 226 A7
Lee 183 L2
Leigh 274 D7
Lemsford 22 C6
Lessness Heath 164 C5
Letchmore Heath 74 D5
Lett's Green 245 J2
Letty Green 24 B9
Leverstock Green 36 D7
Lewisham 161 H10
Ley Hill 51 N6
Leyton 121 J8
Leytonstone 121 L6
Lightwater 212 B7
Limehouse 140 D9
Limpsfield 261 L3
Limpsfield Chart 262 C7
Limpsfield Common 261 N6
Linford 169 J1
Lippitts Hill 81 L6
Lisson Grove 10 B3
Little Berkhamsted 42 B5
Little Bookham 253 M1
Little Chalfont 69 N6
Little End 67 M10
Littlefield Common 248 G5
Little Heath 34 D4
Little Heath 59 L5
Little Heath 123 M2
Little Heath 217 N10
Little Ilford 122 D10
Little Laver 49 N1
Little Missenden 68 A3
Little Parndon 28 E10
Little Stanmore 95 L9
Little Thurrock 167 P3
Littleton 196 C3
Littleton 267 M6
Littleton Common 174 C10
Little Warley 107 L10
Littlewick 231 L2
Little Woodcote 222 B7
Littleworth Common 108 C8
Locksbottom 206 E10
Logmore Green 272 A7
London Colney 57 K2
Longcross 193 N10
Long Ditton 198 G8
Longfield 211 L3
Longford 151 L7
Longford 246 E6
Longlands 184 F6
Loudwater 71 N7
Loughton 82 C8
Love Green 130 G7
Lower Ashtead 237 H5
Lower Bobbingworth Green 49 J10
Lower Bois 51 H10
Lower Clapton 120 B9
Lower Edmonton 99 M3
Lower Feltham 174 F6
Lower Green 198 A9
Lower Halliford 196 E7
Lower Holloway 118 G10
Lower Kingswood 257 K2
Lower Nazeing 45 J9
Lower Place 135 P4
Lower Sheering 30 B2
Lower Sunbury 197 H3
Lower Sydenham 182 C7
Lower Woodside 41 J8
Lowfield Heath 280 A10
Low Street 169 J5
Loxford 122 F10
Loyter's Green 30 G10
Lucas End 61 K3
Lucas Green 230 C1
Luxted 226 D10
Lye Green 51 L4
Magdalen Laver 48 E4
Maida Vale 2 G9
Maidenbower 284 D9
Maitland Park 4 A1
Malden Rushett 218 G8
Manor Park 122 B9
Manor Park 129 H6
Manor Royal 283 P3
Mantles Green 68 F4
Manwood Green 31 M6
Maple Cross 90 G5
Marden Ash 67 N6
Margery 257 K5
Mark Hall North 29 K8
Mark Hall South 29 K9
Marks Gate 103 P10
Marshalswick 38 F3
Marshmoor 40 G8
Martyr's Green 234 F6
Marylebone 10 C4
Matching 31 H7
Matching Green 31 L8
Matching Tye 30 G8
Maybury 232 E3
Mayfair 10 E8
Mayford 231 P8
Maypole 186 F4
Maypole 228 A3
May's Green 234 G6
Mead Vale 275 M3
Meath Green 279 N2
Meriden 73 M2
Merrow 250 F9
Merry Hill 94 A2
Merstham 258 C4
Merton 201 K1
Merton Park 201 J2
Micklefield Green 71 K4
Mickleham 255 H4
Middle Green 130 B9
Mid Holmwood 272 G8
Mile End 140 D6
Mill End 91 J2
Mill Green 41 H1
Mill Hill 96 D6
Mill Meads 141 J4
Millwall 160 F2
Milton 190 G2
Mimbridge 213 N9
Mitcham 202 B3
Mogador 256 G5
Moneyhill 91 L2
Monken Hadley 77 H6
Monks Orchard 204 B7
Moorhouse Bank 262 D4
Moor Park 92 D5
Morden 201 K4
Morden Park 201 H6
Moreton 49 K7
Mortlake 155 P8
Motspur Park 200 D6
Mottingham 183 P5
Mount End 66 A8
Mount Hermon 232 C5
Mount Pleasant 91 L9
Muckingford 169 J2
Mugswell 257 L1
Muswell Hill 98 B10
Nalderswood 274 F10
Nash 225 N3
Nash Mills 54 B1
Nast Hyde 40 A5
Navestock Heath 85 K6
Navestock Side 86 B6
Nazeing 45 N8
Nazeing Gate 63 P1
Nazeing Long Green 63 M1

Nazeing Mead 45 J4
Neasden 116 A9
Netherne on the Hill 240 E8
Netteswell 28 G10
New Addington 225 J4
New Ash Green 211 M9
New Barn 211 N2
New Barnet 77 L9
New Beckenham 182 D9
Newbury Park 122 G4
New Charlton 162 A3
New Cross 160 D8
New Cross Gate 160 D7
New Denham 131 K1
New Eltham 184 E5
Newgate Street 42 F10
New Greens 38 B1
New Haw 215 M4
New House 190 B5
Newington 18 B4
Newlands Corner 269 L2
New Malden 200 C3
Newman's End 30 G6
New Southgate 98 D5
New Town 187 N2
Newtown 51 H5
Newyears Green 112 B5
Noah's Arks 247 P5
Noak Hill 105 M3
Noel Park 99 J10
Nomansland 21 H5
Norbiton 199 L2
Norbury 203 J2
Nork 238 G2
Normandy 248 A7
North Acton 135 P6
Northaw 60 B6
North Cheam 200 G10
Northchurch 33 J3
North Cray 186 B6
North End 117 M6
North End 164 G7
North Feltham 175 J1
North Finchley 97 M7
Northfleet 189 P1
Northfleet Green 189 P8
Northgate 284 A5
North Harrow 113 N4
North Hillingdon 132 C2
North Holmwood 272 G7
North Hyde 153 M3
North Kensington 136 G7
North Looe 220 F9
North Ockendon 126 G10
Northolt 133 P2
North Sheen 155 N8
North Stifford 147 K9
Northumberland Heath 164 D6
North Watford 73 J3
North Weald Bassett 66 C3
North Wembley 114 G6
Northwood 92 D9
Northwood Hills 92 E10
North Woolwich 162 B1
Norwood Green 153 P3
Norwood Hill 279 H4
Norwood New Town 181 L9
Notting Hill 8 B7
Nunhead 160 B10
Nuper's Hatch 104 F1
Nutfield 258 G10
Oakhurst 265 P9
Oakleigh Park 97 N3
Oakwood 78 E10
Oatlands Park 216 F1
Ockham 234 B8
Old Bexley 186 B5
Old Coulsdon 241 J6
Old Ford 140 D3
Old Harlow 29 N7
Old Hatfield 40 G3
Old Malden 200 A7
Old Oak Common 136 C6
Old Windsor 171 N2
Old Woking 232 E6
Onslow Village 267 K2
Orchard Leigh 51 N3
Orpington 207 K9
Orsett Heath 168 C1
Osidge 98 D3
Osterley 154 B6
Otford 247 H3
Ottershaw 214 F2
Otterspool 73 N3
Outwood 277 K9
Oxhey 73 L10
Oxlease 40 E5
Oxshott 218 B9
Oxted 261 K5
Pachesham Park 236 F2
Paddington 9 L4
Pains Hill 261 P7
Palmers Green 98 F4
Panshanger 23 K4
Park Barn 249 K9
Parkgate 278 A3
Park Langley 205 H6
Park Royal 135 M5
Park Street 56 B2
Parrock Farm 190 G6
Parsons Green 157 K8
Passingford Bridge 84 E5
Passmores 46 G4
Patchetts Green 74 B5
Peartree 23 H6
Peartree Green 87 J3
Peasmarsh 267 P8
Peckham 160 A8
Pedlars End 49 J7
Pednor Bottom 50 B5
Pednormead End 50 E8
Penge 182 B10
Penn Street 68 A8
Pentonville 5 P7
Perivale 135 H3
Perry Street 190 C3
Petersham 177 K4
Petts Wood 206 G4
Piccotts End 35 M2
Piercing Hill 82 G1
Pilgrims Hatch 86 G8
Pimlico 16 G7
Pimlico 36 F10
Pinnacles 46 D1
Pinner 113 L2
Pinner Green 93 K10
Pinnerwood Park 93 K8
Pirbright 230 E9
Pitch Place 249 L5
Pixham 255 H9
Plaistow 141 L5
Plaistow 183 M9
Plashet 142 A1
Plumstead 162 F4
Plumstead Common 163 J5
Ponders End 80 B9
Pond Park 50 G5
Poplar 140 F9
Potten End 34 D3
Potters Bar 59 N9
Potters Crouch 37 L10
Potter Street 47 N3
Pouchen End 34 G7
Pound Hill 284 D5
Poverest 207 K4
Povey Cross 279 M6
Poyle 151 H7
Pratt's Bottom 227 L6
Presdales 26 D4
Preston 115 J6
Prey Heath 231 N9
Primrose Hill 4 D6
Puddledock 186 E9
Puddledock 263 K9
Pudds Cross 52 B4
Purfleet 165 P4
Purley 223 H8
Putney 178 G1
Putney Heath 178 F3
Putney Vale 178 D6
Puttenham 266 A4
Pyle Hill 250 A1
Pyrford 233 J1
Pyrford Green 233 L3
Pyrford Village 233 H4
Queensbury 115 J1
Queen's Park 2 A7
Radlett 75 H1
Rainham 145 J5
Ramsden 207 M8
Ranmore Common 254 B9
Rayners Lane 113 N6
Raynes Park 200 F3
Redbridge 121 P3
Redhill 258 B8
Regent's Park 4 F8
Reigate 257 J10
Reigate Hill 257 J8
Richings Park 151 H2
Richmond 177 K1
Richmond Hill 177 K2
Rickmansworth 91 K1
Ridge 58 C10
Ridge Green 276 F3
The Ridgeway 60 C3
Ripley 233 L7
Rise Park 104 F9
The Rise 192 D6
Riverhead 246 E8
Riverview Park 191 K7
Roe Green 40 D4
Roehampton 178 C1
Roestock 40 A9
Romford 124 D3
Romney Street 229 N8
The Rookery 93 H1
Rosedale 61 N4
Rose Hill 272 F2
Rosehill 201 L8
Rosherville 190 C1
Rotherhithe 160 C2
Round Bush 74 C4
Roundshaw 222 G3
Rowley Green 76 C8
Row Town 215 J3
Roxeth 114 B7
Roydon 27 N10
Roydon Hamlet 45 P5
Rucklers Lane 53 P2
Ruislip 112 F4
Ruislip Common 112 D2
Ruislip Gardens 112 F8
Ruislip Manor 113 H7
Rush Green 26 B5
Rush Green 124 E5
Rushmore Hill 227 M9
Russell Hill 222 G6
Russ Hill 278 F10
Ruxley 185 P9
Rydens 197 K9
Rydeshill 249 J8
The Ryde 40 F1
Rye Meads 27 J10
Rye Park 44 G2
Sabine's Green 85 L6
St Albans 38 E4
St George in the East 13 N8
St George's Hill 216 D5
St Giles 11 K5
St Helier 201 M8
St James's 11 J10
St Johns 160 F8
St Johns 231 M5
St John's 247 H8
St John's Wood 3 K6
St Julians 38 B10
St Luke's 12 F1
St Margarets 26 F7
St Margarets 177 H2
St Mary Cray 207 M5
St Pancras 5 M10
St Paul's Cray 207 K2
St Stephens 37 P8
St Vincent's Hamlet 105 P2
Salfords 276 C8
Salt Hill 129 J10
Sanderstead 223 P7
Sandridge 21 H10
Sands End 157 M7
Sarratt 71 K1
Sarratt Bottom 71 H2
Sawbridgeworth 29 L1
Scotswood 192 C8
Seal 247 P7
Seer Green 88 G7
Seething Wells 198 G6
Selhurst 203 L5
Selsdon 224 B6
Send 232 F10
Send Grove 250 E2
Send Marsh 233 J9
Seven Kings 123 H6
Sevenoaks 247 K10
Sevenoaks Common 265 H5
Sevenoaks Weald 265 H8
Sewardstone 81 H6
Sewardstonebury 81 K9
Shackleford 266 C10
Shacklewell 119 P9
Shadwell 140 B9
Shalford 268 C7
Sheering 30 E3
Sheerwater 214 F9
Sheets Heath 230 E5
Shelley 49 P10
Shellwood Cross 274 B9
Shenfield 107 K1
Shenley 57 L10
Shenleybury 57 J7
Shepherd's Bush 136 E10
Shepperton 196 B6
Shepperton Green 196 B4
Shere 270 B4
Sherrardspark 22 E3
Shipley Bridge 280 C9
Shirley 204 B9
Shooters Hill 162 F7
Shootersway 33 K5
Shoreditch 7 H10
Shoreham 228 F7
Shorne 191 P8
Shorne Ridgeway 191 N10
Shortlands 205 K3
Shreding Green 130 E8
Shrubs Hill 193 H6
Sidcup 185 L7
Sidlow 275 L7
Silvertown 161 P1
Singlewell 190 F9
Sipson 152 A4
Slade Green 165 H8
Sleapshyde 39 P7
Slough 129 N10
Slyfield 250 A7
Smallfield 281 H5
Smallford 39 N5
Smug Oak 56 A6
Soho 11 J6
Somers Town 5 J8
Sopwell 38 D9
Southall 153 L1
South Beddington 222 E3
South Borough 206 C6
South Bromley 141 J8
South Croydon 223 J3
South Darenth 210 C1
South Earlswood 275 P5
Southend 183 H7
South Field 148 C4
Southfields 179 K4
Southfleet 189 N9
Southgate 98 F2
Southgate 283 N9
South Hackney 140 B3
South Hampstead 3 K3
South Harefield 111 N2
South Harrow 114 A8
South Hatfield 40 E7
South Hornchurch 144 E3
South Kensington 15 J6
South Lambeth 158 F6
South Merstham 258 E6
South Mimms 58 E8
South Norwood 203 L3
South Nutfield 276 F2
South Ockendon 147 H6
South Oxhey 93 J4
South Park 275 H3
South Ruislip 113 L9
South Stifford 167 J4
South Street 244 C5
South Tottenham 119 M3
South Weald 106 D3
South Wimbledon 179 M8
South Woodford 101 M10
Speed Gate 210 E9
Spital 148 G10
Spitalbrook 44 F5
Spitalfields 13 L3
Spring Grove 154 C7
Spring Park 204 F9
Staines 173 J7
Staines Green 24 D7
Stamford Hill 119 N5
Stanborough 22 C8
Stanford Rivers 67 J9
Stanmore 94 G6
Stanstead Abbotts 27 K7
Stanwell 173 N2
Stanwell Moor 173 K2
Stapleford Abbotts 84 D10
Stapleford Tawney 84 D2
Stepney 140 B7
Stewards 47 H6
Steward's Green 65 L8
Stockwell 158 F9
Stoke D'Abernon 235 M1
Stoke Green 129 M6
Stoke Newington 119 N7
Stoke Poges 129 K2
Stone 188 E1
Stonebridge 273 J5
Stonehill 214 B3
Stonehill Green 186 D9
Stoneleigh 220 C2
Stonewood 189 J6
Stoughton 249 N7
Strand 11 L7
Stratford 141 H2
Stratford Marsh 140 G3
Stratford New Town 141 H1
Strawberry Hill 176 G6
Streatham 180 F8
Streatham Hill 180 F4
Streatham Park 180 D7
Streatham Vale 180 C10
Stroude 194 C2
Stroud Green 119 H4
Sudbury 114 E10
Summerstown 179 N5
Sumners 46 D5
Sunbury 196 F1
Sunbury Common 174 G10
Sundridge 183 P9
Sundridge 246 A10
Sunningdale 192 F5
Sunninghill 192 C5
Sunnymeads 150 B10
Surbiton 199 H8
Sutton 150 F4
Sutton 221 K2
Sutton Abinger 271 J9
Sutton at Hone 187 P10
Sutton Green 250 C1
Swallows Cross 87 L3
Swanley 208 F1
Swanley Bar 59 L4
Swanley Village 209 H2
Swanscombe 189 L1
The Swillett 90 F1
Swiss Cottage 3 M5
Sydenham 182 C8
Tadworth 238 F8
Tandridge 260 F9
Tatling End 110 E6
Tatsfield 244 A6
Teddington 176 C9
Temple Fields 29 K7
Temple Hill 165 L10
Temple Mills 120 G10
Thames Ditton 198 F7
Thamesmead 143 J9
Theydon Bois 82 G3
Theydon Garnon 83 M2
Theydon Mount 84 B2
Thong 191 K9
Thorney 151 L1
Thornton Heath 203 J3
Thornwood Common 65 L1
Thorpe 194 F3
Thorpe Green 194 D4
Thorpe Lea 172 F10
Three Bridges 284 A6
Three Households 89 L4
Threshers Bush 48 B2
Tilbury 168 D7
Tilegate Green 48 E3
Tilgate 283 N10
Timberden Bottom 228 F6
Tinsley Green 284 D1
Titsey 261 P1
Tittenhurst 192 F4
Tokyngton 135 N1
Tolmers 60 F2
Tolworth 199 M8
Toot Hill 66 G6
Tooting 180 A8
Tooting Graveney 179 N8
Tottenham 99 M10
Tottenham Hale 119 N1
Totteridge 97 K2
Totteridge Green 96 F2
Tower Hill 53 J5
Tower Hill 272 G4
Townsend 38 A4
Toy's Hill 263 M8
Trumpsgreen 193 P6
Tufnell Park 118 D9
Tulse Hill 181 J4
Turners Hill 285 P9
Turnford 62 D1
Twickenham 176 D4
Twitton 246 F2
Two Waters 35 M9
Tye Green 46 G3
Tylers Causeway 42 C8
Tyler's Green 48 E10
Tyler's Green 260 A6
Tyler's Hill 51 M7
Tyrrell's Wood 237 M10
Tyttenhanger 39 K9
Underhill 77 K10
Underriver 265 P6
Upminster 126 B7
Upper Clapton 119 P6
Upper Edmonton 99 P5
Upper Elmers End 204 E5
Upper Halliford 196 E4
Upper Holloway 118 D6
Upper Norwood 203 L1
Upper Shirley 224 B1
Upper Sydenham 181 P7
Upper Tooting 179 P6
Upper Walthamstow 121 H2
Upshire 63 P8
Upton 141 N2
Upton 149 M2
Upton Lea 129 M8
Upton Park 141 P3
Uxbridge 131 M3
Uxbridge Moor 131 L3
Vale of Health 117 N8
Valley End 212 F2
Vauxhall 17 M8
Venus Hill 52 E7
The Village 170 G6
Virginia Water 193 P3
Waddon 202 F9
Walham Green 157 K7
Wallend 142 D3
Wallington 222 B2
Waltham Abbey 63 J8
Waltham Cross 62 B9
Walthamstow 120 E2
Walton-on-Thames 197 H8
Walton on the Hill 238 C10
Walworth 18 F8
Wanborough 266 A3
Wandle Park 203 H9
Wandsworth 157 K10
Wanstead 121 N5
Wapping 140 A10
Ware 26 E1
Warley 106 G6
Warlingham 242 C4
Warners End 35 H5
Warwick Wold 259 H5
Wasp Green 277 K10
Waterdale 55 K6
Water End 58 F2
Waterend 21 P3
Waterford 24 C1
Waterhales 85 L10
Waterside 51 J9
Watford 72 G7
Watford Heath 93 M1
Watton's Green 85 J10
Wealdstone 114 F1
Weatherhill 281 H3
Welham Green 40 E9
Well End 75 P4
Well Hill 228 C2
Welling 163 L9
The Wells 219 L10
Welsh Harp 116 A6
Welwyn Garden City 23 L3
Wembley 115 K9
Wembley Park 115 M8
Wennington 145 M9
West Acton 135 M8
West Barnes 200 F5
West Bedfont 174 A3
Westbourne Green 8 D2
West Brompton 14 G9
Westbrook Hay 34 F10
West Byfleet 215 L9
West Clandon 251 L5
Westcott 272 A3
West Court 191 H5
West Drayton 151 N2
West Dulwich 181 L5
West Ealing 134 F10
Wested 208 F7
West End 41 N4
West End 212 E10
West End 217 N2
Westerham 262 C3
West Ewell 220 A3
Westfield 232 C8
West Green 119 K1
West Green 283 M6
West Hampstead 117 K10
West Harrow 114 B5
West Heath 117 L7
West Heath 163 N5
West Hendon 116 D5
West Hill 179 H3
West Horndon 127 P4
West Horsley 252 D4
Westhumble 254 F7
West Hyde 91 H8
West Kensington 156 G4
West Kilburn 2 B9
Westminster 17 H4
West Molesey 197 N4
West Norwood 181 K7
Weston Green 198 D8
West Ruislip 112 D6
West Thurrock 166 F4
West Tilbury 169 H5
West Watford 73 H9
West Wickham 205 J8
Westwick Row 36 F7
Westwood 189 H10
West Yoke 211 J10
Wexham Street 129 P3
Weybridge 216 B1
Wheathampstead 21 J2
Whelpley Hill 52 A2
Whetstone 97 L3
Whippendell Bottom 53 M6
Whitebushes 276 C5
Whitechapel 13 M7
Whiteley Village 216 G5
White Oak 208 F2
Whitley Row 264 C5
Whitton 176 B2
Whyteleafe 241 N4
Widmore 206 A2
Wigginton Bottom 32 D1
Wildernesse 247 M8
Wildhill 41 M7
Willesden 136 D1
Willesden Green 136 E2
Willey Green 248 C7
Willowbank 111 M10
Wilmington 187 J7
Wilton Park 88 G9
Wimbledon 179 H8
Winchmore Hill 88 C1
Winchmore Hill 99 K2
Windlesham 212 A3
Windsor 149 K7
Wisley 233 P1
Woking 232 C4
Woldingham 242 F9
Woldingham Garden Village 242 E7
Wonersh 268 F10
Woodbridge Hill 249 M8
Woodcock Hill 91 P5
Woodcote 222 F7
Woodcote 238 A2
Woodcote Green 222 C6
Wood End 132 F8
Wood End 170 B9
Wood End Green 132 F7
Woodford 101 N7
Woodford Bridge 102 C8
Woodford Green 101 M8
Woodford Wells 101 N4
Wood Green 63 P10
Wood Green 99 H9
Woodhall 23 H7
Woodham 215 K6
Woodhatch 275 K3
Woodlands 154 C9
Woodmansterne 239 N1
Woodrow 68 B8
Woodside 41 K7
Woodside 55 J8
Woodside 65 N2
Woodside 170 A7
Woodside 203 P6
Woodside Park 97 K5
Wood Street Village 248 F8
Woollensbrook 26 C10
Woolwich 162 D5
Worcester Park 200 E9
World's End 79 H8
Wormley 44 D10
Wormleybury 44 A9
Wormley West End 43 P8
Worplesdon 249 J3
Worth 284 F8
Wotton 271 M5
Wray Common 257 N8
Wraysbury 172 C2
The Wrythe 201 P9
Yeading 133 K6
Yiewsley 131 P9

USING THE STREET INDEX

Street names are listed alphabetically. Each street name is followed by its postal town or area locality, the Postcode District, the page number, and the reference to the square in which the name is found.

Standard index entries are shown as follows:

Aaron Hill Rd *EHAM* E6 **142** D7

Street names and selected addresses not shown on the map due to scale restrictions are shown in the index with an asterisk:

Abbeville Ms *CLAP* SW4 * **180** E1

GENERAL ABBREVIATIONS

Abbreviation	Meaning
ACC	ACCESS
ALY	ALLEY
AP	APPROACH
AR	ARCADE
ASS	ASSOCIATION
AV	AVENUE
BCH	BEACH
BLDS	BUILDINGS
BND	BEND
BNK	BANK
BR	BRIDGE
BRK	BROOK
BTM	BOTTOM
BUS	BUSINESS
BVD	BOULEVARD
BY	BYPASS
CATH	CATHEDRAL
CEM	CEMETERY
CEN	CENTRE
CFT	CROFT
CH	CHURCH
CHA	CHASE
CHYD	CHURCHYARD
CIR	CIRCLE
CIRC	CIRCUS
CL	CLOSE
CLFS	CLIFFS
CMP	CAMP
CNR	CORNER
CO	COUNTY
COLL	COLLEGE
COM	COMMON
COMM	COMMISSION
CON	CONVENT
COT	COTTAGE
COTS	COTTAGES
CP	CAPE
CPS	COPSE
CR	CREEK
CREM	CREMATORIUM
CRS	CRESCENT
CSWY	CAUSEWAY
CT	COURT
CTRL	CENTRAL
CTS	COURTS
CTYD	COURTYARD
CUTT	CUTTINGS
CV	COVE
CYN	CANYON
DEPT	DEPARTMENT
DL	DALE
DM	DAM
DR	DRIVE
DRO	DROVE
DRY	DRIVEWAY
DWGS	DWELLINGS
E	EAST
EMB	EMBANKMENT
EMBY	EMBASSY
ESP	ESPLANADE
EST	ESTATE
EX	EXCHANGE
EXPY	EXPRESSWAY
EXT	EXTENSION
F/O	FLYOVER
FC	FOOTBALL CLUB
FK	FORK
FLD	FIELD
FLDS	FIELDS
FLS	FALLS
FM	FARM
FT	FORT
FTS	FLATS
FWY	FREEWAY
FY	FERRY
GA	GATE
GAL	GALLERY
GDN	GARDEN
GDNS	GARDENS
GLD	GLADE
GLN	GLEN
GN	GREEN
GND	GROUND
GRA	GRANGE
GRG	GARAGE
GT	GREAT
GTWY	GATEWAY
GV	GROVE
HGR	HIGHER
HL	HILL
HLS	HILLS
HO	HOUSE
HOL	HOLLOW
HOSP	HOSPITAL
HRB	HARBOUR
HTH	HEATH
HTS	HEIGHTS
HVN	HAVEN
HWY	HIGHWAY
IMP	IMPERIAL
IN	INLET
IND EST	INDUSTRIAL ESTATE
INF	INFIRMARY
INFO	INFORMATION
INT	INTERCHANGE
IS	ISLAND
JCT	JUNCTION
JTY	JETTY
KG	KING
KNL	KNOLL
L	LAKE
LA	LANE
LDG	LODGE
LGT	LIGHT
LK	LOCK
LKS	LAKES
LNDG	LANDING
LTL	LITTLE
LWR	LOWER
MAG	MAGISTRATE
MAN	MANSIONS
MD	MEAD
MDW	MEADOWS
MEM	MEMORIAL
MI	MILL
MKT	MARKET
MKTS	MARKETS
ML	MALL
MNR	MANOR
MS	MEWS
MSN	MISSION
MT	MOUNT
MTN	MOUNTAIN
MTS	MOUNTAINS
MUS	MUSEUM
MWY	MOTORWAY
N	NORTH
NE	NORTH EAST
NW	NORTH WEST
O/P	OVERPASS
OFF	OFFICE
ORCH	ORCHARD
OV	OVAL
PAL	PALACE
PAS	PASSAGE
PAV	PAVILION
PDE	PARADE
PH	PUBLIC HOUSE
PK	PARK
PKWY	PARKWAY
PL	PLACE
PLN	PLAIN
PLNS	PLAINS
PLZ	PLAZA
POL	POLICE STATION
PR	PRINCE
PREC	PRECINCT
PREP	PREPARATORY
PRIM	PRIMARY
PROM	PROMENADE
PRS	PRINCESS
PRT	PORT
PT	POINT
PTH	PATH
PZ	PIAZZA
QD	QUADRANT
QU	QUEEN
QY	QUAY
R	RIVER
RBT	ROUNDABOUT
RD	ROAD
RDG	RIDGE
REP	REPUBLIC
RES	RESERVOIR
RFC	RUGBY FOOTBALL CLUB
RI	RISE
RP	RAMP
RW	ROW
S	SOUTH
SCH	SCHOOL
SE	SOUTH EAST
SER	SERVICE AREA
SH	SHORE
SHOP	SHOPPING
SKWY	SKYWAY
SMT	SUMMIT

SOC SOCIETY
SP SPUR
SPR SPRING
SQ SQUARE
ST STREET
STN STATION
STR STREAM
STRD STRAND
SW SOUTH WEST
TDG TRADING
TER TERRACE
THWY THROUGHWAY
TNL TUNNEL
TOLL TOLLWAY
TPK TURNPIKE
TR TRACK
TRL TRAIL
TWR TOWER
U/P UNDERPASS
UNI UNIVERSITY
UPR UPPER
V VALE
VA VALLEY
VIAD VIADUCT
VIL VILLA
VIS VISTA
VLG VILLAGE
VLS VILLAS
VW VIEW
W WEST
WD WOOD
WHF WHARF
WK WALK
WKS WALKS
WLS WELLS
WY WAY
YD YARD
YHA YOUTH HOSTEL

POSTCODE TOWNS AND AREA ABBREVIATIONS

ABLGY Abbots Langley
ABR/ST Abridge/Stapleford Abbotts
ABYW Abbey Wood
ACT Acton
ADL/WDHM Addlestone/Woodham
ALP/SUD Alperton/Sudbury
AMS Amersham
AMSS Amersham south
ARCH Archway
ASC Ascot
ASHF Ashford (Surrey)
ASHTD Ashtead
BAGS Bagshot
BAL Balham
BANK Bank
BAR Barnet
BARB Barbican
BARK Barking
BARK/HLT Barkingside/Hainault
BARN Barnes
BAY/PAD Bayswater/Paddington
BCTR Becontree
BEAC Beaconsfield
BECK Beckenham
BELMT Belmont
BELV Belvedere
BERK Berkhamsted
BERM/RHTH Bermondsey/Rotherhithe
BETH Bethnal Green
BF/WBF Byfleet/West Byfleet
BFN/LL Blackfen/Longlands
BFOR Bracknell Forest/Windlesham
BGR/WK Borough Green/West Kingsdown
BGVA Belgravia
BH/WHM Biggin Hill/Westerham
BKHH Buckhurst Hill
BKHTH/KID Blackheath/Kidbrooke
BLKFR Blackfriars
BMLY Bromley
BMSBY Bloomsbury
BNSTD Banstead
BORE Borehamwood
BOW Bow
BRKHM/BTCW Brockham/Betchworth
BRKMPK Brookmans Park
BROCKY Brockley
BROX Broxbourne
BRW Brentwood
BRWN Brentwood north
BRXN/ST Brixton north/Stockwell
BRXS/STRHM Brixton south/Streatham Hill
BRYLDS Berrylands
BTFD Brentford
BTSEA Battersea
BUSH Bushey
BXLY Bexley
BXLYHN Bexleyheath north
BXLYHS Bexleyheath south
CAMTN Camden Town
CAN/RD Canning Town/Royal Docks
CANST Cannon Street station
CAR Carshalton
CAT Catford
CAVSQ/HST Cavendish Square/Harley Street
CDALE/KGS Colindale/Kingsbury
CDW/CHF Chadwell St Mary/Chafford Hundred
CEND/HSY/T Crouch End/Hornsey/Turnpike Lane
CFSP/GDCR Chalfont St Peter/Gerrards Cross
CHARL Charlton
CHCR Charing Cross
CHDH Chadwell Heath
CHEAM Cheam
CHEL Chelsea
CHERT Chertsey
CHES/WCR Cheshunt/Waltham Cross
CHESW Cheshunt west
CHIG Chigwell
CHING Chingford
CHOB/PIR Chobham/Pirbright
CHONG Chipping Ongar
CHSGTN Chessington
CHST Chislehurst
CHSWK Chiswick
CITYW City of London west
CLAP Clapham
CLAY Clayhall
CLKNW Clerkenwell
CLPT Clapton
CMBW Camberwell
COB Cobham
CONDST Conduit Street
COUL/CHIP Coulsdon/Chipstead
COVGDN Covent Garden
CRAWE Crawley east
CRAWW Crawley west
CRICK Cricklewood
CROY/NA Croydon/New Addington
CRW Collier Row
CSHM Chesham
CSTG Chalfont St Giles
CTHM Caterham
DAGE Dagenham east
DAGW Dagenham west
DART Dartford
DEN/HRF Denham/Harefield
DEN/HRF Denham/Harefield
DEPT Deptford
DORK Dorking
DTCH/LGLY Datchet/Langley
DUL Dulwich
E/WMO/HCT East & West Molesey/Hampton Court
EA Ealing
EBAR East Barnet
EBED/NFELT East Bedfont/North Feltham
ECT Earl's Court
ED Edmonton
EDEN Edenbridge
EDGW Edgware
EDUL East Dulwich
EFNCH East Finchley
EGH Egham
EHAM East Ham
EHSLY East Horsley
ELTH/MOT Eltham/Mottingham
EMB Embankment
EMPK Emerson Park
EN Enfield
ENC/FH Enfield Chase/Forty Hill
EPP Epping
EPSOM Epsom
ERITH Erith
ERITHM Erith Marshes
ESH/CLAY Esher/Claygate
EW Ewell
EYN Eynsford
FARR Farringdon
FBAR/BDGN Friern Barnet/Bounds Green
FELT Feltham
FENCHST Fenchurch Street
FITZ Fitzrovia
FLKWH/TG Flackwell Heath/Tylers Green
FLST/FETLN Fleet Street/Fetter Lane
FNCH Finchley
FRIM Frimley
FSBYE Finsbury east
FSBYPK Finsbury Park
FSBYW Finsbury west
FSTGT Forest Gate
FSTH Forest Hill
FUL/PGN Fulham/Parsons Green
GDMY/SEVK Goodmayes/Seven Kings
GDST Godstone
GFD/PVL Greenford/Perivale
GINN Gray's Inn
GLDGN Golders Green
GNTH/NBYPK Gants Hill/Newbury Park
GNWCH Greenwich
GODL Godalming
GPK Gidea Park
GRAYS Grays
GSTN Garston
GT/LBKH Great Bookham/Little Bookham
GTDUN Great Dunmow
GTMIS/PWD Great Missenden/Prestwood
GTPST Great Portland Street
GU Guildford
GUW Guildford west
GVE Gravesend east
GVW Gravesend west
GWRST Gower Street
HACK Hackney
HAMP Hampstead
HARH Harold Hill
HARP Harpenden
HART Hartley
HAT Hatfield
HAYES Hayes
HBRY Highbury
HCH Hornchurch
HCIRC Holborn Circus
HDN Hendon
HDTCH Houndsditch
HERT/BAY Hertford/Bayford
HERT/WAT Hertford/Watton at Stone
HEST Heston
HGDN/ICK Hillingdon/Ickenham
HGT Highgate
HHNE Hemel Hempstead northeast
HHOL High Holborn
HHS/BOV Hemel Hempstead south/Bovingdon
HHW Hemel Hempstead west
HLW Harlow
HLWE Harlow east
HLWS Harlow south
HLWW/ROY Harlow west/Roydon
HMSMTH Hammersmith
HNHL Herne Hill
HNWL Hanwell
HOD Hoddesdon
HOL/ALD Holborn/Aldwych
HOLWY Holloway
HOM Homerton
HOR/WEW Horton/West Ewell
HORL Horley
HORS Horsham
HPTN Hampton
HRW Harrow
HSLW Hounslow
HSLWW Hounslow west
HTHAIR Heathrow Airport
HYS/HAR Hayes/Harlington
IL Ilford
ING Ingatestone
IS Islington
ISLW Isleworth
IVER Iver
KENS Kensington
KGLGY Kings Langley
KIL/WHAMP Kilburn/West Hampstead
KTBR Knightsbridge
KTN/HRWW/WS Kenton/Harrow Weald/Wealdstone
KTTN Kentish Town
KUT/HW Kingston upon Thames/Hampton Wick
KUTN/CMB Kingston upon Thames north/Coombe
KWD/TDW/WH Kingswood/Tadworth/Walton on the Hill
LBTH Lambeth
LCOL/BKTW London Colney/Bricket Wood
LEE/GVPK Lee/Grove Park
LEW Lewisham
LEY Leyton
LHD/OX Leatherhead/Oxshott
LING Lingfield
LINN Lincoln's Inn
LOTH Lothbury
LOU Loughton
LSQ/SEVD Leicester Square/Seven Dials
LTWR Lightwater
LVPST Liverpool Street
MANHO Mansion House
MBLAR Marble Arch
MDHD Maidenhead
MEO Meopham
MFD/CHID Milford/Chiddingfold
MHST Marylebone High Street
MLHL Mill Hill
MNPK Manor Park
MON Monument
MORT/ESHN Mortlake/East Sheen
MRDN Morden
MTCM Mitcham
MUSWH Muswell Hill
MV/WKIL Maida Vale/West Kilburn
MYFR/PICC Mayfair/Piccadilly
MYFR/PKLN Mayfair/Park Lane
NFNCH/WDSPK North Finchley/Woodside Park
NKENS North Kensington
NOXST/BSQ New Oxford Street/Bloomsbury Square
NRWD Norwood
NTGHL Notting Hill
NTHLT Northolt
NTHWD Northwood
NWCR New Cross
NWDGN Norwood Green
NWMAL New Malden
OBST Old Broad Street
ORP Orpington
OXHEY Oxhey
OXSTW Oxford Street west
OXTED Oxted
PECK Peckham
PEND Ponders End
PGE/AN Penge/Anerley
PIM Pimlico
PIN Pinner
PLMGR Palmers Green
PLSTW Plaistow
POP/IOD Poplar/Isle of Dogs
POTB/CUF Potters Bar/Cuffley
PUR Purfleet
PUR/KEN Purley/Kenley
PUT/ROE Putney/Roehampton
RAD Radlett
RAIN Rainham (Gt Lon)
RBRW/HUT Rural Brentwood/Hutton
RBSF Rural Bishop's Stortford
RCH/KEW Richmond/Kew
RCHPK/HAM Richmond Park/Ham
RDART Rural Dartford
RDKG Rural Dorking
REDBR Redbridge
REDH Redhill
REGST Regent Street
REIG Reigate
RFNM Rural Farnham
RGUE Rural Guildford east
RGUW Rural Guildford west
RKW/CH/CXG Rickmansworth/Chorleywood/Croxley Green
ROM Romford
ROMW/RG Romford west/Rush Green
RPLY/SEND Ripley/Send
RSEV Rural Sevenoaks
RSLP Ruislip
RSQ Russell Square
RTON Rural Tonbridge
RYLN/HDSTN Rayners Lane/Headstone
RYNPK Raynes Park
SAND/SEL Sanderstead/Selsdon
SBW Sawbridgeworth
SCUP Sidcup
SDTCH Shoreditch
SEV Sevenoaks
SEVS/STOTM Seven Sisters/South Tottenham
SHB Shepherd's Bush
SHGR Shamley Green
SHPTN Shepperton
SKENS South Kensington
SL Slough
SLH/COR Stanford-le-Hope/Corringham
SLN Slough north
SNWD South Norwood
SOCK/AV South Ockendon/Aveley
SOHO/CST Soho/Carnaby Street
SOHO/SHAV Soho/Shaftesbury Avenue
SRTFD Stratford
STA Staines
STAL St Albans
STALE/WH St Albans east/Wheathampstead
STALW/RED St Albans west/Redbourn
STAN Stanmore
STBT St Bart's
STHGT/OAK Southgate/Oakwood
STHL Southall
STHWK Southwark
STJS St James's
STJSPK St James's Park
STJWD St John's Wood
STKPK Stockley Park
STLK St Luke's
STMC/STPC St Mary Cray/St Paul's Cray
STNW/STAM Stoke Newington/Stamford Hill
STP St Paul's
STPAN St Pancras
STRHM/NOR Streatham/Norbury
STWL/WRAY Stanwell/Wraysbury
SUN Sunbury
SURB Surbiton
SUT Sutton
SWCM Swanscombe
SWFD South Woodford
SWLY Swanley
SYD Sydenham
TEDD Teddington
THDIT Thames Ditton
THHTH Thornton Heath
THMD Thamesmead
TIL Tilbury
TOOT Tooting
TOTM Tottenham
TPL/STR Temple/Strand
TRDG/WHET Totteridge/Whetstone
TRING Tring
TWK Twickenham
TWRH Tower Hill
UED Upper Edmonton
UPMR Upminster
UX/CGN Uxbridge/Colham Green
VW Virginia Water
VX/NE Vauxhall/Nine Elms
WAB Waltham Abbey
WALTH Walthamstow
WALW Walworth
WAN Wanstead
WAND/EARL Wandsworth/Earlsfield
WAP Wapping
WARE Ware
WARL Warlingham
WAT Watford
WATN Watford north
WATW Watford west
WBLY Wembley
WBPTN West Brompton
WCHMH Winchmore Hill
WCHPL Whitechapel
WDGN Wood Green
WDR/YW West Drayton/Yiewsley
WDSR Windsor
WEA West Ealing
WELL Welling
WEST Westminster
WESTW Westminster west
WEY Weybridge
WFD Woodford
WGCE Welwyn Garden City east
WGCW Welwyn Garden City west
WHALL Whitehall
WHTN Whitton
WIM/MER Wimbledon/Merton
WKENS West Kensington
WLGTN Wallington
WLSDN Willesden
WLYN Welwyn
WNWD West Norwood
WOKN/KNAP Woking north/Knaphill
WOKS/MYFD Woking south/Mayford
WOOL/PLUM Woolwich/Plumstead
WOT/HER Walton-on-Thames/Hersham
WPK Worcester Park
WTHK West Thurrock
WWKM West Wickham
YEAD Yeading

Index - streets

1

1 Av *WOOL/PLUM* SE18 162 E2
1st Av *KWD/TDW/WH* KT20 257 H1
2nd Av *KWD/TDW/WH* KT20 257 H1
3rd Av *KWD/TDW/WH* KT20 257 H1
4th Av *KWD/TDW/WH* KT20 257 H1
5th Av *KWD/TDW/WH* KT20 257 H1
6th Av *KWD/TDW/WH* KT20 257 H1
7th Av *KWD/TDW/WH* KT20 257 H2
8th Av *KWD/TDW/WH* KT20 257 H2
9th Av *KWD/TDW/WH* KT20 257 H1
10th Av *KWD/TDW/WH* KT20 257 H2
11th Av *KWD/TDW/WH* KT20 257 H1
12th Av *KWD/TDW/WH* KT20 257 H2
13th Av *KWD/TDW/WH* KT20 257 H2
14th Av *KWD/TDW/WH* KT20 257 H2
15th Av *KWD/TDW/WH* KT20 257 J2
16th Av *KWD/TDW/WH* KT20 257 H2

A

Aaron Hill Rd *EHAM* E6 142 D7
Abberley Ms *BTSEA* SW11 158 C9
Abbess Cl *BRXS/STRHM* SW2 181 J4
Abbeville Ms *CLAP* SW4 * 180 E1
Abbeville Rd *CEND/HSY/T* N8 118 E2
CLAP SW4 180 D2
Abbey Av *ALP/SUD* HA0 135 K4
STALW/RED AL3 37 P9
Abbey Cha *CHERT* KT16 * 195 L6
Abbey Cl *HYS/HAR* UB3 133 J10
NTHLT UB5 133 N5
PIN HA5 113 K1
ROM RM1 124 G4
SL SL1 128 D9
WOKS/MYFD GU22 233 H2
Abbey Ct *CHERT* KT16 * 195 L7
WAB EN9 62 G10
Abbey Crs *BELV* DA17 164 B3
Abbey Dale Cl *HLWE* CM17 47 M2
Abbeydale Rd *ALP/SUD* HA0 135 L3
Abbey Dr *ABLGY* WD5 55 H8
RDART DA2 186 F5
STA TW18 * 195 M4
TOOT SW17 180 B8
Abbeyfield Cl *MTCM* CR4 201 P2
Abbeyfield Est
BERM/RHTH SE16 160 B3
Abbeyfield Rd *BERM/RHTH* SE16 160 B3
Abbeyfields Cl *WLSDN* NW10 135 M5
Abbey Gdns *BERM/RHTH* SE16 19 P5
CHERT KT16 195 K6
CHST BR7 206 D1
HMSMTH W6 14 A10
STJWD NW8 3 J8
Abbey Gn *CHERT* KT16 195 K6
Abbey Gv *ABYW* SE2 163 L3
Abbeyhill Rd *BFN/LL* DA15 185 M5
Abbey La *BECK* BR3 182 F10
SRTFD E15 141 H4
SRTFD E15 141 J4
Abbey Mdw *CHERT* KT16 195 M7
Abbey Ms *ISLW* TW7 154 G7
STA TW18 * 195 M3
STAL AL1 * 38 C7
WALTH E17 120 F3
Abbey Mill End *STALW/RED* AL3 38 B7
Abbey Mill La *STALW/RED* AL3 38 B7
Abbey Mt *BELV* DA17 164 A4
Abbey Orchard St *WEST* SW1P 17 K3
Abbey Pk *BECK* BR3 182 F10
Abbey Park La *SL* SL1 108 D7
Abbey Pl *CHERT* KT16 195 K3
DART DA1 * 187 L1
Abbey Rd *BARK* IG11 142 F3
BELV DA17 163 N3
BXLYHN DA7 163 P10
CHERT KT16 195 L7
CHES/WCR EN8 62 D10
CROY/NA CR0 203 J10
EN EN1 79 M9
GNTH/NBYPK IG2 122 E4
GVE DA12 191 H4
KIL/WHAMP NW6 2 G5
SAND/SEL CR2 224 C6
SHPTN TW17 196 B8
SRTFD E15 141 J4
SWCM DA10 189 H1
VW GU25 194 A5
WIM/MER SW19 201 M1
WLSDN NW10 135 N4
WOKN/KNAP GU21 231 P3
Abbey St *PLSTW* E13 141 M6
STHWK SE1 19 L3
Abbey Ter *ABYW* SE2 163 M2
Abbey Vw *MLHL* NW7 96 C4
RAD WD7 74 E1
Abbeyview *WAB* EN9 62 G9
Abbey View Rd *STALW/RED* AL3 38 B6
Abbey Wk *E/WMO/HCT* KT8 198 A3
Abbey Wd *ASC* SL5 192 F7
Abbey Wood La *RAIN* RM13 145 L4
Abbey Wood Rd *ABYW* SE2 163 L3
Abbot Cl *BF/WBF* KT14 215 N6
RSLP HA4 113 L8
STA TW18 173 N10
Abbot John Ms *STALE/WH* AL4 21 J2
Abbot Rd *GU* GU1 268 A2
Abbots Av *HOR/WEW* KT19 219 M7
STAL AL1 38 D9
Abbots Av West *STAL* AL1 38 D9
Abbotsbury Cl *SRTFD* E15 141 H4
WKENS W14 14 C2
Abbotsbury Gdns *PIN* HA5 113 K4
Abbotsbury Ms *PECK* SE15 160 B9
Abbotsbury Rd *MRDN* SM4 201 L4
NTGHL W11 14 B1
WWKM BR4 205 L9
Abbot's Cl *GUW* GU2 267 K3
BRWN CM15 107 M2
RAIN RM13 145 K4
STMC/STPC BR5 206 F8
Abbots Dr *RYLN/HDSTN* HA2 113 P7
VW GU25 193 P4
Abbotsfield Rd *CRAWW* RH11 282 C8
Abbotsford Av *SEVS/STOTM* N15 119 K2
Abbotsford Cl
WOKS/MYFD GU22 232 D3
Abbotsford Gdns *WFD* IG8 101 M8
Abbotsford Rd *GDMY/SEVK* IG3 123 K7
Abbots Gdns *EFNCH* N2 117 N2
Abbots Gn *CROY/NA* CR0 224 C3
Abbotshade Rd
BERM/RHTH SE16 * 140 C10
Abbotshall Av *STHGT/OAK* N14 98 D4
Abbotshall Rd *CAT* SE6 183 J4
Abbots Hl *HHS/BOV* HP3 * 54 C1
Abbots La *PUR/KEN* CR8 241 K2
STHWK SE1 13 K10
Abbotsleigh Cl *BELMT* SM2 221 L4
Abbotsleigh Rd
STRHM/NOR SW16 180 D7
Abbots Mnr *PIM* SW1V 16 E7
Abbots Manor Est *PIM* SW1V 16 E7
Abbotsmede Cl *TWK* TW1 176 E5
Abbots Pk *BRXS/STRHM* SW2 181 H4
STAL AL1 38 E9
Abbots Pl *BORE* WD6 75 N4
KIL/WHAMP NW6 2 G5
Abbots Ri *KGLGY* WD4 54 A3
REDH RH1 258 A2
Abbots Rd *ABLGY* WD5 54 B9
EDGW HA8 96 A8
EHAM E6 142 A3
Abbots Ter *CEND/HSY/T* N8 118 F4
Abbotstone Rd *PUT/ROE* SW15 156 F9
Abbot St *HACK* E8 7 L1
Abbots Vw *KGLGY* WD4 54 A3
Abbot's Wk *WDSR* SL4 148 D8
CTHM CR3 242 A8
EN EN1 79 H4
Abbot's Wy *GU* GU1 250 G9
BECK BR3 204 D5
CHERT KT16 195 J7
Abbotswell *HLWS* CM18 46 G4
Abbotswell Rd *BROCKY* SE4 182 E1
Abbotswood *GU* GU1 250 C8
Abbotswood Cl *BELV* DA17 163 P2
GU GU1 250 C8
Abbotswood Dr *WEY* KT13 216 E6
Abbotswood Gdns *CLAY* IG5 122 E1
Abbotswood Rd *EDUL* SE22 159 M10
STRHM/NOR SW16 180 E6
Abbotswood Wy *HYS/HAR* UB3 133 J10
Abbott Av *RYNPK* SW20 200 G2
Abbott Cl *HPTN* TW12 175 M9
NTHLT UB5 133 N1
Abbott Rd *POP/IOD* E14 141 J8
Abbott's Cl *UX/CGN* UB8 131 N7
IS N1 * 6 E3
ROMW/RG RM7 124 C1
SWLY BR8 209 H4
THMD SE28 143 M9
Abbotts Ct *WARE* SG12 27 J7
Abbotts Crs *CHING* E4 101 J5
ENC/FH EN2 79 J6
Abbotts Dr *ALP/SUD* HA0 114 G7
WAB EN9 63 M10
Abbotts Md *RCHPK/HAM* TW10 * 177 H7
Abbotts Park Rd *LEY* E10 121 H5
Abbotts Ri *REDH* RH1 258 B8
WARE SG12 27 J7
Abbotts Rd *BAR* EN5 77 L8
CHEAM SM3 221 H1
MTCM CR4 202 D4
STHL UB1 133 M10
Abbotts Tilt *WOT/HER* KT12 197 M10
Abbotts V *CSHM* HP5 51 H4
Abbott's Wk *BXLYHN* DA7 163 N6
Abbotts Wy *SL* SL1 128 C10
WARE SG12 27 J7
Abbs Cross Gdns *HCH* RM12 125 K6
Abbs Cross La *HCH* RM12 125 K8
Abchurch La *MANHO* EC4N 13 H7
Abdale La *BRKMPK* AL9 58 E3
Abdale Rd *SHB* W12 136 E10
Abel Cl *HHNE* HP2 36 B6
Abelia Cl *CHOB/PIR* GU24 212 D9
Abenberg Wy *RBRW/HUT* CM13 107 M3
Aberavon Rd *BOW* E3 140 E5
Abercairn Rd *STRHM/NOR* SW16 180 D10
Aberconway Rd *MRDN* SM4 201 L3
Abercorn Cl *MLHL* NW7 97 H8
SAND/SEL CR2 222 F2
STJWD NW8 3 J8
Abercorn Crs *RYLN/HDSTN* HA2 114 A6
Abercorn Gdns *CHDH* RM6 123 L5
KTN/HRWW/WS HA3 115 J5
Abercorn Gv *RSLP* HA4 112 F5
Abercorn Ms *RCHPK/HAM* TW10 177 L1
Abercorn Pl *STJWD* NW8 3 J9
Abercorn Rd *MLHL* NW7 97 H8
STAN HA7 95 H8
Abercorn Wy *STHWK* SE1 19 N7
WOKN/KNAP GU21 231 M4
Abercrombie Dr *EN* EN1 79 P5
Abercrombie St *BTSEA* SW11 157 P8
Abercrombie Wy
HLWW/ROY CM19 46 C3
Aberdale Gdns *POTB/CUF* EN6 59 J9
Aberdare Cl *WWKM* BR4 205 H9
Aberdare Gdns *KIL/WHAMP* NW6 3 H4
MLHL NW7 96 G8
Aberdare Rd *PEND* EN3 80 B8
Aberdeen Av *SL* SL1 128 F9
Aberdeen Cottages *STAN* HA7 * 95 H8
Aberdeen La *HBRY* N5 119 J10
Aberdeen Pde *UED* N18 * 100 A6
Aberdeen Pk *HBRY* N5 119 K10
Aberdeen Pl *BAY/PAD* W2 9 L2
Aberdeen Rd *CROY/NA* CR0 223 L1
HBRY N5 119 K9
KTN/HRWW/WS HA3 94 E10
KTN/HRWW/WS HA3 114 E1
UED N18 99 P6
UED N18 100 A6
WLSDN NW10 116 C10
Aberdeen Ter *BKHTH/KID* SE3 161 J8
Aberdour Rd *GDMY/SEVK* IG3 123 L8
Aberdour St *STHWK* SE1 19 J5
Aberfeldy St *POP/IOD* E14 141 H8
Aberford Gdns
WOOL/PLUM SE18 162 B7
Aberford Rd *BORE* WD6 75 M6
Aberfoyle Rd *STRHM/NOR* SW16 180 E10
Abergeldie Rd *LEE/GVPK* SE12 183 N2
Abernethy Rd *LEW* SE13 161 K10
Abersham Rd *HACK* E8 119 N10
Abery St *WOOL/PLUM* SE18 163 H3
Abigail Ms *HARH* RM3 105 P10
Abingdon Cl *CAMTN* NW1 5 J2
HGDN/ICK UB10 132 A3
STHWK SE1 * 19 M6
WIM/MER SW19 179 M9
WOKN/KNAP GU21 231 N4
Abingdon Pl *POTB/CUF* EN6 59 L8
Abingdon Rd *FNCH* N3 97 M10
KENS W8 14 F4
STRHM/NOR SW16 202 F1
Abingdon St *WEST* SW1P 17 L2
Abingdon Vls *KENS* W8 14 F5
Abingdon Wy *ORP* BR6 227 L1
Abinger Av *BELMT* SM2 220 G6
Abinger Cl *BMLY* BR1 206 B3
CROY/NA CR0 225 H3
GDMY/SEVK IG3 123 K9
RDKG RH5 273 H6
WLGTN SM6 222 F2
Abinger Common Rd *RDKG* RH5 271 N10
Abinger Dr *NRWD* SE19 181 K10
REDH RH1 275 P2
Abinger Gdns *ISLW* TW7 154 D9
Abinger Gv *DEPT* SE8 160 E5
Abinger La *RDKG* RH5 271 K8
Abinger Ms *MV/WKIL* W9 8 E1
Abinger Rd *CHSWK* W4 156 C2
REDH RH1 275 P3
Abinger Wy *RGUE* GU4 250 E5
Ablett St *BERM/RHTH* SE16 160 B4
Abney Park Ter
STNW/STAM N16 * 119 N7
Aboyne Dr *RYNPK* SW20 200 D2
Aboyne Rd *TOOT* SW17 179 M6
WLSDN NW10 116 B8
Abraham Cl *OXHEY* WD19 93 J5
Abraham Ct *UPMR* RM14 125 P7
Abridge Cl *CHES/WCR* EN8 80 C1
Abridge Gdns *CRW* RM5 104 B7
Abridge Rd *CHIG* IG7 83 H10
EPP CM16 83 K3
Abridge Wy *BARK* IG11 143 L4
Abyssinia Cl *BTSEA* SW11 157 P10
Abyssinia Rd *BTSEA* SW11 * 157 P10
Acacia Av *BTFD* TW8 154 G6
HCH RM12 124 G7
HYS/HAR UB3 132 G8
RSLP HA4 113 H6
SHPTN TW17 196 B5
STWL/WRAY TW19 150 B10
TOTM N17 99 L8
WBLY HA9 115 K10
WDR/YW UB7 132 A9
WOKS/MYFD GU22 232 A6
Acacia Cl *ADL/WDHM* KT15 215 J6
CHESW EN7 61 M3
CHSM HP5 50 F6
DEPT SE8 160 D3
STAN HA7 94 D7
STMC/STPC BR5 206 G5
Acacia Dr *ADL/WDHM* KT15 215 J7
BNSTD SM7 220 G10
CHEAM SM3 201 J8
UPMR RM14 125 P9
Acacia Gdns *STJWD* NW8 3 M7
UPMR RM14 126 E5
WWKM BR4 205 H9
Acacia Gv *BERK* HP4 33 N6
DUL SE21 181 L5
NWMAL KT3 200 B3
Acacia Ms *WDR/YW* UB7 151 N5
Acacia Pl *STJWD* NW8 3 M7
Acacia Rd *ACT* W3 135 P9
BECK BR3 204 E3
DART DA1 187 K4
ENC/FH EN2 79 L5
GU GU1 250 A10
HPTN TW12 175 P9
MTCM CR4 202 B2
RDART DA2 188 D2
STA TW18 173 L8
STJWD NW8 3 M7
STRHM/NOR SW16 202 F1
WALTH E17 120 D4
WAN E11 121 K7
WDGN N22 99 H9
The Acacias *EBAR* EN4 * 77 N9
Acacia St *HAT* AL10 40 D7
Acacia Wk *HARP* AL5 20 C5
Acacia Wy *BFN/LL* DA15 185 J3
Academy Fields Rd *GPK* RM2 125 J3
Academy Gdns *CROY/NA* CR0 203 N8
NTHLT UB5 133 L4
Academy Pl *WOOL/PLUM* SE18 162 C7
Academy Rd *WOOL/PLUM* SE18 162 C6
Acanthus Dr *STHWK* SE1 19 N7
Acanthus Rd *BTSEA* SW11 158 B9
Accommodation La
WDR/YW UB7 151 M5
Accommodation Rd *CHERT* KT16 214 B1
GLDGN NW11 117 J5
Ace Pde *CHSGTN* KT9 199 K10
Acer Av *RAIN* RM13 145 L5
YEAD UB4 133 M6
Acer Dr *CHOB/PIR* GU24 212 E9
Acer Rd *BH/WHM* TN16 244 A2
Acers *LCOL/BKTW* AL2 56 B4
Acfold Rd *FUL/PGN* SW6 157 L7
Achilles Cl *HHNE* HP2 36 A4
STHWK SE1 19 P7
Achilles Pl *WOKN/KNAP* GU21 231 P3
Achilles Rd *KIL/WHAMP* NW6 117 K10
Achilles St *NWCR* SE14 160 D6
Acklam Rd *NKENS* W10 8 C4
Acklington Dr *CDALE/KGS* NW9 96 B9
Ackmar Rd *FUL/PGN* SW6 157 K7
Ackroyd Dr *BOW* E3 140 E7
Ackroyd Rd *FSTH* SE23 182 D3
Acland Cl *WOOL/PLUM* SE18 162 G6
Acland Crs *CMBW* SE5 159 L10

Acland Rd CRICK NW2 136 E1
Acle Cl BARK/HLT IG6 102 E9
Acme Rd WATN WD24 73 H4
Acock Gv NTHLT UB5 114 A9
Acol Crs RSLP HA4 113 J10
Acol Rd KIL/WHAMP NW6 2 F4
Acorn Cl CHING E4 100 G6
CHST BR7 184 F8
ENC/FH EN2 79 H5
HORL RH6 280 D3
HPTN TW12 176 A9
STAN HA7 94 G8
Acorn Gdns ACT W3 136 A7
NRWD SE19 203 N1
Acorn Gv HYS/HAR UB3 152 G6
KWD/TDW/WH KT20 239 J10
RSLP HA4 112 G9
WOKS/MYFD GU22 * 232 B7
Acorn La POTB/CUF EN6 60 F6
Acorn Pde PECK SE15 * 160 A6
Acorn Pl WATN WD24 73 H5
Acorn Rd DART DA1 186 G1
HHS/BOV HP3 36 B7
The Acorns HORL RH6 281 J5
SEV TN13 247 H9
STALE/WH AL4 * 39 J6
Acorn St WARE SG12 28 A4
Acorns Wy ESH/CLAY KT10 218 B2
Acorn Wy BECK BR3 205 H5
FSTH SE23 182 C6
ORP BR6 226 E1
Acre Dr EDUL SE22 159 P10
Acrefield Rd CFSP/GDCR SL9 110 A2
Acre La BRXS/STRHM SW2 158 G10
CAR SM5 222 B1
Acre Rd DAGE RM10 144 C2
KUTN/CMB KT2 199 K1
WIM/MER SW19 179 N9
Acres Av CHONG CM5 67 N2
Acres End AMSS HP7 69 K5
Acres Gdns KWD/TDW/WH KT20 238 F5
Acre Wy NTHWD HA6 92 G9
Acre Wd HHNE HP2 35 P7
Acrewood Wy STALE/WH AL4 39 L6
Acris St WAND/EARL SW18 179 M1
Acton Cl CHES/WCR EN8 62 D7
ED N9 99 P3
Acton Hill Ms ACT W3 * 135 N10
Acton La ACT W3 155 P1
CHSWK W4 155 P2
WLSDN NW10 135 P4
WLSDN NW10 136 A4
Acton Ms HACK E8 7 L5
Acton St FSBYW WC1X 5 N10
Acuba Rd WAND/EARL SW18 179 L5
Acworth Cl ED N9 100 B1
Acworth Pl DART DA1 * 187 K2
Ada Ct MV/WKIL W9 3 K10
Ada Gdns POP/IOD E14 141 J8
SRTFD E15 141 L3
Adair Cl SNWD SE25 204 A3
Adair Gdns CTHM CR3 241 K7
Adair Rd NKENS W10 8 B2
NKENS W10 137 H6
Adam Cl CAT SE6 182 E7
FSTH SE23 182 B5
SL SL1 128 F10
Adam & Eve Ms KENS W8 14 F3
Adam Rd CHING E4 100 E7
Adams Cl BRYLDS KT5 199 L6
FNCH N3 97 K8
WBLY HA9 115 N7
Adams Ct OBST EC2N 13 H5
Adams Cft CHOB/PIR GU24 230 B6
Adamsfield CHESW EN7 61 N2
Adams House HLW CM20 28 G10
Adams Ms TOOT SW17 180 A5
WDGN N22 98 G8
Adamson Rd CAN/RD E16 141 M8
HAMP NW3 3 M3
Adamson Wy BECK BR3 205 H5
Adams Pl HOLWY N7 118 G10
Adamsrill Cl EN EN1 79 L10
Adamsrill Rd SYD SE26 182 C7
Adams Rd BECK BR3 204 D5
TOTM N17 99 L10
Adam's Rw MYFR/PKLN W1K 10 D8
Adams Sq BXLYHS DA6 163 P9
Adam St CHCR WC2N 11 M8
Adams Wk KUT/HW KT1 199 K2
Adams Wy CROY/NA CR0 203 N6
Adam Wk FUL/PGN SW6 * 156 F6
Ada Pl BETH E2 7 P6
Adare Wk STRHM/NOR SW16 180 F5
Ada Rd ALP/SUD HA0 * 115 H8
CMBW SE5 159 M6
Ada St HACK E8 140 A3
Adderley Gdns ELTH/MOT SE9 184 D7
Adderley Gv BTSEA SW11 180 B1
Adderley Rd
KTN/HRWW/WS HA3 94 E9
Adderley St POP/IOD E14 141 H8
Addington Cl WDSR SL4 148 F9
Addington Dr
NFNCH/WDSPK N12 97 N7
Addington Gv SYD SE26 182 D7
Addington Rd BOW E3 140 F5
CAN/RD E16 141 K6
CROY/NA CR0 203 J8
FSBYPK N4 119 H5
SAND/SEL CR2 223 P7
WWKM BR4 205 K10
WWKM BR4 225 H1
Addington Sq CMBW SE5 159 K6
Addington St STHWK SE1 17 P2
Addington Village Rd
CROY/NA CR0 224 F3
Addis Cl PEND EN3 80 C5
Addiscombe Av CROY/NA CR0 203 P7
Addiscombe Cl
KTN/HRWW/WS HA3 115 H3
Addiscombe Court Rd
CROY/NA CR0 203 M9
Addiscombe Gv CROY/NA CR0 203 L9
Addiscombe Rd CROY/NA CR0 203 M9
CROY/NA CR0 203 P9
WATW WD18 73 J8
Addison Av HSLW TW3 154 B7
NTGHL W11 8 A10
NTGHL W11 137 H10
STHGT/OAK N14 78 C10
Addison Bridge Pl WKENS W14 14 B5
Addison Cl CTHM CR3 241 L8
IVER SL0 131 H9
NTHWD HA6 93 H9
STMC/STPC BR5 206 F6
Addison Ct EPP CM16 65 K7
Addison Crs WKENS W14 14 B3
WKENS W14 157 H2
Addison Dr LEE/GVPK SE12 183 N1
Addison Gdns BRYLDS KT5 199 L4
GRAYS RM17 167 P3
WKENS W14 156 G2
Addison Gv CHSWK W4 156 B3
Addison Pl NTGHL W11 8 A10
NTGHL W11 137 H10
Addison Rd BARK/HLT IG6 102 F9
CSHM HP5 51 H5
CTHM CR3 241 L7
GU GU1 268 C2
HAYES BR2 206 A5
PEND EN3 80 B5
SNWD SE25 203 P4
TEDD TW11 176 G9
WALTH E17 120 G3
WAN E11 121 M4
WKENS W14 14 C3
Addison's Cl CROY/NA CR0 204 E9
Addison Ter CHSWK W4 * 155 P3
Addison Wy GLDGN NW11 117 J2
HYS/HAR UB3 133 H8
NTHWD HA6 92 G9
Addle Hl BLKFR EC4V 12 D7
Addlestone Moor
ADL/WDHM KT15 195 M9
Addlestone Pk ADL/WDHM KT15 215 L2
Addlestone Rd ADL/WDHM KT15 215 P1
Addle St CITYW EC2V * 12 F5
Adecroft Wy E/WMO/HCT KT8 198 B3
Adela Av NWMAL KT3 200 E5
Adelaide Av BROCKY SE4 160 F10
Adelaide Cl CRAWW RH11 283 N4
EN EN1 79 M4
SL SL1 148 F1
STAN HA7 94 F5
Adelaide Ct HNWL W7 154 E1
Adelaide Gdns CHDH RM6 123 P3
Adelaide Gv SHB W12 136 D10
Adelaide Pl WEY KT13 216 E1
Adelaide Rd ASHF TW15 173 N8
CHST BR7 184 E8
HEST TW5 153 M7
IL IG1 122 E7
LEY E10 121 H8
PUT/ROE SW15 179 K1
RCH/KEW TW9 155 L10
STJWD NW8 3 L4
SURB KT6 199 K5
TEDD TW11 176 E9
TIL RM18 168 C7
WDSR SL4 149 L7
WEA W13 154 F1
WOT/HER KT12 197 H10
Adelaide Sq WDSR SL4 149 J8
Adelaide St CHCR WC2N * 11 L8
STALW/RED AL3 38 C5
Adelaide Ter BTFD TW8 * 155 J4
Adela St NKENS W10 8 A1
NKENS W10 137 H6
Adelina Gv WCHPL E1 140 B7
Adelina Ms BAL SW12 180 E4
Adeline Pl RSQ WC1B 11 K4
Adeliza Cl BARK IG11 142 F2
Adelphi Cl CRAWE RH10 284 E9
Adelphi Crs HCH RM12 125 H7
YEAD UB4 132 F5
Adelphi Gdns SL SL1 149 K1
Adelphi Rd EW KT17 220 A9
Adelphi Ter CHCR WC2N 11 M8
Adelphi Wy YEAD UB4 132 G5
Adeney Cl HMSMTH W6 156 G5
Aden Gv STNW/STAM N16 119 L9
Adenmore Rd CAT SE6 182 F3
Aden Rd IL IG1 122 E5
PEND EN3 80 D8
Adeyfield Gdns HHNE HP2 36 A5
Adeyfield Rd HHNE HP2 36 A6
Adhara Rd NTHWD HA6 93 H6
Adie Rd HMSMTH W6 156 F2
Adine Rd PLSTW E13 141 M6
Adlers La RDKG RH5 254 F7
Adler St WCHPL E1 13 N5
Adley St CLPT E5 120 D10
Adlington Cl UED N18 99 L6
Admaston Rd WOOL/PLUM SE18 162 F6
Admiral Cl STMC/STPC BR5 207 N4
Admiral Ms NKENS W10 136 G6
Admiral Pl BERM/RHTH SE16 140 D10
Admiral Rd CRAWW RH11 283 K10
Admirals Cl STALE/WH AL4 40 B9
SWFD E18 121 N2
Admirals Ct GU GU1 250 E9
Admiral Seymour Rd
ELTH/MOT SE9 162 C10
Admiral's Ga GNWCH SE10 160 G7
Admiral Sq WBPTN SW10 * 157 M7
Admiral St DEPT SE8 160 F7
HERT/BAY SG13 25 P5
Admiral's Wk HAMP NW3 117 M8
HOD EN11 44 G5
RDART DA2 188 G1
STAL AL1 38 F9
Admirals Wy POP/IOD E14 160 G1
Admiralty Cl DEPT SE8 * 160 F7
Admiralty Rd TEDD TW11 176 E10
Admiral Wk MV/WKIL W9 8 F3
Admiral Wy BERK HP4 33 L3
Adnams Wk RAIN RM13 125 H10
Adolf St CAT SE6 182 F7
Adolphus Rd FSBYPK N4 119 J7
Adolphus St DEPT SE8 160 E6
Adomar Rd BCTR RM8 123 N8
Adpar St BAY/PAD W2 9 L3
Adrian Cl BAR EN5 76 G10
DEN/HRF UB9 91 N9
Adrian Ms WBPTN SW10 15 H9
Adrian Rd ABLGY WD5 54 F7
Adrians Wk SLN SL2 129 L10
Adrienne Av STHL UB1 133 N6
Adstock Ms CFSP/GDCR SL9 * 90 A9
Adstock Wy GRAYS RM17 167 L3
Advance Rd WNWD SE27 181 K7
Advent Wy UED N18 100 C6
Advice Av CDW/CHF RM16 167 M1
Adys Lawn CRICK NW2 136 E1
Adys Rd PECK SE15 159 N9
Aerodrome Rd CDALE/KGS NW9 96 C10
Aerodrome Wy HEST TW5 153 K5
Affleck St IS N1 * 5 P8
Afghan Rd BTSEA SW11 157 P8
Aftab Ter WCHPL E1 * 140 A6
Afton Dr SOCK/AV RM15 146 G8
Agamemnon Rd
KIL/WHAMP NW6 117 J10
Agar Cl SURB KT6 199 L9
Agar Gv CAMTN NW1 5 K3
Agar Pl CAMTN NW1 5 H4
Agars Pl DTCH/LGLY SL3 149 M5
Agar St CHCR WC2N 11 L8
Agate Cl CAN/RD E16 142 A8
Agate Rd HMSMTH W6 156 F2
Agates La ASHTD KT21 237 J4
Agatha Cl WAP E1W 140 A10
Agaton Rd ELTH/MOT SE9 184 F5
Agave Rd CRICK NW2 116 F9
Agdon St FSBYE EC1V 12 C1
Agincourt Pl ASC SL5 192 B3
Agincourt Rd HAMP NW3 118 A9
Agister Rd CHIG IG7 103 K6
Agnes Av IL IG1 122 D9
Agnes Cl EHAM E6 142 D9
Agnesfield Cl
NFNCH/WDSPK N12 97 P7
Agnes Gdns BCTR RM8 123 N9
Agnes Riley Gdns CLAP SW4 * 180 D3
Agnes Rd ACT W3 156 C1
Agnes Scott Ct WEY KT13 * 196 C10
Agnes St POP/IOD E14 140 E8
Agnew Rd FSTH SE23 182 D3
Agraria Rd GUW GU2 267 N1
Agricola Pl EN EN1 79 N9
Aidan Cl BCTR RM8 123 P9
Ailsa Av TWK TW1 176 F1
Ailsa Cl CRAWW RH11 283 L10
Ailsa Rd TWK TW1 176 G1
Ailsa St POP/IOD E14 141 H7
Ainger Rd HAMP NW3 4 B4
Ainsdale Cl ORP BR6 200 G0
Ainsdale Crs PIN HA5 113 P1
Ainsdale Dr STHWK SE1 19 N8
Ainsdale Rd EA W5 135 J6
OXHEY WD19 93 K4
Ainsdale Wy WOKN/KNAP GU21 231 M3
Ainsley Av ROMW/RG RM7 124 D4
Ainsley Cl ED N9 99 M2
Ainsley St BETH E2 140 A5
Ainslie Wood Crs CHING E4 100 G6
Ainslie Wood Gdns CHING E4 100 G5
Ainslie Wood Rd CHING E4 100 F6
Ainsty St BERM/RHTH SE16 * 160 B1
Ainsworth Cl CMBW SE5 * 159 M8
CRICK NW2 116 D8
Ainsworth Rd CROY/NA CR0 203 J9
HOM E9 140 B2
Ainsworth Wy STJWD NW8 3 J5
Aintree Av EHAM E6 142 B3
Aintree Cl DTCH/LGLY SL3 151 H7
GVE DA12 190 E6
UX/CGN UB8 132 C8
Aintree Crs BARK/HLT IG6 102 F10
Aintree Gv UPMR RM14 125 N8
Aintree Rd CRAWE RH10 284 B9
GFD/PVL UB6 134 G4
Aintree St FUL/PGN SW6 157 H6
Airco Cl CDALE/KGS NW9 115 P1
Airdrie Cl IS N1 5 N4
YEAD UB4 133 M7
Airedale HHNE HP2 35 P3
Airedale Av CHSWK W4 156 C4
Airedale Av South CHSWK W4 * 156 C4
Airedale Cl RDART DA2 188 B4
Airedale Rd BAL SW12 180 A3
EA W5 155 H2
Aire Dr SOCK/AV RM15 146 G6
Airfield Wy GSTN WD25 54 G10
HCH RM12 145 J1
Airlie Gdns IL IG1 122 E6
KENS W8 8 E10
Airport Wy HORL RH6 280 B7
STWL/WRAY TW19 151 K10
Air St REGST W1B 11 H8
Airthrie Rd GDMY/SEVK IG3 123 L7
Aisgill Av WKENS W14 14 D8
Aisher Rd THMD SE28 143 M9
Aisher Wy SEV TN13 246 F7
Aislibie Rd LEE/GVPK SE12 161 K10
Aiten Pl HMSMTH W6 156 D3
Aitken Cl HACK E8 7 N5
MTCM CR4 202 A7
Aitken Rd BAR EN5 76 F9
CAT SE6 182 G5
Aitman Dr BTFD TW8 * 155 M4
Ajax Av CDALE/KGS NW9 116 B1
SL SL1 128 G9
Ajax Rd KIL/WHAMP NW6 117 J9
Akabusi Cl CROY/NA CR0 203 P6
Akehurst Cl CRAWE RH10 285 H2
Akehurst La SEV TN13 265 K1
Akehurst St PUT/ROE SW15 178 D2
Akeman Cl STALW/RED AL3 * 37 N8
Akenside Rd HAMP NW3 117 N10
Akerman Rd BRXN/ST SW9 159 J7
SURB KT6 199 H6
Alabama St WOOL/PLUM SE18 162 G6
Alacross Rd EA W5 155 H1
Alamein Cl BROX EN10 44 C6
Alamein Gdns RDART DA2 188 C3
Alamein Rd SWCM DA10 189 K2
Alanbrooke GVE DA12 190 F3
Alanbrooke Cl
WOKN/KNAP GU21 230 G4
Alan Cl DART DA1 165 K10
Alandale Dr PIN HA5 93 J9
Alander Ms WALTH E17 120 G2
Alan Dr BAR EN5 77 H10
Alan Gdns ROMW/RG RM7 124 B5
Alan Hilton Ct CHERT KT16 * 214 G3
Alan Hocken Wy SRTFD E15 141 K4
Alan Rd WIM/MER SW19 179 H8
Alanthus Cl LEE/GVPK SE12 183 L2
Alan Turing Rd GUW GU2 249 J10
Alan Wy DTCH/LGLY SL3 130 B8
Alaska St STHWK SE1 12 A10
Alba Cl YEAD UB4 133 L6
Albacore Crs LEW SE13 182 G2
Alba Gdns GLDGN NW11 117 H4
Albain Crs ASHF TW15 173 P5
Alban Av STALW/RED AL3 38 C4
Alban Crs BORE WD6 75 N5
EYN DA4 209 P8
Alban Pk STALE/WH AL4 * 39 L6
Albans Vw GSTN WD25 55 J9
Albany Cl BUSH WD23 74 C10
BXLY DA5 185 M3
ESH/CLAY KT10 217 P5
HGDN/ICK UB10 112 B10
MORT/ESHN SW14 155 N10
SEVS/STOTM N15 119 J2
Albany Cottages HNWL W7 * 134 D10
Albany Ct EPP CM16 65 J6
Albany Ctyd MYFR/PICC W1J 10 G8
Albany Crs EDGW HA8 95 M8
ESH/CLAY KT10 218 D3
Albany Ga CSHM HP5 50 G6
Albany Ms BMLY BR1 183 M9
CMBW SE5 18 F10
CMBW SE5 159 K5
IS N1 6 B3
KUTN/CMB KT2 * 177 J9
LCOL/BKTW AL2 * 55 P3
SUT SM1 221 L2
WARE SG12 26 D2
Albany Pde BTFD TW8 * 155 K5
PEND EN3 80 C4
Albany Pk DTCH/LGLY SL3 150 G6
PEND EN3 * 80 C4
Albany Park Av PEND EN3 80 B5
Albany Park Rd KUTN/CMB KT2 177 J9
LHD/OX KT22 236 F5
Albany Pl BTFD TW8 155 J5
EGH TW20 172 D7
Albany Rd BELV DA17 164 A5
BRWN CM15 86 G10
BTFD TW8 155 J5
BXLY DA5 185 M3
CHDH RM6 124 A4
CHST BR7 184 E8
CMBW SE5 18 G10
CRAWW RH11 283 M7
FSBYPK N4 118 G4
FSBYPK N4 119 H4
HCH RM12 125 H6
LEY E10 120 F5
MNPK E12 122 A9
NWMAL KT3 200 A4
PEND EN3 80 C3
RCHPK/HAM TW10 * 177 L1
TIL RM18 168 D8
UED N18 100 A6
WALTH E17 120 D4
WDSR SL4 149 J8
WDSR SL4 171 M1
WEA W13 134 G9
WGCE AL7 * 23 H5
WIM/MER SW19 179 L8
WOT/HER KT12 217 L1
Albany Rw EFNCH N2 * 117 P2
The Albanys REIG RH2 257 K8
Albany St CAMTN NW1 4 F9
Albany Ter RCHPK/HAM TW10 * 177 L1
The Albany KUTN/CMB KT2 177 J9
Albany Vw BKHH IG9 101 M2
Alba Pl NTGHL W11 8 C5
Albatross Cl EHAM E6 142 C6
Albatross Gdns SAND/SEL CR2 224 C7
Albatross St WOOL/PLUM SE18 163 H6
Albemarle Ap GNTH/NBYPK IG2 122 E4
Albemarle Av CHES/WCR EN8 62 B4
POTB/CUF EN6 59 L9
WHTN TW2 175 N4
Albemarle Cl GRAYS RM17 167 M1
Albemarle Gdns
GNTH/NBYPK IG2 122 E4
NWMAL KT3 200 A4
Albemarle Pk BECK BR3 * 204 G1
STAN HA7 95 H6
Albemarle Rd BECK BR3 204 G1
EBAR EN4 97 P1
Albemarle St CONDST W1S 10 G8
Albemarle Wy FSBYE EC1V 12 C2
Albeny Ga STAL AL1 38 C7
Alberon Gdns GLDGN NW11 117 J2
Alberta Av SUT SM1 221 H1
Alberta Dr HORL RH6 281 H4
Alberta Est WALW SE17 18 D7
Alberta Rd EN EN1 79 N10
ERITH DA8 164 D7
Alberta St WALW SE17 18 D7
Albert Av CHERT KT16 195 K3
CHING E4 100 F5
VX/NE SW8 158 G6
Albert Br CHEL SW3 15 P10
BTSEA SW11 157 P6
WDSR SL4 149 N9
Albert Bridge Ga BTSEA SW11 158 A6
Albert Bridge Rd BTSEA SW11 157 P6
BTSEA SW11 158 A7
Albert Carr Gdns
STRHM/NOR SW16 180 F8
Albert Cl CDW/CHF RM16 167 P2
HOM E9 140 A3
WDGN N22 98 E9
Albert Cottages WCHPL E1 * 13 N3
Albert Crs CHING E4 100 F5
Albert Dr STA TW18 173 J8
WIM/MER SW19 179 H5
WOKN/KNAP GU21 232 E1
Albert Emb STHWK SE1 17 M7
Albert Gdns HLWE CM17 47 N2
WCHPL E1 140 C8
Albert Ga KTBR SW1X 16 B1
Albert Gv RYNPK SW20 200 G1
Albertine Cl EW KT17 238 E2
Albert Ms BROCKY SE4 * 160 E10
FSBYPK N4 * 118 G6
KENS W8 15 J3
POP/IOD E14 * 140 D9
Albert Murray Cl GVE DA12 190 F3
Albert Pl FNCH N3 97 K9
KENS W8 * 15 H2
WDSR SL4 148 F4
Albert Rd ADL/WDHM KT15 195 N10
ASHF TW15 174 A8
ASHTD KT21 237 L4
BCTR RM8 124 A6
BELV DA17 164 A4
BKHH IG9 102 A3
BXLY DA5 186 B2
CAN/RD E16 142 B10
CAN/RD E16 162 D1
CSHM HP5 51 H7
EA W5 134 G6
EBAR EN4 77 N8
EGH TW20 172 A9
ELTH/MOT SE9 184 B6
EW KT17 220 C9
FSBYPK N4 118 G6
HAYES BR2 206 A5
HDN NW4 116 G2
HORL RH6 280 B4
HPTN TW12 176 B8
HSLW TW3 153 P10
HYS/HAR UB3 152 G2
IL IG1 122 F8
KIL/WHAMP NW6 2 D8
KUT/HW KT1 199 L2
LEY E10 121 H7
MLHL NW7 96 C6
MTCM CR4 202 A3
NWDGN UB2 153 L2
NWMAL KT3 200 C4
ORP BR6 227 K2
PGE/AN SE20 182 C10
RCHPK/HAM TW10 177 K1
RDART DA2 187 K6
REDH RH1 258 D5
ROM RM1 124 G4
RYLN/HDSTN HA2 114 B1
SEVS/STOTM N15 119 M4
SNWD SE25 204 A4
STMC/STPC BR5 207 L6
SUT SM1 221 N2
SWCM DA10 189 L2
SWFD E18 121 N1
TEDD TW11 176 E9
TWK TW1 176 E4
WALTH E17 120 F3
WARL CR6 242 D3
WDGN N22 98 E9
WDR/YW UB7 131 P10
WDSR SL4 149 K10
Albert Rd North REIG RH2 257 J9
WAT WD17 73 J6
Albert Rd South WAT WD17 * 73 J7
Albert Sq SRTFD E15 121 K10
VX/NE SW8 158 G6
Albert St BRW CM14 107 H6
CAMTN NW1 4 F6
NFNCH/WDSPK N12 97 M6
SL SL1 149 L2
STAL AL1 38 C7
WDSR SL4 148 G7
Albert Ter CAMTN NW1 4 C5
EA W5 * 134 G6
WLSDN NW10 * 136 A3
Albert Terrace Ms CAMTN NW1 4 C6
Albert Wy PECK SE15 160 A6
Albion Av MUSWH N10 98 B9
VX/NE SW8 158 E8
Albion Cl BAY/PAD W2 9 P7
CRAWE RH10 284 E8
HERT/BAY SG13 25 M5
ROMW/RG RM7 124 E4
SLN SL2 129 M10
Albion Crs CSTG HP8 89 N4
Albion Dr HACK E8 7 M4
Albion Est BERM/RHTH SE16 * 160 B1
Albion Gdns HMSMTH W6 156 E3
Albion Ga BAY/PAD W2 9 P7
Albion Gv STNW/STAM N16 119 M9
Albion Hl HHNE HP2 35 N7
LOU IG10 81 P9
Albion Ms BAY/PAD W2 9 P7
IS N1 6 A5
REIG RH2 * 275 M2
Albion Pde WOKN/KNAP GU21 * 231 H3
Albion Pk LOU IG10 82 A9
Albion Pl FARR EC1M 12 C3
HMSMTH W6 156 E3
SNWD SE25 203 P3
WDSR SL4 148 F8
Albion Riverside BTSEA SW11 157 P6
Albion Rd BELMT SM2 221 N3
BXLYHS DA6 164 A10
CSTG HP8 89 N3
GVE DA12 190 F3
HSLW TW3 153 P10
HYS/HAR UB3 132 F8
KUTN/CMB KT2 199 P1
REIG RH2 275 M1
STAL AL1 38 E6
STNW/STAM N16 119 L10
TOTM N17 99 N10
WALTH E17 121 H1
WHTN TW2 176 D4
Albion Sq HACK E8 7 L4
Albion St BAY/PAD W2 9 P6
BERM/RHTH SE16 160 B1
CROY/NA CR0 203 J8
Albion Ter CHING E4 * 80 G8
GVE DA12 190 G2
HACK E8 7 L4
Albion Villas Rd SYD SE26 182 B6
Albion Wk IS N1 5 M8
Albion Wy LEW SE13 161 H10
STBT EC1A 12 E4
WBLY HA9 115 M8
Albion Yd IS N1 5 M8
Albrighton Rd EDUL SE22 159 M9
Albuhera Cl ENC/FH EN2 79 H5
Albury Av BELMT SM2 220 F5
BXLYHN DA7 163 P8
ISLW TW7 154 E6
Albury Cl CHERT KT16 193 M10
HOR/WEW KT19 219 N5
HPTN TW12 175 P9
Albury Dr PIN HA5 93 L8
Albury Grove Rd CHES/WCR EN8 62 C6
Albury Keep HORL RH6 280 C3
Albury Ms MNPK E12 121 P6
Albury Ride CHES/WCR EN8 62 C7
Albury Rd CHSGTN KT9 219 K2
GU GU1 268 C1
REDH RH1 258 D5
WOT/HER KT12 216 G3
Albury St DEPT SE8 160 F5
SHGR GU5 269 M5
Albury Wk CHES/WCR EN8 62 B6
Albyfield BMLY BR1 206 C3
Albyn Rd DEPT SE8 160 G8
Albyns La ABR/ST RM4 84 E6
Alcester Crs CLPT E5 120 A7
Alcester Rd WLGTN SM6 222 C1
Alcock Cl WLGTN SM6 222 E4
Alcock Rd HEST TW5 153 L6
Alcocks Cl KWD/TDW/WH KT20 239 H6
Alcocks La KWD/TDW/WH KT20 239 H6
Alconbury WGCE AL7 23 P5
Alconbury Cl BORE WD6 75 L5
Alconbury Rd CLPT E5 119 P7
Alcorn Cl CHEAM SM3 201 K9
Alcott Cl HNWL W7 134 E7
Aldborough Rd DAGE RM10 144 D1
UPMR RM14 125 N7
Aldborough Rd North
GNTH/NBYPK IG2 123 J3
Aldborough Rd South
GDMY/SEVK IG3 123 H4
Aldborough Sp SL SL1 129 K8
Aldbourne Rd SHB W12 136 C10
SL SL1 128 A7
Aldbridge St WALW SE17 19 K7
Aldburgh Ms MHST W1U 10 D5
Aldbury Av WBLY HA9 135 N2
Aldbury Cl GSTN WD25 73 L2
STALE/WH AL4 39 H1
Aldbury Gv WGCE AL7 23 L5
Aldbury Ms ED N9 99 L1
Aldbury Rd RKW/CH/CXG WD3 91 J1
Aldebert Ter VX/NE SW8 158 G6
Aldeburgh Pl WFD IG8 101 M5
Aldeburgh St GNWCH SE10 161 M4
Alden Av SRTFD E15 141 L5
Aldenham Av RAD WD7 74 F3
Aldenham Dr UX/CGN UB8 132 C6
Aldenham Gv RAD WD7 56 G10
Aldenham Rd BORE WD6 74 E6
BUSH WD23 73 N8
OXHEY WD19 73 M10
RAD WD7 74 F1
Aldenham St CAMTN NW1 5 H8
Aldenholme WEY KT13 216 F3
Alden Md PIN HA5 * 93 P8
Aldensley Rd HMSMTH W6 156 E2
Alden Vw WDSR SL4 148 C7
Alder Av UPMR RM14 125 N9
Alderbourne La DTCH/LGLY SL3 110 B9
Alderbrook Rd BAL SW12 180 C2
Alderbury Rd BARN SW13 156 D5
DTCH/LGLY SL3 150 C1
Alderbury Rd West
DTCH/LGLY SL3 150 C1
Alder Cl EGH TW20 172 B8
HOD EN11 44 G1
LCOL/BKTW AL2 56 A4
PECK SE15 19 L10
SL SL1 128 E10
Aldercombe La CTHM CR3 259 M3
Alder Cft COUL/CHIP CR5 240 F3
Alder Dr SOCK/AV RM15 147 H6
Alder Gv CRICK NW2 116 D7
Alderholt Wy PECK SE15 * 159 M6
Alderley Ct BERK HP4 33 N6
Alderman Av BARK IG11 143 K5
Aldermanbury CITYW EC2V * 12 F5
Aldermanbury Sq CITYW EC2V 12 F4
Alderman Cl BRKMPK AL9 40 F10
DART DA1 186 F3
Alderman Judge Ml
KUT/HW KT1 * 199 K2
Alderman's Hl PLMGR N13 98 F5
Aldermary Rd BMLY BR1 205 M1
Alder Ms ARCH N19 118 D7
Aldermoor Rd CAT SE6 182 E6
Alderney Av HEST TW5 154 A6
Alderney Gdns NTHLT UB5 133 N2
Alderney Ms STHWK SE1 18 G3
Alderney Rd ERITH DA8 165 H6
WCHPL E1 140 C6
Alderney St PIM SW1V 16 F7
Alder Rd DEN/HRF UB9 131 M1
IVER SL0 130 G4
MORT/ESHN SW14 156 A9
SCUP DA14 185 H6
Alders Av WFD IG8 101 K7
Aldersbrook Av EN EN1 79 M6
Aldersbrook Dr KUTN/CMB KT2 177 L9
Aldersbrook La MNPK E12 122 C8
Aldersbrook Rd MNPK E12 121 P7
Alders Cl EA W5 155 J2
EDGW HA8 95 P6
WAN E11 121 N7
Aldersey Gdns BARK IG11 142 G1
Aldersey Rd GU GU1 250 C10
Aldersford Cl BROCKY SE4 160 C10
Aldersgate St STBT EC1A 12 E3
Aldersgrove E/WMO/HCT KT8 198 C5
Aldersgrove Av ELTH/MOT SE9 183 P6
Aldershot Rd GUW GU2 249 L8
KIL/WHAMP NW6 2 D5
RGUW GU3 248 D6
RGUW GU3 249 J6
Aldershot Ter
WOOL/PLUM SE18 * 162 D6
Alderside Wk EGH TW20 172 B8
Aldersmead Av CROY/NA CR0 204 C6
Aldersmead Rd BECK BR3 182 D10
Alderson Pl NWDGN UB2 134 B10
Alderson St NKENS W10 * 8 B1
NKENS W10 137 H6
Alders Rd EDGW HA8 95 P6
REIG RH2 257 L8
Alderstead La REDH RH1 258 E1
The Alders BF/WBF KT14 215 M8
DEN/HRF UB9 * 131 M1
FELT TW13 175 M8
HEST TW5 153 N5
STRHM/NOR SW16 * 180 D7
WCHMH N21 79 H10
WWKM BR4 204 G8
Alders Wk SBW CM21 29 P1
Alderton Cl BRWN CM15 86 G9
WLSDN NW10 116 A7
Alderton Crs HDN NW4 116 E3
Alderton Hall La LOU IG10 82 D8
Alderton Hl LOU IG10 82 C9
Alderton Ri LOU IG10 82 D8
Alderton Rd CROY/NA CR0 203 N7
HNHL SE24 159 K9
Alderton Wy HDN NW4 116 E3
LOU IG10 82 C9
Alderville Rd FUL/PGN SW6 157 J8
Alder Wk GSTN WD25 73 J1
Alder Wy SWLY BR8 208 E2
Alderwick Dr HSLW TW3 154 C9
Alderwood Cl CTHM CR3 259 M1
Alderwood Dr ABR/ST RM4 83 L8
Alderwood Ms EBAR EN4 77 M4
Alderwood Rd ELTH/MOT SE9 184 C2
Aldford St MYFR/PKLN W1K 10 C9
Aldgate FENCHST EC3M 13 K6
Aldgate Barrs WCHPL E1 * 13 M5
Aldgate High St TWRH EC3N 13 L6
Aldham Dr SOCK/AV RM15 146 G7
Aldin Av North SL SL1 149 M1
Aldin Av South SL SL1 149 M1
Aldine St SHB W12 156 F1
Aldingbourne Cl CRAWW RH11 283 J6
Aldingham Gdns HCH RM12 125 H10
Aldington Cl BCTR RM8 123 M5
Aldington Rd CHARL SE7 162 A2
Aldis Ms TOOT SW17 179 P8
Aldis St TOOT SW17 179 P8
Aldock WGCE AL7 23 K7
Aldred Rd KIL/WHAMP NW6 117 K10
Aldren Rd TOOT SW17 179 M6
Aldrich Crs CROY/NA CR0 225 H5
Aldriche Wy CHING E4 101 H7
Aldrich Gdns CHEAM SM3 201 J10
Aldrich Ter WAND/EARL SW18 179 M5
Aldridge Av EDGW HA8 95 N4
PEND EN3 80 F4
RSLP HA4 113 K7
STAN HA7 95 K10
Aldridge Ri NWMAL KT3 200 B7
Aldridge Rd SLN SL2 128 F6
Aldridge Road Vls NTGHL W11 8 D4
Aldridge Wk STHGT/OAK N14 98 F1
Aldrington Rd
STRHM/NOR SW16 180 D8
Aldsworth Cl MV/WKIL W9 8 G2
Aldwick STAL AL1 38 F8
Aldwickbury Crs HARP AL5 20 C2
Aldwick Cl ELTH/MOT SE9 184 G6
Aldwick Rd CROY/NA CR0 202 G10
HARP AL5 20 D3
Aldworth Gv LEW SE13 183 H2
Aldworth Rd SRTFD E15 141 K2
Aldwych HOL/ALD WC2B 11 N6
Aldwych Av BARK/HLT IG6 122 F3
Aldwych Cl HCH RM12 125 H7
Aldykes HAT AL10 40 C4
Alers Rd BXLYHS DA6 185 N1
Alesia Cl WDGN N22 98 F8
Alestan Beck Rd CAN/RD E16 142 A8
Alexander Av WLSDN NW10 136 E2
Alexander Cl BFN/LL DA15 185 H1
EBAR EN4 77 N8
HAYES BR2 205 M8
NWDGN UB2 134 B10
WHTN TW2 176 D5
Alexander Crs CTHM CR3 241 K8
Alexander Evans Ms FSTH SE23 182 C5
Alexander Godley Cl ASHTD KT21 237 L5
Alexander La BRWN CM15 87 M9
Alexander Ms BAY/PAD W2 8 G5
HLWE CM17 47 N3
Alexander Pl OXTED RH8 261 K4
SKENS SW7 15 N5
Alexander Rd ARCH N19 118 F8
BXLYHN DA7 163 N8
CHST BR7 184 E9
COUL/CHIP CR5 240 C1
EGH TW20 172 E8
HERT/WAT SG14 25 H5
LCOL/BKTW AL2 57 H1
REIG RH2 275 K3
SWCM DA10 189 H1
Alexander Sq CHEL SW3 15 N5
Alexander St BAY/PAD W2 8 F5
CSHM HP5 51 H6
Alexanders Wk CTHM CR3 259 N2
Alexander Ter ABYW SE2 * 163 L4
Alexandra Av BTSEA SW11 * 158 B7
RYLN/HDSTN HA2 113 N6
RYLN/HDSTN HA2 113 P8
STHL UB1 133 N9
SUT SM1 201 K10
WARL CR6 242 E3
WDGN N22 98 E9
Alexandra Cl ASHF TW15 174 E10
CDW/CHF RM16 168 E1
RYLN/HDSTN HA2 113 P8
STA TW18 173 N9
SWLY BR8 208 F2
WOT/HER KT12 197 H9
Alexandra Cottages NWCR SE14 160 E7
Alexandra Ct CRAWE RH10 * 283 N8
STHGT/OAK N14 78 D9
Alexandra Crs BMLY BR1 183 L9
Alexandra Dr BRYLDS KT5 199 M7
NRWD SE19 181 M8
Alexandra Gdns CAR SM5 222 B5
HSLW TW3 154 A8
MUSWH N10 118 C2
WOKN/KNAP GU21 231 J4
Alexandra Ga SKENS SW7 15 L1
Alexandra Gv FSBYPK N4 119 J6
NFNCH/WDSPK N12 97 L6
Alexandra Ms EFNCH N2 118 A1
WAT WD17 73 H6
Alexandra Palace Wy
CEND/HSY/T N8 118 D2
Alexandra Pde
RYLN/HDSTN HA2 * 114 A9
Alexandra Park Rd MUSWH N10 98 C10
Alexandra Pl CROY/NA CR0 203 M8
GU GU1 268 C2
SNWD SE25 203 L5
STJWD NW8 3 K5
Alexandra Rd ADL/WDHM KT15 215 N1
ASHF TW15 174 E10
BH/WHM TN16 243 N5
BORE WD6 76 A4
BTFD TW8 * 155 J5
CEND/HSY/T N8 119 H1
CHDH RM6 123 N4
CHSWK W4 156 A1
CROY/NA CR0 203 M8
ED N9 * 100 A1
EGH TW20 171 P9
EHAM E6 142 D5
ERITH DA8 164 G5
EW KT17 220 C9
GVE DA12 191 H3
HDN NW4 116 G2
HHNE HP2 35 N6
HSLW TW3 154 A8
KGLGY WD4 53 K6
KGLGY WD4 54 C6
KUTN/CMB KT2 177 M10
LEY E10 121 H8
MORT/ESHN SW14 156 A9
MTCM CR4 179 P10
MUSWH N10 98 C9
PEND EN3 80 C8
RAIN RM13 144 G3
RCH/KEW TW9 155 L8
RKW/CH/CXG WD3 71 K2
ROM RM1 124 G4
SEVS/STOTM N15 119 L3
SL SL1 149 J2
STAL AL1 38 D6
STJWD NW8 3 K5
SWFD E18 121 N1
SYD SE26 182 C9
THDIT KT7 198 E5
TIL RM18 168 C8
TWK TW1 177 J2
UX/CGN UB8 131 N4
WALTH E17 120 E4
WARL CR6 242 D3
WAT WD17 73 H6
WDSR SL4 149 J8
WIM/MER SW19 179 K8
Alexandra Sq MRDN SM4 201 K5
Alexandra St CAN/RD E16 141 M7
NWCR SE14 160 D6
Alexandra Ter GU GU1 268 B1
Alexandra Wk EYN DA4 * 210 C2
Alexandra Wy CHES/WCR EN8 62 E10
HOR/WEW KT19 219 M8
TIL RM18 169 L3
Alexandria Rd WEA W13 134 G9
Alexis St BERM/RHTH SE16 19 N5
Alfan La RDART DA2 186 E8
Alfearn Rd CLPT E5 120 B9
Alford Cl RGUE GU4 250 D7
Alford Gn CROY/NA CR0 225 J3
Alford Pl IS N1 * 6 F8
Alford Rd ERITH DA8 164 D4
Alfoxton Av SEVS/STOTM N15 119 J2
Alfreda St BTSEA SW11 158 C7
Alfred Cl CHSWK W4 156 A3
CRAWE RH10 284 F8
Alfred Gdns STHL UB1 133 M10
Alfred Ms GWRST WC1E 11 J3
Alfred Pl GVW DA11 190 C4
GWRST WC1E 11 J3
Alfred Rd ACT W3 135 P10
BAY/PAD W2 8 F3
BELV DA17 164 A4
BKHH IG9 102 A3
BRW CM14 107 J3
FELT TW13 175 K5
GVW DA11 190 E5
KUT/HW KT1 199 K3
RDART DA2 187 N7
SNWD SE25 203 P5
SOCK/AV RM15 146 B10

SRTFD E15 121 L10
SUT SM1 221 M2
Alfred's Gdns BARK IG11 143 H4
Alfred St BOW E3 140 E5
GRAYS RM17 167 P5
Alfred's Wy (East Ham and Barking By-Pass) BARK IG11 143 H4
Alfred Vls WALTH E17 * 121 H2
Alfreton Cl WIM/MER SW19 178 G6
Alfriston BRYLDS KT5 199 L6
Alfriston Av CROY/NA CR0 202 F7
RYLN/HDSTN HA2 113 P4
Alfriston Cl BRYLDS KT5 199 L6
DART DA1 186 F2
Alfriston Rd BTSEA SW11 180 A1
Algar Cl STAN HA7 94 E6
Algar Rd ISLW TW7 154 F9
Algarve Rd WAND/EARL SW18 179 L4
Algernon Rd HDN NW4 116 D4
KIL/WHAMP NW6 2 E6
LEW SE13 160 G10
Algers Cl LOU IG10 82 A9
Algers Rd LOU IG10 82 B9
Alghers Md LOU IG10 82 A9
Algiers Rd LEW SE13 160 F10
Alguin Ct STAN HA7 * 95 H7
Alibon Gdns DAGE RM10 124 B10
Alibon Rd DAGE RM10 124 B10
Alice La BOW E3 140 E3
SL SL1 128 A6
Alice Ruston Pl
WOKS/MYFD GU22 231 P5
Alice St STHWK SE1 19 J4
Alice Thompson Cl
LEE/GVPK SE12 183 P5
Alice Walker Cl HNHL SE24 * 159 J10
Alice Wy HSLW TW3 154 A10
Alicia Av CRAWE RH10 284 C7
KTN/HRWW/WS HA3 114 G2
Alicia Cl KTN/HRWW/WS HA3 115 H2
Alicia Gdns KTN/HRWW/WS HA3 114 G2
Alie St WCHPL E1 13 M6
Alington Crs CDALE/KGS NW9 115 P6
Alington Gv WLGTN SM6 222 E5
Alison Cl CROY/NA CR0 204 C8
EHAM E6 142 D8
WOKN/KNAP GU21 232 B1
Aliwal Ms BTSEA SW11 * 157 P10
Aliwal Rd BTSEA SW11 157 P10
Alkerden La SWCM DA10 189 H2
Alkerden Rd CHSWK W4 156 B4
Alkham Rd STNW/STAM N16 119 N7
Allan Barclay Cl
SEVS/STOTM N15 119 N4
Allan Cl NWMAL KT3 200 A5
Allandale HHNE HP2 35 N4
STALW/RED AL3 38 A9
Allandale Av FNCH N3 117 H1
Allandale Crs POTB/CUF EN6 59 H8
Allandale Pl ORP BR6 207 N10
Allandale Rd EMPK RM11 124 G5
PEND EN3 80 C2
Allan Wy ACT W3 135 P7
Allard Cl STMC/STPC BR5 207 M7
Allard Crs BUSH WD23 94 B3
Allard Wy BROX EN10 44 D7
Allardyce St CLAP SW4 158 G10
Allbrook Cl TEDD TW11 176 D8
Allcot Cl CRAWW RH11 283 H10
EBED/NFELT TW14 174 G4
Allcroft Rd KTTN NW5 4 D1
Allder Wy SAND/SEL CR2 223 J4
Alldicks Rd HHS/BOV HP3 36 A8
Allenby Av SAND/SEL CR2 223 K5
Allenby Cl GFD/PVL UB6 133 P5
Allenby Crs GRAYS RM17 167 N4
Allenby Dr EMPK RM11 125 M6
Allenby Rd BH/WHM TN16 244 B3
FSTH SE23 182 D6
STHL UB1 133 P6
STHL UB1 133 P8
WOOL/PLUM SE18 162 F2
Allen Cl MTCM CR4 202 C1
RAD WD7 57 K8
STALE/WH AL4 21 J4
SUN TW16 197 J1
Allen Ct HAT AL10 * 40 E6
Allendale Av STHL UB1 133 P8
Allendale Cl CMBW SE5 159 L8
RDART DA2 188 C4
SYD SE26 182 C8
Allendale Rd GFD/PVL UB6 134 G1
Allen Edwards Dr VX/NE SW8 158 F7
Allen House Pk
WOKS/MYFD GU22 231 P6
Allen Rd BECK BR3 204 C2
BOW E3 140 E4
CROY/NA CR0 202 G7
GT/LBKH KT23 254 A2
RAIN RM13 145 K5
STNW/STAM N16 119 M9
SUN TW16 197 J1
Allensbury Pl CAMTN NW1 5 K4
Allens Md GVE DA12 191 J4
Allens Rd PEND EN3 80 B9
Allen St KENS W8 14 F4
Allenswood Rd ELTH/MOT SE9 162 C9
Allerds Rd SLN SL2 128 E3
Allerford Ct HRW HA1 114 A3
Allerford Rd CAT SE6 182 G7
Allerton Cl BORE WD6 75 L4
Allerton Rd BORE WD6 75 L4
STNW/STAM N16 119 K7
Allerton St IS N1 6 G9
Allestree Rd FUL/PGN SW6 157 H6
Alleyn Crs DUL SE21 181 L6
Alleyndale Rd BCTR RM8 123 M7
Alleyn Pk DUL SE21 181 L5
DUL SE21 * 181 M7
NWDGN UB2 153 N4
Alleyn Rd DUL SE21 181 L6
Allfarthing La WAND/EARL SW18 179 M2
Allgood Cl MRDN SM4 200 G6
Allgood St BETH E2 7 M8
Allhallows La CANST EC4R 12 G8
Allhallows Rd EHAM E6 142 B8
All Hallows Rd TOTM N17 99 M9
Alliance Cl ALP/SUD HA0 115 J9
HSLWW TW4 175 N1
Alliance Rd ACT W3 135 N6
PLSTW E13 141 P7
WOOL/PLUM SE18 163 K5
Allied Wy ACT W3 * 156 B1
Allingham Cl HNWL W7 134 E9
Allingham Rd REIG RH2 275 K3
Allington Av TOTM N17 99 M7
Allington Cl GFD/PVL UB6 134 B2
WIM/MER SW19 178 G8
Allington Rd HDN NW4 116 E3
NKENS W10 2 A9
NKENS W10 137 H5
ORP BR6 207 H9
RYLN/HDSTN HA2 114 A3
Allington St BGVA SW1W 16 F4
Allis Ms HLWE CM17 29 M10
Allison Cl GNWCH SE10 161 H7
WAB EN9 63 M9
Allison Gv DUL SE21 181 M4
Allison Rd ACT W3 135 P8
CEND/HSY/T N8 119 H3
Allitsen Rd STJWD NW8 3 N8
Allitson Rd STJWD NW8 3 N8
Allkins Ct WDSR SL4 149 J8
Allmains Cl WAB EN9 63 N1
Allnutts Rd EPP CM16 65 K9
Allnutt Wy CLAP SW4 180 E1
Alloa Rd DEPT SE8 160 C4
GDMY/SEVK IG3 123 L7
Allonby Dr RSLP HA4 112 C5
Allonby Gdns WBLY HA9 115 H6
Allotment La SEV TN13 247 K8
Alloway Cl WOKN/KNAP GU21 231 N4
Alloway Rd BOW E3 140 D5
Allport Ms WCHPL E1 * 140 B7
All Saints' Cl ED N9 99 N3
BRWN CM15 86 G2
CHIG IG7 103 L4
SWCM DA10 189 L1
Allsaints Crs GSTN WD25 55 L9
All Saints Dr BKHTH/KID SE3 161 L8
SAND/SEL CR2 223 N8
All Saints La RKW/CH/CXG WD3 72 B10
All Saints Ms STAN HA7 94 D7
All Saints Pas
WAND/EARL SW18 * 179 K1
All Saints' Rd ACT W3 155 P2
GVW DA11 190 C4
LTWR GU18 212 B6
NTGHL W11 8 C4
SUT SM1 201 M10
WIM/MER SW19 179 M10
All Saints St IS N1 5 N7
Allsop Pl CAMTN NW1 10 B2
All Souls Av CHOB/PIR GU24 230 G7
WLSDN NW10 136 E4
All Souls' Pl REGST W1B 10 F4
Allum Gv KWD/TDW/WH KT20 238 E7
Allum La BORE WD6 75 L8
Allum Wy TRDG/WHET N20 97 M2
Allwood Cl SYD SE26 182 C7
Allwood Rd CHESW EN7 61 N3
Allyington Wy CRAWE RH10 284 E8
Allyn Cl STA TW18 173 J9
Alma Av CHING E4 101 H8
HCH RM12 125 M8
Almack Rd CLPT E5 120 B9
Alma Cl MUSWH N10 * 98 C9
WOKN/KNAP GU21 231 K3
Alma Ct RYLN/HDSTN HA2 * 114 C7
Alma Crs SUT SM1 221 H2
Alma Cut STAL AL1 38 D7
Alma Gv STHWK SE1 19 M6
Alma Pl NRWD SE19 181 N10
THHTH CR7 203 H5
WLSDN NW10 136 E5
Alma Rd BERK HP4 33 K3
BFN/LL DA15 185 K6
CAR SM5 221 P2
CSHM HP5 51 H5
ESH/CLAY KT10 198 D8
MUSWH N10 98 B8
PEND EN3 80 D9
REIG RH2 257 L9
STAL AL1 38 D7
STHL UB1 133 M9
STMC/STPC BR5 207 N9
SWCM DA10 189 K1
WAND/EARL SW18 179 M1
WDSR SL4 148 E3
Alma Rw KTN/HRWW/WS HA3 * 94 C9
Alma Sq STJWD NW8 3 K9
Alma St KTTN NW5 4 F1
SRTFD E15 141 J1
Alma Ter BOW E3 140 E3
KENS W8 14 F4
WAND/EARL SW18 179 N3
The Alma GVE DA12 * 191 J7
Almeida St IS N1 6 C5
Almeric Rd BTSEA SW11 158 A10
Almer Rd RYNPK SW20 178 D10
Almington St FSBYPK N4 * 118 F6
Almners Rd CHERT KT16 194 F7
Almond Av CAR SM5 202 A9
EA W5 155 K2
HGDN/ICK UB10 112 C8
WDR/YW UB7 152 B2
WOKS/MYFD GU22 232 A7
Almond Cl CDW/CHF RM16 168 D2
CRAWW RH11 283 K8
EGH TW20 171 N9
FELT TW13 175 H4
GU GU1 250 A6
HAYES BR2 206 D7
HYS/HAR UB3 132 F9
PECK SE15 159 P8
RSLP HA4 112 G8
SHPTN TW17 196 D2
WDSR SL4 148 G8
Almond Dr SWLY BR8 208 E3
Almond Gv BTFD TW8 154 G6
Almond Rd BERM/RHTH SE16 160 A3
HOR/WEW KT19 220 A7
RDART DA2 188 B3
SL SL1 128 A5
TOTM N17 99 P8
Almonds Av BKHH IG9 101 M3
The Almonds STAL AL1 38 G10
Almond Wy BORE WD6 75 N8
HAYES BR2 206 D7
MTCM CR4 202 E5
RYLN/HDSTN HA2 94 A10
Almons Wy SLN SL2 129 N7
Almorah Rd HEST TW5 153 L7
IS N1 6 G4
Almsgate RGUW GU3 267 H7
Alms Heath RPLY/SEND GU23 234 C7
Almshouse La CHSGTN KT9 219 J5
EN EN1 80 A3
Alnwick Gv MRDN SM4 201 L4
Alnwick Rd CAN/RD E16 141 P8
LEE/GVPK SE12 183 N3
Alnwick Ter LEE/GVPK SE12 183 N3
Alperton La ALP/SUD HA0 135 J5
Alperton St NKENS W10 8 B1
NKENS W10 137 H6
Alphabet Gdns CAR SM5 201 N6
Alpha Cl CAMTN NW1 9 P1
Alpha Ct CTHM CR3 241 P4
Alpha Est HYS/HAR UB3 * 152 F1
Alpha Gv POP/IOD E14 160 F1
Alpha Pl CHEL SW3 15 P9
KIL/WHAMP NW6 2 F7
MRDN SM4 * 200 G7
Alpha Rd BRYLDS KT5 199 L6
CHING E4 100 F4
CHOB/PIR GU24 213 L6
CRAWW RH11 283 M7
CROY/NA CR0 203 M8
HGDN/ICK UB10 132 C6
NWCR SE14 160 E7
PEND EN3 80 D8
TEDD TW11 176 C8
UED N18 99 P7
WOKS/MYFD GU22 232 E2
Alpha St PECK SE15 159 P8
Alpha St North SL SL1 149 M1
Alpha St South SL SL1 149 M2
Alpha Wy EGH TW20 194 F1
Alphea Cl WIM/MER SW19 179 P10
Alpine Av BRYLDS KT5 199 P9
Alpine Cl CROY/NA CR0 203 M10
Alpine Copse BMLY BR1 206 D2
Alpine Gv HOM E9 140 B2
Alpine Rd BERM/RHTH SE16 160 B3
LEY E10 120 G7
REDH RH1 258 B7
WOT/HER KT12 197 H7
Alpine Vw CAR SM5 221 P2
Alpine Wk BUSH WD23 94 D3
Alpine Wy EHAM E6 142 D7
Alresford Rd GUW GU2 267 M1
Alric Av NWMAL KT3 200 B3
WLSDN NW10 136 A2
Alroy Rd FSBYPK N4 119 H5
Alsace Rd WALW SE17 19 J7
Alscot Rd STHWK SE1 19 M4
Alscot Wy STHWK SE1 19 L5
Alsike Rd ERITHM DA18 163 N2
Alsom Av WPK KT4 220 C1
Alsop Cl LCOL/BKTW AL2 57 K4
Alston Cl SURB KT6 198 G7
Alston Rd BAR EN5 77 H7
HHW HP1 35 K7
TOOT SW17 179 N7
UED N18 100 A6
Altair Cl TOTM N17 99 N7
Altair Wy NTHWD HA6 92 G6
Altash Wy ELTH/MOT SE9 184 C5
Altenburg Av WEA W13 154 G2
Altenburg Gdns BTSEA SW11 158 A10
Alterton Cl WOKN/KNAP GU21 231 M3
Alt Gv WIM/MER SW19 179 J10
Altham Ct RYLN/HDSTN HA2 * 94 A9
Altham Gdns OXHEY WD19 93 L5
Altham Gv HLW CM20 29 J9
Altham Rd PIN HA5 93 M9
Althea St FUL/PGN SW6 157 L8
Althorne Gdns SWFD E18 121 L2
Althorne Rd REDH RH1 276 B2
Althorne Wy DAGE RM10 124 B7
Althorp Cl BAR EN5 96 D1
Althorpe Rd HRW HA1 * 114 B3
Althorp Rd STAL AL1 38 D5
TOOT SW17 180 A4
Altmore Av EHAM E6 142 C2
Alton Av STAN HA7 94 E8
Altona Wy SL SL1 128 G8
Alton Cl BXLY DA5 185 P4
ISLW TW7 154 E8
Alton Ct STA TW18 195 H1
Alton Gdns BECK BR3 182 F10
WHTN TW2 176 C2
Alton Rd CROY/NA CR0 223 H1
PUT/ROE SW15 178 D4
RCH/KEW TW9 155 K10
TOTM N17 119 L1
Alton St POP/IOD E14 140 G8
Altwood HARP AL5 20 C2
Altwood Cl SL SL1 128 D7
Altyre Cl BECK BR3 204 E5
Altyre Rd CROY/NA CR0 203 L9
Altyre Wy BECK BR3 204 E5
Aluric Cl CDW/CHF RM16 168 E3
Alvanley Gdns KIL/WHAMP NW6 117 L10
Alva Wy OXHEY WD19 93 L3
Alverstoke Rd HARH RM3 105 M8
Alverstone Av EBAR EN4 97 N1
WAND/EARL SW18 179 K5
Alverstone Gdns ELTH/MOT SE9 184 E4
Alverstone Rd CRICK NW2 136 F2
MNPK E12 122 D9
NWMAL KT3 200 C4
WBLY HA9 115 L6
Alverston Gdns SNWD SE25 203 M5
Alverton STALW/RED AL3 38 B3
Alverton St DEPT SE8 160 E4
Alveston Av KTN/HRWW/WS HA3 114 G1
Alveston Sq SWFD E18 * 101 M10
Alvey St WALW SE17 19 J7
Alvia Gdns SUT SM1 221 M1
Alvington Crs HACK E8 119 N10
Alvista Av MDHD SL6 128 A8
Alway Av HOR/WEW KT19 219 P2
Alwen Gv SOCK/AV RM15 146 G7
Alwin Pl WATW WD18 72 F8
Alwold Crs LEE/GVPK SE12 183 P2
Alwyn Av CHSWK W4 156 A4
Alwyn Cl BORE WD6 75 L10
CROY/NA CR0 224 G4
Alwyne Av BRWN CM15 87 L10
Alwyne Ct WOKN/KNAP GU21 232 B2
Alwyne La IS N1 6 D3
Alwyne Pl IS N1 6 E3
Alwyne Rd HNWL W7 134 D9
IS N1 6 E3
WIM/MER SW19 179 J9
Alwyne Sq IS N1 6 E1
Alwyne Vls IS N1 6 D3
Alwyn Gdns ACT W3 135 N8
HDN NW4 116 D2
Alwyns Cl CHERT KT16 195 K6
Alwyns La CHERT KT16 195 J6
Alyn Bank CEND/HSY/T N8 * 118 E4
Alyngton BERK HP4 33 K2
Alyth Gdns GLDGN NW11 117 J4
Alzey Gdns HARP AL5 20 C3
Amalgamated Dr BTFD TW8 154 F5
Amanda Cl CHIG IG7 102 G7
Amanda Ct DTCH/LGLY SL3 150 A2
Amanda Ms ROMW/RG RM7 124 D3
Amar Ct WOOL/PLUM SE18 163 J3
Amardeep Ct WOOL/PLUM SE18 163 J4
Amazon St WCHPL E1 140 A8
Ambassador Cl HSLW TW3 153 M8
Ambassador Gdns EHAM E6 142 C7
Ambassador Sq POP/IOD E14 160 G3
Amber Av WALTH E17 100 D9
Ambercroft Wy COUL/CHIP CR5 241 J5
Amberden Av FNCH N3 117 K1
Ambergate St WALW SE17 18 C8
Amber Gv CRICK NW2 116 G6
Amberleigh Gdns
RKW/CH/CXG WD3 71 J2
Amberley Cl CRAWE RH10 284 D7
HARP AL5 20 A1
ORP BR6 227 J2
PIN HA5 113 N1
RPLY/SEND GU23 251 J1
Amberley Ct CRAWW RH11 * 283 N2
SCUP DA14 185 M8
Amberley Dr ADL/WDHM KT15 215 J6
Amberley Gdns HOR/WEW KT19 220 C1
Amberley Gv CROY/NA CR0 203 N7
SYD SE26 182 A7
Amberley Pl WDSR SL4 149 J7
Amberley Rd ABYW SE2 163 N5
BKHH IG9 101 P2
EN EN1 99 N1
LEY E10 120 F5
MV/WKIL W9 8 F3
PLMGR N13 98 G3
SLN SL2 128 D7
Amberley Wy HGDN/ICK UB10 131 P4
HSLWW TW4 175 K1
MRDN SM4 201 K7
ROMW/RG RM7 124 C2
Amberry Ct HLW CM20 28 G10
Amberside Cl ISLW TW7 176 C2
Amber St SRTFD E15 * 141 J1
Amberwood Cl WLGTN SM6 222 F2
Amberwood Ri NWMAL KT3 200 B6
Amblecote COB KT11 217 L7
Amblecote Cl LEE/GVPK SE12 183 N6
Amblecote Meadow
LEE/GVPK SE12 183 N6
Amblecote Rd LEE/GVPK SE12 183 N6
Ambler Rd FSBYPK N4 119 J8
Ambleside BMLY BR1 183 J9
EPP CM16 65 K7
HARP AL5 20 C1
Ambleside Av BECK BR3 204 D5
HCH RM12 125 J10
STRHM/NOR SW16 180 E7
WOT/HER KT12 197 K8
Ambleside Cl CRAWW RH11 282 G9
LEY E10 120 G5
REDH RH1 276 C5
SEVS/STOTM N15 119 N1
Ambleside Crs PEND EN3 80 C7
Ambleside Dr EBED/NFELT TW14 174 G4
Ambleside Gdns BELMT SM2 221 M3
REDBR IG4 122 B2
SAND/SEL CR2 224 C6
WBLY HA9 115 J6
Ambleside Rd BXLYHN DA7 164 B8
LTWR GU18 212 A7
WLSDN NW10 136 C2
Ambleside Wy EGH TW20 172 E10
Ambrey Wy WLGTN SM6 222 E5
Ambrook Rd BELV DA17 164 B2
Ambrosden Av WEST SW1P 17 H4
Ambrose Av GLDGN NW11 117 J4
Ambrose Cl DART DA1 164 G10
ORP BR6 207 J10
Ambrose St BERM/RHTH SE16 160 A3
Amelia Cl ACT W3 135 N10
Amelia St WALW SE17 18 D7
Amen Cnr STP EC4M 12 D6
TOOT SW17 180 B9
Amen Ct STP EC4M 12 D6
Amenity Wy MRDN SM4 200 F7
Amerden Wy SL SL1 148 F1
America Sq TWRH EC3N 13 L7
America St STHWK SE1 12 E10
Amerland Rd PUT/ROE SW15 179 J2
Amersham Av UED N18 99 L7
Amersham Cl HARH RM3 105 N7
Amersham Gv NWCR SE14 160 E6
Amersham Pl AMSS HP7 69 P5
Amersham Rd AMS HP6 51 H10
AMSS HP7 70 A5
BEAC HP9 88 F6
CFSP/GDCR SL9 90 A5
CFSP/GDCR SL9 90 B10
CFSP/GDCR SL9 110 C2
CFSP/GDCR SL9 110 D5
CROY/NA CR0 203 K6
CSTG HP8 69 N10
HARH RM3 105 M7
NWCR SE14 160 E7
RKW/CH/CXG WD3 70 E5
Amersham V NWCR SE14 160 E6
Amersham Wk HARH RM3 105 N7
Amersham Wy AMS HP6 70 B5
Amery Gdns GPK RM2 105 L10
GPK RM2 125 L1
WLSDN NW10 136 E3
Amery Rd HRW HA1 114 F7
Amesbury WAB EN9 63 M8
Amesbury Av BRXS/STRHM SW2 180 F5
Amesbury Cl WPK KT4 200 F8
Amesbury Dr CHING E4 80 G10
Amesbury Rd BMLY BR1 206 A3
DAGW RM9 143 N2
EPP CM16 65 J7
FELT TW13 175 L5
Ames Cottages POP/IOD E14 * 140 D7
Ames Rd SWCM DA10 189 K2
Amethyst Ct ORP BR6 227 H3
Amethyst Rd SRTFD E15 121 J9
Amey Dr GT/LBKH KT23 236 B10
Amherst Av WEA W13 135 H8
Amherst Cl STMC/STPC BR5 207 K4
Amherst Dr STMC/STPC BR5 207 J4
Amherst Gdns WEA W13 * 135 H8
Amherst Hl SEV TN13 246 F8
Amherst Pl SEV TN13 246 G8
Amherst Rd SEV TN13 247 J8
WEA W13 135 H8
Amhurst Gdns ISLW TW7 154 E7
Amhurst Pde STNW/STAM N16 * 119 N5
Amhurst Pk STNW/STAM N16 119 M5
Amhurst Rd HACK E8 140 A1
STNW/STAM N16 119 N9
Amhurst Ter HACK E8 119 P9
Amidas Gdns BCTR RM8 123 L9
Amiel St WCHPL E1 140 B6
Amies St BTSEA SW11 158 A9
Amina Wy BERM/RHTH SE16 19 N4
Amis Av ADL/WDHM KT15 215 K7
HOR/WEW KT19 219 M3
Amity Gv RYNPK SW20 200 F1
Amity Rd SRTFD E15 141 L2
Ammanford Gn
CDALE/KGS NW9 * 116 B4
Amner Rd BTSEA SW11 180 B2
Amor Rd HMSMTH W6 156 F2
Amott Rd PECK SE15 159 P9
Ampere Wy CROY/NA CR0 202 F7
Ampleforth Cl ORP BR6 227 M1
Ampleforth Rd ABYW SE2 163 L1
Ampthill Est CAMTN NW1 4 G8
Ampthill Sq CAMTN NW1 5 H8
Ampton St FSBYW WC1X 5 N10
Amroth Cl FSTH SE23 182 A4
Amroth Gn CDALE/KGS NW9 * 116 B4
Amstel Wy WOKN/KNAP GU21 231 L4
Amsterdam Rd POP/IOD E14 161 H2
Amwell Cl ENC/FH EN2 79 L9
GSTN WD25 73 M1
Amwell Common WGCE AL7 23 L6
Amwell Ct HOD EN11 44 F2
WAB EN9 63 K9
Amwell End WARE SG12 26 C3
Amwell Hl WARE SG12 26 E5
Amwell La STALE/WH AL4 20 G4
WARE SG12 26 F5
Amwell St CLKNW EC1R 6 A9
HOD EN11 44 F3
Amyand Cottages TWK TW1 176 G2
Amyand Park Gdns TWK TW1 176 G3
Amyand Park Rd TWK TW1 176 G3
Amy Cl WLGTN SM6 222 F4
Amy La CSHM HP5 50 G8
Amy Rd OXTED RH8 261 K5
Amyruth Rd BROCKY SE4 182 F1
Amy Warne Cl EHAM E6 142 B7
Anatola Rd ARCH N19 118 C7
Ancaster Crs NWMAL KT3 200 D6
Ancaster Ms BECK BR3 204 C3
Ancaster Rd BECK BR3 204 C3
Ancaster St WOOL/PLUM SE18 163 H6
Anchorage Cl WIM/MER SW19 179 K8
Anchor Bvd RDART DA2 166 B10
RDART DA2 * 188 A2
Anchor Cl BARK IG11 143 L5
CHES/WCR EN8 62 C4
RGUW GU3 248 B7
Anchor Dr RAIN RM13 145 J6
Anchor Hl WOKN/KNAP GU21 231 J3
Anchor & Hope La CHARL SE7 161 N2
Anchor La HHW HP1 35 L8
Anchor St BERM/RHTH SE16 160 A3
Anchor Ter WCHPL E1 * 140 B6
Anchor Yd FSBYE EC1V * 12 F1
Ancill Cl HMSMTH W6 14 A10
HMSMTH W6 156 G5
Ancona Rd WLSDN NW10 136 D4
WOOL/PLUM SE18 162 G4
Andace Park Gdns BMLY BR1 * 205 P1
Andalus Rd BRXN/ST SW9 158 F9
Ander Cl ALP/SUD HA0 115 J9
Andermans WDSR SL4 * 148 C7
Anderson Cl ACT W3 136 A8
CHEAM SM3 201 K8
DEN/HRF UB9 91 K9
HOR/WEW KT19 219 N8
WCHMH N21 78 G9
Anderson Dr ASHF TW15 174 D7
Anderson Rd HOM E9 140 C1
RAD WD7 57 M9
WEY KT13 * 196 E10
WFD IG8 122 A1
Anderson's Pl HSLW TW3 154 A10
Anderson Sq IS N1 6 C6
Anderson St CHEL SW3 16 A7
Anderson Wy BELV DA17 164 C1
Andover Av CAN/RD E16 142 A8
Andover Cl EBED/NFELT TW14 174 G4
GFD/PVL UB6 134 A6
HOR/WEW KT19 220 A7
UX/CGN UB8 131 L4
Andover Pl KIL/WHAMP NW6 2 G8
Andover Rd HOLWY N7 118 G7
ORP BR6 207 H8
WHTN TW2 176 C4
Andover Ter HMSMTH W6 * 156 E3
Andrea Av CDW/CHF RM16 167 M1
Andre St HACK E8 119 P10
Andrew Borde St
LSQ/SEVD WC2H * 11 K5
Andrew Cl BARK/HLT IG6 102 G8
DART DA1 186 E1
RAD WD7 57 L9
Andrewes Gdns EHAM E6 142 B8
Andrew Hill La SLN SL2 109 H6
Andrew Pl VX/NE SW8 158 E7
Andrew's Cl EW KT17 220 C10
BKHH IG9 101 P3
HHNE HP2 35 N4
HRW HA1 114 C5
STMC/STPC BR5 207 N3
WPK KT4 200 G9
Andrewsfield WGCE AL7 23 M5
Andrew's La CHESW EN7 61 M4
CHESW EN7 62 A4
Andrews Pl RDART DA2 186 F5
RDART DA2 187 H7
Andrews Rd BETH E2 140 A3
Andrew St POP/IOD E14 141 H8
Andrews Wk WALW SE17 18 D10
Andromeda Cl CRAWW RH11 283 H9
Andwell Cl ABYW SE2 163 L1
Anelle Ri HHS/BOV HP3 36 A10
Anerley Gv NRWD SE19 181 N10
Anerley Hl NRWD SE19 181 N9
Anerley Pk PGE/AN SE20 182 A10
Anerley Park Rd PGE/AN SE20 182 A10
Anerley Rd PGE/AN SE20 203 P1
Anerley Station Rd PGE/AN SE20 204 A1
Anerley V NRWD SE19 181 N10
Anfield Cl BAL SW12 180 D3
Angas Ct WEY KT13 216 D2
Angel Aly WCHPL E1 13 M4
Angel Cl UED N18 99 N6
Angel Corner Pde UED N18 * 99 P6
Angel Ct LOTH EC2R 13 H5
Angelfield HSLW TW3 154 A10
Angel Ga GU GU1 268 A1
Angel Hl SUT SM1 201 L10
Angel Hill Dr SUT SM1 201 L10
Angelica Cl WDR/YW UB7 132 A8
Angelica Dr EHAM E6 142 D7
Angelica Gdns CROY/NA CR0 204 C8
Angelica Rd CHOB/PIR GU24 230 F1
GUW GU2 249 M6
Angel La HYS/HAR UB3 132 E7
SRTFD E15 141 J1
Angell Park Gdns BRXN/ST SW9 159 H9
Angell Rd BRXN/ST SW9 159 J9
Angell Town Est BRXN/ST SW9 * 159 H8
Angel Ms PUT/ROE SW15 178 D3
WCHPL E1 140 A9
Angel Pas CANST EC4R 12 G8
Angel Pl REIG RH2 * 275 L2
Angel Rd HRW HA1 114 D4
THDIT KT7 198 F8
Angel Rd (North Circular)
UED N18 99 P6
Angel Sq FSBYE EC1V * 6 C8
Angel St STBT EC1A 12 E5
Angel Wk HMSMTH W6 156 F3
Angel Wy ROM RM1 124 F3
Angerstein La BKHTH/KID SE3 161 L6
Angle Cl HGDN/ICK UB10 132 B3
Anglefield Rd BERK HP4 33 M5
Angle Rd WTHK RM20 167 J5
Anglers La KTTN NW5 4 F2
Anglers Reach SURB KT6 * 199 J5
Anglesea Ms WOOL/PLUM SE18 162 E3
Anglesea Pl GVW DA11 190 E2
Anglesea Rd KUT/HW KT1 199 J4
STMC/STPC BR5 207 M6
WOOL/PLUM SE18 162 E3
Anglesey Cl ASHF TW15 174 B7
CRAWW RH11 283 M10
Anglesey Court Rd CAR SM5 222 B3
Anglesey Dr RAIN RM13 145 H6
Anglesey Gdns CAR SM5 222 B3
Anglesey Rd OXHEY WD19 93 K6
PEND EN3 80 A8
Anglesmede Crs PIN HA5 113 P1
Anglesmede Wy PIN HA5 113 N1
Angles Rd STRHM/NOR SW16 180 F7
Anglia Cl TOTM N17 100 A8
Anglian Cl WATN WD24 73 K6
Anglian Rd WAN E11 121 J8
Anglo Rd BOW E3 140 E4
Angus Cl CHSGTN KT9 219 M2
Angus Dr RSLP HA4 113 K9
Angus Gdns CDALE/KGS NW9 96 A9
Angus Rd PLSTW E13 141 P5
Angus St NWCR SE14 160 D6
Anhalt Rd BTSEA SW11 157 P6
Ankerdine Crs WOOL/PLUM SE18 162 E7
Anlaby Rd TEDD TW11 176 D8
Anley Rd HMSMTH W6 156 G1
Anmersh Gv STAN HA7 95 J9
Annabel Cl POP/IOD E14 140 G8
Anna Cl HACK E8 7 M5
Annalee Gdns SOCK/AV RM15 146 G7
Annalee Rd SOCK/AV RM15 146 G7
Annandale Gv HGDN/ICK UB10 112 D8
Annandale Rd BFN/LL DA15 185 H3
CHSWK W4 156 B3
CROY/NA CR0 203 P9
GNWCH SE10 161 L5
GUW GU2 267 N2
Anna Neagle Cl FSTGT E7 121 M9
Annan Wy ROM RM1 104 E9
Anne Boleyn's Wk CHEAM SM3 220 G4
KUTN/CMB KT2 177 K8
Anne Case Ms NWMAL KT3 * 200 A3
Anne Compton Ms
LEE/GVPK SE12 183 L3
Anne Heart Cl CDW/CHF RM16 167 J3
Anne of Cleves Rd DART DA1 187 L1
Anners Cl EGH TW20 194 F3
Annesley Av CDALE/KGS NW9 116 A1
Annesley Cl WLSDN NW10 116 B8
Annesley Dr CROY/NA CR0 224 E1
Annesley Rd BKHTH/KID SE3 161 N7
Annesmere Gdns
BKHTH/KID SE3 162 A9
Anne St PLSTW E13 141 M6
Anne's Wk CTHM CR3 241 M6
Annett Cl SHPTN TW17 196 F4
Annette Cl KTN/HRWW/WS HA3 94 D10
Annette Rd HOLWY N7 118 G9
Annett Rd WOT/HER KT12 197 H7
Anne Wy BARK/HLT IG6 102 F7
Annexe Market WCHPL E1 * 13 L3
Annie Besant Cl BOW E3 * 140 E3
Annie Brookes Cl STA TW18 172 G6
Anningsley Pk CHERT KT16 214 E6
Anning St WCHPL E1 13 K1
Annington Rd EFNCH N2 118 A1
Annisdowne Cl RDKG RH5 270 G8
Annis Rd HOM E9 140 D1
Ann La WBPTN SW10 157 N6
Ann Moss Wy BERM/RHTH SE16 160 B2
Ann's Cl KTBR SW1X 16 B2
Ann St WOOL/PLUM SE18 162 G3
Annsworthy Av THHTH CR7 203 L3
Annsworthy Crs SNWD SE25 203 L3
Ansar Gdns WALTH E17 120 D3
Ansculf Rd SLN SL2 128 F5
Ansdell Rd PECK SE15 160 B8
Ansdell St KENS W8 15 H3
Ansdell Ter KENS W8 15 H3
Ansell Gv CAR SM5 202 A8
Ansell Rd DORK RH4 272 G1
TOOT SW17 179 P6
Anselm Cl CROY/NA CR0 203 N10
Anselm Rd FUL/PGN SW6 14 E10
PIN HA5 93 N8
Ansford Rd BMLY BR1 183 H8
Ansleigh Pl NTGHL W11 136 G9
Ansley Cl SAND/SEL CR2 224 A10
Anslow Gdns IVER SL0 130 G4
Anslow Pl SL SL1 128 B7
Anson Cl CTHM CR3 241 L6
HHS/BOV HP3 52 C3
ROMW/RG RM7 104 C10
STAL AL1 38 G8
STALE/WH AL4 21 H10
Anson Rd ARCH N19 118 D9
CRICK NW2 116 E10
CRICK NW2 116 G10
Anson Wk NTHWD HA6 92 D5
Anstead Dr RAIN RM13 145 H4
Anstey Rd PECK SE15 159 P9
Anstice Cl CHSWK W4 156 B6
Anstridge Rd ELTH/MOT SE9 184 G2
Antelope Av CDW/CHF RM16 167 M2
Antelope Rd WOOL/PLUM SE18 162 C2
Anthony Cl MLHL NW7 96 B5
OXHEY WD19 93 L2
SEV TN13 246 F7
Anthony Rd BORE WD6 75 K6
GFD/PVL UB6 134 D4
SNWD SE25 203 P6
WELL DA16 163 K7
Anthony's Cl WAP E1W 13 N9
Anthonys La SWLY BR8 209 J1
Anthony St WCHPL E1 140 A8
Anthony Wy SL SL1 128 C9
Anthorne Cl POTB/CUF EN6 59 L7
Anthus Ms NTHWD HA6 92 E8
Antill Rd BOW E3 140 D5
SEVS/STOTM N15 119 P2
Antill Ter WCHPL E1 140 C8
Antlands La HORL RH6 280 G10
Antlands La East HORL RH6 280 F10
Antlands La West HORL RH6 280 F9
Antlers Hl CHING E4 80 G9
Antoinette Ct ABLGY WD5 * 54 G5
Anton Crs SUT SM1 201 K10
Antoneys Cl PIN HA5 93 L10
Antonine Ga STALW/RED AL3 37 P7
Anton Pl WBLY HA9 115 N8
Anton Rd SOCK/AV RM15 146 G6
Anton St HACK E8 119 P10
Antrim Gv HAMP NW3 4 A1
Antrim Rd HAMP NW3 4 A1
Antrobus Cl SUT SM1 221 J2
Antrobus Rd CHSWK W4 155 P3
Anvil Cl HHS/BOV HP3 52 E4
STRHM/NOR SW16 180 D10
Anvil La COB KT11 235 H1
Anvil Pl LCOL/BKTW AL2 * 55 P2
Anvil Rd SUN TW16 197 H3
Anvil Ter RDART DA2 186 F5
Anworth Cl WFD IG8 101 N7
Anyards Rd COB KT11 217 J10
Anzio Gdns CTHM CR3 241 K7
Aostle Wy THHTH CR7 203 J2
Apeldoorn Dr WLGTN SM6 222 F5
Aperdele Rd LHD/OX KT22 236 F4
Aperfield Rd BH/WHM TN16 244 B3
ERITH DA8 164 G5
Apers Av WOKS/MYFD GU22 232 C7
Apex Cl BECK BR3 204 G1
Apex Pde MLHL NW7 * 96 A5
Apex Point BRKMPK AL9 * 40 F8
Apley Rd REIG RH2 275 K3
Aplin Wy ISLW TW7 154 D7
Apollo Av BMLY BR1 205 N1
NTHWD HA6 93 H6
Apollo Cl HCH RM12 125 J7
Apollo Pl WAN E11 121 K8
WBPTN SW10 * 157 N6
WOKN/KNAP GU21 * 231 M5
Apollo Wy ERITH DA8 164 E3
HHNE HP2 35 P4
THMD SE28 162 G2
Apothecary St BLKFR EC4V * 12 C6
Appach Rd BRXS/STRHM SW2 181 H1
Apperlie Dr BRKHM/BTCW RH3 273 P1
Apple Blossom Ct VX/NE SW8 158 E6
Appleby Cl CHING E4 101 H7
SEVS/STOTM N15 119 L3
STMC/STPC BR5 207 H7
UX/CGN UB8 132 D8
WHTN TW2 176 C5
Appleby Dr HARH RM3 105 K6
Appleby Gdns
EBED/NFELT TW14 * 174 G4
Appleby Rd CAN/RD E16 141 M8
HACK E8 7 P3
Appleby St BETH E2 7 L7
CHESW EN7 61 M2
Apple Cottages HHS/BOV HP3 52 D3
Applecroft BERK HP4 33 K3
LCOL/BKTW AL2 56 A4
Applecroft Rd WGCW AL8 22 E5
Appledore Av BXLYHN DA7 164 D7
RSLP HA4 113 J8
Appledore Cl EDGW HA8 95 M9
HARH RM3 105 K9
HAYES BR2 205 L5
TOOT SW17 180 A5
Appledore Crs SCUP DA14 185 H6
Appledore Wy MLHL NW7 96 G8
Appledown Ri COUL/CHIP CR5 240 D1
Applefield AMSS HP7 69 P5
CRAWE RH10 283 P6
Appleford Rd NKENS W10 8 B2
NKENS W10 137 H6
Appleford's Cl HOD EN11 44 E1
Apple Garth BTFD TW8 155 J3
Applegarth CROY/NA CR0 224 G4
ESH/CLAY KT10 218 E2
Apple Garth GODL GU7 267 H10
Applegarth Av GUW GU2 249 J10
Applegarth Dr DART DA1 187 M5
GNTH/NBYPK IG2 123 J2
Applegarth Rd THMD SE28 143 L10
WKENS W14 * 156 G2
Apple Ga BRW CM14 86 E9
Apple Gv CHSGTN KT9 219 K1
EN EN1 79 M7
Apple Ldg ALP/SUD HA0 * 115 H8
Apple Market KUT/HW KT1 199 J2
Apple Orch SWLY BR8 208 E4
The Apple Orch HHNE HP2 36 A4
Apple Rd WAN E11 121 K8
Appleshaw Cl GVW DA11 190 D8
Appleton Cl AMSS HP7 69 N6
BXLYHN DA7 164 D8
HLWW/ROY CM19 46 F2
Appleton Dr RDART DA2 187 J6
Appleton Gdns NWMAL KT3 200 D6
Appleton Rd ELTH/MOT SE9 162 B9
LOU IG10 82 E7
Appleton Wy HCH RM12 125 L6
Apple Tree Av WDR/YW UB7 132 A8
Apple Tree Cl LHD/OX KT22 236 B10
Appletree Cl PGE/AN SE20 204 A1
Appletree Ct RGUE GU4 250 G8
Apple Tree Crs BRWN CM15 87 H4
Appletree Dell
RKW/CH/CXG WD3 * 71 J8
Appletree Gdns EBAR EN4 77 P8
Appletree La DTCH/LGLY SL3 149 P2
Apple Trees Pl
WOKS/MYFD GU22 * 231 P5
Appletree Wk CSHM HP5 51 J10
GSTN WD25 73 J1
Apple Tree Yd STJS SW1Y 11 H9
Applewood Cl CRICK NW2 116 E8
HGDN/ICK UB10 111 P9
TRDG/WHET N20 97 P2
Applewood Dr PLSTW E13 141 N6
Appleyard Ter PEND EN3 * 80 B3
Appold St ERITH DA8 164 G5
SDTCH EC2A 13 J3
Apprentice Wy CLPT E5 120 A9
Approach La MLHL NW7 97 H6
Approach Rd ASHF TW15 174 D9
BETH E2 140 B4
BH/WHM TN16 243 N8
E/WMO/HCT KT8 197 P5
EBAR EN4 77 M8
PUR/KEN CR8 223 H8
RYNPK SW20 200 F2
STAL AL1 38 D7
The Approach ACT W3 136 A8
EN EN1 80 A6
HDN NW4 116 G3
ORP BR6 207 J9
POTB/CUF EN6 59 J8
UPMR RM14 126 A8
Appspond La LCOL/BKTW AL2 37 K10
Aprey Gdns HDN NW4 116 F2
April Cl ASHTD KT21 237 L4
FELT TW13 175 H6
HNWL W7 134 D9
ORP BR6 227 J2
April Gln FSTH SE23 182 C6
April St HACK E8 119 N9
Aprilwood Cl ADL/WDHM KT15 215 J7
Apsley Cl HRW HA1 114 B3
Apsley Rd NWMAL KT3 199 P3
SNWD SE25 204 A4
Apsley Wy CRICK NW2 116 D7
MYFR/PICC W1J * 10 E10
Aquarius TWK TW1 * 176 G4
Aquarius Wy NTHWD HA6 93 H6
Aquila Cl LHD/OX KT22 237 K7

Aquila St STJWD NW8 3 M7
Aquinas St STHWK SE1 12 B10
Arabella Dr PUT/ROE SW15 156 B10
Arabia Cl CHING E4 101 J1
Arabin Rd BROCKY SE4 160 D10
Araby Cnr SHPTN TW17 196 D6
Araglen Av SOCK/AV RM15 146 G7
Aragon Av EW KT17 220 E5
THDIT KT7 198 E5
Aragon Cl CROY/NA CR0 225 K6
ENC/FH EN2 78 G4
HAYES BR2 206 C8
HHNE HP2 36 D1
LOU IG10 82 B10
SUN TW16 174 G10
Aragon Dr BARK/HLT IG6 102 F8
RSLP HA4 113 L6
Aragon Pl MRDN SM4 200 G7
Aragon Rd KUTN/CMB KT2 177 K8
MRDN SM4 200 G7
Aram Ct WOKS/MYFD GU22 * 232 E1
Aran Cl HARP AL5 20 C5
Arandora Crs CHDH RM6 123 L5
Aran Hts CSTG HP8 89 N4
Arbery Rd BOW E3 140 D5
Arbor Cl BECK BR3 204 G2
Arborfield Cl BRXS/STRHM SW2 180 G4
SL SL1 149 K2
Arbor Rd CHING E4 101 J4
Arbour Cl BRW CM14 107 J6
LHD/OX KT22 236 E9
Arbour Rd PEND EN3 80 C8
Arbour Sq WCHPL E1 140 C8
The Arbour GODL GU7 266 E8
HERT/BAY SG13 25 L7
Arbour Vw AMSS HP7 69 N5
Arbour Wy HCH RM12 125 J10
Arbroath Gn OXHEY WD19 93 H4
Arbroath Rd ELTH/MOT SE9 162 B9
Arbrook Cl STMC/STPC BR5 207 K3
Arbrook La ESH/CLAY KT10 218 C3
Arbuthnot La BXLY DA5 185 P2
Arbuthnot Rd NWCR SE14 160 C8
Arbutus Cl REDH RH1 275 M2
Arbutus Rd REDH RH1 275 M2
Arbutus St HACK E8 7 L5
Arcade Chambers
ELTH/MOT SE9 * 184 D2
Arcade Pde CHSGTN KT9 * 219 K1
The Arcade BEAC HP9 88 D9
ELTH/MOT SE9 * 184 D2
LVPST EC2M * 13 J4
REDH RH1 * 258 B9
WALTH E17 * 120 F2
Arcadia Av FNCH N3 97 K9
Arcadia Cl CAR SM5 222 B1
Arcadian Av BXLY DA5 185 P2
Arcadian Cl BXLY DA5 185 P2
Arcadian Gdns WDGN N22 99 H8
Arcadian Pl WAND/EARL SW18 179 H3
Arcadian Rd BXLY DA5 185 P3
Arcadia St POP/IOD E14 140 F8
Arcany Rd SOCK/AV RM15 146 G6
Archangel St BERM/RHTH SE16 160 C1
Archates Av CDW/CHF RM16 167 M2
Archbishop's Pl
BRXS/STRHM SW2 180 G3
Archdale Ct SHB W12 136 E10
Archdale Pl NWMAL KT3 199 N3
Archdale Rd EDUL SE22 181 N1
Archel Rd WKENS W14 14 C9
Archer Cl KGLGY WD4 54 A5
KUTN/CMB KT2 177 K10
Archer Ct FELT TW13 175 H4
Archer Ms HPTN TW12 176 B9
Archer Rd SNWD SE25 204 A4
STMC/STPC BR5 207 K6
Archers HLWW/ROY CM19 46 D6
Archers Cl HERT/WAT SG14 25 K4
Archers Dr PEND EN3 80 B6
Archers Flds STAL AL1 38 E4
Archers Green La WLYN AL6 23 N3
Archer Sq NWCR SE14 160 D5
Archers Ride WGCE AL7 23 L8
Archer St SOHO/SHAV W1D 11 J7
Archer Wy SWLY BR8 208 G3
SWLY BR8 209 H3
Archery Cl BAY/PAD W2 9 P6
KTN/HRWW/WS HA3 114 E1
Archery Rd ELTH/MOT SE9 184 C1
The Arches CHCR WC2N * 11 M9
RYLN/HDSTN HA2 114 A7
WDSR SL4 * 149 H7
Archfield WGCE AL7 23 H2
Archibald Ms MYFR/PKLN W1K 10 D8
Archibald Rd HARH RM3 105 P9
HOLWY N7 118 E9
Archibold St BOW E3 140 F5
Archie Cl WDR/YW UB7 152 B1
Arch Rd WOT/HER KT12 197 L10
Arch St STHWK SE1 18 E4
Archway HARH RM3 105 J7
Archway Cl ARCH N19 * 118 D7
NKENS W10 136 G7
WIM/MER SW19 179 L7
WLGTN SM6 * 202 F10
Archway Ms DORK RH4 272 F1
Archway Rd HGT N6 118 A3
HGT N6 118 C4
HGT N6 118 D6
Archway St BARN SW13 156 B9
Arcola St HACK E8 119 N10
Arcon Dr NTHLT UB5 133 M6
Arctic St KTTN NW5 118 C10
Arcturus Rd CRAWW RH11 282 G10
Arcus Rd BMLY BR1 183 K9
Ardbeg Rd HNHL SE24 181 L2
Arden Cl BUSH WD23 94 E1
HHS/BOV HP3 52 D4
HRW HA1 114 C8
REIG RH2 275 L4
THMD SE28 143 N8
Arden Court Gdns EFNCH N2 117 N5
Arden Crs DAGW RM9 143 N2
POP/IOD E14 160 F3
Arden Est IS N1 7 J8
Arden Gv HARP AL5 20 A2
ORP BR6 226 E1
Arden Mhor PIN HA5 113 J2
Arden Rd CRAWE RH10 284 A9
FNCH N3 117 J1
WEA W13 135 H9
Ardens Marsh STALE/WH AL4 * 39 K4
Ardens Wy STALE/WH AL4 39 J4
Ardent Cl SNWD SE25 203 M3
Ardesley Wd WEY KT13 216 F1
Ardfern Av STRHM/NOR SW16 203 H3
Ardfillan Rd CAT SE6 183 J4
Ardgowan Rd CAT SE6 183 K3
Ardilaun Rd HBRY N5 119 K9
Ardingly Cl CRAWW RH11 283 L5
CROY/NA CR0 204 C10
Ardleigh Cl EMPK RM11 125 L1
Ardleigh Ct BRWN CM15 107 L1
Ardleigh Gdns CHEAM SM3 201 K8
Ardleigh Green Rd EMPK RM11 125 L3
Ardleigh Rd IS N1 7 J2
WALTH E17 100 E9
Ardleigh Ter WALTH E17 100 E9
Ardley Cl CAT SE6 182 D6
WLSDN NW10 116 B8
Ardley Crs RBSF CM22 31 J1
Ardlui Rd WNWD SE27 181 K5
Ardmay Gdns SURB KT6 * 199 K5
Ardmere Rd LEW SE13 183 J2
Ardmore Av GUW GU2 249 N8
Ardmore La BKHH IG9 101 N2
Ardmore Pl BKHH IG9 * 101 N1
Ardmore Rd SOCK/AV RM15 146 G6
Ardmore Wy GUW GU2 249 N8
Ardoch Rd CAT SE6 183 J5
Ardra Rd ED N9 100 C4
Ardrossan Cl SLN SL2 129 H6
Ardrossan Gdns WPK KT4 200 D10
Ardross Av NTHWD HA6 92 F6
Ardshiel Cl PUT/ROE SW15 156 G9
Ardshiel Dr REDH RH1 275 P2
Ardwell Av BARK/HLT IG6 122 F3
Ardwell Rd BRXS/STRHM SW2 180 F5
Ardwick Rd CRICK NW2 117 K9
Arena Est FSBYPK N4 * 119 J4
The Arena STKPK UB11 * 132 D10
Arethusa Pl SWCM DA10 * 166 G10
Arethusa Wy CHOB/PIR GU24 230 E2
Argall Av LEY E10 120 D5
Argall Wy LEY E10 120 D6
Argenta Wy WLSDN NW10 135 N2
Argent Centre HYS/HAR UB3 * 153 H1
Argent Cl EGH TW20 172 F9
Argent Ct SURB KT6 * 199 M9
Argent St GRAYS RM17 167 K5
Argent Wy CHESW EN7 61 L3
Argles Cl RDART DA2 188 F1
Argon Ms FUL/PGN SW6 157 K6
Argon Rd UED N18 100 B6
Argosy Gdns STA TW18 173 J9
Argosy La STWL/WRAY TW19 173 N3
Argus Cl ROMW/RG RM7 104 C9
Argus Wk CRAWW RH11 283 K10
Argus Wy NTHLT UB5 133 M5
Argyle Av HSLW TW3 175 P2
Argyle Cl WEA W13 134 E6
Argyle Cnr WEA W13 * 134 G9
Argyle Ct WATW WD18 * 72 G8
Argyle Gdns UPMR RM14 126 C8
Argyle Pl HMSMTH W6 156 E3
Argyle Rd BAR EN5 76 F8
CAN/RD E16 141 N8
GFD/PVL UB6 134 E5
HSLW TW3 176 A1
IL IG1 122 D7
NFNCH/WDSPK N12 97 K6
RYLN/HDSTN HA2 114 A4
SEV TN13 265 J1
SRTFD E15 121 K9
TOTM N17 99 P9
UED N18 99 P5
UED N18 100 A5
WCHPL E1 140 C6
WEA W13 134 F7
Argyle Sq STPAN WC1H 5 M9
Argyle St STPAN WC1H 5 L9
Argyle Wk STPAN WC1H * 5 L10
Argyle Wy BERM/RHTH SE16 19 P8
Argyll Av SL SL1 128 F9
STHL UB1 134 A10
Argyll Cl BRXN/ST SW9 158 G9
Argyll Gdns EDGW HA8 95 N10
Argyll Rd GRAYS RM17 167 M4
HHNE HP2 35 P1
KENS W8 14 E2
WOOL/PLUM SE18 162 F2
Argyll St REGST W1B 10 G6
Arhchie St STHWK SE1 19 K2
Arica Rd BROCKY SE4 160 D10
Ariel Cl GVE DA12 191 J7
Ariel Rd KIL/WHAMP NW6 2 E2
Ariel Wy HSLWW TW4 153 J9
SHB W12 136 F10
Arisdale Av SOCK/AV RM15 146 G5
SOCK/AV RM15 146 G7
Aristotle Rd CLAP SW4 158 E10
Ark Av CDW/CHF RM16 167 M2
Arkell Gv NRWD SE19 181 J10
Arkindale Rd CAT SE6 183 H6
Arkley Crs WALTH E17 120 E3
Arkley Dr BAR EN5 76 D8
Arkley La BAR EN5 76 D7
Arkley Rd HHNE HP2 36 C1
WALTH E17 120 E3
Arkley Vw BAR EN5 76 E8
Arklow Rd NWCR SE14 160 E5
Arkwright Rd DTCH/LGLY SL3 151 H8
HAMP NW3 117 M10
SAND/SEL CR2 223 N6
TIL RM18 168 D8
Arkwrights HLW CM20 29 J10
Arlesford Rd BRXN/ST SW9 158 F9
Arlingford Rd BRXS/STRHM SW2 181 H2
Arlington NFNCH/WDSPK N12 97 K4
Arlington Av IS N1 6 F6
Arlington Cl BFN/LL DA15 185 H3
LEW SE13 183 J1
SUT SM1 201 K9
TWK TW1 * 177 H2
Arlington Ct HYS/HAR UB3 152 E4
Arlington Crs CHES/WCR EN8 62 D10
Arlington Dr CAR SM5 202 A9
RSLP HA4 112 E4
Arlington Gdns CHSWK W4 155 P4
HARH RM3 105 M9
IL IG1 122 C5
Arlington Ldg WEY KT13 216 C1
Arlington Pde
BRXS/STRHM SW2 * 158 G10
Arlington Rd ASHF TW15 174 A8
CAMTN NW1 4 F6
STHGT/OAK N14 98 C3
SURB KT6 199 J6
TEDD TW11 176 E7
TWK TW1 177 H2
WEA W13 134 G8
WFD IG8 101 M9
Arlington Sq IS N1 6 F6
Arlington St MYFR/PICC W1J 10 G9
Arlington Wy CLKNW EC1R 6 B9
Arliss Wy NTHLT UB5 133 K3
Arlow Rd WCHMH N21 99 H2
Armadale Cl TOTM N17 120 A2
Armadale Rd EBED/NFELT TW14 175 H1
FUL/PGN SW6 157 K6
WOKN/KNAP GU21 231 M3
Armada St DEPT SE8 160 F5
Armada Wy EHAM E6 142 F7
Armagh Rd BOW E3 140 E3
Armand Cl WAT WD17 72 G4
Armfield Cl E/WMO/HCT KT8 197 N5
Armfield Crs MTCM CR4 202 A2
Armfield Rd ENC/FH EN2 79 L5
Arminger Rd SHB W12 136 E10
Armistice Gdns SNWD SE25 203 P3
Armitage Cl RKW/CH/CXG WD3 71 N8
Armitage Ct ASC SL5 192 B6
Armitage Rd GLDGN NW11 117 H6
GNWCH SE10 161 L3
Armor Rd PUR RM19 166 C3
Armour Cl HOLWY N7 5 N2
Armoury Dr GVE DA12 190 F3
Armoury Rd DEPT SE8 160 G8
Armoury Wy WAND/EARL SW18 179 K1
Armstead Wk DAGE RM10 144 B2
Armstrong Av WFD IG8 101 K7
Armstrong Cl BCTR RM8 123 N5
BMLY BR1 206 B3
BORE WD6 75 P7
EHAM E6 142 C8
LCOL/BKTW AL2 57 K3
PSEV TN14 246 C1
RSLP HA4 113 H4
WOT/HER KT12 197 H6
Armstrong Crs EBAR EN4 77 N7
Armstrong Gdns RAD WD7 57 K8
Armstrong Pl HHW HP1 35 M4
Armstrong Rd ACT W3 136 C10
EGH TW20 171 P9
FELT TW13 175 M8
WOOL/PLUM SE18 162 F2
Armstrong Wy NWDGN UB2 154 A1
Armytage Rd HEST TW5 153 L6
Arnal Crs WAND/EARL SW18 179 H3
Arncliffe Cl FBAR/BDGN N11 98 B7
Arndale Wy EGH TW20 172 D8
Arne Cl CRAWW RH11 283 J10
Arne Gv HORL RH6 279 P2
ORP BR6 207 J10
Arne St COVGDN WC2E 11 M6
Arnett Cl RKW/CH/CXG WD3 71 K10
Arnett Sq CHING E4 100 E7
Arnett Wy RKW/CH/CXG WD3 91 K1
Arne Wk LEW SE13 161 L10
Arneways Av CHDH RM6 123 N2
Arneway St WEST SW1P 17 K4
Arnewood Cl LHD/OX KT22 218 A10
PUT/ROE SW15 178 D4
Arney's La MTCM CR4 202 B6
Arnfield Cl CRAWW RH11 283 H8
Arngask Rd CAT SE6 183 J3
Arnheim Pl POP/IOD E14 160 F2
Arnhem Av SOCK/AV RM15 146 B10
Arnhem Dr CROY/NA CR0 225 J7
Arnison Rd E/WMO/HCT KT8 198 C4
Arnold Av East PEND EN3 80 F4
Arnold Av West PEND EN3 80 E4
Arnold Circ BETH E2 7 L10
Arnold Cl KTN/HRWW/WS HA3 115 L5
Arnold Crs ISLW TW7 176 C1
Arnold Dr CHSGTN KT9 219 J3
Arnold Est STHWK SE1 19 M2
Arnold Gdns PLMGR N13 99 J6
Arnold Pl TIL RM18 168 F7
Arnold Rd BOW E3 140 F5
DAGW RM9 144 A2
GVE DA12 190 F5
NTHLT UB5 133 M1
SEVS/STOTM N15 119 N1
STA TW18 173 M10
TOOT SW17 180 A10
WAB EN9 81 H1
WOKN/KNAP GU21 232 E2
Arnolds Av RBRW/HUT CM13 87 P9
Arnolds Cl RBRW/HUT CM13 87 P9
Arnolds La EYN DA4 187 P9
Arnold Ter STAN HA7 * 94 E6
Arnos Gv STHGT/OAK N14 98 E5
Arnos Rd FBAR/BDGN N11 98 D6
Arnott Cl CHSWK W4 156 A3
THMD SE28 143 M10
Arnould Av CMBW SE5 159 L10
Arnsberg Wy BXLYHN DA7 164 B10
Arnside Gdns WBLY HA9 115 J6
Arnside Rd BXLYHN DA7 164 B7
Arnside St WALW SE17 18 F9
Arnulf St CAT SE6 182 G7
Arnull's Rd STRHM/NOR SW16 181 J9
Arodene Rd BRXS/STRHM SW2 180 G2
Arosa Rd TWK TW1 177 J2
Arragon Gdns STRHM/NOR SW16 180 F10
WWKM BR4 204 G10
Arragon Rd EHAM E6 142 A3
TWK TW1 176 F4
WAND/EARL SW18 179 K4
Arragon Wk BF/WBF KT14 216 A9
Arran Cl CRAWW RH11 283 L10
ERITH DA8 164 E5
HHS/BOV HP3 36 D8
WLGTN SM6 222 D1
Arran Dr MNPK E12 122 A6
STAN HA7 95 H5
Arran Gn OXHEY WD19 * 93 L5
Arran Ms EA W5 135 L10
Arranmore Ct BUSH WD23 * 73 M8
Arran Rd CAT SE6 182 G5
Arran Wk IS N1 6 E3
Arran Wy ESH/CLAY KT10 198 A9
Arras Av MRDN SM4 201 M5
Arretine Cl STALW/RED AL3 37 N8
Arreton Md WOKN/KNAP GU21 214 B10
Arrivals Rd HORL RH6 280 A7
Arrol Rd BECK BR3 204 B3
Arrow Rd BOW E3 140 G5
Arrowsmith Rd CHIG IG7 103 J6
Arsenal Rd ELTH/MOT SE9 162 C8
Arsenal Wy CAN/RD E16 162 D1
WOOL/PLUM SE18 162 F3
Artel Cft CRAWE RH10 284 A7
Artemis Cl GVE DA12 191 H3
Artemis Pl WAND/EARL SW18 179 J3
Arterberry Rd RYNPK SW20 178 F10
Arterial Av RAIN RM13 145 K6
Arterial Rd North Stifford
CDW/CHF RM16 167 K1
Arterial Rd Purfleet PUR RM19 166 B3
SOCK/AV RM15 165 P2
Arterial Road (West Thurrock)
PUR RM19 166 G2
Arterial Road West Thurrock
WTHK RM20 166 E2
Artesian Cl ROM RM1 124 G4
WLSDN NW10 136 A2
Artesian Gv BAR EN5 77 M8
Artesian Houses BAY/PAD W2 * 8 E6
Artesian Rd BAY/PAD W2 8 E6
Arthingworth St SRTFD E15 141 K3
Arthurdon Rd BROCKY SE4 182 F1
Arthur Gv WOOL/PLUM SE18 162 F3
Arthur Rd BH/WHM TN16 243 P1
CHDH RM6 123 M5
CRAWW RH11 283 H7
ED N9 99 N3
EHAM E6 142 C4
HOLWY N7 118 G8
KUTN/CMB KT2 177 M10
NWMAL KT3 200 E5
STAL AL1 38 G6
WDSR SL4 149 H7
WIM/MER SW19 179 J7
Arthur's Bridge Rd
WOKN/KNAP GU21 231 P3
Arthur St BUSH WD23 73 L7
CANST EC4R 13 H8
ERITH DA8 164 G6
GRAYS RM17 167 P5
GVW DA11 190 D3
Arthur St West GVW DA11 190 D3
Artichoke Dell
RKW/CH/CXG WD3 * 71 H8
Artichoke Hl WAP E1W 140 A9
Artichoke Pl CMBW SE5 * 159 L7
Artillery Cl GNTH/NBYPK IG2 122 F4
Artillery La LVPST EC2M 13 K4
SHB W12 136 D8
Artillery Pas WCHPL E1 * 13 K4
Artillery Pl WOOL/PLUM SE18 162 C4
Artillery Rd GU GU1 268 A1
Artillery Rw GVE DA12 190 F3
WEST SW1P 17 J4
Artillery Ter GU GU1 268 A1
Artington Cl ORP BR6 226 F1
Artington Wk GUW GU2 267 P3
Artisan Crs STALW/RED AL3 38 B5
Artizan St WCHPL E1 13 K5
Artwell Cl LEY E10 120 G4
Arun TIL RM18 169 M3
Arundel Av EW KT17 220 E6
MRDN SM4 201 J4
SAND/SEL CR2 223 P6
Arundel Cl BTSEA SW11 179 P1
BXLY DA5 186 A2
CHES/WCR EN8 62 A4
CRAWE RH10 284 D7
CROY/NA CR0 * 203 J10
HHNE HP2 36 C5
HPTN TW12 176 A8
SRTFD E15 121 K9
Arundel Ct DTCH/LGLY SL3 150 A3
Arundel Dr BORE WD6 75 P8
ORP BR6 227 L2
RYLN/HDSTN HA2 113 N9
WFD IG8 101 M8
Arundel Gdns EDGW HA8 96 A8
GDMY/SEVK IG3 123 K7
NTGHL W11 8 C7
WCHMH N21 99 H2
Arundel Gv IS N1 119 M10
STALW/RED AL3 38 C2
Arundell Rd ABLGY WD5 55 H8
Arundel Pl HOLWY N7 6 A2
Arundel Rd BELMT SM2 221 J4
CROY/NA CR0 203 L6
DART DA1 165 K10
DORK RH4 272 F2
EBAR EN4 77 P7
HARH RM3 105 N8
HSLWW TW4 153 K9
UX/CGN UB8 131 L4
Arundel Sq HOLWY N7 6 A2
Arundel St TPL/STR WC2R 11 P7
Arundel Ter BARN SW13 156 E5
Arvon Rd HBRY N5 119 H10
Asbaston Ter IL IG1 122 F10
Ascalon St VX/NE SW8 158 D6
Ascension Rd CRW RM5 104 D7
Ascham Dr CHING E4 100 G8
Ascham End WALTH E17 100 D9
Ascham St KTTN NW5 118 D10
Aschurch Rd CROY/NA CR0 203 N7
Ascot Cl BARK/HLT IG6 103 H7
BORE WD6 75 M9
NTHLT UB5 113 P10
Ascot Ct RKW/CH/CXG WD3 * 72 C10
Ascot Gdns HCH RM12 125 M9
PEND EN3 80 B3
STHL UB1 133 N7
Ascot Ga ASC SL5 * 170 E10
Ascot Ms WLGTN SM6 222 D5
Ascot Pde CLAP SW4 * 158 F10
Ascot Rd EBED/NFELT TW14 174 B4
EHAM E6 142 C5
GVW DA11 190 E6
SEVS/STOTM N15 119 L3
STMC/STPC BR5 207 J4
TOOT SW17 180 B9
UED N18 99 P5
WATW WD18 72 F9
Ascots La BRKMPK AL9 23 H10
WGCE AL7 23 J9
Ascott Av EA W5 155 K1
Ascott Ct PIN HA5 * 113 H2
Ashanti Ms HACK E8 * 140 A1
Ashbeam Cl RBRW/HUT CM13 107 H7
Ashborurne Sq NTHWD HA6 92 F7
Ashbourne Av BXLYHN DA7 163 P6
GLDGN NW11 117 J3
RYLN/HDSTN HA2 * 114 C7
SWFD E18 121 N2
TRDG/WHET N20 98 A3
Ashbourne Cl COUL/CHIP CR5 240 D4
EA W5 135 L7
NFNCH/WDSPK N12 97 L5
Ashbourne Ct STALE/WH AL4 39 H8
Ashbourne Gv CHSWK W4 156 B4
EDUL SE22 181 N1
MLHL NW7 96 A6
Ashbourne Pde EA W5 * 135 L6
GLDGN NW11 * 117 J2
Ashbourne Ri ORP BR6 226 G1
Ashbourne Rd BROX EN10 44 E7
EA W5 135 L6
HARH RM3 105 K5
MTCM CR4 180 B9
Ashbourne Ter WIM/MER SW19 179 K10
Ashbourne Wy GLDGN NW11 117 J3
Ashbridge Rd WAN E11 121 K5
Ashbridge St STJWD NW8 9 N2
Ashbrook EDGW HA8 * 95 L7
Ashbrook Rd ARCH N19 118 E6
DAGE RM10 124 C8
WDSR SL4 171 N3
Ashburn Gdns SKENS SW7 15 J5
Ashburnham Av HRW HA1 114 E5
Ashburnham Cl EFNCH N2 117 N1
OXHEY WD19 * 93 H4
SEV TN13 265 K3
Ashburnham Dr OXHEY WD19 93 H4
Ashburnham Gdns HRW HA1 114 E4
UPMR RM14 126 B6
Ashburnham Gv GNWCH SE10 160 G6
Ashburnham Pk ESH/CLAY KT10 218 B1
Ashburnham Pl GNWCH SE10 160 G6
Ashburnham Retreat
GNWCH SE10 160 G6
Ashburnham Rd BELV DA17 164 D3
CRAWE RH10 284 B9
RCHPK/HAM TW10 176 G6
WBPTN SW10 * 157 M6
WLSDN NW10 136 F5
Ashburn Pl SKENS SW7 15 J6
Ashburton Av CROY/NA CR0 204 A8
GDMY/SEVK IG3 123 J9
Ashburton Cl CROY/NA CR0 203 P8
Ashburton Gdns CROY/NA CR0 203 P9
Ashburton Rd CAN/RD E16 141 M8
CROY/NA CR0 203 P9
RSLP HA4 113 H7
Ashbury Cl HAT AL10 40 B4
Ashbury Crs RGUE GU4 250 F8
Ashbury Dr HGDN/ICK UB10 112 C8
Ashbury Gdns CHDH RM6 123 N3
Ashbury Pl WIM/MER SW19 179 M9
Ashbury Rd BTSEA SW11 158 A9
Ashby Av CHSGTN KT9 219 M3
Ashby Cl EMPK RM11 125 P6
Ashby Gdns STAL AL1 38 C10
Ashby Gv IS N1 6 F3
Ashby Ms BROCKY SE4 160 E9
Ashby Rd BERK HP4 33 J2
BROCKY SE4 160 E8
SEVS/STOTM N15 119 P3
WATN WD24 73 H4
Ashby St FSBYE EC1V 6 D10
Ashby Wk CROY/NA CR0 203 K6
Ashby Wy WDR/YW UB7 152 B6
Ashchurch Gv SHB W12 156 D2
Ashchurch Park Vls SHB W12 156 D2
Ashchurch Ter SHB W12 156 C2
Ash Cl ABLGY WD5 54 E8
BRKMPK AL9 59 K1
BRWN CM15 86 E9
CAR SM5 202 A9
CRW RM5 104 C8
DEN/HRF UB9 91 N9
DTCH/LGLY SL3 150 E2
EDGW HA8 95 P5
GSTN WD25 73 J1
KWD/TDW/WH KT20 255 P7
NWMAL KT3 200 A2
PGE/AN SE20 204 B2
REDH RH1 258 D6
SCUP DA14 185 L6
STAN HA7 94 F7
STMC/STPC BR5 206 G5
SWLY BR8 208 D2
WOKS/MYFD GU22 232 B6
WOKS/MYFD GU22 233 K1
Ashcombe WGCW AL8 23 H1
Ashcombe Av SURB KT6 199 J7
Ashcombe Gdns EDGW HA8 95 M5
Ashcombe Pde
WOKS/MYFD GU22 * 232 D6
Ashcombe Pk CRICK NW2 116 B8
Ashcombe Rd CAR SM5 222 B3
DORK RH4 254 F10
REDH RH1 258 D3
WIM/MER SW19 179 K8
Ashcombe Sq NWMAL KT3 199 P3
Ashcombe St FUL/PGN SW6 * 157 L8
Ashcombe Ter
KWD/TDW/WH KT20 238 E6
Ash Copse LCOL/BKTW AL2 55 N7
Ash Ct HOR/WEW KT19 219 P1
Ashcroft PIN HA5 93 P7
RGUE GU4 268 B7
Ashcroft Av BFN/LL DA15 185 K2
Ashcroft Cl HARP AL5 20 D3
Ashcroft Ct SL SL1 128 A4
Ashcroft Crs BFN/LL DA15 185 K2
Ashcroft Dr DEN/HRF UB9 111 J4
Ashcroft Pk COB KT11 217 M8
Ashcroft Ri COUL/CHIP CR5 240 F2
Ashcroft Rd BOW E3 140 D5
CHSGTN KT9 199 L10
Ashdale GT/LBKH KT23 254 B2
Ashdale Cl STWL/WRAY TW19 173 P5
WHTN TW2 176 A3
Ashdale Gv STAN HA7 94 F7
Ashdale Rd LEE/GVPK SE12 183 N4
Ashdales STAL AL1 38 C10
Ashdene PIN HA5 113 K1
Ashdene Cl ASHF TW15 * 174 D10
Ashdon Cl RBRW/HUT CM13 87 P10
SOCK/AV RM15 146 G8
WFD IG8 101 N7
Ashdon Rd BUSH WD23 73 L7
Ashdown WEA W13 * 134 G7
Ashdown Cl BECK BR3 204 G2
BXLY DA5 186 D3
REIG RH2 275 L4
WOKS/MYFD GU22 232 B5
Ashdown Ct CRAWE RH10 * 284 A10
Ashdown Crs CHES/WCR EN8 62 D4
KTTN NW5 * 118 B10
Ashdown Dr BORE WD6 75 L6
Ashdown Gdns SAND/SEL CR2 242 A1
Ashdown Pl THDIT KT7 198 F6
Ashdown Rd EW KT17 220 C9
HGDN/ICK UB10 132 B5
KUT/HW KT1 199 K2
PEND EN3 80 B7
REIG RH2 275 L4
WLSDN NW10 136 C3
Ashdown Wk ROMW/RG RM7 104 C9
Ashdown Wy AMS HP6 69 J3
TOOT SW17 180 B5
Ash Dr HAT AL10 40 D8
REDH RH1 276 B2
Ashen EHAM E6 142 D8
Ashendene Rd CHESW EN7 61 J1
HERT/BAY SG13 42 G4
Ashenden Rd CLPT E5 120 D10
GUW GU2 249 L10
Ashenden Wk SLN SL2 109 J9
Ashen Dr DART DA1 187 H2
Ashen Gv WIM/MER SW19 179 K6
Ashen V SAND/SEL CR2 224 C5
Asheridge Rd CSHM HP5 50 E4
Asher Loftus Wy
FBAR/BDGN N11 98 A7
Asher Wy WAP E1W 13 P9
Ashfield Av BUSH WD23 74 A10
FELT TW13 175 J4
Ashfield Cl BECK BR3 182 F10
RCHPK/HAM TW10 177 K4
Ashfield Ct EA W5 * 135 K9
Ashfield La CHST BR7 184 F9
Ashfield Rd ACT W3 136 C10
CSHM HP5 51 J5
FSBYPK N4 119 K4
STHGT/OAK N14 98 D4
Ashfields GSTN WD25 72 G1
LOU IG10 82 C6
Ashfield St WCHPL E1 140 B7
Ashfield Yd WCHPL E1 * 140 B7
Ashford Av ASHF TW15 174 C9
BRW CM14 106 G4
CEND/HSY/T N8 118 F2
YEAD UB4 133 L8
Ashford Cl ASHF TW15 173 P7
WALTH E17 120 E4
Ashford Crs ASHF TW15 173 P6
PEND EN3 80 B6
Ashford Gdns COB KT11 235 L2
Ashford Gn OXHEY WD19 93 L6
Ashford La WDSR SL4 148 A1
Ashford Ms TOTM N17 99 P9
Ashford Rd ASHF TW15 174 D10
CRICK NW2 116 G9
EHAM E6 142 C1
FELT TW13 174 E7
IVER SL0 130 F3
STA TW18 195 N1
SWFD E18 101 N10
Ashford St IS N1 7 J9
Ash Gn DEN/HRF UB9 131 L1
Ash Gv ALP/SUD HA0 114 F9
AMS HP6 68 F2
CRICK NW2 116 G9
DEN/HRF UB9 91 N9
EA W5 155 K1
EBED/NFELT TW14 174 F4
EN EN1 99 M1
GUW GU2 249 M10
HACK E8 140 A3
HEST TW5 153 L7
HHS/BOV HP3 36 A10
HYS/HAR UB3 132 E9
PLMGR N13 99 K4
SLN SL2 129 L2
STA TW18 173 M9
STALE/WH AL4 21 H2
STHL UB1 133 P7
WDR/YW UB7 132 A9
WWKM BR4 205 H9
PGE/AN SE20 204 B2
Ashgrove RSEV TN14 * 245 P1
Ashgrove Rd ASHF TW15 174 D8
BMLY BR1 183 J9
GDMY/SEVK IG3 123 J6
SEV TN13 265 J4
Ash Groves SBW CM21 30 B1
Ash Hill Cl BUSH WD23 94 A2
Ash Hill Dr PIN HA5 113 K1
Ashingdon Cl CHING E4 101 H5
Ashington Rd FUL/PGN SW6 * 157 J8
Ash Keys CRAWE RH10 283 P8
Ashlake Rd STRHM/NOR SW16 180 F7
Ashland Pl MHST W1U 10 C3
Ash La WDSR SL4 148 C8
Ashlar Pl WOOL/PLUM SE18 162 E3
Ashlea Rd CFSP/GDCR SL9 90 B10
Ashleigh Av EGH TW20 172 F10
Ashleigh Cl HORL RH6 280 A4
Ashleigh Gdns SUT SM1 201 L9
UPMR RM14 126 C8
Ashleigh Rd MORT/ESHN SW14 156 B9
PGE/AN SE20 204 A3
Ashley Av BARK/HLT IG6 102 E10
EPSOM KT18 220 A9
MRDN SM4 201 K5
Ashley Cl GT/LBKH KT23 253 N1
HDN NW4 96 F10
HHS/BOV HP3 36 A8
PIN HA5 93 J10
SEV TN13 247 J10
WGCW AL8 22 F3
WOT/HER KT12 196 F8
Ashley Cottages ASHTD KT21 * 237 L5
Ashley Ct EPSOM KT18 220 A9
WOKN/KNAP GU21 * 231 L4
Ashley Crs BTSEA SW11 158 B9
WDGN N22 99 H10
Ashley Dr BNSTD SM7 221 K10
BORE WD6 75 P9
ISLW TW7 154 D5
WHTN TW2 176 A4
WOT/HER KT12 197 H10
Ashley Gdns CDW/CHF RM16 147 P10
ORP BR6 227 H2
PLMGR N13 99 K5
RCHPK/HAM TW10 177 J6
WBLY HA9 115 K7
Ashley Green Rd CSHM HP5 51 K2
Ashley La CROY/NA CR0 223 J1
HDN NW4 96 F10
MLHL NW7 96 F8
Ashley Park Av WOT/HER KT12 196 G9
Ashley Park Crs WOT/HER KT12 197 H8
Ashley Park Rd WOT/HER KT12 197 H10
Ashley Pl WEST SW1P 16 G4
Ashley Ri WOT/HER KT12 197 H10
Ashley Rd ARCH N19 118 F6
CHING E4 100 F7
DORK RH4 272 B3
EPSOM KT18 238 B1
EPSOM KT18 238 C3
FSTGT E7 141 P2
HERT/WAT SG14 25 H6
HOR/WEW KT19 220 A9
HPTN TW12 197 P1
PEND EN3 80 B6
RCH/KEW TW9 155 K9
SEV TN13 247 J10
STAL AL1 39 H6
THDIT KT7 198 E6
THHTH CR7 202 G4
TOTM N17 * 100 A10
TOTM N17 119 P1
UX/CGN UB8 131 L4
WIM/MER SW19 179 L9
WOKN/KNAP GU21 231 L4
WOT/HER KT12 197 H8
WOT/HER KT12 216 G1
Ashleys RKW/CH/CXG WD3 91 J1
Ashley Wy CHOB/PIR GU24 212 C9
Ashling Rd CROY/NA CR0 203 P8
Ashlin Rd SRTFD E15 121 J9
Ashlone Rd PUT/ROE SW15 156 F9
Ashlyn Cl BUSH WD23 73 M8
Ashlyn Gv EMPK RM11 125 L1
Ashlyns Ct BERK HP4 33 N6
Ashlyns La CHONG CM5 48 G7
Ashlyn's Pk COB KT11 217 M9
Ashlyns Rd BERK HP4 33 N6
EPP CM16 65 J6
Ashlyns Wy CHSGTN KT9 219 J3
Ashmead STHGT/OAK N14 78 D9
Ash Mead Dr DEN/HRF UB9 111 K7
Ashmead Ga BMLY BR1 205 P1
Ashmead La DEN/HRF UB9 111 K7
Ashmead Ms DEPT SE8 * 160 F7
Ashmead Pl AMSS HP7 69 P5
Ashmead Rd DEPT SE8 160 F8
EBED/NFELT TW14 175 H4
Ashmere Av BECK BR3 205 J2
Ashmere Cl CHEAM SM3 220 G2
Ashmere Gv BRXS/STRHM SW2 158 F10
Ash Ms EPSOM KT18 220 B10
KTTN NW5 * 118 D10
Ashmill St STJWD NW8 9 N3
Ashmole St VX/NE SW8 17 P10
Ashmore Cl PECK SE15 159 N6
Ashmore Gdns GVW DA11 190 A7
HHS/BOV HP3 36 C7
Ashmore Gv WELL DA16 162 G9
Ashmore La HAYES BR2 225 P7
Ashmore Rd MV/WKIL W9 2 C8
Ashmount Rd ARCH N19 118 D5
SEVS/STOTM N15 119 N3
Ashmount Ter EA W5 * 155 J3
Ashmour Gdns ROM RM1 104 E10
Ashneal Gdns HRW HA1 114 C8
Ashness Gdns GFD/PVL UB6 134 G1
Ashness Rd BTSEA SW11 180 A1
Ashotts La CSHM HP5 50 A1
Ash Platt Rd BGR/WK TN15 247 M7
Ash Ride ENC/FH EN2 79 H1
Ashridge Cl HHS/BOV HP3 52 D4
KTN/HRWW/WS HA3 115 H4
Ashridge Crs WOOL/PLUM SE18 162 F6
Ashridge Dr LCOL/BKTW AL2 55 M6
OXHEY WD19 93 K6
Ashridge Gdns PIN HA5 113 M2
PLMGR N13 98 F6
Ashridge La CSHM HP5 52 A7
Ashridge Ri BERK HP4 33 L4
Ashridge Wy MRDN SM4 201 J4
SUN TW16 175 H9
Ash Rd BGR/WK TN15 211 K10
BH/WHM TN16 262 G1
CHEAM SM3 201 H8
CHOB/PIR GU24 248 F2
CRAWE RH10 284 B5
CROY/NA CR0 204 F9
DART DA1 187 L4
GVE DA12 190 F7
HART DA3 211 K5
ORP BR6 227 K4
RDART DA2 187 N7
SHPTN TW17 196 B4
SRTFD E15 121 K10
WOKS/MYFD GU22 232 B6
Ash Rw HAYES BR2 206 D6
Ashtead Rd CLPT E5 119 P5
Ashtead Woods Rd ASHTD KT21 237 J2
Ashton Cl SUT SM1 221 K1
WOT/HER KT12 217 J3
Ashton Gdns CHDH RM6 123 P4
HSLWW TW4 153 N10
Ashton Rd HARH RM3 105 L9
PEND EN3 80 D2
SRTFD E15 121 J10
WOKN/KNAP GU21 231 L3
Ashton St POP/IOD E14 141 H9
Ashtree Av MTCM CR4 201 N2
Ash Tree Cl CROY/NA CR0 204 D6
Ashtree Cl ORP BR6 226 E1
Ash Tree Cl SURB KT6 199 K8
Ashtree Ct STAL AL1 38 E6
Ash Tree Dell CDALE/KGS NW9 115 P3
CDALE/KGS NW9 116 A3
Ash Tree Fld HLW CM20 28 D9
Ash Tree Rd WATN WD24 73 J2
Ash Tree Wy CROY/NA CR0 204 D5
Ashtree Wy HHW HP1 35 K7
Ashurst Cl DART DA1 164 G9
LHD/OX KT22 236 F7
NTHWD HA6 92 F8
PGE/AN SE20 204 A1
PUR/KEN CR8 241 L1
Ashurst Dr CRAWE RH10 284 E7
GNTH/NBYPK IG2 122 E4
KWD/TDW/WH KT20 255 N6
SHPTN TW17 195 P5
Ashurst Gdns
BRXS/STRHM SW2 * 181 H4
Ashurst Pk ASC SL5 * 192 C3
Ashurst Pl DORK RH4 273 H1
Ashurst Rd EBAR EN4 78 A9
KWD/TDW/WH KT20 238 E7
NFNCH/WDSPK N12 97 P6
Ashurst Wk CROY/NA CR0 204 A9
Ash V RKW/CH/CXG WD3 90 G6
Ashvale Dr UPMR RM14 126 D7
Ashvale Gdns CRW RM5 104 E6
UPMR RM14 126 D7
Ashvale Rd TOOT SW17 180 A8
Ashview Cl ASHF TW15 173 P9
Ashview Gdns ASHF TW15 173 P9
Ashville Rd WAN E11 121 J7
Ash Wk ALP/SUD HA0 115 H9
SOCK/AV RM15 147 J5
Ashwater Rd LEE/GVPK SE12 183 M4
Ashwell Cl EHAM E6 142 C8
Ashwell Pk HARP AL5 20 C2
Ashwells Rd BRWN CM15 86 E7
Ashwell St STALW/RED AL3 * 38 C5
Ashwells Wy CSTG HP8 89 P3
Ashwick Cl CTHM CR3 259 P1
Ashwin St HACK E8 7 L1
Ashwood WARL CR6 242 B6
Ashwood Av RAIN RM13 145 J5
UX/CGN UB8 132 B8
Ashwood Dr CSHM HP5 50 G6
Ashwood Gdns CROY/NA CR0 224 G3
HYS/HAR UB3 152 G3
Ashwood Ms STAL AL1 38 C8
Ashwood Pk LHD/OX KT22 236 B9
WOKS/MYFD GU22 232 D4
Ashwood Rd CHING E4 101 J4
EGH TW20 171 N9
POTB/CUF EN6 59 L10
WOKS/MYFD GU22 232 C4
Ashworth Cl CMBW SE5 159 L8
Ashworth Pl GUW GU2 * 249 L10
HLWE CM17 47 N1
Ashworth Rd MV/WKIL W9 3 H9
Askern Cl BXLYHS DA6 163 N10
Aske St IS N1 7 J9
Askew Crs SHB W12 156 C1
Askew Rd NTHWD HA6 92 E3
SHB W12 156 C1
Askews Farm La GRAYS RM17 167 K5
Askew Vls PLMGR N13 * 99 J4
Askham Rd SHB W12 136 D10
Askill Dr PUT/ROE SW15 179 H1
Askwith Rd RAIN RM13 144 E4
Asland Rd SRTFD E15 141 J3
Aslett St WAND/EARL SW18 179 L3
Asmara Rd CRICK NW2 117 H10
Asmar Cl COUL/CHIP CR5 240 F1
Asmuns Hl GLDGN NW11 117 K3

Asmuns Pl GLDGN NW11 117 J3
Asolando Dr WALW SE17 18 F7
Aspasia Cl STAL AL1 38 E7
Aspdin Rd GVW DA11 190 A6
Aspen Cl COB KT11 235 M2
EA W5 155 L1
ORP BR6 227 K2
RGUE GU4 250 G7
SLN SL2 128 G7
STA TW18 173 J6
SWLY BR8 208 E1
WDR/YW UB7 132 A10
Aspen Copse BMLY BR1 206 C2
Aspen Ct RBRW/HUT CM13 107 M4
Aspen Dr ALP/SUD HA0 114 F9
Aspen Gdns ASHF TW15 174 D8
MTCM CR4 202 B5
Aspen Gn ERITHM DA18 164 A2
Aspen Gv PIN HA5 112 G1
UPMR RM14 125 P9
Aspen La NTHLT UB5 133 M5
Aspenlea Rd HMSMTH W6 156 G5
Aspen Park Dr GSTN WD25 73 J1
Aspens WAB EN9 81 P1
Aspen V CTHM CR3 241 N4
Aspen Wy BNSTD SM7 220 G10
FELT TW13 175 J6
PEND EN3 80 C1
POP/IOD E14 141 H9
SOCK/AV RM15 147 J5
WGCE AL7 23 M6
Aspern Gv HAMP NW3 117 P10
Aspfield Rw HHW HP1 35 L4
Aspinall Rd BROCKY SE4 160 C9
Aspinden Rd BERM/RHTH SE16 160 A3
Aspley Rd WAND/EARL SW18 179 L1
Asplins Rd TOTM N17 99 P9
Asplins Vls TOTM N17 * 99 P9
Asprey Gv CTHM CR3 241 P10
Asprey Ms BECK BR3 204 E5
Asquith Cl BCTR RM8 123 M6
Assam St WCHPL E1 13 N5
Assembly Pas WCHPL E1 140 B7
Assembly Wk CAR SM5 201 P7
Assher Rd WOT/HER KT12 197 M10
Assheton Rd BEAC HP9 88 C7
Ass House La
KTN/HRWW/WS HA3 94 A5
Astall Cl KTN/HRWW/WS HA3 94 D9
Astbury Rd PECK SE15 160 B7
Astede Pl ASHTD KT21 237 L4
Astell St CHEL SW3 15 P7
The Asters CHESW EN7 61 L4
Asteys Rw IS N1 6 D4
Astleham Wy SHPTN TW17 195 P3
Astle St BTSEA SW11 158 B8
Astley GRAYS RM17 167 L5
Astley Av CRICK NW2 116 F10
Astley Rd HHW HP1 35 M6
Aston Av KTN/HRWW/WS HA3 115 H5
Aston Cl ASHTD KT21 237 H4
BUSH WD23 74 B10
SCUP DA14 185 K6
WATN WD24 73 K6
Aston Gn HSLWW TW4 153 K8
Aston Md WDSR SL4 148 D7
Astonplace STRHM/NOR SW16 181 J9
Aston Rd EA W5 135 J8
ESH/CLAY KT10 218 D2
RYNPK SW20 200 F2
Astons Rd NTHWD HA6 92 D5
Aston St POP/IOD E14 140 D8
Aston Ter BAL SW12 * 180 C2
Astonville St WAND/EARL SW18 179 K4
Aston Wy EPSOM KT18 238 C2
POTB/CUF EN6 59 N8
Astor Av ROMW/RG RM7 124 C4
Astor Cl ADL/WDHM KT15 215 N1
KUTN/CMB KT2 177 N9
Astoria Pde ASHF TW15 * 174 B7
STRHM/NOR SW16 * 180 F6
Astoria Wk BRXN/ST SW9 159 H9
Astra Cl HCH RM12 145 J1
Astra Dr GVE DA12 191 H8
Astrop Ms HMSMTH W6 156 F2
Astrop Ter HMSMTH W6 156 F2
Astwick Av HAT AL10 40 C1
Astwood Ms SKENS SW7 15 H5
Asylum Arch Rd REDH RH1 276 A3
Asylum Rd PECK SE15 160 A6
Atalanta Cl PUR/KEN CR8 223 H6
Atalanta St FUL/PGN SW6 156 G7
Atbara Rd TEDD TW11 176 G9
Atcham Rd HSLW TW3 154 B10
Atcost Rd BARK IG11 143 K7
Atfield Gv BFOR GU20 212 C3
Athelden Rd WAND/EARL SW18 179 M4
Athelney St CAT SE6 182 F6
Athelstan Cl CRAWE RH10 284 F7
HARH RM3 105 N9
Athelstane Gv BOW E3 140 E4
Athelstane Ms FSBYPK N4 119 H6
Athelstan Gdns
KIL/WHAMP NW6 * 2 B4
Athelstan Rd HARH RM3 105 N9
HHS/BOV HP3 35 P9
KUT/HW KT1 199 L4
Athelstan Wk North WGCE AL7 23 H6
Athelstan Wk South WGCE AL7 22 G6
Athelstan Wy STMC/STPC BR5 207 K1
Athelstone Rd
KTN/HRWW/WS HA3 94 C10
Athena Cl KUT/HW KT1 199 L3
RYLN/HDSTN HA2 114 C7
Athenaeum Pl MUSWH N10 118 C1
Athenaeum Rd TRDG/WHET N20 97 M2
Athena Pl NTHWD HA6 92 G9
Athenia Cl CHESW EN7 61 J5
Athenlay Rd PECK SE15 182 C1
Athens Gdns MV/WKIL W9 * 8 E2
Atherden Rd CLPT E5 120 B9
Atherfield Rd REIG RH2 275 M3
Atherfold Rd BRXN/ST SW9 158 F9
Atherley Wy HSLWW TW4 175 N3
Atherstone Ms SKENS SW7 15 K5
Atherton Cl RGUE GU4 268 B6
STWL/WRAY TW19 173 N2
Atherton Dr WIM/MER SW19 178 G7
Atherton Gdns CDW/CHF RM16 168 F3
Atherton Hts ALP/SUD HA0 135 H1
Atherton Ms FSTGT E7 141 L1
Atherton Pl RYLN/HDSTN HA2 114 B1
STHL UB1 133 P9
Atherton Rd BARN SW13 156 D6
CLAY IG5 102 B10
FSTGT E7 121 L10
Atherton St BTSEA SW11 157 P8
Athlone ESH/CLAY KT10 218 D3
Athlone Cl CLPT E5 120 A10
RAD WD7 * 74 G2
Athlone Ct WALTH E17 121 J1
Athlone Rd BRXS/STRHM SW2 180 G3
Athlone St KTTN NW5 4 D1
Athlon Rd ALP/SUD HA0 135 J4
Athol Cl PIN HA5 93 J9
Athole Gdns EN EN1 79 M9
Athol Gdns PIN HA5 93 J9
Atholl Rd GDMY/SEVK IG3 123 K5
Athol Rd ERITH DA8 164 D4
Athol Sq POP/IOD E14 141 H8
Athol Wy HGDN/ICK UB10 132 B5
Atkins Cl WOKN/KNAP GU21 231 M4
Atkins Dr WWKM BR4 205 J10
Atkinson Cl ORP BR6 227 K2
Atkinson Ct HORL RH6 * 280 C5
Atkinson Rd CAN/RD E16 141 P7
CRAWE RH10 284 D9
Atkins Rd BAL SW12 180 E3
LEY E10 120 G4
Atlanta Bvd ROM RM1 124 F4
Atlantic Cl SWCM DA10 189 K1
Atlantic Rd BRXN/ST SW9 159 H10
Atlantis Cl BARK IG11 143 L5
Atlas Gdns CHARL SE7 161 P3
Atlas Ms HACK E8 7 M1
Atlas Rd DART DA1 165 N9
FBAR/BDGN N11 98 B7
PLSTW E13 141 M4
WBLY HA9 115 P9
WLSDN NW10 136 B5
Atley Rd BOW E3 140 F3
Atlip Rd ALP/SUD HA0 135 K3
Atney Rd PUT/ROE SW15 157 H10
Atria Rd NTHWD HA6 93 H6
Attenborough Cl OXHEY WD19 93 M4
Atterbury Cl BH/WHM TN16 262 G2
Atterbury Rd FSBYPK N4 119 H4
Atterbury St WEST SW1P 17 K6
Attewood Av WLSDN NW10 116 B8
Attewood Rd NTHLT UB5 133 M1
Attfield Cl TRDG/WHET N20 97 N3
Attimore Cl WGCW AL8 22 E6
Attimore Rd WGCW AL8 22 E6
Attle Cl HGDN/ICK UB10 132 B4
Attlee Cl THHTH CR7 203 K6
YEAD UB4 * 133 J5
Attlee Ct GRAYS RM17 167 M2
Attlee Dr DART DA1 187 P1
Attlee Rd THMD SE28 143 L9
YEAD UB4 133 H5
Attlee Ter WALTH E17 120 G2
Attneave St CLKNW EC1R 12 A1
Attwood Cl SAND/SEL CR2 224 A10
Atwell Pl THDIT KT7 198 F8
Atwell Rd PECK SE15 * 159 P8
Atwood GT/LBKH KT23 235 M10
Atwood Av RCH/KEW TW9 155 M8
Atwood Rd HMSMTH W6 156 E3
Auber Cl HOD EN11 26 E10
Aubert Pk HBRY N5 119 J9
Aubert Rd HBRY N5 119 J9
Aubrey Av LCOL/BKTW AL2 57 H2
Aubrey Pl STJWD NW8 3 J8
Aubrey Rd CEND/HSY/T N8 * 118 F3
KENS W8 8 D10
WALTH E17 120 F1
Aubreys Rd HHW HP1 35 H7
Aubrey Wk KENS W8 8 D10
Aubrietia Cl HARH RM3 105 M9
Auburn Cl NWCR SE14 160 D6
Aubyn Hl WNWD SE27 181 K7
Aubyn Sq PUT/ROE SW15 178 D1
Auckland Av RAIN RM13 144 G5
Auckland Cl CRAWW RH11 283 N4
EN EN1 80 A3
NRWD SE19 203 N1
TIL RM18 168 D8
Auckland Gdns NRWD SE19 203 M1
Auckland Hl WNWD SE27 181 K7
Auckland Ri NRWD SE19 203 M1
Auckland Rd BTSEA SW11 157 P10
CTHM CR3 241 M8
IL IG1 122 E6
KUT/HW KT1 199 L4
LEY E10 120 G8
NRWD SE19 203 N1
POTB/CUF EN6 58 G8
Auckland St LBTH SE11 17 N8
Aucuba Vls WELL DA16 * 163 L9
Audax CDALE/KGS NW9 * 96 C10
Auden Dr BORE WD6 75 M9
Auden Pl CAMTN NW1 4 C5
CHEAM SM3 * 220 F1
Audleigh Pl CHIG IG7 102 D7
Audley Cl ADL/WDHM KT15 215 L2
BORE WD6 75 M7
BTSEA SW11 158 B9
MUSWH N10 98 C8
Audley Ct PIN HA5 93 K10
WAN E11 121 L2
Audley Dr CAN/RD E16 141 N10
WARL CR6 242 B1
Audley Firs WOT/HER KT12 217 J1
Audley Gdns GDMY/SEVK IG3 123 J7
LOU IG10 82 G6
WAB EN9 63 H10
Audley Pl BELMT SM2 221 L4
Audley Rd EA W5 135 L7
ENC/FH EN2 79 J6
HDN NW4 116 D4
RCHPK/HAM TW10 177 L1
Audley Sq MYFR/PKLN W1K * 10 D9
Audley St MYFR/PKLN W1K 10 D9
Audrey Cl BECK BR3 204 G6
Audrey Gdns ALP/SUD HA0 114 G7
Audrey Rd IL IG1 122 E8
Audric Cl KUTN/CMB KT2 199 M1
Audwick Cl CHES/WCR EN8 62 D4
Augur Cl STA TW18 173 J8
Augurs La PLSTW E13 141 N5
Augusta Cl E/WMO/HCT KT8 197 N3
Augusta Rd WHTN TW2 176 B5
August End DTCH/LGLY SL3 130 B8
Augustine Cl DTCH/LGLY SL3 151 H9
Augustine Ct WAB EN9 62 G9
Augustine Rd GVE DA12 190 G3
HMSMTH W6 156 G2
KTN/HRWW/WS HA3 94 A9
STMC/STPC BR5 207 N3
August La SHGR GU5 269 N10
Augustus Cl BTFD TW8 155 J6
SHB W12 156 E1
STALW/RED AL3 37 P8
STAN HA7 95 J4
Augustus Rd WIM/MER SW19 179 H4
Augustus St CAMTN NW1 4 F8
Aukingford Gdns CHONG CM5 67 N2
Aukingford Gn CHONG CM5 67 N3
Aultone Wy CAR SM5 202 A10
SUT SM1 201 M9
Aulton Pl LBTH SE11 18 B8
Aurelia Gdns CROY/NA CR0 202 G5
Aurelia Rd CROY/NA CR0 202 F6
Auriel Av DAGE RM10 144 E1
Auriga Ms IS N1 119 L10
Auriol Cl WPK KT4 200 B10
Auriol Dr GFD/PVL UB6 134 C2
HGDN/ICK UB10 132 C1
Auriol Park Rd WPK KT4 200 B10
Auriol Rd WKENS W14 14 A6
Aurum Cl HORL RH6 280 C5
Austell Gdns MLHL NW7 96 B4
Austen Cl LOU IG10 82 G7
SWCM DA10 * 189 H2
THMD SE28 143 L10
TIL RM18 168 F8
Austen Rd ERITH DA8 164 C6
GU GU1 268 C2
RYLN/HDSTN HA2 114 A7
Austenway CFSP/GDCR SL9 110 B1
Austenwood Cl CFSP/GDCR SL9 89 P10
Austenwood La CFSP/GDCR SL9 110 B1
Austin Av HAYES BR2 206 B6
Austin Cl COUL/CHIP CR5 241 J4
FSTH SE23 182 D3
TWK TW1 177 H1
Austin Friars OBST EC2N 13 H5
Austin Friars Sq OBST EC2N * 13 H5
Austin Rd BTSEA SW11 158 B7
GVW DA11 190 C4
HYS/HAR UB3 152 G1
STMC/STPC BR5 207 K6
Austins La HGDN/ICK UB10 112 D8
Austins Md HHS/BOV HP3 52 E4
Austins Pl HHNE HP2 35 N5
Austin St BETH E2 7 L10
Austin Vls GSTN WD25 * 55 J7
Austin Wy DTCH/LGLY SL3 150 C5
Austral Cl BFN/LL DA15 185 J6
Austral Dr EMPK RM11 125 L5
Australia Rd SHB W12 136 E9
SL SL1 149 N1
Austral St LBTH SE11 18 C5
Austyn Gdns BRYLDS KT5 * 199 N8
Autumn Cl CRAWW RH11 283 M8
EN EN1 80 A6
SL SL1 128 E10
WIM/MER SW19 179 M9
Autumn Dr BELMT SM2 221 L5
Autumn Glades HHS/BOV HP3 36 D8
Autumn Gv BMLY BR1 183 N9
WGCE AL7 23 L7
Autumn St BOW E3 140 F3
Avalon Cl ENC/FH EN2 79 H6
GSTN WD25 55 M8
ORP BR6 207 N9
RYNPK SW20 201 H2
WEA W13 134 F7
Avalon Rd FUL/PGN SW6 157 L7
ORP BR6 207 M9
WEA W13 134 F6
Avard Gdns ORP BR6 226 F1
Avarn Rd TOOT SW17 180 A9
Avebury SL SL1 128 F10
Avebury Ct HHNE HP2 36 B3
Avebury Pk SURB KT6 * 199 J6
Avebury Rd ORP BR6 206 G10
WAN E11 121 J6
WIM/MER SW19 201 J1
Avebury St IS N1 6 G6
Aveley By-Pass SOCK/AV RM15 146 B9
Aveley Cl ERITH DA8 164 G5
SOCK/AV RM15 146 C10
Aveley Rd UPMR RM14 146 A2
UPMR RM14 146 B4
Aveline St LBTH SE11 17 P7
Aveling Cl CRAWE RH10 284 D9
PUR/KEN CR8 222 G9
Aveling Park Rd WALTH E17 100 F10
Avelon Rd CRW RM5 104 E7
RAIN RM13 145 H3
Ave Marie La STP EC4M 12 D6
Avenell Rd HBRY N5 119 J8
Avening Rd WAND/EARL SW18 179 K3
Avening Ter WAND/EARL SW18 179 K2
Avenons Rd PLSTW E13 141 M7
Avenue All Hallows
WOKS/MYFD GU22 230 G8
Avenue All Saints
WOKS/MYFD GU22 230 G8
Avenue Ap KGLGY WD4 54 B6
Avenue C ADL/WDHM KT15 195 P10
Avenue Cl HARH RM3 105 N8
HEST TW5 153 J7
KWD/TDW/WH KT20 238 E8
STHGT/OAK N14 78 D10
STJWD NW8 3 P6
WDR/YW UB7 151 N2
Avenue Crs ACT W3 155 N1
HEST TW5 153 J7
Avenue De Cagny
CHOB/PIR GU24 230 E8
Avenue Dr DTCH/LGLY SL3 130 C7
Avenue Elmers SURB KT6 199 K5
Avenue Gdns ACT W3 155 N1
HEST TW5 * 153 H6
HORL RH6 280 D5
MORT/ESHN SW14 156 B9
SNWD SE25 203 P3
TEDD TW11 176 E10
Avenue Ga LOU IG10 81 P10
Avenue Ldg GRAYS RM17 * 167 N4
Avenue Ms MUSWH N10 118 C1
Avenue One ADL/WDHM KT15 215 P1
Avenue Pde SUN TW16 197 J3
WCHMH N21 * 99 L1
Avenue Park Rd WNWD SE27 181 J5
Avenue Ri BUSH WD23 73 P9
Avenue Rd ACT W3 155 N1
BELMT SM2 221 K6
BH/WHM TN16 244 B6
BNSTD SM7 239 L1
BRW CM14 107 H5
BTFD TW8 155 H4
BXLYHN DA7 163 P9
CHDH RM6 123 M5
COB KT11 235 L2
CTHM CR3 241 L8
EPP CM16 82 G2
EPSOM KT18 220 A10
ERITH DA8 164 D6
FELT TW13 174 G6
FSTGT E7 121 N10
HAMP NW3 3 L3
HARH RM3 105 N8
HGT N6 118 D5
HOD EN11 45 J5
HPTN TW12 198 A1
ISLW TW7 154 D7
KUT/HW KT1 199 K3
NFNCH/WDSPK N12 97 M5
NWMAL KT3 200 B3
PGE/AN SE20 204 B1
PIN HA5 113 M1
SEV TN13 247 K10
SEVS/STOTM N15 119 L3
SNWD SE25 203 P2
STA TW18 172 G8
STAL AL1 38 D5
STHGT/OAK N14 98 D1
STHL UB1 133 N10
STRHM/NOR SW16 202 E2
TEDD TW11 176 F10
WFD IG8 101 P7
WLGTN SM6 222 D4
WLSDN NW10 136 C4
Avenue St Andrew
CHOB/PIR GU24 230 G7
Avenue St Barnabas
CHOB/PIR GU24 230 G8
Avenue St Bartholomew
WOKS/MYFD GU22 231 H8
Avenue St Chad
WOKS/MYFD GU22 231 H8
Avenue St David
WOKS/MYFD GU22 230 G8
Avenue St George
WOKS/MYFD GU22 230 G8
Avenue St Margaret
WOKS/MYFD GU22 230 G8
Avenue St Mark CHOB/PIR GU24 230 G8
WOKS/MYFD GU22 231 H8
Avenue St Saviour
CHOB/PIR GU24 230 G7
Avenue South BRYLDS KT5 199 L7
Avenue Ter NWMAL KT3 199 P3
OXHEY WD19 73 M10
The Avenue ADL/WDHM KT15 215 K6
AMSS HP7 69 H4
BAR EN5 77 H7
BECK BR3 204 G1
BELMT SM2 221 J5
BH/WHM TN16 244 D9
BMLY BR1 206 A3
BRKHM/BTCW RH3 255 M10
BRYLDS KT5 199 L6
BUSH WD23 73 N8
BXLY DA5 185 N3
CAR SM5 222 B4
CEND/HSY/T N8 119 H1
CHING E4 101 J7
CHOB/PIR GU24 213 L5
CHSWK W4 156 B2
CLAP SW4 158 B10
COUL/CHIP CR5 240 E1
CROY/NA CR0 203 M10
CTHM CR3 241 P5
DTCH/LGLY SL3 149 N7
EGH TW20 172 E7
ESH/CLAY KT10 218 D3
EW KT17 220 F4
FBAR/BDGN N11 98 C6
GNWCH SE10 161 J6
GVW DA11 190 D4
HCH RM12 125 L7
HERT/WAT SG14 25 J3
HEST TW5 153 H7
HGDN/ICK UB10 112 C8
HHW HP1 35 H5
HOD EN11 44 E5
HORL RH6 280 A5
HPTN TW12 175 N9
HSLW TW3 176 A1
KIL/WHAMP NW6 137 H3
KTN/HRWW/WS HA3 94 E9
KWD/TDW/WH KT20 238 E8
LHD/OX KT22 218 E8
LOU IG10 82 B10
MUSWH N10 98 D10
NTHWD HA6 92 D7
ORP BR6 207 J9
PIN HA5 93 N7
PIN HA5 113 N4
POTB/CUF EN6 59 J6
RAD WD7 56 F10
RBRW/HUT CM13 107 K7
RCH/KEW TW9 155 L8
REDH RH1 276 F3
RGUW GU3 249 K3
RGUW GU3 267 H8
ROM RM1 124 E2
SLN SL2 108 G10
STA TW18 195 L1
STMC/STPC BR5 185 L10
STWL/WRAY TW19 150 A9
SUN TW16 197 J2
SWCM DA10 166 G10
TOTM N17 99 N10
TWK TW1 176 G2
UX/CGN UB8 131 N6
WAB EN9 63 P1
WAN E11 121 N4
WAT WD17 73 H6
WBLY HA9 115 L7
WDSR SL4 171 N2
WEA W13 134 G9
WPK KT4 200 C9
WWKM BR4 205 J7
Avenue Three ADL/WDHM KT15 195 P10
Avenue Two ADL/WDHM KT15 215 P1
Averil Ct MDHD SL6 128 B8
Averil Gv STRHM/NOR SW16 181 J9
Averill St HMSMTH W6 156 G5
Avern Gdns E/WMO/HCT KT8 198 A4
Avern Rd E/WMO/HCT KT8 198 A4
Avery Farm Rw BGVA SW1W * 16 E6
Avery Gdns GNTH/NBYPK IG2 122 C3
Avery Hill Rd ELTH/MOT SE9 184 F4
Avery Rw MYFR/PKLN W1K 10 E7
Avery Wy DART DA1 187 N5
Avey La LOU IG10 81 M4
Avia Cl HHS/BOV HP3 35 N10
Aviary Cl CAN/RD E16 141 L7
Aviary Rd WOKS/MYFD GU22 233 K2
Aviemore Cl BECK BR3 204 E5
Aviemore Wy BECK BR3 204 D5
Avignon Rd BROCKY SE4 160 C9
Avington Cl GU GU1 250 B10
Avington Gv PGE/AN SE20 182 B10
Avington Wy PECK SE15 * 159 N6
Avion Crs CDALE/KGS NW9 96 D10
Avior Dr NTHWD HA6 92 G5
Avis Sq WCHPL E1 140 C8
Avoca Rd TOOT SW17 180 B7
Avocet Cl STALW/RED AL3 38 B3
STHWK SE1 19 N7
Avocet Ms THMD SE28 162 G2
Avon Cl ADL/WDHM KT15 215 K3
GSTN WD25 55 K10
GVE DA12 190 G5
SL SL1 128 D9
SUT SM1 221 M1
WPK KT4 200 D9
YEAD UB4 133 K6
Avon Ct PIN HA5 * 93 P8
Avondale Av CRICK NW2 116 B8
EBAR EN4 98 A2
ESH/CLAY KT10 198 F10
NFNCH/WDSPK N12 97 L6
STA TW18 173 J10
WPK KT4 200 C8
Avondale Cl HORL RH6 280 A2
LOU IG10 102 C1
WOT/HER KT12 217 K2
Avondale Ct SWFD E18 101 N9
Avondale Crs PEND EN3 80 D7
REDBR IG4 122 A3
Avondale Dr HYS/HAR UB3 133 H10
LOU IG10 82 C10
Avondale Est STHWK SE1 19 N7
Avondale Gdns HSLWW TW4 175 N1
Avondale Park Gdns NTGHL W11 8 A8
Avondale Park Rd NTGHL W11 8 A7
Avondale Pavement STHWK SE1 19 N8
Avondale Ri PECK SE15 159 N9
Avondale Rd ASHF TW15 173 N6
BMLY BR1 183 L9
CAN/RD E16 141 K7
ELTH/MOT SE9 184 B6
FNCH N3 97 M9
KTN/HRWW/WS HA3 114 E1
MORT/ESHN SW14 156 A9
PLMGR N13 99 H3
SAND/SEL CR2 223 K3
SEVS/STOTM N15 119 J3
WALTH E17 120 F5
WELL DA16 163 M8
WIM/MER SW19 179 L8
Avondale Sq STHWK SE1 19 N8
Avon Gn SOCK/AV RM15 146 G8
Avonley Rd NWCR SE14 160 B6
Avonmead WOKN/KNAP GU21 231 P4
Avon Ms PIN HA5 93 N9
Avonmore Av GU GU1 250 C9
Avonmore Gdns WKENS W14 14 C5
Avonmore Pl WKENS W14 14 B5
Avonmore Rd WKENS W14 14 C5
Avonmouth Rd DART DA1 187 L1
Avonmouth St STHWK SE1 18 E3
Avon Rd BROCKY SE4 160 F9
GFD/PVL UB6 133 P6
SUN TW16 174 G10
UPMR RM14 126 C4
WALTH E17 121 J1
Avon Sq HHNE HP2 36 A1
Avonstowe Cl ORP BR6 206 F10
Avontar Rd SOCK/AV RM15 146 G6
Avon Wk CRAWW RH11 283 J8
Avon Wy SWFD E18 121 M2
Avonwick Rd HSLW TW3 154 A8
Avril Wy CHING E4 101 J6
Avro Wy BF/WBF KT14 215 P6
WLGTN SM6 222 F4
Awberry Ct WATW WD18 * 72 E10
Awlfield Av TOTM N17 99 L9
Awliscombe Rd WELL DA16 163 J8
Axeholm Av EDGW HA8 95 N9
Axes La REDH RH1 276 D7
Axe St BARK IG11 142 F3
Axholme Av EDGW HA8 95 M9
Axis Ct GNWCH SE10 161 K5
Axminster Crs WELL DA16 163 M7
Axminster Rd HOLWY N7 118 F8
Axon Pl IL IG1 122 F7
Axtaine Rd STMC/STPC BR5 207 N7
Axtane MEO DA13 * 189 L10
Axtane Cl EYN DA4 210 B2
Axwood EPSOM KT18 237 P1
Aybrook St MHST W1U 10 C4
Aycliff Ct KUT/HW KT1 * 199 M2
Aycliffe Cl BMLY BR1 206 C4
Aycliffe Dr HHNE HP2 35 P2
Aycliffe Rd BORE WD6 75 L5
SHB W12 136 C10
Ayebridges Av EGH TW20 172 F10
Ayelands HART DA3 211 K9
Ayelands La HART DA3 211 K9
Aylands Cl WBLY HA9 115 K7
Aylands Rd PEND EN3 80 C2
Aylesbury Cl FSTGT E7 141 L1
Aylesbury Crs SL SL1 129 J8
Aylesbury End BEAC HP9 88 D10
Aylesbury Est WALW SE17 19 J8
Aylesbury Rd HAYES BR2 205 M3
WALW SE17 19 H8
Aylesbury St CLKNW EC1R 12 C2
WLSDN NW10 116 A8
Aylesford Av BECK BR3 204 D5
Aylesford St PIM SW1V 17 J7
Aylesham Cl MLHL NW7 96 D8
Aylesham Rd ORP BR6 207 H7
Ayles Rd YEAD UB4 133 J5
Aylestone Av KIL/WHAMP NW6 136 G2
Aylesworth Av SLN SL2 128 G5
Aylesworth Sp WDSR SL4 171 N3
Aylets Fld HLWS CM18 47 H4
Aylett Rd ISLW TW7 154 D8
SNWD SE25 204 A4
UPMR RM14 126 B7
Ayley Cft EN EN1 79 P9
Ayliffe Cl KUT/HW KT1 199 M2
Aylmer Cl STAN HA7 94 F5
Aylmer Dr STAN HA7 94 F5
Aylmer Pde EFNCH N2 * 118 A3
Aylmer Rd BCTR RM8 123 P8
EFNCH N2 117 P3
SHB W12 156 B1
WAN E11 121 L6
Ayloffe Rd DAGW RM9 144 A1
Ayloffs Cl EMPK RM11 125 M2
Ayloff's Wk EMPK RM11 125 M3
Aylsham Dr HGDN/ICK UB10 112 D7
Aylsham La HARH RM3 105 K5
Aylsham Rd HOD EN11 45 H2
Aylton Est BERM/RHTH SE16 * 160 B1
Aylward Gdns CSHM HP5 50 F6
Aylward Rd FSTH SE23 182 C5
RYNPK SW20 201 J2
Aylwards Ri STAN HA7 94 F5
Aylward St WCHPL E1 * 140 B8
Aymer Cl STA TW18 195 H1
Aymer Dr STA TW18 195 H1
Aynhoe Rd WKENS W14 156 G3
Aynho St WATW WD18 73 J9
Aynscombe Angle ORP BR6 207 K7
Aynsley Gdns HLWE CM17 47 M1
Ayot Gn WLYN AL6 22 C4
Ayot Little Green La WLYN AL6 22 C2
Ayres Cl PLSTW E13 141 M5
Ayres Crs WLSDN NW10 136 A2
Ayres End La HARP AL5 20 C7
Ayres St STHWK SE1 18 F1
Ayr Gn ROM RM1 104 F9
Ayron Rd SOCK/AV RM15 146 G6
Ayrsome Rd STNW/STAM N16 119 M8
Ayrton Rd SKENS SW7 15 L3
Ayr Wy ROM RM1 104 F9
Aysgarth Cl HARP AL5 20 A3
Aysgarth Rd DUL SE21 181 L2
Aytoun Pl BRXN/ST SW9 158 G8
Aytoun Rd BRXN/ST SW9 158 G8
Azalea Cl HNWL W7 134 E10
IL IG1 122 E10
LCOL/BKTW AL2 57 H3
Azalea Ct WFD IG8 * 101 K8
WOKS/MYFD GU22 232 A5
Azalea Dr SWLY BR8 208 E4
Azalea Wk PIN HA5 113 J4
Azalea Wy DTCH/LGLY SL3 130 B8
Azania Ms KTTN NW5 4 E1
Azenby Rd PECK SE15 159 N8
Azof St GNWCH SE10 161 K3

B

Baalbec Rd HBRY N5 119 J10
Baas Hl BROX EN10 44 C7
Baas Hill Cl BROX EN10 44 D7
Baas La BROX EN10 44 D7
Babbacombe Cl CHSGTN KT9 219 J2
Babbacombe Gdns REDBR IG4 122 B2
Babbacombe Rd BMLY BR1 205 N1
Baber Bridge Pde
EBED/NFELT TW14 * 175 K2
Baber Dr EBED/NFELT TW14 175 K2
Babington Ri WBLY HA9 135 M1
Babington Rd BCTR RM8 123 M10
HCH RM12 125 J6
HDN NW4 116 E2
STRHM/NOR SW16 180 E8
Babmaes St STJS SW1Y 11 J9
Babylon La KWD/TDW/WH KT20 257 L3
Bachelors Acre WDSR SL4 149 J7
Bachelor's La RPLY/SEND GU23 234 B10
Bache's St IS N1 7 H10
Back Church La WCHPL E1 13 N6
Back Gn WOT/HER KT12 217 K3
Back Hl CLKNW EC1R 12 B2
Back La BGR/WK TN15 247 P10
BTFD TW8 155 J6
BXLY DA5 186 B3
CDW/CHF RM16 167 H1
CEND/HSY/T N8 118 F3
CHDH RM6 123 N5
EDGW HA8 95 P9
GSTN WD25 74 D5
HAMP NW3 117 M9
PUR RM19 166 D3
RBSF CM22 30 D3
RCHPK/HAM TW10 177 H6
RGUE GU4 251 N7
RSEV TN14 264 C4
SEV TN13 246 E10
WAB EN9 45 P9
WLYN AL6 23 P1
WTHK RM20 166 G2
Backley Gdns CROY/NA CR0 203 P6
Back Rd SCUP DA14 185 K7
TEDD TW11 176 D10
The Backs CSHM HP5 51 H7
The Back BERK HP4 34 E2
Bacon Gv STHWK SE1 19 L5
Bacon La CDALE/KGS NW9 115 N3
EDGW HA8 95 M9
Bacon Link CRW RM5 104 C7
Bacons Dr POTB/CUF EN6 60 F4
Bacon's La HGT N6 118 B6
Baconsmead DEN/HRF UB9 111 K7
Bacon St BETH E2 13 M1
Bacton St BETH E2 140 B5
Badburgham Ct WAB EN9 63 L9
Baddeley Cl PEND EN3 80 F3
Baddow Cl DAGE RM10 144 B3
WFD IG8 102 A7
Baden Cl STA TW18 173 K10
Baden Dr HORL RH6 279 P3
Baden Pl STHWK SE1 18 G1
Baden Powell Cl DAGW RM9 143 P3
SURB KT6 199 L9
Baden Powell Rd SEV TN13 246 F8
Baden Rd CEND/HSY/T N8 118 E2
GUW GU2 249 N8
IL IG1 122 E10
Bader Cl PUR/KEN CR8 241 L1
WGCE AL7 23 M5
Bader Gdns SL SL1 148 F1
Bader Wk GVW DA11 190 B6
Bader Wy RAIN RM13 145 H1
Badger Cl FELT TW13 175 J6
GUW GU2 249 N7
HSLWW TW4 153 K9
Badgers Cl ASHF TW15 * 174 A8
BORE WD6 * 75 L6
ENC/FH EN2 79 J7
GODL GU7 267 J9
HERT/BAY SG13 26 A5
HRW HA1 114 C4
HYS/HAR UB3 132 F10
WOKN/KNAP GU21 231 P4
Badgers Copse ORP BR6 207 J9
WPK KT4 200 C9
Badgers Ct WPK KT4 * 200 C9
Badgers Cft BROX EN10 44 D7
ELTH/MOT SE9 184 D6
HHNE HP2 36 E7
TRDG/WHET N20 97 H2
Badgers Hl VW GU25 193 P5
Badgers La WARL CR6 242 B5
Badgers Mt CDW/CHF RM16 168 C1
Badgers Ri RSEV TN14 228 B6
Badgers Rd RSEV TN14 228 D6
Badgers Wk CTHM CR3 241 N4
NWMAL KT3 200 B2
PUR/KEN CR8 222 D7
RKW/CH/CXG WD3 71 J8
Badgers Wd CTHM CR3 259 K1
SLN SL2 109 J10
Badger Wy HAT AL10 40 E6
Badingham Dr LHD/OX KT22 236 D10
Badlis Rd WALTH E17 100 F10
Badlow Cl ERITH DA8 164 F6
Badminton Cl BORE WD6 75 M6
HRW HA1 * 114 D2
NTHLT UB5 133 P1
Badminton Ms CAN/RD E16 141 M10
Badminton Pl BROX EN10 44 D6
Badminton Rd BAL SW12 180 B2
Badsworth Rd CMBW SE5 159 K6
Bafton Ga HAYES BR2 205 N8
Bagden Hl RDKG RH5 254 C6
Bagley Cl WDR/YW UB7 151 P1
Bagley House
WOOL/PLUM SE18 * 162 B6
Bagley's La FUL/PGN SW6 157 M7
Bagleys Spring CHDH RM6 123 P2
Bagot Cl ASHTD KT21 237 L2
Bagshot Ct WOOL/PLUM SE18 * 162 D7
Bagshot Rd ASC SL5 192 A8
CHOB/PIR GU24 212 G7
EGH TW20 171 P10
EN EN1 99 N1
WOKN/KNAP GU21 230 G5
Bagshot St WALW SE17 19 K8
Bahram Rd HOR/WEW KT19 220 A6
Baigents La BFOR GU20 212 C3
Baildon St DEPT SE8 160 E6
Bailes La RGUW GU3 248 C9
Bailey Cl FBAR/BDGN N11 98 F8
PUR RM19 166 C3
THMD SE28 143 H10
WDSR SL4 148 F8
Bailey Cottages POP/IOD E14 * 140 D7
Bailey Crs CHSGTN KT9 219 J4
Bailey House
WOOL/PLUM SE18 * 162 B6
Bailey Ms BRXS/STRHM SW2 181 H1
CHSWK W4 155 N5
Bailey Pl SYD SE26 182 B9
Bailey Rd DORK RH4 272 B3
Baillie Cl RAIN RM13 145 J6
Baillie Rd GU GU1 268 C1
Bainbridge Cl RCHPK/HAM TW10 177 K8
Bainbridge Rd DAGW RM9 124 A9
Bainbridge St NOXST/BSQ WC1A 11 K5
Baines Cl SAND/SEL CR2 223 L2
Bainton Md WOKN/KNAP GU21 231 M3
Baird Av STHL UB1 134 A9
Baird Cl BUSH WD23 74 A10
CDALE/KGS NW9 115 P4
CRAWE RH10 284 B4
LEY E10 120 F6
SL SL1 148 G1
Baird Dr RGUW GU3 248 G9
Baird Gdns NRWD SE19 181 M7
Baird Memorial Cottages
STHGT/OAK N14 * 98 E3
Baird Rd EN EN1 80 A8
Baird St STLK EC1Y 12 F1
Bairstow Cl BORE WD6 75 K5
Baizdon Rd BKHTH/KID SE3 161 K8
Bakeham La EGH TW20 171 P10
Bakehouse Rd HORL RH6 280 A2
Baker Cl CRAWE RH10 283 N9
Baker Crs DART DA1 187 L3
Baker Hill Cl GVW DA11 190 C7
Baker La MTCM CR4 202 B2
Baker Ms ORP BR6 227 J3
Baker Rd WLSDN NW10 136 B3
WOOL/PLUM SE18 162 B6
Bakers Av WALTH E17 120 G4
Bakers Cl DART DA1 187 L3
PUR/KEN CR8 223 K10
STAL AL1 38 F7
Bakerscroft CHES/WCR EN8 * 62 C4
Bakers End RYNPK SW20 201 H2
Bakers Fld HOLWY N7 118 F9
Bakers Gdns CAR SM5 201 P9
Bakers Gv WGCE AL7 23 M4
Bakers Hl BAR EN5 77 L6
CLPT E5 120 A6
Bakers La EPP CM16 65 J6
Bakers Md GDST RH9 260 B6
Bakers Meadow BRWN CM15 87 H3
Baker's Ms MHST W1U 10 C5
Bakers Rents BETH E2 7 L9
Bakers Rd CHESW EN7 62 A6
UX/CGN UB8 131 N2
Baker's Rw CLKNW EC1R 12 A2
SRTFD E15 141 K4
Baker St BAR EN5 77 H1
CAMTN NW1 10 B2
EN EN1 79 L6
HERT/BAY SG13 25 M5
MHST W1U 10 C4
POTB/CUF EN6 59 J9
WEY KT13 216 B1
Bakers Wd DEN/HRF UB9 110 G6
Baker's Yd CLKNW EC1R 12 A2
Bakery Cl BRXN/ST SW9 * 158 G6
HLWW/ROY CM19 45 P1
Bakery Pl BTSEA SW11 158 A10
Bakewell Wy NWMAL KT3 200 B2
Balaams La STHGT/OAK N14 98 E3
Balaam St PLSTW E13 141 M5
Balaclava Rd STHWK SE1 19 M6
SURB KT6 199 H7
Bala Gn CDALE/KGS NW9 * 116 B4
Balantyne Cl ELTH/MOT SE9 184 B7
Balcary Gdns BERK HP4 33 K6
Balcaskie Rd ELTH/MOT SE9 184 C1
Balchier Rd EDUL SE22 182 A2
Balchins La DORK RH4 271 P3
Balcombe Cl BXLYHS DA6 163 N10
Balcombe Gdns HORL RH6 280 D5
Balcombe Rd CRAWE RH10 284 E6
HORL RH6 280 C3
Balcombe St CAMTN NW1 10 A1
Balcon Wy BORE WD6 75 P5
Balcorne St HOM E9 140 B2
Balder Ri LEE/GVPK SE12 183 N5
Balderton St MYFR/PKLN W1K 10 D6
Baldocks Rd EPP CM16 83 H1
Baldock St BOW E3 140 G4
WARE SG12 26 C1
Baldock Wy BORE WD6 75 L5
Baldry Gdns STRHM/NOR SW16 180 F9
Baldwin Cl CRAWE RH10 * 284 D10
Baldwin Crs CMBW SE5 159 K7
RGUE GU4 250 F8
Baldwin Gdns HSLW TW3 154 B7
Baldwin Rd BEAC HP9 88 G10
SL SL1 128 B5
Baldwins WGCE AL7 23 L5
Baldwin's Gdns FSBYW WC1X 12 A3
Baldwin's Hl LOU IG10 82 C5
Baldwins La RKW/CH/CXG WD3 72 C8
Baldwin's Shore WDSR SL4 149 J5
Baldwin St FSBYE EC1V 6 G10
Baldwin Ter IS N1 6 E7
Baldwyn Gdns ACT W3 135 P9
Baldwyn's Pk BXLY DA5 186 E5
Baldwyn's Rd BXLY DA5 186 E5
Bale Rd WCHPL E1 140 D7
Bales Ter ED N9 * 99 N4
Balfern Gv CHSWK W4 156 B4
Balfern St BTSEA SW11 157 P8
Balfe St IS N1 5 M8
Balfont Cl SAND/SEL CR2 223 P9
Balfour Av HNWL W7 134 E10
WOKS/MYFD GU22 232 B8
Balfour Gv TRDG/WHET N20 98 A4
Balfour Ms ED N9 99 P4
HHS/BOV HP3 52 C3
MYFR/PKLN W1K 10 D9
Balfour Pl MYFR/PKLN W1K 10 D8
PUT/ROE SW15 156 E10
Balfour Rd ACT W3 135 P7

CAR SM5 222 A4
GRAYS RM17 167 P3
HAYES BR2 206 A5
HBRY N5 119 K9
HRW HA1 114 C3
HSLW TW3 154 A9
IL IG1 122 E7
NWDGN UB2 153 L2
SNWD SE25 203 P4
WEA W13 154 G1
WEY KT13 216 A1
WIM/MER SW19 179 L10
Balfour St HERT/WAT SG14 25 K4
STHWK SE1 18 G5
Balgonie Rd CHING E4 101 J3
Balgores Crs GPK RM2 125 J1
Balgores La GPK RM2 125 J2
Balgores Sq GPK RM2 125 J2
Balgowan Cl NWMAL KT3 200 B4
Balgowan Rd BECK BR3 204 E3
Balgowan St WOOL/PLUM SE18 163 J3
Balham Gv BAL SW12 180 B3
Balham High Rd BAL SW12 180 C3
Balham Hl BAL SW12 180 C3
Balham Park Rd BAL SW12 180 A4
Balham Rd ED N9 99 P3
Balham Station Rd BAL SW12 180 B4
Balkan Wk WAP E1W * 140 A9
Balladier Wk POP/IOD E14 140 G7
Ballamore Rd BMLY BR1 183 M6
Ballance Rd HOM E9 140 C1
The Ballands North
LHD/OX KT22 236 D8
The Ballands' South
LHD/OX KT22 236 D9
Ballantine St WAND/EARL SW18 157 M10
Ballantyne Dr
KWD/TDW/WH KT20 239 J7
Ballard Cl KUTN/CMB KT2 178 A10
Ballard Gn WDSR SL4 148 D6
Ballards Cl DAGE RM10 144 D2
Ballards Farm Rd CROY/NA CR0 224 A3
SAND/SEL CR2 224 A3
Ballards Gn KWD/TDW/WH KT20 239 H5
Ballards La FNCH N3 97 L8
OXTED RH8 261 P5
Ballards Ms EDGW HA8 95 M7
Ballards Ri SAND/SEL CR2 223 P3
Ballards Rd CRICK NW2 116 D7
DAGE RM10 144 D2
Ballards Wy CROY/NA CR0 224 B3
SAND/SEL CR2 223 P3
Ballast Quay GNWCH SE10 161 J4
Ballater Cl OXHEY WD19 93 K5
Ballater Rd BRXS/STRHM SW2 158 F10
SAND/SEL CR2 223 N2
Ballencrieff Rd ASC SL5 192 E7
Ballina St FSTH SE23 182 C3
Ballingdon Rd BTSEA SW11 180 B2
Ballinger Ct BERK HP4 33 N6
Ballinger Wy NTHLT UB5 133 M6
Balliol Av CHING E4 101 J5
Balliol Cl CRAWE RH10 284 D4
Balliol Rd NKENS W10 136 F8
TOTM N17 99 M9
WELL DA16 163 L8
Balloch Rd CAT SE6 183 J4
Ballogie Av WLSDN NW10 116 B9
Ballow Cl CMBW SE5 * 159 L6
Ball's Pond Pl IS N1 * 7 H1
Balls Pond Rd IS N1 7 J1
Balmain Cl EA W5 135 J10
Balmer Rd BOW E3 140 E4
Balmes Rd IS N1 7 H5
Balmoral Av BECK BR3 204 D4
FBAR/BDGN N11 98 B7
Balmoral Cl CHES/WCR EN8 62 C10
PUT/ROE SW15 * 178 G2
SL SL1 128 D8
Balmoral Crs E/WMO/HCT KT8 197 P3
Balmoral Dr BORE WD6 76 A8
STHL UB1 133 N6
WOKS/MYFD GU22 232 F2
YEAD UB4 132 F6
YEAD UB4 133 H7
Balmoral Gdns BXLY DA5 186 A3
SAND/SEL CR2 223 L6
WDSR SL4 149 J9
WEA W13 154 F2
Balmoral Gv HOLWY N7 5 N2
Balmoral Ms SHB W12 156 C2
Balmoral Rd ABLGY WD5 55 H8
BRWN CM15 86 G10
CRICK NW2 136 E1
EYN DA4 187 P10
EYN DA4 188 A10
FSTGT E7 121 P9
HCH RM12 125 L8
KUT/HW KT1 199 L4
LEY E10 120 G7
PEND EN3 80 C2
RYLN/HDSTN HA2 113 P9
WATN WD24 73 K4
WPK KT4 200 E10
Balmoral Wy BELMT SM2 221 K6
Balmore Crs EBAR EN4 78 B9
Balmore St ARCH N19 118 C7
Balmuir Gdns PUT/ROE SW15 156 F10
Balnacraig Av WLSDN NW10 116 B9
Balquhain Cl ASHTD KT21 237 J3
Balsams Cl HERT/BAY SG13 25 L7
Baltic Cl WIM/MER SW19 179 N10
Baltic Pl IS N1 7 K5
Baltic St East STLK EC1Y 12 E2
Baltic St West FARR EC1M 12 E2
Baltimore Pl WELL DA16 163 J8
Balvaird Pl PIM SW1V 17 K8
Balvernie Gv WAND/EARL SW18 179 J3
Bamber Rd PECK SE15 159 N7
Bamborough Gdns SHB W12 156 F1
Bamford Av ALP/SUD HA0 135 L3
Bamford Rd BMLY BR1 183 J8
Bamford Wy CRW RM5 104 C6
Bampfylde Cl WLGTN SM6 202 D10
Bampton Dr MLHL NW7 96 D8
Bampton Rd FSTH SE23 182 C6
HARH RM3 105 M9
Bampton Wy WOKN/KNAP GU21 231 M4
Bamville Wd HARP AL5 * 20 B6
Banavie Gdns BECK BR3 204 G1
Banbury Av SL SL1 128 E7
Banbury Cl ENC/FH EN2 79 J5
Banbury Ct BELMT SM2 * 221 K4
COVGDN WC2E * 11 L7
Banbury Rd HOM E9 140 C2
WALTH E17 100 D8
Banbury St BTSEA SW11 * 157 P8
WATW WD18 73 H9
Banbury Vls MEO DA13 189 L9
Banchory Rd BKHTH/KID SE3 161 N6
Bankside HART DA3 211 K4
Bancroft Av EFNCH N2 117 P3
Bancroft Cha HCH RM12 124 G7
Bancroft Cl ASHF TW15 * 174 B8
Bancroft Ct NTHLT UB5 133 K3
REIG RH2 257 L10
Bancroft Gdns
KTN/HRWW/WS HA3 94 B9
ORP BR6 207 J8
Bancroft Rd CRAWE RH10 284 E8
KTN/HRWW/WS HA3 94 B10
REIG RH2 257 K10
WCHPL E1 140 B6
Banders Ri GU GU1 250 F9
Band La EGH TW20 172 C8
Bandon Cl HGDN/ICK UB10 132 A4
Bandon Ri WLGTN SM6 222 E3
Banes Down WAB EN9 45 K8
Banfield Rd PECK SE15 160 A10
Bangalore St PUT/ROE SW15 156 F9
Bangor Cl NTHLT UB5 114 A10
Bangors Cl IVER SL0 131 J8
Bangors Pk IVER SL0 * 131 H6
Bangors Rd North IVER SL0 130 G4
Bangors Rd South IVER SL0 131 H6
Banim St HMSMTH W6 156 E3
Banister Rd NKENS W10 136 G5
Bank Av MTCM CR4 201 N2
Bank Buildings CHING E4 * 101 J7
Bank End STHWK SE1 12 F9
Bankfoot GRAYS RM17 167 L3
Bankfoot Rd BMLY BR1 183 K7
Bank Gn CSHM HP5 32 B9
Bankhurst Rd CAT SE6 182 E3
Bank La BGR/WK TN15 265 P8
CRAWE RH10 283 N7
KUTN/CMB KT2 177 K10
PUT/ROE SW15 178 B1
Bank Ms SUT SM1 221 M3
Bank Ml BERK HP4 34 B5
Bankmill Br BERK HP4 34 C6
Bank Mill La BERK HP4 34 B6
Bank Prec CRAWE RH10 * 284 B4
Banksia Rd UED N18 100 B8
Bankside ENC/FH EN2 79 N5
SAND/SEL CR2 223 N3
SEV TN13 246 E7
STHL UB1 133 L10
STHWK SE1 12 E8
WOKN/KNAP GU21 231 N4
Bankside Av LEW SE13 161 H9
NTHLT UB5 133 H4
Bankside Cl BH/WHM TN16 243 P4
BXLY DA5 186 E7
CAR SM5 221 P2
DEN/HRF UB9 91 K7
ISLW TW7 154 E10
Bankside Down
RKW/CH/CXG WD3 * 71 N10
Bankside Dr THDIT KT7 198 G9
Bankside Rd IL IG1 122 F10
Banks La BXLYHS DA6 164 A10
EHSLY KT24 235 J8
EPP CM16 65 P8
Banks Rd BORE WD6 75 P6
CRAWE RH10 284 D8
Banks Sp SL SL1 148 G1
Bank St GVW DA11 190 E2
Banks Wy MNPK E12 122 D9
RGUE GU4 250 C7
Bank Ter CRAWE RH10 * 283 N8
The Bank CRAWE RH10 * 285 P9
HGT N6 118 C6
Bankton Rd BRXS/STRHM SW2 159 H10
Bankwell Rd LEW SE13 161 K10
Bann Cl SOCK/AV RM15 146 G9
Banner Cl PUR RM19 166 C3
Banner St STLK EC1Y 12 F2
Banning St GNWCH SE10 161 K4
Bannister Cl BRXS/STRHM SW2 181 H4
DTCH/LGLY SL3 150 B1
GFD/PVL UB6 114 C10
Bannister Dr RBRW/HUT CM13 87 P10
Bannister Gdns STMC/STPC BR5 207 M3
Bannister's Rd GUW GU2 267 M2
Bannockburn Rd
WOOL/PLUM SE18 163 H3
Bannow Cl HOR/WEW KT19 220 B1
Banson's La CHONG CM5 67 P4
Bansons Wy CHONG CM5 67 P4
Banstead Gdns ED N9 99 L4
Banstead Rd BNSTD SM7 221 H9
CTHM CR3 241 L8
EW KT17 220 E6
PUR/KEN CR8 223 H7
Banstead Rd South BELMT SM2 221 M6
Banstead St PECK SE15 160 B9
Banstead Wy WLGTN SM6 222 F2
Banstock Rd EDGW HA8 95 N7
Banting Dr WCHMH N21 78 G9
Banton Cl EN EN1 80 A6
Bantry St CMBW SE5 159 L6
Banwell Rd BXLY DA5 185 N2
Banyard Rd BERM/RHTH SE16 160 A2
Banyards EMPK RM11 125 M3
Bapchild Pl STMC/STPC BR5 207 M4
Baptist Gdns KTTN NW5 4 C1
Barandon Wk NTGHL W11 * 136 G9
Barbara Castle Cl FUL/PGN SW6 14 D10
Barbara Cl SHPTN TW17 196 C5
Barbara Hucklesbury Cl
WDGN N22 99 J10
Barbaraville Camp
BRKMPK AL9 * 41 J1
Barbauld Rd STNW/STAM N16 119 M8
Barbel Cl CHES/WCR EN8 62 F10
Barber Cl WCHMH N21 99 H1
Barberry Cl HARH RM3 105 K7
Barberry Rd HHW HP1 35 K6
Barbers Rd SRTFD E15 140 G4
Barbican Rd GFD/PVL UB6 134 A8
Barb Ms HMSMTH W6 156 F2
Barbon Cl BMSBY WC1N 11 N3
Barbot Cl ED N9 99 P4
Barchard St WAND/EARL SW18 179 L1
Barchester Cl HNWL W7 134 E10
UX/CGN UB8 131 M6
Barchester Rd DTCH/LGLY SL3 150 C1
KTN/HRWW/WS HA3 94 C9
Barchester St POP/IOD E14 140 G7
Barclay Cl FUL/PGN SW6 * 157 K6
HERT/BAY SG13 26 A7
LHD/OX KT22 236 A9
WATW WD18 73 H10
Barclay Ct HOD EN11 44 F4
Barclay Ov WFD IG8 101 M5
Barclay Rd CROY/NA CR0 203 L10
FUL/PGN SW6 157 K6
PLSTW E13 141 P6
UED N18 99 L7
WALTH E17 121 H3
WAN E11 121 L6
Barclay Wy WTHK RM20 166 E4
Barcombe Av BRXS/STRHM SW2 180 F5
Barcombe Cl STMC/STPC BR5 207 K3
Barden Cl DEN/HRF UB9 91 M9
Barden St WOOL/PLUM SE18 163 H6
Bardeswell Cl BRW CM14 107 M4
Bardfield Av CHDH RM6 123 N1
Bardney Rd MRDN SM4 201 L4
Bardolph Av CROY/NA CR0 224 E5
Bardolph Rd HOLWY N7 118 F9
RCH/KEW TW9 155 L10
Bardon Wk WOKN/KNAP GU21 * 231 N3
Bard Rd NKENS W10 136 G9
Bardsey Pl WCHPL E1 140 B7
Bardsey Wk IS N1 * 6 F1
Bardsley Cl CROY/NA CR0 203 N10
Bardsley La GNWCH SE10 161 H5
Bardwell Ct STAL AL1 * 38 C7
Bardwell Rd STAL AL1 38 C7
Barfett St NKENS W10 8 C1
Barfield EYN DA4 210 A1
Barfield Av TRDG/WHET N20 98 A3
Barfield Rd BMLY BR1 206 D3
WAN E11 * 121 L6
Barfields LOU IG10 82 D8
REDH RH1 259 J9
Barfields Gdns LOU IG10 82 D8
Barfields Pth LOU IG10 82 D8
Barford Cl HDN NW4 96 D10
Barford St IS N1 6 B6
Barforth Rd PECK SE15 160 A9
Barfreston Wy PGE/AN SE20 204 A1
Bargate Cl NWMAL KT3 200 D7
WOOL/PLUM SE18 163 J4
Barge House Rd CAN/RD E16 162 E1
Barge House St STHWK SE1 12 B9
Barge La BOW E3 140 E3
Bargery Rd CAT SE6 182 G4
Barge Wk KUT/HW KT1 199 J2
Bargrove Av HHW HP1 35 K9
Bargrove Cl PGE/AN SE20 181 P10
Bargrove Crs CAT SE6 182 E5
Barham Av BORE WD6 75 L7
Barham Cl ALP/SUD HA0 134 G1
CHST BR7 184 E8
GVE DA12 191 J4
HAYES BR2 206 B8
ROMW/RG RM7 104 C10
WEY KT13 216 D1
Barham Ct ALP/SUD HA0 135 H1
Barham Rd CHST BR7 184 E8
DART DA1 187 P3
RYNPK SW20 178 D10
SAND/SEL CR2 223 K1
Baring Cl LEE/GVPK SE12 183 M5
Baring Rd BEAC HP9 88 B8
CROY/NA CR0 203 P8
EBAR EN4 77 N7
LEE/GVPK SE12 183 N5
LEE/GVPK SE12 183 N7
Baring St IS N1 6 G6
Barington Ct RBRW/HUT CM13 87 P10
Bark Burr Rd CDW/CHF RM16 167 L1
Barker Cl CHERT KT16 195 H7
NTHWD HA6 92 G8
NWMAL KT3 199 N4
RCH/KEW TW9 155 N8
Barker Dr CAMTN NW1 5 H4
Barker Rd CHERT KT16 195 H7
Barker St WBPTN SW10 15 J9
Barker Wk STRHM/NOR SW16 180 E6
Barkham Rd TOTM N17 99 L8
Bark Hart Rd ORP BR6 207 L8
Barking Rd CAN/RD E16 141 L7
EHAM E6 142 C3
PLSTW E13 141 N6
POP/IOD E14 141 K8
Bark Pl BAY/PAD W2 8 G7
Barkston Gdns ECT SW5 14 G7
Barkway Dr ORP BR6 226 D1
Barkwood Cl ROMW/RG RM7 124 D3
Barkworth Rd BERM/RHTH SE16 160 A4
Barlborough St NWCR SE14 160 C6
Barlby Gdns NKENS W10 136 G5
Barlby Rd NKENS W10 136 F7
Barley Crs UX/CGN UB8 131 M7
Barle Gdns SOCK/AV RM15 146 G8
Barley Brow GSTN WD25 55 J7
Barley Cl ALP/SUD HA0 115 J9
BUSH WD23 74 A9
CRAWE RH10 283 N8
RBSF CM22 31 M1
Barleycorn Wy EMPK RM11 125 N4
Barley Cft HERT/WAT SG14 25 L3
HHNE HP2 36 D6
HLWS CM18 46 C5
Barleycroft Gn WGCW AL8 22 F5
Barleycroft Rd WGCW AL8 22 F6
Barley Fld BRWN CM15 86 E3
Barley La GDMY/SEVK IG3 123 K4
Barley Mow Cl
WOKN/KNAP GU21 231 J3
Barley Mow Ct
BRKHM/BTCW RH3 255 P10
Barley Mow La STALE/WH AL4 39 L9
WOKN/KNAP GU21 231 J3
Barley Mow Pas CHSWK W4 156 A4
Barley Mow Rd EGH TW20 171 P8
Barley Mow Wy SHPTN TW17 196 B4
Barley Ponds Cl WARE SG12 26 E2
Barley Ponds Rd WARE SG12 26 E2
Barlings Rd HARP AL5 20 A6
Barlow Cl WLGTN SM6 222 F3
Barlow Dr BKHTH/KID SE3 162 B7
Barlow Pl MYFR/PICC W1J 10 F8
Barlow Rd ACT W3 135 N10
CRAWW RH11 283 H10
HPTN TW12 175 P10
KIL/WHAMP NW6 2 D1
Barlow St WALW SE17 19 H6
Barlow Wy RAIN RM13 144 E8
Barlow Wy South RAIN RM13 144 F8
Barmeston Rd CAT SE6 182 G5
Barmor Cl RYLN/HDSTN HA2 94 A10
Barmouth Av GFD/PVL UB6 134 E4
Barmouth Rd CROY/NA CR0 204 C9
WAND/EARL SW18 179 M2
Barnabas Rd HOM E9 140 L1
Barnaby Cl RYLN/HDSTN HA2 114 B7
Barnaby Pl SKENS SW7 15 L6
Barnaby Wy CHIG IG7 102 D4
Barnacre Cl UX/CGN UB8 131 N8
Barnacres Rd HHS/BOV HP3 36 A10
Barnard Acres WAB EN9 45 K9
Barnard Cl CHST BR7 206 G1
SUN TW16 175 J10
WLGTN SM6 222 E4
WOOL/PLUM SE18 162 D3
Barnard Gdns NWMAL KT3 200 D4
YEAD UB4 133 J6
Barnard Gn WGCE AL7 23 J6
Barnard Hl MUSWH N10 98 C10
Barnard Ms BTSEA SW11 157 P10
Barnardo Dr BARK/HLT IG6 122 F2
Barnardo Gdns WCHPL E1 * 140 C8
Barnardo St WCHPL E1 140 C8
Barnard Pl EW KT17 220 F6
Barnard Rd BTSEA SW11 157 P10
EN EN1 80 A6
MTCM CR4 202 B3
WARL CR6 242 G5
Barnards Pl SAND/SEL CR2 223 J5
Barnard Wy HHS/BOV HP3 35 P8
Barnato Cl BF/WBF KT14 215 P8
Barnby Rd WOKN/KNAP GU21 231 J3
Barnby St CAMTN NW1 5 H8
SRTFD E15 141 K3
Barn Cl ASHF TW15 174 E8
BNSTD SM7 239 N1
HHS/BOV HP3 36 A9
HTN NW5 * 118 E10
KWD/TDW/WH KT20 255 L8
NTHLT UB5 133 K4
RAD WD7 74 F1
SLN SL2 108 G9
WGCW AL8 22 F5
Barn Crs PUR/KEN CR8 223 P9
STAN HA7 95 H7
Barncroft Cl LOU IG10 82 D9
UX/CGN UB8 132 C7
Barncroft Gn LOU IG10 82 D9
Barncroft Rd BERK HP4 33 L6
LOU IG10 82 D9
Barncroft Wy STAL AL1 38 F7
Barndale Ct GVE DA12 191 P8
Barndicott WGCE AL7 23 M5
Barneby Cl WHTN TW2 176 D4
Barnehurst Av BXLYHN DA7 164 D7
Barnehurst Cl ERITH DA8 164 D7
Barnehurst Rd BXLYHN DA7 164 D8
Barn End Dr RDART DA2 187 K7
Barn End La RDART DA2 187 K9
Barnes Av BARN SW13 156 D6
NWDGN UB2 153 N3
Barnes Br CHSWK W4 156 B8
Barnes Cl MNPK E12 122 A9
Barnes Cray Rd DART DA1 165 H10
Barnesdale Crs STMC/STPC BR5 207 N8
Barnes End NWMAL KT3 200 D5
Barnes High St BARN SW13 156 C8
Barnes La KGLGY WD4 53 M4
Barnes Ri KGLGY WD4 54 A3
Barnes Rd GODL GU7 267 K9
IL IG1 122 F10
UED N18 100 B5
Barnes St POP/IOD E14 140 D8
Barnes Ter DEPT SE8 160 E4
Barnes Wallis Cl EHSLY KT24 253 L3
Barnes Wallis Dr BF/WBF KT14 215 P7
Barnes Wy IVER SL0 131 J9
Barnet By-Pass BORE WD6 76 B9
Barnet Dr HAYES BR2 206 B9
Barnet Ga BAR EN5 96 G1
Barnet Gv BETH E2 7 N9
Barnet Hl BAR EN5 77 J8
Barnet La BORE WD6 75 L10
TRDG/WHET N20 97 J2
Barnet Rd BAR EN5 76 C10
BAR EN5 76 B10
BAR EN5 76 F8
BAR EN5 77 K3
LCOL/BKTW AL2 57 L4
POTB/CUF EN6 59 L9
Barnett Cl ERITH DA8 164 G8
LHD/OX KT22 236 G5
SHGR GU5 268 F9
Barnett La SHGR GU5 268 E10
Barnett Rw RGUE GU4 250 A5
Barnetts Ct RYLN/HDSTN HA2 * 114 A8
Barnett's Shaw OXTED RH8 261 J3
Barnett St WCHPL E1 140 A8
Barnetts Wy OXTED RH8 261 J3
Barnett Wood La ASHTD KT21 237 J3
LHD/OX KT22 236 G5
Barnet Wy (Barnet By-Pass)
MLHL NW7 96 A2
Barnet Wood Rd HAYES BR2 205 P9
Barney Cl CHARL SE7 161 P4
Barn Fld BNSTD SM7 221 L10
Barnfield EPP CM16 65 K4
GVW DA11 190 D5
Barn Fld HAMP NW3 * 118 A10
Barnfield HHS/BOV HP3 36 A9
IVER SL0 131 H8
NWMAL KT3 200 B6
SL SL1 128 C10
Barnfield Av CROY/NA CR0 204 B9
KUTN/CMB KT2 177 J7
MTCM CR4 202 C4
Barnfield Cl COUL/CHIP CR5 241 K5
FSBYPK N4 118 F5
HOD EN11 44 F1
RDART DA2 188 E2
SWLY BR8 208 D7
TOOT SW17 179 M6
WAB EN9 45 L8
Barnfield Ct HARP AL5 20 B3
Barnfield Crs BGR/WK TN15 247 M3
Barnfield Gdns KUTN/CMB KT2 177 K8
WOOL/PLUM SE18 * 162 E5
Barnfield Pl POP/IOD E14 160 G3
Barnfield Rd BELV DA17 164 A5
BH/WHM TN16 244 A7
CRAWE RH10 283 N6
EA W5 135 H6
EDGW HA8 95 P9
HARP AL5 20 B3
SAND/SEL CR2 223 M5
SEV TN13 246 E9
STALE/WH AL4 39 H4
STMC/STPC BR5 207 N3
WGCE AL7 23 H7
WOOL/PLUM SE18 162 E5
Barnfield Wy OXTED RH8 261 M9
Barnfield Wood Cl BECK BR3 205 J6
Barnfield Wood Rd BECK BR3 205 J6
Barnham Dr THMD SE28 143 J10
Barnham Rd GFD/PVL UB6 134 B5
Barnham St STHWK SE1 19 K1
Barn Hl HLWW/ROY CM19 45 N5
Barnhill PIN HA5 113 K3
Barn Hl WBLY HA9 115 N7
Barnhill Av HAYES BR2 205 M5
Barnhill La YEAD UB4 133 J5
Barnhill Rd WBLY HA9 115 P8
YEAD UB4 133 J6
Barnhurst Pth OXHEY WD19 93 K6
Barningham Wy
CDALE/KGS NW9 115 P4
Barn Lea RKW/CH/CXG WD3 91 K2
Barnlea Cl FELT TW13 175 M5
Barn Md BRWN CM15 87 H2
EHAM E6 142 B5
Barnmead CHOB/PIR GU24 213 L6
EPP CM16 83 H2
Barn Md HLWS CM18 46 G3
Barnmead Gdns DAGW RM9 124 A10
Barn Meadow La GT/LBKH KT23 235 N10
Barnmead Rd BECK BR3 204 C1
DAGW RM9 124 A10
Barnock Cl DART DA1 186 F3
Barn Ri WBLY HA9 115 M6
Barn Rd ADL/WDHM KT15 215 L5
Barnsbury Cl NWMAL KT3 199 P4
Barnsbury Crs BRYLDS KT5 199 P8
Barnsbury Est IS N1 5 P6
Barnsbury Gv HOLWY N7 5 P3
Barnsbury La BRYLDS KT5 199 N9
Barnsbury Pk IS N1 6 A3
Barnsbury Rd IS N1 6 A7
Barnsbury Sq IS N1 6 A4
Barnsbury St IS N1 6 B4
Barnsbury Ter IS N1 5 P4
Barns Ct CRAWE RH10 285 M3
HLWW/ROY CM19 46 E6
Barnscroft RYNPK SW20 200 E3
Barnsdale Av POP/IOD E14 160 G3
Barnsdale Cl BORE WD6 75 L5
Barnsdale Rd MV/WKIL W9 8 D1
Barnsfield Pl UX/CGN UB8 131 M3
Barnsford Crs CHOB/PIR GU24 212 F8
Barnside Ct WGCW AL8 22 F5
Barnsley Rd HARH RM3 105 N8
Barnsley St WCHPL E1 140 A6
Barnstaple La LEW SE13 161 H10
Barnstaple Rd HARH RM3 105 N8
RSLP HA4 113 K8
The Barns MFD/CHID GU8 266 B9
Barnston Wk IS N1 * 6 E5
Barnston Wy RBRW/HUT CM13 87 P9
Barn St STNW/STAM N16 119 M7
Barnsway KGLGY WD4 53 P4
The Barn GRAYS RM17 * 167 N3
Barnway EGH TW20 171 P8
Barn Wy WBLY HA9 115 M6
Barnwell Rd BRXS/STRHM SW2 181 H1
DART DA1 165 N9
Barnwood CRAWE RH10 284 D6
Barnwood Cl GUW GU2 249 K8
MV/WKIL W9 8 G2
RSLP HA4 112 E7
Barnwood Ct GUW GU2 249 K8
Barnwood Rd GUW GU2 249 K9
The Barnyard
KWD/TDW/WH KT20 238 D10
Baron Cl BELMT SM2 221 L6
FBAR/BDGN N11 98 B6
Baron Ct HARH RM3 105 N9
Baroness Rd BETH E2 7 M9
Baronet Gv TOTM N17 99 P9
Baronet Rd TOTM N17 99 P9
Baron Gdns BARK/HLT IG6 122 G1
Baron Gv MTCM CR4 201 P4
Baron Rd BCTR RM8 123 N6
Barons Cl IS N1 * 6 A7
Baron's Court Rd WKENS W14 14 A7
Baronsfield Rd TWK TW1 * 176 G2
Barons Ga EBAR EN4 77 P10
Baron's Hurst EPSOM KT18 237 P2
Barons Keep WKENS W14 * 157 H4
Barons Md HRW HA1 114 D2
Baronsmead Rd BARN SW13 156 D7
Baronsmede EA W5 155 L1
Baronsmere Ct BAR EN5 * 77 H8
Baronsmere Rd EFNCH N2 117 P2
Baron's Pl STHWK SE1 18 B2
The Barons TWK TW1 176 G2
Baron St IS N1 6 B8
Baron's Wk CROY/NA CR0 204 D6
Barons Wy EGH TW20 172 G9
REIG RH2 275 K4
Barque Ms DEPT SE8 160 F5
Barrack La WDSR SL4 149 J7
Barrack Pth WOKN/KNAP GU21 231 L5
Barrack Rd GUW GU2 249 M8
HSLWW TW4 153 L10
Barrack Rw GVW DA11 190 E2
Barracks Hl AMSS HP7 88 E1
Barracks La BAR EN5 76 G10
Barrack Rd GUW GU2 249 M8
HSLWW TW4 153 L10
Barrack Rw GVW DA11 190 E2
Barracks Hl AMSS HP7 88 E1
Barrack Pth WOKN/KNAP GU21 231 L5
Barra Cl HHS/BOV HP3 36 C9
Barra Hall Rd HYS/HAR UB3 132 F9
Barrards Wy BEAC HP9 89 H7
Barrass Cl PEND EN3 80 E3
Barratt Av WDGN N22 98 G10
Barratt Wy KTN/HRWW/WS HA3 114 C1
Barrenger Rd MUSWH N10 98 A9
Barrens Brae WOKS/MYFD GU22 232 D4
Barrens Cl WOKS/MYFD GU22 232 D5
Barrens Pk WOKS/MYFD GU22 232 D4
Barrett Cl HARH RM3 105 J8
Barrett Rd LHD/OX KT22 254 B1
WALTH E17 121 J3
Barrett's Green Rd WLSDN NW10 135 P4
Barrett's Gv STNW/STAM N16 119 M10
Barretts Rd SEV TN13 246 E6
Barrett St MHST W1U 10 D6
Barrhill Rd BRXS/STRHM SW2 180 F5
Barricane WOKN/KNAP GU21 231 N5
Barrie Cl COUL/CHIP CR5 240 D2
Barriedale NWCR SE14 160 D7
Barrier Point Rd CAN/RD E16 161 P1
Barringer Sq TOOT SW17 180 B7
Barrington Cl CLAY IG5 102 C9
KTTN NW5 118 B10
Barrington Ct DORK RH4 272 F3
Barrington Dr DEN/HRF UB9 91 K8
Barrington Gn LOU IG10 82 G9
Barrington Ldg WEY KT13 216 D2
Barrington Park Gdns CSTG HP8 90 A2
Barrington Rd BRXN/ST SW9 159 J9
BXLYHN DA7 163 N8
CEND/HSY/T N8 118 E3
CHEAM SM3 201 K8
CRAWE RH10 283 N9
DORK RH4 * 272 F3
LOU IG10 82 F7
MNPK E12 142 D1
PUR/KEN CR8 222 D8
Barrington Vls
WOOL/PLUM SE18 162 D7
Barrington Wk NRWD SE19 * 181 M9
Barron's Cl CHONG CM5 67 N3
Barrons Rw HARP AL5 20 C4
Barrow Av CAR SM5 222 A4
Barrow Cl WCHMH N21 99 J4
Barrowdene Cl PIN HA5 93 M10
Barrowell Gn WCHMH N21 99 J3
Barrowgate Rd CHSWK W4 155 P4
Barrow Green Rd OXTED RH8 260 F7
OXTED RH8 261 J4
Barrow Hedges Cl CAR SM5 221 P4
Barrow Hedges Wy CAR SM5 221 P4
Barrow Hl WPK KT4 200 B9
Barrow Hill Cl WPK KT4 200 B9
Barrow Hill Est STJWD NW8 3 N8
Barrow Hill Rd STJWD NW8 3 N8
Barrow La CHESW EN7 61 N7
Barrow Point Av PIN HA5 93 M10
Barrow Point La PIN HA5 93 M10
Barrow Rd CROY/NA CR0 223 H2
STRHM/NOR SW16 180 E9
Barrows Rd HLWW/ROY CM19 46 C1
Barr Rd GVE DA12 191 J5
POTB/CUF EN6 59 M9
Barrsbrook Farm Rd
CHERT KT16 195 H8
Barr's La WOKN/KNAP GU21 231 K2
Barr's Rd MDHD SL6 128 A8
WLSDN NW10 136 A2
Barry Av BXLYHN DA7 163 P6
SEVS/STOTM N15 119 N4
WDSR SL4 148 G6
Barry Cl CDW/CHF RM16 168 D2
CRAWE RH10 283 P10
LCOL/BKTW AL2 56 A1
ORP BR6 207 H10
Barry Pde EDUL SE22 * 159 P10
Barry Rd EDUL SE22 181 P2
EHAM E6 142 B8
WLSDN NW10 135 P2
Barry Ter ASHF TW15 * 174 A5
Barset Rd PECK SE15 160 B9
Barson Cl PGE/AN SE20 182 B10
The Bars GU GU1 268 A1
Barston Rd WNWD SE27 181 K5
Barstow Crs BRXS/STRHM SW2 180 G4
Bartel Cl HHS/BOV HP3 36 E8
Bartelotts Rd SLN SL2 128 C6
Barter St NOXST/BSQ WC1A 11 M4
Barth Ms WOOL/PLUM SE18 163 H3
Bartholomew Ct DORK RH4 * 272 F3
Bartholomew Cl STBT EC1A 12 E4
WAND/EARL SW18 157 M10
Bartholomew Dr HARH RM3 105 L10
Bartholomew La OBST EC2N 13 H5
Bartholomew Pl STBT EC1A 12 E4
Bartholomew Rd KTTN NW5 4 G2
Bartholomew Sq FSBYE EC1V * 12 F1
Bartholomew St STHWK SE1 18 G4
Bartholomew Vls KTTN NW5 4 G2
Bartholomew Wy SWLY BR8 208 F3
Barth Rd WOOL/PLUM SE18 163 H3
Bartle Av EHAM E6 142 B4
Bartle Rd NTGHL W11 136 G8
Bartlett Cl POP/IOD E14 140 F8
Bartlett Ct FLST/FETLN EC4A * 12 B5
Bartlett Rd BH/WHM TN16 262 F2
GVW DA11 190 D4
Bartletts Md HERT/WAT SG14 25 L2
Bartlett St SAND/SEL CR2 223 K2
Bartlow Gdns CRW RM5 104 E9
Barton Av ROMW/RG RM7 124 D6
Barton Cl ADL/WDHM KT15 215 K3
BXLYHS DA6 185 P1
CHIG IG7 102 F3
EHAM E6 142 C8
HDN NW4 116 D3
HOM E9 120 B10
PECK SE15 160 A9
SHPTN TW17 196 C6
WOKN/KNAP GU21 231 H4
Barton Gn NWMAL KT3 200 A2
Barton Meadow BARK/HLT IG6 122 E2
Barton Pl RGUE GU4 * 250 E7
Barton Rd DTCH/LGLY SL3 150 C1
EYN DA4 210 A1
HCH RM12 125 H6
SCUP DA14 185 P9
SHGR GU5 268 D10
STALE/WH AL4 39 L2
WKENS W14 14 A8
The Bartons BORE WD6 75 J10
Barton St WEST SW1P 17 L4
The Barton COB KT11 217 L8
Barton Wk CRAWE RH10 284 C9
Barton Wy BORE WD6 75 M6
RKW/CH/CXG WD3 72 C9
Bartram Cl UX/CGN UB8 132 C6
Bartram Rd BROCKY SE4 182 D1
Bartrams La EBAR EN4 77 M4
Bartrip St HOM E9 140 D1
Bartrop Cl CHESW EN7 61 L4
Barts Cl BECK BR3 204 F5
Barwell Ct CHSGTN KT9 * 219 H4
Barwell La CHSGTN KT9 219 H4
Barwick Dr UX/CGN UB8 132 C7
Barwick Rd FSTGT E7 121 N9
Barwood Av WWKM BR4 204 G8
Bascombe Gv DART DA1 186 F3
Bascombe St BRXS/STRHM SW2 181 H3
Basden Gv FELT TW13 175 P5
Basedale Rd DAGW RM9 143 L2
Baseing Cl EHAM E6 142 D9
Basevi Wy DEPT SE8 160 F5
Basford Wy WDSR SL4 148 C9
Bashford Wy CRAWE RH10 284 E5
Bashley Rd WLSDN NW10 136 A6
Basil Av EHAM E6 142 B5
Basildene Rd HSLWW TW4 153 L9
Basildon Av CLAY IG5 102 D9
Basildon Cl BELMT SM2 221 L5
WATW WD18 72 D10
Basildon Rd ABYW SE2 163 K4
Basildon Sq HHNE HP2 36 A2
Basildon Wy CRAWW RH11 283 H10
Basil Gdns CROY/NA CR0 204 C8
WNWD SE27 181 K8
Basil Ms HLWE CM17 29 M10
Basilon Rd BXLYHN DA7 163 P8
Basil St CHEL SW3 16 A3
Basin Ap POP/IOD E14 140 D8
Basing Cl THDIT KT7 198 E7
Basing Ct PECK SE15 159 N7
Basingdon Wy CMBW SE5 159 L10
Basing Dr BXLY DA5 186 A2
Basingfield Rd THDIT KT7 198 E7
Basinghall Av CITYW EC2V 12 G5
Basinghall Gdns BELMT SM2 221 L5
Basinghall St CITYW EC2V 12 G5
Basing Hl GLDGN NW11 117 J6
WBLY HA9 115 L7
Basing Pl BETH E2 7 K9
Basing Rd BNSTD SM7 239 J1
RKW/CH/CXG WD3 91 J2
Basing St NTGHL W11 8 C5
Basing Wy FNCH N3 117 H4
THDIT KT7 198 E7
Basire St IS N1 6 F5
Baskerville Gdns WLSDN NW10 116 B9
Baskerville Rd WAND/EARL SW18 179 P3
Basket Gdns ELTH/MOT SE9 184 B1
Baslow Cl KTN/HRWW/WS HA3 94 C9
Baslow Wk CLPT E5 120 C9
Basnett Rd BTSEA SW11 * 158 B9
Basque Ct BERM/RHTH SE16 * 160 C2
Bassano St EDUL SE22 181 N1
Bassant Rd WOOL/PLUM SE18 163 J5
Bassein Park Rd SHB W12 156 C1
Basset Cl ADL/WDHM KT15 215 L6
Basset Dr REIG RH2 257 K9
Bassett Cl BELMT SM2 221 L6
Bassett Gdns EPP CM16 66 C2
ISLW TW7 154 B6
Bassett Rd CRAWE RH10 284 E10
NKENS W10 136 G8
UX/CGN UB8 131 M2
WOKS/MYFD GU22 232 F2
Bassetts Cl ORP BR6 226 E1
Bassetts St KTTN NW5 4 C1
Bassetts Wy ORP BR6 226 E1
Bassett Wy GFD/PVL UB6 134 A8
Bassil Rd HHNE HP2 35 N7
Bassingbourne Cl BROX EN10 44 E6
Bassingburn Wk WGCE AL7 23 J6
Bassingham Rd ALP/SUD HA0 135 J1
WAND/EARL SW18 179 M3
Basswood Cl PECK SE15 160 A9
Bastable Av BARK IG11 143 K4
Bastion Rd ABYW SE2 163 K4
Baston Manor Rd WWKM BR4 205 N10
Baston Rd HAYES BR2 205 N9
HAYES BR2 225 P1
Bastwick St FSBYE EC1V 12 D1
Basuto Rd FUL/PGN SW6 157 K7
Bata Av TIL RM18 169 L4
Batavia Rd NWCR SE14 160 D6
SUN TW16 197 J1
Batchelor St IS N1 6 A7
Batchelors Wy AMSS HP7 69 J5
CSHM HP5 50 G5
Batchwood Dr STALW/RED AL3 38 B3
Batchwood Gdns
STALW/RED AL3 38 C3
Batchwood Gn STMC/STPC BR5 207 K4
Batchwood Vw STALW/RED AL3 38 B4
Batchworth Hl
RKW/CH/CXG WD3 * 91 P3
Batchworth La NTHWD HA6 92 D6
Bateman Cl BARK IG11 142 F1
Bateman Ct CRAWE RH10 * 284 B10
Bateman Rd CHING E4 100 F7
RKW/CH/CXG WD3 72 B10
Bateman's Buildings
SOHO/SHAV W1D 11 J6
Batemans Cnr CHSWK W4 * 156 A4
Batemans Ct CRAWE RH10 284 B10
Bateman's Rw SDTCH EC2A 13 K1
Bateman St SOHO/SHAV W1D 11 K6
Bates Cl DTCH/LGLY SL3 130 B8
Bates Crs CROY/NA CR0 223 H3
STRHM/NOR SW16 180 D10
Bateson Wy WOKN/KNAP GU21 214 F10
Bates Rd HARH RM3 105 P8
Bate St POP/IOD E14 140 E9
Bates Wk ADL/WDHM KT15 215 M3
Batford Cl WGCE AL7 23 L6
Batford Ml HARP AL5 * 20 C1
Bath Cl PECK SE15 160 B7
Bathgate Rd WIM/MER SW19 178 G6
Bath Gv BETH E2 7 N8
Bath House Rd CROY/NA CR0 202 F8
Bath Pas KUT/HW KT1 199 J2
Bath Pl BAR EN5 77 J7
SDTCH EC2A * 7 J10
Bath Rd CHSWK W4 156 B3
DART DA1 187 J3
DTCH/LGLY SL3 151 J7
ED N9 100 A3
FSTGT E7 142 A1
HSLW TW3 153 N9
HSLW TW3 154 A9
HSLWW TW4 153 H7
HSLWW TW4 153 L8
HYS/HAR UB3 152 C7
SL SL1 128 G9
WDR/YW UB7 151 L7
WDR/YW UB7 152 A7
Baths Ap FUL/PGN SW6 * 157 J6
Bath St FSBYE EC1V 6 F10
GVW DA11 190 E2
Bath Ter STHWK SE1 18 E4
Bathurst Av WIM/MER SW19 201 L1
Bathurst Cl WDR/YW UB7 151 J1
Bathurst Gdns WLSDN NW10 136 E4
Bathurst Ms BAY/PAD W2 9 M7
Bathurst Rd HHNE HP2 35 N3
IL IG1 122 E6
Bathurst St BAY/PAD W2 9 M7
Bathurst Wk DTCH/LGLY SL3 151 H1
Bathway WOOL/PLUM SE18 162 D3
Batley Cl CAR SM5 202 A7
Batley Pl STNW/STAM N16 119 N8
Batley Rd ENC/FH EN2 79 K5
STNW/STAM N16 119 N8
Batman Cl SHB W12 136 E10
Baton Cl PUR RM19 166 C3
Batoum Gdns HMSMTH W6 156 F2
Batson St SHB W12 156 D1
Batsworth Rd MTCM CR4 201 N3
Batten Av WOKN/KNAP GU21 231 K5
Batten Cl EHAM E6 142 C8
Batten Cottages POP/IOD E14 * 140 D7
Batten St BTSEA SW11 157 P9
Battersby Rd CAT SE6 183 J5
Battersea Br WBPTN SW10 157 N6
Battersea Bridge Rd
BTSEA SW11 157 P6
Battersea Church Rd
BTSEA SW11 157 N7
Battersea High St BTSEA SW11 157 N8
Battersea Park Rd BTSEA SW11 158 B7
VX/NE SW8 158 C6
Battersea Ri BTSEA SW11 179 P1
Battersea Sq BTSEA SW11 * 157 P6
Battery Rd THMD SE28 143 J10
THMD SE28 163 H1
Battishill St IS N1 6 C4
Battlebridge La REDH RH1 258 C6
Battle Bridge La STHWK SE1 13 J10
Battle Bridge Rd CAMTN NW1 5 L8
Battle Cl WIM/MER SW19 179 M9
Battledean Rd HBRY N5 119 J10
Battlefield Rd STAL AL1 38 E4
Battle Rd ERITH DA8 164 D3
Battlers Green Dr RAD WD7 74 D3
Battleview STALE/WH AL4 21 K3
Batts Hl REIG RH2 257 N8
Batty St WCHPL E1 13 P6
Batty St SCHPL E1 13 P6
Baudwin Rd CAT SE6 183 K5
Baugh Rd SCUP DA14 185 M8
The Baulk WAND/EARL SW18 179 K3
Bavant Rd STRHM/NOR SW16 202 F2
Bavaria Rd ARCH N19 118 F7
Bavdene Ms HDN NW4 116 E2
Bavent Rd CMBW SE5 159 K8
Bawdale Rd EDUL SE22 181 N1
Bawdsey Av GNTH/NBYPK IG2 123 J2
Bawtree Cl BELMT SM2 221 M6
Bawtree Rd NWCR SE14 160 D6

UX/CGN UB8 131 M1
Bawtry Rd TRDG/WHET N20 98 A4
Baxendale TRDG/WHET N20 97 M3
Baxendale St BETH E2 7 N9
Baxter Av REDH RH1 257 P10
Baxter Cl CRAWE RH10 284 C9
HGDN/ICK UB10 132 C5
NWDGN UB2 154 A2
SL SL1 149 K2
Baxter Rd CAN/RD E16 141 P8
IL IG1 122 E10
IS N1 7 H2
UED N18 100 A5
Bayards WARL CR6 242 B4
Bay Cl HORL RH6 279 P1
Bay Ct EA W5 * 155 K2
Baycroft Cl PIN HA5 * 113 K1
Bayeux KWD/TDW/WH KT20 238 G8
Bayfield Rd ELTH/MOT SE9 162 A10
HORL RH6 279 P3
Bayford Cl HERT/BAY SG13 25 K7
HHNE HP2 36 D1
Bayford Gn HERT/BAY SG13 43 H3
Bayford La HERT/BAY SG13 42 G1
Bayford Ms HACK E8 * 140 A2
Bayford Rd WLSDN NW10 136 G5
Bayford St HACK E8 140 A2
Bayham Pl CAMTN NW1 4 G6
Bayham Rd CHSWK W4 156 A2
MRDN SM4 201 L4
SEV TN13 247 K9
WEA W13 134 G9
Bayham St CAMTN NW1 4 G6
Bayhorne La HORL RH6 280 D6
Bayhurst Dr NTHWD HA6 92 G7
Bayleaf Cl HPTN TW12 176 C8
Bayley Md HHW HP1 * 35 L8
Bayley's Hl RSEV TN14 264 F8
Bayleys Md RBRW/HUT CM13 107 P3
Bayley St FITZ W1T 11 J4
Baylie Ct HHNE HP2 35 P5
Baylie La HHNE HP2 35 P5
Baylis Ms TWK TW1 176 F3
Baylis Pde SL SL1 129 K8
Baylis Rd SL SL1 129 J9
STHWK SE1 18 A3
Bayliss Av THMD SE28 143 N9
Bayliss Cl ENC/FH EN2 78 F9
Bayliss Ct GU GU1 267 P1
Bayly Rd DART DA1 187 P2
Bay Manor La WTHK RM20 166 E5
Baymans Wd BRWN CM15 107 L3
Bayne Cl EHAM E6 142 C8
Bayne Hl BEAC HP9 89 J8
Bayne Hill Cl BEAC HP9 89 J8
Baynes Cl EN EN1 79 P5
Baynes Ms HAMP NW3 3 M1
Baynes St CAMTN NW1 5 H4
Baynham Cl BXLY DA5 186 A2
Bayonne Rd HMSMTH W6 14 A10
Bays Cl SYD SE26 182 B8
Baysfarm Ct WDR/YW UB7 151 M7
Bayshill Ri NTHLT UB5 134 A1
Bayston Rd STNW/STAM N16 119 N8
Bayswater Rd BAY/PAD W2 9 K8
Baythorne St BOW E3 140 E7
Baythorn La HORL RH6 280 D6
Bay Tree Av LHD/OX KT22 236 F6
Baytree Cl BFN/LL DA15 185 J4
BMLY BR1 206 A1
Bay Tree Cl CHESW EN7 * 61 N3
LCOL/BKTW AL2 56 A3
Bay Tree Ct SL SL1 128 B5
Baytree Rd BRXS/STRHM SW2 158 G10
Bay Tree Wk WAT WD17 72 G4
Baywood Sq CHIG IG7 103 L5
Bazalgette Cl NWMAL KT3 199 P5
Bazalgette Gdns NWMAL KT3 200 A5
Bazely St POP/IOD E14 141 H9
Bazes Shaw HART DA3 211 L9
Bazile Rd WCHMH N21 79 H10
Beacham Cl CHARL SE7 162 A5
Beachborough Rd BMLY BR1 183 H7
Beachcroft Rd WAN E11 121 K8
Beach Gv FELT TW13 175 P6
Beachy Rd BOW E3 140 F2
Beacon Cl BNSTD SM7 238 G2
CFSP/GDCR SL9 90 B8
UX/CGN UB8 111 N10
Beacon Ct DTCH/LGLY SL3 150 F6
HERT/BAY SG13 * 26 B8
Beacon Dr RDART DA2 189 H6
Beaconfield Av EPP CM16 65 K5
Beaconfield Rd EPP CM16 65 J5
Beaconfields SEV TN13 264 G2
Beaconfield Wy EPP CM16 65 J5
Beacon Ga NWCR SE14 160 C9
Beacon Hl BRW CM14 86 B3
HOLWY N7 118 F10
PUR RM19 166 A4
WOKN/KNAP GU21 231 P5
Beacon Hill Rd BRW CM14 86 B3
Beacon Pl CROY/NA CR0 202 F10
Beacon Ri SEV TN13 265 H2
Beacon Rd ERITH DA8 165 J6
HTHAIR TW6 174 B2
LEW SE13 183 J2
WARE SG12 26 F1
Beaconsfield Cl BKHTH/KID SE3 161 M5
CHSWK W4 155 P4
Beaconsfield Common La
BEAC HP9 109 H4
Beaconsfield Cottages
TRDG/WHET N20 * 97 K4
Beaconsfield Ct HAT AL10 * 40 F2
Beaconsfield Gdns
ESH/CLAY KT10 218 D4
Beaconsfield Pl EW KT17 220 B8
Beaconsfield Rd BKHTH/KID SE3 161 M5
BMLY BR1 206 A3
BXLY DA5 186 F5
CAN/RD E16 141 L6
CHSWK W4 156 A2
CROY/NA CR0 203 L6
EA W5 155 H1
ED N9 99 P4
ELTH/MOT SE9 184 B6
EPSOM KT18 238 A5
ESH/CLAY KT10 218 D4
FBAR/BDGN N11 98 B4
HAT AL10 40 F3
LEY E10 * 121 H8
NWMAL KT3 200 A2
PEND EN3 80 C3
SEVS/STOTM N15 119 M2
SLN SL2 129 H3
STAL AL1 38 E6
STHL UB1 133 L10
SURB KT6 199 L7
TWK TW1 176 G3
WALTH E17 120 E5
WALW SE17 19 H9
WLSDN NW10 136 C1
WOKS/MYFD GU22 232 C6
YEAD UB4 133 K10
Beaconsfield Terrace Rd
WKENS W14 157 H2
Beaconsfield Wk FUL/PGN SW6 157 J7
The Beacons LOU IG10 82 D4
Beacontree Av WALTH E17 101 J9
Beacontree Rd WAN E11 121 L6
Beacon Wy BNSTD SM7 238 G2
RKW/CH/CXG WD3 91 L1
Beadles La OXTED RH8 261 J6
Beadlow Cl CAR SM5 201 N6
Beadman Pl WNWD SE27 * 181 J7
Beadman St WNWD SE27 181 J7
Beadnell Rd FSTH SE23 182 C4
Beadon Rd HAYES BR2 205 M4
HMSMTH W6 156 F3
Beads Hall La BRWN CM15 86 G8
Beaford Gv RYNPK SW20 201 H3
Beagle Cl FELT TW13 175 J7
RAD WD7 74 E3
Beagles Cl STMC/STPC BR5 207 N9
Beak St REGST W1B 10 G7
Beal Cl WELL DA16 163 K7
Beale Cl PLMGR N13 99 J6
Beale Pl BOW E3 140 E4
Beale Rd BOW E3 140 E3
Beales La WEY KT13 196 C10
Beales Rd GT/LBKH KT23 254 A3
Bealings End BEAC HP9 88 C6
Beal Rd IL IG1 122 D7
Beam Av DAGE RM10 144 C3
Beames Rd WLSDN NW10 136 A3
Beaminster Gdns BARK/HLT IG6 122 E1
Beamish Cl EPP CM16 66 D1
Beamish Dr BUSH WD23 94 B2
Beamish Rd ED N9 99 P2
STMC/STPC BR5 207 M7
Beamway DAGE RM10 144 E2
Beanacre Cl HOM E9 140 E1
Beane Cft GVE DA12 191 J4
Beane River Vw HERT/WAT SG14 25 K5
Beane Rd HERT/WAT SG14 25 J5
Bean La RDART DA2 188 G6
Bean Rd BXLYHS DA6 163 N10
SWCM DA10 188 G2
Beanshaw ELTH/MOT SE9 184 D7
Beansland Gv CHDH RM6 103 P10
Bear Cl ROMW/RG RM7 124 C4
Beardell St NRWD SE19 181 N9
Beardow Gv STHGT/OAK N14 * 78 D10
Beard Rd KUTN/CMB KT2 177 L8
Beardsfield PLSTW E13 141 M3
Beard's Hl HPTN TW12 197 P1
Beard's Hill Cl HPTN TW12 197 P1
Beardsley Wy ACT W3 156 A1
Beards Rd ASHF TW15 174 F9
Bearfield Rd KUTN/CMB KT2 177 K10
Bear Gdns STHWK SE1 12 E9
Bearing Cl CHIG IG7 103 K5
Bearing Wy CHIG IG7 103 K5
Bear La STHWK SE1 12 D9
Bear Rd FELT TW13 175 L7
Bears Den KWD/TDW/WH KT20 239 J8
Bearstead Ri BROCKY SE4 182 E1
Bearstead Ter BECK BR3 * 204 F1
Bear St LSQ/SEVD WC2H 11 K7
Bearswood End BEAC HP9 88 D7
Bearwood Cl ADL/WDHM KT15 215 K3
POTB/CUF EN6 59 N7
Beasant House WATN WD24 * 73 L6
Beasley's Ait SUN TW16 196 G6
Beasley's Ait La SUN TW16 196 G6
Beaton Cl SWCM DA10 188 G1
Beatrice Av STRHM/NOR SW16 202 G3
WBLY HA9 115 K10
Beatrice Cl PIN HA5 113 H2
PLSTW E13 141 M6
Beatrice Pl KENS W8 14 G4
Beatrice Rd ED N9 100 B1
FSBYPK N4 119 H5
OXTED RH8 261 K5
RCHPK/HAM TW10 177 L1
STHL UB1 133 N10
STHWK SE1 19 P6
WALTH E17 120 F3
Beattie Cl EBED/NFELT TW14 174 G4
GT/LBKH KT23 235 N10
Beattock Ri MUSWH N10 118 C2
Beatty Av GU GU1 250 D9
Beatty Rd CHES/WCR EN8 62 E10
STAN HA7 95 H7
STNW/STAM N16 119 M9
Beatty St CAMTN NW1 * 4 G7
Beattyville Gdns CLAY IG5 122 D1
Beauchamp Gdns
RKW/CH/CXG WD3 91 K2
Beauchamp Pl CHEL SW3 15 P4
Beauchamp Rd BTSEA SW11 157 P10
E/WMO/HCT KT8 198 A5
FSTGT E7 141 N2
NRWD SE19 203 L1
SUT SM1 221 K2
TWK TW1 176 F3
Beauchamps WGCE AL7 23 L6
Beauchamp St HCIRC EC1N 12 A4
Beauchamp Ter BARN SW13 156 E9
Beauclare Cl LHD/OX KT22 237 J7
Beauclerc Rd HMSMTH W6 156 E2
Beauclerk Cl FELT TW13 175 J4
Beaufort EHAM E6 142 D7
Beaufort Av
KTN/HRWW/WS HA3 114 F2
Beaufort Cl CDW/CHF RM16 167 L2
CHING E4 100 G7
EA W5 135 L7
EPP CM16 66 B3
PUT/ROE SW15 178 F4
REIG RH2 257 J9
ROMW/RG RM7 124 D2
WOKS/MYFD GU22 232 F2
Beaufort Ct RCHPK/HAM TW10 177 H7
Beaufort Dr GLDGN NW11 117 K2
Beaufort Gdns CHEL SW3 15 P3
HDN NW4 116 F4
HEST TW5 153 M7
IL IG1 122 D6
STRHM/NOR SW16 180 G10
Beaufort Rd EA W5 135 L7
KUT/HW KT1 199 K4
RCHPK/HAM TW10 177 H7
REIG RH2 257 J9
RSLP HA4 * 112 E7
TWK TW1 177 H3
WOKS/MYFD GU22 232 F2
Beauforts EGH TW20 171 P8
Beaufort St CHEL SW3 15 L9
Beaufort Wy EW KT17 220 D4
Beaufoy Rd TOTM N17 99 N8
Beaufoy Wk LBTH SE11 17 P6
Beaulah Pl WDSR SL4 * 170 A5
Beaulieu Av CAN/RD E16 141 N10
SYD SE26 182 A7
Beaulieu Cl CDALE/KGS NW9 116 B2
CMBW SE5 159 L9
DTCH/LGLY SL3 149 N7
HSLWW TW4 175 N1
MTCM CR4 202 B1
OXHEY WD19 93 K2
TWK TW1 177 J2
Beaulieu Dr PIN HA5 113 L4
WAB EN9 62 G9
Beaulieu Gdns WCHMH N21 99 K1
Beaulieu Pl CHSWK W4 155 P2
Beauly Ct ROM RM1 104 F9
Beauly Wy ROM RM1 104 F9
Beaumaris Gn CDALE/KGS NW9 * 116 B4
Beaumayes Cl HHW HP1 35 L7
Beaumonds STAL AL1 * 38 D6
Beaumont Av ALP/SUD HA0 115 H10
RCH/KEW TW9 155 L9
RYLN/HDSTN HA2 114 A4
STAL AL1 38 G5
WKENS W14 14 C7
Beaumont Cl CRAWW RH11 283 H8
GPK RM2 105 K10
KUTN/CMB KT2 177 M10
Beaumont Ct ALP/SUD HA0 115 H10
Beaumont Crs RAIN RM13 145 H1
WKENS W14 14 C7
Beaumont Dr ASHF TW15 174 E8
GVW DA11 190 C3
Beaumont Gdns HAMP NW3 117 K7
RBRW/HUT CM13 87 P10
Beaumont Ga RAD WD7 74 F1
Beaumont Gv WCHPL E1 140 C6
Beaumont Ms MHST W1U * 10 D3
PIN HA5 * 113 M1
Beaumont Park Dr
HLWW/ROY CM19 45 N1
Beaumont Pl BAR EN5 77 J5
FITZ W1T 11 H1
ISLW TW7 176 E1
Beaumont Ri ARCH N19 118 F6
Beaumont Rd BROX EN10 43 N10
CHSWK W4 155 P2
LEY E10 120 G5
NRWD SE19 181 K9
PLSTW E13 141 N5
PUR/KEN CR8 223 H9
SLN SL2 129 J7
STMC/STPC BR5 206 G6
WDSR SL4 * 149 H8
WIM/MER SW19 179 H3
Beaumonts REDH RH1 276 A8
Beaumont Sq WCHPL E1 140 C7
Beaumont St CAVSQ/HST W1G 10 D3
Beaumont Ter LEW SE13 * 183 K3
Beaumont Vw CHESW EN7 61 L2
Beaumont Wk HAMP NW3 4 B3
Beauvais Ter NTHLT UB5 133 L5
Beauval Rd EDUL SE22 181 N2
Beaverbank Rd ELTH/MOT SE9 184 G4
Beaver Cl HPTN TW12 198 A1
MRDN SM4 200 F7
PGE/AN SE20 * 181 P10
Beaver Rd BARK/HLT IG6 103 M6
Beavers Cl RGUW GU3 249 K9
Beavers Crs HSLWW TW4 153 L10
Beavers La HSLWW TW4 153 K9
Beaverwood Rd CHST BR7 185 H8
Beavor La HMSMTH W6 156 D3
Beazley Cl WARE SG12 26 D1
Bebbington Rd
WOOL/PLUM SE18 * 163 H3
Beblets Cl ORP BR6 227 J2
Beccles Dr BARK IG11 143 J1
Beccles St POP/IOD E14 140 E8
Bec Cl RSLP HA4 113 L8
Beck Cl LEW SE13 160 G7
Beckenham Gdns ED N9 99 M4
Beckenham Gv HAYES BR2 205 J2
Beckenham Hill Rd BECK BR3 182 G9
Beckenham La HAYES BR2 205 K2
Beckenham Place Pk BECK BR3 182 G10
Beckenham Rd BECK BR3 204 C1
Beckenshaw Gdns BNSTD SM7 239 P1
Becket Av EHAM E6 142 D5
Becket Cl RBRW/HUT CM13 107 H7
SNWD SE25 203 P6
WIM/MER SW19 * 201 L1
Becket Fold HRW HA1 * 114 E3
Becket Rd UED N18 100 B5
Beckets Sq BERK HP4 * 33 M3
Becket St STHWK SE1 18 G3
Beckets Wk WARE SG12 * 26 C2
Beckett Av PUR/KEN CR8 241 J1
Beckett Cha DTCH/LGLY SL3 150 C4
Beckett Cl BELV DA17 163 P2
STRHM/NOR SW16 180 E5
WLSDN NW10 136 A1
Beckett La CRAWW RH11 283 N4
Becketts HERT/WAT SG14 25 H6
Beckett's Av STALW/RED AL3 38 B3
Becketts Cl EBED/NFELT TW14 175 J2
ORP BR6 207 J10
Becketts Pl KUT/HW KT1 199 J1
Beckett Wk BECK BR3 182 D9
Beckford Cl WKENS W14 14 D6
Beckford Dr STMC/STPC BR5 206 G7
Beckford Pl WALW SE17 * 18 F8
Beckford Rd CROY/NA CR0 203 N6
Beckingham Rd GUW GU2 249 M9
Beck La BECK BR3 204 C3
Beckley Cl GVE DA12 191 L5
Becklow Rd SHB W12 156 C1
Beckman Cl RSEV TN14 246 D1
Beck River Pk BECK BR3 204 E1
Beck Rd HACK E8 140 A3
Becks Rd SCUP DA14 185 K6
Beckton Rd CAN/RD E16 141 L7
Beck Wy BECK BR3 204 E3
Beckway Rd STRHM/NOR SW16 202 E2
Beckway St WALW SE17 19 J6
Beckwell Rd SL SL1 149 H1
Beckwith Rd HNHL SE24 181 L2
Beclands Rd TOOT SW17 180 B9
Becmead Av
KTN/HRWW/WS HA3 114 G3
STRHM/NOR SW16 180 E7
Becondale Rd NRWD SE19 181 M8
Becontree Av BCTR RM8 123 L9
BCTR RM8 123 N7
Bective Rd FSTGT E7 121 M9
PUT/ROE SW15 157 J10
Becton Pl ERITH DA8 164 C7
Bedale Cl CRAWW RH11 283 M9
Bedale Rd ENC/FH EN2 79 K4
HARH RM3 105 P6
Bedale St STHWK SE1 * 12 G10
Beddington Cross CROY/NA CR0 202 F7
Beddington Farm Rd
CROY/NA CR0 202 F9
Beddington Gdns CAR SM5 222 B3
Beddington Gn STMC/STPC BR5 207 J1
Beddington Gv WLGTN SM6 222 E2
Beddington La CROY/NA CR0 202 E8
Beddington Rd GDMY/SEVK IG3 123 J5
STMC/STPC BR5 207 H1
Beddington Ter CROY/NA CR0 * 202 G7
Beddlestead La BH/WHM TN16 243 M7
WARL CR6 243 L4
Bede Cl PIN HA5 93 L9
Bedens Rd SCUP DA14 185 P9
Bede Rd CHDH RM6 123 M4
Bedevere Rd ED N9 99 P4
Bedfont Cl EBED/NFELT TW14 174 D3
MTCM CR4 202 B2
Bedfont Ct STWL/WRAY TW19 151 L9
Bedfont Court Est
STWL/WRAY TW19 * 151 L10
Bedfont Green Cl
EBED/NFELT TW14 174 D4
Bedfont La EBED/NFELT TW14 174 F3
EBED/NFELT TW14 175 H4
Bedfont Rd EBED/NFELT TW14 174 D4
FELT TW13 174 G6
STWL/WRAY TW19 174 A2
Bedford Av AMS HP6 69 P5
BAR EN5 77 J9
RSQ WC1B 11 K4
SL SL1 128 F8
YEAD UB4 133 J8
Bedfordbury CHCR WC2N 11 L7
Bedford Cl CHSWK W4 156 C6
MUSWH N10 98 B8
RKW/CH/CXG WD3 70 E4
WOKN/KNAP GU21 231 P1
Bedford Cnr CHSWK W4 * 156 B3
Bedford Ct CHCR WC2N 11 L8
Bedford Crs PEND EN3 80 D1
Bedford Dr SLN SL2 108 G10
Bedford Gdns HCH RM12 125 K7
KENS W8 8 E10
Bedford Hl BAL SW12 180 C5
Bedford La ASC SL5 192 G5
Bedford Pk CROY/NA CR0 203 K8
Bedford Park Rd STAL AL1 38 D6
Bedford Pl CROY/NA CR0 203 L8
RSQ WC1B 11 L3
Bedford Rd BFN/LL DA15 185 H6
CEND/HSY/T N8 118 E4
CHSWK W4 156 A2
CLAP SW4 158 F10
DART DA1 187 P3
ED N9 100 A1
EFNCH N2 117 P1
EHAM E6 142 D3
GRAYS RM17 * 167 N4
GU GU1 267 P1
GVW DA11 190 C5
HRW HA1 114 B4
IL IG1 122 E8
MLHL NW7 96 B3
NTHWD HA6 92 E5
ORP BR6 207 L9
RSLP HA4 112 G9
SEVS/STOTM N15 119 L2
STAL AL1 38 D7
SWFD E18 101 M10
WALTH E17 100 F10
WDGN N22 98 F9
WEA W13 134 G10
WHTN TW2 176 C6
WPK KT4 200 F9
Bedford Rw GINN WC1R 11 P3
Bedford Sq RSQ WC1B 11 K4
Bedford St BERK HP4 34 A5
COVGDN WC2E 11 L7
WATN WD24 73 J5
Bedford Vls KUT/HW KT1 * 199 L2
Bedford Wy STPAN WC1H 11 K2
Bedgebury Gdns
WIM/MER SW19 179 H5
Bedgebury Rd ELTH/MOT SE9 162 A10
Bedivere Rd BMLY BR1 183 M6
Bedlow Cl STJWD NW8 9 M2
Bedlow Wy CROY/NA CR0 222 G1
Bedmond La ABLGY WD5 55 H2
LCOL/BKTW AL2 37 K10
Bedmond Rd ABLGY WD5 54 G5
HHS/BOV HP3 36 E8
Bedonwell Rd BELV DA17 163 P5
BELV DA17 164 A5
BXLYHN DA7 164 A7
Bedser Cl LBTH SE11 17 P9
THHTH CR7 203 K3
WOKN/KNAP GU21 232 D2
Bedser Dr GFD/PVL UB6 114 C10
Bedster Gdns E/WMO/HCT KT8 198 A2
Bedwardine Rd NRWD SE19 181 M10
Bedwell Av BRKMPK AL9 42 B2
Bedwell Cl WGCE AL7 23 H6
Bedwell Gdns HYS/HAR UB3 152 F4
Bedwell Rd BELV DA17 164 B4
TOTM N17 99 M9
Beeby Rd CAN/RD E16 141 N7
Beech Av ACT W3 136 B10
BFN/LL DA15 185 K3
BH/WHM TN16 244 A5
BKHH IG9 101 N3
BTFD TW8 154 G6
EHSLY KT24 253 L6
ENC/FH EN2 79 H1
RAD WD7 56 F9
RBRW/HUT CM13 107 L4
RSLP HA4 113 J6
SAND/SEL CR2 223 L7
SWLY BR8 208 G4
TRDG/WHET N20 97 P2
UPMR RM14 126 A8
Beech Bottom STALW/RED AL3 38 C3
Beech Cl ASHF TW15 174 E8
BF/WBF KT14 215 P8
CAR SM5 202 A9
COB KT11 217 P8
DEPT SE8 160 E5
DORK RH4 272 E1
ED N9 79 P10
EHSLY KT24 253 L4
HARP AL5 20 B6
HAT AL10 40 D5
HCH RM12 125 J8
LOU IG10 82 E7
PUT/ROE SW15 178 D3
SUN TW16 197 L2
WARE SG12 26 C3
WDR/YW UB7 152 B2
WOT/HER KT12 217 K1
Beech Close Ct COB KT11 217 N7
Beech Copse BMLY BR1 206 C2
SAND/SEL CR2 223 M2
Beech Ct ELTH/MOT SE9 * 184 B2
Beech Crs KWD/TDW/WH KT20 255 P6
STALE/WH AL4 21 J4
Beechcroft ASHTD KT21 237 L5
BERK HP4 33 P6
CHST BR7 184 D10
Beechcroft Av BXLYHN DA7 164 E8
GLDGN NW11 117 J5
NWMAL KT3 199 P1
PUR/KEN CR8 241 L1
RKW/CH/CXG WD3 72 D10
RYLN/HDSTN HA2 113 P5
SLH/COR SS17 169 K3
STHL UB1 133 N10
Beechcroft Cl ASC SL5 192 C4
HEST TW5 153 M6
ORP BR6 226 G1
STRHM/NOR SW16 180 G8
Beechcroft Dr GUW GU2 267 J3
Beechcroft Gdns WBLY HA9 115 L8
Beechcroft Mnr WEY KT13 196 E10
Beechcroft Rd BUSH WD23 73 M9
CHSGTN KT9 219 L1
CSHM HP5 50 G6
MORT/ESHN SW14 * 155 P9
ORP BR6 226 G1
SWFD E18 101 N10
TOOT SW17 180 A6
Beechdale WCHMH N21 98 G3
Beechdale Rd BRXS/STRHM SW2 180 G2
Beech Dell HAYES BR2 226 C1
Beechdene KWD/TDW/WH KT20 238 E8
Beech Dr BERK HP4 33 P6
BORE WD6 75 L6
EFNCH N2 118 A1
KWD/TDW/WH KT20 239 J8
REIG RH2 257 N10
RPLY/SEND GU23 233 J10
SBW CM21 29 N3
Beechen Cliff Wy ISLW TW7 154 E8
Beechengrove PIN HA5 113 N1
Beechen Gv WAT WD17 73 K8
Beechen La KWD/TDW/WH KT20 257 J1
Beechenlea La SWLY BR8 209 H4
Beechen Pl FSTH SE23 182 B5
Beechen Wd RKW/CH/CXG WD3 90 G5
Beeches Av CAR SM5 221 P4
Beeches Cl KWD/TDW/WH KT20 239 K9
PGE/AN SE20 204 B1
Beeches Crs CRAWE RH10 283 P9
Beeches Dr SLN SL2 108 G9
Beeches Pk BEAC HP9 88 C9
Beeches Rd CHEAM SM3 201 H8
SLN SL2 108 G10
TOOT SW17 179 P6
The Beeches AMS HP6 68 F2
BNSTD SM7 239 L2
BRW CM14 106 G4
CHING E4 * 101 J2
HART DA3 211 P2
HNWL W7 * 154 E1
LCOL/BKTW AL2 56 C3
LHD/OX KT22 236 D10
RKW/CH/CXG WD3 71 J9
STA TW18 * 173 K8
SWLY BR8 186 G10
TIL RM18 168 E8
WATW WD18 * 73 J7
Beeches Wk BELMT SM2 221 N5
Beeches Wd KWD/TDW/WH KT20 239 K8
Beechey Cl CRAWE RH10 285 J2
Beechey Wy CRAWE RH10 285 J2
Beech Farm Dr STALE/WH AL4 39 L2
Beech Farm Rd WARL CR6 243 J6
Beechfield BNSTD SM7 221 L9
HOD EN11 26 G9
KGLGY WD4 54 A6
SBW CM21 30 A1
Beechfield Cl BORE WD6 75 K6
Beechfield Gdns ROMW/RG RM7 124 D5
Beechfield Rd BMLY BR1 205 P2
CAT SE6 182 E4
ERITH DA8 164 F6
FSBYPK N4 119 K4
HHW HP1 35 L7
WARE SG12 26 E1
WGCE AL7 23 H7
Beechfield Wk WAB EN9 81 J1
Beech Gdns CRAWE RH10 285 P6
DAGE RM10 144 C2
EA W5 155 K1
WOKN/KNAP GU21 232 B1
Beech Gv ADL/WDHM KT15 215 L1
AMSS HP7 69 H5
BARK/HLT IG6 103 H7
CHOB/PIR GU24 230 B6
CTHM CR3 259 L2
EPSOM KT18 238 E3
GT/LBKH KT23 253 P3
GUW GU2 249 L10
MTCM CR4 202 E5
NWMAL KT3 200 A3
SOCK/AV RM15 166 B1
WOKS/MYFD GU22 232 A9
Beech Hall CHERT KT16 * 214 F4
Beech Hall Crs CHING E4 101 J8
Beech Hall Rd CHING E4 101 H8
Beech Hl EBAR EN4 77 N4
WOKS/MYFD GU22 232 A9
Beech Hill Av EBAR EN4 77 N5
Beech Hill Ct BERK HP4 34 A5
Beech Hill Gdns WAB EN9 81 N3
Beech Hill Rd ASC SL5 192 D6
Beechhill Rd ELTH/MOT SE9 184 D1
Beech Holme CRAWE RH10 285 P6
Beech Holt LHD/OX KT22 237 H8
Beech House Rd CROY/NA CR0 203 L10
Beech Hyde La STALE/WH AL4 21 L4
Beechlands Cl HART DA3 211 M5
Beech La BEAC HP9 89 K8
GUW GU2 267 P3
Beechlawn GU GU1 268 C1
Beech Lawns
NFNCH/WDSPK N12 * 97 N6
Beechmeads COB KT11 * 217 L9
Beech Ms WARE SG12 26 C4
Beechmont Av VW GU25 194 A6
Beechmont Cl BMLY BR1 183 K8
Beechmont Rd SEV TN13 265 J5
Beechmore Gdns CHEAM SM3 200 G9
Beechmore Rd BTSEA SW11 158 A7
Beechmount Av HNWL W7 134 C7
Beecholme BNSTD SM7 * 221 H10
Beecholme Av MTCM CR4 202 C1
Beecholme Est CLPT E5 * 120 B8
Beech Pk TRING HP23 * 32 E4
Beechpark Wy WAT WD17 72 F3
Beech Pl EPP CM16 65 J7
STALW/RED AL3 * 38 C3
Beech Rd BH/WHM TN16 243 P3
DART DA1 187 L4
DTCH/LGLY SL3 150 B1
EBED/NFELT TW14 174 F3
EW KT17 238 C1
FBAR/BDGN N11 98 F7
ORP BR6 227 K4
REDH RH1 258 D2
REIG RH2 257 K8
SEV TN13 265 J1
STALW/RED AL3 38 D3
STRHM/NOR SW16 202 F2
WATN WD24 73 H3
WEY KT13 216 E1
Beechrow KUTN/CMB KT2 177 K7
Beechside CRAWE RH10 283 P8
Beech St ROMW/RG RM7 124 D2
Beech St (Below) BARB EC2Y 12 E3
Beechtree Av EGH TW20 171 N9
Beech Tree Cl CRAWE RH10 * 283 N6
IS N1 6 A3
STAN HA7 95 H6
Beech Tree Gld CHING E4 101 L2
Beech Tree La STA TW18 * 195 L2
Beechtree La STALW/RED AL3 37 J8
Beech Tree Pl SUT SM1 221 L2
Beech V WOKS/MYFD GU22 * 232 B4
Beechvale Cl
NFNCH/WDSPK N12 97 P6
Beech Wk DART DA1 165 H10
EW KT17 220 D7
MLHL NW7 96 A7
Beechway BXLY DA5 185 N2
Beech Wy EW KT17 238 C1
Beechway GU GU1 250 E9
Beech Wy SAND/SEL CR2 224 C9
WHTN TW2 175 P6
WLSDN NW10 136 A2
Beech Waye CFSP/GDCR SL9 110 D5
Beechwood
KWD/TDW/WH KT20 * 255 N7
Beechwood Av AMS HP6 69 P4
COUL/CHIP CR5 240 C1
FNCH N3 117 J1
GFD/PVL UB6 134 A5
HYS/HAR UB3 132 E9
KWD/TDW/WH KT20 239 K7
ORP BR6 227 H3
POTB/CUF EN6 59 L9
RCH/KEW TW9 155 M7
RKW/CH/CXG WD3 70 E8
RSLP HA4 112 G7
RYLN/HDSTN HA2 114 A8
STA TW18 173 L9
STAL AL1 38 G4
SUN TW16 175 H9
THHTH CR7 203 J4
UX/CGN UB8 132 A8
WEY KT13 216 F1
Beechwood Cl AMS HP6 69 P5
CHESW EN7 61 M2
EFNCH N2 * 118 A2
HERT/BAY SG13 25 N5
MLHL NW7 96 B6
SURB KT6 199 H7
WEY KT13 216 F1
WOKN/KNAP GU21 231 K3
Beechwood Crs BXLYHN DA7 163 N9
Beechwood Dr COB KT11 217 P7
HAYES BR2 226 A1
WFD IG8 101 L6
Beechwood Gdns CLAY IG5 122 C3
CTHM CR3 241 P8
RAIN RM13 145 J7
RYLN/HDSTN HA2 114 A8
SL SL1 149 K1
Beechwood Gv ACT W3 136 B9
Beechwood La WARL CR6 242 C5
Beechwood Mnr WEY KT13 216 F1
Beechwood Ms ED N9 99 P3
Beechwood Pk HHS/BOV HP3 35 J10
LHD/OX KT22 237 H8
RKW/CH/CXG WD3 71 J8
SWFD E18 121 M1
Beechwood Ri CHST BR7 184 E7
WATN WD24 73 J2
Beechwood Rd BEAC HP9 88 B9
CEND/HSY/T N8 118 E2
CTHM CR3 241 P8
HACK E8 7 L2
SAND/SEL CR2 223 M5
SLN SL2 129 J7
VW GU25 193 N7
WOKN/KNAP GU21 231 K4
Beechwood Vls REDH RH1 276 B10
Beechworth Cl HAMP NW3 117 L7
Beechy Lees Rd RSEV TN14 247 L3
Beecot La WOT/HER KT12 197 K9
Beecroft La BROCKY SE4 182 D1
Beecroft Ms BROCKY SE4 182 D1
Beecroft Rd BROCKY SE4 182 D1
Beehive Cha BRWN CM15 87 J1
Beehive Cl BORE WD6 75 J10
HACK E8 7 L3
HGDN/ICK UB10 132 A2
Beehive Gn WGCE AL7 23 K7
Beehive La REDBR IG4 122 C3
WGCE AL7 23 K8
Beehive Pl BRXN/ST SW9 159 H9
Beehive Ring Rd HORL RH6 284 C1
Beehive Rd CHESW EN7 61 J4
STA TW18 173 J8
Beehive Wy REIG RH2 275 L4
Beeken Dene ORP BR6 226 F1
Beel Cl AMSS HP7 69 P5
Beeleigh Rd MRDN SM4 201 L4
Beesfield La EYN DA4 209 P8
Beeston Cl HACK E8 119 P10
OXHEY WD19 93 L5
Beeston Dr CHES/WCR EN8 62 C3
Beeston Pl BGVA SW1W 16 F4
Beeston Rd EBAR EN4 77 N10
Beeston Wy EBED/NFELT TW14 175 K2
Beethoven Rd BORE WD6 95 H1
Beethoven St NKENS W10 2 B9
Beeton Cl PIN HA5 93 P8
Begbie Rd BKHTH/KID SE3 161 P7
Beggars Bush La WATW WD18 72 E9
Beggarshouse La HORL RH6 278 F7
Beggars La BH/WHM TN16 262 G1
CHOB/PIR GU24 213 H7
RDKG RH5 270 F5
Beggar's Roost La SUT SM1 221 K3
Begonia Cl EHAM E6 142 B7
Begonia Pl HPTN TW12 175 P9
Behenna Cl CRAWW RH11 283 H8
Beira St BAL SW12 180 C3
Beken Ct GSTN WD25 * 73 K1
Bekesbourne St POP/IOD E14 * 140 D8
Belcher Rd HOD EN11 44 F2
Belchers La WAB EN9 45 P10
Belcroft Cl BMLY BR1 183 L10
Beldam Bridge Rd
CHOB/PIR GU24 212 F9
Beldam Haw RSEV TN14 228 B7
Beldham Gdns E/WMO/HCT KT8 198 A3
Belfairs Dr CHDH RM6 123 M5
Belfairs Gdn OXHEY WD19 93 L6
Belfairs Gn OXHEY WD19 93 L6
Belfast Av SL SL1 129 J8
Belfast Rd SNWD SE25 204 A4
STNW/STAM N16 119 N7
Belfield Rd HOR/WEW KT19 220 A5
Belford Gv WOOL/PLUM SE18 162 D3
Belford Rd BORE WD6 75 L4
Belfort Rd PECK SE15 160 B8
Belfry Av DEN/HRF UB9 91 K9
Belfry Cl BERM/RHTH SE16 160 A4
BMLY BR1 206 E4
Belfry La RKW/CH/CXG WD3 91 M2
The Belfry REDH RH1 258 A9
Belgrade Rd HPTN TW12 198 A1
STNW/STAM N16 119 M9
Belgrave Av GPK RM2 125 K1
Belgrave Cl ACT W3 155 P1
MLHL NW7 96 A6
STALE/WH AL4 39 H2
STHGT/OAK N14 78 D9
STMC/STPC BR5 207 M4
WOT/HER KT12 217 J1
Belgrave Crs SUN TW16 197 J1
Belgrave Dr KGLGY WD4 54 D4
Belgrave Gdns STAN HA7 95 H6
STHGT/OAK N14 78 E9
STJWD NW8 3 J6
Belgrave Mnr WOKS/MYFD GU22 232 B5
Belgrave Ms UX/CGN UB8 131 N6
Belgrave Ms South KTBR SW1X 16 D3
Belgrave Ms West KTBR SW1X 16 C3
Belgrave Pde SL SL1 * 129 K9
Belgrave Pl KTBR SW1X 16 D4
Belgrave Rd BARN SW13 156 C6
HSLWW TW4 153 N9
IL IG1 122 C6
MTCM CR4 201 N3
PIM SW1V 17 H6
PLSTW E13 141 P6
SL SL1 129 L9
SNWD SE25 203 N4
SUN TW16 197 J1
WALTH E17 120 F4
WAN E11 121 M6
Belgrave Sq KTBR SW1X 16 C3
Belgrave St WCHPL E1 140 C8
Belgrave Wk MTCM CR4 201 N3
Belgravia Cl BAR EN5 77 J7
Belgravia Gdns BMLY BR1 183 K9
Belgravia Ms KUT/HW KT1 199 J4
Belgrove St CAMTN NW1 5 L9
Belham Rd KGLGY WD4 54 A4
Belinda Rd BRXN/ST SW9 159 J9
Belitha Vls IS N1 5 P3
Bellamaine Cl THMD SE28 163 J1
Bellamy Cl EDGW HA8 95 P4
HGDN/ICK UB10 112 B9
POP/IOD E14 160 F1
WAT WD17 73 H5
WKENS W14 14 D8
Bellamy Dr STAN HA7 94 G9
Bellamy Rd CHES/WCR EN8 62 D5
CHING E4 100 G7
ENC/FH EN2 * 79 L6
Bellamy St BAL SW12 180 C3
Bel La FELT TW13 175 M6
Bellarmine Cl THMD SE28 143 J10
Bellasis Av BRXS/STRHM SW2 180 F4
Bell Av HARH RM3 105 J9
WDR/YW UB7 152 A2
Bell Bridge Rd CHERT KT16 195 J8
The Bell Centre CRAWE RH10 * 284 A3
Bellchambers Cl LCOL/BKTW AL2 57 H2
Bell Cl ABLGY WD5 54 G3
PIN HA5 113 K1
RDART DA2 188 E1
SLN SL2 129 N7
Bellclose Rd WDR/YW UB7 151 P1
Bell Common EPP CM16 65 H8
Bell Crs COUL/CHIP CR5 240 C7
Bell Dr WAND/EARL SW18 179 H3
Bellefield Rd STMC/STPC BR5 207 L5
Bellefields Rd BRXN/ST SW9 158 G9
Bellegrove Cl WELL DA16 163 J8
Bellegrove Rd WELL DA16 163 H8
Bellenden Rd PECK SE15 159 N8
Belle Staines Pleasaunce
CHING E4 100 F3
Belleville Rd BTSEA SW11 179 P1
Belle Vue GFD/PVL UB6 134 C3
Belle Vue Cl STA TW18 195 K1
Belle Vue La BUSH WD23 94 C2
Bellevue Pk THHTH CR7 203 K3
Belle Vue Pl SL SL1 * 149 L2
Bellevue Pl WCHPL E1 * 140 B6
Belle Vue Rd CRW RM5 104 D7
HDN NW4 116 G2
ORP BR6 226 D6
WALTH E17 101 J10
Bellevue Rd BARN SW13 156 D8
BXLYHS DA6 186 A1
EMPK RM11 125 N6
FBAR/BDGN N11 98 B5
KUT/HW KT1 199 K3
TOOT SW17 180 A3
WARE SG12 26 D2
WEA W13 134 G6
Belle Vue Ter DEN/HRF UB9 * 91 K8
Bellew St TOOT SW17 179 M6
Bell Farm Av DAGE RM10 124 D8
Bellfield CROY/NA CR0 224 D5
Bellfield Av KTN/HRWW/WS HA3 94 C7
Bellfield Cl BKHTH/KID SE3 161 N6
Bellfield Gdns HLWE CM17 47 M2
Bellfields Rd GU GU1 250 A8
Bell Gdns LEY E10 * 120 F6
STMC/STPC BR5 207 M5
Bellgate HHNE HP2 35 P3
Bellgate Ms KTTN NW5 118 C9
Bell Gn HHS/BOV HP3 * 52 E3
SYD SE26 182 E7
Bell Green La SYD SE26 182 E8
Bellhouse La BRW CM14 86 D9
Bell House Rd ROMW/RG RM7 124 D6
Bellina Ms KTTN NW5 118 C9
Bellingdon Rd CSHM HP5 50 G7
Bellingham Dr REIG RH2 257 J10
Bellingham Gn CAT SE6 182 F6
Bellingham Rd CAT SE6 183 H6
Bell La ABLGY WD5 55 H4
AMSS HP7 69 N5
BERK HP4 33 K4
BRKMPK AL9 41 K10
BROX EN10 44 D7
CAN/RD E16 141 L10
HDN NW4 116 G2
HERT/WAT SG14 25 L5
LCOL/BKTW AL2 57 L5

LHD/OX KT22 236 C9
PEND EN3 80 C4
TWK TW1 176 F4
WBLY HA9 * 115 J7
WCHPL E1 13 L4
WDSR SL4 148 E3
Bell Lane Cl LHD/OX KT22 236 C9
Bellman Av GVE DA12 191 H4
Bellmarsh Rd ADL/WDHM KT15 215 L1
Bell Md SBW CM21 29 P1
Bell Meadow GDST RH9 260 B8
NRWD SE19 181 M7
Bellmount Wood Av WAT WD17 72 F5
Belloc Cl CRAWE RH10 284 C6
Bello Cl HNHL SE24 181 J4
Bellot St GNWCH SE10 161 K4
Bell Pde HSLW TW3 * 154 A10
WWKM BR4 * 205 H9
Bellridge Pl BEAC HP9 88 A5
Bellring Cl BELV DA17 164 B5
Bell Rd E/WMO/HCT KT8 198 C5
EN EN1 79 L5
The Bell Rbt LCOL/BKTW AL2 57 M3
Bells Hl BAR EN5 76 G9
SLN SL2 129 M3
Bells Hill Gn SLN SL2 129 M2
Bells La DTCH/LGLY SL3 150 E9
Bell St BAY/PAD W2 9 N3
REIG RH2 257 K10
SBW CM21 29 P1
WOOL/PLUM SE18 162 B7
Bellswood La IVER SL0 130 E7
Belltrees Gv STRHM/NOR SW16 180 G8
Bell Vw STALE/WH AL4 39 J6
WDSR SL4 148 E9
Bell View Cl WDSR SL4 148 E8
Bell Water Ga WOOL/PLUM SE18 162 D2
Bellweir Cl STWL/WRAY TW19 172 E5
Bellwether La REDH RH1 277 J9
Bell Wharf La CANST EC4R 12 F8
Bellwood Rd PECK SE15 160 C10
Bell Yd LINN WC2A 12 A6
Bell Yard Ms STHWK SE1 19 K2
Belmont SLN SL2 128 F7
Belmont Av ALP/SUD HA0 135 L3
EBAR EN4 78 A9
ED N9 99 P2
GUW GU2 249 L7
NWDGN UB2 153 M2
NWMAL KT3 200 D5
PLMGR N13 98 F6
TOTM N17 119 K1
UPMR RM14 125 N7
WELL DA16 163 H8
Belmont Cir
KTN/HRWW/WS HA3 * 94 G9
Belmont Cl CHING E4 101 J6
CLAP SW4 158 D9
EBAR EN4 78 A8
TRDG/WHET N20 97 L2
UX/CGN UB8 131 N1
Belmont Gv CHSWK W4 156 A3
LEW SE13 161 J9
Belmont Hl LEW SE13 161 J9
STAL AL1 38 C7
Belmont La CHST BR7 184 F8
STAN HA7 95 H8
Belmont Pde CHST BR7 * 184 E8
GLDGN NW11 * 117 J3
Belmont Pk LEW SE13 161 J10
Belmont Park Cl LEW SE13 161 K10
Belmont Park Rd LEY E10 120 G4
Belmont Ri BELMT SM2 221 J5
Belmont Rd BELMT SM2 221 K6
BUSH WD23 73 M9
CHST BR7 184 E8
CLAP SW4 158 D9
CSHM HP5 50 G5
ERITH DA8 164 C6
GRAYS RM17 167 L4
HCH RM12 125 L8
HHS/BOV HP3 35 P9
IL IG1 122 F8
KTN/HRWW/WS HA3 114 E1
LHD/OX KT22 236 F8
REIG RH2 275 M1
SEVS/STOTM N15 119 K2
SNWD SE25 204 A5
UX/CGN UB8 131 N2
WHTN TW2 176 C5
WLGTN SM6 222 D2
Belmont St CAMTN NW1 4 D3
Belmont Ter CHSWK W4 156 A3
Belmor BORE WD6 75 M9
Belmore Av WOKS/MYFD GU22 232 G2
YEAD UB4 133 H8
Belmore La HOLWY N7 118 E10
Belmore St VX/NE SW8 158 E7
Beloe Cl PUT/ROE SW15 156 D10
Belsham Cl CSHM HP5 50 G4
Belsham St HOM E9 140 B1
Belsize RKW/CH/CXG WD3 * 52 G9
Belsize Av HAMP NW3 3 N1
PLMGR N13 98 G7
WEA W13 154 G2
Belsize Cl HHS/BOV HP3 36 B7
STALE/WH AL4 39 H1
Belsize Court Gdns HAMP NW3 117 N10
Belsize Crs HAMP NW3 3 M1
Belsize Gdns SUT SM1 221 L1
Belsize Gv HAMP NW3 3 P1
Belsize La HAMP NW3 3 L2
Belsize Pk HAMP NW3 3 L2
Belsize Park Gdns HAMP NW3 3 N2
Belsize Park Ms HAMP NW3 * 3 M1
Belsize Pl HAMP NW3 117 N10
Belsize Rd HHS/BOV HP3 36 B7
KIL/WHAMP NW6 2 G5
KTN/HRWW/WS HA3 94 C8
Belsize Sq HAMP NW3 3 M2
Belsize Ter HAMP NW3 3 M1
Belson Rd WOOL/PLUM SE18 162 C3
Belswains La HHS/BOV HP3 35 P10
Beltana Dr GVE DA12 191 H7
Beltane Dr WIM/MER SW19 178 G6
Belthorn Crs BAL SW12 180 D3
Beltinge Rd HARH RM3 125 N1
Beltona Gdns CHES/WCR EN8 62 C3
Belton Rd BERK HP4 33 M4
FSTGT E7 141 N2
SCUP DA14 185 K7
TOTM N17 119 M1
WAN E11 121 K9
WLSDN NW10 136 D1
Belton Wy BOW E3 140 F7
Beltran Rd FUL/PGN SW6 157 L8
Beltwood Rd BELV DA17 164 D3
Belvedere Av BARK/HLT IG6 102 E10
WIM/MER SW19 179 H8
Belvedere Buildings STHWK SE1 18 D2
Belvedere Cl AMS HP6 69 L3
ESH/CLAY KT10 218 A2
GUW GU2 249 N8
GVE DA12 190 F4
TEDD TW11 176 D8
WEY KT13 216 B2
Belvedere Ct BELV DA17 164 A2
OXHEY WD19 73 M10
Belvedere Dr WIM/MER SW19 179 H8
Belvedere Gdns
E/WMO/HCT KT8 197 N5
LCOL/BKTW AL2 55 N3
Belvedere Gv WIM/MER SW19 179 H8
Belvedere Ms PECK SE15 160 B9
Belvedere Pl BRXS/STRHM SW2 158 G10
Belvedere Rd ABYW SE2 143 N10
BH/WHM TN16 244 C4
BRW CM14 106 E4
BXLYHN DA7 164 A9
HNWL W7 154 D2
LEY E10 120 D6
NRWD SE19 181 N10
STHWK SE1 17 N1
Belvedere Sq WIM/MER SW19 179 H8
Belvedere Strd CDALE/KGS NW9 96 C10
The Belvedere WBPTN SW10 * 157 M7
Belvedere Wy
KTN/HRWW/WS HA3 115 K4
Belvoir Rd EDUL SE22 181 P3
Belvue Cl NTHLT UB5 133 P2
Belvue Rd NTHLT UB5 133 P2
Bembridge Cl KIL/WHAMP NW6 2 A3
Bembridge Gdns RSLP HA4 112 E7
Bembridge Pl GSTN WD25 * 55 H9
Bemerton Est IS N1 5 N5
Bemerton St IS N1 5 N5
Bemish Rd PUT/ROE SW15 156 G9
Bempton Dr RSLP HA4 113 J7
Bemsted Rd WALTH E17 120 E1
Benares Rd WOOL/PLUM SE18 163 J3
Benbow Cl STAL AL1 38 G8
Benbow Moorings
UX/CGN UB8 * 131 M7
Benbow Rd HMSMTH W6 156 E2
Benbow St DEPT SE8 160 F5
Benbow Wy UX/CGN UB8 131 M7
Benbrick Rd GUW GU2 267 M1
Benbury Cl BMLY BR1 183 H8
The Bence EGH TW20 194 E3
Bench Fld SAND/SEL CR2 223 N3
Benchleys Rd HHW HP1 35 J7
Bench Manor Crs
CFSP/GDCR SL9 89 P10
The Bench RCHPK/HAM TW10 * 177 H6
Bencombe Rd PUR/KEN CR8 223 H10
Bencroft CHESW EN7 61 P2
Bencroft Rd HHNE HP2 35 P6
STRHM/NOR SW16 180 D10
Bencurtis Pk WWKM BR4 205 J10
Bendall Ms CAMTN NW1 9 P3
Bendemeer Rd PUT/ROE SW15 156 G9
Bendish Rd EHAM E6 142 B2
Bendmore Av ABYW SE2 163 K4
Bendon Va WAND/EARL SW18 179 L3
Bendysh Rd BUSH WD23 73 M7
Benedict Cl ORP BR6 207 H10
Benedict Dr EBED/NFELT TW14 174 E3
Benedictine Ga CHES/WCR EN8 62 D4
Benedict Rd BRXN/ST SW9 158 G9
MTCM CR4 201 N3
Benedict Wy EFNCH N2 * 117 M1
Benedict Whf MTCM CR4 201 P3
Benenden Gn HAYES BR2 205 M5
Benen-Stock Rd
STWL/WRAY TW19 173 K2
Benets Rd EMPK RM11 125 P6
Benett Gdns STRHM/NOR SW16 202 F2
Benfleet Cl COB KT11 217 M8
SUT SM1 201 M10
Benfleet Wy FBAR/BDGN N11 98 B3
Benford Rd HOD EN11 44 E5
Bengal Rd IL IG1 122 E9
Bengarth Dr
KTN/HRWW/WS HA3 94 C10
Bengarth Rd NTHLT UB5 133 L3
Bengeo Mdw HERT/WAT SG14 * 25 K2
Bengeo Ms HERT/WAT SG14 * 25 K2
Bengeo St HERT/WAT SG14 25 K4
Bengeworth Rd CMBW SE5 159 K9
HRW HA1 114 F7
Ben Hale Cl STAN HA7 94 F6
Benham Cl CHSGTN KT9 219 H3
COUL/CHIP CR5 241 J4
CSHM HP5 50 G6
Benham Gdns HSLWW TW4 175 N1
Benham Rd HNWL W7 134 D7
Benhams Dr HORL RH6 280 B2
Benhill Av SUT SM1 221 M1
Benhill Rd CMBW SE5 159 L6
SUT SM1 201 M10
Benhill Wood Rd SUT SM1 221 M1
Benhilton Gdns SUT SM1 201 L10
Benhurst Av HCH RM12 125 J9
Benhurst Cl SAND/SEL CR2 224 C6
Benhurst Gdns SAND/SEL CR2 224 B6
Benhurst La STRHM/NOR SW16 181 H8
Beningfield Dr LCOL/BKTW AL2 56 G3
Benin St LEW SE13 183 J3
Benjafield Cl UED N18 100 A5
Benjamin Cl EMPK RM11 125 H4
HACK E8 7 P5
Benjamin Ms BAL SW12 180 D3
Benjamin Rd CRAWE RH10 284 E9
Benjamin St FARR EC1M 12 C3
Ben Jonson Rd WCHPL E1 140 D7
Benledi St POP/IOD E14 141 J8
Benn Cl OXTED RH8 261 M10
Bennelong Cl SHB W12 136 E9
Benner La CHOB/PIR GU24 212 E8
Bennerley Rd BTSEA SW11 179 P1
Bennet Cl KUT/HW KT1 199 H1
Bennetsfield Rd STKPK UB11 132 C10
Bennet's Hl BLKFR EC4V 12 D7
Bennett Cl COB KT11 217 H9
HSLWW TW4 175 M1
NTHWD HA6 92 G8
WELL DA16 163 K8
WGCE AL7 23 J9
Bennett Gv LEW SE13 160 G7
Bennett Pk BKHTH/KID SE3 161 L9
Bennett Rd BRXN/ST SW9 159 H8
CHDH RM6 123 P4
PLSTW E13 141 P6
Bennetts CSHM HP5 51 J6
Bennetts Av CROY/NA CR0 204 D9
GFD/PVL UB6 134 D3
Bennett's Castle La BCTR RM8 123 M9
Bennetts Cl MTCM CR4 202 C1
SL SL1 128 F10
STALE/WH AL4 40 A9
TOTM N17 99 N7
Bennetts Copse CHST BR7 184 B9
Bennetts End Cl HHS/BOV HP3 * 36 A8
Bennetts End Rd HHS/BOV HP3 36 B8
Bennetts Farm Pl
GT/LBKH KT23 253 N1
Bennett St CHSWK W4 156 B5
WHALL SW1A 10 G9
Bennetts Wy CROY/NA CR0 204 D9
Bennetts Yd UX/CGN UB8 131 N2
Bennett Wy RDART DA2 188 C7
RGUE GU4 251 K5
Benning Dr WDSR SL4 148 C9
Benningfield Gdns BERK HP4 34 B2
Benningholme Rd EDGW HA8 96 B7
Bennington Rd TOTM N17 99 M9
WFD IG8 * 101 K8
Bennions Cl HCH RM12 145 L1
Bennison Dr HARH RM3 105 L10
Benn St HOM E9 140 D1
Benrek Cl BARK/HLT IG6 102 F8
Bensbury Cl PUT/ROE SW15 178 E3
Bensham Cl THHTH CR7 203 K4
Bensham Gv THHTH CR7 203 K2
Bensham La THHTH CR7 203 J6
Bensham Manor Rd THHTH CR7 203 L5
Benskin Rd WATW WD18 73 H9
Benskins La ABR/ST RM4 105 L2
Bensley Cl FBAR/BDGN N11 98 A6
Ben Smith Wy BERM/RHTH SE16 19 P3
Benson Av PLSTW E13 141 P4
Benson Cl HSLW TW3 153 P10
SLN SL2 129 M10
UX/CGN UB8 131 P7
Benson Quay WAP E1W 140 B9
Benson Rd CROY/NA CR0 203 H10
FSTH SE23 182 B4
GRAYS RM17 167 N5
Benthall Gdns PUR/KEN CR8 241 K2
Benthal Rd STNW/STAM N16 119 N7
Bentham Av WOKN/KNAP GU21 232 F1
Bentham Rd HOM E9 140 C1
THMD SE28 143 L10
Ben Tillet Cl BARK IG11 143 K2
CAN/RD E16 * 142 C10
Bentinck Cl CFSP/GDCR SL9 110 A3
Bentinck Ms MHST W1U 10 D5
Bentinck Rd WDR/YW UB7 131 N10
Bentinck St MHST W1U 10 D5
Bentley Cl HART DA3 211 P3
WIM/MER SW19 179 K7
Bentley Dr CRICK NW2 117 J8
GNTH/NBYPK IG2 122 F4
HLWE CM17 47 N2
WEY KT13 216 B5
Bentley Heath La BAR EN5 77 H1
Bentley Ms EN EN1 79 L10
Bentley Pk SL SL1 128 C4
Bentley Rd HERT/WAT SG14 24 F4
IS N1 * 7 K2
SL SL1 128 E10
Bentley's Meadow
BGR/WK TN15 247 N6
Bentley St GVE DA12 190 F2
Bentley Wy STAN HA7 94 F6
WFD IG8 101 M4
Benton Rd IL IG1 122 G6
OXHEY WD19 93 L6
Bentons WAB EN9 * 45 K8
Benton's La WNWD SE27 181 K7
Benton's Ri WNWD SE27 181 L8
Bentry Cl BCTR RM8 123 P7
Bentry Rd BCTR RM8 123 P7
Bentsbrook Cl RDKG RH5 272 G6
Bentsbrook Pk RDKG RH5 272 G6
Bentsbrook Rd RDKG RH5 272 G6
Bentsley Cl STALE/WH AL4 38 G2
Bentworth Rd SHB W12 136 E8
Benwell Ct SUN TW16 * 197 H1
Benwell Rd CHOB/PIR GU24 230 F5
HOLWY N7 119 H9
Benwick Cl BERM/RHTH SE16 160 A3
Benwood Ct SUT SM1 201 M10
Benworth St BOW E3 140 E5
Benyon Ct SOCK/AV RM15 147 H4
Benyon Pth SOCK/AV RM15 147 H4
Benyon Rd IS N1 7 H5
Benyon Whf IS N1 7 K5
Beomonds Rw CHERT KT16 195 K7
Berberis Cl GU GU1 249 P8
Berberis Wk WDR/YW UB7 151 P3
Berber Pde WOOL/PLUM SE18 * 162 B6
Berber Rd BTSEA SW11 * 180 A1
Berceau Wk WAT WD17 72 F5
Bercta Rd ELTH/MOT SE9 184 F5
Bere Cl SWCM DA10 189 H1
Berecroft HLWS CM18 46 G6
Beredens La RBRW/HUT CM13 106 E10
Berefeld HHNE HP2 35 N4
Berenger Wk WBPTN SW10 * 157 N6
Berens Rd STMC/STPC BR5 207 M5
WLSDN NW10 136 G5
Berens Wy CHST BR7 207 J4
Beresford Av ALP/SUD HA0 135 M3
BRYLDS KT5 199 N8
HNWL W7 134 C7
SLN SL2 129 P9
TRDG/WHET N20 98 A3
TWK TW1 177 H2
Beresford Dr BMLY BR1 206 B3
WFD IG8 101 P5
Beresford Gdns CHDH RM6 123 P3
EN EN1 79 M8
HSLWW TW4 175 N1
Beresford Rd BELMT SM2 221 J4
CEND/HSY/T N8 119 H3
CHING E4 101 K2
DORK RH4 272 G2
EFNCH N2 117 P1
GVW DA11 190 B3
HBRY N5 119 L10
HRW HA1 114 C3
KUTN/CMB KT2 199 L1
RKW/CH/CXG WD3 91 J5
STAL AL1 39 H7
STHL UB1 133 L10
WALTH E17 100 G9
Beresford Sq WOOL/PLUM SE18 162 E3
Beresford St WOOL/PLUM SE18 162 E2
Beresford Ter HBRY N5 119 K10
Berestede Rd HMSMTH W6 156 C4
Bere St WAP E1W 140 C9
Bergenia Ct CHOB/PIR GU24 212 D9
Berger Cl STMC/STPC BR5 206 G6
Berger Rd HOM E9 140 C1
Berghem Ms WKENS W14 156 G2
Bergholt Av REDBR IG4 122 B3
Bergholt Crs STNW/STAM N16 119 M5
Bergholt Ms CAMTN NW1 5 H4
Bericot Wy WGCE AL7 23 N5
Bering Sq POP/IOD E14 160 F4
Bering Wk CAN/RD E16 142 A8
Berisford Ms WAND/EARL SW18 179 M2
Berkeley Av BXLYHN DA7 163 N7
CLAY IG5 102 D10
CRW RM5 104 D8
CSHM HP5 50 E5
GFD/PVL UB6 134 D1
HSLWW TW4 153 H7
Berkeley Cl ABLGY WD5 54 G8
BORE WD6 75 M9
CSHM HP5 50 F6
EMPK RM11 126 A7
KUTN/CMB KT2 177 K10
POTB/CUF EN6 59 L8
RSLP HA4 112 G8
STMC/STPC BR5 207 H7
STWL/WRAY TW19 172 G5
WARE SG12 26 B1
Berkeley Ct RKW/CH/CXG WD3 * 72 E9
WEY KT13 196 E9
WLGTN SM6 202 D10
Berkeley Crs DART DA1 187 N4
EBAR EN4 77 N9
Berkeley Dr E/WMO/HCT KT8 197 N3
EMPK RM11 125 P6
WDSR SL4 170 A4
Berkeley Gdns BF/WBF KT14 215 J10
ESH/CLAY KT10 218 F4
KENS W8 8 F10
WCHMH N21 99 L1
WOT/HER KT12 196 G7
Berkeley Ms MBLAR W1H 10 B5
SUN TW16 197 K3
Berkeley Pl EPSOM KT18 238 A2
WIM/MER SW19 178 G9
Berkeley Rd BARN SW13 156 D7
CDALE/KGS NW9 115 M2
CEND/HSY/T N8 118 E3
HGDN/ICK UB10 132 D3
MNPK E12 122 B10
SEVS/STOTM N15 119 L4
Berkeley Sq MYFR/PICC W1J 10 F8
Berkeley St MYFR/PICC W1J 10 F8
The Berkeleys LHD/OX KT22 236 D10
SNWD SE25 * 203 P4
Berkeley Ter TIL RM18 168 D6
Berkeley Waye HEST TW5 153 M6
Berkhampstead Rd BELV DA17 164 B4
CSHM HP5 51 H6
Berkhamsted Av WBLY HA9 135 L1
Berkhamsted Rd HHW HP1 34 G4
Berkley Av CHES/WCR EN8 62 C10
Berkley Cl STALE/WH AL4 39 H2
WHTN TW2 * 176 D6
Berkley Ct GU GU1 250 B10
Berkley Gv CAMTN NW1 4 C4
Berkley Pl CHES/WCR EN8 * 62 C10
Berkley Rd BEAC HP9 88 C5
CAMTN NW1 4 B4
GVE DA12 190 E2
Berkley Rw GVE DA12 * 190 E2
Berks Hl RKW/CH/CXG WD3 70 F9
Berkshire Av SL SL1 128 G8
Berkshire Cl CTHM CR3 241 L8
Berkshire Gdns PLMGR N13 99 H7
UED N18 100 A6
Berkshire Rd HOM E9 140 E1
Berkshire Wy EMPK RM11 125 P3
MTCM CR4 202 F4
Bermans Wy WLSDN NW10 116 C9
Bermer Rd WATN WD24 73 K5
Bermondsey Sq STHWK SE1 19 M3
Bermondsey St STHWK SE1 13 J10
Bermondsey Wall East
BERM/RHTH SE16 19 P2
Bermondsey Wall West
STHWK SE1 19 N1
Bermuda Rd TIL RM18 168 D8
Bernal Cl THMD SE28 143 N9
Bernard Ashley Dr CHARL SE7 161 N4
Bernard Av WEA W13 154 G2
Bernard Cassidy St CAN/RD E16 141 L7
Bernard Gdns WIM/MER SW19 179 J8
Bernard Gv WAB EN9 62 G9
Bernard Rd ROMW/RG RM7 124 D5
SEVS/STOTM N15 119 N3
WLGTN SM6 222 C2
Bernards Cl BARK/HLT IG6 102 F8
Bernard St BMSBY WC1N 11 L2
GVE DA12 190 E2
STALW/RED AL3 38 D5
Bernays Cl STAN HA7 95 H7
Bernay's Gv BRXN/ST SW9 158 G10
Bernel Dr CROY/NA CR0 204 E10
Berne Rd THHTH CR7 203 J5
Berners Cl SL SL1 128 D9
Berners Dr STAL AL1 38 E6
WEA W13 134 F9
Berners Ms FITZ W1T 11 H5
Berners Pl FITZ W1T 11 H5
Berners Rd IS N1 6 C7
WDGN N22 99 H9
Berners St FITZ W1T 11 H4
Berners Wy BROX EN10 44 E9
Berner Ter WCHPL E1 * 13 N6
Berney Rd CROY/NA CR0 203 L7
Bernhardt Crs STJWD NW8 9 N1
Bernhart Cl EDGW HA8 95 P8
Bernice Cl RAIN RM13 145 K6
Bernwell Rd CHING E4 101 K4
Berridge Gn EDGW HA8 95 M8
Berridge Ms KIL/WHAMP NW6 117 K10
Berridge Rd NRWD SE19 181 L8
The Berries STALE/WH AL4 38 F2
Berriman Rd HOLWY N7 118 G8
Berrington Dr EHSLY KT24 234 G10
Berriton Rd RYLN/HDSTN HA2 113 N6
Berry Av WATN WD24 73 J2
Berrybank Cl CHING E4 101 H3
Berry Cl DAGE RM10 124 B10
HCH RM12 125 K10
RKW/CH/CXG WD3 91 L1
WCHMH N21 99 J2
Berry Cottages POP/IOD E14 * 140 D8
Berry Ct HSLWW TW4 175 N1
Berrydale Rd YEAD UB4 133 M6
Berry Fld SLN SL2 129 P8
Berryfield Cl BMLY BR1 206 B1
Berry Field Cl WALTH E17 120 G2
Berry Field Pk AMS HP6 68 G3
Berryfield Rd WALW SE17 18 D7
Berry Grove La GSTN WD25 73 N4
Berrygrove La GSTN WD25 73 P5
Berryhill ELTH/MOT SE9 162 E10
Berry Hl STAN HA7 95 J5
Berryhill Gdns ELTH/MOT SE9 162 E10
Berrylands BRYLDS KT5 199 M5
HART DA3 211 M6
ORP BR6 207 M10
RYNPK SW20 200 F3
Berrylands Rd BRYLDS KT5 199 L6
Berry La DUL SE21 181 L7
RGUW GU3 231 J10
RKW/CH/CXG WD3 70 G10
RKW/CH/CXG WD3 91 L2
Berryman Cl BCTR RM8 123 M8
Berryman's La SYD SE26 182 C7
Berrymead HHNE HP2 36 A4
Berry Meade ASHTD KT21 237 L3
Berry Meade Cl ASHTD KT21 237 L3
Berrymead Gdns ACT W3 135 P10
Berrymede Rd CHSWK W4 156 A2
Berry Pl FSBYE EC1V 6 D10
Berryscroft Rd STA TW18 173 M10
Berry's Green Rd BH/WHM TN16 244 E2
Berry's Hl BH/WHM TN16 244 E1
Berry's La BF/WBF KT14 215 N7
Berry St FSBYE EC1V 12 D2
Berry Wk ASHTD KT21 237 L5
Berry Wy EA W5 155 K2
RKW/CH/CXG WD3 91 L1
Bersham La GRAYS RM17 167 L3
Bertal Rd TOOT SW17 179 N7
Berther Rd EMPK RM11 125 M5
Berthold Ms WAB EN9 62 G9
Berthons Gdns WALTH E17 * 121 J3
Berthon St DEPT SE8 160 F6
Bertie Rd SYD SE26 182 C9
WLSDN NW10 136 D1
Bertram Rd EN EN1 79 P8
HDN NW4 116 E4
KUTN/CMB KT2 177 M10
Bertram St KTTN NW5 118 C8
Bertrand St LEW SE13 160 G9
Bertrand Wy THMD SE28 143 L9
Bert Rd THHTH CR7 203 K5
Bert Wy EN EN1 79 N8
Berwick Av SL SL1 128 G9
YEAD UB4 133 L8
Berwick Cl BEAC HP9 88 G10
CHES/WCR EN8 62 F10
STAN HA7 94 E7
WHTN TW2 175 P4
Berwick Crs BFN/LL DA15 185 H2
Berwick Gdns SUT SM1 201 M10
Berwick La CHONG CM5 66 F9
CHONG CM5 85 H2
Berwick Pond Cl RAIN RM13 145 L4
Berwick Pond Rd RAIN RM13 145 M2
Berwick Rd BORE WD6 75 L4
CAN/RD E16 141 N8
RAIN RM13 145 L4
WDGN N22 99 J9
WELL DA16 163 L7
Berwick St SOHO/CST W1F 11 J6
Berwick Wy RSEV TN14 247 J7
Berwyn Av HSLW TW3 154 A7
Berwyn Rd HNHL SE24 181 J4
RCHPK/HAM TW10 155 N10
Beryl Av EHAM E6 142 B7
Beryl Rd HMSMTH W6 156 G4
Berystede KUTN/CMB KT2 177 N10
Besant Cl CRICK NW2 * 117 J7
Besant Pl EDUL SE22 159 N10
Besant Rd CRICK NW2 117 H9
Besant Wy WLSDN NW10 115 P10
Besley St STRHM/NOR SW16 180 D9
Bessant Dr RCH/KEW TW9 155 N7
Bessborough Gdns PIM SW1V 17 K7
Bessborough Pl PIM SW1V 17 J8
Bessborough Rd HRW HA1 114 C6
PUT/ROE SW15 178 D4
Bessborough St PIM SW1V 17 J7
Bessels Green Rd SEV TN13 246 E10
Bessels Meadow SEV TN13 246 E10
Bessemer Cl DTCH/LGLY SL3 150 C4
Bessemer Rd CMBW SE5 159 K8
WGCW AL8 23 H1
Bessie Lansbury Cl EHAM E6 142 D8
Bessingby Rd RSLP HA4 113 H8
Besson St NWCR SE14 160 B7
Bessy St BETH E2 * 140 B5
Bestobell Rd SL SL1 129 H8
Best Ter SWLY BR8 * 208 D5
Beswick Ms KIL/WHAMP NW6 117 L10
Betam Rd HYS/HAR UB3 152 E1
Beta Rd CHOB/PIR GU24 213 L6
WOKS/MYFD GU22 232 E2
Beta Wy EGH TW20 194 F1
Betchworth Cl SUT SM1 221 N2
Betchworth Rd GDMY/SEVK IG3 123 H7
Betchworth Wy CROY/NA CR0 225 H5
Betenson Av SEV TN13 246 G8
Betham Rd GFD/PVL UB6 134 C5
Bethany Pl WOKN/KNAP GU21 * 232 A4
Bethany Waye
EBED/NFELT TW14 174 F3
Bethecar Rd HRW HA1 114 D3
Bethel Cl HDN NW4 116 G3
Bethell Av CAN/RD E16 141 L6
IL IG1 122 D5
Bethel Rd SEV TN13 247 K9
WELL DA16 163 M9
Bethersden Cl BECK BR3 182 E10
Bethnal Green Rd BETH E2 13 M1
Bethune Av FBAR/BDGN N11 98 A5
Bethune Cl CRAWE RH10 284 E8
Bethune Rd STNW/STAM N16 119 L5
WLSDN NW10 136 A6
Bethwin Rd CMBW SE5 159 J6
Betjeman Cl CHESW EN7 61 P4
COUL/CHIP CR5 240 G3
HARP AL5 * 20 B2
RYLN/HDSTN HA2 113 P2
Betjeman Ct WDR/YW UB7 * 131 N10
Betjeman Wy CHONG CM5 67 N2
HHW HP1 35 L4
Betley Ct WOT/HER KT12 197 J10
Betony Cl CROY/NA CR0 204 C8
Betoyne Av CHING E4 101 K5
Betsham Rd ERITH DA8 164 G6
MEO DA13 189 K8
Betstyle Rd FBAR/BDGN N11 98 C5
Betterton Dr SCUP DA14 185 P5
Betterton Rd RAIN RM13 144 F4
Betterton St LSQ/SEVD WC2H 11 L6
Bettles Cl UX/CGN UB8 131 M4
Bettons Pk SRTFD E15 141 K3
Bettridge Rd FUL/PGN SW6 157 J8
Betts Cl BECK BR3 204 D2
Betts La WAB EN9 45 P7
Betts Ms WALTH E17 120 E4
Betts Rd CAN/RD E16 141 N8
Betts St WAP E1W 140 A9
Betts Wy CRAWE RH10 283 N3
PGE/AN SE20 204 A2
SURB KT6 198 G8
Betula Cl PUR/KEN CR8 241 L1
Betula Ter CHES/WCR EN8 * 62 D8
Between Streets COB KT11 217 J10
Beulah Av THHTH CR7 * 203 K2
Beulah Cl EDGW HA8 95 N4
Beulah Crs THHTH CR7 203 K2
Beulah Gv CROY/NA CR0 203 K6
Beulah Hl NRWD SE19 181 K9
NRWD SE19 203 L1
Beulah Rd EPP CM16 65 K5
HCH RM12 125 K8
SUT SM1 221 K1
THHTH CR7 203 K3
WALTH E17 120 G3
WIM/MER SW19 179 J10
Beulah Wk CTHM CR3 242 D6
Beult Rd DART DA1 165 H9
Bevan Av BARK IG11 143 K2
Bevan Cl HHS/BOV HP3 35 N8
Bevan Ct CROY/NA CR0 223 H2
Bevan Hl CSHM HP5 50 G5
Bevan House WATN WD24 73 L6
Bevan Pk EW KT17 220 C7
Bevan Pl SWLY BR8 208 G4
Bevan Rd ABYW SE2 163 L4
EBAR EN4 78 A8
Bevans Cl SWCM DA10 189 H2
Bevan St IS N1 6 F6
Bevan Wy HCH RM12 125 N9
Bev Callender Cl VX/NE SW8 158 C9
Bevenden St IS N1 7 H9
Beveridge Rd WLSDN NW10 136 B2
Beverley Av BFN/LL DA15 185 J3
HSLWW TW4 153 N10
RYNPK SW20 200 C1
Beverley Cl ADL/WDHM KT15 215 N2
BARN SW13 156 D8
BTSEA SW11 157 N10
CHSGTN KT9 219 H1
EMPK RM11 125 N5
EW KT17 220 F7
WCHMH N21 99 K2
WEY KT13 196 F9
Beverley Ct BROCKY SE4 160 E9
Beverley Crs WFD IG8 101 N9
Beverley Dr EDGW HA8 115 L1
Beverley Gdns BARN SW13 156 C9
CHESW EN7 61 N7
EMPK RM11 125 N5
GLDGN NW11 117 H5
STALE/WH AL4 39 J2
STAN HA7 94 F9
WBLY HA9 115 L6
WGCE AL7 23 M5
WPK KT4 200 D8
Beverley Hts REIG RH2 257 L8
Beverley La KUTN/CMB KT2 178 B10
Beverley Ms CRAWE RH10 284 B8
Beverley Rd BXLYHN DA7 164 D8
CHING E4 101 J7
CHSWK W4 156 C4
CTHM CR3 241 M3
DAGW RM9 123 P9
EHAM E6 142 A5
HAYES BR2 206 B9
KUT/HW KT1 199 H1
MTCM CR4 202 E4
NWDGN UB2 153 M3
NWMAL KT3 200 D4
PGE/AN SE20 204 A2
RSLP HA4 113 J7
SUN TW16 196 C1
Beverley Wy KUTN/CMB KT2 200 C1
Beverley Wy (Kingston By-Pass)
RYNPK SW20 200 C1
NWMAL KT3 200 C2
Beverly Cl BROX EN10 44 D7
Beversbrook Rd ARCH N19 118 E8
Beverstone Rd
BRXS/STRHM SW2 180 G1
THHTH CR7 203 H4
Beverston Ms MBLAR W1H 10 A4
Bevill Allen Cl TOOT SW17 180 A9
Bevill Cl SNWD SE25 203 P3
Bevin Cl BERM/RHTH SE16 140 D10
Bevington Rd BECK BR3 204 G2
NKENS W10 8 B3
Bevington St BERM/RHTH SE16 19 P2
Bevin Rd YEAD UB4 133 H5
Bevin Sq TOOT SW17 180 A6
Bevin Wy FSBYW WC1X 6 A8
Bevis Cl RDART DA2 188 B3
Bevis Marks HDTCH EC3A 13 K5
Bewbush Dr CRAWW RH11 283 J10
Bewcastle Gdns ENC/FH EN2 78 F8
Bewdley Cl HARP AL5 20 C5
Bewdley St IS N1 6 A3
Bewick Ms PECK SE15 160 A6
Bewick St VX/NE SW8 158 C8
Bewley Cl CHES/WCR EN8 62 C7
Bewley St WCHPL E1 140 A9
WIM/MER SW19 179 N9
Bewlys Rd WNWD SE27 181 J8
Bexhill Cl FELT TW13 175 M5
Bexhill Dr GRAYS RM17 167 K3
Bexhill Rd BROCKY SE4 182 E2
FBAR/BDGN N11 98 E6
MORT/ESHN SW14 155 P9
Bexley Cl DART DA1 186 F1
Bexley Gdns CHDH RM6 123 L3
ED N9 99 L4
Bexley High St BXLY DA5 186 B3
Bexley La DART DA1 186 F1
SCUP DA14 185 M5
Bexley Rd ELTH/MOT SE9 184 D2
ERITH DA8 164 E5
ERITH DA8 * 164 G4
Bexley St WDSR SL4 148 G7
Beyers Gdns HOD EN11 26 F10
Beyers Prospect HOD EN11 26 F10
Beyers Ride HOD EN11 26 F10
Beynon Rd CAR SM5 222 A2
Bianca Rd PECK SE15 19 M10
Bibsworth Rd FNCH N3 97 J10
Bibury Cl PECK SE15 19 K10
Bicester Rd RCH/KEW TW9 155 M9
Bickenhall St MHST W1U 10 B3
Bickersteth Rd TOOT SW17 180 A9
Bickerton Rd ARCH N19 118 C7
Bickles Yd STHWK SE1 19 K2
Bickley Crs BMLY BR1 206 B4
Bickley Park Rd BMLY BR1 206 C3
Bickley Rd BMLY BR1 206 A2
LEY E10 120 G5
Bickley St TOOT SW17 179 P8
Bicknell Cl GU GU1 249 P9
Bicknell Rd CMBW SE5 159 K9
Bickney Wy LHD/OX KT22 236 B8
Bicknoller Cl BELMT SM2 221 L6
Bicknoller Rd EN EN1 79 N5
Bicknor Rd ORP BR6 207 H7
Bidborough Cl HAYES BR2 * 205 L5
Bidborough St STPAN WC1H 5 L10
Biddenden Wy ELTH/MOT SE9 184 D7
Biddenham Turn GSTN WD25 73 K1
Bidder St CAN/RD E16 141 K7
Biddestone Rd HOLWY N7 118 G9
Biddles Cl SL SL1 128 D10
Biddulph Rd MV/WKIL W9 3 H10
SAND/SEL CR2 223 K5
Bideford Av GFD/PVL UB6 134 G5
Bideford Cl EDGW HA8 95 M9
FELT TW13 175 N6
HARH RM3 105 L9
Bideford Gdns EN EN1 99 M1
Bideford Rd BMLY BR1 183 L6
PEND EN3 80 E4
RSLP HA4 113 J8
WELL DA16 163 L6
Bideford Sp SLN SL2 128 G5
Bidhams Crs
KWD/TDW/WH KT20 238 F7
Bidwell Gdns FBAR/BDGN N11 98 D9
Bidwell St PECK SE15 * 160 A7
The Bield REIG RH2 275 K2
Big Common La REDH RH1 259 J9
Biggerstaff Rd SRTFD E15 141 H3
Biggerstaff St FSBYPK N4 119 H7
Biggin Av MTCM CR4 202 A1
Biggin Cl CRAWW RH11 283 M9
Biggin Hl NRWD SE19 181 J10
Biggin La CDW/CHF RM16 168 E5
Biggin Wy NRWD SE19 181 J10
Bigginwood Rd
STRHM/NOR SW16 181 J10
Biggs Grove Rd CHESW EN7 61 M3
Bigg's Rw PUT/ROE SW15 156 G9
Bigland St WCHPL E1 140 A8
Bignell Rd WOOL/PLUM SE18 162 E4
Bignolds Cnr POTB/CUF EN6 58 E10
Bignold Rd FSTGT E7 121 M9
Big St CLPT E5 120 A6
Bigwood Rd GLDGN NW11 117 L4
Biko Cl UX/CGN UB8 131 M8
Bilberry Cl CRAWW RH11 283 L10
Billesden Rd CHOB/PIR GU24 230 B7
Billet La BERK HP4 33 M4
DTCH/LGLY SL3 130 E8
EMPK RM11 125 L6
IVER SL0 130 E5
Billet Rd CHDH RM6 123 M1
WALTH E17 100 C9
WALTH E17 100 F9
Billetts Hart Cl HNWL W7 154 D1
Bill Hamling Cl ELTH/MOT SE9 184 C5
Billingford Cl BROCKY SE4 160 C10
Billing Pl WBPTN SW10 * 157 L6
Billing Rd WBPTN SW10 157 L6
Billings HART DA3 211 L6
Billings Cl DAGW RM9 143 M2
Billing St WBPTN SW10 * 157 L6
Billington Hl CROY/NA CR0 203 L9
Billington Rd NWCR SE14 160 C6
Billinton Dr CRAWE RH10 284 C8
Billiter Sq FENCHST EC3M * 13 K6
Billiter St FENCHST EC3M 13 K6
Bill Nicholson Wy TOTM N17 99 N8
Billockby Cl CHSGTN KT9 219 L3
Billson St POP/IOD E14 161 H3
Billy Lows La POTB/CUF EN6 59 M7
Bilton Centre LHD/OX KT22 * 236 E5
Bilton Rd ERITH DA8 165 H6
GFD/PVL UB6 134 G3
Bilton Wy HYS/HAR UB3 153 J1
PEND EN3 80 E5
Bina Gdns ECT SW5 15 J6
Bincote Rd ENC/FH EN2 78 G7
Binden Rd SHB W12 156 C2
Binfield Rd BF/WBF KT14 215 P8
CLAP SW4 158 F7
SAND/SEL CR2 223 N2
Bingfield St IS N1 5 N5
Bingham Cl HHW HP1 35 J4
SOCK/AV RM15 146 G8
Bingham Ct IS N1 * 6 D3
Bingham Dr STA TW18 173 N10
WOKN/KNAP GU21 231 L4
Bingham Pl CAMTN NW1 10 C3
Bingham Rd CROY/NA CR0 203 P8
Bingham St IS N1 6 G1
Bingley Rd CAN/RD E16 141 P8
GFD/PVL UB6 134 B6
HOD EN11 45 H3
SUN TW16 175 H10
Binney Ct CRAWE RH10 284 F4
Binney St MYFR/PKLN W1K 10 D7
Binns Rd CHSWK W4 156 B4
Binscombe GODL GU7 267 J9
Binscombe Crs GODL GU7 267 K10
Binscombe La GODL GU7 267 J9
Binsey Wk ABYW SE2 163 M1
Binstead Cl CRAWW RH11 283 L5
YEAD UB4 133 M7
Binyon Crs STAN HA7 94 E6
Birbetts Rd ELTH/MOT SE9 184 C5
Birchall La HERT/WAT SG14 23 P7
Birchall Wd WGCE AL7 23 M6
Birchanger Rd SNWD SE25 203 P5
Birch Av CTHM CR3 241 L10
LHD/OX KT22 236 E6
PLMGR N13 99 K4
WDR/YW UB7 132 A8
Birch Cl GODL GU7 267 L9
Birch Cl ADL/WDHM KT15 215 N5
AMS HP6 69 K3
BKHH IG9 102 A4
CAN/RD E16 141 K7
EYN DA4 209 L10
HART DA3 211 P2
HSLW TW3 154 C9
IVER SL0 130 G4
ROMW/RG RM7 124 C1
RPLY/SEND GU23 251 J1
SEV TN13 247 J9
SOCK/AV RM15 147 J6
TEDD TW11 176 F8
WOKN/KNAP GU21 231 P5
Birch Copse LCOL/BKTW AL2 55 M6
Birch Ct WLGTN SM6 222 C1
Birch Crs EMPK RM11 125 M2
HGDN/ICK UB10 132 A3
SOCK/AV RM15 147 K5
Birchcroft Cl CTHM CR3 259 K1
Birchdale CFSP/GDCR SL9 110 A6
Birchdale Cl BF/WBF KT14 215 M7
Birchdale Gdns CHDH RM6 123 N5
Birchdale Rd FSTGT E7 121 P10
Birchdene Dr THMD SE28 163 K1
Birch Dr HAT AL10 40 D5
RKW/CH/CXG WD3 90 G6
Birchen Cl CDALE/KGS NW9 116 A7
Birchend Cl SAND/SEL CR2 223 L3
Birchen Gv CDALE/KGS NW9 116 A7
Bircherley Ct HERT/WAT SG14 * 25 L5
Bircherley St HERT/WAT SG14 25 L5
Birches Cl EPSOM KT18 238 B1
MTCM CR4 202 A3
PIN HA5 113 M3
The Birches BUSH WD23 74 B9
CHARL SE7 161 N5
CMBW SE5 * 159 M9

CRAWE RH10 284 C6
EHSLY KT24 252 F2
EPP CM16 66 C2
HHS/BOV HP3 35 J9
HSLWW TW4 * 175 N3
ORP BR6 226 D1
RBRW/HUT CM13 107 K4
SWLY BR8 208 F2
WAB EN9 63 L10
WCHMH N21 78 G10
WOKS/MYFD GU22 232 C4
Birchfield CDW/CHF RM16 167 J1
Birchfield Cl ADL/WDHM KT15 215 L1
COUL/CHIP CR5 240 G2
Birchfield Est HORL RH6 * 282 G1
Birchfield Gv EW KT17 220 F6
Birchfield Rd CHES/WCR EN8 62 A5
Birchfield St POP/IOD E14 140 F9
Birch Gdns AMSS HP7 69 K5
DAGE RM10 124 D8
Birchgate Ms
KWD/TDW/WH KT20 * 238 F7
Birch Gn HHW HP1 35 J5
STA TW18 173 J7
Birch Gv ACT W3 135 M10
Birchgrove COB KT11 217 K10
Birch Gv COB KT11 235 L1
GU GU1 * 249 P7
KWD/TDW/WH KT20 239 J10
LEE/GVPK SE12 183 L3
POTB/CUF EN6 59 K8
SHPTN TW17 196 F2
SLN SL2 128 G7
WAN E11 121 K8
WDSR SL4 148 C7
WELL DA16 163 K10
WOKS/MYFD GU22 232 G1
Birch Hl CROY/NA CR0 224 C2
Birchin Cross Rd BGR/WK TN15 229 P10
BGR/WK TN15 247 N1
Birchington Cl BXLYHN DA7 164 C7
Birchington Rd BRYLDS KT5 199 L7
CEND/HSY/T N8 118 E4
KIL/WHAMP NW6 2 F5
WDSR SL4 148 F8
Birchin La BANK EC3V 13 H6
Birchlands Av BAL SW12 180 A3
Birch La CHOB/PIR GU24 212 C8
HHS/BOV HP3 52 E9
PUR/KEN CR8 222 F7
Birch Lea CRAWE RH10 284 B4
Birch Leys HHNE HP2 36 D1
Birch Md ORP BR6 206 D9
Birchmead WAT WD17 72 G4
Birchmead Av PIN HA5 113 K2
Birchmead Cl STALW/RED AL3 * 38 C3
Birchmere Rw BKHTH/KID SE3 161 L8
Birchmore Wk HBRY N5 119 K8
Birch Pk KTN/HRWW/WS HA3 94 B8
Birch Pl RDART DA2 188 D2
Birch Platt CHOB/PIR GU24 212 C9
Birch Rd BERK HP4 33 J2
BFOR GU20 212 D3
FELT TW13 175 L8
GODL GU7 267 L9
ROMW/RG RM7 124 C1
Birch Rw HAYES BR2 206 D7
Birch Tree Av WWKM BR4 225 L1
Birch Tree Gv CSHM HP5 51 N6
Birch Tree Wk WAT WD17 72 G3
Birch Tree Wy CROY/NA CR0 204 A9
Birch V COB KT11 217 P9
Birch Wk BORE WD6 * 75 M5
MTCM CR4 202 C1
Birch Wy CSHM HP5 51 J5
HARP AL5 20 B3
Birchway HAT AL10 40 D2
HYS/HAR UB3 133 H10
Birch Wy LCOL/BKTW AL2 57 J3
Birchway REDH RH1 276 C2
Birch Wy WARL CR6 242 D4
Birchwood RAD WD7 57 M10
Birchwood Av BECK BR3 204 E4
HAT AL10 40 D2
MUSWH N10 118 B1
SCUP DA14 185 L6
WLGTN SM6 202 B10
Birchwood Cl CRAWE RH10 284 D10
HAT AL10 40 D2
HORL RH6 280 C3
MRDN SM4 201 L4
RBRW/HUT CM13 * 107 H7
Birchwood Ct EDGW HA8 95 P10
Birchwood Dr BF/WBF KT14 215 K8
HAMP NW3 117 L8
LTWR GU18 212 B6
RDART DA2 186 F7
Birchwood Gv HPTN TW12 175 P9
Birchwood La CTHM CR3 259 J1
ESH/CLAY KT10 218 C5
RSEV TN14 246 A1
Birchwood Park Av SWLY BR8 208 G3
Birchwood Rd BF/WBF KT14 215 K8
RDART DA2 186 E8
STMC/STPC BR5 206 G4
SWLY BR8 186 D10
TOOT SW17 180 C8
Birchwood Ter SWLY BR8 * 208 D1
Birchwood Wy LCOL/BKTW AL2 56 A4
Birdbrook Cl DAGE RM10 144 D2
RBRW/HUT CM13 87 N10
Birdbrook Rd BKHTH/KID SE3 161 P9
Birdcage Wk WESTW SW1E 17 H2
Birdcroft Rd WGCW AL8 22 G6
Birdham Cl BMLY BR1 206 B5
CRAWW RH11 283 L5
Bird House La ORP BR6 226 D10
Birdhurst Av SAND/SEL CR2 223 L1
Birdhurst Gdns SAND/SEL CR2 223 L1
Birdhurst Ri SAND/SEL CR2 223 M2
Birdhurst Rd SAND/SEL CR2 223 M2
WAND/EARL SW18 179 M1
Birdie Wy HERT/BAY SG13 26 A4
Bird in Bush Rd PECK SE15 159 P6
Bird-in-Hand La BMLY BR1 206 A2
Bird-in-Hand Ms FSTH SE23 182 B5
Bird-in-Hand Pas FSTH SE23 182 B5
Bird La RBRW/HUT CM13 107 H10
UPMR RM14 126 C3
Birds Cl WGCE AL7 23 L7
Birds Farm Av CRW RM5 104 C9
Birdsfield La BOW E3 140 E3
Birds Gv WOKN/KNAP GU21 230 G4
Birds Hill Dr LHD/OX KT22 218 D9
Birds Hill Ri LHD/OX KT22 218 C9
Birds Hill Rd LHD/OX KT22 218 C8
Bird St MHST W1U 10 D6
Birdswood Dr WOKN/KNAP GU21 231 K6
Bird Wk WHTN TW2 175 N4
Birdwood Cl SAND/SEL CR2 224 B7
TEDD TW11 176 D7
Birkbeck Av ACT W3 135 P9
GFD/PVL UB6 134 B3
Birkbeck Gv ACT W3 156 A1
Birkbeck Hl DUL SE21 181 J5
Birkbeck Ms ACT W3 * 136 A9
HACK E8 119 N10
Birkbeck Pl DUL SE21 181 J4
Birkbeck Rd ACT W3 136 A10
BECK BR3 204 C2
CEND/HSY/T N8 118 F2
EA W5 155 H3
ENC/FH EN2 79 L5
GNTH/NBYPK IG2 122 G3
HACK E8 119 N10
MLHL NW7 96 C6
NFNCH/WDSPK N12 97 M6
ROMW/RG RM7 124 E6
SCUP DA14 185 K6
TOTM N17 99 N9
WIM/MER SW19 179 L9
Birkbeck St BETH E2 140 A5
Birkbeck Wy GFD/PVL UB6 134 C3
Birkdale Av HARH RM3 105 P8
PIN HA5 113 P1
Birkdale Cl BERM/RHTH SE16 160 A4
ORP BR6 206 G8
THMD SE28 143 M8
Birkdale Dr CRAWW RH11 282 G8
Birkdale Gdns CROY/NA CR0 224 C1
OXHEY WD19 93 L4
Birkdale Rd ABYW SE2 163 K3
EA W5 135 K6
Birkenhead Av KUTN/CMB KT2 199 L2
Birkenhead St CAMTN NW1 5 M9
Birkett Wy CSTG HP8 70 A7
Birkhall Rd CAT SE6 183 J4
Birkheads Rd REIG RH2 257 K9
Birklands La STAL AL1 38 G10
Birklands Pk STAL AL1 * 38 G10
Birkwood Cl BAL SW12 180 E3
Birley Rd SL SL1 129 J8
TRDG/WHET N20 97 M3
Birley St BTSEA SW11 158 B8
Birling Rd ERITH DA8 164 E6
Birnam Rd FSBYPK N4 118 G7
Birnham Cl RPLY/SEND GU23 233 K10
Birse Crs WLSDN NW10 116 B9
Birstal Gn OXHEY WD19 93 L5
Birstall Rd SEVS/STOTM N15 119 M3
Biscay Rd HMSMTH W6 156 G4
Biscoe Cl HEST TW5 153 P5
Biscoe Wy LEW SE13 * 161 J10
Bisenden Rd CROY/NA CR0 203 M9
Bisham Cl CAR SM5 202 A8
CRAWE RH10 284 E9
Bisham Gdns HGT N6 118 B6
Bishop Butt Cl ORP BR6 207 J10
Bishop Ct ABLGY WD5 54 G7
Bishop Duppas Pk SHPTN TW17 196 E7
Bishop Fox Wy E/WMO/HCT KT8 197 N4
Bishop Ken Rd
KTN/HRWW/WS HA3 94 E10
Bishop Kings Rd WKENS W14 14 B5
Bishop Rd STHGT/OAK N14 98 C2
Bishops Av BMLY BR1 205 P3
BORE WD6 75 L9
CHDH RM6 123 M4
FUL/PGN SW6 156 G8
NTHWD HA6 92 F5
PLSTW E13 141 N3
The Bishops Av EFNCH N2 117 N4
Bishop's Bridge Rd BAY/PAD W2 9 H5
Bishop's Cl HGDN/ICK UB10 132 B4
ARCH N19 118 D8
STALE/WH AL4 38 F2
WALTH E17 120 G2
BAR EN5 76 G10
CHSWK W4 155 P4
COUL/CHIP CR5 241 H4
ELTH/MOT SE9 184 F5
EN EN1 80 A6
HAT AL10 40 C4
RCHPK/HAM TW10 177 J6
SUT SM1 201 K10
Bishops Ct CHES/WCR EN8 * 62 A6
RDART DA2 188 E1
STP EC4M 12 C5
Bishops Dr EBED/NFELT TW14 174 E2
NTHLT UB5 133 M3
Bishops Farm Cl WDSR SL4 148 A8
Bishopsfield HLWS CM18 47 H4
Bishopsford Rd MRDN SM4 201 N6
Bishopsgate LVPST EC2M 13 K4
Bishopsgate Ar LVPST EC2M 13 K3
Bishopsgate Rd EGH TW20 171 M6
Bishops Gn BMLY BR1 * 205 P1
Bishops Gv BFOR GU20 212 B3
EFNCH N2 117 N4
HPTN TW12 175 N7
Bishop's Hall KUT/HW KT1 199 J2
Bishop's Hall Rd BRWN CM15 86 G10
Bishops Hl WOT/HER KT12 197 H7
Bishops Md CMBW SE5 * 159 K6
HHW HP1 35 L8
Bishopsmead Cl EHSLY KT24 252 G4
HOR/WEW KT19 220 A6
Bishopsmead Dr EHSLY KT24 252 G5
Bishops Orch SLN SL2 128 G5
Bishop's Park Rd FUL/PGN SW6 156 G8
STRHM/NOR SW16 202 F1
Bishop's Pl SUT SM1 221 M2
Bishop Sq HAT AL10 40 B3
Bishops Ri HAT AL10 40 C5
Bishop's Rd CROY/NA CR0 203 J7
FUL/PGN SW6 157 J7
HGT N6 118 B4
HNWL W7 154 D1
HYS/HAR UB3 132 D8
SL SL1 149 M1
Bishops Ter LBTH SE11 18 B5
Bishopsthorpe Rd SYD SE26 182 B7
Bishop St IS N1 6 E5
Bishops Wk BRWN CM15 107 L3
CHST BR7 206 F1
CROY/NA CR0 224 C2
Bishop's Wy BETH E2 140 B4
EGH TW20 172 G9
Bishops Wd WOKN/KNAP GU21 231 L3
Bishopswood Rd HGT N6 118 A5
Bishop Wy WLSDN NW10 136 B2
Biskra WAT WD17 73 H5
Bisley Cl CHES/WCR EN8 62 C9
WPK KT4 200 F8
Bispham Rd WLSDN NW10 135 L5
Bisson Rd SRTFD E15 141 H4
Bistern Av WALTH E17 121 J1
Bitmead Cl CRAWW RH11 * 283 H8
Bittacy Cl MLHL NW7 96 G7
Bittacy Hl MLHL NW7 96 G7
Bittacy Park Av MLHL NW7 96 G7
Bittacy Ri MLHL NW7 96 G7
Bittacy Rd MLHL NW7 96 G7
Bittams La CHERT KT16 214 G1
Bittern Cl CHESW EN7 61 J1
CRAWW RH11 282 G8
HHS/BOV HP3 53 P1
YEAD UB4 133 L7
Bitterne Dr WOKN/KNAP GU21 231 L3
Bittern Pl WDGN N22 * 98 G10
Bittern St STHWK SE1 18 E2
The Bit AMSS HP7 * 68 E10
Bittoms Ct KUT/HW KT1 * 199 J3
The Bittoms KUT/HW KT1 199 J3
Bixley Cl NWDGN UB2 153 N3
Black Acre Cl AMSS HP7 69 K5
Blackacre Rd EPP CM16 83 H3
Blackall St SDTCH EC2A 13 J1
Blackberry Cl GU GU1 249 N7
SHPTN TW17 196 F4
Blackberry Farm Cl HEST TW5 153 M6
Blackberry Fld STMC/STPC BR5 207 K1
Blackbird Hl WBLY HA9 115 P7
Blackbirds La GSTN WD25 74 C1
Blackbird Yd BETH E2 7 M9
Blackborne Rd DAGE RM10 144 B1
Blackborough Cl REIG RH2 257 M10
Blackborough Rd REIG RH2 257 N10
Black Boy La SEVS/STOTM N15 119 K3
Black Boy Wd LCOL/BKTW AL2 55 P6
Blackbridge Rd
WOKS/MYFD GU22 232 A6
Blackbrook La HAYES BR2 206 D5
Blackbrook Rd RDKG RH5 273 K7
Blackburne's Ms
MYFR/PKLN W1K 10 C7
Blackburn Rd KIL/WHAMP NW6 2 G2
The Blackburn GT/LBKH KT23 235 N10
Blackbury Cl POTB/CUF EN6 59 M7
Blackbush Av CHDH RM6 123 N3
Blackbush Cl BELMT SM2 221 L4
Blackbush Spring HLW CM20 29 K10
Blackcap Cl CRAWW RH11 283 M9
Black Cut STAL AL1 38 D7
Blackdale CHESW EN7 61 P3
Black Ditch Rd WAB EN9 * 81 H2
Black Ditch Wy WAB EN9 80 G2
Black Dog Wk CRAWE RH10 283 P5
Blackdown Av
WOKS/MYFD GU22 233 H1
Blackdown Cl EFNCH N2 97 M10
WOKS/MYFD GU22 232 F2
Blackdown Ter
WOOL/PLUM SE18 * 162 C7
Black Eagle Cl BH/WHM TN16 262 F3
Blackenham Rd TOOT SW17 180 A7
Blackett Cl EGH TW20 195 J2
Blackett Rd CRAWE RH10 284 D8
Blackett St PUT/ROE SW15 156 C9
Blacketts Wood Dr
RKW/CH/CXG WD3 70 F8
Black Fan Cl ENC/FH EN2 79 K5
Black Fan Rd WGCE AL7 23 K4
Blackfen Pde BFN/LL DA15 * 185 K2
Blackfen Rd BFN/LL DA15 185 J1
Blackfold Rd CRAWE RH10 284 B8
Blackford Cl SAND/SEL CR2 223 J5
Blackford Rd OXHEY WD19 93 L6
Blackfriars Br STHWK SE1 12 C8
Black Friars La BLKFR EC4V 12 C6
Blackfriars Pas BLKFR EC4V 12 C7
Blackfriars Rd STHWK SE1 12 C9
Blackfriars U/P BLKFR EC4V 12 D7
Black Green Wood Cl
LCOL/BKTW AL2 56 A5
Blackhall La BGR/WK TN15 247 M9
Blackheath CRAWE RH10 284 E5
Blackheath Av GNWCH SE10 161 J6
Blackheath Gv BKHTH/KID SE3 161 L8
SHGR GU5 268 E9
Blackheath Hl GNWCH SE10 161 H7
Blackheath La SHGR GU5 268 F9
Blackheath Pk BKHTH/KID SE3 161 M8
Blackheath Ri LEW SE13 161 H8
Blackheath Rd GNWCH SE10 160 G7
Blackheath V BKHTH/KID SE3 161 K8
Blackhills ESH/CLAY KT10 217 N5
Black Horse Av CSHM HP5 51 J9
Black Horse Cl WDSR SL4 148 C8
Black Horse Ct STHWK SE1 * 19 H4
Blackhorse Crs AMS HP6 69 K4
Blackhorse La CROY/NA CR0 203 P7
EPP CM16 66 E1
KWD/TDW/WH KT20 257 L5
POTB/CUF EN6 58 B6
WALTH E17 100 C10
WALTH E17 120 C1
Black Horse Pde PIN HA5 * 113 J3
Blackhorse Pl UX/CGN UB8 131 L3
Blackhorse Rd DEPT SE8 160 D5
Black Horse Rd SCUP DA14 185 K7
Blackhorse Rd WALTH E17 120 C2
WOKS/MYFD GU22 231 J6
Blacklands Dr YEAD UB4 132 D6
Blacklands Meadow REDH RH1 258 F9
Blacklands Rd CAT SE6 183 H7
Blacklands Ter CHEL SW3 16 A6
Blackley Cl WAT WD17 72 G3
Black Lion Ct HLWE CM17 * 29 M7
Black Lion Ga BAY/PAD W2 9 H8
Black Lion Hl RAD WD7 57 K8
Black Lion La HMSMTH W6 156 D3
Blackmans Cl DART DA1 187 K4
Blackman's La WARL CR6 225 K10
Blackmans Yd WCHPL E1 * 13 M1
Blackmead SEV TN13 246 F7
Blackmoor La WATW WD18 72 E9
Blackmore Av STHL UB1 134 C10
Blackmore Ct WAB EN9 63 M9
Blackmore Crs
WOKN/KNAP GU21 232 E1
Blackmore Dr WLSDN NW10 135 N2
Blackmore Rd BKHH IG9 102 B1
BRWN CM15 86 D4
GRAYS RM17 167 P4
Blackmore's Gv TEDD TW11 176 F9
Blackmore Wy UX/CGN UB8 131 N1
Blackness Cottages HAYES BR2 * 226 A5
Blackness La HAYES BR2 226 A5
WOKS/MYFD GU22 232 B5
Blacknest Gate Rd ASC SL5 192 G3
Blacknest Rd ASC SL5 193 J3
Black Park Rd DTCH/LGLY SL3 130 C5
Blackpond La SLN SL2 128 G3
Blackpool Gdns YEAD UB4 132 F6
Blackpool Rd PECK SE15 160 A8
Black Potts Copse
WOKS/MYFD GU22 231 N5
Black Prince Cl BF/WBF KT14 216 A10
Black Prince Rd LBTH SE11 17 N6
Black Rod Cl HYS/HAR UB3 152 G2
Blackrurn Wy HSLWW TW4 175 M1
Blackshaw Rd TOOT SW17 179 N8
Blackshots La CDW/CHF RM16 147 P9
Blacksmith Cl ASHTD KT21 237 L5
CHDH RM6 123 M4
Blacksmith La RGUE GU4 268 F5
Blacksmith Rw DTCH/LGLY SL3 150 D3
Black Smiths Cl WARE SG12 26 F4
Blacksmiths Hl SAND/SEL CR2 224 A9
Blacksmiths La CHERT KT16 195 K7
DEN/HRF UB9 110 G7
RAIN RM13 144 G3
STA TW18 195 L3
STALW/RED AL3 38 A6
STMC/STPC BR5 207 M5
Blacksmiths Wy SBW CM21 29 L2
Black's Rd HMSMTH W6 156 F4
Blackstock Rd FSBYPK N4 119 J7
Blackstone Cl REDH RH1 275 P1
Blackstone Est HACK E8 7 P3
Blackstone Hl REDH RH1 257 P10
Blackstone Rd CRICK NW2 116 F10
Blackstroud La East LTWR GU18 212 D7
Blackstroud La West LTWR GU18 212 C7
Black Swan Ct WARE SG12 * 26 C2
Black Swan Yd STHWK SE1 19 J1
Blacks Yd SEV TN13 * 265 J1
Blackthorn Av WDR/YW UB7 152 B3
Blackthorn Cl CRAWW RH11 283 M5
GSTN WD25 55 J8
REIG RH2 275 M2
STALE/WH AL4 39 H3
Blackthorn Ct HEST TW5 153 M6
Blackthorn Dell DTCH/LGLY SL3 149 P2
Blackthorn Dr LTWR GU18 212 A8
Blackthorne Av CROY/NA CR0 204 B8
Blackthorne Cl HAT AL10 40 C7
Blackthorne Crs DTCH/LGLY SL3 151 H8
Blackthorne Dr CHING E4 101 J5
Blackthorne Rd DTCH/LGLY SL3 151 H9
GT/LBKH KT23 254 B2
Blackthorn Gv BXLYHN DA7 163 P9
Blackthorn Pl GU GU1 * 249 P7
Blackthorn Rd BH/WHM TN16 244 B2
CDW/CHF RM16 147 N10
IL IG1 122 G10
REIG RH2 275 M2
WGCE AL7 23 K6
Blackthorn St BOW E3 140 F6
Blackthorn Wy BRW CM14 107 J6
Blacktree Ms BRXN/ST SW9 * 159 H9
Blackwall La GNWCH SE10 161 K4
Blackwall Tunnel Ap
POP/IOD E14 141 H9
Blackwall Tunnel Northern Ap
BOW E3 140 F3
POP/IOD E14 141 H8
Blackwall Wy POP/IOD E14 141 H9
Blackwater Cl FSTGT E7 121 L9
RAIN RM13 144 E7
Blackwater La CRAWE RH10 284 D8
HHS/BOV HP3 36 F9
Blackwater St EDUL SE22 181 N1
Blackwell Av GUW GU2 249 J10
Blackwell Cl CLPT E5 120 D9
KTN/HRWW/WS HA3 94 C8
Blackwell Dr OXHEY WD19 73 K10
Blackwell Gdns EDGW HA8 95 M5
Blackwellhall La CSHM HP5 51 P7
Blackwell Hall La CSHM HP5 69 M1
Blackwell Rd KGLGY WD4 54 B5
Blackwood Cl BF/WBF KT14 215 M8
Blackwood St WALW SE17 18 G7
Bladen Cl WEY KT13 216 E3
Blades Cl LHD/OX KT22 237 J6
Bladindon Dr BXLY DA5 185 N3
Bladon Cl GU GU1 250 D9
Bladon Gdns RYLN/HDSTN HA2 114 A4
Blagden's La STHGT/OAK N14 98 E3
Blagdon Rd CAT SE6 182 G2
NWMAL KT3 200 C4
Blagdon Wk TEDD TW11 177 H9
Blagrove Rd NKENS W10 8 B4
Blair Av CDALE/KGS NW9 116 B5
ESH/CLAY KT10 198 B9
Blair Cl BFN/LL DA15 185 H1
HYS/HAR UB3 153 H3
IS N1 6 F1
Blairderry Rd BRXS/STRHM SW2 180 F5
Blair Dr SEV TN13 247 J9
Blairhead Dr OXHEY WD19 93 J4
Blair Rd SL SL1 129 K10
Blair St POP/IOD E14 141 H8
Blake Av BARK IG11 143 H3
Blake Cl CAR SM5 201 P8
NKENS W10 136 F7
RAIN RM13 144 G3
STAL AL1 38 F9
WELL DA16 163 H7
Blakeden Dr ESH/CLAY KT10 218 E4
Blake Gdns DART DA1 165 N10
FUL/PGN SW6 157 K7
Blakehall Rd CAR SM5 222 A3
Blake Hall Rd CHONG CM5 67 H2
WAN E11 121 M6
Blakemere Rd WGCW AL8 22 G3
Blake Ms RCH/KEW TW9 155 M7
Blakemore Gdns BARN SW13 156 E5
Blakemore Rd
STRHM/NOR SW16 180 F6
THHTH CR7 202 G5
Blakemore Wy BELV DA17 163 P2
Blakeney Av BECK BR3 204 E1
Blakeney Cl CAMTN NW1 5 J4
CAMTN NW1 5 J7
HACK E8 119 P10
HOR/WEW KT19 220 A7
TRDG/WHET N20 97 M2
Blakeney Rd BECK BR3 204 E1
Blaker Ct CHARL SE7 * 161 P6
Blake Rd CAN/RD E16 141 L6
CROY/NA CR0 203 M9
FBAR/BDGN N11 98 D8
MTCM CR4 201 P3
Blaker Rd SRTFD E15 141 H3
Blakes Av NWMAL KT3 200 C5
Blakes Cl WLSDN NW10 136 D1
Blake's Gn WWKM BR4 205 H8
Blake's La EHSLY KT24 252 A7
NWMAL KT3 200 C5
Blakesley Av EA W5 135 H8
Blakes Rd PECK SE15 159 M6
Blakes Ter NWMAL KT3 200 D5
Blakesware Gdns ED N9 99 L1
Blakewood Cl FELT TW13 175 K7
Blanchard Cl ELTH/MOT SE9 184 B6
Blanchard Dr WATW WD18 72 F8
Blanchard Gv PEND EN3 80 F4
Blanchard Ms HARH RM3 105 N8
Blanchards Hl RGUE GU4 250 B3
Blanchard Wy HACK E8 7 P2
Blanch Cl PECK SE15 160 B6
Blanchedowne CMBW SE5 159 L10
Blanche La BAR EN5 76 D1
POTB/CUF EN6 58 C10
Blanche St CAN/RD E16 141 L6
Blanchland Rd MRDN SM4 201 L5
Blanchman's Rd WARL CR6 242 D4
Blandfield Rd BAL SW12 180 B3
Blandford Av BECK BR3 204 D2
WHTN TW2 176 A4
Blandford Cl CROY/NA CR0 202 F10
DTCH/LGLY SL3 150 A2
EFNCH N2 117 M3
ROMW/RG RM7 124 C2
WOKS/MYFD GU22 232 E3
Blandford Crs CHING E4 101 H1
Blandford Ms REIG RH2 257 N10
Blandford Rd BECK BR3 204 C2
CHSWK W4 156 B2
EA W5 155 J1
NWDGN UB2 153 N3
STAL AL1 38 F5
TEDD TW11 176 C8
Blandford Rd North
DTCH/LGLY SL3 150 A2
Blandford Rd South
DTCH/LGLY SL3 150 A3
Blandford Sq CAMTN NW1 9 P2
Blandford St MHST W1U 10 B5
Blandford Waye YEAD UB4 133 K8
Bland St ELTH/MOT SE9 162 A10
Blaney Crs EHAM E6 142 E5
Blanford Rd REIG RH2 275 M1
Blanks La HORL RH6 278 D4
Blanmerle Rd ELTH/MOT SE9 184 E4
Blann Cl ELTH/MOT SE9 184 A2
Blantyre St WBPTN SW10 157 N6
Blantyre Wk WBPTN SW10 * 157 N6
Blashford St CAT SE6 183 J3
Blattner Cl BORE WD6 75 K8
Blawith Rd HRW HA1 114 D2
Blaydon Cl RSLP HA4 112 F5
TOTM N17 * 100 A8
Blaydon Wk TOTM N17 100 A8
Blays Cl EGH TW20 171 P9
Blay's La EGH TW20 171 N9
Bleak Hill La WOOL/PLUM SE18 163 J5
Blean Gv PGE/AN SE20 182 B10
Bleasdale Av GFD/PVL UB6 134 F4
Blechynden Gdns NKENS W10 136 G9
Blechynden St NKENS W10 * 136 G9
Bledlow Cl THMD SE28 143 M9
Bledlow Ri GFD/PVL UB6 134 B4
Bleeding Heart Yd HCIRC EC1N * 12 B4
Blegberry Gdns BERK HP4 33 K6
Blegborough Rd
STRHM/NOR SW16 180 D9
Blencarn Cl WOKN/KNAP GU21 231 M2
Blendon Dr BXLY DA5 185 N2
Blendon Rd BXLY DA5 185 N2
Blendon Ter WOOL/PLUM SE18 162 F5
Blendworth Wy PECK SE15 159 M6
Blenheim CDALE/KGS NW9 * 96 C10
Blenheim Av GNTH/NBYPK IG2 122 D4
Blenheim Cl BF/WBF KT14 215 J9
CRAWE RH10 284 E3
DART DA1 187 K2
GFD/PVL UB6 * 134 C4
OXHEY WD19 93 L1
ROMW/RG RM7 124 D2
RYNPK SW20 200 F3
SBW CM21 29 L3
UPMR RM14 126 D6
WCHMH N21 99 K2
WLGTN SM6 222 D4
Blenheim Ct ARCH N19 118 F7
BFN/LL DA15 184 G6
WFD IG8 101 N8
WGCE AL7 23 J4
Blenheim Crs NTGHL W11 8 B6
RSLP HA4 112 E7
SAND/SEL CR2 223 K4
Blenheim Dr WELL DA16 163 J7
Blenheim Gdns
BRXS/STRHM SW2 180 G2
CRICK NW2 116 F10
KUTN/CMB KT2 199 N1
SAND/SEL CR2 223 P8
SOCK/AV RM15 146 A10
WBLY HA9 115 K8
WLGTN SM6 222 D3
WOKS/MYFD GU22 231 N5
Blenheim Gv GVE DA12 190 F3
PECK SE15 159 N8
Blenheim Pde HGDN/ICK UB10 * 132 C6
Blenheim Park Rd
SAND/SEL CR2 223 K5
Blenheim Pas STJWD NW8 * 3 J7
Blenheim Pl TEDD TW11 176 E8
Blenheim Ri SEVS/STOTM N15 * 119 N2
Blenheim Rd BAR EN5 76 G7
BFN/LL DA15 185 M4
BMLY BR1 206 B4
BRWN CM15 86 F10
CHSWK W4 156 B2
DART DA1 187 K2
DTCH/LGLY SL3 150 A3
EHAM E6 142 A5
HOR/WEW KT19 220 A7
NTHLT UB5 134 A1
ORP BR6 207 M9
PGE/AN SE20 182 B10
RYLN/HDSTN HA2 114 A4
RYNPK SW20 200 F3
STAL AL1 38 E5
STJWD NW8 3 K7
SUT SM1 201 K10
WALTH E17 120 C1
WAN E11 121 K9
Blenheim St CONDST W1S 10 E6
Blenheim Ter STJWD NW8 3 J7
Blenheim Wy EPP CM16 66 B3
ISLW TW7 154 F7
Blenhiem Ct WGCE AL7 * 23 J4
Blenhiem Rd ABLGY WD5 55 H9
Blenkarne Rd BTSEA SW11 180 A2
Blenkin Cl STALW/RED AL3 38 B2
Bleriot Rd HEST TW5 153 K6
Blessbury Rd EDGW HA8 95 P9
Blessington Rd LEW SE13 161 J10
Blessing Wy BARK IG11 143 M4
Bletchingley Cl REDH RH1 258 D5
THHTH CR7 203 J4
Bletchingley Rd GDST RH9 259 P7
REDH RH1 258 D5
REDH RH1 259 H9
Bletchley St IS N1 6 F8
Bletchmore Cl HYS/HAR UB3 152 E5
Bletsoe Wk IS N1 6 F7
Bligh Cl CRAWE RH10 284 A9
Bligh Rd GVW DA11 190 D2
Blighs Ct SEV TN13 * 265 J1
Blighs Wk SEV TN13 * 265 J1
Blincoe Cl WIM/MER SW19 178 G5
Blinco La DTCH/LGLY SL3 130 B8
Blind La GTMIS/PWD HP16 50 B6
Blindley Rd CRAWE RH10 284 E4
Blindman's La CHES/WCR EN8 62 C6
Blissett St GNWCH SE10 161 H7
Bliss Ms NKENS W10 * 2 B9
NKENS W10 137 H5
Blisworth Cl YEAD UB4 133 M6
Blithbury Rd DAGW RM9 143 L1
Blithdale Rd ABYW SE2 163 K3
Blithfield St KENS W8 14 G4
Blockhouse Rd GRAYS RM17 167 P5
Blockley Rd ALP/SUD HA0 114 G7
Bloemfontein Av SHB W12 136 E10
Bloemfontein Rd SHB W12 136 E9
Blomfield Rd MV/WKIL W9 9 H3
Blomfield St LVPST EC2M 13 H4
Blomfield Vls BAY/PAD W2 9 J3
Blomville Rd BCTR RM8 123 P7
Blondell Cl WDR/YW UB7 151 N5
Blondel St BTSEA SW11 158 B8
Blondin Av EA W5 155 H3
Blondin St BOW E3 140 F4
Bloomfield Cl WOKN/KNAP GU21 231 K4
Bloomfield Crs GNTH/NBYPK IG2 122 E4
Bloomfield Pl MYFR/PKLN W1K 10 F7
Bloomfield Rd CHESW EN7 61 K1
HAYES BR2 206 A5
HGT N6 118 B4
KUT/HW KT1 199 K4
WOOL/PLUM SE18 162 E4
Bloomfield Ter BGVA SW1W 16 D7
Bloom Gv WNWD SE27 181 J6
Bloomhall Rd NRWD SE19 181 L8
Bloom Park Rd FUL/PGN SW6 157 J6
Bloomsbury Cl EA W5 135 L9
HOR/WEW KT19 220 A6
Bloomsbury Pl
NOXST/BSQ WC1A 11 M4
Bloomsbury Sq
NOXST/BSQ WC1A 11 M4
Bloomsbury St GWRST WC1E 11 K3
Bloomsbury Wy
NOXST/BSQ WC1A 11 L4
Blore Cl VX/NE SW8 158 E7
Blossom Cl DAGW RM9 144 A3
EA W5 155 K1
SAND/SEL CR2 223 N2
Blossom La ENC/FH EN2 79 K5
Blossom St WCHPL E1 13 K2
Blossom Wy HGDN/ICK UB10 132 A2
WDR/YW UB7 152 B3
Blossom Waye HEST TW5 153 M5
Blount St POP/IOD E14 140 D8
Bloxam Gdns ELTH/MOT SE9 184 B1
Bloxhall Rd LEY E10 120 E6
Bloxham Crs HPTN TW12 197 N1
Bloxworth Cl WLGTN SM6 202 D10
Blucher Rd CMBW SE5 159 K6
Blucher St CSHM HP5 50 G7
Blue Anchor La
BERM/RHTH SE16 19 P5
TIL RM18 169 H4
Blue Anchor Yd WCHPL E1 13 N7
Blue Ball La EGH TW20 172 C8
Blue Ball Yd WHALL SW1A 10 G10
Blue Barn La WEY KT13 216 B7
Bluebell Av MNPK E12 122 B10
Bluebell Cl CRAWW RH11 * 283 L10
HERT/BAY SG13 25 P5
HHW HP1 * 35 H7
HOM E9 140 B3
NTHLT UB5 133 N1
ORP BR6 206 F9
ROMW/RG RM7 124 F7
SYD SE26 181 N7
WLGTN SM6 202 C8
Bluebell Ct WOKS/MYFD GU22 232 A5
Bluebell Dr ABLGY WD5 54 G3
CHESW EN7 61 L4
Bluebell La EHSLY KT24 252 F5
Bluebell Ri LTWR GU18 212 A7
Bluebell Wy HAT AL10 22 C10
IL IG1 142 E1
Blueberry Cl STALW/RED AL3 38 C2
WFD IG8 101 M7
Blueberry Gdns COUL/CHIP CR5 240 G2
Blueberry La RSEV TN14 245 M2
Bluebird La DAGE RM10 144 B2
Bluebird Wy LCOL/BKTW AL2 55 N6
THMD SE28 162 G1
Bluebridge Av BRKMPK AL9 59 H3
Blue Bridge Rd BRKMPK AL9 59 H4
Blue Cedars BNSTD SM7 220 G10
Blue Cedars Pl COB KT11 217 L8
Bluecoats Av HERT/WAT SG14 25 L5
Bluecoat Yd WARE SG12 26 C2
Bluefield Cl HPTN TW12 175 P8
Bluegates EW KT17 220 D4
Bluehouse Gdns OXTED RH8 261 M4
Bluehouse Hill
Hemel Hempstead Rd
STALW/RED AL3 37 P7
Bluehouse La OXTED RH8 261 K4
OXTED RH8 261 M4
Bluehouse Rd CHING E4 101 K4
Blue Leaves Av COUL/CHIP CR5 240 E8
Blue Lion Pl STHWK SE1 19 J3
Bluemans EPP CM16 48 E10
Bluemans End EPP CM16 48 E10
Blue Riband Est CROY/NA CR0 * 203 J9
Bluett Rd LCOL/BKTW AL2 57 J3
Bluewater Pkwy RDART DA2 188 F3
Blumfield Crs SL SL1 128 C7
Blundel La COB KT11 218 A10
COB KT11 235 N2
Blundell Av HORL RH6 280 A4
Blundell Cl HACK E8 119 P9
STALW/RED AL3 38 C2
Blundell Rd EDGW HA8 96 B8
Blundell St HOLWY N7 5 M3
Blunden Cl BCTR RM8 123 M6
Blunden Dr DTCH/LGLY SL3 150 E3
Blunesfield POTB/CUF EN6 59 N7
Blunt Rd SAND/SEL CR2 223 L2
Blunts Av WDR/YW UB7 152 B6
Blunts La LCOL/BKTW AL2 55 L2
Blunts Rd ELTH/MOT SE9 184 D1
Blurton Rd CLPT E5 120 C9
Blyth Cl BORE WD6 75 L5
TWK TW1 176 E2
Blythe Cl CAT SE6 182 E3
IVER SL0 131 J8
Blythe Hl CAT SE6 182 E3
STMC/STPC BR5 207 J1
Blythe Hill La CAT SE6 182 E3
Blythe Hill Pl FSTH SE23 * 182 D3
Blythe Ms WKENS W14 * 156 G2
Blythe Rd HOD EN11 45 J5
WKENS W14 156 G2
Blythe St BETH E2 140 A5
Blytheswood Pl
STRHM/NOR SW16 180 G7
Blythe V CAT SE6 182 E4
Blyth Rd BMLY BR1 205 L1
HYS/HAR UB3 152 F1
THMD SE28 143 M9
WALTH E17 120 E5
Blyth's Whf POP/IOD E14 * 140 D9
Blythswood Rd GDMY/SEVK IG3 123 K6
Blyth Wk UPMR RM14 126 D5
Blythway WGCE AL7 23 J2
Blythwood Rd FSBYPK N4 118 F5
PIN HA5 93 L9
Blyton Cl BEAC HP9 88 C7
Boadicea Cl SL SL1 128 D10
Boadicea St IS N1 5 N6
Boakes Cl CDALE/KGS NW9 115 P2
Boakes Meadow RSEV TN14 228 G7
Boardman Av CHING E4 80 G9
Boardman Cl BAR EN5 77 H9
Board School Rd
WOKN/KNAP GU21 232 C2
Boardwalk Pl POP/IOD E14 141 H10
Boar Hl DORK RH4 272 D8
Boarlands Cl SL SL1 128 E9
Boar's Head Yd BTFD TW8 155 J6
Boathouse Wk PECK SE15 159 N6
RCH/KEW TW9 155 J7
Boat Lifter Wy
BERM/RHTH SE16 160 D3
Boat Quay CAN/RD E16 141 P9
Bob Anker Cl PLSTW E13 141 M5
Bobbin Cl CLAP SW4 158 D9
Bobbingworth Ml CHONG CM5 49 H10
Bob Marley Wy HNHL SE24 159 H10
Bockhampton Rd
KUTN/CMB KT2 177 L10
Bocking St HACK E8 140 A3
Boddicott Cl WIM/MER SW19 179 H5
Boddington Gdns ACT W3 155 M1
Bodell Cl CDW/CHF RM16 167 N2
Bodiam Cl CRAWE RH10 284 D7
EN EN1 79 L6
Bodiam Rd STRHM/NOR SW16 202 E1
Bodiam Wy WLSDN NW10 135 L5
Bodicea Ms HSLWW TW4 175 N2
Bodle Av SWCM DA10 189 K2
Bodley Cl EPP CM16 65 J6
NWMAL KT3 200 B5
Bodley Rd NWMAL KT3 200 B6
Bodmin Av SLN SL2 128 F7
Bodmin Cl RYLN/HDSTN HA2 113 N8
STMC/STPC BR5 207 M8
Bodmin Gv MRDN SM4 201 L5
Bodmin St WAND/EARL SW18 179 K5
Bodnant Gdns RYNPK SW20 200 D3
Bodney Rd CLPT E5 120 A10
Bodwell Cl HHW HP1 35 K5
Boeing Wy NWDGN UB2 153 J2
Bofors House CHARL SE7 * 162 B6
Bognor Gdns OXHEY WD19 * 93 K6
Bognor Rd WELL DA16 163 N7
Bohemia HHNE HP2 35 P5
Bohemia Pl HACK E8 140 B1
Bohn Rd WCHPL E1 140 D7
Bohun Gv EBAR EN4 77 P10
Boileau Rd BARN SW13 156 D6
EA W5 135 L8
Bois Av AMS HP6 68 G2
Bois Hall Rd ADL/WDHM KT15 215 N2
Bois Hl CSHM HP5 51 K10
Bois La AMS HP6 69 J2
Bois Ml CSHM HP5 * 69 M2
Bois Moor Rd CSHM HP5 51 J10
Boissy Cl STALE/WH AL4 39 L7
Bolden St DEPT SE8 160 G8
Boldero Pl STJWD NW8 * 9 N2
Bolderwood Wy WWKM BR4 204 G9
Bolding House La
CHOB/PIR GU24 212 E9
Boldmere Rd PIN HA5 113 K5
Boleyn Av EN EN1 80 A5
EW KT17 220 E6
Boleyn Cl CDW/CHF RM16 167 L2
CRAWE RH10 284 E10
HHNE HP2 36 D1
LOU IG10 82 B10
STA TW18 173 H8
WALTH E17 120 F2
Boleyn Ct BKHH IG9 101 N2
BROX EN10 44 D7
Boleyn Dr E/WMO/HCT KT8 197 N3
RSLP HA4 113 L7
STAL AL1 38 D8
Boleyn Gdns DAGE RM10 144 D2
RBRW/HUT CM13 107 M4
WWKM BR4 204 G9
Boleyn Rd BGR/WK TN15 247 M3
EHAM E6 142 A4
FSTGT E7 141 M2
STNW/STAM N16 119 M10
Boleyn Wk LHD/OX KT22 236 E6
Boleyn Wy BAR EN5 77 M7
BARK/HLT IG6 102 F7
SWCM DA10 189 K3
Bolina Rd BERM/RHTH SE16 160 B4
Bolingbroke Gv BTSEA SW11 179 P1
BTSEA SW11 180 A2
Bolingbroke Rd WKENS W14 156 G2
Bolingbroke Wk BTSEA SW11 * 157 N6
Bolingbroke Wy HYS/HAR UB3 132 E10
Bolingbrook STALE/WH AL4 38 F2
Bollo Bridge Rd ACT W3 155 N2
Bollo La ACT W3 155 N2
Bolney Ct CRAWW RH11 283 J10
Bolney Ga SKENS SW7 15 N2
Bolney St VX/NE SW8 158 G6
Bolsover Gv REDH RH1 258 F5
Bolsover St GTPST W1W 10 F2
Bolstead Rd MTCM CR4 202 C1
Bolster Gv WDGN N22 * 98 E9
Bolt Ct FLST/FETLN EC4A 12 B6
Bolters La BNSTD SM7 239 K1
Bolters Rd HORL RH6 280 B2
Bolters Rd South HORL RH6 280 A2
Boltmore Cl HDN NW4 116 G1
Bolton Av WDSR SL4 149 J9
Bolton Cl CHSGTN KT9 219 J3
Bolton Crs CMBW SE5 18 B10
WDSR SL4 149 H9
Bolton Dr MRDN SM4 201 N7
Bolton Gdns BMLY BR1 183 L9
ECT SW5 15 H7
TEDD TW11 176 F9
WLSDN NW10 136 G4
Bolton Gardens Ms
WBPTN SW10 15 H8
Bolton Pl IS N1 6 C4
Bolton Rd CHSGTN KT9 219 J3
CHSWK W4 155 P6
HRW HA1 114 B2
SRTFD E15 141 L1
STJWD NW8 3 H6

UED N18 99 N6
WDSR SL4 149 H9
WLSDN NW10 136 B3
Boltons Cl WOKS/MYFD GU22 233 K1
Bolton's La HYS/HAR UB3 152 D6
WOKS/MYFD GU22 233 K2
Boltons Pl ECT SW5 15 J7
The Boltons ALP/SUD HA0 114 E9
WBPTN SW10 15 J7
WFD IG8 * 101 M5
Bolton St MYFR/PICC W1J 10 F9
Bombay St BERM/RHTH SE16 160 A3
Bombers La BH/WHM TN16 244 G6
Bomer Cl WDR/YW UB7 152 B6
Bomore Rd NTGHL W11 8 A7
Bonaparte Ms PIM SW1V 17 J7
Bonar Pl CHST BR7 184 B10
Bonar Rd PECK SE15 159 P6
Bonaventure Ct GVE DA12 191 J7
Bonchester Cl CHST BR7 184 D10
Bonchurch Cl BELMT SM2 221 L4
Bonchurch Rd NKENS W10 8 A3
WEA W13 134 G10
Bond Cl IVER SL0 130 E2
RSEV TN14 245 N1
WDR/YW UB7 132 A8
Bondfield Av YEAD UB4 133 H5
Bond Gdns WLGTN SM6 222 D1
Bond Rd MTCM CR4 202 A2
SURB KT6 199 L9
WARL CR6 242 C4
Bond's La RDKG RH5 272 G8
Bond St EA W5 135 J9
EGH TW20 171 N9
GRAYS RM17 167 P5
SRTFD E15 121 K10
Bondway VX/NE SW8 17 M10
Bonehurst Rd HORL RH6 276 B10
Bone Mill La GDST RH9 260 D10
Bones La HORL RH6 281 P3
Boneta Rd WOOL/PLUM SE18 162 C2
Bonfield Rd LEW SE13 161 H10
Bonham Gdns BCTR RM8 123 N7
Bonham Rd BCTR RM8 123 N7
BRXS/STRHM SW2 180 G1
Bonheur Rd CHSWK W4 156 A1
Bonhill St SDTCH EC2A 13 H2
Boniface Gdns
KTN/HRWW/WS HA3 94 A8
Boniface Rd HGDN/ICK UB10 112 C8
Boniface Wk
KTN/HRWW/WS HA3 94 A8
Bonington Rd HCH RM12 125 L10
Bonita Ms BROCKY SE4 160 C9
Bonks Hl SBW CM21 29 N2
Bonner Hill Rd KUT/HW KT1 199 L3
Bonner Rd BETH E2 140 B4
Bonners Cl WOKS/MYFD GU22 232 C8
Bonnersfield Cl HRW HA1 114 F4
Bonnersfield La HRW HA1 114 F4
Bonner St BETH E2 * 140 B4
Bonner Wk CDW/CHF RM16 * 167 L2
Bonnetts La CRAWW RH11 283 K2
Bonneville Gdns CLAP SW4 180 D2
Bonney Gv CHESW EN7 61 P6
Bonney Wy SWLY BR8 208 F2
Bonningtons RBRW/HUT CM13 107 N4
Bonnington Sq VX/NE SW8 17 N9
Bonnys Rd REIG RH2 256 G10
Bonny St CAMTN NW1 4 G4
Bonser Rd TWK TW1 176 E5
Bonsey Cl WOKS/MYFD GU22 232 B7
Bonsey La WOKS/MYFD GU22 232 B7
Bonsey's La CHOB/PIR GU24 214 B5
Bonsor Dr KWD/TDW/WH KT20 239 H8
Bonsor St CMBW SE5 159 M6
Bonville Gdns HDN NW4 116 D2
Bonville Rd BMLY BR1 183 L8
Booker Rd UED N18 99 P6
Bookham Ct GT/LBKH KT23 235 N9
Bookham Gv GT/LBKH KT23 254 A2
Bookham Rd COB KT11 235 L6
Boones Rd LEW SE13 161 K10
Boone St LEW SE13 161 K10
Boord St GNWCH SE10 161 K2
Boothby Rd ARCH N19 118 E7
Booth Cl HOM E9 140 A3
THMD SE28 143 L10
Booth Dr STA TW18 173 N9
Booth La BLKFR EC4V 12 E7
Booth Rd CDALE/KGS NW9 96 A9
CRAWW RH11 283 H10
CROY/NA CR0 * 203 J9
Booths Cl BRKMPK AL9 40 G10
Boot Pde EDGW HA8 * 95 M7
Boot St FSBYE EC1V 7 J10
Borage Cl CRAWW RH11 283 K10
Bordars Rd HNWL W7 134 D7
Bordars Wk HNWL W7 134 D7
Borden Av EN EN1 79 L10
Border Cha CRAWE RH10 285 H3
Border Crs SYD SE26 182 A8
Border Gdns CROY/NA CR0 224 G1
Border Ga MTCM CR4 201 P1
Border Rd SYD SE26 182 B8
Borders Cl CRAWE RH10 285 K1
Borderside SLN SL2 129 M8
Border's La LOU IG10 82 D8
Bordesley Rd MRDN SM4 201 L4
Bordon Wk PUT/ROE SW15 178 D3
Boreas Wk IS N1 6 D8
Boreham Av CAN/RD E16 141 M8
Boreham Cl WAN E11 121 H6
Boreham Ms HOD EN11 26 F10
Boreham Rd WDGN N22 99 K9
Borers Arms Rd CRAWE RH10 285 K2
Borers Cl CRAWE RH10 * 285 K2
Borgard House CHARL SE7 * 162 B6
Borgard Rd WOOL/PLUM SE18 162 C3
Borkwood Pk ORP BR6 227 J1
Borkwood Wy ORP BR6 227 H1
Borland Cl RDART DA2 188 F1
Borland Rd PECK SE15 160 B10
TEDD TW11 176 G9
Bornedene POTB/CUF EN6 59 H7
Borneo St PUT/ROE SW15 156 F9
Borough High St STHWK SE1 18 F2
Borough Hl CROY/NA CR0 203 J10
Borough Rd BH/WHM TN16 244 A7
ISLW TW7 154 D7
KUTN/CMB KT2 199 M1
MTCM CR4 201 P2
STHWK SE1 18 C3
Borough Sq STHWK SE1 18 E2
The Borough BRKHM/BTCW RH3 273 M1
CHONG CM5 67 N5
Borough Wy POTB/CUF EN6 59 H8
Borrell Cl BROX EN10 44 E6
Borrett Cl WALW SE17 18 E8
Borrodaile Rd WAND/EARL SW18 179 L2
Borrowdale Av
KTN/HRWW/WS HA3 94 F10
Borrowdale Cl CRAWW RH11 283 L9
EGH TW20 172 E10
REDBR IG4 122 B2
SAND/SEL CR2 223 N9
Borrowdale Ct HHNE HP2 35 P3
Borrowdale Dr SAND/SEL CR2 223 N8
Borthwick Ms WAN E11 * 121 K9
Borthwick Rd CDALE/KGS NW9 116 C4
SRTFD E15 121 K9
Borthwick St DEPT SE8 160 F4
Borwick Av WALTH E17 120 E1
Bosanquet Cl UX/CGN UB8 131 N7
Bosanquet Rd HOD EN11 45 H1
Bosbury Rd CAT SE6 183 H6
Boscastle Rd KTTN NW5 118 C8
Boscobel Cl BMLY BR1 206 C2
Boscobel Pl BGVA SW1W 16 D5
Boscobel St BAY/PAD W2 9 M3
Boscombe Av EMPK RM11 125 L5
GRAYS RM17 168 A3
LEY E10 121 J5
Boscombe Cl CLPT E5 120 D10
EGH TW20 194 F1
Boscombe Rd SHB W12 156 D1
WIM/MER SW19 201 K1
WPK KT4 200 F8
Bose Cl FNCH N3 97 H9
Bosgrove CHING E4 101 H2
Bosham Rd CRAWE RH10 284 D10
Boshers Gdns EGH TW20 172 C9
Bosman Dr BFOR GU20 192 A10
Boss St STHWK SE1 19 L1
Bostall Heath ABYW SE2 * 163 M4
Bostall Hl ABYW SE2 163 L4
Bostall La ABYW SE2 163 L4
Bostall Manorway ABYW SE2 163 L3
Bostall Park Av BXLYHN DA7 163 P6
Bostall Rd STMC/STPC BR5 185 L10
Boston Gdns BTFD TW8 154 F3
CHSWK W4 156 B5
Boston Gv RSLP HA4 112 D4
SL SL1 129 H8
Boston Manor Rd BTFD TW8 154 F3
Boston Pde HNWL W7 * 154 F3
Boston Park Rd BTFD TW8 * 155 H5
Boston Pl CAMTN NW1 10 A2
Boston Rd CROY/NA CR0 202 G6
EDGW HA8 95 P8
EHAM E6 142 B5
HNWL W7 134 D10
HNWL W7 154 E1
Bostonthorpe Rd HNWL W7 * 154 D1
Boston V HNWL W7 154 F3
Bosville Dr SEV TN13 247 H9
Bosville Rd SEV TN13 247 H9
Boswell Cl RAD WD7 57 K8
STMC/STPC BR5 207 M6
Boswell Ct BMSBY WC1N 11 M3
Boswell Rd CRAWE RH10 283 P10
THHTH CR7 203 K4
Boswell St BMSBY WC1N 11 M3
Boswick La BERK HP4 33 J1
Bosworth Cl WALTH E17 100 E9
Bosworth Crs HARH RM3 105 K7
Bosworth Rd BAR EN5 77 K7
DAGE RM10 124 B9
FBAR/BDGN N11 98 E7
NKENS W10 8 B2
Botany Bay La CHST BR7 206 F2
Botany Cl EBAR EN4 77 P8
Botany Ter PUR RM19 * 165 P4
Botany Wy PUR RM19 166 A4
Boteley Cl CHING E4 101 J3
Botery's Cross REDH RH1 259 J9
Botham Cl EDGW HA8 95 P8
Botham Dr SL SL1 149 K2
Botha Rd PLSTW E13 141 N7
Bothwell Cl CAN/RD E16 141 M7
Bothwell Rd CROY/NA CR0 225 H6
Bothwell St HMSMTH W6 156 G5
Botley La CSHM HP5 51 M6
Botley Rd CSHM HP5 51 K6
HHNE HP2 36 B1
Botleys Pk CHERT KT16 * 214 F2
Botolph Aly MON EC3R 13 J8
Botolph La MON EC3R 13 J8
Botsford Rd RYNPK SW20 201 H2
Bottom House Farm La
CSTG HP8 69 M10
CSTG HP8 89 J2
Bottom La BEAC HP9 89 H7
KGLGY WD4 71 M1
Bottrells La CSTG HP8 89 M3
Bott Rd RDART DA2 187 N7
Bott's Ms BAY/PAD W2 8 F6
Botwell Common Rd
HYS/HAR UB3 132 E9
Botwell Crs HYS/HAR UB3 132 F8
Botwell La HYS/HAR UB3 132 F9
HYS/HAR UB3 152 G1
Boucher Cl TEDD TW11 176 E8
Boucher Dr GVW DA11 190 C7
Boughton Av HAYES BR2 205 L7
Boughton Hall Av
RPLY/SEND GU23 233 J10
Boughton Rd THMD SE28 163 H2
Boughton Wy AMS HP6 69 P5
Boulcott St WCHPL E1 140 C8
Boulevard WATW WD18 * 72 E9
The Boulevard CRAWE RH10 283 N7
FUL/PGN SW6 157 M8
WATW WD18 72 E9
WFD IG8 102 D8
WGCE AL7 23 J3
Boulmer Rd UX/CGN UB8 131 M5
Boulogne Rd CROY/NA CR0 203 L6
Boulter Gdns RAIN RM13 145 H1
Boulters Cl SL SL1 148 F1
Boulthurst Wy OXTED RH8 261 N8
Boulton Rd BCTR RM8 123 P7
Boultwood Rd EHAM E6 142 C8
Bounces La ED N9 100 A3
Bounces Rd ED N9 100 A3
The Bounce HHNE HP2 35 N4
Boundaries Rd BAL SW12 180 A5
FELT TW13 175 K4
Boundary Av WALTH E17 120 E5
Boundary Business Ct
MTCM CR4 201 N3
Boundary Cl BAR EN5 77 J5
CRAWE RH10 283 P6
GDMY/SEVK IG3 123 H9
KUT/HW KT1 199 M3
NWDGN UB2 153 P4
Boundary Dr HERT/WAT SG14 25 L3
Boundary La CMBW SE5 18 F10
PLSTW E13 142 A6
WGCE AL7 23 H9
Boundary Ms STJWD NW8 * 3 K5
Boundary Pk HHNE HP2 * 35 N7
WEY KT13 196 F10
Boundary Pass WCHPL E1 13 K1
Boundary Rd ASHF TW15 173 M8
BARK IG11 142 F4
BFN/LL DA15 185 H1
CAR SM5 222 B5
CFSP/GDCR SL9 90 A8
CRAWE RH10 283 P6
ED N9 80 B10
EFNCH N2 97 N9
PIN HA5 113 L4
PLSTW E13 141 P4
ROM RM1 125 H4
STAL AL1 38 D4
STJWD NW8 3 J6
UPMR RM14 125 P8
WALTH E17 120 E5
WBLY HA9 115 K8
WDGN N22 99 K10
WIM/MER SW19 179 N9
WLGTN SM6 222 C3
WOKN/KNAP GU21 232 D2
Boundary Rd East
ADL/WDHM KT15 215 L5
Boundary Rd North
ADL/WDHM KT15 215 L5
Boundary Rd West
ADL/WDHM KT15 215 L5
Boundary Rw STHWK SE1 18 C1
Boundary St BETH E2 7 L10
ERITH DA8 164 G6
The Boundary HERT/BAY SG13 42 D5
Boundary Wy CROY/NA CR0 224 F2
GSTN WD25 55 K8
HHNE HP2 36 E4
WOKN/KNAP GU21 232 E1
Boundfield Rd CAT SE6 183 L5
Bounds Green Rd
FBAR/BDGN N11 98 F8
Bourchier Cl SEV TN13 265 J2
Bourchier St SOHO/SHAV W1D 11 J7
Bourdon Pl MYFR/PKLN W1K 10 F7
Bourdon Rd PGE/AN SE20 204 B2
Bourdon St MYFR/PICC W1J 10 E8
Bourke Cl CLAP SW4 180 F2
WLSDN NW10 136 B1
Bourke Hl COUL/CHIP CR5 240 A4
Bourlet Cl FITZ W1T 10 G4
Bourn Av EBAR EN4 77 N9
SEVS/STOTM N15 119 L2
UX/CGN UB8 132 B6
Bournbrook Rd BKHTH/KID SE3 162 A9
Bourne Av CHERT KT16 195 K3
HYS/HAR UB3 152 D2
RSLP HA4 113 K10
STHGT/OAK N14 98 F3
WDSR SL4 149 H10
Bournebridge La ABR/ST RM4 104 C1
Bourne Cl BF/WBF KT14 215 L9
BROX EN10 44 E6
ISLW TW7 154 D9
RGUE GU4 268 E6
THDIT KT7 198 E9
WARE SG12 26 C1
Bourne Ct BF/WBF KT14 * 215 P9
RSLP HA4 113 J10
Bourne Dr MTCM CR4 201 N2
Bourne End EMPK RM11 125 P5
Bourne End La HHW HP1 34 F8
Bourne End Rd NTHWD HA6 92 F5
Bourne Est HCIRC EC1N * 12 A3
Bournefield Rd CTHM CR3 241 N4
Bourne Gdns CHING E4 100 G5
Bourne Gv ASHTD KT21 237 J5
Bournehall BUSH WD23 73 P10
Bournehall Av BUSH WD23 73 P9
Bournehall La BUSH WD23 73 P10
Bournehall Rd BUSH WD23 73 P10
Bourne Hl PLMGR N13 98 F3
Bourne Hill Cl PLMGR N13 * 98 G3
Bourne La CTHM CR3 241 L7
Bourne Md BXLY DA5 186 D1
Bournemead Av NTHLT UB5 133 H4
Bournemead Cl NTHLT UB5 133 H5
Bourne Meadow EGH TW20 194 E4
Bournemouth Cl PECK SE15 159 P8
Bournemouth Rd PECK SE15 159 P8
WIM/MER SW19 201 K1
Bourne Pde BXLY DA5 * 186 C3
Bourne Park Cl PUR/KEN CR8 241 M2
Bourne Rd ADL/WDHM KT15 215 L5
BERK HP4 33 L4
BUSH WD23 73 P9
BXLY DA5 186 D2
CEND/HSY/T N8 118 F4
GODL GU7 267 L9
GVE DA12 191 J5
HAYES BR2 206 A4
REDH RH1 258 D6
SL SL1 149 H1
VW GU25 194 A5
WAN E11 121 L8
Bourneside VW GU25 193 M7
Bourneside Crs STHGT/OAK N14 98 E2
Bourneside Gdns CAT SE6 183 H8
Bourneside Rd ADL/WDHM KT15 215 N2
Bourne St BGVA SW1W 16 C6
CROY/NA CR0 203 J9
Bourne Ter BAY/PAD W2 8 G3
The Bourne HHS/BOV HP3 52 D3
STHGT/OAK N14 98 F2
WARE SG12 26 C1
Bourne V HAYES BR2 205 M8
Bournevale Rd
STRHM/NOR SW16 180 F7
Bourne Vw GFD/PVL UB6 134 E1
PUR/KEN CR8 241 L1
Bourne Wy ADL/WDHM KT15 215 M2
HAYES BR2 205 M9
HOR/WEW KT19 219 P1
SUT SM1 221 J2
SWLY BR8 208 D3
WOKS/MYFD GU22 232 A8
Bournewood Rd
STMC/STPC BR5 207 L7
WOOL/PLUM SE18 163 K6
Bournville Rd CAT SE6 182 F3
Bournwell Cl EBAR EN4 78 A6
Bourton Cl HYS/HAR UB3 133 H10
Bousfield Rd NWCR SE14 160 C8
Bousley Ri CHERT KT16 214 G4
Boutflower Rd BTSEA SW11 157 P10
Boutique Hall LEW SE13 * 161 H10
Bouverie Gdns
KTN/HRWW/WS HA3 115 J4
PUR/KEN CR8 222 F10
Bouverie Ms STNW/STAM N16 119 M7
Bouverie Pl BAY/PAD W2 9 M5
Bouverie Rd COUL/CHIP CR5 240 B4
HRW HA1 114 B4
STNW/STAM N16 119 M7
Bouverie St EMB EC4Y 12 B6
Bouverie Wy DTCH/LGLY SL3 150 B4
Bouvier Rd PEND EN3 80 B4
Boveney Cl SL SL1 148 F1
Boveney New Rd WDSR SL4 148 D3
Boveney Rd FSTH SE23 182 C3
WDSR SL4 148 B3
Boveney Wood La SL SL1 108 C8
Bovey Wy SOCK/AV RM15 146 G7
Bovill Rd FSTH SE23 182 C3
Bovingdon Av WBLY HA9 135 M1
Bovingdon Crs GSTN WD25 55 L10
Bovingdon La CDALE/KGS NW9 96 B9
Bovingdon Rd FUL/PGN SW6 157 L7
Bovington Dr ARCH N19 118 D7
Bow Arrow La DART DA1 187 P2
RDART DA2 188 A2
Bowater Cl BRXS/STRHM SW2 180 F2
CDALE/KGS NW9 116 A3
Bowater Gdns SUN TW16 197 K1
Bowater Pl BKHTH/KID SE3 161 N6
Bowater Rdg WEY KT13 216 E6
Bowater Rd CRAWE RH10 284 D10
WBLY HA9 115 N8
WOOL/PLUM SE18 162 A2
Bow Br STALW/RED AL3 37 M3
Bow Bridge Est BOW E3 140 G5
Bow Churchyard STP EC4M * 12 F6
Bow Common La BOW E3 140 E6
Bowden Cl EBED/NFELT TW14 174 F4
Bowden Dr EMPK RM11 125 M6
Bowden Rd ASC SL5 192 B5
Bowden St LBTH SE11 18 B7
Bowditch DEPT SE8 160 E4
Bowdon Rd WALTH E17 120 F5
Bowen Dr DUL SE21 181 M6
Bowen Rd HRW HA1 114 B5
Bowen St POP/IOD E14 140 G8
Bowens Wd CROY/NA CR0 * 224 E5
Bowenswood CROY/NA CR0 224 E5
Bowen Wy COUL/CHIP CR5 240 E8
Bower Av GNWCH SE10 161 K7
Bower Cl CRW RM5 104 E8
NTHLT UB5 133 K4
Bower Ct WOKS/MYFD GU22 232 E2
Bowerdean St FUL/PGN SW6 157 L8
Bower Farm Rd ABR/ST RM4 104 D4
Bower Hl EPP CM16 65 K8
Bower Hill Cl REDH RH1 276 F2
Bower Hill La REDH RH1 276 E1
Bower La BGR/WK TN15 229 P7
EYN DA4 209 M10
EYN DA4 229 P4
Bowerman Av NWCR SE14 160 D5
Bowerman Rd CDW/CHF RM16 168 D3
Bower Rd SWLY BR8 187 H10
Bowers Av GVW DA11 190 C7
Bowers Cl RGUE GU4 250 D6
Bowers Farm Dr RGUE GU4 250 D6
Bowers La RGUE GU4 250 D5
Bowers Rd RSEV TN14 228 G7
Bower St WCHPL E1 * 140 C8
Bower V EPP CM16 65 K8
Bower Wy SL SL1 128 D9
Bowes Cl BFN/LL DA15 185 L2
Bowes Dr CHONG CM5 67 N3
Bowes Lyon Cl WDSR SL4 149 H7
Bowes Lyon Ms STALW/RED AL3 38 C6
Bowes Rd ACT W3 136 B9
BCTR RM8 123 M9
FBAR/BDGN N11 98 C6
STA TW18 173 H9
WOT/HER KT12 197 J9
Bowes Rd (North Circular)
PLMGR N13 98 F6
Bowes Wd HART DA3 211 L10
Bowfell Rd HMSMTH W6 156 F5
Bowford Av BXLYHN DA7 163 P7
Bowgate STAL AL1 38 D5
Bowhay RBRW/HUT CM13 107 N3
Bowhill Cl BRXN/ST SW9 159 H6
Bowie Cl CLAP SW4 180 E3
Bowland Rd CLAP SW4 158 E10
WFD IG8 101 P7
Bowland Yd KTBR SW1X * 16 B2
Bow La NFNCH/WDSPK N12 97 M8
STP EC4M 12 F6
Bowl Ct WCHPL E1 13 K2
Bowler's Orch CSTG HP8 89 M4
Bowles Gdn EN EN1 80 A2
Bowley Cl NRWD SE19 181 N9
Bowley La NRWD SE19 181 N8
Bowley St POP/IOD E14 140 E9
Bowling Cl HARP AL5 20 B4
HGDN/ICK UB10 132 A3
Bowling Green Cl
PUT/ROE SW15 178 E3
Bowling Green Ct WBLY HA9 115 L7
Bowling Green La CLKNW EC1R 12 B2
Bowling Green Pl STHWK SE1 * 18 G1
Bowling Green Rd
CHOB/PIR GU24 213 K5
Bowling Green Rw
WOOL/PLUM SE18 * 162 C3
Bowling Green St LBTH SE11 18 A9
Bowling Green Wk IS N1 7 J10
Bowling Rd WARE SG12 26 D2
Bow Locks BOW E3 * 141 H6
Bowls Cl STAN HA7 94 G6
Bowman Av CAN/RD E16 141 M8
Bowman Ct CRAWE RH10 * 283 N6
Bowman Ms WAND/EARL SW18 179 J4
Bowmans Cl POTB/CUF EN6 59 N8
SL SL1 128 A4
WEA W13 134 G10
Bowmans Ct HHNE HP2 35 N4
Bowmans Gn GSTN WD25 73 M2
Bowmans Lea FSTH SE23 182 B3
Bowman's Meadow WLGTN SM6 202 C10
Bowman's Ms HOLWY N7 118 F8
WCHPL E1 13 N7
Bowman's Pl HOLWY N7 118 F8
Bowmans Rd DART DA1 186 G3
Bowmead ELTH/MOT SE9 184 C5
Bowmont Cl RBRW/HUT CM13 87 N10
Bowmore Wk CAMTN NW1 5 K4
Bown Cl TIL RM18 168 E8
Bowness Cl HACK E8 7 L2
Bowness Crs PUT/ROE SW15 178 B8
Bowness Dr HSLWW TW4 153 M10
Bowness Rd BXLYHN DA7 164 C8
CAT SE6 182 G3
Bowness Wy HCH RM12 125 H10
Bowood Rd CLAP SW4 158 B10
PEND EN3 80 C6
Bowring Gn OXHEY WD19 93 K6
Bow Rd BOW E3 140 F5
Bowrons Av ALP/SUD HA0 135 J2
Bowry Dr STWL/WRAY TW19 172 C2
Bowsley Ct FELT TW13 175 H5
The Bowsprit COB KT11 235 K1
Bow St COVGDN WC2E 11 M6
SRTFD E15 121 K10
Bowstridge La CSTG HP8 89 P7
Bowyer Cl EHAM E6 142 C7
Bowyer Crs DEN/HRF UB9 111 J4
Bowyer Dr SL SL1 128 D9
Bowyer Pl CMBW SE5 159 K6
Bowyers HHNE HP2 35 N4
Bowyers Cl ASHTD KT21 237 L4
Bowyers Ct TWK TW1 154 G10
Bowyer St CMBW SE5 159 K6
Bowzell Rd RSEV TN14 264 G9
Boxall Rd DUL SE21 181 M2
Boxelder Cl EDGW HA8 95 P6
Boxfield WGCE AL7 23 L8
Boxford Cl SAND/SEL CR2 224 C8
Boxgrove Av GU GU1 250 D8
Boxgrove La GU GU1 250 D9
Boxgrove Rd ABYW SE2 163 M2
GU GU1 250 D9
Boxhill HHNE HP2 35 N4
Boxhill Rd DORK RH4 255 K10
KWD/TDW/WH KT20 255 L8
Boxhill Wy BRKHM/BTCW RH3 273 N4
Box La BARK IG11 143 M4
HHS/BOV HP3 52 G1
HHW HP1 35 J9
HOD EN11 44 D3
Boxley Rd MRDN SM4 201 M4
Boxley St CAN/RD E16 141 N10
Boxmoor Rd CRW RM5 104 D6
KTN/HRWW/WS HA3 114 G2
Boxoll Rd DAGW RM9 124 A9
Box Ridge Av PUR/KEN CR8 222 G8
Boxted Cl BKHH IG9 102 B2
Boxted Rd HHW HP1 35 J4
Box Tree Cl CSHM HP5 * 51 J9
Boxtree La KTN/HRWW/WS HA3 94 B9
Boxtree Rd KTN/HRWW/WS HA3 94 C8
Box Tree Wk REDH RH1 275 M3
Boxwell Rd BERK HP4 33 N5
Boxwood Cl WDR/YW UB7 152 A1
Boxwood Wy WARL CR6 242 C3
Boxworth Cl NFNCH/WDSPK N12 97 N6
Boxworth Gv IS N1 5 P5
Boyard Rd WOOL/PLUM SE18 162 E4
Boyce Cl BORE WD6 75 K5
Boyce Wy PLSTW E13 141 M6
Boycroft Av CDALE/KGS NW9 115 P4
Boyd Av STHL UB1 133 N10
Boyd Cl KUTN/CMB KT2 177 M10
Boydell Ct STJWD NW8 3 L4
Boyd Rd WIM/MER SW19 179 N9
Boyd St WCHPL E1 13 N6
Boyes Crs LCOL/BKTW AL2 56 G2
Boyfield St STHWK SE1 18 D2
Boyland Rd BMLY BR1 183 L8
Boyle Av STAN HA7 94 F7
Boyle Cl HGDN/ICK UB10 132 A4
Boyle Farm Rd THDIT KT7 198 F6
Boyne Av HDN NW4 116 G2
Boyne Rd DAGE RM10 124 B8
LEW SE13 161 J9
Boyne Terrace Ms NTGHL W11 8 C9
Boyson Rd WALW SE17 18 F9
Boyton Cl CEND/HSY/T N8 118 F1
WCHPL E1 140 C6
Boyton Rd CEND/HSY/T N8 118 F1
Brabant Rd WDGN N22 98 G10
Brabazon Av WLGTN SM6 222 F4
Brabazon Rd HEST TW5 153 K6
NTHLT UB5 133 P4
Brabazon St POP/IOD E14 140 G8
Brabourne Cl NRWD SE19 181 M8
Brabourne Crs BXLYHN DA7 164 A5
Brabourne Ri BECK BR3 205 J5
Brabourn Gv PECK SE15 160 B8
Brace Cl CHESW EN7 61 J1
Bracewell Av GFD/PVL UB6 114 E10
Bracewell Rd NKENS W10 136 F7
Bracewood Gdns CROY/NA CR0 203 N10
Bracey St FSBYPK N4 * 118 F7
Bracken Av BAL SW12 180 B2
CROY/NA CR0 204 F10
Brackenbridge Dr RSLP HA4 113 L8
Brackenbury Gdns HMSMTH W6 156 E2
Brackenbury Rd EFNCH N2 117 M1
HMSMTH W6 156 E2
Bracken Cl BORE WD6 75 N5
CRAWE RH10 283 P5
CRAWE RH10 285 J3
EHAM E6 142 C7
GT/LBKH KT23 235 N10
LOU IG10 82 E6
SLN SL2 109 J9
SUN TW16 * 174 G9
WHTN TW2 175 P3
WOKS/MYFD GU22 232 C4
Brackendale POTB/CUF EN6 59 K9
WCHMH N21 98 G3
Brackendale Cl HSLW TW3 154 A7
Brackendale Gdns UPMR RM14 126 B9
Brackendene LCOL/BKTW AL2 55 N6
RDART DA2 186 F7
Brackendene Cl
WOKN/KNAP GU21 232 D1
Bracken Dr CHIG IG7 102 E7
Bracken End ISLW TW7 176 C1
Brackenforde DTCH/LGLY SL3 149 P1
Bracken Gdns BARN SW13 156 D8
Bracken Hl BERK HP4 34 B4
Brackenhill COB KT11 217 P8
RSLP HA4 * 113 M9
Bracken Hill Cl BMLY BR1 205 L1
Bracken Hill La BMLY BR1 205 L1
Brackenlea GODL GU7 267 J10
Bracken Ms ROMW/RG RM7 124 C4
Bracken Pth EPSOM KT18 219 N9
Brackens Dr BRW CM14 107 J6
The Brackens EN EN1 99 M1
HHNE HP2 * 35 N5
ORP BR6 227 K2
The Bracken CHING E4 101 H3
Bracken Wy CHOB/PIR GU24 213 L6
RGUW GU3 249 L8
Brackenwood SUN TW16 197 H1
Brackenwood Rd
WOKN/KNAP GU21 231 J5
Brackley WEY KT13 216 E2
Brackley Av PECK SE15 160 B9
Brackley Cl WLGTN SM6 222 F4
Brackley Rd BECK BR3 182 E10
CHSWK W4 156 B3
Brackley Sq WFD IG8 102 A8
Brackley St BARB EC2Y 12 F3
Brackley Ter CHSWK W4 156 B4
Bracklyn St IS N1 6 G7
Bracknell Cl WDGN N22 99 H9
Bracknell Gdns HAMP NW3 117 L10
Bracknell Pl HHNE HP2 36 A2
Bracknell Wy HAMP NW3 117 L9
Bracondale ESH/CLAY KT10 218 B2
Bracondale Rd ABYW SE2 163 K3
Bracton La RDART DA2 186 G6
Bradbery RKW/CH/CXG WD3 90 G6
Bradbourne Park Rd SEV TN13 247 H9
Bradbourne Rd BXLY DA5 186 B3
GRAYS RM17 167 N5
SEV TN13 247 J8
Bradbourne St FUL/PGN SW6 157 K8
Bradbourne Vale Rd SEV TN13 246 G8
Bradbury Cl BORE WD6 75 N5
NWDGN UB2 153 N3
Bradbury Rd CRAWE RH10 284 D10
Bradbury St STNW/STAM N16 119 M10
Bradd Cl SOCK/AV RM15 147 H5
Braddock Cl CRW RM5 104 D7
ISLW TW7 154 E9
Braddon Ct BAR EN5 * 77 H7
Braddon Rd RCH/KEW TW9 155 L9
Braddyll St GNWCH SE10 161 K4
Bradenham Av WELL DA16 163 K10
Bradenham Cl WALW SE17 18 G9
Bradenham Rd
KTN/HRWW/WS HA3 114 G2
YEAD UB4 132 F5
Bradenhurst Cl CTHM CR3 259 N2
Braden St MV/WKIL W9 * 8 G2
Bradfield Cl RGUE GU4 250 D7
WOKS/MYFD GU22 232 B4
Bradfield Dr BARK IG11 123 K10
Bradfield Rd CAN/RD E16 161 M1
RSLP HA4 113 M10
Bradford Cl HAYES BR2 206 C8
SYD SE26 182 A7
TOTM N17 99 N7
Bradford Dr HOR/WEW KT19 220 C3
Bradford Rd ACT W3 156 B1
IL IG1 122 G6
RKW/CH/CXG WD3 90 F1
SL SL1 128 F8
Bradgate POTB/CUF EN6 60 E3
Bradgate Cl POTB/CUF EN6 60 E4
Bradgate Rd CAT SE6 182 G2
Brading Crs WAN E11 121 N7
Brading Rd BRXS/STRHM SW2 180 G3
CROY/NA CR0 202 G6
Brading Ter SHB W12 156 D2
Bradiston Rd MV/WKIL W9 2 D9
Bradleigh Av GRAYS RM17 167 P3
Bradley Cl BELMT SM2 221 L6
HOLWY N7 5 M3
Bradley Gdns WEA W13 134 G8
Bradley La RDKG RH5 254 G8
Bradley Rd NRWD SE19 181 K9
PEND EN3 80 D4
SL SL1 129 J9
WAB EN9 81 H1
WDGN N22 98 G10
Bradley's Cl IS N1 6 A7
Bradley Stone Rd EHAM E6 142 C8
Bradman Rw EDGW HA8 * 95 P8
Bradmead VX/NE SW8 * 158 C7
Bradmore Gn BRKMPK AL9 59 H2
Bradmore La BRKMPK AL9 58 G2
Bradmore Park Rd HMSMTH W6 156 E2
Bradmore Wy BRKMPK AL9 59 H2
COUL/CHIP CR5 240 F4
Bradshaw Cl WDSR SL4 148 D7
WIM/MER SW19 179 K9
Bradshaw Cottages
POP/IOD E14 * 140 D8
Bradshaw Dr MLHL NW7 96 G8
Bradshaw Rd CDW/CHF RM16 147 M10
WATN WD24 73 K5
Bradshaws HAT AL10 40 C8
Bradshaws Cl SNWD SE25 203 P3
Bradstock Rd EW KT17 220 E2
HOM E9 140 C1
Brad St STHWK SE1 12 B10
Bradwell Av DAGE RM10 124 B7
Bradwell Cl HCH RM12 145 J1
SWFD E18 121 L2
Bradwell Gn RBRW/HUT CM13 87 P10
Bradwell Ms UED N18 99 P5
Bradwell Rd BKHH IG9 102 B2
Brady Av LOU IG10 82 F6
Brady Dr BMLY BR1 206 D3
Bradymead EHAM E6 142 D8
Brady St WCHPL E1 140 A6
Braemar Av ALP/SUD HA0 135 J2
BXLYHN DA7 164 D10
SAND/SEL CR2 223 K6
THHTH CR7 203 J3
WDGN N22 98 F9
WIM/MER SW19 179 K5
WLSDN NW10 116 A8
Braemar Gdns BFN/LL DA15 184 G6
CDALE/KGS NW9 90 A9
EMPK RM11 125 P4
SL SL1 148 F1
WWKM BR4 205 H8
Braemar Rd BTFD TW8 155 J5
PLSTW E13 141 L6
SEVS/STOTM N15 119 M3
WPK KT4 200 E10
Braeside ADL/WDHM KT15 215 L7
BECK BR3 182 F8
Braeside Av RYNPK SW20 201 H1
SEV TN13 246 G10
Braeside Cl PIN HA5 93 P8
SEV TN13 246 G10
Braeside Crs BXLYHN DA7 164 D10
Braeside Rd STRHM/NOR SW16 180 D10
Braes Md REDH RH1 276 F1
Braes St IS N1 6 D4
Braesyde Cl BELV DA17 164 A3
Brafferton Rd CROY/NA CR0 223 K1
Braganza St WALW SE17 18 C8
Bragg Cl BCTR RM8 143 L1
Bragg Rd TEDD TW11 176 D10
Bragmans La RKW/CH/CXG WD3 52 G9
Braham St WCHPL E1 13 M6
Braid Av ACT W3 136 B8
Braid Cl FELT TW13 175 N5
The Braid CSHM HP5 51 K6
Braidwood Rd CAT SE6 183 J4
Braidwood St STHWK SE1 13 J10
Brailsford Cl WIM/MER SW19 179 P10
Brailsford Rd BRXS/STRHM SW2 181 H2
Brain Cl HAT AL10 40 E3
Brainton Av EBED/NFELT TW14 175 J3
Braintree Av REDBR IG4 122 B3
Braintree Rd DAGE RM10 124 B8
RSLP HA4 113 J9
Braintree St BETH E2 * 140 B5
Braithwaite Av ROMW/RG RM7 124 B5
Braithwaite Gdns STAN HA7 95 H9
Braithwaite Rd PEND EN3 80 E7
Brakefield Rd MEO DA13 189 N9
Brakey Hl REDH RH1 259 M10
Brakynbery BERK HP4 33 K2
Brallings La CFSP/GDCR SL9 90 D5
Bramalea Cl HGT N6 118 B4
Bramall Cl SRTFD E15 121 L10
Bramber Cl CRAWE RH10 283 P5
Bramber Ct BTFD TW8 155 K3
SL SL1 128 F10
Bramber Rd NFNCH/WDSPK N12 97 P6
WKENS W14 14 C9
Bramber Wy WARL CR6 242 E2
Bramble Acres Cl BELMT SM2 221 K4
Bramble Av RDART DA2 189 H6
Bramble Banks CAR SM5 222 B5
Bramblebury Rd
WOOL/PLUM SE18 162 G4
Bramble Cl BECK BR3 205 H5
CFSP/GDCR SL9 90 B7
CHIG IG7 102 F2
CRAWE RH10 285 J3
CROY/NA CR0 224 F1
GSTN WD25 55 H10
REDH RH1 276 B2
RGUW GU3 249 K8
SEVS/STOTM N15 119 P2
SHPTN TW17 196 E4
STAN HA7 95 J8
UX/CGN UB8 132 A7
Bramble Cft ERITH DA8 164 D3
Brambledene Cl
WOKN/KNAP GU21 231 P4
Brambledown HART DA3 211 L4
STA TW18 195 L1
Brambledown Cl WWKM BR4 205 K6
Brambledown Rd CAR SM5 222 B4
SAND/SEL CR2 223 M5
Bramblefield Cl HART DA3 211 K3
Bramble Gdns SHB W12 136 C9
Bramblehall La
KWD/TDW/WH KT20 255 L8
Bramble La AMSS HP7 69 K7
HPTN TW12 175 N9
SEV TN13 265 J4
UPMR RM14 146 B3
Bramble Md CSTG HP8 89 M4
Bramble Ri COB KT11 217 K10
HLW CM20 28 F10
Bramble Rd HAT AL10 39 P5
Brambles Cl CTHM CR3 241 M8
ISLW TW7 154 G6
Brambles Farm Dr
HGDN/ICK UB10 132 C5
The Brambles CHES/WCR EN8 62 C7
CHIG IG7 102 F7
GODL GU7 267 J10
STAL AL1 38 C8
SUT SM1 201 N9
WDR/YW UB7 151 N4
WIM/MER SW19 * 179 J8
Brambletye Park Rd REDH RH1 276 A2
Brambletye Rd CRAWE RH10 284 B8
Bramble Wk EPSOM KT18 219 N10
REDH RH1 * 276 B2
Bramble Wy RPLY/SEND GU23 233 J10
Bramblewood REDH RH1 258 C5
Bramblewood Cl CAR SM5 201 P8
Brambling Cl BUSH WD23 73 M8
Brambling Ri HHNE HP2 35 P3
The Bramblings CHING E4 101 J5
Bramcote Av MTCM CR4 202 A4
Bramcote Gv BERM/RHTH SE16 160 B4
Bramcote Rd PUT/ROE SW15 156 E10
Bramdean Crs LEE/GVPK SE12 183 M4
Bramdean Gdns LEE/GVPK SE12 183 M4
Bramerton Rd BECK BR3 204 E3
Bramerton St CHEL SW3 15 N9
Bramfield GSTN WD25 55 M10
Bramfield Rd BTSEA SW11 179 P2
HERT/WAT SG14 24 F3
Bramford Rd WAND/EARL SW18 157 M10
Bramham Ct NTHWD HA6 * 92 F6
Bramham Gdns CHSGTN KT9 * 219 J2
ECT SW5 14 G7
Bramhope La CHARL SE7 161 N5
Bramlands Cl BTSEA SW11 157 P9
Bramleas WATW WD18 72 G9
Bramley Av COUL/CHIP CR5 240 D1
Bramley Cl CHERT KT16 195 L8
CRAWE RH10 284 A7
HYS/HAR UB3 133 H9
MEO DA13 190 C10
ORP BR6 206 E8
PIN HA5 112 G1
REDH RH1 275 P2
SAND/SEL CR2 223 K2
STA TW18 173 M9
STHGT/OAK N14 78 C9
SWLY BR8 208 F4
WALTH E17 100 D10
WFD IG8 101 P8
WHTN TW2 176 B2
Bramley Ct GSTN WD25 55 J8
Bramley Crs GNTH/NBYPK IG2 122 D4
VX/NE SW8 158 E6
Bramley Gdns OXHEY WD19 93 K7
Bramley Gv ASHTD KT21 237 K5
Bramley Hl SAND/SEL CR2 223 K1
Bramley House Ct ENC/FH EN2 * 79 L3
Bramley Hyrst SAND/SEL CR2 * 223 K2
Bramley Ldg ALP/SUD HA0 115 J10
Bramley Pde STHGT/OAK N14 78 D8
Bramley Pl DART DA1 165 H10
Bramley Rd BELMT SM2 220 G5
EA W5 155 H2
NKENS W10 136 G8
STHGT/OAK N14 78 C9
SUT SM1 221 N2
Bramley Shaw WAB EN9 63 L9
Bramley Wk HORL RH6 280 D4
Bramley Wy ASHTD KT21 237 L3
HSLWW TW4 175 N1
STALE/WH AL4 39 H7
WWKM BR4 204 G9
Brammas Cl SL SL1 140 H2
Brampton Cl CHESW EN7 61 P4
CLPT E5 120 A7
HARP AL5 20 C2
Brampton Gdns WOT/HER KT12 217 K2
Brampton Gv HDN NW4 116 E2
KTN/HRWW/WS HA3 114 F2
WBLY HA9 115 M6
Brampton La HDN NW4 116 F2
Brampton Park Rd WDGN N22 119 H1
Brampton Rd BXLYHN DA7 163 N5
BXLYHN DA7 163 N9
CDALE/KGS NW9 115 M2
CROY/NA CR0 203 N7
EHAM E6 142 A6
HGDN/ICK UB10 132 C4
OXHEY WD19 93 H4
SEVS/STOTM N15 119 K3
STAL AL1 38 F5
Brampton Ter BORE WD6 75 M4
Bramshaw Gdns OXHEY WD19 93 L6
Bramshaw Ri NWMAL KT3 200 B6
Bramshaw Rd HOM E9 140 C1

Bramshill Gdns KTTN NW5 118 C8
Bramshill Rd WLSDN NW10 136 B4
Bramshot Av CHARL SE7 161 N5
Bramshot Wy OXHEY WD19 93 H3
Bramston Cl BARK/HLT IG6 103 J7
Bramston Rd MTCM CR4 180 A10
WLSDN NW10 136 D4
Bramwell Cl SUN TW16 197 L2
Bramwell Ms IS N1 5 P5
Brancaster Dr MLHL NW7 96 D8
Brancaster La PUR/KEN CR8 223 K7
Brancaster Rd GNTH/NBYPK IG2 122 G4
STRHM/NOR SW16 180 F6
Brancepeth Gdns BKHH IG9 101 M3
Branch Cl HAT AL10 40 F2
Branch Hl HAMP NW3 117 M8
Branch Pl IS N1 7 H5
Branch Rd BARK/HLT IG6 103 L6
LCOL/BKTW AL2 56 C3
POP/IOD E14 140 D8
STALW/RED AL3 38 A5
Branch St CMBW SE5 159 M6
Brancker Rd
KTN/HRWW/WS HA3 115 J1
Brancroft Wy PEND EN3 80 D5
Brand Cl FSBYPK N4 119 J6
Brandesbury Sq WFD IG8 102 D8
Brandlehow Rd PUT/ROE SW15 157 J10
Brandon Cl CDW/CHF RM16 167 L1
CHESW EN7 61 M2
CRAWE RH10 284 E9
Brandon Est WALW SE17 18 C10
WALW SE17 18 E9
Brandon Groves Av
SOCK/AV RM15 147 J6
Brandon Ms BARB EC2Y * 12 G3
Brandon Rd DART DA1 187 P3
HOLWY N7 5 L3
NWDGN UB2 153 N4
SUT SM1 221 L1
WALTH E17 121 H2
Brandon St GVW DA11 190 E3
WALW SE17 18 F6
Brandram Ms LEW SE13 * 161 K10
Brandram Rd LEW SE13 161 K9
Brandreth Ct HRW HA1 * 114 E4
Brandreth Rd EHAM E6 142 C8
TOOT SW17 180 C5
The Brandries WLGTN SM6 202 E10
Brands Hatch Pk HART DA3 * 210 E10
Brands Hatch Rd HART DA3 210 F10
Brandsland REIG RH2 275 L4
Brands Rd DTCH/LGLY SL3 150 E5
Brand St GNWCH SE10 161 H6
Brandville Gdns BARK/HLT IG6 122 E2
Brandville Rd WDR/YW UB7 151 P1
Brandy Wy BELMT SM2 221 K4
Branfill Rd UPMR RM14 126 A7
Brangbourne Rd BMLY BR1 183 H8
Brangton Rd LBTH SE11 17 P8
Brangwyn Crs WIM/MER SW19 201 N2
Branksea St FUL/PGN SW6 157 H6
Branksome Av UED N18 99 N7
Branksome Cl HHNE HP2 36 B5
TEDD TW11 176 C7
WOT/HER KT12 197 L9
Branksome Rd
BRXS/STRHM SW2 180 F1
WIM/MER SW19 201 K1
Branksome Wy
KTN/HRWW/WS HA3 115 L4
NWMAL KT3 199 P2
Bransby Rd CHSGTN KT9 219 K4
Branscombe Gdns WCHMH N21 99 H1
Branscombe St LEW SE13 160 G9
Bransdale Cl KIL/WHAMP NW6 2 F5
Bransell Cl SWLY BR8 208 D6
Bransgrove Rd EDGW HA8 95 L9
Branston Crs STMC/STPC BR5 206 G8
Branstone Rd RCH/KEW TW9 155 L7
Branton Rd RDART DA2 188 E2
Brantridge Rd CRAWE RH10 284 A9
Brants Wk HNWL W7 134 D6
Brantwood Av ERITH DA8 164 D6
ISLW TW7 154 F10
Brantwood Cl WALTH E17 * 120 G1
Brantwood Dr BF/WBF KT14 215 J9
Brantwood Gdns BF/WBF KT14 215 J9
ENC/FH EN2 78 F9
REDBR IG4 122 B3
Brantwood Rd BXLYHN DA7 164 C8
HNHL SE24 181 K1
SAND/SEL CR2 223 K5
TOTM N17 99 P7
Brantwood Wy STMC/STPC BR5 207 M3
Brasenose Dr BARN SW13 156 F5
Brasher Cl GFD/PVL UB6 114 C10
Brassey Cl EBED/NFELT TW14 * 175 H4
OXTED RH8 261 M5
Brassey Hl OXTED RH8 261 M6
Brassey Rd KIL/WHAMP NW6 2 D1
OXTED RH8 261 M5
Brassey Sq BTSEA SW11 158 B9
Brassie Av ACT W3 136 B8
Brasted Cl BELMT SM2 221 K6
BXLYHS DA6 185 N1
SYD SE26 182 B7
Brasted Hl RSEV TN14 245 K6
Brasted Hill Rd BH/WHM TN16 245 M9
Brasted La RSEV TN14 245 K5
Brasted Rd BH/WHM TN16 263 H2
ERITH DA8 164 F6
Brathway Rd WAND/EARL SW18 179 K3
Bratley St WCHPL E1 13 N2
Brattle Wd SEV TN13 265 K5
Braund Av GFD/PVL UB6 134 A6
Braundton Av BFN/LL DA15 185 J4
Braunston Dr YEAD UB4 133 M6
Bravington Cl SHPTN TW17 196 A5
Bravington Pl MV/WKIL W9 * 8 C1
Bravington Rd MV/WKIL W9 2 C9
Bravingtons Wk IS N1 5 M8
Braxfield Rd BROCKY SE4 160 D10
Braxted Pk STRHM/NOR SW16 180 G9
Brayard's Rd PECK SE15 160 A8
Braybourne Cl UX/CGN UB8 131 M1
Braybourne Dr ISLW TW7 154 E6
Braybrooke Gdns NRWD SE19 181 M10
Braybrook St SHB W12 136 C7
Brayburne Av VX/NE SW8 158 D8
Bray Cl BORE WD6 75 P5
CRAWE RH10 284 E9
Braycourt Av WOT/HER KT12 197 K7
Bray Crs BERM/RHTH SE16 160 C1
Braydon Rd STNW/STAM N16 119 N6
Bray Dr CAN/RD E16 141 L9
Brayfield Ter IS N1 6 A4
Brayford Sq WCHPL E1 * 140 B8
Bray Gdns WOKS/MYFD GU22 233 H2
Bray Ldg CHES/WCR EN8 * 62 D3
Bray Pl CHEL SW3 16 A7
Bray Rd COB KT11 235 M2
GUW GU2 267 N1
MLHL NW7 96 G7
Brays Cl AMS HP6 68 A1
Brays Green La AMS HP6 68 B1
Brays La AMS HP6 50 B10
Brays Md HLWS CM18 47 J3
Brays Meadow AMS HP6 68 B1
Brayton Gdns ENC/FH EN2 78 E8
Braywood Av EGH TW20 172 C9
Braywood Rd ELTH/MOT SE9 162 G10
Braziers Fld HERT/BAY SG13 25 N5
Brazil Cl CROY/NA CR0 202 F7
Breach Barns La WAB EN9 63 M6
Breach La DAGW RM9 144 B5
Breach Rd WTHK RM20 166 E5
Bread & Cheese La CHESW EN7 61 M1
Breadcroft La HARP AL5 20 A1
Bread St STP EC4M 12 F7
Breakfield COUL/CHIP CR5 240 F2
Breakmead WGCE AL7 23 L7
Breakneck Hl RDART DA2 188 G1
Breakspear Av STAL AL1 38 E7
Breakspear Ct ABLGY WD5 54 G6
Breakspeare Cl WATN WD24 73 J4
Breakspeare Rd ABLGY WD5 54 F7
Breakspear Rd RSLP HA4 112 C4
Breakspear Rd North
DEN/HRF UB9 111 N1
DEN/HRF UB9 112 B3
Breakspear Rd South
HGDN/ICK UB10 112 A8
DEN/HRF UB9 112 C5
Breakspears Dr STMC/STPC BR5 207 K1
Breakspears Ms BROCKY SE4 160 F8
Breakspears Rd BROCKY SE4 160 E9
Breakspear Wy HHNE HP2 36 D6
Breaks Rd HAT AL10 40 E4
Bream Cl TOTM N17 120 A2
Bream Gdns EHAM E6 142 D5
Breamore Cl PUT/ROE SW15 178 D4
Breamore Rd GDMY/SEVK IG3 123 J7
Bream's Buildings LINN WC2A 12 A5
Bream St BOW E3 140 F2
Breamwater Gdns
RCHPK/HAM TW10 176 G6
Brearley Cl EDGW HA8 95 P8
UX/CGN UB8 131 P1
Breasley Cl PUT/ROE SW15 156 E10
Breasy Pl HDN NW4 * 116 E2
Brechin Pl SKENS SW7 15 K7
Brecken Cl STALE/WH AL4 38 F2
Brecknock Rd ARCH N19 118 D9
Brecknock Road Est ARCH N19 * 118 E10
Brecon Cl MTCM CR4 202 F4
WPK KT4 200 F9
Brecon Gn CDALE/KGS NW9 * 116 B4
Brecon Ms HOLWY N7 118 E10
KTTN NW5 5 J1
Brecon Rd HMSMTH W6 14 A10
PEND EN3 80 B8
Brede Cl EHAM E6 142 D5
Bredgar Rd ARCH N19 118 C7
Bredhurst Cl PGE/AN SE20 182 B9
Bredon Rd CROY/NA CR0 203 N7
Bredune PUR/KEN CR8 241 L1
Bredward Cl SL SL1 128 A5
Breech La KWD/TDW/WH KT20 256 D1
Breer St FUL/PGN SW6 157 L9
Breezehurst Dr CRAWW RH11 283 J10
Breezer's Hl WAP E1W 13 P8
Bremans Rw WAND/EARL SW18 179 M5
Bember Rd RYLN/HDSTN HA2 114 B7
Bremer Ms WALTH E17 120 G2
Bremer Rd STA TW18 173 K6
Bremner Av HORL RH6 280 A3
Bremner Cl SWLY BR8 209 H4
Bremner Rd SKENS SW7 15 K3
Brenchley Av GVW DA11 190 E8
Brenchley Cl CHST BR7 206 D1
HAYES BR2 205 L5
Brenchley Gdns EDUL SE22 182 B2
Brenchley Rd STMC/STPC BR5 207 H2
Brendans Cl EMPK RM11 125 M6
Brenda Rd TOOT SW17 180 A5
Brende Gdns E/WMO/HCT KT8 198 A5
Brendon SCUP DA14 * 185 K7
Brendon Av WLSDN NW10 116 B9
Brendon Cl ERITH DA8 164 F7
ESH/CLAY KT10 218 B3
HYS/HAR UB3 152 D6
Brendon Ct RAD WD7 * 56 G10
Brendon Dr ESH/CLAY KT10 218 B3
Brendon Gdns RYLN/HDSTN HA2 114 A9
Brendon Gv EFNCH N2 97 M10
Brendon Rd BCTR RM8 124 A6
ELTH/MOT SE9 184 G5
Brendon St MBLAR W1H 9 P5
Brendon Vls WCHMH N21 * 99 K2
Brendon Wy EN EN1 99 M1
Brenley Cl MTCM CR4 202 B3
Brenley Gdns ELTH/MOT SE9 162 A10
Brennan Rd TIL RM18 168 E8
Brent Cl BXLY DA5 185 P4
RDART DA2 188 A2
Brentcot Cl WEA W13 134 G6
Brent Crs WLSDN NW10 135 L4
Brent Cross F/O HDN NW4 116 F4
Brentfield WLSDN NW10 135 N2
Brentfield Cl WLSDN NW10 136 A1
Brentfield Gdns CRICK NW2 * 116 G5
Brentfield Rd DART DA1 187 P2
WLSDN NW10 136 A1
Brentford Cl YEAD UB4 133 L6
Brent Gn HDN NW4 116 G3
Brentham Wy EA W5 135 J6
Brenthouse Rd HACK E8 140 A2
Brenthurst Rd WLSDN NW10 136 C1
Brentlands Dr DART DA1 187 P4
Brent La DART DA1 187 N3
Brent Lea BTFD TW8 155 H6
Brentmead Cl HNWL W7 134 D9
Brentmead Gdns WLSDN NW10 135 L4
Brentmoor Rd CHOB/PIR GU24 212 B9
Brenton St POP/IOD E14 140 D8
Brent Park Rd CDALE/KGS NW9 116 D6
Brent Pl BAR EN5 77 K9
Brent River Park Wk
GFD/PVL UB6 134 G5
Brent Rd BTFD TW8 155 H5
CAN/RD E16 141 M8
NWDGN UB2 153 K2
SAND/SEL CR2 224 A5
WOOL/PLUM SE18 162 E6
Brentside BTFD TW8 155 H5
Brentside Cl WEA W13 134 E6
Brent St HDN NW4 116 G3
Brent Ter CRICK NW2 116 F7
The Brent DART DA1 187 P3
Brentvale Av ALP/SUD HA0 135 L3
STHL UB1 134 C10
Brent View Rd CDALE/KGS NW9 116 D4
Brent Wy BTFD TW8 155 J6
FNCH N3 97 K7
RDART DA2 188 A2
WBLY HA9 135 N1
Brentwick Gdns BTFD TW8 155 K3
Brentwood Cl ELTH/MOT SE9 184 F4
Brentwood Pl BRWN CM15 107 J2
Brentwood Rd CDW/CHF RM16 168 E3
CHONG CM5 67 P7
GPK RM2 125 K3
RBRW/HUT CM13 107 N6
ROM RM1 124 G4
Brereton Rd TOTM N17 99 N8
Bressenden Pl WESTW SW1E 16 G4
Bressey Av EN EN1 79 P5
Bressey Gv SWFD E18 101 L10
Bretlands Rd CHERT KT16 195 H9
Brett Cl NTHLT UB5 133 L5
STNW/STAM N16 119 M7
Brett Crs WLSDN NW10 136 A3
Brettell St WALW SE17 19 H8
Brettenham Av WALTH E17 100 F9
Brettenham Rd UED N18 99 P5
WALTH E17 100 F10
Brett Gdns DAGW RM9 143 P2
Brettgrave HOR/WEW KT19 219 P6
Brettingham Cl CRAWW RH11 * 283 H10
Brett Pas HACK E8 120 A10
Brett Pl WATN WD24 73 H3
Brett Rd BAR EN5 76 F10
HACK E8 120 A10
Brett Vls ACT W3 * 136 A7
Brevet Cl PUR RM19 166 C3
Brewer Rd CRAWE RH10 283 N9
Brewers Fld RDART DA2 187 K7
Brewer St REDH RH1 259 K7
REGST W1B 11 H7
Brewery Cl ALP/SUD HA0 114 F10
Brewery La BF/WBF KT14 215 P9
SEV TN13 265 J1
Brewery Ms Centre ISLW TW7 * 154 F9
Brewery Rd HAYES BR2 206 B8
HOD EN11 44 F3
HOLWY N7 5 L2
WOKN/KNAP GU21 232 B3
WOOL/PLUM SE18 162 G4
Brewery Sq FSBYE EC1V 12 D2
STHWK SE1 13 L10
Brewhouse Hl STALE/WH AL4 21 H3
Brewhouse La HERT/WAT SG14 25 K5
WAP E1W 140 A10
Brew House Rd
BRKHM/BTCW RH3 273 N4
Brewhouse Rd
WOOL/PLUM SE18 162 C3
Brewhouse St PUT/ROE SW15 157 H10
Brewhouse Wk
BERM/RHTH SE16 140 D10
Brewhouse Yd FSBYE EC1V 12 C1
GVE DA12 190 E2
Brewood Rd BCTR RM8 143 L1
Brewster Gdns NKENS W10 136 F7
Brewster Rd LEY E10 120 G6
Breydon Wk CRAWE RH10 284 C9
Brian Av SAND/SEL CR2 223 M8
Brian Cl HCH RM12 125 J9
Briane Rd HOR/WEW KT19 219 P6
Brian Rd CHDH RM6 123 M3
Briants Cl PIN HA5 93 M10
Briant St NWCR SE14 160 C7
Briar Av STRHM/NOR SW16 180 G10
Briar Bank CAR SM5 222 B5
Briarbank Rd WEA W13 134 F8
Briarcliff HHW HP1 35 H5
Briar Cl BERK HP4 34 D2
BF/WBF KT14 215 L7
BKHH IG9 102 A3
CHES/WCR EN8 62 B5
CRAWW RH11 283 M4
EFNCH N2 97 M10
EFNCH N2 * 117 L1
HPTN TW12 175 N8
ISLW TW7 176 E1
MDHD SL6 128 A8
PLMGR N13 99 K4
WARL CR6 242 F2
Briar Crs NTHLT UB5 134 A1
Briardale Gdns HAMP NW3 117 K8
Briarfield Av EFNCH N2 117 L1
FNCH N3 97 L10
Briarfield Cl BXLYHN DA7 164 B8
Briar Gdns HAYES BR2 205 L8
Briar Gv SAND/SEL CR2 223 P9
Briar Hl PUR/KEN CR8 222 F7
Briar La CAR SM5 222 B5
CROY/NA CR0 224 G1
Briarleas Gdns UPMR RM14 126 D5
Briarley Cl BROX EN10 44 E8
Briar Rd BXLY DA5 186 E6
CRICK NW2 116 F9
GSTN WD25 55 J10
GSTN WD25 73 J1
HARH RM3 105 L8
KTN/HRWW/WS HA3 115 H3
RPLY/SEND GU23 232 E10
SHPTN TW17 196 A5
STALE/WH AL4 39 H3
STRHM/NOR SW16 202 F3
WHTN TW2 176 D4
Briars Cl HAT AL10 40 D4
Briars Ct LHD/OX KT22 218 C10
Briars La HAT AL10 40 D4
The Briars CHES/WCR EN8 62 D7
DTCH/LGLY SL3 150 C4
HERT/BAY SG13 25 P5
HLWS CM18 47 H4
RKW/CH/CXG WD3 71 K2
Briars Wk HARH RM3 105 M10
Briars Wy HART DA3 211 M5
Briarswood CHESW EN7 61 M4
Briars Wd HAT AL10 40 D4
HORL RH6 280 D3
Briarswood Cl CRAWE RH10 284 E6
Briarswood Wy ORP BR6 227 J2
Briar Wk BF/WBF KT14 215 K8
EDGW HA8 95 P8
NKENS W10 8 A1
PUT/ROE SW15 156 E10
Briar Wy BERK HP4 33 P6
RGUE GU4 250 E6
SLN SL2 128 G7
WDR/YW UB7 152 B1
Briarwood BRWN CM15 86 E3
Briarwood Cl CDALE/KGS NW9 * 115 P4
FELT TW13 174 F6
Briarwood Ct WPK KT4 * 200 D8
Briarwood Dr NTHWD HA6 93 H10
Briarwood Rd CLAP SW4 180 E1
EW KT17 220 D3
WOKN/KNAP GU21 231 K5
Briary Cl EDGW HA8 95 N10
HAMP NW3 3 N3
Briary Ct SCUP DA14 185 L8
Briary Gdns BMLY BR1 183 N8
Briary La ED N9 99 M4
Brickbarn Cl WBPTN SW10 * 157 M6
Brick Ct EMB EC4Y * 12 A6
GRAYS RM17 * 167 M5
Brickcroft BROX EN10 62 D2
Brickenden Ct WAB EN9 63 L9
Brickendon La HERT/BAY SG13 25 L9
HERT/BAY SG13 43 L4
Bricket Rd STAL AL1 38 D6
Brickett Cl RSLP HA4 112 D3
Brick Farm Cl RCH/KEW TW9 155 N7
Brickfield HAT AL10 40 D7
Brickfield Av HHS/BOV HP3 36 C7
Brickfield Cl BTFD TW8 155 H6
Brickfield Cottages
WOOL/PLUM SE18 163 J5
Brickfield Farm HART DA3 211 M3
Brickfield Farm Gdns ORP BR6 226 F1
Brickfield La BAR EN5 76 C10
HORL RH6 279 N6
HYS/HAR UB3 152 E5
Brickfield Rd BOW E3 140 G6
EPP CM16 65 N5
REDH RH1 277 K9
THHTH CR7 203 J1
WIM/MER SW19 179 L7
Brickfields RYLN/HDSTN HA2 114 C7
The Brickfields WARE SG12 26 A1
Brickfields Wy WDR/YW UB7 152 A2
Brickfield Vls CAR SM5 * 201 P10
Brick Kiln Cl OXHEY WD19 73 M10
Brick Kiln La OXTED RH8 261 P6
Brick Knoll Pk STAL AL1 39 H7
Brick La BETH E2 7 M10
EN EN1 80 A6
NTHLT UB5 133 N5
STAN HA7 95 J8
WCHPL E1 13 M2
Brickmakers La HHS/BOV HP3 36 C7
Brickstock Furze BRWN CM15 * 107 M2
Brick St MYFR/PKLN W1K 10 E10
Brickwall Cl WLYN AL6 22 D3
Brickwall La RSLP HA4 112 F6
Brickwood Cl SYD SE26 182 A6
Brickwood Rd CROY/NA CR0 203 M9
Brickyard La RDKG RH5 271 L7
Brideake Cl CRAWW RH11 283 K10
Brideale Cl PECK SE15 19 M10
Bride Ct EMB EC4Y 12 C6
Bride La EMB EC4Y 12 C6
Bridel Ms FSBYE EC1V 6 C8
Bride St HOLWY N7 5 P2
Bridewain St STHWK SE1 19 L3
Bridewell Pl BLKFR EC4V 12 C6
Bridford Ms GTPST W1W 10 F3
Bridge Ap CAMTN NW1 4 C3
Bridge Av HMSMTH W6 156 F4
HNWL W7 134 C7
UPMR RM14 125 P8
Bridge Barn La
WOKN/KNAP GU21 231 P4
Bridge Cl BF/WBF KT14 216 A8
EN EN1 80 A6
NKENS W10 136 G8
RBRW/HUT CM13 107 K4
RDART DA2 166 C9
ROMW/RG RM7 124 F4
SL SL1 128 E9
STA TW18 173 H7
WOKN/KNAP GU21 231 P3
WOT/HER KT12 196 G7
Bridge Ct GRAYS RM17 * 167 N5
RAD WD7 * 74 G1
WOKN/KNAP GU21 232 A3
Bridge Dr PLMGR N13 98 G5
Bridge End WALTH E17 101 H9
Bridge End Cl KUTN/CMB KT2 199 M1
Bridgefield Cl BNSTD SM7 238 F1
Bridgefield Rd SUT SM1 221 K3
Bridgefields WGCE AL7 23 J4
Bridge Foot WARE SG12 * 26 C2
Bridgefoot La POTB/CUF EN6 58 G9
Bridge Gdns ASHF TW15 174 D10
E/WMO/HCT KT8 198 C4
Bridge Ga WCHMH N21 99 K1
Bridge Gate Centre WGCE AL7 * 23 J4
Bridgeham Cl WEY KT13 216 B2
Bridgeham Wy HORL RH6 281 J5
Bridge Hl EPP CM16 65 J9
Bridgehill Cl GUW GU2 249 M8
Bridge House Quay
POP/IOD E14 141 H10
Bridgeland Rd CAN/RD E16 141 M9
Bridgelands CRAWE RH10 284 G2
Bridgelands Cl BECK BR3 182 E10
Bridge La BTSEA SW11 157 P7
GLDGN NW11 117 H3
HDN NW4 116 G2
VW GU25 194 B6
Bridgeman Dr WDSR SL4 148 F8
Bridgeman Rd IS N1 5 P4
TEDD TW11 176 F9
Bridgeman St STJWD NW8 3 N8
Bridge Mdw NWCR SE14 160 C5
Bridge Ms WOKN/KNAP GU21 232 A3
Bridgend Rd EN EN1 80 B1
Bridgenhall Rd EN EN1 79 N5
Bridgen Rd BXLY DA5 185 P3
Bridge Pde STRHM/NOR SW16 * 180 F8
WCHMH N21 * 99 K1
Bridge Pk RGUE GU4 * 250 F7
WAND/EARL SW18 179 K1
Bridge Pl AMS HP6 69 K4
CROY/NA CR0 203 L8
PIM SW1V 16 F5
WAT WD17 73 L9
Bridgepoint Pl HGT N6 118 C6
Bridgeport Pl WAP E1W * 13 P9
Bridger Cl GSTN WD25 55 L9
Bridge Rd ASC SL5 192 C5
BECK BR3 182 E10
BXLYHN DA7 163 P9
CHERT KT16 195 L7
CHONG CM5 49 K7
CHSGTN KT9 219 K2
COB KT11 235 J1
E/WMO/HCT KT8 198 D4
ED N9 99 P4
EHAM E6 142 C2
ERITH DA8 164 G7
EW KT17 220 C8
GRAYS RM17 167 N5
HSLW TW3 154 C9
KGLGY WD4 54 D9
NWDGN UB2 153 N1
RAIN RM13 145 H6
SRTFD E15 141 J3
STMC/STPC BR5 207 L6
SUT SM1 221 L3
TWK TW1 176 G2
UX/CGN UB8 131 M4
WALTH E17 120 E5
WBLY HA9 115 M8
WDGN N22 98 F9
WEY KT13 216 A1
WGCW AL8 22 F4
WLGTN SM6 222 C2
WLSDN NW10 136 B1
Bridge Rd East WGCE AL7 23 J5
Bridge Rw CROY/NA CR0 * 203 L8
Bridges Cl HORL RH6 280 E4
Bridges Ct BTSEA SW11 157 N9
HERT/WAT SG14 25 K5
Bridges Dr DART DA1 188 A1
Bridges La CROY/NA CR0 222 F1
Bridges Rd STAN HA7 94 E6
Bridges Road Ms
WIM/MER SW19 179 L9
Bridge St BERK HP4 34 A5
CHSWK W4 156 A3
DTCH/LGLY SL3 150 G6
GU GU1 267 P2
HHW HP1 35 M7
LHD/OX KT22 236 F8
PIN HA5 113 L1
TWK TW1 177 J2
WHALL SW1A 17 L2
WOT/HER KT12 196 G8
Bridge Ter LEW SE13 * 161 J10
SRTFD E15 141 J2
The Bridge EA W5 * 135 L10
KTN/HRWW/WS HA3 114 E1
Bridgetown Cl NRWD SE19 181 M8
Bridge Vw ASC SL5 192 G7
SWCM DA10 166 G10
Bridgeview HMSMTH W6 156 F4
Bridge Vls WIM/MER SW19 * 179 K8
Bridgewater Cl STMC/STPC BR5 207 H2
Bridgewater Ct DTCH/LGLY SL3 150 D4
Bridgewater Gdns EDGW HA8 95 L10
Bridgewater Hl BERK HP4 33 L2
Bridgewater Rd ALP/SUD HA0 134 G1
BERK HP4 33 N3
SRTFD E15 141 H3
WEY KT13 216 E3
Bridgewater Sq BARB EC2Y * 12 E3
Bridgewater St BARB EC2Y 12 E3
Bridgewater Ter WDSR SL4 149 J7
Bridgewater Wy BUSH WD23 74 A10
WDSR SL4 149 J7
Bridgeway ALP/SUD HA0 135 K2
BARK IG11 143 J2
Bridge Wy COUL/CHIP CR5 239 P5
GLDGN NW11 117 J3
HGDN/ICK UB10 112 C10
WHTN TW2 176 B3
Bridgeways HOD EN11 44 G3
Bridgeway St CAMTN NW1 5 H8
Bridge Wharf Rd ISLW TW7 154 G9
Bridgewood Cl PGE/AN SE20 182 A10
Bridgewood Rd
STRHM/NOR SW16 180 E10
WPK KT4 220 D1
Bridgford St WAND/EARL SW18 179 M6
Bridgman Rd CHSWK W4 155 P2
Bridgwater Rd HARH RM3 105 K6
RSLP HA4 113 H9
Bridgwater Wk HARH RM3 105 L6
Bridle Cl HOD EN11 26 F9
HOR/WEW KT19 219 P1
KUT/HW KT1 199 J4
PEND EN3 80 E3
STALW/RED AL3 38 D4
SUN TW16 197 H3
Bridle La COB KT11 236 A1
RKW/CH/CXG WD3 71 M7
SOHO/CST W1F 11 H7
TWK TW1 176 G2
Bridle Pth CROY/NA CR0 202 F10
WAT WD17 73 J6
The Bridle Pth EW KT17 220 F6
WFD IG8 101 K8
Bridlepath Wy
EBED/NFELT TW14 174 F3
Bridle Rd CROY/NA CR0 204 F9
CROY/NA CR0 224 F1
ESH/CLAY KT10 218 G3
EW KT17 220 C9
PIN HA5 113 K4
The Bridle Rd PUR/KEN CR8 222 F6
Bridle Wy BERK HP4 33 M3
CRAWE RH10 284 E6
CROY/NA CR0 224 F2
HOD EN11 26 F10
ORP BR6 226 F1
Bridleway Cl EW KT17 220 F6
Bridle Way (North) HOD EN11 26 G9
Bridle Way (South) HOD EN11 26 G10
The Bridle Wy WLGTN SM6 222 D1
Bridlington Cl BH/WHM TN16 243 N5
Bridlington Rd ED N9 100 A1
OXHEY WD19 93 L4
Bridlington Sp SL SL1 148 G2
Bridport Av ROMW/RG RM7 124 C4
Bridport Pl IS N1 7 H7
Bridport Rd GFD/PVL UB6 134 A3
THHTH CR7 203 H3
UED N18 99 M6
Bridport Wy SLN SL2 128 G6
Bridstow Pl BAY/PAD W2 8 F5
Brief St BRXN/ST SW9 159 J7
Brier Lea KWD/TDW/WH KT20 257 J2
Brierley CROY/NA CR0 224 C3
Brierley Av ED N9 100 B2
Brierley Cl EMPK RM11 125 K4
SNWD SE25 203 P4
Brierley Rd BAL SW12 180 D5
WAN E11 121 J9
Brierly Cl GUW GU2 249 M8
Brierly Gdns BETH E2 * 140 B4
Brier Rd KWD/TDW/WH KT20 238 E5
Briery Fld RKW/CH/CXG WD3 71 K8
Briery Wy AMS HP6 69 K3
HHNE HP2 36 B4
Brigade Cl RYLN/HDSTN HA2 114 C7
Brigade Pl CTHM CR3 241 K8
Brigade St BKHTH/KID SE3 * 161 L8
Brigadier Av ENC/FH EN2 79 K5
Brigadier Hl ENC/FH EN2 79 K4
Briggeford Cl CLPT E5 119 P7
Briggs Cl MTCM CR4 202 C1
Bright Cl BELV DA17 163 N3
Brightfield Rd LEE/GVPK SE12 183 K1
Bright Hl GU GU1 268 A2
Brightlands GVW DA11 190 B7
Brightlands Rd REIG RH2 257 M8
Brightling Rd BROCKY SE4 182 E2
Brightlingsea Pl POP/IOD E14 140 E9
Brightman Rd WAND/EARL SW18 179 N4
Brighton Av WALTH E17 120 E3
Brighton Cl ADL/WDHM KT15 215 M2
HGDN/ICK UB10 132 C2
Brighton Dr NTHLT UB5 * 133 P1
Brighton Rd ADL/WDHM KT15 215 M1
BELMT SM2 221 M4
BNSTD SM7 221 J10
COUL/CHIP CR5 240 C7
COUL/CHIP CR5 240 E1
CRAWE RH10 283 N10
EFNCH N2 97 M10
EHAM E6 142 D5
HORL RH6 280 A4
KWD/TDW/WH KT20 257 K3
PUR/KEN CR8 222 F10
REDH RH1 276 B8
SAND/SEL CR2 223 K5
STNW/STAM N16 119 M9
SURB KT6 199 H6
WATN WD24 73 H4
Brighton Sp SLN SL2 128 G6
Brighton Ter BRXN/ST SW9 158 G10
REDH RH1 * 276 A1
Brights Av RAIN RM13 145 J6
Brightside Av STA TW18 173 M10
Brightside Rd LEW SE13 183 J2
The Brightside PEND EN3 80 C5
Bright St POP/IOD E14 140 G8
Brightview Cl LCOL/BKTW AL2 55 M5
Brightwell Cl CROY/NA CR0 203 H8
Brightwell Crs TOOT SW17 180 A8
Brightwell Rd WATW WD18 73 H9
Brig Ms DEPT SE8 160 F5
Brigstock Rd BELV DA17 164 C3
COUL/CHIP CR5 240 C1
THHTH CR7 203 J5
Brill Pl CAMTN NW1 5 K8
Brimfield Rd PUR RM19 166 C3
Brim Hl EFNCH N2 117 M2
Brimpsfield Cl ABYW SE2 163 L2
Brimsdown Av PEND EN3 80 D5
Brimshot La CHOB/PIR GU24 213 K5
Brimstone Cl ORP BR6 227 M4
Brimstone Wy BERK HP4 33 L3
Brindle Ga BFN/LL DA15 185 H5
Brindles EMPK RM11 125 M2
Brindles Cl RBRW/HUT CM13 107 P3
SLH/COR SS17 169 K3
The Brindles BNSTD SM7 239 J3
Brindley Cl ALP/SUD HA0 135 H3
BXLYHN DA7 164 B9
Brindley St BROCKY SE4 160 E7
Brindley Wy BMLY BR1 183 M8
STHL UB1 134 A9
Brindwood Rd CHING E4 100 F4
Brinkburn Cl ABYW SE2 163 K3
EDGW HA8 115 N1
Brinkburn Gdns EDGW HA8 115 M1
Brinkley Rd WPK KT4 200 E9
Brinklow Ct STALW/RED AL3 38 A9
Brinklow Crs WOOL/PLUM SE18 162 E6
Brinkworth Rd CLAY IG5 122 B1
Brinkworth Wy HOM E9 140 E1
Brinley Cl CHES/WCR EN8 62 C7
Brinsdale Rd HDN NW4 116 G1
Brinsley Rd KTN/HRWW/WS HA3 94 C10
Brinsley St WCHPL E1 * 140 A8
Brinsmead LCOL/BKTW AL2 56 C3
Brinsmead Rd HARH RM3 105 P10
Brinsworth Cl WHTN TW2 176 C5
Brinton Wk STHWK SE1 12 C10
Brion Pl POP/IOD E14 141 H7
Brisbane Av WIM/MER SW19 201 L1
Brisbane Cl CRAWW RH11 283 N4
Brisbane Rd IL IG1 122 F5
LEY E10 120 G7
Brisbane St CMBW SE5 159 L6
Briscoe Cl HOD EN11 44 E1
WAN E11 121 L7
Briscoe Rd HOD EN11 44 E1
RAIN RM13 145 K4
WIM/MER SW19 179 N9
Briset Rd ELTH/MOT SE9 162 A9
Briset St FARR EC1M 12 C3
Briset Wy HOLWY N7 118 G7
Brisson Cl ESH/CLAY KT10 217 N3
Bristol Cl CRAWE RH10 284 E4
STWL/WRAY TW19 173 P2
WLGTN SM6 222 F5
Bristol Gdns MV/WKIL W9 9 H2
Bristol Ms MV/WKIL W9 9 H2
Bristol Park Rd WALTH E17 * 120 D2
Bristol Rd FSTGT E7 141 P1
GFD/PVL UB6 134 A3
GVE DA12 190 G6
MRDN SM4 201 M5
Bristol Wy SL SL1 129 L10
Briston Gv CEND/HSY/T N8 118 F4
Bristowe Cl BRXS/STRHM SW2 181 H2
Bristow Rd BXLYHN DA7 163 P7
CROY/NA CR0 222 F1
HSLW TW3 154 A9
NRWD SE19 181 M8
Britannia Cl CLAP SW4 158 E10
ERITH DA8 164 G5
NTHLT UB5 133 L5
Britannia Dr GVE DA12 191 J8
Britannia Ga CAN/RD E16 141 M10
Britannia La WHTN TW2 176 B3
Britannia Rd BRW CM14 107 H6
BRYLDS KT5 199 L7
CHES/WCR EN8 62 E10
CSHM HP5 51 H5
FUL/PGN SW6 157 L6
IL IG1 122 E8
NFNCH/WDSPK N12 97 M5
POP/IOD E14 160 F3
Britannia Rw IS N1 6 D5
Britannia St FSBYW WC1X 5 N9
Britannia Wk IS N1 6 G9
Britannia Wy FUL/PGN SW6 157 L6
STWL/WRAY TW19 173 N3
WLSDN NW10 135 N6
British Est BOW E3 140 E5
British Gv HMSMTH W6 156 C4
British Grove Pas CHSWK W4 * 156 C4
British Legion Rd CHING E4 101 L3
British St BOW E3 140 E5
Briton Cl SAND/SEL CR2 223 M7
Briton Crs SAND/SEL CR2 223 M7
Briton Hill Rd SAND/SEL CR2 223 N6
Brittain Rd BCTR RM8 123 P8
WOT/HER KT12 217 L2
Brittains La SEV TN13 246 G10
Britten Cl BORE WD6 75 J10
CRAWW RH11 283 J10
GLDGN NW11 117 L6
Brittenden Pde ORP BR6 * 227 J3
Britten Dr STHL UB1 133 P8
Brittens Cl GUW GU2 249 M5
Britten St CHEL SW3 15 N8
Brittidge Rd WLSDN NW10 * 136 B2
Britton Av STALW/RED AL3 38 C6
Britton Cl CAT SE6 183 J3
Britton St FARR EC1M 12 C2
Britwell Dr BERK HP4 34 B3
Britwell Rd SL SL1 128 B5
Brixham Crs RSLP HA4 113 H6
Brixham Gdns GDMY/SEVK IG3 123 H10
Brixham Rd WELL DA16 163 N7
Brixham St CAN/RD E16 142 C10
Brixton Hl BRXS/STRHM SW2 180 G2
Brixton Hill Pl BRXS/STRHM SW2 180 F3
Brixton Ov BRXS/STRHM SW2 159 H10
Brixton Rd BRXN/ST SW9 159 H10
LBTH SE11 18 A10
WATN WD24 73 J5
Brixton Station Rd
BRXN/ST SW9 159 H9
Brixton Water La
BRXS/STRHM SW2 180 G1
BRXS/STRHM SW2 181 H1
Broad Acre LCOL/BKTW AL2 55 M6
Broadacre STA TW18 173 K8
Broadacre Cl HGDN/ICK UB10 112 C8
Broad Acres GODL GU7 267 K9
HAT AL10 40 C1
Broadacres RGUW GU3 249 K8
Broadbent Cl HGT N6 118 C6
Broadbent St MYFR/PKLN W1K * 10 E7
Broadberry Ct UED N18 100 A6
Broad Bridge Cl BKHTH/KID SE3 161 M6
Broadbridge La HORL RH6 281 H5
Broad Cl WOT/HER KT12 197 L10
Broad Common Est
STNW/STAM N16 * 119 P6
Broadcoombe SAND/SEL CR2 224 C4
Broad Ct COVGDN WC2E * 11 M6
WGCE AL7 23 H5
Broadcroft HHNE HP2 35 N4
Broadcroft Av STAN HA7 95 J10
Broadcroft Rd STMC/STPC BR5 206 G7
Broad Ditch Rd MEO DA13 189 P10
Broadeaves Cl SAND/SEL CR2 223 M2
Broadfield HLW CM20 29 H10
Broadfield Cl CRICK NW2 116 F8
KWD/TDW/WH KT20 238 F6
ROM RM1 124 G3
Broadfield Ct BUSH WD23 94 D3
Broadfield Dr CRAWW RH11 283 L10
Broadfield La CAMTN NW1 5 L4
Broadfield Pde EDGW HA8 * 95 N4
Broadfield Pl WGCW AL8 22 E6
Broadfield Rd CAT SE6 183 K4
HHNE HP2 36 A6
SHGR GU5 270 E8
Broadfields CHESW EN7 61 J5
E/WMO/HCT KT8 198 C6
RYLN/HDSTN HA2 94 A10
SBW CM21 29 L2
Broadfields Av EDGW HA8 95 N5
WCHMH N21 99 H1
Broadfields Hts EDGW HA8 95 N5
Broadfields La OXHEY WD19 93 J2
Broadfield Sq EN EN1 80 A7
Broadfields Wy WLSDN NW10 116 C10
Broadfield Wy BKHH IG9 101 P4
Broadford La CHOB/PIR GU24 213 L8
Broadford Pk RGUE GU4 268 A7
Broadford Rd RGUE GU4 268 A7
Broadgate WAB EN9 63 L9
Broadgates Av EBAR EN4 77 L5
Broadgates Rd
WAND/EARL SW18 179 N4
Broad Gn HERT/BAY SG13 42 G1
Broad Green Av CROY/NA CR0 203 J7
Broadgreen Rd CHESW EN7 61 L2
Broad Green Wd HERT/BAY SG13 42 G1
Broadham Green Rd OXTED RH8 261 J9
Broadham Pl OXTED RH8 261 J8
Broadhead Strd
CDALE/KGS NW9 96 C10
Broadheath Dr CHST BR7 184 C8
Broad Hwy COB KT11 217 L10
Broadhinton Rd CLAP SW4 158 C9
Broadhurst ASHTD KT21 237 K2
Broadhurst Av EDGW HA8 95 N5
GDMY/SEVK IG3 123 J9
Broadhurst Cl KIL/WHAMP NW6 3 J2
Broadhurst Gdns
KIL/WHAMP NW6 3 H2
KIL/WHAMP NW6 3 K2
REIG RH2 275 L3
RSLP HA4 113 K7
Broadhusrt Cl
RCHPK/HAM TW10 177 L1
Broadlake Cl LCOL/BKTW AL2 57 J3
Broadlands FELT TW13 175 N6
GRAYS RM17 167 L4
HORL RH6 280 D3
Broadlands Av CSHM HP5 51 H6
PEND EN3 80 A7
SHPTN TW17 196 D6
STRHM/NOR SW16 180 F5
Broadlands Cl HGT N6 118 B5
PEND EN3 80 A7
STRHM/NOR SW16 180 F5
Broadlands Dr ASC SL5 192 B7
WARL CR6 242 B5
Broadlands Rd BMLY BR1 183 N7
HGT N6 118 A5
Broadlands Wy NWMAL KT3 200 C6
Broad La CEND/HSY/T N8 118 G3
HPTN TW12 175 N10
RDART DA2 187 J7
RDKG RH5 278 A2
SEVS/STOTM N15 119 N3
Broad Lawn ELTH/MOT SE9 184 D5
Broadlawns Ct
KTN/HRWW/WS HA3 94 E9
Broadleaf Gv WGCW AL8 22 E2
Broadley Gn BFOR GU20 212 C4
Broadley Rd HLWW/ROY CM19 46 C5
Broadley St STJWD NW8 9 N3
Broadley Ter CAMTN NW1 9 P2
Broadmark Rd SLN SL2 129 N10
Broadmead ASHTD KT21 237 K4
CAT SE6 182 F6
HORL RH6 280 D3
REDH RH1 * 258 D4
Broadmead Av WPK KT4 200 D7
Broadmead Cl HPTN TW12 175 P9
PIN HA5 * 93 M8
Broad Meadow BRWN CM15 86 E4
Broadmead Rd WFD IG8 101 M7
WFD IG8 102 A8
YEAD UB4 133 M6
Broadmeads RPLY/SEND GU23 232 E8
WARE SG12 26 C2
Broad Oak SLN SL2 129 H6
SUN TW16 174 G9
WFD IG8 101 N6
Broadoak Av PEND EN3 80 C1
Broad Oak Cl CHING E4 100 G6

Broadoak Cl EYN DA4 187 P9
Broad Oak Cl STMC/STPC BR5 207 K2
Broad Oak Ct SLN SL2 129 H6
Broadoak End HERT/WAT SG14 * 24 G2
Broadoak Rd ERITH DA8 164 E6
Broadoaks EPP CM16 65 J8
Broad Oaks SURB KT6 199 N8
Broadoaks Crs BF/WBF KT14 215 L10
Broad Oaks Wy HAYES BR2 205 L5
Broad Platts DTCH/LGLY SL3 150 A2
Broad Rd SWCM DA10 189 K2
Broadstone Pl MHST W1U 10 C4
Broadstone Rd HARP AL5 20 B5
HCH RM12 125 H7
Broad St CHOB/PIR GU24 212 C8
CSHM HP5 51 H6
DAGE RM10 144 B2
HHNE HP2 35 N6
RGUW GU3 249 J8
TEDD TW11 176 E9
Broad Street Av LVPST EC2M 13 J4
Broad Street Pl LVPST EC2M 13 H4
Broadstrood LOU IG10 82 D4
Broadview CDALE/KGS NW9 115 M4
Broadview Av CDW/CHF RM16 168 A1
Broadview Rd CSHM HP5 50 G3
STRHM/NOR SW16 180 E10
Broad Wk BGR/WK TN15 265 M4
BKHTH/KID SE3 161 P8
BKHTH/KID SE3 162 B8
COUL/CHIP CR5 240 B8
CTHM CR3 241 N8
EPSOM KT18 238 F5
HEST TW5 153 L7
HLW CM20 * 28 G10
ORP BR6 207 N10
RCH/KEW TW9 155 L6
WCHMH N21 99 H2
Broadwalk CRAWE RH10 283 N7
RYLN/HDSTN HA2 * 114 A3
SWFD E18 121 M1
Broadwalk La GLDGN NW11 117 J5
The Broad Wk (North)
RBRW/HUT CM13 107 M4
The Broadwalk (South)
RBRW/HUT CM13 107 M5
The Broad Wk BAY/PAD W2 9 H9
KENS W8 15 J1
The Broadwalk NTHWD HA6 92 D10
Broadwall STHWK SE1 12 B9
Broadwater BERK HP4 33 P4
POTB/CUF EN6 59 L6
Broadwater Cl
WOKN/KNAP GU21 214 G8
WOT/HER KT12 217 H2
Broadwater Crs WGCE AL7 22 G6
Broadwater Gdns DEN/HRF UB9 111 M2
ORP BR6 226 E1
Broadwater La DEN/HRF UB9 111 L2
Broadwater Pk DEN/HRF UB9 * 111 K4
Broadwater Ri GU GU1 268 D1
Broadwater Rd THMD SE28 162 G2
TOOT SW17 179 P7
TOTM N17 99 M10
WGCE AL7 23 H6
WGCW AL8 22 G6
Broadway BARK IG11 142 F3
BXLYHS DA6 163 P10
BXLYHS DA6 164 B10
DEN/HRF UB9 * 111 K5
GPK RM2 125 H1
GRAYS RM17 167 P5
HNWL W7 134 D10
RAIN RM13 145 H6
SRTFD E15 141 J2
STA TW18 * 173 L8
STJSPK SW1H 17 J3
SURB KT6 199 N8
SWLY BR8 208 D6
TIL RM18 168 C8
WDSR SL4 170 A4
WOKN/KNAP GU21 230 G5
Broadway Av CROY/NA CR0 203 L5
HLWE CM17 29 L7
TWK TW1 176 G2
Broadway Cl AMSS HP7 68 G6
SAND/SEL CR2 224 A10
WFD IG8 101 N7
Broadway Ct WIM/MER SW19 179 K9
Broadway Gdns MTCM CR4 201 P4
Broadway Market HACK E8 140 A3
Broadway Market Ms HACK E8 7 P6
Broadway Ms PLMGR N13 98 G6
STNW/STAM N16 119 N5
WCHMH N21 99 J2
Broadway Pde CHING E4 * 101 H7
HYS/HAR UB3 * 152 G1
RYLN/HDSTN HA2 * 114 A3
WDR/YW UB7 * 151 P1
Broadway Rd LTWR GU18 212 C5
The Broadway ACT W3 * 155 M1
ADL/WDHM KT15 215 K6
AMSS HP7 68 G6
BCTR RM8 124 A7
BEAC HP9 * 88 C8
BRKMPK AL9 40 F4
CDALE/KGS NW9 116 C4
CEND/HSY/T N8 118 F4
CFSP/GDCR SL9 90 B9
CHEAM SM3 221 H3
CRAWE RH10 283 N7
CSHM HP5 50 G7
EA W5 135 J9
ED N9 99 P4
FBAR/BDGN N11 * 98 A6
HCH RM12 125 J9
KTN/HRWW/WS HA3 94 D10
LOU IG10 82 F7
MLHL NW7 96 B6
PIN HA5 93 N8
PLSTW E13 141 M4
POTB/CUF EN6 59 J8
RYLN/HDSTN HA2 * 114 C7
STA TW18 195 M3
STAL AL1 * 38 C6
STAN HA7 95 H6
SUT SM1 221 M1
THDIT KT7 198 D8
WAT WD17 73 K7
WFD IG8 101 N7
WIM/MER SW19 179 J9
WOKN/KNAP GU21 232 C3
Broadwell Pde
KIL/WHAMP NW6 * 3 K2
Broadwick St SOHO/CST W1F 11 H7
Broadwood GVW DA11 190 E8
Broadwood Av RSLP HA4 112 G4
Broadwood Rd COUL/CHIP CR5 240 E7
Broadwood Ter WKENS W14 14 D5
Broad Yd FARR EC1M 12 C2
Brocas Cl HAMP NW3 3 P3
Brocas St WDSR SL4 149 J6
Brocas Ter WDSR SL4 149 H6
Brockdene Dr HAYES BR2 226 A1
Brockdish Av BARK IG11 123 J10
Brockenhurst E/WMO/HCT KT8 197 N5
Brockenhurst Av WPK KT4 200 B8
Brockenhurst Cl
WOKN/KNAP GU21 214 C10
Brockenhurst Gdns IL IG1 122 F10
MLHL NW7 96 B7
Brockenhurst Ms UED N18 99 P5
Brockenhurst Rd ASC SL5 192 A5
CROY/NA CR0 204 A7
Brockenhurst Wy
STRHM/NOR SW16 202 E2
Brocket Cl CHIG IG7 103 J5
Brocket Rd HOD EN11 44 F3
WGCW AL8 22 C7
Brockett Cl WGCW AL8 22 E5
Brockett Rd CDW/CHF RM16 168 D2
Brocket Vw STALE/WH AL4 21 J3
Brocket Wy CHIG IG7 103 H6
Brock Gn SOCK/AV RM15 146 G8
Brockham Cl WIM/MER SW19 179 J8
Brockham Crs CROY/NA CR0 225 J4
Brockham Dr BRXS/STRHM SW2 180 G3
GNTH/NBYPK IG2 122 F4
Brockham Hill Pk
KWD/TDW/WH KT20 255 P7
Brockhamhurst Rd
BRKHM/BTCW RH3 273 N7
Brockham La BRKHM/BTCW RH3 255 M10
Brockham St STHWK SE1 18 F3
Brockhill WOKN/KNAP GU21 * 231 M3
Brockhurst Cl STAN HA7 94 E7
Brockhurst Rd CSHM HP5 51 H5
Brockill Crs BROCKY SE4 160 D10
Brocklebank Rd CHARL SE7 161 N3
WAND/EARL SW18 179 M3
Brocklehurst St NWCR SE14 160 C6
Brocklesbury Cl WATN WD24 73 K7
Brocklesby Rd SNWD SE25 204 A4
Brockles Md HLWW/ROY CM19 46 F5
Brockley Av STAN HA7 95 K4
Brockley Cl STAN HA7 95 K5
Brockley Combe WEY KT13 216 E2
Brockley Crs CRW RM5 104 D8
Brockley Cross BROCKY SE4 160 E9
Brockley Gv BROCKY SE4 182 E1
RBRW/HUT CM13 107 M2
Brockley Hall Rd BROCKY SE4 182 D2
Brockley Hl STAN HA7 95 H3
Brockley Ms BROCKY SE4 182 D1
Brockley Pk FSTH SE23 182 D3
Brockley Ri FSTH SE23 182 D3
Brockley Rd BROCKY SE4 182 E1
Brockleyside STAN HA7 95 J5
Brockley Vw FSTH SE23 182 D3
Brockley Wy FSTH SE23 182 C1
Brockman Ri BMLY BR1 183 J7
Brock Pl BOW E3 140 G6
Brock Rd CRAWW RH11 283 L4
PLSTW E13 141 N7
Brocks Dr CHEAM SM3 201 H10
RGUW GU3 249 H6
Brockshot Cl BTFD TW8 155 J5
Brocksparkwood
RBRW/HUT CM13 107 N4
Brock St PECK SE15 160 B9
Brockswood La WGCW AL8 22 E4
Brockton Cl ROM RM1 124 G2
Brock Wy VW GU25 193 P5
Brockway Cl GU GU1 250 E9
WAN E11 121 K7
Brockwell Av BECK BR3 204 G5
BECK BR3 205 H5
Brockwell Cl STMC/STPC BR5 207 J5
Brockwell Park Gdns HNHL SE24 181 J3
Brockwell Park Rw
BRXS/STRHM SW2 181 H3
Brockworth Cl PECK SE15 19 J10
Brodewater Rd BORE WD6 75 N6
Brodia Rd STNW/STAM N16 119 M8
Brodie Rd CHING E4 101 H2
ENC/FH EN2 79 K4
GU GU1 268 B1
Brodie St STHWK SE1 19 M7
Brodlove La WAP E1W 140 C9
Brodrick Gv ABYW SE2 163 L3
GT/LBKH KT23 253 P2
Brodrick Rd TOOT SW17 179 P5
Brograve Gdns BECK BR3 204 G2
Broke Ct RGUE GU4 250 F7
Broke Farm Dr ORP BR6 227 M5
Broken Furlong WDSR SL4 149 H4
Broken Gate La DEN/HRF UB9 110 F6
Broken Whf BLKFR EC4V 12 E7
Brokes Crs REIG RH2 257 K8
Brokesley St BOW E3 140 E6
Brokes Rd REIG RH2 257 K8
Broke Wk HACK E8 7 N5
Bromar Rd CMBW SE5 159 M9
Bromborough Gn OXHEY WD19 93 K6
Bromefield STAN HA7 95 J8
Bromefield Ct WAB EN9 63 M9
Bromehead St WCHPL E1 140 B8
Brome House CHARL SE7 * 162 B6
Bromell's Rd CLAP SW4 158 D10
Brome Rd ELTH/MOT SE9 162 C9
Bromet Cl WAT WD17 72 G4
Bromfelde Rd CLAP SW4 158 E9
Bromfield St IS N1 6 B7
Bromford Cl OXTED RH8 261 M9
Bromhall Rd BCTR RM8 143 L1
Bromhedge ELTH/MOT SE9 184 C6
Bromholm Rd ABYW SE2 163 L2
Bromleigh Cl CHES/WCR EN8 62 D4
Bromley GRAYS RM17 167 L5
Bromley Av BMLY BR1 183 K10
Bromley Common HAYES BR2 206 B7
Bromley Ct BMLY BR1 183 K10
Bromley Crs HAYES BR2 205 L3
RSLP HA4 112 G9
Bromley Gdns HAYES BR2 205 L2
Bromley Gv HAYES BR2 205 J2
Bromley Hall Rd POP/IOD E14 141 H7
Bromley High St BOW E3 140 G5
Bromley Hl BMLY BR1 183 K9
Bromley La AMS HP6 50 B10
CHST BR7 184 F10
Bromley Pk BMLY BR1 * 183 K10
Bromley Rd BECK BR3 204 F1
BECK BR3 205 H2
CAT SE6 182 G6
CAT SE6 183 H7
CHST BR7 206 E1
HAYES BR2 205 K2
UED N18 99 L5
WALTH E17 120 F1
Bromley St WCHPL E1 140 C7
Brompton Ar CHEL SW3 * 16 A2
Brompton Cl HSLWW TW4 175 N1
Brompton Dr ERITH DA8 165 J6
Brompton Gv EFNCH N2 117 P2
Brompton Park Crs
FUL/PGN SW6 14 G10
Brompton Pl CHEL SW3 15 P3
Brompton Rd CHEL SW3 15 N5
Brompton Sq CHEL SW3 15 N3
Brompton Ter
WOOL/PLUM SE18 * 162 D7
Bromwich Av HGT N6 118 B7
Bromyard Av ACT W3 136 B10
Bromycroft Rd SLN SL2 128 F5
Brondesbury Ms
KIL/WHAMP NW6 * 2 E4
Brondesbury Pk
KIL/WHAMP NW6 136 F2
Brondesbury Rd
KIL/WHAMP NW6 2 D7
Brondesbury Vls
KIL/WHAMP NW6 2 D7
Bronhill Ter TOTM N17 * 99 P9
Bronsart Rd FUL/PGN SW6 157 H6
Bronson Rd RYNPK SW20 200 G2
Bronte Cl ERITH DA8 164 C7
FSTGT E7 121 M9
GNTH/NBYPK IG2 122 D3
TIL RM18 168 F8
Bronte Gv DART DA1 165 N10
Bronte Vw GVE DA12 190 F4
Bronti Cl WALW SE17 18 F7
Bronze Age Wy BELV DA17 164 D2
Bronze St DEPT SE8 160 F6
Brook Av DAGE RM10 144 C2
EDGW HA8 95 N7
WBLY HA9 115 L8
Brookbank Av HNWL W7 134 C7
Brookbank Rd LEW SE13 160 G9
Brook Cl ACT W3 135 M10
BORE WD6 75 N7
DORK RH4 255 H10
GPK RM2 104 G9
HOR/WEW KT19 220 B5
RSLP HA4 112 F5
RYNPK SW20 200 E3
STWL/WRAY TW19 174 A3
TOOT SW17 180 B5
Brook Ct BECK BR3 * 204 E1
RAD WD7 * 56 F9
Brook Crs ED N9 100 A5
SL SL1 128 D8
Brookdale FBAR/BDGN N11 98 D5
Brookdale Av UPMR RM14 125 P8
Brookdale Cl UPMR RM14 126 A8
Brookdale Rd BXLY DA5 185 P2
CAT SE6 182 G3
WALTH E17 120 F1
Brookdene Av OXHEY WD19 93 J1
Brookdene Dr NTHWD HA6 92 G8
Brookdene Rd
WOOL/PLUM SE18 163 H3
Brook Dr HRW HA1 114 B2
LBTH SE11 18 C5
RAD WD7 56 E9
RSLP HA4 112 F5
Brooke Av RYLN/HDSTN HA2 114 B8
Brooke Cl BUSH WD23 94 B1
Brooke Dr GVE DA12 191 L4
Brooke End OXTED RH8 * 261 M9
Brooke Forest RGUW GU3 249 H6
Brookehowse Rd CAT SE6 182 G6
Brook End SBW CM21 29 N1
Brookend Rd BFN/LL DA15 185 H4
Brooker Cl POP/IOD E14 140 E7
Brooke Rd GRAYS RM17 167 M4
STNW/STAM N16 119 P8
WALTH E17 121 H2
Brooker Rd WAB EN9 63 H10
Brookers Cl ASHTD KT21 237 H3
Brooke's Market HCIRC EC1N * 12 A3
Brooke St HCIRC EC1N 12 A4
Brooke Wy BUSH WD23 94 B1
Brook Farm Rd COB KT11 235 L1
Brookfield BGR/WK TN15 247 M3
EPP CM16 65 M1
GODL GU7 267 M9
WOKN/KNAP GU21 231 N2
Brookfield Av EA W5 135 J6
MLHL NW7 96 E7
SUT SM1 201 P10
WALTH E17 121 H2
Brookfield Cl ASHTD KT21 237 K6
CHERT KT16 214 G3
MLHL NW7 96 E7
RBRW/HUT CM13 87 P10
REDH RH1 276 B6
Brookfield Crs
KTN/HRWW/WS HA3 115 J3
MLHL NW7 96 E7
Brookfield Gdns CHES/WCR EN8 62 C3
ESH/CLAY KT10 218 E3
Brookfield La CHES/WCR EN8 62 A4
Brookfield La East
CHES/WCR EN8 62 C4
Brookfield La West
CHES/WCR EN8 62 B4
Brookfield Pk KTTN NW5 118 C8
Brookfield Pth WFD IG8 101 J7
Brookfield Pl COB KT11 235 M1
Brookfield Rd CHSWK W4 156 B2
ED N9 99 P4
HOM E9 140 D1
Brookfields CHONG CM5 67 N2
PEND EN3 80 C8
SBW CM21 29 N1
Brookfields Av MTCM CR4 201 P5
Brook Gdns BARN SW13 156 C9
CHING E4 100 G5
KUTN/CMB KT2 199 P1
Brook Ga MYFR/PKLN W1K 10 B8
Brook Gn HMSMTH W6 156 F2
Brook Hl OXTED RH8 261 H6
SHGR GU5 269 N9
Brookhill Cl CRAWE RH10 285 H2
EBAR EN4 77 P9
Brook Hill Cl WOOL/PLUM SE18 162 E4
Brookhill Rd CRAWE RH10 285 H3
EBAR EN4 77 N9
WOOL/PLUM SE18 162 E4
Brookhouse Gdns CHING E4 101 K5
Brookhurst Rd ADL/WDHM KT15 215 L3
Brooking Cl BCTR RM8 123 M8
Brooking Rd FSTGT E7 121 M10
Brookland Cl GLDGN NW11 117 K2
Brookland Garth GLDGN NW11 117 K2
Brookland Hl GLDGN NW11 117 K2
Brookland Ri GLDGN NW11 117 K2
Brooklands DART DA1 187 M4
Brooklands Ap ROM RM1 124 E2
Brooklands Av BFN/LL DA15 184 G5
WIM/MER SW19 179 L5
Brooklands Cl COB KT11 235 M1
ROMW/RG RM7 124 E2
SUN TW16 196 F1
Brooklands Ct KIL/WHAMP NW6 * 2 C3
STAL AL1 * 38 D6
WCHMH N21 79 L9
Brooklands Dr GFD/PVL UB6 135 H3
Brooklands Gdns EMPK RM11 125 K3
POTB/CUF EN6 59 H8
Brooklands La ROMW/RG RM7 124 E2
WEY KT13 216 A3
Brooklands Pk BKHTH/KID SE3 161 M9
Brooklands Pl HPTN TW12 176 A8
Brooklands Rd ROMW/RG RM7 124 E2
THDIT KT7 198 E8
WEY KT13 216 B7
Brooklands Ter SUN TW16 * 197 H4
The Brooklands ISLW TW7 * 154 C7
Brooklands Wy REDH RH1 257 P8
Brook La BERK HP4 33 N4
BKHTH/KID SE3 161 N8
BMLY BR1 183 M9
BRWN CM15 87 J3
BXLY DA5 185 N2
CHOB/PIR GU24 213 J7
RPLY/SEND GU23 233 H8
SBW CM21 29 N1
SHGR GU5 269 P8
Brooklane Fld HLWS CM18 47 L4
Brook La North BTFD TW8 155 J4
Brooklea Cl CDALE/KGS NW9 96 B9
Brookleys CHOB/PIR GU24 213 L6
Brooklyn Av LOU IG10 82 B8
SNWD SE25 204 A4
Brooklyn Cl CAR SM5 201 P9
WOKS/MYFD GU22 232 B5
Brooklyn Gv SNWD SE25 204 A4
Brooklyn Rd HAYES BR2 206 A5
SNWD SE25 204 A4
WOKS/MYFD GU22 232 B4
Brooklyn Wy WDR/YW UB7 151 N2
Brookmans Av BRKMPK AL9 59 J2
CDW/CHF RM16 147 P10
Brookmans Cl UPMR RM14 126 D5
Brookmans Park Dr UPMR RM14 126 D3
Brookmead CROY/NA CR0 202 D6
Brook Md HOR/WEW KT19 220 B3
Brookmead Av BMLY BR1 206 C5
Brookmead Cl STMC/STPC BR5 207 L7
Brook Meadow
NFNCH/WDSPK N12 97 L5
Brook Meadow Cl WFD IG8 101 K7
Brookmead Rd CROY/NA CR0 202 D6
Brook Ms North BAY/PAD W2 9 L7
Brookmill Cl OXHEY WD19 * 93 J1
Brookmill Rd DEPT SE8 160 F7
Brook Pk DART DA1 187 P5
Brook Park Cl WCHMH N21 79 J10
Brook Pth SL SL1 128 E9
Brook Pl BAR EN5 77 K9
Brook Ri CHIG IG7 102 D4
Brook Rd BKHH IG9 101 M3
BORE WD6 75 M5
BRW CM14 106 E4
CEND/HSY/T N8 118 F2
CHES/WCR EN8 62 E10
CRICK NW2 116 D7
EPP CM16 65 K9
GNTH/NBYPK IG2 123 H4
GPK RM2 104 G10
GVW DA11 190 C4
LOU IG10 82 B9
REDH RH1 276 A1
RGUE GU4 268 F6
SBW CM21 29 N2
SURB KT6 199 K9
SWLY BR8 208 E3
THHTH CR7 203 K4
TWK TW1 176 F2
WDGN N22 * 98 G10
Brook Rd South BTFD TW8 155 K5
Brooks Av EHAM E6 142 C6
Brooksbank St HOM E9 * 140 C1
Brooksby Ms IS N1 6 A3
Brooksby St IS N1 6 A4
Brooksby's Wk HOM E9 120 C10
Brooks Cl WEY KT13 216 B6
Brooks Ct HERT/WAT SG14 * 24 G4
Brookscroft CROY/NA CR0 224 E6
Brookscroft Rd WALTH E17 100 G9
Brooksfield WGCE AL7 23 L4
Brookshill KTN/HRWW/WS HA3 94 D7
Brookshill Av
KTN/HRWW/WS HA3 94 C6
Brookshill Dr
KTN/HRWW/WS HA3 94 C6
Brookside BARK/HLT IG6 102 F7
CAR SM5 222 B2
CHERT KT16 195 H7
CRAWE RH10 285 H2
DTCH/LGLY SL3 150 F6
EBAR EN4 77 P10
EMPK RM11 125 M3
HAT AL10 40 A4
HERT/BAY SG13 25 M6
HGDN/ICK UB10 132 A2
HLWW/ROY CM19 46 D4
HOD EN11 44 F3
ORP BR6 207 J7
POTB/CUF EN6 58 D8
RGUE GU4 250 A5
WAB EN9 63 K8
WATN WD24 * 73 L2
WCHMH N21 78 G10
Brookside Av ASHF TW15 173 M8
STWL/WRAY TW19 150 B9
Brookside Cl BAR EN5 76 G10
BAR EN5 77 H10
FELT TW13 175 H6
KTN/HRWW/WS HA3 115 J3
RSLP HA4 113 M9
Brookside Crs POTB/CUF EN6 60 F3
WPK KT4 200 D8
Brookside Gdns EN EN1 80 A3
Brookside Rd ARCH N19 118 D7
GLDGN NW11 117 H4
MEO DA13 190 C10
OXHEY WD19 93 J1
UED N18 100 A5
YEAD UB4 133 K9
Brookside South EBAR EN4 98 B1
Brookside Wy CROY/NA CR0 204 C6
Brooks La CHSWK W4 155 M5
Brook's Ms MYFR/PKLN W1K 10 E7
Brooks Rd CHSWK W4 155 M4
PLSTW E13 141 M3
Brook St BAY/PAD W2 9 M7
BELV DA17 164 C4
BRW CM14 106 D5
KUT/HW KT1 199 K2
MYFR/PKLN W1K 10 D7
TOTM N17 99 N10
WDSR SL4 149 J8
Brooksville Av KIL/WHAMP NW6 2 B6
Brookswood RGUE GU4 268 F7
The Brook CRAWE RH10 283 N6
Brook Va RDKG RH5 272 G8
Brookview CRAWE RH10 285 H2
Brookview Rd
STRHM/NOR SW16 180 C8
Brookville Rd FUL/PGN SW6 157 J6
Brook Wk EDGW HA8 96 A7
EFNCH N2 97 N9
Brook Water La HDN NW4 * 116 G3
Brook Wy CHIG IG7 102 D4
LHD/OX KT22 236 F4
Brookway BKHTH/KID SE3 161 M9
RAIN RM13 145 J7
Brookwood HORL RH6 280 C3
Brookwood Av BARN SW13 156 C9
Brookwood Br CHOB/PIR GU24 230 G6
Brookwood Cl HAYES BR2 205 L4
Brookwood Lye Rd
CHOB/PIR GU24 231 H6
Brookwood Pk HORL RH6 280 C5
Brookwood Rd HSLW TW3 154 A8
WAND/EARL SW18 179 J4
Broom Av STMC/STPC BR5 207 L2
Broom Bank WARL CR6 243 H5
Broom Cl CHESW EN7 61 P3
ESH/CLAY KT10 218 A2
HAT AL10 40 C7
HAYES BR2 206 B6
TEDD TW11 177 J10
Broom Cnr HARP AL5 * 20 B3
Broomcroft Av NTHLT UB5 133 K5
Broomcroft Dr
WOKS/MYFD GU22 232 G1
Broomdashers Rd CRAWE RH10 284 A6
Broome Cl EPSOM KT18 256 A2
Broome Pl SOCK/AV RM15 146 C10
Broome Rd HPTN TW12 197 N1
Broomer Pl CHES/WCR EN8 62 B6
Broome Wy CMBW SE5 159 L6
Broomfield GUW GU2 249 K9
HLW CM20 29 L8
LCOL/BKTW AL2 56 B3
SUN TW16 197 H1
WALTH E17 120 E5
Broomfield Av BROX EN10 62 D2
LOU IG10 82 C10
PLMGR N13 98 G6
Broomfield Cl ASC SL5 192 G7
CRW RM5 104 E8
RGUW GU3 249 K8
WOKS/MYFD GU22 232 G2
Broomfield Cottages WEA W13 * 134 G10
Broomfield Ct WEY KT13 216 B3
Broomfield Ga SLN SL2 128 G6
Broomfield La PLMGR N13 98 F5
Broomfield Pk ASC SL5 192 G7
DORK RH4 272 B3
Broomfield Pl WEA W13 134 G10
Broomfield Ride LHD/OX KT22 218 C8
Broomfield Ri ABLGY WD5 54 E8
Broomfield Rd ADL/WDHM KT15 215 L7
BECK BR3 204 D4
BXLYHS DA6 186 B1
CHDH RM6 123 N5
PLMGR N13 98 F6
RCH/KEW TW9 155 L7
SEV TN13 246 G8
SURB KT6 199 L8
SWCM DA10 189 K2
TEDD TW11 177 H9
WEA W13 134 G10
Broomfields ESH/CLAY KT10 218 B2
HART DA3 211 K5
Broomfield St POP/IOD E14 140 F7
Broom Gdns CROY/NA CR0 204 F10
Broom Gv WAT WD17 73 H4
Broomgrove Gdns EDGW HA8 95 M9
Broomgrove Rd BRXN/ST SW9 158 G8
Broom Hall LHD/OX KT22 218 B10
Broomhall End
WOKN/KNAP GU21 232 B2
Broomhall La ASC SL5 192 E6
WOKN/KNAP GU21 232 B2
Broomhall Rd SAND/SEL CR2 223 L5
WOKN/KNAP GU21 232 B2
Broom Hl HHW HP1 35 H7
SLN SL2 129 M2
Broomhill Ri BXLYHS DA6 186 B1
Broomhill Rd DART DA1 187 J2
GDMY/SEVK IG3 123 K7
ORP BR6 207 K7
WAND/EARL SW18 179 K1
WFD IG8 101 M7
Broomhills MEO DA13 189 K7
WGCE AL7 23 K4
Broomhouse La FUL/PGN SW6 157 K8
Broomhouse Rd FUL/PGN SW6 157 K8
Broomhurst Ct DORK RH4 272 G4
Broomlands La OXTED RH8 262 B3
Broom La CHOB/PIR GU24 213 K5
Broomleys STALE/WH AL4 39 H3
Broomloan La SUT SM1 201 K9
Broom Lock TEDD TW11 * 177 H8
Broom Md BXLYHS DA6 186 B2
Broom Pk TEDD TW11 177 J10
Broom Rd CROY/NA CR0 204 F10
TEDD TW11 176 G8
TEDD TW11 177 H9
Brooms Cl WGCW AL8 22 G2
Broomsleigh St
KIL/WHAMP NW6 * 117 K10
Broomstick Hall Rd WAB EN9 63 K9
Broomstick La CSHM HP5 51 M6
Broom Water TEDD TW11 177 H9
Broom Water West TEDD TW11 177 H8
Broom Wy WEY KT13 216 E1
Broomwood Cl BXLY DA5 186 E5
CROY/NA CR0 204 C5
Broomwood Gdns BRWN CM15 86 F10
Broomwood Rd STMC/STPC BR5 207 L2
Broseley Gdns HARH RM3 105 M5
Broseley Gv SYD SE26 182 D8
Broseley Rd HARH RM3 105 M5
Broster Gdns SNWD SE25 203 N3
Brougham Rd ACT W3 135 P8
HACK E8 7 P5
Brougham St BTSEA SW11 158 A8
Brough Cl KUTN/CMB KT2 * 177 J8
VX/NE SW8 158 F6
Broughinge Rd BORE WD6 75 N6
Broughton Av FNCH N3 117 H1
RCHPK/HAM TW10 177 H7
Broughton Dr BRXN/ST SW9 159 H10
Broughton Gdns HGT N6 118 D4
Broughton Rd FUL/PGN SW6 157 L8
ORP BR6 206 G10
RSEV TN14 247 H2
THHTH CR7 203 H6
WEA W13 134 G9
Broughton Road Ap
FUL/PGN SW6 * 157 L8
Broughton St VX/NE SW8 158 C8
Broughton Wy
RKW/CH/CXG WD3 91 K1
Brouncker Rd ACT W3 155 P1
Brow Cl STMC/STPC BR5 207 N7
Brow Crs STMC/STPC BR5 207 M8
Browell's La FELT TW13 175 K5
Brown Cl WLGTN SM6 222 F4
Browne Cl BRW CM14 106 G2
Brownfields WGCE AL7 23 J4
Brownfields Ct WGCE AL7 23 K4
Brownfield St POP/IOD E14 141 H8
Browngraves Rd HYS/HAR UB3 152 D6
Brown Hart Gdns
MYFR/PKLN W1K 10 D7
Brownhill Rd CAT SE6 183 H3
Browning Av HNWL W7 134 E8
SUT SM1 221 P1
WPK KT4 200 E8
Browning Cl CRAWE RH10 284 D6
HPTN TW12 175 N7
MV/WKIL W9 * 9 K2
WALTH E17 121 H2
WELL DA16 163 H7
Browning Ms CAVSQ/HST W1G * 10 D4
Browning Rd DART DA1 165 N10
ENC/FH EN2 79 L4
HARP AL5 20 B1
LHD/OX KT22 254 C1
MNPK E12 142 C1
WAN E11 121 L5
Browning St WALW SE17 18 F7
Browning Wy HEST TW5 153 L7
Brownlea Gdns GDMY/SEVK IG3 123 K7
Brownlow Cl EBAR EN4 77 N9
Brownlow Ms BMSBY WC1N 11 P2
Brownlow Rd BERK HP4 33 P4
BORE WD6 75 M8
CROY/NA CR0 223 M1
FBAR/BDGN N11 98 F7
FNCH N3 97 L8
FSTGT E7 121 M9
HACK E8 7 N5
REDH RH1 257 P10
WEA W13 * 134 F10
WLSDN NW10 136 B2
Brownlow St GINN WC1R 11 P4
Brownrigg Rd ASHF TW15 174 B7
Brown Rd GVE DA12 191 H5
Brown's Hl REDH RH1 277 L7
Browns La EHSLY KT24 253 L3
Brownspring Dr ELTH/MOT SE9 184 E7
Brown's Rd BRYLDS KT5 199 L7
WALTH E17 120 F1
Browns Spring BERK HP4 34 F2
Brown St MBLAR W1H 10 A5
Brownswell Rd EFNCH N2 97 N10
Brownswood Rd BEAC HP9 88 C7
FSBYPK N4 119 K7
The Brow CSTG HP8 90 A4
GSTN WD25 55 J9
REDH RH1 276 B5
Broxash Rd BTSEA SW11 180 B2
Broxbourne Av SWFD E18 121 N2
Broxbourne House BOW E3 140 G6
Broxbourne Rd FSTGT E7 121 M8
ORP BR6 207 J8
Broxburn Dr SOCK/AV RM15 146 G9
SOCK/AV RM15 147 H8
Broxhill Rd ABR/ST RM4 105 H4
Broxholm Rd WNWD SE27 181 H6
Brox La CHERT KT16 214 G5
Brox Rd CHERT KT16 214 F5
Broxted Rd CAT SE6 182 E5
Broxwood Wy STJWD NW8 3 P6
Bruce Av HCH RM12 125 L7
SHPTN TW17 196 D6
Bruce Castle Rd TOTM N17 99 N9
Bruce Cl BF/WBF KT14 215 N9
NKENS W10 136 G7
SL SL1 128 F10
WELL DA16 163 L7
Bruce Dr SAND/SEL CR2 224 C5
Bruce Gdns TRDG/WHET N20 98 A4
Bruce Gv ORP BR6 207 K8
TOTM N17 99 N10
WATN WD24 73 K4
Bruce Rd BAR EN5 77 H7
BOW E3 140 G5
KTN/HRWW/WS HA3 94 D10
MTCM CR4 180 B10
SNWD SE25 203 L4
WLSDN NW10 136 A2
Bruces Wharf Rd GRAYS RM17 167 M5
Bruce Wy CHES/WCR EN8 62 C9
Bruckner St NKENS W10 2 C10
Brudenell WDSR SL4 148 E9
Brudenell Rd TOOT SW17 180 A6
Bruffs Meadow NTHLT UB5 133 M1
Bruford Ct DEPT SE8 160 F5
Bruges Pl CAMTN NW1 5 H4
Brumana Cl WEY KT13 216 C3
Brumfield Rd HOR/WEW KT19 219 P2
The Brunel Centre
CRAWE RH10 * 284 A4
Brunel Cl HEST TW5 153 J6
NRWD SE19 181 N9
NTHLT UB5 133 N5
ROM RM1 124 F2
TIL RM18 168 E8
Brunel Ct WLSDN NW10 136 D5
Brunel Est BAY/PAD W2 8 E4
Brunel House
WOOL/PLUM SE18 * 162 B6
Brunel Ms NKENS W10 136 G5
Brunel Pl CRAWE RH10 283 P8
Brunel Rd ACT W3 136 B7
BERM/RHTH SE16 160 B1
WALTH E17 120 D4
WFD IG8 102 C6
Brunel St CAN/RD E16 141 L8
Brunel Wk WHTN TW2 175 P3
Brunel Wy SL SL1 129 L10
Brune St WCHPL E1 13 L4
Brunner Cl GLDGN NW11 117 L3
Brunner Ct CHERT KT16 214 F2
Brunner Rd EA W5 135 J6
WALTH E17 120 E3
Bruno Pl CDALE/KGS NW9 115 P7
Brunswick Av FBAR/BDGN N11 98 B4
UPMR RM14 126 D5
Brunswick Cl BXLYHS DA6 163 N10
CRAWE RH10 284 B9
PIN HA5 113 N5
THDIT KT7 198 E8
WHTN TW2 176 C6
WOT/HER KT12 197 K9
Brunswick Ct STHWK SE1 19 K2
Brunswick Crs FBAR/BDGN N11 98 B4
Brunswick Dr CHOB/PIR GU24 230 C6
Brunswick Gdns BARK/HLT IG6 102 F8
EA W5 135 K6
KENS W8 8 F10
Brunswick Gv COB KT11 217 K9
FBAR/BDGN N11 98 B4
Brunswick Ms MBLAR W1H 10 B5
STRHM/NOR SW16 180 E9
Brunswick Pk CMBW SE5 159 L7
Brunswick Park Gdns
FBAR/BDGN N11 98 B3
Brunswick Park Rd
FBAR/BDGN N11 98 C4
Brunswick Pl CAMTN NW1 10 D2
IS N1 7 H10
NRWD SE19 181 P10
Brunswick Quay
BERM/RHTH SE16 160 D2
Brunswick Rd BXLYHS DA6 163 N10
CHOB/PIR GU24 230 C7
EA W5 135 J6
KUTN/CMB KT2 199 M1
LEY E10 121 H6
PEND EN3 80 F4
SEVS/STOTM N15 119 M3
SUT SM1 221 L1
Brunswick Sq BMSBY WC1N 11 M1
TOTM N17 99 N7
Brunswick St WALTH E17 121 H3
Brunswick Vls CMBW SE5 159 M7
Brunswick Wk GVE DA12 190 G2
Brunswick Wy FBAR/BDGN N11 98 C5
Brunton Pl POP/IOD E14 140 D8
Brushfield St WCHPL E1 13 K3
Brushfield Wy
WOKN/KNAP GU21 231 H5
Brushmakers Ct CSHM HP5 51 H6
Brushrise WATN WD24 73 H2
Brushwood Cl POP/IOD E14 140 G7
Brushwood Dr
RKW/CH/CXG WD3 70 F8
Brushwood Rd CSHM HP5 51 K5
Brussels Rd BTSEA SW11 157 N10
Bruton Cl CHST BR7 184 C10
Bruton La MYFR/PICC W1J 10 F8
Bruton Pl MYFR/PICC W1J 10 E8
Bruton Rd MRDN SM4 201 M4
Bruton St MYFR/PICC W1J 10 F8
Bruton Wy WEA W13 134 F7
Bryan Av WLSDN NW10 136 E2
Bryan Cl SUN TW16 175 H10
Bryan Rd BERM/RHTH SE16 160 E1
Bryanston Av WHTN TW2 176 A4
Bryanston Cl NWDGN UB2 153 N3
Bryanstone Av GUW GU2 249 M6
Bryanstone Cl GUW GU2 249 L7
Bryanstone Gv GUW GU2 249 L6
Bryanstone Rd CEND/HSY/T N8 118 E3
CHES/WCR EN8 62 E10
Bryanston Ms East MBLAR W1H 10 A4
Bryanston Ms West MBLAR W1H 10 A4
Bryanston Pl MBLAR W1H 10 A4
Bryanston Rd TIL RM18 168 F8
Bryanston Sq MBLAR W1H 10 A5
Bryanston St MBLAR W1H 10 A6
Bryant Av HARH RM3 105 L10
SLN SL2 129 J7
Bryant Cl BAR EN5 77 J9
Bryant Rd NTHLT UB5 133 K5
Bryant Rw HARH RM3 105 K3
Bryant St SRTFD E15 141 J2
Bryantwood Rd HOLWY N7 119 H10
Brycedale Crs STHGT/OAK N14 98 E5
Bryce Rd BCTR RM8 123 M9
Bryden Cl SYD SE26 182 D8
Brydges Pl CHCR WC2N 11 L8
Brydges Rd SRTFD E15 121 J10
Brydon Wk IS N1 5 M5
Bryer Pl WDSR SL4 148 C9
Bryett Rd HOLWY N7 118 F8
Brymay Cl BOW E3 140 F4
Brympton Cl DORK RH4 272 F4
Brynford Cl WOKN/KNAP GU21 232 B1
Brynmaer Rd BTSEA SW11 158 A7
Bryn Wy STALE/WH AL4 39 J8
Bryn-y-Mawr Rd EN EN1 79 N8
Bryony Cl LOU IG10 82 E8
UX/CGN UB8 132 A7
Bryony Rd GU GU1 250 E7
SHB W12 136 D9
Bryony Wy SUN TW16 175 H9
Bubblestone Rd RSEV TN14 247 J2
Bubsy Ms CAMTN NW1 5 J1
Buccleuch Rd DTCH/LGLY SL3 149 M6
Buchanan Cl SOCK/AV RM15 146 B9
WCHMH N21 78 G9
Buchanan Ct BORE WD6 * 75 P6
Buchanan Gdns WLSDN NW10 136 E4
Buchan Cl UX/CGN UB8 131 M5
Buchan Rd PECK SE15 160 B9
Bucharest Rd WAND/EARL SW18 179 M3
Buckden Cl LEE/GVPK SE12 183 L2
Buckettsland La BORE WD6 76 A4
Buckfast Rd MRDN SM4 201 L4
Buckfast St BETH E2 7 N10
Buckham Thorns Rd
BH/WHM TN16 262 F2
Buckhold Rd WAND/EARL SW18 179 K2
Buckhurst Av CAR SM5 201 P8
Buckhurst Cl REDH RH1 257 P8
Buckhurst La ASC SL5 192 E3
SEV TN13 265 K1
Buckhurst Rd ASC SL5 192 E2
BH/WHM TN16 244 E7
Buckhurst St WCHPL E1 140 A6
Buckhurst Wy BKHH IG9 102 A4
Buckingham Av
E/WMO/HCT KT8 198 A2
EBED/NFELT TW14 175 J2
GFD/PVL UB6 134 F3
SL SL1 128 D8
THHTH CR7 203 H1
TRDG/WHET N20 97 M1
WELL DA16 163 H10
Buckingham Av East SL SL1 129 H9
Buckingham Cl EA W5 135 H7
EMPK RM11 125 L3
EN EN1 79 M6
GU GU1 250 C9
HPTN TW12 175 N8
STMC/STPC BR5 207 H7
Buckingham Ct BELMT SM2 * 221 K5
Buckingham Dr CHST BR7 184 E8
Buckingham Gdns
E/WMO/HCT KT8 198 A2
SL SL1 149 L1
STAN HA7 95 K8
THHTH CR7 203 H2
Buckingham Ga HORL RH6 280 D7
WESTW SW1E 16 G3
Buckingham Gv HGDN/ICK UB10 132 B4
Buckingham La FSTH SE23 182 D3
Buckingham Ms IS N1 7 K2

WESTW SW1E * 16 G3
WLSDN NW10 136 C4
Buckingham Palace Rd
BGVA SW1W 16 F4
Buckingham Pde
CFSP/GDCR SL9 90 B9
STAN HA7 * 95 H6
Buckingham Pl WESTW SW1E 16 G3
Buckingham Rd BORE WD6 76 A8
EDGW HA8 95 L8
GVW DA11 190 A3
HPTN TW12 175 N7
HRW HA1 114 C3
IL IG1 122 G7
IS N1 7 J2
KUT/HW KT1 199 L4
LEY E10 120 G8
MTCM CR4 202 F5
RCHPK/HAM TW10 177 J5
RDKG RH5 273 H10
SRTFD E15 121 L10
SWFD E18 101 L9
WATN WD24 73 K3
WDGN N22 98 F9
WLSDN NW10 136 C4
Buckingham St CHCR WC2N 11 M8
Buckingham Wy WLGTN SM6 222 D5
Buckland Av DTCH/LGLY SL3 149 N2
Buckland Crs HAMP NW3 3 L3
WDSR SL4 148 E7
Buckland Ga DTCH/LGLY SL3 129 N5
Buckland La BRKHM/BTCW RH3 256 E7
Buckland Ri PIN HA5 93 K9
Buckland Rd BELMT SM2 220 F6
CHSGTN KT9 219 L2
KWD/TDW/WH KT20 257 J5
LEY E10 121 H7
ORP BR6 227 H1
REIG RH2 256 G9
Bucklands OXHEY WD19 * 93 L4
Bucklands Rd TEDD TW11 177 H9
Buckland St IS N1 7 H8
Bucklands Whf KUT/HW KT1 * 199 J2
Buckland Wk MRDN SM4 201 M4
Buckland Wy WPK KT4 200 F8
Buck La CDALE/KGS NW9 116 A3
Buckleigh Av RYNPK SW20 201 J3
Buckleigh Rd STRHM/NOR SW16 180 E9
Buckleigh Wy NRWD SE19 203 N1
Bucklersbury MANHO EC4N * 12 G6
Bucklers Cl BROX EN10 44 E8
Bucklers Ct BRW CM14 107 H6
Bucklers' Wy CAR SM5 202 A10
Buckles La SOCK/AV RM15 147 H7
Buckle St WCHPL E1 13 N5
Buckles Wy BNSTD SM7 239 H2
Buckley Cl DART DA1 164 G8
FSTH SE23 182 A3
Buckley Pl CRAWE RH10 285 P5
Buckley Rd KIL/WHAMP NW6 2 D4
Buckmans Rd CRAWW RH11 283 N7
Buckmaster Cl BRXN/ST SW9 159 H9
Buckmaster Rd BTSEA SW11 157 P10
Bucknalls Cl GSTN WD25 55 M8
Bucknalls Dr LCOL/BKTW AL2 55 N7
Bucknalls La GSTN WD25 55 M8
Bucknall St NOXST/BSQ WC1A 11 L5
Bucknall Wy BECK BR3 204 G4
Bucknell Cl BRXS/STRHM SW2 158 G10
Buckner Rd BRXS/STRHM SW2 158 G10
Bucknills Cl EPSOM KT18 219 P10
Buckrell Rd CHING E4 101 J3
Buck's Aly HERT/BAY SG13 42 F5
Bucks Av OXHEY WD19 93 M1
Bucks Cl BF/WBF KT14 215 L10
Bucks Cross Rd GVW DA11 190 C6
ORP BR6 227 P2
Bucks Hl KGLGY WD4 53 M9
KGLGY WD4 71 N1
Buckstone Cl FSTH SE23 182 B2
Buckstone Rd UED N18 99 P7
Buck St CAMTN NW1 4 F5
Buckswood Dr CRAWW RH11 283 K9
Buckters Rents
BERM/RHTH SE16 140 D10
Buckthorne Rd BROCKY SE4 182 D2
Buckton Rd BORE WD6 75 L4
Budd Cl NFNCH/WDSPK N12 97 L5
Buddcroft WGCE AL7 23 L4
Buddings Cir WBLY HA9 115 P8
Budebury Rd STA TW18 173 J8
Bude Cl WALTH E17 120 E3
Budge La MTCM CR4 202 A7
Budgen Cl CRAWE RH10 284 E4
Budgen Dr REDH RH1 258 B7
Budge Rw MANHO EC4N 12 G7
Budgin's Hl ORP BR6 227 L8
Budleigh Crs WELL DA16 163 M7
Budoch Dr GDMY/SEVK IG3 123 K7
Buer Rd FUL/PGN SW6 157 H8
Buff Av BNSTD SM7 239 L1
Buffers La LHD/OX KT22 236 F5
Bug Hl WARL CR6 242 C6
Bugsby's Wy GNWCH SE10 161 L3
Bulbourne Cl BERK HP4 33 L3
HHW HP1 35 K7
Bulganak Rd THHTH CR7 203 K4
Bulinca St WEST SW1P * 17 L6
Bulkeley Av WDSR SL4 148 G9
Bulkeley Cl EGH TW20 171 P8
Bullace Cl HHW HP1 35 J5
Bullace Rw CMBW SE5 159 L7
Bull Aly WELL DA16 163 L9
Bullard Rd TEDD TW11 176 D9
Bullards Pl BETH E2 140 C5
Bullbaiters La AMS HP6 50 A10
Bullbanks Rd BELV DA17 164 D3
Bullbeggars La BERK HP4 34 D5
GDST RH9 260 B8
WOKN/KNAP GU21 231 N2
Bull Cl CDW/CHF RM16 167 L1
Bulleid Wy BGVA SW1W 16 F6
Bullen's Green La STALE/WH AL4 40 B9
Bullen St BTSEA SW11 157 P8
Buller Cl PECK SE15 159 P6
Buller Rd BARK IG11 143 H2
THHTH CR7 203 L3
TOTM N17 99 P10
WDGN N22 99 H10
WLSDN NW10 136 G5
Bullers Cl SCUP DA14 185 P8
Bullers Wood Dr CHST BR7 206 B1
Bullescroft Rd EDGW HA8 95 N4
Bullfinch Cl HORL RH6 279 P3
SEV TN13 246 E8
Bullfinch Dene SEV TN13 246 E8
Bullfinch La SEV TN13 246 F8
Bullfinch Rd SAND/SEL CR2 224 C6
Bullhead Rd BORE WD6 75 P8
Bull Hl EYN DA4 210 B4
LHD/OX KT22 236 F7
Bullivant Cl RDART DA2 188 F1
Bullivant St POP/IOD E14 141 H9
Bull La CFSP/GDCR SL9 110 A2
CHST BR7 184 G10
DAGE RM10 124 C8
RGUE GU4 250 C2
STALE/WH AL4 20 F5
UED N18 99 M6
Bullock's La HERT/BAY SG13 25 K7
Bull Pln HERT/WAT SG14 25 L5
Bull Rd HARP AL5 20 A3
SRTFD E15 141 L4
Bullrush Cl CAR SM5 201 P9
CROY/NA CR0 203 M6
HAT AL10 40 E5
Bullrush Gv UX/CGN UB8 131 M6
Bulls Aly MORT/ESHN SW14 * 156 A9
Bull's Br NWDGN UB2 153 H2
Bulls Bridge Centre
HYS/HAR UB3 * 152 G2
Bulls Bridge Rd NWDGN UB2 153 J2
Bullsbrook Rd YEAD UB4 133 K10
Bull's Cross EN EN1 79 P2
Bulls Cross Ride CHESW EN7 61 P10
ENC/FH EN2 79 P1
Bull's Gdns CHEL SW3 15 P5
Bullsland Gdns
RKW/CH/CXG WD3 70 E10
Bullsland La RKW/CH/CXG WD3 90 E1
Bulls La BRKMPK AL9 41 H10
Bullsmoor Cl CHES/WCR EN8 80 B1
Bullsmoor Gdns CHES/WCR EN8 80 A1
Bullsmoor La ENC/FH EN2 79 P1
CHES/WCR EN8 80 A1
PEND EN3 80 C1
Bullsmoor Ride CHES/WCR EN8 80 B1
Bullsmoor Wy CHES/WCR EN8 80 A1
Bull Stag Gn BRKMPK AL9 40 F2
Bullswater Common Rd
CHOB/PIR GU24 248 F1
Bullswater La CHOB/PIR GU24 248 F1
Bullwell Crs CHES/WCR EN8 62 D5
Bull Yd GVE DA12 * 190 E2
PECK SE15 159 P7
Bulmer Gdns
KTN/HRWW/WS HA3 115 J5
Bulmer Ms NTGHL W11 8 E9
Bulstrode Av HSLW TW3 153 N9
Bulstrode Cl KGLGY WD4 53 H5
Bulstrode Gdns HSLW TW3 153 P9
Bulstrode La KGLGY WD4 53 H5
Bulstrode Pl MHST W1U 10 D4
Bulstrode Rd HSLW TW3 153 P9
Bulstrode St MHST W1U 10 D5
Bulstrode Wy CFSP/GDCR SL9 110 A3
Bulwer Court Rd WAN E11 121 J6
Bulwer Gdns BAR EN5 77 M8
Bulwer Rd BAR EN5 77 L8
UED N18 99 M5
WAN E11 121 J6
Bulwer St SHB W12 136 F10
Bumbles Green La WAB EN9 63 N1
Bunbury Wy EW KT17 238 E2
Bunby Rd SLN SL2 129 L2
Bunce Common Rd REIG RH2 274 B7
Bunce Dr CTHM CR3 241 L9
Buncefield Terminal HHNE HP2 * 36 E4
Bunces Cl WDSR SL4 148 G4
Bunces La WFD IG8 101 L8
Bundys Wy STA TW18 173 J9
Bungalow Rd SNWD SE25 203 M4
The Bungalows
RYLN/HDSTN HA2 * 113 N8
STRHM/NOR SW16 180 C10
WTHK RM20 * 166 F5
Bunhill Rw STLK EC1Y 12 G1
Bunhouse Pl BGVA SW1W 16 C7
Bunker's Hl BELV DA17 164 B3
GLDGN NW11 117 M5
SCUP DA14 186 A6
Bunkers La HHS/BOV HP3 54 B1
Bunning Wy HOLWY N7 5 M3
Bunnsfield WGCE AL7 23 M4
Bunn's La MLHL NW7 96 B7
Bunny Hl GVE DA12 * 191 P9
Bunsen St BOW E3 140 D4
Bunten Meade SL SL1 128 G10
Buntingbridge Rd BARK/HLT IG6 122 G3
Bunting Cl ED N9 100 C2
MTCM CR4 202 A5
Bunton St WOOL/PLUM SE18 162 D2
Bunyan Cl CRAWW RH11 283 H10
Bunyan Rd WALTH E17 120 D1
Bunyard Dr WOKN/KNAP GU21 214 F10
Burbage Cl CHES/WCR EN8 62 D7
HYS/HAR UB3 132 E8
STHWK SE1 18 G4
Burbage Rd HNHL SE24 181 L2
Burbeach Cl CRAWW RH11 283 L10
Burberry Cl NWMAL KT3 200 B2
Burbidge Rd SHPTN TW17 196 B4
Burbridge Wy TOTM N17 99 P10
Burcham St POP/IOD E14 140 G8
Burcharbro Rd ABYW SE2 163 N5
Burchell Ct BUSH WD23 94 B1
Burchell Rd LEY E10 120 G6
PECK SE15 160 A7
Burcher Gale Gv PECK SE15 159 N6
Burchets Hollow SHGR GU5 270 E10
Burchetts Wy SHPTN TW17 196 C6
Burchwall Cl CRW RM5 104 D8
Burcote WEY KT13 216 E3
Burcote Rd WAND/EARL SW18 179 N4
Burcott Gdns ADL/WDHM KT15 215 N3
Burcott Rd PUR/KEN CR8 223 H10
Burden Cl BTFD TW8 155 H4
Burdenshot Hl RGUW GU3 249 M1
Burdenshott Av
RCHPK/HAM TW10 155 N10
Burdenshott Rd RGUW GU3 249 P3
Burden Wy GUW GU2 249 N5
WAN E11 121 N7
Burder Cl IS N1 7 K1
Burder Rd IS N1 7 K1
Burdett Av GVE DA12 191 P7
RYNPK SW20 200 D1
Burdett Cl CRAWE RH10 284 E8
HNWL W7 * 134 E10
SCUP DA14 185 P8
Burdett Rd BOW E3 140 E6
CROY/NA CR0 203 L6
POP/IOD E14 140 E8
RCH/KEW TW9 155 L8
Burdetts Rd DAGW RM9 144 A3
Burdock Cl CROY/NA CR0 204 C8
LTWR GU18 212 A7
Burdock Rd TOTM N17 119 P1
Burdon La BELMT SM2 221 K7
Burdon Pk BELMT SM2 221 J5
Bure TIL RM18 169 M2
Burfield Cl HAT AL10 40 D2
TOOT SW17 179 M7
Burfield Dr WARL CR6 242 B5
Burfield Rd RKW/CH/CXG WD3 70 E9
WDSR SL4 171 M3
Burford Cl BARK/HLT IG6 122 F2
BCTR RM8 123 M8
HGDN/ICK UB10 111 P9
Burford Gdns HOD EN11 44 G2
PLMGR N13 98 G4
SL SL1 128 B7
Burford La EW KT17 220 F7
Burford Rd BMLY BR1 206 B4
BTFD TW8 155 K4
CAT SE6 182 E5
EHAM E6 142 B5
SRTFD E15 141 J2
SUT SM1 201 K9
WPK KT4 200 D7
Burford St HOD EN11 44 F3
Burford Wk FUL/PGN SW6 * 157 L6
Burford Wy CROY/NA CR0 225 H4
Burgage Ct WARE SG12 * 26 C2
Burgage La WARE SG12 26 C2
Burgate Cl DART DA1 164 G9
Burges Cl EMPK RM11 125 N4
Burges Gv BARN SW13 156 E6
Burges Rd EHAM E6 142 D2
STA TW18 173 K9
Burgess Av CDALE/KGS NW9 116 A4
Burgess Cl CHESW EN7 61 K1
FELT TW13 175 M7
Burgess Hl CRICK NW2 117 K9
Burgess Ms WIM/MER SW19 179 L9
Burgess Rd SRTFD E15 121 K9
SUT SM1 221 L1
Burgess St POP/IOD E14 140 F7
Burgess Wood Rd BEAC HP9 88 B9
Burgess Wood Rd South
BEAC HP9 88 A10
Burge St STHWK SE1 19 H4
Burges Wy STA TW18 173 K8
Burgett Rd SL SL1 148 G2
Burgh Cl CRAWE RH10 284 E4
Burghfield EW KT17 238 C1
Burghfield Rd MEO DA13 190 C10
Burgh Heath Rd EW KT17 238 D2
Burghill Rd SYD SE26 182 C7
Burghley Av BORE WD6 75 P9
NWMAL KT3 200 A1
Burghley Hall Cl
WIM/MER SW19 * 179 H4
Burghley Pl MTCM CR4 202 A4
Burghley Rd CDW/CHF RM16 167 J2
CEND/HSY/T N8 119 H1
KTTN NW5 118 C9
WAN E11 * 121 K6
WIM/MER SW19 178 G7
Burgh Mt BNSTD SM7 239 J1
Burgh St IS N1 6 E7
Burgh Wd BNSTD SM7 239 H1
Burgon St BLKFR EC4V 12 D6
Burgos Cl CROY/NA CR0 223 H3
Burgos Gv GNWCH SE10 160 G7
Burgoyne Rd BRXN/ST SW9 158 G9
FSBYPK N4 119 J4
SNWD SE25 203 N4
SUN TW16 174 G9
Burgundy Cft WGCE AL7 23 J7
Burham Cl PGE/AN SE20 182 B10
Burhill Gv PIN HA5 93 M10
Burhill Rd WOT/HER KT12 217 J5
WOT/HER KT12 217 K3
Burke Cl PUT/ROE SW15 156 B10
Burkes Cl BEAC HP9 108 A1
Burkes Ct BEAC HP9 * 88 C8
Burkes Crs BEAC HP9 88 C9
Burkes Rd BEAC HP9 108 B1
Burke St CAN/RD E16 141 L7
Burket Cl NWDGN UB2 153 M3
Burland Rd BRWN CM15 107 J2
BTSEA SW11 180 A1
CRW RM5 104 D7
Burlands CRAWW RH11 283 K4
Burlea Cl WOT/HER KT12 217 J2
Burleigh Av BFN/LL DA15 185 J1
WLGTN SM6 202 B10
Burleigh Cl ADL/WDHM KT15 215 L2
Burleigh Ct BUSH WD23 * 73 M8
Burleigh Gdns ASHF TW15 174 D8
STHGT/OAK N14 98 D2
WOKN/KNAP GU21 232 C3
Burleigh Md BRKMPK AL9 40 F2
Burleigh Pde STHGT/OAK N14 * 98 E2
Burleigh Pk COB KT11 217 M8
Burleigh Pl PUT/ROE SW15 178 G1
Burleigh Rd ADL/WDHM KT15 215 L1
CHEAM SM3 201 H8
CHES/WCR EN8 * 62 D8
EN EN1 79 M8
HERT/BAY SG13 25 P4
HGDN/ICK UB10 132 C3
HHNE HP2 36 D7
STAL AL1 38 G6
Burleigh St COVGDN WC2E 11 M7
Burleigh Wk CAT SE6 183 H4
Burleigh Wy ENC/FH EN2 79 L7
POTB/CUF EN6 60 F6
Burley Cl CHING E4 100 F6
STRHM/NOR SW16 202 E2
Burley Hl HLWE CM17 47 N2
Burley Rd CAN/RD E16 141 P8
Burleys Rd CRAWE RH10 284 E7
Burlingham Cl RGUE GU4 250 G8
Burlings La RSEV TN14 245 J3
Burlington Ar CONDST W1S 10 G8
Burlington Av RCH/KEW TW9 155 M7
ROMW/RG RM7 124 C4
SL SL1 149 K1
Burlington Cl EBED/NFELT TW14 174 E3
EHAM E6 142 B8
MV/WKIL W9 8 E1
ORP BR6 206 E9
PIN HA5 113 J1
Burlington Ct SL SL1 149 K1
Burlington Gdns ACT W3 135 P10
CHDH RM6 123 P5
CHSWK W4 155 P4
CONDST W1S 10 G8
Burlington La CHSWK W4 155 P6
CHSWK W4 156 B5
Burlington Ms ACT W3 135 P10
Burlington Pde CRICK NW2 * 116 G8
Burlington Pl FUL/PGN SW6 157 H8
REIG RH2 257 K9
WFD IG8 101 M4
Burlington Ri EBAR EN4 97 P2
Burlington Rd CHSWK W4 * 155 P4
ENC/FH EN2 79 L5
FUL/PGN SW6 157 H8
ISLW TW7 154 C7
MUSWH N10 118 B1
NWMAL KT3 200 C4
SL SL1 149 K1
THHTH CR7 203 K2
TOTM N17 99 P9
Burman Cl RDART DA2 188 B3
Burma Rd CHERT KT16 193 L9
STNW/STAM N16 119 L9
Burma Ter NRWD SE19 * 181 M8
Burmester Rd TOOT SW17 179 M6
Burnaby Crs CHSWK W4 155 N5
Burnaby Gdns CHSWK W4 155 N5
Burnaby Rd GVW DA11 190 B3
Burnaby St WBPTN SW10 157 M6
Burnbrae Cl NFNCH/WDSPK N12 97 L7
Burnbury Rd BAL SW12 180 D4
Burn Cl ADL/WDHM KT15 215 N1
GSTN WD25 * 74 C8
LHD/OX KT22 236 B1
Burncroft Av PEND EN3 80 B6
Burndell Wy YEAD UB4 133 L7
Burnell Av RCHPK/HAM TW10 177 H8
WELL DA16 163 K8
Burnell Gdns STAN HA7 95 J10
Burnell Rd SUT SM1 221 L1
Burnell Wk RBRW/HUT CM13 107 H7
STHWK SE1 * 19 M7
Burnels Av EHAM E6 142 D5
Burness Cl HOLWY N7 5 N1
UX/CGN UB8 131 N4
Burne St CAMTN NW1 9 N3
Burnet Av GU GU1 250 E7
Burnet Cl CHOB/PIR GU24 212 D9
HHS/BOV HP3 35 P7
HOM E9 120 B10
Burnet Gv HOR/WEW KT19 219 P9
Burnett La BARK/HLT IG6 102 E8
Burnett Pk HLWW/ROY CM19 46 E6
Burnett Rd ERITH DA8 165 L5
Burnett Sq HERT/WAT SG14 24 G4
Burnetts Rd WDSR SL4 148 D7
Burney Av BRYLDS KT5 199 L5
Burney Cl LHD/OX KT22 254 B1
Burney Dr LOU IG10 82 F7
Burney Rd RDKG RH5 254 F7
Burney St GNWCH SE10 161 H6
Burnfoot Av FUL/PGN SW6 157 H7
Burnham Av BEAC HP9 108 F1
HGDN/ICK UB10 112 D9
Burnham Cl EN EN1 79 M4
KTN/HRWW/WS HA3 114 F2
MLHL NW7 96 D8
STHWK SE1 19 M7
WDSR SL4 148 C8
WOKN/KNAP GU21 231 J4
Burnham Crs DART DA1 165 K10
WAN E11 121 P2
Burnham Dr REIG RH2 257 K9
WPK KT4 200 G9
Burnham Gdns CROY/NA CR0 203 N7
HSLWW TW4 153 J7
HYS/HAR UB3 152 E2
Burnham La SL SL1 128 D8
Burnham Rd BEAC HP9 108 D4
CHING E4 100 E6
DAGW RM9 143 L2
DART DA1 187 L1
MRDN SM4 201 L5
ROMW/RG RM7 124 D1
SCUP DA14 185 P6
STAL AL1 38 F6
WOKN/KNAP GU21 231 J4
Burnhams Rd GT/LBKH KT23 235 N10
Burnham St BETH E2 140 B5
KUTN/CMB KT2 199 M1
Burnham Ter DART DA1 * 187 L1
Burnham Wy SYD SE26 182 E8
WEA W13 154 G3
Burnhill Rd BECK BR3 204 F2
Burnley Cl OXHEY WD19 93 K6
Burnley Rd BRXN/ST SW9 158 G8
WLSDN NW10 116 C10
WTHK RM20 166 E7
Burnsall Pl HARP AL5 20 B5
Burnsall St CHEL SW3 15 P8
Burns Av BFN/LL DA15 185 L2
CHDH RM6 123 M5
EBED/NFELT TW14 175 H2
STHL UB1 133 P9
Burns Cl CAR SM5 222 B5
ERITH DA8 164 C7
WALTH E17 121 H2
WELL DA16 163 J7
WIM/MER SW19 179 N9
YEAD UB4 133 H7
Burns Dr BNSTD SM7 221 H10
HHNE HP2 36 C1
Burnside ASHTD KT21 237 L4
HERT/WAT SG14 25 H6
HOD EN11 44 E3
SBW CM21 29 N1
STAL AL1 38 G8
Burnside Av CHING E4 100 E7
Burnside Cl BAR EN5 77 K7
BERM/RHTH SE16 140 C10
TWK TW1 176 F2
Burnside Crs ALP/SUD HA0 135 J3
Burnside Rd BCTR RM8 123 M7
Burns Pl TIL RM18 168 E7
Burns Rd ALP/SUD HA0 135 K4
BTSEA SW11 158 A8
CRAWE RH10 284 D5
WEA W13 * 154 G1
WLSDN NW10 136 C3
Burns Wy HEST TW5 153 L7
Burnt Ash Hl LEE/GVPK SE12 183 L2
Burnt Ash La BMLY BR1 183 M9
Burnt Ash Rd LEE/GVPK SE12 183 L2
Burnt Common Cl
RPLY/SEND GU23 251 J1
Burntcommon La
RPLY/SEND GU23 251 K1
Burntfarm Ride ENC/FH EN2 61 J10
Burnt House La HORS RH12 282 D6
RDART DA2 187 N7
Burnthwaite Rd FUL/PGN SW6 157 J6
Burnt Ml HLW CM20 28 F9
Burntmill Cl HLW CM20 28 F8
Burntmill La HLW CM20 28 F8
Burnt Oak Broadway EDGW HA8 95 N9
Burnt Oak Flds EDGW HA8 95 P9
Burnt Oak La BFN/LL DA15 185 L3
RDKG RH5 278 B7
Burnt Pollard La LTWR GU18 212 D6
Burntwood Av EMPK RM11 125 L4
Burntwood Cl CTHM CR3 241 P7
WAND/EARL SW18 * 179 N4
Burntwood Grange Rd
WAND/EARL SW18 179 N4
Burntwood Gv SEV TN13 265 J3
Burntwood La CTHM CR3 241 P7
TOOT SW17 179 N5
Burntwood Rd SEV TN13 265 J4
Burntwood Vw NRWD SE19 * 181 N8
Burnway EMPK RM11 125 M5
Burnwood Park Rd
WOT/HER KT12 217 J1
Buross St WCHPL E1 140 A8
Burpham Cl YEAD UB4 133 L7
Burpham La RGUE GU4 250 D6
Burrage Gv WOOL/PLUM SE18 162 F3
Burrage Pl WOOL/PLUM SE18 162 E4
Burrage Rd WOOL/PLUM SE18 162 F3
Burrard Rd CAN/RD E16 141 M8
KIL/WHAMP NW6 117 K10
Burr Bank Ter RDART DA2 * 187 K7
Burr Cl BXLYHN DA7 164 A9
LCOL/BKTW AL2 57 K3
WAP E1W 13 N9
Burrell Cl CROY/NA CR0 204 D6
EDGW HA8 95 N3
Burrell Rw BECK BR3 204 F2
Burrell St STHWK SE1 12 C9
The Burrell DORK RH4 272 B3
Burrels Whf POP/IOD E14 160 G4
The Burren AMS HP6 * 69 J3
Burrfield Dr STMC/STPC BR5 207 N5
Burr Hill La CHOB/PIR GU24 213 L5
Burritt Rd KUT/HW KT1 199 M2
Burroughs Cottages
POP/IOD E14 * 140 D7
Burroughs Gdns HDN NW4 116 E2
The Burroughs HDN NW4 116 E2
Burroway Rd DTCH/LGLY SL3 150 E2
Burrowfield WGCE AL7 22 G7
Burrow Gn CHIG IG7 103 J6
Burrow Hill Gn CHOB/PIR GU24 213 J5
Burrow Rd CHIG IG7 103 K6
EDUL SE22 159 M10
Burrows Cha WAB EN9 81 J2
Burrows Cl GT/LBKH KT23 235 N10
GUW GU2 249 L9
Burrows Cross SHGR GU5 270 D7
Burrows Hill Cl
STWL/WRAY TW19 151 M10
Burrows La SHGR GU5 270 D6
Burrows Ms STHWK SE1 18 C1
Burrows Rd WLSDN NW10 136 F5
Burr Rd WAND/EARL SW18 179 K4
Bursar St STHWK SE1 * 13 J10
Bursdon Cl BFN/LL DA15 185 J5
Burses Wy RBRW/HUT CM13 107 N1
Bursland Rd PEND EN3 80 C8
Burslem Av BARK/HLT IG6 103 K7
Burslem St WCHPL E1 13 P6
WCHPL E1 * 140 A8
Burstead Cl COB KT11 217 L9
Burstock Rd PUT/ROE SW15 157 H10
Burston Dr LCOL/BKTW AL2 56 B4
Burston Rd PUT/ROE SW15 178 G1
Burstow Rd RYNPK SW20 201 H1
Burtenshaw Rd THDIT KT7 198 F7
Burtley Cl FSBYPK N4 119 K6
Burton Av WATW WD18 73 H8
Burton Bank IS N1 * 6 G4
Burton Cl CHSGTN KT9 219 J4
HORL RH6 280 B5
THHTH CR7 203 L3
Burton Dr PEND EN3 80 F3
RGUW GU3 248 F5
Burton Gdns HEST TW5 153 N7
Burton Gv WALW SE17 18 G8
Burtonhole Cl MLHL NW7 96 G5
Burtonhole La MLHL NW7 96 G6
Burton La BRXN/ST SW9 * 159 H8
CHESW EN7 61 M4
Burton Ms BGVA SW1W 16 D6
Burton Pl STPAN WC1H 11 K1
Burton Rd BRXN/ST SW9 159 J8
KIL/WHAMP NW6 2 D4
KUTN/CMB KT2 177 K10
LOU IG10 82 F8
SWFD E18 121 N1
Burtons Ct SRTFD E15 141 J2
Burtons La CSTG HP8 70 C9
Burton's Rd HPTN TW12 176 A7
Burton St STPAN WC1H 11 K1
Burton's Wy CSTG HP8 69 P6
Burton Wy WDSR SL4 148 D9
Burt Rd CAN/RD E16 141 P10
Burtwell La DUL SE21 181 L7
Burvale Ct WATW WD18 73 J7
Burwash Ct STMC/STPC BR5 207 M5
Burwash Rd CRAWE RH10 284 B8
WOOL/PLUM SE18 162 G4
Burway Crs CHERT KT16 195 K4
Burwell Av GFD/PVL UB6 134 D1
Burwell Cl WCHPL E1 140 A8
Burwell Rd LEY E10 120 D6
Burwood Av HAYES BR2 205 N9
PIN HA5 113 K3
PUR/KEN CR8 223 J10
Burwood Cl GU GU1 250 F9
REIG RH2 257 N10
SURB KT6 199 M8
WOT/HER KT12 217 K3
Burwood Gdns RAIN RM13 144 G5
Burwood Pl BAY/PAD W2 9 P5
EBAR EN4 77 M5
Burwood Rd WEY KT13 216 E4
WOT/HER KT12 217 H3
Bury Av RSLP HA4 112 D4
YEAD UB4 132 F4
Bury Cl BERM/RHTH SE16 140 C10
WOKN/KNAP GU21 232 A2
Bury Ct HDTCH EC3A 13 K5
Burycroft WGCW AL8 23 H2
Burydell La LCOL/BKTW AL2 56 C3
Bury Farm AMSS HP7 69 H6
Bury Flds GUW GU2 267 P2
Buryfield Wy WARE SG12 26 B1
Bury Gn HHW HP1 35 M5
STALE/WH AL4 21 H3
Bury Green Rd CHESW EN7 61 P8
CHESW EN7 62 A6
Bury Gv MRDN SM4 201 L5
Bury Hl HHW HP1 35 M5
Bury Hill Cl HHW HP1 35 M5
Bury Holme BROX EN10 44 E9
Bury La CSHM HP5 50 G7
EPP CM16 64 G6
RKW/CH/CXG WD3 91 N2
WOKN/KNAP GU21 231 P2
Bury Mdw RKW/CH/CXG WD3 91 N2
Bury Pl NOXST/BSQ WC1A 11 L4
Bury Ri HHS/BOV HP3 52 G1
Bury Rd CHING E4 81 J8
DAGE RM10 124 D10
EPP CM16 65 H7
HAT AL10 40 F3
HHW HP1 35 M6
HLWE CM17 29 M7
WDGN N22 99 H10
Buryside Cl GNTH/NBYPK IG2 123 J3
Bury St ED N9 99 N1
GUW GU2 267 P2
HDTCH EC3A 13 K6
RSLP HA4 112 E4
STJS SW1Y 10 G9
Bury St West ED N9 99 M1
The Bury CSHM HP5 * 50 G8
Bury Wk CHEL SW3 15 N6
Burywick HARP AL5 20 A6
Busby Pl KTTN NW5 5 J1
Busch Cl ISLW TW7 154 G7
Bushbaby Cl STHWK SE1 19 J4
Bushbarns CHESW EN7 61 P5
Bushberry Rd HOM E9 140 D1
Bushbury La BRKHM/BTCW RH3 273 M5
Bushby Av BROX EN10 44 E8
Bush Cl ADL/WDHM KT15 215 M2
GNTH/NBYPK IG2 122 G3
Bush Cottages
WAND/EARL SW18 179 K1
Bushell Cl BRXS/STRHM SW2 180 G5
Bushell Gn BUSH WD23 94 C3
Bushell Wy CHST BR7 184 D8
Bush Elms Rd EMPK RM11 125 H5
Bushetts Gv REDH RH1 258 C5
Bushey Av STMC/STPC BR5 206 G7
SWFD E18 121 L1
Bushey Cl CHING E4 101 H4
HGDN/ICK UB10 112 B7
PUR/KEN CR8 241 N2
WGCE AL7 23 L6
Bushey Cft HLWS CM18 47 H3
OXTED RH8 261 H6
Bushey Gn WGCE AL7 23 L6
Bushey Grove Rd BUSH WD23 73 M8
Bushey Hall Dr BUSH WD23 73 M8
Bushey Hall Pk BUSH WD23 * 73 M8
Bushey Hall Rd BUSH WD23 73 M8
Bushey Hill Rd CMBW SE5 159 N7
Bushey La SUT SM1 201 K10
Bushey Lees BFN/LL DA15 * 185 J2
Bushey Ley WGCE AL7 23 L6
Busheymill Br WATN WD24 73 M4
Bushey Mill Crs WATN WD24 73 K3
Bushey Mill La BUSH WD23 73 N6
WATN WD24 73 K3
Bushey Rd CROY/NA CR0 204 F9
HGDN/ICK UB10 112 B7
HYS/HAR UB3 152 F3
PLSTW E13 141 P4
RYNPK SW20 200 F2
SEVS/STOTM N15 119 M4
SUT SM1 221 K1
Bushey Wy BECK BR3 205 J6
Bushfield Cl EDGW HA8 95 N3
Bushfield Crs EDGW HA8 95 N3
Bushfield Dr REDH RH1 276 B5
Bushfield Rd HHS/BOV HP3 52 F1
Bushfields LOU IG10 82 D9
Bush Gv CDALE/KGS NW9 115 P5
STAN HA7 95 J9
Bushgrove Rd BCTR RM8 123 N9
Bush Hall La BRKMPK AL9 40 G1
Bush Hl WCHMH N21 99 K1
Bush Hill Pde ED N9 99 L1
Bush Hill Rd KTN/HRWW/WS HA3 115 L4
WCHMH N21 99 L1
Bush House WOOL/PLUM SE18 * 162 B6
Bush La CANST EC4R 12 G7
RPLY/SEND GU23 232 G10
Bushmead Cl SEVS/STOTM N15 * 119 N2
Bushmoor Crs WOOL/PLUM SE18 162 E7
Bushnell Rd TOOT SW17 180 C5
Bush Rd BKHH IG9 102 A5
DEPT SE8 160 C3
HACK E8 140 A3
RCH/KEW TW9 155 L5
SHPTN TW17 196 A5
WAN E11 121 L5
Bushway BCTR RM8 123 N9
Bushwood WAN E11 121 L6
Bushwood Cl BRKMPK AL9 40 E9
Bushwood Dr STHWK SE1 19 M6
Bushwood Rd RCH/KEW TW9 155 M5
Bushy Hill Dr GU GU1 250 F9
Bushy Lea CHONG CM5 67 P5
Bushy Park Gdns HPTN TW12 176 C8
Bushy Park Rd TEDD TW11 176 G10
Bushy Rd LHD/OX KT22 236 A8
TEDD TW11 176 D9
Bushy Shaw ASHTD KT21 237 H3
Buslins La CSHM HP5 50 D4
Butcher Rw WAP E1W 140 C8
Butchers La BGR/WK TN15 211 J9
Butchers Rd CAN/RD E16 141 M8
Butchers Yd ORP BR6 226 D7
Bute Av RCHPK/HAM TW10 177 K5
Bute Gdns HMSMTH W6 156 G3
RCHPK/HAM TW10 * 177 K4
WLGTN SM6 222 D2
Bute Gdns West WLGTN SM6 222 D2
Bute Ms GLDGN NW11 117 L3
Bute Rd BARK/HLT IG6 122 E3
CROY/NA CR0 203 H8
WLGTN SM6 222 D1
Bute St SKENS SW7 15 L5
Bute Wk IS N1 6 G2
Butler Av HRW HA1 114 C5
Butler Cl EDGW HA8 95 N10
Butler Rd BCTR RM8 123 L9
HRW HA1 114 B5
WLSDN NW10 136 C2
Butlers Cl AMS HP6 68 F3
HSLWW TW4 153 N10
WDSR SL4 148 C8
Butlers & Colonial Whf
STHWK SE1 19 M1
Butlers Court Rd BEAC HP9 88 C10
Butlers Dene Rd CTHM CR3 242 F6
Butlers Dr CHING E4 81 H4
Butlers Hl EHSLY KT24 252 C6
Butlers Pl BGR/WK TN15 * 211 K10
Butler St BETH E2 * 140 B5
HGDN/ICK UB10 132 C6
Buttell Cl GRAYS RM17 168 A4
Buttercross La EPP CM16 * 65 K6
Buttercup Cl HARH RM3 105 L9
HAT AL10 22 C10
NTHLT UB5 133 N1
Buttercup Sq
STWL/WRAY TW19 * 173 N4
Butterfield Cl BERM/RHTH SE16 19 P2
TOTM N17 99 K7
TWK TW1 176 E2
Butterfield House CHARL SE7 * 162 B6
Butterfield La STAL AL1 38 D10
Butterfield Rd STALE/WH AL4 21 H4
Butterfields WALTH E17 121 H3
Butterfield Sq EHAM E6 142 C8
Butterfly Av DART DA1 187 N6
Butterfly La BORE WD6 74 G7
ELTH/MOT SE9 184 E2
Butterfly Wk CMBW SE5 * 159 L7
WARL CR6 242 B6
Butter Hl CAR SM5 202 B10
DORK RH4 272 F2
Butteridges Cl DAGW RM9 144 A3
Butterly Av DART DA1 * 187 N5
Buttermere Av SL SL1 128 B7
Buttermere Cl
EBED/NFELT TW14 174 G4
MRDN SM4 200 G6
SRTFD E15 121 J9
STAL AL1 38 G7
STHWK SE1 19 L6
Buttermere Dr PUT/ROE SW15 179 H1
Buttermere Gdns PUR/KEN CR8 223 L10
Buttermere Pl GSTN WD25 * 55 H9
Buttermere Rd STMC/STPC BR5 207 N4
Buttermere Wk HACK E8 7 M2
Buttermere Wy EGH TW20 172 E10
Buttersweet Ri SBW CM21 29 P2
Butterwick GSTN WD25 73 M2
HMSMTH W6 156 F3
Butterworth Gdns WFD IG8 101 M7
Buttesland St IS N1 7 H9
Buttfield Cl DAGE RM10 144 C1
Butt Field Vw STAL AL1 38 B10
Buttlehide RKW/CH/CXG WD3 90 G6
Buttmarsh Cl WOOL/PLUM SE18 162 E4
Buttondene Crs BROX EN10 44 G8
Button Rd GRAYS RM17 167 L3
Button St SWLY BR8 209 K4
Buttsbury Rd IL IG1 122 F10
Butts Cl CRAWW RH11 283 L6
Butts Crs FELT TW13 175 P6
Butts End HHW HP1 35 K5
Butts Green Rd EMPK RM11 125 L4
Buttsmead NTHWD HA6 92 D8
Butts Piece NTHLT UB5 133 J4
Butts Rd BMLY BR1 183 K8
WOKN/KNAP GU21 232 B4
The Butts BROX EN10 44 D10
BTFD TW8 155 J5
RSEV TN14 247 J3
Buxhall Crs HOM E9 140 E1
Buxted Rd EDUL SE22 159 M10
HACK E8 7 L3
NFNCH/WDSPK N12 97 P6
Buxton Av CTHM CR3 241 M7
Buxton Cl HOR/WEW KT19 219 N7
STALE/WH AL4 39 J3
WFD IG8 102 A7
Buxton Crs CHEAM SM3 221 H1
Buxton Dr NWMAL KT3 200 A2
WAN E11 121 K2
Buxton Gdns ACT W3 135 N9
Buxton La CTHM CR3 241 M7
Buxton Ms CLAP SW4 158 F8
Buxton Pth OXHEY WD19 * 93 K4
Buxton Rd ARCH N19 118 E6
ASHF TW15 173 N8
CDW/CHF RM16 168 B1
CHING E4 101 J1
CRICK NW2 136 E1
EHAM E6 142 B5
EPP CM16 83 H2
ERITH DA8 164 E6
GNTH/NBYPK IG2 123 H4
MORT/ESHN SW14 156 B9
SRTFD E15 121 K10
THHTH CR7 203 J5
WAB EN9 63 M8
WALTH E17 120 D2
Buxton St WCHPL E1 13 N2
Byam St FUL/PGN SW6 157 M8
Byards Cft STRHM/NOR SW16 202 E1
Bybend Cl SLN SL2 128 G3
Bychurch End TEDD TW11 * 176 E8
Bycliffe Ms GVW DA11 * 190 C3
Bycliffe Ter GVW DA11 * 190 C3
Bycroft Rd STHL UB1 133 P7
Bycroft St PGE/AN SE20 182 C10
Bycroft Wy CRAWE RH10 284 C5
Bycullah Av ENC/FH EN2 79 J7
Bycullah Rd ENC/FH EN2 79 J7
Byde St HERT/WAT SG14 25 K4
Byelands Cl BERM/RHTH SE16 140 C10
Byerley Wy CRAWE RH10 284 F6
Byers Cl POTB/CUF EN6 59 M10
The Bye ACT W3 136 B8
Byewaters WATW WD18 72 E10
Bye Ways WHTN TW2 176 A6
The Byeways BRYLDS KT5 199 M5
The Bye Wy KTN/HRWW/WS HA3 94 D9
The Byeway MORT/ESHN SW14 155 P9
RKW/CH/CXG WD3 91 P3
Byfeld Gdns BARN SW13 156 D7
Byfield WGCW AL8 23 H2
Byfield Cl BERM/RHTH SE16 160 D1
Byfield Ct RBRW/HUT CM13 * 127 P4
Byfield Rd ISLW TW7 154 F9
Byfleet Rd ADL/WDHM KT15 215 N5
COB KT11 216 C8
COB KT11 216 F9
Byford Cl SRTFD E15 141 K2
Bygrove CROY/NA CR0 224 G3
Bygrove Rd WIM/MER SW19 179 N9
Bygrove St POP/IOD E14 140 G8
Byland Cl ABYW SE2 163 L2
CAR SM5 201 N7
STHGT/OAK N14 98 G1
Bylands WOKS/MYFD GU22 232 D4
Byne Rd CAR SM5 201 P9
SYD SE26 182 B9
Bynes Rd SAND/SEL CR2 223 L4
Byng Dr POTB/CUF EN6 59 K7
Bynghams HLWW/ROY CM19 46 C3
Byng Pl GWRST WC1E 11 K2
Byng Rd BAR EN5 76 G7
Byng St POP/IOD E14 160 F1
Bynon Av BXLYHN DA7 163 P9
Byrd Rd CRAWW RH11 283 J10
Byrefield Rd GUW GU2 249 L7
Byre Rd STHGT/OAK N14 78 C10
Byrne Rd BAL SW12 180 C4
Byron Av BORE WD6 75 M9
CDALE/KGS NW9 115 N2
COUL/CHIP CR5 240 F1
HSLWW TW4 153 J8
MNPK E12 142 B1
NWMAL KT3 200 D5
SUT SM1 221 N1
SWFD E18 121 L1
WATN WD24 73 L5
Byron Av East SUT SM1 221 N1
Byron Cl CHESW EN7 61 N3
CRAWE RH10 284 C6
HACK E8 7 N5
HPTN TW12 175 N7
PGE/AN SE20 * 204 A3
STRHM/NOR SW16 180 F9
SYD SE26 * 182 D7
THMD SE28 143 M10

WOKN/KNAP GU21 231 K3
WOT/HER KT12 197 M8
Byron Ct ENC/FH EN2 79 J6
WDSR SL4 148 F9
Byron Dr EFNCH N2 117 N4
ERITH DA8 164 C6
Byron Gdns SUT SM1 221 N1
TIL RM18 168 F7
Byron Hill Rd RYLN/HDSTN HA2 114 D7
Byron Ms HAMP NW3 117 P10
MV/WKIL W9 8 F1
Byron Pde HGDN/ICK UB10 * 132 C6
Byron Pl LHD/OX KT22 236 C8
Byron Rd ADL/WDHM KT15 215 N1
ALP/SUD HA0 115 H7
CRICK NW2 116 E7
DART DA1 166 A10
EA W5 135 L10
HRW HA1 114 D4
KTN/HRWW/WS HA3 94 E10
KTN/HRWW/WS HA3 114 E1
MLHL NW7 96 D6
SAND/SEL CR2 224 A6
WALTH E17 120 F1
Byron St POP/IOD E14 141 H8
Byron Ter ED N9 * 100 B1
Byron Wy HARH RM3 105 K9
NTHLT UB5 133 M5
WDR/YW UB7 152 A3
YEAD UB4 132 G6
Bysouth Cl CLAY IG5 102 E9
SEVS/STOTM N15 119 L2
By The Wd OXHEY WD19 93 M3
Bythorn St BRXN/ST SW9 158 G9
Byton Rd TOOT SW17 180 A9
Byttom Hl RDKG RH5 255 H3
Byward Av EBED/NFELT TW14 175 K2
Byward St MON EC3R 13 K8
Bywater Pl BERM/RHTH SE16 140 D10
Bywater St CHEL SW3 16 A7
Byways BERK HP4 34 B4
The Byway BELMT SM2 221 N5
HOR/WEW KT19 220 C1
POTB/CUF EN6 59 K9
Bywell Pl GTPST W1W * 10 G4
Bywood Av CROY/NA CR0 204 B6
Bywood Cl PUR/KEN CR8 241 J1
By-Wood End CFSP/GDCR SL9 90 D6

C

Cabbell Pl ADL/WDHM KT15 215 M1
Cabbell St BAY/PAD W2 9 N4
Cabell Rd GUW GU2 249 K9
Caberfeigh Cl REDH RH1 257 P10
Caberfeigh Pl REDH RH1 * 257 N10
Cabinet Wy CHING E4 100 E7
Cable Pl GNWCH SE10 161 H7
Cables Cl ERITH DA8 164 D2
Cable St WCHPL E1 13 P7
Cable Trade Pk CHARL SE7 * 161 M4
Cabot Sq POP/IOD E14 140 F10
Cabot Wy EHAM E6 142 A3
Cabrera Av VW GU25 194 A5
Cabrera Cl VW GU25 193 P6
Cabul Rd BTSEA SW11 157 P8
Caburn Ct CRAWW RH11 283 M9
Caburn Hts CRAWW RH11 283 M9
Cacket's La RSEV TN14 244 G1
The Cackstones CRAWE RH10 * 284 E6
Cactus Cl CMBW SE5 * 159 M8
Cadbury Cl ISLW TW7 154 F7
SUN TW16 174 F10
Cadbury Rd SUN TW16 174 F10
Cadbury Wy BERM/RHTH SE16 19 M5
Caddington Cl EBAR EN4 77 P9
Caddington Rd CRICK NW2 117 H8
Caddis Cl STAN HA7 * 94 E8
Caddy Cl EGH TW20 172 D8
Cade La SEV TN13 265 K4
Cadell Cl BETH E2 7 M8
Cade Rd GNWCH SE10 161 J7
Cader Rd WAND/EARL SW18 179 M2
Cadet Dr STHWK SE1 19 N7
Cadet Pl GNWCH SE10 161 K4
Cadiz Rd DAGE RM10 144 D2
Cadiz St WALW SE17 18 F8
Cadlocks Hl RSEV TN14 228 A6
Cadman Cl BRXN/ST SW9 159 J6
Cadmer Cl NWMAL KT3 200 B4
Cadmore La CHES/WCR EN8 62 E5
Cadmus Cl CLAP SW4 158 E10
Cadogan Av RDART DA2 188 C3
Cadogan Cl HOM E9 * 140 E2
RYLN/HDSTN HA2 114 A9
TEDD TW11 176 D8
Cadogan Ct BELMT SM2 221 L3
Cadogan Gdns CHEL SW3 16 B6
FNCH N3 * 97 L9
SWFD E18 121 N1
WCHMH N21 79 H9
Cadogan Ga KTBR SW1X 16 B5
Cadogan La KTBR SW1X 16 C4
Cadogan Pl KTBR SW1X 16 B3
PUR/KEN CR8 241 K3
Cadogan Rd SURB KT6 199 J5
WOOL/PLUM SE18 162 F2
Cadogan Sq KTBR SW1X 16 B4
Cadogan St CHEL SW3 16 A6
Cadogan Ter HOM E9 140 E1
Cadoxton Av SEVS/STOTM N15 119 N4
Cadwallon Rd ELTH/MOT SE9 184 E5
Caedmon Rd HOLWY N7 118 G9
Caenshill Pl WEY KT13 * 216 B4
Caenshill Rd WEY KT13 216 B4
Caenswood Hl WEY KT13 216 B6
Caenwood Cl WEY KT13 216 B3
Caen Wood Rd ASHTD KT21 237 H4
Caerleon Cl ESH/CLAY KT10 218 G4
SCUP DA14 185 M8
Caernarvon Cl EMPK RM11 125 P6
HHNE HP2 35 N6
MTCM CR4 202 F3
Caernarvon Dr CLAY IG5 102 D9
Caesars Rd STALE/WH AL4 21 J3
Caesars Wk MTCM CR4 202 A5
Caesar's Wy SHPTN TW17 196 E6
Caffins Cl CRAWE RH10 283 P5
Cage Farm Cottages
OXTED RH8 * 260 G10
Cage Pond Rd RAD WD7 57 M9
Cages Wood Dr SLN SL2 108 G9
Cage Yd REIG RH2 * 257 K10
Cahill St STLK EC1Y * 12 F2
Cahir St POP/IOD E14 160 G3
Caillard Rd BF/WBF KT14 215 N7
Cain's La EBED/NFELT TW14 174 E1
Caird St NKENS W10 2 B10
Cairn Av EA W5 135 J10
Cairndale Cl BMLY BR1 183 L10
Cairnfield Av CRICK NW2 116 B8
Cairngorm Cl TEDD TW11 176 F8
Cairns Av WFD IG8 102 C7
Cairns Cl DART DA1 187 L1
STALE/WH AL4 39 J7
Cairns Rd BTSEA SW11 179 P1
Cairn Wy STAN HA7 94 E7
Cairo New Rd CROY/NA CR0 203 J9
Cairo Rd WALTH E17 * 120 F2
Caishowe Rd BORE WD6 75 N5
Caister Cl HHNE HP2 35 P7
Caister Ms BAL SW12 180 C3
Caistor Park Rd SRTFD E15 141 L3
Caistor Rd BAL SW12 180 C3
Caithness Dr EPSOM KT18 220 A10
Caithness Gdns BFN/LL DA15 185 J2
Caithness Rd MTCM CR4 180 C10
WKENS W14 156 G2
Calabria Rd HBRY N5 6 D1
Calais Cl CHESW EN7 61 L2
Calais St CMBW SE5 159 J7
Calbourne Av HCH RM12 125 J10
Calbourne Rd BAL SW12 180 A3
Calbroke Rd SLN SL2 128 E6
Calbury Cl STAL AL1 38 G7
Calcott Cl BRW CM14 106 G2
Calcroft Av SWCM DA10 189 H1
Calcutta Rd TIL RM18 168 C8
Caldbeck WAB EN9 63 J10
Caldbeck Av WPK KT4 200 E9
Caldecot Av CHESW EN7 61 N5
Caldecote Gdns BUSH WD23 74 D10
Caldecote La BUSH WD23 94 E1
Caldecot Rd CMBW SE5 159 K8
Caldecott Wy CLPT E5 120 C8
Caldecot Wy BROX EN10 44 E8
Calder Av BRKMPK AL9 59 L2
GFD/PVL UB6 134 E4
Calder Ct DTCH/LGLY SL3 150 C4
Calderdale Cl CRAWW RH11 283 L9
Calder Gdns EDGW HA8 115 M1
Calderon Rd WAN E11 121 H9
Calder Rd MRDN SM4 201 M5
Caldervale Rd CLAP SW4 180 E1
Calder Wy DTCH/LGLY SL3 151 H9
Calderwood GVE DA12 191 H9
Calderwood St
WOOL/PLUM SE18 162 D3
Caldew St CMBW SE5 159 L6
Caldicote Gn CDALE/KGS NW9 * 116 B4
Caldwell Rd BFOR GU20 212 D2
OXHEY WD19 93 L5
Caldwell St BRXN/ST SW9 158 G6
Caldy Rd BELV DA17 164 C2
Caldy Wk IS N1 6 F2
Caledonian Cl GDMY/SEVK IG3 * 123 L6
Caledonian Rd HOLWY N7 118 G10
IS N1 5 N4
Caledonian Sq CAMTN NW1 5 J1
Caledonian Wy HORL RH6 * 280 C7
Caledonian Wharf Rd
POP/IOD E14 161 J3
Caledonia Rd STWL/WRAY TW19 173 P4
Caledonia St IS N1 5 M8
Caledon Pl RGUE GU4 250 D7
Caledon Rd BEAC HP9 88 D8
EHAM E6 142 C3
LCOL/BKTW AL2 57 H2
WLGTN SM6 222 B1
Cale St CHEL SW3 15 N7
Calfstock La EYN DA4 209 M4
Calidore Cl BRXS/STRHM SW2 * 180 G2
California Cl BELMT SM2 221 K6
California La BUSH WD23 94 C2
California Rd NWMAL KT3 199 P4
Caling Cft HART DA3 211 L8
Caliph Cl GVE DA12 191 J6
Callaby Ter IS N1 6 G2
Callaghan Cl LEW SE13 161 K10
Callaghan Cottages WCHPL E1 * 140 B7
Callander Rd CAT SE6 182 G5
The Callanders BUSH WD23 * 94 D2
Callan Gv SOCK/AV RM15 147 H9
Callard Av PLMGR N13 99 J5
Callcott Rd KIL/WHAMP NW6 2 C4
Callcott St KENS W8 8 E9
Callendar Rd SKENS SW7 15 L3
Calley Down Crs CROY/NA CR0 225 J6
Callingham Cl POP/IOD E14 140 E7
Callingham Pl BEAC HP9 88 D8
Callis Farm Cl STWL/WRAY TW19 173 P2
Callisons Pl GNWCH SE10 161 K4
Callis Rd WALTH E17 120 E4
Callisto Cl CRAWW RH11 283 H10
Callisto Ct HHNE HP2 36 A3
Callow Fld PUR/KEN CR8 223 H9
Callow Hl VW GU25 193 P2
Callowland Pl WATN WD24 73 J4
Callow St CHEL SW3 15 L9
Calluna Ct WOKS/MYFD GU22 232 C4
Calluna Dr CRAWE RH10 285 H3
Calmington Rd CMBW SE5 19 K9
Calmont Rd BMLY BR1 183 J9
Calmore Cl HCH RM12 125 K10
Calne Av CLAY IG5 102 E9
Calonne Rd WIM/MER SW19 178 G7
Calshot Av CDW/CHF RM16 167 L1
Calshot Rd HTHAIR TW6 152 C8
Calshot St IS N1 5 N7
Calshot Wy ENC/FH EN2 79 J7
HTHAIR TW6 152 C8
Calthorpe Gdns EDGW HA8 95 L6
SUT SM1 201 M10
Calthorpe St FSBYW WC1X 11 P1
Calton Av DUL SE21 181 M2
Calton Rd BAR EN5 77 M10
Calumet BEAC HP9 88 C8
Calverley Cl BECK BR3 182 G9
Calverley Crs DAGE RM10 124 B7
Calverley Gv ARCH N19 118 E6
Calverley Rd EW KT17 220 D3
Calvert Av WCHPL E1 7 K10
Calvert Cl BELV DA17 164 B3
SCUP DA14 185 P9
Calvert Crs DORK RH4 254 G10
Calvert Dr RDART DA2 186 F5
Calverton Rd EHAM E6 142 D3
Calvert Rd BAR EN5 76 G6
DORK RH4 254 G10
EHSLY KT24 253 J4
GNWCH SE10 161 L4
Calvert St CAMTN NW1 4 C5
Calvin Cl STMC/STPC BR5 207 N3
Calvin St WCHPL E1 13 L2
Calydon Rd CHARL SE7 161 N4
Calypso Crs PECK SE15 159 M6
Calypso Wy BERM/RHTH SE16 160 E2
Camac Rd WHTN TW2 176 C5
Camarthen Gn
CDALE/KGS NW9 * 116 B4
Cambalt Rd PUT/ROE SW15 178 G1
Camber Cl CRAWE RH10 284 D7
Camberley Av EN EN1 79 M8
RYNPK SW20 200 E2
Camberley Cl CHEAM SM3 200 G10
Camberley Ct HHNE HP2 * 35 L6
Camberley Pl HARP AL5 20 C5
Camberley Rd HTHAIR TW6 152 B9
Cambert Wy BKHTH/KID SE3 161 N10
Camberwell Church St
CMBW SE5 159 L7
Camberwell Glebe CMBW SE5 159 L7
Camberwell Gn CMBW SE5 159 L7
Camberwell Gv CMBW SE5 159 L7
Camberwell La RSEV TN14 264 A7
Camberwell New Rd CMBW SE5 159 J6
Camberwell Pas CMBW SE5 18 F10
Camberwell Station Rd
CMBW SE5 159 K7
Cambeys Rd DAGE RM10 124 D10
Camborne Av HARH RM3 105 M8
WEA W13 154 G1
Camborne Cl HTHAIR TW6 152 B9
Camborne Crs HTHAIR TW6 152 B9
Camborne Dr HHNE HP2 35 P2
Camborne Ms WAND/EARL SW18 179 K4
Camborne Rd BELMT SM2 221 K4
CROY/NA CR0 203 P7
MRDN SM4 200 G6
SCUP DA14 185 M6
WAND/EARL SW18 179 K3
WELL DA16 163 H8
Camborne Wy HARH RM3 105 N8
HEST TW5 153 P7
Cambourne Av ED N9 100 C1
Cambourne Ms NTGHL W11 8 A6
Cambourne Wy HARH RM3 105 M8
Cambray Rd BAL SW12 180 D4
ORP BR6 207 J7
Cambria Cl BFN/LL DA15 184 G4
HSLW TW3 153 P10
Cambria Ct EBED/NFELT TW14 175 J3
Cambria Crs GVE DA12 191 H7
Cambria Gdns STWL/WRAY TW19 173 P3
Cambrian Av GNTH/NBYPK IG2 123 H3
Cambrian Cl WNWD SE27 181 J6
Cambrian Gn CDALE/KGS NW9 116 B3
Cambrian Gv GVW DA11 190 D3
Cambrian Rd LEY E10 120 F5
RCHPK/HAM TW10 177 L2
Cambrian Wy HHNE HP2 35 P3
Cambria Rd CMBW SE5 159 K9
Cambria St FUL/PGN SW6 157 L6
Cambridge Av GFD/PVL UB6 134 E1
GPK RM2 105 K10
GPK RM2 125 K1
KIL/WHAMP NW6 2 F7
NWMAL KT3 200 C2
SL SL1 128 A4
WELL DA16 163 J10
Cambridge Barracks Rd
WOOL/PLUM SE18 162 C3
Cambridge Circ
SOHO/SHAV W1D 11 K6
Cambridge Cl CHES/WCR EN8 62 B5
HSLWW TW4 153 M10
RYNPK SW20 200 E1
WALTH E17 120 E4
WDGN N22 * 99 H9
WDR/YW UB7 151 N5
WLSDN NW10 115 P8
WOKN/KNAP GU21 231 L4
Cambridge Cottages RCH/KEW TW9 156 A5
Cambridge Crs BETH E2 140 A4
TEDD TW11 * 176 F8
Cambridge Dr LEE/GVPK SE12 183 M1
POTB/CUF EN6 59 H7
RSLP HA4 113 L7
Cambridge Gdns
CDW/CHF RM16 168 E3
EN EN1 79 P6
KIL/WHAMP NW6 2 F7
KUT/HW KT1 199 M2
MUSWH N10 98 B9
NKENS W10 8 B5
TOTM N17 99 L8
Cambridge Ga CAMTN NW1 4 E10
Cambridge Gate Ms CAMTN NW1 4 F10
Cambridge Gn ELTH/MOT SE9 184 E4
Cambridge Gv HMSMTH W6 156 E3
PGE/AN SE20 * 204 A1
Cambridge Grove Rd
KUT/HW KT1 199 M3
Cambridge Heath Rd BETH E2 140 A5
Cambridge Lodge Pk
HORL RH6 * 280 B1
Cambridge Pde EN EN1 * 79 P6
Cambridge Pk TWK TW1 177 J3
WAN E11 121 M4
Cambridge Park Rd WAN E11 121 M5
Cambridge Pas HOM E9 140 B2
Cambridge Pl KENS W8 * 15 H2
Cambridge Rd ASHF TW15 174 D10
BARK IG11 142 F2
BARN SW13 156 C8
BEAC HP9 88 B9
BMLY BR1 183 M10
BTSEA SW11 158 A7
CAR SM5 221 P3
CHING E4 101 J2
GDMY/SEVK IG3 123 H6
HLW CM20 29 M5
HNWL W7 154 E1
HPTN TW12 175 N10
HSLWW TW4 153 M10
KIL/WHAMP NW6 2 F9
KUT/HW KT1 199 M2
MTCM CR4 202 D2
NWMAL KT3 200 A4
PGE/AN SE20 203 P4
RCH/KEW TW9 155 M6
RYLN/HDSTN HA2 113 P3
SCUP DA14 185 H7
STAL AL1 38 G7
STHL UB1 * 133 N10
TEDD TW11 176 F7
TWK TW1 177 J2
UX/CGN UB8 131 N1
WAN E11 121 L5
WATW WD18 * 73 K8
WOT/HER KT12 197 J6
Cambridge Rd North CHSWK W4 155 N4
Cambridge Rd South CHSWK W4 155 N4
Cambridge Rw
WOOL/PLUM SE18 162 E4
Cambridge Sq BAY/PAD W2 9 N5
REDH RH1 276 B3
Cambridge St PIM SW1V 16 F7
Cambridge Ter BERK HP4 34 A5
CAMTN NW1 4 E10
ED N9 * 99 N1
Cambridge Terrace Ms
CAMTN NW1 * 4 F10
Cambridge Yd HNWL W7 * 154 E1
Cambus Cl YEAD UB4 133 M7
Cambus Rd CAN/RD E16 141 M7
Camdale Rd WOOL/PLUM SE18 163 J6
Camden Av FELT TW13 175 K5
YEAD UB4 133 K9
Camden Cl CDW/CHF RM16 168 E3
CHST BR7 206 F1
GVW DA11 189 P5
Camden Gdns CAMTN NW1 4 F4
SUT SM1 221 L2
THHTH CR7 203 J3
Camden Gv CHST BR7 184 E9
Camden High St CAMTN NW1 4 F4
Camden Hill Rd NRWD SE19 181 M9
Camdenhurst St POP/IOD E14 140 D8
Camden Lock Pl CAMTN NW1 4 E4
Camden Ms CAMTN NW1 5 J3
Camden Park Rd CAMTN NW1 5 K1
CHST BR7 184 C10
Camden Pas IS N1 6 C7
Camden Rd BXLY DA5 186 A4
CAMTN NW1 4 G4
CAR SM5 222 A1
CDW/CHF RM16 167 K2
HOLWY N7 118 F9
SEV TN13 247 J8
SUT SM1 221 L2
WALTH E17 120 E4
WAN E11 121 N4
Camden Rd Permanent Wy
CAMTN NW1 * 5 J6
Camden Rw BKHTH/KID SE3 161 K8
PIN HA5 * 113 K1
Camden Sq CAMTN NW1 5 J3
Camden St CAMTN NW1 4 F4
Camden Ter CAMTN NW1 5 J2
Camden Wk IS N1 6 C6
Camden Wy CHST BR7 184 C10
THHTH CR7 203 J3
Camelford Wk NTGHL W11 8 A6
Camel Gv KUTN/CMB KT2 177 J8
Camellia Cl HARH RM3 105 M9
Camellia Ct CHOB/PIR GU24 212 E9
Camellia Pl WHTN TW2 176 A3
Camellia St VX/NE SW8 158 F6
Camelot Cl BH/WHM TN16 243 P2
THMD SE28 162 G2
WIM/MER SW19 179 J7
Camel Rd CAN/RD E16 142 B10
Camera Pl WBPTN SW10 15 L10
Cameron Cl BRW CM14 107 J5
BXLY DA5 186 F6
TRDG/WHET N20 97 P3
UED N18 100 A6
Cameron Ct WARE SG12 26 C1
Cameron Dr CHES/WCR EN8 62 C10
Cameron Pl STRHM/NOR SW16 181 H6
Cameron Rd CAT SE6 * 182 E5
CROY/NA CR0 203 J6
CSHM HP5 51 J6
GDMY/SEVK IG3 123 H6
HAYES BR2 205 M5
Cameron Sq MTCM CR4 201 P1
Cameron Ter LEE/GVPK SE12 * 183 N6
Camerton Cl HACK E8 7 M2
Camfield WGCE AL7 23 J9
Cam Gn SOCK/AV RM15 146 G8
Camilla Cl GT/LBKH KT23 254 A1
SUN TW16 174 G9
Camilla Dr RDKG RH5 254 F6
Camilla Rd BERM/RHTH SE16 160 A3
Camille Cl SNWD SE25 203 P3
Camlan Rd BMLY BR1 183 L7
Camlet St BETH E2 13 L1
Camlet Wy EBAR EN4 77 K6
STALW/RED AL3 38 A5
Camley St CAMTN NW1 5 J4
Camm Av WDSR SL4 148 D9
Camm Gdns KUT/HW KT1 * 199 L2
THDIT KT7 198 D7
Camomile Av MTCM CR4 202 A1
Camomile St HDTCH EC3A 13 K5
Camomile Wy WDR/YW UB7 131 P8
Camomile Rd ROMW/RG RM7 124 E7
Campana Rd FUL/PGN SW6 157 K7
Campbell Av BARK/HLT IG6 122 F2
WOKS/MYFD GU22 232 C7
Campbell Cl BF/WBF KT14 215 N8
HLWE CM17 47 L2
ROM RM1 104 F7
RSLP HA4 113 H4
STRHM/NOR SW16 * 180 E8
WHTN TW2 176 C4
WOOL/PLUM SE18 162 D7
Campbell Cottages MTCM CR4 * 202 B2
Campbell Cft EDGW HA8 95 M6
Campbell Gordon Wy
CRICK NW2 116 E9
Campbell Rd BOW E3 140 F5
CRAWE RH10 284 D9
CROY/NA CR0 203 J7
CTHM CR3 241 L7
EHAM E6 142 B3
GVW DA11 190 C4
HNWL W7 134 D9
SRTFD E15 121 K9
TOTM N17 99 N9
WALTH E17 120 E2
WEY KT13 216 B4
WHTN TW2 176 C5
Campbell Wk IS N1 * 5 M5
Campdale Rd HOLWY N7 118 E8
Campden Crs ALP/SUD HA0 114 G8
BCTR RM8 123 M9
Campden Gv KENS W8 14 F1
Campden Hl KENS W8 14 E1
Campden Hill Gdns KENS W8 8 E9
Campden Hill Pl NTGHL W11 8 D9
Campden Hill Rd KENS W8 8 E9
Campden Hill Sq NTGHL W11 8 D9
Campden House Cl KENS W8 14 F1
Campden House Ter KENS W8 * 8 F10
Campden Rd HGDN/ICK UB10 112 A8
SAND/SEL CR2 223 M2
Campden St KENS W8 8 E10
Campden Ter CHSWK W4 * 156 B4
Campen Cl WIM/MER SW19 179 H5
Camp End Rd WEY KT13 216 D8
Camperdown St WCHPL E1 13 M6
Campfield Rd ELTH/MOT SE9 184 A3
HERT/WAT SG14 25 J5
STAL AL1 38 G8
Camphill Ct BF/WBF KT14 215 K8
Camphill Rd BF/WBF KT14 215 L8
Campine Cl CHES/WCR EN8 62 C4
Campion Cl CROY/NA CR0 223 M1
DEN/HRF UB9 111 K8
EHAM E6 142 C9
GSTN WD25 55 H9
GVW DA11 190 B7
KTN/HRWW/WS HA3 115 L4
ROMW/RG RM7 124 E7
UX/CGN UB8 132 A7
Campion Ct ALP/SUD HA0 * 135 H2
Campion Dr KWD/TDW/WH KT20 238 E6
Campion Gdns WFD IG8 101 M6
Campion Pl THMD SE28 143 L10
Campion Rd HAT AL10 40 C1
HHW HP1 35 H7
ISLW TW7 154 E7
PUT/ROE SW15 156 F10
Campions EPP CM16 65 K4
LOU IG10 82 D4
Campions Ct BERK HP4 33 M6
The Campions BORE WD6 75 L4
Campion Ter CRICK NW2 116 G8
Campion Wy EDGW HA8 95 P5
Cample La SOCK/AV RM15 146 F9
Camplin Rd KTN/HRWW/WS HA3 115 K3
Camplin St NWCR SE14 160 C6
Camp Rd CFSP/GDCR SL9 110 A5
CTHM CR3 242 D7
STAL AL1 38 E7
WIM/MER SW19 178 E8
Campsbourne Pde
CEND/HSY/T N8 * 118 F2
Campsbourne Rd
CEND/HSY/T N8 118 F1
The Campsbourne
CEND/HSY/T N8 118 F2
Campsey Gdns DAGW RM9 143 L2
Campsey Rd DAGW RM9 143 L2
Campshill Pl LEW SE13 183 H1
Campshill Rd LEW SE13 183 H1
Campus Rd WALTH E17 120 E4
The Campus HHNE HP2 * 36 C4
WGCW AL8 22 G4
Camp Vw WIM/MER SW19 178 E8
Camp View Rd STAL AL1 38 G7
Cam Rd SRTFD E15 141 J3
Camrose Av EDGW HA8 95 K10
ERITH DA8 164 D5
FELT TW13 175 J9
Camrose Cl CROY/NA CR0 204 D7
MRDN SM4 201 K4
Camrose St WOOL/PLUM SE18 163 K4
Canada Av REDH RH1 276 B4
UED N18 99 K7
Canada Crs ACT W3 135 P7
Canada Dr REDH RH1 276 B4
Canada Farm Rd EYN DA4 210 G5
Canada La BROX EN10 62 D1
Canada Park Pde EDGW HA8 * 95 N9
Canada Rd ACT W3 135 P7
BF/WBF KT14 215 N7
COB KT11 217 K9
ERITH DA8 165 J6
SL SL1 149 N1
Canada Sq POP/IOD E14 140 G10
The Canadas BROX EN10 62 D2
Canada St BERM/RHTH SE16 160 C1
Canada Wy SHB W12 136 E9
Canadian Av CAT SE6 182 G4
Canal App DEPT SE8 160 D5
Canal Basin GVE DA12 190 G2
Canal Bvd CAMTN NW1 5 J1
Canal Cl NKENS W10 136 G6
WCHPL E1 140 D6
Canal Est DTCH/LGLY SL3 * 150 D1
Canal Gv PECK SE15 19 P9
Canal Pth BETH E2 7 L6
Canal Rd GVE DA12 190 G2
Canalside BERK HP4 33 L3
Canal St CMBW SE5 18 G10
Canal Wk CROY/NA CR0 203 M6
IS N1 7 H5
WLSDN NW10 * 135 P2
Canal Wy DEN/HRF UB9 91 K7
NKENS W10 136 G6
Canal Whf DTCH/LGLY SL3 150 D1
GFD/PVL UB6 * 134 F3
Canal Yd NWDGN UB2 * 153 J3
Canberra Cl CRAWW RH11 283 N4
DAGE RM10 144 E2
HCH RM12 125 K9
HDN NW4 116 D1
STALW/RED AL3 38 E2
Canberra Crs DAGE RM10 144 E2
Canberra Dr NTHLT UB5 133 L5
Canberra Rd HTHAIR TW6 152 B9
ABYW SE2 163 N5
CHARL SE7 161 P5
EHAM E6 142 C3
WEA W13 134 F10
Canberra Sq TIL RM18 * 168 D8
Canbury Av KUTN/CMB KT2 199 L1
Canbury Ms SYD SE26 181 P6
Canbury Park Rd KUTN/CMB KT2 199 K1
Canbury Pth STMC/STPC BR5 207 K4
Cancell Rd BRXN/ST SW9 159 H7
Candahar Rd BTSEA SW11 157 P8
Cander Wy SOCK/AV RM15 146 G9
Candlefield Rd HHS/BOV HP3 36 B9
Candle Gv PECK SE15 160 A9
Candlelight Ct SRTFD E15 141 L1
Candlemas La BEAC HP9 88 D9
Candlemas Md BEAC HP9 88 D9
Candler Ms TWK TW1 176 F3
Candler St SEVS/STOTM N15 * 119 L4
Candlerush Cl WOKS/MYFD GU22 232 E3
Candover Cl WDR/YW UB7 151 N6
Candover Rd HCH RM12 125 J6
Candover St GTPST W1W * 10 G4
Candy Cft GT/LBKH KT23 254 A2
Candy St BOW E3 140 E3
Cane Hl HARH RM3 105 L10
Canes La HLWE CM17 47 M6
Canewden Cl WOKS/MYFD GU22 232 B5
Caney Ms CRICK NW2 116 G7
Canfield Dr RSLP HA4 113 J10
Canfield Gdns KIL/WHAMP NW6 3 H3
Canfield Pl KIL/WHAMP NW6 3 J2
Canfield Rd RAIN RM13 144 G3
WFD IG8 102 B8
Canford Av NTHLT UB5 133 N3
Canford Cl ENC/FH EN2 79 H6
Canford Dr ADL/WDHM KT15 195 L9
Canford Gdns NWMAL KT3 200 B6
Canford Pl TEDD TW11 177 H9
Canford Rd CLAP SW4 158 B10
Cangels Cl HHW HP1 35 K8
Canham Rd CHSWK W4 156 B1
SNWD SE25 203 M3
Can Hatch KWD/TDW/WH KT20 239 H4
Canmore Gdns
STRHM/NOR SW16 180 D10
Cann Hall Rd WAN E11 121 L9
Canning Crs WDGN N22 98 G9
Canning Cross CMBW SE5 159 M8
Canning Pas KENS W8 * 15 J3
Canning Pl KENS W8 15 J3
Canning Place Ms KENS W8 * 15 J3
Canning Rd CROY/NA CR0 203 N9
HBRY N5 119 J8
KTN/HRWW/WS HA3 114 D1
SRTFD E15 141 K4
WALTH E17 120 D2
Cannington Rd DAGW RM9 143 M1
Cannizaro Rd WIM/MER SW19 178 F9
Cannonbury Av PIN HA5 113 L4
Cannon Cl HPTN TW12 176 A9
RYNPK SW20 200 F3
Cannon Crs CHOB/PIR GU24 213 K7
Cannon Dr POP/IOD E14 140 F9
Cannon Ga SLN SL2 129 P6
Cannon Gv LHD/OX KT22 236 D8
Cannon Hl KIL/WHAMP NW6 117 L10
STHGT/OAK N14 98 F4
Cannon Hill La RYNPK SW20 200 G5
Cannon Hill Ms STHGT/OAK N14 98 F4
Cannon La HAMP NW3 117 N8
PIN HA5 113 M3
PIN HA5 113 M5
Cannon Ms WAB EN9 62 G9
Cannon Mill Av CSHM HP5 51 J9
Cannon Pl CHARL SE7 162 B4
HAMP NW3 117 M8
Cannon Rd BXLYHN DA7 163 P7
STHGT/OAK N14 98 F4
WATW WD18 73 K9
Cannon Side LHD/OX KT22 236 D8
Cannons Meadow WLYN AL6 23 P2
Cannon St BLKFR EC4V 12 E6
STALW/RED AL3 38 C5
Cannon Street Rd WCHPL E1 140 A8
Cannon Wy E/WMO/HCT KT8 197 P4
LHD/OX KT22 236 D7
Canon Av CHDH RM6 123 M3
Canon Beck Rd
BERM/RHTH SE16 160 B1
Canonbie Rd FSTH SE23 182 B3
Canonbury Crs IS N1 6 F3
Canonbury Gv IS N1 6 E3
Canonbury La IS N1 6 C3
Canonbury Pk North IS N1 6 E2
Canonbury Pk South IS N1 6 F2
Canonbury Pl IS N1 6 E2
Canonbury Rd EN EN1 79 M5
IS N1 6 D3
Canonbury Sq IS N1 6 D3
Canonbury St IS N1 6 E3
Canonbury Vls IS N1 6 D4
Canonbury Yd East IS N1 6 D2
Canon Mohan Cl
STHGT/OAK N14 78 B10
Canon Murnane Rd STHWK SE1 19 L4
Canon Rd BMLY BR1 205 P3
Canon Rw WHALL SW1A 17 L2
Canons Brook HLWW/ROY CM19 46 D1
Canons Cl EDGW HA8 95 L7
EFNCH N2 117 N5
RAD WD7 74 C1
REIG RH2 257 J9
Canons Cottages EDGW HA8 * 95 L7
Canons Ct EDGW HA8 * 95 L7
Canons Dr EDGW HA8 95 J7
Canons Fld STALE/WH AL4 21 J2
Canons Ga CHES/WCR EN8 62 E2
HLW CM20 28 D10
Canon's Hl COUL/CHIP CR5 241 H4
Canons La KWD/TDW/WH KT20 239 H5
Canonsleigh Rd DAGW RM9 143 L2
Canons Rd WARE SG12 26 B1
Canon St IS N1 6 E6
Canons Wk BH/WHM TN16 263 L5
CROY/NA CR0 204 C10
Canopus Wy NTHWD HA6 93 H5
STWL/WRAY TW19 173 P3
Canopy La HLWE CM17 29 M10
Canrobert St BETH E2 * 140 A5
Cantelowes Rd CAMTN NW1 5 K2
Canterbury Av BFN/LL DA15 185 M5
IL IG1 122 B5
SLN SL2 129 H6
UPMR RM14 126 E6
Canterbury Cl AMSS HP7 69 K5
BECK BR3 204 G1
CHIG IG7 103 J4
CMBW SE5 * 159 K8
DART DA1 187 P3
EHAM E6 142 C8
GFD/PVL UB6 134 A7
NTHWD HA6 92 F7
Canterbury Ct DORK RH4 * 272 F1
Canterbury Crs BRXN/ST SW9 159 H9
Canterbury Gv WNWD SE27 181 J6
Canterbury Pde SOCK/AV RM15 147 H5
Canterbury Pl WALW SE17 18 D6
Canterbury Rd BORE WD6 75 M6
CROY/NA CR0 202 G7
FELT TW13 175 M5
GUW GU2 249 L8
GVE DA12 190 F5
KIL/WHAMP NW6 2 E8
LEY E10 121 H5
MRDN SM4 201 M6
RYLN/HDSTN HA2 114 A3
WAT WD17 * 73 J6
Canterbury Ter KIL/WHAMP NW6 2 E7
Canterbury Wy
RBRW/HUT CM13 107 H7
RKW/CH/CXG WD3 72 D7
WTHK RM20 166 D6
The Canter CRAWE RH10 284 F6
Cantley Gdns GNTH/NBYPK IG2 122 F4
NRWD SE19 203 N1
Cantley Rd HNWL W7 154 F2
Canton St POP/IOD E14 140 F8
Cantrell Rd BOW E3 140 F6
Cantwell Rd WOOL/PLUM SE18 162 E6
Canvey Cl CRAWW RH11 283 M10
Canvey St STHWK SE1 12 E9
Capability Wy SWCM DA10 167 H10
Cape Cl BARK IG11 142 E2
Capel Av WLGTN SM6 222 G2
Capel Cl HAYES BR2 206 B8
TRDG/WHET N20 97 M4
Capel Gdns GDMY/SEVK IG3 123 J9
PIN HA5 113 N2
Capel La CRAWW RH11 283 K8
Capella Rd NTHWD HA6 92 G6
Capell Av RKW/CH/CXG WD3 70 F9
Capell Rd RKW/CH/CXG WD3 70 G9
Capell Wy RKW/CH/CXG WD3 70 G9
Capel Pl RDART DA2 187 K7
Capel Rd EBAR EN4 77 P10
EN EN1 80 A2
FSTGT E7 121 N9
OXHEY WD19 73 M10
Capelvere Wk WAT WD17 72 F5
Capener's Cl KTBR SW1X 16 C2
Capern Rd WAND/EARL SW18 179 M4
Cape Rd STAL AL1 38 G6
TOTM N17 119 P1
Cape Yd WAP E1W 13 P9
Capital Interchange Wy
BTFD TW8 155 M4
Capital Pl HLWW/ROY CM19 46 D2
Capitol Wy CDALE/KGS NW9 115 P1
Capland St STJWD NW8 9 N1
Caple Pde WLSDN NW10 * 136 C4
Caple Rd WLSDN NW10 136 C4
Capon Cl BRW CM14 106 G2
Caponfield WGCE AL7 23 L7
Cappell La WARE SG12 27 H6
Caprea Cl YEAD UB4 133 L7
Capricorn Cl CRAWW RH11 283 H9
Capri Rd CROY/NA CR0 203 N7
Capsey Rd CRAWW RH11 283 H8
Capstan Cl CHDH RM6 123 L4
Capstan Ct RDART DA2 166 B10
Capstan Dr RAIN RM13 145 H7
Capstan Ride ENC/FH EN2 79 H6
Capstan Rd DEPT SE8 160 E3
Capstan Sq POP/IOD E14 161 H1
Capstans Whf WOKN/KNAP GU21 231 L4
Capstan Wy BERM/RHTH SE16 140 D10
Capstone Rd BMLY BR1 183 L7
Captain Cook Cl CSTG HP8 89 M5
Captain's Cl CSHM HP5 50 F3
Captains Wk BERK HP4 34 A6
Capthorne Av RYLN/HDSTN HA2 113 M6
Capuchin Cl STAN HA7 94 G7
Capulet Ms CAN/RD E16 141 M10
Capulet Sq LEY E10 120 G5
Caractacus Cottage Vw
WATW WD18 93 H1
Caractacus Gn WATW WD18 72 G10
Caradoc Cl BAY/PAD W2 8 E5
Caradoc Evans Cl
FBAR/BDGN N11 * 98 C6
Caradoc St GNWCH SE10 161 K4
Caradon Cl WOKN/KNAP GU21 231 N4
Caradon Ct WAN E11 121 K6
Caradon Wy SEVS/STOTM N15 119 L2
Caravan La RKW/CH/CXG WD3 91 P1
The Caravan Site PUR RM19 166 C2
Caravel Cl CDW/CHF RM16 167 L2
Caravel Ms DEPT SE8 * 160 F5
Caraway Cl PLSTW E13 141 N7
Caraway Pl GUW GU2 249 M5
WLGTN SM6 202 C10
Carberry Rd NRWD SE19 181 M9
Carbery Av ACT W3 155 L1
Carbery La ASC SL5 192 A3
Carbis Cl CHING E4 101 J2
Carbis Rd POP/IOD E14 140 E8
Carbone Hl POTB/CUF EN6 60 E2
Carburton St GTPST W1W 10 F3
Carbury Cl HCH RM12 145 K1
Cardale St POP/IOD E14 161 H2
Cardamom Cl GUW GU2 249 M6
Carde Cl HERT/WAT SG14 24 G4
Carden Rd PECK SE15 160 A9
Cardiff Rd HNWL W7 154 F2
PEND EN3 80 A8
WATW WD18 73 J10
Cardiff St WOOL/PLUM SE18 163 K6
Cardiff Wy ABLGY WD5 55 H8
Cardigan Cl SL SL1 128 E9
WOKN/KNAP GU21 231 L4
Cardigan Gdns GDMY/SEVK IG3 123 K7
Cardigan Pl LEW SE13 * 161 J8
Cardigan Rd BARN SW13 156 D8
BOW E3 140 E4
RCHPK/HAM TW10 177 K2
WIM/MER SW19 179 M9
Cardigan St LBTH SE11 18 A7
Cardigan Wk IS N1 6 F3
Cardinal Av BORE WD6 75 N7
KUTN/CMB KT2 177 K8
MRDN SM4 201 H6
Cardinal Bourne St STHWK SE1 * 19 H4
Cardinal Cl CHESW EN7 61 N2
CHST BR7 206 G1
EDGW HA8 95 P8
MRDN SM4 201 H6
SAND/SEL CR2 223 P9
WPK KT4 220 D1
Cardinal Crs NWMAL KT3 199 P2
Cardinal Dr BARK/HLT IG6 102 F7
WOT/HER KT12 197 L8
Cardinal Gv STALW/RED AL3 38 A8
Cardinal Hinsey Cl WLSDN NW10 136 D4
Cardinal Pl PUT/ROE SW15 156 G10
Cardinal Rd CDW/CHF RM16 167 K2
FELT TW13 175 J4
RSLP HA4 113 L6
Cardinal's Wk HPTN TW12 176 B10
MDHD SL6 128 B8
SUN TW16 174 F9
Cardinals Wy ARCH N19 118 E6
Cardinal Wy
KTN/HRWW/WS HA3 * 114 D1
RAIN RM13 145 L4
Cardine Ms PECK SE15 160 A6
Cardingham WOKN/KNAP GU21 231 M3
Cardington Sq HSLWW TW4 153 L10
Cardington St CAMTN NW1 5 H10
Cardozo Rd HOLWY N7 118 F10
Cardrew Av NFNCH/WDSPK N12 97 N6
Cardross St HMSMTH W6 156 E2
Cardwell Crs ASC SL5 192 B5
Cardwell Rd HOLWY N7 * 118 F9
Cardwells Keep GUW GU2 249 M7
Cardwell Ter HOLWY N7 * 118 F9
Cardy Rd HHW HP1 35 L7
Carew Cl CDW/CHF RM16 167 K2
COUL/CHIP CR5 241 J5
HOLWY N7 118 G7
Carew Rd ASHF TW15 174 D9
MTCM CR4 202 B2
NTHWD HA6 92 F7
THHTH CR7 203 J3
TOTM N17 99 P10
WEA W13 155 H1
WLGTN SM6 222 D3
Carew St CMBW SE5 159 K8
Carew Wy OXHEY WD19 93 N4
STMC/STPC BR5 207 M8
Carey Cl WDSR SL4 148 G9
Carey Gdns VX/NE SW8 158 D7
Carey La CITYW EC2V 12 E5
Carey Pl PIM SW1V 17 J7
Carey Rd DAGW RM9 123 P9
Careys Copse HORL RH6 * 281 J4
Careys Cft BERK HP4 33 M2
Carey's Fld SEV TN13 246 F6
Carey St LINN WC2A 11 P6
Carey's Wd HORL RH6 281 J4
Carey Wy WBLY HA9 115 N9
Carfax Pl CLAP SW4 158 E10
Carfax Rd HCH RM12 124 G9
HYS/HAR UB3 153 H4

The Carfax SYD SE26 * ...182 B6
Carfree Cl IS N1 ...6 B3
Cargill Rd WAND/EARL SW18 ...179 M4
Cargo Forecourt Rd HORL RH6 ...279 N8
Cargo Rd HORL RH6 ...279 N8
Cargreen Rd SNWD SE25 ...205 N4
Carholme Rd FSTH SE23 ...182 E6
Carisbrook Ct STAN HA7 * ...95 N5
Carisbrooke Av BXLY DA5 ...185 N4
  WATN WD24 ...B4
Carisbrooke Cl EMPK RM11 ...125 P6
  HSLWW TW4 ...J5
  STAN HA7 ...95 J10
Carisbrooke Ct NTHLT UB5 * ...L8
  SL SL1 ...129 L9
Carisbrooke Gdns PECK SE15 * ...159 N6
Carisbrooke Rd HARP AL5 ...D2
  HAYES BR2 ...205 P4
  MTCM CR4 ...202 F4
  WALTH E17 * ...120 D2
Carisbrook Rd BRWN CM15 ...B9
  LCOL/BKTW AL2 ...56 A2
Carker's La KTTN NW5 ...118 C10
Carleton Av WLGTN SM6 ...222 E5
Carleton Cl ESH/CLAY KT10 ...198 C8
Carleton Gdns ARCH N19 * ...C1
Carleton Pl FLYN DA4 ...210 B4
Carleton Rd CHES/WCR EN8. ...62 C3
  HOLWY N7 ...N1
Carleton Vls KTTN NW5 * ...118 D10
Carlile Cl BOW E3 ...140 E4
Carlina Gdns WFD IG8 ...101 N6
Carlingford Rd HAMP NW3 ...117 N9
  MRDN SM4 ...200 G6
  SEVS/STOTM N15 ...119 J1
Carlisle Av ACT W3 ...B6
  STALW/RED AL3 ...38 C4
  TWRH EC3N ...13 L6
Carlisle Cl KUTN/CMB KT2 ...199 M1
  PIN HA5 ...113 M5
Carlisle Gdns IL IG1 ...122 B4
  KTN/HRWW/WS HA3 ...115 J5
Carlisle Pl FBAR/BDGN N11 ...98 C5
  WEST SW1P ...16 C4
Carlisle La STHWK SE1 ...17 P3
  DART DA1 ...P2
  FSBYPK N4 ...119 H6
  HPTN TW12 ...176 A10
  KIL/WHAMP NW6 ...2 C1
  LEY E10 ...F6
  ROM RM1 ...124 C3
  SL SL1 ...129 J9
  SUT SM1 ...221 J3
Carlisle Wk SOHO/SHAV W1D ...H1
Carlisle Wk HACK E8 ...L2
Carlos Pl MYFR/PKLN W1K ...10 D8
Carlow St CAMTN NW1 ...G7
Carlton Av EBED/NFELT TW14 ...175 K2
  HYS/HAR UB3 ...152 F3
  KTN/HRWW/WS HA3 ...114 F5
  RDART DA2 ...188 D2
  SAND/SEL CR2 ...223 L4
  STHGT/OAK N14 ...78 E9
Carlton Av East WBLY HA9 ...J3
Carlton Av West ALP/SUD HA0 ...114 G7
Carlton Bank HARP AL5 * ...20 A2
Carlton Cl BORE WD6. ...A8
  CHSGTN KT9 ...219 J3
  EDGW HA8 ...95 M6
  HAMP NW3 ...117 H4
  UPMR RM14 ...126 A7
  WOKN/KNAP GU21 ...214 C10
Carlton Ct HORL RH6 ...280 C2
Carlton Crs CHEAM SM3 ...221 H1
Carlton Dene EW KT17 * ...220 E2
Carlton Dr BARK/HLT IG6. ...E1
  PUT/ROE SW15 ...178 C1
Carlton Ga MV/WKIL W9 ...8 C3
Carlton Gn REDH RH1 * ...135 H8
  SCUP DA14 * ...185 J7
Carlton Gv PECK SE15 ...160 A7
Carlton Hl STJWD NW8 ...N7
Carlton House Ter STJS SW1Y ...11 J10
Carlton Ms KIL/WHAMP NW6 * ...2 F1
Carlton Pde SEV TN13 * ...247 K8
  WBLY HA9 ...H5
Carlton Pk Av RYNPK SW20 ...200 F2
Carlton Pl WEY KT13 * ...216 C1
Carlton Rd CDW/CHF RM16 ...168 C1
  CHSWK W4 ...156 A1
  EA W5 ...135 H9
  ERITH DA8 ...164 D6
  FBAR/BDGN N11 ...98 B6
  FSBYPK N4 ...119 H5
  GPK RM2 ...J2
  MNPK E12 ...122 A9
  MORT/ESHN SW14 ...155 P9
  NWMAL KT3 ...200 B2
  REIG RH2 ...257 N6
  SAND/SEL CR2 ...223 L4
  SCUP DA14 ...185 J7
  SLN SL2 ...129 N9
  SUN TW16 ...174 C10
  WALTH E17 ...100 D9
  WAN E11 ...L8
  WELL DA16 ...165 L9
  WOKN/KNAP GU21 ...214 D10
  WOT/HER KT12 ...197 J7
Carlton Sq WCHPL E1 * ...140 C6
Carlton St STJS SW1Y ...11 J9
Carlton Ter SYD SE26 ...182 B7
  UED N18 * ...99 L5
  WAN E11 ...121 N3
Carlton Tower Pl KTBR SW1X ...16 E1
Carlton Tye HORL RH6 ...280 E4
Carlton V KIL/WHAMP NW6 ...2 F2
Carlwell St TOOT SW17 ...179 P8
Carlyle Av BMLY BR1 ...206 A3
  STHL UB1 ...133 M9
Carlyle Cl E/WMO/HCT KT8. ...198 A3
  EFNCH N2 ...117 M4
  WLSDN NW10 ...J1
Carlyle Ct WBPTN SW10 * ...157 M7
Carlyle Gdns STHL UB1 ...133 N9
Carlyle Rd CROY/NA CR0. ...203 P9
  EA W5 ...155 H5
  MNPK E12 ...122 A9
  STA TW18 ...173 J10
  THMD SE28 ...143 L9
Carlyle Sq CHEL SW3 ...M8
Carlyon Av RYLN/HDSTN HA2 ...113 N9
Carlyon Cl ALP/SUD HA0 ...135 K4
Carlyon Rd ALP/SUD HA0 ...135 K4
  YEAD UB4 ...133 K8
Carlys Cl BECK BR3 ...C1
Carmalt Gdns PUT/ROE SW15 ...156 F10
  WEY KT13 * ...217 K2
Carmarthen Rd SL SL1 ...129 K9
Carmel Cl WOKS/MYFD GU22 * ...232 B4
Carmel Ct KENS W8. ...L1
Carmelite Rd KTN/HRWW/WS HA3 ...94 B9
Carmelite St EMB EC4Y ...L7
Carmelite Wy HART DA3 ...211 L5
Carmel Wy RCH/KEW TW9 ...155 N8
Carmen St POP/IOD E14 ...140 G9
Carmichael Cl BTSEA SW11 * ...157 N1
  RSLP HA4 ...113 H9
Carmichael Ms WAND/EARL SW18 ...179 N3
Carmichael Rd SNWD SE25 ...203 N4
Carminia Rd TOOT SW17 ...180 C5
Carnaby Rd BROX EN10 ...44 D6
Carnac St WNWD SE27 ...181 L7
Carnanton Rd WALTH E17 ...101 J2
Carnarvon Av EN EN1 ...N6
Carnarvon Dr HYS/HAR UB3 ...152 D2
Carnarvon Rd BAR EN5 ...H1
  LEY E10 ...H4

SRTFD E15 ...141 L1
SWFD E18 ...101 L10
Carnation Cl ROMW/RG RM7 ...124 F7
Carnation St ABYW SE2 ...163 L4
Carnbrook Rd BKHTH/KID SE3. ...162 A9
Carnecke Gdns ELTH/MOT SE9 ...184 B1
Carnegie Cl PEND EN3 ...H3
  SURB KT6. ...199 L9
Carnegie Pl WIM/MER SW19 ...178 G6
Carnegie Rd STALW/RED AL3 ...38 C2
Carnegie St IS N1 ...5 N6
Carnet Cl DART DA1 ...186 F3
Carnforth Cl HOR/WEW KT19 ...219 N3
Carnforth Gdns HCH RM12 ...125 H10
Carnforth Rd STRHM/NOR SW16 ...180 E10
  STMC/STPC BR5 ...A4
Carnoustie Dr IS N1 ...5 N4
Carnoustie Cl THMD SE28 ...143 N8
Carnwath Rd FUL/PGN SW6 ...157 X9
Caro La HDN HP3 ...36 B8
Carol Cl HDN NW4 ...116 C2
Carolina Cl SRTFD E15 ...121 K10
Carolina Rd THHTH CR7 ...203 J3
Caroline Cl BAY/PAD W2 ...9 H8
  CROY/NA CR0. ...223 J1
  ISLW TW7 ...154 D10
  MUSWH N10 ...98 C10
  STRHM/NOR SW16 ...180 G6
  WDR/YW UB7 ...151 N1
Caroline Ct ASHF TW15 ...174 C9
  CRAWW RH11 ...283 N8
  STAN HA7 * ...94 F7
Caroline Pl BAY/PAD W2 ...9 H7
  BTSEA SW11 ...158 B8
  HYS/HAR UB3 ...152 F6
  OXHEY WD19 ...73 M10
Caroline Place Ms BAY/PAD W2 * ...9 H8
  WIM/MER SW19 ...179 J7
Caroline St WCHPL E1 ...140 C8
Caroline Ter BGVA SW1W ...16 C6
Caroline Wk FUL/PGN SW6 * ...14 A10
Carol St CAMTN NW1 ...4 C5
Carolyn Cl WOKN/KNAP GU21. ...231 L5
Carolyn Dr ORP BR6 ...207 K10
Caroon Dr RKW/CH/CXG WD3 * ...71 L2
Carpenders Av OXHEY WD19 ...93 M4
Carpenter Cl EW KT17 ...220 C5
Carpenters Gdns WCHMH N21 ...99 J1
Carpenters Arms La EPP CM16 ...65 L1
Carpenters Cl BAR EN5 ...77 L10
Carpenters Ms HOLWY N7 * ...118 F10
Carpenter's Pl CLAP SW4 ...158 E10
Carpenters Rd EN EN1 ...80 B2
  SRTFD E15 ...140 G2
Carpenter St MYFR/PKLN W1K ...10 E8
Carpenters Wood Dr
  RKW/CH/CXG WD3 ...70 E8
Carrara Ms HACK E8 ...7 N1
Carrara Whf FUL/PGN SW6 ...157 H9
Carr Cl STAN HA7 ...94 F7
Carre Ms CMBW SE5 ...159 J7
Carr Gv WOOL/PLUM SE18 ...162 B3
Carriage Dr North BTSEA SW11 ...158 A7
Carriage Dr South BTSEA SW11 ...158 A7
Carriage Dr West BTSEA SW11 ...158 A7
Carriage Ms IL IG1 ...122 D7
The Carriageway BW/WHM TN16. ...245 N10
Carrick Cl ISLW TW7 ...154 F9
Carrick Dr BARK/HLT IG6. ...102 F9
  SEV TN13 ...247 J9
Carrick Gdns TOTM N17 ...99 M8
Carrick Ga ESH/CLAY KT10 ...198 B10
Carrill Wy BELV DA17 ...163 N5
Carrington Av BORE WD6. ...75 N9
  HSLW TW3 ...176 A1
Carrington Cl BAR EN5 ...76 D9
  CROY/NA CR0. ...204 D7
  REDH RH1 ...B8
Carrington Gdns FSTGT E7 ...121 M9
Carrington Pl ESH/CLAY KT10 ...218 A1
Carrington Rd DART DA1 ...187 N2
  RCHPK/HAM TW10 ...155 M10
  SL SL1 ...129 K9
Carrington Sq
  KTN/HRWW/WS HA3 ...94 B8
Carrington St MYFR/PICC W1J. ...10 E10
Carroll Cl KTTN NW5 ...118 C9
Carrol Cl GU GU1 ...250 E10
Carroll Cl SRTFD E15 ...121 L10
Carroll Hl LOU IG10 ...82 C7
Carronade Pl THMD SE28 ...162 F2
Carron Cl POP/IOD E14 ...140 G8
Carroun Rd VX/NE SW8 ...17 P10
Carroway La GFD/PVL UB6. ...154 C1
Carrow Rd DAGW RM9 ...143 L2
  WOT/HER KT12 ...197 L10
Carr Rd NTHLT UB5 ...134 A2
  WALTH E17 ...100 E10
Carrs La WCHMH N21 ...79 L9
Carr St POP/IOD E14 ...140 D8
Carshalton Gv SUT SM1 ...221 N1
Carshalton Park Rd CAR SM5. ...222 A9
Carshalton Pl CAR SM5. ...222 A9
Carshalton Rd BNSTD SM7 ...222 A9
  MTCM CR4 ...202 B5
  SUT SM1 ...221 M2
Carsington Gdns DART DA1 ...187 L5
Carslake Rd PUT/ROE SW15 ...178 F2
Carson Rd CAN/RD E16 ...141 M1
  DUL SE21 ...181 N2
  EBAR EN4 ...78 A1
Carstairs Rd CAT SE6 ...183 H6
Carston Cl LEE/GVPK SE12 ...183 L1
Carswell Cl REDBR IG4. ...F2
Carswell Rd CAT SE6 ...183 H3
Cartbridge Cl RPLY/SEND GU23 ...232 F3
Cartel Cl PUR RM19 ...166 C3
Carter Cl CDALE/KGS NW9 ...F4
  CRW RM5. ...F8
  WDSR SL4 ...148 F8
  WLGTN SM6 ...222 E4
Carter Dr CRW RM5. ...C5
Carteret St STJSPK SW1H ...11 J2
Carteret Wy DEPT SE8 ...160 D3
Carterhatch La EN EN1 ...N5
  PEND EN3 ...80 B6
Carterhatch Rd PEND EN3 ...80 D6
Carter La BLKFR EC4V ...12 D6
Carter Pl WALW SE17 ...18 F8
Carter Rd CRAWE RH10 ...284 E10
  PLSTW E13 ...141 N5
  WIM/MER SW19 ...179 N9
Carters Cl GU GU1 ...250 B6
  KTTN NW5 ...5 J1
  WPK KT4. ...200 G9
Cartersfield Rd WAB EN9 ...63 H10
Carters Hill Cl ELTH/MOT SE9 ...183 P4
Carters La EPP CM16 ...46 E10
  WOKS/MYFD GU22. ...232 F6
Carters Md HLWE CM17 ...47 L2
Cartersmead Cl HORL RH6. ...280 C3
Carters Rw CDW/CHF RM16 ...168 B3
Carter St WALW SE17 ...18 E9
Carthew Rd HMSMTH W6 ...156 F1
Carthew Vls HMSMTH W6 ...156 F1
Carthouse La WOKN/KNAP GU21 ...213 K10
  WOKN/KNAP GU21 ...231 M1
Carthusian St FARR EC1M ...12 E3
Cart La CHING E4 ...K2
  GRAYS RM17 ...167 N4
Cartmel Cl REIG RH2 ...257 P7
  TOTM N17 ...100 A9
Cartmel Ct NTHLT UB5 ...133 M1
Cartmel Gdns MRDN SM4 ...201 M5
Cartmel Rd BXLYHN DA7 ...164 E7
Carton Cl BNSTD SM7 ...C6
  CROY/NA CR0. ...204 D6
Cartwright Gdns STPAN WC1H ...5 L1
Cartwright St WCHPL E1 ...13 N2
Cartwright Wy BARN SW13 ...156 E6

Carve Ley WGCE AL7 ...23 L6
Carver Cl CHSWK W4. ...155 P2
Carver Rd HNHL SE24 ...181 K2
Carville Crs BTFD TW8 ...155 K4
Cary Rd WAN E11 ...121 K9
Carysfort Rd CEND/HSY/T N8. ...118 C2
  STNW/STAM N16 ...M2
Cary Wk RAD WD7 ...56 G10
Cascade Av MUSWH N10 ...118 D2
Cascade Cl STMC/STPC BR5. ...207 M3
Cascade Rd BKHH IG9 ...102 A3
Cascades CROY/NA CR0. ...224 E6
Caselden Cl ADL/WDHM KT15. ...215 M6
Casella Rd NWCR SE14 ...160 C6
Casewick Rd WNWD SE27 ...181 J4
Casey Cl STJWD NW8 ...3 N10
  STJWD NW8 ...9 P2
Casher Rd CRAWE RH10 ...284 D10
Casimir Rd CLPT E5 ...120 A8
Casino Av HNHL SE24 ...181 K1
Caspian St CMBW SE5 ...159 L6
Caspian Wk CAN/RD E16 ...142 A8
Caspian Wy PUR RM19 ...165 P4
  SWCM DA10 ...189 K1
Cassandra Cl NTHLT UB5 ...114 C9
Cassandra Ga CHES/WCR EN8. ...62 C3
Casselden Rd WLSDN NW10 ...136 A2
Cassidy Rd FUL/PGN SW6 ...157 K5
Cassilda Rd ABYW SE2 ...163 K5
Cassilis Rd POP/IOD E14 ...160 F1
  TWK TW1 ...176 C2
Cassiobridge Rd WATW WD18. ...72 F8
Cassiobury Ter
  RKW/CH/CXG WD3 * ...72 F2
Cassiobury Av
  EBED/NFELT TW14 ...174 C3
Cassiobury Park Av WATW WD18. ...72 C7
Cassiobury Rd WALTH E17 ...E2
Cassio Pl WATW WD18 ...72 C8
Cassio Rd WATW WD18 ...73 J8
Cassio Whf WATW WD18 * ...72 D8
Cassland Rd HOM E9 ...140 D1
  THHTH CR7 ...203 L4
Casslee Rd CAT SE6 ...182 E3
Casson St WCHPL E1 ...13 N4
Casstine Cl SWLY BR8 ...208 C1
Castellain Rd MV/WKIL W9 ...8 C1
Castellan Av GPK RM2 ...125 J1
Castellane Cl STAN HA7 ...94 B8
Castello Av PUT/ROE SW15 ...178 F1
Castell Rd LOU IG10 ...82 F5
Castelnau BARN SW13 ...156 E6
Casterbridge Rd BKHTH/KID SE3. ...161 M9
Casterton St HACK E8. ...140 A1
Castile Gdns KGLGY WD4. ...54 A5
Castillon Rd CAT SE6 ...183 K5
Castlands Rd CAT SE6 ...182 E5
Castle Av CHING E4 ...101 J1
  DTCH/LGLY SL3 ...149 M5
  EW KT17 ...220 D5
  RAIN RM13 ...144 F2
  WDR/YW UB7 ...131 P9
  WEA W13 ...135 H7
Castlebar HI EA W5 ...135 H4
Castlebar Ms EA W5 ...135 G4
Castlebar Pk EA W5 ...134 G4
Castlebar Rd EA W5 ...135 H5
Castle Baynard St BLKFR EC4V ...12 C5
Castlebrook Cl LBTH SE11 ...18 G6
Castle Cl ACT W3 ...155 N1
  BUSH WD23 ...74 A10
  HARH RM3 ...105 K4
  HAYES BR2 ...205 K3
  HOD EN11 ...27 H10
  REDH RH1 ...259 K9
  REIG RH2 ...257 H8
  SUN TW16 ...174 F10
  WIM/MER SW19 ...178 G6
Castlecombe Dr WIM/MER SW19 ...178 C5
Castlecombe Rd ELTH/MOT SE9 ...184 B8
Castle Ct BANK EC3V * ...13 H6
  SYD SE26 ...182 D7
Castledine Rd PGE/AN SE20 ...182 A10
Castle Dr BGR/WK TN15 ...247 N4
  HORL RH6 ...280 D6
  REDBR IG4 ...122 B4
  REIG RH2 ...275 K4
Castle Farm Rd RSEV TN14 ...228 G5
Castlefield Rd REIG RH2 ...257 L4
Castleford Av ELTH/MOT SE9 ...184 E4
Castleford Cl BORE WD6 ...75 L4
  TOTM N17 ...99 N7
Castle Gdns DORK RH4 ...255 L10
Castle Gandolph HERT/WAT SC14 * ...25 K6
Castlegate RCH/KEW TW9 ...155 L9
Castle Gate Wy BERK HP4 ...33 P5
Castle Gn WEY KT13 ...196 F10
Castle Grove Rd CHOB/PIR GU24. ...213 K8
Castlehaven Rd CAMTN NW1 ...4 B3
Castle Hl BERK HP4 ...33 P5
  GU GU1 ...268 A2
  HART DA3 ...211 K5
  WDSR SL4 ...149 J2
Castle Hill Av BERK HP4 ...33 P4
  CROY/NA CR0. ...224 C5
Castle Hill Cl BERK HP4 ...33 N4
Castle Hill Pde WEA W13 * ...134 C9
Castle Hill Rd EGH TW20. ...171 N7
Castle La BER DA12 ...191 L5
  WESTW SW1E ...11 H3
Castleleigh Ct ENC/FH EN2 ...79 J9
Castlemaine Av EW KT17 ...220 E5
  SAND/SEL CR2 ...223 N2
Castlemaine St WCHPL E1 ...140 K6
  HHW HP1 ...35 L8
Castle Mead Gdns
  HERT/WAT SC14 * ...25 K5
Castle Ms BERK HP4 * ...34 A5
  CAMTN NW1 ...4 B2
  NFNCH/WDSPK N12 ...97 N6
  TOOT SW17 ...179 P7
  WEY KT13. ...196 E10
Castle Pde EW KT17 * ...220 D4
Castle Pl CAMTN NW1 ...4 F2
  CHSWK W4 ...156 B3
Castle Rd ACT W3 ...135 P7
  CAMTN NW1 ...4 B2
  DAGW RM9 ...143 J3
  EPSOM KT18 ...237 N1
  EYN DA4 ...199 J9
  GRAYS RM17 ...167 K5
  HOD EN11 ...26 G10
  ISLW TW7 ...154 E8
  NFNCH/WDSPK N12 ...97 M4
  NTHLT UB5 ...134 A1
  NWDGN UB2 * ...D5
  PEND EN3 ...80 D5
  STAL AL1 ...38 E6
  WEY KT13 ...196 F10
  WOKN/KNAP GU21 ...211 K6
Castle Rw CHSWK W4 * ...156 A4
Castle Sq BERK HP4 ...33 P5
Castle St BERK HP4 ...33 P5
  CHONG CM5. ...66 A6
  EHAM E6 ...141 H4
  GU GU1 ...268 A2
  HERT/WAT SC14 ...25 L6
  KUT/HW KT1 ...199 C2
  RDART DA2 ...188 F3
  SWCM DA10 ...189 J1
Castleton Av BXLYHN DA7 ...164 E7
  WBLY HA9 ...115 K9
Castleton Cl BNSTD SM7 ...C6
  CROY/NA CR0. ...204 D6
Castleton Gdns WBLY HA9 ...115 K8
Castleton Rd CLAY IG5 ...103 N7
  ELTH/MOT SE9 ...C8
  CDMY/SEVK IG3 ...123 L6

MTCM CR4 ...202 E4
RSLP HA4 ...113 L6
WALTH E17 ...101 J10
Castletown Rd WKENS W14 ...14 B1
Castleview Cl FSBYPK N4 ...119 K7
Castleview Gdns IL IG1 ...122 B4
  WEY KT13. ...216 C1
Castle Vw CRICK NW2 ...136 D1
Castle Wk SUN TW16 ...197 K3
Castle Wy EW KT17 ...220 D6
  FELT TW13. ...175 K7
  WIM/MER SW19 ...178 G6
Castlewood Dr ELTH/MOT SE9 ...162 C8
Castlewood Rd EBAR EN4 ...77 N1
  STNW/STAM N16 ...119 P4
Castle Yd HGT N6 ...118 B5
  RCH/KEW TW9 ...177 J1
  STHWK SE1 ...12 D9
Castor La POP/IOD E14 ...140 G9
Catalina Gv CDW/CHF RM16 ...167 L1
Catalina Rd HTHAIR TW6 ...152 C9
Catalpa Cl GU GU1 * ...249 P8
Catalpa Ct LEW SE13 ...183 J2
Catena Ri LTWR GU18 ...212 A6
Cater Gdns RGUW GU3 ...249 L6
Caterham Av CLAY IG5 ...102 D10
Caterham-by-Pass CTHM CR5 ...242 A8
Caterham Cl CHOB/PIR GU24. ...230 D7
Caterham Ct WAB EN9 ...63 L8
Caterham Dr COUL/CHIP CR5. ...241 K5
Caterham Rd LEW SE13 ...161 K9
Catesby St WALW SE17 ...19 H6
Catford Broadway CAT SE6 ...182 C3
Catford HI CAT SE6 ...182 A4
Catford Island CAT SE6 ...182 C3
Catford Rd CAT SE6 ...182 B1
Cathall Rd WAN E11 ...121 K8
Catham Cl STAL AL1 ...38 D8
Catharine St CMBW SE5 ...159 H4
Cathay St BERM/RHTH SE16 ...160 A7
Cathcart Dr ORP BR6 ...207 H9
Cathcart HI ARCH N19 ...118 D8
Cathcart Rd WBPTN SW10 ...15 J8
Cathcart St KTTN NW5 ...4 E1
Cathedral Cl GUW GU2 ...267 N1
Cathedral HI GUW GU2 ...249 N9
Cathedral St STHWK SE1 ...12 G9
Catherall Rd HBRY N5 ...119 H6
Catherine Cl BF/WBF KT14 ...215 P10
  BRWN CM15 ...E9
  HHNE HP2 ...36 D1
  LOU IG10 ...82 C10
Catherine Ct RCH/KEW TW9 ...155 K10
  SUN TW16 ...174 D10
Catherine Gdns HSLW TW3 ...154 C10
Catherine Griffiths Ct
  CLKNW EC1R ...12 B1
Catherine Gv GNWCH SE10 ...160 G7
Catherine Howard Ct WEY KT13 ...196 C10
Catherine Pl HRW HA1 ...114 E3
  WESTW SW1E ...16 G3
Catherine Rd GPK RM2 ...125 J3
  KUT/HW KT1 ...199 L2
  PEND EN3 ...80 D3
  SURB KT6. ...199 J5
Catherine St CHEL SW3 ...16 A9
  HOL/ALD WC2B * ...11 N7
  STALW/RED AL3 ...38 C5
Catherine Vls RYNPK SW20 * ...178 E10
Catherine Wheel Aly
  LVPST EC2M ...13 K4
Catherine Wheel Rd BTFD TW8 ...155 J6
Catherine Wheel Yd
  WHALL SW1A ...10 G10
Cat HI EBAR EN4 ...77 P10
  EBAR EN4 ...78 A9
Cathles Rd BAL SW12 ...180 C2
Cathnor Rd SHB W12 ...156 E1
Cathrow Ms HOD EN11 ...26 E10
Catisfield Rd PEND EN3 ...80 D3
Catkin Cl HHW HP1 ...35 L5
Catlin Crs SHPTN TW17 ...196 E6
Catlin Gdns GDST RH9 ...260 A7
Catling Cl FSTH SE23 ...182 B4
Catlin's La PIN HA5 ...113 J1
Catlin St BERM/RHTH SE16 ...19 M5
  HHS/BOV HP3 ...35 L9
Cator Cl CROY/NA CR0. ...225 K7
Cator Cr CROY/NA CR0. ...225 K7
Cator La BECK BR3 ...204 D2
Cator Rd CAR SM5 ...222 A2
  SYD SE26 ...182 C9
Cator St PECK SE15 ...19 L10
Cato St MBLAR W1H ...9 P5
Catsdell Bottom HHS/BOV HP3 ...36 C9
Catsey La BUSH WD23 ...94 B1
Catsey Wd BUSH WD23 ...94 B1
Catterick Cl FBAR/BDGN N11 ...98 A7
Catterick Wy BORE WD6. ...75 L5
Cattistock Rd ELTH/MOT SE9 ...184 B8
Cattlegate Rd POTB/CUF EN6. ...60 E7
  ENC/FH EN2 ...60 E10
Cattley Cl BAR EN5 ...77 H8
Cattlins Cl CHESW EN7 ...61 M5
Catton St RSQ WC1B ...11 M4
Cattsdell HHNE HP2 ...35 P4
Caudwell Ter
  WAND/EARL SW18 ...179 J1
Caulfield Rd EHAM E6 ...142 C2
  PECK SE15 ...159 L2
Causeway EBED/NFELT TW14 ...153 J10
Causeway Br PUR RM19 ...166 D2
Causeway Cl POTB/CUF EN6 ...59 N7
The Causeway BELMT SM2 ...221 M5
  CAR SM5. ...202 B10
  CHSGTN KT9 ...219 K1
  EFNCH N2 ...117 N2
  ESH/CLAY KT10 ...218 A4
  IL IG1 * ...123 N10
  STA TW18 ...172 F7
  TEDD TW11 ...176 A1
  WAND/EARL SW18 ...160 A10
  WIM/MER SW19 ...178 D6
Causeyware Rd ED N9 ...90 B10
Causton Cottages
  POP/IOD E14 * ...140 C7
Causton Rd HGT N6 ...118 C5
Causton Sq DAGE RM10 ...144 B2
Causton St WEST SW1P ...17 H6
Cautherly La WARE SG12 ...26 B1
Cautley Av CLAP SW4 ...180 D1
Cavalier Cl CHDH RM6 ...123 M2
Cavalier Ct BERK HP4. ...33 P5
Cavalier Gdns HYS/HAR UB3 ...132 B8
Cavalry Crs HSLWW TW4 ...153 L10
  WDSR SL4 ...148 G9
Cavalry Gdns PUT/ROE SW15 ...179 J1
Cavan Dr STALW/RED AL3. ...38 C1
Cavan Pl PIN HA5 ...93 N9
Cavaye Pl WBPTN SW10. ...15 K8
Cavell Ct BROX EN10 * ...29 H6
Cavell Dr ENC/FH EN2 ...79 H1
Cavell Rd CHESW EN7 ...61 N1
  TOTM N17 ...99 J6
Cavell St WCHPL E1 ...140 C4
Cavell Wy HAYES BR2 ...205 M8
  SLN SL2 ...128 E8
Cavendish Av BFN/LL DA15 ...185 K5
  ERITH DA8 ...164 D5
  FNCH N3 ...97 H2
  HCH RM12 ...145 J1
  HRW HA1 ...114 C9
  NWMAL KT3 ...200 E3
  RSLP HA4 ...113 P7
  RYNPK SW20 ...200 F5
  SEV TN13 ...247 H8
  STHGT/OAK N14 ...98 C2
  WELL DA16 ...164 G4
  WLSDN NW10 ...D1
Cavendish Cl AMS HP6 ...69 C7

KIL/WHAMP NW6 ...2 C2
STJWD NW8 ...3 M9
SUN TW16 ...174 Q9
UED N18 * ...100 A6
YEAD UB4 ...132 F7
Cavendish Crs BORE WD6. ...75 M8
  HCH RM12 ...145 J1
Cavendish Dr EDGW HA8 ...95 L7
  ESH/CLAY KT10 ...218 D2
  WAN E11 ...121 J6
Cavendish Gdns BARK IG11 ...123 J10
  CHDH RM6 ...123 P3
  CLAP SW4 ...180 D2
  IL IG1 ...122 B2
  REDH RH1 ...258 B9
Cavendish Meads ASC SL5 ...192 C6
Cavendish Ms North GTPST W1W ...10 F3
Cavendish Ms South
  GTPST W1W * ...10 F4
Cavendish Pde CLAP SW4 * ...158 D10
  HSLWW TW4 ...153 M8
Cavendish Pl BMLY BR1 ...206 C3
  CAVSQ/HST W1G. ...10 F5
Cavendish Rd BAL SW12 ...180 D3
  BAR EN5 ...76 F2
  BELMT SM2 ...221 M4
  CHING E4 ...100 B1
  CHSWK W4 ...156 A6
  CLAP SW4 ...180 C2
  CROY/NA CR0. ...203 J8
  FELT TW13. ...175 L7
  KIL/WHAMP NW6 ...2 C1
  NWMAL KT3 ...200 C4
  REDH RH1 ...258 B10
  STAL AL1 ...38 E4
  SUN TW16 ...174 C9
  UED N18 ...100 A6
  WEY KT13 ...216 D4
  WIM/MER SW19 ...179 P10
  WOKS/MYFD GU22 ...232 C6
Cavendish Sq CAVSQ/HST W1G ...10 F5
  HART DA3. ...211 J3
Cavendish St IS N1 ...6 G8
Cavendish Ter FELT TW13 * ...175 K5
  FELT TW13 * ...175 N7
Cavendish Wy HAYES BR2 ...205 K9
  WWKM BR4 ...204 C4
Cavenham Cl WOKS/MYFD GU22 ...232 B5
Cavenham Gdns EMPK RM11 ...125 K3
  IL IG1 ...122 D8
Caverleigh Wy WPK KT4 ...200 D8
Caverley Gdns
  KTN/HRWW/WS HA3 ...115 J5
Cave St IS N1 ...5 M6
Caversham Av CHEAM SM3 ...201 H9
  PLMGR N13 ...99 J1
Caversham Rd KTTN NW5 ...4 G1
  KUT/HW KT1 ...199 L2
  SEVS/STOTM N15 ...119 K2
Caversham St CHEL SW3 ...16 A9
Caverswall St SHB W12 ...136 F6
Cawcott Dr WDSR SL4 ...148 D7
Cawdor Av SOCK/AV RM15 ...146 F9
Cawdor Crs HNWL W7 ...154 A4
Cawley Hatch HLWW/ROY CM19. ...46 A4
Cawnpore St NRWD SE19 ...181 M8
Cawsey Wy WOKS/MYFD GU22 ...232 B3
Caxton Av ADL/WDHM KT15 ...215 K3
The Caxton Centre
  STALW/RED AL3 * ...38 E1
Caxton Cl CRAWE RH10 ...283 N10
  HART DA3. ...211 L4
Caxton Dr UX/CGN UB8 ...131 M4
Caxton Gdns GUW GU2 ...249 N9
Caxton Gv BOW E3 ...140 A8
Caxton Ms BTFD TW8 * ...155 J6
Caxton Ri REDH RH1 ...258 E5
Caxton Rd HOD EN11 ...26 C9
  NWDGN UB2 ...132 E3
  SHB W12 ...136 G10
  WDGN N22 ...98 D10
  WIM/MER SW19 ...179 M8
The Caxtons BRXN/ST SW9 * ...17 J3
Caxton St STJSPK SW1H ...17 J3
Caxton St North CAN/RD E16 ...141 L8
Caxton Wy ROM RM1 ...124 F2
  WATW WD18 ...92 E1
Cayenne Ct STHWK SE1 * ...19 N1
Caygill Cl HAYES BR2 ...205 L4
Cayley Rd NWDGN UB2 ...154 A2
Cayton Pl CLKNW EC1R ...6 F8
Cayton Rd COUL/CHIP CR5. ...240 E8
  GFD/PVL UB6. ...134 D4
Cayton St FSBYE EC1V ...6 F8
Cazenove Rd STNW/STAM N16. ...119 N7
  WALTH E17 ...101 J10
Cearn Wy COUL/CHIP CR5. ...240 G2
Cecil Av BARK IG11 ...142 C2
  EN EN1 ...C7
  HCH RM12 ...125 J1
  WBLY HA9 ...115 L10
Cecil Cl ASHF TW15 ...174 D10
  CHSGTN KT9 ...219 J1
  EA W5 ...135 J7
Cecil Ct BAR EN5 ...L3
  CHCR WC2N ...11 L8
  HLWS CM18 ...M5
Cecil Crs HART AL10 ...40 E2
Cecile Pk CEND/HSY/T N8. ...118 F4
Cecilia Cl EFNCH N2 ...117 M1
Cecilia Rd HACK E8. ...119 N10
Cecil Pk PIN HA5 ...113 N2
Cecil Pl MTCM CR4 ...202 A5
Cecil Rd ACT W3 ...135 P7
  CDALE/KGS NW9 ...96 C10
  CHDH RM6 ...123 P6
  CHES/WCR EN8 ...62 C3
  CROY/NA CR0. ...202 G7
  ENC/FH EN2 ...79 J4
  GVW DA11 ...190 C4
  HERT/BAY SG13 ...25 H1
  HOD EN11 ...45 H1
  HSLW TW3 ...154 C8
  IL IG1 ...122 E9
  IVER SL0 ...131 H1
  KTN/HRWW/WS HA3 ...94 B9
  PLSTW E13 ...141 M3
  POTB/CUF EN6 ...58 E6
  STAL AL1 ...38 E6
  SUT SM1 ...221 J4
  WALTH E17 ...100 G2
  WAN E11 ...121 J6
  WIM/MER SW19 ...179 K3
  WLSDN NW10 ...H1
Cecil St WATN WD24 ...J3
Cecil Wy HAYES BR2 ...205 N9
  SLN SL2 ...128 B6
Cedar Av BFN/LL DA15 ...185 K5
  BAR EN5 ...C4
  CRICK NW2 ...A1
  EN EN1 ...C7
  HYS/HAR UB3 ...132 C4
  RDART DA2 ...187 M2
  RKW/CH/CXG WD3. ...M2
  WALTH E17 ...120 F3
Cedar Cl ASC SL5 ...192 E7
  CSHM HP5 ...P2
  CHOB/PIR GU24. ...F1
  CSHM HP5 ...32
  STHL UB1 ...133 P7
Cedar Copse BMLY BR1 ...206 C5
Cedar Cl CHARL SE7 * ...161 P5
  CSHM HP5 ...C9
  ELTH/MOT SE9 ...184 B2
  STALE/WH AL4 ...39 J6
  WIM/MER SW19 ...178 A9
Cedar Crs HAYES BR2 ...206 B10
Cedarcroft Rd CHSGTN KT9 ...219 L1
Cedar Dr ASC SL5 ...192 F7
  CSHM HP5 ...P5
  EFNCH N2 ...117 P2
  EYN DA4 ...210 A2
  LHD/OX KT22 ...236 D9
  PIN HA5 ...94 C10
  SL SL1 ...E6
Cedar Gdns BELMT SM2 ...221 M3
  UPMR RM14 ...126 B8
  WOKN/KNAP GU21 ...231 N4
Cedar Gv AMSS HP7 ...J5
  BXLY DA5 ...185 L5
  CHOB/PIR GU24. ...230 F1
  CSHM HP5 ...C5
  STHL UB1 ...133 P7
Cedar Hts RCHPK/HAM TW10 ...177 K4
Cedar La EPSOM KT18 ...237 P1
Cedarhurst BMLY BR1 * ...183 K10
Cedarhurst Dr ELTH/MOT SE9 ...183 P5
Cedar Lawn Av BAR EN5 ...77 H9
Cedar Ldg CHEL SW3 ...M8
Cedar Mt ELTH/MOT SE9 ...184 A4
Cedarne Rd FUL/PGN SW6 ...157 K6
Cedar Park Gdns CHDH RM6. ...123 N5
Cedar Park Rd ENC/FH EN2 ...79 J4
Cedar Pl CHARL SE7 * ...161 P4
Cedar Rdg AMS HP6 ...50 B10
Cedar Ri STHGT/OAK N14 ...98 B1
  SOCK/AV RM15 ...147 L6
Cedar Rd BELMT SM2 ...221 M3
  BERK HP4 ...34 A6
  BMLY BR1 ...205 B6
  CRICK NW2 ...A1
  CROY/NA CR0. ...J8
  DART DA1 ...187 L5
  E/WMO/HCT KT8 ...E4
  EBED/NFELT TW14 ...174 E4
  ENC/FH EN2 ...79 J1
  ERITH DA8 ...165 H7
  HAT AL10 ...40 D6
  HCH RM12 ...125 K8
  HSLWW TW4 ...153 K8
  OXHEY WD19 ...73 K10
  ROMW/RG RM7 ...124 D2
  TEDD TW11 ...176 B1
  TOTM N17 ...99 N9
  WEY KT13 ...216 B1
  WOKS/MYFD GU22 ...231 N6
Cedars BNSTD SM7 ...222 A10
  WAB EN9 ...P1
Cedars Av MTCM CR4 ...202 B4
  RKW/CH/CXG WD3. ...M2
  WALTH E17 ...F3
Cedars Cl BORE WD6. ...75 N8
  CFSP/GDCR SL9. ...90 B6
  HDN NW4 ...L6
  LEW SE13 ...161 J9
Cedars Cottages
  PUT/ROE SW15 * ...178 D2
Cedars Ct ED N9 ...D4
  GU GU1 ...250 D7
Cedars Dr HGDN/ICK UB10. ...132 B4
Cedars Ms CLAP SW4 * ...158 C10
Cedars Rd BARN SW13 ...156 C8
  BECK BR3 ...204 D2
  CHSWK W4 ...155 N4
  CLAP SW4 ...158 C10
  CROY/NA CR0. ...202 F10
  ED N9 ...H3
  KUT/HW KT1 ...199 H1
  MRDN SM4 ...201 K4
  SRTFD E15 ...141 K1
The Cedars BERK HP4 * ...34 B5
  BF/WBF KT14 ...216 A8
  BKHH IG9 ...101 M2
  BRKHM/BTCW RH3 ...255 M10
  GU GU1 ...250 D7
  HARP AL5 ...20 A2
  HOM E9 * ...C2
  LHD/OX KT22 ...237 K7
  REIG RH2 ...257 N10
  SRTFD E15 * ...141 L3
  TEDD TW11 * ...176 E9
Cedar Ter RCH/KEW TW9 ...155 L10
Cedar Terrace Rd SEV TN13 ...247 J8
Cedar Tree Gv WNWD SE27 ...181 J8
Cedarville Gdns
  STRHM/NOR SW16 ...180 C9
Cedar Wk ESH/CLAY KT10 ...218 E3
  HHS/BOV HP3 ...35 N8
  KWD/TDW/WH KT20 ...239 J7
  PUR/KEN CR8 ...241 K2
Cedar Wy BERK HP4 ...A6
  CAMTN NW1 ...5 J4
  DTCH/LGLY SL3 ...150 B3
  GU GU1 ...249 P7
  SUN TW16 ...174 F10
Cedar Wood Dr GSTN WD25. ...73 K1
Cedarwood Dr STALE/WH AL4 ...39 K1
Cedric Av ROM RM1 ...J6
Cedric Rd ELTH/MOT SE9 ...184 F6
Celadon Cl PEND EN3 ...81 J2
Celandine Cl POP/IOD E14 * ...140 H6
  SOCK/AV RM15 ...147 H6
  THMD SE28 ...143 L10
Celandine Gv STHGT/OAK N14 ...78 D10
Celandine Rd WOT/HER KT12 ...217 M1
Celandine Wy SRTFD E15 ...141 K5
Celbridge Ms BAY/PAD W2 ...9 H5
Celedon Cl CDW/CHF RM16 ...167 L1
Celestial Gdns LEW SE13 ...161 J2
Celia Cl STALE/WH AL4 ...39 H6
Celia Crs ASHF TW15 ...173 N9
Celia Rd ARCH N19 ...118 C10
Cell Barnes Cl STAL AL1 ...38 G8
Cell Barnes La STAL AL1 ...38 G8
Cell Farm Av WDSR SL4 ...171 N1
Celtic Av HAYES BR2 ...205 P7
Celtic Rd BF/WBF KT14 ...215 P10
Celtic St POP/IOD E14 ...140 F4
Cement Block Cottages
  GRAYS RM17 * ...167 P4
Cemetery HI HHW HP1 ...35 M7
Cemetery La CHARL SE7 ...162 D5
Cemetery Pales CHOB/PIR GU24. ...230 F8
Cemetery Rd ABYW SE2 ...163 L5
  FSTGT E7 ...121 L2
  TOTM N17 ...99 P6
Cemmaes Court Rd HHW HP1 ...35 M5
Cemmaes Meadow HHW HP1 ...35 M5
Cenacle Cl HAMP NW3. ...117 K8

Centaur Ct BTFD TW8 * 155 K4
Centaur St STHWK SE1 17 P3
Centenary Rd PEND EN3 80 E8
Centenary Wk CHING E4 101 L4
EPP CM16 64 F10
LOU IG10 81 N10
WALTH E17 121 K1
WAN E11 121 M7
Centennial Av BORE WD6 94 G1
Centennial Pk BORE WD6 95 H1
Central Ar ASHF TW15 * 174 A7
Central Av CHES/WCR EN8 62 D9
E/WMO/HCT KT8 197 N5
ED N9 99 N4
EFNCH N2 97 N10
EN EN1 79 P6
GVE DA12 190 E5
HSLW TW3 154 B10
HYS/HAR UB3 133 H9
PIN HA5 113 N4
SOCK/AV RM15 166 B1
TIL RM18 168 D7
WAN E11 121 J7
WELL DA16 163 K8
WLGTN SM6 222 F2
Central Buildings EA W5 * 135 J9
Central Circ HDN NW4 116 E3
Central Ct CHIG IG7 103 H6
Central Dr HCH RM12 125 N8
SL SL1 128 E9
STAL AL1 39 H5
WGCE AL7 23 J3
Central Hall Buildings
ARCH N19 * 118 D7
Central Hl NRWD SE19 181 K8
Central La WDSR SL4 170 A4
Central Pde ACT W3 * 155 M1
BFN/LL DA15 * 185 K6
CROY/NA CR0 225 H6
E/WMO/HCT KT8 * 197 N4
GFD/PVL UB6 * 134 F5
HORL RH6 * 280 B5
HRW HA1 114 E3
PEND EN3 * 80 B6
PGE/AN SE20 * 182 C10
STRHM/NOR SW16 * 180 F7
SURB KT6 * 199 K6
WALTH E17 * 120 F2
Central Park Av DAGE RM10 124 D9
Central Park Est HSLWW TW4 * 153 L10
Central Park Rd EHAM E6 142 B4
Central Pl SNWD SE25 * 203 P4
Central Rd ALP/SUD HA0 114 G10
DART DA1 187 M1
HLW CM20 29 K7
MRDN SM4 201 L5
WPK KT4 200 D9
Central Sq E/WMO/HCT KT8 197 N4
GLDGN NW11 117 K4
Central St FSBYE EC1V 6 E10
Central Ter BECK BR3 * 204 C3
Central Wy CAR SM5 221 P4
EBED/NFELT TW14 175 J1
NTHWD HA6 92 F8
OXTED RH8 261 J3
THMD SE28 143 L9
WLSDN NW10 135 P5
Centre Av ACT W3 136 A10
EPP CM16 65 J8
Centre Common Rd CHST BR7 184 F10
Centre Dr EPP CM16 65 J8
Centre Gn EPP CM16 65 J8
Centre Rd DAGE RM10 144 C4
HART DA3 211 K10
WAN E11 121 M7
WDSR SL4 * 148 B6
Centre St BETH E2 140 A4
The Centre FELT TW13 175 H5
Centre Wy ED N9 100 B3
WAB EN9 81 H1
Centric Cl CAMTN NW1 * 4 E5
Centro HHNE HP2 36 D4
Centurian Wy ERITHM DA18 164 A2
Centurion Cl HOLWY N7 5 N3
Centurion Ct WLGTN SM6 * 202 C9
Centurion La BOW E3 140 E4
Centurion Sq CHARL SE7 * 162 B6
Centurion Wy PUR RM19 165 N3
Century Cl HDN NW4 116 G3
Century Ct WATW WD18 * 92 D1
WOKN/KNAP GU21 232 C2
Century Ms CLPT E5 * 120 B9
Century Pk WAT WD17 * 73 K9
Century Rd EGH TW20 172 F8
HOD EN11 44 F2
WALTH E17 120 D1
WARE SG12 26 C1
Cephas Av WCHPL E1 140 B6
Cephas St WCHPL E1 140 B6
Ceres Rd WOOL/PLUM SE18 163 J3
Cerise Rd PECK SE15 159 P7
Cerne Cl YEAD UB4 133 K9
Cerne Rd GVE DA12 191 H7
MRDN SM4 201 M6
Cerotus Pl CHERT KT16 195 J7
Cervantes Ct BAY/PAD W2 9 H6
NTHWD HA6 92 G8
Cervia Wy GVE DA12 191 J6
Cestreham Crs CSHM HP5 51 J5
Ceylon Rd WKENS W14 14 A4
Chabot Dr PECK SE15 160 A9
Chace Av POTB/CUF EN6 59 N8
Chacombe Pl BEAC HP9 88 C6
Chadacre Av CLAY IG5 122 C1
Chadacre Rd EW KT17 220 E2
Chadbourn St POP/IOD E14 140 G7
Chad Crs ED N9 100 B4
Chadd Dr BMLY BR1 206 B3
Chadfields TIL RM18 168 D6
Chadhurst Cl RDKG RH5 273 J5
Chadville Gdns CHDH RM6 123 N3
Chadway BCTR RM8 123 M7
Chadwell WARE SG12 26 B3
Chadwell Av CHDH RM6 123 L5
CHES/WCR EN8 62 B4
Chadwell By-Pass
CDW/CHF RM16 168 D4
Chadwell Heath La CHDH RM6 123 M3
Chadwell Hl CDW/CHF RM16 168 E4
Chadwell Ri WARE SG12 26 B3
Chadwell Rd GRAYS RM17 167 P3
Chadwell St CLKNW EC1R 6 B9
Chadwick Av CHING E4 101 J5
WCHMH N21 * 78 G9
WIM/MER SW19 179 K9
Chadwick Cl GVW DA11 190 B5
PUT/ROE SW15 178 C3
TEDD TW11 176 F9
Chadwick Dr HARH RM3 105 L10
Chadwick Pl SURB KT6 199 H6
Chadwick Rd IL IG1 122 E8
PECK SE15 159 N8
WAN E11 121 K5
WLSDN NW10 136 C3
Chadwick St WEST SW1P 17 J4
Chadwick Wy THMD SE28 143 N9
Chadwin Rd PLSTW E13 141 N7
Chadworth Wy ESH/CLAY KT10 218 C2
Chaffers Md ASHTD KT21 237 L2
Chaffinch Av CROY/NA CR0 204 C6
Chaffinch Cl CRAWW RH11 283 N5
CROY/NA CR0 204 C5
ED N9 100 C2
SURB KT6 199 M10
Chaffinch Ct ORP BR6 207 K7
Chaffinches Gn HHS/BOV HP3 36 B10
Chaffinch La WATW WD18 92 G1
Chaffinch Rd BECK BR3 204 D1
Chaffinch Wy HORL RH6 279 P3
Chafford Wy CDW/CHF RM16 147 M10
CHDH RM6 123 M2
Chagford St CAMTN NW1 10 A2
Chailey Av EN EN1 79 N6
Chailey Cl CRAWW RH11 283 K10
HEST TW5 153 L7
Chailey Pl WOT/HER KT12 217 M1
Chailey St CLPT E5 120 B8
Chain Wk CHESW EN7 61 K6
ENC/FH EN2 61 M10
ENC/FH EN2 79 H2
HERT/BAY SG13 42 C3
HERT/WAT SG14 24 B1
POTB/CUF EN6 60 E3
Chalbury Wk IS N1 5 P7
Chalcombe Rd ABYW SE2 163 L2
Chalcot Cl BELMT SM2 221 K4
Chalcot Crs CAMTN NW1 4 B5
Chalcot Gdns HAMP NW3 4 A2
Chalcot Ms STRHM/NOR SW16 180 F6
Chalcot Rd CAMTN NW1 4 C5
Chalcot Sq CAMTN NW1 4 C4
Chalcott Gdns SURB KT6 * 199 H8
Chalcroft Rd LEW SE13 183 K1
Chaldon Cl REDH RH1 275 P2
Chaldon Common Rd CTHM CR3 241 K10
Chaldon Rd CTHM CR3 241 L9
FUL/PGN SW6 157 H6
Chaldon Wy COUL/CHIP CR5 240 F3
Chale Rd BRXS/STRHM SW2 180 F2
Chalet Cl BERK HP4 33 L5
BXLY DA5 186 E7
Chalet Est MLHL NW7 * 96 D5
Chalfont Av AMS HP6 70 A5
WBLY HA9 135 N1
Chalfont Cl HHNE HP2 36 C1
Chalfont Gn ED N9 99 M4
Chalfont La RKW/CH/CXG WD3 70 E9
RKW/CH/CXG WD3 90 F8
Chalfont Ms WAND/EARL SW18 179 J4
Chalfont Pl STAL AL1 * 38 D6
Chalfont Rd BEAC HP9 89 J6
CSTG HP8 90 E4
ED N9 99 M4
HYS/HAR UB3 153 H1
SNWD SE25 203 N3
Chalfont Station Rd AMSS HP7 69 P6
Chalfont Wk PIN HA5 * 93 K10
Chalfont Wy WEA W13 154 G2
Chalford Cl E/WMO/HCT KT8 197 P4
Chalforde Gdns GPK RM2 125 J2
Chalford Rd DUL SE21 181 L7
Chalford Wk WFD IG8 102 A9
Chalgrove WGCE AL7 23 N4
Chalgrove Av MRDN SM4 201 K5
Chalgrove Crs CLAY IG5 102 B10
Chalgrove Gdns FNCH N3 117 H1
Chalgrove Rd BELMT SM2 221 N4
HACK E8 140 B1
TOTM N17 100 A9
Chalice Cl WLGTN SM6 222 E3
Chalice Wy RDART DA2 188 D1
Chalk Ct GRAYS RM17 * 167 M5
Chalk Dl WGCE AL7 23 L4
Chalkdell Flds STALE/WH AL4 38 F3
Chalkdell Hl HHNE HP2 35 P6
Chalkenden Cl PGE/AN SE20 182 A10
Chalk Farm Pde HAMP NW3 * 4 C3
Chalk Farm Rd CAMTN NW1 4 C3
Chalk Hl AMSS HP7 88 E1
CSHM HP5 50 G6
OXHEY WD19 73 M10
Chalk Hill Rd HMSMTH W6 156 G3
Chalkhill Rd WBLY HA9 115 M8
Chalklands WBLY HA9 115 P8
Chalk La ASHTD KT21 237 M5
EBAR EN4 78 A7
EHSLY KT24 252 G7
EPSOM KT18 238 B2
HLWE CM17 30 B9
MFD/CHID GU8 266 C9
Chalkley Cl MTCM CR4 202 A2
Chalkmill Dr EN EN1 80 A7
Chalk Paddock EPSOM KT18 238 A1
Chalk Pit Av STMC/STPC BR5 207 N3
Chalkpit La BRKHM/BTCW RH3 255 N9
DORK RH4 254 F10
Chalk Pit La GT/LBKH KT23 253 N3
Chalkpit La OXTED RH8 261 H3
Chalk Pit La SL SL1 128 A3
Chalk Pit Rd BNSTD SM7 239 K3
EPSOM KT18 237 P5
SUT SM1 221 M2
Chalkpit Ter DORK RH4 254 F10
Chalkpit Wd OXTED RH8 261 J3
Chalk Rd GVE DA12 191 K4
PLSTW E13 141 N7
Chalkstone Cl WELL DA16 163 K7
Chalkways BGR/WK TN15 247 M2
Chalkwell Park Av EN EN1 79 M8
Chalky Bank GVW DA11 190 D7
Chalky La CHSGTN KT9 219 J6
Challacombe Cl
RBRW/HUT CM13 107 N2
Challenge Cl GVE DA12 191 J7
WLSDN NW10 136 B3
Challenge Ct LHD/OX KT22 236 G5
Challenge Rd ASHF TW15 174 D6
Challice Wy BRXS/STRHM SW2 180 G4
Challinor HLWE CM17 47 P1
Challin St PGE/AN SE20 204 B1
Challis Rd BTFD TW8 155 J4
Challock Cl BH/WHM TN16 243 P2
Challoner Cl EFNCH N2 97 N10
Challoner Crs WKENS W14 14 C8
Challoners Cl E/WMO/HCT KT8 198 C4
Challoner St WKENS W14 14 C7
Chalmers Cl HORL RH6 279 H9
Chalmers Rd ASHF TW15 174 C7
BNSTD SM7 239 M1
Chalmers Rd East ASHF TW15 174 C7
Chalmers Wy EBED/NFELT TW14 175 J1
TWK TW1 154 G10
Chalsey Rd BROCKY SE4 160 E10
Chalton Dr EFNCH N2 117 M4
Chalton St CAMTN NW1 5 J7
Chalvey Gv SL SL1 148 G2
Chalvey Pk SL SL1 149 K1
Chalvey Rd East SL SL1 149 K2
Chalvey Rd West SL SL1 149 J1
Chamberlain Cl HLWE CM17 47 M1
IL IG1 122 F8
THMD SE28 162 G2
Chamberlain Cottages
CMBW SE5 * 159 L7
Chamberlain Crs WWKM BR4 204 G8
Chamberlain Gdns HSLW TW3 154 B7
Chamberlain La PIN HA5 113 H2
Chamberlain Pl WALTH E17 120 D1
Chamberlain Rd EFNCH N2 97 M10
WEA W13 154 F1
Chamberlain St HAMP NW3 4 B4
Chamberlain Wy PIN HA5 113 J1
SURB KT6 199 K7
Chamberlayne Av WBLY HA9 115 K8
Chamberlayne Rd WLSDN NW10 136 F3
Chamberlens Garages
HMSMTH W6 * 156 E3
Chambersbury La HHS/BOV HP3 54 B1
Chambers Cl RDART DA2 188 F1
Chambers Gdns EFNCH N2 97 N9
Chambers Gv WGCE AL7 23 H8
Chambers La WLSDN NW10 136 E2
Chambers Pl SAND/SEL CR2 223 L4
Chambers Rd HOLWY N7 118 F9
Chambers St BERM/RHTH SE16 19 N1
HERT/WAT SG14 25 K5
Chamber St WCHPL E1 13 M7
Chambon Pl HMSMTH W6 156 D3
Chambord St BETH E2 7 M10
Champa Cl TOTM N17 99 N10
Champion Crs SYD SE26 182 D7
Champion Down EHSLY KT24 253 M4
Champion Gv CMBW SE5 159 L9
Champion Hl CMBW SE5 159 L10
Champion Pk CMBW SE5 159 L8
Champion Rd SYD SE26 182 D7
UPMR RM14 126 A7
Champions Cl BORE WD6 75 N3
Champions Wy HOD EN11 26 F10
Champness Cl WNWD SE27 181 L7
Champness Rd BARK IG11 143 J2
Champney Cl DTCH/LGLY SL3 150 D9
Champneys OXHEY WD19 * 93 M3
Champneys Cl BELMT SM2 221 J4
Chance Cl CDW/CHF RM16 167 L2
Chancellor Gdns SAND/SEL CR2 223 J5
Chancellor Gv DUL SE21 181 K5
Chancellor Pl CDALE/KGS NW9 96 C10
Chancellors AMSS HP7 68 A8
Chancellor's Rd HMSMTH W6 156 F4
Chancellors St HMSMTH W6 156 F4
Chancellors Whf HMSMTH W6 156 F5
Chancelot Rd ABYW SE2 163 L3
Chancel St STHWK SE1 12 C9
Chancery Cl STALE/WH AL4 39 J1
Chancery La BECK BR3 204 G2
LINN WC2A 11 P4
Chancery Ms TOOT SW17 179 P5
Chance St BETH E2 13 L1
Chanctonbury Cha REDH RH1 276 C1
Chanctonbury Cl ELTH/MOT SE9 184 E6
Chanctonbury Dr ASC SL5 192 D8
Chanctonbury Gdns BELMT SM2 221 L4
Chanctonbury Wy CRAWW RH11 283 M9
NFNCH/WDSPK N12 97 K5
Chandler Av CAN/RD E16 141 M7
Chandler Cl CRAWE RH10 283 N9
HPTN TW12 197 N1
Chandler Rd LOU IG10 82 E5
Chandlers Cl EBED/NFELT TW14 174 G4
Chandlers Ct LEE/GVPK SE12 * 183 N5
Chandlers Dr ERITH DA8 164 F3
Chandler's La RKW/CH/CXG WD3 71 P2
Chandlers Ms POP/IOD E14 160 F1
Chandlers Rd STALE/WH AL4 39 H3
Chandler St WAP E1W 140 A10
Chandlers Wk BRWN CM15 86 D3
Chandlers Wy HERT/WAT SG14 25 H5
ROM RM1 124 F3
Chandler Wy PECK SE15 19 K10
Chandos Av EA W5 155 H3
STHGT/OAK N14 98 D4
TRDG/WHET N20 97 N2
WALTH E17 * 100 F10
Chandos Cl AMS HP6 69 P4
BKHH IG9 101 N3
Chandos Ct STAN HA7 94 G7
Chandos Crs EDGW HA8 95 L8
Chandos Gdns COUL/CHIP CR5 241 J5
Chandos Pl CHCR WC2N 11 L8
Chandos Rd BORE WD6 75 L6
CRICK NW2 116 F10
EFNCH N2 97 N10
HRW HA1 114 B3
PIN HA5 113 K5
SRTFD E15 121 J10
STA TW18 172 G8
TOTM N17 99 M10
WLSDN NW10 136 B6
Chandos St CAVSQ/HST W1G 10 F5
Chandos Wy GLDGN NW11 117 L6
Chanlock Pth SOCK/AV RM15 146 G9
Channel Cl HEST TW5 153 P7
Channel Gate Rd WLSDN NW10 136 B5
Channel Islands Est IS N1 6 F2
Channelsea Rd SRTFD E15 141 J3
Channing Cl EMPK RM11 125 N5
Channings WOKN/KNAP GU21 232 B1
Chanton Dr BELMT SM2 220 F6
Chantress Cl DAGE RM10 144 D3
Chantrey Cl ASHTD KT21 237 H5
SCUP DA14 185 P8
Chantrey Rd BRXN/ST SW9 158 G9
CRAWE RH10 283 P10
Chantreywood
RBRW/HUT CM13 107 M4
Chantry Av HART DA3 211 K6
Chantry Cl ABYW SE2 163 M2
BAR EN5 76 C10
ENC/FH EN2 79 K5
HORL RH6 280 A3
KGLGY WD4 54 B5
KTN/HRWW/WS HA3 115 L3
MLHL NW7 96 C1
MV/WKIL W9 8 D2
SUN TW16 175 H10
WDR/YW UB7 131 N9
WDSR SL4 148 F7
Chantry Crs WLSDN NW10 116 B10
Chantry Hurst EPSOM KT18 238 A1
Chantry La HAT AL10 40 D5
HAYES BR2 206 A5
LCOL/BKTW AL2 57 J2
SHGR GU5 270 A5
Chantry Pl KTN/HRWW/WS HA3 94 A9
SEV TN13 246 G8
Chantry Rd CHERT KT16 195 L8
CHSGTN KT9 219 L2
KTN/HRWW/WS HA3 94 A9
RGUE GU4 268 E6
Chantry Sq KENS W8 14 G4
Chantry St IS N1 6 D6
The Chantry CHING E4 * 101 H2
HLW CM20 29 K9
UX/CGN UB8 132 A5
Chantry View Rd GU GU1 268 B3
Chantry Wy MTCM CR4 201 N3
Chant Sq SRTFD E15 * 141 J2
Chant St SRTFD E15 141 J2
Chapel Av ADL/WDHM KT15 215 L1
CHOB/PIR GU24 230 G7
Chapel Cl DART DA1 186 F1
GSTN WD25 54 G10
STAL AL1 38 C9
WLSDN NW10 116 C10
WTHK RM20 166 G5
Chapel Cottages HHNE HP2 35 N4
Chapel Ct DORK RH4 * 272 F2
EFNCH N2 117 P1
STHWK SE1 18 G1
WOOL/PLUM SE18 163 J5
Chapel Cft KGLGY WD4 53 K7
Chapel Crofts BERK HP4 33 K3
Chapel End CFSP/GDCR SL9 * 90 A10
HOD EN11 44 F4
Chapel Farm Rd ELTH/MOT SE9 184 C6
Chapel Flds HLWE CM17 47 M3
Chapelfields WARE SG12 27 J6
Chapel Gv ADL/WDHM KT15 215 L1
EPSOM KT18 238 F5
Chapel Hl DART DA1 186 F1
EHSLY KT24 253 L3
Chapelhouse Cl GUW GU2 249 K10
Chapel House St POP/IOD E14 160 G3
Chapel La CHIG IG7 103 J4
CHOB/PIR GU24 230 G9
CRAWE RH10 285 N1
DORK RH4 272 B3
GT/LBKH KT23 254 B4
HERT/WAT SG14 24 C9
HLWE CM17 47 M3
PIN HA5 113 L1
SLN SL2 129 N2
UX/CGN UB8 132 B8
Chapel Market IS N1 6 A7
Chapel Mill Rd KUT/HW KT1 199 L3
Chapel Park Rd
ADL/WDHM KT15 215 L1
Chapel Pl CAVSQ/HST W1G 10 E6
IS N1 6 B7
STAL AL1 * 38 C9
TOTM N17 99 N8
Chapel Rd BXLYHN DA7 164 B10
EPP CM16 65 J6
HORL RH6 279 H8
HORL RH6 281 J4
HSLW TW3 154 A9
IL IG1 122 E8
KWD/TDW/WH KT20 238 F9
OXTED RH8 261 P6
REDH RH1 258 A10
TWK TW1 176 G3
WARL CR6 242 C4
WEA W13 134 G10
WNWD SE27 181 J7
Chapel Rw DEN/HRF UB9 91 M9
Chapels Cl SL SL1 128 D10
Chapel Side BAY/PAD W2 8 G8
Chapel Sq VW GU25 194 B3
Chapel St BAY/PAD W2 9 N4
BERK HP4 33 P5
ENC/FH EN2 79 K7
GU GU1 268 A2
HHNE HP2 35 N5
KTBR SW1X 16 D3
SL SL1 149 L1
WOKN/KNAP GU21 232 C3
Chapel Vw SAND/SEL CR2 224 B4
Chapel Wk COUL/CHIP CR5 240 E8
Chapel Wy ABLGY WD5 54 G3
EPSOM KT18 238 F5
Chapel Wd HART DA3 211 K9
Chapel Wood Rd HART DA3 211 K9
Chaplaincy Gdns EMPK RM11 125 M6
Chaplemount Rd WFD IG8 * 102 C7
Chaplin Cl ALP/SUD HA0 * 135 J1
STHWK SE1 18 C1
Chaplin Crs SUN TW16 174 F9
Chaplin Ms LBTH SE11 18 B8
Chaplin Rd ALP/SUD HA0 135 H1
CRICK NW2 136 D1
SRTFD E15 141 K4
TOTM N17 * 119 N1
Chapman Cl WDR/YW UB7 152 A2
Chapman Crs
KTN/HRWW/WS HA3 115 K3
Chapman Rd BELV DA17 164 B4
CROY/NA CR0 203 H8
HOM E9 140 E1
Chapmans Crs CSHM HP5 50 F5
Chapmans Gn WDGN N22 * 99 H9
Chapman's La STMC/STPC BR5 207 N2
SWLY BR8 208 B2
Chapman Sq WIM/MER SW19 178 C5
Chapmans Rd RSEV TN14 245 P10
Chapman St WCHPL E1 140 A9
Chapmans Yd WAT WD17 73 K8
Chapman Ter WDGN N22 * 99 J9
Chapter Cl HGDN/ICK UB10 132 A2
Chapter Ms WDSR SL4 149 J6
Chapter Rd CRICK NW2 116 E10
WALW SE17 18 D8
Chapter St WEST SW1P 17 J6
Chapter Wy HPTN TW12 175 P7
WIM/MER SW19 201 N1
Chara Pl CHSWK W4 156 A5
Charcroft Gdns PEND EN3 80 C8
Chardia Ter CHES/WCR EN8 * 62 C6
Chardin Rd CHSWK W4 * 156 B3
Chardins Cl HHW HP1 35 J5
Chardmore Rd STNW/STAM N16 119 P6
Chardwell Cl EHAM E6 142 B8
Charecroft Wy WKENS W14 156 G1
Charford Rd CAN/RD E16 141 M7
Chargate Cl WOT/HER KT12 216 G3
Chargeable La PLSTW E13 141 M6
Chargeable St CAN/RD E16 141 L6
Chargrove Cl BERM/RHTH SE16 160 C1
Charing Cl ORP BR6 227 J1
Charing Cross CHCR WC2N * 11 L9
Charing Cross Rd
LSQ/SEVD WC2H 11 K5
Chariot Cl BOW E3 140 F3
Chariotts Pl WDSR SL4 * 149 J7
Charkham Ms BRKMPK AL9 40 F10
Charlbert St STJWD NW8 3 N7
Charlbury Av STAN HA7 95 J6
Charlbury Cl HARH RM3 105 K7
Charlbury Crs HARH RM3 105 K7
Charlbury Gdns GDMY/SEVK IG3 123 J7
Charlbury Gv EA W5 135 H8
Charlbury Rd HGDN/ICK UB10 112 A9
Charldane Rd ELTH/MOT SE9 184 E6
Charlecote Gv SYD SE26 182 A6
Charlecote Rd BCTR RM8 123 P8
Charlemont Rd EHAM E6 142 C5
Charles Babbage Cl CHSGTN KT9 219 H4
Charles Barry Cl CLAP SW4 158 D9
Charles Cl SCUP DA14 185 L7
Charles Cobb Gdns
CROY/NA CR0 223 H2
Charles Coveney Rd PECK SE15 159 N7
Charles Crs HRW HA1 114 C5
Charles Dickens Ter
PGE/AN SE20 * 182 B10
Charlesfield ELTH/MOT SE9 183 P6
Charlesfield Rd HORL RH6 280 A3
Charles Flemwell Ms
CAN/RD E16 * 141 M10
Charles Gdns SLN SL2 129 M8
Charles Grinling Wk
WOOL/PLUM SE18 162 D3
Charles Haller St
BRXS/STRHM SW2 181 H3
Charles II Pl CHEL SW3 15 P8
Charles II St STJS SW1Y 11 J9
Charles La STJWD NW8 3 N8
Charles Pl CAMTN NW1 * 5 H10
Charles Rd CHDH RM6 123 N5
DAGE RM10 144 E1
FSTGT E7 141 P2
RSEV TN14 228 C6
STA TW18 173 N9
WEA W13 134 F8
WIM/MER SW19 201 K1
Charles Sevright Dr MLHL NW7 96 G6
Charles Sq IS N1 7 H10
Charles Square Est IS N1 7 H10
Charles St BARN SW13 156 B9
BERK HP4 33 N5
CAN/RD E16 141 P10
CHERT KT16 195 J8
CROY/NA CR0 203 K10
EN EN1 79 N9
EPP CM16 65 K8
GRAYS RM17 167 N5
HGDN/ICK UB10 132 C6
HHW HP1 35 M7
HSLW TW3 153 N8
MYFR/PICC W1J 10 F9
RDART DA2 188 E1
WDSR SL4 149 H7
Charleston Cl FELT TW13 175 H6
Charleston Ct CRAWE RH10 284 C10
Charleston St WALW SE17 18 F6
Charles Whincup Rd
CAN/RD E16 141 N10
Charlesworth Cl HHS/BOV HP3 35 N8
Charleville Circ SYD SE26 181 P8
Charleville Rd WKENS W14 14 B8
Charlieville Rd ERITH DA8 164 D6
Charlmont Rd TOOT SW17 179 P9
Charlock Wy GU GU1 250 E8
WATW WD18 72 G10
Charlotte Av SLN SL2 129 L9
Charlotte Cl BXLYHS DA6 185 P1
STALE/WH AL4 39 K6
Charlotte Ct ESH/CLAY KT10 218 B2
Charlotte Despard Av
BTSEA SW11 158 C7
Charlotte Gdns CRW RM5 104 C7
Charlotte Gv HORL RH6 281 H3
Charlotte Ms ESH/CLAY KT10 * 218 A1
FITZ W1T 11 H3
NKENS W10 136 G8
Charlotte Pde FSTH SE23 * 182 D5
Charlotte Park Av BMLY BR1 206 B3
Charlotte Pl FITZ W1T 11 H4
PIM SW1V 16 G6
WTHK RM20 166 G5
Charlotte Rd BARN SW13 156 C7
SDTCH EC2A 7 J10
WLGTN SM6 222 D3
Charlotte Rw CLAP SW4 158 D9
Charlotte St FITZ W1T 11 H3
Charlotte Ter IS N1 5 P6
Charlow Cl FUL/PGN SW6 157 M8
Charlton WDSR SL4 148 B8
Charlton Av WOT/HER KT12 217 J1
Charlton Church La CHARL SE7 161 P4
Charlton Cl HGDN/ICK UB10 112 C7
HOD EN11 44 F3
SL SL1 148 G1
Charlton Crs BARK IG11 143 J4
Charlton Dene CHARL SE7 161 P6
Charlton Dr BH/WHM TN16 244 A3
Charlton Gdns COUL/CHIP CR5 240 D4
Charlton Kings WEY KT13 216 F1
Charlton King's Rd KTTN NW5 118 E10
Charlton La CHARL SE7 162 A4
SHPTN TW17 196 D3
Charlton Mead La HOD EN11 45 H4
Charlton Park La CHARL SE7 162 A6
Charlton Park Rd CHARL SE7 162 A5
Charlton Pl IS N1 6 C7
Charlton Rd BKHTH/KID SE3 161 M6
ED N9 100 C2
KTN/HRWW/WS HA3 115 J2
SHPTN TW17 196 D2
WLSDN NW10 136 B3
Charlton St WTHK RM20 167 J5
Charlton Wy BKHTH/KID SE3 161 L6
HOD EN11 44 F4
Charlwood CROY/NA CR0 224 E5
Charlwood Cl CRAWE RH10 285 J1
GT/LBKH KT23 236 A10
KTN/HRWW/WS HA3 94 D7
Charlwood Dr LHD/OX KT22 236 C1
Charlwood La RDKG RH5 278 D10
Charlwood Pl PIM SW1V 17 H6
REIG RH2 257 J10
Charlwood Rd CRAWW RH11 283 J3
HORL RH6 279 M7
PUT/ROE SW15 156 G10
Charlwood St PIM SW1V 16 G8
Charlwood Ter PUT/ROE SW15 156 G10
Charlwood Wk CRAWW RH11 283 L4
Charman Rd REDH RH1 257 P10
Charm Cl HORL RH6 279 P3
Charmian Av STAN HA7 115 J1
Charminster Av WIM/MER SW19 201 K2
Charminster Rd ELTH/MOT SE9 184 A7
WPK KT4 200 G8
Charmouth Ct STAL AL1 38 F3
Charmouth Rd STAL AL1 38 F4
WELL DA16 163 M7
Charmwood La ORP BR6 227 L6
The Charne RSEV TN14 247 H3
Charnock SWLY BR8 208 F4
Charnock Rd CLPT E5 120 A8
Charnwood ASC SL5 192 E6
Charnwood Av WIM/MER SW19 201 K2
Charnwood Cl NWMAL KT3 200 B4
Charnwood Dr SWFD E18 121 N1
Charnwood Gdns POP/IOD E14 160 F3
Charnwood Pl TRDG/WHET N20 97 M4
Charnwood Rd EN EN1 80 A2
HGDN/ICK UB10 132 B4
SNWD SE25 203 L5
Charnwood St CLPT E5 * 119 P7
Charnwood Vls SWFD E18 121 N1
Charrington Rd CROY/NA CR0 203 J9
Charrington St CAMTN NW1 5 J7
Charsley Cl AMS HP6 69 P5
Charsley Rd CAT SE6 182 G5
Charta Rd EGH TW20 172 F8
Chart Cl CROY/NA CR0 204 B6
HAYES BR2 205 K1
MTCM CR4 202 A4
RDKG RH5 273 H4
Chart Downs RDKG RH5 273 H4
Charter Av GNTH/NBYPK IG2 122 G6
Charter Cl SL SL1 149 L2
Charter Crs HSLWW TW4 153 M10
Charter Dr BXLY DA5 185 P3
Charterhouse Av ALP/SUD HA0 115 H10
Charterhouse Buildings
FARR EC1M 12 E2
Charterhouse Dr SEV TN13 247 H9
Charterhouse Ms FARR EC1M 12 D3
Charterhouse Rd HACK E8 119 P10
ORP BR6 207 K10
Charterhouse St HCIRC EC1N 12 B4
The Charterhouse FARR EC1M * 12 D2
Charteris Rd FSBYPK N4 118 G6
KIL/WHAMP NW6 2 D6
WFD IG8 101 N7
Charter Pl STA TW18 173 K9
UX/CGN UB8 131 N3
WAT WD17 * 73 J8
Charter Rd KUT/HW KT1 199 N2
SL SL1 128 D9
The Charter Rd WFD IG8 101 K7
Charters Cl NRWD SE19 181 M8
Charters Cross HLWS CM18 46 G4
Charters La ASC SL5 192 C5
Charter Sq KUT/HW KT1 199 N2
Charters Rd ASC SL5 192 E7
Charters Wy ASC SL5 192 E7
Charter Wy FNCH N3 117 J2
STHGT/OAK N14 78 E10
Chartfield Av PUT/ROE SW15 178 E1
Chartfield Rd REIG RH2 275 M1
Chartfield Sq PUT/ROE SW15 * 178 G1
Chart Gdns RDKG RH5 273 H5
Chartham Gv WNWD SE27 181 H6
Chartham Rd SNWD SE25 204 A3
Chart Hills Cl THMD SE28 143 P8
Chart La BH/WHM TN16 263 M1
DORK RH4 272 G2
REIG RH2 257 L10
Chart La South RDKG RH5 273 J5
Chartley Av CRICK NW2 116 B8
STAN HA7 94 E7
Chartley Pde CRICK NW2 * 116 B8
Charton Cl BELV DA17 164 A5
Chartridge OXHEY WD19 * 93 L3
Chartridge Cl BAR EN5 76 D9
BUSH WD23 74 B10
Chartridge Grange Dr
CSHM HP5 50 C3
Chartridge La CSHM HP5 50 C4
Chartridge Wy HHNE HP2 36 D6
Chart St IS N1 7 H9
Chart Vw BGR/WK TN15 247 P3
Chartway REIG RH2 257 L10
SEV TN13 247 K10
Chartwell Cl CROY/NA CR0 203 L8
ELTH/MOT SE9 184 G5
GFD/PVL UB6 134 A3
WAB EN9 63 K9
Chartwell Dr ORP BR6 226 G2
Chartwell Gdns CHEAM SM3 201 H10
Chartwell Pl CHEAM SM3 221 H1
EPSOM KT18 220 B10
RYLN/HDSTN HA2 114 C7
Chartwell Rd NTHWD HA6 92 G7
Chartwell Wy PGE/AN SE20 204 A1
Chartwood Pl DORK RH4 272 F2
Charville La HGDN/ICK UB10 132 D5
Charville La West
HGDN/ICK UB10 132 C5
Charwood STRHM/NOR SW16 181 H7
Charwood Cl RAD WD7 57 K9
Chasden Rd HHW HP1 35 J4
Chase Cl AMSS HP7 68 F9
Chase Ct RYNPK SW20 201 H2
Chase Court Gdns ENC/FH EN2 79 K7
Chase Cross Rd CRW RM5 104 E7
Chase End HOR/WEW KT19 220 A8
Chasefield Cl RGUE GU4 250 D7
Chasefield Rd TOOT SW17 180 A7
Chase Gdns CHING E4 100 F5
WHTN TW2 176 C2
Chase Gn ENC/FH EN2 79 K7
Chase Green Av ENC/FH EN2 79 J6
Chase Hl ENC/FH EN2 79 K7
Chase House Gdns EMPK RM11 125 N3
Chase La BARK/HLT IG6 122 G3
CHIG IG7 103 K4
Chaseley Ct CHSWK W4 155 N4
Chaseley Dr SAND/SEL CR2 223 L6
Chaseley St POP/IOD E14 * 140 D8
Chasemore Cl MTCM CR4 202 A7
Chasemore Gdns CROY/NA CR0 223 H2
Chase Ridings ENC/FH EN2 79 H6
Chase Rd ACT W3 136 A6
BRW CM14 107 H4
HOR/WEW KT19 220 A8
STHGT/OAK N14 78 D9
STHGT/OAK N14 98 E2
Chase Side ENC/FH EN2 79 K6
STHGT/OAK N14 78 B10
Chase Side Av ENC/FH EN2 79 L6
Chaseside Av RYNPK SW20 201 H1
Chaseside Cl ROM RM1 * 104 F7
Chase Side Crs ENC/FH EN2 79 L5
Chaseside Gdns CHERT KT16 195 L7
Chase Side Pl ENC/FH EN2 79 K7
Chase Sq GVW DA11 * 190 E2
The Chase ASHTD KT21 237 H4
BGR/WK TN15 247 M2
BMLY BR1 205 N3
BRW CM14 106 G5
BXLYHN DA7 164 C9
CHESW EN7 61 J4
CHIG IG7 102 E5
CLAP SW4 158 C9
COUL/CHIP CR5 222 D10
CRAWE RH10 284 B8
CSHM HP5 50 G5
EDGW HA8 95 N9
EHSLY KT24 252 G2
FSTGT E7 122 A9
GUW GU2 249 M10
HERT/BAY SG13 25 N6
HGDN/ICK UB10 112 B10
HHNE HP2 35 P7
HLWE CM17 29 M10
KWD/TDW/WH KT20 239 M7
LHD/OX KT22 236 B1
LOU IG10 101 P1
ORP BR6 227 K7
PIN HA5 113 K4
PIN HA5 113 N2
RAD WD7 74 E1
RBRW/HUT CM13 107 P6
REIG RH2 257 N10
ROM RM1 124 F1
ROMW/RG RM7 124 E8
STAN HA7 94 F7
STRHM/NOR SW16 180 G10
SUN TW16 197 J1
UPMR RM14 126 D8
WARE SG12 26 F5
WATW WD18 72 F8
WLGTN SM6 222 F2
WTHK RM20 167 J5
Chaseville Pde WCHMH N21 * 78 G9
Chaseville Park Rd
STHGT/OAK N14 78 F9
Chase Wy STHGT/OAK N14 98 C2
Chaseways SBW CM21 29 L3
Chasewood Av ENC/FH EN2 79 J6
Chasewood Pk HRW HA1 * 114 D8
Chastilian Rd DART DA1 187 H3
Chatelet Cl HORL RH6 280 C3
Chatfield SLN SL2 128 F7
Chatfield Ct CTHM CR3 241 L8
Chatfield Dr RGUE GU4 250 F8
Chatfield Rd BTSEA SW11 157 M9
CROY/NA CR0 203 J8
Chatfields CRAWW RH11 283 L9
Chatham Av HAYES BR2 205 M7
Chatham Cl CHEAM SM3 201 J7
GLDGN NW11 117 K3
Chatham Hill Rd RSEV TN14 247 K7
Chatham Ms GUW GU2 249 M7
Chatham Pl HOM E9 140 B1
Chatham Rd BTSEA SW11 180 A1
KUT/HW KT1 199 M2
SWFD E18 101 L10
WALTH E17 120 D1
Chatham St WALW SE17 18 G5
WOOL/PLUM SE18 162 E2
Chatham Wy BRW CM14 107 H3
Chatsfield EW KT17 220 D6
Chatsfield Pl EA W5 135 K8
Chatsworth Av BFN/LL DA15 185 K4
BMLY BR1 183 N8
HDN NW4 96 F10
RYNPK SW20 201 H1
WBLY HA9 115 L10
Chatsworth Cl BORE WD6 75 M7
CHSWK W4 * 155 P5
HDN NW4 96 F10
WWKM BR4 205 L9
Chatsworth Crs HSLW TW3 154 C10
Chatsworth Dr EN EN1 99 P1
Chatsworth Est CLPT E5 * 120 C9
Chatsworth Gdns ACT W3 135 N9
NWMAL KT3 * 200 C5
RYLN/HDSTN HA2 114 A6
Chatsworth Pl LHD/OX KT22 218 C8
MTCM CR4 202 A3
TEDD TW11 176 F7
Chatsworth Ri EA W5 135 L6
Chatsworth Rd CHEAM SM3 220 G1
CHSWK W4 155 P5
CLPT E5 120 B8
CRICK NW2 136 G1
CROY/NA CR0 223 L1
DART DA1 187 K1
EA W5 135 L6
SRTFD E15 121 L10
YEAD UB4 133 J6
Chatsworth Wy WNWD SE27 181 K5
Chatteris Av HARH RM3 105 K7
Chattern Hl ASHF TW15 174 C7
Chattern Rd ASHF TW15 174 D7
Chatterton Ms FSBYPK N4 * 119 J8
Chatterton Rd FSBYPK N4 119 J8
HAYES BR2 206 A5
Chatton Rw CHOB/PIR GU24 230 F3
Chatto Rd BTSEA SW11 180 A1
Chaucer Av HSLWW TW4 153 J8
RCH/KEW TW9 155 M8
WEY KT13 216 B4
YEAD UB4 133 H7
Chaucer Cl BERK HP4 33 L4
BNSTD SM7 221 H10
FBAR/BDGN N11 98 D6
TIL RM18 168 F8
WDSR SL4 149 J9
Chaucer Ct GUW GU2 * 267 P2
Chaucer Dr STHWK SE1 19 M7
Chaucer Gdns SUT SM1 221 K1
Chaucer Gn CROY/NA CR0 204 B7
Chaucer Pk DART DA1 187 N3
Chaucer Rd ACT W3 135 P10
ASHF TW15 173 P7
BFN/LL DA15 185 M4
CRAWE RH10 284 C5
FSTGT E7 141 M1
GVW DA11 190 A6
HARH RM3 105 J8
HNHL SE24 181 J1
SUT SM1 221 K1
WALTH E17 121 H9
WAN E11 121 M4
WELL DA16 163 J7
Chaucer Wy ADL/WDHM KT15 215 K3
DART DA1 165 P10
HOD EN11 26 F9
SL SL1 129 L10
WIM/MER SW19 179 N9
Chaulden House Gdns HHW HP1 35 J8
Chaulden La HHW HP1 35 H8
Chaulden Ter HHW HP1 35 J7
Chauncey Cl ED N9 99 P4
Chauncy Av POTB/CUF EN6 59 M9
Chaundrye Cl ELTH/MOT SE9 184 C2
Chauntler Rd CAN/RD E16 141 N8
Chave Cft EPSOM KT18 * 238 F5
Chavecroft Ter EPSOM KT18 * 238 F5
Chave Rd RDART DA2 187 M6
Chaworth Cl CHERT KT16 214 F3
Chaworth Rd CHERT KT16 214 F3
Cheam Cl KWD/TDW/WH KT20 238 E7
Cheam Common Rd WPK KT4 200 E9

Cheam Man CHEAM SM3 * 221 H3
Cheam Park Wy CHEAM SM3 220 G3
Cheam Rd EW KT17 220 E6
SUT SM1 221 J3
Cheam St PECK SE15 * 160 A9
Cheapside CITYW EC2V 12 F6
EFNCH N2 * 118 A1
PLMGR N13 99 K5
WDGN N22 * 119 H1
WOKN/KNAP GU21 214 A10
Cheapside La DEN/HRF UB9 111 J7
Cheapside Rd ASC SL5 192 B3
Chedburgh WGCE AL7 23 N4
Cheddar Cl FBAR/BDGN N11 98 A7
Cheddar Waye YEAD UB4 133 J8
Cheddington Rd UED N18 99 M5
Cheelson Rd SOCK/AV RM15 147 H4
Cheeseman Cl HPTN TW12 175 M9
Cheesemans Ter WKENS W14 14 C8
Cheffins Rd HOD EN11 26 E10
Chelford Rd BMLY BR1 183 J8
Chelmer Crs BARK IG11 143 L4
Chelmer Dr SOCK/AV RM15 147 H9
Chelmer Rd CDW/CHF RM16 168 D4
HOM E9 120 C10
UPMR RM14 126 C4
Chelmsford Av CRW RM5 104 E8
Chelmsford Cl BELMT SM2 221 K5
EHAM E6 142 C8
HMSMTH W6 156 G5
Chelmsford Dr UPMR RM14 125 N8
Chelmsford Gdns IL IG1 122 B5
Chelmsford Rd BRWN CM15 87 M9
HERT/WAT SG14 25 H6
RBSF CM22 31 J1
STHGT/OAK N14 98 D1
SWFD E18 101 L9
WALTH E17 120 F4
WAN E11 121 J6
Chelmsford Sq WLSDN NW10 136 F3
Chelsea Br BGVA SW1W 16 D9
Chelsea Bridge Ga VX/NE SW8 16 E10
Chelsea Bridge Rd BGVA SW1W 16 C7
Chelsea Cl EDGW HA8 95 M10
HPTN TW12 176 B8
WLSDN NW10 136 A3
WPK KT4 200 D7
Chelsea Crs CRICK NW2 * 2 C1
WBPTN SW10 * 157 M7
Chelsea Emb CHEL SW3 16 A10
Chelsea Flds HOD EN11 26 G9
Chelsea Gdns CHEAM SM3 221 H1
HLWE CM17 47 P2
WEA W13 134 E7
Chelsea Harbour Dr
WBPTN SW10 157 M7
Chelsea Manor Gdns CHEL SW3 15 N9
Chelsea Manor St CHEL SW3 15 N7
Chelsea Ms EMPK RM11 125 J6
Chelsea Park Gdns CHEL SW3 15 L9
Chelsea Sq CAR SM5 222 A5
CHEL SW3 15 M8
Chelsea Village FUL/PGN SW6 * 157 L6
Chelsfield Av ED N9 100 C1
Chelsfield Gdns SYD SE26 182 B6
Chelsfield Hl ORP BR6 227 M5
Chelsfield La ORP BR6 228 B4
STMC/STPC BR5 207 N7
Chelsfield Rd STMC/STPC BR5 207 M6
Chelsham Common Rd
WARL CR6 242 F3
Chelsham Court Rd WARL CR6 243 J4
Chelsham Rd CLAP SW4 158 E9
SAND/SEL CR2 223 L4
Chelsing Ri HHNE HP2 36 D7
Chelston Rd RSLP HA4 113 H7
Chelsworth Dr HARH RM3 105 M9
WOOL/PLUM SE18 162 G5
Cheltenham Av TWK TW1 176 F3
Cheltenham Cl GVE DA12 190 F8
NTHLT UB5 134 A1
NWMAL KT3 199 P3
Cheltenham Gdns EHAM E6 142 B4
LOU IG10 82 B10
Cheltenham Pl ACT W3 155 P1
KTN/HRWW/WS HA3 115 K2
Cheltenham Rd LEY E10 121 H4
ORP BR6 207 K10
PECK SE15 160 B10
Cheltenham Ter CHEL SW3 16 B7
Chelton Av MLHL NW7 96 G8
Chelverton Rd PUT/ROE SW15 156 G10
Chelveston WGCE AL7 23 N4
Chelwood Av HAT AL10 40 D2
Chelwood Cl CHING E4 80 G10
COUL/CHIP CR5 240 D5
CRAWE RH10 284 A9
EW KT17 220 C8
NTHWD HA6 92 D8
Chelwood Gdns RCH/KEW TW9 155 M8
Chenappa Cl PLSTW E13 141 M5
Chenduit Wy STAN HA7 94 E6
Chene Dr STALW/RED AL3 38 C4
Cheney Rw WALTH E17 100 E9
Cheneys Rd WAN E11 121 K8
Cheney St PIN HA5 113 K2
Chenies Av AMS HP6 70 A5
Chenies Ct HHNE HP2 36 C1
Chenies Ms GWRST WC1E 11 J2
Chenies Pde AMSS HP7 * 69 P6
Chenies Pl CAMTN NW1 5 K7
Chenies Rd RKW/CH/CXG WD3 70 G6
Chenies St GWRST WC1E 11 J3
The Chenies ORP BR6 207 H6
RDART DA2 186 F7
Chenies Wy WATW WD18 92 F1
Cheniston Cl BF/WBF KT14 215 K9
Cheniston Gdns KENS W8 14 F3
Chennells HAT AL10 40 C5
The Chennies HARP AL5 * 20 B4
Chepstow Av HCH RM12 125 M8
Chepstow Cl CRAWE RH10 284 F7
PUT/ROE SW15 179 H1
Chepstow Cnr BAY/PAD W2 * 8 F6
Chepstow Crs GDMY/SEVK IG3 123 H4
NTGHL W11 8 E7
Chepstow Gdns STHL UB1 133 N8
Chepstow Pl BAY/PAD W2 8 F6
Chepstow Ri CROY/NA CR0 203 N10
Chepstow Rd BAY/PAD W2 8 F5
CROY/NA CR0 203 M10
HNWL W7 154 F2
Chepstow Vls NTGHL W11 8 D7
Chequers BKHH IG9 101 N2
BRKMPK AL9 40 C1
WGCE AL7 22 C7
Chequers Cl CDALE/KGS NW9 116 B1
HORL RH6 280 B3
KWD/TDW/WH KT20 256 D1
STMC/STPC BR5 207 J4
Chequers Dr HORL RH6 280 B3
Chequersfield WGCE AL7 22 G8
Chequers La DAGW RM9 144 A6
GSTN WD25 55 J6
KWD/TDW/WH KT20 256 D1
Chequers Orch IVER SL0 131 J8
Chequers Pde PLMGR N13 * 99 K6
Chequers Pl DORK RH4 272 G2
Chequers Rd HARH RM3 105 M3
LOU IG10 82 D9
The Chequers PIN HA5 * 113 L1
Chequer St STAL AL1 38 C6
STLK EC1Y 12 G2
Chequers Wy PLMGR N13 99 K6
Chequer Tree Cl
WOKN/KNAP GU21 231 K2
Cherbury Cl THMD SE28 143 N8
Cherbury St IS N1 7 H8
Cherimoya Gdns
E/WMO/HCT KT8 198 A3
Cherington Rd HNWL W7 * 134 E10
Cheriton Av CLAY IG5 102 D10
HAYES BR2 205 M5
Cheriton Cl EA W5 135 H7
EBAR EN4 78 A7
STALE/WH AL4 39 J2
Cheriton Ct WOT/HER KT12 197 K8
Cheriton Dr WOOL/PLUM SE18 162 G6
Cheriton Sq TOOT SW17 180 B5
Cherkley LHD/OX KT22 * 255 J2
Cherkley Hl LHD/OX KT22 255 H2
The Cherries SLN SL2 129 N8
Cherry Acre CFSP/GDCR SL9 90 A5
Cherry Av DTCH/LGLY SL3 150 A1
RBRW/HUT CM13 107 L4
STHL UB1 133 L10
SWLY BR8 208 E3
Cherry Bank HHNE HP2 * 35 N4
Cherry Blossom Cl HLWE CM17 29 M7
PLMGR N13 99 J6
Cherry Cl BNSTD SM7 220 G10
BRXS/STRHM SW2 * 181 H3
CAR SM5 202 A9
CDALE/KGS NW9 96 C10
EA W5 155 J2
MRDN SM4 201 H4
RSLP HA4 112 G8
Cherrycot Ri ORP BR6 226 F1
Cherry Ct PIN HA5 93 L10
Cherry Crs BTFD TW8 154 G6
Cherry Cft RKW/CH/CXG WD3 72 C10
WGCW AL8 22 G1
Cherry Croft Gdns PIN HA5 * 93 N8
Cherrydale WATW WD18 72 G8
Cherrydown Av CHING E4 100 E4
Cherrydown Cl CHING E4 100 F4
Cherrydown Rd SCUP DA14 185 N5
Cherrydown Wk ROMW/RG RM7 104 C10
Cherry Dr BEAC HP9 88 A7
Cherry Gdns DAGW RM9 124 A10
NTHLT UB5 134 A2
Cherry Garden St
BERM/RHTH SE16 160 A1
Cherry Garth BTFD TW8 155 J3
Cherry Green Cl REDH RH1 276 C2
Cherry Gv HYS/HAR UB3 133 J10
UX/CGN UB8 132 D7
Cherry Hl BAR EN5 77 L10
KTN/HRWW/WS HA3 94 D8
LCOL/BKTW AL2 55 P1
RKW/CH/CXG WD3 71 L7
Cherry Hill Gdns CROY/NA CR0 222 G1
Cherry Hills OXHEY WD19 93 M6
Cherry Hollow ABLGY WD5 54 G7
Cherrylands Cl
CDALE/KGS NW9 * 115 P7
Cherry La AMSS HP7 68 F6
CRAWW RH11 283 M4
WDR/YW UB7 152 A3
Cherry Orch AMS HP6 69 K3
ASHTD KT21 237 N4
CHARL SE7 161 P5
HHW HP1 35 K4
SLN SL2 129 N2
STA TW18 173 K8
WDR/YW UB7 151 P1
Cherry Orchard Cl
STMC/STPC BR5 207 M5
Cherry Orchard Gdns
CROY/NA CR0 203 L8
E/WMO/HCT KT8 197 N3
Cherry Orchard Rd
CROY/NA CR0 203 L8
E/WMO/HCT KT8 197 P3
HAYES BR2 206 B9
Cherry Ri CSTG HP8 90 A3
Cherry Rd PEND EN3 80 B4
Cherry St ROMW/RG RM7 124 E3
WOKN/KNAP GU21 232 B4
Cherry Tree Av GUW GU2 249 L10
LCOL/BKTW AL2 57 J2
STA TW18 173 L9
WDR/YW UB7 132 A8
Cherry Tree Cl ALP/SUD HA0 114 F9
CRAWE RH10 284 E5
HOM E9 140 B3
RAIN RM13 145 H4
Cherry Tree Cnr BEAC HP9 * 89 K7
Cherry Tree Ct CHARL SE7 * 161 P5
COUL/CHIP CR5 240 G4
Cherry Tree Dr SOCK/AV RM15 147 J6
STRHM/NOR SW16 180 F6
Cherry Tree Gn HERT/WAT SG14 24 G3
SAND/SEL CR2 224 A10
Cherry Tree Hl EFNCH N2 117 P3
Cherry Tree La DTCH/LGLY SL3 130 C1
GODL GU7 267 J9
HHNE HP2 36 E3
RAIN RM13 144 G5
RDART DA2 186 G6
RKW/CH/CXG WD3 90 F2
STALE/WH AL4 20 F1
Cherrytree La CFSP/GDCR SL9 90 A10
HHNE HP2 36 D1
IVER SL0 131 K3
Cherry Tree Ri BKHH IG9 101 P5
Cherry Tree Rd BEAC HP9 108 A1
EFNCH N2 118 A2
HOD EN11 44 F2
SLN SL2 128 G2
SRTFD E15 121 K10
WATN WD24 73 J2
Cherry Trees COUL/CHIP CR5 240 E7
HART DA3 211 L6
Cherry Tree Wk BECK BR3 204 E4
CSHM HP5 51 J5
STLK EC1Y 12 F2
WWKM BR4 225 L1
Cherry Tree Wy STAN HA7 94 G7
Cherry Wk CDW/CHF RM16 168 D2
HAYES BR2 205 M8
RAIN RM13 144 G4
RKW/CH/CXG WD3 71 M6
Cherry Wy DTCH/LGLY SL3 150 F9
HAT AL10 40 D7
HOR/WEW KT19 220 A3
SHPTN TW17 196 E4
Cherrywood Av EGH TW20 171 N9
Cherrywood Cl BEAC HP9 89 J7
BOW E3 140 D5
KUTN/CMB KT2 177 M10
Cherrywood Dr GVW DA11 190 B7
PUT/ROE SW15 178 G1
Cherrywood La RYNPK SW20 201 H4
Cherston Gdns LOU IG10 82 D8
Cherston Rd LOU IG10 82 D8
Chertsey Bridge Rd CHERT KT16 195 N7
Chertsey Cl PUR/KEN CR8 241 J1
Chertsey Crs CROY/NA CR0 225 H6
Chertsey Dr CHEAM SM3 201 H9
Chertsey La HOR/WEW KT19 219 M8
STA TW18 195 H1
Chertsey Rd ASHF TW15 174 E10
BF/WBF KT14 215 N8
BFOR GU20 212 D3
CHOB/PIR GU24 213 M6
IL IG1 122 G9
SHPTN TW17 195 P7
SHPTN TW17 196 B7
SUN TW16 174 F9
WAN E11 121 J7
WHTN TW2 176 B4
WOKN/KNAP GU21 214 D9
WOKN/KNAP GU21 232 C3
Chertsey St GU GU1 268 A1
TOOT SW17 180 B8
Chertsey Wk CHERT KT16 * 195 K7
Chervil Cl FELT TW13 175 H6
Chervil Ms THMD SE28 143 L10
Cherwell Cl DTCH/LGLY SL3 150 E5
RKW/CH/CXG WD3 72 B9
Cherwell Ct HOR/WEW KT19 219 P1
Cherwell Gv SOCK/AV RM15 146 G9
Cherwell Wk CRAWW RH11 283 J8
Cherwell Wy RSLP HA4 112 D4
Cheryls Cl FUL/PGN SW6 157 L7
Cheselden Rd GU GU1 268 B1
Cheseman St SYD SE26 182 A6
Chesfield Rd KUTN/CMB KT2 177 K10
Chesham Av STMC/STPC BR5 206 E6
Chesham Cl BELMT SM2 221 H6
KTBR SW1X * 16 C4
ROMW/RG RM7 124 E2
Chesham Crs PGE/AN SE20 204 B1
Chesham La CFSP/GDCR SL9 90 B5
Chesham Ms GU GU1 268 B1
KTBR SW1X 16 C3
Chesham Pl KTBR SW1X 16 C4
Chesham Rd AMS HP6 69 H3
CSHM HP5 32 B8
GU GU1 268 B1
KUT/HW KT1 199 M2
KWD/TDW/WH KT20 257 J2
PGE/AN SE20 204 B2
WARL CR6 242 F2
WIM/MER SW19 179 N9
Chesham St KTBR SW1X 16 C4
WLSDN NW10 116 A8
Chesham Ter WEA W13 154 G1
Chesham Wy WATW WD18 72 F10
Cheshire Cl CHERT KT16 214 G3
EMPK RM11 125 P3
MTCM CR4 202 F3
WALTH E17 100 G9
Cheshire Dr GSTN WD25 54 G10
Cheshire Gdns CHSGTN KT9 219 J3
Cheshire Rd WDGN N22 98 G8
Cheshire St BETH E2 13 N1
Chesholm Rd STNW/STAM N16 119 M8
Cheshunt Rd BELV DA17 164 B4
FSTGT E7 141 N1
Cheshunt Wash CHES/WCR EN8 62 D3
Chesilton Rd FUL/PGN SW6 157 J7
Chesil Wy YEAD UB4 132 G5
Chesley Gdns EHAM E6 142 A4
Chesney Crs CROY/NA CR0 225 H4
Chesney St BTSEA SW11 158 B7
Chesnut Av North WALTH E17 121 J2
Chesnut Gv TOTM N17 119 N1
Chesnut Rw FNCH N3 * 97 K8
The Chesnuts ABR/ST RM4 83 L7
Chessbury Rd CSHM HP5 50 G8
Chess Cl CSHM HP5 70 A2
RKW/CH/CXG WD3 71 N8
Chessell Cl THHTH CR7 203 J4
Chessfield Pk AMS HP6 70 B5
Chess Hl RKW/CH/CXG WD3 71 N8
Chessholme Rd ASHF TW15 174 D9
Chessington Av BXLYHN DA7 163 P6
FNCH N3 117 J1
Chessington Cl HOR/WEW KT19 219 P3
Chessington Ct PIN HA5 113 N2
Chessington Hall Gdns
CHSGTN KT9 219 J4
Chessington Hill Pk CHSGTN KT9 219 M3
Chessington Pde CHSGTN KT9 * 219 J2
Chessington Rd CHSGTN KT9 219 M3
HOR/WEW KT19 219 P3
HOR/WEW KT19 220 A5
Chessington Wy WWKM BR4 204 G9
Chess La RKW/CH/CXG WD3 71 N8
Chessmount Ri CSHM HP5 51 J9
Chesson Rd WKENS W14 14 C9
Chess Vale Ri RKW/CH/CXG WD3 72 A10
Chess Valley Wk CSHM HP5 70 C3
Chess Wy RKW/CH/CXG WD3 71 K7
Chesswood Ct
RKW/CH/CXG WD3 * 91 N2
Chesswood Wy PIN HA5 93 L10
Chester Av RCHPK/HAM TW10 177 L2
UPMR RM14 126 D7
WHTN TW2 175 N4
Chester Cl ASHF TW15 174 E8
BARN SW13 * 156 E9
CDW/CHF RM16 167 K2
DORK RH4 255 H10
GUW GU2 249 L8
KTBR SW1X 16 D2
SUT SM1 201 K9
Chester Cl North CAMTN NW1 4 F9
Chester Cl South CAMTN NW1 4 F10
Chester Crs HACK E8 119 N10
Chester Dr RYLN/HDSTN HA2 113 P4
Chesterfield Cl STMC/STPC BR5 207 N4
Chesterfield Dr DART DA1 187 J1
ESH/CLAY KT10 198 F9
SEV TN13 246 E8
Chesterfield Gdns FSBYPK N4 119 J3
GNWCH SE10 * 161 J6
MYFR/PICC W1J * 10 E9
Chesterfield Gv EDUL SE22 181 N1
Chesterfield Hl MYFR/PICC W1J 10 E9
Chesterfield Ms FSBYPK N4 119 J3
Chesterfield Rd ASHF TW15 173 P8
BAR EN5 76 G9
CHSWK W4 155 P5
FNCH N3 97 K7
HOR/WEW KT19 220 A4
LEY E10 121 H5
PEND EN3 80 D3
Chesterfield St MYFR/PICC W1J 10 E9
Chesterfield Wy HYS/HAR UB3 * 153 H1
PECK SE15 160 B6
Chesterford Gdns HAMP NW3 117 L9
Chesterford Rd MNPK E12 142 D1
Chester Gdns MRDN SM4 201 M5
PEND EN3 80 A10
WEA W13 * 134 G8
Chester Ga CAMTN NW1 4 E10
Chester Gibbons Gn
LCOL/BKTW AL2 57 J2
Chester Ms KTBR SW1X 16 E3
Chester Pl CAMTN NW1 4 E9
NTHWD HA6 * 92 F8
Chester Rd ARCH N19 118 C7
BFN/LL DA15 185 H1
BORE WD6 75 P7
CAMTN NW1 4 D10
CAN/RD E16 141 K6
CHIG IG7 102 D4
ED N9 100 A2
EHSLY KT24 253 J4
FSTGT E7 142 A2
GDMY/SEVK IG3 123 J6
HSLWW TW4 153 J9
HTHAIR TW6 152 B9
LOU IG10 82 F5
NTHWD HA6 92 G8
SL SL1 129 J8
TOTM N17 119 L1
WALTH E17 120 C3
WAN E11 121 N4
WATW WD18 73 H9
WIM/MER SW19 178 F9
Chester Rw BGVA SW1W 16 C6
Chesters HORL RH6 279 P2
Chester Sq BGVA SW1W 16 D5
Chester Square Ms
BGVA SW1W * 16 E4
The Chesters NWMAL KT3 200 B1
Chester St BETH E2 * 7 N6
BETH E2 13 P1
KTBR SW1X 16 D3
Chester Ter CAMTN NW1 4 E9
Chesterton Av HARP AL5 20 C2
Chesterton Cl CSHM HP5 50 G5
GFD/PVL UB6 134 A4
WAND/EARL SW18 179 K1
Chesterton Ct EA W5 * 135 J8
Chesterton Dr REDH RH1 258 F4
STWL/WRAY TW19 174 A4
Chesterton Gn BEAC HP9 88 D9
Chesterton Rd NKENS W10 136 G7
PLSTW E13 141 M5
Chesterton Sq KENS W8 14 D5
Chesterton Ter KUT/HW KT1 199 M2
PLSTW E13 141 M5
Chester Wy LBTH SE11 18 B6
Chesthunte Rd TOTM N17 99 K9
Chestnut Aly FUL/PGN SW6 * 14 D10
Chestnut Av ALP/SUD HA0 114 G10
BH/WHM TN16 244 A8
BH/WHM TN16 244 D7
BKHH IG9 102 A4
BTFD TW8 155 J4
CDW/CHF RM16 167 N1
CEND/HSY/T N8 118 F3
CSHM HP5 51 J5
DTCH/LGLY SL3 150 B1
EDGW HA8 95 K7
ESH/CLAY KT10 198 C7
FSTGT E7 121 N9
GUW GU2 267 P4
HCH RM12 124 G7
HOR/WEW KT19 220 B1
HPTN TW12 175 P10
MORT/ESHN SW14 156 A9
NTHWD HA6 92 G10
RDART DA2 188 F3
RKW/CH/CXG WD3 71 K9
TEDD TW11 176 E10
VW GU25 193 L4
WDR/YW UB7 132 A9
WEY KT13 216 D4
WWKM BR4 225 K2
Chestnut Av South WALTH E17 121 H3
Chestnut Cl ADL/WDHM KT15 215 N2
AMS HP6 69 K3
ASHF TW15 174 C7
BERK HP4 34 E3
BFN/LL DA15 185 K5
BKHH IG9 102 A4
CAR SM5 202 A8
CAT SE6 183 H7
CFSP/GDCR SL9 90 C9
EGH TW20 171 N9
GVW DA11 190 C2
HCH RM12 125 K9
HYS/HAR UB3 132 F9
HYS/HAR UB3 152 C6
KWD/TDW/WH KT20 239 K9
NWCR SE14 160 E7
ORP BR6 227 K2
REDH RH1 276 C2
RPLY/SEND GU23 251 K1
STHGT/OAK N14 78 D9
STNW/STAM N16 119 L7
STRHM/NOR SW16 181 H7
WARE SG12 28 A2
Chestnut Copse OXTED RH8 261 N9
Chestnut Cottages
TRDG/WHET N20 * 97 H2
Chestnut Dr BERK HP4 34 A6
BXLYHN DA7 163 N9
EGH TW20 172 A9
KTN/HRWW/WS HA3 94 E8
PIN HA5 113 L4
STAL AL1 38 G4
WAN E11 121 M4
WDSR SL4 148 D10
Chestnut Gln HCH RM12 124 G7
Chestnut Gv ALP/SUD HA0 114 G10
BAL SW12 180 B3
BARK/HLT IG6 103 H7
BRW CM14 107 H3
EA W5 155 J2
EBAR EN4 78 A9
HOD EN11 26 G9
ISLW TW7 154 F10
MTCM CR4 202 E5
NWMAL KT3 200 A3
RDART DA2 186 E8
SAND/SEL CR2 224 A4
STA TW18 173 M9
WOKS/MYFD GU22 232 B7
Chestnut La AMS HP6 69 K3
CHOB/PIR GU24 213 H3
HLW CM20 28 E10
SEV TN13 247 J10
TRDG/WHET N20 97 H2
WEY KT13 216 C2
Chestnut Manor Cl STA TW18 173 L8
Chestnut Md REDH RH1 257 P9
Chestnut Ms WFD IG8 101 M6
Chestnut Pl ASHTD KT21 237 K5
NRWD SE19 181 N7
WEY KT13 * 216 C2
Chestnut Ri BUSH WD23 94 A1
WOOL/PLUM SE18 163 H4
Chestnut Rd ASHF TW15 174 B7
BEAC HP9 88 A10
DART DA1 187 L4
GU GU1 250 A10
HORL RH6 280 C2
KUTN/CMB KT2 177 K10
PEND EN3 80 D2
RYNPK SW20 200 G2
WHTN TW2 176 D5
WNWD SE27 181 K6
Chestnuts RBRW/HUT CM13 107 N2
The Chestnuts BECK BR3 * 204 C3
HERT/BAY SG13 25 L6
HHS/BOV HP3 35 J10
PIN HA5 * 93 N8
WOT/HER KT12 197 H9
Chestnut Ter SUT SM1 * 221 L1
Chestnut Wk BGR/WK TN15 265 N4
CFSP/GDCR SL9 * 90 B8
CRAWW RH11 283 M4
EPP CM16 64 E1
SHPTN TW17 196 F5
WATN WD24 73 H3
Chestnut Wy FELT TW13 175 J6
Cheston Av CROY/NA CR0 204 D8
Chestwood Gv HGDN/ICK UB10 132 A3
Cheswick Cl DART DA1 164 G10
Chesworth Cl ERITH DA8 164 F7
Chettle Cl STHWK SE1 18 G3
Chetwode Dr EPSOM KT18 238 G4
Chetwode Rd EPSOM KT18 238 F5
TOOT SW17 180 A6
Chetwynd Av EBAR EN4 98 A2
Chetwynd Dr HGDN/ICK UB10 132 A4
Chetwynd Rd KTTN NW5 118 C9
Chetwynd Vls KTTN NW5 * 118 C9
Chevalier Cl STAN HA7 95 J4
Cheval Pl SKENS SW7 15 P3
Cheval St POP/IOD E14 160 F2
Cheveley Gdns SL SL1 128 B4
Chevely Cl EPP CM16 65 N5
Cheveney Wk HAYES BR2 205 M3
Chevening La RSEV TN14 245 P2
Chevening Rd GNWCH SE10 161 L4
KIL/WHAMP NW6 136 G4
NRWD SE19 181 L10
RSEV TN14 246 A5
RSEV TN14 246 A9
The Chevenings SCUP DA14 185 M6
Cheverton Rd ARCH N19 118 E6
Chevet St HOM E9 120 D10
Chevington CRICK NW2 * 2 C1
Chevington Pl HCH RM12 125 L10
Chevington Vls REDH RH1 259 N9
Chevington Wy HCH RM12 125 L9
Cheviot Cl BELMT SM2 221 N5
BNSTD SM7 239 L1
BUSH WD23 74 B10
BXLYHN DA7 164 F8
ENC/FH EN2 79 L6
HYS/HAR UB3 152 E6
Cheviot Gdns CRICK NW2 116 G7
Cheviot Rd DTCH/LGLY SL3 150 D4
EMPK RM11 125 H5
WNWD SE27 181 J8
Cheviots HAT AL10 40 D7
HHNE HP2 36 A3
Cheviot Wk CRAWW RH11 * 283 L7
Cheviot Wy GNTH/NBYPK IG2 123 H3
Chevron Cl CAN/RD E16 141 M8
Chevy Rd NWDGN UB2 154 B1
Chewter La BFOR GU20 212 A1
Chewton Rd WALTH E17 120 D2
Cheyham Gdns BELMT SM2 220 G6
Cheyham Wy BELMT SM2 221 H6
Cheyne Av SWFD E18 121 L1
WHTN TW2 175 N4
Cheyne Cl CFSP/GDCR SL9 110 B6
HAYES BR2 206 B10
WARE SG12 26 C1
Cheyne Ct BNSTD SM7 239 L1
BUSH WD23 * 73 M8
Cheyne Gdns CHEL SW3 15 P9
Cheyne Hl BRYLDS KT5 199 L4
Cheyne Ms CHEL SW3 15 P10
Cheyne Park Dr WWKM BR4 205 H10
Cheyne Pth HNWL W7 134 E7
Cheyne Pl CHEL SW3 16 A9
Cheyne Rd ASHF TW15 174 E9
Cheyne Rw CHEL SW3 15 N10
Cheyne Wk CHEL SW3 15 N10
CROY/NA CR0 203 P9
CSHM HP5 51 J7
HDN NW4 116 F4
HORL RH6 280 B5
WBPTN SW10 157 N6
WCHMH N21 79 H9
Cheyneys Av EDGW HA8 95 J7
Chichele Gdns CROY/NA CR0 223 M1
Chichele Rd CRICK NW2 116 G10
OXTED RH8 261 K4
Chicheley Rd
KTN/HRWW/WS HA3 94 B8
Chicheley St STHWK SE1 17 P1
Chichester Av RSLP HA4 112 E7
Chichester Cl BKHTH/KID SE3 161 P6
CDW/CHF RM16 167 J3
DORK RH4 254 G10
EHAM E6 142 B8
HPTN TW12 175 N9
SOCK/AV RM15 146 B10
Chichester Ct EW KT17 * 220 C5
SL SL1 149 N2
STAN HA7 115 K1
Chichester Dr PUR/KEN CR8 222 G8
SEV TN13 264 G1
Chichester Gdns IL IG1 122 C5
Chichester Ri GVE DA12 190 G7
Chichester Rd BAY/PAD W2 9 H3
CROY/NA CR0 203 M10
DORK RH4 254 G9
ED N9 99 N2
KIL/WHAMP NW6 2 E8
RDART DA2 188 E1
WAN E11 121 K8
Chichester St PIM SW1V 17 H8
Chichester Wy
EBED/NFELT TW14 175 K3
GSTN WD25 55 M9
POP/IOD E14 161 J3
Chichester Whf ERITH DA8 164 F4
Chicken La LCOL/BKTW AL2 * 57 J3
Chicksand Est WCHPL E1 13 N3
Chicksand St WCHPL E1 13 M4
Chiddingfold
NFNCH/WDSPK N12 97 K4
Chiddingly Cl CRAWE RH10 284 C8
Chiddingstone Av BXLYHN DA7 164 A6
Chiddingstone Cl BELMT SM2 221 K6
Chiddingstone St FUL/PGN SW6 157 K8
Chieftan Dr PUR RM19 165 P3
Chieveley Pde BXLYHN DA7 * 164 C9
Chieveley Rd BXLYHN DA7 164 C10
Chiffinch Gdns GVW DA11 190 B6
Chignell Pl WEA W13 134 F10
Chigwell Hl WAP E1W 140 A9
Chigwell La LOU IG10 82 F10
Chigwell Park Dr CHIG IG7 102 D5
Chigwell Ri CHIG IG7 102 D3
Chigwell Rd SWFD E18 101 P10
SWFD E18 121 N1
WFD IG8 102 B7
Chilberton Dr REDH RH1 258 D6
Chilbrook Rd COB KT11 235 H4
Chilcote La AMSS HP7 69 N5
Chilcott Cl ALP/SUD HA0 115 H9
Chilcott Rd WATN WD24 72 F2
Childebert Rd TOOT SW17 180 C5
Childerditch Hall Dr
RBRW/HUT CM13 127 M2
Childerditch La
RBRW/HUT CM13 127 M1
Childerditch St RBRW/HUT CM13 127 M1
Childeric Rd NWCR SE14 160 D6
Childerley St FUL/PGN SW6 157 H7
Childers St DEPT SE8 160 D5
The Childers WFD IG8 102 C6
Child La GNWCH SE10 161 L2
Childs Av DEN/HRF UB9 91 M10
Childsbridge La BGR/WK TN15 247 N3
Childsbridge Wy BGR/WK TN15 247 N6
Childs Cl EMPK RM11 125 K4
Childs Ct HYS/HAR UB3 133 H9
Childs Crs SWCM DA10 189 J2
Childs Hall Dr GT/LBKH KT23 253 N1
Childs Hall Rd GT/LBKH KT23 253 N2
Childs La NRWD SE19 * 181 M9
Child's Ms ECT SW5 * 14 G6
Child's Pl ECT SW5 14 F6
Child's St ECT SW5 14 F5
Child's Wk ECT SW5 * 14 F5
Childs Wy GLDGN NW11 117 J3
Childwick Ct HHS/BOV HP3 36 C9
Chilham Cl BXLY DA5 186 A3
GFD/PVL UB6 134 F4
HHNE HP2 35 P7
Chilham Rd ELTH/MOT SE9 184 B7
Chilham Wy HAYES BR2 205 M7
Chillerton Rd TOOT SW17 180 B8
Chillington Dr BTSEA SW11 157 M10
Chillingworth Gdns TWK TW1 * 176 E5
Chillingworth Rd HOLWY N7 118 G10
Chilmans Dr GT/LBKH KT23 254 A1
Chilmark Gdns NWMAL KT3 200 C6
REDH RH1 258 F5
Chilmark Rd STRHM/NOR SW16 202 E2
Chilmead REDH RH1 * 258 A9
Chilmead La REDH RH1 258 E8
Chilsey Green Rd CHERT KT16 195 H6
Chiltern Av AMS HP6 69 J4
BUSH WD23 74 B10
WHTN TW2 175 P4
Chiltern Cl BERK HP4 33 M4
BORE WD6 75 L6
BUSH WD23 74 A10
BXLYHN DA7 164 F7
CHESW EN7 61 J3
CRAWW RH11 283 L7
CROY/NA CR0 203 M10
HGDN/ICK UB10 112 C7
STA TW18 173 K8
WOKS/MYFD GU22 231 P8
WPK KT4 200 F9
Chiltern Ct UX/CGN UB8 132 C6
Chiltern Dene ENC/FH EN2 78 G8
Chiltern Dr BRYLDS KT5 199 N6
RKW/CH/CXG WD3 91 J1
Chiltern Est WATN WD24 * 73 K5
Chiltern Gdns CRICK NW2 116 G8
HAYES BR2 205 L4
HCH RM12 125 K8
Chiltern Hts AMSS HP7 69 M5
Chiltern Hl CFSP/GDCR SL9 90 C9
Chiltern Hills Rd BEAC HP9 88 B9
Chiltern Pde AMS HP6 69 H3
Chiltern Park Av BERK HP4 33 M3
Chiltern Rd AMS HP6 50 G10
BELMT SM2 221 M6
BOW E3 140 F6
GNTH/NBYPK IG2 123 H2
GVW DA11 190 B6
PIN HA5 113 K3
SL SL1 128 A7
STALE/WH AL4 39 H2
Chilterns HAT AL10 40 D7
HHNE HP2 35 P3
The Chilterns BELMT SM2 * 221 L5
Chiltern St MHST W1U 10 C4
Chiltern View Rd UX/CGN UB8 131 M4
Chiltern Wy WFD IG8 101 M4
Chilthorne Cl CAT SE6 182 E3
Chilton Av EA W5 155 J3
Chilton Gn WGCE AL7 23 M6
Chilton Gv DEPT SE8 160 C3
Chilton Rd CDW/CHF RM16 168 D2
CSHM HP5 51 H5
EDGW HA8 95 M7
RCH/KEW TW9 155 M9
Chiltons Cl BNSTD SM7 239 L1
Chilton St BETH E2 13 M1
Chilvers Cl WHTN TW2 176 D5
Chilver St GNWCH SE10 161 L4
Chilwell Gdns OXHEY WD19 93 K5
Chilwick Rd SLN SL2 128 E6
Chilworth Gdns SUT SM1 201 M10
Chilworth Ga BROX EN10 44 E8
Chilworth Ms BAY/PAD W2 9 K6
Chilworth Rd SHGR GU5 269 K5
Chilworth St BAY/PAD W2 9 K6
Chimes Av PLMGR N13 99 H5
Chime Sq STALW/RED AL3 38 D5
China Hall Ms BERM/RHTH SE16 160 B3
China Ms BRXS/STRHM SW2 180 G3
Chinbrook Crs LEE/GVPK SE12 183 N6
Chinbrook Rd LEE/GVPK SE12 183 N6
Chinchilla Dr HSLWW TW4 153 K8
Chindit Cl BROX EN10 44 D6
Chindits La RBRW/HUT CM13 107 H6
The Chine ALP/SUD HA0 114 G10
DORK RH4 272 G1
MUSWH N10 118 C2
MUSWH N10 118 D2
WCHMH N21 79 J10
Chingdale Rd CHING E4 101 K4
Chingford Av CHING E4 100 G4
Chingford La WFD IG8 101 L6
Chingford Mount Rd CHING E4 100 F6
Chingford Rd CHING E4 100 F8
WALTH E17 100 F10
Chingley Cl BMLY BR1 183 K9
Ching Wy CHING E4 100 E7
Chinnery Cl EN EN1 79 N4
Chinnor Crs GFD/PVL UB6 134 B4
Chinthurst La RGUE GU4 268 B7
Chinthurst Ms COUL/CHIP CR5 240 D1
Chinthurst Pk RGUE GU4 268 B8
Chipka St POP/IOD E14 161 H1
Chipley St NWCR SE14 160 D5
Chipmunk Cha HAT AL10 40 A2
Chippendale St CLPT E5 120 C8
Chippendale Waye UX/CGN UB8 131 N2
Chippenham Cl PIN HA5 * 112 G2
Chippenham Gdns HARH RM3 105 L6
Chippenham Ms MV/WKIL W9 8 E2
Chippenham Rd HARH RM3 105 L7
MV/WKIL W9 8 E1
Chipperfield Cl UPMR RM14 126 D6
Chipperfield Rd HHS/BOV HP3 35 M10
HHS/BOV HP3 52 E4
KGLGY WD4 53 N5
STMC/STPC BR5 207 L3
Chipping Cl BAR EN5 77 H7
Chippingfield HLWE CM17 29 M8
Chipstead CFSP/GDCR SL9 89 P9
Chipstead Av THHTH CR7 203 J4
Chipstead Cl BELMT SM2 221 L5
COUL/CHIP CR5 240 B3
NRWD SE19 181 N10
REDH RH1 276 A1
Chipstead Ct WOKN/KNAP GU21 231 K3
Chipstead Gdns CRICK NW2 116 E7
Chipstead La COUL/CHIP CR5 239 L10
SEV TN13 246 E8
Chipstead Pk SEV TN13 246 E8
Chipstead Park Cl SEV TN13 246 D8
Chipstead Place Gdns SEV TN13 246 D9
Chipstead Rd BNSTD SM7 239 J3
ERITH DA8 164 F6
HTHAIR TW6 152 B9
Chipstead Station Pde
COUL/CHIP CR5 240 A4
Chipstead St FUL/PGN SW6 157 K8
Chipstead Valley Rd
COUL/CHIP CR5 240 C2
Chipstead Wy BNSTD SM7 240 A3
Chirk Cl YEAD UB4 133 M6
Chirton Wk WOKN/KNAP GU21 231 M4
Chisenhale Rd BOW E3 140 D4
Chisholm Rd CROY/NA CR0 203 M9
RCHPK/HAM TW10 177 L2
Chislehurst Av
NFNCH/WDSPK N12 97 M8
Chislehurst High St CHST BR7 184 E9
Chislehurst Rd BMLY BR1 206 B2
ORP BR6 207 J7
RCHPK/HAM TW10 177 K2
SCUP DA14 185 K8
STMC/STPC BR5 207 H4
Chislet Cl BECK BR3 182 F10
Chisley Rd SEVS/STOTM N15 119 M4
Chiswell Ct WATN WD24 73 K4
Chiswell Green La
LCOL/BKTW AL2 55 M1
Chiswell Sq BKHTH/KID SE3 161 N8
Chiswell St CMBW SE5 * 159 L6
STLK EC1Y 12 G3
Chiswick Br CHSWK W4 155 P8
Chiswick Cl CROY/NA CR0 202 G10
Chiswick Common Rd
CHSWK W4 156 A3
Chiswick High Rd CHSWK W4 155 M4
CHSWK W4 156 A4
CHSWK W4 156 C3
Chiswick House Grounds
CHSWK W4 * 156 A5
Chiswick La CHSWK W4 156 B4
Chiswick La South CHSWK W4 156 C5
Chiswick Ml CHSWK W4 156 C5
Chiswick Pk CHSWK W4 * 155 P2
Chiswick Pier CHSWK W4 * 156 C6
Chiswick Quay CHSWK W4 155 P7
Chiswick Rd CHSWK W4 155 P3
ED N9 99 P3
Chiswick Sq CHSWK W4 156 B5
Chiswick Staithe RCH/KEW TW9 155 N7
Chiswick Village CHSWK W4 155 N5
Chiswick Whf CHSWK W4 156 C5
Chithurst La HORL RH6 281 N5
Chittenden Cl HOD EN11 26 G10
Chitterfield Ga WDR/YW UB7 152 B6
Chitty's La BCTR RM8 123 N7
Chitty St FITZ W1T 11 H3
Chitty's Wk RGUW GU3 249 L6
Chivalry Rd BTSEA SW11 179 P1
Chivenor Gv KUTN/CMB KT2 177 J8
Chivenor Pl STALE/WH AL4 39 H8
Chivers Rd BRWN CM15 86 E1
CHING E4 100 G4
Choats Manor Wy DAGW RM9 144 A5
Choats Rd BARK IG11 143 M4
Chobham Cl CHERT KT16 214 E3
Chobham Gdns WIM/MER SW19 178 G5
Chobham La CHERT KT16 193 M9
Chobham Park La
CHOB/PIR GU24 213 N6
Chobham Rd ASC SL5 193 H9
CHERT KT16 214 D4
SRTFD E15 121 J10
WOKN/KNAP GU21 232 C3
Choir Gn WOKN/KNAP GU21 231 K3
Cholesbury La TRING HP23 32 B6
Cholesbury Rd TRING HP23 32 B6
Cholmeley Cl HGT N6 * 118 C5
Cholmeley Crs HGT N6 118 C5
Cholmeley Pk HGT N6 118 C6
Cholmley Gdns KIL/WHAMP NW6 117 K10
Cholmley Rd THDIT KT7 198 G6
Cholmley Ter THDIT KT7 * 198 G7
Cholmley Vls THDIT KT7 * 198 G7
Cholmondeley Av WLSDN NW10 136 D4
Chopwell Cl SRTFD E15 * 141 J2
Chorleywood Bottom
RKW/CH/CXG WD3 70 G9
Chorleywood Cl
RKW/CH/CXG WD3 91 N1
Chorleywood Crs
STMC/STPC BR5 207 J2
Chorleywood House Dr
RKW/CH/CXG WD3 71 H7
Chorleywood Rd
RKW/CH/CXG WD3 71 M9

Choumert Gv PECK SE15 159 P8
Choumert Ms PECK SE15 159 P8
Choumert Rd PECK SE15 159 N9
Chow Sq HACK E8 119 N10
Chrislaine Cl STWL/WRAY TW19 173 N2
Chrisp St POP/IOD E14 140 G8
Christabel Cl ISLW TW7 154 D9
Christchurch Av ALP/SUD HA0 135 K1
Christ Church Av ERITH DA8 164 E5
Christchurch Av KIL/WHAMP NW6 2 B3
KTN/HRWW/WS HA3 114 F2
NFNCH/WDSPK N12 97 M7
RAIN RM13 144 G4
TEDD TW11 176 F8
Christchurch Cl ENC/FH EN2 79 K6
NFNCH/WDSPK N12 * 97 N8
WIM/MER SW19 179 N10
Christchurch Crs RAD WD7 74 F2
Christchurch Gdns
KTN/HRWW/WS HA3 114 F2
Christchurch Hl HAMP NW3 117 N8
Christ Church La BAR EN5 77 H6
Christchurch Ldg EBAR EN4 * 78 A8
Christ Church Mt
HOR/WEW KT19 219 N8
Christchurch Pk BELMT SM2 221 M4
Christ Church Rd BECK BR3 * 204 F2
BRYLDS KT5 199 L7
CEND/HSY/T N8 118 F4
EPSOM KT18 219 L9
GVE DA12 190 F4
HOR/WEW KT19 219 M9
Christchurch Rd BFN/LL DA15 185 J7
BRXS/STRHM SW2 180 G4
DART DA1 187 K3
HHNE HP2 35 N5
IL IG1 122 E6
MORT/ESHN SW14 177 N1
PUR/KEN CR8 223 H6
TIL RM18 168 D7
VW GU25 194 B4
WIM/MER SW19 201 N1
Christchurch Sq HOM E9 140 B3
Christchurch St CHEL SW3 16 A9
Christchurch Ter CHEL SW3 * 16 A9
Christchurch Wy GNWCH SE10 161 K4
WOKN/KNAP GU21 232 C3
Christian Flds STRHM/NOR SW16 181 H10
Christian Fields Av GVE DA12 190 F7
Christian St WCHPL E1 13 P5
Christie Cl BROX EN10 44 E7
GT/LBKH KT23 253 N1
LTWR GU18 212 A6
Christie Ct WATW WD18 73 H9
Christie Dr CROY/NA CR0 203 P5
Christie Rd HOM E9 140 D1
WAB EN9 80 G1
Christies Av RSEV TN14 228 B6
Christie Wk COUL/CHIP CR5 241 J5
Christina Sq FSBYPK N4 119 J6
Christina St SDTCH EC2A 13 J1
Christine Worsley Cl
WCHMH N21 99 J2
Christmas Hl SHGR GU5 268 E9
Christmas La SLN SL2 109 H8
Christmaspie Av RGUW GU3 248 A10
Christopher Av HNWL W7 154 F2
Christopher Cl BERM/RHTH SE16 160 C1
BFN/LL DA15 185 J1
HCH RM12 125 L9
Christopher Ct WARE SG12 * 26 C2
Christopher Gdns DAGW RM9 123 N10
Christopher Pl CAMTN NW1 * 5 K9
STALW/RED AL3 * 38 C6
Christopher Rd NWDGN UB2 153 J3
Christophers Ms NTGHL W11 8 A9
Christopher St SDTCH EC2A 13 H2
Christy Rd BH/WHM TN16 243 P1
Christy Ter WFD IG8 102 B8
Chryssell Rd BRXN/ST SW9 159 H6
Chrystie La GT/LBKH KT23 254 A2
Chubworthy St NWCR SE14 160 D5
Chuck's La KWD/TDW/WH KT20 238 E10
Chudleigh Crs GDMY/SEVK IG3 123 H9
Chudleigh Gdns SUT SM1 201 M10
Chudleigh Rd BROCKY SE4 182 E1
HARH RM3 105 M5
KIL/WHAMP NW6 136 F2
WHTN TW2 176 D2
Chudleigh St WCHPL E1 140 C8
Chudleigh Wy RSLP HA4 113 H6
Chulsa Rd SYD SE26 182 A8
Chumleigh St CMBW SE5 19 J9
Chumleigh Wk BRYLDS KT5 199 L4
Church Aly GVW DA11 * 190 E2
Church Ap DUL SE21 181 L6
EGH TW20 194 F3
Church Av BECK BR3 204 F1
CAMTN NW1 4 F2
CHING E4 101 J7
MORT/ESHN SW14 156 A10
NTHLT UB5 133 N2
NWDGN UB2 153 M2
PIN HA5 113 M4
RSLP HA4 112 E6
SCUP DA14 185 K8
Churchbury Cl EN EN1 79 M6
Churchbury La EN EN1 79 M5
EN EN1 79 M7
Churchbury Rd ELTH/MOT SE9 184 A3
EN EN1 79 M6
Church Cl ADL/WDHM KT15 215 L1
BRW CM14 86 C3
CHOB/PIR GU24 230 E6
EDGW HA8 95 P6
EW KT17 * 220 B9
HSLW TW3 153 N8
HYS/HAR UB3 132 E7
KWD/TDW/WH KT20 257 J3
LHD/OX KT22 236 C10
NTHWD HA6 92 G8
POTB/CUF EN6 60 F5
RAD WD7 74 F2
STA TW18 195 M3
TRDG/WHET N20 97 P4
UX/CGN UB8 131 L4
WDR/YW UB7 151 P2
WDSR SL4 149 J5
WOKN/KNAP GU21 232 A2
Church Ct BROX EN10 * 44 F6
REIG RH2 257 L10
Church Crs FNCH N3 97 J9
HOM E9 140 C2
MUSWH N10 118 C2
SOCK/AV RM15 147 H5
STALW/RED AL3 38 B5
TRDG/WHET N20 97 P4
Church Cft STALE/WH AL4 39 H8
Churchcroft Cl BAL SW12 * 180 B3
Churchdown BMLY BR1 183 K7
Church Dr CDALE/KGS NW9 116 A6
RYLN/HDSTN HA2 113 P4
WWKM BR4 205 K10
Church Elm La DAGE RM10 144 C1
Church End HDN NW4 116 E1
HLWW/ROY CM19 46 D3
STALE/WH AL4 21 H9
WALTH E17 * 120 G2
Church Farm EBAR EN4 * 98 A1
Church Farm La CHEAM SM3 221 H3
Church Farm Wy GSTN WD25 74 A4
Church Fld EPP CM16 65 K5
RDART DA2 187 L5
SEV TN13 246 G8
Churchfield HARP AL5 20 B3
HLW CM20 29 L9
Churchfield Av
NFNCH/WDSPK N12 97 N7
Churchfield Cl HYS/HAR UB3 132 G9
RYLN/HDSTN HA2 114 B2
Churchfield Ms SLN SL2 129 N8
Church Field Pth CHES/WCR EN8 62 C5
Churchfield Rd ACT W3 135 P10
CFSP/GDCR SL9 90 A9
HNWL W7 154 D1
REIG RH2 257 J9
WEA W13 134 G10
WELL DA16 163 K9
WEY KT13 216 B1
WLYN AL6 23 M2
WOT/HER KT12 197 H8
Church Flds RAD WD7 * 74 F2
Churchfields BROX EN10 44 F6
E/WMO/HCT KT8 197 P3
GNWCH SE10 161 H5
HERT/BAY SG13 25 L6
LOU IG10 82 B8
RGUE GU4 250 D5
SWFD E18 101 M9
WOKN/KNAP GU21 232 A2
Churchfields Av FELT TW13 175 N6
WEY KT13 216 C1
Churchfields La BROX EN10 44 F6
Churchfields Rd BECK BR3 204 C2
Churchfield Wy
NFNCH/WDSPK N12 97 M7
Church Gdns ALP/SUD HA0 114 F9
EA W5 155 J1
LHD/OX KT22 * 236 G6
Church Garth ARCH N19 * 118 E7
Churchgate CHES/WCR EN8 62 A6
Church Ga FUL/PGN SW6 157 H9
Churchgate Rd CHES/WCR EN8 62 A5
Churchgate St HLWE CM17 29 P7
Church Gn BRXN/ST SW9 * 159 H8
HYS/HAR UB3 132 G8
KWD/TDW/WH KT20 * 238 D10
WOT/HER KT12 217 K3
Church Gv AMS HP6 70 B5
DTCH/LGLY SL3 129 P7
KUT/HW KT1 199 H2
LEW SE13 160 G10
Church Hl ABLGY WD5 54 G2
BH/WHM TN16 244 A8
CAR SM5 222 A2
CTHM CR3 241 N10
DART DA1 164 F10
DEN/HRF UB9 111 M2
EPP CM16 65 K5
HERT/BAY SG13 26 B7
HRW HA1 114 D6
LOU IG10 82 C7
ORP BR6 207 L8
PUR/KEN CR8 222 F6
RDART DA2 188 D1
REDH RH1 258 C2
SHGR GU5 270 B5
WALTH E17 120 F2
WCHMH N21 98 G1
WIM/MER SW19 179 J8
WOKN/KNAP GU21 232 A2
WOKS/MYFD GU22 233 J3
WOOL/PLUM SE18 162 C2
Church Hill Rd CHEAM SM3 220 G1
EBAR EN4 77 P10
EBAR EN4 98 A2
SURB KT6 199 K5
WALTH E17 120 G2
Church Hill Wd STMC/STPC BR5 207 K5
Church Hollow PUR RM19 165 P4
Church Hyde WOOL/PLUM SE18 163 H5
Churchill Av HGDN/ICK UB10 132 C5
KTN/HRWW/WS HA3 114 G4
Churchill Cl CHONG CM5 67 P3
DART DA1 188 A4
EBED/NFELT TW14 174 G4
LHD/OX KT22 236 D9
WARL CR6 242 B3
Churchill Ct CRAWE RH10 284 A4
Churchill Dr BEAC HP9 88 B6
WEY KT13 216 D1
Churchill Gdns ACT W3 135 M8
PIM SW1V 16 G8
Churchill Gardens Rd PIM SW1V 16 G9
Churchill Ms WFD IG8 101 L7
Churchill Pl POP/IOD E14 140 G10
Churchill Rd CAN/RD E16 141 P8
CRICK NW2 136 E1
DTCH/LGLY SL3 150 C3
EDGW HA8 95 L7
EYN DA4 210 B4
GRAYS RM17 168 A5
GU GU1 268 C1
GVW DA11 190 C4
HOR/WEW KT19 219 M7
HORL RH6 281 J4
KTTN NW5 118 C9
SAND/SEL CR2 223 K5
STAL AL1 38 F4
Churchill Ter CHING E4 100 F5
Churchill Wk HOM E9 120 B10
Churchill Wy BH/WHM TN16 244 A1
BMLY BR1 205 M2
SUN TW16 175 H9
Church La ASC SL5 192 C4
BERK HP4 33 P5
BRKMPK AL9 40 F4
BRWN CM15 86 G3
CDALE/KGS NW9 115 P6
CEND/HSY/T N8 118 G2
CFSP/GDCR SL9 90 B9
CHES/WCR EN8 62 B5
CHOB/PIR GU24 230 C8
CHONG CM5 49 P10
CHSGTN KT9 219 L3
CHST BR7 206 F1
COUL/CHIP CR5 240 B8
CTHM CR3 241 H9
DAGE RM10 144 D2
DTCH/LGLY SL3 129 N6
EA W5 155 H1
ED N9 99 P3
EFNCH N2 117 N1
EN EN1 79 L7
EPP CM16 66 B1
EPSOM KT18 255 P1
GDST RH9 260 C8
GSTN WD25 74 A4
GVE DA12 191 M6
HAYES BR2 206 B8
HHS/BOV HP3 52 E3
HORL RH6 280 F9
KGLGY WD4 54 B6
KTN/HRWW/WS HA3 94 E9
KWD/TDW/WH KT20 238 G3
LOU IG10 81 N5
OXTED RH8 261 J6
PIN HA5 113 M1
POTB/CUF EN6 60 B6
PUR RM19 * 165 P4
RAIN RM13 145 L9
RBRW/HUT CM13 127 J4
RBSF CM22 30 E3
REDH RH1 259 L9
RGUW GU3 249 K3
RKW/CH/CXG WD3 71 K3
RKW/CH/CXG WD3 91 K2
ROM RM1 124 F2
RPLY/SEND GU23 250 F2
SHGR GU5 269 L5
SLN SL2 129 L6
STALE/WH AL4 39 N8
TEDD TW11 176 E8
THDIT KT7 198 F6
TOOT SW17 180 A8
TOOT SW17 180 C7
TOTM N17 99 M9
TWK TW1 176 F4
UPMR RM14 126 G10
WALTH E17 120 G2
WAN E11 121 K6
WARL CR6 242 C3
WARL CR6 243 H2
WDSR SL4 149 J7
WEY KT13 216 B1
WIM/MER SW19 201 K2
WLGTN SM6 202 E10
Church Lane Av COUL/CHIP CR5 240 C8
Church Lane Dr COUL/CHIP CR5 240 C8
Church Langley Wy HLWE CM17 47 M1
Churchley Rd SYD SE26 182 A7
Church Leys HLWS CM18 47 J2
Church Manor Wy ABYW SE2 163 K3
Church Manorway ERITH DA8 164 E2
Church Md CMBW SE5 * 159 K6
HLWW/ROY CM19 27 N10
Churchmead WAB EN9 * 45 H8
Churchmead Cl EBAR EN4 77 P10
Church Meadow SURB KT6 199 H9
Churchmead Rd WLSDN NW10 136 D1
Church Ms ADL/WDHM KT15 215 M1
Churchmore Rd
STRHM/NOR SW16 202 D1
Church Mt EFNCH N2 117 N3
Church Paddock Ct WLGTN SM6 202 E10
Church Pde ASHF TW15 * 174 A7
Church Pk CRAWW RH11 * 283 K6
Church Pas BAR EN5 * 77 J7
Church Pth CHSWK W4 155 P2
COUL/CHIP CR5 241 H4
GVW DA11 189 P2
MTCM CR4 201 P3
NFNCH/WDSPK N12 97 M6
RDART DA2 188 E2
RYNPK SW20 201 J2
WAN E11 121 M3
WOKN/KNAP GU21 * 232 C3
Church Pl EA W5 155 J1
MTCM CR4 201 P3
Church Ri CHSGTN KT9 219 L3
FSTH SE23 182 C4
Church Rd ABR/ST RM4 85 L5
ABR/ST RM4 105 L2
ACT W3 155 P1
ADL/WDHM KT15 215 L2
ASC SL5 192 F6
ASHF TW15 174 A7
ASHTD KT21 237 J4
BARK IG11 142 F1
BARN SW13 156 D8
BEAC HP9 89 J7
BF/WBF KT14 215 P9
BFOR GU20 212 A3
BGR/WK TN15 247 N7
BH/WHM TN16 245 L10
BKHH IG9 101 N2
BRW CM14 86 B3
BXLYHN DA7 164 A8
CHEAM SM3 221 H3
CHOB/PIR GU24 212 E8
CHONG CM5 49 K7
CRAWE RH10 284 F8
CROY/NA CR0 * 223 K1
CTHM CR3 241 N9
CTHM CR3 242 D9
DEN/HRF UB9 111 M1
E/WMO/HCT KT8 198 C4
EGH TW20 172 D8
ERITH DA8 164 D4
ESH/CLAY KT10 218 E3
EW KT17 220 B9
EYN DA4 187 P9
FELT TW13 175 K8
GNTH/NBYPK IG2 123 H4
GT/LBKH KT23 235 N9
GT/LBKH KT23 253 P1
GU GU1 268 A1
GVE DA12 190 F9
HARH RM3 105 P9
HART DA3 211 L5
HAYES BR2 205 K3
HAYES BR2 205 M2
HAYES BR2 226 A4
HDN NW4 116 E2
HERT/BAY SG13 42 D5
HERT/WAT SG14 25 J4
HEST TW5 153 J4
HEST TW5 153 P6
HGT N6 118 B4
HHS/BOV HP3 * 36 D8
HLWE CM17 47 M4
HNWL W7 134 D9
HOR/WEW KT19 220 A4
HYS/HAR UB3 132 G10
IS N1 6 F2
ISLW TW7 154 C7
IVER SL0 130 F4
KUT/HW KT1 199 L2
LEY E10 120 F6
LHD/OX KT22 236 G8
LOU IG10 81 M7
MEO DA13 190 F10
MNPK E12 122 C10
NRWD SE19 181 M10
NTHLT UB5 133 M4
NTHWD HA6 92 G8
NWDGN UB2 153 N2
ORP BR6 226 F2
ORP BR6 227 N3
PEND EN3 80 B10
POTB/CUF EN6 59 M6
PUR/KEN CR8 222 F6
PUR/KEN CR8 241 L1
RCHPK/HAM TW10 177 K1
RCHPK/HAM TW10 177 K7
RDART DA2 188 D1
REDH RH1 275 P2
REIG RH2 275 K2
WAND/EARL SW18 179 L1
RSEV TN14 263 P2
RSEV TN14 265 J8
SCUP DA14 185 K7
SHPTN TW17 196 C7
SLN SL2 129 H5
STAN HA7 94 G6
SURB KT6 199 H9
SWCM DA10 189 L2
SWLY BR8 208 E7
SWLY BR8 209 L1
TEDD TW11 176 D7
TIL RM18 168 B7
TOTM N17 99 N8
UX/CGN UB8 131 N6
WALTH E17 100 D10
WARL CR6 242 C3
WAT WD17 73 H5
WDR/YW UB7 151 N1
WDSR SL4 171 N1
WELL DA16 163 L8
WGCW AL8 22 G5
WIM/MER SW19 179 H6
WIM/MER SW19 201 N2
WLGTN SM6 202 D10
WLSDN NW10 136 B2
WOKN/KNAP GU21 232 A2
WPK KT4 200 B8
Church Rw CHST BR7 206 F1
FUL/PGN SW6 * 157 L6
HAMP NW3 117 M9
RPLY/SEND GU23 * 233 M7
WAND/EARL SW18 * 179 K1
Church Row Ms CHST BR7 184 F10
Church Side EPSOM KT18 219 N9
Churchside Cl BH/WHM TN16 245 P4
Church Sq SHPTN TW17 196 C7
Church St AMSS HP7 68 G6
BAY/PAD W2 9 M3
BGR/WK TN15 247 P6
BRKHM/BTCW RH3 274 B1
BRKMPK AL9 40 F3
BRKMPK AL9 41 P3
CHSWK W4 156 C5
COB KT11 235 J1
CRAWW RH11 283 M7
CROY/NA CR0 203 J10
CSHM HP5 50 G8
DAGE RM10 144 C2
DORK RH4 272 F2
ED N9 99 L2
EHSLY KT24 253 L3
ENC/FH EN2 79 L7
ESH/CLAY KT10 218 A1
EW KT17 220 B9
GRAYS RM17 167 P5
GVW DA11 190 E2
HART DA3 211 L9
HERT/WAT SG14 25 L5
HHNE HP2 35 N4
HHS/BOV HP3 52 E3
HPTN TW12 198 B1
HSLW TW3 176 B1
ISLW TW7 154 G9
KUT/HW KT1 199 J2
LHD/OX KT22 236 G8
MEO DA13 189 M8
REIG RH2 257 L10
RKW/CH/CXG WD3 91 P2
RSEV TN14 228 G7
SBW CM21 29 P1
SL SL1 149 J1
SRTFD E15 141 K3
STA TW18 172 G7
STALE/WH AL4 21 J3
STALW/RED AL3 38 C5
SUN TW16 197 J3
TWK TW1 176 F4
WAB EN9 63 H9
WARE SG12 26 C2
WATW WD18 * 73 K8
WDSR SL4 149 J7
WEY KT13 216 B1
WOKS/MYFD GU22 232 F7
WOT/HER KT12 197 H8
Church St East
WOKN/KNAP GU21 232 C3
Church Street Est STJWD NW8 9 M2
Church St North SRTFD E15 141 K3
Church St West
WOKN/KNAP GU21 232 B3
Church Ter BGR/WK TN15 * 247 N7
BKHTH/KID SE3 161 K9
FUL/PGN SW6 * 157 L8
HDN NW4 116 E1
RCHPK/HAM TW10 177 J1
WDSR SL4 148 D8
Church V EFNCH N2 118 A1
FSTH SE23 182 B5
Church Vw BROX EN10 44 E6
FSTH SE23 182 C5
SOCK/AV RM15 166 B1
STALE/WH AL4 * 21 J3
UPMR RM14 126 A7
Church View Cl HORL RH6 280 A5
Churchview Rd WHTN TW2 176 C4
Church Wk BTFD TW8 155 H5
BUSH WD23 73 P10
CDALE/KGS NW9 116 A7
CRAWE RH10 283 N7
CRICK NW2 117 J8
CTHM CR3 241 P10
GVE DA12 190 G3
HORL RH6 280 A5
HYS/HAR UB3 132 F8
RDART DA2 187 L6
REIG RH2 257 M10
RYNPK SW20 200 F3
SBW CM21 30 A1
STNW/STAM N16 119 L9
STRHM/NOR SW16 202 D2
THDIT KT7 198 E6
WEY KT13 196 B10
WOT/HER KT12 197 H8
Churchway CAMTN NW1 5 K9
Church Wy OXTED RH8 261 L8
SAND/SEL CR2 223 N6
TRDG/WHET N20 97 P4
Churchyard Rw LBTH SE11 18 D5
Churston Av PLSTW E13 141 N3
Churston Cl BRXS/STRHM SW2 * 181 J4
Churston Dr MRDN SM4 200 G5
Churston Gdns FBAR/BDGN N11 98 D7
Churton Pl CHSWK W4 * 155 N5
PIM SW1V 17 H6
Churton St PIM SW1V 17 H6
Chuters Cl BF/WBF KT14 216 A8
Chuters Gv EW KT17 220 C8
The Chyne CFSP/GDCR SL9 110 C3
Chyngton Cl BFN/LL DA15 185 J6
Cibber Rd FSTH SE23 182 C5
Cicada Rd WAND/EARL SW18 179 M2
Cicely Rd PECK SE15 159 P7
Cidermill Rd RDKG RH5 278 B4
Cillocks Cl HOD EN11 44 F2
Cimba Wd GVE DA12 191 H7
Cinderella Pth GLDGN NW11 117 L6
Cinderford Wy BMLY BR1 183 K7
Cinder Pth WOKS/MYFD GU22 231 P5
Cinema Pde EDGW HA8 * 95 M7
Cinnamon Cl CROY/NA CR0 * 202 F7
PECK SE15 159 N6
WDSR SL4 148 E7
Cinnamon Gdns GUW GU2 249 M5
Cinnamon St WAP E1W 140 A10
Cintra Pk NRWD SE19 181 N10
Cippenham Cl SL SL1 128 E9
Cippenham La SL SL1 128 E9
Circle Gdns BF/WBF KT14 216 A9
WIM/MER SW19 201 K3
Circle Rd WOT/HER KT12 216 F6
The Circle CRICK NW2 116 B8
MLHL NW7 96 A7
Circuit Centre WEY KT13 * 215 P7
The Circuit Centre WEY KT13 * 215 P7
The Circuits PIN HA5 113 K2
Circular Rd TOTM N17 119 N1
Circular Wy WOOL/PLUM SE18 162 C5
Circus Ms MBLAR W1H * 10 A3
Circus Pl LVPST EC2M * 13 H4
Circus Rd STJWD NW8 3 L9
Circus St GNWCH SE10 161 H6
The Circus LHD/OX KT22 * 236 G6
Cirencester St BAY/PAD W2 8 G3
Cirrus Crs GVE DA12 191 H8
Cissbury Hl CRAWW RH11 283 M9
Cissbury Ring North
NFNCH/WDSPK N12 97 K6
Cissbury Ring South
NFNCH/WDSPK N12 97 K6
Cissbury Rd SEVS/STOTM N15 119 L3
Citadel Pl LBTH SE11 17 N7
Citizen Rd HOLWY N7 119 H8
Citron Ter PECK SE15 * 160 A9
City Barracks SHB W12 * 136 F10
City Garden Rw FSBYE EC1V 6 E9
City Pk WGCE AL7 * 23 K4
City Rd FSBYE EC1V 6 C8
SDTCH EC2A 13 H3
City Wk STHWK SE1 19 J3
Civic Centre STAL AL1 * 38 C6
Civic Sq TIL RM18 168 D8
Civic Wy BARK/HLT IG6 122 F2
RSLP HA4 113 L10
Clabon Ms KTBR SW1X 16 A4
Clacket La BH/WHM TN16 244 B10
BH/WHM TN16 262 C3
Clack St BERM/RHTH SE16 160 B1
Clacton Rd TOTM N17 * 99 N10
WALTH E17 120 D4
Claire Cswy RDART DA2 * 166 D10
Claire Cl RBRW/HUT CM13 107 M5
Claire Ct NFNCH/WDSPK N12 97 M5
Claire Gdns STAN HA7 95 H6
Claire Pl POP/IOD E14 160 F2
Clairvale EMPK RM11 125 M5
Clairvale Rd HEST TW5 153 L7
Clairview Rd STRHM/NOR SW16 180 C8
Clairville Gdns HNWL W7 134 D10
Clammas Wy UX/CGN UB8 131 M7
Clamp Hl STAN HA7 94 C5
Clancarty Rd FUL/PGN SW6 157 K8
Clandon Av EGH TW20 172 F10
Clandon Cl ACT W3 155 N1
EW KT17 220 C3
Clandon Gdns FNCH N3 117 K1
Clandon Rd GDMY/SEVK IG3 123 H7
GU GU1 268 B1
RGUE GU4 251 K2
Clandon St DEPT SE8 160 F8
Clandon Ter RYNPK SW20 * 200 G2
Clanricarde Gdns BAY/PAD W2 8 F8
Clapgate Rd BUSH WD23 74 A10
Clapham Common North Side
CLAP SW4 158 C10
Clapham Common South Side
CLAP SW4 180 C2
Clapham Common West Side
CLAP SW4 180 B1
Clapham Court Ter CLAP SW4 * 180 F1
Clapham Crs CLAP SW4 158 E10
Clapham High St CLAP SW4 158 E10
Clapham Manor St CLAP SW4 158 D9
Clapham Park Est CLAP SW4 * 180 E3
Clapham Park Rd CLAP SW4 158 D10
Clapham Park Ter
BRXS/STRHM SW2 * 180 F1
Clapham Rd BRXN/ST SW9 158 F8
Clappers Ga CRAWE RH10 283 N6
Clappers La CHOB/PIR GU24 213 H7
Claps Gate La EHAM E6 142 E6
Clapton Common CLPT E5 119 P5
Clapton Pas CLPT E5 120 B10
Clapton Sq CLPT E5 120 B10
Clapton Ter CLPT E5 119 P5
Clapton Wy CLPT E5 119 P9
Clara Pl WOOL/PLUM SE18 162 D3
Clare Cswy RDART DA2 166 D10
Clare Cl BF/WBF KT14 215 K9
BORE WD6 75 L10
CRAWE RH10 284 D4
EFNCH N2 117 M1
Clare Cnr ELTH/MOT SE9 184 E3
Clare Ct CTHM CR3 242 F9
NTHWD HA6 92 F6
Clare Crs LHD/OX KT22 236 F4
Claredale WOKS/MYFD GU22 232 B5
Claredale St BETH E2 7 P8
Clare Dr SLN SL2 108 G9
Clare Gdns BARK IG11 143 J1
EGH TW20 172 D8
FSTGT E7 121 M9
NTGHL W11 8 B6
Clare Hl ESH/CLAY KT10 218 A2
Clare La IS N1 6 F4
Clare Lawn Av
MORT/ESHN SW14 178 A1
Clare Ms CHONG CM5 67 P2
FUL/PGN SW6 157 L6
Claremont CHESW EN7 61 N5
LCOL/BKTW AL2 55 P7
Claremont Av
KTN/HRWW/WS HA3 115 K3
NWMAL KT3 200 E5
SUN TW16 197 J1
WOKS/MYFD GU22 232 B5
WOT/HER KT12 217 L1
Claremont Cl BRXS/STRHM SW2 180 G4
CAN/RD E16 142 D10
CDW/CHF RM16 167 P2
IS N1 6 B8
ORP BR6 226 D1
SAND/SEL CR2 242 A1
WOT/HER KT12 217 K2
Claremont Ct DORK RH4 272 G3
Claremont Crs DART DA1 164 F10
RKW/CH/CXG WD3 72 D9
Claremont Dr ESH/CLAY KT10 218 A4
SHPTN TW17 196 C6
WOKS/MYFD GU22 232 B5
Claremont End ESH/CLAY KT10 218 A3
Claremont Gdns GDMY/SEVK IG3 123 H7
SURB KT6 199 K5
UPMR RM14 126 C6
Claremont Gv CHSWK W4 156 B6
WFD IG8 101 P7
Claremont House WATW WD18 * 72 E10
Claremont La ESH/CLAY KT10 218 A2
Claremont Pk FNCH N3 97 H9
Claremont Park Rd
ESH/CLAY KT10 217 P3
Claremont Rd BF/WBF KT14 215 K8
BMLY BR1 206 B4
CRICK NW2 116 F5
CROY/NA CR0 203 P8
EBAR EN4 77 M4
EMPK RM11 125 H4
ESH/CLAY KT10 218 D4
HGT N6 118 C5
KTN/HRWW/WS HA3 94 D10
MV/WKIL W9 2 B8
REDH RH1 258 B7
STA TW18 172 G8
SURB KT6 199 K5
SWLY BR8 186 F10
TWK TW1 176 G3
WALTH E17 100 D10
WAN E11 121 J8
WDSR SL4 149 H8
WEA W13 134 F7
Claremont Sq IS N1 6 A8
Claremont St GNWCH SE10 160 G5
UED N18 99 P7
Claremont Ter THDIT KT7 * 198 G7
Claremont Vls CMBW SE5 * 159 L6
KUT/HW KT1 * 199 L2
Claremont Wy CRICK NW2 116 F6
Claremount Cl EPSOM KT18 238 F3
Claremount Gdns EPSOM KT18 238 G3
Clarence Av BMLY BR1 206 B4
CLAP SW4 180 E3
IL IG1 122 C4
NWMAL KT3 199 P2
UPMR RM14 125 P7
Clarence Cl BUSH WD23 94 E1
EBAR EN4 77 N9
WOT/HER KT12 217 J1
Clarence Ct HORL RH6 280 E4
MLHL NW7 96 C6
Clarence Crs CLAP SW4 180 E2
SCUP DA14 185 L6
WDSR SL4 149 H7
Clarence Dr EGH TW20 171 P7
Clarence Gdns CAMTN NW1 4 F10
Clarence Ga CAMTN NW1 10 B2
CHIG IG7 102 D7
Clarence La PUT/ROE SW15 178 C2
Clarence Ms BERM/RHTH SE16 140 C10
CLPT E5 120 A10
TOOT SW17 179 M6
Clarence Pas CAMTN NW1 * 5 L8
Clarence Pl CLPT E5 120 B10
GVE DA12 190 E3
Clarence Rd BERK HP4 33 L5
BH/WHM TN16 244 C4
BMLY BR1 206 B3
BRWN CM15 86 G10
BXLYHS DA6 163 P10
CAN/RD E16 141 K6
CLPT E5 120 A9
CROY/NA CR0 203 L7
DEPT SE8 160 G5
ELTH/MOT SE9 184 B5
GRAYS RM17 167 N5
KIL/WHAMP NW6 2 C4
MNPK E12 121 P9
PEND EN3 80 B9
RCH/KEW TW9 155 L7
REDH RH1 275 N3
SCUP DA14 185 L6
SEVS/STOTM N15 119 K3
STAL AL1 38 F6
SUT SM1 221 L1
TEDD TW11 176 E9
WALTH E17 100 C10
WDGN N22 98 F8
WDSR SL4 148 G7
WIM/MER SW19 179 L9
WLGTN SM6 222 C2
WOT/HER KT12 217 J1
Clarence Rw GVE DA12 190 E3
Clarence St EGH TW20 172 C9
KUT/HW KT1 199 K2
NWDGN UB2 153 L2
RCH/KEW TW9 155 K10
STA TW18 173 H7
Clarence Ter CAMTN NW1 10 B1
HSLW TW3 154 A10
Clarence Vls KUT/HW KT1 * 199 L2
Clarence Wk CLAP SW4 158 F8
REDH RH1 275 N3
Clarence Wy CAMTN NW1 4 F3
HORL RH6 280 E4
Clarenden Flds
RKW/CH/CXG WD3 72 A4
Clarendon Cl BAY/PAD W2 * 9 N7
HHNE HP2 35 N5
HOM E9 140 B2
STMC/STPC BR5 207 K3
Clarendon Ct SLN SL2 129 N9
Clarendon Crs WHTN TW2 176 C6
Clarendon Cross NTGHL W11 137 H9
Clarendon Dr PUT/ROE SW15 156 F10
Clarendon Gdns HDN NW4 116 D1
IL IG1 122 C6
MV/WKIL W9 9 K2
RDART DA2 188 C4
WBLY HA9 115 K9
Clarendon Ga BAY/PAD W2 9 N7
CHERT KT16 214 G3
Clarendon Gn STMC/STPC BR5 207 K3
Clarendon Gv MTCM CR4 202 A3
STMC/STPC BR5 207 K4
Clarendon Ms ASHTD KT21 237 K5
BAY/PAD W2 9 N7
BORE WD6 * 75 M7
Clarendon Pth STMC/STPC BR5 207 K4
Clarendon Pl BAY/PAD W2 9 N7
RDART DA2 186 E8
SEV TN13 * 265 H1
Clarendon Ri LEW SE13 161 H9
Clarendon Rd ASHF TW15 174 A7
BORE WD6 75 M7
CEND/HSY/T N8 118 G1
CHES/WCR EN8 62 C5
CROY/NA CR0 203 J9
EA W5 135 K5
GVE DA12 190 F2
HRW HA1 114 D4
HYS/HAR UB3 152 G1
NTGHL W11 8 A7
REDH RH1 258 A9
SEV TN13 247 H10
SEVS/STOTM N15 119 K2
SWFD E18 121 M1
UED N18 99 P7
WALTH E17 120 G4
WAN E11 121 J6
WAT WD17 73 J7
WDGN N22 * 98 G10
WIM/MER SW19 179 P10
WLGTN SM6 222 D3
Clarendon St PIM SW1V 16 F7
Clarendon Ter MV/WKIL W9 9 K1
Clarendon Wk NTGHL W11 8 A6
Clarendon Wy CHST BR7 207 J3
WCHMH N21 99 K1
Clarens St CAT SE6 182 E5
Clare Pde GFD/PVL UB6 * 134 C1
Clare Pk AMSS HP7 69 K6
Clare Rd GFD/PVL UB6 134 C1
HSLWW TW4 153 N9
MDHD SL6 128 B8
NWCR SE14 160 E8
STWL/WRAY TW19 173 N4
WAN E11 121 J4
WLSDN NW10 136 D2
The Clares CTHM CR3 241 P10
Clare St BETH E2 140 A4
Claret Gdns SNWD SE25 203 M4
Clareville Gv SKENS SW7 15 K6
Clareville Rd CTHM CR3 241 P10
STMC/STPC BR5 206 F9
Clareville St SKENS SW7 15 K6
Clare Wy BXLYHN DA7 163 P7
SEV TN13 265 K4
Clare Wd LHD/OX KT22 236 F4
Clarges Ms MYFR/PICC W1J 10 E9
Clarges St MYFR/PICC W1J 10 F10
Claribel Rd BRXN/ST SW9 159 J8
Clarice Wy WLGTN SM6 222 F5
Claridge Rd BCTR RM8 123 N6
Clarissa Rd CHDH RM6 123 N4
Clarissa St HACK E8 7 L5
Clarkbourne Dr GRAYS RM17 168 A5
Clark Cl ERITH DA8 165 H7
Clarke Gn GSTN WD25 73 H1
Clarke Ms ED N9 100 A4
Clarkers La KTTN NW5 118 C10
Clarkes Av WPK KT4 200 G8
Clarkes Dr UX/CGN UB8 131 P7
Clarkes Green Road
BGR/WK TN15 229 P10
Clarkes Ms CAVSQ/HST W1G 10 D3
Clarke's Rd HAT AL10 40 E3
Clarke Wy GSTN WD25 73 H1
Clarkfield RKW/CH/CXG WD3 91 K2
Clarkhill HLWS CM18 47 H4
Clarks La EPP CM16 65 J7
OXTED RH8 243 N9
RSEV TN14 228 A8
Clarks Md BUSH WD23 94 B1
Clarkson Rd CAN/RD E16 141 L8
Clarkson Rw CAMTN NW1 4 G8
Clarkson St BETH E2 140 A5
Clark's Rd IL IG1 122 G7
Clark St WCHPL E1 140 B8
Clark Wy HEST TW5 153 L6
Classon Cl WDR/YW UB7 151 P1
Claston Cl DART DA1 164 F10
Claude Monet Ct EDUL SE22 * 181 P1
Claude Rd LEY E10 121 H6
PECK SE15 160 A8
PLSTW E13 141 N3
Claude St POP/IOD E14 160 F3
Claudian Pl STALW/RED AL3 37 P8
Claudian Wy CDW/CHF RM16 168 E2
Claudia Pl WIM/MER SW19 179 H4
Claudius Cl STAN HA7 95 J4
Claughton Rd PLSTW E13 141 P4
Clauson Av NTHLT UB5 114 A10
Clavell St GNWCH SE10 161 H5
Claverdale Rd BRXS/STRHM SW2 180 G3
Claverhambury Rd WAB EN9 63 M4
Clavering Av BARN SW13 156 E5
Clavering Cl TEDD TW11 176 F7
Clavering Rd MNPK E12 122 A6
Clavering Wy RBRW/HUT CM13 87 P10
Claverley Gv FNCH N3 97 K9
Claverley Vls FNCH N3 97 L8
Claverton Cl HHS/BOV HP3 52 D4
Claverton St PIM SW1V 17 H8
Clave St WAP E1W 140 B10
Claxton Gv HMSMTH W6 156 G4
Clay Acre CSHM HP5 51 J6
Clay Av MTCM CR4 202 C2
Claybank Gv LEW SE13 160 G9
Claybridge Rd LEE/GVPK SE12 183 P7
Claybrook Cl EFNCH N2 117 N1
Claybrook Rd HMSMTH W6 156 G5
Clayburn Gdns SOCK/AV RM15 146 G10
Claybury BUSH WD23 94 A1
Claybury Rd WFD IG8 102 B8
Clay Cnr CHERT KT16 195 L8
Claycroft WGCE AL7 23 L4
Claydon Dr CROY/NA CR0 222 F1
Claydon End CFSP/GDCR SL9 110 B1
Claydon La CFSP/GDCR SL9 110 B1
Claydon Rd WOKN/KNAP GU21 231 M2
Claydown Ms WOOL/PLUM SE18 162 D4
Clayfarm Rd ELTH/MOT SE9 184 F5
Claygate Cl HCH RM12 125 H9
Claygate Crs CROY/NA CR0 225 J3
Claygate La ESH/CLAY KT10 198 F9
Claygate Lodge Cl
ESH/CLAY KT10 218 D4
Claygate Rd DORK RH4 272 G4
WEA W13 154 G2
Clayhall Av CLAY IG5 102 C10
Clay Hall La CRAWE RH10 285 K1
Clayhall La REIG RH2 275 H3
WDSR SL4 171 L1

Clayhanger RGUE GU4 .....250 F8
Clay HI ENC/FH EN2 .....79 K3
Clayhill Cl REIG RH2 .....274 D7
Clayhill Crs RYN/HRT/MOT SL6 .....184 A7
Clayhill Rd REIG RH2 .....274 C8
Claylands Pl VX/NE SW8 .....159 H6
Claylands Rd VX/NE SW8 .....17 P10
Clay La BUSH WD23 .....94 A3
EPSOM KT18 .....237 N10
REDH RH1 .....276 D7
RGUE GU4 .....250 A4
STWL/WRAY TW19 .....174 A3
Claymore HHNE HP2 .....35 P2
Claymore Cl MRDN SM4 .....201 K7
Claypole HI WAB EN9 .....81 P7
Claypole Dr HEST TW5 .....153 M7
Claypole Rd SRTFD E15 .....141 H4
Clayponds Av BTFD TW8 .....106 C2
Clayponds Gdns EA W5 .....155 J5
Clayponds La BTFD TW8 .....155 K4
Clayside CHIG IG7 .....102 C7
Clay's La LOU IG10 .....82 E5
SRTFD E15 .....120 C10
Clays Lane Cl SRTFD E15 .....120 C10
Clay St MHST W1U 10 B4
Clayton Av ALP/SUD HA0 .....135 K2
UPMR RM14 .....126 A10
Clayton Cl EHAM E6 .....142 C8
Clayton Crs BTFD TW8 .....155 J4
IS N1 .....5 N6
Clayton Croft Rd RDART DA2 .....187 H6
Clayton Dr DEPT SE8 .....160 D4
GUW GU2 .....249 L2
Clayton Fld CDALE/KGS NW9 .....96 B9
Clayton HI CRAWW RH11 .....283 M9
Clayton Rd GDST RH9 .....260 A6
Clayton Ms GNWCH SE10 .....161 J7
Clayton Pde CHES/WCR EN8 * 62 C6
DTCH/LGLY SL3 * 150 D2
Clayton Rd CHSGTN KT9 .....219 H1
EW KT17 .....220 B8
HYS/HAR UB3 .....152 F1
ISLW TW7 .....154 D9
PECK SE15 .....159 P8
ROMW/RG RM7 .....124 D6
Clayton St LBTH SE11 .....18 A9
Clayton Ter YEAD UB4 .....133 L7
Claytonville Ter BELV DA17 * 164 C1
Clayton Wk AMSS HP7 .....34 D7
Clay Tye Rd UPMR RM14 .....127 H10
Claywood La RDART DA2 .....189 J6
Clayworth Cl BFN/LL DA15 .....185 L2
Cleall Av WAB EN9 .....81 L1
Cleanthus Cl WOOL/PLUM SE18 .....162 F7
Cleanthus Rd WOOL/PLUM SE18 .....162 F7
Clearbrook Wy WCHPL E1 .....140 B8
Cleardene DORK RH4 .....272 G6
Cleardown WOKS/MYFD GU22 .....232 E4
Cleares Pasture SL SL1 .....128 A5
The Clears REIG RH2 .....257 H8
Clearwater Pl SURB KT6 .....199 H6
Clearwater Ter NTGHL W11 .....156 E1
Clearwell Dr MV/WKIL W9 .....8 G2
Cleave Av HYS/HAR UB3 .....152 F3
ORP BR6 .....227 H3
Cleaveland Rd SURB KT6 .....199 J5
Cleave Prior COUL/CHIP CR5 .....289 P5
Cleaverholme Cl SNWD SE25 .....204 A5
Cleaver Sq LBTH SE11 .....18 A7
Cleaver St LBTH SE11 .....18 A7
The Cleave HARP AL5 .....20 C2
Cleeve Ct EBED/NFELT TW14 .....174 F4
Cleeve HI FSTH SE23 .....162 G3
Cleeve Park Gdns SCUP DA14 .....185 L5
The Cleeve GU GU1 .....250 D10
Cleeve Wy PUT/ROE SW15 .....178 G2
SUT SM1 .....201 L8
Clegg St PLSTW E13 .....141 M4
WAP E1W 140 A10
Cleland Pth LOU IG10 .....82 E5
Clematis Cl HARH RM3 .....105 K8
Clematis Cottages SHB W12 * 136 F7
Clematis Gdns WFD IG8 .....96 E5
Clematis St SHB W12 .....136 C9
Clem Attlee Pde FUL/PGN SW6 .....14 D9
Clemence Rd DAGE RM10 .....144 E3
Clemence St POP/IOD E14 .....140 E7
Clement Av CLAP SW4 .....158 G3
Clement Cl CHSWK W4 .....156 A3
KIL/WHAMP NW6 .....137 H6
PUR/KEN CR8 .....241 J2
Clement Gdns HYS/HAR UB3 .....152 F3
Clementhorpe Rd DAGW RM9 .....143 M1
Clementina Rd LEY E10 .....120 E6
Clementine Cl WEA W13 .....154 G1
Clementine Wy HHW HP1 .....35 N5
Clement Rd BECK BR3 .....204 C2
CHES/WCR EN8 .....62 D3
WIM/MER SW19 .....178 A8
Clements Av CAN/RD E16 .....141 M9
Clements Cl NFNCH/WDSPK N12 .....97 L1
SL SL1 .....149 N1
Clements Inn LINN WC2A 11 M6
Clements La IL IG1 .....122 E8
MANHO EC4R 11 H6
Clements Rd BTFD TW8 * 155 J4
Clement's Rd BERM/RHTH SE16 .....19 P4
EHAM E6 .....142 C2
IL IG1 .....122 E8
RKW/CH/CXG WD3 .....70 G3
WOT/HER KT12 .....197 J9
Clements St WARE SG12 .....26 D2
Clement St SWLY BR8 .....187 L9
Clement Wy UPMR RM14 .....124 F1
Clenches Farm Rd SEV TN13 .....265 H2
Clendon Wy WOOL/PLUM SE18 .....162 G3
Clennam St STHWK SE1 * 19 H1
Clensham La SUT SM1 .....201 K9
Clenshaw Cl SUT SM1 .....201 K9
Clenston Ms MBLAR W1H 10 A5
Cleopatra Cl STAN HA7 .....95 J4
Clephane Rd IS N1 .....6 F1
Clephane Rd North IS N1 .....6 F1
Clephane Rd South IS N1 .....6 G2
Clere Pl SDTCH EC2A 13 J1
Clere St SDTCH EC2A 13 H1
Clerkenwell Cl CLKNW EC1R 12 C2
Clerkenwell Gn CLKNW EC1R 12 C2
Clerkenwell Rd CLKNW EC1R 12 A2
Clerks Cft REDH RH1 .....259 L6
Clerks Piece LOU IG10 .....82 G7
Clermont Rd HOM E9 .....140 B3
Clevedon WEY KT13 .....216 D4
Clevedon Gdns HEST TW5 .....153 J8
HYS/HAR UB3 .....152 E2
Clevedon Rd KUT/HW KT1 .....199 M2
PGE/AN SE20 .....200 C1
TWK TW1 .....177 J2
Clevehurst Cl SLN SL2 .....129 L1
Cleveland Av CHSWK W4 .....156 A3
HPTN TW12 .....175 H4
Cleveland Cl WOT/HER KT12 .....197 J10
Cleveland Crs BORE WD6 .....75 P9
Cleveland Dr STA TW18 .....195 L2
Cleveland Gdns BARN SW13 .....158 D3
BAY/PAD W2 .....9 K1
CRICK NW2 .....116 C7
SEVS/STOTM N15 .....119 K2
WPK KT4 .....200 B9
Cleveland Gv WCHPL E1 .....140 E6
Cleveland Ms FITZ W1T 10 E3
Cleveland Park Av WALTH E17 .....120 C9
Cleveland Park Crs WALTH E17 .....120 C9
Cleveland Pl GODL GU7 .....267 K10
STJS SW1Y 11 J8
Cleveland Ri MRDN SM4 .....201 G7
Cleveland Rd BARN SW13 .....158 C3
CHSWK W4 .....155 P2
ED N9 .....102 C6
HHNE HP2 .....36 A1
IL IG1 .....122 E8
IS N1 .....7 H4

ISLW TW7 .....154 F10
SWFD E18 .....121 M1
UX/CGN UB8 .....131 N3
WEA W13 .....134 F7
WELL DA16 .....163 J8
WPK KT4 .....200 B9
Cleveland Rw WHALL SW1A 11 H10
Cleveland Sq BAY/PAD W2 .....9 K1
Cleveland St FITZ W1T 10 E2
Cleveland Ter BAY/PAD W2 .....9 J1
Cleveland Wy HHNE HP2 .....36 A1
WCHPL E1 .....140 E6
Cleveley Crs EA W5 .....135 K4
Cleveleys Rd CLPT E5 .....120 A8
Clevely Cl CHARL SE7 .....162 A3
Cleverly Est SHB W12 .....136 D10
Cleve Rd KIL/WHAMP NW6 .....2 E1
SCUP DA14 .....185 N6
Cleves Av BRW CM14 .....106 C2
EW KT17 .....220 E5
Cleves Cl COB KT11 .....217 G10
LOU IG10 .....82 B10
Cleves Ct WDSR SL4 .....148 E9
Cleves Crs CROY/NA CR0 .....225 H7
Cleves Rd BGR/WK TN15 .....247 M3
EHAM E6 .....142 A3
HHNE HP2 .....36 C1
RCHPK/HAM TW10 .....177 H6
Cleves Wk BARK/HLT IG6 .....102 F7
Cleves Wd WEY KT13 .....216 F1
Cleves Wy HPTN TW12 .....175 N10
RSLP HA4 .....113 L6
SUN TW16 .....174 D9
Clewer Court Rd WDSR SL4 .....148 H8
Clewer Crs KTN/HRWW/WS HA3 .....94 C9
Clewer Flds WDSR SL4 .....149 H7
Clewer Hill Rd WDSR SL4 .....148 D9
Clewer New Town WDSR SL4 .....148 E9
Clewer La CHOB/PIR GU24 .....230 F2
Clifden Ms CLPT E5 .....120 C9
Clifden Rd BTFD TW8 .....155 J5
CLPT E5 .....120 B10
TWK TW1 .....176 E4
Cliff End PUR/KEN CR8 .....223 J8
Cliffe Rd SAND/SEL CR2 .....223 L2
Clifford Av CHST BR7 .....184 C9
CLAY IG5 .....102 E9
RCH/KEW TW9 .....155 N9
WLGTN SM6 .....222 D1
Clifford Cl NTHLT UB5 .....133 M5
Clifford Dr BRXN/ST SW9 .....159 J10
Clifford Gdns HYS/HAR UB3 .....152 E2
WLSDN NW10 .....136 F4
Clifford Gv ASHF TW15 .....174 B7
Clifford Manor Rd RGUE GU4 .....268 B4
Clifford Rd ALP/SUD HA0 .....135 J3
BAR EN5 .....77 L7
CAN/RD E16 .....141 L6
CDW/CHF RM16 .....167 L2
ED N9 .....80 B10
HSLWW TW4 .....153 L9
RCHPK/HAM TW10 .....177 J5
SNWD SE25 .....203 P4
WALTH E17 .....101 H10
Clifford St CONDST W1S 10 E7
Clifford Wy WLSDN NW10 .....116 D10
Cliff Pl SOCK/AV RM15 .....147 L5
Cliff Reach RDART DA2 .....188 D2
Cliff Rd CAMTN NW1 .....5 K1
Cliff Ter DEPT SE8 .....160 F8
Cliffview Rd LEW SE13 .....160 F9
Cliff Vls CAMTN NW1 .....5 K1
Cliff Wk CAN/RD E16 .....141 L7
Clifton Av BELMT SM2 .....221 L7
FELT TW13 .....175 K7
FNCH N3 .....97 J7
KTN/HRWW/WS HA3 .....95 L1
SHB W12 .....136 C7
STAN HA7 .....95 J8
WBLY HA9 .....136 B1
Clifton Cl ADL/WDHM KT15 .....195 L9
CHES/WCR EN8 .....62 D5
CTHM CR3 .....241 L9
HORL RH6 .....280 E4
ORP BR6 .....226 F2
Clifton Ct BECK BR3 .....204 C1
Clifton Crs PECK SE15 .....160 A6
Clifton Gdns CHSWK W4 .....156 A3
ENC/FH EN2 .....78 F9
GLDGN NW11 .....117 J4
HGDN/ICK UB10 .....132 C4
MV/WKIL W9 .....8 H3
SEVS/STOTM N15 .....119 N4
UX/CGN UB8 .....131 G7
Clifton Gv HACK E8 .....7 N1
Clifton Hatch HLWS CM18 .....47 K4
Clifton HI STJWD NW8 .....3 A1
Clifton Lawns AMS HP6 .....69 H1
Clifton Marine Pde GRAV DA11 .....190 D2
Clifton Ms SNWD SE25 .....203 M4
Clifton Pde FELT TW13 * 175 K7
Clifton Pk ADL/WDHM KT15 200
Clifton Pl BAY/PAD W2 .....9 M6
BERM/RHTH SE16 .....160 B1
BNSTD SM7 .....239 K7
KUTN/CMB KT2 * 199 L1
Clifton Ri NWCR SE14 .....160 E9
Clifton Rd AMS HP6 .....68 G1
CAN/RD E16 .....141 H6
CEND/HSY/T N8 .....118 B4
COUL/CHIP CR5 .....240 E5
CRAWE RH10 .....284 D8
EMPK RM11 .....125 H4
FNCH N3 .....97 M9
FSTGT E7 .....142 A1
GFD/PVL UB6 .....134 B6
GNTH/NBYPK IG2 .....122 C4
GVW DA11 .....190 D2
HTHAIR TW6 * 152 C10
ISLW TW7 .....154 D8
KTN/HRWW/WS HA3 .....115 L3
KUTN/CMB KT2 .....199 L1
LOU IG10 .....82 B8
MV/WKIL W9 .....8 H4
NWDGN UB2 .....153 M3
SCUP DA14 .....185 H7
SL SL1 .....149 M1
SNWD SE25 .....203 M4
TEDD TW11 .....176 D7
WATW WD18 .....73 P3
WDGN N22 .....98 D9
WELL DA16 .....163 M9
WIM/MER SW19 .....178 C9
WLGTN SM6 .....222 C2
Clifton's La REIG RH2 .....256 G9
Clifton St SDTCH EC2A 13 J3
Clifton Ter DORK RH4 * 272
FSBYPK N4 .....119 H7
Clifton Vls MV/WKIL W9 .....8 H3
Cliftonville AMS HP6 69
Cliftonville Wy ALP/SUD HA0 .....135 K3
BORE WD6 .....75 M5
Clifton Wy PECK SE15 .....160 B6
WOKN/KNAP GU21 .....231 L3
The Climb RKW/CH/CXG WD3 .....71 L10
Climping Rd CRAWW RH11 .....283 H9
Cline Rd FBAR/BDGN N11 .....98 D7
GU GU1 .....268 C2
Clink St STHWK SE1 .....19 K8
Clinton Av E/WMO/HCT KT8 .....198 B4
WELL DA16 .....163 K10
Clinton Cl WEY KT13 .....196 C10
Clinton Crs BARK/HLT IG6 .....103 H7
Clinton End HHNE HP2 .....36 D6
Clinton Rd BOW E3 .....140 D10

Clinton Ter DEPT SE8 * 160 F5
SUT SM1 * 221 M1
Clipper Bvd RDART DA2 .....166 D10
Clipper Bvd West RDART DA2 .....166 C9
Clipper Cl BERM/RHTH SE16 .....160 C1
Clipper Crs GVE DA12 .....191 J7
Clipper Wy LEW SE13 .....161 H10
Clippesby Cl CHSGTN KT9 .....219 L3
Clipstone Ms FITZ W1T 10 E2
Clipstone Rd HSLW TW5 .....153 P9
Clipstone St GTPST W1W 10 E3
Clissold Cl EFNCH N2 .....118 A1
Clissold Ct FSBYPK N4 .....119 J3
Clissold Crs STNW/STAM N16 .....119 L3
Clissold Rd STNW/STAM N16 .....119 L3
Clitheroe Av RYLN/HDSTN HA2 .....113 P6
Clitheroe Gdns OXHEY WD19 .....93 J3
Clitheroe Rd BRXN/ST SW9 .....158 D10
CRW RM5 .....104 D6
Clitherow Av HNWL W7 .....154 F2
Clitherow Gdns CRAWE RH10 .....283 P6
Clitherow Rd BTFD TW8 .....154 D4
Clitterhouse Crs CRICK NW2 .....116 C6
Clitterhouse Rd CRICK NW2 .....116 C6
Clive Av DART DA1 191
UED N18 .....99 P7
Clive Cl POTB/CUF EN6 .....59 J4
Clive Ct SL SL1 .....149 J1
WLSDN NW10 * 136 C1
Cliveden Cl NFNCH/WDSPK N12 .....107 K5
NFNCH/WDSPK N12 .....97 M5
SHPTN TW17 .....196 A1
Cliveden Pl BGVA SW1W 16 C5
Cliveden Rd WIM/MER SW19 .....201 J1
WEA W13 .....134 G7
Cliveden Rd CHING E4 .....101 K6
Clive Rd BELV DA17 .....164 B5
DUL SE21 .....181 L6
EBED/NFELT TW14 .....175 H2
EN EN1 .....79 P8
ESH/CLAY KT10 .....218 A1
GPK RM2 .....125 J3
GVW DA11 .....190 E2
RBRW/HUT CM13 .....107 H8
TWK TW1 .....176 E7
WIM/MER SW19 .....179 K6
Clivesdale Dr HYS/HAR UB3 .....133 H10
Clive Wy CRAWE RH10 .....284 D7
EN EN1 .....79 P8
WATN WD24 .....73 K5
Cloak La CANST EC4R 12 F7
Clockhouse Av BARK IG11 .....142 F3
Clock House Cl BF/WBF KT14 .....216 A8
Clockhouse Cl WIM/MER SW19 .....178 F6
Clockhouse La ASHF TW15 .....174 B7
EBED/NFELT TW14 .....167 K2
CRW RM5 .....104 D8
Clockhouse La East EGH TW20 .....172 E10
Clockhouse La West EGH TW20 .....172 E10
Clock House Md LHD/OX KT22 .....218 A10
Clockhouse Ms RKW/CH/CXG WD3 * 71 H7
Clock House Pde PLMGR N13 * 99
Clockhouse Pl PUT/ROE SW15 .....179 H1
Clock House Rd BECK BR3 .....204 D3
Clock Pde ENC/FH EN2 * 79
IS N1 .....6 F6
Clock Tower Ms THMD SE28 .....143 J9
Clock Tower Pl HOLWY N7 * 5 M1
Clock Tower Rd ISLW TW7 .....154 E9
Clodhouse HI WOKS/MYFD GU22 231
Cloister Cl RAIN RM13 .....145 J6
TEDD TW11 .....176 D8
Cloister Gdns EDGW HA8 .....95 M6
SNWD SE25 .....204 A6
Cloister Garth BERK HP4 .....33 P5
STAL AL1 .....38 D10
Cloister Rd ACT W3 .....135 P8
CRICK NW2 .....117 J8
Cloisters Av HAYES BR2 .....206 C5
The Cloisters HHS/BOV HP3 * 36
RKW/CH/CXG WD3 .....91 H7
WCCW AL8 .....22 G5
WOKS/MYFD GU22 .....232 E7
Cloister Wk HHNE HP2 * 36
Clonard Wy PIN HA5 .....93 P7
Clonbrock Rd STNW/STAM N16 .....119 L9
Cloncurry St FUL/PGN SW6 .....156 G8
Clonmel Cl RYLN/HDSTN HA2 .....114 C6
Clonmel Rd FUL/PGN SW6 .....157 J7
TEDD TW11 .....176 C7
Clonmell Wy SL SL1 .....128 A5
Clonmore St WAND/EARL SW18 .....179 J4
Cloonmore Av ORP BR6 .....227 J2
Clorane Gdns HAMP NW3 .....117 K8
The Close ALP/SUD HA0 .....135 K1
BECK BR3 .....204 D4
BF/WBF KT14 .....215 K9
BH/WHM TN16 * 244 E2
BRKHM/BTCW RH3 .....273 N4
BRKMPK AL9 .....40 C5
BRKMPK AL9 .....59 H2
BRW CM14 .....107 J4
BUSH WD23 * 75 P10
BXLY DA5 .....186 B2
CAR SM5 .....221 N7
CDW/CHF RM16 .....167 N1
CHDH RM6 .....123 P4
CHEAM SM3 .....201 J7
CHING E4 .....101 N8
EBAR EN4 .....78 A10
GNTH/NBYPK IG2 .....123 H4
HART 211 N2
HGDN/ICK UB10 .....131 P2
HGDN/ICK UB10 .....132 B3
HHS/BOV HP3 * 35
HORL RH6 .....280 D6
ISLW TW7 .....154 C8
IVER SL0 .....130 F5
MTCM CR4 .....202 A4
NWMAL KT3 .....199 P2
PIN HA5 .....113 K5
PIN HA5 .....131 N5
POTB/CUF EN6 .....59 K8
PUR/KEN CR8 .....222 D6
RAD WD7 .....56 D9
RCH/KEW TW9 .....155 N9
RDART DA2 .....187 K6
REIG RH2 .....275 L1
RKW/CH/CXG WD3 .....71 H7
SCUP DA14 .....185 L8
SEV TN13 .....265 J8
SL SL1 .....128 C9
SNWD SE25 * 205 P6
STHGT/OAK N14 .....98 E2
STMC/STPC BR5 .....207 H6
SURB KT6 .....199 K7
TRDG/WHET N20 .....97 J3
VW GU25 .....194 A5
WARE SG12 .....26 D2
WBLY HA9 .....115 P9
WOKS/MYFD GU22 .....232 E7
WOT/HER KT12 .....217 H1

HGDN/ICK UB10 .....112 D9
WARL CR6 .....242 A5
Clovelly Cl HGDN/ICK UB10 .....112 D9
PIN HA5 .....113 K1
Clovelly Gdns EN EN1 .....90 M1
ROMW/RG RM7 .....104 C9
Clovelly Rd BXLYHN DA7 .....163 P5
CEND/HSY/T N8 .....118 B4
EA W5 .....155 H1
HSLW TW3 .....153 P8
Clovelly Wy ORP BR6 .....207 L6
RYLN/HDSTN HA2 .....113 N7
WCHPL E1 .....140 F8
Clover Cl WAN E11 * 121 J7
Clover Ct WOKS/MYFD GU22 .....232 A4
Coverdale Gdns BFN/LL DA15 .....185 G2
Clover Fld WCCE AL7 23
Cloverfield WCCE AL7 .....23 H1
Cloverfields HORL RH6 .....280 C3
The Clover Fld BUSH WD23 .....75 N10
Clover HI COUL/CHIP CR5 .....240 C7
Cloverland HAT AL10 .....40 C7
Cloverlands CRAWE RH10 .....284 A5
Clover Leas EPP CM16 .....65 J6
Clover Lea GODL GU7 .....267 K9
Cloverley Rd CHONG CM5 .....67 P6
Clover Ms CHEL SW3 .....16 B9
Clover Wy HHW HP1 .....35 L9
HORL RH6 .....281 K4
WLGTN SM6 .....202 C8
Cobs Wy ADL/WDHM KT15 .....211 J6
Clowders Rd CAT SE6 .....182 C4
Clowser Cl SUT SM1 .....221 M2
Cloyster Wd EDGW HA8 .....95 J8
Club Gardens Rd HAYES BR2 .....205 M7
Club Rw BETH E2 .....13 L1
Clump Av KWD/TDW/WH KT20 .....255 P7
The Clumps ASHF TW15 .....174 E7
The Clump RKW/CH/CXG WD3 .....71 K9
Clunas Gdns GPK RM2 .....125 L1
Clunbury Av NWDGN UB2 .....153 N4
Clunbury St IS N1 .....7 H5
Cluny Est STHWK SE1 .....19 J3
Cluny Ms ECT SW5 .....14 E6
Cluny Pl STHWK SE1 .....19 J3
Clutterbucks RKW/CH/CXG WD3 .....71 K2
Clutton St POP/IOD E14 .....140 G7
Clyde Av SAND/SEL CR2 .....242 A1
Clyde Circ SEVS/STOTM N15 .....119 M2
Clyde Cl REDH RH1 .....258 E9
Clyde Ct CAMTN NW1 .....5 H2
Clyde Crs UPMR RM14 .....126 D4
Clyde Flats FUL/PGN SW6 * 157 J6
Clyde Pl LEY E10 .....120 C5
Clyde Rd CROY/NA CR0 .....203 N10
HOD EN11 .....45 J5
SEVS/STOTM N15 .....119 M2
STWL/WRAY TW19 .....173 N4
SUT SM1 .....221 K2
WDGN N22 .....98 E9
WLGTN SM6 .....222 E3
Clydesdale PEND EN3 .....80 C8
Clydesdale Av STAN HA7 .....115 J1
Clydesdale Cl BORE WD6 .....76 B4
ISLW TW7 .....154 E9
Clydesdale Gdns RCHPK/HAM TW10 .....155 N10
Clydesdale Pth BORE WD6 * 76 A9
Clydesdale Rd EMPK RM11 .....124 C5
NTGHL W11 .....8 C1
Clyde St DEPT SE8 .....160 E5
Clyde Ter FSTH SE23 .....182 B5
HERT/BAY SG13 .....25 P5
Clyde V FSTH SE23 .....182 B5
Clyde Wy ROM RM1 .....104 F1
Clydon Cl ERITH DA8 .....164 F5
Clyfford Rd RSLP HA4 .....112 G9
Clyfton Cl BROX EN10 .....44 E9
Clymping Dene EBED/NFELT TW14 .....175 J3
Clyston Rd WATW WD18 .....72 G10
Clyston St VX/NE SW8 .....158 D8
Clyve Wy STA TW18 .....195 H1
Coach & Horses Yd CONDST W1S * 10 F7
Coach House La HBRY N5 * 119 J9
WIM/MER SW19 .....178 G7
Coach House Ms FSTH SE23 .....182 B2
NWCR SE14 * 160 C7
REDH RH1 * 276 A1
Coachmaster Ms HERT/WAT SG14 * 25 K4
Coach House Yd WAND/EARL SW18 * 157 L10
Coachlads Av GUW GU2 .....249 L6
Coach Ms STAL AL1 .....38 G6
Coach Rd BRKHM/BTCW RH3 .....273 M2
CHERT KT16 .....214 F3
DORK RH4 .....255 K10
HORL RH6 .....280 C8
Coalecroft Rd PUT/ROE SW15 .....178 F1
Coalport Cl HLWE CM17 * 47 P3
Coal Post Cl ORP BR6 * 227 J4
Coast HI DORK RH4 .....271 N4
Coast Hill La DORK RH4 .....271 P4
Coates Av WAND/EARL SW18 .....179 N1
Coates Cl THHTH CR7 .....203 K3
Coates Dell WATN WD24 .....55 M9
Coates Hill Rd BMLY BR1 .....206 D2
Coates Rd BORE WD6 .....95 J1
Coate St BETH E2 .....7 P1
Coates Wy GSTN WD25 .....55 L9
Coat Wicks BEAC HP9 .....49 L6
Cobalt Cl BECK BR3 .....204 C4
Cobb Cl BORE WD6 .....76 B4
DTCH/LGLY SL3 .....150 A7
Cobbett Cl CRAWE RH10 .....284 D5
PEND EN3 .....80 B2
Cobbett Hill Rd RGUW GU3 .....248 A6
Cobbett Rd ELTH/MOT SE9 .....162 G5
GUW GU2 .....249 L6
Cobbetts Av REDBR IG4 .....122 C8
Cobbett's Cl RGUW GU3 .....248 D5
Cobbetts Farm CHOB/PIR GU24 .....230 F1
Cobbetts HI WEY KT13 .....216 C4
Cobbett St VX/NE SW8 .....158 B6
Cobbetts Wk CHOB/PIR GU24 .....230 F2
Cobb Gn GSTN WD25 .....55 J8
Cobbinsbank WAB EN9 * 63 J9
Cobbins Br EPP CM16 .....64 G5
Cobbins Wy HLWE CM17 .....47 P4
Cobble La IS N1 .....6 B1
Cobble Ms HBRY N5 .....119 K6
Cobblers Cl SLN SL2 .....128 G4
Cobbler's Wk TEDD TW11 .....176 D10
Cobbles Crs CRAWE RH10 .....283 P6
The Cobbles BRWN CM15 .....107 K3
Cobblestone Pl CROY/NA CR0 * 203 B8
Cobbold Ms SHB W12 * 156 D1
Cobbold Rd SHB W12 .....156 C1
WAN E11 .....121 L8
WLSDN NW10 .....136 C1
Cobb Rd BERK HP4 .....33 L9
Cobb's Rd HSLWW TW4 .....153 N10
Cobb St WCHPL E1 .....13 L4
Cobden Cl UX/CGN UB8 .....131 M3
Cobden HI RAD WD7 .....74 D2
Cobden Ms SYD SE26 .....182 A8
Cobden Rd ORP BR6 .....226 G1
SEV TN13 .....265 H5
SNWD SE25 .....203 P4
WAN E11 .....121 J8
Cob Dr GVE DA12 .....191 P8

Cobham Av NWMAL KT3 .....200 D5
Cobham Cl BFN/LL DA15 .....185 J2
BTSEA SW11 .....179 P2
EDGW HA8 .....95 H10
EN EN1 .....79 P7
HAYES BR2 .....206 B7
SL SL1 .....128 E10
SWCM DA10 .....188 G2
WLGTN SM6 .....222 F3
Cobham Ms CAMTN NW1 .....5 J5
Cobham Park Rd COB KT11 .....235 K3
Cobham Pl BXLYHS DA6 .....185 N1
Cobham Rd COB KT11 .....235 P4
GDMY/SEVK IG3 .....123 J1
HEST TW5 .....153 K6
KUT/HW KT1 .....199 M2
WALTH E17 .....101 H9
WARE SG12 .....26 E1
Cobham St GVW DA11 .....190 D3
Cobham Ter GVW DA11 * 190 C4
SWCM DA10 .....188 G1
Cobill Cl GPK RM2 .....105 L9
Cobland Rd LEE/GVPK SE12 .....183 P7
Cobmead HAT AL10 .....40 C2
Cobnor Cl CRAWW RH11 .....283 J9
Coborn Rd BOW E3 .....140 E5
Coborn St BOW E3 .....140 E5
Cobourg Rd CMBW SE5 .....19 L9
Cobourg St CAMTN NW1 .....5 H5
Cobsdene GVE DA12 .....190 G9
Cobs Wy ADL/WDHM KT15 .....211 J6
Coburg Cl WEST SW1P 17 H5
Coburg Crs BRXS/STRHM SW2 .....180 A4
Coburg Dwellings WCHPL E1 * 140 B9
Coburg Gdns CLAY IG5 .....102 A10
Coburg Rd WDGN N22 .....98 C10
Cob Wk CRAWW RH11 .....283 K8
Cochrane Pl BFOR GU20 212
Cochrane Rd WIM/MER SW19 .....178 A4
Cochrane St STJWD NW8 .....3 M8
Cockayne Wy DEPT SE8 .....160 D8
Cockbush Av HERT/BAY SG13 .....25 P4
Cockcrow HI SURB KT6 * 199 J8
Cockerell Rd WALTH E17 .....120 C1
Cockerhurst Rd RSEV TN14 .....228 F5
Cocker Rd EN EN1 .....80 A2
Cockett Rd DTCH/LGLY SL3 .....150 B2
Cockfosters Rd EBAR EN4 .....78 B8
Cock Gn HLWW/ROY CM19 .....46 E3
Cock Gv BERK HP4 .....32 F6
Cock La BROX EN10 .....44 B5
CANST EC4R 12 C4
Cockle Wy RAD WD7 .....57 K9
Cockmannings La STMC/STPC BR5 .....207 N8
Cockmannings Rd STMC/STPC BR5 .....207 N7
Cockpit Yd BMSBY WC1N 11 M2
Cockrobin La HLW CM20 .....28 D4
Cocks Crs NWMAL KT3 .....200 C4
Cocksett Av ORP BR6 .....227 H5
Cockshot HI REIG RH2 .....275 L2
Cockshot Rd REIG RH2 .....275 M1
Cockspur Ct WHALL SW1A 11 K9
Cockspur St STJS SW1Y 11 J9
Cocksure La SCUP DA14 .....186 E7
Code St WCHPL E1 .....13 M2
Codham Hall La RBRW/HUT CM13 .....126 G3
Codicote Dr GSTN WD25 .....55 L10
Codicote Rd STALE/WH AL4 .....21 J3
Codicote Rw HHNE HP2 .....36 B1
Codling Cl WAP E1W 13 P9
Codmore Crs CSHM HP5 .....51 K6
Codmore Wood Rd CSHM HP5 .....51 K9
Codrington Ct WOKN/KNAP GU21 .....231 L4
Codrington Gdns GVE DA12 .....190 G8
Codrington HI FSTH SE23 .....182 B5
Codrington Ms NTGHL W11 .....8 B6
Cody Cl KTN/HRWW/WS HA3 .....115 J1
WLGTN SM6 .....222 F5
Cody Rd CAN/RD E16 .....141 H6
Coe Av SNWD SE25 .....203 P6
Coe's Aly BAR EN5 .....77 H4
Coe Sp SL SL1 .....148 G1
Coffey St DEPT SE8 .....160 F6
Coftards SLN SL2 .....129 P8
Cogan Av WALTH E17 .....100 D9
Cogdells La CSHM HP5 .....50 A5
Cogdells Ms CSHM HP5 .....50 A5
Cohen Cl CHES/WCR EN8 .....62 D8
Coity Rd KTTN NW5 .....4 D1
Cokers La DUL SE21 .....181 K4
Coke's Farm La CSTG HP8 .....69 J4
Coke's La CSTG HP8 .....69 J6
Coke St WCHPL E1 .....13 N5
Colbeck Ms SKENS SW7 .....14 F5
Colbeck Rd HRW HA1 .....114 D5
Colberg Pl STNW/STAM N16 * 119 L4
Colborne Wy WPK KT4 .....200 F10
Colbrook Av HYS/HAR UB3 .....152 E2
Colbrook Cl HYS/HAR UB3 .....152 E2
Colburn Crs GU GU1 .....250 D6
Colburn Wy SUT SM1 .....201 N10
Colby Rd NRWD SE19 .....181 M8
WOT/HER KT12 .....197 H8
Colchester Dr PIN HA5 .....113 L3
Colchester Rd EDGW HA8 .....95 M8
HARH RM3 .....105 M8
LEY E10 .....120 A4
NTHWD HA6 .....93 H10
WALTH E17 .....120 F4
Colchester St WCHPL E1 .....13 M5
Colcokes Rd BNSTD SM7 .....239 K7
Cold Arbor Rd SEV TN13 .....246 E10
Coldbath Sq CLKNW EC1R 12 A2
Coldbath St LEW SE13 .....161 L9
Cold Blow Crs BXLY DA5 .....186 E4
Cold Blow La NWCR SE14 .....160 C6
Coldershaw Rd WEA W13 .....154 F1
Coldfall Av MUSWH N10 .....98 A10
Coldham Gv PEND EN3 .....80 D3
Coldharbour La BRXN/ST SW9 .....159 H10
BUSH WD23 .....74 A10
CHOB/PIR GU24 .....212 E7
DORK RH4 .....272 F7
EGH TW20 .....194 A7
HARP AL5 .....20 D4
HYS/HAR UB3 .....133 H10
PUR/KEN CR8 .....223 J6
RAIN RM13 .....145 H10
REDH RH1 .....259 N10
WOKS/MYFD GU22 .....233 J1
Coldharbour Crest ELTH/MOT SE9 * 184 D6
Coldharbour Rd CROY/NA CR0 .....223 H1
CROY/NA CR0 .....204 E10
RDART DA2 .....188 A2
WWKM BR4 .....204 A9
Coldharbour Wy CROY/NA CR0 .....223 H1
Coldhope Cl HRW HA1 .....114 A4
Coldmoreham Yd AMSS HP7 * 68 C3
Coldshott OXTED RH8 .....261 M4
Coldstream Gdns WAND/EARL SW18 .....179 J3
Coldstream Rd CTHM CR3 .....241 M10

Colebrooke Pl CHERT KT16 * 214 F3
IS N1 .....6 D6
Colebrooke Rd REDH RH1 .....257 P5
Colebrooke Rw IS N1 .....6 C5
Colebrook Gdns LOU IG10 .....82 G5
Colebrook La LOU IG10 .....82 G5
Colebrook Rd STRHM/NOR SW16 .....202 A1
Colebrook Wy FBAR/BDGN N11 .....98 A8
Cole Cl THMD SE28 146
Coledale Dr STAN HA7 .....95 L8
Coleford Rd WAND/EARL SW18 .....179 M1
Cole Gdns HEST TW5 .....153 G6
Colegrave Rd SRTFD E15 .....121 J10
Cole Green La WGCE AL7 .....23 H5
Cole Green Wy HERT/WAT SG14 .....24 F2
Colegrove Rd PECK SE15 .....19 M10
Coleherne Ms WBPTN SW10 .....14 C8
Coleherne Rd WBPTN SW10 .....14 C8
Colehill Gdns FUL/PGN SW6 * 157 H7
Colehill La FUL/PGN SW6 .....157 H7
Colekitchen La SHGR GU5 .....270 F8
Coleman Cl SNWD SE25 .....203 P2
Coleman Fids IS N1 .....6 F3
Coleman Green La STALE/WH AL4 .....21 J8
Coleman Rd BELV DA17 .....164 B2
CMBW SE5 .....159 M6
Colemans Heath ELTH/MOT SE9 .....184 D6
Coleman's La WAB EN9 .....63 J3
Coleman St CITYW EC2V 12 G5
Colenorton Crs WDSR SL4 .....148 D3
Colenso Dr MLHL NW7 .....96 D6
Colenso Rd CLPT E5 .....120 B9
GNTH/NBYPK IG2 .....123 H6
Cole Park Gdns TWK TW1 .....176 F3
Cole Park Rd TWK TW1 .....176 F3
Colepits Wood Rd ELTH/MOT SE9 .....184 G1
Coleraine Rd BKHTH/KID SE3 .....161 L5
CEND/HSY/T N8 .....119 H1
Coleridge Av MNPK E12 .....142 B3
SUT SM1 .....221 P1
Coleridge Cl CHESW EN7 .....61 N3
VX/NE SW8 .....158 C8
Coleridge Crs DTCH/LGLY SL3 .....151 N7
Coleridge Gdns KIL/WHAMP NW6 .....3 J4
WBPTN SW10 .....157 M6
Coleridge Rd ASHF TW15 .....175 M7
CEND/HSY/T N8 .....118 E4
CROY/NA CR0 .....204 B7
DART DA1 .....165 P10
FSBYPK N4 .....119 H7
HARH RM3 .....105 J8
NFNCH/WDSPK N12 .....97 M6
TIL RM18 .....168 F8
WALTH E17 .....120 E2
Coleridge Wk GLDGN NW11 .....117 K2
RBRW/HUT CM13 .....75 M8
Coleridge Wy BORE WD6 .....75 M8
ORP BR6 .....207 K6
WDR/YW UB7 .....151 P3
YEAD UB4 .....133 H8
Cole Rd TWK TW1 .....176 F2
WAT WD17 .....73 J5
Colesburg Rd BECK BR3 .....204 E3
Coles Cl CHONG CM5 .....67 P2
Coles Crs RYLN/HDSTN HA2 .....114 B5
Colescroft HI PUR/KEN CR8 .....241 H1
Coles Gn BUSH WD23 .....94 B2
LOU IG10 .....82 G1
Coles Green Rd CRICK NW2 .....116 E7
Coleshill Flats BGVA SW1W * 16 C6
Coleshill La CFSP/GDCR SL9 .....50 C1
Coleshill Rd TEDD TW11 .....176 D9
Coles La BH/WHM TN16 .....245 H9
Colesmead Rd REDH RH1 .....258 A7
Colestown St BTSEA SW11 .....157 P8
Cole St STHWK SE1 .....19 F2
Coleswood Rd HARP AL5 .....20 D4
Colet Cl PLMGR N13 .....99 J5
Colet Gdns WKENS W14 .....156 B1
Colet Rd CRAWE RH10 .....283 N10
Coley Av WOKS/MYFD GU22 .....232 D4
Coley St FSBYW WC1X 11 P2
Colfe & Hatcliffe Glebe LEW SE13 * 182 G1
Colfe Rd FSTH SE23 .....182 D4
Colgate Cl CRAWW RH11 .....283 L5
Colham Av WDR/YW UB7 .....151 P3
Colham Green Rd UX/CGN UB8 .....132 B8
Colham Mill Rd WDR/YW UB7 .....151 N1
Colham Rd UX/CGN UB8 .....132 A6
Colina Ms SEVS/STOTM N15 .....119 J3
Colina Rd CEND/HSY/T N8 .....119 J3
Colin Chapman Wy WAN E11 .....116 E10
Colin Cl CDALE/KGS NW9 .....116 B2
CROY/NA CR0 .....204 E10
WWKM BR4 .....205 G1
Colin Crs CDALE/KGS NW9 .....116 A1
Colindale Av CDALE/KGS NW9 .....116 A1
STAL AL1 .....38 D6
Colindeep Gdns HDN NW4 .....116 A2
Colindeep La CDALE/KGS NW9 .....116 A2
Colin Dr CDALE/KGS NW9 .....116 C2
Colinette Rd PUT/ROE SW15 .....156 F10
Colin Gdns CDALE/KGS NW9 .....116 C1
Colin Park Rd CDALE/KGS NW9 .....116 B1
Colin Rd CTHM CR3 .....241 P9
WLSDN NW10 .....117 J6
Colinsdale IS N1 .....6 C4
Colinton Rd GDMY/SEVK IG3 .....123 P2
Collamore Av WAND/EARL SW18 .....179 P4
Collapit Cl HRW HA1 .....114 A4
Collard Av LOU IG10 .....83 K6
Collard Cl PUR/KEN CR8 .....241 L6
Collard Pl CAMTN NW1 .....4 D2
College Ap GNWCH SE10 .....161 H5
College Av EGH TW20 .....172 C9
EW KT17 .....220 C10
GRAYS RM17 .....168 A9
KTN/HRWW/WS HA3 .....94 F2
SL SL1 .....149 K2
College Cl ADL/WDHM KT15 .....194 D8
KTN/HRWW/WS HA3 .....94 D8
UED N18 .....99 N6
WARE SG12 .....26 C3
WHTN TW2 .....176 B6
College Ct CHES/WCR EN8 .....62 B6
EA W5 * 135 K5
REDH RH1 * 258 B7
WDSR SL4 .....148 G8
College Cross IS N1 .....6 B3
College Dr RSLP HA4 .....113 H5
THDIT KT7 .....198 D7
College East WCHPL E1 * 13 M4
ENC/FH EN2 .....79 P2
NWMAL KT3 .....200 C5
REDBR IG4 .....121 P5
TOOT SW17 .....179 P6
UED N18 .....99 N6
College Gn NRWD SE19 .....181 M10
College HI CANST EC4R 12 F7
College Hill Rd KTN/HRWW/WS HA3 .....94 D8
College La KTTN NW5 .....4 B1
WOKN/KNAP GU21 .....231 G7
College Ms IS N1 * 6 B2
WEST SW1P 17 K3
College Pde KIL/WHAMP NW6 * 2 B3
KIL/WHAMP NW6 * 137 H5

College Park Cl LEW SE13 161 H10
College Pl CAMTN NW1 5 H5
STALW/RED AL3 38 B6
SWCM DA10 167 H10
WALTH E17 121 K2
WBPTN SW10 * 157 M6
College Rd ABLGY WD5 55 H7
BMLY BR1 205 M1
CHES/WCR EN8 62 B6
CRAWE RH10 283 P7
CROY/NA CR0 203 L9
DUL SE21 181 M3
DUL SE21 181 N6
ENC/FH EN2 79 L6
EW KT17 220 D10
GRAYS RM17 167 P3
GU GU1 268 A1
GVW DA11 189 N1
HERT/BAY SG13 26 C9
HOD EN11 44 E1
HRW HA1 114 D4
ISLW TW7 154 E7
KTN/HRWW/WS HA3 94 D9
NRWD SE19 181 N8
SL SL1 128 E10
STAL AL1 38 G7
SWLY BR8 186 F10
TOTM N17 99 N7
WALTH E17 121 H3
WBLY HA9 115 J6
WCHMH N21 99 H3
WEA W13 134 G8
WIM/MER SW19 179 N9
WLSDN NW10 136 F4
WOKS/MYFD GU22 232 E2
College Sq HLW CM20 * 46 C1
College St CANST EC4R * 12 F7
STALW/RED AL3 38 C6
College Ter FNCH N3 97 J9
The College EW KT17 * 238 D1
College Vw ELTH/MOT SE9 184 A4
College Wy ASHF TW15 174 A7
HYS/HAR UB3 133 H9
NTHWD HA6 92 E7
WGCW AL8 22 G4
College Yd KIL/WHAMP NW6 * 2 B5
KTTN NW5 118 C9
Collendean La HORL RH6 279 J3
Collens Fld CHOB/PIR GU24 230 D10
Collens Rd HARP AL5 20 A6
Collent St HOM E9 140 B1
Coller Crs RDART DA2 188 D8
Colless Rd SEVS/STOTM N15 119 N3
Collet Cl CHES/WCR EN8 62 C4
Collet Rd BGR/WK TN15 247 M3
Collett Rd BERM/RHTH SE16 19 P4
HHW HP1 35 M6
WARE SG12 26 C1
Collett Wy NWDGN UB2 154 A1
Colley Hill La SLN SL2 109 L8
Colley Land RKW/CH/CXG WD3 70 G8
Colley La REIG RH2 257 H9
Colley Manor Dr REIG RH2 256 G9
Colley Wy REIG RH2 257 H7
Collier Cl EHAM E6 142 E9
HOR/WEW KT19 219 M3
Collier Dr EDGW HA8 95 M10
Collier Rw CRAWE RH10 283 N10
Collier Row La CRW RM5 104 C9
Collier Row Rd CRW RM5 104 B9
Colliers CTHM CR3 259 P1
Colliers Cl WOKN/KNAP GU21 231 N3
Colliers Shaw HAYES BR2 226 B2
Collier St IS N1 5 N8
Colliers Water La THHTH CR7 203 J4
Collier Wy RGUE GU4 250 G8
Collindale Av BFN/LL DA15 185 K4
CDALE/KGS NW9 116 B1
ERITH DA8 164 C5
Collingbourne Rd SHB W12 136 E10
Collingham Gdns ECT SW5 15 H6
Collingham Pl ECT SW5 14 G6
Collingham Rd ECT SW5 15 H5
Collingsbourne
ADL/WDHM KT15 * 215 L1
Collings Cl WDGN N22 98 G7
Collington Cl GVW DA11 190 B3
Collington St GNWCH SE10 * 161 J4
Collingtree Rd SYD SE26 182 B7
Collingwood Av BRYLDS KT5 199 P8
MUSWH N10 118 B1
Collingwood Cl HORL RH6 280 C3
Colling Wood Cl PGE/AN SE20 204 A1
Collingwood Cl WHTN TW2 175 P3
Collingwood Crs GU GU1 250 D9
Collingwood Dr LCOL/BKTW AL2 57 J1
Collingwood Rd CRAWE RH10 284 E8
MTCM CR4 201 P2
RAIN RM13 144 G4
SEVS/STOTM N15 119 M2
SUT SM1 221 K1
UX/CGN UB8 132 C6
Collingwood St WCHPL E1 140 A6
Collins Av STAN HA7 95 K10
Collins Dr RSLP HA4 113 K7
Collins Meadow
HLWW/ROY CM19 46 E1
Collinson St STHWK SE1 18 E2
Collinson Wk STHWK SE1 18 E2
Collins Rd CRAWW RH11 283 H9
HBRY N5 119 K9
Collins Sq BKHTH/KID SE3 161 L8
Collins St BKHTH/KID SE3 161 K8
Collinswood Rd SLN SL2 108 G7
Collinwood Av PEND EN3 80 B7
Collinwood Gdns
GNTH/NBYPK IG2 122 C3
Collum Green Rd SLN SL2 109 K8
Collyer Av CROY/NA CR0 222 F1
Collyer Pl PECK SE15 159 P7
Collyer Rd CROY/NA CR0 222 F1
LCOL/BKTW AL2 57 J3
Colman Cl EPSOM KT18 238 F3
Colman Pde EN EN1 * 79 M7
Colman Rd CAN/RD E16 141 P7
Colmans Hl SHGR GU5 270 E10
Colman Wy REDH RH1 257 P8
Colmar Cl WCHPL E1 140 C6
Colmer Pl KTN/HRWW/WS HA3 94 G8
Colmer Rd STRHM/NOR SW16 180 F10
Colmore Ms PECK SE15 160 A7
Colmore Rd PEND EN3 80 B8
Colnbrook By-Pass
DTCH/LGLY SL3 150 F5
WDR/YW UB7 151 L6
Colnbrook Cl LCOL/BKTW AL2 57 K3
Colnbrook St STHWK SE1 18 C4
Colndale Rd DTCH/LGLY SL3 151 H8
Colne TIL RM18 169 M2
Colne Av OXHEY WD19 73 J10
RKW/CH/CXG WD3 91 K3
WDR/YW UB7 151 M1
Colne Bank DTCH/LGLY SL3 150 F9
Colne Cl SOCK/AV RM15 147 H9
Colne Ct HOR/WEW KT19 219 P1
Colnedale Rd UX/CGN UB8 111 N10
Colne Dr HARH RM3 105 N7
WOT/HER KT12 197 L10
Colne Gdns LCOL/BKTW AL2 57 K3
Colne Ldg BUSH WD23 * 73 L8
Colne Md RKW/CH/CXG WD3 91 K3
Colne Orch IVER SL0 131 J8
Colne Rd CLPT E5 120 D9
WCHMH N21 99 L1
WHTN TW2 176 D4
Colne St PLSTW E13 141 M5
Colne Va UPMR RM14 126 D4
Colne Valley Trail
HGDN/ICK UB10 111 M8
RKW/CH/CXG WD3 91 M3
Colne Valley Wy IVER SL0 131 K8
STWL/WRAY TW19 173 H4
Colne Wy HHNE HP2 36 A1
STWL/WRAY TW19 172 F6
Colne Way Ct WATN WD24 * 73 L3
Colney Hatch La
FBAR/BDGN N11 98 A7
MUSWH N10 98 C10
Colney Heath La STALE/WH AL4 39 K7
Colney Rd DART DA1 187 N2
Cologne Rd BTSEA SW11 157 N10
Colombo Rd IL IG1 122 F6
Colombo St STHWK SE1 12 C10
Colomb St GNWCH SE10 161 K4
Colonel's La CHERT KT16 195 K6
Colonels Wk ENC/FH EN2 79 J6
Colonial Av WHTN TW2 176 B2
Colonial Dr CHSWK W4 155 P3
Colonial Rd EBED/NFELT TW14 174 F3
SL SL1 149 M1
Colonial Wy WATN WD24 73 K5
Colonnade BMSBY WC1N 11 L2
The Colonnades HAT AL10 * 40 F2
The Colonnade CHES/WCR EN8 62 C4
DEPT SE8 * 160 E3
STALW/RED AL3 * 38 C6
Colonsay HHS/BOV HP3 36 D8
Colonsay Rd CRAWW RH11 283 L10
Colosseum Ter CAMTN NW1 10 F1
Colson Pth LOU IG10 82 D8
Colson Rd CROY/NA CR0 203 L9
LOU IG10 82 E8
Colson Wy STRHM/NOR SW16 180 D7
Colsterworth Rd
SEVS/STOTM N15 119 N2
Colston Av CAR SM5 221 P1
Colston Crs CHESW EN7 61 J3
Colston Rd FSTGT E7 142 A1
MORT/ESHN SW14 155 P10
Coltash Rd CRAWE RH10 284 B8
Colt Hatch HLW CM20 28 E9
Colthurst Crs FSBYPK N4 119 K7
Colthurst Dr ED N9 100 A4
Colthurst Gdns HOD EN11 45 J1
Coltishall Rd HCH RM12 145 K1
Coltness Crs ABYW SE2 163 L4
Colton Gdns TOTM N17 119 K1
Colton Rd HRW HA1 114 D3
Coltsfoot WGCE AL7 23 L7
Coltsfoot Ct GRAYS RM17 168 A5
Coltsfoot Dr GU GU1 250 E7
WDR/YW UB7 131 P8
Coltsfoot La OXTED RH8 261 L10
Coltsfoot Pth HARH RM3 105 L8
The Coltsfoot HHW HP1 35 H7
Coltstead HART DA3 211 K10
Colts Yd WAN E11 * 121 L6
Columbas Dr HAMP NW3 117 N7
Columbia Av EDGW HA8 95 N9
RSLP HA4 113 J6
WPK KT4 200 C7
Columbia Rd BETH E2 7 L9
BROX EN10 62 D2
PLSTW E13 * 141 L6
Columbia Whf PEND EN3 * 80 D9
Columbia Wharf Rd GRAYS RM17 167 M5
Columbine Av EHAM E6 142 B7
SAND/SEL CR2 223 J4
Columbine Wy HARH RM3 105 M9
LEW SE13 * 161 H8
Columbus Gdns NTHWD HA6 93 H9
Colveiw Ct ELTH/MOT SE9 184 A4
Colvers HLWE CM17 31 K9
Colvestone Crs HACK E8 119 N10
Colville Est IS N1 7 H6
Colville Gdns LTWR GU18 212 B7
NTGHL W11 8 D6
Colville Houses NTGHL W11 8 C5
Colville Ms NTGHL W11 8 D6
Colville Pl FITZ W1T 11 H4
Colville Rd ACT W3 155 N2
ED N9 100 A2
NTGHL W11 8 D6
WALTH E17 100 D10
WAN E11 121 H8
Colville Sq NTGHL W11 8 C6
Colville Square Ms NTGHL W11 8 C6
Colville Ter NTGHL W11 8 D6
Colvin Cl SYD SE26 182 B8
Colvin Gdns BARK/HLT IG6 102 F8
CHES/WCR EN8 80 C1
CHING E4 101 H4
SWFD E18 121 N2
Colvin Rd EHAM E6 142 B2
THHTH CR7 203 H5
Colwall Gdns WFD IG8 101 M6
Colwell Rd EDUL SE22 181 N1
Colwick Cl HGT N6 118 E5
Colwith Rd HMSMTH W6 156 F5
Colwood Gdns WIM/MER SW19 180 B10
Colworth Gv WALW SE17 18 F6
Colworth Rd CROY/NA CR0 203 P8
WAN E11 121 K4
Colwyn Av GFD/PVL UB6 134 E4
Colwyn Cl CRAWW RH11 283 H9
STRHM/NOR SW16 180 D8
Colwyn Crs HSLW TW3 154 B7
Colwyn Gn CDALE/KGS NW9 * 116 B4
Colwyn Rd CRICK NW2 116 E8
Colyer Cl ELTH/MOT SE9 184 E5
Colyer Rd GVW DA11 190 A5
Colyers Cl ERITH DA8 164 E7
Colyers La ERITH DA8 164 D7
Colyton Cl ALP/SUD HA0 135 H1
WELL DA16 163 N7
WOKN/KNAP GU21 231 P4
Colyton La STRHM/NOR SW16 181 H8
Colyton Rd EDUL SE22 182 A1
Colyton Wy UED N18 99 P6
Combe Av BKHTH/KID SE3 161 L6
Combe Bank Dr RSEV TN14 245 P9
Combedale Rd GNWCH SE10 161 M4
Combe La SHGR GU5 270 A3
WOT/HER KT12 216 G5
Combemartin Rd
WAND/EARL SW18 179 H3
Comber Cl CRICK NW2 116 E7
Comber Gv CMBW SE5 159 K6
Combermere Cl WDSR SL4 148 G8
Combermere Rd BRXN/ST SW9 158 G10
MRDN SM4 201 L6
Combe Rd GODL GU7 267 K9
WATW WD18 72 G10
Comberton Rd CLPT E5 120 A7
Combeside WOOL/PLUM SE18 163 J6
Combes Rd DAGW RM9 144 A3
Combe St HHW HP1 * 35 M6
Combwell Crs ABYW SE2 163 K2
Comely Bank Rd WALTH E17 121 H3
Comeragh Cl WOKS/MYFD GU22 231 M5
Comeragh Ms WKENS W14 14 B7
Comeragh Rd WKENS W14 14 A8
Comerford Rd BROCKY SE4 160 D10
Comet Cl GSTN WD25 54 G10
MNPK E12 122 A9
PUR RM19 165 P3
Comet Pl DEPT SE8 160 F6
Comet Rd HAT AL10 40 C4
STWL/WRAY TW19 173 N3
Comet St DEPT SE8 160 F6
Comet Wy HAT AL10 40 B4
Comforts Farm Av OXTED RH8 261 L9
Comfrey Ct GRAYS RM17 168 A5
Commerce Rd BTFD TW8 155 H5
WDGN N22 98 G9
Commerce Wy CROY/NA CR0 202 G10
Commercial Pl GVE DA12 190 F2
Commercial Rd GU GU1 268 A1
POP/IOD E14 140 D8
STA TW18 173 K9
UED N18 99 M6
WCHPL E1 13 N5
Commercial St WCHPL E1 13 L2
Commercial Wy WLSDN NW10 135 N4
WOKN/KNAP GU21 232 C3
Commerell Pl GNWCH SE10 161 L4
Commerell St GNWCH SE10 161 K4
Commodore Pde
STRHM/NOR SW16 * 180 G10
Commodore St WCHPL E1 140 D6
Common Cl WOKN/KNAP GU21 214 A10
Commondale PUT/ROE SW15 156 F8
Commonfield Rd BNSTD SM7 221 K10
Commonfields CHOB/PIR GU24 212 E9
HLW CM20 29 H10
Common Gdns BERK HP4 34 E3
Common Gate Rd
RKW/CH/CXG WD3 70 G9
Common La ADL/WDHM KT15 215 M5
ESH/CLAY KT10 218 F4
GSTN WD25 74 D4
KGLGY WD4 54 A4
RDART DA2 188 H5
SL SL1 108 C8
WDSR SL4 149 H4
Common Rd BARN SW13 156 D9
DTCH/LGLY SL3 150 E4
ESH/CLAY KT10 218 F3
RBRW/HUT CM13 107 P6
REDH RH1 276 A2
RKW/CH/CXG WD3 70 G8
STAN HA7 94 C4
WAB EN9 46 B7
WDSR SL4 148 C3
Common Side EPSOM KT18 237 M1
Commonside GT/LBKH KT23 235 P9
HAYES BR2 225 P1
Commonside Cl BELMT SM2 221 L7
COUL/CHIP CR5 241 J6
Commonside East MTCM CR4 202 B3
MTCM CR4 202 E5
Commonside Rd HLWS CM18 47 J5
Commonside West MTCM CR4 202 B3
Commons La HHNE HP2 35 P6
The Commons WGCE AL7 23 K8
The Common BERK HP4 34 C3
EA W5 135 K10
HAT AL10 40 D3
KGLGY WD4 53 K8
NWDGN UB2 153 L3
RAD WD7 56 G7
RKW/CH/CXG WD3 * 71 H9
SRTFD E15 141 L1
STAN HA7 94 B3
WDR/YW UB7 151 M4
Commonwealth Av
HYS/HAR UB3 132 E8
SHB W12 136 E9
Commonwealth Rd CTHM CR3 241 P9
TOTM N17 99 P8
Commonwealth Wy ABYW SE2 163 L4
Common Whf WARE SG12 26 D2
Common Wd SLN SL2 109 H10
Community Cl HEST TW5 153 K7
HGDN/ICK UB10 * 112 C8
Community La HOLWY N7 118 E10
Community Rd GFD/PVL UB6 134 B3
SRTFD E15 121 J10
Community Wy
RKW/CH/CXG WD3 72 C9
Como Rd FSTH SE23 182 D5
Como St ROMW/RG RM7 124 E3
Compass Cl ASHF TW15 174 D10
EDGW HA8 95 L5
Compass Hl RCHPK/HAM TW10 177 J2
Compassion Cl CRAWW RH11 283 H8
Compayne Gdns
KIL/WHAMP NW6 2 G3
Comper Cl CRAWW RH11 283 H9
Comport Gn CROY/NA CR0 225 K8
Compton Av ALP/SUD HA0 114 G9
EHAM E6 142 A4
GPK RM2 125 J1
HGT N6 117 P5
IS N1 6 C2
RBRW/HUT CM13 107 P2
Compton Cl CAMTN NW1 4 F10
EDGW HA8 95 P8
ESH/CLAY KT10 218 C3
GLDGN NW11 116 G8
PECK SE15 159 P6
WEA W13 134 F8
Compton Crs CHSGTN KT9 219 K3
CHSWK W4 155 P5
NTHLT UB5 133 L3
TOTM N17 99 K8
Compton Gdns LCOL/BKTW AL2 56 A2
Compton Hts RGUW GU3 267 J4
Compton Pas FSBYE EC1V 12 D1
Compton Pl ERITH DA8 164 G5
OXHEY WD19 93 M5
STPAN WC1H 11 L1
Compton Ri PIN HA5 113 M3
Compton Rd CROY/NA CR0 204 A8
HYS/HAR UB3 132 F5
IS N1 6 D2
WCHMH N21 99 J2
WIM/MER SW19 179 J9
WLSDN NW10 136 G5
Compton St FSBYE EC1V 12 D1
Compton Ter IS N1 6 C2
WCHMH N21 * 99 H2
Comreddy Cl ENC/FH EN2 79 J5
Comus Pl WALW SE17 19 J6
Comyne Rd WATN WD24 72 G2
Comyn Rd BTSEA SW11 157 P10
Comyns Cl CAN/RD E16 141 L7
Comyns Rd DAGW RM9 144 B4
The Comyns BUSH WD23 94 B2
Conant Ms WCHPL E1 13 N7
Conaways Cl EW KT17 220 D6
Concanon Rd BRXS/STRHM SW2 158 G10
Concert Hall Ap STHWK SE1 11 P10
Concord Cl NTHLT UB5 133 L5
Concorde Cl HGDN/ICK UB10 131 P4
HSLW TW3 154 A8
Concorde Dr EHAM E6 142 C7
HHNE HP2 35 N6
Concorde Wy SL SL1 149 H1
Concord Rd ACT W3 135 N6
PEND EN3 80 B9
Concord Wy BERM/RHTH SE16 160 C3
Condell Rd VX/NE SW8 158 D7
Conder St POP/IOD E14 140 D8
Condor Ct GUW GU2 * 267 P2
Condor Rd STA TW18 195 M3
Condover Crs WOOL/PLUM SE18 162 E6
Condray Pl BTSEA SW11 157 P6
Conduit Ct COVGDN WC2E * 11 L7
Conduit La DTCH/LGLY SL3 150 B4
HOD EN11 44 F3
SAND/SEL CR2 223 P2
UED N18 100 B6
Conduit La East HOD EN11 44 G3
Conduit Ms BAY/PAD W2 9 L6
Conduit Pas BAY/PAD W2 9 L6
Conduit Pl BAY/PAD W2 9 L6
Conduit Rd WOOL/PLUM SE18 162 E4
Conduit St CONDST W1S 10 F7
The Conduit REDH RH1 259 L5
Conduit Wy WLSDN NW10 135 P2
Conegar Ct SL SL1 129 K10
Conewood St HBRY N5 119 J8
Coneyberry REIG RH2 275 M4
Coney Burrows CHING E4 101 K5
Coneybury REDH RH1 259 M10
Coneybury Cl WARL CR6 242 A5
Coney Cl CRAWW RH11 283 L5
HAT AL10 40 E6
Coneydale WGCW AL8 22 G3
Coney Gv HGDN/ICK UB10 132 A5
Coney Hall Pde WWKM BR4 * 205 K10
Coney Hill Rd WWKM BR4 205 K9
Coney Wy VX/NE SW8 17 N10
Conference Cl CHING E4 101 H3
Conference Rd ABYW SE2 163 M3
Conford Dr RGUE GU4 268 B7
Congleton Gv WOOL/PLUM SE18 162 G4
Congo Dr ED N9 100 B4
Congo Rd WOOL/PLUM SE18 162 G4
Congress Rd ABYW SE2 163 M3
Congreve Rd ELTH/MOT SE9 162 C9
WAB EN9 63 K9
Congreve St WALW SE17 19 J6
Conical Cnr ENC/FH EN2 79 K6
Coniers Wy RGUE GU4 250 E7
Conifer Av CRW RM5 104 C6
HART DA3 211 K6
Conifer Cl CHESW EN7 61 N5
ORP BR6 226 C1
REIG RH2 257 K8
Conifer Dr BRW CM14 107 J6
Conifer Gdns EN EN1 79 L10
STRHM/NOR SW16 180 G6
SUT SM1 201 L9
Conifer La EGH TW20 172 F8
Conifer Pk EW KT17 220 B7
Conifers WEY KT13 216 F1
Conifers Cl TEDD TW11 176 G10
The Conifers GSTN WD25 73 K1
HHS/BOV HP3 * 35 J9
Conifer Wk WDSR SL4 * 148 B6
Conifer Wy ALP/SUD HA0 115 H8
HYS/HAR UB3 133 H9
SWLY BR8 208 D1
Coniger Rd FUL/PGN SW6 157 K8
Coningesby Dr WAT WD17 72 F5
Coningham Ms SHB W12 136 D10
Coningham Rd SHB W12 156 E1
Coningsby Av CDALE/KGS NW9 96 B10
Coningsby Bank STAL AL1 38 C10
Coningsby Cl BRKMPK AL9 40 F10
Coningsby Cottages EA W5 155 J1
Coningsby Ct RAD WD7 * 74 F2
Coningsby Dr POTB/CUF EN6 59 N9
Coningsby Gdns CHING E4 100 G7
Coningsby Rd EA W5 155 H1
FSBYPK N4 119 J5
SAND/SEL CR2 223 K5
Conington Rd LEW SE13 160 G8
Conisbee Ct STHGT/OAK N14 78 D9
Conisborough Crs CAT SE6 183 H6
Coniscliffe Cl CHST BR7 206 D1
Coniscliffe Rd PLMGR N13 99 K4
Conista Ct WOKN/KNAP GU21 231 L2
Coniston Av BARK IG11 143 H2
GFD/PVL UB6 134 G5
PUR RM19 166 B5
UPMR RM14 126 B9
WELL DA16 163 H9
Coniston Cl BARN SW13 156 C6
BXLYHN DA7 164 D7
CHSWK W4 155 P7
CRAWW RH11 282 G9
DART DA1 187 J4
HHS/BOV HP3 36 D7
MRDN SM4 200 G6
Coniston Ct BAY/PAD W2 * 9 P6
LTWR GU18 212 A6
Coniston Cresent SL SL1 128 B7
Conistone Wy HOLWY N7 5 M3
Coniston Gdns BELMT SM2 * 221 N3
CDALE/KGS NW9 116 A3
ED N9 100 B2
PIN HA5 113 H2
REDBR IG4 122 B2
WBLY HA9 115 H6
Coniston Rd BMLY BR1 183 K9
BXLYHN DA7 164 D7
COUL/CHIP CR5 240 D2
CROY/NA CR0 203 P7
KGLGY WD4 54 A4
MUSWH N10 98 C10
TOTM N17 99 P7
WHTN TW2 176 A2
WOKS/MYFD GU22 232 E6
Coniston Wk HOM E9 140 B10
Coniston Wy CHSGTN KT9 199 K10
EGH TW20 172 E10
HCH RM12 125 H10
REIG RH2 257 P9
Conlan St NKENS W10 8 A2
NKENS W10 137 H6
Conley Rd WLSDN NW10 136 B1
Conley St GNWCH SE10 * 161 K4
Connaught Av ASHF TW15 173 P7
CDW/CHF RM16 167 N1
CHING E4 101 J1
EBAR EN4 98 A2
EN EN1 79 M6
HSLWW TW4 175 M1
LOU IG10 82 A8
MORT/ESHN SW14 155 P9
Connaught Br CAN/RD E16 142 A10
Connaught Cl BAY/PAD W2 9 N7
EN EN1 79 M6
HHNE HP2 36 B4
LEY E10 120 D7
SUT SM1 201 P9
UX/CGN UB8 * 132 D7
Connaught Crs CHOB/PIR GU24 230 F6
Connaught Dr GLDGN NW11 117 K2
WEY KT13 216 A7
Connaught Gdns BERK HP4 33 L2
CRAWE RH10 283 N5
MRDN SM4 201 M5
MUSWH N10 118 C3
PLMGR N13 99 J5
Connaught Hl LOU IG10 82 A8
Connaught La IL IG1 122 F7
Connaught Ms FUL/PGN SW6 * 157 H7
HAMP NW3 * 117 P10
WOOL/PLUM SE18 162 D4
Connaught Rd BAR EN5 76 G10
CAN/RD E16 142 A10
CHING E4 101 K1
CHOB/PIR GU24 230 F7
FSBYPK N4 119 H5
HARP AL5 20 A1
HCH RM12 125 L8
IL IG1 122 G7
KTN/HRWW/WS HA3 94 E9
NWMAL KT3 200 B4
RCHPK/HAM TW10 * 177 L1
SL SL1 149 N1
STALW/RED AL3 38 B4
SUT SM1 201 N9
TEDD TW11 176 C8
WALTH E17 * 120 F3
WAN E11 121 J6
WEA W13 134 G9
WLSDN NW10 136 B4
WOOL/PLUM SE18 162 D4
Connaught Sq BAY/PAD W2 9 P6
Connaught St BAY/PAD W2 9 P6
Connaught Wy PLMGR N13 99 J5
Connell Crs EA W5 135 L6
Connemara Cl BORE WD6 * 75 P10
Connington Crs CHING E4 101 L4
Connop Rd PEND EN3 80 C4
Connor Cl BARK/HLT IG6 102 C9
WAN E11 121 K6
Connor Rd DAGW RM9 124 B9
Connor St HOM E9 * 140 C3
Conolly Rd HNWL W7 134 D10
Conquerors Hl STALE/WH AL4 21 K9
Conquest Rd ADL/WDHM KT15 215 K3
Conrad Cl CDW/CHF RM16 167 N1
Conrad Dr WPK KT4 200 E8
Conrad Gdns CDW/CHF RM16 167 N1
Conroy Ct SCUP DA14 185 K7
Consfield Av NWMAL KT3 200 D4
Consort Cl BRW CM14 107 H6
FBAR/BDGN N11 98 A6
Consort Ms ISLW TW7 176 C2
Consort Rd PECK SE15 160 A8
Consort Wy DEN/HRF UB9 111 J4
HORL RH6 280 B4
Consort Wy East HORL RH6 280 C5
Cons St STHWK SE1 * 18 B1
Constable Av CAN/RD E16 141 N10
Constable Cl GLDGN NW11 117 L4
YEAD UB4 132 D4
Constable Crs SEVS/STOTM N15 119 P3
Constable Gdns EDGW HA8 95 M9
ISLW TW7 176 C1
Constable Ms BCTR RM8 123 L10
Constable Rd GVW DA11 190 B6
Constable Wk DUL SE21 181 N6
Constance Crs HAYES BR2 205 L8
Constance Rd CROY/NA CR0 203 J7
EN EN1 79 M10
SUT SM1 221 M1
WHTN TW2 176 A3
Constance St CAN/RD E16 142 B10
Constantine Rd HAMP NW3 117 P10
HAMP NW3 118 A9
Constitution Hl GVE DA12 190 F4
MYFR/PICC W1J 16 E1
WOKS/MYFD GU22 232 B4
Constitution Ri
WOOL/PLUM SE18 162 D7
Consul Av DAGW RM9 144 D6
Consul Gdns SWLY BR8 * 187 H10
Content St WALW SE17 18 F6
Contessa Cl ORP BR6 227 H2
Control Tower Rd HORL RH6 279 N9
HTHAIR TW6 152 C9
Convent Cl BECK BR3 183 H10
Convent Gdns EA W5 155 H3
NTGHL W11 8 C6
Convent Hl NRWD SE19 181 K9
Convent La COB KT11 216 G8
Convent Rd ASHF TW15 174 C8
WDSR SL4 148 F8
Convent Wy NWDGN UB2 153 K3
Conway Cl RAIN RM13 145 H2
STAN HA7 94 F7
Conway Crs CHDH RM6 123 M5
GFD/PVL UB6 134 D4
Conway Dr ASHF TW15 174 D9
BELMT SM2 221 L3
HYS/HAR UB3 152 D2
Conway Gdns ENC/FH EN2 79 M4
GRAYS RM17 167 N6
MTCM CR4 202 E4
WBLY HA9 115 H5
Conway Gv ACT W3 136 A7
Conway Ms FITZ W1T 10 G3
Conway Rd CRICK NW2 116 F7
FELT TW13 175 L8
HSLWW TW4 175 N3
MDHD SL6 128 A8
RYNPK SW20 200 F1
SEVS/STOTM N15 119 K3
STHGT/OAK N14 98 F4
WOOL/PLUM SE18 162 G3
Conway St FITZ W1T 10 G2
Conybeare HAMP NW3 3 P3
Conybury Cl WAB EN9 63 M8
Cony Cl CHESW EN7 61 M3
Conyers HLW CM20 28 F9
Conyers Cl WOT/HER KT12 217 L2
Conyers Rd STRHM/NOR SW16 180 E8
Conyer St BOW E3 * 140 D4
Conyers Wy LOU IG10 82 E7
Cooden Cl BMLY BR1 183 N10
Cooke Cl CDW/CHF RM16 167 K2
Cookes Cl WAN E11 121 L7
Cookes La CHEAM SM3 221 H3
Cookham Cl NWDGN UB2 154 A2
Cookham Dene Cl CHST BR7 206 G1
Cookham Rd SCUP DA14 208 B1
Cookhill Rd ABYW SE2 163 L1
Cook Rd CRAWE RH10 283 P9
Cook's Cl CRW RM5 104 D9
Cooks Ferry Rbt UED N18 100 D6
Cook's Hole Rd ENC/FH EN2 79 K4
Cooks Md BUSH WD23 74 A10
HORS RH12 282 A6
Cooks Meadow HORS RH12 282 A6
Cookson Gv ERITH DA8 164 C6
Cook's Rd SRTFD E15 140 G4
WALW SE17 18 C9
Cooks Spinney HLW CM20 29 K9
Cooks Vennel HHW HP1 35 K4
Cooks Wy HAT AL10 40 E6
Coolfin Rd CAN/RD E16 141 M8
Coolgardie Av CHIG IG7 102 D4
CHING E4 101 J6
Coolgardie Rd ASHF TW15 174 D8
Coolhurst Rd HGT N6 118 E4
Cool Oak Br CDALE/KGS NW9 116 C5
Cool Oak La CDALE/KGS NW9 116 C5
Coomassie Rd MV/WKIL W9 8 C1
Coombe Av CROY/NA CR0 223 M1
RSEV TN14 247 J6
Coombe Bank NWMAL KT3 200 B1
Coombe Cl CRAWW RH11 283 N5
EDGW HA8 95 L10
HSLW TW3 153 P10
Coombe Cnr WCHMH N21 99 J2
Coombe Crs HPTN TW12 175 M10
Coombe Dr ADL/WDHM KT15 215 J5
RSLP HA4 113 J6
Coombe End KUTN/CMB KT2 178 A10
Coombefield Cl NWMAL KT3 200 B5
Coombe Gdns BERK HP4 33 L4
RYNPK SW20 200 D2
Coombe Hill Ct WDSR SL4 148 C10
Coombe Hill Gld KUTN/CMB KT2 178 B10
Coombe Hill Rd KUTN/CMB KT2 178 B10
RKW/CH/CXG WD3 91 K4
Coombe House Cha NWMAL KT3 200 A1
Coombehurst Cl EBAR EN4 78 A6
Coombelands La
ADL/WDHM KT15 215 K3
Coombe La CROY/NA CR0 224 A2
RGUW GU3 249 J3
RYNPK SW20 200 C1
Coombe La West KUTN/CMB KT2 178 B10
KUTN/CMB KT2 199 P1
KUTN/CMB KT2 200 B1
Coombe Lea BMLY BR1 206 B3
Coombe Ldg CHARL SE7 161 P5
Coombe Mnr CHOB/PIR GU24 230 G1
Coombe Neville KUTN/CMB KT2 177 P10
Coombe Pk KUTN/CMB KT2 177 P8
KUTN/CMB KT2 178 A8
Coombe Ridings KUTN/CMB KT2 177 P8
Coombe Ri BRWN CM15 107 L2
KUTN/CMB KT2 199 N1
Coombe Rd BUSH WD23 94 C1
CHSWK W4 156 B4
GVE DA12 190 F5
HARH RM3 125 N1
HPTN TW12 175 N10
KUTN/CMB KT2 199 M1
NWMAL KT3 200 B3
RSEV TN14 247 K1
SAND/SEL CR2 223 N1
SYD SE26 182 A7
WDGN N22 99 H10
WEA W13 154 G2
WLSDN NW10 116 A7
Coomber Wy CROY/NA CR0 202 F7
Coombes Rd LCOL/BKTW AL2 57 H2
The Coombe BRKHM/BTCW RH3 256 A7
Coombe V CFSP/GDCR SL9 110 B6
Coombe Vls WAND/EARL SW18 * 179 K3
Coombe Wy BF/WBF KT14 216 A8
Coombewood Dr CHDH RM6 124 A4
Coombe Wood Hl PUR/KEN CR8 223 K8
Coombe Wood Rd
KUTN/CMB KT2 177 P8
Coombfield Dr RDART DA2 188 C7
Coombs St IS N1 6 D8
Coomer Pl FUL/PGN SW6 14 D10
Coomes Wk EDGW HA8 95 N9
Cooperage Cl TOTM N17 99 N7
Cooper Av WALTH E17 100 C9
Cooper Cl HORL RH6 281 H4
RDART DA2 188 D1
STHWK SE1 18 B2
Cooper Crs CAR SM5 202 A10
Cooperdale Cl WFD IG8 101 P8
Cooper Ms CHONG CM5 67 P5
Cooper Rd BFOR GU20 212 C3
CROY/NA CR0 223 H2
GU GU1 268 B2
HDN NW4 116 G4
WLSDN NW10 116 D10
Cooper Rw RWCRE RH10 283 N10
Coopersale Cl WFD IG8 101 P8
Coopersale Common EPP CM16 65 N4
Coopersale La EPP CM16 83 K3
Coopersale Rd HOM E9 120 C10
Coopersale St EPP CM16 65 M8
Coopers Cl CHIG IG7 103 L3
DAGE RM10 144 C1
EYN DA4 210 B1
STA TW18 173 J8
WCHPL E1 140 B6
Coopers Ct WARE SG12 * 26 D2
Coopers Crs BORE WD6 75 P5
Coopers Dr RDART DA2 186 F5
Coopers Ga STALE/WH AL4 39 N8
Coopers Green La HAT AL10 22 C9
STALE/WH AL4 39 L3
Cooper Shaw Rd TIL RM18 168 G6
Coopers Hl CHONG CM5 67 P5
Coopers Hill Dr CHOB/PIR GU24 230 C6
Cooper's Hill La EGH TW20 171 P7
Coopers Hill Rd REDH RH1 258 G9
REDH RH1 277 H1
REDH RH1 277 J4
Coopers La CAMTN NW1 5 K8
LEE/GVPK SE12 183 N5
LEY E10 120 G6
POTB/CUF EN6 59 P5
POTB/CUF EN6 59 P7
Coopers Lane Rd POTB/CUF EN6 60 B9
Coopers Ms BECK BR3 204 F2
Cooper's Rd GVW DA11 190 C4
POTB/CUF EN6 59 M6
STHWK SE1 19 M8
Coopers Rw IVER SL0 130 F6
TWRH EC3N 13 L7
Cooper St CAN/RD E16 141 L7
Coopers Yd IS N1 6 C4
NRWD SE19 181 M9
Cooper Wy BERK HP4 34 A5
SL SL1 148 G2
Coote Rd BCTR RM8 124 A8
BXLYHN DA7 164 A7
Copeland Rd PECK SE15 159 P8
WALTH E17 120 G3
Copeman Cl SYD SE26 182 B8
Copenhagen Gdns CHEL SW3 15 M7
CHSWK W4 156 A1
Copenhagen Pl POP/IOD E14 140 E8
Copenhagen St IS N1 5 M6
Copenhagen Wy WOT/HER KT12 197 J10
Cope Pl KENS W8 14 E4
Copers Cope Rd BECK BR3 182 E10
BECK BR3 204 F1
Cope St BERM/RHTH SE16 160 C3
Copford Wk IS N1 * 6 E5
Copgate Pth STRHM/NOR SW16 180 G9
Copland Av ALP/SUD HA0 115 J10
Copland Cl ALP/SUD HA0 115 H10
Copland Ms ALP/SUD HA0 135 K1
Copland Rd ALP/SUD HA0 135 K1
Copleigh Dr KWD/TDW/WH KT20 239 H6
Copleston Rd PECK SE15 159 N9
Copley Cl CMBW SE5 18 E10
HNWL W7 * 134 D6
REDH RH1 257 P8
WOKN/KNAP GU21 231 K5
Copley Dene BMLY BR1 206 A1
Copley Pk STRHM/NOR SW16 180 G9
Copley Rd STAN HA7 95 H6
Copley Wy KWD/TDW/WH KT20 238 G6
Copmans Wick
RKW/CH/CXG WD3 70 G9
Coppard Gdns CHSGTN KT9 219 H3
Coppelia Rd BKHTH/KID SE3 161 L10
Coppen Rd BCTR RM8 124 A5
Copperas St DEPT SE8 160 G5
Copper Beech Cl CLAY IG5 102 D9
GVE DA12 190 G3
HHS/BOV HP3 35 J9
STMC/STPC BR5 207 M5
WDSR SL4 148 C5
WOKS/MYFD GU22 231 N7
Copper Beeches HARP AL5 20 A2
Copper Beech Rd SOCK/AV RM15 147 H5
Copper Cl NRWD SE19 181 N10
TOTM N17 100 A8
Copperdale Rd HYS/HAR UB3 153 H1
Copperfield BARK/HLT IG6 102 G7
Copperfield Av UX/CGN UB8 132 B6
Copperfield Cl GVE DA12 191 K4
SAND/SEL CR2 223 K7
Copperfield Dr SEVS/STOTM N15 119 N2
Copperfield Gdns BRW CM14 106 G2
Copperfield Ri ADL/WDHM KT15 215 J4
Copperfield Rd BOW E3 140 D6
THMD SE28 143 M8
Copperfields BEAC HP9 88 D6
BGR/WK TN15 247 N3
LHD/OX KT22 236 B8
SUN TW16 * 174 G9
WGCE AL7 23 M6
Copperfield St STHWK SE1 18 D1
Copperfields Wk BGR/WK TN15 247 N3
Copperfields Wy HARH RM3 105 L9
Copperfield Wy CHST BR7 184 F9
PIN HA5 113 N2
Coppergate Ct BMLY BR1 205 N1
Copperkins Gv AMS HP6 68 C2
Copperkins La AMS HP6 68 B2
Coppermead Cl CRICK NW2 116 F8
Copper Mill Dr ISLW TW7 154 E8
Coppermill La RKW/CH/CXG WD3 91 J8
Copper Mill La TOOT SW17 179 M7
Coppermill La WALTH E17 120 B4
Coppermill Lock DEN/HRF UB9 * 91 K8
Coppermill Rd STWL/WRAY TW19 172 E2
Copper Rdg CFSP/GDCR SL9 90 C6
Copper Rw STHWK SE1 13 L10
Copperwood HERT/BAY SG13 25 N5
Coppetts Cl NFNCH/WDSPK N12 98 B8
Coppetts Rd MUSWH N10 98 A9
Coppice Cl BECK BR3 204 G4
GUW GU2 249 J9
HAT AL10 40 C8
RSLP HA4 * 112 D4
RYNPK SW20 200 F3
STAN HA7 94 E7
Coppice Dr PUT/ROE SW15 178 D2
STWL/WRAY TW19 172 A3
Coppice End WOKS/MYFD GU22 233 H2
Coppice Hatch HLWS CM18 46 G3
Coppice La REIG RH2 257 J8
Coppice Pth BARK/HLT IG6 103 L5
Coppice Rw EPP CM16 82 G2
The Coppice ASHF TW15 174 C9
BAR EN5 * 77 L10
BXLY DA5 186 E6
ENC/FH EN2 79 J8
HHNE HP2 36 C5
OXHEY WD19 73 K10
WDR/YW UB7 131 P8
Coppice Wk CRAWE RH10 284 B6
TRDG/WHET N20 97 K4
Coppice Wy SLN SL2 109 J7
SWFD E18 121 L2
Copping Cl CROY/NA CR0 223 M1
Copping Gv FBAR/BDGN N11 98 C5
The Coppings HOD EN11 26 F10
Coppins Cl BERK HP4 33 L5
Coppins La IVER SL0 131 J7
The Coppins CROY/NA CR0 224 G3
KTN/HRWW/WS HA3 94 D7
Coppock Cl BTSEA SW11 157 P8
Copsfield E/WMO/HCT KT8 197 P3
Copse Av WWKM BR4 204 G10
Copse Bank BGR/WK TN15 247 N6
Copse Cl CHARL SE7 161 N5
NTHWD HA6 92 D9
RGUE GU4 268 F6
SL SL1 128 E10
WDR/YW UB7 151 N2
Copse Crs CRAWW RH11 283 M6
Copse Edge RGUE GU4 * 250 F7
Copse Edge Av EW KT17 220 C10
Copse Gld SURB KT6 199 J7
Copse Hl BELMT SM2 221 L4
HLWW/ROY CM19 46 E4
PUR/KEN CR8 222 F9

RYNPK SW20 200 D1
Copse Hill Cl HHS/BOV HP3 52 G4
Copse La BEAC HP9 89 K8
HORL RH6 280 E3
Copsem Dr ESH/CLAY KT10 218 A3
Copsem La ESH/CLAY KT10 218 A3
ESH/CLAY KT10 218 B5
LHD/OX KT22 218 B7
Copsem Wy ESH/CLAY KT10 218 B3
Copsen Wd LHD/OX KT22 218 B7
Copse Rd COB KT11 217 J9
REDH RH1 275 M2
WOKN/KNAP GU21 231 L4
Copse Side GODL GU7 267 J9
HART DA3 211 K3
The Copse AMSS HP7 69 H4
CHING E4 101 L2
CTHM CR3 259 P2
EFNCH N2 * 118 A1
HERT/BAY SG13 25 P5
HHW HP1 35 H4
LHD/OX KT22 236 A9
REDH RH1 276 F2
WDSR SL4 * 170 A4
Copse Vw SAND/SEL CR2 224 D5
Copse Wy CSHM HP5 50 F3
Copse Wd IVER SL0 130 G3
Copsewood Cl BFN/LL DA15 185 H2
Copsewood Rd WATN WD24 73 J5
Copse Wood Wy NTHWD HA6 92 D9
Copshall Cl HLWS CM18 47 H5
Copsleigh Av REDH RH1 276 B7
Copsleigh Cl REDH RH1 276 B6
Copsleigh Wy REDH RH1 276 B6
Coptefield Dr BELV DA17 163 N2
Coptfold Rd BRW CM14 107 H3
Copthall Av LOTH EC2R 13 H5
Copthall Cl CFSP/GDCR SL9 90 C8
Copthall Cnr CFSP/GDCR SL9 90 B8
Copthall Dr MLHL NW7 96 D8
Copthall Gdns MLHL NW7 96 D8
TWK TW1 176 F4
Copthall La CFSP/GDCR SL9 90 B8
Copthall Rd East
HGDN/ICK UB10 112 B7
Copthall Rd West
HGDN/ICK UB10 112 B7
Copthall Wy ADL/WDHM KT15 215 J6
Copt Hill La KWD/TDW/WH KT20 239 J6
Copthorne Av BAL SW12 180 E3
BARK/HLT IG6 102 E7
BROX EN10 44 E6
HAYES BR2 206 C9
Copthorne Bank CRAWE RH10 285 J1
HORL RH6 281 K9
Copthorne Cl RKW/CH/CXG WD3 72 A9
SHPTN TW17 196 D6
Copthorne Common Rd
CRAWE RH10 285 J3
Copthorne Ct LHD/OX KT22 * 236 F7
Copthorne Dr LTWR GU18 212 A6
Copthorne Gdns EMPK RM11 125 P3
Copthorne Ms HYS/HAR UB3 152 F3
Copthorne Ri SAND/SEL CR2 223 L9
Copthorne Rd CRAWE RH10 284 F4
LHD/OX KT22 236 G6
RKW/CH/CXG WD3 72 A10
Copthorne Wy CRAWE RH10 284 G3
Coptic St NOXST/BSQ WC1A 11 L5
Copton Cl BOW E3 140 G7
Copwood Cl NFNCH/WDSPK N12 97 N5
Coral Cl CHDH RM6 123 M1
Coral Gdns HHNE HP2 36 A5
Coraline Cl STHL UB1 133 N5
Coralline Wk ABYW SE2 163 M1
Coral Rw BTSEA SW11 157 M9
Corals Md WGCE AL7 22 G6
Coral St STHWK SE1 18 B2
Coram Cl BERK HP4 33 P6
Coram St BMSBY WC1N 11 L2
Coran Cl ED N9 100 C1
Corban Rd HSLW TW3 153 P9
Corbar Cl EBAR EN4 77 N4
Corbet Cl WLGTN SM6 202 B9
Corbet Pl WCHPL E1 13 L3
Corbet Rd EW KT17 220 B6
Corbets Av UPMR RM14 126 A10
Corbets Tey Rd UPMR RM14 126 A10
Corbett Cl CROY/NA CR0 225 J8
Corbett Gv FBAR/BDGN N11 98 F8
Corbett Rd WALTH E17 101 J10
WAN E11 121 P4
Corbett's La BERM/RHTH SE16 160 B3
Corbicum WAN E11 121 K5
Corbiere Ct WIM/MER SW19 178 G9
Corbin's La RYLN/HDSTN HA2 114 A8
Corbridge Crs BETH E2 140 A4
Corbridge Ms ROM RM1 124 G3
Corby Cl EGH TW20 171 P9
LCOL/BKTW AL2 55 P1
Corby Crs ENC/FH EN2 78 F8
Corby Dr EGH TW20 171 P9
Corbylands Rd BFN/LL DA15 185 H4
Corbyn St FSBYPK N4 118 F6
Corby Rd WLSDN NW10 135 P4
WLSDN NW10 136 A4
Corcorans BRWN CM15 86 G10
Cordelia Cl HNHL SE24 159 J10
Cordelia Gdns STWL/WRAY TW19 173 P3
Cordelia Rd STWL/WRAY TW19 173 P3
Cordelia St POP/IOD E14 140 G8
Cordell Cl CHES/WCR EN8 62 D4
Corder Cl STALW/RED AL3 37 P9
Corderoy Pl CHERT KT16 195 H6
Cordingley Rd RSLP HA4 112 E7
Cording St POP/IOD E14 140 G7
Cordrey Gdns COUL/CHIP CR5 240 F1
Cordwell Rd LEW SE13 183 J1
Corelli Rd BKHTH/KID SE3 162 B7
Coresbrook Wy
WOKN/KNAP GU21 230 F4
Corfe Av RYLN/HDSTN HA2 113 P9
Corfe Cl ASHTD KT21 237 H4
BORE WD6 76 A7
HHS/BOV HP3 35 P8
HSLWW TW4 175 M4
YEAD UB4 133 K8
Corfe Gdns SL SL1 128 F9
Corfield Rd WCHMH N21 78 G9
Corfield St BETH E2 140 A6
Corfton Rd EA W5 135 K8
Coriander Av POP/IOD E14 141 J8
Coriander Crs GUW GU2 249 M5
Cories Cl BCTR RM8 123 N7
Corinium Cl WBLY HA9 115 L9
Corinium Ga STALW/RED AL3 37 P8
Corinne Rd ARCH N19 118 D9
Corinthian Manorway
ERITH DA8 164 E3
Corinthian Rd ERITH DA8 164 E3
Corkran Rd SURB KT6 199 J7
Cork St Mews CONDST W1S 10 G8
Corkscrew Hl WWKM BR4 205 H9
Cork St CONDST W1S 10 G8
Cork Tree Wy CHING E4 100 D6
Corlett St CAMTN NW1 9 N3
Cormongers La REDH RH1 258 E9
Cormont Rd CMBW SE5 159 J7
Cormorant Cl WALTH E17 100 C9
Cormorant Rd FSTGT E7 121 L10
Cornbury Rd EDGW HA8 95 J8
Corncroft HAT AL10 40 E2
Cornelia Dr YEAD UB4 133 K7
Cornelia St HOLWY N7 5 P2
Cornell Cl SCUP DA14 185 P9
Cornell Wy CRW RM5 104 C6
Corner Farm Cl
KWD/TDW/WH KT20 238 F8
Cornerfield HAT AL10 40 E1
Corner Fielde
BRXS/STRHM SW2 * 180 G4
Corner Gn BKHTH/KID SE3 161 M8
Corner Hall HHS/BOV HP3 35 N8
Corner Hall Av HHS/BOV HP3 35 N8
Corner Md CDALE/KGS NW9 96 C8
Corner Meadow HLWS CM18 47 K5
Corners WGCE AL7 23 K4
Cornerside ASHF TW15 174 D10
The Corner EA W5 * 135 K10
Corney Reach Wy CHSWK W4 156 C6
Corney Rd CHSWK W4 156 B5
Cornfield Cl UX/CGN UB8 131 N4
Cornfield Crs BERK HP4 33 J2
Cornfield Rd BUSH WD23 74 A8
REIG RH2 275 M1
Cornfields GODL GU7 267 L9
The Cornfields HHW HP1 35 L7
Cornflower La CROY/NA CR0 204 C8
Cornflower Ter EDUL SE22 182 A2
Cornflower Wy HARH RM3 105 M9
HAT AL10 40 B1
Cornford Cl HAYES BR2 205 M5
Cornford Gv BAL SW12 180 C5
Cornhill BANK EC3V 13 H6
Cornhill Cl ADL/WDHM KT15 195 L9
Cornhill Dr PEND EN3 80 D3
Cornish Ct ED N9 100 A1
Cornish Gv PGE/AN SE20 204 A1
Corn Md WGCW AL8 22 F2
Cornmill WAB EN9 62 G9
Corn Mill Dr ORP BR6 207 J7
Cornmill La LEW SE13 160 G9
Cornmow Dr WLSDN NW10 116 C10
Cornshaw Rd BCTR RM8 123 N6
Cornsland BRW CM14 107 J4
Cornsland Cl UPMR RM14 126 B1
Cornthwaite Rd CLPT E5 120 B8
Cornwall Av BETH E2 140 B5
BF/WBF KT14 216 A10
ESH/CLAY KT10 218 E4
FNCH N3 97 K8
SLN SL2 129 H6
STHL UB1 133 N7
WDGN N22 98 F9
WELL DA16 163 H9
Cornwall Cl BARK IG11 143 J1
CHES/WCR EN8 62 D9
EMPK RM11 125 P2
WDSR SL4 148 D4
Cornwall Crs NTGHL W11 8 A7
Cornwall Dr STMC/STPC BR5 185 M10
Cornwall Gdns SKENS SW7 15 J4
SNWD SE25 * 203 N4
WLSDN NW10 136 E1
Cornwall Gardens Wk
SKENS SW7 15 H4
Cornwall Gv CHSWK W4 156 B4
Cornwallis Av ED N9 100 B3
ELTH/MOT SE9 184 G5
Cornwallis Cl CTHM CR3 241 K8
ERITH DA8 164 G5
Cornwallis Gv ED N9 100 A3
Cornwallis Rd ARCH N19 118 F7
DAGW RM9 123 P9
ED N9 100 A3
WALTH E17 120 C2
WOOL/PLUM SE18 162 E2
Cornwallis Sq ARCH N19 118 F7
Cornwallis Wk ELTH/MOT SE9 162 C9
Cornwall Ms South SKENS SW7 15 J4
Cornwall Ms West SKENS SW7 * 15 H4
Cornwall Rd BELMT SM2 221 J4
BRWN CM15 86 G9
CROY/NA CR0 203 J9
DART DA1 165 N9
FSBYPK N4 119 H5
HARP AL5 20 A1
HRW HA1 114 B4
PIN HA5 93 N8
RSLP HA4 112 C7
SEVS/STOTM N15 119 L3
STAL AL1 38 D8
STHWK SE1 12 A10
TWK TW1 176 F3
UED N18 99 P6
UX/CGN UB8 131 N1
Cornwall St WCHPL E1 140 A9
Cornwall Ter CAMTN NW1 10 B2
Cornwall Terrace Ms
CAMTN NW1 10 B2
Cornwall Wy STA TW18 173 H9
Corn Wy WAN E11 121 J8
Cornwell Av GVE DA12 190 F6
Cornwell Rd WDSR SL4 171 M2
Cornwood Cl EFNCH N2 117 N3
Cornwood Dr WCHPL E1 140 B8
Cornworthy Rd BCTR RM8 123 M10
Corona Rd LEE/GVPK SE12 183 M3
Coronation Av DTCH/LGLY SL3 130 B8
TIL RM18 169 M3
WDSR SL4 149 M9
Coronation Cl BARK/HLT IG6 122 G2
BXLY DA5 185 N2
Coronation Dr HCH RM12 125 J10
Coronation Hl EPP CM16 65 J6
Coronation Rd HYS/HAR UB3 152 G3
PLSTW E13 141 P5
WARE SG12 26 C1
WLSDN NW10 135 N6
Coronation Vls WLSDN NW10 * 135 N6
Coronet Pde ALP/SUD HA0 * 135 K1
Coronet St IS N1 7 J10
The Coronet HORL RH6 280 D6
Corporation Av HSLWW TW4 153 M10
Corporation Rw CLKNW EC1R 12 B1
Corporation St HOLWY N7 5 L1
SRTFD E15 141 K4
Corrance Rd BRXS/STRHM SW2 158 F10
Corran Wy SOCK/AV RM15 146 G9
Corri Av STHGT/OAK N14 98 E5
Corrib Dr SUT SM1 221 P2
Corrie Gdns VW GU25 193 P7
Corrie Rd ADL/WDHM KT15 215 N1
WOKS/MYFD GU22 232 E6
Corrigan Av COUL/CHIP CR5 240 B1
Corrigan Cl HDN NW4 116 F1
Corringham Ct STAL AL1 38 E5
Corringham Rd GLDGN NW11 117 K5
WBLY HA9 115 M7
Corringway EA W5 135 L7
GLDGN NW11 117 L5
Corris Gn CDALE/KGS NW9 * 116 B4
Corry Dr BRXN/ST SW9 159 J10
Corsair Cl STWL/WRAY TW19 173 N3
Corsair Rd STWL/WRAY TW19 173 P3
Corscombe Cl KUTN/CMB KT2 177 P8
Corsehill St STRHM/NOR SW16 180 D9
Corsellis Sq TWK TW1 154 G10
Corsham St IS N1 7 H10
Corsica St HBRY N5 6 D1
Cortayne Rd FUL/PGN SW6 * 157 J8
Cortina Dr DAGW RM9 144 D5
Cortis Rd PUT/ROE SW15 178 E2
Cortis Ter PUT/ROE SW15 178 E1
Cortland Cl DART DA1 186 F2
Corunna Rd VX/NE SW8 158 D7
Corunna Ter VX/NE SW8 158 D7
Corve La SOCK/AV RM15 146 G10
Corwell Gdns UX/CGN UB8 132 D8
Corwell La UX/CGN UB8 132 D8
Cory Dr RBRW/HUT CM13 107 N1
Coryton Pth MV/WKIL W9 8 D1
Cory-Wright Wy STALE/WH AL4 21 K2
Cosbycote Av HNHL SE24 181 K1
Cosdach Av WLGTN SM6 222 E4
Cosedge Crs CROY/NA CR0 223 H2
Cosgrove Cl WCHMH N21 99 K3
YEAD UB4 133 L6
Cosgrove Rd WTHK RM20 166 D6
Cosmo Pl BMSBY WC1N 11 M3
Cosmur Cl SHB W12 156 C2
Cossall Wk PECK SE15 160 A7
Cossar Ms BRXS/STRHM SW2 181 H2
Cosser St STHWK SE1 18 A3
Costa St PECK SE15 159 P8
Costead Manor Rd BRW CM14 106 G2
Costells Meadow BH/WHM TN16 262 G2
Costons Av GFD/PVL UB6 134 C5
Costons La GFD/PVL UB6 134 C5
Cosway St CAMTN NW1 9 P3
Cotall St POP/IOD E14 140 F8
Coteford Cl LOU IG10 82 E6
PIN HA5 113 H3
Coteford St TOOT SW17 180 A7
Cotelands CROY/NA CR0 203 M10
Cotesbach Rd CLPT E5 120 B8
Cotesmore Gdns BCTR RM8 123 M9
Cotesmore Rd HHW HP1 35 H7
Cotford Rd THHTH CR7 203 K4
Cotham St WALW SE17 18 F6
Cotherstone HOR/WEW KT19 220 A5
Cotherstone Rd
BRXS/STRHM SW2 180 G4
Cotland Acres REDH RH1 275 N2
Cotlandswick LCOL/BKTW AL2 57 H1
Cotleigh Av BXLY DA5 185 N5
Cotleigh Rd KIL/WHAMP NW6 2 E3
ROMW/RG RM7 124 E4
Cotman Cl GLDGN NW11 117 M4
Cotmandene Crs
STMC/STPC BR5 207 L2
Cotmans Cl HYS/HAR UB3 133 H10
Coton Rd WELL DA16 163 K9
Cotsford Av NWMAL KT3 199 P5
Cotsmoor STAL AL1 * 38 E6
Cotswold HHNE HP2 35 P3
Cotswold Av BUSH WD23 74 B10
Cotswold Cl BXLYHN DA7 164 F8
CRAWW RH11 283 L7
ESH/CLAY KT10 198 E9
KUTN/CMB KT2 177 P9
SL SL1 148 G2
STA TW18 173 K8
STALE/WH AL4 39 H1
UX/CGN UB8 131 M3
Cotswold Gdns CRICK NW2 116 G7
EHAM E6 142 B4
GNTH/NBYPK IG2 122 G5
Cotswold Ga CRICK NW2 117 H6
Cotswold Gn ENC/FH EN2 78 G8
Cotswold Ms BTSEA SW11 157 N7
Cotswold Ri ORP BR6 207 J6
Cotswold Rd BELMT SM2 221 L6
GVW DA11 190 B6
HARH RM3 105 N10
HPTN TW12 175 P9
Cotswolds HAT AL10 40 D6
Cotswold St WNWD SE27 181 J7
Cotswold Wy ENC/FH EN2 78 G7
WPK KT4 200 F9
Cottage Av HAYES BR2 206 B8
Cottage Cl CHERT KT16 214 F3
RKW/CH/CXG WD3 72 A10
RSLP HA4 112 E6
RYLN/HDSTN HA2 114 C7
Cottage Farm Wy EGH TW20 * 194 F3
Cottage Field Cl SCUP DA14 185 M4
Cottage Gdns CHES/WCR EN8 62 C5
Cottage Gn CMBW SE5 159 L6
Cottage Gv BRXN/ST SW9 158 F9
SURB KT6 199 J6
Cottage Park Rd SLN SL2 109 J7
Cottage Pl CHEL SW3 15 N3
CRAWE RH10 285 M2
Cottage Rd HOLWY N7 5 N1
HOR/WEW KT19 220 A4
The Cottages EDGW HA8 * 95 N8
Cottage St POP/IOD E14 140 G9
Cottenham Dr CDALE/KGS NW9 116 C1
Cottenham Park Rd
RYNPK SW20 178 F10
RYNPK SW20 200 E1
Cottenham Pl RYNPK SW20 178 E10
Cottenham Rd WALTH E17 120 E2
Cotterells HHW HP1 35 M8
Cotterells Hl HHW HP1 35 M6
Cotterill Rd SURB KT6 199 L9
Cottesbrooke Cl DTCH/LGLY SL3 150 G7
Cottesbrook St NWCR SE14 160 D6
Cottesloe Cl CHOB/PIR GU24 230 E2
Cottesloe Ms STHWK SE1 18 B3
Cottesmore Av CLAY IG5 102 C10
Cottesmore Gdns KENS W8 15 H3
Cottimore Av WOT/HER KT12 197 J8
Cottimore Crs WOT/HER KT12 197 J7
Cottimore La WOT/HER KT12 197 K8
Cottimore Ter WOT/HER KT12 197 J7
Cottingham Cha RSLP HA4 113 H8
Cottingham Rd PGE/AN SE20 182 C10
VX/NE SW8 158 G6
Cottington Rd FELT TW13 175 L7
Cottington St LBTH SE11 18 B7
Cottis La EPP CM16 65 J6
Cotton Av ACT W3 136 A8
Cotton Cl DAGW RM9 143 M2
WAN E11 121 K7
Cotton Dr HERT/BAY SG13 26 A4
Cotton Fld HAT AL10 40 E2
Cotton Gardens Est LBTH SE11 18 C6
Cottongrass Cl CROY/NA CR0 204 C8
Cotton Hl BMLY BR1 183 J7
Cotton La RDART DA2 188 C1
Cottonmill Crs STAL AL1 38 C7
Cottonmill La STAL AL1 38 C8
Cotton Rd POTB/CUF EN6 59 M7
Cotton Rw BTSEA SW11 157 N9
Cottons Ap ROMW/RG RM7 124 E3
Cottons Centre STHWK SE1 13 J9
Cotton's Gdns BETH E2 7 K9
Cotton St POP/IOD E14 141 H9
Cotts Wood Dr RGUE GU4 250 D5
Couchmore Av CLAY IG5 102 C10
ESH/CLAY KT10 198 D9
Coulgate St BROCKY SE4 160 D9
Coulsdon Court Rd
COUL/CHIP CR5 240 G2
Coulsdon La COUL/CHIP CR5 240 B5
Coulsdon Pl CTHM CR3 241 L8
Coulsdon Ri COUL/CHIP CR5 240 F3
Coulsdon Rd COUL/CHIP CR5 240 G4
COUL/CHIP CR5 241 H6
CTHM CR3 241 K7
Coulser Cl HHW HP1 35 K3
Coulson Cl BCTR RM8 123 M6
Coulson St CHEL SW3 16 A7
Coulson Wy SL SL1 128 A8
Coulter Cl POTB/CUF EN6 60 E3
YEAD UB4 133 M6
Coulter Rd HMSMTH W6 156 E2
Coulton Av GVW DA11 190 B3
Council Av GVW DA11 189 P2
Councillor St CMBW SE5 159 K6
Counters Cl HHW HP1 35 K6
Counter St STHWK SE1 13 J9
Countess Cl DEN/HRF UB9 91 M10
Countess Rd KTTN NW5 118 D10
Countisbury Av EN EN1 99 N1
Countisbury Gdns
ADL/WDHM KT15 215 L2
Country Wy FELT TW13 175 K8
County Ga BAR EN5 77 L10
ELTH/MOT SE9 184 F6
County Gv CMBW SE5 159 K7
County Oak La CRAWE RH10 283 N2
County Oak Wy CRAWW RH11 283 N3
County Pde BTFD TW8 * 155 J6
County Rd EHAM E6 142 E7
THHTH CR7 203 J2
County St STHWK SE1 18 F4
Coupland Pl WOOL/PLUM SE18 162 F4
Courage Cl EMPK RM11 125 K4
Courcy Rd CEND/HSY/T N8 119 H1
Courier Rd DAGW RM9 144 D6
Courland Gv VX/NE SW8 158 E8
Courland Rd ADL/WDHM KT15 195 L10
Courland St VX/NE SW8 158 E7
Coursers Rd LCOL/BKTW AL2 57 M3
STALE/WH AL4 40 A9
The Course ELTH/MOT SE9 184 D6
Courtauld Rd ARCH N19 118 E6
Courtaulds KGLGY WD4 53 L6
Courtaulds Cl THMD SE28 143 K10
Court Av BELV DA17 164 A4
COUL/CHIP CR5 241 H4
HARH RM3 105 P8
Court Bushes Rd CTHM CR3 241 P5
CTHM CR3 242 A6
Court Cl KTN/HRWW/WS HA3 115 J1
STJWD NW8 * 3 L4
WHTN TW2 176 A6
WLGTN SM6 222 E4
Court Close Av WHTN TW2 176 A6
Court Crs CHSGTN KT9 219 J3
SL SL1 129 J8
SWLY BR8 208 F4
Court Downs Rd BECK BR3 204 G2
Court Dr CROY/NA CR0 222 G1
HGDN/ICK UB10 132 A3
STAN HA7 95 K5
SUT SM1 221 P1
Courtenay Av BELMT SM2 221 K5
HGT N6 117 P5
KTN/HRWW/WS HA3 94 B9
Courtenay Dr BECK BR3 205 J2
CDW/CHF RM16 167 L2
Courtenay Gdns UPMR RM14 126 B7
Courtenay Ms WALTH E17 120 D3
WOKN/KNAP GU21 232 D2
Courtenay Pl WALTH E17 120 D3
Courtenay Rd PGE/AN SE20 182 C10
WALTH E17 120 C3
WAN E11 * 121 L8
WBLY HA9 * 115 J8
WOKN/KNAP GU21 232 D2
WPK KT4 200 F10
Courtenay Sq LBTH SE11 18 A8
Courtenay St LBTH SE11 17 P7
Courten Ms STAN HA7 95 H8
Court Farm Av HOR/WEW KT19 220 B2
Court Farm Cl SL SL1 128 G10
Court Farm Gdns
HOR/WEW KT19 * 220 A7
Court Farm Pk WARL CR6 * 241 P2
Court Farm Rd ELTH/MOT SE9 184 A5
NTHLT UB5 133 P2
WARL CR6 241 P4
Courtfield Av HRW HA1 * 114 E3
Courtfield Cl BROX EN10 * 44 F6
Courtfield Crs HRW HA1 114 E3
Courtfield Gdns DEN/HRF UB9 111 K8
ECT SW5 15 H6
RSLP HA4 112 G7
WEA W13 134 F8
Courtfield Ms ECT SW5 15 J6
Courtfield Ri WWKM BR4 205 J10
Courtfield Rd ASHF TW15 174 C9
SKENS SW7 15 J6
Courtfields HARP AL5 20 C2
Court Gdns HOLWY N7 6 B2
Courtgate Cl MLHL NW7 96 C7
Court Green Hts
WOKS/MYFD GU22 231 P6
Court Haw BNSTD SM7 239 P1
Court Hl SAND/SEL CR2 223 M8
Courthill Rd LEW SE13 183 H1
Courthope Rd GFD/PVL UB6 134 C4
HAMP NW3 118 A9
WIM/MER SW19 179 H8
Courthope Vls WIM/MER SW19 179 H10
Courthouse La
STNW/STAM N16 119 N9
Court House Rd FNCH N3 97 L7
Courtland Av CHING E4 101 L3
IL IG1 122 C7
MLHL NW7 96 A4
STRHM/NOR SW16 180 G10
Courtland Dr CHIG IG7 102 F4
Courtland Gv THMD SE28 143 N9
Courtland Rd EHAM E6 142 B3
Courtlands CHST BR7 184 E10
RCHPK/HAM TW10 177 M1
Courtlands Av DTCH/LGLY SL3 150 A3
ESH/CLAY KT10 217 N3
HAYES BR2 205 K8
HPTN TW12 175 N9
LEE/GVPK SE12 183 N1
RCH/KEW TW9 155 N8
Courtlands Cl RSLP HA4 112 G5
SAND/SEL CR2 223 N6
WATN WD24 72 F1
Courtlands Crs BNSTD SM7 239 K2
Courtlands Dr HOR/WEW KT19 220 B3
WAT WD17 72 F2
Courtlands Rd BRYLDS KT5 199 M7
Court La DUL SE21 181 N3
HOR/WEW KT19 219 P9
IVER SL0 131 K10
SL SL1 128 C5
Court Lane Gdns DUL SE21 181 M3
Courtleas COB KT11 217 P9
Courtleet Dr BXLYHN DA7 164 C7
Courtleigh Av EBAR EN4 77 N4
Courtleigh Gdns GLDGN NW11 117 H2
Court Ldg GVE DA12 191 P9
RAD WD7 * 57 M10
Court Lodge Rd HORL RH6 279 P4
Courtman Rd TOTM N17 99 K8
Court Md NTHLT UB5 133 N5
Courtmead Cl HNHL SE24 181 K2
Courtnell St BAY/PAD W2 8 E5
Courtney Cl NRWD SE19 181 M9
Courtney Crs CAR SM5 222 A4
Courtney Pl COB KT11 217 N8
CROY/NA CR0 203 H10
Courtney Rd CDW/CHF RM16 168 F1
CROY/NA CR0 203 H10
HOLWY N7 119 H10
HTHAIR TW6 152 B9
WIM/MER SW19 179 P10
Courtney Wy HTHAIR TW6 152 B9
Courtoak La HORL RH6 281 K2
Courtrai Rd FSTH SE23 182 D2
Court Rd BNSTD SM7 239 K1
CTHM CR3 241 L9
ELTH/MOT SE9 184 C4
GDST RH9 260 B7
HGDN/ICK UB10 112 C10
NWDGN UB2 153 N3
RDART DA2 188 D8
SNWD SE25 203 N2
Court Rd (Orpington By-Pass)
ORP BR6 207 L10
Courtside HGT N6 118 E4
STALW/RED AL3 * 38 B4
SYD SE26 * 182 B6
The Courts STRHM/NOR SW16 180 F10
Courtstreet BMLY BR1 205 M2
Court St WCHPL E1 140 A7
The Court MUSWH N10 * 118 D2
RSLP HA4 113 M9
WARL CR6 242 D4
Court Vw HGT N6 * 118 C7
Court Wy ACT W3 135 P7
BARK/HLT IG6 122 F1
CDALE/KGS NW9 116 B2
HARH RM3 105 M10
WHTN TW2 176 E3
The Courtway OXHEY WD19 93 M3
Court Wood La CROY/NA CR0 224 E6
Court Yd ELTH/MOT SE9 184 C2
Courtyard Cl AMS HP6 69 H4
Courtyard Ms STMC/STPC BR5 185 K10
The Courtyards WATW WD18 * 92 E1
The Courtyard BF/WBF KT14 215 K8
BH/WHM TN16 * 262 G2
BRWN CM15 106 G1
CRAWE RH10 * 283 N8
HHS/BOV HP3 53 N2
IS N1 5 P3
STALE/WH AL4 39 L6
Cousin La CANST EC4R 12 G8
Cousins Cl WDR/YW UB7 131 P9
Couthurst Rd BKHTH/KID SE3 161 N5
Coutts Av CHSGTN KT9 219 K2
GVE DA12 191 P7
Coutts Crs KTTN NW5 * 118 B8
Coval Gdns MORT/ESHN SW14 155 N10
Coval La MORT/ESHN SW14 155 N10
Coval Rd MORT/ESHN SW14 155 P10
Coveham Crs COB KT11 217 H9
Covelees Wall EHAM E6 142 D8
Covenbrook RBRW/HUT CM13 107 N4
Covent Gdn COVGDN WC2E 11 M7
Covent Gdn Piazza
COVGDN WC2E 11 M7
Coventry Cl EHAM E6 142 C8
KIL/WHAMP NW6 2 F7
Coventry Cross Est BOW E3 141 H6
Coventry Rd IL IG1 122 E6
SNWD SE25 203 P4
WCHPL E1 140 A6
Coventry St SOHO/SHAV W1D 11 J8
Coverack Cl CROY/NA CR0 204 D8
STHGT/OAK N14 78 D10
Coverdale HHNE HP2 35 P3
Coverdale Gdns CROY/NA CR0 203 N10
Coverdale Rd CRICK NW2 2 A2
CRICK NW2 137 H2
FBAR/BDGN N11 98 B7
SHB W12 136 E10
The Coverdales BARK IG11 142 F4
Coverdale Wy SLN SL2 128 D6
Coverley Cl RBRW/HUT CM13 107 H7
WCHPL E1 * 13 P3
Covert Cl BERK HP4 33 J3
CRAWE RH10 283 P6
Coverton Rd TOOT SW17 179 P7
Covert Rd BARK/HLT IG6 103 J7
BERK HP4 33 J2
Coverts Rd ESH/CLAY KT10 218 E4
The Coverts RBRW/HUT CM13 107 M2
The Covert ASC SL5 192 A7
NRWD SE19 * 181 N10
NTHWD HA6 92 D9
ORP BR6 207 H6
Covert Wy EBAR EN4 77 M6
Covesfield GVW DA11 190 C3
Covet Wood Cl STMC/STPC BR5 207 J6
Covey Cl WIM/MER SW19 201 L2
The Covey CRAWE RH10 284 F5
Covington Gdns
STRHM/NOR SW16 181 J10
Covington Wy
STRHM/NOR SW16 181 H10
Cowbridge HERT/WAT SG14 25 K5
Cowbridge La BARK IG11 142 E2
Cowbridge Meadow
CHOB/PIR GU24 230 E9
Cowbridge Rd
KTN/HRWW/WS HA3 115 L2
Cowcross St FARR EC1M 12 C3
Cowdenbeath Pth IS N1 5 N5
Cowden Rd ORP BR6 207 J7
Cowden St CAT SE6 182 F7
Cowdray Cl CRAWE RH10 284 D8
Cowdray Rd HGDN/ICK UB10 132 D3
Cowdray Wy HCH RM12 125 H9
Cowdrey Cl EN EN1 79 M6
Cowdrey Ct DART DA1 187 J3
Cowdrey Rd WIM/MER SW19 179 L9
Cowen Av HRW HA1 114 C7
Cowfold Cl CRAWW RH11 283 J10
Cowgate Rd GFD/PVL UB6 134 C5
Cowick Rd TOOT SW17 180 A7
Cowings Md NTHLT UB5 133 M2
Cowland Av PEND EN3 80 B8
Cow La GSTN WD25 73 K2
Cow Leaze EHAM E6 142 D8
Cowleaze Rd KUTN/CMB KT2 199 K1
Cowles CHESW EN7 61 N3
Cowley Av CHERT KT16 195 J7
RDART DA2 188 E1
Cowley Cl SAND/SEL CR2 224 B6
Cowley Ct WAN E11 * 121 K8
Cowley Crs UX/CGN UB8 131 M7
WOT/HER KT12 217 K1
Cowley Hl BORE WD6 75 N4
Cowley La CHERT KT16 195 J7
WAN E11 * 121 K8
Cowley Mill Rd UX/CGN UB8 131 L4
Cowley Pl HDN NW4 116 F3
Cowley Rd ACT W3 136 C10
BRXN/ST SW9 159 H7
HARH RM3 105 J8
IL IG1 122 C5
MORT/ESHN SW14 156 B9
UX/CGN UB8 131 M5
WAN E11 121 N3
Cowley St WEST SW1P 17 L4
Cowling Cl NTGHL W11 8 A8
Cowlins HLWE CM17 29 N7
Coworth Cl ASC SL5 192 G5
Coworth Pk ASC SL5 * 193 H3
Coworth Rd ASC SL5 192 F5
Cowper Av EHAM E6 142 B2
SUT SM1 221 N1
TIL RM18 168 E7
Cowper Cl CHERT KT16 195 J6
HAYES BR2 206 A4
WELL DA16 185 K1
Cowper Ct WATN WD24 73 H3
Cowper Crs HERT/WAT SG14 25 J2
Cowper Gdns STHGT/OAK N14 78 D10
WLGTN SM6 222 D3
Cowper Rd ACT W3 136 A10
BELV DA17 164 A3
BERK HP4 33 N5
CSHM HP5 50 G5
HARP AL5 20 A2
HAYES BR2 206 A4
HHW HP1 35 L7
HNWL W7 134 E9
KUTN/CMB KT2 177 L8
RAIN RM13 145 H6
SLN SL2 128 F6
STHGT/OAK N14 98 C2
STNW/STAM N16 119 M9
UED N18 99 P6
WGCE AL7 23 J7
WIM/MER SW19 179 M9
Cowper St STLK EC1Y 13 H1
Cowper Ter NKENS W10 * 136 G7
Cowshot Crs CHOB/PIR GU24 230 C6
Cowslip Cl HGDN/ICK UB10 131 P2
Cowslip La RDKG RH5 254 F4
Cowslip Rd SWFD E18 101 N10
SWFD E18 121 N1
Cowthorpe Rd VX/NE SW8 158 E7
Cox Cl RAD WD7 57 K8
Coxdean EPSOM KT18 238 F5
Coxe Pl KTN/HRWW/WS HA3 114 F2
Coxes Av SHPTN TW17 * 196 F3
Coxfield Cl HHNE HP2 35 P7
Cox La CHSGTN KT9 219 L1
Coxley Ri PUR/KEN CR8 223 K9
Coxmount Rd CHARL SE7 162 A4
Coxon Dr CDW/CHF RM16 167 K2
Coxs Cottages WARL CR6 * 225 K10
Coxson Wy STHWK SE1 19 L2
Coxtie Green Rd BRW CM14 86 A8
BRW CM14 105 P1
Coxwell Rd NRWD SE19 181 M10
WOOL/PLUM SE18 162 G4
Cozens La East BROX EN10 44 E8
Cozens La West BROX EN10 44 D8
Cozens Rd WARE SG12 26 E1
Crabbe Crs CSHM HP5 51 J5
Crabbet Rd CRAWE RH10 284 C6
Crabbs Croft Cl ORP BR6 * 226 F2
Crab Hl BECK BR3 183 J10
Crab Hill La REDH RH1 276 G4
Crab La GSTN WD25 74 A1
Crabtree Av ALP/SUD HA0 135 K4
CHDH RM6 123 N2
Crabtree Cl BETH E2 7 L8
BUSH WD23 74 A9
GT/LBKH KT23 254 B2
HHS/BOV HP3 35 N8
Crabtree Dr LHD/OX KT22 255 H1
Crabtree La EPSOM KT18 255 P2
FUL/PGN SW6 156 G6
GT/LBKH KT23 254 B2
HARP AL5 20 A3
HHS/BOV HP3 35 N8
RDKG RH5 254 E6
Crabtree Manorway North
BELV DA17 164 D1
Crabtree Manorway South
BELV DA17 164 D2
Crabtree Office Village
EGH TW20 * 194 F2
Crabtree Rd CRAWW RH11 283 M6
EGH TW20 194 F2
Crabtree Wk BROX EN10 44 D5
Crackley Meadow HHNE HP2 36 C1
Cracknell Cl EN EN1 80 A3
Craddock Rd EN EN1 79 N7
Craddocks Av ASHTD KT21 237 L2
Craddock's Cl ASHTD KT21 237 M2
Craddock St KTTN NW5 4 C2
Cradhurst Cl DORK RH4 272 B3
Cradley Rd ELTH/MOT SE9 184 G4
Cragg Av RAD WD7 74 E2
Cragie Lea MUSWH N10 * 98 C10
Craigans CRAWW RH11 283 K7
Craigavon Rd HHNE HP2 36 A2
Craigdale Rd EMPK RM11 124 G4
Craig Dr UX/CGN UB8 132 C8
Craigen Av CROY/NA CR0 204 A8
Craigerne Rd BKHTH/KID SE3 161 N6
Craig Gdns SWFD E18 101 L10
Craigholm WOOL/PLUM SE18 162 D8
Craiglands STALE/WH AL4 39 J2
Craig Mt RAD WD7 74 G1
Craigmuir Pk ALP/SUD HA0 135 L3
Craignair Rd BRXS/STRHM SW2 180 G3
Craignish Av STRHM/NOR SW16 202 G2
Craig Park Rd UED N18 100 A5
Craig Rd RCHPK/HAM TW10 177 H7
Craig's Ct WHALL SW1A 11 L9
Craigs Wk CHES/WCR EN8 62 C4
Craigton Rd ELTH/MOT SE9 162 C10
Craigweil Av RAD WD7 74 G1
Craigweil Cl STAN HA7 95 J6
Craigweil Dr STAN HA7 95 J6
Craigwell Av FELT TW13 175 H6
Craigwell Cl STA TW18 195 H1
Crail Rw WALW SE17 19 H6
Crakell Rd REIG RH2 275 M1
Crakers Md WATW WD18 * 73 J7
Cramer St MHST W1U 10 D4
Crammavill St CDW/CHF RM16 147 M10
Crammond Cl HMSMTH W6 * 14 A9
Cramond Ct EBED/NFELT TW14 174 F4
Crampshaw La ASHTD KT21 237 L6
Crampton Rd PGE/AN SE20 182 B9
Crampton's Rd RSEV TN14 247 J6
Crampton St WALW SE17 18 E7
Cranberry Cl NTHLT UB5 133 L4
Cranberry La CAN/RD E16 141 K6
Cranborne Av NWDGN UB2 153 P3
SURB KT6 199 M10
Cranborne Cl HERT/BAY SG13 25 K8
POTB/CUF EN6 59 H7
Cranborne Crs POTB/CUF EN6 59 H7
Cranborne Gdns UPMR RM14 126 A7
WGCE AL7 23 J6
Cranborne Pde POTB/CUF EN6 * 58 G7
Cranborne Rd BARK IG11 142 G3
CHES/WCR EN8 62 C8
HAT AL10 40 F3
HOD EN11 44 G2
POTB/CUF EN6 59 H7
Cranborne Wk CRAWE RH10 284 A9
Cranborne Waye YEAD UB4 133 K9
Cranbourne Av POTB/CUF EN6 59 H6
WAN E11 121 N2
WDSR SL4 148 E8
Cranbourne Cl ESH/CLAY KT10 218 A3
HORL RH6 * 280 C2
SL SL1 129 H10
STRHM/NOR SW16 202 F3
WOT/HER KT12 217 K3
Cranbourne Dr HARP AL5 20 B5
HOD EN11 26 G9
PIN HA5 113 L3
Cranbourne Gdns BARK/HLT IG6 122 G1
GLDGN NW11 117 J3
Cranbourne Rd MNPK E12 122 B10
MUSWH N10 98 C10
NTHWD HA6 112 G1
SL SL1 129 H10
SRTFD E15 121 H9
Cranbourn St LSQ/SEVD WC2H 11 K7
Cranbrook Cl HAYES BR2 205 M6
Cranbrook Dr ESH/CLAY KT10 198 B8
GPK RM2 125 K2
STALE/WH AL4 39 K6
WHTN TW2 176 A4
Cranbrook La FBAR/BDGN N11 98 C5
Cranbrook Ms WALTH E17 120 E3
Cranbrook Pk WDGN N22 99 H9
Cranbrook Ri IL IG1 122 C4
Cranbrook Rd BARK/HLT IG6 122 E2
BXLYHN DA7 164 A7
CHSWK W4 156 B4
DEPT SE8 160 F8
EBAR EN4 77 N10
GNTH/NBYPK IG2 122 D4
HSLWW TW4 153 N10
IL IG1 122 D5
THHTH CR7 203 L2
WIM/MER SW19 179 H10
Cranbrook St BETH E2 140 C4
Cranbury Rd FUL/PGN SW6 157 L8
Crandon Wk EYN DA4 * 210 D2
Crane Av ACT W3 135 P9
ISLW TW7 176 F1
Cranebank Ms TWK TW1 * 176 G1
Cranebrook WHTN TW2 176 B5
Crane Cl DAGE RM10 144 B1
Crane Ct FLST/FETLN EC4A 12 B6
MORT/ESHN SW14 * 155 P10
Cranefield Dr GSTN WD25 55 M9
Craneford Cl WHTN TW2 176 E3
Craneford Wy WHTN TW2 176 D3
Crane Gdns HYS/HAR UB3 152 G3
Crane Gv HOLWY N7 6 B1
Cranell Gn SOCK/AV RM15 146 G10
Crane Lodge Rd HEST TW5 153 J5
Crane Md BERM/RHTH SE16 160 C3
WARE SG12 26 D3
Crane Park Rd WHTN TW2 176 A5
Crane Rd STWL/WRAY TW19 174 B2
WHTN TW2 176 D4
Cranesbill Cl CDALE/KGS NW9 116 A1
Cranes Dr BRYLDS KT5 199 K4
Cranes Pk BRYLDS KT5 199 K4
Cranes Park Av BRYLDS KT5 199 L4
Cranes Park Crs BRYLDS KT5 199 L4
Crane St PECK SE15 159 N7
Craneswater HYS/HAR UB3 152 G6
Craneswater Pk NWDGN UB2 153 N4
Cranes Wy BORE WD6 75 P9
Crane Wy WHTN TW2 176 B3
Cranfield Crs POTB/CUF EN6 60 F5
Cranfield Dr CDALE/KGS NW9 96 B9
Cranfield Rd BROCKY SE4 160 E9
Cranfield Rd East CAR SM5 222 B5
Cranfield Rd West CAR SM5 * 222 A5
Cranford Av PLMGR N13 98 F6
STWL/WRAY TW19 173 P3
Cranford Cl PUR/KEN CR8 223 K9
RYNPK SW20 * 200 E1
STWL/WRAY TW19 173 P3
Cranford Cottages WAP E1W * 140 C9
Cranford Dr HYS/HAR UB3 152 G3
Cranford La HEST TW5 153 L6
HTHAIR TW6 152 G8
HYS/HAR UB3 152 E5
Cranford Park Rd HYS/HAR UB3 152 G3
Cranford Ri ESH/CLAY KT10 218 B2
Cranford Rd DART DA1 187 M4
Cranford St WAP E1W 140 C9
Cranford Wy CEND/HSY/T N8 118 G3
Cranham Gdns UPMR RM14 126 E5
Cranham Rd EMPK RM11 125 J4
Cranhurst Rd CRICK NW2 116 F10
Cranleigh Cl BXLY DA5 * 186 C2
CHESW EN7 61 P4

ORP BR6 207 K10
PGE/AN SE20 204 A2
SAND/SEL CR2 223 P8
Cranleigh Dr SWLY BR8 208 F4
Cranleigh Gdns BARK IG11 142 G2
KTN/HRWW/WS HA3 115 K3
KUTN/CMB KT2 177 L9
LOU IG10 82 C10
SAND/SEL CR2 223 P8
SNWD SE25 203 M3
STHL UB1 133 N8
SUT SM1 201 L9
WCHMH N21 79 H9
Cranleigh Ms BTSEA SW11 157 P8
Cranleigh Rd ESH/CLAY KT10 198 B8
FELT TW13 174 G7
SEVS/STOTM N15 119 K3
SHGR GU5 268 F10
WIM/MER SW19 201 K3
Cranleigh St CAMTN NW1 5 H8
Cranley Cl GU GU1 250 D10
Cranley Dene GU GU1 250 D10
Cranley Dr GNTH/NBYPK IG2 122 F5
RSLP HA4 112 G7
Cranley Gdns CHEL SW3 15 L7
MUSWH N10 118 C2
PLMGR N13 98 G4
WLGTN SM6 222 D4
Cranley Ms SKENS SW7 15 K7
Cranley Pl SKENS SW7 15 L6
WOKN/KNAP GU21 * 231 J4
Cranley Rd GNTH/NBYPK IG2 122 F4
GU GU1 250 C10
PLSTW E13 141 N7
WOT/HER KT12 216 G3
Cranley Ter HDN NW4 * 96 G10
Cranmer Av WEA W13 154 G2
Cranmer Cl MRDN SM4 200 G6
POTB/CUF EN6 59 M6
RSLP HA4 113 L6
STAN HA7 95 H8
WARL CR6 242 D3
WEY KT13 216 B4
Cranmer Ct HPTN TW12 176 A8
KUTN/CMB KT2 177 J7
Cranmer Farm Cl MTCM CR4 202 A4
Cranmer Gdns DAGE RM10 124 D9
WARL CR6 242 D3
Cranmer Rd BRXN/ST SW9 159 H6
CROY/NA CR0 203 K10
EDGW HA8 95 N4
FSTGT E7 121 N9
HPTN TW12 176 A8
HYS/HAR UB3 132 E8
KUTN/CMB KT2 177 K8
MTCM CR4 202 A4
SEV TN13 246 F9
Cranmer Ter TOOT SW17 179 N8
Cranmore Av ISLW TW7 154 B6
Cranmore La EHSLY KT24 252 C5
Cranmore Rd BMLY BR1 183 K6
CHST BR7 184 C8
Cranmore Wy MUSWH N10 118 D2
Cranston Cl HGDN/ICK UB10 112 E7
HSLW TW3 153 M8
REIG RH2 275 L1
Cranston Est IS N1 7 H7
Cranston Gdns CHING E4 100 G7
Cranston Park Av UPMR RM14 126 C9
Cranston Rd FSTH SE23 182 D4
Cranstoun Cl RGUW GU3 249 L6
Cranswick Rd BERM/RHTH SE16 160 A4
Crantock Rd CAT SE6 183 H5
Cranwell Cl BOW E3 140 G6
Cranwell Gv SHPTN TW17 196 A4
Cranwich Av WCHMH N21 99 L1
Cranwich Rd STNW/STAM N16 119 M5
Cranwood St FSBYE EC1V 7 H10
Cranworth Crs CHING E4 101 J2
Cranworth Gdns BRXN/ST SW9 159 H7
Craster Rd BRXS/STRHM SW2 180 G3
Crathie Rd LEE/GVPK SE12 183 N2
Cravan Av FELT TW13 175 H5
Cravells Rd HARP AL5 20 B5
Craven Av EA W5 135 H9
STHL UB1 133 N8
Craven Cl STNW/STAM N16 * 119 P5
YEAD UB4 133 H8
Craven Gdns BARK IG11 143 H4
BARK/HLT IG6 102 G10
CRW RM5 104 B6
HARH RM3 106 B7
WIM/MER SW19 179 L8
Craven Hl BAY/PAD W2 9 K7
Craven Hill Gdns BAY/PAD W2 9 J7
Craven Hill Ms BAY/PAD W2 9 K7
Craven Ms BTSEA SW11 158 B9
Craven Pk WLSDN NW10 136 A3
Craven Park Ms WLSDN NW10 136 B3
Craven Park Rd
SEVS/STOTM N15 119 N4
WLSDN NW10 136 B3
Craven Pas CHCR WC2N 11 L9
Craven Rd BAY/PAD W2 9 K7
CRAWE RH10 284 C8
CROY/NA CR0 204 A8
KUTN/CMB KT2 199 L1
ORP BR6 207 N10
WEA W13 135 H9
WLSDN NW10 136 A3
The Cravens HORL RH6 281 H4
Craven St CHCR WC2N 11 L9
Craven Ter BAY/PAD W2 9 K7
Craven Wk CLPT E5 119 P5
Crawford Av ALP/SUD HA0 115 J10
CDW/CHF RM16 147 N10
Crawford Cl ISLW TW7 154 D8
Crawford Gdns NTHLT UB5 133 N5
PLMGR N13 99 J4
Crawford Pas CLKNW EC1R 12 A2
Crawford Pl MBLAR W1H 9 P5
Crawford Rd CMBW SE5 159 K8
HAT AL10 40 D2
Crawfords SWLY BR8 186 F10
Crawford St MBLAR W1H 10 A4
WLSDN NW10 136 A2
Crawley Av CRAWE RH10 283 P5
CRAWW RH11 283 L10
Crawley Dr HHNE HP2 36 A2
Crawley Goods Yd
CRAWE RH10 * 284 C3
Crawley La CRAWE RH10 284 D6
Crawley Market CRAWE RH10 * 283 N7
Crawley Rd ED N9 99 N1
LEY E10 120 G6
WDGN N22 99 K10
Crawley's La TRING HP23 32 D2
Crawshaw Rd CHERT KT16 214 G3
Crawshay Cl SEV TN13 247 H9
Crawters Cl CRAWE RH10 284 A6
Crawthew Gv EDUL SE22 159 N10
Cray Av ASHTD KT21 237 K2
ORP BR6 207 L7
STMC/STPC BR5 207 L5
Craybrooke Rd SCUP DA14 185 L7
Crayburne MEO DA13 189 L8
Craybury End ELTH/MOT SE9 184 F5
Cray Cl DART DA1 187 H1
Craydene Rd ERITH DA8 164 G7
Crayford High St DART DA1 186 F1
Crayford Rd DART DA1 186 G1
HOLWY N7 118 F9
Crayford Wy DART DA1 165 H10
Crayke Hl CHSGTN KT9 219 K4
Craylands STMC/STPC BR5 207 M3
Craylands La SWCM DA10 189 J1
Craylands Sq SWCM DA10 189 J1
Crayleigh Ter SCUP DA14 * 185 M9
Crayle St SLN SL2 128 F5
Crayonne Cl SUN TW16 196 F1
Cray Rd BELV DA17 164 B5
SCUP DA14 185 M9
SWLY BR8 208 D6
Crays Pde STMC/STPC BR5 * 207 M2
Cray Valley Rd STMC/STPC BR5 207 K5
Crealock Gv WFD IG8 101 L6
Crealock St WAND/EARL SW18 179 L2
Creasey Cl EMPK RM11 125 J7
Creasy Cl ABLGY WD5 54 G7
Crebor St EDUL SE22 181 P2
Credenhall Dr HAYES BR2 206 C8
Credenhill St STRHM/NOR SW16 180 D9
Crediton Hl KIL/WHAMP NW6 117 L10
Crediton Rd WLSDN NW10 136 F3
Crediton Wy ESH/CLAY KT10 218 F2
Credon Rd BERM/RHTH SE16 160 A4
PLSTW E13 141 P4
Credo Wy WTHK RM20 166 G5
Creechurch La HDTCH EC3A 13 K6
Creechurch Pl HDTCH EC3A * 13 K6
Creed La BLKFR EC4V 12 D6
Creek Cottages
E/WMO/HCT KT8 * 198 D4
Creek Rd BARK IG11 143 J5
DEPT SE8 160 F5
E/WMO/HCT KT8 198 D4
Creekside DEPT SE8 160 G6
RAIN RM13 144 G6
The Creek GVW DA11 189 N1
SUN TW16 197 H5
Creek Wy RAIN RM13 144 F7
Creeland Gv CAT SE6 182 E4
Cree's Meadow BFOR GU20 * 212 C4
Cree Wy ROM RM1 104 F8
Crefeld Cl HMSMTH W6 14 A10
Creffield Rd EA W5 135 M9
Creighton Av EFNCH N2 98 A10
EHAM E6 142 A4
STAL AL1 38 C10
Creighton Cl SHB W12 136 E9
Creighton Rd EA W5 155 J2
KIL/WHAMP NW6 136 G4
TOTM N17 99 M8
Creigton Av EFNCH N2 117 P1
Cremer St BETH E2 7 L8
Cremorne Est WBPTN SW10 15 L10
Cremorne Gdns HOR/WEW KT19 220 A5
Cremorne Rd GVW DA11 190 C3
WBPTN SW10 157 M6
Crescent TWRH EC3N 13 L7
Crescent Ar GNWCH SE10 161 H5
Crescent Av GRAYS RM17 168 A5
HCH RM12 124 G7
Crescent Cottages SEV TN13 246 F6
Crescent Ct GRAYS RM17 * 168 A5
HORL RH6 * 280 B6
Crescent Dr BRWN CM15 107 K2
STMC/STPC BR5 206 F6
Crescent East EBAR EN4 77 M4
Crescent Gdns RSLP HA4 113 J5
SWLY BR8 208 D2
WIM/MER SW19 179 K6
Crescent Gv CLAP SW4 158 D10
MTCM CR4 201 P4
Crescent La CLAP SW4 180 E1
Crescent Pde HGDN/ICK UB10 * 132 B5
Crescent Pl CHEL SW3 15 N5
Crescent Ri EBAR EN4 77 P9
FNCH N3 * 97 J9
WDGN N22 98 E9
Crescent Rd BECK BR3 204 G2
BFN/LL DA15 185 J6
BMLY BR1 183 M10
BRW CM14 106 G5
CEND/HSY/T N8 118 E4
CHING E4 101 K1
CTHM CR3 241 P10
DAGE RM10 124 C9
EBAR EN4 77 P10
ED N9 99 P2
ENC/FH EN2 79 J8
ERITH DA8 164 C5
FBAR/BDGN N11 98 A5
FNCH N3 97 J9
HHNE HP2 35 N6
KUTN/CMB KT2 177 M10
LEY E10 120 G7
PLSTW E13 141 M3
REDH RH1 259 K9
REIG RH2 275 K2
RYNPK SW20 200 G1
SEVS/STOTM N15 * 119 J1
SHPTN TW17 196 D5
SOCK/AV RM15 166 B1
SWFD E18 101 P10
WDGN N22 98 E9
WOOL/PLUM SE18 162 E4
Crescent Rw STLK EC1Y 12 E2
Crescent St IS N1 5 P3
The Crescent ABLGY WD5 54 G6
ACT W3 136 B8
ALP/SUD HA0 114 G7
ASHF TW15 174 A8
BAR EN5 77 L7
BARN SW13 156 C8
BECK BR3 204 F1
BELMT SM2 221 K7
BXLY DA5 185 M3
CHERT KT16 195 K3
CHOB/PIR GU24 230 F7
CRICK NW2 116 E8
CROY/NA CR0 203 L6
CTHM CR3 242 F9
E/WMO/HCT KT8 197 N4
EGH TW20 172 C9
EPP CM16 65 J8
EPSOM KT18 219 M10
EPSOM KT18 237 M1
FBAR/BDGN N11 98 A5
GNTH/NBYPK IG2 122 D4
GSTN WD25 74 A4
GUW GU2 249 M9
GVW DA11 190 C5
HART DA3 211 K3
HLWE CM17 29 M5
HORL RH6 280 B6
HYS/HAR UB3 152 D6
LCOL/BKTW AL2 55 P6
LHD/OX KT22 236 G8
LOU IG10 82 A10
NWMAL KT3 199 P2
REDH RH1 * 275 N3
REIG RH2 257 L10
RKW/CH/CXG WD3 72 C10
RYLN/HDSTN HA2 114 B6
SCUP DA14 185 J7
SEV TN13 247 L8
SHPTN TW17 196 G7
SL SL1 149 K1
STHL UB1 153 M1
SURB KT6 199 K5
SUT SM1 221 N2
SWCM DA10 189 H2
UPMR RM14 126 D5
WALTH E17 120 D3
WATW WD18 73 K8
WEY KT13 196 B10
WIM/MER SW19 179 K6
WWKM BR4 203 K6
Crescent Vw LOU IG10 82 A10
Crescent Wk SOCK/AV RM15 166 B1
Crescent Wy BROCKY SE4 160 F9
HORL RH6 280 B6
ORP BR6 227 H2
SOCK/AV RM15 146 C10
STRHM/NOR SW16 180 G10
Crescentway
NFNCH/WDSPK N12 97 P7
Crescent West EBAR EN4 77 M4
Crescent Wood Rd SYD SE26 181 P6
Cresford Rd FUL/PGN SW6 157 L7
Crespigny Rd HDN NW4 116 E4
Cressage Cl STHL UB1 133 P6
Cressall Cl LHD/OX KT22 236 G6
Cressall Md LHD/OX KT22 236 G6
Cress End RKW/CH/CXG WD3 91 K2
Cresset Cl WARE SG12 27 H8
Cresset Rd HOM E9 140 B1
Cresset St CLAP SW4 158 E9
Cressfield Cl KTTN NW5 118 B10
Cressida Rd ARCH N19 118 D6
Cressingham Gv SUT SM1 221 M1
Cressingham Rd EDGW HA8 96 A8
LEW SE13 161 H9
The Cressinghams EPSOM KT18 * 220 A9
Cressington Cl STNW/STAM N16 119 M10
Cress Rd SL SL1 148 G1
Cresswell Gdns ECT SW5 * 15 J7
Cresswell Pk BKHTH/KID SE3 161 L9
Cresswell Pl WBPTN SW10 15 J7
Cresswell Rd CSHM HP5 51 J10
FELT TW13 175 M7
SNWD SE25 203 P4
TWK TW1 177 J2
Cresswell Wy WCHMH N21 99 H1
Cressy Ct HMSMTH W6 156 E2
WCHPL E1 140 B7
Cressy Houses WCHPL E1 * 140 B7
Cressy Pl WCHPL E1 140 B7
Cressy Rd HAMP NW3 118 A9
Cressys Cnr HSLW TW3 * 154 A9
Cresta Dr ADL/WDHM KT15 215 J6
Crest Av GRAYS RM17 167 N6
Crestbrook Av PLMGR N13 99 J4
Crestbrook Pl PLMGR N13 * 99 H4
Crest Cl RSEV TN14 228 C7
Crest Dr PEND EN3 80 B4
Crestfield St CAMTN NW1 5 M9
Crest Gdns RSLP HA4 113 K8
Crest Hl SHGR GU5 270 F8
Cresthill Av GRAYS RM17 167 P4
Creston Av WOKN/KNAP GU21 231 K3
Creston Wy WPK KT4 200 G8
Crest Pk HHNE HP2 36 B6
Crest Rd CRICK NW2 116 D7
HAYES BR2 205 L7
SAND/SEL CR2 224 A4
The Crest BRYLDS KT5 199 M5
CHESW EN7 61 J3
HDN NW4 116 F3
HOLWY N7 * 118 E10
PLMGR N13 99 H5
POTB/CUF EN6 * 59 M7
SBW CM21 29 N1
Crest Vw PIN HA5 113 L2
RDART DA2 166 F10
Crest View Dr STMC/STPC BR5 206 E5
Crestway PUT/ROE SW15 178 D2
Crestwood Wy HSLWW TW4 175 N1
Creswell WOKN/KNAP GU21 * 231 J3
Creswell Cnr
WOKN/KNAP GU21 * 231 J3
Creswell Dr BECK BR3 204 G5
Creswick Ct WGCE AL7 * 22 G6
Creswick Rd ACT W3 135 N9
Creswick Wk GLDGN NW11 117 J2
Crete Hall Rd GVW DA11 190 B2
Creukhorne Rd WLSDN NW10 * 136 B2
Crew Curve BERK HP4 33 L2
Crewdson Rd BRXN/ST SW9 158 G6
Crewe Pl WLSDN NW10 136 C5
Crewe's Av WARL CR6 242 B2
Crewe's Cl WARL CR6 242 B2
Crewe's Farm La WARL CR6 242 D3
Crewe's La WARL CR6 242 D2
Crews Hl ENC/FH EN2 60 G10
Crews St POP/IOD E14 160 F3
Crewys Rd CRICK NW2 117 J7
PECK SE15 160 A8
Crib St WARE SG12 26 G1
Crichton Av WLGTN SM6 222 E2
Crichton Rd CAR SM5 222 A4
Crichton St VX/NE SW8 * 158 D8
Cricketers Arms Rd
ENC/FH EN2 * 79 K6
Cricketers Cl CHSGTN KT9 219 J2
ERITH DA8 164 F4
STALW/RED AL3 38 D5
STHGT/OAK N14 98 D1
Cricketers La BFOR GU20 212 C2
Cricketers Ms BAL SW12 180 C5
WAND/EARL SW18 179 L1
Cricketers Wk SYD SE26 182 B8
Cricketfield Rd CLPT E5 120 A9
Cricket Field Rd UX/CGN UB8 131 N3
Cricketfield Rd WDR/YW UB7 151 M3
Cricket Gn MTCM CR4 202 A3
Cricket Ground Rd CHST BR7 206 E1
Cricket Hl REDH RH1 276 E2
Cricket La BECK BR3 182 D9
Cricket Rw EFNCH N2 * 117 N1
Crickets Hl SHGR GU5 270 B6
Cricket Vw WEY KT13 216 C2
Cricket Wy WEY KT13 196 F9
Cricklade Av BRXS/STRHM SW2 180 F6
HARH RM3 105 L7
Cricklewood Broadway
CRICK NW2 116 G9
Cricklewood La CRICK NW2 117 H9
Cridland St SRTFD E15 141 L3
Crieff Ct TEDD TW11 177 H10
Crieff Rd WAND/EARL SW18 179 M2
Criffel Av BRXS/STRHM SW2 180 E5
Crimp Hl WDSR SL4 171 L3
Crimscott St STHWK SE1 19 K4
Crimsworth Rd VX/NE SW8 158 E7
Crinan St IS N1 5 M7
Cringle St VX/NE SW8 158 D6
Cripplegate St BARB EC2Y * 12 E3
Cripsey Av CHONG CM5 67 N2
Crispen Rd FELT TW13 175 M7
Crispian Cl WLSDN NW10 116 B9
Crispin Cl BEAC HP9 88 B7
Crispin Crs CROY/NA CR0 202 E10
Crispin Rd EDGW HA8 95 P7
Crispin St WCHPL E1 13 L4
Crispin Wy SLN SL2 109 J9
UX/CGN UB8 132 A6
Crisp Rd HMSMTH W6 156 F4
Criss Gv CFSP/GDCR SL9 89 P10
Criss La CFSP/GDCR SL9 89 P10
Cristowe Rd FUL/PGN SW6 * 157 J8
Criterion Ms ARCH N19 118 E7
Critten La RDKG RH5 253 L8
Crockenhill Hl STMC/STPC BR5 207 N5
Crockenhill La SWLY BR8 209 H7
Crockenhill Rd STMC/STPC BR5 207 N6
Crockerton Rd TOOT SW17 180 A5
Crockford Cl ADL/WDHM KT15 215 M1
Crockford Park Rd
ADL/WDHM KT15 215 M2
Crockham Cl CRAWW RH11 283 M9
Crockham Wy ELTH/MOT SE9 184 D7
Crocknorth Rd EHSLY KT24 252 G7
RDKG RH5 253 K10
Crocus Cl CROY/NA CR0 204 C8
Crocus Fld BAR EN5 77 J10
Croffets KWD/TDW/WH KT20 238 G7
Croft Av DORK RH4 254 G10
WWKM BR4 205 H8
Croft Cl ABYW SE2 164 A4
CHST BR7 184 C8
HGDN/ICK UB10 132 B2
HYS/HAR UB3 152 D6
KGLGY WD4 53 K6
MLHL NW7 96 B4
Croft Ct BORE WD6 76 A7
HARP AL5 * 20 A2
RSLP HA4 * 112 G6
SUT SM1 * 201 N9
Croftdown Rd KTTN NW5 118 B8
Croft End Rd KGLGY WD4 53 K6
Crofters WDSR SL4 171 M2
Crofters Cl ISLW TW7 176 C1
REDH RH1 276 C2
Crofters Ct DEPT SE8 160 D3
Crofters Md CROY/NA CR0 * 224 E5
Crofters Rd NTHWD HA6 92 F5
The Crofters WDSR SL4 * 171 M2
Crofters Wy CAMTN NW1 5 J5
Croft Fld HAT AL10 40 D4
KGLGY WD4 53 K6
Croft Gdns HNWL W7 154 F1
RSLP HA4 112 F6
Crofthill Rd SLN SL2 128 G6
Croft La KGLGY WD4 53 K6
Croftleigh Av PUR/KEN CR8 241 H2
Croft Lodge Cl WFD IG8 101 N7
Croft Meadow KGLGY WD4 53 K6
Croft Ms NFNCH/WDSPK N12 97 M4
Crofton ASHTD KT21 237 K4
Crofton Av BXLY DA5 185 N3
CHSWK W4 155 P6
CHSWK W4 156 A6
ORP BR6 206 F9
WOT/HER KT12 197 K10
Crofton Cl CHERT KT16 214 F4
Crofton Gate Wy BROCKY SE4 182 D1
Crofton Gv CHING E4 101 J5
Crofton La STMC/STPC BR5 206 G8
Crofton Park Rd BROCKY SE4 182 E2
Crofton Rd CDW/CHF RM16 168 B1
CMBW SE5 159 M8
ORP BR6 226 D1
PLSTW E13 141 N6
Crofton Ter RCH/KEW TW9 155 L10
Crofton Wy BAR EN5 * 77 L10
ENC/FH EN2 79 H6
Croft Rd BH/WHM TN16 262 E2
BMLY BR1 183 M9
CFSP/GDCR SL9 90 B10
CTHM CR3 242 E8
PEND EN3 80 D5
STRHM/NOR SW16 181 H10
SUT SM1 221 N2
WARE SG12 26 B1
WIM/MER SW19 179 M10
Crofts Pth HHS/BOV HP3 36 C8
Crofts Rd HRW HA1 114 F4
Crofts St WAP E1W 13 N8
The Crofts HHS/BOV HP3 36 C7
SHPTN TW17 196 F4
Croft St DEPT SE8 160 D3
The Croft ALP/SUD HA0 115 H10
BAR EN5 77 H8
BROX EN10 44 E9
CHING E4 101 K3
CRAWW RH11 283 K7
EA W5 135 K7
EDGW HA8 95 N9
HEST TW5 153 M6
LCOL/BKTW AL2 55 P1
LOU IG10 82 D6
RSLP HA4 113 K9
SWLY BR8 208 D3
WGCE AL7 3 J8
WLSDN NW10 136 C4
Croft Wy BFN/LL DA15 185 H6
RCHPK/HAM TW10 176 G6
SEV TN13 264 G1
Croftwell HARP AL5 20 E3
Crogsland Rd CAMTN NW1 4 C3
Croham Cl SAND/SEL CR2 223 M4
Croham Manor Rd
SAND/SEL CR2 223 M4
Croham Mt SAND/SEL CR2 223 M4
Croham Park Av SAND/SEL CR2 223 N2
Croham Rd SAND/SEL CR2 223 L2
Croham Valley Rd SAND/SEL CR2 223 P3
SAND/SEL CR2 224 B4
Croindene Rd STRHM/NOR SW16 202 F1
Cromartie Rd ARCH N19 118 E5
Cromarty Rd EDGW HA8 95 N3
Cromarty Vls BAY/PAD W2 * 9 J7
Crombie Cl REDBR IG4 122 C3
Crombie Ms BTSEA SW11 * 157 P8
Crombie Rd BFN/LL DA15 184 G4
Cromer Cl UX/CGN UB8 132 D8
Cromer Hyde MRDN SM4 * 201 L5
Crome Rd WLSDN NW10 136 B1
Cromer Rd BAR EN5 77 M8
CHDH RM6 123 P4
EMPK RM11 125 L5
HTHAIR TW6 152 B9
LEY E10 121 J5
ROMW/RG RM7 124 D4
SNWD SE25 204 A3
TOOT SW17 180 B9
TOTM N17 99 P10
WATN WD24 73 K4
Cromer Rd West HTHAIR TW6 152 B9
Cromer St STPAN WC1H 5 M10
Cromer Ter HACK E8 119 P10
Cromer Villas Rd
WAND/EARL SW18 179 J2
Cromford Cl ORP BR6 207 H10
Cromford Rd PUT/ROE SW15 179 J1
Cromford Wy NWMAL KT3 200 A1
Cromlix Cl CHST BR7 206 E2
Crompton Flds CRAWE RH10 283 P4
Crompton Pl PEND EN3 80 F4
Crompton St BAY/PAD W2 9 L2
Crompton Wy CRAWE RH10 283 P5
Cromwell Av CHESW EN7 62 A6
HAYES BR2 205 N3
HGT N6 118 C6
HMSMTH W6 156 E4
NWMAL KT3 200 C5
Cromwell Cl CHSWK W4 * 155 N4
CSTG HP8 89 P4
EFNCH N2 117 N2
HAYES BR2 205 N4
STALE/WH AL4 39 J1
WOT/HER KT12 197 J8
Cromwell Ct ALP/SUD HA0 135 K4
Cromwell Crs ECT SW5 14 E5
Cromwell Dr SL SL1 129 K8
Cromwell Gdns SKENS SW7 15 M5
Cromwell Gv CTHM CR3 241 K7
HMSMTH W6 156 F2
Cromwell Ms SKENS SW7 15 M5
Cromwell Pde ALP/SUD HA0 * 135 K4
Cromwell Pl ACT W3 135 P10
HGT N6 * 118 C6
MORT/ESHN SW14 155 P9
SKENS SW7 15 M5
Cromwell Rd ALP/SUD HA0 135 J4
ASC SL5 192 A4
BECK BR3 204 D2
BORE WD6 75 K5
BRW CM14 106 G5
BRXN/ST SW9 159 J7
CHESW EN7 62 A5
CROY/NA CR0 203 L7
CTHM CR3 241 K7
ECT SW5 14 F5
FELT TW13 175 J4
FNCH N3 97 M10
FSTGT E7 141 P2
GRAYS RM17 167 M4
HERT/BAY SG13 25 N4
HSLW TW3 153 P10
HYS/HAR UB3 132 E8
KUTN/CMB KT2 199 K1
MUSWH N10 98 B8
REDH RH1 258 A10
SKENS SW7 15 L5
TEDD TW11 176 F9
WALTH E17 121 H3
WARE SG12 26 E2
WIM/MER SW19 179 K8
WOT/HER KT12 197 J9
WPK KT4 200 A10
Cromwell St HSLW TW3 153 P10
Cromwell Ter HSLW TW3 * 153 P10
Crondace Rd FUL/PGN SW6 157 K7
Crondall St IS N1 7 H8
Cronin St PECK SE15 159 N6
Cronks Hl REIG RH2 275 M1
Cronks Hill Cl REDH RH1 275 N2
Cronks Hill Rd REDH RH1 275 N2
Crooked Billet Rbt CHING E4 100 G8
Crooked La GVE DA12 190 E2
Crooked Mile WAB EN9 63 H6
WAB EN9 63 H9
Crooked Usage FNCH N3 117 H1
Crooked Wy WAB EN9 45 K8
Crooke Rd DEPT SE8 160 D4
Crookham Rd FUL/PGN SW6 157 J7
Crookhams WGCE AL7 23 K3
Crook Log BXLYHS DA6 163 N9
Crookston Rd ELTH/MOT SE9 162 E9
Croombs Rd CAN/RD E16 141 P7
Croom's Hl GNWCH SE10 161 J6
Croom's Hill Gv GNWCH SE10 161 H6
Crop Common HAT AL10 40 E2
Cropley St IS N1 6 G7
Croppath Rd DAGE RM10 124 B9
Cropthorne Ct MV/WKIL W9 3 K10
Crosby Cl BEAC HP9 108 E1
FELT TW13 175 M7
STALE/WH AL4 39 H9
Crosby Rd DAGE RM10 144 C4
FSTGT E7 141 M1
Crosby Rw STHWK SE1 18 G2
Crosby Sq HDTCH EC3A 13 J6
Crosby Wk HACK E8 7 L2
Crosier Cl BKHTH/KID SE3 162 B7
Crosier Rd HGDN/ICK UB10 112 D9
Crosier Wy RSLP HA4 112 F8
Crosland Pl BTSEA SW11 158 B9
Crossacres WOKS/MYFD GU22 233 H2
Crossbow Rd CHIG IG7 103 J6
Crossbrook HAT AL10 40 B5
Crossbrook Rd BKHTH/KID SE3 162 B8
Crossbrook St CHES/WCR EN8 62 C7
Cross Deep TWK TW1 176 E6
Cross Deep Gdns TWK TW1 176 E5
Crossett Gn HHS/BOV HP3 36 D8
Crossfell Rd HHS/BOV HP3 36 C8
Crossfield Est DEPT SE8 160 F6
Crossfield Pl WEY KT13 216 C4
Crossfield Rd HAMP NW3 3 M2
HOD EN11 44 C1
TOTM N17 119 K1
Crossfields STALW/RED AL3 38 A9
Crossfields Cl BERK HP4 33 L5
Crossfield St DEPT SE8 160 F6
Crossford St BRXN/ST SW9 158 G8
Crossgate EDGW HA8 95 M4
GFD/PVL UB6 134 G1
Crossing Rd EPP CM16 65 K8
Cross Keys CRAWE RH10 283 N7
Cross Keys Cl ED N9 99 P3
MHST W1U 10 D4
Cross Lances Rd HSLW TW3 154 A10
Crossland Rd REDH RH1 258 B10
THHTH CR7 203 J6
Crosslands CHERT KT16 195 H10
Crosslands Av EA W5 135 L10
NWDGN UB2 153 N4
Crosslands Pde NWDGN UB2 * 153 P4
Crosslands Rd HOR/WEW KT19 220 A3
Cross La BEAC HP9 108 E1
BXLY DA5 186 A3
CEND/HSY/T N8 118 G1
CHERT KT16 214 E3
HARP AL5 20 B6
HERT/WAT SG14 25 J5
HORL RH6 281 K7
MON EC3R 13 J8
Cross La East GVE DA12 190 E5
Cross Lanes CFSP/GDCR SL9 90 C6
GU GU1 268 C1
Cross Lanes Cl CFSP/GDCR SL9 90 C6
Cross La West GVW DA11 190 E5
Crosslet St WALW SE17 19 H5
Crosslet V GNWCH SE10 160 G7
Crossley Cl BH/WHM TN16 244 A1
Crossleys CSTG HP8 89 P5
Crossleys Hl CSTG HP8 89 P4
Crossley St HOLWY N7 6 A1
Crossmead ELTH/MOT SE9 184 C4
OXHEY WD19 73 J10
Crossmead Av GFD/PVL UB6 133 P5
Cross Meadow CSHM HP5 50 E5
Crossness Rd BARK IG11 143 J5
Cross Oak WDSR SL4 148 F8
Cross Oak La REDH RH1 276 E10
Cross Oak Rd BERK HP4 33 M6
Crossoaks La BORE WD6 76 A1
Crosspath CRAWE RH10 * 283 P6
The Crosspath RAD WD7 74 F1
Cross Rd ASC SL5 192 E8
BELMT SM2 221 K6
CHDH RM6 123 M5
CHES/WCR EN8 62 D9
CHING E4 101 J2
CMBW SE5 159 M8
CROY/NA CR0 203 L8
EN EN1 79 N8
FBAR/BDGN N11 98 C6
FELT TW13 175 M7
GVW DA11 190 C2
HAYES BR2 205 P8
HERT/WAT SG14 25 K4
HRW HA1 114 C2
KTN/HRWW/WS HA3 94 F10
KUTN/CMB KT2 177 L10
KWD/TDW/WH KT20 238 F8
OXHEY WD19 73 M10
PUR/KEN CR8 223 J9
RDART DA2 187 N7
ROMW/RG RM7 124 B1
RYLN/HDSTN HA2 113 P8
SCUP DA14 185 L7
STMC/STPC BR5 207 L5
WDGN N22 99 H7
WEY KT13 * 196 E10
WFD IG8 102 C7
WIM/MER SW19 179 K10
Cross Roads LOU IG10 81 N6
The Crossroads EHSLY KT24 253 L4
Cross St BARN SW13 156 B8
ERITH DA8 164 F5
HPTN TW12 176 B8
IS N1 6 D5
STALW/RED AL3 38 C6
UED N18 99 P6
UX/CGN UB8 131 M3
WARE SG12 26 D2
WAT WD17 73 K7
Crossthwaite Av HNHL SE24 159 L10
Crosswall TWRH EC3N 13 L7
Cross Wy HYS/HAR UB3 153 H1
Crossway BCTR RM8 123 M8
CDALE/KGS NW9 116 C2
CHSM HP5 51 K6
EN EN1 99 M1
HLWE CM17 29 N10
NFNCH/WDSPK N12 97 N7
NWMAL KT3 200 F4
PIN HA5 93 J10
RSLP HA4 113 K9
STMC/STPC BR5 206 G4
STNW/STAM N16 119 M10
THMD SE28 143 M9
WEA W13 134 E6
WGCW AL8 22 F1
WOT/HER KT12 197 J9
Crossway Pde WDGN N22 * 99 J8
Crossways BEAC HP9 88 E10
BELMT SM2 221 N5
BERK HP4 33 L6
BH/WHM TN16 243 P6
BRWN CM15 87 M10
CRAWE RH10 284 B6
EGH TW20 172 G9
EHSLY KT24 253 L3
GPK RM2 125 J1
HHS/BOV HP3 36 C6
SAND/SEL CR2 224 E4
SUN TW16 196 G1
Crossways Bvd RDART DA2 166 E10
RDART DA2 188 F1
Crossways Cl CRAWE RH10 284 A6
Crossways La REIG RH2 257 M4
Crossways Rd BECK BR3 204 F4
MTCM CR4 202 C3
Crossways Ter CLPT E5 * 120 B9
The Crossways BRYLDS KT5 * 199 N8
COUL/CHIP CR5 240 C5
GUW GU2 267 L2
HEST TW5 153 N6
REDH RH1 258 C5
WBLY HA9 115 M7
The Cross Wy
KTN/HRWW/WS HA3 94 D10
The Crossway ELTH/MOT SE9 184 A5
WDGN N22 99 J8
Crosswell Cl SHPTN TW17 196 D2
Crossthwaite Wy SL SL1 128 C7
Croston St HACK E8 7 P5
Crosts La WDGN N22 99 H8
Crothall Cl PLMGR N13 98 G4
Crouch Av BARK IG11 143 L4
Crouch Cl BECK BR3 182 F9
Crouch Cft ELTH/MOT SE9 184 D6
Crouch End Hl CEND/HSY/T N8 118 E5
Crouchfield HERT/WAT SG14 25 K2
HHW HP1 35 L7
Crouch Hall Rd CEND/HSY/T N8 118 E4
Crouch Hl CEND/HSY/T N8 118 F5
Crouch La CHESW EN7 61 K3
CHESW EN7 61 M3
Crouchman Cl CDW/CHF RM16 167 P1
Crouchmans Cl SYD SE26 181 N6
Crouch Oak La ADL/WDHM KT15 215 M1
Crouch Rd CDW/CHF RM16 168 D4
WLSDN NW10 136 A2
Crouch Va UPMR RM14 126 D5
Crowborough Cl WARL CR6 242 D4
Crowborough Dr WARL CR6 242 D4
Crowborough Pth OXHEY WD19 93 L5
Crowborough Rd TOOT SW17 180 B8
Crowden Wy THMD SE28 143 M9
Crowder Cl NFNCH/WDSPK N12 97 M8
Crowder St WCHPL E1 140 A9
Crow Dr RSEV TN14 246 D1
Crowfoot Cl HOM E9 120 E10
THMD SE28 143 H10
Crow Gn BRWN CM15 86 F8
Crow Green La BRWN CM15 86 F9
Crow Green Rd BRWN CM15 86 F9
Crow Hl ORP BR6 * 226 C6
Crowhurst Cl BRXN/ST SW9 159 H8
CRAWE RH10 284 F7
Crowhurst Md GDST RH9 260 B6
Crowhurst Wy STMC/STPC BR5 207 M5
Crowland Av HYS/HAR UB3 152 F3
Crowland Gdns STHGT/OAK N14 * 98 F1
Crowland Rd SEVS/STOTM N15 119 N3
THHTH CR7 * 203 L4
Crowlands Av ROMW/RG RM7 124 C4
Crowland Ter IS N1 6 G3
Crowland Wk MRDN SM4 201 L6
Crow La ROMW/RG RM7 124 B5
ROMW/RG RM7 124 D5
Crowley Crs CROY/NA CR0 223 H2
Crowline Wk IS N1 * 6 F1
Crowmarsh Gdns FSTH SE23 182 B3
Crown Ar KUT/HW KT1 * 199 J2
Crownbourne Ct SUT SM1 * 221 L1
Crown Buildings CHING E4 * 101 J2
Crown Cl BOW E3 140 F3
DTCH/LGLY SL3 150 F6
HYS/HAR UB3 152 G1
KIL/WHAMP NW6 2 G1
MLHL NW7 96 C3
ORP BR6 227 K1
RBSF CM22 30 D3
WOT/HER KT12 197 K7
Crown Ct HOL/ALD WC2B 11 M6
Crown Dl NRWD SE19 181 K9
Crowndale Rd CAMTN NW1 5 H7
Crownfield BROX EN10 44 F7
Crownfield Av GNTH/NBYPK IG2 123 H3
Crownfield Rd SRTFD E15 121 J10
Crownfields SEV TN13 265 J1
Crown Ga HLW CM20 46 G1
Crown Gn GVE DA12 191 P8
Crown Hts GU GU1 268 B3
Crown Hl CROY/NA CR0 * 203 K9
WAB EN9 64 C9
Crown Hill Ct ASC SL5 192 A5
Crownhill Rd WFD IG8 102 B8
WLSDN NW10 136 C3
Crown La GVE DA12 191 P7
HAYES BR2 206 A5
MRDN SM4 201 K3
SLN SL2 128 G2
STHGT/OAK N14 98 D2
STRHM/NOR SW16 181 H8
VW GU25 194 A6
Crown Lane Gdns
STRHM/NOR SW16 * 181 H8
Crown Lane Sp HAYES BR2 206 A6
Crown Meadow DTCH/LGLY SL3 150 E6
Crownmead Wy ROMW/RG RM7 124 C2
Crown Office Rw EMB EC4Y 12 A7
Crown Pde MRDN SM4 * 201 L4
STHGT/OAK N14 * 98 D2
Crown Pas STJS SW1Y 11 H10
Crown Pl KTTN NW5 4 F1
SDTCH EC2A 13 J2
Crown Ri CHERT KT16 195 J8
GSTN WD25 55 K10
Crown Rd BARK/HLT IG6 122 G2
BORE WD6 75 M5
BRW CM14 86 C5
EN EN1 79 P7
GRAYS RM17 167 M5
KUTN/CMB KT2 199 P1
MRDN SM4 201 K4
MUSWH N10 98 B8
ORP BR6 227 K2
RSEV TN14 228 G6
RSLP HA4 113 L10
SUT SM1 221 K1
TWK TW1 176 G2
VW GU25 193 P6
Crown Sq WOKN/KNAP GU21 232 C3
Crownstone Rd
BRXS/STRHM SW2 181 H1
Crown St ACT W3 135 N10
BRW CM14 107 H3
CMBW SE5 159 K6
DAGE RM10 124 D10
EGH TW20 172 D8
RYLN/HDSTN HA2 114 C6
Crown Ter CRICK NW2 * 116 G9
RCH/KEW TW9 155 L10
STHGT/OAK N14 * 98 E2
Crowntree Cl ISLW TW7 154 E5
Crown Vls ACT W3 * 155 P1
Crown Wk HHS/BOV HP3 35 P10
WBLY HA9 115 L8
Crown Wy WDR/YW UB7 132 A10
Crown Woods La
WOOL/PLUM SE18 162 E8
Crown Woods Wy
ELTH/MOT SE9 184 G1
Crown Yd HSLW TW3 154 B9
Crow Piece La SLN SL2 128 E2
Crowscroft Cl GUW GU2 249 N6
Crowshott Av STAN HA7 95 H10
Crows Rd BARK IG11 142 E1
BOW E3 141 J5
EPP CM16 65 J6
Crowstone Rd CDW/CHF RM16 167 P1
Crowther Av BTFD TW8 155 K4
Crowther Cl FUL/PGN SW6 14 D10
Crowther Rd SNWD SE25 203 P4
Crowthorne Cl
WAND/EARL SW18 179 J3
Crowthorne Rd NKENS W10 136 G8
Croxdale Rd BORE WD6 75 L6
Croxden Cl EDGW HA8 115 M1
Croxden Wk MRDN SM4 201 M6
Croxford Gdns WDGN N22 99 J8
Croxford Wy ROMW/RG RM7 124 E6
Croxley Cl STMC/STPC BR5 207 L2
Croxley Gn STMC/STPC BR5 207 L1
Croxley Rd MV/WKIL W9 2 D10
Croxley Vw WATW WD18 72 F10
Croxted Cl DUL SE21 181 K3
Croxted Ms HNHL SE24 181 K2
Croxted Rd DUL SE21 181 K3
DUL SE21 181 L5

Croyde Av GFD/PVL UB6 134 B5
HYS/HAR UB3 152 F3
Croyde Cl BFN/LL DA15 184 G3
Croydonbarn La GDST RH9 281 P3
The Croydon F/O CROY/NA CR0 223 J1
Croydon Gv CROY/NA CR0 203 J8
Croydon La BNSTD SM7 221 N9
Croydon La South BNSTD SM7 221 L10
Croydon Rd BECK BR3 204 D3
BH/WHM TN16 262 E2
CROY/NA CR0 222 F1
CTHM CR3 241 P8
MTCM CR4 202 C5
PGE/AN SE20 204 A2
PLSTW E13 141 L6
REIG RH2 257 M9
WARL CR6 243 J8
WLGTN SM6 202 E10
WLGTN SM6 222 C1
WWKM BR4 205 K10
WWKM BR4 205 N10
Croyland Rd ED N9 99 P2
Croylands Dr SURB KT6 199 K7
Croysdale Av SUN TW16 197 H3
Crozier Dr SAND/SEL CR2 224 A6
Crozier Ter HOM E9 120 D10
Crucible Cl CHDH RM6 123 L4
Crucifix La STHWK SE1 19 J1
Cruden Rd GVE DA12 191 J6
Cruden St IS N1 6 D6
Cruick Av SOCK/AV RM15 147 H9
Cruickshank St FSBYW WC1X 6 A9
Cruikshank Rd SRTFD E15 121 K9
Crummock Cl SL SL1 128 B8
Crummock Gdns
CDALE/KGS NW9 116 B3
Crumpsall St ABYW SE2 163 M3
Crundale Av CDALE/KGS NW9 115 M3
Crunden Rd SAND/SEL CR2 223 L4
Crusader Cl PUR RM19 165 P3
Crusader Gdns CROY/NA CR0 203 M10
Crusader Wy WATW WD18 72 G10
Crusoe Ms STNW/STAM N16 119 L7
Crusoe Rd ERITH DA8 164 E4
MTCM CR4 180 A10
Crutched Friars TWRH EC3N 13 K7
Crutchfield La HORL RH6 279 K1
WOT/HER KT12 197 J9
Crutchley Rd CAT SE6 183 L5
Crystal Av HCH RM12 125 M9
Crystal Palace Pde NRWD SE19 * 181 P10
Crystal Palace Park Rd NRWD SE19 181 N9
Crystal Palace Park Rd SYD SE26 181 P8
Crystal Palace Rd EDUL SE22 181 N2
Crystal Palace Station Rd
NRWD SE19 181 P9
Crystal Ter NRWD SE19 181 L9
Crystal Wy BCTR RM8 123 M6
HRW HA1 114 E3
Cuba Dr PEND EN3 80 B6
Cuba St POP/IOD E14 160 F1
Cubitt Sq NWDGN UB2 * 134 B10
Cubitt St FSBYW WC1X 5 P10
Cubitt Ter CLAP SW4 158 D9
Cubitt Wy WOKN/KNAP GU21 231 J4
Cublands HERT/BAY SG13 26 A5
Cuckfield Cl CRAWW RH11 283 J10
Cuckmans Dr LCOL/BKTW AL2 55 P1
Cuckmere Cl CRAWW RH11 283 J8
Cuckmere Wy STMC/STPC BR5 207 N8
Cuckoo Av HNWL W7 134 D6
Cuckoo Dene HNWL W7 134 C7
Cuckoo Hall La ED N9 100 B1
Cuckoo Hl PIN HA5 113 K2
Cuckoo Hill Dr PIN HA5 113 K1
Cuckoo Hill Rd PIN HA5 113 L2
Cuckoo La CDW/CHF RM16 167 L1
CHOB/PIR GU24 212 C9
HNWL W7 134 D9
Cuckoo V CHOB/PIR GU24 212 C9
Cucumber La BRKMPK AL9 42 A7
Cuda's Cl HOR/WEW KT19 220 C1
Cuddington Av WPK KT4 200 C10
Cuddington Cl
KWD/TDW/WH KT20 238 F6
Cuddington Gld HOR/WEW KT19 219 M8
Cuddington Park Cl BNSTD SM7 221 J9
Cuddington Wy BELMT SM2 220 G8
Cudham Cl BELMT SM2 221 K6
Cudham Dr CROY/NA CR0 224 G6
Cudham La North ORP BR6 227 H5
RSEV TN14 226 F10
Cudham La South RSEV TN14 244 G1
Cudham Park Rd RSEV TN14 226 G7
Cudham Rd BH/WHM TN16 244 B5
ORP BR6 226 D7
Cudham St CAT SE6 182 G3
Cudworth Pk RDKG RH5 278 B7
Cudworth St WCHPL E1 140 A6
Cuff Crs ELTH/MOT SE9 184 B2
Cuffley Av GSTN WD25 55 L10
Cuffley Ct HHNE HP2 36 D1
Cuffley Hl CHESW EN7 61 J5
Cugley Rd RDART DA2 188 B3
Culcroft HART DA3 211 L4
Culford Gdns CHEL SW3 16 B6
Culford Gv IS N1 7 J2
Culford Ms IS N1 7 J1
Culford Rd CDW/CHF RM16 167 P1
IS N1 7 J3
Culgaith Gdns ENC/FH EN2 78 F8
Culin Sq SOCK/AV RM15 147 H9
Cullera Cl NTHWD HA6 92 G7
Cullerne Cl EW KT17 220 C6
Cullesden Rd PUR/KEN CR8 241 J1
Culling Rd BERM/RHTH SE16 160 B2
Cullings Ct WAB EN9 63 L9
Cullington Cl
KTN/HRWW/WS HA3 114 F2
Cullingworth Rd WLSDN NW10 116 E10
Culloden Cl BERM/RHTH SE16 19 P8
Culloden Rd ENC/FH EN2 79 J6
Culloden St POP/IOD E14 141 H8
Cull's Rd RGUW GU3 248 A10
Cullum St FENCHST EC3M 13 J7
Culmington Pde WEA W13 * 135 H9
Culmington Rd SAND/SEL CR2 223 K5
WEA W13 135 H10
Culmore Rd PECK SE15 160 A6
Culmstock Rd BTSEA SW11 180 B1
Culpepper Cl CHIG IG7 102 E7
UED N18 100 A6
Culross Cl SEVS/STOTM N15 119 K2
Culross St MYFR/PKLN W1K 10 C8
Culsac Rd SURB KT6 199 K9
Culverden Rd BAL SW12 180 D6
OXHEY WD19 93 J4
Culverden Ter WEY KT13 * 196 E10
Culver Dr OXTED RH8 261 K6
Culver Gv STAN HA7 95 H10
Culverhay ASHTD KT21 237 K2
Culverhouse Gdns
STRHM/NOR SW16 180 G7
Culverlands Cl STAN HA7 94 G5
Culverley Rd CAT SE6 182 G4
Culver Rd STAL AL1 38 D5
Culvers Av CAR SM5 202 A9
Culvers Cft BEAC HP9 89 H7
Culvers Retreat CAR SM5 202 A8
Culverstone Cl HAYES BR2 205 L6
Culvers Wy CAR SM5 202 A10
Culvert La UX/CGN UB8 131 L4
Culvert Pl BTSEA SW11 158 B8
Culvert Rd BTSEA SW11 158 A8
SEVS/STOTM N15 119 M3
Culvey Cl HART DA3 211 K5
Culworth St STJWD NW8 3 N8
Cumberland Av GUW GU2 249 M5
GVE DA12 190 F3
HCH RM12 125 M8
SLN SL2 129 H6
WELL DA16 163 H9
WLSDN NW10 135 N5
Cumberland Cl AMSS HP7 69 N5
BARK/HLT IG6 102 F9
HACK E8 7 L2
HERT/WAT SG14 25 J2
HHS/BOV HP3 36 F10
HOR/WEW KT19 220 B6
RYNPK SW20 178 G10
TWK TW1 176 G2
Cumberland Crs WKENS W14 157 H3
WKENS W14 14 B5
Cumberland Dr BXLYHN DA7 163 P6
CHSGTN KT9 199 K10
DART DA1 187 N3
ESH/CLAY KT10 198 F9
Cumberland Gdns FSBYW WC1X 5 P9
HDN NW4 * 96 G10
Cumberland Ga BAY/PAD W2 10 B7
CAMTN NW1 4 E9
Cumberland House
KUTN/CMB KT2 177 N10
Cumberland Market CAMTN NW1 4 F9
Cumberland Ms LBTH SE11 18 B8
Cumberland Pk ACT W3 135 P9
Cumberland Pl CAMTN NW1 4 E9
CAT SE6 183 L4
SUN TW16 197 H4
Cumberland Rd ACT W3 135 P9
ASHF TW15 173 N6
BARN SW13 156 C7
CDW/CHF RM16 167 K1
ED N9 100 B2
HAYES BR2 205 K4
HNWL W7 154 E1
HRW HA1 114 A3
MNPK E12 122 A9
PLSTW E13 141 N7
RCH/KEW TW9 155 M7
SNWD SE25 204 A6
STAN HA7 115 L1
WDGN N22 98 G10
Cumberlands PUR/KEN CR8 241 L1
Cumberland St PIM SW1V 16 F7
STA TW18 172 G8
Cumberland Ter CAMTN NW1 4 E8
PGE/AN SE20 * 182 A10
Cumberland Terrace Ms
CAMTN NW1 4 E8
Cumberlow Av SNWD SE25 203 P3
Cumberlow Pl HHNE HP2 36 D7
Cumbernauld Gdns SUN TW16 174 G8
Cumberton Rd TOTM N17 99 L9
Cumbrae Cl SLN SL2 129 M10
Cumbrae Gdns SURB KT6 199 J9
Cumbrian Av BXLYHN DA7 164 F8
Cumbrian Gdns CRICK NW2 116 G7
Cumbrian Wy UX/CGN UB8 131 N3
Cumley Rd CHONG CM5 66 F6
Cummings Hall La HARH RM3 105 K4
Cumming St IS N1 5 P8
Cumnor Cl BRXN/ST SW9 * 158 G8
Cumnor Gdns EW KT17 220 D3
Cumnor Ri PUR/KEN CR8 241 K3
Cumnor Rd BELMT SM2 221 M3
Cunard Crs WCHMH N21 79 L10
Cunard Rd WLSDN NW10 136 A5
Cundalls Rd WARE SG12 26 D1
Cundy Rd CAN/RD E16 141 P8
Cundy St BGVA SW1W 16 D6
Cunliffe Cl EPSOM KT18 237 N10
Cunliffe Rd HOR/WEW KT19 220 C1
Cunliffe St STRHM/NOR SW16 180 D9
Cunningham Av GU GU1 250 D9
HAT AL10 40 A3
PEND EN3 80 D2
STAL AL1 38 E8
Cunningham Cl CHDH RM6 123 M3
WWKM BR4 204 G9
Cunningham Hill Rd STAL AL1 38 E8
Cunningham Pk HRW HA1 114 C3
Cunningham Pl STJWD NW8 9 L1
Cunningham Ri EPP CM16 66 D1
Cunningham Rd BNSTD SM7 239 N1
CHES/WCR EN8 62 D3
SEVS/STOTM N15 * 119 P2
Cunnington St CHSWK W4 155 P3
Cupar Rd BTSEA SW11 158 B7
Cupola Cl BMLY BR1 183 N8
Curates Wk RDART DA2 187 L6
Cureton St WEST SW1P 17 K7
Curfew Bell Rd CHERT KT16 195 J7
Curfew Yd WDSR SL4 * 149 J7
Curlew Cl BERK HP4 33 P6
SAND/SEL CR2 224 C7
THMD SE28 143 N9
Curlew Ct BROX EN10 * 44 E9
Curlew Gdns RGUE GU4 250 G8
The Curlews GVE DA12 190 G5
Curlew St STHWK SE1 19 L1
Curlew Wy YEAD UB4 133 H2
Curling Cl COUL/CHIP CR5 240 C6
Curling La GRAYS RM17 167 L4
Curling V GUW GU2 267 M2
Curnick's La WNWD SE27 181 K7
Curo Pk LCOL/BKTW AL2 56 D4
Curran Av BFN/LL DA15 185 J1
WLGTN SM6 202 B10
Curran Cl UX/CGN UB8 131 M6
Currey Rd NTHLT UB5 134 B1
Curricle St ACT W3 136 B10
Currie Hill Cl WIM/MER SW19 179 J7
Curriers La SL SL1 108 C10
Currie St HERT/BAY SG13 25 M4
Curry Ri MLHL NW7 96 G7
Cursitor St FLST/FETLN EC4A 12 A5
Curtain Pl SDTCH EC2A 7 K10
Curtain Rd SDTCH EC2A 13 J2
Curteys HLWE CM17 29 N6
Curthwaite Gdns ENC/FH EN2 78 E8
Curtis Cl RKW/CH/CXG WD3 91 K2
Curtis Dr ACT W3 136 A8
Curtis Field Rd
STRHM/NOR SW16 180 G7
Curtis La ALP/SUD HA0 135 K1
Curtismill Cl STMC/STPC BR5 207 L3
Curtis Mill La ABR/ST RM4 84 G8
ABR/ST RM4 85 H10
Curtismill Wy STMC/STPC BR5 207 L3
Curtis Rd DORK RH4 272 E1
EMPK RM11 125 N6
HHS/BOV HP3 36 E7
HOR/WEW KT19 219 P1
HSLWW TW4 175 N3
Curtiss Dr GSTN WD25 54 G10
Curtis St STHWK SE1 19 L5
Curtis Wy BERK HP4 34 A6
STHWK SE1 19 L5
Curvan Cl EW KT17 220 C6
The Curve SHB W12 136 D9
Curwen Av FSTGT E7 121 N9
Curwen Rd SHB W12 156 D1
Curzon Av BEAC HP9 88 C7
PEND EN3 80 C9
STAN HA7 94 F9
Curzon Cl ORP BR6 226 G1
WEY KT13 216 B1
Curzon Crs BARK IG11 143 J5
WLSDN NW10 136 B2
Curzon Dr GRAYS RM17 167 P6
Curzon Pl PIN HA5 113 K3
Curzon Rd EA W5 134 G6
MUSWH N10 98 C10
THHTH CR7 203 H6
WEY KT13 216 B1
Curzon Sq MYFR/PICC W1J 10 D10
Curzon St MYFR/PKLN W1K 10 D10
Cusack Cl TWK TW1 * 176 E7
Cussons Cl CHESW EN7 61 P5
Custom House Reach
BERM/RHTH SE16 * 160 E2
Cutcombe Rd CMBW SE5 159 K8
Cuthberga Cl BARK IG11 142 F2
Cuthbert Cl CHESW EN7 61 N5
Cuthbert Gdns SNWD SE25 203 M5
Cuthbert Rd CROY/NA CR0 203 J9
UED N18 99 P6
WALTH E17 121 H1
Cuthbert St BAY/PAD W2 9 L2
Cutlers Gardens Ar LVPST EC2M 13 K5
Cutler St HDTCH EC3A 13 K5
Cutmore Dr STALE/WH AL4 39 N8
Cutmore St GVW DA11 190 E3
The Cut STHWK SE1 18 B1
Cuttinglye La CRAWE RH10 285 P4
Cuttsfield Ter HHW HP1 35 J7
Cutty Sark Ct RDART DA2 * 188 F1
Cuxton Cl BXLYHS DA6 185 P1
Cwmbran Ct HHNE HP2 36 A2
Cyclamen Cl HPTN TW12 175 P9
Cyclamen Rd SWLY BR8 208 E4
Cyclamen Wy HOR/WEW KT19 219 P2
Cygnet Av EBED/NFELT TW14 175 L3
Cygnet Cl BORE WD6 75 P5
NTHWD HA6 92 D8
WLSDN NW10 116 A10
WOKN/KNAP GU21 231 N2
Cygnets Cl REDH RH1 258 B8
The Cygnets FELT TW13 175 M7
STA TW18 173 J8
Cygnet St WCHPL E1 13 M1
Cygnet Vw WTHK RM20 166 E3
Cygnet Wy YEAD UB4 133 L8
Cymbeline Ct HRW HA1 * 114 E4
Cynthia St IS N1 5 P8
Cypress Av ENC/FH EN2 79 H1
WGCE AL7 23 M6
WHTN TW2 176 B3
Cypress Cl CLPT E5 119 P7
WAB EN9 * 63 J10
Cypress Ct VW GU25 194 C4
Cypress Gdns BROCKY SE4 182 D1
Cypress Gv BARK/HLT IG6 103 H7
Cypress Rd GU GU1 249 P8
KTN/HRWW/WS HA3 94 C10
SNWD SE25 203 M2
Cypress Tree Cl BFN/LL DA15 185 J4
Cypress Wk EGH TW20 171 N9
GSTN WD25 * 73 J1
Cypress Wy BNSTD SM7 220 G10
Cyprians Av CHOB/PIR GU24 230 G8
Cyprus Av FNCH N3 97 H10
Cyprus Cl FSBYPK N4 119 H4
Cyprus Gdns FNCH N3 97 H10
Cyprus Pl BETH E2 140 B4
EHAM E6 142 D9
Cyprus Rd ED N9 99 N3
FNCH N3 97 J10
Cyprus St BETH E2 140 B4
Cyrena Rd EDUL SE22 181 N2
Cyril Rd BXLYHN DA7 163 P8
ORP BR6 207 K7
Cyrils Wy STAL AL1 38 C9
Cyrus St FSBYE EC1V 12 D1
Czar St DEPT SE8 160 F5

D

Dabbling Cl ERITH DA8 * 165 J6
Dabbs Hill La NTHLT UB5 114 A10
NTHLT UB5 133 N1
D'Abernon Cl ESH/CLAY KT10 217 P1
D'Abernon Dr COB KT11 235 M2
Dabin Crs GNWCH SE10 161 H7
Dacca St DEPT SE8 160 E5
Dace Rd BOW E3 140 F3
Dacorum Wy HHW HP1 35 M6
Dacre Av CLAY IG5 102 D10
SOCK/AV RM15 146 C10
Dacre Cl CHIG IG7 102 F5
GFD/PVL UB6 134 A4
Dacre Crs SOCK/AV RM15 146 C10
Dacre Gdns BORE WD6 76 A9
CHIG IG7 102 F5
LEW SE13 * 161 K10
Dacre Pk LEW SE13 161 K9
Dacre Pl LEW SE13 161 K9
Dacre Rd CROY/NA CR0 202 F7
PLSTW E13 141 N3
WAN E11 121 L6
Dacres Est FSTH SE23 * 182 C6
Dacres Rd FSTH SE23 182 C6
Dacre St STJSPK SW1H 17 J3
Dade Wy NWDGN UB2 153 N4
Dads Wd HLW CM20 46 F1
Daerwood Cl HAYES BR2 206 C8
Daffodil Av BRWN CM15 86 G9
Daffodil Cl CROY/NA CR0 204 C8
HAT AL10 22 C10
HPTN TW12 175 P9
Daffodil Dr CHOB/PIR GU24 230 F2
Daffodil Gdns IL IG1 122 E10
Daffodil St SHB W12 136 C9
Dafforne Rd TOOT SW17 180 A6
Dagden Rd RGUE GU4 268 B6
Dagenham Av DAGW RM9 143 P3
Dagenham Rd DAGE RM10 124 D9
LEY E10 120 E6
RAIN RM13 144 E2
Dagger La BORE WD6 74 F10
BORE WD6 74 F8
Daggs Dell Rd HHW HP1 35 J4
Dagley La RGUE GU4 268 A7
Dagmar Av WBLY HA9 115 L9
Dagmar Gdns WLSDN NW10 136 G4
Dagmar Ms NWDGN UB2 153 M2
Dagmar Pas IS N1 6 C5
Dagmar Rd CMBW SE5 159 M8
DAGE RM10 144 D2
FSBYPK N4 119 H5
KUTN/CMB KT2 199 L1
NWDGN UB2 153 M2
SNWD SE25 203 M4
WDGN N22 98 E9
WDSR SL4 149 J8
Dagmar Ter IS N1 6 D5
Dagnall Crs UX/CGN UB8 131 M7
Dagnall Pk SNWD SE25 203 M5
Dagnall Rd SNWD SE25 203 M5
Dagnall St BTSEA SW11 158 A8
Dagnam Park Cl HARH RM3 105 P6
HARH RM3 106 A6
Dagnam Park Dr HARH RM3 105 M6
Dagnam Park Gdns HARH RM3 105 P7
Dagnam Park Sq HARH RM3 105 P7
Dagnan Rd BAL SW12 180 C3
Dagonet Rd BMLY BR1 183 M6
Dagwood La BRWN CM15 86 G4
Dahlia Cl CHESW EN7 61 K1
Dahlia Dr SWLY BR8 208 G2
Dahlia Gdns IL IG1 142 E1
MTCM CR4 202 E4
Dahlia Rd ABYW SE2 163 L4
Dahomey Rd STRHM/NOR SW16 180 D9
Daiglen Dr SOCK/AV RM15 146 F9
Daimler Wy WLGTN SM6 222 F4
Daines Cl MNPK E12 122 C8
SOCK/AV RM15 146 F6
Dainford Cl BMLY BR1 183 J8
Daintry Cl KTN/HRWW/WS HA3 114 F2
Dairsie Rd ELTH/MOT SE9 162 D9
Dairy Cl BMLY BR1 * 183 N10
EYN DA4 188 A10
THHTH CR7 203 K2
WLSDN NW10 136 D3
Dairyfields CRAWW RH11 283 K8
Dairyglen Av CHES/WCR EN8 62 C7
Dairy La EDEN TN8 262 E10
WOOL/PLUM SE18 162 C3
Dairyman Cl CRICK NW2 * 116 G9
Dairymans Wk RGUE GU4 250 E5
Dairy Wy ABLGY WD5 54 G5
Daisy Cl CROY/NA CR0 204 C8
Daisy Dr HAT AL10 40 C1
Daisy La FUL/PGN SW6 157 K9
Daisy Meadow EGH TW20 172 D8
Daisy Rd SWFD E18 101 N10
Dakin Pl WCHPL E1 140 D7
Dakota Cl WLGTN SM6 222 G4
Dalberg Rd BRXS/STRHM SW2 181 H1
Dalberg Wy ABYW SE2 163 N2
Dalby Rd WAND/EARL SW18 157 M10
Dalbys Crs TOTM N17 99 M7
Dalby St KTTN NW5 4 E2
Dalcross Rd HSLWW TW4 153 M8
Dale Av EDGW HA8 95 L9
HSLWW TW4 153 M9
Dalebury Rd TOOT SW17 180 A5
Dale Cl ADL/WDHM KT15 215 L2
ASC SL5 192 F5
BAR EN5 77 L10
BKHTH/KID SE3 161 M9
DART DA1 186 G2
PIN HA5 93 J9
SOCK/AV RM15 146 F8
Dale Ct GSTN WD25 * 55 H9
SBW CM21 29 N2
Dale Dr YEAD UB4 132 G6
Dale Gdns WFD IG8 101 N5
Dalegarth Gdns PUR/KEN CR8 223 L9
Dale Green Rd FBAR/BDGN N11 98 C4
Dale Gv NFNCH/WDSPK N12 97 M6
Daleham Av EGH TW20 172 D9
Daleham Dr UX/CGN UB8 132 C8
Daleham Gdns HAMP NW3 3 L1
Dale Lodge Rd ASC SL5 192 F5
Dalemain Ms CAN/RD E16 141 M10
Dale Park Av CAR SM5 202 A9
Dale Park Rd NRWD SE19 203 K1
Dale Rd DART DA1 186 G2
KTTN NW5 118 B10
MEO DA13 189 M7
PUR/KEN CR8 223 H8
STHL UB1 134 A7
SUN TW16 * 174 G10
SUT SM1 221 J1
SWLY BR8 208 D3
WALW SE17 18 D10
WOT/HER KT12 196 G7
Dale Rw NTGHL W11 * 8 B6
Dale Side CFSP/GDCR SL9 110 B6
Daleside ORP BR6 227 K2
Daleside Cl ORP BR6 227 K3
Daleside Dr POTB/CUF EN6 59 J9
Daleside Gdns CHIG IG7 102 F4
Daleside Rd HOR/WEW KT19 220 A3
STRHM/NOR SW16 180 C8
Dales Pth BORE WD6 * 76 A9
Dales Rd BORE WD6 76 A9
Dalestone Ms HARH RM3 105 J8
Dale St CHSWK W4 156 B4
The Dale HAYES BR2 226 A1
WAB EN9 63 K10
Dale Vw BAR EN5 * 77 J7
EPSOM KT18 237 N9
ERITH DA8 165 H8
WOKN/KNAP GU21 231 M4
Dale View Av CHING E4 101 H3
Dale View Crs CHING E4 101 H4
Dale View Gdns CHING E4 101 J4
Daleview Rd SEVS/STOTM N15 119 M4
Dalewood HARP AL5 20 C2
WGCE AL7 23 N6
Dalewood Cl EMPK RM11 125 N5
Dalewood Gdns CRAWE RH10 284 A5
WPK KT4 200 E9
Dale Wood Rd ORP BR6 207 H8
Daley St HOM E9 140 C1
Daley Thompson Wy VX/NE SW8 158 C9
Dalgarno Gdns NKENS W10 136 F7
Dalgarno Wy NKENS W10 136 F6
Dalkeith Gv STAN HA7 95 J6
Dalkeith Rd DUL SE21 181 K4
HARP AL5 20 B1
IL IG1 122 F8
Dallas Rd CHEAM SM3 221 H3
EA W5 135 L7
HDN NW4 116 D5
SYD SE26 182 A7
Dallas Ter HYS/HAR UB3 152 G2
Dallega Cl HYS/HAR UB3 132 E9
Dallinger Rd LEE/GVPK SE12 183 L2
Dalling Rd HMSMTH W6 156 E3
Dallington Cl WOT/HER KT12 217 K3
Dallington Sq FSBYE EC1V 12 D1
Dallington St FARR EC1M 12 D2
Dallin Rd BXLYHS DA6 163 N10
WOOL/PLUM SE18 162 E6
Dalmain Rd FSTH SE23 182 C4
Dalmally Rd CROY/NA CR0 203 N7
Dalmeny Av HOLWY N7 118 E9
STRHM/NOR SW16 203 H2
Dalmeny Cl ALP/SUD HA0 135 H3
Dalmeny Crs HSLW TW3 154 C10
Dalmeny Rd BAR EN5 77 M10
CAR SM5 222 B4
ERITH DA8 164 C7
HOLWY N7 118 E9
WPK KT4 200 E10
Dalmeyer Rd WLSDN NW10 136 C1
Dalmore Av ESH/CLAY KT10 218 E3
Dalmore Rd DUL SE21 181 K5
Dalroy Cl SOCK/AV RM15 146 D8
Dalrymple Cl STHGT/OAK N14 98 E1
Dalrymple Rd BROCKY SE4 182 E1
Dalston Gdns STAN HA7 95 K9
Dalston La HACK E8 7 L1
HACK E8 120 A10
Dalton Av MTCM CR4 201 P2
Dalton Cl ORP BR6 207 H10
YEAD UB4 132 E6
Dalton Gn DTCH/LGLY SL3 150 C4
Daltons Rd SWLY BR8 208 D9
Dalton St STALW/RED AL3 38 C5
WNWD SE27 181 J5
Dalton Wy WAT WD17 73 L10
Dalwood St CMBW SE5 159 M7
Dalyell Rd BRXN/ST SW9 158 G9
Damask Cl CHOB/PIR GU24 212 D9
Damask Crs CAN/RD E16 141 K6
Damask Gn HHW HP1 35 H7
Damer Ter WBPTN SW10 157 M6
Dames Rd FSTGT E7 121 M9
Dame St IS N1 6 E7
Damien St WCHPL E1 140 A7
Damigos Rd GVE DA12 191 J4
Damon Cl SCUP DA14 185 L6
Damsel Ct BERM/RHTH SE16 * 19 P2
Damson Dr HYS/HAR UB3 133 H9
Damson Gv SL SL1 149 H1
Damson Wy CAR SM5 222 A5
STAL/WH AL4 39 H4
Damsonwood Rd NWDGN UB2 153 P2
Danbrook Rd STRHM/NOR SW16 202 F1
Danbury Cl BRWN CM15 86 E9
CHDH RM6 123 N1
Danbury Crs SOCK/AV RM15 146 G8
Danbury Ms WLGTN SM6 222 C1
Danbury Rd LOU IG10 82 B10
RAIN RM13 144 G3
Danbury St IS N1 6 D7
Danbury Wy WFD IG8 101 P7
Danby St PECK SE15 159 N9
Dancer Rd FUL/PGN SW6 157 J7
RCH/KEW TW9 155 M9
Dancers Hill Rd BAR EN5 76 G2
Dandelion Cl ROMW/RG RM7 124 F4
Dando Crs BKHTH/KID SE3 161 N9
Dandridge Cl DTCH/LGLY SL3 149 P2
GNWCH SE10 161 L4
Danebury CROY/NA CR0 224 G3
Danebury Av PUT/ROE SW15 178 C3
Daneby Rd CAT SE6 183 H6
Dane Cl AMSS HP7 69 L7
BXLY DA5 186 B3
ORP BR6 226 G2
Dane Ct WOKS/MYFD GU22 233 J1
Danecourt Gdns CROY/NA CR0 203 N10
Danecroft Rd HNHL SE24 181 K1
Danehurst Cl EGH TW20 172 B9
Danehurst Gdns REDBR IG4 122 B3
Danehurst St FUL/PGN SW6 157 H7
Daneland EBAR EN4 78 A10
Danemead Gv NTHLT UB5 114 A10
Danemere St PUT/ROE SW15 156 F9
Dane Pl BOW E3 140 D4
Dane Rd ASHF TW15 174 D9
IL IG1 122 F10
RSEV TN14 246 F3
STHL UB1 133 M9
UED N18 100 B5
WARL CR6 242 C3
WEA W13 135 H9
WIM/MER SW19 201 M1
Danesbury Pk HERT/WAT SG14 25 L4
Danesbury Rd FELT TW13 175 K5
Danes Cl GVW DA11 189 P6
LHD/OX KT22 218 B10
Danescombe LEE/GVPK SE12 183 M4
Danescourt Crs SUT SM1 201 M9
Danescroft Av HDN NW4 * 116 G3
Danescroft Gdns HDN NW4 116 G3
Danesdale Rd HOM E9 140 D1
Danesfield RPLY/SEND GU23 233 J9
Danesfield Cl WOT/HER KT12 197 J10
Danes Ga HRW HA1 114 D1
Daneshill REDH RH1 257 P9
Danes Hl WOKS/MYFD GU22 232 E4
Daneshill Cl REDH RH1 257 P9
Danes Hill School Dr
LHD/OX KT22 * 218 C10
Danesmead COB KT11 217 P7
Danes Rd ROMW/RG RM7 124 D5
The Danes LCOL/BKTW AL2 56 B4
Dane St GINN WC1R 11 N4
Danes Wy BRWN CM15 86 F9
LHD/OX KT22 218 C10
Daneswood Av CAT SE6 183 H6
Daneswood Cl WEY KT13 216 C2
Danethorpe Rd ALP/SUD HA0 135 J1
Danetree Cl HOR/WEW KT19 219 P4
Danetree Rd HOR/WEW KT19 219 P4
Danette Gdns DAGE RM10 124 A7
Daneville Rd CMBW SE5 159 L7
Dangan Rd WAN E11 121 M4
Daniel Bolt Cl POP/IOD E14 140 G7
Daniel Cl CDW/CHF RM16 167 K1
HSLWW TW4 175 N3
TOOT SW17 179 P9
UED N18 100 B5
Daniel Gdns PECK SE15 159 N6
Daniells WGCE AL7 23 K4
Daniel Wy CROY/NA CR0 202 F8
Daniel Pl HDN NW4 116 E4
Daniel Rd EA W5 135 L9
Daniels La WARL CR6 242 E2
Daniel's Rd PECK SE15 160 B9
Daniel Wy BNSTD SM7 221 L10
Dan Leno Wk FUL/PGN SW6 * 157 L6
Dan Manson Dr CHSWK W4 156 A8
Dansey Pl SOHO/SHAV W1D 11 J7
Dansington Rd WELL DA16 163 K10
Danson Crs WELL DA16 163 L9
Danson La WELL DA16 163 L10
Danson Md WELL DA16 163 M9
Danson Rd BXLYHS DA6 185 N1
Danson U/P BFN/LL DA15 185 M2
Dante Rd LBTH SE11 18 C5
Danube St CHEL SW3 15 P7
Danvers Rd CEND/HSY/T N8 118 E2
Danvers St CHEL SW3 15 M10
Danvers Wy CTHM CR3 241 K9
Danyon Cl RAIN RM13 145 K4
Danziger Wy BORE WD6 75 P5
Dapdune Rd GU GU1 250 A10
Daphne Gdns CHING E4 101 K4
Daphne Jackson Rd GUW GU2 267 K1
Daphne St WAND/EARL SW18 179 M2
Daplyn St WCHPL E1 13 N3
Darby Cl STALE/WH AL4 21 L6
D'Arblay St SOHO/CST W1F 11 H6
Darby Cl CTHM CR3 241 K8
Darby Crs SUN TW16 197 K2
Darby Dr WAB EN9 63 H9
Darby Gdns SUN TW16 197 K2
Darcy Av WLGTN SM6 222 D1
Darcy Cl CHES/WCR EN8 62 D7
COUL/CHIP CR5 241 J5
RBRW/HUT CM13 107 N1
TRDG/WHET N20 97 N3
D'Arcy Dr KTN/HRWW/WS HA3 115 J2
D'Arcy Gdns DAGW RM9 144 A3
KTN/HRWW/WS HA3 115 K2
Darcy Pl ASHTD KT21 237 L3
D'Arcy Pl HAYES BR2 205 M4
Darcy Rd ASHTD KT21 237 L2
D'Arcy Rd CHEAM SM3 220 G1
Darcy Rd ISLW TW7 154 F7
STRHM/NOR SW16 202 F2
Darell Rd RCH/KEW TW9 155 M9
Darent Cl SEV TN13 246 D8
Darenth Dr GVE DA12 191 L4
Darenth Gdns BH/WHM TN16 262 G2
Darenth Hl RDART DA2 188 A9
Darenth La SEV TN13 246 F7
SOCK/AV RM15 146 F8
Darenth Park Av RDART DA2 188 D5
Darenth Pl RDART DA2 * 188 C8
Darenth Rd DART DA1 187 P5
STNW/STAM N16 119 N5
WELL DA16 163 K7
Darenth Rd South RDART DA2 188 A7
Darenth Wy HORL RH6 280 A2
RSEV TN14 228 G7
Darenth Wood Rd RDART DA2 188 D3
Darent Md EYN DA4 210 A1
Darent Valley Pth DART DA1 165 L10
ERITH DA8 165 N9
RSEV TN14 229 H5
EYN DA4 229 J2
RSEV TN14 246 F4
EYN DA4 210 A5
RSEV TN14 247 H1
SEV TN13 246 D7
Darfield Rd BROCKY SE4 182 E1
RGUE GU4 250 D7
Darfield Wy NKENS W10 136 G9
Darfur St PUT/ROE SW15 156 G9
Dargate Cl NRWD SE19 181 N10
Darien Rd BTSEA SW11 157 N9
Darkes La POTB/CUF EN6 59 K8
Dark La BRW CM14 106 E6
BRW CM14 106 F9
CHESW EN7 61 P7
HARP AL5 20 A6
RGUW GU3 266 A5
Darlands Dr BAR EN5 76 G9
Darlan Rd FUL/PGN SW6 157 J6
Darlaston Rd WIM/MER SW19 178 G10
Darley Cl ADL/WDHM KT15 215 M2
CROY/NA CR0 204 C6
Darley Cft LCOL/BKTW AL2 * 56 A4
Darley Dene Ct
ADL/WDHM KT15 * 215 M1
Darley Dr NWMAL KT3 200 A2
Darley Gdns MRDN SM4 201 L6
Darley Rd BTSEA SW11 180 B1
ED N9 99 N2
Darling Rd BROCKY SE4 160 F9
Darling Rw WCHPL E1 140 A6
Darlington Ct BRWN CM15 86 F10
Darlington Gdns HARH RM3 105 L6
Darlington Rd WNWD SE27 181 J8
Darlton Cl DART DA1 164 G8
Darmaine Cl SAND/SEL CR2 223 K4
Darndale Cl WALTH E17 100 E10
Darnets Fld RSEV TN14 246 G3
Darnicle Hl CHESW EN7 61 H1
Darnley Pk WEY KT13 196 C10
Darnley Rd GRAYS RM17 * 167 N5
GVW DA11 190 D2
HACK E8 140 A1
WFD IG8 101 M9
Darnley St GVW DA11 190 D3
Darnley Ter NTGHL W11 136 G10
Darns Hl SWLY BR8 208 D7
Darrell Cl DTCH/LGLY SL3 150 C3
Darrell Rd EDUL SE22 181 P1
Darren Cl FSBYPK N4 118 G5
Darrick Wood Rd ORP BR6 206 G9
Darrington Rd BORE WD6 75 K5
Darris Cl YEAD UB4 133 M6
Darr's La BERK HP4 33 J4
Darsley Dr VX/NE SW8 158 E7
Dart Cl DTCH/LGLY SL3 150 E5
UPMR RM14 126 C4
Dartfields HARH RM3 105 L7
Dartford Av ED N9 80 B10
Dartford Gdns CHDH RM6 123 L3
Dartford Rd BXLY DA5 186 D4
DART DA1 187 H2
EYN DA4 209 N6
SEV TN13 247 K10
Dartford St WALW SE17 18 F9
Dart Gn SOCK/AV RM15 146 G8
Dartmoor Wk POP/IOD E14 * 160 F3
Dartmouth Av
WOKN/KNAP GU21 214 F10
Dartmouth Cl NTGHL W11 8 D5
Dartmouth Gv GNWCH SE10 161 H7
Dartmouth Hl GNWCH SE10 161 H7
Dartmouth Park Av KTTN NW5 118 C8
Dartmouth Park Hl KTTN NW5 118 C8
Dartmouth Park Rd KTTN NW5 118 C8
Dartmouth Pl CHSWK W4 156 B5
FSTH SE23 182 B5
Dartmouth Rd CRICK NW2 2 A1
HAYES BR2 205 M7
HDN NW4 116 D4
RSLP HA4 113 H8
SYD SE26 182 A6
Dartmouth Rw GNWCH SE10 161 H8
Dartmouth St STJSPK SW1H 17 J2
Dartmouth Ter GNWCH SE10 161 J7
Dartnell Av BF/WBF KT14 215 M8
Dartnell Cl BF/WBF KT14 215 M8
Dartnell Ct BF/WBF KT14 215 M8
Dartnell Crs BF/WBF KT14 215 L8
Dartnell Park Rd BF/WBF KT14 215 L8
Dartnell Pl BF/WBF KT14 215 L8
Dartnell Rd CROY/NA CR0 203 N7
Dartrey Wk WBPTN SW10 * 157 M6
Dart St MV/WKIL W9 2 C9
The Dart HHNE HP2 36 A1
Dartview Cl GRAYS RM17 168 B3
Darvel Cl WOKN/KNAP GU21 231 M2
Darvells Dr CSHM HP5 50 F5
Darvells Yd RKW/CH/CXG WD3 70 G8
Darville Rd STNW/STAM N16 119 N8
Darvill's La SL SL1 149 J1
Darwell Cl EHAM E6 142 D4
Darwin Cl FBAR/BDGN N11 98 C4
ORP BR6 226 G2
STALW/RED AL3 38 D2
Darwin Dr STHL UB1 134 A8
Darwin Gdns OXHEY WD19 93 K6
Darwin Rd DTCH/LGLY SL3 150 C1
EA W5 155 H4
TIL RM18 168 C7
WDGN N22 99 J9
WELL DA16 163 J9
Darwin St WALW SE17 19 H5
Darylngton Dr GFD/PVL UB6 134 C4
GU GU1 250 E10
The Dashes HLW CM20 29 H10
Dashwood Cl BF/WBF KT14 215 M8
BXLYHS DA6 186 B1
DTCH/LGLY SL3 149 P3
Dashwood Lang Rd
ADL/WDHM KT15 * 215 M2
ADL/WDHM KT15 215 P1
Dashwood Rd CEND/HSY/T N8 118 G4
GVW DA11 190 D4
Dassett Rd WNWD SE27 181 J8
Datchelor Pl CMBW SE5 * 159 L7
Datchet Cl HHNE HP2 36 C1
Datchet Pl DTCH/LGLY SL3 149 N7
Datchet Rd CAT SE6 182 E6
DTCH/LGLY SL3 149 L3
WDSR SL4 149 J6
Datchworth Turn HHNE HP2 36 D6
Date St WALW SE17 18 G8
Daubeney Gdns TOTM N17 99 K8
Daubeney Rd CLPT E5 120 D10
TOTM N17 99 K8
Dault Rd WAND/EARL SW18 179 M2
Davema Cl CHST BR7 206 D1
Davenant Rd ARCH N19 118 E7
Davenant St WCHPL E1 13 P4
Davenham Av NTHWD HA6 92 G5
Davenport Cl TEDD TW11 * 176 F9
Davenport Rd CAT SE6 182 G2
SCUP DA14 185 N5
Daventer Dr STAN HA7 94 E8
Daventry Av WALTH E17 120 F4
Daventry Cl DTCH/LGLY SL3 151 J7
Daventry Gdns HARH RM3 105 K6
Daventry Rd HARH RM3 105 K6
Daventry St CAMTN NW1 9 N3
Davern Cl GNWCH SE10 161 L3
Davey Cl HOLWY N7 5 P2
PLMGR N13 98 G6
Davey Rd HOM E9 140 F2
Davey St PECK SE15 19 M10
David Av GFD/PVL UB6 134 D5
David Cl HYS/HAR UB3 152 E6
David Dr HARH RM3 105 P7
Davidge Pl BEAC HP9 88 B6
Davidge St STHWK SE1 18 C2
David Ms MHST W1U 10 B3
David Rd BCTR RM8 123 P7
DTCH/LGLY SL3 151 J8
Davidson Gdns VX/NE SW8 158 F6
Davidson Rd CROY/NA CR0 203 M8
DTCH/LGLY SL3 150 C4
Davidson Wy ROMW/RG RM7 124 F4
David's Rd FSTH SE23 182 B4
David St SRTFD E15 141 J1
Davids Wy BARK/HLT IG6 103 H8
David Twigg Cl KUTN/CMB KT2 199 K1
Davies Cl CROY/NA CR0 203 N6
GODL GU7 267 J10
RAIN RM13 145 K5
Davies La WAN E11 121 K7
Davies Ms MYFR/PKLN W1K 10 D8
Davies St HERT/BAY SG13 25 M5
MYFR/PKLN W1K 10 D7
Davies Wk ISLW TW7 154 C7
Davington Gdns BCTR RM8 123 L10
Davington Rd BCTR RM8 143 L1
Davinia Cl WFD IG8 102 C7
Davis Av GVW DA11 190 B4
Davis Cl SEV TN13 247 K8
Davis Ct STAL AL1 * 38 D6
Davison Cl CHES/WCR EN8 62 C4
Davison Dr CHES/WCR EN8 62 C4
Davis Rd ACT W3 136 C10
CDW/CHF RM16 167 L2
CHSGTN KT9 219 M1
SOCK/AV RM15 146 C10
WEY KT13 216 A6
Davis St PLSTW E13 141 N4
Davisville Rd SHB W12 156 D1
Davos Cl WOKS/MYFD GU22 232 B5
Davys Cl STALE/WH AL4 21 K4
Davy's Pl GVE DA12 191 H9
Dawell Dr BH/WHM TN16 243 P3
Dawes Av HCH RM12 125 N8
ISLW TW7 176 F1
Dawes Cl CSHM HP5 50 G8
HGDN/ICK UB10 131 P4
RDART DA2 188 E1
Dawes Ct ESH/CLAY KT10 218 A1
Dawes East Rd SL SL1 128 B6
Dawes La RKW/CH/CXG WD3 71 J2
STALE/WH AL4 21 J2
Dawes Moor Cl SLN SL2 129 P8
Dawes Rd FUL/PGN SW6 157 J6
HGDN/ICK UB10 131 P4
Dawes St WALW SE17 19 H7
Dawley WGCE AL7 23 J2
Dawley Av UX/CGN UB8 132 C7

Dawley Ct HHNE HP2 36 B2
Dawley Gn SOCK/AV RM15 146 F8
Dawley Pde HYS/HAR UB3 132 E9
Dawley Ride DTCH/LGLY SL3 151 H7
Dawley Rd HYS/HAR UB3 132 E9
HYS/HAR UB3 152 E1
Dawlish Av GFD/PVL UB6 134 F4
PLMGR N13 98 F5
WAND/EARL SW18 179 L5
Dawlish Dr GDMY/SEVK IG3 123 J9
RSLP HA4 113 H7
Dawlish Rd CRICK NW2 136 G1
LEY E10 121 H7
TOTM N17 119 P1
Dawnay Gdns WAND/EARL SW18 179 N5
Dawnay Rd GT/LBKH KT23 254 A2
WAND/EARL SW18 179 M5
Dawn Cl HSLWW TW4 153 M9
Dawn Crs SRTFD E15 141 J3
Dawney Hl CHOB/PIR GU24 230 D7
Dawneys Rd CHOB/PIR GU24 230 D8
Dawn Redwood Cl
DTCH/LGLY SL3 150 D9
Dawn Ri CRAWE RH10 285 H2
Dawpool Rd CRICK NW2 116 C7
Daws Hl CHING E4 81 H7
Daws La MLHL NW7 96 C6
Dawson Av BARK IG11 143 J2
STMC/STPC BR5 207 L2
Dawson Cl HYS/HAR UB3 132 E7
WDSR SL4 148 F8
WOOL/PLUM SE18 162 F3
Dawson Dr RAIN RM13 145 J2
SWLY BR8 186 F10
Dawson Gdns BARK IG11 143 J2
Dawson Pl BAY/PAD W2 8 E7
Dawson Rd BF/WBF KT14 215 N7
CRICK NW2 116 F10
KUT/HW KT1 199 L3
Dawson St BETH E2 7 M8
Dawson Ter ED N9 * 100 B1
Daybrook Rd WIM/MER SW19 201 L2
Dayemead WGCE AL7 23 L8
Daylesford Av PUT/ROE SW15 156 D10
Daylop Dr CHIG IG7 103 L4
Daymer Gdns PIN HA5 113 K2
Daymerslea Rdg LHD/OX KT22 237 H7
Day's Acre SAND/SEL CR2 223 N6
Daysbrook Rd BRXS/STRHM SW2 180 G4
Days Cl HAT AL10 40 C4
Dayseys Hl REDH RH1 277 H9
Days La BFN/LL DA15 185 H3
BRWN CM15 86 F8
Days Md HAT AL10 40 C4
Dayspring GUW GU2 249 N6
Dayton Dr ERITH DA8 165 L5
Dayton Gv PECK SE15 160 B7
Deacon Cl COB KT11 235 J5
PUR/KEN CR8 222 F5
STAL AL1 38 C10
The Deacon Est CHING E4 * 100 E7
Deacon Fld GUW GU2 249 M9
Deacon Ms IS N1 7 H4
Deacon Pl CTHM CR3 241 K9
Deacon Rd CRICK NW2 136 D1
KUTN/CMB KT2 199 L1
Deacons Cl BORE WD6 75 M8
PIN HA5 93 J10
Deaconsfield Rd HHS/BOV HP3 35 N9
Deacons Hts BORE WD6 75 M10
Deacons Hl OXHEY WD19 73 K10
Deacon's Hill Rd BORE WD6 75 L9
Deacons Leas ORP BR6 226 G1
Deacons Ri EFNCH N2 117 N3
Deacons Ter IS N1 * 6 F1
Deacons Wk HPTN TW12 175 P7
Deacon Wy WALW SE17 18 F5
WFD IG8 102 C8
Deadhearn La CSTG HP8 90 B2
Deadman's Ash La
RKW/CH/CXG WD3 71 L1
Deakin Cl WATW WD18 92 F1
Deakins Ter ORP BR6 207 K7
Deal Av SL SL1 128 E8
Deal Porters Wy
BERM/RHTH SE16 160 B2
Deal Rd TOOT SW17 180 B9
Deals Gtwy LEW SE13 160 G7
Deal St WCHPL E1 13 N3
Dealtree Cl BRWN CM15 86 G1
Dealtry Rd PUT/ROE SW15 156 F10
Deal Wk BRXN/ST SW9 159 H6
Deanacre Cl CFSP/GDCR SL9 90 B7
Dean Bradley St WEST SW1P 17 L4
Dean Cl BERM/RHTH SE16 140 C10
HGDN/ICK UB10 132 A2
HOM E9 120 B10
WDSR SL4 148 C9
WOKS/MYFD GU22 233 H2
Dean Ct ALP/SUD HA0 114 G8
GSTN WD25 * 55 L9
Deancroft Rd CFSP/GDCR SL9 90 B7
Deancross St WCHPL E1 140 B8
Dean Dr STAN HA7 95 K10
Deane Av RSLP HA4 113 J10
Deane Ct NTHWD HA6 * 92 F9
Deane Croft Rd PIN HA5 113 K4
Deanery Cl EFNCH N2 117 P2
Deanery Ms MYFR/PKLN W1K * 10 D9
Deanery Rd EDEN TN8 262 F10
SRTFD E15 141 K1
Deanery St MYFR/PKLN W1K 10 D9
Deane Wy RSLP HA4 113 J4
Dean Farrar St STJSPK SW1H 17 K3
Dean Fld HHS/BOV HP3 52 D3
Deanfield Gdns CROY/NA CR0 * 223 L2
Dean Gdns WALTH E17 121 J2
Deanhill Ct MORT/ESHN SW14 * 155 N10
Deanhill Rd MORT/ESHN SW14 155 N10
Dean La REDH RH1 240 D10
REDH RH1 240 F10
Dean Moore Cl STAL AL1 38 C7
Deanoak La REIG RH2 274 G10
Dean Rd CRICK NW2 136 F1
CROY/NA CR0 223 L1
HPTN TW12 175 P8
HSLW TW3 176 A1
THMD SE28 143 K10
Dean Ryle St WEST SW1P 17 L5
Deansbrook Cl EDGW HA8 95 P8
Deansbrook Rd EDGW HA8 95 N8
EDGW HA8 96 A7
Dean's Buildings WALW SE17 19 H7
Deans Cl ABLGY WD5 54 E8
AMS HP6 69 L3
CHSWK W4 155 N5
CROY/NA CR0 203 N10
EDGW HA8 95 P7
KWD/TDW/WH KT20 238 E10
SLN SL2 129 N3
Deans Ct BFOR GU20 212 C4
STP EC4M 12 D6
Deanscroft Av CDALE/KGS NW9 115 P7
Dean's Dr EDGW HA8 96 A6
PLMGR N13 99 J7
Deansfield CTHM CR3 259 N1
Dean's Gdns STALE/WH AL4 38 F2
Deans Gate Cl FSTH SE23 182 C6
Dean's La EDGW HA8 95 P7
KWD/TDW/WH KT20 256 E1
REDH RH1 259 H9
Dean's Ms CAVSQ/HST W1G * 10 F5
Deans Rd BRW CM14 106 G4
HNWL W7 154 E1
REDH RH1 258 D6
SUT SM1 201 L10
Dean Stanley St WEST SW1P 17 L4
Dean St FSTGT E7 121 M10
SOHO/SHAV W1D 11 J5
Deans Wk COUL/CHIP CR5 241 H4
Deans Wy EDGW HA8 95 P6
Deansway CSHM HP5 50 G5
ED N9 99 M4
EFNCH N2 117 N2
HHS/BOV HP3 36 A9
Deans Yd WEST SW1P 17 K3
Dean Trench St WEST SW1P 17 L4
Dean Vls COB KT11 * 217 K9
Dean Wk GT/LBKH KT23 254 A2
Dean Wy CSTG HP8 89 M4
NWDGN UB2 154 A1
Deanway CSTG HP8 89 N4
Dean Wood Rd BEAC HP9 89 J9
Dearne Cl STAN HA7 94 F6
De'Arn Gdns MTCM CR4 201 P3
Dearsley Rd EN EN1 79 P7
Deason St SRTFD E15 * 141 H3
De Barowe Ms HBRY N5 119 J9
Debden Cl CDALE/KGS NW9 96 B9
KUTN/CMB KT2 177 J8
WFD IG8 102 A8
Debden La LOU IG10 82 E5
Debden Rd LOU IG10 82 E4
De Beauvoir Crs IS N1 7 J5
De Beauvoir Est IS N1 7 J5
De Beauvoir Rd IS N1 7 J4
De Beauvoir Sq IS N1 7 K4
Debenham Rd CHESW EN7 62 A3
Debnams Rd BERM/RHTH SE16 160 B3
De Bohun Av STHGT/OAK N14 78 C10
Deborah Cl ISLW TW7 154 D7
Deborah Crs RSLP HA4 112 E5
Debrabant Cl ERITH DA8 164 E5
De Broome Rd FELT TW13 175 K4
De Burgh Gdns
KWD/TDW/WH KT20 238 G5
De Burgh Pk BNSTD SM7 239 L2
Deburgh Rd WIM/MER SW19 179 M10
Decies Wy SLN SL2 129 M3
Decima St STHWK SE1 19 J3
Decimus Cl THHTH CR7 203 L4
Deck Cl BERM/RHTH SE16 140 C10
Decoy Av GLDGN NW11 117 H3
De Crespigny Pk CMBW SE5 159 L8
Dedisham Cl CRAWE RH10 284 B8
Dedswell Dr RGUE GU4 251 K5
Dedworth Dr WDSR SL4 148 D7
Dedworth Rd WDSR SL4 148 A8
Dee Cl UPMR RM14 126 D4
Deeley Rd VX/NE SW8 158 E7
Deena Cl ACT W3 135 L8
SL SL1 128 D9
Deep Acres AMS HP6 68 F2
Deepdale WIM/MER SW19 178 G7
Deepdale Av HAYES BR2 205 L4
Deepdale Cl FBAR/BDGN N11 98 B7
Deepdene POTB/CUF EN6 58 G7
Deepdene Av CROY/NA CR0 203 N10
RDKG RH5 273 H2
Deepdene Avenue Rd DORK RH4 255 H10
Deepdene Cl WAN E11 121 M2
Deepdene Ct WCHMH N21 79 J10
Deepdene Dr RDKG RH5 273 H2
Deepdene Gdns
BRXS/STRHM SW2 180 G3
DORK RH4 272 G1
Deepdene Park Rd RDKG RH5 273 J1
Deepdene Pth LOU IG10 82 E8
Deepdene Rd HNHL SE24 159 K10
LOU IG10 82 D8
WELL DA16 163 K9
Deepdene V DORK RH4 255 H10
Deepdene Wd RDKG RH5 273 J2
Deep Fld DTCH/LGLY SL3 149 N6
Deepfields HORL RH6 280 A2
Deepfield Wy COUL/CHIP CR5 240 F2
Deep Pool La CHOB/PIR GU24 213 M9
Deeprose Cl GUW GU2 249 N6
Deepwell Cl ISLW TW7 154 F7
Deepwood La GFD/PVL UB6 134 C5
Deerbarn Rd GUW GU2 249 N9
Deerbrook Rd HNHL SE24 181 J4
Deer Cl HERT/BAY SG13 25 N5
Deerdale Rd HNHL SE24 159 K10
Deere Av RAIN RM13 145 H1
Deerfield Cl CDALE/KGS NW9 116 C3
WARE SG12 26 C1
Deerhurst Cl FELT TW13 175 H7
HART DA3 211 P3
Deerhurst Crs HPTN TW12 176 B8
Deerhurst Rd KIL/WHAMP NW6 136 G2
STRHM/NOR SW16 180 G8
Deerings Dr PIN HA5 113 H3
Deerings Rd REIG RH2 257 L10
Deerleap Gv CHING E4 80 G9
Deerleap La RSEV TN14 227 N9
Deerleap Rd DORK RH4 272 A3
Dee Rd RCH/KEW TW9 155 L10
WDSR SL4 * 148 B6
Deer Pk HLWW/ROY CM19 46 D4
Deer Park Cl KUTN/CMB KT2 177 N10
Deer Park Gdns MTCM CR4 * 201 N4
Deer Park Rd WIM/MER SW19 201 M2
Deer Park Wk CSHM HP5 51 K4
Deer Park Wy WAB EN9 80 G2
WWKM BR4 205 L9
Deers Farm Cl RPLY/SEND GU23 233 P2
Deerswood Av HAT AL10 40 E6
Deerswood Cl CRAWW RH11 283 L6
CTHM CR3 241 P10
Deerswood Rd CRAWW RH11 283 L6
Deeside Rd TOOT SW17 179 N6
Dee St POP/IOD E14 141 H8
The Dee HHNE HP2 36 A1
Deeves Hall La POTB/CUF EN6 58 B9
Dee Wy HOR/WEW KT19 220 B6
ROM RM1 104 F9
Defence Cl THMD SE28 143 H10
Defiant Wy WLGTN SM6 222 F4
Defoe Av RCH/KEW TW9 155 M6
Defoe Cl TOOT SW17 179 P9
Defoe Pde CDW/CHF RM16 168 E2
Defoe Pl TOOT SW17 179 P5
TOOT SW17 180 A7
Defoe Rd BERM/RHTH SE16 160 E1
STNW/STAM N16 119 M7
Defoe Wy CRW RM5 104 B7
De Frene Rd SYD SE26 182 D7
Degema Rd CHST BR7 184 E8
Dehar Crs CDALE/KGS NW9 116 C5
De Haviland Dr
WOOL/PLUM SE18 162 E5
De Havilland Cl HAT AL10 40 C3
Dehavilland Cl NTHLT UB5 133 L5
De Havilland Cl STALE/WH AL4 39 P5
De Havilland Ct IL IG1 122 G6
RAD WD7 * 57 K8
De Havilland Dr WEY KT13 215 P7
De Havilland Rd EDGW HA8 95 N10
HEST TW5 153 K6
De Havilland Wy ABLGY WD5 54 G8
STWL/WRAY TW19 173 N2
Deimos Dr HHNE HP2 36 B3
Dekker Rd DUL SE21 181 M2
Delabole Rd REDH RH1 258 F5
Delacourt Rd BKHTH/KID SE3 161 N6
Delafield Rd CHARL SE7 161 N4
GRAYS RM17 168 A4
Delaford Cl IVER SL0 * 131 J8
Delaford Rd BERM/RHTH SE16 160 A4
Delaford St FUL/PGN SW6 157 H6
Delagarde Rd BH/WHM TN16 262 F2
Delahay Ri BERK HP4 33 N3
Delamare Crs CROY/NA CR0 204 B6
Delamare Rd CHES/WCR EN8 62 E5
Delamere Gdns MLHL NW7 96 A6
Delamere Rd BORE WD6 75 N5
EA W5 155 K1
REIG RH2 275 L4
RYNPK SW20 200 G1
YEAD UB4 133 L9
Delamere St BAY/PAD W2 9 J4
Delamere Ter BAY/PAD W2 9 H3
Delancey Pas CAMTN NW1 4 F6
Delancey St CAMTN NW1 4 F6
Delaporte Cl EW KT17 220 B8
De Lapre Cl STMC/STPC BR5 207 N7
De Lara Wy WOKN/KNAP GU21 232 A4
Delargy Cl CDW/CHF RM16 168 E2
De Laune St WALW SE17 18 C8
Delaware Rd MV/WKIL W9 8 G1
Delawyk Crs HNHL SE24 181 L2
Delcombe Av WPK KT4 200 F8
Delderfield ASHTD KT21 237 J6
Delfont Cl CRAWE RH10 284 E9
Delhi Rd EN EN1 99 N1
Delhi St IS N1 5 M6
Delia St WAND/EARL SW18 179 L3
Delisle Rd THMD SE28 163 H1
Delius Cl BORE WD6 75 H10
Delius Gv SRTFD E15 141 H4
Della Pth CLPT E5 119 P8
Dellbow Rd EBED/NFELT TW14 175 J1
Dell Cl CSHM HP5 50 E5
LHD/OX KT22 236 C9
RDKG RH5 255 H3
SLN SL2 109 H10
SRTFD E15 141 J3
WFD IG8 101 N4
WLGTN SM6 222 D1
Dellcott Cl WGCW AL8 22 F4
Dellcut Rd HHNE HP2 36 B4
Dell Farm Rd RSLP HA4 112 E3
Dellfield CSHM HP5 50 F5
STAL AL1 38 E7
Dellfield Av BERK HP4 33 N3
Dellfield Cl BECK BR3 205 H1
BERK HP4 33 M3
RAD WD7 74 D1
WAT WD17 73 H6
Dellfield Crs UX/CGN UB8 131 M6
Dellfield Pde UX/CGN UB8 * 131 M6
Dellfield Rd HAT AL10 40 D4
Dell La EW KT17 220 D2
Dell Lees BEAC HP9 89 H7
Dellmeadow ABLGY WD5 54 F6
Dell Meadow HHS/BOV HP3 35 P10
Dellors Cl BAR EN5 76 G9
Dellow Cl GNTH/NBYPK IG2 122 G5
Dellow St WCHPL E1 140 A9
Dell Ri LCOL/BKTW AL2 56 A2
Dell Rd BERK HP4 33 J2
EW KT17 220 D3
GRAYS RM17 167 N3
PEND EN3 80 B4
WATN WD24 73 H3
WDR/YW UB7 152 A2
Dells Cl CHING E4 100 G1
TEDD TW11 176 E9
Dellside DEN/HRF UB9 111 M3
Dell Side WATN WD24 73 H3
Dell's Ms PIM SW1V * 17 H6
Dellsome La STALE/WH AL4 40 C9
The Dells HHS/BOV HP3 36 C7
Dellswood Cl HERT/BAY SG13 25 M6
Dells Wood Cl HOD EN11 26 E10
The Dell ABYW SE2 163 K4
ALP/SUD HA0 114 G10
BECK BR3 * 182 F10
BTFD TW8 155 H5
BXLY DA5 186 F4
CFSP/GDCR SL9 90 B7
EBED/NFELT TW14 175 J3
HERT/BAY SG13 25 K8
HORL RH6 279 M2
HORL RH6 280 C3
KWD/TDW/WH KT20 238 F7
NRWD SE19 203 N1
NTHWD HA6 92 F3
PIN HA5 93 L10
RAD WD7 74 F2
RBRW/HUT CM13 106 G7
REIG RH2 * 257 K9
STAL AL1 38 F4
SWCM DA10 188 G1
WAB EN9 81 H2
WFD IG8 101 N4
WOKN/KNAP GU21 231 P5
Dell Wk NWMAL KT3 200 B2
Dell Wy WEA W13 135 H8
Dellwood RKW/CH/CXG WD3 91 L2
Dellwood Gdns CLAY IG5 122 D1
Delmar Av HHNE HP2 36 E7
Delmeade Rd CSHM HP5 50 F8
Delme Crs BKHTH/KID SE3 161 N8
Delmey Cl CROY/NA CR0 203 N10
Deloraine St DEPT SE8 160 F7
Delorme St HMSMTH W6 156 G5
Delta Centre ALP/SUD HA0 * 135 L3
Delta Cl CHOB/PIR GU24 213 L6
WPK KT4 200 B10
Delta Dr HORL RH6 280 B6
Delta Est BETH E2 * 7 N9
Delta Gain OXHEY WD19 93 L3
Delta Gv NTHLT UB5 133 L5
Delta Rd CHOB/PIR GU24 213 L6
WOKN/KNAP GU21 232 D2
WPK KT4 200 B10
Delta St BETH E2 7 N9
Delta Wy EGH TW20 194 F1
De Luci Rd ERITH DA8 164 D4
De Lucy St ABYW SE2 163 L3
Delvers Md DAGE RM10 124 D9
Delverton Rd WALW SE17 18 D8
Delves KWD/TDW/WH KT20 238 G7
Delvino Rd FUL/PGN SW6 157 K7
De Mandeville Ga EN EN1 79 P8
Demesne Rd WLGTN SM6 222 E1
Demeta Cl WBLY HA9 115 P8
De Montfort Pde
STRHM/NOR SW16 * 180 F6
De Montfort Rd
STRHM/NOR SW16 180 F6
De Morgan Rd FUL/PGN SW6 157 L9
Dempster Cl SURB KT6 199 H8
Dempster Rd WAND/EARL SW18 179 M1
Denbar Pde ROMW/RG RM7 124 D2
Denberry Dr SCUP DA14 185 L6
Denbigh Cl CHST BR7 184 C9
EMPK RM11 125 N2
HHNE HP2 35 P7
NTGHL W11 8 D7
STHL UB1 133 N8
SUT SM1 221 J2
WLSDN NW10 136 B2
Denbigh Dr HYS/HAR UB3 152 D1
Denbigh Gdns
RCHPK/HAM TW10 177 L1
Denbigh Pl PIM SW1V 16 G7
Denbigh Rd EHAM E6 142 A5
HSLW TW3 154 A8
NTGHL W11 8 D7
STHL UB1 133 N8
WEA W13 134 G9
Denbigh St PIM SW1V 16 G6
Denbigh Ter NTGHL W11 8 D7
Denbridge Rd BMLY BR1 206 C2
Denby Gra HLWE CM17 47 P1
Denby Rd COB KT11 217 K8
Denchers Plat CRAWW RH11 283 N4
Dencliffe ASHF TW15 * 174 B8
Den Cl BECK BR3 205 J4
Dendridge Cl EN EN1 80 A3
Dendy St BAL SW12 180 B4
Dene Av BFN/LL DA15 185 L3
HSLW TW3 153 N9
Dene Cl BROCKY SE4 160 D9
COUL/CHIP CR5 239 P5
HAYES BR2 205 L8
HORL RH6 279 P2
RDART DA2 186 F7
WPK KT4 200 C9
Denecroft Crs HGDN/ICK UB10 132 C3
Denecroft Gdns GRAYS RM17 168 A2
Dene Dr HART DA3 211 N2
ORP BR6 207 L10
Denefield Dr PUR/KEN CR8 241 L1
Dene Gdns STAN HA7 95 H6
THDIT KT7 198 F9
Dene Holm Rd GVW DA11 190 B6
Denehurst Gdns ACT W3 135 N10
HDN NW4 116 F4
RCHPK/HAM TW10 155 M10
WFD IG8 101 N5
WHTN TW2 176 C3
Dene Pth SOCK/AV RM15 146 F8
Dene Pl WOKN/KNAP GU21 231 N4
Dene Rd ASHTD KT21 237 L5
BKHH IG9 102 B2
DART DA1 187 N3
GU GU1 268 B1
NTHWD HA6 92 D7
NTHWD HA6 92 F7
TRDG/WHET N20 98 A2
Dene St DORK RH4 272 G2
Dene Street Gdns DORK RH4 272 G2
The Dene BELMT SM2 221 J7
CROY/NA CR0 224 C1
E/WMO/HCT KT8 197 N5
SEV TN13 265 J2
WBLY HA9 115 K9
WEA W13 134 G7
Dene Tye CRAWE RH10 284 D6
Dene Wk HART DA3 211 K3
Denewood BAR EN5 77 M9
EW KT17 * 220 B9
Denewood Cl WAT WD17 72 G3
Denewood Rd HGT N6 117 P4
Denfield DORK RH4 272 G4
Dengie Wk IS N1 6 E5
Denham Av DEN/HRF UB9 111 J7
Denham Cl DEN/HRF UB9 111 K8
HHNE HP2 36 B1
Denham Court Dr DEN/HRF UB9 111 M7
Denham Crs MTCM CR4 202 A4
Denham Dr GNTH/NBYPK IG2 122 F4
Denham Green Cl DEN/HRF UB9 111 K5
Denham Green La DEN/HRF UB9 111 J4
Denham La CFSP/GDCR SL9 90 C7
Denham Ldg DEN/HRF UB9 * 131 M1
Denham Pde DEN/HRF UB9 * 111 J8
Denham Pl DEN/HRF UB9 111 J10
DEN/HRF UB9 * 111 K6
Denham Rd EBED/NFELT TW14 175 K3
EGH TW20 172 D7
EW KT17 220 C8
IVER SL0 130 G3
TRDG/WHET N20 98 A4
Denham Wk CFSP/GDCR SL9 90 C7
Denham Wy BARK IG11 143 H3
BORE WD6 75 P5
DEN/HRF UB9 111 K8
Denham Wy (North Orbital Road) RKW/CH/CXG WD3 91 H2
Denholme Rd MV/WKIL W9 2 D9
Denholme Wk RAIN RM13 144 G1
Denholm Gdns RGUE GU4 250 D7
Denison Cl EFNCH N2 117 M1
Denison Rd EA W5 135 H6
FELT TW13 174 G7
WIM/MER SW19 179 N9
Deniston Av BXLY DA5 185 N4
Denleigh Gdns THDIT KT7 * 198 D6
WCHMH N21 99 H1
Denly Wy LTWR GU18 212 B6
Denman Dr ASHF TW15 174 C9
ESH/CLAY KT10 218 F3
GLDGN NW11 117 K3
Denman Dr North GLDGN NW11 117 K3
Denman Dr South GLDGN NW11 117 K3
Denman Rd PECK SE15 159 N7
Denmans CRAWE RH10 284 E6
Denman St SOHO/SHAV W1D 11 J8
Denmark Av WIM/MER SW19 179 H10
Denmark Ct MRDN SM4 201 K5
Denmark Gdns CAR SM5 202 A10
Denmark Gv IS N1 6 A7
Denmark Hl HNHL SE24 159 L10
Denmark Hill Dr
CDALE/KGS NW9 116 D1
Denmark Rd BMLY BR1 205 N1
CAR SM5 202 A10
CEND/HSY/T N8 118 G2
CMBW SE5 159 K7
KIL/WHAMP NW6 2 E8
KUT/HW KT1 199 K3
SNWD SE25 204 A5
WEA W13 134 G9
WHTN TW2 176 C6
WIM/MER SW19 178 G9
Denmark St LSQ/SEVD WC2H 11 K6
PLSTW E13 141 N7
TOTM N17 100 A9
WAN E11 121 K8
WAT WD17 73 J6
Denmark Ter EFNCH N2 * 118 A1
Denmead Cl CFSP/GDCR SL9 110 B5
Denmead Rd CROY/NA CR0 203 J8
Dennan Rd SURB KT6 199 L8
Denne Rd CRAWW RH11 283 N8
Denner Rd CHING E4 100 F3
Denne Ter HACK E8 7 M6
Dennett Rd CROY/NA CR0 203 H7
Dennett's Gv NWCR SE14 160 C8
Dennettsland Rd EDEN TN8 262 F10
Dennett's Rd NWCR SE14 160 B7
Denning Av CROY/NA CR0 223 H2
Denning Cl HPTN TW12 175 N9
STJWD NW8 3 K9
Denning Rd HAMP NW3 117 N9
Dennington Park Rd
KIL/WHAMP NW6 2 F1
The Denningtons WPK KT4 200 B9
Dennis Av WBLY HA9 115 L10
Dennis Cl ASHF TW15 174 E10
REDH RH1 257 P8
Dennises La UPMR RM14 146 E2
Dennis Gdns STAN HA7 95 H6
Dennis La STAN HA7 94 G5
Dennis Pde STHGT/OAK N14 * 98 E2
Dennis Park Crs RYNPK SW20 201 H1
Dennis Reeve Cl MTCM CR4 202 A1
Dennis Rd E/WMO/HCT KT8 198 B4
GVW DA11 190 D6
UPMR RM14 146 F3
Dennis Wy CLAP SW4 158 E9
GU GU1 250 B5
SL SL1 128 C9
Denny Av WAB EN9 63 J10
Denny Crs LBTH SE11 18 B7
Denny Gdns DAGW RM9 143 L2
Denny Ga CHES/WCR EN8 62 E3
Denny Rd DTCH/LGLY SL3 * 150 C3
ED N9 100 A2
Denny's La BERK HP4 33 L7
Denny St LBTH SE11 18 B7
Den Rd HAYES BR2 205 J3
Densham Dr PUR/KEN CR8 223 H10
Densham Rd SRTFD E15 141 K3
Densley Cl WGCW AL8 22 F3
Densole Cl BECK BR3 * 204 D1
Densworth Gv ED N9 100 B3
Dent Cl SOCK/AV RM15 146 F8
Denton Cl BAR EN5 76 F9
REDH RH1 276 B5
Denton Court Rd GVE DA12 191 H4
Denton Gv WOT/HER KT12 197 M9
Denton Rd CEND/HSY/T N8 118 G3
DART DA1 186 F3
TWK TW1 177 J2
UED N18 99 N5
WELL DA16 163 M6
Denton St GVE DA12 191 H3
WAND/EARL SW18 179 L2
Denton Ter BXLY DA5 * 186 F5
Denton Wy CLPT E5 120 C8
WOKN/KNAP GU21 231 M3
Denton Whf GVE DA12 * 191 J2
Dents Gv KWD/TDW/WH KT20 257 J4
Dents Rd BTSEA SW11 180 A2
Denvale Trade Pk MTCM CR4 201 N4
Denvale Wk WOKN/KNAP GU21 231 M4
Denver Cl ORP BR6 207 H6
Denver Rd DART DA1 187 H3
STNW/STAM N16 119 M5
Denyer St CHEL SW3 15 P5
Denziloe Av HGDN/ICK UB10 132 C5
Denzil Rd GUW GU2 267 N1
WLSDN NW10 116 C10
Deodar Rd PUT/ROE SW15 157 J10
Deodora Cl TRDG/WHET N20 97 P4
Departures Rd HORL RH6 280 A7
Depot Ap CRICK NW2 116 G9
Depot Rd CRAWW RH11 283 N4
EW KT17 220 B9
HSLW TW3 154 C9
Depot St CMBW SE5 18 G10
Deptford Br DEPT SE8 160 F7
Deptford Broadway NWCR SE14 160 F7
Deptford Church St DEPT SE8 160 F5
Deptford Gn DEPT SE8 160 F5
Deptford High St DEPT SE8 160 F5
Deptford Market DEPT SE8 * 160 F6
Deptford Whf DEPT SE8 160 E3
De Quincey Ms CAN/RD E16 141 M10
De Quincey Rd TOTM N17 99 L9
Derby Arms Rd EPSOM KT18 238 C3
Derby Av KTN/HRWW/WS HA3 94 C9
NFNCH/WDSPK N12 97 M6
ROMW/RG RM7 124 D4
UPMR RM14 125 N8
Derby Cl EPSOM KT18 238 E5
Derby Ga WHALL SW1A 17 L1
Derby Hl FSTH SE23 182 B5
Derby Hill Crs FSTH SE23 182 B5
Derby Rd BRYLDS KT5 199 M8
CROY/NA CR0 203 J9
FSTGT E7 142 A2
GFD/PVL UB6 134 A3
GUW GU2 249 L10
HOD EN11 45 J5
HOM E9 140 C3
HSLW TW3 154 A10
MORT/ESHN SW14 155 N10
PEND EN3 80 A9
SUT SM1 221 J3
SWFD E18 101 L9
UED N18 100 B6
UX/CGN UB8 131 M4
WAT WD17 73 K8
WIM/MER SW19 179 K10
Derby Road Br GRAYS RM17 167 N4
Derbyshire St BETH E2 7 P10
Derby Stables Rd EPSOM KT18 238 B3
Derby St MYFR/PICC W1J 10 D10
Dereham Pl CRW RM5 104 C7
SDTCH EC2A 13 K1
Dereham Rd BARK IG11 143 J1
Derek Av HOR/WEW KT19 219 M3
WBLY HA9 135 N2
WLGTN SM6 202 C10
Derek Cl HOR/WEW KT19 219 N2
Derek Walcott Cl HNHL SE24 * 181 J1
Derham Gdns UPMR RM14 126 B8
Deri Av RAIN RM13 145 J6
Dericote St HACK E8 7 P5
Deri Dene Cl STWL/WRAY TW19 * 173 P2
Derifall Cl EHAM E6 142 C7
Dering Pl CROY/NA CR0 223 K1
Dering Rd CROY/NA CR0 223 K1
Dering St OXSTW W1C 10 E6
Dering Wy GVE DA12 191 J4
Derinton Rd TOOT SW17 180 B7
Derley Rd NWDGN UB2 153 K2
Dermody Gdns LEW SE13 * 183 J1
Dermody Rd LEW SE13 183 J1
Deronda Rd HNHL SE24 181 J4
De Ros Pl EGH TW20 172 D9
Deroy Cl CAR SM5 222 A3
Derrick Av SAND/SEL CR2 223 K6
Derrick Gdns CHARL SE7 161 P2
Derrick Rd BECK BR3 204 E3
Derry Av SOCK/AV RM15 146 F7
Derrydown WOKS/MYFD GU22 231 N7
Derry Downs STMC/STPC BR5 207 M6
Derry Leys HAT AL10 40 B2
Derry Rd CROY/NA CR0 202 F10
Derry St KENS W8 14 G2
Dersingham Av MNPK E12 122 C9
Dersingham Rd CRICK NW2 117 H8
Derwent Av CDALE/KGS NW9 116 B3
EBAR EN4 98 A2
HGDN/ICK UB10 112 B7
MLHL NW7 96 A6
PIN HA5 93 M7
PUT/ROE SW15 178 B7
UED N18 99 L6
Derwent Cl ADL/WDHM KT15 215 N2
AMSS HP7 69 N5
CRAWW RH11 283 J8
DART DA1 187 J4
EBED/NFELT TW14 174 G4
ESH/CLAY KT10 218 D3
GSTN WD25 55 K9
Derwent Crs BXLYHN DA7 164 B8
STAN HA7 95 H10
TRDG/WHET N20 97 M4
Derwent Dr PUR/KEN CR8 223 L10
SL SL1 128 B7
STMC/STPC BR5 206 G7
YEAD UB4 132 F7
Derwent Gdns REDBR IG4 122 B2
WBLY HA9 115 H6
Derwent Gv EDUL SE22 159 N10
Derwent Pde SOCK/AV RM15 146 F8
Derwent Ri CDALE/KGS NW9 116 B4
Derwent Rd EA W5 155 H2
EGH TW20 172 E9
HHS/BOV HP3 36 D7
LTWR GU18 212 A7
PGE/AN SE20 203 P2
PLMGR N13 98 G5
RYNPK SW20 200 G6
STHL UB1 133 N7
WHTN TW2 176 A2
Derwent St GNWCH SE10 161 K4
Derwentwater Rd ACT W3 135 P10
Derwent Wy HCH RM12 125 J10
Derwent Yd EA W5 * 155 H2
De Salis Rd HGDN/ICK UB10 132 D6
Desborough Cl HERT/WAT SG14 25 K2
SHPTN TW17 196 B7
WGCE AL7 23 L8
Desenfans Rd DUL SE21 181 M2
Deseronto Est DTCH/LGLY SL3 * 150 B1
Desford Rd CAN/RD E16 141 K6
Desford Wy ASHF TW15 174 A5
Desmond Rd WATN WD24 72 G2
Desmond St NWCR SE14 160 D5
Desmond Tutu Dr FSTH SE23 182 D4
Despard Rd ARCH N19 118 D6
De Tany Ct STAL AL1 38 C7
Detillens La OXTED RH8 261 M5
Detling Cl HCH RM12 125 K10
Detling Rd BMLY BR1 183 M8
ERITH DA8 164 E6
GVW DA11 190 A4
Detmold Rd CLPT E5 120 B7
Deva Cl STALW/RED AL3 37 P8
Devalls Cl EHAM E6 142 E9
Devana End CAR SM5 202 A10
Devas Rd RYNPK SW20 200 F1
Devas St BOW E3 140 G6
Devenay Rd SRTFD E15 141 L2
Devenish La ASC SL5 192 D8
Devenish Rd ABYW SE2 163 K1
ASC SL5 192 C6
Deveraux Cl BECK BR3 205 H5
De Vere Cl WLGTN SM6 222 F4
De Vere Gdns IL IG1 122 C6
KENS W8 15 J2
Deverell St STHWK SE1 18 G4
De Vere Ms KENS W8 15 J3
Devereux Ct TPL/STR WC2R 12 A7
Devereux Dr WAT WD17 72 F4
Devereux La BARN SW13 156 E6
Devereux Rd BTSEA SW11 180 A2
CDW/CHF RM16 167 L2
WDSR SL4 149 J8
De Vere Wk WAT WD17 72 F6
Deverills Wy DTCH/LGLY SL3 150 F3
Deveron Gdns SOCK/AV RM15 146 F8
Deveron Wy ROM RM1 104 F9
Devey Cl KUTN/CMB KT2 178 C10
Devil's La EGH TW20 172 F9
Devitt Cl ASHTD KT21 237 M2
Devizes St IS N1 * 7 H6
Devoil Cl RGUE GU4 250 E6
Devoke Wy WOT/HER KT12 197 L9
Devon Av SL SL1 129 H8
WHTN TW2 176 B4
Devon Bank GUW GU2 267 P3
Devon Cl BKHH IG9 101 N3
GFD/PVL UB6 135 H3
HOR/WEW KT19 219 M8
PUR/KEN CR8 241 M2
TOTM N17 119 N1
Devon Ct STAL AL1 * 38 D7
Devon Crs REDH RH1 257 N10
Devoncroft Gdns TWK TW1 176 F3
Devon Gdns FSBYPK N4 119 J4
Devonhurst Pl CHSWK W4 * 156 A4
Devonia Gdns UED N18 99 K7
Devonia Rd IS N1 6 D7
Devon Man
KTN/HRWW/WS HA3 * 115 H3
Devon Md HAT AL10 40 A2
Devonport Gdns IL IG1 122 C4
Devonport Ms SHB W12 * 136 E10
Devonport Rd SHB W12 156 E1
Devonport St WCHPL E1 140 B8
Devon Ri EFNCH N2 117 N2
Devon Rd BARK IG11 143 H3
BELMT SM2 221 H5
EYN DA4 210 A1
REDH RH1 258 D6
WATN WD24 73 L5
WOT/HER KT12 217 K1
Devons Est BOW E3 140 G5
Devonshire Av AMS HP6 68 G3
BELMT SM2 221 M4
DART DA1 187 J2
KWD/TDW/WH KT20 255 P7
WOKN/KNAP GU21 214 F10
Devonshire Cl CAVSQ/HST W1G 10 E3
SRTFD E15 121 K9
Devonshire Ct FELT TW13 * 175 J5
Devonshire Crs MLHL NW7 96 G8
Devonshire Dr GNWCH SE10 160 G7
SURB KT6 199 J8
Devonshire Gdns CHSWK W4 155 P6
SLH/COR SS17 169 K2
TOTM N17 99 K7
Devonshire Gn SLN SL2 128 G4
Devonshire Gv PECK SE15 160 A5
Devonshire Hill La TOTM N17 99 L8
Devonshire Ms South
CAVSQ/HST W1G 10 E3
Devonshire Ms West
CAVSQ/HST W1G 10 E3
Devonshire Pl CAVSQ/HST W1G 10 D2
CRICK NW2 117 K8
KENS W8 * 14 G4
Devonshire Place Ms
CAVSQ/HST W1G 10 D3
Devonshire Rd BELMT SM2 221 M4
BXLYHS DA6 163 P10
CAN/RD E16 141 N8
CAR SM5 222 B1
CDW/CHF RM16 167 K3
CHSWK W4 156 B4
CROY/NA CR0 203 L7
EA W5 155 H2
ED N9 100 B2
ELTH/MOT SE9 184 B5
FELT TW13 175 M6
FSTH SE23 182 C3
GNTH/NBYPK IG2 122 G5
GVW DA11 190 E4
HARP AL5 20 A1
HCH RM12 125 L7
HRW HA1 114 C4
MLHL NW7 96 G8
ORP BR6 207 K7
PIN HA5 93 N9
PIN HA5 113 K5
PLMGR N13 98 G5
STHL UB1 133 P7
TOTM N17 99 K7
WALTH E17 120 F4
WEY KT13 * 216 B1
WIM/MER SW19 179 P10
Devonshire Rw LVPST EC2M 13 K4
Devonshire Row Ms GTPST W1W 10 F2
Devonshire Sq HAYES BR2 205 N4
LVPST EC2M 13 K5
Devonshire St CAVSQ/HST W1G 10 E3
CHSWK W4 156 B5
Devonshire Ter BAY/PAD W2 9 K7
EDUL SE22 * 159 P10
Devonshire Wy CROY/NA CR0 204 E9
YEAD UB4 133 J8
Devons Rd BOW E3 140 F7
Devon St PECK SE15 160 A5
Devon Wy HGDN/ICK UB10 132 A4
HOR/WEW KT19 219 N2
Devon Waye HEST TW5 153 N6
De Walden St CAVSQ/HST W1G 10 D4
Dewar Cl CRAWW RH11 * 283 H8
Dewar Sp DTCH/LGLY SL3 150 C5
Dewar St PECK SE15 159 P9
Dewberry Gdns EHAM E6 142 B7
Dewberry St POP/IOD E14 141 H8
Dewey La BRXS/STRHM SW2 181 H2
Dewey Rd DAGE RM10 144 D1
IS N1 6 A7
Dewey St TOOT SW17 180 A8
Dewgrass Gv CHES/WCR EN8 80 C1
Dewhurst Rd CHES/WCR EN8 62 B5
HMSMTH W6 156 G2
Dewlands GDST RH9 260 B7
Dewlands Av RDART DA2 188 A3
Dewsbury Cl PIN HA5 113 M4
Dewsbury Gdns HARH RM3 105 L7
WPK KT4 200 D10
Dewsbury Rd HARH RM3 105 M7
WLSDN NW10 116 D10
Dexter Cl GRAYS RM17 167 M2
STAL AL1 38 F7
Dexter Rd BAR EN5 76 G10
DEN/HRF UB9 91 M10
Deyncourt Gdns UPMR RM14 126 B7
Deyncourt Rd TOTM N17 99 K9
Deynecourt Gdns WAN E11 121 P2
D'Eynsford Rd CMBW SE5 159 L6
Dharam Marg GSTN WD25 * 74 D5
Diadem Ct SOHO/CST W1F 11 J5
Dial Cl SWCM DA10 189 H1
Diamedes Av STWL/WRAY TW19 173 N3
Diameter Rd STMC/STPC BR5 206 E7
Diamond Cl BCTR RM8 123 M6
CDW/CHF RM16 167 L2
Diamond Rd RSLP HA4 113 L9
SL SL1 149 M1
WATN WD24 73 H4
Diamond St PECK SE15 159 M6
WLSDN NW10 136 A2
Diamond Ter GNWCH SE10 161 H7
Diana Cl CDW/CHF RM16 167 L2
DEPT SE8 160 E5
DTCH/LGLY SL3 130 B8
SCUP DA14 185 P5
SWFD E18 101 N9
Diana Gdns SURB KT6 199 L9
Diana Pl CAMTN NW1 10 F1
Diana Rd WALTH E17 120 E1
Dianne Wy EBAR EN4 77 P8
Dianthus Cl ABYW SE2 * 163 L4
CHERT KT16 195 H7
Dianthus Ct WOKS/MYFD GU22 232 A4
Diban Av HCH RM12 125 J9
Dibden Hl CSTG HP8 89 N5
Dibden La RSEV TN14 264 F3
Dibden St IS N1 6 E5
Dibdin Cl SUT SM1 201 K10
Dibdin Rd SUT SM1 201 K10
Diceland Rd BNSTD SM7 239 J2
Dicey Av CRICK NW2 116 F10
Dickens Av DART DA1 165 P10
FNCH N3 97 M9

TIL RM18 168 E7
UX/CGN UB8 132 C8
Dickens Cl ERITH DA8 164 C6
HART DA3 211 K5
HYS/HAR UB3 152 F3
RCHPK/HAM TW10 177 K5
STALW/RED AL3 38 C5
Dickens Dr ADL/WDHM KT15 215 J3
CHST BR7 184 F9
Dickens Est BERM/RHTH SE16 19 N3
Dickens La UED N18 99 M6
Dickens Ms FARR EC1M 12 C2
Dickenson Cl ED N9 99 P2
Dickenson Rd CEND/HSY/T N8 118 F5
FELT TW13 175 K8
Dickenson's La SNWD SE25 203 P6
Dickenson's Pl SNWD SE25 203 P6
Dickenson Wy WARE SG12 26 C2
Dickens Pl DTCH/LGLY SL3 151 H7
Dickens Ri CHIG IG7 102 D4
Dickens Rd CRAWE RH10 283 N10
EHAM E6 142 A4
GVE DA12 191 H4
Dickens Sq STHWK SE1 18 F3
Dickens St VX/NE SW8 158 C8
Dickens Wy ROM RM1 124 F2
Dickens Wood Cl NRWD SE19 181 J10
Dickerage La NWMAL KT3 199 P3
Dickerage Rd KUT/HW KT1 199 P1
Dicker Ml HERT/BAY SG13 25 L4
Dickins Cl CHESW EN7 61 P3
Dickinson Av RKW/CH/CXG WD3 72 B10
Dickinson Quay HHS/BOV HP3 53 P1
Dickinsons Fld HARP AL5 20 B4
Dickinson Sq RKW/CH/CXG WD3 72 C10
Dickson CHESW EN7 61 N3
Dickson Fold PIN HA5 113 L2
Dickson House CHARL SE7 * 162 B6
Dickson Rd ELTH/MOT SE9 162 B9
Dick Turpin Wy
EBED/NFELT TW14 152 G10
Didsbury Cl EHAM E6 142 C3
Digby Crs FSBYPK N4 119 K7
Digby Gdns DAGE RM10 144 B3
Digby Pl CROY/NA CR0 203 N10
Digby Rd BARK IG11 143 J2
HOM E9 140 C1
Digby St BETH E2 140 B5
Digby Wy BF/WBF KT14 216 A8
Dig Dag Hl CHESW EN7 61 N3
Digdens Ri EPSOM KT18 237 P1
Diggon St WCHPL E1 140 C7
Dighton Rd WAND/EARL SW18 179 M1
Dignum St IS N1 * 6 A7
Digswell Cl BORE WD6 75 M4
Digswell Hl WGCW AL8 22 D2
Digswell La WGCE AL7 23 J1
Digswell Ri WGCW AL8 22 G3
Digswell Rd WGCW AL8 22 G3
Digswell St HOLWY N7 6 B1
Dilhorne Cl LEE/GVPK SE12 183 N6
Dilke St CHEL SW3 16 B9
Dillwyn Cl SYD SE26 182 D7
Dilston Cl NTHLT UB5 133 K5
Dilston Rd LHD/OX KT22 236 F5
Dilton Gdns PUT/ROE SW15 178 D4
Dimes Pl HMSMTH W6 156 E3
Dimmock Dr GFD/PVL UB6 114 C10
Dimmocks La RKW/CH/CXG WD3 71 K2
Dimond Cl FSTGT E7 121 M10
Dimsdale Dr CDALE/KGS NW9 115 P6
EN EN1 99 P1
Dimsdale St HERT/WAT SG14 25 K5
Dimson Crs BOW E3 140 F6
Dinant Link Rd HOD EN11 44 G2
Dingle Cl BAR EN5 76 C10
CRAWW RH11 283 L6
Dingle Gdns POP/IOD E14 * 140 F9
Dingle Rd ASHF TW15 174 C8
The Dingle CRAWW RH11 283 L7
HGDN/ICK UB10 132 C5
Dingley La STRHM/NOR SW16 180 E5
Dingley Pl FSBYE EC1V 6 F10
Dingley Rd FSBYE EC1V 6 E10
Dingwall Av CROY/NA CR0 203 K9
Dingwall Gdns GLDGN NW11 117 K4
Dingwall Rd CAR SM5 222 A5
CROY/NA CR0 203 L9
WAND/EARL SW18 179 M3
Dinmont Est BETH E2 7 P7
Dinmont St BETH E2 140 A4
Dinmore HHS/BOV HP3 52 C4
Dinsdale Cl WOKS/MYFD GU22 232 C4
Dinsdale Gdns BAR EN5 77 L9
SNWD SE25 203 M5
Dinsdale Rd BKHTH/KID SE3 161 L5
Dinsmore Rd BAL SW12 180 C3
Dinton Rd KUTN/CMB KT2 177 L10
WIM/MER SW19 179 N9
Dione Rd HHNE HP2 36 A3
Diploma Av EFNCH N2 117 P2
Dippers Cl BGR/WK TN15 247 N3
Dirdene Cl EW KT17 220 C8
Dirdene Gdns EW KT17 220 C8
Dirdene Gv EW KT17 220 B8
Dirleton Rd SRTFD E15 141 L3
Dirtham La EHSLY KT24 253 J5
Disbrowe Rd HMSMTH W6 14 A10
HMSMTH W6 157 H5
Discovery Wk WAP E1W 140 A9
Dishforth La CDALE/KGS NW9 96 B9
Disney Pl STHWK SE1 18 F1
Disney St STHWK SE1 18 F1
Dison Cl PEND EN3 80 C5
Disraeli Cl THMD SE28 143 L10
Disraeli Ct DTCH/LGLY SL3 150 E5
Disraeli Pk BEAC HP9 88 C7
Disraeli Rd EA W5 135 J10
FSTGT E7 141 M1
PUT/ROE SW15 157 H10
WLSDN NW10 135 P4
Diss St BETH E2 7 L9
Distaff La BLKFR EC4V 12 E7
Distillery La HMSMTH W6 156 F4
Distillery Rd HMSMTH W6 156 F4
Distin St LBTH SE11 18 A6
District Rd ALP/SUD HA0 114 G10
Ditchburn St POP/IOD E14 141 H9
Ditches La COUL/CHIP CR5 240 E3
COUL/CHIP CR5 240 F6
Ditchfield Rd HOD EN11 44 F1
YEAD UB4 133 M6
Ditchling Hl CRAWW RH11 283 M10
Dittisham Rd ELTH/MOT SE9 184 B7
Ditton Cl THDIT KT7 198 F7
Dittoncroft Cl CROY/NA CR0 223 M1
Ditton Grange Cl SURB KT6 199 J8
Ditton Grange Dr SURB KT6 199 J8
Ditton Hl SURB KT6 199 H8
Ditton Hill Rd SURB KT6 199 H8
Ditton Lawn THDIT KT7 198 F8
Ditton Park Rd DTCH/LGLY SL3 150 C4
Ditton Pl PGE/AN SE20 * 204 A1
Ditton Reach THDIT KT7 198 G6
Ditton Rd BXLYHS DA6 185 N1
DTCH/LGLY SL3 150 A7
DTCH/LGLY SL3 150 C5
NWDGN UB2 153 N4
SURB KT6 199 K8
Divot Pl HERT/BAY SG13 26 A4
Dixey Cottages EFNCH N2 * 117 P3
Dixon Cl EHAM E6 142 C8
Dixon Dr WEY KT13 216 A6
Dixon Pl WWKM BR4 204 G8
Dixon Rd NWCR SE14 160 D7
SNWD SE25 203 M3
Dixons Ct WARE SG12 * 26 D3
Dixons Hill Cl BRKMPK AL9 58 E1
Dixons Hill Rd BRKMPK AL9 40 E10
Dobbin Cl KTN/HRWW/WS HA3 94 F10
Dobbins Pl CRAWW RH11 282 G8
Dobb's Weir Rd HOD EN11 45 J4
Dobell Rd ELTH/MOT SE9 184 C1
Dobree Av WLSDN NW10 136 E2
Dobson Cl KIL/WHAMP NW6 3 L4
Dobson Rd CRAWW RH11 283 N4
GVE DA12 191 H8
Dock Approach Rd
CDW/CHF RM16 168 C4
Dockers Tanner Rd POP/IOD E14 160 F3
Dockett Eddy La SHPTN TW17 196 A7
Dockett Moorings CHERT KT16 * 196 A8
Dockhead STHWK SE1 19 M2
Dock Hill Av BERM/RHTH SE16 160 C1
Dockland St CAN/RD E16 162 D1
Dockley Rd BERM/RHTH SE16 19 N4
Dock Rd BTFD TW8 * 155 J6
CAN/RD E16 141 L9
GRAYS RM17 168 B6
Dockside Rd CAN/RD E16 142 A9
Dock St WCHPL E1 13 N7
Dockwell Cl EBED/NFELT TW14 153 H10
Doctors Cl SYD SE26 182 B8
Doctor's Commons Rd
BERK HP4 33 N6
Doctors La CTHM CR3 241 H10
Docwra's Buildings IS N1 7 J1
Dodbrooke Rd WNWD SE27 181 H6
Doddinghurst Rd BRWN CM15 87 H9
Doddington Gv WALW SE17 18 C9
Doddington Pl WALW SE17 18 C9
Dodds Crs BF/WBF KT14 215 L10
Doddsfield Rd SLN SL2 128 F5
Dodds La CSTG HP8 89 N3
HHNE HP2 35 M1
WOKS/MYFD GU22 215 K10
Dodds Pk BRKHM/BTCW RH3 273 N2
Dodsley Pl ED N9 100 B4
Dodson St STHWK SE1 18 B2
Dod St POP/IOD E14 140 F8
Dodwood WGCE AL7 23 L6
Doebury Wk WOOL/PLUM SE18 163 K5
Doel Cl WIM/MER SW19 179 M10
Doggett Rd CAT SE6 182 F3
Doggetts Ct EBAR EN4 77 P9
Doggetts Farm Rd
DEN/HRF UB9 110 F5
Doggetts Wy STAL AL1 38 B8
Doggetts Wood Cl CSTG HP8 69 N8
Doggetts Wood La CSTG HP8 69 N7
Doghurst Av WDR/YW UB7 152 C6
Doghurst Dr WDR/YW UB7 152 C6
Doghurst La COUL/CHIP CR5 240 A6
Dog Kennel Hl EDUL SE22 159 M9
Dog Kennel La HAT AL10 40 D3
RKW/CH/CXG WD3 71 J9
Dog La WLSDN NW10 116 B9
Dognell Gn WGCW AL8 22 E4
Dog Rose Ramble YEAD UB4 133 H3
Dog Rose Ramble &
Hillingdon Trail YEAD UB4 132 G3
Dogwood Cl GVW DA11 190 B7
Doherty Rd PLSTW E13 141 M6
Dolben Ct DEPT SE8 * 160 E3
Dolben St STHWK SE1 * 12 D10
Dolby Rd FUL/PGN SW6 157 J8
Dolby Ter HORL RH6 * 279 H9
Doldens Cottages EYN DA4 * 210 A4
Dolland St LBTH SE11 17 P8
Dollary Pde KUT/HW KT1 * 199 N3
Dollis Av FNCH N3 97 J9
Dollis Cl CRAWE RH10 284 D8
Dollis Crs RSLP HA4 113 K6
Dollis Hill Av CRICK NW2 116 E8
Dollis Hill Est CRICK NW2 * 116 D8
Dollis Hill La CRICK NW2 116 C9
CRICK NW2 116 E8
Dollis Pk FNCH N3 97 J9
Dollis Rd MLHL NW7 97 H9
Dollis Valley Dr BAR EN5 77 J10
Dollis Valley Green Wk
GLDGN NW11 117 J2
HDN NW4 97 H10
TRDG/WHET N20 97 L4
Dollis Valley Wy EBAR EN4 77 N8
Dolman Cl FNCH N3 97 M10
Dolman Rd CHSWK W4 156 A3
Dolman St CLAP SW4 158 G10
Dolphin Ap ROM RM1 124 G2
Dolphin Cl BERM/RHTH SE16 160 C1
SURB KT6 199 J6
THMD SE28 143 N8
Dolphin Ct SL SL1 149 N1
STA TW18 173 K6
Dolphin Ct North STA TW18 * 173 K6
Dolphin Est SUN TW16 * 196 F1
Dolphin La POP/IOD E14 140 G9
Dolphin Rd NTHLT UB5 133 N4
SL SL1 149 N1
SUN TW16 196 F1
Dolphin Rd North SUN TW16 196 E1
Dolphin Rd South SUN TW16 196 E1
Dolphin Rd West SUN TW16 196 F1
Dolphin Sq CHSWK W4 * 156 B6
PIM SW1V 17 J8
Dolphin St KUT/HW KT1 199 K2
Dolphin Wy PUR RM19 166 D4
Dolphin Yd STAL AL1 * 38 C6
WARE SG12 * 26 C2
Dombey St BMSBY WC1N 11 N3
Dome Buildings RCH/KEW TW9 * 177 J1
Dome Hl CTHM CR3 259 M3
Dome Hill Pk SYD SE26 181 N7
Dome Hill Peak CTHM CR3 259 M2
Domett Cl CMBW SE5 159 L10
Dome Wy REDH RH1 258 A9
Domingo St FSBYE EC1V 12 E1
Dominica Cl PLSTW E13 142 A5
Dominic Ct WAB EN9 62 G9
Dominion Cl HSLW TW3 154 C8
Dominion Dr CRW RM5 104 C7
Dominion Pde HRW HA1 * 114 E3
Dominion Rd CROY/NA CR0 203 N7
NWDGN UB2 153 M2
Dominion St LVPST EC2M 13 H3
Dominion Wy RAIN RM13 145 H5
Domonic Dr ELTH/MOT SE9 184 E6
Domville Cl TRDG/WHET N20 97 N3
Donald Biggs Dr GVE DA12 190 G3
Donald Dr CHDH RM6 123 M3
Donald Rd CROY/NA CR0 202 G6
PLSTW E13 141 N3
Donaldson Rd KIL/WHAMP NW6 2 D6
WOOL/PLUM SE18 162 D7
Donald Woods Gdns BRYLDS KT5 199 N9
Doncaster Dr NTHLT UB5 113 N10
Doncaster Gdns FSBYPK N4 * 119 K4
NTHLT UB5 113 N10
Doncaster Gn OXHEY WD19 93 K6
Doncaster Rd ED N9 100 A1
Doncaster Wk CRAWE RH10 * 284 B9
Doncaster Wy UPMR RM14 125 N8
Doncella Cl CDW/CHF RM16 167 H3
Donegal St IS N1 5 P8
Doneraile St FUL/PGN SW6 156 G8
Dongola Rd PLSTW E13 141 N5
TOTM N17 119 M1
WCHPL E1 140 D7
Dongola Rd West PLSTW E13 141 N5
Donington Av BARK/HLT IG6 122 F3
Donkey Aly EDUL SE22 181 P3
Donkey La EN EN1 79 P6
EYN DA4 210 A9
HORL RH6 280 E8
RDKG RH5 271 L9
WDR/YW UB7 151 M3
Donnafields CHOB/PIR GU24 230 F2
Donnay Cl CFSP/GDCR SL9 110 A4
Donne Cl CRAWE RH10 284 C5
Donnefield Av EDGW HA8 95 K7
Donne Gdns WOKS/MYFD GU22 233 H1
Donnella Cl CDW/CHF RM16 167 J2
Donne Pl CHEL SW3 15 P5
MTCM CR4 202 C4
Donne Rd BCTR RM8 123 M7
Donnington Ct CRAWW RH11 283 J10
Donnington Rd
KTN/HRWW/WS HA3 115 J4
WLSDN NW10 136 E3
WPK KT4 200 D9
Donnybrook Rd
STRHM/NOR SW16 180 E10
Donoghue Cottages
POP/IOD E14 * 140 D7
Donovan Av MUSWH N10 98 C10
Donovan Cl HOR/WEW KT19 220 A6
Donovan Pl WCHMH N21 78 G9
Don Phelan Cl CMBW SE5 159 L7
Don Wy ROM RM1 104 F8
Doods Park Rd REIG RH2 257 L9
Doods Pl REIG RH2 * 257 M9
Doods Rd REIG RH2 257 M9
Doods Wy REIG RH2 257 N9
Doone Cl TEDD TW11 176 F9
Doon St STHWK SE1 12 A9
Dorado Gdns ORP BR6 207 N10
Doral Wy CAR SM5 222 A2
Dorando Cl SHB W12 * 136 E9
Doran Dr REDH RH1 257 N10
Doran Gdns REDH RH1 * 257 N10
Doran Gv WOOL/PLUM SE18 163 H6
Dora Rd WIM/MER SW19 179 K8
Dora St POP/IOD E14 140 E8
Dora Wy BRXN/ST SW9 159 H8
Dorchester Av BXLY DA5 185 N4
HOD EN11 44 F1
PLMGR N13 99 K5
RYLN/HDSTN HA2 114 B4
Dorchester Cl DART DA1 187 N4
NTHLT UB5 114 A10
STMC/STPC BR5 185 L10
Dorchester Ct CRICK NW2 116 F8
HNHL SE24 181 K1
RKW/CH/CXG WD3 * 72 D9
STHGT/OAK N14 98 C1
WOKS/MYFD GU22 232 D2
Dorchester Dr
EBED/NFELT TW14 174 F2
HNHL SE24 181 K1
Dorchester Gdns CHING E4 100 F5
GLDGN NW11 * 117 K2
Dorchester Gv CHSWK W4 156 C4
Dorchester Ms TWK TW1 177 H2
Dorchester Pde
STRHM/NOR SW16 * 180 F5
Dorchester Rd GVE DA12 190 G6
MRDN SM4 201 M7
NTHLT UB5 114 A10
WEY KT13 196 C10
WPK KT4 200 F8
Dorchester Ter HDN NW4 * 96 G10
Dorchester Wy
KTN/HRWW/WS HA3 115 L4
Dorchester Waye YEAD UB4 133 K8
Dorcis Av BXLYHN DA7 163 P8
Dordrecht Rd ACT W3 136 B10
Dore Av MNPK E12 122 D10
Doreen Av CDALE/KGS NW9 116 A6
Dore Gdns MRDN SM4 201 L7
Dorell Cl STHL UB1 133 N7
Dorian Ct WARL CR6 * 242 A5
Dorian Dr ASC SL5 192 D1
Dorian Rd HCH RM12 125 H6
Doria Rd FUL/PGN SW6 157 J8
Doric Dr KWD/TDW/WH KT20 239 J6
Doric Wy CAMTN NW1 5 J9
Dorie Ms NFNCH/WDSPK N12 97 L5
Dorien Rd RYNPK SW20 200 G2
Dorin Ct WARL CR6 242 A6
WOKS/MYFD GU22 233 H1
Doris Av ERITH DA8 164 D7
Doris Rd ASHF TW15 174 E9
FSTGT E7 141 M2
Dorking Cl DEPT SE8 160 E5
WPK KT4 200 G9
Dorking Ri HARH RM3 105 L5
Dorking Rd ASHTD KT21 237 N1
GT/LBKH KT23 254 A3
HARH RM3 105 L5
KWD/TDW/WH KT20 256 C4
KWD/TDW/WH KT20 256 E2
LHD/OX KT22 254 G1
RGUE GU4 268 G6
SHGR GU5 270 E5
Dorking Wk HARH RM3 105 L5
Dorkins Wy UPMR RM14 126 D6
Dorlcote Rd WAND/EARL SW18 179 N3
Dorling Dr EW KT17 220 C8
Dorly Cl SHPTN TW17 196 F4
Dorman Pl ED N9 99 P3
Dormans CRAWW RH11 283 K8
Dormans Cl NTHWD HA6 92 E8
Dorman Wy STJWD NW8 3 L5
Dormay St WAND/EARL SW18 179 L1
Dormer Cl BAR EN5 76 G9
SRTFD E15 141 L1
Dormers HHS/BOV HP3 * 53 H3
Dormer's Av STHL UB1 133 P8
Dormers Cl GODL GU7 267 J10
Dormers Ri STHL UB1 134 A9
Dormer's Wells La STHL UB1 133 P9
STHL UB1 134 A10
Dormie Cl STALW/RED AL3 38 B4
Dormywood RSLP HA4 112 G3
Dornberg Cl BKHTH/KID SE3 161 M6
Dornberg Rd BKHTH/KID SE3 * 161 N6
Dorncliffe Rd FUL/PGN SW6 157 H8
Dornels SLN SL2 129 P8
Dorney End CSHM HP5 50 F6
Dorney Gv WEY KT13 196 C9
Dorney Hl North BEAC HP9 108 F4
Dorney Hl South SL SL1 108 F5
Dorney Ri STMC/STPC BR5 207 J4
Dorney Wy HSLWW TW4 175 M1
Dorney Wood Rd SL SL1 108 B8
Dornfell St KIL/WHAMP NW6 117 J10
Dornford Gdns COUL/CHIP CR5 241 K5
Dornton Rd BAL SW12 180 C5
SAND/SEL CR2 223 M2
Dorothy Av ALP/SUD HA0 135 K2
Dorothy Evans Cl BXLYHN DA7 164 C10
Dorothy Gdns BCTR RM8 123 L9
Dorothy Rd BTSEA SW11 158 A9
Dorrell Pl BRXN/ST SW9 159 H9
Dorrien's Cft BERK HP4 33 L2
Dorrington Gdns HCH RM12 125 L7
Dorrington St HCIRC EC1N 12 A3
Dorrington Wy BECK BR3 205 H5
Dorrit Crs RGUW GU3 249 K8
Dorrit Ms UED N18 99 N5
Dorrit St STHWK SE1 * 18 F1
Dorrit Wy CHST BR7 184 F9
Dorrofield Cl RKW/CH/CXG WD3 72 D9
Dors Cl CDALE/KGS NW9 116 A6
Dorset Av NWDGN UB2 153 P3
ROM RM1 124 E1
WELL DA16 163 J10
YEAD UB4 132 F5
Dorset Buildings EMB EC4Y * 12 C6
Dorset Cl BERK HP4 33 L4
CAMTN NW1 10 A3
YEAD UB4 * 132 F5
Dorset Crs GVE DA12 191 H7
Dorset Dr EDGW HA8 95 L7
WOKS/MYFD GU22 232 E3
Dorset Gdns MTCM CR4 202 G4
Dorset Ms FNCH N3 97 K9
KTBR SW1X 16 E3
Dorset Pl SRTFD E15 141 J1
Dorset Ri EMB EC4Y 12 C6
Dorset Rd ASHF TW15 173 N6
BECK BR3 204 C3
BELMT SM2 221 K6
EA W5 155 J2
ELTH/MOT SE9 184 B5
FSTGT E7 141 P2
HRW HA1 114 B4
SEVS/STOTM N15 119 L2
VX/NE SW8 158 G6
WDGN N22 98 F9
WDSR SL4 149 H8
WIM/MER SW19 201 K1
Dorset Sq CAMTN NW1 10 A3
Dorset St MHST W1U 10 C4
Dorset Wy BF/WBF KT14 215 N7
HGDN/ICK UB10 132 A4
WHTN TW2 176 B4
Dorset Waye HEST TW5 153 N6
Dorton Cl PECK SE15 159 M6
Dorton Dr BGR/WK TN15 247 N8
Dorton Wy RPLY/SEND GU23 233 L7
Dorville Crs HMSMTH W6 156 E2
Dorville Rd LEE/GVPK SE12 183 M1
Dothill Rd WOOL/PLUM SE18 162 F6
Douai Gv HPTN TW12 198 B1
Doubleday Rd LOU IG10 82 F7
Doughty Ms BMSBY WC1N 11 N2
Doughty St BMSBY WC1N 11 N1
Douglas Av ALP/SUD HA0 135 K2
HARH RM3 105 M10
NWMAL KT3 200 E4
WALTH E17 100 F9
WATN WD24 73 L3
Douglas Cl BARK/HLT IG6 102 E8
CDW/CHF RM16 167 K2
RGUE GU4 250 A4
STAN HA7 94 F6
WLGTN SM6 222 F3
Douglas Ct CTHM CR3 * 241 K8
Douglas Crs YEAD UB4 133 K6
Douglas Dr CROY/NA CR0 204 F10
Douglas Est IS N1 6 F2
Douglas Gdns BERK HP4 33 M4
Douglas La STWL/WRAY TW19 172 C1
Douglas Ms BNSTD SM7 239 J2
CRICK NW2 117 H8
Douglas Pth POP/IOD E14 161 H4
Douglas Pl POP/IOD E14 * 161 H4
Douglas Rd ADL/WDHM KT15 195 L10
CAN/RD E16 141 M7
CHING E4 101 K1
ESH/CLAY KT10 198 A9
GDMY/SEVK IG3 123 K5
HSLW TW3 154 A9
IS N1 6 E3
KIL/WHAMP NW6 2 C5
REIG RH2 257 K9
ROM RM1 124 G4
SLN SL2 129 J7
STWL/WRAY TW19 173 N2
SURB KT6 199 L9
WDGN N22 99 H9
WELL DA16 163 L7
Douglas Rd North IS N1 6 F1
Douglas Rd South IS N1 6 F2
Douglas St WEST SW1P 17 J6
Douglas Ter WALTH E17 100 E9
Douglas Vls KUT/HW KT1 * 199 L2
Douglas Wy DEPT SE8 160 F6
WGCE AL7 23 M5
Doug Siddons Ct GRAYS RM17 167 P5
Doulton Cl HLWE CM17 47 P2
Doulton Ms KIL/WHAMP NW6 3 H1
The Doultons STA TW18 173 K9
Dounesforth Gdns
WAND/EARL SW18 179 L4
Douro Pl KENS W8 15 H3
Douro St BOW E3 140 F4
Douthwaite Sq WAP E1W 13 P9
Dove Ap EHAM E6 142 B7
Dove Cl CDW/CHF RM16 167 K2
CRAWW RH11 283 N5
MLHL NW7 96 D8
NTHLT UB5 133 L6
SAND/SEL CR2 224 C7
WLGTN SM6 222 G4
Dovecot Cl PIN HA5 113 K3
Dovecote Cl WEY KT13 196 C10
Dove Ct BEAC HP9 88 C8
HAT AL10 40 D6
LOTH EC2R * 12 G6
Dovedale Av CLAY IG5 102 D10
KTN/HRWW/WS HA3 115 H4
Dovedale Cl DEN/HRF UB9 91 M10
RGUE GU4 250 D7
WELL DA16 163 K7
Dovedale Crs CRAWW RH11 283 L9
Dovedale Ri MTCM CR4 180 A10
Dovedale Rd EDUL SE22 182 A1
RDART DA2 188 B4
Dovedon Cl STHGT/OAK N14 98 F3
Dove House Crs SLN SL2 128 D5
Dovehouse Cft HLW CM20 29 K9
Dove House Gdns CHING E4 100 F3
Dovehouse Gn WEY KT13 216 E1
Dovehouse Md BARK IG11 142 G4
Dovehouse St CHEL SW3 15 N8
Dove La POTB/CUF EN6 59 M10
Dove Ms ECT SW5 15 J6
Doveney Cl STMC/STPC BR5 207 M3
Dove Pk PIN HA5 93 N8
RKW/CH/CXG WD3 70 E10
Dover Cl CRICK NW2 116 G7
CRW RM5 104 D10
Dovercourt Av THHTH CR7 203 H4
Dovercourt Est IS N1 7 H1
Dovercourt Gdns STAN HA7 95 K6
Dovercourt La SUT SM1 201 M10
Dovercourt Rd DUL SE21 181 M2
Doverfield CHESW EN7 61 K5
Doverfield Rd BRXS/STRHM SW2 180 F3
RGUE GU4 250 D7
Dover Gdns CAR SM5 202 A10
Dover House Rd PUT/ROE SW15 156 D10
PUT/ROE SW15 178 E2
Doveridge Gdns PLMGR N13 99 J5
Dove Rd IS N1 7 H1
Dove Rw BETH E2 7 N7
Dover Park Dr PUT/ROE SW15 178 E2
Dover Patrol BKHTH/KID SE3 161 N8
Dover Rd ED N9 100 B3
GVW DA11 190 A3
MNPK E12 121 P7
NRWD SE19 181 L9
SL SL1 128 E8
WOOL/PLUM SE18 162 E8
Dover Rd East GVW DA11 190 C4
Dovers Green Rd REIG RH2 275 L5
Doversmead WOKN/KNAP GU21 231 K2
Dover St CONDST W1S 10 G9
Dover Ter RCH/KEW TW9 * 155 M8
Dover Wy RKW/CH/CXG WD3 72 D8
Dover Yd MYFR/PICC W1J 10 G9
Doves Cl HAYES BR2 206 B9
Doves Yd IS N1 6 A6
Doveton Rd SAND/SEL CR2 223 L2
Doveton St WCHPL E1 140 B6
Dowanhill Rd CAT SE6 183 J4
Dowd Cl FBAR/BDGN N11 98 B3
Dowdeswell Cl PUT/ROE SW15 156 B10
Dowding Cl HCH RM12 145 J2
Dowding Pl STAN HA7 94 F7
Dowding Rd BH/WHM TN16 244 A1
HGDN/ICK UB10 132 A2
Dowding Wy GSTN WD25 54 G10
Dowdney Cl KTTN NW5 118 D10
Dower Av WLGTN SM6 222 C5
Dower Cl BEAC HP9 88 B6
Dower Pk WDSR SL4 148 D10
Dower Wk CRAWW RH11 283 K8
Dowgate Hl CANST EC4R 12 G7
Dowlands La HORL RH6 281 L5
Dowland St NKENS W10 2 B9
Dowlans Cl GT/LBKH KT23 253 P3
Dowlans Rd GT/LBKH KT23 254 A3
Dowlas St CMBW SE5 159 M6
Dowlerville Rd ORP BR6 227 J3
Dowling Ct HHS/BOV HP3 35 N9
Dowman Cl WIM/MER SW19 201 L1
Downage HDN NW4 116 F1
The Downage GVW DA11 190 D5
Downalong BUSH WD23 94 C2
Downbank Av BXLYHN DA7 164 E8
Down Barns Rd RSLP HA4 113 L9
Down Cl NTHLT UB5 133 J5
Downderry Rd BMLY BR1 183 J6
Downe Av RSEV TN14 226 F8
Downe Cl HORL RH6 279 P2
WELL DA16 163 M6
Downedge STALW/RED AL3 38 A5
Downend WOOL/PLUM SE18 162 E6
Downer Dr RKW/CH/CXG WD3 71 J2
Downer Meadow GODL GU7 267 K9
Downe Rd HAYES BR2 226 B5
MTCM CR4 202 A2
ORP BR6 226 F10
Downer's Cottages CLAP SW4 158 D10
Downes Cl TWK TW1 176 G2
Downes Ct WCHMH N21 99 H2
Downes Rd STALE/WH AL4 38 G2
Downfield WPK KT4 200 C8
Downfield Cl HERT/BAY SG13 26 B7
MV/WKIL W9 8 G2
Downfield Rd CHES/WCR EN8 62 D7
HERT/BAY SG13 26 B7
Downfields WGCW AL8 22 E7
Down Green La STALE/WH AL4 20 G4
Down Hall Rd KUT/HW KT1 199 J1
Downhall Rd RBSF CM22 31 J5
Downham Cl CRW RM5 104 B8
Downham Ct WOT/HER KT12 * 197 K10
Downham Rd IS N1 6 G4
Downham Wy BMLY BR1 183 K8
BMLY BR1 183 M6
BMLY BR1 183 M8
Downhills Av TOTM N17 119 L1
Downhills Park Rd TOTM N17 119 L1
Downhills Wy TOTM N17 99 K10
Downhurst Av MLHL NW7 96 A6
Downing Av GUW GU2 267 L1
Downing Cl RYLN/HDSTN HA2 114 B1
Downing Dr GFD/PVL UB6 134 D3
Downing Rd DAGW RM9 144 A3
Downings EHAM E6 142 D8
Downing St WHALL SW1A 17 L1
Downings Wd
RKW/CH/CXG WD3 90 G6
Downland Cl COUL/CHIP CR5 222 C10
EPSOM KT18 238 E4
TRDG/WHET N20 97 M2
Downland Dr CRAWW RH11 283 M9
Downland Gdns EPSOM KT18 238 E4
Downland Pl CRAWW RH11 283 M9
Downlands WAB EN9 63 K10
Downlands Rd PUR/KEN CR8 222 F9
Downland Wy EPSOM KT18 238 E4
Down La RGUW GU3 266 G4
Downleys Cl ELTH/MOT SE9 184 B5
Downman Rd ELTH/MOT SE9 162 B9
Down Pl HMSMTH W6 156 E3
Down Rd GU GU1 250 E10
TEDD TW11 176 G9
Downs Av CHST BR7 184 C8
DART DA1 187 P3
EPSOM KT18 238 C1
PIN HA5 113 N4
Downs Bridge Rd BECK BR3 205 J1
Downs Court Pde HACK E8 * 120 A10
Downs Court Rd PUR/KEN CR8 223 K9
Downsell Rd SRTFD E15 121 J9
Downsfield HAT AL10 40 D7
Downsfield Rd WALTH E17 120 D4
Downshall Av GDMY/SEVK IG3 123 H4
Downs Hl BECK BR3 205 J1
Downs Hill Rd EPSOM KT18 * 238 B1
Downshire Hl HAMP NW3 117 N9
Downside BECK BR3 * 204 F1
CHERT KT16 * 195 J8
EPSOM KT18 220 B10
HHNE HP2 35 P5
SUN TW16 197 H1
TWK TW1 176 E6
Downside Bridge Rd COB KT11 235 J1
Downside Cl WIM/MER SW19 179 M9
Downside Common COB KT11 235 J4
Downside Common Rd
COB KT11 235 K4
Downside Crs HAMP NW3 117 P10
WEA W13 134 F6
Downside Orch
WOKS/MYFD GU22 232 D3
Downside Rd BELMT SM2 221 N3
COB KT11 235 J4
RGUE GU4 268 E1
Downsland Dr BRW CM14 107 H4
Downs La CLPT E5 120 A9
HAT AL10 40 D6
LHD/OX KT22 236 G9
Downs Link RGUE GU4 269 H5
SHGR GU5 268 C9
Downs Lodge Ct EW KT17 * 220 B10
Downs Park Rd HACK E8 119 P10
Downs Rd BECK BR3 204 G2
BELMT SM2 221 L7
CLPT E5 119 P9
COUL/CHIP CR5 240 E4
DTCH/LGLY SL3 150 A1
EN EN1 79 M8
EPSOM KT18 237 P6
MEO DA13 190 A9
PUR/KEN CR8 223 J7
RDKG RH5 255 H4
THHTH CR7 203 K1
Downs Side BELMT SM2 221 J7
The Downs HAT AL10 40 D6
HLW CM20 47 H1
LHD/OX KT22 254 C1
RYNPK SW20 178 G10
Down St E/WMO/HCT KT8 197 P5
MYFR/PICC W1J 10 E10
Downs Va HART DA3 211 K4
Downs Vw DORK RH4 255 H10
ISLW TW7 154 E7
KWD/TDW/WH KT20 238 E7
Downsview Av
WOKS/MYFD GU22 232 C7
Downs View Cl ORP BR6 227 M6
Downsview Cl COB KT11 235 J5
SWLY BR8 208 G3
Downsview Gdns DORK RH4 272 G3
NRWD SE19 181 K10
Downs View Rd GT/LBKH KT23 254 B3
Downsview Rd NRWD SE19 181 K10
SEV TN13 264 G1
Downs Wy EPSOM KT18 238 C2
GT/LBKH KT23 254 B2
OXTED RH8 261 K3
Downsway CTHM CR3 241 N2
GU GU1 250 G10
ORP BR6 227 H2
SAND/SEL CR2 223 M7
Downsway Cl
KWD/TDW/WH KT20 238 D7
The Downsway BELMT SM2 221 M5
Downs Wd EPSOM KT18 238 E3
Downswood REIG RH2 257 N8
Downton Av BRXS/STRHM SW2 180 G5
Downtown Rd
BERM/RHTH SE16 160 D1
Downway NFNCH/WDSPK N12 97 P8
Down Wy NTHLT UB5 133 J5
Dowrey St IS N1 * 6 A5
Dowry Wk WAT WD17 72 G4
Dowsett Rd TOTM N17 99 P10
Dowson Cl CMBW SE5 * 159 L10
Doyce St STHWK SE1 * 18 E1
Doyle Cl ERITH DA8 164 F7
Doyle Gdns WLSDN NW10 136 E3
Doyle Rd SNWD SE25 203 P4
D'Oyley St BGVA SW1W 16 C5
Doynton St ARCH N19 * 118 C7
Draco Ga PUT/ROE SW15 * 156 F9
Draco St WALW SE17 18 E9
Dragonfly Cl PLSTW E13 141 N5
Dragon La WEY KT13 216 B6
Dragon Rd HAT AL10 40 B3
LBTH SE11 17 P6
PECK SE15 19 K10
Dragoon Rd DEPT SE8 160 E4
Dragor Rd WLSDN NW10 135 P6
Drake Av CTHM CR3 241 K8
DTCH/LGLY SL3 150 A3
STA TW18 173 J8
Drake Cl BERM/RHTH SE16 160 C1
BRW CM14 107 J6
Drake Crs THMD SE28 143 M8
Drakefell Rd NWCR SE14 160 C8
Drakefield Rd TOOT SW17 180 B6
Drake Ms HAYES BR2 205 P4
HCH RM12 145 H2
Drake Rd BROCKY SE4 160 F9
CDW/CHF RM16 167 K1
CHSGTN KT9 219 M2
CRAWE RH10 283 P10
CROY/NA CR0 202 G7
HORL RH6 279 P4
MTCM CR4 202 B6
RYLN/HDSTN HA2 113 N7
Drakes Cl CHES/WCR EN8 62 C4
ESH/CLAY KT10 217 P2
Drakes Ctyd KIL/WHAMP NW6 2 D3
Drakes Dr NTHWD HA6 92 C9
STAL AL1 38 G9
Drakes Rd AMSS HP7 69 J5
Drake St ENC/FH EN2 79 L5
FSBYW WC1X 11 N4
Drakes Wy HAT AL10 40 E6
WOKS/MYFD GU22 232 A8
Drakewood Rd
STRHM/NOR SW16 180 E10
Draper Cl BELV DA17 164 A3
ISLW TW7 154 C8
Draper Est STHWK SE1 18 D5
Draper Pl IS N1 6 D5
Drapers Cnr CHONG CM5 67 K6
Drapers Rd ENC/FH EN2 79 J6
SRTFD E15 121 H9
TOTM N17 119 N1
Drappers Wy BERM/RHTH SE16 19 P5
Draven Cl HAYES BR2 205 L7
Drawell Cl WOOL/PLUM SE18 163 H4
Drax Av RYNPK SW20 178 D10
Draxmont WIM/MER SW19 179 H9
Draycot Rd SURB KT6 199 M8
WAN E11 121 N4
Draycott Av CHEL SW3 15 P6
KTN/HRWW/WS HA3 114 G4
Draycott Cl CMBW SE5 159 L6
CRICK NW2 116 G8
KTN/HRWW/WS HA3 114 G4
Draycott Pl CHEL SW3 16 A6
Draycott Ter CHEL SW3 16 A5
Dray Ct ALP/SUD HA0 * 135 H1
GUW GU2 267 N1
Drayford Cl MV/WKIL W9 8 D1
Dray Gdns BRXS/STRHM SW2 180 G1
Draymans Ms PECK SE15 159 N8
Draymans Wy ISLW TW7 154 E9
Drayson Cl WAB EN9 63 J8
Drayson Ms KENS W8 14 F2
Drayton Av LOU IG10 102 C1
ORP BR6 206 E8
POTB/CUF EN6 59 H8
WEA W13 134 F9
Drayton Bridge Rd HNWL W7 134 E9
Drayton Cl HSLWW TW4 175 N1
IL IG1 122 G6
LHD/OX KT22 236 C10
Drayton Ct WDR/YW UB7 * 152 A3
Drayton Court Chambers
WEA W13 * 134 G9
Drayton Gdns WBPTN SW10 15 K7
WCHMH N21 99 J1
WDR/YW UB7 151 N1
WEA W13 134 F9
Drayton Gn WEA W13 134 F9
Drayton Green Rd WEA W13 134 G9
Drayton Gv WEA W13 134 F9
Drayton Pk HBRY N5 119 H10
HBRY N5 119 H8
Drayton Park Ms HOLWY N7 * 119 H10
Drayton Rd BORE WD6 75 M8
CROY/NA CR0 203 J9
TOTM N17 99 M10
WAN E11 121 J6
WEA W13 134 F9
WLSDN NW10 136 C3
Dreadnought St GNWCH SE10 161 K2
Drenon Sq HYS/HAR UB3 132 G9
Dresden Cl KIL/WHAMP NW6 3 H1
Dresden Rd ARCH N19 118 D6
Dresden Wy WEY KT13 216 D2
Dressington Av BROCKY SE4 182 F2
Drew Av MLHL NW7 97 H7
Drewery Ct BKHTH/KID SE3 * 161 K9
Drew Gdns GFD/PVL UB6 134 E1
Drew Meadow SLN SL2 109 H9
Drew Pl CTHM CR3 241 L9
Drew Rd CAN/RD E16 142 B10
Drews Cottages
STRHM/NOR SW16 * 180 E5
Drews Pk BEAC HP9 88 B5
Drewstead Rd
STRHM/NOR SW16 180 E5
The Drey CFSP/GDCR SL9 90 B6
Driffield Rd BOW E3 140 D4
The Drift EHSLY KT24 234 F10
HAYES BR2 206 A10
Drift Wy DTCH/LGLY SL3 150 F7
The Driftway BNSTD SM7 238 F1
HHNE HP2 36 A6
LHD/OX KT22 237 H9
MTCM CR4 202 B1
Driftwood Av LCOL/BKTW AL2 55 P2
Driftwood Dr PUR/KEN CR8 241 K3
Drill Hall Rd CHERT KT16 195 K7
Drinkwater Rd RYLN/HDSTN HA2 114 A7
Drive Ct EDGW HA8 * 95 M6
Drive Md COUL/CHIP CR5 222 F10
Drive Rd COUL/CHIP CR5 240 D6
Drive Sp KWD/TDW/WH KT20 239 L7
The Drive ACT W3 135 P8
AMSS HP7 69 J4
ASHF TW15 174 E10
BAR EN5 77 H7
BAR EN5 77 M10
BARK IG11 143 J2
BECK BR3 204 F2
BELMT SM2 221 J8
BKHH IG9 101 P1
BNSTD SM7 239 H3
BRKMPK AL9 59 L1
BXLY DA5 185 N3
CFSP/GDCR SL9 90 B8
CHESW EN7 61 J4
CHESW EN7 62 A4
CHING E4 101 J1
CHST BR7 185 J10
CHST BR7 207 J1
COB KT11 217 M10
COUL/CHIP CR5 222 F10
CRAWE RH10 285 K2
CRW RM5 104 E9
DTCH/LGLY SL3 149 N7
DTCH/LGLY SL3 150 B1
EBED/NFELT TW14 175 K3
EDGW HA8 95 M6
ENC/FH EN2 79 L5
ERITH DA8 164 C6
ESH/CLAY KT10 198 B8
FBAR/BDGN N11 98 D7
FNCH N3 97 K8
GLDGN NW11 117 H5
GUW GU2 249 L10
GUW GU2 267 M2
GVE DA12 190 G7
HARH RM3 105 M9
HART DA3 211 N3
HERT/BAY SG13 * 42 F10
HERT/WAT SG14 25 K3
HGDN/ICK UB10 111 P9
HGT N6 118 A3
HLW CM20 29 H10
HOD EN11 44 F1
HOLWY N7 5 N2
HOR/WEW KT19 220 C3
HORL RH6 280 C6
HSLW TW3 154 C8
IL IG1 122 B4
KUTN/CMB KT2 177 P10

KWD/TDW/WH KT20 * 239 K10
LCOL/BKTW AL2 56 F1
LHD/OX KT22 236 D8
LHD/OX KT22 237 K9
LOU IG10 82 B7
MRDN SM4 201 M5
NTHWD HA6 92 F9
ORP BR6 207 J9
POTB/CUF EN6 59 J9
RAD WD7 56 F10
RBRW/HUT CM13 107 H7
RGUW GU3 267 N4
RKW/CH/CXG WD3 71 L9
RYLN/HDSTN HA2 113 P5
RYNPK SW20 178 F10
SBW CM21 29 P1
SCUP DA14 185 L6
SEV TN13 247 J10
STWL/WRAY TW19 172 A1
SURB KT6 199 K7
SWFD E18 121 M1
THHTH CR7 203 L4
VW GU25 194 C5
WALTH E17 120 G1
WAT WD17 72 E3
WBLY HA9 115 P7
WLGTN SM6 222 D6
WOKS/MYFD GU22 231 N6
WWKM BR4 205 J7
The Driveway HHW HP1 35 L8
POTB/CUF EN6 60 F4
Dr Johnson Av TOOT SW17 180 C6
Drodges Cl SHGR GU5 268 C9
Droitwich Cl SYD SE26 181 P6
Dromey Gdns
KTN/HRWW/WS HA3 94 E8
Dromore Rd PUT/ROE SW15 179 H2
Dronfield Gdns BCTR RM8 123 M10
Droop St NKENS W10 8 A1
NKENS W10 137 H6
Drop La LCOL/BKTW AL2 56 A7
Dropmore Pk SL SL1 * 108 A8
Dropmore Rd SL SL1 128 B4
Drove Rd RGUE GU4 269 K2
Drovers Md BRW CM14 106 G5
Drovers Pl PECK SE15 160 A6
Drovers Rd SAND/SEL CR2 223 L2
Drovers Wy BEAC HP9 89 H7
HAT AL10 40 E1
STALW/RED AL3 38 C6
The Drove Wy MEO DA13 190 C10
Druce Rd DUL SE21 181 M2
Drudgeon Wy RDART DA2 188 G6
Druid's Cl ASHTD KT21 237 L6
Druid St STHWK SE1 19 L2
Druids Wy HAYES BR2 205 J4
Drumaline Rdg WPK KT4 200 B9
Drummond Av ROMW/RG RM7 124 E2
Drummond Cl ERITH DA8 164 F7
Drummond Crs CAMTN NW1 5 J9
Drummond Dr STAN HA7 94 E8
Drummond Ga PIM SW1V 17 K7
Drummond Rd
BERM/RHTH SE16 160 A2
CRAWW RH11 283 H8
CROY/NA CR0 203 K9
GU GU1 250 A10
ROMW/RG RM7 124 D2
WAN E11 121 N4
Drummonds Pl RCH/KEW TW9 155 K10
The Drummonds EPP CM16 65 K6
Drummond St CAMTN NW1 10 G1
Drum St WCHPL E1 13 M5
Drury Cl CRAWE RH10 284 E9
Drury Crs CROY/NA CR0 203 H9
Drury La COVGDN WC2E 11 M6
WARE SG12 28 B2
Drury Rd HRW HA1 114 B5
Drury Wy WLSDN NW10 116 A10
Dryad St PUT/ROE SW15 156 G9
Dry Arch Rd ASC SL5 192 E7
Dryburgh Gdns CDALE/KGS NW9 115 M1
Dryburgh Rd PUT/ROE SW15 156 E9
Drycroft WGCE AL7 23 H9
Drydell La CSHM HP5 50 E7
Dryden Av HNWL W7 134 E8
Dryden Cl BARK/HLT IG6 103 J7
Dryden Pl TIL RM18 168 E7
Dryden Rd EN EN1 79 M10
KTN/HRWW/WS HA3 94 E9
WELL DA16 163 J7
WIM/MER SW19 179 M9
Dryden St COVGDN WC2E 11 M6
Dryden Wy ORP BR6 207 K8
Dryfield Cl WLSDN NW10 135 P1
Dryfield Rd EDGW HA8 95 P7
Dryhill La RSEV TN14 246 C9
Dryhill Rd BELV DA17 164 A5
Dryland Av ORP BR6 227 J1
Drylands Rd CEND/HSY/T N8 118 F4
Drynham Pk WEY KT13 196 F10
Drysdale Av CHING E4 80 G10
Drysdale Cl NTHWD HA6 92 F8
Drysdale Dwellings HACK E8 * 119 N10
Drysdale Pl IS N1 7 K9
Drysdale St IS N1 7 K10
Duarte Pl CDW/CHF RM16 167 L2
Dublin Av HACK E8 7 P5
Dubrae Cl STALW/RED AL3 37 P8
Du Burstow Ter HNWL W7 154 D1
Ducal St BETH E2 7 M10
Du Cane Cl SHB W12 * 136 F8
Du Cane Rd SHB W12 136 E8
Duchess Cl FBAR/BDGN N11 98 C6
SUT SM1 221 M1
Duchess Ct WEY KT13 196 E10
Duchess Gv BKHH IG9 * 101 N3
Duchess Ms CAVSQ/HST W1G 10 F4
Duchess of Bedford's Wk
KENS W8 14 E2
Duchess of Kent Cl GUW GU2 249 M6
Duchess St REGST W1B 10 F4
SL SL1 128 D10
Duchess' Wk BGR/WK TN15 265 M1
Duchy Rd EBAR EN4 77 N4
Duchy St STHWK SE1 12 B9
Ducie St CLAP SW4 158 F10
Duck Aly CSHM HP5 50 C8
Duckett Rd FSBYPK N4 119 J4
Ducketts Md HLWW/ROY CM19 27 N10
Ducketts Rd DART DA1 186 G1
Duckett St WCHPL E1 140 C7
Ducking Stool Ct ROM RM1 124 F2
Duck La EPP CM16 65 M2
SOHO/CST W1F 11 J6
Duck Lees La PEND EN3 80 D8
Duckling La SBW CM21 29 P1
Ducks Hill Rd NTHWD HA6 92 C10
NTHWD HA6 92 C8
Du Cros Dr STAN HA7 95 J7
Du Cros Rd ACT W3 136 B10
Dudbrook Rd BRW CM14 85 P4
Dudden Hill La WLSDN NW10 116 C10
Dudden Hill Pde WLSDN NW10 * 116 C9
Duddington Cl ELTH/MOT SE9 184 A7
Dudely Rd GVW DA11 190 A3
Dudley Av CHES/WCR EN8 62 C8
KTN/HRWW/WS HA3 115 H1
Dudley Cl ADL/WDHM KT15 195 M10
CDW/CHF RM16 167 K1
Dudley Dr MRDN SM4 201 H8
RSLP HA4 113 J10
Dudley Gdns RYLN/HDSTN HA2 114 C6
WEA W13 154 G1
Dudley Gv EPSOM KT18 219 P10
Dudley Pl HYS/HAR UB3 152 E3
Dudley Rd ASHF TW15 174 A8
FNCH N3 97 L10
HARH RM3 105 L7
IL IG1 122 E9
KIL/WHAMP NW6 2 B7
KIL/WHAMP NW6 137 H4
KUT/HW KT1 199 L3
NWDGN UB2 153 L1
RCH/KEW TW9 155 L8
RYLN/HDSTN HA2 114 B7
WALTH E17 100 F10
WIM/MER SW19 179 K9
WOT/HER KT12 197 H6
Dudley St BAY/PAD W2 * 9 L4
Dudley Whf IVER SL0 * 130 F10
Dudlington Rd CLPT E5 120 B7
Dudmaston Ms CHEL SW3 15 M7
Dudrich Ms EDUL SE22 181 N1
Dudsbury Rd DART DA1 187 J2
Dudset La HEST TW5 153 H7
Dudswell La BERK HP4 33 J1
Dudswell Ml BERK HP4 * 33 H1
Dufferin Av STLK EC1Y 12 G2
Dufferin St STLK EC1Y 12 F2
Duffield Cl CDW/CHF RM16 167 L2
HRW HA1 114 E3
Duffield Dr SEVS/STOTM N15 119 N2
Duffield La SLN SL2 129 L2
Duffield Pk SLN SL2 129 L5
Duffield Rd KWD/TDW/WH KT20 238 E10
Duffins Orch CHERT KT16 214 F4
Duff St POP/IOD E14 140 G8
Dufour's Pl SOHO/CST W1F 11 H6
Dufrey Pl CMBW SE5 * 159 L6
Dugard Wy LBTH SE11 18 C6
Dugdale Hill La POTB/CUF EN6 59 H9
Dugdales RKW/CH/CXG WD3 72 B8
Duggan Dr CHST BR7 184 B9
Dugolly Av WBLY HA9 115 N8
Duke Humphrey Rd
BKHTH/KID SE3 161 K8
Duke of Cambridge Cl
WHTN TW2 176 C2
Duke of Edinburgh Rd SUT SM1 201 N10
The Duke of Wellington Av
WOOL/PLUM SE18 162 E2
Duke of Wellington Pl
KTBR SW1X 16 D2
Duke of York Sq CHEL SW3 16 B7
Duke of York St STJS SW1Y 11 H9
Duke Rd BARK/HLT IG6 122 G2
CHSWK W4 156 A4
Duke's Av CHSWK W4 156 A4
EDGW HA8 95 L7
EPP CM16 83 H1
FNCH N3 97 L9
GRAYS RM17 167 M2
HRW HA1 114 D2
HSLWW TW4 153 M10
MUSWH N10 118 D1
NTHLT UB5 133 M2
NWMAL KT3 200 B3
PIN HA5 113 N4
RCHPK/HAM TW10 177 H7
Dukes Cl ASHF TW15 174 D7
CFSP/GDCR SL9 110 A6
EPP CM16 66 C3
HPTN TW12 175 N8
Duke's Dr GODL GU7 266 G10
SL SL1 108 E10
Dukes Ga CHSWK W4 * 155 P3
Dukes Green Av
EBED/NFELT TW14 175 H2
Dukes Hl CTHM CR3 242 D6
Dukes Kiln Dr CFSP/GDCR SL9 109 P7
Duke's La ASC SL5 170 F10
KENS W8 14 G1
Duke's Ms MHST W1U 10 D5
MUSWH N10 118 C1
Dukes Orch BXLY DA5 186 D4
Dukes Pl HDTCH EC3A 13 L6
Dukes Point HGT N6 118 C6
Dukes Ride CFSP/GDCR SL9 110 B6
HGDN/ICK UB10 111 P9
RDKG RH5 273 J5
Dukes Rd ACT W3 135 M6
RDKG RH5 278 C10
CAMTN NW1 5 K10
EHAM E6 142 D3
WOT/HER KT12 217 L2
Dukesthorpe Rd SYD SE26 182 C7
Duke St HOD EN11 44 F2
MHST W1U 10 D5
RCH/KEW TW9 155 J10
SUT SM1 221 N1
WAT WD17 73 K7
WDSR SL4 148 G6
WOKN/KNAP GU21 232 C3
Duke Street Hl STHWK SE1 13 H9
Duke Street St James's
MYFR/PICC W1J 11 H9
Dukes Va CFSP/GDCR SL9 109 N7
Dukes Wy BERK HP4 * 33 M3
UX/CGN UB8 131 L3
WWKM BR4 205 K10
Dukes Wood Av CFSP/GDCR SL9 110 B6
Dukes Wood Dr CFSP/GDCR SL9 109 P6
Duke's Yd MYFR/PKLN W1K 10 D7
Dulas St FSBYPK N4 118 G6
Dulford St NTGHL W11 8 A7
Dulka Rd BTSEA SW11 180 A1
Dulverton Rd ELTH/MOT SE9 184 F5
HARH RM3 105 L7
RSLP HA4 113 H7
SAND/SEL CR2 224 B6
Dulwich Common DUL SE21 181 L4
The Dulwich Oaks DUL SE21 * 181 N6
Dulwich Rd HNHL SE24 181 H1
Dulwich Village DUL SE21 181 L2
Dulwich Wy RKW/CH/CXG WD3 72 B9
Dulwich Wood Av NRWD SE19 181 N8
Dulwich Wood Pk NRWD SE19 181 M7
Dumbarton Av CHES/WCR EN8 62 C10
Dumbarton Rd
BRXS/STRHM SW2 180 F2
Dumbleton Cl KUT/HW KT1 199 N1
Dumbletons RKW/CH/CXG WD3 91 H5
Dumbreck Rd ELTH/MOT SE9 162 D10
Dumfries Cl OXHEY WD19 93 H4
Dumont Rd STNW/STAM N16 119 M8
Dumpton Pl CAMTN NW1 4 C4
Dumville Dr GDST RH9 260 A7
Dunally Pk SHPTN TW17 196 E7
Dunbar Av BECK BR3 204 D4
DAGE RM10 124 B8
STRHM/NOR SW16 203 H2
Dunbar Cl SLN SL2 129 M9
YEAD UB4 133 H7
Dunbar Ct WOT/HER KT12 197 K9
Dunbar Gdns DAGE RM10 124 B10
Dunbar Rd FSTGT E7 141 M1
NWMAL KT3 199 P4
WDGN N22 99 H9
Dunbar St WNWD SE27 181 K6
Dunblane Rd ELTH/MOT SE9 162 B9
Dunboe Pl SHPTN TW17 196 D7
Dunboyne Rd HAMP NW3 118 A10
Dunbridge St BETH E2 13 P1
Duncan Cl BAR EN5 77 M8
WGCE AL7 23 H6
Duncan Dr GU GU1 250 D9
Duncan Gdns STA TW18 173 K9
Duncan Gv ACT W3 136 B8
Duncannon Crs WDSR SL4 148 C9
Duncannon St CHCR WC2N 11 L8
Duncan Rd HACK E8 140 A3
KWD/TDW/WH KT20 239 H5
RCH/KEW TW9 155 K10
Duncan St IS N1 6 C7
Duncan Ter IS N1 6 C8
Duncan Wy BUSH WD23 73 N6
Dunch St WCHPL E1 140 A8
Duncombe Cl AMS HP6 69 K4
HERT/WAT SG14 25 K3
Duncombe Hl FSTH SE23 182 D3
Duncombe Rd ARCH N19 118 E6
BERK HP4 33 K3
HERT/WAT SG14 25 K4
Duncrievie Rd LEW SE13 183 J2
Duncroft WDSR SL4 148 E9
WOOL/PLUM SE18 163 H6
Duncroft Cl REIG RH2 257 J10
Dunction Cl CRAWW RH11 283 L5
Dundalk Rd BROCKY SE4 160 D9
Dundas Gdns E/WMO/HCT KT8 198 A3
Dundas Rd PECK SE15 160 B8
Dundee Rd PLSTW E13 141 N4
SL SL1 128 E8
SNWD SE25 204 A5
Dundee St WAP E1W 140 A10
Dundee Wy PEND EN3 80 D7
Dundela Gdns WPK KT4 220 E1
Dundonald Cl EHAM E6 142 B8
Dundonald Rd WIM/MER SW19 179 J10
WLSDN NW10 136 G3
Dundrey Crs REDH RH1 258 F5
Dunedin Dr CTHM CR3 259 M1
Dunedin Rd IL IG1 122 F6
LEY E10 120 G8
RAIN RM13 144 G5
Dunedin Wy YEAD UB4 133 K6
Dunelm St WCHPL E1 140 C8
Dunfee Wy BF/WBF KT14 215 P8
Dunfield Rd CAT SE6 182 G8
Dunford Br CHERT KT16 214 E7
Dunford Rd HOLWY N7 118 G9
Dungarvan Av PUT/ROE SW15 156 D10
Dungates La BRKHM/BTCW RH3 256 D10
Dunheved Cl THHTH CR7 203 H6
Dunheved Rd North THHTH CR7 203 H6
Dunheved Rd South THHTH CR7 203 H6
Dunheved Rd West THHTH CR7 203 H6
Dunholme Gn ED N9 99 N4
Dunholme La ED N9 99 N4
Dunholme Rd ED N9 99 N4
Dunkeld Rd BCTR RM8 123 L7
SNWD SE25 203 L4
Dunkellin Gv SOCK/AV RM15 146 F8
Dunkellin Wy SOCK/AV RM15 146 F8
Dunkery Rd ELTH/MOT SE9 184 A7
Dunkin Rd DART DA1 165 P10
Dunkirk Cl GVE DA12 190 F8
Dunkirk St WNWD SE27 * 181 K7
Dunlace Rd CLPT E5 120 B10
Dunleary Cl HSLWW TW4 175 N3
Dunley Dr CROY/NA CR0 225 H3
Dunlin Cl REDH RH1 275 P5
Dunlin Ri RGUE GU4 250 G8
Dunlin Rd HHNE HP2 35 P1
Dunloe Av TOTM N17 119 L1
Dunloe St BETH E2 7 M8
Dunlop Pl BERM/RHTH SE16 19 M4
Dunlop Rd TIL RM18 168 C7
Dunmail Dr SAND/SEL CR2 223 M9
Dunmore GUW GU2 249 J9
Dunmore Rd KIL/WHAMP NW6 2 A6
RYNPK SW20 200 F1
Dunmow Cl CHDH RM6 123 M3
FELT TW13 * 175 M7
LOU IG10 82 B10
Dunmow Dr RAIN RM13 144 G3
Dunmow Rd SRTFD E15 121 J9
Dunmow Wk IS N1 * 6 E5
Dunnage Crs BERM/RHTH SE16 160 D3
Dunnets WOKN/KNAP GU21 231 K3
Dunning Cl SOCK/AV RM15 146 F8
Dunningford Cl HCH RM12 124 C10
Dunnings La RBRW/HUT CM13 127 N7
Dunn Md CDALE/KGS NW9 96 C8
Dunnock Cl BORE WD6 75 M8
ED N9 100 C2
Dunnock Rd EHAM E6 142 B8
Dunn St HACK E8 119 N10
Dunny La KGLGY WD4 53 J8
Dunnymans Rd BNSTD SM7 239 J1
Dunollie Pl KTTN NW5 118 D10
Dunollie Rd KTTN NW5 118 D10
Dunoon Gdns FSTH SE23 * 182 D3
Dunoon Rd FSTH SE23 182 B3
Dunottar Cl REDH RH1 275 M3
Dunraven Av REDH RH1 276 C8
Dunraven Dr ENC/FH EN2 79 H6
Dunraven Rd SHB W12 136 D10
Dunraven St MYFR/PKLN W1K 10 B7
Dunsany Rd HMSMTH W6 156 G2
Dunsbury Cl BELMT SM2 221 M6
Dunsdon Av GUW GU2 267 N1
Dunsfold Cl CRAWW RH11 283 K8
Dunsfold Ri COUL/CHIP CR5 222 E9
Dunsfold Wy CROY/NA CR0 224 G4
Dunsford Wy PUT/ROE SW15 178 E3
Dunsmore OXHEY WD19 * 93 L3
Dunsmore Cl BUSH WD23 74 C10
YEAD UB4 133 L6
Dunsmore Rd WOT/HER KT12 197 J5
Dunsmore Wy BUSH WD23 74 C10
Dunsmure Rd STNW/STAM N16 119 M6
Dunspring La CLAY IG5 102 E10
Dunstable Ms CAVSQ/HST W1G 10 E3
Dunstable Rd E/WMO/HCT KT8 197 N4
HARH RM3 105 L7
RCH/KEW TW9 155 K9
Dunstall Rd RYNPK SW20 178 E9
Dunstalls HLWW/ROY CM19 46 D5
Dunstall Wy E/WMO/HCT KT8 198 A2
Dunstall Welling Est
WELL DA16 * 163 L8
Dunstan Cl EFNCH N2 * 117 M1
Dunstan Gld STMC/STPC BR5 * 206 G6
Dunstan Houses WCHPL E1 * 140 B7
Dunstan Rd COUL/CHIP CR5 240 E3
GLDGN NW11 117 J6
Dunstan's Gv EDUL SE22 182 A1
Dunstan's Rd EDUL SE22 181 P3
Dunster Av MRDN SM4 200 G8
Dunster Cl BAR EN5 76 G8
CRW RM5 104 D10
DEN/HRF UB9 91 L9
Dunster Ct BORE WD6 76 A7
MON EC3R 13 J7
Dunster Crs EMPK RM11 125 P7
EMPK RM11 126 A7
Dunster Dr CDALE/KGS NW9 115 P6
Dunster Gdns KIL/WHAMP NW6 2 D3
SL SL1 128 F9
Dunsters Md WGCE AL7 23 K7
Dunsterville Wy STHWK SE1 19 H2
Dunster Wy RYLN/HDSTN HA2 113 M8
Dunston Rd BTSEA SW11 158 B8
HACK E8 7 L6
Dunston St HACK E8 7 K5
Dunton Cl SURB KT6 199 K8
Dunton Rd LEY E10 120 G5
ROM RM1 124 F2
STHWK SE1 19 L6
Duntshill Rd WAND/EARL SW18 179 L4
Dunvegan Cl E/WMO/HCT KT8 198 A4
Dunvegan Rd ELTH/MOT SE9 162 C10
Dunwich Rd BXLYHN DA7 164 A7
Dunworth Ms NTGHL W11 8 C6
Duplex Ride KTBR SW1X 16 B2
Dupont Rd RYNPK SW20 200 G2
Duppas Av CROY/NA CR0 223 J1
Duppas Cl SHPTN TW17 196 E5
Duppas Hill Rd CROY/NA CR0 223 J1
Duppas Hill Ter CROY/NA CR0 223 J10
Duppas Rd CROY/NA CR0 203 H10
Dupre Cl CDW/CHF RM16 167 K2
SL SL1 148 D1
Dupree Rd CHARL SE7 161 N4
Dura Den Cl BECK BR3 182 G10
Durand Gdns BRXN/ST SW9 158 G7
Durand Wy WLSDN NW10 135 P2
Durant Rd SWLY BR8 187 H10
Durants Park Av PEND EN3 80 C8
Durants Rd PEND EN3 80 B8
Durant St BETH E2 7 N9
Durban Gdns DAGE RM10 144 D2
Durban Rd BECK BR3 204 E2
GNTH/NBYPK IG2 123 H6
SRTFD E15 141 K5
TOTM N17 99 N7
WALTH E17 100 E10
WNWD SE27 181 K7
Durban Rd East WATW WD18 73 H8
Durban Rd West WATW WD18 73 H8
Durbin Rd CHSCTN KT9 219 K1
Durdans Rd STHL UB1 133 N8
Durell Gdns DAGW RM9 123 N10
Durell Rd DAGW RM9 123 N10
Durfey Pl WALW SE17 159 L6
Durfold Dr REIG RH2 257 M10
Durford Crs PUT/ROE SW15 178 E4
Durham Av GPK RM2 125 K2
HAYES BR2 205 L4
HEST TW5 153 N5
SL SL1 128 F8
WFD IG8 102 A6
Durham Cl GUW GU2 249 L8
SBW CM21 29 M2
WARE SG12 26 G6
Durham Hl BMLY BR1 183 L7
Durham House St CHCR WC2N * 11 M8
Durham Pl CHEL SW3 16 A8
Durham Ri WOOL/PLUM SE18 162 F4
Durham Rd BORE WD6 75 P7
CAN/RD E16 141 K6
DAGE RM10 124 D10
EA W5 155 J2
EBED/NFELT TW14 175 L5
ED N9 99 P3
EFNCH N2 117 P1
HAYES BR2 205 M4
HOLWY N7 118 G7
HRW HA1 114 A3
MNPK E12 122 A9
RYNPK SW20 200 E1
SCUP DA14 185 L8
Durham Rw WCHPL E1 140 C7
Durham St LBTH SE11 17 N8
Durham Ter BAY/PAD W2 8 G5
PGE/AN SE20 * 182 A10
Durham Wharf Dr BTFD TW8 155 H6
Durham Yd BETH E2 * 140 A6
Duriun Wy ERITH DA8 165 J6
Durleston Park Dr GT/LBKH KT23 254 B1
Durley Av PIN HA5 113 M4
Durley Gdns ORP BR6 227 L1
Durley Rd STNW/STAM N16 119 M5
Durlston Rd CLPT E5 119 P7
KUTN/CMB KT2 177 K9
Durndale La GVW DA11 190 C7
Durnell Wy LOU IG10 82 D7
Durnford St SEVS/STOTM N15 119 M3
Durning Rd NRWD SE19 181 L8
Durnsford Av WIM/MER SW19 179 K5
Durnsford Rd FBAR/BDGN N11 98 E8
WIM/MER SW19 179 K6
Durpe Crs BEAC HP9 88 G10
Durrants Cl RAIN RM13 145 K4
Durrants Dr RKW/CH/CXG WD3 72 D7
Durrants Hill Rd HHS/BOV HP3 35 N9
Durrants La BERK HP4 33 L4
Durrants Rd BERK HP4 33 L4
Durrant Wy ORP BR6 226 G2
SWCM DA10 189 K3
Durrell Rd FUL/PGN SW6 157 H8
Durrell Wy SHPTN TW17 196 E6
Durrington Av RYNPK SW20 * 200 F1
Durrington Park Rd
RYNPK SW20 200 F1
Durrington Rd CLPT E5 120 D9
Dursley Cl BKHTH/KID SE3 161 P8
Dursley Gdns BKHTH/KID SE3 162 A7
Dursley Rd BKHTH/KID SE3 161 P8
Durward St WCHPL E1 13 P3
Durweston Ms MHST W1U * 10 B3
Durweston St MBLAR W1H 10 A4
Dury Falls Cl EMPK RM11 125 N6
Dury Rd BAR EN5 77 J5
Dutch Barn Cl STWL/WRAY TW19 173 N2
Dutch Gdns KUTN/CMB KT2 177 N9
Dutch Yd WAND/EARL SW18 179 K1
Duthie St POP/IOD E14 141 H9
Dutton St GNWCH SE10 161 H7
Dutton Wy IVER SL0 131 H8
Duxberry Cl HAYES BR2 206 B5
Duxford Cl HCH RM12 145 K1
Duxhurst La REIG RH2 275 L10
Duxons Turn HHNE HP2 36 C5
Dwight Rd WATW WD18 92 E1
Dye House La BOW E3 140 F3
Dyer's Buildings
FLST/FETLN EC4A 12 A4
Dyer's Fld HORL RH6 281 J4
Dyers Hall Rd WAN E11 121 K6
Dyer's La PUT/ROE SW15 156 E9
Dyers Wy HARH RM3 105 H8
Dyke Dr STMC/STPC BR5 207 M7
Dyke La STALE/WH AL4 21 K4
Dykes Pth WOKN/KNAP GU21 232 F1
Dykes Wy HAYES BR2 205 L3
Dykewood Cl BXLY DA5 186 E6
Dylan Cl BORE WD6 * 95 J1
Dylan Rd BELV DA17 164 B4
HNHL SE24 159 J10
Dylways CMBW SE5 159 L10
Dymchurch Cl CLAY IG5 122 D1
ORP BR6 227 H1
Dymock St FUL/PGN SW6 157 L9
Dymoke Gn STALE/WH AL4 38 F3
Dymoke Rd EMPK RM11 124 G5
Dymokes Wy HOD EN11 26 F10
Dyneley Rd LEE/GVPK SE12 183 P7
Dyne Rd KIL/WHAMP NW6 2 C4
Dynes Rd BGR/WK TN15 247 M3
Dynevor Pl RGUW GU3 249 H6
Dynevor Rd RCHPK/HAM TW10 177 K1
STNW/STAM N16 119 M8
Dynham Rd KIL/WHAMP NW6 2 E3
Dyott St LSQ/SEVD WC2H 11 L5
Dyrham La BAR EN5 76 D2
Dysart Av KUTN/CMB KT2 177 H8
Dysart St SDTCH EC2A 13 J2
Dyson Cl WDSR SL4 148 G9
Dyson Ct ALP/SUD HA0 114 G10
DORK RH4 * 272 F2
Dyson Rd SRTFD E15 141 L1
WAN E11 121 K4
Dysons Cl CHES/WCR EN8 62 C9
Dyson's Rd UED N18 100 A7
Dytchleys Rd BRW CM14 85 N8

E

Eade Rd FSBYPK N4 119 K5
Eagans Cl EFNCH N2 * 117 N1
Eagle Av CHDH RM6 123 P4
Eagle Cl AMS HP6 69 L3
BERM/RHTH SE16 160 A5
HCH RM12 145 J1
PEND EN3 80 B8
WAB EN9 63 M10
WLGTN SM6 222 F3
Eagle Ct FARR EC1M 12 C3
HERT/BAY SG13 26 A4
Eagle Dr CDALE/KGS NW9 96 B10
Eagle Hl NRWD SE19 181 L9
Eagle House Ms CLAP SW4 180 D1
Eagle La BRWN CM15 86 D3
WAN E11 121 M2
Eagle Ms IS N1 7 J1
Eagle Pl SKENS SW7 15 K7
Eagle Rd ALP/SUD HA0 135 J2
GU GU1 268 A1
HTHAIR TW6 152 C9
Eagles Dr BH/WHM TN16 244 A4
Eaglesfield Rd
WOOL/PLUM SE18 162 E7
Eagles Rd RDART DA2 166 G10
Eagle St GINN WC1R 11 N4
Eagle Ter WFD IG8 101 N8
Eagle Wy GVW DA11 189 M1
HAT AL10 40 D6
RBRW/HUT CM13 107 H7
Eagle Wharf Rd IS N1 6 F7
Eagling Cl BOW E3 140 F5
Ealdham Sq ELTH/MOT SE9 161 P10
Ealing Broadway Centre
EA W5 * 135 J9
Ealing Cl BORE WD6 76 A5
Ealing Gn EA W5 135 J10
Ealing Park Gdns EA W5 155 H3
Ealing Rd ALP/SUD HA0 135 K1
ALP/SUD HA0 135 K4
BOW E3 140 G5
BTFD TW8 155 K5
EA W5 155 J3
NTHLT UB5 133 P3
Ealing Village EA W5 135 K8
Eamont Cl RSLP HA4 112 C5
Eamont St STJWD NW8 3 N7
Eardemont Cl DART DA1 164 G10
Eardley Crs ECT SW5 14 F7
Eardley Rd BELV DA17 164 B4
SEV TN13 247 J10
STRHM/NOR SW16 180 D9
Earl Cl FBAR/BDGN N11 98 C6
Earldom Rd PUT/ROE SW15 156 F10
Earle Gdns KUTN/CMB KT2 177 K10
Earleswood COB KT11 217 L8
Earleydene ASC SL5 192 A8
Earlham Gv FSTGT E7 121 L10
WDGN N22 98 G8
Earlham St LSQ/SEVD WC2H 11 K6
Earl Ri WOOL/PLUM SE18 162 G4
Earl Rd GVW DA11 190 B5
MORT/ESHN SW14 155 P10
Earlsbrook Rd REDH RH1 276 A2
Earls Cnr POTB/CUF EN6 * 58 D9
Earl's Court Gdns ECT SW5 14 G6
Earl's Court Rd ECT SW5 14 F5
Earl's Court Sq ECT SW5 14 G7
Earls Crs HRW HA1 114 D2
Earlsferry Wy IS N1 5 N4
Earlsfield Rd WAND/EARL SW18 179 M4
Earlshall Rd ELTH/MOT SE9 162 C10
Earls La POTB/CUF EN6 58 B8
SL SL1 128 E10
Earlsmead RYLN/HDSTN HA2 113 N9
Earlsmead Rd SEVS/STOTM N15 119 N3
WLSDN NW10 136 F5
Earls Ms WAND/EARL SW18 179 M3
Earl's Pth LOU IG10 81 P7
Earls Ter KENS W8 14 E4
Earlsthorpe Ms BAL SW12 180 B2
Earlsthorpe Rd SYD SE26 182 C7
Earlstoke Est FSBYE EC1V 6 C9
Earlstoke St FSBYE EC1V 6 C9
Earlston Gv HOM E9 140 A3
Earl St SDTCH EC2A 13 J3
WAT WD17 73 K7
Earls Wk BCTR RM8 123 L9
KENS W8 14 E4
Earlswood Av THHTH CR7 203 H5
Earlswood Gdns CLAY IG5 122 D1
Earlswood Rd REDH RH1 276 A2
Earlswood St GNWCH SE10 161 K4
Early Commons CRAWE RH10 284 A6
Early Ms CAMTN NW1 4 F5
Earnshaw St NOXST/BSQ WC1A 11 K5
Earsby St WKENS W14 14 B5
Easby Crs MRDN SM4 201 L6
Easebourne Rd BCTR RM8 123 M10
Easedale Dr HCH RM12 125 J10
Easington Pl GU GU1 268 C1
Easington Wy SOCK/AV RM15 146 F7
Easleys Ms MHST W1U 10 D5
East Acton Av ACT W3 * 136 C8
East Acton La ACT W3 136 B9
East Arbour St WCHPL E1 140 C8
East Av EHAM E6 142 B2
HYS/HAR UB3 152 G1
WALTH E17 120 G3
WLGTN SM6 222 G2
East Bank STNW/STAM N16 119 M5
Eastbank Rd HPTN TW12 176 B8
East Barnet Rd BAR EN5 77 M8
EBAR EN4 77 P10
Eastbourne Av ACT W3 136 A8
Eastbourne Gdns
MORT/ESHN SW14 155 P9
Eastbourne Ms BAY/PAD W2 9 K5
Eastbourne Rd BTFD TW8 155 J4
EHAM E6 142 D5
FELT TW13 175 L5
GDST RH9 260 B8
GDST RH9 260 D10
SEVS/STOTM N15 119 M4
SL SL1 128 F8
SRTFD E15 141 K3
TOOT SW17 180 B9
Eastbourne Ter BAY/PAD W2 9 L5
Eastbournia Av ED N9 100 B4
Eastbridge SL SL1 149 N1
Eastbrook Av DAGE RM10 124 D8
ED N9 100 B1
Eastbrook Cl WOKN/KNAP GU21 232 D2
Eastbrook Dr ROMW/RG RM7 124 F8
Eastbrook Rd BKHTH/KID SE3 161 N7
WAB EN9 63 K9
Eastbrook Wy HHNE HP2 35 P6
East Burnham La SLN SL2 128 F3
East Burrowfield WGCE AL7 22 G7
Eastbury Av BARK IG11 143 H3
EN EN1 79 M5
NTHWD HA6 92 F6
Eastbury Ct OXHEY WD19 * 93 K1
STAL AL1 38 E5
Eastbury Gv CHSWK W4 156 B4
Eastbury La RGUW GU3 266 F6
Eastbury Rd EHAM E6 142 D6
KUTN/CMB KT2 177 K10
NTHWD HA6 92 F7
OXHEY WD19 93 K1
ROMW/RG RM7 124 E4
STMC/STPC BR5 206 G6
Eastbury Sq BARK IG11 143 J3
Eastbury Ter WCHPL E1 140 C6
Eastcastle St GTPST W1W 10 G5
Eastcheap FENCHST EC3M 13 H7
East Churchfield Rd ACT W3 136 A10
Eastchurch Rd HTHAIR TW6 152 F9
East Cl EA W5 135 M6
EBAR EN4 78 B8
GFD/PVL UB6 134 B4
LCOL/BKTW AL2 56 A1
RAIN RM13 145 J6
Eastcombe Av CHARL SE7 161 N5
East Common CFSP/GDCR SL9 110 B4
Eastcote ORP BR6 207 J8
Eastcote Av E/WMO/HCT KT8 197 N5
RYLN/HDSTN HA2 114 A7
Eastcote Dr HARP AL5 20 C5
Eastcote La NTHLT UB5 133 P2
RYLN/HDSTN HA2 113 N9
RYLN/HDSTN HA2 114 A8
Eastcote La North NTHLT UB5 133 N1
Eastcote Rd RSLP HA4 112 F5
RSLP HA4 113 H4
PIN HA5 113 L3
RYLN/HDSTN HA2 114 B8
WELL DA16 162 G8
Eastcote St BRXN/ST SW9 158 F8
Eastcote Vw PIN HA5 113 K2
East Ct ALP/SUD HA0 115 H7
East Crs EN EN1 79 M9
FBAR/BDGN N11 98 A5
WDSR SL4 148 E7
Eastcroft SLN SL2 128 G6
Eastcroft Rd HOR/WEW KT19 220 B4
East Cross Centre SRTFD E15 * 140 F1
East Cross Route HOM E9 140 E2
Eastdean Av EPSOM KT18 219 N9
East Dene Dr HARH RM3 105 L6
Eastdown Pk LEW SE13 161 J10
East Dr CAR SM5 221 P5
GSTN WD25 73 J2
LCOL/BKTW AL2 56 G2
NTHWD HA6 92 F3
SBW CM21 29 P2
SLN SL2 129 K6
STALE/WH AL4 39 K5
STMC/STPC BR5 207 L6
VW GU25 193 N6
East Duck Lees La PEND EN3 80 E8
East Dulwich Gv EDUL SE22 181 M1
East Dulwich Rd EDUL SE22 159 N10
East End Rd EFNCH N2 117 M1
EFNCH N2 117 P2
FNCH N3 97 K10
FNCH N3 117 L1
East End Wy PIN HA5 113 M1
East Entrance DAGE RM10 144 C4
Eastergate BEAC HP9 88 B7
Eastern Av CHERT KT16 195 K3
CHES/WCR EN8 62 E9
CHOB/PIR GU24 230 G7
GNTH/NBYPK IG2 122 F4
PIN HA5 113 L5
REDBR IG4 122 A4
SOCK/AV RM15 166 B1
WAN E11 121 P4
Eastern Av East ROM RM1 124 E1
Eastern Av West CHDH RM6 123 P2
ROMW/RG RM7 124 D2
Eastern Gtwy CAN/RD E16 141 P9
Eastern Perimeter Rd
HTHAIR TW6 152 F8
Eastern Rd BROCKY SE4 160 F10
EFNCH N2 118 A1
PLSTW E13 141 N4
ROM RM1 124 G3
WALTH E17 121 H3
WDGN N22 98 F9
Eastern Wy BH/WHM TN16 243 P3
Easternville Gdns
GNTH/NBYPK IG2 122 F4
Eastern Wy GRAYS RM17 167 M5
THMD SE28 143 N10
THMD SE28 163 K1
East Ferry Rd POP/IOD E14 160 G3
Eastfield Av WATN WD24 73 L5
Eastfield Cl SL SL1 * 149 M2
Eastfield Ct STALE/WH AL4 39 J3
Eastfield Gdns DAGE RM10 124 B9
Eastfield Rd BRW CM14 107 J5
CEND/HSY/T N8 118 F1
CHES/WCR EN8 62 E8
DAGE RM10 124 B9
PEND EN3 80 C4
REDH RH1 276 C1
WALTH E17 120 F2
Eastfields PIN HA5 113 K3
Eastfields Av WAND/EARL SW18 157 K10
Eastfields Rd ACT W3 135 P7
MTCM CR4 202 B2
Eastfield St POP/IOD E14 140 D7
East Flexford La RGUW GU3 266 E3
East Flint HHW HP1 35 H5
East Gdns TOOT SW17 179 P9
WOKS/MYFD GU22 232 F3
Eastgate BNSTD SM7 221 J10
East Ga HLW CM20 28 G10
Eastgate Cl THMD SE28 143 N8
Eastgate Ct GU GU1 * 268 B1
Eastgate Gdns GU GU1 268 B1
Eastglade NTHWD HA6 92 F6
PIN HA5 113 N1
East Hall La RAIN RM13 145 L8
East Hall Rd STMC/STPC BR5 207 P7
Eastham Cl BAR EN5 77 J9
East Ham Crs RBRW/HUT CM13 107 M5
East Ham Manor Wy EHAM E6 142 D8
East Harding St
FLST/FETLN EC4A 12 B5
East Heath Rd HAMP NW3 117 N8
East Hl BH/WHM TN16 243 N4
DART DA1 187 N3
EYN DA4 210 C1
OXTED RH8 261 L5
SAND/SEL CR2 223 M6
WAND/EARL SW18 179 M1
WBLY HA9 115 M7
WOKS/MYFD GU22 232 F2
East Hill Dr DART DA1 187 N3
East Hill La CRAWE RH10 281 L9
East Hill Rd OXTED RH8 261 K5
Eastholm GLDGN NW11 117 L2
East Holme ERITH DA8 164 E7
Eastholme HYS/HAR UB3 133 H10
East India Dock Rd POP/IOD E14 140 F8
East India Wy CROY/NA CR0 203 N8
East Kent Av GVW DA11 189 P2
Eastlake Rd CMBW SE5 159 J8
Eastlands Cl OXTED RH8 261 J3
Eastlands Crs EDUL SE22 181 N2
Eastlands Wy OXTED RH8 261 J3
East La ABLGY WD5 55 H4
ABLGY WD5 55 J6
ALP/SUD HA0 115 H8
EHSLY KT24 252 D2
KUT/HW KT1 199 J3
STALE/WH AL4 21 J2
Eastlea Av GSTN WD25 73 M3
Eastlea Ms CAN/RD E16 141 K6
Eastleigh Av RYLN/HDSTN HA2 114 A7
Eastleigh Cl BELMT SM2 221 L4
CRICK NW2 116 B8
Eastleigh Rd BXLYHN DA7 164 D8
WALTH E17 100 E10
Eastleigh Wy EBED/NFELT TW14 175 H4
East Lodge La ENC/FH EN2 78 E2
Eastman Rd ACT W3 156 A1
Eastman Wy HHNE HP2 36 B3
East Md RSLP HA4 113 L8
WGCE AL7 23 L8
Eastmead WOKN/KNAP GU21 231 N3
Eastmead Av GFD/PVL UB6 134 A5
Eastmead Cl BMLY BR1 206 B2
East Meads GUW GU2 267 L1
Eastmearn Rd DUL SE21 181 K5
East Ml GVW DA11 190 C2
East Milton Rd GVE DA12 190 G3
East Mimms HHNE HP2 35 P5
Eastmont Rd ESH/CLAY KT10 198 D9
Eastmoor Pk HARP AL5 20 B5
Eastmoor Pl CHARL SE7 162 A2
Eastmoor St CHARL SE7 162 A2
East Mt STALE/WH AL4 21 J2
East Mount St WCHPL E1 140 A7
Eastney Rd CROY/NA CR0 203 J8
Eastney St GNWCH SE10 161 J4
Eastnor HHS/BOV HP3 52 D4
Eastnor Pl REIG RH2 * 275 K2
Eastnor Rd ELTH/MOT SE9 184 F4
REIG RH2 275 J2
Easton Gdns BORE WD6 76 B8
Easton St FSBYW WC1X 12 A1
Eastor WGCE AL7 23 K2
East Pk CRAWE RH10 283 N8
HLWE CM17 29 L8
East Park Cl CHDH RM6 123 N3
East Parkside GNWCH SE10 161 K1
WARL CR6 242 F2
East Pas STBT EC1A 12 E3
East Pl WNWD SE27 181 K7
East Pole Cottages
STHGT/OAK N14 * 78 E8
East Poultry Av FARR EC1M 12 C4
East Rp HTHAIR TW6 152 C7
East Ridgeway POTB/CUF EN6 60 F5
East Rd CHDH RM6 123 P3
CHEL SW3 16 C8
EBAR EN4 98 B2
EBED/NFELT TW14 174 E3
EDGW HA8 95 N9
HLW CM20 29 L7
IS N1 7 H9
KUTN/CMB KT2 199 K1
PEND EN3 80 B4
REIG RH2 257 J9
ROMW/RG RM7 124 E5
SRTFD E15 141 M3
WDR/YW UB7 152 A3
WELL DA16 163 L8
WEY KT13 216 E5
WIM/MER SW19 179 M9
East Rochester Wy BFN/LL DA15 185 H1
BFN/LL DA15 185 M2
DART DA1 186 E3

East Rw NKENS W10 8 B2
WAN E11 121 M4
Eastry Av HAYES BR2 205 L6
Eastry Rd ERITH DA8 164 B6
East Shalford La RGUE GU4 268 D5
East Sheen Av
MORT/ESHN SW14 178 A1
Eastside Rd GLDGN NW11 117 J2
East Smithfield WAP E1W 13 M8
East St BARK IG11 142 F2
BMLY BR1 205 M2
BTFD TW8 155 H6
BXLYHN DA7 164 B10
CSHM HP5 50 G8
EW KT17 220 B8
GT/LBKH KT23 254 A1
HHNE HP2 35 N6
HORS RH12 282 B6
WALW SE17 18 F7
WALW SE17 19 J6
WARE SG12 26 C2
WTHK RM20 167 K5
East Surrey Gv PECK SE15 159 N6
East Tenter St WCHPL E1 13 M6
East Ter BFN/LL DA15 * 185 H4
GVE DA12 190 F2
East Thurrock Rd GRAYS RM17 167 N5
East Tilbury Rd SLH/COR SS17 169 K1
East Towers PIN HA5 113 L4
East V ACT W3 * 136 C10
East Vw BAR EN5 77 J7
BRKMPK AL9 42 A3
CHING E4 101 H6
Eastview Av WOOL/PLUM SE18 163 H6
Eastville Av GLDGN NW11 117 J4
East Wk EBAR EN4 98 B2
HLW CM20 * 28 G10
HYS/HAR UB3 153 H1
REIG RH2 257 L10
East Wy CROY/NA CR0 204 D9
HYS/HAR UB3 133 H10
RSLP HA4 113 H6
WAB EN9 81 J2
Eastway GUW GU2 249 L10
HAYES BR2 205 M7
HOM E9 140 D3
HOM E9 140 E1
HOR/WEW KT19 219 P8
HORL RH6 280 C8
LEY E10 120 F9
MRDN SM4 200 G5
WAN E11 121 N3
WLGTN SM6 222 D1
Eastway Crs RYLN/HDSTN HA2 114 A7
Eastwell Cl BECK BR3 204 D1
Eastwick Crs RKW/CH/CXG WD3 91 J3
Eastwick Dr GT/LBKH KT23 236 A10
Eastwick Hall La HLW CM20 28 D7
Eastwick Park Av GT/LBKH KT23 254 A1
Eastwick Rd GT/LBKH KT23 254 A1
HLW CM20 28 E7
WARE SG12 27 N8
WOT/HER KT12 217 J3
Eastwick Rw HHNE HP2 36 B7
Eastwood CRAWE RH10 284 A7
Eastwood Cl HOLWY N7 119 H10
SWFD E18 101 M10
TOTM N17 * 100 A8
Eastwood Dr RAIN RM13 145 J8
Eastwood Ldg SHGR GU5 * 268 C10
Eastwood Rd GDMY/SEVK IG3 123 K5
MUSWH N10 98 B10
SHGR GU5 268 C10
SWFD E18 101 M10
WDR/YW UB7 152 B1
Eastwood St STRHM/NOR SW16 180 D9
Eastworth Rd CHERT KT16 195 J8
Eatington Rd LEY E10 121 J3
Eaton Cl BGVA SW1W 16 C5
STAN HA7 94 G5
Eaton Dr BRXN/ST SW9 159 J10
CRW RM5 104 C8
KUTN/CMB KT2 177 M10
Eaton Gdns DAGW RM9 143 P2
Eaton Ga BGVA SW1W 16 C5
NTHWD HA6 92 D7
Eaton La BGVA SW1W 16 F4
Eaton Ms North KTBR SW1X 16 D4
Eaton Ms South BGVA SW1W 16 D5
Eaton Ms West BGVA SW1W 16 D5
Eaton Pk COB KT11 217 M10
Eaton Park Rd COB KT11 217 N10
PLMGR N13 99 H3
Eaton Pl KTBR SW1X 16 C5
Eaton Ri EA W5 135 J8
WAN E11 121 P3
Eaton Rd BELMT SM2 221 N3
EN EN1 79 M7
HDN NW4 116 F3
HHNE HP2 36 C3
HSLW TW3 154 C10
SCUP DA14 185 N5
STAL AL1 38 G6
UPMR RM14 126 D7
Eaton Rw BGVA SW1W 16 E3
Eatons Md CHING E4 100 F3
Eaton Sq BGVA SW1W 16 E4
Eaton Ter BGVA SW1W 16 C5
BOW E3 * 140 D5
Eaton Terrace Ms BGVA SW1W 16 C5
Eatonville Rd TOOT SW17 180 A5
Eatonville Vls TOOT SW17 180 A5
Eaton Wy BORE WD6 75 L5
Eaves Cl ADL/WDHM KT15 215 M3
Ebba's Wy EPSOM KT18 237 N1
Ebberns Rd HHS/BOV HP3 35 P9
Ebbisham Cl DORK RH4 272 F2
Ebbisham Dr VX/NE SW8 17 N9
Ebbisham La
KWD/TDW/WH KT20 238 C7
KWD/TDW/WH KT20 238 D10
Ebbisham Rd EPSOM KT18 237 N1
WPK KT4 200 F9
Ebbsfleet Rd CRICK NW2 117 H10
Ebdon Wy BKHTH/KID SE3 161 N9
Ebenezer St FSBYE EC1V 6 G9
Ebenezer Wk STRHM/NOR SW16 202 D1
Ebley Cl PECK SE15 19 L10
Ebner St WAND/EARL SW18 179 L1
Ebor St WCHPL E1 13 L1
Ebrington Rd
KTN/HRWW/WS HA3 115 H4
Ebsworth St FSTH SE23 182 C3
Eburne Rd HOLWY N7 118 F8
Ebury Ap RKW/CH/CXG WD3 91 N2
Ebury Br BGVA SW1W 16 E7
Ebury Bridge Rd BGVA SW1W 16 D8
Ebury Cl HAYES BR2 206 B10
NTHWD HA6 92 D6
Ebury Ms BGVA SW1W 16 D5
Ebury Ms East BGVA SW1W 16 E5
Ebury Rd RKW/CH/CXG WD3 91 N2
WAT WD17 73 L7
Ebury Sq BGVA SW1W 16 E6
Ebury St BGVA SW1W 16 D6
Ecclesbourne Cl PLMGR N13 99 H6
Ecclesbourne Gdns PLMGR N13 99 H6
Ecclesbourne Rd IS N1 6 F4
THHTH CR7 203 K5
Eccles Hl RDKG RH5 273 H6
Eccles Rd BTSEA SW11 158 A10
Eccleston Cl EBAR EN4 77 P9
ORP BR6 * 206 G8
Eccleston Crs CHDH RM6 123 L5
Ecclestone Ct WBLY HA9 115 K10
Ecclestone Ms WBLY HA9 115 K10
Ecclestone Pl WBLY HA9 115 L10
Eccleston Ms KTBR SW1X 16 D4
Eccleston Pl BGVA SW1W 16 E4
Eccleston Rd WEA W13 134 F9
Eccleston Sq PIM SW1V 16 F6
Eccleston Square Ms PIM SW1V 16 F6
Eccleston St BGVA SW1W 16 D4
Echelforde Dr ASHF TW15 174 B7
Echo Ct GVE DA12 190 F5
Echo Hts CHING E4 * 100 G2
Echo Pit Rd GU GU1 268 B4
Eckford St IS N1 6 A7
Eckstein Rd BTSEA SW11 157 P10
Eclipse Rd PLSTW E13 141 N7
Ecob Cl RGUW GU3 249 L6
Ecton Rd ADL/WDHM KT15 215 L1
Ector Rd CAT SE6 183 K5
Edans Ct SHB W12 156 C1
Edbrooke Rd MV/WKIL W9 8 E2
Eddington Crs WGCE AL7 22 G8
Eddiscombe Rd FUL/PGN SW6 157 J8
Eddy Cl ROMW/RG RM7 124 C4
Eddystone Rd BROCKY SE4 182 D1
Eddy St BERK HP4 33 M4
Ede Cl HSLW TW3 153 N9
Edenbridge Cl BERM/RHTH SE16 160 A4
STMC/STPC BR5 207 N4
Edenbridge Rd EN EN1 79 M10
HOM E9 * 140 C2
Eden Cl ADL/WDHM KT15 215 L6
ALP/SUD HA0 135 J3
BXLY DA5 186 E7
DTCH/LGLY SL3 150 D4
HAMP NW3 117 K7
KENS W8 14 F3
PEND EN3 80 F4
Edencourt Rd STRHM/NOR SW16 180 C9
Edencroft SHGR GU5 268 D10
Edendale Rd BXLYHN DA7 164 E7
Edenfield Gdns WPK KT4 200 C10
Eden Gn SOCK/AV RM15 146 G7
Eden Gv HOLWY N7 118 G10
WLSDN NW10 136 E1
Eden Grove Rd BF/WBF KT14 215 P9
Edenhall Cl HHNE HP2 36 E7
Edenhall Rd HARH RM3 105 K6
Edenham Wy NKENS W10 8 C3
Edenhurst Av FUL/PGN SW6 157 J9
Eden Pde BECK BR3 * 204 D4
Eden Park Av BECK BR3 204 F4
Eden Rd BECK BR3 204 D4
BXLY DA5 186 D7
CRAWW RH11 283 J9
CROY/NA CR0 223 L1
WALTH E17 120 G3
WNWD SE27 181 J8
Edenside Rd GT/LBKH KT23 235 N10
Edensor Rd CHSWK W4 156 B6
Eden St KUT/HW KT1 199 J2
Edenvale CHESW EN7 62 A5
Edenvale Rd MTCM CR4 180 B10
Edenvale St FUL/PGN SW6 157 L8
Eden Wk KUT/HW KT1 * 199 K2
Eden Wy BECK BR3 204 F5
BOW E3 140 E3
WARL CR6 242 D4
Ederline Av STRHM/NOR SW16 202 G3
Edes Cottages ASHTD KT21 * 237 J5
Edgar Cl CRAWE RH10 284 F8
SWLY BR8 208 G3
Edgar Kail Wy CMBW SE5 159 M9
Edgarley Ter FUL/PGN SW6 * 157 H7
Edgar Rd BGR/WK TN15 247 M3
BH/WHM TN16 244 A7
BOW E3 140 G5
HSLWW TW4 175 N3
SAND/SEL CR2 223 L6
WDR/YW UB7 131 P9
Edgars Ct WGCE AL7 23 H6
Edgar Wallace Cl PECK SE15 159 M6
Edgbaston Dr RAD WD7 57 K8
Edgeborough Ct GU GU1 * 268 C1
Edgeborough Wy BMLY BR1 206 A1
Edgebury CHST BR7 184 E7
Edge Cl WEY KT13 216 B4
Edgecombe Cl KUTN/CMB KT2 178 A10
Edgecoombe SAND/SEL CR2 224 C5
Edgecote Cl ACT W3 135 P10
Edgefield Av BARK IG11 143 J2
Edgefield Cl DART DA1 188 A4
REDH RH1 276 B5
Edge Hl WIM/MER SW19 178 G10
WOOL/PLUM SE18 162 E5
Edge Hill Av FNCH N3 117 K2
Edge Hill Ct WIM/MER SW19 178 G10
Edgehill Ct WOT/HER KT12 * 197 K8
Edgehill Gdns DAGE RM10 124 B9
Edgehill Rd CHST BR7 184 F6
MTCM CR4 202 C1
PUR/KEN CR8 223 H6
WEA W13 135 H8
Edgeley GT/LBKH KT23 235 M10
Edgeley La CLAP SW4 158 E9
Edgeley Rd CLAP SW4 158 D9
Edgell Cl VW GU25 194 C3
Edgell Rd STA TW18 173 J9
Edgel St WAND/EARL SW18 179 L1
Edge Point Cl STRHM/NOR SW16 181 J8
Edgepoint Cl WNWD SE27 * 181 J8
Edge St KENS W8 8 F9
Edgewood Dr ORP BR6 227 J2
Edgewood Gn CROY/NA CR0 204 C8
Edgeworth Av HDN NW4 116 D3
Edgeworth Cl CTHM CR3 241 P4
HDN NW4 116 D3
Edgeworth Crs HDN NW4 116 D3
Edgeworth Rd EBAR EN4 77 P8
ELTH/MOT SE9 161 P10
Edgington Rd STRHM/NOR SW16 180 E9
Edgington Wy SCUP DA14 185 M10
Edgwarebury Gdns EDGW HA8 95 M6
Edgwarebury La BORE WD6 95 L1
EDGW HA8 95 M3
Edgware Rd BAY/PAD W2 9 L2
CDALE/KGS NW9 116 A2
CRICK NW2 116 F8
Edgware Rd
Burnt Oak Broadway
EDGW HA8 95 N8
Edgware Rd High St EDGW HA8 95 M7
Edgware Rd The Hyde
CDALE/KGS NW9 116 B2
Edgware Road Wy CRICK NW2 116 C7
Edgware Wy (Watford By-Pass)
EDGW HA8 95 K3
Edinburgh Av RKW/CH/CXG WD3 91 K1
SL SL1 128 F8
Edinburgh Cl BETH E2 140 B4
HGDN/ICK UB10 112 C9
PIN HA5 113 M5
Edinburgh Ct KUT/HW KT1 * 199 K3
Edinburgh Crs CHES/WCR EN8 62 D9
Edinburgh Dr ABLGY WD5 55 H8
HGDN/ICK UB10 112 C9
STA TW18 173 N9
Edinburgh Gdns WDSR SL4 149 J8
Edinburgh Ga DEN/HRF UB9 111 J4
KTBR SW1X 16 A1
Edinburgh Ms TIL RM18 168 E8
Edinburgh Pl HLW CM20 29 K7
Edinburgh Rd HNWL W7 154 E1
PLSTW E13 141 N4
SUT SM1 201 M10
UED N18 * 99 P6
WALTH E17 120 F3
Edinburgh Wy HLW CM20 28 G8
Edington Rd ABYW SE2 163 L2
PEND EN3 80 B6
Edison Av HCH RM12 124 G6
Edison Cl HCH RM12 124 G6
STALE/WH AL4 39 H7
WDR/YW UB7 152 A1
Edison Dr STHL UB1 134 A8
WBLY HA9 115 K7
Edison Gv WOOL/PLUM SE18 163 J6
Edison Rd CEND/HSY/T N8 118 E4
HAYES BR2 205 M2
PEND EN3 80 E6
WELL DA16 163 J7
Edis St CAMTN NW1 4 C5
Edith Cavell Wy
WOOL/PLUM SE18 162 B7
Edith Gdns BRYLDS KT5 199 N7
Edith Gv WBPTN SW10 15 J10
Edithna St BRXN/ST SW9 158 F9
Edith Nesbit Wk ELTH/MOT SE9 162 B10
Edith Neville Cottages
CAMTN NW1 5 J9
Edith Rd CHDH RM6 123 N5
EHAM E6 142 A2
FBAR/BDGN N11 98 E8
ORP BR6 227 K2
SNWD SE25 203 L5
SRTFD E15 121 J10
WIM/MER SW19 179 L9
WKENS W14 14 B6
WKENS W14 157 H3
Edith Rw FUL/PGN SW6 157 L7
Edith St BETH E2 7 M7
Edith Ter WBPTN SW10 * 157 M6
Edith Vls WKENS W14 14 C6
Edith Yd WBPTN SW10 157 N6
Edlson Cl WALTH E17 120 F3
Edlyn Cl BERK HP4 33 L4
Edmansons Cl TOTM N17 99 N10
Edmeston Cl HOM E9 140 D1
Edmund Beaufort Dr
STALW/RED AL3 38 C4
Edmund Gv FELT TW13 175 N5
Edmund Halley Wy GNWCH SE10 161 K1
Edmund Hurst Dr EHAM E6 142 E7
Edmund Ms KGLGY WD4 54 B5
Edmund Rd CDW/CHF RM16 167 J1
MTCM CR4 201 P3
RAIN RM13 144 F5
STMC/STPC BR5 207 M6
WELL DA16 163 K9
Edmunds Av STMC/STPC BR5 207 N3
Edmunds Cl YEAD UB4 133 K7
Edmunds Rd HERT/WAT SG14 24 G4
Edmund St CMBW SE5 159 L6
Edmunds Wk EFNCH N2 117 P2
Edmunds Wy SLN SL2 129 N7
Edna Rd RYNPK SW20 200 G2
Edna St BTSEA SW11 157 P7
Edrick Rd EDGW HA8 95 P7
Edrick Wk EDGW HA8 95 P7
Edric Rd NWCR SE14 160 C6
Edridge Cl BUSH WD23 74 A9
HCH RM12 125 L10
Edridge Rd CROY/NA CR0 203 K10
Edulf Rd BORE WD6 75 N6
Edward Amey Cl GSTN WD25 73 K2
Edward Av CHING E4 100 G6
MRDN SM4 201 N5
Edward Cl ABLGY WD5 54 G8
CDW/CHF RM16 167 J1
ED N9 99 N1
GPK RM2 125 K1
HPTN TW12 176 B8
STAL AL1 38 E7
Edward Ct CAN/RD E16 141 M7
HHS/BOV HP3 35 N10
STA TW18 173 M9
WAB EN9 63 L9
Edwardes Pl KENS W8 * 14 D4
Edwardes Sq KENS W8 14 E4
Edward Gv EBAR EN4 77 N9
Edward II Av BF/WBF KT14 216 A10
Edward Mann Cl East
WCHPL E1 * 140 C8
Edward Mann Cl West
WCHPL E1 * 140 C8
Edward Ms CAMTN NW1 * 4 F9
Edward Pl DEPT SE8 160 E5
Edward Rd BFOR GU20 212 C3
BH/WHM TN16 244 B4
BMLY BR1 183 N10
CHDH RM6 123 P4
CHST BR7 184 E8
COUL/CHIP CR5 240 E1
CROY/NA CR0 203 M7
EBAR EN4 77 N9
EBED/NFELT TW14 174 E1
HPTN TW12 176 B8
NTHLT UB5 133 K4
PGE/AN SE20 182 C10
RYLN/HDSTN HA2 114 B1
WALTH E17 120 C2
Edwards Av RSLP HA4 113 K10
Edwards Cl WPK KT4 200 G9
Edward's Cottages IS N1 6 C2
Edwards Ct EYN DA4 209 M10
SL SL1 149 K1
Edwards Dr FBAR/BDGN N11 98 E8
Edwards Gdns SWLY BR8 208 E4
Edward's La STNW/STAM N16 119 L7
Edwards Ms IS N1 6 B3
MHST W1U 10 C6
Edwards Pl FBAR/BDGN N11 98 E8
Edward Sq IS N1 5 N6
Edwards Rd BELV DA17 164 B3
Edward St CAN/RD E16 141 M6
DEPT SE8 160 E5
Edward's Wy BROCKY SE4 182 F1
Edward Temme Av SRTFD E15 141 L2
Edward Tyler Rd LEE/GVPK SE12 183 N5
Edward Wy ASHF TW15 174 A5
Edwina Gdns REDBR IG4 122 B3
Edwin Av EHAM E6 142 D4
Edwin Cl BXLYHN DA7 164 A5
EHSLY KT24 252 E1
RAIN RM13 144 G5
Edwin Hall Pl LEW SE13 183 J2
Edwin Petty Pl RDART DA2 * 188 B3
Edwin Pl CROY/NA CR0 203 L8
Edwin Rd EDGW HA8 96 A7
EHSLY KT24 252 D1
RDART DA2 187 J6
WHTN TW2 176 D4
Edwin's Md HOM E9 120 D9
Edwin St CAN/RD E16 141 M7
GVE DA12 190 E3
WCHPL E1 140 B6
Edwin Ware Ct PIN HA5 * 93 K10
Edwyn Cl BAR EN5 76 F10
Effie Pl FUL/PGN SW6 157 K6
Effie Rd FUL/PGN SW6 157 K6
Effingham Cl BELMT SM2 221 L4
Effingham Common Rd
EHSLY KT24 253 K1
Effingham Ct
WOKS/MYFD GU22 * 232 B5
Effingham La CRAWE RH10 281 M10
Effingham Pl EHSLY KT24 253 L3
Effingham Rd CEND/HSY/T N8 119 H3
CROY/NA CR0 202 G7
HORL RH6 281 K9
LEE/GVPK SE12 183 K1
REIG RH2 275 L1
SURB KT6 198 G7
Effort St TOOT SW17 179 P8
Effra Pde BRXS/STRHM SW2 181 H1
Effra Rd BRXS/STRHM SW2 158 G10
WIM/MER SW19 179 L9
Egan Cl PUR/KEN CR8 241 L6
Egan Wy HYS/HAR UB3 132 F9
Egbert St CAMTN NW1 4 C5
Egerton Av SWLY BR8 208 G1
Egerton Cl DART DA1 187 J4
PIN HA5 113 H2
Egerton Crs CHEL SW3 15 P5
Egerton Dr GNWCH SE10 160 G7
Egerton Gdns CHEL SW3 15 N5
GDMY/SEVK IG3 123 J8
HDN NW4 116 E2
WEA W13 134 G8
WLSDN NW10 * 136 F3
Egerton Gardens Ms CHEL SW3 15 P4
Egerton Pl CHEL SW3 * 15 P4
WEY KT13 216 D3
Egerton Rd ALP/SUD HA0 135 L2
BERK HP4 33 M3
GUW GU2 267 L1
NWMAL KT3 200 C4
SLN SL2 128 D6
SNWD SE25 203 M3
STNW/STAM N16 119 N5
WEY KT13 216 D3
WHTN TW2 176 D3
Egerton Ter CHEL SW3 15 P4
Egerton Wy HYS/HAR UB3 152 C6
Egg Farm La KGLGY WD4 54 D6
Egg Hall EPP CM16 65 K5
Egglesfield Cl BERK HP4 33 K3
Egham By-Pass EGH TW20 172 C7
Egham Cl CHEAM SM3 201 H9
Egham Crs CHEAM SM3 200 G10
Egham Hl EGH TW20 172 B8
Egham Rd PLSTW E13 141 N7
Eghams Cl BEAC HP9 88 B7
Eghams Wood Rd BEAC HP9 88 B7
Eglantine La EYN DA4 210 A6
Eglantine Rd WAND/EARL SW18 179 M1
Egleston Rd MRDN SM4 201 L6
Egley Dr WOKS/MYFD GU22 232 A8
Egley Rd WOKS/MYFD GU22 232 A6
WOKS/MYFD GU22 232 A8
Eglington Rd CHING E4 101 J1
Eglinton Hl WOOL/PLUM SE18 162 E5
Eglinton Rd SWCM DA10 189 L2
WOOL/PLUM SE18 162 D5
Eglise Rd WARL CR6 242 D3
Egliston Ms PUT/ROE SW15 156 F9
Egliston Rd PUT/ROE SW15 156 F9
Eglon Ms CAMTN NW1 4 B4
Egmont Av SURB KT6 199 L8
Egmont Park Rd
KWD/TDW/WH KT20 256 D1
Egmont Rd BELMT SM2 221 M4
NWMAL KT3 200 C4
SURB KT6 199 L8
WOT/HER KT12 197 J7
Egmont St NWCR SE14 160 C6
Egmont Wy KWD/TDW/WH KT20 239 H5
Egremont Gdns SL SL1 128 F9
Egremont Rd WNWD SE27 181 H6
Egret Wy YEAD UB4 133 L7
Egypt La SLN SL2 108 G8
Eider Cl SRTFD E15 121 L10
Eight Acres SL SL1 128 A6
Eighteenth Rd MTCM CR4 202 F4
Eighth Av HYS/HAR UB3 133 H10
KWD/TDW/WH KT20 * 257 J2
MNPK E12 122 C9
Eileen Rd SNWD SE25 203 L5
Eindhoven Cl CAR SM5 202 B8
WIM/MER SW19 201 N1
Eisenhower Dr EHAM E6 142 B7
Elaine Gv KTTN NW5 118 B10
Elam Cl CMBW SE5 159 J8
Elam St CMBW SE5 159 J8
Eland Rd BTSEA SW11 158 A9
CROY/NA CR0 203 J10
Elan Rd SOCK/AV RM15 146 F7
Elba Pl WALW SE17 * 18 F5
Elberon Av CROY/NA CR0 202 D6
Elbe St FUL/PGN SW6 157 M8
Elborough Rd SNWD SE25 203 P5
Elborough St WAND/EARL SW18 179 K4
Elbow La HERT/BAY SG13 26 A10
HOD EN11 44 A2
Elbow Meadow DTCH/LGLY SL3 * 151 J7
Elbury Dr CAN/RD E16 141 M8
Elcho Rd CHOB/PIR GU24 230 C5
Elcho St BTSEA SW11 157 P6
Elcot Av PECK SE15 159 P6
Elder Av CEND/HSY/T N8 118 F3
Elderbeck Cl CHESW EN7 61 P4
Elderberry Cl BARK/HLT IG6 102 E8
Elderberry Rd EA W5 155 K1
Elderberry Wy GSTN WD25 73 J1
Elder Cl BFN/LL DA15 185 J4
RGUE GU4 250 D7
TRDG/WHET N20 97 L3
WDR/YW UB7 131 P9
Elder Ct BUSH WD23 94 D3
Elderfield HLWE CM17 29 N7
Elderfield Rd CLPT E5 120 C9
SLN SL2 129 L1
Elderfield Wk WAN E11 121 N3
Elderflower Wy SRTFD E15 141 K2
Elder Oak Cl PGE/AN SE20 204 A1
Elder Rd CHOB/PIR GU24 230 F1
WNWD SE27 181 K8
Eldersley Cl REDH RH1 258 A8
Eldersley Gdns REDH RH1 258 A8
Elderslie Cl BECK BR3 204 G6
Elderslie Rd ELTH/MOT SE9 184 D1
Elder St WCHPL E1 13 L3
Elderton Rd SYD SE26 182 D7
Eldertree Wy MTCM CR4 202 C1
Elder Wk IS N1 6 E5
Elder Wy DTCH/LGLY SL3 * 150 C1
RAIN RM13 145 L5
RDKG RH5 273 H6
Eldon Av BORE WD6 75 M6
CROY/NA CR0 204 B9
HEST TW5 153 P6
Eldon Gv HAMP NW3 117 N10
Eldon Pde WDGN N22 * 99 J9
Eldon Pk SNWD SE25 204 A4
Eldon Rd CTHM CR3 241 L7
ED N9 100 B2
HOD EN11 45 J5
KENS W8 15 H4
WALTH E17 120 E2
WDGN N22 99 J9
Eldon St LVPST EC2M 13 H4
Eldon Wy WLSDN NW10 135 N4
Eldred Dr STMC/STPC BR5 207 N9
Eldred Gdns UPMR RM14 126 D5
Eldridge Cl EBED/NFELT TW14 175 H4
Eleanora Ter SUT SM1 * 221 M2
Eleanor Av HOR/WEW KT19 220 A6
STALW/RED AL3 38 C4
Eleanor Cl BERM/RHTH SE16 160 C1
SEVS/STOTM N15 119 N1
Eleanor Crs MLHL NW7 96 G5
Eleanor Cross Rd
CHES/WCR EN8 62 D10
Eleanor Gdns BAR EN5 76 G9
BCTR RM8 124 A8
Eleanor Gv BARN SW13 156 B9
HGDN/ICK UB10 112 C8
Eleanor Rd CFSP/GDCR SL9 89 P9
CHES/WCR EN8 62 D9
FBAR/BDGN N11 98 F7
HACK E8 140 A2
HERT/WAT SG14 25 K4
SRTFD E15 141 L1
Eleanor St BOW E3 140 F5
Eleanor Wy BRW CM14 107 J6
CHES/WCR EN8 62 E10
Electra Av HTHAIR TW6 152 G9
Electric Av BRXN/ST SW9 159 H10
PEND EN3 80 E2
Electric La BRXN/ST SW9 * 159 H10
Electric Pde SURB KT6 199 J6
Elephant & Castle STHWK SE1 18 D5
Elephant La BERM/RHTH SE16 160 B1
Elephant Rd WALW SE17 18 E5
Elers Rd HYS/HAR UB3 152 D3
WEA W13 155 H1
Eleven Acre Ri LOU IG10 82 C7
Eleventh Av
KWD/TDW/WH KT20 * 257 J2
Eley Rd UED N18 100 C6
Elfindale Rd HNHL SE24 181 K1
Elfin Gv TEDD TW11 176 E8
Elford Cl BKHTH/KID SE3 161 P10
Elfort Rd HBRY N5 119 H9
Elfrida Crs CAT SE6 182 F7
Elfrida Rd WATW WD18 73 K9
Elf Rw WAP E1W 140 B9
Elfwine Rd HNWL W7 134 D7
Elgal Cl ORP BR6 226 E2
Elgar Av BRYLDS KT5 199 N8
EA W5 155 K1
STRHM/NOR SW16 202 F3
WLSDN NW10 136 A1
Elgar Cl BKHH IG9 102 A3
BORE WD6 95 H1
DEPT SE8 160 F6
HGDN/ICK UB10 112 B7
PLSTW E13 141 P4
Elgar Gdns TIL RM18 168 D7
Elgar St BERM/RHTH SE16 160 D1
Elger Wy CRAWE RH10 285 H1
Elgin Av ASHF TW15 174 D9
HARH RM3 106 A8
KTN/HRWW/WS HA3 94 G10
MV/WKIL W9 8 E2
SHB W12 156 E2
Elgin Cl SHB W12 156 E1
Elgin Crs CTHM CR3 241 P8
HTHAIR TW6 152 F8
NTGHL W11 8 C6
Elgin Dr NTHWD HA6 92 F8
Elgin Est MV/WKIL W9 8 E2
Elgin Gdns GU GU1 250 D9
Elgin Ms NTGHL W11 8 B6
NTGHL W11 137 H8
Elgin Ms North MV/WKIL W9 3 H9
Elgin Ms South MV/WKIL W9 3 H10
Elgin Pl WEY KT13 * 216 D3
Elgin Rd BROX EN10 44 E10
CHES/WCR EN8 62 B6
CROY/NA CR0 203 N9
GDMY/SEVK IG3 123 H6
SUT SM1 201 M10
WDGN N22 98 D10
WEY KT13 216 B3
WLGTN SM6 222 D3
Elgiva La CSHM HP5 50 G7
Elgood Av NTHWD HA6 93 H8
Elgood Cl NTGHL W11 8 A8
Elham Cl BMLY BR1 184 A10
Elia Ms IS N1 6 C8
Elias Pl VX/NE SW8 18 A10
Elia St IS N1 6 C8
Elibank Rd ELTH/MOT SE9 162 D10
Elim St STHWK SE1 19 J3
Elim Wy PLSTW E13 141 L5
Eliot Bank FSTH SE23 182 A5
Eliot Dr RYLN/HDSTN HA2 114 A7
Eliot Gdns PUT/ROE SW15 156 D10
Eliot Hl LEW SE13 161 H8
Eliot Ms STJWD NW8 3 J8
Eliot Pk LEW SE13 161 H8
Eliot Pl BKHTH/KID SE3 161 K8
Eliot Rd DAGW RM9 123 N9
DART DA1 188 A1
Eliot V BKHTH/KID SE3 161 J8
Elizabethan Wy CRAWE RH10 284 D8
STWL/WRAY TW19 173 N3
Elizabeth Av AMS HP6 69 P5
ENC/FH EN2 79 J7
IL IG1 122 G7
IS N1 6 F4
STA TW18 173 M9
Elizabeth Barnes Ct
FUL/PGN SW6 * 157 L8
Elizabeth Br BGVA SW1W 16 E6
Elizabeth Cl BAR EN5 76 G7
HERT/WAT SG14 24 G4
MV/WKIL W9 * 9 K2
ROMW/RG RM7 104 C9
SUT SM1 221 J1
TIL RM18 168 E8
WAB EN9 45 J9
WGCE AL7 23 M5
Elizabeth Clyde Cl
SEVS/STOTM N15 119 M2
Elizabeth Cottages
RCH/KEW TW9 155 L7
Elizabeth Ct GODL GU7 267 K10
HORL RH6 * 280 B4
STALE/WH AL4 39 J3
Elizabeth Dr EPP CM16 83 H2
Elizabeth Fry Pl
WOOL/PLUM SE18 162 B7
Elizabeth Gdns ACT W3 136 C10
ASC SL5 192 A5
ISLW TW7 154 F10
STAN HA7 95 H7
SUN TW16 197 K3
Elizabeth Huggins Cottages
GVW DA11 * 190 E5
Elizabeth Ms HAMP NW3 3 P2
Elizabeth Pl EYN DA4 * 209 N6
SEVS/STOTM N15 119 L2
Elizabeth Ride ED N9 100 A1
Elizabeth Rd BRWN CM15 86 G10
CDW/CHF RM16 167 L2
EHAM E6 142 A3
GODL GU7 267 K10
RAIN RM13 145 J7
SEVS/STOTM N15 119 M3
Elizabeth Sq BERM/RHTH SE16 140 D9
Elizabeth St BGVA SW1W 16 D5
RDART DA2 188 D1
Elizabeth Wy FELT TW13 175 K7
HLW CM20 28 D9
HLWW/ROY CM19 46 C2
NRWD SE19 181 L10
SLN SL2 129 L3
STMC/STPC BR5 207 M5
Eliza Cook Cl SWCM DA10 166 G10
Elkanette Ms TRDG/WHET N20 97 M3
Elkington Rd PLSTW E13 141 N6
Elkins Gdns RGUE GU4 250 D7
Elkins Rd SLN SL2 109 K7
The Elkins ROM RM1 104 F10
Elkstone Rd NKENS W10 8 C3
Ellaline Rd HMSMTH W6 156 G5
Ella Ms HAMP NW3 118 A9
Ellanby Crs UED N18 100 A6
Elland Rd PECK SE15 160 B10
WOT/HER KT12 197 L9
Ella Rd CEND/HSY/T N8 118 F5
Ellement Cl PIN HA5 113 L3
Ellenborough Pl PUT/ROE SW15 156 D10
Ellenborough Rd SCUP DA14 185 N9
WDGN N22 99 K9
Ellenbridge Wy SAND/SEL CR2 223 M5
Ellenbrook Cl WATN WD24 * 73 K5
Ellenbrook Crs HAT AL10 40 A4
Ellenbrook La HAT AL10 40 B5
Ellen Cl BMLY BR1 206 A3
HHNE HP2 36 A5
Ellen Ct ED N9 100 B3
Ellen Ms HHNE HP2 * 36 A5
Ellen St WCHPL E1 13 P6
Ellen Webb Dr
KTN/HRWW/WS HA3 114 D1
Elleray Rd TEDD TW11 176 E9
Ellerby St FUL/PGN SW6 156 G7
Ellerdale Cl HAMP NW3 117 M10
Ellerdale Rd HAMP NW3 117 M10
Ellerdale St LEW SE13 160 G10
Ellerdine Rd HSLW TW3 154 B10
Ellerker Gdns RCHPK/HAM TW10 177 K2
Ellerman Av WHTN TW2 175 N4
Ellerman Rd TIL RM18 168 C8
Ellerslie GVE DA12 190 G3
Ellerslie Rd SHB W12 136 E10
Ellerton Gdns DAGW RM9 143 M2
Ellerton Rd BARN SW13 * 156 D7
DAGW RM9 143 M2
RYNPK SW20 178 D10
SURB KT6 199 L9
WAND/EARL SW18 179 N4
Ellery Rd NRWD SE19 181 L10
Ellery St PECK SE15 160 A8
Elles Av GU GU1 250 E10
Ellesborough Cl OXHEY WD19 93 K6
Ellesmere Av BECK BR3 204 G2
MLHL NW7 96 A4
Ellesmere Cl DTCH/LGLY SL3 149 M5
RSLP HA4 112 D5
WAN E11 121 L3
Ellesmere Dr SAND/SEL CR2 224 A10
Ellesmere Gdns REDBR IG4 122 B4
Ellesmere Gv BAR EN5 77 J9
Ellesmere Pl WOT/HER KT12 216 F2
Ellesmere Rd BERK HP4 34 A5
BOW E3 140 D4
GFD/PVL UB6 134 B6
TWK TW1 177 H2
WEY KT13 216 F3
WLSDN NW10 116 D10
Ellesmere St POP/IOD E14 140 G8
Ellice Rd OXTED RH8 261 L5
Ellies Ms ASHF TW15 173 P5
Elliman Av SLN SL2 129 K9
Ellingfort Rd HACK E8 140 A2
Ellingham Cl HHNE HP2 36 B4
Ellingham Rd CHSGTN KT9 219 J3
HHNE HP2 36 A5
SHB W12 156 D1
SRTFD E15 121 J9
Ellington Rd FELT TW13 174 G7
HSLW TW3 154 A8
MUSWH N10 118 C2
Ellington St HOLWY N7 6 A2
Ellington Wy EPSOM KT18 238 E3
Elliot Cl CRAWE RH10 284 D8
SRTFD E15 141 K2
WBLY HA9 115 L8
WFD IG8 102 A7
Elliot Rd HDN NW4 116 E4
Elliott Av RSLP HA4 113 J7
Elliott Cl WGCE AL7 22 G8
Elliott Ct WOKN/KNAP GU21 * 232 D2
Elliott Gdns HARH RM3 105 J9
SHPTN TW17 196 B4
Elliott Rd BRXN/ST SW9 159 J6
CHSWK W4 156 B3
HAYES BR2 206 A4
STAN HA7 94 F7
THHTH CR7 203 J4
Elliotts La BH/WHM TN16 245 M10
Elliott's Pl IS N1 6 D6
Elliott Sq HAMP NW3 3 P4
Elliott's Rw LBTH SE11 18 D5
Elliott St GVE DA12 190 G3
Ellis Av CFSP/GDCR SL9 90 C9
GUW GU2 267 L2
RAIN RM13 145 H7
SL SL1 149 K1
Ellis Cl COUL/CHIP CR5 240 G6
EDGW HA8 96 B7
ELTH/MOT SE9 184 F5
HOD EN11 26 E9
SWLY BR8 208 E4
WLSDN NW10 136 F1
Elliscombe Mt CHARL SE7 * 161 P5
Elliscombe Rd CHARL SE7 161 P5
Ellis Farm Cl WOKS/MYFD GU22 232 A8
Ellisfield Dr PUT/ROE SW15 178 C3
Ellis Flds STALW/RED AL3 38 D3
Ellison Cl WDSR SL4 148 E9
Ellison Gdns NWDGN UB2 153 N3
Ellison Rd BARN SW13 156 C8
BFN/LL DA15 184 G4
STRHM/NOR SW16 180 E10
Ellis Rd COUL/CHIP CR5 240 G6
MTCM CR4 202 A6
NWDGN UB2 134 B10
Ellis St KTBR SW1X 16 B5
Ellis Waterton Cl SWLY BR8 208 E4
Ellis Wy DART DA1 * 187 N5
Elliswick Rd HARP AL5 20 A1
Ellman Rd CRAWW RH11 283 J9
Ellmore Cl HARH RM3 105 J9
Ellora Rd STRHM/NOR SW16 180 E8
Ellson Cl CRAWE RH10 284 D9
Ellsworth St BETH E2 * 140 A5
Ellwood Gdns GSTN WD25 55 J10
Ellwood Pl CRAWW RH11 * 283 J7
Ellwood Ri CSTG HP8 89 P3
Ellwood Rd BEAC HP9 88 A10
Elmar Gn SLN SL2 128 F5
Elmar Rd SEVS/STOTM N15 119 L2
Elm Av EA W5 135 K10
OXHEY WD19 93 M1
RSLP HA4 113 H6
UPMR RM14 126 A8
Elm Bank CHOB/PIR GU24 * 213 K7
Elmbank STHGT/OAK N14 98 F1
Elmbank Av BAR EN5 76 F8
EGH TW20 171 N10
GUW GU2 267 M1
Elmbank Dr BMLY BR1 206 A2
Elm Bank Gdns BARN SW13 156 B8
Elmbank Wy HNWL W7 134 C7
Elmbourne Dr BELV DA17 164 C3
Elmbourne Rd TOOT SW17 180 C6
Elmbridge HLWE CM17 30 A8
Elmbridge Av BRYLDS KT5 199 P6
Elmbridge Cl RSLP HA4 113 H4
Elmbridge Dr RSLP HA4 113 H4
Elmbridge La WOKS/MYFD GU22 232 C5
Elmbridge Rd BARK/HLT IG6 103 K7
Elmbridge Wk HACK E8 * 7 P4
Elmbrook Cl SUN TW16 197 J1
Elmbrook Gdns ELTH/MOT SE9 162 B10
Elmbrook Rd SUT SM1 221 J1
Elm Cl AMS HP6 69 J4
BKHH IG9 102 A3
BRYLDS KT5 199 P7
CAR SM5 202 A8
DART DA1 187 K4
EPP CM16 46 E10
HDN NW4 116 G3
HYS/HAR UB3 133 H8
KWD/TDW/WH KT20 255 P6
LHD/OX KT22 236 G8
ROMW/RG RM7 104 C9
RPLY/SEND GU23 233 K10
RYLN/HDSTN HA2 114 A4
RYNPK SW20 200 F4
SAND/SEL CR2 223 L3
SLN SL2 129 H1
STWL/WRAY TW19 173 N4
WAB EN9 63 J10
WAN E11 121 N4
WARL CR6 242 C3
WHTN TW2 176 A5
WOKN/KNAP GU21 232 A1
Elmcote Wy RKW/CH/CXG WD3 72 A10
Elm Cottages GDST RH9 * 260 A6
MTCM CR4 * 202 A2
Elm Ct WAT WD17 * 73 J7
WOKN/KNAP GU21 231 J3
Elmcourt Rd WNWD SE27 181 J5
Elm Crs EA W5 155 K1
KUTN/CMB KT2 199 K1
Elmcroft CEND/HSY/T N8 118 G3
Elm Cft DTCH/LGLY SL3 149 P7
Elmcroft GT/LBKH KT23 * 235 P10
Elmcroft Av BFN/LL DA15 185 J3
ED N9 80 A10
GLDGN NW11 117 J5
WAN E11 121 N3
Elmcroft Cl CHSGTN KT9 * 199 K10
EA W5 135 J8
EBED/NFELT TW14 174 G2
Elmcroft Crs GLDGN NW11 116 G5
RYLN/HDSTN HA2 113 P1
Elmcroft Dr ASHF TW15 * 174 B8
CHSGTN KT9 199 K10
Elmcroft Gdns CDALE/KGS NW9 115 M3
Elmcroft Rd ORP BR6 207 K7
Elmcroft St CLPT E5 120 B9
Elmcroft Ter UX/CGN UB8 * 132 B8
Elmdale Rd PLMGR N13 98 G6
Elmdene BRYLDS KT5 199 P8
Elmdene Av EMPK RM11 125 N3
Elmdene Cl BECK BR3 204 E5
Elmdene Ct WOKS/MYFD GU22 232 B5
Elmdene Rd WOOL/PLUM SE18 162 E4
Elmdon Rd HSLWW TW4 153 L8
HTHAIR TW6 152 G9
SOCK/AV RM15 146 F7
Elm Dr CHES/WCR EN8 62 D4
CHOB/PIR GU24 213 L6
HAT AL10 40 D5
LHD/OX KT22 236 G8
RYLN/HDSTN HA2 114 A4
STALE/WH AL4 39 H6
SUN TW16 197 K2
SWLY BR8 208 E2

RCH/KEW TW9 155 K9
RCHPK/HAM TW10 177 H6
RSEV TN14 247 K2
WALTH E17 121 H2
WIM/MER SW19 179 L8
Evelyns Cl UX/CGN UB8 132 B8
Evelyn Sharp Cl GPK RM2 * 125 L1
Evelyn St DEPT SE8 160 E5
GNWCH SE10 161 H5
Evelyn Ter RCH/KEW TW9 155 K9
Evelyn Wk CRAWE RH10 283 P10
IS N1 6 G8
Evelyn Wy COB KT11 235 N2
HOR/WEW KT19 219 M7
SUN TW16 196 G1
WLGTN SM6 222 E1
Evensyde WATW WD18 72 D10
Evenwood Cl PUT/ROE SW15 * 179 H1
Everard Av HAYES BR2 205 M8
SL SL1 149 K1
Everard Cl STAL AL1 38 C8
Everard Wy WBLY HA9 115 K8
Everatt Cl WAND/EARL SW18 * 179 J2
Everdon Rd BARN SW13 156 D5
Everest Cl GVW DA11 190 B6
Everest Ct WOKN/KNAP GU21 231 K2
Everest Pl POP/IOD E14 141 H7
SWLY BR8 208 E4
Everest Rd ELTH/MOT SE9 184 B1
STWL/WRAY TW19 173 N3
Everest Wy HHNE HP2 36 B6
Everett Cl BUSH WD23 94 D2
CHESW EN7 61 K1
PIN HA5 112 G1
Everglade BH/WHM TN16 244 A4
Everglade Cl HART DA3 211 L4
The Everglades HSLW TW3 * 154 B9
Everglade Strd CDALE/KGS NW9 96 C9
Evergreen Cl PGE/AN SE20 182 B10
Evergreen Ct
STWL/WRAY TW19 * 173 N3
Evergreen Oak Av WDSR SL4 149 M9
Evergreen Sq HACK E8 7 L3
Evergreen Wk HHS/BOV HP3 35 P8
Evergreen Wy HYS/HAR UB3 132 G9
STWL/WRAY TW19 173 N3
Everilda St IS N1 5 P6
Evering Rd STNW/STAM N16 119 N8
Everington Rd MUSWH N10 98 A10
Everington St HMSMTH W6 156 G5
Everitt Rd WLSDN NW10 136 A5
Everlands Cl WOKS/MYFD GU22 232 B4
Everlasting La STALW/RED AL3 38 B5
Everleigh St FSBYPK N4 118 G6
Eve Rd ISLW TW7 154 F10
SRTFD E15 141 K4
TOTM N17 119 M1
WAN E11 121 K9
WOKN/KNAP GU21 232 E1
Eversfield Gdns EDGW HA8 96 B8
Eversfield Rd RCH/KEW TW9 155 L8
REIG RH2 257 L10
Evershed Wk CHSWK W4 155 P2
Eversholt St CAMTN NW1 4 G7
Evershot Rd FSBYPK N4 118 G6
Eversleigh Gdns UPMR RM14 126 C6
Eversleigh Rd BAR EN5 77 M9
BTSEA SW11 158 A9
EHAM E6 142 A3
FNCH N3 97 J8
Eversley Av BXLYHN DA7 164 F8
WBLY HA9 115 M7
Eversley Cl LOU IG10 82 F7
WCHMH N21 78 G10
Eversley Crs ISLW TW7 154 C7
RSLP HA4 112 F7
WCHMH N21 78 G10
Eversley Cross BXLYHN DA7 164 F8
Eversley Mt WCHMH N21 78 G10
Eversley Pk WIM/MER SW19 178 E8
Eversley Park Rd WCHMH N21 78 G10
Eversley Rd BRYLDS KT5 199 L4
CHARL SE7 161 N5
NRWD SE19 181 L10
Eversley Wy CROY/NA CR0 224 F1
EGH TW20 194 F2
Everthorpe Rd PECK SE15 159 N9
Everton Buildings CAMTN NW1 4 G10
Everton Dr STAN HA7 115 L1
Everton Rd CROY/NA CR0 203 P8
Evesham Av WALTH E17 100 F10
Evesham Cl BELMT SM2 221 K4
GFD/PVL UB6 134 A4
REIG RH2 257 J9
Evesham Gn MRDN SM4 201 L6
Evesham Rd FBAR/BDGN N11 98 D6
GVE DA12 190 G5
MRDN SM4 201 L6
REIG RH2 257 J9
SRTFD E15 141 L2
Evesham Rd North REIG RH2 257 J9
Evesham St NTGHL W11 136 G9
Evesham Ter SURB KT6 * 199 J6
Evesham Wk BRXN/ST SW9 159 H8
Evesham Wy BTSEA SW11 158 B9
CLAY IG5 122 D1
Evreham Rd IVER SL0 131 H8
Evry Rd SCUP DA14 185 M9
Ewald Rd FUL/PGN SW6 157 J8
Ewanrigg Ter WFD IG8 101 P6
Ewan Rd HARH RM3 105 L10
Ewart Gv WDGN N22 99 H9
Ewart Pl BOW E3 * 140 E4
Ewart Rd FSTH SE23 182 C3
Ewe Cl HOLWY N7 5 M1
Ewelands HORL RH6 280 D3
Ewell By-Pass EW KT17 220 D4
Ewell Court Av HOR/WEW KT19 220 B2
Ewell Downs Rd EW KT17 220 D7
Ewell House EW KT17 * 220 C6
Ewell House Gv EW KT17 220 C6
Ewell House Pde EW KT17 * 220 C6
Ewellhurst Rd CLAY IG5 102 B10
Ewell Park Gdns EW KT17 220 D4
Ewell Park Wy EW KT17 220 D3
Ewell Rd CHEAM SM3 220 G3
SURB KT6 198 G7
SURB KT6 199 L6
SURB KT6 199 N8
Ewelme Rd FSTH SE23 182 B4
Ewen Crs BRXS/STRHM SW2 181 H3
Ewer St STHWK SE1 12 E10
Ewhurst Av SAND/SEL CR2 223 N6
Ewhurst Cl BELMT SM2 220 F5
CRAWW RH11 283 M7
WCHPL E1 140 B7
Ewhurst Rd BROCKY SE4 182 E2
CRAWW RH11 283 L7
Ewood La RDKG RH5 278 A1
Exbury Rd CAT SE6 182 F5
Excalibur Cl CRAWW RH11 283 H7
Excel Ct LSQ/SEVD WC2H 11 K8
Excel Marina CAN/RD E16 141 M9
Excelsior Cl KUT/HW KT1 199 M2
Excel Waterfront CAN/RD E16 141 N9
Exchange Ar LVPST EC2M 13 J4
Exchange Ct COVGDN WC2E * 11 M8
Exchange Rd ASC SL5 192 B5
CRAWE RH10 283 P7
WATW WD18 73 J8
Exchange Sq SDTCH EC2A * 13 K3
Exchange St ROM RM1 124 F3
Exchange Wk PIN HA5 113 M5
Executive Pk STAL AL1 * 38 G6
Exeforde Av ASHF TW15 174 B7
Exeter Cl EHAM E6 142 C8
WATN WD24 73 K6
Exeter Gdns IL IG1 122 C6
Exeter Ms FUL/PGN SW6 157 K6
Exeter Pde CRICK NW2 * 2 B1
Exeter Pl GUW GU2 * 249 L8
Exeter Rd CAN/RD E16 141 M7
CRICK NW2 117 H10
CROY/NA CR0 203 M7
DAGE RM10 144 C1
ED N9 100 B3
FELT TW13 175 N6
GVE DA12 190 G6
HTHAIR TW6 152 F9
PEND EN3 80 C7
RYLN/HDSTN HA2 113 M7
STHGT/OAK N14 98 C2
WALTH E17 120 F3
WELL DA16 163 J8
Exeter St COVGDN WC2E 11 N7
Exeter Wy HTHAIR TW6 152 F8
NWCR SE14 160 E6
Exford Gdns LEE/GVPK SE12 183 N4
Exford Rd LEE/GVPK SE12 183 N5
Exhibition Grounds WBLY HA9 * 115 N9
Exhibition Rd SKENS SW7 15 M2
Exit Rd EFNCH N2 97 N10
Exmoor Cl BARK/HLT IG6 102 F9
Exmoor St NKENS W10 136 G7
Exmouth Market CLKNW EC1R 12 B1
Exmouth Ms CAMTN NW1 * 5 H10
Exmouth Pl HACK E8 140 A3
Exmouth Rd GRAYS RM17 167 N5
RSLP HA4 113 K8
WALTH E17 120 E3
WELL DA16 163 M7
YEAD UB4 132 F5
Exmouth St WCHPL E1 140 B8
Exning Rd CAN/RD E16 141 L6
Exon St WALW SE17 19 J6
Explorer Av STWL/WRAY TW19 173 P4
Explorer Dr WATW WD18 72 G10
Express Dr GDMY/SEVK IG3 123 L6
Extension Rd HERT/BAY SG13 25 N5
Exton Gdns BCTR RM8 123 N10
Exton Rd WLSDN NW10 135 P2
Exton St STHWK SE1 12 A10
Eyhurst Av HCH RM12 125 H8
Eyhurst Cl CRICK NW2 116 E7
KWD/TDW/WH KT20 239 J10
Eyhurst Pk
KWD/TDW/WH KT20 * 239 M9
Eyhurst Sp KWD/TDW/WH KT20 239 J10
Eylewood Rd WNWD SE27 181 K8
Eynella Rd DUL SE21 181 N3
Eynham Rd SHB W12 136 F8
Eynsford Cl STMC/STPC BR5 206 F7
Eynsford Crs SCUP DA14 185 M4
Eynsford Ri EYN DA4 229 L1
Eynsford Rd EYN DA4 209 N8
GDMY/SEVK IG3 123 H7
SWCM DA10 189 H1
SWLY BR8 208 F6
Eynsford Ter WDR/YW UB7 * 132 A8
Eynsham Dr ABYW SE2 163 L2
Eynswood Dr SCUP DA14 185 L8
Eyot Gdns HMSMTH W6 156 C4
Eyre Cl GPK RM2 125 J2
Eyre Street Hl CLKNW EC1R 12 A2
Eyston Dr WEY KT13 216 B6
Eythorne Rd BRXN/ST SW9 159 H7
Eywood Rd STAL AL1 38 B8
Ezra St BETH E2 7 M9

F

Faber Gdns HDN NW4 116 D3
Fabian Rd FUL/PGN SW6 157 J6
Fabian St EHAM E6 142 C6
The Facade FSTH SE23 * 182 B5
REIG RH2 257 K9
Fackenden La BGR/WK TN15 229 L9
Factory La CROY/NA CR0 203 H9
TOTM N17 99 N10
Factory Pl POP/IOD E14 161 H4
Factory Rd CAN/RD E16 142 A10
CAN/RD E16 162 C1
GVW DA11 189 P2
Factory Yd BEAC HP9 * 88 D10
HNWL W7 134 D10
Faesten Wy BXLY DA5 186 F6
Faggoters La CHONG CM5 49 H2
Faggots Cl RAD WD7 75 H1
Faggotters La HLWE CM17 30 F10
Faggs Rd EBED/NFELT TW14 152 G10
EBED/NFELT TW14 175 H1
Fagnall La AMSS HP7 88 B1
Fagus Av RAIN RM13 145 L5
Faints Cl CHESW EN7 61 N5
Fairacre HHS/BOV HP3 36 A10
ISLW TW7 * 154 C7
NWMAL KT3 200 B3
Fair Acres HAYES BR2 205 M5
Fairacres COB KT11 217 L8
CROY/NA CR0 224 E5
KWD/TDW/WH KT20 238 F7
PUT/ROE SW15 156 C10
RSLP HA4 112 G5
Fairacres Cl POTB/CUF EN6 59 J9
Fairbairn Cl PUR/KEN CR8 223 H9
Fairbank Av ORP BR6 206 E9
Fairbank Cl CHONG CM5 67 N5
Fairbank Est IS N1 6 G8
Fairbanks Rd TOTM N17 119 P1
Fairborne Wy GUW GU2 249 M7
Fairbourne COB KT11 217 L9
Fairbourne Cl WOKN/KNAP GU21 231 M4
Fairbourne La CTHM CR3 241 K8
Fairbourne Rd TOTM N17 119 M1
Fairbridge Rd ARCH N19 118 E7
Fairbrook Cl PLMGR N13 99 H6
Fairburn Cl BORE WD6 75 M5
Fairby Hl HART DA3 * 211 K5
Fairby La HART DA3 211 K6
Fairby Rd LEE/GVPK SE12 183 N1
Fairchild Cl BTSEA SW11 157 N8
Fairchildes Av CROY/NA CR0 225 J8
Fairchildes Rd WARL CR6 243 J1
Fairchild Pl SDTCH EC2A * 13 K2
Fairchild St SDTCH EC2A 13 K2
Fair Cl BUSH WD23 94 A1
Fairclough St WCHPL E1 13 P6
Faircroft SLN SL2 128 G6
Faircross Av BARK IG11 142 F1
CRW RM5 104 E8
Faircross Wy STAL AL1 38 F4
Fairdale Gdns HYS/HAR UB3 153 H1
PUT/ROE SW15 156 E10
Fairdene Rd COUL/CHIP CR5 240 E4
Fairey CDALE/KGS NW9 * 96 C10
Fairey Av HYS/HAR UB3 152 G2
Fairfax Av EW KT17 220 E5
REDH RH1 258 A9
Fairfax Cl OXTED RH8 261 J6
WOT/HER KT12 197 J8
Fairfax Gdns BKHTH/KID SE3 161 P7
Fairfax Ms CAN/RD E16 141 N10
CEND/HSY/T N8 * 119 J2
PUT/ROE SW15 156 F10
Fairfax Pl KIL/WHAMP NW6 3 K4
WKENS W14 14 B4
Fairfax Rd CEND/HSY/T N8 119 H2
CHSWK W4 156 B2
GRAYS RM17 167 N4
HERT/BAY SG13 25 N4
KIL/WHAMP NW6 3 K4
TEDD TW11 176 F10
TIL RM18 168 C7
WOKS/MYFD GU22 232 E6
Fairfax Wy MUSWH N10 98 B8
Fairfield GVE DA12 191 H8
Fairfield Ap STWL/WRAY TW19 172 A2
Fairfield Av CDW/CHF RM16 147 P10
DTCH/LGLY SL3 149 P6
EDGW HA8 95 N7
HDN NW4 116 E4
HORL RH6 280 B6
OXHEY WD19 93 K4
RSLP HA4 112 D5
STA TW18 173 J7
UPMR RM14 126 B8
WHTN TW2 176 A4
Fairfield Cl BFN/LL DA15 185 J2
BGR/WK TN15 247 P4
GT/LBKH KT23 254 A1
GUW GU2 249 L9
HARP AL5 20 C2
HCH RM12 125 H6
HOR/WEW KT19 220 B2
MTCM CR4 179 P10
NFNCH/WDSPK N12 97 M5
PEND EN3 80 C8
RAD WD7 74 D3
Fairfield Cnr KUT/HW KT1 * 199 L2
Fairfield Ct RSLP HA4 112 E6
Fairfield Crs EDGW HA8 95 N7
Fairfield Dr BROX EN10 44 E10
DORK RH4 254 G10
GFD/PVL UB6 135 H3
RYLN/HDSTN HA2 114 B1
WAND/EARL SW18 179 L1
Fairfield East KUT/HW KT1 199 K2
Fairfield Gdns CEND/HSY/T N8 118 F3
Fairfield Gv CHARL SE7 162 A5
Fairfield La CHOB/PIR GU24 212 E8
SLN SL2 128 G4
Fairfield North KUTN/CMB KT2 199 K2
Fairfield Pk COB KT11 217 L10
Fairfield Pth CROY/NA CR0 203 L10
Fairfield Pl KUT/HW KT1 199 K3
Fairfield Ri GUW GU2 249 L9
Fairfield Rd BECK BR3 204 F2
BMLY BR1 183 M10
BOW E3 140 F4
BRW CM14 107 H4
BXLYHN DA7 164 A8
CEND/HSY/T N8 118 F3
CHONG CM5 67 N5
CROY/NA CR0 203 L10
EPP CM16 65 L5
HOD EN11 44 F1
IL IG1 142 E1
KUT/HW KT1 199 K2
LHD/OX KT22 236 G7
SL SL1 128 B5
STHL UB1 133 N8
STMC/STPC BR5 206 G6
STWL/WRAY TW19 172 A2
UED N18 99 P6
UX/CGN UB8 131 N1
WALTH E17 100 D10
WFD IG8 101 M7
Fairfields CAT SE6 182 G3
CHERT KT16 195 L8
Fairfields Cl CDALE/KGS NW9 115 P3
Fairfields Crs CDALE/KGS NW9 115 P3
Fairfield South KUT/HW KT1 199 K3
Fairfield St WAND/EARL SW18 179 L1
Fairfield Wk LHD/OX KT22 236 G7
Fairfield Wy BAR EN5 77 K9
COUL/CHIP CR5 222 E10
HOR/WEW KT19 220 B2
Fairfield West KUT/HW KT1 199 K2
Fairfolds GSTN WD25 73 M1
Fairfoot Rd BOW E3 * 140 F6
Fairford Av BXLYHN DA7 164 D7
CROY/NA CR0 204 C5
Fairford Cl BF/WBF KT14 215 J10
CROY/NA CR0 204 C5
HARH RM3 106 A7
REIG RH2 257 M8
Fairford Ct BELMT SM2 * 221 L4
Fairford Gdns WPK KT4 200 C10
Fairford Wy HARH RM3 106 A7
Fairgreen EBAR EN4 78 A7
Fairgreen Ct EBAR EN4 * 78 A7
Fairgreen Rd THHTH CR7 203 J5
Fairham Av SOCK/AV RM15 146 F9
Fairhaven EGH TW20 172 C8
LCOL/BKTW AL2 * 56 C3
Fairhaven Av CROY/NA CR0 204 C7
Fairhaven Crs OXHEY WD19 93 H4
Fairhaven Rd REDH RH1 258 B6
Fairhazel Gdns KIL/WHAMP NW6 3 J3
Fairhill HHS/BOV HP3 36 A10
Fairholme EBED/NFELT TW14 174 E3
Fairholme Av GPK RM2 125 H3
Fairholme Cl FNCH N3 117 H2
Fairholme Ct PIN HA5 * 93 P7
Fairholme Crs ASHTD KT21 237 H3
YEAD UB4 132 G6
Fairholme Gdns FNCH N3 117 H1
UPMR RM14 126 F5
Fairholme Rd ASHF TW15 173 P8
CROY/NA CR0 203 H7
HRW HA1 114 D3
IL IG1 122 C5
SUT SM1 221 J3
WKENS W14 14 C8
Fairholt Rd STNW/STAM N16 119 L6
Fairholt St SKENS SW7 15 P3
Fairkytes Av EMPK RM11 125 L6
Fairland Rd SRTFD E15 141 L1
Fairlands Av BKHH IG9 101 M3
RGUW GU3 249 H6
SUT SM1 201 K9
THHTH CR7 202 G4
Fairlands Rd RGUW GU3 249 H5
Fair La COUL/CHIP CR5 257 M1
Fairlawn CHARL SE7 161 P6
GT/LBKH KT23 235 N10
WEY KT13 * 216 F2
Fairlawn Av BXLYHN DA7 163 N8
CHSWK W4 155 P3
EFNCH N2 117 P2
Fairlawn Cl ESH/CLAY KT10 218 E3
FELT TW13 175 N7
KUTN/CMB KT2 177 P9
STHGT/OAK N14 78 E10
Fairlawn Ct CHARL SE7 * 161 P6
Fairlawn Dr REDH RH1 275 P2
WFD IG8 101 M8
Fairlawn Gdns STHL UB1 * 133 N9
Fairlawn Gv BNSTD SM7 221 N9
CHSWK W4 155 P3
Fairlawn Pk SYD SE26 182 D8
WDSR SL4 148 D10
WOKN/KNAP GU21 232 B1
Fairlawn Rd CAR SM5 221 M7
WIM/MER SW19 179 J10
Fairlawns ADL/WDHM KT15 215 J7
HORL RH6 280 C5
PIN HA5 93 K10
SUN TW16 197 H3
TWK TW1 177 H2
WAT WD17 72 G5
Fairlawns Cl EMPK RM11 125 N5
STA TW18 173 L9
Fairlea Pl EA W5 135 H7
Fair Leas CSHM HP5 50 F5
Fairley Wy CHESW EN7 62 A4
Fairlie Gdns FSTH SE23 182 B3
Fairlie Rd SL SL1 128 F8
Fairlight Av CHING E4 101 J3
WDSR SL4 149 J8
WLSDN NW10 136 B4
Fairlight Cl CHING E4 101 J3
WPK KT4 220 F1
Fairlight Cross HART DA3 211 N3
Fairlight Dr UX/CGN UB8 131 N1
Fairlight Rd TOOT SW17 179 N7
Fairlop Cl HCH RM12 145 J1
Fairlop Gdns BARK/HLT IG6 102 F8
Fairlop Rd BARK/HLT IG6 102 F10
WAN E11 121 J5
Fairmark Dr HGDN/ICK UB10 132 B1
Fairmead BMLY BR1 206 C4
BRYLDS KT5 199 N8
WOKN/KNAP GU21 231 P4
Fairmead Av HARP AL5 20 B3
Fairmead Cl BMLY BR1 206 C4
HEST TW5 153 L6
NWMAL KT3 200 A3
Fairmead Crs EDGW HA8 95 P5
Fairmead Gdns REDBR IG4 122 B3
Fairmead Rd ARCH N19 118 F8
CROY/NA CR0 * 202 G7
LOU IG10 81 N8
Fairmeads COB KT11 217 M9
LOU IG10 82 E6
Fairmile Av COB KT11 217 M10
STRHM/NOR SW16 180 E8
Fairmile Ct COB KT11 217 M9
Fairmile Hts COB KT11 217 P9
Fairmile La COB KT11 217 L8
COB KT11 235 M1
Fairmile Park Copse COB KT11 217 N8
Fairmile Park Rd COB KT11 217 N9
Fairmont Cl BELV DA17 164 A5
Fairmount Rd BRXS/STRHM SW2 180 G2
Fair Oak Cl LHD/OX KT22 218 C7
Fairoak Cl PUR/KEN CR8 241 J1
STMC/STPC BR5 206 E7
Fairoak Dr ELTH/MOT SE9 184 G1
Fairoak Gdns ROM RM1 104 F10
Fairoak La LHD/OX KT22 218 D7
Fair Oak Pl BARK/HLT IG6 102 F10
Fairoaks RGUW GU3 * 248 F5
Fairoaks Gv PEND EN3 80 C3
Fairseat Cl BUSH WD23 94 D3
Fairs Rd LHD/OX KT22 236 F5
Fairstead Wk IS N1 * 6 E5
Fairstone Ct HORL RH6 280 C3
Fair St HSLW TW3 154 B9
STHWK SE1 19 L1
Fairthorn Rd CHARL SE7 161 M4
Fairtrough Rd ORP BR6 227 L9
Fair Vw POTB/CUF EN6 59 L6
Fairview ERITH DA8 164 G6
EW KT17 220 F7
HART DA3 * 210 G10
Fairview Av ALP/SUD HA0 135 J1
RAIN RM13 145 L4
WOKS/MYFD GU22 232 C4
Fair View Cl WALTH E17 100 D9
Fairview Cl CHIG IG7 103 H5
SYD SE26 182 D8
WOKS/MYFD GU22 232 C4
Fairview Ct HDN NW4 * 96 G10
Fairview Crs RYLN/HDSTN HA2 113 P6
Fairview Dr CHIG IG7 103 H6
ORP BR6 226 G1
SHPTN TW17 196 A5
WAT WD17 72 F2
Fairview Gdns WFD IG8 101 N9
Fairview Pl BRXS/STRHM SW2 180 G3
Fairview Rd CHIG IG7 103 H5
ENC/FH EN2 79 H5
EW KT17 220 C7
MEO DA13 190 A10
SEVS/STOTM N15 119 N4
SLN SL2 128 E6
STRHM/NOR SW16 202 G1
SUT SM1 221 N2
Fairview Vls CHING E4 * 100 F8
Fairview Wy EDGW HA8 95 M5
Fairwater Av WELL DA16 163 K10
Fairwater Dr ADL/WDHM KT15 215 N5
Fairway BXLYHS DA6 185 P1
CAR SM5 221 M7
CDW/CHF RM16 167 N1
CHERT KT16 195 L8
CRAWE RH10 285 J3
CRAWW RH11 282 G9
GU GU1 250 G10
HHS/BOV HP3 36 A10
RYNPK SW20 200 F3
SBW CM21 30 A1
STMC/STPC BR5 206 G6
WARE SG12 26 B3
WFD IG8 101 P6
Fairway Av BORE WD6 75 N6
CDALE/KGS NW9 115 N1
WDR/YW UB7 131 M10
Fairway Cl CRAWE RH10 285 H3
CROY/NA CR0 204 D5
GLDGN NW11 117 M5
HOR/WEW KT19 219 P1
HSLWW TW4 175 L1
LCOL/BKTW AL2 56 B3
WOKS/MYFD GU22 231 N5
Fairway Ct MLHL NW7 * 96 A4
Fairway Dr GFD/PVL UB6 134 A2
RDART DA2 188 A3
THMD SE28 143 N8
Fairway Gdns BECK BR3 205 J6
IL IG1 122 F10
Fairways ASHF TW15 174 B9
CHES/WCR EN8 62 C2
ISLW TW7 * 154 D7
PUR/KEN CR8 241 K3
STAN HA7 95 K10
TEDD TW11 177 J10
WALTH E17 * 121 H2
The Fairways CHES/WCR EN8 * 62 C2
REDH RH1 275 N3
The Fairway ABLGY WD5 54 E8
ACT W3 136 B8
ALP/SUD HA0 114 G7
BAR EN5 77 L10
E/WMO/HCT KT8 198 A3
GVW DA11 190 D5
HAYES BR2 206 C5
HGDN/ICK UB10 132 A5
HLWS CM18 47 J4
HNWL W7 * 134 D9
LHD/OX KT22 236 F4
MLHL NW7 96 A4
NTHLT UB5 134 B1
NTHWD HA6 92 F5
NWMAL KT3 200 A1
PLMGR N13 99 K4
RGUW GU3 231 H10
RSLP HA4 113 K9
SL SL1 128 B5
STHGT/OAK N14 78 C10
UPMR RM14 126 B5
WEY KT13 216 B7
Fairweather Cl SEVS/STOTM N15 119 M2
Fairweather Rd
STNW/STAM N16 119 P4
Fairwell La EHSLY KT24 252 C4
Fairwyn Rd SYD SE26 182 D7
Faithfield BUSH WD23 * 73 M10
Faithorn Cl CSHM HP5 50 F6
Fakenham Cl MLHL NW7 96 D8
NTHLT UB5 133 P1
Fakruddin St WCHPL E1 13 P2
Falaise EGH TW20 172 B8
Falaize Av IL IG1 122 E9
Falcon Av BMLY BR1 206 B3
GRAYS RM17 167 N6
Falconberg Ct
SOHO/SHAV W1D * 11 J5
Falcon Cl CHSWK W4 155 N5
CRAWW RH11 283 N5
DART DA1 187 N1
HAT AL10 40 D6
NTHWD HA6 92 F8
SBW CM21 29 M2
STHWK SE1 12 D9
Falcon Ct IS N1 6 D8
Falcon Crs PEND EN3 80 C9
Falcon Dr STWL/WRAY TW19 173 N2
Falconer Rd BARK/HLT IG6 103 M6
BUSH WD23 73 P10
Falconers Pk SBW CM21 29 N2
Falcon Gv BTSEA SW11 157 P9
Falconhurst LHD/OX KT22 236 C1
Falcon La BTSEA SW11 157 P9
Falcon Ms GVW DA11 190 B4
Falcon Rdg BERK HP4 33 P6
Falcon Rd BTSEA SW11 157 P9
GU GU1 250 A10
HPTN TW12 175 N10
PEND EN3 80 C9
Falcons Cl BH/WHM TN16 244 A3
Falcon St PLSTW E13 141 M6
Falcon Ter BTSEA SW11 * 157 P9
Falcon Wy CDALE/KGS NW9 96 B10
GSTN WD25 55 M10
KTN/HRWW/WS HA3 115 K3
POP/IOD E14 160 G3
SUN TW16 196 F2
WAN E11 121 M2
WGCE AL7 23 J3
Falconwood EGH TW20 172 B8
EHSLY KT24 234 G10
Falcon Wd LHD/OX KT22 236 E6
Falconwood Av WELL DA16 162 G8
Falconwood Pde WELL DA16 163 H10
Falconwood Rd CROY/NA CR0 224 F5
Falcourt Cl SUT SM1 221 L2
Falkirk Cl EMPK RM11 125 P6
Falkirk Gdns OXHEY WD19 93 L6
Falkirk St IS N1 7 K8
Falkland Av FBAR/BDGN N11 98 B5
FNCH N3 97 K8
Falkland Gv DORK RH4 272 F3
Falkland Park Av SNWD SE25 203 M2
Falkland Pl KTTN NW5 118 D10
Falkland Rd BAR EN5 77 H6
CEND/HSY/T N8 119 J2
DORK RH4 272 F3
KTTN NW5 118 D10
Falling La WDR/YW UB7 131 P9
Falloden Wy GLDGN NW11 117 K2
Fallow Cl CHIG IG7 103 J6
Fallow Court Av
NFNCH/WDSPK N12 97 M8
Fallowfield RDART DA2 188 G6
STAN HA7 94 F4
WGCE AL7 23 J2
Fallowfield Cl DEN/HRF UB9 91 M9
Fallowfield Ct STAN HA7 94 F4
Fallow Flds LOU IG10 101 P1
Fallowfields Dr
NFNCH/WDSPK N12 97 P7
Fallowfield Wy HORL RH6 280 C3
Fallow Ri HERT/BAY SG13 25 N5
Fallows Cl EFNCH N2 97 N10
Fallsbrook Rd STRHM/NOR SW16 180 C9
Falman Cl ED N9 99 P2
Falmer Cl CRAWW RH11 283 N9
Falmer Rd EN EN1 79 M8
SEVS/STOTM N15 119 K3
WALTH E17 120 G1
Falmouth Av CHING E4 101 J6
Falmouth Cl LEE/GVPK SE12 183 L1
WDGN N22 98 G8
Falmouth Ct STALW/RED AL3 38 C4
Falmouth Gdns REDBR IG4 122 A2
Falmouth Rd SL SL1 128 F8
STHWK SE1 18 F4
WOT/HER KT12 217 K1
Falmouth St SRTFD E15 121 J10
Falstaff Cl DART DA1 186 F3
Falstaff Gdns STAL AL1 38 B9
Falstaff Ms HPTN TW12 176 C8
Falstone WOKN/KNAP GU21 231 N4
Fambridge Cl SYD SE26 182 E7
Fambridge Rd BCTR RM8 124 B6
Famet Av PUR/KEN CR8 223 K9
Famet Cl PUR/KEN CR8 223 K9
Famet Wk PUR/KEN CR8 223 K9
Fane St WKENS W14 14 D9
Fanhams Rd WARE SG12 26 D1
Fanns Ri PUR RM19 165 P3
Fann St FARR EC1M 12 E2
Fanshaw Ct HERT/WAT SG14 25 J4
Fanshawe Av BARK IG11 142 F1
Fanshawe Crs DAGW RM9 123 P10
EMPK RM11 125 L4
WARE SG12 26 B1
Fanshawe Rd CDW/CHF RM16 * 168 D2
RCHPK/HAM TW10 177 H7
Fanshawe St HERT/WAT SG14 25 J4
Fanshaws La HERT/BAY SG13 43 K4
Fanshaw St IS N1 7 J9
Fantail Cl THMD SE28 143 M8
Fantasia Ct BRW CM14 106 G6
Fanthorpe St PUT/ROE SW15 156 F9
Faraday Av SCUP DA14 185 L5
Faraday Cl HOLWY N7 5 P2
SLN SL2 * 128 G7
WATW WD18 72 E10
Faraday Pl E/WMO/HCT KT8 197 P4
Faraday Rd ACT W3 135 P9
CRAWE RH10 284 A3
E/WMO/HCT KT8 197 P4
GU GU1 249 P10
NKENS W10 8 A3
SLN SL2 128 G7
SRTFD E15 141 L1
STHL UB1 134 A9
WELL DA16 163 K9
WIM/MER SW19 179 L9
Faraday Wy STMC/STPC BR5 207 L4
WOOL/PLUM SE18 162 A2
Fareham Rd EBED/NFELT TW14 175 K3
Fareham St SOHO/CST W1F * 11 J5
Far End HAT AL10 40 E7
Farewell Pl MTCM CR4 201 N1
Faringdon Av HARH RM3 105 K9
HAYES BR2 206 E6
Faringford Cl POTB/CUF EN6 59 N7
Faringford Rd SRTFD E15 141 K2
Faris Barn Dr ADL/WDHM KT15 215 K8
Faris La ADL/WDHM KT15 215 J7
Farjeon Rd BKHTH/KID SE3 162 A7
Farland Rd HHNE HP2 36 B6
Farleigh Av HAYES BR2 205 M7
Farleigh Court Rd CROY/NA CR0 202 G9
WARL CR6 242 G1
Farleigh Dean Crs CROY/NA CR0 224 G7
Farleigh Pl STNW/STAM N16 119 N9
Farleigh Rd ADL/WDHM KT15 215 K7
STNW/STAM N16 119 N9
WARL CR6 242 D3
Farleton Cl WEY KT13 216 E3
Farleycroft BH/WHM TN16 262 E2
Farley Dr GDMY/SEVK IG3 123 H6
Farley La BH/WHM TN16 262 E3
Farley Nursery BH/WHM TN16 262 F3
Farley Pk OXTED RH8 261 J6
Farley Pl SNWD SE25 203 P4
Farley Rd CAT SE6 183 H3
GVE DA12 191 J3
SAND/SEL CR2 224 A4
Farleys Cl EHSLY KT24 252 D2
Farlington Pl PUT/ROE SW15 178 E3
Farlow Cl GVW DA11 190 C6
Farlow Rd PUT/ROE SW15 156 G9
Farlton Rd WAND/EARL SW18 179 L3
Farman Ter
KTN/HRWW/WS HA3 * 115 J2
Farm Av ALP/SUD HA0 135 H1
CRICK NW2 117 H8
RYLN/HDSTN HA2 113 P5
STRHM/NOR SW16 180 F7
SWLY BR8 208 D3
Farmborough Cl HRW HA1 114 C5
Farm Cl AMS HP6 70 A5
ASC SL5 192 B5
BAR EN5 76 E9
BELMT SM2 221 N4
BF/WBF KT14 216 A8
BKHH IG9 101 P4
BORE WD6 75 K4
CAR SM5 221 P4
CHERT KT16 194 D6
CHES/WCR EN8 62 B7
COUL/CHIP CR5 240 A6
CRAWE RH10 284 A6
DAGE RM10 144 D2
EHSLY KT24 252 G4
FUL/PGN SW6 * 157 K6
GU GU1 250 A7
HERT/WAT SG14 25 H5
HGDN/ICK UB10 112 C8
HLWW/ROY CM19 27 N10
LHD/OX KT22 236 C10
POTB/CUF EN6 60 F3
RAD WD7 57 K6
RBRW/HUT CM13 107 P1
RGUW GU3 249 H5
SHPTN TW17 196 B7
STA TW18 173 H8
STHL UB1 134 A9
WGCW AL8 22 F5
WLGTN SM6 222 D6
WWKM BR4 205 L10
Farmcote Rd LEE/GVPK SE12 183 M4
Farm Cottages
E/WMO/HCT KT8 * 198 F4
Farm Crs LCOL/BKTW AL2 56 G2
SLN SL2 129 N7
Farmcroft GVW DA11 190 D5
Farmdale Rd CAR SM5 221 P4
CHARL SE7 161 M4
Farm Dr CROY/NA CR0 204 E9
PUR/KEN CR8 222 F7
WDSR SL4 171 N2
Farm End CHING E4 81 K9
Farmer Ct WAB EN9 63 M9
Farmer Rd LEY E10 120 G6
Farmers Cl GSTN WD25 55 J9
Farmers Rd CMBW SE5 159 J6
STA TW18 173 H8
Farmer St KENS W8 8 E9
Farmers Wy BEAC HP9 89 H7
Farmfield Dr HORL RH6 279 L7
Farmfield Rd BMLY BR1 183 K8
Farm Flds SAND/SEL CR2 223 N7
Farm Gv BEAC HP9 88 B6
Farm Hill Rd WAB EN9 63 J10
Farm Holt HART DA3 211 L8
Farmhouse Cl BROX EN10 * 62 E1
WOKS/MYFD GU22 232 G1
Farmhouse La HHNE HP2 36 B4
Farmhouse Rd
STRHM/NOR SW16 180 D10
Farmilo Rd WALTH E17 120 F5
Farmington Av SUT SM1 201 N10
Farmlands ENC/FH EN2 79 H5
PIN HA5 113 H2
The Farmlands NTHLT UB5 133 N1
Farmland Wk CHST BR7 184 E8
Farm La ADL/WDHM KT15 215 K3
ASHTD KT21 237 N4
BEAC HP9 89 J9
CROY/NA CR0 204 E9
EHSLY KT24 252 G4
FUL/PGN SW6 14 F10
HOD EN11 45 H2
PUR/KEN CR8 222 D6
RKW/CH/CXG WD3 71 L7
RPLY/SEND GU23 232 F10
STHGT/OAK N14 78 C10
Farmleigh STHGT/OAK N14 98 D1
Farmleigh Cl CRAWE RH10 284 D5
Farmleigh Gv WOT/HER KT12 216 G3
Farm Pl BERK HP4 33 L4
DART DA1 165 H10
KENS W8 8 E9
Farm Rd ADL/WDHM KT15 215 L5
BELMT SM2 221 N4
CDW/CHF RM16 168 C1
EDGW HA8 95 P6
ESH/CLAY KT10 197 P8
HSLWW TW4 175 M4
MRDN SM4 201 L5
NTHWD HA6 92 D6
RAIN RM13 145 K5
RKW/CH/CXG WD3 70 D8
RSEV TN14 247 K6
STA TW18 173 L9
STAL AL1 38 G5
TIL RM18 169 M3
WARL CR6 242 D5
WCHMH N21 99 K2
WLSDN NW10 136 A3
WOKS/MYFD GU22 232 E6
Farmstead Rd CAT SE6 182 G7
KTN/HRWW/WS HA3 94 C9
Farm St MYFR/PICC W1J 10 E8
The Farm WIM/MER SW19 * 178 G3
Farm V BXLY DA5 186 C2
Farmview COB KT11 235 L2
Farm Wk GLDGN NW11 117 J4
GUW GU2 267 L2
Farmway BCTR RM8 123 M9
Farm Wy BKHH IG9 101 P5
BUSH WD23 74 A8
HCH RM12 125 J9
NTHWD HA6 92 F5
STWL/WRAY TW19 173 J2
WPK KT4 200 F10
Farm Yd WDSR SL4 149 J6
Farnaby Dr SEV TN13 264 G2
Farnaby Rd BMLY BR1 205 K1
ELTH/MOT SE9 161 P10
Farnan Av WALTH E17 100 F10
Farnan Rd STRHM/NOR SW16 180 F8
Farnborough Av SAND/SEL CR2 224 D4
WALTH E17 * 120 D1
Farnborough Cl WBLY HA9 115 N7
Farnborough Common ORP BR6 226 D1
Farnborough Crs HAYES BR2 205 L8
SAND/SEL CR2 224 D5
Farnborough Hl ORP BR6 226 G2
Farnborough Wy ORP BR6 226 E2
PECK SE15 * 159 M6
Farnburn Av SL SL1 128 G7
Farncombe Hl GODL GU7 267 J10
Farncombe St BERM/RHTH SE16 19 P2
GODL GU7 267 K10
Farndale Av PLMGR N13 99 J4
Farndale Crs GFD/PVL UB6 134 B5
Farnell Ms ECT SW5 14 G7
Farnell Pl ACT W3 135 N9
Farnell Rd ISLW TW7 154 C9
STA TW18 173 K6
Farnes Dr GPK RM2 105 K10
Farnham Cl HHS/BOV HP3 52 D4
SBW CM21 29 M2
TRDG/WHET N20 97 M1
Farnham Gdns RYNPK SW20 200 E2
Farnham La SLN SL2 128 F4
Farnham Park La SLN SL2 129 H3
Farnham Pl STHWK SE1 12 D10
Farnham Rd GDMY/SEVK IG3 123 J5
GUW GU2 267 J3
HARH RM3 105 L6
SL SL1 129 H10
SLN SL2 128 G5
WELL DA16 163 M8
Farnham Royal LBTH SE11 17 P8
Farningham Crs CTHM CR3 241 P9
Farningham Hill Rd EYN DA4 209 K5
Farningham Rd CTHM CR3 241 P9
TOTM N17 99 P8
Farnley WOKN/KNAP GU21 231 L3
Farnley Rd CHING E4 101 K1
SNWD SE25 203 L4
Farnol Rd DART DA1 187 P1
Faro Cl BMLY BR1 206 D2
Faroe Rd WKENS W14 156 G2
Farorna Wk ENC/FH EN2 79 H5
Farquhar Rd NRWD SE19 181 N8
WIM/MER SW19 179 K6
Farquharson Rd CROY/NA CR0 203 K7
Farquhar St HERT/WAT SG14 25 K4
Farraline Rd WATW WD18 73 J8
Farrance Rd CHDH RM6 123 P4
Farrance St POP/IOD E14 140 F8
Farrant Av WDGN N22 99 H10
Farrant Cl ORP BR6 227 K4
Farrant Wy BORE WD6 75 K5
Farr Av BARK IG11 143 K4
Farren Rd FSTH SE23 182 D5
Farrer Ms CEND/HSY/T N8 118 D2
Farrer Rd CEND/HSY/T N8 118 D2
KTN/HRWW/WS HA3 115 K3
Farriday Cl STALW/RED AL3 38 D2
Farrier Cl BMLY BR1 206 A3
UX/CGN UB8 132 B8
Farrier Pl SUT SM1 201 L10
Farrier Rd NTHLT UB5 133 P4
Farriers WARE SG12 26 F5
Farriers Cl EW KT17 220 B8
GVE DA12 191 J4

HHS/BOV HP3 52 E4
Farriers End BROX EN10 62 E2
Farrier St CAMTN NW1 4 F3
Farriers Wy BORE WD6 76 A10
CSHM HP5 50 F4
Farrier Wk WBPTN SW10 15 J9
Farringdon La CLKNW EC1R 12 B2
Farringdon Rd CLKNW EC1R 12 A1
Farringdon St FLST/FETLN EC4A 12 C5
Farringford Cl LCOL/BKTW AL2 55 P2
Farrington Acres WEY KT13 * 196 E10
Farrington Av STMC/STPC BR5 207 L3
Farrington Pl CHST BR7 184 G10
Farrins Rents BERM/RHTH SE16 140 D10
Farrlers Rd EW KT17 220 B7
Farrow Gdns CDW/CHF RM16 147 N10
Farrow La NWCR SE14 160 B6
Farrow Pl BERM/RHTH SE16 160 D2
Farr Rd ENC/FH EN2 79 L5
Farthingale La WAB EN9 63 M10
Farthingale Wk SRTFD E15 141 J2
Farthing Aly STHWK SE1 19 N2
Farthing Cl WATW WD18 73 K9
Farthing Flds WAP E1W 140 A10
Farthing Green La SLN SL2 129 N3
Farthings WOKN/KNAP GU21 231 K2
Farthings Cl CHING E4 101 K4
PIN HA5 113 J4
The Farthings HHW HP1 35 L6
KUTN/CMB KT2 199 M1
Farthing St HAYES BR2 226 C4
Farwell Rd SCUP DA14 185 L7
Farwig La BMLY BR1 205 M1
Fashion St WCHPL E1 13 L4
Fashoda Rd HAYES BR2 206 A4
Fassett Rd HACK E8 7 N1
KUT/HW KT1 199 K4
Fassett Sq HACK E8 7 N1
Fauconberg Rd CHSWK W4 155 P5
Faulkner Cl BCTR RM8 123 N5
Faulkner's Rd WOT/HER KT12 217 K2
Faulkner St NWCR SE14 160 B7
Fauna Cl CHDH RM6 123 M4
STAN HA7 95 J5
Faunce St WALW SE17 18 C8
Favart Rd FUL/PGN SW6 157 K7
Faverolle Gn CHES/WCR EN8 62 C4
Faversham Av CHING E4 101 K2
EN EN1 79 L10
Faversham Cl CHIG IG7 103 L3
Faversham Rd BECK BR3 204 E2
CAT SE6 182 E3
MRDN SM4 201 L6
Fawcett Cl BTSEA SW11 157 N8
STRHM/NOR SW16 181 H7
Fawcett Est CLPT E5 * 119 P6
Fawcett Rd CROY/NA CR0 203 J10
WDSR SL4 148 G7
WLSDN NW10 136 C2
Fawcett St WBPTN SW10 15 J9
Fawcus Cl ESH/CLAY KT10 218 D3
Fawe Park Rd PUT/ROE SW15 157 J10
Fawe St POP/IOD E14 140 G7
Fawkes Av DART DA1 187 N5
Fawkham Av HART DA3 211 P3
Fawkham Green Rd HART DA3 210 G10
Fawkham Rd HART DA3 211 J4
Fawley Rd KIL/WHAMP NW6 117 L10
Fawnbrake Av HNHL SE24 181 J1
Fawn Ct BRKMPK AL9 40 F2
Fawn Rd CHIG IG7 103 J6
PLSTW E13 141 P4
Fawns Manor Rd
EBED/NFELT TW14 174 E4
Fawood Av WLSDN NW10 136 A2
Fawsley Cl DTCH/LGLY SL3 151 H6
Faygate Crs BXLYHS DA6 186 B1
Faygate La HORS RH12 282 B6
Faygate Rd BRXS/STRHM SW2 180 G5
Fay Gn ABLGY WD5 54 E9
Fayland Av STRHM/NOR SW16 180 D8
Faymore Gdns SOCK/AV RM15 146 F9
Fays Pas GU GU1 * 267 P1
Feacey Down HHW HP1 35 K4
Fearn Cl EHSLY KT24 252 F5
Fearney Md RKW/CH/CXG WD3 91 K2
Fearnley Crs HPTN TW12 175 N9
Fearnley Rd WGCW AL8 22 F6
Fearnley St WATW WD18 73 J8
Fearns Md BRW CM14 107 H6
Fearon St GNWCH SE10 161 M4
Featherbed La ABLGY WD5 55 J2
CROY/NA CR0 224 G6
HHS/BOV HP3 35 M10
SAND/SEL CR2 224 E4
Feather Dell HAT AL10 40 C4
Feathers La STWL/WRAY TW19 172 D5
Feathers Pl GNWCH SE10 161 J5
Featherstone Av FSTH SE23 182 A5
Featherstone Gdns BORE WD6 76 A8
Featherstone Rd MLHL NW7 96 E7
NWDGN UB2 153 M2
Featherstone St STLK EC1Y 12 G1
Featherstone Ter NWDGN UB2 153 M2
Featley Rd BRXN/ST SW9 159 J9
Federal Rd GFD/PVL UB6 135 H4
Federal Wy WATN WD24 73 K5
Federation Rd ABYW SE2 163 M3
Fee Farm Rd ESH/CLAY KT10 218 E4
Feenan Hwy TIL RM18 168 E7
Feeny Cl WLSDN NW10 116 C9
Felbridge Av CRAWE RH10 284 E6
STAN HA7 94 F9
Felbridge Cl BELMT SM2 221 L5
STRHM/NOR SW16 181 H7
Felbrigge Rd GDMY/SEVK IG3 123 J7
Felcott Cl WOT/HER KT12 197 K10
Felcott Rd WOT/HER KT12 197 K10
Felday Rd LEW SE13 182 G2
RDKG RH5 270 G6
Felden Cl GSTN WD25 55 L10
PIN HA5 93 M8
Felden Dr HHS/BOV HP3 35 K10
Felden La HHS/BOV HP3 35 K9
Felden Lawns HHS/BOV HP3 35 K10
Felden St FUL/PGN SW6 157 J7
Feldman Cl STNW/STAM N16 119 P6
Felgate Ms HMSMTH W6 156 E3
Felhampton Rd ELTH/MOT SE9 184 E6
Felicia Wy CDW/CHF RM16 168 E3
Felipe Rd CDW/CHF RM16 167 H3
Felix Av CEND/HSY/T N8 118 F4
Felix Dr RGUE GU4 251 K4
Felix La SHPTN TW17 196 G7
Felix Pl BRXS/STRHM SW2 181 H1
Felix Rd WEA W13 134 F9
WOT/HER KT12 197 H6
Felixstowe Rd ABYW SE2 163 M2
ED N9 99 P5
SEVS/STOTM N15 119 N1
WLSDN NW10 136 E5
Felix St BETH E2 * 140 A4
Felland Wy REIG RH2 275 N4
Fellbrigg Rd EDUL SE22 181 N1
Fellbrigg St WCHPL E1 140 A6
Fellbrook RCHPK/HAM TW10 176 G6
Fellmongers Yd CROY/NA CR0 203 K10
Fellowes Cl YEAD UB4 133 L6
Fellowes La STALE/WH AL4 40 A9
Fellowes Rd CAR SM5 201 P10
Fellow Gn CHOB/PIR GU24 212 E9
Fellow Green Rd
CHOB/PIR GU24 212 F9
Fellows Rd HAMP NW3 3 M3
Fell Pth BORE WD6 * 76 A9
Fell Rd CROY/NA CR0 203 K10
Felltram Wy CHARL SE7 161 M4
Felmersham Cl CLAP SW4 158 F10
Felmingham Rd PGE/AN SE20 204 B2
Felmongers HLW CM20 29 L9
Felsberg Rd BRXS/STRHM SW2 180 F3
Fels Cl DAGE RM10 124 C8
Fels Farm Av DAGE RM10 124 D8
Felsham Ms PUT/ROE SW15 156 G9
Felsham Rd PUT/ROE SW15 156 F9
Felspar Cl WOOL/PLUM SE18 163 J4
Felstead Av CLAY IG5 102 D9
Felstead Cl RBRW/HUT CM13 87 P10
Felstead Rd CHES/WCR EN8 62 D8
CRW RM5 104 D7
HOM E9 140 F1
HOR/WEW KT19 220 A7
LOU IG10 102 B1
ORP BR6 207 L9
WAN E11 121 M5
Felstead St HOM E9 140 E1
Felsted Rd CAN/RD E16 142 A8
Feltham Av E/WMO/HCT KT8 198 D4
Felthambrook Wy FELT TW13 175 J7
Feltham Hill Rd ASHF TW15 174 B8
ASHF TW15 174 D9
Feltham Rd ASHF TW15 174 C7
MTCM CR4 202 A2
REDH RH1 276 A5
Felton Cl BORE WD6 * 75 K4
BROX EN10 62 E1
STMC/STPC BR5 206 E6
Felton Lea SCUP DA14 185 J8
Felton Rd BARK IG11 143 H4
WEA W13 155 H1
Felton St IS N1 7 H6
Fencepiece Rd BARK/HLT IG6 102 F7
Fenchurch Av FENCHST EC3M 13 J6
Fenchurch Buildings
FENCHST EC3M 13 K6
Fenchurch Pl FENCHST EC3M * 13 K7
Fenchurch Rd CRAWE RH10 284 C9
Fenchurch St FENCHST EC3M 13 J7
Fen Cl BRWN CM15 87 P8
Fendall Rd HOR/WEW KT19 219 P2
Fendall St STHWK SE1 19 K4
Fendt Cl CAN/RD E16 141 L8
Fendyke Rd BELV DA17 163 N3
Fenelon Pl WKENS W14 14 D6
Fengates Rd REDH RH1 257 P10
Fen Gv BFN/LL DA15 185 J2
Fenham Rd PECK SE15 159 P6
Fen La UPMR RM14 127 J10
Fenman Ct TOTM N17 100 A9
Fenman Gdns GDMY/SEVK IG3 123 L6
Fenmore Rd PUR/KEN CR8 241 L5
Fenn Cl BMLY BR1 183 M9
Fennel Cl CAN/RD E16 141 K6
CROY/NA CR0 204 C8
GU GU1 250 E7
Fennel Crs CRAWW RH11 283 L10
Fennells HLWW/ROY CM19 46 F6
Fennells Md EW KT17 220 B5
Fennell St WOOL/PLUM SE18 162 D5
Fenner Cl BERM/RHTH SE16 160 A3
Fenner Rd CDW/CHF RM16 167 H2
Fenners Marsh GVE DA12 191 J4
Fenner Sq BTSEA SW11 * 157 N9
The Fennings AMS HP6 69 J2
Fenning St STHWK SE1 19 J1
Fennscombe Ct CHOB/PIR GU24 212 D9
Fenns La CHOB/PIR GU24 212 D9
Fenn St HOM E9 120 C10
Fenn's Wy WOKN/KNAP GU21 232 B1
Fennycroft Rd HHW HP1 35 J3
Fensomes Aly HHNE HP2 35 N5
Fensom's Cl HHNE HP2 35 N5
Fenstanton Av
NFNCH/WDSPK N12 97 N7
Fen St CAN/RD E16 141 L9
Fens Wy SWLY BR8 187 H9
Fentiman Rd VX/NE SW8 17 N10
Fentiman Wy EMPK RM11 125 M6
RYLN/HDSTN HA2 114 A7
Fenton Av STA TW18 173 M9
Fenton Cl BRXN/ST SW9 * 158 G8
CHST BR7 184 C8
HACK E8 7 M2
REDH RH1 258 B10
Fenton Gra HLWE CM17 47 M2
Fenton Rd CDW/CHF RM16 167 K2
REDH RH1 258 B10
TOTM N17 99 K8
Fenton's Av PLSTW E13 141 N5
Fenton St WCHPL E1 140 A8
Fentum Rd GUW GU2 249 M8
Fenwick Cl WOKN/KNAP GU21 231 N4
Fenwick Gv PECK SE15 159 P9
Fenwick Pl BRXN/ST SW9 158 F9
SAND/SEL CR2 223 J4
Fenwick Rd PECK SE15 159 P9
Ferdinand Pl CAMTN NW1 4 D3
Ferdinand St CAMTN NW1 4 D3
Ferguson Av BRYLDS KT5 199 L5
GPK RM2 105 K10
GVE DA12 190 G7
Ferguson Cl BECK BR3 205 H3
Ferguson Ct GPK RM2 105 L10
Ferguson Dr ACT W3 136 A8
Ferguson Gv CHES/WCR EN8 * 62 C5
Ferguson's Cl POP/IOD E14 160 F3
Fergus Rd HBRY N5 119 J10
Fermandy La CRAWE RH10 285 P4
Ferme Park Rd CEND/HSY/T N8 118 F3
Fermor Rd FSTH SE23 182 D4
Fermoy Rd GFD/PVL UB6 134 A7
MV/WKIL W9 8 C2
Fern Av MTCM CR4 202 E4
Fernbank BKHH IG9 101 N2
EYN DA4 * 209 N9
Fernbank Av ALP/SUD HA0 114 E9
HCH RM12 125 K9
WOT/HER KT12 197 M7
Fernbank Ms BAL SW12 180 C2
Fernbank Rd ADL/WDHM KT15 215 K2
Fernbrook Dr RYLN/HDSTN HA2 114 A5
Fernbrook Rd LEW SE13 183 K2
Ferncliff Rd HACK E8 119 P10
Fern Cl BROX EN10 44 E9
ERITH DA8 165 J7
IS N1 7 J7
WARL CR6 242 D4
Fern Ct NWCR SE14 160 C8
Ferncroft Av HAMP NW3 117 K8
NFNCH/WDSPK N12 97 P7
RSLP HA4 113 K7
Ferndale BMLY BR1 205 P2
RGUW GU3 249 K8
Ferndale Av CHERT KT16 195 H10
HSLWW TW4 153 M9
WALTH E17 121 J3
Ferndale Cl BXLYHN DA7 163 P7
Ferndale Crs UX/CGN UB8 131 M5
Ferndale Rd ASHF TW15 173 N8
BNSTD SM7 239 J2
CLAP SW4 158 F10
CRW RM5 104 D10
FSTGT E7 141 N2
GVE DA12 190 E5
PEND EN3 80 D3
SEVS/STOTM N15 119 N4
SNWD SE25 204 A5
WAN E11 121 L7
WOKN/KNAP GU21 232 C2
Ferndale St EHAM E6 142 E9
Ferndale Ter HRW HA1 114 E2
Ferndale Wy ORP BR6 226 G2
Ferndell Av BXLY DA5 186 E6
Fern Dells HAT AL10 40 C5
Ferndene LCOL/BKTW AL2 55 N7
Fern Dene WEA W13 134 G7
Ferndene Rd HNHL SE24 159 K10
Fernden Ri GODL GU7 267 K10
Fernden Wy ROMW/RG RM7 124 C4
Ferndown CRAWE RH10 284 E3
EMPK RM11 125 P4
HORL RH6 280 B2
NTHWD HA6 93 H10
Ferndown Av ORP BR6 206 G8
Ferndown Cl BELMT SM2 221 N3
GU GU1 268 D1
PIN HA5 93 M8
Ferndown Gdns COB KT11 217 K10
Ferndown Rd ELTH/MOT SE9 184 A3
OXHEY WD19 93 K5
Fern Dr HHS/BOV HP3 35 P7
MDHD SL6 128 A8
Fernecroft STAL AL1 38 B9
The Fernery STA TW18 173 H8
Fernes Cl UX/CGN UB8 131 M8
Ferney Ct BF/WBF KT14 215 N8
Ferney Meade Wy ISLW TW7 154 F8
Ferney Rd CHESW EN7 61 L2
EBAR EN4 98 B2
Fern Gv EBED/NFELT TW14 175 J3
WGCW AL8 22 G1
Fernhall Dr REDBR IG4 122 A3
Fernhall La WAB EN9 64 A7
Fernham Rd THHTH CR7 203 K3
Fernhead Rd MV/WKIL W9 2 D9
Fernheath Wy RDART DA2 186 E8
Fernhill HLWS CM18 47 H5
LHD/OX KT22 218 C10
Fernhill Cl WOKS/MYFD GU22 231 P6
Fernhill Ct WALTH E17 101 J10
Fernhill Gdns KUTN/CMB KT2 177 J8
Fern Hill La HLWS CM18 47 J6
Fernhill La WOKS/MYFD GU22 231 P6
Fernhill Pk WOKS/MYFD GU22 231 P6
Fernhill Rd HORL RH6 280 E8
Fernhills KGLGY WD4 54 E10
Fernhill St CAN/RD E16 142 C10
Fernholme Rd PECK SE15 182 C1
Fernhurst Cl BEAC HP9 88 E9
CRAWW RH11 283 L5
Fernhurst Gdns EDGW HA8 95 M7
Fernhurst Rd ASHF TW15 174 D7
CROY/NA CR0 203 P7
FUL/PGN SW6 157 H7
Fernihough Cl WEY KT13 216 B7
Fernlands Cl CHERT KT16 195 H10
Fern La HEST TW5 153 N4
Fernlea GT/LBKH KT23 236 A10
Fernlea Pl COB KT11 217 L8
Fernlea Rd BAL SW12 180 C4
MTCM CR4 202 B2
Fernleigh Cl CROY/NA CR0 223 H1
MV/WKIL W9 2 D9
WOT/HER KT12 197 J10
Fernleigh Ct RYLN/HDSTN HA2 94 A10
WBLY HA9 115 K6
Fernleigh Rd WCHMH N21 99 H3
Fernley Cl PIN HA5 113 H2
Fernleys STALE/WH AL4 39 H3
Fernsbury St FSBYW WC1X 6 A10
Ferns Cl PEND EN3 80 D2
SAND/SEL CR2 224 A6
Fernshaw Rd WBPTN SW10 15 J10
Fernside BKHH IG9 101 N2
GLDGN NW11 117 K7
Fernside Av FELT TW13 175 J7
MLHL NW7 96 A4
Fernside La SEV TN13 265 K5
Fernside Rd BAL SW12 180 A4
Fernsleigh Cl CFSP/GDCR SL9 90 B7
Ferns Rd SRTFD E15 141 K1
Fern St BOW E3 140 F6
Fernthorpe Rd
STRHM/NOR SW16 180 D9
Ferntower Rd HBRY N5 119 L10
Fern Towers CTHM CR3 259 P1
Fernville La HHNE HP2 35 N6
Fern Wk ASHF TW15 173 N8
BERM/RHTH SE16 19 P8
Fern Wy GSTN WD25 73 J1
Fernways IL IG1 122 E8
Fernwood Av ALP/SUD HA0 135 H1
STRHM/NOR SW16 180 E7
Fernwood Cl BMLY BR1 205 P2
Fernwood Crs TRDG/WHET N20 98 A4
Ferny Hl EBAR EN4 78 A4
EBAR EN4 78 C4
Feroners Cl CRAWE RH10 284 B9
Ferranti Cl WOOL/PLUM SE18 162 A2
Ferraro Cl HEST TW5 153 P5
Ferrers Av WDR/YW UB7 151 N1
WLGTN SM6 222 E1
Ferrers Cl SL SL1 128 D10
Ferrers La HARP AL5 20 E6
STALE/WH AL4 21 J6
Ferrers Rd STRHM/NOR SW16 180 E8
Ferrestone Rd CEND/HSY/T N8 118 G2
Ferrey Ms BRXN/ST SW9 159 H8
Ferriby Cl IS N1 6 A3
Ferrier St WAND/EARL SW18 157 L10
Ferriers Wy EPSOM KT18 238 F5
Ferring Cl RYLN/HDSTN HA2 114 B6
Ferrings DUL SE21 181 M5
Ferris Av CROY/NA CR0 204 E10
Ferris Rd EDUL SE22 159 P10
Ferron Rd CLPT E5 * 120 A8
Ferro Rd RAIN RM13 145 H6
Ferry Av STA TW18 173 H10
Ferryhills Cl OXHEY WD19 93 K4
Ferry La BARN SW13 156 C5
BTFD TW8 155 K5
CHERT KT16 195 K6
GUW GU2 267 P4
RAIN RM13 144 G7
SHPTN TW17 196 B8
STWL/WRAY TW19 172 E6
TOTM N17 120 A2
Ferrymead Av GFD/PVL UB6 133 P4
Ferrymead Dr GFD/PVL UB6 133 P5
Ferrymead Gdns GFD/PVL UB6 134 B4
Ferrymoor RCHPK/HAM TW10 176 G6
Ferry Rd BARN SW13 156 D6
E/WMO/HCT KT8 197 P3
TEDD TW11 176 G8
THDIT KT7 198 G6
TIL RM18 168 D10
Ferry Sq BTFD TW8 155 K5
SHPTN TW17 196 C7
Ferry St POP/IOD E14 161 H4
Feryby Rd CDW/CHF RM16 168 E2
Fesants Cft HLW CM20 29 L8
Festing Rd PUT/ROE SW15 156 G9
Festival Cl BXLY DA5 185 N4
ERITH DA8 164 G6
HGDN/ICK UB10 132 C3
Festoon Wy CAN/RD E16 142 A9
Fetcham Common La
LHD/OX KT22 236 A7
Fetcham Park Dr LHD/OX KT22 236 D9
Fetherstone Cl POTB/CUF EN6 59 N8
Fetter La FLST/FETLN EC4A 12 B6
Ffinch St DEPT SE8 160 F6
Fiddicroft Av BNSTD SM7 239 L1
Fiddle Bridge La HAT AL10 40 C3
Fiddlers Cl RDART DA2 166 G10
Fidler Pl BUSH WD23 74 A10
Field Cl ABR/ST RM4 83 L7
BKHH IG9 101 P4
BMLY BR1 205 P2
CHING E4 100 G7
CHSGTN KT9 219 H2
CRICK NW2 116 D7
CSHM HP5 51 K4
E/WMO/HCT KT8 198 A5
HARP AL5 20 C4
HGDN/ICK UB10 112 B7
HSLWW TW4 153 J7
HYS/HAR UB3 152 D6
RGUE GU4 250 G8
SAND/SEL CR2 224 A10
STALE/WH AL4 38 F2
Fieldcommon La WOT/HER KT12 197 M8
Field Cottages EFNCH N2 * 118 A1
FUL/PGN SW6 * 157 J8
Field Ct GINN WC1R 11 P4
OXTED RH8 261 K4
Field End BAR EN5 76 E8
CHOB/PIR GU24 212 E9
COUL/CHIP CR5 222 E10
RSLP HA4 133 L1
Fieldend TEDD TW11 176 E7
Field End Cl OXHEY WD19 93 M1
Field End Rd PIN HA5 113 J4
RSLP HA4 113 M10
Fieldend Rd STRHM/NOR SW16 202 D1
Fielders Cl EN EN1 79 M8
RYLN/HDSTN HA2 114 C6
Fielders Gn GU GU1 250 D10
Fielders Wy RAD WD7 57 K9
Fieldfare Rd THMD SE28 143 M9
Fieldfares LCOL/BKTW AL2 57 J3
Field Gdns CHONG CM5 67 M10
Fieldgate St WCHPL E1 13 P4
Fieldhouse Cl SWFD E18 101 N9
Fieldhouse Rd BAL SW12 180 D4
Fieldhouse Vls BNSTD SM7 * 239 P1
Field Hurst DTCH/LGLY SL3 150 C3
Fieldhurst Cl ADL/WDHM KT15 215 L2
Fielding Av TIL RM18 168 E7
WHTN TW2 176 B6
Fielding Gdns DTCH/LGLY SL3 149 P1
Fielding La HAYES BR2 205 P4
Fielding Rd CHSWK W4 156 B2
Fieldings Rd CHES/WCR EN8 62 E5
The Fieldings BNSTD SM7 239 J3
FSTH SE23 182 B4
HORL RH6 280 C3
WOKN/KNAP GU21 231 L2
Fielding St WALW SE17 18 E9
Fielding Ter EA W5 * 135 L9
Fielding Wy RBRW/HUT CM13 87 P10
Field La BTFD TW8 155 H6
GODL GU7 267 L10
TEDD TW11 176 F8
Field Md CDALE/KGS NW9 96 B8
Fieldpark Gdns CROY/NA CR0 204 D8
Field Pl NWMAL KT3 200 C6
Field Rd DEN/HRF UB9 111 H9
EBED/NFELT TW14 175 J2
FSTGT E7 121 M9
HHNE HP2 36 B7
HMSMTH W6 14 A9
OXHEY WD19 73 M10
SOCK/AV RM15 146 B10
TOTM N17 119 L1
Fields End La HHW HP1 34 G4
Fieldsend Rd CHEAM SM3 221 H2
Fields Est HACK E8 * 7 P4
Fieldside Cl ORP BR6 226 F1
Fieldside Cottages
TRDG/WHET N20 * 97 J1
Fieldside Rd BMLY BR1 183 J8
Fields Park Crs CHDH RM6 123 N3
Field St FSBYW WC1X 5 N9
Field Vw EGH TW20 172 F8
FELT TW13 174 E7
Fieldview HORL RH6 280 C3
WAND/EARL SW18 179 N4
Fieldview Cottages
STHGT/OAK N14 * 98 E3
Field View Ri LCOL/BKTW AL2 55 M5
Field View Rd POTB/CUF EN6 59 K9
Field Wk HORL RH6 281 K3
Field Wy AMSS HP7 68 G7
CFSP/GDCR SL9 90 A8
CROY/NA CR0 224 G4
GFD/PVL UB6 134 A3
HHS/BOV HP3 52 D3
HOD EN11 26 G9
RKW/CH/CXG WD3 91 L2
RPLY/SEND GU23 251 J1
RSLP HA4 112 D6
UX/CGN UB8 131 N6
WLSDN NW10 135 P2
Fieldway BCTR RM8 123 L9
BERK HP4 34 B7
CDW/CHF RM16 147 M10
STMC/STPC BR5 206 G6
WARE SG12 26 G7
Fieldway Crs HBRY N5 119 H10
Fiennes Cl BCTR RM8 123 M6
Fiennes Wy SEV TN13 265 K3
Fiesta Dr RAIN RM13 144 D6
Fifehead Cl ASHF TW15 173 P9
Fife Rd CAN/RD E16 141 M7
KUT/HW KT1 199 K2
MORT/ESHN SW14 177 P1
WDGN N22 99 J9
Fife Ter IS N1 5 P7
Fife Wy GT/LBKH KT23 253 P1
Fifield Pth FSTH SE23 182 C6
Fifteenth Av
KWD/TDW/WH KT20 * 257 J2
Fifth Av GSTN WD25 73 L1
HYS/HAR UB3 132 G10
KWD/TDW/WH KT20 * 257 J2
MNPK E12 122 C9
NKENS W10 2 A10
WTHK RM20 166 F5
Fifth Avenue Allende Av
HLW CM20 28 F9
Fifth Cross Rd WHTN TW2 176 C5
Fifth Wy WBLY HA9 115 N9
Figge's Rd MTCM CR4 180 B10
Figgswood COUL/CHIP CR5 240 D8
Fig Tree Cl WLSDN NW10 136 B3
Figtree Hl HHW HP1 35 N5
Filbert Crs CRAWW RH11 283 K8
Filborough Wy GVE DA12 191 L4
Filby Rd CHSGTN KT9 219 L3
Filey Av STNW/STAM N16 119 P6
Filey Cl BELMT SM2 221 M4
BH/WHM TN16 243 N5
CRAWW RH11 283 J9
Filey Sp SL SL1 148 G2
Filey Waye RSLP HA4 113 H7
Fillebrook Av EN EN1 79 M6
Fillebrook Rd WAN E11 121 J6
Fillingham Wy HAT AL10 40 B2
Filmer Chambers
FUL/PGN SW6 * 157 J7
Filmer La RSEV TN14 247 M7
Filmer Rd FUL/PGN SW6 157 J7
WDSR SL4 148 C8
Filston La RSEV TN14 228 F9
RSEV TN14 246 E2
Filton Cl CDALE/KGS NW9 96 B10
Finborough Rd TOOT SW17 180 A10
WBPTN SW10 15 H9
Finchale Rd ABYW SE2 163 L2
Fincham Cl HGDN/ICK UB10 112 D8
Finch Av WNWD SE27 181 L7
Finch Cl BAR EN5 77 K9
HAT AL10 40 D6
WOKN/KNAP GU21 231 H3
Finchdale HHW HP1 35 K6
Finch Dr EBED/NFELT TW14 175 L3
Finches Ri GU GU1 250 E8
The Finches HERT/BAY SG13 26 A5
Finch Gdns CHING E4 100 F6
Finch Gn RKW/CH/CXG WD3 71 J8
Finchingfield Av WFD IG8 101 P8
The Finchingfields BRWN CM15 86 D3
Finch La AMSS HP7 69 M7
BANK EC3V 13 H6
BEAC HP9 88 B6
BUSH WD23 73 P9
Finchley Cl DART DA1 187 P2
Finchley La HDN NW4 116 G2
Finchley Pk NFNCH/WDSPK N12 97 M5
Finchley Pl STJWD NW8 3 L7
Finchley Rd GLDGN NW11 117 J3
GLDGN NW11 117 J3
GLDGN NW11 117 K7
GRAYS RM17 167 N5
HAMP NW3 3 K2
STJWD NW8 3 L6
Finchley Vls
NFNCH/WDSPK N12 * 97 N5
Finchley Wy FNCH N3 97 K7
Finch Ms PECK SE15 * 159 N7
Finchmoor HLWS CM18 46 G4
Finch Rd BERK HP4 33 M5
GU GU1 * 250 A10
Finden Rd FSTGT E7 121 N10
Findhorn Av YEAD UB4 133 J7
Findhorn St POP/IOD E14 141 H8
Findlay Dr RGUW GU3 249 L6
Findon Cl RYLN/HDSTN HA2 * 114 A8
WAND/EARL SW18 179 K2
Findon Gdns RAIN RM13 145 H7
Findon Rd CRAWW RH11 283 L5
ED N9 100 A2
SHB W12 156 D1
Fine Bush La DEN/HRF UB9 112 C4
Fingal St GNWCH SE10 161 L4
Finglesham Cl STMC/STPC BR5 207 N8
Finians Cl HGDN/ICK UB10 132 A2
Finland Rd BROCKY SE4 160 D9
Finland St BERM/RHTH SE16 160 D2
Finlay Gdns ADL/WDHM KT15 215 M1
Finlays Cl CHSGTN KT9 219 M2
Finlay St FUL/PGN SW6 156 G7
Finnart Cl WEY KT13 216 D1
Finney Dr BFOR GU20 212 C3
Finney La ISLW TW7 154 F7
Finnis St BETH E2 140 A5
Finnymore Rd DAGW RM9 143 P2
Finsbury Av LVPST EC2M * 13 H4
Finsbury Circ LVPST EC2M 13 H4
Finsbury Cottages WDGN N22 98 F8
Finsbury Est CLKNW EC1R 6 B10
Finsbury Market SDTCH EC2A 13 J3
Finsbury Park Av FSBYPK N4 119 K4
Finsbury Park Rd FSBYPK N4 119 J8
Finsbury Pavement LVPST EC2M 13 H3
Finsbury Rd WDGN N22 98 G9
Finsbury Sq SDTCH EC2A 13 H3
Finsbury St STLK EC1Y 12 G3
Finsbury Wy BXLY DA5 186 A2
Finsen Rd CMBW SE5 159 K10
Finstock Rd NKENS W10 136 G8
Finucane Dr STMC/STPC BR5 207 M7
Finucane Gdns RAIN RM13 145 H1
Finucane Ri BUSH WD23 94 B3
Finway Ct WATW WD18 * 72 G9
Finway Rd HHNE HP2 36 C2
Fiona Cl GT/LBKH KT23 235 P10
Fiona Ct ENC/FH EN2 * 79 J7
Firbank WGCW AL8 * 22 F5
Firbank Cl CAN/RD E16 142 A7
ENC/FH EN2 79 K8
Firbank Dr OXHEY WD19 93 M1
WOKN/KNAP GU21 231 N5
Firbank La WOKN/KNAP GU21 231 N5
Firbank Pl EGH TW20 171 N9
Firbank Rd CRW RM5 104 C6
PECK SE15 160 A8
STALW/RED AL3 38 E2
Fir Cl WOT/HER KT12 197 H7
Fircroft Cl SLN SL2 129 M1
WOKS/MYFD GU22 232 C4
Fircroft Ct WOKS/MYFD GU22 * 232 C4
Fircroft Gdns HRW HA1 114 D8
Fircroft Rd CHSGTN KT9 219 L1
EGH TW20 171 P10
TOOT SW17 180 A6
Firdene BRYLDS KT5 199 P8
Fir Dene ORP BR6 206 C10
Fireball Hl ASC SL5 192 C7
Fire Bell Aly SURB KT6 199 K6
Firebell Ms SURB KT6 199 K6
Firecrest Cl HART DA3 211 N3
Firecrest Dr HAMP NW3 117 L8
Firefly Cl WLGTN SM6 * 222 F4
Firefly Gdns EHAM E6 142 B6
Firethorn Cl EDGW HA8 95 P5
Firfield Rd ADL/WDHM KT15 215 K1
Firfields WEY KT13 216 C4
Fir Grange Av WEY KT13 216 C2
Fir Gv NWMAL KT3 200 C6
Firgrove WOKN/KNAP GU21 231 M5
Fir Grove Rd BRXN/ST SW9 * 159 H8
Firham Park Av HARH RM3 105 P8
Firhill Rd CAT SE6 182 F6
Firlands HORL RH6 280 C3
WEY KT13 216 F3
Firle Cl CRAWE RH10 283 P5
Firle Ct EW KT17 * 220 C8
Firle Pl WAND/EARL SW18 179 M3
Firmingers Rd ORP BR6 228 D2
Firmin Rd DART DA1 187 K1
Fir Pk HLWW/ROY CM19 46 E4
Fir Rd CHEAM SM3 201 J8
FELT TW13 175 L8
Firs WAB EN9 81 P1
Firs Av FBAR/BDGN N11 98 B7
MORT/ESHN SW14 155 P10
MUSWH N10 118 B1
WDSR SL4 148 E9
Firsby Av CROY/NA CR0 204 C8
Firsby Rd STNW/STAM N16 119 N6
Firs Cl DORK RH4 272 F4
ESH/CLAY KT10 218 D3
FSTH SE23 182 C3
HAT AL10 40 E5
IVER SL0 130 F2
MTCM CR4 202 C2
MUSWH N10 118 B1
Firscroft PLMGR N13 99 K4
Firsdene Cl CHERT KT16 214 G3
Firs Dr DTCH/LGLY SL3 130 C10
HEST TW5 153 J7
LOU IG10 82 D5
Firsgrove Crs BRW CM14 106 G5
Firside Gv BFN/LL DA15 185 J4
Firs La PLMGR N13 99 K4
POTB/CUF EN6 59 L9
WCHMH N21 99 K1
Firs Park Av WCHMH N21 99 L2
Firs Park Gdns WCHMH N21 99 L2
The Firs Pk BRKMPK AL9 * 41 K9
Firs Rd PUR/KEN CR8 241 J1
First Av ACT W3 136 C10
ADL/WDHM KT15 215 L5
AMSS HP7 69 H6
BXLYHN DA7 163 M6
CHDH RM6 123 M3
DAGE RM10 144 C4
EN EN1 79 N9
GSTN WD25 73 K1
GVW DA11 190 B4
HDN NW4 116 F2
HOR/WEW KT19 220 B5
HYS/HAR UB3 132 G10
KWD/TDW/WH KT20 * 257 J2
MNPK E12 122 B9
MORT/ESHN SW14 156 B8
NKENS W10 8 C1
PLSTW E13 141 M5
UED N18 100 B5
WALTH E17 120 C3
WBLY HA9 115 J7
WOT/HER KT12 197 J6
WTHK RM20 166 F5
First Avenue Mandela Av
HLW CM20 29 K9
First Cl E/WMO/HCT KT8 198 B4
First Crs SL SL1 129 H7
First Cross Rd WHTN TW2 176 D5
First Dr WLSDN NW10 135 P2
The Firs BF/WBF KT14 * 215 N8
BRWN CM15 86 F10
DXLY DA5 186 F4
CDW/CHF RM16 147 P10
CHESW EN7 61 M3
EA W5 135 J7
EBED/NFELT TW14 * 174 F2
EDGW HA8 * 96 A5
GT/LBKH KT23 * 254 A1
HARP AL5 * 20 C1
ORP BR6 * 228 B3
RGUW GU3 267 N4
STAL AL1 38 G10
TRDG/WHET N20 97 N2
WGCW AL8 22 F1
First Quarter HOR/WEW KT19 * 220 B7
First St CHEL SW3 15 P5
Firstway RYNPK SW20 200 F2
First Wy WBLY HA9 115 N9
Firs Wk NTHWD HA6 92 E7
WFD IG8 101 M6
Firsway GUW GU2 249 L9
Firswood Av HOR/WEW KT19 220 B2
Firth Gdns FUL/PGN SW6 157 H7
Firtree Av MTCM CR4 202 B2
Fir Tree Av SLN SL2 129 L6
WDR/YW UB7 152 B2
Fir Tree Cl CRAWW RH11 283 L4
EA W5 135 K8
ESH/CLAY KT10 218 B2
EW KT17 238 F1
HHS/BOV HP3 36 C7
HOR/WEW KT19 220 C1
LHD/OX KT22 237 H9
ORP BR6 227 J2
ROM RM1 124 E1
STRHM/NOR SW16 180 D8
Fir Tree Ct BORE WD6 75 L8
Fir Tree Gdns CROY/NA CR0 224 F1
Fir Tree Gv CAR SM5 222 A4
Fir Tree Hl RKW/CH/CXG WD3 72 B3
Fir Tree Pl ASHF TW15 * 174 B7
Fir Tree Rd BNSTD SM7 220 F10
EW KT17 238 E2
GU GU1 249 P7
HSLWW TW4 153 M10
LHD/OX KT22 237 H9
Fir Trees ABR/ST RM4 83 L7
Fir Trees Cl BERM/RHTH SE16 140 D10
Fir Tree Wk EN EN1 79 M7
REIG RH2 257 N10
Fir Wk CHEAM SM3 220 G3
Firwood Av STALE/WH AL4 39 K6
Firwood Cl WOKN/KNAP GU21 231 K6
Firwood Rd VW GU25 193 K6
Fisher Cl CRAWE RH10 283 P9
CROY/NA CR0 203 N8
GFD/PVL UB6 133 P5
KGLGY WD4 54 B5
PEND EN3 80 F3
WOT/HER KT12 217 J1
Fisherdene ESH/CLAY KT10 218 F4
Fisherman Cl RCHPK/HAM TW10 177 H7
Fishermans Dr
BERM/RHTH SE16 160 C1
Fishermans Wy HOD EN11 45 J1
Fishermen's Hl GVW DA11 189 N1
Fisher Rd KTN/HRWW/WS HA3 94 E10
Fishers Cl BUSH WD23 73 M8
CHES/WCR EN8 62 F10
STRHM/NOR SW16 180 E6
Fishers Ct NWCR SE14 160 C7
Fisher's La CHSWK W4 156 A3
Fisher St CAN/RD E16 141 M7
HHOL WC1V 11 N4
Fisher's Wy BELV DA17 144 D10
Fishers Wd ASC SL5 193 H8
Fisherton St STJWD NW8 9 L2
Fishery Pas HHW HP1 35 L8
Fishery Rd HHW HP1 35 K8
Fishguard Sp SL SL1 149 N1
Fishguard Wy CAN/RD E16 142 E10
Fishponds Rd HAYES BR2 226 A2
TOOT SW17 179 P7
Fishpool St STALW/RED AL3 38 B6
Fish Street Hl MON EC3R 13 H8
Fisk Cl SUN TW16 174 G9
Fisons Rd CAN/RD E16 141 M10
Fitchet Cl CRAWW RH11 283 L5
Fitzalan Rd ESH/CLAY KT10 218 D4
FNCH N3 117 H1
Fitzalan St LBTH SE11 17 P5
Fitzgeorge Av NWMAL KT3 200 A1
WKENS W14 14 A6
Fitzgerald Av MORT/ESHN SW14 156 B9
Fitzgerald Rd MORT/ESHN SW14 156 A9
THDIT KT7 198 F6
WAN E11 121 M3
Fitzhardinge St MBLAR W1H 10 C5
Fitzhugh Gv WAND/EARL SW18 179 N2
Fitzilian Av HARH RM3 105 N9
Fitzjames Av CROY/NA CR0 203 P9
WKENS W14 14 B6
Fitzjohn Av BAR EN5 77 H9
Fitzjohn Cl RGUE GU4 250 F7
Fitzjohn's Av HAMP NW3 117 N10
Fitzmaurice Pl MYFR/PICC W1J * 10 F9
Fitzneal St SHB W12 136 C8
Fitzrobert Pl EGH TW20 172 D9
Fitzroy Cl HGT N6 118 A6
Fitzroy Crs CHSWK W4 * 156 A6
Fitzroy Gdns NRWD SE19 181 M10
Fitzroy Ms FITZ W1T 10 G2
Fitzroy Pk HGT N6 118 A6
Fitzroy Pl REIG RH2 257 N10
Fitzroy Rd CAMTN NW1 4 C5
Fitzroy Sq FITZ W1T 10 G2
Fitzroy St CAMTN NW1 10 G2
Fitzstephen Rd BCTR RM8 123 L10
Fitzwarren Gdns HGT N6 118 D6
Fitzwilliam Av RCH/KEW TW9 155 L8
Fitzwilliam Ms CAN/RD E16 141 M10
Fitzwilliam Rd CLAP SW4 158 D9
Fitzwilliams Ct HLWE CM17 29 P7
Fitz Wygram Cl HPTN TW12 176 B8
Five Acre CDALE/KGS NW9 96 C10
Fiveacre Cl CROY/NA CR0 203 H6
Five Acres CRAWE RH10 283 P5
CSHM HP5 51 J9
HLWS CM18 47 H4
KGLGY WD4 54 A5
LCOL/BKTW AL2 57 J1
Five Acres Av LCOL/BKTW AL2 55 N5
Fiveash Rd GVW DA11 190 C3
Five Elms Rd DAGW RM9 124 A8
HAYES BR2 205 P10
Five Fields Cl OXHEY WD19 93 N4
Five Oak Ms BMLY BR1 183 M6
Five Oaks HAT AL10 * 40 E7
Five Oaks Cl WOKN/KNAP GU21 231 K5
Five Oaks La CHIG IG7 103 P7
Fiveways Cnr ELTH/MOT SE9 184 E5
Five Ways Jct HDN NW4 96 D9
Fiveways Rd BRXN/ST SW9 159 H8
Five Wents SWLY BR8 209 H2
Fladbury Rd SEVS/STOTM N15 119 L4
Fladgate Rd WAN E11 121 K4
Flag Cl CROY/NA CR0 204 C8
Flagstaff Cl WAB EN9 62 G9
Flagstaff Rd WAB EN9 62 G9
The Flags HHNE HP2 36 C6
Flag Wk PIN HA5 113 H4
Flambard Rd HRW HA1 114 F4
Flamborough Cl BH/WHM TN16 243 N5
Flamborough Rd RSLP HA4 113 H8
Flamborough Sp SL SL1 148 F1
Flamborough St POP/IOD E14 140 D8
Flamborough Wk
POP/IOD E14 * 140 D8
Flamingo Wk HCH RM12 145 H2
Flamstead End Rd
CHES/WCR EN8 62 A4
Flamstead Gdns DAGW RM9 143 M2
Flamstead Rd DAGW RM9 143 M2
Flamsted Av WBLY HA9 135 M1
Flamsteed Rd CHARL SE7 162 B4
Flanchford Rd REIG RH2 256 G10
REIG RH2 274 F5
SHB W12 156 C2
Flanders Crs TOOT SW17 180 A10
Flanders Rd CHSWK W4 156 B3
EHAM E6 142 C4
Flanders Wy HOM E9 140 C1
Flandrian Cl PEND EN3 80 F5
Flank St WCHPL E1 13 N7
Flash La ENC/FH EN2 79 K3
Flask Wk HAMP NW3 117 M9
Flatfield Rd HHS/BOV HP3 36 B8
Flather Cl STRHM/NOR SW16 180 D9
Flaunden Bottom CSHM HP5 70 B3
HHS/BOV HP3 52 C10
Flaunden Hl HHS/BOV HP3 52 C9
Flaunden La HHS/BOV HP3 52 E8
RKW/CH/CXG WD3 53 H9
Flavell Ms GNWCH SE10 161 K4
Flavian Cl STALW/RED AL3 37 N8
Flaxen Cl CHING E4 100 G4
Flaxen Rd CHING E4 100 G4
Flaxley Rd MRDN SM4 201 L6

Flaxman Rd CMBW SE5 159 J8
Flaxman Ter STPAN WC1H 5 K10
Flaxton Rd WOOL/PLUM SE18 162 G7
Flecker Cl STAN HA7 94 E6
Fleece Dr ED N9 99 P5
Fleece Rd SURB KT6 199 H8
Fleece Wk HOLWY N7 5 M1
Fleeming Cl WALTH E17 100 E10
Fleeming Rd WALTH E17 100 E10
Fleet Av RDART DA2 188 B4
UPMR RM14 126 C4
Fleet Cl E/WMO/HCT KT8 197 N5
RSLP HA4 112 D4
UPMR RM14 126 C4
Fleetdale Pde RDART DA2 * 188 B4
Fleethall Gv CDW/CHF RM16 147 M10
Fleet Pl FLST/FETLN EC4A 12 C5
Fleet Rd GVW DA11 189 P6
HAMP NW3 117 P10
RDART DA2 188 B4
Fleetside E/WMO/HCT KT8 197 N6
Fleet Sq FSBYW WC1X 5 N10
Fleet St EMB EC4Y 12 B6
Fleet Street Hl WCHPL E1 13 N2
Fleet Ter CAT SE6 * 183 H3
Fleetway EGH TW20 194 F3
Fleetwood Cl CAN/RD E16 142 A7
CHSGTN KT9 219 J4
CROY/NA CR0 203 N10
CSTG HP8 89 M5
KWD/TDW/WH KT20 238 G7
Fleetwood Ct BF/WBF KT14 215 K9
Fleetwood Rd KUT/HW KT1 199 N3
SLN SL2 129 L10
WLSDN NW10 116 D10
Fleetwood Sq KUT/HW KT1 199 N3
Fleetwood St STNW/STAM N16 119 M7
Fleetwood Wy OXHEY WD19 93 K5
Fleming Cl CHESW EN7 61 P3
MV/WKIL W9 8 E2
Fleming Ct CROY/NA CR0 223 H2
Fleming Crs HERT/WAT SG14 25 H5
Fleming Dr WCHMH N21 78 G9
Fleming Gdns TIL RM18 168 F7
Fleming Md MTCM CR4 179 P10
Fleming Rd CDW/CHF RM16 167 H3
STHL UB1 134 A8
WAB EN9 80 G1
WALW SE17 18 D9
Flemings RBRW/HUT CM13 107 H7
Fleming Wk CDALE/KGS NW9 * 96 B10
Fleming Wy CRAWE RH10 283 P3
ISLW TW7 154 E9
THMD SE28 143 N9
Flemish Flds CHERT KT16 195 K7
Flemming Av RSLP HA4 113 J7
Flempton Rd LEY E10 120 D6
Fletcher Cl CHERT KT16 214 G3
CRAWE RH10 283 P9
EHAM E6 142 E9
Fletcher La LEY E10 121 H5
Fletcher Rd CHERT KT16 214 G3
CHIG IG7 103 J6
CHSWK W4 155 P2
Fletchers Cl HAYES BR2 205 N4
Fletcher St WCHPL E1 13 P7
Fletcher Wy HHNE HP2 35 M4
Fletching Rd CHARL SE7 162 A5
CLPT E5 120 B8
Fletton Rd FBAR/BDGN N11 98 F8
Fleur De Lis St WCHPL E1 13 L2
Fleur Gates WIM/MER SW19 178 G3
Flexford Rd RGUW GU3 266 A1
Flexley Wd WGCE AL7 23 J2
Flex Meadow HLWW/ROY CM19 46 B2
Flexmere Rd TOTM N17 99 L9
Flight Ap CDALE/KGS NW9 * 96 C9
Flimwell Cl BMLY BR1 183 K8
Flinders Cl STAL AL1 38 F8
Flint Cl BNSTD SM7 221 L10
CRAWE RH10 284 D10
GT/LBKH KT23 254 B2
ORP BR6 * 227 J3
REDH RH1 258 A9
SRTFD E15 141 L1
Flint Cottages LHD/OX KT22 * 236 G7
Flint Down Cl STMC/STPC BR5 * 207 K1
Flint Hl DORK RH4 272 G4
Flint Hill Cl DORK RH4 272 G5
Flintlock Cl STWL/WRAY TW19 151 K10
Flintmill Crs ELTH/MOT SE9 162 B9
Flinton St WALW SE17 19 K7
Flint St WALW SE17 19 H6
WTHK RM20 166 G5
Flint Wy STALW/RED AL3 38 B2
Flitcroft St LSQ/SEVD WC2H 11 K6
Floathaven Cl THMD SE28 143 K10
The Floats SEV TN13 246 F7
Flock Mill Pl WAND/EARL SW18 179 L4
Flockton St BERM/RHTH SE16 19 N2
Flodden Rd CMBW SE5 159 K7
Flood La TWK TW1 * 176 F4
Flood St CHEL SW3 15 P8
Flood Wk CHEL SW3 15 P9
Flora Cl POP/IOD E14 140 G8
STAN HA7 95 J4
Flora Gdns CHDH RM6 123 M4
CROY/NA CR0 225 H7
Flora Gv STAL AL1 38 E7
Floral Dr LCOL/BKTW AL2 57 J2
Floral Pl IS N1 119 L10
Floral St COVGDN WC2E 11 M7
Flora St BELV DA17 164 A4
Florence Av ADL/WDHM KT15 215 K7
ENC/FH EN2 79 K7
MRDN SM4 201 M5
Florence Cl GSTN WD25 73 H1
HCH RM12 125 M7
HLWE CM17 47 M3
WOT/HER KT12 197 J7
WTHK RM20 167 K5
Florence Ct WAN E11 121 N2
Florence Dr ENC/FH EN2 79 K7
Florence Elson Cl MNPK E12 122 D9
Florence Gdns CHSWK W4 155 P5
STA TW18 173 L10
Florence Rd ABYW SE2 163 M3
BECK BR3 204 C2
BMLY BR1 205 M1
CHSWK W4 156 A2
EA W5 135 K9
FELT TW13 175 J4
FSBYPK N4 118 G5
KUTN/CMB KT2 177 L10
NWCR SE14 160 E7
NWDGN UB2 153 L3
PLSTW E13 141 M4
SAND/SEL CR2 223 L5
WIM/MER SW19 179 L9
WOT/HER KT12 197 J7
Florence St CAN/RD E16 141 L6
HDN NW4 116 F2
IS N1 6 C4
Florence Ter NWCR SE14 160 E7
Florence Vls HGT N6 * 118 C5
Florence Wy BAL SW12 180 A4
UX/CGN UB8 131 M2
WOKN/KNAP GU21 231 H4
Florey Sq WCHMH N21 78 G9
Florfield Rd HACK E8 140 A1
Florian Av SUT SM1 221 N1
Florian Rd PUT/ROE SW15 157 H10
Florida Cl BUSH WD23 94 C3
Florida Rd RGUE GU4 268 B6
THHTH CR7 203 J1
Florida St BETH E2 7 P10
Florin Ct UED N18 99 M5
Floris Pl CLAP SW4 158 D9
Floriston Av HGDN/ICK UB10 132 D2
Floriston Cl STAN HA7 94 G9
Floriston Gdns STAN HA7 94 G9
Floss St PUT/ROE SW15 156 F8
Flower Crs CHERT KT16 214 E3
Flower & Dean Wk WCHPL E1 13 M4
Flowerfield RSEV TN14 246 G3
Flowerhill Wy MEO DA13 190 B10
Flower La GDST RH9 260 C5
MLHL NW7 96 C6
Flower Ms GLDGN NW11 117 H4
Flowerpot Cl SEVS/STOTM N15 119 N4
Flowers Cl CRICK NW2 116 D8
Flowers Ms ARCH N19 118 D7
Flower Wk GUW GU2 267 P3
Floyd Rd CHARL SE7 161 P4
Floyds La WOKS/MYFD GU22 233 K2
Floyer Cl RCHPK/HAM TW10 177 L1
Fludyer St LEW SE13 161 K10
Flux's La EPP CM16 65 K9
The Flyers Wy BH/WHM TN16 262 G2
Fogerty Cl PEND EN3 80 G3
Fold Cft HLW CM20 28 D10
Foley Cl BEAC HP9 88 B7
Foley Ms ESH/CLAY KT10 218 D3
Foley Rd BH/WHM TN16 244 A4
ESH/CLAY KT10 218 D4
Foley St GTPST W1W 10 G4
Folgate St WCHPL E1 13 K3
Foliot St SHB W12 136 C8
Folkes La UPMR RM14 126 E3
Folkestone Ct DTCH/LGLY SL3 150 D4
Folkestone Rd EHAM E6 142 D4
UED N18 99 P5
WALTH E17 120 G2
Folkingham La CDALE/KGS NW9 96 A9
Folkington Cnr
NFNCH/WDSPK N12 97 J6
Follet Cl WDSR SL4 171 N2
Follett Dr ABLGY WD5 54 G7
Follett St POP/IOD E14 141 H8
Folly Av STALW/RED AL3 38 B5
Folly Cl RAD WD7 74 E2
Follyfield Rd BNSTD SM7 221 K10
Folly Flds STALE/WH AL4 20 G1
Folly La RDKG RH5 272 G10
STALW/RED AL3 38 B5
WALTH E17 100 D9
Folly Pathway RAD WD7 74 E1
The Folly HERT/WAT SG14 25 L5
LTWR GU18 * 212 A8
Folly Vw WARE SG12 26 G6
Folly Wall POP/IOD E14 161 H1
Fontaine Rd STRHM/NOR SW16 180 G9
Fontana Cl CRAWE RH10 284 E8
Fontarabia Rd BTSEA SW11 158 B10
Fontayne Av CHIG IG7 102 F5
RAIN RM13 144 F2
ROM RM1 104 F10
Fontenoy Rd BAL SW12 180 C5
Fonteyne Gdns WFD IG8 102 A10
Fonthill Ms FSBYPK N4 118 G7
Fonthill Rd FSBYPK N4 118 G7
Font Hills EFNCH N2 97 M10
Fontley Wy PUT/ROE SW15 178 D3
Fontmell Cl ASHF TW15 174 B8
STALW/RED AL3 38 D3
Fontmell Pk ASHF TW15 174 A8
Fontwell Cl KTN/HRWW/WS HA3 94 D8
NTHLT UB5 133 P1
Fontwell Dr HAYES BR2 206 D5
Fontwell Park Gdns HCH RM12 125 M9
Fontwell Rd CRAWE RH10 284 B10
Foord Cl RDART DA2 188 D5
Football La HRW HA1 114 E6
Footbury Hill Rd ORP BR6 207 K7
The Footpath PUT/ROE SW15 * 178 D1
Foots Cray High St SCUP DA14 185 M9
Foots Cray La SCUP DA14 185 M4
Footscray Rd ELTH/MOT SE9 184 D2
ELTH/MOT SE9 184 E4
Forbes Av POTB/CUF EN6 59 N9
Forbes Cl CRICK NW2 116 D8
HCH RM12 125 J6
Forbes St WCHPL E1 13 N6
Forbes Wy RSLP HA4 113 J7
Forburg Rd STNW/STAM N16 119 P6
Force Green La BH/WHM TN16 244 G10
Fordbridge Cl CHERT KT16 195 L8
Fordbridge Rd ASHF TW15 173 P9
SUN TW16 196 F6
Ford Cl ASHF TW15 173 P9
BUSH WD23 74 B8
HRW HA1 114 C5
RAIN RM13 144 G2
SHPTN TW17 196 B5
THHTH CR7 203 J6
Fordcroft Rd STMC/STPC BR5 207 L5
Forde Av BMLY BR1 205 P3
Fordel Rd CAT SE6 183 J4
Ford End DEN/HRF UB9 111 J7
WFD IG8 101 N7
Fordham Cl EMPK RM11 125 P5
Fordham Rd EBAR EN4 77 N7
Fordham St WCHPL E1 13 P5
Fordhook Av EA W5 135 L9
Fordingbridge Cl CHERT KT16 * 195 L8
Fordingley Rd MV/WKIL W9 2 D10
Fordington Rd HGT N6 118 A2
Ford La IVER SL0 131 K8
RAIN RM13 144 G2
Fordmill Rd CAT SE6 182 F5
Ford Rd ASHF TW15 174 A7
BOW E3 140 D4
CHERT KT16 195 L8
CHOB/PIR GU24 230 E1
DAGE RM10 144 B2
GVW DA11 189 N1
WOKS/MYFD GU22 232 E6
Ford's Gv WCHMH N21 99 K2
Fords Park Rd CAN/RD E16 141 M8
Ford Sq WCHPL E1 140 A7
Ford St BOW E3 140 D3
CAN/RD E16 141 L8
Fordwater Rd CHERT KT16 195 L8
Fordwich Cl HERT/WAT SG14 25 H5
ORP BR6 207 J7
Fordwich Hl HERT/WAT SG14 25 H5
Fordwich Ri HERT/WAT SG14 25 H5
Fordwich Rd WGCW AL8 22 F6
Fordwych Rd CRICK NW2 117 H10
Fordyce Cl EMPK RM11 125 P5
Fordyce Rd LEW SE13 183 H2
Fordyke Rd BCTR RM8 123 P7
Forebury Av SBW CM21 30 A1
The Forebury SBW CM21 30 A1
Forefield LCOL/BKTW AL2 55 P3
Foreland Ct HDN NW4 97 H9
Foreland St WOOL/PLUM SE18 162 G3
Forelands Wy CSHM HP5 51 H8
Foremark Cl BARK/HLT IG6 103 J7
Foreshore DEPT SE8 160 E4
Forest Ap CHING E4 101 K1
Forest Av CHIG IG7 102 D6
CHING E4 101 K1
HHS/BOV HP3 35 N8
Forest Cl CHST BR7 206 D2
EHSLY KT24 252 G1
WAB EN9 81 N3
WAN E11 121 L3
WFD IG8 101 N5
WOKS/MYFD GU22 232 G1
Forest Ct CHING E4 101 L2
WAN E11 121 K2
Forest Crs ASHTD KT21 237 M2
Forestdale STHGT/OAK N14 98 E5
Forest Dr EPP CM16 83 H2
HAYES BR2 226 B1
KWD/TDW/WH KT20 239 K7
MNPK E12 122 A8
SUN TW16 174 G10
WFD IG8 101 J8
Forest Dr East WAN E11 121 J5
Forest Dr West WAN E11 121 H5
Forest Edge BKHH IG9 101 P4
Forester Rd CRAWE RH10 283 P9
GUW GU2 249 M6
PECK SE15 160 A10
Foresters Cl CHESW EN7 61 M3
WLGTN SM6 222 E4
WOKN/KNAP GU21 231 L4
Foresters Crs BXLYHN DA7 164 C10
Foresters Dr WALTH E17 121 J2
WLGTN SM6 222 E4
Forestfield CRAWE RH10 284 C9
Forest Gdns TOTM N17 99 N10
Forest Ga CDALE/KGS NW9 116 B2
Forest Gld CHING E4 101 K6
EPP CM16 65 P3
WAN E11 121 K4
Forest Gv HACK E8 7 L2
Forest Hill Rd EDUL SE22 182 A2
Forestholme Cl FSTH SE23 182 B5
SYD SE26 * 182 B8
Forest La CHIG IG7 102 D6
EHSLY KT24 234 G10
FSTGT E7 121 M10
RAD WD7 56 G7
Forest Mount Rd WFD IG8 101 J8
Forest Pk WDSR SL4 170 D2
Fore St BARB EC2Y 12 G4
BRKMPK AL9 40 F3
HERT/WAT SG14 25 L5
HLWE CM17 29 M7
PIN HA5 112 G2
UED N18 99 P5
Forest Rdg BECK BR3 204 F3
HAYES BR2 226 B1
Forest Ri WALTH E17 121 J2
Forest Rd BARK/HLT IG6 103 H9
BARK/HLT IG6 103 L7
CHEAM SM3 201 K8
CHES/WCR EN8 62 C5
ED N9 100 A2
EHSLY KT24 252 G1
EPP CM16 82 D1
ERITH DA8 165 H7
FELT TW13 175 K6
FSTGT E7 121 M9
GSTN WD25 55 J9
HACK E8 7 L2
LOU IG10 82 A8
PEND EN3 80 D2
RCH/KEW TW9 155 M6
ROMW/RG RM7 124 C1
WALTH E17 101 J10
WALTH E17 120 D2
WALTH E17 120 F1
WAN E11 121 J5
WDSR SL4 170 C3
WFD IG8 101 M4
WOKS/MYFD GU22 232 G1
Forest Side CHING E4 101 L1
BKHH IG9 101 P2
EPP CM16 64 G9
FSTGT E7 121 N9
WPK KT4 200 C8
Forest St FSTGT E7 121 M10
The Forest WAN E11 121 K2
Forest Vw CHING E4 101 J1
CRAWE RH10 284 A10
WAN E11 121 L5
Forest View Av LEY E10 121 J3
Forest View Rd LOU IG10 82 A8
MNPK E12 122 B9
WALTH E17 101 H9
Forest Wk BUSH WD23 73 N5
Forest Wy ASHTD KT21 237 M3
BFN/LL DA15 184 G3
HLWE CM17 30 C10
HLWS CM18 47 L5
LOU IG10 81 P4
LOU IG10 82 A5
STMC/STPC BR5 207 K5
WAB EN9 64 B7
WFD IG8 101 N5
Forfar Rd BTSEA SW11 158 B7
WDGN N22 99 J9
Forge Av COUL/CHIP CR5 241 H6
Forge Bridge La COUL/CHIP CR5 240 C8
Forge Cl HAYES BR2 205 M8
KGLGY WD4 53 K7
Forge Cottages EA W5 * 135 J10
Forge Dr ESH/CLAY KT10 218 F4
SLN SL2 129 H1
Forge End LCOL/BKTW AL2 55 P2
WOKN/KNAP GU21 232 B3
Forgefield BH/WHM TN16 244 A2
Forge La CHEAM SM3 221 H4
CRAWE RH10 * 284 B6
EYN DA4 210 B4
FELT TW13 175 M8
GVE DA12 191 J5
NTHWD HA6 92 F8
RCHPK/HAM TW10 177 K4
SUN TW16 197 H3
Forge Ms CROY/NA CR0 224 F2
SUN TW16 * 197 H3
Forge Pl CAMTN NW1 4 D2
GVE DA12 * 191 J4
HORL RH6 279 P6
Forge Rd CRAWE RH10 284 B6
The Forge HORL RH6 * 279 H8
Forge Wy RSEV TN14 228 G7
Forge Wd CRAWE RH10 284 E2
Forman Pl STNW/STAM N16 119 N9
Formby Av KTN/HRWW/WS HA3 115 H1
Formby Cl DTCH/LGLY SL3 150 F3
Form Cl RAD WD7 57 K7
Formosa St MV/WKIL W9 9 H2
Formunt Cl CAN/RD E16 141 L7
Forres Cl HOD EN11 44 F1
Forres Gdns GLDGN NW11 117 K4
Forrester Pth SYD SE26 182 B7
Forresters Dr WGCE AL7 23 M6
Forrest Gdns
STRHM/NOR SW16 202 G3
Forris Av HYS/HAR UB3 132 G10
Forset St MBLAR W1H 9 P5
Forstal Cl HAYES BR2 205 M3
Forster Cl CHING E4 101 J8
Forster Rd BECK BR3 204 D3
BRXS/STRHM SW2 180 F3
TOTM N17 119 N1
WALTH E17 120 D4
Forsters Cl CHDH RM6 124 A4
Forston St IS N1 6 G7
Forsyte Crs NRWD SE19 203 M1
Forsyth Gdns WALW SE17 18 D9
Forsythia Cl IL IG1 122 E10
Forsythia Pl GU GU1 * 249 P8
Forsyth Pl EN EN1 79 M9
Forsyth Rd WOKN/KNAP GU21 232 F1
Forterie Gdns GDMY/SEVK IG3 123 K8
Fortescue Av WHTN TW2 176 B6
Fortescue Rd EDGW HA8 96 A9
WEY KT13 216 A1
WIM/MER SW19 179 N10
Fortess Gv KTTN NW5 118 D10
Fortess Rd KTTN NW5 118 C10
Fortess Wk KTTN NW5 118 C10
Forthbridge Rd BTSEA SW11 158 B10
Forth Rd UPMR RM14 126 C4
Fortin Cl SOCK/AV RM15 146 F9
Fortin Wy SOCK/AV RM15 146 F9
Fortis Cl CAN/RD E16 141 P8
Fortis Gn EFNCH N2 118 A1
Fortis Green Av EFNCH N2 118 B1
Fortis Green Rd MUSWH N10 118 B1
Fortismere Av MUSWH N10 118 B1
Fort La REIG RH2 257 L6
Fortnam Rd ARCH N19 118 E7
Fortnums Acre STAN HA7 94 E7
Fort Rd GU GU1 268 B3
KWD/TDW/WH KT20 255 N7
NTHLT UB5 133 P2
RSEV TN14 246 D1
STHWK SE1 19 M6
TIL RM18 168 E10
Fortrose Cl POP/IOD E14 141 J8
Fortrose Gdns
BRXS/STRHM SW2 180 F4
Fortrye Cl GVW DA11 190 B5
Fort St CAN/RD E16 141 N10
WCHPL E1 * 13 K4
Fortuna Cl HOLWY N7 5 P1
Fortunegate Rd WLSDN NW10 136 C2
Fortune Green Rd
KIL/WHAMP NW6 117 K10
Fortune La BORE WD6 75 J10
Fortune Pl STHWK SE1 19 M8
Fortunes Md NTHLT UB5 133 M1
The Fortunes HLWS CM18 47 J3
Fortune St STLK EC1Y 12 F2
Fortune Wy WLSDN NW10 136 D5
Forty Acre La CAN/RD E16 141 M7
Forty Av WBLY HA9 115 L8
Forty Cl WBLY HA9 115 L7
Fortyfoot Rd LHD/OX KT22 237 J8
Forty Green Rd BEAC HP9 88 B6
Forty Hl ENC/FH EN2 79 N3
Forty La WBLY HA9 115 N7
Forum Cl BOW E3 140 F3
Forum Magnum Sq STHWK SE1 17 N1
Forum Pl HAT AL10 * 40 D3
Forumside EDGW HA8 95 M7
The Forum E/WMO/HCT KT8 198 A4
Forum Wy EDGW HA8 95 M7
Forval Cl MTCM CR4 202 A5
Forward Dr KTN/HRWW/WS HA3 114 F2
Fosbury Ms BAY/PAD W2 9 H8
Foscote Ms MV/WKIL W9 8 F3
Foscote Rd HDN NW4 116 E4
Foskett Rd FUL/PGN SW6 157 J8
Foss Av CROY/NA CR0 223 H2
Fossdene Rd CHARL SE7 161 N4
Fossdyke Cl YEAD UB4 133 M7
Fosse Wy BF/WBF KT14 215 J9
WEA W13 134 F7
Fossil Rd LEW SE13 160 F9
Fossington Rd BELV DA17 163 N3
Foss Rd TOOT SW17 179 N7
Fossway BCTR RM8 123 M7
Foster Av WDSR SL4 148 D9
Foster Cl CHES/WCR EN8 62 C6
Fosterdown GDST RH9 260 A5
Foster La CITYW EC2V 12 E5
Foster Rd ACT W3 136 B9
CHSWK W4 156 A4
HHW HP1 35 L8
PLSTW E13 141 M6
Fosters Cl CHST BR7 184 C8
SWFD E18 101 N9
Fosters Gv BFOR GU20 212 A1
Fosters La WOKN/KNAP GU21 231 H3
Fosters Ms HART DA3 211 K3
Fosters Pth SLN SL2 128 E6
Foster St HDN NW4 116 F2
HLWE CM17 48 A3
Foster Wk HDN NW4 116 F2
Fothergill Cl PLSTW E13 141 M3
Fothergill Dr WCHMH N21 78 F9
Fotheringay Gdns SL SL1 128 F9
Fotheringham Rd EN EN1 79 N8
Fotherley Rd RKW/CH/CXG WD3 91 J3
Fouberts Pl SOHO/CST W1F 10 G6
Foulden Rd STNW/STAM N16 119 N9
Foulden Ter STNW/STAM N16 119 N9
Foulis Ter SKENS SW7 15 L6
Foulser Rd TOOT SW17 180 A6
Foulsham Rd THHTH CR7 203 K3
Foundary Ga CHES/WCR EN8 62 D9
Foundation Pl ELTH/MOT SE9 * 184 D1
Founder Cl EHAM E6 142 E8
Founders Cl NTHLT UB5 133 N5
Founders Gdns NRWD SE19 181 K10
Founders Rd HOD EN11 26 G10
Foundry Cl BERM/RHTH SE16 140 D10
Foundry Ct CHERT KT16 195 K7
Foundry La DTCH/LGLY SL3 150 E9
Foundry Ms CAMTN NW1 10 G1
HSLW TW3 154 A10
Foundry Pl WAND/EARL SW18 * 179 L3
Founes Dr CDW/CHF RM16 167 K2
Fountain Cl UX/CGN UB8 132 D7
Fountain Dr CAR SM5 222 A5
HERT/BAY SG13 25 N4
NRWD SE19 181 N7
Fountain Farm HLWS CM18 47 J3
Fountain Gdns WDSR SL4 149 J9
Fountain Green Sq
BERM/RHTH SE16 19 P2
Fountain Ms HAMP NW3 4 A1
Fountain Pl BRXN/ST SW9 159 H7
WAB EN9 63 H10
Fountain Rd REDH RH1 275 P2
THHTH CR7 203 K2
TOOT SW17 179 N8
Fountains Av FELT TW13 175 N6
Fountains Cl CRAWW RH11 283 K9
FELT TW13 175 N5
Fountains Crs STHGT/OAK N14 98 F1
Fountain Wk GVW DA11 190 B2
Fountayne Rd SEVS/STOTM N15 119 N2
STNW/STAM N16 119 P7
Fount St VX/NE SW8 158 E6
Four Acres COB KT11 217 M9
GU GU1 250 F8
WGCE AL7 23 H7
Fouracres PEND EN3 80 D5
Fouracres Dr HHS/BOV HP3 36 A8
The Four Acres SBW CM21 30 B1
Fouracres Wk HHS/BOV HP3 36 A9
Fourdrinier Wy HHS/BOV HP3 35 N10
Fourland Wk EDGW HA8 95 P7
Four Limes STALE/WH AL4 21 J3
Fournier St WCHPL E1 13 L3
Four Oaks BRWN CM15 * 107 K4
CSHM HP5 50 F3
Four Seasons Cl BOW E3 140 F4
Four Seasons Crs CHEAM SM3 201 J9
Fourteenth Av
KWD/TDW/WH KT20 * 257 J2
Fourth Av GSTN WD25 73 L1
HLW CM20 28 F10
HLWW/ROY CM19 46 D1
HYS/HAR UB3 132 G10
KWD/TDW/WH KT20 * 257 J2
MNPK E12 122 C9
NKENS W10 8 A1
ROMW/RG RM7 124 D6
WTHK RM20 166 F5
Fourth Cross Rd WHTN TW2 176 C5
Fourth Dr COUL/CHIP CR5 240 E2
Fourth Wy WBLY HA9 115 N9
The Four Tubs BUSH WD23 94 C1
Four Wents COB KT11 217 J9
The Four Wents CHING E4 101 J3
Fovant Cl HARP AL5 20 B5
Fowey Av REDBR IG4 122 A3
Fowey Cl WAP E1W 140 A10
Fowler Cl BTSEA SW11 157 N9
CRAWE RH10 284 D9
SCUP DA14 185 P8
Fowler Rd BARK/HLT IG6 103 M6
FSTGT E7 121 M9
IS N1 6 D5
Fowlerscroft RGUW GU3 266 G7
Fowlers Md CHOB/PIR GU24 213 K5
Fowler's Wk EA W5 135 J6
Fowley Cl CHES/WCR EN8 62 E10
Fowley Mead Pk
CHES/WCR EN8 * 62 E10
Fownes St BTSEA SW11 157 P9
Foxacre CTHM CR3 241 M8
Fox And Knot St FARR EC1M * 12 D3
Foxberry Rd BROCKY SE4 160 D10
Foxborough Cl DTCH/LGLY SL3 150 D4
Foxborough Gdns BROCKY SE4 182 F2
Foxborough Hill Rd SHGR GU5 268 B9
Foxbourne Rd TOOT SW17 180 B5
Fox Burrow Rd BARK/HLT IG6 103 M6
Foxburrows Av GUW GU2 249 L10
Foxbury Av CHST BR7 184 G9
Foxbury Cl BMLY BR1 183 N9
ORP BR6 227 K2
Foxbury Dr ORP BR6 227 K3
Foxbury Rd BMLY BR1 183 M9
Fox Cl BORE WD6 75 J10
BUSH WD23 74 A9
CAN/RD E16 141 M7
CRAWW RH11 283 L5
CRW RM5 104 C6
ORP BR6 227 K2
WCHPL E1 140 B6
WEY KT13 216 E2
WOKS/MYFD GU22 232 G1
Foxcombe CROY/NA CR0 224 G3
Fox Covert LHD/OX KT22 236 C10
Fox Covert Cl ASC SL5 192 B5
Foxcroft STAL AL1 38 F8
Foxcroft Rd WOOL/PLUM SE18 162 E7
Foxdell NTHWD HA6 92 E7
Foxdells HERT/WAT SG14 24 D8
Foxdell Wy CFSP/GDCR SL9 90 B6
Foxearth Cl BH/WHM TN16 244 B4
Foxearth Rd SAND/SEL CR2 224 B6
Foxearth Sp SAND/SEL CR2 224 B5
Foxenden Rd GU GU1 268 B1
Foxes Cl HERT/BAY SG13 26 A5
Foxes Dl BKHTH/KID SE3 161 M9
HAYES BR2 205 J3
Foxes Dr CHESW EN7 61 N5
Foxes Gn CDW/CHF RM16 168 D1
Foxes La POTB/CUF EN6 60 F4
Foxes Pde WAB EN9 * 63 H9
Foxes Pth RGUE GU4 250 C2
Foxfield Cl NTHWD HA6 92 G7
Foxfield Rd ORP BR6 206 G9
Foxglove Cl BFN/LL DA15 185 K2
ED N9 100 B2
HAT AL10 40 E5
HOD EN11 27 H10
STHL UB1 133 M9
STWL/WRAY TW19 173 N4
Foxglove Gdns PUR/KEN CR8 222 F7
RGUE GU4 250 F8
WAN E11 121 P2
Foxglove La CHSGTN KT9 219 M1
Foxglove Pth THMD SE28 163 H1
Foxglove Rd ROMW/RG RM7 124 F7
SOCK/AV RM15 147 H8
The Foxgloves HHW HP1 35 H7
Foxglove St ACT W3 136 C9
Foxglove Wy WLGTN SM6 202 B8
Foxgrove STHGT/OAK N14 98 F4
Fox Gv WOT/HER KT12 197 J7
Foxgrove Av BECK BR3 182 G10
Foxgrove Dr WOKN/KNAP GU21 232 D1
Foxgrove Pth OXHEY WD19 93 L6
Foxgrove Rd BECK BR3 182 G10
Foxhall Rd UPMR RM14 126 B10
Foxham Rd ARCH N19 118 E8
Foxhanger Gdns
WOKS/MYFD GU22 232 D3
Fox Hatch BRWN CM15 86 D3
Foxherne DTCH/LGLY SL3 149 P1
Fox Hl HAYES BR2 225 P2
NRWD SE19 181 N10
Foxhill WATN WD24 73 H2
Fox Hill Gdns NRWD SE19 181 N10
Foxhill Ms CHERT KT16 194 E10
Foxhills WOKN/KNAP GU21 231 P4
Foxhills Cl CHERT KT16 214 E3
Fox Hills Rd CHERT KT16 214 E2
Foxhole Rd ELTH/MOT SE9 184 B1
Foxholes WEY KT13 216 E2
Foxholes Av HERT/BAY SG13 25 N5
Fox Hollow Cl WOOL/PLUM SE18 163 H4
Fox Hollow Dr BXLYHN DA7 163 N9
Foxhollow Dr SLN SL2 109 H10
Foxhollows HAT AL10 40 E2
Foxholt Gdns WLSDN NW10 135 P2
Foxhome Cl CHST BR7 184 D9
Fox House Rd BELV DA17 164 C3
Foxlake Rd BF/WBF KT14 216 A8
Foxlands Cl GSTN WD25 55 H10
Foxlands Crs DAGE RM10 124 D10
Foxlands Rd DAGE RM10 124 D10
Fox La EA W5 135 K7
GT/LBKH KT23 235 N10
HAYES BR2 225 N2
PLMGR N13 98 G3
REIG RH2 257 L7
Fox La North CHERT KT16 195 J8
Fox La South CHERT KT16 * 195 J8
Foxlees ALP/SUD HA0 114 F9
Foxley Cl HACK E8 119 P10
REDH RH1 276 B5
Foxley Gdns PUR/KEN CR8 223 J9
Foxley Hill Rd PUR/KEN CR8 223 H8
Foxley La PUR/KEN CR8 222 F6
Foxley Rd CMBW SE5 159 H6
PUR/KEN CR8 223 J10
THHTH CR7 203 J4
Foxleys OXHEY WD19 93 M4
Foxley Sq BRXN/ST SW9 * 159 J6
Fox Manor Wy WTHK RM20 166 G5
Foxmead Cl ENC/FH EN2 78 G7
Foxmore St BTSEA SW11 158 A7
Foxoak Hl WOT/HER KT12 216 F6
Foxon Cl CTHM CR3 241 M7
Foxon La CTHM CR3 241 L7
Foxon Lane Gdns CTHM CR3 241 M7
Fox Rd CAN/RD E16 141 L7
DTCH/LGLY SL3 150 A3
Fox's La BRKMPK AL9 41 H10
Foxton Gv MTCM CR4 201 N2
Foxton Rd HOD EN11 44 E3
WTHK RM20 167 J5
Foxwarren ESH/CLAY KT10 218 E5
Foxwell St BROCKY SE4 160 D9
Fox Wd WOT/HER KT12 216 G4
Foxwood Cha WAB EN9 81 H2
Foxwood Cl FELT TW13 175 J6
MLHL NW7 96 B5
Foxwood Green Cl EN EN1 79 M10
Foxwood Gv GVW DA11 190 B4
ORP BR6 227 M6
Foxwood Rd BKHTH/KID SE3 161 L10
RDART DA2 188 G6
Foyle Dr SOCK/AV RM15 146 F8
Foyle Rd BKHTH/KID SE3 161 L5
TOTM N17 99 P9
Frailey Cl WOKS/MYFD GU22 232 E2
Frailey Hl WOKS/MYFD GU22 232 E2
Framewood Rd SLN SL2 129 P2
Framfield Cl CRAWW RH11 283 K5
NFNCH/WDSPK N12 97 K5
Framfield Rd HBRY N5 119 J10
HNWL W7 134 E8
MTCM CR4 180 B10
Framlingham Crs ELTH/MOT SE9 184 B7
Frampton Cl BELMT SM2 221 K4
Frampton Park Rd HOM E9 140 B1
Frampton Rd EPP CM16 65 K4
HSLWW TW4 175 M1
POTB/CUF EN6 59 M6
Frampton St HERT/WAT SG14 25 L5
STJWD NW8 9 M2
Francemary Rd LEW SE13 182 F1
Frances Av CDW/CHF RM16 167 H3
Frances Gdns SOCK/AV RM15 146 E9
Frances Rd CHING E4 100 F7
WDSR SL4 149 J8
Frances St CSHM HP5 51 H6
WOOL/PLUM SE18 162 C3
Franche Court Rd TOOT SW17 179 M6
Franchise St CSHM HP5 51 H6
Francis Av BXLYHN DA7 164 B8
FELT TW13 175 H6
IL IG1 122 G7
STALW/RED AL3 38 C3
Francis Barber Cl
STRHM/NOR SW16 * 180 G7
Franciscan Rd TOOT SW17 180 B7
Francis Chichester Cl ASC SL5 192 A5
Francis Chichester Wy
BTSEA SW11 * 158 B7
Francis Cl HOR/WEW KT19 220 A1
SHPTN TW17 196 B4
Francis Ct GUW GU2 * 249 N8
Francis Gv WIM/MER SW19 179 J10
Francis Ms LEE/GVPK SE12 * 183 L2
Francis Rd CROY/NA CR0 203 J7
CTHM CR3 241 L8
DART DA1 187 L1
EFNCH N2 * 118 A2
GFD/PVL UB6 135 H4
HRW HA1 114 F3
HSLWW TW4 153 L8
LEY E10 121 H7
PIN HA5 113 K3
STMC/STPC BR5 207 N3
WARE SG12 26 C1
WATW WD18 73 J8
WLGTN SM6 222 D3
Francis St SRTFD E15 121 K10
WEST SW1P 17 H5
Francis Ter ARCH N19 118 D8
Francis Wk IS N1 5 N5
Francis Wy SL SL1 128 C9
Francis Yd CSHM HP5 * 50 G7
Francklyn Gdns EDGW HA8 95 M4
Francombe Gdns ROM RM1 125 H4
Franconia Rd CLAP SW4 180 D1
Frank Burton Cl CHARL SE7 161 N4
Frank Dixon Cl DUL SE21 181 M3
Frank Dixon Wy DUL SE21 181 M4
Frankfurt Rd HNHL SE24 181 K1
Frankham St DEPT SE8 160 F6
Frankland Cl BERM/RHTH SE16 160 A2
RKW/CH/CXG WD3 92 B1
WFD IG8 101 P6
Frankland Rd CHING E4 100 F6
RKW/CH/CXG WD3 72 C10
SKENS SW7 15 L4
Franklands Dr ADL/WDHM KT15 215 J4
Franklin Av CHESW EN7 61 P6
SLN SL2 128 G7
Franklin Cl HHS/BOV HP3 * 35 P9
KUT/HW KT1 199 M3
LEW SE13 160 G7
STALE/WH AL4 40 B8
TRDG/WHET N20 97 M1
WNWD SE27 181 J7
Franklin Ct GUW GU2 249 L10
Franklin Crs MTCM CR4 202 D4
Franklin Rd BXLYHN DA7 163 P7
CRAWE RH10 284 D8
GVE DA12 190 G8
HCH RM12 145 K1
PGE/AN SE20 182 B10
RDART DA2 186 F5
WAT WD17 73 J6
Franklins Ms RYLN/HDSTN HA2 114 B7
Franklin Sq WKENS W14 14 D8
Franklins Rw CHEL SW3 16 B7
Franklin St BOW E3 140 G5
SEVS/STOTM N15 119 M4
Franklin Wy CROY/NA CR0 202 F8
Franklyn Crs WDSR SL4 148 C9
Franklyn Gdns BARK/HLT IG6 102 G7
Franklyn Rd WLSDN NW10 136 C2
WOT/HER KT12 197 J6
Frank Martin Ct CHESW EN7 61 P6
Franks Av NWMAL KT3 199 P4
Franksfield SHGR GU5 270 F10
Franks La EYN DA4 210 A5
Franks Rd GUW GU2 249 M7
Frank Sutton Wy SL SL1 129 H9
Franks Wood Av
STMC/STPC BR5 206 E5
Frankswood Av WDR/YW UB7 132 A8
Franlaw Crs PLMGR N13 99 K5
Franmil Rd HCH RM12 124 G5
Fransfield Gv SYD SE26 182 A6
Franshams BUSH WD23 * 94 D3
Frant Cl PGE/AN SE20 182 B10
Frant Rd THHTH CR7 203 J5
Fraser Cl BXLY DA5 186 D4
Fraser Rd CHES/WCR EN8 62 D4
ED N9 100 A4
ERITH DA8 164 D4
GFD/PVL UB6 135 H3
WALTH E17 120 G3
Fraser St CHSWK W4 156 B4
Frating Crs WFD IG8 101 M7
Frays Av WDR/YW UB7 151 N1
Frays Cl WDR/YW UB7 151 N2
Frayslea UX/CGN UB8 131 M4
Fray's Waye UX/CGN UB8 131 M3
Frazer Av RSLP HA4 113 K10
Frazer Cl ROM RM1 124 G5
Frazier St STHWK SE1 18 B2
Frean St BERM/RHTH SE16 19 N3
Freda Corbett Cl PECK SE15 159 P6
Frederica Rd CHING E4 101 J1
Frederica St HOLWY N7 5 N3
Frederick Cl BAY/PAD W2 9 P7
SUT SM1 221 J1
Frederick Crs BRXN/ST SW9 159 J6
PEND EN3 80 B6
Frederick Gdns CROY/NA CR0 203 J6
SUT SM1 221 J2
Frederick Pl WOOL/PLUM SE18 162 E4
Frederick Rd RAIN RM13 144 E4
SUT SM1 221 J2
WALW SE17 * 18 D8
Frederick Sanger Rd GUW GU2 267 J1
Frederick's Pl LOTH EC2R * 12 G6
NFNCH/WDSPK N12 97 M5
Frederick Sq BERM/RHTH SE16 140 D9
Frederick's Rw FSBYE EC1V 6 C9
Frederick St FSBYW WC1X 5 N10
Frederick Ter HACK E8 7 L4
Frederic Ms KTBR SW1X * 16 C2
Frederic St WALTH E17 120 D3
Fredora Av YEAD UB4 132 G6
Freeborne Gdns RAIN RM13 145 H1
Freedom Cl WALTH E17 120 C2
Freedom Rd TOTM N17 99 L10
TOTM N17 119 L1
Freedom St BTSEA SW11 158 A8
Freedown La BNSTD SM7 221 L9
BNSTD SM7 221 N8
Freegrove Rd HOLWY N7 118 F10
Freeland Pk HDN NW4 97 H10
Freeland Rd EA W5 135 L9
Freelands Av SAND/SEL CR2 224 C5
Freelands Gv BMLY BR1 205 N1
Freelands Rd BMLY BR1 205 N1
COB KT11 217 J10
Freeland Wy ERITH DA8 165 H7
Freeling St IS N1 * 5 N4
Freeman Cl NTHLT UB5 133 M2
SHPTN TW17 196 F4
Freeman Ct CSHM HP5 51 H6
Freeman Dr E/WMO/HCT KT8 197 N4
Freeman Rd GVE DA12 191 H6
MRDN SM4 201 N5
Freemans Cl SLN SL2 129 L1
Freemans La HYS/HAR UB3 132 F9
Freemantle Av PEND EN3 80 C9
Freemantle St WALW SE17 19 J7
Freeman Wy EMPK RM11 125 M4
Freemasons Pl CROY/NA CR0 203 M8
Freemasons Rd CAN/RD E16 141 N8
CROY/NA CR0 203 M8
Free Prae Rd CHERT KT16 195 K8
Freesia Cl ORP BR6 227 J2
Freesia Dr CHOB/PIR GU24 230 F2
Freestone Yd DTCH/LGLY SL3 * 150 G6
Freethorpe Cl NRWD SE19 203 M1
Freezeland Wy HGDN/ICK UB10 132 C1
Freightmaster Est RAIN RM13 * 165 H3
Freke Rd BTSEA SW11 158 B9
Fremantle Rd BARK/HLT IG6 102 E10
BELV DA17 164 B3
Fremont St HOM E9 140 B3
Frenchaye ADL/WDHM KT15 215 M2
Frenches Rd REDH RH1 258 C7
The Frenches REDH RH1 258 B8
French Gdns COB KT11 217 K10
French Horn Ct WARE SG12 * 26 C2
French Horn La HAT AL10 40 F3
Frenchlands Hatch EHSLY KT24 252 F3
French Pl SDTCH EC2A 7 K10
French's Cl WARE SG12 26 G6
French St SUN TW16 197 K2
French's Wls WOKN/KNAP GU21 231 N3
Frenchum Gdns SL SL1 128 D10

Frendsbury Rd BROCKY SE4 160 D10
Frensham CHESW EN7 61 N3
Frensham Cl STHL UB1 133 N6
Frensham Dr CROY/NA CR0 225 H4
PUT/ROE SW15 178 D6
Frensham Rd ELTH/MOT SE9 184 G5
PUR/KEN CR8 223 J10
Frensham St PECK SE15 19 P10
Frensham Wk SLN SL2 109 H10
Frensham Wy EW KT17 238 F2
Frere St BTSEA SW11 157 P8
Freshborough Ct GU GU1 268 C1
Freshfield Av HACK E8 7 L3
Freshfield Cl CRAWE RH10 284 B8
LEW SE13 161 J10
Freshfield Dr STHGT/OAK N14 98 C1
Freshfield Flats
KWD/TDW/WH KT20 * 257 J3
Freshfields CROY/NA CR0 204 E7
Freshfields Av UPMR RM14 126 B10
Freshford St TOOT SW17 179 M6
Freshmount Gdns
HOR/WEW KT19 219 N7
Freshwater Cl TOOT SW17 180 B9
Freshwater Rd BCTR RM8 123 N6
TOOT SW17 180 B9
Freshwaters HLW CM20 29 H10
Freshwell Av CHDH RM6 123 M2
Fresh Wharf Rd BARK IG11 142 E3
Freshwood Cl BECK BR3 204 G1
Freshwood Wy WLGTN SM6 222 D5
Freston Gdns EBAR EN4 78 B9
Freston Pk FNCH N3 97 J10
Freston Rd NKENS W10 136 G9
Freta Rd BXLYHS DA6 186 A1
Fretherne Chambers
WGCW AL8 * 22 G5
Fretherne Rd WGCW AL8 22 G5
Frewin Rd WAND/EARL SW18 179 N4
Friar Ms WNWD SE27 181 J6
Friar Rd STMC/STPC BR5 207 K5
YEAD UB4 133 L6
Friar's Av BRWN CM15 107 M1
PUT/ROE SW15 178 C6
TRDG/WHET N20 97 P4
Friar's Cl BRWN CM15 107 M1
CHING E4 101 H4
IL IG1 122 G6
NTHLT UB5 133 K5
STHWK SE1 * 12 D9
Friarscroft BROX EN10 44 F6
Friars Cft RGUE GU4 250 F7
Friars Fld BERK HP4 33 K2
Friars Gdns ACT W3 136 A8
Friar's Ga GUW GU2 267 M2
Friars Gate Cl WFD IG8 101 M5
Friars La RBSF CM22 31 K1
RCH/KEW TW9 177 J1
Friars Md POP/IOD E14 161 H2
Friars Ms ELTH/MOT SE9 184 D1
Friars Orch LHD/OX KT22 236 C7
Friars Place La ACT W3 136 B9
Friars Ri WOKS/MYFD GU22 232 D4
Friar's Rd EHAM E6 142 A3
VW GU25 194 A4
Friars Rookery CRAWE RH10 283 P7
Friars Stile Rd
RCHPK/HAM TW10 177 K2
The Friars CHIG IG7 103 H5
HLWW/ROY CM19 46 E3
Friars Wk ABYW SE2 163 N4
STHGT/OAK N14 98 C2
Friars Wy ACT W3 136 A8
BUSH WD23 73 N5
CHERT KT16 195 K6
KGLGY WD4 54 B6
Friars Wd CROY/NA CR0 224 D5
Friary Br GU GU1 267 P2
Friary Cl NFNCH/WDSPK N12 97 P6
Friary Ct WOKN/KNAP GU21 231 L4
Friary Est PECK SE15 * 159 P6
Friary Island STWL/WRAY TW19 171 P2
Friary La WFD IG8 101 M5
Friary Pk NFNCH/WDSPK N12 * 97 P5
Friary Park Ct ACT W3 * 135 P8
Friary Rd ACT W3 135 P8
ACT W3 136 A8
ASC SL5 192 A6
NFNCH/WDSPK N12 97 N5
PECK SE15 159 P6
STWL/WRAY TW19 171 P2
The Friary CHES/WCR EN8 * 62 E9
WDSR SL4 171 P3
Friary Wy CRAWE RH10 283 N8
NFNCH/WDSPK N12 97 P5
Friday Hl CHING E4 101 K4
Friday Hl East CHING E4 101 K4
Friday Hl West CHING E4 101 K3
Friday Rd ERITH DA8 164 E4
MTCM CR4 180 A10
Friday St RDKG RH5 271 M9
STP EC4M 12 E7
Frideswide Pl KTTN NW5 118 D10
Friendly Pl LEW SE13 160 G7
Friendly St DEPT SE8 160 F7
Friendly Street Ms DEPT SE8 160 F8
Friends Av CHES/WCR EN8 62 C8
Friends Cl CRAWW RH11 283 N4
Friendship Wy SRTFD E15 * 141 H3
Friends' Rd CROY/NA CR0 203 L10
PUR/KEN CR8 223 J8
Friend St FSBYE EC1V 6 C9
Friern Barnet La
FBAR/BDGN N11 98 A5
TRDG/WHET N20 97 N4
Friern Barnet Rd
FBAR/BDGN N11 98 B6
Friern Cl CHESW EN7 61 M2
Friern Mount Dr
TRDG/WHET N20 97 M1
Friern Pk NFNCH/WDSPK N12 97 N6
Friern Rd EDUL SE22 181 P2
Friern Watch Av
NFNCH/WDSPK N12 97 N5
Frigate Ms DEPT SE8 160 F5
Frimley Av EMPK RM11 125 P6
WLGTN SM6 222 F2
Frimley Cl CROY/NA CR0 225 H4
WIM/MER SW19 179 H5
Frimley Ct SCUP DA14 185 M8
Frimley Crs CROY/NA CR0 225 H4
Frimley Gdns MTCM CR4 201 P3
Frimley Rd CHSGTN KT9 219 J2
GDMY/SEVK IG3 123 H8
HHW HP1 35 H5
Frimley Wy WCHPL E1 * 140 C6
Fringewood Cl NTHWD HA6 92 C9
Frinstead Gv STMC/STPC BR5 207 N4
Frinsted Rd ERITH DA8 164 E6
Frinton Cl OXHEY WD19 93 J3
Frinton Dr WFD IG8 101 J8
Frinton Ms GNTH/NBYPK IG2 122 D4
Frinton Rd CRW RM5 104 B8
EHAM E6 142 A3
SCUP DA14 185 P5
SEVS/STOTM N15 119 M4
TOOT SW17 180 B9
Friston St FUL/PGN SW6 157 L8
Friston Wk CRAWW RH11 283 K6
Friswell Pl BXLYHN DA7 164 B10
Fritham Cl NWMAL KT3 200 B6
Frith Ct MLHL NW7 97 H8
The Frithe SLN SL2 129 N9
Frith Knowle WOT/HER KT12 217 J3
Frith La MLHL NW7 97 H7
Frith Manor Farm Cotts
MLHL NW7 * 97 H6
Frith Rd CROY/NA CR0 203 K9
WAN E11 121 H9
Frithsden Copse BERK HP4 34 C1
Friths Dr REIG RH2 257 L7
Frith St SOHO/SHAV W1D 11 J6
Frithville Gdns SHB W12 136 F10
Frithwald Rd CHERT KT16 195 J7
Frithwood Av NTHWD HA6 92 G7

Frizlands La DAGE RM10 124 C8
Frobisher Cl BUSH WD23 73 P10
PIN HA5 113 L5
PUR/KEN CR8 241 K3
Frobisher Crs BARB EC2Y * 12 F3
STWL/WRAY TW19 173 P3
Frobisher Gdns CDW/CHF RM16 167 K2
GU GU1 250 D9
LEY E10 * 120 G4
Frobisher Ms ENC/FH EN2 79 L8
Frobisher Rd CEND/HSY/T N8 119 H2
EHAM E6 142 C8
ERITH DA8 165 H6
STAL AL1 39 H8
Frobisher Wy GVE DA12 191 H8
HAT AL10 40 A1
RDART DA2 166 G10
Frog Grove La RGUW GU3 248 F6
Froggy La DEN/HRF UB9 110 G8
Froghole La EDEN TN8 263 H9
Frog La RGUE GU4 250 B1
Frogley Rd EDUL SE22 159 N10
Frogmoor La RKW/CH/CXG WD3 91 N3
Frogmore LCOL/BKTW AL2 56 D3
WAND/EARL SW18 179 K1
Frogmore Av YEAD UB4 132 F6
Frogmore Cl CHEAM SM3 200 G10
SL SL1 148 F1
Frogmore Dr WDSR SL4 149 L8
Frogmore Est HBRY N5 * 119 K9
Frogmore Gdns CHEAM SM3 221 H1
YEAD UB4 132 F6
Frogmore Rd HHS/BOV HP3 * 35 N9
Frognal HAMP NW3 117 M10
Frognal Av HRW HA1 114 E2
SCUP DA14 185 K9
Frognal Cl HAMP NW3 117 M10
Frognal Gdns HAMP NW3 117 M9
Frognal La HAMP NW3 117 L10
Frognal Man HAMP NW3 * 117 M9
Frognal Pde HAMP NW3 3 J1
Frognal Pl SCUP DA14 185 L8
Frognal Ri HAMP NW3 117 M8
Frognal Wy HAMP NW3 117 M9
Frog St BRWN CM15 86 D5
Froissart Rd ELTH/MOT SE9 184 B1
Frome TIL RM18 169 M3
Frome Rd SEVS/STOTM N15 119 J1
Frome Sq HHNE HP2 36 B1
Frome St IS N1 6 E7
Fromondes Rd CHEAM SM3 221 H2
Fromow Gdns BFOR GU20 212 C3
Fromows Cnr CHSWK W4 * 155 P4
Front La UPMR RM14 126 D7
The Front BERK HP4 34 E2
Frostic Wk WCHPL E1 13 M4
Froude St VX/NE SW8 158 C8
Frowick Cl BRKMPK AL9 40 E9
Frowycke Crs POTB/CUF EN6 58 D8
Fruen Rd EBED/NFELT TW14 174 G3
Fryatt Rd TOTM N17 99 L8
Fry Cl CRW RM5 104 B6
Fryday Grove Ms BAL SW12 180 D3
Fryent Cl KTN/HRWW/WS HA3 115 M4
Fryent Crs CDALE/KGS NW9 116 B4
Fryent Flds CDALE/KGS NW9 116 B4
Fryent Gv CDALE/KGS NW9 116 B4
Fryent Wy CDALE/KGS NW9 115 M4
Fryer Cl CSHM HP5 51 J9
Fryern Wd CTHM CR3 241 K10
Frying Pan Aly WCHPL E1 13 K4
Frymley Vw WDSR SL4 148 C7
Fry Rd EHAM E6 142 A2
WLSDN NW10 136 C3
Fryston Av COUL/CHIP CR5 222 C10
CROY/NA CR0 203 P9
Fryth Md STALW/RED AL3 38 A5
Fuchsia Cl ROMW/RG RM7 124 F7
Fuchsia St ABYW SE2 163 L4
Fuchsia Wy CHOB/PIR GU24 212 D9
Fuel Farm Rd HORL RH6 279 P7
Fulbeck Dr CDALE/KGS NW9 96 B9
Fulbeck Wy RYLN/HDSTN HA2 94 B10
Fulbourne Cl REDH RH1 257 P8
Fulbourne Est WCHPL E1 13 P2
Fulbourne Rd WALTH E17 101 H10
Fulbourne St WCHPL E1 140 A7
Fulbrook La SOCK/AV RM15 146 E9
Fulbrook Ms ARCH N19 118 D9
Fulbrook Rd ARCH N19 118 D9
Fulford Gv OXHEY WD19 93 J3
Fulford Rd CTHM CR3 241 L7
HOR/WEW KT19 220 A4
Fulford St BERM/RHTH SE16 160 A1
Fulham Broadway
FUL/PGN SW6 157 K6
Fulham Cl HGDN/ICK UB10 132 D6
Fulham Est FUL/PGN SW6 14 D9
Fulham High St FUL/PGN SW6 157 H8
Fulham Palace Rd FUL/PGN SW6 156 G7
Fulham Park Gdns
FUL/PGN SW6 157 J8
Fulham Park Rd FUL/PGN SW6 157 J8
Fulham Rd FUL/PGN SW6 157 H8
FUL/PGN SW6 157 L6
WBPTN SW10 15 K9
Fullarton Crs SOCK/AV RM15 146 E8
Fullbrook Av ADL/WDHM KT15 215 K7
Fullbrooks Av WPK KT4 200 C8
Fuller Cl BETH E2 13 N1
BUSH WD23 94 C1
ORP BR6 227 J2
Fuller Gdns WATN WD24 73 J3
Fuller Rd BCTR RM8 123 M8
WATN WD24 73 J3
Fullers Av SURB KT6 199 L9
SWFD E18 101 L8
Fullers Cl CRW RM5 104 D8
CSHM HP5 50 G9
WAB EN9 63 M9
Fullers Farm Rd EHSLY KT24 252 C10
Fuller's Hl AMS HP6 50 E10
BH/WHM TN16 262 G2
Fullers Md HLWE CM17 47 M3
Fuller's Rd SWFD E18 101 L9
Fuller St HDN NW4 116 F2
Fullers Wy North SURB KT6 199 L10
Fullers Wy South CHSGTN KT9 219 K1
Fuller's Wd CROY/NA CR0 224 F1
Fullers Wood La REDH RH1 258 D10
Fullerton Cl BF/WBF KT14 216 A10
Fullerton Dr BF/WBF KT14 215 P10
Fullerton Rd BF/WBF KT14 215 P10
CAR SM5 221 P5
CROY/NA CR0 203 N7
WAND/EARL SW18 179 M1
Fullerton Wy BF/WBF KT14 215 P10
Fuller Wy HYS/HAR UB3 152 G4
RKW/CH/CXG WD3 72 B9
Fullmer Wy ADL/WDHM KT15 215 J6
Fullwell Av CLAY IG5 102 D9
Fullwood Pl GINN WC1R 11 P4
Fullwood's Ms IS N1 7 H9
Fulmar Cl CRAWW RH11 * 282 G8
Fulmar Ct BRYLDS KT5 199 L6
Fulmar Crs HHW HP1 35 K7
Fulmar Rd HCH RM12 145 J2
Fulmead St FUL/PGN SW6 157 L7
Fulmer Cl HPTN TW12 175 M8
Fulmer Common Rd
DTCH/LGLY SL3 130 C1
Fulmer Cnr CFSP/GDCR SL9 * 110 E6
Fulmer Dr CFSP/GDCR SL9 110 B7
Fulmer La DTCH/LGLY SL3 110 C8
CFSP/GDCR SL9 110 D6
Fulmer Pl DTCH/LGLY SL3 * 110 B9
Fulmer Rd CAN/RD E16 142 A7
DTCH/LGLY SL3 110 B9
Fulmer Wy CFSP/GDCR SL9 110 B4
WEA W13 154 G2
Fulready Rd LEY E10 121 J3
Fulstone Cl HSLWW TW4 153 N10
Fulthorp Rd BKHTH/KID SE3 161 L8
Fulton Ms BAY/PAD W2 9 J7
Fulton Rd WBLY HA9 115 M8

Fulvens SHGR GU5 270 F9
Fulwell Park Av WHTN TW2 176 B5
Fulwell Rd TEDD TW11 176 C7
Fulwich Rd DART DA1 187 N2
Fulwood Av ALP/SUD HA0 135 L4
Fulwood Gdns TWK TW1 176 E2
Fulwood Wk WIM/MER SW19 179 H4
Furber St HMSMTH W6 156 E2
Furham Fld PIN HA5 93 P8
Furley Rd PECK SE15 159 P6
Furlong Cl WLGTN SM6 202 C8
Furlong Rd DORK RH4 272 B3
HOLWY N7 6 B1
Furlongs HHW HP1 35 K5
Furlong Wy HORL RH6 280 A7
WARE SG12 26 F4
The Furlough WOKS/MYFD GU22 232 D3
Furmage St WAND/EARL SW18 179 L3
Furnace Dr CRAWE RH10 284 A9
Furnace Farm Rd CRAWE RH10 * 284 B9
Furnace Pde CRAWE RH10 284 B9
Furnace Pl CRAWE RH10 284 B9
Furneaux Av WNWD SE27 181 J8
Furner Cl DART DA1 164 G9
Furness WDSR SL4 148 B8
Furness Cl CDW/CHF RM16 168 E4
Furness Rd FUL/PGN SW6 157 L8
MRDN SM4 201 L6
RYLN/HDSTN HA2 114 A6
WLSDN NW10 136 D4
Furness Wy HCH RM12 125 H10
Furnival Av SLN SL2 128 G7
Furnival Cl VW GU25 194 A6
Furnival St FLST/FETLN EC4A 12 A5
Furrow La HOM E9 120 B10
Furrows Pl CTHM CR3 241 N9
The Furrows WOT/HER KT12 197 K9
Fursby Av FNCH N3 97 K7
Furse Av STALE/WH AL4 38 F3
Further Acre CDALE/KGS NW9 96 C10
Furtherfield ABLGY WD5 54 F8
Furtherfield Cl CROY/NA CR0 203 H6
Further Green Rd CAT SE6 183 K3
Furtherground HHNE HP2 35 P7
Furzebank ASC SL5 192 C4
Furzebushes La LCOL/BKTW AL2 55 M1
Furze Cl HORL RH6 280 E4
OXHEY WD19 93 K6
REDH RH1 258 A9
Furzedown Cl EGH TW20 172 B9
Furzedown Ct HARP AL5 20 A3
Furzedown Dr TOOT SW17 180 C8
Furzedown Rd BELMT SM2 221 M7
STRHM/NOR SW16 180 C7
Furze Farm Cl CHDH RM6 103 P10
Furzefield CHES/WCR EN8 62 A4
CRAWW RH11 283 L6
Furze Fld LHD/OX KT22 218 C9
Furzefield Cl CHST BR7 184 E9
Furzefield Ct POTB/CUF EN6 * 59 H7
Furzefield Crs REIG RH2 275 M2
Furzefield Rd BEAC HP9 88 C9
BKHTH/KID SE3 161 N5
REIG RH2 275 M2
WGCE AL7 23 H7
Furzeground Wy STKPK UB11 * 152 D1
Furze Gv KWD/TDW/WH KT20 239 J7
Furzeham Rd WDR/YW UB7 151 P1
Furze Hl KWD/TDW/WH KT20 239 J7
PUR/KEN CR8 222 F7
Furzehill REDH RH1 257 P9
Furzehill Pde BORE WD6 * 75 M8
Furzehill Rd BORE WD6 75 N8
Furzehill Sq STMC/STPC BR5 207 L4
Furze La GODL GU7 267 L9
PUR/KEN CR8 222 F7
Furzen Cl SLN SL2 128 F5
Furzen Crs HAT AL10 40 C7
Furze Pl REDH RH1 * 258 A9
Furze Rd ADL/WDHM KT15 215 J3
HHW HP1 35 H7
THHTH CR7 203 K3
Furze St BOW E3 * 140 F7
Furze Vw RKW/CH/CXG WD3 70 F10
Furzewood SUN TW16 197 H1
Fusedale Wy SOCK/AV RM15 146 E9
Fuzzens Wk WDSR SL4 148 D8
Fydlers Cl WDSR SL4 170 A9
Fye Foot La BLKFR EC4V 12 E7
Fyfe Wy BMLY BR1 205 M2
Fyfield Cl HAYES BR2 205 J4
Fyfield Dr SOCK/AV RM15 146 E9
Fyfield Rd BRXN/ST SW9 159 H9
CHONG CM5 49 N6
EN EN1 79 M7
RAIN RM13 144 G3
WALTH E17 121 J1
WFD IG8 101 P8
Fynes St WEST SW1P 17 J5

G

Gabion Av PUR RM19 166 C3
Gable Cl ABLGY WD5 54 F8
DART DA1 187 H1
PIN HA5 93 P8
Gable Ct SYD SE26 182 A7
Gable Ms HAYES BR2 206 B9
Gables Av ASHF TW15 174 A8
BORE WD6 75 L7
Gables Cl CFSP/GDCR SL9 90 B5
CMBW SE5 159 M7
DTCH/LGLY SL3 149 M5
LEE/GVPK SE12 183 M4
WOKS/MYFD GU22 232 C6
The Gables BNSTD SM7 239 J3
CHONG CM5 67 P2
GRAYS RM17 * 167 L3
HART DA3 211 P3
LHD/OX KT22 218 B8
NRWD SE19 * 203 M1
WBLY HA9 115 L8
WEY KT13 216 D2
WOKS/MYFD GU22 * 232 A5
Gables Wy BNSTD SM7 239 J2
Gabriel Cl CDW/CHF RM16 167 H2
CRW RM5 104 D8
FELT TW13 175 M7
Gabriel Gdns GVE DA12 191 H8
Gabrielle Cl WBLY HA9 115 L8
Gabrielspring Rd HART DA3 210 C9
Gabriel Spring Road (East)
HART DA3 210 E9
Gabriel St FSTH SE23 182 C3
Gabriel's Whf STHWK SE1 12 A9
Gadbrook Rd BRKHM/BTCW RH3 273 P6
Gad Cl PLSTW E13 141 N5
Gaddesden Av WBLY HA9 135 L1
Gaddesden Crs GSTN WD25 55 L10
Gaddesden Gv WGCE AL7 23 L6
Gade Av WATW WD18 72 F8
Gade Bank RKW/CH/CXG WD3 72 E8
Gadebridge La HHW HP1 35 M4
Gadebridge Rd HHW HP1 35 L5
Gade Cl HHW HP1 35 L3
HYS/HAR UB3 133 J10
WATW WD18 72 F8
Gadesden Rd HOR/WEW KT19 219 P3
Gade Valley Cl KGLGY WD4 54 B4
Gade View Gdns KGLGY WD4 54 D8
Gade View Rd HHS/BOV HP3 35 M10
Gadsbury Cl CDALE/KGS NW9 116 C4
Gadsden Cl UPMR RM14 126 D4
Gadswell Cl GSTN WD25 73 M2
Gadwall Cl CAN/RD E16 141 N8
Gage Rd CAN/RD E16 141 K7
Gage St BMSBY WC1N 11 M3
Gainford St IS N1 6 A5
Gainsboro Gdns GFD/PVL UB6 114 D10
Gainsborough Av DART DA1 187 K1
MNPK E12 122 D10
STAL AL1 38 E5

TIL RM18 168 D7
Gainsborough Cl BECK BR3 182 F10
ESH/CLAY KT10 198 D8
Gainsborough Ct SHB W12 156 F1
WOT/HER KT12 217 H1
Gainsborough Dr GVW DA11 190 A6
SAND/SEL CR2 223 P9
Gainsborough Gdns EDGW HA8 95 L10
GLDGN NW11 117 J5
HSLW TW3 176 C1
Gainsborough Ms DUL SE21 181 K4
SYD SE26 * 182 A6
Gainsborough Pl CHIG IG7 103 J4
Gainsborough Rd BCTR RM8 123 L9
CHSWK W4 156 C3
HOR/WEW KT19 219 P6
NFNCH/WDSPK N12 97 L6
NWMAL KT3 200 A6
RAIN RM13 145 H3
RCH/KEW TW9 155 L8
SRTFD E15 141 K5
WAN E11 121 K5
WFD IG8 102 B7
YEAD UB4 132 D4
Gainsborough Sq BXLYHS DA6 163 N9
Gainsborough St HOM E9 140 E1
Gainsborough Ter BELMT SM2 * 221 J4
Gainsford Rd WALTH E17 120 E2
Gainsford St STHWK SE1 13 L10
Gainsthorpe Rd CHONG CM5 49 L9
Gainswood WGCE AL7 23 H6
Gairloch Rd CMBW SE5 159 M8
Gaisford St KTTN NW5 4 G1
Gaist Av CTHM CR3 242 A8
Gaitskell Rd ELTH/MOT SE9 184 F4
Gaitskell Wy STHWK SE1 18 E1
Galahad Cl SL SL1 148 F1
Galahad Rd BMLY BR1 183 M6
CRAWW RH11 283 H7
ED N9 99 P4
Galata Rd BARN SW13 156 D6
Galatea Sq PECK SE15 160 A9
Galbraith St POP/IOD E14 161 H2
Galdana Av BAR EN5 77 M7
Galeborough Av WFD IG8 101 J8
Gale Cl HPTN TW12 175 M9
MTCM CR4 201 N3
Gale Crs BNSTD SM7 239 K3
Galena Rd HMSMTH W6 156 E3
Galen Cl HOR/WEW KT19 219 M7
Galen Pl NOXST/BSQ WC1A 11 M4
Galesbury Rd WAND/EARL SW18 179 M2
Gales Cl RGUE GU4 * 250 G7
Gales Dr CRAWE RH10 284 A7
Gales Gdns BETH E2 140 A5
Gales Pl CRAWE RH10 284 A7
Gale St BOW E3 140 F7
DAGW RM9 143 N1
Gales Wy WFD IG8 102 B8
Galey Gn SOCK/AV RM15 146 G7
Galgate Cl WIM/MER SW19 178 G4
Gallants Farm Rd EBAR EN4 97 P2
Galleon Bvd RDART DA2 188 C1
Galleon Cl BERM/RHTH SE16 160 B1
ERITH DA8 164 E3
Galleon Rd CDW/CHF RM16 166 G3
Galleons Dr BARK IG11 143 K5
Galleons La DTCH/LGLY SL3 130 A5
The Galleons AMSS HP7 * 69 H4
The Galleria HAT AL10 * 40 C3
The Galleries IS N1 * 6 C7
Gallery Gdns NTHLT UB5 133 L4
Gallery Rd DUL SE21 181 L4
Galley Gn HERT/BAY SG13 26 F9
Galley Hl HHW HP1 35 K4
Galley Hill Rd GVW DA11 189 L1
Galleyhill Rd WAB EN9 63 K9
WAB EN9 63 L6
Galley La BAR EN5 76 D4
Galleymead Rd DTCH/LGLY SL3 151 J7
Galleywall Rd BERM/RHTH SE16 160 A3
Galleywood Crs CRW RM5 104 E7
Galliard Rd ED N9 99 P1
Gallia Rd HBRY N5 119 J10
Gallions Cl BARK IG11 143 K5
Gallions Rd CAN/RD E16 142 E9
CHARL SE7 161 N3
Gallions View Rd THMD SE28 163 H1
Gallon Cl CHARL SE7 161 P3
The Gallop BELMT SM2 221 N5
SAND/SEL CR2 224 A4
Gallosson Rd WOOL/PLUM SE18 163 H3
Galloway Cha SLN SL2 129 M9
Galloway Cl BROX EN10 62 E2
Galloway Dr DART DA1 186 F3
Galloway Pth CROY/NA CR0 223 L1
Galloway Rd SHB W12 136 D10
Gallows Hl KGLGY WD4 54 D7
Gallows Hill La ABLGY WD5 54 D8
Gallus Cl WCHMH N21 78 G10
Gallus Sq BKHTH/KID SE3 161 N9
Gallys Rd WDSR SL4 148 C7
Galpin's Rd THHTH CR7 202 F4
Galsworthy Av CHDH RM6 123 L5
POP/IOD E14 140 D8
Galsworthy Cl THMD SE28 143 L10
Galsworthy Crs BKHTH/KID SE3 161 P7
Galsworthy Rd CHERT KT16 195 K7
CRICK NW2 117 H9
KUTN/CMB KT2 199 N1
TIL RM18 168 F7
Galton Rd ASC SL5 192 E6
Galton St NKENS W10 2 A10
Galva Cl EBAR EN4 78 B8
Galveston Rd PUT/ROE SW15 179 J1
Galvin Rd SL SL1 129 H10
Galvins Cl GUW GU2 249 M8
Galway Cl BERM/RHTH SE16 160 A4
Galway St FSBYE EC1V 6 F10
Gambetta St VX/NE SW8 158 C8
Gambia St STHWK SE1 12 D10
Gambles La RPLY/SEND GU23 251 M1
Gambole Rd TOOT SW17 179 P7
Games Rd EBAR EN4 77 P7
Gamlen Rd PUT/ROE SW15 156 G10
Gammon Cl HHS/BOV HP3 36 B7
Gammons Farm Cl WATN WD24 72 G2
Gammons La WATN WD24 73 H3
Gamuel Cl WALTH E17 120 F4
Gander Green Crs HPTN TW12 197 P1
Gander Green La CHEAM SM3 201 H9
SUT SM1 221 J1
Ganders Ash GSTN WD25 55 H9
Gandhi Cl WALTH E17 120 F4
Gandhi Ct WATN WD24 73 L6
Gandolfi St PECK SE15 19 J10
Gangers Hl GDST RH9 260 E3
Ganghill GU GU1 250 D8
Gant Ct WAB EN9 63 L10
Ganton St REGST W1B 10 G7
Ganton Wk OXHEY WD19 * 93 M5
Gantshill Crs GNTH/NBYPK IG2 122 D3
Ganymede Pl HHNE HP2 36 A3
Gape Mouth Rd CHOB/PIR GU24 230 A8
Gap Rd WIM/MER SW19 179 K8
Garage Rd ACT W3 135 M8
Garbrand Wk EW KT17 220 C5
Garbutt Pl MHST W1U * 10 D3
Garbutt Rd UPMR RM14 126 B7
Garden Av BXLYHN DA7 164 A9
HAT AL10 40 D8
MTCM CR4 180 C10
Garden City EDGW HA8 95 M7
Garden Cl ADL/WDHM KT15 215 N1
ASHF TW15 174 D9
BAR EN5 76 F8
BH/WHM TN16 263 M8
BNSTD SM7 239 K1
CHING E4 100 F6
HPTN TW12 175 N8
LEE/GVPK SE12 183 N6
LHD/OX KT22 237 H10
NTHLT UB5 133 M3
PUT/ROE SW15 178 E3
RSLP HA4 112 F7

STAL AL1 38 G5
WAT WD17 72 G6
WLGTN SM6 222 F2
Garden Ct CHSWK W4 155 P2
EMB EC4Y * 12 A7
HPTN TW12 175 N8
SEV TN13 * 247 L8
STALE/WH AL4 21 J2
WGCE AL7 23 H4
Garden End AMS HP6 69 K3
Gardeners Rd CROY/NA CR0 203 J8
Gardener's Wk GT/LBKH KT23 254 A2
Garden Field La BERK HP4 34 C7
Garden Flats HMSMTH W6 * 156 G5
Gardenia Ct CHOB/PIR GU24 212 E9
Gardenia Rd BMLY BR1 206 D3
EN EN1 79 M10
Gardenia Wy WFD IG8 101 M7
Garden La BMLY BR1 183 N9
BRXS/STRHM SW2 180 G4
Garden Lodge Ct EFNCH N2 * 117 N1
Garden Pl HACK E8 7 L5
RDART DA2 187 L6
Garden Reach CSTG HP8 70 A7
Garden Rd ABLGY WD5 54 F7
BMLY BR1 183 N10
PGE/AN SE20 204 B1
RCH/KEW TW9 155 M9
SEV TN13 247 L8
STJWD NW8 3 K9
WOT/HER KT12 197 J6
Garden Rw GVW DA11 190 C6
STHWK SE1 18 C4
The Gardens BECK BR3 205 H2
BRKMPK AL9 59 H3
BRWN CM15 86 G2
CEND/HSY/T N8 * 118 F2
CHOB/PIR GU24 230 E8
CLPT E5 * 119 N5
COB KT11 * 234 D5
EBED/NFELT TW14 174 E2
EDUL SE22 159 P10
ESH/CLAY KT10 217 P1
HGDN/ICK UB10 111 P7
HRW HA1 114 B4
PIN HA5 * 113 N4
WAT WD17 72 G6
Garden St WCHPL E1 140 C7
Garden Studios BAY/PAD W2 * 9 J4
Garden Ter PIM SW1V 17 J7
Garden Terrace Rd HLWE CM17 29 M7
Garden Vls ESH/CLAY KT10 * 218 E4
Garden Wk BECK BR3 204 E1
COUL/CHIP CR5 240 C9
CRAWW RH11 283 M7
SDTCH EC2A 13 J1
Garden Wy LOU IG10 82 D4
WLSDN NW10 135 P1
Gardiner Av CRICK NW2 * 116 F10
Gardiner Cl BCTR RM8 123 N9
PEND EN3 80 C10
STMC/STPC BR5 207 M2
The Gardiners HLWE CM17 47 L2
Gardner Cl WAN E11 121 N4
Gardner La CRAWE RH10 285 P5
Gardner Pl EBED/NFELT TW14 175 J2
Gardner Rd GU GU1 249 P10
PLSTW E13 141 N6
Gardners Cl FBAR/BDGN N11 98 B3
Gardners La BLKFR EC4V 12 E7
Gardnor Rd HAMP NW3 117 N9
Gard St FSBYE EC1V 6 D9
Garendon Gdns MRDN SM4 201 L7
Garendon Rd MRDN SM4 201 L7
Gareth Cl WPK KT4 200 G9
Gareth Dr ED N9 99 P4
Gareth Gv BMLY BR1 183 M7
Garfield Ms BTSEA SW11 158 C9
Garfield Pl WDSR SL4 * 149 H8
Garfield Rd ADL/WDHM KT15 215 M2
BTSEA SW11 158 B9
CHING E4 101 J2
PEND EN3 80 B8
PLSTW E13 141 L6
TWK TW1 176 F4
WIM/MER SW19 179 M9
Garfield St WATN WD24 73 J4
Garford St POP/IOD E14 140 F9
Garganey Wk THMD SE28 143 N9
Gargery Cl GVE DA12 191 J4
Garibaldi Rd REDH RH1 276 A1
Garibaldi St WOOL/PLUM SE18 163 H3
Garland Cl CHES/WCR EN8 62 D7
HHNE HP2 * 35 N5
Garland Dr HSLW TW3 154 B8
Garland Rd STAN HA7 95 J9
WARE SG12 26 D2
WOOL/PLUM SE18 162 G6
Garlands Rd LHD/OX KT22 236 G7
REDH RH1 258 A10
Garland Wy CTHM CR3 241 L8
EMPK RM11 125 M2
Garlichill Rd EPSOM KT18 238 E3
Garlick Hl BLKFR EC4V 12 F7
Garlies Rd FSTH SE23 182 D6
Garlinge Rd CRICK NW2 2 C2
Garman Cl UED N18 99 L6
Garman Rd TOTM N17 100 B8
Garnault Ms CLKNW EC1R 6 B10
Garnault Pl CLKNW EC1R 6 B10
Garnault Rd EN EN1 79 N4
Garner Cl BCTR RM8 123 N6
Garner Dr BROX EN10 62 D2
Garner Rd WALTH E17 101 H9
Garners Cl CFSP/GDCR SL9 90 B7
Garners End CFSP/GDCR SL9 90 B7
Garners Rd CFSP/GDCR SL9 90 B7
Garner St BETH E2 7 P8
Garnet Cl SL SL1 148 F1
Garnet Rd THHTH CR7 203 K4
WLSDN NW10 136 B1
Garnet St WAP E1W 140 B9
Garnett Cl ELTH/MOT SE9 162 C9
WATN WD24 73 L3
Garnett Dr LCOL/BKTW AL2 55 N5
Garnett Rd HAMP NW3 118 A10
Garnham St STNW/STAM N16 119 N7
Garnies Cl PECK SE15 159 N6
Garnon Md EPP CM16 65 N4
Garrad's Rd STRHM/NOR SW16 180 E6
Garrard Cl BXLYHN DA7 164 B9
CHST BR7 184 E8
Garrard Rd BNSTD SM7 239 K2
SLN SL2 128 D6
Garrard Wk WLSDN NW10 * 136 B1
Garrard Wy STALE/WH AL4 21 J3
Garratt Cl CROY/NA CR0 222 F1
Garratt La TOOT SW17 179 N7
WAND/EARL SW18 179 L1
Garratt Rd EDGW HA8 95 M8
Garratts La BNSTD SM7 239 J2
Garratts Rd BUSH WD23 94 B1
Garratt Ter TOOT SW17 179 P7
Garrett Cl ACT W3 136 A7
CRAWE RH10 284 D9
CSHM HP5 51 H9
Garretts Cl HERT/WAT SG14 25 K5
Garrett St STLK EC1Y 12 E1
Garrick Av GLDGN NW11 117 J4
Garrick Cl EA W5 135 K6
RCH/KEW TW9 177 H1
STA TW18 173 K10
WAND/EARL SW18 157 M10
WOT/HER KT12 217 J1
Garrick Crs CROY/NA CR0 203 M9
Garrick Dr HDN NW4 96 F10
THMD SE28 162 G2
Garrick Gdns E/WMO/HCT KT8 197 P3
Garrick Pk HDN NW4 96 G10
Garrick Rd CDALE/KGS NW9 116 C4
GFD/PVL UB6 134 A6
RCH/KEW TW9 155 M8
Garrick St COVGDN WC2E 11 L7
GVW DA11 190 E2
Garrick Wk CRAWE RH10 283 P10

Garrick Wy HDN NW4 116 G2
Garrick Yd CHCR WC2N 11 L7
Garrison Cl HSLWW TW4 175 N1
WOOL/PLUM SE18 162 D6
Garrison La CHSGTN KT9 219 K4
Garrison Rd BOW E3 140 F3
Garrolds Cl SWLY BR8 208 E2
The Garrones CRAWE RH10 * 284 F6
Garron La SOCK/AV RM15 146 E8
Garrow HART DA3 211 N3
Garry Cl ROM RM1 104 F8
Garry Wy ROM RM1 104 F8
Garside Cl HPTN TW12 176 A10
THMD SE28 162 G2
Garsington Ms BROCKY SE4 160 E9
Garsmouth Wy GSTN WD25 73 L2
Garson Gv CSHM HP5 50 F5
Garson La STWL/WRAY TW19 172 A3
Garson Rd ESH/CLAY KT10 217 N3
Garston Crs GSTN WD25 55 K10
Garston Dr GSTN WD25 55 K10
Garston La GSTN WD25 73 L1
PUR/KEN CR8 241 L1
The Garstons GT/LBKH KT23 253 N1
Garter Wy BERM/RHTH SE16 160 C1
Garth Cl KUTN/CMB KT2 177 L8
MRDN SM4 200 G7
RSLP HA4 113 L6
Garthland Dr BAR EN5 76 E9
Garth Ms EA W5 * 135 K6
Garthorne Rd FSTH SE23 182 C3
Garth Rd CHSWK W4 156 A4
CRICK NW2 117 J7
KUTN/CMB KT2 177 L8
MRDN SM4 200 G8
SEV TN13 265 K4
SOCK/AV RM15 147 H6
Garthside KUTN/CMB KT2 177 K8
The Garth ABLGY WD5 54 E9
COB KT11 217 M9
HPTN TW12 176 A9
KTN/HRWW/WS HA3 115 L4
NFNCH/WDSPK N12 * 97 L6
Garthway NFNCH/WDSPK N12 97 P7
Gartlet Rd WAT WD17 73 K7
Gartmoor Gdns WIM/MER SW19 179 J4
Gartmore Rd GDMY/SEVK IG3 123 J6
Garton Cl CRAWW RH11 283 H8
Garton Pl WAND/EARL SW18 179 M2
Gartons Cl PEND EN3 80 B9
Gartons Wy BTSEA SW11 157 M9
Garvary Rd CAN/RD E16 141 N8
Garvin Av BEAC HP9 88 D8
Garvock Dr SEV TN13 265 H2
Garway Rd BAY/PAD W2 8 G6
Gascoigne Gdns WFD IG8 101 K8
Gascoigne Pl BETH E2 7 L10
Gascoigne Rd BARK IG11 142 F3
CROY/NA CR0 225 H6
WEY KT13 196 C10
Gascon's Gv SLN SL2 128 G6
Gascony Av KIL/WHAMP NW6 2 E4
Gascoyne Cl HARH RM3 105 L9
POTB/CUF EN6 58 D8
Gascoyne Dr DART DA1 164 G9
Gascoyne Rd HOM E9 140 C2
Gascoyne Wy HERT/BAY SG13 25 L6
Gaselee St POP/IOD E14 141 H9
Gasholder Pl LBTH SE11 17 P8
Gaskarth Rd BAL SW12 180 C2
EDGW HA8 95 P10
Gaskell Rd HGT N6 118 A4
Gaskell St CLAP SW4 158 F8
Gaskin St IS N1 6 C5
Gaspar Cl ECT SW5 * 15 H5
Gaspar Ms ECT SW5 15 H5
Gassiot Rd TOOT SW17 180 A7
Gassiot Wy SUT SM1 201 N10
Gasson Rd SWCM DA10 189 K2
Gasson Wood Rd CRAWW RH11 283 H10
Gastein Rd HMSMTH W6 156 G5
Gaston Bell Cl RCH/KEW TW9 155 L9
Gaston Bridge Rd SHPTN TW17 196 F5
Gaston Rd MTCM CR4 202 B3
Gaston Wy SHPTN TW17 196 E5
Gataker St BERM/RHTH SE16 160 A2
Gatcombe Ms EA W5 135 L9
Gatcombe Rd ARCH N19 118 E8
Gatcombe Wy EBAR EN4 78 A7
Gate Cl BORE WD6 75 P5
Gate Cottages EDGW HA8 * 95 M3
Gatecroft HHS/BOV HP3 36 A8
Gate End NTHWD HA6 93 H8
Gateforth St STJWD NW8 9 N2
Gatehill Rd NTHWD HA6 92 G8
Gatehope Dr SOCK/AV RM15 146 E8
Gatehouse Cl KUTN/CMB KT2 177 P10
WDSR SL4 148 G9
Gatehouse Ldg REDH RH1 276 B3
Gatehouse Sq STHWK SE1 12 F9
Gateley Rd BRXN/ST SW9 158 G9
Gate Ms SKENS SW7 15 P2
Gater Dr ENC/FH EN2 79 L5
Gatesden Cl LHD/OX KT22 236 B9
Gatesden Rd LHD/OX KT22 236 B9
Gates Green Rd WWKM BR4 225 M1
Gateshead Rd BORE WD6 75 L6
Gateside Rd TOOT SW17 180 A6
Gatestone Rd NRWD SE19 181 M9
Gate St HOL/ALD WC2B 11 N5
Gateway WALW SE17 18 F9
Gateway Ar IS N1 * 6 C7
Gateway Cl NTHWD HA6 92 D7
Gateway Gdns EHAM E6 142 C5
Gateway Ms HACK E8 * 119 N10
Gateway Pde GVE DA12 * 191 J7
Gateways GU GU1 268 E1
The Gateways CHESW EN7 61 L4
RCH/KEW TW9 * 155 J10
The Gateway WATW WD18 72 F9
WOKN/KNAP GU21 214 E10
Gatewick Cl SL SL1 129 K10
Gatfield Gv FELT TW13 175 P5
Gathorne Rd WDGN N22 99 H10
Gathorne St BETH E2 140 C4
Gatley Av HOR/WEW KT19 219 N2
Gatley Dr RGUE GU4 250 C7
Gatliff Rd BGVA SW1W 16 E9
Gatling Rd ABYW SE2 163 K4
Gatonby St PECK SE15 159 N7
Gatting Wy UX/CGN UB8 131 P1
Gatton Bottom REIG RH2 258 A4
Gatton Cl BELMT SM2 * 221 L5
REIG RH2 257 M7
Gatton Park Rd REIG RH2 257 N7
Gatton Rd REIG RH2 257 M7
TOOT SW17 179 P7
Gattons Wy SCUP DA14 186 A7
Gatward Cl WCHMH N21 79 J10
Gatward Gn ED N9 99 N3
Gatwick Rd CRAWE RH10 284 B4
GVE DA12 190 E5
WAND/EARL SW18 179 J3
Gatwick Wy HORL RH6 280 A7
Gauden Cl CLAP SW4 158 E9
Gauden Rd CLAP SW4 158 E9
Gaumont Ap WAT WD17 73 J7
Gaumont Ter SHB W12 * 156 F1
Gauntlet Cl NTHLT UB5 133 M2
Gauntlet Crs COUL/CHIP CR5 241 L6
Gauntlett Ct ALP/SUD HA0 114 G10
Gauntlett Rd SUT SM1 221 N2
Gaunt St STHWK SE1 18 D3
Gautrey Rd PECK SE15 160 B8
Gavell Rd COB KT11 217 H9
Gavel St WALW SE17 * 19 H5
Gavenny Pth SOCK/AV RM15 146 E8
Gaverick St POP/IOD E14 160 F3
Gaveston Cl BF/WBF KT14 216 A9
Gaveston Dr BERK HP4 33 N3
Gavestone Crs LEE/GVPK SE12 183 N4
Gavestone Rd LEE/GVPK SE12 183 N3
Gaveston Rd LHD/OX KT22 236 F6
SLN SL2 128 E5
Gavina Cl MRDN SM4 201 P5

Gaviots Cl CFSP/GDCR SL9 110 C6
Gaviots Gn CFSP/GDCR SL9 110 B6
Gaviots Wy CFSP/GDCR SL9 110 B5
Gawain Wk ED N9 99 P4
Gawber St BETH E2 140 B5
Gawdrey Cl CSHM HP5 51 J9
Gawsworth Cl SRTFD E15 121 L10
Gawthorne Av MLHL NW7 97 H6
Gawton Crs COUL/CHIP CR5 240 D7
Gay Cl CRICK NW2 116 E10
Gaydon La CDALE/KGS NW9 96 B9
Gayfere Rd CLAY IG5 122 C1
EW KT17 220 D2
Gayfere St WEST SW1P 17 L4
Gayford Rd SHB W12 156 C1
Gay Gdns DAGE RM10 124 D9
Gayhouse La REDH RH1 277 M10
Gayhurst Rd HACK E8 7 N3
Gayler Cl REDH RH1 259 N10
Gaylor Rd NTHLT UB5 113 N10
TIL RM18 168 B7
Gaynes Ct UPMR RM14 126 A9
Gaynesford Rd CAR SM5 222 A4
FSTH SE23 182 C5
Gaynes Hill Rd WFD IG8 102 B8
Gaynes Park Rd UPMR RM14 125 P9
UPMR RM14 126 A9
Gaynes Rd UPMR RM14 126 A7
Gay Rd SRTFD E15 141 J4
Gaysham Av GNTH/NBYPK IG2 122 D3
Gayton Cl AMS HP6 69 K1
ASHTD KT21 237 K4
Gayton Crs HAMP NW3 117 N9
Gayton Rd HAMP NW3 117 N9
HRW HA1 114 F4
Gayville Rd BTSEA SW11 180 A2
Gaywood Av CHES/WCR EN8 62 C6
Gaywood Cl BRXS/STRHM SW2 180 G4
Gaywood Rd ASHTD KT21 237 L4
WALTH E17 120 F1
Gaywood St STHWK SE1 18 D4
Gaza St WALW SE17 18 C8
Gazelle Gld GVE DA12 191 J8
Geariesville Gdns BARK/HLT IG6 122 E2
Gearing Cl TOOT SW17 180 C7
Geary Cl HORL RH6 281 J6
Geary Dr BRW CM14 107 H2
Geary Rd WLSDN NW10 116 D10
Geary St HOLWY N7 118 G10
Geddes Pl BXLYHS DA6 164 B10
Geddes Rd BUSH WD23 * 74 B8
Geddings Rd HOD EN11 44 G3
Gedeney Rd TOTM N17 99 K9
Gedling Pl STHWK SE1 19 L3
Geere Rd SRTFD E15 141 L3
Gees Ct MHST W1U 10 D6
Gee St FSBYE EC1V 12 E1
Geffrye Est IS N1 7 K8
Geffrye St BETH E2 7 L7
Geisthorp Ct WAB EN9 63 M9
Geldart Rd PECK SE15 160 A6
Geldeston Rd CLPT E5 119 P7
Gellatly Rd NWCR SE14 160 B8
Gelsthorpe Rd CRW RM5 104 C8
Gemini Cl CRAWW RH11 282 G9
Gemmell Cl PUR/KEN CR8 222 G10
General Gordon Pl
WOOL/PLUM SE18 162 E2
The Generals Wk PEND EN3 80 D3
General Wolfe Rd GNWCH SE10 161 J7
Genesis Cl STWL/WRAY TW19 174 A4
Genesta Gld GVE DA12 191 K8
Genesta Rd WOOL/PLUM SE18 162 E5
Geneva Cl SHPTN TW17 196 F2
Geneva Dr BRXN/ST SW9 159 H10
Geneva Gdns CHDH RM6 123 P3
Geneva Rd KUT/HW KT1 199 K4
THHTH CR7 203 K5
Genever Cl CHING E4 100 F6
Genista Rd UED N18 100 A6
Genoa Av PUT/ROE SW15 178 F1
Genoa Rd PGE/AN SE20 204 B1
Genotin Rd EN EN1 79 L7
Gentleman's Rw ENC/FH EN2 79 K7
Genyn Rd GUW GU2 267 N1
Geoffrey Av HARH RM3 105 P7
Geoffrey Cl CMBW SE5 159 K8
Geoffrey Gdns EHAM E6 142 B4
Geoffrey Rd BROCKY SE4 160 E9
George Avey Cft EPP CM16 66 C2
George Beard Rd DEPT SE8 160 E3
George Crs MUSWH N10 98 B8
George Downing Est
STNW/STAM N16 119 N7
George Gange Wy
KTN/HRWW/WS HA3 114 D1
George Green Dr DTCH/LGLY SL3 130 C8
George Green Rd DTCH/LGLY SL3 130 B8
George Groves Rd PGE/AN SE20 203 P1
Georgelands RPLY/SEND GU23 233 L7
George La HAYES BR2 205 N8
LEW SE13 183 H2
SWFD E18 101 M10
SWFD E18 121 N1
George Lovell Dr PEND EN3 80 F3
George Lowe Ct BAY/PAD W2 8 G3
George Mathers Rd LBTH SE11 * 18 C5
George Ms BRXN/ST SW9 159 H8
CAMTN NW1 4 G10
George Rd CHING E4 100 F7
GODL GU7 267 K10
GU GU1 250 A10
KUTN/CMB KT2 177 N10
NWMAL KT3 200 C5
George Rw BERM/RHTH SE16 19 N2
Georges Dr BRWN CM15 86 E9
Georges Md BORE WD6 75 K10
George's Rd BH/WHM TN16 244 A6
HOLWY N7 5 N1
Georges Ter CTHM CR3 241 L8
George St BARK IG11 142 F2
BERK HP4 34 B5
CAN/RD E16 141 L8
CROY/NA CR0 203 L9
CSHM HP5 51 H6
GRAYS RM17 167 M5
HERT/WAT SG14 25 K5
HHNE HP2 35 N5
HNWL W7 134 D10
MBLAR W1H 10 A5
NWDGN UB2 153 M3
RCH/KEW TW9 177 J1
ROM RM1 124 G4
STA TW18 173 J7
STALW/RED AL3 38 C6
UX/CGN UB8 131 N2
WATW WD18 73 K8
George's Wood Rd BRKMPK AL9 59 L2
Georgetown Cl NRWD SE19 181 M8
Georgette Pl GNWCH SE10 161 H6
George V Av PIN HA5 93 N10
PIN HA5 113 P1
Georgeville Gdns BARK/HLT IG6 122 E2
George V Wy GFD/PVL UB6 134 G2
RKW/CH/CXG WD3 71 K2
George Wk WARE SG12 26 C2
Georgewood Rd HHS/BOV HP3 54 A1
George Wyver Cl
WIM/MER SW19 179 H3
George Yd BANK EC3V 13 H6
MYFR/PKLN W1K 10 D7
Georgiana St CAMTN NW1 4 G5
Georgian Cl CRAWE RH10 284 E8
HAYES BR2 205 N8
HGDN/ICK UB10 111 P9
STA TW18 173 L7
STAN HA7 94 F8
Georgian Ct WBLY HA9 135 M1
Georgian Wy HRW HA1 114 C7
Georgia Rd NWMAL KT3 199 P4
THHTH CR7 203 J1
Georgina Gdns BETH E2 * 7 M9
Geraint Rd BMLY BR1 183 M6
Geraldine Rd CHSWK W4 155 M5
WAND/EARL SW18 179 M1
Geraldine St LBTH SE11 18 C4
Gerald Rd BCTR RM8 124 A7
BGVA SW1W 16 D5
CAN/RD E16 141 L6
GVE DA12 191 H4
Gerald's Gv BNSTD SM7 220 G10
Gerard Av HSLWW TW4 175 P3
Gerard Gdns RAIN RM13 144 F4
Gerard Rd BARN SW13 156 C7
HRW HA1 114 F4
Gerards Cl BERM/RHTH SE16 160 B5
Gerda Rd ELTH/MOT SE9 184 E5
Gerdview Dr RDART DA2 187 K7
Germains Cl CSHM HP5 50 G8
Germain St CSHM HP5 50 G8
Germander Dr CHOB/PIR GU24 230 F2
Germander Wy SRTFD E15 141 K5
Gernon Cl RAIN RM13 145 L4
Gernon Rd BOW E3 140 D4
Geron Wy CRICK NW2 116 F7
Gerpins La RAIN RM13 145 N4
Gerrard Crs BRW CM14 107 H4
Gerrard Gdns PIN HA5 113 H3
Gerrard Pl SOHO/SHAV W1D * 11 K7
Gerrard Rd IS N1 6 C7
Gerrards Cl STHGT/OAK N14 78 D9
Gerrards Cross Rd SLN SL2 129 M1
Gerrards Md BNSTD SM7 239 J2
Gerrard St SOHO/SHAV W1D 11 K7
Gerridge St STHWK SE1 18 B2
Gertrude Rd BELV DA17 164 B3
Gertrude St WBPTN SW10 15 K10
Gervaise Cl SL SL1 128 E10
Gervase Cl WBLY HA9 115 P8
Gervase Rd EDGW HA8 95 P9
Gervase St PECK SE15 160 A6
Gew's Cnr CHES/WCR EN8 62 C5
Ghent St CAT SE6 182 F5
Ghent Wy HACK E8 * 7 M1
Ghyll Gdns BERK HP4 * 33 J2
Giant Arches Rd HNHL SE24 181 K3
Giant Tree Hl BUSH WD23 94 C3
Gibb Cft HLWS CM18 47 H5
Gibbfield Cl CHDH RM6 123 P1
Gibbins Rd SRTFD E15 141 H2
Gibbon Rd ACT W3 136 B9
KUTN/CMB KT2 199 K1
PECK SE15 160 B8
Gibbons Cl BORE WD6 75 K5
CRAWE RH10 * 284 D10
STALE/WH AL4 21 H10
Gibbons Ms GLDGN NW11 117 J3
Gibbons Rd WLSDN NW10 136 A2
Gibbon Wk PUT/ROE SW15 * 156 D10
Gibb's Acre CHOB/PIR GU24 230 E9
Gibbs Av NRWD SE19 181 L9
Gibbs Brook La OXTED RH8 261 J10
Gibbs Cl CHES/WCR EN8 62 C5
NRWD SE19 * 181 L8
Gibbs Couch OXHEY WD19 93 L4
Gibbs Gn EDGW HA8 95 P5
WKENS W14 14 C7
Gibbs Green Cl WKENS W14 14 D8
Gibbs Rd UED N18 100 B5
Gibbs Sq NRWD SE19 * 181 L8
Gibraltar Cl RBRW/HUT CM13 107 H7
Gibraltar Crs HOR/WEW KT19 220 B6
Gibraltar Wk BETH E2 7 M10
Gibson Cl CHSGTN KT9 219 H2
EPP CM16 * 66 D1
GVW DA11 190 C6
ISLW TW7 154 C9
WCHMH N21 79 H10
WCHPL E1 140 B6
Gibson Ct DTCH/LGLY SL3 150 C4
Gibson Gdns STNW/STAM N16 * 119 N7
Gibson Pl STWL/WRAY TW19 173 M2
Gibson Rd BCTR RM8 123 M6
HGDN/ICK UB10 112 A9
LBTH SE11 17 P6
SUT SM1 221 L2
Gibson's Hl STRHM/NOR SW16 181 H10
Gibson Sq IS N1 6 B5
Gibson St GNWCH SE10 161 K4
Gidd Hl COUL/CHIP CR5 240 B2
Gidea Av GPK RM2 125 H1
Gidea Cl GPK RM2 125 H1
Gideon Cl BELV DA17 164 C3
Gideon Ms EA W5 * 155 J1
Gideon Rd BTSEA SW11 158 B9
Gidian Ct LCOL/BKTW AL2 56 C3
Giesbach Rd ARCH N19 118 D7
Giffard Rd UED N18 99 M6
Giffard Wy GUW GU2 249 M7
Giffin St DEPT SE8 160 F6
Gifford Gdns HNWL W7 134 C7
Giffordside CDW/CHF RM16 168 E4
Gifford St IS N1 5 M4
Gift La SRTFD E15 141 K3
Giggs Hl STMC/STPC BR5 207 K2
Giggs Hill Gdns THDIT KT7 198 F8
Giggs Hill Rd THDIT KT7 198 F8
Gilbert Cl SWCM DA10 189 J2
WIM/MER SW19 * 201 L1
WOOL/PLUM SE18 162 C7
Gilbert Gv EDGW HA8 95 P9
Gilbert Pl NOXST/BSQ WC1A 11 L4
Gilbert Rd BELV DA17 164 B2
BMLY BR1 183 M10
CDW/CHF RM16 167 H2
DEN/HRF UB9 91 N10
LBTH SE11 18 C5
PIN HA5 113 L2
ROM RM1 124 G2
WIM/MER SW19 179 M10
Gilbert Rw GVW DA11 * 190 C5
Gilbert St HSLW TW3 154 B9
MYFR/PKLN W1K 10 D6
PEND EN3 80 B3
SRTFD E15 121 K9
Gilbert Wy BERK HP4 33 M5
Gilbey Cl HGDN/ICK UB10 112 C9
Gilbey Rd TOOT SW17 179 P7
Gilbeys Yd CAMTN NW1 4 D4
Gilbourne Rd WOOL/PLUM SE18 163 J5
Gilda Av PEND EN3 80 D9
Gilda Crs STNW/STAM N16 119 P6
Gildea Cl PIN HA5 93 P8
Gildea St GTPST W1W 10 F4
Gilden Cl HLWE CM17 * 29 P7
Gilden Crs KTTN NW5 118 B10
Gildenhill Rd SWLY BR8 187 K10
Gilden Wy HLWE CM17 29 N8
Gilders SBW CM21 29 N1
Gildersome St WOOL/PLUM SE18 162 D5
Gilders Rd CHSGTN KT9 219 L4
Giles Cl RAIN RM13 145 L4
STALE/WH AL4 21 H10
Giles Coppice NRWD SE19 181 N7
Giles Fld GVE DA12 191 J4
Giles Md EPSOM KT18 * 220 B10
Giles Travers Cl EGH TW20 194 F3
Gilfrid Cl UX/CGN UB8 132 C8
Gilham's Av BNSTD SM7 220 G8
Gilhams Cottages BNSTD SM7 * 221 H8
Gilkes Crs DUL SE21 181 M2
Gilkes Pl DUL SE21 181 M2
Gillam Wy RAIN RM13 145 H1
Gillan Gn BUSH WD23 94 B3
Gillards Ms WALTH E17 120 F2
Gillards Wy WALTH E17 120 F2
Gill Av CAN/RD E16 141 M8
GUW GU2 267 K1
Gill Cl WATW WD18 72 D10
Gill Crs GVW DA11 190 C6
Gillender St BOW E3 141 H6
Gillespie Rd HBRY N5 119 H8
Gillett Av EHAM E6 142 B4
Gillett Pl HACK E8 119 N10
Gillett Rd THHTH CR7 203 L4
Gillett St STNW/STAM N16 119 M10
Gillham Ter TOTM N17 99 P7
Gilliam Gv PUR/KEN CR8 223 H6
Gillian Av STAL AL1 38 B10
Gillian Crs GPK RM2 105 K10
Gillian Park Rd CHEAM SM3 201 J8
Gillian St LEW SE13 182 G1
Gillian Ter BRYLDS KT5 * 199 L6
Gilliat Dr RGUE GU4 250 G8
Gilliat Rd SL SL1 129 K9
Gilliat's Gn RKW/CH/CXG WD3 70 G8
Gilliatt Cl IVER SL0 131 H8
Gillies St KTTN NW5 118 B10
Gillingham Ms PIM SW1V 16 G5
Gillingham Rd CRICK NW2 117 H8
Gillingham Rw PIM SW1V 16 G5
Gillingham St PIM SW1V 16 G5
Gillison Wk BERM/RHTH SE16 19 P3
Gillman Dr SRTFD E15 141 K3
Gillmans Rd STMC/STPC BR5 207 L8
Gills Hl RAD WD7 74 E1
Gills Hill La RAD WD7 74 E2
Gills Hollow RAD WD7 74 E2
Gill's Rd EYN DA4 210 D1
Gill St POP/IOD E14 140 E8
Gillum Cl EBAR EN4 98 A2
Gilmais GT/LBKH KT23 254 B1
Gilman Crs WDSR SL4 148 C9
Gilmore Cl DTCH/LGLY SL3 149 P1
HGDN/ICK UB10 112 B8
Gilmore Crs ASHF TW15 174 B8
Gilmore Rd LEW SE13 161 J10
Gilmour Cl CHESW EN7 79 P1
Gilpin Av MORT/ESHN SW14 156 A10
Gilpin Cl BAY/PAD W2 9 K4
MTCM CR4 201 P2
Gilpin Crs UED N18 99 N6
WHTN TW2 176 A3
Gilpin Gn HARP AL5 20 B2
Gilpin Rd CLPT E5 120 D9
WARE SG12 26 D3
Gilpin's Gallop WARE SG12 26 G7
Gilpin's Ride BERK HP4 34 B4
Gilpin Wy HYS/HAR UB3 152 E6
Gilroy Cl RAIN RM13 144 G1
Gilroy Wy STMC/STPC BR5 207 L7
Gilsland WAB EN9 81 K1
Gilsland Rd THHTH CR7 203 L4
Gilson Ct WDSR SL4 171 P3
Gilstead Rd FUL/PGN SW6 157 L8
Gilsted Ct STALW/RED AL3 38 C2
Gilston Pk HLW CM20 28 F4
Gilston Rd WBPTN SW10 15 K8
Gilton Rd CAT SE6 183 K6
Giltspur St STBT EC1A 12 D5
Gilwell Cl CHING E4 80 G8
Gilwell La CHING E4 81 J8
Gimcrack Hl LHD/OX KT22 236 G8
Ginhams Rd CRAWW RH11 283 L7
Gippeswyck Cl PIN HA5 93 L9
Gipsy Hl NRWD SE19 181 M8
Gipsy La GRAYS RM17 167 P5
PUT/ROE SW15 156 D9
Gipsy Rd WELL DA16 163 N8
WNWD SE27 181 L7
Gipsy Road Gdns WNWD SE27 181 K7
Giralda Cl CAN/RD E16 142 A7
Giraud St POP/IOD E14 140 G8
Girdlers Rd HMSMTH W6 156 G3
Girdwood Rd WAND/EARL SW18 179 H3
Girling Wy EBED/NFELT TW14 153 H9
Girona Cl CDW/CHF RM16 167 H2
Gironde Rd FUL/PGN SW6 157 J6
Girtin Rd BUSH WD23 74 A9
Girton Av CDALE/KGS NW9 115 M1
Girton Cl NTHLT UB5 134 B1
Girton Ct CHES/WCR EN8 62 D6
Girton Gdns CROY/NA CR0 204 F10
Girton Rd NTHLT UB5 134 B1
SYD SE26 182 C8
Girton Wy RKW/CH/CXG WD3 72 D9
Gisbourne Cl WLGTN SM6 202 E10
Gisburne Wy WATN WD24 73 H3
Gisburn Rd CEND/HSY/T N8 118 G2
Gissing Wk IS N1 6 B4
Gittens Cl BMLY BR1 183 L7
Glacier Wy ALP/SUD HA0 135 J4
Gladbeck Wy ENC/FH EN2 79 K8
Gladden Ct HLWS CM18 47 H5
Gladding Rd CHESW EN7 61 K2
MNPK E12 122 A9
Glade Cl SURB KT6 * 199 J9
Glade Gdns CROY/NA CR0 204 D7
Glade La NWDGN UB2 154 A1
Glade Ms GU GU1 268 C1
Gladeside CROY/NA CR0 204 C7
STALE/WH AL4 39 J3
WCHMH N21 98 G1
Gladesmore Rd
SEVS/STOTM N15 119 N4
Glade Sp KWD/TDW/WH KT20 239 L7
The Glades GVE DA12 190 G9
HHW HP1 35 H5
The Glade ASC SL5 192 B5
BELMT SM2 221 H5
BF/WBF KT14 215 H9
BMLY BR1 206 A2
CFSP/GDCR SL9 110 A6
CHARL SE7 161 P6
CLAY IG5 102 C10
COUL/CHIP CR5 241 H5
CRAWE RH10 284 B9
CROY/NA CR0 204 D6
ENC/FH EN2 79 H7
EW KT17 220 D3
HACK E8 * 7 M2
KWD/TDW/WH KT20 239 L7
LHD/OX KT22 235 P8
NFNCH/WDSPK N12 * 97 N5
RBRW/HUT CM13 107 M2
SEV TN13 247 J9
SHB W12 156 E1
STA TW18 173 L10
UPMR RM14 126 B10
WCHMH N21 78 G10
WFD IG8 101 N4
WGCW AL8 22 F3
WWKM BR4 204 G10
The Gladeway WAB EN9 63 J9
Gladiator St FSTH SE23 182 D3
Glading Ter STNW/STAM N16 119 N8
Gladioli Cl HPTN TW12 175 P9
Gladsdale Dr PIN HA5 113 H2
Gladsmuir Cl WOT/HER KT12 197 K9
Gladsmuir Rd ARCH N19 118 D6
BAR EN5 77 H6
Gladstone Av EBED/NFELT TW14 175 H2
MNPK E12 142 B2
WDGN N22 99 J10
WHTN TW2 176 C3
Gladstone Gdns HSLW TW3 154 B7
Gladstone Ms KIL/WHAMP NW6 * 2 C3
PGE/AN SE20 182 B10
WDGN N22 99 H10
Gladstone Pde CRICK NW2 * 116 F8
Gladstone Park Gdns CRICK NW2 116 E8
Gladstone Pl BAR EN5 * 76 G8
E/WMO/HCT KT8 * 198 D5
Gladstone Rd ASHTD KT21 237 J4
BKHH IG9 101 P2
CHSWK W4 * 156 A2
CROY/NA CR0 203 L7
CSHM HP5 51 H7
DART DA1 187 N2
HOD EN11 44 G2
NWDGN UB2 153 M1
ORP BR6 226 F2
SURB KT6 199 J9
WARE SG12 26 B1
WAT WD17 73 K7
WIM/MER SW19 179 K10
Gladstone St STHWK SE1 18 C3
Gladstone Ter VX/NE SW8 158 C7
WNWD SE27 * 181 K7
Gladstone Wy
KTN/HRWW/WS HA3 114 D1
SL SL1 148 F1
Gladwell Rd BMLY BR1 183 M9
CEND/HSY/T N8 118 G4
Gladwyn Rd PUT/ROE SW15 156 G9
Gladys Rd KIL/WHAMP NW6 2 F3
Glaisher St DEPT SE8 160 G5
Glaisyer Wy IVER SL0 130 F4
Glamis Cl CHESW EN7 61 P5
Glamis Crs HYS/HAR UB3 152 D2
Glamis Dr EMPK RM11 125 M6
Glamis Pl HHNE HP2 35 P5
WAP E1W 140 B9
Glamis Rd WAP E1W 140 B9
Glamis Wy NTHLT UB5 134 B1
Glamorgan Cl MTCM CR4 202 F3
Glamorgan Rd KUT/HW KT1 177 H10
Glandford Wy CHDH RM6 123 L3
Glanfield HHNE HP2 35 P3
Glanfield Rd BECK BR3 204 E4
Glanleam Rd STAN HA7 95 J5
Glanmead BRWN CM15 107 K2
Glanmor Rd SLN SL2 129 N9
Glanthams Rd BRWN CM15 107 L3
The Glanty EGH TW20 172 F7
Glanville Dr EMPK RM11 125 N6
Glanville Ms STAN HA7 94 F6
Glanville Rd BRXS/STRHM SW2 180 F1
HAYES BR2 205 N3
Glasbrook Av WHTN TW2 175 N4
Glasbrook Rd ELTH/MOT SE9 184 A3
Glaserton Rd STNW/STAM N16 119 M5
Glasford St TOOT SW17 180 A9
Glasgow Rd PLSTW E13 141 N4
SL SL1 128 F8
UED N18 100 A6
Glasgow Ter PIM SW1V 16 G8
Glaskin Ms HOM E9 140 D1
Glasse Cl WEA W13 134 F9
Glasshill St STHWK SE1 18 D1
Glasshouse Cl UX/CGN UB8 132 C7
Glasshouse Flds WAP E1W 140 C9
Glasshouse St REGST W1B 11 H8
Glasshouse Wk LBTH SE11 17 M7
Glasshouse Yd FARR EC1M 12 E2
Glasslyn Rd CEND/HSY/T N8 118 E3
Glassmill La HAYES BR2 205 L2
Glass St BETH E2 * 140 A6
Glass Yd WOOL/PLUM SE18 162 D2
Glastonbury Av WFD IG8 102 A8
Glastonbury Cl STMC/STPC BR5 207 M8
Glastonbury Pl WCHPL E1 140 B8
Glastonbury Rd ED N9 99 P2
MRDN SM4 201 K7
Glastonbury St KIL/WHAMP NW6 117 J10
Glaston Ct EA W5 * 135 J10
Glaucus St BOW E3 140 G7
Glazbury Rd WKENS W14 14 B7
Glazebrook Cl DUL SE21 181 L5
Glazebrook Rd TEDD TW11 176 E10
Glaziers La RGUW GU3 248 B9
Gleave Cl STAL AL1 38 G5
Glebe Av ENC/FH EN2 79 J7
HGDN/ICK UB10 112 D9
KTN/HRWW/WS HA3 115 K1
MTCM CR4 201 P2
RSLP HA4 133 J1
WFD IG8 101 M7
Glebe Cl BRKMPK AL9 42 A3
CFSP/GDCR SL9 90 A9
CHSWK W4 * 156 B4
CRAWE RH10 283 N6
GT/LBKH KT23 253 P2
HERT/WAT SG14 25 L3
HGDN/ICK UB10 112 D9
HHS/BOV HP3 35 P10
LTWR GU18 212 B7
SAND/SEL CR2 223 N8
Glebe Cottages BRKMPK AL9 42 A3
RGUE GU4 251 L8
Glebe Ct BKHTH/KID SE3 * 161 K9
EA W5 * 135 J10
GU GU1 250 C10
STAN HA7 95 H6
Glebe Crs HDN NW4 116 F2
KTN/HRWW/WS HA3 115 K1
The Glebefield SEV TN13 246 G9
Glebe Gdns BF/WBF KT14 215 N10
NWMAL KT3 200 B7
Glebe House Dr HAYES BR2 205 N8
Glebe Hyrst SAND/SEL CR2 223 N8
Glebeland Gdns SHPTN TW17 196 D6
Glebelands CHIG IG7 103 L4
CRAWE RH10 285 P5
DART DA1 164 G10
E/WMO/HCT KT8 198 A5
ESH/CLAY KT10 218 E5
HLW CM20 29 J8
Glebelands Av GNTH/NBYPK IG2 122 G5
SWFD E18 101 M10
Glebelands Cl
NFNCH/WDSPK N12 97 N9
CMBW SE5 159 M9
Glebelands Rd
EBED/NFELT TW14 175 H3
Glebe La BAR EN5 76 D10
KTN/HRWW/WS HA3 115 K2
RDKG RH5 271 L9
SEV TN13 265 J2
Glebe Pth MTCM CR4 202 A3
Glebe Pl CHEL SW3 15 N9
EYN DA4 210 B4
Glebe Rd ASHTD KT21 237 J4
BARN SW13 156 D8
BELMT SM2 221 H5
BMLY BR1 205 M1
CAR SM5 222 A3
CEND/HSY/T N8 118 G2
CFSP/GDCR SL9 89 P9
CHONG CM5 67 N5
DAGE RM10 144 C1
DORK RH4 272 E2
EGH TW20 172 F9
FNCH N3 97 M9
GVW DA11 190 C4
HACK E8 7 L4
HERT/WAT SG14 25 L3
RAIN RM13 145 J5
REDH RH1 240 B10
RSEV TN14 265 J8
STA TW18 173 L8
STAN HA7 95 H6
UX/CGN UB8 131 M4
WARL CR6 242 C3
WDSR SL4 171 N1
WLSDN NW10 136 D1
Glebe Side TWK TW1 176 E2
Glebe Sq MTCM CR4 * 202 A3
Glebe St CHSWK W4 156 A4
The Glebe BKHTH/KID SE3 161 K9
CHST BR7 206 F1
CRAWE RH10 285 J2
GSTN WD25 55 K9
HLW CM20 29 H10
HORL RH6 280 A4
KGLGY WD4 54 B5
REIG RH2 274 D7
STRHM/NOR SW16 * 180 E7
WDR/YW UB7 151 P3
WPK KT4 200 C8
Glebe Wy AMS HP6 69 J2
EMPK RM11 125 M5
ERITH DA8 164 F5
FELT TW13 175 P6
SAND/SEL CR2 223 N8
Glebeway WFD IG8 101 P6
Glebe Wy WWKM BR4 205 J9
Gledhow Gdns ECT SW5 15 J6
Gledhow Wd
KWD/TDW/WH KT20 239 L8
Gledstanes Rd WKENS W14 14 B8
Gledwood Av YEAD UB4 132 G7
Gledwood Crs YEAD UB4 132 G7
Gledwood Dr YEAD UB4 132 G7
Gledwood Gdns YEAD UB4 133 H7
Gleed Av BUSH WD23 94 C3
Gleeson Dr ORP BR6 227 J2
Gleeson Ms ADL/WDHM KT15 215 M1
Glegg Pl PUT/ROE SW15 * 156 G10
Glemsford Dr HARP AL5 20 C1
Glenaffric Av POP/IOD E14 161 H3
Glen Albyn Rd WIM/MER SW19 178 G5
Glenalla Rd RSLP HA4 112 G5
Glenalmond Rd
KTN/HRWW/WS HA3 115 K2
Glenalvon Wy WOOL/PLUM SE18 162 B3
Glena Mt SUT SM1 221 M1
Glenarm Rd CLPT E5 120 B9
Glen Av ASHF TW15 174 B7
Glenavon Cl ESH/CLAY KT10 218 F3
Glenavon Gdns DTCH/LGLY SL3 149 P3
Glenavon Rd SRTFD E15 141 K2
Glenbarr Cl ELTH/MOT SE9 162 E9
Glenbow Rd BMLY BR1 183 K9
Glenbrook North ENC/FH EN2 78 G8
Glenbrook Rd KIL/WHAMP NW6 117 K10
Glenbrook South ENC/FH EN2 78 G8
Glenbuck Rd SURB KT6 199 J6
Glenburnie Rd TOOT SW17 180 A6
Glencairn Dr EA W5 134 G6
Glencairne Cl CAN/RD E16 142 A7
Glencairn Rd STRHM/NOR SW16 180 F10
Glen Cl KWD/TDW/WH KT20 239 H9
SHPTN TW17 196 B4
Glencoe Av GNTH/NBYPK IG2 123 H5
Glencoe Rd BUSH WD23 73 P10
DAGE RM10 124 B9
WEY KT13 196 B10
YEAD UB4 133 M7
Glencorse Gn OXHEY WD19 * 93 L5
Glen Ct ADL/WDHM KT15 * 215 J2
Glen Crs WFD IG8 101 N7
Glendale HHW HP1 35 L6
SWLY BR8 208 G5
Glendale Av CHDH RM6 123 M5
EDGW HA8 95 L5
WDGN N22 99 H8
Glendale Cl BRWN CM15 107 K2
ELTH/MOT SE9 162 D9
WOKN/KNAP GU21 231 P4
Glendale Dr RGUE GU4 250 F6
WIM/MER SW19 179 J8
Glendale Gdns WBLY HA9 115 J6
Glendale Ms BECK BR3 204 G1
Glendale Ri PUR/KEN CR8 241 J1
Glendale Rd ERITH DA8 164 D3
GVW DA11 190 B7
Glendale Wy THMD SE28 143 M10
Glendall St BRXN/ST SW9 158 G9
Glendarvon St PUT/ROE SW15 156 G9
Glendene Av EHSLY KT24 252 F2
Glendevon Cl EDGW HA8 95 N4
Glendish Rd TOTM N17 99 P9
Glendor Gdns MLHL NW7 96 A5
Glendower Crs ORP BR6 207 K6
Glendower Gdns
MORT/ESHN SW14 156 A9
Glendower Pl SKENS SW7 15 L5
Glendower Rd CHING E4 101 J2
MORT/ESHN SW14 156 A9
Glendown Rd ABYW SE2 163 K4
Glendun Rd ACT W3 136 B9
Gleneagle Ms STRHM/NOR SW16 180 E8
Gleneagle Rd STRHM/NOR SW16 180 E8
Gleneagles STAN HA7 94 G7
Gleneagles Cl BERM/RHTH SE16 160 A4
HARH RM3 105 N8
ORP BR6 206 G8
OXHEY WD19 * 93 L6
STWL/WRAY TW19 173 M2
Gleneagles Ct CRAWE RH10 * 283 N8
Gleneldon Ms STRHM/NOR SW16 180 F8
Gleneldon Rd STRHM/NOR SW16 180 F7
Glenelg Rd BRXS/STRHM SW2 180 F1
Glenesk Rd ELTH/MOT SE9 162 D10
Glenester Cl HOD EN11 26 F10
Glen Faba Rd HLWW/ROY CM19 45 L3
Glenfarg Rd CAT SE6 183 J4
Glenferrie Rd STAL AL1 38 F6
Glenfield Cl BRKHM/BTCW RH3 273 N4
Glenfield Ct HERT/WAT SG14 24 G4
Glenfield Crs RSLP HA4 112 E5
Glenfield Rd ASHF TW15 174 C9
BAL SW12 180 D4
BNSTD SM7 239 L1
BRKHM/BTCW RH3 273 N4
WEA W13 154 G1
Glenfinlas Wy CMBW SE5 159 J6
Glenforth St GNWCH SE10 161 L3
Glengall Br POP/IOD E14 160 G2
Glengall Gv POP/IOD E14 160 G2
Glengall Pl STAL AL1 * 38 D9
Glengall Rd BXLYHN DA7 163 P9
EDGW HA8 95 N4
KIL/WHAMP NW6 2 D6
PECK SE15 19 M9
WFD IG8 101 M7
Glengall Ter PECK SE15 19 M9
Glen Gdns CROY/NA CR0 203 H10
Glengarnock Av POP/IOD E14 161 H3
Glengarry Rd EDUL SE22 159 M10
Glenham Dr GNTH/NBYPK IG2 122 E3
Glenhaven Av BORE WD6 75 M7
Glen Hazel BRWN CM15 87 J1
Glenhead Cl ELTH/MOT SE9 162 E9
Glenheadon Cl LHD/OX KT22 237 J9
Glenheadon Ri LHD/OX KT22 237 J9
Glenhill Cl FNCH N3 97 K10
Glenhouse Rd ELTH/MOT SE9 184 D1
Glenhurst Av BXLY DA5 186 A4
KTTN NW5 118 B9
RSLP HA4 112 D6
Glenhurst Ri NRWD SE19 181 K10
Glenhurst Rd BTFD TW8 155 H5
NFNCH/WDSPK N12 97 N5
Glenilla Rd HAMP NW3 3 N1
Glenister Park Rd
STRHM/NOR SW16 180 E10
Glenister Rd CSHM HP5 51 H4
GNWCH SE10 161 L4
Glenlea Rd ELTH/MOT SE9 184 D1
Glenlee WOKS/MYFD GU22 231 P5
Glenloch Rd HAMP NW3 3 N1
PEND EN3 80 B6
Glen Luce CHES/WCR EN8 62 C7
Glenluce Rd BKHTH/KID SE3 161 N9
Glenluge Rd BKHTH/KID SE3 161 M5
Glenlyn Av STAL AL1 38 G7
Glenlyon Rd ELTH/MOT SE9 184 D1
Glenmere Av MLHL NW7 96 D8
Glenmill HPTN TW12 175 N8
Glenmore Cl ADL/WDHM KT15 195 L10
Glenmore Gdns ABLGY WD5 55 H7
Glenmore Lawns WEA W13 * 134 F8
Glenmore Pde ALP/SUD HA0 * 135 K3
Glenmore Rd HAMP NW3 3 N1
WELL DA16 163 J7
Glenmore Wy BARK IG11 143 K4
Glenn Av PUR/KEN CR8 223 J7
Glennie Rd WNWD SE27 181 H6
Glenny Rd BARK IG11 142 F1
Glenorchy Cl YEAD UB4 133 M7
Glenparke Rd FSTGT E7 141 N1
Glen Ri WFD IG8 101 N7
Glen Rd CHSGTN KT9 199 K10
PLSTW E13 141 P6
WALTH E17 120 E3
Glen Rd End WLGTN SM6 222 C5
Glenrosa Gdns GVE DA12 191 J8
Glenrosa St FUL/PGN SW6 157 M8
Glenroy St SHB W12 136 F8
Glensdale Rd BROCKY SE4 160 E9
Glenshiel Rd ELTH/MOT SE9 184 D1
Glenside CHIG IG7 102 E7
Glenside Cl PUR/KEN CR8 241 L1
Glentanner Wy TOOT SW17 179 N6
Glentham Cottages
BARN SW13 * 156 D5
Glentham Gdns BARN SW13 156 E5
Glentham Rd BARN SW13 156 D5
The Glen ADL/WDHM KT15 215 J2
ASC SL5 * 192 C4
BELMT SM2 * 221 M3
CROY/NA CR0 204 C10
DTCH/LGLY SL3 149 P3
ENC/FH EN2 79 J8
HAYES BR2 205 K2
NTHWD HA6 92 E8
NWDGN UB2 153 N4
ORP BR6 206 C10
PIN HA5 113 J3
PIN HA5 113 M5
RAIN RM13 145 K6
WBLY HA9 115 J9
Glenthorne Av CROY/NA CR0 204 B8
Glenthorne Cl CHEAM SM3 201 K8
Glenthorne Gdns BARK/HLT IG6 122 D1
CHEAM SM3 201 K8
Glenthorne Rd FBAR/BDGN N11 98 A6
HMSMTH W6 156 F3
KUT/HW KT1 199 L4
WALTH E17 120 D3
Glenthorpe Rd MRDN SM4 200 G5
Glenton Cl ROM RM1 104 F8
Glenton Rd LEW SE13 161 K10
Glenton Wy ROM RM1 104 F8
Glentrammon Av ORP BR6 227 J3
Glentrammon Cl ORP BR6 227 J3
Glentrammon Gdns ORP BR6 227 J3
Glentrammon Rd ORP BR6 227 J3
Glentworth Pl SL SL1 129 H10
Glentworth St CAMTN NW1 10 B2
Glenure Rd ELTH/MOT SE9 184 D1
Glenview ABYW SE2 163 N5
Glen Vw GVE DA12 190 F4
Glenview Cl CRAWE RH10 284 A5
Glen View Rd BMLY BR1 206 A2
Glenview Rd HHW HP1 35 L6
Glenville Av ENC/FH EN2 79 K4
Glenville Gv DEPT SE8 160 E6
Glenville Ms WAND/EARL SW18 179 L3
Glenville Rd KUTN/CMB KT2 199 M1
Glen Wy WAT WD17 72 F4
Glenwood BROX EN10 44 E5
RDKG RH5 273 H4
WGCE AL7 23 N6
Glenwood Av CDALE/KGS NW9 116 B6
RAIN RM13 145 H6
Glenwood Cl HRW HA1 114 E3
Glenwood Dr GPK RM2 125 H3
Glenwood Gdns
GNTH/NBYPK IG2 122 D3
Glenwood Gv CDALE/KGS NW9 115 P6
Glenwood Rd CAT SE6 182 E4
EW KT17 220 D3
HSLW TW3 154 C9
MLHL NW7 96 B4
SEVS/STOTM N15 119 J3
Glenwood Rw NRWD SE19 * 203 N1
Glenwood Wy CROY/NA CR0 204 C6
Glenworth Av POP/IOD E14 161 J3
Glevum Cl STALW/RED AL3 37 N8
Gliddon Dr CLPT E5 120 A9
Gliddon Rd WKENS W14 14 A7
Glimpsing Gn ERITHM DA18 163 P2
Glisson Rd HGDN/ICK UB10 132 B4
Gload Crs STMC/STPC BR5 207 N9
Globe Cl HARP AL5 20 B2
Globe Pond Rd
BERM/RHTH SE16 140 D10
Globe Rd EMPK RM11 125 H4
SRTFD E15 121 L10
WCHPL E1 140 B5
WFD IG8 101 P7
Globe St STHWK SE1 18 G2
Globe Ter BETH E2 140 B5
Glory Md DORK RH4 273 H5
Glossop Rd SAND/SEL CR2 223 L5
Gloster Rd NWMAL KT3 200 B4
WOKS/MYFD GU22 232 D6
Gloucester Av BFN/LL DA15 185 H5
CAMTN NW1 4 C4
CDW/CHF RM16 167 P1
CHES/WCR EN8 62 D9
EMPK RM11 125 P3
SL SL1 129 H7
TIL RM18 169 M4
Gloucester Circ GNWCH SE10 161 H6
Gloucester Cl THDIT KT7 * 198 F8
WLSDN NW10 136 A2
Gloucester Ct MTCM CR4 * 202 F5
RCH/KEW TW9 * 155 M6
Gloucester Crs CAMTN NW1 4 E5
STA TW18 173 N9
Gloucester Dr FSBYPK N4 119 J7
GLDGN NW11 117 K2
STA TW18 172 F6
Gloucester Gdns BAY/PAD W2 9 J5
EBAR EN4 78 B8
GLDGN NW11 117 J5
IL IG1 122 B5
SUT SM1 201 L9
Gloucester Ga CAMTN NW1 4 E7
Gloucester Gate Ms CAMTN NW1 4 E7
Gloucester Gv EDGW HA8 96 A9
Gloucester Ms BAY/PAD W2 9 K6
LEY E10 120 F5
Gloucester Ms West BAY/PAD W2 9 J6
Gloucester Pde BFN/LL DA15 * 185 K1
HYS/HAR UB3 * 152 D2
Gloucester Pl CAMTN NW1 10 A1
MHST W1U 10 B4
WDSR SL4 149 J8
Gloucester Place Ms
MBLAR W1H 10 B4
Gloucester Rd ACT W3 155 P1
BAR EN5 77 L9
BELV DA17 164 A4
BRWN CM15 86 G9
CROY/NA CR0 203 L7
DART DA1 187 J2
EA W5 155 H1
ENC/FH EN2 79 K4
FELT TW13 175 K4
GUW GU2 249 L8
GVE DA12 190 F7
HPTN TW12 176 A10
HRW HA1 114 A3
HSLWW TW4 153 M10
KUT/HW KT1 199 M2
LEY E10 120 F5
MNPK E12 122 C8
RCH/KEW TW9 155 M6
REDH RH1 258 A9
ROM RM1 124 G4
SKENS SW7 15 J3
TEDD TW11 176 D8
TOTM N17 99 L10
TOTM N17 119 L1
UED N18 99 N6
WALTH E17 100 C10
WAN E11 121 N3
WHTN TW2 176 B4
Gloucester Sq BAY/PAD W2 9 M7
BETH E2 7 N6
Gloucester St PIM SW1V 16 G8
Gloucester Ter BAY/PAD W2 9 H5
STHGT/OAK N14 * 98 E2
Gloucester Wk KENS W8 14 F1
Gloucester Wy CLKNW EC1R 6 B10
Glover Cl ABYW SE2 163 M3
CHESW EN7 * 61 N3
Glover Dr UED N18 100 B7
Glover Rd PIN HA5 113 L4
Glovers Cl BH/WHM TN16 243 N2
HERT/BAY SG13 25 K7
Glovers Fld BRWN CM15 86 E3
Glovers Gv RSLP HA4 112 C5
Glovers La HLWE CM17 47 P6
Glover's Rd HORL RH6 278 G8
REIG RH2 275 L1
Gloxinia Rd MEO DA13 189 N9
Glycena Rd BTSEA SW11 158 A9
Glyn Av EBAR EN4 77 N8
Glyn Cl EW KT17 220 D5
SNWD SE25 203 M2
Glyn Ct STAN HA7 94 G7
Glyn Davies Cl SEV TN13 246 F6
Glyndebourne Pk ORP BR6 206 E10
Glynde Ms CHEL SW3 15 P4

Glynde Rd BXLYHN DA7 163 N9
Glynde St BROCKY SE4 182 E2
Glyndon Rd WOOL/PLUM SE18 162 F3
Glyn Dr SCUP DA14 185 L7
Glynfield Rd WLSDN NW10 136 B2
Glynne Rd WDGN N22 99 H10
Glyn Rd CLPT E5 120 C9
PEND EN3 80 B8
WPK KT4 200 G9
Glyn St LBTH SE11 17 N8
Glynswood CFSP/GDCR SL9 90 C8
Glynswood Pl NTHWD HA6 92 C9
Goat La EN EN1 79 N4
Goat Rd MTCM CR4 202 B7
Goatsfield Rd BH/WHM TN16 243 P6
Goatswood La ABR/ST RM4 105 J1
Goat Whf BTFD TW8 155 K5
Gobions Av CRW RM5 104 E8
Gobions Wy POTB/CUF EN6 59 L4
Goblins Gn WGCE AL7 22 G6
Godalming Av WLGTN SM6 222 F4
Godalming Rd POP/IOD E14 140 G7
Godbold Rd SRTFD E15 141 K6
Goddard Cl CRAWE RH10 284 C10
GUW GU2 249 M6
SHPTN TW17 196 A3
Goddard Pl ARCH N19 118 D8
Goddard Rd BECK BR3 204 D4
CDW/CHF RM16 147 M10
Goddards Cl HERT/BAY SG13 42 D5
Goddards Wy IL IG1 122 G6
Goddington Cha ORP BR6 227 L1
Goddington La ORP BR6 207 K10
Godfrey Av NTHLT UB5 133 M3
WHTN TW2 176 C3
Godfrey Hl WOOL/PLUM SE18 162 B3
Godfrey Rd WOOL/PLUM SE18 162 B3
Godfrey St CHEL SW3 15 P7
SRTFD E15 141 H4
Godfrey Wy HSLWW TW4 175 M3
Goding St LBTH SE11 17 M8
Godley Rd BF/WBF KT14 216 A9
WAND/EARL SW18 179 N4
Godliman St BLKFR EC4V 12 D6
Godman Rd CDW/CHF RM16 168 E2
PECK SE15 * 160 A8
Godolphin Cl BELMT SM2 221 J7
PLMGR N13 99 J7
Godolphin Ct CRAWE RH10 * 283 N8
Godolphin Pl ACT W3 136 A9
Godolphin Rd BEAC HP9 89 H7
SHB W12 156 E1
SL SL1 129 J9
WEY KT13 216 E3
Godric Crs CROY/NA CR0 225 J6
Godson Rd CROY/NA CR0 203 H10
Godson St IS N1 6 A7
Godstone Green Rd GDST RH9 260 A7
Godstone Hl GDST RH9 260 A4
GDST RH9 260 B6
Godstone Mt PUR/KEN CR8 * 223 J8
Godstone Rd CTHM CR3 241 P10
OXTED RH8 260 G7
PUR/KEN CR8 223 J9
PUR/KEN CR8 241 M1
REDH RH1 259 M9
SUT SM1 221 M3
TWK TW1 176 G2
Godstow Rd ABYW SE2 163 M1
Godwin Cl CHING E4 81 H4
HOR/WEW KT19 219 P3
IS N1 6 F7
Godwin Rd FSTGT E7 121 N9
HAYES BR2 205 P3
Goffers Rd BKHTH/KID SE3 161 K8
Goffs Cl CRAWW RH11 283 M8
Goffs Crs CHESW EN7 61 K5
Goff's La CHESW EN7 61 K5
CHESW EN7 61 N5
CRAWW RH11 283 L7
Goff's Oak Av CHESW EN7 61 K4
Goffs Park Rd CRAWW RH11 283 M9
Goffs Rd ASHF TW15 174 E9
Gogmore Farm Cl CHERT KT16 195 H7
Gogmore La CHERT KT16 195 K7
Goidel Cl WLGTN SM6 222 E1
Golborne Gdns NKENS W10 8 C2
Golborne Ms NKENS W10 * 8 B3
Golborne Rd NKENS W10 8 B3
Goldace GRAYS RM17 167 L5
Golda Cl BAR EN5 76 G10
Goldbeaters Gv EDGW HA8 96 B8
Goldcliff Cl MRDN SM4 201 K7
Gold Cl BROX EN10 44 D6
Goldcrest Cl CAN/RD E16 142 A7
HORL RH6 279 N3
THMD SE28 143 M9
Goldcrest Ms EA W5 * 135 J7
Goldcrest Wy BUSH WD23 94 B2
CROY/NA CR0 225 J5
PUR/KEN CR8 222 E6
Goldcroft HHS/BOV HP3 36 B8
Golden Ct HSLW TW3 154 C8
Golden Crs HYS/HAR UB3 132 G10
Golden Cross Ms NTGHL W11 8 C5
Golden Dell WGCE AL7 23 J9
Golden Hind Pl DEPT SE8 * 160 E3
Golden Jubilee Br STHWK SE1 11 N9
Golden La STLK EC1Y 12 E1
Golden Lane Est STLK EC1Y 12 E2
Golden Mnr HNWL W7 134 D9
Golden Oak Cl SLN SL2 128 C1
Golden Pde WALTH E17 * 121 H1
Golden Plover Cl CAN/RD E16 141 M8
Golden Sq SOHO/CST W1F 11 H7
Golden Yd HAMP NW3 117 M9
Golders Cl EDGW HA8 95 N6
Golders Gdns GLDGN NW11 117 H5
Golders Green Crs GLDGN NW11 117 H5
Golders Green Rd GLDGN NW11 117 H4
GLDGN NW11 117 J6
Golders Hl HAMP NW3 * 117 L7
Golderslea GLDGN NW11 * 117 K6
Golders Manor Dr GLDGN NW11 116 G4
Golders Park Cl GLDGN NW11 117 K6
Golders Ri HDN NW4 116 G3
Golders Wy GLDGN NW11 117 J5
Goldfinch Cl CRAWW RH11 283 N5
ORP BR6 227 K2
Goldfinch Gdns RGUE GU4 250 G9
Goldfinch Rd SAND/SEL CR2 224 D6
THMD SE28 162 G2
Goldfinch Wy BORE WD6 75 M8
Goldhawk Ms SHB W12 156 E1
Goldhawk Rd HMSMTH W6 156 C3
Goldhaze Cl WFD IG8 101 P8
Gold Hl EDGW HA8 96 A7
Gold Hl East CFSP/GDCR SL9 90 A10
Gold Hl North CFSP/GDCR SL9 89 P9
Gold Hl West CFSP/GDCR SL9 89 P9
Goldhurst Ter KIL/WHAMP NW6 3 H4
Golding Cl CRAWE RH10 284 D8
Goldingham Av LOU IG10 82 F6
Golding Rd SEV TN13 247 K8
Goldings Crs HAT AL10 40 E3
Golding's Hl LOU IG10 82 C4
Goldings La HERT/WAT SG14 25 H2
Goldings Ri LOU IG10 82 D5
Goldings Rd LOU IG10 82 D5
The Goldings WOKN/KNAP GU21 231 L2
Golding St WCHPL E1 13 P6
Goldington Cl HOD EN11 26 E10
Goldington Crs CAMTN NW1 5 J3
Goldington St CAMTN NW1 5 J3
Gold La EDGW HA8 96 A7
Goldman Cl BETH E2 13 N1
Goldney Rd MV/WKIL W9 8 E1
Goldrill Dr FBAR/BDGN N11 98 B3
Goldrings Rd LHD/OX KT22 218 B9
Goldring Wy LCOL/BKTW AL2 56 E3
Goldsboro Rd VX/NE SW8 158 E7
Goldsborough Crs CHING E4 100 G3
Goldsdown Cl PEND EN3 80 D5
Goldsdown Rd PEND EN3 80 C6
Goldsel Rd SWLY BR8 208 F4
Goldsmid St WOOL/PLUM SE18 163 H4
Goldsmith GRAYS RM17 167 L5
Goldsmith Av ACT W3 136 A9
CDALE/KGS NW9 116 B3
MNPK E12 142 B1
ROMW/RG RM7 124 B5
Goldsmith Cl RYLN/HDSTN HA2 113 P6
Goldsmith La CDALE/KGS NW9 115 P3
Goldsmith Pl KIL/WHAMP NW6 * 2 G6
Goldsmith Rd ACT W3 136 A10
FBAR/BDGN N11 98 A6
LEY E10 120 G6
PECK SE15 159 P7
WALTH E17 100 C10
Goldsmiths Cl ACT W3 * 136 A10
WOKN/KNAP GU21 231 P4
Goldsmith's Rw BETH E2 7 P7
Goldsmith St CITYW EC2V 12 F5
Goldsmiths Whf GRAYS RM17 * 167 M6
Goldsmith Wy STALW/RED AL3 38 B4
Goldstone Cl WARE SG12 26 C1
Goldstone Farm Vw
GT/LBKH KT23 253 P3
Goldsworth Orch
WOKN/KNAP GU21 231 M4
Goldsworth Rd
WOKN/KNAP GU21 231 P4
WOKN/KNAP GU21 232 B3
Goldsworthy Wy SL SL1 128 B8
Goldwell Rd THHTH CR7 202 G4
Goldwing Cl CAN/RD E16 141 M8
Gole Rd CHOB/PIR GU24 230 C7
Golf Cl BUSH WD23 73 L7
STAN HA7 95 H8
THHTH CR7 203 H1
WOKS/MYFD GU22 215 H10
Golf Club Dr KUTN/CMB KT2 178 A10
Golf Club Rd BRKMPK AL9 59 K2
WEY KT13 216 D6
WOKS/MYFD GU22 231 N6
Golfe Rd IL IG1 122 G8
Golf House La OXTED RH8 261 P5
Golf Links Av GVW DA11 190 E8
Golf Ride ENC/FH EN2 79 H1
Golf Rd BMLY BR1 206 D3
EA W5 * 135 L8
PUR/KEN CR8 241 L4
Golf Side BELMT SM2 221 H7
WHTN TW2 176 C6
Golf Side Cl NWMAL KT3 200 B2
Golfside Cl TRDG/WHET N20 97 P4
Gollogly Ter CHARL SE7 161 P4
Gombards STALW/RED AL3 38 C5
Gomer Gdns TEDD TW11 176 F9
Gomer Pl TEDD TW11 176 F9
Gomm Rd BERM/RHTH SE16 160 B3
Gomms Wood Cl BEAC HP9 88 A7
Gomshall Av WLGTN SM6 222 F2
Gomshall Gdns PUR/KEN CR8 241 M1
Gomshall La SHGR GU5 270 B5
Gomshall Rd BELMT SM2 220 F6
Gondar Gdns CRICK NW2 117 J10
Gonson St DEPT SE8 160 G5
Gonston Cl WIM/MER SW19 179 H5
Gonville Av RKW/CH/CXG WD3 72 C10
Gonville Crs NTHLT UB5 134 A1
Gonville Rd THHTH CR7 202 G5
Gonville St FUL/PGN SW6 157 H9
Goodacre Cl POTB/CUF EN6 59 L8
Goodall Rd WAN E11 121 H8
Gooden Ct HRW HA1 114 D8
Goodenough Cl COUL/CHIP CR5 241 H6
Goodenough Rd
WIM/MER SW19 179 J10
Goodenough Wy
COUL/CHIP CR5 240 G6
Goodey Rd BARK IG11 143 J2
Goodge Pl FITZ W1T 11 H4
Goodge St FITZ W1T 11 H4
Goodhall Cl STAN HA7 94 G7
Goodhall St WLSDN NW10 136 C5
Goodhart Wy WWKM BR4 205 K6
Goodhew Rd CROY/NA CR0 203 P6
Gooding Cl NWMAL KT3 199 P4
Goodinge Cl HOLWY N7 5 L1
Goodinge Rd HOLWY N7 5 L1
Goodison Cl BUSH WD23 74 B9
Goodlake Ct DEN/HRF UB9 111 J5
Goodley Stock Rd
BH/WHM TN16 262 E5
Goodman Ct ALP/SUD HA0 * 115 J9
Goodman Crs BRXS/STRHM SW2 180 F5
Goodman Pk SLN SL2 149 P1
Goodman Rd LEY E10 121 H5
Goodmans Ct ALP/SUD HA0 115 J9
Goodman's Yd TWRH EC3N 13 L7
Goodmayes Av GDMY/SEVK IG3 123 K6
Goodmayes La GDMY/SEVK IG3 123 K9
Goodmayes Rd GDMY/SEVK IG3 123 K6
Goodmead Rd ORP BR6 207 L6
Goodrich Cl GSTN WD25 73 H1
Goodrich Rd EDUL SE22 181 N2
Goodson Rd WLSDN NW10 136 B2
Goods Wy CAMTN NW1 5 L7
Goodway Gdns POP/IOD E14 141 J8
Goodwin Cl BERM/RHTH SE16 19 M4
CRAWW RH11 283 H10
MTCM CR4 201 N3
Goodwin Ct CHES/WCR EN8 62 D4
Goodwin Dr SCUP DA14 185 N5
Goodwin Gdns CROY/NA CR0 223 J3
Goodwin Rd CROY/NA CR0 223 J2
ED N9 100 B2
SHB W12 156 D1
SLN SL2 128 E5
Goodwins Ct CHCR WC2N 11 K8
Goodwin St FSBYPK N4 119 H7
Goodwood Av HCH RM12 125 M9
PEND EN3 80 B3
WATN WD24 72 F1
Goodwood Cl CRAWE RH10 284 B10
HOD EN11 44 F2
MRDN SM4 201 K4
Goodwood Crs GVE DA12 190 F9
Goodwood Dr NTHLT UB5 133 P1
Goodwood Pde BECK BR3 * 204 D4
Goodwood Rd NWCR SE14 160 D6
REDH RH1 257 P8
Goodwyn Av MLHL NW7 96 B6
Goodwyns Rd DORK RH4 272 G5
Goodwyn's V MUSWH N10 98 B9
Goodyers Av RAD WD7 56 E9
Goodyers Gdns HDN NW4 116 G3
Goosander Wy THMD SE28 162 G2
Goose Acre CSHM HP5 51 K6
Gooseacre WGCE AL7 23 J7
Gooseacre La
KTN/HRWW/WS HA3 115 J3
Goosecroft HHW HP1 35 J5
Goosefields RKW/CH/CXG WD3 71 M10
Goose Gn SHGR GU5 270 D5
SLN SL2 128 G4
Goose Green Cl STMC/STPC BR5 207 K2
Goose La WOKS/MYFD GU22 231 N8
Gooseley La EHAM E6 142 D5
Goose Rye Rd RGUW GU3 249 K2
Gooshays Dr HARH RM3 105 M7
Gooshays Gdns HARH RM3 105 M7
Goossens Cl SUT SM1 221 M2
Gophir La CANST EC4R * 12 G7
Gopsall St IS N1 7 H6
Goral Md RKW/CH/CXG WD3 91 N2
Gordon Av CHING E4 101 K7
HCH RM12 124 G7
MORT/ESHN SW14 156 B10
SAND/SEL CR2 223 K6
STAN HA7 94 E7
TWK TW1 176 F1
Gordonbrock Rd BROCKY SE4 182 F1
Gordon Cl CHERT KT16 195 H10
STA TW18 173 L9
STAL AL1 38 G7
TIL RM18 169 N6
WALTH E17 120 F4
Gordon Ct REDH RH1 * 276 A2
Gordon Crs CROY/NA CR0 203 M8
HYS/HAR UB3 153 H3
Gordondale Rd WIM/MER SW19 179 K5
Gordon Dr CHERT KT16 195 H10
SHPTN TW17 196 E6
Gordon Gdns EDGW HA8 95 N10
Gordon Gv CMBW SE5 159 J8
Gordon Hl ENC/FH EN2 79 K5
Gordon House Rd KTTN NW5 118 B9
Gordon Pl GVE DA12 190 F2
KENS W8 14 F1
Gordon Prom East GVE DA12 190 G2
Gordon Rd ASHF TW15 173 P6
BARK IG11 143 H3
BECK BR3 204 E3
BELV DA17 164 D3
BFN/LL DA15 185 H1
BRWN CM15 107 M2
BRYLDS KT5 199 L7
CAR SM5 222 A3
CDW/CHF RM16 168 B1
CHDH RM6 124 A4
CHING E4 101 K1
CHSWK W4 155 N5
CSHM HP5 51 H9
CTHM CR3 241 L7
DART DA1 187 L3
EA W5 135 H9
ED N9 100 A3
ENC/FH EN2 79 L5
ESH/CLAY KT10 218 D4
FBAR/BDGN N11 98 E8
FNCH N3 97 J8
GVW DA11 190 B3
HSLW TW3 154 B10
IL IG1 122 G8
KTN/HRWW/WS HA3 114 D1
KUTN/CMB KT2 199 L1
NWDGN UB2 153 M3
PECK SE15 160 A8
RCH/KEW TW9 155 L8
REDH RH1 258 B7
SEV TN13 265 J1
SHPTN TW17 196 E6
SRTFD E15 121 H9
STA TW18 172 F7
SWFD E18 101 N9
WAB EN9 62 F10
WAN E11 121 M4
WDR/YW UB7 131 N9
WDSR SL4 148 E9
Gordon Sq STPAN WC1H 11 K2
Gordon St PLSTW E13 141 M5
STPAN WC1H 11 J1
Gordons Wk HARP AL5 20 B3
Gordons Wy OXTED RH8 261 J4
Gordon Wy BAR EN5 77 J8
BMLY BR1 205 M1
CSTG HP8 89 N4
Gore Cl DEN/HRF UB9 111 L2
Gorefield Pl KIL/WHAMP NW6 2 F7
Gore Hl AMSS HP7 68 G8
Gorelands La CSTG HP8 90 B3
Gorell Rd BEAC HP9 88 G10
Gore Rd HOM E9 140 B3
RDART DA2 188 C5
RYNPK SW20 200 F2
SL SL1 128 A5
Goresbrook Rd DAGW RM9 143 M3
Gore St SKENS SW7 15 K3
Gorham Dr STAL AL1 38 D9
Gorham Pl NTGHL W11 8 A8
NTGHL W11 137 H9
Goring Cl CRW RM5 104 D9
Goring Gdns BCTR RM8 123 M9
Goring Rd DAGE RM10 144 E1
FBAR/BDGN N11 * 98 F7
STA TW18 172 G8
Goring St HDTCH EC3A 13 K5
Goring Wy GFD/PVL UB6 134 B4
Gorle Cl GSTN WD25 55 H10
Gorleston Rd SEVS/STOTM N15 119 L3
Gorleston St WKENS W14 14 B5
Gorling Cl CRAWW RH11 283 H8
Gorman Rd WOOL/PLUM SE18 162 C3
Gorringe Av EYN DA4 210 C2
Gorringe Park Av MTCM CR4 180 A10
Gorse Cl CAN/RD E16 141 M8
CRAWE RH10 285 J3
HAT AL10 40 D4
KWD/TDW/WH KT20 238 E6
Gorse Cnr HARP AL5 * 20 A3
STALW/RED AL3 38 C4
Gorse Ct RGUE GU4 250 F8
Gorse Dr HORL RH6 281 J3
Gorse Hill La VW GU25 194 A4
Gorse Hill Rd VW GU25 194 A4
Gorselands HARP AL5 20 A4
Gorselands Cl BF/WBF KT14 215 M7
Gorse La CHOB/PIR GU24 213 K4
Gorse Meade SL SL1 128 G10
Gorse Ri TOOT SW17 180 B8
Gorse Rd CROY/NA CR0 204 F10
STMC/STPC BR5 208 B9
Gorse Wk WDR/YW UB7 131 P8
Gorse Wy HART DA3 211 L5
Gorseway HAT AL10 40 C1
ROMW/RG RM7 124 F7
Gorse Wood Rd HART DA3 211 M4
Gorsewood Rd
WOKN/KNAP GU21 231 J5
Gorst Rd BTSEA SW11 180 A2
WLSDN NW10 135 P6
Gorsuch Pl BETH E2 7 L9
Gorsuch St BETH E2 7 L9
Gosberton Rd BAL SW12 180 A4
Gosbury Hl CHSGTN KT9 219 K1
Gosden Cl CRAWE RH10 284 B8
SHGR GU5 268 C9
Gosden Hill Rd RGUE GU4 250 F6
Gosden Rd CHOB/PIR GU24 212 E9
Gosfield Rd BCTR RM8 124 B6
HOR/WEW KT19 220 A8
Gosfield St GTPST W1W 10 F3
Gosford Gdns REDBR IG4 122 C3
Gosforth La OXHEY WD19 93 H4
Gosforth Pth OXHEY WD19 93 H4
Goshawk Gdns YEAD UB4 132 F5
Goslar Wy WDSR SL4 148 G8
Goslett Yd SOHO/SHAV W1D 11 K6
Gosling Cl GFD/PVL UB6 133 P5
Gosling Gn DTCH/LGLY SL3 150 B2
Gosling Rd DTCH/LGLY SL3 150 B2
Gosling Wy BRXN/ST SW9 159 H7
Gospatrick Rd TOTM N17 99 K9
Gosport Dr HCH RM12 145 K1
Gosport Rd WALTH E17 120 E3
Gosport Wy PECK SE15 159 N6
Gossage Rd HGDN/ICK UB10 132 A2
WOOL/PLUM SE18 162 G4
The Gossamers GSTN WD25 73 M1
Gosse Cl HOD EN11 26 E10
Gosselin Rd HERT/WAT SG14 25 K3
Gosset St BETH E2 7 N10
Gosshill Rd BMLY BR1 206 D2
Gossington Cl CHST BR7 184 E7
Gossoms Ryde BERK HP4 33 M4
Gossoms's End BERK HP4 33 M4
Gossops Dr CRAWW RH11 283 K8
Gossops Green La CRAWW RH11 283 K8
Gosterwood St DEPT SE8 160 D5
Gostling Rd WHTN TW2 175 P4
Goston Gdns THHTH CR7 203 H3
Goswell Hl WDSR SL4 149 J7
Goswell Pl FSBYE EC1V 6 D10
Goswell Rd FSBYE EC1V 6 D9
WDSR SL4 149 J7
Gothic Cl DART DA1 187 L6
Gothic Ct HYS/HAR UB3 152 E5
Gothic Rd WHTN TW2 176 C5
Gottfried Ms KTTN NW5 118 D9
Goudhurst Cl CRAWE RH10 284 F7
Goudhurst Rd BMLY BR1 183 L8
Gouge Av GVW DA11 190 B4
Gough Rd EN EN1 80 A6
SRTFD E15 121 L9
Gough Sq FLST/FETLN EC4A 12 B5
Gough St FSBYW WC1X 11 P1
Gould Cl BRKMPK AL9 40 E10
CHONG CM5 49 K7
Gould Ct RGUE GU4 250 G8
Goulding Gdns THHTH CR7 203 K2
Gould Rd EBED/NFELT TW14 174 F3
WHTN TW2 176 D4
Goulds Gn UX/CGN UB8 132 C9
Gould's Ter HACK E8 120 A10
Goulston St WCHPL E1 13 L5
Goulton Rd CLPT E5 120 A10
Gourley Pl SEVS/STOTM N15 119 M3
Gourley St SEVS/STOTM N15 119 M3
Gourney Gv CDW/CHF RM16 147 N9
Gourock Rd ELTH/MOT SE9 184 D1
Govan St BETH E2 7 P6
Government Rw PEND EN3 80 F3
Governors Av DEN/HRF UB9 111 J3
Governors Cl AMS HP6 69 L4
Govett Av SHPTN TW17 * 196 D5
Govett Gv BFOR GU20 212 C2
Govier Cl SRTFD E15 141 K2
Gowan Av FUL/PGN SW6 157 H7
Gowan Rd WLSDN NW10 136 E2
Gowar Fld POTB/CUF EN6 58 F7
Gower Cl CLAP SW4 180 D2
Gower Ms GWRST WC1E 11 K4
Gower Pl GWRST WC1E 11 H1
Gower Rd FSTGT E7 141 M1
HORL RH6 279 P4
ISLW TW7 154 E5
WEY KT13 216 E3
Gowers La CDW/CHF RM16 168 C1
The Gowers AMS HP6 69 K3
HLW CM20 29 K9
Gower St GWRST WC1E 11 J2
Gower's Wk WCHPL E1 13 N5
The Gower EGH TW20 194 E3
Gowings Gn SL SL1 148 D1
Gowland Pl BECK BR3 204 E2
Gowlett Rd PECK SE15 159 P9
Gowlland Cl CROY/NA CR0 203 P7
Gowrie Pl CTHM CR3 241 K8
Gowrie Rd BTSEA SW11 158 B9
Graburn Wy E/WMO/HCT KT8 198 C3
Grace Av BXLYHN DA7 164 A8
RAD WD7 57 K9
Gracechurch St BANK EC3V 13 H7
Grace Cl BARK/HLT IG6 103 J7
BORE WD6 76 A5
EDGW HA8 95 P8
ELTH/MOT SE9 184 A6
Grace Ct SL SL1 129 H10
Gracedale Rd STRHM/NOR SW16 180 C8
Gracefield Gdns
STRHM/NOR SW16 180 F6
Grace Jones Cl HACK E8 7 M2
Grace Pl BOW E3 140 G5
Grace Rd CROY/NA CR0 203 K6
Grace's Aly WCHPL E1 13 N7
Grace's Ms CMBW SE5 159 L8
STJWD NW8 * 3 K8
Grace's Rd CMBW SE5 159 M8
Grace St BOW E3 140 G5
Gracious La SEV TN13 265 H6
Gracious Lane Br BGR/WK TN15 247 P2
Gracious Lane End RSEV TN14 264 G6
Gracious Pond Rd
CHOB/PIR GU24 213 M4
The Gradient SYD SE26 181 P7
Graduate Pl STHWK SE1 19 J3
Graeme Rd EN EN1 79 M6
Graemesdyke Av
MORT/ESHN SW14 155 N9
Graemes Dyke Rd BERK HP4 33 M6
Graffham Cl CRAWW RH11 283 L5
Grafton Cl BF/WBF KT14 215 J9
DTCH/LGLY SL3 130 B8
HSLWW TW4 175 M4
STALE/WH AL4 39 J7
WEA W13 134 F8
WPK KT4 200 B10
Grafton Ct EBED/NFELT TW14 174 E4
Grafton Crs CAMTN NW1 4 F2
Grafton Gdns BCTR RM8 123 P7
FSBYPK N4 119 K4
Grafton Ms FITZ W1T 10 G2
Grafton Park Rd WPK KT4 200 B10
Grafton Pl CAMTN NW1 5 K10
Grafton Rd ACT W3 135 P9
BCTR RM8 123 P7
CROY/NA CR0 203 J8
ENC/FH EN2 78 G7
HRW HA1 114 B3
KTTN NW5 118 B10
NWMAL KT3 200 B4
WPK KT4 200 A10
Grafton Sq CLAP SW4 158 D10
Grafton St CONDST W1S 10 F8
Grafton Ter HAMP NW3 118 A10
Grafton Wy E/WMO/HCT KT8 197 N4
FITZ W1T 10 G3
Grafton Yd KTTN NW5 4 F2
Graham Av BROX EN10 44 D6
MTCM CR4 202 B1
WEA W13 154 G1
Graham Cl CROY/NA CR0 204 F9
RBRW/HUT CM13 87 P9
STAL AL1 38 C9
Grahame Park Wy MLHL NW7 96 C8
Graham Gdns SURB KT6 199 K8
Graham Rd BFOR GU20 212 B3
BXLYHS DA6 164 A10
CHSWK W4 156 A2
HACK E8 7 P1
HDN NW4 116 E4
HPTN TW12 175 P7
KTN/HRWW/WS HA3 114 D1
MTCM CR4 202 B1
PLSTW E13 141 M6
PUR/KEN CR8 223 H9
SEVS/STOTM N15 119 J1
WIM/MER SW19 179 J10
Graham St IS N1 6 D8
Graham Ter BFN/LL DA15 * 185 L2
BGVA SW1W 16 D6
Grainger Cl NTHLT UB5 114 B10
Grainger Rd ISLW TW7 154 E8
WDGN N22 99 K9
Gramer Cl WAN E11 121 J7
Grampian Cl BELMT SM2 221 M6
HYS/HAR UB3 152 E6
ORP BR6 207 J6
Grampian Gdns CRICK NW2 117 H6
Grampian Wy DTCH/LGLY SL3 150 D4
Gramsci Wy CAT SE6 182 G6
Granada St TOOT SW17 180 A8
Granard Av PUT/ROE SW15 178 E1
Granard Rd BTSEA SW11 180 A3
The Granaries WAB EN9 63 K10
Granary Cl ED N9 100 B1
HORL RH6 280 B2
STALE/WH AL4 21 J3
Granary La HARP AL5 20 A2
Granary Ms WCHPL E1 140 A6
Granary Sq IS N1 6 B2
Granary St CAMTN NW1 5 J6
The Granary WARE SG12 27 H8
Granby Av HARP AL5 20 B1
Granby Park Rd CHESW EN7 61 N4
Granby Rd ELTH/MOT SE9 162 C8
GVW DA11 190 A2
Granby St BETH E2 13 N1
Granby Ter CAMTN NW1 4 G8
Grand Av BRYLDS KT5 199 N6
FARR EC1M 12 D3
MUSWH N10 118 B2
WBLY HA9 115 M10
Grand Av East WBLY HA9 115 N10
Grand Depot Rd
WOOL/PLUM SE18 162 D4
Grand Dr NWDGN UB2 154 B1
RYNPK SW20 200 F2
RYNPK SW20 200 G2
Granden Rd STRHM/NOR SW16 * 202 F2
Grandfield Av WAT WD17 72 G5
Grandison Rd BTSEA SW11 180 A1
WPK KT4 200 F9
Grand Junction Whf IS N1 * 6 E8
Grand Pde CRAWE RH10 * 283 N7
FSBYPK N4 * 119 J4
MORT/ESHN SW14 * 155 P10
SURB KT6 * 199 M8
WBLY HA9 * 115 N7
Grand Stand Rd EPSOM KT18 238 D3
Grand Union Canal Wk
BERK HP4 33 K2
BTFD TW8 155 H5
DEN/HRF UB9 111 L3
DEN/HRF UB9 111 M9
DTCH/LGLY SL3 150 C1
HHS/BOV HP3 54 A1
HHW HP1 34 G8
HNWL W7 154 D2
HYS/HAR UB3 153 H2
IVER SL0 130 F10
KGLGY WD4 54 C5
NKENS W10 8 B1
NWDGN UB2 153 J2
NWDGN UB2 154 B1
RKW/CH/CXG WD3 91 K6
RKW/CH/CXG WD3 91 L4
RKW/CH/CXG WD3 91 N3
RKW/CH/CXG WD3 92 C1
SLN SL2 129 N10
STHL UB1 133 N6
UX/CGN UB8 131 M5
UX/CGN UB8 131 M9
WDR/YW UB7 152 C1
WLSDN NW10 135 N4
WLSDN NW10 136 B5
WLSDN NW10 136 D6
Grand Union Cl MV/WKIL W9 8 D3
Grand Union Crs HACK E8 7 P5
Grand Union Wk CAMTN NW1 * 4 F4
Grand View Av BH/WHM TN16 243 P3
Grand Wk WCHPL E1 * 140 D6
Granfield St BTSEA SW11 * 157 N7
Grange Av EBAR EN4 97 P2
KTN/HRWW/WS HA3 94 G10
NFNCH/WDSPK N12 97 M6
SNWD SE25 203 M2
TRDG/WHET N20 97 H1
WFD IG8 101 M7
WHTN TW2 176 D5
Grangecliffe Gdns SNWD SE25 203 M2
Grange Cl BFN/LL DA15 185 K6
BH/WHM TN16 262 G2
CFSP/GDCR SL9 90 B9
CRAWE RH10 284 B5
E/WMO/HCT KT8 198 A4
GUW GU2 249 N6
HERT/WAT SG14 25 J5
HEST TW5 153 N4
HHNE HP2 36 B7
HYS/HAR UB3 132 F7
LHD/OX KT22 237 J6
RBRW/HUT CM13 107 P6
REDH RH1 259 L9
STWL/WRAY TW19 172 B2
WAT WD17 73 H5
WFD IG8 101 M8
Grange Ct ALP/SUD HA0 * 115 H10
BELMT SM2 * 221 L4
EGH TW20 * 172 C8
GUW GU2 * 249 N6
HERT/WAT SG14 * 25 K4
HRW HA1 * 114 E8
NTHLT UB5 133 K4
PIN HA5 * 113 M1
WAB EN9 62 G10
WLGTN SM6 * 202 C10
WOT/HER KT12 197 H9
Grange Court Rd HARP AL5 20 B5
Grangecourt Rd
STNW/STAM N16 119 M6
Grange Crs CHIG IG7 102 G6
RDART DA2 188 A2
THMD SE28 143 M8
Grangedale Cl NTHWD HA6 92 F9
Grange Dr CHST BR7 184 B9
ORP BR6 227 M5
REDH RH1 258 C4
WOKN/KNAP GU21 232 B1
Grange End HORL RH6 281 H4
Grange Farm Cl
RYLN/HDSTN HA2 114 B7
Grange Flds CFSP/GDCR SL9 90 B9
Grangefields Rd RGUE GU4 250 A4
Grange Gdns BNSTD SM7 221 L9
HAMP NW3 117 L8
PIN HA5 113 N2
SLN SL2 109 J10
SNWD SE25 203 M2
STHGT/OAK N14 98 E2
WARE SG12 26 D3
Grange Gv IS N1 6 E1
Grange Hl EDGW HA8 95 P6
SNWD SE25 203 M2
Grangehill Pl ELTH/MOT SE9 162 C9
Grangehill Rd ELTH/MOT SE9 162 C10
Grange Houses HBRY N5 * 119 K9
Grange La DUL SE21 181 N5
GSTN WD25 74 C5
HART DA3 211 N7
HLWW/ROY CM19 45 P1
Grange Meadow BNSTD SM7 221 L9
Grange Ms FELT TW13 * 174 E6
Grangemill Rd CAT SE6 182 F6
Grangemill Wy CAT SE6 182 F5
Grangemount LHD/OX KT22 237 J6
Grange Pk EA W5 135 K10
WOKN/KNAP GU21 * 214 C10
Grange Park Av WCHMH N21 99 K1
Grange Park Pl RYNPK SW20 178 E10
Grange Park Rd LEY E10 120 G7
THHTH CR7 203 L3
Grange Pl KIL/WHAMP NW6 2 E4
STA TW18 195 M2
WOT/HER KT12 197 H9
Grange Rd ADL/WDHM KT15 215 K6
BARN SW13 156 D7
BELMT SM2 221 K4
BORE WD6 75 L9
BUSH WD23 73 M9
CFSP/GDCR SL9 90 B9
CHOB/PIR GU24 230 C8
CHSGTN KT9 219 K1
CHSWK W4 156 A3
CRAWE RH10 285 P6
CTHM CR3 259 N1
E/WMO/HCT KT8 198 A4
EA W5 135 J10
EDGW HA8 96 A7
EGH TW20 172 C8
GRAYS RM17 167 N6
GUW GU2 249 N7
GVW DA11 190 D3
HARH RM3 105 J7
HGT N6 118 B4
HRW HA1 114 F4
HYS/HAR UB3 132 F8
IL IG1 122 F9
KUT/HW KT1 199 K3
LEY E10 120 F6
LHD/OX KT22 237 J6
ORP BR6 206 F9
PLSTW E13 141 L5
RYLN/HDSTN HA2 114 C7
SAND/SEL CR2 223 K6
SEV TN13 265 H3
SNWD SE25 203 L4
SOCK/AV RM15 146 B10
STHL UB1 153 M1
STHWK SE1 19 K4
TOTM N17 99 P7
WALTH E17 120 D3
WLSDN NW10 136 E1
WOKN/KNAP GU21 232 B1
WOT/HER KT12 217 M1
Granger Wy EMPK RM11 125 H4
Grange St IS N1 7 H6
STALW/RED AL3 38 C5
The Grange ALP/SUD HA0 135 M2
CHOB/PIR GU24 213 K6
CROY/NA CR0 204 E9
EYN DA4 210 C1
HOD EN11 * 44 F4
NWMAL KT3 * 200 D5
SL SL1 * 128 B5
STALE/WH AL4 * 40 A9
STHWK SE1 19 L3
WDSR SL4 171 N1
WIM/MER SW19 178 G9
WOT/HER KT12 197 J9
WPK KT4 220 A1
Grange V BELMT SM2 221 L4
Grangeview Rd TRDG/WHET N20 97 M2
Grange Wk STHWK SE1 19 L4
Grange Walk Ms STHWK SE1 19 K4
Grange Wy ERITH DA8 165 J6
HART DA3 211 L6
IVER SL0 131 J8
Grangeway HORL RH6 281 H4
KIL/WHAMP NW6 2 E4
NFNCH/WDSPK N12 97 L5
WFD IG8 101 P5
Grangeway Gdns REDBR IG4 122 B3
Grangeways Cl GVW DA11 190 C7
The Grangeway WCHMH N21 79 J10
Grangewood BXLY DA5 186 A4
DTCH/LGLY SL3 129 P7
POTB/CUF EN6 59 L6
Grangewood Av CDW/CHF RM16 168 B2
RAIN RM13 145 K6
Grangewood Cl PIN HA5 113 H3
RBRW/HUT CM13 107 M4
Grangewood La BECK BR3 182 E9
Grangewood St EHAM E6 142 A3
Grange Yd STHWK SE1 19 L4
Granham Gdns ED N9 99 N3
Granite St WOOL/PLUM SE18 163 J4
Granleigh Rd WAN E11 121 K7
Gransden Av HACK E8 140 A2
Gransden Rd SHB W12 156 C1
Grant Av SL SL1 129 K8
Grantbridge St IS N1 6 D7
Grantchester KUT/HW KT1 * 199 M2
Grantchester Cl HRW HA1 114 E8
Grant Cl SHPTN TW17 196 C6
STHGT/OAK N14 98 D1
TOTM N17 99 M10
Grant Gdns HARP AL5 20 A1
Grantham Cl EDGW HA8 95 K4
Grantham Gdns CHDH RM6 124 A4
WARE SG12 26 D1
Grantham Gn BORE WD6 75 P9
Grantham Ms BERK HP4 34 A5
Grantham Pl MYFR/PKLN W1K 10 E10
Grantham Rd BRXN/ST SW9 158 F8
CHSWK W4 156 B6
MNPK E12 122 D8
Grantham Wy CDW/CHF RM16 147 M10
Grantley Cl RGUE GU4 268 B8
Grantley Gdns GUW GU2 249 M9
Grantley Pl ESH/CLAY KT10 218 A2
Grantley Rd GUW GU2 249 M9
HSLWW TW4 153 K8
Grantley St WCHPL E1 140 C5
Grantock Rd WALTH E17 101 J9
Granton Av UPMR RM14 125 N7
Granton Rd GDMY/SEVK IG3 123 K6
SCUP DA14 185 M9
STRHM/NOR SW16 202 D1
Grant Pl CROY/NA CR0 203 N8
Grant Rd BTSEA SW11 157 N9
CROY/NA CR0 203 N8
KTN/HRWW/WS HA3 114 D1
Grants Cl MLHL NW7 96 F8
Grants La OXTED RH8 261 P9
Grant St IS N1 6 A7
PLSTW E13 141 M5
Grant Ter STNW/STAM N16 * 119 P5
Grantully Rd MV/WKIL W9 2 G10
Grant Wk ASC SL5 192 D8
Grant Wy ISLW TW7 154 F5
Grantwood Cl REDH RH1 276 B5
Granville Ar BRXN/ST SW9 * 159 H10
Granville Av ED N9 100 B4
FELT TW13 175 H5
HSLW TW3 175 P1
SLN SL2 129 J7
Granville Cl BF/WBF KT14 216 A9
CROY/NA CR0 203 M9
Granville Dene HHS/BOV HP3 52 D3
Granville Gdns EA W5 135 L10
HOD EN11 26 F9
STRHM/NOR SW16 202 G1
Granville Gv LEW SE13 161 H9
Granville Ms SCUP DA14 185 K7
Granville Pk LEW SE13 161 H9
Granville Pl FUL/PGN SW6 * 157 L6
MBLAR W1H 10 C6
NFNCH/WDSPK N12 * 97 M8
PIN HA5 113 L1
Granville Rd BAR EN5 76 F8
BERK HP4 33 K3
BH/WHM TN16 262 F2
CEND/HSY/T N8 118 G4
CRICK NW2 117 J7
EPP CM16 65 L5
GVW DA11 190 C3
HGDN/ICK UB10 132 C1
HYS/HAR UB3 152 G3
IL IG1 122 E6
KIL/WHAMP NW6 2 E8
NFNCH/WDSPK N12 97 M8
OXTED RH8 261 L5
PLMGR N13 98 G7
SCUP DA14 185 K7
SEV TN13 247 H10
STAL AL1 38 E6
SWFD E18 101 N10
WALTH E17 120 G4
WAND/EARL SW18 179 J3
WATW WD18 * 73 K8
WDGN N22 99 J9
WELL DA16 163 M9
WEY KT13 216 D4
WOKS/MYFD GU22 232 C6
Granville Sq PECK SE15 * 159 M6
Granville St FSBYW WC1X 5 P10
Grape St LSQ/SEVD WC2H 11 L5
Graphite Sq LBTH SE11 17 N7
Grapsome Cl CHSGTN KT9 219 H4
Grasdene Rd WOOL/PLUM SE18 163 K6
Grasholm Wy DTCH/LGLY SL3 150 F3
Grasmere Av ACT W3 135 P9
ACT W3 136 A9
HARP AL5 20 B1
HSLW TW3 176 A2
ORP BR6 206 E10
PUT/ROE SW15 178 A7
RSLP HA4 112 D5
SLN SL2 129 M9
WBLY HA9 115 J5
WIM/MER SW19 201 K3
Grasmere Cl EBED/NFELT TW14 174 G4
EGH TW20 172 E10
GSTN WD25 55 J8
GU GU1 250 E9
HHS/BOV HP3 36 C8
LOU IG10 82 C6
Grasmere Ct WDGN N22 98 G7
Grasmere Gdns
KTN/HRWW/WS HA3 94 F10
ORP BR6 206 E10
REDBR IG4 122 B3
Grasmere Pde SLN SL2 * 129 N9
Grasmere Rd BMLY BR1 205 L1
BXLYHN DA7 164 D7
LTWR GU18 212 A6

MUSWH N10 98 C9
ORP BR6 206 E10
PLSTW E13 141 M4
PUR/KEN CR8 223 J7
SNWD SE25 204 A6
STAL AL1 38 G8
STRHM/NOR SW16 180 G8
TOTM N17 99 P7
Grasmere Wy BF/WBF KT14 216 A8
Grassfield Cl COUL/CHIP CR5 240 C5
Grasshaven Wy THMD SE28 143 J10
Grassingham End
CFSP/GDCR SL9 90 B8
Grassingham Rd CFSP/GDCR SL9 90 B8
Grassington Cl FBAR/BDGN N11 98 B7
LCOL/BKTW AL2 55 P6
Grassington Rd SCUP DA14 185 K7
Grasslands HORL RH6 281 H4
Grassmere HORL RH6 280 C3
Grassmere Rd EMPK RM11 125 N2
Grassmount FSTH SE23 182 A5
WLGTN SM6 222 D6
Grass Pk FNCH N3 97 J9
Grass Warren WLYN AL6 23 P2
Grassway WLGTN SM6 222 D1
Grassy Cl HHW HP1 35 K5
Grassy La SEV TN13 265 J3
Grasvenor Av BAR EN5 77 K10
Grately Wy PECK SE15 * 159 M6
Gratton Dr WDSR SL4 148 D10
Gratton Rd WKENS W14 14 A4
Grattons Dr CRAWE RH10 284 D4
Gratton Ter CRICK NW2 116 G8
Gravel Cl CHIG IG7 103 K3
Graveley Av BORE WD6 75 P9
Graveley Dell WGCE AL7 23 L6
Gravel Hl BXLYHS DA6 186 C1
CFSP/GDCR SL9 90 B8
CROY/NA CR0 224 D3
FNCH N3 97 J10
LHD/OX KT22 236 F7
UX/CGN UB8 111 N10
Gravel Hill Cl BXLYHS DA6 186 C2
Gravelhill Ter HHW HP1 35 K7
Gravel La CHIG IG7 83 K10
HHW HP1 35 K6
WCHPL E1 13 L5
Gravelly Hl CTHM CR3 259 N4
Gravel Pth BERK HP4 34 B4
Gravel Pits La SHGR GU5 270 D5
Gravel Pit Wy ORP BR6 207 K9
Gravel Rd EYN DA4 188 A10
HAYES BR2 206 B9
WHTN TW2 176 D4
Gravelwood Cl CHST BR7 184 F6
Gravely Ct HHNE HP2 36 D7
Gravenel Gdns TOOT SW17 * 179 P8
Graveney Gv PGE/AN SE20 182 B10
Graveney Rd CRAWE RH10 284 D8
TOOT SW17 179 P7
Gravesend Rd GVE DA12 191 P7
SHB W12 136 D9
Gravetts La RGUW GU3 249 K7
Gravetye Cl CRAWE RH10 284 B9
Gray Av BCTR RM8 124 A6
Grayburn Cl CSTG HP8 89 M3
Gray Gdns RAIN RM13 145 H1
Grayham Crs NWMAL KT3 200 A4
Grayham Rd NWMAL KT3 200 A4
Grayland Cl BMLY BR1 206 A1
Graylands GRAYS RM17 * 167 K5
WOKN/KNAP GU21 232 B2
Graylands Cl WOKN/KNAP GU21 232 B2
Grayling Cl CAN/RD E16 141 K6
Grayling Ct BERK HP4 33 L3
EA W5 * 135 J10
Grayling Rd STNW/STAM N16 119 L7
Grayling Sq BETH E2 7 P9
The Graylings ABLGY WD5 54 E9
Gray Pl CHERT KT16 214 G3
Grays Cottages
STMC/STPC BR5 * 207 M1
Grayscroft Rd
STRHM/NOR SW16 180 E10
Grays End Cl GRAYS RM17 167 M2
Grays Farm Rd STMC/STPC BR5 207 L1
Graysfield WGCE AL7 23 K8
Grayshott Rd BTSEA SW11 158 B9
Gray's Inn Rd FSBYW WC1X 5 M9
Gray's Inn Sq GINN WC1R 12 A3
Grays La ASHF TW15 174 C7
ASHTD KT21 237 L5
Grays Park Rd SLN SL2 129 M5
Grays Pl SLN SL2 129 L10
Grays Rd BH/WHM TN16 244 E7
GODL GU7 267 L10
HGDN/ICK UB10 131 P2
SL SL1 129 L10
Grays Wk CSHM HP5 50 G5
Grays Wd HORL RH6 280 D4
Grayswood Gdns RYNPK SW20 200 E2
Gray's Yd MHST W1U * 10 D6
Graywood Ct
NFNCH/WDSPK N12 97 M8
Grazebrook Rd STNW/STAM N16 119 L7
Grazeley Cl BXLYHS DA6 186 D1
The Grazings HHNE HP2 36 A4
Greatacre CSHM HP5 51 J6
Great Augur St HLWE CM17 29 N10
Great Benty WDR/YW UB7 151 P3
Great Braitch La HAT AL10 22 B10
Great Brays HLWS CM18 47 K2
Great Break WGCE AL7 23 L6
Great Brownings DUL SE21 181 N7
Great Bushey Dr
TRDG/WHET N20 97 L2
Great Cambridge Jct
PLMGR N13 99 K6
Great Cambridge Rd
CHES/WCR EN8 62 C4
BROX EN10 62 D2
CHES/WCR EN8 80 A1
EN EN1 79 P10
EN EN1 79 P5
UED N18 99 L6
Great Castle St REGST W1B 10 G5
Great Central Av RSLP HA4 113 K10
Great Central St CAMTN NW1 10 A3
Great Central Wy WBLY HA9 115 P10
WLSDN NW10 116 B10
Great Chapel St
SOHO/SHAV W1D 11 J5
Great Chart St BTSEA SW11 157 M9
Great Chertsey Rd CHSWK W4 156 A7
FELT TW13 175 N6
Great Church La HMSMTH W6 156 G4
Great College St WEST SW1P 17 L3
Great Conduit WGCE AL7 23 M4
Great Cross Av GNWCH SE10 161 K6
Great Cullings ROMW/RG RM7 124 F7
Great Cumberland Ms
MBLAR W1H 10 A6
Great Cumberland Pl
MBLAR W1H 10 A5
Great Dell WGCW AL8 22 G3
Great Dover St STHWK SE1 18 G3
Greatdown Rd HNWL W7 134 E7
Great Eastern Rd BRW CM14 107 H5
SRTFD E15 141 J2
Great Eastern St SDTCH EC2A 7 J10
Great Eastern Whf BTSEA SW11 157 P6
Great Ellshams BNSTD SM7 239 K2
Great Elms EW KT17 * 220 C7
Great Elms Rd HAYES BR2 205 P4
HHS/BOV HP3 36 A10
Great Fld CDALE/KGS NW9 96 B9
Greatfield Av EHAM E6 142 C6
Greatfield Cl ARCH N19 118 D9
BROCKY SE4 160 F10
Greatfields Dr UX/CGN UB8 132 B7
Greatfields Rd BARK IG11 142 G3
Greatford Dr GU GU1 250 G10
Great Fox Meadow BRWN CM15 86 E4
Great Galley Cl BARK IG11 143 L5
Great Ganett WGCE AL7 23 L7
Great Gardens Rd EMPK RM11 125 K4
Great Gatton Cl CROY/NA CR0 204 D7
Great George St STJSPK SW1H 17 K2
Great Goodwin Dr GU GU1 250 E8
Great Gregories La EPP CM16 65 H9
Great Gv BUSH WD23 74 A8
Great Groves CHESW EN7 61 M4
Great Guildford St STHWK SE1 12 E10
Greatham Rd BUSH WD23 73 L7
CRAWE RH10 284 D10
Great Harry Dr ELTH/MOT SE9 184 D7
Great Heart HHNE HP2 35 P4
Great Heath HAT AL10 40 E1
Great Hivings CSHM HP5 50 F3
Great James St BMSBY WC1N 11 N3
Greatlake Ct HORL RH6 280 C3
Great Lawn CHONG CM5 67 P3
Great Ley WGCE AL7 23 H7
Great Leylands HLWS CM18 47 K2
Great Marlborough St
REGST W1B 10 G6
Great Maze Pond STHWK SE1 13 H10
Great Meadow BROX EN10 44 F8
Great Molewood
HERT/WAT SG14 25 J2
Great Nelmes Cha EMPK RM11 125 N3
Greatness La RSEV TN14 247 K7
Greatness Rd RSEV TN14 247 K7
Great New St FLST/FETLN EC4A * 12 B5
Great North Leisure Pk
NFNCH/WDSPK N12 * 97 N8
Great North Rd BAR EN5 77 J6
BRKMPK AL9 22 E10
EFNCH N2 117 P3
HAT AL10 40 E5
WGCW AL8 22 D7
Great North Wy (Barnet By-Pass)
HDN NW4 96 E9
HDN NW4 116 G1
Great Oaks CHIG IG7 102 F5
RBRW/HUT CM13 87 N10
Great Oaks Pk RGUE GU4 250 F6
Greatorex St WCHPL E1 13 N3
Great Ormond St BMSBY WC1N 11 M3
Great Owl Rd CHIG IG7 102 D4
Great Palmers HHNE HP2 36 A1
Great Pk KGLGY WD4 54 B6
Great Percy St FSBYW WC1X 5 P9
Great Peter St WEST SW1P 17 K4
Great Plumtree HLW CM20 29 J9
Great Portland St GTPST W1W 10 F3
Great Pulteney St
SOHO/CST W1F 11 H7
Great Quarry GU GU1 268 A3
Great Queen St DART DA1 187 N2
HOL/ALD WC2B 11 M5
Great Rd HHNE HP2 36 A5
Great Ropers La
RBRW/HUT CM13 106 G7
Great Russell St
NOXST/BSQ WC1A 11 L4
Great St Thomas Apostle
BLKFR EC4V 12 F7
Great Scotland Yd WHALL SW1A 11 L10
Great Slades POTB/CUF EN6 59 J9
Great Smith St WEST SW1P 17 K3
Great South-west Rd
EBED/NFELT TW14 153 H9
EBED/NFELT TW14 174 D3
Great Spilmans EDUL SE22 181 M1
Great Stockwood Rd
CHESW EN7 61 L2
Great Strd CDALE/KGS NW9 96 C10
Great Sturgess Rd HHW HP1 35 J6
Great Suffolk St STHWK SE1 12 D10
Great Sutton St FSBYE EC1V 12 D2
Great Swan Aly LOTH EC2R 12 G5
Great Tattenhams EPSOM KT18 238 F5
Great Thrift STMC/STPC BR5 206 F4
Great Till Cl RSEV TN14 246 G2
Great Titchfield St GTPST W1W 10 G3
Great Tower St MON EC3R 13 J8
Great Trinity La BLKFR EC4V 12 F7
Great Turnstile HHOL WC1V * 11 P4
Great Warley St
RBRW/HUT CM13 106 F9
Great Western Rd NTGHL W11 8 D4
Great West Rd BTFD TW8 155 H4
HEST TW5 153 M8
HEST TW5 154 A7
HMSMTH W6 156 E4
ISLW TW7 154 D6
Great West Rd Chiswick
CHSWK W4 156 C5
Great West Rd Ellesmere Rd
CHSWK W4 155 P5
Great West Rd Hogarth La
CHSWK W4 156 A5
Great Westwood KGLGY WD4 * 71 P1
Great Whites Rd HHS/BOV HP3 36 A8
Great Winchester St OBST EC2N 13 H5
Great Windmill St
SOHO/SHAV W1D 11 J8
Greatwood CHST BR7 184 D10
Greatwood Cl CHERT KT16 214 F5
Great Woodcote Dr
PUR/KEN CR8 222 E6
Great Woodcote Pk
PUR/KEN CR8 222 F6
Great Yd STHWK SE1 19 K1
Greaves Cl BARK IG11 142 G2
Greaves Cottages
POP/IOD E14 * 140 D7
Greaves Pl TOOT SW17 179 P7
Grebe Av YEAD UB4 133 L8
Grebe Cl BARK IG11 143 K6
FSTGT E7 121 L10
WALTH E17 100 D8
Grebe Ct SUT SM1 221 J2
Grebe Crest WTHK RM20 166 F3
Grebe Ter KUT/HW KT1 * 199 K3
Grecian Crs NRWD SE19 181 J9
Greding Wk RBRW/HUT CM13 107 N3
Greek St SOHO/SHAV W1D 11 K6
Greenacre WDSR SL4 148 D8
Greenacre Cl BAR EN5 77 J4
NTHLT UB5 113 N10
SWLY BR8 208 F4
Greenacre Ct EGH TW20 * 171 P9
Greenacre Gdns WALTH E17 121 H2
Greenacre Pl WLGTN SM6 202 C9
Green Acres CROY/NA CR0 203 N10
SCUP DA14 * 185 J7
WGCE AL7 * 23 J8
Greenacres BUSH WD23 94 C3
CRAWE RH10 284 C8
ELTH/MOT SE9 184 D2
EPP CM16 65 J4
GT/LBKH KT23 235 P10
HHNE HP2 36 E8
KWD/TDW/WH KT20 257 J4
OXTED RH8 261 K3
Greenacres Av HGDN/ICK UB10 112 B8
Greenacres Cl ORP BR6 226 F1
RAIN RM13 145 M5
Greenacres Dr STAN HA7 94 G8
Greenacre Sq
BERM/RHTH SE16 * 160 C1
Greenacre Wk STHGT/OAK N14 98 E4
Greenall Cl CHES/WCR EN8 62 D6
Green Arbour Ct STBT EC1A * 12 C5
Green Av MLHL NW7 96 A5
WEA W13 154 G2
Greenaway Av UED N18 * 100 C6
Greenaway Gdns HAMP NW3 117 L9
Green Bank NFNCH/WDSPK N12 97 L5
WAP E1W 140 A10
Greenbank CHES/WCR EN8 62 A4
Greenbank Av ALP/SUD HA0 114 F10
Greenbank Cl CHING E4 101 H3
HARH RM3 105 L4
Greenbank Crs HDN NW4 117 H2
Greenbank Rd WAT WD17 72 E2
Greenbanks DART DA1 187 M5
STAL AL1 38 E8
UPMR RM14 126 D7
Greenbay Rd CHARL SE7 162 A6
Greenberry St STJWD NW8 3 N8
Greenbrook Av EBAR EN4 77 M5
Greenbury Cl RKW/CH/CXG WD3 70 F7
Green Chain Wk BMLY BR1 183 H8
BMLY BR1 183 K6
CHARL SE7 162 A3
ELTH/MOT SE9 184 A8
ELTH/MOT SE9 184 E1
SYD SE26 182 C9
THMD SE28 143 N10
WOOL/PLUM SE18 162 C5
Green Cl BRKMPK AL9 59 H2
CAR SM5 202 A9
CDALE/KGS NW9 115 P4
CHES/WCR EN8 62 D8
EPP CM16 46 E10
FELT TW13 175 M8
GLDGN NW11 117 M5
HAYES BR2 205 K3
Greencoates HERT/BAY SG13 25 M6
Greencoat Pl WEST SW1P 17 H5
Greencoat Rw WEST SW1P 17 H4
Green Common La BEAC HP9 108 C5
Green Court Av CROY/NA CR0 204 A9
Greencourt Av EDGW HA8 95 N9
Green Court Gdns CROY/NA CR0 204 A9
Greencourt Rd STMC/STPC BR5 207 H5
Green Court Rd SWLY BR8 208 E6
Green Cft HAT AL10 40 D1
Greencroft EDGW HA8 95 P6
GU GU1 250 E10
Greencroft Av RSLP HA4 113 K7
Greencroft Gdns EN EN1 79 M7
KIL/WHAMP NW6 3 J3
Greencroft Rd HEST TW5 153 N7
Green Curve BNSTD SM7 239 J1
Green Dl EDUL SE22 181 M1
Greendale Ms SLN SL2 129 M9
Greendale Wk GVW DA11 190 B6
Green Dell Wy HHS/BOV HP3 36 D6
Green Dene EHSLY KT24 270 D1
Green Dragon La BTFD TW8 155 K4
WCHMH N21 78 G9
Green Dragon Yd WCHPL E1 13 N4
Green Dr RPLY/SEND GU23 233 J9
STHL UB1 133 P10
Green East Rd BEAC HP9 89 K8
Greene Fielde End STA TW18 173 N10
Greene Field Rd BERK HP4 33 P5
Green End CHSGTN KT9 219 J1
WCHMH N21 99 J3
Green End Gdns HHW HP1 35 K7
Green End La HHW HP1 35 J6
Greenend Rd CHSWK W4 156 B1
Green End Rd HHW HP1 35 K7
Greenes Ct BERK HP4 33 P4
Greene Wk BERK HP4 34 A6
Green Farm Cl ORP BR6 227 J2
Green Farm La GVE DA12 191 P6
Greenfell Man DEPT SE8 * 160 E4
Greenfern Av SL SL1 128 B8
Greenfield BRKMPK AL9 40 G1
WGCW AL8 22 G2
Greenfield Av BRYLDS KT5 199 N7
OXHEY WD19 93 M3
Greenfield Ct ELTH/MOT SE9 184 B6
Greenfield Dr BMLY BR1 205 P2
EFNCH N2 118 A2
Greenfield End CFSP/GDCR SL9 90 C8
Greenfield Gdns CRICK NW2 117 H7
DAGW RM9 143 M3
STMC/STPC BR5 206 F7
Greenfield Link COUL/CHIP CR5 240 F1
Greenfield Rd DAGW RM9 143 N3
RDART DA2 186 E8
SEVS/STOTM N15 119 M3
WCHPL E1 13 P5
Greenfields LOU IG10 82 D8
POTB/CUF EN6 * 60 F6
STHL UB1 133 P9
Greenfields Cl HORL RH6 279 P2
Greenfields Rd HORL RH6 279 P2
Greenfield St WAB EN9 63 H10
Greenfield Wy RYLN/HDSTN HA2 114 A1
Greenfinches HART DA3 211 N3
Greenford Av HNWL W7 134 D7
STHL UB1 133 N9
Greenford Gdns GFD/PVL UB6 134 A5
Greenford Rd HRW HA1 114 D9
STHL UB1 134 B9
SUT SM1 221 L1
Green Gdns ORP BR6 226 F2
Greengate GFD/PVL UB6 134 G1
Greengate St PLSTW E13 141 N4
Green Gld EPP CM16 83 H3
Green Glades EMPK RM11 125 N4
Greenhalgh Wk EFNCH N2 117 M2
Greenham Cl STHWK SE1 18 A2
Greenham Crs CHING E4 100 E7
Greenham Rd MUSWH N10 98 B10
Greenham Wk
WOKN/KNAP GU21 231 P4
Greenhaven Dr THMD SE28 143 M8
Greenhayes Av BNSTD SM7 239 K1
Greenhayes Cl REIG RH2 257 M10
Greenhayes Gdns BNSTD SM7 239 K1
Greenheys Cl NTHWD HA6 92 F9
Greenheys Dr SWFD E18 121 L1
Greenheys Pl WOKS/MYFD GU22 232 C4
Green Hl ORP BR6 226 B8
WOOL/PLUM SE18 162 C4
Greenhill BKHH IG9 101 P2
HAMP NW3 117 N9
SUT SM1 201 M9
WBLY HA9 115 N7
Greenhill Av CTHM CR3 242 A7
Greenhill Ct BAR EN5 * 77 L9
Greenhill Crs WATW WD18 72 F10
Greenhill Gdns NTHLT UB5 133 N4
RGUE GU4 250 F7
Greenhill Gv MNPK E12 122 B9
Greenhill La WARL CR6 242 D3
Greenhill Pde BAR EN5 * 77 L9
Greenhill Pk BAR EN5 77 M9
WLSDN NW10 136 B3
Greenhill Rd GVW DA11 190 C5
HRW HA1 114 D4
RSEV TN14 247 K1
WLSDN NW10 136 B3
Greenhills HLW CM20 47 H1
Greenhills Cl RKW/CH/CXG WD3 71 L9
Greenhill's Rents FARR EC1M * 12 C3
Greenhills Ter IS N1 7 H2
Greenhill Ter NTHLT UB5 * 133 N4
WOOL/PLUM SE18 162 C4
Greenhill Wy HRW HA1 114 D4
WBLY HA9 115 N7
Greenhithe Cl BFN/LL DA15 185 H3
Greenholm Rd ELTH/MOT SE9 184 E1
Green Hundred Rd PECK SE15 19 P10
Greenhurst La OXTED RH8 261 M8
Greenhurst Rd WNWD SE27 181 H8
Greening St ABYW SE2 163 M3
Greenlake Ter STA TW18 * 173 K10
Greenland Crs NWDGN UB2 153 K2
Greenland Ms DEPT SE8 160 C4
Greenland Pl CAMTN NW1 4 F5
Greenland Quay
BERM/RHTH SE16 160 D3
Greenland Rd BAR EN5 76 F10
CAMTN NW1 4 G5
Greenlands CHERT KT16 194 F10
HOR/WEW KT19 219 N2
Greenlands Rd BGR/WK TN15 247 P5
STA TW18 173 K7
WEY KT13 196 C10
Greenland St CAMTN NW1 4 F5
Greenland Wy CROY/NA CR0 202 E7
Green La AMS HP6 69 J1
ASC SL5 192 D1
ASHTD KT21 237 H3
BCTR RM8 124 A7
BF/WBF KT14 216 A8
BROX EN10 44 G9
BRW CM14 106 F2
BRW CM14 106 F8
BRWN CM15 87 H10
CDW/CHF RM16 147 P7
CHERT KT16 195 H9
CHIG IG7 102 F2
CHIG IG7 103 H4
CHING E4 * 81 K7
CHOB/PIR GU24 213 L6
CHSGTN KT9 219 K5
COB KT11 217 M8
CRAWE RH10 285 N1
CSHM HP5 51 N9
CTHM CR3 241 K9
DTCH/LGLY SL3 149 N7
E/WMO/HCT KT8 198 A5
EDGW HA8 95 L5
EGH TW20 172 E8
EGH TW20 194 F2
ELTH/MOT SE9 184 E5
ELTH/MOT SE9 184 E7
FELT TW13 175 M8
GODL GU7 267 K8
GU GU1 250 E10
HDN NW4 116 G3
HHNE HP2 36 D7
HHS/BOV HP3 52 D4
HLWE CM17 48 C2
HNWL W7 154 D1
HORL RH6 280 G9
HSLWW TW4 175 K1
IL IG1 122 G7
KWD/TDW/WH KT20 257 J2
LHD/OX KT22 237 J7
MRDN SM4 201 L7
NTHWD HA6 92 E8
NWMAL KT3 199 P5
OXHEY WD19 93 K2
PGE/AN SE20 182 C10
PUR/KEN CR8 222 D7
RDKG RH5 278 A7
REDH RH1 257 P8
REDH RH1 276 B5
REIG RH2 257 J10
RGUE GU4 251 K3
RGUW GU3 248 F8
RKW/CH/CXG WD3 72 A9
RPLY/SEND GU23 234 C10
SHPTN TW17 196 E6
SL SL1 128 C4
STA TW18 195 H1
STALW/RED AL3 38 B3
STAN HA7 94 G5
SUN TW16 174 G10
THHTH CR7 203 J1
UX/CGN UB8 132 D7
WAB EN9 82 A1
WDSR SL4 148 F8
WGCE AL7 23 M7
WOT/HER KT12 217 J2
WPK KT4 200 E7
Green Lane Av WOT/HER KT12 217 J2
Green Lane Cl BF/WBF KT14 216 A8
CHERT KT16 195 H9
HARP AL5 20 D3
Green La Cottages STAN HA7 * 94 G5
Green Lane Ct SL SL1 128 B5
Green Lane Gdns THHTH CR7 203 K2
Green Lanes FSBYPK N4 119 K6
HAT AL10 40 C1
HOR/WEW KT19 220 B5
PLMGR N13 98 G6
SEVS/STOTM N15 119 J1
WCHMH N21 99 K2
WGCW AL8 22 C7
Green La West EHSLY KT24 252 B1
Greenlaw Ct EA W5 * 135 J8
Greenlaw Gdns NWMAL KT3 200 C7
Greenlawn La BTFD TW8 155 J4
Green Lawns
NFNCH/WDSPK N12 * 97 L7
RSLP HA4 * 113 K6
Greenlaw St WOOL/PLUM SE18 162 D2
Green Leaf Av WLGTN SM6 222 E1
Greenleaf Cl BRXS/STRHM SW2 * 181 H3
Greenleaf Ct DTCH/LGLY SL3 149 M5
Greenleafe Dr BARK/HLT IG6 122 E1
Greenleaf Rd EHAM E6 141 P3
WALTH E17 120 E1
Greenlea Pk WIM/MER SW19 * 201 P1
Green Leas SUN TW16 174 G10
Green Leas Cl SUN TW16 174 G9
Greenleaves Ct ASHF TW15 * 174 C9
Greenleigh Av STMC/STPC BR5 207 L4
Greenlink Wk RCH/KEW TW9 155 N7
Green Man La EBED/NFELT TW14 153 H10
WEA W13 134 F9
Greenman St IS N1 6 E4
Green Md ESH/CLAY KT10 217 N3
Greenmead Cl SNWD SE25 203 P5
Green Meadow POTB/CUF EN6 59 K6
Greenmeads WOKS/MYFD GU22 232 B8
Green Moor Link WCHMH N21 99 J1
Greenmoor Rd PEND EN3 80 B6
Green North Rd BEAC HP9 89 K7
Greenoak Pl EBAR EN4 78 A6
Greenoak Ri BH/WHM TN16 243 P4
Green Oaks NWDGN UB2 * 153 L3
Greenoak Wy WIM/MER SW19 178 G7
Greenock Rd ACT W3 155 N2
SL SL1 128 F8
STRHM/NOR SW16 202 E1
Greenock Wy ROM RM1 104 F8
Greeno Crs SHPTN TW17 196 B5
Green Pde HSLW TW3 * 176 A2
Green Pk STA TW18 173 H6
Greenpark Wy GFD/PVL UB6 134 D3
Green Pond Cl WALTH E17 120 E1
Green Pond Rd WALTH E17 120 D1
Green Ride CHING E4 81 M10
LOU IG10 81 N8
Green Rd EGH TW20 194 E4
STHGT/OAK N14 78 C10
TRDG/WHET N20 97 M4
Greenroof Wy GNWCH SE10 161 L2
Greensand Cl REDH RH1 258 E4
Greensand Rd REDH RH1 258 B9
Greensand Wy BH/WHM TN16 263 H7
BRKHM/BTCW RH3 256 D10
DORK RH4 272 D3
EDEN TN8 262 F7
GDST RH9 260 C10
OXTED RH8 261 K2
OXTED RH8 261 K7
OXTED RH8 261 M6
OXTED RH8 262 A7
OXTED RH8 262 C7
RDKG RH5 254 C10
REDH RH1 259 J10
REDH RH1 275 P3
REDH RH1 276 A3
REDH RH1 277 J2
REIG RH2 257 H8
RSEV TN14 264 E8
SEV TN13 265 K2
The Greens Cl LOU IG10 82 D6
Greens Ct NTGHL W11 * 8 C10
SOHO/CST W1F 11 J7
Greens End WOOL/PLUM SE18 162 E3
Greenshank Cl WALTH E17 100 D8
Greenshaw BRW CM14 106 G2
Greenside BCTR RM8 123 M7
BORE WD6 75 M4
BXLY DA5 185 P4
RPLY/SEND GU23 * 233 M7
SLN SL2 128 F7
SWLY BR8 208 E2
Greenside Cl CAT SE6 183 J5
RGUE GU4 250 F8
TRDG/WHET N20 97 N3
Greenside Dr ASHTD KT21 236 C4
Greenside Rd CROY/NA CR0 203 H7
SHB W12 156 D2
Greenslade Rd BARK IG11 142 G2
Greensleeves Cl STALE/WH AL4 39 H7
Green Sleeves Dr BRW CM14 106 G6
Greenstead SBW CM21 29 P2
Greenstead Av WFD IG8 101 P7
Greenstead Gdns
PUT/ROE SW15 178 D1
WFD IG8 101 P7
Greensted Rd CHONG CM5 67 H4
LOU IG10 102 C1
Greenstone Ms WAN E11 121 M4
Green St BORE WD6 75 M3
BRKMPK AL9 41 L6
FSTGT E7 121 N10
HLWE CM17 29 N10
MYFR/PKLN W1K 10 B7
PEND EN3 80 C7
RAD WD7 75 M1
RKW/CH/CXG WD3 70 F6
SUN TW16 197 H1
Green Street Green Rd
RDART DA2 188 C7
RDART DA2 210 G1
Greenstreet Hl NWCR SE14 * 160 C9
Greensward BUSH WD23 74 A10
Green Ter CLKNW EC1R 6 B10
The Green ACT W3 136 B8
ASHF TW15 * 173 N8
BERK HP4 34 E3
BH/WHM TN16 * 245 M10
BH/WHM TN16 262 G2
BKHH IG9 * 101 N2
BXLYHN DA7 164 B7
CAR SM5 * 222 B1
CHES/WCR EN8 62 B4
CRAWE RH10 285 J2
CRAWW RH11 283 M6
CROY/NA CR0 224 E5
CTHM CR3 242 F9
ED N9 99 P3
EGH TW20 171 P7
EPP CM16 82 G2
EPP CM16 83 H3
EW KT17 220 D8
FELT TW13 175 J5
GDST RH9 260 A8
HARH RM3 105 K4
HAYES BR2 205 M7
HEST TW5 153 P5
HGDN/ICK UB10 112 D7
HRW HA1 114 F7
KWD/TDW/WH KT20 238 G9
KWD/TDW/WH KT20 239 H5
LCOL/BKTW AL2 * 57 J3
LHD/OX KT22 236 C10
MRDN SM4 201 H4
NWDGN UB2 153 N1
NWMAL KT3 199 P3
ORP BR6 * 227 M6
RAIN RM13 145 M9
RCH/KEW TW9 177 J1
RDART DA2 188 C5
RKW/CH/CXG WD3 72 A10
SCUP DA14 185 K8
SEV TN13 247 L8
SL SL1 149 J1
SRTFD E15 141 L1
STHGT/OAK N14 98 E4
STMC/STPC BR5 185 L10
STWL/WRAY TW19 172 B2
SUT SM1 201 L10
TOTM N17 99 K7
WAB EN9 63 H10
WAN E11 121 N4
WCHMH N21 99 H1
WDR/YW UB7 151 N2
WELL DA16 163 H10
WHTN TW2 176 D4
WLGTN SM6 202 B9
Green Tiles DEN/HRF UB9 * 111 J5
Green Tiles La DEN/HRF UB9 111 J4
Green Trees EPP CM16 65 K7
Green V BXLYHS DA6 185 N1
EA W5 135 L8
WGCE AL7 23 K6
Greenvale Rd ELTH/MOT SE9 162 C10
WOKN/KNAP GU21 231 J5
Green Verges STAN HA7 95 J8
Green Vw CHSGTN KT9 219 L4
Greenview Av BECK BR3 204 D6
Greenview Cl ACT W3 136 B10
Green View Cl HHS/BOV HP3 52 D5
Green Wk CHONG CM5 67 N6
CRAWE RH10 283 P5
DART DA1 164 G10
HDN NW4 116 G3
NWDGN UB2 153 P4
RSLP HA4 112 G6
STHWK SE1 19 J4
WFD IG8 102 B7
The Green Wk CHING E4 101 H2
Green Wy ELTH/MOT SE9 184 A1
HART DA3 211 K5
HAYES BR2 206 B6
REDH RH1 257 P8
SL SL1 128 A5
SUN TW16 197 H4
Greenway BCTR RM8 123 M7
BERK HP4 33 M5
BH/WHM TN16 243 P6
CHST BR7 184 D8
CSHM HP5 50 G4
GT/LBKH KT23 236 A9
HARH RM3 106 A7
HARP AL5 20 C3
HHNE HP2 36 C6
HLWW/ROY CM19 46 B1
KTN/HRWW/WS HA3 115 K3
PIN HA5 93 J10
RBRW/HUT CM13 107 M1
RYNPK SW20 200 F4
STHGT/OAK N14 98 F3
TRDG/WHET N20 97 K3
WLGTN SM6 222 D1
YEAD UB4 133 J6
Greenway Av WALTH E17 121 J2
Greenway Cl BF/WBF KT14 215 K9
CDALE/KGS NW9 96 A10
FBAR/BDGN N11 98 B7
FSBYPK N4 119 K7
TRDG/WHET N20 97 K3
Greenway Ct IL IG1 122 D6
SRTFD E15 141 K4
Greenway Dr STA TW18 195 M1
Greenway Gdns CDALE/KGS NW9 95 P10
CDALE/KGS NW9 96 A10
CROY/NA CR0 204 E10
GFD/PVL UB6 133 P5
Green Way Gdns
KTN/HRWW/WS HA3 94 D10
Greenways ABLGY WD5 54 E7
BECK BR3 204 F2
CHESW EN7 61 J5
EGH TW20 172 B9
ESH/CLAY KT10 218 D1
HERT/WAT SG14 25 J5
KWD/TDW/WH KT20 256 D1
NFNCH/WDSPK N12 * 97 M7
Greenways Dr ASC SL5 192 D8
The Greenways TWK TW1 * 176 F2
The Green Wy
KTN/HRWW/WS HA3 94 D9
The Greenway CDALE/KGS NW9 96 A10
CFSP/GDCR SL9 110 A1
EPSOM KT18 219 M10
HGDN/ICK UB10 112 C7
HSLWW TW4 * 153 N10
OXTED RH8 261 M9
PEND EN3 80 C1
PIN HA5 113 N4
POTB/CUF EN6 59 K9
RKW/CH/CXG WD3 91 K1
SL SL1 128 C10
UX/CGN UB8 131 N4
Greenwell Cl GDST RH9 260 A6
Greenwell St GTPST W1W 10 F2
Green West Rd BEAC HP9 89 K8
Greenwich Church St
GNWCH SE10 * 161 H5
Greenwich Crs EHAM E6 142 B7
Greenwich Foot Tnl
GNWCH SE10 161 H4
Greenwich Hts CHARL SE7 * 162 B6
Greenwich High Rd
GNWCH SE10 160 G6
Greenwich Park St
GNWCH SE10 * 161 J5
Greenwich Quay DEPT SE8 160 G5
Greenwich South St
GNWCH SE10 160 G7
Greenwich Vw POP/IOD E14 160 G2
Greenwich Wy WAB EN9 81 J2
Greenwood Av CHESW EN7 62 A7
DAGE RM10 124 C9
PEND EN3 80 D5
Greenwood Cl ADL/WDHM KT15 215 J7
AMS HP6 * 69 K4
BEAC HP9 89 J7
BFN/LL DA15 185 K5
CHESW EN7 62 A7
MRDN SM4 201 H4
STMC/STPC BR5 207 H6
THDIT KT7 198 F8
Greenwood Cottages ASC SL5 193 H6
Greenwood Dr CHING E4 101 H6
GSTN WD25 55 J10
REDH RH1 276 B5
Greenwood Gdns BARK/HLT IG6 102 F8
CTHM CR3 259 P1
OXTED RH8 261 M10
PLMGR N13 99 J4
RAD WD7 57 K9
Greenwood La HPTN TW12 176 A8
Greenwood Pk KUTN/CMB KT2 178 B10
Greenwood Pl KTTN NW5 118 C10
Greenwood Rd BXLY DA5 186 E7
CHIG IG7 103 L5
CHOB/PIR GU24 230 A7
CROY/NA CR0 203 J7
HACK E8 7 P1
ISLW TW7 154 D9
MTCM CR4 202 E3
PLSTW E13 141 L4
THDIT KT7 198 F8
WOKN/KNAP GU21 231 K6
Greenwood Ter WLSDN NW10 * 136 A3
The Greenwood GU GU1 250 D10
Greenwood Wy SEV TN13 264 G1
Green Wrythe Crs CAR SM5 201 P8
Green Wrythe La CAR SM5 201 N6
CAR SM5 201 P8
Green Yd FSBYW WC1X 11 P1
Greenyard WAB EN9 63 H9
Greer Rd KTN/HRWW/WS HA3 94 B9
Greet St STHWK SE1 12 B10
Greg Cl LEY E10 121 H4
Gregories Farm La BEAC HP9 88 C9
Gregories Rd BEAC HP9 88 B8
Gregor Ms BKHTH/KID SE3 161 M6
Gregory Av POTB/CUF EN6 59 M9
Gregory Cl WOKN/KNAP GU21 231 P3
Gregory Crs ELTH/MOT SE9 184 A3
Gregory Dr WDSR SL4 171 N2
Gregory Ms WAB EN9 62 G8
Gregory Pl KENS W8 14 G1
Gregory Rd CHDH RM6 123 N2
NWDGN UB2 153 P2
SLN SL2 109 J7
Gregson Cl BORE WD6 75 P6
Greig Cl CEND/HSY/T N8 118 F3
Greig Ter WALW SE17 18 D9
Grenaby Av CROY/NA CR0 203 L7
Grenaby Rd CROY/NA CR0 203 L7
Grenada Rd BKHTH/KID SE3 161 P6
Grenade St POP/IOD E14 140 E9
Grenadier Cl STALE/WH AL4 39 H7
Grenadier Pl CTHM CR3 241 K8
Grenadier St CAN/RD E16 142 D10
Grenadine Cl CHESW EN7 61 N3
Grena Gdns RCH/KEW TW9 155 L10
Grenard Cl PECK SE15 * 159 P6
Grena Rd RCH/KEW TW9 155 L10
Grendon Cl HORL RH6 280 A2
Grendon Gdns WBLY HA9 115 M7
Grendon St STJWD NW8 9 N1
Grenfell Av HCH RM12 124 G6
Grenfell Cl BORE WD6 75 P5
Grenfell Ct MLHL NW7 * 96 E7
Grenfell Gdns
KTN/HRWW/WS HA3 115 K5
Grenfell Rd BEAC HP9 88 D8
MTCM CR4 180 A10
NTGHL W11 136 G9
Grennell Cl SUT SM1 201 N9
Grennell Rd SUT SM1 201 M9
Grenoble Gdns PLMGR N13 99 H7
Grenside Rd WEY KT13 196 C10
Grenville Av BROX EN10 44 E7
Grenville Cl BRYLDS KT5 199 P8
CHES/WCR EN8 62 C8
COB KT11 217 L9
FNCH N3 97 J9
SL SL1 128 A4
Grenville Gdns WFD IG8 101 P8
Grenville Ms ARCH N19 118 F6
HPTN TW12 176 A8
Grenville Pl MLHL NW7 96 A6
SKENS SW7 15 J5
Grenville Rd ARCH N19 118 F6
CDW/CHF RM16 166 G4
CROY/NA CR0 225 H6
MFD/CHID GU8 266 C10
Grenville St BMSBY WC1N 11 M2
Gresford Cl STALE/WH AL4 39 J6
Gresham Almshouses
BRXN/ST SW9 * 158 G10
Gresham Av HART DA3 211 L5
TRDG/WHET N20 98 A5
WARL CR6 242 D4
Gresham Cl BXLY DA5 185 P2
ENC/FH EN2 79 K7
OXTED RH8 261 L5
Gresham Ct BERK HP4 33 N6
BRW CM14 107 H4
Gresham Dr CHDH RM6 123 L3
Gresham Gdns GLDGN NW11 117 H6
Gresham Rd BECK BR3 204 D2
BRW CM14 107 H4
BRXN/ST SW9 159 H9
CAN/RD E16 141 N8
EDGW HA8 95 L7
EHAM E6 142 C4
HGDN/ICK UB10 132 B4
HPTN TW12 175 P9
HSLW TW3 154 B7
OXTED RH8 261 L5
SL SL1 128 F8
SNWD SE25 * 203 P4
STA TW18 173 J8
WLSDN NW10 116 A10
Gresham St CITYW EC2V 12 E5
Gresham Wk CRAWE RH10 283 P10
Gresham Wy WIM/MER SW19 179 K6
Gresley Cl SEVS/STOTM N15 * 119 L2
WALTH E17 120 D4
WGCW AL8 23 H4
Gresley Rd ARCH N19 118 D6
Gressenhall Rd
WAND/EARL SW18 179 J2
Gresse St FITZ W1T 11 J4
Gresswell Cl SCUP DA14 185 K6
Greswell St FUL/PGN SW6 156 G7
Greta Bank EHSLY KT24 252 D2
Gretton Rd TOTM N17 99 M8
Greville Av SAND/SEL CR2 224 C6
Greville Cl ASHTD KT21 237 K5
BRKMPK AL9 40 E10
GUW GU2 249 K10
TWK TW1 176 G3
Greville Ct GT/LBKH KT23 254 B1
Greville Ms KIL/WHAMP NW6 2 G6

Greville Park Av ASHTD KT21 237 K4
Greville Park Rd ASHTD KT21 237 K4
Greville Pl KIL/WHAMP NW6 3 H7
Greville Rd KIL/WHAMP NW6 2 G6
RCHPK/HAM TW10 177 L2
WALTH E17 121 H2
Greville St HCIRC EC1N 12 B4
Grey Alders BNSTD SM7 220 F10
Greycaine Rd WATN WD24 73 L3
Grey Cl GLDGN NW11 117 M4
Greycoat Pl WEST SW1P 17 J4
Greycoat St WEST SW1P 17 J4
Greycot Rd BECK BR3 182 F8
Grey Eagle St WCHPL E1 13 M3
Greyfell Cl STAN HA7 94 G6
Greyfields Cl PUR/KEN CR8 223 J9
Greyfriars RBRW/HUT CM13 107 N1
Greyfriars Dr ASC SL5 192 A6
CHOB/PIR GU24 230 F1
Greyfriars Rd RPLY/SEND GU23 233 K10
Greygoose Pk HLWW/ROY CM19 46 D4
Greyhound Hl HDN NW4 116 D1
Greyhound La CDW/CHF RM16 168 D1
POTB/CUF EN6 58 D9
STRHM/NOR SW16 180 F9
Greyhound Rd HMSMTH W6 156 G5
SUT SM1 221 M2
TOTM N17 119 M1
WLSDN NW10 136 E5
Greyhound Slip CRAWE RH10 284 E6
Greyhound Ter
STRHM/NOR SW16 202 D1
Greyhound Wy DART DA1 186 F1
Greyladies Gdns GNWCH SE10 * 161 H8
Greys Park Cl HAYES BR2 225 P2
Greystead Rd FSTH SE23 182 B3
Greystoke Av PIN HA5 113 P1
Greystoke Cl BERK HP4 33 M6
Greystoke Cottages EA W5 * 135 K6
Greystoke Dr RSLP HA4 112 C5
Greystoke Gdns EA W5 135 K6
ENC/FH EN2 78 E8
Greystoke Rd SLN SL2 128 E7
Greystone Cl SAND/SEL CR2 224 B7
Greystone Gdns BARK/HLT IG6 102 F10
KTN/HRWW/WS HA3 115 H4
Greystone Pk RSEV TN14 263 P1
Greystones Av UED N18 * 100 C6
Greystones Cl BGR/WK TN15 247 M3
REDH RH1 275 N2
Greystones Dr REIG RH2 257 M8
Greyswood St
STRHM/NOR SW16 180 C9
Greythorne Rd
WOKN/KNAP GU21 231 M4
Grey Towers Av EMPK RM11 125 L6
Grey Towers Gdns EMPK RM11 125 K6
Grice Av BH/WHM TN16 225 N9
Gridiron Pl UPMR RM14 126 A7
Grier Cl CRAWW RH11 283 H8
Grierson Rd FSTH SE23 182 D2
Grieves Rd GVW DA11 190 C6
Griffin Av UPMR RM14 126 D4
Griffin Centre
EBED/NFELT TW14 * 175 J2
Griffin Cl SL SL1 149 H1
WLSDN NW10 116 E10
Griffin Ct ASHTD KT21 * 237 K5
Griffin Manor Wy THMD SE28 162 G2
Griffin Rd TOTM N17 99 M10
WOOL/PLUM SE18 162 G4
Griffins Cl WCHMH N21 99 L2
The Griffins CDW/CHF RM16 167 N1
Griffin Wk RDART DA2 188 E1
Griffin Wy GT/LBKH KT23 253 P2
SUN TW16 197 H2
THMD SE28 163 H2
Griffith Cl BCTR RM8 123 M5
Griffiths Rd WIM/MER SW19 179 K10
Griffiths Wy STAL AL1 38 B8
Griffon Wy GSTN WD25 54 G10
Grifon Cl CDW/CHF RM16 167 H2
Grifon Rd CDW/CHF RM16 167 J2
Griggs Ap IL IG1 122 F7
Griggs Gdns HCH RM12 125 K10
Grigg's Pl STHWK SE1 19 K4
Griggs Rd LEY E10 121 H4
Grimsby Gv CAN/RD E16 162 E1
Grimsby St BETH E2 13 M1
Grimsdells Cnr AMS HP6 * 69 J3
Grimsdell's La AMS HP6 69 J3
Grimsdyke Crs BAR EN5 76 F7
Grimsdyke Rd PIN HA5 93 M8
Grimsel Pth CMBW SE5 159 J6
Grimshaw Cl HGT N6 * 118 B5
Grimshaw Wy ROM RM1 124 F3
Grimston Rd FUL/PGN SW6 157 J8
STAL AL1 38 E7
Grimthorpe Cl STALW/RED AL3 38 B3
Grimwade Av CROY/NA CR0 203 P10
Grimwade Cl PECK SE15 160 A8
Grimwood Rd TWK TW1 176 E3
Grindall Cl CROY/NA CR0 223 J1
Grindal St STHWK SE1 18 A2
Grindcobbe Cl STAL AL1 38 C9
Grindleford Av FBAR/BDGN N11 98 B3
Grindley Gdns CROY/NA CR0 * 203 N6
Grindstone Crs
WOKN/KNAP GU21 230 G4
Grinling Pl DEPT SE8 160 F5
Grinstead Rd DEPT SE8 160 D4
Grisedale Cl CRAWW RH11 283 M9
PUR/KEN CR8 223 M10
Grisedale Gdns PUR/KEN CR8 223 M10
Grisle Cl ED N9 100 A5
Grittleton Av WBLY HA9 135 N1
Grittleton Rd MV/WKIL W9 8 E1
Grobars Av WOKN/KNAP GU21 231 P1
Grocers' Hall Ct LOTH EC2R * 12 G6
Groombridge Cl WELL DA16 185 K1
WOT/HER KT12 217 J2
Groombridge Rd HOM E9 140 C2
Groom Cl HAYES BR2 205 N4
Groom Crs WAND/EARL SW18 179 N3
Groomfield Cl TOOT SW17 180 B7
Groom Pl KTBR SW1X 16 D3
Groom Rd BROX EN10 62 E2
Grooms Cottages CSHM HP5 51 N6
Grooms Dr PIN HA5 113 H3
The Grooms CRAWE RH10 284 E6
Grosmont Rd
WOOL/PLUM SE18 163 J4
Grosse Wy PUT/ROE SW15 178 E2
Grosvenor Av CAR SM5 222 A3
HBRY N5 119 K10
KGLGY WD4 54 D4
MORT/ESHN SW14 156 B9
RYLN/HDSTN HA2 114 A5
YEAD UB4 132 G4
Grosvenor Br PIM SW1V 16 F9
Grosvenor Cl HORL RH6 280 B6
LOU IG10 82 E5
Grosvenor Cottages KTBR SW1X 16 C5
Grosvenor Ct
RKW/CH/CXG WD3 * 72 E9
Grosvenor Crs CDALE/KGS NW9 115 M2
DART DA1 187 L1
HGDN/ICK UB10 132 C2
KTBR SW1X 16 D2
Grosvenor Crescent Ms
KTBR SW1X 16 D2
Grosvenor Dr EMPK RM11 125 K6
LOU IG10 82 E6
Grosvenor Gdns BGVA SW1W 16 F4
CRICK NW2 136 F1
GLDGN NW11 117 J4
KUTN/CMB KT2 177 J9
MORT/ESHN SW14 156 B9
MUSWH N10 118 D1
STHGT/OAK N14 78 E9
UPMR RM14 126 C7
WFD IG8 101 M7
WLGTN SM6 222 D4
Grosvenor Gardens Ms East
BGVA SW1W * 16 F3
Grosvenor Gardens Ms North
BGVA SW1W 16 E4
Grosvenor Ga MYFR/PKLN W1K 10 B8
Grosvenor Hl MYFR/PKLN W1K 10 E7
WIM/MER SW19 179 H9
Grosvenor Ms REIG RH2 275 L3
Grosvenor Pde EA W5 * 135 M10
Grosvenor Pk CMBW SE5 18 E10
Grosvenor Park Rd WALTH E17 120 G3
Grosvenor Pl KTBR SW1X 16 E2
WEY KT13 196 E10
Grosvenor Ri East WALTH E17 120 G3
Grosvenor Rd BCTR RM8 124 A6
BELV DA17 164 A5
BORE WD6 75 M7
BROX EN10 44 E6
BTFD TW8 155 J5
BXLYHS DA6 185 N1
CHOB/PIR GU24 213 J9
CHSWK W4 155 P4
ED N9 100 A2
EHAM E6 142 A3
EPSOM KT18 238 B5
FNCH N3 97 J8
FSTGT E7 141 N1
HNWL W7 134 F10
HSLWW TW4 153 N9
IL IG1 122 F8
LEY E10 121 H6
MUSWH N10 98 C9
NTHWD HA6 92 G6
NWDGN UB2 153 N2
PIM SW1V 16 F9
RCHPK/HAM TW10 177 K1
SNWD SE25 203 P4
STA TW18 173 K10
STAL AL1 38 D7
STMC/STPC BR5 207 H6
TWK TW1 176 F3
WAN E11 121 N3
WAT WD17 73 K8
WLGTN SM6 222 C3
WWKM BR4 204 G9
Grosvenor Sq HART DA3 * 211 K3
KGLGY WD4 54 D4
MYFR/PKLN W1K 10 D7
Grosvenor St MYFR/PKLN W1K 10 D7
Grosvenor Ter CMBW SE5 18 E10
HHW HP1 35 K7
Grosvenor V RSLP HA4 112 G7
Grosvenor Wy CLPT E5 120 B7
Grosvenor Wharf Rd
POP/IOD E14 161 J3
Grote's Buildings BKHTH/KID SE3 161 K8
Grote's Pl BKHTH/KID SE3 161 K8
Groton Rd WAND/EARL SW18 179 L5
Grotto Ct STHWK SE1 * 18 E1
Grotto Pas MHST W1U 10 C3
Grotto Rd TWK TW1 176 E5
WEY KT13 196 C10
The Grotto WARE SG12 26 C3
Ground La HAT AL10 40 E2
Grove Av EW KT17 220 B9
HARP AL5 20 C4
HNWL W7 134 D8
MUSWH N10 98 D10
PIN HA5 113 M2
SUT SM1 221 K3
TWK TW1 176 E4
Grove Bank OXHEY WD19 * 93 L2
Grovebury Cl ERITH DA8 164 E5
Grovebury Ct STHGT/OAK N14 98 D1
Grovebury Gdns LCOL/BKTW AL2 56 B3
Grovebury Rd ABYW SE2 163 L1
Grove Cl CFSP/GDCR SL9 89 P9
FSTH SE23 182 C4
HAYES BR2 205 M9
HGDN/ICK UB10 112 B10
HOR/WEW KT19 219 M6
KUT/HW KT1 199 L4
SL SL1 149 M2
STHGT/OAK N14 * 98 C1
WDSR SL4 171 N3
Grove Cottages CHEL SW3 15 P9
CHSWK W4 * 156 B5
COB KT11 * 235 L2
Grove Ct E/WMO/HCT KT8 198 C5
EA W5 * 135 K10
EGH TW20 172 D8
WAB EN9 62 G9
Grove Crs CDALE/KGS NW9 115 P2
FELT TW13 175 M7
KUT/HW KT1 199 K3
RKW/CH/CXG WD3 72 B8
SWFD E18 101 L10
WOT/HER KT12 197 J7
Grove Crescent Rd SRTFD E15 141 K1
Grovedale Cl CHESW EN7 61 N6
Grovedale Rd ARCH N19 118 E7
Grove Dwellings WCHPL E1 * 140 B7
Grove End CFSP/GDCR SL9 89 P9
KTTN NW5 118 C9
SWFD E18 101 L10
Grove End La ESH/CLAY KT10 198 C8
Grove End Rd STJWD NW8 3 L10
Grove Farm Pk NTHWD HA6 92 E6
Grove Footpath BRYLDS KT5 199 K4
Grove Gdns HDN NW4 * 116 D3
PEND EN3 80 C5
STJWD NW8 3 P10
TEDD TW11 176 F7
Grove Green Rd WAN E11 121 H8
WAN E11 121 J6
Grove Hall Rd BUSH WD23 73 M8
Grove Heath La
RPLY/SEND GU23 233 M10
Grove Heath North
RPLY/SEND GU23 233 L9
Grove Heath Rd
RPLY/SEND GU23 233 L9
Groveherst Rd DART DA1 165 N9
Grove Hl CFSP/GDCR SL9 89 P8
HRW HA1 114 D5
SWFD E18 101 L10
Grove Hill Rd CMBW SE5 159 M9
HRW HA1 114 E5
Grovehill Rd REDH RH1 257 P10
Grove House Rd CEND/HSY/T N8 118 F2
Groveland Av STRHM/NOR SW16 180 G10
Groveland Ct STP EC4M 12 F6
Groveland Rd BECK BR3 204 E3
Grovelands E/WMO/HCT KT8 197 P4
HHNE HP2 36 D4
LCOL/BKTW AL2 56 A3
Grovelands Cl CMBW SE5 159 M8
RYLN/HDSTN HA2 114 A8
Grovelands Ct STHGT/OAK N14 98 E1
Grovelands Rd PLMGR N13 98 G5
PUR/KEN CR8 222 G8
SEVS/STOTM N15 119 P4
STMC/STPC BR5 185 L10
Grovelands Wy GRAYS RM17 167 L4
Groveland Wy NWMAL KT3 199 P5
Grove La CFSP/GDCR SL9 89 N9
CHIG IG7 103 J4
CMBW SE5 159 L7
COUL/CHIP CR5 240 C1
CSHM HP5 51 N3
EPP CM16 65 K6
KUT/HW KT1 199 K4
UX/CGN UB8 132 A6
Grove Lea HAT AL10 40 D7
Groveley Rd SUN TW16 174 G8
Grove Market Pl
ELTH/MOT SE9 * 184 C2
Grove Md HAT AL10 40 C4
Grove Meadow WGCE AL7 23 M5
Grove Ms HMSMTH W6 156 F2
Grove Mill La RKW/CH/CXG WD3 72 D4
Grove Mill Pl CAR SM5 202 B10
Grove Pk CDALE/KGS NW9 115 P2
CMBW SE5 159 M8
WAN E11 121 N3
Grove Park Av CHING E4 100 G8
Grove Park Br CHSWK W4 155 P6
Grove Park Gdns CHSWK W4 155 N6
Grove Park Rd CHSWK W4 155 N6
ELTH/MOT SE9 184 B5
RAIN RM13 145 H3
SEVS/STOTM N15 119 M2
Grove Park Ter CHSWK W4 155 N6
Grove Pl ACT W3 135 P10
BAL SW12 180 C2
BRKMPK AL9 40 F10
GSTN WD25 * 74 A5
HAMP NW3 117 N8
WEY KT13 216 D2
Grover Cl HHNE HP2 35 N5
Grove Rd ACT W3 135 P10
AMS HP6 69 L3
ASHTD KT21 237 L4
BARN SW13 156 C8
BEAC HP9 88 C9
BELV DA17 164 A5
BGR/WK TN15 247 P8
BH/WHM TN16 243 P6
BORE WD6 75 M5
BOW E3 140 D4
BTFD TW8 155 H4
BXLYHN DA7 164 D10
CHDH RM6 123 M5
CHERT KT16 195 J6
CHING E4 101 H4
CRICK NW2 136 F1
E/WMO/HCT KT8 198 C4
EA W5 135 J9
EBAR EN4 77 P7
EDGW HA8 95 M7
EW KT17 220 B9
FBAR/BDGN N11 98 C6
GRAYS RM17 167 P5
GU GU1 250 F10
GVW DA11 189 N1
HARP AL5 20 C4
HHW HP1 35 K8
HOM E9 140 C3
HORL RH6 279 P3
HSLW TW3 153 P10
ISLW TW7 154 D7
MTCM CR4 202 C2
NFNCH/WDSPK N12 97 N6
NTHWD HA6 92 E6
OXTED RH8 261 H9
PIN HA5 113 N3
RCHPK/HAM TW10 177 L2
RKW/CH/CXG WD3 91 K3
RSEV TN14 247 K7
SEVS/STOTM N15 119 M3
SHPTN TW17 196 D6
SL SL1 128 D2
STAL AL1 38 C7
SURB KT6 199 J5
SUT SM1 221 K3
SWFD E18 101 L10
THHTH CR7 203 H4
UX/CGN UB8 131 N2
WALTH E17 120 G3
WAN E11 121 L6
WARE SG12 26 E1
WDSR SL4 149 J8
WHTN TW2 176 C6
WIM/MER SW19 179 M10
WOKN/KNAP GU21 232 C2
Grove Rd West PEND EN3 80 B3
Grover Rd OXHEY WD19 73 L10
Grovers Farm Cottages
ADL/WDHM KT15 * 215 H7
Groves Cl SOCK/AV RM15 146 E9
Grove Shaw KWD/TDW/WH KT20 239 H10
Groveside GT/LBKH KT23 253 P3
Groveside Cl ACT W3 135 M8
CAR SM5 201 P9
GT/LBKH KT23 253 P3
Groveside Rd CHING E4 101 K4
Grovestile Waye
EBED/NFELT TW14 174 F4
Grove St BERM/RHTH SE16 160 E3
UED N18 99 N7
Grove Ter KTTN NW5 118 B8
STHL UB1 * 133 P9
TEDD TW11 176 F7
Grove Terrace Ms KTTN NW5 118 C8
The Grove ADL/WDHM KT15 215 L2
AMS HP6 69 J1
BH/WHM TN16 244 A4
BRKMPK AL9 59 K3
BRW CM14 106 E5
BXLYHS DA6 163 N10
CDALE/KGS NW9 116 A3
CEND/HSY/T N8 118 E3
COUL/CHIP CR5 240 E1
CRAWW RH11 283 M7
CSHM HP5 70 A3
CTHM CR3 241 J7
EA W5 135 J10
EDGW HA8 95 N5
EGH TW20 172 D8
ENC/FH EN2 79 H6
EW KT17 220 B9
FNCH N3 97 K8
FSBYPK N4 118 G5
GFD/PVL UB6 134 B8
GLDGN NW11 117 H5
GU GU1 * 268 C2
GVE DA12 190 E3
HARP AL5 * 20 D4
HGDN/ICK UB10 112 B10
HGT N6 118 B6
HORL RH6 280 C5
ISLW TW7 154 D7
KGLGY WD4 * 53 M6
PLMGR N13 99 H5
POTB/CUF EN6 59 M8
RAD WD7 56 F10
RKW/CH/CXG WD3 * 72 B8
SCUP DA14 185 P7
SL SL1 149 M1
SRTFD E15 141 K2
SWCM DA10 189 L1
SWLY BR8 208 G3
TEDD TW11 176 F7
UPMR RM14 125 P9
WOKN/KNAP GU21 232 C2
WOT/HER KT12 197 J7
WWKM BR4 205 H10
Grove V CHST BR7 184 D9
EDUL SE22 159 M10
Grove Wk HERT/WAT SG14 25 K3
Groveway BCTR RM8 123 N9
BRXN/ST SW9 158 G7
Grove Wy ESH/CLAY KT10 198 B8
RKW/CH/CXG WD3 70 E9
UX/CGN UB8 131 N2
WBLY HA9 115 P10
Grovewood Cl
RKW/CH/CXG WD3 70 E9
Grove Wood Hl COUL/CHIP CR5 222 E10
Grovewood Pl WFD IG8 102 C7
Grubbs La BRKMPK AL9 41 K8
Grub St OXTED RH8 261 P4
Grummant Rd PECK SE15 159 N7
Grundy St POP/IOD E14 140 G8
Gruneisen Rd FNCH N3 97 L8
Guardian Av CDW/CHF RM16 167 J1
Guardian Cl EMPK RM11 125 J7
Guards Av CTHM CR3 241 K8
Guards Ct ASC SL5 192 G7
Guardsman Cl BRW CM14 107 J6
Guards Rd WDSR SL4 148 B8
Gubbins La HARH RM3 105 N9
Gubyon Av HNHL SE24 181 K1
Guernsey Cl HEST TW5 153 P7
RGUE GU4 250 D5
Guernsey Farm Dr
WOKN/KNAP GU21 * 232 A1
Guernsey Gv HNHL SE24 181 K3
Guernsey Rd IS N1 6 F2
LEY E10 121 J6
Guessens Gv WGCW AL8 22 F5
Guessens Rd WGCW AL8 22 F5
Guessens Wk WGCW AL8 22 F4
Guibal Rd LEE/GVPK SE12 183 N4
Guildables Lane EDEN TN8 262 B10
Guildcroft GU GU1 250 D10
Guildersfield Rd
STRHM/NOR SW16 180 F10
Guildford Av FELT TW13 174 G5
Guildford Business Park Rd
GUW GU2 249 N9
Guildford Gv GNWCH SE10 160 G7
Guildford La SHGR GU5 269 K4
Guildford Park Av GUW GU2 267 N1
Guildford Park Rd GUW GU2 267 N1
Guildford Rd CHERT KT16 194 G10
CHERT KT16 195 J8
CHERT KT16 214 E6
CHERT KT16 214 F3
CHOB/PIR GU24 212 D8
CROY/NA CR0 203 L6
DORK RH4 272 A4
EHAM E6 142 B8
EHSLY KT24 253 K4
GDMY/SEVK IG3 123 H7
GT/LBKH KT23 253 N4
HARH RM3 105 M7
LHD/OX KT22 236 D10
LHD/OX KT22 236 F8
LTWR GU18 212 A6
RDKG RH5 270 G6
RGUE GU4 249 P1
STAL AL1 38 G7
VX/NE SW8 158 F7
WALTH E17 101 H9
WOKS/MYFD GU22 232 A10
WOKS/MYFD GU22 232 B4
Guildford St CHERT KT16 195 K7
STA TW18 173 K9
Guildford Wy WLGTN SM6 222 F2
Guildhall Buildings CITYW EC2V 12 F5
Guildhall Yd CITYW EC2V 12 F5
Guildhouse St PIM SW1V 16 G6
Guildown Av GUW GU2 267 N3
NFNCH/WDSPK N12 97 L5
Guildown Rd GUW GU2 267 N3
Guild Rd CHARL SE7 162 A4
ERITH DA8 164 G6
Guildsway WALTH E17 100 E9
Guileshill La RPLY/SEND GU23 233 P8
Guilford Av BRYLDS KT5 199 L5
Guilford Pl BMSBY WC1N 11 N2
Guilfords HLWE CM17 29 N6
Guilford St BMSBY WC1N 11 N2
Guillemot Pl WDGN N22 * 98 G10
Guilsborough Cl WLSDN NW10 136 B2
Guinery Gv HHS/BOV HP3 36 A10
Guinevere Gdns CHES/WCR EN8 62 C6
Guinevere Rd CRAWW RH11 283 H7
Guinness Cl HOM E9 140 D2
HYS/HAR UB3 152 E2
Guinness Ct CROY/NA CR0 * 203 N9
Guinness Sq STHWK SE1 19 J5
Guinness Trust
STNW/STAM N16 * 119 N6
Guinness Trust Est CHEL SW3 16 A6
SRTFD E15 * 141 L3
Guion Rd FUL/PGN SW6 157 J8
Gulland Cl BUSH WD23 74 B9
Gulland Wk IS N1 * 6 F2
Gullbrook HHW HP1 35 K6
Gullet Wood Rd GSTN WD25 73 H1
Gulliver Cl NTHLT UB5 133 N3
Gulliver Rd BFN/LL DA15 184 G5
Gulliver St BERM/RHTH SE16 160 E2
The Gulphs HERT/BAY SG13 25 L6
Gumbrells Cl RGUW GU3 249 H6
Gumleigh Rd EA W5 155 H3
Gumley Gdns ISLW TW7 154 F9
Gumley Rd WTHK RM20 167 J5
Gumping Rd STMC/STPC BR5 206 F9
Gundulph Rd HAYES BR2 205 P3
Gunfleet Cl GVE DA12 191 H3
Gun Hl TIL RM18 168 G5
Gunmakers La BOW E3 140 D3
Gunnell Cl CROY/NA CR0 203 N6
SYD SE26 * 181 P7
Gunner Dr PEND EN3 80 F3
Gunner La WOOL/PLUM SE18 162 D4
Gunnersbury Av ACT W3 155 M3
Gunnersbury Av
(North Circular Rd) ACT W3 155 M2
EA W5 135 L9
Gunnersbury Cl CHSWK W4 * 155 N4
Gunnersbury Crs ACT W3 155 M1
Gunnersbury Dr EA W5 155 L1
Gunnersbury Gdns ACT W3 155 M1
Gunnersbury La ACT W3 155 M1
Gunnersbury Ms CHSWK W4 155 N4
Gunners Gv CHING E4 101 H4
Gunners Rd TOOT SW17 179 N5
Gunning Cl CRAWW RH11 283 K10
Gunning Rd GRAYS RM17 167 P4
Gunning St WOOL/PLUM SE18 163 H3
Gunn Rd SWCM DA10 189 K2
Gunstor Rd STNW/STAM N16 * 119 M9
Gun St WCHPL E1 13 L4
Gunter Gv EDGW HA8 96 A9
WBPTN SW10 15 J10
Gunters Md LHD/OX KT22 * 218 B7
Gunterstone Rd WKENS W14 14 B7
WKENS W14 157 H4
Gunthorpe St WCHPL E1 13 M4
Gunton Rd CLPT E5 120 A8
TOOT SW17 180 B9
Gunwhale Cl BERM/RHTH SE16 140 C10
Gunyard Ms WOOL/PLUM SE18 * 162 B6
Gurdon Rd CHARL SE7 161 M4
Gurnard Cl WDR/YW UB7 131 N9
Gurnell Gv WEA W13 134 E6
Gurnells Rd BEAC HP9 89 H6
Gurney Cl BARK IG11 142 E1
BEAC HP9 88 B9
SRTFD E15 121 K10
WALTH E17 100 C9
Gurney Court Rd STAL AL1 38 E4
Gurney Crs CROY/NA CR0 202 G8
Gurney Dr EFNCH N2 117 N2
Gurney Rd CAR SM5 222 B1
FUL/PGN SW6 157 M9
NTHLT UB5 133 J5
SRTFD E15 121 K10
Gurney's Cl REDH RH1 276 A1
Guthrie St CHEL SW3 15 N7
Gutteridge La ABR/ST RM4 84 D10
Gutter La CITYW EC2V 12 E5
Guyatt Gdns MTCM CR4 202 B2
Guy Barnett Gv BKHTH/KID SE3 161 M9
Guy Rd WLGTN SM6 202 F10
Guyscliff Rd LEW SE13 183 H1
Guysfield Cl RAIN RM13 145 H3
Guysfield Dr RAIN RM13 145 H3
Guy St STHWK SE1 19 H1
Gwalior Rd PUT/ROE SW15 156 G10
Gwendolen Av PUT/ROE SW15 178 G1
Gwendoline Av PLSTW E13 141 N3
Gwendwr Rd WKENS W14 14 B7
WKENS W14 157 H4
Gweneth Cottages EDGW HA8 * 95 M7
Gwent Cl GSTN WD25 55 L10
Gwillim Cl BFN/LL DA15 185 K2
Gwydor Rd BECK BR3 204 C3
Gwydyr Rd HAYES BR2 205 L3
Gwyn Cl FUL/PGN SW6 157 M6
Gwynne Av CROY/NA CR0 204 C7
Gwynne Cl WDSR SL4 148 D7
Gwynne Park Av WFD IG8 102 C7
Gwynne Rd BTSEA SW11 157 N8
CTHM CR3 241 L9
Gwynne Whf CHSWK W4 156 C5
Gwynn Rd GVW DA11 189 P5
Gwynns Wk HERT/BAY SG13 25 M5
Gylcote Cl CMBW SE5 159 L10
Gyles Pk STAN HA7 95 H9
Gyllyngdune Gdns
GDMY/SEVK IG3 123 J8
Gypsy Cl WARE SG12 26 E7
Gypsy La KGLGY WD4 72 E1
SLN SL2 109 K9
WARE SG12 26 E7
WGCE AL7 23 J10
Gypsy Moth Av HAT AL10 40 B2
Gywnne Pl FSBYW WC1X 5 P10

H

Haarlem Rd WKENS W14 156 G2
Haberdasher Pl IS N1 7 H9
Haberdasher St IS N1 7 H9
Habgood Rd LOU IG10 82 B7
Habington Cl CMBW SE5 * 159 L6
Habitat Cl PECK SE15 160 A8
Haccombe Rd WIM/MER SW19 179 M9
Hackbridge Park Gdns CAR SM5 202 A9
Hackbridge Rd CAR SM5 202 B9
Hacketts La WOKS/MYFD GU22 233 J1
Hackford Rd BRXN/ST SW9 158 G7
Hackford Wk BRXN/ST SW9 158 G7
Hackforth Cl BAR EN5 76 E9
Hackhurst La RDKG RH5 270 G5
Hackington Crs BECK BR3 182 F9
Hackney Cl BORE WD6 76 A9
Hackney Gv HACK E8 * 140 A1
Hackney Rd BETH E2 7 L9
Hackney Wick HOM E9 140 E1
Hacton Dr HCH RM12 125 M9
Hacton La HCH RM12 125 N7
UPMR RM14 125 N10
Hadar Cl TRDG/WHET N20 97 K2
Haddenham Ct OXHEY WD19 * 93 L4
Hadden Rd THMD SE28 163 H2
Hadden Wy GFD/PVL UB6 134 C1
Haddestoke Ga CHES/WCR EN8 62 E2
Haddington Rd BMLY BR1 183 J6
Haddon Cl BORE WD6 75 M7
EN EN1 79 P10
HHS/BOV HP3 36 B7
NWMAL KT3 200 C5
WEY KT13 196 F10
Haddon Gv BFN/LL DA15 185 K3
Haddon Rd RKW/CH/CXG WD3 70 F9
STMC/STPC BR5 207 N5
SUT SM1 221 L1
Haddo St GNWCH SE10 160 G5
Hadfield Cl STHL UB1 133 N5
Hadfield Rd STWL/WRAY TW19 173 N3
Hadland Cl HHS/BOV HP3 52 D2
Hadleigh Cl RYNPK SW20 201 J2
WCHPL E1 140 B6
Hadleigh Ct BROX EN10 44 E8
HARP AL5 20 D5
Hadleigh Dr BELMT SM2 221 K5
Hadleigh Rd ED N9 100 A1
Hadleigh St BETH E2 140 B6
Hadley Cl BORE WD6 75 L9
WCHMH N21 79 H10
Hadley Common BAR EN5 77 M6
Hadley Gdns CHSWK W4 156 A4
NWDGN UB2 153 N4
Hadley Gra HLWE CM17 47 M2
Hadley Gn BAR EN5 77 J7
Hadley Green Rd BAR EN5 77 J6
Hadley Gn West BAR EN5 77 H6
Hadley Gv BAR EN5 77 H6
Hadley Highstone BAR EN5 77 J5
Hadley Pde BAR EN5 * 77 H7
Hadley Pl WEY KT13 216 B4
Hadley Rdg BAR EN5 77 J7
Hadley Rd BAR EN5 77 L8
BELV DA17 164 A3
EBAR EN4 78 B4
ENC/FH EN2 78 F4
MTCM CR4 202 E4
Hadley St CAMTN NW1 4 E2
Hadley Wy WCHMH N21 79 H10
Hadley Wood Ri PUR/KEN CR8 241 J1
Hadley Wood Rd BAR EN5 77 K6
Hadlow Ct SL SL1 129 H10
Hadlow Pl NRWD SE19 181 P10
Hadlow Rd SCUP DA14 185 K7
WELL DA16 163 M6
Hadlow Wy MEO DA13 190 B10
Hadrian Cl BOW E3 140 F3
STALW/RED AL3 37 N8
STWL/WRAY TW19 173 P3
Hadrian Est BETH E2 7 P8
Hadrian's Ride EN EN1 79 N9
Hadrian St GNWCH SE10 161 K4
Hadrian Wy STWL/WRAY TW19 173 N3
Hadyn Park Rd SHB W12 156 D1
Hafer Rd BTSEA SW11 158 A10
Hafton Rd CAT SE6 183 K4
Hagden La WATW WD18 72 G8
Haggard Rd TWK TW1 176 G3
Hagger Ct WALTH E17 * 121 J1
Haggerston Rd BORE WD6 75 K4
HACK E8 7 L4
Hagsdell Rd HERT/BAY SG13 25 L6
Hague St BETH E2 7 P10
Ha-Ha Rd WOOL/PLUM SE18 162 C5
Haig Cl STAL AL1 38 G7
Haig Dr SL SL1 148 G1
Haig Gdns GVE DA12 190 F3
Haigh Crs REDH RH1 276 C2
Haig Rd BH/WHM TN16 244 B3
CDW/CHF RM16 168 D2
STAN HA7 95 H6
UX/CGN UB8 132 C7
Haig Rd East PLSTW E13 141 P5
Haig Rd West PLSTW E13 141 P5
Haigville Gdns BARK/HLT IG6 122 E2
Hailes Cl WIM/MER SW19 179 M9
Hailey Av HOD EN11 26 F9
Haileybury Av EN EN1 79 N10
Haileybury Rd ORP BR6 227 K1
Hailey Cl HERT/BAY SG13 26 D9
Hailey La HERT/BAY SG13 26 C10
Hailey Pl SBW CM21 29 P1
Hailey Rd ERITHM DA18 164 B1
Hailsham Av BRXS/STRHM SW2 180 G5
Hailsham Cl HARH RM3 105 K6
SURB KT6 199 J7
Hailsham Dr HRW HA1 114 C1
Hailsham Rd HARH RM3 105 K6
TOOT SW17 180 B9
Hailsham Ter UED N18 * 99 L6
Haimo Rd ELTH/MOT SE9 184 A1
Hainault Buildings LEY E10 * 121 H6
Hainault Gore CHDH RM6 123 P3
Hainault Gv CHIG IG7 102 F5
Hainault Rd BARK/HLT IG6 103 L8
CHDH RM6 123 L1
CHDH RM6 124 A4
CHIG IG7 102 F5
CRW RM5 124 D1
WAN E11 121 H6
Hainault St ELTH/MOT SE9 184 E4
IL IG1 122 E7
Haines Ct WEY KT13 216 E2
Haines Wk MRDN SM4 201 L7
Haines Wy GSTN WD25 55 H10
Hainford Cl PECK SE15 160 C10
Haining Cl CHSWK W4 155 M4
Hainthorpe Rd WNWD SE27 181 J6
Hainton Cl WCHPL E1 140 A8
Halberd Ms CLPT E5 120 A7
Halbutt St DAGW RM9 124 A9
Halcomb St IS N1 7 J6
Halcot Av BXLYHS DA6 186 C1
Halcrow St WCHPL E1 140 B7
Halcyon Wy EMPK RM11 125 N6
Haldane Cl MUSWH N10 98 C8
PEND EN3 80 G4
Haldane Gdns GVW DA11 189 P4
Haldane Pl WAND/EARL SW18 179 L4
Haldane Rd EHAM E6 142 A5
FUL/PGN SW6 157 J6
STHL UB1 134 B9
THMD SE28 143 N9
Haldan Rd CHING E4 101 H7
Haldens WGCE AL7 23 J2
Haldon Rd WAND/EARL SW18 179 J2
Halebourne La CHOB/PIR GU24 212 F6
Hale Cl CHING E4 101 H4
EDGW HA8 95 P6
ORP BR6 226 F1
Hale Dr MLHL NW7 95 P7
MLHL NW7 96 A7
Hale End HARH RM3 105 J7
Hale End Cl RSLP HA4 113 H4
Hale End Rd CHING E4 101 J7
WALTH E17 101 J10
Hale Ends WOKS/MYFD GU22 231 N7
Halefield Rd TOTM N17 99 P9
Hale Gdns ACT W3 135 M10
SEVS/STOTM N15 119 P2
Hale Grove Gdns MLHL NW7 96 A6
Hale House WOOL/PLUM SE18 * 162 B6
Hale La EDGW HA8 95 P6
MLHL NW7 96 A6
RSEV TN14 246 G3
Hale Oak Rd RSEV TN14 265 J10
Halepit Rd GT/LBKH KT23 254 B2
Hale Rd EHAM E6 142 B6
HERT/BAY SG13 25 L6
TOTM N17 119 P1
Hales Oak GT/LBKH KT23 254 B2
Halesowen Rd MRDN SM4 201 L7
Hales Pk HHNE HP2 36 D5
Hales Park Cl HHNE HP2 36 D5
Hales St DEPT SE8 160 F6
Hale St POP/IOD E14 140 G9
STA TW18 173 H7
Haleswood COB KT11 217 J10
Haleswood Rd HHNE HP2 36 C5
Halesworth Cl HARH RM3 105 M8
Halesworth Rd HARH RM3 105 M7
LEW SE13 160 G9
The Hale CHING E4 101 J8
TOTM N17 119 P1
Haley Rd HDN NW4 116 F4
Half Acre BTFD TW8 155 J5
Halfacre Hl CFSP/GDCR SL9 90 C9
Half Acre Ms BTFD TW8 155 J6
Half Acre Rd HNWL W7 134 D10
Halfhide La CHES/WCR EN8 62 C3
Halfhides WAB EN9 63 J9
Half Moon Crs IS N1 5 P7
Half Moon La EPP CM16 65 J7
HNHL SE24 181 K2
Half Moon Meadow HHNE HP2 36 D1
Half Moon Ms STAL AL1 38 C6
Half Moon Pas WCHPL E1 13 M6
Half Moon St MYFR/PICC W1J 10 F9
Halford Cl EDGW HA8 95 N10
Halford Ct HAT AL10 40 B3
Halford Rd FUL/PGN SW6 14 F10
HGDN/ICK UB10 112 B10
LEY E10 121 J3
RCHPK/HAM TW10 177 K1
Halfpenny Cl RGUE GU4 268 G6
Halfpenny La ASC SL5 192 G7
RGUE GU4 268 F3
Halfway Ct PUR RM19 165 P3
Halfway Gn WOT/HER KT12 197 J10
Halfway St BFN/LL DA15 185 H4
Haliburton Rd TWK TW1 176 F1
Haliday Wk IS N1 * 7 H1
Halidon Ri HARH RM3 106 A7
Halifax Cl CRAWE RH10 284 F4
GSTN WD25 54 G10
LCOL/BKTW AL2 55 N7
TEDD TW11 176 D9
Halifax Rd ENC/FH EN2 79 K6
GFD/PVL UB6 134 A3
RKW/CH/CXG WD3 90 F1
Halifax St SYD SE26 182 A6
Halifax Wy WGCE AL7 23 P5
Halifield Dr BELV DA17 163 P2
Haling Gv SAND/SEL CR2 223 K4
Haling Park Gdns SAND/SEL CR2 223 J3
Haling Park Rd SAND/SEL CR2 223 K3
Haling Rd SAND/SEL CR2 223 L3
Halings La DEN/HRF UB9 110 G2
Halkin Ar KTBR SW1X 16 C3
Halkingcroft DTCH/LGLY SL3 149 P1
Halkin Ms KTBR SW1X * 16 C3
Halkin Pl KTBR SW1X 16 C3
Halkin St KTBR SW1X 16 D2
Hallam Cl BRWN CM15 86 G3
CHST BR7 184 C8
WATN WD24 73 K6
Hallam Gdns PIN HA5 93 M8
Hallam Ms GTPST W1W 10 F3
Hallam Rd BARN SW13 156 E9
SEVS/STOTM N15 119 J2
Hallam St GTPST W1W 10 F3
Halland Cl CRAWE RH10 284 B6
Halland Wy NTHWD HA6 92 E7
Hall Av SOCK/AV RM15 146 B10
Hall Cl EA W5 135 K7
GODL GU7 267 K10
RKW/CH/CXG WD3 91 K2
Hall Ct DTCH/LGLY SL3 149 N6
TEDD TW11 176 E8
Hall Crs SOCK/AV RM15 166 B1
Hall Dene Cl GU GU1 250 F9
Hall Dr DEN/HRF UB9 91 M9
SYD SE26 182 B8
Halley Gdns LEW SE13 161 J10
Halley Rd FSTGT E7 141 P1
MNPK E12 142 A1
WAB EN9 80 G2
Halley's Ap WOKN/KNAP GU21 231 M4
Halley's Ct WOKN/KNAP GU21 * 231 M4
Halleys Rdg HERT/WAT SG14 25 H6
Halley St POP/IOD E14 140 D7
Halley's Wk ADL/WDHM KT15 215 M4
Hall Farm Cl STAN HA7 94 G5
Hall Farm Dr WHTN TW2 176 C3
Hallfield Est BAY/PAD W2 9 H6
Hallford Wy DART DA1 187 K2
Hall Gdns CHING E4 100 E5
STALE/WH AL4 40 A9
Hall Ga STJWD NW8 3 K10
Hall Gv WGCE AL7 23 L7
Hall Heath Cl STAL AL1 38 G4
Hall Hl OXTED RH8 261 J8
The Halliards WOT/HER KT12 197 H6
Halliday Cl RAD WD7 57 K8
Halliday Sq NWDGN UB2 134 C10
Halliford Cl SHPTN TW17 196 F3
Halliford Rd SHPTN TW17 196 F5
Halliford St IS N1 6 F3
Hallillo Valley Rd CTHM CR3 242 E6
Halling Hl HLW CM20 29 J9
Hallington Cl WOKN/KNAP GU21 231 N3
Halliwell Rd BRXS/STRHM SW2 180 G2
Halliwick Court Pde
NFNCH/WDSPK N12 * 98 A6
Halliwick Rd MUSWH N10 98 B9
Hall La BRWN CM15 87 L10
CHING E4 100 E6
HDN NW4 96 D10
HYS/HAR UB3 152 E6
SOCK/AV RM15 147 K4
UPMR RM14 106 B10
UPMR RM14 126 B2
UPMR RM14 126 B6
Hall Meadow SL SL1 128 B4
Hallmead Rd SUT SM1 201 L10
Hallmores BROX EN10 44 F5
Hall Oak Wk KIL/WHAMP NW6 2 D1
Hallowell Av CROY/NA CR0 222 F1
Hallowell Cl MTCM CR4 202 B3
Hallowell Rd NTHWD HA6 92 F8
Hallowes Cl GUW GU2 249 N5
Hallowes Crs OXHEY WD19 93 H4
Hallowfield Wy MTCM CR4 201 N3
Hallows Gv SUN TW16 174 G8
Hall Pk BERK HP4 34 B6
Hall Park Ga BERK HP4 34 B7
Hall Park Hl BERK HP4 34 B7
Hall Park Rd UPMR RM14 126 B10

Hall Pl BAY/PAD W2 9 L2
STAL AL1 * 38 D5
WOKN/KNAP GU21 232 D2
Hall Place Cl STAL AL1 38 D5
Hall Place Crs BXLY DA5 186 D1
Hall Place Dr WEY KT13 216 F2
Hall Place Gdns STAL AL1 38 D5
Hall Rd CHDH RM6 123 M4
DART DA1 165 N10
EHAM E6 142 C3
GPK RM2 125 J1
GVW DA11 189 P6
HHNE HP2 36 C4
ISLW TW7 176 C1
MV/WKIL W9 3 K10
SHGR GU5 268 C10
SOCK/AV RM15 166 B1
SRTFD E15 121 J9
WLGTN SM6 222 C5
Halls Farm Cl WOKN/KNAP GU21 231 J3
Hallside Rd EN EN1 79 N4
Hallsland Wy OXTED RH8 261 L9
Halls Ter HGDN/ICK UB10 * 132 C6
Hall St FSBYE EC1V 6 D9
NFNCH/WDSPK N12 97 M6
Hallsville Rd CAN/RD E16 141 L8
Hallswelle Pde GLDGN NW11 * 117 J3
Hallswelle Rd GLDGN NW11 117 J3
Hall Ter SOCK/AV RM15 166 C1
The Hall BKHTH/KID SE3 161 M9
Hall Vw ELTH/MOT SE9 184 A5
The Hall Wk BERK HP4 * 34 A5
Hallwood Crs BRWN CM15 107 K1
Hallywell Crs EHAM E6 142 C7
Halnaker Wk CRAWW RH11 * 283 J10
Halons Rd ELTH/MOT SE9 184 D3
Halpin Pl WALW SE17 19 H6
Halsbrook Rd BKHTH/KID SE3 161 P9
Halsbury Cl STAN HA7 94 G6
Halsbury Rd SHB W12 136 E10
Halsbury Rd East NTHLT UB5 114 B9
Halsbury Rd West NTHLT UB5 114 A10
Halse Dr SL SL1 108 E9
Halsend HYS/HAR UB3 * 133 J10
Halsey Dr HHW HP1 35 J4
Halsey Pk LCOL/BKTW AL2 57 L3
Halsey Pl WATN WD24 * 73 J4
Halsey Rd WATW WD18 73 J7
Halsey St CHEL SW3 16 A5
Halsham Crs BARK IG11 143 J1
Halsmere Rd CMBW SE5 159 J7
Halstead Cl CROY/NA CR0 203 K10
Halstead Gdns WCHMH N21 99 L2
Halstead Hl CHESW EN7 61 M6
Halstead La RSEV TN14 245 P1
Halstead Rd EN EN1 79 M8
ERITH DA8 164 F7
WAN E11 121 N3
WCHMH N21 99 L2
Halstead Wy RBRW/HUT CM13 87 P10
Halston Cl BTSEA SW11 180 A2
Halstow Rd GNWCH SE10 161 M4
WLSDN NW10 136 G5
Halsway HYS/HAR UB3 133 H10
Halt Dr SLH/COR SS17 169 K3
Halter Cl BORE WD6 76 A9
Halton Cl FBAR/BDGN N11 98 A7
LCOL/BKTW AL2 56 B4
Halton Cross St IS N1 * 6 D5
Halton Pl IS N1 * 6 E5
Halton Rd CDW/CHF RM16 168 E2
IS N1 6 D4
PUR/KEN CR8 241 M6
Halt Pde CDALE/KGS NW9 * 116 A2
Halt Robin Rd BELV DA17 164 C3
Haltside HAT AL10 40 A5
Halwick Cl HHW HP1 35 L8
Hambalt Rd CLAP SW4 180 D1
Hamberlins La TRING HP23 32 G2
Hamble Cl RSLP HA4 112 F7
WOKN/KNAP GU21 231 M3
Hambledon Cl UX/CGN UB8 132 C6
Hambledon Ct EA W5 * 135 K9
Hambledon Gdns SNWD SE25 203 N3
Hambledon Hl EPSOM KT18 237 P2
Hambledon Pl DUL SE21 181 N4
GT/LBKH KT23 235 P9
Hambledon Rd CTHM CR3 241 L9
WAND/EARL SW18 179 J3
Hambledon V EPSOM KT18 237 P2
Hambledown Rd BFN/LL DA15 * 184 G3
Hamble La SOCK/AV RM15 146 E7
Hamble St FUL/PGN SW6 157 L9
Hambleton WDSR SL4 * 171 P4
Hambleton Cl WPK KT4 200 F9
Hambleton Hl CRAWW RH11 283 M9
Hamblings Cl RAD WD7 57 J9
Hambro Av HAYES BR2 205 M8
Hambrook Rd SNWD SE25 204 A3
Hambro Rd BRW CM14 107 J3
STRHM/NOR SW16 180 E9
Hambrough Rd STHL UB1 133 M10
Hamburgh Ct CHES/WCR EN8 62 C4
Ham Common
RCHPK/HAM TW10 177 J6
Ham Croft Cl FELT TW13 175 H6
Hamden Crs DAGE RM10 124 C8
Hamel Cl KTN/HRWW/WS HA3 115 J2
Hamels Dr HERT/BAY SG13 26 A4
Hamer Cl HHS/BOV HP3 52 D4
Hamerton Rd GVW DA11 189 N1
Hameway EHAM E6 142 D6
Ham Farm Rd RCHPK/HAM TW10 177 J7
Hamfield Cl OXTED RH8 261 H3
Hamfrith Rd SRTFD E15 141 L1
Ham Gate Av RCHPK/HAM TW10 177 L7
Hamilton Av BARK/HLT IG6 122 E2
CHEAM SM3 201 H9
COB KT11 217 H9
ED N9 99 P1
HOD EN11 44 F1
ROM RM1 104 E10
SURB KT6 199 M9
WOKS/MYFD GU22 233 H2
Hamilton Cl BERM/RHTH SE16 160 D1
CHERT KT16 195 J8
EBAR EN4 77 P8
FELT TW13 174 G8
GUW GU2 * 249 M5
HOR/WEW KT19 219 P8
LCOL/BKTW AL2 55 P7
POTB/CUF EN6 58 D9
PUR/KEN CR8 223 J8
STJWD NW8 3 L10
TEDD TW11 176 G9
TOTM N17 119 N1
Hamilton Ct EA W5 135 L9
HAT AL10 * 40 E6
Hamilton Crs BRW CM14 107 H6
HSLW TW3 176 A1
PLMGR N13 99 H5
RYLN/HDSTN HA2 113 N8
Hamilton Dr ASC SL5 192 D7
GUW GU2 249 M5
HARH RM3 105 M10
Hamilton Gdns SL SL1 128 A5
STJWD NW8 3 K9
Hamilton Gordon Ct GU GU1 * 249 P9
Hamilton La HBRY N5 119 J9
Hamilton Md HHS/BOV HP3 * 52 D3
Hamilton Ms MYFR/PICC W1J 16 E1
WEY KT13 * 216 B1
Hamilton Pde FELT TW13 * 175 H7
Hamilton Pk HBRY N5 119 J9
Hamilton Pk West HBRY N5 119 J9
Hamilton Pl GUW GU2 249 M5
KWD/TDW/WH KT20 239 J9
MYFR/PKLN W1K 10 D10
SUN TW16 175 J10
Hamilton Rd BERK HP4 33 N5
BTFD TW8 155 J5
BXLYHN DA7 163 P8
CHSWK W4 156 B2
EA W5 135 K9
EBAR EN4 77 P8
ED N9 99 P1
EFNCH N2 117 M1
FELT TW13 174 F8
GPK RM2 125 J3
HRW HA1 114 D3
HYS/HAR UB3 133 J9
IL IG1 122 E9
KGLGY WD4 54 D9
OXHEY WD19 93 J4
SCUP DA14 185 K7
SL SL1 128 F8
SRTFD E15 141 K5
STAL AL1 38 F5
THHTH CR7 203 L3
UX/CGN UB8 131 N6
WALTH E17 100 D10
WHTN TW2 176 D4
WIM/MER SW19 179 L10
WLSDN NW10 116 D10
WNWD SE27 181 L7
Hamilton Road Ms
WIM/MER SW19 179 L10
Hamilton Sq
NFNCH/WDSPK N12 * 97 M7
Hamilton St DEPT SE8 160 F5
WATW WD18 73 K9
Hamilton Ter STJWD NW8 3 J8
Hamilton Wy FNCH N3 97 K7
PLMGR N13 99 J5
WLGTN SM6 222 E5
Ham La EGH TW20 171 N7
WDSR SL4 149 P10
Hamlea Cl LEE/GVPK SE12 183 M1
Hamlet Cl CRW RM5 104 B8
LCOL/BKTW AL2 55 N6
LEW SE13 161 K10
Hamlet Gdns HMSMTH W6 156 D3
Hamlet Hl HLWW/ROY CM19 45 M5
Hamlet Rd CRW RM5 104 B8
NRWD SE19 181 N10
Hamlet Sq CRICK NW2 117 H8
Hamlets Wy BOW E3 140 E6
The Hamlet BERK HP4 34 D2
CMBW SE5 159 L9
Hamlet Wy STHWK SE1 19 H2
Hamlin Crs PIN HA5 113 K3
Hamlin Rd SEV TN13 246 F7
Hamlyn Cl EDGW HA8 95 K4
Hamlyn Gdns NRWD SE19 181 M10
Hammarskjold Rd HLW CM20 28 F10
Hamm Ct WEY KT13 196 A10
Hamm Court Est WEY KT13 196 A9
Hammelton Rd BMLY BR1 205 M1
Hammerfield Dr RDKG RH5 270 G7
Hammer La HHNE HP2 36 A5
Hammer Pde GSTN WD25 * 55 H9
Hammers Ga LCOL/BKTW AL2 55 P2
Hammers La MLHL NW7 96 D5
Hammersmith Br HMSMTH W6 156 E4
Hammersmith Bridge Rd
BARN SW13 156 E5
Hammersmith Broadway
HMSMTH W6 156 F3
Hammersmith Emb
HMSMTH W6 * 156 F5
Hammersmith Flyover
HMSMTH W6 156 F4
Hammersmith Gv HMSMTH W6 156 F3
Hammersmith Rd HMSMTH W6 156 G3
Hammersmith Ter HMSMTH W6 * 156 D4
Hammerton Cl BXLY DA5 186 F6
Hammer Yd CRAWE RH10 * 283 N8
Hammet Cl YEAD UB4 133 L7
Hammett St TWRH EC3N 13 L7
Hamm Moor La
ADL/WDHM KT15 215 P2
Hammond Av MTCM CR4 202 C2
Hammond Cl BAR EN5 77 J9
CHESW EN7 61 N2
GFD/PVL UB6 114 C10
HPTN TW12 197 P1
WOKN/KNAP GU21 231 P1
Hammond End SLN SL2 108 G9
Hammond Rd EN EN1 80 A7
NWDGN UB2 153 M2
WOKN/KNAP GU21 231 P1
Hammonds Cl BCTR RM8 123 M8
Hammonds La RBRW/HUT CM13 106 G7
STALE/WH AL4 21 M8
Hammond St KTTN NW5 4 G1
Hammondstreet Rd CHESW EN7 61 K1
Hammond Wy LTWR GU18 212 A6
Hamond Cl SAND/SEL CR2 223 J5
Hamonde Cl EDGW HA8 95 N3
Hamond Sq IS N1 7 J7
Ham Park Rd FSTGT E7 141 M2
Hampden Av BECK BR3 204 D2
CSHM HP5 50 F6
Hampden Cl CAMTN NW1 5 K8
CRAWE RH10 284 F4
EPP CM16 66 B3
SLN SL2 129 M5
Hampden Crs BRW CM14 107 H6
CHESW EN7 62 A7
Hampden Gurney St
MBLAR W1H 10 A6
Hampden Hl BEAC HP9 88 A9
WARE SG12 26 E2
Hampden Hill Cl WARE SG12 26 E1
Hampden La TOTM N17 99 N9
Hampden Pl LCOL/BKTW AL2 56 D5
Hampden Rd ARCH N19 118 E7
BECK BR3 204 D2
CEND/HSY/T N8 119 H2
CFSP/GDCR SL9 90 A9
DTCH/LGLY SL3 150 C2
GRAYS RM17 167 N4
KTN/HRWW/WS HA3 94 B9
KUT/HW KT1 199 M3
MUSWH N10 98 B8
TOTM N17 99 P9
Hampden Wy STHGT/OAK N14 98 C2
WAT WD17 72 F2
Hampermill La OXHEY WD19 93 H2
Hampshire Av SL SL1 129 H7
Hampshire Cl UED N18 100 A6
Hampshire Gdns SLH/COR SS17 169 K1
Hampshire Hog La
HMSMTH W6 * 156 E3
Hampshire Rd EMPK RM11 125 P2
WDGN N22 98 G8
Hampshire St KTTN NW5 5 J1
Hampson Wy VX/NE SW8 158 G7
Hampstead Av WFD IG8 102 D8
Hampstead Cl LCOL/BKTW AL2 55 N7
THMD SE28 143 L10
Hampstead Gdns GLDGN NW11 117 K4
Hampstead Ga HAMP NW3 117 M10
Hampstead Gn HAMP NW3 117 P10
Hampstead Gv HAMP NW3 117 M9
Hampstead Hill Gdns
HAMP NW3 117 P9
Hampstead La DORK RH4 272 E3
HGT N6 118 A5
Hampstead Rd CAMTN NW1 4 G10
DORK RH4 272 F3
Hampstead Sq HAMP NW3 117 M8
Hampstead Wy GLDGN NW11 117 K3
GLDGN NW11 117 L5
Hampton Cl BORE WD6 75 P9
CDW/CHF RM16 167 H2
FBAR/BDGN N11 98 B6
KIL/WHAMP NW6 2 E10
RYNPK SW20 * 178 F10
WOKN/KNAP GU21 230 G5
Hampton Ct IS N1 6 C2
Hampton Court Av
E/WMO/HCT KT8 198 C6
Hampton Court Crs
E/WMO/HCT KT8 * 198 C3
Hampton Court Cresent
E/WMO/HCT KT8 198 C3
Hampton Court Est THDIT KT7 * 198 D5
Hampton Court Rd
E/WMO/HCT KT8 198 D3
E/WMO/HCT KT8 198 F3
KUT/HW KT1 199 H2
Hampton Court Wy
E/WMO/HCT KT8 198 D4
ESH/CLAY KT10 198 D9
THDIT KT7 198 D7
THDIT KT7 198 D8
Hampton Crs GVE DA12 191 H5
Hampton Gdns SBW CM21 29 L4
Hampton Gv EW KT17 220 C7
Hampton La FELT TW13 175 M7
Hampton Ri KTN/HRWW/WS HA3 115 K4
Hampton Rd CHING E4 100 E6
CROY/NA CR0 203 K6
IL IG1 122 F9
REDH RH1 276 A5
TEDD TW11 176 C8
WAN E11 121 J6
WHTN TW2 176 C6
WPK KT4 200 D9
Hampton Rd East FELT TW13 175 N7
Hampton Rd West FELT TW13 175 M5
Hampton St WALW SE17 18 D6
Ham Ridings RCHPK/HAM TW10 177 L8
Hamsey Green Gdns WARL CR6 242 B2
Hamsey Wy SAND/SEL CR2 242 A1
Ham Shades Cl BFN/LL DA15 185 J6
Hamstel Rd HLW CM20 28 E9
Ham St RCHPK/HAM TW10 177 H5
The Ham BTFD TW8 155 H6
Ham Vw CROY/NA CR0 204 D6
Ham Yd SOHO/SHAV W1D * 11 J7
Hanameel St CAN/RD E16 141 M10
Hanbury Cl CHES/WCR EN8 62 C6
HDN NW4 116 F1
Hanbury Ct HRW HA1 * 114 E4
Hanbury Dr BH/WHM TN16 225 N9
WCHMH N21 78 G8
Hanbury Rd ACT W3 155 N1
CRAWW RH11 283 H8
TOTM N17 100 A10
Hanbury St WCHPL E1 13 N3
Hancock Ct BORE WD6 75 P5
Hancock Rd BOW E3 141 H5
NRWD SE19 181 L9
Hancocks Mt ASC SL5 192 C6
Hancroft Rd HHS/BOV HP3 36 A8
Handa Cl HHS/BOV HP3 36 C9
Handa Wk IS N1 6 F1
Hand Ct HHOL WC1V 11 P4
Handcroft Rd CROY/NA CR0 203 J8
Handel Cl EDGW HA8 95 L7
Handel Crs TIL RM18 168 D6
Handel Pde EDGW HA8 * 95 M7
Handel Pl WLSDN NW10 136 A1
Handel St BMSBY WC1N 11 M1
Handel Wy EDGW HA8 95 M8
Handen Rd LEE/GVPK SE12 183 K1
Handforth Rd BRXN/ST SW9 159 H6
IL IG1 122 E8
Hand La SBW CM21 29 M2
Handley Gv CRICK NW2 116 G8
Handley Page Rd WLGTN SM6 222 G4
Handley Page Wy
LCOL/BKTW AL2 56 E6
Handley Rd HOM E9 140 B2
Handowe Cl HDN NW4 116 D2
Handpost Lodge Gdns HHNE HP2 36 E7
Handside Cl WGCW AL8 22 F5
WPK KT4 200 G8
Handside Gn WGCW AL8 22 F4
Handside La WGCW AL8 22 F5
Handsworth Av CHING E4 101 J7
Handsworth Cl OXHEY WD19 93 H4
Handsworth Rd TOTM N17 119 L1
Handtrough Wy BARK IG11 142 E4
Hanford Cl WAND/EARL SW18 179 K4
Hanford Rd SOCK/AV RM15 146 B10
Hangar La (North Circular Rd)
EA W5 135 L8
Hangar Rd DEN/HRF UB9 111 H2
Hangar Ruding OXHEY WD19 93 N4
Hanger Cl HHW HP1 35 L7
Hanger Gn EA W5 135 M6
Hanger Hl WEY KT13 216 C2
Hanger La EA W5 135 K5
Hanger Lane
(North Circular Road) EA W5 135 K5
Hanger Vale La EA W5 135 L8
Hanger View Wy ACT W3 135 M8
Hang Grove Hl ORP BR6 226 E9
Hanging Hill La
RBRW/HUT CM13 107 N4
Haning Hill La RBRW/HUT CM13 87 P10
Hankey Pl STHWK SE1 19 H2
Hankins La MLHL NW7 96 B3
Hanley Cl WDSR SL4 148 C7
Hanley Gdns FSBYPK N4 118 G6
Hanley Pl BECK BR3 182 F10
Hanley Rd FSBYPK N4 118 F6
Hanmer Wk HOLWY N7 118 G7
Hannah Cl BECK BR3 204 G3
WLSDN NW10 115 P9
Hannah Mary Wy STHWK SE1 19 P6
Hannards Wy BARK/HLT IG6 103 L6
Hannay La ARCH N19 118 E5
Hannell Rd FUL/PGN SW6 157 H6
Hannen Rd WNWD SE27 * 181 J6
Hannibal Rd STWL/WRAY TW19 173 P3
WCHPL E1 140 B7
Hannibal Wy CROY/NA CR0 222 G2
Hannington Rd CLAP SW4 158 C9
Hanover Av CAN/RD E16 141 M10
FELT TW13 175 H4
Hanover Cir HYS/HAR UB3 132 D8
Hanover Cl CHEAM SM3 221 H1
CRAWE RH10 284 A10
EGH TW20 171 N9
RCH/KEW TW9 155 M6
REDH RH1 258 D4
SL SL1 149 M2
WDSR SL4 148 E7
Hanover Ct DORK RH4 272 E2
WOKS/MYFD GU22 232 B5
Hanover Dr CHST BR7 184 F7
Hanover Gdns ABLGY WD5 * 54 G6
BARK/HLT IG6 102 F8
LBTH SE11 18 A10
Hanover Ga SL SL1 128 E10
Hanover Gn HHW HP1 35 K8
Hanover Pk PECK SE15 159 P7
Hanover Pl BRW CM14 106 G6
COVGDN WC2E 11 M6
Hanover Rd SEVS/STOTM N15 119 N2
WIM/MER SW19 179 M10
WLSDN NW10 136 F2
Hanover Sq CONDST W1S 10 F6
Hanover Steps BAY/PAD W2 * 9 P6
Hanover St CONDST W1S 10 F6
CROY/NA CR0 203 J10
Hanover Ter CAMTN NW1 4 A10
Hanover Terrace Ms CAMTN NW1 3 P10
Hanover Wk HAT AL10 40 C7
WEY KT13 196 E10
Hanover Wy BXLYHS DA6 163 N9
WDSR SL4 148 E8
Hanover Yd IS N1 * 6 D7
Hansard Ms WKENS W14 156 G1
Hansart Wy ENC/FH EN2 79 H5
Hans Crs KTBR SW1X 16 A3
Hanselin Cl STAN HA7 94 E6
Hansells Md HLWW/ROY CM19 45 M1
Hansen Dr WCHMH N21 78 G9
Hanshaw Dr EDGW HA8 96 A9
Hansler Gv E/WMO/HCT KT8 198 C5
Hansler Rd EDUL SE22 181 N1
Hansol Rd BXLYHS DA6 185 P1
Hansom Ter BMLY BR1 * 205 N1
Hanson Cl BAL SW12 180 C3
BECK BR3 * 182 G9
MORT/ESHN SW14 155 P9
RGUE GU4 250 C7
WDR/YW UB7 152 A2
Hanson Dr LOU IG10 82 F6
Hanson Gdns STHL UB1 153 M1
Hanson St GTPST W1W 10 G3
Hans Pl KTBR SW1X 16 A3
Hans Rd CHEL SW3 16 A3
Hans St KTBR SW1X 16 B4
Hanway Pl FITZ W1T 11 J5
Hanway Rd HNWL W7 134 C8
Hanway St FITZ W1T 11 J5
Hanworth La CHERT KT16 195 J8
Hanworth Rd FELT TW13 175 J4
HPTN TW12 175 N7
HSLW TW3 154 A9
HSLWW TW4 175 N3
REDH RH1 276 A5
SUN TW16 175 H10
Hanworth Ter HSLW TW3 154 A10
Hanyards La POTB/CUF EN6 60 E4
Hapgood Cl GFD/PVL UB6 114 C10
Harben Pde HAMP NW3 * 3 L3
Harben Rd KIL/WHAMP NW6 3 K3
Harberson Rd BAL SW12 180 C4
SRTFD E15 141 L3
Harbert Gdns LCOL/BKTW AL2 56 A5
Harberton Rd ARCH N19 118 D6
Harberts Rd HLWW/ROY CM19 46 E2
Harbet Rd BAY/PAD W2 9 M4
UED N18 100 C6
Harbex Cl BXLY DA5 186 C3
Harbinger Rd POP/IOD E14 160 G3
Harbledown Pl STMC/STPC BR5 207 M4
Harbledown Rd FUL/PGN SW6 157 K7
SAND/SEL CR2 223 P7
Harbord Cl CMBW SE5 159 L8
Harbord St FUL/PGN SW6 156 G7
Harborne Cl OXHEY WD19 93 K6
Harborough Av BFN/LL DA15 185 H3
Harborough Rd
STRHM/NOR SW16 180 G7
Harbour Av WBPTN SW10 157 M7
Harbourer Rd BARK/HLT IG6 103 L6
Harbour Exchange Sq
POP/IOD E14 160 G1
Harbourfield Rd BNSTD SM7 239 L1
Harbour Rd CMBW SE5 159 K9
Harbour Yd WBPTN SW10 * 157 M7
Harbridge Av PUT/ROE SW15 178 C3
Harbury Rd CAR SM5 221 P5
Harbut Rd BTSEA SW11 157 N10
Harcamlow Wy SBW CM21 29 P3
WARE SG12 27 M6
Harcastle Cl YEAD UB4 133 M6
Harcombe Rd STNW/STAM N16 119 M8
Harcourt STWL/WRAY TW19 172 B2
Harcourt Av BFN/LL DA15 185 M2
EDGW HA8 95 P4
MNPK E12 122 C9
WLGTN SM6 222 C1
Harcourt Buildings EMB EC4Y * 12 A7
Harcourt Cl EGH TW20 172 F9
ISLW TW7 154 F9
Harcourt Fld WLGTN SM6 222 C1
Harcourt Ms GPK RM2 124 G3
Harcourt Rd BROCKY SE4 160 E10
BUSH WD23 74 B9
BXLYHS DA6 163 P10
SRTFD E15 141 L4
THHTH CR7 202 G6
WDGN N22 98 E9
WDSR SL4 148 D7
WIM/MER SW19 179 K10
WLGTN SM6 222 C1
Harcourt St MBLAR W1H 9 P4
Harcourt Ter WBPTN SW10 15 H8
Hardcastle Cl CROY/NA CR0 203 P6
Hardcourts Cl WWKM BR4 224 G1
Hardell Cl EGH TW20 172 D8
Hardel Wk BRXS/STRHM SW2 181 H3
Harden Farm Cl COUL/CHIP CR5 240 D7
Harden Rd GVW DA11 190 C5
Hardens Manorway
WOOL/PLUM SE18 162 A2
Harders Rd PECK SE15 160 A8
Hardess St HNHL SE24 159 K9
Hardham Cl CRAWW RH11 283 K5
Hardie Cl WLSDN NW10 116 A10
Hardie Rd DAGE RM10 124 D8
Harding Cl CROY/NA CR0 203 N10
GSTN WD25 55 K9
KUTN/CMB KT2 199 L1
WALW SE17 18 E10
Hardinge Rd UED N18 99 M6
WLSDN NW10 136 F3
Hardinge St WCHPL E1 140 B8
WOOL/PLUM SE18 162 E2
Harding Pde HARP AL5 * 20 A2
Harding Rd BXLYHN DA7 164 A8
CDW/CHF RM16 168 D2
CSHM HP5 51 J6
EPSOM KT18 238 B5
Hardings WGCE AL7 23 M4
Hardings Cl HHS/BOV HP3 35 L9
Hardings La PGE/AN SE20 182 C9
Harding Sp DTCH/LGLY SL3 150 C4
Hardings Rw IVER SL0 130 G5
Hardley Crs EMPK RM11 125 L2
Hardinge Crs WOOL/PLUM SE18 162 F2
Hardman Rd CHARL SE7 161 N4
KUTN/CMB KT2 199 K2
Hardres Ter STMC/STPC BR5 * 207 N9
Hardwick Cl LHD/OX KT22 236 B1
STAN HA7 95 H6
Hardwick Crs RDART DA2 188 A2
Hardwicke Av HEST TW5 * 153 P7
Hardwicke Gdns AMS HP6 69 K4
Hardwicke Ms FSBYW WC1X * 5 P10
Hardwicke Pl LCOL/BKTW AL2 57 J3
Hardwicke Rd CHSWK W4 155 P3
PLMGR N13 98 F6
RCHPK/HAM TW10 177 H7
REIG RH2 257 K9
Hardwicke St BARK IG11 142 F3
Hardwick Gn WEA W13 134 G7
Hardwick La CHERT KT16 194 F7
Hardwick Pl STRHM/NOR SW16 180 D10
Hardwick Rd REDH RH1 275 N2
Hardwick St CLKNW EC1R 6 B10
Hardwick's Wy
WAND/EARL SW18 179 K1
Hardwidge St STHWK SE1 19 J1
Hardy Av CAN/RD E16 141 M10
GVW DA11 190 B5
RSLP HA4 113 J10
Hardy Cl BAR EN5 77 H9
BERM/RHTH SE16 160 C1
CRAWE RH10 284 D6
HORL RH6 279 P4
PIN HA5 113 L5
RDKG RH5 272 G7
SL SL1 128 F10
Hardy Cottages GNWCH SE10 * 161 J5
Hardy Gv DART DA1 165 P10
Hardy Pas WDGN N22 98 G9
Hardy Rd BKHTH/KID SE3 161 L5
CHING E4 100 E7
HHNE HP2 36 A5
WIM/MER SW19 179 L10
Hardys Ms E/WMO/HCT KT8 198 D4
Hardy Wy ENC/FH EN2 79 H5
Harebell WGCE AL7 23 H9
Harebell Cl HERT/BAY SG13 26 A5
Harebell Dr EHAM E6 142 D7
Harebell Hl COB KT11 217 L10
Harebell Wy HARH RM3 105 L8
Hare & Billet Rd BKHTH/KID SE3 161 J7
The Harebreaks WATN WD24 73 J3
Hare Ct EMB EC4Y * 12 A6
Harecourt Rd IS N1 6 E1
Hare Crs GSTN WD25 55 H8
Harecroft DORK RH4 273 H5
LHD/OX KT22 236 A9
Haredale Rd HNHL SE24 159 K10
Haredon Cl FSTH SE23 182 B3
Harefield ESH/CLAY KT10 198 D10
HLW CM20 29 K10
Harefield Av BELMT SM2 221 H5
Harefield Cl ENC/FH EN2 79 H5
Harefield Ms BROCKY SE4 160 E9
Harefield Pl STALE/WH AL4 39 J3
Harefield Rd BROCKY SE4 160 E9
CEND/HSY/T N8 118 E3
RKW/CH/CXG WD3 91 P3
SCUP DA14 185 N6
STRHM/NOR SW16 180 G10
UX/CGN UB8 131 N1
Hare Hall La GPK RM2 125 J2
Harehatch La SLN SL2 108 F6
Hare Hl ADL/WDHM KT15 215 J3
Hare Hill Cl WOKS/MYFD GU22 233 K1
Harelands Cl WOKN/KNAP GU21 231 P3
Hare La CRAWW RH11 283 L4
ESH/CLAY KT10 218 D3
HAT AL10 40 E6
Hare Marsh BETH E2 * 13 N1
Harendon KWD/TDW/WH KT20 238 F7
Harepark Cl HHW HP1 35 J5
Hare Rw BETH E2 140 A4
Hares Bank CROY/NA CR0 225 J6
Haresfield Rd DAGE RM10 144 B1
Harestone Dr CTHM CR3 241 N10
CTHM CR3 259 N1
Harestone Hl CTHM CR3 259 N2
Harestone La CTHM CR3 259 M1
Harestone Valley Rd CTHM CR3 259 N1
CTHM CR3 259 P3
Hare St HLWW/ROY CM19 46 E1
WOOL/PLUM SE18 162 D2
Hare St Springs
HLWW/ROY CM19 46 F1
Hare Ter WTHK RM20 * 167 J4
Hare Wk IS N1 7 K8
Harewood RKW/CH/CXG WD3 71 M9
Harewood Av CAMTN NW1 9 P2
NTHLT UB5 133 M2
Harewood Cl CRAWE RH10 284 B4
NTHLT UB5 133 N2
REIG RH2 257 M8
Harewood Dr CLAY IG5 102 C10
Harewood Gdns SAND/SEL CR2 242 A1
Harewood Hl EPP CM16 83 H1
Harewood Pl CONDST W1S 10 F6
SL SL1 149 M2
Harewood Rd BRWN CM15 86 G10
CSTG HP8 69 P7
ISLW TW7 154 E6
OXHEY WD19 93 J4
RGUE GU4 250 F7
SAND/SEL CR2 223 M3
WIM/MER SW19 179 P9
Harewood Rw CAMTN NW1 9 P3
Harewood Ter NWDGN UB2 153 N3
Harfield Gdns CMBW SE5 * 159 M9
Harfield Rd SUN TW16 197 L2
Harford Cl CHING E4 100 G1
Harford Dr WAT WD17 72 F4
Harforde Ct HERT/BAY SG13 * 25 P5
Harford Rd CHING E4 100 G1
Harford St WCHPL E1 140 D6
Harford Wk EFNCH N2 117 N2
Harfst Wy SWLY BR8 208 D1
Harglaze Ter CDALE/KGS NW9 * 116 B1
Hargood Cl KTN/HRWW/WS HA3 115 K4
Hargood Rd BKHTH/KID SE3 161 P7
Hargrave Pk ARCH N19 118 D7
Hargrave Pl KTTN NW5 118 E10
Hargrave Rd ARCH N19 118 D7
Hargreaves Av CHESW EN7 62 A7
Hargreaves Cl CHESW EN7 62 A7
Hargwyne St BRXN/ST SW9 158 G9
Haringey Pk CEND/HSY/T N8 118 F4
Haringey Rd CEND/HSY/T N8 118 F2
Harington Ter UED N18 * 99 L5
Harkett Cl KTN/HRWW/WS HA3 94 E10
Harkness CHESW EN7 62 A5
Harkness Cl EW KT17 238 F2
HARH RM3 105 N6
Harkness Rd SL SL1 128 A7
Harland Av BFN/LL DA15 184 G6
CROY/NA CR0 203 N10
Harland Cl WIM/MER SW19 201 L3
Harland Rd LEE/GVPK SE12 183 M4
Harlands Gv ORP BR6 226 E1
Harlech Gdns HEST TW5 153 L5
PIN HA5 113 L5
Harlech Rd ABLGY WD5 55 H7
STHGT/OAK N14 98 F4
Harlequin Av BTFD TW8 154 F5
Harlequin Centre NWDGN UB2 * 153 K3
Harlequin Cl ISLW TW7 176 D1
YEAD UB4 133 L7
Harlequin Ct EA W5 * 135 H9
Harlequin Rd TEDD TW11 * 176 G10
The Harlequin WAT WD17 * 73 K8
Harlescott Rd PECK SE15 160 C10
Harlesden Cl HARH RM3 105 N8
Harlesden Gdns WLSDN NW10 136 C3
Harlesden Rd HARH RM3 105 N7
STAL AL1 38 F6
WLSDN NW10 136 E3
Harley Cl ALP/SUD HA0 * 135 J1
Harley Ct STALE/WH AL4 * 39 J2
Harley Crs HRW HA1 114 C2
Harleyford BMLY BR1 205 P1
Harleyford Rd LBTH SE11 17 N9
Harleyford St LBTH SE11 18 A10
Harley Gdns ORP BR6 227 H1
WBPTN SW10 15 K8
Harley Gv BOW E3 140 E5
Harley Pl CAVSQ/HST W1G 10 E4
Harley Rd HAMP NW3 3 M4
HRW HA1 114 C2
WLSDN NW10 136 B4
Harley St CAVSQ/HST W1G 10 E3
Harley Vls WLSDN NW10 * 136 B4
Harlinger St WOOL/PLUM SE18 162 B2
The Harlings HERT/BAY SG13 26 B9
Harlington Cl HYS/HAR UB3 152 D6
Harlington Rd BXLYHN DA7 163 P9
UX/CGN UB8 132 B5
UX/CGN UB8 132 C8
Harlington Rd East
EBED/NFELT TW14 175 J3
Harlington Rd West
EBED/NFELT TW14 175 J2
Harlow Common HLWE CM17 47 N4
Harlow Ct HHNE HP2 36 A2
Harlow Gdns CRW RM5 104 D7
Harlow Rd CHONG CM5 49 K6
HLWW/ROY CM19 27 P10
PLMGR N13 99 L4
RAIN RM13 144 G3
RBSF CM22 30 C4
SBW CM21 29 M3
Harlyn Dr PIN HA5 113 J1
Harman Av GVW DA11 190 E8
WFD IG8 101 L8
Harman Cl CHING E4 101 J5
CRICK NW2 117 H8
Harman Dr BFN/LL DA15 185 J2
CRICK NW2 117 H8
Harman Pl PUR/KEN CR8 223 J7
Harman Rd EN EN1 79 N9
Harmer Rd SWCM DA10 189 L2
Harmer St GVE DA12 190 F2
Harmondsworth La
WDR/YW UB7 151 P5
Harmondsworth Rd
WDR/YW UB7 151 P3
Harmony Cl CRAWW RH11 283 H9
GLDGN NW11 117 H3
HAT AL10 40 D2
WLGTN SM6 222 F5
Harmony Pl STHWK SE1 19 M7
Harmony Wy BMLY BR1 205 M2
HDN NW4 116 F2
Harmood Gv CAMTN NW1 * 4 E3
Harmood St CAMTN NW1 4 E3
Harms Gv RGUE GU4 250 F7
Harmsworth Ms STHWK SE1 18 B4
Harmsworth St WALW SE17 18 C8
Harmsworth Wy
TRDG/WHET N20 97 J2
Harness Rd THMD SE28 163 K1
Harness Wy STALE/WH AL4 39 J3
Harnetts Cl SWLY BR8 * 208 E7
Harold Av BELV DA17 164 A4
HYS/HAR UB3 152 G2
Harold Cl HLWW/ROY CM19 46 C2
Harold Court Rd HARH RM3 106 A7
Harold Crs WAB EN9 63 H8
Harold Rd CEND/HSY/T N8 118 G3
CHING E4 101 H4
CRAWE RH10 284 F8
NRWD SE19 181 L10
PLSTW E13 141 N3
RDART DA2 187 N7
SEVS/STOTM N15 119 N3
SUT SM1 221 N1
SWFD E18 101 M9
WAN E11 121 K6
WLSDN NW10 136 A5
Haroldslea HORL RH6 280 F5
Haroldslea Cl HORL RH6 280 D6
Haroldslea Dr HORL RH6 280 D6
Harolds Rd HLWW/ROY CM19 46 C2
Haroldstone Rd WALTH E17 120 C3
Harold Vw HARH RM3 105 N10
Harpenden Rd MNPK E12 121 P7
STALW/RED AL3 38 C1
WNWD SE27 181 J5
Harper Cl CDW/CHF RM16 167 H4
STHGT/OAK N14 78 D9
Harper La RAD WD7 56 F7
Harper Rd EHAM E6 142 C8
STHWK SE1 18 F3
Harpers La BRWN CM15 87 J3
Harpers Yd ISLW TW7 * 154 E8
TOTM N17 99 N9
Harpesford Av VW GU25 193 P5
Harp Island Cl WLSDN NW10 116 A7
Harp La MON EC3R 13 J8
Harpley Sq WCHPL E1 140 B6
Harpour Rd BARK IG11 142 F1
Harp Rd HNWL W7 134 E6
Harpsden St BTSEA SW11 158 B7
Harpsfield Broadway HAT AL10 40 C3
Harps Oak La REDH RH1 258 B1
Harpswood Cl COUL/CHIP CR5 240 D8
Harptree Wy STAL AL1 38 E4
Harpur Ms BMSBY WC1N 11 N3
Harpurs KWD/TDW/WH KT20 238 G7
Harpur St BMSBY WC1N 11 N3
Harraden Rd BKHTH/KID SE3 161 P7
Harrap Cha GRAYS RM17 167 L4
Harrier Cl HCH RM12 145 J1
Harrier Ms THMD SE28 162 G1
Harrier Rd CDALE/KGS NW9 96 B10
Harriers Cl EA W5 135 K9
Harrier Wy EHAM E6 142 C7
WAB EN9 63 M10
Harries Cl CSHM HP5 50 G6
Harriescourt WAB EN9 63 M8
Harries Rd YEAD UB4 133 K6
Harriet Cl HACK E8 7 N5
Harriet Gdns CROY/NA CR0 203 P9
Harriet St KTBR SW1X 16 B2
Harriet Tubman Cl
BRXS/STRHM SW2 181 H3
Harriet Wk KTBR SW1X 16 B2
Harriet Walker Wy
RKW/CH/CXG WD3 91 J1
Harriet Wy BUSH WD23 94 C1
Harringay Gdns CEND/HSY/T N8 119 J2
Harringay Rd SEVS/STOTM N15 119 J3
Harrington Cl CROY/NA CR0 202 F9
REIG RH2 274 D7
WDSR SL4 148 E10
WLSDN NW10 116 A8
Harrington Ct NKENS W10 2 C9
Harrington Crs CDW/CHF RM16 167 J1
Harrington Cresent
CDW/CHF RM16 147 J10
Harrington Gdns SKENS SW7 15 J6
Harrington Hl CLPT E5 120 A6
Harrington Rd SKENS SW7 15 L5
SNWD SE25 203 P4
WAN E11 121 K6
Harrington Sq CAMTN NW1 4 G7
Harrington St CAMTN NW1 4 G9
Harrington Wy
WOOL/PLUM SE18 162 A2
Harriott Cl GNWCH SE10 161 L3
Harriotts Cl ASHTD KT21 237 J6
Harriotts La ASHTD KT21 237 H5
Harris Cl CRAWW RH11 283 L10
ENC/FH EN2 79 J5
GVW DA11 190 B6
HARH RM3 105 M8
HSLW TW3 153 P7
Harris Gdns SL SL1 149 H1
Harris La RAD WD7 57 M10
Harrison Cl NTHWD HA6 92 D7
REIG RH2 275 L1
TRDG/WHET N20 97 P2
Harrison Ct SHPTN TW17 * 196 C5
Harrison Dr EPP CM16 66 C2
Harrison Rd DAGE RM10 144 C1
WAB EN9 81 H1
WLSDN NW10 136 A3
Harrison's Ri CROY/NA CR0 203 J10
Harrison St STPAN WC1H 5 M10
Harrisons Whf PUR RM19 165 P4
Harrison Wk CHES/WCR EN8 62 C6
Harrison Wy SEV TN13 247 H8
SHPTN TW17 196 C5
SL SL1 128 C10
Harris Rd BXLYHN DA7 163 P7
DAGW RM9 124 A10
GSTN WD25 73 H1
Harriss La WARE SG12 26 B1
Harris St CMBW SE5 159 L6
WALTH E17 120 E5
Harris Wy SUN TW16 196 F1
Harrods Gn EDGW HA8 95 M6
Harrogate Ct DTCH/LGLY SL3 150 D4
Harrogate Rd OXHEY WD19 93 K4
Harrold Rd BCTR RM8 123 L10
Harrow Av EN EN1 79 N10
Harroway Rd BTSEA SW11 157 N8
Harrowband Rd HLWE CM17 29 M10
Harrow Bottom Rd VW GU25 194 C6
Harrowby Gdns GVW DA11 190 B5
Harrowby St MBLAR W1H 9 P5
Harrow Cl ADL/WDHM KT15 195 L9
CHSGTN KT9 219 J4
DORK RH4 272 F3
Harrow Crs HARH RM3 105 J8
Harrowdene Cl ALP/SUD HA0 115 J9
Harrowdene Gdns TEDD TW11 176 F10
Harrowdene Rd ALP/SUD HA0 115 J9
Harrow Dr ED N9 99 N2
EMPK RM11 125 K5
Harrowes Meade EDGW HA8 95 M4
Harrow Fields Gdns HRW HA1 114 D8
Harrow Gdns ORP BR6 227 L1
WARL CR6 242 E2
Harrowgate Rd HOM E9 140 D2
Harrow Gn WAN E11 121 K8
Harrowlands Pk DORK RH4 272 G3
Harrow La GODL GU7 267 K10
POP/IOD E14 141 H9
Harrow Manor Wy ABYW SE2 143 M10
ABYW SE2 163 M2
Harrow Pk HRW HA1 114 D7
Harrow Pl WCHPL E1 13 K5
Harrow Rd ALP/SUD HA0 114 F9
ALP/SUD HA0 115 H10
ALP/SUD HA0 135 H1
BARK IG11 143 H3
CAR SM5 221 P3
DTCH/LGLY SL3 150 C2
EBED/NFELT TW14 174 B5
IL IG1 122 F9
RSEV TN14 245 P1
UPMR RM14 127 P10
WAN E11 121 L8
WARL CR6 242 E1

WBLY HA9 115 L10
WBLY HA9 135 N1
WLSDN NW10 136 E5
Harrow Rd East DORK RH4 272 G4
Harrow Road F/O BAY/PAD W2 9 M4
Harrow Rd West DORK RH4 272 F4
Harrowsley Ct HORL RH6 280 C3
Harrow St CAMTN NW1 * 9 P3
Harrow Vw HGDN/ICK UB10 132 D5
HYS/HAR UB3 133 H9
RYLN/HDSTN HA2 114 C1
Harrow View Rd EA W5 134 G6
Harrow Wy OXHEY WD19 93 M4
SHPTN TW17 196 D2
Harrow Weald Pk
KTN/HRWW/WS HA3 94 C7
Harston Dr PEND EN3 80 F4
Hartcliff Ct HNWL W7 * 154 E1
Hart Cl REDH RH1 259 N9
Hart Cnr WTHK RM20 * 167 J4
Hart Crs CHIG IG7 103 J6
Hart Dyke Rd STMC/STPC BR5 207 M9
SWLY BR8 208 E4
Harte Rd HSLW TW3 153 N8
Hartfield Av BORE WD6 75 M8
NTHLT UB5 133 J4
Hartfield Cl BORE WD6 75 M9
Hartfield Crs WIM/MER SW19 179 J10
WWKM BR4 205 M10
Hartfield Gv PGE/AN SE20 204 A1
Hartfield Pl GVW DA11 190 A3
Hartfield Rd CHSGTN KT9 219 J2
WIM/MER SW19 179 J10
WWKM BR4 225 M1
Hartfield Ter BOW E3 140 F4
Hartford Av KTN/HRWW/WS HA3 114 F1
Hartforde Rd BORE WD6 75 M6
Hartford Rd BXLY DA5 186 B2
HOR/WEW KT19 219 N3
Hart Gdns DORK RH4 272 G1
Hart Gv EA W5 135 M10
STHL UB1 133 P7
Harthall La KGLGY WD4 54 D4
Hartham Cl HOLWY N7 118 F10
ISLW TW7 154 F7
Hartham Common
HERT/WAT SG14 * 25 L4
Hartham La HERT/WAT SG14 25 K5
Hartham Rd HOLWY N7 118 F10
ISLW TW7 154 E7
TOTM N17 99 N10
Harting Ct CRAWW RH11 283 J10
Harting Rd ELTH/MOT SE9 184 B7
Hartington Cl HRW HA1 114 D9
ORP BR6 226 F2
REIG RH2 257 K8
Hartington Pl REIG RH2 * 257 K8
Hartington Rd CAN/RD E16 141 N8
CHSWK W4 155 N6
NWDGN UB2 * 153 M2
TWK TW1 176 G3
VX/NE SW8 158 F7
WALTH E17 120 D4
WEA W13 134 G9
Hartismere Rd FUL/PGN SW6 157 J6
Hartlake Rd HOM E9 140 C1
Hartland Cl ADL/WDHM KT15 215 M6
EDGW HA8 95 M3
SL SL1 129 J10
WCHMH N21 79 K10
Hartland Dr EDGW HA8 95 M3
RSLP HA4 113 J8
Hartland Rd ADL/WDHM KT15 215 K4
CAMTN NW1 4 E3
CHES/WCR EN8 62 C6
EPP CM16 65 K7
FBAR/BDGN N11 98 A6
HCH RM12 125 H7
HPTN TW12 176 A7
ISLW TW7 154 F9
KIL/WHAMP NW6 2 C7
MRDN SM4 201 K7
SRTFD E15 141 L2
Hartland Rd Arches
CAMTN NW1 * 4 D3
Hartlands Cl BXLY DA5 186 A2
The Hartlands HEST TW5 153 J5
Hartland Wy CROY/NA CR0 204 D9
MRDN SM4 201 K7
Hartley Av EHAM E6 142 B3
MLHL NW7 96 C6
Hartley Bottom Rd HART DA3 211 N8
Hartley Cl BMLY BR1 206 C2
MLHL NW7 96 C6
SLN SL2 129 P3
Hartley Copse WDSR SL4 171 M2
Hartley Down PUR/KEN CR8 222 G10
Hartley Farm PUR/KEN CR8 240 G1
Hartley Hl HART DA3 211 M8
PUR/KEN CR8 240 G1
Hartley Old Rd PUR/KEN CR8 222 G10
Hartley Rd BH/WHM TN16 262 G1
CROY/NA CR0 203 K7
HART DA3 211 K2
WAN E11 121 L6
WELL DA16 163 M6
Hartley St BETH E2 140 B5
Hartley Wy PUR/KEN CR8 240 G1
Hartmann Rd CAN/RD E16 142 A10
Hartmoor Ms PEND EN3 80 C3
Hartnoll St HOLWY N7 118 G10
Harton Cl BMLY BR1 206 A1
Harton Rd ED N9 100 A3
Harton St DEPT SE8 160 F7
Hart Rd BF/WBF KT14 215 P9
DORK RH4 272 G1
HLWE CM17 29 M6
STAL AL1 38 C7
Hartsbourne Av BUSH WD23 94 B3
Hartsbourne Cl BUSH WD23 94 C3
Hartsbourne Rd BUSH WD23 94 C3
Hartsbourne Wy HHNE HP2 36 D7
Harts Cl BUSH WD23 73 P6
Hartscroft CROY/NA CR0 224 D5
Harts Gdns GUW GU2 249 N7
Harts Gv WFD IG8 101 M6
Hart Shaw HART DA3 211 N2
Hartshill GUW GU2 249 J9
Hartshill Cl HGDN/ICK UB10 132 B1
Hartshill Rd GVW DA11 190 C5
Hartshorn Gdns EHAM E6 142 D6
Hartsland Rd SEV TN13 247 K9
Harts La BARK IG11 142 E2
NWCR SE14 160 D6
Hartslock Dr ABYW SE2 163 N1
Hartsmead Rd ELTH/MOT SE9 184 C5
Hartspiece Rd REDH RH1 276 C2
Hartspring La BUSH WD23 73 P6
GSTN WD25 74 A5
Hart Sq MRDN SM4 * 201 L5
Hart St BRW CM14 107 H3
MON EC3R 13 K7
Hartsway PEND EN3 80 A8
Hartswood RDKG RH5 273 J5
Hartswood Av REIG RH2 275 K4
Hartswood Cl BRW CM14 107 K5
Hartswood Gdns SHB W12 * 156 C2
Hartswood Gn BUSH WD23 94 C3
Hartswood Rd BRW CM14 107 K5
SHB W12 156 C2
Hartsworth Cl PLSTW E13 141 L4
Hartville Rd WOOL/PLUM SE18 163 H3
Hartwell Dr BEAC HP9 88 C9
CHING E4 101 H7
Hartwell St HACK E8 * 7 L1
Harty Cl CDW/CHF RM16 147 N10
Harvard Hl CHSWK W4 155 N4
Harvard Rd CHSWK W4 155 N4
ISLW TW7 154 D7
LEW SE13 183 H1
Harvel Cl CHST BR7 207 K3
Harvel Crs ABYW SE2 163 N4
Harvest Bank AMS HP6 68 B1
Harvest Bank Rd WWKM BR4 205 M10
Harvest Ct STALE/WH AL4 39 H2
Harvest End GSTN WD25 73 L2
Harvester Rd HOR/WEW KT19 220 A6
Harvesters Cl ISLW TW7 176 C1
Harvesters Ms STALE/WH AL4 * 39 J2
Harvest La LOU IG10 102 A1
THDIT KT7 198 F6
Harvest Md HAT AL10 40 E3
Harvest Rd BUSH WD23 74 A8
CRAWE RH10 284 D9
EGH TW20 172 A8
FELT TW13 175 H7
Harvestside HORL RH6 280 D3
Harvest Wy SWLY BR8 208 D7
Harvey CDW/CHF RM16 167 N1
Harvey Dr HPTN TW12 198 A1
Harveyfields WAB EN9 63 H10
Harvey Gdns CHARL SE7 161 P4
CHARL SE7 162 A4
GU GU1 * 268 B1
LOU IG10 82 E7
Harvey Rd CEND/HSY/T N8 118 G3
CMBW SE5 159 L7
GU GU1 268 B2
HGDN/ICK UB10 132 B4
HSLWW TW4 175 N3
IL IG1 122 E10
LCOL/BKTW AL2 57 H2
NTHLT UB5 133 K2
RKW/CH/CXG WD3 72 B10
WAN E11 121 K6
WOT/HER KT12 197 H7
Harvey's La ROMW/RG RM7 124 F7
Harvey St IS N1 7 H6
Harvill Rd SCUP DA14 185 N8
Harvil Rd DEN/HRF UB9 111 M2
Harvington Wk HACK E8 * 7 P4
Harvist Rd KIL/WHAMP NW6 137 H4
Harwater Dr LOU IG10 82 C6
Harwell Cl RSLP HA4 112 E6
Harwich Rd SL SL1 128 F8
Harwood Av BMLY BR1 205 N2
EMPK RM11 125 M1
MTCM CR4 201 P3
Harwood Cl ALP/SUD HA0 115 J9
NFNCH/WDSPK N12 97 P7
WGCW AL8 23 H1
Harwood Dr HGDN/ICK UB10 132 A3
Harwood Gdns WDSR SL4 171 N3
Harwood Hall La UPMR RM14 146 A1
Harwood Hl WGCW AL8 23 H2
Harwood Ms FUL/PGN SW6 * 157 L6
Harwood Pk REDH RH1 276 B9
Harwood Rd FUL/PGN SW6 157 K6
Harwoods Rd WATW WD18 73 H8
Harwood Ter FUL/PGN SW6 157 L7
Hascombe Ter CMBW SE5 * 159 L8
Hasedines Rd HHW HP1 35 K5
Haselbury Rd ED N9 99 M4
Haseldine Mdw HAT AL10 40 C5
Haseldine Rd LCOL/BKTW AL2 57 J2
Haseley End FSTH SE23 * 182 B3
Haselrigge Rd CLAP SW4 158 E10
Haseltine Rd SYD SE26 182 E7
Haselwood Dr ENC/FH EN2 79 J8
Haskard Rd DAGW RM9 123 N9
Hasker St CHEL SW3 15 P5
Haslam Av CHEAM SM3 201 H8
Haslam Cl HGDN/ICK UB10 112 D7
IS N1 6 B3
Haslam St PECK SE15 159 N7
Haslemere Av EBAR EN4 98 A2
HDN NW4 116 G4
HEST TW5 153 K8
HNWL W7 154 F2
MTCM CR4 201 N2
WAND/EARL SW18 179 L5
Haslemere Cl HPTN TW12 175 N8
WLGTN SM6 222 F2
Haslemere Gdns FNCH N3 117 H2
Haslemere Heathrow Est
HSLWW TW4 * 153 J8
Haslemere Rd BXLYHN DA7 164 A8
CEND/HSY/T N8 118 F5
GDMY/SEVK IG3 123 J7
THHTH CR7 203 J5
WCHMH N21 99 J3
WDSR SL4 148 F7
Hasler Cl THMD SE28 143 M9
Haslett Av CRAWE RH10 284 A7
Haslett Av East CRAWE RH10 284 B7
Haslett Av West CRAWE RH10 283 N8
Haslett Rd SHPTN TW17 196 F2
Haslewood Av HOD EN11 44 F2
Hasluck Gdns BAR EN5 77 M10
Hassard St BETH E2 7 M8
Hassendean Rd BKHTH/KID SE3 161 N5
Hassett Rd HOM E9 140 C1
Hassocks Cl SYD SE26 182 A6
Hassocks Ct CRAWW RH11 283 J10
Hassocks Rd STRHM/NOR SW16 202 E1
Hassock Wd HAYES BR2 226 A1
Hassop Rd CRICK NW2 116 G9
Hasted Cl SWCM DA10 189 H2
Hasted Rd CHARL SE7 162 A4
Hastings Av BARK/HLT IG6 122 F2
Hastings Cl ALP/SUD HA0 115 H9
BAR EN5 77 M8
GRAYS RM17 167 K5
PECK SE15 * 159 P6
Hastings Dr SURB KT6 199 H6
Hastings Meadow SLN SL2 * 129 M3
Hastings Pl CROY/NA CR0 203 N8
Hastings Rd CRAWE RH10 284 C7
CROY/NA CR0 203 N8
FBAR/BDGN N11 98 D6
GPK RM2 125 J3
HAYES BR2 206 B9
TOTM N17 * 119 L1
WEA W13 134 G9
Hastings St STPAN WC1H 5 L10
Hastings Ter SEVS/STOTM N15 * 119 K3
Hastings Wy BUSH WD23 73 M8
RKW/CH/CXG WD3 72 C8
Hastingwood Rd HLWE CM17 47 P6
Hastings St WOOL/PLUM SE18 162 F2
Hastoe Cl YEAD UB4 133 M6
Hatcham Park Ms NWCR SE14 160 C7
Hatcham Park Rd NWCR SE14 160 C7
Hatcham Rd PECK SE15 160 B5
Hatchard Rd ARCH N19 118 E7
Hatch Cl ADL/WDHM KT15 195 L10
Hatchcroft HDN NW4 116 E1
Hatch End BFOR GU20 212 B3
Hatchers Ms STHWK SE1 19 K2
Hatchet La WDSR SL4 170 A6
Hatchett Rd EBED/NFELT TW14 174 D4
Hatch Gdns KWD/TDW/WH KT20 238 G6
Hatchgate HORL RH6 280 A5
Hatchgate Gdns SL SL1 128 C5
Hatch Gv CHDH RM6 123 P2
Hatch La BNSTD SM7 240 B1
CHING E4 101 J5
REDH RH1 276 G6
RPLY/SEND GU23 234 C6
WDR/YW UB7 151 N6
WDSR SL4 148 F9
Hatch Pl KUTN/CMB KT2 177 L8
Hatch Rd BRWN CM15 86 F9
STRHM/NOR SW16 202 F2
Hatch Side CHIG IG7 102 D6
The Hatch PEND EN3 80 C5
WDSR SL4 148 B6
Hatchwoods WFD IG8 101 L5
Hatcliffe Almshouses
GNWCH SE10 * 161 K4
Hatcliffe Cl BKHTH/KID SE3 161 L9
Hatcliffe St GNWCH SE10 161 L4
Hatfield Av HAT AL10 40 C1
Hatfield Cl BARK/HLT IG6 122 E1
BELMT SM2 221 K5
BF/WBF KT14 * 215 L8
HCH RM12 125 L10
MTCM CR4 * 201 N4
Hatfield Ct BKHTH/KID SE3 * 161 M6
Hatfield Crs HHNE HP2 36 A2
Hatfield Rd ASHTD KT21 237 L5
BRKMPK AL9 23 P10
CDW/CHF RM16 167 J4
CHSWK W4 156 A1
HNWL W7 134 F10
POTB/CUF EN6 59 M7
SL SL1 149 M1
SRTFD E15 121 K10
STAL AL1 38 G6
STALE/WH AL4 39 H6
WATN WD24 73 J5
Hatfields LOU IG10 82 E7
STHWK SE1 12 B9
Hatfield Tnl HAT AL10 40 C3
Hathaway Cl BARK/HLT IG6 102 E7
HAYES BR2 206 C8
RSLP HA4 112 G9
STAN HA7 94 F6
Hathaway Ct STALE/WH AL4 39 K6
Hathaway Crs MNPK E12 142 C1
Hathaway Gdns CHDH RM6 123 N3
WEA W13 134 F7
Hathaway Rd CROY/NA CR0 203 J7
GRAYS RM17 167 N3
Hatherleigh Cl CHSGTN KT9 219 J2
EBAR EN4 77 L5
MRDN SM4 201 K4
Hatherleigh Gdns
POTB/CUF EN6 59 N8
Hatherleigh Rd RSLP HA4 113 H7
Hatherleigh Wy HARH RM3 105 L9
Hatherley Crs BFN/LL DA15 185 K5
Hatherley Gdns CEND/HSY/T N8 118 F4
EHAM E6 142 A5
Hatherley Gv BAY/PAD W2 8 G5
Hatherley Ms WALTH E17 120 F2
Hatherley Rd RCH/KEW TW9 155 L7
SCUP DA14 185 K6
WALTH E17 120 E2
Hatherley St WEST SW1P 17 H6
Hathern Gdns ELTH/MOT SE9 184 D7
Hatherop Rd HPTN TW12 175 N10
Hathersham Cl HORL RH6 281 H3
Hathersham La HORL RH6 280 G1
Hatherwood LHD/OX KT22 237 J7
Hathorne Cl PECK SE15 160 A8
Hathorne Ter ARCH N19 * 118 E6
Hathway St PECK SE15 160 B8
Hatley Av BARK/HLT IG6 122 F2
Hatley Cl FBAR/BDGN N11 98 A6
Hatley Rd FSBYPK N4 118 G7
Hat & Mitre Ct FARR EC1M 12 D2
Hatteraick St BERM/RHTH SE16 160 B1
Hattersfield Cl BELV DA17 164 A3
Hatters La WATW WD18 72 E10
Hatton Av SLN SL2 129 J6
Hatton Cl CDW/CHF RM16 167 J2
GVW DA11 190 B6
WOOL/PLUM SE18 162 G6
Hatton Ct WDSR SL4 149 H8
Hatton Cross Est HTHAIR TW6 * 152 G10
Hatton Gdn HCIRC EC1N 12 B3
Hatton Gdns MTCM CR4 202 A5
Hatton Gn EBED/NFELT TW14 153 H10
Hatton Gv WDR/YW UB7 * 151 N1
Hatton Hl BFOR GU20 212 B2
Hatton Ms SWCM DA10 167 H10
Hatton Pl HCIRC EC1N 12 B2
Hatton Rd CHES/WCR EN8 62 C5
CROY/NA CR0 203 H8
EBED/NFELT TW14 174 D3
HTHAIR TW6 152 G10
Hatton Rw STJWD NW8 * 9 M2
Hatton St STJWD NW8 9 M2
Hatton Wall HCIRC EC1N 12 A3
Haunch of Venison Yd
OXSTW W1C * 10 E6
Havana Cl ROM RM1 124 F3
Havana Rd WIM/MER SW19 179 K5
Havannah St POP/IOD E14 160 F1
Havant Rd WALTH E17 121 H1
Havelock Cl SHB W12 * 136 E9
Havelock Pl HRW HA1 114 D4
Havelock Rd BELV DA17 * 164 A3
CROY/NA CR0 203 N9
DART DA1 187 J3
GVW DA11 190 C4
HAYES BR2 205 P4
KGLGY WD4 54 B4
KTN/HRWW/WS HA3 114 D1
NWDGN UB2 153 M2
NWDGN UB2 153 P2
TOTM N17 99 P10
WIM/MER SW19 179 M8
Havelock St IS N1 5 M5
Havelock Ter VX/NE SW8 158 C6
Havelock Wk FSTH SE23 182 B4
Haven Cl ELTH/MOT SE9 184 C6
HAT AL10 40 D3
SCUP DA14 185 M9
SWLY BR8 208 G2
WIM/MER SW19 178 G6
YEAD UB4 132 F7
Haven Ct BRYLDS KT5 * 199 L6
Havenfield KGLGY WD4 53 L7
Haven Gdns CRAWE RH10 285 P4
Havengore Av GVE DA12 191 H3
Haven Gn EA W5 135 J9
Havenhurst Ri ENC/FH EN2 79 H6
Haven La EA W5 135 K8
Haven Pl CDW/CHF RM16 167 P1
Haven Rd ASHF TW15 174 C7
Havens Ms BOW E3 140 E7
Haven St CAMTN NW1 * 4 E4
Havenswood Ct KUTN/CMB KT2 177 N9
The Haven CDW/CHF RM16 168 C3
RCH/KEW TW9 155 M9
SUN TW16 175 H10
Havenwood WBLY HA9 115 N8
Havercroft Cl STALW/RED AL3 38 A8
Haverfield Est BTFD TW8 155 K5
Haverfield Gdns RCH/KEW TW9 155 M6
Haverfield Rd BOW E3 140 C5
Haverford Wy EDGW HA8 95 L9
Havergal Vls SEVS/STOTM N15 * 119 J2
Haverhill Rd BAL SW12 180 D4
CHING E4 101 H2
Havering Dr ROM RM1 124 F2
Havering Gdns CHDH RM6 123 M3
Havering Rd ROM RM1 104 E6
ROM RM1 104 E8
ROM RM1 124 E1
Havering St WCHPL E1 140 C8
Havering Wy BARK IG11 143 L5
Havers Av WOT/HER KT12 217 L2
Haversham Cl CRAWE RH10 284 A7
TWK TW1 177 J3
Haversham Pl HGT N6 118 A7
Haverstock Hl HAMP NW3 3 P1
Haverstock Pl FSBYE EC1V 6 B8
Haverstock Rd KTTN NW5 118 B10
Haverstock St IS N1 6 D8
Haverthwaite Rd ORP BR6 206 G10
Havil St CMBW SE5 159 M7
Havisham Pl NRWD SE19 181 J9
Havisham Rd GVE DA12 191 K4
Hawarden Gv HNHL SE24 181 K3
Hawarden Hl CRICK NW2 116 D8
Hawarden Rd CTHM CR3 241 K7
WALTH E17 120 C2
Haward Rd HOD EN11 45 H1
Hawbridge Rd WAN E11 121 J6
Hawes Cl NTHWD HA6 92 G8
Hawes La CHING E4 81 H4
WWKM BR4 205 J9
Hawes Rd BMLY BR1 205 N1
KWD/TDW/WH KT20 238 G6
UED N18 100 A7
Hawes St IS N1 6 D4
Haweswater Dr GSTN WD25 55 K9
Hawfield Bank ORP BR6 207 M10
Hawfield Gdns LCOL/BKTW AL2 56 C2
Hawgood St BOW E3 140 F7
Hawk Cl WAB EN9 63 M10
Hawk Cnr WTHK RM20 * 167 J4
Hawkdene CHING E4 80 G10
Hawkenbury HLWW/ROY CM19 46 D3
Hawke Park Rd WDGN N22 119 J1
Hawke Pl BERM/RHTH SE16 * 160 C1
Hawke Rd NRWD SE19 181 L9
Hawker Rd CROY/NA CR0 223 H3
Hawkesbury Cl BARK/HLT IG6 103 L5
Hawkesbury Rd PUT/ROE SW15 178 E1
Hawkes Cl GRAYS RM17 167 N5
Hawkesfield Rd FSTH SE23 182 E5
Hawkes Leap BFOR GU20 212 A1
Hawkesley Cl TWK TW1 176 F7
Hawkesley Ct RAD WD7 74 E1
Hawkesmoor Rd CRAWW RH11 283 H9
Hawkes Pl SEV TN13 265 H3
Hawkes Rd EBED/NFELT TW14 175 H3
MTCM CR4 201 P1
Hawkesworth Cl NTHWD HA6 92 F8
Hawkewood Rd SUN TW16 197 H3
Hawkhirst Rd PUR/KEN CR8 241 L2
Hawkhurst COB KT11 217 P10
Hawkhurst Gdns CRW RM5 104 E7
Hawkhurst Rd
STRHM/NOR SW16 202 E1
Hawkhurst Wk CRAWE RH10 284 C9
Hawkhurst Wy NWMAL KT3 200 A5
WWKM BR4 204 G9
Hawkinge Wy HCH RM12 145 K1
Hawkings Wy HHS/BOV HP3 52 D2
Hawkins Av GVE DA12 190 F7
Hawkins Cl BORE WD6 75 P6
EDGW HA8 96 A6
HRW HA1 114 C5
Hawkins Dr CDW/CHF RM16 167 J1
Hawkins Rd CRAWE RH10 283 P9
TEDD TW11 176 G9
WLSDN NW10 136 B2
Hawkins Ter CHARL SE7 162 B4
Hawkins Wy CAT SE6 182 F8
Hawkley Gdns WNWD SE27 181 J6
Hawkridge Cl CHDH RM6 123 M4
Hawkridge Dr GRAYS RM17 168 A4
Hawksbrook La BECK BR3 204 G6
Hawkshaw Cl BRXS/STRHM SW2 180 F3
Hawkshead Cl BMLY BR1 183 K10
Hawkshead La BRKMPK AL9 59 H4
Hawkshead Rd CHSWK W4 156 B2
POTB/CUF EN6 59 K5
WLSDN NW10 * 136 C2
Hawks Hl EPP CM16 66 B3
LHD/OX KT22 236 E9
Hawkshill STAL AL1 38 F7
Hawkshill Cl ESH/CLAY KT10 217 P3
Hawks Hill Cl LHD/OX KT22 236 E9
Hawks Hill Ct LHD/OX KT22 236 E9
Hawkshill Dr HHS/BOV HP3 35 J9
Hawkshill Pl ESH/CLAY KT10 * 217 P3
Hawkshill Rd SLN SL2 128 F5
Hawkshill Wy ESH/CLAY KT10 217 N3
Hawkslade Rd PECK SE15 182 C1
Hawksley Rd STNW/STAM N16 119 L8
Hawksmead Cl PEND EN3 80 C2
Hawks Ms GNWCH SE10 * 161 H6
Hawksmoor RAD WD7 57 M9
Hawksmoor Cl EHAM E6 142 B8
WOOL/PLUM SE18 163 H4
Hawksmoor Ms WCHPL E1 140 A9
Hawksmoor St HMSMTH W6 156 G5
Hawksmouth CHING E4 100 G1
Hawks Rd KUT/HW KT1 199 L2
Hawkstone Est
BERM/RHTH SE16 160 B3
Hawkstone Rd
BERM/RHTH SE16 160 B3
Hawksview COB KT11 217 N9
Hawksway STA TW18 173 J6
Hawkswell Cl WOKN/KNAP GU21 231 L3
Hawkswood Gv DTCH/LGLY SL3 130 C1
Hawkswood La DTCH/LGLY SL3 110 C10
Hawkwell Wk IS N1 * 6 F5
Hawkwood Crs CHING E4 80 G10
Hawkwood Dell GT/LBKH KT23 253 P2
Hawkwood La CHST BR7 206 F1
Hawkwood Mt CLPT E5 120 A6
Hawkwood Ri GT/LBKH KT23 253 P2
Hawlands Dr PIN HA5 113 M5
Hawley Cl HPTN TW12 175 N9
Hawley Crs CAMTN NW1 4 F4
Hawley Ms CAMTN NW1 4 E3
Hawley Rd CAMTN NW1 4 F3
DART DA1 187 M5
UED N18 100 C6
Hawley St CAMTN NW1 4 E4
Hawley Ter RDART DA2 * 187 P7
Hawley V RDART DA2 * 187 P8
Hawley Wy ASHF TW15 174 B8
Haworth Rd CRAWE RH10 284 C8
Hawridge La CSHM HP5 32 D9
Hawridge V CSHM HP5 32 E8
Hawstead La ORP BR6 228 A2
Hawstead Rd CAT SE6 182 G2
Hawsted BKHH IG9 101 N1
Hawth Av CRAWE RH10 284 B8
Hawth Cl CRAWE RH10 283 P9
Hawthorn Av PLMGR N13 98 F6
RAIN RM13 145 J6
RBRW/HUT CM13 107 L4
THHTH CR7 203 J1
Hawthorn Centre HRW HA1 114 E2
Hawthorn Cl ABLGY WD5 54 G8
BNSTD SM7 221 H10
CRAWW RH11 283 M4
GVE DA12 190 E7
HARP AL5 20 C4
HERT/WAT SG14 25 H4
HEST TW5 153 J6
HPTN TW12 175 P8
IVER SL0 130 F5
REDH RH1 276 B5
STMC/STPC BR5 206 G6
WAT WD17 72 G4
WOKS/MYFD GU22 232 B6
Hawthorn Ct ASHF TW15 174 D10
Hawthorn Crs SAND/SEL CR2 224 B7
TOOT SW17 180 B8
Hawthornden Cl
NFNCH/WDSPK N12 97 P7
Hawthorndene Cl HAYES BR2 * 205 L9
Hawthorndene Rd HAYES BR2 205 M9
Hawthorn Dr DEN/HRF UB9 131 M1
RYLN/HDSTN HA2 113 P4
WWKM BR4 225 K1
Hawthorne Av BH/WHM TN16 244 A1
BOW E3 140 E3
CAR SM5 222 B4
CHESW EN7 62 A6
HRW HA1 114 F4
MTCM CR4 201 N2
RSLP HA4 113 J4
WDSR SL4 170 A5
Hawthorne Cl BMLY BR1 206 C3
CHESW EN7 62 A7
IS N1 7 J1
Hawthorne Ct
STWL/WRAY TW19 * 173 N3
Hawthorne Crs SL SL1 129 K8
WDR/YW UB7 152 A1
Hawthorne Dr WDSR SL4 * 170 A4
Hawthorne Gv CDALE/KGS NW9 115 P5
Hawthorne Pl EW KT17 220 B8
Hawthorne Rd BMLY BR1 206 C3
RAD WD7 56 F10
STA TW18 172 F8
UED N18 99 N7
WALTH E17 120 F1
Hawthornes HAT AL10 40 C6
Hawthorne Wy ED N9 99 N3
RGUE GU4 250 E6
STWL/WRAY TW19 173 N3
Hawthorn Farm Av NTHLT UB5 133 M3
Hawthorn Gdns EA W5 155 J2
Hawthorn Gv ENC/FH EN2 79 L4
PGE/AN SE20 204 A1
Hawthorn Hatch BTFD TW8 154 G6
Hawthorn La HHW HP1 35 J5
SEV TN13 246 G8
SLN SL2 128 E2
Hawthorn Ms MLHL NW7 97 H9
Hawthorn Pl ERITH DA8 164 D4
HYS/HAR UB3 * 132 G9
RGUE GU4 * 250 A5
Hawthorn Rd BTFD TW8 154 G6
BXLYHS DA6 * 164 A10
CEND/HSY/T N8 118 E1
DART DA1 187 L5
FELT TW13 175 H4
HOD EN11 44 G1
RPLY/SEND GU23 233 J10
SUT SM1 221 N2
WFD IG8 101 P5
WLGTN SM6 222 C4
WLSDN NW10 136 D2
WOKS/MYFD GU22 232 B6
Hawthorns HART DA3 211 L4
HLWS CM18 47 J5
WFD IG8 101 M4
WGCW AL8 22 G3
The Hawthorns BERK HP4 33 M4
CSTG HP8 69 P6
DTCH/LGLY SL3 151 J7
EW KT17 220 C3
HHS/BOV HP3 35 J10
OXTED RH8 261 M9
RKW/CH/CXG WD3 90 G6
Hawthorn Ter BFN/LL DA15 185 J2
WEY KT13 * 216 B7
Hawthorn Wk NKENS W10 8 A1
Hawthorn Wy ADL/WDHM KT15 215 L6
CHOB/PIR GU24 230 F2
CSHM HP5 51 J5
LCOL/BKTW AL2 37 P10
REDH RH1 276 C2
SHPTN TW17 196 E4
Hawtrees RAD WD7 74 E1
Hawtrey Av NTHLT UB5 133 L4
Hawtrey Cl SL SL1 149 N1
Hawtrey Dr RSLP HA4 113 H5
Hawtrey Rd HAMP NW3 3 N4
WDSR SL4 149 H8
Haxted Rd BMLY BR1 205 N1
Haybourn Md HHW HP1 35 L7
Hayburn Wy HCH RM12 124 G6
Hay Cl BORE WD6 75 P6
SRTFD E15 141 K2
Haycroft Cl COUL/CHIP CR5 241 J5
Haycroft Gdns WLSDN NW10 136 D3
Haycroft Rd BRXS/STRHM SW2 180 F1
SURB KT6 199 J9
Hay Currie St POP/IOD E14 140 G8
Hayday Rd CAN/RD E16 141 M7
Hayden Ct ADL/WDHM KT15 215 L6
Hayden Dell BUSH WD23 73 N10
Hayden Rd WAB EN9 81 H1
Haydens Cl STMC/STPC BR5 207 M7
Hayden's Pl NTGHL W11 8 C5
Haydens Rd HLW CM20 46 F1
Hayden Wy CRW RM5 104 D10
Haydn Av PUR/KEN CR8 241 H1
Haydock Av NTHLT UB5 133 P1
Haydock Cl HCH RM12 125 N9
Haydock Gn NTHLT UB5 133 P1
Haydon Cl CDALE/KGS NW9 115 P2
EN EN1 79 M10
HARH RM3 105 J8
Haydon Dr PIN HA5 113 H2
Haydon Park Rd
WIM/MER SW19 179 K8
Haydon Pl GU GU1 268 A1
Haydon Rd BCTR RM8 123 M7
OXHEY WD19 73 M10
Haydon's Rd WIM/MER SW19 179 L8
Haydon St TWRH EC3N 13 L7
Haydon Wk WCHPL E1 13 L6
Haydon Wy WAND/EARL SW18 157 M10
Hayes Barton WOKS/MYFD GU22 232 G2
Hayes Cha WWKM BR4 205 J6
Hayes Cl HAYES BR2 205 M9
WTHK RM20 167 H5
Hayes Crs CHEAM SM3 220 G1
GLDGN NW11 117 J3
Hayes Dr RAIN RM13 145 J2
Hayes End Dr YEAD UB4 132 E7
Hayes End Rd YEAD UB4 132 E7
Hayesford Park Dr HAYES BR2 205 L5
Hayes Gdn HAYES BR2 205 M9
Hayes Gv EDUL SE22 159 N10
Hayes Hl HAYES BR2 205 K8
Hayes Hill Rd HAYES BR2 205 L8
HAYES BR2 205 M6
Hayes La BECK BR3 205 J3
PUR/KEN CR8 241 J2
Hayes Mead Rd HAYES BR2 205 K8
Hayes Metro Centre YEAD UB4 * 133 K10
Hayes Pl CAMTN NW1 9 P3
Hayes Rd HAYES BR2 205 M4
NWDGN UB2 153 K3
RDART DA2 188 D3
Hayes St HAYES BR2 205 N8
Hayes Ter GVE DA12 * 191 P8
The Hayes EPSOM KT18 238 A5
Hayes Wk HORL RH6 281 H3
Hayes Wy BECK BR3 205 H4
Hayes Wood Av HAYES BR2 205 N8
Hayfield Cl BUSH WD23 74 A8
Hayfield Pas WCHPL E1 140 B6
Hayfield Rd STMC/STPC BR5 207 K5
Hayfields HORL RH6 280 D3
Haygarth Pl WIM/MER SW19 178 G8
Haygreen Cl KUTN/CMB KT2 177 N9
Hay Green La BRWN CM15 87 K1
Hay Hl MYFR/PICC W1J 10 F8
Hayland Cl CDALE/KGS NW9 116 A2
Hay La CDALE/KGS NW9 116 A2
DTCH/LGLY SL3 110 A9
Hayle TIL RM18 169 M2
Hayles St LBTH SE11 18 C5
Haylett Gdns KUT/HW KT1 * 199 J4
Hayley Cl CDW/CHF RM16 167 H2
Hayling Av FELT TW13 175 H6
Hayling Cl STNW/STAM N16 119 M10
Hayling Rd OXHEY WD19 92 G4
OXHEY WD19 93 J3
Hayman Crs YEAD UB4 132 E4
Haymarket STJS SW1Y 11 J8
Haymeads WGCW AL8 23 H2
Haymeads Dr ESH/CLAY KT10 218 B3
Haymer Gdns WPK KT4 200 D10
Haymerle Rd PECK SE15 19 N10
Haymill Cl GFD/PVL UB6 134 E5
Haymill Rd SL SL1 128 C6
Hayne Rd BECK BR3 204 E2
Haynes Cl BKHTH/KID SE3 161 K9
DTCH/LGLY SL3 150 C4
FBAR/BDGN N11 98 B4
RPLY/SEND GU23 233 L8
TOTM N17 100 A8
WGCE AL7 23 K6
Haynes Dr ED N9 100 A4
Haynes La NRWD SE19 181 M9
Haynes Md BERK HP4 33 M3
Haynes Rd ALP/SUD HA0 135 K2
EMPK RM11 125 L3
GVW DA11 190 C6
Hayne St STBT EC1A 12 D3
Haynt Wk RYNPK SW20 201 H3
Hay Pl SWLY BR8 * 208 D6
Hayse Hl WDSR SL4 148 C7
Hay's La STHWK SE1 13 J9
Haysleigh Gdns PGE/AN SE20 203 P2
Hay's Ms MYFR/PICC W1J 10 E9
Haysoms Cl ROM RM1 124 F2
Haystall Cl YEAD UB4 132 F4
Hay St BETH E2 7 P6
Hays Wk BELMT SM2 220 G6
Hayter Rd BRXS/STRHM SW2 180 F1
Hayton Cl HACK E8 7 M2
Haywain CTHM CR3 241 K8
The Haywain OXTED RH8 261 J6
Hayward Cl DART DA1 186 E1
WIM/MER SW19 179 L10
Hayward Dr DART DA1 187 N6
Hayward Gdns PUT/ROE SW15 178 F2
Hayward Rd THDIT KT7 198 E8
TRDG/WHET N20 97 M3
Haywards CRAWE RH10 284 E4
Haywards Cl CHDH RM6 123 M3
Haywards Md WDSR SL4 148 E4
Hayward's Pl CLKNW EC1R * 12 C2
Haywood Cl PIN HA5 93 L10
Haywood Copse
RKW/CH/CXG WD3 71 N8
Haywood Ct WAB EN9 63 L10
Haywood Dr RKW/CH/CXG WD3 71 J9
Haywood Pk RKW/CH/CXG WD3 71 J9
Haywood Pl CDW/CHF RM16 * 168 F1
Haywood Ri ORP BR6 227 H2
Haywood Rd HAYES BR2 206 A4
Haywoods Dr HHS/BOV HP3 35 J9
Hazel Av GU GU1 249 P6
WDR/YW UB7 152 B2
Hazelbank BRYLDS KT5 199 P8
Hazelbank Rd CAT SE6 183 J5
CHERT KT16 195 M7
Hazelbourne Rd BAL SW12 180 C2
Hazelbrouck Gdns BARK/HLT IG6 102 G8
Hazelbury Av ABLGY WD5 54 D8
Hazelbury Cl WIM/MER SW19 201 K2
Hazelbury Gn ED N9 99 M4
Hazelbury La ED N9 99 M4
Hazel Cl BTFD TW8 * 154 G6
CDALE/KGS NW9 96 C10
CHESW EN7 61 M2
CRAWW RH11 283 M5
CROY/NA CR0 204 C7
EGH TW20 171 N9
HCH RM12 125 J8
MTCM CR4 202 E4
PLMGR N13 99 L4
REIG RH2 275 M2
WHTN TW2 176 C3
Hazel Ct COB KT11 217 H9
RKW/CH/CXG WD3 * 91 H5
Hazelcroft PIN HA5 93 P7
Hazelcroft Cl HGDN/ICK UB10 132 A2
Hazeldean Rd WLSDN NW10 136 A2
Hazeldell Link HHW HP1 * 35 H7
Hazeldell Rd HHW HP1 35 H7
Hazeldene ADL/WDHM KT15 215 M2
CHES/WCR EN8 62 D8
Hazeldene Ct PUR/KEN CR8 241 L1
Hazeldene Dr PIN HA5 113 K1
Hazeldene Gdns HGDN/ICK UB10 132 D3
Hazeldene Rd GDMY/SEVK IG3 123 L7
WELL DA16 163 M8
Hazeldon Rd BROCKY SE4 182 D1
Hazel Dr ERITH DA8 165 J7
RPLY/SEND GU23 251 J1
SOCK/AV RM15 147 H5
Hazeleigh RBRW/HUT CM13 107 N4
Hazeleigh Gdns WFD IG8 102 B7
Hazel End SWLY BR8 208 F5
Hazel Gdns CDW/CHF RM16 168 B2
EDGW HA8 95 N5
Hazelgreen Cl WCHMH N21 99 J2
Hazel Gv ALP/SUD HA0 135 K3
CHDH RM6 123 P1
EN EN1 * 79 P10
GSTN WD25 73 J1
HAT AL10 40 C7
ORP BR6 206 E9
STA TW18 173 L9
SYD SE26 182 C7
WGCE AL7 23 L4
Hazelhurst BECK BR3 205 J1
HORL RH6 280 D3
Hazelhurst Cl RGUE GU4 250 E5
Hazelhurst Dr CRAWE RH10 284 F7
Hazelhurst Rd SL SL1 128 B4
TOOT SW17 179 M7
Hazel La BARK/HLT IG6 102 E8
Hazell Crs CRW RM5 104 C9
Hazell Pk AMSS HP7 69 H5
Hazellville Rd ARCH N19 118 E5
Hazell Wy SLN SL2 129 L1
Hazel Md BAR EN5 76 E9
EW KT17 220 D6
Hazelmere Cl
EBED/NFELT TW14 174 E2
LHD/OX KT22 236 G5
NTHLT UB5 133 N4
Hazelmere Dr NTHLT UB5 133 N4
Hazelmere Gdns EMPK RM11 125 J3
Hazelmere Rd KIL/WHAMP NW6 2 D5
NTHLT UB5 133 N4
STALE/WH AL4 39 H3
STMC/STPC BR5 206 F4
Hazelmere Wk NTHLT UB5 133 N4
Hazelmere Wy HAYES BR2 205 M6
Hazel Pde LHD/OX KT22 * 236 B8
Hazel Ri EMPK RM11 125 K4
Hazel Rd BERK HP4 34 A6
BF/WBF KT14 215 J10
DART DA1 187 L5
ERITH DA8 165 H7
LCOL/BKTW AL2 56 A4
REIG RH2 275 M3
SRTFD E15 * 121 K10
WLSDN NW10 136 E5
Hazel Rw NFNCH/WDSPK N12 * 97 N6
The Hazels WLYN AL6 * 23 P1
Hazeltree La NTHLT UB5 133 M5
Hazel Tree Rd WATN WD24 73 J3
Hazel Wk HAYES BR2 206 D6
Hazel Wy CHING E4 100 E7
COUL/CHIP CR5 240 A5
LHD/OX KT22 236 B8
STHWK SE1 19 L5
Hazelway Cl LHD/OX KT22 236 B9
Hazelwick Av CRAWE RH10 284 C6
Hazelwick Mill La CRAWE RH10 284 C5
CRAWW RH11 283 N3
Hazelwick Rd CRAWE RH10 284 B6
Hazelwood CRAWW RH11 283 K7
DORK RH4 * 272 G3
SLH/COR SS17 169 K3
Hazelwood Av MRDN SM4 201 L4
Hazelwood Cl CLPT E5 120 D8
CRAWE RH10 285 N5
CSHM HP5 51 J5
EA W5 155 K1
RYLN/HDSTN HA2 114 A2
Hazelwood Ct SURB KT6 199 K6
Hazelwood Dr PIN HA5 93 J10
STALE/WH AL4 39 H5
Hazelwood Gdns BRWN CM15 86 F9
Hazelwood Gv SAND/SEL CR2 224 A10
Hazelwood Hts OXTED RH8 261 M7
Hazelwood La ABLGY WD5 54 E8
COUL/CHIP CR5 240 A5
PLMGR N13 99 H5
Hazelwood Park Cl CHIG IG7 103 H6
Hazelwood Rd EN EN1 79 N10
OXTED RH8 261 N8
RKW/CH/CXG WD3 72 D10
RSEV TN14 226 G8
WALTH E17 120 D3
WOKN/KNAP GU21 231 K4
Hazlebury Rd FUL/PGN SW6 157 L8
Hazledean Rd CROY/NA CR0 203 L9
Hazledene Rd CHSWK W4 155 P5
Hazlemere Gdns WPK KT4 200 D8
Hazlemere Rd SLN SL2 129 N10
Hazlewell Rd PUT/ROE SW15 178 F1
Hazlewood Crs NKENS W10 8 B2
Hazlitt Cl FELT TW13 175 M7
Hazlitt Ms WKENS W14 14 A4
Hazlitt Rd WKENS W14 14 A4
Hazon Wy HOR/WEW KT19 220 A8
Heacham Av HGDN/ICK UB10 112 D8
Headcorn Rd BMLY BR1 183 L8
THHTH CR7 202 G4
TOTM N17 99 N8
Headfort Pl KTBR SW1X 16 D2
Headingley Cl CHESW EN7 61 N2
RAD WD7 57 K8

Headington Rd
WAND/EARL SW18 179 M4
Headlam Rd CLAP SW4 180 E3
Headlam St WCHPL E1 140 A6
Headlands Dr BERK HP4 34 B4
Headley Ap GNTH/NBYPK IG2 122 D3
Headley Av WLGTN SM6 222 G2
Headley Cha BRW CM14 107 H5
Headley Cl CHSGTN KT9 219 M3
CRAWE RH10 284 E4
Headley Common
RBRW/HUT CM13 106 G8
Headley Common Rd
EPSOM KT18 256 A4
Headley Dr CROY/NA CR0 225 H4
EPSOM KT18 238 F5
GNTH/NBYPK IG2 122 E4
Headley Gv EPSOM KT18 256 A4
KWD/TDW/WH KT20 238 E6
Headley Heath Ap
KWD/TDW/WH KT20 255 N7
Headley La RDKG RH5 255 H5
Headley Pde EPSOM KT18 * 238 A5
Headley Rd EPSOM KT18 237 P4
LHD/OX KT22 237 H8
Heads Ms NTGHL W11 8 E6
Headstone Dr HRW HA1 114 D1
Headstone Gdns
RYLN/HDSTN HA2 114 B2
Headstone La RYLN/HDSTN HA2 94 A10
Headstone Pde HRW HA1 * 114 C2
Headstone Rd HRW HA1 114 D4
Head St WCHPL E1 140 C8
Headway Cl RCHPK/HAM TW10 177 H7
The Headway EW KT17 220 C5
Heald St NWCR SE14 160 E7
Healey Rd WATW WD18 72 G10
Healey St CAMTN NW1 4 E2
Healy Dr ORP BR6 227 J1
Heard's La BRWN CM15 87 L7
Hearleway HAT AL10 40 B2
Hearne Rd CHSWK W4 155 M4
Hearnes Cl BEAC HP9 89 J6
Hearn Ri NTHLT UB5 133 L3
Hearn Rd ROM RM1 124 G4
Hearn's Buildings WALW SE17 19 H6
Hearns Cl STMC/STPC BR5 207 M4
Hearnshaw St POP/IOD E14 140 D8
Hearns Rd STMC/STPC BR5 207 M4
Hearn St SDTCH EC2A 13 K2
Hearnville Rd BAL SW12 180 B4
Heatham Pk WHTN TW2 176 E3
Heath Av BXLYHN DA7 163 N5
STALW/RED AL3 38 D5
Heathbourne Rd BUSH WD23 94 D3
Heathbridge WEY KT13 * 216 B3
Heath Brow HAMP NW3 117 M8
HHW HP1 35 M8
Heath Cl BNSTD SM7 221 L10
EA W5 135 L6
GLDGN NW11 117 L5
GPK RM2 125 H1
HARP AL5 20 B4
HHW HP1 35 M7
HYS/HAR UB3 152 E6
POTB/CUF EN6 59 L6
SAND/SEL CR2 223 J3
STMC/STPC BR5 207 M6
STWL/WRAY TW19 173 M2
SWLY BR8 208 F2
VW GU25 194 A4
Heathclose Av DART DA1 187 J3
Heathclose Rd DART DA1 187 H4
Heathcote KWD/TDW/WH KT20 238 G8
Heathcote Av CLAY IG5 102 C10
HAT AL10 40 D2
Heathcote Gdns HLWE CM17 47 P1
Heathcote Gv CHING E4 101 H4
Heathcote Rd EPSOM KT18 220 A10
TWK TW1 176 G2
Heathcote St BMSBY WC1N 11 N1
Heathcote Wy WDR/YW UB7 131 N10
Heathcroft EA W5 135 L6
WGCE AL7 23 M4
Heathcroft Av SUN TW16 174 G10
Heathcroft Gdns WALTH E17 101 J9
Heathdale Av HSLWW TW4 153 M9
Heathdene KWD/TDW/WH KT20 239 H5
Heathdene Dr BELV DA17 164 C3
Heathdene Mnr WAT WD17 * 72 G5
Heathdene Rd
STRHM/NOR SW16 180 G10
WLGTN SM6 222 C4
Heathdown Rd
WOKS/MYFD GU22 232 G1
Heath Dr BELMT SM2 221 M5
CHOB/PIR GU24 230 F6
EPP CM16 83 H1
GPK RM2 105 H9
HAMP NW3 117 L9
KWD/TDW/WH KT20 256 E2
POTB/CUF EN6 59 K6
RPLY/SEND GU23 232 E9
RYNPK SW20 200 F4
Heathedge SYD SE26 * 182 A5
Heathend Rd BXLY DA5 186 F4
Heather Av ROM RM1 104 E10
Heatherbank CHST BR7 206 D2
ELTH/MOT SE9 162 C8
Heatherbank Cl COB KT11 217 L7
DART DA1 186 F2
Heather Cl ABLGY WD5 55 H8
ADL/WDHM KT15 215 L6
BRWN CM15 86 G9
CRAWE RH10 285 J3
EHAM E6 142 E8
GUW GU2 249 N8
HPTN TW12 197 N1
ISLW TW7 176 C1
KWD/TDW/WH KT20 239 H8
LEW SE13 183 J2
REDH RH1 258 C7
ROM RM1 104 E9
UX/CGN UB8 132 A7
VX/NE SW8 158 C9
WOKN/KNAP GU21 231 P1
Heatherdale Cl KUTN/CMB KT2 177 M9
Heatherdene EHSLY KT24 252 E1
Heatherdene Cl MTCM CR4 201 N4
NFNCH/WDSPK N12 97 M9
Heatherden Gn IVER SL0 130 F3
Heather Dr ASC SL5 192 G7
DART DA1 187 H3
ENC/FH EN2 79 J6
ROM RM1 104 E10
Heather End SWLY BR8 208 E5
Heatherfold Wy PIN HA5 112 G1
Heather Gdns BELMT SM2 221 K3
GLDGN NW11 117 H4
ROM RM1 104 E10
WAB EN9 81 H2
Heather Gln ROM RM1 104 E10
Heatherlands HORL RH6 * 280 D3
SUN TW16 175 H9
Heather La WDR/YW UB7 131 P8
Heatherley Dr CLAY IG5 122 C1
Heather Park Dr ALP/SUD HA0 135 M3
Heather Park Pde
ALP/SUD HA0 * 135 L2
Heather Pl ESH/CLAY KT10 218 A1
Heather Ri BUSH WD23 73 N6
Heather Rd CHING E4 100 E7
CRICK NW2 116 C7
LEE/GVPK SE12 183 M5
WGCW AL8 22 F7
Heatherset Cl ESH/CLAY KT10 218 B2
Heatherset Gdns
STRHM/NOR SW16 180 G10
Heatherside Cl GT/LBKH KT23 * 253 N1
Heatherside Dr VW GU25 193 M6
Heatherside Gdns SLN SL2 109 J8
Heatherside Rd HOR/WEW KT19 220 A4
SCUP DA14 185 M6
Heathers Land DORK RH4 273 H5
The Heathers STWL/WRAY TW19 174 A3
Heatherton Pk AMS HP6 68 G2
Heathervale Rd
ADL/WDHM KT15 215 L6
Heathervale Wy
ADL/WDHM KT15 215 M6
Heather Wk CHOB/PIR GU24 230 C7
EDGW HA8 95 N6
HORL RH6 281 K4
NKENS W10 8 B1
Heather Wy CHOB/PIR GU24 213 K4
HHNE HP2 35 N5
POTB/CUF EN6 59 J8
ROM RM1 104 E9
SAND/SEL CR2 224 C5
STAN HA7 94 E7
Heatherwood Cl MNPK E12 121 N7
Heatherwood Dr YEAD UB4 132 E4
Heath Farm La STALW/RED AL3 38 D4
Heathfield CHING E4 101 H4
CHST BR7 184 F9
COB KT11 217 P10
CRAWE RH10 284 E5
HRW HA1 * 114 E5
Heathfield Av ASC SL5 192 D5
WAND/EARL SW18 179 N3
Heathfield Cl ASHTD KT21 237 H5
CAN/RD E16 142 A7
HAYES BR2 225 P2
OXHEY WD19 93 K1
POTB/CUF EN6 59 L6
WOKS/MYFD GU22 232 D4
Heathfield Cottages
GRAYS RM17 * 167 K5
Heathfield Dr MTCM CR4 201 P1
REDH RH1 275 P5
Heathfield Gdns CHSWK W4 155 P4
CROY/NA CR0 * 223 K1
GLDGN NW11 116 G4
WAND/EARL SW18 179 N2
Heathfield La CHST BR7 184 F9
Heathfield North WHTN TW2 176 D3
Heathfield Pk CRICK NW2 136 F1
Heathfield Park Dr CHDH RM6 123 L3
Heathfield Ri RSLP HA4 112 D5
Heathfield Rd ACT W3 155 N1
BMLY BR1 183 L10
BUSH WD23 73 M8
BXLYHS DA6 164 A10
HAYES BR2 225 P2
SAND/SEL CR2 223 L2
SEV TN13 246 G8
WAND/EARL SW18 179 M2
WOKS/MYFD GU22 232 D4
WOT/HER KT12 217 M1
Heathfield South WHTN TW2 176 E3
Heathfield Sq WAND/EARL SW18 179 N3
Heathfield Ter CHSWK W4 155 P4
SWLY BR8 * 208 E2
WOOL/PLUM SE18 163 H5
Heathfield V SAND/SEL CR2 224 C5
Heath Gdns DART DA1 * 187 K4
TWK TW1 176 E4
Heathgate GLDGN NW11 117 L4
HERT/BAY SG13 26 A8
Heathgate Pl HAMP NW3 118 A9
Heath Gv PGE/AN SE20 182 B10
SUN TW16 174 G10
Heath Hl DORK RH4 272 G2
Heath House Rd
WOKS/MYFD GU22 231 J8
Heath Hurst Rd HAMP NW3 117 P9
Heathhurst Rd SAND/SEL CR2 223 M5
Heathland Rd STNW/STAM N16 119 M6
Heathlands KWD/TDW/WH KT20 238 G8
Heathlands Cl SUN TW16 197 H2
TWK TW1 176 E5
WOKN/KNAP GU21 214 B10
Heathlands Ct HSLWW TW4 175 M1
Heathlands Dr STALW/RED AL3 38 D4
Heathlands Ri DART DA1 187 J3
Heathlands Wy HSLWW TW4 175 M1
Heath La BKHTH/KID SE3 161 J8
DART DA1 187 J4
HERT/BAY SG13 26 B9
HHW HP1 35 M8
SHGR GU5 269 P7
Heathlee Rd BKHTH/KID SE3 161 L10
DART DA1 186 F2
Heathley End CHST BR7 184 F9
Heath Ldg BUSH WD23 * 94 C2
Heathman's Rd FUL/PGN SW6 157 J7
Heath Md WIM/MER SW19 178 G6
Heath Ms RPLY/SEND GU23 233 L9
Heath Mill La RGUW GU3 249 H1
Heathpark Dr BFOR GU20 212 D3
Heath Park Dr BMLY BR1 206 B3
Heath Park Rd GPK RM2 125 H3
Heath Ridge Gn COB KT11 217 P9
Heath Ri DORK RH4 272 B4
HAYES BR2 205 M6
PUT/ROE SW15 178 G2
VW GU25 194 A4
Heathrise RPLY/SEND GU23 233 L9
Heath Rd AMS HP6 50 B10
BXLY DA5 186 D4
CDW/CHF RM16 168 C1
CHDH RM6 123 N5
CTHM CR3 241 L9
HGDN/ICK UB10 132 D6
HRW HA1 114 B5
HSLW TW3 154 B10
LHD/OX KT22 218 B8
OXHEY WD19 93 L1
POTB/CUF EN6 59 L6
STAL AL1 38 D5
THHTH CR7 203 K3
TWK TW1 176 E4
VX/NE SW8 158 C8
WEY KT13 216 B2
WOKN/KNAP GU21 232 C1
Heathrow SHGR GU5 270 D5
Heathrow Cl WDR/YW UB7 151 L7
Heath's Cl EN EN1 79 L6
Heath Side STMC/STPC BR5 206 G8
Heathside ESH/CLAY KT10 198 D10
HAMP NW3 117 N9
HSLWW TW4 175 N3
STALE/WH AL4 39 N9
STALW/RED AL3 38 D4
WEY KT13 216 C2
Heathside Av BXLYHN DA7 163 P8
Heathside Cl ESH/CLAY KT10 198 D10
GNTH/NBYPK IG2 122 G3
NTHWD HA6 92 E6
Heathside Ct
KWD/TDW/WH KT20 238 E9
Heathside Crs WOKS/MYFD GU22 232 C3
Heathside Gdns
WOKS/MYFD GU22 232 D3
Heathside Park Rd
WOKS/MYFD GU22 232 C4
Heathside Pl EPSOM KT18 238 G4
Heathside Rd NTHWD HA6 92 E5
WOKS/MYFD GU22 232 C4
Heathstan Rd SHB W12 136 D8
Heath St DART DA1 187 L3
HAMP NW3 117 M8
The Heath CTHM CR3 241 K10
HNWL W7 * 154 D1
RAD WD7 56 F9
Heath Vw EFNCH N2 117 M2
EHSLY KT24 252 G1
Heathview Av DART DA1 186 F2
Heath View Cl EFNCH N2 117 M2
Heathview Crs DART DA1 187 H3
Heath View Dr ABYW SE2 163 N5
Heath View Gdns
CDW/CHF RM16 167 P2
Heathview Gdns PUT/ROE SW15 178 F3
Heath View Rd CDW/CHF RM16 167 P1
Heathview Rd THHTH CR7 203 H4
Heath Vls WAND/EARL SW18 * 179 M4
WOOL/PLUM SE18 163 J4
Heathville Rd ARCH N19 118 F5
Heathwall St BTSEA SW11 158 A9
Heath Wy ERITH DA8 164 D7
IVER SL0 130 G4
RAD WD7 57 H6
Heathway BKHTH/KID SE3 161 M6
CROY/NA CR0 204 E10
CTHM CR3 259 K1
DAGW RM9 124 A10
DAGW RM9 144 B2
EHSLY KT24 234 G10
NWDGN UB2 * 153 L3
WFD IG8 101 P5
Heathwood Gdns CHARL SE7 162 B3
SWLY BR8 208 D2
Heathwood Pde SWLY BR8 * 208 D2
Heathwood Wk BXLY DA5 186 F4
Heaton Av HARH RM3 105 J8
Heaton Cl CHING E4 101 H4
HARH RM3 105 K8
Heaton Grange Rd GPK RM2 104 G9
Heaton Rd MTCM CR4 180 B10
PECK SE15 160 A9
Heaton Wy HARH RM3 105 K8
Heaven Tree Cl IS N1 119 K10
Heaver Rd BTSEA SW11 * 157 N9
Heavitree Cl WOOL/PLUM SE18 162 G4
Heavitree Rd WOOL/PLUM SE18 162 G4
Heay Flds WGCE AL7 23 M4
Hebden Ter TOTM N17 99 M7
Hebdon Rd TOOT SW17 179 P6
Heber Rd CRICK NW2 116 G10
EDUL SE22 181 N2
Hebron Rd HMSMTH W6 156 E2
Hecham Cl WALTH E17 100 D10
Heckfield Pl FUL/PGN SW6 157 K6
Heckford Cl WATW WD18 72 D10
Heckford St WAP E1W 140 C9
Hector St WOOL/PLUM SE18 * 163 H3
Heddington Gv HOLWY N7 118 G10
Heddon Cl ISLW TW7 154 F10
Heddon Court Av EBAR EN4 78 A9
Heddon Court Pde EBAR EN4 * 78 B9
Heddon Rd EBAR EN4 78 A9
Heddon St CONDST W1S 10 G8
Hedgebrooms WGCE AL7 23 M4
Hedge Hl ENC/FH EN2 79 J5
Hedge La PLMGR N13 99 K5
Hedgeley REDBR IG4 122 C2
Hedgemans Rd DAGW RM9 143 N2
Hedgemans Wy DAGW RM9 143 P1
Hedge Place Rd RDART DA2 188 E2
Hedgerley Ct WOKN/KNAP GU21 231 P3
Hedgerley Gdns GFD/PVL UB6 134 B4
Hedgerley Hl SLN SL2 109 J8
Hedgerley La BEAC HP9 108 F1
SLN SL2 109 K4
Hedgerow CFSP/GDCR SL9 90 B7
Hedge Rw HHW HP1 35 K4
Hedgerow La BAR EN5 76 E9
Hedgerows SBW CM21 30 A1
The Hedgerows GVW DA11 190 B5
Hedgerow Wk CHES/WCR EN8 62 C6
Hedger's Gv HOM E9 * 140 D1
Hedger St LBTH SE11 18 C5
Hedges Cl HAT AL10 40 E3
Hedgeside BERK HP4 34 D2
Hedgeway GUW GU2 267 M2
Hedgewood Gdns CLAY IG5 122 D3
Hedgley St LEE/GVPK SE12 183 L1
Hedingham Cl HORL RH6 280 D3
IS N1 6 E4
Hedingham Rd BCTR RM8 123 L10
CDW/CHF RM16 167 H4
EMPK RM11 125 P6
Hedley Av WTHK RM20 167 H5
Hedley Rd STAL AL1 38 G6
WHTN TW2 175 P3
Hedley Rw HBRY N5 119 L10
Hedworth Av CHES/WCR EN8 62 C9
Heenan Cl BARK IG11 142 F1
Heene Rd ENC/FH EN2 79 L6
Heidegger Crs BARN SW13 156 E6
Heigham Rd EHAM E6 142 B2
Heighams HLWW/ROY CM19 46 C4
Heighton Gdns CROY/NA CR0 223 J2
Heights Cl BNSTD SM7 239 H2
RYNPK SW20 178 E10
The Heights BECK BR3 * 183 H10
CHARL SE7 161 P4
LOU IG10 82 C6
NTHLT UB5 113 P10
SEV TN13 * 246 F8
WAB EN9 63 N1
WEY KT13 * 216 B6
Heiron St WALW SE17 18 D10
Helby Rd CLAP SW4 180 E2
Helder Gv LEE/GVPK SE12 183 L3
Helder St SAND/SEL CR2 223 L3
Heldmann Cl HSLW TW3 154 C10
Helegan Cl ORP BR6 227 J1
Helena Cl EBAR EN4 77 N3
Helena Pl HACK E8 140 A3
Helena Rd EA W5 135 J7
PLSTW E13 141 L4
WALTH E17 120 F3
WDSR SL4 149 J8
WLSDN NW10 116 E10
Helena Sq BERM/RHTH SE16 140 D9
Helen Av EBED/NFELT TW14 175 J3
Helen Cl DART DA1 187 J3
E/WMO/HCT KT8 198 A4
EFNCH N2 117 M1
Helen Rd EMPK RM11 125 L1
Helens Ga CHES/WCR EN8 62 E2
Helenslea Av GLDGN NW11 117 J6
Helen's Pl BETH E2 140 B5
Helen St WOOL/PLUM SE18 * 162 E3
Helford Cl RSLP HA4 112 F7
Helford Wk WOKN/KNAP GU21 231 M4
Helford Wy UPMR RM14 126 C4
Helgiford Gdns SUN TW16 174 F10
Helions Rd HLWW/ROY CM19 46 E1
Helios Rd WLGTN SM6 202 B8
Helix Gdns BRXS/STRHM SW2 180 G2
Helix Rd BRXS/STRHM SW2 180 G2
Helleborine GRAYS RM17 167 L4
Hellings St WAP E1W 13 P10
Helm Cl HOR/WEW KT19 219 M8
Helme Cl WIM/MER SW19 179 J8
Helmet Rw FSBYE EC1V 12 F1
Helmore Rd BARK IG11 143 J2
Helmsdale WOKN/KNAP GU21 231 N4
Helmsdale Cl ROM RM1 104 F8
YEAD UB4 * 133 M6
Helmsdale Rd ROM RM1 104 F8
STRHM/NOR SW16 202 D1
Helmsley Pl HACK E8 140 A2
Helmsley St HACK E8 140 A3
Helperby Rd WLSDN NW10 136 B2
Helsinki Sq BERM/RHTH SE16 160 E2
Helston Cl PIN HA5 93 N8
Helston Gv HHNE HP2 * 35 N1
Helston La WDSR SL4 148 G7
Helston Pl ABLGY WD5 54 G8
Helvellyn Cl EGH TW20 172 E10
Helvetia St CAT SE6 182 E5
Hemans St VX/NE SW8 158 E6
Hemel Hempstead Rd
HHS/BOV HP3 36 F8
LCOL/BKTW AL2 37 L8
Hemery Rd GFD/PVL UB6 114 C10
Hemingford Cl
NFNCH/WDSPK N12 97 N6
Hemingford Rd CHEAM SM3 220 F1
IS N1 5 P5
WAT WD17 72 F2
Heming Rd EDGW HA8 95 N7
Hemington Av FBAR/BDGN N11 98 A6
Hemlock Cl KWD/TDW/WH KT20 239 H9
Hemlock Rd SHB W12 136 C9
Hemmen La HYS/HAR UB3 132 G9
Hemming Cl HPTN TW12 197 P1
Hemmings Cl SCUP DA14 185 L5
Hemmingsmead
HOR/WEW KT19 219 P3
The Hemmings BERK HP4 33 K6
Hemming St WCHPL E1 13 P2
Hemming Wy GSTN WD25 73 H1
SLN SL2 128 G5
Hemmingway Cl KTTN NW5 118 B9
Hemnall St EPP CM16 65 J7
Hempshaw Av BNSTD SM7 240 A2
Hempson Av DTCH/LGLY SL3 149 P2
Hempstall WGCE AL7 23 L7
Hempstead Cl BKHH IG9 101 M3
Hempstead La BERK HP4 34 F3
Hempstead Rd HHS/BOV HP3 52 E2
KGLGY WD4 54 B4
WALTH E17 121 J1
WAT WD17 72 E2
WAT WD17 73 H6
Hemp Wk WALW SE17 19 H5
Hemsby Rd CHSGTN KT9 219 L3
Hemsby Wk CRAWE RH10 284 C9
Hemstal Rd KIL/WHAMP NW6 2 E3
Hemsted Rd ERITH DA8 164 F7
Hemswell Dr CDALE/KGS NW9 96 B9
Hemsworth St IS N1 7 J7
Hemwood Rd WDSR SL4 148 C9
Henbit Cl KWD/TDW/WH KT20 238 E5
Henbury Wy OXHEY WD19 93 L4
Henchley Dene RGUE GU4 250 G7
Henchman St SHB W12 136 C8
Hencroft St North SL SL1 149 L1
Hencroft St South SL SL1 149 L2
Hendale Av HDN NW4 116 D1
Henderson Av GUW GU2 249 N6
Henderson Cl EMPK RM11 125 J7
STALW/RED AL3 38 B2
WLSDN NW10 135 P1
Henderson Dr DART DA1 165 P10
STJWD NW8 9 L1
Henderson Pl ABLGY WD5 54 G3
Henderson Rd BH/WHM TN16 225 P8
CROY/NA CR0 203 L6
ED N9 100 A2
FSTGT E7 141 P1
WAND/EARL SW18 179 P3
YEAD UB4 133 H5
Hendham Rd TOOT SW17 179 P5
Hendon Av FNCH N3 97 H10
Hendon Gdns CRW RM5 104 D7
Hendon Gv HOR/WEW KT19 219 M5
Hendon Hall Ct HDN NW4 * 116 G1
Hendon La FNCH N3 117 H1
Hendon Park Rw GLDGN NW11 * 117 J4
Hendon Rd ED N9 99 P3
Hendon Ter ASHF TW15 * 174 E9
Hendon Wy CRICK NW2 116 G5
CRICK NW2 117 J8
STWL/WRAY TW19 173 N1
Hendon Wood La MLHL NW7 96 D2
Hendren Cl GFD/PVL UB6 114 C10
Hendre Rd STHWK SE1 19 K6
Hendrick Av BAL SW12 180 A2
Heneage Crs CROY/NA CR0 225 H6
Heneage La HDTCH EC3A 13 K6
Heneage St WCHPL E1 13 M3
Henfield Cl ARCH N19 118 D6
BXLY DA5 186 B2
Henfield Rd WIM/MER SW19 201 J1
Henfold La RDKG RH5 273 K10
Hengelo Gdns MTCM CR4 201 N4
Hengist Rd ERITH DA8 164 D6
LEE/GVPK SE12 183 N3
Hengist Wy HAYES BR2 205 J4
Hengrave Rd FSTH SE23 182 B3
Hengrove Ct BXLY DA5 185 P4
Hengrove Crs ASHF TW15 173 N6
Henhurst Rd GVE DA12 191 H10
Henley Av CHEAM SM3 201 H10
Henley Bank GUW GU2 267 M2
Henley Cl BERM/RHTH SE16 * 160 B1
CRAWE RH10 284 E10
GFD/PVL UB6 * 134 B4
ISLW TW7 154 E7
Henley Ct WOKS/MYFD GU22 232 D6
Henley Deane GVW DA11 190 B7
Henley Dr KUTN/CMB KT2 178 C10
STHWK SE1 19 M5
Henley Gdns CHDH RM6 123 P3
PIN HA5 113 J1
Henley Ga CHOB/PIR GU24 248 B3
Henley Pk RGUW GU3 * 248 C5
Henley Rd CAN/RD E16 162 C1
IL IG1 122 F9
SL SL1 128 D8
UED N18 99 M5
WLSDN NW10 136 F3
Henley St BTSEA SW11 158 B8
Henley Wy FELT TW13 175 L8
Hennel Cl FSTH SE23 182 B6
Hennessy Ct WOKN/KNAP GU21 214 F9
Hennessy Rd ED N9 100 B3
Henniker Gdns EHAM E6 142 A5
Henniker Ms CHEL SW3 15 L9
Henniker Rd SRTFD E15 121 J10
Henningham Rd TOTM N17 99 L9
Henning St BTSEA SW11 157 P7
Henrietta Cl DEPT SE8 160 F5
Henrietta Ms BMSBY WC1N 11 M1
Henrietta Pl CAVSQ/HST W1G 10 E6
Henrietta St COVGDN WC2E 11 M7
SRTFD E15 121 H10
Henriques St WCHPL E1 13 P6
Henry Addlington Cl EHAM E6 142 E7
Henry Cl ENC/FH EN2 79 M4
Henry Cooper Wy
ELTH/MOT SE9 184 A6
Henry Darlot Dr MLHL NW7 96 G6
Henry De Grey Cl GRAYS RM17 167 L3
Henry Dent Cl CMBW SE5 159 L9
Henry Dickens Ct NTGHL W11 136 G9
Henry Doulton Dr TOOT SW17 180 B7
Henry Jackson Rd
PUT/ROE SW15 156 G9
Henry Macaulay Av
KUTN/CMB KT2 199 J1
Henry Peters Dr TEDD TW11 * 176 D8
Henry Rd EBAR EN4 77 N9
EHAM E6 142 B4
FSBYPK N4 119 K6
SL SL1 149 J1
Henry's Av WFD IG8 101 L6
Henrys Grant STAL AL1 38 D7
Henryson Rd BROCKY SE4 182 F1
Henry St BMLY BR1 205 N1
GRAYS RM17 167 P5
HHS/BOV HP3 35 N10
Henry Tate Ms
STRHM/NOR SW16 181 H8
Henry Wells Sq HHNE HP2 * 36 A2
Hensford Gdns SYD SE26 182 A7
Henshall St IS N1 7 H2
Henshaw Cl CRAWW RH11 283 J9
Henshawe Rd BCTR RM8 123 N8
Henshaw St WALW SE17 18 G5
Henslowe Rd EDUL SE22 181 P1
Henslow Wy WOKN/KNAP GU21 214 G10
Henson Av CRICK NW2 116 F10
Henson Cl ORP BR6 206 E9
Henson Pl NTHLT UB5 133 K3
Henson Rd CRAWE RH10 284 C6
Henstridge Pl STJWD NW8 3 N7
Hensworth Rd ASHF TW15 173 N9
Henty Cl BTSEA SW11 157 P6
CRAWW RH11 283 H10
Henty Wk PUT/ROE SW15 178 E1
Henville Rd BMLY BR1 205 N1
Henwick Rd ELTH/MOT SE9 162 A9
Henwood Side WFD IG8 102 C7
Hepburn Cl CDW/CHF RM16 167 J3
Hepburn Gdns HAYES BR2 205 L8
Hepple Cl ISLW TW7 154 G8
Hepscott Rd HOM E9 140 F1
Hepworth Gdns BARK IG11 123 K10
Hepworth Rd STRHM/NOR SW16 180 F10
Hepworth Wy WOT/HER KT12 196 G8
Heracles Cl LCOL/BKTW AL2 56 B4
Herald Gdns WLGTN SM6 202 C10
Heralds Pl LBTH SE11 18 C5
Herald St BETH E2 140 A6
Herbal Hl CLKNW EC1R 12 B2
Herbert Crs KTBR SW1X 16 B3
WOKN/KNAP GU21 231 K4
Herbert Gdns CHDH RM6 123 N5
CHSWK W4 155 N5
WLSDN NW10 136 E4
Herbert Ms BRXS/STRHM SW2 181 H2
Herbert Pl ISLW TW7 154 C8
WOOL/PLUM SE18 162 E5
Herbert Rd BXLYHN DA7 163 P8
CDALE/KGS NW9 116 D4
EMPK RM11 125 M5
FBAR/BDGN N11 98 F8
GDMY/SEVK IG3 123 H7
HAYES BR2 206 A5
KUT/HW KT1 199 L3
MNPK E12 122 B9
SEVS/STOTM N15 119 N3
STHL UB1 133 N10
SWCM DA10 189 L2
SWLY BR8 187 J9
WALTH E17 120 E5
WIM/MER SW19 179 J10
WOOL/PLUM SE18 162 E6
Herberts Hole CSHM HP5 50 C6
Herbert St HHNE HP2 35 N5
KTTN NW5 4 C1
PLSTW E13 141 M4
Herbrand St BMSBY WC1N 11 L2
Hercies Rd HGDN/ICK UB10 132 A1
Hercules Pl HOLWY N7 118 F8
Hercules Rd STHWK SE1 17 P4
Hercules St HOLWY N7 118 F8
Hereford Av EBAR EN4 98 A2
Hereford Cl EPSOM KT18 220 A9
GUW GU2 249 L8
STA TW18 195 L1
Hereford Copse
WOKS/MYFD GU22 231 N5
Hereford Gdns IL IG1 122 B5
PIN HA5 113 M3
WHTN TW2 * 176 B4
Hereford Ms BAY/PAD W2 8 F5
Hereford Pl NWCR SE14 * 160 E6
Hereford Retreat PECK SE15 159 P6
Hereford Rd ACT W3 135 P9
BAY/PAD W2 8 F6
BOW E3 140 E4
EA W5 155 H2
FELT TW13 175 K4
WAN E11 121 N3
Hereford Sq SKENS SW7 15 K6
Hereford St BETH E2 13 N1
Hereford Wy CHSGTN KT9 219 H2
Herent Dr CLAY IG5 122 C1
Heretage Cl BRXN/ST SW9 159 J9
Hereward Av PUR/KEN CR8 223 H6
Hereward Cl WAB EN9 63 H8
Hereward Gdns PLMGR N13 99 H6
Hereward Gn LOU IG10 82 F5
Hereward Rd TOOT SW17 179 P7
Herga Ct WAT WD17 73 H6
Herga Rd KTN/HRWW/WS HA3 114 E2
Herington Gv RBRW/HUT CM13 107 M1
Heriot Av CHING E4 100 F3
Heriot Rd CHERT KT16 195 K7
HDN NW4 116 F3
Heriots Cl STAN HA7 94 F5
Heritage Cl STALW/RED AL3 * 38 C6
SUN TW16 197 H1
UX/CGN UB8 131 M6
Heritage Ct EGH TW20 172 C8
Heritage Hl HAYES BR2 225 P2
Heritage Lawn HORL RH6 280 D3
Heritage Pl WAND/EARL SW18 * 179 N2
Heritage Vw HRW HA1 114 E8
Heritage Wk
RKW/CH/CXG WD3 * 71 H7
Herkomer Cl BUSH WD23 74 A10
Herkomer Rd BUSH WD23 73 P9
Herlwyn Av RSLP HA4 112 F8
Herlwyn Gdns TOOT SW17 180 A7
Herm Cl ISLW TW7 154 B6
Hermes Cl MV/WKIL W9 8 E2
Hermes St IS N1 6 A8
Hermes Wy WLGTN SM6 222 E4
Hermiston Av CEND/HSY/T N8 118 F3
Hermitage Cl ABYW SE2 163 M2
DTCH/LGLY SL3 149 P2
ENC/FH EN2 79 J6
ESH/CLAY KT10 218 F3
RCHPK/HAM TW10 * 177 J1
SHPTN TW17 196 B4
SWFD E18 121 L2
Hermitage Cottages STAN HA7 * 94 D6
Hermitage Ct POTB/CUF EN6 59 M9
Hermitage Gdns CRICK NW2 117 K8
NRWD SE19 181 K10
Hermitage La CRICK NW2 117 K8
CROY/NA CR0 203 N7
STRHM/NOR SW16 180 G10
UED N18 99 L6
WDSR SL4 148 F9
Hermitage Rd FSBYPK N4 119 K5
NRWD SE19 181 K10
PUR/KEN CR8 241 K2
WOKN/KNAP GU21 231 L5
Hermitage Rw HACK E8 * 119 P10
Hermitage St BAY/PAD W2 9 L4
The Hermitage BARN SW13 * 156 C7
FELT TW13 * 174 G6
FSTH SE23 182 B4
KUT/HW KT1 * 199 J4
LEW SE13 * 161 H8
RCHPK/HAM TW10 177 J1
UX/CGN UB8 * 131 N1
Hermitage Wk SWFD E18 121 L2
Hermitage Wall WAP E1W 13 P10
Hermitage Wy STAN HA7 94 F9
Hermitage Woods Crs
WOKN/KNAP GU21 231 K6
Hermit Pl KIL/WHAMP NW6 2 G6
Hermit Rd CAN/RD E16 141 L7
Hermits Rd CRAWE RH10 284 A6
Hermit St FSBYE EC1V 6 C9
Hermon Gv HYS/HAR UB3 133 H10
Hermon Hl WAN E11 121 M2
Herndon Cl EGH TW20 172 D7
Herndon Rd WAND/EARL SW18 179 M1
Herne Cl HYS/HAR UB3 132 G8
WLSDN NW10 116 A10
Herne Ct BUSH WD23 * 94 B2
Herne Hl HNHL SE24 181 K1
Herne Hill Rd HNHL SE24 159 K10
Herne Ms UED N18 99 P5
Herne Pl HNHL SE24 181 J1
Herne Rd BUSH WD23 74 A10
SURB KT6 199 J9
Herneshaw HAT AL10 40 C6
Herns La WGCE AL7 23 L5
Herns Wy WGCE AL7 23 K3
Heron Cl BKHH IG9 101 M2
CRAWW RH11 283 M5
GUW GU2 249 N7
HHS/BOV HP3 54 A1
RKW/CH/CXG WD3 91 N3
SBW CM21 29 N2
UX/CGN UB8 131 N1
WALTH E17 100 E10
WLSDN NW10 136 B1
Heron Ct DORK RH4 * 272 F1
HAYES BR2 205 P4
KUT/HW KT1 * 199 K3
Heron Crs SCUP DA14 185 H7
Heron Dl ADL/WDHM KT15 215 N2
Herondale SAND/SEL CR2 224 C5
Herondale Av WAND/EARL SW18 179 N4
Heron Dr DTCH/LGLY SL3 150 E3
FSBYPK N4 119 K7
WARE SG12 27 H8
Heronfield EGH TW20 171 N9
POTB/CUF EN6 59 M6
Heron Flight Av HCH RM12 145 H2
Herongate Rd CHES/WCR EN8 62 D3
MNPK E12 121 P7
SWLY BR8 186 F9
Heron Hl BELV DA17 164 A3
Heron Md PEND EN3 80 F4
Heron Ms IL IG1 122 E7
Heron Pl DEN/HRF UB9 91 K7
Heron Quays POP/IOD E14 140 F10
Heron Rd CROY/NA CR0 * 203 M8
HNHL SE24 159 K10
TWK TW1 154 G10
The Heronry WOT/HER KT12 217 H3
Herons Cl CRAWE RH10 281 P10
Heronscourt LTWR GU18 212 B7
Herons Cft WEY KT13 216 D3
Herons Elm BERK HP4 33 K2
Heronsforde WEA W13 135 H8
Heronsgate EDGW HA8 95 M6
Heronsgate Rd
RKW/CH/CXG WD3 70 E10
Herons Lea CRAWE RH10 281 P10
Heronslea GSTN WD25 73 K2
Herons Lea HGT N6 * 118 A4
Heronslea Dr STAN HA7 95 K6
Herons Pl ISLW TW7 154 G9
Herons Ri EBAR EN4 77 P8
Herons Wy CHOB/PIR GU24 230 C7
STAL AL1 38 F10
Herons Wd HLW CM20 28 E9
Heronswood Cl HORL RH6 280 C3
Herons Wood Ct HORL RH6 * 280 C3
Heronswood Pl WGCE AL7 23 K6
Heronswood Rd WGCE AL7 23 J5
Heron Wk NTHWD HA6 92 F5
Heron Wy EBED/NFELT TW14 153 H10
HAT AL10 40 D6
UPMR RM14 126 D6
WTHK RM20 166 G4
Heronway RBRW/HUT CM13 107 N2
Herrick Cl CRAWE RH10 284 D5
Herrick Rd HBRY N5 119 K8
Herrick St WEST SW1P 17 K6
Herries St NKENS W10 2 B8
Herringham Rd CHARL SE7 161 P2
Herrings La BFOR GU20 212 C2
CHERT KT16 195 K6
Herrongate Cl EN EN1 79 N6
Hersant Cl WLSDN NW10 136 D3
Herschell Rd FSTH SE23 182 C3
Herschel Park Dr SL SL1 149 L2
Herschel St SL SL1 149 L1
Hersham Centre
WOT/HER KT12 * 217 L2
Hersham Cl PUT/ROE SW15 178 D3
Hersham Gdns WOT/HER KT12 217 J1
Hersham Pl WOT/HER KT12 * 217 L2
Hersham Rd WOT/HER KT12 197 J9
WOT/HER KT12 217 K1
Hershell Ct MORT/ESHN SW14 * 155 N10
Hertford Av MORT/ESHN SW14 178 A1
Hertford Cl EBAR EN4 77 N7
Hertford Ct STAN HA7 * 95 J8
Hertford End Ct NTHWD HA6 * 92 F6
Hertford Pl FITZ W1T 10 G2
Hertford Rd BARK IG11 142 D2
BRKMPK AL9 23 L10
BRKMPK AL9 40 G2
EBAR EN4 77 M7
ED N9 100 A2
EFNCH N2 117 P1
GNTH/NBYPK IG2 123 H4
HOD EN11 44 D1
IS N1 7 K3
PEND EN3 80 B4
PEND EN3 80 B6
PEND EN3 80 C1
WARE SG12 26 C3
WGCE AL7 23 L3
WLYN AL6 24 A1
Hertford Road High St PEND EN3 80 B10
Hertfordshire Wy
HERT/WAT SG14 25 H1
Hertford St MYFR/PICC W1J 10 E10
Hertford Wy MTCM CR4 202 F4
Hertingfordbury Rd
HERT/WAT SG14 24 G6
Hertslet Rd HOLWY N7 118 G8
Hertsmere Rd POP/IOD E14 140 F10
Hertswood Ct BAR EN5 * 77 H8
Hervey Cl FNCH N3 97 K9
Hervey Park Rd WALTH E17 120 D2
Hervines Ct AMS HP6 69 H3
Hervines Rd AMS HP6 68 G3
Hesa Rd HYS/HAR UB3 133 H8
Hesewall Cl CLAP SW4 158 D8
Hesiers Hl WARL CR6 243 K3
Hesiers Rd WARL CR6 243 K2
Hesketh Av RDART DA2 188 A4
Hesketh Pl NTGHL W11 8 A8
NTGHL W11 137 H9
Hesketh Rd FSTGT E7 121 M8
Heslop Rd BAL SW12 180 A4
Hesper Ms ECT SW5 14 G7
Hesperus Crs POP/IOD E14 160 G3
Hessel Rd WEA W13 154 F1
Hessel St WCHPL E1 140 A8
Hesselyn Dr RAIN RM13 145 J2
Hessle Gv EW KT17 220 C7
Hestercombe Av FUL/PGN SW6 157 H8
Hesterman Wy CROY/NA CR0 202 F8
Hester Rd BTSEA SW11 157 P6
UED N18 99 P6
Hester Ter RCH/KEW TW9 155 M9
Heston Av HEST TW5 153 M6
Heston Grange La HEST TW5 153 N5
Heston Rd HEST TW5 153 P6
REDH RH1 276 A5
Heston St DEPT SE8 160 F7
Heswell Gn OXHEY WD19 * 93 H4
Hetchleys HHW HP1 35 K3
Hetherington Cl SLN SL2 128 E5
Hetherington Rd CLAP SW4 158 F10
SHPTN TW17 196 D2
Hetherington Wy
HGDN/ICK UB10 111 P9
Hethersett Cl REIG RH2 257 N7
Hetley Rd SHB W12 136 E10
Heton Gdns HDN NW4 116 D2
Hevelius Cl GNWCH SE10 161 L4
Hever Court Rd GVE DA12 190 F9
Hever Cft ELTH/MOT SE9 184 D7
Hever Gdns BMLY BR1 206 D2
Heverham Rd WOOL/PLUM SE18 163 H3
Hevers Av HORL RH6 280 A3
Heversham Rd BXLYHN DA7 164 B8
Hevingham Dr CHDH RM6 123 M4
Hewens Rd HGDN/ICK UB10 132 D5
Hewer St NKENS W10 136 G7
Hewers Wy KWD/TDW/WH KT20 238 E6
Hewett Cl STAN HA7 94 G5
Hewett Pl SWLY BR8 208 E4
Hewetts Quay BARK IG11 142 E3
Hewett St SDTCH EC2A 13 K2
Hewins Cl WAB EN9 63 K8
Hewish Rd UED N18 99 M5
Hewison St BOW E3 140 E4
Hewitt Av WDGN N22 99 J10
Hewitt Cl CROY/NA CR0 204 F10
STALE/WH AL4 21 J4
Hewitt Rd CEND/HSY/T N8 119 H3
Hewitts Rd ORP BR6 228 A4
Hewlett Rd BOW E3 140 D4
The Hexagon HGT N6 118 A6
Hexal Rd CAT SE6 183 K6
Hexham Cl CRAWE RH10 284 F7
Hexham Gdns ISLW TW7 154 F6
Hexham Rd BAR EN5 77 L8
MRDN SM4 201 L8
WNWD SE27 181 K5
Hextalls La REDH RH1 259 L4
Heybourne Rd TOTM N17 100 A8
Heybridge Av STRHM/NOR SW16 180 G9
Heybridge Ct HERT/WAT SG14 24 G4
Heybridge Dr BARK/HLT IG6 122 G1
Heybridge Wy LEY E10 120 E6
Heydons Cl STALW/RED AL3 38 C4

Heyford Av RYNPK SW20 201 J3
VX/NE SW8 158 F6
Heyford End LCOL/BKTW AL2 56 C3
Heyford Rd MTCM CR4 201 P2
RAD WD7 74 E3
Heyford Ter VX/NE SW8 158 F6
Heyford Wy HAT AL10 40 F2
Heygate Est WALW SE17 18 F5
Heygate St WALW SE17 18 E6
Heymede LHD/OX KT22 237 H9
Heynes Rd BCTR RM8 123 M9
Heysham Dr OXHEY WD19 93 K6
Heysham La HAMP NW3 117 M8
Heysham Rd SEVS/STOTM N15 119 L4
Heythorpe Cl WOKN/KNAP GU21 231 L3
Heythorp St WAND/EARL SW18 179 J5
Heythrop Dr HGDN/ICK UB10 112 A9
Heywood Av CDALE/KGS NW9 96 B9
Heyworth Rd CLPT E5 120 A9
SRTFD E15 121 L10
Hibbert Av WATN WD24 73 L4
Hibbert Rd KTN/HRWW/WS HA3 94 E10
WALTH E17 120 E5
Hibbert St BTSEA SW11 157 M9
Hibberts Wy CFSP/GDCR SL9 110 B1
Hibbs Cl SWLY BR8 208 E2
Hibernia Dr GVE DA12 191 J6
Hibernia Gdns HSLW TW3 175 P1
Hibernia Rd HSLW TW3 153 P10
Hichisson Rd PECK SE15 182 B1
Hickin Cl CHARL SE7 162 A3
Hickin St POP/IOD E14 161 H2
Hickling Rd IL IG1 122 E10
Hickling Wk CRAWE RH10 284 C9
Hickman Av CHING E4 101 H7
Hickman Cl BROX EN10 44 D6
CAN/RD E16 142 A7
Hickman Rd CHDH RM6 123 M5
Hickmans Cl GDST RH9 260 B8
Hickory Cl ED N9 99 P1
Hicks Av GFD/PVL UB6 134 C5
Hicks Cl BTSEA SW11 157 P9
Hicks St DEPT SE8 160 D4
Hidalgo Ct HHNE HP2 36 A4
Hidcote Cl WOKS/MYFD GU22 232 E2
Hidcote Gdns RYNPK SW20 200 E3
The Hideaway ABLGY WD5 54 G7
Hide Pl WEST SW1P 17 J6
Hide Rd HRW HA1 114 C2
The Hides HLW CM20 28 G10
Higgins Rd CHESW EN7 61 L3
Highacre DORK RH4 272 G5
High Acres ABLGY WD5 54 E8
Higham Hill Rd WALTH E17 100 D10
WALTH E17 120 D1
Higham Md CSHM HP5 51 H6
Higham Ms NTHLT UB5 133 N6
Higham Pl WALTH E17 120 D1
Higham Rd CSHM HP5 51 H6
TOTM N17 119 L1
WFD IG8 101 M7
Highams Hl CRAWW RH11 283 J8
Highams Hill Cottages
WARL CR6 * 225 M8
Highams La CHOB/PIR GU24 212 F3
Higham Station Av CHING E4 100 G7
The Highams WALTH E17 * 101 H9
Higham St WALTH E17 120 D1
Higham Vw EPP CM16 66 D2
High Ash Cl SLH/COR SS17 169 K2
High Ash Rd STALE/WH AL4 21 H4
Highbank Pl WAND/EARL SW18 * 179 L4
Highbanks Cl WELL DA16 163 K6
Highbanks Rd PIN HA5 94 A7
Highbank Wy CEND/HSY/T N8 119 H4
High Barn Rd RDKG RH5 253 L10
Highbarns HHS/BOV HP3 54 B1
Highbarrow Rd CROY/NA CR0 203 N8
High Beech SAND/SEL CR2 223 M4
High Beeches BNSTD SM7 220 G10
CFSP/GDCR SL9 110 A6
ORP BR6 227 K3
SCUP DA14 185 P8
WEY KT13 216 F3
High Beeches Cl PUR/KEN CR8 222 E6
High Beech Rd LOU IG10 82 B8
High Bois La AMS HP6 69 J1
Highbridge Rd BARK IG11 142 E3
Highbridge St WAB EN9 62 F10
Highbrook Rd BKHTH/KID SE3 162 A9
High Broom Crs WWKM BR4 204 G7
Highbury Av HOD EN11 44 F1
THHTH CR7 203 H2
Highbury Cl NWMAL KT3 199 P4
WWKM BR4 204 G9
Highbury Cnr IS N1 6 C2
Highbury Crs HBRY N5 119 J10
Highbury Est HBRY N5 119 K10
Highbury Gdns GDMY/SEVK IG3 123 H7
Highbury Gra HBRY N5 119 K9
Highbury Gv HBRY N5 119 J10
Highbury Hl HBRY N5 6 D1
HBRY N5 119 J9
Highbury New Pk HBRY N5 6 D1
Highbury Pk HBRY N5 119 J9
Highbury Pl HBRY N5 6 C1
Highbury Qd HBRY N5 119 K8
Highbury Rd WIM/MER SW19 179 H8
Highbury Station Pde HBRY N5 * 6 C1
Highbury Station Rd IS N1 6 C2
Highbury Ter HBRY N5 119 J10
Highbury Terrace Ms HBRY N5 119 J10
High Canons BORE WD6 75 P3
High Cedar Dr RYNPK SW20 178 E10
Highclere ASC SL5 192 C5
GU GU1 250 D8
Highclere Cl PUR/KEN CR8 241 K1
Highclere Ct WOKN/KNAP GU21 231 H3
Highclere Dr HHS/BOV HP3 36 C10
Highclere Gdns
WOKN/KNAP GU21 231 H3
Highclere Rd NWMAL KT3 200 A3
WOKN/KNAP GU21 231 H3
Highclere St SYD SE26 182 D7
Highcliffe Dr PUT/ROE SW15 178 C2
Highcliffe Gdns REDBR IG4 122 B3
High Cl RKW/CH/CXG WD3 71 M9
Highcombe CHARL SE7 161 N5
Highcombe Cl ELTH/MOT SE9 184 B5
High Coombe Pl KUTN/CMB KT2 178 A10
High Coppice AMSS HP7 69 H5
Highcotts La RGUE GU4 251 K2
Highcroft CDALE/KGS NW9 116 B3
Highcroft Av ALP/SUD HA0 135 L2
Highcroft Ct GT/LBKH KT23 235 P9
Highcroft Gdns GLDGN NW11 117 J4
Highcroft Rd ARCH N19 118 F5
HHS/BOV HP3 53 K1
Highcroft Trailer Gdns
HHS/BOV HP3 * 52 E2
High Cross GSTN WD25 74 C3
Highcross Rd MEO DA13 189 J9
High Cross Rd TOTM N17 119 M1
Highcross Wy PUT/ROE SW15 178 D4
Highdaun Dr STRHM/NOR SW16 202 G4
High Dells HAT AL10 40 C5
Highdown WPK KT4 200 B9
Highdown Ct CRAWE RH10 284 C10
High Down La BELMT SM2 221 M7
Highdown Rd PUT/ROE SW15 178 E2
High Dr CTHM CR3 242 E8
LHD/OX KT22 218 C10
NWMAL KT3 199 P1
High Elms CHIC IG7 103 H5
UPMR RM14 126 D6
WFD IG8 101 M6
High Elms Cl NTHWD HA6 92 D7
High Elms La GSTN WD25 55 K7
High Elms Rd ORP BR6 226 F5
Higher Dr BNSTD SM7 220 G9
EHSLY KT24 252 F3
PUR/KEN CR8 223 H9
Higher Gn EW KT17 220 D9
Highfield BNSTD SM7 239 P3
CSTG HP8 90 A3
HLWS CM18 47 K2
KGLGY WD4 53 P4
OXHEY WD19 93 N4
RGUE GU4 268 C8
Highfield Av ERITH DA8 164 D5
GFD/PVL UB6 114 D10
GLDGN NW11 116 G5
HARP AL5 20 B3
ORP BR6 227 J3
PIN HA5 113 N3
WBLY HA9 115 K8
Highfield Cl AMS HP6 69 J3
BF/WBF KT14 215 K9
CDALE/KGS NW9 115 P3
CRW RM5 104 D7
LEW SE13 183 J3
LHD/OX KT22 218 C7
NTHWD HA6 92 F9
SURB KT6 199 H8
WDGN N22 99 H9
Highfield Cottages RDART DA2 * 187 J9
Highfield Ct EGH TW20 171 P9
STHGT/OAK N14 78 D10
Highfield Crs HCH RM12 125 N7
NTHWD HA6 92 F9
Highfield Dr BROX EN10 44 D7
HAYES BR2 205 K4
HGDN/ICK UB10 111 P8
HOR/WEW KT19 220 C4
WWKM BR4 204 G10
Highfield Gdns CDW/CHF RM16 168 A1
EPP CM16 65 H7
GLDGN NW11 117 H4
Highfield Hl NRWD SE19 181 L10
Highfield La HHNE HP2 36 B4
STALE/WH AL4 39 H8
Highfield Link CRW RM5 104 D7
Highfield Park Dr STALE/WH AL4 39 J9
Highfield Pl EPP CM16 65 H7
Highfield Rd ACT W3 135 N7
BERK HP4 34 A6
BF/WBF KT14 215 K9
BGR/WK TN15 247 M2
BH/WHM TN16 243 P3
BMLY BR1 206 C4
BRYLDS KT5 199 N7
BUSH WD23 73 M9
BXLYHS DA6 186 A1
CHERT KT16 195 K8
CHESW EN7 61 M2
CHST BR7 207 J3
CRW RM5 104 D7
CSHM HP5 50 G5
CTHM CR3 241 P8
DART DA1 187 L3
EGH TW20 172 A9
FELT TW13 175 H4
GLDGN NW11 * 117 H4
HCH RM12 125 N7
HERT/BAY SG13 25 L7
ISLW TW7 154 E7
NTHWD HA6 92 F9
PUR/KEN CR8 222 G6
STALE/WH AL4 20 G10
SUN TW16 196 G5
SUT SM1 221 P2
WCHMH N21 99 J3
WDSR SL4 148 E9
WFD IG8 102 B8
WOT/HER KT12 197 H8
Highfield Rd North DART DA1 187 L2
Highfield Rd South DART DA1 187 L4
High Flds ASC SL5 192 E5
Highfields ASHTD KT21 237 J5
EHSLY KT24 252 G4
KGLGY WD4 * 53 P4
LHD/OX KT22 236 C10
POTB/CUF EN6 60 F4
RAD WD7 74 E1
Highfields Gv HGT N6 118 B6
Highfield Wy POTB/CUF EN6 59 L8
RKW/CH/CXG WD3 71 L10
RKW/CH/CXG WD3 91 M1
High Firs RAD WD7 74 F1
SWLY BR8 208 F4
High Firs Crs HARP AL5 20 C3
High Foleys ESH/CLAY KT10 218 G4
High Gdns WOKS/MYFD GU22 231 N6
High Garth ESH/CLAY KT10 218 B3
Highgate Av HGT N6 118 C5
Highgate Cl HGT N6 118 B5
Highgate Edge EFNCH N2 * 117 P3
Highgate Gv SBW CM21 29 N1
Highgate High St HGT N6 118 B6
Highgate Hl ARCH N19 118 C6
Highgate Rd KTTN NW5 118 B8
Highgate Spinney
CEND/HSY/T N8 * 118 E4
Highgate Wk FSTH SE23 182 B5
Highgate West Hl HGT N6 118 B6
High Gv BMLY BR1 205 P1
STALW/RED AL3 38 C4
WGCW AL8 22 F4
WOOL/PLUM SE18 162 G6
Highgrove BRWN CM15 86 G10
Highgrove Cl CHST BR7 206 B1
FBAR/BDGN N11 98 B6
Highgrove Ms CAR SM5 201 P10
Highgrove Rd BCTR RM8 123 M10
Highgrove Wy RSLP HA4 113 H5
High Hill Ferry CLPT E5 120 A6
High Hill Rd WARL CR6 225 J10
High Holborn HHOL WC1V 11 M5
High House La TIL RM18 168 G2
Highland Av BRWN CM15 107 H2
DAGE RM10 124 D8
HNWL W7 134 D8
LOU IG10 82 C10
Highland Cottages WLGTN SM6 * 222 C1
Highland Cft BECK BR3 182 G9
Highland Dr BUSH WD23 94 A1
HHS/BOV HP3 36 C6
Highland Pk FELT TW13 174 G7
Highland Rd AMSS HP7 69 J5
BMLY BR1 205 L1
BXLYHS DA6 186 B1
NRWD SE19 181 M9
NTHWD HA6 93 H10
PUR/KEN CR8 223 H10
RSEV TN14 228 C7
WAB EN9 45 K8
Highlands BRKMPK AL9 40 F1
OXHEY WD19 93 K2
Highlands Av ACT W3 135 P9
LHD/OX KT22 237 H8
WCHMH N21 78 G9
Highlands Cl CFSP/GDCR SL9 90 C8
HSLW TW3 154 A7
LHD/OX KT22 236 G8
Highlands End CFSP/GDCR SL9 90 C8
Highlands Gdns IL IG1 122 C6
Highlands Hl SWLY BR8 209 H2
Highlands La CFSP/GDCR SL9 90 C7
WOKS/MYFD GU22 232 B8
Highlands Pk BGR/WK TN15 247 M7
LHD/OX KT22 237 J9
Highlands Rd BAR EN5 77 K9
BEAC HP9 89 H6
LHD/OX KT22 237 H8
REIG RH2 257 N9
STMC/STPC BR5 207 L7
The Highlands BAR EN5 77 K9
EDGW HA8 95 N10
EHSLY KT24 252 F1
POTB/CUF EN6 59 M7
RKW/CH/CXG WD3 91 L1
SLN SL2 109 H9
Highland Ter LEW SE13 * 160 G9
High La CTHM CR3 242 E5
HNWL W7 134 C8
RBSF CM22 30 F5
Highlea Cl CDALE/KGS NW9 96 B9
High Level Dr SYD SE26 181 P7
Highlever Rd NKENS W10 136 F7
High Limes NRWD SE19 * 181 M9
High Md CHIC IG7 102 F3
HRW HA1 114 D3
Highmead WOOL/PLUM SE18 163 J6
High Md WWKM BR4 205 J9
Highmead Crs ALP/SUD HA0 135 L2
High Meadow Cl DORK RH4 272 G3
PIN HA5 113 J2
High Meadow Crs
CDALE/KGS NW9 116 A3
High Meadow Pl CHERT KT16 195 J6
High Mdw CHIG IG7 102 G6
High Meads STALE/WH AL4 21 H3
High Meads Rd CAN/RD E16 142 A8
Highmoor AMSS HP7 69 J5
Highmore Rd BKHTH/KID SE3 161 K6
High Mt HDN NW4 * 116 D4
High Oak Rd WARE SG12 26 C1
High Oaks CRAWW RH11 283 L9
ENC/FH EN2 78 G4
STALW/RED AL3 38 B1
High Oaks Rd WGCW AL8 22 E4
Highover Pk AMSS HP7 69 H6
The High Pde
STRHM/NOR SW16 * 180 F6
High Park Av EHSLY KT24 252 G2
High Park Rd RCH/KEW TW9 155 M7
High Pastures RBSF CM22 30 E3
High Pth WIM/MER SW19 201 L1
High Path Rd GU GU1 250 F10
High Pewley GU GU1 268 B2
High Pine Cl WEY KT13 216 D2
High Pines WARL CR6 242 B5
High Point ELTH/MOT SE9 184 E6
Highpoint WEY KT13 216 B2
High Rdg MUSWH N10 * 98 C9
POTB/CUF EN6 60 F3
Highridge Cl EPSOM KT18 * 238 B1
High Ridge Cl HHS/BOV HP3 53 N1
Highridge Pl ENC/FH EN2 * 78 G4
High Ridge Rd HHS/BOV HP3 53 N1
High Rd BF/WBF KT14 215 P8
BKHH IG9 101 N2
BRKMPK AL9 41 P4
BROX EN10 44 E6
BUSH WD23 94 C2
CDW/CHF RM16 147 K10
CHDH RM6 124 A4
CHIC IG7 102 E4
COUL/CHIP CR5 239 P10
EFNCH N2 97 N10
EFNCH N2 117 P1
EPP CM16 66 D2
FBAR/BDGN N11 98 C6
IL IG1 122 E8
GDMY/SEVK IG3 123 K6
GSTN WD25 54 G10
GSTN WD25 72 G1
KTN/HRWW/WS HA3 94 D9
LEY E10 120 G4
LOU IG10 81 P10
NFNCH/WDSPK N12 97 M4
NFNCH/WDSPK N12 97 M8
RDART DA2 187 K6
SEVS/STOTM N15 119 N3
TOTM N17 119 N1
TRDG/WHET N20 97 M1
UX/CGN UB8 131 M7
WBLY HA9 115 K10
WDGN N22 98 G9
WDGN N22 99 H10
WDGN N22 119 H1
WLSDN NW10 136 D1
High Rd Broxbourne BROX EN10 44 E7
High Rd Eastcote PIN HA5 113 K2
High Rd Ickenham
HGDN/ICK UB10 112 D8
High Rd Leyton LEY E10 120 G7
LEY E10 121 H6
SRTFD E15 121 H9
High Rd Turnford
CHES/WCR EN8 62 D2
High Rd Woodford Gn
SWFD E18 101 M9
WFD IG8 101 M4
High Rd Wormley BROX EN10 44 E10
Highshore Rd PECK SE15 159 N8
High Silver LOU IG10 82 A8
High St IVER SL0 131 J8
High Standing CTHM CR3 259 K1
Highstead Crs ERITH DA8 164 F7
Highstone Av WAN E11 121 M4
High St ABLGY WD5 54 G3
ABLGY WD5 54 G6
ACT W3 135 N10
ADL/WDHM KT15 215 L1
AMSS HP7 68 F6
ASC SL5 192 C5
BAR EN5 77 J8
BARK/HLT IG6 102 F10
BARK/HLT IG6 122 F1
BECK BR3 204 F2
BELMT SM2 221 M4
BERK HP4 33 K3
BGR/WK TN15 247 N7
BGR/WK TN15 247 P3
BH/WHM TN16 245 M10
BH/WHM TN16 262 F3
BMLY BR1 205 M3
BNSTD SM7 239 K1
BORE WD6 75 J10
BRW CM14 107 H3
BTFD TW8 155 K5
BUSH WD23 73 P10
CAR SM5 222 A2
CEND/HSY/T N8 118 F2
CFSP/GDCR SL9 90 B9
CHEAM SM3 221 H3
CHES/WCR EN8 62 C4
CHES/WCR EN8 62 D10
CHES/WCR EN8 62 D3
CHOB/PIR GU24 212 D8
CHOB/PIR GU24 213 K7
CHONG CM5 67 P5
COB KT11 235 J1
CRAWE RH10 283 N8
CROY/NA CR0 203 K10
CSHM HP5 50 G7
CSTG HP8 89 P4
CTHM CR3 241 M9
DART DA1 187 M3
DEN/HRF UB9 91 M10
DORK RH4 272 G2
DTCH/LGLY SL3 149 N7
DTCH/LGLY SL3 150 D2
EA W5 135 J9
EGH TW20 172 D8
EPP CM16 65 J7
ESH/CLAY KT10 218 A2
ESH/CLAY KT10 218 E3
EW KT17 220 D5
EYN DA4 209 M9
EYN DA4 209 N6
FBAR/BDGN N11 98 C6
FELT TW13 174 G6
GDST RH9 260 B7
GRAYS RM17 167 M5
GT/LBKH KT23 253 P1
GT/LBKH KT23 254 A1
GU GU1 268 A2
GUW GU2 267 P2
GVW DA11 189 N2
GVW DA11 190 E2
HCH RM12 125 L6
HEST TW5 153 J6
HHS/BOV HP3 52 D3
HHW HP1 35 M5
HLWE CM17 29 M7
HLWW/ROY CM19 27 N10
HOD EN11 44 F5
HOR/WEW KT19 220 A9
HORL RH6 280 C4
HPTN TW12 176 B9
HPTN TW12 198 A1
HRW HA1 114 D7
HSLW TW3 154 A9
HYS/HAR UB3 152 E5
IVER SL0 131 J8
KGLGY WD4 54 B5
KTN/HRWW/WS HA3 94 D10
KTN/HRWW/WS HA3 114 D1
KUT/HW KT1 199 H1
KWD/TDW/WH KT20 238 F9
LCOL/BKTW AL2 57 H1
LHD/OX KT22 218 C9
LHD/OX KT22 236 G8
MLHL NW7 96 E6
NTHWD HA6 92 G9
NWMAL KT3 200 B4
ORP BR6 226 D7
OXTED RH8 261 J6
PGE/AN SE20 182 B10
PIN HA5 113 M1
PLSTW E13 141 M4
POTB/CUF EN6 59 M8
PUR RM19 165 P4
PUR/KEN CR8 223 H7
RDART DA2 166 G10
RDART DA2 188 G6
REDH RH1 258 A9
REDH RH1 258 C4
REDH RH1 258 G10
REIG RH2 257 K10
RKW/CH/CXG WD3 91 N2
ROM RM1 124 F3
RPLY/SEND GU23 233 M7
RSEV TN14 228 G6
RSEV TN14 247 H2
RSLP HA4 112 F6
SCUP DA14 185 K7
SEV TN13 246 D8
SHPTN TW17 196 D6
SL SL1 128 B5
SNWD SE25 203 N4
SOCK/AV RM15 146 B10
SRTFD E15 141 H4
SRTFD E15 141 J2
STA TW18 173 J7
STALE/WH AL4 20 G10
STALE/WH AL4 39 N8
STALW/RED AL3 38 C6
STHGT/OAK N14 98 E2
STMC/STPC BR5 207 M4
STMC/STPC BR5 207 M6
STWL/WRAY TW19 172 C2
STWL/WRAY TW19 173 N2
SUT SM1 221 L1
SWCM DA10 189 L1
SWLY BR8 208 F3
TEDD TW11 176 F8
THDIT KT7 198 F7
THHTH CR7 203 K4
UX/CGN UB8 131 M2
WALTH E17 120 E2
WAN E11 121 N4
WARE SG12 28 A2
WAT WD17 73 K8
WBLY HA9 115 L9
WDR/YW UB7 131 P10
WDR/YW UB7 151 N5
WDSR SL4 149 J7
WEY KT13 216 B1
WHTN TW2 176 B3
WIM/MER SW19 178 G8
WOKN/KNAP GU21 231 P2
WOKN/KNAP GU21 232 C3
WOKS/MYFD GU22 232 D7
WOT/HER KT12 197 H8
WWKM BR4 204 G8
High St Collier's Wd
WIM/MER SW19 179 N10
High St Gn HHNE HP2 36 B4
High St Harlesden WLSDN NW10 136 C4
High Str Harlington HTHAIR TW6 152 E7
High Street Ms WIM/MER SW19 179 H8
High St North MNPK E12 142 B1
The High HLW CM20 * 28 F10
High Timber St BLKFR EC4V 12 E7
High Tor Cl BMLY BR1 183 N10
High Tree Cl ADL/WDHM KT15 215 K2
High Trees BRXS/STRHM SW2 181 H4
CROY/NA CR0 204 D8
EBAR EN4 77 P9
RDART DA2 188 A2
High Trees Cl CTHM CR3 241 N8
High Trees Rd REIG RH2 275 N1
High Vw BELMT SM2 221 J7
CSTG HP8 90 A3
HAT AL10 40 D6
PIN HA5 113 K2
RKW/CH/CXG WD3 71 K8
SHGR GU5 270 D5
WATW WD18 72 G10
Highview CTHM CR3 241 M10
WOKN/KNAP GU21 * 231 K3
Highview Av EDGW HA8 95 P5
High View Av GRAYS RM17 167 P4
WLGTN SM6 222 G2
High View Cl LOU IG10 81 P9
NRWD SE19 203 N2
Highview Cl POTB/CUF EN6 59 M9
High View Ct REIG RH2 * 257 N10
Highview Crs RBRW/HUT CM13 87 P10
High View Gdns GRAYS RM17 167 P4
Highview Gdns EDGW HA8 95 P6
FBAR/BDGN N11 98 D6
FNCH N3 117 H1
POTB/CUF EN6 59 M9
STALE/WH AL4 39 H1
UPMR RM14 126 A7
High View Rd GUW GU2 267 K3
NRWD SE19 181 L9
SWFD E18 101 L10
Highview Rd SCUP DA14 185 L7
WEA W13 134 F8
Highview Ter DART DA1 * 187 L1
Highwayman's Rdg BFOR GU20 212 A1
The Highway BELMT SM2 221 M5
ORP BR6 227 L2
STAN HA7 94 E9
High Wickfield WGCE AL7 23 M6
Highwold COUL/CHIP CR5 240 B4
Highwood Av BUSH WD23 73 N5
NFNCH/WDSPK N12 97 M5
Highwood Cl BRW CM14 106 G1
FSTH SE23 181 P4
ORP BR6 206 F9
PUR/KEN CR8 241 K3
Highwood Dr ORP BR6 206 F9
Highwood Gdns CLAY IG5 122 C3
Highwood Gv MLHL NW7 96 A6
Highwoodhall La HHS/BOV HP3 54 B1
Highwood Hl MLHL NW7 96 C4
Highwood La LOU IG10 82 E10
Highwood Rd ARCH N19 118 F8
High Wood Rd HOD EN11 26 E10
Highwoods CTHM CR3 259 M1
LHD/OX KT22 237 H7
High Worple RYLN/HDSTN HA2 113 M5
Highworth Rd FBAR/BDGN N11 98 E7
Highworth St CAMTN NW1 * 9 P3
High Wych La SBW CM21 29 K2
High Wych Rd SBW CM21 29 H5
Hilary Av MTCM CR4 202 B3
Hilary Cl ERITH DA8 164 C7
FUL/PGN SW6 * 157 L6
HCH RM12 125 L10
Hilary Rd SHB W12 136 C9
Hilberry Ct BUSH WD23 * 94 A1
Hilbert Rd CHEAM SM3 220 G1
Hilborough Cl WIM/MER SW19 179 M10
Hilborough Rd HACK E8 * 7 M4
Hilborough Wy ORP BR6 226 G2
Hilbury HAT AL10 40 C5
Hilbury Cl AMS HP6 69 H1
Hilda Lockert Wk BRXN/ST SW9 159 J8
Hilda May Av SWLY BR8 208 F2
Hilda Rd CAN/RD E16 141 K6
EHAM E6 142 A2
Hilda Ter BRXN/ST SW9 * 159 H8
Hilda Vale Rd ORP BR6 226 D1
Hildenborough Gdns BMLY BR1 183 K9
Hilden Dr ERITH DA8 165 J6
Hildenlea Pl HAYES BR2 205 K2
Hildenley Cl REDH RH1 258 E4
The Hildens DORK RH4 272 B4
The Hilders ASHTD KT21 237 N3
Hildreth St BAL SW12 180 C4
Hildyard Rd FUL/PGN SW6 14 F9
Hiley Rd WLSDN NW10 136 F5
Hilfield La GSTN WD25 74 A5
Hilgay GU GU1 250 C10
Hilgay Cl GU GU1 250 C10
Hilgrove Rd KIL/WHAMP NW6 3 K4
Hiliary Gdns STAN HA7 95 H10
Hiljon Crs CFSP/GDCR SL9 90 B9
Hillars Heath Rd COUL/CHIP CR5 240 F1
Hillary Av GVW DA11 190 B6
Hillary Crs WOT/HER KT12 197 K8
Hillary Dr ISLW TW7 154 E10
Hillary Ri BAR EN5 77 K8
Hillary Rd DTCH/LGLY SL3 150 B2
HHNE HP2 36 B5
NWDGN UB2 153 P2
Hill Av AMS HP6 69 H4
Hillbarn SAND/SEL CR2 223 M7
Hillbeck Cl PECK SE15 160 B6
Hillbeck Wy GFD/PVL UB6 134 C3
Hillborne Cl HYS/HAR UB3 153 H4
Hillborough Cl WIM/MER SW19 * 179 M10
Hillbrook Gdns WEY KT13 216 B4
Hillbrook Rd TOOT SW17 180 A6
Hill Brow BMLY BR1 206 A1
DART DA1 186 G2
Hillbrow NWMAL KT3 200 C3
Hillbrow Cl BXLY DA5 186 E7
RGUW GU3 248 G9
Hillbrow Rd BMLY BR1 183 K10
ESH/CLAY KT10 218 B1
Hillbury Av KTN/HRWW/WS HA3 114 G3
Hillbury Cl WARL CR6 242 A4
Hillbury Gdns WARL CR6 242 B4
Hillbury Rd TOOT SW17 180 C6
WARL CR6 241 P3
Hill Cl BAR EN5 76 F9
CHST BR7 184 E8
COB KT11 217 P8
CRICK NW2 116 E8
GLDGN NW11 117 K4
HRW HA1 114 D8
MEO DA13 190 B10
PUR/KEN CR8 223 K9
STAN HA7 94 G5
WOKN/KNAP GU21 232 A2
Hill Common HHS/BOV HP3 36 B10
Hillcote Av STRHM/NOR SW16 181 H10
Hillcourt Av NFNCH/WDSPK N12 97 L7
Hillcourt Rd EDUL SE22 182 A2
Hill Crs BRYLDS KT5 199 L5
BXLY DA5 186 D4
EMPK RM11 125 K4
HRW HA1 114 F3
TRDG/WHET N20 97 L3
WPK KT4 200 F9
Hill Crest BFN/LL DA15 185 K3
POTB/CUF EN6 59 M10
SEV TN13 247 H8
SURB KT6 * 199 K7
Hillcrest HAT AL10 40 D5
HGT N6 118 B5
HNHL SE24 * 159 L10
KWD/TDW/WH KT20 * 255 N7
STALW/RED AL3 * 38 A8
WCHMH N21 99 J1
WEY KT13 216 C1
Hillcrest Av CHERT KT16 195 H10
EDGW HA8 95 N5
GLDGN NW11 117 H3
PIN HA5 113 L2
WTHK RM20 166 F5
Hillcrest Cl BECK BR3 204 E6
CRAWE RH10 284 E7
EPSOM KT18 238 C1
SYD SE26 181 P7
Hillcrest Dr RDART DA2 188 F1
Hill Crest Gdns CRICK NW2 116 D8
Hillcrest Gdns ESH/CLAY KT10 218 E1
FNCH N3 117 H2
Hill Crest Rd CHONG CM5 66 F6
Hillcrest Rd BH/WHM TN16 244 A2
BMLY BR1 183 M7
CTHM CR3 241 N3
DART DA1 186 G3
EA W5 135 K7
EMPK RM11 125 H5
GUW GU2 249 L9
LOU IG10 82 A10
ORP BR6 207 K9
PUR/KEN CR8 222 G6
RAD WD7 57 M9
WALTH E17 101 J10
Hillcrest Vw BECK BR3 204 E6
Hillcrest Wy EPP CM16 65 K7
Hillcroft LOU IG10 82 D6
Hillcroft Av PIN HA5 113 N4
PUR/KEN CR8 222 D9
Hillcroft Crs EA W5 135 J8
OXHEY WD19 93 J2
RSLP HA4 113 L8
WBLY HA9 115 L9
Hillcroft Rd CSHM HP5 51 J5
EHAM E6 142 E7
Hillcroome Rd BELMT SM2 221 N3
Hillcross Av MRDN SM4 201 H6
Hilldale Rd SUT SM1 221 J1
Hilldeane Rd PUR/KEN CR8 223 H6
Hilldene Av HARH RM3 105 K7
Hilldene Cl HARH RM3 105 L6
Hilldown Rd HAYES BR2 205 K8
HHW HP1 35 K4
STRHM/NOR SW16 180 F10
Hill Dr STRHM/NOR SW16 202 G3
WBLY HA9 115 N6
Hilldrop Crs HOLWY N7 118 E10
Hilldrop Est HOLWY N7 118 E10
Hilldrop La HOLWY N7 118 E10
Hilldrop Rd BMLY BR1 183 N9
HOLWY N7 118 E10
Hill Dyke Rd STALE/WH AL4 21 K4
Hill End ORP BR6 207 J9
WOOL/PLUM SE18 162 D7
Hill End La STALE/WH AL4 39 H9
Hill End Rd DEN/HRF UB9 91 L7
Hillersdon SLN SL2 129 N7
Hillersdon Av BARN SW13 156 D8
EDGW HA8 95 L6
Hillery Cl WALW SE17 19 H6
Hilley Field La LHD/OX KT22 236 C8
Hill Farm Av GSTN WD25 55 H9
Hill Farm La CSTG HP8 89 M2
Hill Farm Rd CFSP/GDCR SL9 90 B8
CSHM HP5 51 J10
NKENS W10 136 F7
Hillfield HAT AL10 40 E1
Hillfield Av ALP/SUD HA0 135 K2
CDALE/KGS NW9 116 B3
CEND/HSY/T N8 118 G2
MRDN SM4 201 P6
Hillfield Cl GU GU1 250 F8
REDH RH1 258 B10
RYLN/HDSTN HA2 114 B2
Hillfield Ct HHNE HP2 35 P6
Hillfield La South BUSH WD23 74 D10
Hillfield Ms CEND/HSY/T N8 118 G2
Hillfield Pde MRDN SM4 * 201 N6
Hillfield Pk MUSWH N10 118 C2
WCHMH N21 99 H3
Hillfield Park Ms MUSWH N10 118 C1
Hillfield Pl SEV TN13 246 E6
Hill Field Rd HPTN TW12 175 N10
Hillfield Rd CFSP/GDCR SL9 90 B8
HHNE HP2 35 N6
KIL/WHAMP NW6 117 J10
REDH RH1 258 B10
SEV TN13 246 F6
Hillfield Sq CFSP/GDCR SL9 90 B8
Hillfoot Av CRW RM5 104 D9
Hillfoot Rd CRW RM5 104 D9
Hillford Pl REDH RH1 276 B6
Hill Gardens Craven
BAY/PAD W2 * 9 J7
Hillgate Pl BAL SW12 180 C2
KENS W8 8 E9
Hillgate St KENS W8 8 E9
Hill Gv FELT TW13 175 N5
ROM RM1 124 F1
Hillhampton ASC SL5 192 E7
Hillhouse WAB EN9 63 L9
Hill House Av STAN HA7 94 E8
Hill House Cl CFSP/GDCR SL9 90 B8
CRAWE RH10 285 P9
WCHMH N21 99 H1
Hill House Dr CDW/CHF RM16 168 E4
GRAYS RM17 167 M5
HPTN TW12 197 P1
REIG RH2 275 L2
WEY KT13 216 B7
Hill House Rd RDART DA2 188 B3
STRHM/NOR SW16 180 G8
Hillhurst Gdns CTHM CR3 241 M6
Hilliard Rd NTHWD HA6 92 G9
Hilliard's Ct WAP E1W * 140 B10
Hilliards Rd UX/CGN UB8 131 N8
Hillier Cl BAR EN5 77 L10
Hillier Gdns CROY/NA CR0 223 H2
Hillier Pl CHSGTN KT9 219 J3
Hillier Rd BTSEA SW11 180 A2
GU GU1 250 D10
Hilliers Av UX/CGN UB8 132 B5
Hillier's La CROY/NA CR0 202 F10
Hillingdale BH/WHM TN16 243 N4
Hillingdon Av SEV TN13 247 K7
STWL/WRAY TW19 173 P4
Hillingdon Hl HGDN/ICK UB10 131 P5
Hillingdon Pde HGDN/ICK UB10 * 132 C6
Hillingdon Ri SEV TN13 247 L8
Hillingdon Rd BXLYHN DA7 164 D9
GSTN WD25 55 H10
GVW DA11 190 E5
HGDN/ICK UB10 131 P3
Hillingdon St WALW SE17 18 D10
Hillingdon Trail DEN/HRF UB9 91 K8
DEN/HRF UB9 111 N1
HYS/HAR UB3 153 H4
Hill La KWD/TDW/WH KT20 239 H7
RSLP HA4 112 D6
Hill Ley HAT AL10 40 C4
Hill Leys POTB/CUF EN6 60 F4
Hillman Cl EMPK RM11 125 L1
Hillman Dr NKENS W10 136 F6
Hillman St HACK E8 140 A1
Hillmarton Rd HOLWY N7 118 F10
Hillmarton Ter HOLWY N7 * 118 F10
Hill Md BERK HP4 33 M6
Hillmead CRAWW RH11 283 J7
Hillmead Dr BRXN/ST SW9 159 J10
Hill Meadow AMSS HP7 68 E9
Hillmont Rd ESH/CLAY KT10 198 D10
Hillmore Gv SYD SE26 182 C8
Hillmount WOKS/MYFD GU22 * 232 B4
Hill Pk LHD/OX KT22 * 236 F5
Hill Park Ct LHD/OX KT22 * 236 E5
Hill Park Dr LHD/OX KT22 236 E5
Hill Pl CRAWW RH11 283 M8
SLN SL2 128 G2
Hillpoint RKW/CH/CXG WD3 71 M9
Hillreach WOOL/PLUM SE18 162 C4
Hillrise DTCH/LGLY SL3 150 D5
Hill Ri CFSP/GDCR SL9 90 B10
DORK RH4 254 F10
ED N9 80 A10
ESH/CLAY KT10 198 G9
FSTH SE23 182 A4
GFD/PVL UB6 134 B2
GLDGN NW11 117 L2
POTB/CUF EN6 59 M10
POTB/CUF EN6 60 F4
RCHPK/HAM TW10 177 J1
RDART DA2 188 C8
RKW/CH/CXG WD3 91 L1
RSLP HA4 112 D6
UPMR RM14 125 P7
Hillrise Av WATN WD24 73 L4
Hill Rise Crs CFSP/GDCR SL9 90 B10
Hillrise Rd ARCH N19 118 F5
CRW RM5 104 D7
Hill Rd BRW CM14 106 F4
CAR SM5 221 P3
EPP CM16 83 H3
HRW HA1 114 F3
LHD/OX KT22 236 A8
MTCM CR4 202 C1
MUSWH N10 98 A9
NTHWD HA6 92 E7
PIN HA5 113 M4
PUR/KEN CR8 222 G8
RDART DA2 187 M5
STJWD NW8 3 K8
SUT SM1 221 L2
Hillsboro Rd EDUL SE22 181 M1
Hillsborough Gn OXHEY WD19 * 93 H4
Hill's Chace BRW CM14 107 H5
Hillsgrove Cl WELL DA16 163 M6
Hill Shaw HART DA3 211 L6
Hill Side BAR EN5 77 M9
Hillside ASC SL5 * 192 B5
BAR EN5 * 76 D9
BNSTD SM7 239 H1
CDALE/KGS NW9 116 A2
CSHM HP5 50 F4
DEN/HRF UB9 111 M3
ESH/CLAY KT10 * 218 A2
EYN DA4 209 N7
GRAYS RM17 168 A3
HAT AL10 40 D4
HLWE CM17 47 M3
HOD EN11 44 E2
RDART DA2 188 D8
SL SL1 149 K1
VW GU25 193 P6
WARE SG12 26 C3
WGCE AL7 23 L8
WIM/MER SW19 178 G9
WLSDN NW10 135 P3
WOKS/MYFD GU22 232 A6
Hillside Av BORE WD6 75 N8
CHES/WCR EN8 62 C7
FBAR/BDGN N11 98 A7
GVE DA12 190 G5
PUR/KEN CR8 223 J9
WBLY HA9 115 L9
WFD IG8 101 P6
Hillside Cl ABLGY WD5 54 F8
BNSTD SM7 239 H2
BRKHM/BTCW RH3 273 M1
CFSP/GDCR SL9 90 B7
CRAWW RH11 283 L9
CSTG HP8 89 N4
MRDN SM4 201 H4
STJWD NW8 3 H7
WFD IG8 101 P6
WOKN/KNAP GU21 231 J3
Hillside Cottages BNSTD SM7 * 222 A9
Hillside Ct SWLY BR8 209 H4
Hillside Crs CHES/WCR EN8 62 C7
ENC/FH EN2 79 L4
NTHWD HA6 93 H9
OXHEY WD19 73 L10
RYLN/HDSTN HA2 114 B7
WARE SG12 26 G7
Hillside Dr EDGW HA8 95 M7
GVE DA12 190 G5
Hillside Gdns ADL/WDHM KT15 215 J2
AMSS HP7 69 K6
BAR EN5 77 H9
BERK HP4 34 A6
BRKHM/BTCW RH3 255 M10
BRXS/STRHM SW2 * 181 H5
EDGW HA8 95 L5
FBAR/BDGN N11 * 98 D7
HGT N6 118 B4

KTN/HRWW/WS HA3 115 K5
NTHWD HA6 93 H8
WALTH E17 121 J1
WLGTN SM6 222 D4
Hillside Gv MLHL NW7 96 D8
STHGT/OAK N14 98 E1
Hillside La HAYES BR2 205 M9
WARE SG12 26 F6
Hillside Pk ASC SL5 192 E8
Hillside Ri NTHWD HA6 93 H8
Hillside Rd ASHTD KT21 237 L3
BELMT SM2 221 J4
BH/WHM TN16 244 B5
BRXS/STRHM SW2 180 G5
BUSH WD23 73 M9
COUL/CHIP CR5 240 F4
CROY/NA CR0 223 J2
CTHM CR3 241 P4
DART DA1 187 H2
EA W5 135 K7
EW KT17 220 F6
HAYES BR2 205 L3
NTHWD HA6 93 H8
RAD WD7 74 G1
RKW/CH/CXG WD3 70 F9
SEV TN13 247 L9
SEVS/STOTM N15 119 M5
STAL AL1 38 D5
STHL UB1 133 P6
Hillside Ter GVE DA12 * 190 E4
HERT/BAY SG13 25 K7
The Hillside ORP BR6 227 L5
Hillside Wk BRW CM14 106 F4
Hillside Wy GODL GU7 267 J10
Hills La NTHWD HA6 92 F9
Hillsleigh Rd KENS W8 8 D9
Hillsmead Wy SAND/SEL CR2 223 P10
Hills Ms EA W5 * 135 K9
Hills Pl SOHO/SHAV W1D 10 G6
Hillspur Cl GUW GU2 249 L9
Hillspur Rd GUW GU2 249 L9
Hill's Rd BKHH IG9 101 N2
Hillstowe St CLPT E5 120 B7
Hill St MYFR/PICC W1J 10 E9
RCH/KEW TW9 177 J1
STALW/RED AL3 38 B6
Hillswood Dr CHERT KT16 214 F1
The Hill AMSS HP7 68 B10
CTHM CR3 241 N10
GVW DA11 189 P2
HLWE CM17 29 M7
STALE/WH AL4 21 J3
Hill Top CHEAM SM3 201 J7
GLDGN NW11 117 L2
LOU IG10 82 D7
Hilltop WALTH E17 * 120 G1
Hilltop Av WLSDN NW10 135 P2
Hilltop Cl ASC SL5 192 D2
CHESW EN7 61 N2
LHD/OX KT22 237 H9
Hill Top Cl LOU IG10 82 D7
Hilltop Cl RGUW GU3 249 L6
Hilltop Cottages SYD SE26 * 182 A7
Hilltop Gdns DART DA1 187 N1
HDN NW4 96 E10
ORP BR6 207 H9
Hilltop La CTHM CR3 259 H1
Hilltop Ri GT/LBKH KT23 254 B2
Hilltop Rd BERK HP4 33 P6
CTHM CR3 241 M3
KGLGY WD4 54 E3
KIL/WHAMP NW6 2 F3
REIG RH2 275 L2
WTHK RM20 166 F5
Hill Top Vw WFD IG8 * 102 C7
Hilltop Wk CTHM CR3 242 D6
HARP AL5 20 C3
Hilltop Wy STAN HA7 94 F4
Hill Tree Cl SBW CM21 29 N2
Hill Vw BERK HP4 33 M3
CHOB/PIR GU24 * 213 H1
RDKG RH5 273 H1
Hillview CTHM CR3 241 N3
RYNPK SW20 * 200 E1
Hillview Av EMPK RM11 125 K4
KTN/HRWW/WS HA3 115 K3
Hill View Cl KWD/TDW/WH KT20 238 F7
PUR/KEN CR8 223 J7
Hillview Cl PIN HA5 93 N7
WBLY HA9 115 L7
Hillview Ct WOKS/MYFD GU22 * 232 B4
Hill View Crs GUW GU2 249 L8
Hillview Crs IL IG1 122 C4
ORP BR6 207 H8
Hillview Dr REDH RH1 276 B1
Hill View Dr THMD SE28 143 H10
WELL DA16 163 H8
Hill View Gdns CDALE/KGS NW9 116 A3
Hillview Gdns CHES/WCR EN8 62 D3
HDN NW4 116 G2
RYLN/HDSTN HA2 113 P1
Hill View Rd ESH/CLAY KT10 218 F4
HART DA3 211 N3
ORP BR6 207 J8
STWL/WRAY TW19 172 A2
TWK TW1 176 F2
WOKS/MYFD GU22 232 C4
Hillview Rd CHST BR7 184 D8
MLHL NW7 96 G5
PIN HA5 93 N8
SUT SM1 201 M10
Hill Wy AMSS HP7 68 G7
Hillway CDALE/KGS NW9 116 B6
HGT N6 118 B7
Hill Waye CFSP/GDCR SL9 110 C4
Hillwood Cl RBRW/HUT CM13 107 N2
Hillwood Gv RBRW/HUT CM13 107 N2
Hillworth BECK BR3 * 204 G2
Hillworth Rd BRXS/STRHM SW2 181 H3
Hillyard Rd HNWL W7 134 D7
Hillyard St BRXN/ST SW9 159 H7
Hillybarn Rd CRAWW RH11 282 F4
Hillydeal Rd RSEV TN14 247 K1
Hilly Fld HLWS CM18 47 J5
Hillyfield WALTH E17 100 D10
Hillyfield Cl HOM E9 120 D10
Hilly Flds BROCKY SE4 * 160 F10
Hillyfields LOU IG10 82 D6
Hilly Flds WGCE AL7 23 M4
Hilly Fields Crs BROCKY SE4 160 F10
Hilmay Dr HHW HP1 35 L7
Hilperton Rd SL SL1 149 K1
Hilsea St CLPT E5 120 B9
Hilton Av NFNCH/WDSPK N12 97 N6
Hilton Cl UX/CGN UB8 131 L4
Hilton Wy SAND/SEL CR2 242 A1
Himalayan Wy WATW WD18 72 G10
Himley Rd TOOT SW17 179 P8
Hinchley Cl ESH/CLAY KT10 198 E10
Hinchley Dr ESH/CLAY KT10 198 E10
Hinchley Wy ESH/CLAY KT10 198 F10
Hinckley Rd EDUL SE22 159 P10
Hind Cl CHIG IG7 103 J6
Hind Ct FLST/FETLN EC4A 12 B6
Hind Crs ERITH DA8 164 D6
Hinde Ms MHST W1U * 10 D5
Hindes Rd HRW HA1 114 D3
Hinde St MHST W1U 10 D5
Hind Gv POP/IOD E14 140 F8
Hindhead Cl CRAWW RH11 283 M9
UX/CGN UB8 132 C7
Hindhead Gdns NTHLT UB5 133 M3
Hindhead Gn OXHEY WD19 93 K6
Hindhead Wy WLGTN SM6 222 F2
Hindmans Rd EDUL SE22 181 P1
Hindmans Wy DAGW RM9 144 A6
Hindmarsh Cl WCHPL E1 13 P7
Hindrey Rd CLPT E5 120 A10
Hindsley's Pl FSTH SE23 182 B5
Hind Ter WTHK RM20 * 167 J5
Hine Cl COUL/CHIP CR5 240 D8
Hinkler Rd KTN/HRWW/WS HA3 115 J1
Hinkley Cl DEN/HRF UB9 111 M2
Hinksey Cl DTCH/LGLY SL3 150 E2
Hinksey Pth ABYW SE2 163 N2
Hinstock Rd WOOL/PLUM SE18 162 F6
Hinton Av HSLWW TW4 153 L10
Hinton Cl ELTH/MOT SE9 184 B4
Hinton Rd BRXN/ST SW9 159 J9
SL SL1 128 D9
UED N18 99 M5
UX/CGN UB8 131 M3
WLGTN SM6 222 D3
Hipkins Pl BROX EN10 44 D6
Hipley St WOKS/MYFD GU22 232 E6
Hippodrome Pl NTGHL W11 8 A8
NTGHL W11 137 H9
Hirst Crs WBLY HA9 115 K8
Hitcham Rd WALTH E17 120 E5
Hitchcock Cl SHPTN TW17 196 A3
Hitchen Hatch La SEV TN13 247 J9
Hitchens Cl HHW HP1 35 J5
Hitches Yd WARE SG12 * 26 C2
Hitchin Cl HARH RM3 105 K5
Hitchings Wy REIG RH2 275 K4
Hitherbaulk WGCE AL7 22 G7
Hitherbroom Rd HYS/HAR UB3 133 H10
Hitherbury Cl GUW GU2 267 P3
Hither Farm Rd BKHTH/KID SE3 161 P9
Hitherfield Rd BCTR RM8 123 P7
STRHM/NOR SW16 180 G5
Hither Green La LEW SE13 183 H1
Hither Meadow
CFSP/GDCR SL9 * 90 B9
Hithermoor Rd
STWL/WRAY TW19 173 K2
Hitherway WGCW AL8 22 G1
Hitherwell Dr
KTN/HRWW/WS HA3 94 C9
Hitherwood Cl HCH RM12 125 L9
REIG RH2 257 N8
Hitherwood Dr NRWD SE19 181 N7
Hive Cl BRW CM14 106 F3
BUSH WD23 94 C3
Hive La GVW DA11 189 N2
Hive Rd BUSH WD23 94 C3
Hiving's Hl CSHM HP5 50 F4
Hivings Pk CSHM HP5 50 G4
Hoadly Rd STRHM/NOR SW16 180 E6
Hobart Cl TRDG/WHET N20 97 P3
YEAD UB4 133 L6
Hobart Dr YEAD UB4 133 L6
Hobart Gdns THHTH CR7 203 L3
Hobart La YEAD UB4 133 L6
Hobart Pl BGVA SW1W 16 E4
RCHPK/HAM TW10 177 L3
Hobart Rd BARK/HLT IG6 102 F10
DAGW RM9 123 N9
TIL RM18 168 D7
WPK KT4 200 E10
YEAD UB4 133 L6
Hobarts Dr DEN/HRF UB9 111 J4
Hobart Wk STALW/RED AL3 38 E2
Hobbayne Rd HNWL W7 134 C8
Hobbes Wk PUT/ROE SW15 178 E1
Hobbs Cl BF/WBF KT14 215 L9
CHES/WCR EN8 62 C5
STALE/WH AL4 39 K7
Hobbs Cross Rd EPP CM16 83 N2
HLWE CM17 30 A9
Hobbs Gn EFNCH N2 117 M1
Hobbs Hill Rd HHS/BOV HP3 36 A9
Hobbs Pl IS N1 7 J6
Hobbs Place Est IS N1 7 J7
Hobbs Rd WNWD SE27 181 K7
Hobbs Wy WGCW AL8 22 F6
Hobby Horse Cl CHESW EN7 61 L2
Hobby St PEND EN3 80 C9
Hobday St POP/IOD E14 140 G8
Hoblands End CHST BR7 185 H9
Hobletts Rd HHNE HP2 36 A5
Hobsons Cl HOD EN11 26 E10
Hobsons Pl WCHPL E1 13 N3
Hobtoe Rd HLW CM20 28 D10
Hobury St WBPTN SW10 15 K10
Hockenden La SWLY BR8 208 B3
Hocken Md CRAWE RH10 284 E5
Hockeridge Vw BERK HP4 33 L6
Hockering Gdns
WOKS/MYFD GU22 232 E4
Hockering Rd WOKS/MYFD GU22 232 D4
Hocker St BETH E2 * 7 L10
Hockford Cl CHOB/PIR GU24 248 G2
Hocklands WGCE AL7 23 M4
Hockley Av EHAM E6 142 B4
Hockley Dr GPK RM2 105 K10
Hockley La SLN SL2 129 N2
Hockley Ms BARK IG11 143 H4
Hocroft Av CRICK NW2 117 J8
Hocroft Rd CRICK NW2 117 J9
Hocroft Wk CRICK NW2 117 J8
Hodder Dr GFD/PVL UB6 134 E4
Hoddesdon Rd BELV DA17 164 B4
WARE SG12 27 H7
Hodds Wood Rd CSHM HP5 51 H9
Hodes Rw HAMP NW3 118 A9
Hodford Rd GLDGN NW11 117 J6
Hodge La WDSR SL4 * 149 H10
Hodgemoor Vw CSTG HP8 89 L4
Hodges Cl CDW/CHF RM16 167 J4
Hodges Wy WATW WD18 73 H10
Hodgkin Cl CRAWE RH10 284 D8
Hodgkins Cl THMD SE28 143 N9
Hodgkins Ms STAN HA7 94 G6
Hodgson Gdns RGUE GU4 250 D7
Hodings Rd HLW CM20 28 E10
Hodister Cl CMBW SE5 159 K6
Hodson Cl RYLN/HDSTN HA2 113 N8
Hodson Crs STMC/STPC BR5 207 N6
Hodson Pl PEND EN3 80 F4
Hoebrook Cl WOKS/MYFD GU22 232 B7
Hoecroft WAB EN9 45 L8
Hoe La ABR/ST RM4 83 L7
EN EN1 80 A4
SHGR GU5 270 F10
WAB EN9 45 L8
WARE SG12 26 C5
Hoe Meadow BEAC HP9 88 B7
Hoestock Rd SBW CM21 29 N1
Hoe St WALTH E17 120 F3
The Hoe OXHEY WD19 93 L3
Hoffmann Gdns SAND/SEL CR2 223 P3
Hoffman Sq IS N1 * 7 H9
Hofland Rd WKENS W14 157 H2
Hogan Ms BAY/PAD W2 9 L3
Hogarth Av ASHF TW15 174 D9
BRWN CM15 107 K4
Hogarth Cl CAN/RD E16 142 A7
EA W5 135 K7
SL SL1 128 D9
UX/CGN UB8 131 M5
Hogarth Crs CROY/NA CR0 203 K7
WIM/MER SW19 201 N1
Hogarth Gdns HEST TW5 153 P6
Hogarth Hl GLDGN NW11 117 J2
Hogarth Pl ECT SW5 * 14 G6
Hogarth Reach LOU IG10 82 C9
Hogarth Rd BCTR RM8 123 L10
CDW/CHF RM16 147 M10
CRAWE RH10 284 A10
ECT SW5 14 G6
EDGW HA8 95 M10
Hogarth Ter CHSWK W4 * 156 B5
Hogarth Wy HPTN TW12 198 B1
Hogback Wood Rd BEAC HP9 88 A7
Hogden La EHSLY KT24 253 M7
Hogden Rd RDKG RH5 253 M10
Hogfair La SL SL1 128 B6
Hogg End La STALW/RED AL3 37 H4
Hogg La BORE WD6 74 F8
CDW/CHF RM16 167 M3
Hog Hill Rd CRW RM5 104 A8
Hog La CSHM HP5 32 G8
Hogpits Bottom HHS/BOV HP3 52 D8
Hogscross La COUL/CHIP CR5 240 A8
Hogsdell La HERT/BAY SG13 26 A7
Hogshead Pas WAP E1W * 140 A9
Hogshill La COB KT11 217 K10
Hogsmill Wy HOR/WEW KT19 219 P2
Hogtrough Hl BH/WHM TN16 245 K8
Hogtrough La OXTED RH8 260 G4
REDH RH1 276 E1
Holbeach Cl CDALE/KGS NW9 96 B9
Holbeach Gdns BFN/LL DA15 185 H2
Holbeach Rd CAT SE6 182 G3
Holbeck La CHESW EN7 61 N2
Holbeck Rw PECK SE15 159 P6
Holbein Ga NTHWD HA6 92 F6
Holbein Ms BGVA SW1W 16 C7
Holbein Pl BGVA SW1W 16 C6
Holbein Rd CRAWE RH10 284 A10
Holberton Gdns WLSDN NW10 136 E5
Holborn HCIRC EC1N 12 A4
Holborn Circ HCIRC EC1N 12 B4
Holborn Cl STALE/WH AL4 39 J1
Holborn Pl HHOL WC1V 11 N4
Holborn Rd PLSTW E13 141 N7
Holborn Viad STBT EC1A 12 C5
Holborn Wy MTCM CR4 202 A2
Holbreck Pl WOKS/MYFD GU22 232 C4
Holbrook Cl EN EN1 79 N5
Holbrooke Ct HOLWY N7 118 F8
Holbrook Gdns GSTN WD25 74 A2
Holbrook La CHST BR7 184 G10
Holbrook Meadow EGH TW20 172 F9
Holbrook Rd SRTFD E15 141 L4
Holbrook Wy HAYES BR2 206 C6
Holburn GINN WC1R 12 A4
Holburne Cl BKHTH/KID SE3 161 P7
Holburne Gdns BKHTH/KID SE3 162 A7
Holburne Rd BKHTH/KID SE3 161 P7
Holcombe Cl BH/WHM TN16 262 G2
Holcombe Hl MLHL NW7 96 D4
Holcombe Rd IL IG1 122 D5
TOTM N17 119 N1
Holcombe St HMSMTH W6 156 E4
Holcon Ct REDH RH1 258 B7
Holcote Cl BELV DA17 163 P2
Holcroft Rd HOM E9 140 B2
Holdbrook Wy HARH RM3 105 N10
Holden Av CDALE/KGS NW9 115 P6
NFNCH/WDSPK N12 97 L6
Holdenby Rd BROCKY SE4 182 D1
Holden Cl BCTR RM8 123 L8
HERT/BAY SG13 25 M4
Holden Gdns BRW CM14 107 J6
Holdenhurst Av FNCH N3 97 L8
Holden Rd NFNCH/WDSPK N12 97 L5
Holden St BTSEA SW11 158 B8
Holden Wy UPMR RM14 126 C6
Holdernesse Rd ISLW TW7 154 F7
TOOT SW17 180 A6
Holderness Wy WNWD SE27 181 K8
Holder Rd CRAWE RH10 284 C10
Holders Hill Av HDN NW4 96 G10
Holders Hill Crs HDN NW4 96 G10
Holders Hill Dr HDN NW4 96 G10
Holders Hill Gdns HDN NW4 96 G10
Holders Hill Pde MLHL NW7 * 97 H9
Holders Hill Rd HDN NW4 96 G10
The Holdings BRKMPK AL9 40 G2
Holecroft WAB EN9 63 K10
Hole Hl DORK RH4 272 A2
Holford Ms FSBYW WC1X * 5 N9
Holford Rd GU GU1 250 F10
HAMP NW3 117 M8
TIL RM18 168 G3
Holford St FSBYW WC1X 6 A9
Holford Yd FSBYW WC1X * 6 A8
Holgate Av BTSEA SW11 157 N9
Holgate Rd DAGE RM10 124 B10
Holgate St CHARL SE7 162 A2
Holland Av BELMT SM2 221 K4
RYNPK SW20 200 C1
Holland Cl HAYES BR2 205 L9
REDH RH1 258 A10
ROMW/RG RM7 124 D3
STAN HA7 94 G6
TRDG/WHET N20 97 N1
Holland Crs OXTED RH8 261 M9
Holland Dr FSTH SE23 182 D6
Holland Gdns BTFD TW8 155 L4
EGH TW20 195 J2
GSTN WD25 73 K1
WKENS W14 14 B3
WKENS W14 157 H2
Holland Gv BRXN/ST SW9 159 H6
Holland La OXTED RH8 261 M9
Holland Pk NTGHL W11 8 B10
NTGHL W11 14 C1
Holland Park Av GDMY/SEVK IG3 123 H4
NTGHL W11 14 A1
Holland Park Gdns NTGHL W11 8 A10
Holland Park Ms NTGHL W11 8 C10
Holland Park Rd WKENS W14 14 C4
Holland Park Ter NTGHL W11 8 B10
Holland Pas IS N1 6 E5
Holland Pl KENS W8 14 G1
Holland Rd ALP/SUD HA0 135 J1
EHAM E6 142 C3
OXTED RH8 261 M9
SNWD SE25 203 P5
SRTFD E15 141 K4
WKENS W14 14 A2
WLSDN NW10 136 D3
Hollands Cl GVE DA12 191 P8
Holland's Cft WARE SG12 28 A2
The Hollands WOKS/MYFD GU22 232 B4
WPK KT4 200 C8
Holland St KENS W8 14 F2
STHWK SE1 12 D9
Holland Villas Rd WKENS W14 14 B2
Holland Wk STAN HA7 94 F6
Holland Wy HAYES BR2 205 L9
HLWE CM17 29 N10
Hollar Rd STNW/STAM N16 119 N8
Hollen St SOHO/CST W1F 11 H6
Holles Cl HPTN TW12 175 P9
Holles St CAVSQ/HST W1G 10 F5
Holley Rd ACT W3 156 B1
Hollickwood Av
NFNCH/WDSPK N12 98 A7
Holliday Sq BTSEA SW11 157 N9
Holliday St BERK HP4 34 A5
Hollidge Wy DAGE RM10 144 C2
Holliers Wy HAT AL10 40 D4
Hollies WAB EN9 81 P1
Hollies Av BF/WBF KT14 215 J9
BFN/LL DA15 185 J5
Hollies Cl STRHM/NOR SW16 181 H9
TWK TW1 176 E5
Hollies Ct ADL/WDHM KT15 215 M2
Hollies End MLHL NW7 96 E6
Hollies Rd EA W5 155 H3
The Hollies ADL/WDHM KT15 * 215 M2
BAR EN5 * 76 D9
GVE DA12 190 G9
HART DA3 211 P3
HHS/BOV HP3 52 D5
KTN/HRWW/WS HA3 114 F2
OXTED RH8 261 N9
STAL AL1 * 38 D5
WOKN/KNAP GU21 * 231 J3
Hollies Wy BAL SW12 * 180 B3
POTB/CUF EN6 59 M7
Holligrave Rd BMLY BR1 205 M1
Hollin Ct CRAWE RH10 283 P4
Hollingbourne Av BXLYHN DA7 164 A7
Hollingbourne Gdns WEA W13 134 G7
Hollingbourne Rd HNHL SE24 181 K1
Hollingsworth Rd CROY/NA CR0 224 A3
Hollington Crs NWMAL KT3 200 C6
Hollington Rd EHAM E6 142 C5
TOTM N17 99 P10
Hollingworth Cl
E/WMO/HCT KT8 197 N4
Hollingworth Rd
STMC/STPC BR5 206 E7
Hollingworth Wy BH/WHM TN16 262 G2
Hollis Pl GRAYS RM17 167 M3
Hollis Rw REDH RH1 * 276 A2
Hollman Gdns
STRHM/NOR SW16 181 J9
Holloway Cl WDR/YW UB7 151 P4
Holloway Dr VW GU25 194 B4
Holloway Hl CHERT KT16 194 F10
Holloway La RKW/CH/CXG WD3 70 E4
WDR/YW UB7 152 A4
Holloway Rd ARCH N19 118 E7
EHAM E6 142 C5
WAN E11 121 J8
Holloways La BRKMPK AL9 40 G9
Holloway St HSLW TW3 154 A9
Hollow Cl GUW GU2 267 N1
Hollowfield Av GRAYS RM17 168 A3
Hollow Hill La IVER SL0 130 E10
Hollow La RDKG RH5 271 L7
VW GU25 193 P3
The Hollow CRAWW RH11 283 J8
WFD IG8 101 L5
Hollow Wy CSHM HP5 50 D6
Hollow Way La AMS HP6 69 K1
Holly Av ADL/WDHM KT15 215 K6
STAN HA7 95 K10
WOT/HER KT12 197 L8
Hollybank CHOB/PIR GU24 212 E9
Holly Bank MUSWH N10 * 118 D2
Hollybank Cl HPTN TW12 175 P8
Hollybank Rd BF/WBF KT14 215 K10
Holly Bank Rd
WOKS/MYFD GU22 231 N6
Hollybrake Cl CHST BR7 184 G10
Hollybush Av LCOL/BKTW AL2 55 P1
Hollybush Cl BERK HP4 34 G2
CRAWE RH10 283 P6
KTN/HRWW/WS HA3 94 D9
OXHEY WD19 93 K1
SEV TN13 247 K10
WAN E11 121 M3
Hollybush Gdns BETH E2 140 A5
Hollybush Hl SLN SL2 129 N2
WAN E11 121 L5
Holly Bush La HPTN TW12 175 N10
SEV TN13 247 K10
Hollybush La DEN/HRF UB9 110 F7
HHW HP1 35 J5
IVER SL0 130 E8
AMS HP6 69 J3
ORP BR6 228 B3
WGCE AL7 23 J9
Hollybush Pl BETH E2 140 A5
Hollybush Rd CRAWE RH10 283 P6
CSHM HP5 50 F3
GVE DA12 190 F5
KUTN/CMB KT2 177 K9
Hollybush Rw TRING HP23 * 32 C1
Hollybush St PLSTW E13 141 N5
Hollybush Ter NRWD SE19 * 181 M9
Holly Bush V HAMP NW3 * 117 M9
Hollybush Wy CHESW EN7 61 P4
Holly Cl BECK BR3 205 H4
BKHH IG9 102 A4
CHERT KT16 193 M10
CRAWE RH10 284 B5
EGH TW20 171 N9
FELT TW13 175 M8
HAT AL10 40 C5
SLN SL2 109 H9
WLGTN SM6 222 C4
WLSDN NW10 136 B2
WOKN/KNAP GU21 231 N5
Hollycombe EGH TW20 171 P7
Holly Crs BECK BR3 204 E5
WDSR SL4 148 C8
WFD IG8 101 J8
Holly Cft HERT/WAT SG14 24 G4
Hollycroft Av HAMP NW3 117 K8
WBLY HA9 115 K7
Hollycroft Cl SAND/SEL CR2 223 M2
WDR/YW UB7 152 B5
Hollycroft Gdns WDR/YW UB7 152 B5
Hollycross Rd WARE SG12 26 E3
Hollydale Cl NTHLT UB5 114 A10
Hollydale Dr HAYES BR2 206 C10
Hollydale Rd PECK SE15 160 B8
Holly Dell HERT/BAY SG13 25 K7
Hollydown Wy WAN E11 121 J8
Holly Dr BERK HP4 34 A6
CHING E4 100 G1
POTB/CUF EN6 59 L9
SOCK/AV RM15 147 K5
WDSR SL4 171 K1
Holly Farm Rd NWDGN UB2 153 M4
Hollyfield HAT AL10 40 D7
Holly Fld HLWW/ROY CM19 46 F4
Hollyfield Av FBAR/BDGN N11 98 A6
Hollyfield Rd BRYLDS KT5 199 L7
Hollyfields BROX EN10 62 D2
Holly Gdns BXLYHN DA7 164 D10
WDR/YW UB7 152 A1
Holly Gn WEY KT13 216 E1
Hollygrove BUSH WD23 94 C1
Holly Gv CDALE/KGS NW9 115 P5
PECK SE15 159 N8
PIN HA5 93 M9
Hollygrove Cl HSLW TW3 153 N10
Holly Hedge Rd COB KT11 217 J10
Holly Hedges La HHS/BOV HP3 52 F7
Holly Hedge Ter LEW SE13 183 H1
Holly Hl HAMP NW3 117 M9
WCHMH N21 78 G10
Holly Hill Rd BELV DA17 164 C4
Hollyhock Cl HHW HP1 35 H5
Holly Hock Dr CHOB/PIR GU24 230 F1
Holly Hough
KWD/TDW/WH KT20 255 N6
Holly La BNSTD SM7 239 N4
RGUW GU3 249 J5
Holly La East BNSTD SM7 239 L2
Holly La West BNSTD SM7 239 L3
Holly Lea RGUE GU4 250 A4
Holly Ldg WOKN/KNAP GU21 * 231 K3
Holly Lodge Gdns HGT N6 118 B7
Hollymead CAR SM5 202 A10
Hollymead Rd COUL/CHIP CR5 240 B4
Holly Ms WBPTN SW10 15 K8
Hollymoor La HOR/WEW KT19 220 A6
Holly Mt HAMP NW3 * 117 M9
Hollymount Cl GNWCH SE10 161 H7
Holly Pde COB KT11 * 235 J1
Holly Pk FNCH N3 117 J1
FSBYPK N4 118 G5
Holly Park Gdns FNCH N3 117 K1
Holly Park Rd FBAR/BDGN N11 98 B5
HNWL W7 134 E10
Holly Rd CHSWK W4 * 156 A3
DART DA1 187 L4
HPTN TW12 176 B9
HSLW TW3 154 A10
ORP BR6 227 K4
PEND EN3 80 C2
REIG RH2 275 L2
TWK TW1 176 F4
WAN E11 121 L5
Holly St HACK E8 7 M2
Hollytree Av SWLY BR8 208 F2
Hollytree Cl CFSP/GDCR SL9 90 B6
CSHM HP5 51 N7
WIM/MER SW19 178 G4
Holly Tree Ct HHNE HP2 36 C6
Hollytree Pde SCUP DA14 * 185 M8
Holly Tree Rd CTHM CR3 241 M8
Hollyview Cl HDN NW4 116 D4
Holly Vls HMSMTH W6 * 156 E2
Holly Wk HAMP NW3 117 M9
HARP AL5 20 C2
WDSR SL4 170 D7
WGCW AL8 22 F1
Holly Wy MTCM CR4 202 E4
Hollywood Gdns YEAD UB4 133 J8
Hollywood Ms WBPTN SW10 15 J9
Hollywood Rd CHING E4 100 D6
WBPTN SW10 15 J9
Hollywoods CROY/NA CR0 224 E6
Hollywood Wy ERITH DA8 165 J7
WFD IG8 101 J8
Holman Ct EW KT17 * 220 D5
Holman Rd BTSEA SW11 157 N8
HOR/WEW KT19 219 P2
Holmbank Dr SHPTN TW17 196 F4
Holmbridge Gdns PEND EN3 80 C8
Holmbrook Dr HDN NW4 116 G3
Holmbury Cl BUSH WD23 94 D3
CRAWW RH11 283 M9
Holmbury Ct WIM/MER SW19 179 P10
Holmbury Dr RDKG RH5 273 H5
Holmbury Gdns HYS/HAR UB3 132 G10
Holmbury Gv CROY/NA CR0 224 E4
Holmbury Keep HORL RH6 280 D3
Holmbury Mnr SCUP DA14 * 185 K7
Holmbury Pk BMLY BR1 184 B10
Holmbury Vw CLPT E5 120 A6
Holmbush Rd PUT/ROE SW15 179 H2
Holm Cl ADL/WDHM KT15 215 H8
Holmcote Gdns HBRY N5 119 K10
Holmcroft CRAWE RH10 283 P8
KWD/TDW/WH KT20 256 E1
Holmcroft Wy HAYES BR2 206 C5
Holmdale Cl BORE WD6 75 L6
Holmdale Gdns HDN NW4 116 G3
Holmdale Rd CHST BR7 184 F8
KIL/WHAMP NW6 117 K10
Holmdale Ter SEVS/STOTM N15 119 M4
Holmdene Av HNHL SE24 181 K1
MLHL NW7 96 D7
RYLN/HDSTN HA2 114 A1
Holmdene Cl BECK BR3 205 H2
Holmdene Ct BMLY BR1 206 B3
Holmead Rd FUL/PGN SW6 157 L6
Holmebury Cl BUSH WD23 * 94 D3
Holme Cl CHES/WCR EN8 62 D7
HAT AL10 40 C1
WEY KT13 216 D3
Holme Ct ISLW TW7 154 F9
Holmedale SLN SL2 129 P9
Holme Lacey Rd LEE/GVPK SE12 183 L2
Holme Lea GSTN WD25 55 K10
Holme Pk BORE WD6 75 L6
Holme Pl HHNE HP2 36 D5
Holme Rd EHAM E6 142 B3
EMPK RM11 125 P6
HAT AL10 40 C1
Holmes Av MLHL NW7 97 H6
WALTH E17 120 E1
Holmes Cl ASC SL5 192 B6
EDUL SE22 159 P10
PUR/KEN CR8 222 G9
WOKS/MYFD GU22 232 C7
Holmesdale CHES/WCR EN8 80 B1
Holmesdale Av
MORT/ESHN SW14 155 N9
Holmesdale Cl GU GU1 250 E9
SNWD SE25 203 N3
Holmesdale Hl EYN DA4 210 C1
Holmesdale Pk REDH RH1 * 258 G10
Holmesdale Rd BXLYHN DA7 163 N8
EYN DA4 210 B1
HGT N6 118 C5
RCH/KEW TW9 155 L7
RDKG RH5 272 G6
REDH RH1 276 G2
REIG RH2 257 L9
SNWD SE25 203 L5
TEDD TW11 177 H10
Holmesdale Ter RDKG RH5 * 272 G6
Holmesley Rd FSTH SE23 182 D2
Holmes Meadow
HLWW/ROY CM19 46 E7
Holmes Rd KTTN NW5 4 E1
TWK TW1 176 E5
WIM/MER SW19 179 M10
Holmes Ter STHWK SE1 18 A1
Holmethorpe Av REDH RH1 258 C7
Holme Wy STAN HA7 94 E7
Holmewood Gdns
BRXS/STRHM SW2 180 G3
Holmewood Rd
BRXS/STRHM SW2 180 F3
SNWD SE25 203 M3
Holmfield Av HDN NW4 116 G3
Holm Gv HGDN/ICK UB10 132 B2
Holmhurst Rd BELV DA17 164 C4
Holmlea Rd DTCH/LGLY SL3 150 A7
Holmlea Wk DTCH/LGLY SL3 149 P7
Holmleigh Av DART DA1 165 K10
Holmleigh Rd STNW/STAM N16 119 M6
Holm Oak Cl PUT/ROE SW15 179 J2
Holm Oak Pk WATW WD18 * 73 H9
Holmsdale Cl IVER SL0 131 J8
Holmsdale Gv BXLYHN DA7 164 F8
Holmshaw Cl SYD SE26 182 D7
Holmshill La BORE WD6 76 C3
Holmside Ri OXHEY WD19 93 J4
Holmside Rd BAL SW12 180 B2
Holmsley Cl NWMAL KT3 200 C6
Holmstall Av CDALE/KGS NW9 115 P1
EDGW HA8 95 P10
Holmstall Pde EDGW HA8 * 95 P10
Holmwood Av BRWN CM15 87 M9
SAND/SEL CR2 223 N9
Holmwood Cl ADL/WDHM KT15 215 K2
BELMT SM2 220 G5
EHSLY KT24 252 F4
NTHLT UB5 134 A1
RYLN/HDSTN HA2 114 B1
Holmwood Gdns FNCH N3 97 K10
WLGTN SM6 222 C3
Holmwood Gv MLHL NW7 96 A6
Holmwood Rd BELMT SM2 220 F5
CHSGTN KT9 219 K2
GDMY/SEVK IG3 123 H7
PEND EN3 80 C2
Holmwood View Rd RDKG RH5 272 G8
Holne Cha EFNCH N2 117 M4
MRDN SM4 201 K6
Holness Rd SRTFD E15 141 L1
Holroyd Rd ESH/CLAY KT10 218 F5
PUT/ROE SW15 156 F10
Holsart Cl KWD/TDW/WH KT20 238 E8
Holstein Av WEY KT13 216 B1
Holstein Wy ERITHM DA18 163 N2
Holstock Rd IL IG1 122 F7
Holsworth Cl RYLN/HDSTN HA2 114 B3
Holsworthy Sq FSBYW WC1X 11 P2
Holsworthy Wy CHSGTN KT9 219 H2
Holt Cl BORE WD6 75 L8
CHIG IG7 103 J6
MUSWH N10 118 B2
THMD SE28 143 L9
Holton St WCHPL E1 140 C6
Holt Rd ALP/SUD HA0 114 G8
CAN/RD E16 142 B10
HARH RM3 105 M8
Holtsmere Cl GSTN WD25 73 K1
The Holt BARK/HLT IG6 102 F7
HHNE HP2 35 P7
MRDN SM4 * 201 K4
WGCE AL7 23 N6
WLGTN SM6 222 D1
Holt Wy CHIG IG7 103 J6
Holtwhite Av ENC/FH EN2 79 K6
Holtwhite's Hl ENC/FH EN2 79 K6
Holtwood Rd LHD/OX KT22 218 B9
Holtye Wk CRAWE RH10 * 284 B9
Holwell Hyde WGCE AL7 23 M7
Holwell La BRKMPK AL9 41 P1
Holwell Pl PIN HA5 113 M2
Holwell Rd WGCE AL7 23 H6
Holwood Cl WOT/HER KT12 197 K9
Holwood Park Av ORP BR6 226 C1
Holwood Pl CLAP SW4 158 E10
Holybourne Av PUT/ROE SW15 178 D3
Holy Cross Hl BROX EN10 43 P9
Holyfield Rd WAB EN9 63 H5
Holyhead Cl BOW E3 140 F5
Holyoake Av WOKN/KNAP GU21 231 P3
Holyoake Ct BERM/RHTH SE16 160 D1
Holyoake Crs WOKN/KNAP GU21 231 P3
Holyoake Ter SEV TN13 247 H10
Holyoake Wk EA W5 135 H6
EFNCH N2 117 M1
Holyoak Rd LBTH SE11 18 C5
Holyport Rd FUL/PGN SW6 156 F6
Holyrood Av RYLN/HDSTN HA2 113 M9
Holyrood Crs STAL AL1 38 C10
Holyrood Gdns CDW/CHF RM16 168 F3
EDGW HA8 95 N10
Holyrood Ms CAN/RD E16 141 M10
Holyrood Rd BAR EN5 77 M10
Holyrood St STHWK SE1 13 J10
Holywell WOKS/MYFD GU22 231 N7
Holywell Cl BERM/RHTH SE16 160 A4
BKHTH/KID SE3 161 M5
ORP BR6 227 K1
STWL/WRAY TW19 173 P4
Holywell Hl STAL AL1 38 C7
Holywell La SDTCH EC2A 13 K1
Holywell Rd WATW WD18 73 H9
Holywell Rw SDTCH EC2A 13 J2
Holywell Wy STWL/WRAY TW19 173 P4
Home Cl BROX EN10 44 E10
CAR SM5 202 A9
CRAWE RH10 284 D5
HLW CM20 47 J1
LHD/OX KT22 236 C7
NTHLT UB5 133 N5
VW GU25 194 A6
Home Ct FELT TW13 * 175 H4
SURB KT6 * 199 J5
Homecroft Gdns LOU IG10 82 E8
Homecroft Rd SYD SE26 182 B8
WDGN N22 99 J9
Homedean Rd SEV TN13 246 D8
Home Farm Cl
BRKHM/BTCW RH3 274 B1
CHERT KT16 214 D4
EPSOM KT18 238 G3
ESH/CLAY KT10 218 A3
SHPTN TW17 196 F4
THDIT KT7 198 E7
Home Farm Ct CSTG HP8 * 89 M4
Home Farm Gdns
WOT/HER KT12 197 K10
Home Farm Rd BERK HP4 33 J2
Homefarm Rd HNWL W7 134 D8
Home Farm Rd
RBRW/HUT CM13 107 K9
RKW/CH/CXG WD3 92 B5
Home Farm Wy DTCH/LGLY SL3 129 P3
Homefield BERK HP4 34 E2
HHS/BOV HP3 52 E4
WAB EN9 63 M8
Homefield Av GNTH/NBYPK IG2 123 H3
Homefield Cl ADL/WDHM KT15 215 H8
EPP CM16 65 K5
HORL RH6 280 C3
LHD/OX KT22 237 H7
STMC/STPC BR5 207 L4
SWLY BR8 208 G3
WLSDN NW10 135 P1
YEAD UB4 133 L6
Homefield Gdns EFNCH N2 117 N1
KWD/TDW/WH KT20 238 F6
WIM/MER SW19 201 M2
Homefield Ms BECK BR3 * 204 F1
Homefield Pk SUT SM1 221 L3
Homefield Ri ORP BR6 207 L9
Homefield Rd ALP/SUD HA0 114 F9
BMLY BR1 205 P1
BUSH WD23 73 P9
CHSWK W4 156 C3
COUL/CHIP CR5 241 J6
EDGW HA8 96 A7
HHNE HP2 36 B7
RAD WD7 74 E3
RKW/CH/CXG WD3 70 G8
SEV TN13 246 F8
WARE SG12 26 D1
WARL CR6 242 B6
WIM/MER SW19 179 H9
WOT/HER KT12 197 N7
Homefield St IS N1 * 7 J8
The Homefield MRDN SM4 * 201 K4
Home Gdns DAGE RM10 124 D8
DART DA1 187 M2
Home Hl SWLY BR8 186 G10
Homeland Dr BELMT SM2 221 L5
Homelands LHD/OX KT22 237 H7
Homelands Dr NRWD SE19 181 M10
Home Lea ORP BR6 227 J2
Homeleigh Ct CHES/WCR EN8 62 A6
Homeleigh Rd PECK SE15 182 C1
Home Ley WGCE AL7 23 H5
Home Md STAN HA7 95 H9
Home Mead Cl GVE DA12 190 E3
Home Meadow BNSTD SM7 239 K2
SLN SL2 129 H4
WGCE AL7 23 H5
Homemead Rd CROY/NA CR0 202 D6
HAYES BR2 206 C5
Home Pk OXTED RH8 261 M7
Home Park Ct KUT/HW KT1 * 199 J4
Home Park Mill Link Rd
KGLGY WD4 54 C7
Home Park Rd WIM/MER SW19 179 J7
Home Park Ter KUT/HW KT1 199 J2
Home Park Wk KUT/HW KT1 199 J4
Homer Cl BXLYHN DA7 164 D7
Homer Dr POP/IOD E14 160 F3
Homerfield WGCW AL8 22 F5
Home Rd BTSEA SW11 157 P8
Homer Rd CROY/NA CR0 204 C6
HOM E9 140 D1
Homer Rw CAMTN NW1 9 P4
Homersham Rd KUT/HW KT1 199 M2
Homers Rd WDSR SL4 148 C7
Homer St MBLAR W1H 9 P4
Homerswood La WLYN AL6 22 D1
Homerton Gv HOM E9 120 C10
Homerton High St HOM E9 120 C10
Homerton Rd HOM E9 120 E10
Homerton Rw HOM E9 120 B10
Homerton Ter HOM E9 140 B1
Homesdale Cl WAN E11 121 M3
Homesdale Rd CTHM CR3 241 L9
HAYES BR2 205 P4
ORP BR6 207 H7
Homesfield GLDGN NW11 117 K3
Homestall GUW GU2 249 J10
Homestall Rd EDUL SE22 182 B1
Homestead Cl LCOL/BKTW AL2 56 B3
Homestead Ct WGCE AL7 23 J7
Homestead Gdns ESH/CLAY KT10 218 D2
Homestead La WGCE AL7 23 J8
Homestead Paddock
STHGT/OAK N14 78 C9
Homestead Pk CRICK NW2 116 C8
Homestead Rd BCTR RM8 124 A7
CTHM CR3 241 L9
FUL/PGN SW6 157 J6
HAT AL10 40 E2
ORP BR6 227 L4
RKW/CH/CXG WD3 91 N1
STA TW18 173 L9
The Homestead DART DA1 187 K2
Homestead Wy CROY/NA CR0 225 H7
Homewaters Av SUN TW16 196 G1
Homeway HARH RM3 106 A7
Home Wy RKW/CH/CXG WD3 91 J2
Homewillow Cl WCHMH N21 79 J10
Homewood DTCH/LGLY SL3 130 A8
Homewood Av POTB/CUF EN6 60 F3
Homewood Cl HPTN TW12 175 N9
Homewood Crs CHST BR7 185 H9
Homewood Gdns SNWD SE25 * 203 M5
Homewood La POTB/CUF EN6 60 D3
Homewood Rd STAL AL1 38 G3
Honduras St FSBYE EC1V 12 E1
Honeybourne Rd
KIL/WHAMP NW6 117 L10
Honeybourne Wy
STMC/STPC BR5 206 F8
Honey Brook WAB EN9 63 K9
Honeybrook Rd BAL SW12 180 D3
Honey Cl BRWN CM15 87 J1
DAGE RM10 144 D1
Honeycrock La REDH RH1 276 B7
Honeycroft LOU IG10 82 D8
WGCW AL8 22 F6
Honeycroft Dr STALE/WH AL4 39 H9

Honeycroft Hl *HGDN/ICK* UB10 131 P2
Honeycross Rd *HHW* HP1 35 H7
Honeyden Rd *SCUP* DA14 185 P9
Honey Hl *HGDN/ICK* UB10 132 A2
Honey La *WAB* EN9 63 L10
Honeyman Cl *CRICK* NW2 136 G2
Honeymeade *SBW* CM21 29 M4
Honeypot Cl *CDALE/KGS* NW9 115 L2
Honeypot La *BRW* CM14 106 F4
CDALE/KGS NW9 115 L2
STAN HA7 95 K9
WAB EN9 63 P10
Honeypots Rd
WOKS/MYFD GU22 232 A8
Honeysett Rd *TOTM* N17 99 N10
Honeysuckle Bottom
EHSLY KT24 252 F10
Honeysuckle Cl *BRWN* CM15 86 G9
HARH RM3 105 K7
HERT/BAY SG13 25 P5
HORL RH6 280 D3
IVER SL0 130 F8
STHL UB1 133 M9
Honeysuckle Fld *CSHM* HP5 51 H6
Honeysuckle Gdns *CROY/NA* CR0 204 C7
HAT AL10 40 E5
Honeysuckle La *CRAWW* RH11 283 M4
Honeywell Rd *BTSEA* SW11 179 P2
Honeywood Cl *POTB/CUF* EN6 59 N9
Honeywood Rd *ISLW* TW7 * 154 F10
WLSDN NW10 136 C4
Honeywood Wk *CAR* SM5 222 A1
Honister Cl *STAN* HA7 94 G9
Honister Gdns *STAN* HA7 94 G8
Honister Hts *PUR/KEN* CR8 223 L10
Honister Pl *STAN* HA7 94 G9
Honiton Gdns *MLHL* NW7 96 G8
PECK SE15 * 160 B8
Honiton Rd *KIL/WHAMP* NW6 2 C7
ROMW/RG RM7 124 E4
WELL DA16 163 J8
Honley Rd *CAT* SE6 182 G3
Honnor Gdns *ISLW* TW7 154 C8
Honnor Rd *STA* TW18 173 N10
Honor Oak Pk *FSTH* SE23 182 B3
Honor Oak Ri *FSTH* SE23 182 B2
Honor Oak Rd *FSTH* SE23 182 B3
Honor St *HLWE* CM17 29 N10
Honours Md *HHS/BOV* HP3 * 52 D3
Hood Av *MORT/ESHN* SW14 177 P1
STHGT/OAK N14 78 C10
STMC/STPC BR5 207 L5
Hood Cl *CROY/NA* CR0 203 J8
Hoodcote Gdns *WCHMH* N21 99 J1
Hood Rd *RAIN* RM13 144 F3
RYNPK SW20 178 C10
Hood Wk *ROMW/RG* RM7 104 C9
Hook End Rd *BRWN* CM15 86 G1
Hooke Rd *EHSLY* KT24 252 G1
Hooker's Rd *WALTH* E17 120 C1
Hook Farm Rd *HAYES* BR2 206 A5
Hook Fld *HLWS* CM18 47 H3
Hookfield *HOR/WEW* KT19 219 P9
Hookfields *GVW* DA11 190 B6
Hook Ga *EN* EN1 80 A3
Hook Green La *RDART* DA2 186 F7
Hook Green Rd *MEO* DA13 189 K10
Hook Heath Av
WOKS/MYFD GU22 231 N5
Hook Heath Gdns
WOKS/MYFD GU22 231 L7
Hook Heath Rd
WOKS/MYFD GU22 231 L7
Hook Hl *SAND/SEL* CR2 223 M6
Hook Hill La *WOKS/MYFD* GU22 231 N7
Hook Hill Pk *WOKS/MYFD* GU22 231 N7
Hooking Gn *RYLN/HDSTN* HA2 114 A3
Hook La *ABR/ST* RM4 84 A10
CHOB/PIR GU24 212 B9
POTB/CUF EN6 60 B7
RGUW GU3 266 C7
SHGR GU5 270 C7
WELL DA16 185 J1
Hook Mill La *LTWR* GU18 212 C5
Hook Ri North *SURB* KT6 199 L10
Hook Ri South *CHSGTN* KT9 199 L10
Hook Rd *CHSGTN* KT9 219 J2
HOR/WEW KT19 219 P4
Hooks Hall Dr *DAGE* RM10 124 D8
Hookstone La *CHOB/PIR* GU24 212 E7
Hookstone Wy *WFD* IG8 102 A8
The Hook *BAR* EN5 77 N10
Hook Underpass (Kingston By-Pass) *CHSGTN* KT9 199 J10
Hook Wk *EDGW* HA8 95 P7
Hookwood Cnr *OXTED* RH8 261 N4
Hooley La *REDH* RH1 276 A1
Hooper Dr *UX/CGN* UB8 132 C7
Hooper Rd *CAN/RD* E16 141 M8
Hooper's Ms *ACT* W3 135 P10
BUSH WD23 94 A2
Hooper St *WCHPL* E1 13 N7
Hoop La *GLDGN* NW11 117 J5
The Hoo *HLWE* CM17 29 M6
Hop Ct *ALP/SUD* HA0 * 135 H1
Hope Cl *BTFD* TW8 155 K4
CHDH RM6 123 N2
IS N1 6 F1
LEE/GVPK SE12 183 N6
SUT SM1 221 M2
Hopedale Rd *CHARL* SE7 161 N5
Hopefield Av *KIL/WHAMP* NW6 2 B7
Hope Gdns *ACT* W3 155 N1
Hope Gn *GSTN* WD25 55 H9
Hope La *ELTH/MOT* SE9 184 E6
Hope Pk *BMLY* BR1 183 L10
Hope Rd *SWCM* DA10 189 L2
Hopes Cl *HEST* TW5 153 P5
Hope Sq *LVPST* EC2M 13 J4
Hope St *BTSEA* SW11 157 N10
Hope Ter *WTHK* RM20 * 167 J4
Hopetown St *WCHPL* E1 13 N4
Hopewell Cl *CDW/CHF* RM16 167 J4
Hopewell Dr *GVE* DA12 191 J8
Hopewell St *CMBW* SE5 159 L6
Hopewell Yd *CMBW* SE5 159 L6
Hopfield Av *BF/WBF* KT14 215 P8
Hopgarden La *SEV* TN13 265 H4
Hop Gdns *CHCR* WC2N 11 L8
Hop Garden Wy *GSTN* WD25 55 K7
Hopgood St *SHB* W12 136 F10
Hopground Cl *STAL* AL1 38 F8
Hopkin Cl *GUW* GU2 249 N6
Hopkins Cl *GPK* RM2 125 K1
MUSWH N10 98 B8
Hopkins Crs *STALE/WH* AL4 20 G10
Hopkins Ms *SRTFD* E15 141 L3
Hopkinsons Pl *CAMTN* NW1 4 B5
Hopkins Rd *LEY* E10 120 G5
Hopkins St *SOHO/CST* W1F 11 H6
Hopkins Yd *STAL* AL1 38 D7
Hoppers Rd *WCHMH* N21 99 H3
Hoppett Rd *CHING* E4 101 K4
The Hoppety
KWD/TDW/WH KT20 238 G8
Hopping La *IS* N1 6 D2
Hoppingwood Av *NWMAL* KT3 200 B3
Hoppit Rd *WAB* EN9 62 G8
The Hoppitt *CHONG* CM5 49 K6
Hoppner Rd *YEAD* UB4 132 E4
Hop St *GNWCH* SE10 161 L3
Hopton Gdns *NWMAL* KT3 200 D6
Hopton Pde *STRHM/NOR* SW16 * 180 F8
Hopton Rd *STRHM/NOR* SW16 180 F8
WOOL/PLUM SE18 162 E2
Hoptons Gdns *STHWK* SE1 * 12 D9
Hopton St *STHWK* SE1 12 D9
Hoptree Cl *NFNCH/WDSPK* N12 * 97 L5
Hopwood Cl *TOOT* SW17 179 M6
WAT WD17 72 E2
Hopwood Rd *WALW* SE17 19 H9
Hopwood Wk *HACK* E8 * 7 P4
Horace Av *ROMW/RG* RM7 124 E6
Horace Rd *BARK/HLT* IG6 122 F1
FSTGT E7 121 N9
KUT/HW KT1 199 L3
Horatio Pl *POP/IOD* E14 161 H1
Horatio St *BETH* E2 7 N9
Horatius Wy *CROY/NA* CR0 222 G3
Horbury Crs *NTGHL* W11 8 E8
Horbury Ms *NTGHL* W11 8 D8
Horder Rd *FUL/PGN* SW6 157 H7
Hordle Gdns *STAL* AL1 38 E8
Hordle Prom East *PECK* SE15 159 N6
Hordle Prom North *PECK* SE15 159 N6
Hordle Prom West *PECK* SE15 159 M6
Horksley Gdns *RBRW/HUT* CM13 87 P10
Horley Cl *BXLYHS* DA6 186 B1
Horley Lodge La *REDH* RH1 276 B9
Horley Rd *ELTH/MOT* SE9 184 B7
HORL RH6 279 K8
REDH RH1 276 A5
Horley Rw *HORL* RH6 280 A3
Hormead Rd *MV/WKIL* W9 8 C2
Hornbeam Av *UPMR* RM14 125 N9
Hornbeam Cha *SOCK/AV* RM15 147 J5
Hornbeam Cl *BORE* WD6 75 M5
EPP CM16 83 H3
IL IG1 122 G10
LBTH SE11 18 A5
MLHL NW7 96 C4
NTHLT UB5 113 N10
RBRW/HUT CM13 107 N4
Hornbeam Crs *BTFD* TW8 154 G6
Hornbeam Gdns *DTCH/LGLY* SL3 149 M2
NWMAL KT3 200 D6
Hornbeam Gv *CHING* E4 101 L4
Hornbeam La *BRKMPK* AL9 41 P7
CHING E4 81 K9
Hornbeam Rd *BKHH* IG9 102 A4
EPP CM16 82 G3
GU GU1 249 P7
REIG RH2 275 M3
YEAD UB4 133 K7
Hornbeams *HLW* CM20 28 F9
LCOL/BKTW AL2 55 N6
WGCE AL7 * 23 L6
Hornbeams Av *EN* EN1 80 B1
Hornbeam Sq *BOW* E3 140 E3
Hornbeams Ri *FBAR/BDGN* N11 98 B7
The Hornbeams *HLW* CM20 28 E9
Hornbeam Wy *CHESW* EN7 61 N5
HAYES BR2 206 D6
Hornbill Cl *UX/CGN* UB8 131 N8
Hornbuckle Cl *RYLN/HDSTN* HA2 114 C7
Hornby Cl *HAMP* NW3 3 M3
Horncastle Cl *LEE/GVPK* SE12 183 M3
Horncastle Rd *LEE/GVPK* SE12 183 M3
Hornchurch Cl *KUTN/CMB* KT2 177 J8
Hornchurch Hl *CTHM* CR3 241 N3
Hornchurch Rd *HCH* RM12 125 H6
Horndean Cl *CRAWE* RH10 284 E3
PUT/ROE SW15 178 D4
Horndon Cl *CRW* RM5 104 D9
Horndon Gn *CRW* RM5 104 D9
Horndon Rd *CRW* RM5 104 D9
Horne Court Hl *HORL* RH6 277 N10
Horne House *CHARL* SE7 * 162 B6
Horner La *MTCM* CR4 201 N2
Horne Rd *SHPTN* TW17 196 A4
The Hornets *WATW* WD18 73 J8
Horne Wy *PUT/ROE* SW15 156 F8
Hornfair Rd *CHARL* SE7 162 A5
Hornford Wy *ROMW/RG* RM7 124 F5
Hornhatch *RGUE* GU4 268 F7
Hornhatch Cl *RGUE* GU4 268 E6
Hornhatch La *RGUE* GU4 268 D6
Hornhill Rd *RKW/CH/CXG* WD3 90 F6
Horniman Dr *FSTH* SE23 182 A4
Horniman Gdns *FSTH* SE23 * 182 A4
Horning Cl *ELTH/MOT* SE9 184 B7
Horn La *ACT* W3 135 P10
GNWCH SE10 161 M3
WFD IG8 101 M7
Horn Link Wy *GNWCH* SE10 161 M3
Hornminster Gln *EMPK* RM11 125 P7
Horn Park Cl *LEE/GVPK* SE12 183 N1
Horn Park La *LEE/GVPK* SE12 183 N1
Horns Cl *HERT/BAY* SG13 25 K7
Horns Cft *BARK* IG11 143 H2
Horns End Pl *PIN* HA5 113 K3
Hornsey Chambers *CLPT* E5 * 120 A7
Hornsey La *HGT* N6 118 D5
Hornsey Lane Est *ARCH* N19 118 F5
Hornsey Lane Gdns *HGT* N6 118 D5
Hornsey Park Rd
CEND/HSY/T N8 118 G1
Hornsey Ri *ARCH* N19 118 E5
Hornsey Rise Gdns *ARCH* N19 118 F5
Hornsey Rd *ARCH* N19 118 F6
Hornsey St *HOLWY* N7 118 G10
Hornsfield *WGCE* AL7 23 M4
Hornshay St *PECK* SE15 160 B5
Horns Mill Rd *HERT/BAY* SG13 25 K7
Horns Rd *BARK/HLT* IG6 122 F3
HERT/BAY SG13 25 K6
Hornton Pl *KENS* W8 14 G2
Hornton St *KENS* W8 14 F1
Horsa Gdns *HAT* AL10 40 A3
Horsa Rd *ERITH* DA8 164 D6
LEE/GVPK SE12 183 P3
Horsebridges Cl *DAGW* RM9 143 P3
Horsecroft *BNSTD* SM7 239 J3
Horsecroft Cl *ORP* BR6 207 L8
Horsecroft Mdw *BNSTD* SM7 * 239 K2
Horsecroft Rd *EDGW* HA8 96 A8
HHW HP1 35 K8
HLWW/ROY CM19 46 B2
Horse Fair *KUT/HW* KT1 199 J2
Horseferry Pl *GNWCH* SE10 161 H5
Horseferry Rd *POP/IOD* E14 140 D9
WEST SW1P 17 J4
Horse Guards Av *WHALL* SW1A 11 L10
Horse Guards Rd *WHALL* SW1A 11 K10
Horse Hl *CSHM* HP5 52 A8
HORL RH6 279 L3
Horse Leaze *EHAM* E6 142 E8
Horselers *HHS/BOV* HP3 36 B9
Horsell Birch *WOKN/KNAP* GU21 231 N1
Horsell Common Rd
WOKN/KNAP GU21 213 P10
Horsell Ct *CHERT* KT16 195 L7
Horsell Moor *WOKN/KNAP* GU21 232 B3
Horsell Pk *WOKN/KNAP* GU21 232 B3
Horsell Park Cl
WOKN/KNAP GU21 232 A3
Horsell Ri *WOKN/KNAP* GU21 232 B1
Horsell Rise Cl
WOKN/KNAP GU21 232 A1
Horsell Rd *HBRY* N5 119 H10
STMC/STPC BR5 207 K1
Horsell V *WOKN/KNAP* GU21 232 B1
Horsell Wy *WOKN/KNAP* GU21 231 P2
Horselydown La *STHWK* SE1 13 L10
Horseman Ct *BRWN* CM15 86 D3
Horsemans Dr *LCOL/BKTW* AL2 55 P2
Horseman Side *BRW* CM14 85 L10
Horsemoor Cl *DTCH/LGLY* SL3 150 D3
Horsemoor La *AMSS* HP7 68 A10
Horsenden Av *GFD/PVL* UB6 114 D10
Horsenden Crs *GFD/PVL* UB6 114 E10
Horsenden La North
GFD/PVL UB6 134 E1
Horsenden La South
GFD/PVL UB6 134 F3
Horseshoe Cl *CRAWE* RH10 284 F6
CRICK NW2 116 E7
POP/IOD E14 161 H4
WAB EN9 63 M10
Horse Shoe Crs *NTHLT* UB5 133 P4
Horseshoe Dr *UX/CGN* UB8 132 B8
Horseshoe Hl *SL* SL1 108 B9
WAB EN9 63 P9
Horseshoe La *ENC/FH* EN2 79 K2
GSTN WD25 55 K9
TRDG/WHET N20 96 G2
Horseshoe La East *GU* GU1 250 F9
Horseshoe La West *GU* GU1 250 E9
Horseshoe Ms *BRXS/STRHM* SW2 158 F10
Horseshoe Rdg *WEY* KT13 216 D7
The Horseshoe *BNSTD* SM7 239 J1
COUL/CHIP CR5 222 E9
HHS/BOV HP3 36 D8
Horse Yd *IS* N1 6 D5
Horsfeld Gdns *ELTH/MOT* SE9 184 B1
Horsfeld Rd *ELTH/MOT* SE9 184 A1
Horsfield Cl *RDART* DA2 188 B3
Horsford Rd *BRXS/STRHM* SW2 180 C1
Horsham Av *NFNCH/WDSPK* N12 97 P6
Horsham Rd *BXLYHS* DA6 186 A2
DORK RH4 272 F3
EBED/NFELT TW14 174 D2
RDKG RH5 270 G8
RDKG RH5 273 H10
SHGR GU5 268 B9
Horsley Cl *HOR/WEW* KT19 220 A9
Horsley Dr *CROY/NA* CR0 225 H4
KUTN/CMB KT2 177 J8
Horsley Rd *BMLY* BR1 205 N1
CHING E4 101 H3
COB KT11 235 J5
Horsleys *RKW/CH/CXG* WD3 90 G6
Horsley St *WALW* SE17 18 G9
Horsmans Pl *DART* DA1 * 187 M3
Horsman St *CMBW* SE5 18 F10
Horsmonden Cl *ORP* BR6 207 H7
Horsmonden Rd *BROCKY* SE4 182 E1
Horticultural Pl *CHSWK* W4 156 A4
Horton Av *CRICK* NW2 117 H9
Horton Bridge Rd *WDR/YW* UB7 132 A10
Horton Cl *WDR/YW* UB7 132 A10
Horton Crs *HOR/WEW* KT19 219 N7
Horton Gdns *DTCH/LGLY* SL3 * 150 C9
HOR/WEW KT19 219 P7
Horton Hl *HOR/WEW* KT19 219 P7
Horton La *HOR/WEW* KT19 219 M8
Horton Pde *WDR/YW* UB7 * 131 P10
Horton Pl *BH/WHM* TN16 262 G2
Horton Rd *DTCH/LGLY* SL3 149 P7
DTCH/LGLY SL3 150 E7
DTCH/LGLY SL3 151 H9
EYN DA4 210 B3
HACK E8 140 A1
STWL/WRAY TW19 173 K1
WDR/YW UB7 131 P10
Horton St *LEW* SE13 160 G9
Hortons Wy *BH/WHM* TN16 262 G2
Horton Wy *CROY/NA* CR0 204 C5
EYN DA4 209 N7
Hortus Rd *NWDGN* UB2 153 N1
Horvath Cl *WEY* KT13 216 E1
Hosack Rd *TOOT* SW17 180 A5
Hoselands Vw *HART* DA3 211 L4
Hoser Av *LEE/GVPK* SE12 183 M5
Hosey Common La
BH/WHM TN16 263 H6
Hosey Common Rd
BH/WHM TN16 263 H5
Hosey Hl *BH/WHM* TN16 263 H3
Hosier La *STBT* EC1A 12 D4
Hoskin's Cl *CAN/RD* E16 141 P8
HYS/HAR UB3 152 G4
Hoskins Rd *OXTED* RH8 261 K5
Hoskins St *GNWCH* SE10 161 J4
Hoskins Wk *OXTED* RH8 261 K5
Hospital Bridge Rd *WHTN* TW2 176 A5
Hospital Hl *CSHM* HP5 51 H8
Hospital Rd *HSLW* TW3 153 P9
SEV TN13 247 K7
Hospital Wy *LEW* SE13 183 J2
Hotham Cl *E/WMO/HCT* KT8 197 P3
EYN DA4 187 P10
SWLY BR8 209 J1
Hotham Rd *PUT/ROE* SW15 156 F9
Hotham Road Ms
WIM/MER SW19 179 M10
Hotham St *SRTFD* E15 141 K3
Hothfield Pl *BERM/RHTH* SE16 160 B2
Hotspur Rd *NTHLT* UB5 133 P4
Hotspur St *LBTH* SE11 18 A7
Hottsfield *HART* DA3 211 K3
Houblon Rd *RCHPK/HAM* TW10 177 K1
Houblons Hl *EPP* CM16 65 N7
Houghton Cl *HACK* E8 7 M2
HPTN TW12 175 M9
Houghton Rd *CRAWE* RH10 * 284 D10
SEVS/STOTM N15 119 N2
Houghton St *LINN* WC2A * 11 P6
Houlder Crs *CROY/NA* CR0 223 J5
Hound House Rd *SHGR* GU5 270 B10
Houndsden Rd *WCHMH* N21 78 G10
Houndsditch *HDTCH* EC3A 13 K5
Houndsfield Rd *ED* N9 100 A1
Hounslow Av *HSLW* TW3 176 A1
Hounslow Gdns *HSLW* TW3 176 A1
Hounslow Rd *EBED/NFELT* TW14 175 J3
WHTN TW2 176 A2
Housden Cl *STALE/WH* AL4 21 M4
Housefield Wy *STALE/WH* AL4 39 H9
House La *STALE/WH* AL4 39 J1
Houseman Wy *CMBW* SE5 159 L6
Housewood End *HHW* HP1 35 L3
Houston Rd *FSTH* SE23 182 D5
SURB KT6 198 G6
Hove Av *WALTH* E17 120 E3
Hove Cl *GRAYS* RM17 167 M5
RBRW/HUT CM13 107 P3
Hoveden Rd *CRICK* NW2 116 G10
Hove Gdns *SUT* SM1 201 L8
Hoveton Rd *THMD* SE28 143 M8
Howard Agne Cl *HHS/BOV* HP3 52 D3
Howard Av *BXLY* DA5 185 M4
EW KT17 220 D6
SLN SL2 129 J7
Howard Cl *ACT* W3 135 N8
ASHTD KT21 237 L5
BUSH WD23 94 D1
CRICK NW2 * 117 H9
EHSLY KT24 252 E1
FBAR/BDGN N11 98 B3
HPTN TW12 176 B10
KWD/TDW/WH KT20 256 C1
LHD/OX KT22 237 H9
LOU IG10 82 B10
STAL AL1 39 H9
SUN TW16 174 G9
WAB EN9 63 J10
WATN WD24 73 H3
Howard Crs *BEAC* HP9 89 H6
Howard Dr *BORE* WD6 76 A8
Howard Gdns *GU* GU1 250 D9
Howard Pl *REIG* RH2 257 K9
Howard Rdg *RGUE* GU4 250 D6
Howard Rd *BEAC* HP9 89 H6
BMLY BR1 183 M10
CDW/CHF RM16 167 H2
COUL/CHIP CR5 240 D1
CRICK NW2 116 G9
CSHM HP5 50 G4
DART DA1 187 P2
DORK RH4 272 D2
EHAM E6 142 C4
EHSLY KT24 235 H8
GT/LBKH KT23 254 A3
IL IG1 122 E9
ISLW TW7 154 E9
NWMAL KT3 200 B3
PGE/AN SE20 204 B1
RDKG RH5 * 273 H6
REIG RH2 275 L1
SNWD SE25 203 P5
STHL UB1 134 A8
STNW/STAM N16 119 L9
SURB KT6 199 L6
UPMR RM14 126 B7
WALTH E17 120 F1
WAN E11 121 K8
Howards Cl *PIN* HA5 * 93 J10
WOKS/MYFD GU22 232 D6
Howards Crest Cl *BECK* BR3 205 H2
Howards Dr *HHW* HP1 35 J3
Howardsgate *WGCW* AL8 22 G5
Howards La *ADL/WDHM* KT15 215 H3
PUT/ROE SW15 156 F10
Howard's Rd *PLSTW* E13 141 M5
WOKS/MYFD GU22 232 C6
Howards Thicket
CFSP/GDCR SL9 109 P7
Howard St *THDIT* KT7 198 G7
Howards Wood Dr
CFSP/GDCR SL9 110 A7
Howards Yd *WAND/EARL* SW18 179 L3
Howard Wk *EFNCH* N2 117 M2
Howard Wy *BAR* EN5 76 G9
HLW CM20 29 J9
HLWS CM18 47 K1
Howarth Rd *ABYW* SE2 163 K4
Howberry Cl *EDGW* HA8 95 J7
Howberry Rd *EDGW* HA8 95 J8
THHTH CR7 203 L1
Howbury La *ERITH* DA8 165 H8
Howbury Rd *PECK* SE15 160 B9
Howcroft Crs *FNCH* N3 97 K8
Howcroft La *GFD/PVL* UB6 134 C5
Howden Cl *THMD* SE28 143 N9
Howden Rd *SNWD* SE25 203 N2
Howden St *PECK* SE15 159 P9
Howe Cl *RAD* WD7 57 K9
ROMW/RG RM7 104 B9
Howe Dell *HAT* AL10 40 F4
Howe Dr *BEAC* HP9 88 D6
CTHM CR3 241 L8
Howell Cl *CHDH* RM6 123 N3
Howell Hl *BELMT* SM2 * 220 F6
Howell Hill Cl *EW* KT17 220 F7
Howell Hill Gv *EW* KT17 220 F7
Howell Wk *STHWK* SE1 18 D6
Howerd Wy *BKHTH/KID* SE3 162 B7
Howe Rd *HHS/BOV* HP3 36 B8
Howes Cl *FNCH* N3 117 K1
Howfield Gn *HOD* EN11 26 E10
Howfield Pl *TOTM* N17 * 119 N1
Howgate Rd *MORT/ESHN* SW14 156 A9
Howick Pl *WESTW* SW1E 17 H4
Howicks Gn *WGCE* AL7 23 K8
Howie St *BTSEA* SW11 157 P6
Howitt Cl *HAMP* NW3 3 N1
Howitt Rd *HAMP* NW3 3 P1
Howitts Cl *ESH/CLAY* KT10 217 P3
Howland Ct *PIN* HA5 * 93 P7
Howland Garth *STAL* AL1 38 B10
Howland Ms East *FITZ* W1T 11 H3
Howlands *WGCE* AL7 23 J9
Howland St *FITZ* W1T 11 H3
Howland Wy *BERM/RHTH* SE16 160 D1
How La *COUL/CHIP* CR5 240 B4
Howletts La *RSLP* HA4 112 D4
Howletts Rd *HNHL* SE24 181 K2
Howley Pl *BAY/PAD* W2 9 K3
Howley Rd *CROY/NA* CR0 203 J10
Hownslow Centre *HSLW* TW3 * 154 A9
Howse Rd *WAB* EN9 80 G1
Howsman Rd *BARN* SW13 156 D5
Hows Md *EPP* CM16 48 E10
Howson Rd *BROCKY* SE4 160 D10
Howson Ter *RCHPK/HAM* TW10 * 177 J2
How's Rd *UX/CGN* UB8 131 M3
Hows St *BETH* E2 7 L7
Howton Pl *BUSH* WD23 94 C2
How Wd *LCOL/BKTW* AL2 56 A4
Hoxton Market *IS* N1 7 J10
Hoxton Sq *IS* N1 7 J10
Hoxton St *IS* N1 7 J6
Hoylake Cl *CRAWW* RH11 282 G8
Hoylake Crs *HGDN/ICK* UB10 112 B6
Hoylake Gdns *HARH* RM3 105 P9
MTCM CR4 202 D3
OXHEY WD19 93 L5
RSLP HA4 113 J6
Hoylake Rd *ACT* W3 136 B8
Hoyland Cl *PECK* SE15 * 160 A6
Hoyle Rd *TOOT* SW17 179 P8
Hoy St *CAN/RD* E16 141 L8
Hoy Ter *WTHK* RM20 * 167 J4
Hubbard Dr *CHSGTN* KT9 219 H3
Hubbard Rd *WNWD* SE27 181 K7
Hubbards Cha *EMPK* RM11 125 P3
Hubbards Cl *EMPK* RM11 125 P3
UX/CGN UB8 132 C8
Hubbard's Hl *RSEV* TN14 265 J7
Hubbards Rd *RKW/CH/CXG* WD3 70 G9
Hubbard St *SRTFD* E15 141 K3
Hubert Cl *WIM/MER* SW19 * 201 M1
Hubert Day Cl *BEAC* HP9 88 C8
Hubert Gv *BRXN/ST* SW9 158 F9
Hubert Rd *BRW* CM14 106 G4
DTCH/LGLY SL3 150 A2
EHAM E6 142 A5
RAIN RM13 144 G5
Hucknall Cl *HARH* RM3 105 N7
Huddart St *BOW* E3 140 E7
Huddleston Cl *BETH* E2 * 140 B4
Huddlestone Crs *REDH* RH1 258 E4
Huddlestone Rd *CRICK* NW2 136 E1
FSTGT E7 121 L9
Huddleston Rd *HOLWY* N7 118 D8
Hudson Cl *SHB* W12 * 136 E9
STAL AL1 38 B9
WATN WD24 72 G2
Hudson Ct *GUW* GU2 249 L10
Hudson Pl *DTCH/LGLY* SL3 150 C4
WOOL/PLUM SE18 162 F4
Hudson Rd *BXLYHN* DA7 164 A8
CRAWE RH10 283 P9
HYS/HAR UB3 152 E5
Hudsons *KWD/TDW/WH* KT20 238 G7
Hudsons Av *DEN/HRF* UB9 111 J4
Huesden Wy *CFSP/GDCR* SL9 110 C6
Huggens College *GVW* DA11 * 189 N1
Huggin Hl *BLKFR* EC4V 12 F7
Huggins La *BRKMPK* AL9 40 E9
Huggins Pl *BRXS/STRHM* SW2 180 G4
Hughan Rd *SRTFD* E15 121 J10
Hugh Dalton Av *FUL/PGN* SW6 14 C10
Hughenden Av
KTN/HRWW/WS HA3 114 G3
Hughenden Gdns *NTHLT* UB5 133 K5
Hughenden Rd *SL* SL1 129 J8
STALE/WH AL4 38 G3
WPK KT4 200 D7
Hughes Cl *NFNCH/WDSPK* N12 97 M6
Hughes Rd *ASHF* TW15 174 D10
CDW/CHF RM16 168 D2
HYS/HAR UB3 133 J9
Hughes Ter *CAN/RD* E16 * 141 L7
Hughes Wk *CROY/NA* CR0 203 K7
Hugh Gaitskell Cl *FUL/PGN* SW6 14 C10
Hugh Ms *PIM* SW1V 16 F6
Hugh Pl *WEST* SW1P 17 J5
Hugh St *PIM* SW1V 16 F6
Hugo Cl *WATW* WD18 72 F8
Hugo Gdns *RAIN* RM13 144 G1
Hugon Rd *FUL/PGN* SW6 157 L9
Hugo Rd *ARCH* N19 118 D9
Huguenot Pl *WAND/EARL* SW18 179 M1
WCHPL E1 13 M3
Huguenot Sq *PECK* SE15 160 A10
Hullbridge Ms *IS* N1 6 G5
Hull Cl *BERM/RHTH* SE16 * 140 C10
CHESW EN7 61 L2
SL SL1 149 H1
Hullett's La *BRWN* CM15 86 E8
Hull Gn *HLWE* CM17 31 L9
Hull Gv *HLWW/ROY* CM19 46 D6
Hull St *FSBYE* EC1V 6 E10
Hulme Pl *STHWK* SE1 18 F2
Hulse Av *BARK* IG11 142 G1
ROMW/RG RM7 104 C9
Hulsewood Cl *RDART* DA2 187 J6
Hulton Cl *LHD/OX* KT22 237 H9
Hulverston Cl *BELMT* SM2 221 L6
Humber Av *SOCK/AV* RM15 146 E8
Humber Cl *WDR/YW* UB7 131 N10
Humber Dr *NKENS* W10 136 G6
UPMR RM14 126 C4
Humber Rd *BKHTH/KID* SE3 161 M5
CRICK NW2 116 F7
DART DA1 187 L1
Humberstone Rd *PLSTW* E13 141 P5
Humber Wy *DTCH/LGLY* SL3 150 D3
Humbolt Cl *GUW* GU2 249 K10
Humbolt Rd *HMSMTH* W6 14 A10
Hume Av *TIL* RM18 168 E9
Hume Cl *TIL* RM18 168 D9
Humes Av *HNWL* W7 154 E2
Hume Wy *RSLP* HA4 113 H4
Hummer Rd *EGH* TW20 172 D7
Humphrey Cl *CLAY* IG5 * 102 C9
LHD/OX KT22 236 B8
Humphrey St *STHWK* SE1 19 L7
Humphries Cl *DAGW* RM9 124 A9
Hundred Acre *CDALE/KGS* NW9 96 C10
Hundred Acres *CHES/WCR* EN8 * 62 F10
Hundred Acres La *AMSS* HP7 69 J6
Hungerdown *CHING* E4 101 H2
Hungerford Av *SLN* SL2 129 K7
Hungerford Sq *WEY* KT13 216 E1
Hungerford St *WCHPL* E1 * 140 A8
Hungry Hill La *RPLY/SEND* GU23 251 M2
Hunsdon *WGCE* AL7 23 N5
Hunsdon Cl *DAGW* RM9 143 P1
Hunsdon Dr *SEV* TN13 247 K9
Hunsdon Rd *NWCR* SE14 160 C6
WARE SG12 27 K7
Hunslett St *BETH* E2 * 140 B4
Hunstanton Cl *CRAWW* RH11 282 G8
DTCH/LGLY SL3 150 F6
Hunston Rd *MRDN* SM4 201 L8
Hunt Cl *BKHTH/KID* SE3 * 161 M8
NTGHL W11 136 G10
STALE/WH AL4 39 J3
Hunter Av *BRWN* CM15 87 M10
Hunter Cl *BAL* SW12 180 B4
BORE WD6 75 P9
POTB/CUF EN6 59 L9
STHWK SE1 19 H4
TOOT SW17 180 B4
WLGTN SM6 222 F4
Huntercombe Cl *MDHD* SL6 128 A8
Huntercombe La North *SL* SL1 128 B7
Huntercombe La South
MDHD SL6 128 B10
Hunter Ct *CMBW* SE5 * 159 L10
Huntercrombe Gdns
OXHEY WD19 93 K6
Hunter Dr *HCH* RM12 125 K9
Hunter Rd *CRAWE* RH10 283 N10
GU GU1 268 B1
RYNPK SW20 200 F1
THHTH CR7 203 L3
Hunters Cha *CHONG* CM5 67 P6
Hunters Cl *BXLY* DA5 186 F6
CSHM HP5 50 F6
HHS/BOV HP3 52 D5
HOR/WEW KT19 219 P9
Hunters Ct *RCH/KEW* TW9 177 J1
Huntersfield Cl *REIG* RH2 257 M7
Hunters Ga *REDH* RH1 258 G9
Hunter's Gv *CRW* RM5 104 C6
HYS/HAR UB3 133 H10
KTN/HRWW/WS HA3 115 H2
ORP BR6 226 F1
Hunters Hall Rd *DAGE* RM10 124 B10
Hunters Hl *RSLP* HA4 113 K8
Hunter's La *GSTN* WD25 54 G10
Hunters Meadow *NRWD* SE19 181 M7
Hunters Oak *HHNE* HP2 36 C1
Hunters Pk *BERK* HP4 34 B4
Hunters Reach *CHESW* EN7 61 N5
Hunters Ride *LCOL/BKTW* AL2 55 P7
Hunters Rd *CHSGTN* KT9 199 K10
IL IG1 122 E10
Hunters Sq *DAGE* RM10 124 B9
Hunter St *BMSBY* WC1N 11 M1
Hunters Wk *RSEV* TN14 227 P10
Hunters Wy *CROY/NA* CR0 223 M1
ENC/FH EN2 79 H5
SL SL1 148 D1
WGCE AL7 23 J8
Hunting Cl *ESH/CLAY* KT10 217 P1
Huntingdon Cl *BROX* EN10 44 D10
MTCM CR4 202 F4
NTHLT UB5 133 N2
Huntingdon Gdns *CHSWK* W4 155 P6
WPK KT4 200 F10
Huntingdon Rd *ED* N9 100 B2
EFNCH N2 117 P1
REDH RH1 258 A10
WOKN/KNAP GU21 231 K3
Huntingdon St *CAN/RD* E16 141 L8
IS N1 5 P3
Huntingfield *CROY/NA* CR0 224 E4
Huntingfield Rd *PUT/ROE* SW15 156 D10
Huntingfield Wy *EGH* TW20 172 G10
Hunting Ga *HHNE* HP2 35 P2
Hunting Gate Cl *ENC/FH* EN2 79 H7
Hunting Gate Dr *CHSGTN* KT9 219 K4
Hunting Gate Ms *WHTN* TW2 * 176 D4
Huntings Rd *DAGE* RM10 144 B1
Huntington Pl *DTCH/LGLY* SL3 150 E2
Huntland Cl *RAIN* RM13 145 J7
Huntley Av *GVW* DA11 189 N2
Huntley Cl *STWL/WRAY* TW19 173 P3
Huntley St *GWRST* WC1E 11 J3
Huntley Wy *RYNPK* SW20 * 200 D2
Huntly Dr *FNCH* N3 97 K7
Huntly Rd *SNWD* SE25 203 M3
Hunton Bridge Hl *KGLGY* WD4 54 E9
Hunton St *WCHPL* E1 13 N3
Hunt Rd *GVW* DA11 190 B6
NWDGN UB2 153 P2
Hunts Cl *BKHTH/KID* SE3 161 M8
GUW GU2 249 J9
Hunts Hill Rd *RGUW* GU3 248 A7
Hunt's La *SRTFD* E15 141 H4
Huntsman Cl *FELT* TW13 175 J7
Huntsman Rd *BARK/HLT* IG6 103 L7
Huntsmans Cl *WARL* CR6 242 B5
Huntsmans Dr *UPMR* RM14 126 B10
Huntsman St *WALW* SE17 19 J6
Hunts Md *PEND* EN3 80 C7
Hunts Medde Cl *CHST* BR7 184 B10
Hunts Mede Cl *CHST* BR7 184 C10
Huntsmill Rd *HHW* HP1 35 H7
Huntsmoor Rd *HOR/WEW* KT19 220 A2
Huntspill St *TOOT* SW17 179 M6
Hunts Slip Rd *DUL* SE21 181 M6
Huntsworth Ms *CAMTN* NW1 10 A1
Hurdwick Pl *CAMTN* NW1 * 4 G7
Hurley Cl *WOT/HER* KT12 197 J9
Hurley Crs *BERM/RHTH* SE16 140 C10
Hurley Gdns *RGUE* GU4 250 D7
Hurley Rd *GFD/PVL* UB6 134 A7
Hurlfield *RDART* DA2 187 K6
Hurlford *WOKN/KNAP* GU21 231 M3
Hurlingham Gdns *FUL/PGN* SW6 157 J9
Hurlingham Pk *FUL/PGN* SW6 157 J9
Hurlingham Rd *BXLYHN* DA7 164 A6
FUL/PGN SW6 157 J8
Hurlingham Sq *FUL/PGN* SW6 * 157 K9
Hurlock St *HBRY* N5 119 J8
Hurlstone Rd *SNWD* SE25 203 L5
Hurn Court Rd *HSLWW* TW4 153 L8
Hurnford Cl *SAND/SEL* CR2 223 M6
Huron Cl *ORP* BR6 227 H3
Huron Rd *BROX* EN10 62 D2
TOOT SW17 180 B5
Hurren Cl *BKHTH/KID* SE3 161 K9
Hurricane House
WOOL/PLUM SE18 * 162 B6
Hurricane Rd *WLGTN* SM6 222 F4
Hurricane Wy *ABLGY* WD5 55 H9
DTCH/LGLY SL3 150 F4
EPP CM16 66 A3
Hurry Cl *SRTFD* E15 141 K3
Hursley Rd *CHIG* IG7 103 J6
Hurst Av *CHING* E4 100 F4
HGT N6 118 D4
Hurstbourne *ESH/CLAY* KT10 218 E3
Hurstbourne Gdns *BARK* IG11 142 G1
Hurstbourne Rd *FSTH* SE23 182 D4
Hurst Cl *CHING* E4 100 F4
CHSGTN KT9 219 M2
CRAWW RH11 283 J9
EPSOM KT18 237 P10
GLDGN NW11 117 L4
HAYES BR2 205 L8
NTHLT UB5 133 N1
WGCE AL7 23 M6
WOKS/MYFD GU22 231 P6
Hurstcourt Rd *SUT* SM1 201 L8
Hurst Cft *GU* GU1 268 B3
Hurstdene Av *HAYES* BR2 205 L8
STA TW18 173 L9
Hurstdene Gdns
SEVS/STOTM N15 119 M5
Hurst Dr *CHES/WCR* EN8 62 C10
KWD/TDW/WH KT20 256 D2
Hurst Farm Rd *RSEV* TN14 265 K8
Hurstfield *HAYES* BR2 205 M5
Hurstfield Crs *YEAD* UB4 132 F7
Hurstfield Dr *MDHD* SL6 128 A8
Hurstfield Rd *E/WMO/HCT* KT8 197 P3
Hurst Green Cl *OXTED* RH8 261 M8
Hurst Green Rd *OXTED* RH8 261 M9
Hurst Gv *WOT/HER* KT12 196 G8
Hurstlands *OXTED* RH8 261 M8
Hurstlands Cl *EMPK* RM11 125 K5
Hurst La *ABYW* SE2 163 N4
E/WMO/HCT KT8 198 B4
EGH TW20 194 C3
EPSOM KT18 238 A8
RSEV TN14 265 J9
Hurstleigh Cl *REDH* RH1 258 A8
Hurstleigh Dr *REDH* RH1 258 A8
Hurstleigh Gdns *CLAY* IG5 102 C9
Hurstlings *WGCE* AL7 23 L7
Hurst Park Av *HCH* RM12 125 M9
Hurst Pl *ABYW* SE2 163 M4
DART DA1 * 187 K2
POTB/CUF EN6 59 K10
NTHWD HA6 92 C9
Hurst Ri *BAR* EN5 77 K7
Hurst Rd *BFN/LL* DA15 185 L5
BKHH IG9 102 A2
CROY/NA CR0 223 L2
E/WMO/HCT KT8 198 B3
EPSOM KT18 238 B9
ERITH DA8 164 D6
HOR/WEW KT19 220 A7
HORL RH6 279 P3
SL SL1 128 C7
WALTH E17 120 G1
WCHMH N21 99 H2
WOT/HER KT12 197 L4
Hurst Springs *BXLY* DA5 185 P4
Hurst St *HNHL* SE24 181 J2
Hurst View Rd *SAND/SEL* CR2 223 M4
Hurst Wy *SAND/SEL* CR2 223 M3
SEV TN13 265 K3
WOKS/MYFD GU22 215 H10
Hurstway Rd *NTGHL* W11 * 136 G9
Hurstway Wk *NTGHL* W11 * 136 G9
Hurstwood Av *BRWN* CM15 106 G1
BXLY DA5 185 P4
ERITH DA8 164 F7
SWFD E18 121 N2
Hurstwood Dr *BMLY* BR1 206 C3
Hurstwood Rd *GLDGN* NW11 117 H2
Hurtmore Cha *GODL* GU7 266 G9
Hurtmore Rd *GODL* GU7 266 E10
Hurtwood Rd *WOT/HER* KT12 197 N7
Hurworth Av *DTCH/LGLY* SL3 149 P2
Huson Cl *HAMP* NW3 3 N3
Hussain Cl *HRW* HA1 114 E9
Hussars Cl *HSLWW* TW4 153 M9
Husseywell Crs *HAYES* BR2 205 M8
Hutchingson's Rd *CROY/NA* CR0 225 H7
Hutching's St *POP/IOD* E14 160 F1
Hutchings Wk *GLDGN* NW11 117 L2
Hutchins Cl *HCH* RM12 125 M8
SRTFD E15 141 H2
Hutchinson Ter *WBLY* HA9 115 J8
Hutchins Rd *THMD* SE28 143 K9
Hutchins Wy *HORL* RH6 280 A2
Hutton Cl *BFOR* GU20 212 C4
GFD/PVL UB6 114 C10
HERT/WAT SG14 25 H5
WFD IG8 101 N7
WOT/HER KT12 217 J2
Hutton Ga *RBRW/HUT* CM13 107 N1
Hutton Gv *NFNCH/WDSPK* N12 97 L7
Hutton La *KTN/HRWW/WS* HA3 94 B8
Hutton Pl *RBRW/HUT* CM13 87 N10
Hutton Rd *BRWN* CM15 107 M1
Hutton Rw *EDGW* HA8 95 P8
Hutton St *EMB* EC4Y 12 B6
Hutton Wk *KTN/HRWW/WS* HA3 94 B8
Huxbear St *BROCKY* SE4 182 E1
Huxley *UED* N18 * 99 L6
Huxley Cl *GODL* GU7 267 J10
NTHLT UB5 133 M4
Huxley Dr *CHDH* RM6 123 L5
Huxley Gdns *WLSDN* NW10 135 L5
Huxley Pde *UED* N18 * 99 L6
Huxley Pl *PLMGR* N13 99 J5
Huxley Rd *GUW* GU2 267 J1
LEY E10 121 H7
UED N18 99 L5
WELL DA16 163 J9
Huxley Sayze *UED* N18 * 99 L6
Huxley St *NKENS* W10 2 A10
Hyacinth Cl *HPTN* TW12 175 P9
IL IG1 142 E1
Hyacinth Dr *HGDN/ICK* UB10 131 P2
Hyacinth Rd *PUT/ROE* SW15 178 D4
Hyatts Yd *CSHM* HP5 * 50 G8
Hyburn Cl *HHS/BOV* HP3 36 C7
LCOL/BKTW AL2 55 N6
Hycliffe Gdns *CHIG* IG7 102 F5
Hyde Av *POTB/CUF* EN6 59 L9
Hyde Cl *BAR* EN5 77 J7
CDW/CHF RM16 167 J2
PLSTW E13 141 M4
Hyde Crs *CDALE/KGS* NW9 116 B3
Hyde Dr *CRAWW* RH11 283 H8
STMC/STPC BR5 207 L4
Hyde Estate Rd *CDALE/KGS* NW9 116 C3
Hyde Farm Ms *BAL* SW12 180 E4
Hydefield Cl *WCHMH* N21 99 L2
Hydefield Ct *ED* N9 99 M3
Hyde Gn *BEAC* HP9 88 E9
Hyde La *BTSEA* SW11 157 P7
HHS/BOV HP3 54 C3
LCOL/BKTW AL2 56 D4
Hyde Md *WAB* EN9 45 K9
Hyde Mdw *HHS/BOV* HP3 52 D4
Hyde Park Av *WCHMH* N21 99 L2
Hyde Park Cnr *MYFR/PICC* W1J 16 D1
Hyde Park Crs *BAY/PAD* W2 9 N6
Hyde Park Gdns *BAY/PAD* W2 9 M7
WCHMH N21 99 K2
Hyde Park Gardens Ms
BAY/PAD W2 9 M7
Hyde Park Ga *SKENS* SW7 15 K2
Hyde Park Gate Ms *SKENS* SW7 * 15 K2
Hyde Park Pl *BAY/PAD* W2 9 P7
Hyde Park Sq *BAY/PAD* W2 9 N6
Hyde Park St *BAY/PAD* W2 9 N7
Hyderabad Wy *SRTFD* E15 141 K2
Hyde Rd *BXLYHN* DA7 164 A8
IS N1 7 J6
RCHPK/HAM TW10 177 L1
SAND/SEL CR2 223 M9
WAT WD17 73 H7
Hyder Rd *CDW/CHF* RM16 168 F2
Hydeside Gdns *ED* N9 99 N3
Hyde's Pl *IS* N1 6 C3
Hyde St *DEPT* SE8 160 F5
Hyde Ter *ASHF* TW15 174 F9
The Hyde *CDALE/KGS* NW9 116 A2
WARE SG12 26 A1
Hydethorpe Av *ED* N9 99 N3
Hydethorpe Rd *BAL* SW12 180 D4
Hyde V *GNWCH* SE10 161 H6
Hyde Va *WGCE* AL7 23 J7
Hyde Wk *MRDN* SM4 201 K7
Hyde Wy *ED* N9 99 N3
HYS/HAR UB3 152 G3
WGCE AL7 23 H5
Hyland Cl *EMPK* RM11 125 J5

Hylands Cl CRAWE RH10 284 B8
Hylands Ms EPSOM KT18 237 P1
Hylands Rd EPSOM KT18 237 P1
WALTH E17 101 J10
Hyland Wy EMPK RM11 125 J5
Hylle Cl WDSR SL4 148 D7
Hylton St WOOL/PLUM SE18 163 J3
Hyndewood FSTH SE23 182 C6
Hyndford Crs SWCM DA10 189 H1
Hyndman St PECK SE15 160 A5
Hynton Rd BCTR RM8 123 M7
Hyperion Ct CRAWW RH11 283 H9
HHNE HP2 36 A3
Hyperion Pl HOR/WEW KT19 220 A5
Hyrons Cl AMS HP6 69 K4
Hyrons La AMS HP6 69 J4
Hyrstdene SAND/SEL CR2 223 J1
Hyson Rd BERM/RHTH SE16 160 A4
Hythe Av BXLYHN DA7 163 P6
Hythe Cl STMC/STPC BR5 207 M4
UED N18 99 P5
Hythe End Rd STWL/WRAY TW19 172 E6
Hythe Field Av EGH TW20 172 G9
Hythe Park Rd EGH TW20 172 F8
Hythe Rd STA TW18 172 G8
THHTH CR7 203 L2
WLSDN NW10 136 C5
Hythe St DART DA1 187 M2
The Hythe STA TW18 173 H8
Hyver Hl BAR EN5 76 A10

I

Ibbetson Pth LOU IG10 82 E7
Ibbotson Av CAN/RD E16 141 L8
Ibbott St WCHPL E1 140 B6
Iberian Av WLGTN SM6 222 E1
Ibis La CHSWK W4 155 P7
Ibis Wy YEAD UB4 133 L8
Ibscott Cl DAGE RM10 144 D1
Ibsley Gdns PUT/ROE SW15 178 D4
Ibsley Wy EBAR EN4 77 P9
Icehouse Wd OXTED RH8 261 L7
Iceland Rd BOW E3 140 F3
Ickburgh Est CLPT E5 * 120 A7
Ickburgh Rd CLPT E5 120 A8
Ickenham Cl RSLP HA4 112 E7
Ickenham Rd RSLP HA4 112 E6
Ickleton Rd ELTH/MOT SE9 184 B7
Icklingham Ga COB KT11 217 K8
Icklingham Rd COB KT11 217 K8
Icknield Cl STALW/RED AL3 37 N8
Icknield Dr GNTH/NBYPK IG2 122 E3
Ickworth Park Rd WALTH E17 120 D2
Ida Rd SEVS/STOTM N15 119 L3
Ida St POP/IOD E14 141 H8
Ide Hill Rd RSEV TN14 264 A8
Iden Cl HAYES BR2 205 K3
Idlecombe Rd TOOT SW17 180 B9
Idleigh Court Rd MEO DA13 211 N10
Idmiston Rd SRTFD E15 121 L10
WNWD SE27 181 K6
WPK KT4 200 C7
Idmiston Sq WPK KT4 200 C7
Idol La MON EC3R 13 J8
Idonia St DEPT SE8 160 E6
Iffley Cl UX/CGN UB8 131 N2
Iffley Rd HMSMTH W6 156 E2
Ifield Av CRAWW RH11 283 K4
Ifield Cl REDH RH1 275 P3
Ifield Dr CRAWW RH11 283 K6
Ifield Gn CRAWW RH11 283 K4
Ifield Pk CRAWW RH11 * 283 J7
Ifield Rd CRAWW RH11 283 L6
HORL RH6 279 H10
WBPTN SW10 15 H9
Ifield St CRAWW RH11 283 J5
Ifield Wy GVE DA12 190 G9
Ifield Wd CRAWW RH11 282 G4
Ifold Rd REDH RH1 276 B2
Ightham Rd ERITH DA8 164 B6
Ikona Ct WEY KT13 * 216 D2
Ilbert St NKENS W10 2 A10
Ilchester Gdns BAY/PAD W2 8 G7
Ilchester Pl WKENS W14 14 D3
Ilchester Rd BCTR RM8 123 L10
Ildersly Gv DUL SE21 181 L5
Ilderton Rd BERM/RHTH SE16 160 B4
Ilex Cl EGH TW20 171 N10
SUN TW16 197 K2
Ilex Rd WLSDN NW10 136 C1
Ilex Wy STRHM/NOR SW16 181 H8
Ilford Hl IL IG1 122 D8
Ilford La IL IG1 122 E9
Ilfracombe Crs HCH RM12 125 K9
Ilfracombe Gdns CHDH RM6 123 L5
Ilfracombe Rd BMLY BR1 183 L6
Iliffe St WALW SE17 18 D7
Iliffe Yd WALW SE17 18 D7
Ilkley Cl NRWD SE19 * 181 L9
Ilkley Ct FBAR/BDGN N11 98 B7
Ilkley Rd CAN/RD E16 141 P7
OXHEY WD19 93 L6
Illingworth WDSR SL4 148 D9
Illingworth Wy EN EN1 79 M9
Ilmington Rd
KTN/HRWW/WS HA3 115 J4
Ilminster Gdns BTSEA SW11 157 P10
Imber Cl STHGT/OAK N14 98 D1
Imber Cross THDIT KT7 * 198 E7
Imber Gv ESH/CLAY KT10 198 C7
Imber Park Rd ESH/CLAY KT10 198 C8
Imber St IS N1 6 G6
Imperial Av STNW/STAM N16 * 119 M9
Imperial Cl RYLN/HDSTN HA2 113 P4
Imperial College Rd SKENS SW7 15 M3
Imperial Ct WDSR SL4 148 F9
Imperial Crs FUL/PGN SW6 157 M8
Imperial Dr GVE DA12 191 J8
RYLN/HDSTN HA2 113 P5
Imperial Gdns MTCM CR4 202 C3
Imperial Ms EHAM E6 142 A4
Imperial Pk LHD/OX KT22 * 236 F6
Imperial Pl BORE WD6 * 75 N7
CHST BR7 206 D1
Imperial Rd EBED/NFELT TW14 174 F3
FUL/PGN SW6 157 L7
WDGN N22 98 F8
WDSR SL4 148 F9
Imperial Sq FUL/PGN SW6 157 L7
Imperial St BOW E3 141 H5
Imperial Wy CHST BR7 184 F6
CROY/NA CR0 222 G3
KTN/HRWW/WS HA3 115 K4
WATN WD24 73 K5
Imre Cl SHB W12 136 E10
Inca Dr ELTH/MOT SE9 184 E3
Ince Rd WOT/HER KT12 216 F4
Inchmery Rd CAT SE6 182 G5
Inchwood CROY/NA CR0 224 G1
Indells HAT AL10 40 C5
Independent Pl HACK E8 119 N10
Independents Rd
BKHTH/KID SE3 161 L9
Inderwick Rd CEND/HSY/T N8 118 G4
Indescon Ct POP/IOD E14 160 G1
India Rd SL SL1 149 N1
India St TWRH EC3N 13 L6
India Wy SHB W12 136 E9
Indigo Ms POP/IOD E14 * 141 H9
STNW/STAM N16 119 L8
Indus Rd CHARL SE7 161 P6
Infant House
WOOL/PLUM SE18 * 162 B6
Ingal Rd PLSTW E13 141 M6
Ingate Pl VX/NE SW8 158 C7
Ingatestone Rd MNPK E12 121 P6
SNWD SE25 204 A5
WFD IG8 101 N8
Ingelow Rd VX/NE SW8 158 C8
Ingels Md EPP CM16 65 J5
Ingersoll Rd PEND EN3 80 B4
SHB W12 136 E10
Ingestre Pl SOHO/CST W1F 11 H6
Ingestre Rd FSTGT E7 121 M9
KTTN NW5 118 C9
Ingham Cl SAND/SEL CR2 224 C5
Ingham Rd KIL/WHAMP NW6 117 K9
SAND/SEL CR2 224 B5
Inglebert St CLKNW EC1R 6 A9
Ingleboro Dr PUR/KEN CR8 223 L9
Ingleborough St BRXN/ST SW9 159 H8
Ingleby Dr HRW HA1 114 C8
Ingleby Gdns CHIG IG7 103 L4
Ingleby Rd CDW/CHF RM16 168 E2
DAGE RM10 144 C1
HOLWY N7 118 F8
IL IG1 122 E6
Ingleby Wy CHST BR7 184 D8
WLGTN SM6 222 E5
Ingle Cl PIN HA5 113 N1
Ingledew Rd WOOL/PLUM SE18 162 G4
Inglefield POTB/CUF EN6 59 K6
Inglefield Sq WAP E1W * 140 A10
Ingleglen EMPK RM11 125 P5
SLN SL2 108 G10
Inglehurst ADL/WDHM KT15 215 L6
Inglehurst Gdns REDBR IG4 122 C3
Inglemere Rd FSTH SE23 182 C6
MTCM CR4 180 A10
Ingles WGCW AL8 23 H2
Ingleside DTCH/LGLY SL3 151 H7
Ingleside Cl BECK BR3 182 F10
Ingleside Gv BKHTH/KID SE3 161 L5
Inglethorpe St FUL/PGN SW6 156 G7
Ingleton Av WELL DA16 185 K1
Ingleton Rd CAR SM5 221 P5
UED N18 99 P7
Ingleton St BRXN/ST SW9 159 H8
Ingleway NFNCH/WDSPK N12 97 N7
Inglewood CHERT KT16 195 J10
CROY/NA CR0 224 D5
SWLY BR8 * 208 F2
WOKN/KNAP GU21 231 N4
Inglewood Cl BARK/HLT IG6 103 J7
HCH RM12 125 L9
POP/IOD E14 160 F3
Inglewood Copse BMLY BR1 206 B2
Inglewood Gdns LCOL/BKTW AL2 56 E1
Inglewood Rd BXLYHN DA7 164 E10
KIL/WHAMP NW6 117 K10
Inglis Rd CROY/NA CR0 203 N8
EA W5 135 L9
Inglis St CMBW SE5 159 J7
Ingoldsby Rd GVE DA12 191 H4
Ingram Av GLDGN NW11 117 M5
Ingram Cl LBTH SE11 17 P5
STAN HA7 95 H6
Ingram Rd DART DA1 187 M4
EFNCH N2 117 P2
GRAYS RM17 167 P3
THHTH CR7 203 K1
Ingrams Cl WOT/HER KT12 217 K2
Ingram Wy GFD/PVL UB6 134 C3
Ingrave Rd BRWN CM15 107 K4
ROM RM1 124 E2
Ingrave St BTSEA SW11 157 N9
Ingrebourne Gdns UPMR RM14 126 B6
Ingrebourne Rd RAIN RM13 145 J6
Ingress Park Av SWCM DA10 189 H1
Ingress St CHSWK W4 156 B4
Ingress Ter MEO DA13 * 189 L7
Ingreway HARH RM3 106 A7
Inholms La RDKG RH5 273 H6
Inigo Jones Rd CHARL SE7 162 B6
Inkerman Pde
WOKN/KNAP GU21 * 231 K4
Inkerman Rd KTTN NW5 4 E1
STAL AL1 38 D7
WDSR SL4 148 E3
WOKN/KNAP GU21 231 K4
Inkerman Ter CSHM HP5 51 H9
Inkerman Wy WOKN/KNAP GU21 231 K4
Inks Gn CHING E4 101 H6
Inkwell Cl NFNCH/WDSPK N12 97 M4
Inman Rd WAND/EARL SW18 179 M3
WLSDN NW10 136 B3
Inmans Rw WFD IG8 101 M5
Inner Cir CAMTN NW1 4 C10
Inner Park Rd WIM/MER SW19 178 G5
Inner Ring East HTHAIR TW6 152 C9
Innes Cl RYNPK SW20 201 H2
Innes Ct HHS/BOV HP3 35 N8
Innes Gdns PUT/ROE SW15 178 E2
Innes St PECK SE15 159 M6
Innes Yd CROY/NA CR0 203 K10
Inniskilling Rd PLSTW E13 141 P4
Innovation Cl ALP/SUD HA0 135 K3
Innova Wy PEND EN3 80 E2
Inskip Cl LEY E10 120 G7
Inskip Dr EMPK RM11 125 M6
Inskip Rd BCTR RM8 123 N6
Institute Pl HACK E8 120 A10
Institute Rd DORK RH4 272 B3
EPP CM16 65 N5
Instone Rd DART DA1 187 L3
Integer Gdns WAN E11 * 121 J5
International Av HEST TW5 153 K4
International Wy SUN TW16 196 F1
Inver Ct BAY/PAD W2 9 H6
Inveresk Gdns WPK KT4 200 D10
Inverforth Cl HAMP NW3 117 M7
Inverforth Rd FBAR/BDGN N11 98 C6
Inverine Rd CHARL SE7 161 N4
Invermore Pl WOOL/PLUM SE18 162 F3
Inverness Av EN EN1 79 M5
Inverness Dr BARK/HLT IG6 103 H7
Inverness Gdns KENS W8 8 G10
Inverness Ms BAY/PAD W2 9 H7
Inverness Pl BAY/PAD W2 9 H7
Inverness Rd NWDGN UB2 153 M3
UED N18 100 A6
WPK KT4 200 G8
Inverness St CAMTN NW1 4 E5
Inverness Ter BAY/PAD W2 9 H6
WDGN N22 * 99 J9
Inverton Rd PECK SE15 160 C10
Invicta Cl CHST BR7 184 D8
EBED/NFELT TW14 174 G4
Invicta Gv NTHLT UB5 133 N5
Invicta Pde SCUP DA14 * 185 L7
Invicta Plaza STHWK SE1 12 C9
Invicta Rd BKHTH/KID SE3 161 M6
RDART DA2 188 A2
Inville Rd WALW SE17 19 H8
Inwood Av COUL/CHIP CR5 241 H6
HSLW TW3 154 B9
Inwood Cl CROY/NA CR0 204 D9
Inwood Rd HSLW TW3 154 B10
Inworth St BTSEA SW11 157 P8
Inworth Wk IS N1 * 6 E5
Iona Cl CAT SE6 182 F3
CRAWW RH11 283 L10
MRDN SM4 201 L7
Iona Crs SL SL1 128 D8
Ionian Wy HHNE HP2 36 A3
Ionia Wk GVE DA12 191 J6
Ion Sq BETH E2 * 7 N8
Ipswich Rd SL SL1 128 E8
TOOT SW17 180 C9
Ireland Cl EHAM E6 142 C7
Ireland Pl WDGN N22 98 F8
Irene Ms HNWL W7 * 134 E10
Irene Rd COB KT11 217 P10
FUL/PGN SW6 157 K7
ORP BR6 207 J7
Ireton Av WOT/HER KT12 196 G9
Ireton Cl MUSWH N10 98 B8
Ireton Pl GRAYS RM17 167 M3
Ireton St BOW E3 140 F6
Iris Av BXLY DA5 185 P2
Iris Cl BRWN CM15 86 G9
CROY/NA CR0 204 C8
EHAM E6 142 B7
SURB KT6 * 199 L7
Iris Crs BXLYHN DA7 164 A5
Iris Rd CHOB/PIR GU24 230 F1
HOR/WEW KT19 219 N2
Iris Wy CHING E4 100 E7
Irkdale Av EN EN1 79 N5
Iron Bridge Cl NWDGN UB2 134 B10
WLSDN NW10 116 B10
Ironbridge Rd STKPK UB11 * 132 B10
Iron Bridge Rd STKPK UB11 * 132 C10
Iron Bridge Rd North
STKPK UB11 132 B10
Iron Bridge Rd South
WDR/YW UB7 152 C1
Iron Dr HERT/BAY SG13 26 A4
Iron Mill La DART DA1 164 G10
Iron Mill Pl DART DA1 164 G10
WAND/EARL SW18 * 179 L2
Iron Mill Rd WAND/EARL SW18 179 L2
Ironmonger La CITYW EC2V 12 G6
Ironmonger Rw FSBYE EC1V 6 F10
Ironmongers Pl POP/IOD E14 160 F3
Ironsbottom REIG RH2 275 J10
Ironside Cl BERM/RHTH SE16 160 C1
Irons Wy CRW RM5 104 D8
Irvine Av KTN/HRWW/WS HA3 114 F1
Irvine Cl TRDG/WHET N20 97 P3
Irvine Gdns SOCK/AV RM15 146 E8
Irvine Pl VW GU25 194 B5
Irvine Wy ORP BR6 207 J7
Irving Av NTHLT UB5 133 L3
Irving Gv BRXN/ST SW9 158 G8
Irving Ms IS N1 6 E2
Irving Rd WKENS W14 156 G2
Irving St LSQ/SEVD WC2H 11 K8
Irving Wk CRAWE RH10 283 P10
Irving Wy CDALE/KGS NW9 116 C3
SWLY BR8 208 E2
Irwell Est BERM/RHTH SE16 * 160 B1
Irwin Av WOOL/PLUM SE18 163 H6
Irwin Cl HGDN/ICK UB10 112 B8
Irwin Gdns WLSDN NW10 136 E3
Irwin Rd GUW GU2 267 M1
Isaac Wy STHWK SE1 18 F1
Isabel Ga CHES/WCR EN8 62 E2
Isabella Cl STHGT/OAK N14 98 D1
Isabella Ct RCHPK/HAM TW10 177 L2
Isabella Dr ORP BR6 226 F1
Isabella Ms IS N1 7 J1
Isabella Pl KUTN/CMB KT2 177 L8
Isabella Rd HOM E9 * 120 B10
Isabella St STHWK SE1 12 C10
Isabelle Cl CHESW EN7 61 K5
Isabel St BRXN/ST SW9 158 G7
Isambard Ms POP/IOD E14 161 H2
Isambard Pl BERM/RHTH SE16 140 B10
Isbells Dr REIG RH2 275 L2
Isenburg Wy HHNE HP2 35 N1
Isham Rd STRHM/NOR SW16 202 F2
Isis Cl PUT/ROE SW15 156 F10
RSLP HA4 112 D4
Isis Dr UPMR RM14 126 D4
Isis St WAND/EARL SW18 179 M5
Island Centre Wy PEND EN3 80 F4
Island Cl STA TW18 173 H7
Island Farm Av E/WMO/HCT KT8 197 N5
Island Farm Rd E/WMO/HCT KT8 197 N5
Island Rd BERM/RHTH SE16 160 C3
MTCM CR4 180 A10
Island Rw POP/IOD E14 140 E8
Isla Rd WOOL/PLUM SE18 162 F5
Islay Gdns HSLWW TW4 175 L1
Islay Wk IS N1 6 F2
Islay Whf POP/IOD E14 * 141 H7
Isledon Rd HOLWY N7 119 H8
Islehurst Cl CHST BR7 206 D1
Islington Gn IS N1 6 C6
Islington High St IS N1 6 C7
Islington Park Ms IS N1 6 C3
Islington Park St IS N1 6 B3
Islip Gdns EDGW HA8 96 A7
NTHLT UB5 133 M2
Islip Manor Rd NTHLT UB5 133 M2
Islip St KTTN NW5 118 D10
Ismailia Rd FSTGT E7 141 N2
Ismay Cl SLN SL2 * 129 K8
Isom Cl PLSTW E13 141 N5
Istead Ri MEO DA13 190 C10
Itchingwood Common Rd
OXTED RH8 261 P9
Ivanhoe Cl CRAWW RH11 283 N4
UX/CGN UB8 131 N7
Ivanhoe Dr KTN/HRWW/WS HA3 94 G10
Ivanhoe Rd CMBW SE5 159 N9
HSLWW TW4 153 L9
Ivatt Pl WKENS W14 14 D8
Ivatt Wy SEVS/STOTM N15 119 J1
Iveagh Av WLSDN NW10 135 M4
Iveagh Cl HOM E9 140 C3
NTHWD HA6 92 C9
WLSDN NW10 135 M4
Iveagh Rd GUW GU2 267 N1
Ivedon Rd WELL DA16 163 M8
Ive Farm Cl LEY E10 120 F7
Ive Farm La LEY E10 120 F7
Iveley Rd CLAP SW4 158 D8
Iverdale Cl IVER SL0 130 F9
Ivere Dr BAR EN5 77 L10
Iverhurst Cl BXLYHS DA6 185 N1
Iver La IVER SL0 131 L7
Iver Ldg IVER SL0 131 J7
Iverna Ct KENS W8 14 F3
Iverna Gdns EBED/NFELT TW14 174 E1
KENS W8 14 F3
Iverson Rd KIL/WHAMP NW6 2 D2
Ivers Wy CROY/NA CR0 224 G4
Ives Gdns ROM RM1 124 G2
Ives Rd CAN/RD E16 141 K7
DTCH/LGLY SL3 150 D2
HERT/WAT SG14 25 J4
Ives St CHEL SW3 15 P5
Ivimey St BETH E2 7 P9
Ivinghoe Cl EN EN1 79 M6
GSTN WD25 73 L1
STALE/WH AL4 39 H1
Ivinghoe Rd BCTR RM8 123 L10
BUSH WD23 94 C1
RKW/CH/CXG WD3 91 J1
Ivor Cl GU GU1 268 C1
Ivor Gv ELTH/MOT SE9 184 E4
Ivor Pl CAMTN NW1 10 A2
Ivor St CAMTN NW1 4 G4
Ivory Cl STALE/WH AL4 39 H9
Ivory Ct FELT TW13 175 H4
HHS/BOV HP3 35 P9
Ivorydown BMLY BR1 183 M7
Ivory Wk CRAWW RH11 283 H10
Ivy Bower Cl RDART DA2 188 C1
Ivybridge BROX EN10 44 F5
Ivybridge Cl TWK TW1 176 F2
Ivy Bridge Cl UX/CGN UB8 131 P5
Ivy Chimneys Rd EPP CM16 65 H9
Ivychurch Cl PGE/AN SE20 182 A10
Ivy Church La WALW SE17 * 19 L7
Ivy Cl DART DA1 187 P2
GVE DA12 190 F7
PIN HA5 113 K5
RYLN/HDSTN HA2 113 N9
SUN TW16 197 K2
Ivy Cottages HGDN/ICK UB10 * 132 B5
Ivy Crs CHSWK W4 155 P3
SL SL1 128 E9
Ivydale Rd CAR SM5 202 A9
PECK SE15 160 C9
Ivyday Gv STRHM/NOR SW16 180 G6
Ivydene E/WMO/HCT KT8 197 N5
WOKN/KNAP GU21 230 G4
Ivydene Cl REDH RH1 276 C5
SUT SM1 221 M1
Ivy Gdns CEND/HSY/T N8 118 F4
MTCM CR4 202 E3
Ivy House La BERK HP4 34 B5
RSEV TN14 246 F3
Ivyhouse Rd DAGW RM9 143 N1
HGDN/ICK UB10 112 C8
Ivy La HSLWW TW4 153 N10
RSEV TN14 245 P2
WOKS/MYFD GU22 232 E4
Ivy Lea RKW/CH/CXG WD3 * 91 K2
Ivy Lodge La HARH RM3 106 B10
Ivy Mill Cl GDST RH9 260 A8
Ivy Mill La GDST RH9 259 P8
Ivymount Rd WNWD SE27 181 H6
Ivy Rd BROCKY SE4 160 E10
CAN/RD E16 141 M8
CRICK NW2 116 F9
HSLW TW3 154 A10
STHGT/OAK N14 98 E1
SURB KT6 * 199 M9
TOOT SW17 179 P8
WALTH E17 120 F4
Ivy St IS N1 7 J7
Ivy Ter HOD EN11 45 H2
Ivy Wk DAGW RM9 143 P1
NTHWD HA6 * 92 F9
Ixworth Pl CHEL SW3 15 N6
Izane Rd BXLYHS DA6 164 A10

J

Jacaranda Cl NWMAL KT3 200 B3
Jacaranda Gv HACK E8 7 M3
Jackass La GDST RH9 260 E7
HAYES BR2 225 N3
Jack Clow Rd SRTFD E15 141 K4
Jack Cornwell St MNPK E12 122 D9
Jack Dash Wy EHAM E6 142 B6
Jackdaw Cl CRAWW RH11 283 M5
Jackdaws WGCE AL7 23 M5
Jackets La DEN/HRF UB9 92 B8
Jacketts Fld ABLGY WD5 54 G7
Jack Evans Ct SOCK/AV RM15 146 F8
Jackman Ms WLSDN NW10 116 B8
Jackman's La WOKN/KNAP GU21 231 N5
Jackman St HACK E8 140 A3
Jacks La DEN/HRF UB9 91 K9
Jackson Cl EMPK RM11 125 N2
EPSOM KT18 220 A10
HOM E9 140 C2
RDART DA2 188 E1
Jackson Rd BARK IG11 142 G3
EBAR EN4 77 P10
HAYES BR2 206 C8
HGDN/ICK UB10 131 P2
HOLWY N7 118 G9
Jacksons Cl CHONG CM5 * 67 P5
Jacksons Dr CHESW EN7 61 P4
Jackson's La HGT N6 118 B5
Jackson's Pl CROY/NA CR0 203 L8
Jackson St WOOL/PLUM SE18 162 D5
Jackson's Wy CROY/NA CR0 204 F10
Jackson Wy HOR/WEW KT19 219 M5
NWDGN UB2 154 A1
Jack Stevens Cl HLWE CM17 * 47 M3
Jack Walker Ct HBRY N5 119 J9
Jacob Cl WDSR SL4 148 D7
Jacobean Cl CRAWE RH10 284 D8
Jacobs Av HARH RM3 105 M10
Jacobs Cl DAGE RM10 124 C9
Jacob St STHWK SE1 19 N1
Jacob's Well Ms MHST W1U 10 D5
Jacobs Well Rd RGUE GU4 250 A5
Jacqueline Cl NTHLT UB5 133 M3
Jacqueline Creft Ter HGT N6 * 118 B4
Jacqueline Vls WALTH E17 * 121 H3
Jade Cl BCTR RM8 123 M6
CAN/RD E16 142 A8
CRICK NW2 116 G5
Jade Ter KIL/WHAMP NW6 * 3 K3
Jaffe Rd IL IG1 122 F6
Jaffray Rd HAYES BR2 206 A4
Jaggard Wy BAL SW12 180 A3
Jagger Cl RDART DA2 188 B3
Jago Cl WOOL/PLUM SE18 162 F5
Jago Wk CMBW SE5 159 L6
Jail La BH/WHM TN16 244 A1
Jamaica Rd BERM/RHTH SE16 160 A2
THHTH CR7 203 J6
Jamaica St WCHPL E1 140 B7
James Av BCTR RM8 124 A6
CRICK NW2 116 F10
James Bedford Cl PIN HA5 93 K10
James Cl BUSH WD23 73 M9
GLDGN NW11 * 117 H4
GPK RM2 125 H3
PLSTW E13 141 M4
James Collins Cl MV/WKIL W9 8 C2
James Gdns TOTM N17 99 K8
James Joyce Wk BRXN/ST SW9 159 J10
James Joyes Wk HNHL SE24 * 159 J10
James La WAN E11 121 H5
James Lee Sq PEND EN3 80 F4
James Martin Cl DEN/HRF UB9 111 K4
James Meadow DTCH/LGLY SL3 150 C5
Jameson St KENS W8 8 F9
James Pl TOTM N17 99 N9
James Rd DART DA1 187 H3
RGUW GU3 267 P8
James St BARK IG11 142 F2
COVGDN WC2E 11 M7
EN EN1 79 N9
EPP CM16 65 J4
HSLW TW3 154 C9
MHST W1U 10 D6
WDSR SL4 149 J7
Jamestown Rd CAMTN NW1 4 E5
Jamestown Wy POP/IOD E14 141 J9
James Watt Wy CRAWE RH10 284 B1
ERITH DA8 164 G5
James Wy OXHEY WD19 93 L5
James Yd CHING E4 * 101 J7
Jamnagar Cl STA TW18 173 J9
Jamuna Cl POP/IOD E14 140 D7
Jane Cl HHNE HP2 36 D1
Jane St WCHPL E1 140 A8
Janet St POP/IOD E14 160 F2
Janeway Pl BERM/RHTH SE16 19 P2
Janeway St BERM/RHTH SE16 19 P2
Janmead RBRW/HUT CM13 107 N1
Janoway Hill La
WOKN/KNAP GU21 231 P5
Janson Cl SRTFD E15 121 K10
WLSDN NW10 116 A8
Janson Rd SRTFD E15 121 K10
Jansons Rd SEVS/STOTM N15 119 M1
Japan Crs FSBYPK N4 118 G6
Japan Rd CHDH RM6 123 N4
Japonica Cl WOKN/KNAP GU21 231 P4
Jardine Rd WAP E1W 140 C9
Jarman Cl HHS/BOV HP3 35 P8
Jarrah Cottages PUR RM19 * 166 C5
Jarrett Cl BRXS/STRHM SW2 181 J4
Jarrow Cl MRDN SM4 201 L5
Jarrow Rd BERM/RHTH SE16 160 B3
CHDH RM6 123 M4
TOTM N17 120 A2
Jarrow Wy HOM E9 120 E9
Jarvis Cleys CHESW EN7 61 N2
Jarvis Cl BAR EN5 76 G9
Jarvis Rd EDUL SE22 159 M10
SAND/SEL CR2 223 L3
Jarvis Wy HARH RM3 105 M10
Jasmin Cl NTHWD HA6 92 G9
Jasmine Cl IL IG1 122 E10
ORP BR6 206 E9
REDH RH1 276 B5
STHL UB1 133 M9
WOKN/KNAP GU21 231 L2
Jasmine Ct LEE/GVPK SE12 183 M2
Jasmine Dr HERT/BAY SG13 25 P5
Jasmine Gdns CROY/NA CR0 204 G10
HAT AL10 40 C2
RYLN/HDSTN HA2 113 P7
Jasmine Gv PGE/AN SE20 204 A1
Jasmine Rd HOR/WEW KT19 219 N3
ROMW/RG RM7 124 F7
Jasmine Ter WDR/YW UB7 152 B1
Jasmine Wk CSHM HP5 50 F6
Jasmin Rd HOR/WEW KT19 219 N3
Jasmin Wy HHW HP1 35 H5
Jason Cl REDH RH1 275 P5
WEY KT13 216 D2
Jasons Cl BRW CM14 106 E5
Jasons Dr RGUE GU4 250 F7
Jasons Hl CSHM HP5 51 N5
Jason Wk ELTH/MOT SE9 184 D7
Jasper Cl PEND EN3 80 B4
Jasper Rd CAN/RD E16 142 A8
NRWD SE19 181 N9
Javelin Wy NTHLT UB5 133 L5
Jay Av ADL/WDHM KT15 * 195 P10
Jaycroft ENC/FH EN2 79 H5
Jay Gdns CHST BR7 184 C7
Jay Ms SKENS SW7 15 K2
Jean Batten Cl WLGTN SM6 222 G4
Jebb Av BRXS/STRHM SW2 180 F2
Jebb St BOW E3 140 F4
Jedburgh Rd PLSTW E13 141 P5
Jedburgh St BTSEA SW11 158 B10
Jeddo Ms SHB W12 156 C1
Jeddo Rd SHB W12 156 C1
Jefferson Cl DTCH/LGLY SL3 150 D3
GNTH/NBYPK IG2 122 E3
WEA W13 154 G2
Jefferson Rd CHOB/PIR GU24 230 B6
Jeffrey's Pl CAMTN NW1 4 G3
Jeffreys Rd CLAP SW4 158 F8
PEND EN3 80 E8
Jeffrey's St CAMTN NW1 4 G3
Jeffries Pas GU GU1 * 268 A1
Jeffries Rd EHSLY KT24 252 D7
WARE SG12 26 D2
Jeffs Cl HPTN TW12 * 176 A9
Jeffs Rd SUT SM1 221 J1
Jeger Av BETH E2 7 L6
Jeken Rd ELTH/MOT SE9 161 P10
Jelf Rd BRXS/STRHM SW2 181 H1
Jellicoe Av GVE DA12 190 F6
Jellicoe Cl SL SL1 148 G1
Jellicoe Gdns STAN HA7 94 F7
Jellicoe Rd TOTM N17 99 L8
WATW WD18 73 H10
Jemmett Cl KUTN/CMB KT2 199 N1
Jem Paterson Ct HRW HA1 * 114 D9
Jengar Cl SUT SM1 221 L1
Jenkins Av LCOL/BKTW AL2 55 M6
Jenkins La BARK IG11 142 F5
Jenkins Rd PLSTW E13 141 N6
Jenner Av ACT W3 136 A7
Jenner Cl SCUP DA14 185 K7
Jenner Dr CHOB/PIR GU24 212 F9
Jenner Rd CRAWE RH10 284 A2
GU GU1 268 B1
STNW/STAM N16 119 N7
Jenner Wy HOR/WEW KT19 219 M5
Jennery La SL SL1 128 B5
Jennett Rd CROY/NA CR0 203 H10
Jennifer Rd BMLY BR1 183 L6
Jenningham Dr CDW/CHF RM16 147 M10
Jennings Cl ADL/WDHM KT15 215 M5
SURB KT6 199 H7
Jennings Rd EDUL SE22 181 N2
STAL AL1 38 F5
Jennings Wy BAR EN5 76 F7
HHS/BOV HP3 35 P8
HORL RH6 280 E4
Jenningtree Rd ERITH DA8 165 J6
Jenningtree Wy BELV DA17 164 D1
Jenny Hammond Cl WAN E11 121 L8
Jennys Wy COUL/CHIP CR5 240 D8
Jenson Wy NRWD SE19 181 N10
Jenton Av BXLYHN DA7 163 P8
Jephson Rd FSTGT E7 141 P2
Jephson St CMBW SE5 159 L7
Jephtha Rd WAND/EARL SW18 179 K2
Jeppo's La MTCM CR4 202 A4
Jepps Cl CHESW EN7 61 M3
Jerdan Pl FUL/PGN SW6 157 K6
Jeremiah St POP/IOD E14 140 G8
Jeremy's Gn UED N18 100 A5
Jermyn St STJS SW1Y 10 G9
Jerningham Av CLAY IG5 102 E10
Jerningham Rd NWCR SE14 160 D8
Jerome Crs STJWD NW8 9 N1
Jerome Dr STALW/RED AL3 37 P8
Jerome St WCHPL E1 13 L3
Jerounds HLWW/ROY CM19 46 E3
Jerrard St LEW SE13 160 G9
Jerrold St IS N1 * 7 K8
Jersey Av KTN/HRWW/WS HA3 94 G10
Jersey Cl CHERT KT16 195 J10
HOD EN11 44 F2
RGUE GU4 250 E5
Jersey Dr STMC/STPC BR5 206 G6
Jersey La STAL AL1 38 G4
STALE/WH AL4 21 H10
Jersey Pl ASC SL5 192 C6
Jersey Rd CAN/RD E16 141 P7
HEST TW5 154 A7
HNWL W7 154 F1
HSLW TW3 154 A7
IL IG1 122 E9
IS N1 6 F2
LEY E10 121 J6
RAIN RM13 145 H2
TOOT SW17 180 C10
Jersey St BETH E2 140 A5
Jersey Vls HNWL W7 * 154 D1
Jerusalem Pas CLKNW EC1R 12 C2
Jervis Av PEND EN3 80 D1
Jerviston Gdns
STRHM/NOR SW16 181 H9
Jervois House
WOOL/PLUM SE18 * 162 B6
Jesmond Av WBLY HA9 135 L1
Jesmond Cl MTCM CR4 202 C3
Jesmond Dene HAMP NW3 * 3 J1
Jesmond Rd CROY/NA CR0 203 N7
Jesmond Wy STAN HA7 95 K6
Jessam Av CLPT E5 120 A6
Jessamine Pl RDART DA2 188 B3
Jessamine Rd HNWL W7 134 D10
Jessamine Ter SWLY BR8 * 208 D1
Jessamy Rd WEY KT13 196 B9
Jessel Dr LOU IG10 82 F6
Jesse Rd LEY E10 121 H6
Jesses La SHGR GU5 270 D9
Jessett Cl ERITH DA8 164 E3
Jessica Rd WAND/EARL SW18 179 M1
Jessiman Ter SHPTN TW17 196 B5
Jessop Av NWDGN UB2 153 N3
Jessops Wy CROY/NA CR0 202 D6
Jessup Cl WOOL/PLUM SE18 162 F3
Jetstar Wy NTHLT UB5 133 M5
Jetty Wk GRAYS RM17 167 M5
Jevington Wy LEE/GVPK SE12 183 N4
Jewel Rd WALTH E17 120 F1
Jewels Hl WARL CR6 225 M8
Jewry St TWRH EC3N 13 L6
Jews Rw WAND/EARL SW18 157 L10
Jews Wk SYD SE26 182 A7
Jeymer Av WLSDN NW10 116 E10
Jeymer Dr GFD/PVL UB6 134 B3
Jeypore Rd WAND/EARL SW18 179 M3
Jillian Cl HPTN TW12 175 P10
Jim Bradley Cl WOOL/PLUM SE18 162 D3
The Jinnings WGCE AL7 23 L8
Joan Crs ELTH/MOT SE9 184 A3
Joan Gdns BCTR RM8 123 P7
Joan Rd BCTR RM8 123 P7
Joan St STHWK SE1 12 C10
Jocelyn Rd RCH/KEW TW9 155 K9
Jocelyns HLWE CM17 29 M7
Jocelyn St PECK SE15 159 P7
Jocketts Hl HHW HP1 35 J6
Jocketts Rd HHW HP1 35 J7
Jockey's Flds FSBYW WC1X 11 P3
Jodane Rd DEPT SE8 160 E3
Jodrell Cl ISLW TW7 154 F7
Jodrell Rd BOW E3 140 E3
Jodrell Wy WTHK RM20 166 F4
Joel St NTHWD HA6 93 H10
PIN HA5 113 H1
Johanna St STHWK SE1 * 18 A2
John Adam St CHCR WC2N 11 M9
John Aird Ct BAY/PAD W2 9 K3
John Archer Wy
WAND/EARL SW18 179 N2
John Ashby Cl BRXS/STRHM SW2 180 F2
John Austin Cl KUTN/CMB KT2 199 L1
John Bradshaw Rd
STHGT/OAK N14 98 E2
John Burns Dr BARK IG11 143 H3
Johnby Cl PEND EN3 80 D3
John Campbell Rd
STNW/STAM N16 119 M10
John Carpenter St EMB EC4Y 12 C7
John Cobb Rd WEY KT13 216 B4
John Eliot Cl WAB EN9 45 K8
John Felton Rd
BERM/RHTH SE16 19 N2
John Fisher St WCHPL E1 13 N7
John Gooch Dr ENC/FH EN2 79 J6
John Goodchild Wy KUT/HW KT1 199 N3
John Harrison Wy
BERM/RHTH SE16 160 C2
GNWCH SE10 161 L2
John Islip St WEST SW1P 17 L6
John Lamb Ct
KTN/HRWW/WS HA3 94 D9
John Maurice Cl WALW SE17 18 G5
John McKenna Wk
BERM/RHTH SE16 19 P3
John Parker Sq BTSEA SW11 * 157 N9
John Penn St LEW SE13 160 G7
John Perrin Pl
KTN/HRWW/WS HA3 115 K5
John Prince's St CAVSQ/HST W1G 10 F5
John Rennie Wk WAP E1W 140 A9
John Roll Wy BERM/RHTH SE16 19 P3
John Ruskin St CMBW SE5 159 J6
John Russell Cl GUW GU2 249 M7
John's Av HDN NW4 116 F2
John's Cl ASHF TW15 174 D7
HART DA3 211 L5
Johnsdale OXTED RH8 261 L5
John Silkin La DEPT SE8 160 C4
Johns La CSHM HP5 33 J8
MRDN SM4 201 M5
John's Ms BMSBY WC1N 11 P2
John Smith Av FUL/PGN SW6 157 J6
John Smith Ms POP/IOD E14 141 J9
Johnson Cl GVW DA11 190 B6
HACK E8 7 N5
Johnson Ct HHS/BOV HP3 35 P8
Johnson Rd CROY/NA CR0 203 L7
HAYES BR2 206 A5
HEST TW5 153 K6
WLSDN NW10 136 A3
Johnsons Av RSEV TN14 228 C6
Johnson's Cl CAR SM5 202 A10
Johnson's Ct FLST/FETLN EC4A 12 B6
Johnsons Dr HPTN TW12 198 B1
Johnson's Pl PIM SW1V 17 H8
Johnson St NWDGN UB2 153 K2
WCHPL E1 140 B8
Johnsons Wy SWCM DA10 189 H2
WLSDN NW10 135 N6
Johnsons Whf RDART DA2 * 166 F10
Johnson Wk CRAWE RH10 283 N10
John Spencer Sq IS N1 6 D2
Johns Pl WCHPL E1 140 A8
John's Rd BH/WHM TN16 244 A6
John's Ter CROY/NA CR0 203 M8
The Johns CHONG CM5 67 P3
Johnston Cl BRXN/ST SW9 158 G7
Johnstone Rd EHAM E6 142 C5
Johnstone Ter CRICK NW2 116 G8
Johnston Rd WFD IG8 101 M6
Johnston Wk GUW GU2 249 M6
John St BMSBY WC1N 11 P2
EN EN1 79 N9
GRAYS RM17 167 P5
HSLW TW3 153 M8
SNWD SE25 203 P4
SRTFD E15 141 L3
Johns Wk CTHM CR3 241 P5
John Tate Rd HERT/BAY SG13 25 N6
John Taylor Ct SL SL1 129 H10
John Trundle Highwalk
BARB EC2Y * 12 E3
John Watkin Cl HOR/WEW KT19 219 N5
John William Cl CDW/CHF RM16 167 J4
John Williams Cl NWCR SE14 160 C5
John Wilson St
WOOL/PLUM SE18 162 D3
John Wooley Cl LEW SE13 * 161 K10
Joiners Arms Yd CMBW SE5 * 159 L7
Joiner's Cl CFSP/GDCR SL9 90 C8
Joiners La CFSP/GDCR SL9 90 B9
Joiner St STHWK SE1 13 H10
Joiners Wy CFSP/GDCR SL9 90 B8
Joinville Pl ADL/WDHM KT15 215 N1
Jolesfield Ct CRAWW RH11 283 J10
Jolive Ct GU GU1 * 268 D1
Jolliffe Rd REDH RH1 258 D2
Jollys La YEAD UB4 133 M7
Jonathan St LBTH SE11 17 N7
Jones Rd CHESW EN7 61 J6
PLSTW E13 141 N6
Jones Wy SLN SL2 109 J7
Jonquil Cl WGCE AL7 23 L7
Jonson Cl MTCM CR4 202 C4
YEAD UB4 133 H7
Jordan Cl GSTN WD25 72 G1
RYLN/HDSTN HA2 113 N8
SAND/SEL CR2 223 N7
Jordan Rd GFD/PVL UB6 134 G3
Jordans Cl CRAWW RH11 283 N5
DAGE RM10 124 C9
GU GU1 250 D9
REDH RH1 276 B5
STWL/WRAY TW19 173 M3
Jordans Crs CRAWW RH11 283 N4
Jordans La BEAC HP9 89 L7
Jordans Ms WHTN TW2 176 D5
Jordans Rd RKW/CH/CXG WD3 91 K2
Jordans Wy BEAC HP9 89 L7
LCOL/BKTW AL2 55 M6
RAIN RM13 145 L4
Joseph Av ACT W3 136 A8
Joseph Hardcastle Cl
NWCR SE14 160 C6
Josephine Av BRXS/STRHM SW2 180 G1
KWD/TDW/WH KT20 257 J3
Josephine Cl
KWD/TDW/WH KT20 257 J3
Joseph Locke Wy
ESH/CLAY KT10 197 P9
Joseph Powell Cl BAL SW12 180 D2
Joseph Ray Rd WAN E11 121 K7
Joseph's Rd GU GU1 250 A9
Joseph St BOW E3 140 E7
Joseph Trotter Cl CLKNW EC1R 6 B10
Joshua Cl MUSWH N10 98 C8
SAND/SEL CR2 223 J4
Joshua St POP/IOD E14 141 H8
Joshua Wk CHES/WCR EN8 62 F10
Josling Cl GRAYS RM17 167 L5
Joslings Cl SHB W12 136 D9
Joslin Rd PUR RM19 166 C5
Joslyn Cl PEND EN3 80 F4
Joubert St BTSEA SW11 158 A8
Journeys End SLN SL2 129 K7
Jowett St PECK SE15 159 N6
Joyce Av UED N18 99 N6
Joyce Ct WAB EN9 63 J10
Joyce Green La ERITH DA8 165 L7
Joyden's Wood Rd BXLY DA5 186 F6
Joydon Dr CHDH RM6 123 L4
Joyners Cl DAGW RM9 124 A9
Joyners Fld HLWS CM18 46 F5
Joy Rd GVE DA12 190 F4
Jubilee Arch WDSR SL4 * 149 J7
Jubilee Av CHING E4 101 H7
LCOL/BKTW AL2 57 J2
ROMW/RG RM7 124 D3
WARE SG12 26 E1
WHTN TW2 176 B4
Jubilee Cl CDALE/KGS NW9 116 A4

KUT/HW KT1 199 H1
ROMW/RG RM7 124 C3
STWL/WRAY TW19 173 M3
SWCM DA10 189 H2
WLSDN NW10 136 B4
Jubilee Crs ADL/WDHM KT15 215 N2
ED N9 99 P2
GVE DA12 191 H5
Jubilee Dr RSLP HA4 113 L9
Jubilee Gdns STHL UB1 133 P7
STHWK SE1 * 11 P10
Jubilee Pl CHEL SW3 15 P7
Jubilee Ri BGR/WK TN15 247 N7
Jubilee Rd CHEAM SM3 220 G4
GFD/PVL UB6 134 G3
ORP BR6 228 B3
WATN WD24 73 H4
WTHK RM20 166 G5
Jubilee St WCHPL E1 140 B8
Jubilee Ter BRKHM/BTCW RH3 273 P4
DORK RH4 272 G1
FUL/PGN SW6 * 157 H8
The Jubilee GNWCH SE10 * 160 G6
Jubilee Vls ESH/CLAY KT10 * 198 D8
Jubilee Wk CRAWE RH10 284 B7
Jubilee Wy CHSGTN KT9 199 N10
DTCH/LGLY SL3 149 P6
EBED/NFELT TW14 175 H4
SCUP DA14 185 K5
WIM/MER SW19 201 L1
Judd St STPAN WC1H 5 L10
Jude St CAN/RD E16 141 L8
Judeth Gdns GVE DA12 191 H8
Judge Heath La HYS/HAR UB3 132 D8
Judge's Hl POTB/CUF EN6 60 A5
Judge St WATN WD24 73 J4
Judges' Wk HAMP NW3 117 M8
Judge Wk ESH/CLAY KT10 218 D3
Judith Av CRW RM5 104 C7
Juer St BTSEA SW11 157 P6
Juglans Rd ORP BR6 207 K8
Jules Thorn Av EN EN1 79 P7
Julia Gdns BARK IG11 143 N4
Juliana Cl EFNCH N2 117 M1
Julian Av ACT W3 135 N9
Julian Cl BAR EN5 77 L7
WOKN/KNAP GU21 231 P4
Julian Hl HRW HA1 114 D7
WEY KT13 216 B4
Julian Pl POP/IOD E14 160 G4
Julian Rd ORP BR6 227 K3
Julians Cl SEV TN13 265 H3
Julians Wy SEV TN13 265 H3
Julian Tayler Pth FSTH SE23 * 182 A5
Julien Rd COUL/CHIP CR5 240 D1
EA W5 155 H2
Juliette Rd PLSTW E13 141 M4
Juliette Wy SOCK/AV RM15 165 N1
Julius Caesar Wy STAN HA7 95 J5
Julius Nyerere Cl IS N1 5 P6
Junction Ap BTSEA SW11 157 P9
Junction Ms BAY/PAD W2 9 N5
Junction Pl BAY/PAD W2 * 9 M5
Junction Rd ARCH N19 118 D8
ASHF TW15 174 D8
BRW CM14 107 H5
DART DA1 187 L2
DORK RH4 272 F2
EA W5 155 H3
ED N9 99 P2
HRW HA1 114 D4
LTWR GU18 212 A6
PLSTW E13 141 N3
ROM RM1 124 G2
SAND/SEL CR2 223 L3
TOTM N17 119 P1
Junction Rd East CHDH RM6 123 P5
Junction Rd West CHDH RM6 123 N5
June Cl COUL/CHIP CR5 222 C10
June La REDH RH1 276 C7
Junewood Cl ADL/WDHM KT15 215 J7
Juniper Av LCOL/BKTW AL2 55 P7
Juniper Cl BAR EN5 76 G9
BH/WHM TN16 244 B3
BROX EN10 62 E1
CHSGTN KT9 219 L2
GU GU1 249 N5
OXTED RH8 261 N9
REIG RH2 275 M2
RKW/CH/CXG WD3 91 N4
WBLY HA9 115 L10
Juniper Ct CHDH RM6 123 L4
KTN/HRWW/WS HA3 * 94 E9
NTHWD HA6 * 93 H9
RBRW/HUT CM13 * 107 L4
SL SL1 149 M1
Juniper Crs CAMTN NW1 4 D4
Juniper Dr CHOB/PIR GU24 230 F1
SOCK/AV RM15 147 K5
WAND/EARL SW18 157 M10
Juniper Gdns MTCM CR4 202 D1
RAD WD7 57 K9
SUN TW16 174 G9
Juniper Ga RKW/CH/CXG WD3 91 N3
Juniper Gn HHW HP1 35 H6
Juniper Gv WAT WD17 73 H4
Juniper La EHAM E6 142 B7
Juniper Rd CRAWW RH11 283 M4
IL IG1 122 D9
REIG RH2 275 M2
Juniper St WCHPL E1 * 140 B9
Juniper Wy HARH RM3 105 L9
HYS/HAR UB3 132 E9
Juno Wy NWCR SE14 160 C5
Jupiter Dr HHNE HP2 36 A4
Jupiter Wy HOLWY N7 5 P1
Jupp Rd SRTFD E15 141 J2
Jupp Rd West SRTFD E15 141 J3
Jura Cl CRAWW RH11 283 L10
Jurgens Rd PUR RM19 * 166 B3
Jury St GVW DA11 190 E2
Justice Wk CHEL SW3 15 N10
Justin Cl BTFD TW8 155 J6
Justin Rd CHING E4 100 E7
Jute La PEND EN3 80 D6
Jutland Pl EGH TW20 172 F8
Jutland Rd CAT SE6 183 H3
PLSTW E13 141 M6
Jutsums Av ROMW/RG RM7 124 C4
Jutsums La ROMW/RG RM7 124 C4
Juxon Cl CRAWW RH11 283 J9
KTN/HRWW/WS HA3 94 A9
Juxon St LBTH SE11 17 P5

K

Kaduna Cl PIN HA5 113 H3
Kale Rd ERITHM DA18 163 N1
Kambala Rd BTSEA SW11 157 N8
Kandlewood RBRW/HUT CM13 107 N1
Kangley Bridge Rd SYD SE26 182 E7
Kaplan Dr WCHMH N21 78 G9
Kara Wy CRICK NW2 116 G9
Karen Cl BRWN CM15 107 H1
RAIN RM13 144 F4
Karen Ct BMLY BR1 205 L1
ELTH/MOT SE9 183 P1
Karenza Ct WBLY HA9 * 115 H5
Karina Cl CHIG IG7 103 H6
Karma Wy RYLN/HDSTN HA2 113 P6
Kashgar Rd WOOL/PLUM SE18 163 J4
Kashmir Cl ADL/WDHM KT15 215 N5
Kashmir Rd CHARL SE7 162 A6
Kassala Rd BTSEA SW11 158 A7
Kates Cl BAR EN5 76 D9
Katescroft WGCE AL7 23 H9
Katharine St CROY/NA CR0 203 K10
Katherine Cl ADL/WDHM KT15 215 K3
BERM/RHTH SE16 140 C10
HHS/BOV HP3 35 P9
Katherine Gdns BARK/HLT IG6 102 F8
ELTH/MOT SE9 162 A10
Katherine Ms CTHM CR3 241 N3
Katherine Pl ABLGY WD5 55 H8
Katherine Rd EHAM E6 142 A2
Katherine Sq NTGHL W11 8 A9
Katherine's Wy HLWW/ROY CM19 46 D4
Kathleen Av ACT W3 135 P7
ALP/SUD HA0 135 K2
Kathleen Rd BTSEA SW11 158 A9
Katrine Sq HHNE HP2 35 N2
Kavanaghs Rd BRW CM14 106 G5
Kavanaghs Ter BRW CM14 106 G4
Kay Av ADL/WDHM KT15 195 P10
Kaye Don Wy WEY KT13 216 B6
Kayemoor Rd BELMT SM2 221 P4
Kay Rd BRXN/ST SW9 158 F8
Kays Ter SWFD E18 * 101 L10
Kay St BETH E2 7 P7
SRTFD E15 141 J2
WELL DA16 163 L7
Kay Wk STALE/WH AL4 39 J6
Kaywood Cl DTCH/LGLY SL3 149 P2
Kean St HOL/ALD WC2B 11 N6
Kearton Cl PUR/KEN CR8 241 K3
Keary Rd SWCM DA10 189 L3
Keatley Gn CHING E4 100 E7
Keats Av CAN/RD E16 141 N10
HARH RM3 105 J8
REDH RH1 258 B8
Keats Cl CHIG IG7 102 F7
PEND EN3 80 C9
STHWK SE1 19 L6
WAN E11 121 N3
WIM/MER SW19 179 N9
YEAD UB4 133 H7
Keats Est STNW/STAM N16 * 119 N7
Keats Gdns TIL RM18 168 E8
Keats Gv HAMP NW3 117 P9
Keats La WDSR SL4 149 J5
Keats Pde ED N9 99 P3
Keats Rd BELV DA17 164 D2
WELL DA16 163 H7
Keats Wy CROY/NA CR0 204 B6
GFD/PVL UB6 134 A7
WDR/YW UB7 152 A3
Keble Cl CRAWE RH10 284 E4
NTHLT UB5 114 B10
WPK KT4 200 C8
Keble Pl BARN SW13 156 E5
Keble St TOOT SW17 179 M7
Keble Ter ABLGY WD5 54 G8
Kechill Gdns HAYES BR2 205 M7
Kedleston Dr STMC/STPC BR5 207 J6
Kedleston Wk BETH E2 140 A5
Keeble Cl WOOL/PLUM SE18 * 162 E5
Keedonwood Rd BMLY BR1 183 L8
Keel Cl BARK IG11 143 M4
BERM/RHTH SE16 140 C10
Keel Dr SL SL1 149 H1
Keele Cl WATN WD24 73 K6
Keeler Cl WDSR SL4 148 D9
Keeley Rd CROY/NA CR0 203 K9
Keeley St HOL/ALD WC2B 11 N6
Keeling Rd ELTH/MOT SE9 184 A1
Keely Cl EBAR EN4 77 P9
Keemor Cl WOOL/PLUM SE18 * 162 D6
Keensacre IVER SL0 130 G4
Keens Cl STRHM/NOR SW16 180 E8
Keens La RGUW GU3 249 L6
Keens Park Rd RGUW GU3 249 L6
Keen's Rd CROY/NA CR0 223 K1
Keen's Yd IS N1 6 D2
Keepers Cl RGUE GU4 250 G7
Keepers Farm Cl WDSR SL4 148 D8
Keepers Ms TEDD TW11 177 H9
Keepers Wk VW GU25 194 A5
The Keep BKHTH/KID SE3 161 M8
KUTN/CMB KT2 177 L9
Keesey St WALW SE17 18 G9
Keetons Rd BERM/RHTH SE16 160 A2
Keevil Dr WIM/MER SW19 178 G3
Keighley Cl HOLWY N7 118 F9
Keightley Dr ELTH/MOT SE9 184 F4
Keilder Cl HGDN/ICK UB10 132 B4
Keildon Rd BTSEA SW11 158 A10
Keir Hardie Est CLPT E5 * 120 A6
Keir Hardie Wy BARK IG11 143 K2
YEAD UB4 * 133 H5
Keith Av EYN DA4 188 A9
Keith Connor Cl VX/NE SW8 158 C9
Keith Gv SHB W12 156 D1
Keith Park Crs BH/WHM TN16 225 P8
Keith Park Rd HGDN/ICK UB10 132 A2
Keith Rd BARK IG11 142 G4
HYS/HAR UB3 152 F2
WALTH E17 100 E9
Keiths Rd HHS/BOV HP3 36 B7
Keith Wy EMPK RM11 125 M5
Kelbrook Rd BKHTH/KID SE3 162 B8
Kelburn Wy RAIN RM13 145 H5
Kelbys WGCE AL7 23 M4
Kelceda Cl CRICK NW2 116 D7
Kelf Gv HYS/HAR UB3 132 G8
Kelfield Gdns NKENS W10 136 G8
Kelfield Ms NKENS W10 136 G7
Kelland Cl CEND/HSY/T N8 * 118 E3
Kelland Rd PLSTW E13 141 M6
Kellaway Rd BKHTH/KID SE3 161 P8
Keller Cresent MNPK E12 122 A9
Kellerton Rd LEW SE13 183 K1
Kellett Rd BRXS/STRHM SW2 159 H10
Kelling Gdns CROY/NA CR0 203 J7
Kellino St TOOT SW17 180 A7
Kellner Rd THMD SE28 163 J2
Kell St STHWK SE1 18 D3
Kelly Av PECK SE15 159 N7
Kelly Cl BORE WD6 76 A6
SHPTN TW17 196 F2
WLSDN NW10 116 A8
Kelly Ms MV/WKIL W9 8 D2
Kelly Rd MLHL NW7 97 H7
Kelly St CAMTN NW1 4 F2
Kelly Wy CHDH RM6 123 P3
Kelman Cl CHES/WCR EN8 62 C7
CLAP SW4 158 E8
Kelmore Gv EDUL SE22 159 P10
Kelmscott Cl WALTH E17 100 E9
WATW WD18 73 H10
Kelmscott Crs WATW WD18 73 H9
Kelmscott Gdns SHB W12 156 D2
Kelmscott Rd BTSEA SW11 179 P1
Kelpatrick Rd SL SL1 128 C8
Kelross Rd HBRY N5 119 J9
Kelsall Cl BKHTH/KID SE3 161 N8
Kelsall Ms RCH/KEW TW9 155 N7
Kelsey Cl HORL RH6 280 A4
Kelsey La BECK BR3 204 F3
Kelsey Park Av BECK BR3 204 G3
Kelsey Park Rd BECK BR3 204 F2
Kelsey Rd STMC/STPC BR5 207 L2
Kelsey Sq BECK BR3 204 F2
Kelsey St BETH E2 13 P1
Kelsey Wy BECK BR3 204 F3
Kelshall GSTN WD25 73 M2
Kelsie Wy BARK/HLT IG6 103 H7
Kelso Cl CRAWE RH10 284 F6
Kelso Dr GVE DA12 191 J7
Kelso Pl KENS W8 14 G3
Kelso Rd CAR SM5 201 M7
Kelston Rd BARK/HLT IG6 102 E10
Kelton Vls KUT/HW KT1 * 199 L2
Kelvedon Av WOT/HER KT12 216 G4
Kelvedon Cl KUTN/CMB KT2 177 M9
Kelvedon Gn BRWN CM15 86 E3
Kelvedon Hall La BRW CM14 86 B1
Kelvedon Rd FUL/PGN SW6 157 J6
Kelvedon Wy WFD IG8 102 C7
Kelvin Av LHD/OX KT22 236 D5
WDGN N22 98 G7
Kelvinbrook E/WMO/HCT KT8 198 A3
Kelvin Cl HOR/WEW KT19 219 M3
Kelvin Crs KTN/HRWW/WS HA3 94 D8
Kelvin Dr TWK TW1 176 G2
Kelvin Gdns CROY/NA CR0 202 F7
STHL UB1 133 P8
Kelvin Gv CHSGTN KT9 199 J10
SYD SE26 182 A6
Kelvington Cl CROY/NA CR0 204 D7
Kelvington Rd PECK SE15 182 C1
Kelvin La CRAWE RH10 284 A3
Kelvin Pde ORP BR6 207 H8
Kelvin Rd HBRY N5 119 J9
TIL RM18 168 D8
WELL DA16 163 K9
Kelvin Wy CRAWE RH10 284 A3
Kember St IS N1 * 5 N4
Kemble Cl POTB/CUF EN6 59 N9
WEY KT13 216 E1
Kemble Dr HAYES BR2 206 B10
Kemble Pde POTB/CUF EN6 * 59 M8
Kemble Rd CROY/NA CR0 203 J10
FSTH SE23 182 C4
TOTM N17 99 P9
Kembleside Rd BH/WHM TN16 243 P4
Kemble St HOL/ALD WC2B 11 N6
Kemerton Rd BECK BR3 204 G2
CMBW SE5 159 K9
CROY/NA CR0 203 N7
Kemey's St HOM E9 120 D10
Kemishford WOKS/MYFD GU22 231 M9
Kemnal Rd CHST BR7 184 F9
Kempe Cl DTCH/LGLY SL3 150 F3
STAL AL1 38 B10
Kempe Rd EN EN1 80 A2
KIL/WHAMP NW6 136 G4
Kemp Gdns CROY/NA CR0 203 K6
Kemplay Rd HAMP NW3 117 N9
Kemp Pl BUSH WD23 73 P10
Kemprow GSTN WD25 74 C2
Kemps Dr NTHWD HA6 92 G8
POP/IOD E14 140 F9
Kempsford Gdns ECT SW5 14 F8
Kempsford Rd LBTH SE11 18 B6
Kempshott Rd STRHM/NOR SW16 180 F10
Kempson Rd FUL/PGN SW6 157 K7
Kempthorne Rd DEPT SE8 160 D3
Kempton Av HCH RM12 125 N9
NTHLT UB5 133 P1
SUN TW16 197 J1
Kempton Cl ERITH DA8 164 D5
HGDN/ICK UB10 112 D9
Kempton Ct SUN TW16 197 J1
Kempton Pk SUN TW16 * 197 K1
Kempton Rd EHAM E6 142 C3
HPTN TW12 197 N2
Kempton Wk CROY/NA CR0 204 D6
Kempt St WOOL/PLUM SE18 162 D5
Kemsing Cl BXLY DA5 185 P3
THHTH CR7 * 203 K4
Kemsing Rd GNWCH SE10 161 M4
Kemsley Cha SLN SL2 129 H3
Kemsley Cl GVW DA11 190 C7
SWCM DA10 188 G2
Kemsley Rd BH/WHM TN16 244 A5
Kenbury Cl HGDN/ICK UB10 112 B8
Kenbury St CMBW SE5 159 K8
Kenchester Cl VX/NE SW8 158 F6
Kendal Av ACT W3 135 N7
BARK IG11 143 H3
EPP CM16 65 K7
UED N18 99 L5
Kendal Cl BRXN/ST SW9 159 J6
EBED/NFELT TW14 174 G4
REIG RH2 257 N9
SLN SL2 129 M9
WFD IG8 101 L3
YEAD UB4 132 F4
Kendal Ct ACT W3 135 M7
Kendal Cft HCH RM12 125 H10
Kendal Dr SLN SL2 129 M9
Kendale CDW/CHF RM16 168 E2
HHS/BOV HP3 36 C7
Kendale Rd BMLY BR1 183 K8
Kendal Gdns SUT SM1 201 M9
UED N18 99 L5
Kendall Av BECK BR3 204 D2
SAND/SEL CR2 223 L5
Kendall Av South SAND/SEL CR2 223 L6
Kendall Cl WGCE AL7 23 J9
Kendall Gdns GVW DA11 190 C3
Kendall Pl MHST W1U 10 C4
Kendall Rd BECK BR3 204 D2
ISLW TW7 154 F8
WOOL/PLUM SE18 162 B7
Kendalmere Cl MUSWH N10 98 C9
Kendal Ms UX/CGN UB8 131 M3
Kendal Pde UED N18 99 L5
Kendal Pl PUT/ROE SW15 179 J1
Kendal Rd WAB EN9 81 H1
WLSDN NW10 116 D9
Kendals Cl RAD WD7 74 D2
Kendal Steps BAY/PAD W2 * 9 P6
Kendal St BAY/PAD W2 9 P6
Kender St NWCR SE14 160 B6
Kendoa Rd CLAP SW4 158 E10
Kendon Cl WAN E11 121 N3
Kendor Av HOR/WEW KT19 219 P7
Kendra Hall Rd SAND/SEL CR2 223 J4
Kendrey Gdns WHTN TW2 176 D2
Kendrick Ms SKENS SW7 15 L5
Kendrick Pl SKENS SW7 * 15 L6
Kendrick Rd DTCH/LGLY SL3 149 N2
Kenelm Cl HRW HA1 114 F8
Kenerne Dr BAR EN5 77 H9
Kenford Cl GSTN WD25 55 J8
Kenilford Rd BAL SW12 180 C3
Kenilworth Av COB KT11 218 A10
HARH RM3 106 A6
RYLN/HDSTN HA2 113 N9
WALTH E17 100 F10
WIM/MER SW19 179 K8
Kenilworth Cl BNSTD SM7 239 L2
HHNE HP2 35 P7
SL SL1 149 L2
Kenilworth Ct WAT WD17 73 H5
Kenilworth Crs EN EN1 79 M5
Kenilworth Dr BORE WD6 75 P7
RKW/CH/CXG WD3 72 C8
WOT/HER KT12 197 L10
Kenilworth Gdns GDMY/SEVK IG3 123 J7
HCH RM12 125 K8
LOU IG10 82 C10
OXHEY WD19 93 K6
STA TW18 173 M8
STHL UB1 * 133 N5
WOOL/PLUM SE18 162 E8
YEAD UB4 132 G7
Kenilworth Rd ASHF TW15 173 N6
BOW E3 140 D4
EA W5 135 K10
EDGW HA8 95 P3
EW KT17 220 D3
KIL/WHAMP NW6 2 D5
PGE/AN SE20 204 C1
STMC/STPC BR5 206 F6
Kenilworth Ter BELMT SM2 221 K4
Kenley Av CDALE/KGS NW9 90 D10
Kenley Cl BXLY DA5 186 B3
CHST BR7 207 H3
EBAR EN4 77 P8
PUR/KEN CR8 241 L6
Kenley Gdns HCH RM12 125 N7
THHTH CR7 203 J4
Kenley La PUR/KEN CR8 241 K1
Kenley Rd KUT/HW KT1 199 N2
TWK TW1 176 G2
WIM/MER SW19 201 K3
Kenley Wk CHEAM SM3 220 G1
NTGHL W11 8 A8
Kenlor Rd TOOT SW17 179 N8
Kenmara Cl CRAWE RH10 284 C4
Kenmara Ct CRAWE RH10 284 B3
Kenmare Dr MTCM CR4 180 A10
TOTM N17 99 N10
Kenmare Gdns PLMGR N13 99 K5
Kenmare Rd THHTH CR7 203 H6
Kenmere Gdns ALP/SUD HA0 135 M3
Kenmere Rd WELL DA16 163 M8
Kenmont Gdns WLSDN NW10 136 E5
Kenmore Av KTN/HRWW/WS HA3 114 F3
Kenmore Crs YEAD UB4 132 G5
Kenmore Gdns EDGW HA8 95 N10
Kenmore Rd KTN/HRWW/WS HA3 115 J1
PUR/KEN CR8 223 J10
Kenmure Rd HACK E8 * 120 A10
Kenmure Yd HACK E8 * 120 A10
Kennacraig Cl CAN/RD E16 141 N10
Kennard Rd FBAR/BDGN N11 98 A6
SRTFD E15 141 J2
Kennard St BTSEA SW11 158 B7
CAN/RD E16 142 C10
Kenneally WDSR SL4 148 B8
Kennedy Av HOD EN11 44 E3
PEND EN3 80 B10
Kennedy Cl CHES/WCR EN8 62 D4
LCOL/BKTW AL2 57 J2
MTCM CR4 202 B2
PIN HA5 93 N7
PLSTW E13 141 M4
SLN SL2 129 H1
STMC/STPC BR5 206 G8
Kennedy Gdns SEV TN13 247 L9
Kennedy Rd BARK IG11 143 H3
HNWL W7 134 D7
Kennedy Wk WALW SE17 19 H6
Kennel Cl LHD/OX KT22 236 B10
Kennel La BFOR GU20 212 B2
HORL RH6 279 N5
LHD/OX KT22 236 B9
Kennel Wood Crs CROY/NA CR0 225 J8
Kennelwood La HAT AL10 40 E3
Kennet Cl BTSEA SW11 157 N10
CRAWW RH11 283 J8
UPMR RM14 126 D4
Kennet Dr YEAD UB4 133 M7
Kenneth Av IL IG1 122 E9
Kenneth Crs CRICK NW2 116 E10
Kenneth Gdns STAN HA7 94 F7
Kenneth More Rd IL IG1 122 E8
Kenneth Rd BNSTD SM7 239 N1
CHDH RM6 123 P5
Kennet Rd DART DA1 165 H9
ISLW TW7 154 E9
MV/WKIL W9 8 D1
Kennet Sq MTCM CR4 201 P1
Kennet St WAP E1W 13 P9
Kennett Rd DTCH/LGLY SL3 150 E2
Kennett Wharf La BLKFR EC4V 12 F7
Kenninghall Rd CLPT E5 120 A8
UED N18 100 B6
Kenning Rd HOD EN11 44 F1
Kenning St BERM/RHTH SE16 160 B1
Kennings Wy LBTH SE11 18 B7
Kennington Gdns KUT/HW KT1 199 J3
Kennington La LBTH SE11 17 P8
Kennington Ov LBTH SE11 17 P9
Kennington Park Gdns LBTH SE11 18 C9
Kennington Park Pl LBTH SE11 18 B8
Kennington Park Rd LBTH SE11 18 A10
Kennington Rd LBTH SE11 18 A4
Kenny Dr CAR SM5 222 B5
Kennylands Rd BARK/HLT IG6 103 K8
Kenny Rd MLHL NW7 97 H7
Kenrick Pl MHST W1U 10 C4
Kenrick Sq REDH RH1 259 M10
Kensal Rd NKENS W10 137 H6
Kensal Whf NKENS W10 * 8 A1
Kensington Av MNPK E12 142 C1
THHTH CR7 203 H1
WATW WD18 72 G8
Kensington Church Ct KENS W8 14 G2
Kensington Church St KENS W8 14 F1
Kensington Church Wk KENS W8 * 14 G1
Kensington Cl FBAR/BDGN N11 * 98 B6
STAL AL1 38 F8
Kensington Ct GRAYS RM17 * 167 P5
KENS W8 15 H2
Kensington Court Gdns KENS W8 * 15 H3
Kensington Court Ms KENS W8 * 15 H3
Kensington Court Pl KENS W8 15 H3
Kensington Dr WFD IG8 102 A10
Kensington Gdns IL IG1 122 C6
Kensington Gardens Sq BAY/PAD W2 8 G6
Kensington Ga KENS W8 15 J3
Kensington High St KENS W8 14 D4
Kensington Ml KENS W8 8 F9
Kensington Palace KENS W8 * 9 H10
Kensington Palace Gdns KENS W8 14 G1
Kensington Park Gdns NTGHL W11 8 C8
Kensington Park Ms NTGHL W11 * 8 C6
Kensington Park Rd NTGHL W11 8 D7
Kensington Pl KENS W8 8 E10
Kensington Rd BRWN CM15 86 F10
KENS W8 15 H2
NTHLT UB5 133 P4
ROMW/RG RM7 124 D4
Kensington Sq KENS W8 14 G2
Kensington Ter SAND/SEL CR2 223 L4
Kensington Wy BORE WD6 76 A7
Kent Av DAGW RM9 144 B6
SL SL1 129 H7
WEA W13 134 G7
WELL DA16 185 J1
Kent Cl BORE WD6 76 A4
MTCM CR4 202 F4
ORP BR6 227 H3
STA TW18 173 N9
UX/CGN UB8 131 M1
Kent Ct CDALE/KGS NW9 * 96 B10
Kent Dr EBAR EN4 78 B8
HCH RM12 125 L9
TEDD TW11 176 D8
Kentford Wy NTHLT UB5 133 M3
Kent Gdns RSLP HA4 113 H4
WEA W13 134 G7
Kent Gate Wy CROY/NA CR0 224 E3
Kent Hatch Rd OXTED RH8 261 P6
Kent House La BECK BR3 182 D9
Kent House Rd BECK BR3 182 C10
Kentish La BRKMPK AL9 41 M10
Kentish Rd BELV DA17 164 B3
Kentish Town Rd CAMTN NW1 4 F2
Kentish Wy BMLY BR1 205 N2
Kentlea Rd THMD SE28 163 H1
Kentmere Rd WOOL/PLUM SE18 163 H3
Kenton Av HRW HA1 114 E5
STHL UB1 133 P9
SUN TW16 197 L2
Kenton Gdns KTN/HRWW/WS HA3 115 H3
STAL AL1 38 E7
Kenton La KTN/HRWW/WS HA3 94 F9
Kenton Park Av KTN/HRWW/WS HA3 115 J2
Kenton Park Cl KTN/HRWW/WS HA3 115 H3
Kenton Park Crs KTN/HRWW/WS HA3 115 J2
Kenton Park Pde KTN/HRWW/WS HA3 * 115 H3
Kenton Park Rd KTN/HRWW/WS HA3 115 H2
Kenton Rd HOM E9 140 C1
HRW HA1 114 E5
Kentons La WDSR SL4 148 D8
Kenton St STPAN WC1H 11 L1
Kenton Wy WOKN/KNAP GU21 231 L3
YEAD UB4 132 F5
Kent Pas CAMTN NW1 10 A1
Kent Rd BFOR GU20 212 C2
CHSWK W4 155 P2
DAGE RM10 124 C10
DART DA1 187 M2
E/WMO/HCT KT8 198 B4
GRAYS RM17 167 P5
GVW DA11 190 D4
HART DA3 211 J2
KUT/HW KT1 199 J3
RCH/KEW TW9 155 M6
STMC/STPC BR5 207 L6
WCHMH N21 99 L2
WOKS/MYFD GU22 232 E2
WWKM BR4 204 G8
Kents Av HHS/BOV HP3 35 N10
Kents La EPP CM16 48 E7
Kent St BETH E2 7 M7
PLSTW E13 141 N5
Kent Ter CAMTN NW1 3 P10
Kent Vw SOCK/AV RM15 166 B1
Kent View Gdns GDMY/SEVK IG3 123 H7
Kent Wy SURB KT6 199 K10
Kentwell Cl BROCKY SE4 * 160 D10
Kentwode Gn BARN SW13 156 D6
Kentwyns Ri REDH RH1 276 G1
Kent Yd SKENS SW7 15 P2
Kenver Av NFNCH/WDSPK N12 97 N7
Kenward Rd ELTH/MOT SE9 183 P1
Kenway CRW RM5 104 D10
RAIN RM13 145 K5
Ken Wy WBLY HA9 115 P7
Kenway Cl RAIN RM13 145 K5
Kenway Dr AMSS HP7 69 N5
Kenway Rd ECT SW5 14 G6
Kenway Wk RAIN RM13 145 L5
Kenwood Av HART DA3 211 P3
Kenwood Cl HAMP NW3 117 N6
WDR/YW UB7 152 B5
Kenwood Dr BECK BR3 205 H3
RKW/CH/CXG WD3 91 J3
WOT/HER KT12 217 J3
Kenwood Gdns CLAY IG5 122 D2
SWFD E18 121 N1
Kenwood Pk WEY KT13 216 E3
Kenwood Rdg PUR/KEN CR8 241 J3
Kenwood Rd ED N9 99 P3
HGT N6 118 A4
Kenworth Cl CHES/WCR EN8 62 C9
Kenworthy Rd HOM E9 140 D1
Kenwyn Dr CRICK NW2 116 B8
Kenwyn Rd CLAP SW4 158 E10
DART DA1 187 L1
RYNPK SW20 200 F1
Kenya Ct HORL RH6 * 280 A3
Kenya Rd CHARL SE7 162 A6
Kenyngton Dr SUN TW16 175 H8
Kenyngton Pl KTN/HRWW/WS HA3 115 H3
Kenyon Pl WGCE AL7 23 H8
Kenyons EHSLY KT24 252 C4
Kenyon St FUL/PGN SW6 156 G7
Keogh Rd SRTFD E15 141 K1
Kepler Rd CLAP SW4 158 F10
Keppel Rd DAGW RM9 123 P9
DORK RH4 254 G10
EHAM E6 142 C2
Keppel Sp WDSR SL4 171 N3
Keppel St GWRST WC1E 11 K3
WDSR SL4 149 J8
Kerbela St BETH E2 13 N1
Kerbey St POP/IOD E14 140 G8
Kerdistone Cl POTB/CUF EN6 59 L6
Kerfield Crs CMBW SE5 159 L7
Kerfield Pl CMBW SE5 159 L7
Kernel Ct GU GU1 * 249 P10
Kerria Wy CHOB/PIR GU24 212 E9
Kerri Cl BAR EN5 76 F8
Kerril Cft HLW CM20 28 D10
Kerrill Av COUL/CHIP CR5 241 H5
Kerrison Pl EA W5 135 J10
Kerrison Rd BTSEA SW11 157 P9
EA W5 135 J10
SRTFD E15 141 J3
Kerry Av SOCK/AV RM15 165 N1
STAN HA7 95 H5
Kerry Cl CAN/RD E16 141 N8
PLMGR N13 98 G3
UPMR RM14 126 E5
Kerry Ct STAN HA7 95 J5
Kerry Dr UPMR RM14 126 E5
Kerry Pth NWCR SE14 160 E5
Kerry Rd NWCR SE14 160 E5
Kerry Ter WOKN/KNAP GU21 232 E2
Kersey Dr SAND/SEL CR2 224 B8
Kersey Gdns HARH RM3 105 M8
Kersfield Rd PUT/ROE SW15 178 G2
Kershaw Cl CDW/CHF RM16 167 H2
EMPK RM11 125 L5
WAND/EARL SW18 179 M2
Kershaw Rd DAGE RM10 124 B8
Kersley Ms BTSEA SW11 * 158 A7
Kersley Rd STNW/STAM N16 119 M8
Kersley St BTSEA SW11 158 A8
Kerstin Cl HYS/HAR UB3 132 G9
Kerswell Cl SEVS/STOTM N15 119 M3
Kerwick Cl HOLWY N7 5 M3
Keslake Rd KIL/WHAMP NW6 136 G4
Kessock Cl TOTM N17 120 A3
Kesters Rd CSHM HP5 51 J8
Kesteven Cl BARK/HLT IG6 103 J7
Keston Av ADL/WDHM KT15 215 K7
COUL/CHIP CR5 241 H5
HAYES BR2 225 P2
Keston Cl UED N18 99 L4
WELL DA16 163 M6
Keston Gdns HAYES BR2 225 P1
Keston Ms WAT WD17 73 J6
Keston Park Cl HAYES BR2 226 C1
Keston Rd PECK SE15 159 P9
THHTH CR7 202 G6
TOTM N17 119 L1
Kestrel Av EHAM E6 142 B7
HNHL SE24 181 J1
STA TW18 173 J6
Kestrel Cl BARK/HLT IG6 103 L5
BERK HP4 33 P6
CDALE/KGS NW9 96 B10
CRAWW RH11 283 M5
GSTN WD25 55 M10
HCH RM12 145 J2
HOR/WEW KT19 219 M7
KUTN/CMB KT2 177 J7
RGUE GU4 250 G8
WLSDN NW10 116 A10
Kestrel Gn HAT AL10 40 D5
Kestrel Pl NWCR SE14 * 160 D5
Kestrel Rd WAB EN9 63 M10
The Kestrels LCOL/BKTW AL2 55 N7
Kestrel Wy CROY/NA CR0 225 J5
HYS/HAR UB3 152 E1
WGCE AL7 23 J3
WOKN/KNAP GU21 231 N1
Keswick Av EMPK RM11 125 L6
PUT/ROE SW15 178 B8
WIM/MER SW19 201 K2
Keswick Cl CRAWW RH11 282 G9
STAL AL1 38 G8
SUT SM1 221 M1
Keswick Ct SLN SL2 129 L9
Keswick Dr LTWR GU18 212 A7
PEND EN3 80 B2
Keswick Gdns PUR RM19 166 B5
REDBR IG4 122 B3
RSLP HA4 112 E4
WBLY HA9 115 K10
Keswick Ms EA W5 135 K10
Keswick Rd BXLYHN DA7 164 B8
EGH TW20 172 E10
GT/LBKH KT23 254 B1
ORP BR6 207 J8
PUT/ROE SW15 179 H1
WHTN TW2 176 B2
WWKM BR4 205 K9
Kettering Rd HARH RM3 105 M8
PEND EN3 80 C3
Kettering St STRHM/NOR SW16 180 C9
Kett Gdns BRXS/STRHM SW2 180 G1
Kettlebaston Rd LEY E10 120 E6
Kettlebury Wy CHONG CM5 67 N6
Kettlewell Cl FBAR/BDGN N11 98 B7
WOKN/KNAP GU21 232 B1
Kettlewell Ct SWLY BR8 208 G2
Kettlewell Hl WOKN/KNAP GU21 232 B1
Kevan Dr RPLY/SEND GU23 251 H1
Kevelioc Rd TOTM N17 99 K9
Kevin Cl HSLWW TW4 153 L8
Kevington Cl STMC/STPC BR5 207 J4
Kevington Dr CHST BR7 207 J4
Kew Br RCH/KEW TW9 155 M5
Kew Bridge Arches CHSWK W4 * 155 M5
Kew Bridge Ct BTFD TW8 155 M4
Kew Bridge Rd BTFD TW8 155 L5
Kew Cl UX/CGN UB8 131 M4
Kew Crs CHEAM SM3 201 J10
Kewferry Dr NTHWD HA6 92 D6
Kewferry Rd NTHWD HA6 92 D7
Kew Foot Rd RCH/KEW TW9 155 K10
Kew Gardens Rd RCH/KEW TW9 155 L6
Kew Gn RCH/KEW TW9 155 L5
Kew Meadow Pth RCH/KEW TW9 155 M7
Kew Riverside Pk RCH/KEW TW9 155 N7
Kew Rd RCH/KEW TW9 155 K10
Key Cl WCHPL E1 140 A6
Keyes Rd CRICK NW2 116 G10
DART DA1 187 N1
Keyfield STAL AL1 38 C7
Keymer Cl BH/WHM TN16 243 P2
Keymer Rd BRXS/STRHM SW2 180 G5
CRAWW RH11 283 N9
Keynes Cl EFNCH N2 118 A1
Keynsham Av WFD IG8 101 K5
Keynsham Gdns ELTH/MOT SE9 184 B1
Keynsham Rd ELTH/MOT SE9 184 B1
MRDN SM4 201 L8
Keynton Cl HERT/WAT SG14 24 G4
Keyse Rd STHWK SE1 19 L4
Keysers Rd BROX EN10 44 F8
Keysham Av HEST TW5 153 H7
Keystone Crs IS N1 5 M8
Keywood Dr SUN TW16 175 H9
Keyworth Cl CLPT E5 120 D9
Keyworth St STHWK SE1 18 D3
Kezia St DEPT SE8 160 D4
Khalsa Av GVE DA12 190 F3
Khama Rd TOOT SW17 179 P7
Khartoum Pl GVE DA12 190 F2
Khartoum Rd IL IG1 122 E10
PLSTW E13 141 N5
TOOT SW17 179 N7
Khyber Rd BTSEA SW11 157 P8
Kibes La WARE SG12 26 D2
Kibworth St VX/NE SW8 158 G6
Kidborough Down GT/LBKH KT23 253 P3
Kidborough Rd CRAWW RH11 283 J9
Kidbrooke Gdns BKHTH/KID SE3 161 M8
Kidbrooke Gv BKHTH/KID SE3 161 M7
Kidbrooke La ELTH/MOT SE9 162 B10
Kidbrooke Park Cl BKHTH/KID SE3 161 N7
Kidbrooke Park Rd LEE/GVPK SE12 183 N1
Kidbrooke Wy BKHTH/KID SE3 161 N8
Kidderminster Pl CROY/NA CR0 203 J8
Kidderminster Rd CROY/NA CR0 203 K7
SLN SL2 128 F5
Kidderpore Av HAMP NW3 117 K9
Kidderpore Gdns HAMP NW3 117 K9
Kidd Pl CHARL SE7 162 B4
Kidworth Cl HORL RH6 280 A3
Kielder Cl BARK/HLT IG6 103 J7
Kier Pk ASC SL5 192 B3
Kiffen St SDTCH EC2A 13 H1
Kilberry Cl ISLW TW7 154 C7
Kilbride Ct HHNE HP2 36 A2
Kilburn Br KIL/WHAMP NW6 2 F6
Kilburn High Rd KIL/WHAMP NW6 2 C2
Kilburn La NKENS W10 2 A9
Kilburn Park Rd MV/WKIL W9 2 E10
Kilburn Pl KIL/WHAMP NW6 2 F6
Kilburn Priory KIL/WHAMP NW6 2 G6
Kilburn Sq KIL/WHAMP NW6 2 E6
Kilburn V KIL/WHAMP NW6 2 F6
Kilby Cl GSTN WD25 73 L1
Kilcorral Cl EW KT17 220 D10
Kildare Cl RSLP HA4 113 K6
Kildare Gdns BAY/PAD W2 8 F5
Kildare Rd CAN/RD E16 141 M7
Kildare Ter BAY/PAD W2 8 F5
Kildoran Rd CLAP SW4 180 F1
Kildowan Rd GDMY/SEVK IG3 123 K6
Kilfillan Gdns BERK HP4 33 M6
Kilgour Rd FSTH SE23 182 D2
Kilkie St FUL/PGN SW6 157 M8
Killarney Rd WAND/EARL SW18 179 M2
Killburns Mill Cl WLGTN SM6 202 C10
Killearn Rd CAT SE6 183 J4
Killester Gdns WPK KT4 220 E1
Killewarren Wy STMC/STPC BR5 207 M7
Killick Cl SEV TN13 246 F7
Killick St IS N1 5 N7
Killieser Av BRXS/STRHM SW2 180 F5
Killip Cl CAN/RD E16 141 L8
Killowen Av NTHLT UB5 114 B10
Killowen Rd HOM E9 * 140 C1
Killyon Rd VX/NE SW8 158 D8
Kilmaine Rd FUL/PGN SW6 157 H6
Kilmarnock Gdns BCTR RM8 123 M8
Kilmarnock Pk REIG RH2 257 L9
Kilmarnock Rd OXHEY WD19 93 L5
Kilmarsh Rd HMSMTH W6 156 F3
Kilmartin Av STRHM/NOR SW16 203 H3
Kilmartin Rd GDMY/SEVK IG3 123 K7
Kilmartin Wy HCH RM12 125 J10
Kilmington Cl RBRW/HUT CM13 107 N3
Kilmington Rd BARN SW13 156 D5
Kilmiston Av SHPTN TW17 196 D6
Kilmorey Gdns TWK TW1 176 G1
Kilmorey Rd TWK TW1 154 G10
Kilmorie Rd FSTH SE23 182 D4
Kiln Av AMS HP6 69 P4
Kiln Cl BERK HP4 34 E3
HYS/HAR UB3 152 E5
Kilncroft HHS/BOV HP3 36 C8
Kilndown GVE DA12 190 F9
Kilner St POP/IOD E14 140 F7
Kilnfield BRWN CM15 87 J1
CHONG CM5 67 N5
WGCE AL7 23 J2
Kiln Gnd HHS/BOV HP3 36 B8
Kiln House Cl WARE SG12 26 D1
Kiln La ASC SL5 192 F5
BRKHM/BTCW RH3 273 N1
CSHM HP5 51 N7
EW KT17 220 B8
HLWE CM17 47 N2
HORL RH6 280 A2
RPLY/SEND GU23 233 L10
SLN SL2 109 H6
WDSR SL4 170 A9
Kilnmead CRAWE RH10 283 P6
Kilnmead Cl CRAWE RH10 283 P6
Kiln Mdw RGUW GU3 249 H6
Kiln Ms TOOT SW17 179 N8
Kiln Pl KTTN NW5 118 B9
Kiln Rd EPP CM16 66 B4
Kilnside ESH/CLAY KT10 218 F4
Kiln Wy GRAYS RM17 167 L4
NTHWD HA6 92 F7
Kilnwood RSEV TN14 228 A9
Kiln Wood La ABR/ST RM4 104 E6
Kilnwood La HORS RH12 282 D10
Kilpatrick Wy YEAD UB4 133 M7
Kilravock St NKENS W10 2 A10
Kilross Rd EBED/NFELT TW14 174 E4
Kilrue La WOT/HER KT12 216 G1
Kilrush Ter WOKN/KNAP GU21 232 D2
Kilsha Rd WOT/HER KT12 197 J6
Kilsmore La CHES/WCR EN8 62 C4
Kilvinton Dr ENC/FH EN2 79 L4
Kilworth Av BRWN CM15 87 M10
Kilworth Cl WGCE AL7 23 L7
Kimbell Gdns FUL/PGN SW6 157 H7
Kimbell Pl BKHTH/KID SE3 161 P10
Kimber Cl WDSR SL4 148 F9

Kimber Ct RGUE GU4 * 250 G8
Kimberley Av EHAM E6 142 B4
GNTH/NBYPK IG2 122 G5
PECK SE15 160 A8
PECK SE15 160 B9
Kimberley Cl DTCH/LGLY SL3 150 C3
HORL RH6 279 P4
Kimberley Ct KIL/WHAMP NW6 2 B4
Kimberley Dr SCUP DA14 185 N5
Kimberley Gdns EN EN1 79 N7
FSBYPK N4 119 J3
Kimberley Pl PUR/KEN CR8 223 H7
Kimberley Ride COB KT11 218 A9
Kimberley Rd BECK BR3 204 C2
BRXN/ST SW9 158 F8
CAN/RD E16 141 L6
CHING E4 101 K2
CRAWE RH10 284 C6
CROY/NA CR0 203 J6
KIL/WHAMP NW6 2 B5
STALW/RED AL3 38 B5
TOTM N17 99 P10
UED N18 100 A7
WALTH E17 100 D9
WAN E11 121 J7
Kimberley Wy CHING E4 101 K2
Kimber Rd WAND/EARL SW18 179 K3
Kimbers Dr SL SL1 128 C5
Kimble Cl WATW WD18 * 72 F10
Kimble Crs BUSH WD23 94 B1
Kimble Rd WIM/MER SW19 179 N9
Kimbolton Cl LEE/GVPK SE12 183 L3
Kimbolton Gn BORE WD6 75 P8
Kimmeridge Gdns
ELTH/MOT SE9 184 B7
Kimmeridge Rd ELTH/MOT SE9 184 B7
Kimps Wy HHS/BOV HP3 36 B9
Kimpton Av BRWN CM15 106 G1
Kimpton Cl HHNE HP2 36 C1
Kimpton Park Wy CHEAM SM3 201 J9
Kimpton Pl GSTN WD25 55 L10
Kimpton Rd CHEAM SM3 201 J10
CMBW SE5 159 L7
Kimpton's Cl CHONG CM5 67 N2
POTB/CUF EN6 58 G9
Kimptons Md POTB/CUF EN6 58 G9
Kinburn Dr EGH TW20 172 B8
Kinburn St BERM/RHTH SE16 * 160 C1
Kincaid Rd PECK SE15 160 A6
Kincardine Gdns MV/WKIL W9 * 8 E2
Kinch Gv WBLY HA9 115 L5
Kincraig Dr SEV TN13 247 H9
Kinder Cl THMD SE28 143 N9
Kinderscout HHS/BOV HP3 36 B8
Kindersley Wy ABLGY WD5 54 D7
Kinder St WCHPL E1 140 A8
Kinderton Cl STHGT/OAK N14 98 D2
Kinfauns Av EMPK RM11 125 K4
Kinfauns Rd BRXS/STRHM SW2 181 H5
GDMY/SEVK IG3 123 L6
Kingaby Gdns RAIN RM13 145 H2
King Alfred Av CAT SE6 182 F7
King Alfred Rd HARH RM3 105 N10
King Arthur Cl PECK SE15 160 B6
King Arthur Ct CHES/WCR EN8 62 D7
King Charles Crs BRYLDS KT5 199 L7
King Charles I Island
WHALL SW1A 11 L9
King Charles' Rd BRYLDS KT5 199 L6
RAD WD7 57 K8
King Charles St WHALL SW1A 17 K1
King Charles Ter WAP E1W * 140 A9
King Charles Wk
WIM/MER SW19 * 179 H4
King Croft Rd HARP AL5 20 C4
Kingcup Cl CROY/NA CR0 204 C8
Kingcup Dr CHOB/PIR GU24 230 F1
King David La WCHPL E1 140 B9
Kingdon Rd KIL/WHAMP NW6 2 F1
King Edward Av DART DA1 187 L2
RAIN RM13 145 L4
King Edward Dr CHSGTN KT9 199 K10
GRAYS RM17 168 B3
King Edward III Ms
BERM/RHTH SE16 160 A1
King Edward Pl STALE/WH AL4 21 J2
King Edward Rd BAR EN5 77 K8
BRW CM14 107 H4
CHES/WCR EN8 62 D9
LEY E10 121 H6
OXHEY WD19 73 M10
RAD WD7 57 L9
RDART DA2 188 F1
ROM RM1 124 G4
WALTH E17 120 D1
King Edward's Gdns ACT W3 135 M10
King Edward's Gv TEDD TW11 176 G9
King Edward's Rd BARK IG11 142 G3
ED N9 100 A1
HACK E8 140 A3
PEND EN3 80 C8
RSLP HA4 112 E6
WARE SG12 26 D1
King Edward St HHS/BOV HP3 35 N10
SL SL1 149 J1
STBT EC1A 12 E5
King Edward VII Av WDSR SL4 149 K6
King Edward Wk STHWK SE1 18 B3
Kingfield Cl WOKS/MYFD GU22 232 C6
Kingfield Dr WOKS/MYFD GU22 232 C6
Kingfield Gdns
WOKS/MYFD GU22 232 C6
Kingfield Rd EA W5 135 J6
WOKS/MYFD GU22 232 C6
Kingfield St POP/IOD E14 161 H3
Kingfisher Cl CRAWE RH10 284 B4
KTN/HRWW/WS HA3 94 E8
NTHWD HA6 92 C9
RBRW/HUT CM13 107 N1
STALE/WH AL4 21 J2
STMC/STPC BR5 207 N4
THMD SE28 143 M9
WARE SG12 27 H8
WOT/HER KT12 217 M2
Kingfisher Ct DORK RH4 * 272 F1
RGUE GU4 250 G8
Kingfisher Dr HHS/BOV HP3 54 A1
RCHPK/HAM TW10 177 H7
RDART DA2 188 F2
REDH RH1 258 B7
RGUE GU4 250 F8
STA TW18 173 J7
Kingfisher Gdns SAND/SEL CR2 224 C6
Kingfisher Lure KGLGY WD4 * 54 C5
RKW/CH/CXG WD3 71 L8
Kingfisher Ms LEW SE13 182 G1
Kingfisher Pl WDGN N22 * 98 G10
Kingfisher Rd UPMR RM14 126 E6
Kingfisher St EHAM E6 142 B7
Kingfisher Wy BECK BR3 204 C5
HLWW/ROY CM19 27 M10
WLSDN NW10 * 136 A1
King Gdns CROY/NA CR0 223 J2
King Garth Ms FSTH SE23 182 B5
King George Av BUSH WD23 74 A10
CAN/RD E16 142 A8
GNTH/NBYPK IG2 122 G4
WOT/HER KT12 197 L8
King George Cl ROMW/RG RM7 124 D1
SUN TW16 174 F8
King George Rd WAB EN9 * 63 H10
WARE SG12 26 D1
King Georges Av WATW WD18 72 G8
King George's Dr
ADL/WDHM KT15 215 K6
King George Sq
RCHPK/HAM TW10 177 L2
King George's Rd BRWN CM15 86 G10
King George St GNWCH SE10 161 H6
King George VI Av MTCM CR4 202 A4
TIL RM18 169 L3
Kingham Cl NTGHL W11 157 H1
WAND/EARL SW18 179 M3
King Harolds Wy BXLYHN DA7 163 N6
King Harry La STALW/RED AL3 37 P7
King Harry St HHNE HP2 35 N7
King Henry Ct WAB EN9 * 81 H2
King Henry Ms HRW HA1 114 D6
ORP BR6 227 J2
King Henry's Dr CROY/NA CR0 225 H5
King Henry's Ms PEND EN3 80 F3
King Henry's Reach
HMSMTH W6 156 F5
King Henry's Rd HAMP NW3 3 N4
KUT/HW KT1 199 N3
King Henry St STNW/STAM N16 119 M10
King Henry's Wk IS N1 7 J1
King Henry Ter WAP E1W * 140 A9
Kinghorn St STBT EC1A 12 E4
King James Av POTB/CUF EN6 60 F5
King James Ct STHWK SE1 18 D2
King James St STHWK SE1 18 D2
King John Ct SDTCH EC2A 13 K1
King John's Cl STWL/WRAY TW19 171 P2
King John St WCHPL E1 140 C7
King John's Wk ELTH/MOT SE9 184 B3
Kinglake Est WALW SE17 * 19 J7
Kinglake St WALW SE17 19 K7
Kinglet Cl FSTGT E7 141 M1
Kingly Ct REGST W1B * 11 H7
Kingly St REGST W1B 10 G6
Kingpost Pde RGUE GU4 * 250 E6
King & Queen Cl ELTH/MOT SE9 184 B7
King & Queen St WALW SE17 * 18 F7
King & Queen Whf
BERM/RHTH SE16 * 140 C10
Kingsand Rd LEE/GVPK SE12 183 M5
King's Arms Yd LOTH EC2R 12 G5
Kingsash Dr YEAD UB4 133 M6
King's Av GFD/PVL UB6 134 A8
HSLW TW3 154 A7
SUN TW16 174 G8
WCHMH N21 99 J2
WFD IG8 101 P6
BAL SW12 180 E4
BF/WBF KT14 215 N8
BMLY BR1 183 L9
CAR SM5 221 P4
CHDH RM6 124 A4
EA W5 135 J8
HHS/BOV HP3 36 A10
MUSWH N10 118 B1
NWMAL KT3 200 C4
REDH RH1 275 P2
WATW WD18 73 H8
King's Bench St STHWK SE1 18 D1
King's Bench Wk EMB EC4Y * 12 B7
Kingsbridge Av ACT W3 155 L1
Kingsbridge Ct POP/IOD E14 160 F3
Kingsbridge Crs STHL UB1 133 N7
Kingsbridge Dr MLHL NW7 96 G8
Kingsbridge Rd BARK IG11 142 G4
HARH RM3 105 M7
MRDN SM4 200 G7
NKENS W10 136 F8
NWDGN UB2 153 N3
WOT/HER KT12 197 J7
Kingsbrook LHD/OX KT22 236 F4
Kingsbury Av STALW/RED AL3 38 A5
Kingsbury Crs STA TW18 172 G7
Kingsbury Dr WDSR SL4 171 N3
Kingsbury Gn CDALE/KGS NW9 * 115 P3
Kingsbury Rd CDALE/KGS NW9 115 M3
IS N1 7 K1
Kingsbury Ter IS N1 7 K1
King's Cha BRW CM14 107 H4
E/WMO/HCT KT8 198 B3
Kingsclere Cl PUT/ROE SW15 178 D3
Kingsclere Pl ENC/FH EN2 79 K6
Kingscliffe Gdns
WIM/MER SW19 179 J5
King's Cl KGLGY WD4 53 L7
LEY E10 120 G5
STA TW18 173 N10
CSTG HP8 90 A3
DART DA1 164 F10
HDN NW4 116 G2
NTHWD HA6 92 G7
THDIT KT7 198 F6
WATW WD18 73 K8
WOT/HER KT12 197 J8
King's College Rd HAMP NW3 3 N3
RSLP HA4 112 G4
Kingscote Hl CRAWW RH11 283 L9
Kingscote Rd CHSWK W4 156 A2
CROY/NA CR0 204 A7
NWMAL KT3 200 A3
Kingscote St BLKFR EC4V 12 C7
Kings Ct KWD/TDW/WH KT20 238 F8
PLSTW E13 141 N3
STHWK SE1 * 18 D1
Kingscourt Rd
STRHM/NOR SW16 180 F6
King's Crs FSBYPK N4 119 K8
Kingscroft WGCE AL7 23 L4
Kingscroft Rd BNSTD SM7 239 N1
CRICK NW2 2 C1
LHD/OX KT22 236 G6
King's Cross Br IS N1 * 5 M9
Kings Cross La REDH RH1 276 G3
King's Cross Rd FSBYW WC1X 5 N9
Kingsdale Gdns NTGHL W11 136 G10
Kingsdale Rd BERK HP4 33 M6
PGE/AN SE20 204 C1
WOOL/PLUM SE18 163 J5
Kingsdene KWD/TDW/WH KT20 238 E7
Kingsdon La HLWE CM17 47 M2
Kingsdown Av ACT W3 136 B9
SAND/SEL CR2 223 K5
WEA W13 154 G1
Kingsdown Cl
BERM/RHTH SE16 * 160 A4
GVE DA12 191 J4
NKENS W10 136 G8
Kingsdowne Ct EA W5 * 135 K9
Kingsdowne Rd SURB KT6 199 K7
Kingsdown Rd ARCH N19 118 F8
CHEAM SM3 221 H2
EW KT17 220 D9
WAN E11 121 K8
Kingsdown Wy HAYES BR2 205 M6
Kings Dr BRYLDS KT5 199 M7
EDGW HA8 95 L5
GVE DA12 190 E6
THDIT KT7 198 G6
WBLY HA9 115 N7
The Kings Dr WOT/HER KT12 216 G5
Kingsend RSLP HA4 112 F6
Kingsend Ct RSLP HA4 * 112 F6
Kings Farm WALTH E17 * 100 G9
Kings Farm Av
RCHPK/HAM TW10 155 M10
Kings Farm Rd
RKW/CH/CXG WD3 70 G10
Kingsfield HOD EN11 44 F1
WDSR SL4 148 C7
Kingsfield Av RYLN/HDSTN HA2 114 A3
Kingsfield Ct OXHEY WD19 93 L1
Kingsfield Dr PEND EN3 80 C1
Kingsfield Rd HRW HA1 * 114 C5
OXHEY WD19 93 L1
Kingsfield Ter DART DA1 * 187 L2
Kingsfield Wy PEND EN3 80 C1
Kingsford St KTTN NW5 118 A10
Kingsford Wy EHAM E6 142 C7
Kings Gdns IL IG1 122 G6
KIL/WHAMP NW6 2 F4
UPMR RM14 126 D5
Kingsgate CRAWE RH10 * 283 P7
STALW/RED AL3 38 A8
WBLY HA9 115 P8
Kingsgate Av FNCH N3 117 K1
Kingsgate Cl BXLYHN DA7 163 P7
STMC/STPC BR5 207 M3
Kingsgate Est IS N1 * 7 K2
Kingsgate Pl KIL/WHAMP NW6 2 E4
Kingsgate Rd KIL/WHAMP NW6 2 E3
KUT/HW KT1 199 K1
King's Gn LOU IG10 82 B7
Kingsground ELTH/MOT SE9 184 B3
King's Gv PECK SE15 160 A7
ROM RM1 125 H3
Kings Hall Ms LEW SE13 * 161 H9
Kings Hall Rd BECK BR3 182 C10
Kings Head Hl CHING E4 100 G1
King's Head La BF/WBF KT14 215 N7
King's Hwy WOOL/PLUM SE18 163 H5
Kingshill Av CRW RM5 104 D7
KTN/HRWW/WS HA3 114 G2
NTHLT UB5 133 J5
STALE/WH AL4 38 G3
WPK KT4 200 D7
YEAD UB4 132 F5
Kingshill Cl YEAD UB4 133 H5
Kingshill Ct BAR EN5 * 77 H8
Kingshill Dr KTN/HRWW/WS HA3 114 G1
Kingshill Wy BERK HP4 33 M7
Kingshold Rd HOM E9 140 B2
Kingsholm Gdns ELTH/MOT SE9 162 A10
Kingshurst Rd LEE/GVPK SE12 183 M3
Kings Keep HAYES BR2 * 205 K3
KUT/HW KT1 * 199 K4
Kingsland HLWS CM18 46 F3
Kingsland Ct CRAWE RH10 * 284 B7
Kingsland Gn STNW/STAM N16 7 K1
Kingsland Pas HACK E8 * 7 L1
Kingsland Rd BETH E2 7 K8
HHW HP1 35 K8
PLSTW E13 141 P5
Kings La BFOR GU20 212 D2
EGH TW20 171 M8
KGLGY WD4 53 K7
SUT SM1 221 N2
Kingslawn Cl PUT/ROE SW15 178 E1
Kingslea LHD/OX KT22 236 F6
Kingsleigh Cl BTFD TW8 155 J5
Kingsleigh Pl MTCM CR4 202 A3
Kingsleigh Wk HAYES BR2 205 L4
Kingsley Av BNSTD SM7 239 K1
BORE WD6 75 L6
CHES/WCR EN8 62 A5
DART DA1 187 P1
EGH TW20 171 N9
HSLW TW3 154 B8
STHL UB1 133 P9
SUT SM1 221 N1
WEA W13 134 F8
Kingsley Cl DAGE RM10 124 C9
EFNCH N2 117 M3
HORL RH6 280 A2
Kingsley Ct EDGW HA8 * 95 N3
GPK RM2 125 J4
WGCE AL7 23 J9
Kingsley Dr WPK KT4 200 C9
Kingsley Gdns CHING E4 100 F6
EMPK RM11 125 L2
Kingsley Gv REIG RH2 275 K3
Kingsley Ms CHST BR7 184 E9
IL IG1 122 E7
KENS W8 15 H4
WAP E1W * 140 A9
Kingsley Pl HGT N6 118 C5
Kingsley Rd BARK/HLT IG6 102 F9
CRAWW RH11 283 K10
CROY/NA CR0 203 H8
FSTGT E7 141 M2
HORL RH6 280 A2
HSLW TW3 154 B8
KIL/WHAMP NW6 2 D5
LOU IG10 82 G7
ORP BR6 227 J4
PIN HA5 113 N2
PLMGR N13 99 J5
RYLN/HDSTN HA2 114 B9
WALTH E17 101 H10
WIM/MER SW19 179 L8
Kingsley St BTSEA SW11 158 A9
Kingsley Wk CDW/CHF RM16 168 D3
Kingsley Wy EFNCH N2 117 M4
Kingsley Wood Dr
ELTH/MOT SE9 184 C6
Kingslyn Crs NRWD SE19 203 M2
Kings Lynn Dr HARH RM3 105 L7
Kings Ml HMSMTH W6 * 156 F3
Kingsman Dr CDW/CHF RM16 147 N9
Kingsman St WOOL/PLUM SE18 162 C3
Kingsmead BAR EN5 77 K8
BH/WHM TN16 244 A2
CHES/WCR EN8 62 C4
Kings Md HORL RH6 281 J4
Kingsmead POTB/CUF EN6 60 F4
RCHPK/HAM TW10 177 L2
Kings Md REDH RH1 276 F2
Kingsmead SBW CM21 29 P2
STALE/WH AL4 39 J3
WAB EN9 * 45 H8
WOKN/KNAP GU21 232 D2
Kingsmead Av CDALE/KGS NW9 116 A5
ED N9 100 A2
MTCM CR4 202 D3
ROM RM1 124 F4
SUN TW16 197 K3
SURB KT6 199 M9
WPK KT4 200 E10
Kingsmead Cl BFN/LL DA15 185 K5
HLWW/ROY CM19 45 N2
HOR/WEW KT19 220 A4
TEDD TW11 176 G9
Kingsmead Dr NTHLT UB5 133 N2
Kings Meadow KGLGY WD4 54 B4
Kingsmead Pde NTHLT UB5 * 133 N2
Kings Mead Pk ESH/CLAY KT10 218 D4
Kingsmead Rd
BRXS/STRHM SW2 181 H5
Kingsmead Wy CLPT E5 120 D9
Kingsmere Cl PUT/ROE SW15 156 G9
Kingsmere Pk CDALE/KGS NW9 115 P6
Kingsmere Pl STNW/STAM N16 * 119 L6
Kingsmere Rd WIM/MER SW19 178 G5
King's Ms BMSBY WC1N 11 P2
CHIG IG7 102 F3
CLAP SW4 180 F1
HHNE HP2 * 35 N5
Kingsmill Ct HAT AL10 40 E6
Kingsmill Gdns DAGW RM9 124 A10
Kings Mill La REDH RH1 276 E4
Kingsmill Rd DAGW RM9 124 A10
Kingsmill Ter STJWD NW8 3 M7
Kingsmoor Rd HLWW/ROY CM19 46 E4
Kingsnympton Pk
KUTN/CMB KT2 177 N10
Kings Oak ROMW/RG RM7 124 B1
King's Orch ELTH/MOT SE9 184 B2
King's Paddock HPTN TW12 198 B1
Kings Pde CAR SM5 * 201 P10
SHB W12 * 156 D2
TOTM N17 * 119 N1
WLSDN NW10 * 136 F3
Kingspark Ct SWFD E18 121 M1
Kings Pas WAN E11 * 121 K5
Kings Pl CHSWK W4 155 P4
LOU IG10 102 A1
STHWK SE1 18 E2
King Sq FSBYE EC1V 6 E10
King's Quay WBPTN SW10 * 157 M7
Kings Reach EMB EC4Y * 12 B7
WHALL SW1A 11 M10
Kings Ride Ga RCHPK/HAM TW10 155 M10
Kingsridge Gdns DART DA1 187 L2
King's Rd ASC SL5 192 D5
BARK IG11 142 F2
BRW CM14 107 H4
CHES/WCR EN8 62 D10
CHING E4 101 J2
ADL/WDHM KT15 215 L6
EGH TW20 172 D7
FUL/PGN SW6 157 M6
HERT/BAY SG13 25 P4
KUTN/CMB KT2 177 L10
LCOL/BKTW AL2 57 H2
MORT/ESHN SW14 156 A9
PLSTW E13 141 P3
RGUE GU4 268 B7
ROM RM1 125 H3
SL SL1 149 K2
SNWD SE25 203 P3
STALW/RED AL3 38 A5
SURB KT6 199 H8
TEDD TW11 176 C8
TOTM N17 99 N9
TWK TW1 176 G2
UED N18 * 99 P6
UX/CGN UB8 131 N4
WAN E11 121 K5
WDGN N22 98 G9
WIM/MER SW19 179 K9
BAR EN5 76 F7
BELMT SM2 221 K6
BERK HP4 33 N6
BH/WHM TN16 243 P3
CHOB/PIR GU24 212 F10
CSTG HP8 90 A3
EA W5 135 J7
FELT TW13 175 K4
HORL RH6 280 B4
MTCM CR4 202 B3
ORP BR6 227 J1
RCHPK/HAM TW10 177 L1
RYLN/HDSTN HA2 113 N7
SHGR GU5 268 E8
WBPTN SW10 15 L10
WDR/YW UB7 152 A1
WDSR SL4 149 J9
WLSDN NW10 136 E2
WOKN/KNAP GU21 232 D2
WOT/HER KT12 197 J9
King's Scholars' Pas PIM SW1V 16 G5
Kings Shade Wk
HOR/WEW KT19 * 220 A9
Kings Sq HAT AL10 * 40 A1
Kings's Rd GU GU1 250 A10
King Stable St WDSR SL4 149 J6
King Stairs Cl BERM/RHTH SE16 160 A1
King's Ter CAMTN NW1 4 G6
Kingsthorpe Rd SYD SE26 182 C7
Kingston Av CHEAM SM3 201 H10
EBED/NFELT TW14 174 F2
EHSLY KT24 252 F2
LHD/OX KT22 236 G7
WDR/YW UB7 132 A9
Kingston By-Pass
ESH/CLAY KT10 198 D10
RYNPK SW20 178 C9
RYNPK SW20 200 D2
Kingston Cl CHDH RM6 123 P1
NTHLT UB5 133 N2
TEDD TW11 176 G9
Kingston Ct GVW DA11 189 N2
Kingston Crs ASHF TW15 173 M8
BECK BR3 204 E1
Kingston Gdns CROY/NA CR0 202 F10
Kingston Hall Rd KUT/HW KT1 199 J3
Kingston Hl KUTN/CMB KT2 199 M1
Kingston Hill Av CHDH RM6 123 P1
Kingston Hill Pl KUTN/CMB KT2 177 P7
Kingston House Est SURB KT6 * 198 G6
Kingston House Gdns
LHD/OX KT22 * 236 G7
Kingston La EHSLY KT24 252 B3
TEDD TW11 176 G9
UX/CGN UB8 131 P5
WDR/YW UB7 152 A1
Kingston Ldg NWMAL KT3 200 B4
Kingston Pde GRAYS RM17 * 167 N3
Kingston Pl KTN/HRWW/WS HA3 94 E8
Kingston Ri ADL/WDHM KT15 215 K6
Kingston Rd ASHF TW15 173 P9
BRYLDS KT5 199 N9
EBAR EN4 77 N9
ED N9 99 P3
HOR/WEW KT19 220 A1
IL IG1 122 F9
LHD/OX KT22 236 F7
NWDGN UB2 153 N1
NWMAL KT3 200 A4
PUT/ROE SW15 178 E4
ROM RM1 124 G2
RYNPK SW20 201 H2
STA TW18 173 K7
TEDD TW11 176 G9
WIM/MER SW19 179 K10
Kingston Sq NRWD SE19 181 L8
Kingston V PUT/ROE SW15 178 A7
Kingstown St CAMTN NW1 4 C5
King St ACT W3 135 N10
CHERT KT16 195 K8
CITYW EC2V 12 F6
COVGDN WC2E 11 L7
CSHM HP5 50 G8
EFNCH N2 * 97 N10
EFNCH N2 117 N1
GVE DA12 190 E2
HMSMTH W6 156 D3
NWDGN UB2 153 M2
PLSTW E13 141 M6
RCH/KEW TW9 177 J1
TOTM N17 99 N9
TWK TW1 176 F4
WATW WD18 73 K8
WHALL SW1A 11 H10
King St Cloisters HMSMTH W6 * 156 E3
King Street Pde TWK TW1 * 176 F4
Kings Wk SAND/SEL CR2 224 A10
Kings Warren LHD/OX KT22 218 B7
Kingswater Pl BTSEA SW11 * 157 P6
King's Wy CHOB/PIR GU24 230 C5
CROY/NA CR0 222 G2
HRW HA1 114 D2
Kingsway CFSP/GDCR SL9 110 B1
HOL/ALD WC2B 11 N6
HYS/HAR UB3 132 D7
MORT/ESHN SW14 155 N9
NFNCH/WDSPK N12 97 M7
NWMAL KT3 200 F4
PEND EN3 80 A9
POTB/CUF EN6 60 F6
SLN SL2 128 G1
STMC/STPC BR5 206 G5
STWL/WRAY TW19 173 N4
WBLY HA9 115 K9
WOKN/KNAP GU21 232 A4
WWKM BR4 205 L10
Kingsway Av SAND/SEL CR2 224 B5
WOKN/KNAP GU21 232 A4
Kingsway Crs RYLN/HDSTN HA2 114 B2
Kingsway North Orbital Rd
GSTN WD25 55 J10
Kingsway Pde
STNW/STAM N16 * 119 L8
Kingsway Pl CLKNW EC1R * 12 B1
Kingsway Rd CHEAM SM3 221 H4
Kingsway Ter WEY KT13 216 B5
The Kingsway EW KT17 220 C6
Kingswear Rd KTTN NW5 118 C8
RSLP HA4 113 H7
Kingswell Ride POTB/CUF EN6 60 F6
Kingswick Cl ASC SL5 192 D4
Kingswick Dr ASC SL5 192 C4
Kingswood Av BELV DA17 164 A3
HAYES BR2 205 K3
HPTN TW12 176 A9
HSLW TW3 153 N8
KIL/WHAMP NW6 2 A6
SAND/SEL CR2 242 B1
SWLY BR8 208 G4
THHTH CR7 203 H5
Kingswood Cl ASHF TW15 174 D7
BAR EN5 77 M10
DART DA1 187 K2
EGH TW20 172 A7
EN EN1 79 M9
GU GU1 250 F9
NWMAL KT3 200 C6
STMC/STPC BR5 206 G7
SURB KT6 199 K7
VX/NE SW8 158 F6
WEY KT13 216 C4
Kingswood Ct LEW SE13 183 J2
Kingswood Creek
STWL/WRAY TW19 172 A1
Kingswood Dr BELMT SM2 221 L5
CAR SM5 202 A8
DUL SE21 181 M7
Kingswood La WARL CR6 242 B1
Kingswood Pk FNCH N3 97 J10
Kingswood Pl LEW SE13 161 K10
Kingswood Ri EGH TW20 172 A8
Kingswood Rd
BRXS/STRHM SW2 180 F2
CHSWK W4 155 P2
GDMY/SEVK IG3 123 K6
GSTN WD25 55 J10
HAYES BR2 205 K3
KWD/TDW/WH KT20 238 E7
PGE/AN SE20 182 B9
SEV TN13 246 F7
WAN E11 121 K5
WBLY HA9 115 M8
WIM/MER SW19 201 J1
Kingswood Ter CHSWK W4 155 P2
Kingswood Wy SAND/SEL CR2 224 C8
WLGTN SM6 222 F2
Kingsworth Cl BECK BR3 204 D5
Kingsworthy Cl KUT/HW KT1 199 L2
Kings Yd PUT/ROE SW15 * 156 G10
RKW/CH/CXG WD3 * 91 P2
SRTFD E15 * 140 F1
Kingthorpe Rd WLSDN NW10 136 A2
Kingthorpe Ter WLSDN NW10 * 136 A2
Kingwell Rd EBAR EN4 77 N4
Kingweston Cl CRICK NW2 117 H8
King William Ct WAB EN9 * 81 H1
King William La GNWCH SE10 161 K4
King William St CANST EC4R 13 H8
King William Wk GNWCH SE10 161 H5
Kingwood Rd FUL/PGN SW6 157 H6
Kinlet Rd WOOL/PLUM SE18 162 F7
Kinloch Dr CDALE/KGS NW9 116 B5
Kinloch St HOLWY N7 118 G8
Kinloss Gdns FNCH N3 117 J1
Kinloss Rd CAR SM5 201 M7
Kinnaird Av BMLY BR1 183 L9
CHSWK W4 155 P6
Kinnaird Cl BMLY BR1 183 L9
SL SL1 128 B8
Kinnaird Wy WFD IG8 102 C7
Kinnear Rd SHB W12 156 C1
Kinnersley Mnr REIG RH2 * 275 M8
Kinnersley Wk REIG RH2 275 K5
Kinnerton Pl North KTBR SW1X * 16 B2
Kinnerton Pl South KTBR SW1X * 16 B2
Kinnerton St KTBR SW1X 16 C2
Kinnerton Yd KTBR SW1X * 16 C2
Kinnoul Rd HMSMTH W6 14 A9
Kinross Av WPK KT4 200 D9
Kinross Cl KTN/HRWW/WS HA3 115 L3
SUN TW16 174 G8
Kinross Dr SUN TW16 174 G8
Kinross Ter WALTH E17 100 E10
Kinsale Rd PECK SE15 159 P9
Kinsella Gdns WIM/MER SW19 178 E9
Kintyre Cl STRHM/NOR SW16 202 G2
Kinveachy Gdns CHARL SE7 162 B4
Kinver Rd SYD SE26 182 B7
Kipings KWD/TDW/WH KT20 238 G8
Kipling Av TIL RM18 168 E7
Kipling Cl BRW CM14 106 G6
CRAWE RH10 284 D5
Kipling Dr WIM/MER SW19 179 N9
Kipling Est STHWK SE1 19 H2
Kipling Rd BXLYHN DA7 163 P7
DART DA1 188 A1
Kipling St STHWK SE1 19 H2
Kipling Ter ED N9 * 99 L4
Kipling Wy HARP AL5 20 A2
Kippington Cl SEV TN13 246 G10
Kippington Dr ELTH/MOT SE9 184 A4
Kippington Rd SEV TN13 246 G10
Kirby Cl BARK/HLT IG6 103 H7
HARH RM3 105 P6
HOR/WEW KT19 220 C2
LOU IG10 102 B1
NTHWD HA6 92 G7
Kirby Est BERM/RHTH SE16 * 160 A2
WDR/YW UB7 * 131 N9
Kirby Gv STHWK SE1 19 J1
Kirby Rd RDART DA2 188 B3
WOKN/KNAP GU21 231 P2
Kirby St HCIRC EC1N 12 B3
Kirchen Rd WEA W13 134 G9
Kirdford Cl CRAWW RH11 283 K5
Kirkcaldy Gn OXHEY WD19 93 K4
Kirkdale SYD SE26 182 A5
Kirkdale Cnr SYD SE26 * 182 B7
Kirkdale Rd WAN E11 121 K6
Kirkefields GUW GU2 249 M7
Kirkfield Cl WEA W13 134 G10
Kirkham Rd EHAM E6 142 B8
Kirkham St WOOL/PLUM SE18 163 H5
Kirkland Av CLAY IG5 102 D10
WOKN/KNAP GU21 231 K2
Kirkland Cl BFN/LL DA15 185 H2
Kirkland Drive ENC/FH EN2 79 K5
Kirklands WGCW AL8 23 H1
Kirkland Ter BECK BR3 182 F9
Kirkland Wk HACK E8 7 L2
Kirk La WOOL/PLUM SE18 162 F5
Kirkleas Rd SURB KT6 199 K8
Kirklees Rd BCTR RM8 123 M10
THHTH CR7 203 H5
Kirkley Rd WIM/MER SW19 201 K1
Kirkly Cl SAND/SEL CR2 223 M5
Kirkmichael Rd POP/IOD E14 141 H8
Kirk Rd WALTH E17 120 E4
Kirkside Rd BKHTH/KID SE3 161 M5
Kirkstall Av SEVS/STOTM N15 119 L2
Kirkstall Gdns BRXS/STRHM SW2 180 E4
Kirkstall Rd BRXS/STRHM SW2 180 F4
Kirksted Rd MRDN SM4 201 L8
Kirkstone Wy BMLY BR1 183 K10
Kirkton Rd SEVS/STOTM N15 119 M2
Kirkwall Pl BETH E2 * 140 B5
Kirkwall Sp SL SL1 129 K7
Kirkwood Rd PECK SE15 160 A8
Kirn Rd WEA W13 134 G9
Kirrane Cl NWMAL KT3 200 C5
Kirtle Rd CSHM HP5 51 H7
Kirtley Rd SYD SE26 182 D7
Kirtling St VX/NE SW8 158 D6
Kirton Cl CHSWK W4 156 A3
HCH RM12 145 K1
Kirton Gdns BETH E2 7 M10
Kirton Ldg WAND/EARL SW18 * 179 L2
Kirton Rd PLSTW E13 141 P4
Kirton Wk EDGW HA8 95 P8
Kirwyn Wy CMBW SE5 159 K6
Kitcat Ter BOW E3 140 F5
Kitchener Av GVE DA12 190 F7
Kitchener Cl STAL AL1 38 F7
Kitchener Rd EFNCH N2 117 P1
FSTGT E7 141 N1
THHTH CR7 203 L3
TOTM N17 119 M1
WALTH E17 100 G9
Kite Fld BERK HP4 33 K2
Kite Pl BETH E2 7 P9
Kites Cl CRAWW RH11 283 M7
Kite Yd BTSEA SW11 * 158 A7
Kithurst Cl CRAWW RH11 283 M9
Kitley Gdns NRWD SE19 203 N1
Kitsbury Rd BERK HP4 33 N5
Kitsbury Ter BERK HP4 33 N5
Kitsmead CRAWE RH10 285 H3
Kitsmead La CHERT KT16 194 A9
VW GU25 193 P8
Kitson Rd BARN SW13 156 D7
CMBW SE5 159 K6
Kitson Wy HLW CM20 28 F10
Kitswell Wy RAD WD7 56 E9
Kittiwake Cl CRAWW RH11 282 G9
SAND/SEL CR2 224 D6
Kittiwake Rd NTHLT UB5 133 L5
Kittiwake Wy YEAD UB4 133 L7
Kitto Rd NWCR SE14 160 C8
Kitt's End Rd BAR EN5 77 H3
Kiver Rd ARCH N19 118 F7
Kiwi Ter EHAM E6 142 D5
Klea Av CLAP SW4 180 D2
Knapdale Cl FSTH SE23 182 A5
Knapmill Rd CAT SE6 182 F5
Knapmill Wy CAT SE6 182 F5
Knapp Cl WLSDN NW10 136 B1
Knapp Rd ASHF TW15 174 A7
BOW E3 140 F6
Knapton Ms TOOT SW17 180 B9
Knaresborough Dr
WAND/EARL SW18 179 L4
Knaresborough Pl ECT SW5 14 G6
Knatchbull Rd WALW SE17 159 K7
WLSDN NW10 136 A3
Knave Wood Rd BGR/WK TN15 247 M3
Knebworth Av WALTH E17 100 F9
Knebworth Pth BORE WD6 76 A8
Knebworth Rd
STNW/STAM N16 * 119 M9
Knee Hl ABYW SE2 163 M4
Knee Hill Crs ABYW SE2 163 M3
Knella Gn WGCE AL7 23 K5
Knella Rd WGCE AL7 23 J6
Kneller Gdns ISLW TW7 176 C2
Kneller Rd BROCKY SE4 160 D10
NWMAL KT3 200 B7
WHTN TW2 176 B2
Knepp Cl CRAWE RH10 284 D8
Knevett Ter HSLW TW3 153 P10
Knifton Ct POTB/CUF EN6 * 58 G7
Knight Cl BCTR RM8 123 M7
Knighten St WAP E1W 140 A10
Knighthead Point
POP/IOD E14 * 160 F1
Knightland Rd CLPT E5 120 A7
Knighton Cl CRAWE RH10 284 E3
ROMW/RG RM7 124 E4
SAND/SEL CR2 223 J5
WFD IG8 101 N5
Knighton Dr WFD IG8 101 N5
Knighton La BKHH IG9 101 N3
Knighton Park Rd SYD SE26 182 C8
Knighton Rd FSTGT E7 121 M8
REDH RH1 276 B2
ROMW/RG RM7 124 D4
RSEV TN14 246 G3
Knighton-way La DEN/HRF UB9 111 L10
Knightrider Ct BLKFR EC4V 12 D7
Knightrider St BLKFR EC4V 12 E7
Knight's Av EA W5 155 K1
Knightsbridge SKENS SW7 15 P2
Knightsbridge Crs STA TW18 173 L10
Knightsbridge Gdns
ROMW/RG RM7 124 E3
Knightsbridge Gn KTBR SW1X * 16 A2
Knightsbridge Wy HHNE HP2 35 P5
Knights Chambers ED N9 * 99 P4
Knights Cl E/WMO/HCT KT8 197 N5
EGH TW20 * 172 G9
WDSR SL4 148 C7
Knightscote Cl DEN/HRF UB9 91 N10
Knightsfield WGCW AL8 22 G1
Knights Hl WNWD SE27 181 J8
Knight's Hill Sq WNWD SE27 181 J7
Knight's La ED N9 99 P4
Knights Manor Wy DART DA1 187 N2
Knights Orch HHW HP1 35 J4
STALW/RED AL3 38 B6
Knight's Pk KUT/HW KT1 199 K3
Knights Pl REDH RH1 258 B9
WDSR SL4 149 H9
WHTN TW2 176 D4
Knights Rdg ORP BR6 227 L2
Knights Rd CAN/RD E16 141 M10
STAN HA7 95 H5
Knight St SBW CM21 29 P1
Knights Wk ABR/ST RM4 83 L7
LBTH SE11 18 C6
Knights Wy BARK/HLT IG6 102 F7
RBRW/HUT CM13 107 M5
Knightswood WOKN/KNAP GU21 231 L4
Knightswood Cl EDGW HA8 95 P3
Knightswood Rd RAIN RM13 144 G4
Knightwood Cl REIG RH2 275 K2
Knightwood Crs NWMAL KT3 200 B6
Knipp Hl COB KT11 217 N9
Knivet Rd FUL/PGN SW6 14 E10
Knobfield RDKG RH5 270 G9
Knobs Hill Rd SRTFD E15 140 G3
Knockhall Cha SWCM DA10 189 H1
Knockhall Rd SWCM DA10 189 H2
Knockholt Cl BELMT SM2 221 L6
Knockholt Rd ELTH/MOT SE9 184 A1
RSEV TN14 228 A10
Knole Cl CRAWE RH10 284 E6
CROY/NA CR0 * 204 B6
Knole La SEV TN13 265 K2
Knole Rd DART DA1 187 H3
SEV TN13 247 L9
The Knole ELTH/MOT SE9 184 D7
MEO DA13 190 B10
Knole Wy SEV TN13 265 K1
Knole Wd ASC SL5 * 192 D8
Knoll Crs NTHWD HA6 92 G10
Knoll Dr STHGT/OAK N14 98 B1
Knolles Crs BRKMPK AL9 40 E10
Knoll Gn HHNE HP2 * 35 P4
Knollmead BRYLDS KT5 199 P8
Knoll Park Rd CHERT KT16 195 J8
Knoll Ri ORP BR6 207 J8
Knoll Rd BXLY DA5 186 B3
DORK RH4 272 F4
SCUP DA14 185 L8
WAND/EARL SW18 179 L1
Knolls Cl WPK KT4 200 E10
The Knolls EW KT17 238 F2
The Knoll BECK BR3 204 G1
CHERT KT16 195 J8
COB KT11 217 P9
EA W5 135 H7
HAYES BR2 205 M9
HERT/BAY SG13 26 A4
LHD/OX KT22 237 H7
PIN HA5 * 93 L10
Knollys Cl STRHM/NOR SW16 181 J6
Knolly's Rd STRHM/NOR SW16 181 H6
Knolton Wy SLN SL2 129 N8
Knottisford St BETH E2 140 C5
Knottocks Cl BEAC HP9 88 C6
Knottocks Dr BEAC HP9 88 C6
Knottocks End BEAC HP9 88 C6
Knotts Green Ms LEY E10 120 G4
Knotts Green Rd LEY E10 120 G4
Knotts Pl SEV TN13 247 H10
Knowle Av BXLYHN DA7 163 P6
Knowle Cl BRXN/ST SW9 159 H9
CRAWE RH10 285 K2
Knowle Dr CRAWE RH10 285 J2
HARP AL5 20 C4
Knowle Gdns BF/WBF KT14 215 J9
Knowle Gn STA TW18 173 K8
Knowle Gv VW GU25 193 P7
Knowle Grove Cl VW GU25 193 P7
Knowle Hl VW GU25 193 N7
Knowle Pk COB KT11 235 M1
Knowle Park Av STA TW18 173 L9
Knowle Rd HAYES BR2 206 B9
WHTN TW2 176 D4
Knowles Cl WDR/YW UB7 131 P10
Knowles Hill Crs LEW SE13 183 J1
The Knowle HOD EN11 44 F4
KWD/TDW/WH KT20 * 238 E7
Knowl Hl WOKS/MYFD GU22 232 E5
Knowlton Gn HAYES BR2 205 L5
Knowl Wy BORE WD6 75 L9
Knowsley Av STHL UB1 134 A10
Knowsley Rd BTSEA SW11 158 A8
Knox Rd FSTGT E7 141 M1
GUW GU2 249 M5
Knox St CAMTN NW1 10 A3
Knoyle St NWCR SE14 160 D5
Knutsford Av WATN WD24 73 L4
Kohat Rd WIM/MER SW19 179 M8
Koh-i-Noor Av BUSH WD23 73 P10

Koonowla Cl BH/WHM TN16 244 A1
Kooringa WARL CR6 242 A5
Korda Cl SHPTN TW17 196 A3
Korea Cottages COB KT11 * 235 L2
Kossuth St GNWCH SE10 161 K4
Kramer Ms ECT SW5 14 F8
Kreedman Wk HACK E8 * 119 P10
Kuala Gdns STRHM/NOR SW16 202 C1
Kydbrook Cl STMC/STPC BR5 206 F7
Kylemore Cl EHAM E6 142 A4
Kylemore Rd KIL/WHAMP NW6 2 E3
Kymberley Rd HRW HA1 * 114 D4
Kyme Rd ROM RM1 124 G4
Kynance Cl HARH RM3 105 K5
Kynance Gdns STAN HA7 95 H9
Kynance Ms SKENS SW7 15 H4
Kynance Pl KENS W8 15 J4
Kynaston Av THHTH CR7 203 K5
Kynaston Cl KTN/HRWW/WS HA3 94 C8
Kynaston Ct CTHM CR3 259 M1
Kynaston Crs THHTH CR7 203 K5
Kynaston Rd BMLY BR1 183 M8
ENC/FH EN2 79 L5
STMC/STPC BR5 207 L7
STNW/STAM N16 119 M8
THHTH CR7 203 K5
Kynaston Wd
KTN/HRWW/WS HA3 94 C8
Kynersley Cl CAR SM5 202 A10
Kyngeshene Gdns GU GU1 268 D1
Kynoch Rd UED N18 100 C5
Kyrle Rd BTSEA SW11 180 B2
Kytes Dr GSTN WD25 55 L9
Kyverdale Rd STNW/STAM N16 119 N5

L

Laburnham Cl UPMR RM14 126 F5
Laburnham Gdns UPMR RM14 126 E5
Laburnum Av DART DA1 187 K4
ED N9 99 M3
HCH RM12 125 H7
SUT SM1 201 P10
SWLY BR8 208 E3
TOTM N17 99 L8
WDR/YW UB7 132 A9
Laburnum Cl ALP/SUD HA0 135 M3
CHES/WCR EN8 62 C7
CHING E4 100 E7
GU GU1 249 P7
PECK SE15 160 B6
RBSF CM22 30 D3
Laburnum Ct STAN HA7 95 H5
Laburnum Crs SUN TW16 197 J1
Laburnum Gdns CROY/NA CR0 204 C7
Laburnum Gv CDALE/KGS NW9 115 P5
DTCH/LGLY SL3 150 D5
GVW DA11 190 A3
HSLW TW3 153 N10
LCOL/BKTW AL2 55 P1
NWMAL KT3 200 A2
RSLP HA4 112 E4
SOCK/AV RM15 147 J6
STHL UB1 133 N6
WCHMH N21 99 K3
Laburnum Pl EGH TW20 171 N9
ELTH/MOT SE9 * 184 D1
Laburnum Rd CHERT KT16 195 K8
EPP CM16 65 M5
EPSOM KT18 220 B9
HOD EN11 44 G1
HYS/HAR UB3 152 G3
MTCM CR4 202 B2
WIM/MER SW19 179 M10
WOKS/MYFD GU22 232 A6
Laburnum St BETH E2 7 L6
Laburnum Wk HCH RM12 125 K10
Laburnum Wy CHESW EN7 61 I4
HAYES BR2 206 E7
STWL/WRAY TW19 174 A4
Lacebark Cl BFN/LL DA15 185 J3
Lacemaker Ct AMSS HP7 * 69 H6
Lacewing Cl PLSTW E13 141 M5
Lacey Av COUL/CHIP CR5 241 H6
Lacey Cl ED N9 99 P3
EGH TW20 172 G10
Lacey Dr BCTR RM8 123 M8
COUL/CHIP CR5 241 H6
EDGW HA8 95 K5
HPTN TW12 197 N1
Laceys Yd CSHM HP5 * 50 G7
Lackford Rd COUL/CHIP CR5 240 A4
Lackington St SDTCH EC2A 13 H3
Lackmore Rd EN EN1 80 B1
Lacock Cl WIM/MER SW19 179 M9
Lacon Rd EDUL SE22 159 P10
Lacrosse Wy STRHM/NOR SW16 202 E1
Lacy Gn COUL/CHIP CR5 241 H6
Lacy Rd PUT/ROE SW15 156 G10
Ladas Rd WNWD SE27 181 K8
Ladbroke Crs NTGHL W11 8 B6
Ladbroke Gdns NTGHL W11 8 C7
Ladbroke Gv NKENS W10 8 A4
REDH RH1 258 B9
Ladbroke Ms NTGHL W11 8 B10
Ladbroke Rd EN EN1 79 N10
EPSOM KT18 220 A10
HORL RH6 280 C2
REDH RH1 258 B8
Ladbroke Sq NTGHL W11 8 D8
Ladbroke Ter NTGHL W11 8 D9
Ladbroke Wk NTGHL W11 8 D9
Ladbrook Cl PIN HA5 113 N3
Ladbrooke Cl POTB/CUF EN6 59 K8
Ladbrooke Crs SCUP DA14 185 N6
Ladbrooke Dr POTB/CUF EN6 59 K8
Ladbrooke Rd SL SL1 149 J2
Ladbrook Rd SNWD SE25 203 L3
Ladderstile Ride KUTN/CMB KT2 177 N8
Ladderswood Wy
FBAR/BDGN N11 98 D6
Ladds Wy SWLY BR8 208 E4
Ladies Gv STALW/RED AL3 38 B4
Lady Alesford Av STAN HA7 94 G6
Lady Booth Rd KUT/HW KT1 199 K2
Ladycroft Gdns ORP BR6 226 F2
Ladycroft Rd LEW SE13 160 G9
Ladycroft Wk STAN HA7 95 J9
Ladycroft Wy ORP BR6 226 F2
Ladyday Pl SL SL1 * 129 H10
Ladyegate Cl RDKG RH5 273 J1
Ladyegate Rd RDKG RH5 273 J1
Ladyfields GVW DA11 190 C7
LOU IG10 82 E8
Lady Forsdyke Wy
HOR/WEW KT19 219 M5
Ladygate La RSLP HA4 112 D4
Ladygrove CROY/NA CR0 224 D5
Lady Gv WGCE AL7 23 H9
Ladygrove Dr RGUE GU4 250 F5
Lady Harewood Wy
HOR/WEW KT19 219 M5
Lady Hay WPK KT4 200 C9
Lady Margaret Rd ASC SL5 192 E8
CRAWW RH11 283 K6
KTTN NW5 118 D10
STHL UB1 133 N9
Ladymead GU GU1 249 P9
Ladymead Cl CRAWE RH10 284 D10
Lady Meadow KGLGY WD4 53 N3
Ladymount WLGTN SM6 222 E1
Lady St John Sq
HERT/WAT SG14 * 25 H5
Lady's Cl WATW WD18 73 K8
Ladyship Ter EDUL SE22 * 182 A3
Ladyshot HLW CM20 29 L10
Ladysmith Av EHAM E6 142 B4
GNTH/NBYPK IG2 122 G5
Ladysmith Cl MLHL NW7 96 D8
Ladysmith Rd CAN/RD E16 141 L5
ELTH/MOT SE9 184 D2
EN EN1 79 N6
KTN/HRWW/WS HA3 94 D10
STALW/RED AL3 38 C5
TOTM N17 99 P10
UED N18 100 A6
Lady Somerset Rd KTTN NW5 118 C9
Ladythorpe Cl ADL/WDHM KT15 215 L1
Ladywalk RKW/CH/CXG WD3 91 H6
Ladywell Cl BROCKY SE4 182 F1
Ladywell Prospect SBW CM21 30 A2
Ladywell Rd LEW SE13 182 G1
Ladywell St SRTFD E15 141 L3
Ladywell Water Tower
BROCKY SE4 * 160 E9
Ladywood Av STMC/STPC BR5 207 H5
Ladywood Cl RKW/CH/CXG WD3 71 L7
Ladywood Rd HERT/WAT SG14 24 G6
RDART DA2 188 D8
SURB KT6 199 M9
Lafone Av FELT TW13 175 K4
Lafone St STHWK SE1 19 L1
Lagado Ms BERM/RHTH SE16 140 C10
Lagger Cl CSTG HP8 89 N4
The Lagger CSTG HP8 89 N4
Laglands Cl REIG RH2 257 M8
Lagley Meadow BERK HP4 * 33 M4
Lagonda Av BARK/HLT IG6 103 J7
Lagonda Wy DART DA1 165 K10
Lagoon Rd STMC/STPC BR5 207 L5
Laidlaw Dr WCHMH N21 78 G9
Laidon Sq HHNE HP2 35 N2
Laing Cl BARK/HLT IG6 102 G7
Laing Dean NTHLT UB5 133 K3
Laings Av MTCM CR4 201 P2
Lainlock Pl HSLW TW3 154 A7
Lainson St WAND/EARL SW18 179 K3
Lairdale Cl DUL SE21 181 K4
Laird Av CDW/CHF RM16 168 A1
Lairs Cl HOLWY N7 5 M1
Laitwood Rd BAL SW12 180 C4
Lake Av BMLY BR1 183 M9
RAIN RM13 145 L4
SL SL1 129 J9
Lake Cl BCTR RM8 123 N8
BF/WBF KT14 215 N8
Lakedale Rd WOOL/PLUM SE18 163 H4
Lake Dr BUSH WD23 94 B3
Lake End Ct MDHD SL6 * 128 A8
Lake End Rd MDHD SL6 128 A9
WDSR SL4 148 A2
Lakefield Rd WDGN N22 99 J10
Lakefields Cl RAIN RM13 145 L4
Lake Gdns DAGE RM10 124 B10
RCHPK/HAM TW10 176 G6
WLGTN SM6 202 C10
Lakehall Gdns THHTH CR7 203 J5
Lakehall Rd THHTH CR7 203 J5
Lake House Rd WAN E11 121 M7
Lakehurst Rd HOR/WEW KT19 220 B2
Lakeland Cl CHIG IG7 103 L5
KTN/HRWW/WS HA3 94 C7
Lake La HORL RH6 280 D2
Lakenheath STHGT/OAK N14 78 E9
Lake Ri ROM RM1 124 G1
WTHK RM20 166 F3
Lake Rd CHDH RM6 123 N2
CROY/NA CR0 204 E9
DAGW RM9 144 C5
LEY E10 120 G5
VW GU25 193 N5
WAB EN9 45 K7
WIM/MER SW19 179 J8
Lakers Ri BNSTD SM7 239 P2
Lakes Cl RGUE GU4 268 E6
Lakeside BECK BR3 204 G3
ENC/FH EN2 78 E8
HOR/WEW KT19 220 B3
RAIN RM13 145 M4
REDH RH1 258 B8
WEA W13 135 H8
WEY KT13 196 F9
WLGTN SM6 222 C1
WOKN/KNAP GU21 231 K5
Lakeside Av REDBR IG4 122 A2
THMD SE28 143 K10
Lakeside Cl BFN/LL DA15 185 M1
CHIG IG7 103 J5
RSLP HA4 112 E2
SNWD SE25 203 P2
WOKN/KNAP GU21 231 K5
Lakeside Crs BRW CM14 107 J4
EBAR EN4 78 A10
Lakeside Dr ESH/CLAY KT10 218 B3
HAYES BR2 206 B10
SLN SL2 129 K3
WLSDN NW10 135 L5
Lakeside Gra WEY KT13 196 D10
Lakeside Leisure Pk
WTHK RM20 * 166 F3
Lakeside Pl LCOL/BKTW AL2 57 J4
Lakeside Rd CHES/WCR EN8 62 B4
DTCH/LGLY SL3 151 J6
PLMGR N13 98 G5
WKENS W14 156 G2
Lakeside Wy WBLY HA9 115 M9
Lakes La BEAC HP9 108 E1
Lakes Rd HAYES BR2 225 P2
Lakeswood Rd STMC/STPC BR5 206 E6
The Lake BUSH WD23 94 C2
Lake Vw EDGW HA8 95 L6
KGLGY WD4 * 54 C4
POTB/CUF EN6 59 M9
RDKG RH5 273 H5
Lake View Est BOW E3 * 140 C4
Lake View Rd SEV TN13 247 H9
Lakeview Rd WELL DA16 163 L10
WNWD SE27 181 J8
Lake View Ter UED N18 * 99 N5
Lakis Cl HAMP NW3 117 M9
Laleham Abbey STA TW18 * 195 M4
Laleham Av MLHL NW7 96 A4
Laleham Cl STA TW18 195 L1
Laleham Ct SUT SM1 * 221 M2
WOKN/KNAP GU21 * 232 B2
Laleham Reach CHERT KT16 195 L2
Laleham Rd CAT SE6 183 H3
SHPTN TW17 195 P4
STA TW18 173 J9
Lalor St FUL/PGN SW6 157 H8
Lambarde Av ELTH/MOT SE9 184 D7
Lambarde Dr SEV TN13 247 H9
Lambarde Rd SEV TN13 247 H8
Lambardes HART DA3 211 L10
Lambardes Cl ORP BR6 227 M7
Lamb Cl GSTN WD25 55 K10
HAT AL10 40 E5
NTHLT UB5 133 M5
TIL RM18 168 F8
Lamb Ct STALE/WH AL4 * 21 K4
Lamberhurst Cl STMC/STPC BR5 207 N8
Lamberhurst Rd BCTR RM8 123 P6
WNWD SE27 181 H7
Lamberhurst Wk CRAWE RH10 284 B8
Lambert Av DTCH/LGLY SL3 150 B2
RCH/KEW TW9 155 M9
Lambert Cl BH/WHM TN16 244 A2
Lambert Ct BUSH WD23 73 L8
Lambert Jones Ms BARB EC2Y * 12 E3
Lambert Rd BNSTD SM7 221 K10
BRXS/STRHM SW2 180 F1
CAN/RD E16 141 N8
NFNCH/WDSPK N12 97 N6
Lambert's Pl CROY/NA CR0 203 L8
Lambert's Rd BRYLDS KT5 199 L5
Lambert St IS N1 6 A4
Lambert Wy NFNCH/WDSPK N12 97 M6
Lambeth Br WEST SW1P 17 M5
Lambeth High St LBTH SE11 17 N5
Lambeth Hl BLKFR EC4V 12 E7
Lambeth Palace Rd STHWK SE1 17 N4
Lambeth Rd CROY/NA CR0 203 H8
STHWK SE1 18 A4
Lambeth Wk LBTH SE11 17 P5
PECK SE15 159 N8
Lambkins Ms WALTH E17 121 H2
Lamb La HACK E8 140 A2
Lamble St KTTN NW5 118 B9
Lambley Rd DAGW RM9 143 L1
Lambly Hl VW GU25 194 B3
Lambolle Pl HAMP NW3 3 P2
Lambolle Rd HAMP NW3 3 N2
Lambourn Cha RAD WD7 74 D2
Lambourn Cl HNWL W7 154 E1
KTTN NW5 * 118 D9
SAND/SEL CR2 223 J5
Lambourne Av WIM/MER SW19 179 J7
Lambourne Cl CHIG IG7 103 L4
CRAWE RH10 284 A9
Lambourne Ct UX/CGN UB8 131 L3
Lambourne Crs CHIG IG7 103 M3
WOKN/KNAP GU21 214 G9
Lambourne Dr COB KT11 235 K1
Lambourne Gdns BARK IG11 143 J2
CHING E4 100 F3
EN EN1 79 N6
HCH RM12 125 L7
Lambourne Gv
BERM/RHTH SE16 160 C4
KUT/HW KT1 199 N2
Lambourne Pl BKHTH/KID SE3 161 N7
Lambourne Rd BARK IG11 143 H2
CHIG IG7 103 J5
GDMY/SEVK IG3 123 H7
WAN E11 121 H5
Lambourn Rd CLAP SW4 158 C9
Lambrook Ter FUL/PGN SW6 157 H7
Lambs Cl ED N9 99 P3
POTB/CUF EN6 60 G5
Lamb's Conduit Pas
FSBYW WC1X 11 N3
Lamb's Conduit St BMSBY WC1N 11 N2
Lambscroft Av ELTH/MOT SE9 183 P6
Lambscroft Wy CFSP/GDCR SL9 90 B10
Lambs Green Rd HORS RH12 282 C8
Lambs Gv BARK IG11 143 H2
Lamb's La North RAIN RM13 145 L6
Lamb's La South RAIN RM13 145 K7
Lambs Meadow WFD IG8 102 A10
Lambs Ms IS N1 6 C6
Lamb's Pas STLK EC1Y 12 G2
Lambs Ter ED N9 * 99 L3
Lamb St WCHPL E1 13 L3
Lambs Wk ENC/FH EN2 79 K6
Lambton Av CHES/WCR EN8 62 C9
Lambton Pl NTGHL W11 8 D7
Lambton Rd ARCH N19 118 F6
RYNPK SW20 200 F2
Lamb Wk STHWK SE1 19 J2
Lambyn Cft HORL RH6 280 D3
Lamerock Rd BMLY BR1 183 L7
Lamerton Rd BARK/HLT IG6 102 E10
Lamerton St DEPT SE8 160 F5
Lamford Cl TOTM N17 99 L8
Lamlash St LBTH SE11 18 C5
Lammas Av MTCM CR4 202 B2
Lammas Cl STA TW18 173 H6
Lammas Ct WDSR SL4 149 H8
Lammas Dr STA TW18 172 G7
Lammas La ESH/CLAY KT10 217 P1
Lammasmead BROX EN10 44 E9
Lammas Park Gdns EA W5 135 H10
Lammas Rd HOM E9 140 C2
LEY E10 120 D7
RCHPK/HAM TW10 177 H7
SL SL1 128 C7
WATW WD18 73 K9
Lammermoor Rd BAL SW12 * 180 C3
Lamont Rd WBPTN SW10 15 K10
Lamont Road Pas WBPTN SW10 15 L10
Lamorbey Cl BFN/LL DA15 185 J5
Lamorbey Pk BFN/LL DA15 * 185 L4
Lamorna WOKS/MYFD GU22 * 232 B4
Lamorna Av GVE DA12 190 G6
Lamorna Cl ORP BR6 207 K7
RAD WD7 56 G10
WALTH E17 101 J10
Lamorna Gv STAN HA7 95 J10
Lampard Gv STNW/STAM N16 119 N6
Lampern Sq BETH E2 7 P9
Lampeter Cl WOKS/MYFD GU22 232 B4
Lampeter Sq HMSMTH W6 14 A10
Lampits HOD EN11 44 G3
Lamplighter Cl WCHPL E1 140 B6
Lamplighters Cl DART DA1 187 N2
WAB EN9 63 M10
Lampmead Rd LEE/GVPK SE12 183 K1
Lamport Cl WOOL/PLUM SE18 162 C3
Lampton Av HSLW TW3 153 P7
Lampton House Cl
WIM/MER SW19 178 G7
Lampton Park Rd HSLW TW3 154 A8
Lampton Rd HEST TW5 154 A7
Lamsey Rd HHS/BOV HP3 35 N8
Lamson Rd RAIN RM13 144 G7
Lanacre Av CDALE/KGS NW9 96 B9
Lanark Cl EA W5 135 H7
Lanark Pl MV/WKIL W9 9 K1
Lanark Rd MV/WKIL W9 3 J9
Lanbury Rd PECK SE15 160 C10
Lancashire Ct MYFR/PKLN W1K 10 E7
Lancaster Av BARK IG11 143 H2
EBAR EN4 77 N4
GU GU1 268 C2
MTCM CR4 202 F5
SLN SL2 129 H6
WAN E11 121 N2
WIM/MER SW19 178 G8
WNWD SE27 181 J5
Lancaster Cl ASHF TW15 173 P7
BRWN CM15 86 F9
CDALE/KGS NW9 96 C8
CRAWE RH10 284 E4
EGH TW20 172 A8
HAYES BR2 205 L4
IS N1 7 K4
STWL/WRAY TW19 173 P2
TOTM N17 * 99 P8
WOKN/KNAP GU21 232 D2
WPK KT4 200 E7
Lancaster Ct BAY/PAD W2 9 K7
WOT/HER KT12 197 J7
Lancaster Dr HAMP NW3 3 N2
HCH RM12 125 J10
HHS/BOV HP3 52 C3
LOU IG10 82 B9
POP/IOD E14 141 H10
Lancaster Garde BMLY BR1 206 B5
Lancaster Gdn KUTN/CMB KT2 177 J8
Lancaster Gdns KUTN/CMB KT2 177 K8
WIM/MER SW19 179 H8
Lancaster Ga BAY/PAD W2 9 K8
Lancaster Gv HAMP NW3 3 M2
Lancaster House
WOOL/PLUM SE18 * 162 B6
Lancaster Ms BAY/PAD W2 9 K7
RCHPK/HAM TW10 177 K2
WAND/EARL SW18 * 179 L1
Lancaster Pk RCHPK/HAM TW10 177 K1
Lancaster Pl COVGDN WC2E 11 N8
TWK TW1 176 F3
WIM/MER SW19 178 G8
Lancaster Rd UX/CGN UB8 131 N1
CDW/CHF RM16 167 J3
EBAR EN4 77 N9
ENC/FH EN2 79 L5
EPP CM16 66 B2
FBAR/BDGN N11 98 E7
FSBYPK N4 119 H5
FSTGT E7 141 M2
NTGHL W11 8 B5
NTHLT UB5 134 B1
RYLN/HDSTN HA2 113 P3
SNWD SE25 203 N2
STAL AL1 38 E4
STHL UB1 133 M9
UED N18 99 N6
WALTH E17 100 C10
WAN E11 121 K7
WIM/MER SW19 178 G8
WLSDN NW10 116 C10
Lancaster Stables HAMP NW3 3 P2
Lancaster St STHWK SE1 18 C2
Lancaster Ter BAY/PAD W2 9 L7
Lancaster Wk HYS/HAR UB3 132 D8
Lancaster Wy ABLGY WD5 54 G7
WPK KT4 200 F7
Lancaster West NTGHL W11 8 A7
Lancastrian Rd WLGTN SM6 222 F4
Lancefield St NKENS W10 2 C10
Lancell St STNW/STAM N16 119 M7
Lancelot Av ALP/SUD HA0 115 J9
Lancelot Cl CRAWW RH11 283 H7
SL SL1 148 F1
Lancelot Crs ALP/SUD HA0 115 J9
Lancelot Gdns EBAR EN4 98 B1
Lancelot Pde ALP/SUD HA0 * 115 K10
Lancelot Pl SKENS SW7 16 A3
Lancelot Rd ALP/SUD HA0 115 J9
BARK/HLT IG6 103 H7
WELL DA16 163 K10
Lance Rd HRW HA1 114 B5
Lancer Sq KENS W8 14 G1
Lancey Cl CHARL SE7 162 A3
Lanchester Rd HGT N6 118 A3
Lancing Cl CRAWW RH11 283 K6
Lancing Gdns ED N9 99 N2
Lancing Rd CROY/NA CR0 202 G6
FELT TW13 174 G5
GNTH/NBYPK IG2 122 G4
HARH RM3 105 M8
ORP BR6 207 L9
WEA W13 134 G9
Lancing St CAMTN NW1 5 J10
Lancing Wy RKW/CH/CXG WD3 72 C9
Lancresse Cl UX/CGN UB8 131 N1
Landale Gdns DART DA1 187 K4
Landau Ter HAYES BR2 226 B1
Landau Wy BROX EN10 62 E2
ERITH DA8 165 L4
Landcroft Rd EDUL SE22 181 N2
Landells Rd EDUL SE22 181 N2
Landen Pk HORL RH6 279 P2
Lander Rd GRAYS RM17 168 A4
Landford Cl RKW/CH/CXG WD3 91 P3
Landford Rd PUT/ROE SW15 156 F9
Landgrove Rd WIM/MER SW19 179 K8
Landleys Flds HOLWY N7 * 118 E10
Landmann Wy NWCR SE14 160 C5
Landmead Rd CHES/WCR EN8 62 D5
Landon Pl KTBR SW1X 16 A3
Landons Cl POP/IOD E14 141 H10
Landon Wy ASHF TW15 * 174 C9
Landor Rd BRXN/ST SW9 158 F9
Landor Wk SHB W12 156 D1
Landra Gdns WCHMH N21 79 J10
Landridge Dr EN EN1 80 A4
Landridge Rd FUL/PGN SW6 157 H8
Landrock Rd CEND/HSY/T N8 118 F4
Landscape Rd WARL CR6 242 A5
WFD IG8 101 N8
Landseer Av GVW DA11 190 A6
MNPK E12 122 D10
Landseer Cl EDGW HA8 95 M10
EMPK RM11 125 J6
WIM/MER SW19 201 M1
Landseer Rd ARCH N19 118 F8
EN EN1 79 P9
NWMAL KT3 200 A7
SUT SM1 221 K3
Lands' End BORE WD6 75 J10
Landstead Rd WOOL/PLUM SE18 162 G6
Landview Gdns CHONG CM5 67 N6
Landway BGR/WK TN15 247 N6
The Landway BGR/WK TN15 247 P3
STMC/STPC BR5 207 M3
Lane Ap MLHL NW7 97 H6
Lane Av SWCM DA10 189 H2
Lane Cl ADL/WDHM KT15 215 K2
CRICK NW2 116 E8
Lane End BERK HP4 33 L5
BXLYHN DA7 164 C9
EPSOM KT18 219 N10
HAT AL10 40 C7
HLWE CM17 47 P2
Lane End Dr WOKN/KNAP GU21 231 H3
Lanefield Wk WGCW AL8 22 F5
Lane Gdns BUSH WD23 94 D2
ESH/CLAY KT10 218 E4
Lane Ms MNPK E12 122 C8
Lanercost Gdns STHGT/OAK N14 78 F10
Lanercost Rd BRXS/STRHM SW2 181 H5
CRAWW RH11 283 M9
Lanes Av GVW DA11 190 D6
Laneside CHST BR7 184 E8
EDGW HA8 95 P6
Laneside Av BCTR RM8 124 A5
The Lane BKHTH/KID SE3 161 M9
CHERT KT16 195 K3
STJWD NW8 3 J8
VW GU25 194 B3
Laneway PUT/ROE SW15 178 E1
Lane Wood Cl AMSS HP7 69 L5
Lanfranc Rd BOW E3 140 D4
Lanfrey Pl WKENS W14 14 C8
Langafel Cl HART DA3 211 K3
Langaller La LHD/OX KT22 236 A7
Langbourne Av HGT N6 118 B7
Langbourne Wy ESH/CLAY KT10 218 F3
Langbrook Rd BKHTH/KID SE3 162 A9
Lang Cl LHD/OX KT22 236 A9
Langcroft Cl CAR SM5 202 A10
Langdale Av HARP AL5 20 C1
MTCM CR4 202 A3
Langdale Cl BCTR RM8 123 M6
MORT/ESHN SW14 155 N10
ORP BR6 206 E10
WALW SE17 18 E9
WOKN/KNAP GU21 231 P2
Langdale Ct HHNE HP2 35 P3
Langdale Crs BXLYHN DA7 164 B7
Langdale Dr YEAD UB4 132 F4
Langdale Gdns HCH RM12 125 H10
PEND EN3 80 C1
Langdale Pde MTCM CR4 * 202 A2
Langdale Rd CRAWW RH11 282 G9
GNWCH SE10 161 H6
THHTH CR7 203 H4
Langdale St WCHPL E1 * 140 A8
Langdale Ter BORE WD6 * 76 A7
Langdon Ct WLSDN NW10 136 B3
Langdon Crs EHAM E6 142 D4
Langdon Dr CDALE/KGS NW9 115 P6
Langdon House
WOOL/PLUM SE18 * 162 B6
Langdon Pk TEDD TW11 177 H10
Langdon Park Rd HGT N6 118 C5
Langdon Pl MORT/ESHN SW14 155 P9
Langdon Rd EHAM E6 142 D3
HAYES BR2 205 N3
MRDN SM4 201 M5
Langdon Shaw SCUP DA14 185 J8
Langdon Wk MRDN SM4 201 M5
Langdon Wy STHWK SE1 19 P6
Langfield Cl WAB EN9 45 K8
Langford Cl HACK E8 119 P10
SEVS/STOTM N15 119 M4
STALE/WH AL4 39 H4
STJWD NW8 3 K7
Langford Crs EBAR EN4 78 A8
Langford Gn CMBW SE5 159 M9
RBRW/HUT CM13 87 P10
Langford Pl SCUP DA14 185 K6
STJWD NW8 3 K8
Langford Rd EBAR EN4 78 A8
FUL/PGN SW6 157 L8
WFD IG8 101 P7
Langfords BKHH IG9 102 A3
Langham Cl STALE/WH AL4 39 H1
Langham Ct EMPK RM11 125 L5
RSLP HA4 * 113 J10
Langham Dene PUR/KEN CR8 241 J1
Langham Dr GDMY/SEVK IG3 123 L4
Langham Gdns ALP/SUD HA0 115 H7
EDGW HA8 95 P8
RCHPK/HAM TW10 177 H7
WCHMH N21 79 H9
WEA W13 134 G9
Langham House Cl
RCHPK/HAM TW10 177 J7
Langham Pde
SEVS/STOTM N15 * 119 J1
Langham Park Pl HAYES BR2 205 L4
Langham Pl CHSWK W4 156 B5
EGH TW20 172 C8
REGST W1B 10 F5
SEVS/STOTM N15 119 J1
Langham Rd EDGW HA8 95 P7
RYNPK SW20 200 F1
SEVS/STOTM N15 119 K2
TEDD TW11 176 G8
Langham St GTPST W1W 10 G4
Langhedge Cl UED N18 99 N7
Langhedge La UED N18 99 N7
Langholm Cl BAL SW12 180 E3
Langholme BUSH WD23 94 B2
Langhorn Dr WHTN TW2 176 D3
Langhorne Rd DAGE RM10 144 B2
Langhurst La CRAWW RH11 282 D5
Langland Ct NTHWD HA6 92 D8
Langland Crs STAN HA7 95 J10
Langland Dr PIN HA5 93 M8
Langland Gdns CROY/NA CR0 204 E9
HAMP NW3 117 L10
Langlands Dr RDART DA2 188 D8
Langlands Ri HOR/WEW KT19 219 P9
Langler Rd WLSDN NW10 136 F4
Langley CRAWW RH11 283 M3
Langley Av HHS/BOV HP3 35 P9
RSLP HA4 113 J7
SURB KT6 199 J8
WPK KT4 200 G9
Langley Broom DTCH/LGLY SL3 150 C4
Langleybury La KGLGY WD4 54 C10
Langley Cl EPSOM KT18 238 A5
GU GU1 249 P9
HARH RM3 105 L8
Langley Ct BECK BR3 * 204 G4
CHESW EN7 * 61 K4
COVGDN WC2E 11 L7
Langley Crs DAGW RM9 143 M2
EDGW HA8 95 P4
HYS/HAR UB3 152 G6
KGLGY WD4 54 B6
STALW/RED AL3 38 B4
WAN E11 121 N5
Langley Dr ACT W3 155 N1
BRW CM14 106 F4
CRAWW RH11 283 M5
WAN E11 121 N5
Langley Gdns DAGW RM9 143 N2
STMC/STPC BR5 206 E6
Langley Gn WAB EN9 * 45 J8
Langley Gv NWMAL KT3 200 A2
STALE/WH AL4 21 H9
Langley Hl KGLGY WD4 54 A5
Langley Hill Cl KGLGY WD4 54 B5
Langley La ABLGY WD5 54 G7
CRAWW RH11 283 K5
EPSOM KT18 255 N1
VX/NE SW8 17 M9
Langley Lodge La KGLGY WD4 53 P7
Langley Oaks Av SAND/SEL CR2 223 P6
Langley Pde CRAWW RH11 283 M4
Langley Pk DTCH/LGLY SL3 * 130 D7
MLHL NW7 96 B7
Langley Park Rd BELMT SM2 221 N4
DTCH/LGLY SL3 130 D10
Langley Pl CRAWW RH11 283 M4
WPK KT4 200 G9
Langley Quay DTCH/LGLY SL3 * 150 D1
Langley Rd ABLGY WD5 54 F7
BECK BR3 204 C4
DTCH/LGLY SL3 149 P2
DTCH/LGLY SL3 150 C2
ISLW TW7 154 E8
KGLGY WD4 53 M6
SAND/SEL CR2 224 C5
STA TW18 173 J9
SURB KT6 199 K7
WAT WD17 72 G5
WELL DA16 163 M5
WIM/MER SW19 201 J1
Langley Rw BAR EN5 77 J5
Langley St LSQ/SEVD WC2H 11 L6
Langley Vale Rd EPSOM KT18 238 B4
Langley Wk CRAWW RH11 283 M4
Langley Wy WAT WD17 72 G5
WWKM BR4 205 J8
Langley Whf KGLGY WD4 * 54 B3
Langley Wd BECK BR3 * 205 K5
Langmans Wy
WOKN/KNAP GU21 231 K2
Langmead Dr BUSH WD23 94 C2
Langmead St WNWD SE27 181 J7
Langport Ct WOT/HER KT12 197 K8
Langridge Ms HPTN TW12 175 N9
Langroyd Rd TOOT SW17 180 A5
Langshott HORL RH6 280 E3
Langshott Cl ADL/WDHM KT15 215 H7
Langshott La HORL RH6 280 D3
Langside Av PUT/ROE SW15 156 D10
Langside Crs STHGT/OAK N14 98 E4
Langstone Cl CRAWE RH10 284 D10
Langstone Ley WGCE AL7 23 L6
Langston Hughes Cl
HNHL SE24 * 159 J10
Langston Rd LOU IG10 82 G8
Lang St WCHPL E1 140 B6
Langthorn Ct LOTH EC2R * 13 H5
Langthorne Crs GRAYS RM17 167 P3
Langthorne Rd WAN E11 121 J8
Langthorne St FUL/PGN SW6 156 G7
Langton Av EHAM E6 142 D5
EW KT17 220 C7
TRDG/WHET N20 97 M1
Langton Cl ADL/WDHM KT15 195 L10
FSBYW WC1X 5 P10
SL SL1 128 C10
WOKN/KNAP GU21 231 L3
Langton Gv NTHWD HA6 92 D6
Langton Ri EDUL SE22 182 A3
Langton Rd BRXN/ST SW9 159 J7
CRICK NW2 116 F8
E/WMO/HCT KT8 198 B5
HOD EN11 44 E3
KTN/HRWW/WS HA3 94 B8
Langton's Meadow SLN SL2 129 H1
Langton St WBPTN SW10 15 K10
Langton Vls TOTM N17 * 99 P9
Langton Wy BKHTH/KID SE3 161 M7
CDW/CHF RM16 168 F3
CROY/NA CR0 223 N1
EGH TW20 172 F9
Langtry Pl FUL/PGN SW6 14 F9
Langtry Rd KIL/WHAMP NW6 2 G6
NTHLT UB5 133 L4
Langtry Wk STJWD NW8 3 K4
Langwood Cha TEDD TW11 177 H9
Langwood Cl ASHTD KT21 237 M3
Langwood Gdns WAT WD17 73 H5
Langworth Cl RDART DA2 187 L6
Langworth Dr YEAD UB4 133 J8
Lanhill Rd MV/WKIL W9 8 E1
Lanier Rd LEW SE13 183 H2
Lanigan Dr HSLW TW3 176 A1
Lankaster Gdns EFNCH N2 97 N9
Lankers Dr RYLN/HDSTN HA2 113 N4
Lankton Cl BECK BR3 205 H1
Lannock Rd HYS/HAR UB3 132 G10
Lannoy Rd ELTH/MOT SE9 184 F4
Lanrick Copse BERK HP4 34 B4
Lanrick Rd POP/IOD E14 141 J8
Lanridge Rd ABYW SE2 163 N2
Lansbury Av BARK IG11 143 K2
CHDH RM6 123 P3
EBED/NFELT TW14 175 J2
UED N18 99 L6
Lansbury Cl WLSDN NW10 115 P10
Lansbury Crs DART DA1 187 P1
Lansbury Dr YEAD UB4 132 G5
Lansbury Gdns POP/IOD E14 * 141 J8
Lansbury Rd PEND EN3 80 C5
Lansbury Wy UED N18 99 M6
Lanscombe Wk VX/NE SW8 * 158 F6
Lansdell Rd MTCM CR4 202 B2
Lansdown GU GU1 250 D10
Lansdown Cl WOKN/KNAP GU21 231 L5
WOT/HER KT12 197 K8
Lansdowne Av BXLYHN DA7 163 M6
ORP BR6 206 E8
SL SL1 129 K10
Lansdowne Cl BRYLDS KT5 199 N9
TWK TW1 176 E4
Lansdowne Copse WPK KT4 * 200 D9
Lansdowne Ct BROX EN10 * 44 F6
SL SL1 129 K10
WPK KT4 200 D9
Lansdowne Crs NTGHL W11 8 B8
Lansdowne Dr HACK E8 7 P3
Lansdowne Gdns VX/NE SW8 158 F7
Lansdowne Gn VX/NE SW8 158 F6
Lansdowne Gv WLSDN NW10 116 B9
Lansdowne Hl WNWD SE27 181 J6
Lansdowne La CHARL SE7 162 A4
Lansdowne Ms CHARL SE7 162 A4
NTGHL W11 8 C10
Lansdowne Pl NRWD SE19 181 N10
STHWK SE1 19 H3
Lansdowne Ri NTGHL W11 8 B8
Lansdowne Rd BMLY BR1 183 M10
CHING E4 100 F3
CROY/NA CR0 203 L9
CSHM HP5 51 H5
FNCH N3 97 J8
GDMY/SEVK IG3 123 J6
HOR/WEW KT19 219 P4
HSLW TW3 154 A9
MUSWH N10 98 D10
NTGHL W11 8 C9
PUR/KEN CR8 223 H8
RYNPK SW20 178 F10
SEV TN13 247 L8
STA TW18 173 L10
STAN HA7 95 H7
SWFD E18 121 M1
TOTM N17 99 P9
UX/CGN UB8 132 C8
WALTH E17 120 F4
WAN E11 121 L7
Lansdowne Sq GVW DA11 190 C2
Lansdowne Ter BMSBY WC1N 11 M2
Lansdowne Wk NTGHL W11 8 B9
Lansdowne Wy VX/NE SW8 158 F7
Lansdowne Wood Cl
WNWD SE27 181 J6
Lansdown Pl GVW DA11 190 C4
Lansdown Rd CFSP/GDCR SL9 90 A9
FSTGT E7 141 P2
SCUP DA14 185 L6
TIL RM18 168 D8
Lansfield Av UED N18 99 P5
Lantern Cl ALP/SUD HA0 115 J10
ORP BR6 226 E1
PUT/ROE SW15 156 D10
Lanterns LOU IG10 82 C5
Lanterns Ct POP/IOD E14 160 G2
Lantern Wy WDR/YW UB7 151 P1
Lanthorn Cl BROX EN10 44 D5
Lant St STHWK SE1 18 E1
Lanvanor Rd PECK SE15 160 B8
Lapford Cl MV/WKIL W9 8 D1
Lapis Cl GVE DA12 191 L4
La Plata Gv BRW CM14 106 G4
Lapse Wood Wk FSTH SE23 182 A4
Lapstone Gdns
KTN/HRWW/WS HA3 115 H4
Lapwing Cl ERITH DA8 * 165 J6
HHNE HP2 35 P3
SAND/SEL CR2 224 D6
Lapwing Gv RGUE GU4 250 G8
Lapwing Pl GSTN WD25 * 55 K8
Lapwings HART DA3 211 N3
Lapwing Ter FSTGT E7 122 A10
Lapwing Wy ABLGY WD5 55 H7
YEAD UB4 133 L8
Lapworth Cl ORP BR6 207 M9
Lapworth Ct BAY/PAD W2 9 H3
Lara Cl CHSGTN KT9 219 K4
LEW SE13 183 H2
Larbert Rd STRHM/NOR SW16 202 D1
Larby Pl EW KT17 220 B6
Larch Av ACT W3 136 B10
ASC SL5 192 D5
GU GU1 249 P7
LCOL/BKTW AL2 55 M6
Larch Cl BAL SW12 180 C5
CHESW EN7 61 M3
DEPT SE8 160 E5
FBAR/BDGN N11 98 B8
KWD/TDW/WH KT20 239 M7
REDH RH1 275 M2
SLN SL2 128 G7
WARL CR6 242 D5
Larch Crs HOR/WEW KT19 219 N3
YEAD UB4 133 K7
Larch Dene ORP BR6 206 D9
Larch Dr CHSWK W4 * 155 M4
Larches Av EN EN1 80 B1
MORT/ESHN SW14 156 A10
The Larches BERK HP4 33 J4
BUSH WD23 73 M9
HGDN/ICK UB10 132 C4
PLMGR N13 99 K4
STALE/WH AL4 39 J2
WOKN/KNAP GU21 232 B2
Larch Gv BFN/LL DA15 185 J4
Larchmoor Pk SLN SL2 109 M10
Larch Ri BERK HP4 33 M4
Larch Rd CRICK NW2 116 F9
DART DA1 187 L4
LEY E10 120 F7
Larch Tree Wy CROY/NA CR0 204 F10
Larch Wy HAYES BR2 206 D7
Larchwood Av CRW RM5 104 C7
Larchwood Cl BNSTD SM7 239 H2
CRW RM5 104 D7
Larchwood Dr EGH TW20 171 N9
Larchwood Gdns BRWN CM15 86 F10
Larchwood Rd ELTH/MOT SE9 184 E5
HHNE HP2 36 B4
WOKN/KNAP GU21 231 J6
Larcombe Cl CROY/NA CR0 223 N1
Larcom St WALW SE17 18 F6
Larden Rd ACT W3 156 B1
Largewood Av SURB KT6 199 M9
Larissa St WALW SE17 * 19 H6
Lark Av STA TW18 173 J6
Larkbere Rd SYD SE26 182 D7
Lark Cl BRW CM14 106 G5
Larken Cl BUSH WD23 94 B2
Larken Dr BUSH WD23 94 B2
Larkfield COB KT11 217 H9
Larkfield Av KTN/HRWW/WS HA3 114 G1
Larkfield Ct HORL RH6 281 H4
Larkfield Rd RCH/KEW TW9 155 K10
SCUP DA14 185 J6
SEV TN13 246 D9
Larkfields GVW DA11 190 B6
Larkhall Cl WOT/HER KT12 217 K3
Larkhall La CLAP SW4 158 F8
Larkhall Ri CLAP SW4 158 D9
Larkham Cl FELT TW13 174 F6
Larkhill Ter WOOL/PLUM SE18 * 162 D6
Larkin Cl COUL/CHIP CR5 240 G3
RBRW/HUT CM13 107 P1
Larkings La SLN SL2 129 N3
Larkins Rd HORL RH6 279 N8
Lark Ri CRAWW RH11 283 M5
EHSLY KT24 252 F7
HAT AL10 40 D6
Lark Rw BETH E2 140 B3
Larksfield EGH TW20 171 N10
Larks Fld HART DA3 211 L4
Larksfield HORL RH6 280 C3
Larksfield Gv EN EN1 80 A5
Larkshall Crs CHING E4 101 H5

Larkshall Rd CHING E4 101 J7
Larkspur Cl CDALE/KGS NW9 115 N3
HHW HP1 35 H5
ORP BR6 207 M9
RSLP HA4 112 C5
SOCK/AV RM15 147 H5
TOTM N17 99 L8
Larkspur Gv EDGW HA8 95 P5
Larkspur Wy HOR/WEW KT19 219 P2
RDKG RH5 273 J5
Larks Rdg LCOL/BKTW AL2 55 P2
Larks Ri CSHM HP5 51 J9
Larks Wy WOKN/KNAP GU21 231 H2
Larkswood HLWE CM17 47 M3
Larkswood Cl ERITH DA8 165 H7
Larkswood Ri PIN HA5 113 K2
STALE/WH AL4 39 H1
Larkswood Rd CHING E4 100 F5
Lark Wy CAR SM5 201 P7
Larkway Cl CDALE/KGS NW9 116 A2
Larkwell La HART DA3 211 L4
Larmans Rd PEND EN3 80 C2
Larnach Rd HMSMTH W6 156 G5
Larne Rd RSLP HA4 112 G5
Larner Rd ERITH DA8 164 F6
La Roche Cl DTCH/LGLY SL3 149 P2
Larpent Av PUT/ROE SW15 178 F1
Larsen Dr WAB EN9 63 J10
Larwood Cl GFD/PVL UB6 114 C10
Lascelles Av HRW HA1 114 C5
Lascelles Cl BRWN CM15 86 G9
WAN E11 121 J7
Lascelles Rd DTCH/LGLY SL3 149 N2
Lascott's Rd WDGN N22 98 G7
Lashmere CRAWE RH10 285 L2
Lassa Rd ELTH/MOT SE9 184 B1
Lassell St GNWCH SE10 161 J4
Lasseter Pl BKHTH/KID SE3 161 K5
Lasswade Rd CHERT KT16 195 J7
Latchett Rd SWFD E18 101 N9
Latchford Ms STALE/WH AL4 21 J2
Latchford Pl CHIG IG7 103 L5
Latchingdon Gdns WFD IG8 102 B7
Latchmere Cl RCHPK/HAM TW10 177 K8
Latchmere La KUTN/CMB KT2 177 L9
Latchmere Rd BTSEA SW11 158 A8
KUTN/CMB KT2 177 K9
Latchmere St BTSEA SW11 158 A8
Latchmoor Av CFSP/GDCR SL9 110 A2
Latchmoor Gv CFSP/GDCR SL9 110 A2
Latchmoor Wy CFSP/GDCR SL9 110 A2
Lateward Rd BTFD TW8 155 J5
Latham Cl BH/WHM TN16 243 P2
EHAM E6 142 B8
RDART DA2 188 D5
Latham Rd BXLYHS DA6 186 B1
TWK TW1 176 E3
Latham's Wy CROY/NA CR0 202 G9
Lathkill Cl EN EN1 99 P1
Lathom Rd EHAM E6 142 C2
Latimer Av EHAM E6 142 C3
Latimer Cl AMS HP6 69 P5
CRAWW RH11 283 N4
HHNE HP2 36 C1
PIN HA5 93 K9
WATW WD18 92 F1
WOKS/MYFD GU22 232 E2
WPK KT4 220 E1
Latimer Ct REDH RH1 276 A2
Latimer Dr HCH RM12 125 L8
Latimer Gdns PIN HA5 93 K9
WGCE AL7 23 L5
Latimer Pl NKENS W10 136 F8
Latimer Rd BAR EN5 77 L7
CROY/NA CR0 * 203 J10
CSHM HP5 51 K10
FSTGT E7 121 N9
NKENS W10 136 F7
RKW/CH/CXG WD3 70 C4
SEVS/STOTM N15 119 M4
TEDD TW11 176 E8
WIM/MER SW19 179 L9
Latimer Wy BEAC HP9 88 B5
Latium Cl STAL AL1 38 C7
Latona Dr GVE DA12 191 J8
Latona Rd PECK SE15 159 N10
La Tourne Gdns ORP BR6 206 F10
Lattimer Pl CHSWK W4 156 B6
Lattimore Rd STAL AL1 38 D7
STALE/WH AL4 21 H3
Latton Cl ESH/CLAY KT10 218 A1
WOT/HER KT12 197 N7
Latton Gn HLWS CM18 47 J5
Latton Hall Cl HLW CM20 29 K10
Latton House HLWS CM18 47 L4
Latton St HLW CM20 47 L1
HLWE CM17 47 L2
HLWE CM17 47 M4
Latymer Cl WEY KT13 216 D1
Latymer Gdns FNCH N3 * 97 H10
Latymer Rd ED N9 99 N3
Latymer Wy ED N9 99 L3
Laubin Cl TWK TW1 154 G10
Laud Dr CRAWE RH10 284 E8
Lauder Cl NTHLT UB5 133 L4
Lauderdale Dr
RCHPK/HAM TW10 177 J6
Lauderdale Pde MV/WKIL W9 * 2 G10
Lauderdale Pl BARB EC2Y * 12 F4
Lauderdale Rd KGLGY WD4 54 D9
MV/WKIL W9 3 H10
Laud St CROY/NA CR0 203 K10
LBTH SE11 17 N7
Laughton Rd NTHLT UB5 133 L4
Launcelot Rd BMLY BR1 183 M7
Launcelot St STHWK SE1 18 A2
Launceston RKW/CH/CXG WD3 70 E10
Launceston Cl HARH RM3 105 K9
Launceston Gdns GFD/PVL UB6 135 H3
Launceston Pl KENS W8 15 J3
Launceston Rd GFD/PVL UB6 135 H3
Launch St POP/IOD E14 161 H2
Launders Ga ACT W3 * 155 N1
Launder's La RAIN RM13 145 M7
Laundress La STNW/STAM N16 119 P8
Laundry La WAB EN9 63 L1
Laundry Rd GU GU1 267 P1
HMSMTH W6 14 A10
Laura Cl EN EN1 79 M9
WAN E11 121 P3
Lauradale Rd EFNCH N2 118 A2
Laura Dr SWLY BR8 187 H10
Laura Pl CLPT E5 120 B9
Laura Ter FSBYPK N4 * 119 J7
Laureate Wy HHW HP1 35 L4
Laurel Av DTCH/LGLY SL3 150 B1
EGH TW20 171 N8
GVE DA12 190 F5
POTB/CUF EN6 59 J8
TWK TW1 176 E4
Laurel Bank CHOB/PIR GU24 * 213 K7
HHS/BOV HP3 35 J9
NFNCH/WDSPK N12 * 97 M5
Laurel Bank Gdns FUL/PGN SW6 157 J8
Laurel Bank Rd ENC/FH EN2 79 K5
Laurel Cl BARK/HLT IG6 102 F7
BFN/LL DA15 185 K6
CRAWE RH10 284 B10
DART DA1 187 K4
DTCH/LGLY SL3 151 H6
HHNE HP2 36 A5
OXHEY WD19 93 L1
RBRW/HUT CM13 87 N9
TOOT SW17 179 P8
Laurel Ct AMS HP6 69 H2
IVER SL0 * 130 G2
RBRW/HUT CM13 * 87 P10
Laurel Crs CROY/NA CR0 204 F10
ROMW/RG RM7 124 F6
WOKN/KNAP GU21 214 F9
Laureldene RGUW GU3 248 A10
Laurel Dr OXTED RH8 261 L7
SOCK/AV RM15 147 J6
WCHMH N21 99 H1
Laurel Flds POTB/CUF EN6 59 J7
Laurel Gdns CHING E4 100 G1
HNWL W7 134 D10
HSLWW TW4 153 M10
MLHL NW7 96 A4
Laurel Gv PGE/AN SE20 182 B10
SYD SE26 182 C8
Laurel La WDR/YW UB7 151 P3
Laurel Pk KTN/HRWW/WS HA3 94 E8
Laurel Rd BARN SW13 156 D8
CFSP/GDCR SL9 90 A9
HPTN TW12 176 C8
RYNPK SW20 200 E1
STAL AL1 38 E6
Laurels Cl STALW/RED AL3 38 A9
Laurels Rd IVER SL0 130 G4
The Laurels BERK HP4 34 F3
BNSTD SM7 239 J3
BORE WD6 * 75 M5
BRXN/ST SW9 * 159 J6
BUSH WD23 * 94 D3
CHESW EN7 61 M3
COB KT11 235 M1
CRAWE RH10 * 284 B4
HART DA3 211 P3
RDART DA2 * 187 K6
Laurel St HACK E8 7 M2
Laurel Vw NFNCH/WDSPK N12 97 L4
Laurel Vls HNWL W7 * 154 D1
Laurel Wy SWFD E18 121 L2
TRDG/WHET N20 97 K4
Laurence Ms SHB W12 156 D1
Laurence Pountney Hl
CANST EC4R 12 G7
Laurence Pountney La
CANST EC4R 12 G7
Laurie Gv NWCR SE14 160 D7
Laurie Rd HNWL W7 134 D7
Laurier Rd CROY/NA CR0 203 N7
KTTN NW5 118 C8
Lauries Cl HHW HP1 34 E8
Laurimel Cl STAN HA7 94 G7
Laurino Pl BUSH WD23 94 B3
Lauriston Cl WOKN/KNAP GU21 231 J3
Lauriston Rd HOM E9 140 C3
WIM/MER SW19 178 G9
Lausanne Rd CEND/HSY/T N8 119 H2
PECK SE15 160 B8
Lauser Rd STWL/WRAY TW19 173 M3
Laustan Cl GU GU1 250 F10
Lavant Cl CRAWW RH11 283 J8
Lavender Av BRWN CM15 86 G9
CDALE/KGS NW9 115 P6
MTCM CR4 201 P1
WPK KT4 200 F10
Lavender Cl CAR SM5 220 D1
CHEL SW3 15 M10
CHESW EN7 61 N3
COUL/CHIP CR5 * 240 D5
CTHM CR3 259 K1
HARH RM3 105 L8
HAT AL10 40 C1
HAYES BR2 206 B6
HLW CM20 29 H10
LHD/OX KT22 237 H8
REDH RH1 276 C5
SOCK/AV RM15 147 K5
Lavender Cottages
LHD/OX KT22 * 237 H8
Lavender Ct E/WMO/HCT KT8 198 A3
Lavender Crs STALW/RED AL3 38 B4
Lavender Gdns BTSEA SW11 158 A10
ENC/FH EN2 79 J4
KTN/HRWW/WS HA3 94 D7
Lavender Ga LHD/OX KT22 218 A10
Lavender Gv HACK E8 7 N4
MTCM CR4 201 P1
Lavender Hl BTSEA SW11 158 A9
ENC/FH EN2 79 J5
SWLY BR8 208 E3
Lavender Park Rd
BF/WBF KT14 * 215 K9
Lavender Pl IL IG1 122 E10
Lavender Ri WDR/YW UB7 152 B1
Lavender Rd BERM/RHTH SE16 140 D10
BTSEA SW11 157 N9
CROY/NA CR0 202 G6
ENC/FH EN2 79 L5
HOR/WEW KT19 219 N3
SUT SM1 221 M3
UX/CGN UB8 132 A7
WLGTN SM6 222 B2
WOKS/MYFD GU22 232 E2
Lavender St SRTFD E15 141 K2
Lavender Sweep BTSEA SW11 158 A10
Lavender Ter BTSEA SW11 * 157 P9
Lavender V WLGTN SM6 222 E3
Lavender Wk BTSEA SW11 158 A10
HHNE HP2 35 N4
Lavender Wy CROY/NA CR0 204 C6
Lavengro Rd WNWD SE27 181 K5
Lavenham Rd WAND/EARL SW18 179 J5
Lavernock Rd BXLYHN DA7 164 B8
Lavers Rd STNW/STAM N16 119 M8
Laverstoke Gdns PUT/ROE SW15 178 C3
Laverton Ms ECT SW5 * 15 H6
Laverton Pl ECT SW5 15 H6
Lavidge Rd ELTH/MOT SE9 184 B5
Lavina Gv IS N1 5 N7
Lavington Cl CRAWW RH11 283 K6
HOM E9 140 E1
Lavington Rd CROY/NA CR0 202 G10
WEA W13 134 G10
Lavington St STHWK SE1 12 D10
Lavinia Av GSTN WD25 55 K10
Lavinia Rd DART DA1 187 N2
Lavrock La RKW/CH/CXG WD3 92 A1
Lawbrook La SHGR GU5 270 D9
Lawdon Gdns CROY/NA CR0 223 J1
Lawford Av RKW/CH/CXG WD3 70 F10
Lawford Cl HCH RM12 125 K9
RKW/CH/CXG WD3 70 F10
Lawford Gdns DART DA1 187 K1
PUR/KEN CR8 241 K2
Lawford Rd CHSWK W4 155 P6
IS N1 7 J4
KTTN NW5 4 G2
Lawford's Hill Rd RGUW GU3 231 H10
Lawkland SLN SL2 129 H5
Lawless St POP/IOD E14 * 140 G9
Lawley Rd STHGT/OAK N14 98 C1
Lawley St CLPT E5 120 B9
Lawn Av WDR/YW UB7 151 M1
Lawn Cl BMLY BR1 183 N10
DTCH/LGLY SL3 149 P6
EN EN1 99 N1
NWMAL KT3 200 B2
RSLP HA4 112 G8
SWLY BR8 208 D2
Lawn Crs RCH/KEW TW9 155 M8
Lawn Farm Gv CHDH RM6 123 P2
Lawn Gdns HNWL W7 134 D10
Lawn House Cl POP/IOD E14 161 H1
Lawn La HHS/BOV HP3 35 N9
VX/NE SW8 17 M9
Lawn Pk SEV TN13 265 J3
Lawn Rd BECK BR3 182 F10
GUW GU2 267 P3
GVW DA11 189 P2
HAMP NW3 118 A10
UX/CGN UB8 131 M2
Lawns Ct WBLY HA9 * 115 M7
Lawns Crs GRAYS RM17 168 A5
The Lawns Dr BROX EN10 44 E8
Lawnsmead SHGR GU5 268 E10
Lawns Pl GRAYS RM17 * 168 A5
The Lawns BELMT SM2 221 H4
BKHTH/KID SE3 * 161 L9
BRW CM14 * 107 K6
CHING E4 100 F6
DTCH/LGLY SL3 * 151 H7
HHW HP1 35 H5
NRWD SE19 203 L1
PIN HA5 94 A8
RAD WD7 57 K9
SCUP DA14 185 L7
STALW/RED AL3 38 B5
WGCW AL8 22 G2
Lawns Wy CRW RM5 104 D8
Lawnswood BAR EN5 * 77 H9
Lawn Ter BKHTH/KID SE3 161 L9
The Lawn DTCH/LGLY SL3 * 149 P7
NWDGN UB2 153 P4
Lawn V PIN HA5 93 M10
Lawrance Gdns CHES/WCR EN8 62 C4
Lawrance Rd STALW/RED AL3 38 B2
Lawrance Sq GVW DA11 * 190 C6
Lawrence Av MLHL NW7 96 B5
MNPK E12 122 D9
NWMAL KT3 200 B7
PLMGR N13 99 J5
WALTH E17 100 D9
WARE SG12 27 H8
WLSDN NW10 136 A3
Lawrence Buildings
STNW/STAM N16 119 N8
Lawrence Campe Cl
TRDG/WHET N20 97 N4
Lawrence Cl HERT/WAT SG14 24 F4
RGUE GU4 250 E5
SEVS/STOTM N15 119 M2
SHB W12 136 E9
Lawrence Ct MLHL NW7 96 B6
OXHEY WD19 * 93 L4
Lawrence Crs BFOR GU20 212 C3
DAGE RM10 124 C8
EDGW HA8 95 M10
Lawrence Dr HGDN/ICK UB10 112 D9
Lawrence Gdns MLHL NW7 96 C4
TIL RM18 168 E6
Lawrence Hl CHING E4 100 F3
Lawrence Hill Gdns DART DA1 187 K2
Lawrence Hill Rd DART DA1 187 K2
Lawrence La BRKHM/BTCW RH3 256 E8
CITYW EC2V 12 F6
Lawrence Moorings SBW CM21 30 A2
Lawrence Pde ISLW TW7 * 154 G9
Lawrence Pl IS N1 5 M5
Lawrence Rd EA W5 155 H3
ERITH DA8 164 C6
GPK RM2 125 J3
HPTN TW12 175 N10
HSLWW TW4 153 K10
PIN HA5 113 L3
PLSTW E13 141 N3
RCHPK/HAM TW10 177 H7
SEVS/STOTM N15 119 M2
SNWD SE25 203 N4
UED N18 100 A5
WWKM BR4 225 H4
YEAD UB4 132 D4
Lawrence St CAN/RD E16 141 L7
CHEL SW3 15 N10
MLHL NW7 96 C5
Lawrence Wy SL SL1 128 B7
WLSDN NW10 115 P8
Lawrence Yd SEVS/STOTM N15 119 M2
Lawrie Park Av SYD SE26 182 A8
Lawrie Park Crs SYD SE26 182 B8
Lawrie Park Gdns SYD SE26 182 A8
Lawrie Park Rd SYD SE26 182 B9
Laws Cl CRAWW RH11 283 H8
SNWD SE25 203 L4
Lawson Cl CAN/RD E16 141 P8
IL IG1 122 G10
WIM/MER SW19 178 G6
Lawson Gdns DART DA1 187 L1
PIN HA5 113 J1
Lawson Rd DART DA1 165 L10
PEND EN3 80 B5
STHL UB1 133 N6
Lawson Ter SHGR GU5 * 268 E10
Lawson Wk CAR SM5 222 A6
Lawson Wy ASC SL5 192 G6
Law St STHWK SE1 19 H3
Lawton Rd BOW E3 140 D5
EBAR EN4 77 N7
LEY E10 121 H6
LOU IG10 82 E7
Laxcon Cl WLSDN NW10 116 A10
Laxey Rd ORP BR6 227 J5
Laxley Cl CMBW SE5 159 J6
Laxton Gdns REDH RH1 258 E4
Laxton Pl CAMTN NW1 10 F1
Layard Rd BERM/RHTH SE16 160 A3
EN EN1 79 N5
THHTH CR7 203 L2
Layard Sq BERM/RHTH SE16 160 A3
Layborne Av HARH RM3 105 K3
Lay Brook STALE/WH AL4 38 F2
Layburn Crs DTCH/LGLY SL3 150 E5
Laycock St IS N1 6 B2
Layer Gdns ACT W3 135 M9
Layfield Cl HDN NW4 116 E5
Layfield Crs HDN NW4 116 E5
Layfield Rd HDN NW4 116 E5
Layhams Rd WWKM BR4 225 K1
Layhill HHNE HP2 35 N4
Laymarsh Cl BELV DA17 164 A2
Laymead Cl NTHLT UB5 133 M1
Laystall St FSBYW WC1X 12 A2
Layter's Av CFSP/GDCR SL9 89 P10
Layter's Av South
CFSP/GDCR SL9 89 P10
Layter's Cl CFSP/GDCR SL9 89 P10
Layter's End CFSP/GDCR SL9 89 P10
Layter's Green La
CFSP/GDCR SL9 89 N10
Layters Wy CFSP/GDCR SL9 110 A3
Layton Ct WEY KT13 216 C1
Layton Crs CROY/NA CR0 223 H2
Layton Pl RCH/KEW TW9 155 M7
Layton Rd BTFD TW8 155 J4
HSLW TW3 154 A10
Layton's La SUN TW16 196 G2
Layzell Wk ELTH/MOT SE9 184 A4
Lazell Gdns BRKHM/BTCW RH3 273 P6
Lazenby Ct COVGDN WC2E * 11 L7
Leabank Cl HRW HA1 114 D8
Leabank Sq HOM E9 140 F1
Leabank Vw SEVS/STOTM N15 119 P4
Leabourne Rd STNW/STAM N16 119 P4
Lea Bridge Rd LEY E10 120 C7
WALTH E17 121 H3
Lea Bushes GSTN WD25 73 M1
Leachcroft CFSP/GDCR SL9 89 N9
Leach Gv LHD/OX KT22 237 H8
Lea Cl BUSH WD23 74 A9
CRAWW RH11 283 J8
WHTN TW2 175 N3
Lea Cottages MTCM CR4 * 202 B2
Lea Crs RSLP HA4 112 G9
Leacroft ASC SL5 192 F5
STA TW18 173 L8
Leacroft Av BAL SW12 180 A3
Leacroft Cl PUR/KEN CR8 241 K2
STA TW18 173 L7
WCHMH N21 99 J3
WDR/YW UB7 131 P9
Leacroft Rd IVER SL0 130 G9
Leadale Av CHING E4 100 F3
Leadale Rd STNW/STAM N16 119 P4
Leadbeaters Cl FBAR/BDGN N11 98 A6
Leadenhall Pl BANK EC3V 13 J6
Leadenhall St BANK EC3V 13 J6
Leader Av MNPK E12 122 D10
The Leadings WBLY HA9 115 P8
Leaf Cl NTHWD HA6 92 E8
THDIT KT7 198 D5
Leaf Gv WNWD SE27 181 H8
Leafield Cl STRHM/NOR SW16 181 J9
WOKN/KNAP GU21 231 N4
Leafield La SCUP DA14 186 A7
Leafield Rd RYNPK SW20 201 J3
SUT SM1 201 K9
Leaford Crs WATN WD24 72 G3
Leaforis Rd CHESW EN7 61 P4
Leafy Gv HAYES BR2 225 P2
Leafy Oak Rd LEE/GVPK SE12 183 P7
Leafy Wy CROY/NA CR0 203 N9
Lea Gdns WBLY HA9 115 L10
Leagrave St CLPT E5 120 B8
Lea Gn BRKMPK AL9 * 41 H1
Lea Hall Gdns LEY E10 * 120 F6
Lea Hall Rd LEY E10 120 F6
Leahoe Gdns HERT/BAY SG13 25 K6
Leaholme Gdns SL SL1 128 B7
Leaholme Waye RSLP HA4 112 C4
Leahurst Rd LEW SE13 * 183 K2
Leake St STHWK SE1 17 P1
Lealand Rd SEVS/STOTM N15 119 N4
Leaming Cl MNPK E12 122 B10
Leamington Av BMLY BR1 183 P8
MRDN SM4 201 J4
ORP BR6 227 H1
WALTH E17 120 F3
Leamington Cl BMLY BR1 183 P7
HARH RM3 105 N7
HSLW TW3 176 B1
Leamington Crs
RYLN/HDSTN HA2 113 M8
Leamington Gdns
GDMY/SEVK IG3 123 J7
Leamington Pk ACT W3 136 A7
Leamington Pl YEAD UB4 132 G6
Leamington Rd HARH RM3 105 P6
NWDGN UB2 153 L3
Leamington Road Vls NTGHL W11 8 D4
Leamore St HMSMTH W6 156 E3
Lea Mt CHESW EN7 61 M4
Leamouth Rd EHAM E6 142 B8
POP/IOD E14 141 J8
Leander Dr GVE DA12 191 J7
Leander Gdns GSTN WD25 * 73 M3
Leander Rd BRXS/STRHM SW2 180 G2
NTHLT UB5 133 P4
THHTH CR7 202 G4
Leapale La GU GU1 268 A1
Leapale Rd GU GU1 268 A1
Learner Dr RYLN/HDSTN HA2 113 P7
Lea Rd BECK BR3 204 F2
CDW/CHF RM16 168 D4
ENC/FH EN2 79 L5
HOD EN11 45 H1
NWDGN UB2 153 M3
SEV TN13 265 K3
WAB EN9 62 F10
WATN WD24 * 73 J4
Learoyd Gdns EHAM E6 142 D9
Leas Cl CHSGTN KT9 219 L4
Leas Dl ELTH/MOT SE9 184 D6
Leas Dr IVER SL0 131 H8
Leasey Bridge La HARP AL5 20 E2
Leasey Dell Dr STALE/WH AL4 20 F1
Leas Gn CHST BR7 185 J9
Leaside GT/LBKH KT23 235 P9
HHNE HP2 36 D7
Leaside Av MUSWH N10 118 B1
Leaside Ct HGDN/ICK UB10 132 C5
Leaside Rd CLPT E5 120 B6
Leas La WARL CR6 242 C4
Leasowes Rd LEY E10 120 F6
Leas Rd GU GU1 267 P1
WARL CR6 242 C4
The Leas BUSH WD23 73 N6
HHS/BOV HP3 36 B10
STA TW18 * 173 K7
UPMR RM14 126 C5
Leasway BRW CM14 107 J4
CDW/CHF RM16 147 P10
UPMR RM14 126 B8
Leathart Cl HCH RM12 145 J2
The Lea EGH TW20 172 E10
Leatherbottle Gn ERITHM DA18 164 A2
Leather Cl MTCM CR4 202 B2
Leatherdale St WCHPL E1 * 140 C5
Leather Gdns SRTFD E15 141 K3
Leatherhead By-Pass Rd
LHD/OX KT22 236 G6
Leatherhead Cl STNW/STAM N16 119 M6
Leatherhead Rd CHSGTN KT9 218 G10
GT/LBKH KT23 254 B2
LHD/OX KT22 218 C10
LHD/OX KT22 237 J7
Leather La CLKNW EC1R 12 A2
EMPK RM11 125 L6
SHGR GU5 270 D5
Leathermarket Ct STHWK SE1 19 J2
Leathermarket St STHWK SE1 19 J2
Leather Rd BERM/RHTH SE16 160 C3
Leathersellers Cl BAR EN5 * 77 K7
Leather St WAP E1W 140 C9
Leathsale Rd RYLN/HDSTN HA2 114 A8
Leathwaite Rd BTSEA SW11 158 A10
Leathwell Rd DEPT SE8 160 G8
Lea V DART DA1 164 E10
Lea Valley Rd CHING E4 80 E10
Lea Valley Wk BRKMPK AL9 22 F9
BRKMPK AL9 24 A10
BRKMPK AL9 41 H1
CLPT E5 120 A5
HERT/BAY SG13 25 N3
HOD EN11 45 J4
TOTM N17 100 A10
WAB EN9 62 F9
WARE SG12 26 F5
WGCW AL8 22 C5
Leaveland Cl BECK BR3 204 F4
Leaver Gdns GFD/PVL UB6 134 C4
Leavesden Rd STAN HA7 94 F7
WATN WD24 73 J4
WEY KT13 216 C2
Leaves Green Crs HAYES BR2 225 P7
Leaves Green Rd HAYES BR2 226 A6
Leaview WAB EN9 62 F9
Leaway CLPT E5 * 120 B6
Leazes Av CTHM CR3 241 H9
Lebanon Av FELT TW13 175 L8
Lebanon Cl WAT WD17 72 E2
Lebanon Dr COB KT11 217 P9
Lebanon Gdns BH/WHM TN16 244 A3
WAND/EARL SW18 179 K2
Lebanon Pk TWK TW1 176 G4
Lebanon Rd CROY/NA CR0 203 M8
WAND/EARL SW18 179 K1
Lebrun Sq BKHTH/KID SE3 161 N10
Lechford Rd HORL RH6 280 A6
Lechmere Ap WFD IG8 101 P10
Lechmere Av CHIG IG7 102 F5
Lechmere Rd CRICK NW2 136 E1
Leckford Rd WAND/EARL SW18 179 M5
Leckhampton Pl
BRXS/STRHM SW2 181 H3
Leckwith Av ABYW SE2 163 P5
Lecky St SKENS SW7 15 L7
Leconfield Av BARN SW13 156 C9
Leconfield Rd HBRY N5 119 L10
Le Corte Cl KGLGY WD4 54 A5
Lectern La STAL AL1 38 D10
Leda Av PEND EN3 80 C5
Leda Rd WOOL/PLUM SE18 162 C2
Ledborough Ga BEAC HP9 88 E8
Ledborough La BEAC HP9 88 F6
Ledborough Wd BEAC HP9 88 D7
Ledbury Ms North NTGHL W11 8 E7
Ledbury Ms West NTGHL W11 * 8 E7
Ledbury Rd CROY/NA CR0 223 L1
NTGHL W11 8 D5
REIG RH2 257 K10
Ledbury St PECK SE15 159 P6
Ledger Cl GU GU1 250 E8
Ledger Dr ADL/WDHM KT15 215 J3
Ledger's Rd SL SL1 149 J1
WARL CR6 242 F2
Ledrington Rd NRWD SE19 181 N9
Ledway Dr WBLY HA9 115 L5
Lee Acre DORK RH4 * 273 H5
Lee Av CHDH RM6 123 P4
Leechcroft Av BFN/LL DA15 185 J1
SWLY BR8 208 G3
Leechcroft Rd WLGTN SM6 202 B10
Leech La EPSOM KT18 255 P2
Lee Church St LEW SE13 161 K10
Lee Cl HERT/BAY SG13 25 K7
WALTH E17 100 C9
WARE SG12 27 H7
Lee Conservancy Rd HOM E9 120 E9
Leecroft Rd BAR EN5 77 H9
Leeds Cl ORP BR6 207 N9
Leeds Rd IL IG1 122 G6
SL SL1 129 K9
Leeds St UED N18 99 P6
Lee Farm Cl CSHM HP5 51 L6
Leefe Wy POTB/CUF EN6 60 E4
Lee Gardens Av EMPK RM11 125 P6
Leegate Cl WOKN/KNAP GU21 231 N3
Lee Gn STMC/STPC BR5 207 K5
Lee Gv CHIG IG7 102 E3
Lee High Rd LEW SE13 161 J10
Leeke St FSBYW WC1X 5 N9
Leeland Rd WEA W13 134 F10
Leeland Ter WEA W13 134 F10
Leeland Wy WLSDN NW10 116 B9
Leeming Rd BORE WD6 75 L5
Leemount Cl HDN NW4 * 116 G2
Lee Pk BKHTH/KID SE3 161 L10
Lee Park Wy UED N18 100 C6
Lee Rd BKHTH/KID SE3 161 L9
EN EN1 79 P10
GFD/PVL UB6 135 H3
MLHL NW7 96 G8
WIM/MER SW19 201 L1
Lees Av NTHWD HA6 92 G9
Leeside BAR EN5 77 H10
POTB/CUF EN6 59 N8
Leeside Crs GLDGN NW11 117 H4
Leeside Rd TOTM N17 100 B8
Leeson Gdns WDSR SL4 148 D3
Leeson Rd HNHL SE24 * 181 H1
Leesons Hl CHST BR7 207 H3
Leesons Wy STMC/STPC BR5 207 J2
Lees Pde HGDN/ICK UB10 * 132 C6
Lees Pl MYFR/PKLN W1K 10 C7
Lees Rd UX/CGN UB8 132 C6
The Lees CROY/NA CR0 204 E9
Lee St HACK E8 7 L5
HORL RH6 279 N4
Lee Ter BKHTH/KID SE3 161 K9
The Lee NTHWD HA6 92 G6
Lee Vw ENC/FH EN2 79 J5
Leeward Gdns WIM/MER SW19 179 J9
Leeway DEPT SE8 160 E4
The Leeways CHEAM SM3 * 221 H3
Leewood Cl LEE/GVPK SE12 * 183 L2
Leewood Pl SWLY BR8 208 E4
Leewood Wy EHSLY KT24 253 K3
Lefevre Wk BOW E3 140 E3
Leffern Rd SHB W12 156 D1
Lefroy Rd SHB W12 156 C1
Left Side STHGT/OAK N14 * 98 E2
Legard Rd HBRY N5 119 J8
Legatt Rd ELTH/MOT SE9 184 A1
Leggatt Rd SRTFD E15 141 H4
Leggatts Cl WATN WD24 72 G2
Leggatts Ri GSTN WD25 73 H2
Leggatts Wy WATN WD24 73 H2
Leggatts Wood Av WATN WD24 73 J2
Legge St LEW SE13 183 H1
Leggfield Ter HHW HP1 35 J6
Leghorn Rd WLSDN NW10 136 D4
WOOL/PLUM SE18 162 G4
Legion Cl IS N1 6 B3
Legion Ct MRDN SM4 201 K6
Legion Ter BOW E3 140 E3
Legion Wy NFNCH/WDSPK N12 97 P8
Legon Av ROMW/RG RM7 124 D6
Legra Av HOD EN11 44 F3
Legrace Av HSLWW TW4 153 L8
Leicester Av MTCM CR4 202 F4
Leicester Cl WPK KT4 220 F1
Leicester Gdns GDMY/SEVK IG3 123 H5
Leicester Pl LSQ/SEVD WC2H * 11 K7
Leicester Rd BAR EN5 77 L9
CROY/NA CR0 203 M7
EFNCH N2 117 P1
TIL RM18 168 C7
WAN E11 121 N3
WLSDN NW10 136 A2
Leicester Sq LSQ/SEVD WC2H 11 K8
Leicester St LSQ/SEVD WC2H 11 K7
Leigham Av STRHM/NOR SW16 180 F6
Leigham Cl STRHM/NOR SW16 181 H6
Leigham Court Rd
STRHM/NOR SW16 180 G6
Leigham Dr ISLW TW7 154 D6
Leigham Hall Pde
STRHM/NOR SW16 * 180 F6
Leigham V STRHM/NOR SW16 181 H6
Leigh Av REDBR IG4 122 A2
Leigh Cl ADL/WDHM KT15 215 J4
NWMAL KT3 200 A4
Leigh Common WGCE AL7 23 H7
Leigh Ct BORE WD6 * 76 A6
RYLN/HDSTN HA2 * 114 D6
Leigh Court Cl COB KT11 217 L10
Leigh Crs CROY/NA CR0 224 G4
Leigh Dr HARH RM3 105 L5
Leigh Gdns WLSDN NW10 136 F4
Leigh Hill Rd COB KT11 235 K1
Leigh Hunt Dr STHGT/OAK N14 98 E3
Leigh Jenkins Wy HORL RH6 280 B8
Leighlands CRAWE RH10 284 D5
Leigh Orchard Cl
STRHM/NOR SW16 180 G6
Leigh Pk DTCH/LGLY SL3 * 149 P6
Leigh Pl COB KT11 217 K10
FELT TW13 175 K4
RDART DA2 * 187 P8
WELL DA16 163 K8
Leigh Place La GDST RH9 260 D8
Leigh Place Rd REIG RH2 274 D6
Leigh Rd BRKHM/BTCW RH3 273 P6
COB KT11 217 J9
EHAM E6 142 D2
GVW DA11 190 E5
HBRY N5 119 J9
HSLW TW3 154 C10
LEY E10 121 H5
SL SL1 128 G9
Leigh Rodd OXHEY WD19 93 M4
Leigh Sq WDSR SL4 148 C8
Leigh St STPAN WC1H 5 L10
Leigh Ter STMC/STPC BR5 * 207 L3
The Leigh KUTN/CMB KT2 178 B9
Leighton Av MNPK E12 122 D10
PIN HA5 113 L1
Leighton Buzzard Rd HHW HP1 35 L1
Leighton Cl EDGW HA8 95 M10
Leighton Crs KTTN NW5 118 D10
Leighton Gdns SAND/SEL CR2 224 A9
TIL RM18 168 D6
WLSDN NW10 136 F4
Leighton Gv KTTN NW5 118 D10
Leighton Pl KTTN NW5 118 D10
Leighton Rd EN EN1 79 N9
KTN/HRWW/WS HA3 94 C10
KTTN NW5 118 D10
WEA W13 154 F1
Leighton St CROY/NA CR0 203 J8
Leighton Wy EPSOM KT18 220 A10
Leila Parnell Pl CHARL SE7 161 P5
Leinster Av MORT/ESHN SW14 155 P9
Leinster Gdns BAY/PAD W2 9 J6
Leinster Ms BAY/PAD W2 9 J8
Leinster Pl BAY/PAD W2 9 J6
Leinster Rd MUSWH N10 118 C2
Leinster Sq BAY/PAD W2 8 F7
Leinster Ter BAY/PAD W2 9 J8
Leiston Sp SL SL1 129 K8
Leisure La BF/WBF KT14 * 215 L8
Leisure Wy NFNCH/WDSPK N12 97 N8
Leith Cl CDALE/KGS NW9 116 A6
SL SL1 129 M10
Leithcote Gdns
STRHM/NOR SW16 180 G7
Leithcote Pth STRHM/NOR SW16 180 G6
Leith Hl STMC/STPC BR5 207 K1
Leith Hill Rd RDKG RH5 271 M10
Leith Park Rd GVE DA12 190 D4
Leith Rd EW KT17 220 B8
WDGN N22 99 J9
Leith Towers BELMT SM2 * 221 L4
Leith Vw RDKG RH5 273 H6
Leith Yd KIL/WHAMP NW6 * 2 F5
Lela Av HSLWW TW4 153 K8
Lelitia Cl HACK E8 7 N6
Leman St WCHPL E1 13 M6
Lemark Cl STAN HA7 95 H7
Le May Av LEE/GVPK SE12 183 N6
Le May Cl HORL RH6 280 B3
Lemmon Rd GNWCH SE10 161 K5
Lemna Rd WAN E11 121 K5
Lemonfield Dr GSTN WD25 55 M8
Lemon Field Dr GSTN WD25 55 M9
Lemonwell Dr ELTH/MOT SE9 184 E1
Lemsford Cl SEVS/STOTM N15 119 P4
Lemsford Ct BORE WD6 75 P8
Lemsford La WGCW AL8 22 E6
Lemsford Rd HAT AL10 40 D2
STAL AL1 38 E6
Lemsford Village WGCW AL8 22 D6
Lena Crs ED N9 100 B3
Lena Gdns HMSMTH W6 156 F2
Lena Kennedy Cl CHING E4 101 H7
Lendal Ter CLAP SW4 158 E9
Lenelby Rd SURB KT6 199 M8
Len Freeman Pl FUL/PGN SW6 14 C10
Lenham Rd BXLYHN DA7 164 A5
LEE/GVPK SE12 161 L10
SUT SM1 221 L1
THHTH CR7 203 L2
Lenmore Av GRAYS RM17 167 P2
Lennard Av WWKM BR4 205 K9
Lennard Cl WWKM BR4 205 K9
Lennard Rd CROY/NA CR0 203 K8
HAYES BR2 206 C8
SEV TN13 246 F6
SYD SE26 182 B9
Lennard Rw SOCK/AV RM15 146 C10
Lennard Ter PGE/AN SE20 * 182 C9
Lennon Rd CRICK NW2 116 F10
Lennox Av GVW DA11 190 D2
Lennox Cl CDW/CHF RM16 167 H3
ROM RM1 124 G4
Lennox Gdns CROY/NA CR0 223 J1
IL IG1 122 C6
KTBR SW1X 16 A5
WLSDN NW10 116 C9
Lennox Gardens Ms CHEL SW3 16 A4
Lennox Rd FSBYPK N4 118 G7
GVW DA11 190 C2
WALTH E17 120 E4
Lennox Rd East GVW DA11 190 D3
Lenor Cl BXLYHS DA6 163 P10
Lensbury Cl CHES/WCR EN8 62 D4
Lensbury Wy ABYW SE2 163 N2
Lens Rd FSTGT E7 141 P2
Lenten Cl SHGR GU5 270 E8
Lent Green La SL SL1 128 A6
Lenthall Av GRAYS RM17 167 M1
Lenthall Rd HACK E8 7 M3
LOU IG10 82 G8
Lenthorp Rd GNWCH SE10 161 L3
Lentmead Rd BMLY BR1 183 L6
Lenton Ri RCH/KEW TW9 155 K9
Lenton St WOOL/PLUM SE18 162 G3
Lenton Ter FSBYPK N4 * 119 H7
Lent Rise Rd MDHD SL6 128 A8
Leof Crs CAT SE6 182 G8
Leominster Rd MRDN SM4 201 M6
Leominster Wk MRDN SM4 201 M6
Leonard Av MRDN SM4 201 M5
ROMW/RG RM7 124 E6
RSEV TN14 247 J2
SWCM DA10 189 K3
Leonard Ct KENS W8 * 14 E3
Leonard Pl HAYES BR2 * 206 B10
STNW/STAM N16 119 M9
Leonard Rd CHING E4 100 F7
ED N9 99 N4
FSTGT E7 121 M9
NWDGN UB2 153 L3
STRHM/NOR SW16 202 D1
Leonardslee Ct CRAWE RH10 * 284 C10
Leonard St CAN/RD E16 142 B10
SDTCH EC2A 13 J1
Leonard Wy BRW CM14 106 E5
Leontine Cl PECK SE15 159 P6
Leopold Av WIM/MER SW19 179 J8
Leopold Ms HOM E9 140 B3
Leopold Rd CRAWW RH11 283 M7
EA W5 135 L10
EFNCH N2 117 N1
UED N18 100 A6
WALTH E17 120 F3
WIM/MER SW19 179 J7
WLSDN NW10 136 B2
Leopold St BOW E3 140 E7
Leo St PECK SE15 160 B6
Le Personne Rd CTHM CR3 241 L8
Leppoc Rd CLAP SW4 180 E1
Leret Wy LHD/OX KT22 236 F7
Leroy St STHWK SE1 19 J5
Lerry Cl WKENS W14 14 D9
Lerwick Dr SL SL1 129 K7
Lesbourne Rd REIG RH2 275 L1
Lescombe Cl CAT SE6 182 D6
Lescombe Rd FSTH SE23 182 D6
Lesley Cl BXLY DA5 186 C3
SWLY BR8 208 E3
Leslie Gdns BELMT SM2 221 K4
Leslie Gv CROY/NA CR0 203 L8
Leslie Grove Pl CROY/NA CR0 203 M8
Leslie Park Rd CROY/NA CR0 203 M8
Leslie Rd CAN/RD E16 141 N8
CHOB/PIR GU24 213 J6
DORK RH4 255 J10
EFNCH N2 117 N1
WAN E11 121 H8
Lesney Pk ERITH DA8 164 E5
Lesney Park Rd ERITH DA8 164 E5
Lessar Av CLAP SW4 180 D1
Lessingham Av TOOT SW17 180 A7
Lessing St FSTH SE23 182 D3
Lessington Av ROMW/RG RM7 124 E4
Lessness Av BXLYHN DA7 163 N6
Lessness Pk BELV DA17 164 A4
Lessness Rd MRDN SM4 201 M6
Lester Av CAN/RD E16 141 K6
Lestock Cl SNWD SE25 203 P3
Leston Cl RAIN RM13 145 J5
Leswin Pl STNW/STAM N16 119 N8
Leswin Rd STNW/STAM N16 119 N8
Letchfield CSHM HP5 51 N7
Letchford Gdns WLSDN NW10 136 D5
Letchford Ms WLSDN NW10 * 136 D5
Letchford Ter
KTN/HRWW/WS HA3 * 94 A9
Letchmore Rd RAD WD7 74 F2
Letchworth Av
EBED/NFELT TW14 174 G3
Letchworth Cl HAYES BR2 205 M5
OXHEY WD19 93 L6
Letchworth Dr HAYES BR2 205 M5
Letchworth St TOOT SW17 180 A7
Letter Box La SEV TN13 265 K5
Letterstone Rd FUL/PGN SW6 157 J6
Lettice St FUL/PGN SW6 157 J8
Lett Rd SRTFD E15 141 J2
Leucha Rd WALTH E17 120 D3
Levana Cl WIM/MER SW19 179 H4
Levehurst Wy CLAP SW4 158 F8
Leven Cl CHES/WCR EN8 * 62 C9
OXHEY WD19 * 93 L6
Levendale Rd FSTH SE23 182 D5
Leven Dr CHES/WCR EN8 62 C9
Leven Rd POP/IOD E14 141 H7
Leven Wy HHNE HP2 35 N2
HYS/HAR UB3 132 F8
Leveret Cl CROY/NA CR0 225 J7
GSTN WD25 55 H10
Leveret La CRAWW RH11 283 L5
Leverett St CHEL SW3 15 P5
Leverholme Gdns ELTH/MOT SE9 184 D7
Leverson St STRHM/NOR SW16 180 D9
Lever Sq CDW/CHF RM16 168 D3

Leverstock Green Rd HHNE HP2 36 C6
HHS/BOV HP3 36 E8
Lever St FSBYE EC1V 6 E10
Leverton Pl KTTN NW5 118 D10
Leverton St KTTN NW5 118 D10
Leverton Wy WAB EN9 63 H9
Leveson Rd CDW/CHF RM16 168 E2
Levett Gdns GDMY/SEVK IG3 123 J9
Levett Rd BARK IG11 143 H1
LHD/OX KT22 236 G6
Levine Gdns BARK IG11 143 N4
Levison Wy ARCH N19 118 E7
Levylsdene GU GU1 250 G10
Lewes Cl CRAWE RH10 284 D8
GRAYS RM17 167 M5
NTHLT UB5 133 P1
Lewes Ct SL SL1 149 H1
Lewesdon Cl WIM/MER SW19 178 G4
Lewes Rd BMLY BR1 206 A2
HARH RM3 105 L5
NFNCH/WDSPK N12 97 P6
Leweston Pl STNW/STAM N16 119 N5
Lewes Wy RKW/CH/CXG WD3 72 C8
Lewgars Av CDALE/KGS NW9 115 P4
Lewing Cl ORP BR6 207 H8
Lewin Rd BXLYHS DA6 163 P10
MORT/ESHN SW14 156 A9
STRHM/NOR SW16 180 E9
Lewins Rd CFSP/GDCR SL9 110 A1
EPSOM KT18 219 N10
Lewins Wy SL SL1 128 E9
Lewis Av WALTH E17 100 F9
Lewis Cl ADL/WDHM KT15 215 M1
BRWN CM15 107 L1
DEN/HRF UB9 91 M10
STHGT/OAK N14 98 D1
Lewis Crs WLSDN NW10 116 A10
Lewis Gdns EFNCH N2 97 N10
Lewis Gv LEW SE13 161 H10
Lewisham High St LEW SE13 182 C2
Lewisham Hl LEW SE13 161 H8
Lewisham Pk LEW SE13 182 C2
LEW SE13 183 H1
Lewisham Rd LEW SE13 161 H8
Lewisham Wy BROCKY SE4 160 E8
Lewis La CFSP/GDCR SL9 90 B9
Lewis Pl HACK E8 119 P10
Lewis Rd EMPK RM11 125 K4
MTCM CR4 201 P2
RCH/KEW TW9 * 177 J1
SCUP DA14 185 M6
STHL UB1 153 M1
SUT SM1 221 L1
SWCM DA10 189 K2
WELL DA16 163 M9
Lewis St CAMTN NW1 4 F3
Lewiston Cl WPK KT4 200 E7
Lewis Wy DAGE RM10 144 C1
Lexden Dr CHDH RM6 123 L4
Lexden Rd ACT W3 135 N9
MTCM CR4 202 E4
Lexden Ter WAB EN9 * 63 H10
Lexham Gdns AMS HP6 69 H3
KENS W8 14 F5
Lexham Ms KENS W8 14 F5
Lexington Cl BORE WD6 75 L7
Lexington Ct POTB/CUF EN6 58 G7
PUR/KEN CR8 223 K6
Lexington St SOHO/CST W1F 11 H6
Lexington Wy BAR EN5 76 G8
UPMR RM14 126 E4
Lexton Gdns BAL SW12 180 E4
Leyborne Av WEA W13 155 H1
Leyborne Pk RCH/KEW TW9 155 M7
Leybourne Av BF/WBF KT14 216 A9
Leybourne Cl BF/WBF KT14 216 A9
HAYES BR2 205 M5
Leybourne Rd CAMTN NW1 4 F4
CDALE/KGS NW9 115 M3
HGDN/ICK UB10 132 D3
WAN E11 121 L6
Leybourne St CAMTN NW1 4 E4
Leyburn Cl WALTH E17 121 H2
Leyburn Crs HARH RM3 105 M8
Leyburn Gdns CROY/NA CR0 203 M9
Leyburn Gv UED N18 99 P7
Leyburn House CHARL SE7 * 162 B6
Leyburn Rd HARH RM3 105 M8
UED N18 99 P7
Leycester Cl BFOR GU20 212 A1
Leycroft Gdns ERITH DA8 165 J7
Leycroft Wy HARP AL5 20 D4
Leydenhatch La SWLY BR8 208 E1
Leyden St WCHPL E1 13 L4
Leydon Cl BERM/RHTH SE16 140 C10
Leyes Rd CAN/RD E16 141 P9
Leyfield WPK KT4 200 B9
Leyhill Cl SWLY BR8 208 F5
Leyland Av PEND EN3 80 D6
STAL AL1 38 C8
Leyland Cl CHES/WCR EN8 62 B5
Leyland Gdns WFD IG8 101 P6
Leyland Rd LEE/GVPK SE12 183 L1
Leylands La STWL/WRAY TW19 151 J10
Leylang Rd NWCR SE14 160 C6
Leys Av DAGE RM10 144 D3
Leys Cl DAGE RM10 144 D2
DEN/HRF UB9 91 N9
HRW HA1 114 C3
Leysdown WGCE AL7 23 N5
Leysdown Av BXLYHN DA7 164 D10
Leysdown Rd ELTH/MOT SE9 184 B5
Leysfield Rd SHB W12 156 D1
Leys Gdns EBAR EN4 78 B9
Leyspring Rd WAN E11 121 L6
Leys Rd HHS/BOV HP3 36 A8
LHD/OX KT22 218 C8
Leys Rd East PEND EN3 80 D5
The Leys AMS HP6 68 G1
EFNCH N2 117 M2
KTN/HRWW/WS HA3 115 L4
RAD WD7 74 F5
STALE/WH AL4 39 J3
WOT/HER KT12 * 217 M1
Ley St IL IG1 122 E7
Leyswood Dr GNTH/NBYPK IG2 123 H3
Leythe Rd ACT W3 155 P1
Leyton Cross Rd RDART DA2 186 G6
Leyton Gra LEY E10 120 F7
Leyton Green Rd LEY E10 121 H4
Leyton Park Rd LEY E10 121 H7
Leyton Rd SRTFD E15 121 H10
WIM/MER SW19 179 M10
Leytonstone Rd SRTFD E15 121 K10
Ley Wk WGCE AL7 23 M5
Leywick St SRTFD E15 141 K4
Leywood Cl AMSS HP7 69 J6
Lezayre Rd ORP BR6 227 J3
Liardet St NWCR SE14 160 D5
Liberia Rd HBRY N5 6 D1
Liberty Av WIM/MER SW19 201 N1
Liberty Cl HERT/BAY SG13 25 K7
UED N18 99 N5
Liberty Hall Rd ADL/WDHM KT15 215 K2
Liberty La ADL/WDHM KT15 215 L2
Liberty Ms WDGN N22 * 99 J9
Liberty Ri ADL/WDHM KT15 215 K3
Liberty St BRXN/ST SW9 158 G7
Liberty Wk STAL AL1 * 38 G7
Libra Rd BOW E3 140 E4
PLSTW E13 141 M4
Library Ct SEVS/STOTM N15 119 N1
Library Pde WLSDN NW10 * 136 B3
Library St STHWK SE1 18 D2
Lichfield Cl EBAR EN4 78 A7
Lichfield Gdns RCH/KEW TW9 * 177 K1
Lichfield Gv FNCH N3 97 K9
Lichfield Pl STAL AL1 * 38 E5
Lichfield Rd BCTR RM8 123 L9
BOW E3 140 D5
CRICK NW2 117 H9
ED N9 99 P3
EHAM E6 142 A5
HSLWW TW4 153 K9
NTHWD HA6 113 H1
RCH/KEW TW9 155 L7
WFD IG8 101 K5
Lichfield Ter RCH/KEW TW9 * 177 K1
UPMR RM14 126 D7
Lichfield Wy BROX EN10 44 E8
SAND/SEL CR2 224 C6
Lidbury Rd MLHL NW7 97 H7
Lidcote Gdns BRXN/ST SW9 * 159 H8
Liddall Wy WDR/YW UB7 132 A10
Liddell WDSR SL4 148 B9
Liddell Cl KTN/HRWW/WS HA3 115 J1
Liddell Gdns WLSDN NW10 136 F4
Liddell Rd KIL/WHAMP NW6 2 E1
Lidding Rd KTN/HRWW/WS HA3 115 J3
Liddington Hall Dr RGUW GU3 249 K7
Liddington New Rd RGUW GU3 249 K7
Liddington Rd SRTFD E15 141 L3
Liddon Rd BMLY BR1 205 P3
PLSTW E13 141 M5
Liden Cl LEY E10 120 E5
Lidfield Rd STNW/STAM N16 119 L9
Lidgate Rd CMBW SE5 * 159 N6
Lidiard Rd WAND/EARL SW18 179 M5
Lidlington Pl CAMTN NW1 5 H8
Lido Rd GU GU1 250 A9
Lido Sq TOTM N17 99 L10
Lidsey Cl CRAWE RH10 284 D9
Lidstone Cl WOKN/KNAP GU21 231 N3
Lidyard Rd ARCH N19 118 D6
Lieutenant Ellis Wy CHESW EN7 61 N7
Liffler Rd WOOL/PLUM SE18 163 H4
Lifford St PUT/ROE SW15 156 G10
Lightcliffe Rd PLMGR N13 99 H5
Lighter Cl BERM/RHTH SE16 160 D3
Lighterman Ms WCHPL E1 140 C8
Lighterman's Ms GVW DA11 190 B3
Lighterman's Rd POP/IOD E14 160 F1
Lightermans Wy SWCM DA10 167 H10
Lightfoot Rd CEND/HSY/T N8 118 F3
Lightswood Cl CHESW EN7 61 L3
Lightwater Meadow LTWR GU18 212 A7
Lightwater Rd LTWR GU18 212 A7
Ligonier St BETH E2 13 L1
Lilac Av EN EN1 80 B2
WOKS/MYFD GU22 232 A7
Lilac Cl BRWN CM15 86 G9
CHESW EN7 62 A7
CHING E4 100 E7
GU GU1 249 P6
Lilac Gdns CROY/NA CR0 204 F10
EA W5 155 J2
HYS/HAR UB3 132 F8
ROMW/RG RM7 124 F6
SWLY BR8 208 E3
Lilac Pl LBTH SE11 17 N6
WDR/YW UB7 132 A9
Lilac Rd HOD EN11 44 G1
Lilac St SHB W12 136 D9
Lilac Wy HARP AL5 20 C5
Lilah Ms HAYES BR2 205 L2
Lila Pl SWLY BR8 208 F4
Lilbourne Dr HERT/BAY SG13 25 P4
Lilburne Gdns ELTH/MOT SE9 184 B1
Lilburne Rd ELTH/MOT SE9 184 B1
Lile Crs HNWL W7 134 D7
Lilestone St STJWD NW8 9 N1
Lilford Rd CMBW SE5 159 J8
Lilian Barker Cl LEE/GVPK SE12 183 M1
Lilian Board Wy GFD/PVL UB6 114 C10
Lilian Crs RBRW/HUT CM13 107 N3
Lilian Gdns WFD IG8 101 N9
Lilian Rd STRHM/NOR SW16 202 D1
Lillechurch Rd BCTR RM8 143 L1
Lilleshall Rd MRDN SM4 201 N5
Lilley Cl BRWN CM14 106 E5
WAP E1W 13 P10
Lilley Dr KWD/TDW/WH KT20 239 L8
Lilley La MLHL NW7 * 96 B6
Lilley Wy SL SL1 128 D10
Lillian Av ACT W3 155 M1
Lillian Rd BARN SW13 156 D5
Lilliard Cl HOD EN11 26 G9
Lillie Rd BH/WHM TN16 244 A4
FUL/PGN SW6 156 G4
Lillieshall Rd CLAP SW4 158 C9
Lillie Yd FUL/PGN SW6 14 E9
Lillington Gardens Est PIM SW1V 17 H6
Lilliott's La LHD/OX KT22 236 F5
Lilliput Av NTHLT UB5 133 M3
Lilliput Rd ROMW/RG RM7 124 E8
Lillyfee Farm La FLKWH/TG HP10 108 A4
Lilly La HHNE HP2 36 E2
Lily Cl WKENS W14 14 A6
WKENS W14 157 H3
Lily Dr WDR/YW UB7 151 N3
Lily Gdns ALP/SUD HA0 135 H4
Lily Pl FARR EC1M 12 B3
Lily Rd WALTH E17 120 F4
Lilyville Rd FUL/PGN SW6 157 J7
Limbourne Av BCTR RM8 124 A5
Limbrick Rd HARP AL5 20 A5
Limburg Rd BTSEA SW11 157 P10
Lime Av GVW DA11 190 A3
RBRW/HUT CM13 107 L4
UPMR RM14 125 P9
WDR/YW UB7 132 A9
WDSR SL4 149 L6
WDSR SL4 170 E6
Limeburner La STP EC4M 12 C5
Limebush Cl ADL/WDHM KT15 215 M5
Lime Cl BKHH IG9 102 A3
BMLY BR1 206 B4
CRAWE RH10 285 J2
CRAWW RH11 283 M4
KTN/HRWW/WS HA3 94 F10
OXHEY WD19 93 L1
PIN HA5 112 G1
REIG RH2 275 L3
RGUE GU4 251 L4
ROMW/RG RM7 124 D5
SOCK/AV RM15 147 H5
WAP E1W 13 P9
WARE SG12 26 D1
Lime Crs SUN TW16 197 K2
Limecroft Cl HOR/WEW KT19 220 A4
Limecroft Rd WOKN/KNAP GU21 230 G3
Limedene Cl PIN HA5 93 L9
Lime Gv ADL/WDHM KT15 215 K1
BARK/HLT IG6 103 J7
BFN/LL DA15 185 J2
BRWN CM15 87 H4
CHING E4 100 E7
GU GU1 249 N6
HYS/HAR UB3 132 E9
NWMAL KT3 200 A3
ORP BR6 206 E9
RGUE GU4 251 L4
RSLP HA4 113 J4
SHB W12 156 F1
TRDG/WHET N20 97 H2
TWK TW1 176 E2
WARL CR6 242 D4
WOKS/MYFD GU22 232 B7
Limeharbour POP/IOD E14 160 G2
Limehouse POP/IOD E14 * 140 F9
Limehouse Cswy POP/IOD E14 140 E9
Limehouse Link POP/IOD E14 140 D9
Limehouse Link (Tunnel)
POP/IOD E14 140 E9
Lime Kiln Dr CHARL SE7 161 N5
Limekiln Pl NRWD SE19 181 N10
Lime Meadow Av SAND/SEL CR2 223 P9
Lime Pit La SEV TN13 246 D3
Limerick Cl BAL SW12 180 D3
Limerick Gdns UPMR RM14 126 E5
Lime Rd SWLY BR8 208 E3
Limerston St WBPTN SW10 15 K9
Limes Av BARN SW13 156 C8
CAR SM5 202 A8
CHIG IG7 102 G7
CROY/NA CR0 202 G10
GLDGN NW11 117 H5
HORL RH6 280 C6
MLHL NW7 96 B7
NFNCH/WDSPK N12 97 M5
PGE/AN SE20 182 A10
WAN E11 121 N2
The Limes Av FBAR/BDGN N11 98 C6
Limes Cl ASHF TW15 174 B8
CAR SM5 202 A9
FBAR/BDGN N11 * 98 D6
Limes Ct HOD EN11 44 F3
Limesdale Gdns EDGW HA8 95 P10
Limes Field Rd
MORT/ESHN SW14 156 B9
Limesford Rd PECK SE15 160 C10
Limes Gdns WAND/EARL SW18 179 K2
Limes Gv LEW SE13 161 H10
Limes Rd BECK BR3 204 G2
CHES/WCR EN8 62 C8
CROY/NA CR0 203 L6
EGH TW20 172 G4
WEY KT13 216 B1
Limes Rw ORP BR6 226 E2
The Limes AMS HP6 68 G1
CMBW SE5 * 159 M9
EMPK RM11 125 L1
EYN DA4 * 209 N7
LHD/OX KT22 236 G9
PUR RM19 165 P4
RBRW/HUT CM13 107 L4
RKW/CH/CXG WD3 * 91 M2
STAL AL1 38 D4
WAND/EARL SW18 * 179 K2
WDSR SL4 148 B8
WGCE AL7 23 K7
WOKN/KNAP GU21 232 A1
Limestone Wk ERITHM DA18 163 N1
Lime St FENCHST EC3M 13 J7
WALTH E17 120 D1
Lime Street Pas BANK EC3V * 13 J6
Limes Wk EA W5 155 J1
PECK SE15 * 160 B10
Lime Tree Av ESH/CLAY KT10 198 C8
RDART DA2 188 F4
Limetree Cl BRXS/STRHM SW2 180 G4
Lime Tree Ct GT/LBKH KT23 235 P10
Lime Tree Ct LCOL/BKTW AL2 56 G2
PIN HA5 * 93 P8
Lime Tree Ct PIN HA5 93 P8
Lime Tree Gv CROY/NA CR0 204 E10
Limetree Pl MTCM CR4 202 C1
Lime Tree Pl STAL AL1 38 D7
Lime Tree Rd HEST TW5 154 A7
Lime Tree Ter CAT SE6 * 182 E4
Lime Tree Wk AMSS HP7 69 L5
BUSH WD23 94 D2
ENC/FH EN2 79 K4
RKW/CH/CXG WD3 71 L9
SEV TN13 265 J1
VW GU25 194 B4
WWKM BR4 225 L1
Lime Wk DEN/HRF UB9 111 M10
HHS/BOV HP3 36 A8
SRTFD E15 * 141 K3
Limeway Ter DORK RH4 254 F10
Limewood Cl BECK BR3 205 K5
WALTH E17 120 E2
WEA W13 134 G8
WOKN/KNAP GU21 231 J6
Limewood Rd ERITH DA8 164 D6
Limpsfield Av THHTH CR7 202 G5
WIM/MER SW19 178 G5
Limpsfield Rd SAND/SEL CR2 223 P8
WARL CR6 242 B2
Linacre Cl PECK SE15 160 A9
Linacre Rd CRICK NW2 136 E1
Linale House IS N1 * 6 G7
Lince La DORK RH4 272 C2
Linces Wy WGCE AL7 23 L7
Linchfield Rd DTCH/LGLY SL3 149 P7
Linchmere Pl CRAWW RH11 283 K6
Linchmere Rd LEE/GVPK SE12 183 K3
Lincoln Av ROMW/RG RM7 124 F6
STHGT/OAK N14 98 D4
WHTN TW2 176 B5
WIM/MER SW19 178 G6
Lincoln Cl CRAWE RH10 283 P10
EMPK RM11 125 M2
ERITH DA8 164 G8
GFD/PVL UB6 134 B3
HORL RH6 280 B5
RYLN/HDSTN HA2 113 N3
WGCE AL7 23 M4
Lincoln Ct BERK HP4 33 N5
BORE WD6 76 A9
Lincoln Crs EN EN1 79 M9
Lincoln Dr OXHEY WD19 93 K4
RKW/CH/CXG WD3 72 C8
WOKS/MYFD GU22 233 H4
Lincoln Est BOW E3 140 F6
Lincoln Gdns IL IG1 122 B5
Lincoln Green Rd
STMC/STPC BR5 207 J5
Lincoln Hatch La SL SL1 128 B6
Lincoln Ms KIL/WHAMP NW6 2 C5
SEVS/STOTM N15 119 K2
Lincoln Pde EFNCH N2 * 117 P1
Lincoln Pk AMSS HP7 69 K5
Lincoln Rd ALP/SUD HA0 135 J1
CFSP/GDCR SL9 90 B9
DORK RH4 255 H10
EFNCH N2 117 P1
EN EN1 79 M8
ERITH DA8 164 G8
FELT TW13 175 N6
FSTGT E7 142 A1
GUW GU2 249 L8
MTCM CR4 202 F5
NTHWD HA6 112 G1
NWMAL KT3 199 P3
PLSTW E13 141 N6
RYLN/HDSTN HA2 113 M3
SCUP DA14 185 L8
SNWD SE25 204 A3
SWFD E18 101 P9
WPK KT4 200 E8
Lincoln's Cl STALE/WH AL4 39 J1
Lincolns Fld EPP CM16 65 J5
Lincoln's Inn Flds LINN WC2A 11 N5
Lincolns La BRW CM14 86 B10
The Lincolns MLHL NW7 96 C4
Lincoln St CHEL SW3 16 A6
WAN E11 121 K7
Lincoln Ter BELMT SM2 * 221 K4
Lincoln Wy EN EN1 80 A9
RKW/CH/CXG WD3 72 E8
SL SL1 128 C9
SUN TW16 196 F1
Lincombe Rd BMLY BR1 183 L6
Lindal Crs ENC/FH EN2 78 F9
Lindale Cl VW GU25 193 L4
The Lindales TOTM N17 99 P7
Lindal Rd BROCKY SE4 182 E1
Lindbergh WGCE AL7 23 M5
Linden Av COUL/CHIP CR5 240 C2
DART DA1 187 K4
EN EN1 79 P5
HSLW TW3 176 A1
RSLP HA4 113 M6
THHTH CR7 203 J4
WATW WD18 72 G8
WBLY HA9 115 L10
WLSDN NW10 136 G4
Linden Chase Rd SEV TN13 247 J8
Linden Cl ADL/WDHM KT15 215 K7
CHESW EN7 62 A6
CRAWE RH10 284 B10
KWD/TDW/WH KT20 238 C6
ORP BR6 227 K2
PUR RM19 166 B5
RSLP HA4 113 H6
STAN HA7 94 G6
STHGT/OAK N14 78 D10
THDIT KT7 198 F7
Linden Cottages
WIM/MER SW19 * 179 H9
Linden Ct EGH TW20 171 N9
HARP AL5 20 A3
LHD/OX KT22 236 G7
Linden Crs GFD/PVL UB6 134 E1
KUT/HW KT1 199 L2
STAL AL1 39 H6
WFD IG8 101 N7
Linden Dr CFSP/GDCR SL9 90 B9
CTHM CR3 241 K10
SLN SL2 129 H3
Lindenfield CHST BR7 206 E2
Linden Gdns BAY/PAD W2 8 F8
CHSWK W4 156 A4
EN EN1 79 P5
LHD/OX KT22 237 H7
Linden Gld HHW HP1 35 L7
Linden Gv NWMAL KT3 200 B3
PECK SE15 160 A9
PGE/AN SE20 182 B9
TEDD TW11 176 E8
WARL CR6 242 D4
WOT/HER KT12 196 G9
Linden Lea DORK RH4 * 273 H4
EFNCH N2 117 M3
GSTN WD25 55 H9
PIN HA5 * 93 N8
Linden Leas WWKM BR4 205 J9
Linden Ms BAY/PAD W2 8 F8
IS N1 119 L10
Linden Pit Pth LHD/OX KT22 236 G7
Linden Pl EHSLY KT24 * 252 F2
EW KT17 220 B8
MTCM CR4 201 P4
Linden Ri BRW CM14 107 J6
Linden Rd FBAR/BDGN N11 98 A3
GU GU1 249 P10
HPTN TW12 197 P1
LHD/OX KT22 236 G7
MUSWH N10 118 C2
SEVS/STOTM N15 119 K2
WEY KT13 216 D5
Lindens WAB EN9 81 P1
Lindens Cl EHSLY KT24 253 M4
Lindens Sq DEN/HRF UB9 91 K7
SEV TN13 246 F8
The Lindens CHSWK W4 155 P7
CRAWE RH10 285 J2
CROY/NA CR0 225 H3
HAT AL10 * 40 C3
HHS/BOV HP3 35 J9
LOU IG10 82 D9
NFNCH/WDSPK N12 * 97 N6
WAB EN9 * 81 P1
WALTH E17 * 120 G2
Linden St ROMW/RG RM7 124 E2
Linden Ter UX/CGN UB8 * 131 N8
Linden Wy PUR/KEN CR8 222 D6
RPLY/SEND GU23 233 J10
SHPTN TW17 196 D5
STHGT/OAK N14 78 D10
WOKS/MYFD GU22 232 C7
Lindfield Gdns GU GU1 250 C9
HAMP NW3 117 M10
Lindfield Rd CROY/NA CR0 203 N6
EA W5 135 H6
HARH RM3 105 M6
Lindfield St POP/IOD E14 140 E8
Lindfield Ter WOKN/KNAP GU21 * 231 P2
Lindhill Cl PEND EN3 80 C6
Lindisfarne Cl GVE DA12 191 H5
Lindisfarne Md HOM E9 120 D9
Lindisfarne Rd BCTR RM8 123 M8
RYNPK SW20 178 D10
Lindiswara Ct
RKW/CH/CXG WD3 * 72 B10
Lindley Est PECK SE15 159 P6
Lindley Pl RCH/KEW TW9 155 M7
Lindley Rd GDST RH9 260 B6
LEY E10 121 H7
WOT/HER KT12 197 M10
Lindley St WCHPL E1 140 B7
Lindlings HHW HP1 35 H7
Lindo Cl CSHM HP5 50 G6
Lindore Rd BTSEA SW11 158 A10
Lindores Rd CAR SM5 201 N8
Lindo St PECK SE15 160 B8
Lind Rd SUT SM1 221 M2
Lindrop St FUL/PGN SW6 157 M8
Lindsay Cl CHSGTN KT9 219 K4
HOR/WEW KT19 219 P8
STWL/WRAY TW19 173 N1
Lindsay Dr KTN/HRWW/WS HA3 115 K4
SHPTN TW17 196 E6
Lindsay Pl CHESW EN7 62 A6
Lindsay Rd ADL/WDHM KT15 215 K7
HPTN TW12 176 A7
WPK KT4 200 E9
Lindsay Sq PIM SW1V 17 K8
Lindsell St GNWCH SE10 161 H7
Lindsey Cl BMLY BR1 206 A3
BRW CM14 106 F4
MTCM CR4 202 F4
Lindsey Gdns
EBED/NFELT TW14 * 174 E3
Lindsey Ms IS N1 6 F3
Lindsey Rd BCTR RM8 123 M8
DEN/HRF UB9 111 K8
Lindsey St EPP CM16 65 H4
FARR EC1M 12 D3
Lindsey Wy EMPK RM11 125 K3
Lind St DEPT SE8 160 G8
Lindum Pl STALW/RED AL3 37 N8
Lindum Rd TEDD TW11 177 H10
Lindvale WOKN/KNAP GU21 232 B1
Lindway WNWD SE27 181 J8
Linfield Cl HDN NW4 116 F1
WOT/HER KT12 * 217 J2
Linfields AMSS HP7 69 P6
Linford Cl HLWW/ROY CM19 46 F3
Linford End HLWW/ROY CM19 46 F3
Linford Rd CDW/CHF RM16 168 F3
WALTH E17 121 H1
Linford St VX/NE SW8 158 D7
Lingards Rd LEW SE13 161 H10
Lingey Cl BFN/LL DA15 185 J5
Lingfield Av RDART DA2 188 A3
UPMR RM14 125 N8
Lingfield Cl EN EN1 79 M10
NTHWD HA6 92 F8
Lingfield Ct NTHLT UB5 * 133 P4
Lingfield Crs ELTH/MOT SE9 162 G10
Lingfield Dr CRAWE RH10 284 F4
Lingfield Gdns COUL/CHIP CR5 241 J5
ED N9 100 A1
Lingfield Rd GVW DA11 190 E5
WIM/MER SW19 178 G9
WPK KT4 200 F10
Lingfield Wy WAT WD17 72 G4
Lingham St BRXN/ST SW9 158 F8
Lingholm Wy BAR EN5 76 G9
Lingmere Cl CHIG IG7 102 F3
Lingmoor Dr GSTN WD25 55 K9
Ling Rd CAN/RD E16 141 M7
ERITH DA8 164 D5
Lingwell Rd TOOT SW17 179 P6
Lingwood Gdns ISLW TW7 154 D6
Lingwood Rd CLPT E5 119 P5
Linhope St CAMTN NW1 10 A1
Linington Av CSHM HP5 51 M6
Link 10 CRAWE RH10 284 B4
Link Cl HAT AL10 40 E4
Link Dr HAT AL10 40 E4
Linkfield E/WMO/HCT KT8 197 P3
Link Fld HAYES BR2 205 M6
Linkfield WGCE AL7 23 H9
Linkfield Cnr REDH RH1 257 P10
Linkfield Gdns REDH RH1 257 P10
Linkfield La REDH RH1 258 A9
Linkfield Rd ISLW TW7 154 E8
Linkfield St REDH RH1 257 P10
Link La WLGTN SM6 222 E3
Linklea Cl CDALE/KGS NW9 96 B8
Link Rd ADL/WDHM KT15 215 P1
DAGW RM9 144 C4
DTCH/LGLY SL3 149 P6
EBED/NFELT TW14 174 G3
FBAR/BDGN N11 98 B5
HHW HP1 35 M3
WATN WD24 73 L6
WLGTN SM6 202 B8
Links Av GPK RM2 105 J10
HERT/BAY SG13 26 A4
MRDN SM4 201 K4
Links Brow LHD/OX KT22 236 D10
Links Cl ASHTD KT21 237 H3
Linkscroft Av ASHF TW15 174 C9
Links Dr BORE WD6 75 L8
RAD WD7 56 E9
TRDG/WHET N20 97 K2
Links Gdns STRHM/NOR SW16 181 H10
Links Green Wy COB KT11 217 P10
Linkside CHIG IG7 102 F6
NFNCH/WDSPK N12 97 J7
NWMAL KT3 200 B2
Linkside Cl ENC/FH EN2 78 G7
Linkside Gdns ENC/FH EN2 78 G7
Links Pl ASHTD KT21 237 J3
Links Rd ACT W3 135 M8
ASHF TW15 173 P8
ASHTD KT21 237 H3
CRICK NW2 116 C7
EW KT17 220 D9
SHGR GU5 268 B10
TOOT SW17 180 B9
WFD IG8 101 M6
WWKM BR4 205 H8
Links Side ENC/FH EN2 78 G7
The Links CHES/WCR EN8 62 C2
WALTH E17 120 D2
WOT/HER KT12 197 H9
Link St HOM E9 140 B1
Links Vw DART DA1 187 K4
FNCH N3 97 J8
STALW/RED AL3 38 A4
Links View Av
BRKHM/BTCW RH3 255 M10
Links View Cl STAN HA7 94 F7
Linksview Ct HPTN TW12 * 176 C7
Links View Rd CROY/NA CR0 204 F10
HPTN TW12 176 B8
Links Wy BECK BR3 204 F6
EHSLY KT24 253 M4
NTHWD HA6 92 D9
RKW/CH/CXG WD3 72 D7
TOOT SW17 180 A9
Linksway HDN NW4 96 G10
NTHWD HA6 92 E9
Linkswood Rd SL SL1 128 B4
Links Yd WCHPL E1 13 M3
The Link ACT W3 135 N8
ALP/SUD HA0 115 H6
CRAWW RH11 283 N7
CRICK NW2 116 D6
NTHLT UB5 * 113 N10
PEND EN3 80 D5
PIN HA5 113 K4
SLN SL2 129 N8
TEDD TW11 176 E10
Link Wy DEN/HRF UB9 111 K4
EMPK RM11 125 M6
HAYES BR2 206 B7
RCHPK/HAM TW10 176 G5
STA TW18 173 L9
Linkway BCTR RM8 123 M9
FSBYPK N4 119 K5
GUW GU2 249 L10
HORL RH6 280 D8
PIN HA5 93 L9
RYNPK SW20 200 E3
WOKS/MYFD GU22 232 F3
Linkway Rd BRW CM14 106 E4
The Linkway BAR EN5 77 K10
BELMT SM2 221 M5
Linkwood Wk CAMTN NW1 5 K3
Linley Cl TIL RM18 169 N6
Linley Crs ROMW/RG RM7 124 C1
Linley Rd TOTM N17 99 M10
Linnell Cl GLDGN NW11 117 L4
Linnell Dr GLDGN NW11 117 L4
Linnell Rd CMBW SE5 159 M8
REDH RH1 276 B1
UED N18 99 P6
Linnet Cl BUSH WD23 94 B2
ED N9 100 C2
SAND/SEL CR2 224 C6
THMD SE28 143 M9
Linnet Gv RGUE GU4 250 G8
Linnet Ms BAL SW12 180 B3
Linnet Rd ABLGY WD5 55 H7
Linnett Cl CHING E4 101 H5
Linnet Wy PUR RM19 166 A4
Linom Rd CLAP SW4 158 F10
Linscott Rd CLPT E5 120 B9
Linsdell Rd BARK IG11 142 F3
Linsey Cl HHS/BOV HP3 36 B10
Linsey St BERM/RHTH SE16 19 N5
BERM/RHTH SE16 159 P3
Linslade Cl HSLWW TW4 175 M1
PIN HA5 113 J1
Linslade Rd ORP BR6 227 K3
Linstead St KIL/WHAMP NW6 2 E3
Linstead Wy WAND/EARL SW18 179 H3
Linster Gv BORE WD6 75 P9
Lintaine Cl HMSMTH W6 * 157 H5
Linthorpe Av ALP/SUD HA0 135 H1
Linthorpe Rd EBAR EN4 77 P7
STNW/STAM N16 119 M5
Linton Av BORE WD6 75 L6
Linton Cl CAR SM5 202 A7
CHARL SE7 161 P4
WELL DA16 163 L7
Linton Ct ROM RM1 104 F10
Linton Gdns EHAM E6 142 B8
Linton Gld CROY/NA CR0 224 D6
Linton Gv WNWD SE27 181 J8
Linton Rd BARK IG11 142 F2
Linton's La EW KT17 220 B8
Linton St IS N1 6 F6
Lintott Ct STWL/WRAY TW19 173 N2
Linver Rd FUL/PGN SW6 157 J8
Linwood SBW CM21 * 29 P1
Linwood Cl CMBW SE5 159 N8
Linwood Crs EN EN1 79 P5
Linwood Rd HARP AL5 20 B4
Linzee Rd CEND/HSY/T N8 118 F2
Lion Av TWK TW1 176 E4
Lion Cl BROCKY SE4 182 F2
SHPTN TW17 195 P3
Lion Ct BORE WD6 75 P5
Lionel Gdns ELTH/MOT SE9 184 A1
Lionel Ms NKENS W10 8 A3
NKENS W10 * 137 H7
Lionel Rd ELTH/MOT SE9 184 A1
Lionel Rd North BTFD TW8 155 K2
Lionel Rd South BTFD TW8 155 L4
Lion Gate Gdns RCH/KEW TW9 155 L9
Lion Gate Ms WAND/EARL SW18 179 K3
Lion Green Rd COUL/CHIP CR5 240 E1
Lion La CRAWE RH10 285 P9
Lion Mills BETH E2 * 7 P8
Lion Park Av CHSGTN KT9 219 M1
Lion Rd BXLYHS DA6 163 P10
CROY/NA CR0 203 K5
ED N9 99 P3
EHAM E6 142 C7
TWK TW1 176 E4
Lions Cl LEE/GVPK SE12 183 P6
Lion Wy BTFD TW8 155 J6
Lion Wharf Rd ISLW TW7 154 G9
Liphook Cl HCH RM12 124 G9
Liphook Crs FSTH SE23 182 B3
Liphook Rd OXHEY WD19 93 L5
Lippitts Hl LOU IG10 81 K6
Lipsham Cl BNSTD SM7 221 N9
Lipton Rd WCHPL E1 140 C8
Lisbon Av WHTN TW2 176 B5
Lisbon Cl WALTH E17 100 E10
Lisburne Rd HAMP NW3 118 A9
Lisford St PECK SE15 159 N7
Lisgar Ter WKENS W14 14 C5
Liskeard Cl CHST BR7 184 F9
Liskeard Gdns BKHTH/KID SE3 161 M7
Lisle Cl GVE DA12 191 L5
TOOT SW17 180 C7
Lisle Pl GRAYS RM17 167 M2
Lisle St LSQ/SEVD WC2H 11 K7
Lismore HHS/BOV HP3 36 D8
WIM/MER SW19 * 179 J8
Lismore Circ KTTN NW5 118 A10
Lismore Cl ISLW TW7 154 F8
Lismore Crs CRAWW RH11 283 L10
Lismore Pk SLN SL2 129 L9
Lismore Rd SAND/SEL CR2 223 M3
TOTM N17 119 L1
Lismore Wk IS N1 6 F2
Lissant Cl SURB KT6 199 H7
Lissenden Gdns KTTN NW5 118 B9
Lissoms Rd COUL/CHIP CR5 240 B4
Lisson Gv CAMTN NW1 9 N2
Lisson St CAMTN NW1 9 N3
Lister Av HARH RM3 105 L10
Lister Cl ACT W3 136 A7
MTCM CR4 179 P10
Lister Gdns UED N18 99 K6
Lister Rd TIL RM18 168 D8
WAN E11 121 K6
Liston Rd CLAP SW4 158 D9
TOTM N17 99 P9
Liston Wy WFD IG8 101 P8
Listowel Cl BRXN/ST SW9 159 H6
Listowel Rd DAGE RM10 124 B8
Listria Pk STNW/STAM N16 119 M7
Litcham Sp SL SL1 129 J8
Litchfield Av MRDN SM4 201 J7
SRTFD E15 * 141 K1
Litchfield Gdns WLSDN NW10 136 D1
Litchfield Rd SUT SM1 221 M1
Litchfield St LSQ/SEVD WC2H 11 K7
Litchfield Wy GLDGN NW11 117 M3
GUW GU2 267 L2
Lithgow's Rd HTHAIR TW6 152 F10
Lithos Rd HAMP NW3 3 J1
Little Acre BECK BR3 204 F3
STALW/RED AL3 38 C6
Little Acres WARE SG12 26 C3
Little Albany St CAMTN NW1 10 F1
Little Argyll St REGST W1B * 10 G6
Little Aston Rd HARH RM3 105 N8
Little Belhus Cl SOCK/AV RM15 146 F6
Little Benty WDR/YW UB7 151 N4
Little Berkhamsted La
BRKMPK AL9 42 B6
Little Birch Cl ADL/WDHM KT15 215 N5
Little Birches BFN/LL DA15 185 H5
The Little Boltons WBPTN SW10 15 H7
Little Bookham St GT/LBKH KT23 235 N10
Little Bornes DUL SE21 181 M7
Little Borough
BRKHM/BTCW RH3 273 M1
Little Brays HLWS CM18 47 K3
Little Bridge Rd BERK HP4 * 34 A5
Little Britain STBT EC1A 12 E5
Littlebrook Av SLN SL2 128 D7
Littlebrook Cl CROY/NA CR0 204 C6
Littlebrook Gdns CHES/WCR EN8 62 C6
Littlebrook Manor Wy DART DA1 187 P1
Little Brook Rd
HLWW/ROY CM19 45 P1
Little Brownings FSTH SE23 182 A5
Little Buntings WDSR SL4 148 E9
Little Burrow WGCE AL7 22 G7
Littlebury Ct BRWN CM15 86 E3
Littlebury Rd CLAP SW4 * 158 E9
Little Bury St ED N9 99 M1
Little Bushey La BUSH WD23 73 P7
Little Catherells HHW HP1 35 H4
Little Cattins HLWW/ROY CM19 46 C5
Little Cedars NFNCH/WDSPK N12 97 M5
Little Chesters
KWD/TDW/WH KT20 256 D1
Little Chester St KTBR SW1X 16 E3
Little Cloisters WEST SW1P 17 L3
Little Collins REDH RH1 * 277 J10
Littlecombe Cl PUT/ROE SW15 * 178 G2
Little Common STAN HA7 94 F4
Little Common La REDH RH1 259 K8
Littlecote Cl WIM/MER SW19 178 G3
Littlecote Pl PIN HA5 93 M9
Little Cottage Pl GNWCH SE10 * 160 G6
Little Ct WWKM BR4 205 K9
Littlecourt Rd SEV TN13 247 H10
Little Crabtree CRAWW RH11 283 M6
Little Cranmore La EHSLY KT24 252 C4
Littlecroft ELTH/MOT SE9 162 D9
MEO DA13 190 B10
Littlecroft Rd EGH TW20 172 C8
Littledale ABYW SE2 163 K5
Little Deans Yd WEST SW1P 17 L3
Little Dell WGCW AL8 22 G3
Little Dimocks BAL SW12 180 C5
Little Dorrit Ct STHWK SE1 18 F1
Littledown Rd SL SL1 129 L10
Little Dragons LOU IG10 82 A8
Little Ealing La EA W5 155 H3
Little East Fld COUL/CHIP CR5 240 E7
Little Edward St CAMTN NW1 * 4 F9
Little Elms HYS/HAR UB3 152 E6
Little Essex St TPL/STR WC2R * 12 A7
Little Ferry Rd TWK TW1 * 176 G4
Littlefield Cl ARCH N19 118 D9
KUT/HW KT1 199 K2
RGUW GU3 249 J6
Littlefield Rd EDGW HA8 95 P8
Little Friday Rd CHING E4 101 K3
Little Gaynes Gdns UPMR RM14 126 A9
Little Gaynes La UPMR RM14 * 125 N9
Little Gearies BARK/HLT IG6 122 E2
Little George St WEST SW1P 17 L2
Little Gerpins La RAIN RM13 145 N3
Little Graylings ABLGY WD5 54 F9
Little Greencroft CSHM HP5 50 F3
Little Green La CHERT KT16 195 H10
RKW/CH/CXG WD3 72 A7
Little Green St KTTN NW5 * 118 C9
Little Gregories La EPP CM16 82 C1
Little Gv BUSH WD23 74 A8
DORK RH4 * 273 H4
Littlegrove EBAR EN4 77 P10
Little Grove Av CHESW EN7 61 M3
Little Grove Fld
HLWW/ROY CM19 46 F1
Little Halliards WOT/HER KT12 197 H6
Little Hardings WGCE AL7 23 M4
Little Hayes KGLGY WD4 54 B5
Little Heath CHARL SE7 162 B5
CHDH RM6 123 L2
Littleheath La COB KT11 217 P10
Little Heath La HHW HP1 34 E7
Little Heath Rd BXLYHN DA7 164 A7
CHOB/PIR GU24 213 K5
Littleheath Rd SAND/SEL CR2 224 A5
Little Hide GU GU1 250 E8
Little Hl RKW/CH/CXG WD3 70 F10
Little Hivings CSHM HP5 50 F3
Little How Cft ABLGY WD5 54 D7
Little Ilford La MNPK E12 122 C9
Littlejohn Rd HNWL W7 134 E8
STMC/STPC BR5 207 K6
Little Julians Hl SEV TN13 265 H3
Little Kiln GODL GU7 267 K9
Little Lake WGCE AL7 23 L8
Little La HARP AL5 20 B5
Little Laver Rd CHONG CM5 49 N3
HLWE CM17 31 M10
Little Ley WGCE AL7 23 H8
Little London SHGR GU5 269 P7
Little London Cl UX/CGN UB8 132 C7
Little Marlborough St
REGST W1B * 10 G6
Little Martins BUSH WD23 74 A9
Littlemead ESH/CLAY KT10 218 C1
Little Md HAT AL10 40 E1
WOKN/KNAP GU21 231 L2
Littlemede ELTH/MOT SE9 184 C6

Little Mimms HHNE HP2 35 N5
Littlemoor Rd IL IG1 122 G8
Littlemore Rd ABYW SE2 163 K1
Little Moreton Cl BF/WBF KT14 * 215 L8
Little Moss La PIN HA5 93 M10
Little Mundells WGCE AL7 23 J4
Little Newport St
LSQ/SEVD WC2H 11 K7
Little New St FLST/FETLN EC4A 12 B5
Little Oak Cl SHPTN TW17 196 A4
Little Orch ADL/WDHM KT15 215 K7
HHNE HP2 36 B5
WOKN/KNAP GU21 214 D10
Little Orchard Cl ABLGY WD5 54 E7
PIN HA5 * 93 M10
Little Orchards EPSOM KT18 220 B10
Little Orchard Wy RGUE GU4 268 B7
Little Oxhey La OXHEY WD19 93 M6
Little Pk HHS/BOV HP3 52 D4
Little Park Dr FELT TW13 175 L5
Little Park Gdns ENC/FH EN2 79 L7
Little Piper's Cl CHESW EN7 61 J5
Little Platt GUW GU2 249 J9
Little Pluckett's Wy BKHH IG9 102 A2
Little Portland St REGST W1B 10 F5
Littleport Sp SL SL1 129 K8
Little Potters BUSH WD23 94 C1
Little Pynchons HLWS CM18 47 J4
Little Queens Rd TEDD TW11 176 E9
Little Queen St DART DA1 187 N3
Little Redlands BMLY BR1 206 B2
Little Reeves Av AMSS HP7 69 L5
Little Rdg WGCE AL7 23 K5
Little Riding WOKS/MYFD GU22 232 E2
Little Rivers WGCE AL7 23 K4
Little Rd HHNE HP2 35 P5
HYS/HAR UB3 152 G1
SL SL1 108 B8
Little Roke Av PUR/KEN CR8 223 J10
Little Roke Rd PUR/KEN CR8 223 K10
Littlers Cl WIM/MER SW19 201 N1
Little Russell St
NOXST/BSQ WC1A 11 L4
Little St James's St WHALL SW1A 10 G10
Little St Leonards
MORT/ESHN SW14 155 P9
Little Shardeloes AMSS HP7 68 F6
Little Smith St WEST SW1P 17 K3
Little Somerset St TWRH EC3N 13 L6
Little Spring CSHM HP5 50 G4
Little Stock Rd CHESW EN7 61 L2
Littlestone Cl BECK BR3 182 F9
Little Strd CDALE/KGS NW9 96 C10
Little Stream Cl NTHWD HA6 92 F6
Little St GUW GU2 249 N6
WAB EN9 81 H2
Little Sutton La DTCH/LGLY SL3 150 F4
Little Thistle WGCE AL7 23 M7
Little Thrift STMC/STPC BR5 206 F4
Little Titchfield St GTPST W1W 10 G4
Littleton Av CHING E4 101 L2
Littleton Crs HRW HA1 114 E7
Littleton La REIG RH2 275 H2
RGUW GU3 267 M6
SHPTN TW17 195 P5
Littleton Rd ASHF TW15 174 D10
HRW HA1 114 E7
Littleton St WAND/EARL SW18 179 M5
Little Trinity La BLKFR EC4V 12 F7
Little Tumners Ct GODL GU7 267 K10
Little Turnstile HHOL WC1V 11 N4
Little Wade WGCE AL7 23 J8
Little Wk HLW CM20 * 28 G10
Little Warley Hall La
RBRW/HUT CM13 127 K3
Little Warren Cl RGUE GU4 268 F2
Littlewick Rd WOKN/KNAP GU21 231 J2
Little Widbury WARE SG12 26 E2
Little Widbury La WARE SG12 26 E2
Little Windmill Hl KGLGY WD4 53 H8
Littlewood LEW SE13 183 H1
Little Wd SEV TN13 247 K8
Little Wood Cl STMC/STPC BR5 207 K1
Littlewood Cl WEA W13 154 G2
Little Woodcote Est
WLGTN SM6 * 222 C6
Little Woodcote La CAR SM5 222 C8
Little Woodlands WDSR SL4 148 E9
Littleworth Av ESH/CLAY KT10 218 C2
Littleworth Common Rd
ESH/CLAY KT10 198 C10
Littleworth La ESH/CLAY KT10 218 C1
Littleworth Pl ESH/CLAY KT10 218 C1
Littleworth Rd ESH/CLAY KT10 218 C2
Little Youngs WGCW AL8 22 F5
Littlt Halliards WOT/HER KT12 * 197 H6
Livermere Rd HACK E8 7 M5
Liverpool Gv WALW SE17 18 G8
Liverpool Rd CAN/RD E16 141 K7
EA W5 155 J1
HOLWY N7 6 A1
KUTN/CMB KT2 177 M10
LEY E10 121 H4
SL SL1 128 G8
STAL AL1 38 D6
THHTH CR7 203 K3
WATW WD18 73 J9
Liverpool St LVPST EC2M 13 J4
Livesey Cl KUT/HW KT1 199 L3
THMD SE28 162 F2
Livesey Pl PECK SE15 19 P9
Livingstone Cl CHONG CM5 67 P5
Livingstone Gdns GVE DA12 190 G9
Livingstone Rd BTSEA SW11 157 N9
CRAWE RH10 283 P9
CTHM CR3 241 L8
GVE DA12 190 G8
HSLW TW3 154 B10
PLMGR N13 98 F7
SRTFD E15 141 H3
STHL UB1 133 L9
THHTH CR7 203 L2
WALTH E17 120 G4
Livingstone Wk HHNE HP2 36 A2
Lizard St FSBYE EC1V 6 F10
Lizban St BKHTH/KID SE3 161 N6
Llanbury Cl CFSP/GDCR SL9 90 C8
Llanelly Rd CRICK NW2 117 J7
Llanover Rd WBLY HA9 115 J8
WOOL/PLUM SE18 162 D6
Llanthony Rd MRDN SM4 201 N6
Llanvanor Rd CRICK NW2 117 J7
Llewellyn St BERM/RHTH SE16 19 P2
Lloyd Av COUL/CHIP CR5 222 B10
STRHM/NOR SW16 202 F1
Lloyd Baker St FSBYW WC1X 6 A10
Lloyd Ct PIN HA5 113 L3
Lloyd Ms PEND EN3 80 F4
Lloyd Park Av CROY/NA CR0 223 N1
Lloyd Rd DAGW RM9 144 A1
EHAM E6 142 C3
WALTH E17 120 C2
WPK KT4 200 F10
Lloyd's Av FENCHST EC3M 13 K6
Lloyds Ct CRAWE RH10 * 283 P4
Lloyd's Pl BKHTH/KID SE3 * 161 K8
Lloyd Sq FSBYW WC1X 6 A10
Lloyd's Rw CLKNW EC1R 6 B10
Lloyd St FSBYW WC1X 6 A9
Lloyds Wy BECK BR3 204 D5
Lloyd Thomas Ct WDGN N22 * 98 G8
Lloyd Vls BROCKY SE4 160 F8
Loampit Hl LEW SE13 160 F8
Loampit V LEW SE13 160 G9
Loanda Cl HACK E8 7 L5
Loates La WAT WD17 73 K7
Loats Rd BRXS/STRHM SW2 180 F2
Lobelia Rd CHOB/PIR GU24 230 F1
Local Board Rd WAT WD17 73 L9
Locarno Rd ACT W3 135 P10
GFD/PVL UB6 134 B6
Lochaber Rd LEW SE13 161 K10
Lochaline St HMSMTH W6 156 F5
Lochan Cl YEAD UB4 133 M6
Lochinvar Cl SL SL1 148 G1
Lochinvar St BAL SW12 180 C3
Lochmere Cl ERITH DA8 164 C5
Lochnagar St POP/IOD E14 141 H7
Lochnell Rd BERK HP4 33 L3
Lock Cha BKHTH/KID SE3 161 K9
Lock Cl ADL/WDHM KT15 215 H8
NWDGN UB2 154 B1
Locke Cl RAIN RM13 144 G1
Locke Gdns DTCH/LGLY SL3 149 P1
Locke-King Cl WEY KT13 216 B4
Locke King Rd WEY KT13 216 B4
Lockers Park La HHW HP1 35 M6
Lockesley Dr STMC/STPC BR5 207 J6
Lockesley Sq SURB KT6 * 199 J6
Lockestone Cl WEY KT13 216 A3
Locket Rd KTN/HRWW/WS HA3 94 E10
Locket Road Ms
KTN/HRWW/WS HA3 94 D10
Lockets Cl WDSR SL4 148 C7
Locke Wy WOKN/KNAP GU21 232 C3
Lockfield Av PEND EN3 80 D6
Lockfield Dr WOKN/KNAP GU21 231 K3
Lockgate Cl HOM E9 120 E10
Lockhart Cl HOLWY N7 5 N1
PEND EN3 80 A9
Lockhart Rd COB KT11 217 K9
Lockhart St BOW E3 140 E6
Lockhurst St CLPT E5 120 C9
Lockington Rd VX/NE SW8 158 C7
Lock Keepers Cottages
TOTM N17 * 120 A2
Lock La WOKS/MYFD GU22 233 L2
Lockley Crs HAT AL10 40 E2
Lockmead Rd LEW SE13 161 H9
SEVS/STOTM N15 119 P4
Lock Pth WDSR SL4 148 C5
Lock Rd GU GU1 250 A6
RCHPK/HAM TW10 177 H7
Lock's La MTCM CR4 202 B1
Locksley Dr WOKN/KNAP GU21 231 L3
Locksley Est POP/IOD E14 140 E8
Locksley St POP/IOD E14 140 E7
Locksmeade Rd
RCHPK/HAM TW10 176 G7
Lockstone WEY KT13 216 A3
Lockswood CHOB/PIR GU24 230 G6
Locks Yd SEV TN13 * 265 K1
Lockton St NTGHL W11 * 136 G9
Lockwell Rd DAGE RM10 124 A8
Lockwood Cl SYD SE26 182 C7
Lockwood Ct CRAWE RH10 * 284 A5
Lockwood Pth
WOKN/KNAP GU21 214 G9
Lockwood Pl CHING E4 100 F7
Lockwood Sq BERM/RHTH SE16 160 A2
Lockwood Wy CHSGTN KT9 219 M2
WALTH E17 100 C10
Lockyer Cl PEND EN3 80 G4
Lockyer Pl BH/WHM TN16 * 262 G2
Lockyer Rd PUR RM19 166 B5
Lockyer St STHWK SE1 19 H2
Locomotive Dr
EBED/NFELT TW14 175 H3
Locton Gn BOW E3 * 140 E3
Loddiges Rd HOM E9 140 B2
Loddon Sp SL SL1 129 K9
Loder Cl WOKN/KNAP GU21 214 G9
Loder St PECK SE15 160 B6
Lodge Av BORE WD6 75 L9
CROY/NA CR0 202 G10
DAGW RM9 143 L3
DART DA1 187 K2
GPK RM2 125 H3
KTN/HRWW/WS HA3 115 K2
Lodgebottom Rd RDKG RH5 255 M3
Lodge Cl CHIC IG7 103 K4
COB KT11 235 N2
CRAWW RH11 283 M7
EDGW HA8 * 95 L7
EGH TW20 172 A8
EW KT17 220 F6
HERT/WAT SG14 25 K3
ISLW TW7 154 G7
LHD/OX KT22 236 C8
ORP BR6 207 L8
RDKG RH5 273 H6
SL SL1 149 H1
UED N18 99 K6
UX/CGN UB8 131 M6
WLGTN SM6 202 B8
Lodge Ct ALP/SUD HA0 * 115 K10
Lodge Crs CHES/WCR EN8 62 C10
ORP BR6 207 L8
Lodge Dr BRKMPK AL9 40 G1
PLMGR N13 99 H5
RKW/CH/CXG WD3 71 M8
Lodge End RAD WD7 56 G10
RKW/CH/CXG WD3 72 E8
Lodge Fld WGCE AL7 23 H2
Lodge Gdns BECK BR3 204 E5
Lodge Hall HLWS CM18 47 H5
Lodge Hl PUR/KEN CR8 241 H1
REDBR IG4 122 B2
WELL DA16 163 L6
Lodgehill Park Cl
RYLN/HDSTN HA2 114 A7
Lodge La BH/WHM TN16 262 F3
BXLY DA5 185 N2
CDW/CHF RM16 167 N2
CROY/NA CR0 224 G4
CRW RM5 104 B7
CSTG HP8 70 C6
GRAYS RM17 167 M1
NFNCH/WDSPK N12 97 M6
RDKG RH5 273 L10
REDH RH1 275 P8
WAB EN9 81 J1
Lodge Mansions Pde
PLMGR N13 * 99 H5
Lodge Ms HBRY N5 * 119 K9
Lodge Pl SUT SM1 221 L2
Lodge Rd BMLY BR1 183 P10
CROY/NA CR0 203 J6
EPP CM16 64 D10
HDN NW4 116 F2
LHD/OX KT22 236 B8
RKW/CH/CXG WD3 72 E8
STJWD NW8 3 M10
SUT SM1 221 L2
WLGTN SM6 222 C2
The Lodge SHB W12 * 156 G1
Lodge Vls WFD IG8 101 L8
Lodge Wk WARL CR6 242 F2
Lodge Wy ASHF TW15 173 P5
SHPTN TW17 196 D2
WDSR SL4 148 D9
Lodore Gdns CDALE/KGS NW9 116 B3
Lodore Gn HGDN/ICK UB10 111 P8
Lodore St POP/IOD E14 141 H8
Loewen Rd CDW/CHF RM16 168 D2
Lofthouse Pl CHSGTN KT9 219 H3
Loftie St BERM/RHTH SE16 19 P2
BERM/RHTH SE16 159 P1
Lofting Rd IS N1 6 A4
Loftus Rd BARK IG11 142 F1
SHB W12 136 E10
Loftus Vls SHB W12 * 136 E10
Logan Cl HSLWW TW4 153 N9
PEND EN3 80 C5
Logan Ms KENS W8 14 E5
ROM RM1 124 F3
Logan Pl ECT SW5 14 E5
Logan Rd ED N9 100 A3
WBLY HA9 115 K7
The Logans BAR EN5 * 76 G7
Logmore La DORK RH4 272 D7
Logs Hl CHST BR7 206 B1
Logs Hill Cl CHST BR7 206 B1
Lois Dr SHPTN TW17 196 C5
Lolesworth Cl WCHPL E1 13 M4
Lollards Cl AMS HP6 69 H3
Lollard St LBTH SE11 17 P5
Lollesworth La EHSLY KT24 252 D2
Loman Pth SOCK/AV RM15 146 E8
Loman St STHWK SE1 18 D1
Lomas Cl CROY/NA CR0 225 H4
Lomas St WCHPL E1 13 P3
Lombard Av GDMY/SEVK IG3 123 H6
PEND EN3 80 B5
Lombard La EMB EC4Y 12 B6
Lombard Rd BTSEA SW11 157 N8
FBAR/BDGN N11 98 C6
WIM/MER SW19 201 L2
The Lombards EMPK RM11 125 N5
Lombard St BANK EC3V 13 H6
EYN DA4 210 B4
MFD/CHID GU8 266 A10
Lombard Vls FBAR/BDGN N11 * 98 C6
Lombard Wall CHARL SE7 161 N2
Lombardy Cl HHNE HP2 36 E7
WFD IG8 102 E8
WOKN/KNAP GU21 231 L3
Lombardy Dr BERK HP4 34 A6
Lombardy Pl BAY/PAD W2 8 G8
Lombardy Wy BORE WD6 75 K5
Lomond Cl ALP/SUD HA0 135 L2
SEVS/STOTM N15 119 M2
Lomond Gdns SAND/SEL CR2 224 D4
Lomond Gv CMBW SE5 159 L6
Lomond Rd HHNE HP2 35 N2
Loncin Mead Av
ADL/WDHM KT15 215 M5
Loncroft Rd CMBW SE5 19 K9
Londesborough Rd
STNW/STAM N16 119 M9
London Br CANST EC4R 13 H8
London Bridge St STHWK SE1 13 H10
London Bridge Wk STHWK SE1 * 13 H9
London City Airport Link
CAN/RD E16 141 L9
Londonderry Pde ERITH DA8 * 164 E6
London End BEAC HP9 88 E10
London Flds HACK E8 * 140 A2
London Flds East Side HACK E8 140 A2
London Flds West Side HACK E8 7 P3
London La BMLY BR1 183 M10
HACK E8 140 A2
SHGR GU5 270 B5
London Loop BNSTD SM7 221 K9
BORE WD6 75 N10
COUL/CHIP CR5 240 F5
CROY/NA CR0 204 C10
ENC/FH EN2 78 F3
ORP BR6 206 E8
PUR/KEN CR8 223 M10
SAND/SEL CR2 224 C5
WWKM BR4 205 J10
London Ms BAY/PAD W2 9 M6
London Rd ABR/ST RM4 83 K7
ABR/ST RM4 84 D5
ASC SL5 192 B3
BARK IG11 142 E2
BEAC HP9 109 H1
BERK HP4 34 B6
BFOR GU20 192 B10
BGR/WK TN15 265 N9
BH/WHM TN16 244 F9
BMLY BR1 183 K9
BRW CM14 106 F4
BUSH WD23 73 M10
CHEAM SM3 200 G9
CHONG CM5 67 L10
CRAWE RH10 283 N6
CSTG HP8 89 P3
CTHM CR3 241 L9
DART DA1 186 E1
DORK RH4 254 G10
DORK RH4 272 G1
DTCH/LGLY SL3 149 N6
DTCH/LGLY SL3 149 P2
EGH TW20 171 P10
ENC/FH EN2 79 L9
EW KT17 220 C5
EYN DA4 209 L6
EYN DA4 209 M6
FSTH SE23 182 B4
GRAYS RM17 167 M5
GU GU1 250 D8
GVW DA11 190 A2
HERT/BAY SG13 25 N6
HHS/BOV HP3 53 P1
HHW HP1 34 E8
HLWE CM17 29 M8
HLWE CM17 47 L2
HORL RH6 280 B7
HRW HA1 114 D7
ISLW TW7 154 D8
ISLW TW7 154 E8
KUTN/CMB KT2 199 L2
MRDN SM4 201 K5
MTCM CR4 201 P4
MTCM CR4 202 B7
PLSTW E13 141 M4
PUR RM19 165 P4
RAD WD7 57 L9
RDART DA2 188 B3
RDKG RH5 255 H8
REDH RH1 258 B9
REIG RH2 257 K9
RGUE GU4 250 E7
ROMW/RG RM7 124 B4
RPLY/SEND GU23 251 H2
RSEV TN14 228 A5
SBW CM21 29 P1
SEV TN13 246 E4
SEV TN13 246 F7
SOCK/AV RM15 145 N10
STA TW18 173 J7
STAL AL1 38 F9
STAN HA7 95 J5
STHWK SE1 18 D3
STRHM/NOR SW16 202 C2
SWCM DA10 189 H1
SWLY BR8 208 D2
THHTH CR7 203 H4
TIL RM18 168 E8
TWK TW1 176 F3
WARE SG12 26 D4
WBLY HA9 115 K10
WLGTN SM6 202 C10
WTHK RM20 167 K5
London Rd East AMSS HP7 69 K7
London Rd North REDH RH1 240 C10
London Rd Purfleet PUR RM19 166 B5
London Rd South REDH RH1 258 C6
London Rd West AMSS HP7 69 H6
London Rd West Thurrock
WTHK RM20 166 D5
Londons Cl UPMR RM14 126 B10
London Sq GU GU1 * 250 B10
London Stile CHSWK W4 155 M4
London St BAY/PAD W2 9 M6
CHERT KT16 195 K7
FENCHST EC3M * 13 K7
London Ter BETH E2 * 7 N8
London Wall CITYW EC2V 12 F4
LVPST EC2M 13 H5
London Wall Buildings
LVPST EC2M 13 H4
Loneacre BFOR GU20 * 212 D3
Lone Oak HORL RH6 281 J6
Lonesome La REIG RH2 275 M4
Lonesome Wy MTCM CR4 202 C1
Long Acre COVGDN WC2E 11 L6
CRAWE RH10 285 P5
HLWE CM17 29 L7
ORP BR6 207 N9
Long Acre Ct WEA W13 * 134 F7
Longacre Pl CAR SM5 * 222 B3
Longacre Rd WALTH E17 101 J9
Longacres STALE/WH AL4 39 J6
Longaford Wy RBRW/HUT CM13 107 P2
Long Arrotts HHW HP1 35 L4
Long Av CHOB/PIR GU24 230 F7
Long Banks HLWS CM18 46 G5
Long Barn Cl GSTN WD25 55 H8
Long Barn Rd RSEV TN14 265 J9
Longbeach Rd BTSEA SW11 158 A9
Longboat Rw STHL UB1 133 N8
Longbottom La BEAC HP9 88 G8
Longbourn WDSR SL4 148 F9
Longbourne Wy CHERT KT16 195 J6
Longboyds COB KT11 217 J10
Longbridge Rd BARK IG11 142 G1
HORL RH6 280 A6
Longbridge Wk HORL RH6 280 A6
Longbridge Wy HORL RH6 280 A6
LEW SE13 183 H1
UX/CGN UB8 131 L4
Long Buftlers HARP AL5 20 E3
Longbury Cl STMC/STPC BR5 207 L3
Longbury Dr STMC/STPC BR5 207 L3
Longchamp Cl HORL RH6 280 D4
Long Chaulden HHW HP1 35 H7
Longcliffe Pth OXHEY WD19 93 H4
Long Cl SLN SL2 128 G2
Long Copse Cl GT/LBKH KT23 236 A9
Long Ct PUR RM19 165 P3
Longcroft ELTH/MOT SE9 184 D6
Long Cft OXHEY WD19 93 J1
Longcroft Av BNSTD SM7 221 M10
Long Croft Dr CHES/WCR EN8 62 E10
Longcrofte Rd EDGW HA8 95 J8
Longcroft Gdns WGCW AL8 22 G6
Longcroft Gn WGCW AL8 22 G7
Longcroft La HHS/BOV HP3 52 F4
WGCW AL8 22 G6
Longcroft Ri LOU IG10 82 E9
Long Croft Rd
RKW/CH/CXG WD3 90 G6
Longcross Rd CHERT KT16 193 N10
Long Deacon Rd CHING E4 101 K2
Longdean Pk HHS/BOV HP3 36 B10
Longdon Wd HAYES BR2 226 B1
Longdown La North EW KT17 220 D9
Longdown La South EW KT17 238 D1
Longdown Rd CAT SE6 182 F7
EW KT17 220 D10
RGUE GU4 268 E3
Long Dr ACT W3 136 B8
GFD/PVL UB6 134 A3
RSLP HA4 113 L9
SL SL1 128 B5
WDR/YW UB7 * 151 P1
Long Dyke GU GU1 250 E8
Long Elmes KTN/HRWW/WS HA3 94 A9
Long Elms ABLGY WD5 54 E9
Long Elms Cl ABLGY WD5 54 E9
Long Fallow LCOL/BKTW AL2 55 P3
Longfellow Dr RBRW/HUT CM13 107 P1
Longfellow Rd WALTH E17 120 E4
WCHPL E1 * 140 D5
WPK KT4 200 D8
Longfellow Wy STHWK SE1 * 19 M6
Longfield BMLY BR1 205 L1
Long Fld CDALE/KGS NW9 96 B9
Longfield HHS/BOV HP3 36 C8
HLWS CM18 47 K3
LOU IG10 81 P9
SLN SL2 109 J8
Longfield Av EA W5 135 H9
EMPK RM11 124 G5
HART DA3 211 P2
MLHL NW7 96 D8
PEND EN3 80 B3
WALTH E17 120 D2
WBLY HA9 115 K6
WLGTN SM6 202 B8
Longfield Crs
KWD/TDW/WH KT20 238 F6
SYD SE26 182 B6
Longfield Dr AMS HP6 68 G4
MORT/ESHN SW14 177 N1
MTCM CR4 201 P1
Longfield Est STHWK SE1 19 M5
Longfield La CHESW EN7 61 N3
Longfield Rd CSHM HP5 50 E5
DORK RH4 272 E3
EA W5 135 H8
HARP AL5 20 B4
Long Flds CHONG CM5 67 P6
Longfield St WAND/EARL SW18 179 K3
Longford Av EBED/NFELT TW14 174 G2
STHL UB1 133 P9
STWL/WRAY TW19 173 P4
Longford Cl FELT TW13 175 M6
Londford Cl HPTN TW12 175 P7
Longford Cl YEAD UB4 133 L9
Longford Ct HOR/WEW KT19 219 P1
HPTN TW12 176 A9
Longford Gdns SUT SM1 201 M10
YEAD UB4 133 L9
Longford Rd WHTN TW2 175 P4
Longford St CAMTN NW1 10 F1
Longford Wy STWL/WRAY TW19 173 P4
Long Furlong Dr SLN SL2 128 D6
Long Gore GODL GU7 267 K9
Long Gn CHIG IG7 103 H5
Long Gv BEAC HP9 89 H7
HARH RM3 105 M10
Long Grove Cl BROX EN10 44 D5
Long Grove Rd HOR/WEW KT19 219 N6
PUR/KEN CR8 222 F7
Longhayes Av CHDH RM6 123 N1
Longheath Dr GT/LBKH KT23 235 M10
Longheath Gdns CROY/NA CR0 204 B5
Longhedge St BTSEA SW11 158 B8
Long Hl CTHM CR3 242 D7
Longhill Rd CAT SE6 183 J5
Longhook Gdns NTHLT UB5 133 H5
Longhope Cl PECK SE15 19 K10
Longhouse Rd CDW/CHF RM16 168 E2
Longhurst Rd CROY/NA CR0 204 A6
EHSLY KT24 252 F5
LEW SE13 183 K1
Long John HHS/BOV HP3 36 A8
Longland Dr TRDG/WHET N20 97 L4
Longlands HHNE HP2 36 B6
Longlands Av COUL/CHIP CR5 222 C10
Longlands Cl CHES/WCR EN8 62 C8
Longlands Park Crs
BFN/LL DA15 185 H6
Longlands Rd BFN/LL DA15 185 H6
WGCE AL7 23 J7
Long La BXLYHN DA7 163 P6
CDW/CHF RM16 167 N1
CROY/NA CR0 204 B6
FNCH N3 97 L9
HGDN/ICK UB10 112 C9
HHS/BOV HP3 52 C7
RKW/CH/CXG WD3 70 F10
RKW/CH/CXG WD3 91 J2
STBT EC1A 12 D3
STHWK SE1 19 H2
STWL/WRAY TW19 174 A2
Longleat Rd EN EN1 79 M9
Longleat Wy EBED/NFELT TW14 174 D3
Longleigh La ABYW SE2 163 M5
Long Ley HLW CM20 47 J1
WGCE AL7 23 M5
Longley Av ALP/SUD HA0 135 L3
Longley Ms CDW/CHF RM16 168 C1
Longley Rd CROY/NA CR0 203 J7
HRW HA1 114 C3
TOOT SW17 179 P9
Long Leys CHING E4 100 G7
Longley St STHWK SE1 19 N6
Longley Wy CRICK NW2 116 F8
Long Lodge Dr WOT/HER KT12 197 K10
Longmans Cl WATW WD18 72 D10
Long Mark Rd CAN/RD E16 142 A8
Longmarsh La THMD SE28 143 H10
Longmarsh Vw EYN DA4 210 A1
Long Md CDALE/KGS NW9 96 C9
Longmead CHST BR7 206 D2
GU GU1 250 F10
HAT AL10 40 E1
WDSR SL4 148 D7
Longmead Cl BRWN CM15 107 K2
CTHM CR3 241 M8
Longmead Dr SCUP DA14 185 N5
Longmeade GVE DA12 191 J4
Longmead La SL SL1 128 C2
Long Meadow CSHM HP5 51 H4
Longmeadow GT/LBKH KT23 253 N1
Long Meadow HARH RM3 105 K4
KTTN NW5 * 5 J1
RBRW/HUT CM13 107 P3
Longmeadow SEV TN13 246 E7
Long Meadow Cl WWKM BR4 205 H7
Longmeadow Rd BFN/LL DA15 185 H4
Longmeadow Vls HORL RH6 * 279 H10
Longmead Rd HOR/WEW KT19 220 B6
HYS/HAR UB3 132 G9
THDIT KT7 198 D7
TOOT SW17 180 A7
Longmere Gdns
KWD/TDW/WH KT20 238 F5
Longmere Rd CRAWE RH10 283 N5
Long Mimms HHNE HP2 35 P5
Long Moor CHES/WCR EN8 62 D5
Longmoore St PIM SW1V 16 G6
Longmore Av BAR EN5 77 M10
Longmore Cl RKW/CH/CXG WD3 91 J5
Longmore Gdns WGCE AL7 23 J5
Longmore Rd WOT/HER KT12 217 M1
Longnor Rd WCHPL E1 140 C5
Long Pk AMS HP6 69 H2
Long Park Cl AMS HP6 69 H2
Long Park Wy AMS HP6 69 H2
Long Pond Rd BKHTH/KID SE3 161 K7
Longport Cl BARK/HLT IG6 103 K7
Long Reach RPLY/SEND GU23 234 C10
Long Reach Rd BARK IG11 143 J6
Longreach Rd ERITH DA8 165 J6
Long Readings La SLN SL2 128 G6
Longridge RAD WD7 56 G10
Longridge Gv
WOKS/MYFD GU22 215 H10
Longridge La STHL UB1 134 A9
Longridge Rd ECT SW5 14 E6
Long Ridings Av
RBRW/HUT CM13 87 N9
Long Rd CLAP SW4 158 D10
Longs Cl WOKS/MYFD GU22 233 K2
Longsdon Wy CTHM CR3 241 P10
Long Shaw LHD/OX KT22 236 F5
Longshaw Rd CHING E4 101 J4
Longshore DEPT SE8 160 E3
Longside Cl EGH TW20 194 F1
Long Spring STALW/RED AL3 38 E2
Longspring WATN WD24 73 J3
Longstaff Crs WAND/EARL SW18 179 K3
Longstaff Rd WAND/EARL SW18 179 K2
Longstone Av WLSDN NW10 136 C2
Longstone Rd IVER SL0 130 F4
TOOT SW17 180 C8
Long St BETH E2 7 L9
WAB EN9 64 B6
Longthornton Rd
STRHM/NOR SW16 202 D2
Longton Av SYD SE26 181 P7
Longton Gv SYD SE26 182 A7
Longtown Cl HARH RM3 105 K6
Longtown Rd HARH RM3 105 K6
Long Vw BERK HP4 33 M3
Longview Wy CRW RM5 104 E9
Longville Rd LBTH SE11 18 C5
Long Wk CSTG HP8 70 B7
EPSOM KT18 238 G5
NWMAL KT3 199 P3
STHWK SE1 19 K3
WDSR SL4 * 171 J1
Longwalk Rd STKPK UB11 132 C10
The Long Wk WDSR SL4 171 J1
Long Wd HLWS CM18 46 G6
Longwood Av DTCH/LGLY SL3 150 E4
Longwood Cl UPMR RM14 126 B10
Longwood Ct WPK KT4 200 D9
Long Wood Dr BEAC HP9 89 L7
Longwood Dr PUT/ROE SW15 178 E3
Longwood Gdns CLAY IG5 122 C2
Longwood La AMSS HP7 69 J5
Longwood Rd HERT/WAT SG14 24 G4
PUR/KEN CR8 241 L2
Longwood Vw CRAWE RH10 284 B10
Longworth Cl THMD SE28 143 N8
Long Yd BMSBY WC1N 11 N2
The Loning CDALE/KGS NW9 116 C2
PEND EN3 80 B4
Lonsdale HHNE HP2 35 P3
Lonsdale Av EHAM E6 142 A6
ROMW/RG RM7 124 D4
WBLY HA9 115 K10
Lonsdale Cl EHAM E6 142 B6
ELTH/MOT SE9 184 A6
UX/CGN UB8 132 D8
Lonsdale Crs GNTH/NBYPK IG2 122 E4
RDART DA2 188 B5
Lonsdale Dr ENC/FH EN2 78 F9
Lonsdale Dr North ENC/FH EN2 78 F9
Lonsdale Gdns THHTH CR7 202 G4
Lonsdale Ms NTGHL W11 8 D6
RCH/KEW TW9 * 155 M7
Lonsdale Pl IS N1 6 B4
Lonsdale Rd BXLYHN DA7 164 A8
CHSWK W4 156 C3
DORK RH4 272 G1
KIL/WHAMP NW6 2 C7
NTGHL W11 8 C6
NWDGN UB2 153 L2
SNWD SE25 204 A4
WAN E11 121 L5
WEY KT13 216 B4
Lonsdale Sq IS N1 6 B4
Loobert Rd SEVS/STOTM N15 119 M1
Looe Gdns BARK/HLT IG6 122 E1
Loom La RAD WD7 74 F3
Loop Rd CHST BR7 184 F9
EPSOM KT18 237 P2
WAB EN9 62 G8
WOKS/MYFD GU22 232 C6
Lopen Rd UED N18 99 M5
Loppets Rd CRAWE RH10 284 A9
Loraine Cl PEND EN3 80 B9
Loraine Cottages HOLWY N7 * 118 G9
Loraine Gdns ASHTD KT21 237 K3
Loraine Rd CHSWK W4 155 N5
HOLWY N7 118 G9
Lord Av CLAY IG5 122 C2
Lord Chancellor Wk
KUTN/CMB KT2 199 P1
Lord Chathman's Ride
RSEV TN14 245 P4
Lorden Wk BETH E2 7 N10
Lord Gdns CLAY IG5 122 B2
Lord Hills Rd BAY/PAD W2 9 H3
Lord Holland La BRXN/ST SW9 * 159 H8
Lord Knyvett Cl
STWL/WRAY TW19 173 N2
Lord Knyvetts Ct
STWL/WRAY TW19 * 173 P2
Lord Mayors Dr SLN SL2 128 E1
Lord Napier Pl HMSMTH W6 156 D4
Lord North St WEST SW1P 17 L4
Lord Roberts Ms
FUL/PGN SW6 * 157 L6
Lordsbury Fld WLGTN SM6 222 D6
Lords Cl DUL SE21 181 K5
FELT TW13 175 M5
RAD WD7 57 K8
Lordsgrove Cl
KWD/TDW/WH KT20 238 E6
Lordship Gv STNW/STAM N16 119 L7
Lordship La EDUL SE22 181 N2
WDGN N22 99 H10
Lordship Pk STNW/STAM N16 119 L7
Lordship Park Ms
STNW/STAM N16 119 K7
Lordship Pl CHEL SW3 15 N10
Lordship Rd CHESW EN7 62 A6
NTHLT UB5 133 M2
STNW/STAM N16 119 L7
Lordship Ter STNW/STAM N16 119 L7
Lordsmead Rd TOTM N17 99 M9
Lords Mill Ct CSHM HP5 51 H8
Lord St CAN/RD E16 142 B10
GVE DA12 190 E3
HOD EN11 44 D3
WAT WD17 73 K7
Lords Vw STJWD NW8 3 N10
Lords Wd WGCE AL7 23 M5
Lordswood Cl RDART DA2 188 D7
Lord Warwick St
WOOL/PLUM SE18 162 C2
Lorenzo St FSBYW WC1X 5 N9
Loretto Gdns
KTN/HRWW/WS HA3 115 K2
Lorian Cl NFNCH/WDSPK N12 97 L5
Lorian Dr REIG RH2 257 M9
Loriners CRAWE RH10 283 N10
Loriners Cl COB KT11 217 H10
Loring Rd BERK HP4 33 P6
ISLW TW7 154 E8
TRDG/WHET N20 97 P3
WDSR SL4 148 E7
Loris Rd HMSMTH W6 156 F2
Lorn Ct BRXN/ST SW9 159 H8
Lorne Av CROY/NA CR0 204 C7
Lorne Cl SL SL1 148 G2
STJWD NW8 3 P10
Lorne Gdns CROY/NA CR0 204 D7
NTGHL W11 156 G1
WAN E11 121 P2
WOKN/KNAP GU21 231 J5
Lorne Rd BRW CM14 107 H5
FSBYPK N4 118 G6
FSTGT E7 121 N9
KTN/HRWW/WS HA3 94 E10
RCHPK/HAM TW10 177 L1
WALTH E17 120 F3
Lorne Ter FNCH N3 * 97 J10
The Lorne GT/LBKH KT23 253 P2
Lorn Rd BRXN/ST SW9 158 G8
Lorraine Pk KTN/HRWW/WS HA3 94 D8
Lorrimore Rd WALW SE17 18 D10
Lorrimore Sq WALW SE17 18 D9
Lorton Cl GVE DA12 191 H5
Loseberry Rd ESH/CLAY KT10 218 C2
Loseley Rd GODL GU7 267 K9
Losfield Rd WDSR SL4 148 E7
Lossie Dr IVER SL0 130 E9
Lothair Rd EA W5 155 J1
Lothair Rd North FSBYPK N4 119 J4
Lothair Rd South FSBYPK N4 119 H5
Lothbury LOTH EC2R 12 G5
Lothian Av YEAD UB4 133 J7
Lothian Cl ALP/SUD HA0 114 F9
Lothian Rd BRXN/ST SW9 159 J7
Lothian Wd KWD/TDW/WH KT20 238 E8
Lothrop St NKENS W10 2 A10
Lots Rd WBPTN SW10 157 M6
Lotus Rd BH/WHM TN16 244 C4
Loubet St TOOT SW17 180 A9
Loudhams Rd AMSS HP7 69 P5
Loudhams Wood La CSTG HP8 70 A6
Loudoun Av BARK/HLT IG6 122 E3
Loudoun Rd STJWD NW8 3 K6
Loudwater Cl SUN TW16 197 H4
Loudwater Dr
RKW/CH/CXG WD3 71 M8
Loudwater Hts
RKW/CH/CXG WD3 71 L7
Loudwater La RKW/CH/CXG WD3 71 M9
Loudwater Rdg
RKW/CH/CXG WD3 71 M8
Loughborough Pk
BRXN/ST SW9 159 J10
Loughborough Rd
BRXN/ST SW9 159 J8
Loughborough St LBTH SE11 17 P8
Lough Rd HOLWY N7 5 P1
Loughton La EPP CM16 82 G3
Loughton Wy BKHH IG9 102 A2
Louisa Cl HOM E9 140 B2
Louisa St WCHPL E1 140 C7
Louis Cl CHST BR7 184 C7
Louise Bennett Cl HNHL SE24 * 159 J10
Louise Gdns RAIN RM13 144 F5
Louise Rd SRTFD E15 141 K1
Louise Wk HHS/BOV HP3 52 D4
Louis Flds RGUW GU3 249 H6
Louisville Cl WARE SG12 27 H7
Louisville Rd TOOT SW17 180 B6
Louvaine Rd BTSEA SW11 157 N10
Louvain Rd RDART DA2 188 D3
Louvain Wy GSTN WD25 55 J8
Lovage Ap EHAM E6 142 B7
Lovat Cl CRICK NW2 116 C8
Lovat La FENCHST EC3M 13 J7
Lovatt Cl EDGW HA8 95 N7
Lovatts RKW/CH/CXG WD3 72 B8
Loveday Rd WEA W13 134 G10
Love Green La IVER SL0 130 G7
Lovegrove Dr SLN SL2 128 E6
Lovegrove St STHWK SE1 19 P9
Lovegrove Wk POP/IOD E14 141 H10
Love Hill La DTCH/LGLY SL3 130 D9
Lovejoy La WDSR SL4 148 C8
Lovekyn Cl KUTN/CMB KT2 199 L2
Lovelace Av HAYES BR2 206 D6
Lovelace Cl EHSLY KT24 235 H9
Lovelace Dr WOKS/MYFD GU22 233 J1
Lovelace Gdns BARK IG11 123 K10
SURB KT6 199 J7
WOT/HER KT12 217 K2
Lovelace Gn ELTH/MOT SE9 162 C9
Lovelace Rd DUL SE21 181 K5
EBAR EN4 97 P1
SURB KT6 199 H7
Lovelace Vls THDIT KT7 * 198 G7
Lovelands La CHOB/PIR GU24 213 H9
KWD/TDW/WH KT20 257 L3
Love La ABLGY WD5 54 G6
BXLY DA5 186 B2
CHEAM SM3 221 H3
CHONG CM5 67 P4
CITYW EC2V 12 F5
GDST RH9 260 B8
IVER SL0 130 G8
KGLGY WD4 53 P5
KWD/TDW/WH KT20 256 D2
MRDN SM4 201 K7
MTCM CR4 201 P3
PIN HA5 113 M1
SNWD SE25 204 A3
SOCK/AV RM15 166 B1
SURB KT6 199 J9
TIL RM18 169 M5
TOTM N17 99 N8
WFD IG8 102 C7
WOOL/PLUM SE18 162 D3
Lovel Av WELL DA16 163 K8
Lovel Cl HHW HP1 35 K7
Lovel End CFSP/GDCR SL9 89 P8
Loveletts CRAWW RH11 283 K8
Lovel Hl WDSR SL4 * 170 A8
Lovelinch Cl PECK SE15 160 B5
Lovel La WDSR SL4 170 A8
Lovell Pl BERM/RHTH SE16 160 D2
Lovell Rd EN EN1 80 A1
RCHPK/HAM TW10 177 H6
STHL UB1 134 A8
Lovells Cl LTWR GU18 212 A6
Lovell Wk RAIN RM13 145 H1
Lovel Md CFSP/GDCR SL9 89 P8
Lovelock Cl PUR/KEN CR8 241 K3
Lovel Rd CFSP/GDCR SL9 89 P8
Loveridge Ms KIL/WHAMP NW6 2 C2
Loveridge Rd KIL/WHAMP NW6 2 D2
Lovering Rd CHESW EN7 61 K1
Lover's La SWCM DA10 167 J10
Lovet Rd HLWW/ROY CM19 46 D2
Lovett Dr CAR SM5 201 M7
Lovett Rd DEN/HRF UB9 111 M1
LCOL/BKTW AL2 56 F2
STA TW18 172 E7
Lovetts Pl WAND/EARL SW18 157 M10
Lovett Wy WLSDN NW10 115 P10
Love Wk CMBW SE5 159 L8
Lovibonds Av ORP BR6 206 E10
WDR/YW UB7 132 A8
Lowbell La LCOL/BKTW AL2 57 L3
Lowbrook Rd IL IG1 122 E9
Lowburys DORK RH4 272 F5

Low Cl RDART DA2 188 F1
Lowdell Cl WDR/YW UB7 131 P8
Lowden Rd ED N9 100 A2
HNHL SE24 159 J10
STHL UB1 133 M9
Lowe Av CAN/RD E16 141 M7
Lowe Cl CHIG IG7 103 K6
Lowell St POP/IOD E14 140 D8
Lowen Rd RAIN RM13 144 E4
Lower Addiscombe Rd
CROY/NA CR0 203 L8
Lower Addison Gdns
WKENS W14 14 A2
Lower Adeyfield Rd HHNE HP2 35 N5
Lower Barn HHS/BOV HP3 36 A9
Lower Barn Rd PUR/KEN CR8 223 L9
Lower Bedfords Rd ROM RM1 105 H7
Lower Belgrave St BGVA SW1W 16 E4
Lower Boston Rd HNWL W7 134 D10
Lower Bridge Rd REDH RH1 258 A10
Lower Britwell Rd SLN SL2 128 C6
Lower Broad St DAGE RM10 144 B3
Lower Bury La EPP CM16 65 H7
Lower Camden CHST BR7 206 C1
Lower Church St CROY/NA CR0 * 203 J9
Lower Cippenham La SL SL1 128 E10
Lower Clabdens WARE SG12 26 E2
Lower Clapton Rd CLPT E5 120 A9
Lower Clarendon Wk NKENS W10 8 A6
Lower Common South
PUT/ROE SW15 156 E9
Lower Coombe St CROY/NA CR0 223 K1
Lower Court Rd HOR/WEW KT19 219 P7
Lower Crs SLH/COR SS17 169 K2
Lower Cft SWLY BR8 208 G4
Lower Dagnall St
STALW/RED AL3 38 B6
Lower Derby Rd WAT WD17 73 K8
Lower Downs Rd RYNPK SW20 200 G1
Lower Dr BEAC HP9 88 C6
Lower Dunnymans BNSTD SM7 221 P7
Lower Edgeborough Rd GU GU1 268 C1
Lower Emms HHNE HP2 36 D1
Lower Farm Rd EHSLY KT24 235 J10
Lowerfield WCCE AL7 23 K6
Lower Forecourt HORL RH6 280 C8
Lower Gravel Rd HAYES BR2 206 B8
Lower Green Gdns WPK KT4 200 D8
Lower Green Rd ESH/CLAY KT10 198 A9
Lower Gn West MTCM CR4 201 P3
Lower Grosvenor Pl BGVA SW1W 16 E3
Lower Grove Rd
RCHPK/HAM TW10 177 L2
Lower Guildford Rd
WOKN/KNAP GU21 231 J3
Lower Hall La CHING E4 100 D6
Lower Hampton Rd SUN TW16 197 L2
Lower Ham Rd KUTN/CMB KT2 177 J9
Lower Hatfield Rd
HERT/BAY SG13 42 F1
Lower Higham Rd GVE DA12 191 J4
Lower High St WAT WD17 73 L9
Lower Hill Rd HOR/WEW KT19 219 N8
Lower Island Wy WAB EN9 80 G1
Lower James St
SOHO/CST W1F * 11 H7
Lower John St SOHO/CST W1F 11 H7
Lower Kenwood Av ENC/FH EN2 78 F9
Lower Kings Rd BERK HP4 33 N5
KUTN/CMB KT2 199 K1
Lower Lea Crossing
POP/IOD E14 141 K9
Lower Lees Rd SLN SL2 128 F5
Lower Luton Rd STALE/WH AL4 20 E1
Lower Maidstone Rd
FBAR/BDGN N11 98 D7
Lower Mardyke Av RAIN RM13 144 D4
Lower Marsh STHWK SE1 18 A2
Lower Marsh La BRYLDS KT5 199 L4
Lower Md IVER SL0 130 G5
Lower Meadow CHES/WCR EN8 62 C3
HLWS CM18 47 H5
Lower Merton Ri HAMP NW3 3 N4
Lower Morden La MRDN SM4 200 G6
Lower Mortlake Rd
RCH/KEW TW9 155 K10
Lower Noke Cl BRW CM14 105 N3
Lower Northfield BNSTD SM7 221 J10
Lower Nursery ASC SL5 192 E1
Lower Paddock Rd OXHEY WD19 73 M10
Lower Park Rd BELV DA17 164 B3
COUL/CHIP CR5 239 P4
FBAR/BDGN N11 98 D6
LOU IG10 82 B9
Lower Paxton Rd STAL AL1 38 D7
Lower Peryers EHSLY KT24 252 F4
Lower Pillory Down CAR SM5 222 C8
Lower Plantation
RKW/CH/CXG WD3 71 M7
Lower Queen's Rd BKHH IG9 102 B3
Lower Range Rd GVE DA12 191 H3
Lower Richmond Rd
PUT/ROE SW15 156 F9
RCH/KEW TW9 155 N9
Lower Riding BEAC HP9 88 A10
Lower Rd BELV DA17 164 D2
BERM/RHTH SE16 160 B2
CFSP/GDCR SL9 110 B1
DEN/HRF UB9 110 F5
GT/LBKH KT23 253 N2
GVE DA12 191 P5
GVW DA11 167 M10
HHS/BOV HP3 54 B2
LHD/OX KT22 236 D9
LOU IG10 82 D5
PUR/KEN CR8 223 J9
REDH RH1 275 N2
RKW/CH/CXG WD3 70 G8
RYLN/HDSTN HA2 114 C7
STMC/STPC BR5 207 L6
SUT SM1 221 N2
SWLY BR8 187 J10
TIL RM18 168 D9
WARE SG12 26 E5
Lower Sales HHW HP1 35 J7
Lower Sandfields
RPLY/SEND GU23 232 G9
Lower Sand Hills SURB KT6 199 H7
Lower Sawleywood BNSTD SM7 221 J10
Lower Shott CHESW EN7 61 N2
GT/LBKH KT23 253 P2
Lower Sloane St BGVA SW1W 16 B6
Lower Sq ISLW TW7 154 G9
Lower Station Rd DART DA1 186 F2
Lower Strd CDALE/KGS NW9 96 C10
Lower St SHGR GU5 270 B5
Lower Sunbury Rd
E/WMO/HCT KT8 197 N2
Lower Swaines EPP CM16 65 H6
Lower Tail OXHEY WD19 93 M4
Lower Teddington Rd
KUT/HW KT1 199 J1
Lower Ter HAMP NW3 117 M8
Lower Thames St MON EC3R 13 K8
Lower Tub BUSH WD23 94 C1
Lower Village Rd ASC SL5 192 C4
Lower Wood Rd ESH/CLAY KT10 218 G3
Lower Yott HHNE HP2 35 P7
Lowestoft Dr SL SL1 128 B8
Lowestoft Rd WATN WD24 73 J5
Loweswater Cl GSTN WD25 55 K9
WBLY HA9 115 J7
The Lowe CHIG IG7 103 K6
Lowfield SBW CM21 29 N4
Lowfield Heath Rd HORL RH6 279 J10
Lowfield La HOD EN11 44 F3
Lowfield Rd KIL/WHAMP NW6 2 E3
Lowfield St DART DA1 187 M3
Lowfield Wy HORL RH6 279 P10
Low Hall Cl CHING E4 100 F1
Low Hall La WALTH E17 120 D4
Low Hill Rd HLWW/ROY CM19 45 L3
Lowick Rd HRW HA1 114 D2
Lowland Gdns ROMW/RG RM7 124 D4
Lowlands BRKMPK AL9 40 F1
Lowlands Dr STWL/WRAY TW19 173 N1
Lowlands Rd HRW HA1 114 D5
PIN HA5 113 K5
SOCK/AV RM15 146 B10
Lowman Rd HOLWY N7 118 G9
Lowndes Av CSHM HP5 50 G6
Lowndes Cl KTBR SW1X 16 D4
Lowndes Ct SOHO/CST W1F * 10 G6
Lowndes Pl KTBR SW1X * 16 D4
Lowndes Sq KTBR SW1X 16 B2
Lowndes St KTBR SW1X 16 C3
Lowood St WCHPL E1 140 A9
Low Rd BRKMPK AL9 42 A1
Lowry Cl ERITH DA8 164 E3
Lowry Crs MTCM CR4 201 P2
Lowry Rd BCTR RM8 123 L10
Lowshoe La CRW RM5 104 C9
Lowson Gv OXHEY WD19 93 M1
Low Street La TIL RM18 169 J5
Lowswood Cl NTHWD HA6 92 D9
Lowther Cl BORE WD6 75 L9
Lowther Dr ENC/FH EN2 78 F9
Lowther Hl FSTH SE23 182 D3
Lowther Man BARN SW13 * 156 D6
Lowther Rd BARN SW13 156 C6
HOLWY N7 * 119 H10
KUTN/CMB KT2 199 L1
STAN HA7 115 L1
WALTH E17 100 D10
Lowth Rd CMBW SE5 159 K8
Loxford Av EHAM E6 142 A4
Loxford La IL IG1 122 F10
Loxford Rd BARK IG11 142 E1
CTHM CR3 259 N1
Loxford Wy CTHM CR3 259 N1
Loxham Rd CHING E4 100 G8
Loxham St STPAN WC1H * 5 M10
Loxley Cl SYD SE26 182 C8
Loxley Ct WARE SG12 * 26 G2
Loxley Rd BERK HP4 33 K3
HPTN TW12 175 N7
WAND/EARL SW18 179 N4
Loxton Rd FSTH SE23 182 D5
Loxwood Cl EBED/NFELT TW14 174 E4
STMC/STPC BR5 207 N9
Loxwood Rd SEVS/STOTM N15 119 M1
Loxwood Wk CRAWW RH11 283 J6
Lubbock Rd CHST BR7 206 D1
Lubbock St NWCR SE14 160 B6
Lucan Dr STA TW18 173 N10
Lucan Pl CHEL SW3 15 N6
Lucan Rd BAR EN5 77 H7
Lucas Av PLSTW E13 141 N3
RYLN/HDSTN HA2 113 P7
Lucas Cl WAB EN9 63 L9
Lucas Crs SWCM DA10 188 G1
Lucas Gdns EFNCH N2 97 M10
Lucas Green Rd CHOB/PIR GU24 230 C1
Lucas Rd GRAYS RM17 167 M2
PGE/AN SE20 182 B9
Lucas Sq GLDGN NW11 117 K4
Lucas St BROCKY SE4 160 F8
Lucern Cl CHESW EN7 61 M3
Lucerne Cl PLMGR N13 98 F4
WOKS/MYFD GU22 232 B5
Lucerne Ct ERITH DA8 * 164 C2
Lucerne Dr CRAWE RH10 284 E9
Lucerne Gv WALTH E17 121 J2
Lucerne Ms KENS W8 * 8 F9
Lucerne Rd HBRY N5 119 J9
ORP BR6 207 J8
THHTH CR7 203 J5
Lucerne Wy HARH RM3 105 L7
Lucey Rd BERM/RHTH SE16 19 N4
Lucey Wy BERM/RHTH SE16 19 P4
BERM/RHTH SE16 159 P2
Lucie Av ASHF TW15 174 C9
Lucien Rd TOOT SW17 180 B7
WIM/MER SW19 179 L5
Lucinda Ct EN EN1 * 79 L5
Lucknow St WOOL/PLUM SE18 163 H6
Lucks Hl HHW HP1 35 H6
Lucorn Cl LEE/GVPK SE12 183 L2
Luctons Av BKHH IG9 101 P2
Luddesdon Rd ERITH DA8 164 B6
Luddington Av VW GU25 194 C2
Ludford Cl CROY/NA CR0 223 J1
Ludgate Broadway
BLKFR EC4V * 12 D6
Ludgate Circ STP EC4M 12 C6
Ludgate Hl STP EC4M 12 C6
Ludgate Sq STP EC4M * 12 D6
Ludham Cl BARK/HLT IG6 102 F9
THMD SE28 143 M8
Ludlow Cl HAYES BR2 * 205 M3
RYLN/HDSTN HA2 113 N8
Ludlow Md OXHEY WD19 93 J4
Ludlow Pl GRAYS RM17 167 N2
Ludlow Rd EA W5 135 H6
FELT TW13 175 H6
GUW GU2 267 N1
Ludlow St FSBYE EC1V * 12 E1
Ludlow Wy EFNCH N2 117 M2
RKW/CH/CXG WD3 72 D8
Ludovick Wk PUT/ROE SW15 156 B10
Ludwick Cl WGCE AL7 * 23 J7
Ludwick Gn WGCE AL7 * 23 J6
Ludwick Wy WGCE AL7 23 J5
Luff Cl WDSR SL4 148 D9
Luffield Rd ABYW SE2 163 L2
Luffman Rd LEE/GVPK SE12 183 N6
Lugard Rd PECK SE15 160 A8
Lugg Ap MNPK E12 122 D8
Luke St SDTCH EC2A 13 J1
Lukin Crs CHING E4 101 J4
Lukin St WCHPL E1 140 B9
Lullarook Cl BH/WHM TN16 243 P2
Lullingstone Av SWLY BR8 208 G3
Lullingstone Cl STMC/STPC BR5 185 L10
Lullingstone Crs STMC/STPC BR5 185 K10
Lullingstone La EYN DA4 209 K10
LEW SE13 183 J2
Lullingstone Rd BELV DA17 164 A5
Lullington Garth BMLY BR1 183 K10
BORE WD6 * 75 P9
NFNCH/WDSPK N12 97 J6
Lullington Rd DAGW RM9 143 P2
PGE/AN SE20 181 P10
Lulot Gdns ARCH N19 118 C7
Lulworth Av CHESW EN7 61 J5
HEST TW5 154 A7
WBLY HA9 115 H5
Lulworth Cl CRAWW RH11 283 K10
RYLN/HDSTN HA2 113 N8
Lulworth Crs MTCM CR4 201 P2
Lulworth Dr CRW RM5 104 C6
PIN HA5 113 L5
Lulworth Gdns RYLN/HDSTN HA2 113 M7
Lulworth Rd ELTH/MOT SE9 184 B5
PECK SE15 * 160 A8
WELL DA16 163 J8
Lulworth Waye YEAD UB4 133 J8
Lumbards WGCE AL7 23 K2
Lumen Rd WBLY HA9 115 J7
Lumley Cl BELV DA17 164 D5
Lumley Gdns CHEAM SM3 221 H2
Lumley Rd CHEAM SM3 221 H3
HORL RH6 280 B4
Lumley St OXSTW W1C 10 D6
Luna Cl BH/WHM TN16 244 A2
Luna Rd THHTH CR7 203 K3
Lundin Wk OXHEY WD19 * 93 L5
Lundy Cl CRAWW RH11 283 M10
Lundy Dr HYS/HAR UB3 152 G3
Lundy Wk IS N1 6 F2
Lunedale Rd RDART DA2 188 B4
Lunghurst Rd CTHM CR3 242 F7
Lunham Rd NRWD SE19 181 M9
Lupin Cl BRXS/STRHM SW2 181 J5
CROY/NA CR0 204 C8
ROMW/RG RM7 124 E7
WDR/YW UB7 151 N4
Luppits Cl RBRW/HUT CM13 107 M2
Lupton Cl LEE/GVPK SE12 183 N7
Lupton St KTTN NW5 118 D9
Lupus St PIM SW1V 16 F8
Lurgan Av HMSMTH W6 156 G5
Lurline Gdns BTSEA SW11 158 B7
Luscombe Wy VX/NE SW8 158 F6
Lushes Ct LOU IG10 82 E9
Lushes Rd LOU IG10 82 E9
Lushington Dr COB KT11 217 J10
Lushington Rd CAT SE6 182 G8
WLSDN NW10 136 E4
Lushington Ter HACK E8 * 119 P10
Lusted Hall La BH/WHM TN16 243 P7
Lusteds Cl DORK RH4 273 H5
Luther Cl EDGW HA8 95 P3
Luther King Cl WALTH E17 120 E4
Luther King Rd HLW CM20 46 C1
Luther Ms TEDD TW11 176 E8
Luther Rd TEDD TW11 176 E8
Luthers Cl BRWN CM15 86 D3
Luton Pl GNWCH SE10 161 H6
Luton Rd PLSTW E13 141 M6
SCUP DA14 185 M6
WALTH E17 120 D1
Luton St STJWD NW8 9 M2
Luttrell Av PUT/ROE SW15 178 E1
Lutwyche Rd FSTH SE23 182 E5
Lutyens Cl CRAWW RH11 283 H9
Luxborough La CHIG IG7 102 C5
Luxborough St CAMTN NW1 10 C2
Luxembourg Ms SRTFD E15 121 K10
Luxemburg Gdns HMSMTH W6 156 G3
Luxfield Rd ELTH/MOT SE9 184 B4
Luxford Pl SBW CM21 30 A2
Luxford St BERM/RHTH SE16 160 C3
Luxmore St BROCKY SE4 160 E7
Luxor St CMBW SE5 159 K9
Luxted Rd ORP BR6 226 D8
Lyall Av DUL SE21 181 M7
Lyall Ms KTBR SW1X 16 C4
Lyall Ms West KTBR SW1X * 16 C4
Lyall St KTBR SW1X 16 C4
Lyal Rd BOW E3 140 D4
Lycaste Cl STAL AL1 38 E7
Lycett Pl SHB W12 156 D1
Lych Ga GSTN WD25 55 L9
Lych Gate Rd ORP BR6 207 K8
Lych Gate Wk HYS/HAR UB3 132 G9
Lych Wy WOKN/KNAP GU21 232 A2
Lychony Gdns CROY/NA CR0 204 D7
Lycrome La CSHM HP5 51 K4
Lycrome Rd CSHM HP5 51 K4
Lydd Cl BFN/LL DA15 185 H6
Lydden Gv WAND/EARL SW18 179 L3
Lydden Rd WAND/EARL SW18 179 L3
Lydd Rd BXLYHN DA7 164 A6
Lydeard Rd EHAM E6 142 C2
Lydele Cl WOKN/KNAP GU21 232 C1
Lydford Av SLN SL2 129 J7
Lydford Cl STNW/STAM N16 119 M10
Lydford Rd MV/WKIL W9 8 D1
SEVS/STOTM N15 119 L3
Lydhurst Av BRXS/STRHM SW2 180 G5
Lydia Ms BRKMPK AL9 40 F10
Lydia Rd ERITH DA8 164 G5
Lydney Cl WIM/MER SW19 179 H5
Lydon Rd CLAP SW4 158 D9
Lydsey Cl SLN SL2 128 F5
Lydstep Rd CHST BR7 184 D7
Lye Green Rd CSHM HP5 51 K6
Lye La LCOL/BKTW AL2 55 N4
Lyell Rd WDSR SL4 148 B9
The Lye KWD/TDW/WH KT20 238 F8
Lyfield LHD/OX KT22 218 A10
Lyford Rd WAND/EARL SW18 179 N3
Lyford St WOOL/PLUM SE18 162 D3
Lygean Av WARE SG12 26 D2
Lygon Pl BGVA SW1W * 16 D4
Lyham Cl BRXS/STRHM SW2 180 F2
Lyham Rd BRXS/STRHM SW2 180 F1
Lyle Cl MTCM CR4 202 B7
Lyle Pk SEV TN13 247 K9
Lyles La WGCW AL8 23 H3
Lymbourne Cl BELMT SM2 221 K6
Lymden Gdns REIG RH2 275 L2
Lyme Av BERK HP4 33 J2
Lyme Farm Rd LEE/GVPK SE12 161 M10
Lyme Gv HOM E9 140 B1
Lymer Av NRWD SE19 181 N8
Lyme Regis Rd BNSTD SM7 239 J3
Lyme Rd WELL DA16 163 L7
Lymescote Gdns SUT SM1 201 K9
Lyme St CAMTN NW1 4 G4
Lyme Ter CAMTN NW1 4 G4
Lyminge Cl SCUP DA14 185 J7
Lyminge Gdns WAND/EARL SW18 179 P4
Lymington Av WDGN N22 99 H10
Lymington Cl STRHM/NOR SW16 202 E2
Lymington Ct GSTN WD25 * 55 H10
Lymington Dr RSLP HA4 112 E7
Lymington Gdns HOR/WEW KT19 220 C2
Lymington Rd BCTR RM8 123 N6
KIL/WHAMP NW6 2 G1
Lyminster Cl YEAD UB4 133 M7
Lympstone Gdns PECK SE15 159 P6
Lynbridge Gdns PLMGR N13 99 J5
Lynbrook Cl RAIN RM13 144 E4
Lynbrook Gv PECK SE15 159 M6
Lynceley Gra EPP CM16 65 K5
Lynch Cl UX/CGN UB8 131 M2
Lynchen Cl HEST TW5 153 H7
Lynch Hill La SLN SL2 128 D6
Lynchmere Pl GUW GU2 249 M7
The Lynch HOD EN11 44 G3
UX/CGN UB8 131 M2
Lyncourt BKHTH/KID SE3 * 161 J8
Lyncroft Av PIN HA5 113 L3
Lyncroft Gdns EW KT17 220 E6
HSLW TW3 176 B1
KIL/WHAMP NW6 117 K10
WEA W13 155 H1
Lyndale BRWN CM15 86 E3
CRICK NW2 117 J8
THDIT KT7 198 D7
Lyndale Av CRICK NW2 117 J8
Lyndale Cl BKHTH/KID SE3 161 K5
Lyndale Hampton Court Wy
ESH/CLAY KT10 198 D7
Lyndale Rd REDH RH1 258 B7
Lynden Wy SWLY BR8 208 D3
Lyndhurst Av BRYLDS KT5 199 N8
MLHL NW7 96 B7
NFNCH/WDSPK N12 98 A7
PIN HA5 93 J9
STHL UB1 134 A10
STRHM/NOR SW16 202 E1
SUN TW16 197 H3
WHTN TW2 175 N4
Lyndhurst Cl BXLYHN DA7 164 C9
CRAWW RH11 283 N8
CROY/NA CR0 203 N10
HARP AL5 20 B1
ORP BR6 226 E1
WLSDN NW10 116 E8
WOKN/KNAP GU21 232 A1
Lyndhurst Ct BELMT SM2 * 221 K6
Lyndhurst Dr EMPK RM11 125 K6
HARP AL5 4 B1
LEY E10 121 H5
NWMAL KT3 200 B6
SEV TN13 246 F10
Lyndhurst Gdns BARK IG11 143 H1
EN EN1 79 M8
FNCH N3 97 H9
GNTH/NBYPK IG2 122 G4
HAMP NW3 117 N10
PIN HA5 93 J9
Lyndhurst Gv CMBW SE5 159 M8
Lyndhurst Leys HAYES BR2 * 205 M5
Lyndhurst Prior SNWD SE25 * 203 M3
Lyndhurst Ri CHIG IG7 102 D5
Lyndhurst Rd BXLYHN DA7 164 C9
CHING E4 100 G8
COUL/CHIP CR5 240 B2
CSHM HP5 50 E2
GFD/PVL UB6 134 A6
HAMP NW3 117 N10
REIG RH2 275 K3
THHTH CR7 203 H4
UED N18 99 P5
WDGN N22 99 H7
Lyndhurst Sq PECK SE15 159 N7
Lyndhurst Ter HAMP NW3 117 N10
Lyndhurst Wy BELMT SM2 221 K5
CHERT KT16 195 H10
PECK SE15 159 N7
RBRW/HUT CM13 107 P2
Lyndon Av BFN/LL DA15 185 J1
PIN HA5 93 M7
WLGTN SM6 202 B10
Lyndon Md STALE/WH AL4 21 H9
Lyndon Rd BELV DA17 164 B3
Lyndon Yd TOOT SW17 179 L7
Lyndsey Pl CHESW EN7 * 62 A6
Lyndwood Dr WDSR SL4 171 M2
Lyndwood Pde WDSR SL4 * 171 M2
Lyne Cl VW GU25 194 C6
Lyne Crs WALTH E17 100 E9
Lyne Crossing Rd CHERT KT16 194 D6
Lynegrove Av ASHF TW15 174 D8
Lyneham Wk CLPT E5 * 120 D10
Lyne La EGH TW20 194 D5
Lyne Rd VW GU25 194 B6
Lynette Av CLAP SW4 180 C2
Lyne Wy HHW HP1 35 J4
Lynford Cl BAR EN5 76 G9
EDGW HA8 95 P9
Lynford Gdns EDGW HA8 95 N5
GDMY/SEVK IG3 123 J7
Lynford Ter ED N9 * 99 N2
Lynhurst Crs HGDN/ICK UB10 132 D2
Lynhurst Rd HGDN/ICK UB10 132 D2
Lynmere Rd WELL DA16 163 L8
Lyn Ms STNW/STAM N16 * 119 N9
Lynmouth Av EN EN1 79 N10
MRDN SM4 200 G7
Lynmouth Dr RSLP HA4 113 J7
Lynmouth Gdns GFD/PVL UB6 134 G3
HEST TW5 153 L7
Lynmouth Ri STMC/STPC BR5 207 L4
Lynmouth Rd EFNCH N2 118 A1
GFD/PVL UB6 134 G3
STNW/STAM N16 119 N6
WALTH E17 120 D4
WCCE AL7 23 J5
Lynn Cl ASHF TW15 174 E8
KTN/HRWW/WS HA3 94 C10
Lynne Cl ORP BR6 227 J3
SAND/SEL CR2 224 B7
Lynnett Rd BCTR RM8 123 N7
Lynne Wk ESH/CLAY KT10 218 B2
Lynne Wy NTHLT UB5 133 L4
Lynn Ms WAN E11 121 K7
Lynn Rd BAL SW12 180 C3
GNTH/NBYPK IG2 122 G5
WAN E11 121 K7
Lynn St EN/CH EN2 79 L5
Lynn Wk REIG RH2 275 L4
Lynross Cl HARH RM3 105 M10
Lynscott Wy SAND/SEL CR2 223 J5
Lynstead Cl BMLY BR1 205 P2
Lynsted Cl BXLYHS DA6 186 C1
Lynsted Ct BECK BR3 204 D2
Lynsted Gdns ELTH/MOT SE9 162 A10
Lynton Av CDALE/KGS NW9 116 C2
NFNCH/WDSPK N12 97 N5
ROMW/RG RM7 104 C9
STAL AL1 39 H8
STMC/STPC BR5 207 L4
WEA W13 134 F8
Lynton Cl CHSGTN KT9 219 K1
ISLW TW7 154 E10
WLSDN NW10 116 B10
Lynton Crs GNTH/NBYPK IG2 122 E4
Lynton Est STHWK SE1 19 M6
STHWK SE1 * 159 P3
Lynton Gdns EN EN1 99 M1
FBAR/BDGN N11 98 E7
Lynton Md TRDG/WHET N20 97 K4
Lynton Pde CHES/WCR EN8 62 C6
Lynton Rd ACT W3 135 M9
CEND/HSY/T N8 118 E3
CHING E4 100 G6
CROY/NA CR0 203 H6
CSHM HP5 50 G4
GVW DA11 190 C2
KIL/WHAMP NW6 2 D6
NWMAL KT3 200 A5
RYLN/HDSTN HA2 113 M7
STHWK SE1 19 M6
Lynton Rd South GVW DA11 190 D4
Lynton Ter ACT W3 * 135 P8
Lynwood GUW GU2 267 N1
Lynwood Av COUL/CHIP CR5 240 C1
DTCH/LGLY SL3 150 A2
EGH TW20 172 B9
EW KT17 220 C10
Lynwood Cl CRW RM5 104 C7
RYLN/HDSTN HA2 113 M8
SWFD E18 101 P9
WOKN/KNAP GU21 214 G9
Lynwood Crs ASC SL5 192 D6
Lynwood Dr CRW RM5 104 C7
NTHWD HA6 92 F9
WPK KT4 200 D9
Lynwood Gdns CROY/NA CR0 222 G1
STHL UB1 133 N8
Lynwood Gv ORP BR6 207 H7
WCHMH N21 99 H2
Lynwood Hts RKW/CH/CXG WD3 71 L9
Lynwood Rd EA W5 135 J5
EW KT17 220 C10
REDH RH1 258 B8
THDIT KT7 198 E9
TOOT SW17 180 A6
Lynwood Ter WIM/MER SW19 * 201 J1
Lynx Hl EHSLY KT24 252 G4
Lyon Meade STAN HA7 95 H9
Lyon Park Av ALP/SUD HA0 135 L2
Lyon Rd HRW HA1 114 E4
ROM RM1 124 G5
WIM/MER SW19 201 M1
WOT/HER KT12 197 M9
Lyons Ct DORK RH4 272 G2
Lyonsdene KWD/TDW/WH KT20 257 J3
Lyonsdown Av BAR EN5 77 M10
Lyonsdown Rd BAR EN5 77 M10
Lyons Dr GUW GU2 249 M5
Lyons Pl STJWD NW8 9 L2
Lyon St IS N1 5 N4
Lyons Wk WKENS W14 14 A5
Lyon Wy GFD/PVL UB6 134 D3
STALE/WH AL4 39 M6
Lyoth Rd STMC/STPC BR5 206 F9
Lyrical Wy HHW HP1 35 L4
Lyric Cl CRAWE RH10 284 E9
Lyric Dr GFD/PVL UB6 134 A6
Lyric Ms SYD SE26 182 B7
Lyric Rd BARN SW13 156 C7
Lysander CDALE/KGS NW9 * 96 C9
Lysander Cl HHS/BOV HP3 52 C3
Lysander Gdns SURB KT6 199 L6
Lysander Gv ARCH N19 118 E6
Lysander Ms ARCH N19 * 118 F6
Lysander Rd CROY/NA CR0 222 G3
RSLP HA4 112 E7
Lysander Wy ABLGY WD5 55 H8
ORP BR6 206 F10
WCCE AL7 23 N4
Lys Hill Gdns HERT/WAT SG14 25 J3
Lysias Rd BAL SW12 180 B2
Lysia St FUL/PGN SW6 156 G6
Lysley Pl BRKMPK AL9 59 M3
Lysons Wk PUT/ROE SW15 * 178 D1
Lyster Ms COB KT11 217 K9
Lytchet Rd BMLY BR1 183 M10
Lytchet Wy PEND EN3 80 B5
Lytchgate Cl SAND/SEL CR2 223 M4
Lytcott Dr E/WMO/HCT KT8 197 N3
Lytcott Gv EDUL SE22 181 N1
Lytham Av OXHEY WD19 93 L6
Lytham Cl THMD SE28 143 P8
Lytham Gv EA W5 135 J6
Lytham St WALW SE17 18 G8
Lyttelton Rd EFNCH N2 117 M3
LEY E10 120 G8
Lyttleton Cl HAMP NW3 3 N4
Lyttleton Rd CEND/HSY/T N8 * 119 H1
Lytton Av PEND EN3 80 D4
PLMGR N13 99 H3
Lytton Cl EFNCH N2 117 N3
LOU IG10 82 G7
NTHLT UB5 133 N2
Lytton Dr CRAWE RH10 284 F6
Lytton Gdns WGCW AL8 22 G5
WLGTN SM6 222 E1
Lytton Gv PUT/ROE SW15 178 G1
Lytton Pk COB KT11 217 N8
Lytton Rd BAR EN5 77 M8
CDW/CHF RM16 168 D3
GPK RM2 125 J3
PIN HA5 93 M8
WAN E11 121 K5
WOKS/MYFD GU22 232 E3
Lyttons Wy HOD EN11 26 F10
Lyveden Rd BKHTH/KID SE3 161 N6
TOOT SW17 179 P9
Lywood Cl KWD/TDW/WH KT20 238 F8

M

Mabbotts KWD/TDW/WH KT20 238 G7
Mabbutt Cl LCOL/BKTW AL2 55 M6
Mabel Rd SWLY BR8 187 H9
Mabel St WOKN/KNAP GU21 232 A4
Maberley Crs NRWD SE19 181 P10
Maberley Rd BECK BR3 204 C3
BMLY BR1 205 L1
NRWD SE19 203 N1
Mabey's Wk SBW CM21 29 L2
Mabledon Pl CAMTN NW1 5 K10
Mablethorpe Rd FUL/PGN SW6 157 H6
Mabley St HOM E9 120 D10
Macaret Cl TRDG/WHET N20 97 L1
Macarthur Cl FSTGT E7 141 M1
WBLY HA9 135 N1
Macarthur Ter CHARL SE7 * 162 A5
Macaulay Av ESH/CLAY KT10 198 D9
Macaulay Rd CLAP SW4 158 C9
CTHM CR3 241 M8
EHAM E6 142 A4
Macbean St WOOL/PLUM SE18 162 D2
Macbeth St HMSMTH W6 156 E4
Macclesfield Br STJWD NW8 3 P7
Macclesfield Rd FSBYE EC1V 6 E9
SNWD SE25 204 B5
Macclesfield St
SOHO/SHAV W1D * 11 K7
Macdonald Av DAGE RM10 124 C8
EMPK RM11 125 M2
Macdonald Cl AMS HP6 69 H1
Macdonald Rd ARCH N19 118 D7
FBAR/BDGN N11 98 A6
FSTGT E7 121 M9
WALTH E17 101 H10
Macdonald Wy EMPK RM11 125 M2
Macdonnell Gdns GSTN WD25 72 G1
Macdowall Rd GUW GU2 249 M5
Macduff Rd BTSEA SW11 158 B7
Mace Cl WAP E1W 140 A10
Mace La RSEV TN14 226 G9
Macer's La BROX EN10 44 E10
Mace St BETH E2 140 C4
Macfarlane La ISLW TW7 154 E5
Macfarlane Rd SHB W12 136 F10
Mac Farren Pl CAMTN NW1 10 D2
Macgregor Rd CAN/RD E16 141 P7
Machell Rd PECK SE15 160 B9
Macintosh Cl CHESW EN7 61 L2
Mackay Rd VX/NE SW8 158 C9
Mackennal St STJWD NW8 3 P8
Mackenzie Cl SHB W12 136 E9
Mackenzie Rd BECK BR3 204 D1
HOLWY N7 5 N1
Mackenzie St SL SL1 149 L1
Mackenzie Wy GVE DA12 190 G9
Mackeson Rd HAMP NW3 * 118 A9
Mackie Rd BRXS/STRHM SW2 181 H3
Mackies Hl SHGR GU5 270 E10
Mackintosh La HOM E9 120 C10
Macklin St HOL/ALD WC2B * 11 M5
Macks Rd BERM/RHTH SE16 19 P5
Mackworth St CAMTN NW1 4 G9
Maclean Rd FSTH SE23 182 D2
Maclean Ter GVE DA12 * 191 J5
Maclennan Av RAIN RM13 145 L5
Macleod Cl GRAYS RM17 168 A3
Macleod House CHARL SE7 * 162 B6
Macleod Rd WCHMH N21 78 F9
Macleod St WALW SE17 18 F8
Maclise Rd WKENS W14 14 A4
Macmahon Cl CHOB/PIR GU24 213 K6
Macmillan Wy TOOT SW17 180 C7
Macoma Rd WOOL/PLUM SE18 162 G5
Macoma Ter WOOL/PLUM SE18 162 G5
Maconochies Rd POP/IOD E14 * 160 G4
Macon Wy UPMR RM14 126 E4
Macquarie Wy POP/IOD E14 160 G3
Macroom Rd MV/WKIL W9 2 D9
Madan Cl BH/WHM TN16 263 H1
Madan Rd BH/WHM TN16 262 G1
Madans Wk EPSOM KT18 220 A10
Mada Rd ORP BR6 206 E10
Maddams St BOW E3 140 G6
Madden Cl SWCM DA10 189 K2
Maddesfield Ct RAD WD7 57 K9
Maddison Cl EFNCH N2 97 M10
TEDD TW11 176 E9
Maddocks Cl SCUP DA14 185 N9
Maddock Wy WALW SE17 18 C10
Maddox Dr CRAWE RH10 284 F8
Maddox La GT/LBKH KT23 235 N10
Maddox Pk GT/LBKH KT23 235 M9
Maddox Rd HHNE HP2 36 C6
HLW CM20 29 H10
Maddox St CONDST W1S 10 F7
Madehurst Ct CRAWW RH11 283 J10
Madeira Av BMLY BR1 205 K1
Madeira Cl BF/WBF KT14 215 J9
Madeira Gv WFD IG8 101 P7
Madeira Rd BF/WBF KT14 215 J9
MTCM CR4 202 A4
PLMGR N13 99 J5
STRHM/NOR SW16 180 F8
WAN E11 121 J7
Madeira Wk EPSOM KT18 220 A10
REIG RH2 257 N9
WDSR SL4 149 J7
Madeleine Ct CHDH RM6 123 M4
Madeley Cl AMS HP6 69 J2
Madeley Rd EA W5 135 J9
Madeline Gv IL IG1 122 G10
Madeline Rd PGE/AN SE20 181 P10
Madells EPP CM16 65 J7
Madge Gill Wy EHAM E6 142 B3
Madge Hl HNWL W7 * 134 D9
Madgeways Cl WARE SG12 * 26 E6
Madgeways La WARE SG12 26 E6
Madinah Rd HACK E8 119 P10
Madison Crs BXLYHN DA7 163 M6
Madison Gdns BXLYHN DA7 163 M6
Madison Wy SEV TN13 246 G9
Madras Pl HOLWY N7 6 A1
Madras Rd IL IG1 122 E9
Madrid Rd BARN SW13 156 D7
Madron St WALW SE17 19 K7
Maesmaur Rd BH/WHM TN16 244 A7
Mafeking Av BTFD TW8 155 K5
EHAM E6 142 A4
GNTH/NBYPK IG2 122 G5
Mafeking Rd CAN/RD E16 141 L6
EN EN1 79 N7
STWL/WRAY TW19 172 E5
TOTM N17 99 P10
Magazine Ga BAY/PAD W2 * 9 P9
Magazine Pl LHD/OX KT22 236 G8
Magazine Rd CTHM CR3 241 J8
Magdala Av ARCH N19 118 D7
Magdala Rd ISLW TW7 154 F9
SAND/SEL CR2 223 L4
Magdalen Cl BF/WBF KT14 215 P10
Magdalen Crs BF/WBF KT14 215 P10
Magdalene Cl CRAWE RH10 284 D4
Magdalene Gdns EHAM E6 142 D6
Magdalene Rd SHPTN TW17 196 A4
Magdalen Rd WAND/EARL SW18 179 M4
Magdalen St STHWK SE1 13 J10
Magdalen Gv ORP BR6 227 L1
Magee St LBTH SE11 18 A9
Magellan Pl POP/IOD E14 160 F3
Magellan Ter CRAWE RH10 * 284 B3
Magna Carta La
STWL/WRAY TW19 172 B4
Magna Cl HARP AL5 20 C5
Magna Rd EGH TW20 171 N9
Magnaville Rd BUSH WD23 94 D1
Magnet Rd WBLY HA9 115 J7
WTHK RM20 167 H5
Magnin Cl HACK E8 * 7 P5
Magnolia Av ABLGY WD5 54 G8
Magnolia Cl HERT/BAY SG13 25 P5
KUTN/CMB KT2 177 N9
LCOL/BKTW AL2 56 C2
LEY E10 120 F7
SOCK/AV RM15 147 K6
Magnolia Ct HGDN/ICK UB10 * 132 C1
HORL RH6 * 280 B4
KTN/HRWW/WS HA3 115 L5
Magnolia Dr BH/WHM TN16 244 A2
Magnolia Gdns DTCH/LGLY SL3 149 N2
EDGW HA8 95 P5
Magnolia Pl CLAP SW4 * 180 F1
EA W5 * 135 J7
GU GU1 * 249 P7
Magnolia Rd CHSWK W4 155 N5
Magnolia St WDR/YW UB7 151 N3
Magnolia Wy BRWN CM15 86 G9
HOR/WEW KT19 219 P2
RDKG RH5 273 J5
Magnolia Whf CHSWK W4 * 155 N6
Magnum Cl RAIN RM13 145 K6
Magpie Bottom BGR/WK TN15 229 M8
Magpie Cl CDALE/KGS NW9 96 B10
COUL/CHIP CR5 240 D4
EN EN1 79 P5
FSTGT E7 121 L10
Magpie Hall Cl HAYES BR2 206 B6
Magpie Hall La HAYES BR2 206 C6
Magpie Hall Rd STAN HA7 94 D3
Magpie La AMSS HP7 88 F2
RBRW/HUT CM13 107 J10
Magpie Pl GSTN WD25 * 55 K8
NWCR SE14 * 160 D5
Magpies EPP CM16 46 D10
Magpie Wk CRAWE RH10 284 A5
Magri Wk WCHPL E1 140 B7
Maguire Dr RCHPK/HAM TW10 177 H7
Maguire St STHWK SE1 19 M1
Mahlon Av RSLP HA4 113 J10
Mahogany Cl BERM/RHTH SE16 140 D10
Mahon Cl EN EN1 79 N5
Mahonia Cl CHOB/PIR GU24 * 212 E9
Maida Av BAY/PAD W2 9 K3
CHING E4 100 G1
Maida Rd BELV DA17 164 B2
Maida V MV/WKIL W9 3 H8
Maida Vale Rd DART DA1 187 H1
Maida Wy CHING E4 100 G1
Maidenbower Dr CRAWE RH10 284 E9
Maidenbower La CRAWE RH10 284 D9
Maidenbower Pl CRAWE RH10 284 D9
Maiden Erlegh Av BXLY DA5 185 P4
Maidenhead Rd WDSR SL4 148 B6
Maidenhead St HERT/WAT SG14 25 L5
Maidenhead Yd HERT/WAT SG14 25 L5
Maiden La CAMTN NW1 5 K3
COVGDN WC2E 11 M8
CRAWW RH11 283 M5
DART DA1 164 D9
STHWK SE1 12 F10
Maiden Rd SRTFD E15 141 K2
Maidens Br ENC/FH EN2 * 79 P3
Maidensfield WGCW AL8 22 G2
Maidenshaw Rd HOR/WEW KT19 220 A8
Maidenstone Hl GNWCH SE10 161 H7
Maidstone Av CRW RM5 104 D10
Maidstone Buildings Ms
STHWK SE1 12 F10
Maidstone Rd FBAR/BDGN N11 98 E7
SCUP DA14 185 N9
SEV TN13 246 F8
SWLY BR8 208 C1
Main Av EN EN1 79 N9
NTHWD HA6 92 E3
Main Barracks
WOOL/PLUM SE18 * 162 C4
Main Dr CFSP/GDCR SL9 109 P3
DTCH/LGLY SL3 151 H2
GFD/PVL UB6 * 134 F5
WBLY HA9 115 J8
Main Ga TIL RM18 * 168 C8
Mainridge Rd CHST BR7 184 D7
Main Rd BH/WHM TN16 225 P9
EDEN TN8 262 F10
EYN DA4 188 A9
EYN DA4 209 M6
GPK RM2 105 K10
HART DA3 211 P4
ORP BR6 * 227 M5
RDART DA2 211 H1
ROM RM1 124 G2
RSEV TN14 245 K4
RSEV TN14 245 P10
SCUP DA14 185 H6
STMC/STPC BR5 207 M1
SWLY BR8 208 D6
SWLY BR8 208 G1
WDSR SL4 * 148 B6
Main Road Gorse Hl EYN DA4 210 A8
Mainstone Crs CHOB/PIR GU24 230 C7
Mainstone Rd CHOB/PIR GU24 230 E2
Main St ADL/WDHM KT15 195 P10
FELT TW13 175 L8
Maise Webster Cl
STWL/WRAY TW19 * 173 N3
Maismore St PECK SE15 19 N10
The Maisonettes SUT SM1 * 221 J2
Maitland Cl BF/WBF KT14 215 K9
GNWCH SE10 160 G6
HSLWW TW4 153 N9
WOT/HER KT12 197 M9
Maitland Park Rd HAMP NW3 4 B1
Maitland Park Vls HAMP NW3 4 B1
Maitland Rd PGE/AN SE20 182 C9
SRTFD E15 141 L1
Maizecroft HORL RH6 280 D3
Maizey Ct BRWN CM15 86 F9
Majendie Rd WOOL/PLUM SE18 162 G4
Major Cl BRXN/ST SW9 159 J9
Major Rd BERM/RHTH SE16 19 P3
SRTFD E15 121 J10
Major's Farm Rd DTCH/LGLY SL3 150 B6
Major's Hl CRAWE RH10 285 L9
Makepeace Av HGT N6 118 B7
Makepeace Rd NTHLT UB5 133 M4
WAN E11 121 M2
Makins St CHEL SW3 15 P6
Malabar St POP/IOD E14 160 F1
Malacca Farm RGUE GU4 251 L4
Malam Gdns POP/IOD E14 140 G9
Malan Cl BH/WHM TN16 244 B3
Malan Sq RAIN RM13 145 J1
Malbrook Rd PUT/ROE SW15 156 E10
Malcolm Cl PGE/AN SE20 * 182 B10
Malcolm Ct STAN HA7 95 H6
Malcolm Crs HDN NW4 116 D4
Malcolm Dr SURB KT6 199 J8
Malcolm Gdns HORL RH6 279 N6
Malcolm Pl BETH E2 140 B6
Malcolm Rd COUL/CHIP CR5 240 E1
HGDN/ICK UB10 112 A9

338 Mal - Mar

PGE/AN SE20 182 B10
SNWD SE25 203 P6
WCHPL E1 140 B6
WIM/MER SW19 179 H9
Malcolms Wy STHGT/OAK N14 * 78 D9
Malcolm Wy WAN E11 121 M3
Malden Av GFD/PVL UB6 134 D1
SNWD SE25 204 A4
Malden Crs CAMTN NW1 4 D2
Malden Flds BUSH WD23 73 L9
Malden Green Av WPK KT4 200 D8
Malden Hl NWMAL KT3 200 C4
Malden Hill Gdns NWMAL KT3 200 C3
Malden Pk NWMAL KT3 200 C6
Malden Pl KTTN NW5 118 B10
Malden Rd BORE WD6 75 M7
CHEAM SM3 220 G1
KTTN NW5 118 A10
NWMAL KT3 200 C7
WAT WD17 73 J6
Malden Wy NWMAL KT3 200 B6
Maldon Cl CMBW SE5 * 159 M9
IS N1 6 E5
Maldon Ct HARP AL5 20 A1
Maldon Rd ACT W3 135 P9
ED N9 99 N4
ROMW/RG RM7 124 D5
WLGTN SM6 222 C2
Maldon Wk WFD IG8 101 P7
Malet Cl EGH TW20 * 172 G9
Malet St GWRST WC1E 11 J2
Maley Av WNWD SE27 181 J5
Malford Gv SWFD E18 121 L1
Malfort Rd CMBW SE5 159 M9
Malham Cl CRAWE RH10 284 D10
FBAR/BDGN N11 98 B7
Malham Rd FSTH SE23 182 C4
Malham Ter UED N18 * 100 A7
Malins Cl BAR EN5 * 76 E9
Malkin Dr BEAC HP9 88 B8
HLWE CM17 47 P3
Malkin Wy WATW WD18 72 F8
Mallams Ms BRXN/ST SW9 159 H9
Mallard Cl BAR EN5 * 77 N10
DART DA1 187 N1
HNWL W7 154 D1
HORL RH6 280 B2
KIL/WHAMP NW6 2 F6
REDH RH1 258 B7
UPMR RM14 126 E5
WHTN TW2 175 P3
Mallard Ct DORK RH4 * 272 F1
WALTH E17 * 121 J1
Mallard Dr SL SL1 128 E9
Mallard Pl TWK TW1 176 F6
WDGN N22 98 G10
Mallard Rd ABLGY WD5 55 H7
SAND/SEL CR2 224 C6
Mallards Ct OXHEY WD19 93 N4
Mallard's Reach WEY KT13 196 E9
Mallards Ri HLWE CM17 47 N1
Mallards Rd BARK IG11 143 K6
WFD IG8 101 N8
The Mallards HHS/BOV HP3 54 A1
STA TW18 195 L2
Mallard Wk BECK BR3 204 C5
Mallard Wy CDALE/KGS NW9 115 P5
GSTN WD25 73 M2
NTHWD HA6 92 D8
RBRW/HUT CM13 107 N1
WLGTN SM6 222 D5
Mall Chambers KENS W8 * 8 F9
Mallet Dr NTHLT UB5 113 N10
Mallet Rd LEW SE13 183 J2
Malling Cl CROY/NA CR0 * 204 B6
Malling Gdns MRDN SM4 201 M6
Malling Wy HAYES BR2 205 L7
Mallinson Cl HCH RM12 125 K10
Mallinson Rd BTSEA SW11 179 P1
CROY/NA CR0 202 E10
Mallion Ct WAB EN9 63 L9
Mallord St CHEL SW3 15 M9
Mallory Cl BROCKY SE4 160 D10
Mallory Gdns EBAR EN4 98 B1
Mallory St STJWD NW8 9 P2
Mallow Cl CROY/NA CR0 204 C8
GVW DA11 190 B7
KWD/TDW/WH KT20 238 E5
Mallow Ct GRAYS RM17 168 A5
Mallow Crs RGUE GU4 250 F7
Mallow Md MLHL NW7 97 H8
Mallows Gn HLWW/ROY CM19 46 D6
The Mallows HGDN/ICK UB10 112 C8
Mallow St FSBYE EC1V 12 G1
Mallow Wk CHESW EN7 61 L4
Mall Rd HMSMTH W6 156 E4
The Mall BXLYHS DA6 * 164 B10
EA W5 135 K9
EMPK RM11 125 J6
KTN/HRWW/WS HA3 115 L4
LCOL/BKTW AL2 56 B3
MORT/ESHN SW14 177 P1
STHGT/OAK N14 98 F4
SURB KT6 199 J5
WHALL SW1A 16 G1
Mall Vls HMSMTH W6 * 156 E4
Mallys Pl EYN DA4 210 B1
Malmains Cl BECK BR3 205 J5
Malmains Wy BECK BR3 205 H4
Malm Cl RKW/CH/CXG WD3 91 N5
Malmesbury Cl PIN HA5 112 G2
Malmesbury Rd BOW E3 140 E5
CAN/RD E16 141 L7
MRDN SM4 201 M7
SWFD E18 101 L9
Malmesbury Ter CAN/RD E16 141 L7
Malmesbury West Est BOW E3 140 E5
Malmes Cft HHS/BOV HP3 36 D8
Malmsdale WGCW AL8 22 G1
Malmstone Av REDH RH1 258 D4
Malory Cl BECK BR3 204 D2
Malpas Dr PIN HA5 113 L3
Malpas Rd BROCKY SE4 160 E8
CDW/CHF RM16 168 F2
DAGW RM9 143 N1
HACK E8 140 A1
SL SL2 129 N9
Malta Rd LEY E10 120 F6
TIL RM18 168 C8
Malta St FSBYE EC1V 12 C1
Maltby Cl ORP BR6 207 K8
Maltby Dr EN EN1 80 A4
Maltby Rd CHSGTN KT9 219 M3
Maltby St STHWK SE1 19 L3
Malt Hl EGH TW20 172 B8
Malt House Cl WDSR SL4 171 N3
Malthouse Ct CHOB/PIR GU24 * 212 E8
RGUE GU4 * 268 B5
Malthouse Dr CHSWK W4 156 C5
FELT TW13 175 L8
Malthouse La CHOB/PIR GU24 212 E8
GVE DA12 191 P8
RGUW GU3 231 H10
Malthouse Ms DEN/HRF UB9 * 91 M9
Malthouse Rd CRAWE RH10 283 N8
Malthouse Sq BEAC HP9 108 E1
The Malthouse
HERT/WAT SG14 * 25 L5
Malting Md HAT AL10 * 40 F3
Malting Ms HERT/BAY SG13 * 25 K6
Maltings Dr STALE/WH AL4 21 H4
Maltings Hl CHONG CM5 49 L6
Maltings La EPP CM16 65 K5
Maltings Pl FUL/PGN SW6 157 L7
STHWK SE1 19 K1
The Maltings AMSS HP7 * 68 G5
BF/WBF KT14 215 P9
HERT/BAY SG13 * 25 M5
HHNE HP2 35 N5
KGLGY WD4 54 D9
ORP BR6 207 J8
OXTED RH8 261 L7
ROM RM1 124 G5
SHGR GU5 * 270 D5
SNWD SE25 * 203 M3
STA TW18 173 H7
Malting Wy ISLW TW7 154 E9
Maltmans La CFSP/GDCR SL9 109 P1
Malton Av SL SL1 128 G8
Malton Ms NKENS W10 * 8 A5
WOOL/PLUM SE18 163 H5
Malton Rd NKENS W10 8 A5
Malton St WOOL/PLUM SE18 163 H5
Maltravers St TPL/STR WC2R 11 P7
Malt St STHWK SE1 19 N9
Malus Cl ADL/WDHM KT15 215 J4
HHNE HP2 36 B6
Malus Dr ADL/WDHM KT15 215 J4
Malva Cl WAND/EARL SW18 179 L1
Malvern Av BXLYHN DA7 163 P6
CHING E4 101 J8
RYLN/HDSTN HA2 113 M8
Malvern Cl BUSH WD23 74 B10
CHERT KT16 214 F3
HAT AL10 40 C3
HGDN/ICK UB10 112 B7
MTCM CR4 202 D3
NKENS W10 8 C4
STALE/WH AL4 38 G2
SURB KT6 199 K8
Malvern Dr FELT TW13 175 L8
GDMY/SEVK IG3 123 J9
WFD IG8 101 P6
Malvern Gdns CRICK NW2 117 H7
KTN/HRWW/WS HA3 115 K2
LOU IG10 82 C10
Malvern Ms KIL/WHAMP NW6 2 E10
Malvern Pl MV/WKIL W9 2 D9
Malvern Rd CEND/HSY/T N8 118 G1
CRAWW RH11 283 M9
EHAM E6 142 B3
EMPK RM11 125 H4
GRAYS RM17 168 B3
HACK E8 7 N4
HPTN TW12 197 P1
HYS/HAR UB3 152 F8
KIL/WHAMP NW6 2 F6
ORP BR6 227 L1
PEND EN3 80 D3
SURB KT6 199 K9
THHTH CR7 203 H4
TOTM N17 119 P1
WAN E11 121 K7
Malvern Ter ED N9 99 N2
IS N1 6 A5
Malvern Wy HHNE HP2 35 P4
RKW/CH/CXG WD3 72 C9
WEA W13 134 G7
Malvina Av GVE DA12 190 E5
Malwood Rd BAL SW12 180 C2
Malyons Rd LEW SE13 182 G1
SWLY BR8 186 G10
Malyons Ter LEW SE13 182 G1
The Malyons SHPTN TW17 * 196 E6
Managers St POP/IOD E14 * 141 H10
Manan Cl HHS/BOV HP3 36 D8
Manaton Cl PECK SE15 160 A9
Manaton Crs STHL UB1 133 P8
Manbey Gv SRTFD E15 141 K1
Manbey Park Rd SRTFD E15 141 K1
Manbey Rd SRTFD E15 * 141 K1
Manbey St SRTFD E15 141 K1
Manbre Rd HMSMTH W6 156 F5
Manbrough Av EHAM E6 142 C5
Manchester Ct CAN/RD E16 141 N8
Manchester Dr NKENS W10 8 A2
Manchester Gv POP/IOD E14 161 H4
Manchester Ms MHST W1U 10 C4
Manchester Rd POP/IOD E14 161 H4
SEVS/STOTM N15 119 L4
THHTH CR7 203 K3
Manchester Sq MBLAR W1H 10 C5
Manchester St MHST W1U 10 C4
Manchester Wy DAGE RM10 * 124 C9
Manchuria Rd BTSEA SW11 180 B2
Manciple St STHWK SE1 19 H2
Mandalay Rd CLAP SW4 180 D1
Mandarin Wy YEAD UB4 133 L8
Mandela Cl WLSDN NW10 135 P2
Mandela Pl WATN WD24 73 L6
Mandela Rd CAN/RD E16 141 M8
Mandela St BRXN/ST SW9 159 H6
CAMTN NW1 5 H5
Mandela Wy STHWK SE1 19 L6
Mandelyns BERK HP4 33 L6
Mandeville Cl BROX EN10 44 E6
GUW GU2 249 M7
HERT/BAY SG13 25 K8
WAT WD17 72 G4
WIM/MER SW19 179 H10
Mandeville Ct CHING E4 100 D5
Mandeville Dr STAL AL1 38 C9
SURB KT6 199 J8
Mandeville Pl MHST W1U 10 D5
Mandeville Ri WGCW AL8 22 G3
Mandeville Rd HERT/BAY SG13 25 K8
ISLW TW7 154 F8
NTHLT UB5 133 P1
PEND EN3 80 D3
POTB/CUF EN6 59 M8
SHPTN TW17 196 B5
STHGT/OAK N14 98 C3
Mandeville St CLPT E5 120 D8
Mandrake Rd TOOT SW17 180 A6
Mandrake Wy SRTFD E15 * 141 K2
Mandrell Rd BRXS/STRHM SW2 180 F1
Manette St LSQ/SEVD WC2H 11 H5
Manfield Cl SLN SL2 128 F5
Manford Cl CHIG IG7 103 K6
Manford Cross CHIG IG7 103 K6
Manford Wy CHIG IG7 103 H6
Manfred Rd PUT/ROE SW15 179 J1
Manger Rd HOLWY N7 5 M1
Mangles Rd GU GU1 250 A8
Mangold Wy ERITHM DA18 163 N2
Mangrove Dr HERT/BAY SG13 25 M7
Mangrove La HERT/BAY SG13 25 M8
Mangrove Rd HERT/BAY SG13 25 M6
Manilla St POP/IOD E14 160 F1
Manister Rd ABYW SE2 163 K2
Manland Av HARP AL5 20 B1
Manland Wy HARP AL5 20 B1
Manley Ct STNW/STAM N16 119 N8
Manley Rd HHNE HP2 35 P5
Manley St CAMTN NW1 4 C5
Manly Dixon Dr PEND EN3 80 D3
Mannamead EPSOM KT18 238 B5
Mannamead Cl EPSOM KT18 238 B5
Mann Cl CROY/NA CR0 203 K10
Mannicotts WGCW AL8 22 E5
Manningford Cl FSBYE EC1V * 6 C9
Manning Gdns
KTN/HRWW/WS HA3 115 J5
Manning Pl RCHPK/HAM TW10 177 L2
Manning Rd DAGE RM10 144 B2
STMC/STPC BR5 207 N5
WALTH E17 120 D4
Mannings Cl CRAWE RH10 284 E4
Manning St SOCK/AV RM15 146 B10
Manningtree Cl WIM/MER SW19 179 H4
Manningtree Rd RSLP HA4 113 J9
Manningtree St WCHPL E1 13 N5
Mannin Rd CHDH RM6 123 L5
Mannock Dr LOU IG10 82 F6
Mannock Ms SWFD E18 101 N9
Mannock Rd DART DA1 165 N9
WDGN N22 119 J1
Mann's Cl ISLW TW7 176 E1
Manns Rd EDGW HA8 95 M7
Manoel Rd WHTN TW2 176 B5
Manor Av BROCKY SE4 160 E8
CTHM CR3 241 M10
EMPK RM11 125 K3
HHS/BOV HP3 35 N9
HSLWW TW4 153 L9
NTHLT UB5 133 N2
Manorbrook BKHTH/KID SE3 161 M10
Manor Cha WEY KT13 216 C2
Manor Cl BAR EN5 77 H8
BERK HP4 * 33 P5
CDALE/KGS NW9 115 N3
DAGE RM10 144 E1
DART DA1 164 E10
EHSLY KT24 252 F4
GVE DA12 191 L5
HAT AL10 40 C1
HERT/WAT SG14 25 L3
HORL RH6 280 A4
MLHL NW7 * 96 A6
RDART DA2 187 H6
ROM RM1 125 H3
RSLP HA4 112 G6
SOCK/AV RM15 146 B10
THMD SE28 143 M8
WARL CR6 242 D3
WOKS/MYFD GU22 233 J2
WPK KT4 200 B8
Manor Cottages NTHWD HA6 92 G9
Manor Cottages Ap EFNCH N2 97 M10
Manor Ct ACT W3 * 155 M3
CHES/WCR EN8 * 62 C7
DEN/HRF UB9 91 M10
E/WMO/HCT KT8 * 197 P4
EN EN1 80 A2
HRW HA1 * 114 E4
KUTN/CMB KT2 * 199 M1
POTB/CUF EN6 * 59 J8
RAD WD7 74 E3
SL SL1 128 E10
WBLY HA9 * 115 K10
WEY KT13 216 C1
Manor Court Rd HNWL W7 134 D9
Manor Crs BEAC HP9 89 J6
BF/WBF KT14 216 A9
BRYLDS KT5 199 M6
CHOB/PIR GU24 230 C6
EMPK RM11 125 K3
GUW GU2 249 N8
HOR/WEW KT19 219 M8
Manor Cft EDGW HA8 * 95 M7
Manor Croft Pde
CHES/WCR EN8 * 62 C6
Manorcrofts Rd EGH TW20 172 D9
Manordene Cl THDIT KT7 198 F8
Manordene Rd THMD SE28 143 M8
Manor Dr ADL/WDHM KT15 215 K6
AMS HP6 68 G2
BRYLDS KT5 199 M6
ESH/CLAY KT10 198 E10
FELT TW13 175 L8
HART DA3 211 L6
HOR/WEW KT19 220 B3
HORL RH6 280 A4
LCOL/BKTW AL2 55 P3
MLHL NW7 96 A6
STHGT/OAK N14 98 C1
SUN TW16 197 H2
TRDG/WHET N20 97 P4
WBLY HA9 115 L9
Manor Dr North NWMAL KT3 200 A7
The Manor Dr WPK KT4 200 C8
Manor Est BERM/RHTH SE16 160 A3
Manor Farm RGUW GU3 266 B3
Manor Farm Av SHPTN TW17 196 C6
Manor Farm Cl RGUW GU3 248 A8
WDSR SL4 148 E9
WPK KT4 200 B8
Manor Farm Cottages WDSR SL4 171 M1
Manor Farm Ct EGH TW20 * 172 D8
Manor Farm Dr CHING E4 101 K4
Manor Farm La EGH TW20 172 D8
Manor Farm Rd ALP/SUD HA0 135 J4
EN EN1 80 A1
STRHM/NOR SW16 203 H2
Manor Fld GVE DA12 191 P8
Manorfield Cl ARCH N19 118 D9
Manorfields Cl CHST BR7 207 J3
Manor Forstal HART DA3 211 L10
Manor Gdns ACT W3 155 M3
CLAP SW4 * 158 D8
EHSLY KT24 253 L4
GODL GU7 267 K10
GUW GU2 249 N8
HOLWY N7 118 F8
HPTN TW12 176 A10
RCH/KEW TW9 155 L10
RSLP HA4 113 K10
RYNPK SW20 201 J2
SAND/SEL CR2 223 N3
SUN TW16 197 H1
Manor Ga NTHLT UB5 133 M2
Manorgate Rd KUTN/CMB KT2 199 M1
Manor Green Rd HOR/WEW KT19 219 P8
Manor Gv BECK BR3 204 G2
PECK SE15 160 B5
RCH/KEW TW9 155 M10
Manor Hall Av HDN NW4 96 G10
Manor Hall Dr HDN NW4 96 G10
Manor Hall Gdns LEY E10 120 F6
Manor Hatch HLWS CM18 47 K2
Manor Hatch Cl HLWS CM18 47 L2
Manor Hl BNSTD SM7 240 A1
Manor House Ct EPSOM KT18 * 219 P9
SHPTN TW17 196 C7
Manor House Dr
KIL/WHAMP NW6 136 G2
NTHWD HA6 92 C8
WOT/HER KT12 216 D2
Manor House Gdns ABLGY WD5 54 E7
Manor House La DTCH/LGLY SL3 149 N7
Manorhouse La GT/LBKH KT23 253 M2
Manor House Wy ISLW TW7 154 G9
Manor La CFSP/GDCR SL9 110 B5
FELT TW13 175 H5
HART DA3 211 H7
HART DA3 211 M6
HYS/HAR UB3 152 E5
KWD/TDW/WH KT20 257 K5
LEW SE13 183 K1
SUN TW16 197 J2
SUT SM1 221 M2
Manor Lane Ter LEW SE13 161 K10
Manor Leaze EGH TW20 172 E8
Manor Ldg GUW GU2 * 249 N8
Manor Ms KIL/WHAMP NW6 2 F7
Manor Mt FSTH SE23 182 B4
Manor Pde HAT AL10 40 C1
HRW HA1 * 114 E4
STNW/STAM N16 * 119 N7
Manor Pk CHST BR7 206 G2
LEW SE13 183 J1
RCH/KEW TW9 155 L10
STA TW18 172 G6
Manor Park Cl WWKM BR4 204 G8
Manor Park Crs EDGW HA8 95 M7
Manor Park Dr RYLN/HDSTN HA2 114 A1
Manor Park Gdns EDGW HA8 95 M6
Manor Park Rd CHST BR7 206 F1
EFNCH N2 117 M1
MNPK E12 122 A9
SUT SM1 221 M2
WLSDN NW10 136 C3
WWKM BR4 204 G8
Manor Pl BORE WD6 * 75 P7
CHST BR7 206 G2
EBED/NFELT TW14 175 H4
GT/LBKH KT23 253 P2
MTCM CR4 202 D3
STA TW18 173 L8
SUT SM1 221 L2
WALW SE17 18 E7
Manor Rd ABR/ST RM4 103 N2
ASHF TW15 174 A8
BAR EN5 77 H8
BARK IG11 143 J1
BEAC HP9 89 J6
BECK BR3 204 F2
BELMT SM2 221 J4
BFN/LL DA15 185 J6
BH/WHM TN16 244 B6
BXLY DA5 186 C4
CAN/RD E16 141 K7
CHDH RM6 123 N4
CHIG IG7 102 D7
CSHM HP5 50 G5
DAGE RM10 144 D1
DART DA1 164 F10
E/WMO/HCT KT8 198 C4
ENC/FH EN2 79 L6
ERITH DA8 164 G5
GRAYS RM17 167 P5
GUW GU2 249 N8
GVE DA12 * 190 E2
HART DA3 211 P5
HAT AL10 40 C1
HLWE CM17 29 M6
HOD EN11 44 F1
HRW HA1 114 F4
HYS/HAR UB3 133 H8
LCOL/BKTW AL2 57 H2
LEY E10 120 F5
LOU IG10 81 N10
LOU IG10 81 N5
MTCM CR4 202 D3
POTB/CUF EN6 59 J7
RCH/KEW TW9 155 L9
REDH RH1 258 D5
REIG RH2 257 J8
ROM RM1 125 H3
RPLY/SEND GU23 233 J9
RSEV TN14 245 N10
RSLP HA4 112 E6
RYNPK SW20 201 J2
SNWD SE25 203 P4
STAL AL1 38 D5
STALE/WH AL4 20 E1
STNW/STAM N16 119 M6
SWCM DA10 189 K3
TEDD TW11 176 F8
TIL RM18 168 D8
TOTM N17 99 P9
WAB EN9 63 J9
WALTH E17 100 D10
WAT WD17 73 J5
WDGN N22 98 F7
WDSR SL4 148 D8
WEA W13 134 G8
WHTN TW2 176 B5
WLGTN SM6 222 C1
WOKN/KNAP GU21 231 P2
WOT/HER KT12 196 G7
WTHK RM20 167 H5
WWKM BR4 204 G9
Manor Rd North ESH/CLAY KT10 198 E10
WLGTN SM6 222 C1
Manor Rd South ESH/CLAY KT10 218 D1
Manor Royal CRAWE RH10 283 P4
Manorside BAR EN5 77 H8
Manor Sq BCTR RM8 123 M7
Manor St BERK HP4 34 A5
Manor V BTFD TW8 155 H4
Manor Vw FNCH N3 97 L10
HART DA3 * 211 M6
Manorville Rd HHS/BOV HP3 35 M10
Manor Wk WEY KT13 216 C2
Manor Wy BECK BR3 204 F3
BKHTH/KID SE3 161 M10
BNSTD SM7 240 A2
BORE WD6 75 P8
BRW CM14 106 F4
BXLY DA5 186 B4
BXLYHN DA7 164 E9
CDALE/KGS NW9 116 B2
CHING E4 101 J5
CSHM HP5 51 J6
EGH TW20 172 C9
GRAYS RM17 167 N6
GUW GU2 267 K3
GVW DA11 167 M9
HAYES BR2 206 B6
LHD/OX KT22 236 B2
MTCM CR4 202 D3
NWDGN UB2 153 L3
POTB/CUF EN6 59 K6
PUR/KEN CR8 222 F8
RAIN RM13 144 F6
RKW/CH/CXG WD3 72 B8
RSLP HA4 112 G6
RYLN/HDSTN HA2 114 A2
SAND/SEL CR2 223 M3
STMC/STPC BR5 206 F4
SWCM DA10 167 K10
TIL RM18 167 P6
WOKS/MYFD GU22 232 E6
WPK KT4 200 B8
Manorway EN EN1 99 M1
WFD IG8 101 P6
Manor Waye UX/CGN UB8 131 N4
The Manor Wy WLGTN SM6 222 C1
Manor Wood Rd PUR/KEN CR8 222 F9
Manresa Rd CHEL SW3 15 N8
Mansard Beeches TOOT SW17 180 B8
Mansard Cl HCH RM12 125 H7
PIN HA5 113 L1
Manscroft Rd HHW HP1 35 L4
Manse Cl HYS/HAR UB3 152 E5
Mansefield Cl CSHM HP5 50 G4
Mansel Cl GUW GU2 249 N5
SLN SL2 129 N7
Mansel Gv WALTH E17 100 F9
Mansell Cl WDSR SL4 148 D8
Mansell Rd ACT W3 136 A10
GFD/PVL UB6 134 A7
Mansell St WCHPL E1 13 M6
Mansell Wy CTHM CR3 241 L8
Mansel Rd WIM/MER SW19 179 H9
Mansergh Cl CHARL SE7 162 B6
Manse Rd STNW/STAM N16 119 N8
Manser Rd RAIN RM13 144 F5
Manse Wy SWLY BR8 209 H4
Mansfield SBW CM21 29 K2
Mansfield Av EBAR EN4 78 A10
RSLP HA4 113 J6
SEVS/STOTM N15 119 L2
Mansfield Cl ED N9 79 P10
STMC/STPC BR5 207 N7
Mansfield Dr REDH RH1 258 E4
YEAD UB4 132 F6
Mansfield Gdns HCH RM12 125 L7
HERT/WAT SG14 25 K3
Mansfield Hl CHING E4 100 G2
Mansfield Ms CAVSQ/HST W1G 10 E4
Mansfield Rd ACT W3 135 N6
CHSGTN KT9 219 H2
HAMP NW3 118 A10
IL IG1 122 D7
SAND/SEL CR2 223 L3
SWLY BR8 186 G9
WALTH E17 120 E2
WAN E11 121 N4
Mansfield St CAVSQ/HST W1G 10 E4
Mansford St BETH E2 7 P8
Manship Rd MTCM CR4 202 B1
Mansion Cl BRXN/ST SW9 159 H7
Mansion Gdns HAMP NW3 117 L8
Mansion House Pl
MANHO EC4N * 12 G6
Mansion La IVER SL0 130 F10
Manson Ms SKENS SW7 15 K6
Manson Pl SKENS SW7 15 L6
Manstead Gdns CHDH RM6 123 M5
RAIN RM13 145 J8
Manston Av NWDGN UB2 153 P3
Manston Cl CHES/WCR EN8 62 B6
PGE/AN SE20 204 B1
Manstone Rd CRICK NW2 117 H10
Manston Gv KUTN/CMB KT2 177 J8
Manston Rd HLW CM20 47 H1
RGUE GU4 250 D6
Manston Wy HCH RM12 145 J1
STALE/WH AL4 39 J7
Manthorpe Rd
WOOL/PLUM SE18 162 F4
Mantilla Rd TOOT SW17 180 B7
Mantle Rd BROCKY SE4 160 D9
Mantlet Cl STRHM/NOR SW16 180 D10
Mantle Wy SRTFD E15 141 K2
Manton Av HNWL W7 154 E1
Manton Cl HYS/HAR UB3 132 F9
Manton Rd ABYW SE2 163 K3
PEND EN3 80 G4
Manton Ter ADL/WDHM KT15 * 215 M1
Mantua St BTSEA SW11 157 N9
Mantus Cl WCHPL E1 140 B6
Mantus Rd WCHPL E1 140 B6
Manus Wy TRDG/WHET N20 97 M3
Manville Gdns TOOT SW17 180 C6
Manville Rd TOOT SW17 180 B5
Manwood Rd BROCKY SE4 182 E2
Manwood St CAN/RD E16 142 C10
Manygate La SHPTN TW17 196 D6
Many Gates BAL SW12 180 C5
Maori Rd GU GU1 268 C1
Mapesbury Ms CDALE/KGS NW9 116 D4
Mapesbury Rd CRICK NW2 2 A2
Mapeshill Pl CRICK NW2 136 F1
Mape St BETH E2 140 A6
Maple Av ACT W3 136 B10
CHING E4 100 E7
RYLN/HDSTN HA2 114 A7
STALW/RED AL3 38 B2
UPMR RM14 126 A8
WDR/YW UB7 131 P9
Maple Cl BARK/HLT IG6 103 H7
BKHH IG9 102 A4
BUSH WD23 73 M6
CLAP SW4 180 E2
CRAWW RH11 283 M4
CTHM CR3 241 N3
FNCH N3 97 K7
HAT AL10 40 D5
HCH RM12 125 J8
HPTN TW12 175 N9
MTCM CR4 202 C1
RBRW/HUT CM13 107 L4
RSLP HA4 113 J4
STMC/STPC BR5 206 G5
STNW/STAM N16 119 P4
SWLY BR8 208 F2
YEAD UB4 133 L5
Maple Ct ASHF TW15 174 E10
EGH TW20 171 N9
HACK E8 7 N1
NWMAL KT3 200 A3
Maple Crs BFN/LL DA15 185 K2
SLN SL2 129 N9
Maplecroft Cl EHAM E6 142 A8
Maplecroft La WAB EN9 45 K7
Mapledale Av CROY/NA CR0 204 A10
Mapledene Est HACK E8 * 7 N3
Mapledene Rd HACK E8 7 M3
Maple Dr SOCK/AV RM15 147 J6
Maplefield LCOL/BKTW AL2 56 B5
Maplefield La CSTG HP8 69 N7
Maple Gdns ASHF TW15 173 P5
EDGW HA8 96 B8
Maple Ga LOU IG10 82 D6
Maple Gn HHW HP1 35 H4
Maple Gv BTFD TW8 154 G6
CDALE/KGS NW9 115 P5
EA W5 155 J2
GU GU1 250 A8
STHL UB1 133 N7
WAT WD17 73 H5
WGCE AL7 23 J2
WOKS/MYFD GU22 232 B7
Maplehurst LHD/OX KT22 236 C9
Maplehurst Cl KUT/HW KT1 199 K4
Maple Leaf Cl ABLGY WD5 55 H8
BH/WHM TN16 244 A2
Maple Leaf Dr BFN/LL DA15 185 J4
Mapleleafe Gdns BARK/HLT IG6 122 E1
Maple Leaf Sq
BERM/RHTH SE16 * 160 C1
Maple Lodge Cl
RKW/CH/CXG WD3 91 J5
Maple Ms KIL/WHAMP NW6 * 2 G7
STRHM/NOR SW16 180 G8
Maple Pl BNSTD SM7 220 G10
FITZ W1T 11 H3
TOTM N17 99 P8
WDR/YW UB7 131 P10
Maple Rd ASHTD KT21 237 J5
CTHM CR3 241 N3
DART DA1 187 K4
GRAYS RM17 167 P5
GVE DA12 190 F7
PGE/AN SE20 204 B1
REDH RH1 276 A4
RPLY/SEND GU23 233 K10
SURB KT6 199 J5
WAN E11 121 L4
YEAD UB4 133 K5
Maples WAB EN9 81 P1
Maplescombe La EYN DA4 209 P10
Maples Pl WCHPL E1 * 140 A7
Maple Springs WAB EN9 63 M9
Maplestead Rd
BRXS/STRHM SW2 180 G3
DAGW RM9 143 L3
The Maples BNSTD SM7 221 L9
CHERT KT16 214 E3
CHESW EN7 61 M4
ESH/CLAY KT10 * 218 F4
HART DA3 211 N3
HLWW/ROY CM19 46 E6
KUT/HW KT1 * 177 H10
Maple St BETH E2 7 P8
FITZ W1T 10 G3
ROMW/RG RM7 124 D2
Maplethorpe Rd THHTH CR7 203 H4
Mapleton Cl HAYES BR2 205 M5
Mapleton Crs PEND EN3 80 B4
WAND/EARL SW18 179 L2
Mapleton Rd BH/WHM TN16 263 H6
CHING E4 101 H5
EN EN1 80 A6
WAND/EARL SW18 179 K2
Maple Tree Pl BKHTH/KID SE3 162 B7
Maple Wk NKENS W10 * 136 G6
Maple Wy COUL/CHIP CR5 240 C7
FELT TW13 175 H6
Maplewood Gdns BEAC HP9 88 A10
Maplin Cl WCHMH N21 78 C10
Maplin Pk DTCH/LGLY SL3 150 E2
Maplin Rd CAN/RD E16 141 M8
Maplin St BOW E3 140 E5
Mapperley Dr WFD IG8 101 K8
Marabou Cl MNPK E12 122 B10
Maran Wy ERITHM DA18 163 N2
Marathon Wy THMD SE28 143 J10
Marban Rd MV/WKIL W9 2 C9
Marbeck Cl WDSR SL4 148 C7
Marble Cl ACT W3 135 N10
Marble Dr CRICK NW2 116 G6
Marble Hill Cl TWK TW1 176 G3
Marble Hill Gdns TWK TW1 176 G3
Marble Quay WAP E1W 13 M9
Marbles Wy KWD/TDW/WH KT20 238 C5
Marbrook Ct LEE/GVPK SE12 183 P6
Marcella Rd BRXN/ST SW9 159 H8
Marcellina Wy ORP BR6 207 H10
Marcet Rd DART DA1 187 K1
Marchant Rd WAN E11 121 J7
Marchant St NWCR SE14 160 D5
Marchbank Rd WKENS W14 14 D9
Marchmant Cl HCH RM12 125 K8
Marchmont Gn HHNE HP2 35 N4
Marchmont Rd
RCHPK/HAM TW10 177 L1
WLGTN SM6 222 D5
Marchmont St BMSBY WC1N 11 L1
March Rd TWK TW1 176 E3
WEY KT13 216 B2
Marchside Cl HEST TW5 153 L7
Marchwood Cl CMBW SE5 159 M6
Marchwood Crs EA W5 135 J8
Marcia Ct SL SL1 128 E10
Marcia Rd STHWK SE1 19 K6
Marcilly Rd WAND/EARL SW18 179 N1
Marconi Gdns BRWN CM15 87 H9
Marconi Pl FBAR/BDGN N11 98 C5
Marconi Rd GVW DA11 190 A6
LEY E10 120 F6
Marconi Wy STALE/WH AL4 39 J6
STHL UB1 134 A8
Marco Pl HACK E8 7 P1
Marco Rd HMSMTH W6 156 E2
Marcus Ct WOKS/MYFD GU22 232 C4
Marcuse Rd CTHM CR3 241 L9
Marcus Garvey Ms EDUL SE22 182 A2
Marcus Garvey Wy HNHL SE24 159 H10
Marcus Rd DART DA1 187 H3
Marcus St SRTFD E15 141 K3
WAND/EARL SW18 179 L2
Marcus Ter WAND/EARL SW18 179 L2
Mardale Dr CDALE/KGS NW9 116 A3
Mardell Rd CROY/NA CR0 204 C5
Marden Av HAYES BR2 205 M6
Marden Crs BXLY DA5 186 D1
CROY/NA CR0 202 G6
Marden Rd CROY/NA CR0 202 G6
ROM RM1 124 F4
TOTM N17 99 M10
Marden Sq BERM/RHTH SE16 160 A2
The Mardens CRAWW RH11 283 L6
Marder Rd WEA W13 154 F1
Mardyke Cl RAIN RM13 144 D4
Mardyke Rd HLW CM20 29 K9
Mardyke Vw PUR RM19 * 166 D2
Marechal Niel Av BFN/LL DA15 184 G6
Marechal Niel Pde SCUP DA14 * 184 G6
Mareschal Rd GUW GU2 267 P2
Marescroft Rd SLN SL2 128 D6
Maresfield CROY/NA CR0 203 M10
Maresfield Gdns HAMP NW3 117 M10
Mare St HACK E8 120 A10
Marfield Cl WPK KT4 200 D8
Marfleet Cl CAR SM5 201 P9
Marford Rd STALE/WH AL4 21 M3
STALE/WH AL4 22 A4
Margaret Av BRWN CM15 * 107 M1
CHING E4 80 G10
STALW/RED AL3 38 C4
Margaret Bondfield Av
BARK IG11 143 K2
Margaret Cl ABLGY WD5 54 G8
GPK RM2 125 J3
POTB/CUF EN6 59 M9
STA TW18 173 N10
WAB EN9 63 J9
Margaret Dr EMPK RM11 125 N6
Margaret Gardner Dr
ELTH/MOT SE9 184 C5
Margaret Ingram Cl
FUL/PGN SW6 * 14 C10
Margaret Lockwood Cl
KUT/HW KT1 * 199 L4
Margaret Rd BXLY DA5 185 N2
EBAR EN4 77 N9
EPP CM16 65 K5
GPK RM2 125 J3
GU GU1 267 P1
STNW/STAM N16 * 119 N6
Margaret St CAVSQ/HST W1G 10 F5
Margaretta Ter CHEL SW3 15 N9
Margaretting Rd MNPK E12 121 P7
Margaret Wy COUL/CHIP CR5 241 J5
REDBR IG4 122 B4
Margate Rd BRXS/STRHM SW2 180 F1
Margeholes OXHEY WD19 93 M3
Margery Gv KWD/TDW/WH KT20 257 H5
Margery La KWD/TDW/WH KT20 257 J5
Margery Park Rd FSTGT E7 141 M1
Margery Rd BCTR RM8 123 N8
Margery St CLKNW EC1R 6 A10
Margery Wd WGCE AL7 23 K2
Margherita Pl WAB EN9 63 L10
Margin Dr WIM/MER SW19 178 G7
Margravine Gdns HMSMTH W6 156 G4
Margravine Rd HMSMTH W6 156 G5
Marguerite Vls RYNPK SW20 * 178 E10
Marham Gdns MRDN SM4 201 M6
WAND/EARL SW18 179 P4
Maria Cl STHWK SE1 19 P5
Mariam Gdns HCH RM12 125 N7
Marian Cl CDW/CHF RM16 147 K10
YEAD UB4 133 L6
Marian Gdns GSTN WD25 55 J9
Marian Pl BETH E2 140 A4
Marian Rd STRHM/NOR SW16 202 D1
Marian Sq BETH E2 7 P7
Marian St BETH E2 * 140 A4
Marian Wy WLSDN NW10 136 C2
Maria Ter WCHPL E1 140 C7
Maria Theresa Cl NWMAL KT3 200 A5
Maricas Av KTN/HRWW/WS HA3 94 C9
Marie Curie CMBW SE5 * 159 M7
Marie Lloyd Wk HACK E8 * 7 N2
Marie Manor Wy RDART DA2 * 188 B6
Mariette Wy WLGTN SM6 222 F5
Marigold Aly STHWK SE1 12 C8
Marigold Cl STHL UB1 133 M9
Marigold Ct GU GU1 250 B7
Marigold Dr CHOB/PIR GU24 250 F1
Marigold Pl HLWE CM17 * 29 L7
Marigold Rd TOTM N17 100 B9
Marigold St BERM/RHTH SE16 160 A1
Marigold Wy CROY/NA CR0 204 C8
Marina Ap YEAD UB4 133 M7
Marina Av NWMAL KT3 200 E6
Marina Cl CHERT KT16 195 L8
Marina Dr DART DA1 187 P4
GVW DA11 190 C3
WELL DA16 163 H8
Marina Gdns CHES/WCR EN8 62 B6
ROMW/RG RM7 124 C3
Marina Pde STA TW18 * 195 L1
Marina Wy IVER SL0 131 J9
SL SL1 128 C9
TEDD TW11 177 J10
Marine Ct PUR RM19 165 N3
Marine Dr BARK IG11 143 K5
WOOL/PLUM SE18 162 C3
Marinefield Rd FUL/PGN SW6 157 L8
Mariner Gdns RCHPK/HAM TW10 176 G6
Mariner Rd MNPK E12 122 D9
Mariners Dr RGUW GU3 248 A8
Mariners Ms POP/IOD E14 161 J3
Mariners Wy GVW DA11 190 B3
Mariner Wy HHNE HP2 36 B7
Marine St BERM/RHTH SE16 19 N3
Marion Av SHPTN TW17 196 C5
Marion Cl BARK/HLT IG6 102 G8
BUSH WD23 73 N5
Marion Crs STMC/STPC BR5 207 L5
Marion Gv WFD IG8 101 K6
Marion Ms DUL SE21 181 L6
Marion Rd CRAWE RH10 284 C10
MLHL NW7 96 D6
THHTH CR7 203 K5
Marion Wk HHNE HP2 * 36 A1
Marischal Rd LEW SE13 161 J9
Marisco Cl CDW/CHF RM16 168 E3
Marish La DEN/HRF UB9 110 G2
Marish Whf DTCH/LGLY SL3 * 150 B1
Maritime Cl RDART DA2 188 G1
Maritime Ga GVW DA11 190 B3
Maritime Quay POP/IOD E14 160 F4
Maritime St BOW E3 140 E6
Marius Rd TOOT SW17 180 B5
Marjoram Cl GUW GU2 249 M6
Marjorams Av LOU IG10 82 D6
Marjorie Gv BTSEA SW11 158 A10
Mark Av CHING E4 80 G10
Mark Cl BXLYHN DA7 163 P7
HAYES BR2 226 B1
STHL UB1 133 P10
Mark Dr CFSP/GDCR SL9 90 A5
Markedge La COUL/CHIP CR5 240 A10
REDH RH1 258 A3
Markenfield Rd GU GU1 250 A10
Markenhorn GODL GU7 267 J10
Markeston Gn OXHEY WD19 93 L5
Market Chambers ENC/FH EN2 * 79 L7
Market Est HOLWY N7 5 L1
Market Field Rd REDH RH1 258 A9
Marketfield Wy REDH RH1 258 B10
Market La DTCH/LGLY SL3 150 F2
EDGW HA8 95 P9

Market Link ROM RM1 124 F3
Market Meadow
STMC/STPC BR5 207 M4
Market Ms MYFR/PICC W1J 10 E10
Market Oak La HHS/BOV HP3 36 B10
Market Pde BMLY BR1 * 205 M1
ED N9 * 99 P3
EW KT17 * 220 C5
FELT TW13 * 175 M5
SCUP DA14 * 185 K7
SNWD SE25 * 203 P4
STNW/STAM N16 * 119 P6
WALTH E17 * 120 E1
Market Pl ABR/ST RM4 83 L7
ACT W3 135 P10
BERM/RHTH SE16 19 P5
BTFD TW8 155 H6
BXLYHS DA6 164 B10
CFSP/GDCR SL9 90 A9
DART DA1 187 M3
DTCH/LGLY SL3 * 150 F6
EFNCH N2 117 N1
GTPST W1W 10 G5
HAT AL10 40 E3
HERT/WAT SG14 25 L5
KUT/HW KT1 * 199 J2
ROM RM1 124 F3
STALW/RED AL3 38 C6
TIL RM18 * 168 D8
WAT WD17 73 K8
Market Rd HOLWY N7 5 L2
RCH/KEW TW9 155 M9
Market Sq BH/WHM TN16 262 F3
ED N9 100 A3
HLW CM20 * 28 G10
Market St EHAM E6 142 C4
GU GU1 268 A1
HERT/WAT SG14 25 L5
HLWE CM17 29 M7
WATW WD18 73 J8
WOOL/PLUM SE18 162 D3
Market Ter BTFD TW8 * 155 K5
The Market CAR SM5 * 201 M8
COVGDN WC2E 11 M7
HNWL W7 * 154 E1
PECK SE15 * 159 P8
RCH/KEW TW9 * 177 J1
SUT SM1 * 201 M8
Market Wk AMSS HP7 * 68 G6
Market Wy BH/WHM TN16 262 G2
Market Yard Ms STHWK SE1 19 J3
Markfield CROY/NA CR0 224 E6
Markfield Gdns CHING E4 100 G1
Markfield Rd CTHM CR3 260 A2
SEVS/STOTM N15 119 P2
Mark Hall Moors HLW CM20 29 L8
Markham Cl BORE WD6 75 L7
Markham Pl CHEL SW3 * 16 A7
Markham Rd CHESW EN7 61 K2
Markham Sq CHEL SW3 16 A7
Markham St CHEL SW3 15 P7
Markhole Cl HPTN TW12 175 N10
Markhouse Av WALTH E17 120 D4
Markhouse Rd WALTH E17 120 E4
Mark La GVE DA12 191 H3
MON EC3R 13 K7
Markmanor Av WALTH E17 120 D5
Mark Oak La LHD/OX KT22 235 P7
Mark Rd HHNE HP2 36 B4
WDGN N22 99 J10
Mark's Av CHONG CM5 67 N3
Marksbury Av RCH/KEW TW9 155 M9
Marks Rd ROMW/RG RM7 124 D3
WARL CR6 242 D4
Marks Sq GVW DA11 190 C7
Markstone Ter ORP BR6 * 207 K7
Mark St REIG RH2 257 L9
SDTCH EC2A 13 J1
SRTFD E15 141 K2
Mark Ter RYNPK SW20 * 178 F10
Markville Gdns CTHM CR3 259 P1
Markwade Cl MNPK E12 122 A6
Mark Wy GODL GU7 266 G9
SWLY BR8 209 H5
The Markway SUN TW16 197 K2
Markwell Cl SYD SE26 182 A7
Markwell Wd HLWW/ROY CM19 46 E7
Markyate Rd BCTR RM8 123 M10
Marlands Rd CLAY IG5 102 C10
Marlborogh Rd ISLW TW7 154 G6
Marlborough Av EDGW HA8 95 N4
HACK E8 7 N5
RSLP HA4 112 D4
STHGT/OAK N14 98 D4
Marlborough Cl CDW/CHF RM16 167 P1
ORP BR6 207 J7
TRDG/WHET N20 98 A4
UPMR RM14 126 D6
WALW SE17 18 D6
WIM/MER SW19 179 P9
WOT/HER KT12 197 L10
Marlborough Ct REGST W1B * 10 G7
Marlborough Crs CHSWK W4 156 B2
HYS/HAR UB3 152 E6
SEV TN13 246 F10
Marlborough Dr CLAY IG5 122 B1
WEY KT13 196 D10
Marlborough Gdns
TRDG/WHET N20 98 A4
UPMR RM14 126 D6
Marlborough Ga BAY/PAD W2 9 L8
STAL AL1 38 D6
Marlborough Gv STHWK SE1 19 N8
Marlborough Hl DORK RH4 272 G2
HRW HA1 114 D2
STJWD NW8 3 K6
Marlborough La CHARL SE7 161 P5
Marlborough Ms BNSTD SM7 239 K1
BRXS/STRHM SW2 158 G10
Marlborough Pde FSBYPK N4 * 119 K6
HGDN/ICK UB10 * 132 C6
Marlborough Pk HARP AL5 20 B4
Marlborough Park Av
BFN/LL DA15 185 K4
Marlborough Pl STJWD NW8 3 K7
Marlborough Ri HHNE HP2 35 P3
Marlborough Rd ARCH N19 118 F7
ASHF TW15 173 P8
BCTR RM8 123 M9
BRWN CM15 86 F10
CHING E4 100 G7
CHSWK W4 155 P4
DART DA1 187 K2
DTCH/LGLY SL3 150 A3
EA W5 155 J1
ED N9 99 N2
FELT TW13 175 L5
FSTGT E7 141 P2
HAYES BR2 205 P4
HGDN/ICK UB10 132 C6
HPTN TW12 175 P9
NWDGN UB2 153 K2
RCHPK/HAM TW10 177 L2
ROMW/RG RM7 124 B2
SAND/SEL CR2 223 K4
SRTFD E15 * 121 K9
STAL AL1 38 D6
SUT SM1 201 K10
SWFD E18 121 M1
WATW WD18 73 J8
WDGN N22 98 G8
WELL DA16 163 N9
WHALL SW1A 11 H10
WIM/MER SW19 179 P9
WOKN/KNAP GU21 232 D2
WOOL/PLUM SE18 162 E2
Marlborough St CHEL SW3 15 N6
Marlborough Yd ARCH N19 118 E7
The Marld ASHTD KT21 237 L4
Marle Gdns WAB EN9 63 H8
Marler Rd FSTH SE23 182 E4
Marlescroft Wy LOU IG10 82 E9
Marley Av BXLYHN DA7 163 N5
Marley Cl ADL/WDHM KT15 215 J3
GFD/PVL UB6 133 P5
SEVS/STOTM N15 119 J2
Marley Ri DORK RH4 272 F5
Marley Rd BERM/RHTH SE16 * 160 C3
WGCE AL7 23 K7
Marlin Cl BERK HP4 33 L4
SUN TW16 174 F9
Marlin Copse BERK HP4 33 M6
Marlingdene Cl HPTN TW12 175 P9
Marlings Cl CHST BR7 207 H4
CTHM CR3 241 M3
Marlings Park Av CHST BR7 207 H3
Marling Wy GVE DA12 191 H8
Marlins Cl RKW/CH/CXG WD3 71 H6
SUT SM1 * 221 M2
Marlins End BERK HP4 33 L6
Marlins Meadow WATW WD18 72 E10
Marlin Sq ABLGY WD5 54 G7
The Marlins NTHWD HA6 92 G7
Marlins Turn HHW HP1 35 L3
Marloes Cl ALP/SUD HA0 115 J9
Marloes Rd KENS W8 14 G3
Marlow Av PUR RM19 165 P3
Marlow Cl PGE/AN SE20 204 A3
Marlow Ct CDALE/KGS NW9 116 C1
CRAWE RH10 283 N6
Marlow Crs TWK TW1 176 E2
Marlow Dr CHEAM SM3 200 G10
Marlowe Cl BARK/HLT IG6 102 F9
CHST BR7 184 G10
Marlowe Rd WALTH E17 121 H2
Marlowes HHW HP1 35 N6
Marlowe Sq MTCM CR4 202 D4
The Marlowes DART DA1 164 E10
STJWD NW8 3 L6
Marlowe Wy CROY/NA CR0 202 F9
Marlow Gdns HYS/HAR UB3 152 E2
Marlow Rd EHAM E6 142 C5
NWDGN UB2 153 N2
PGE/AN SE20 204 A3
Marlow Wy BERM/RHTH SE16 160 C1
Marlpit Av COUL/CHIP CR5 240 F3
Marlpit La COUL/CHIP CR5 240 F3
Marl Rd WAND/EARL SW18 157 L10
Marlton St GNWCH SE10 161 L4
Marlwood Cl BFN/LL DA15 185 H5
Marlyns Cl RGUE GU4 250 D7
Marlyns Dr RGUE GU4 250 D7
Marlyon Rd BARK/HLT IG6 103 L6
Marmadon Rd
WOOL/PLUM SE18 163 J3
Marmion Ap CHING E4 100 F5
Marmion Av CHING E4 100 E5
Marmion Cl CHING E4 100 E5
Marmion Ms BTSEA SW11 * 158 B9
Marmion Rd BTSEA SW11 158 B10
Marmont Rd PECK SE15 159 P7
Marmora Rd EDUL SE22 182 B2
Marmot Rd HSLWW TW4 153 L9
Marne Av FBAR/BDGN N11 98 C5
WELL DA16 163 K9
Marnell Wy HSLWW TW4 153 L9
Marne St NKENS W10 2 A9
Marney Rd BTSEA SW11 158 B10
Marneys Cl EPSOM KT18 237 M1
Marnfield Crs BRXS/STRHM SW2 180 G4
Marnham Av CRICK NW2 117 H9
Marnham Crs GFD/PVL UB6 134 A4
Marnham Pl ADL/WDHM KT15 215 M1
Marnham Ri HHW HP1 35 K4
Marnock Rd BROCKY SE4 182 E1
Maroon St POP/IOD E14 140 D7
Maroons Wy CAT SE6 182 F8
Marquess Rd North IS N1 6 F2
Marquis Cl ALP/SUD HA0 135 L2
HARP AL5 20 C1
Marquis La HARP AL5 20 C1
Marquis Rd CAMTN NW1 5 K2
FSBYPK N4 118 G6
WDGN N22 98 G7
Marrabon Cl BFN/LL DA15 185 K4
Marrick Cl PUT/ROE SW15 156 D10
Married Quarters EDGW HA8 * 95 N8
Marrilyne Av PEND EN3 80 E4
Marriner Ct HYS/HAR UB3 * 132 F9
Marriot Rd MUSWH N10 98 A9
Marriott Cl EBED/NFELT TW14 174 E2
Marriott Lodge Cl
ADL/WDHM KT15 195 M10
Marriott Rd BAR EN5 76 G7
DART DA1 187 P3
FSBYPK N4 118 G6
SRTFD E15 141 K3
Marriotts Cl CDALE/KGS NW9 116 C4
Marriotts Wy HHS/BOV HP3 35 N8
Marriotts Yd BAR EN5 * 76 G7
Marriott Ter RKW/CH/CXG WD3 71 J8
Mar Rd SOCK/AV RM15 147 H6
Marrod's Bottom AMSS HP7 88 B3
Marrowells WEY KT13 196 F10
Marryat Cl HSLWW TW4 153 N10
Marryat Pl WIM/MER SW19 179 H7
Marryat Rd EN EN1 80 A1
WIM/MER SW19 178 G8
Marsala Rd LEW SE13 160 G10
Marsden Cl WGCW AL8 22 E7
Marsden Gn WGCW AL8 22 F7
Marsden Rd ED N9 100 A3
PECK SE15 159 N9
WGCW AL8 22 E6
Marsden St KTTN NW5 4 C2
Marsden Wy ORP BR6 227 J1
Marshall Av STALW/RED AL3 38 D3
Marshall Cl FBAR/BDGN N11 98 C5
HRW HA1 114 C5
HSLWW TW4 175 N1
SAND/SEL CR2 223 P9
WAND/EARL SW18 179 M2
Marshall Dr YEAD UB4 132 G7
Marshall Est MLHL NW7 * 96 D5
Marshall Pde
WOKS/MYFD GU22 * 233 J1
Marshall Pl ADL/WDHM KT15 215 M5
Marshall Rd CRAWE RH10 284 D9
LEY E10 120 G9
TOTM N17 99 L9
Marshalls Cl HOR/WEW KT19 219 P9
Marshalls Dr ROM RM1 124 F1
Marshalls Gv WOOL/PLUM SE18 162 B3
Marshall's Pl BERM/RHTH SE16 19 M4
Marshalls Rd ROMW/RG RM7 124 E2
SUT SM1 221 L1
Marshall St SOHO/CST W1F 11 H6
Marshalls Wy STALE/WH AL4 20 E1
Marshal's Dr STAL AL1 38 F3
Marshalsea Rd STHWK SE1 18 F1
Marshalswick La STAL AL1 38 F3
Marsham Cl CHST BR7 * 184 E8
Marsham La CFSP/GDCR SL9 110 C3
Marsham Ldg CFSP/GDCR SL9 110 B4
Marsham St WEST SW1P 17 L6
Marsham Wy CFSP/GDCR SL9 110 B3
Marsh Av HOR/WEW KT19 220 B6
MTCM CR4 202 A2
Marshbrook Cl BKHTH/KID SE3 162 A9
Marsh Cl CHES/WCR EN8 62 E9
MLHL NW7 96 C4
Marshcroft Dr CHES/WCR EN8 62 D6
Marsh Dr CDALE/KGS NW9 116 C4
Marshe Cl POTB/CUF EN6 59 N8
Marsh Farm Rd WHTN TW2 176 E4
Marshfield DTCH/LGLY SL3 149 P7
Marshfield St POP/IOD E14 161 H2
Marshfoot Rd CDW/CHF RM16 168 D4
Marshgate Dr HERT/BAY SG13 25 M4
Marshgate La SRTFD E15 140 G3
Marsh Green Rd DAGE RM10 144 B3
Marsh Hl HOM E9 120 D10
WAB EN9 63 K3
Marsh La ADL/WDHM KT15 215 L1
HLWE CM17 29 P6
LEY E10 120 E7
MLHL NW7 96 B4
STAN HA7 95 J7
TOTM N17 100 A8
WARE SG12 26 D3
WARE SG12 27 J8
Marshmoor Crs BRKMPK AL9 40 G8
Marshmoor La BRKMPK AL9 40 G9
Marsh Rd ALP/SUD HA0 135 J5
PIN HA5 113 N2
Marshside Cl ED N9 100 B3
Marsh St DART DA1 165 P8
POP/IOD E14 * 160 G3
Marsh Ter STMC/STPC BR5 * 207 N4
Marsh Vw GVE DA12 191 J4
Marsh Wall POP/IOD E14 160 F1
Marsh Wy RAIN RM13 144 E5
Marshwood Rd LTWR GU18 212 C7
Marsland Cl WALW SE17 18 D8
Marston HOR/WEW KT19 219 P7
Marston Av CHSGTN KT9 219 K3
DAGE RM10 124 B8
Marston Cl CSHM HP5 50 F3
DAGE RM10 124 B8
HHS/BOV HP3 36 B7
KIL/WHAMP NW6 3 K3
Marston Ct WOT/HER KT12 * 197 K8
Marston Dr WARL CR6 242 D4
Marston Rd CLAY IG5 102 B10
HOD EN11 44 G2
TEDD TW11 176 G8
WOKN/KNAP GU21 231 N3
Marston Wy NRWD SE19 181 J10
Marsworth Av PIN HA5 93 L9
Marsworth Cl WATW WD18 * 72 F10
YEAD UB4 133 M7
Martaban Rd STNW/STAM N16 119 M7
Martello St HACK E8 140 A2
Martell Rd DUL SE21 181 L6
Martel Pl HACK E8 7 M1
Marten Ga STALE/WH AL4 38 F2
Marten Rd WALTH E17 100 F10
Martens Av BXLYHN DA7 164 D10
Martens Cl BXLYHN DA7 164 D10
Martham Cl BARK/HLT IG6 102 E9
THMD SE28 143 N9
Martha Rd SRTFD E15 141 K1
Martha's Buildings FSBYE EC1V 12 G1
Martha St WCHPL E1 140 B8
Marthorne Crs
KTN/HRWW/WS HA3 94 C10
Martian Av HHNE HP2 36 A3
Martin Bowes Rd ELTH/MOT SE9 162 C9
Martin Cl CRAWW RH11 283 N5
ED N9 100 C2
HAT AL10 40 D6
HGDN/ICK UB10 131 P4
SAND/SEL CR2 224 C7
WARL CR6 242 A2
WDSR SL4 148 C7
Martin Crs CROY/NA CR0 202 G8
Martindale IVER SL0 130 F6
MORT/ESHN SW14 177 P1
Martindale Av CAN/RD E16 141 M9
ORP BR6 227 K2
Martindale Cl RGUE GU4 250 G8
Martindale Rd BAL SW12 180 C3
HHW HP1 35 J5
HSLWW TW4 153 M10
WOKN/KNAP GU21 231 L4
Martin Dene BXLYHS DA6 186 A1
Martin Dr NTHLT UB5 113 N10
RAIN RM13 145 J6
RDART DA2 188 B2
Martineau Cl ESH/CLAY KT10 218 C1
Martineau Dr DORK RH4 272 G4
TWK TW1 154 G10
Martineau Rd HBRY N5 119 J9
Martineau St WCHPL E1 140 B9
Martinfield WGCE AL7 23 J4
Martingale Cl SUN TW16 197 H4
Martingales Cl
RCHPK/HAM TW10 177 J6
Martin Gdns BCTR RM8 123 M9
Martin Gv MRDN SM4 201 K3
Martini Dr PEND EN3 80 F3
Martin La CANST EC4R 13 H7
Martin Ri BXLYHS DA6 186 A1
Martin Rd BCTR RM8 123 M9
GUW GU2 249 M8
RDART DA2 187 K6
SL SL1 149 K2
SOCK/AV RM15 146 C10
Martins Cl GU GU1 250 F9
RAD WD7 74 D2
STMC/STPC BR5 207 N3
WWKM BR4 205 J9
Martins Dr CHES/WCR EN8 62 D4
HERT/BAY SG13 26 A5
Martins Mt BAR EN5 77 K8
Martins Pl THMD SE28 143 H10
Martin's Pln SLN SL2 129 L5
Martin's Rd HAYES BR2 205 K2
Martin's Shaw SEV TN13 246 D8
The Martins SYD SE26 182 A8
WBLY HA9 * 115 L8
Martinstown Cl EMPK RM11 125 P4
Martin St THMD SE28 143 H10
Martins Wk MUSWH N10 * 98 B9
THMD SE28 143 H10
Martinsyde WOKS/MYFD GU22 232 F3
Martin Wy MRDN SM4 201 H3
WOKN/KNAP GU21 231 M4
Martlesham WGCE AL7 23 P5
Martlesham Cl HCH RM12 125 K10
Martlet Gv NTHLT UB5 133 L5
The Martlets CRAWE RH10 283 P7
Martlett Ct HOL/ALD WC2B 11 M6
Martley Dr GNTH/NBYPK IG2 122 E3
Martock Cl KTN/HRWW/WS HA3 114 F2
Martock Gdns FBAR/BDGN N11 98 A6
Marton Cl CAT SE6 182 F6
Marton Rd STNW/STAM N16 * 119 M7
Martyr Cl STAL AL1 38 C10
Martyr Rd GU GU1 268 A1
Martyrs Av CRAWW RH11 283 M4
Martyrs La WOKN/KNAP GU21 214 E8
Martys Yd HAMP NW3 * 117 N9
Marunden Gn SLN SL2 128 E5
Marvell Av YEAD UB4 133 H7
Marvell Cl CRAWE RH10 284 D5
Marvels Cl LEE/GVPK SE12 183 N5
Marvels La LEE/GVPK SE12 183 N5
Marville Rd FUL/PGN SW6 157 J6
Marvin St HACK E8 * 140 A1
Marwell BH/WHM TN16 262 E2
Marwell Cl ROM RM1 125 H4
WWKM BR4 205 L9
Marwood Cl KGLGY WD4 54 A5
WELL DA16 163 L9
Marwood Dr MLHL NW7 96 G8
Mary Adelaide Cl PUT/ROE SW15 178 B7
Mary Ann Buildings DEPT SE8 160 F5
Maryat Sq FUL/PGN SW6 157 H7
Maryatt Av RYLN/HDSTN HA2 114 A7
Marybank WOOL/PLUM SE18 162 C3
Mary Cl KTN/HRWW/WS HA3 115 L2
Mary Datchelor Cl CMBW SE5 159 L7
Maryfield Cl BXLY DA5 186 F6
Marygold Wk AMS HP6 69 P5
Mary Gn STJWD NW8 * 3 H5
Maryhill Cl PUR/KEN CR8 241 K3
Maryland HAT AL10 40 D4
Maryland Pk SRTFD E15 121 K10
Maryland Rd MV/WKIL W9 8 F2
SRTFD E15 121 J10
THHTH CR7 203 J1
WDGN N22 99 H7
Maryland Sq SRTFD E15 121 K10
Marylands Rd MV/WKIL W9 8 G2
Maryland St SRTFD E15 121 J10
Maryland Wk IS N1 * 6 E5
Maryland Wy SUN TW16 197 H2
Mary Lawrencson Pl
BKHTH/KID SE3 161 L6
Marylebone F/O BAY/PAD W2 9 N4
Marylebone High St
CAVSQ/HST W1G 10 D4
Marylebone La MHST W1U 10 D5
Marylebone Ms CAVSQ/HST W1G 10 D4
Marylebone Pas GTPST W1W 11 H5
Marylebone Rd CAMTN NW1 9 P3
Marylebone St CAVSQ/HST W1G 10 D4
Marylee Wy LBTH SE11 17 P6
Maryon Gv CHARL SE7 162 B3
Maryon Ms HAMP NW3 117 P9
Maryon Rd CHARL SE7 162 B3
Mary Peters Dr GFD/PVL UB6 114 C10
Mary Pl NTGHL W11 8 A8
Mary Rd GU GU1 267 P1
Mary Rose Cl CDW/CHF RM16 167 H3
DART DA1 166 B10
HPTN TW12 197 P1
Maryrose Wy TRDG/WHET N20 97 N2
Mary Seacole Cl HACK E8 * 7 L5
Mary Secole Cl HACK E8 * 7 L5
Maryside DTCH/LGLY SL3 150 B1
Mary's Ter TWK TW1 176 F3
Mary St CAN/RD E16 141 L7
IS N1 6 F6
Mary Ter CAMTN NW1 4 F6
Mary Wy OXHEY WD19 93 K5
Masbro' Rd WKENS W14 156 G2
Mascalls Gdns BRW CM14 106 E5
Mascalls La BRW CM14 106 E5
Mascalls Rd CHARL SE7 161 P5
Mascotts Cl CRICK NW2 116 E8
Masefield Av BORE WD6 75 N9
STAN HA7 94 E6
STHL UB1 133 P9
Masefield Cl ERITH DA8 164 G7
HARH RM3 105 J9
Masefield Crs HARH RM3 105 K9
STHGT/OAK N14 78 D9
Masefield Dr UPMR RM14 126 B5
Masefield Gdns EHAM E6 142 D6
Masefield La YEAD UB4 133 J6
Masefield Rd CDW/CHF RM16 168 B1
CRAWW RH11 283 H10
DART DA1 188 A1
GVW DA11 190 A6
HPTN TW12 175 N7
Masefield Vw ORP BR6 206 F10
Masefield Wy STWL/WRAY TW19 174 A4
Mashie Rd ACT W3 136 B8
Mashiters Hl ROM RM1 104 E9
Mashiters Wk ROM RM1 124 F1
Maskall Cl BRXS/STRHM SW2 * 181 H4
Maskell Rd TOOT SW17 179 M6
Maskelyne Cl BTSEA SW11 157 P7
Mason Cl BERM/RHTH SE16 19 P7
BORE WD6 76 A6
BXLYHN DA7 164 C9
CAN/RD E16 141 M9
HPTN TW12 197 N1
RYNPK SW20 200 G1
Mason Ct WBLY HA9 * 115 M7
Mason Dr HARH RM3 105 M10
Masonic Hall Rd CHERT KT16 195 J6
Mason Rd CRAWE RH10 283 P9
SUT SM1 221 L2
WFD IG8 101 K5
Mason's Arms Ms CONDST W1S * 10 F6
Mason's Av CITYW EC2V 12 G5
CROY/NA CR0 223 K1
KTN/HRWW/WS HA3 114 D1
Mason's Bridge Rd REDH RH1 276 D6
Masons Ct EW KT17 * 220 D5
Masons Hl BMLY BR1 205 M3
WOOL/PLUM SE18 162 E3
Masons Paddock DORK RH4 254 F10
Masons Pde CHESW EN7 * 61 K4
Mason's Pl FSBYE EC1V 6 D9
MTCM CR4 202 A1
Masons Rd EN EN1 80 A2
HHNE HP2 36 C5
SL SL1 128 D9
Mason St WALW SE17 19 H6
Masons Yd FSBYE EC1V 12 E1
STJS SW1Y 11 H9
Mason Wy WAB EN9 63 K9
Massetts Rd HORL RH6 280 A5
Massey Cl FBAR/BDGN N11 98 C6
Massie Rd HACK E8 7 N2
Massingberd Wy TOOT SW17 180 C7
Massinger St WALW SE17 19 J6
Massingham St WCHPL E1 140 C6
Masson Av RSLP HA4 133 K1
Master Cl OXTED RH8 261 K5
Masterman Rd EHAM E6 142 B5
Masters Cl STRHM/NOR SW16 180 D9
Masters Dr BERM/RHTH SE16 160 A4
Master's St WCHPL E1 140 C7
Masthead Cl RDART DA2 166 B10
Mast House Ter POP/IOD E14 * 160 F3
Masthouse Ter POP/IOD E14 160 F3
Mastmaker Rd POP/IOD E14 160 F1
Mast Quay WOOL/PLUM SE18 162 C2
Maswell Park Crs HSLW TW3 154 B10
Maswell Park Rd HSLW TW3 176 A1
Matara Ms WALW SE17 18 E8
Matcham Rd WAN E11 121 K8
Matching Fld BRWN CM15 86 E3
Matching Rd HLWE CM17 30 C7
RBSF CM22 31 H4
Matchless Dr WOOL/PLUM SE18 162 D6
Matfield Cl HAYES BR2 205 M5
Matfield Rd BELV DA17 164 B5
Matham Gv EDUL SE22 159 N10
Matham Rd E/WMO/HCT KT8 198 C5
Matheson Rd WKENS W14 14 C6
Mathews Av EHAM E6 142 D4
Mathews Park Av SRTFD E15 141 L1
Mathews Yd LSQ/SEVD WC2H * 11 L6
Mathias Cl EPSOM KT18 219 P9
Mathieson Ct STHWK SE1 18 D2
Mathisen Wy DTCH/LGLY SL3 151 H8
Mathon Ct GU GU1 250 C10
Matilda Cl NRWD SE19 181 L10
Matilda St IS N1 5 P6
Matlock Cl BAR EN5 76 G9
HNHL SE24 159 K10
Matlock Crs CHEAM SM3 221 H1
OXHEY WD19 93 K4
Matlock Gdns CHEAM SM3 221 H1
HCH RM12 125 M8
Matlock Pl CHEAM SM3 221 H1
Matlock Rd CTHM CR3 241 M8
LEY E10 121 H4
Matlock St POP/IOD E14 140 D8
Matlock Wy NWMAL KT3 200 A1
Matthew Arnold Cl COB KT11 217 H10
STA TW18 173 M9
Matthew Cl NKENS W10 * 136 G6
Matthew Ct MTCM CR4 202 E5
Matthews Ct ASC SL5 192 C4
Matthew's Gdns CROY/NA CR0 225 J7
Matthews La STA TW18 173 J7
Matthews Rd GFD/PVL UB6 114 C10
Matthews St BTSEA SW11 * 158 A8
REIG RH2 275 K4
Matthey Pl CRAWE RH10 284 E4
Matthias Rd STNW/STAM N16 119 L10
Mattingly Wy PECK SE15 159 N6
Mattison Rd FSBYPK N4 119 H4
Mattock La WEA W13 134 G10
Maud Cashmore Wy
WOOL/PLUM SE18 162 C2
Maude Cl BEAC HP9 88 F10
Maude Crs WATN WD24 73 J4
Maude Rd BEAC HP9 88 F10
CMBW SE5 159 M8
SWLY BR8 187 H9
WALTH E17 120 D3
Maudesville Cottages HNWL W7 134 D10
Maude Ter WALTH E17 120 D3
Maud Gdns BARK IG11 143 J4
PLSTW E13 141 L4
Maud Rd LEY E10 121 H8
PLSTW E13 141 L4
Maudslay Rd ELTH/MOT SE9 162 C9
Maud St CAN/RD E16 141 L7
Maud Wilkes Cl KTTN NW5 118 D10
Mauleverer Rd
BRXS/STRHM SW2 180 F1
Maundeby Wk WLSDN NW10 * 116 B10
Maunder Cl CDW/CHF RM16 167 J3
Maunder Rd HNWL W7 134 D10
Maunds Hatch HLWS CM18 46 G5
Maunsell Pk CRAWE RH10 284 C7
Maunsel St WEST SW1P 17 J5
Maurice Av CTHM CR3 241 L8
WDGN N22 99 J10
Maurice Brown Cl MLHL NW7 * 96 G6
Maurice Browne Cl MLHL NW7 96 G6
Maurice St SHB W12 136 E8
Maurice Wk GLDGN NW11 117 M2
Maurier Cl NTHLT UB5 133 K3
Mauritius Rd GNWCH SE10 161 K3
Maury Rd STNW/STAM N16 119 P7
Mauveine Gdns HSLW TW3 153 P10
Mavelstone Rd BMLY BR1 206 A1
Maverton Rd BOW E3 * 140 F3
Mavis Av HOR/WEW KT19 220 B2
Mavis Cl HOR/WEW KT19 220 B2
Mavis Gv HCH RM12 125 M7
Mawbey Est STHWK SE1 19 N8
Mawbey Pl STHWK SE1 19 M8
Mawbey Rd CHERT KT16 214 G3
STHWK SE1 19 M8
Mawbey St VX/NE SW8 158 F6
Mawney Cl ROMW/RG RM7 124 C1
Mawney Rd ROMW/RG RM7 104 C10
Mawson Cl RYNPK SW20 201 H2
Mawson La CHSWK W4 156 C5
Maxey Gdns DAGW RM9 123 P9
Maxey Rd DAGW RM9 123 P9
WOOL/PLUM SE18 162 F3
Maxfield Cl TRDG/WHET N20 97 M1
Maxilla Wk NKENS W10 136 G8
Maximfeldt Rd ERITH DA8 164 F4
Maxim Rd DART DA1 186 F1
ERITH DA8 164 F4
WCHMH N21 79 H10
Maxted Cl HHNE HP2 36 D4
Maxted Cnr HHNE HP2 36 C3
Maxted Pk HRW HA1 114 D5
Maxted Rd HHNE HP2 36 C4
PECK SE15 159 N9
Maxwell Cl CROY/NA CR0 202 F8
HYS/HAR UB3 133 H9
RKW/CH/CXG WD3 91 K3
Maxwell Dr BF/WBF KT14 215 M7
Maxwell Gdns ORP BR6 207 J10
Maxwell Ri OXHEY WD19 93 M1
Maxwell Rd ASHF TW15 174 D9
BEAC HP9 88 D8
BORE WD6 75 N7
FUL/PGN SW6 157 L6
NTHWD HA6 92 E8
STAL AL1 38 G7
WDR/YW UB7 151 P3
WELL DA16 163 K10
Maxwell Wy CRAWE RH10 284 B4
Maxwelton Av MLHL NW7 96 A6
Maxwelton Cl MLHL NW7 96 A6
Maya Cl PECK SE15 160 A8
Mayall Cl PEND EN3 80 F4
STHWK SE1 12 F10
Mayall Rd HNHL SE24 181 J1
Maya Pl FBAR/BDGN N11 98 E8
Maya Rd EFNCH N2 117 M2
May Av GVW DA11 190 C4
STMC/STPC BR5 207 L5
Maybank Av ALP/SUD HA0 114 F9
HCH RM12 125 J10
SWFD E18 101 N10
Maybank Gdns PIN HA5 113 H2
Maybank Rd SWFD E18 101 P9
May Bate Av KUTN/CMB KT2 199 J1
Mayberry Pl BRYLDS KT5 199 L7
Maybourne Cl SYD SE26 182 A9
Maybourne Ri
WOKS/MYFD GU22 232 A10
Maybrick Rd EMPK RM11 125 K3
Maybury Av CHES/WCR EN8 62 A4
RDART DA2 188 A4
Maybury Cl EN EN1 80 A4
KWD/TDW/WH KT20 239 H5
SL SL1 128 C8
STMC/STPC BR5 206 E5
Maybury Gdns WLSDN NW10 136 D2
Maybury Hl WOKS/MYFD GU22 232 E3
Maybury Ms HGT N6 118 D5
Maybury Rd BARK IG11 143 K4
PLSTW E13 141 P6
WOKN/KNAP GU21 232 D2
Maybury St TOOT SW17 179 P8
Maybush Rd EMPK RM11 125 M5
Maychurch Cl STAN HA7 95 J9
May Cl CHSGTN KT9 219 L3
STALW/RED AL3 38 C4
Maycock Gv NTHWD HA6 92 G7
Maycroft PIN HA5 93 J10
Maycroft Av GRAYS RM17 168 A4
Maycroft Gdns GRAYS RM17 168 A4
Maycroft Rd CHESW EN7 61 M2
Maycross Av MRDN SM4 201 J4
Mayday Gdns BKHTH/KID SE3 162 B8
Mayday Rd THHTH CR7 203 J6
Maydwell Ldg BORE WD6 75 L6
Mayefield Rd THHTH CR7 202 G4
Mayell Cl LHD/OX KT22 237 H9
Mayerne Rd ELTH/MOT SE9 184 A1
Mayesbrook Rd BARK IG11 143 J3
GDMY/SEVK IG3 123 K8
Mayes Cl CRAWE RH10 284 D8
SWLY BR8 209 H4
WARL CR6 242 C4
Mayesford Rd CHDH RM6 123 M5
Mayes Rd WDGN N22 98 G10
Mayeswood Rd LEE/GVPK SE12 183 P7
Mayfair Av BXLYHN DA7 163 N7
CHDH RM6 123 N4
IL IG1 122 C7
WHTN TW2 176 B3
WPK KT4 200 D8
Mayfair Cl BECK BR3 204 G1
STALE/WH AL4 39 H1
SURB KT6 199 K8
Mayfair Ct EDGW HA8 95 L6
Mayfair Gdns TOTM N17 99 L7
WFD IG8 101 M8
Mayfair Ms CAMTN NW1 * 4 B4
Mayfair Pl MYFR/PICC W1J 10 F9
Mayfair Rd DART DA1 187 L1
Mayfair Ter STHGT/OAK N14 98 E1
Mayfare RKW/CH/CXG WD3 72 E9
Mayfield BXLYHN DA7 164 A9
CRAWE RH10 284 E7
LHD/OX KT22 237 H7
SWCM DA10 189 K2
WGCW AL8 22 F1
Mayfield Av ADL/WDHM KT15 215 L6
CHSWK W4 156 B3
KTN/HRWW/WS HA3 114 G3
NFNCH/WDSPK N12 97 M5
ORP BR6 207 J8
STHGT/OAK N14 98 D3
WEA W13 154 G2
WFD IG8 101 M7
Mayfield Cl ADL/WDHM KT15 215 M6
ASHF TW15 174 C9
CLAP SW4 180 E1
HACK E8 7 L2
HGDN/ICK UB10 132 C5
HLWE CM17 30 A7
PGE/AN SE20 204 A1
REDH RH1 276 B6
THDIT KT7 198 G8
WOT/HER KT12 217 H1
Mayfield Crs ED N9 80 A10
THHTH CR7 202 G4
Mayfield Dr PIN HA5 113 N2
WDSR SL4 148 F9
Mayfield Gdns ADL/WDHM KT15 215 L6
BRW CM14 106 G2
HDN NW4 116 G4
HNWL W7 134 C8
STA TW18 173 J10
WOT/HER KT12 217 H1
Mayfield Gn GT/LBKH KT23 253 P3
Mayfield Rd ACT W3 135 N9
BCTR RM8 123 M6
BELMT SM2 221 N3
BELV DA17 164 D3
BMLY BR1 206 B5
CEND/HSY/T N8 118 G4
CHING E4 101 H3
GVW DA11 190 C4
HACK E8 7 L4
PEND EN3 80 C6
PLSTW E13 141 L6
SAND/SEL CR2 223 L5
SHB W12 156 B1
WALTH E17 100 D10
WEY KT13 216 A2
WIM/MER SW19 201 J1
WOT/HER KT12 217 H1
Mayfields CDW/CHF RM16 167 P1
WBLY HA9 115 M7
Mayfields Cl WBLY HA9 115 M7
Mayfield Vls SCUP DA14 * 185 M9
Mayflower Av HHNE HP2 35 N6
Mayflower Cl BERM/RHTH SE16 160 C3
CRAWE RH10 284 E8
HERT/WAT SG14 24 F7
RSLP HA4 112 D4
SOCK/AV RM15 147 H6
WAB EN9 45 K9
Mayflower Rd BRXN/ST SW9 158 F9
CDW/CHF RM16 167 H4
LCOL/BKTW AL2 56 A3
Mayflower St BERM/RHTH SE16 160 B1
Mayflower Wy CHONG CM5 67 P3
SLN SL2 109 H10
Mayfly Cl PIN HA5 113 K5
STMC/STPC BR5 207 N4
Mayford Cl BAL SW12 180 A3
BECK BR3 204 C3
WOKS/MYFD GU22 232 A8
Mayford Gn WOKS/MYFD GU22 231 P8
Mayford Rd BAL SW12 180 A3
May Gdns ALP/SUD HA0 135 H5
BORE WD6 75 J10
Maygoods Cl UX/CGN UB8 131 N7
Maygoods Gn UX/CGN UB8 131 N7
Maygoods La UX/CGN UB8 131 N7
Maygood St IS N1 5 P7
Maygoods Vw UX/CGN UB8 * 131 M7
Maygreen Crs EMPK RM11 125 H5
Maygrove Rd KIL/WHAMP NW6 2 D2
Mayhall La AMS HP6 68 G1
Mayhew Cl CHING E4 100 F4
Mayhill Rd BAR EN5 77 H10
CHARL SE7 161 N5
Mayhurst Av WOKS/MYFD GU22 232 F2
Mayhurst Crs WOKS/MYFD GU22 232 F2
Maylands Av HCH RM12 125 J9
HHNE HP2 36 C4
Maylands Dr SCUP DA14 185 N6
UX/CGN UB8 131 N1
Maylands Rd OXHEY WD19 93 K5
Maylands Wy HARH RM3 106 B7
Maylins Dr SBW CM21 29 N1
Maynard Cl CRAWE RH10 285 K1
ERITH DA8 164 G6
FUL/PGN SW6 157 M6
SEVS/STOTM N15 119 M3
Maynard Dr STAL AL1 38 C9
Maynard Pl POTB/CUF EN6 60 F5
Maynard Rd HHNE HP2 35 N7
WALTH E17 121 H3
Maynards EMPK RM11 125 M5
Maynards Quay WAP E1W * 140 B9
Mayne Av STALW/RED AL3 37 N8
Maynooth Gdns CAR SM5 202 A7
Mayo Cl CHES/WCR EN8 62 B4
Mayo Gdns HHW HP1 35 L7
Mayola Rd CLPT E5 120 B9
Mayo Rd CROY/NA CR0 203 L5
WLSDN NW10 136 B1
WOT/HER KT12 197 H7
Mayors La RDART DA2 187 K8
Mayow Rd SYD SE26 182 C7
Mayplace Av DART DA1 165 H10
Mayplace Cl BXLYHN DA7 164 C9
Mayplace La WOOL/PLUM SE18 162 E5
Mayplace Rd BXLYHN DA7 164 D9
Mayplace Rd East BXLYHN DA7 164 D9
Mayplace Rd West BXLYHN DA7 164 B10
Maypole Crs BARK/HLT IG6 102 G8
ERITH DA8 165 L5
Maypole Dr CHIG IG7 103 K4
Maypole Rd GVE DA12 191 J4
ORP BR6 228 A3
Maypole St HLWE CM17 29 M10
May Rd CHING E4 100 F7
PLSTW E13 141 M4
RDART DA2 187 N7
WHTN TW2 176 D4
Mayroyd Av SURB KT6 199 M9
May's Buildings Ms GNWCH SE10 161 J6
Mays Cl WEY KT13 216 A6
Mays Ct CHCR WC2N 11 L8
Maysfield Rd RPLY/SEND GU23 232 G9
Mays Gn COB KT11 * 234 G6
Mays Gv RPLY/SEND GU23 232 G9
May's Hill Rd HAYES BR2 205 L3
May's La BAR EN5 96 E1
Maysoule Rd BTSEA SW11 157 N10
Mays Rd TEDD TW11 176 C8
May St WKENS W14 14 C8
Mayswood Gdns DAGE RM10 144 D1
Maythorne Cl WATW WD18 72 F8
Maythorne Cottages LEW SE13 183 J2
Mayton St HOLWY N7 118 G8
Maytree Cl EDGW HA8 95 P4
GU GU1 249 N7
RAIN RM13 144 F4
Maytree Ct MTCM CR4 202 B3
Maytree Crs WATN WD24 72 G2
Maytree La STAN HA7 94 E8
Maytrees RAD WD7 74 F3
WOKN/KNAP GU21 231 H3
Maytree Wk BRXS/STRHM SW2 * 181 H5
Mayville Est STNW/STAM N16 * 119 M10
Mayville Rd IL IG1 122 E10
WAN E11 121 K8
Maywater Cl SAND/SEL CR2 223 L7
Maywin Dr EMPK RM11 125 N6
Maywood Cl BECK BR3 * 182 G10
Maze Hl BKHTH/KID SE3 161 L6
Mazenod Av KIL/WHAMP NW6 2 F4
Maze Rd RCH/KEW TW9 155 M6
McAdam Cl HOD EN11 44 F1
McAdam Dr ENC/FH EN2 79 J6
McAlmont Rdg GODL GU7 267 J10
McAuley Cl ELTH/MOT SE9 184 D1
STHWK SE1 18 A3
McAuliffe Dr SL SL1 108 E9
McCall Cl CLAP SW4 158 F8
McCall Crs CHARL SE7 162 B4
McCarthy Rd FELT TW13 175 L8
McCoid Wy STHWK SE1 18 E2
McCrone Ms HAMP NW3 * 3 M1
McCudden Rd DART DA1 165 N9
McCullum Rd BOW E3 140 E3
McDermott Cl BTSEA SW11 157 P8
McDermott Rd PECK SE15 159 P9
McDonald Ct HAT AL10 40 D7
McDonough Cl CHSGTN KT9 219 K1
McDougall Ct RCH/KEW TW9 155 M8
McDougall Rd BERK HP4 34 A5
McDowall Cl CAN/RD E16 141 M7
McDowall Rd CMBW SE5 159 K7
McEntee Av WALTH E17 100 D9
McEwan Wy SRTFD E15 * 141 J3
McGrath Rd SRTFD E15 121 L10
McGredy CHESW EN7 62 A5
McGregor Rd NTGHL W11 8 C5
McIntosh Cl ROM RM1 124 F1
WLGTN SM6 222 F4
McIntosh Rd ROM RM1 124 F1
McKay Rd RYNPK SW20 178 E10

Mc Kellar Cl *BUSH* WD23 94 B3
Mc Kenzie Rd *BROX* EN10 44 F6
McKenzie Wy *HOR/WEW* KT19 219 M6
McKerrell Rd *PECK* SE15 159 P7
McKillop Wy *SCUP* DA14 185 M10
McLeod Rd *ABYW* SE2 163 M3
McLeod's Ms *SKENS* SW7 15 H4
McMillan Cl *GVE* DA12 190 F7
McMillan St *DEPT* SE8 * 160 F5
McNair Rd *NWDGN* UB2 153 P2
McNeil Rd *CMBW* SE5 159 M8
McNicol Dr *WLSDN* NW10 135 P4
McRae La *MTCM* CR4 202 A7
Mead Av *DTCH/LGLY* SL3 150 E2
REDH RH1 276 B8
Mead Cl *CAMTN* NW1 4 D3
CDW/CHF RM16 167 N1
DEN/HRF UB9 111 K7
DTCH/LGLY SL3 150 E1
EGH TW20 172 E9
GPK RM2 105 H10
KTN/HRWW/WS HA3 94 C9
LOU IG10 82 E6
REDH RH1 258 B7
SWLY BR8 209 H5
Mead Ct *CDALE/KGS* NW9 115 P3
EGH TW20 172 F9
WAB EN9 62 G10
WOKN/KNAP GU21 231 K3
Mead Crs *CHING* E4 101 H5
DART DA1 187 L4
GT/LBKH KT23 253 P1
SUT SM1 221 P1
Meadcroft Rd *LBTH* SE11 18 C10
Meade Cl *CHSWK* W4 155 M5
Mead End *ASHTD* KT21 237 L2
Meades La *CSHM* HP5 50 G8
The Meades *WEY* KT13 * 216 E3
Meadfield *EDGW* HA8 95 N3
Mead Fld *RYLN/HDSTN* HA2 * 113 N8
Meadfield Av *DTCH/LGLY* SL3 150 D2
Meadfield Rd *DTCH/LGLY* SL3 150 E2
Meadfoot Rd *STRHM/NOR* SW16 202 D1
Meadgate Av *WFD* IG8 102 B6
Meadgate Rd *WAB* EN9 45 J6
Mead Gv *CHDH* RM6 123 N1
Mead House La *YEAD* UB4 132 E6
Meadhurst Pk *SUN* TW16 174 F9
Meadhurst Rd *CHERT* KT16 * 195 L8
Meadlands Dr *RCHPK/HAM* TW10 177 J5
Mead La *CHERT* KT16 195 M8
HERT/BAY SG13 25 M4
Meadow Ap *CRAWE* RH10 285 H2
Meadow Av *CROY/NA* CR0 204 C6
RAD WD7 57 H7
Meadowbank *BKHTH/KID* SE3 161 L9
BRYLDS KT5 199 L6
Meadow Bank *EHSLY* KT24 252 G3
Meadowbank *HAMP* NW3 4 A4
KGLGY WD4 54 B6
OXHEY WD19 93 K1
WCHMH N21 78 G10
Meadowbank Cl *FUL/PGN* SW6 156 F6
HHS/BOV HP3 52 E4
Meadowbank Gdns *HEST* TW5 153 H7
Meadowbank Rd
CDALE/KGS NW9 116 A5
LTWR GU18 212 B6
Meadowbanks *BAR* EN5 76 C9
Meadowbrook *OXTED* RH8 261 H6
Meadowbrook Cl *DTCH/LGLY* SL3 151 H8
Meadowbrook Rd *DORK* RH4 272 F1
Meadow Cl *BAR* EN5 77 J10
BARK IG11 143 K2
BRKMPK AL9 40 G10
BXLYHS DA6 186 A1
CAT SE6 182 F8
CHING E4 100 G2
CHST BR7 184 E8
CRAWE RH10 285 H2
CSHM HP5 * 50 F3
ESH/CLAY KT10 198 E10
GODL GU7 267 K10
HERT/BAY SG13 25 N4
HOM E9 120 E10
HSLWW TW4 175 P3
LCOL/BKTW AL2 * 55 P6
LCOL/BKTW AL2 57 J3
NTHLT UB5 133 P4
PEND EN3 80 D5
PUR/KEN CR8 222 E9
RAD WD7 57 H6
RCHPK/HAM TW10 177 K4
RSLP HA4 112 G4
RYNPK SW20 200 G4
SEV TN13 247 H9
SLH/COR SS17 169 K2
STALE/WH AL4 39 H3
WDSR SL4 171 N2
WOT/HER KT12 217 N1
Meadowcot La *AMSS* HP7 68 E10
Meadow Ct *EPSOM* KT18 219 P9
STA TW18 173 H6
Meadowcourt Rd
BKHTH/KID SE3 161 L10
Meadowcroft *BERK* HP4 33 J2
Meadow Cft *BMLY* BR1 206 C5
Meadowcroft *BUSH* WD23 * 74 A10
CFSP/GDCR SL9 90 A10
Meadow Cft *HAT* AL10 40 C4
Meadowcroft *STAL* AL1 38 F10
Meadowcroft Cl *CRAWW* RH11 283 J8
Meadow Croft Cl *HORL* RH6 280 D7
Meadowcroft Cl *PLMGR* N13 * 99 J3
Meadowcroft Farm
RDART DA2 * 188 G10
Meadowcroft Rd *PLMGR* N13 99 H3
Meadowcross *WAB* EN9 63 K10
Meadow Dell *HAT* AL10 40 C4
Meadow Dr *AMS* HP6 69 K3
HDN NW4 96 F10
MUSWH N10 118 C1
RPLY/SEND GU23 233 J9
Meadowford Cl *THMD* SE28 143 K9
Meadow Gdns *EDGW* HA8 95 N7
STA TW18 172 G8
Meadow Garth *WLSDN* NW10 135 P1
Meadow Gn *WGCW* AL8 22 F5
Meadow Hl *COUL/CHIP* CR5 222 D9
NWMAL KT3 200 B6
Meadowlands *BAR* EN5 76 C9
BGR/WK TN15 247 N6
COB KT11 217 H9
CRAWW RH11 283 M7
EMPK RM11 125 M5
OXTED RH8 261 M10
RGUE GU4 251 L6
Meadow La *BEAC* HP9 88 E9
LEE/GVPK SE12 183 N6
LHD/OX KT22 236 B8
WDSR SL4 148 G5
Meadowlea Cl *WDR/YW* UB7 151 N5
Meadow Ms *VX/NE* SW8 17 N10
Meadow Pl *CHSWK* W4 * 156 B6
VX/NE SW8 158 F6
Meadow Ri *COUL/CHIP* CR5 222 E9
WOKN/KNAP GU21 231 H3
Meadow Rd *ASHF* TW15 174 E8
ASHTD KT21 237 K3
BARK IG11 143 K2
BERK HP4 33 N3
BORE WD6 75 N6
BUSH WD23 74 A9
CDW/CHF RM16 147 P10
DAGW RM9 144 A1
DTCH/LGLY SL3 150 B2
EPP CM16 65 J5
ESH/CLAY KT10 218 D3
FELT TW13 175 M5
GSTN WD25 55 H10
GVW DA11 189 P4
GVW DA11 190 D5
HAYES BR2 205 K1
HHS/BOV HP3 54 B1
LOU IG10 82 B9
PIN HA5 113 L2
RGUE GU4 250 D6
ROMW/RG RM7 124 D6
STHL UB1 133 N9
SUT SM1 221 P1
VW GU25 193 K5
VX/NE SW8 17 N10
WIM/MER SW19 179 M10
Meadow Road Cl *BERK* HP4 33 M3
Meadow Rw *STHWK* SE1 18 E4
Meadows Cl *LEY* E10 120 F7
RBRW/HUT CM13 107 P7
Meadows End *SUN* TW16 197 H1
Meadowside *BEAC* HP9 89 L8
BKHTH/KID SE3 161 P10
DART DA1 187 M4
GSTN WD25 55 J7
GT/LBKH KT23 235 P9
HORL RH6 280 C3
TWK TW1 177 J3
WOT/HER KT12 197 K9
Meadowside Rd *BELMT* SM2 221 H5
UPMR RM14 126 B10
Meadows Leigh Cl *WEY* KT13 196 D10
The Meadows *AMSS* HP7 69 K5
GUW GU2 267 P3
HHW HP1 35 H5
ORP BR6 227 M3
RBRW/HUT CM13 107 P7
RSEV TN14 228 A9
SBW CM21 30 B1
WARL CR6 242 C3
Meadow Stile *CROY/NA* CR0 203 K10
Meadowsweet Cl *CAN/RD* E16 142 A7
NWMAL KT3 200 F5
The Meadow *CHST* BR7 184 F9
CRAWE RH10 285 H2
HERT/BAY SG13 26 D9
WGCE AL7 23 M5
Meadow Vw *BFN/LL* DA15 185 L2
CHERT KT16 195 M8
CSTG HP8 89 M4
EPP CM16 65 K5
HORL RH6 281 K4
HRW HA1 114 D6
STMC/STPC BR5 207 M3
STWL/WRAY TW19 173 J1
SWLY BR8 * 208 E6
UX/CGN UB8 * 131 M7
Meadowview Rd *BXLY* DA5 185 P2
CAT SE6 182 F7
HOR/WEW KT19 220 B5
Meadow View Rd *THHTH* CR7 203 J5
YEAD UB4 132 E6
Meadow Wk *DAGW* RM9 144 A1
HARP AL5 20 B3
HOR/WEW KT19 220 B3
KWD/TDW/WH KT20 238 E10
RDART DA2 187 K7
SWFD E18 121 M2
WLGTN SM6 202 C10
Meadow Wy *ABLGY* WD5 54 G3
ADL/WDHM KT15 215 L1
AMS HP6 68 B1
CDALE/KGS NW9 116 A3
CHIG IG7 102 F3
CHOB/PIR GU24 212 E9
CHSGTN KT9 219 K2
EHSLY KT24 252 E1
GT/LBKH KT23 236 A9
HHS/BOV HP3 35 J9
KGLGY WD4 54 B6
KWD/TDW/WH KT20 239 H3
ORP BR6 206 D10
POTB/CUF EN6 59 K10
RDART DA2 188 B3
REIG RH2 275 L4
RKW/CH/CXG WD3 91 M1
RSLP HA4 113 J5
SBW CM21 30 B2
UPMR RM14 126 B8
WBLY HA9 115 J9
WDSR SL4 171 N2
Meadow Waye *HEST* TW5 153 M6
The Meadow Wy
KTN/HRWW/WS HA3 94 D9
Mead Pl *CROY/NA* CR0 203 J8
HOM E9 140 B1
HORL RH6 281 K4
RKW/CH/CXG WD3 91 L2
Mead Plat *WLSDN* NW10 135 P1
Mead Rd *CHST* BR7 184 F9
CRAWE RH10 284 A6
CTHM CR3 241 N9
DART DA1 187 L4
EDGW HA8 95 M7
GVW DA11 190 E5
RAD WD7 57 M9
RCHPK/HAM TW10 177 H6
UX/CGN UB8 131 N1
WOT/HER KT12 217 M1
Mead Rw *STHWK* SE1 18 A3
Meadside Cl *BECK* BR3 204 D1
Meads La *GDMY/SEVK* IG3 123 J5
STALE/WH AL4 21 J2
Meads Rd *GU* GU1 250 E10
PEND EN3 80 D5
WDGN N22 99 J10
The Meads *BERK* HP4 33 L3
CHEAM SM3 200 G10
EDGW HA8 96 A7
LCOL/BKTW AL2 55 N5
MRDN SM4 * 201 P5
UPMR RM14 126 D7
UX/CGN UB8 131 P6
WEY KT13 216 D3
Meadsway *RBRW/HUT* CM13 106 G7
The Mead *ABR/ST* RM4 83 L7
ASHTD KT21 237 K5
BEAC HP9 * 88 D9
BECK BR3 205 H2
BROX EN10 * 44 G7
CHES/WCR EN8 62 B5
DORK RH4 * 273 H5
EFNCH N2 97 M10
HART DA3 211 K9
HGDN/ICK UB10 112 B7
OXHEY WD19 93 M4
WEA W13 134 G7
WLGTN SM6 222 E3
WWKM BR4 205 J8
Meadvale Rd *CROY/NA* CR0 203 N7
EA W5 134 G6
Meadview Rd *WARE* SG12 26 C3
Mead Wk *CHONG* CM5 67 N6
DTCH/LGLY SL3 150 E1
Mead Wy *BUSH* WD23 73 M6
COUL/CHIP CR5 240 F4
CROY/NA CR0 204 D9
HAYES BR2 205 M6
RGUE GU4 250 F5
RSLP HA4 112 E4
SL SL1 128 C7
Meadway *ASHF* TW15 174 B7
BAR EN5 77 K8
BECK BR3 205 H1
BERK HP4 34 B5
BRYLDS KT5 199 P8
EHSLY KT24 253 M4
ESH/CLAY KT10 218 A5
GDMY/SEVK IG3 123 H9
GLDGN NW11 117 L4
GPK RM2 105 H10
GRAYS RM17 168 A3
HARP AL5 20 D4
HOD EN11 44 F5
HOR/WEW KT19 219 P9
LHD/OX KT22 218 C10
PEND EN3 80 C2
RSEV TN14 228 A9
RYNPK SW20 200 F4
STA TW18 173 K10
STALE/WH AL4 40 A9
STHGT/OAK N14 98 E3
WARL CR6 242 B2
WFD IG8 101 P6
WGCE AL7 23 J7
WHTN TW2 176 C4
Meadway Cl *BAR* EN5 77 K7
GLDGN NW11 117 L4
PIN HA5 94 A7
STA TW18 173 J10
Meadway Ct *EA* W5 * 135 L7
Meadway Dr *ADL/WDHM* KT15 215 M4
WOKN/KNAP GU21 231 P2
Meadway Gdns *RSLP* HA4 112 E4
Meadway Pk *CFSP/GDCR* SL9 110 A6
The Meadway *BKHH* IG9 102 A2
BKHTH/KID SE3 161 J8
HORL RH6 280 D4
ORP BR6 227 L2
POTB/CUF EN6 60 G4
SEV TN13 246 G8
Meaford Wy *PGE/AN* SE20 182 A10
Meanley Rd *MNPK* E12 122 B10
Meard St *SOHO/CST* W1F 11 J6
Meare Cl *KWD/TDW/WH* KT20 238 F9
Meath Cl *STMC/STPC* BR5 207 L5
Meath Green Av *HORL* RH6 280 A3
Meath Green La *HORL* RH6 275 P9
Meath Rd *IL* IG1 122 F8
SRTFD E15 141 L4
Meath St *BTSEA* SW11 158 C7
Meautys *STALW/RED* AL3 37 N8
Mecklenburgh Pl *BMSBY* WC1N 11 N1
Mecklenburgh Sq *BMSBY* WC1N 11 N1
Mecklenburgh St *BMSBY* WC1N 11 N1
Medawar Rd *GUW* GU2 267 J1
Medburn St *CAMTN* NW1 5 J7
Medbury Rd *GVE* DA12 191 J4
Medcalf Rd *PEND* EN3 80 E3
Medcroft Gdns
MORT/ESHN SW14 155 P10
Medebourne Cl *BKHTH/KID* SE3 161 M9
Medebridge Rd *CDW/CHF* RM16 147 M7
Mede Cl *STWL/WRAY* TW19 172 A4
Mede Fld *LHD/OX* KT22 236 C10
Medesenge Wy *PLMGR* N13 99 J7
Medfield St *PUT/ROE* SW15 178 D3
Medhurst Cl *BOW* E3 140 D4
CHOB/PIR GU24 213 L6
Medhurst Crs *GVE* DA12 191 J6
Medhurst Gdns *GVE* DA12 191 J6
Median Rd *CLPT* E5 120 B10
Medick Ct *GRAYS* RM17 168 B5
Medina Av *ESH/CLAY* KT10 198 D10
Medina Rd *GRAYS* RM17 168 A4
HOLWY N7 119 H8
Medlake Rd *EGH* TW20 172 F9
Medland Cl *WLGTN* SM6 202 B8
Medlar Cl *CRAWW* RH11 283 M4
GU GU1 249 P8
NTHLT UB5 133 L4
Medlar Dr *SOCK/AV* RM15 147 K6
Medlar Rd *GRAYS* RM17 168 B5
Medlar St *CMBW* SE5 159 K7
Medley Rd *KIL/WHAMP* NW6 2 E2
Medman Cl *UX/CGN* UB8 131 M4
Medora Rd *BRXS/STRHM* SW2 180 G3
ROMW/RG RM7 124 E2
Medow Md *RAD* WD7 56 E9
Medusa Rd *CAT* SE6 182 G2
Medway *CRAWE* RH10 285 P8
Medway Cl *CROY/NA* CR0 204 B6
GSTN WD25 55 K10
IL IG1 122 F10
Medway Dr *GFD/PVL* UB6 134 E4
Medway Gdns *ALP/SUD* HA0 114 F9
Medway Pde *GFD/PVL* UB6 * 134 E4
Medway Rd *BOW* E3 140 D4
CRAWW RH11 283 J8
DART DA1 165 H9
HHNE HP2 36 A1
Medway St *WEST* SW1P 17 J4
Medwick Ms *HHNE* HP2 36 C1
Medwin St *CLAP* SW4 158 G10
Meerbrook Rd *BKHTH/KID* SE3 161 P9
Meeson Rd *SRTFD* E15 141 L2
Meesons La *GRAYS* RM17 167 L3
Meeson St *CLPT* E5 120 D9
Meesons Whf *SRTFD* E15 * 141 H4
Meeting Aly *WAT* WD17 * 73 K8
Meeting Field Pth *HOM* E9 * 140 B1
Meeting House Aly *WAP* E1W * 140 A10
Meeting House La *PECK* SE15 160 A7
Megg La *KGLGY* WD4 53 L5
Mehetabel Rd *HOM* E9 140 B1
Meister Cl *IL* IG1 122 G6
Melanda Cl *CHST* BR7 184 C8
Melanie Cl *BXLYHN* DA7 163 P7
Melba Gdns *TIL* RM18 168 D6
Melbourne Av *PIN* HA5 114 A1
SL SL1 129 H8
WDGN N22 98 G7
WEA W13 134 F10
Melbourne Cl *ORP* BR6 207 H7
STALW/RED AL3 38 E2
WLGTN SM6 222 D2
Melbourne Ct *WGCW* AL8 22 E6
Melbourne Gdns *CHDH* RM6 123 P3
Melbourne Gv *EDUL* SE22 159 N10
Melbourne Ms *BRXN/ST* SW9 159 H7
CAT SE6 183 H3
Melbourne Pl *HOL/ALD* WC2B 11 P6
Melbourne Rd *BUSH* WD23 74 A10
EHAM E6 142 C3
IL IG1 122 E6
TEDD TW11 177 H9
TIL RM18 168 B7
WALTH E17 120 E2
WIM/MER SW19 201 K1
WLGTN SM6 222 C2
Melbourne Sq *BRXN/ST* SW9 159 H7
Melbourne Ter *EDUL* SE22 * 159 M10
FUL/PGN SW6 * 157 L6
Melbourne Wy *EN* EN1 79 N10
Melbury Av *NWDGN* UB2 154 A2
Melbury Cl *BF/WBF* KT14 215 K10
CHERT KT16 195 K7
CHST BR7 184 C9
ESH/CLAY KT10 218 G3
Melbury Ct *KENS* W8 14 D3
Melbury Dr *CMBW* SE5 159 M6
Melbury Gdns *RYNPK* SW20 200 E1
Melbury Rd *KTN/HRWW/WS* HA3 115 L3
WKENS W14 14 C3
Melbury Ter *CAMTN* NW1 9 P2
Melcombe Gdns
KTN/HRWW/WS HA3 115 L4
Melcombe Pl *CAMTN* NW1 10 A3
Melcombe St *CAMTN* NW1 10 B2
Meldex Cl *MLHL* NW7 96 F7
Meldon Cl *FUL/PGN* SW6 * 157 L7
Meldone Cl *BRYLDS* KT5 199 N6
Meldrum Cl *OXTED* RH8 261 L8
STMC/STPC BR5 207 M6
Meldrum Rd *GDMY/SEVK* IG3 123 K7
Melfield Gdns *CAT* SE6 182 G7
Melford Av *BARK* IG11 143 H1
Melford Cl *CHSGTN* KT9 219 L2
Melford Rd *EDUL* SE22 181 P4
EHAM E6 142 C6
IL IG1 122 G7
WALTH E17 120 E2
WAN E11 121 K7
Melfort Av *THHTH* CR7 203 J3
Melfort Rd *THHTH* CR7 203 J3
Melgund Rd *HBRY* N5 119 H10
Melia Cl *GSTN* WD25 73 K1
Melina Cl *HYS/HAR* UB3 132 E7
Melina Pl *STJWD* NW8 3 L10
Melina Rd *SHB* W12 156 E1
The Melings *HHNE* HP2 36 C1
Melior Pl *STHWK* SE1 * 19 J1
Melior St *STHWK* SE1 19 H1
Meliot Rd *CAT* SE6 183 J5
Melksham Cl *HARH* RM3 105 N8
Melksham Gdns *HARH* RM3 105 N8
Meller Cl *CROY/NA* CR0 202 F10
Melling Dr *EN* EN1 79 P5
Melling St *WOOL/PLUM* SE18 163 H5
Mellish Gdns *WFD* IG8 101 M6
Mellish St *POP/IOD* E14 160 F2
Mellish Wy *EMPK* RM11 125 K3
Mellison Rd *TOOT* SW17 179 P8
Melliss Av *RCH/KEW* TW9 155 N7
Mellitus St *SHB* W12 136 C8
Mellor Cl *WOT/HER* KT12 197 N7
Mellor Wk *WDSR* SL4 149 J7
Mellow Cl *BNSTD* SM7 221 L10
Mellow La East *HGDN/ICK* UB10 132 D6
Mellows Rd *CLAY* IG5 122 C1
WLGTN SM6 222 E2
Mells Crs *ELTH/MOT* SE9 184 C7
Mell St *GNWCH* SE10 161 K4
Melody La *HBRY* N5 119 J10
Melody Rd *BH/WHM* TN16 243 P4
WAND/EARL SW18 179 M2
Melon Pl *KENS* W8 * 14 F1
Melon Rd *PECK* SE15 159 P7
WAN E11 121 K8
Melrose Av *BORE* WD6 75 N9
CRICK NW2 116 F10
DART DA1 186 F3
GFD/PVL UB6 134 A4
MTCM CR4 180 C10
POTB/CUF EN6 59 L9
STRHM/NOR SW16 202 G3
WDGN N22 99 J9
WHTN TW2 176 A3
WIM/MER SW19 179 J5
Melrose Cl *GFD/PVL* UB6 134 A4
LEE/GVPK SE12 183 M4
YEAD UB4 133 H7
Melrose Crs *ORP* BR6 226 G1
Melrose Dr *STHL* UB1 133 P10
Melrose Gdns *EDGW* HA8 115 N1
HMSMTH W6 156 F2
NWMAL KT3 200 A3
WOT/HER KT12 217 K2
Melrose Pl *WAT* WD17 72 G4
Melrose Rd *BARN* SW13 156 C8
BH/WHM TN16 243 P2
COUL/CHIP CR5 240 C1
PIN HA5 113 N2
WAND/EARL SW18 179 J2
WEY KT13 216 B2
WIM/MER SW19 201 K2
Melrose Ter *HMSMTH* W6 156 F1
Melrose Vls *BECK* BR3 * 204 F2
Melsa Rd *MRDN* SM4 201 M6
Melsted Rd *HHW* HP1 35 L6
Melstock Av *UPMR* RM14 126 B9
Melthorne Dr *RSLP* HA4 113 K8
Melthorpe Gdns *BKHTH/KID* SE3 162 A7
Melton Cl *RSLP* HA4 113 K6
Melton Flds *HOR/WEW* KT19 220 A5
Melton Gdns *ROM* RM1 124 G5
Melton Pl *HOR/WEW* KT19 220 A5
Melton Rd *REDH* RH1 258 D6
Melton St *CAMTN* NW1 5 H10
Melville Av *GFD/PVL* UB6 114 E10
RYNPK SW20 178 D10
SAND/SEL CR2 223 N2
Melville Cl *HGDN/ICK* UB10 112 E8
Melville Ct *DEPT* SE8 160 C3
Melville Gdns *PLMGR* N13 99 J7
Melville Pl *IS* N1 6 E4
Melville Rd *BARN* SW13 156 D7
CRW RM5 104 C8
RAIN RM13 145 H6
SCUP DA14 185 M5
WALTH E17 120 E2
WLSDN NW10 136 A2
Melville Villas Rd *ACT* W3 * 136 A10
Melvin Rd *PGE/AN* SE20 204 B1
Melvinshaw *LHD/OX* KT22 237 H7
Melvyn Cl *CHESW* EN7 61 J4
Memel St *STLK* EC1Y 12 E2
Memorial Av *SRTFD* E15 141 K5
Memorial Cl *HEST* TW5 153 N5
OXTED RH8 261 J3
Memorial Sq *KUT/HW* KT1 199 J2
Mendip Cl *DTCH/LGLY* SL3 150 D4
HYS/HAR UB3 152 E6
STALE/WH AL4 39 H1
SYD SE26 182 B7
WPK KT4 200 F9
Mendip Dr *CRICK* NW2 117 H7
Mendip Houses *BETH* E2 * 140 B5
Mendip Rd *BTSEA* SW11 157 M9
BUSH WD23 74 B10
EMPK RM11 125 H5
ERITH DA8 164 F7
GNTH/NBYPK IG2 123 H3
Mendip Wk *CRAWW* RH11 283 L7
Mendip Wy *HHNE* HP2 35 P3
Mendlesham *WGCE* AL7 23 P5
Mendora Rd *FUL/PGN* SW6 157 H6
Mendoza Cl *EMPK* RM11 125 M3
Menelik Rd *CRICK* NW2 117 H9
Menlo Gdns *NRWD* SE19 181 L10
Menon Dr *ED* N9 100 A4
Menotti St *BETH* E2 13 P1
Mentmore Cl
KTN/HRWW/WS HA3 115 H4
Mentmore Rd *STAL* AL1 38 D8
Mentmore Ter *HACK* E8 140 A2
Meon Cl *KWD/TDW/WH* KT20 238 E8
Meon Rd *ACT* W3 155 P1
Meopham Rd *MTCM* CR4 202 D1
Mepham Crs
KTN/HRWW/WS HA3 94 B8
Mepham Gdns
KTN/HRWW/WS HA3 94 B8
Mepham St *STHWK* SE1 11 P10
Mera Dr *BXLYHN* DA7 164 C10
Merantum Wy *WIM/MER* SW19 201 M1
Merbury Cl *LEW* SE13 183 H1
THMD SE28 142 G10
Merbury Rd *THMD* SE28 142 G10
Merbury St *WOOL/PLUM* SE18 162 E2
Mercator Pl *POP/IOD* E14 160 F4
Mercator Rd *LEW* SE13 161 J10
Mercer Cl *CRAWE* RH10 284 D10
THDIT KT7 198 E7
Merceron Houses *BETH* E2 * 140 B5
Merceron St *WCHPL* E1 140 A6
Mercer Pl *PIN* HA5 93 K10
Mercers *HHNE* HP2 35 P4
HLWW/ROY CM19 46 D4
Mercers Cl *GNWCH* SE10 161 L3
Mercers Cottages *WCHPL* E1 * 140 D8
Mercers Ms *ARCH* N19 118 E9
Mercers Pl *HMSMTH* W6 156 F3
Mercers Rd *ARCH* N19 118 E8
Mercers Rw *STAL* AL1 38 B8
Mercer St *LSQ/SEVD* WC2H 11 L6
Merchant Dr *HERT/BAY* SG13 25 N4
Merchants Cl *SNWD* SE25 203 P4
WOKN/KNAP GU21 231 H3
Merchant St *BOW* E3 * 140 E5
Merchiston Rd *CAT* SE6 183 J5
Merchland Rd *ELTH/MOT* SE9 184 F4
Mercia Gv *LEW* SE13 161 H10
Mercian Wy *SL* SL1 128 D10
Mercier Rd *PUT/ROE* SW15 179 H1
Mercury Cl *CRAWW* RH11 283 H10
Mercury Gdns *ROM* RM1 124 G3
Mercury House *HYS/HAR* UB3 * 152 G1
Mercury Rd *BTFD* TW8 155 H4
Mercury Wk *HHNE* HP2 36 A3
Mercury Wy *NWCR* SE14 160 C5
Mercy Ter *LEW* SE13 182 G1
Merebank La *WLGTN* SM6 222 G2
Mere Cl *ORP* BR6 206 E9
PUT/ROE SW15 178 G3
Meredith Av *CRICK* NW2 116 F10
Meredith Cl *PIN* HA5 93 L8
Meredith Ms *BROCKY* SE4 * 160 E10
Meredith Rd *CDW/CHF* RM16 168 D3
Meredith St *CLKNW* EC1R 6 C10
PLSTW E13 141 M5
Meredyth Rd *BARN* SW13 156 D8
Mere End *CROY/NA* CR0 204 C7
Merefield *SBW* CM21 29 P2
Merefield Gdns
KWD/TDW/WH KT20 238 G5
Mere Rd *KWD/TDW/WH* KT20 238 E10
SHPTN TW17 * 196 C6
SL SL1 149 L2
WEY KT13 196 E10
Mereside *ORP* BR6 206 D9
Mereside Pk *ASHF* TW15 * 174 D7
Meretone Cl *BROCKY* SE4 160 D10
Merevale Crs *MRDN* SM4 201 M6
Mereway Rd *WHTN* TW2 176 C4
Merewood Cl *BMLY* BR1 206 D2
Merewood Gdns *CROY/NA* CR0 204 C7
Merewood Rd *BXLYHN* DA7 164 D8
Mereworth Cl *HAYES* BR2 205 L5
Mereworth Dr *CRAWE* RH10 284 E5
WOOL/PLUM SE18 162 E6
Meriden Cl *BARK/HLT* IG6 102 F9
BMLY BR1 184 A10
Meriden Wy *GSTN* WD25 73 M3
Meridian Cl *CRAWW* RH11 283 J10
Meridian Gv *HORL* RH6 280 D3
Meridian Rd *CHARL* SE7 162 A6
Meridian Sq *SRTFD* E15 141 J2
Meridian Wy *UED* N18 100 B5
WAB EN9 62 G10
WARE SG12 26 G6
Merifield Rd *ELTH/MOT* SE9 161 P10
Merileys Cl *HART* DA3 211 P3
Merino Cl *WAN* E11 121 P2
Merivale Rd *HRW* HA1 114 C5
PUT/ROE SW15 157 H10
Merland Cl *KWD/TDW/WH* KT20 238 F6
Merland Gn *KWD/TDW/WH* KT20 238 F6
Merland Ri *EPSOM* KT18 238 F5
Merle Av *DEN/HRF* UB9 91 M10
Merlewood *SEV* TN13 247 J9
Merlewood Cl *CTHM* CR3 241 L6
Merlewood Dr *CHST* BR7 206 C1
Merley Ct *CDALE/KGS* NW9 115 P6
Merlin Centre *CRAWW* RH11 * 283 N3
Merlin Cl *BARK/HLT* IG6 103 L5
CDW/CHF RM16 167 K2
CRAWW RH11 283 H7
CROY/NA CR0 223 M1
CRW RM5 104 E7
DTCH/LGLY SL3 * 150 E5
MTCM CR4 201 P3
NTHLT UB5 133 K5
WAB EN9 63 M10
WLGTN SM6 222 G3
Merlin Crs *EDGW* HA8 95 L9
Merlin Gdns *CRW* RM5 104 E7
Merling Cl *CHSGTN* KT9 219 J2
Merling Cft *BERK* HP4 33 K3
Merlin Gv *BARK/HLT* IG6 102 E8
BECK BR3 204 E4
Merlin Rd *CRW* RM5 104 E7
MNPK E12 122 A7
WELL DA16 163 K10
Merlin Rd North *WELL* DA16 163 K10
Merlins Av *RYLN/HDSTN* HA2 113 N8
Merlin St *FSBYW* WC1X 6 A10
Merlin Wy *EPP* CM16 66 B1
GSTN WD25 54 G10
Mermagen Dr *RAIN* RM13 145 J2
Mermaid Cl *GVW* DA11 190 B3
Mermaid Ct *STHWK* SE1 18 G1
Mermerus Gdns *GVE* DA12 191 J7
Merredene St *BRXS/STRHM* SW2 180 G2
Merriam Av *HOM* E9 140 E1
Merriam Cl *CHING* E4 101 H6
Merrick Rd *NWDGN* UB2 153 N3
Merrick Sq *STHWK* SE1 18 G3
Merridene *WCHMH* N21 79 J10
Merrielands Crs *DAGW* RM9 144 A4
Merrilands Rd *WPK* KT4 200 F8
Merrilees Rd *BFN/LL* DA15 185 H3
Merrilyn Cl *ESH/CLAY* KT10 218 F3
Merriman Rd *BKHTH/KID* SE3 161 P7
Merrington Rd *FUL/PGN* SW6 14 F9
Merring Wy *HLWW/ROY* CM19 46 C2
WAB EN9 46 C7
Merrin Hl *SAND/SEL* CR2 223 M8
Merrion Av *STAN* HA7 95 J6
Merritt Gdns *CHSGTN* KT9 219 J3
Merritt Rd *BROCKY* SE4 182 E1
Merritt Wk *BRKMPK* AL9 40 E10
Merrivale *STHGT/OAK* N14 78 E10
Merrivale Av *REDBR* IG4 122 A2
Merrivale Gdns
WOKN/KNAP GU21 231 P3
Merrivale Ms *WDR/YW* UB7 * 131 N10
Merrow Cha *GU* GU1 250 F10
Merrow Common Rd *RGUE* GU4 250 G7
Merrow Copse *GU* GU1 250 E9
Merrow Ct *GU* GU1 * 250 G10
Merrow Cft *GU* GU1 250 F9
Merrow Dr *HHW* HP1 35 H5
Merrow La *RGUE* GU4 250 F5
Merrow Pl *RGUE* GU4 250 G8
Merrow Rd *BELMT* SM2 220 G5
Merrows Cl *NTHWD* HA6 92 D7
Merrow St *RGUE* GU4 250 G8
WALW SE17 18 G8
Merrow Wk *WALW* SE17 19 H7
Merrow Wy *CROY/NA* CR0 225 H3
GU GU1 * 250 G9
Merrow Woods *GU* GU1 250 E8
Merrydown Wy *CHST* BR7 206 C1
Merryfield *BKHTH/KID* SE3 161 L8
Merryfield Gdns *STAN* HA7 95 H6
Merryfields *STALE/WH* AL4 39 K6
UX/CGN UB8 131 N4
Merryfields Cl *HART* DA3 211 L4
Merryfield Wy *CAT* SE6 182 G3
Merryhill Cl *CHING* E4 100 G1
Merry Hill Mt *BUSH* WD23 94 A2
Merry Hill Rd *BUSH* WD23 93 P1
Merryhills Cl *BH/WHM* TN16 244 A2
Merryhills Dr *ENC/FH* EN2 78 F8
Merrylands *CHERT* KT16 195 H10
Merrylands Farm *GT/LBKH* KT23 235 N10
Merrylands Rd *GT/LBKH* KT23 235 N9
Merrymeade Cha *BRWN* CM15 107 J2
Merrymeet *BNSTD* SM7 222 A10
Merryweather Cl *DART* DA1 187 N2
Merryweather Ct *NWMAL* KT3 200 B5
Merrywood Gv
KWD/TDW/WH KT20 256 G6
Merrywood Pk *REIG* RH2 257 L8
Mersey Av *UPMR* RM14 126 C4
Mersey Pl *HHNE* HP2 36 A1
Mersey Rd *WALTH* E17 120 E1
Mersham Dr *CDALE/KGS* NW9 115 N3
Mersham Pl *PGE/AN* SE20 204 A1
THHTH CR7 203 L2
Mersham Rd *THHTH* CR7 203 L3
Merstham Rd *REDH* RH1 259 H6
Merten Rd *CHDH* RM6 123 P5
Merthyr Ter *BARN* SW13 156 E5
Merton Av *CHSWK* W4 156 C3
HART DA3 211 L4
HGDN/ICK UB10 132 C2
NTHLT UB5 114 B10
Merton Gdns
KWD/TDW/WH KT20 238 G5
STMC/STPC BR5 206 E5
Merton Hall Gdns *RYNPK* SW20 201 H1
Merton Hall Rd *WIM/MER* SW19 201 J1
Merton High St *WIM/MER* SW19 179 M10
Merton La *HGT* N6 118 A7
Merton Pl *CDW/CHF* RM16 168 D3
WIM/MER SW19 * 201 M1
Merton Ri *HAMP* NW3 3 N3
Merton Rd *BARK* IG11 143 J2
ENC/FH EN2 79 L4
GDMY/SEVK IG3 123 J5
RYLN/HDSTN HA2 114 B6
SL SL1 149 M2
SNWD SE25 203 N5
WALTH E17 121 H3
WAND/EARL SW18 179 K3
WAND/EARL SW18 179 K4
WATW WD18 73 J8
WIM/MER SW19 179 L10
Merton Wy *E/WMO/HCT* KT8 198 B4
HGDN/ICK UB10 132 C2
LHD/OX KT22 236 G5
Mertoun Ter *MBLAR* W1H * 10 A5
Merttins Rd *PECK* SE15 160 C10
Meru Cl *KTTN* NW5 118 B10
Mervan Rd *BRXS/STRHM* SW2 159 H10
Mervyn Av *ELTH/MOT* SE9 184 F6
Mervyn Rd *SHPTN* TW17 196 D7
WEA W13 154 F2
Merwin Wy *WDSR* SL4 * 148 C9
Meryfield Cl *BORE* WD6 75 L6
Mesne Wy *RSEV* TN14 228 G8
Messaline Av *ACT* W3 135 P8
Messant Cl *HARH* RM3 105 L10
Messenger Cl *CRAWW* RH11 283 K5
Messent Rd *ELTH/MOT* SE9 183 P1
Messeter Pl *ELTH/MOT* SE9 184 D2
Messina Av *KIL/WHAMP* NW6 2 E4
Metcalf Rd *ASHF* TW15 174 C8
Metcalf Wy *CRAWW* RH11 283 N3
Meteor St *BTSEA* SW11 158 B10
Meteor Wy *WLGTN* SM6 222 F4
Metford Crs *PEND* EN3 80 F4
Methley St *LBTH* SE11 18 B8
Methuen Cl *EDGW* HA8 95 M8
Methuen Pk *MUSWH* N10 98 C10
Methuen Rd *BELV* DA17 164 C3
BXLYHS DA6 164 A10
EDGW HA8 95 M8
Methwold Rd *NKENS* W10 136 G7
Metro Centre *STALE/WH* AL4 * 38 E2
Metropolitan Cl *POP/IOD* E14 140 F7
Metropolitan Ms *WATW* WD18 72 F8
Metropolitan Station Ap
WATW WD18 72 G8
Metropolitan Whf *WAP* E1W * 140 B10
Meux Cl *CHESW* EN7 61 P7
Mewsend *BH/WHM* TN16 244 A4
Mews North *BGVA* SW1W 16 E4
Mews Pl *WFD* IG8 101 M5
Mews St *WAP* E1W 13 M9
The Mews *BECK* BR3 204 F1
CEND/HSY/T N8 119 H2
GU GU1 * 250 G10
GVE DA12 190 G5
HARP AL5 * 20 A2
NFNCH/WDSPK N12 * 97 L6
REDBR IG4 122 A3
REIG RH2 * 257 L9
ROM RM1 124 F2
SEV TN13 * 247 H10
SEVS/STOTM N15 119 M2
STRHM/NOR SW16 * 202 G1
TWK TW1 * 176 G2
WATW WD18 * 73 K8
Mexfield Rd *PUT/ROE* SW15 179 J1
Meyer Gn *EN* EN1 79 P4
Meyer Rd *ERITH* DA8 164 D5
Meymott St *STHWK* SE1 12 C10
Meynell Crs *HOM* E9 140 C2
Meynell Gdns *HOM* E9 140 C2
Meynell Rd *HARH* RM3 105 J8
HOM E9 140 C2
Meyrick Cl *WOKN/KNAP* GU21 231 K2
Meyrick Rd *BTSEA* SW11 157 N9
WLSDN NW10 136 D1
Mezen Cl *NTHWD* HA6 92 E6
Miah Ter *WAP* E1W * 13 P10
Micawber Av *UX/CGN* UB8 132 B6
Micawber St *IS* N1 6 F9
Michael Crs *HORL* RH6 280 B6
Michael Gdns *EMPK* RM11 125 L2
GVE DA12 191 H9
Michael Gaynor Cl *HNWL* W7 134 E10
Michael La *GUW* GU2 249 N6
Michaelmas Cl *RYNPK* SW20 200 F3
Michael Rd *FUL/PGN* SW6 157 L7
SNWD SE25 203 M3
WAN E11 121 K6
Michaels Cl *LEW* SE13 161 K9
Michaels La *HART* DA3 210 G9
Micheldever Rd *LEE/GVPK* SE12 183 K2
Michelet Cl *LTWR* GU18 212 A6
Michelham Gdns
KWD/TDW/WH KT20 * 238 F6
TWK TW1 176 E6
Michelsdale Dr *RCH/KEW* TW9 155 K10
Michel Wk *WOOL/PLUM* SE18 162 E4
Michigan Av *MNPK* E12 122 B9
Michigan Cl *BROX* EN10 62 D2
Michleham Down
NFNCH/WDSPK N12 97 J5
Micholls Av *CFSP/GDCR* SL9 90 B6
Micklefield Rd *HHNE* HP2 36 D7
Micklefield Wy *BORE* WD6 75 K4
Mickleham Cl *STMC/STPC* BR5 207 J2
Mickleham Dr *LHD/OX* KT22 255 H2
Mickleham Gdns *CHEAM* SM3 221 H3
Mickleham Rd *STMC/STPC* BR5 207 J1
Mickleham Wy *CROY/NA* CR0 225 J4
Micklem Dr *HHW* HP1 35 J5
Micklethwaite Rd *FUL/PGN* SW6 14 F10
Midcot Wy *BERK* HP4 33 L3
Midcroft *RSLP* HA4 112 F6
SLN SL2 128 G6
Mid Cross La *CFSP/GDCR* SL9 90 C6
Middle Boy *ABR/ST* RM4 83 M7
Middle Cl *COUL/CHIP* CR5 241 H6
EW KT17 220 B8
Middle Dartrey Wk
WBPTN SW10 * 157 M6
Middle Dene *MLHL* NW7 96 A4
Middle Down *GSTN* WD25 74 A2
Middle Dr *BEAC* HP9 88 C6
Middle Farm Cl *EHSLY* KT24 253 L3
Middle Farm Pl *EHSLY* KT24 253 L3
Middlefield *HAT* AL10 40 D3
HORL RH6 280 D3
STJWD NW8 3 L5
WGCE AL7 23 H9
Middlefield Av *HOD* EN11 44 F1
Middlefield Cl *HOD* EN11 44 F1
STALE/WH AL4 39 H3
Middlefielde *WEA* W13 134 G7
Middlefield Rd *HOD* EN11 44 F1
Middlefields *CROY/NA* CR0 224 D5
WEA W13 134 G7
Middle Furlong *BUSH* WD23 74 A8
Middle Gn *BRWN* CM15 87 H3
DTCH/LGLY SL3 130 B9
Middle Green Cl *BRYLDS* KT5 199 L6
Middlegreen Rd *DTCH/LGLY* SL3 130 A10
Middleham Gdns *UED* N18 99 P7
Middleham Rd *UED* N18 99 P7
Middle Hl *EGH* TW20 171 P8
Middlehill *HHW* HP1 35 H6
Middleknights Hl *HHW* HP1 35 K4
Middle La *BGR/WK* TN15 247 N7
CEND/HSY/T N8 118 F3
EW KT17 220 B8
HHS/BOV HP3 52 D5
TEDD TW11 176 E9
Middle Lane Ms *CEND/HSY/T* N8 118 F3
Middlemead Cl *GT/LBKH* KT23 253 P1
Middle Meadow *CSTG* HP8 89 N4
Middlemead Rd *GT/LBKH* KT23 253 N1
Middle Ope *WATN* WD24 73 J3
Middle Park Av *ELTH/MOT* SE9 184 A3
Middle Rd *BERK* HP4 33 N5
DEN/HRF UB9 110 F5
EBAR EN4 77 P10
LHD/OX KT22 236 G7
PLSTW E13 141 M5
RBRW/HUT CM13 107 P5
RYLN/HDSTN HA2 114 C7
STRHM/NOR SW16 202 D2
WAB EN9 62 G8
Middle Rw *NKENS* W10 8 A2
Middlesborough Rd *UED* N18 99 P7
Middlesex Cl *STHL* UB1 134 A6
Middlesex Pl *HOM* E9 140 B1
Middlesex Rd *MTCM* CR4 202 F5

Middlesex St WCHPL E1 13 K4
Middle St BRKHM/BTCW RH3 273 N2
CROY/NA CR0 203 K9
SHGR GU5 270 B5
STBT EC1A 12 E3
WAB EN9 45 K8
Middle Temple La EMB EC4Y 12 A6
Middleton Av CHING E4 100 E5
GFD/PVL UB6 134 C4
SCUP DA14 185 M9
Middleton Cl CHING E4 100 E4
Middleton Dr BERM/RHTH SE16 160 C1
PIN HA5 113 H1
Middleton Gdns
GNTH/NBYPK IG2 122 E4
Middleton Gv HOLWY N7 118 F10
Middleton Hall La BRWN CM15 107 K3
Middleton Ms HOLWY N7 118 F10
Middleton Pl GTPST W1W 10 G4
Middleton Rd BRWN CM15 107 K2
COB KT11 235 J5
GLDGN NW11 117 K5
HACK E8 7 L4
HOR/WEW KT19 * 220 A6
HYS/HAR UB3 132 E7
MRDN SM4 201 M6
NWMAL KT3 199 P3
RKW/CH/CXG WD3 91 K2
Middleton St BETH E2 140 A5
Middleton Wy CRAWW RH11 283 H8
LEW SE13 161 J10
Middle Wk SL SL1 128 A5
WOKN/KNAP GU21 * 232 B3
Middleway GLDGN NW11 117 L3
Middle Wy STRHM/NOR SW16 202 E2
WATN WD24 73 J3
The Middle Wy
KTN/HRWW/WS HA3 94 E10
Middle Yd STHWK SE1 13 H9
The Middlings SEV TN13 264 G2
Middlings Wd SEV TN13 264 G1
Midfield Av BXLYHN DA7 164 D9
SWLY BR8 187 H9
Midfield Wy STMC/STPC BR5 207 L1
Midford Pl FITZ W1T * 11 H2
Midgarth Cl LHD/OX KT22 218 B9
Midgley Rd CRAWE RH10 284 A5
Midholm GLDGN NW11 117 L2
WBLY HA9 115 M6
Midholm Cl GLDGN NW11 * 117 L2
Midholm Rd CROY/NA CR0 204 D10
Mid Holmwood La RDKG RH5 272 G8
Midhope Cl WOKS/MYFD GU22 232 B5
Midhope Gdns
WOKS/MYFD GU22 232 B5
Midhope Rd WOKS/MYFD GU22 232 B5
Midhope St STPAN WC1H 5 M10
Midhurst Av CROY/NA CR0 203 H7
MUSWH N10 118 B1
Midhurst Cl CRAWW RH11 283 K6
HCH RM12 125 H9
Midhurst Gdns HGDN/ICK UB10 132 D2
Midhurst Hl BXLYHS DA6 186 B1
Midhurst Pde MUSWH N10 * 118 B1
Midhurst Rd WEA W13 154 F1
Midhurst Wy CLPT E5 119 P9
Midland Arches CRICK NW2 * 116 E7
Midland Crs HAMP NW3 3 J1
Midland Rd CAMTN NW1 5 L9
HHNE HP2 35 N6
LEY E10 121 H6
Midland Ter CRICK NW2 116 G8
WLSDN NW10 136 B6
Midleton Industrial Estate Rd
GUW GU2 249 N9
Midleton Rd GUW GU2 249 L10
Midlothian Rd BOW E3 140 E6
Midmoor Rd BAL SW12 180 D4
WIM/MER SW19 200 G1
Midship Cl BERM/RHTH SE16 * 140 C10
Midship Point POP/IOD E14 * 160 F1
Midstrath Rd WLSDN NW10 116 B9
Mid St REDH RH1 258 G10
Midsummer Av HSLWW TW4 153 N10
Midsummer Wk
WOKN/KNAP GU21 232 A2
Midway CHEAM SM3 201 J7
STALW/RED AL3 38 A9
WOT/HER KT12 197 J9
Midway Av CHERT KT16 195 L3
EGH TW20 194 E3
Midway Cl STA TW18 173 L6
Midwinter Cl WELL DA16 163 K9
Midwood Cl CRICK NW2 116 D8
Miena Wy ASHTD KT21 237 J3
Mighell Av REDBR IG4 122 A3
Milan Rd STHL UB1 153 N1
Milborne Gv WBPTN SW10 15 K8
Milborne St HOM E9 140 B1
Milborough Crs LEE/GVPK SE12 183 K3
Milbourne La ESH/CLAY KT10 218 B3
Milbrook ESH/CLAY KT10 218 B3
Milburn Dr WDR/YW UB7 131 P9
Milburn Wk EPSOM KT18 238 B1
Milcote St STHWK SE1 18 C2
Mildenhall Rd CLPT E5 120 B9
SL SL1 129 K8
Mildmay Av IS N1 7 H1
Mildmay Gv North IS N1 119 L10
Mildmay Gv South IS N1 119 L10
Mildmay Pk IS N1 119 L10
Mildmay Pl RSEV TN14 228 G7
STNW/STAM N16 * 119 M10
Mildmay Rd IL IG1 122 E8
IS N1 119 L10
ROMW/RG RM7 124 D3
Mildmay St IS N1 7 H1
Mildred Av BORE WD6 75 M8
HYS/HAR UB3 152 E3
NTHLT UB5 114 A10
WATW WD18 73 H8
Mildred Cl DART DA1 187 P2
Mildred Rd ERITH DA8 164 F4
Mile Cl WAB EN9 63 H9
Mile End Pl WCHPL E1 140 C6
Mile End Rd WCHPL E1 140 B7
The Mile End WALTH E17 100 C9
Mile House Cl STAL AL1 38 F9
Mile House La STAL AL1 38 E10
Mile Pth WOKS/MYFD GU22 231 N6
Mile Rd WLGTN SM6 202 B8
Miles Cl HLWW/ROY CM19 46 E2
Miles Dr THMD SE28 143 H10
Miles La COB KT11 217 M9
Milespit Hl MLHL NW7 96 E6
Miles Pl BRYLDS KT5 * 199 L4
Miles Rd CEND/HSY/T N8 118 F1
HOR/WEW KT19 220 A8
MTCM CR4 201 P3
Miles St VX/NE SW8 17 L10
Milestone Cl BELMT SM2 221 N3
ED N9 99 P3
RPLY/SEND GU23 233 K8
Milestone Rd NRWD SE19 101 N9
Mile Stone Rd RDART DA2 188 A3
Miles Wy TRDG/WHET N20 97 P3
Milfoil St SHB W12 136 D9
Milford Cl ABYW SE2 163 P5
STALE/WH AL4 39 J2
Milford Ct SL SL1 149 M1
Milford Gdns ALP/SUD HA0 115 J10
CROY/NA CR0 204 B5
EDGW HA8 95 M8
Milford Gv SUT SM1 221 M1
Milford La TPL/STR WC2R 12 A7
Milford Ms STRHM/NOR SW16 180 G7
Milford Rd STHL UB1 133 P9
WEA W13 134 G10
Milkhouse Ga GU GU1 * 268 A2
Milking La ORP BR6 226 B8
Milk St BMLY BR1 183 N9
CAN/RD E16 142 E10
CITYW EC2V 12 F5
Milkwell Gdns WFD IG8 101 N8
Milkwell Yd CMBW SE5 159 K7
Milkwood RGUE GU4 * 268 C7
Milkwood Rd HNHL SE24 181 J1
Milk Yd WAP E1W 140 B9
Millacres WARE SG12 * 26 D2
Millais Av MNPK E12 122 D10
Millais Crs HOR/WEW KT19 220 B2
Millais Gdns EDGW HA8 95 M10
Millais Pl TIL RM18 168 D6
Millais Rd EN EN1 79 N9
NWMAL KT3 200 B7
WAN E11 121 H9
Millais Wy HOR/WEW KT19 219 P1
Millan Cl ADL/WDHM KT15 215 L6
Milland Ct BORE WD6 76 A5
Millard Cl STNW/STAM N16 119 M10
Millars Meadow BKHTH/KID SE3 161 L10
Mill Av UX/CGN UB8 131 M4
Millbank HHS/BOV HP3 35 N10
WEST SW1P 17 L5
Millbank Av CHONG CM5 67 N5
Millbank Est WEST SW1P 17 K6
The Millbank CRAWW RH11 283 J8
Millbank Wy LEE/GVPK SE12 183 M1
Millbottom La RDKG RH5 273 J10
Millbourne Rd FELT TW13 175 M7
Mill Br BAR EN5 * 77 J9
HERT/WAT SG14 25 K5
Mill Bridge Pl UX/CGN UB8 131 L4
Millbro SWLY BR8 209 H1
Millbrook GU GU1 268 A2
WEY KT13 216 F1
Millbrook Av ELTH/MOT SE9 162 G10
Millbrook Gdns CHDH RM6 123 P4
GPK RM2 104 F10
Millbrook Rd BRXN/ST SW9 159 J9
BUSH WD23 73 N5
ED N9 100 A2
Mill Brook Rd STMC/STPC BR5 207 M4
Millbrook Wy DTCH/LGLY SL3 151 H8
Mill Cl CAR SM5 * 202 B9
CSHM HP5 51 K10
GT/LBKH KT23 235 P10
HHS/BOV HP3 54 B1
HHW HP1 35 L2
HORL RH6 279 P3
WARE SG12 26 C2
WDR/YW UB7 151 N2
WGCW AL8 22 D6
Millcombe Cl WOKN/KNAP GU21 231 N4
Mill Cnr BAR EN5 77 J5
Mill Ct WDR/YW UB7 151 N2
Millcrest Rd CHESW EN7 61 J4
Millen Ct EYN DA4 210 B4
Millennium Br STHWK SE1 12 E8
Millennium Cl CAN/RD E16 141 M8
UX/CGN UB8 131 L4
Millennium Dr POP/IOD E14 161 J2
Millennium Pl BETH E2 * 140 A4
Millennium Sq STHWK SE1 19 L1
Millennium Wy GNWCH SE10 161 K1
Millennium Whf POP/IOD E14 161 J3
RKW/CH/CXG WD3 * 91 P2
Miller Av PEND EN3 80 F4
Miller Cl BMLY BR1 183 M8
CRW RM5 104 B8
MTCM CR4 202 A7
Miller Pl CFSP/GDCR SL9 110 A3
Miller Rd CROY/NA CR0 202 G8
GVE DA12 191 K5
RGUE GU4 250 F7
WIM/MER SW19 179 N9
Miller's Av HACK E8 119 N10
Millers Cl CHIG IG7 103 L3
MLHL NW7 96 D5
STA TW18 173 L8
Millers Copse EPSOM KT18 238 A5
REDH RH1 277 J10
Miller's Ct CHSWK W4 156 C4
Millersdale HLWW/ROY CM19 46 E5
Millers Green Cl ENC/FH EN2 79 J7
Miller's La CHIG IG7 103 L2
REDH RH1 277 J10
WARE SG12 27 H7
Millers Ri STAL AL1 38 D7
Miller's Ter HACK E8 119 N10
Miller St CAMTN NW1 4 G7
Miller's Wy HMSMTH W6 156 F1
Millers Yd FNCH N3 97 L9
HERT/WAT SG14 25 L5
Miller Wk STHWK SE1 12 B10
Millet Rd GFD/PVL UB6 134 A5
Mill Farm Av SUN TW16 174 F10
Mill Farm Cl PIN HA5 93 K10
Mill Farm Crs HSLWW TW4 175 M4
Millfield BERK HP4 34 A4
HART DA3 211 K9
Mill Fld HLWE CM17 29 M7
Millfield SUN TW16 196 E1
WGCE AL7 23 M4
Millfield Av WALTH E17 100 E9
Millfield Dr GVW DA11 190 B5
Millfield La HART DA3 211 K9
HGT N6 118 A7
KWD/TDW/WH KT20 257 K1
Millfield Pl HGT N6 118 B7
Millfield Rd EDGW HA8 95 P10
HSLWW TW4 175 M4
Millfields CSHM HP5 51 H9
Millfields Cl STMC/STPC BR5 207 L4
Millfields Crs HORL RH6 278 G9
Millfields Rd CLPT E5 120 B9
Millfield Wk HHS/BOV HP3 36 B9
Millford WOKN/KNAP GU21 231 N3
Mill Gdns SYD SE26 182 A7
Mill Gn MTCM CR4 * 202 B7
Mill Green La BRKMPK AL9 23 H10
Mill Green Rd MTCM CR4 202 B7
WGCE AL7 23 H7
Millgrove St BTSEA SW11 158 B7
Millharbour POP/IOD E14 160 G2
Millhaven Cl CHDH RM6 123 L4
Millhedge Cl COB KT11 235 M2
Mill Hl BARN SW13 156 D9
BRKHM/BTCW RH3 273 N1
BRWN CM15 107 K1
Mill Hill Gv ACT W3 * 135 N10
Mill Hill La BRKHM/BTCW RH3 255 N10
GVE DA12 191 N8
Mill Hill Rd ACT W3 155 N1
BARN SW13 156 E9
Mill Hill Ter ACT W3 135 N10
Millhouse La ABLGY WD5 55 H3
Mill House La EGH TW20 194 E4
Millhouse Pl WNWD SE27 181 J7
Millhurst Ms HLWE CM17 29 P7
Millicent Rd LEY E10 * 120 E6
Milligan St POP/IOD E14 140 E9
Milliners Ct STAL AL1 * 38 D6
Milling Rd EDGW HA8 96 A8
Millington Rd HYS/HAR UB3 152 F2
Mill La ABR/ST RM4 85 K6
AMSS HP7 68 F5
ASC SL5 192 G2
BF/WBF KT14 216 B9
BH/WHM TN16 262 F3
BROX EN10 44 E7
BRWN CM15 86 D3
BRWN CM15 87 J1
CAR SM5 222 B1
CFSP/GDCR SL9 110 C4
CHDH RM6 123 P4
CHES/WCR EN8 62 D4
CHING E4 80 G7
CHOB/PIR GU24 230 C10
CHONG CM5 49 K4
CHONG CM5 66 F5
CRAWE RH10 285 M2
CRAWW RH11 283 K5
CRICK NW2 117 H10
CROY/NA CR0 203 H10
CSTG HP8 89 M3
DORK RH4 272 G1
DTCH/LGLY SL3 150 E9
EGH TW20 194 F4
EW KT17 220 C5
EYN DA4 209 M8
GU GU1 268 A2
HLWE CM17 29 P7
HORL RH6 279 N4
KGLGY WD4 54 B5
KWD/TDW/WH KT20 238 G9
LHD/OX KT22 236 F8
ORP BR6 226 D6
OXTED RH8 261 L8
OXTED RH8 262 C7
RDKG RH5 278 A2
REDH RH1 258 D7
RGUW GU3 267 P8
RPLY/SEND GU23 233 N5
RSEV TN14 228 G6
RSEV TN14 247 K7
SHGR GU5 269 K4
WDSR SL4 148 F6
WFD IG8 101 L6
WOOL/PLUM SE18 162 D4
WTHK RM20 167 J4
Mill Lane Cl BROX EN10 44 E7
Millman Ms BMSBY WC1N * 11 N2
Millman Pl BMSBY WC1N 11 N2
Millman St BMSBY WC1N 11 N2
Millmark Gv NWCR SE14 160 D8
Millmarsh La PEND EN3 80 D6
Millmead BF/WBF KT14 216 A8
GUW GU2 267 P2
Mill Md STA TW18 173 J7
Mill Mead Rd TOTM N17 120 A1
Millmead Ter GUW GU2 267 P2
Millmead Wy HERT/WAT SG14 25 J4
Mill Park Av HCH RM12 125 M7
Mill Pl CHST BR7 206 D1
DART DA1 165 H10
DTCH/LGLY SL3 150 A8
KUT/HW KT1 199 L3
POP/IOD E14 140 D8
Mill Plat ISLW TW7 154 F9
Mill Plat Av ISLW TW7 154 F8
Mill Pond Cl RSEV TN14 247 L7
VX/NE SW8 158 E6
Millpond Ct ADL/WDHM KT15 215 P2
Millpond Est BERM/RHTH SE16 * 160 A1
Mill Pond Rd BFOR GU20 212 A2
DART DA1 187 M2
Mill Race WARE SG12 27 J7
Mill Reach SHGR GU5 269 J5
Mill Rdg EDGW HA8 95 L6
Mill Rd CAN/RD E16 141 N10
COB KT11 235 K1
CRAWE RH10 284 C6
ERITH DA8 164 D6
ESH/CLAY KT10 197 P9
EW KT17 220 C8
GVW DA11 190 B3
HERT/BAY SG13 25 L4
IL IG1 122 D8
KWD/TDW/WH KT20 238 G9
PUR RM19 166 A5
RDART DA2 187 N7
RDKG RH5 273 H10
SEV TN13 246 F7
SOCK/AV RM15 146 B9
WDR/YW UB7 151 N2
WHTN TW2 176 B5
WIM/MER SW19 179 M10
Mill Rw BXLY DA5 * 186 C3
IS N1 7 K6
Mills Cl HGDN/ICK UB10 132 B4
Mills Crs BGR/WK TN15 247 N6
Mills Gv HDN NW4 116 G1
POP/IOD E14 141 H7
Mill Shaw OXTED RH8 261 L8
Millshot Cl FUL/PGN SW6 156 F7
Millshott Cl WHALL SW1A 11 K9
Millside CAR SM5 202 A9
Millside Ct GT/LBKH KT23 * 253 P1
Millside Pk WDSR SL4 * 148 C8
Millside Pl ISLW TW7 154 G8
Millsmead Wy LOU IG10 82 C6
Millson Cl TRDG/WHET N20 97 N3
Mills Rd WOT/HER KT12 217 K2
Mills Rw CHSWK W4 156 A3
Mills Sp WDSR SL4 171 N3
Millstead Cl KWD/TDW/WH KT20 238 E9
Mill Stone Cl EYN DA4 210 B2
Millstone Ms EYN DA4 210 B1
Millstream Cl HERT/WAT SG14 25 J5
PLMGR N13 99 H6
Millstream La SL SL1 128 D10
Millstream Rd STHWK SE1 19 L3
Mill St BERK HP4 33 P5
BH/WHM TN16 262 G3
CONDST W1S 10 F7
DTCH/LGLY SL3 150 G6
HHS/BOV HP3 35 N10
HLWE CM17 47 P4
KUT/HW KT1 199 K3
REDH RH1 275 P1
SLN SL2 129 L10
STHWK SE1 19 M2
Mills Wy RBRW/HUT CM13 107 P2
Millthorne Cl RKW/CH/CXG WD3 72 A9
Mill V HAYES BR2 205 M3
Mill View Cl EW KT17 220 C4
Millview Cl REIG RH2 257 N8
Mill View Gdns CROY/NA CR0 204 C10
Millwall Dock Rd POP/IOD E14 160 F2
Millwards HAT AL10 40 E7
Mill Wy BUSH WD23 73 M6
EBED/NFELT TW14 175 J1
LHD/OX KT22 255 L1
MLHL NW7 96 B6
RKW/CH/CXG WD3 91 J2
Millway REIG RH2 257 N10
Millway Gdns NTHLT UB5 133 N1
Millwell Crs CHIG IG7 102 G6
Millwood Rd HSLW TW3 176 B1
STMC/STPC BR5 207 M3
Millwood St NKENS W10 137 H7
Mill Yd WCHPL E1 13 N7
Milman Cl PIN HA5 113 L1
Milman Rd KIL/WHAMP NW6 136 G4
Milman's St WBPTN SW10 15 L10
Milne Cl CRAWW RH11 283 H10
Milne Fld PIN HA5 93 P8
Milne Gdns ELTH/MOT SE9 184 B1
Milne Pk East CROY/NA CR0 225 J7
Milne Pk West CROY/NA CR0 225 J7
Milner Ap CTHM CR3 241 P7
Milner Cl CTHM CR3 241 P8
GSTN WD25 55 J10
Milner Ct BUSH WD23 74 A10
Milner Dr COB KT11 217 N8
WHTN TW2 176 C3
Milner Pl IS N1 6 B5
Milner Rd BCTR RM8 123 M7
CTHM CR3 241 P8
KUT/HW KT1 199 J3
MRDN SM4 201 N5
SRTFD E15 141 K5
THHTH CR7 203 K3
WIM/MER SW19 201 L1
Milner Sq IS N1 6 C4
Milner St CHEL SW3 16 A5
Milneway DEN/HRF UB9 91 L9
Milnthorpe Rd CHSWK W4 156 A5
Milo Rd EDUL SE22 181 N2
Milroy Av GVW DA11 190 B5
Milroy Wk STHWK SE1 12 B9
Milson Rd WKENS W14 157 H2
Milton Av BAR EN5 77 J9
CDALE/KGS NW9 115 N1
CFSP/GDCR SL9 110 A2
CROY/NA CR0 203 L7
DORK RH4 272 C3
EHAM E6 142 A2
GVE DA12 190 G4
HCH RM12 124 G7
HCT N6 118 D5
RSEV TN14 228 C6
SUT SM1 201 N10
WLSDN NW10 136 A3
Milton Cl DTCH/LGLY SL3 150 D9
EFNCH N2 117 M4
STHWK SE1 19 L6
SUT SM1 201 N10
YEAD UB4 133 H8
Milton Ct BARB EC2Y 12 G3
HGDN/ICK UB10 112 C8
WAB EN9 63 H10
Miltoncourt La DORK RH4 272 D2
Milton Court Rd NWCR SE14 160 D5
Milton Crs CHONG CM5 67 N2
GNTH/NBYPK IG2 122 F5
Milton Dene HHNE HP2 36 C1
Milton Dr BORE WD6 75 N9
SHPTN TW17 195 P4
Milton Flds CSTG HP8 89 N4
Milton Gdns EPSOM KT18 220 B10
STWL/WRAY TW19 174 A4
TIL RM18 168 E7
Milton Gv FBAR/BDGN N11 98 D6
STNW/STAM N16 119 L9
Milton Hall Rd GVE DA12 190 G4
Milton Lawns AMS HP6 69 J2
Milton Mount Av CRAWE RH10 284 E4
Milton Pk EGH TW20 * 172 D10
HGT N6 118 D5
Milton Pl GVE DA12 190 F2
Milton Rd ACT W3 136 A10
ADL/WDHM KT15 215 K3
BELV DA17 164 B3
BRW CM14 106 G4
CDALE/KGS NW9 * 116 D5
CRAWE RH10 284 D6
CROY/NA CR0 203 L7
CSHM HP5 50 G5
CTHM CR3 241 L7
EGH TW20 172 C8
GRAYS RM17 167 N3
GVE DA12 190 E2
HARP AL5 20 B3
HGDN/ICK UB10 112 C9
HGT N6 118 D5
HNHL SE24 181 J1
HNWL W7 134 E9
HPTN TW12 175 P10
HRW HA1 114 D2
MLHL NW7 96 D6
MORT/ESHN SW14 156 A9
ROM RM1 125 H4
SEV TN13 246 F7
SEVS/STOTM N15 119 J1
SLN SL2 129 J6
SUT SM1 201 K10
SWCM DA10 189 K2
WALTH E17 120 F2
WARE SG12 26 C1
WELL DA16 163 J7
WIM/MER SW19 179 M9
WLGTN SM6 222 D3
WOT/HER KT12 197 L10
Milton St BARB EC2Y 12 G3
DORK RH4 272 C3
SWCM DA10 189 K2
WATN WD24 73 J5
Milton Wy LHD/OX KT22 254 B1
WDR/YW UB7 152 A3
Milverton Dr HGDN/ICK UB10 112 D9
Milverton Gdns GDMY/SEVK IG3 123 J7
Milverton Rd KIL/WHAMP NW6 136 F2
Milverton St LBTH SE11 18 B8
Milverton Wy ELTH/MOT SE9 184 D7
Milwards HLWW/ROY CM19 46 E5
Milward St WCHPL E1 140 A7
Mimas Rd HHNE HP2 36 A3
Mimms Hall Rd POTB/CUF EN6 58 G7
Mimms La RAD WD7 57 M9
Mimosa Cl BRWN CM15 86 G9
HARH RM3 105 K8
ORP BR6 207 M9
Mimosa Rd YEAD UB4 133 K7
Mimosa St FUL/PGN SW6 157 J7
Mimram Rd HERT/WAT SG14 25 J6
Mina Av DTCH/LGLY SL3 150 A1
Minard Rd CAT SE6 183 K3
Mina Rd WALW SE17 19 K8
WIM/MER SW19 201 K1
Minchenden Crs STHGT/OAK N14 98 E4
Minchen Rd HLW CM20 29 K10
Minchin Cl LHD/OX KT22 236 F8
Mincing La CHOB/PIR GU24 213 L5
MON EC3R 13 J7
Minden Rd CHEAM SM3 201 H9
PGE/AN SE20 204 A1
Minehead Rd RYLN/HDSTN HA2 113 P8
STRHM/NOR SW16 180 G8
Mineral Cl BAR EN5 76 F10
Mineral La CSHM HP5 51 H8
Mineral St WOOL/PLUM SE18 163 H3
Minera Ms BGVA SW1W 16 D5
Minerva Cl BRXN/ST SW9 159 H6
SCUP DA14 185 H7
STWL/WRAY TW19 * 173 K1
Minerva Dr WAT WD17 72 F2
Minerva Rd CHING E4 100 G8
KUT/HW KT1 199 L2
WLSDN NW10 135 P6
Minerva St BETH E2 140 A4
Minerva Wy BEAC HP9 88 G9
Minet Av WLSDN NW10 136 B4
Minet Dr HYS/HAR UB3 133 H10
Minet Gdns HYS/HAR UB3 133 J10
WLSDN NW10 136 B4
Minet Rd BRXN/ST SW9 159 J8
Minford Gdns WKENS W14 156 G1
Ming St POP/IOD E14 140 F9
Minimax Cl EBED/NFELT TW14 175 H2
The Minims HAT AL10 40 D3
Minister Ct LCOL/BKTW AL2 56 D4
Ministry Wy ELTH/MOT SE9 184 C5
Mink Ct HSLWW TW4 153 K8
Minniecroft Rd SL SL1 128 A5
Minniedale BRYLDS KT5 199 L5
Minnow Wk WALW SE17 19 K6
Minoan Dr HHS/BOV HP3 35 P10
Minorca Rd WEY KT13 216 B1
Minories TWRH EC3N 13 L6
Minshull Pl BECK BR3 * 182 F10
Minshull St VX/NE SW8 * 158 E7
Minson Rd HOM E9 140 C3
Minstead Gdns PUT/ROE SW15 178 C3
Minstead Wy NWMAL KT3 200 B6
Minster Av SUT SM1 201 K9
Minster Cl HAT AL10 40 D6
Minster Ct EMPK RM11 125 P7
MON EC3R * 13 J7
Minster Dr CROY/NA CR0 223 M1
Minster Gdns E/WMO/HCT KT8 197 N4
Minsterley Av SHPTN TW17 196 F4
Minster Rd BMLY BR1 183 N10
CRICK NW2 117 H10
Minster Wk CEND/HSY/T N8 118 F2
Minster Wy DTCH/LGLY SL3 150 C1
EMPK RM11 125 N6
Minstrel Cl HHW HP1 35 L5
Minstrel Gdns BRYLDS KT5 199 L4
Mint Cl HGDN/ICK UB10 132 C5
Mintern Cl PLMGR N13 99 J4
Minterne Av NWDGN UB2 153 P3
Minterne Rd
KTN/HRWW/WS HA3 115 L3
Minterne Waye YEAD UB4 133 K8
Mintern St IS N1 7 H7
Mint Gdns DORK RH4 272 F1
Mint La KWD/TDW/WH KT20 257 K5
Minton La HLWE CM17 47 M1
Minton Ms KIL/WHAMP NW6 3 H1
Minton Ri MDHD SL6 128 A8
Mint Rd BNSTD SM7 239 M2
WLGTN SM6 222 C2
Mint St STHWK SE1 18 E1
Mint Wk CROY/NA CR0 203 K10
WARL CR6 242 C3
WOKN/KNAP GU21 231 K3
Mirabel Rd FUL/PGN SW6 157 J6
Mirador Crs SLN SL2 129 N9
Miramar Wy HCH RM12 125 L10
Miranda Cl WCHPL E1 140 B7
Miranda Rd ARCH N19 118 D6
Mirfield St CHARL SE7 162 A2
Miriam Rd WOOL/PLUM SE18 163 H4
Mirren Cl RYLN/HDSTN HA2 113 N9
Mirrie La DEN/HRF UB9 110 F3
Misbourne Av CFSP/GDCR SL9 90 B6
Misbourne Cl CFSP/GDCR SL9 90 B6
Misbourne Ct AMSS HP7 * 68 G6
Misbourne Mdw DEN/HRF UB9 110 F6
Misbourne Rd HGDN/ICK UB10 132 B4
Miskin Rd DART DA1 187 K3
Miskin Wy GVE DA12 190 G9
Missden Dr HHS/BOV HP3 36 D8
Missenden Cl EBED/NFELT TW14 174 G4
Missenden Gdns MRDN SM4 201 M6
SL SL1 128 A8
Missenden Rd CSHM HP5 50 E8
Mission Gv WALTH E17 120 E3
Mission Pl PECK SE15 159 P7
Mistletoe Cl CROY/NA CR0 204 C8
Mistley Gdns HORL RH6 279 N5
Mistley Rd HLW CM20 29 K9
Misty's Fld WOT/HER KT12 197 K8
Mitali Pas WCHPL E1 13 N6
Mitcham La STRHM/NOR SW16 180 D8
Mitcham Pk MTCM CR4 201 P4
Mitcham Rd CROY/NA CR0 202 F6
EHAM E6 142 B5
GDMY/SEVK IG3 123 J5
TOOT SW17 180 A8
Mitchell Av GVW DA11 190 A5
Mitchellbrook Wy WLSDN NW10 136 A1
Mitchell Cl ABLGY WD5 55 H8
ABYW SE2 163 M4
BELV DA17 164 D2
DART DA1 187 M5
HHS/BOV HP3 52 C3
RAIN RM13 145 K4
SL SL1 148 F2
STAL AL1 38 C10
WGCE AL7 23 M5
Mitchell Rd ORP BR6 227 J1
PLMGR N13 99 J6
Mitchells Cl RGUE GU4 268 B6
Mitchells Rd CRAWE RH10 284 A7
Mitchell St FSBYE EC1V 12 E1
Mitchell Wk AMS HP6 69 K4
Mitchell Wy BMLY BR1 205 M1
WLSDN NW10 135 P1
Mitchison Rd IS N1 6 G2
Mitchley Av PUR/KEN CR8 223 L9
Mitchley Gv SAND/SEL CR2 223 P9
Mitchley Hl SAND/SEL CR2 223 N9
Mitchley Rd TOTM N17 119 P1
Mitchley Vw SAND/SEL CR2 223 P9
Mitford Rd ARCH N19 118 F7
Mitre Cl BELMT SM2 221 M4
SHPTN TW17 196 E7
Mitre Ct HERT/WAT SG14 * 25 L5
Mitre Rd SRTFD E15 141 K4
STHWK SE1 18 B1
Mitre Sq HDTCH EC3A 13 K6
Mitre St HDTCH EC3A 13 K6
The Mitre POP/IOD E14 140 E9
Mitre Wy NKENS W10 136 E7
Mixbury Gv WEY KT13 216 E3
Mixnams La CHERT KT16 195 K3
Mizen Cl COB KT11 217 L10
Mizen Wy COB KT11 217 M10
Moat Cl BRWN CM15 87 H2
BUSH WD23 74 A9
ORP BR6 227 J3
SEV TN13 246 C9
Moat Ct ASHTD KT21 237 K3
ELTH/MOT SE9 * 184 C2
Moat Crs FNCH N3 117 L1
Moat Cft WELL DA16 163 M9
Moat Dr HRW HA1 114 B2
PLSTW E13 141 P4
RSLP HA4 112 F5
SLN SL2 129 P7
Moated Farm Dr
ADL/WDHM KT15 215 M4
Moat Farm Rd NTHLT UB5 133 N1
Moatfield Rd BUSH WD23 74 A9
Moat La ERITH DA8 165 H7
Moat Pl ACT W3 135 N8
BRXN/ST SW9 158 G9
DEN/HRF UB9 111 L9
Moat Side FELT TW13 175 K7
PEND EN3 80 B8
Moats La REDH RH1 276 G6
The Moat NWMAL KT3 200 B1
Moat Wk CRAWE RH10 284 D6
Moatwood Gn WGCE AL7 23 H6
Moberly Rd CLAP SW4 180 E3
Modbury Gdns HAMP NW3 4 B2
Model Cottages WEA W13 * 154 G1
Model Farm Cl ELTH/MOT SE9 184 B6
Moelyn Ms HRW HA1 114 F3
Moffat Rd PLMGR N13 98 F7
THHTH CR7 203 K2
TOOT SW17 179 P7
Moffats Cl BRKMPK AL9 59 K2
Moffats La BRKMPK AL9 59 H3
Mogador Rd
KWD/TDW/WH KT20 257 H4
Mogden La ISLW TW7 176 E1
Mohmmad Khan Rd WAN E11 * 121 L6
Moiety Rd POP/IOD E14 160 F2
Moira Cl TOTM N17 99 M10
Moira Rd ELTH/MOT SE9 162 C10
Moir Cl SAND/SEL CR2 223 P5
Molash Rd STMC/STPC BR5 207 N4
Mole Abbey Gdns
E/WMO/HCT KT8 197 P3
Mole Cl CRAWW RH11 283 L5
Mole Ct HOR/WEW KT19 219 P1
Molember Ct E/WMO/HCT KT8 198 D5
Molember Rd E/WMO/HCT KT8 198 D5
Mole Rd LHD/OX KT22 236 C7
WOT/HER KT12 217 L2
Molescroft ELTH/MOT SE9 184 F6
Molesey Av E/WMO/HCT KT8 197 N5
Molesey Cl WOT/HER KT12 217 M1
Molesey Dr CHEAM SM3 201 H9
Molesey Park Av
E/WMO/HCT KT8 198 A5
Molesey Park Cl
E/WMO/HCT KT8 198 B5
Molesey Park Rd
E/WMO/HCT KT8 198 A5
Molesey Rd E/WMO/HCT KT8 197 M5
WOT/HER KT12 217 L1
Molesford Rd FUL/PGN SW6 * 157 K7
Molesham Cl E/WMO/HCT KT8 198 A3
Molesham Wy
E/WMO/HCT KT8 198 A4
Moles Hl LHD/OX KT22 218 C7
Molesworth HOD EN11 26 F9
Molesworth St LEW SE13 161 H10
Mole Valley Pl ASHTD KT21 237 J5
Molewood Rd HERT/WAT SG14 25 J4
Mollands Ct SOCK/AV RM15 147 K6
Mollands La SOCK/AV RM15 147 J6
Mollison Av PEND EN3 80 D1
Mollison Dr WLGTN SM6 222 F4
Mollison Ri GVE DA12 191 H8
Mollison Wy EDGW HA8 95 L10
Molly Huggins Cl BAL SW12 180 D3
Molteno Rd WAT WD17 73 H5
Molyneaux Av HHS/BOV HP3 52 C3
Molyneux Dr TOOT SW17 180 C7
Molyneux Rd BFOR GU20 212 B3
GODL GU7 267 L10
WEY KT13 216 B1
Molyneux St MBLAR W1H 9 P4
Molyns Ms SL SL1 128 D10
Momples Rd HLW CM20 29 K10
Monahan Av PUR/KEN CR8 222 G8
Monarch Cl CRAWW RH11 283 K10
EBED/NFELT TW14 174 F3
RAIN RM13 145 H4
TIL RM18 168 E8
WWKM BR4 225 L1
Monarch Dr CAN/RD E16 142 A7
Monarch Ms STRHM/NOR SW16 181 H8
Monarch Pde MTCM CR4 * 202 A2
Monarch Pl BKHH IG9 101 P3
Monarch Rd BELV DA17 164 B2
Monarch's Wy CHES/WCR EN8 62 D9
RSLP HA4 * 112 E6
Monarch Wk RAD WD7 * 57 L9
Monarch Wy GNTH/NBYPK IG2 122 G4
Mona Rd PECK SE15 160 B8
Monastery Cl STALW/RED AL3 * 38 B6
Monastery Gdns
DTCH/LGLY SL3 * 149 N9
ENC/FH EN2 79 L6
Mona St CAN/RD E16 141 L7
Monaveen Gdns
E/WMO/HCT KT8 198 A3
Monck's Rw WAND/EARL SW18 * 179 J2
Monck St WEST SW1P 17 K4
Monclar Rd CMBW SE5 159 L10
Moncorvo Cl SKENS SW7 15 N2
Moncrieff Cl EHAM E6 142 B8
Moncrieff St PECK SE15 159 P8
Monday Aly STNW/STAM N16 119 N8
Mondial Wy HYS/HAR UB3 152 D6
Monega Rd FSTGT E7 141 P1
MNPK E12 142 A1
Money Av CTHM CR3 241 L8
Moneyhill Ct
RKW/CH/CXG WD3 * 91 L2
Money Hill Rd RKW/CH/CXG WD3 91 M2
Money Hole La WLYN AL6 23 P4
Money La WDR/YW UB7 151 N2
Money Rd CTHM CR3 241 L8
Mongers La EW KT17 220 D6
Monica Cl WATN WD24 73 L6
Monier Rd BOW E3 140 F2
Monivea Rd BECK BR3 182 E10
Monkchester Cl LOU IG10 82 D5
Monk Dr CAN/RD E16 141 M9
Monkfrith Av STHGT/OAK N14 78 C10
Monkfrith Wy STHGT/OAK N14 98 C1
Monkham's Av WFD IG8 101 N6
Monkham's Dr WFD IG8 101 N6
Monkham's La WFD IG8 101 N5
Monkleigh Rd MRDN SM4 201 H3
Monks Av BAR EN5 77 M10
E/WMO/HCT KT8 197 N5
Monksbury HLWS CM18 47 K4
Monks Cha RBRW/HUT CM13 107 P6
Monks Cl ABYW SE2 163 N3
ASC SL5 192 A6
BROX EN10 44 F6
ENC/FH EN2 79 K6
RSLP HA4 113 L9
RYLN/HDSTN HA2 * 113 P7
STAL AL1 38 D8
Monks Crs ADL/WDHM KT15 215 L2
WOT/HER KT12 197 J8
Monksdene Gdns SUT SM1 201 L10
Monks Dr ACT W3 135 M7
ASC SL5 192 A6
Monksfield CRAWE RH10 284 A7
Monksfield Wy SLN SL2 128 F6
Monks Gn LHD/OX KT22 236 B7
Monksgrove LOU IG10 82 D9
Monks Horton Wy STAL AL1 38 F4
Monksmead BORE WD6 75 P8
Monks Orch DART DA1 187 K5
Monks Orchard Rd BECK BR3 204 F8
Monks Pk WBLY HA9 135 N1
Monks Park Gdns WBLY HA9 135 N2
Monks Ri WGCW AL8 22 G1
Monks Rd BNSTD SM7 239 K3
ENC/FH EN2 79 J6
VW GU25 194 A4
WDSR SL4 148 C8
Monks Rw WARE SG12 26 C1
Monk St WOOL/PLUM SE18 162 D3
Monks Wk ASC SL5 192 A6
MEO DA13 189 M9
REIG RH2 257 L10
Monks Wy BECK BR3 204 F6
GLDGN NW11 117 J2
STA TW18 173 N10
STMC/STPC BR5 206 F8
Monks Well SWCM DA10 167 H10
Monkswell La COUL/CHIP CR5 239 L10
Monkswick Rd HLW CM20 29 J9
Monkswood WGCW AL8 22 F1
Monkswood Av WAB EN9 63 J9
Monkswood Gdns BORE WD6 76 A9
CLAY IG5 122 D1
Monk Ter FSTH SE23 182 E5
Monkton Rd WELL DA16 163 J8
Monkton St LBTH SE11 18 B5
Monkville Av GLDGN NW11 117 J2
Monkville Pde GLDGN NW11 * 117 J2
Monkwell Sq BARB EC2Y 12 F4
Monkwood Cl ROM RM1 125 H3
Monmouth Av KUT/HW KT1 177 H10
SWFD E18 121 N2
Monmouth Cl CHSWK W4 156 A2
MTCM CR4 202 F4
WELL DA16 163 K10
Monmouth Gv BTFD TW8 155 K3
Monmouth Pl BAY/PAD W2 8 F6
Monmouth Rd BAY/PAD W2 8 F6
DAGW RM9 124 A10
ED N9 100 A3
EHAM E6 142 C5
HYS/HAR UB3 152 F3
WAT WD17 73 J7
Monmouth St LSQ/SEVD WC2H 11 L6
Monnery Rd ARCH N19 118 D8
Monnow Rd SOCK/AV RM15 146 B9
STHWK SE1 19 N6
Mono La FELT TW13 175 J5
Monoux Gv WALTH E17 100 F9
Monro Dr GUW GU2 249 N7
Monroe Crs EN EN1 80 A5
Monroe Dr MORT/ESHN SW14 177 N1
Monro Gdns
KTN/HRWW/WS HA3 94 D8
Monro Pl HOR/WEW KT19 219 M5
Mons Cl HARP AL5 20 C5
Monsell Gdns STA TW18 173 H8
Monsell Rd FSBYPK N4 119 J8
Monson Rd BROX EN10 44 E6
NWCR SE14 160 C6
REDH RH1 258 A7
WLSDN NW10 136 D4
Mons Wk EGH TW20 172 F8
Mons Wy HAYES BR2 206 B6
Montacute Rd BUSH WD23 94 D1
CAT SE6 182 E3
CROY/NA CR0 225 H5
MRDN SM4 201 N6
Montagu Crs UED N18 100 A5
Montague Av BROCKY SE4 160 E10
HNWL W7 134 F10
SAND/SEL CR2 223 M8
Montague Cl STHWK SE1 12 G9
SWLY BR8 208 G4
WOT/HER KT12 197 J7
Montague Dr CTHM CR3 241 K8
Montague Gdns ACT W3 135 M9
Montague Hall Pl BUSH WD23 73 P10
Montague Pl GWRST WC1E 11 K3
SWLY BR8 208 G4
Montague Rd BERK HP4 33 N5
CEND/HSY/T N8 118 G3
CROY/NA CR0 203 J8
HACK E8 119 P10
HSLW TW3 154 A9
NWDGN UB2 153 M3
RCHPK/HAM TW10 177 K2
SEVS/STOTM N15 * 119 P2
SL SL1 129 L9
UX/CGN UB8 131 N2
WAN E11 121 L7
WEA W13 134 G8
WIM/MER SW19 179 L10

Montague Sq PECK SE15 160 B6
Montague St RSQ WC1B 11 L4
STBT EC1A 12 E4
Montague Ter HAYES BR2 205 M4
Montague Waye NWDGN UB2 153 M2
Montagu Gdns UED N18 100 A5
WLGTN SM6 222 D1
Montagu Man MHST W1U 10 B4
Montagu Ms North MBLAR W1H 10 B4
Montagu Ms South MBLAR W1H 10 B5
Montagu Ms West MBLAR W1H 10 B5
Montagu Pl MBLAR W1H 10 A4
Montagu Rd DTCH/LGLY SL3 149 N7
HDN NW4 116 D4
UED N18 100 A6
Montagu Rw MHST W1U 10 B4
Montagu Sq MBLAR W1H 10 B4
Montagu St MBLAR W1H 10 B5
Montalt Rd WFD IG8 101 L6
Montana Cl SAND/SEL CR2 223 L6
Montana Gdns SUT SM1 221 M2
SYD SE26 182 E8
Montana Rd RYNPK SW20 200 F1
TOOT SW17 180 B6
Montayne Rd CHES/WCR EN8 62 C8
Montbelle Rd ELTH/MOT SE9 184 E6
Montbretia Cl STMC/STPC BR5 207 M4
Montcalm Cl HAYES BR2 205 M6
YEAD UB4 133 J5
Montcalm Rd CHARL SE7 162 A6
Montclare St BETH E2 7 L10
Monteagle Av BARK IG11 142 F1
Monteagle Wy PECK SE15 160 A9
Montefiore St VX/NE SW8 158 C8
Montem La SL SL1 149 J1
Montem Rd FSTH SE23 182 E3
NWMAL KT3 200 B4
Montem St FSBYPK N4 118 G6
Montenotte Rd CEND/HSY/T N8 118 D3
Monterey Cl BXLY DA5 186 D5
Montesole Ct PIN HA5 93 K10
Montesquieu Ter CAN/RD E16 * 141 L8
Montford Pl LBTH SE11 18 A9
Montford Rd SUN TW16 197 H4
Montfort Gdns BARK/HLT IG6 102 F7
Montfort Pl WIM/MER SW19 178 G4
Montfort Ri REDH RH1 276 A8
Montfort Rd BGR/WK TN15 247 M3
Montgomerie Cl BERK HP4 33 M3
Montgomerie Dr GUW GU2 249 M5
Montgomerie Ms FSTH SE23 182 B3
Montgomery Av ESH/CLAY KT10 198 D9
HHNE HP2 36 B6
Montgomery Cl BFN/LL DA15 185 H1
MTCM CR4 * 202 F4
Montgomery Crs HARH RM3 105 L6
Montgomery Dr CHES/WCR EN8 62 D4
Montgomery Gdns BELMT SM2 221 N4
Montgomery Pl SLN SL2 129 P8
Montgomery Rd CHSWK W4 155 P3
EDGW HA8 95 L7
EYN DA4 210 C1
WOKS/MYFD GU22 232 B4
Montholme Rd BTSEA SW11 180 A2
Monthope Rd WCHPL E1 13 N4
Montolieu Gdns PUT/ROE SW15 178 E1
Montpelier Av BXLY DA5 185 N3
EA W5 135 H7
Montpelier Cl HGDN/ICK UB10 132 B3
Montpelier Gdns CHDH RM6 123 M5
EHAM E6 142 A5
Montpelier Gv KTTN NW5 118 D10
Montpelier Ms CHEL SW3 15 P3
Montpelier Pl SKENS SW7 15 P3
WCHPL E1 140 B8
Montpelier Ri GLDGN NW11 117 H5
WBLY HA9 115 J6
Montpelier Rd EA W5 135 J7
FNCH N3 97 M9
PECK SE15 160 A7
PUR/KEN CR8 223 J6
SUT SM1 221 M1
Montpelier Rw BKHTH/KID SE3 161 L8
TWK TW1 176 G3
Montpelier Sq SKENS SW7 15 P3
Montpelier St SKENS SW7 15 P2
Montpelier Ter SKENS SW7 15 P2
Montpelier V BKHTH/KID SE3 * 161 L8
Montpelier Wk SKENS SW7 15 P2
Montpelier Wy GLDGN NW11 117 H5
Montpellier Ct WDSR SL4 149 H8
Montrave Rd PGE/AN SE20 182 B9
Montreal Pl HOL/ALD WC2B 11 N7
Montreal Rd IL IG1 122 F5
SEV TN13 246 G9
TIL RM18 168 D9
Montrell Rd BRXS/STRHM SW2 180 F4
Montrose Av BFN/LL DA15 185 K3
DTCH/LGLY SL3 149 P6
EDGW HA8 96 A10
GPK RM2 105 K10
KIL/WHAMP NW6 2 B7
SL SL1 128 G8
WELL DA16 162 G9
WHTN TW2 176 A3
Montrose Cl ASHF TW15 174 D9
WELL DA16 163 J9
WFD IG8 101 M5
Montrose Crs ALP/SUD HA0 135 K1
NFNCH/WDSPK N12 97 L7
Montrose Gdns LHD/OX KT22 218 C8
MTCM CR4 202 A3
SUT SM1 201 L9
Montrose Pl KTBR SW1X 16 D2
Montrose Rd EBED/NFELT TW14 174 E2
KTN/HRWW/WS HA3 94 D10
Montrose Vls HMSMTH W6 * 156 D4
Montrose Wk WEY KT13 196 C10
Montrose Wy DTCH/LGLY SL3 150 A7
FSTH SE23 182 C4
Montrouge Crs EW KT17 238 F2
Montserrat Av WFD IG8 101 J8
Montserrat Cl NRWD SE19 181 L8
Montserrat Rd PUT/ROE SW15 157 H10
Monument Hl WEY KT13 216 C1
Monument La CFSP/GDCR SL9 90 B7
Monument Rd WEY KT13 216 C1
WOKN/KNAP GU21 232 E1
Monument Wy TOTM N17 119 N1
Monument Wy East
WOKN/KNAP GU21 232 E1
Monument Wy West
WOKN/KNAP GU21 232 D1
Monza St WAP E1W 140 B9
Moodkee St BERM/RHTH SE16 160 B2
Moody St WCHPL E1 140 C5
Moolintock Pl PEND EN3 80 G3
Moon Ct LEE/GVPK SE12 * 161 M10
Moon La BAR EN5 77 J7
Moon St IS N1 6 C5
Moorcroft EDGW HA8 * 95 N9
Moorcroft Cl CRAWW RH11 283 L6
Moorcroft Gdns HAYES BR2 206 B5
Moorcroft La UX/CGN UB8 132 B7
Moorcroft Rd STRHM/NOR SW16 180 F6
Moorcroft Wy PIN HA5 113 M3
Moordown WOOL/PLUM SE18 162 E7
Moore Av TIL RM18 168 E8
WTHK RM20 167 K4
Moore Cl ADL/WDHM KT15 215 L2
MORT/ESHN SW14 155 P9
MTCM CR4 * 202 C2
RDART DA2 188 C5
SL SL1 148 G1
Moore Crs DAGW RM9 143 L3
Moorefield Rd TOTM N17 119 N1
Moore Grove Crs EGH TW20 172 C10
Mooreland Rd BMLY BR1 183 L10
Moorend WGCE AL7 23 K8
Moor End Rd HHW HP1 35 M7
Moore Park Rd FUL/PGN SW6 157 L6
Moore Rd BERK HP4 33 L3
CHOB/PIR GU24 230 A7
NRWD SE19 181 K9
SWCM DA10 189 K2
Moorescroft BRWN CM15 86 D3
Moores La WDSR SL4 148 E3
Moores Pl BRW CM14 107 J3
Moore's Rd DORK RH4 272 G1
Moore Wy BELMT SM2 221 K5
Moorey Cl SRTFD E15 141 L3
Moorfield RDKG RH5 * 273 J10
Moorfield Av EA W5 135 J6
Moorfield Point GU GU1 250 B6
Moorfield Rd CHSGTN KT9 219 K2
DEN/HRF UB9 111 K5
GU GU1 250 B6
ORP BR6 207 K7
PEND EN3 80 E5
UX/CGN UB8 131 N8
Moorfields HLWS CM18 46 F6
LVPST EC2M 12 G4
Moorfields Cl STA TW18 195 H1
Moorfields Highwalk BARB EC2Y 12 G4
Moor Furlong SL SL1 128 D10
Moorgate LOTH EC2R 12 G5
Moorgate Pl LOTH EC2R * 12 G5
Moorhall Rd DEN/HRF UB9 111 L3
Moor Hall Rd HLWE CM17 30 B7
Moorhayes Dr STA TW18 195 M3
Moorhead Wy BKHTH/KID SE3 161 N10
Moorhen Cl ERITH DA8 165 J5
Moorhen Wy HLWW/ROY CM19 27 M10
Moorholme WOKS/MYFD GU22 * 232 B5
Moorhouse Rd BAY/PAD W2 8 E5
KTN/HRWW/WS HA3 115 J1
OXTED RH8 262 C6
Moorhurst Av CHESW EN7 61 J5
The Moorings BF/WBF KT14 215 M8
CHSWK W4 * 155 M5
GT/LBKH KT23 253 P1
WDSR SL4 * 148 C6
WDSR SL4 148 F6
Moorland Cl CRW RM5 104 C9
WHTN TW2 175 P3
Moorland Rd BRXN/ST SW9 159 J10
CRAWE RH10 284 D10
HHW HP1 35 J8
WDR/YW UB7 151 M6
Moorlands LCOL/BKTW AL2 * 56 D4
WGCE AL7 23 K8
Moorlands Av MLHL NW7 96 E7
Moorlands Reach SBW CM21 30 A4
The Moorlands
WOKS/MYFD GU22 232 C7
Moor La BARB EC2Y 12 G4
CHSGTN KT9 219 L2
RKW/CH/CXG WD3 71 J1
RKW/CH/CXG WD3 91 P3
STWL/WRAY TW19 172 G5
UPMR RM14 126 E6
WDR/YW UB7 151 M5
WOKS/MYFD GU22 232 B8
Moor Lane Crossing
WATW WD18 92 D1
Moormead Dr HOR/WEW KT19 220 B2
Moor Mead Rd TWK TW1 176 F2
Moormede Crs STA TW18 173 J7
Moor Mill La LCOL/BKTW AL2 56 D6
Moor Pk HORL RH6 * 280 C5
Moor Park Crs CRAWW RH11 282 G8
Moor Park Gdns KUTN/CMB KT2 178 B10
NTHWD HA6 * 92 D3
Moor Park Rd NTHWD HA6 92 E7
Moor Pl BFOR GU20 212 A3
Moor Rd CSHM HP5 51 H9
The Moor Rd RSEV TN14 247 K6
Moorside WGCE AL7 23 K8
Moorside Rd BMLY BR1 183 K7
Moorsom Wy COUL/CHIP CR5 240 E5
The Moors WGCE AL7 23 K4
Moorstown Ct SL SL1 149 K1
Moor St SOHO/SHAV W1D 11 K6
Moors Wk WGCE AL7 23 M5
Moortown Rd OXHEY WD19 93 K5
Moor Vw WATW WD18 93 H1
Moran Cl LCOL/BKTW AL2 55 N7
Morant Gdns CRW RM5 104 C6
Morant Rd CDW/CHF RM16 168 E2
Morants Court Rd SEV TN13 246 D5
Morant St POP/IOD E14 140 F9
Mora Rd CRICK NW2 116 F9
Mora St FSBYE EC1V 6 F10
Morat St BRXN/ST SW9 158 G7
Moravian Pl WBPTN SW10 15 M10
Moravian St BETH E2 140 B4
Moray Av HYS/HAR UB3 132 G10
Moray Cl EDGW HA8 * 95 N3
ROM RM1 104 F8
Moray Dr SLN SL2 129 M8
Moray Ms HOLWY N7 118 G7
Moray Rd HOLWY N7 118 G7
Moray Wy ROM RM1 104 E8
Morcambe St WALW SE17 18 F6
Mordaunt Gdns DAGW RM9 143 P2
Mordaunt Rd WLSDN NW10 136 A3
Mordaunt St BRXN/ST SW9 158 G9
Morden Cl KWD/TDW/WH KT20 238 G6
Morden Ct MRDN SM4 201 L4
Morden Court Pde MRDN SM4 * 201 J3
Morden Gdns GFD/PVL UB6 114 E10
MTCM CR4 201 N4
Morden Hall Rd MRDN SM4 201 L3
Morden Hl LEW SE13 161 H8
Morden La LEW SE13 161 H8
Morden Rd BKHTH/KID SE3 161 M8
CHDH RM6 123 P5
WIM/MER SW19 201 L2
Morden Road Ms
BKHTH/KID SE3 161 M8
Morden St LEW SE13 160 G7
Morden Wy CHEAM SM3 201 K7
Morden Wharf Rd GNWCH SE10 161 K2
Mordon Rd GDMY/SEVK IG3 123 J5
Mordred Rd CAT SE6 183 K5
Moreau Wk DTCH/LGLY SL3 130 B8
Morecambe Cl CRAWW RH11 283 J9
HCH RM12 125 J10
WCHPL E1 * 140 C7
Morecambe Gdns STAN HA7 * 95 J5
Morecambe St POP/IOD E14 160 G4
WALW SE17 19 J9
Morecambe Ter UED N18 * 99 L5
More Cir GODL GU7 267 K10
More Cl CAN/RD E16 141 L8
PUR/KEN CR8 222 G7
WKENS W14 156 G3
Morecoombe Cl KUTN/CMB KT2 177 N10
Moree Wy UED N18 99 P5
Moreland Cl DTCH/LGLY SL3 150 F6
Moreland Cottages BOW E3 * 140 F4
Moreland Dr CFSP/GDCR SL9 110 C5
Morelands Av CDW/CHF RM16 167 P1
Moreland St FSBYE EC1V 6 D9
Moreland Wy CHING E4 100 G4
More La ESH/CLAY KT10 198 A10
Morel Ct SEV TN13 247 K8
Morella Cl VW GU25 193 P2
Morella Rd BAL SW12 180 A3
Morello Av UX/CGN UB8 132 C7
Morello Cl SWLY BR8 208 E4
Morello Dr DTCH/LGLY SL3 130 D10
More London Pl STHWK SE1 13 K10
More London Riverside
STHWK SE1 13 K10
Moremead WAB EN9 63 J9
Moremead Rd CAT SE6 182 E7
Morena St CAT SE6 182 G3
More Rd GODL GU7 267 K10
Moresby Av BRYLDS KT5 199 N7
Moresby Rd CLPT E5 120 A6
Moresby Wk VX/NE SW8 158 C8
Mores La BRW CM14 86 C7
Moretaine Rd ASHF TW15 173 N6
Moreton Av ISLW TW7 154 C7
Moreton Br CHONG CM5 49 K7
Moreton Cl CHESW EN7 62 A3
CLPT E5 120 B7
MLHL NW7 96 F7
SEVS/STOTM N15 119 L4
Moreton Ct DART DA1 164 F9
Moreton Gdns WFD IG8 102 B6
Moreton Pl PIM SW1V 17 H7
Moreton Rd CHONG CM5 49 H9
CHONG CM5 49 L8
SAND/SEL CR2 223 L2
SEVS/STOTM N15 119 L4
WPK KT4 200 D9
Moreton St PIM SW1V 17 H7
Moreton Ter PIM SW1V 17 H7
Moreton Terrace Ms South
PIM SW1V 17 H7
Moreton Wy SL SL1 128 C10
Morewood Cl SEV TN13 246 G9
Morford Cl RSLP HA4 113 J5
Morford Wy RSLP HA4 113 J5
Morgan Av WALTH E17 121 J2
Morgan Cl DAGE RM10 144 B2
NTHWD HA6 92 C6
Morgan Crs EPP CM16 83 H2
Morgan Dr RDART DA2 188 D3
Morgan Gdns GSTN WD25 74 A4
Morgan Rd BMLY BR1 183 M10
HOLWY N7 119 H10
NKENS W10 8 C3
Morgans Cl HERT/BAY SG13 25 L7
Morgan's La HYS/HAR UB3 132 E7
STHWK SE1 13 J10
Morgan's Rd HERT/BAY SG13 25 L7
Morgan St BOW E3 140 E5
CAN/RD E16 141 L7
Morgan's Wk HERT/BAY SG13 25 L8
Morgan Wy RAIN RM13 145 K5
WFD IG8 102 B7
Moriarty Cl BMLY BR1 206 E4
Moriatry Cl HOLWY N7 118 F9
Morice Rd HOD EN11 44 E1
Morie St WAND/EARL SW18 157 L10
Morieux Rd LEY E10 120 E6
Moring Rd TOOT SW17 180 B7
Morkyns Wk DUL SE21 * 181 M6
Morland Av CROY/NA CR0 203 M8
DART DA1 187 J1
Morland Cl GLDGN NW11 117 L6
HPTN TW12 175 M8
MTCM CR4 201 P3
Morland Est HACK E8 * 7 P3
Morland Gdns STHL UB1 134 A10
WLSDN NW10 136 A2
Morland Ms IS N1 6 B4
Morland Rd CROY/NA CR0 203 N7
DAGE RM10 144 B2
IL IG1 122 E7
KTN/HRWW/WS HA3 115 K3
PGE/AN SE20 182 C10
SUT SM1 221 M3
WALTH E17 120 C3
Morland Wy CHES/WCR EN8 62 D4
Morley Av CHING E4 101 J8
UED N18 99 P5
WDGN N22 99 H10
Morley Cl DTCH/LGLY SL3 150 C1
ORP BR6 206 F9
Morley Crs EDGW HA8 95 P3
RSLP HA4 113 K7
Morley Crs East STAN HA7 115 H1
Morley Crs West STAN HA7 115 H1
Morley Gv HLW CM20 28 F10
Morley Hl ENC/FH EN2 79 L4
Morley Rd BARK IG11 142 D3
CHDH RM6 123 P3
CHEAM SM3 201 J8
CHST BR7 206 F1
LEW SE13 161 H10
LEY E10 121 H6
SAND/SEL CR2 223 N6
SRTFD E15 141 L4
TWK TW1 177 J2
Morley Sq CDW/CHF RM16 168 D3
Morley's Rd RSEV TN14 265 L9
Morley St STHWK SE1 18 B2
Morna Rd CMBW SE5 159 K8
Morning La HOM E9 140 B1
Morningside Rd WPK KT4 200 E9
Mornington Av HAYES BR2 205 P3
IL IG1 122 D5
WKENS W14 14 C6
Mornington Cl BH/WHM TN16 244 A3
Mornington Ct BXLY DA5 186 E4
Mornington Crs CAMTN NW1 4 G7
HEST TW5 153 J7
Mornington Gv BOW E3 140 F5
Mornington Ms CMBW SE5 159 K7
Mornington Pl CAMTN NW1 4 F7
Mornington Rd ASHF TW15 174 D8
CHING E4 101 J1
GFD/PVL UB6 134 A7
NWCR SE14 160 E6
RAD WD7 56 G10
WAN E11 121 L4
WFD IG8 101 M5
Morningtons HLWW/ROY CM19 46 F6
Mornington St CAMTN NW1 4 F7
Mornington Ter CAMTN NW1 4 F6
Mornington Wk
RCHPK/HAM TW10 177 H7
Morocco St STHWK SE1 19 J2
Morpeth Av BORE WD6 75 L4
Morpeth Cl HHNE HP2 35 P7
Morpeth Gv HOM E9 140 C3
Morpeth Rd HOM E9 140 B3
Morpeth St BETH E2 140 C5
Morpeth Ter WEST SW1P 16 G4
Morpeth Wk TOTM N17 * 100 A8
Morrab Gdns GDMY/SEVK IG3 123 J8
Morrel Cl BAR EN5 77 M7
Morrell Ct WGCE AL7 * 23 J4
Morrells Yd LBTH SE11 18 B7
Morrice Cl DTCH/LGLY SL3 150 D3
Morris Av MNPK E12 122 C10
Morris Bishop Ter HGT N6 * 118 B4
Morris Cl CFSP/GDCR SL9 90 C9
CROY/NA CR0 204 D6
ORP BR6 207 H10
Morris Ct CHING E4 100 G4
WAB EN9 63 L10
Morris Gdns DART DA1 187 P1
WAND/EARL SW18 179 K3
Morrish Rd BRXS/STRHM SW2 180 F3
Morrison Av CHING E4 100 F7
TOTM N17 119 M1
Morrison Rd BARK IG11 143 P4
YEAD UB4 133 J5
Morrison St BTSEA SW11 158 B9
Morris Pl FSBYPK N4 119 H7
Morris Rd BCTR RM8 124 A7
HARH RM3 105 J8
ISLW TW7 154 E9
POP/IOD E14 140 G7
REDH RH1 276 F2
SRTFD E15 121 K9
Morris St WCHPL E1 140 A8
Morriston Cl OXHEY WD19 93 K6
Morris Wy LCOL/BKTW AL2 57 J2
Morse Cl DEN/HRF UB9 91 M10
PLSTW E13 141 M5
Morshead Rd MV/WKIL W9 2 F10
Morson Rd PEND EN3 80 D10
Morston Cl KWD/TDW/WH KT20 238 E6
Morston Gdns ELTH/MOT SE9 184 E7
Mortain Dr BERK HP4 33 L3
Morten Gdns DEN/HRF UB9 111 K5
Mortens Wd AMSS HP7 69 J6
Morteyne Rd TOTM N17 99 L9
Mortham St SRTFD E15 141 K3
Mortimer Cl BUSH WD23 74 A10
CRICK NW2 117 J8
STRHM/NOR SW16 180 E5
Mortimer Crs KIL/WHAMP NW6 2 G6
WPK KT4 200 A10
Mortimer Dr EN EN1 79 L9
Mortimer Ga CHES/WCR EN8 62 E6
Mortimer Pl KIL/WHAMP NW6 2 G6
Mortimer Rd BH/WHM TN16 225 P8
DTCH/LGLY SL3 150 A2
EHAM E6 142 C5
ERITH DA8 164 E5
IS N1 7 K4
MTCM CR4 202 A1
ORP BR6 207 K9
WEA W13 135 H8
WLSDN NW10 136 F5
Mortimer Sq NTGHL W11 136 G9
Mortimer St GTPST W1W 10 F5
Mortimer Ter KTTN NW5 * 118 C9
Mortlake Cl CROY/NA CR0 202 F10
Mortlake Dr MTCM CR4 201 P1
Mortlake High St
MORT/ESHN SW14 156 A9
Mortlake Rd CAN/RD E16 141 N8
IL IG1 122 F9
RCH/KEW TW9 155 M6
Morton KWD/TDW/WH KT20 238 G7
Morton Cl CLAP SW4 180 E2
UX/CGN UB8 132 A6
WLGTN SM6 222 G4
WOKN/KNAP GU21 231 P1
Morton Crs STHGT/OAK N14 98 E5
Morton Dr SL SL1 108 D10
Morton Gdns WLGTN SM6 222 D2
Morton Ms ECT SW5 14 G6
Morton Pl STHWK SE1 18 A4
Morton Rd IS N1 6 F4
MRDN SM4 201 N5
SRTFD E15 141 L2
WOKN/KNAP GU21 231 P1
Morton Wy STHGT/OAK N14 98 E5
Morvale Cl BELV DA17 164 A3
Morval Rd BRXS/STRHM SW2 181 H1
Morven Cl POTB/CUF EN6 59 N7
Morven Rd TOOT SW17 180 A6
Morville St BOW E3 140 F4
Morwell St RSQ WC1B 11 J4
Mosbach Gdns RBRW/HUT CM13 107 N3
Moscow Pl BAY/PAD W2 8 G7
Moscow Rd BAY/PAD W2 8 G7
Moselle Av WDGN N22 99 H10
Moselle Cl CEND/HSY/T N8 118 G1
Moselle Pl TOTM N17 99 N8
Moselle Rd BH/WHM TN16 244 B4
Moselle St TOTM N17 99 N8
Mosford Cl HORL RH6 280 A2
Mospey Crs EW KT17 238 C1
Mosquito Wy HAT AL10 40 C2
Moss Bank GRAYS RM17 167 L4
Mossborough Cl
NFNCH/WDSPK N12 97 L7
Mossbury Rd BTSEA SW11 157 P9
Moss Cl PIN HA5 93 N10
RKW/CH/CXG WD3 91 N3
WCHPL E1 13 P4
Mossdown Cl BELV DA17 164 B3
Mossendew Cl DEN/HRF UB9 91 N9
Mossfield COB KT11 217 H9
Mossford Gn BARK/HLT IG6 122 E1
Mossford La BARK/HLT IG6 102 F10
Mossford St BOW E3 140 E6
Moss Gdns FELT TW13 175 H5
SAND/SEL CR2 224 C4
Moss Gn WGCE AL7 23 H7
Moss Hall Crs
NFNCH/WDSPK N12 97 L7
Moss Hall Gv NFNCH/WDSPK N12 97 L7
Moss La PIN HA5 93 M10
ROM RM1 124 G4
Mosslea Rd CTHM CR3 241 N2
HAYES BR2 206 A5
ORP BR6 206 F10
PGE/AN SE20 182 B10
Mossop St CHEL SW3 15 P5
Moss Rd DAGE RM10 144 B2
GSTN WD25 55 J10
SOCK/AV RM15 147 H7
Moss Side LCOL/BKTW AL2 55 N6
Mossville Gdns MRDN SM4 201 J3
Moss Wy RDART DA2 188 C7
Mostyn Cl HYS/HAR UB3 152 G4
Mostyn Av WBLY HA9 115 L10
Mostyn Gdns WLSDN NW10 136 G5
Mostyn Gv BOW E3 140 E4
Mostyn Rd BRXN/ST SW9 159 H7
BUSH WD23 74 B9
EDGW HA8 96 B8
WIM/MER SW19 201 J2
Mostyn Ter REDH RH1 276 B1
Mosul Wy HAYES BR2 206 B6
Mosyer Dr STMC/STPC BR5 207 N9
Motcomb St KTBR SW1X 16 C3
Mote End WAB EN9 63 L6
Moth Cl WLGTN SM6 222 F4
The Mothers Sq CLPT E5 * 120 A9
Motherwell Wy WTHK RM20 166 F4
Moth House WOOL/PLUM SE18 * 162 B6
Motley St VX/NE SW8 158 D8
Motspur Pk NWMAL KT3 200 D6
Mottingham Gdns
ELTH/MOT SE9 184 A4
Mottingham La LEE/GVPK SE12 183 P4
Mottingham Rd ED N9 80 C10
ELTH/MOT SE9 184 C6
Mottisfont Rd ABYW SE2 163 L2
Motts Hill La
KWD/TDW/WH KT20 238 E8
Mott St CHING E4 81 K5
Mouchotte Cl BH/WHM TN16 225 N8
Moulins Rd HOM E9 140 B2
Moultain Hl SWLY BR8 209 H4
Moulton Av HSLW TW3 153 M8
Moultrie Wy UPMR RM14 126 D5
Moundfield Rd STNW/STAM N16 119 P4
Mountacre Cl SYD SE26 181 N7
Mount Adon Pk EDUL SE22 181 P3
Montague Pl POP/IOD E14 141 H9
Mount Angelus Rd
PUT/ROE SW15 178 C3
Mount Ararat Rd
RCHPK/HAM TW10 177 K1
Mount Ash Rd SYD SE26 182 A6
Mount Av CHING E4 100 F4
CTHM CR3 241 K10
EA W5 135 J7
HARH RM3 106 B7
RBRW/HUT CM13 107 N1
STHL UB1 133 P8
Mountbatten Cl NRWD SE19 181 M8
SL SL1 149 M2
STAL AL1 38 G9
WOOL/PLUM SE18 163 H5
Mountbatten Ct BKHH IG9 102 A3
Mountbatten Sq WDSR SL4 * 149 H7
Mountbel Rd STAN HA7 * 94 F10
Mount Cl BMLY BR1 206 B1
CAR SM5 222 B5
CRAWE RH10 284 D6
EA W5 * 135 H7
EBAR EN4 78 B8
HHW HP1 35 J6
LHD/OX KT22 236 E9
PUR/KEN CR8 241 K2
SEV TN13 246 G9
SLN SL2 109 H9
WOKS/MYFD GU22 231 N7
The Mount Cl VW GU25 194 A6
Mountcombe Cl SURB KT6 199 K7
Mount Cottages BXLYHS DA6 * 163 P10
Mount Ct WWKM BR4 205 K9
Mount Crs BRW CM14 107 J5
Mount Culver Av SCUP DA14 185 N9
Mount Dr LCOL/BKTW AL2 56 C1
RYLN/HDSTN HA2 113 N3
WBLY HA9 115 P7
The Mount Dr REIG RH2 257 M8
Mountearl Gdns
STRHM/NOR SW16 180 G6
Mount Echo Av CHING E4 100 G2
Mount Echo Dr CHING E4 100 G2
Mount Ephraim La
STRHM/NOR SW16 180 E6
Mount Ephraim Rd
STRHM/NOR SW16 180 E6
Mount Felix WOT/HER KT12 196 G8
Mountfield Cl CAT SE6 183 J3
Mountfield Rd EA W5 135 J8
EHAM E6 142 D4
FNCH N3 117 K1
HHNE HP2 35 P6
Mountfield Ter CAT SE6 183 J3
Mountfield Wy STMC/STPC BR5 207 M4
Mountford St WCHPL E1 13 N5
Mountfort Ter IS N1 6 A4
Mount Gdns SYD SE26 182 A6
Mount Grace Rd POTB/CUF EN6 59 K7
Mount Gv EDGW HA8 95 P4
Mountgrove Rd HBRY N5 119 K8
Mount Harry Rd SEV TN13 247 J9
Mount Hermon Rd
WOKS/MYFD GU22 232 B4
Mount Hill La CFSP/GDCR SL9 109 N7
Mounthurst Rd HAYES BR2 205 M7
Mountington Park Cl
KTN/HRWW/WS HA3 115 J4
Mountjoy Cl ABYW SE2 163 L1
Mount La CRAWE RH10 285 P9
DEN/HRF UB9 110 G7
Mount Lee EGH TW20 172 B8
Mount Ms HPTN TW12 198 A1
Mount Mills FSBYE EC1V 6 D10
Mountnessing La BRWN CM15 87 K4
Mountnessing Rd BRWN CM15 87 M2
Mount Nod Rd
STRHM/NOR SW16 180 G6
Mount Nugent CSHM HP5 50 F3
Mount Pde EBAR EN4 * 77 P8
Mount Pk CAR SM5 222 B5
Mount Park Av HRW HA1 114 D7
SAND/SEL CR2 223 J5
Mount Park Crs EA W5 135 J8
Mount Park Rd EA W5 135 J8
HRW HA1 114 C7
PIN HA5 113 H3
Mount Pl ACT W3 135 N10
Mount Pleasant ALP/SUD HA0 135 K3
BH/WHM TN16 244 A3
DEN/HRF UB9 91 K9
EBAR EN4 78 A8
EHSLY KT24 252 C5
EHSLY KT24 253 M4
EW KT17 220 C6
FSBYW WC1X 11 P2
GUW GU2 267 P2
HERT/BAY SG13 26 B7
HRW HA1 * 114 D7
RDKG RH5 * 270 G6
RSLP HA4 113 K7
STALW/RED AL3 38 B5
WEY KT13 196 B10
WNWD SE27 181 K7
Mount Pleasant Cl BRKMPK AL9 40 F1
Mount Pleasant Cottages
EGH TW20 * 172 A9
Mount Pleasant Crs
FSBYPK N4 * 118 G5
Mount Pleasant Hl CLPT E5 120 A7
Mount Pleasant La BRKMPK AL9 40 F1
CLPT E5 120 A6
LCOL/BKTW AL2 55 N6
Mount Pleasant Pl
WOOL/PLUM SE18 162 G3
Mount Pleasant Rd CHIG IG7 102 G5
CRW RM5 104 E7
CTHM CR3 241 P9
DART DA1 187 N2
EA W5 135 H6
LEW SE13 183 H2
NWMAL KT3 199 P3
RSEV TN14 265 J9
TOTM N17 99 M10
WALTH E17 100 D10
WLSDN NW10 136 F2
Mount Pleasant Vls FSBYPK N4 118 G5
Mount Ri FSTH SE23 182 B5
REDH RH1 275 N2
Mount Rd BCTR RM8 124 A6
BXLYHS DA6 185 P1
CHOB/PIR GU24 213 N8
CHSGTN KT9 219 L2
CRICK NW2 116 E8
CRICK NW2 116 E8
DART DA1 186 G2
EBAR EN4 77 P9
EPP CM16 65 P8
FELT TW13 175 M6
HDN NW4 116 D5
HERT/WAT SG14 25 H6
HYS/HAR UB3 152 G1
IL IG1 122 E10
MTCM CR4 201 N2
NRWD SE19 181 L9
NWMAL KT3 200 A3
STALE/WH AL4 21 J2
WIM/MER SW19 179 K5
WOKS/MYFD GU22 231 N7
Mount Rw MYFR/PKLN W1K 10 E8
Mountsfield Cl
STWL/WRAY TW19 173 K1
Mounts Hl WDSR SL4 170 B5
Mountside GUW GU2 267 N3
KTN/HRWW/WS HA3 94 E9
Mountsorrel HERT/BAY SG13 25 N5
Mounts Pond Rd BKHTH/KID SE3 161 K8
The Mount Sq HAMP NW3 * 117 M8
Mounts Rd SWCM DA10 188 G2
Mount Stewart Av
KTN/HRWW/WS HA3 115 J5
Mount St DORK RH4 272 F2
MYFR/PKLN W1K 10 C8
Mount Ter WCHPL E1 140 A7
The Mount BMLY BR1 * 206 B1
BRW CM14 107 M8
BXLYHS DA6 * 186 C1
CHESW EN7 61 L2
CLPT E5 120 A7
COUL/CHIP CR5 240 B1
CRAWW RH11 282 E4
ESH/CLAY KT10 217 P3
EW KT17 220 C6
EW KT17 220 E1
GUW GU2 267 N3
HAMP NW3 117 M9
HARH RM3 105 K4
KWD/TDW/WH KT20 257 J2
LHD/OX KT22 236 D9
NTHLT UB5 * 114 A10
NWMAL KT3 200 C3
POTB/CUF EN6 59 L6
RKW/CH/CXG WD3 71 M10
TRDG/WHET N20 97 M1
VW GU25 194 A6
WARL CR6 241 P5
WBLY HA9 115 N7
WEY KT13 196 F9
WOKN/KNAP GU21 232 A4
Mount Vw ENC/FH EN2 78 G4
LCOL/BKTW AL2 57 K3
NWDGN UB2 * 153 L3
RKW/CH/CXG WD3 91 L2
Mountview MLHL NW7 96 A4
NTHWD HA6 93 H7
Mountview Cl HAMP NW3 117 M6
REDH RH1 275 P2
Mountview Dr REDH RH1 275 P2
Mount View Rd CDALE/KGS NW9 116 A2
Mountview Rd CHESW EN7 61 M2
Mount View Rd CHING E4 101 J1
CLAY KT10 218 G4
FSBYPK N4 118 G5
Mountview Rd ORP BR6 207 K7
Mount Vls WNWD SE27 181 J6
Mount Wy CAR SM5 222 B5
Mountway POTB/CUF EN6 59 K6
Mount Wy WGCE AL7 23 J8
Mountway Cl WGCE AL7 23 J8
Mountwood E/WMO/HCT KT8 198 A3
Mountwood Cl SAND/SEL CR2 224 A6
Mountwood La EPP CM16 66 C3
Movers La BARK IG11 142 G3
Mowatt Cl ARCH N19 118 E6
Mowbray Av BF/WBF KT14 215 P9
Mowbray Crs EGH TW20 172 D8
Mowbray Dr CRAWW RH11 283 J9
Mowbray Gdns DORK RH4 254 G10
NTHLT UB5 * 133 P3
Mowbray Rd BAR EN5 77 M9
CRICK NW2 2 A3
EDGW HA8 95 M5
HLW CM20 29 J9
KIL/WHAMP NW6 137 H2
NRWD SE19 203 N1
RCHPK/HAM TW10 177 H6
Mowbrays Cl CRW RM5 104 D9
Mowbrays Rd CRW RM5 104 D10
Mowbrey Gdns LOU IG10 82 F6
Mowlem St BETH E2 140 A4
Mowll St BRXN/ST SW9 159 H6
Moxom Av CHES/WCR EN8 62 D6
Moxon Cl PLSTW E13 141 L4
Moxon St BAR EN5 77 J7
MHST W1U 10 C4
Moye Cl BETH E2 7 P7
Moyers Rd LEY E10 121 H6
Moylan Rd HMSMTH W6 14 B10
HMSMTH W6 157 H5
Moyne Pl WLSDN NW10 135 M5
Moynihan Dr WCHMH N21 78 F9
Moys Cl CROY/NA CR0 202 F6
Moyser Rd STRHM/NOR SW16 180 C8
Mozart Est NKENS W10 2 C9
Mozart St NKENS W10 2 C10
Muchelney Rd MRDN SM4 201 M6
Muckhatch La EGH TW20 194 E3
Muckingford Rd TIL RM18 169 J3
Muggeridge Cl SAND/SEL CR2 223 L2
Muggeridge Rd DAGE RM10 124 C9
Muirdown Av MORT/ESHN SW14 155 P10
Muir Dr WAND/EARL SW18 179 N2
Muirfield ACT W3 136 B8
Muirfield Cl BERM/RHTH SE16 160 A4
CRAWW RH11 282 G8
OXHEY WD19 93 K6
Muirfield Crs POP/IOD E14 160 G2
Muirfield Gn OXHEY WD19 93 K5
Muirfield Rd OXHEY WD19 93 K5
WOKN/KNAP GU21 231 M4
Muirkirk Rd CAT SE6 183 H4
Muir Rd CLPT E5 119 P8
Muir St CAN/RD E16 142 C10
Mulberry Av STWL/WRAY TW19 173 P4
WDSR SL4 149 L9
Mulberry Cl BROX EN10 44 E10
CEND/HSY/T N8 118 F3
CHING E4 100 F3
EBAR EN4 77 N8
GPK RM2 125 J2
HDN NW4 116 F1
LCOL/BKTW AL2 56 A4
NTHLT UB5 133 M4
STRHM/NOR SW16 180 D7
WAT WD17 72 F2
WEY KT13 196 C10
WOKN/KNAP GU21 214 B10
Mulberry Crs BTFD TW8 154 G6
WDR/YW UB7 152 B1
Mulberry Dr DTCH/LGLY SL3 150 B4
PUR RM19 165 N3
Mulberry Gdns RAD WD7 57 K9
Mulberry Ga BNSTD SM7 239 J2
Mulberry Gn HLWE CM17 29 N7
Mulberry Hl BRWN CM15 107 L1
Mulberry La CROY/NA CR0 203 N8
Mulberry Md HAT AL10 22 C10
Mulberry Ms NWCR SE14 160 E7
Mulberry Pde WDR/YW UB7 152 B2
Mulberry Pl ELTH/MOT SE9 162 A10
HMSMTH W6 156 D4
Mulberry Rd CRAWW RH11 283 L4
GVW DA11 190 B7
HACK E8 7 L4
Mulberry St WCHPL E1 13 N5
Mulberry Trees SHPTN TW17 196 E7
Mulberry Wk CHEL SW3 15 M9
Mulberry Wy BARK/HLT IG6 122 F2
BELV DA17 164 D1
SWFD E18 101 N10
Mulgrave Rd BELMT SM2 221 J4
CROY/NA CR0 223 L1
EA W5 135 J5
HRW HA1 114 F7
WKENS W14 14 C9
WLSDN NW10 116 C9
WOOL/PLUM SE18 162 C3
Mulgrave Wy WOKN/KNAP GU21 231 K4
Mulholland Cl MTCM CR4 202 C2
Mulkern Rd ARCH N19 118 E6
Mullards Cl MTCM CR4 202 A8
Mullein Ct GRAYS RM17 168 A5
Mullens Rd EGH TW20 172 B8
Mullet Gdns BETH E2 7 P9
Mullins Pth MORT/ESHN SW14 156 A9
Mullion Cl KTN/HRWW/WS HA3 94 A9
Mullion Wk OXHEY WD19 93 L5
Mull Wk IS N1 6 F2
Mulready St STJWD NW8 9 N2
Mulready Wk HHS/BOV HP3 35 P10
Multi Wy ACT W3 156 B1
Multon Rd WAND/EARL SW18 179 N3
Mumford Mills GNWCH SE10 160 F6
Mumford Rd HNHL SE24 181 J1
Mumfords La CFSP/GDCR SL9 109 M1
Muncaster Cl ASHF TW15 174 B7
Muncaster Rd ASHF TW15 174 C8
CLAP SW4 158 A10
Muncies Ms CAT SE6 183 H5
Mundania Rd EDUL SE22 182 A2
Munday Rd CAN/RD E16 141 M8
Munday's Boro Rd RGUW GU3 266 A5
Mundells CHESW EN7 61 P3
WGCE AL7 23 J4
Munden Gv WATN WD24 73 K4
Munden St WKENS W14 14 A5
Mundesley Sp SL SL1 129 K8
Mundesly Cl OXHEY WD19 93 K5
Mundford Rd CLPT E5 120 B7
Mundon Gdns IL IG1 122 G6
Mund St WKENS W14 14 D8
Mundy St IS N1 7 J9
Munford Dr SWCM DA10 189 L3
Mungo-park Cl BUSH WD23 * 94 B3
Mungo Park Rd GVE DA12 190 G8
RAIN RM13 145 H2
Mungo Park Wy STMC/STPC BR5 207 N7
Munnery Wy ORP BR6 206 E10
Munnings Gdns ISLW TW7 176 C1
Munro Dr FBAR/BDGN N11 * 98 D7
Munroe Ter WBPTN SW10 157 N6
Munro Ms NKENS W10 8 B3
Munro Rd BUSH WD23 74 A9
Munro Wy CLPT E5 119 P9
Munslow Gdns SUT SM1 221 M1
Munstead Vw RGUW GU3 267 N5
Munster Av HSLWW TW4 153 M10
Munster Ct FUL/PGN SW6 157 J8
Munster Gdns PLMGR N13 99 K5
Munster Ms FUL/PGN SW6 * 157 J6
Munster Rd FUL/PGN SW6 157 H6
TEDD TW11 177 H9
Munster Sq CAMTN NW1 4 F10
Munton Rd WALW SE17 18 F5
Murchison Av BXLY DA5 185 N4
Murchison Rd HOD EN11 26 G10
LEY E10 121 H7
Murdoch Cl STA TW18 173 K8
Murdock Cl CAN/RD E16 141 L8
Murdock St PECK SE15 160 A5
Murfett Cl WIM/MER SW19 179 H5
Murfitt Wy UPMR RM14 125 P9
Muriel Av WATW WD18 73 K9
Muriel St IS N1 5 P7
Murillo Rd LEW SE13 161 J10
Murphy St STHWK SE1 18 A2
Murray Av BMLY BR1 205 N2
HSLW TW3 176 A1

Murray Cl THMD SE28 143 H10
Murray Ct ASC SL5 192 B6
Murray Crs PIN HA5 93 L9
Murray Gv IS N1 6 G8
Murray House
WOOL/PLUM SE18 * 162 B6
Murray Ms CAMTN NW1 5 J3
Murray Rd BERK HP4 33 P4
CHERT KT16 214 G3
EA W5 155 H3
NTHWD HA6 92 F9
RCHPK/HAM TW10 176 G5
STMC/STPC BR5 207 L3
WIM/MER SW19 178 G9
Murray's La BF/WBF KT14 215 N10
Murray Sq CAN/RD E16 141 M8
Murray St CAMTN NW1 5 H3
Murray Ter HAMP NW3 117 M9
Murrells Wk GT/LBKH KT23 235 P9
The Murreys ASHTD KT21 237 J4
Murthering La ABR/ST RM4 85 H8
Murton Ct STAL AL1 38 D5
Murtwell Dr CHIG IG7 102 F7
Musard Rd HMSMTH W6 14 B9
HMSMTH W6 157 H5
Musbury St WCHPL E1 140 B8
Muscatel Pl CMBW SE5 159 M7
Muschamp Rd CAR SM5 201 P9
PECK SE15 159 N9
Muscovy St MON EC3R 13 K8
Museum St NOXST/BSQ WC1A 11 K3
Musgrave Cl EBAR EN4 77 M5
Musgrave Crs FUL/PGN SW6 157 K6
Musgrave Rd ISLW TW7 154 E7
Musgrove Rd NWCR SE14 160 C7
Musjid Rd BTSEA SW11 157 N8
Muskalls Cl CHESW EN7 61 P3
Muskham Rd HLW CM20 29 K8
Musk Hl HHW HP1 35 H7
Musleigh Mnr WARE SG12 26 E2
Musley Hl WARE SG12 26 D1
Musley La WARE SG12 26 D1
Musquash Wy HSLWW TW4 153 K8
Mussenden Ct WATN WD24 * 73 J5
Mussenden La EYN DA4 210 C6
Mustard Mill Rd STA TW18 173 J7
Muston Rd CLPT E5 120 A7
Muswell Av MUSWH N10 98 C10
Muswell Hl MUSWH N10 118 C1
Muswell Hl Broadway
MUSWH N10 118 C2
Muswell Hill Pl MUSWH N10 118 C2
Muswell Hill Rd MUSWH N10 118 B2
Muswell Ms MUSWH N10 118 C1
Muswell Rd MUSWH N10 98 C10
Mutchetts Cl GSTN WD25 55 M9
Mutrix Rd KIL/WHAMP NW6 2 F5
Mutter Rd CLAP SW4 180 E2
Mutton La POTB/CUF EN6 58 G7
POTB/CUF EN6 59 H8
Mutton Pl CAMTN NW1 4 E2
Mutton Rw CHONG CM5 67 K6
Muybridge Rd NWMAL KT3 199 P2
Myatt Rd BRXN/ST SW9 159 J7
Mycenae Rd BKHTH/KID SE3 161 M5
Myddelton Av EN EN1 79 M4
Myddelton Gdns WCHMH N21 99 K1
Myddelton Pk TRDG/WHET N20 97 N4
Myddelton Pas CLKNW EC1R 6 B9
Myddelton Rd CEND/HSY/T N8 118 F1
Myddelton Sq CLKNW EC1R 6 B9
Myddelton St CLKNW EC1R 6 B10
Myddleton Av FSBYPK N4 119 J7
Myddleton Rd UX/CGN UB8 131 M3
WARE SG12 26 C3
WDGN N22 98 F8
Myers Cl RAD WD7 57 K8
Myers La NWCR SE14 160 C5
Mygrove Cl RAIN RM13 145 L4
Mygrove Gdns RAIN RM13 145 L4
Mygrove Rd RAIN RM13 145 L4
Myles Ct CHESW EN7 61 K5
Mylis Cl SYD SE26 182 A7
Mylne Cl CHES/WCR EN8 62 B3
HMSMTH W6 * 156 D4
Mylne St CLKNW EC1R 6 A9
Mylor Cl WOKN/KNAP GU21 214 B10
Mymms Dr BRKMPK AL9 59 K3
Mynchen End BEAC HP9 88 C5
Mynn's Cl EPSOM KT18 219 N10
Myra St ABYW SE2 163 K4
Myrdle St WCHPL E1 13 P4
The Myrke DTCH/LGLY SL3 149 L3
Myrna Cl WIM/MER SW19 179 P10
Myron Pl LEW SE13 161 H9
Myrtle Aly WOOL/PLUM SE18 162 D2
Myrtle Av EBED/NFELT TW14 152 F10
RSLP HA4 113 H5
Myrtleberry Cl BEAC HP9 * 7 L2
Myrtle Cl DTCH/LGLY SL3 151 H7
EBAR EN4 98 A2
ERITH DA8 164 F6
LTWR GU18 212 A7
UX/CGN UB8 132 A7
WDR/YW UB7 152 A3
Myrtle Cottages DORK RH4 * 272 C5
Myrtle Crs SLN SL2 129 L9
Myrtledene Rd ABYW SE2 163 K4
Myrtle Gdns HNWL W7 134 D10
Myrtle Gv ENC/FH EN2 79 L4
NWMAL KT3 199 P2
SOCK/AV RM15 166 B1
Myrtle Pl RDART DA2 188 C4
Myrtle Rd ACT W3 135 P10
BRW CM14 107 H5
CROY/NA CR0 204 F10
DART DA1 187 L5
DORK RH4 272 F1
EHAM E6 142 B3
HARH RM3 105 K7
HPTN TW12 176 B9
HSLW TW3 154 B8
IL IG1 122 E7
PLMGR N13 99 K4
SUT SM1 221 M2
WALTH E17 120 D4
Myrtleside Cl NTHWD HA6 92 E8
Myrtle St IS N1 7 J8
Myrtle Wk IS N1 7 J8
Mysore Rd BTSEA SW11 158 A10
Myton Rd DUL SE21 181 L6

N

Nadine St CHARL SE7 161 P4
Naffenton Ri LOU IG10 82 A9
Nagle Cl WALTH E17 101 J10
Nag's Head La UPMR RM14 106 B9
WELL DA16 163 L9
Nags Head Rd PEND EN3 80 B8
Nailsworth Crs REDH RH1 258 E5
Nailzee Cl CFSP/GDCR SL9 110 B5
Nairn Cl HARP AL5 20 C5
Nairn Ct TIL RM18 * 168 C8
Nairne Gv CMBW SE5 159 L10
HNHL SE24 181 L1
Nairn Gn OXHEY WD19 93 H4
Nairn Rd RSLP HA4 133 K1
Nairn St POP/IOD E14 141 H7
Nalders Rd CSHM HP5 51 J5
Nallhead Rd FELT TW13 175 K8
Namba Roy Cl
STRHM/NOR SW16 180 G7
Namton Dr THHTH CR7 202 G4
Nan Clark's La MLHL NW7 96 C3
Nancy Downs OXHEY WD19 93 K1
Nankin St POP/IOD E14 140 F8
Nansen Rd BTSEA SW11 158 B10
GVE DA12 190 G7
Nansen Village
NFNCH/WDSPK N12 * 97 L5
Nantes Cl WAND/EARL SW18 157 M10
Nant Rd CRICK NW2 117 J7
Nant St BETH E2 140 A5
Naoroji St FSBYW WC1X 6 A10
Napier Av FUL/PGN SW6 157 J9
POP/IOD E14 160 G4
Napier Cl DEPT SE8 160 E6
EMPK RM11 125 J6
LCOL/BKTW AL2 57 J1
WDR/YW UB7 152 A2
WKENS W14 14 C3
Napier Ct CTHM CR3 241 M8
LEE/GVPK SE12 183 N5
Napier Dr BUSH WD23 73 M8
Napier Gdns GU GU1 250 E9
Napier Gv IS N1 6 F8
Napier Pl WKENS W14 14 C4
Napier Rd ALP/SUD HA0 115 J10
ASHF TW15 174 E10
BELV DA17 164 A3
EHAM E6 142 D5
GVW DA11 190 C4
HAYES BR2 205 N3
ISLW TW7 154 F10
PEND EN3 80 C9
SAND/SEL CR2 223 L4
SNWD SE25 204 A4
SRTFD E15 141 K4
TOTM N17 119 M1
WAN E11 121 K8
WDR/YW UB7 151 N7
WKENS W14 14 C4
WLSDN NW10 136 E5
Napier Ter IS N1 6 C4
Napier Wk ASHF TW15 174 E10
Napier Wy CRAWE RH10 284 B4
Napoleon Rd CLPT E5 120 A8
TWK TW1 * 176 G3
Napsbury Av LCOL/BKTW AL2 57 H2
Napsbury La STAL AL1 38 F9
The Nap KGLGY WD4 54 B5
Napton Cl YEAD UB4 133 M6
Narbonne Av CLAP SW4 180 D1
Narboro Ct ROM RM1 125 H4
Narborough Cl HGDN/ICK UB10 112 D7
Narborough St FUL/PGN SW6 157 L8
Narcissus Rd KIL/WHAMP NW6 117 K10
Narcot La CSTG HP8 89 N6
Narcot Rd CSTG HP8 89 M4
Narcot Wy CSTG HP8 89 M5
Nare Rd SOCK/AV RM15 146 B9
Narford Rd CLPT E5 119 P8
Narrow Boat Cl THMD SE28 162 G1
Narrow La WARL CR6 242 B5
Narrow St ACT W3 135 N10
POP/IOD E14 140 D9
Narrow Wy HAYES BR2 206 B6
Nascot Pl WAT WD17 73 J6
Nascot Rd WAT WD17 73 J6
Nascot St SHB W12 136 F8
WAT WD17 73 J6
Nascot Wood Rd WAT WD17 72 G4
Naseby Cl ISLW TW7 154 D7
KIL/WHAMP NW6 3 K3
Naseby Ct WOT/HER KT12 * 197 K9
Naseby Rd CLAY IG5 102 C9
DAGE RM10 124 B8
NRWD SE19 181 L9
Nash Cl BORE WD6 75 L8
BRKMPK AL9 40 G9
SUT SM1 201 N10
Nash Cft GVW DA11 190 B7
Nash Gdns REDH RH1 258 A8
Nash Gn BMLY BR1 183 M10
Nash La HAYES BR2 225 M3
Nashleigh Hl CSHM HP5 51 J5
Nash Mills La HHS/BOV HP3 54 A2
Nash Rd BROCKY SE4 160 D10
CHDH RM6 123 N2
CRAWE RH10 283 P10
DTCH/LGLY SL3 150 C4
ED N9 100 B3
Nash St CAMTN NW1 4 F9
Nash Wy KTN/HRWW/WS HA3 114 G4
Nasmyth St HMSMTH W6 156 E2
Nassau Rd BARN SW13 156 C7
Nassau St GTPST W1W 10 G4
Nassington Rd HAMP NW3 117 P9
Nasturtium Dr CHOB/PIR GU24 230 F1
Natalie Cl EBED/NFELT TW14 174 E3
Natalie Ms WHTN TW2 176 C6
Natal Rd FBAR/BDGN N11 98 F7
IL IG1 122 E9
STRHM/NOR SW16 180 E9
THHTH CR7 203 L3
Nathan Cl UPMR RM14 126 D6
Nathaniel Cl WCHPL E1 13 M4
Nathans Rd ALP/SUD HA0 115 H7
Nathan Wy ABYW SE2 163 K1
National Ter BERM/RHTH SE16 * 160 A1
Nation Wy CHING E4 101 H2
Natwoke Cl BEAC HP9 88 C6
Naunton Wy HCH RM12 125 L8
Naval Rw POP/IOD E14 141 H9
Navarino Gv HACK E8 7 P1
Navarino Rd HACK E8 7 P1
Navarre Gdns CRW RM5 104 C7
Navarre Rd EHAM E6 142 B4
Navarre St BETH E2 13 L1
Navestock Cl CHING E4 * 101 H4
Navestock Crs WFD IG8 101 P9
Navestock Side BRW CM14 86 B6
Navestock Ter WFD IG8 101 P8
Navigator Dr NWDGN UB2 154 B1
Navy St CLAP SW4 158 E9
Nayim Pl HACK E8 140 A1
Naylor Gv PEND EN3 80 C9
Naylor Rd PECK SE15 160 A6
TRDG/WHET N20 97 M3
Nazareth Cl PECK SE15 160 A8
Nazeingbury Cl WAB EN9 45 J8
Nazeingbury Pde WAB EN9 * 45 J8
Nazeing Common WAB EN9 45 P9
Nazeing New Rd BROX EN10 44 F7
Nazrul St BETH E2 7 L9
Neagle Cl BORE WD6 75 P5
Neal Av STHL UB1 133 N6
Neal Cl CFSP/GDCR SL9 110 E6
NTHWD HA6 93 H9
Neal Ct HERT/WAT SG14 25 K5
WAB EN9 63 L9
Nealden St BRXN/ST SW9 158 G9
Neale Cl EFNCH N2 117 M1
Neal St LSQ/SEVD WC2H 11 L6
WATW WD18 73 K9
Neal Ter FSTH SE23 * 182 C4
Neal Yd LSQ/SEVD WC2H 11 L6
Near Acre CDALE/KGS NW9 96 C9
Neasden Cl WLSDN NW10 116 B10
Neasden La WLSDN NW10 116 B9
Neasden La North WLSDN NW10 116 B8
Neasham Rd BCTR RM8 123 L10
Neate St CMBW SE5 19 L9
Neath Gdns MRDN SM4 201 M6
Neathouse Pl PIM SW1V 16 D5
Neats Acre RSLP HA4 112 E5
Neatscourt Rd EHAM E6 142 A8
Neave Crs HARH RM3 105 K9
Neb La OXTED RH8 261 H7
Neckinger BERM/RHTH SE16 19 M3
Neckinger Est BERM/RHTH SE16 19 M3
Neckinger St STHWK SE1 19 M2
Nectarine Wy LEW SE13 160 G8
Necton Rd STALE/WH AL4 21 K3
Needham Cl WDSR SL4 148 D7
Needham Rd NTGHL W11 8 E6
Needleman St BERM/RHTH SE16 160 C1
Needles Bank GDST RH9 260 A7
Neela Cl HGDN/ICK UB10 112 C9
Neeld Crs HDN NW4 116 E3
WBLY HA9 115 M10
Neil Cl ASHF TW15 174 D8
Neild Wy RKW/CH/CXG WD3 91 J1
Neils Yd LSQ/SEVD WC2H * 11 L6
Nelgarde Rd CAT SE6 182 F3
Nella Rd HMSMTH W6 156 G5
Nelldale Rd BERM/RHTH SE16 160 A3
Nellgrove Rd UX/CGN UB8 132 C6
Nell Gwynn Av SHPTN TW17 196 E6
Nell Gwynn Cl RAD WD7 57 K8
Nell Gwynne Av ASC SL5 192 C4
Nell Gwynne Cl HOR/WEW KT19 219 M7
Nello James Gdns WNWD SE27 181 L7
Nelmes Cl EMPK RM11 125 N3
Nelmes Crs EMPK RM11 125 N3
Nelmes Rd EMPK RM11 125 M5
Nelmes Wy EMPK RM11 125 M2
Nelson Av STAL AL1 38 G9
Nelson Cl AMSS HP7 68 B10
BH/WHM TN16 244 B3
BRW CM14 107 J6
CRAWE RH10 284 D8
CROY/NA CR0 203 J8
DTCH/LGLY SL3 150 A3
EBED/NFELT TW14 * 174 G4
HGDN/ICK UB10 132 C5
KIL/WHAMP NW6 2 E9
ROMW/RG RM7 104 C9
WOT/HER KT12 197 J8
Nelson Gdns BETH E2 7 P10
GU GU1 250 D9
HSLW TW3 175 P2
Nelson Grove Rd
WIM/MER SW19 201 L1
Nelson La HGDN/ICK UB10 132 C6
Nelson Mandela Cl MUSWH N10 98 A10
Nelson Mandela Rd
BKHTH/KID SE3 161 P9
Nelson Pl IS N1 6 D8
Nelson Rd ASHF TW15 173 P8
BELV DA17 164 A4
CEND/HSY/T N8 118 G3
CHING E4 100 G7
CTHM CR3 241 L9
DART DA1 187 K2
ED N9 100 D3
GNWCH SE10 161 H5
GVW DA11 190 C5
HAYES BR2 205 P4
HGDN/ICK UB10 132 C5
HRW HA1 114 D6
HTHAIR TW6 152 A7
NWMAL KT3 200 A5
PEND EN3 80 C10
RAIN RM13 144 G4
SCUP DA14 185 K7
SEVS/STOTM N15 119 M2
SOCK/AV RM15 147 H4
STAN HA7 95 H7
WAN E11 121 M2
WDSR SL4 148 E9
WHTN TW2 175 P2
WIM/MER SW19 179 L10
Nelson Sq STHWK SE1 18 C1
Nelsons Rw CLAP SW4 158 E10
Nelson St CAN/RD E16 141 L9
EHAM E6 142 C4
HERT/WAT SG14 25 J4
WCHPL E1 140 A8
Nelsons Yd CAMTN NW1 4 G7
Nelson Ter FSBYE EC1V 6 D8
Nelson Wk HOR/WEW KT19 219 M5
Nelwyn Av EMPK RM11 125 N3
Nemoure Rd ACT W3 135 P9
Nene Gdns FELT TW13 175 N5
Nene Rd HTHAIR TW6 152 C7
Nepaul Rd BTSEA SW11 157 P8
Nepean St PUT/ROE SW15 178 D3
Neptune Cl CRAWW RH11 283 H9
RAIN RM13 144 G4
Neptune Ct BORE WD6 * 75 M7
Neptune Dr HHNE HP2 35 P4
Neptune Rd HRW HA1 114 C4
HTHAIR TW6 * 152 D7
Neptune St BERM/RHTH SE16 160 B2
Nesbit Cl BKHTH/KID SE3 161 K9
Nesbit Rd ELTH/MOT SE9 162 A10
Nesbitts Aly BAR EN5 * 77 J7
Nesbitt Sq NRWD SE19 * 181 M10
Nesham St WAP E1W 13 N9
Ness Rd ERITH DA8 165 L5
Ness St BERM/RHTH SE16 19 N3
BERM/RHTH SE16 159 P2
Nesta Rd WFD IG8 101 L7
Nestle's Av HYS/HAR UB3 152 G2
Neston Rd WATN WD24 73 K3
Nestor Av WCHMH N21 79 J10
Nethan Dr SOCK/AV RM15 146 B9
Netheravon Rd CHSWK W4 156 C3
HNWL W7 134 E10
Netheravon Rd South
CHSWK W4 156 C5
Netherbury Rd EA W5 155 J2
Netherby Gdns ENC/FH EN2 78 F8
Netherby Rd FSTH SE23 182 B3
Nether Cl FNCH N3 97 K8
Nethercote Av
WOKN/KNAP GU21 231 L3
Nether Ct MLHL NW7 * 97 J7
Nethercourt Av FNCH N3 97 K7
Netherfield Gdns BARK IG11 142 G2
Netherfield La WARE SG12 27 K9
Netherfield Rd HARP AL5 20 A7
NFNCH/WDSPK N12 97 L6
TOOT SW17 180 B6
Netherford Rd CLAP SW4 158 D8
Netherhall Gdns HAMP NW3 117 M10
Netherhall Rd HLWW/ROY CM19 45 L3
Netherhall Wy HAMP NW3 3 J1
Netherlands Rd BAR EN5 77 N10
The Netherlands COUL/CHIP CR5 240 D5
Netherleigh Cl HGT N6 118 C6
Netherleigh Pk REDH RH1 276 F3
Nether Mt GUW GU2 267 N2
Nethern Court Rd CTHM CR3 242 F9
Nethern Dr COUL/CHIP CR5 240 C7
Netherne La COUL/CHIP CR5 240 D8
Netherpark Dr GPK RM2 104 G10
Nether St FNCH N3 97 K9
Netherton Gv WBPTN SW10 15 J10
Netherton Rd SEVS/STOTM N15 119 L4
TWK TW1 176 F1
Netherway STALW/RED AL3 37 P9
Netherwood CRAWW RH11 283 K10
Netherwood Pl HMSMTH W6 * 156 G2
Netherwood Rd BEAC HP9 88 C6
WKENS W14 156 G2
Netherwood St KIL/WHAMP NW6 2 D3
Netley Cl CHEAM SM3 220 G2
CROY/NA CR0 225 H4
SHGR GU5 270 D4
Netley Dr WOT/HER KT12 197 N7
Netley Gdns MRDN SM4 201 M7
Netley Rd BTFD TW8 155 K5
GNTH/NBYPK IG2 122 G3
MRDN SM4 201 M7
WALTH E17 120 E3
Netley St CAMTN NW1 4 G10
Netteswellbury Farm
HLWS CM18 47 J2
Netteswell Orch HLW CM20 28 G10
Netteswell Rd HLW CM20 29 H9
Nettlecombe Cl BELMT SM2 221 L5
Nettlecroft HHW HP1 35 L7
WGCE AL7 23 L4
Nettleden Av WBLY HA9 135 M1
Nettleden Rd BERK HP4 34 D2
Nettlefold Pl WNWD SE27 181 J6
Nettlestead Cl BECK BR3 182 E10
Nettles Ter GU GU1 250 A10
Nettleton Rd HGDN/ICK UB10 112 A9
HTHAIR TW6 152 C7
NWCR SE14 160 C7
Nettlewood Rd
STRHM/NOR SW16 180 E10
Neuchatel Rd CAT SE6 182 E5
Nevada Cl NWMAL KT3 199 P4
Nevada St GNWCH SE10 161 H6
Nevell Rd CDW/CHF RM16 168 E2
Nevern Pl ECT SW5 14 F6
Nevern Rd ECT SW5 14 E6
Nevern Sq ECT SW5 14 F6
Nevil Cl NTHWD HA6 92 E6
Neville Cl CRAWW RH11 283 K10
Neville Av NWMAL KT3 200 A1
Neville Cl ACT W3 155 P1
BFN/LL DA15 185 J7
BNSTD SM7 221 L10
ESH/CLAY KT10 217 N3
HSLW TW3 153 P8
KIL/WHAMP NW6 2 D8
PECK SE15 159 P6
POTB/CUF EN6 59 J8
SLN SL2 129 L1
WAN E11 121 L8
Neville Dr EFNCH N2 117 M4
Neville Gdns BCTR RM8 123 N8
Neville Gill Cl WAND/EARL SW18 179 K2
Neville Pl WDGN N22 98 G9
Neville Rd BARK/HLT IG6 102 F9
BCTR RM8 123 N7
CROY/NA CR0 203 L7
EA W5 135 J6
FSTGT E7 141 M2
KIL/WHAMP NW6 2 D8
KUT/HW KT1 199 M2
RCHPK/HAM TW10 177 H6
Neville St SKENS SW7 15 L7
Neville Ter SKENS SW7 * 15 L7
Neville Wk CAR SM5 201 P7
Nevill Gv WATN WD24 73 J5
Nevill Rd STNW/STAM N16 119 M9
Nevill Wy LOU IG10 82 B10
Nevil Wk CAR SM5 * 201 P7
Nevin Dr CHING E4 100 G2
Nevinson Cl WAND/EARL SW18 179 N2
Nevis Cl ROM RM1 104 F7
Nevis Rd TOOT SW17 180 B5
New Acres Rd THMD SE28 143 H10
Newall Rd HTHAIR TW6 152 D7
New Ar UX/CGN UB8 * 131 N3
The New Ar HERT/WAT SG14 * 25 L5
Newark Cl RGUE GU4 250 E5
RPLY/SEND GU23 233 J7
Newark Ct WOT/HER KT12 197 K8
Newark Crs WLSDN NW10 136 B6
Newark Gn BORE WD6 76 B7
Newark Knok EHAM E6 142 D8
Newark La RPLY/SEND GU23 233 J6
Newark Rd BFOR GU20 212 A1
CRAWE RH10 284 A5
SAND/SEL CR2 223 L3
Newark St WCHPL E1 140 A7
Newark Wy HDN NW4 116 D2
New Ash Cl EFNCH N2 117 N1
New Barn Cl WLGTN SM6 222 G3
New Barnes Av STAL AL1 38 F9
Newbarn La BEAC HP9 89 K5
New Barn La CTHM CR3 241 M3
Newbarn La RSEV TN14 244 G2
New Barn Rd HART DA3 211 N3
MEO DA13 189 N7
SWLY BR8 208 G1
New Barns Av MTCM CR4 202 E4
New Barn St CAN/RD E16 141 N7
New Barns Wy CHIG IG7 102 E6
New Battlebridge La REDH RH1 258 C6
Newberries Av RAD WD7 74 G1
Newberry Crs WDSR SL4 148 C8
New Berry La WOT/HER KT12 217 L1
Newbery Rd ERITH DA8 164 G7
Newbery Wy SL SL1 149 J1
Newbiggin Path OXHEY WD19 93 K5
Newbold Cottages WCHPL E1 * 140 B8
Newbolt Av CHEAM SM3 220 F2
Newbolt Rd STAN HA7 94 F7
New Bond St CONDST W1S 10 F6
Newborough Gn NWMAL KT3 200 A4
New Brent St HDN NW4 116 F3
New Bridge St EMB EC4Y 12 C6
New Broad St LVPST EC2M 13 H4
New Broadway EA W5 135 H9
HGDN/ICK UB10 * 132 C6
Newburgh Rd ACT W3 135 P10
GRAYS RM17 168 A4
Newburgh St SOHO/CST W1F 10 G6
New Burlington Ms
CONDST W1S 10 G7
New Burlington Pl CONDST W1S 10 G7
New Burlington St CONDST W1S 10 G7
Newburn St LBTH SE11 17 P7
Newbury Av PEND EN3 80 E3
Newbury Cl HARH RM3 105 K7
NTHLT UB5 133 N1
RDART DA2 188 A3
Newbury Gdns HARH RM3 105 L7
HOR/WEW KT19 220 C1
UPMR RM14 125 N8
Newbury Ms KTTN NW5 4 D2
Newbury Rd CHING E4 101 H8
CRAWE RH10 284 E7
GNTH/NBYPK IG2 122 G4
HARH RM3 105 K6
HAYES BR2 205 M3
HTHAIR TW6 151 P7
Newbury St STBT EC1A 12 E4
Newbury Wk HARH RM3 105 L6
Newbury Wy NTHLT UB5 133 N1
New Butt La DEPT SE8 * 160 F6
Newby Cl EN EN1 79 M6
Newby Pl POP/IOD E14 141 H9
Newby St VX/NE SW8 158 C9
Newcastle Av BARK/HLT IG6 103 H8
Newcastle Cl FLST/FETLN EC4A 12 B5
Newcastle Pl BAY/PAD W2 9 M4
Newcastle Rw CLKNW EC1R 12 B2
New Cswy REIG RH2 275 L3
New Cavendish St
CAVSQ/HST W1G 10 D4
New Change STP EC4M 12 E6
New Charles St FSBYE EC1V 6 D9
New Chilterns AMSS HP7 * 69 K5
New Church Rd CMBW SE5 19 H10
CMBW SE5 159 K6
Newchurch Rd SLN SL2 128 E7
New City Rd PLSTW E13 141 P5
New Cl FELT TW13 175 M8
WIM/MER SW19 201 M3
New College Ms IS N1 * 6 B3
New College Pde HAMP NW3 3 L2
Newcombe Gdns HSLWW TW4 153 N10
Newcombe Pk ALP/SUD HA0 135 L3
MLHL NW7 96 B6
Newcombe Ri WDR/YW UB7 131 P8
Newcombe St KENS W8 * 8 F9
Newcome Gdns
STRHM/NOR SW16 180 F7
Newcomen Rd BTSEA SW11 157 N9
WAN E11 * 121 L8
Newcomen St STHWK SE1 18 G1
New Compton St
LSQ/SEVD WC2H * 11 K6
New Coppice WOKN/KNAP GU21 231 K5
New Cottages BRKMPK AL9 58 G4
DORK RH4 * 272 E3
REIG RH2 * 256 G8
New Ct EMB EC4Y * 12 A7
NTHLT UB5 114 A10
Newcourt UX/CGN UB8 131 M7
Newcourt St STJWD NW8 3 N8
New Crane Pl WAP E1W * 140 B10
New Crescent Yd
WLSDN NW10 * 136 C4
Newcroft Cl UX/CGN UB8 132 A7
New Cross Rd GUW GU2 249 M8
NWCR SE14 160 B6
Newdales Cl ED N9 99 P3
Newdene Av NTHLT UB5 133 L4
Newdigate STRHM/NOR SW16 * 181 H7
Newdigate Gn DEN/HRF UB9 91 N9
Newdigate Rd DEN/HRF UB9 91 M9
HORS RH12 282 A5
Newdigate Rd East
DEN/HRF UB9 91 N9
Newell Ri HHS/BOV HP3 35 P9
Newell Rd HHS/BOV HP3 35 P9
Newell St POP/IOD E14 140 E9
New End HAMP NW3 117 M9
New End Sq HAMP NW3 117 N9
New England St STALW/RED AL3 38 B6
Newenham Rd GT/LBKH KT23 253 P2
Newent Cl CAR SM5 202 A8
PECK SE15 159 M6
New Era Est IS N1 7 J6
New Farm Av HAYES BR2 205 M4
New Farm Cl STA TW18 195 M1
New Farm Dr ABR/ST RM4 83 M7
New Farm La NTHWD HA6 92 G9
New Ferry Ap WOOL/PLUM SE18 162 D2
New Fetter La FLST/FETLN EC4A 12 B5
Newfield Cl HPTN TW12 197 P1
Newfield La HHNE HP2 36 A6
Newfield Ri CRICK NW2 116 D8
Newfields WGCW AL8 22 E6
Newfield Wy STALW/WH AL4 39 J8
Newford Cl HHNE HP2 36 C5
New Ford Rd CHES/WCR EN8 62 E10
New Forest La CHIG IG7 102 D7
Newgale Gdns EDGW HA8 95 L9
New Garden Dr WDR/YW UB7 151 P1
Newgate CROY/NA CR0 203 K8
Newgate Cl FELT TW13 175 M5
STALE/WH AL4 39 K3
Newgate St CHING E4 101 K4
STBT EC1A 12 D5
Newgatestreet Rd CHESW EN7 61 J2
Newgate St Village
HERT/BAY SG13 42 E9
New Globe Wk STHWK SE1 12 E9
New Goulston St WCHPL E1 13 L5
New Green Pl BRXS/STRHM SW2 181 H3
NRWD SE19 181 M9
New Greens Av STALW/RED AL3 38 C1
New Hall Cl HHS/BOV HP3 52 D3
Newhall Cl HHS/BOV HP3 * 52 D3
Newhall Ct WAB EN9 63 L9
New Hall Dr HARH RM3 105 M9
Newhall Gdns WOT/HER KT12 197 K9
Newham's Rw STHWK SE1 19 K2
Newham Wy CAN/RD E16 141 L7
EHAM E6 142 B6
Newhaven Cl HYS/HAR UB3 152 G3
Newhaven Crs ASHF TW15 174 E8
Newhaven Gdns ELTH/MOT SE9 162 A10
Newhaven La CAN/RD E16 141 M7
Newhaven Rd SNWD SE25 203 L5
Newhaven Sp SLN SL2 * 128 G6
New Haw Rd ADL/WDHM KT15 215 M3
New Heston Rd HEST TW5 153 N6
Newhouse Av CHDH RM6 123 N1
Newhouse Cl NWMAL KT3 200 B7
Newhouse Crs GSTN WD25 55 K9
New House Farm La RGUW GU3 248 G8
Newhouse La CHONG CM5 49 K8
New House La GVW DA11 190 D5
REDH RH1 276 E8
New House Pk STAL AL1 38 F9
Newhouse Rd HHS/BOV HP3 52 D3
Newhouse Wk MRDN SM4 201 M7
Newick Cl BXLY DA5 186 C2
Newick Rd CLPT E5 120 B8
Newing Gn BMLY BR1 184 A10
Newington Barrow Wy
HOLWY N7 118 G8
Newington Butts WALW SE17 18 D6
Newington Cswy STHWK SE1 18 E3
Newington Gn IS N1 119 L10
Newington Green Rd IS N1 119 L10
New Inn Broadway
SDTCH EC2A * 13 K1
New Inn La GU GU1 250 E7
New Inn Sq SDTCH EC2A * 13 K1
New Inn St SDTCH EC2A * 13 K1
New Inn Yd SDTCH EC2A 13 K1
New Kelvin Av TEDD TW11 176 D9
New Kent Rd WALW SE17 18 F5
New King's Rd FUL/PGN SW6 157 K7
New King St DEPT SE8 160 F5
Newland Cl PIN HA5 93 N7
STAL AL1 38 F9
Newland Ct WBLY HA9 115 M7
Newland Dr EN EN1 80 A5
Newland Gdns HERT/BAY SG13 25 M5
WEA W13 154 F1
Newland Rd CEND/HSY/T N8 118 F1
Newlands GU GU1 268 C2
Newlands Av RAD WD7 56 E10
THDIT KT7 198 D8
WOKS/MYFD GU22 232 C8
Newlands Cl ALP/SUD HA0 135 H1
EDGW HA8 95 K2
HORL RH6 280 A2
NWDGN UB2 153 M4
WOT/HER KT12 217 M1
Newlands Dr DTCH/LGLY SL3 151 H9
Newlands Pk ABLGY WD5 * 54 G2
CRAWE RH10 285 M2
SYD SE26 182 B9
Newlands Pl BAR EN5 76 G9
Newlands Quay WAP E1W 140 B9
Newlands Rd CRAWW RH11 283 M8
HHW HP1 35 H5
STRHM/NOR SW16 202 F2
WFD IG8 101 L3
The Newlands WLGTN SM6 222 D4
Newland St CAN/RD E16 142 B10
Newlands Wk GSTN WD25 55 L9
Newlands Wy CHSGTN KT9 219 H2
POTB/CUF EN6 59 L6
Newlands Woods CROY/NA CR0 224 E5
New La RGUE GU4 232 C10
Newling Cl EHAM E6 142 C8
Newling Est BETH E2 7 M10
New Lodge Dr OXTED RH8 261 L4
New London St MON EC3R * 13 K7
New Lydenburg St CHARL SE7 161 P2
Newlyn Cl LCOL/BKTW AL2 55 M6
ORP BR6 227 K1
UX/CGN UB8 132 B7
Newlyn Gdns RYLN/HDSTN HA2 113 N5
Newlyn Rd BAR EN5 77 J8
TOTM N17 99 N9
WELL DA16 163 J8
New Maltings SOCK/AV RM15 146 C10
Newman Cl CRAWE RH10 284 D8
EMPK RM11 125 M3
Newman Ms WDGN N22 98 G8
WDGN N22 99 H8
Newman Rd BMLY BR1 205 M1
CROY/NA CR0 202 G7
HYS/HAR UB3 133 J9
PLSTW E13 141 N5
WALTH E17 120 C3
Newmans Dr RBRW/HUT CM13 107 P1
Newmans La LOU IG10 82 D7
SURB KT6 199 J6
Newmans Pl ASC SL5 192 G7
Newman's Rw LINN WC2A 11 P4
Newman St FITZ W1T 11 H4
Newman's Wy EBAR EN4 77 M6
Newmarket Av NTHLT UB5 113 P10
Newmarket Ct STALW/RED AL3 38 B5
Newmarket Rd CRAWE RH10 284 B10
Newmarket Wy HCH RM12 125 M9
Newmarsh Rd THMD SE28 143 J10
New Mile Rd ASC SL5 192 A2
New Mill Rd STMC/STPC BR5 207 M1
Newminster Ct ENC/FH EN2 * 79 J6
Newminster Rd MRDN SM4 201 M7
New Mount St SRTFD E15 141 J2
Newnham Av RSLP HA4 113 K6
Newnham Cl LOU IG10 82 A10
NTHLT UB5 134 B1
THHTH CR7 203 K2
Newnham Gdns NTHLT UB5 134 B1
Newnham Gn WDGN N22 * 99 H9
Newnham Pde CHES/WCR EN8 * 62 C6
Newnham Pl CDW/CHF RM16 168 D3
Newnham Rd WDGN N22 98 G9
Newnhams Cl BMLY BR1 206 C3
Newnham Ter STHWK SE1 18 A3
Newnham Wy
KTN/HRWW/WS HA3 115 K3
New North Pl SDTCH EC2A 13 J1
New North Rd BARK/HLT IG6 102 G8
IS N1 6 F5
REIG RH2 275 J3
New North St BMSBY WC1N 11 N3
Newnton Cl FSBYPK N4 119 L5
New Oak Rd EFNCH N2 97 N10
New Oxford St
NOXST/BSQ WC1A 11 L5
New Pde ASHF TW15 * 174 A7
DORK RH4 * 272 G2
GT/LBKH KT23 * 254 B2
RKW/CH/CXG WD3 * 72 A10
WDR/YW UB7 * 131 P10
New Park Av PLMGR N13 99 L4
New Park Cl NTHLT UB5 133 M1
New Park Dr HHNE HP2 36 C6
New Park Est UED N18 100 B6
New Park Rd ASHF TW15 174 D8
BRXS/STRHM SW2 180 F3
DEN/HRF UB9 91 M9
HERT/BAY SG13 42 E10
New Peachey La UX/CGN UB8 131 N8
Newpiece LOU IG10 82 E7
New Pl ASC SL5 * 192 D9
New Place Gdns REDH RH1 258 A9
UPMR RM14 126 C7
New Place Sq
BERM/RHTH SE16 * 160 A2
New Plaistow Rd SRTFD E15 141 K3
New Pond Pde RSLP HA4 * 113 H8
New Pond Rd GODL GU7 267 K8
Newport Av PLSTW E13 141 N6
POP/IOD E14 141 J9
Newport Cl PEND EN3 80 D3
Newport Ct LSQ/SEVD WC2H 11 K7
Newport Md OXHEY WD19 * 93 L5
Newport Pl SOHO/SHAV W1D * 11 K7
Newport Rd BARN SW13 156 D7
HTHAIR TW6 152 B7
LEY E10 121 J7
SLN SL2 128 D6
WALTH E17 * 120 D2
YEAD UB4 132 E7
Newports SBW CM21 29 M2
SWLY BR8 208 E7
Newport St LBTH SE11 17 N6
Newquay Crs RYLN/HDSTN HA2 113 M7
Newquay Gdns OXHEY WD19 93 J3
Newquay Rd CAT SE6 182 G5
New Quebec St MBLAR W1H 10 B6
New River Av CEND/HSY/T N8 118 G1
WARE SG12 26 G7
New River Cl HOD EN11 44 G2
New River Crs PLMGR N13 99 J5
New River Wy FSBYPK N4 119 L5
New Rd ABR/ST RM4 83 N10
ABYW SE2 163 N5
AMS HP6 69 K3
AMSS HP7 68 E8
BERK HP4 33 L2
BERK HP4 34 A4
BORE WD6 75 J10
BROX EN10 44 E5
BRW CM14 107 J5
BTFD TW8 155 J5
CEND/HSY/T N8 118 F5
CHING E4 100 G5
CSTG HP8 70 B7
DAGE RM10 144 B4
DTCH/LGLY SL3 150 A7
DTCH/LGLY SL3 150 D2
E/WMO/HCT KT8 197 P3
EBED/NFELT TW14 174 E2
ED N9 100 A3
ESH/CLAY KT10 218 B1
ESH/CLAY KT10 218 E6
EYN DA4 210 B2
FELT TW13 175 M8
GDMY/SEVK IG3 123 H7
GRAYS RM17 167 N5
GSTN WD25 74 D5
GVW DA11 190 E2
HERT/WAT SG14 25 L3
HLWE CM17 29 N7
HORL RH6 281 J4
HRW HA1 114 E9
HSLW TW3 154 A10
HYS/HAR UB3 152 D6
KGLGY WD4 53 J6
KUTN/CMB KT2 177 M10
KWD/TDW/WH KT20 238 F9
LHD/OX KT22 218 E7
MLHL NW7 97 H8
MTCM CR4 202 B8
ORP BR6 207 K7
OXTED RH8 261 N6
POTB/CUF EN6 58 D9
RAD WD7 57 M10
RAD WD7 74 D2
RAIN RM13 145 H5
RCHPK/HAM TW10 177 H7
RGUE GU4 251 P7
RGUE GU4 268 E7
RKW/CH/CXG WD3 71 J5
RKW/CH/CXG WD3 72 B9
RSEV TN14 245 N10
SHGR GU5 268 E9
SHGR GU5 269 N5
SHGR GU5 270 D5
SHPTN TW17 196 B3
SOCK/AV RM15 145 N10
STA TW18 172 F8
SWLY BR8 186 G10
SWLY BR8 208 G3
TOTM N17 99 N9
UX/CGN UB8 132 D6
WARE SG12 26 D2
WAT WD17 73 L8
WDGN N22 99 K9
WELL DA16 163 L9
WEY KT13 216 D2
WGCW AL8 22 D8
EBED/NFELT TW14 175 J4
New Road Hl HAYES BR2 226 B5
New Rw CHCR WC2N 11 L7
Newry Rd TWK TW1 154 F10
Newsam Av SEVS/STOTM N15 119 L3
Newsham Rd WOKN/KNAP GU21 231 L3
Newsholme Dr WCHMH N21 78 G9
New Site ADL/WDHM KT15 * 215 P1
New Spring Gardens Wk
STHWK SE1 * 17 M8
New Sq EBED/NFELT TW14 174 D4
LINN WC2A 11 P5
SL SL1 149 L1
Newstead HAT AL10 40 C7
Newstead Av ORP BR6 206 G10
Newstead Cl NFNCH/WDSPK N12 97 P7
Newstead Ct NTHLT UB5 * 133 M5
Newstead Hall HORL RH6 280 E5
Newstead Ri CTHM CR3 260 A2
Newstead Rd LEE/GVPK SE12 183 L3
Newstead Wk CAR SM5 201 M7
Newstead Wy WIM/MER SW19 178 G7
New St BERK HP4 34 A5
BH/WHM TN16 262 F3
CRAWE RH10 284 B6
LVPST EC2M 13 K4
STA TW18 173 K7
WAT WD17 * 73 K8
New Street Hl BMLY BR1 183 N8
New Street Rd MEO DA13 211 P10
New Street Sq FLST/FETLN EC4A 12 B5
New Swan Yd GVE DA12 190 E2
New Tank Hill Rd PUR RM19 165 P2
Newteswell Dr WAB EN9 63 J8
Newton Abbot Rd GVW DA11 190 C5
Newton Av ACT W3 155 P1
MUSWH N10 98 B9
Newton Cl DTCH/LGLY SL3 150 C2

HARP AL5 20 C5
HOD EN11 26 G9
RYLN/HDSTN HA2 113 P7
WALTH E17 120 D4
Newton Ct WDSR SL4 171 M2
Newton Crs BORE WD6 75 P8
Newton Dr SBW CM21 29 N2
Newton Gv CHSWK W4 156 B3
Newton La WDSR SL4 171 N2
Newton Pl POP/IOD E14 160 F3
Newton Rd ACT W3 155 P1
ALP/SUD HA0 135 L2
BAY/PAD W2 8 F6
CRAWE RH10 284 A3
CRICK NW2 116 F9
ISLW TW7 154 E8
KTN/HRWW/WS HA3 94 D10
PUR/KEN CR8 222 D8
SEVS/STOTM N15 119 N3
SRTFD E15 * 121 J10
TIL RM18 168 D8
WELL DA16 163 K9
WIM/MER SW19 179 H10
Newtons Cl RAIN RM13 144 F2
Newton's Ct RDART DA2 166 C10
Newtonside Orch WDSR SL4 * 171 M2
Newton St HOL/ALD WC2B 11 M5
Newton's Yd WAND/EARL SW18 179 K1
Newton Ter HAYES BR2 206 A6
Newton Wk EDGW HA8 95 P9
Newton Wy UED N18 99 K6
Newton Wood Rd ASHTD KT21 237 L2
New Tower Buildings
WAP E1W * 140 A10
New Town CRAWE RH10 285 J2
Newtown Rd DEN/HRF UB9 131 L1
Newtown St BTSEA SW11 158 C7
New Trinity Rd EFNCH N2 117 N1
New Union Cl POP/IOD E14 161 H2
New Union St BARB EC2Y 12 G4
New Vls TOTM N17 * 99 P9
New Wanstead WAN E11 121 M4
New Way La HLWE CM17 30 E10
New Way Rd CDALE/KGS NW9 116 C2
New Wharf Rd IS N1 5 M7
New Wickham La EGH TW20 172 D10
New Wd WGCE AL7 23 M4
Newyears Green La
DEN/HRF UB9 112 B4
New Years La RSEV TN14 245 J2
New Zealand Av WOT/HER KT12 196 G8
New Zealand Wy RAIN RM13 144 G5
Niagara Av EA W5 155 H3
Niagara Cl CHES/WCR EN8 62 C5
IS N1 6 F7
Nibthwaite Rd HRW HA1 114 D3
Nicholas Cl GFD/PVL UB6 134 A4
SOCK/AV RM15 147 H5
STALW/RED AL3 38 C3
WATN WD24 73 J3
Nicholas Gdns EA W5 135 J10
SL SL1 128 D10
WOKS/MYFD GU22 233 J2
Nicholas La HERT/WAT SG14 25 L5
MANHO EC4N 13 H7
Nicholas Rd BCTR RM8 124 A7
BORE WD6 75 L10
CROY/NA CR0 222 F1
WCHPL E1 140 B6
Nicholas Wy HHNE HP2 36 A4
NTHWD HA6 92 D9
Nicholay Rd ARCH N19 118 E6
Nichol Cl STHGT/OAK N14 98 E2
Nicholes Rd HSLW TW3 153 P10
Nichol La BMLY BR1 183 M10
Nicholl Rd EPP CM16 65 J7
Nicholls WDSR SL4 148 B9
Nicholls Av UX/CGN UB8 132 B6
Nicholls Fld HLWS CM18 47 L2
Nichollsfield Wk HOLWY N7 118 F10
Nicholl St BETH E2 7 N6
Nichols Cl FSBYPK N4 * 119 H6
Nichols Gn EA W5 135 K7
Nicholson Dr BUSH WD23 94 B2
Nicholson House CHARL SE7 * 162 B6
Nicholson Ms EGH TW20 * 172 D8
KUT/HW KT1 199 K4
Nicholson Rd CROY/NA CR0 203 N8
Nicholson St STHWK SE1 12 C10
Nicholson Wk EGH TW20 172 D8
Nickelby Cl THMD SE28 143 M8
Nickleby Cl UX/CGN UB8 132 C8
Nickleby Rd GVE DA12 191 K4
Nickols Wk WAND/EARL SW18 157 L10
Nicky Line HHNE HP2 35 P6
Nicola Cl KTN/HRWW/WS HA3 94 C10
SAND/SEL CR2 223 K3
Nicola Ms BARK/HLT IG6 102 E8
Nicol Cl CFSP/GDCR SL9 89 P9
TWK TW1 176 G2
Nicol End CFSP/GDCR SL9 89 P9
Nicoll Pl HDN NW4 116 E4
Nicoll Rd WLSDN NW10 136 B3
Nicolls Cl CTHM CR3 241 K8
Nicoll Wy BORE WD6 76 A9
Nicol Rd CFSP/GDCR SL9 89 P9
Nicolson Rd STMC/STPC BR5 207 M7
Nicosia Rd WAND/EARL SW18 179 P3
Nidderdale HHNE HP2 36 A3
Niederwald Rd SYD SE26 182 D7
Nield Rd HYS/HAR UB3 152 G1
Nigel Cl NTHLT UB5 133 M3
Nigel Fisher Wy CHSGTN KT9 219 J4
Nigel Ms IL IG1 122 E9
Nigel Playfair Av HMSMTH W6 156 E3
Nigel Rd FSTGT E7 121 P10
PECK SE15 159 P9
Nigeria Rd CHARL SE7 161 P6
Nightingale Av CHING E4 101 K6
EHSLY KT24 252 E1
UPMR RM14 126 E6
Nightingale Cl ABLGY WD5 55 H7
BH/WHM TN16 243 P1
CAR SM5 202 B9
CHING E4 101 K5
CHSWK W4 155 P5
COB KT11 217 L8
CRAWW RH11 283 M5
GVW DA11 190 B7
HOR/WEW KT19 219 M8
PIN HA5 113 K3
RAD WD7 74 E2
Nightingale Cnr
STMC/STPC BR5 * 207 N4
Nightingale Ct SL SL1 149 M2
SUT SM1 221 M2
Nightingale Crs EHSLY KT24 252 E1
HARH RM3 105 M10
Nightingale Dr HOR/WEW KT19 219 N3
Nightingale Gv LEW SE13 183 J1
Nightingale La BAL SW12 180 B2
BMLY BR1 205 P2
CEND/HSY/T N8 118 F2
RCHPK/HAM TW10 177 K3
RSEV TN14 264 C6
STALE/WH AL4 39 H9
WAN E11 121 N3
Nightingale Ms KUT/HW KT1 * 199 J3
LBTH SE11 18 B5
Nightingale Pk SLN SL2 128 E2
Nightingale Pl
RKW/CH/CXG WD3 91 N1
WBPTN SW10 15 K9
WOOL/PLUM SE18 162 D5
Nightingale Rd BGR/WK TN15 247 L3
BUSH WD23 73 P9
CAR SM5 202 A10
CHESW EN7 61 K1
CLPT E5 120 A8
CSHM HP5 * 50 G5
E/WMO/HCT KT8 198 A5
ED N9 100 B1
EHSLY KT24 252 G1
ESH/CLAY KT10 217 N2
GU GU1 250 B10
HNWL W7 134 E10
HPTN TW12 175 P9
RKW/CH/CXG WD3 91 M1
SAND/SEL CR2 224 C7
STMC/STPC BR5 206 F6
WDGN N22 98 F9
WLSDN NW10 136 C4
WOT/HER KT12 * 197 K7
Nightingale Shott EGH TW20 172 C9
Nightingales La CSTG HP8 70 A9
Nightingale Sq BAL SW12 180 B3
The Nightingales
STWL/WRAY TW19 174 A4
Nightingale V WOOL/PLUM SE18 162 E5
Nightingale Wk BAL SW12 180 C2
WDSR SL4 149 H9
Nightingale Wy DEN/HRF UB9 111 J4
EHAM E6 142 B7
REDH RH1 259 M10
SWLY BR8 208 F3
Nigntingale Av HRW HA1 114 G5
Nile Cl STNW/STAM N16 119 N8
Nile Dr ED N9 100 B3
Nile Rd PLSTW E13 141 P4
Nile St IS N1 6 G9
Nile Ter PECK SE15 19 M8
Nimbus Rd HOR/WEW KT19 220 A6
Nimmo Dr BUSH WD23 94 C1
Nimrod Cl NTHLT UB5 133 L5
STALE/WH AL4 39 H4
Nimrod Dr HAT AL10 40 A3
Nimrod Pas IS N1 * 7 K2
Nimrod Rd STRHM/NOR SW16 180 C9
Nina Mackay Cl SRTFD E15 * 141 K3
Nine Acre La HAT AL10 40 C5
Nine Acres SL SL1 128 E10
Nine Acres Cl MNPK E12 122 B10
Nineacres Wy COUL/CHIP CR5 240 F2
Nine Ashes WARE SG12 28 A4
Nine Elms Av UX/CGN UB8 131 N7
Nine Elms Cl EBED/NFELT TW14 174 G4
UX/CGN UB8 131 N7
Nine Elms Gv GVW DA11 190 D3
Nine Elms La VX/NE SW8 17 K10
Ninefields WAB EN9 63 M9
Ninehams Cl CTHM CR3 241 L6
Ninehams Gdns CTHM CR3 241 L6
Ninehams Rd BH/WHM TN16 244 A7
CTHM CR3 241 L7
Nine Stiles Cl DEN/HRF UB9 131 L1
Nineteenth Rd MTCM CR4 202 F4
Ninhams Wd ORP BR6 226 D1
Ninian Rd HHNE HP2 35 P1
Ninnings Rd CFSP/GDCR SL9 90 C8
Ninnings Wy CFSP/GDCR SL9 90 C8
Ninth Av HYS/HAR UB3 133 H9
KWD/TDW/WH KT20 * 257 J2
Nisbett Wk SCUP DA14 185 K7
Nita Rd BRW CM14 107 H6
Nithdale Rd WOOL/PLUM SE18 162 E6
Nithsdale Gv HGDN/ICK UB10 112 D8
Niton Cl BAR EN5 76 G10
Niton Rd RCH/KEW TW9 * 155 M9
Niton St FUL/PGN SW6 156 G6
Niven Cl BORE WD6 75 P5
CRAWE RH10 284 E8
Nixey Cl SL SL1 149 M1
Nizels La RTON TN11 265 N10
No1 St WOOL/PLUM SE18 162 E2
No2 St WOOL/PLUM SE18 162 E2
Noahs Ct CRAWE RH10 * 285 P9
Noake Mill La HHW HP1 35 K1
Noak Hill Rd ABR/ST RM4 105 J6
Nobel Dr HYS/HAR UB3 152 F6
Nobel Rd UED N18 100 B5
Noble Cnr HEST TW5 * 153 P7
Noble St CITYW EC2V 12 E5
Nobles Wy EGH TW20 172 B10
Noel Rd ACT W3 135 M8
EHAM E6 142 B6
IS N1 6 C7
Noel St SOHO/CST W1F 11 H6
Noke Dr REDH RH1 258 B9
Noke La LCOL/BKTW AL2 55 M2
Noke Side LCOL/BKTW AL2 55 P3
The Nokes HHW HP1 35 K4
Nolan Wy CLPT E5 119 P9
Nolton Pl EDGW HA8 95 L9
Nonsuch Cl CHIG IG7 102 E7
Nonsuch Court Av EW KT17 220 E6
Nonsuch Pl CHEAM SM3 * 220 G4
Nonsuch Wk BELMT SM2 220 G6
The Nook WARE SG12 26 G7
Noons Corner Rd RDKG RH5 271 N9
Nora Gdns HDN NW4 116 G2
Norbiton Av KUT/HW KT1 199 M2
Norbiton Common Rd
KUT/HW KT1 199 N3
Norbiton Rd POP/IOD E14 140 E8
Norbreck Pde EA W5 135 K5
Norbroke St SHB W12 136 C9
Norburn St NKENS W10 8 A4
Norbury Av HSLW TW3 176 C1
STRHM/NOR SW16 202 G1
WATN WD24 73 K5
Norbury Cl STRHM/NOR SW16 203 H1
Norbury Court Rd
STRHM/NOR SW16 202 F2
Norbury Crs STRHM/NOR SW16 203 H2
Norbury Cross
STRHM/NOR SW16 202 F3
Norbury Gdns CHDH RM6 123 N3
Norbury Gv MLHL NW7 96 B4
Norbury Hl STRHM/NOR SW16 181 H10
Norbury Ri STRHM/NOR SW16 202 F3
Norbury Rd CHING E4 100 F6
FELT TW13 174 G6
REIG RH2 257 J10
THHTH CR7 203 K2
Norbury Vls KUT/HW KT1 * 199 L2
Norbury Wy GT/LBKH KT23 254 B1
Norcombe Gdns
KTN/HRWW/WS HA3 115 H4
Norcott Cl YEAD UB4 133 K6
Norcott Rd STNW/STAM N16 119 P7
Norcroft Gdns EDUL SE22 181 P3
Norcutt Rd WHTN TW2 176 D4
Nordenfeldt Rd ERITH DA8 164 E4
Nordmann Pl SOCK/AV RM15 147 J6
Norelands Dr SL SL1 128 B4
Norfield Rd RDART DA2 186 D7
Norfolk Av PLMGR N13 99 J7
SAND/SEL CR2 223 P6
SEVS/STOTM N15 119 N4
SL SL1 129 H7
WATN WD24 73 K4
Norfolk Cl DART DA1 187 P2
EBAR EN4 78 B8
EFNCH N2 117 P1
HORL RH6 280 B5
PLMGR N13 99 J7
TWK TW1 * 176 G2
Norfolk Ct BAR EN5 * 77 H8
Norfolk Crs BAY/PAD W2 9 N5
BFN/LL DA15 185 H3
Norfolk Farm Cl
WOKS/MYFD GU22 232 G2
Norfolk Farm Rd
WOKS/MYFD GU22 232 G2
Norfolk Gdns BORE WD6 76 A8
BXLYHN DA7 164 A7
WOKN/KNAP GU21 * 231 L5
Norfolk House
RKW/CH/CXG WD3 * 91 P2
Norfolk House Rd
STRHM/NOR SW16 180 E6
Norfolk La RDKG RH5 272 G8
Norfolk Ms NKENS W10 8 B4
Norfolk Pl BAY/PAD W2 9 M5
CDW/CHF RM16 167 H4
WELL DA16 163 K8
Norfolk Rd BAR EN5 77 K7
BARK IG11 143 H2
DAGE RM10 124 C10
DORK RH4 272 F2
EHAM E6 142 C3
ESH/CLAY KT10 218 D2
FELT TW13 175 K4
GDMY/SEVK IG3 123 H6
GVE DA12 190 G3
HRW HA1 114 A3
PEND EN3 80 A10
RKW/CH/CXG WD3 91 P2
ROMW/RG RM7 124 D4
STJWD NW8 3 M6
THHTH CR7 203 K3
UPMR RM14 125 P8
UX/CGN UB8 131 N1
WALTH E17 100 C9
WIM/MER SW19 179 P10
WLSDN NW10 136 B2
Norfolk Rw STHWK SE1 17 N5
Norfolk Sq BAY/PAD W2 9 M6
Norfolk Square Ms BAY/PAD W2 9 M6
Norfolk St FSTGT E7 121 M10
Norgrove Pk CFSP/GDCR SL9 110 B2
Norgrove St BAL SW12 180 B4
Norheads La BH/WHM TN16 243 N3
Norhyrst Av SNWD SE25 203 N3
Nork Gdns BNSTD SM7 221 H10
Nork Ri BNSTD SM7 238 G2
Nork Wy BNSTD SM7 238 G1
Norland Pl NTGHL W11 8 B10
Norland Rd NTGHL W11 136 G10
Norlands Crs CHST BR7 206 E1
Norlands Ga CHST BR7 * 206 E1
Norlands La EGH TW20 195 H2
Norland Sq NTGHL W11 8 B10
Norley V PUT/ROE SW15 178 D4
Norlington Rd LEY E10 121 H6
Norman Av EW KT17 220 C8
FELT TW13 175 M5
SAND/SEL CR2 223 K6
STHL UB1 133 M9
TWK TW1 176 G3
WDGN N22 99 K9
Normanby Cl PUT/ROE SW15 179 J1
Normanby Rd WLSDN NW10 116 C10
Norman Cl BGR/WK TN15 247 L3
EPSOM KT18 238 E5
ORP BR6 206 F10
ROMW/RG RM7 104 C10
STAL AL1 38 D9
WAB EN9 63 J9
Norman Colyer Ct
HOR/WEW KT19 * 220 A6
Norman Ct POTB/CUF EN6 59 M7
Norman Crs HEST TW5 153 L6
PIN HA5 93 K9
RBRW/HUT CM13 107 M4
Normand Gdns WKENS W14 * 157 H5
Normand Ms WKENS W14 14 B9
Normand Rd WKENS W14 14 C9
Normandy Av BAR EN5 77 J9
Normandy Cl CRAWE RH10 284 C9
SYD SE26 182 D6
Normandy Common La
RGUW GU3 248 A7
Normandy Ct HHNE HP2 35 N5
Normandy Dr BERK HP4 33 M4
HYS/HAR UB3 132 D8
Normandy Rd BRXN/ST SW9 159 H7
STALW/RED AL3 38 C5
Normandy Ter CAN/RD E16 141 N8
Normandy Wk EGH TW20 * 172 F8
Normandy Wy ERITH DA8 164 F7
HOD EN11 45 J1
Norman Gv BOW E3 140 D4
Normanhurst RBRW/HUT CM13 87 P10
Normanhurst Av WELL DA16 163 N7
Normanhurst Cl CRAWE RH10 284 A7
Normanhurst Dr TWK TW1 176 G1
Normanhurst Rd
BRXS/STRHM SW2 180 G5
STMC/STPC BR5 207 L2
WOT/HER KT12 197 L9
Norman Pde SCUP DA14 * 185 P6
Norman Rd ASHF TW15 174 E10
BELV DA17 144 C10
DART DA1 187 M4
EHAM E6 142 C6
EMPK RM11 125 H5
GNWCH SE10 160 G6
IL IG1 122 E10
SEVS/STOTM N15 119 N3
SUT SM1 221 K2
THHTH CR7 203 J5
WAN E11 121 K7
WIM/MER SW19 179 M10
Normans Cl GVW DA11 190 D3
UX/CGN UB8 131 P7
WDGN N22 * 99 K9
WLSDN NW10 136 A1
Normansfield Av KUT/HW KT1 177 H10
Normansfield Cl BUSH WD23 94 A1
Normanshire Dr CHING E4 100 F5
Normans Md WLSDN NW10 136 A1
Norman's Rd HORL RH6 281 K2
The Normans SLN SL2 129 N8
Norman St FSBYE EC1V 6 E10
RSEV TN14 263 P6
Norman Ter KIL/WHAMP NW6 * 117 J10
Normanton Av
WAND/EARL SW18 179 K5
Normanton Pk CHING E4 101 K4
Normanton Rd SAND/SEL CR2 223 M3
Normanton St FSTH SE23 182 C5
Norman Wy ACT W3 135 N7
STHGT/OAK N14 98 F3
Normington Cl
STRHM/NOR SW16 181 H8
Norrels Dr EHSLY KT24 252 G2
Norrels Ride EHSLY KT24 252 G2
Norrice Lea EFNCH N2 117 N3
Norris Cl LCOL/BKTW AL2 56 G2
Norris Gv BROX EN10 44 D6
Norris La HOD EN11 44 F2
Norris Ri HOD EN11 44 E2
Norris Rd HOD EN11 44 F3
Norris St STJS SW1Y 11 J8
Norris Wy DART DA1 164 G9
Norroy Rd PUT/ROE SW15 156 G10
Norrys Cl EBAR EN4 78 A9
Norrys Rd EBAR EN4 78 A8
Norseman Cl GDMY/SEVK IG3 123 L6
Norseman Wy GFD/PVL UB6 134 A3
Norstead Pl PUT/ROE SW15 178 D5
Norsted La ORP BR6 227 L7
North Access Rd WALTH E17 120 D4
North Acre BNSTD SM7 239 J2
CDALE/KGS NW9 96 B9
North Acton Rd WLSDN NW10 136 A4
Northallerton Wy HARH RM3 105 L6
Northall Rd BXLYHN DA7 164 D8
Northampton Avevue SL SL1 129 H8
Northampton Gv IS N1 119 L10
Northampton Pk IS N1 6 F1
Northampton Rd CLKNW EC1R 12 B1
CROY/NA CR0 203 P9
PEND EN3 80 D8
Northampton Rw CLKNW EC1R * 12 B1
Northampton Sq FSBYE EC1V 6 C10
Northampton St IS N1 6 E3
Northanger Rd
STRHM/NOR SW16 180 F9
North Ap GSTN WD25 55 H10
NTHWD HA6 92 D3
North Ash Rd HART DA3 211 M10
North Audley St
MYFR/PKLN W1K 10 C7
North Av CAR SM5 222 B4
HYS/HAR UB3 133 H9
RAD WD7 57 K8
RCH/KEW TW9 155 M7
RYLN/HDSTN HA2 114 A4
STHL UB1 133 N9
UED N18 99 P5
WEA W13 134 G8
WOT/HER KT12 216 G5
Northaw Cl HHNE HP2 36 C1
Northaw Pl POTB/CUF EN6 * 59 P6
Northaw Rd West POTB/CUF EN6 60 C7
North Bank STJWD NW8 3 N10
Northbank Rd WALTH E17 101 H10
North Barn BROX EN10 44 G8
North Birkbeck Rd WAN E11 121 J8
Northborough Rd SLN SL2 128 F6
STRHM/NOR SW16 202 F2
Northbourne GODL GU7 267 L9
HAYES BR2 205 M7
Northbourne Rd CLAP SW4 158 E10
North Bridge Rd BERK HP4 33 L3
Northbrook Dr NTHWD HA6 92 F9
Northbrook Rd BAR EN5 77 H10
CROY/NA CR0 203 L5
IL IG1 122 D7
LEW SE13 183 J1
WDGN N22 98 F8
Northbrooks HLWW/ROY CM19 46 F2
Northburgh St FSBYE EC1V 12 D2
North Burnham Cl SL SL1 128 A4
North Carriage Dr BAY/PAD W2 9 P7
Northchurch La CSHM HP5 33 H7
Northchurch Rd IS N1 6 G3
WBLY HA9 135 M1
Northchurch Ter IS N1 7 J4
North Circular PLMGR N13 99 J6
WALTH E17 100 G9
North Circular Rd BARK IG11 142 D2
CHING E4 * 100 D7
CRICK NW2 116 B8
GLDGN NW11 117 H4
NFNCH/WDSPK N12 97 P8
REDBR IG4 121 P1
WLSDN NW10 135 L4
Northcliffe Cl WPK KT4 200 B10
Northcliffe Dr TRDG/WHET N20 97 J2
North Cl BAR EN5 76 F9
BXLYHS DA6 163 N10
CHIG IG7 103 K6
CRAWE RH10 284 A6
DAGE RM10 144 B3
EBED/NFELT TW14 174 E2
LCOL/BKTW AL2 56 A1
MRDN SM4 201 H4
RDKG RH5 273 H6
WDSR SL4 148 E7
The North Colonnade
POP/IOD E14 140 G10
North Common WEY KT13 * 216 D1
North Common Rd EA W5 135 K9
UX/CGN UB8 111 N10
Northcote ADL/WDHM KT15 215 N1
Northcote Av BRYLDS KT5 199 M7
EA W5 135 K9
ISLW TW7 176 F1
STHL UB1 133 M9
Northcote Crs EHSLY KT24 252 D1
Northcote Rd BTSEA SW11 157 P10
CROY/NA CR0 203 L6
EHSLY KT24 252 D1
GVW DA11 190 C4
NWMAL KT3 199 P3
SCUP DA14 185 H7
TWK TW1 176 F1
WALTH E17 120 D2
WLSDN NW10 136 B2
Northcott Av WDGN N22 98 F9
North Countess Rd WALTH E17 100 E10
Northcourt FITZ W1T 11 H3
RKW/CH/CXG WD3 * 91 K2
North Cray Rd BXLY DA5 186 B5
SCUP DA14 185 P9
North Crs CAN/RD E16 141 J6
FNCH N3 97 J10
GWRST WC1E 11 J3
Northcroft SLN SL2 128 G6
Northcroft Cl EGH TW20 171 N8
Northcroft Gdns EGH TW20 171 N8
Northcroft Rd EGH TW20 171 N8
HOR/WEW KT19 220 B4
WEA W13 154 G1
Northcroft Vls EGH TW20 171 N8
North Cross Rd BARK/HLT IG6 122 F2
EDUL SE22 181 N1
Northdene CHIG IG7 102 G6
North Dene HSLW TW3 154 A7
MLHL NW7 96 A4
Northdene Gdns
SEVS/STOTM N15 119 N4
North Down SAND/SEL CR2 223 M7
Northdown Cl RSLP HA4 112 G8
Northdown Ct GDST RH9 260 B6
Northdown Gdns
GNTH/NBYPK IG2 123 H3
Northdown La GU GU1 268 B3
Northdown Rd BELMT SM2 221 K6
BGR/WK TN15 247 M3
CFSP/GDCR SL9 90 B7
CTHM CR3 260 F1
EMPK RM11 125 J5
HART DA3 211 K2
HAT AL10 40 D7
WELL DA16 163 L8
North Downs Crs CROY/NA CR0 224 G6
North Downs Rd CROY/NA CR0 224 G6
Northdown St IS N1 5 N8
North Downs Wy
BRKHM/BTCW RH3 256 A7
CTHM CR3 258 G2
GDST RH9 260 E4
KWD/TDW/WH KT20 255 L8
KWD/TDW/WH KT20 256 G6
RDKG RH5 254 D9
REDH RH1 258 F2
RGUE GU4 268 D4
RGUW GU3 266 D5
RSEV TN14 247 L1
SEV TN13 246 E4
SHGR GU5 269 H4
WARL CR6 243 M9
North Dr BECK BR3 204 G4
CHOB/PIR GU24 230 B7
GPK RM2 125 K1
HAT AL10 40 F2
HSLW TW3 154 B8
ORP BR6 227 H1
RSLP HA4 112 F5
STALE/WH AL4 39 K4
STRHM/NOR SW16 180 D7
VW GU25 193 K5
North End CROY/NA CR0 203 K9
HAMP NW3 117 M7
HARH RM3 105 K3
BKHH IG9 101 P1
Northend BRW CM14 107 H6
HHS/BOV HP3 36 C8
North End Av HAMP NW3 117 M7
North End Crs WKENS W14 14 C6
North End La ASC SL5 192 G7
ORP BR6 226 E5
Northend Rd ERITH DA8 164 G7
North End Rd FUL/PGN SW6 157 K6
GLDGN NW11 117 K6
WBLY HA9 115 N8
WKENS W14 14 B6
North End Wy HAMP NW3 117 M7
Northern Av ED N9 99 N3
Northernhay Wk MRDN SM4 201 H4
Northern Perimeter Rd
HTHAIR TW6 152 D7
Northern Perimeter Road
(West) WDR/YW UB7 151 M7
Northern Relief Rd BARK IG11 142 F2
Northern Rd SLN SL2 129 J6
Northey Av BELMT SM2 220 G6
North Eyot Gdns HMSMTH W6 * 156 C4
Northey St POP/IOD E14 140 D9
North Farm LOU IG10 81 P10
Northfield HART DA3 211 L3
LTWR GU18 212 A7
RGUE GU4 268 B8
Northfield Av PIN HA5 113 L2
STMC/STPC BR5 207 M6
WEA W13 134 G10
Northfield Cl BMLY BR1 206 B1
HYS/HAR UB3 152 G2
Northfield Ct STA TW18 195 L1
Northfield Crs CHEAM SM3 221 H1
Northfield Farm Ms COB KT11 217 H9
Northfield Gdns WATN WD24 73 K3
Northfield Pde HYS/HAR UB3 * 152 G2
Northfield Pk HYS/HAR UB3 152 G2
Northfield Pl WEY KT13 216 C4
Northfield Rd BORE WD6 75 N5
CHES/WCR EN8 62 D8
COB KT11 217 H9
DAGW RM9 124 A9
EBAR EN4 77 P7
ED N9 * 80 A9
EHAM E6 142 C1
HEST TW5 153 L5
STA TW18 195 L1
STNW/STAM N16 119 M5
WDSR SL4 148 E3
WEA W13 154 G1
Northfields ASHTD KT21 237 K5
EW KT17 220 B7
GRAYS RM17 167 P3
WAND/EARL SW18 157 K10
Northfields Rd ACT W3 135 P7
North Gdns WIM/MER SW19 179 N10
North Ga HLW CM20 28 F10
Northgate NTHWD HA6 92 D8
Northgate Av CRAWE RH10 284 A6
Northgate Dr CDALE/KGS NW9 116 B4
Northgate Pth BORE WD6 75 L4
Northgate Pl CRAWE RH10 283 P6
Northgate Rd CRAWE RH10 283 N7
HORL RH6 280 A6
North Gower St CAMTN NW1 4 G10
North Gn SL SL1 129 K9
North Gv CHERT KT16 195 J6
HGT N6 118 B5
HLWS CM18 47 K2
SEVS/STOTM N15 119 L3
North Hl HGT N6 118 A4
RKW/CH/CXG WD3 71 H6
North Hill Av HGT N6 118 A4
North Hill Dr HARH RM3 105 L5
North Hyde Gdns HYS/HAR UB3 153 H2
North Hyde La NWDGN UB2 153 M4
North Hyde Rd HYS/HAR UB3 152 F2
North Hyde Whf NWDGN UB2 * 153 K3
Northiam NFNCH/WDSPK N12 97 K5
Northiam St HACK E8 140 A3
Northington St BMSBY WC1N 11 N3
North Kent Av GVW DA11 189 P2
North Kent Aveune GVW DA11 189 P2
Northlands POTB/CUF EN6 59 N7
Northlands Av ORP BR6 227 H1
Northlands St CMBW SE5 159 K8
North La TEDD TW11 176 E9
North Lodge Cl PUT/ROE SW15 * 178 G1
North Looe EW KT17 * 220 F9
North Md CRAWE RH10 283 P5
REDH RH1 258 A7
Northmead Rd SLN SL2 128 E6
North Ms BMSBY WC1N 11 P2
North Moors GU GU1 250 B6
North Mt TRDG/WHET N20 * 97 M3
Northolm EDGW HA8 96 A5
Northolme Cl CDW/CHF RM16 * 167 P2
Northolme Gdns EDGW HA8 95 M9
Northolme Ri ORP BR6 207 H9
Northolme Rd HBRY N5 119 K9
Northolt Av RSLP HA4 113 J10
Northolt Gdns GFD/PVL UB6 114 E10
Northolt Rd RYLN/HDSTN HA2 114 A9
WDR/YW UB7 151 N7
Northolt Wy HCH RM12 125 K10
North Orbital Rd DEN/HRF UB9 111 J3
LCOL/BKTW AL2 55 M6
North Orbital Rd St Albans Rd
GSTN WD25 55 L8
Northover BMLY BR1 183 L7
North Pde CHSGTN KT9 219 L2
EDGW HA8 * 95 M10
STHL UB1 * 133 P8
North Pk CFSP/GDCR SL9 110 B2
DTCH/LGLY SL3 150 G2
ELTH/MOT SE9 184 C2
North Park La GDST RH9 259 P6
North Pas WAND/EARL SW18 179 K1
North Peckham Est PECK SE15 159 N6
North Pl HLW CM20 29 L6
MTCM CR4 180 A10
TEDD TW11 176 E9
WAB EN9 62 G9
Northpoint Cl SUT SM1 201 M10
North Pole La HAYES BR2 225 M3
North Pole Rd SHB W12 136 F8
Northport St IS N1 7 H6
Northridge Rd GVE DA12 190 F6
Northridge Wy HHW HP1 35 J7
North Riding LCOL/BKTW AL2 55 P6
North Ri BAY/PAD W2 * 9 P6
North Rd ABR/ST RM4 104 F3
AMS HP6 69 H2
BELV DA17 164 C2
BERK HP4 33 N5
BMLY BR1 205 N1
BRW CM14 107 H2
CHDH RM6 123 P3
CHES/WCR EN8 62 D9
CRAWE RH10 284 B6
DART DA1 186 G2
EA W5 155 J2
EBED/NFELT TW14 174 E2
ED N9 100 A2
EDGW HA8 95 N9
GDMY/SEVK IG3 123 H7
GUW GU2 249 N7
HERT/WAT SG14 25 H4
HEST TW5 153 K5
HGT N6 118 B5
HOD EN11 44 F2
HOLWY N7 5 L1
HYS/HAR UB3 132 E7
PUR RM19 166 B3
RCH/KEW TW9 155 M8
REIG RH2 275 J3
RKW/CH/CXG WD3 70 G9
SOCK/AV RM15 147 J3
STHL UB1 133 P9
SURB KT6 199 J6
WDR/YW UB7 152 A2
WIM/MER SW19 179 N9
WOKN/KNAP GU21 232 D2
WOOL/PLUM SE18 163 H3
WOT/HER KT12 217 K2
WWKM BR4 204 G8
North Road Av BRW CM14 107 H3
HERT/WAT SG14 25 H4
North Road Gdns
HERT/WAT SG14 25 J5
Northrop Rd HTHAIR TW6 152 F7
North Rw DTCH/LGLY SL3 * 110 B9
MYFR/PKLN W1K 10 B7
North Several BKHTH/KID SE3 * 161 J8
Northside Rd BMLY BR1 205 M1
North Side Wandsworth
Common WAND/EARL SW18 179 M1
Northspur Rd SUT SM1 201 K10
North Sq ED N9 100 A3
GLDGN NW11 117 K4
North Station Ap REDH RH1 * 276 G2
Northstead Rd
BRXS/STRHM SW2 181 H5
North St BARK IG11 142 E2
BMLY BR1 205 M1
BXLYHN DA7 164 B10
CAR SM5 222 A1
CLAP SW4 158 C9
CRAWE RH10 285 P9
DART DA1 187 L3
DORK RH4 272 F2
EGH TW20 172 C8
EMPK RM11 125 L5
GODL GU7 267 K10
GU GU1 268 A1
GVE DA12 190 E3
HDN NW4 116 F3
ISLW TW7 154 F9
LHD/OX KT22 236 F8
PLSTW E13 141 N4
REDH RH1 258 A9
ROM RM1 124 E2
WAB EN9 45 K8
North Tenter St WCHPL E1 13 M6
North Ter CHEL SW3 15 N4
Northumberland Aly
FENCHST EC3M * 13 K6
Northumberland Av CHCR WC2N 11 L9
EMPK RM11 125 K3
EN EN1 80 A4
ISLW TW7 154 E7
MNPK E12 121 P6
WELL DA16 163 H10
Northumberland Cl ERITH DA8 164 D6
STWL/WRAY TW19 173 P2
Northumberland Crs
EBED/NFELT TW14 174 F2
Northumberland Gdns
BMLY BR1 206 D4
ED N9 99 N4
MTCM CR4 202 F5
Northumberland Gv TOTM N17 100 A8
Northumberland Pk ERITH DA8 164 D6
TOTM N17 99 P8
Northumberland Pl BAY/PAD W2 8 E5
Northumberland Rd BAR EN5 77 M10
EHAM E6 142 B8
MEO DA13 190 C10
RYLN/HDSTN HA2 113 N3
SLH/COR SS17 169 K1
WALTH E17 120 F5
Northumberland St CHCR WC2N 11 L9
Northumberland Wy ERITH DA8 164 D7
Northumbria St POP/IOD E14 140 F8
North Verbena Gdns
HMSMTH W6 * 156 D4
North Vw EA W5 135 H6
PIN HA5 113 K5
WIM/MER SW19 178 E8
Northview SWLY BR8 208 F2
North View Av TIL RM18 168 D7
North View Crs EPSOM KT18 238 F3
Northview Crs WLSDN NW10 116 C9
Northview Dr WFD IG8 102 A10
Northview Pde HOLWY N7 * 118 F8
North View Rd CEND/HSY/T N8 118 E1
SEV TN13 247 K7
North Vls CAMTN NW1 5 J2
North Wk CROY/NA CR0 224 G3
North Wy CDALE/KGS NW9 115 N1
ED N9 100 B3
FBAR/BDGN N11 98 D7
HGDN/ICK UB10 131 P2
PIN HA5 113 K1
Northway GLDGN NW11 117 L3
GODL GU7 266 G10
GUW GU2 249 M8
HORL RH6 280 A7
MRDN SM4 201 H3
RKW/CH/CXG WD3 91 N1
WGCE AL7 23 J2
WLGTN SM6 222 D1
Northway Crs MLHL NW7 96 B5
Northway Rd CMBW SE5 159 K9
CROY/NA CR0 203 N6
Northways Pde HAMP NW3 3 L3
North Weald Cl HCH RM12 145 J2
North Weald La KUTN/CMB KT2 177 J8
North Western Av WATN WD24 72 G1
North Western Av Coln
WATN WD24 73 K2
North Western Av Gade Side
KGLGY WD4 72 D1
North Western Av
Otterspool Wy GSTN WD25 73 N4
North Wharf Rd BAY/PAD W2 9 L4
Northwick Av
KTN/HRWW/WS HA3 114 F4
Northwick Cir
KTN/HRWW/WS HA3 115 H4
Northwick Cl STJWD NW8 9 L1
Northwick Park Rd HRW HA1 114 E4
Northwick Rd ALP/SUD HA0 135 J3
OXHEY WD19 93 K5
Northwick Ter STJWD NW8 9 L1
Northwold Dr PIN HA5 113 K1
Northwold Rd STNW/STAM N16 119 N7
Northwood CDW/CHF RM16 168 E1
WGCE AL7 23 N5
Northwood Av HCH RM12 125 H9
PUR/KEN CR8 223 H9
WOKN/KNAP GU21 231 J4
Northwood Cl CHESW EN7 61 N3
Northwood Gdns CLAY IG5 122 D2
GFD/PVL UB6 114 E10
NFNCH/WDSPK N12 97 N6
Northwood Pk CRAWE RH10 * 284 B3
Northwood Pl ERITHM DA18 164 A2
Northwood Rd CAR SM5 222 B3
DEN/HRF UB9 91 P9
FSTH SE23 182 E4
HGT N6 118 C5
HTHAIR TW6 151 N7
THHTH CR7 203 K2
Northwood Wy DEN/HRF UB9 91 N9
NTHWD HA6 93 H9
North Woolwich Rd CAN/RD E16 141 M10
North Worple Wy
MORT/ESHN SW14 156 A9
Nortoft Rd CFSP/GDCR SL9 90 C7
Norton Av BRYLDS KT5 199 N7
Norton Cl BORE WD6 75 M5
CHING E4 100 F6
RGUW GU3 249 J3
Norton Folgate WCHPL E1 13 K2
Norton Gdns STRHM/NOR SW16 202 F2
Norton La COB KT11 234 G5
Norton Pk ASC SL5 192 B5
Norton Rd ALP/SUD HA0 135 J1
DAGE RM10 144 E1
LEY E10 120 E6
UX/CGN UB8 131 N5
Norval Gn BRXN/ST SW9 * 159 H8
Norval Rd ALP/SUD HA0 114 G7
Norway Dr SLN SL2 129 N7
Norway Ga BERM/RHTH SE16 160 D2
Norway Pl POP/IOD E14 140 E8
Norway St GNWCH SE10 160 G5
Norwich Crs CHDH RM6 123 L3
Norwich Ms GDMY/SEVK IG3 123 K6
Norwich Rd CRAWE RH10 284 B9
FSTGT E7 121 M10
GFD/PVL UB6 134 A3
NTHWD HA6 112 G1
THHTH CR7 203 K3
Norwich St FLST/FETLN EC4A 12 A5
Norwich Wk EDGW HA8 95 P8
Norwich Wy RKW/CH/CXG WD3 72 C8
Norwood Av ALP/SUD HA0 135 L3
ROMW/RG RM7 124 E5
Norwood Cl CRICK NW2 117 H8
EHSLY KT24 253 M4
HERT/WAT SG14 24 G4
NWDGN UB2 153 P3
WHTN TW2 176 C5
Norwood Ct AMSS HP7 * 68 G6
Norwood Dr RYLN/HDSTN HA2 113 N4
Norwood Farm La COB KT11 217 J7
Norwood Gdns NWDGN UB2 153 N3
YEAD UB4 133 K6
Norwood Green Rd NWDGN UB2 153 P3
Norwood High St WNWD SE27 181 K7
Norwood Hl HORL RH6 278 G4
Norwoodhill Rd HORL RH6 279 J6
Norwood La IVER SL0 130 G6
Norwood Park Rd WNWD SE27 181 K8
Norwood Rd CHES/WCR EN8 62 D6
EHSLY KT24 253 M4
HNHL SE24 181 J4

NWDGN UB2 153 M2
Notley End EGH TW20 * 171 P10
Notley St CMBW SE5 159 L6
Notson Rd SNWD SE25 204 A4
Notting Barn Rd NKENS W10 136 G6
Nottingdale Sq NTGHL W11 8 A9
Nottingham Av CAN/RD E16 141 P7
Nottingham Cl GSTN WD25 55 H10
WOKN/KNAP GU21 231 L4
Nottingham Ct LSQ/SEVD WC2H 11 L6
Nottingham Pl CAMTN NW1 10 C2
Nottingham Rd ISLW TW7 154 E8
LEY E10 121 H4
RKW/CH/CXG WD3 90 F2
SAND/SEL CR2 223 K1
TOOT SW17 180 A4
Nottingham St MHST W1U 10 C3
Nottingham Ter CAMTN NW1 10 C2
Notting Hill Ga NTGHL W11 8 F9
Nova Ms CHEAM SM3 201 H7
Novar Cl ORP BR6 207 J7
Nova Rd CROY/NA CR0 203 J8
Novar Rd ELTH/MOT SE9 184 F4
Novello St FUL/PGN SW6 157 K7
Novello Wy BORE WD6 76 A5
Nowell Rd BARN SW13 156 D5
Nower Hl PIN HA5 113 N2
Nower Rd DORK RH4 272 F2
The Nower BH/WHM TN16 245 J6
RSEV TN14 245 N2
Noyna Rd TOOT SW17 180 A6
Nubia Wy BMLY BR1 183 K7
Nuding Cl LEW SE13 160 F9
Nuffield Rd SWLY BR8 187 H9
Nugent Rd ARCH N19 118 F6
GUW GU2 267 J1
SNWD SE25 203 N3
Nugents Ct PIN HA5 * 93 M9
Nugent's Pk PIN HA5 93 N9
Nugent Ter STJWD NW8 3 K8
Numbers Farm KGLGY WD4 * 54 D5
Nunappleton Wy OXTED RH8 261 M8
Nuneaton Rd DAGW RM9 143 N2
Nunhead Crs PECK SE15 160 A9
Nunhead Gv PECK SE15 160 B9
Nunhead La PECK SE15 160 A9
Nunnery Cl STAL AL1 38 D8
Nunnery Stables STAL AL1 38 C8
Nunnington Cl ELTH/MOT SE9 184 B6
Nunn's Rd ENC/FH EN2 79 K6
Nunns Wy GRAYS RM17 168 A3
Nunsbury Dr BROX EN10 62 D1
Nuns La STAL AL1 38 D10
Nuns Wk VW GU25 194 A5
Nupton Dr BAR EN5 76 F10
Nurse Cl EDGW HA8 95 P9
Nurseries Rd STALE/WH AL4 21 K4
Nursery Av BXLYHN DA7 164 A9
CROY/NA CR0 204 C9
FNCH N3 97 L10
Nursery Cl ADL/WDHM KT15 215 J6
AMSS HP7 69 K5
BROCKY SE4 160 E8
CHDH RM6 123 N4
CROY/NA CR0 204 C9
EBED/NFELT TW14 175 J3
EW KT17 220 B6
KWD/TDW/WH KT20 256 E1
ORP BR6 207 J7
OXHEY WD19 93 J2
PEND EN3 80 C5
PUT/ROE SW15 178 G1
RDART DA2 188 B3
SEV TN13 247 K8
SOCK/AV RM15 147 H6
SWLY BR8 208 D2
WFD IG8 101 N6
WOKN/KNAP GU21 231 P2
Nursery Flds SBW CM21 29 N1
Nursery Gdns CHESW EN7 61 L4
CHST BR7 184 E9
HPTN TW12 175 N7
HSLWW TW4 175 N1
PEND EN3 80 C5
RGUE GU4 268 E6
STA TW18 173 L10
SUN TW16 196 G2
WARE SG12 26 D2
WGCE AL7 23 H2
Nursery Hl WGCE AL7 23 H2
Nurserylands CRAWW RH11 283 K7
Nursery La BETH E2 7 L6
DTCH/LGLY SL3 129 P10
FSTGT E7 141 M1
HORL RH6 279 N5
NKENS W10 136 F7
Nurserymans Rd
FBAR/BDGN N11 98 B3
Nursery Pl SEV TN13 246 E8
WDSR SL4 171 N2
Nursery Rd BROX EN10 * 62 D1
BRXN/ST SW9 158 G10
EFNCH N2 97 N9
GODL GU7 267 L10
HOD EN11 26 G10
HOM E9 140 B1
KWD/TDW/WH KT20 256 E1
LOU IG10 82 A8
MDHD SL6 128 A8
MTCM CR4 201 P3
PIN HA5 113 K1
STHGT/OAK N14 98 D1
SUN TW16 196 F2
SUT SM1 221 M1
THHTH CR7 203 L4
WAB EN9 45 J8
WIM/MER SW19 179 H10
WOKN/KNAP GU21 231 J3
Nursery Rw BAR EN5 * 77 H7
WALW SE17 18 G6
Nursery St TOTM N17 99 N8
The Nursery ERITH DA8 164 G6
Nursery Wk HDN NW4 116 E1
Nursery Wy OXTED RH8 * 261 K5
STWL/WRAY TW19 172 A2
Nursery Waye UX/CGN UB8 131 N3
Nurstead Rd ERITH DA8 164 B6
Nutberry Av CDW/CHF RM16 167 M1
Nutberry Cl CDW/CHF RM16 167 M1
Nutbourne St NKENS W10 2 A9
NKENS W10 137 H5
Nutbrook St PECK SE15 159 N9
Nutbrowne Rd DAGW RM9 144 A3
Nutcombe La DORK RH4 272 E2
Nutcroft Gv LHD/OX KT22 236 D8
Nutcroft Rd PECK SE15 160 A6
Nutfield WGCE AL7 23 K2
Nutfield Cl CAR SM5 201 P10
UED N18 99 P7
Nutfield Gdns GDMY/SEVK IG3 123 J7
NTHLT UB5 133 K4
Nutfield Marsh Rd REDH RH1 258 F8
Nutfield Pk REDH RH1 277 H4
Nutfield Rd COUL/CHIP CR5 240 D2
CRICK NW2 116 D7
EDUL SE22 159 N10
REDH RH1 258 C10
REDH RH1 258 D6
SRTFD E15 121 H9
THHTH CR7 203 J4
Nutfield Wy ORP BR6 206 D9
Nutford Pl MBLAR W1H 9 P5
Nut Gv WGCW AL8 22 G2
Nuthatch HART DA3 211 N3
Nuthatch Cl STWL/WRAY TW19 174 A4
Nuthatch Gdns REIG RH2 275 M4
THMD SE28 162 G1
Nuthurst Av BRXS/STRHM SW2 180 G5
Nuthurst Cl CRAWW RH11 283 K6
Nutkins Wy CSHM HP5 51 H5
Nutley Cl SWLY BR8 208 G1
Nutley La REIG RH2 257 J9
Nutley Ter HAMP NW3 3 K1
Nutmead Cl BXLY DA5 186 D4
Nutmeg Cl CAN/RD E16 141 K6
Nutmeg La POP/IOD E14 141 J8
Nuttall St IS N1 7 K7
Nutter La WAN E11 121 P3
Nuttfield Cl RKW/CH/CXG WD3 * 72 C10
Nutt Gv EDGW HA8 95 J3
Nut Tree Cl ORP BR6 207 N10
Nutt St PECK SE15 159 N6
Nutty La SHPTN TW17 196 D4
Nutwell St TOOT SW17 179 P8
Nutwood Av BRKHM/BTCW RH3 273 P1
Nutwood Cl BRKHM/BTCW RH3 273 P1
Nutwood Gdns CHESW EN7 61 M2
Nuxley Rd BELV DA17 164 A5
Nyanza St WOOL/PLUM SE18 162 G5
Nyefield Pk KWD/TDW/WH KT20 256 D2
Nye Wy HHS/BOV HP3 52 D4
Nylands Av RCH/KEW TW9 155 M8
Nymans Ct CRAWE RH10 * 284 C10
Nymans Gdns RYNPK SW20 200 E3
Nynehead St NWCR SE14 160 D6
Nyon Gv CAT SE6 182 E5
Nyssa Cl WFD IG8 102 C7
Nyth Cl UPMR RM14 126 C4
Nyton Cl ARCH N19 118 F6

O

Oakapple Cl SAND/SEL CR2 224 A10
Oak Av CEND/HSY/T N8 118 F2
CHOB/PIR GU24 230 F7
CROY/NA CR0 204 F9
EGH TW20 172 G10
ENC/FH EN2 78 G5
HEST TW5 153 L6
HGDN/ICK UB10 112 C7
HPTN TW12 175 M8
LCOL/BKTW AL2 55 P6
MUSWH N10 98 C8
SEV TN13 265 J4
TOTM N17 99 L8
UPMR RM14 126 A8
WDR/YW UB7 152 B2
Oakbank CROY/NA CR0 225 H3
LHD/OX KT22 236 B9
WOKS/MYFD GU22 232 B5
Oakbank Av WOT/HER KT12 197 N7
Oakbank Gv HNHL SE24 159 K10
Oakbrook Cl BMLY BR1 183 N7
Oakbury Rd FUL/PGN SW6 157 L8
Oak Cl CRAWE RH10 284 G2
DART DA1 164 F10
GODL GU7 267 K9
HHS/BOV HP3 36 A10
KWD/TDW/WH KT20 255 N6
STHGT/OAK N14 98 C1
WAB EN9 63 J10
Oakcombe Cl NWMAL KT3 200 B1
Oak Cottage Cl CAT SE6 183 K4
RGUW GU3 249 H9
Oak Cottages HNWL W7 * 154 D1
ORP BR6 * 228 C2
Oak Ct CRAWE RH10 * 283 N3
Oak Crs CAN/RD E16 141 K7
Oakcroft Cl BF/WBF KT14 215 J10
PIN HA5 93 J10
Oakcroft Rd BF/WBF KT14 215 J10
CHSGTN KT9 219 L1
LEW SE13 161 J8
Oakcroft Vls CHSGTN KT9 219 L1
Oakdale STHGT/OAK N14 98 C2
WGCW AL8 22 G2
Oakdale Av KTN/HRWW/WS HA3 115 K3
NTHWD HA6 93 H10
Oakdale Cl OXHEY WD19 93 K5
Oakdale Gdns CHING E4 101 H6
Oakdale La EDEN TN8 262 F9
Oakdale Rd FSBYPK N4 119 K4
FSTGT E7 141 N2
HOR/WEW KT19 220 A5
OXHEY WD19 93 K4
PECK SE15 160 B9
STRHM/NOR SW16 180 F8
SWFD E18 101 N10
WAN E11 121 J7
WEY KT13 196 B10
Oakdale Wy MTCM CR4 202 B7
Oak Dell CRAWE RH10 284 D6
Oakdene ASC SL5 192 E6
BEAC HP9 88 D8
CHES/WCR EN8 62 D6
CHOB/PIR GU24 213 L6
KWD/TDW/WH KT20 239 H6
WEA W13 134 G7
Oakdene Av CHST BR7 184 D8
ERITH DA8 164 D5
THDIT KT7 198 F8
Oakdene Cl BRKHM/BTCW RH3 273 P2
Oak Dene Cl EMPK RM11 125 J4
Oakdene Cl GT/LBKH KT23 254 B3
PIN HA5 93 N8
Oakdene Dr BRYLDS KT5 199 P8
Oakdene Ms CHEAM SM3 201 J8
Oakdene Pk FNCH N3 97 J8
Oakdene Pl RGUW GU3 267 P8
Oakdene Rd BRKHM/BTCW RH3 273 N2
COB KT11 217 J10
GT/LBKH KT23 235 N10
HGDN/ICK UB10 132 C4
HHS/BOV HP3 36 A10
REDH RH1 258 A10
RGUW GU3 267 P8
SEV TN13 247 H8
STMC/STPC BR5 207 K6
WATN WD24 73 J2
Oakdene Wy STAL AL1 39 H6
Oakden St LBTH SE11 18 B5
Oak Dr BERK HP4 34 A6
KWD/TDW/WH KT20 255 N6
SBW CM21 29 M3
Oaken Coppice ASHTD KT21 237 M5
Oak End HLWS CM18 * 47 J3
Oak End Dr IVER SL0 130 F4
Oaken Dr ESH/CLAY KT10 218 E3
Oak End Wy ADL/WDHM KT15 215 J8
CFSP/GDCR SL9 110 C3
Oaken Gv WGCE AL7 23 H8
Oaken La ESH/CLAY KT10 218 D1
Oakenshaw Cl SURB KT6 199 K7
Oakeshott Av HGT N6 118 B7
Oakey La STHWK SE1 18 A3
Oak Farm BORE WD6 75 P9
Oakfield CHING E4 100 G6
Oak Fld CSHM HP5 50 G6
Oakfield RKW/CH/CXG WD3 91 K1
WOKN/KNAP GU21 231 K2
Oakfield Av KTN/HRWW/WS HA3 114 G1
SL SL1 128 G10
Oakfield Cl NWMAL KT3 200 C5
POTB/CUF EN6 59 J7
RSLP HA4 112 G4
WEY KT13 210 D1
Oakfield Ct BORE WD6 * 75 N8
Oakfield Dr REIG RH2 257 K8
Oakfield Gdns BECK BR3 204 G5
CAR SM5 201 P8
GFD/PVL UB6 134 C6
UED N18 99 M5
Oakfield Gld WEY KT13 216 D1
Oakfield La HAYES BR2 225 P1
RDART DA2 186 G5
Oakfield Park Rd DART DA1 187 L5
Oakfield Pl DART DA1 187 L5
Oakfield Rd ASHF TW15 174 C8
ASHTD KT21 237 K4
COB KT11 217 J9
CROY/NA CR0 203 K8
EHAM E6 142 B3
FNCH N3 97 L9
FSBYPK N4 119 H4
IL IG1 122 E8
PGE/AN SE20 182 A10
STHGT/OAK N14 98 F3
WALTH E17 100 D10
WIM/MER SW19 178 G6
Oakfields BF/WBF KT14 215 L10
CRAWE RH10 284 E6
RGUW GU3 249 K8
SEV TN13 265 J2
WOT/HER KT12 197 H8
Oakfields Rd GLDGN NW11 117 H4
Oakfield St WBPTN SW10 15 J9
Oakford Rd KTTN NW5 118 D9
Oak Gdns CROY/NA CR0 204 F9
EDGW HA8 95 P10
Oak Gld EPP CM16 65 N5
NTHWD HA6 92 C9
Oak Gln EMPK RM11 125 M1
Oak Grange Rd RGUE GU4 251 L5
Oak Gn ABLGY WD5 54 G8
Oak Gv CRICK NW2 116 G9
HAT AL10 40 C4
HERT/BAY SG13 25 M7
RSLP HA4 113 J6
SUN TW16 175 J10
WWKM BR4 205 H9
Oak Grove Rd PGE/AN SE20 204 B1
Oakhall Dr SUN TW16 174 G8
Oak Hall Rd WAN E11 121 N4
Oakham Cl CAT SE6 * 182 E5
Oakham Dr HAYES BR2 205 M4
Oakhampton Rd MLHL NW7 96 G9
Oakhaven CRAWE RH10 283 N9
Oak Hl EPSOM KT18 238 A2
Oakhill ESH/CLAY KT10 218 F3
Oak Hl RGUE GU4 250 F6
RGUW GU3 248 F8
SURB KT6 199 K7
WFD IG8 101 J8
Oakhill Av HAMP NW3 117 L9
PIN HA5 93 M10
Oakhill Cl ASHTD KT21 237 H4
RKW/CH/CXG WD3 91 H5
Oak Hill Crs SURB KT6 199 K7
WFD IG8 101 K8
Oakhill Gdns WEY KT13 196 F9
Oak Hill Gdns WFD IG8 101 K9
Oak Hill Gv SURB KT6 199 K6
Oak Hill Pk HAMP NW3 117 L9
Oak Hill Park Ms HAMP NW3 117 M9
Oakhill Pl PUT/ROE SW15 179 K1
Oak Hill Rd ABR/ST RM4 104 F2
Oakhill Rd ADL/WDHM KT15 215 J3
ASHTD KT21 237 H4
BECK BR3 205 H2
ORP BR6 207 J9
PUR RM19 166 A4
PUT/ROE SW15 179 J1
REIG RH2 275 L1
RKW/CH/CXG WD3 90 G5
Oak Hill Rd SEV TN13 265 H1
Oakhill Rd STRHM/NOR SW16 202 F1
Oak Hill Rd SURB KT6 * 199 K6
Oakhill Rd SUT SM1 201 L10
Oak Hill Wy HAMP NW3 117 M8
Oakhouse Rd BXLYHS DA6 186 B1
Oakhurst CHOB/PIR GU24 213 K5
Oakhurst Av BXLYHN DA7 163 P6
EBAR EN4 97 P1
Oakhurst Cl BARK/HLT IG6 102 F9
CHST BR7 206 C1
TEDD TW11 176 D8
WALTH E17 121 K2
Oakhurst Gdns BXLYHN DA7 163 P6
CHING E4 101 L2
WALTH E17 121 K2
Oakhurst Gv EDUL SE22 159 P10
Oakhurst Pl WATW WD18 * 72 G8
Oakhurst Ri CAR SM5 221 P6
Oakhurst Rd HOR/WEW KT19 219 P3
PEND EN3 80 C2
Oakington WGCE AL7 23 N5
Oakington Av AMS HP6 70 B5
HYS/HAR UB3 152 E3
RYLN/HDSTN HA2 113 P5
WBLY HA9 115 L8
Oakington Cl SUN TW16 197 K2
Oakington Dr SUN TW16 197 K2
Oakington Manor Dr WBLY HA9 115 M10
Oakington Rd MV/WKIL W9 8 F1
Oakington Wy CEND/HSY/T N8 118 F4
Oakland Gdns RBRW/HUT CM13 87 P9
Oakland Pl BKHH IG9 101 M3
Oakland Rd SRTFD E15 121 K9
Oaklands BERK HP4 33 M5
HORL RH6 280 D4
LHD/OX KT22 236 C10
PUR/KEN CR8 223 K10
WCHMH N21 98 G3
Oaklands Av BFN/LL DA15 185 J3
BRKMPK AL9 59 H3
ED N9 80 A10
ESH/CLAY KT10 198 C8
ISLW TW7 154 E5
OXHEY WD19 93 J2
ROM RM1 124 F1
THHTH CR7 203 H4
WWKM BR4 204 G10
Oaklands Cl ALP/SUD HA0 115 J10
BXLYHS DA6 186 A1
CHSGTN KT9 219 H1
RGUE GU4 268 B8
STMC/STPC BR5 207 H6
Oaklands Ct ADL/WDHM KT15 195 L10
WAT WD17 73 H5
Oaklands Dr HLWE CM17 47 M2
REDH RH1 276 C2
SOCK/AV RM15 147 H7
WHTN TW2 176 B3
Oaklands Gdns PUR/KEN CR8 223 K10
Oaklands Ga NTHWD HA6 92 F7
Oaklands Gv BROX EN10 44 D10
SHB W12 136 D10
Oaklands La BAR EN5 76 E8
BH/WHM TN16 243 P1
STALE/WH AL4 39 L4
Oaklands Ms CRICK NW2 116 G9
Oaklands Pk RBRW/HUT CM13 107 N2
Oaklands Park Av IL IG1 122 F7
Oaklands Pl CLAP SW4 158 E10
Oaklands Rd BMLY BR1 183 K10
BXLYHS DA6 164 A10
CHESW EN7 61 M2
CRICK NW2 116 G9
GVW DA11 190 C7
HNWL W7 154 E1
MORT/ESHN SW14 156 A9
RDART DA2 188 B4
TRDG/WHET N20 97 J1
Oaklands Wy
KWD/TDW/WH KT20 238 F8
WLGTN SM6 222 E4
Oaklands Wd HAT AL10 40 D4
Oakland Wy HOR/WEW KT19 220 B3
Oak La EFNCH N2 97 N10
EGH TW20 171 P6
FBAR/BDGN N11 98 E7
ISLW TW7 154 D10
POP/IOD E14 140 E9
POTB/CUF EN6 60 G4
SEV TN13 264 G5
WDSR SL4 148 F7
WFD IG8 101 L5
WOKS/MYFD GU22 232 E2
Oaklawn Rd LHD/OX KT22 236 D4
Oak Leaf Cl HOR/WEW KT19 219 P8
Oakleafe Gdns BARK/HLT IG6 122 E1
Oakleigh Av EDGW HA8 95 N10
SURB KT6 199 M8
TRDG/WHET N20 97 N2
Oakleigh Cl SWLY BR8 208 F3
TRDG/WHET N20 98 A4
Oakleigh Ct EDGW HA8 * 95 P10
OXTED RH8 * 261 K5
Oakleigh Crs TRDG/WHET N20 97 P4
Oakleigh Dr RKW/CH/CXG WD3 72 D10
Oakleigh Gdns EDGW HA8 95 L6
ORP BR6 227 H1
TRDG/WHET N20 97 M2
Oakleigh Ms TRDG/WHET N20 97 N3
Oakleigh Park Av CHST BR7 206 D2
Oakleigh Pk North
TRDG/WHET N20 97 N2
Oakleigh Pk South
TRDG/WHET N20 97 P2
Oakleigh Ri EPP CM16 65 K8
Oakleigh Rd HGDN/ICK UB10 132 D2
PIN HA5 93 N7
Oakleigh Rd North
TRDG/WHET N20 97 N3
Oakleigh Rd South
FBAR/BDGN N11 98 B5
Oakleigh Wy MTCM CR4 202 C1
SURB KT6 199 M8
Oakley Av BARK IG11 143 J2
CROY/NA CR0 222 F1
EA W5 135 M9
Oakley Cl ADL/WDHM KT15 215 N1
CHING E4 101 H4
EHAM E6 142 B8
HNWL W7 134 D9
ISLW TW7 154 C7
WTHK RM20 167 H5
Oakley Ct MTCM CR4 202 B7
Oakley Crs FSBYE EC1V * 6 D8
SL SL1 129 K9
Oakley Dell RGUE GU4 250 F8
Oakley Dr CAT SE6 183 J2
ELTH/MOT SE9 184 G5
HARH RM3 105 P6
HAYES BR2 206 B10
Oakley Gdns BNSTD SM7 239 L1
BRKHM/BTCW RH3 273 P6
CEND/HSY/T N8 118 G3
CHEL SW3 15 P9
Oakley Green Rd WDSR SL4 148 A7
Oakley Pk BXLY DA5 185 M3
Oakley Pl STHWK SE1 19 L8
Oakley Rd HARP AL5 20 C4
HAYES BR2 206 B10
HRW HA1 114 D4
IS N1 6 G3
SNWD SE25 204 A5
WARL CR6 241 P4
Oakley Sq CAMTN NW1 5 H7
Oakley St CHEL SW3 15 N9
Oakley Yd BETH E2 * 13 M1
Oak Lodge Av CHIG IG7 102 G6
Oak Lodge Cl STAN HA7 95 H6
WOT/HER KT12 217 K2
Oak Lodge Dr REDH RH1 276 B8
WWKM BR4 204 G7
Oak Lodge La BH/WHM TN16 262 G1
Oaklodge Wy MLHL NW7 96 C7
Oak Md GODL GU7 267 J9
Oakmead Av HAYES BR2 205 M6
Oakmeade PIN HA5 93 P7
Oakmead Gdns EDGW HA8 96 A5
Oakmead Gn EPSOM KT18 237 P1
Oakmead Pl MTCM CR4 201 P1
Oakmead Rd BAL SW12 180 C4
CROY/NA CR0 202 E6
Oakmere Av POTB/CUF EN6 59 M9
Oakmere Cl POTB/CUF EN6 59 N7
Oakmere La POTB/CUF EN6 59 M8
Oakmere Rd ABYW SE2 163 K5
Oakmoor Wy CHIG IG7 103 H6
Oakmore Gdns STMC/STPC BR5 207 N4
Oak Pk BF/WBF KT14 215 H9
Oak Park Gdns WIM/MER SW19 178 G4
Oak Piece EPP CM16 66 D1
Oakridge CHOB/PIR GU24 212 E9
Oak Rdg DORK RH4 272 G5
Oakridge LCOL/BKTW AL2 55 N5
Oakridge Av RAD WD7 56 E9
Oakridge Dr EFNCH N2 117 N1
Oakridge La GSTN WD25 56 D10
Oakridge Pl SLN SL2 109 H9
Oakridge Rd BMLY BR1 183 K7
Oak Ri BKHH IG9 102 A4
Oak Rd BH/WHM TN16 262 G1
COB KT11 235 L1
CRAWW RH11 283 M8
CTHM CR3 241 M8
EA W5 135 J9
EPP CM16 65 J6
ERITH DA8 164 D6
GRAYS RM17 167 P5
GVE DA12 190 E6
HARH RM3 105 N9
LHD/OX KT22 236 F5
NWMAL KT3 200 A2
ORP BR6 227 K4
RDART DA2 188 D2
REIG RH2 257 L9
Oak Rw MTCM CR4 202 D2
Oakroyd Av POTB/CUF EN6 59 J9
Oakroyd Cl POTB/CUF EN6 59 J10
Oaks Av CRW RM5 104 D10
FELT TW13 175 M5
NRWD SE19 181 M8
WPK KT4 220 E1
Oaks Cl LHD/OX KT22 236 F7
RAD WD7 74 E1
Oaksford Av SYD SE26 182 A6
Oaks Gv CHING E4 101 K3
Oakshade Rd BMLY BR1 183 J7
LHD/OX KT22 218 B10
Oakshaw OXTED RH8 261 J3
Oakshaw Rd WAND/EARL SW18 179 L3
Oakside DEN/HRF UB9 131 L1
Oakside Ct HORL RH6 280 D3
Oakside La HORL RH6 280 D3
Oaks La CROY/NA CR0 204 B10
GNTH/NBYPK IG2 123 H3
RDKG RH5 272 G8
Oaks Pk BNSTD SM7 * 222 A8
Oaks Rd CROY/NA CR0 224 A2
PUR/KEN CR8 223 J10
REIG RH2 257 N9
STWL/WRAY TW19 173 N1
WOKN/KNAP GU21 232 B3
The Oaks BERK HP4 33 M5
BF/WBF KT14 215 K10
BORE WD6 * 75 M5
CHSGTN KT9 199 H10
DORK RH4 * 272 G5
EPSOM KT18 220 B10
FELT TW13 * 175 M5
HAYES BR2 * 206 D6
MRDN SM4 * 201 H4
NFNCH/WDSPK N12 97 L5
OXHEY WD19 93 K2
RDART DA2 188 A2
RSLP HA4 112 E5
STA TW18 * 173 J7
SWLY BR8 208 F2
WFD IG8 101 K8
WOKN/KNAP GU21 * 232 B3
WOOL/PLUM SE18 162 F4
YEAD UB4 132 D4
Oaks Tl CAR SM5 222 B6
Oak St HHS/BOV HP3 36 A10
ROMW/RG RM7 124 D3
Oaks Wy CAR SM5 222 A4
EPSOM KT18 238 E5
PUR/KEN CR8 223 K10
RPLY/SEND GU23 233 K10
SURB KT6 199 J9
Oakthorpe Rd PLMGR N13 99 H6
Oaktree Av PLMGR N13 99 H4
Oak Tree Av RDART DA2 188 E3
Oak Tree Cl ABLGY WD5 54 E8
Oaktree Cl CHESW EN7 61 K4
Oak Tree Cl EA W5 * 135 H8
HAT AL10 40 D3
HERT/BAY SG13 26 B8
LOU IG10 82 F5
Oaktree Cl RBRW/HUT CM13 107 L4
Oak Tree Cl RGUE GU4 249 P4
RGUE GU4 250 F5
STAN HA7 95 H8
VW GU25 194 A6
WOKN/KNAP GU21 230 G4
Oak Tree Ct BORE WD6 * 75 J10
Oak Tree Dell CDALE/KGS NW9 115 P3
Oak Tree Dr DTCH/LGLY SL3 150 E4
EGH TW20 171 P8
GU GU1 249 P6
TRDG/WHET N20 97 L2
Oak Tree Gdns BMLY BR1 183 N8
Oaktree Garth WGCE AL7 23 H6
Oaktree Gv IL IG1 122 G10
Oak Tree Rd STJWD NW8 3 M10
WOKN/KNAP GU21 230 G4
Oaktree Wk CTHM CR3 241 M8
Oakview WATW WD18 72 F7
Oakview Cl CHES/WCR EN8 62 A4
OXHEY WD19 73 K10
Oakview Gdns EFNCH N2 117 N2
Oakview Gv CROY/NA CR0 204 D8
Oakview Rd CAT SE6 182 G8
Oak Village HAMP NW3 118 B9
Oak Vls GLDGN NW11 * 117 J4
Oak Warren SEV TN13 265 H5
Oakway AMS HP6 68 G1
Oak Wy ASHTD KT21 237 M2
CRAWE RH10 283 P5
CROY/NA CR0 204 C6
ACT W3 136 B10
EBED/NFELT TW14 174 F4
REIG RH2 275 N1
STHGT/OAK N14 98 C1
Oakway CDW/CHF RM16 147 N10
HAYES BR2 205 J2
RYNPK SW20 200 F4
WOKN/KNAP GU21 231 K5
Oakway Cl BXLY DA5 185 P2
Oakway Pl RAD WD7 56 F10
Oakways ELTH/MOT SE9 184 E2
Oakwell Dr POTB/CUF EN6 60 C9
Oak Wd BERK HP4 33 L6
Oakwood GUW GU2 249 M5
WLGTN SM6 222 C5
Oakwood Av BECK BR3 205 H2
BORE WD6 75 N8
CHSGTN KT9 219 L4
HAYES BR2 205 N3
MTCM CR4 201 N2
PUR/KEN CR8 223 J8
STHGT/OAK N14 98 E1
STHL UB1 133 P9
Oakwood Cha EMPK RM11 125 N5
Oakwood Cl CHST BR7 184 C9
DART DA1 188 A4
EHSLY KT24 252 F3
LEW SE13 183 J2
REDH RH1 258 B10
REDH RH1 * 276 G2
STHGT/OAK N14 78 D10
WFD IG8 102 B7
Oakwood Ct CHOB/PIR GU24 230 F2
WKENS W14 14 C3
Oakwood Crs GFD/PVL UB6 134 F1
WCHMH N21 78 F10
Oakwood Dr BXLYHN DA7 164 D10
EDGW HA8 95 P7
EHSLY KT24 252 F3
NRWD SE19 181 L9
STALE/WH AL4 39 H5
Oakwood Gdns GDMY/SEVK IG3 123 J7
ORP BR6 206 F9
SUT SM1 201 K9
WOKN/KNAP GU21 230 F4
Oakwood Hl LOU IG10 82 D10
Oakwood Hill Industrial Est
LOU IG10 82 E9
Oakwood La WKENS W14 14 C3
Oakwood Ms HLWE CM17 29 M7
Oakwood Pde STHGT/OAK N14 * 78 D9
Oakwood Park Cottages
WCHMH N21 * 78 G10
Oakwood Park Rd
STHGT/OAK N14 78 F10
Oakwood Pl CROY/NA CR0 203 H6
Oakwood Ri CTHM CR3 259 M1
HART DA3 211 K3
Oakwood Rd BFOR GU20 212 D3
CROY/NA CR0 203 H6
GLDGN NW11 117 K3
HORL RH6 280 B3
LCOL/BKTW AL2 55 N5
ORP BR6 206 F9
PIN HA5 93 J10
REDH RH1 259 H5
RYNPK SW20 200 D1
VW GU25 193 P5
WOKN/KNAP GU21 231 K5
Oakworth Rd NKENS W10 136 F7
Oak Yd WAT WD17 * 73 K8
Oarsman Pl E/WMO/HCT KT8 198 D4
Oast House Cl STWL/WRAY TW19 172 B3
Oast House Wy STMC/STPC BR5 207 L4
Oast Rd OXTED RH8 261 L7
Oast Wy HART DA3 211 K6
Oates Cl HAYES BR2 205 J3
Oates Rd CRW RM5 104 C6
Oates Wk CRAWE RH10 284 A10
Oatfield Rd KWD/TDW/WH KT20 238 E7
ORP BR6 207 J8
Oatland Ri WALTH E17 100 D10
Oatlands CRAWW RH11 283 K8
HORL RH6 280 C3
Oatlands Av WEY KT13 216 E2
Oatlands Cha WEY KT13 196 F10
Oatlands Cl WEY KT13 216 E1
Oatlands Dr SL SL1 129 J8
WEY KT13 216 C1
Oatlands Gn WEY KT13 196 E10
Oatlands Mere WEY KT13 196 E10
Oatlands Rd KWD/TDW/WH KT20 239 H5
PEND EN3 80 B5
Oat La CITYW EC2V 12 E5
Oban Cl PLSTW E13 141 P6
Oban Ct SL SL1 149 J1
Oban Rd PLSTW E13 141 P5
THHTH CR7 203 L4
Oban St POP/IOD E14 141 J8
Oberon Cl BORE WD6 75 P5
Oberon Wy CRAWW RH11 283 H10
SHPTN TW17 195 P3
Oberstein Rd BTSEA SW11 157 N10
Oborne Cl HNHL SE24 181 J1
Observatory Gdns KENS W8 14 F1
Observatory Rd
MORT/ESHN SW14 155 P10
SKENS SW7 15 M4
The Observatory SL SL1 * 149 M1
Observer Dr WATW WD18 72 F8
Occam Rd GUW GU2 249 J10
Occupation La EA W5 155 J3
WOOL/PLUM SE18 162 E7
Occupation Rd WALW SE17 18 E7
WATW WD18 73 J9
WEA W13 154 G1
Ocean Est WCHPL E1 140 C6
Ocean St WCHPL E1 140 C7
Ockenden Cl WOKS/MYFD GU22 232 C4
Ockenden Gdns
WOKS/MYFD GU22 232 C5
Ockenden Rd WOKS/MYFD GU22 232 C4
Ockendon Ms IS N1 * 7 H2
Ockendon Rd IS N1 6 G2
UPMR RM14 146 C1
Ockham Dr EHSLY KT24 234 E10
STMC/STPC BR5 185 K10
Ockham La COB KT11 234 E6
Ockham Rd North
RPLY/SEND GU23 234 C9
Ockham Rd South EHSLY KT24 252 F3
Ockley Ct RGUE GU4 250 E5
Ockley Rd CROY/NA CR0 202 G7
STRHM/NOR SW16 180 F7
Ockleys Md GDST RH9 260 B5
Octagon Ar LVPST EC2M * 13 J4
Octagon Rd WOT/HER KT12 216 G6
Octavia Cl MTCM CR4 201 P5
Octavia Ct WATN WD24 73 K6
Octavia Ms CRICK NW2 * 136 E1
Octavia Rd ISLW TW7 154 E9
Octavia St BTSEA SW11 157 P7
Octavia Wy STA TW18 173 K9
Octavius St DEPT SE8 160 F6
October Pl HDN NW4 * 116 G1
Odard Rd E/WMO/HCT KT8 197 P4
Odds Farm Est
FLKWH/TG HP10 * 108 A5
Odell Cl BARK IG11 143 J2
Odell Wk LEW SE13 160 G9
Odencroft Rd SLN SL2 128 F5
Odeon Pde ELTH/MOT SE9 * 162 B10
GFD/PVL UB6 134 G1
HOLWY N7 * 118 F8
ISLW TW7 * 154 D8
RKW/CH/CXG WD3 * 91 P2
Odessa Rd FSTGT E7 121 L9
WLSDN NW10 136 D4
Odessa St BERM/RHTH SE16 160 E2
Odger St BTSEA SW11 158 A8
Odhams Wk LSQ/SEVD WC2H * 11 L6
Odsey Vls FSBYPK N4 * 119 H4
Odyssey Rd BORE WD6 75 N5
Offa Rd STALW/RED AL3 38 B6
Offa's Md HOM E9 120 D9
Offas Wy STALE/WH AL4 21 J3
Offenham Rd ELTH/MOT SE9 184 C7
Offerton Rd CLAP SW4 158 D9
Offham Slope
NFNCH/WDSPK N12 97 J6
The Office Village SRTFD E15 * 141 K2
Offley Pl ISLW TW7 154 C8
Offley Rd BRXN/ST SW9 159 H6
Offord Cl TOTM N17 99 P8
Offord Rd IS N1 5 P3
Offord St HOLWY N7 5 N3
Ogard Rd HOD EN11 45 H1
Ogilby St WOOL/PLUM SE18 162 C3
Oglander Rd PECK SE15 159 N10
Ogle St GTPST W1W 10 G3
Oglethorpe Rd DAGE RM10 124 A8
Ohio Rd PLSTW E13 141 L6
Oil Mill La HMSMTH W6 156 D4
Okeburn Rd TOOT SW17 180 B8
Okehampton Crs WELL DA16 163 L7
Okehampton Rd WLSDN NW10 136 F3
Okehampton Sq HARH RM3 * 105 K7
Olaf St NTGHL W11 136 G9
Old Acre BF/WBF KT14 215 K10
Oldacre CHOB/PIR GU24 212 E8
Old Amersham Rd
CFSP/GDCR SL9 110 E6
Old Av BF/WBF KT14 214 G10
WEY KT13 216 E3
Old Avenue Cl
WOKN/KNAP GU21 215 H9
Old Bailey STP EC4M 12 D6
Old Barn Cl BELMT SM2 221 H4
BGR/WK TN15 247 P3
Old Barn La CTHM CR3 241 N2
RKW/CH/CXG WD3 72 A9
Old Barn Rd EPSOM KT18 237 P3
Old Barn Wy BXLYHN DA7 164 E10
Old Barrack Yd KTBR SW1X 16 C2
Old Bellgate Whf POP/IOD E14 160 F2
Old Bells Ct CSHM HP5 50 G8
Oldberry Rd EDGW HA8 96 A7
Old Bethnal Green Rd BETH E2 7 P9
BETH E2 140 A5
Old Bexley La BXLY DA5 186 E5
Old Bond St CONDST W1S 10 G8
Oldborough Rd ALP/SUD HA0 115 H7
Old Brewery Ms HAMP NW3 117 N9
Old Bridge Cl NTHLT UB5 133 P4
Old Bridge St KUT/HW KT1 199 J2
Old Brighton Rd South
HORL RH6 279 P10
Old Broad St LVPST EC2M 13 J5
Old Bromley Rd BMLY BR1 183 J8
Old Brompton Rd ECT SW5 14 F8
Old Buildings LINN WC2A 12 A5
Old Burlington St CONDST W1S 10 G7
Oldbury Cl STMC/STPC BR5 207 N4
Oldbury Gv BEAC HP9 88 C6
Oldbury Pl MHST W1U 10 D3
Oldbury Rd CHERT KT16 195 H7
EN EN1 79 P6
The Old Carriageway SEV TN13 246 D9
Old Castle St WCHPL E1 13 M5
Old Cavendish St
CAVSQ/HST W1G 10 E5
Old Chapel Rd SWLY BR8 208 D7
Old Charlton Rd SHPTN TW17 196 D5
Old Char Whf DORK RH4 272 E1
Old Chertsey Rd CHOB/PIR GU24 213 N6
Old Chestnut Av ESH/CLAY KT10 217 P3
Old Chorleywood Rd
RKW/CH/CXG WD3 71 N10
Old Church La CDALE/KGS NW9 115 P7
GFD/PVL UB6 134 F5
STAN HA7 94 G7
Old Church Pth ESH/CLAY KT10 218 A1
Oldchurch Ri ROMW/RG RM7 124 F4
Old Church Rd CHING E4 100 F4
Oldchurch Rd ROMW/RG RM7 124 F4
Old Church Rd WCHPL E1 * 140 C8
Old Church St CHEL SW3 15 M9
Old Claygate La ESH/CLAY KT10 218 F3
The Old Coach Rd
HERT/WAT SG14 24 B8
Old Common COB KT11 * 217 J8
Old Common Rd COB KT11 217 J8
RKW/CH/CXG WD3 70 G8
Old Compton St
SOHO/SHAV W1D 11 J7
Old Cote Dr HEST TW5 153 P5
Old Ct ASHTD KT21 237 K5
Old Court Pl KENS W8 14 G1
Old Court Rd GUW GU2 267 M1
The Old Ctyd BMLY BR1 205 N1
Old Crabtree La HHNE HP2 35 P7
Old Cross HERT/WAT SG14 25 K5
Old Crown SL SL1 * 149 L1
Old Crown La BRW CM14 86 C6
Old Dairy Ms BAL SW12 180 B4
KTTN NW5 4 F1
Old Dartford Rd EYN DA4 209 N6
Old Dean HHS/BOV HP3 52 D4
Old Deer Pk RCH/KEW TW9 * 155 L9
Old Deer Park Gdns
RCH/KEW TW9 155 K9
Old Devonshire Rd BAL SW12 180 C3
Old Dock Cl RCH/KEW TW9 155 M5
Old Dover Rd BKHTH/KID SE3 161 M6
Old Downs HART DA3 211 K5
Old Dr SHGR GU5 270 D4
The Old Dr WGCW AL8 22 E6
Old Earls La POTB/CUF EN6 58 D9
Olden La PUR/KEN CR8 223 H8
Old Esher Cl WOT/HER KT12 * 217 L2
Old Esher Rd WOT/HER KT12 217 L2
Old Farleigh Rd SAND/SEL CR2 224 B6
Old Farm Av BFN/LL DA15 184 G4
STHGT/OAK N14 98 D1
Old Farm Cl BEAC HP9 88 B6
HSLWW TW4 153 N10
Old Farm Gdns SWLY BR8 208 G3
Old Farmhouse Dr LHD/OX KT22 236 C1
Old Farm La AMSS HP7 69 K7
Old Farm Rd EFNCH N2 97 N9
GU GU1 250 A7
HPTN TW12 175 N9
WDR/YW UB7 151 N1
Old Farm Rd East BFN/LL DA15 185 K5
Old Farm Rd West BFN/LL DA15 185 J5
Old Farm Yd RBSF CM22 30 D3
Old Ferry Dr STWL/WRAY TW19 171 P2
Old Field Cl AMS HP6 70 B5
Oldfield Cl BMLY BR1 206 C4
GFD/PVL UB6 114 D10
STAN HA7 94 F6
Oldfield Farm Gdns
GFD/PVL UB6 134 C3
Oldfield Gdns ASHTD KT21 237 J5

346 Old - Ous

Oldfield Gv BERM/RHTH SE16 160 C3
Oldfield La North GFD/PVL UB6 134 C2
Oldfield La South GFD/PVL UB6 134 B5
Oldfield Ms HGT N6 118 D5
Oldfield Rd ACT W3 156 C1
BMLY BR1 206 C4
BXLYHN DA7 163 P8
HHW HP1 35 H7
HORL RH6 280 A6
HPTN TW12 197 P1
LCOL/BKTW AL2 57 J1
STNW/STAM N16 119 M8
WIM/MER SW19 179 H9
WLSDN NW10 136 C2
Oldfields Circ NTHLT UB5 134 B1
Oldfields Rd SUT SM1 201 J10
Oldfieldwood WOKS/MYFD GU22 232 E3
Old Fishery La HHW HP1 35 J8
Old Fish Street Hl BLKFR EC4V * 12 E7
Old Fives Ct SL SL1 128 A5
Old Fleet La FLST/FETLN EC4A 12 C5
Old Fold Cl BAR EN5 * 77 J5
Old Fold La BAR EN5 77 J5
Old Fold Vw BAR EN5 76 F7
Old Ford Lock BOW E3 * 140 F2
Old Ford Rd BETH E2 140 B4
Old Forge Cl GSTN WD25 55 H9
STAN HA7 94 F5
WLYN AL6 23 J1
Old Forge Crs SHPTN TW17 196 C6
Old Forge Rd ARCH N19 118 E7
EN EN1 79 N4
Old Forge Rw HERT/BAY SG13 * 26 A8
Old Forge Wy SCUP DA14 185 L7
Old Fox Cl CTHM CR3 241 K7
Old French Horn La HAT AL10 40 E3
Old Gannon Cl NTHWD HA6 92 D5
Old Garden Ct STALW/RED AL3 38 B6
The Old Gdn SEV TN13 246 E9
Old Gloucester St BMSBY WC1N 11 M3
Old Grove Cl CHESW EN7 61 L2
Old Hall Cl PIN HA5 93 M9
Old Hall Dr PIN HA5 93 M9
Old Hall Ri HLWE CM17 47 P1
Oldhall St HERT/WAT SG14 25 L5
Oldham Ter ACT W3 135 P10
Old Harpenden Rd
STALW/RED AL3 38 D2
Old Herns La WGCE AL7 23 M3
Old Hertford Rd BRKMPK AL9 40 F2
Old Hwy HOD EN11 44 G1
Old Hl CHST BR7 206 D1
ORP BR6 227 H3
WOKS/MYFD GU22 232 A6
Oldhill St STNW/STAM N16 119 P6
Old Hollow CRAWE RH10 284 G5
Old Homesdale Rd HAYES BR2 205 P4
Old Horsham Rd CRAWW RH11 283 L9
Old Hospital Cl BAL SW12 * 180 A4
Old House Cl EW KT17 220 C6
WIM/MER SW19 179 H8
Old House Ct DTCH/LGLY SL3 * 130 A8
Oldhouse Ct HHNE HP2 36 A6
Oldhouse Cft HLW CM20 29 H9
Old House Gdns TWK TW1 * 177 H2
Old House La BFOR GU20 212 A4
Oldhouse La BFOR GU20 212 B5
CHOB/PIR GU24 212 F10
Old House La HLWW/ROY CM19 46 B4
KGLGY WD4 72 B1
Old House Rd HHNE HP2 36 A6
Old Howletts La RSLP HA4 112 E4
Oldings Cnr BRKMPK AL9 22 E10
Old Jamaica Rd
BERM/RHTH SE16 19 N3
Old James St PECK SE15 160 A9
Old Jewry LOTH EC2R * 12 G6
Old Kenton La CDALE/KGS NW9 115 N3
Old Kent Rd PECK SE15 160 A5
STHWK SE1 19 P9
Old Kiln La BRKHM/BTCW RH3 255 P10
Old Kingston Rd WPK KT4 199 P10
Old La BH/WHM TN16 244 A7
COB KT11 234 E5
OXTED RH8 261 L6
Old Lane Gdns EHSLY KT24 234 G8
Old Leys HAT AL10 40 D8
Old Lodge Dr BEAC HP9 88 D10
Old Lodge La PUR/KEN CR8 222 G10
Old Lodge Wy STAN HA7 94 F6
Old London Rd EPSOM KT18 238 D4
HERT/BAY SG13 25 M5
KUTN/CMB KT2 199 L2
RDKG RH5 255 H4
RSEV TN14 228 B6
RSEV TN14 245 P1
STAL AL1 38 D7
Old Maidstone Rd SCUP DA14 186 A10
Old Malden La WPK KT4 200 B9
The Old Maltings
HERT/BAY SG13 * 25 K6
Old Malt Wy WOKN/KNAP GU21 232 A3
Old Manor Cl CRAWW RH11 283 K5
Old Manor Dr ISLW TW7 176 B2
Old Manor Gdns RGUE GU4 268 F6
Old Manor Rd NWDGN UB2 153 L3
Old Manor Wy BXLYHN DA7 164 E8
CHST BR7 184 C8
Old Manor Yd ECT SW5 14 G7
Old Market Sq BETH E2 7 L9
Old Martyrs CRAWW RH11 283 N4
Old Marylebone Rd CAMTN NW1 9 P4
Old Md CFSP/GDCR SL9 90 B7
Old Meadow Cl BERK HP4 33 M7
Old Merrow St RGUE GU4 250 F7
Old Mill Cl EYN DA4 209 M8
Old Mill Ct SWFD E18 121 P1
Old Mill Gdns BERK HP4 34 A5
Old Mill La REDH RH1 258 C4
UX/CGN UB8 131 L7
Old Mill Pl STWL/WRAY TW19 172 E2
Old Mill Rd DEN/HRF UB9 111 K8
KGLGY WD4 54 D10
WOOL/PLUM SE18 162 G5
Old Mitre Ct EMB EC4Y * 12 B6
Old Montague St WCHPL E1 13 N4
Old Nazeing Rd BROX EN10 44 F8
Old Nichol St BETH E2 13 L1
Old North St FSBYW WC1X * 11 N3
Old Nursery Ct SLN SL2 109 H7
Old Nursery Pl ASHF TW15 174 C8
Old Oak STAL AL1 38 D9
Old Oak Av COUL/CHIP CR5 239 P5
Old Oak Cl COB KT11 217 J9
Old Oak Common La
WLSDN NW10 136 B6
Old Oak Gdns BERK HP4 * 33 K2
Old Oak La WLSDN NW10 136 C5
Old Oak Rd ACT W3 136 C10
Old Oaks WAB EN9 63 K8
Old Orch BF/WBF KT14 216 A8
HLWS CM18 46 G3
IVER SL0 131 J8
LCOL/BKTW AL2 56 C2
SUN TW16 197 K2
Old Orchard Cl EBAR EN4 77 N4
UX/CGN UB8 132 B8
Old Orchard Ms BERK HP4 33 P6
Old Orchards CRAWE RH10 284 F7
The Old Orch HAMP NW3 * 118 A9
Old Otford Rd RSEV TN14 247 J4
Old Palace Rd CROY/NA CR0 203 K10
GUW GU2 267 M1
WEY KT13 196 C10
Old Palace Yd RCH/KEW TW9 177 H1
Old Paradise St LBTH SE11 17 N5
Old Park Av BAL SW12 180 B2
ENC/FH EN2 79 K8
Old Parkbury La LCOL/BKTW AL2 56 E6
Old Park Gv ENC/FH EN2 79 K8
Old Park La MYFR/PKLN W1K 10 E10
Old Park Ms HEST TW5 153 N6
Oldpark Ride CHESW EN7 61 L8
Old Park Ridings WCHMH N21 79 K10
Old Park Rd ABYW SE2 163 K4
ENC/FH EN2 79 J7
PLMGR N13 98 G4
Old Park Rd South ENC/FH EN2 79 J8
Old Park Vw ENC/FH EN2 79 H7
Old Parvis Rd BF/WBF KT14 215 M8
Old Pearson St GNWCH SE10 * 160 G6
Old Perry St CHST BR7 185 H10
GVW DA11 190 B5
Old Polhill RSEV TN14 246 E1
Old Portsmouth Rd RGUW GU3 267 N8
Old Post Office La
BKHTH/KID SE3 161 N9
Old Pottery Cl REIG RH2 275 L2
Old Pound Cl ISLW TW7 154 F7
Old Priory DEN/HRF UB9 112 C5
Old Pye St WEST SW1P 17 J3
Old Quebec St MBLAR W1H 10 B6
Old Queen St STJSPK SW1H 17 K2
Old Rectory Cl
KWD/TDW/WH KT20 238 D10
Old Rectory Dr HAT AL10 40 E4
Old Rectory Gdns EDGW HA8 95 M7
STALE/WH AL4 21 J2
Old Rectory La DEN/HRF UB9 111 H5
EHSLY KT24 252 F3
Old Rectory Rd CHONG CM5 67 J9
Old Redding
KTN/HRWW/WS HA3 94 A6
Old Redstone Dr REDH RH1 276 B1
Old Reigate Rd DORK RH4 255 K10
Oldridge Rd BAL SW12 180 B3
Old Rd ABR/ST RM4 85 L6
ADL/WDHM KT15 215 J4
BRKHM/BTCW RH3 256 C9
DART DA1 164 E10
HLWE CM17 29 M5
LEW SE13 161 K10
PEND EN3 80 B5
Old Rd East GVE DA12 190 G4
Old Rd West GVW DA11 190 D4
Old Royal Free Sq IS N1 6 B6
Old Ruislip Rd NTHLT UB5 133 L4
Old St Mary's EHSLY KT24 252 C5
Old's Ap WATW WD18 92 D2
Old Sax La CSHM HP5 50 C3
Old School Cl BECK BR3 204 D2
GU GU1 250 A10
Old School Ct STWL/WRAY TW19 172 C3
SWLY BR8 208 F2
Old School Crs FSTGT E7 141 M1
Old School La BRKHM/BTCW RH3 273 N2
Old School Ms WEY KT13 216 E1
Old School Pl CROY/NA CR0 223 H1
WOKS/MYFD GU22 232 C7
Old School Rd UX/CGN UB8 132 A6
Old Schools La EW KT17 220 C5
Old School Sq THDIT KT7 198 E6
Old School Ter CHEAM SM3 * 220 G4
Old's Cl WATW WD18 92 C2
Old Seacoal La STP EC4M 12 C6
Old Shire La RKW/CH/CXG WD3 70 E10
WAB EN9 63 M10
Old Shire Lane Circular Wk
RKW/CH/CXG WD3 90 F1
Old Slade La DTCH/LGLY SL3 151 J3
Old Solesbridge La
RKW/CH/CXG WD3 71 K7
Old Sopwell Gdns STAL AL1 38 D8
Old South Cl PIN HA5 93 L9
Old South Lambeth Rd
VX/NE SW8 * 158 F6
Old Sq LINN WC2A 11 P5
Old Stable Ms HBRY N5 * 119 K8
Old Station Ap LHD/OX KT22 236 F7
Old Station Cl CRAWE RH10 285 P6
Old Station Gdns TEDD TW11 * 176 F9
Old Station La STWL/WRAY TW19 172 C2
Old Station Rd HYS/HAR UB3 152 G2
LOU IG10 82 B9
The Old Station Yd WALTH E17 121 H2
Oldstead Rd BMLY BR1 183 J7
Old St FSBYE EC1V 7 K10
FSBYE EC1V 12 E1
PLSTW E13 141 N4
STLK EC1Y 13 H1
Old Studio Cl CROY/NA CR0 203 L7
The Old Surrey Ms GDST RH9 * 260 B6
Old Swan Yd CAR SM5 222 A1
Old Town CLAP SW4 158 D9
CROY/NA CR0 203 J10
Old Tramyard WOOL/PLUM SE18 163 H3
Old Tye Av BH/WHM TN16 244 B2
Old Uxbridge Rd
RKW/CH/CXG WD3 91 H8
The Old Wk RSEV TN14 247 J3
Old Watford Rd LCOL/BKTW AL2 55 M7
Oldway La SL SL1 128 B9
Old Westhall Cl WARL CR6 242 B5
Old Wharf Wy WEY KT13 216 A1
Old Woking Rd
WOKS/MYFD GU22 232 E4
Old Woolwich Rd GNWCH SE10 161 J5
The Old Yd REDH RH1 259 K9
The Old Yews HART DA3 211 N3
Old York Rd WAND/EARL SW18 157 L10
Oleander Cl ORP BR6 226 G2
O'Leary Sq WCHPL E1 140 B7
Olga St BOW E3 140 D4
Olinda Rd STNW/STAM N16 119 N4
Oliphant St NKENS W10 2 A9
NKENS W10 137 H5
Olive Cl STAL AL1 38 G7
Olive Gv SEVS/STOTM N15 119 K2
Oliver Av SNWD SE25 203 N4
Oliver Cl ADL/WDHM KT15 215 L1
CHSWK W4 155 N5
HHS/BOV HP3 35 P10
HOD EN11 44 G1
LCOL/BKTW AL2 56 C3
WTHK RM20 166 E6
Oliver Crs EYN DA4 209 N7
Oliver Gdns EHAM E6 142 B7
Oliver Gv SNWD SE25 203 N4
Oliver Ms PECK SE15 159 P8
Olive Rd CRICK NW2 116 F9
DART DA1 187 L4
EA W5 155 J2
PLSTW E13 141 P5
WIM/MER SW19 * 179 M10
Oliver Ri HHS/BOV HP3 35 P10
Oliver Rd ASC SL5 192 A4
BRWN CM15 87 M9
HHS/BOV HP3 36 A10
LEY E10 120 G8
NWMAL KT3 199 P2
RAIN RM13 144 G3
SUT SM1 221 N1
SWLY BR8 208 E3
WALTH E17 121 H3
WTHK RM20 166 F6
Olivers Cl BERK HP4 34 F2
Oliver's Yd STLK EC1Y 13 H1
Olive St ROMW/RG RM7 124 E3
Olivia Dr DTCH/LGLY SL3 150 C4
Olivia Gdns DEN/HRF UB9 91 M9
Olivier Rd CRAWE RH10 284 E8
Ollard's Gv LOU IG10 82 A8
Olleberrie La RKW/CH/CXG WD3 53 H8
Ollerton Gn BOW E3 140 E3
Ollerton Rd FBAR/BDGN N11 98 E6
Olley Cl WLGTN SM6 222 F4
Ollgar Cl SHB W12 136 C10
Olliffe St POP/IOD E14 161 H2
Olmar St STHWK SE1 19 N9
Olney Rd WALW SE17 18 D10
Olron Crs BXLYHS DA6 185 N1
Olven Rd WOOL/PLUM SE18 162 F6
Olveston Wk CAR SM5 201 N6
Olwen Ms PIN HA5 93 L10
Olyffe Av WELL DA16 163 K8
Olyffe Dr BECK BR3 205 H1
Olympia Wy WKENS W14 14 B4
WKENS W14 157 H2
Olympic Wy GFD/PVL UB6 134 A3
WBLY HA9 115 M9
Olympus Gv WDGN N22 99 H9
Olympus Sq CLPT E5 120 A8
Oman Av CRICK NW2 116 F10
O'Meara St STHWK SE1 12 F10
Omega Ct WARE SG12 * 26 C1
Omega Maltings WARE SG12 * 26 D2
Omega Pl IS N1 5 M8
Omega Rd WOKN/KNAP GU21 232 D1
Omega St NWCR SE14 160 E7
Omega Wy EGH TW20 194 F1
Ommaney Rd NWCR SE14 160 C7
Omnibus Wy WALTH E17 100 F10
Ondine Rd PECK SE15 159 N10
Onega Ga BERM/RHTH SE16 160 D2
One Pin La SLN SL2 109 J8
One Tree Cl FSTH SE23 182 B2
One Tree Hill Rd RGUE GU4 268 E2
One Tree La BEAC HP9 88 D8
One Tree Pl AMS HP6 * 69 H4
Ongar Cl ADL/WDHM KT15 215 J3
CHDH RM6 123 M3
Ongar Hl ADL/WDHM KT15 215 K3
Ongar Pl ADL/WDHM KT15 215 K3
BRW CM14 107 J3
Ongar Rd ABR/ST RM4 83 M6
ADL/WDHM KT15 215 K2
BRWN CM15 86 F10
FUL/PGN SW6 14 F9
Ongar Wy RAIN RM13 144 G3
Onra Rd WALTH E17 120 F5
Onslow Av BELMT SM2 221 J6
RCHPK/HAM TW10 177 K1
Onslow Cl CHING E4 101 J3
HAT AL10 40 E4
Onslow Crs CHST BR7 206 E1
SKENS SW7 15 M6
WOKS/MYFD GU22 232 D3
Onslow Dr SCUP DA14 185 N6
Onslow Gdns CHONG CM5 67 P3
MUSWH N10 118 C3
SAND/SEL CR2 223 P8
SKENS SW7 15 L7
SWFD E18 121 N1
THDIT KT7 198 D8
WCHMH N21 79 H9
WLGTN SM6 222 D4
Onslow Ms CHERT KT16 195 J6
Onslow Ms East SKENS SW7 15 L6
Onslow Ms West SKENS SW7 15 L6
Onslow Pde STHGT/OAK N14 * 98 C2
Onslow Rd ASC SL5 192 G7
CROY/NA CR0 203 H7
GU GU1 250 A10
NWMAL KT3 200 D4
RCHPK/HAM TW10 177 K2
WOT/HER KT12 217 H1
Onslow Sq SKENS SW7 15 M6
Onslow St CLKNW EC1R 12 B2
GU GU1 267 P1
Onslow Wy THDIT KT7 198 D8
WOKS/MYFD GU22 233 J1
Ontario Cl BROX EN10 62 D1
HORL RH6 281 H5
Ontario St STHWK SE1 18 D4
Ontario Wy POP/IOD E14 140 F10
On The Hl OXHEY WD19 93 M3
Onyx Ms SRTFD E15 141 K1
Opal Cl CAN/RD E16 142 A8
Opal Ct DTCH/LGLY SL3 129 P6
Opal Ms IL IG1 122 E7
KIL/WHAMP NW6 2 D5
Opal St LBTH SE11 18 C7
Opendale Rd SL SL1 128 A7
Openshaw Rd ABYW SE2 163 L3
Openview WAND/EARL SW18 179 M4
Ophir Ter PECK SE15 159 P7
Opossum Wy HSLWW TW4 153 K9
Oppenheim Rd LEW SE13 161 H8
Oppidans Rd HAMP NW3 4 A4
Optima Pk DART DA1 * 165 H9
Opus Pk GU GU1 * 250 A6
Oram Pl HHS/BOV HP3 35 N9
Orange Court La ORP BR6 226 D5
Orange Gv CHIG IG7 102 F7
WAN E11 121 K8
Orange Hill Rd EDGW HA8 95 P8
Orange Pl BERM/RHTH SE16 160 B2
Orangery La ELTH/MOT SE9 184 C1
The Orangery RCHPK/HAM TW10 177 H5
Orange St LSQ/SEVD WC2H 11 K8
WAP E1W 13 P10
Orange Tree Hl ABR/ST RM4 104 E6
Oransay Rd IS N1 6 F2
Oratory La CHEL SW3 * 15 M7
Orbain Rd FUL/PGN SW6 157 H6
Orbel St BTSEA SW11 157 P7
Orbital Crs GSTN WD25 72 G1
Orbital One DART DA1 * 188 A5
Orb St WALW SE17 18 G6
Orchard Av ADL/WDHM KT15 215 J7
ASHF TW15 174 D9
BELV DA17 163 P5
BERK HP4 33 M5
CROY/NA CR0 204 D9
DART DA1 187 J4
EBED/NFELT TW14 174 E1
FNCH N3 117 K1
GSTN WD25 55 J7
GVW DA11 190 E8
HEST TW5 153 M6
MTCM CR4 202 B8
NWMAL KT3 200 B2
RAIN RM13 145 K6
RBRW/HUT CM13 107 L4
SL SL1 128 C7
STHGT/OAK N14 78 D10
STHL UB1 133 M10
THDIT KT7 198 F8
TRDG/WHET N20 97 N3
WDSR SL4 148 F7
Orchard Cl ABR/ST RM4 83 L7
ALP/SUD HA0 135 K3
ASHF TW15 174 D9
BNSTD SM7 221 L10
BORE WD6 75 L8
BUSH WD23 94 C2
BXLYHN DA7 163 P7
CHING E4 100 F5
CHOB/PIR GU24 212 C9
CRICK NW2 116 D8
DEN/HRF UB9 131 L1
EDGW HA8 95 K7
EGH TW20 172 E8
EHSLY KT24 234 G10
FSTH SE23 182 B2
GU GU1 250 E10
HART DA3 211 N2
HERT/BAY SG13 42 D5
HHNE HP2 36 A4
HOR/WEW KT19 * 219 N3
HORL RH6 280 A3
IS N1 6 F4
LHD/OX KT22 236 C8
LHD/OX KT22 236 E5
NKENS W10 8 B3
POTB/CUF EN6 60 F4
RAD WD7 74 D3
RBSF CM22 30 D3
RGUW GU3 248 A10
RKW/CH/CXG WD3 70 G7
RSEV TN14 247 K7
RSLP HA4 112 D5
RYNPK SW20 200 F4
SOCK/AV RM15 147 H6
STAL AL1 38 E7
THDIT KT7 198 G8
WARE SG12 26 C1
WARE SG12 27 H7
WAT WD17 72 G6
WOKS/MYFD GU22 232 E2
WOT/HER KT12 197 J7
Orchard Cottages
HYS/HAR UB3 * 152 F1
KUTN/CMB KT2 * 199 M1
Orchard Ct BEAC HP9 89 H6
WLGTN SM6 * 222 C2
WPK KT4 * 200 D8
Orchard Crs EDGW HA8 95 P6
EN EN1 79 N5
Orchard Cft HLW CM20 29 K9
Orchard Dr ASHTD KT21 237 J6
BKHTH/KID SE3 161 K8
EDGW HA8 95 L6
EPP CM16 83 H2
GRAYS RM17 167 M1
LCOL/BKTW AL2 56 A2
RKW/CH/CXG WD3 70 F8
UX/CGN UB8 131 N6
WAT WD17 72 G5
WOKN/KNAP GU21 232 B1
Orchard End CTHM CR3 241 M8
LHD/OX KT22 236 B10
WEY KT13 196 F9
Orchard End Av AMSS HP7 69 L5
Orchardfield Rd GODL GU7 267 L10
Orchard Gdns CHSGTN KT9 219 K1
EHSLY KT24 253 M4
EPSOM KT18 237 P1
WAB EN9 62 G10
Orchard Ga CDALE/KGS NW9 116 B2
ESH/CLAY KT10 198 C8
GFD/PVL UB6 134 G1
SLN SL2 109 H10
Orchard Gn ORP BR6 207 H9
Orchard Gv CFSP/GDCR SL9 89 P9
CROY/NA CR0 204 D7
EDGW HA8 95 M9
KTN/HRWW/WS HA3 115 L3
ORP BR6 207 J9
PGE/AN SE20 181 P10
Orchard Hl BFOR GU20 212 C4
DART DA1 186 F1
LEW SE13 160 G8
Orchard House La STAL AL1 38 C7
Orchard La AMS HP6 69 J4
BRWN CM15 86 E9
E/WMO/HCT KT8 198 C6
RYNPK SW20 200 E1
WFD IG8 101 P5
Orchard Lea MEO DA13 * 189 L7
Orchard Lea Cl
WOKS/MYFD GU22 233 H1
Orchardleigh LHD/OX KT22 236 G8
Orchardleigh Av PEND EN3 80 B6
Orchard Mains
WOKS/MYFD GU22 231 P6
Orchard Md HAT AL10 40 C4
Orchardmede WCHMH N21 79 L10
Orchard Mew
WOKN/KNAP GU21 230 G4
Orchard Ms IS N1 7 H4
TOOT SW17 179 M6
The Orchard on the Gn
RKW/CH/CXG WD3 72 A9
Orchard Pde POTB/CUF EN6 * 58 G7
Orchard Pl CHES/WCR EN8 62 C6
POP/IOD E14 141 K9
STMC/STPC BR5 * 207 M3
TOTM N17 99 N8
UX/CGN UB8 * 131 M7
Orchard Ri CROY/NA CR0 204 D8
KUTN/CMB KT2 199 P1
PIN HA5 112 G1
RCHPK/HAM TW10 155 N10
Orchard Ri East BFN/LL DA15 185 H1
Orchard Ri West BFN/LL DA15 185 H1
Orchard Rd BAR EN5 77 H8
BEAC HP9 88 E10
BEAC HP9 89 H6
BELV DA17 164 B3
BMLY BR1 205 P1
BTFD TW8 155 H5
CHSGTN KT9 219 K1
CSTG HP8 89 P3
DAGE RM10 144 B3
DORK RH4 272 G3
FELT TW13 175 H5
GUW GU2 267 L2
GVW DA11 189 P5
HGT N6 118 C5
HORL RH6 281 J4
HPTN TW12 175 N10
HYS/HAR UB3 133 H9
KUT/HW KT1 199 K2
ORP BR6 226 E2
ORP BR6 227 M5
PEND EN3 80 B9
RCH/KEW TW9 155 M9
REIG RH2 257 L10
RGUE GU4 250 E6
RGUE GU4 268 B6
ROMW/RG RM7 104 C10
RSEV TN14 246 G2
SAND/SEL CR2 224 A10
SCUP DA14 185 H7
SEV TN13 246 F8
SHGR GU5 270 B5
SOCK/AV RM15 147 H7
SUN TW16 175 J10
SUT SM1 221 K2
SWCM DA10 189 K1
TWK TW1 176 F1
WDSR SL4 171 N3
WELL DA16 163 L9
Orchards Cl BF/WBF KT14 215 K10
Orchardson St STJWD NW8 9 L2
Orchard Sq BROX EN10 44 E10
WKENS W14 14 C8
The Orchards CRAWW RH11 282 G8
EPP CM16 65 K8
Orchard St CRAWW RH11 283 N7
DART DA1 187 M2
HHS/BOV HP3 35 N10
MBLAR W1H 10 C6
STALW/RED AL3 38 B7
WALTH E17 120 D2
Orchard Ter EN EN1 * 79 P10
RDART DA2 * 188 D1
WLSDN NW10 * 116 C9
The Orchard BKHTH/KID SE3 161 J8
BNSTD SM7 239 K1
BROX EN10 * 44 F6
CHSWK W4 156 B3
EW KT17 220 C4
GLDGN NW11 117 K3
HERT/WAT SG14 25 J2
HORL RH6 * 280 B4
HSLW TW3 154 B8
KGLGY WD4 54 B5
LTWR GU18 212 A7
RDKG RH5 273 H6
SEV TN13 246 F7
SWLY BR8 208 E2
TRDG/WHET N20 97 L2
VW GU25 194 B5
WCHMH N21 79 L10
WEY KT13 216 C1
WGCW AL8 22 G3
WOKN/KNAP GU21 231 N2
WOKS/MYFD GU22 232 B8
Orchard Vw CHERT KT16 195 K6
Orchard Vls SCUP DA14 * 185 M9
Orchardville SL SL1 128 A6
Orchard Wy ADL/WDHM KT15 215 L2
ASHF TW15 174 A5
BGR/WK TN15 247 P3
CHESW EN7 61 J3
CHIG IG7 103 K4
CROY/NA CR0 204 D7
DORK RH4 272 G3
DTCH/LGLY SL3 130 C10
EN EN1 79 M7
ESH/CLAY KT10 218 B3
HHS/BOV HP3 52 D4
KWD/TDW/WH KT20 257 H2
OXTED RH8 261 M9
POTB/CUF EN6 59 L5
RDART DA2 187 L6
REIG RH2 275 L4
RGUW GU3 * 231 J10
RGUW GU3 248 A10
RKW/CH/CXG WD3 91 K1
RPLY/SEND GU23 250 G1
SUT SM1 221 N1
Orchard Waye UX/CGN UB8 131 N4
Orchehill Av CFSP/GDCR SL9 110 A2
Orchehill Ri CFSP/GDCR SL9 110 B3
Orchid Cl CHESW EN7 61 K6
CHSGTN KT9 219 H4
EHAM E6 142 B7
HAT AL10 22 C10
STHL UB1 133 M8
Orchid Ct EGH TW20 172 E7
Orchid Dr CHOB/PIR GU24 230 F1
Orchid Gdns HSLWW TW4 153 N10
Orchid Rd STHGT/OAK N14 98 D1
Orchid St SHB W12 136 D9
Orchis Gv GRAYS RM17 167 L3
Orchis Wy HARH RM3 105 N7
Orde Cl CRAWE RH10 284 E4
Orde Hall St BMSBY WC1N * 11 N3
Ordell Rd BOW E3 140 E4
Ordnance Cl FELT TW13 175 H5
Ordnance Crs GNWCH SE10 161 K1
Ordnance Hl STJWD NW8 3 M6
Ordnance Ms STJWD NW8 3 M7
Ordnance Rd CAN/RD E16 141 L7
GVE DA12 190 F2
PEND EN3 80 C3
WOOL/PLUM SE18 162 D5
Oregano Cl WDR/YW UB7 132 A9
Oregano Dr POP/IOD E14 141 J8
Oregano Wy GUW GU2 249 M5
Oregon Av MNPK E12 122 C9
Oregon Cl NWMAL KT3 199 P4
Oregon Sq ORP BR6 206 G8
Orestan La EHSLY KT24 253 K3
Orestes Ms KIL/WHAMP NW6 117 K10
Oreston Rd RAIN RM13 145 L5
Orford Gdns TWK TW1 176 E5
Orford Rd CAT SE6 182 G6
SWFD E18 121 N1
WALTH E17 120 G3
Organ Hall Rd BORE WD6 75 K5
Oriel Cl CRAWE RH10 284 D4
MTCM CR4 202 E4
Oriel Ct HAMP NW3 117 M9
Oriel Dr BARN SW13 156 F5
Oriel Gdns CLAY IG5 122 C1
Oriel Rd HOM E9 140 C1
Oriel Wy NTHLT UB5 134 A2
Oriental Cl WOKS/MYFD GU22 232 C3
Oriental Rd ASC SL5 192 C4
CAN/RD E16 142 A10
WOKS/MYFD GU22 232 E2
Orient Cl STAL AL1 38 E8
Orient St LBTH SE11 18 C5
Orient Wy CLPT E5 120 C8
Oriole Cl ABLGY WD5 55 H7
Oriole Wy THMD SE28 143 L9
Orion Rd MUSWH N10 98 B7
Orion Wy NTHWD HA6 92 G5
Orissa Rd WOOL/PLUM SE18 163 H4
Orkney St BTSEA SW11 158 B8
Orlando Gdns HOR/WEW KT19 220 A6
Orlando Rd CLAP SW4 158 D9
Orleans Rd NRWD SE19 181 L9
TWK TW1 176 G3
Orlestone Gdns ORP BR6 227 P2
Orleston Ms HOLWY N7 6 B1
Orleston Rd HOLWY N7 6 B1
Orley Farm Rd HRW HA1 114 D9
Orlick Rd GVE DA12 191 L5
Orltons La HORS RH12 282 C3
Ormanton Rd SYD SE26 181 P7
Orme Ct BAY/PAD W2 8 G8
Orme Court Ms BAY/PAD W2 * 9 H8
Orme La BAY/PAD W2 8 G8
Ormeley Rd BAL SW12 180 C3
Orme Rd KUT/HW KT1 199 N2
SUT SM1 221 L3
Ormerod Gdns MTCM CR4 202 B2
Ormesby Cl THMD SE28 143 N9
Ormesby Dr POTB/CUF EN6 58 G8
Ormesby Wk CRAWE RH10 284 C9
Ormesby Wy
KTN/HRWW/WS HA3 115 L4
Orme Sq BAY/PAD W2 8 G8
Orme Square Ga BAY/PAD W2 8 G8
Ormiston Gv SHB W12 136 E10
Ormiston Rd GNWCH SE10 161 M4
Ormond Av HPTN TW12 198 A1
Ormond Cl BMSBY WC1N 11 M3
Ormond Crs HPTN TW12 176 A10
Ormond Dr HPTN TW12 176 A10
Ormonde Av HOR/WEW KT19 220 A5
ORP BR6 206 F9
Ormonde Ct STJWD NW8 * 4 A6
Ormonde Ga CHEL SW3 16 B8
Ormonde Pl BGVA SW1W 16 D6
WEY KT13 * 216 E3
Ormonde Ri BKHH IG9 101 P2
Ormonde Rd MORT/ESHN SW14 155 N9
NTHWD HA6 92 E5
WOKN/KNAP GU21 231 P2
Ormonde Ter STJWD NW8 4 A6
Ormond Rd ARCH N19 118 F6
RCHPK/HAM TW10 177 J1
Ormond Yd STJS SW1Y 11 H9
Ormsby BELMT SM2 * 221 L4
Ormsby Gdns GFD/PVL UB6 134 B4
Ormsby Pl STNW/STAM N16 119 N8
Ormsby St BETH E2 7 L7
Ormside St PECK SE15 160 B5
Ormside Wy REDH RH1 258 C7
Ormskirk Rd OXHEY WD19 93 L5
Ornan Rd HAMP NW3 117 P10
Oronsay HHS/BOV HP3 36 C8
Oronsay Wk IS N1 6 F2
Orphanage Rd WAT WD17 73 K6
Orpheus St CMBW SE5 159 L7
Orpington By-Pass ORP BR6 227 M1
RSEV TN14 228 B5
Orpington Gdns UED N18 99 M4
Orpington Rd CHST BR7 207 H3
WCHMH N21 99 H2
Orpin Rd REDH RH1 258 D6
Orpwood Cl HPTN TW12 175 N9
Orsett Heath Crs
CDW/CHF RM16 168 D2
Orsett Ms BAY/PAD W2 9 J5
Orsett Rd GRAYS RM17 167 N4
Orsett St LBTH SE11 17 P7
Orsett Ter BAY/PAD W2 9 J5
WFD IG8 101 P9
Orsman Rd IS N1 7 J6
Orton Cl STALE/WH AL4 38 F2
Orton Gv EN EN1 79 N5
Orton St WAP E1W 13 N10
Orville Rd BTSEA SW11 157 N8
Orwell Cl HYS/HAR UB3 132 F9
WDSR SL4 149 J9
Orwell Ct WATN WD24 73 L7
Orwell Gdns REIG RH2 275 L2
Orwell Rd PLSTW E13 141 P4
Osbaldeston Rd
STNW/STAM N16 119 P7
Osberton Rd LEE/GVPK SE12 183 M1
Osbert St WEST SW1P 17 J6
Osborn Cl HACK E8 7 N5
Osborne Av STWL/WRAY TW19 173 P4
Osborne Cl BECK BR3 204 D4
EBAR EN4 78 A7
EMPK RM11 125 J4
FELT TW13 175 L8
Osborne Ct EA W5 * 135 K7
WDSR SL4 149 H8
Osborne Gdns POTB/CUF EN6 59 L6
THHTH CR7 203 K2
Osborne Gv WALTH E17 120 E2
Osborne Hts BRW CM14 106 G5
Osborne Ms WALTH E17 120 E3
WDSR SL4 * 149 H8
Osborne Rd ACT W3 155 N1
BELV DA17 164 A4
BKHH IG9 101 N2
BROX EN10 44 F5
BRWN CM15 86 G10
CHES/WCR EN8 62 D3
CRICK NW2 136 E1
EGH TW20 172 C9
EMPK RM11 125 J4
FSBYPK N4 119 H6
FSTGT E7 121 N10
HOM E9 140 E1
HSLW TW3 153 N9
KUTN/CMB KT2 177 K10
LEY E10 120 G8
PEND EN3 80 D6
PLMGR N13 99 H4
POTB/CUF EN6 59 L6
REDH RH1 258 B7
STHL UB1 134 B8
THHTH CR7 203 K2
WATN WD24 73 K4
WDSR SL4 149 J9
WOT/HER KT12 197 H8
Osborne Sq DAGW RM9 124 A9
Osborne St SL SL1 149 L1
Osborne Ter TOOT SW17 * 180 B8
Osborne Wy CHSGTN KT9 219 L2
Osborn Gdns MLHL NW7 96 G8
Osborn La FSTH SE23 182 D3
Osborn Rd UX/CGN UB8 * 131 M2
Osborn St WCHPL E1 13 M4
Osborn Ter BKHTH/KID SE3 161 L10
Osborn Wy WGCW AL8 22 G4
Osbourne Av KGLGY WD4 54 A4
Osbourne Ct RYLN/HDSTN HA2 * 114 A2
Osbourne Rd RDART DA2 188 A2
Oscar Faber Pl IS N1 * 7 K4
Oscar St BROCKY SE4 160 F8
Oseney Crs KTTN NW5 5 H1
Osgood Av ORP BR6 227 J2
Osgood Gdns ORP BR6 227 J2
Osidge La STHGT/OAK N14 98 B2
Osier Crs MUSWH N10 98 A9
Osier Pl EGH TW20 172 F9
Osiers Rd WAND/EARL SW18 157 K10
The Osiers WATW WD18 72 D10
Osier St WCHPL E1 140 B6
Osier Wy BNSTD SM7 221 H10
LEY E10 120 G8
MTCM CR4 201 P5
Oslac Rd CAT SE6 182 G8
Oslow Cl NKENS W10 2 C9
Osman Rd ED N9 99 P4
HMSMTH W6 * 156 F2
Osmond Cl RYLN/HDSTN HA2 114 B7
Osmond Gdns WLGTN SM6 222 D2
Osmund Cl CRAWE RH10 284 F7
Osmund St SHB W12 136 C8
Osnaburgh St CAMTN NW1 10 F2
Osnaburgh Ter CAMTN NW1 10 F1
Osney Cl CRAWW RH11 283 M8
Osney Wk MRDN SM4 201 N6
Osney Wy GVE DA12 191 J5
Osprey Cl EHAM E6 142 B7
GSTN WD25 55 M10
HAYES BR2 206 B8
SUT SM1 221 J2
WALTH E17 100 D8
WAN E11 121 M2
WDR/YW UB7 151 N1
Osprey Est BERM/RHTH SE16 160 C3
Osprey Gdns SAND/SEL CR2 224 D6
Osprey Ms PEND EN3 80 B9
Osprey Rd WAB EN9 63 M10
Ospringe Cl PGE/AN SE20 182 B10
Ospringe Rd KTTN NW5 118 D9
Osram Rd WBLY HA9 115 J8
Ossian Rd FSBYPK N4 118 G5
Ossier Ms CHSWK W4 156 C5
Ossington Buildings
MHST W1U * 10 C3
Ossington Cl BAY/PAD W2 * 8 F8
Ossington St BAY/PAD W2 8 G8
Ossory Rd STHWK SE1 19 N8
Ossulston St CAMTN NW1 5 K8
Ossulton Pl EFNCH N2 * 117 M1
Ossulton Wy EFNCH N2 117 M2
Ostade Rd BRXS/STRHM SW2 180 G3
Ostell Crs PEND EN3 80 F4
Osten Ms SKENS SW7 15 H4
Osterberg Rd DART DA1 165 N10
Osterley Av ISLW TW7 154 C6
Osterley Cl STMC/STPC BR5 207 K1
Osterley Crs ISLW TW7 154 D7
Osterley Gdns THHTH CR7 203 K2
Osterley La ISLW TW7 154 B3
Osterley Park Rd NWDGN UB2 153 N2
Osterley Park View Rd
HNWL W7 154 D1
Osterley Rd ISLW TW7 154 D7
STNW/STAM N16 119 M9
Oster St STALW/RED AL3 38 B5
Ostlers Dr ASHF TW15 174 D8
Ostliffe Rd PLMGR N13 99 J6
Oswald Cl LHD/OX KT22 236 B8
Oswald Rd LHD/OX KT22 236 B8
STAL AL1 38 D7
STHL UB1 133 M10
Oswald's Md HOM E9 120 D9
Oswald St CLPT E5 120 C8
Oswald Ter CRICK NW2 * 116 F8
Osward CROY/NA CR0 224 E6
Osward Pl ED N9 99 P3
Osward Rd BAL SW12 180 A5
Oswin St LBTH SE11 18 D5
Oswyth Rd CMBW SE5 159 M8
Otford Cl BMLY BR1 206 D3
BXLY DA5 186 C2
PGE/AN SE20 204 B1
Otford Crs BROCKY SE4 182 E2
Otford La RSEV TN14 228 A9
Otford Rd RSEV TN14 247 J4
Othello Cl LBTH SE11 18 C7
Otis St BOW E3 141 H5
Otley Ct FBAR/BDGN N11 98 B7
Otley Dr GNTH/NBYPK IG2 122 E4
Otley Rd CAN/RD E16 141 P8
Otley Ter CLPT E5 120 B7
Otley Wy OXHEY WD19 93 K4
Otlinge Rd STMC/STPC BR5 207 N4
Ottawa Ct BROX EN10 62 D1
Ottawa Gdns DAGE RM10 144 E2
Ottawa Rd TIL RM18 168 D8
Ottaway St CLPT E5 119 P8
Otterbourne Rd CHING E4 101 J4
CROY/NA CR0 203 K9
Otterburn Gdns ISLW TW7 154 F6
Otterburn St TOOT SW17 180 A9
Otter Cl CHERT KT16 214 E3
SRTFD E15 141 H3
Otterden Cl ORP BR6 227 H1
Otterden St CAT SE6 182 F7
Otterfield Rd WDR/YW UB7 131 P9
Otter Gdns HAT AL10 40 E5
Ottermead La CHERT KT16 214 F3
Otter Meadow LHD/OX KT22 236 E5
Otter Rd GFD/PVL UB6 134 B6
Otters Cl STMC/STPC BR5 207 N4
Otterspool La GSTN WD25 73 M4
Otterspool Wy GSTN WD25 73 N5
Otto Cl SYD SE26 182 A6
Ottoman Ter WAT WD17 73 K7
Otto St WALW SE17 18 C10
Ottways Av ASHTD KT21 237 J5
Ottways La ASHTD KT21 237 J6
Otway Cl CRAWW RH11 283 J9
Otway Gdns BUSH WD23 94 D1
Otways Cl POTB/CUF EN6 59 L9
Oulton Cl THMD SE28 143 M8
Oulton Crs BARK IG11 143 J1
POTB/CUF EN6 58 G8
Oulton Rd SEVS/STOTM N15 119 L3
Oulton Wk CRAWE RH10 284 C9
Oulton Wy OXHEY WD19 93 N5
Oundle Av BUSH WD23 74 B10
Ousden Cl CHES/WCR EN8 62 D6

Ousden Dr CHES/WCR EN8 62 D6
Ouseley Rd BAL SW12 180 A4
STWL/WRAY TW19 171 P3
Outdowns EHSLY KT24 253 J6
Outer Cir CAMTN NW1 4 B7
Outfield Rd CFSP/GDCR SL9 90 A8
Outgate Rd WLSDN NW10 136 C2
Outing's La BRWN CM15 86 G2
Outlook Dr CSTG HP8 90 A4
Outram Pl IS N1 5 M5
WEY KT13 216 D2
Outram Rd CROY/NA CR0 203 N9
EHAM E6 142 B3
WDGN N22 98 E9
Outwich St HDTCH EC3A * 13 K5
Outwood La COUL/CHIP CR5 240 B2
KWD/TDW/WH KT20 239 L8
REDH RH1 259 L10
REDH RH1 277 L9
Oval Ct EDGW HA8 * 95 P8
Oval Gdns GRAYS RM17 167 P2
Oval Pl VX/NE SW8 158 G6
Oval Rd CAMTN NW1 4 E5
CROY/NA CR0 203 L9
Oval Rd North DAGE RM10 144 D3
Oval Rd South DAGE RM10 144 D4
The Oval BETH E2 140 A4
BFN/LL DA15 185 K3
BNSTD SM7 221 K10
BROX EN10 62 D1
GODL GU7 267 L10
HART DA3 211 P3
RGUW GU3 248 G9
Oval Wy CFSP/GDCR SL9 110 B2
LBTH SE11 17 P9
Ovenden Rd RSEV TN14 245 N6
Overbrae BECK BR3 182 F9
Overbrook EHSLY KT24 252 C5
Overbrook Wk EDGW HA8 95 M8
Overbury Av BECK BR3 204 G3
Overbury Crs CROY/NA CR0 225 H6
Overbury Rd FSBYPK N4 119 L4
Overbury St CLPT E5 120 C9
Overcliffe GVW DA11 190 D2
Overcliff Rd GRAYS RM17 168 A4
LEW SE13 160 F9
Overcourt Cl BFN/LL DA15 185 L2
Overdale ASHTD KT21 237 K2
RDKG RH5 273 H1
REDH RH1 259 K9
RSEV TN14 265 J9
Overdale Av NWMAL KT3 199 P2
Overdale Rd CSHM HP5 50 G4
EA W5 155 H2
Overdene Dr CRAWW RH11 283 K7
Overdown Rd CAT SE6 182 F7
Overhill WARL CR6 242 B5
Overhill Cottages MTCM CR4 * 202 B2
Overhill Rd EDUL SE22 181 P3
PUR/KEN CR8 223 H5
Overhill Wy BECK BR3 205 J5
Overlea Rd CLPT E5 119 P5
Overlord Cl BROX EN10 44 D6
Overlord Ct LHD/OX KT22 236 C7
Overmead ELTH/MOT SE9 184 G3
SWLY BR8 208 F5
Over Minnis HART DA3 211 L10
Overstand Cl BECK BR3 204 F5
Overstone Gdns CROY/NA CR0 204 E7
Overstone Rd HARP AL5 20 B2
HMSMTH W6 156 F3
Overstream RKW/CH/CXG WD3 71 L8
Over the Misbourne
CFSP/GDCR SL9 110 D4
Over the Misbourne Rd
DEN/HRF UB9 110 F4
Overthorpe Cl
WOKN/KNAP GU21 231 K3
Overton Cl ISLW TW7 154 E7
WLSDN NW10 135 P1
Overton Dr CHDH RM6 123 M5
WAN E11 121 N5
Overton Rd ABYW SE2 163 M2
BELMT SM2 221 K4
BRXN/ST SW9 159 H8
LEY E10 120 D6
STHGT/OAK N14 78 F9
Overton's Yd CROY/NA CR0 203 K10
Overy Liberty DART DA1 187 M3
Overy St DART DA1 187 N2
Ovesdon Av RYLN/HDSTN HA2 113 N6
Oveton Wy GT/LBKH KT23 253 P2
Ovett Cl NRWD SE19 181 M9
Ovex Cl POP/IOD E14 161 H2
Ovington Ct WOKN/KNAP GU21 231 L2
Ovington Gdns CHEL SW3 15 P4
Ovington Ms CHEL SW3 15 P4
Ovington Sq CHEL SW3 15 P4
Ovington St CHEL SW3 15 P4
Owen Cl CROY/NA CR0 203 L6
CRW RM5 104 B7
DTCH/LGLY SL3 150 C4
NTHLT UB5 133 M1
THMD SE28 143 M10
YEAD UB4 * 133 J5
Owen Gdns WFD IG8 102 B7
Owenite St ABYW SE2 163 L3
Owen Pl LHD/OX KT22 * 236 G8
Owen Rd BFOR GU20 212 C2
PLMGR N13 99 K6
Owens Ms WAN E11 121 K7
Owen's Rw FSBYE EC1V 6 C9
Owen St FSBYE EC1V 6 C8
Owens Wy FSTH SE23 182 D3
RKW/CH/CXG WD3 72 B9
Owen Wk PGE/AN SE20 181 P10
Owen Wy WLSDN NW10 135 P1
Owgan Cl CMBW SE5 159 L6
Owl Cl SAND/SEL CR2 224 C6
Owlets Hall Cl EMPK RM11 125 N1
Owletts CRAWE RH10 284 E6
Owl Pk LOU IG10 * 81 L6
Owlsears Cl BEAC HP9 88 C7
Ownstead Gdns SAND/SEL CR2 223 N7
Ownsted Hl CROY/NA CR0 225 H6
Oxberry Av FUL/PGN SW6 157 H8
Oxdowne Cl COB KT11 218 A10
Oxenden Wood Rd ORP BR6 227 L3
Oxendon Dr HOD EN11 44 F4
Oxendon St SOHO/SHAV W1D * 11 J8
Oxenford St PECK SE15 159 N9
Oxenhill Rd BGR/WK TN15 247 M3
Oxenpark Av WBLY HA9 115 K5
Oxestalls Rd DEPT SE8 160 D4
Oxfield Cl BERK HP4 33 M6
Oxford Av CDW/CHF RM16 168 D3
EMPK RM11 125 P2
HEST TW5 153 P4
HYS/HAR UB3 152 G6
RYNPK SW20 201 H2
SL SL1 128 E7
STAL AL1 39 H7
STHGT/OAK N14 98 D2
Oxford Cl ASHF TW15 174 D10
CHES/WCR EN8 62 B5
ED N9 100 A3
GPK RM2 125 J3
GVE DA12 191 J5
MTCM CR4 202 D3
NTHWD HA6 92 D5
Oxford Ct BRW CM14 107 J5
MANHO EC4N 12 G7
Oxford Crs NWMAL KT3 200 A6
Oxford Dr RSLP HA4 113 K7
Oxford Gdns CHSWK W4 155 M4
DEN/HRF UB9 111 K8
NKENS W10 136 G8
TRDG/WHET N20 97 N2
WCHMH N21 99 K1
Oxford Ga HMSMTH W6 156 G3
Oxford Ms BXLY DA5 186 B4
Oxford Pl HAT AL10 40 B2
Oxford Rd CAR SM5 221 P3
CFSP/GDCR SL9 109 M2
DEN/HRF UB9 110 G7
EA W5 135 J9
ED N9 100 A3
FSBYPK N4 119 H6
GU GU1 268 A2
HARH RM3 105 N7
HRW HA1 114 B4
IL IG1 122 F10
KIL/WHAMP NW6 2 F7
KTN/HRWW/WS HA3 114 E1
NRWD SE19 181 L9
PEND EN3 80 A9
PUT/ROE SW15 157 H10
REDH RH1 257 P9
SCUP DA14 185 L8
SRTFD E15 141 J1
TEDD TW11 176 C8
WDSR SL4 149 H7
WFD IG8 102 A6
WLGTN SM6 * 222 D2
Oxford Rd East WDSR SL4 149 H7
Oxford Rd North CHSWK W4 155 N4
Oxford Rd South CHSWK W4 155 N4
Oxford Rw SUN TW16 * 197 K3
Oxford Sq BAY/PAD W2 9 N6
Oxford St OXSTW W1C 10 C6
WATW WD18 73 J9
Oxford Ter GU GU1 268 A2
Oxford Wk STHL UB1 133 N10
Oxford Wy FELT TW13 175 L7
Oxgate Court Pde CRICK NW2 * 116 E7
Oxgate Gdns CRICK NW2 116 E8
Oxgate La CRICK NW2 116 E7
Oxhawth Crs HAYES BR2 206 D5
Oxhey Av OXHEY WD19 93 L1
Oxhey Dr NTHWD HA6 93 J6
Oxhey La OXHEY WD19 93 L2
PIN HA5 93 P6
Oxhey Ridge Cl NTHWD HA6 93 H6
Oxhey Rd OXHEY WD19 93 K1
Oxleas EHAM E6 142 E8
Oxleas Cl WELL DA16 162 G8
Oxlease Dr HAT AL10 40 E5
Oxleay Rd RYLN/HDSTN HA2 113 P6
Oxleigh Cl NWMAL KT3 200 B5
Oxley Cl GPK RM2 105 K10
STHWK SE1 19 M7
Oxleys Rd CRICK NW2 116 E8
WAB EN9 63 M9
The Oxleys HLWE CM17 29 N7
Oxlow La DAGE RM10 124 B9
Oxonian St EDUL SE22 159 N10
Oxshott Ri COB KT11 217 M10
Oxshott Rd LHD/OX KT22 236 E2
Oxshott Wy COB KT11 235 M1
Oxted Cl MTCM CR4 201 N3
Oxted Rd GDST RH9 260 E7
Oxtoby Wy STRHM/NOR SW16 202 E1
Oyster Catchers Cl CAN/RD E16 141 N8
Oysterfields STALW/RED AL3 38 A5
Oyster La BF/WBF KT14 215 N7
Oyster Rw WCHPL E1 140 B8
Ozolins Wy CAN/RD E16 141 L8

P

Pablo Neruda HNHL SE24 159 J10
Paceheath Cl CRW RM5 104 E7
Pace Pl WCHPL E1 140 A8
Pacific Cl EBED/NFELT TW14 174 G4
SWCM DA10 189 K1
Pacific Rd CAN/RD E16 141 M8
Packet Boat La IVER SL0 131 L8
Packham Cl ORP BR6 207 M10
Packham Rd GVW DA11 190 C6
Packhorse Cl STALE/WH AL4 39 H3
Packhorse La POTB/CUF EN6 58 A7
Packhorse Rd CFSP/GDCR SL9 110 B4
SEV TN13 246 E9
Packington Sq IS N1 6 E6
Packington St IS N1 6 D6
Packmores Rd ELTH/MOT SE9 184 G1
Padbrook OXTED RH8 261 M5
Padbury Cl EBED/NFELT TW14 174 E4
Padbury Ct BETH E2 7 M10
Padcroft Rd WDR/YW UB7 131 N10
Paddenswick Rd HMSMTH W6 156 D2
Paddick Cl HOD EN11 44 E2
Paddington Cl YEAD UB4 133 L6
Paddington Gn BAY/PAD W2 9 L4
Paddington St MHST W1U 10 C3
Paddock Cl BKHTH/KID SE3 161 M9
EYN DA4 210 B1
NTHLT UB5 133 P4
ORP BR6 226 E1
OXHEY WD19 73 M10
OXTED RH8 261 L7
SYD SE26 182 C7
WARE SG12 28 A2
WPK KT4 200 B8
Paddock Gdns NRWD SE19 181 M9
Paddockhurst Rd CRAWW RH11 283 K8
Paddock La BAR EN5 76 B8
Paddock Md HLWS CM18 46 F6
Paddock Rd BXLYHS DA6 163 P10
CRICK NW2 116 D8
RSLP HA4 113 L8
Paddocks Cl COB KT11 217 K10
RYLN/HDSTN HA2 114 A9
STMC/STPC BR5 207 N9
Paddocks Md WOKN/KNAP GU21 231 K2
Paddocks Rd RGUE GU4 250 D6
The Paddocks ABR/ST RM4 84 G10
ADL/WDHM KT15 215 L6
EA W5 * 155 J2
EBAR EN4 78 A7
GT/LBKH KT23 254 A2
HERT/BAY SG13 26 A8
MLHL NW7 * 97 J7
RGUW GU3 248 B10
RKW/CH/CXG WD3 71 J8
STALE/WH AL4 * 39 N8
WBLY HA9 115 N7
WEY KT13 196 F10
WEY KT13 * 215 P7
WGCE AL7 23 L4
Paddocks Wy ASHTD KT21 237 K4
CHERT KT16 195 L8
The Paddock BH/WHM TN16 262 F2
BROX EN10 44 F6
CFSP/GDCR SL9 90 B6
CRAWE RH10 284 E6
DORK RH4 272 A3
DTCH/LGLY SL3 149 N7
GU GU1 250 G9
HAT AL10 40 D3
HGDN/ICK UB10 112 C9
VW GU25 * 194 B6
WDSR SL4 * 148 B6
WDSR SL4 * 170 A4
Paddock Wk WARL CR6 242 A5
Paddock Wy CHST BR7 184 G10
OXTED RH8 261 L7
PUT/ROE SW15 178 F3
WOKN/KNAP GU21 214 E10
Paddock Wd HARP AL5 20 D4
Padfield Rd BRXN/ST SW9 159 K9
Padley Cl CHSGTN KT9 219 L2
Padnall Rd CHDH RM6 123 N1
Padstow Cl DTCH/LGLY SL3 * 150 B2
ORP BR6 227 J1
Padstow Rd ENC/FH EN2 79 J6
Padstow Wk EBED/NFELT TW14 174 G4
Padua Rd PGE/AN SE20 204 B1
Pagden St VX/NE SW8 158 C7
Pageant Cl TIL RM18 168 F7
Pageant Crs BERM/RHTH SE16 140 E10
Pageant Rd STAL AL1 38 C7
Pageant Wk CROY/NA CR0 203 M10
Page Av WBLY HA9 115 P8
Page Cl DAGW RM9 123 P10
HPTN TW12 175 M9
KTN/HRWW/WS HA3 115 L4
RDART DA2 189 H6
Page Crs CROY/NA CR0 223 J2
ERITH DA8 164 G6
Page Green Rd
SEVS/STOTM N15 * 119 P3
Page Green Ter
SEVS/STOTM N15 119 N3
Page Heath La BMLY BR1 206 A3
Page Heath Vls BMLY BR1 206 A3
Page Hl WARE SG12 26 A1
Pagehurst Rd CROY/NA CR0 203 P7
Page Meadow MLHL NW7 96 D8
Page Rd EBED/NFELT TW14 174 E2
HERT/BAY SG13 25 P5
Pages Cft BERK HP4 33 M3
Page's Hl MUSWH N10 98 B10
Pages La HARH RM3 106 A10
MUSWH N10 98 B10
UX/CGN UB8 131 M1
Page St MLHL NW7 96 D9
WEST SW1P 17 K5
Pages Wk STHWK SE1 19 K4
Pages Yd CHSWK W4 * 156 B5
Paget Av SUT SM1 201 N10
Paget Cl HPTN TW12 176 C7
Paget Gdns CHST BR7 206 E1
Paget La ISLW TW7 154 C9
Paget Pl KUTN/CMB KT2 * 177 P9
THDIT KT7 198 E8
Paget Ri WOOL/PLUM SE18 162 D6
Paget Rd DTCH/LGLY SL3 150 C3
HGDN/ICK UB10 132 D6
IL IG1 122 E9
STNW/STAM N16 119 L6
Paget St FSBYE EC1V 6 C9
Paget Ter WOOL/PLUM SE18 162 E5
Pagette Wy GRAYS RM17 167 M4
Pagewood Cl CRAWE RH10 284 E9
Pagitts Gv EBAR EN4 77 L5
Paglesfield RBRW/HUT CM13 87 P10
Pagnell St NWCR SE14 160 E6
Pagoda Av RCH/KEW TW9 155 L9
Pagoda Gdns BKHTH/KID SE3 161 J8
Pagoda Gv WNWD SE27 181 K5
Paiges Farm Cl RSEV TN14 265 K9
Paignton Rd RSLP HA4 113 H8
SEVS/STOTM N15 119 M4
Paines Brook Wy HARH RM3 105 N7
Paines Cl PIN HA5 113 M1
Painesfield Dr CHERT KT16 195 L9
Paine's La PIN HA5 93 M10
Pain's Cl MTCM CR4 202 C2
Pains Hl COB KT11 * 216 G10
OXTED RH8 261 P8
Pains Hill Pk COB KT11 * 216 G9
Painsthorpe Rd
STNW/STAM N16 119 M8
Painters Ash La GVW DA11 190 A6
Painters La PEND EN3 80 D1
Painters Ms BERM/RHTH SE16 19 P5
Painters Rd GNTH/NBYPK IG2 123 K1
Paisley Rd CAR SM5 201 N8
WDGN N22 99 J9
Paisley Ter CAR SM5 201 N8
Pakeman St HOLWY N7 118 G8
Pakenham Cl BAL SW12 180 B4
Pakenham St FSBYW WC1X 5 P10
Pakes Wy EPP CM16 83 H3
Palace Av KENS W8 9 H10
Palace Cl KGLGY WD4 54 A6
SL SL1 128 E10
Palace Ct BAY/PAD W2 8 G7
KTN/HRWW/WS HA3 115 K4
Palace Court Gdns MUSWH N10 118 D1
Palace Dr WEY KT13 196 C10
Palace Gdns BKHH IG9 102 A2
Palace Gardens Ms KENS W8 8 G9
Palace Gardens Ter KENS W8 8 F9
Palace Ga KENS W8 15 J2
Palace Gates Rd WDGN N22 98 F9
Palace Gn CROY/NA CR0 224 E4
KENS W8 8 G10
Palace Gv BMLY BR1 205 N1
NRWD SE19 181 N10
Palace Ms FUL/PGN SW6 * 157 J6
WALTH E17 120 E2
Palace Pde WALTH E17 * 120 E2
Palace Pl WESTW SW1E 16 G3
Palace Rd ADL/WDHM KT15 215 L5
BH/WHM TN16 244 D7
BMLY BR1 205 N1
BRXS/STRHM SW2 180 G4
CEND/HSY/T N8 118 F3
E/WMO/HCT KT8 198 C3
FBAR/BDGN N11 98 F8
KUT/HW KT1 199 J4
NRWD SE19 181 N10
RSLP HA4 113 M9
Palace Sq NRWD SE19 181 N10
Palace St WESTW SW1E 16 G3
Palace Vw BMLY BR1 205 N3
CROY/NA CR0 224 E1
LEE/GVPK SE12 183 M5
Palace View Rd CHING E4 100 G6
Palace Wy WOKS/MYFD GU22 232 E6
Palamos Rd LEY E10 120 F6
Palatine Av STNW/STAM N16 119 M9
Palatine Rd STNW/STAM N16 119 M9
Palemead Cl FUL/PGN SW6 156 G7
Palermo Rd WLSDN NW10 136 D4
Palestine Gv WIM/MER SW19 201 N1
Palewell Cl STMC/STPC BR5 207 L2
Palewell Common Dr
MORT/ESHN SW14 178 A1
Palewell Pk MORT/ESHN SW14 178 A1
Paley Gdns LOU IG10 82 E7
Palfrey Cl STALW/RED AL3 38 C4
Palfrey Pl VX/NE SW8 158 G6
Palgrave Av STHL UB1 133 P9
Palgrave Gdns CAMTN NW1 9 P1
Palgrave Rd SHB W12 156 C2
Palins Wy CDW/CHF RM16 147 M10
Palissy St BETH E2 7 L10
Pallant Wy ORP BR6 206 D10
Pallas Rd HHNE HP2 36 A4
Pallett Ct HOD EN11 44 G5
Pallet Wy WOOL/PLUM SE18 162 B7
Pallingham Dr CRAWE RH10 284 D10
Palliser Dr RAIN RM13 145 H7
Palliser Rd CSTG HP8 89 M4
WKENS W14 14 A7
WKENS W14 157 H4
Pall Ml STJS SW1Y 11 J10
Pall Mall East STJS SW1Y 11 J9
Pall Mall Pl STJS SW1Y 11 H10
Palmar Crs BXLYHN DA7 164 B9
Palmar Rd BXLYHN DA7 164 B8
Palmarsh Rd STMC/STPC BR5 207 N4
Palm Av SCUP DA14 185 N9
Palm Cl LEY E10 120 G8
Palmeira Rd BXLYHN DA7 163 N9
Palmer Av BUSH WD23 74 A10
CHEAM SM3 220 F1
GVE DA12 190 G7
Palmer Cl HERT/WAT SG14 25 K3
HEST TW5 153 P7
HORL RH6 280 A2
NTHLT UB5 133 M1
REDH RH1 276 B1
WWKM BR4 205 J9
Palmer Crs CHERT KT16 214 G3
KUT/HW KT1 199 K3
Palmer Dr BMLY BR1 206 E4
Palmer Gdns BAR EN5 76 G9
Palmer Pl HOLWY N7 119 H10
Palmer Rd BCTR RM8 123 N6
CRAWE RH10 284 D10
HERT/WAT SG14 25 L3
PLSTW E13 141 N6
Palmer's Av GRAYS RM17 167 P4
Palmers Dr GRAYS RM17 167 P3
Palmersfield Rd BNSTD SM7 221 K10
Palmers Gv E/WMO/HCT KT8 197 P4
WAB EN9 45 L8
Palmers Hl EPP CM16 65 L5
Palmers La PEND EN3 80 B5
Palmer's Ldg GUW GU2 267 M1
Palmer's Moor La IVER SL0 131 L6
Palmers Orch RSEV TN14 228 G7
Palmers Rd BETH E2 140 C4
BORE WD6 75 P5
FBAR/BDGN N11 98 D6
MORT/ESHN SW14 155 P9
STRHM/NOR SW16 202 G2
Palmerston Av DTCH/LGLY SL3 149 N2
Palmerston Cl REDH RH1 275 P3
WGCW AL8 22 F5
WOKN/KNAP GU21 214 D10
Palmerston Crs PLMGR N13 98 G6
WOOL/PLUM SE18 162 F5
Palmerston Dr STALE/WH AL4 21 J2
Palmerstone Rd RAIN RM13 145 K4
Palmerston Gdns WTHK RM20 167 J4
Palmerston Gv WIM/MER SW19 179 K10
Palmerston Rd ACT W3 155 P2
BKHH IG9 101 P3
CROY/NA CR0 203 L5
FSTGT E7 121 N10
HSLW TW3 154 B7
KIL/WHAMP NW6 2 E3
KTN/HRWW/WS HA3 * 114 D1
MORT/ESHN SW14 155 P10
ORP BR6 226 F1
SUT SM1 221 M2
WALTH E17 120 E2
WDGN N22 98 G8
WHTN TW2 176 D2
WIM/MER SW19 179 K10
WTHK RM20 167 J4
Palmerston Wy VX/NE SW8 * 158 C6
Palmer St STJSPK SW1H 17 J3
Palmers Wy CHES/WCR EN8 62 D5
Palmers Whf KUT/HW KT1 * 199 J2
Palm Gv EA W5 155 K2
GU GU1 249 P5
Palm Rd ROMW/RG RM7 124 D3
Pamela Av HHS/BOV HP3 36 A9
Pamela Ct NFNCH/WDSPK N12 * 97 L7
Pamela Gdns PIN HA5 113 J3
Pampisford Rd PUR/KEN CR8 223 H7
Pams Wy HOR/WEW KT19 220 A2
Pancake La HHNE HP2 36 E7
Pancras La MANHO EC4N 12 F6
Pancras Rd CAMTN NW1 5 K7
Pancroft ABR/ST RM4 83 L7
Pandian Wy KTTN NW5 5 J1
Pandora Rd KIL/WHAMP NW6 2 E1
Panfield Ms GNTH/NBYPK IG2 122 D4
Panfield Rd ABYW SE2 163 K2
Pangbourne Av NKENS W10 * 136 F7
Pangbourne Dr STAN HA7 95 J6
Panhard Pl STHL UB1 134 A9
Pank Av BAR EN5 77 N9
Pankhurst Av CAN/RD E16 141 N10
Pankhurst Cl ISLW TW7 154 E9
NWCR SE14 160 C7
Pankhurst Pl WATN WD24 73 L7
Pankhurst Rd WOT/HER KT12 197 K7
Pankridge OXHEY WD19 * 93 L3
Panmuir Rd RYNPK SW20 200 E1
Panmure Cl HBRY N5 119 J9
Panmure Rd SYD SE26 182 A6
Pannells Cl CHERT KT16 195 J8
Pannells Ct GU GU1 268 A1
Panshanger Dr WGCE AL7 23 M5
Pansy Gdns SHB W12 136 D9
Panter's SWLY BR8 186 G10
Panther Dr WLSDN NW10 116 A10
Pantile Rd WEY KT13 216 E1
Pantile Rw DTCH/LGLY SL3 150 D3
Pantiles Cl PLMGR N13 99 J6
WOKN/KNAP GU21 231 N4
The Pantiles BMLY BR1 206 B3
BUSH WD23 94 C2
BXLYHN DA7 164 A6
Panton Cl CROY/NA CR0 203 J8
Panton St STJS SW1Y 11 K8
Panxworth Rd HHS/BOV HP3 35 N8
Paper Buildings EMB EC4Y * 12 B7
Papercourt La RPLY/SEND GU23 233 J8
Paper Ms DORK RH4 272 C1
Papermill Cl CAR SM5 222 B1
Papillons Wk BKHTH/KID SE3 161 M8
Papworth Gdns HOLWY N7 118 G10
Papworth Wy BRXS/STRHM SW2 181 H3
Parade Cl RPLY/SEND GU23 232 F9
Parade Ct EHSLY KT24 * 252 F2
Parade Ms BRXS/STRHM SW2 181 J5
Parade Ter CDALE/KGS NW9 * 116 D4
The Parade BH/WHM TN16 * 243 P7
BROCKY SE4 * 160 E7
BRW CM14 107 H4
BTSEA SW11 * 157 N10
CAR SM5 222 A2
CRAWE RH10 283 P6
CROY/NA CR0 * 202 F6
DART DA1 * 186 G1
EA W5 * 135 J8
EDUL SE22 * 159 M9
EPSOM KT18 220 A9
ESH/CLAY KT10 218 D3
FSBYPK N4 * 119 H7
GFD/PVL UB6 * 134 G1
GUW GU2 * 249 N5
GVE DA12 * 190 G5
HARH RM3 * 106 A7
HART DA3 * 211 K5
HAT AL10 * 40 F2
KUT/HW KT1 * 199 K2
KWD/TDW/WH KT20 * 239 H5
LHD/OX KT22 * 236 G6
OXHEY WD19 93 M4
PGE/AN SE20 * 204 B1
RCH/KEW TW9 * 155 M9
SOCK/AV RM15 * 166 B1
STA TW18 * 172 G8
SUN TW16 174 G10
SUT SM1 * 201 J10
SWCM DA10 * 189 L1
SYD SE26 * 182 A7
UX/CGN UB8 * 131 M7
VW GU25 * 194 A6
WAT WD17 73 J7
WLGTN SM6 * 222 G2
WOKN/KNAP GU21 * 232 B3
Paradise HHNE HP2 35 N7
Paradise Cl CHESW EN7 62 A4
Paradise Pas HOLWY N7 118 G10
Paradise Rd CLAP SW4 158 F8
RCH/KEW TW9 177 K1
WAB EN9 63 H10
Paradise Rw BETH E2 * 140 A5
Paradise St BERM/RHTH SE16 160 A1
Paradise Wk CHEL SW3 16 A9
Paragon Cl CAN/RD E16 141 M8
Paragon Gv BRYLDS KT5 199 L6
Paragon Ms STHWK SE1 19 H5
Paragon Pl BKHTH/KID SE3 161 L8
Paragon Rd HACK E8 140 A1
The Paragon BKHTH/KID SE3 161 L8
Parbury Ri CHSGTN KT9 219 K3
Parbury Rd FSTH SE23 182 D2
Parchment Cl AMS HP6 69 K3
Parchmore Rd THHTH CR7 203 J2
Parchmore Wy THHTH CR7 203 J2
Par Cl HERT/BAY SG13 26 A4
Pardoe Rd LEY E10 120 G5
Pardoner St STHWK SE1 19 H3
Pardon St FSBYE EC1V 12 D1
Pares Cl WOKN/KNAP GU21 232 A2
Parfett St WCHPL E1 13 P4
Parfitt Cl HAMP NW3 117 M6
Parfour Dr PUR/KEN CR8 241 K2
Parfrey St HMSMTH W6 156 F5
Parham Dr GNTH/NBYPK IG2 122 E4
Parham Rd CRAWW RH11 283 J6
Paringdon Rd HLWW/ROY CM19 46 E5
Paris Gdn STHWK SE1 12 C9
Parish Cl GSTN WD25 55 K10
HCH RM12 125 J7
Parish Gate Dr BFN/LL DA15 185 H2
Parish La PGE/AN SE20 182 C10
SLN SL2 109 H8
Parish Whf WOOL/PLUM SE18 162 B3
Park Ap BERM/RHTH SE16 * 160 B2
WELL DA16 163 L10
Park Av BARK IG11 142 F1
BMLY BR1 183 M9
BUSH WD23 73 L6
CAR SM5 222 B3
CRICK NW2 136 E1
CTHM CR3 241 M10
EGH TW20 172 F10
EHAM E6 142 D3
EN EN1 79 L9
FNCH N3 97 L9
GLDGN NW11 117 L6
GVE DA12 190 F4
GVW DA11 190 B4
HLWE CM17 47 M4
HSLW TW3 176 A2
IL IG1 122 D7
MORT/ESHN SW14 156 A10
ORP BR6 206 C9
ORP BR6 207 K10
PLMGR N13 99 H4
POTB/CUF EN6 59 M10
RAD WD7 56 G9
RBRW/HUT CM13 107 P2
REDH RH1 276 A8
RKW/CH/CXG WD3 71 K9
RSLP HA4 112 F4
SRTFD E15 141 K1
STA TW18 173 J9
STAL AL1 38 F5
STHL UB1 153 N1
STWL/WRAY TW19 172 A1
UED N18 99 P5
UPMR RM14 126 D5
WATW WD18 73 H7
WDGN N22 98 F10
WFD IG8 101 N6
WLSDN NW10 135 L5
WTHK RM20 166 F5
WWKM BR4 205 H9
Park Av East EW KT17 220 D3
Park Avenue Ms MTCM CR4 180 C10
Park Av North CEND/HSY/T N8 118 E2
WLSDN NW10 116 E10
Park Avenue Rd TOTM N17 100 A8
Park Av South CEND/HSY/T N8 118 E2
Park Av West EW KT17 220 D3
Park Barn Dr GUW GU2 249 K9
Park Barn East GUW GU2 249 L9
Park Barn Pde GUW GU2 * 249 K10
Park Bvd GPK RM2 104 G9
Park Cha GU GU1 250 B10
WBLY HA9 115 L9
Park Cliff Rd SWCM DA10 167 H10
Park Cl ADL/WDHM KT15 215 L6
BRKHM/BTCW RH3 273 N5
BRKMPK AL9 40 F3
BRKMPK AL9 59 J2
BUSH WD23 73 L7
CAR SM5 222 A3
CRICK NW2 116 D8
EGH TW20 * 171 L8
EPP CM16 66 B3
ESH/CLAY KT10 217 N3
HOM E9 140 B3
HPTN TW12 198 B1
HSLW TW3 176 B1
KTN/HRWW/WS HA3 94 D9
KUTN/CMB KT2 199 M1
LHD/OX KT22 236 C10
NFNCH/WDSPK N12 * 97 N5
OXTED RH8 261 L4
RKW/CH/CXG WD3 92 C5
SKENS SW7 * 16 A2
WDSR SL4 149 J8
WKENS W14 14 D3
WLSDN NW10 135 L5
WOT/HER KT12 196 G9
Park Copse RDKG RH5 273 J2
Park Cnr WDSR SL4 148 D9
Park Corner Dr EHSLY KT24 252 F4
Park Corner Rd MEO DA13 189 L7
Park Cottages FNCH N3 * 97 J10
Park Ct BF/WBF KT14 * 215 K9
DUL SE21 * 181 L6
HLW CM20 28 G10
NWMAL KT3 200 A4
SYD SE26 * 182 A9
WBLY HA9 115 K10
WOKS/MYFD GU22 232 C4
Park Crs ASC SL5 192 E5
BORE WD6 75 L7
EMPK RM11 125 H5
ENC/FH EN2 79 L8
ERITH DA8 164 E5
FNCH N3 97 L8
KTN/HRWW/WS HA3 94 D9
REGST W1B 10 E2
WHTN TW2 176 C4
Park Crs Ms East GTPST W1W 10 F2
Park Crs Ms West
CAVSQ/HST W1G 10 E2
Park Cft EDGW HA8 95 P9
Parkcroft Rd LEE/GVPK SE12 183 L3
Parkdale Crs WPK KT4 200 A10
Parkdale Rd WOOL/PLUM SE18 163 H4
Park Dr ACT W3 155 M2
ASC SL5 192 E6
CHARL SE7 162 B5
DAGE RM10 124 D8
GLDGN NW11 117 L6
HART DA3 211 K3
KTN/HRWW/WS HA3 94 C7
MORT/ESHN SW14 178 A1
POTB/CUF EN6 59 L7
RBSF CM22 31 J1
ROM RM1 124 E2
RYLN/HDSTN HA2 113 P5
UPMR RM14 126 B9
WCHMH N21 79 K10
WEY KT13 216 C2
WOKS/MYFD GU22 232 C4
Park End BMLY BR1 205 L1
HAMP NW3 117 P9
Park End Rd ROM RM1 124 F2
Parker Av HERT/WAT SG14 25 L3
TIL RM18 168 F7
Parker Cl CAN/RD E16 142 B10
CAR SM5 222 A3
CRAWE RH10 284 E8
Parker Ms HOL/ALD WC2B * 11 M5
Parke Rd BARN SW13 156 D7
SUN TW16 197 H4
Parker Rd CROY/NA CR0 223 K1
GRAYS RM17 167 L4
Parker's Cl ASHTD KT21 237 K5
Parker's Hl ASHTD KT21 237 K5
Parker's La ASHTD KT21 237 L5
Parkers Rw STHWK SE1 19 N2
Parker St CAN/RD E16 142 B10
HOL/ALD WC2B 11 M5
WATN WD24 73 J5
Parker Ter FSTH SE23 182 E5
Parkes Rd CHIG IG7 103 J6
Park Farm Cl EFNCH N2 117 M1
PIN HA5 113 J3
Park Farm Rd BMLY BR1 206 B1
KUTN/CMB KT2 177 K10
UPMR RM14 125 N10
Parkfield BGR/WK TN15 247 N9
RKW/CH/CXG WD3 71 J8
Parkfield Av AMS HP6 69 J3
FELT TW13 175 H6
HGDN/ICK UB10 132 C5
MORT/ESHN SW14 156 B10
NTHLT UB5 133 L4
RYLN/HDSTN HA2 94 B10
Parkfield Cl CRAWW RH11 283 J7
EDGW HA8 95 N7
NTHLT UB5 133 M4
Parkfield Crs FELT TW13 175 H6
RSLP HA4 113 M7
RYLN/HDSTN HA2 94 B10
Parkfield Dr NTHLT UB5 133 L4
Parkfield Gdns RYLN/HDSTN HA2 114 A1
Parkfield Pde FELT TW13 * 175 H6
Parkfield Rd FELT TW13 175 H6
HGDN/ICK UB10 112 C7
NTHLT UB5 133 M4
NWCR SE14 160 E7
RYLN/HDSTN HA2 114 B8
WLSDN NW10 136 D2
Parkfields CROY/NA CR0 204 E8
Park Flds HLWW/ROY CM19 45 M1
Parkfields LHD/OX KT22 218 C7
PUT/ROE SW15 156 F10
WGCW AL8 22 G5
Parkfields Av CDALE/KGS NW9 116 A6
RYNPK SW20 200 E1
Parkfields Cl CAR SM5 222 B1
Parkfields Rd KUTN/CMB KT2 177 L8
Parkfield St IS N1 6 B7
Parkfield Vw POTB/CUF EN6 59 L8
Parkfield Wy HAYES BR2 206 C6
Park Gdns CDALE/KGS NW9 115 N1
ERITH DA8 164 E3
KUTN/CMB KT2 177 L8
Parkgate BKHTH/KID SE3 161 L9
Park Ga EA W5 135 J7
EFNCH N2 117 N1
Parkgate SL SL1 128 B6
Park Ga WCHMH N21 98 G1
Parkgate Av EBAR EN4 77 M5
Parkgate Cl KUTN/CMB KT2 177 N9
Park Gate Ct HPTN TW12 * 176 B8
WOKS/MYFD GU22 * 232 B4
Parkgate Crs EBAR EN4 77 M5
Parkgate Gdns
MORT/ESHN SW14 178 A1
Parkgate Ms HGT N6 118 D5
Parkgate Rd BTSEA SW11 157 P6
ORP BR6 228 D1
REIG RH2 275 L1
WATN WD24 73 K3
WLGTN SM6 222 B2
Park Gates RYLN/HDSTN HA2 * 113 P9
Park Gn GT/LBKH KT23 235 P10
Park Gv BMLY BR1 205 N1
BXLYHN DA7 164 D10
CSTG HP8 70 A7
EDGW HA8 95 L6
FBAR/BDGN N11 98 E8
SRTFD E15 141 M3
Park Grove Rd WAN E11 121 K7
Park Hall Rd DUL SE21 181 L6
EFNCH N2 117 P2
REIG RH2 257 K8
Parkham St BTSEA SW11 157 N7
Park Hl BMLY BR1 206 B4
CAR SM5 222 A3
CLAP SW4 180 E1
EA W5 135 J7
FSTH SE23 182 B5
HLWE CM17 29 L8
LOU IG10 82 A9
RCHPK/HAM TW10 177 L2
Park Hill Cl CAR SM5 221 P2
Parkhill Cl HCH RM12 125 K7
Park Hill Ri CROY/NA CR0 203 N10
Parkhill Rd BFN/LL DA15 185 H6
BXLY DA5 186 A3
CHING E4 101 H1
Park Hill Rd CROY/NA CR0 223 M1
EW KT17 220 C7
Parkhill Rd HAMP NW3 118 A10
Park Hill Rd HAYES BR2 205 K2
HHW HP1 35 L6
RSEV TN14 247 M3
WLGTN SM6 222 C4
Park Hill Wk HAMP NW3 118 A10
Parkholme Rd HACK E8 7 N2
Park Horsley EHSLY KT24 253 H5
Park House Dr REIG RH2 275 J2
Park House Gdns TWK TW1 177 H1
Parkhouse St CMBW SE5 159 L6
Parkhurst HOR/WEW KT19 219 P6
Parkhurst Gdns BXLY DA5 186 B3
Parkhurst Gv HORL RH6 279 P3
Parkhurst Rd BXLY DA5 186 B3
FBAR/BDGN N11 98 B5
GUW GU2 249 M9
HERT/WAT SG14 25 J4
HOLWY N7 118 F9
HORL RH6 279 P3
MNPK E12 122 D9
SUT SM1 221 N1
TOTM N17 99 P10
WALTH E17 * 120 D2
WDGN N22 98 G8
Parkinson Cl STALE/WH AL4 21 J3
Parkland Av DTCH/LGLY SL3 150 A4
ROM RM1 104 G10
UPMR RM14 126 A10
Parkland Cl HOD EN11 26 G10
SEV TN13 265 K5
Parkland Gv ASHF TW15 174 B7
ISLW TW7 154 E7
Parkland Md BMLY BR1 206 E3
Parkland Rd ASHF TW15 174 B7
WDGN N22 98 G10
WFD IG8 101 N8
Parklands ADL/WDHM KT15 215 M2
BRYLDS KT5 199 L5
BUSH WD23 * 74 B10
CHIG IG7 102 F4
GT/LBKH KT23 235 P9
HGT N6 118 C5
HHW HP1 35 J4
OXTED RH8 261 K7
RDKG RH5 272 G6
WAB EN9 63 K8
Parklands Cl EBAR EN4 77 N4
GNTH/NBYPK IG2 122 F5
MORT/ESHN SW14 177 P1
Parklands Dr FNCH N3 117 H1
STALW/RED AL3 37 P7
Parklands Pde HEST TW5 * 153 L8
Parklands Pl GU GU1 250 E10
Parklands Rd STRHM/NOR SW16 180 C8
Parklands Wy WPK KT4 200 B9
Parkland Wy CHONG CM5 67 N6
Park La ASHTD KT21 237 L4
BEAC HP9 88 E10
BGR/WK TN15 247 P4
BGR/WK TN15 247 P9
BROX EN10 44 D5
CAR SM5 222 B1
CHDH RM6 123 N4
CHEAM SM3 221 H3
CHES/WCR EN8 62 C9
CHESW EN7 61 P3
COUL/CHIP CR5 240 E7
CROY/NA CR0 203 L10
DEN/HRF UB9 91 K9
DTCH/LGLY SL3 149 N2
DTCH/LGLY SL3 150 D9
EMPK RM11 125 H5
HCH RM12 145 J1
HEST TW5 153 H6
HHNE HP2 35 N7
HLW CM20 28 G9
MYFR/PICC W1J 16 D1
MYFR/PKLN W1K 10 C8
RCH/KEW TW9 155 J10
REIG RH2 257 J10
RGUE GU4 250 G7
RYLN/HDSTN HA2 114 A8
SEV TN13 247 K10
SL SL1 108 D10
SOCK/AV RM15 146 C10
SRTFD E15 * 141 H3
STALE/WH AL4 39 P9
STAN HA7 94 F4
SWLY BR8 209 K2
TEDD TW11 176 E9

TOTM N17 99 P8
UED N18 99 N4
WBLY HA9 115 L9
WDSR SL4 170 A4
YEAD UB4 132 F7
Park Lane Cl TOTM N17 99 P8
Park La East REIG RH2 275 K2
Park Lane Paradise CHESW EN7 43 P10
Parklawn Av EPSOM KT18 219 N9
HORL RH6 280 A2
Park Lawn Rd WEY KT13 216 D1
Parklea Cl CDALE/KGS NW9 96 B9
Parkleigh Rd WIM/MER SW19 201 L2
Park Ley Rd CTHM CR3 242 C7
Parkleys RCHPK/HAM TW10 177 J7
Parkleys Pde
RCHPK/HAM TW10 * 177 J7
Park Md BFN/LL DA15 185 K1
HLW CM20 28 E10
Parkmead LOU IG10 82 D9
PUT/ROE SW15 178 E2
Park Md RYLN/HDSTN HA2 114 A8
Parkmead Gdns MLHL NW7 96 C7
Park Meadow BRKMPK AL9 40 F3
BRWN CM15 87 J4
Park Ms BRKMPK AL9 * 40 F3
GNWCH SE10 161 L4
NKENS W10 2 B8
NKENS W10 137 H4
RAIN RM13 145 H1
STWL/WRAY TW19 174 A3
Park Nook Gdns ENC/FH EN2 79 L3
Parkpale La BRKHM/BTCW RH3 273 M5
Park Pde ACT W3 * 155 M2
HYS/HAR UB3 * 132 F8
WLSDN NW10 136 C4
Park Piazza LEW SE13 183 J2
Park Pl ACT W3 155 M3
AMS HP6 69 K4
BMLY BR1 * 205 N1
DEN/HRF UB9 * 91 M9
EA W5 135 J10
GVE DA12 190 F3
HPTN TW12 176 B9
IS N1 7 H5
LCOL/BKTW AL2 56 C3
POP/IOD E14 140 F10
SEV TN13 246 E9
WBLY HA9 115 L9
WHALL SW1A 10 G10
WOKS/MYFD GU22 * 232 C4
Park Place Vls BAY/PAD W2 9 K3
Park Rd MNPK E12 122 A9
Park Ridings CEND/HSY/T N8 119 H1
Park Ri BERK HP4 33 K3
KTN/HRWW/WS HA3 94 D9
LHD/OX KT22 236 F7
Park Rise Cl LHD/OX KT22 236 G7
Park Rise Rd FSTH SE23 182 D4
Park Rd ALP/SUD HA0 135 K1
AMS HP6 69 L3
ASHF TW15 174 C8
ASHTD KT21 237 K4
BAR EN5 77 J8
BECK BR3 182 E10
BMLY BR1 205 N1
BNSTD SM7 239 M2
BRW CM14 106 G2
BRYLDS KT5 199 L6
BUSH WD23 73 P10
CAMTN NW1 10 B2
CDALE/KGS NW9 116 A5
CDALE/KGS NW9 116 D5
CEND/HSY/T N8 118 F4
CEND/HSY/T N8 119 J2
CHEAM SM3 221 H3
CHES/WCR EN8 62 C9
CHST BR7 184 E9
CHSWK W4 156 A5
CSHM HP5 50 G7
CTHM CR3 241 M9
DART DA1 187 P3
E/WMO/HCT KT8 198 B4
EBAR EN4 77 N8
EFNCH N2 117 N1
EGH TW20 172 D7
ESH/CLAY KT10 218 A1
FBAR/BDGN N11 98 E8
FELT TW13 175 L7
GU GU1 250 A10
GVW DA11 190 E5
HERT/BAY SG13 25 M5
HHW HP1 35 M8
HNWL W7 134 E9
HOD EN11 44 F3
HORL RH6 281 K6
HPTN TW12 176 B8
HSLW TW3 176 B1
IL IG1 122 G8
ISLW TW7 154 G7
KUT/HW KT1 199 H1
KUTN/CMB KT2 177 L8
LEY E10 120 F6
MNPK E12 121 N7
NWMAL KT3 200 A4
OXTED RH8 261 L4
PEND EN3 80 D2
PLSTW E13 141 P3
POTB/CUF EN6 60 B6
PUR/KEN CR8 223 K10
RAD WD7 74 F1
RCHPK/HAM TW10 177 L2
REDH RH1 258 A8
RKW/CH/CXG WD3 91 P1
SHGR GU5 269 P7
SHPTN TW17 196 B8
SLN SL2 129 J4
SNWD SE25 203 M4
SRTFD E15 141 M3
STHGT/OAK N14 98 E1
STJWD NW8 3 P10
STMC/STPC BR5 207 M6
STWL/WRAY TW19 173 M2
SUN TW16 175 J10
SWCM DA10 189 K2
SWLY BR8 208 G4
TEDD TW11 176 E10
TWK TW1 177 H2
UED N18 99 N5
UPMR RM14 125 P9
UX/CGN UB8 131 N2
WALTH E17 120 E3
WARE SG12 26 B1
WARL CR6 225 K10
WAT WD17 73 H5
WIM/MER SW19 179 N9
WLGTN SM6 202 C9
WLGTN SM6 222 C2
WLSDN NW10 * 136 B3
WOKS/MYFD GU22 232 C3
YEAD UB4 132 F7
Park Rd East ACT W3 155 P1
HGDN/ICK UB10 131 N4
Park Rd North ACT W3 155 N1
CHSWK W4 156 A5
Park Rw GNWCH SE10 161 J5
Park Royal Rd WLSDN NW10 135 P5
Parkshot RCH/KEW TW9 155 J10
Park Side BKHH IG9 101 N3
CRICK NW2 116 D8
EPP CM16 65 L5
HYS/HAR UB3 * 132 F9
Parkside ADL/WDHM KT15 215 L6
BECK BR3 * 204 G2
BKHTH/KID SE3 * 161 L6
CDW/CHF RM16 168 A2
CFSP/GDCR SL9 110 C3
CHEAM SM3 221 H3
CHES/WCR EN8 62 D10
CRAWE RH10 283 P7
FNCH N3 97 L9
HHS/BOV HP3 * 54 B3
HPTN TW12 176 C8
MLHL NW7 96 D7
OXHEY WD19 * 73 K10
RSEV TN14 227 P9
SCUP DA14 185 L5
WIM/MER SW19 178 G8
Parkside Av BMLY BR1 206 B4
BXLYHN DA7 164 E8
ROM RM1 104 E10
TIL RM18 168 E8
WIM/MER SW19 178 G8
Parkside Cl EHSLY KT24 252 G1
PGE/AN SE20 182 B10
Parkside Crs BRYLDS KT5 199 P6
HOLWY N7 119 H8
Parkside Cross BXLYHN DA7 164 F8
Parkside Dr EDGW HA8 95 M4
WAT WD17 72 F6
Parkside Est HOM E9 * 140 C3
Parkside Gdns COUL/CHIP CR5 240 C3
EBAR EN4 98 A2
WIM/MER SW19 178 G7
Parkside Ms WARL CR6 242 F2
Parkside Pde DART DA1 * 164 G8
Parkside Pl EHSLY KT24 252 F1
STA TW18 173 K9
Parkside Rd ASC SL5 192 F6
BELV DA17 164 C3
HSLW TW3 176 A1
NTHWD HA6 92 G6
Parkside St BTSEA SW11 158 B7
Parkside Ter ORP BR6 * 207 K8
UED N18 * 99 L5
Parkside Wk SL SL1 149 M2
Parkside Wy RYLN/HDSTN HA2 114 A2
Park Sq WDSR SL4 * 170 A4
Park Sq East CAMTN NW1 10 E1
Park Square Ms CAMTN NW1 10 E2
Park Sq West CAMTN NW1 10 E1
Parkstead Rd PUT/ROE SW15 178 D1
Park Steps BAY/PAD W2 * 9 P7
Parkstone Av EMPK RM11 125 M4
UED N18 99 N6
Parkstone Rd PECK SE15 * 159 P8
WALTH E17 121 H1
Park St BERK HP4 33 N4
BRKMPK AL9 40 F3
CROY/NA CR0 203 K10
DTCH/LGLY SL3 150 G7
GU GU1 267 P2
LCOL/BKTW AL2 56 C3
MYFR/PKLN W1K 10 C8
SL SL1 149 L2
STHWK SE1 12 E9
TEDD TW11 176 D9
WDSR SL4 149 J7
Park Street La LCOL/BKTW AL2 56 A5
Park Ter CAR SM5 * 201 P10
GSTN WD25 * 55 L9
PEND EN3 * 80 D4
RSEV TN14 * 245 N10
SWCM DA10 189 H1
WPK KT4 200 D8
The Park CAR SM5 222 A2
EA W5 135 J10
GLDGN NW11 117 L6
GT/LBKH KT23 235 P10
HGT N6 118 B5
SCUP DA14 185 J8
STAL AL1 38 F4
Parkthorne Cl
RYLN/HDSTN HA2 * 114 A4
Parkthorne Dr RYLN/HDSTN HA2 113 P4
Parkthorne Rd BAL SW12 180 E3
Park Vw ACT W3 135 P7
ADL/WDHM KT15 * 215 M2
BRKMPK AL9 40 F2
CRAWW RH11 283 M8
CTHM CR3 259 P1
EW KT17 * 220 C9
GT/LBKH KT23 253 P1
HOD EN11 44 F4
HORL RH6 280 B4
NWMAL KT3 200 C3
PIN HA5 93 N9
POTB/CUF EN6 59 M9
SOCK/AV RM15 146 C10
WBLY HA9 115 N10
WCHMH N21 98 G1
Parkview WDR/YW UB7 * 131 P9
Parkview Cha SL SL1 128 D8
Park View Cl STAL AL1 38 F7
Park View Ct
NFNCH/WDSPK N12 * 97 P5
WOKS/MYFD GU22 * 232 C5
Park View Crs FBAR/BDGN N11 98 C5
Park View Dr MTCM CR4 201 N2
Park View Est HBRY N5 * 119 K9
Parkview Gdns CLAY IG5 122 C2
Park View Gdns GRAYS RM17 167 N4
HDN NW4 116 F3
WDGN N22 * 99 H9
Parkview Ms RAIN RM13 145 J7
Park View Rd BERK HP4 33 N5
CRICK NW2 116 C9
Parkview Rd CROY/NA CR0 203 P8
Park View Rd CTHM CR3 242 E9
EA W5 135 K7
ELTH/MOT SE9 184 E5
FNCH N3 97 L9
PIN HA5 93 J7
REDH RH1 276 B7
STHL UB1 133 P10
TOTM N17 99 P10
UX/CGN UB8 132 B8
WELL DA16 163 N9
Parkview V RGUE GU4 250 F8
Park Village East CAMTN NW1 4 F7
Park Village West CAMTN NW1 4 E7
Park Vls TOOT SW17 * 179 P8
Parkville Rd FUL/PGN SW6 157 J6
Park Vis GNWCH SE10 161 J5
Park Vista Apartments
CAN/RD E16 141 L5
Park Wk WBPTN SW10 15 K9
Park Wy BRWN CM15 107 L2
BXLY DA5 186 G6
CRAWE RH10 284 D5
E/WMO/HCT KT8 198 A3
EBED/NFELT TW14 175 J3
EDGW HA8 95 N9
ENC/FH EN2 79 H6
GLDGN NW11 117 H3
GT/LBKH KT23 235 P9
RKW/CH/CXG WD3 91 M2
RSLP HA4 113 H6
TRDG/WHET N20 98 A5
Parkway CAMTN NW1 4 F5
CROY/NA CR0 224 G6
DORK RH4 272 F1
ERITHM DA18 163 P2
GDMY/SEVK IG3 123 J8
GPK RM2 104 G10
GU GU1 250 B9
HGDN/ICK UB10 132 B2
HLWW/ROY CM19 46 B1
RAIN RM13 145 H6
RYNPK SW20 200 G4
SBW CM21 29 P2
STHGT/OAK N14 98 F3
WEY KT13 216 E1
WFD IG8 101 P6
WGCW AL8 22 F7
Parkway Cl WGCW AL8 22 F5
Parkway Ct STAL AL1 38 G9
Parkway Gdns WGCW AL8 22 F6
The Parkway HEST TW5 153 H5
IVER SL0 130 F3
NTHLT UB5 133 L5
NWDGN UB2 153 J2
Park West BAY/PAD W2 9 P5
Park West Pl BAY/PAD W2 9 P5
Parkwood BECK BR3 182 F10
Parkwood Av ESH/CLAY KT10 198 B8
Park Wood Cl BNSTD SM7 238 G1
Parkwood Cl BROX EN10 44 D5
Parkwood Dr HHW HP1 35 J6
Parkwood Gv SUN TW16 197 H3
Parkwood Ms HGT N6 118 C4
Parkwood Rd BH/WHM TN16 244 B7
Park Wood Rd BNSTD SM7 238 G1
Parkwood Rd BXLY DA5 186 A3
ISLW TW7 154 E7
REDH RH1 258 F9
WIM/MER SW19 179 J8
Park Wood Vw BNSTD SM7 238 G2
Park Works Rd REDH RH1 258 G9
Parlaunt Rd DTCH/LGLY SL3 150 E3
Parley Dr WOKN/KNAP GU21 231 P4
Parliament Ct WCHPL E1 * 13 K4
Parliament Hl HAMP NW3 117 P9
Parliament Hill Flds KTTN NW5 * 118 B8
Parliament Sq WEST SW1P 17 L2
HERT/WAT SG14 25 L5
Parliament St WHALL SW1A 17 L1
Parma Crs BTSEA SW11 158 A10
Parmiter St BETH E2 140 A4
Parnall Rd HLWS CM18 46 G5
Parndon Mill La HLW CM20 28 E8
Parndon Wood Rd HLWS CM18 46 F6
Parnell Cl ABLGY WD5 54 G6
CDW/CHF RM16 167 H4
CRAWE RH10 284 E9
EDGW HA8 95 N5
SHB W12 156 E2
Parnell Gdns WEY KT13 216 A7
Parnell Rd BOW E3 140 E3
Parnel Rd WARE SG12 26 E1
Parnham Av LTWR GU18 212 C7
Parnham St POP/IOD E14 * 140 D8
Parolles Rd ARCH N19 118 D6
Paroma Rd BELV DA17 164 B2
Parpins KGLGY WD4 * 53 P4
Parr Av EW KT17 220 E5
Parr Cl CDW/CHF RM16 167 H3
ED N9 100 A5
LHD/OX KT22 236 E6
Parr Crs HHNE HP2 36 C1
Parris Cft DORK RH4 273 H5
Parrock Av GVE DA12 190 F4
Parrock Rd GVE DA12 190 F4
Parrock St GVE DA12 190 E3
Parrotts Cl RKW/CH/CXG WD3 72 B8
Parrotts Fld HOD EN11 44 G2
Parrott's La TRING HP23 32 A6
Parr Rd EHAM E6 142 A3
STAN HA7 95 J9
Parrs Cl SAND/SEL CR2 223 L5
Parr's Pl HPTN TW12 175 P10
Parr St IS N1 6 G7
Parry Av EHAM E6 142 C8
Parry Cl EW KT17 220 E4
Parry Dr WEY KT13 216 B6
Parry Gn North DTCH/LGLY SL3 150 C3
Parry Gn South DTCH/LGLY SL3 150 C3
Parry Pl WOOL/PLUM SE18 162 E3
Parry Rd NKENS W10 2 B9
SNWD SE25 203 M3
Parry St VX/NE SW8 17 M9
Parsifal Rd KIL/WHAMP NW6 117 K10
Parsloe Rd EPP CM16 46 D7
Parsloes Av DAGW RM9 123 P10
Parsonage Bank EYN DA4 209 M10
Parsonage Cl ABLGY WD5 54 F6
HYS/HAR UB3 132 G8
WARL CR6 242 D2
Parsonage Fld BRWN CM15 87 J3
Parsonage Gdns ENC/FH EN2 79 K6
Parsonage La BRKMPK AL9 40 E9
DORK RH4 272 B3
ENC/FH EN2 79 L6
EYN DA4 188 A9
SCUP DA14 186 A7
SLN SL2 129 H1
WDSR SL4 148 F7
Parsonage Leys HLW CM20 47 J1
Parsonage Manorway
BELV DA17 164 B5
Parsonage Pl AMSS HP7 * 69 H5
Parsonage Rd BRKMPK AL9 40 E9
CSTG HP8 89 N4
EGH TW20 172 A8
RAIN RM13 145 K4
RKW/CH/CXG WD3 91 N1
WTHK RM20 167 J5
Parsonage Sq DORK RH4 272 F1
Parsonage St POP/IOD E14 161 H3
Parsons Cl HORL RH6 279 P3
Parsons Crs EDGW HA8 95 M4
Parsonsfield Cl BNSTD SM7 238 G1
Parsonsfield Rd BNSTD SM7 238 G2
Parsons Gn FUL/PGN SW6 157 K7
GU GU1 250 A8
Parsons Green La FUL/PGN SW6 157 K7
Parsons Gv EDGW HA8 95 M4
Parsons La RDART DA2 187 J6
Parson's Md CROY/NA CR0 203 J8
E/WMO/HCT KT8 198 B3
Parsons Rd DTCH/LGLY SL3 150 C5
PLSTW E13 141 P4
Parson St HDN NW4 116 F1
Parson's Wood La SLN SL2 129 J2
Parthenia Rd FUL/PGN SW6 157 K7
Parthia Cl KWD/TDW/WH KT20 238 E5
Partingdale La MLHL NW7 96 G6
Partington Cl ARCH N19 118 E6
Partridge Cl BAR EN5 76 F10
BUSH WD23 * 94 B2
CAN/RD E16 142 A7
CSHM HP5 51 K4
STAN HA7 95 K5
Partridge Ct HLWS CM18 47 H3
Partridge Dr ORP BR6 206 F10
Partridge Gn ELTH/MOT SE9 184 D6
Partridge Knoll PUR/KEN CR8 223 J8
Partridge La HORS RH12 282 B3
RDKG RH5 278 A3
RDKG RH5 278 C7
Partridge Md BNSTD SM7 238 F1
Partridge Rd HLWS CM18 46 G3
HPTN TW12 175 N9
HPTN TW12 175 P9
SCUP DA14 185 H6
STALW/RED AL3 38 C2
Partridge Sq EHAM E6 142 B7
Partridge Wy RGUE GU4 250 G8
WDGN N22 98 F9
Parva Cl HARP AL5 20 C5
Parvills WAB EN9 63 J8
Parvis Rd BF/WBF KT14 215 M8
Pasadena Cl HYS/HAR UB3 153 H1
Pascal St VX/NE SW8 158 E6
Pascoe Rd LEW SE13 183 J1
Pasfield WAB EN9 63 J9
Pasley Cl WALW SE17 18 D8
Pasquier Rd WALTH E17 120 D1
Passey Pl ELTH/MOT SE9 184 C2
Passfield Dr POP/IOD E14 140 G7
Passmore Gdns FBAR/BDGN N11 98 E7
Passmore St BGVA SW1W 16 C6
Pastens Rd OXTED RH8 261 P7
Pasteur Cl CDALE/KGS NW9 96 B10
Pasteur Dr HARH RM3 105 L10
Pasteur Gdns UED N18 99 K6
Paston Cl WLGTN SM6 202 D10
Paston Crs LEE/GVPK SE12 183 N3
Paston Rd HHNE HP2 35 N4
Pastoral Wy BRW CM14 106 G6
Pastor St LBTH SE11 18 D5
Pasture Cl ALP/SUD HA0 114 G8
BUSH WD23 94 B1
Pasture Rd ALP/SUD HA0 114 G7
CAT SE6 183 L4
DAGW RM9 124 A10
Pastures Md HGDN/ICK UB10 132 B1
The Pastures HAT AL10 40 E5
HHW HP1 35 H5
LCOL/BKTW AL2 37 P10
OXHEY WD19 93 J1
TRDG/WHET N20 97 J2
WGCE AL7 23 K7
The Pasture CRAWE RH10 284 D7
Pasture Wood Rd RDKG RH5 271 M10
Patcham Ter VX/NE SW8 158 C7
Patching Cl CRAWW RH11 283 J6
Patching Wy YEAD UB4 133 M7
The Patch SEV TN13 246 F8
Paternoster Cl WAB EN9 63 L9
Paternoster Hl WAB EN9 63 L8
Paternoster Rw ABR/ST RM4 105 K3
STP EC4M 12 E6
Paternoster Sq STP EC4M 12 D6
Pater St KENS W8 14 E4
Pates Manor Dr
EBED/NFELT TW14 174 E3
Pathfield Rd STRHM/NOR SW16 180 E9
Pathfields SHGR GU5 270 B6
Path Link CRAWE RH10 283 P6
Path Stort Valley Wy
HERT/BAY SG13 43 J8
The Path WIM/MER SW19 201 L1
The Pathway OXHEY WD19 93 L2
RAD WD7 74 E2
RPLY/SEND GU23 251 J1
Patience Rd BTSEA SW11 157 P8
Patio Cl CLAP SW4 180 E2
Patmore La WOT/HER KT12 216 G3
Patmore Link Rd HHNE HP2 36 D6
Patmore Rd WAB EN9 63 K10
Patmore St VX/NE SW8 158 D7
Patmore Wy CRW RM5 104 C6
Patmos Rd BRXN/ST SW9 159 J6
Paton Cl BOW E3 140 F5
Patricia Cl SL SL1 128 D9
Patricia Ct WELL DA16 163 L6
Patricia Dr EMPK RM11 125 M6
Patricia Vls TOTM N17 * 100 A9
Patrick Gv WAB EN9 62 G9
Patrick Rd PLSTW E13 141 P5
Patrington Cl CRAWW RH11 283 K10
UX/CGN UB8 131 M5
Patriot Sq BETH E2 140 A4
Patrol Pl CAT SE6 182 G2
Patrons Dr DEN/HRF UB9 111 J4
Patrons Wy West DEN/HRF UB9 111 J4
Patshull Pl KTTN NW5 4 G2
Patshull Rd KTTN NW5 4 G1
Pattenden Rd CAT SE6 182 E4
Patten Rd WAND/EARL SW18 179 P3
Patterdale Cl BMLY BR1 183 K9
CRAWW RH11 283 M10
Patterdale Rd PECK SE15 160 B6
RDART DA2 188 C4
Patterson Rd CSHM HP5 50 G4
NRWD SE19 181 N9
Pattina Wk BERM/RHTH SE16 140 D10
Pattison Rd CRICK NW2 117 K8
Paul Cl CHESW EN7 61 K1
SRTFD E15 141 K2
Paulet Rd CMBW SE5 159 J8
Paulet Wy WLSDN NW10 * 136 B2
Paul Gdns CROY/NA CR0 203 N9
Paulhan Rd
KTN/HRWW/WS HA3 115 J2
Paulin Dr WCHMH N21 99 H1
Pauline Crs WHTN TW2 176 B4
Paulinus Cl STMC/STPC BR5 207 M3
Paul Julius Cl POP/IOD E14 141 J9
Paul Robeson Cl EHAM E6 142 D5
Pauls Ct HOD EN11 * 44 F3
Pauls La HOD EN11 44 F3
Paul's Pl ASHTD KT21 237 N5
Paul St SDTCH EC2A 13 J1
SRTFD E15 141 K3
Paultons Sq CHEL SW3 15 M9
Paultons St CHEL SW3 15 M10
Pauntley St ARCH N19 118 D6
Paveley Dr BTSEA SW11 157 P6
Paveley St STJWD NW8 3 P10
Pavement Sq CROY/NA CR0 203 P8
The Pavement CLAP SW4 158 D10
EA W5 * 155 K2
REDH RH1 * 258 A10
TEDD TW11 * 176 G10
WAN E11 * 121 H6
WIM/MER SW19 * 179 J9
WNWD SE27 * 181 K7
Pavet Cl DAGE RM10 144 C1
Pavilion Gdns STA TW18 173 L10
Pavilion Ldg RYLN/HDSTN HA2 * 114 C6
Pavilion Ms FNCH N3 117 K1
Pavilion Pde SHB W12 * 136 F8
Pavilion Rd IL IG1 122 C5
KTBR SW1X 16 B2
The Pavilions EPP CM16 66 D1
Pavilion St KTBR SW1X 16 B4
The Pavilion CHES/WCR EN8 62 D10
VX/NE SW8 * 158 E6
Pavilion Wy AMS HP6 69 P5
EDGW HA8 95 P8
RSLP HA4 113 K7
Pavillion Sq TOOT SW17 179 P6
Pavillion Ter SHB W12 * 136 F8
Pawleyne Cl PGE/AN SE20 182 B10
Pawsey Cl PLSTW E13 141 M3
Pawson's Rd THHTH CR7 203 K6
Pax Cl CRAWW RH11 283 H9
Paxford Rd ALP/SUD HA0 114 G7
Paxton Av SL SL1 149 H2
Paxton Cl RCH/KEW TW9 155 L8
WOT/HER KT12 197 K7
Paxton Gdns WOKN/KNAP GU21 215 H9
Paxton Pl WNWD SE27 181 M7
Paxton Rd BERK HP4 * 34 B5
BMLY BR1 183 M10
CHSWK W4 156 B5
FSTH SE23 182 D6
STAL AL1 38 D7
TOTM N17 99 P8
Paxton Ter PIM SW1V 16 F9
Paycock Rd HLWW/ROY CM19 46 D3
Payne Cl BARK IG11 143 H2
CRAWE RH10 284 E5
Paynell Ct BKHTH/KID SE3 161 K9
Payne Rd BOW E3 140 G4
Paynesfield Av
MORT/ESHN SW14 156 A9
Paynes Field Cl BERK HP4 33 J3
Paynesfield Rd BH/WHM TN16 243 P6
BUSH WD23 94 E1
Paynes La WAB EN9 45 H10
Payne St DEPT SE8 160 E5
Paynes Wk HMSMTH W6 14 A10
HMSMTH W6 157 H5
Paynetts Ct WEY KT13 216 E2
Payzes Gdns WFD IG8 * 101 L7
Peabody Av PIM SW1V 16 F8
Peabody Cl CROY/NA CR0 204 B8
GNWCH SE10 * 160 G7
PIM SW1V 16 F8
Peabody Cottages HNHL SE24 * 181 K3
Peabody Est BTSEA SW11 * 157 P10
CLKNW EC1R * 12 B2
CMBW SE5 * 159 L7
HMSMTH W6 * 156 F4
HNHL SE24 181 K3
NKENS W10 * 136 F7
STHWK SE1 * 12 B9
STHWK SE1 * 12 E9
STLK EC1Y * 12 F2
TOTM N17 * 99 M9
Peabody Hl DUL SE21 181 J4
Peabody Sq IS N1 * 6 E5
Peabody Ter CLKNW EC1R * 12 B2
Peace Cl CHESW EN7 62 A5
GFD/PVL UB6 134 C3
SNWD SE25 203 M4
STHGT/OAK N14 78 C9
Peace Dr WAT WD17 73 H7
Peace Gv WBLY HA9 115 N8
Peacemaker Cl CRAWW RH11 283 H9
Peace Rd IVER SL0 130 D3
Peace St WOOL/PLUM SE18 162 D5
Peach Cft GVW DA11 190 B6
Peaches Cl BELMT SM2 221 H4
Peachey Cl UX/CGN UB8 131 N8
Peachey La UX/CGN UB8 131 N7
Peach Gv WAN E11 121 J8
Peach Rd FELT TW13 175 H4
NKENS W10 136 G5
Peachum Rd BKHTH/KID SE3 161 L5
Peacock Av EBED/NFELT TW14 174 E4
Peacock Cl CHING E4 100 E8
EMPK RM11 125 M2
Peacock Gdns SAND/SEL CR2 224 D6
Peacocks HLWW/ROY CM19 46 C3
Peacocks Cl BERK HP4 33 L2
Peacock St GVE DA12 190 F3
WALW SE17 18 D6
Peacock Yd WALW SE17 18 D6
Peakes La CHESW EN7 61 N3
Peakes Pl STAL AL1 * 38 E6
Peakes Wy CHESW EN7 61 N3
Peaketon Av REDBR IG4 122 A3
Peak Hl SYD SE26 182 B7
Peak Hill Av SYD SE26 182 B7
Peak Hill Gdns SYD SE26 182 B7
Peaks Hl PUR/KEN CR8 222 F6
Peaks Hill Ri PUR/KEN CR8 222 F6
The Peak SYD SE26 182 B6
Pea La BERK HP4 33 J3
UPMR RM14 146 F1
Peal Gdns WEA W13 134 F5
Peall Rd CROY/NA CR0 202 G6
Pearce Cl MTCM CR4 202 B2
Pearcefield Av FSTH SE23 182 B4
Pearce Rd CSHM HP5 50 G5
Pearces Wk STAL AL1 * 38 C7
Pear Cl CDALE/KGS NW9 116 A2
NWCR SE14 160 D6
Pearcroft Rd WAN E11 121 J7
Pearcy Cl HARH RM3 105 M8
Peardon St VX/NE SW8 158 C9
Peareswood Gdns STAN HA7 95 J9
Peareswood Rd ERITH DA8 164 G7
Pearfield Rd FSTH SE23 182 D6
Pearl Cl CRICK NW2 116 G5
EHAM E6 142 D8
Pearl Ct WOKN/KNAP GU21 231 K2
Pearl Gdns SL SL1 128 G10
Pearl Rd WALTH E17 120 F1
Pearl St WAP E1W 140 A10
Pearmain Cl SHPTN TW17 196 C5
Pearman St STHWK SE1 18 B3
Pear Pl STHWK SE1 18 A1
Pear Rd WAN E11 121 J8
Pears Av SHPTN TW17 * 196 F3
Pearscroft Ct FUL/PGN SW6 157 L7
Pearscroft Rd FUL/PGN SW6 157 L8
Pearse St PECK SE15 19 K10
Pearson Av HERT/BAY SG13 25 K7
Pearson Cl BAR EN5 77 L7
Pearson Rd CRAWE RH10 284 C7
Pearson's NWCR SE14 160 F7
Pearsons Cl HERT/BAY SG13 25 K7
Pearson's Rd NWCR SE14 * 160 F7
Pearson St BETH E2 7 L7
Pearson Wy DART DA1 187 N5
MTCM CR4 202 B1
Pears Rd HSLW TW3 154 C9
Peartree Av TOOT SW17 180 A9
Pear Tree Av WDR/YW UB7 132 A8
Pear Tree Cl ADL/WDHM KT15 215 K2
AMSS HP7 69 L5
BEAC HP9 89 H7
Peartree Cl BRWN CM15 87 J4
Pear Tree Cl CHSGTN KT9 219 M2
ERITH DA8 164 E7
Peartree Cl HAYES BR2 206 A5
HHW HP1 35 K5
Pear Tree Cl MTCM CR4 201 P3
Peartree Cl SAND/SEL CR2 224 A10
SL SL1 128 E10
SOCK/AV RM15 147 H5
Pear Tree Cl SWLY BR8 208 E2
Peartree Cl WGCE AL7 23 H5
Pear Tree Ct CLKNW EC1R 12 B2
Peartree Ct WGCE AL7 23 H6
Peartree Gdns BCTR RM8 123 L10
ROMW/RG RM7 104 C10
Pear Tree Hl REDH RH1 * 276 B9
Peartree La BRWN CM15 87 H3
WAP E1W * 140 B9
WGCE AL7 23 J5
Pear Tree Md HLWS CM18 47 K3
Pear Tree Rd ADL/WDHM KT15 215 K2
ASHF TW15 174 D8
Peartree Rd EN EN1 79 M7
HHW HP1 35 K5
Peartrees RBRW/HUT CM13 107 P7
The Pear Trees WDR/YW UB7 * 131 N9
Peartree St FSBYE EC1V 12 D1
Pear Tree Wk CHESW EN7 61 M2
Peartree Wy GNWCH SE10 161 M3
Pearwood Cottages STAN HA7 * 95 H3
Peary Pl BETH E2 140 B5
Peascod St WDSR SL4 149 J7
Peascroft Rd HHS/BOV HP3 36 B9
Pease Cl HCH RM12 145 J2
Peasmead Ter CHING E4 * 101 H5
Peatfield Cl BFN/LL DA15 185 H6
Peatmore Av WOKS/MYFD GU22 233 K2
Peatmore Cl WOKS/MYFD GU22 233 K2
Peatmore Dr CHOB/PIR GU24 230 B7
Pebble Cl EPSOM KT18 256 B4
Pebble Hl EHSLY KT24 252 D9
Pebblehill Rd BRKHM/BTCW RH3 256 B6
Pebble La LHD/OX KT22 237 M8
Pebworth Rd HRW HA1 114 F7
Peckarmans Wd SYD SE26 181 P6
Peckett Sq HBRY N5 * 119 K9
Peckford Pl BRXN/ST SW9 159 H8
Peckham Gv PECK SE15 159 M6
Peckham High St PECK SE15 159 P7
Peckham Hill St PECK SE15 159 P6
Peckham Park Rd PECK SE15 159 P6
Peckham Rd CMBW SE5 159 M7
Peckham Rye PECK SE15 159 P9
Peck's Hl WAB EN9 45 K7
Pecks Yd WCHPL E1 * 13 L3
Peckwater St KTTN NW5 118 D10
Pedlars End CHONG CM5 49 J7
Pedlars Wk HOLWY N7 * 118 F10
Pedley Rd BCTR RM8 123 M6
Pedley St WCHPL E1 13 M2
Pednor Bottom CSHM HP5 50 A4
Pednormead End CSHM HP5 50 G8
Pednor Rd CSHM HP5 50 D5
Pedro St CLPT E5 120 C8
Peek Crs WIM/MER SW19 178 G8
Peeks Brook La HORL RH6 280 F8
HORL RH6 280 G5
Peel Cl CHING E4 100 G3
ED N9 99 P4
WDSR SL4 148 G9
Peel Ct SL SL1 128 G7
Peel Crs HERT/WAT SG14 25 J2
Peel Dr CDALE/KGS NW9 116 C1
CLAY IG5 122 B1
Peel Gv BETH E2 140 B4
Peel Pas KENS W8 * 8 E10
Peel Pl CLAY IG5 102 B10
Peel Prec KIL/WHAMP NW6 2 D8
Peel Rd ALP/SUD HA0 115 H8
KIL/WHAMP NW6 2 D9
KTN/HRWW/WS HA3 114 D1
ORP BR6 226 F1
SWFD E18 101 L9
Peel St KENS W8 8 E10
Peel Wy HARH RM3 105 N10
UX/CGN UB8 131 P7
Peerage Wy EMPK RM11 125 M5
Peerglow Centre WARE SG12 * 26 D3
Peerglow Est PEND EN3 * 80 B9
Peerless Dr DEN/HRF UB9 111 M3
Peerless St FSBYE EC1V 6 G10
Pegamoid Rd UED N18 100 B4
Pegasus Cl STNW/STAM N16 * 119 L9
Pegasus Ct BTFD TW8 155 L4
GVE DA12 190 F6
Pegasus Pl FUL/PGN SW6 * 157 K7
LBTH SE11 18 A9
STALW/RED AL3 38 C4
Pegasus Rd CROY/NA CR0 223 H3
Pegasus Wy FBAR/BDGN N11 98 C7
Pegelm Gdns EMPK RM11 125 N6
Peggotty Wy UX/CGN UB8 132 C8
Pegg Rd HEST TW5 153 L6
Pegler Wy CRAWW RH11 283 N7
Pegley Gdns LEE/GVPK SE12 183 M5
Pegmire La GSTN WD25 74 B5
Pegrams Rd HLWS CM18 46 F4
Pegrum Dr LCOL/BKTW AL2 56 G3
Peg's La HERT/BAY SG13 25 L7
Pegwell Cl CRAWW RH11 283 J10
Pegwell St WOOL/PLUM SE18 163 H6
Peket Cl STA TW18 195 H2
Pekin St POP/IOD E14 140 F8
Peldon Rd HLWW/ROY CM19 46 D3
Peldon Wk IS N1 * 6 D5
Pelham Av BARK IG11 143 J3
Pelham Cl CMBW SE5 159 M9
Pelham Cottages BXLY DA5 * 186 C4
Pelham Ct HHNE HP2 36 D6
WGCE AL7 23 M6
Pelham Crs SKENS SW7 15 N6
Pelham Pl SKENS SW7 15 N5
Pelham Rd BXLYHN DA7 164 B9
GVW DA11 190 D3
IL IG1 122 G7
PGE/AN SE20 204 B2
SEVS/STOTM N15 119 N2
SWFD E18 121 N1
WDGN N22 99 H10
WIM/MER SW19 179 K10
Pelham Rd South GVW DA11 190 C4
Pelhams Cl ESH/CLAY KT10 217 P1
The Pelhams GSTN WD25 73 L1
Pelham St SKENS SW7 15 M5
Pelhams Wk ESH/CLAY KT10 197 P10
Pelham Wy GT/LBKH KT23 254 A2
Pelier St WALW SE17 18 F9
Pelinore Rd CAT SE6 183 K5
Pellant Rd FUL/PGN SW6 14 B10
FUL/PGN SW6 157 H6
Pellatt Gv WDGN N22 99 H9
Pellatt Rd EDUL SE22 181 N1
WBLY HA9 115 K7
Pellerin Rd STNW/STAM N16 119 M10
Pelling Hl WDSR SL4 171 N4
Pellings Cl HAYES BR2 205 K3
Pelling St POP/IOD E14 140 E8
Pellipar Cl PLMGR N13 99 H4
Pellipar Rd WOOL/PLUM SE18 162 C4
Pelly Ct EPP CM16 65 J7
Pelly Rd PLSTW E13 141 M4
Pelter St BETH E2 7 L9
Pelton Av BELMT SM2 221 L6
Pelton Rd GNWCH SE10 161 K4
Pembar Av WALTH E17 * 120 D1
Pemberley Cha HOR/WEW KT19 219 N2
Pemberley Cl HOR/WEW KT19 219 N2
Pember Rd WLSDN NW10 136 G5
Pemberton Av GPK RM2 125 J1
Pemberton Cl STAL AL1 38 C9
Pemberton Gdns ARCH N19 118 D8
CHDH RM6 123 P3
SWLY BR8 208 F3
Pemberton Pl ESH/CLAY KT10 198 B10
HACK E8 140 A2
Pemberton Rd E/WMO/HCT KT8 198 B4
FSBYPK N4 119 J3
SLN SL2 128 E6
Pemberton Rw
FLST/FETLN EC4A 12 B5
Pemberton Ter ARCH N19 118 D8
Pembley Gn CRAWE RH10 285 M2
Pembrey Wy HCH RM12 145 K1
Pembridge Av WHTN TW2 175 N4
Pembridge Cha HHS/BOV HP3 52 C4
Pembridge Cl HHS/BOV HP3 52 C4
Pembridge Crs NTGHL W11 8 D7
Pembridge Gdns BAY/PAD W2 8 E8
Pembridge La BROX EN10 43 N7
Pembridge Ms NTGHL W11 8 E7
Pembridge Pl NTGHL W11 8 F7
Pembridge Rd HHS/BOV HP3 52 D4
NTGHL W11 8 E8
Pembridge Sq BAY/PAD W2 8 F8
Pembridge Vls BAY/PAD W2 8 E7
Pembroke Av BRYLDS KT5 199 N5
EN EN1 80 A5
IS N1 5 M5
KTN/HRWW/WS HA3 114 G1
PIN HA5 113 L6
WOT/HER KT12 217 L1
Pembroke Cl ASC SL5 192 C5
BNSTD SM7 239 L3
BROX EN10 44 D10
EMPK RM11 125 P2
ERITH DA8 164 D3
KTBR SW1X 16 D2
Pembroke Dr CHESW EN7 61 J5
SOCK/AV RM15 166 B1
Pembroke Gdns DAGE RM10 124 C8
KENS W8 14 D5
WOKS/MYFD GU22 232 D4
Pembroke Gardens Cl KENS W8 14 E5
Pembroke Ldg STAN HA7 * 95 H7
Pembroke Ms KENS W8 * 14 E4
MUSWH N10 98 B9
SEV TN13 * 265 K1
Pembroke Pde ERITH DA8 * 164 D4
Pembroke Pl EDGW HA8 95 M8
EYN DA4 210 A1
ISLW TW7 154 D8
KENS W8 * 14 E4
Pembroke Rd BMLY BR1 205 P2
CEND/HSY/T N8 118 F2
CRAWE RH10 284 D5
EHAM E6 142 C7
ERITH DA8 164 D4
GDMY/SEVK IG3 123 J6
GFD/PVL UB6 134 A6
KENS W8 14 E5
MTCM CR4 202 B2
MUSWH N10 98 B9
NTHWD HA6 92 D4
PLMGR N13 99 K4
RSLP HA4 112 F6
SEV TN13 265 J1
SEVS/STOTM N15 119 N3
SNWD SE25 203 M4
WALTH E17 120 G3
WBLY HA9 115 J8
WOKS/MYFD GU22 232 D3
Pembroke Sq KENS W8 14 E4
Pembroke St IS N1 5 M4
Pembroke Ter STJWD NW8 * 3 L6
Pembroke Vls KENS W8 14 E5
Pembroke Wk KENS W8 14 E5
Pembrook Ms BTSEA SW11 * 157 N10
Pembry Cl BRXN/ST SW9 159 H7
Pembury Av WPK KT4 200 D8
Pembury Cl CLPT E5 * 120 A10
COUL/CHIP CR5 222 B10
HAYES BR2 205 L7
Pembury Ct HYS/HAR UB3 152 E5
Pembury Crs SCUP DA14 185 P5
Pembury Rd BXLYHN DA7 163 P6
CLPT E5 120 A10
SNWD SE25 203 P4
TOTM N17 99 N10
Pemdevon Rd CROY/NA CR0 203 H7
Pemell Cl WCHPL E1 140 B6
Pemerich Cl HYS/HAR UB3 * 152 G4
Pempath Pl WBLY HA9 115 J7
Pemsel Ct HHS/BOV HP3 35 P8
Penally Pl IS N1 7 H5
Penang St WAP E1W 140 A10
Penard Rd NWDGN UB2 153 P2
Penarth St PECK SE15 160 B5
Penates ESH/CLAY KT10 218 C1
Penberth Rd CAT SE6 183 H5
Penbury Rd NWDGN UB2 153 N4
Pencombe Ms NTGHL W11 8 D7
Pencraig Wy PECK SE15 160 A5
Pencroft Dr DART DA1 187 K3

Pendall Cl EBAR EN4 77 P8
Penda Rd ERITH DA8 164 C6
Pendarves Rd RYNPK SW20 200 F1
Penda's Md HOM E9 120 D9
Pendell Av HYS/HAR UB3 152 G6
Pendell Ms REDH RH1 * 276 A1
Pendell Rd REDH RH1 259 J7
Pendennis Cl BF/WBF KT14 215 K10
Pendennis Ct HARP AL5 20 C4
Pendennis Rd ORP BR6 207 M9
SEV TN13 247 J9
STRHM/NOR SW16 180 F7
TOTM N17 119 L1
Penderel Rd HSLW TW3 175 P1
Penderry Ri CAT SE6 183 J5
Penderyn Wy HOLWY N7 118 E9
Pendlebury House CHARL SE7 * 162 B6
Pendle Ct HGDN/ICK UB10 * 132 C3
Pendle Rd STRHM/NOR SW16 180 C9
Pendlestone Rd WALTH E17 120 G4
Pendleton Cl REDH RH1 276 A2
Pendleton Rd REDH RH1 275 N3
Pendragon Rd BMLY BR1 183 M6
Pendrell Rd NWCR SE14 160 D9
Pendrell St WOOL/PLUM SE18 162 G5
Pendula Dr YEAD UB4 133 L7
Pendulum Ms HACK E8 * 119 N10
Penenden HART DA3 211 L9
Penerley Rd CAT SE6 182 G4
RAIN RM13 145 J7
Penfold Cl CROY/NA CR0 203 H10
Penfold La BXLY DA5 185 N4
Penfold Pl BAY/PAD W2 9 N3
Penfold Rd ED N9 100 C2
Penfold St STJWD NW8 9 M2
Penford Gdns ELTH/MOT SE9 162 A10
Penford St CMBW SE5 159 J8
Pengarth Rd BXLY DA5 185 N1
Penge La PGE/AN SE20 182 B10
Pengelly Cl CHESW EN7 62 A6
Penge Rd PLSTW E13 141 P2
SNWD SE25 203 P3
Penhale Cl ORP BR6 227 K1
Penhall Rd CHARL SE7 162 A3
Penhill Rd BXLY DA5 185 M3
Penhurst WOKN/KNAP GU21 214 C10
Penhurst Rd BARK/HLT IG6 102 E8
Penifather La GFD/PVL UB6 134 C5
Penington Rd BEAC HP9 108 A1
Peninsular Cl EBED/NFELT TW14 174 E2
Peninsular Park Rd CHARL SE7 161 M4
Penistone Rd STRHM/NOR SW16 180 F10
Penketh Dr HRW HA1 114 C8
Penlow Rd HLWS CM18 46 F4
Penman Cl LCOL/BKTW AL2 55 P3
Penmon Rd ABYW SE2 163 K2
Pennack Rd PECK SE15 19 M10
Pennant Ms KENS W8 14 G5
Pennant Ter WALTH E17 100 E10
Pennard Rd SHB W12 156 F1
The Pennards SUN TW16 197 K3
Penn Av CSHM HP5 50 F6
Penn Cl CRAWW RH11 283 N4
GFD/PVL UB6 134 A4
KTN/HRWW/WS HA3 115 H2
RKW/CH/CXG WD3 70 G10
UX/CGN UB8 131 N6
Penn Ct CRAWW RH11 * 283 J7
Penn Dr DEN/HRF UB9 111 J4
Penne Cl RAD WD7 56 F10
Penner Cl WIM/MER SW19 179 H5
Penners Gdns SURB KT6 199 K7
Pennethorne Cl HOM E9 140 B3
Pennethorne Rd PECK SE15 160 A6
Penney Cl DART DA1 187 L3
Penn Gdns CHST BR7 206 E2
CRW RM5 104 B8
Penn Gaskell La CFSP/GDCR SL9 90 C6
Penn Gn BEAC HP9 88 C7
Pennine Cl CRAWW RH11 283 L7
Pennine Dr CRICK NW2 116 G7
Pennine La CRICK NW2 117 H7
Pennine Pde CRICK NW2 * 117 H7
Pennine Rd SLN SL2 128 F7
Pennine Wy BXLYHN DA7 164 F7
GVW DA11 190 B6
HHNE HP2 36 A3
HYS/HAR UB3 152 E6
Pennings Av GUW GU2 249 L7
Pennington Cl CRW RM5 104 B7
Pennington Dr WCHMH N21 78 F9
WEY KT13 196 F10
Pennington Rd CFSP/GDCR SL9 90 A8
The Penningtons AMS HP6 69 K3
Pennington St WAP E1W 140 A9
Pennington Wy LEE/GVPK SE12 183 N5
Penniston Cl TOTM N17 99 K10
Penn La BXLY DA5 185 N2
RSEV TN14 263 P4
Penn Meadow SLN SL2 129 L3
Penn Rd BEAC HP9 88 B6
DTCH/LGLY SL3 150 A7
HOLWY N7 118 F10
LCOL/BKTW AL2 56 B3
RKW/CH/CXG WD3 91 J2
SLN SL2 129 J6
Penn St IS N1 7 H6
Penn Wy RKW/CH/CXG WD3 70 G10
Penny Cl RAIN RM13 145 J5
Pennycroft CROY/NA CR0 224 D5
Penny Dr RGUW GU3 248 G9
Pennyfield COB KT11 217 H9
Penny Flds BRW CM14 107 H5
Pennyfields POP/IOD E14 140 F9
Penny La SHPTN TW17 196 F7
Pennylets Gn SLN SL2 129 L2
Pennymead HLW CM20 29 K10
Pennymead Dr EHSLY KT24 252 G3
Pennymead Pl ESH/CLAY KT10 217 N3
Penny Ms WAND/EARL SW18 179 K1
Pennymoor Wk MV/WKIL W9 * 8 D1
Pennypot La CHOB/PIR GU24 212 G9
Penny Rd WLSDN NW10 135 N5
Pennyroyal Av EHAM E6 142 D8
Penpoll Rd HACK E8 140 A1
Penpool La WELL DA16 163 L9
Penrhyn Av WALTH E17 100 F9
Penrhyn Cl CTHM CR3 241 L6
Penrhyn Crs MORT/ESHN SW14 155 P10
WALTH E17 100 F9
Penrhyn Gdns KUT/HW KT1 199 J4
Penrhyn Gv WALTH E17 100 F9
Penrhyn Rd KUT/HW KT1 199 K4
Penrith Cl BECK BR3 204 G1
PUT/ROE SW15 179 H1
REIG RH2 257 P9
Penrith Crs HCH RM12 125 H10
Penrith Pl WNWD SE27 181 J5
Penrith Rd BARK/HLT IG6 103 J7
HARH RM3 105 P7
NWMAL KT3 200 A4
SEVS/STOTM N15 119 L3
THHTH CR7 203 K2
Penrith St STRHM/NOR SW16 180 D9
Penrose Av OXHEY WD19 93 M3
Penrose Ct EGH TW20 171 P9
HHNE HP2 35 P2
Penrose Gv WALW SE17 18 E8
Penrose Rd LHD/OX KT22 236 B8
Penrose St WALW SE17 18 E8
Penryn St CAMTN NW1 5 J7
Penry St STHWK SE1 19 K6
Pensbury Pl VX/NE SW8 158 D8
Pensbury St VX/NE SW8 158 D8
Penscroft Gdns BORE WD6 76 A8
Pensford Av RCH/KEW TW9 155 M8
Penshurst HLWE CM17 29 L8
Penshurst Av BFN/LL DA15 185 K2
Penshurst Cl CFSP/GDCR SL9 90 A10
CRAWE RH10 284 E6
Penshurst Gdns EDGW HA8 95 N6
Penshurst Gn HAYES BR2 205 L5
Penshurst Rd BXLYHN DA7 164 A7
HOM E9 140 C2
POTB/CUF EN6 59 N7
THHTH CR7 203 J5
TOTM N17 99 N8
Penshurst Wy BELMT SM2 221 K4
STMC/STPC BR5 207 M4
Pensilver Cl EBAR EN4 * 77 P8
Penson's La CHONG CM5 67 H4
Penstemon Cl FNCH N3 97 K7
Penta Ct BORE WD6 * 75 M8
Pentelow Gdns
EBED/NFELT TW14 175 H2
Pentire Cl UPMR RM14 126 D4
WOKN/KNAP GU21 214 B10
Pentire Rd WALTH E17 101 J9
Pentland HHNE HP2 36 A3
Pentland Av EDGW HA8 95 N3
SHPTN TW17 196 B5
Pentland Cl ED N9 100 B3
GLDGN NW11 117 H7
Pentland Pl NTHLT UB5 133 M3
Pentland Rd BUSH WD23 74 B10
KIL/WHAMP NW6 2 E9
SLN SL2 128 F7
Pentlands Cl MTCM CR4 202 C3
Pentland St WAND/EARL SW18 179 M2
Pentland Wy HGDN/ICK UB10 112 D8
Pentley Pk WGCW AL8 22 G3
Pentlow St PUT/ROE SW15 156 F8
Pentlow Wy BKHH IG9 102 B1
Pentney Rd BAL SW12 180 D4
CHING E4 101 J2
RYNPK SW20 201 H1
Penton Av STA TW18 173 J10
Penton Dr CHES/WCR EN8 62 C5
Penton Gv IS N1 6 A8
Penton Hall Dr STA TW18 195 K1
Penton Hook Rd STA TW18 173 K10
Penton Pl WALW SE17 18 E7
Penton Ri FSBYW WC1X 5 P9
Penton Rd STA TW18 173 J10
Penton St IS N1 6 A7
Pentonville Rd IS N1 5 N8
Pentreath Av GUW GU2 267 M1
Pentrich Av EN EN1 79 P4
Pentridge St PECK SE15 159 N6
Pentstemon Dr SWCM DA10 189 K1
Pentyre Av UED N18 99 L6
Penventon Ct TIL RM18 * 168 D8
Penwerris Av ISLW TW7 154 B6
Penwith Rd WAND/EARL SW18 179 L5
Penwith Wk WOKS/MYFD GU22 * 232 A5
Penwood End
WOKS/MYFD GU22 231 N7
Penwortham Rd SAND/SEL CR2 223 L6
STRHM/NOR SW16 180 C9
Penylan Pl EDGW HA8 95 M9
Penywern Rd ECT SW5 14 F7
Penzance Cl DEN/HRF UB9 * 91 N9
Penzance Gdns HARH RM3 105 P7
Penzance Pl NTGHL W11 8 A9
NTGHL W11 137 H10
Penzance Rd HARH RM3 105 P7
Penzance Sp SLN SL2 128 G6
Penzance St NTGHL W11 8 A9
NTGHL W11 137 H10
Peony Gdns SHB W12 136 D9
Pepler Ms CMBW SE5 19 L8
Pepler Wy SL SL1 128 A5
Peplins Cl BRKMPK AL9 59 H2
Peplins Wy BRKMPK AL9 59 H1
Peploe Rd KIL/WHAMP NW6 136 G4
Peplow Cl WDR/YW UB7 131 N10
Peppard Rd CRAWE RH10 284 E10
Pepper Cl CTHM CR3 259 M1
EHAM E6 142 C7
Peppercorn Cl THHTH CR7 203 L2
Pepper Hl GVW DA11 189 P6
WARE SG12 26 E6
Pepperhill La GVW DA11 189 P6
Peppermead Sq LEW SE13 182 F1
Peppermint Cl CROY/NA CR0 202 F7
Peppermint Pl WAN E11 121 K8
Pepper St POP/IOD E14 160 G2
STHWK SE1 18 E1
Peppett's Gn CSHM HP5 32 C9
Peppie Cl STNW/STAM N16 119 M7
Pepys Cl ASHTD KT21 237 M3
DTCH/LGLY SL3 150 E5
GVW DA11 190 A6
HGDN/ICK UB10 112 C9
TIL RM18 168 F7
Pepys Crs BAR EN5 76 F9
CAN/RD E16 141 M10
Pepys Est DEPT SE8 160 D3
Pepys Park Est DEPT SE8 160 E3
Pepys Ri ORP BR6 207 J8
Pepys Rd NWCR SE14 160 C8
RYNPK SW20 200 F2
Pepys St TWRH EC3N 13 K7
Perceval Av HAMP NW3 117 P10
Percheron Dr WOKN/KNAP GU21 230 G5
Percheron Rd BORE WD6 76 A10
Perch St HACK E8 119 N9
Percival Cl LHD/OX KT22 218 A7
Percival Ct TOTM N17 99 N8
Percival Gdns CHDH RM6 123 M4
Percival Rd EMPK RM11 125 K4
EN EN1 79 N8
FELT TW13 174 G5
MORT/ESHN SW14 155 P10
ORP BR6 206 E9
Percival St FSBYE EC1V 12 C1
Percival Wy HOR/WEW KT19 219 P1
Percy Av ASHF TW15 174 B8
Percy Bryant Rd SUN TW16 174 F10
Percy Bush Rd WDR/YW UB7 152 A2
Percy Gdns PEND EN3 80 C9
WPK KT4 200 A8
YEAD UB4 132 F5
Percy Ms FITZ W1T 11 J4
Percy Rd BXLYHN DA7 163 P8
CAN/RD E16 141 K7
GDMY/SEVK IG3 123 K5
GUW GU2 249 N8
HPTN TW12 175 P10
ISLW TW7 154 F10
MTCM CR4 202 B7
NFNCH/WDSPK N12 97 M6
PGE/AN SE20 204 C1
ROMW/RG RM7 124 D1
SHB W12 156 D1
SNWD SE25 203 N5
WAN E11 121 K5
WATW WD18 73 J8
WCHMH N21 99 K1
WHTN TW2 176 A4
Percy St FITZ W1T 11 J4
GRAYS RM17 167 P5
Percy Ter CSTG HP8 89 M4
Percy Wy WHTN TW2 176 B4
Peregrine Cl GSTN WD25 55 M10
WLSDN NW10 116 A10
Peregrine Ct WELL DA16 163 J7
Peregrine Gdns CROY/NA CR0 204 D9
Peregrine Rd BARK/HLT IG6 103 L6
SUN TW16 196 F2
TOTM N17 99 K8
Peregrine Wy WIM/MER SW19 178 F10
Peregrin Rd WAB EN9 63 M10
Perham Rd WKENS W14 14 C8
WKENS W14 157 H4
Perham Wy LCOL/BKTW AL2 57 J2
Peridot St EHAM E6 142 B7
Perifield DUL SE21 181 K4
Perimeade Rd ALP/SUD HA0 135 H4
Perimeter Rd East HORL RH6 280 C8
Perimeter Rd North HORL RH6 279 N8
HORL RH6 279 P6
Perimeter Rd South
CRAWW RH11 283 M1
HORL RH6 280 A10
Periton Rd ELTH/MOT SE9 162 A10
Perivale Gdns GSTN WD25 55 J10
WEA W13 134 G6
Perivale La GFD/PVL UB6 134 F5
Perivale Village GFD/PVL UB6 * 135 H5
Perkin Cl ALP/SUD HA0 114 G10
HSLW TW3 154 A10
Perkins Cl RDART DA2 188 E1
Perkin's Rents WEST SW1P 17 J3
Perkins Rd BARK/HLT IG6 122 G3
Perkins Sq STHWK SE1 12 F9
Perks Cl BKHTH/KID SE3 161 K8
Perleybrooke La
WOKN/KNAP GU21 231 M3
Permain Cl RAD WD7 57 K9
Perpins Rd ELTH/MOT SE9 185 H2
Perram Cl BROX EN10 62 D2
Perran Cl HART DA3 211 L4
Perran Rd BRXS/STRHM SW2 181 J5
Perren St KTTN NW5 * 4 E1
Perrers Rd HMSMTH W6 156 E2
Perrin Cl ASHF TW15 174 A8
Perrin Ct WOKN/KNAP GU21 232 E1
Perrin Rd ALP/SUD HA0 114 G9
Perrin's Ct HAMP NW3 * 117 M9
Perrin's Wk HAMP NW3 117 M9
Perrior Rd GODL GU7 267 K10
Perriors Cl CHESW EN7 61 P3
Perry Av ACT W3 136 A8
Perry Cl RAIN RM13 144 E4
UX/CGN UB8 132 C8
Perry Ct SEVS/STOTM N15 * 119 M4
Perrycroft WDSR SL4 148 E9
Perryfield HLWE CM17 31 K9
Perryfield Rd CRAWW RH11 283 N8
Perryfields Wy SL SL1 128 A6
Perryfield Wy CDALE/KGS NW9 116 C4
RCHPK/HAM TW10 176 G6
Perry Gdns ED N9 99 M4
Perry Garth NTHLT UB5 133 K3
Perry Gv DART DA1 165 P10
Perry Hall Cl ORP BR6 207 K7
Perry Hall Rd ORP BR6 207 K7
Perry Hl CAT SE6 182 E5
RGUW GU3 249 K4
WAB EN9 45 L9
Perry How WPK KT4 200 C8
Perrylands HORL RH6 279 J8
Perrylands La HORL RH6 280 G5
Perry Mnr CHST BR7 185 H9
Perrymans Farm Rd
GNTH/NBYPK IG2 122 G4
Perryman Wy SLN SL2 128 E5
Perry Md BUSH WD23 74 B10
ENC/FH EN2 79 J6
Perrymead St FUL/PGN SW6 157 K7
Perryn Rd ACT W3 136 A9
BERM/RHTH SE16 160 A2
Perry Oak Dr HTHAIR TW6 151 L8
Perry Ri FSTH SE23 182 D6
Perry Rd DAGW RM9 144 B7
HLWS CM18 46 F4
Perrysfield Rd CHES/WCR EN8 62 D3
Perrys La ORP BR6 227 L9
Perry Spring HLWE CM17 47 M3
Perry St CHST BR7 185 H9
DART DA1 164 F9
GVW DA11 190 B4
Perry V FSTH SE23 182 B5
Perry Wy SOCK/AV RM15 146 B9
Perrywood WGCW AL8 * 22 G3
Persant Rd CAT SE6 183 K6
Perseverance Pl BRXN/ST SW9 159 H6
Persfield Cl EW KT17 220 D6
Persfield Ms EW KT17 * 220 C6
Pershore Cl GNTH/NBYPK IG2 122 E3
Pershore Gv CAR SM5 201 N6
Pert Cl MUSWH N10 98 C8
Perth Av CDALE/KGS NW9 116 A5
SL SL1 128 G8
YEAD UB4 133 K6
Perth Cl CRAWW RH11 283 N4
NTHLT UB5 133 P1
NWMAL KT3 200 C2
Perth Rd BARK IG11 142 G4
BECK BR3 205 H2
FSBYPK N4 119 H6
GNTH/NBYPK IG2 122 E4
LEY E10 120 D6
PLSTW E13 141 N4
WDGN N22 99 J9
Perth Ter GNTH/NBYPK IG2 122 F5
Perwell Av RYLN/HDSTN HA2 113 N6
Pescot Av HART DA3 211 M3
Pescot Hl HHW HP1 35 L4
Petauel Rd TEDD TW11 176 D9
Petavel Rd TEDD TW11 176 D9
Peter Av OXTED RH8 261 J5
WLSDN NW10 136 E2
Peterboat Cl GNWCH SE10 161 K3
Peterborough Av UPMR RM14 126 D6
Peterborough Ms FUL/PGN SW6 157 K8
Peterborough Rd CAR SM5 201 P6
FUL/PGN SW6 157 K8
GUW GU2 249 L8
HRW HA1 114 D6
LEY E10 121 H3
Peterborough Vls FUL/PGN SW6 157 L7
Petergate BTSEA SW11 157 M10
Peterhead Ms DTCH/LGLY SL3 150 D4
Peterhill Cl CFSP/GDCR SL9 90 B6
Peterhouse Pde CRAWE RH10 284 D4
Peterlee Ct HHNE HP2 36 A2
Peters Av LCOL/BKTW AL2 57 H2
Peters Cl BCTR RM8 123 N6
STAN HA7 95 J7
WELL DA16 163 H8
Petersfield STALW/RED AL3 38 D2
Petersfield Av HARH RM3 105 M7
SLN SL2 129 M10
STA TW18 173 M9
Petersfield Cl HARH RM3 105 P7
UED N18 99 K6
Petersfield Crs COUL/CHIP CR5 240 F1
Petersfield Ri PUT/ROE SW15 178 E4
Petersfield Rd ACT W3 155 P1
STA TW18 173 M8
Petersham Av BF/WBF KT14 215 P8
Petersham Cl BF/WBF KT14 215 P8
RCHPK/HAM TW10 177 J5
SUT SM1 221 K2
Petersham Dr STMC/STPC BR5 207 J2
Petersham La SKENS SW7 15 J3
Petersham Ms SKENS SW7 15 J4
Petersham Pl SKENS SW7 15 J4
Petersham Rd
RCHPK/HAM TW10 177 J6
Petersham Ter CROY/NA CR0 * 202 F10
Peter's Hl BLKFR EC4V 12 E7
Petersmead Cl
KWD/TDW/WH KT20 238 F9
Peter's Pl BERK HP4 33 K3
Peterstone Rd ABYW SE2 163 L1
Peterstow Cl WIM/MER SW19 179 H5
Peter St SOHO/CST W1F 11 J7
Peterswood HLWS CM18 46 G5
Peters Wood Hl WARE SG12 26 C4
Peterwood Wy CROY/NA CR0 202 G9
Petherton Rd HBRY N5 119 K10
Petiver Cl HOM E9 * 140 B2
Petley Rd HMSMTH W6 156 F5
Peto Pl CAMTN NW1 10 F1
Peto St North CAN/RD E16 141 L8
Petre Cl RBRW/HUT CM13 127 P4
Petresfield Wy RBRW/HUT CM13 127 P4
Petridge Rd REDH RH1 276 A5
Petrie Cl CRICK NW2 * 2 B1
CRICK NW2 * 137 H1
Petros Gdns HAMP NW3 3 H1
KIL/WHAMP NW6 * 117 L10
Petro St South CAN/RD E16 141 L9
Pettacre Cl THMD SE28 162 F2
Pett Cl EMPK RM11 125 J7
Petten Cl STMC/STPC BR5 207 N8
Petten Gv STMC/STPC BR5 207 M8
Petters Rd ASHTD KT21 237 L2
Petticoat La WCHPL E1 13 K4
Petticoat Sq WCHPL E1 13 L5
Petticoat Tower WCHPL E1 * 13 L5
Pettits Bvd ROM RM1 104 F10
Pettits Cl ROM RM1 104 F10
Pettits La BRWN CM15 87 K3
ROM RM1 104 F10
Pettits La North ROM RM1 104 F9
Pettit's Pl DAGE RM10 124 B10
Pettit's Rd DAGE RM10 124 B10
Pettiward Cl PUT/ROE SW15 156 F10
Pettley Gdns ROMW/RG RM7 124 E3
Pettman Crs THMD SE28 162 G2
Pettsgrove Av ALP/SUD HA0 115 H10
Pett's Hl NTHLT UB5 114 A10
Petts La SHPTN TW17 196 B4
Pett St WOOL/PLUM SE18 162 B3
Petts Wood Rd STMC/STPC BR5 206 G5
Petty Cross SL SL1 128 C8
Petty France WESTW SW1E 17 H3
Pettys Cl CHES/WCR EN8 62 C5
Petty Wales MON EC3R 13 K8
Petworth Cl COUL/CHIP CR5 240 D5
NTHLT UB5 133 N2
Petworth Ct CRAWW RH11 283 J10
Petworth Gdns HGDN/ICK UB10 132 D3
RYNPK SW20 200 E3
Petworth Rd BXLYHS DA6 186 B1
NFNCH/WDSPK N12 97 P6
Petworth St BTSEA SW11 157 P7
Petworth Wy HCH RM12 124 G9
Petyt Pl CHEL SW3 15 N10
Petyward CHEL SW3 15 P6
Pevensey Av EN EN1 79 M6
FBAR/BDGN N11 98 E6
Pevensey Cl CRAWE RH10 284 D8
ISLW TW7 154 B6
Pevensey Rd FELT TW13 175 M4
FSTGT E7 121 M9
SLN SL2 128 F7
TOOT SW17 179 N7
Peverel EHAM E6 142 D8
Peverel Rd CRAWW RH11 283 H8
Peveret Cl FBAR/BDGN N11 * 98 C6
Peveril Dr TEDD TW11 176 C8
Pewley Bank GU GU1 268 B2
Pewley Hl GU GU1 268 B2
Pewley Point GU GU1 268 B2
Pewley Wy GU GU1 268 B2
Pewsey Cl CHING E4 100 F6
Peyton Pl GNWCH SE10 161 H6
Pharaoh Cl MTCM CR4 202 A7
Pheasant Cl BERK HP4 33 P6
CAN/RD E16 141 N8
PUR/KEN CR8 223 J9
Pheasant Hl CSTG HP8 89 P3
Pheasant Ri CSHM HP5 51 J9
Pheasants Wy
RKW/CH/CXG WD3 91 L1
Pheasant Wk CFSP/GDCR SL9 90 A5
Phelips Rd HLWW/ROY CM19 46 D6
Phelp St WALW SE17 18 G9
Phelps Wy HYS/HAR UB3 152 G3
Phene St CHEL SW3 15 P9
Philanthropic Rd REDH RH1 276 C2
Philan Wy CRW RM5 104 E7
Philbeach Gdns ECT SW5 14 E7
Philbye Ms SL SL1 148 E1
Philchurch Pl WCHPL E1 13 P6
Philimore Cl WOOL/PLUM SE18 163 H4
Philip Av ROMW/RG RM7 124 F6
Philip Cl BRWN CM15 86 G10
Philip Gdns CROY/NA CR0 204 E9
Philip La SEVS/STOTM N15 119 L2
Philippa Gdns ELTH/MOT SE9 184 A1
Philip Rd RAIN RM13 144 F5
STA TW18 173 N9
Philips Cl CAR SM5 202 B8
Philip St PLSTW E13 141 M6
Philip Sydney Rd
CDW/CHF RM16 167 J4
Philip Wk PECK SE15 159 P9
Phillida Rd HARH RM3 105 P10
Phillimore Ct RAD WD7 * 74 D2
Phillimore Gdns KENS W8 14 E2
WLSDN NW10 136 F3
Phillimore Gardens Cl KENS W8 * 14 E3
Phillimore Pl KENS W8 14 E2
RAD WD7 74 D2
Phillimore Wk KENS W8 14 E3
Phillip Av SWLY BR8 208 E4
Phillipers GSTN WD25 73 L2
Phillipp St IS N1 7 K6
Phillips Cl DART DA1 187 J2
Phillips Hatch SHGR GU5 268 F9
Philpot La CHOB/PIR GU24 213 P8
FENCHST EC3M 13 J7
Philpots Cl WDR/YW UB7 131 N9
Philpot St WCHPL E1 * 140 A8
Phineas Pett Rd ELTH/MOT SE9 162 B9
Phipp's Bridge Rd MTCM CR4 201 M2
Phipps Hatch La ENC/FH EN2 79 K4
Phipp's Ms BGVA SW1W 16 F4
Phipps Rd SL SL1 128 C7
Phipp St SDTCH EC2A 13 J1
Phoebe Rd HHNE HP2 36 A3
Phoebeth Rd LEW SE13 182 F1
Phoenix Cl HACK E8 * 7 L5
HOR/WEW KT19 219 M8
NTHWD HA6 92 G5
WALTH E17 100 E10
WWKM BR4 205 K9
Phoenix Ct BTFD TW8 155 K4
GU GU1 * 267 P2
POP/IOD E14 160 F3
Phoenix Dr HAYES BR2 206 A10
Phoenix Pk BTFD TW8 * 155 J4
Phoenix Pl DART DA1 187 L3
FSBYW WC1X 11 P1
Phoenix Rd CAMTN NW1 5 J9
PGE/AN SE20 182 B9
Phoenix St LSQ/SEVD WC2H 11 K6
Phoenix Wy HEST TW5 153 L5
Phoenix Wharf Rd STHWK SE1 19 M2
The Phygtle CFSP/GDCR SL9 90 B7
Phyllis Av NWMAL KT3 200 E5
Picardy Manorway BELV DA17 164 C2
Picardy Rd BELV DA17 164 B3
Picardy St BELV DA17 164 B2
Piccadilly MYFR/PICC W1J 10 G9
Piccadilly Ar MYFR/PICC W1J 10 G9
Piccadilly Circ REGST W1B 11 H8
Piccotts End La HHNE HP2 35 N2
Piccotts End Rd HHW HP1 35 M2
Pickard Cl STHGT/OAK N14 98 E2
Pickard St FSBYE EC1V 6 D9
Pickering Av EHAM E6 142 D4
Pickering Gdns CROY/NA CR0 203 N6
FBAR/BDGN N11 98 B7
Pickering Ms BAY/PAD W2 9 H5
Pickering Pl GUW GU2 249 M8
WHALL SW1A * 11 H10
Pickering St IS N1 6 D5
Pickets Cl BUSH WD23 94 C2
Pickets St BAL SW12 180 B3
Pickett Cft STAN HA7 95 J9
Picketts WGCW AL8 22 G2
Picketts La REDH RH1 276 D9
Pickett's Lock La ED N9 100 B3
Pickford Cl BXLYHN DA7 163 P8
Pickford Dr DTCH/LGLY SL3 130 C10
Pickford La BXLYHN DA7 163 P8
Pickford Rd BXLYHN DA7 163 P9
Pickfords Gdns SL SL1 129 K10
Pickfords Whf IS N1 * 6 E8
Pick Hl WAB EN9 63 M8
Pickhurst Gn HAYES BR2 205 L7
Pickhurst La WWKM BR4 205 L6
Pickhurst Md HAYES BR2 205 L7
Pickhurst Pk HAYES BR2 205 K6
Pickhurst Ri WWKM BR4 205 J8
Pickins Piece DTCH/LGLY SL3 150 D8
Pickmoss La RSEV TN14 247 H2
Pickwick Cl HSLWW TW4 175 M1
Pickwick Gdns GVW DA11 190 A6
Pickwick Ms UED N18 99 M6
Pickwick Pl HRW HA1 114 D5
Pickwick Rd DUL SE21 181 L3
Pickwick St STHWK SE1 18 E2
Pickwick Wy CHST BR7 184 F9
Pickworth Cl VX/NE SW8 * 158 F6
Picquets Wy BNSTD SM7 239 J3
Picton Mt WARL CR6 241 P5
Picton Pl MHST W1U 10 D6
Picton St CMBW SE5 159 L6
Pied Bull Yd IS N1 6 C6
Piedmont Rd WOOL/PLUM SE18 162 G4
Pield Heath Av UX/CGN UB8 132 B6
Pield Heath Rd UX/CGN UB8 132 B7
Piercing Hl EPP CM16 82 G1
Pier Four Rd North HORL RH6 280 A7
Pier Head WAP E1W * 140 A10
Pierian Spring HHW HP1 35 L4
Piermont Pl BMLY BR1 206 A2
Piermont Rd EDUL SE22 182 A1
Pierrepoint Ar IS N1 * 6 C7
Pierrepoint Rd ACT W3 135 N9
Pierrepoint Rw IS N1 6 C7
Pier Rd CAN/RD E16 162 C1
EBED/NFELT TW14 175 J1
ERITH DA8 164 F5
GVW DA11 190 C2
SWCM DA10 166 G10
Pierson Rd WDSR SL4 148 C8
Pier St POP/IOD E14 161 H3
Pier Ter WAND/EARL SW18 157 M10
Pier Wy THMD SE28 162 G2
Pier Whf GRAYS RM17 * 167 M6
Pigeonhouse La COUL/CHIP CR5 257 M1
Pigeon La HPTN TW12 175 P7
Piggottshill La HARP AL5 20 C3
Piggotts Orch AMSS HP7 68 C6
Piggs Cnr GRAYS RM17 * 167 P2
Piggy La RKW/CH/CXG WD3 70 E10
Pigott St POP/IOD E14 140 F8
Pike Cl BMLY BR1 183 N8
HGDN/ICK UB10 132 A3
Pike La UPMR RM14 126 E10
Pike Rd MLHL NW7 96 A5
Pike's End PIN HA5 113 J2
Pikes Hl EW KT17 220 B9
Pikes Leap STALE/WH AL4 21 J2
Pikestone Cl YEAD UB4 * 133 M6
Pike Wy EPP CM16 66 B3
Pilgrimage St STHWK SE1 18 G2
Pilgrim Cl GSTN WD25 55 L9
LCOL/BKTW AL2 56 B3
MRDN SM4 201 L7
Pilgrim Hl WNWD SE27 181 K7
Pilgrims Cl BRWN CM15 86 E9
NTHLT UB5 114 B10
PLMGR N13 98 G5
RDKG RH5 254 F8
SHGR GU5 270 B5
Pilgrims Ct DART DA1 187 P1
Pilgrim's La BRW CM14 86 D8
CDW/CHF RM16 147 H10
CTHM CR3 258 G2
HAMP NW3 117 N9
OXTED RH8 243 P10
Pilgrims Ms POP/IOD E14 141 J9
Pilgrims Pl ASHF TW15 * 174 A7
REIG RH2 257 K8
Pilgrim's Ri EBAR EN4 77 P9
Pilgrims' Rd SWCM DA10 167 K10
Pilgrim St BLKFR EC4V * 12 C6
Pilgrims Vw SWCM DA10 189 H2
Pilgrims Wy ARCH N19 118 E6
BGR/WK TN15 247 N2
BH/WHM TN16 244 E9
CHOB/PIR GU24 230 F2
DART DA1 188 A4
RDKG RH5 254 G7
REIG RH2 257 K8
RGUE GU4 268 B4
SAND/SEL CR2 223 N3
SHGR GU5 270 B5
WBLY HA9 115 N6
Pilgrims Wy East RSEV TN14 247 L2
Pilgrims Wy West RSEV TN14 246 G2
Pilkington Rd ORP BR6 206 F10
PECK SE15 160 A8
Pilkingtons HLWE CM17 47 N1
Pilot Cl DEPT SE8 160 E5
Pilots Pl GVE DA12 190 F2
Pilsden Cl WIM/MER SW19 * 178 G4
Piltdown Rd OXHEY WD19 93 L5
Pilton Pl WALW SE17 18 F7
Pimlico Rd BGVA SW1W 16 D7
Pimms Cl RGUE GU4 250 D6
Pinceybrook Rd HLWS CM18 46 F5
Pinchbeck Rd ORP BR6 227 J3
Pinchfield RKW/CH/CXG WD3 90 G6
Pinchin & Johnsons Yd
WCHPL E1 13 P7
Pinchin St WCHPL E1 13 P7
Pincott La EHSLY KT24 252 C5
Pincott Pl BROCKY SE4 160 C9
Pincott Rd BXLYHS DA6 186 B1
WIM/MER SW19 179 M10
Pincroft Wd HART DA3 211 P4
Pindar Rd HOD EN11 45 H2
Pindar St SDTCH EC2A 13 J3
Pindock Ms MV/WKIL W9 9 H2
Pine Apple Ct WESTW SW1E * 16 G3
Pineapple Rd AMSS HP7 69 L5
Pine Av CHOB/PIR GU24 230 F7
GVE DA12 190 G4
SRTFD E15 121 J10
WWKM BR4 204 G8
Pine Cl ADL/WDHM KT15 215 L7
BERK HP4 33 N5
CHES/WCR EN8 62 B4
CRAWW RH11 283 M4
LEY E10 120 F7
PGE/AN SE20 204 B1
PUR/KEN CR8 241 K3
STAN HA7 94 G5
STHGT/OAK N14 98 D1
SWLY BR8 208 G4
WOKN/KNAP GU21 231 P3
Pine Coombe CROY/NA CR0 224 C1
Pinecote Dr ASC SL5 192 E7
Pine Ct UPMR RM14 125 P9
Pine Crs CAR SM5 221 N7
Pinecrest Gdns ORP BR6 226 E1
Pinecroft GPK RM2 125 K2
HHS/BOV HP3 36 A10
KTN/HRWW/WS HA3 115 L3
RBRW/HUT CM13 107 N1
WOOL/PLUM SE18 163 K6
Pinecroft Crs BAR EN5 77 H8
Pine Dean GT/LBKH KT23 254 A1
Pinefield Cl POP/IOD E14 * 140 F9
Pinefields ADL/WDHM KT15 * 215 L1
Pine Gdns BRYLDS KT5 199 M6
HORL RH6 280 B5
RSLP HA4 113 J6
Pine Gld ORP BR6 226 C1
Pine Gv BFOR GU20 212 C3
BRKMPK AL9 59 L1
BUSH WD23 73 N5
FSBYPK N4 118 F7
LCOL/BKTW AL2 55 N6
TRDG/WHET N20 97 J2
WEY KT13 216 C2
WIM/MER SW19 179 J8
Pine Grove Ms WEY KT13 * 216 D2
Pine Hl EPSOM KT18 238 A2
Pinehurst ASC SL5 192 C5
RSEV TN14 247 M7
Pinehurst Cl ABLGY WD5 54 F8
KWD/TDW/WH KT20 239 K8
Pinelands Cl BKHTH/KID SE3 * 161 L6
Pinel Cl VW GU25 194 B4
Pinelees Ct MORT/ESHN SW14 * 155 P10
Pinemartin Cl CRICK NW2 116 F8
Pineneedle La SEV TN13 247 J9
Pine Pk RGUW GU3 * 248 F5
Pine Pl BNSTD SM7 220 G10
Pine Rdg CAR SM5 222 B5
STAL AL1 * 38 F9
Pineridge Cl WEY KT13 216 F1
Pine Rd CRICK NW2 116 F9
FBAR/BDGN N11 98 B3
WOKS/MYFD GU22 231 P6
Pines Av EN EN1 80 B2
Pines Cl AMS HP6 68 C3
NTHWD HA6 92 F7
Pine Shaw CRAWE RH10 284 D6
Pines Rd BMLY BR1 206 B2
The Pines BORE WD6 75 L6
CDW/CHF RM16 147 N10
HHS/BOV HP3 35 J10
NRWD SE19 * 181 J9
PUR/KEN CR8 223 J9
STHGT/OAK N14 78 D9
SUN TW16 197 H3
WFD IG8 101 M4
WOKN/KNAP GU21 214 C10
Pine St CLKNW EC1R 12 A1
Pinetree Cl CFSP/GDCR SL9 89 P8
Pine Tree Cl HEST TW5 153 J7
HHNE HP2 35 N5
Pine Tree Hl WOKS/MYFD GU22 232 G2
Pine Trees STA TW18 * 173 H8
Pinetrees Cl CRAWE RH10 285 J2
Pine Trees Dr HGDN/ICK UB10 111 P9
Pine View Cl RGUE GU4 269 J6
Pine Wk BERK HP4 33 J2
BNSTD SM7 240 A3
BRYLDS KT5 199 M6
CAR SM5 221 N6
COB KT11 217 L10
CTHM CR3 241 M8
EHSLY KT24 252 G4
GT/LBKH KT23 254 A1
Pine Wy EGH TW20 171 N9
Pine Wd SUN TW16 197 H1
Pinewood WGCE AL7 23 H7
Pinewood Av ADL/WDHM KT15 215 M5
BFN/LL DA15 185 H4
PIN HA5 94 A7
RAIN RM13 145 J6
RSEV TN14 247 L7
UX/CGN UB8 132 A8
Pinewood Cl BORE WD6 76 A5
CFSP/GDCR SL9 110 B5
CROY/NA CR0 204 D10
HLWE CM17 47 M3
IVER SL0 130 F2
NTHWD HA6 93 H6
ORP BR6 206 G8
PIN HA5 94 A7
SLH/COR SS17 169 L2
STALE/WH AL4 39 H6
WAT WD17 73 H5
WOKN/KNAP GU21 232 D1
Pinewood Dr ORP BR6 227 H2
POTB/CUF EN6 59 J7
STA TW18 * 173 K8
Pinewood Gdns HHS/BOV HP3 35 P8
HHW HP1 35 L6
Pinewood Gn IVER SL0 130 F2
Pinewood Gv ADL/WDHM KT15 215 L6
EA W5 135 H8
Pinewood Ldg BUSH WD23 * 94 C2
Pinewood Ms STWL/WRAY TW19 173 N2
Pinewood Pk ADL/WDHM KT15 215 L7
Pinewood Pl RDART DA2 186 F5
Pinewood Rd ABR/ST RM4 104 D5
ABYW SE2 163 N5
FELT TW13 175 J6
HAYES BR2 205 M4
IVER SL0 130 E1
VW GU25 193 M3
Pinfold Rd BUSH WD23 73 N6
STRHM/NOR SW16 180 F7
Pinglestone Cl WDR/YW UB7 151 P6
Pinkcoat Cl FELT TW13 175 J6
Pinkham Wy North Circular Rd
NFNCH/WDSPK N12 98 A8
Pink La SL SL1 128 A4
Pinks Hl SWLY BR8 208 F5
Pinkwell Av HYS/HAR UB3 152 E3
Pinkwell La HYS/HAR UB3 152 E3
Pinley Gdns DAGW RM9 143 L3
Pinnacle Hl BXLYHN DA7 164 C10
Pinnacle Hl North BXLYHN DA7 164 C9
Pinnacles WAB EN9 63 K10
Pinnate Pl WGCE AL7 23 H9
Pinn Cl UX/CGN UB8 131 N8
Pinnell Rd ELTH/MOT SE9 162 A10
Pinner Ct PIN HA5 113 P2
Pinner Gn PIN HA5 93 K10
Pinner Gv PIN HA5 113 M2
Pinner Hl PIN HA5 93 K8
Pinner Hill Rd PIN HA5 93 K10
Pinner Park Av
RYLN/HDSTN HA2 94 B10
Pinner Park Gdns
RYLN/HDSTN HA2 94 B10
Pinner Rd NTHWD HA6 92 G9
OXHEY WD19 73 L10
PIN HA5 113 N2
Pinner Vw RYLN/HDSTN HA2 114 B2
Pinnock's Av GVW DA11 190 E4
Pinn Wy RSLP HA4 112 E5
Pinstone Wy CFSP/GDCR SL9 110 E7
Pintail Cl EHAM E6 142 B7
Pintail Rd WFD IG8 101 N8
Pintail Wy YEAD UB4 133 L7
Pinto Cl BORE WD6 * 76 A10
Pinto Wy BKHTH/KID SE3 161 N10
Pioneer Cl SHB W12 136 E8
Pioneer St PECK SE15 159 P7
Pioneer Wy SHB W12 136 F8
SWLY BR8 208 F3
WATW WD18 72 G10
Piper Cl HOLWY N7 5 N1
Piper Rd KUT/HW KT1 199 M3
Pipers Av HARP AL5 20 C4
Pipers Cl COB KT11 235 L1
SL SL1 128 B5
Piper's End VW GU25 194 A3
Pipers Gdns CROY/NA CR0 204 D7
Pipers Gn CDALE/KGS NW9 115 P3
Pipers Green La STAN HA7 95 K4
Piper's Green Rd BH/WHM TN16 263 K4
Pipers La BH/WHM TN16 263 L3
HARP AL5 20 D4
Piper Wy IL IG1 122 G6
Pipewell Rd CAR SM5 201 P6
Pippbrook Gdns DORK RH4 272 G1
Pippens WGCW AL8 23 H2
Pippin Cl CRICK NW2 116 D8
CROY/NA CR0 204 E8
RAD WD7 57 K9
Pippins Cl WDR/YW UB7 151 N2
Pippins Ct ASHF TW15 174 C9
The Pippins DTCH/LGLY SL3 130 C10
GSTN WD25 * 55 K10
Piquet Rd PGE/AN SE20 204 B2
Pirbright Crs CROY/NA CR0 225 H3
Pirbright Rd RGUW GU3 248 B5
WAND/EARL SW18 179 J4
Pirbright Ter CHOB/PIR GU24 * 230 E9
Pirie St CAN/RD E16 141 N10
Pirrip Cl GVE DA12 191 J4
Pirton Cl STALE/WH AL4 39 H1
Pishiobury Dr SBW CM21 29 N3
Pitcairn Cl ROMW/RG RM7 124 B2
Pitcairn Rd MTCM CR4 180 A10
Pitchfont La OXTED RH8 261 M2
WARL CR6 243 L10
Pitchford St SRTFD E15 141 J2
Pitch Pond Cl BEAC HP9 88 B6
Pit Farm Rd GU GU1 250 D10
Pitfield HART DA3 211 L4
Pitfield Crs THMD SE28 143 K10
Pitfield St IS N1 7 J7
Pitfield Wy PEND EN3 80 B5
WLSDN NW10 135 P1
Pitfold Rd LEE/GVPK SE12 183 M3
Pitlake CROY/NA CR0 203 J9
Pitman St CMBW SE5 159 K6
Pitsea Pl WCHPL E1 140 C8
Pitsea St WCHPL E1 140 C8
Pitsfield WGCW AL8 22 G2

Pitshanger La EA W5 134 G6
Pitson Cl ADL/WDHM KT15 215 N1
Pitstone Cl STALE/WH AL4 39 H1
Pitt Crs WIM/MER SW19 179 L7
Pitt Dr STALE/WH AL4 39 H9
Pittman Cl RBRW/HUT CM13 107 P6
Pittman Gdns IL IG1 122 F10
Pittman's Fld HLW CM20 29 J10
Pitt Pl EW KT17 * 220 B10
Pitt Rd EW KT17 220 B10
ORP BR6 226 F1
RYLN/HDSTN HA2 114 B7
THHTH CR7 203 K5
Pitts Head Ms MYFR/PICC W1J 10 D10
Pittsmead Av HAYES BR2 205 M7
Pitts Rd SL SL1 129 H10
Pitt St KENS W8 14 F1
Pittville Gdns SNWD SE25 203 P3
Pit Wood Gn
KWD/TDW/WH KT20 238 F6
Pix Farm La HHW HP1 34 F7
Pixham La DORK RH4 255 H9
Pixholme Gv DORK RH4 255 H10
Pixies Hill Crs HHW HP1 35 J8
Pixies Hill Rd HHW HP1 35 J7
Pixley St POP/IOD E14 140 E8
Pixton Wy CROY/NA CR0 224 E4
Place Farm Av ORP BR6 206 G8
Place Farm La BRWN CM15 86 F3
Place Farm Rd REDH RH1 259 L7
Placehouse La COUL/CHIP CR5 240 G5
Plackett Wy SL SL1 128 C10
Plaines Cl SL SL1 128 E10
The Plain EPP CM16 65 L5
Plaistow Gv BMLY BR1 183 N10
SRTFD E15 141 L3
Plaistow La BMLY BR1 183 M10
Plaistow Park Rd PLSTW E13 141 N4
Plaistow Rd PLSTW E13 141 M4
Plaitford Cl RKW/CH/CXG WD3 91 P3
Plane Av GVW DA11 190 A3
The Planes CHERT KT16 195 M7
Plane St SYD SE26 182 A6
Plane Tree Crs FELT TW13 175 J6
Plantaganet Pl WAB EN9 62 G9
Plantagenet Cl WPK KT4 220 A1
Plantagenet Gdns CHDH RM6 123 N5
Plantagenet Pl CHDH RM6 123 N5
Plantagenet Rd BAR EN5 77 M8
Plantain Gdns WAN E11 * 121 J8
Plantain Pl STHWK SE1 18 G1
Plantation Cl RDART DA2 188 E2
Plantation Dr STMC/STPC BR5 207 N8
Plantation La FENCHST EC3M 13 J7
WARL CR6 242 D5
Plantation Rd AMS HP6 69 K3
ERITH DA8 165 H7
SWLY BR8 187 H10
The Plantation BKHTH/KID SE3 161 M8
Plantation Wk HHW HP1 35 K4
Plantation Wy AMS HP6 69 K3
Plashet Gdns RBRW/HUT CM13 107 M5
Plashet Gv EHAM E6 141 P3
Plashet Rd PLSTW E13 141 M3
Plashets RBSF CM22 30 D2
The Plashets RBSF CM22 30 D3
Plassy Rd CAT SE6 182 G3
Platford Gn EMPK RM11 125 M2
Platina St SDTCH EC2A 13 H2
Plato Rd BRXS/STRHM SW2 158 F10
Platt Meadow RGUE GU4 250 G7
Platt's La HAMP NW3 117 K8
Platts Rd PEND EN3 80 B5
Platt St CAMTN NW1 5 J7
The Platt AMSS HP7 68 G6
Plawsfield Rd BECK BR3 204 C1
Plaxtol Cl BMLY BR1 205 P1
Plaxtol Rd ERITH DA8 164 B6
Playfair St HMSMTH W6 * 156 F4
Playfield Av CRW RM5 104 D9
Playfield Crs EDUL SE22 181 M1
Playfield Rd EDGW HA8 95 P10
Playford Rd FSBYPK N4 118 G7
Playgreen Wy CAT SE6 182 F7
Playground Cl BECK BR3 204 C2
Playhouse Ct STHWK SE1 18 E1
Playhouse Sq HLWW/ROY CM19 46 F1
Playhouse Yd BLKFR EC4V 12 D6
Plaza Pde ALP/SUD HA0 * 135 K1
Plaza Wk CDALE/KGS NW9 115 P1
Pleasance Rd PUT/ROE SW15 178 E1
STMC/STPC BR5 207 L2
The Pleasance PUT/ROE SW15 156 E10
Pleasant Gv CROY/NA CR0 204 E10
Pleasant Pl IS N1 6 D4
RKW/CH/CXG WD3 * 91 H8
WOT/HER KT12 217 L3
Pleasant Ri BRKMPK AL9 40 F1
Pleasant Vw ERITH DA8 164 F4
ORP BR6 226 F2
Pleasant Wy ALP/SUD HA0 135 H4
Pleasure Pit Rd ASHTD KT21 237 N4
Plender St CAMTN NW1 4 G6
Pleshey Rd ARCH N19 118 E9
Plesman Wy WLGTN SM6 * 222 F5
Plevna Crs SEVS/STOTM N15 119 M4
Plevna Rd ED N9 99 P4
HPTN TW12 198 A1
Plevna St POP/IOD E14 161 H2
Pleydell Av HMSMTH W6 156 C2
NRWD SE19 181 N10
Pleydell Est FSBYE EC1V 6 F10
Pleydell Gdns NRWD SE19 * 181 N9
Pleydell St EMB EC4Y 12 B6
Plimsoll Cl POP/IOD E14 140 G8
Plimsoll Rd FSBYPK N4 119 J8
Plomer Av HOD EN11 26 E10
Plough Cl CRAWW RH11 283 J5
Plough Farm Cl RSLP HA4 112 E4
Plough Hl POTB/CUF EN6 60 F6
Plough La BERK HP4 34 E2
COB KT11 235 H2
CROY/NA CR0 222 F1
DEN/HRF UB9 91 M7
EDUL SE22 181 N2
PUR/KEN CR8 222 G6
RKW/CH/CXG WD3 53 J9
SLN SL2 129 N3
TEDD TW11 * 176 F8
WIM/MER SW19 179 L8
Plough Lane Cl WLGTN SM6 222 F2
Ploughlees La SL SL1 129 K10
Ploughmans Cl CAMTN NW1 5 J5
Ploughmans End ISLW TW7 176 C1
WGCE AL7 23 M6
Plough Pl FLST/FETLN EC4A 12 B5
Plough Ri UPMR RM14 126 D6
Plough Rd BTSEA SW11 157 N9
HOR/WEW KT19 220 A4
HORL RH6 281 K4
Plough St WCHPL E1 * 13 N5
Plough Ter BTSEA SW11 157 N10
Plough Wy BERM/RHTH SE16 160 C3
Plough Yd SDTCH EC2A 13 K2
Plover Cl BERK HP4 33 P6
CRAWW RH11 283 M5
STA TW18 173 J6
Plover Gdns UPMR RM14 126 E6
Plovers Barron BRWN CM15 87 J2
Plovers Md BRWN CM15 87 J2
Plovers Ri CHOB/PIR GU24 230 D6
Plover Wy BERM/RHTH SE16 160 D2
YEAD UB4 133 L8
Plowden Buildings EMB EC4Y * 12 A7
Plowman Cl UED N18 99 L6
Plowman Wy BCTR RM8 123 N6
Ployters Rd HLWS CM18 46 F5
Plumbers Rw WCHPL E1 13 N4
Plumbridge St GNWCH SE10 * 161 H7
Plum Cl FELT TW13 175 H4
Plum Garth BTFD TW8 155 J3
Plum La WOOL/PLUM SE18 162 E6
Plummer La MTCM CR4 202 A2
Plummer Rd CLAP SW4 180 D2
Plumpton Av HCH RM12 125 N9
Plumpton Rd HOD EN11 45 H1
Plumpton Wy CAR SM5 201 P10
Plumstead Common Rd
WOOL/PLUM SE18 162 E5
Plumstead High St
WOOL/PLUM SE18 162 G3
Plumstead Rd WOOL/PLUM SE18 162 F3
Plumtree Cl DAGE RM10 144 D1
WLGTN SM6 222 E4
Plumtree Ct FLST/FETLN EC4A 12 B5
Pluto Ri HHNE HP2 35 P4
Plymouth Dr SEV TN13 247 K10
Plymouth Pk SEV TN13 247 K10
Plymouth Rd BMLY BR1 205 N1
CAN/RD E16 141 M8
CDW/CHF RM16 167 H4
SL SL1 128 D8
Plymouth Whf POP/IOD E14 161 J3
Plympton Av KIL/WHAMP NW6 2 C4
Plympton Cl BELV DA17 163 P2
Plympton Pl STJWD NW8 * 9 N2
Plympton Rd KIL/WHAMP NW6 2 C4
Plympton St STJWD NW8 9 N2
Plymstock Rd WELL DA16 163 M6
Pocket Hl SEV TN13 265 H4
Pocklington Cl CDALE/KGS NW9 96 B10
Pocock Av WDR/YW UB7 152 A2
Pococks La WDSR SL4 149 K4
Pocock St STHWK SE1 18 C1
Podmore Rd WAND/EARL SW18 157 M10
Poets Cha HHW HP1 35 L4
Poets Ct HARP AL5 20 A2
Poets Ga CHESW EN7 61 M4
Poet's Rd HBRY N5 119 L10
Poets Wy HRW HA1 114 D2
Pointalls Cl FNCH N3 97 M10
Point Cl GNWCH SE10 161 H7
Pointer Cl THMD SE28 143 N8
Pointers Cl POP/IOD E14 160 G4
Pointers Hl DORK RH4 272 B4
Pointers Rd COB KT11 234 E3
The Pointers ASHTD KT21 237 K6
Point Hl GNWCH SE10 161 H7
Point Pl WBLY HA9 135 N2
Point Pleasant
WAND/EARL SW18 157 K10
Point Wharf La BTFD TW8 155 J6
Poland St SOHO/SHAV W1D 11 H5
Polayn Garth WGCW AL8 22 F4
Polebrook Rd BKHTH/KID SE3 161 P9
Polecroft La CAT SE6 182 E5
Polegate Cottages
GRAYS RM17 * 167 K5
Polehanger La HHW HP1 35 H4
Pole Hill Rd CHING E4 101 H1
HGDN/ICK UB10 132 D5
Polesden Gdns RYNPK SW20 200 E2
Polesden La RPLY/SEND GU23 233 J9
Polesden Rd RDKG RH5 254 A5
Polesden Vw GT/LBKH KT23 254 A3
Poles Hl CSHM HP5 50 F5
RKW/CH/CXG WD3 53 H9
Poles La CRAWW RH11 283 M2
Polesteeple Hl BH/WHM TN16 244 A3
Polesworth Rd DAGW RM9 144 A4
Polhill RSEV TN14 246 D1
Police Station Rd
WOT/HER KT12 217 K3
Polish War Memorial Rbt
RSLP HA4 133 K1
Pollard Av DEN/HRF UB9 111 J4
Pollard Cl CAN/RD E16 141 M9
CHIG IG7 103 K6
HOLWY N7 118 G10
WDSR SL4 171 N1
Pollard Hatch HLWW/ROY CM19 46 E4
Pollard Rd MRDN SM4 201 N5
TRDG/WHET N20 97 P3
WOKS/MYFD GU22 232 E2
Pollard Rw BETH E2 7 P9
Pollards CRAWW RH11 283 K8
RKW/CH/CXG WD3 90 G6
Pollards Cl CHESW EN7 61 K5
LOU IG10 81 P9
Pollards Crs STRHM/NOR SW16 202 F3
Pollards Hl East
STRHM/NOR SW16 202 G3
Pollards Hl North
STRHM/NOR SW16 202 G3
Pollards Hl South
STRHM/NOR SW16 202 F3
Pollards Hl West
STRHM/NOR SW16 202 F3
Pollards Oak Crs OXTED RH8 261 M8
Pollards Oak Rd OXTED RH8 261 M8
Pollard St BETH E2 7 P9
Pollards Wood Hl OXTED RH8 261 N7
Pollards Wood Rd OXTED RH8 261 N7
STRHM/NOR SW16 202 F2
Pollen St CONDST W1S 10 F6
Pollitt Dr STJWD NW8 9 L1
Pollyhaugh EYN DA4 209 M10
Polperro Cl ORP BR6 207 J6
Polperro Ms LBTH SE11 18 B5
Polsted La RGUW GU3 267 J6
Polsted Rd CAT SE6 182 E3
Polthorne Gv WOOL/PLUM SE18 162 F3
Poltimore Rd GUW GU2 267 M2
Polworth Rd STRHM/NOR SW16 180 F8
Polygon Rd CAMTN NW1 5 J8
The Polygon CLAP SW4 * 158 D10
Polytechnic St
WOOL/PLUM SE18 162 D3
Pomell Wy WCHPL E1 13 M5
Pomeroy Cl AMSS HP7 69 J6
Pomeroy Crs WATN WD24 73 J2
Pomeroy St PECK SE15 160 B6
Pomfret Rd CMBW SE5 159 J9
Pomoja La ARCH N19 118 F7
Pompadour Cl BRW CM14 107 H6
Pond Cl AMSS HP7 68 B10
BKHTH/KID SE3 161 M8
DEN/HRF UB9 91 M10
NFNCH/WDSPK N12 97 P7
WOT/HER KT12 216 G3
Pond Cottage La BECK BR3 204 F8
Pond Cft HAT AL10 40 C3
WGCE AL7 23 H6
Ponder St HOLWY N7 * 5 N3
Pond Farm Cl
KWD/TDW/WH KT20 238 E10
Pond Farm Est CLPT E5 * 120 B8
Pondfield Crs STALE/WH AL4 38 G3
Pondfield La GVE DA12 191 P10
RBRW/HUT CM13 107 M5
Pondfield Rd DAGE RM10 124 C10
HAYES BR2 205 K8
ORP BR6 206 E10
PUR/KEN CR8 241 J2
Pond Gn RSLP HA4 112 F7
Pond Hill Gdns CHEAM SM3 * 221 H3
Pond La CFSP/GDCR SL9 89 N9
SHGR GU5 270 D10
Pond Lees Cl DAGE RM10 144 E2
Pond Md DUL SE21 181 L2
Pond Meadow GUW GU2 249 K10
Pond Park Rd CSHM HP5 50 G5
Pond Piece LHD/OX KT22 218 A9
Pond Pl CHEL SW3 15 N6
Pond Rd BKHTH/KID SE3 161 L9
EGH TW20 172 F9
HHS/BOV HP3 54 B1
SRTFD E15 141 K4
WOKS/MYFD GU22 231 M6
Pondside Cl HYS/HAR UB3 152 E6
Ponds La SHGR GU5 269 P8
The Ponds WEY KT13 216 E3
Pond St HAMP NW3 117 P10
Pond Wk UPMR RM14 126 D7
Pond Wy TEDD TW11 177 H9
Pondwicks AMSS HP7 68 G5
Pondwicks Cl STAL AL1 38 B7
Pondwood Ri ORP BR6 207 H8
Pond Wood Rd CRAWE RH10 284 B5
Ponler St WCHPL E1 140 A8
Ponsard Rd WLSDN NW10 136 E5
Ponsford St HOM E9 140 B1
Ponsonby Pl WEST SW1P 17 K7
Ponsonby Rd PUT/ROE SW15 178 E3
Ponsonby Ter WEST SW1P 17 K7
Pontefract Rd BMLY BR1 183 M8
Pontoise Cl SEV TN13 246 G8
Ponton Rd VX/NE SW8 158 E6
Pont St KTBR SW1X 16 A4
Pont Street Ms KTBR SW1X 16 A4
Pony Cha COB KT11 217 N9
Pool Cl BECK BR3 182 F8
E/WMO/HCT KT8 197 N5
Pool Ct CAT SE6 182 F5
Poole Cl RSLP HA4 112 F7
Poole Court Rd HSLW TW3 153 M8
Pool End Cl SHPTN TW17 196 B5
Poole Rd EMPK RM11 125 N5
HOM E9 140 C1
HOR/WEW KT19 220 A3
WOKN/KNAP GU21 232 B4
Pooles Buildings FSBYW WC1X 12 A2
Pooles La WBPTN SW10 157 M6
Pooles Pk FSBYPK N4 119 H7
Poole St IS N1 6 G6
Poole Wy YEAD UB4 * 132 F5
Pooley Av EGH TW20 172 E8
Pooley Dr MORT/ESHN SW14 155 P9
Pooley Green Rd EGH TW20 172 F9
Pooleys La BRKMPK AL9 40 E9
Pool La SL SL1 129 K9
Poolmans Rd WDSR SL4 148 D9
Poolmans St BERM/RHTH SE16 160 C1
Pool Rd E/WMO/HCT KT8 197 N5
HRW HA1 114 C5
Poolsford Rd CDALE/KGS NW9 116 B2
Poonah St WCHPL E1 140 B8
Pope Cl EBED/NFELT TW14 174 G4
WIM/MER SW19 * 179 N9
Pope Rd HAYES BR2 206 A5
Pope's Av WHTN TW2 176 D5
Popes Cl DTCH/LGLY SL3 150 F6
Popes Dr FNCH N3 97 K9
Popes Gv CROY/NA CR0 204 E10
WHTN TW2 176 D5
Pope's La EA W5 155 J2
WATN WD24 73 J3
Pope's Rd ABLGY WD5 54 F7
BRXN/ST SW9 * 159 H9
Pope St STHWK SE1 19 K2
Popham Cl FELT TW13 175 M6
Popham Gdns RCH/KEW TW9 * 155 N9
Popham Rd IS N1 6 E5
Popham St IS N1 6 E5
Popinjays Rw CHEAM SM3 * 220 G2
Popis Gdns WARE SG12 26 D1
Poplar Av AMSS HP7 69 L5
GVE DA12 190 F7
HAT AL10 40 A4
LHD/OX KT22 236 G8
MTCM CR4 202 A1
NWDGN UB2 154 A2
ORP BR6 206 E9
WDR/YW UB7 132 A9
Poplar Bath St POP/IOD E14 140 G9
Poplar Cl CRAWW RH11 283 M4
CSHM HP5 51 H4
DTCH/LGLY SL3 151 H7
HOM E9 120 E10
PIN HA5 93 L9
SOCK/AV RM15 147 J6
Poplar Court Pde TWK TW1 * 177 H2
Poplar Crs HOR/WEW KT19 219 P3
Poplar Dr BNSTD SM7 220 G10
RBRW/HUT CM13 87 P10
Poplar Farm Cl HOR/WEW KT19 219 P3
Poplar Gdns NWMAL KT3 200 A2
Poplar Gn WOKS/MYFD GU22 232 B5
Poplar Gv FBAR/BDGN N11 98 B7
HMSMTH W6 156 F1
NWMAL KT3 200 A3
WBLY HA9 115 P8
Poplar High St POP/IOD E14 140 G9
Poplar La BECK BR3 204 G5
Poplar Ms SHB W12 136 F10
Poplar Mt BELV DA17 164 C3
Poplar Pl BAY/PAD W2 8 G7
HYS/HAR UB3 133 H10
THMD SE28 143 M9
Poplar Rd ASHF TW15 174 D8
CHEAM SM3 201 J8
DEN/HRF UB9 131 M1
HNHL SE24 159 K10
LHD/OX KT22 236 G8
RGUE GU4 268 B7
WIM/MER SW19 201 K2
Poplar Rd South
WIM/MER SW19 201 K3
Poplar Rw EPP CM16 83 H3
Poplars WGCE AL7 23 L4
Poplars Cl GSTN WD25 55 J8
HART DA3 211 P3
HAT AL10 40 A4
RSLP HA4 112 F6
Poplar Shaw WAB EN9 63 L9
Poplars Rd WALTH E17 120 G4
The Poplars ABR/ST RM4 83 L7
BORE WD6 * 75 M5
CHESW EN7 61 M2
DEN/HRF UB9 * 91 M9
GVE DA12 191 H2
HHW HP1 35 L7
RDKG RH5 278 B7
STAL AL1 38 G10
STHGT/OAK N14 78 C9
Poplar St ROMW/RG RM7 124 D2
Poplar Vw WBLY HA9 * 115 J7
Poplar Wk CROY/NA CR0 203 K9
CTHM CR3 241 M9
HNHL SE24 159 K10
Poplar Wy BARK/HLT IG6 122 F2
FELT TW13 175 H6
Poppins Ct FLST/FETLN EC4A 12 C6
Poppleton Rd WAN E11 121 K4
Poppy Cl BELV DA17 164 C2
HHW HP1 35 H5
NTHLT UB5 133 N1
WLGTN SM6 202 B8
Poppyfields WGCE AL7 23 M6
Poppy La CROY/NA CR0 204 B7
Poppy Wk CHESW EN7 61 L4
Porchester Cl EMPK RM11 125 M4
HART DA3 211 L4
Porchester Garden Ms
BAY/PAD W2 9 H6
Porchester Gdns BAY/PAD W2 9 H7
Porchester Ga BAY/PAD W2 * 9 J8
Porchester Md BECK BR3 182 G9
Porchester Pl BAY/PAD W2 9 P6
Porchester Rd BAY/PAD W2 9 H5
KUT/HW KT1 199 N2
Porchester Sq BAY/PAD W2 9 H5
Porchester Square Ms
BAY/PAD W2 9 H5
Porchester Ter BAY/PAD W2 9 J7
Porchester Ter North
BAY/PAD W2 9 H5
Porchfield Cl BELMT SM2 221 L6
GVE DA12 190 F5
Porch Wy TRDG/WHET N20 98 A4
Porcupine Cl ELTH/MOT SE9 184 B5
Porden Rd BRXS/STRHM SW2 158 G10
Porlock Av RYLN/HDSTN HA2 114 B6
Porlock Rd EN EN1 99 N1
Porlock St STHWK SE1 19 H2
Porridge Pot Aly GUW GU2 268 A2
Porrington Cl CHST BR7 206 C1
Portal Cl HGDN/ICK UB10 132 A2
RSLP HA4 113 H9
WNWD SE27 181 H6
Portal Wy ACT W3 136 A7
Port Av SWCM DA10 188 G2
Portbury Cl PECK SE15 159 P7
Portchester Cl HNHL SE24 159 K10
Portchester Ga BAY/PAD W2 9 J8
Portcullis Lodge Rd EN EN1 79 L7
Portelet Rd WCHPL E1 140 C5
Porten Houses WKENS W14 * 157 H2
Porten Rd WKENS W14 14 A4
WKENS W14 157 H2
Porter Cl WTHK RM20 167 H5
Porter Rd EHAM E6 142 C8
Porters Av DAGW RM9 143 L1
Porters Cl BRW CM14 106 F2
Porters Park Dr RAD WD7 57 L9
Porter Sq ARCH N19 118 F6
Porter St MHST W1U 10 B3
STHWK SE1 12 F9
Porters Wk WAP E1W * 140 A9
Porters Wy WDR/YW UB7 152 A2
Porters Wd STALW/RED AL3 38 E2
Porteus Rd BAY/PAD W2 9 L3
Portgate Cl MV/WKIL W9 8 D1
Porthallow Cl ORP BR6 227 J1
Porthcawe Rd SYD SE26 182 D7
Port Hl HERT/WAT SG14 25 K5
ORP BR6 227 L8
Porthkerry Av WELL DA16 163 K10
Portia Wy BOW E3 140 E6
Portinscale Rd PUT/ROE SW15 179 H1
Portland Av BFN/LL DA15 185 K2
GVE DA12 190 E5
NWMAL KT3 200 C7
STNW/STAM N16 119 N6
Portland Cl CHDH RM6 123 P3
SLN SL2 128 C6
WPK KT4 200 E7
Portland Cottages
CROY/NA CR0 * 202 E7
Portland Crs ELTH/MOT SE9 184 B5
FELT TW13 174 E7
GFD/PVL UB6 134 A7
STAN HA7 95 J10
Portland Crs West STAN HA7 115 J1
Portland Dr CHESW EN7 61 P7
ENC/FH EN2 79 M4
REDH RH1 258 E5
Portland Gdns CHDH RM6 123 N3
FSBYPK N4 119 J4
Portland Gv VX/NE SW8 158 G7
Portland Ms SOHO/CST W1F 11 H6
Portland Pk CFSP/GDCR SL9 110 A4
Portland Pl EW KT17 220 B8
HART DA3 * 211 K3
HERT/BAY SG13 26 B7
REGST W1B 10 E2
SNWD SE25 203 P4
Portland Pl Flats EW KT17 * 220 B8
Portland Ri FSBYPK N4 119 J6
Portland Rd ASHF TW15 173 P6
BMLY BR1 183 P7
DORK RH4 272 F1
ELTH/MOT SE9 184 B5
GVW DA11 190 A2
KUT/HW KT1 199 K3
MTCM CR4 201 P2
NTGHL W11 8 A7
NTGHL W11 137 H10
NWDGN UB2 153 N2
SEVS/STOTM N15 119 M2
SNWD SE25 204 A4
YEAD UB4 132 F5
Portland Sq WAP E1W 140 A10
Portland St STALW/RED AL3 38 B6
WALW SE17 18 G8
Portland Ter GU GU1 * 268 B1
RCH/KEW TW9 * 155 J10
Portley La CTHM CR3 241 M7
Portley Wood Rd CTHM CR3 241 N7
Portman Av MORT/ESHN SW14 156 A9
Portman Cl BXLY DA5 186 F4
BXLYHS DA6 163 N9
MBLAR W1H 10 C5
STALE/WH AL4 39 H1
Portman Dr WFD IG8 102 A10
Portman Gdns CDALE/KGS NW9 116 A1
HGDN/ICK UB10 132 B2
Portman Ga CAMTN NW1 9 P2
Portman Ms South MBLAR W1H 10 C6
Portman Pl BETH E2 140 B5
Portman Rd KUT/HW KT1 199 L2
Portman Sq MBLAR W1H 10 C6
Portman St MBLAR W1H 10 C6
Portman Towers MBLAR W1H 10 B5
Portmeadow Wk ABYW SE2 163 N1
Portmeers Cl WALTH E17 * 120 E4
Portmore Gdns CRW RM5 104 B6
Portmore Park Rd WEY KT13 196 B10
Portmore Quays WEY KT13 216 A1
Portmore Wy WEY KT13 * 196 B10
Portnall Dr VW GU25 193 K6
Portnall Ri VW GU25 193 L5
Portnall Rd MV/WKIL W9 2 C9
VW GU25 193 L5
Portnalls Cl COUL/CHIP CR5 240 C2
Portnalls Ri COUL/CHIP CR5 240 C2
Portnalls Rd COUL/CHIP CR5 240 C3
Portnoi Cl ROM RM1 104 E10
Portobello Cl CSHM HP5 50 G5
Portobello Ct NTGHL W11 * 8 D7
Portobello Ms NTGHL W11 * 8 E8
Portobello Rd NKENS W10 137 H7
NTGHL W11 8 C6
Portpool La FSBYW WC1X 12 A3
Portree St POP/IOD E14 141 J8
Portsdown Av GLDGN NW11 117 J4
Portsdown Ms GLDGN NW11 117 J4
Portsea Ms BAY/PAD W2 9 P6
Portsea Pl BAY/PAD W2 9 P6
Portsea Rd TIL RM18 168 F7
Portslade Rd VX/NE SW8 158 D8
Portsmouth Av THDIT KT7 198 F7
Portsmouth Ms CAN/RD E16 141 N9
Portsmouth Rd COB KT11 216 G9
ESH/CLAY KT10 217 P3
KUT/HW KT1 199 J3
PUT/ROE SW15 178 F3
RPLY/SEND GU23 233 K10
Portsmouth St LINN WC2A 11 N5
Portsoken St TWRH EC3N 13 L7
Portugal Gdns WHTN TW2 * 176 B5
Portugal Rd WOKN/KNAP GU21 232 C2
Portugal St LINN WC2A 11 P6
Port V HERT/WAT SG14 25 K5
Port Wy CHOB/PIR GU24 230 F3
Portway EW KT17 220 D6
RAIN RM13 145 H3
SRTFD E15 141 L3
Portway Crs EW KT17 220 D6
Portway Gdns
WOOL/PLUM SE18 162 A7
Postboys Rw COB KT11 * 217 H10
Postern Gn ENC/FH EN2 79 H6
The Postern BARB EC2Y * 12 F4
Postfield WGCE AL7 23 K2
Post House La GT/LBKH KT23 253 P1
Post La WHTN TW2 176 C4
Post Meadow IVER SL0 130 G5
Postmill Cl CROY/NA CR0 204 B10
Post Office Ap FSTGT E7 121 N10
Post Office La BEAC HP9 88 C8
DTCH/LGLY SL3 130 A8
Post Office Rd HLW CM20 28 F10
Post Office Wk
HERT/WAT SG14 * 25 L5
Post Office Wy VX/NE SW8 17 J10
VX/NE SW8 158 E6
Post Rd NWDGN UB2 154 A2
Postway Ms IL IG1 122 E8
Postwood Gn HERT/BAY SG13 26 B8
Post Wood Rd WARE SG12 26 D4
Potash Rd HLWE CM17 31 L8
Potier St STHWK SE1 19 H4
Potiphar Pl BRW CM14 106 G5
Potkiln La BEAC HP9 109 H1
Potten End Hl HHW HP1 35 H1
Potter Cl MTCM CR4 * 202 C2
Potterells BRKMPK AL9 * 58 G1
The Potteries BAR EN5 * 77 K9
CHERT KT16 215 H3
Potterne Cl WIM/MER SW19 178 G3
Potters Bar Station Yd
POTB/CUF EN6 * 59 K7
Potters Cl CROY/NA CR0 204 D8
LOU IG10 82 B6
PECK SE15 * 159 M6
Potters Cross IVER SL0 131 H5
Potterscrouch La
LCOL/BKTW AL2 37 L10
Potters Fld EN EN1 * 79 M8
HLWE CM17 47 N3
STALW/RED AL3 38 D2
Potters Flds STHWK SE1 13 K10
Potters Gv NWMAL KT3 199 P4
Potters Heights Cl PIN HA5 93 J8
Potter's La BAR EN5 77 K8
BORE WD6 75 P5
RPLY/SEND GU23 250 E1
STRHM/NOR SW16 * 180 E9
Potter's Rd BAR EN5 77 L8
FUL/PGN SW6 157 M8
Potter St HLWE CM17 47 M2
NTHWD HA6 93 H9
Potter Street Hl PIN HA5 93 J8
Potters Wy REIG RH2 275 M4
Pottery Cl WDSR SL4 170 A9
Pottery La NTGHL W11 8 A8
NTGHL W11 137 H10
Pottery Rd BTFD TW8 155 K5
BXLY DA5 186 D5
Pottery St BERM/RHTH SE16 * 160 A1
Pott St BETH E2 140 A5
Pouchen End La HHW HP1 34 G4
Poulcott STWL/WRAY TW19 172 B2
Poulett Gdns TWK TW1 176 E5
Poulett Rd EHAM E6 142 C4
Poulter Pk MRDN SM4 * 201 P6
Poulters Wd HAYES BR2 226 A2
Poultney Cl RAD WD7 57 L9
Poulton Av SUT SM1 201 N10
Poulton Cl HACK E8 140 A1
Poultry LOTH EC2R 12 G6
Pound Cl ORP BR6 206 G9
STALE/WH AL4 * 21 H9
SURB KT6 199 H8
WAB EN9 45 K9
Pound Ct ASHTD KT21 237 L4
RGUW GU3 248 G8
Pound Court Dr ORP BR6 206 G9
Pound Crs LHD/OX KT22 236 C7
Pound Farm Cl ESH/CLAY KT10 198 C8
Pound Fld GSTN WD25 72 G1
GU GU1 250 A10
Poundfield Gdns
WOKS/MYFD GU22 232 F6
Poundfield Rd LOU IG10 82 D9
Pound Hl RGUW GU3 248 G9
Pound Hill Pl CRAWE RH10 284 D7
Pound La BFOR GU20 212 B3
HOR/WEW KT19 220 A7
RAD WD7 57 L9
RGUW GU3 248 G9
RSEV TN14 245 N1
SEV TN13 247 K10
WLSDN NW10 136 D1
Pound Park Rd CHARL SE7 162 A3
Pound Pl ELTH/MOT SE9 184 D2
RGUE GU4 268 C7
Pound Place Cl RGUE GU4 268 C6
Pound Rd BNSTD SM7 239 K3
CHERT KT16 195 L7
Pound St CAR SM5 222 A2
Poundwell WGCE AL7 23 K6
Pounsley Rd SEV TN13 246 F7
Pountney Rd BTSEA SW11 158 B9
Poverest Rd STMC/STPC BR5 207 J5
Povey Cross Rd HORL RH6 279 N6
Powderham Ct
WOKN/KNAP GU21 231 J4
Powder Mill La DART DA1 187 N5
Powdermill La WAB EN9 62 G9
Powder Mill La WHTN TW2 175 N4
Powdermill Ms WAB EN9 62 G9
Powdermill Wy WAB EN9 62 G9
Powell Av RDART DA2 188 D5
Powell Cl EDGW HA8 95 L7
GUW GU2 267 L2
HORL RH6 279 P3
Powell Gdns DAGE RM10 124 B9
Powell Rd BKHH IG9 101 P1
CLPT E5 120 A8
Powells Cl DORK RH4 273 H5
Power Cl GU GU1 249 P9
Power Dr PEND EN3 80 E2
Power Rd CHSWK W4 155 M3
Powers Ct TWK TW1 177 J3
Powerscroft Rd CLPT E5 120 B9
SCUP DA14 185 M10
Powis Ct BUSH WD23 * 94 C2
POTB/CUF EN6 59 M10
Powis Gdns GLDGN NW11 117 J5
NTGHL W11 8 D5
Powis Ms NTGHL W11 8 D5
Powis Pl BMSBY WC1N 11 M2
Powis Rd BOW E3 140 G5
Powis Sq NTGHL W11 8 D6
Powis St WOOL/PLUM SE18 162 D2
Powis Ter NTGHL W11 8 D5
Powlett Pl CAMTN NW1 4 D3
Pownall Gdns HSLW TW3 154 A10
Pownall Rd HACK E8 7 N6
HSLW TW3 154 A10
Pownsett Ter IL IG1 * 122 F10
Powster Rd BMLY BR1 183 M8
Powys Cl BXLYHN DA7 163 N5
Powys Ct BORE WD6 76 A7
Powys La STHGT/OAK N14 98 F5
Poyle La SL SL1 128 A3
Poyle Pk DTCH/LGLY SL3 * 151 H9
Poyle Rd DTCH/LGLY SL3 151 H8
GU GU1 268 B2
Poynder Rd TIL RM18 168 E7
Poynders Hl HHNE HP2 36 D7
Poynders Rd CLAP SW4 180 D3
Poynes Rd HORL RH6 279 P2
Poynings Cl HARP AL5 20 E3
ORP BR6 207 M9
Poynings Rd ARCH N19 118 D8
CRAWW RH11 282 G8
The Poynings DTCH/LGLY SL3 151 J3
Poynings Wy HARH RM3 105 M9
NFNCH/WDSPK N12 97 K6
Poyntell Crs CHST BR7 206 G1
Poynter Rd EN EN1 79 N9
Poynton Rd TOTM N17 99 P10
Poyntz Rd BTSEA SW11 158 A8
Poyser St BETH E2 140 A4
Prae Cl STALW/RED AL3 38 A5
Praed Ms BAY/PAD W2 9 M5
Praed St BAY/PAD W2 9 M5
Praetorian Ct STAL AL1 38 B9
Pragel St PLSTW E13 141 N4
Pragnell Rd LEE/GVPK SE12 183 N5
Prague Pl BRXS/STRHM SW2 180 F1
Prah Rd FSBYPK N4 119 H7
Prairie Cl ADL/WDHM KT15 195 L10
Prairie Rd ADL/WDHM KT15 195 L10
Prairie St VX/NE SW8 158 B8
Pratt Ms CAMTN NW1 4 G6
Pratts La WOT/HER KT12 217 L1
Pratt St CAMTN NW1 4 G6
Pratt Wk LBTH SE11 17 P5
Prayle Gv CRICK NW2 116 G6
Prebend Gdns HMSMTH W6 156 C3
Prebend St IS N1 6 E6
Precinct Rd HYS/HAR UB3 133 H9
The Precincts SL SL1 128 A6
The Precinct BROX EN10 * 44 E6
EGH TW20 * 172 D8
IS N1 * 6 E6
Premier Av CDW/CHF RM16 167 P1
Premiere Pl POP/IOD E14 140 F9
Premier Pde HORL RH6 * 280 C4
Premier Park Rd WLSDN NW10 135 N4
Premier Pl WATW WD18 72 G9
Prendergast Rd BKHTH/KID SE3 161 K9
Prentis Rd STRHM/NOR SW16 180 E7
Prentiss Ct CHARL SE7 162 A3
Presburg Rd NWMAL KT3 200 B5
Prescelly Pl EDGW HA8 95 L9
Prescot St WCHPL E1 13 M7
Prescott Av STMC/STPC BR5 206 E6
Prescott Cl EMPK RM11 125 J6
Prescott Gn LOU IG10 82 F7
Prescott Pl CLAP SW4 158 E9
Prescott Rd CHES/WCR EN8 62 D3
DTCH/LGLY SL3 151 H8
Presdales Dr WARE SG12 26 D3
Presentation Ms
BRXS/STRHM SW2 180 G5
Presidents Dr WAP E1W 140 A10
President St FSBYE EC1V * 6 E9
Prespa Cl ED N9 100 B3
Press Rd UX/CGN UB8 131 N2
WLSDN NW10 116 A8
Prestage Wy POP/IOD E14 141 H9
Prestbury Crs BNSTD SM7 240 A2
Prestbury Rd FSTGT E7 141 P2
Prestbury Sq ELTH/MOT SE9 184 C7
Prested Rd BTSEA SW11 157 P10
Preston Av CHING E4 101 J7
Preston Cl STHWK SE1 19 J5
WHTN TW2 176 D6
Preston Ct BAR EN5 77 M8
WOT/HER KT12 197 K8
Preston Dr BXLYHN DA7 163 N7
HOR/WEW KT19 220 B3
WAN E11 121 P3
Preston Gdns IL IG1 122 B4
PEND EN3 80 D3
WLSDN NW10 * 136 B1
Preston Gv ASHTD KT21 237 H3
Preston Hl CSHM HP5 51 J5
KTN/HRWW/WS HA3 115 K5
Preston La KWD/TDW/WH KT20 238 F6
Preston Pl CRICK NW2 136 D1
Preston Rd GVW DA11 190 B4
HARH RM3 105 L5
KTN/HRWW/WS HA3 115 K5
NRWD SE19 181 J9
RYNPK SW20 178 D10
SHPTN TW17 196 B5
SLN SL2 129 P9
WAN E11 121 K4
Preston's Rd POP/IOD E14 141 H10
WWKM BR4 205 M10
Preston Vls KUT/HW KT1 * 199 L2
Preston Waye
KTN/HRWW/WS HA3 115 K6
Prestwich Ter CLAP SW4 * 180 E1
Prestwick Cl CRAWW RH11 282 G8
NWDGN UB2 153 M4
Prestwick Rd OXHEY WD19 93 L4
Prestwood OXHEY WD19 * 93 M3
SLN SL2 129 N8
Prestwood Av
KTN/HRWW/WS HA3 114 G2
Prestwood Cl CRAWW RH11 283 L4
KTN/HRWW/WS HA3 114 G2
WOOL/PLUM SE18 163 K6
Prestwood Dr CRW RM5 104 D6
Prestwood Gdns CROY/NA CR0 203 K7
Prestwood La CRAWW RH11 282 F3
Prestwood St IS N1 * 6 F8
Pretoria Av WALTH E17 120 D2
Pretoria Crs CHING E4 101 H2
Pretoria Pde BROCKY SE4 * 160 F8
Pretoria Rd CAN/RD E16 141 L5
CHERT KT16 195 J8
CHING E4 101 H2
IL IG1 122 E9
LEY E10 121 J6
ROMW/RG RM7 124 D2
STRHM/NOR SW16 180 C9
TOTM N17 99 N7
WATW WD18 73 H8
Pretoria Rd North UED N18 99 N7
Pretty La COUL/CHIP CR5 240 D7
Prevost Rd FBAR/BDGN N11 98 B3
Prey Heath Cl
WOKS/MYFD GU22 231 P10
Prey Heath Rd
WOKS/MYFD GU22 231 N10
Price Cl MLHL NW7 97 H7
TOOT SW17 180 A6
Price Rd CROY/NA CR0 223 J2
Prices La REIG RH2 275 K3
Prices Ms IS N1 5 P5
Price's St STHWK SE1 12 D10
Pricklers Hl BAR EN5 77 L9
Prickley Wd HAYES BR2 205 L8
Priddy's Yd CROY/NA CR0 203 K9
Prideaux Pl ACT W3 136 A9
FSBYW WC1X 5 P9
Prideaux Rd BRXN/ST SW9 158 F9
Pridham Rd THHTH CR7 203 L4
Priest Croft Cl CRAWW RH11 283 K7
Priestfield Rd FSTH SE23 182 D6
Priest Hl OXTED RH8 261 N5
WDSR SL4 171 P5
Priestland Gdns BERK HP4 34 B3
Priestlands Cl HORL RH6 280 A3
Priestlands Park Rd
BFN/LL DA15 185 J6
Priest La CHOB/PIR GU24 230 B1
Priestley Cl STNW/STAM N16 * 119 N5
Priestley Gdns CHDH RM6 123 L4
WOKS/MYFD GU22 232 D6
Priestley Rd GUW GU2 249 J10
MTCM CR4 202 B2
Priestley Wy CRAWE RH10 284 B3
CRICK NW2 116 D6
WALTH E17 120 C1
Priest Park Av RYLN/HDSTN HA2 113 P7
Priests Av ROM RM1 104 E10
Priests Br MORT/ESHN SW14 156 B9
Priests Fld RBRW/HUT CM13 107 P6
Priest's La BRWN CM15 107 K3
Priests Paddock BEAC HP9 88 A6
Prima Rd BRXN/ST SW9 159 H6
Primley La RBSF CM22 30 D2
Primrose Av ENC/FH EN2 79 L5
GDMY/SEVK IG3 123 K5
HORL RH6 280 C6
Primrose Cl BOW E3 140 F4
CAT SE6 183 H8
CRAWW RH11 283 L10
FNCH N3 97 L10
HAT AL10 40 E5
HHW HP1 35 H7
RYLN/HDSTN HA2 113 N8
WLGTN SM6 202 C8
Primrose Dr CHOB/PIR GU24 230 F1
HERT/BAY SG13 26 A5
WDR/YW UB7 151 N3
Primrose Fld HLWS CM18 47 J4
Primrose Gdns BUSH WD23 94 A1
HAMP NW3 3 P2
RSLP HA4 113 K10
Primrose Gln EMPK RM11 125 M2
Primrose Hl BRW CM14 107 H4
EMB EC4Y 12 C6
KGLGY WD4 54 C4
Primrose Hill Rd HAMP NW3 4 A5
Primrose Hill Studios
CAMTN NW1 4 C5
Primrose La CROY/NA CR0 204 B8
GSTN WD25 74 C4
Primrose Ms CAMTN NW1 * 4 B4
Primrose Pth CHESW EN7 61 P7
Primrose Pl ISLW TW7 154 E8
Primrose Rd LEY E10 120 G6
SWFD E18 101 N10
WOT/HER KT12 217 K2
Primrose Sq HOM E9 140 B2
Primrose St SDTCH EC2A 13 J3
Primrose Ter GVE DA12 * 190 F4
Primrose Wk EW KT17 220 C4
NWCR SE14 160 D6
Primrose Wy ALP/SUD HA0 135 J4

Primula St SHB W12 136 D9
Prince Albert Rd CAMTN NW1 4 C6
STJWD NW8 3 N9
Prince Albert Sq REDH RH1 276 B5
Prince Albert's Wk
DTCH/LGLY SL3 149 M8
Prince Arthur Ms HAMP NW3 117 M9
Prince Arthur Rd HAMP NW3 117 M9
Prince Charles Av EYN DA4 210 C2
Prince Charles Dr HDN NW4 116 F5
Prince Charles Rd
BKHTH/KID SE3 161 L7
Prince Charles Wy WLGTN SM6 202 C10
Prince Consort Cottages
WDSR SL4 149 J8
Prince Consort Dr CHST BR7 206 G1
Prince Consort Rd SKENS SW7 15 L3
Prince Consort's Dr WDSR SL4 170 F3
Princedale Rd NTGHL W11 8 B9
NTGHL W11 137 H10
Prince Edward Rd HOM E9 140 E1
Prince Edward St BERK HP4 33 P5
Prince George Av
STHGT/OAK N14 78 E9
Prince George Rd
STNW/STAM N16 119 M9
Prince George's Av RYNPK SW20 200 F2
Prince Georges Rd
WIM/MER SW19 201 N1
Prince Henry Rd CHARL SE7 162 A6
Prince Imperial Rd CHST BR7 184 E10
WOOL/PLUM SE18 162 C7
Prince John Rd ELTH/MOT SE9 184 B1
Princelet St WCHPL E1 13 M3
Prince of Orange La
GNWCH SE10 * 161 H6
Prince of Wales Cl HDN NW4 116 E2
Prince of Wales Dr BTSEA SW11 157 P7
Prince of Wales Ga SKENS SW7 15 N1
Prince of Wales Pas
CAMTN NW1 * 4 G10
Prince of Wales Rd
BKHTH/KID SE3 161 L7
CAN/RD E16 141 P8
KTTN NW5 4 C2
REDH RH1 277 H8
SUT SM1 201 N9
Prince of Wales Ter CHSWK W4 156 B4
KENS W8 15 H2
Prince Pk HHW HP1 35 K7
Prince Philip Av CDW/CHF RM16 147 M10
Prince Regent La PLSTW E13 141 P6
Prince Regent Ms CAMTN NW1 4 G10
Prince Regent Rd HSLW TW3 154 B9
Prince Rd SNWD SE25 203 M5
Prince Rupert Rd ELTH/MOT SE9 162 C10
Princes Ar MYFR/PICC W1J 11 H9
Princes Av ACT W3 155 M2
CAR SM5 222 A4
CDALE/KGS NW9 115 M2
FNCH N3 97 L9
GFD/PVL UB6 134 A8
GODL GU7 267 H10
MUSWH N10 118 C1
PEND EN3 80 D2
PLMGR N13 99 H6
RDART DA2 188 A4
SAND/SEL CR2 242 A1
STMC/STPC BR5 207 H5
SURB KT6 199 M9
WATW WD18 73 H9
WDGN N22 98 E9
WFD IG8 101 N5
Princes Cl BERK HP4 33 M3
CDALE/KGS NW9 115 M2
EDGW HA8 95 M6
EPP CM16 66 D1
FSBYPK N4 119 J6
HPTN TW12 176 C7
SAND/SEL CR2 242 A1
SCUP DA14 185 N6
WDSR SL4 148 E4
Princes Ct WAP E1W 140 A9
WBLY HA9 115 K10
Princes Dr HRW HA1 114 D1
LHD/OX KT22 218 D8
Princesfield Rd WAB EN9 63 N9
Princes Gdns ACT W3 135 M8
EA W5 135 H6
RGUW GU3 * 249 K3
SKENS SW7 15 M3
Prince's Ga SKENS SW7 15 N2
Princes Gate Ct SKENS SW7 15 L2
Princes Gate Ms SKENS SW7 15 M3
Princes La MUSWH N10 118 B1
Prince's Ms BAY/PAD W2 8 G7
HMSMTH W6 * 156 E4
HSLW TW3 153 P10
Princes Pde GLDGN NW11 * 117 H4
POTB/CUF EN6 * 59 L9
Princes Pk RAIN RM13 145 H2
Princes Park Av GLDGN NW11 117 H4
HYS/HAR UB3 132 E9
Princes Park Cir HYS/HAR UB3 132 E9
Princes Park Cl HYS/HAR UB3 132 E9
Princes Park La HYS/HAR UB3 132 E9
Princes Park Pde HYS/HAR UB3 132 E9
Princes Pl NTGHL W11 8 A9
NTGHL W11 137 H10
Prince's Pln HAYES BR2 206 B7
Princes Ri LEW SE13 161 H8
Princes Riverside Rd
BERM/RHTH SE16 140 C10
Princes Rd ASHF TW15 174 A8
BARK/HLT IG6 122 G2
BKHH IG9 101 P3
BRW CM14 85 P6
DART DA1 187 J4
EGH TW20 172 C9
FELT TW13 174 G6
GVE DA12 190 F7
KUTN/CMB KT2 199 M1
MORT/ESHN SW14 156 A9
PGE/AN SE20 182 C9
RCH/KEW TW9 155 L7
RCHPK/HAM TW10 177 L1
RDART DA2 188 B4
REDH RH1 276 B3
ROM RM1 125 H3
SWLY BR8 187 H9
TEDD TW11 176 C7
UED N18 100 B5
WEA W13 134 G10
WEY KT13 216 C2
WIM/MER SW19 179 K9
Princess Alice Wy THMD SE28 162 G1
Princess Av TIL RM18 169 M3
WBLY HA9 115 K7
WDSR SL4 148 G9
Princess Crs FSBYPK N4 119 J7
Princess Diana Dr STALE/WH AL4 39 J7
Princesses Pde DART DA1 * 186 G1
Princess Gdns
WOKS/MYFD GU22 232 E2
Princess La RSLP HA4 112 F6
Princess Louise Cl BAY/PAD W2 9 M3
Princess Margaret Rd TIL RM18 169 L3
Princess Mary Cl GUW GU2 249 N6
Princess Mary's Rd
ADL/WDHM KT15 215 M1
Princess May Rd
STNW/STAM N16 119 M9
Princess Ms HAMP NW3 3 M1
Princess Pde ORP BR6 * 206 D10
Prince's Sq BAY/PAD W2 8 G7
Princess Rd CAMTN NW1 4 C5
CRAWW RH11 283 M7
CROY/NA CR0 203 K6
KIL/WHAMP NW6 2 E8
WOKS/MYFD GU22 232 E2
Princess St BXLYHN DA7 164 A9
STHWK SE1 18 D4
Princes St GVW DA11 190 E2
LOTH EC2R 12 G6
RCH/KEW TW9 155 K10
REGST W1B 10 F6
SL SL1 149 N1
SUT SM1 221 N1
TOTM N17 99 M7
WARE SG12 26 C1
Princess Wy REDH RH1 258 B9
Prince's Ter PLSTW E13 141 N3
Prince St DEPT SE8 160 E5
WAT WD17 73 K7
Princes Vw DART DA1 187 P4
Princes Wy BKHH IG9 101 P3
CROY/NA CR0 222 G2
RBRW/HUT CM13 107 M3
RSLP HA4 113 M9
WIM/MER SW19 178 G3
WWKM BR4 225 L1
Prince's Yd NTGHL W11 * 8 B10
Princethorpe Rd SYD SE26 182 C7
Princeton St GINN WC1R 11 N4
Pringle Gdns PUR/KEN CR8 222 G6
STRHM/NOR SW16 180 D7
Printers Inn Ct FLST/FETLN EC4A 12 A5
Printers Wy HLW CM20 29 K6
Printinghouse La HYS/HAR UB3 152 F1
Printing House Yd BETH E2 * 7 K10
Priolo Rd CHARL SE7 161 P4
Prior Av BELMT SM2 221 P4
Prior Bolton St IS N1 6 D2
Prior Cha GRAYS RM17 167 L3
Prioress Crs SWCM DA10 167 H10
Prioress Rd WNWD SE27 181 J6
Prioress St STHWK SE1 19 J4
Prior Gv CSHM HP5 51 H6
Prior Rd IL IG1 122 D8
Priors Cl GODL GU7 266 F8
HERT/BAY SG13 26 A8
SL SL1 149 M2
Priors Ct WOKN/KNAP GU21 231 M4
Priors Cft WALTH E17 100 D10
WOKS/MYFD GU22 232 D6
Priors Fld NTHLT UB5 133 M1
Priorsfield Rd GODL GU7 266 F9
Priorsford Av STMC/STPC BR5 207 K4
Priors Gdns RSLP HA4 113 K10
Priors Hatch La GODL GU7 266 E8
Priors Md EN EN1 79 M5
GT/LBKH KT23 254 B1
Priors Pk HCH RM12 125 K8
Priors Rd WDSR SL4 148 C9
The Priors ASHTD KT21 237 J5
Prior St GNWCH SE10 161 H6
Priors Wk CRAWE RH10 284 A7
Priorswood RGUW GU3 266 E7
Priors Wood Rd HERT/BAY SG13 26 B8
Priory Av ALP/SUD HA0 114 E9
CEND/HSY/T N8 118 E2
CHEAM SM3 220 G1
CHING E4 100 E4
CHSWK W4 156 B2
DEN/HRF UB9 111 M2
HLWE CM17 29 M6
STMC/STPC BR5 206 G6
WALTH E17 120 F3
Priory Cl ALP/SUD HA0 114 E9
ASC SL5 192 F7
BECK BR3 204 D3
BROX EN10 44 D10
BRWN CM15 86 F9
CHING E4 100 E4
CHST BR7 206 C1
DART DA1 187 K1
DEN/HRF UB9 111 K8
DEN/HRF UB9 111 L2
DORK RH4 272 F4
FNCH N3 97 J9
HOD EN11 44 F4
HORL RH6 280 A3
HPTN TW12 197 N1
HYS/HAR UB3 133 J9
RSLP HA4 112 G6
STAN HA7 94 E4
STHGT/OAK N14 78 C9
SUN TW16 175 H10
SWFD E18 101 M9
TRDG/WHET N20 97 J1
WIM/MER SW19 * 201 L1
WOKN/KNAP GU21 214 G9
WOT/HER KT12 197 H10
Priory Cottages EA W5 * 135 L7
Priory Ct BLKFR EC4V * 12 D6
DORK RH4 * 272 G4
HLWS CM18 47 L4
VX/NE SW8 158 E7
WALTH E17 100 E10
Priory Crs ALP/SUD HA0 114 F8
CHEAM SM3 220 G1
NRWD SE19 181 K10
Priory Dr ABYW SE2 163 N4
REIG RH2 275 K2
STAN HA7 94 E4
Priory Field Dr EDGW HA8 95 N5
Priory Flds EYN DA4 209 N9
Priory Gdns ALP/SUD HA0 114 F9
ASHF TW15 174 E8
BARN SW13 156 C9
BERK HP4 33 P5
CHSWK W4 * 156 B3
DART DA1 187 L1
DEN/HRF UB9 111 M2
HGT N6 118 C4
HPTN TW12 197 N1
SNWD SE25 203 N4
Priory Ga CHES/WCR EN8 62 E3
Priory Gn STA TW18 173 L8
Priory Green Est IS N1 5 N7
Priory Gv HARH RM3 105 M5
VX/NE SW8 158 F7
Priory Hl ALP/SUD HA0 114 F9
DART DA1 187 L2
Priory La E/WMO/HCT KT8 197 P4
EYN DA4 209 N8
PUT/ROE SW15 178 C1
Priory Leas ELTH/MOT SE9 * 184 B4
Priory Market Pl DART DA1 * 187 M3
Priory Md BRWN CM15 87 H2
Priory Ms HCH RM12 125 J6
STA TW18 173 L8
Priory Pk BKHTH/KID SE3 161 L9
Priory Park Rd ALP/SUD HA0 114 F9
KIL/WHAMP NW6 2 D5
Priory Pth HARH RM3 105 M4
Priory Pl DART DA1 187 L2
Priory Rd ASC SL5 192 F7
BARK IG11 142 G2
CFSP/GDCR SL9 109 P1
CHEAM SM3 220 G1
CHSGTN KT9 199 K10
CHSWK W4 156 A2
CROY/NA CR0 203 H7
DART DA1 165 L10
EHAM E6 142 A3
HARH RM3 105 M4
HPTN TW12 175 N10
HSLW TW3 176 B1
KIL/WHAMP NW6 2 G5
LOU IG10 82 B8
MUSWH N10 118 D2
RCH/KEW TW9 155 M5
REIG RH2 275 K2
SL SL1 128 B7
Priory St BOW E3 140 G5
HERT/WAT SG14 25 L5
WARE SG12 26 B2
Priory Ter KIL/WHAMP NW6 2 G5
The Priory BKHTH/KID SE3 161 L10
CROY/NA CR0 * 203 H10
GDST RH9 260 A7
ORP BR6 * 207 L7
Priory Vw BUSH WD23 94 D1
Priory Vls FBAR/BDGN N11 * 98 A7
Priory Wk STAL AL1 38 D9
WBPTN SW10 15 K8
Priory Wy CFSP/GDCR SL9 110 A1
DTCH/LGLY SL3 149 N6
NWDGN UB2 153 L2
RYLN/HDSTN HA2 114 A2
WDR/YW UB7 151 P5
Pritchard's Rd BETH E2 7 P7
Pritchett Cl PEND EN3 80 G3
Priter Rd BERM/RHTH SE16 19 P4
Private Rd EN EN1 79 L9
Probert Rd BRXS/STRHM SW2 181 H1
Probyn Rd BRXS/STRHM SW2 181 J5
Procter St GINN WC1R 11 N4
Proctor Cl CRAWE RH10 284 D9
MTCM CR4 202 B1
Proctor Gdns GT/LBKH KT23 254 A1
Proctors Cl EBED/NFELT TW14 175 H4
Profumo Rd WOT/HER KT12 217 L2
The Progression Centre
HHNE HP2 * 36 B3
Progress Wy CROY/NA CR0 202 G9
EN EN1 79 P10
WDGN N22 99 H9
Promenade Approach Rd
CHSWK W4 156 B6
Promenade De Verdun
PUR/KEN CR8 222 E7
The Promenade CHSWK W4 156 B7
EDGW HA8 * 95 M6
Prospect Cl BELV DA17 164 B3
HSLW TW3 153 N7
RSLP HA4 113 L5
SYD SE26 182 A7
Prospect Cottages
WAND/EARL SW18 157 K10
Prospect Crs WHTN TW2 176 B2
Prospect Gv GVE DA12 190 G3
Prospect Hl WALTH E17 120 G2
Prospect La EGH TW20 171 M8
Prospect Pl CHSWK W4 156 A4
CRAWW RH11 283 M7
CRICK NW2 117 J8
CRW RM5 104 D10
EFNCH N2 117 N2
EW KT17 220 B9
GRAYS RM17 * 167 N5
GVE DA12 190 G3
HAYES BR2 205 N3
RYNPK SW20 178 E10
STA TW18 173 J8
WAP E1W 140 B10
Prospect Rd BAR EN5 77 K8
CHES/WCR EN8 62 B5
CRICK NW2 117 J8
EMPK RM11 125 N1
SEV TN13 247 K9
STAL AL1 38 C8
SURB KT6 199 H6
WFD IG8 101 P6
Prospect St BERM/RHTH SE16 160 A1
Prospect V WOOL/PLUM SE18 162 B3
Prospero Rd ARCH N19 118 E6
Prossers KWD/TDW/WH KT20 238 G7
Protea Cl CAN/RD E16 141 L6
Prothero Gdns HDN NW4 116 E3
Prothero Rd FUL/PGN SW6 157 H6
Prout Gv WLSDN NW10 116 B9
Prout Rd CLPT E5 120 A8
Provence St IS N1 6 E7
Providence Av RYLN/HDSTN HA2 113 P6
Providence Cl HOM E9 * 140 C3
Providence Ct MYFR/PKLN W1K 10 D7
Providence La HYS/HAR UB3 152 E6
Providence Pl CRW RM5 104 A9
IS N1 6 C6
WOKS/MYFD GU22 * 215 K10
Providence Rd WDR/YW UB7 131 P10
Providence Row Cl BETH E2 140 A5
Providence Sq STHWK SE1 19 J1
Providence St RDART DA2 188 F1
Providence Ter CRAWE RH10 * 285 P9
Providence Yd BETH E2 * 7 N9
Provincial Ter PGE/AN SE20 * 182 C10
Provost Est IS N1 6 G9
Provost Rd HAMP NW3 4 B3
Provost St IS N1 6 G8
Prowse Av BUSH WD23 94 B3
Prowse Pl CAMTN NW1 4 G3
Pruden Cl STHGT/OAK N14 * 98 D3
Prune Hl EGH TW20 172 B10
Prunus Cl CHOB/PIR GU24 212 D9
Prusom St WAP E1W 140 A10
Pryor Cl ABLGY WD5 54 G8
Pucknells Cl SWLY BR8 208 D1
Puckshill WOKN/KNAP GU21 231 J3
Pudding La CHIG IG7 83 H10
HHW HP1 35 K4
HORL RH6 279 H7
MON EC3R 13 H8
Pudding Mill La SRTFD E15 140 G3
Puddingstone Dr STALE/WH AL4 39 H8
Puddle Dock BLKFR EC4V 12 D7
Puddledock La BH/WHM TN16 263 K8
RDART DA2 186 F8
Puers La BEAC HP9 89 K7
Puffin Cl BARK IG11 143 L5
BECK BR3 204 C5
Puffin Rd CRAWW RH11 * 282 G8
Pulborough Rd
WAND/EARL SW18 179 J3
Pulborough Wy HSLWW TW4 153 K10
Pulford Rd SEVS/STOTM N15 119 L4
Pulham Av BROX EN10 44 D6
EFNCH N2 117 N2
Puller Rd BAR EN5 76 G6
HHW HP1 35 K7
Pulleyns Av EHAM E6 142 B5
Pulleys Cl HHW HP1 35 J5
Pulleys La HHW HP1 35 J5
Pullfields CSHM HP5 50 F6
Pullman Cl STAL AL1 38 D8
Pullman Gdns PUT/ROE SW15 178 F2
Pullman Ms LEE/GVPK SE12 183 N6
Pullman Pl ELTH/MOT SE9 184 B1
Pullmans Pl STA TW18 173 K8
Pulpit Cl CSHM HP5 50 F5
Pulross Rd BRXN/ST SW9 158 G9
Pulteney Cl BOW E3 140 E3
ISLW TW7 154 F9
Pulteney Rd SWFD E18 121 N1
Pulton Pl FUL/PGN SW6 157 K6
Puma Ct WCHPL E1 13 L3
Pump Aly BTFD TW8 155 J6
Pump Cl NTHLT UB5 133 P4
Pump Ct EMB EC4Y * 12 A6
Pump Hl LOU IG10 82 C6
Pump House Cl HAYES BR2 205 L2
Pump House Ms WCHPL E1 13 N7
Pumping Station Rd CHSWK W4 156 B6
Pumpkin Hl SL SL1 128 D1
Pump La ASC SL5 192 D1
CSHM HP5 51 K9
EPP CM16 46 E10
HYS/HAR UB3 153 H1
NWCR SE14 160 B6
ORP BR6 228 C2
Punchard Crs PEND EN3 80 G4
Punch Bowl La CSHM HP5 51 H8
HHNE HP2 36 E3
Punchbowl La RDKG RH5 273 J1
Punch Bowl La STALW/RED AL3 37 H2
Punchbowl Pk HHNE HP2 * 36 E3
Punch Copse Rd CRAWE RH10 284 A6
Punch Cft HART DA3 211 L10
Punderson's Gdns BETH E2 140 A5
Purbeck Av NWMAL KT3 200 C6
Purbeck Cl REDH RH1 258 E5
Purbeck Dr CRICK NW2 116 G7
WOKN/KNAP GU21 214 C10
Purbeck Rd EMPK RM11 125 H5
Purberry Gv EW KT17 220 C6
Purberry Shot EW KT17 * 220 C6
Purbrock Av GSTN WD25 73 K2
Purbrook St STHWK SE1 19 K3
Purcell Cl BORE WD6 75 J5
PUR/KEN CR8 223 K10
Purcell Crs FUL/PGN SW6 * 156 G5
Purcell Cresent FUL/PGN SW6 156 G6
Purcell Ms WLSDN NW10 * 136 B2
Purcell Rd CRAWW RH11 283 J10
GFD/PVL UB6 134 A7
Purcell St IS N1 7 J7
Purcers Cross Rd FUL/PGN SW6 157 J7
Purchese St CAMTN NW1 5 J7
Purdom Rd WGCE AL7 23 H8
Purdy St BOW E3 140 G6
Purelake Ms LEW SE13 * 161 J9
Purfleet By-Pass PUR RM19 166 A3
Purfleet Deep Whf PUR RM19 * 166 B5
Purfleet Industrial Access Rd
SOCK/AV RM15 165 P2
Purfleet Rd SOCK/AV RM15 146 A10
Purford Gn HLWS CM18 47 K2
Purkis Cl UX/CGN UB8 132 D9
Purkiss Rd HERT/BAY SG13 25 K8
Purland Cl BCTR RM8 124 A6
Purland Rd THMD SE28 163 K1
Purleigh Av WFD IG8 102 B7
Purley Av CRICK NW2 117 H7
Purley Bury Av PUR/KEN CR8 223 K7
Purley Bury Cl PUR/KEN CR8 223 K7
Purley Cl CLAY IG5 102 D10
CRAWE RH10 284 E10
Purley Downs Rd SAND/SEL CR2 223 K6
Purley Hl PUR/KEN CR8 223 J8
Purley Knoll PUR/KEN CR8 222 G7
Purley Oaks Rd SAND/SEL CR2 223 M6
Purley Pde PUR/KEN CR8 * 223 H7
Purley Park Rd PUR/KEN CR8 223 J7
Purley Pl IS N1 6 C3
Purley Ri PUR/KEN CR8 222 G8
Purley Rd ED N9 99 L4
SAND/SEL CR2 223 L4
Purley V PUR/KEN CR8 223 J9
Purley Wy CROY/NA CR0 202 G8
PUR/KEN CR8 223 H7
Purlieu Wy EPP CM16 83 H1
Purlings Rd BUSH WD23 74 A9
Purneys Rd ELTH/MOT SE9 162 A10
Purrett Rd WOOL/PLUM SE18 163 J4
Pursers Ct SLN SL2 129 K9
Pursers Cross Rd FUL/PGN SW6 * 157 J7
Pursers Hollow SHGR GU5 270 E10
Pursers La SHGR GU5 270 E10
Pursers Lea SHGR GU5 270 E10
Pursewardens Cl WEA W13 135 H10
Pursley Gdns BORE WD6 75 M4
Pursley Rd MLHL NW7 96 E8
Purton Ct SLN SL2 129 H2
Purton La SLN SL2 129 H2
Purves Rd WLSDN NW10 136 E5
Putney Br PUT/ROE SW15 157 H9
Putney Bridge Ap FUL/PGN SW6 157 H9
Putney Bridge Rd
PUT/ROE SW15 157 J10
Putney Common PUT/ROE SW15 156 F9
Putney Ex PUT/ROE SW15 * 156 G10
Putney Gdns CHDH RM6 123 L3
Putney Heath PUT/ROE SW15 178 E2
Putney Heath La PUT/ROE SW15 178 G2
Putney High St PUT/ROE SW15 157 H10
Putney Hl PUT/ROE SW15 178 G3
Putney Park Av PUT/ROE SW15 156 D10
Putney Park La PUT/ROE SW15 156 E10
Putney Rd PEND EN3 80 C2
Puttenham Cl OXHEY WD19 93 K4
Puttenham Heath Rd
RGUW GU3 266 D6
Puttenham Hl RGUW GU3 266 C4
Puttenham La MFD/CHID GU8 266 B8
Putters Cft HHNE HP2 36 A1
Puttocks Cl BRKMPK AL9 40 F9
Puttocks Dr BRKMPK AL9 40 F9
Pycombe Cnr
NFNCH/WDSPK N12 97 J5
Pycroft Wy ED N9 99 P5
Pyebush La BEAC HP9 108 F2
Pye Cl CTHM CR3 241 L9
Pyecombe Ct CRAWW RH11 283 J10
Pyenest Rd HLWW/ROY CM19 46 E4
Pylbrook Rd SUT SM1 201 K10
Pyle Hl WOKS/MYFD GU22 232 A10
Pylon Wy CROY/NA CR0 202 F8
Pym Cl EBAR EN4 77 N9
Pymers Md DUL SE21 181 K4
Pymmes Brook Trail EBAR EN4 77 P9
ED N9 100 A4
PLMGR N13 98 G5
STHGT/OAK N14 98 C3
Pymmes Cl PLMGR N13 98 G6
TOTM N17 100 A9
Pymmes Gdns North ED N9 99 N4
Pymmes Gdns South ED N9 99 N4
Pymmes Green Rd
FBAR/BDGN N11 98 C5
Pymmes Rd PLMGR N13 98 F7
Pymms Brook Dr EBAR EN4 77 P8
Pym Orch BH/WHM TN16 245 M10
Pym Pl GRAYS RM17 167 M3
Pynchester Cl HGDN/ICK UB10 112 B7
Pyne Rd SURB KT6 199 M8
Pynest Green La LOU IG10 81 M3
Pynham Cl ABYW SE2 163 K2
Pynnacles Cl STAN HA7 94 G6
Pyot Pth BORE WD6 75 M3
Pyrcroft La WEY KT13 216 C2
Pyrcroft Rd CHERT KT16 195 J7
Pyrford Common Rd
WOKS/MYFD GU22 233 H2
Pyrford Heath
WOKS/MYFD GU22 233 J2
Pyrford Rd BF/WBF KT14 215 K10
Pyrford Woods Cl
WOKS/MYFD GU22 233 J1
Pyrford Woods Rd
WOKS/MYFD GU22 233 J1
Pyrian Cl WOKS/MYFD GU22 232 G3
Pyrland Rd HBRY N5 119 L10
RCHPK/HAM TW10 177 L2
Pyrles Gn LOU IG10 82 E6
Pyrles La LOU IG10 82 E6
Pyrmont Gv WNWD SE27 181 J6
Pyrmont Rd CHSWK W4 155 M5
Pytchley Crs NRWD SE19 181 K9
Pytchley Rd EDUL SE22 159 M9
Pytt Fld HLWE CM17 47 L2

Q

The Quadrangle BAY/PAD W2 9 N5
GUW GU2 267 M1
HNHL SE24 * 181 K1
WBPTN SW10 * 157 M7
WGCW AL8 22 F4
Quadrant Ar REGST W1B 11 H8
Quadrant Cl HDN NW4 * 116 E3
Quadrant Gv KTTN NW5 118 A10
Quadrant Rd RCH/KEW TW9 155 J10
THHTH CR7 203 J4
The Quadrant BELMT SM2 221 M3
BXLYHN DA7 163 N6
EDGW HA8 * 95 M7
NKENS W10 * 136 G5
PUR RM19 166 B3
RCH/KEW TW9 177 J1
RYLN/HDSTN HA2 * 114 C1
RYNPK SW20 201 H1
STALE/WH AL4 38 G3
Quadrant Wy WEY KT13 216 B1
Quad Rd WBLY HA9 * 115 J8
Quaggy Wk BKHTH/KID SE3 161 M10
Quail Gdns SAND/SEL CR2 224 D6
Quainton St WLSDN NW10 116 A8
Quaker Cl SEV TN13 247 L9
Quaker La NWDGN UB2 153 P2
WAB EN9 63 H10
Quakers Cl HART DA3 211 L3
Quakers Course CDALE/KGS NW9 96 C9
Quaker's Hall La SEV TN13 247 K9
Quakers La ISLW TW7 154 F6
POTB/CUF EN6 59 L6
Quakers Pl FSTGT E7 122 A10
Quaker St WCHPL E1 13 L2
Quakers Wk WCHMH N21 79 L10
Quakers Wy RGUW GU3 249 H6
Quality Ct LINN WC2A 12 A5
Quality St REDH RH1 258 C4
Quantock Cl CRAWW RH11 283 L7
DTCH/LGLY SL3 150 D4
HYS/HAR UB3 152 E6
STALE/WH AL4 39 H2
Quantock Gdns CRICK NW2 * 116 G7
Quantock Ms PECK SE15 159 P8
Quantock Rd BXLYHN DA7 164 F8
Quantocks HHNE HP2 36 A3
Quarles Cl CRW RM5 104 B8
Quarles Park Rd CHDH RM6 123 L4
Quarrendon Rd AMSS HP7 69 J6
Quarrendon St FUL/PGN SW6 157 K8
Quarr Rd CAR SM5 201 N6
Quarry Cl OXTED RH8 261 K6
Quarry Gdns LHD/OX KT22 237 J7
Quarry Hl BGR/WK TN15 247 L9
GRAYS RM17 167 M4
Quarry Hill Pk REIG RH2 257 M7
Quarry Ms PUR RM19 165 P3
Quarry Park Rd SUT SM1 221 J3
Quarry Ri SUT SM1 221 J3
Quarry Rd GDST RH9 260 B4
GODL GU7 266 F10
OXTED RH8 261 K6
WAND/EARL SW18 179 M2
Quarry Spring HLW CM20 47 K1
Quarry Springs HLW CM20 47 K1
Quarry St GU GU1 268 A2
The Quarry BRKHM/BTCW RH3 256 A8
Quartermaine Av
WOKS/MYFD GU22 232 C8
Quartermass Cl HHW HP1 35 K5
Quartermass Rd HHW HP1 35 K5
Quartermile La LEY E10 120 G9
Quatre Ports CHING E4 * 101 J6
Quaves Rd DTCH/LGLY SL3 149 N2
Quay House POP/IOD E14 * 160 F1
Quay La RDART DA2 166 G10
Quebec Av BH/WHM TN16 262 G2
Quebec Cl HORL RH6 281 H4
Quebec Ms MBLAR W1H 10 B6
Quebec Rd GNTH/NBYPK IG2 122 F5
TIL RM18 168 D8
YEAD UB4 133 K9
Quebec Wy BERM/RHTH SE16 160 C1
Queen Adelaide Rd
PGE/AN SE20 182 B10
Queen Alexandra's Wy
HOR/WEW KT19 219 M7
Queen Anne Av HAYES BR2 205 M3
Queen Anne Dr ESH/CLAY KT10 218 D4
Queen Anne Ga BXLYHN DA7 163 N9
Queen Anne Ms CAVSQ/HST W1G 10 F4
Queen Anne Rd HOM E9 140 C1
Queen Anne's Cl WDSR SL4 170 G6
WHTN TW2 176 C6
Queen Annes Ct LHD/OX KT22 236 C7
Queen Anne's Gdns CHSWK W4 156 B2
EA W5 155 K1
EN EN1 79 M10
LHD/OX KT22 236 G7
MTCM CR4 * 202 A3
Queen Anne's Ga STJSPK SW1H 17 J2
Queen Anne's Gv CHSWK W4 156 B2
EA W5 155 K1
ED N9 99 L1
Queen Annes Ms LHD/OX KT22 * 236 G7
Queen Anne's Pl EN EN1 79 M10
Queen Annes Ride WDSR SL4 * 170 C6
Queen Anne's Rd WDSR SL4 149 H10
Queen Anne's Ter LHD/OX KT22 * 236 G7
Queen Anne St CAVSQ/HST W1G 10 E4
Queen Anne Ter WAP E1W * 140 A9
Queen Borough Gdns CHST BR7 184 G9
Queenborough Gdns
GNTH/NBYPK IG2 122 D2
Queen Caroline Est HMSMTH W6 156 F4
Queen Caroline St HMSMTH W6 156 F4
Queendale Ct WOKN/KNAP GU21 231 L2
Queen Eleanor's Rd GUW GU2 267 L1
Queen Elizabeth Av TIL RM18 169 M3
Queen Elizabeth Buildings
EMB EC4Y * 12 A7
Queen Elizabeth College
GNWCH SE10 * 161 H6
Queen Elizabeth Ct WAB EN9 * 81 J1
Queen Elizabeth Gdns
MRDN SM4 201 K4
Queen Elizabeth II Br
WTHK RM20 166 D8
Queen Elizabeth Rd
KUTN/CMB KT2 199 L2
WALTH E17 120 D1
Queen Elizabeth's Cl
STNW/STAM N16 119 L7
Queen Elizabeth's Dr
CROY/NA CR0 225 J6
STHGT/OAK N14 98 F2
Queen Elizabeth's Gdns
CROY/NA CR0 225 J6
Queen Elizabeth St STHWK SE1 19 L1
Queen Elizabeth's Wk
STNW/STAM N16 119 L7
WDSR SL4 149 M8
WLGTN SM6 222 E1
Queen Elizabeth Wk BARN SW13 156 E7
Queen Elizabeth Wy
WOKS/MYFD GU22 232 C5
Queenhill Rd SAND/SEL CR2 224 A6
Queenhithe BLKFR EC4V 12 F8
Queenhythe Crs RGUE GU4 250 A4
Queenhythe Rd RGUE GU4 250 A5
Queen Isabella Wy STBT EC1A 12 D5
Queen Margaret's Gv IS N1 119 M10
Queen Mary Av RYNPK SW20 200 G5
TIL RM18 169 M3
Queen Mary Cl ROM RM1 124 G4
SURB KT6 199 M10
WOKS/MYFD GU22 * 232 F2
Queen Mary Rd NRWD SE19 181 J9
SHPTN TW17 196 D2
Queen Mary's Av CAR SM5 222 A4
WATW WD18 72 F8
Queen Marys Ct WAB EN9 * 81 H1
Queen Mary's Dr
ADL/WDHM KT15 215 J6
Queen Mother Ga
MYFR/PICC W1J 10 D10
Queen Mother's Dr
DEN/HRF UB9 111 J4
Queens Acre CHEAM SM3 220 G4
WDSR SL4 149 J10
Queens Av BF/WBF KT14 215 N8
FELT TW13 175 K7
FNCH N3 97 M8
GFD/PVL UB6 134 A8
KTN/HRWW/WS HA3 114 G1
MUSWH N10 118 B1
TRDG/WHET N20 97 N3
WATW WD18 72 G8
WCHMH N21 99 J2
WFD IG8 101 N6
Queensberry Ms West
SKENS SW7 * 15 L5
Queensberry Pl MNPK E12 122 A10
SKENS SW7 15 L5
Queensberry Wy SKENS SW7 * 15 L5
Queensborough Ms
BAY/PAD W2 * 9 J7
Queensborough Pas BAY/PAD W2 9 J7
Queensborough Studios
BAY/PAD W2 9 J7
Queensborough Ter BAY/PAD W2 9 J8
Queensbridge Pk ISLW TW7 176 D2
Queensbridge Rd HACK E8 7 M1
Queensbury Rd ALP/SUD HA0 135 L4
CDALE/KGS NW9 116 A5
Queensbury St IS N1 6 F4
Queens Circ VX/NE SW8 158 C6
Queens Cl CHOB/PIR GU24 230 F2
EDGW HA8 95 M6
ESH/CLAY KT10 * 218 A1
KWD/TDW/WH KT20 238 D10
WDSR SL4 171 M1
WLGTN SM6 222 C2
Queen's Club Gdns WKENS W14 14 B10
WKENS W14 157 H5
Queens Ct BELMT SM2 * 221 K7
SL SL1 * 129 L9
Queenscourt WBLY HA9 115 K9
Queens Ct WEY KT13 216 F2
WOKS/MYFD GU22 * 232 C4
Queens Court Ride COB KT11 217 H9
Queen's Crs DORK RH4 272 F3
HAMP NW3 4 C2
KTTN NW5 118 B10
RCHPK/HAM TW10 177 L1
STALE/WH AL4 38 G3
Queenscroft Rd ELTH/MOT SE9 184 A1
Queensdale Crs NTGHL W11 136 G10
Queensdale Pl NTGHL W11 8 A10
Queensdale Rd NTGHL W11 8 A10
Queensdale Wk NTGHL W11 8 A10
Queens Down Rd CLPT E5 120 A9
Queens Dr ABLGY WD5 54 G8
BRYLDS KT5 199 M7
CHES/WCR EN8 62 F10
DTCH/LGLY SL3 130 C3
EA W5 135 L8
FSBYPK N4 119 J7
GODL GU7 266 G10
GUW GU2 249 M7
LEY E10 120 F5
LHD/OX KT22 218 B7
RSEV TN14 247 K6
THDIT KT7 198 F6
The Queen's Dr
RKW/CH/CXG WD3 71 J10
Queen's Elm Sq CHEL SW3 15 M8
Queen's Farm Rd GVE DA12 191 P5
Queen's Gdns BAY/PAD W2 9 J7
EA W5 135 H7
HDN NW4 116 F3
HEST TW5 153 M7
RAIN RM13 144 E4
RDART DA2 188 A4
UPMR RM14 126 E4
Queens Garth FSTH SE23 * 182 B5
Queensgate COB KT11 217 L8
Queens Ga SKENS SW7 15 K2
Queensgate Centre
GRAYS RM17 * 167 M4
Queens Gate Gdns CHST BR7 206 G1
Queensgate Gdns
PUT/ROE SW15 156 E10
Queen's Gate Gdns SKENS SW7 15 K4
Queen's Gate Ms SKENS SW7 15 K2
Queensgate Pl KIL/WHAMP NW6 2 E4
Queen's Gate Pl SKENS SW7 15 K4
Queen's Gate Place Ms
SKENS SW7 15 K5
Queen's Gate Ter SKENS SW7 15 K3
Queen's Gv STJWD NW8 3 L6
Queen's Grove Rd CHING E4 101 J2
Queen's Head St IS N1 6 D6
Queenshill Ldg ASC SL5 192 A3
Queens Hill Ri ASC SL5 192 B3
Queens Keep TWK TW1 * 177 H2
Queensland Av UED N18 99 K7
WIM/MER SW19 201 L1
Queensland Cl WALTH E17 100 E10
Queensland Rd HOLWY N7 119 H9
Queens La MUSWH N10 118 C1
Queensmead DTCH/LGLY SL3 149 N7
Queens Md EDGW HA8 95 L7
Queensmead LHD/OX KT22 * 218 B7
STJWD NW8 3 M5
Queensmead Av EW KT17 220 E6
Queen's Mead Rd HAYES BR2 205 L2
Queensmere Cl WIM/MER SW19 178 G5
Queensmere Rd SL SL1 149 L1
WIM/MER SW19 178 G5
Queen's Ms BAY/PAD W2 8 G7
Queensmill Rd FUL/PGN SW6 156 G6
Queens Pde CEND/HSY/T N8 * 119 J2
CRICK NW2 * 136 F1
EA W5 * 135 L8
FBAR/BDGN N11 * 98 A6
FBAR/BDGN N11 * 98 F8
HDN NW4 * 116 E3
Queens Parade Cl
FBAR/BDGN N11 98 A6
Queens Park Gdns FELT TW13 174 G6
Queen's Park Rd CTHM CR3 241 M9
HARH RM3 105 N9
Queen's Pl MRDN SM4 201 K4
WAT WD17 73 K7
WOT/HER KT12 216 F2
Queens Prom KUT/HW KT1 199 J4
Queen Sq BMSBY WC1N 11 M2
Queen's Ride PUT/ROE SW15 156 D10
Queen's Ri RCHPK/HAM TW10 177 L2
Queen's Rd ASC SL5 192 C5
BAR EN5 76 G7
BARK IG11 142 F2
BECK BR3 204 D2
BELMT SM2 221 K6
BERK HP4 33 M4
BKHH IG9 101 N3
BMLY BR1 205 M2
BRW CM14 107 H4
CHES/WCR EN8 62 D10
CHOB/PIR GU24 230 D6
CHST BR7 184 E9
CROY/NA CR0 203 J6
CSHM HP5 * 51 H6
DTCH/LGLY SL3 149 N7
EA W5 135 K8
ED N9 100 A3
EGH TW20 172 C9
EN EN1 79 M8
EPP CM16 66 D1
ERITH DA8 164 F5
FBAR/BDGN N11 98 F8
FELT TW13 175 J4
FNCH N3 97 M9
GU GU1 250 A10
GVE DA12 190 F6
HARP AL5 20 A4
HDN NW4 116 F3
HERT/BAY SG13 25 L7
HORL RH6 280 B4
HPTN TW12 176 A7
HSLW TW3 154 A9
HYS/HAR UB3 132 F8
KUTN/CMB KT2 177 M10
LOU IG10 82 C7
MORT/ESHN SW14 156 A9
MTCM CR4 201 N3
NWDGN UB2 153 L1
NWMAL KT3 200 C4
PECK SE15 160 B7
PLSTW E13 141 N3
RCHPK/HAM TW10 177 L2
SL SL1 129 L9
TEDD TW11 176 E9
THDIT KT7 198 E5
TWK TW1 176 E4
UX/CGN UB8 131 M5
WALTH E17 120 E4
WAN E11 121 K5
WARE SG12 26 E1
WAT WD17 73 K7
WDR/YW UB7 152 A1
WDSR SL4 148 D4
WDSR SL4 149 H8
WELL DA16 163 L8
WIM/MER SW19 179 K9
WLGTN SM6 222 C2
WOKN/KNAP GU21 231 H4
WOT/HER KT12 216 G1
Queen's Rd West PLSTW E13 141 M4
Queens Rw WALW SE17 18 G9
Queens Sq CRAWE RH10 283 N7

The Queen's Sq HHNE HP2 36 A6
Queens Ter ISLW TW7 154 F10
PLSTW E13 141 N3
STJWD NW8 3 L6
THDIT KT7 * 198 F6
WCHPL E1 * 140 B6
Queens Ter Cottages
HNWL W7 * 154 D1
Queensthorpe Ms SYD SE26 * 182 C7
Queensthorpe Rd SYD SE26 182 C7
Queenstown Gdns RAIN RM13 144 G5
Queenstown Rd VX/NE SW8 16 E10
Queen St BRW CM14 107 H6
BXLYHN DA7 164 A9
CHERT KT16 195 K8
CROY/NA CR0 223 K1
ERITH DA8 * 164 F5
GVE DA12 190 E2
KGLGY WD4 53 K8
MYFR/PICC W1J 10 E9
ROMW/RG RM7 124 E4
SHGR GU5 270 D5
STALW/RED AL3 38 B6
STP EC4M 12 F6
TOTM N17 99 M7
Queen Street Pl CANST EC4R 12 F8
Queensville Rd BAL SW12 180 E3
Queens Wk ASHF TW15 173 N7
CDALE/KGS NW9 115 P7
CHING E4 101 J2
EA W5 135 H6
HRW HA1 114 D2
RSLP HA4 113 K8
Queens Walk Ter RSLP HA4 * 113 K8
The Queens Wk STHWK SE1 13 K9
Queens Wy CHES/WCR EN8 62 E10
FELT TW13 175 K7
HDN NW4 116 F3
RAD WD7 57 K7
Queensway BAY/PAD W2 9 H6
CHONG CM5 67 N2
CRAWE RH10 283 P7
CROY/NA CR0 222 G3
HAT AL10 40 D4
HHNE HP2 35 P5
PEND EN3 80 B8
REDH RH1 258 A9
STMC/STPC BR5 206 F5
SUN TW16 197 J2
WWKM BR4 225 M1
Queensway North
WOT/HER KT12 217 K1
Queensway South
WOT/HER KT12 217 K2
The Queensway CFSP/GDCR SL9 110 A2
Queens Well Av
TRDG/WHET N20 97 P5
Queen's Whf HMSMTH W6 156 F4
Queenswood Av HPTN TW12 176 A9
HSLW TW3 153 N8
THHTH CR7 203 H5
WALTH E17 101 H9
WLGTN SM6 222 E1
Queenswood Crs GSTN WD25 55 H9
Queenswood Gdns WAN E11 121 M6
Queenswood Pk FNCH N3 97 H10
Queenswood Rd BFN/LL DA15 185 J2
FSTH SE23 182 D6
Queen's Wood Rd HGT N6 118 C4
Queenswood Rd
WOKN/KNAP GU21 231 J5
Queen's Yd FITZ W1T 11 H2
Queen Victoria Av ALP/SUD HA0 135 J2
Queen Victoria St BLKFR EC4V 12 D7
Queen Victoria's Wk WDSR SL4 149 K6
Queen Victoria Ter WAP E1W * 140 A9
Quemerford Rd HOLWY N7 118 G10
Quendell Wk HHNE HP2 35 P6
Quendon Dr WAB EN9 63 J9
Quennell Cl ASHTD KT21 237 L5
Quennell Wy RBRW/HUT CM13 107 P1
Quentin Pl LEW SE13 161 K9
Quentin Rd LEW SE13 161 K9
Quentins Dr BH/WHM TN16 * 244 E2
Quentins Wk BH/WHM TN16 * 244 E2
Quentin Wy VW GU25 193 N4
Quernmore Cl BMLY BR1 183 M9
Quernmore Rd BMLY BR1 183 M9
FSBYPK N4 119 H4
Querrin St FUL/PGN SW6 157 M8
Questor DART DA1 * 187 N5
Quex Ms KIL/WHAMP NW6 2 F5
Quex Rd KIL/WHAMP NW6 2 F5
Quickbeams WGCE AL7 23 K2
Quickberry Pl AMSS HP7 * 69 H5
Quickley Brow
RKW/CH/CXG WD3 * 70 E10
Quickley La RKW/CH/CXG WD3 70 F10
Quickley Ri RKW/CH/CXG WD3 70 E10
Quickly Brow RKW/CH/CXG WD3 70 E10
Quickmoor La KGLGY WD4 53 L9
Quick Rd CHSWK W4 156 B4
Quicks Rd WIM/MER SW19 179 L10
Quick St IS N1 6 D8
Quickswood HAMP NW3 3 P3
Quickwood Cl RKW/CH/CXG WD3 71 J10
Quiet Cl ADL/WDHM KT15 215 K1
Quiet Nook HAYES BR2 206 A10
Quill Hall La AMS HP6 69 L3
The Quillot WOT/HER KT12 216 G2
Quill St EA W5 135 K5
FSBYPK N4 119 H8
Quilp St STHWK SE1 18 E1
Quilter Rd STMC/STPC BR5 207 N8
Quilter St BETH E2 7 N9
WOOL/PLUM SE18 163 J4
Quinbrookes SLN SL2 129 P8
Quince Cl ASC SL5 192 C4
Quince Dr CHOB/PIR GU24 230 G1
Quince Rd LEW SE13 160 G8
Quinces Cft HHW HP1 35 K4
Quince Tree Cl SOCK/AV RM15 147 H6
Quincy Rd EGH TW20 172 D8
Quinnell Cl WOOL/PLUM SE18 163 J4
Quinta Dr BAR EN5 76 E9
Quintin Av RYNPK SW20 201 H1
Quinton Cl BECK BR3 205 H3
HEST TW5 153 J6
WLGTN SM6 222 C1
Quinton Rd THDIT KT7 198 F8
Quinton St WAND/EARL SW18 179 M5
Quinton Wy WAB EN9 81 H1
Quintrell Cl WOKN/KNAP GU21 231 N3
Quixley St POP/IOD E14 141 J9
Quorn Rd EDUL SE22 159 M10

R

Raans Rd AMS HP6 69 L4
Rabbit La WOT/HER KT12 217 H4
Rabbit Rw KENS W8 * 8 F9
Rabbits Rd EYN DA4 210 E2
MNPK E12 122 B9
Rabies Heath Rd REDH RH1 259 P10
Rablus Pl EYN DA4 * 209 N6
Rabournmead Dr NTHLT UB5 113 M10
Raby Rd NWMAL KT3 200 A4
Raby St POP/IOD E14 * 140 D8
Raccoon Wy HSLWW TW4 153 K8
Racecourse Rd HORL RH6 280 B7
Racecourse Wy HORL RH6 280 A8
Racefield Cl GVE DA12 191 P10
Rachel Cl BARK/HLT IG6 122 G2
Rackham Cl CRAWW RH11 283 N9
WELL DA16 163 L8
Rackham Ms STRHM/NOR SW16 180 D9
Racton Rd FUL/PGN SW6 14 E10
Radbourne Av EA W5 155 H3
Radbourne Cl CLPT E5 120 C9
Radbourne Ct
KTN/HRWW/WS HA3 * 114 G4
Radbourne Crs WALTH E17 121 J1
Radbourne Rd BAL SW12 180 D3
Radburn Cl HLWS CM18 47 K5
Radcliffe Av ENC/FH EN2 79 K5
WLSDN NW10 136 D4
Radcliffe Gdns CAR SM5 221 P4
Radcliffe Rd CROY/NA CR0 203 N9
KTN/HRWW/WS HA3 94 F10
STHWK SE1 19 K3
WCHMH N21 99 J2
Radcliffe Sq PUT/ROE SW15 178 G2
Radcliffe Wy NTHLT UB5 133 L5
Radcot Av DTCH/LGLY SL3 150 E2
Radcot St LBTH SE11 18 B8
Raddington Rd NKENS W10 8 B4
NKENS W10 137 H7
Radfield Dr RDART DA2 188 B3
Radfield Wy BFN/LL DA15 184 G3
Radford Est WLSDN NW10 * 136 B5
Radford Rd CRAWE RH10 284 D1
LEW SE13 183 H2
Radford Wy BARK IG11 143 J5
Radipole Rd FUL/PGN SW6 157 J7
Radius Pk EBED/NFELT TW14 * 152 G10
Radland Rd CAN/RD E16 141 M8
Rad La SHGR GU5 270 E8
Radlet Av SYD SE26 182 A6
Radlett Cl FSTGT E7 141 L1
Radlett La RAD WD7 57 J10
Radlett Park Rd RAD WD7 56 G10
Radlett Pl STJWD NW8 3 N6
Radlett Rd GSTN WD25 74 B4
LCOL/BKTW AL2 56 D5
WAT WD17 73 K7
Radley Av GDMY/SEVK IG3 123 J9
Radley Cl EBED/NFELT TW14 174 G4
Radley Ct BERM/RHTH SE16 160 C1
Radley Gdns
KTN/HRWW/WS HA3 115 K2
Radley Ms KENS W8 14 F5
Radley Rd TOTM N17 99 N10
Radley's La SWFD E18 101 M10
Radleys Md DAGE RM10 144 C1
Radley Sq CLPT E5 * 120 B7
Radley Ter CAN/RD E16 141 L7
Radlix Rd LEY E10 120 F6
Radnor Av HRW HA1 114 D3
WELL DA16 185 L1
Radnor Cl CHST BR7 185 H9
MTCM CR4 202 F5
Radnor Ct REDH RH1 257 P10
Radnor Crs REDBR IG4 122 C3
WOOL/PLUM SE18 163 K6
Radnor Gdns EN EN1 79 M5
TWK TW1 176 E5
Radnor Hall BORE WD6 * 75 K9
Radnor La RDKG RH5 271 H10
Radnor Ms BAY/PAD W2 9 M6
Radnor Pl BAY/PAD W2 9 N6
Radnor Rd HRW HA1 114 C3
KIL/WHAMP NW6 2 A6
KIL/WHAMP NW6 137 H3
PECK SE15 159 P6
TWK TW1 176 E5
WEY KT13 196 B10
Radnor St FSBYE EC1V 6 F10
Radnor Ter WKENS W14 14 C5
Radnor Wk CHEL SW3 15 P8
CROY/NA CR0 204 D7
Radnor Wy DTCH/LGLY SL3 150 B3
WLSDN NW10 135 N6
Radolphs KWD/TDW/WH KT20 238 G8
Radstock Av
KTN/HRWW/WS HA3 114 F1
Radstock Cl FBAR/BDGN N11 98 B6
Radstock St BTSEA SW11 * 157 P6
Radstock Wy REDH RH1 258 F5
Radstone Ct WOKS/MYFD GU22 232 C4
Raebarn Gdns BAR EN5 76 E9
Raeburn Av BRYLDS KT5 199 N6
DART DA1 187 J1
Raeburn Cl GLDGN NW11 117 M4
KUT/HW KT1 177 J10
Raeburn Ct WOKN/KNAP GU21 * 231 M5
Raeburn Rd BFN/LL DA15 185 H2
EDGW HA8 95 M10
YEAD UB4 132 E4
Raeburn St BRXS/STRHM SW2 158 F10
Raeside Cl BEAC HP9 89 H7
Rafford Wy BMLY BR1 205 N2
Ragged Hall La LCOL/BKTW AL2 37 M10
Ragge Wy BGR/WK TN15 247 N6
Raggleswood CHST BR7 206 D1
Rag Hill Rd BH/WHM TN16 244 B7
Raglan Av CHES/WCR EN8 62 C10
Raglan Cl HSLWW TW4 175 N1
REIG RH2 257 M8
Raglan Ct SAND/SEL CR2 223 J2
Raglan Gdns OXHEY WD19 93 J2
Raglan Rd BELV DA17 164 A3
EN EN1 99 N1
HAYES BR2 205 P4
REIG RH2 257 M8
WALTH E17 121 H3
WOKN/KNAP GU21 231 K4
WOOL/PLUM SE18 162 F4
Raglan St KTTN NW5 4 F1
Raglan Ter RYLN/HDSTN HA2 * 114 A9
Raglan Vls WALTH E17 * 121 H3
Raglan Wy NTHLT UB5 134 B1
Ragley Cl ACT W3 155 P1
Rags La CHESW EN7 61 N3
Ragstone Rd SL SL1 149 J2
Ragstones BGR/WK TN15 247 N6
Rahn Rd EPP CM16 65 K7
Raider Cl ROMW/RG RM7 104 C9
Raikes La RDKG RH5 271 J8
Railey Ms KTTN NW5 118 D10
Railey Rd CRAWE RH10 283 P7
Railshead Rd ISLW TW7 154 G10
Railton Rd GUW GU2 249 N6
HNHL SE24 181 H1
Railway Ap CHERT KT16 * 195 J8
FSBYPK N4 119 H4
HRW HA1 114 E2
STHWK SE1 12 G9
TWK TW1 176 F3
WLGTN SM6 * 222 C3
Railway Ar BRXN/ST SW9 * 159 H10
Railway Av BERM/RHTH SE16 160 B1
Railway Cottages BNSTD SM7 * 221 J10
HMSMTH W6 * 156 F1
OXTED RH8 * 261 M9
SRTFD E15 * 141 K4
WIM/MER SW19 * 179 L7
Railway Gv NWCR SE14 160 E6
Railway Pl BELV DA17 164 B2
HERT/BAY SG13 25 M5
Railway Ri EDUL SE22 159 M10
Railway Rd CHES/WCR EN8 62 E9
TEDD TW11 176 D7
Railway Side BARN SW13 156 B9
Railway Station Whf LEY E10 * 120 D6
Railway St BCTR RM8 123 M6
GVW DA11 189 M1
HERT/BAY SG13 25 L8
HERT/WAT SG14 25 L5
IS N1 5 M8
Railway Ter BH/WHM TN16 262 G1
FELT TW13 175 H4
KGLGY WD4 54 B3
LEW SE13 182 G1
SLN SL2 129 L10
STA TW18 172 G8
WALTH E17 101 H9
Railway Vw DTCH/LGLY SL3 * 150 C9
Rainborough Cl WBLY HA9 135 P1
Rainbow Av POP/IOD E14 160 G4
Rainbow Ct OXHEY WD19 73 K10
WOKN/KNAP GU21 231 K2
Rainbow Quay
BERM/RHTH SE16 160 D2
Rainbow Rd CDW/CHF RM16 167 J3
HLWE CM17 30 F8
PUR RM19 166 D2
Rainbow St CMBW SE5 159 M6
Rainer Cl CHES/WCR EN8 62 C5
Raine St WAP E1W 140 A10
Rainham Cl BTSEA SW11 179 P2
ELTH/MOT SE9 185 H2
Rainham Rd RAIN RM13 145 H5
WLSDN NW10 136 F5
Rainham Rd North DAGE RM10 124 C7
Rainham Rd South DAGE RM10 144 D2
Rainhill Wy BOW E3 140 F5
Rainsborough Av DEPT SE8 160 D3
Rainsford Cl STAN HA7 95 H6
Rainsford Rd WLSDN NW10 135 N5
Rainsford St BAY/PAD W2 9 N5
Rainsford Wy HCH RM12 125 H6
Rainton Rd CHARL SE7 161 M4
Rainville Rd HMSMTH W6 156 F5
Raisins Hl PIN HA5 113 K1
Raith Av STHGT/OAK N14 98 E4
Raleigh Av WLGTN SM6 222 E1
YEAD UB4 133 J7
Raleigh Cl ERITH DA8 164 G5
HDN NW4 116 F3
PIN HA5 113 L5
RSLP HA4 112 G7
SL SL1 128 F10
Raleigh Ct CRAWE RH10 * 284 B2
STA TW18 173 K7
Raleigh Dr BRYLDS KT5 199 P8
ESH/CLAY KT10 218 C2
HORL RH6 281 J4
TRDG/WHET N20 97 P4
Raleigh Gdns BRXS/STRHM SW2 180 G2
MTCM CR4 202 A3
Raleigh Ms IS N1 6 D6
ORP BR6 227 J2
Raleigh Rd CEND/HSY/T N8 119 H2
ENC/FH EN2 79 L8
FELT TW13 174 G5
NWDGN UB2 153 M4
PGE/AN SE20 182 C10
RCH/KEW TW9 155 L9
Raleigh St IS N1 6 D6
Raleigh Wk CRAWE RH10 283 P9
Raleigh Wy FELT TW13 175 K8
STHGT/OAK N14 98 E2
Ralliwood Rd ASHTD KT21 237 M5
Ralph Perring Ct BECK BR3 204 F4
Ralphs Cross GT/LBKH KT23 * 254 B2
Ralston St CHEL SW3 16 A8
Ralston Wy OXHEY WD19 93 L3
Rama Cl STRHM/NOR SW16 180 F10
Ramac Wy CHARL SE7 161 M4
Rama La NRWD SE19 181 N10
Rambler Cl MDHD SL6 128 A8
STRHM/NOR SW16 180 D7
Rambler La DTCH/LGLY SL3 149 P2
Ramblers La HLWE CM17 29 N10
Ramblers Wy WGCE AL7 23 L6
Rambling Wy BERK HP4 34 F3
Rame Cl TOOT SW17 180 B8
Ram Gorse HLW CM20 28 E9
Ramilles Cl BRXS/STRHM SW2 180 F2
Ramillies Pl SOHO/CST W1F 10 G6
Ramillies Rd BFN/LL DA15 185 L2
CHSWK W4 156 A2
MLHL NW7 96 B3
Ramillies St SOHO/SHAV W1D 10 G6
Ramney Dr PEND EN3 80 D2
Ramones Ter MTCM CR4 * 202 D4
Ramornie Cl WOT/HER KT12 217 N2
The Ramparts STALW/RED AL3 38 A8
Rampart St WCHPL E1 140 A8
Ram Pas KUT/HW KT1 199 J2
Rampayne St PIM SW1V 17 J7
Rampton Cl CHING E4 100 F4
Ramsay Cl BROX EN10 44 E7
Ramsay Gdns HARH RM3 105 K9
Ramsay Ms CHEL SW3 15 N9
Ramsay Rd ACT W3 155 P2
BFOR GU20 212 D2
FSTGT E7 121 M8
Ramsbury Rd STAL AL1 38 D7
Ramscote La CSHM HP5 50 E1
Ramscroft Cl ED N9 99 M1
Ramsdale Rd TOOT SW17 180 B8
Ramsden Cl STMC/STPC BR5 207 M8
Ramsden Dr CRW RM5 104 B8
Ramsden Ga BAL SW12 * 180 C3
Ramsden Rd BAL SW12 180 B3
ERITH DA8 164 E6
FBAR/BDGN N11 98 A6
ORP BR6 207 L7
Ramsey Cl BRKMPK AL9 59 N3
CDALE/KGS NW9 116 C4
GFD/PVL UB6 114 C10
HORL RH6 280 A4
STAL AL1 38 F8
Ramsey Ct SLN SL2 128 C6
Ramsey Lodge Ct STAL AL1 38 D5
Ramsey Pl CTHM CR3 241 K8
Ramsey Rd THHTH CR7 202 G6
Ramsey St BETH E2 13 P1
Ramsey Wk IS N1 6 G2
Ramsey Wy STHGT/OAK N14 98 D1
Ramsgate Cl CAN/RD E16 141 N10
Ramsgate St HACK E8 7 M1
Ramsgill Ap GNTH/NBYPK IG2 123 J2
Ramsgill Dr GNTH/NBYPK IG2 123 J3
Rams Gv CHDH RM6 123 P2
Ramson Ri HHW HP1 35 H7
Ramulis Dr YEAD UB4 133 M6
Ramus Wood Av ORP BR6 227 H2
Rancliffe Gdns ELTH/MOT SE9 162 B10
Rancliffe Rd EHAM E6 142 B4
Randal Crs REIG RH2 275 K2
Randall Av CRICK NW2 116 B7
Randall Cl BTSEA SW11 157 P7
DTCH/LGLY SL3 150 C4
ERITH DA8 164 D5
Randall Dr HCH RM12 125 K9
Randall Pl GNWCH SE10 161 H6
Randall Rd LBTH SE11 17 N7
Randall Rw LBTH SE11 17 N6
Randalls Crs LHD/OX KT22 236 F6
Randalls Park Av LHD/OX KT22 236 F6
Randalls Park Dr LHD/OX KT22 236 F7
Randalls Ride HHNE HP2 35 P4
Randalls Rd LHD/OX KT22 236 D6
Randalls Wk LCOL/BKTW AL2 55 N7
Randalls Wy LHD/OX KT22 236 F7
Randell's Rd IS N1 5 M5
Randisbourne Gdns CAT SE6 * 182 G6
Randle Rd RCHPK/HAM TW10 177 H7
Randlesdown Rd CAT SE6 182 G6
Randle's La RSEV TN14 227 N10
Randolf Rd HAYES BR2 206 C8
Randolph Ap CAN/RD E16 141 P8
Randolph Av MV/WKIL W9 2 G8
Randolph Cl BXLYHN DA7 164 D9
COB KT11 235 P1
KUTN/CMB KT2 * 177 P8
WOKN/KNAP GU21 231 K3
Randolph Crs MV/WKIL W9 9 J2
Randolph Gdns KIL/WHAMP NW6 2 G8
Randolph Gv CHDH RM6 123 M3
Randolph Ms MV/WKIL W9 9 K2
Randolph Rd DTCH/LGLY SL3 150 B3
EW KT17 220 C10
MV/WKIL W9 9 J2
STHL UB1 * 153 N1
WALTH E17 * 120 G3
Randolph St CAMTN NW1 4 G4
Randon Cl RYLN/HDSTN HA2 94 A10
Ranelagh WDSR SL4 * 170 A4
Ranelagh Av BARN SW13 156 D8
FUL/PGN SW6 157 J9
Ranelagh Cl EDGW HA8 95 M5
Ranelagh Dr EDGW HA8 95 M5
TWK TW1 154 G10
Ranelagh Gdns CHSWK W4 155 P6
FUL/PGN SW6 157 H9
GVW DA11 190 C3
IL IG1 122 D6
WAN E11 121 P3
Ranelagh Gv BGVA SW1W 16 D7
Ranelagh Pl NWMAL KT3 200 B5
Ranelagh Rd ALP/SUD HA0 135 J1
EA W5 155 J1
EHAM E6 142 D3
HHNE HP2 36 C6
PIM SW1V 17 H8
REDH RH1 257 P10
SRTFD E15 141 K3
STHL UB1 133 L10
TOTM N17 119 M1
WAN E11 121 K9
WDGN N22 98 G9
WLSDN NW10 136 C4
Ranfurly Rd SUT SM1 201 K9
Rangefield Rd BMLY BR1 183 K8
Rangemoor Rd
SEVS/STOTM N15 119 N3
Range Rd GVE DA12 190 G3
Rangers Rd BKHH IG9 101 M1
Range Wy SHPTN TW17 196 B7
Rangeworth Pl BFN/LL DA15 185 J6
Rangoon St TWRH EC3N * 13 L6
Rankin Cl CDALE/KGS NW9 116 B1
Ranleigh Gdns BXLYHN DA7 164 A6
Ranleigh Wk HARP AL5 20 C5
Ranmere St BAL SW12 180 C4
Ranmoor Cl HRW HA1 114 C2
Ranmoor Gdns HRW HA1 114 C2
Ranmore Av CROY/NA CR0 203 N10
Ranmore Cl REDH RH1 258 B7
Ranmore Common Rd
RDKG RH5 254 D8
Ranmore Pth STMC/STPC BR5 207 K4
Ranmore Pl WEY KT13 * 216 D2
Ranmore Rd BELMT SM2 220 G5
DORK RH4 272 F1
RDKG RH5 254 D10
Rannoch Cl EDGW HA8 95 N3
Rannoch Rd HMSMTH W6 156 F5
Rannoch Wk HHNE HP2 35 N2
Rannock Av CDALE/KGS NW9 116 B5
Ranskill Rd BORE WD6 75 M5
Ransom Cl OXHEY WD19 93 K1
Ransome Cl CRAWW RH11 282 G10
Ransom Rd CHARL SE7 * 161 P4
Ranston Cl DEN/HRF UB9 111 J4
Ranston St CAMTN NW1 9 N3
Rant Meadow HHS/BOV HP3 36 B8
Ranulf Cl HLWE CM17 29 M5
Ranulf Rd CRICK NW2 117 J9
Ranwell Cl BOW E3 * 140 E3
Ranworth Av HOD EN11 26 G9
Ranworth Cl ERITH DA8 164 F8
HHS/BOV HP3 35 N8
Ranworth Gdns POTB/CUF EN6 58 G7
Ranworth Rd ED N9 100 B3
Ranyard Cl CHSGTN KT9 199 L10
Raphael Av ROM RM1 124 G1
TIL RM18 168 D7
Raphael Cl RAD WD7 57 K8
Raphael Dr THDIT KT7 198 E8
WATN WD24 73 L6
Raphael Rd GVE DA12 190 G3
Raphael St SKENS SW7 16 A2
Rapier Cl PUR RM19 165 N3
Rapley's Fld CHOB/PIR GU24 230 D9
Rapsley La WOKN/KNAP GU21 230 G4
Rasehill Cl RKW/CH/CXG WD3 71 M9
Rashleigh Wy EYN DA4 210 B4
Rasper Rd TRDG/WHET N20 97 M3
Rastell Av BRXS/STRHM SW2 180 E5
Ratcliffe Cl LEE/GVPK SE12 183 M3
UX/CGN UB8 131 N5
Ratcliffe Cross St WCHPL E1 * 140 C8
Ratcliffe La POP/IOD E14 140 D8
Ratcliff Rd FSTGT E7 121 P10
Rathbone Market CAN/RD E16 * 141 L7
Rathbone Pl FITZ W1T 11 J4
Rathbone Sq CROY/NA CR0 * 223 K1
Rathbone St CAN/RD E16 141 L7
FITZ W1T 11 H4
Rathcoole Av CEND/HSY/T N8 118 G3
Rathcoole Gdns CEND/HSY/T N8 118 G3
Rathfern Rd CAT SE6 182 E4
Rathgar Av WEA W13 134 G10
Rathgar Cl FNCH N3 97 J10
REDH RH1 276 B5
Rathgar Rd BRXN/ST SW9 159 J9
Rathlin HHS/BOV HP3 36 C8
Rathlin Rd CRAWW RH11 283 L10
Rathmell Dr CLAP SW4 180 E2
Rathmore Rd CHARL SE7 161 N4
GVW DA11 190 E3
Rat's La LOU IG10 81 N4
Rattray Rd BRXS/STRHM SW2 159 H10
Ratty's La HLWW/ROY CM19 45 J2
Raul Rd PECK SE15 159 P8
Raveley St KTTN NW5 118 D9
Ravel Gdns SOCK/AV RM15 146 B8
Ravel Rd SOCK/AV RM15 146 C8
Raven Cl RKW/CH/CXG WD3 91 M1
Raven Ct HAT AL10 40 D6
Ravencroft Crs ELTH/MOT SE9 184 C6
Ravendale Rd SUN TW16 196 G2
Ravenet St BTSEA SW11 158 C7
Ravenfield Rd TOOT SW17 180 A6
Ravenhill Rd PLSTW E13 141 P3
Raven La CRAWW RH11 283 M5
Ravenna Rd PUT/ROE SW15 178 G1
Ravenoak Wy CHIG IG7 103 H6
Ravenor Park Rd GFD/PVL UB6 134 A5
Raven Rd SWFD E18 101 P10
Raven Rw WCHPL E1 140 A7
Ravens Ait SURB KT6 * 199 J5
Ravensbourne Av HAYES BR2 205 J1
STWL/WRAY TW19 173 P4
Ravensbourne Crs HARH RM3 125 N1
Ravensbourne Gdns CLAY IG5 102 D9
WEA W13 134 G7
Ravensbourne Pk CAT SE6 182 F3
Ravensbourne Park Crs CAT SE6 182 E3
Ravensbourne Pl LEW SE13 160 G8
Ravensbourne Rd BMLY BR1 205 M3
CAT SE6 182 E3
DART DA1 165 H9
TWK TW1 177 H2
Ravensbury Av MRDN SM4 201 M5
Ravensbury Gv MTCM CR4 201 N4
Ravensbury La MTCM CR4 201 N4
Ravensbury Rd STMC/STPC BR5 207 J4
WAND/EARL SW18 179 L5
Ravensbury Ter
WAND/EARL SW18 179 L5
Ravenscar Rd BMLY BR1 183 K7
SURB KT6 199 L9
Ravens Cl CDALE/KGS NW9 96 C10
EN EN1 79 M6
HAYES BR2 205 L2
REDH RH1 258 A9
SURB KT6 199 J6
WOKN/KNAP GU21 231 H2
Ravenscourt SUN TW16 196 G1
Ravenscourt Av HMSMTH W6 156 D3
Ravenscourt Cl DEN/HRF UB9 112 D5
HCH RM12 125 M8
Ravenscourt Dr HCH RM12 125 M8
Ravenscourt Gdns HMSMTH W6 156 C3
Ravenscourt Gv HCH RM12 125 M7
Ravenscourt Pk HMSMTH W6 156 D3
Ravenscourt Pl HMSMTH W6 156 E3
Ravenscourt Rd HMSMTH W6 156 E3
STMC/STPC BR5 207 K3
Ravenscourt Sq HMSMTH W6 156 D3
Ravenscraig Rd FBAR/BDGN N11 98 C5
Ravenscroft BROX EN10 * 44 E6
GSTN WD25 73 M1
HARP AL5 20 C5
Ravenscroft Av GLDGN NW11 117 J5
WBLY HA9 115 K6
Ravenscroft Cl CAN/RD E16 141 M7
Ravenscroft Cottages
BAR EN5 * 77 K10
BAR EN5 * 77 K8
Ravenscroft Pk BAR EN5 76 G8
Ravenscroft Rd BECK BR3 204 B2
CAN/RD E16 141 M7
CHSWK W4 155 P3
WEY KT13 216 D7
Ravenscroft St BETH E2 7 M8
Ravensdale Av
NFNCH/WDSPK N12 97 M5
Ravensdale Gdns NRWD SE19 181 L10
Ravensdale Rd HSLWW TW4 153 M9
STNW/STAM N16 119 N5
Ravensdell HHW HP1 35 J5
Ravensdon St LBTH SE11 18 B8
Ravensfield DAGW RM9 123 N9
Ravens Fld DTCH/LGLY SL3 150 A1
Ravensfield EGH TW20 171 N9
Ravensfield Gdns
HOR/WEW KT19 220 B2
Ravenshaw St KIL/WHAMP NW6 117 J10
Ravenshead Cl SAND/SEL CR2 224 B7
Ravenshill CHST BR7 206 E1
Ravenshurst Av HDN NW4 116 F2
Ravenside Cl UED N18 100 C6
Ravens La BERK HP4 34 A5
Ravenslea Rd BAL SW12 180 A3
Ravensleigh Gdns BMLY BR1 183 M8
Ravensmead CFSP/GDCR SL9 90 C6
Ravensmead Rd HAYES BR2 183 J10
Ravensmede Wy CHSWK W4 156 C3
Ravensmere EPP CM16 65 K6
Ravens Ms LEE/GVPK SE12 * 183 M1
Ravenstone Rd
CDALE/KGS NW9 * 116 C4
CEND/HSY/T N8 118 G1
Ravenstone St BAL SW12 180 B4
Ravens Wy LEE/GVPK SE12 183 M1
Ravens Wold PUR/KEN CR8 241 K1
Ravenswood BXLY DA5 185 P4
Ravenswood Av SURB KT6 199 L9
WWKM BR4 205 H8
Ravenswood Cl COB KT11 235 L1
CRW RM5 104 C6
Ravenswood Ct
KUTN/CMB KT2 * 177 N9
WOKS/MYFD GU22 * 232 C4
Ravenswood Crs
RYLN/HDSTN HA2 113 N7
WWKM BR4 205 H8
Ravenswood Gdns ISLW TW7 154 D7
Ravenswood Pk NTHWD HA6 93 H7
Ravenswood Rd BAL SW12 180 C3
CROY/NA CR0 203 J10
WALTH E17 121 H2
Ravensworth Rd ELTH/MOT SE9 184 C7
SLN SL2 128 F5
WLSDN NW10 * 136 E5
Ravey St SDTCH EC2A 13 J1
Ravine Gv WOOL/PLUM SE18 163 H5
Rav Pinter Cl STNW/STAM N16 119 N5
Rawdon Dr HOD EN11 44 F4
Rawlings Cl BECK BR3 205 H5
ORP BR6 227 J2
Rawlings La BEAC HP9 89 J4
Rawlings St CHEL SW3 16 A5
Rawlins Cl FNCH N3 117 H1
SAND/SEL CR2 224 E4
Rawlyn Cl CDW/CHF RM16 167 H4
Rawnsley Av MTCM CR4 201 N5
Raworth Cl CRAWE RH10 * 284 D9
Rawreth Wk IS N1 6 F5
Rawson St BTSEA SW11 158 C7
Rawsthorne Cl CAN/RD E16 142 C10
Rawstorne Pl FSBYE EC1V * 6 C9
Rawstorne St FSBYE EC1V 6 C9
Ray Bell Ct BROCKY SE4 * 160 E8
Rayburn Rd EMPK RM11 125 P5
HHW HP1 35 K4
Raydean Rd BAR EN5 77 K9
Raydons Gdns DAGW RM9 123 P9
Raydons Rd DAGW RM9 123 P10
Raydon St ARCH N19 118 C7
Rayfield EPP CM16 65 J6
WGCW AL8 22 G2
Rayfield Cl HAYES BR2 206 B6
Rayford Av LEE/GVPK SE12 183 L3
Rayford Cl DART DA1 187 K1
Ray Gdns BARK IG11 143 K4
STAN HA7 94 G6
Ray Lamb Wy ERITH DA8 165 J5
Raylands Md CFSP/GDCR SL9 109 P3
Rayleas Cl WOOL/PLUM SE18 162 E7
Rayleigh Av TEDD TW11 176 D9
Rayleigh Cl PLMGR N13 99 L4
RBRW/HUT CM13 107 P1
Rayleigh Ct KUT/HW KT1 199 M2
Rayleigh Pde RBRW/HUT CM13 * 87 P10
Rayleigh Ri SAND/SEL CR2 223 M3
Rayleigh Rd CAN/RD E16 141 N10
PLMGR N13 99 K4
RBRW/HUT CM13 87 P10
WFD IG8 101 P8
WIM/MER SW19 201 J1
Rayley La EPP CM16 48 B10
Ray Lodge Rd WFD IG8 101 P7
Raymead Av THHTH CR7 203 H5
Raymead Cl LHD/OX KT22 236 D8
Raymead Wy LHD/OX KT22 236 D8
Raymer Cl STAL AL1 38 D5
Raymere Gdns
WOOL/PLUM SE18 162 G6
Raymer Wk HORL RH6 280 D3
Raymond Av SWFD E18 121 L1
WEA W13 154 F2
Raymond Buildings
GINN WC1R * 11 P3
Raymond Cl ABLGY WD5 54 E8
DTCH/LGLY SL3 151 H7
SYD SE26 182 B8
Raymond Crs GUW GU2 267 L1
Raymond Gdns CHIG IG7 103 L4
Raymond Rd BECK BR3 204 D4
DTCH/LGLY SL3 150 D3
GNTH/NBYPK IG2 122 G5
PLSTW E13 141 P2
WIM/MER SW19 179 H9
Raymonds Cl WGCE AL7 * 23 H7
Raymonds Pln WGCE AL7 23 H7
Raymond Wy ESH/CLAY KT10 * 218 F3
Raymouth Rd BERM/RHTH SE16 160 B3
Rayne Ct SWFD E18 121 L2
Rayners Cl ALP/SUD HA0 115 J10
DTCH/LGLY SL3 150 F6
Rayners Gdns NTHLT UB5 133 J5
Rayners La PIN HA5 113 N4
Rayner's Rd PUT/ROE SW15 179 H1
Raynes Av WAN E11 121 P5
Raynes Pk RYNPK SW20 200 F2
Raynham Av UED N18 99 P7
Raynham Rd HMSMTH W6 156 E3
UED N18 99 P6
Raynham St HERT/BAY SG13 25 M4
Raynham Ter UED N18 99 P6
Raynor Cl STHL UB1 133 N10
Raynor Pl IS N1 6 F5
Raynsford Rd WARE SG12 26 D2
Raynton Cl RYLN/HDSTN HA2 113 M6
YEAD UB4 132 G6
Raynton Dr YEAD UB4 132 G5
Raynton Rd PEND EN3 80 C3
Ray Rd CRW RM5 104 C6
E/WMO/HCT KT8 198 A5
Rays Av UED N18 100 B5
WDSR SL4 148 E6
Ray's Hl CSHM HP5 32 B7
EYN DA4 210 B4
Rays Rd UED N18 100 B5
WWKM BR4 205 H7
Ray St CLKNW EC1R 12 B2
Ray Street Br CLKNW EC1R * 12 B2
Raywood Cl HYS/HAR UB3 152 D6
Reachview Cl CAMTN NW1 5 H4
Read Cl THDIT KT7 198 F7
Read Ct WAB EN9 63 M9
The Readens BNSTD SM7 239 P2
Reading Arch Rd REDH RH1 258 A10
Reading La HACK E8 140 A1
Reading Rd NTHLT UB5 114 A10
SUT SM1 221 M2
The Readings HLWS CM18 47 J4
RKW/CH/CXG WD3 71 J7
Reading Wy MLHL NW7 96 G6
Read Rd ASHTD KT21 237 J3
Reads Cl IL IG1 122 E8
Reads Rest La
KWD/TDW/WH KT20 239 J5
Read Wy GVE DA12 190 G8
Reapers Cl CAMTN NW1 5 J5
Reapers Wy ISLW TW7 176 C1
Reardon Pth WAP E1W 140 A10
Reardon St WAP E1W 140 A10
Reaston St NWCR SE14 160 B6
Reckitt Rd CHSWK W4 156 B4
Record St PECK SE15 160 B5
Recovery St TOOT SW17 179 P8
Recreation Av HARH RM3 105 N10
ROMW/RG RM7 124 D3
Recreation Rd GU GU1 249 P10
HAYES BR2 205 L2
NWDGN UB2 153 M3
SYD SE26 182 C7
Recreation Wy MTCM CR4 202 F3
Rectar Pl ARCH N19 118 C7
Rector St IS N1 6 E6
Rectory Cha BRWN CM15 87 H3
RBRW/HUT CM13 127 K2
Rectory Cl ASHTD KT21 237 L5
BF/WBF KT14 215 P9
BRKMPK AL9 41 P3
CHING E4 100 F4
DART DA1 164 F10
FNCH N3 97 J9
RGUE GU4 250 G8
RYNPK SW20 200 F2
SCUP DA14 185 L7
SHPTN TW17 196 B3
SLN SL2 129 H5
STAN HA7 94 G7
SURB KT6 199 H9
WARE SG12 28 A3
WDSR SL4 148 F7
Rectory Ct LOU IG10 82 C6
Rectory Fld HLWW/ROY CM19 46 E3
Rectory Field Crs CHARL SE7 161 P6
Rectory Gdns BECK BR3 * 204 F1
CEND/HSY/T N8 118 F2
CHST BR7 * 206 F1
HAT AL10 40 E4
NTHLT UB5 133 N3
UPMR RM14 126 C7
Rectory Gn BECK BR3 204 E1
Rectory Gv CLAP SW4 158 D9
CROY/NA CR0 203 J9
HPTN TW12 175 N7
Rectory Hl AMSS HP7 69 H5
Rectory La AMSS HP7 68 G6
ASHTD KT21 237 L5
BERK HP4 33 P5
BF/WBF KT14 215 P9
BFOR GU20 212 B4
BH/WHM TN16 244 B9
BH/WHM TN16 245 M10
BNSTD SM7 240 A1
BRKHM/BTCW RH3 256 C8
BUSH WD23 73 P10
CRAWW RH11 283 J5
EDGW HA8 95 M7
GT/LBKH KT23 253 N2
HLWW/ROY CM19 46 E3
HORL RH6 278 G8
KGLGY WD4 54 B4
LOU IG10 82 D6
RAD WD7 57 L9
RKW/CH/CXG WD3 91 N2
SCUP DA14 185 L7
SEV TN13 265 K2
SHGR GU5 270 A5
STAN HA7 94 G6
SURB KT6 199 H8
TOOT SW17 180 B8
WLGTN SM6 222 D1
Rectory Meadow MEO DA13 189 M9
Rectory Orch WIM/MER SW19 179 H7
Rectory Pk SAND/SEL CR2 223 M9
Rectory Park Av NTHLT UB5 133 N5
Rectory Pl CHST BR7 * 206 F1
WOOL/PLUM SE18 162 D3
Rectory Rd BARN SW13 156 D8
BECK BR3 204 F1
COUL/CHIP CR5 257 N1
DAGE RM10 144 B2
GRAYS RM17 168 A2
HAYES BR2 226 A4
HSLWW TW4 153 J8
HYS/HAR UB3 133 H8
MNPK E12 122 C10
NWDGN UB2 153 N2
RKW/CH/CXG WD3 91 N1
STNW/STAM N16 119 N8
SUT SM1 201 K10
SWCM DA10 189 K3
TIL RM18 168 G5
WALTH E17 120 G2
WGCW AL8 22 F1
Rectory Sq WCHPL E1 140 C7
Rectory Wy HGDN/ICK UB10 112 C7
Rectory Wd HLW CM20 28 F10
Reculver Ms UED N18 99 P5
Reculver Rd BERM/RHTH SE16 160 C4
Red Anchor Cl CHEL SW3 15 M10
Redan Pl BAY/PAD W2 8 G6
Redan St WKENS W14 156 G2
Redan Ter CMBW SE5 159 J8
Redbarn Cl PUR/KEN CR8 223 J7
Red Barracks Rd
WOOL/PLUM SE18 162 C3
Redberry Gv SYD SE26 182 B6
Redbourne Av FNCH N3 97 K9
Redbourne Dr THMD SE28 143 N8
Redbourn Rd HHNE HP2 36 C1
STALW/RED AL3 37 M2
Redbridge Gdns CMBW SE5 159 M6
Redbridge La East REDBR IG4 122 B3
Redbridge La West WAN E11 121 N4
Redburn St CHEL SW3 16 A9
Redbury Cl RAIN RM13 145 J6
Redcar Cl NTHLT UB5 114 A10
Redcar Rd HARH RM3 105 N6
Redcar St CMBW SE5 * 159 K6
Redcastle Cl WAP E1W 140 B9
Red Cedars Rd ORP BR6 207 H7
Redchurch St BETH E2 13 L1
Redcliffe Cl ECT SW5 14 G8
Redcliffe Gdns IL IG1 122 D6
WBPTN SW10 15 H8
Redcliffe Ms WBPTN SW10 15 H8
Redcliffe Pl WBPTN SW10 15 J10
Redcliffe Rd WBPTN SW10 15 J8
Redcliffe Sq WBPTN SW10 14 G9
WBPTN SW10 15 H9
Redcliffe St WBPTN SW10 15 H9
Redclose Av MRDN SM4 201 K5
Redclyffe Rd PLSTW E13 141 P3
Redcote Pl DORK RH4 255 J10
Red Cottage Ms DTCH/LGLY SL3 149 P2
Red Ct SL SL1 129 K10
Redcourt WOKS/MYFD GU22 232 G1
Redcroft Rd STHL UB1 134 B9
Redcross Wy STHWK SE1 18 F1
Redden Court Rd HARH RM3 125 M1
Redding Cl RDART DA2 188 D5
Redding Dr AMS HP6 68 G3
Reddings HHS/BOV HP3 36 A8
WGCW AL8 22 F4
Reddings Av BUSH WD23 74 A9
Reddings Cl MLHL NW7 96 C5
The Reddings BORE WD6 75 L7
MLHL NW7 96 C4
Reddington Cl SAND/SEL CR2 223 L5
Reddington Dr DTCH/LGLY SL3 150 C3
Redding Wy WOKN/KNAP GU21 230 G5
WOKN/KNAP GU21 231 J4
Reddins Rd PECK SE15 159 P6

Redditch Ct HHNE HP2 36 A2
Reddons Rd BECK BR3 182 D10
Reddown Rd COUL/CHIP CR5 240 E4
Reddy Rd ERITH DA8 164 C5
Rede Ct WEY KT13 196 C10
Redehall Rd HORL RH6 281 J6
Rede Pl BAY/PAD W2 8 F6
Redesdale Gdns ISLW TW7 154 F6
Redesdale St CHEL SW3 16 A9
Redfern Av HSLWW TW4 175 P3
Redfern Cl UX/CGN UB8 131 M3
Redfern Gdns GPK RM2 105 L10
Redfern Rd CAT SE6 183 H3
WLSDN NW10 136 B2
Redfield La ECT SW5 14 C5
Redford Av COUL/CHIP CR5 240 C1
THHTH CR7 202 A4
WLGTN SM6 222 F3
Redford Cl FELT TW13 174 C5
Redford Rd WDSR SL4 148 C7
Redford Wk IS N1 * 6 D5
Redford Wy UX/CGN UB8 131 M2
Redgate Dr HAYES BR2 205 N9
Redgate Ter PUT/ROE SW15 178 G2
Redgrave Cl CROY/NA CR0 203 N6
Redgrave Dr CRAWE RH10 284 E8
Redgrave Rd PUT/ROE SW15 156 G10
Redgrave Ter BETH E2 * 7 P10
Redhall Cl HAT AL10 40 C7
Redhall Dr HAT AL10 40 C8
Redhall La RKW/CH/CXG WD3 71 P5
Redhall Ter EA W5 * 135 M9
Redheath Cl GSTN WD25 72 G1
Red Hl CHST BR7 184 D8
Redhill Dr EDGW HA8 95 N10
Redhill Rd COB KT11 216 C9
HART DA3 211 L10
Redhill St CAMTN NW1 4 F9
Red House Cl BEAC HP9 88 A7
WARE SG12 26 D4
Red House La BXLYHS DA6 163 N10
WOT/HER KT12 197 H9
Redhouse Rd BH/WHM TN16 243 P7
Red House Rd CROY/NA CR0 202 E6
Red House Sq IS N1 6 F3
Redington Gdns HAMP NW3 117 L9
Redington Rd HAMP NW3 117 L8
Red La OXTED RH8 261 N9
Redland Gdns E/WMO/HCT KT8 * 197 N4
Redlands COUL/CHIP CR5 240 F2
Redlands La RDKG RH5 272 F8
Redlands Rd PEND EN3 80 D5
SEV TN13 246 G10
Redlands Wy BRXS/STRHM SW2 180 F3
Red La ESH/CLAY KT10 218 F3
RDKG RH5 273 M7
Redleaf Cl BXLYHN DA7 164 B5
LHD/OX KT22 236 C10
Redleaves Av ASHF TW15 174 C9
Redlees Cl ISLW TW7 154 F10
Red Lion Cl GSTN WD25 74 A3
STMC/STPC BR5 207 M6
WALW SE17 18 G9
Red Lion Ct FLST/FETLN EC4A 12 B5
HSLW TW3 * 154 A9
Red Lion Crs HLWE CM17 47 M3
Red Lion Hl EFNCH N2 97 N10
Red Lion La CHOB/PIR GU24 213 K5
HHS/BOV HP3 54 A2
HLWE CM17 47 M3
RKW/CH/CXG WD3 71 K1
WOOL/PLUM SE18 162 D7
Red Lion Pde PIN HA5 * 113 M1
Red Lion Pl WOOL/PLUM SE18 * 162 D7
Red Lion Rd CHOB/PIR GU24 213 K5
SURB KT6 199 L9
Red Lion Rw CMBW SE5 18 F10
Red Lion Sq GINN WC1R 11 N4
WAND/EARL SW18 * 179 K1
Red Lion St CSHM HP5 50 G8
GINN WC1R 11 N4
RCH/KEW TW9 177 J1
Red Lion Yd MYFR/PKLN W1K * 10 D9
Red Lodge Crs BXLY DA5 186 F6
Redlodge Gdns BERK HP4 33 M6
Red Lodge Rd BXLY DA5 186 E6
WWKM BR4 205 H8
Redman Cl NTHLT UB5 133 K4
Redmans La RSEV TN14 228 G3
Redman's Rd WCHPL E1 140 B7
Redmead La WAP E1W * 13 N10
Redmead Rd HYS/HAR UB3 152 F3
Redmore Rd HMSMTH W6 * 156 E3
Red Oak Cl ORP BR6 206 E10
Red Pl MYFR/PKLN W1K 10 C7
Redpoll Wy ERITHM DA18 163 N2
Red Post Hl HNHL SE24 181 L1
Redricks La SBW CM21 29 J5
Redriffe Rd PLSTW E13 141 L3
Redriff Rd BERM/RHTH SE16 160 D2
ROMW/RG RM7 104 C10
Red Rd BORE WD6 75 L7
BRW CM14 106 G5
Redroofs Cl BECK BR3 204 C1
Redruth Cl WDGN N22 98 G8
Redruth Rd HARH RM3 105 N6
HOM E9 140 B3
Redstart Cl CROY/NA CR0 225 J6
EHAM E6 142 B7
NWCR SE14 * 160 D6
Redstone Hl REDH RH1 258 B10
Redstone Hollow REDH RH1 276 B1
Redstone Mnr REDH RH1 258 B10
Redstone Pk REDH RH1 258 B10
Redstone Rd REDH RH1 276 B1
Redston Rd CEND/HSY/T N8 118 E2
Red St MEO DA13 189 N9
Redvers Rd WARL CR6 242 C4
WDGN N22 99 H10
Redvers St IS N1 7 K9
Redwald Rd CLPT E5 120 C9
Redway Dr WHTN TW2 176 B3
Red Willow HLWW/ROY CM19 46 C4
Redwing Av GODL GU7 267 J9
Redwing Cl SAND/SEL CR2 224 C7
Redwing Ct ORP BR6 207 K7
Redwing Gdns BF/WBF KT14 215 L8
Redwing Gv ABLGY WD5 55 H7
Redwing Ms CMBW SE5 159 K8
Redwing Ri RGUE GU4 250 G8
Redwing Rd WLGTN SM6 222 F4
Redwood EGH TW20 195 H2
Redwood Cha SOCK/AV RM15 147 H6
Redwood Cl BERM/RHTH SE16 140 D10
BFN/LL DA15 185 K4
BOW E3 140 F4
CRAWE RH10 283 P5
HGDN/ICK UB10 132 C4
OXHEY WD19 93 K5
PUR/KEN CR8 223 K10
STHGT/OAK N14 98 E1
Redwood Dr ASC SL5 192 G6
HHS/BOV HP3 35 P8
Redwood Gdns CHIG IG7 103 K6
CHING E4 * 100 C1
SL SL1 129 J9
Redwood Gv EA W5 155 H2
RGUE GU4 268 F6
Redwood Ms ASHF TW15 * 174 E10
VX/NE SW8 158 C9
Redwood Mt REIG RH2 257 K7
Redwood Pl BEAC HP9 88 C10
Redwood Ri BORE WD6 75 M3
Redwoods ADL/WDHM KT15 215 K3
HERT/WAT SG14 25 K4
The Redwoods WDSR SL4 149 J9
Redwood Wy BAR EN5 76 G9
Reece Ms SKENS SW7 15 L5
Reed Av ORP BR6 207 H10
Reed Cl CAN/RD E16 141 M7
IVER SL0 131 H8
LCOL/BKTW AL2 57 J3
LEE/GVPK SE12 183 M1
Reed Ct SWCM DA10 167 H10
Reed Dr REDH RH1 276 B3
Reede Rd DAGE RM10 144 B1
Reede Wy DAGE RM10 144 C1
Reedham Cl LCOL/BKTW AL2 55 P6
TOTM N17 120 A2
Reedham Dr PUR/KEN CR8 222 G9
Reedham Park Av PUR/KEN CR8 241 J2
Reedham St PECK SE15 * 159 P8
Reedholm Vls STNW/STAM N16 119 L9
Reedings CRAWW RH11 282 G9
Reed Pl BF/WBF KT14 215 H9
CLAP SW4 158 E10
SHPTN TW17 196 A8
Reed Pond Wk GPK RM2 104 G10
Reed Rd TOTM N17 99 N10
Reeds Crs WAT WD17 73 K6
Reedsfield Cl ASHF TW15 174 C6
Reedsfield Rd ASHF TW15 174 C7
Reed's Pl CAMTN NW1 4 G3
The Reeds WGCE AL7 22 G6
Reedworth St LBTH SE11 18 B6
Reenglass Rd STAN HA7 * 95 J5
Rees Dr STAN HA7 95 K5
Rees Gdns CROY/NA CR0 203 N6
Reesland Cl MNPK E12 142 A1
Rees St IS N1 6 F6
Reets Farm Cl CDALE/KGS NW9 116 B4
Reeve Rd REIG RH2 275 M4
Reeves Av CDALE/KGS NW9 116 A5
Reeves Cnr CROY/NA CR0 203 J9
Reeves Cresent SWLY BR8 208 D5
Reeves La HLWW/ROY CM19 45 P5
Reeves Ms MYFR/PKLN W1K 10 C8
Reeves Rd BOW E3 140 G6
WOOL/PLUM SE18 162 E5
Reform Rw TOTM N17 99 N10
Reform St BTSEA SW11 158 A8
Regal Cl EA W5 135 J7
WCHPL E1 13 P3
Regal Ct MTCM CR4 202 A3
UED N18 99 N6
Regal Crs WLGTN SM6 202 C10
Regal Dr FBAR/BDGN N11 98 C6
Regalfield Cl GUW GU2 249 M6
Regal La CAMTN NW1 4 D6
Regal Rw PECK SE15 160 B7
Regal Wy KTN/HRWW/WS HA3 115 K4
WATN WD24 73 K4
Regan Cl GUW GU2 249 N5
Regan Wy IS N1 7 J8
Regarder Rd CHIG IG7 103 L6
Regarth Av ROM RM1 124 F4
Regency Cl CHIG IG7 102 F6
EA W5 135 K8
HPTN TW12 175 N8
Regency Ct ADL/WDHM KT15 * 215 N1
BRW CM14 107 H4
EN EN1 79 L9
HLWS CM18 47 K4
Regency Crs HDN NW4 96 G10
Regency Dr BF/WBF KT14 215 J9
RSLP HA4 112 F6
Regency Gdns EMPK RM11 125 L5
WOT/HER KT12 197 L8
Regency Lawn KTTN NW5 * 118 C8
Regency Ms BECK BR3 205 H1
WLSDN NW10 136 D1
Regency Pde HAMP NW3 * 3 L4
Regency Pl WEST SW1P * 17 J5
Regency St WEST SW1P 17 K6
Regency Ter HGT N6 * 118 A5
SEVS/STOTM N15 119 M3
SKENS SW7 * 15 L7
Regency Wk CROY/NA CR0 204 D6
Regency Wy BXLYHS DA6 163 N9
Regeneration Rd
BERM/RHTH SE16 160 C3
Regent Av HGDN/ICK UB10 132 C2
Regent Cl ADL/WDHM KT15 215 M5
CDW/CHF RM16 167 P1
HSLWW TW4 153 J7
KGLGY WD4 54 B5
KTN/HRWW/WS HA3 115 K4
NFNCH/WDSPK N12 97 M6
REDH RH1 258 D5
STALE/WH AL4 39 H2
WGCE AL7 23 H6
Regent Ct GUW GU2 * 249 N8
SL SL1 129 K8
Regent Crs REDH RH1 258 A8
Regent Gdns GDMY/SEVK IG3 123 K4
Regent Pde BELMT SM2 * 221 M3
STNW/STAM N16 * 119 N5
Regent Pk LHD/OX KT22 * 236 F4
Regent Pl CROY/NA CR0 203 N8
WIM/MER SW19 179 M8
Regent Rd BRYLDS KT5 199 L5
EPP CM16 65 J6
HNHL SE24 181 J1
Regents Av PLMGR N13 99 H6
Regents Cl CTHM CR3 241 N4
RAD WD7 56 F10
SAND/SEL CR2 223 M3
YEAD UB4 132 F7
Regents Dr HAYES BR2 226 A2
WFD IG8 102 D8
Regents Ms HORL RH6 280 B4
STJWD NW8 3 K8
Regent's Park Rd CAMTN NW1 4 B5
FNCH N3 117 J2
Regent's Park Ter CAMTN NW1 4 E5
Regents Pl LOU IG10 102 A1
Regents Plaza KIL/WHAMP NW6 * 2 G7
Regent Sq BELV DA17 164 C3
BOW E3 140 G5
STPAN WC1H 5 M10
Regent's Rw HACK E8 7 N6
Regent St CHSWK W4 155 M4
REGST W1B 10 G6
STJS SW1Y 11 J8
WATN WD24 73 J4
WLSDN NW10 136 G5
Regents Wk ASC SL5 192 B7
Regents Whf IS N1 * 5 N7
Regent Whf IS N1 * 5 N7
Reginald Ms HLWE CM17 29 M10
Reginald Rd DEPT SE8 160 F6
FSTGT E7 141 M2
HARH RM3 105 P9
NTHWD HA6 92 G9
Reginald Sq DEPT SE8 160 F6
Regina Rd FSBYPK N4 118 G6
NWDGN UB2 153 M3
SNWD SE25 203 P3
WEA W13 134 F10
Regina Ter WEA W13 134 F10
Regis Rd KTTN NW5 118 C10
Regnart Buildings CAMTN NW1 5 H10
Reid Av CTHM CR3 241 L7
Reid Cl COUL/CHIP CR5 240 C2
HYS/HAR UB3 132 F8
PIN HA5 113 H1
Reidhaven Rd WOOL/PLUM SE18 163 H3
Reigate Av SUT SM1 201 L8
Reigate Cl CRAWE RH10 284 C5
Reigate Hl REIG RH2 257 L6
Reigate Hill Cl REIG RH2 257 K4
Reigate Rd BMLY BR1 183 M6
DORK RH4 255 J10
EW KT17 220 C6
EW KT17 238 F1
GDMY/SEVK IG3 123 J7
HORL RH6 279 N5
LHD/OX KT22 237 H9
REDH RH1 276 B4
REIG RH2 257 M10
REIG RH2 275 M10
Reigate Wy WLGTN SM6 222 F2
Reighton Rd CLPT E5 119 P8
Reinckendorf Av ELTH/MOT SE9 184 F1
Reindorp Cl GUW GU2 267 M1
Relay Rd SHB W12 136 F9
Relf Rd PECK SE15 159 P9
Reliance Ar BRXN/ST SW9 * 159 H10
Reliance Sq SDTCH EC2A 13 K1
Relton Ms SKENS SW7 15 P3
Rembrandt Cl BGVA SW1W 16 C7
POP/IOD E14 161 J2
Rembrandt Ct HOR/WEW KT19 220 C3
Rembrandt Dr GVW DA11 190 A6
Rembrandt Rd EDGW HA8 * 95 M10
LEW SE13 161 K10
Rembrandt Wy WOT/HER KT12 197 J9
Remington Rd EHAM E6 142 B8
SEVS/STOTM N15 119 L4
Remington St FSBYE EC1V 6 D8
Remnant St HOL/ALD WC2B 11 N5
Remus Cl STAL AL1 38 C10
Remus Rd BOW E3 140 F2
Rendle Cl CROY/NA CR0 203 N5
Rendlesham Av RAD WD7 74 E3
Rendlesham Cl WARE SG12 26 A1
Rendlesham Rd CLPT E5 119 P9
ENC/FH EN2 79 J5
Rendlesham Wy
RKW/CH/CXG WD3 70 F10
Renforth St BERM/RHTH SE16 160 B2
Renfree Wy SHPTN TW17 196 B7
Renfrew Cl EHAM E6 142 D9
Renfrew Rd HSLWW TW4 153 L8
KUTN/CMB KT2 177 N10
LBTH SE11 18 C5
The Renmans ASHTD KT21 237 L2
Renmuir St TOOT SW17 180 A9
Rennell St LEW SE13 161 H9
Renness Rd WALTH E17 120 D1
Rennets Cl ELTH/MOT SE9 184 G1
Rennets Wood Rd
ELTH/MOT SE9 184 G1
Rennie Cl ASHF TW15 173 N6
Rennie Est BERM/RHTH SE16 160 A3
Rennie St STHWK SE1 12 C9
Rennie Ter REDH RH1 276 B1
Rennison Cl CHESW EN7 61 N3
Renown Cl CROY/NA CR0 203 J8
ROMW/RG RM7 104 B9
Rensburg Rd WALTH E17 120 C3
Rensburg Vls WALTH E17 * 120 C3
Renshaw Cl BELV DA17 164 A5
Renters Av HDN NW4 116 F4
Renton Cl BRXS/STRHM SW2 * 180 G2
Renton Dr STMC/STPC BR5 207 N7
Renwick Rd BARK IG11 143 L6
Repens Wy YEAD UB4 133 L6
Rephidim St STHWK SE1 19 J4
Replingham Rd
WAND/EARL SW18 179 J4
Reporton Rd FUL/PGN SW6 157 H7
Repository Rd
WOOL/PLUM SE18 162 C5
Repton Av ALP/SUD HA0 115 H9
GPK RM2 125 H1
HYS/HAR UB3 152 E3
Repton Cl CAR SM5 221 P2
Repton Ct BECK BR3 204 G1
Repton Dr GPK RM2 125 H2
Repton Gdns GPK RM2 125 H1
Repton Gn STALW/RED AL3 38 C3
Repton Gv CLAY IG5 102 C9
Repton Pl AMSS HP7 * 69 M5
Repton Rd KTN/HRWW/WS HA3 115 L2
ORP BR6 227 K1
Repton St POP/IOD E14 140 D8
Repton Wy RKW/CH/CXG WD3 72 B9
Repulse Cl CRW RM5 104 C9
Reservoir Cl SWCM DA10 189 H2
THHTH CR7 203 L3
Reservoir Rd BROCKY SE4 160 D8
RSLP HA4 112 D3
STHGT/OAK N14 78 D9
Resham Cl NWDGN UB2 153 K2
Resolution Wy DEPT SE8 160 F6
Reson Wy HHW HP1 35 L7
Restell Cl BKHTH/KID SE3 161 K5
Restmor Wy CAR SM5 202 B9
Reston Cl BORE WD6 75 M4
Reston Pl KENS W8 15 J2
Restons Crs ELTH/MOT SE9 184 G2
Reston Wy CAN/RD E16 142 A9
Restormel Cl HSLW TW3 175 P1
Retford Cl BORE WD6 75 M4
HARH RM3 105 P7
Retford Pth HARH RM3 105 P7
Retford Rd HARH RM3 105 P8
Retford St BETH E2 7 L9
Retingham Wy CHING E4 100 G3
Retreat Cl KTN/HRWW/WS HA3 115 L4
Retreat Pl HOM E9 140 B1
Retreat Rd RCH/KEW TW9 177 J1
The Retreat AMS HP6 70 B5
BRW CM14 106 G2
BRYLDS KT5 199 L6
CDALE/KGS NW9 116 A2
EGH TW20 172 A9
GRAYS RM17 167 N5
MORT/ESHN SW14 156 B9
ORP BR6 227 L3
RBRW/HUT CM13 87 N10
RYLN/HDSTN HA2 113 P5
SEV TN13 * 247 K10
THHTH CR7 203 L4
WPK KT4 200 E9
Retreat Wy CHIG IG7 103 L4
Reubens Rd RBRW/HUT CM13 87 N10
Reunion Rw WAP E1W * 140 A9
Reveley Sq BERM/RHTH SE16 160 D2
Revell Cl LHD/OX KT22 236 A8
Revell Dr LHD/OX KT22 236 A8
Revell Ri WOOL/PLUM SE18 163 J5
Revell Rd KUT/HW KT1 199 N2
SUT SM1 221 J3
Revelon Rd BROCKY SE4 160 D10
Revels Cl HERT/WAT SG14 25 L3
Revels Rd HERT/WAT SG14 25 L3
Revelstoke Rd
WAND/EARL SW18 179 K5
WIM/MER SW19 179 H7
WIM/MER SW19 179 M9
Reventlow Rd ELTH/MOT SE9 184 F4
Reverdy Rd STHWK SE1 19 N6
STHWK SE1 159 P3
Reverend Cl RYLN/HDSTN HA2 114 A8
Revere Wy HOR/WEW KT19 220 B5
Revesby Cl CHOB/PIR GU24 212 C9
Revesby Rd CAR SM5 201 P6
Review Rd CRICK NW2 116 C7
DAGE RM10 144 C4
Rewell St FUL/PGN SW6 * 157 M6
Rewley Rd CAR SM5 201 N6
Rex Av ASHF TW15 174 B9
Rex Pl MYFR/PKLN W1K 10 D9
Reydon Av WAN E11 121 P4
Reynard Cl BMLY BR1 206 C3
Reynard Dr NRWD SE19 181 N10
Reynard Pl NWCR SE14 * 160 D5
Reynardson Rd TOTM N17 99 K8
Reynard's Wy LCOL/BKTW AL2 55 N5
Reynard Wy HERT/BAY SG13 25 P5
Reynolds Gdns CHARL SE7 101 N4
Reynolds Av CHDH RM6 123 M5
CHSGTN KT9 219 K4
MNPK E12 122 D10
Reynolds Cl CAR SM5 202 A5
GLDGN NW11 117 L5
HHW HP1 35 K5
WIM/MER SW19 201 N1
Reynolds Crs STALE/WH AL4 38 G1
Reynolds Dr EDGW HA8 115 L1
Reynolds Pl BKHTH/KID SE3 161 N6
CRAWW RH11 283 M6
RCHPK/HAM TW10 177 L2
Reynolds Rd BEAC HP9 88 B8
CHSWK W4 155 P2
CRAWW RH11 283 M6
NWMAL KT3 200 A7
PECK SE15 182 B1
YEAD UB4 133 K6
Reynolds Wy CROY/NA CR0 223 M1
Reynolds Yd CSHM HP5 50 G8
Rhapsody Crs BRW CM14 106 G6
Rheidol Ms IS N1 6 E7
Rheidol Ter IS N1 6 D7
Rheingold Wy WLGTN SM6 222 F5
Rheola Cl TOTM N17 99 N9
Rhoda St BETH E2 13 M1
Rhodes Av WDGN N22 98 D9
Rhodes Cl EGH TW20 172 F8
Rhodes Ct EGH TW20 * 172 F8
Rhodesia Rd BRXN/ST SW9 158 F8
WAN E11 121 J7
Rhodes St HOLWY N7 118 G10
Rhodes Wy CRAWE RH10 283 P10
WATN WD24 73 L6
Rhodeswell Rd POP/IOD E14 140 E7
Rhododendron Ride EGH TW20 171 L8
Rhodrons Av CHSGTN KT9 219 K2
Rhondda Gv BOW E3 140 D5
Rhyl Rd GFD/PVL UB6 134 E4
Rhyl St KTTN NW5 4 D1
Rhymes HHW HP1 35 L4
Rhys Av FBAR/BDGN N11 98 E8
Rialto Rd MTCM CR4 202 B2
Ribble Cl WFD IG8 101 P7
Ribbledale LCOL/BKTW AL2 57 L3
Ribblesdale HHNE HP2 35 P3
Ribblesdale Av FBAR/BDGN N11 98 A7
NTHLT UB5 134 A1
Ribblesdale Rd CEND/HSY/T N8 118 G2
RDART DA2 188 B4
STRHM/NOR SW16 180 C8
Ribbon Dance Ms CMBW SE5 159 L7
Ribchester Av GFD/PVL UB6 134 E5
Ribston Cl HAYES BR2 206 C8
RAD WD7 57 J9
Rib V HERT/WAT SG14 25 L2
Ricardo Rd WDSR SL4 171 N2
Ricardo St POP/IOD E14 140 G8
Ricards Rd WIM/MER SW19 179 J8
Rice Cl HHNE HP2 36 A5
Rice Pde STMC/STPC BR5 * 206 G5
Richard Cl WOOL/PLUM SE18 162 B3
Richard House Dr CAN/RD E16 142 A8
Richard Meyjes Rd GUW GU2 267 K1
Richards Av ROMW/RG RM7 124 D4
Richards Cl BUSH WD23 94 C1
HGDN/ICK UB10 132 B3
HRW HA1 114 F3
HYS/HAR UB3 152 D5
Richards Cottages CAR SM5 * 222 A2
Richards Fld HOR/WEW KT19 220 A5
Richardson Cl HACK E8 * 7 L5
LCOL/BKTW AL2 57 K3
RDART DA2 188 E1
Richardson Crs CHESW EN7 61 J2
Richardson Gdns DAGE RM10 144 C1
Richardson Pl STALE/WH AL4 39 N8
Richardson Rd SRTFD E15 * 141 K4
Richardson's Ms FITZ W1T 10 G2
Richard's Pl CHEL SW3 15 P5
WALTH E17 120 F1
Richards Rd COB KT11 218 A10
Richards St HAT AL10 40 A2
Richard Stagg Cl STAL AL1 38 G8
Richard St WCHPL E1 140 A8
Richbell Cl ASHTD KT21 237 J4
Richbell Pl BMSBY WC1N 11 N3
Richborne Ter VX/NE SW8 158 G6
Richborough Cl STMC/STPC BR5 207 N4
Richborough Ct CRAWW RH11 * 283 M7
Richborough Rd CRICK NW2 116 G9
Richens Cl HSLW TW3 154 C8
Riches Rd IL IG1 122 F7
Richfield Rd BUSH WD23 94 C2
Richford Ga HMSMTH W6 * 156 F2
Richford Rd SRTFD E15 141 L3
Richford St HMSMTH W6 156 F1
Richings Pl DTCH/LGLY SL3 151 H2
Richings Wy DTCH/LGLY SL3 151 J2
Richland Av COUL/CHIP CR5 222 B10
Richlands Av EW KT17 220 D1
Richmer Rd ERITH DA8 165 H6
Richmond Av CHING E4 101 J6
EBED/NFELT TW14 174 F2
HGDN/ICK UB10 132 C1
IS N1 5 P5
RYNPK SW20 201 H1
Richmond Br TWK TW1 177 J1
Richmond Buildings
SOHO/SHAV W1D 11 J6
Richmond Cl BH/WHM TN16 243 N5
BORE WD6 76 A9
EPSOM KT18 220 B10
LHD/OX KT22 236 B10
WALTH E17 120 E4
Richmond Ct BROX EN10 44 G6
CRAWE RH10 283 P8
POTB/CUF EN6 * 59 M7
Richmond Crs CHING E4 101 J6
ED N9 99 P2
IS N1 5 P5
SL SL1 129 M10
STA TW18 * 173 J8
Richmond Dr GVE DA12 191 H5
SHPTN TW17 196 E6
WAT WD17 72 F6
WFD IG8 102 D8
Richmond Gdns HDN NW4 116 D3
KTN/HRWW/WS HA3 94 E8
Richmond Gn CROY/NA CR0 202 F10
Richmond Gv IS N1 6 D4
Richmond Hl RCHPK/HAM TW10 177 K2
Richmond Ms SOHO/CST W1F 11 J6
Richmond Pde TWK TW1 * 177 H2
Richmond Park Rd
KUTN/CMB KT2 177 K10
MORT/ESHN SW14 156 A10
Richmond Pl WOOL/PLUM SE18 162 F3
Richmond Rd BAR EN5 77 M9
CHING E4 * 101 J2
COUL/CHIP CR5 240 C1
CROY/NA CR0 202 F10
EA W5 155 K1
EFNCH N2 * 97 M10
FBAR/BDGN N11 98 F7
FSTGT E7 121 N10
GRAYS RM17 167 P5
HACK E8 7 L3
IL IG1 123 H8
ISLW TW7 154 F10
KUTN/CMB KT2 177 J8
POTB/CUF EN6 59 M7
ROM RM1 124 G4
RYNPK SW20 200 E1
SEVS/STOTM N15 119 M4
STA TW18 173 J8
THHTH CR7 203 J4
TWK TW1 176 G3
WAN E11 121 J7
Richmond St PLSTW E13 141 M4
Richmond Ter WHALL SW1A 17 M1
Richmond Vls WALTH E17 * 100 G9
Richmond Wk STALE/WH AL4 39 J2
Richmond Wy LHD/OX KT22 236 A9
RKW/CH/CXG WD3 72 D8
SHB W12 156 G1
WAN E11 121 M7
Richmond Wd ASC SL5 192 G8
Richmount Gdns
BKHTH/KID SE3 161 M9
Rich St POP/IOD E14 140 E9
Rickard Cl BRXS/STRHM SW2 181 H4
HDN NW4 116 E2
WDR/YW UB7 151 M2
Rickards Cl SURB KT6 199 K9
Ricketts Hill Rd BH/WHM TN16 244 B5
Rickett St FUL/PGN SW6 14 F9
Rickfield CRAWW RH11 283 K8
Rickfield Cl HAT AL10 40 D6
Rickford Hl RGUW GU3 249 J2
Rickman Crs ADL/WDHM KT15 195 L10
Rickman Hl COUL/CHIP CR5 240 C3
Rickman Hill Rd COUL/CHIP CR5 240 C4
Rickman's La SLN SL2 129 K1
Rickman St WCHPL E1 140 B6
Rickmansworth La
CFSP/GDCR SL9 90 C6
Rickmansworth Rd
DEN/HRF UB9 91 M9
NTHWD HA6 92 C7
PIN HA5 93 J10
RKW/CH/CXG WD3 71 H7
WATW WD18 72 F8
Rick Roberts Wy SRTFD E15 141 J5
Ricksons La EHSLY KT24 252 C3
Rickthorne Rd ARCH N19 118 F7
Rickwood HORL RH6 280 C3
Rickyard GUW GU2 249 J10
Ridding La GFD/PVL UB6 114 E10
Riddings La HLWS CM18 47 K5
The Riddings CTHM CR3 259 N1
Riddlesdown Av PUR/KEN CR8 223 K8
Riddlesdown Rd PUR/KEN CR8 223 K6
Riddons Rd LEE/GVPK SE12 183 P6
Ride La SHGR GU5 269 N10
Rideout St WOOL/PLUM SE18 162 C3
Rider Cl BFN/LL DA15 185 H2
Riders Wy GDST RH9 260 B7
The Ride BTFD TW8 154 G4
PEND EN3 80 B7
Ridgdale St BOW E3 140 G4
Ridge Av DART DA1 186 G2
WCHMH N21 99 K1
Ridgebank SL SL1 128 E9
Ridgebrook Rd BKHTH/KID SE3 161 P10
ELTH/MOT SE9 162 A9
Ridge Cl BRKHM/BTCW RH3 273 N4
CDALE/KGS NW9 116 A2
HDN NW4 96 G10
THMD SE28 162 G1
WOKS/MYFD GU22 231 N7
Ridge Ct CTHM CR3 241 P4
Ridge Crest ENC/FH EN2 78 G5
Ridgecroft Cl BXLY DA5 186 D4
Ridgefield WAT WD17 72 F3
Ridgegate Cl REIG RH2 257 N8
Ridge Gn REDH RH1 276 F3
Ridge Green Cl REDH RH1 276 F3
Ridge Hl GLDGN NW11 117 H6
Ridgehurst Av GSTN WD25 54 G9
Ridgelands LHD/OX KT22 236 C10
Ridge La WAT WD17 72 F2
Ridge Langley SAND/SEL CR2 223 P6
Ridge Lea HHW HP1 35 J7
Ridgemead Cl STHGT/OAK N14 98 F3
Ridgemead Rd EGH TW20 171 N6
Ridgemont Gdns EDGW HA8 95 P5
Ridgemount GUW GU2 267 N1
WEY KT13 196 F9
Ridgemount Av COUL/CHIP CR5 240 C3
CROY/NA CR0 204 D9
Ridgemount Cl PGE/AN SE20 182 A10
Ridgemount End
CFSP/GDCR SL9 90 B6
Ridgemount Gdns ENC/FH EN2 79 J7
Ridge Mount Rd ASC SL5 192 F8
Ridgemount Wy REDH RH1 275 N2
Ridge Pk PUR/KEN CR8 222 E6
Ridge Rd CEND/HSY/T N8 118 G4
CHEAM SM3 201 J8
CRICK NW2 117 J8
MTCM CR4 180 C10
WCHMH N21 99 L2
Ridgeside CRAWE RH10 284 A7
The Ridges RGUW GU3 267 P5
Ridge St WATN WD24 73 J4
Ridges Yd CROY/NA CR0 203 J10
Ridge Ter WCHMH N21 * 99 K1
The Ridge ASC SL5 * 192 F4
BAR EN5 * 77 J9
BRYLDS KT5 199 M5
BXLY DA5 186 A3
COUL/CHIP CR5 222 F10
CTHM CR3 261 K1
EPSOM KT18 237 P4
LHD/OX KT22 236 C10
ORP BR6 206 G9
PUR/KEN CR8 222 E6
WHTN TW2 176 C3
WOKS/MYFD GU22 232 E3
Ridgeview LCOL/BKTW AL2 57 L4
Ridgeview Cl BAR EN5 76 G10
Ridgeview Rd TRDG/WHET N20 97 L4
Ridge Wy DART DA1 186 G2
FELT TW13 175 M6
IVER SL0 131 H10
RKW/CH/CXG WD3 91 L1
VW GU25 194 B5
Ridgeway BERK HP4 33 L5
GRAYS RM17 168 B3
HAYES BR2 205 M9
HOR/WEW KT19 219 P8
RAD WD7 57 H7
RBRW/HUT CM13 107 N2
RDART DA2 188 D8
TRING HP23 32 A1
WFD IG8 101 P5
WGCE AL7 23 L6
WOT/HER KT12 196 G8
Ridgeway Av EBAR EN4 78 A10
GVE DA12 190 E6
Ridgeway Cl CSHM HP5 50 G4
DORK RH4 272 F4
HHS/BOV HP3 54 A1
WOKN/KNAP GU21 232 A2
Ridgeway Ct REDH RH1 * 275 P1
Ridgeway Crs ORP BR6 207 H10
Ridgeway Crescent Gdns
ORP BR6 207 H9
Ridgeway Dr BMLY BR1 183 N7
DORK RH4 272 F5
Ridgeway East BFN/LL DA15 185 J1
Ridgeway Gdns HGT N6 118 D5
REDBR IG4 122 B3
WOKN/KNAP GU21 232 A1
Ridgeway Rd CSHM HP5 50 G4
DORK RH4 272 F4
ISLW TW7 154 D6
REDH RH1 258 A10
Ridgeway Rd North ISLW TW7 154 D6
Ridgeways HLWE CM17 47 P1
The Ridgeway ACT W3 155 M2
AMSS HP7 69 K6
CDALE/KGS NW9 116 A2
CHING E4 101 H2
CHOB/PIR GU24 230 E6
CROY/NA CR0 202 G10
FBAR/BDGN N11 98 A5
FNCH N3 97 L8
GLDGN NW11 117 J6
GPK RM2 125 H2
GU GU1 268 D1
GVE DA12 191 P10
HARH RM3 105 M9
HERT/WAT SG14 24 G4
HORL RH6 280 B6
KTN/HRWW/WS HA3 115 H4
LHD/OX KT22 218 B10
LHD/OX KT22 236 C9
LTWR GU18 212 A6
MLHL NW7 96 E5
POTB/CUF EN6 60 B3
POTB/CUF EN6 78 A1
RAD WD7 74 E3
RYLN/HDSTN HA2 113 N3
The Ridge Wy SAND/SEL CR2 223 M6
The Ridgeway STALE/WH AL4 38 F2
STALE/WH AL4 39 H3
STAN HA7 95 H7
STHGT/OAK N14 98 F3
WAT WD17 72 F3
Ridgeway West BFN/LL DA15 185 H1
Ridgewell Cl DAGE RM10 144 C3
IS N1 6 F5
SYD SE26 182 E7
Ridgewood HART DA3 211 P2
Ridgmont Rd STAL AL1 38 E7
Ridgmount Gdns GWRST WC1E 11 J3
Ridgmount Rd
WAND/EARL SW18 179 L1
Ridgmount St GWRST WC1E 11 J3
Ridgway RCHPK/HAM TW10 * 177 K2
WIM/MER SW19 178 F10
WOKS/MYFD GU22 233 J1
Ridgway Gdns WIM/MER SW19 178 G10
Ridgway Pl WIM/MER SW19 179 H9
Ridgway Rd BRXN/ST SW9 159 J9
WOKS/MYFD GU22 233 J1
The Ridgway BELMT SM2 221 N4
Ridgwell Rd CAN/RD E16 141 P7
Riding Court Rd DTCH/LGLY SL3 149 P6
Riding Hl SAND/SEL CR2 223 P9
Riding House St GTPST W1W 10 G4
Ridings Av WCHMH N21 79 J8
Ridings Cl HGT N6 118 D5
The Ridings ADL/WDHM KT15 215 H3
AMS HP6 69 J1
ASHTD KT21 237 J3
BH/WHM TN16 244 B3
BRYLDS KT5 199 M5
COB KT11 217 P8
CRAWE RH10 284 F6
CSHM HP5 70 A2
DTCH/LGLY SL3 151 J3
EA W5 135 L6
EBAR EN4 * 97 P1
EHSLY KT24 252 F1
EPSOM KT18 238 B1
EW KT17 220 C5
HERT/WAT SG14 25 H6
KWD/TDW/WH KT20 239 J6
REIG RH2 257 N8
RPLY/SEND GU23 233 K9
SUN TW16 197 H1
WDSR SL4 * 148 B6
The Riding GLDGN NW11 117 J5
WOKN/KNAP GU21 214 E10
Ridlands Gv OXTED RH8 262 B6
Ridlands La OXTED RH8 262 B6
Ridlands Ri OXTED RH8 262 B6
Ridler Rd EN EN1 79 M4
Ridley Av WEA W13 154 G2
Ridley Cl BARK IG11 143 J2
HARH RM3 105 J9
Ridley Rd FSTGT E7 121 P9
HACK E8 119 N10
HAYES BR2 205 L3
WARL CR6 242 B4
WELL DA16 163 L7
WIM/MER SW19 179 L10
WLSDN NW10 136 D4
Ridsdale Rd PGE/AN SE20 204 A1
WOKN/KNAP GU21 231 N3
Riefield Rd ELTH/MOT SE9 162 F10
Riesco Dr CROY/NA CR0 224 B3
Riffel Rd CRICK NW2 116 F10
Riffhams RBRW/HUT CM13 107 N4
Rifle Pl NTGHL W11 136 G10
Rifle Range La HRW HA1 114 E6
Rifle St POP/IOD E14 140 G7
Rigault Rd FUL/PGN SW6 157 J8
Rigby Cl CROY/NA CR0 203 H10
Rigby Gdns CDW/CHF RM16 168 E3
Rigby La HYS/HAR UB3 152 E1
Rigby Ms IL IG1 122 D7
Rigby Pl PEND EN3 80 F3
Rigden St POP/IOD E14 140 G8
Rigeley Rd WLSDN NW10 136 D5
Rigg Ap LEY E10 120 C6
Rigge Pl CLAP SW4 158 E10
Riggindale Rd
STRHM/NOR SW16 180 E8
Right Side STHGT/OAK N14 * 98 E2
Riley Rd PEND EN3 80 B4
STHWK SE1 19 L3
Riley St WBPTN SW10 157 N6
Rillside CRAWE RH10 284 B10
Rinaldo Rd BAL SW12 180 C3
Ring Cl BMLY BR1 183 N10
Ringcroft St HOLWY N7 119 H10
Ringer's Rd BMLY BR1 205 M3
Ringford Rd WAND/EARL SW18 179 J1
Ringlet Cl CAN/RD E16 141 N8
Ringlewell Cl EN EN1 80 A6
Ringley Av HORL RH6 280 B4
Ringley Park Av REIG RH2 275 N1
Ringley Park Rd REIG RH2 257 N10
Ringmer Av FUL/PGN SW6 157 H7
Ringmer Pl WCHMH N21 79 L9
Ringmer Wy BMLY BR1 206 C5
Ringmore Dr RGUE GU4 250 F7
Ringmore Ri FSTH SE23 182 A3
Ringmore Rd WOT/HER KT12 197 K10
Ring Rd North HORL RH6 280 D7
Ring Rd South HORL RH6 280 D8
Ringshall Rd STMC/STPC BR5 207 K3
Ringslade Rd WDGN N22 98 G10
Ringstead Rd CAT SE6 182 G3
SUT SM1 221 N1
Ringway NWDGN UB2 153 M4
Ring Wy FBAR/BDGN N11 98 D7
Ringwold Cl BECK BR3 182 D10
Ringwood Av CROY/NA CR0 202 F7
EFNCH N2 118 A1
HCH RM12 125 L7
ORP BR6 227 M6
REDH RH1 258 A7
Ringwood Cl CRAWE RH10 283 P9
PIN HA5 * 113 K1
Ringwood Gdns PUT/ROE SW15 178 D5
Ringwood Rd WALTH E17 120 E4
Ringwood Wy HPTN TW12 175 P7
WCHMH N21 99 J1
Ripley Av EGH TW20 172 B9
Ripley By-Pass RPLY/SEND GU23 251 H2
Ripley Cl BMLY BR1 206 C5
CROY/NA CR0 225 H3
DTCH/LGLY SL3 150 B3
Ripley Gdns MORT/ESHN SW14 156 A9
Ripley La RPLY/SEND GU23 234 A10
Ripley Ms WAN E11 121 K4
Ripley Rd BELV DA17 164 B3
CAN/RD E16 141 P8
ENC/FH EN2 79 K5
GDMY/SEVK IG3 123 H7
HPTN TW12 175 P10
RPLY/SEND GU23 251 M2
Ripley Vw LOU IG10 82 E4
Ripley Vls EA W5 * 135 H8
Ripley Wy CHESW EN7 62 A6
HHW HP1 35 H5
HOR/WEW KT19 219 M7
Ripon Cl GUW GU2 249 L7
NTHLT UB5 113 P10
Ripon Gdns CHSGTN KT9 219 J2
IL IG1 122 B5
Ripon Rd ED N9 100 A1
TOTM N17 119 L1
WOOL/PLUM SE18 162 E5
Ripon Wy BORE WD6 75 P9
STALE/WH AL4 39 J2
Rippersley Rd WELL DA16 163 K7
Ripple Rd BARK IG11 142 F2
BARK IG11 143 M3
Ripplevale Gv IS N1 5 P4
Rippolson Rd WOOL/PLUM SE18 163 J4
Ripston Rd ASHF TW15 174 E8
Risborough Cl MUSWH N10 * 118 C1
Risborough Dr WPK KT4 200 D7
Risborough St STHWK SE1 18 D1
Risdens HLWS CM18 46 F5
Risdon St BERM/RHTH SE16 160 B1
Risebridge Cha ROM RM1 104 G8
Risebridge Rd GPK RM2 104 G10
Risedale Cl HHS/BOV HP3 35 P9
Risedale Hl HHS/BOV HP3 35 P9
Risedale Rd BXLYHN DA7 164 C9
HHS/BOV HP3 35 P9
Riseldine Rd FSTH SE23 182 D2
Rise Park Bvd ROM RM1 104 G9
Rise Park Pde ROM RM1 104 F10
Rise Rd ASC SL5 192 D6
The Rise AMSS HP7 69 H5
BKHH IG9 102 A2

BORE WD6 75 L9
BXLY DA5 185 M3
CRAWE RH10 284 D7
DART DA1 164 G10
EDGW HA8 95 N6
EHSLY KT24 252 F2
EW KT17 220 C6
GFD/PVL UB6 114 F10
GVE DA12 191 H7
HGDN/ICK UB10 132 A4
KWD/TDW/WH KT20 238 F7
LCOL/BKTW AL2 56 C1
MLHL NW7 96 C7
PLMGR N13 99 H5
SAND/SEL CR2 224 B5
SEV TN13 265 K4
WAN E11 121 M3
WLSDN NW10 116 A8
Riseway BRWN CM15 107 K4
Rising Hill Cl NTHWD HA6 * 92 D7
Risinghill St IS N1 6 A7
Risingholme Cl BUSH WD23 94 A1
KTN/HRWW/WS HA3 94 D9
Risingholme Rd
KTN/HRWW/WS HA3 94 D10
The Risings WALTH E17 121 J2
Risley Av TOTM N17 99 K9
Rita Rd VX/NE SW8 158 F6
Ritches Rd SEVS/STOTM N15 119 K3
Ritchie Rd CROY/NA CR0 204 A6
Ritchie St IS N1 6 B7
Ritchings Av WALTH E17 120 D2
Ritcroft Cl HHS/BOV HP3 36 C7
Ritcroft Dr HHS/BOV HP3 36 C7
Ritcroft St HHS/BOV HP3 36 C7
Ritherdon Rd TOOT SW17 180 B5
Ritson Rd HACK E8 7 N1
Ritter St WOOL/PLUM SE18 162 D5
Ritz Ct POTB/CUF EN6 59 K7
Rivaz Pl HOM E9 140 B1
Rivenhall End WGCE AL7 23 M5
Rivenhall Gdns SWFD E18 121 L2
River Av HOD EN11 44 G2
PLMGR N13 99 J4
THDIT KT7 198 F7
Riverbank DORK RH4 * 272 A2
E/WMO/HCT KT8 198 D3
HHW HP1 35 M2
River Bank THDIT KT7 198 E5
WCHMH N21 99 K1
Riverbank Rd BMLY BR1 183 M6
The Riverbank WDSR SL4 148 G6
Riverbank Wy BTFD TW8 155 H5
River Barge Cl POP/IOD E14 161 H1
River Cl CHES/WCR EN8 62 F10
GU GU1 249 P8
NWDGN UB2 154 B1
RAIN RM13 145 J7
RSLP HA4 112 G4
WAN E11 121 P4
River Ct PUR RM19 165 N3
WOKN/KNAP GU21 214 F10
Rivercourt Rd HMSMTH W6 156 E3
Riverdale Dr WAND/EARL SW18 179 L4
WOKS/MYFD GU22 232 C7
Riverdale Gdns TWK TW1 177 H1
Riverdale Rd BXLY DA5 186 A3
ERITH DA8 164 C4
FELT TW13 175 M7
TWK TW1 177 H2
WOOL/PLUM SE18 163 J4
Riverdene EDGW HA8 95 P5
Riverdene Rd IL IG1 122 D8
River Dr UPMR RM14 126 C4
Riverfield Rd STA TW18 173 J9
River Front EN EN1 79 L7
River Gdns CAR SM5 202 B9
EBED/NFELT TW14 175 J1
River Grove Pk BECK BR3 204 E1
Riverhead Cl WALTH E17 100 C10
Riverhead Dr BELMT SM2 221 L6
Riverhill BGR/WK TN15 265 M7
River Hl COB KT11 235 J1
Riverholme Dr HOR/WEW KT19 220 A5
River Island Cl LHD/OX KT22 236 C6
River La COB KT11 235 M2
LHD/OX KT22 236 D6
RCHPK/HAM TW10 177 J4
Rivermead BF/WBF KT14 216 A9
River Md CRAWW RH11 283 K4
Rivermead E/WMO/HCT KT8 198 B3
KUT/HW KT1 * 199 J5
Rivermead Cl ADL/WDHM KT15 * 215 M4
TEDD TW11 176 G8
Rivermead Rd UED N18 * 100 C6
River Meads WARE SG12 27 H6
River Meads Av WHTN TW2 176 A6
Rivermill HLW CM20 28 F9
River Mt WOT/HER KT12 196 G7
River Mount Gdns GUW GU2 267 P3
Rivernook Cl WOT/HER KT12 197 K5
River Pde SEV TN13 * 246 F8
River Pk HHW HP1 35 K8
River Park Av STA TW18 172 G7
Riverpark Gdns HAYES BR2 183 J10
River Park Rd WDGN N22 98 G10
River Park Vw ORP BR6 207 L7
River Pl IS N1 6 E4
River Reach TEDD TW11 177 H9
River Rd BARK IG11 143 H4
BKHH IG9 102 B2
BRW CM14 106 D5
STA TW18 195 J1
WDSR SL4 * 148 B6
Riversdale GVW DA11 190 B5
Riversdale Rd CRW RM5 104 C8
HBRY N5 119 J8
THDIT KT7 198 F5
Riversdell Cl CHERT KT16 195 J7
Riversend Rd HHS/BOV HP3 35 M9
Riversfield Rd EN EN1 79 M7
Riverside CHARL SE7 161 N2
CHERT KT16 * 195 K2
DORK RH4 255 J10
EYN DA4 209 L9
GU GU1 250 A8
HDN NW4 116 E5
HORL RH6 280 B6
LCOL/BKTW AL2 57 K3
RCH/KEW TW9 * 155 M5
RCH/KEW TW9 177 J1
SHPTN TW17 196 F7
STWL/WRAY TW19 171 P3
SUN TW16 * 197 L2
TWK TW1 176 G4
Riverside Av BROX EN10 44 F8
E/WMO/HCT KT8 198 C5
LTWR GU18 212 B7
Riverside Cl CHOB/PIR GU24 230 E6
CLPT E5 120 B6
HNWL W7 134 D6
KGLGY WD4 54 C5
KUT/HW KT1 199 J4
STA TW18 173 J10
STA TW18 195 J1
STAL AL1 38 D8
STMC/STPC BR5 207 M2
WLGTN SM6 202 C10
Riverside Ct CHING E4 * 80 G10
CSHM HP5 * 51 H9
HLW CM20 29 M5
Riverside Dr CHSWK W4 156 B6
ESH/CLAY KT10 217 P1
GLDGN NW11 * 117 H4
MTCM CR4 201 P5
RCHPK/HAM TW10 176 G6
RKW/CH/CXG WD3 91 N2
SHGR GU5 268 D10
STA TW18 173 H8
Riverside Gdns ALP/SUD HA0 135 K4
BERK HP4 33 M4
ENC/FH EN2 79 K6
HMSMTH W6 156 E4
WOKS/MYFD GU22 232 E7
Riverside Ms BROX EN10 * 44 D9
CROY/NA CR0 * 202 F10
WARE SG12 * 26 C2
Riverside Pl FBAR/BDGN N11 * 98 D4
STWL/WRAY TW19 173 N2
Riverside Rd IL IG1 122 E8
OXHEY WD19 73 J10
SCUP DA14 185 P6
SRTFD E15 141 H4
STA TW18 173 J10
STAL AL1 38 D7
STWL/WRAY TW19 173 N1
TOOT SW17 179 L7
WOT/HER KT12 217 L1
The Riverside E/WMO/HCT KT8 198 C3
Riverside Vls SURB KT6 * 199 H6
Riverside Wk KUT/HW KT1 199 J2
WDSR SL4 149 J6
Riverside Wy DART DA1 187 M1
UX/CGN UB8 131 L3
Riverside Yd TOOT SW17 179 L6
Riversmead HOD EN11 44 F4
Riversmeet HERT/WAT SG14 25 J6
Riverstone Cl RYLN/HDSTN HA2 114 C7
River St CLKNW EC1R 6 A9
WARE SG12 26 D2
WDSR SL4 149 J6
River Ter HMSMTH W6 156 F4
Riverton Cl MV/WKIL W9 2 D10
River Vw ADL/WDHM KT15 * 215 M2
CDW/CHF RM16 168 D4
Riverview GU GU1 * 249 P10
River Vw WGCE AL7 23 H1
Riverview Gdns BARN SW13 156 E5
COB KT11 217 H9
River View Gdns TWK TW1 176 E5
Riverview Gv CHSWK W4 155 N5
Riverview Pk CAT SE6 182 F5
Riverview Rd CHSWK W4 155 N6
HOR/WEW KT19 219 P1
RDART DA2 * 188 F1
Riverview Ter PUR RM19 * 166 A4
River Wk DEN/HRF UB9 111 M10
SUN TW16 197 L2
WOT/HER KT12 197 H6
River Wy GNWCH SE10 161 L2
HLW CM20 29 K6
HOR/WEW KT19 220 A2
LOU IG10 82 D10
Riverway PLMGR N13 99 H6
STA TW18 195 L1
River Wy WHTN TW2 176 A5
River Whf BELV DA17 * 164 E1
Riverwood La CHST BR7 206 G2
Rivett-Drake Cl GUW GU2 249 N6
Rivey Cl BF/WBF KT14 215 J10
Rivington Av WFD IG8 102 A10
Rivington Crs MLHL NW7 96 C8
Rivington Pl FSBYE EC1V 7 K10
Rivington St SDTCH EC2A 7 K10
Rivington Wk HACK E8 7 N5
Rivulet Rd TOTM N17 99 K8
Rixon Cl DTCH/LGLY SL3 130 B8
Rixon St HOLWY N7 119 H8
Rixsen Rd MNPK E12 122 B10
Roach Rd BOW E3 140 F2
Road House Est
WOKS/MYFD GU22 * 232 D6
Roads Pl ARCH N19 118 F7
Roakes Av ADL/WDHM KT15 195 L9
Roan St GNWCH SE10 161 H5
Robarts Cl PIN HA5 113 J3
Robb Rd STAN HA7 94 F7
Robbs Cl HHW HP1 35 K4
Robe End HHW HP1 35 J4
Robert Adam St MHST W1U 10 C5
Roberta St BETH E2 7 N9
Robert Av STAL AL1 38 B10
Robert Cl CHIG IG7 103 J6
MV/WKIL W9 9 K2
POTB/CUF EN6 59 H9
WOT/HER KT12 217 J2
Robert Dashwood Wy
WALW SE17 18 E6
Robert Keen Cl PECK SE15 159 P7
Robert Lowe Cl NWCR SE14 160 C6
Roberton Dr BMLY BR1 205 P2
Robert Rd SLN SL2 109 J7
Robertsbridge Rd CAR SM5 201 M7
Roberts Cl CHEAM SM3 220 G4
CHES/WCR EN8 62 D6
DAGE RM10 144 B1
ELTH/MOT SE9 184 G4
HARH RM3 105 J9
STMC/STPC BR5 207 M5
STWL/WRAY TW19 173 M2
THHTH CR7 203 L3
WDR/YW UB7 131 P10
Roberts Ct CHSGTN KT9 219 J2
PGE/AN SE20 204 B1
WLSDN NW10 136 B1
Roberts House
WOOL/PLUM SE18 * 162 B6
Roberts La CFSP/GDCR SL9 90 D6
Roberts Ms KTBR SW1X * 16 C4
Robertson Cl BROX EN10 62 D2
Robertson Rd BERK HP4 34 A5
SRTFD E15 141 H3
Robertson St VX/NE SW8 158 C9
Robert's Pl CLKNW EC1R * 12 B1
Robert Sq LEW SE13 161 H10
Roberts Rd BELV DA17 164 B4
MLHL NW7 97 H6
WALTH E17 100 G9
WATW WD18 73 K9
Robert St CAMTN NW1 4 F10
CHCR WC2N 11 M8
CROY/NA CR0 203 K10
WOOL/PLUM SE18 162 G4
Roberts Wy EGH TW20 171 P10
HAT AL10 40 C6
Roberts Wood Dr
CFSP/GDCR SL9 90 D6
Robeson St BOW E3 140 E7
Robeson Wy BORE WD6 75 P5
Robina Cl BXLYHS DA6 163 N10
NTHWD HA6 92 G10
Robin Cl ADL/WDHM KT15 215 N2
CRAWW RH11 283 M5
CRW RM5 104 E8
FELT TW13 175 M8
MLHL NW7 96 B4
WARE SG12 27 H8
Robin Gdns REDH RH1 258 B8
Robin Gv BTFD TW8 155 H5
HGT N6 118 B7
KTN/HRWW/WS HA3 115 L4
Robin Hl BERK HP4 33 P6
GODL GU7 267 J10
Robin Hill Dr CHST BR7 184 B9
Robinhood Cl MTCM CR4 202 D4
Robin Hood Cl SL SL1 128 D10
WOKN/KNAP GU21 231 L4
Robin Hood Crs
WOKN/KNAP GU21 231 K3
Robin Hood Dr BUSH WD23 73 N5
KTN/HRWW/WS HA3 94 E8
Robin Hood Gdns POP/IOD E14 * 141 H9
Robin Hood Gn STMC/STPC BR5 207 K5
Robin Hood La BXLYHS DA6 185 P1
HAT AL10 40 D3
Robinhood La MTCM CR4 202 D3
Robin Hood La POP/IOD E14 141 H9
PUT/ROE SW15 178 B7
RGUE GU4 232 C10
SUT SM1 221 K2
Robin Hood Meadow HHNE HP2 36 A1
Robin Hood Rd BRWN CM15 106 G1
PUT/ROE SW15 178 B7
WOKN/KNAP GU21 231 L4
Robin Hood Wy GFD/PVL UB6 134 E1
PUT/ROE SW15 178 B7
Robinia Av GVW DA11 190 A3
Robinia Cl BARK/HLT IG6 103 H7
PGE/AN SE20 203 P1
Robinia Crs LEY E10 120 G7
Robin La HDN NW4 116 G1
Robin Md WGCE AL7 23 K2
Robin Pl GSTN WD25 * 55 J8
Robins Cl LCOL/BKTW AL2 57 K3
UX/CGN UB8 131 M7
Robins Dl WOKN/KNAP GU21 231 H3
Robinsfield HHW HP1 35 K6
Robins Gv WWKM BR4 205 M10
Robin's La EPP CM16 82 F2
Robins Nest Hl HERT/BAY SG13 42 E4
Robinson Av CHESW EN7 61 J4
Robinson Cl ENC/FH EN2 79 K7
HCH RM12 145 J2
WAN E11 121 K8
WOKS/MYFD GU22 232 F6
Robinson Crs BUSH WD23 94 B2
Robinson Rd BETH E2 140 B4
DAGE RM10 124 B9
TOOT SW17 179 P9
Robinson's Cl WEA W13 134 F7
Robinson St CHEL SW3 16 A9
Robins Orch CFSP/GDCR SL9 90 B7
Robins Rd HHS/BOV HP3 36 B8
The Robins BRWN CM15 87 J1
Robins Wy HAT AL10 40 C7
Robinsway WOT/HER KT12 217 K1
Robinswood Cl BEAC HP9 88 B6
Robin Wy GUW GU2 249 N6
POTB/CUF EN6 60 F4
STA TW18 173 J7
STMC/STPC BR5 207 L3
Robin Willis Wy WDSR SL4 171 M2
Robinwood Gv UX/CGN UB8 132 A6
Robinwood Pl PUT/ROE SW15 178 A7
Robsart St BRXN/ST SW9 158 G8
Robson Av WLSDN NW10 136 D3
Robson Cl CFSP/GDCR SL9 90 B6
EHAM E6 142 B8
ENC/FH EN2 79 J6
Robson Rd WNWD SE27 181 K6
Robsons Cl CHES/WCR EN8 62 B5
Robyns Cft GVW DA11 190 B7
Robyns Wy SEV TN13 246 G8
Rocastle Rd BROCKY SE4 182 D1
Roch Av EDGW HA8 95 L10
Rochdale Rd ABYW SE2 163 L4
WALTH E17 120 F5
Rochdale Wy DEPT SE8 160 F6
Rochelle Cl BTSEA SW11 157 N10
Rochelle St BETH E2 7 L10
Rochemont Wk HACK E8 * 7 M6
Roche Rd STRHM/NOR SW16 202 F1
Rochester Av BMLY BR1 205 N2
FELT TW13 174 G5
PLSTW E13 141 P3
Rochester Cl BFN/LL DA15 185 L2
EN EN1 79 M5
STRHM/NOR SW16 * 180 F10
Rochester Dr BXLY DA5 186 B2
GSTN WD25 * 73 K1
PIN HA5 113 L3
Rochester Gdns CROY/NA CR0 203 M10
CTHM CR3 241 M8
IL IG1 122 C5
Rochester Ms CAMTN NW1 5 H3
EA W5 * 155 H3
Rochester Pde FELT TW13 * 175 H6
Rochester Pl CAMTN NW1 4 G2
Rochester Rd CAMTN NW1 4 G2
CAR SM5 222 A1
DART DA1 187 P3
EGH TW20 172 G9
GVE DA12 191 H3
HCH RM12 145 J2
NTHWD HA6 112 G1
Rochester Rw WEST SW1P 17 H5
Rochester Sq CAMTN NW1 5 H3
Rochester St WEST SW1P 17 J4
Rochester Ter CAMTN NW1 4 G2
Rochester Wk STHWK SE1 * 12 G9
Rochester Wy BKHTH/KID SE3 161 N7
DART DA1 186 F3
RKW/CH/CXG WD3 72 C8
Rochester Wy Relief Rd
ELTH/MOT SE9 162 E10
Roche Wk CAR SM5 201 N6
Rochford Av BRWN CM15 87 M9
CHDH RM6 123 M3
WAB EN9 63 J10
Rochford Cl BROX EN10 62 D2
EHAM E6 142 A4
HCH RM12 145 J1
Rochford Gn LOU IG10 82 F7
Rochfords Gdns SLN SL2 129 P10
Rochford Wk HACK E8 * 7 P4
Rochford Wy CROY/NA CR0 202 F6
Rockall Ct DTCH/LGLY SL3 150 E2
Rock Av MORT/ESHN SW14 156 A9
Rockbourne Ms FSTH SE23 182 C4
Rockbourne Rd FSTH SE23 182 C4
Rockchase Gdns EMPK RM11 125 M4
Rockcliffe Av KGLGY WD4 54 C6
Rock Cl MTCM CR4 201 N2
Rockdale Gdns SEV TN13 * 265 J1
Rockdale Pleasance SEV TN13 * 265 K1
Rockdale Rd SEV TN13 265 J2
Rockell's Pl EDUL SE22 182 A2
Rockfield Cl OXTED RH8 261 L7
Rockfield Rd OXTED RH8 261 L6
Rockford Av GFD/PVL UB6 134 G4
Rock Grove Wy
BERM/RHTH SE16 19 P5
BERM/RHTH SE16 159 P3
Rockhall Rd CRICK NW2 116 G10
Rockhampton Rd SAND/SEL CR2 223 M3
STRHM/NOR SW16 181 H7
Rock Hl DUL SE21 181 N7
ORP BR6 228 C3
Rockingham Av EMPK RM11 125 J4
Rockingham Cl PUT/ROE SW15 156 C10
UX/CGN UB8 * 131 M3
Rockingham Ga BUSH WD23 74 C10
Rockingham Pde UX/CGN UB8 131 M2
Rockingham Rd UX/CGN UB8 131 M3
Rockingham St STHWK SE1 18 E4
Rockland Rd PUT/ROE SW15 157 H10
Rocklands Dr
KTN/HRWW/WS HA3 94 G10
Rockleigh HERT/WAT SG14 25 K5
Rockleigh Ct BRWN CM15 107 M1
Rockley Rd SHB W12 156 G1
Rockmount Rd NRWD SE19 181 L9
WOOL/PLUM SE18 163 J4
Rockshaw Rd REDH RH1 258 D3
Rocks La BARN SW13 156 D9
Rock St FSBYPK N4 119 J7
Rockware Av GFD/PVL UB6 134 D3
Rockways BAR EN5 76 C10
Rockwell Gdns NRWD SE19 181 M7
Rockwell Rd DAGE RM10 124 C10
Rockwood Gdns LOU IG10 82 F7
Rocky La REDH RH1 258 B5
Rocliffe St IS N1 6 D8
Rocombe Crs FSTH SE23 * 182 B3
Rocque La BKHTH/KID SE3 161 L9
Rodborough Rd GLDGN NW11 117 K6
Roden Cl HLWE CM17 30 A7
Roden Gdns CROY/NA CR0 203 M6
Rodenhurst Rd CLAP SW4 180 D3
Roden St HOLWY N7 118 G8
IL IG1 122 D8
Rodeo Cl ERITH DA8 165 J7
Roderick Rd HAMP NW3 118 A9
Rodgers Cl BORE WD6 75 J10
Roding Dr BRWN CM15 86 E3
Roding Gdns LOU IG10 82 B10
Roding La BKHH IG9 102 B2
Roding La North WFD IG8 102 B10
Roding La South REDBR IG4 122 A3
Roding Ms WAP E1W 13 P9
Roding Rd CLPT E5 120 C9
EHAM E6 142 E7
LOU IG10 82 C9
Rodings Rw BAR EN5 * 77 H8
The Rodings UPMR RM14 126 C5
Roding Vw BKHH IG9 102 A2
Roding Wy RAIN RM13 145 L4
Rodmarton St MHST W1U 10 B4
Rodmell Cl YEAD UB4 133 M6
Rodmell Slope
NFNCH/WDSPK N12 97 J6
Rodmere St GNWCH SE10 161 K4
Rodmill La BRXS/STRHM SW2 180 F3
Rodney Av STAL AL1 38 F8
Rodney Cl CROY/NA CR0 203 J8
NWMAL KT3 200 B5
PIN HA5 113 M5
WOT/HER KT12 * 197 K8
Rodney Crs HOD EN11 44 F1
Rodney Gdns PIN HA5 113 K3
WWKM BR4 225 M1
Rodney Pl STHWK SE1 18 F5
WALTH E17 100 D10
WIM/MER SW19 201 M1
Rodney Rd CHONG CM5 67 N5
MTCM CR4 201 P2
NWMAL KT3 200 B5
WALW SE17 18 F6
WAN E11 121 N2
WHTN TW2 175 P3
WOT/HER KT12 197 K9
Rodney St IS N1 5 P7
Rodney Wy DTCH/LGLY SL3 151 H7
GU GU1 250 D9
ROMW/RG RM7 104 C9
Rodona Rd WEY KT13 216 E7
Rodway Rd BMLY BR1 205 N1
PUT/ROE SW15 178 D3
Rodwell Cl RSLP HA4 * 113 K6
Rodwell Rd EDUL SE22 181 N2
Roebuck Cl ASHTD KT21 237 K6
FELT TW13 175 J7
HERT/BAY SG13 25 P5
REIG RH2 257 K10
Roebuck Gn SL SL1 128 D10
Roebuck La BKHH IG9 101 P2
Roebuck Rd BARK/HLT IG6 103 L7
CHSGTN KT9 219 M2
Roedean Av PEND EN3 80 B5
Roedean Cl ORP BR6 227 L1
PEND EN3 80 B5
Roedean Crs PUT/ROE SW15 178 B2
Roe End CDALE/KGS NW9 115 P2
Roefields Cl HHS/BOV HP3 35 K10
Roe Gn CDALE/KGS NW9 115 P3
Roe Green Centre HAT AL10 * 40 C5
Roe Green Cl HAT AL10 40 B5
Roe Green La HAT AL10 40 C4
Roehampton Cl GVE DA12 191 H3
PUT/ROE SW15 156 D10
Roehampton Dr CHST BR7 184 F9
Roehampton Ga PUT/ROE SW15 178 B2
Roehampton High St
PUT/ROE SW15 178 D3
Roehampton La PUT/ROE SW15 178 D1
Roehampton V PUT/ROE SW15 178 C6
Roe Hill Cl HAT AL10 40 C5
Roehyde Wy HAT AL10 40 B7
Roe La CDALE/KGS NW9 115 N2
Roe Rd WLGTN SM6 222 F3
Roestock Gdns STALE/WH AL4 40 B8
Roestock La STALE/WH AL4 40 A9
Rofant Rd NTHWD HA6 92 F7
Roffe's La CTHM CR3 241 L10
Roffey Cl HORL RH6 280 A4
PUR/KEN CR8 241 J2
Roffey's Cl CRAWE RH10 285 H1
Roffey St POP/IOD E14 161 H1
Roffords WOKN/KNAP GU21 231 N3
Rogers Cl CHESW EN7 61 L3
COUL/CHIP CR5 241 J4
Rogers Ct SWLY BR8 209 H4
Rogers Gdns DAGE RM10 124 B10
Rogers La SLN SL2 129 L3
WARL CR6 242 E4
Rogers Md GDST RH9 260 A8
Rogers Rd CAN/RD E16 141 L8
DAGE RM10 124 B10
GRAYS RM17 167 P3
TOOT SW17 179 N7
Rogers Ruff NTHWD HA6 92 D9
Roger St BMSBY WC1N 11 P2
Rogers Wk NFNCH/WDSPK N12 97 L4
Rojack Rd FSTH SE23 182 C4
Rokeby Gdns WFD IG8 101 M9
Rokeby Pl RYNPK SW20 178 E10
Rokeby Rd BROCKY SE4 * 160 E8
Rokeby St SRTFD E15 141 K3
Roke Cl PUR/KEN CR8 223 K10
Roke Lodge Rd PUR/KEN CR8 223 J9
Roke Rd PUR/KEN CR8 223 J10
Roker Park Av HGDN/ICK UB10 111 P9
Rokers La MFD/CHID GU8 266 C10
Rokesby Cl WELL DA16 162 G8
Rokesby Pl ALP/SUD HA0 115 J10
Rokesby Rd SLN SL2 128 E5
Rokesly Av CEND/HSY/T N8 118 F3
Rokewood Ms WARE SG12 26 C1
Roland Gdns SKENS SW7 15 K7
Roland Ms WCHPL E1 * 140 C7
Roland Rd WALTH E17 121 J2
Roland St STAL AL1 38 F6
Roland Wy SKENS SW7 15 K7
WALW SE17 19 H8
WPK KT4 200 C9
Roles Gv CHDH RM6 123 N2
Rolfe Cl BEAC HP9 88 D10
EBAR EN4 77 P8
Rolinsden Wy HAYES BR2 226 A1
Rollesby Rd CHSGTN KT9 219 M3
Rollesby Wy THMD SE28 143 M9
Rolleston Av STMC/STPC BR5 206 E6
Rolleston Cl STMC/STPC BR5 206 E7
Rolleston Rd SAND/SEL CR2 223 L4
Roll Gdns GNTH/NBYPK IG2 122 D3
Rollins St PECK SE15 160 B5
Rollit Crs HSLW TW3 175 P1
Rollit St HOLWY N7 119 H10
Rollo Rd SWLY BR8 186 G10
Rolls Buildings FLST/FETLN EC4A 12 A5
Rollscourt Av HNHL SE24 181 K1
Rolls Park Av CHING E4 100 G6
Rolls Park Rd CHING E4 100 G6
Rolls Rd STHWK SE1 19 M7
Rolls Royce Cl WLGTN SM6 222 F4
Rollswood WGCE AL7 23 H8
Rolt St NWCR SE14 160 D5
Rolvenden Gdns BMLY BR1 206 A1
Rolvenden Pl TOTM N17 99 P9
Romana Ct STA TW18 * 173 K7
Roman Cl ACT W3 155 N1
DEN/HRF UB9 91 K9
EBED/NFELT TW14 175 K1
RAIN RM13 144 E4
Roman Farm Rd GUW GU2 249 J9
Roman Farm Wy GUW GU2 249 J9
Romanfield Rd
BRXS/STRHM SW2 180 G3
Roman Gdns KGLGY WD4 54 C6
Romanhurst Av HAYES BR2 205 K4
Romanhurst Gdns HAYES BR2 205 K4
Roman Rd BORE WD6 75 J10
CAR SM5 222 A5
Roman Ri NRWD SE19 181 L9
SBW CM21 29 N1
Roman Rd BETH E2 140 C4
BRW CM14 106 C6
CHSWK W4 156 B3
CRICK NW2 116 F8
DORK RH4 272 F4
EHAM E6 142 B6
GVW DA11 189 P6
IL IG1 142 E1
MUSWH N10 98 C8
RAD WD7 74 F1
RDART DA2 188 G5
Romans End STALW/RED AL3 38 B8
Roman Sq THMD SE28 143 K10
Roman St HOD EN11 44 F2
Romans Wy WOKS/MYFD GU22 233 K1
Roman V HLWE CM17 29 M6
Roman Villa Rd EYN DA4 188 B9
Roman Wk RAD WD7 * 74 E2
Roman Wy CROY/NA CR0 203 J9
DART DA1 186 F1
EN EN1 79 N9
HOLWY N7 5 N1
WAB EN9 80 G1
Romany Ct HHNE HP2 36 D5
Romany Gdns CHEAM SM3 201 K7
Romany Ri STMC/STPC BR5 206 F8
Roma Rd WALTH E17 120 D1
Romberg Rd TOOT SW17 180 B6
Romborough Gdns LEW SE13 183 H1
Romborough Wy LEW SE13 183 H1
Rom Crs ROMW/RG RM7 124 F5
Romeland BORE WD6 75 J10
STALW/RED AL3 38 B6
WAB EN9 63 H9
Romeland Hl STALW/RED AL3 38 B6
Romero Cl BRXN/ST SW9 158 G9
Romero Sq BKHTH/KID SE3 161 P10
Romeyn Rd STRHM/NOR SW16 180 G6
Romford Rd CHIG IG7 103 L5
CHONG CM5 67 M9
CRW RM5 103 P8
MNPK E12 122 D8
SOCK/AV RM15 146 B5
SRTFD E15 141 L1
Romford St WCHPL E1 13 P4
Romilly Dr OXHEY WD19 93 M5
Romilly Rd FSBYPK N4 119 J7
Romilly St SOHO/SHAV W1D 11 K7
Rommany Rd WNWD SE27 181 L7
Romney Cha EMPK RM11 125 N4
Romney Cl ASHF TW15 174 D8
CHSGTN KT9 219 K1
GLDGN NW11 117 M6
NWCR SE14 160 B6
RYLN/HDSTN HA2 113 P5
TOTM N17 100 A9
Romney Dr BMLY BR1 184 A10
RYLN/HDSTN HA2 113 P5
Romney Gdns BXLYHN DA7 164 A7
Romney Lock Rd WDSR SL4 149 J6
Romney Rd GNWCH SE10 161 H5
GVW DA11 190 B6
NWMAL KT3 200 A6
WOOL/PLUM SE18 162 F2
YEAD UB4 132 E4
Romney Rw CRICK NW2 * 116 G7
Romney St BGR/WK TN15 229 P8
WEST SW1P 17 K4
Romola Rd HNHL SE24 181 J4
Romsey Cl DTCH/LGLY SL3 150 C2
ORP BR6 226 F1
Romsey Dr SLN SL2 109 J9
Romsey Rd DAGW RM9 143 N3
WEA W13 * 134 F9
Romside Pl ROMW/RG RM7 124 E2
Rom Valley Wy ROMW/RG RM7 124 F4
Rona Cl CRAWW RH11 283 L10
Ronald Av SRTFD E15 141 K5
Ronald Cl BECK BR3 204 E5
Ronald Rd BEAC HP9 88 E9
HARH RM3 105 P9
Ronaldsay Sp SL SL1 129 K7
Ronalds Rd BMLY BR1 205 M1
HBRY N5 119 J10
Ronaldstone Rd BFN/LL DA15 185 H2
Rona Rd HAMP NW3 118 B9
Ronart St KTN/HRWW/WS HA3 114 E1
Rona Wk IS N1 * 6 G2
Rondu Rd CRICK NW2 117 H10
Ronelean Rd SURB KT6 199 L10
Roneo Cnr HCH RM12 124 G6
Roneo Link HCH RM12 124 G6
Ronfearn Av STMC/STPC BR5 207 N5
Ron Green Ct ERITH DA8 164 E4
Ron Leighton Wy EHAM E6 142 B3
Ronneby Cl WEY KT13 196 F10
Ronnie La BCTR RM8 123 M7
Ronsons Wy STALE/WH AL4 38 E2
Ronson Wy LHD/OX KT22 236 F7
Ronver Rd LEE/GVPK SE12 183 M4
Rood La FENCHST EC3M 13 J7
Rookby Ct WCHMH N21 99 J3
Rook Cl RAIN RM13 145 H2
WBLY HA9 115 N8
Rookeries Cl FELT TW13 175 J6
Rookery Cl LHD/OX KT22 236 D10
Rookery Ct WTHK RM20 * 166 F5
Rookery Dr CHST BR7 206 D1
DORK RH4 271 P4
Rookery Gdns STMC/STPC BR5 207 M5
Rookery Hl ASHTD KT21 237 M4
REDH RH1 281 J1
Rookery La HAYES BR2 206 A6
Rookery Md COUL/CHIP CR5 240 E8
Rookery Rd CLAP SW4 158 D10
ORP BR6 226 C6
STA TW18 173 L8
The Rookery
STRHM/NOR SW16 * 180 G9
WTHK RM20 166 F5
Rookery Vw GRAYS RM17 168 A4
Rookery Wy CDALE/KGS NW9 116 C3
KWD/TDW/WH KT20 257 J3
Rookesley Rd STMC/STPC BR5 207 N7
Rookfield Av MUSWH N10 118 D2
Rookfield Cl MUSWH N10 118 D2
Rook La CTHM CR3 241 H10
Rookley Cl BELMT SM2 221 L6
Rooks Cl WGCW AL8 22 G6
Rooks Hl RKW/CH/CXG WD3 71 M8
WGCW AL8 22 F6
Rooksmead Rd SUN TW16 196 G2
Rooks Ter WDR/YW UB7 * 151 P1
Rookstone Rd TOOT SW17 180 A8
Rookwood Av LOU IG10 82 F7
NWMAL KT3 200 D4
WLGTN SM6 222 E1
Rookwood Cl GRAYS RM17 167 N4
REDH RH1 258 C5
Rookwood Ct GUW GU2 267 P3
Rookwood Gdns CHING E4 * 101 L3
Rookwood Rd STNW/STAM N16 119 N4
Roosevelt Wy DAGE RM10 144 E1
Rootes Dr NKENS W10 136 G6
Roothill La BRKHM/BTCW RH3 273 M6
Ropemaker Rd
BERM/RHTH SE16 160 D1
Ropemaker's Flds
POP/IOD E14 * 140 E9
Ropemaker St BARB EC2Y 12 G3
Roper La STHWK SE1 19 K2
Ropers Av CHING E4 101 H6
Roper St ELTH/MOT SE9 184 C1
Roper Wy MTCM CR4 202 B2
Ropery St BOW E3 140 E6
Rope St BERM/RHTH SE16 160 D2
Ropewalk Gdns WCHPL E1 * 13 P5
Rope Yard Rails
WOOL/PLUM SE18 162 E2
Ropley St BETH E2 7 N8
Rosa Alba Ms HBRY N5 119 K9
Rosa Av ASHF TW15 174 B7
Rosalind Franklin Cl GUW GU2 267 K1
Rosaline Rd FUL/PGN SW6 157 H6
Rosaline Ter FUL/PGN SW6 * 157 H6
Rosamond St SYD SE26 182 A6
Rosamond Vls
MORT/ESHN SW14 * 156 A10
Rosamund Cl SAND/SEL CR2 223 L1
Rosamund Rd CRAWE RH10 284 C10
Rosamun Rd NWDGN UB2 153 M3
Rosary Cl HSLW TW3 153 M8
Rosary Ct POTB/CUF EN6 59 L6
Rosary Gdns ASHF TW15 174 C7
BUSH WD23 94 D1
SKENS SW7 15 K7
Rosary Ga BTSEA SW11 158 C6
Rosaville Rd FUL/PGN SW6 157 J6
Roscoe St STLK EC1Y 12 F2
Roscoff Cl EDGW HA8 95 N9
Roseacre OXTED RH8 261 M9
Roseacre Cl EMPK RM11 125 N6
SHPTN TW17 196 B5
WEA W13 134 G7
Roseacre Gdns RGUE GU4 269 J6
WGCE AL7 23 M5
Roseacre Rd WELL DA16 163 L9
Rose Aly LVPST EC2M 13 K4
STHWK SE1 12 F9
Roseary Cl WDR/YW UB7 151 N3
Rose Av GVE DA12 191 H4
MRDN SM4 201 M5
MTCM CR4 202 A1
SWFD E18 101 N10
Rose Bank BRW CM14 107 J4
Rosebank EPSOM KT18 219 P10
PGE/AN SE20 182 A10
WAB EN9 63 K10
Rosebank Av ALP/SUD HA0 114 E9
HCH RM12 125 K10
Rose Bank Cl
NFNCH/WDSPK N12 97 P6
Rosebank Cl TEDD TW11 176 F9
Rosebank Cottages REIG RH2 * 275 L2
Rosebank Est BOW E3 140 E4
Rosebank Gdns ACT W3 * 136 A8
BOW E3 140 E4
GVW DA11 190 B4
Rosebank Gv WALTH E17 120 E1
Rosebank Rd HNWL W7 154 D1
WALTH E17 120 F4
Rosebank Wk CAMTN NW1 5 K4
Rosebank Wy ACT W3 136 A8
Roseberry Cl UPMR RM14 126 E4
Roseberry Ct WAT WD17 73 H5
Roseberry Gdns DART DA1 187 K3
FSBYPK N4 119 J4
ORP BR6 207 H10
UPMR RM14 126 E5
Roseberry Pl HACK E8 7 L2
Roseberry St BERM/RHTH SE16 160 A3
Rosebery Av BFN/LL DA15 185 H3
CLKNW EC1R 12 A2
EW KT17 220 B10
MNPK E12 142 B1
NWMAL KT3 200 C2
RYLN/HDSTN HA2 113 M9
THHTH CR7 203 K2
TOTM N17 99 P10
Rosebery Cl MRDN SM4 200 G6
Rosebery Ct CLKNW EC1R 12 A1
GVW DA11 190 C4
Rosebery Crs WOKS/MYFD GU22 232 C6
Rosebery Gdns
CEND/HSY/T N8 * 118 F3
SUT SM1 221 L1
WEA W13 134 F8
Rosebery Ms MUSWH N10 98 D10
Rosebery Pde EW KT17 * 220 C4
Rosebery Rd BRXS/STRHM SW2 180 F2
BUSH WD23 94 A2
EPSOM KT18 238 A5
GRAYS RM17 167 K5
HSLW TW3 176 B1
KUT/HW KT1 199 N2
MUSWH N10 98 D10
SUT SM1 221 J3
Rosebine Av WHTN TW2 176 C3
Rosebriar Cl WOKS/MYFD GU22 233 K2
Rosebriars CTHM CR3 241 M6
ESH/CLAY KT10 218 B2
Rosebriar Wk WATN WD24 72 G2
Rosebury Dr CHOB/PIR GU24 230 F1
Rosebury Rd FUL/PGN SW6 157 L8
Rosebury Sq WFD IG8 102 D8
Rosebury V RSLP HA4 113 H7
Rose Bushes EW KT17 238 F2
Rose Cottages HAYES BR2 * 225 P7
Rose Ct AMS HP6 69 K3
CHESW EN7 61 P3
WCHPL E1 13 L4
Rosecourt Rd CROY/NA CR0 202 G6
Rosecroft Av HAMP NW3 117 K8
Rosecroft Cl BH/WHM TN16 244 C4
STMC/STPC BR5 207 M6
Rosecroft Ct NTHWD HA6 * 92 D7
Rosecroft Dr WAT WD17 72 F3
Rose Croft Gdns CRICK NW2 116 D8
Rosecroft Gdns WHTN TW2 176 C4
Rosecroft Rd STHL UB1 133 P6
Rosecroft Wk ALP/SUD HA0 115 J10
PIN HA5 113 L3
Rose & Crown Yd STJS SW1Y * 11 H10
Rosedale ASHTD KT21 237 H4
Rose Dl ORP BR6 206 E9
Rosedale WGCE AL7 23 J1
Rosedale Av CHESW EN7 61 N5
HYS/HAR UB3 132 E7
Rosedale Cl ABYW SE2 163 L2
CRAWW RH11 283 K9
HNWL W7 154 E1
LCOL/BKTW AL2 55 M6
RDART DA2 188 A3
STAN HA7 94 G7
Rosedale Dr DAGW RM9 143 L3
Rosedale Gdns DAGW RM9 143 L2
Rosedale Pl CROY/NA CR0 204 C7
Rosedale Rd DAGW RM9 143 L2
EW KT17 220 D2
FSTGT E7 121 P10
GRAYS RM17 168 A4
RCH/KEW TW9 155 K10
ROM RM1 124 D1
Rosedale Wy CHESW EN7 61 P4
Rosedene Av CROY/NA CR0 202 F7
GFD/PVL UB6 133 P5
MRDN SM4 201 K5
STRHM/NOR SW16 180 G6
Rosedene Cl DART DA1 187 K3
Rosedene Gdns
GNTH/NBYPK IG2 122 D2
Rosedene Ter LEY E10 120 G7
Rosedew Rd HMSMTH W6 156 G5
Rose Dr CSHM HP5 51 J8
Rose End WPK KT4 200 G8
Rosefield POP/IOD E14 140 F9
SEV TN13 247 H10
Rosefield Cl CAR SM5 221 P2
Rosefield Gdns CHERT KT16 214 G3
POP/IOD E14 140 F9
Rosefield Rd STA TW18 173 K7
Rose Garden Cl EDGW HA8 95 K7
Rose Gdns EA W5 155 J2
FELT TW13 175 H5
STHL UB1 133 P6
STWL/WRAY TW19 173 N3
WATW WD18 73 H9
Rose Gln CDALE/KGS NW9 116 A2
ROMW/RG RM7 124 F6
Rosehart Ms NTGHL W11 8 E6
Rosehatch Av CHDH RM6 123 N1
Roseheath HHW HP1 35 H5
Roseheath Rd HSLWW TW4 175 N1
Rosehill BERK HP4 33 N5
Rose Hl DORK RH4 272 F3
Rosehill ESH/CLAY KT10 218 F3
HPTN TW12 197 P1
Rose Hl SUT SM1 201 L9
Rose Hill Arch Ms DORK RH4 * 272 F2
Rosehill Av SUT SM1 201 M8
WOKN/KNAP GU21 231 P2
Rosehill Cl HOD EN11 44 E3
Rosehill Court Pde MRDN SM4 * 201 M7
Rosehill Farm Meadow
BNSTD SM7 239 L1
Rosehill Gdns ABLGY WD5 54 E8
GFD/PVL UB6 114 E10
SUT SM1 201 L9
Rose Hill Pk West SUT SM1 201 M9
Rosehill Rd BH/WHM TN16 243 P3
WAND/EARL SW18 179 M2
Roseland Cl TOTM N17 99 L8
Roselands Av HOD EN11 44 E1
Rose La CHDH RM6 123 P2
RPLY/SEND GU23 233 N8

STALE/WH AL4 21 H1
Rose Lawn BUSH WD23 94 B2
Roseleigh Av HBRY N5 119 J9
Roseleigh Cl TWK TW1 177 J2
Rosemary Av E/WMO/HCT KT8 197 P3
ED N9 100 A2
ENC/FH EN2 79 L5
FNCH N3 97 L10
HSLWW TW4 153 L8
ROM RM1 124 G1
Rosemary Cl CROY/NA CR0 202 F7
OXTED RH8 261 M9
SOCK/AV RM15 147 H5
UX/CGN UB8 * 132 B7
Rosemary Ct HORL RH6 * 279 P3
Rosemary Crs RGUW GU3 249 L6
Rosemary Dr LCOL/BKTW AL2 56 F2
POP/IOD E14 141 J8
REDBR IG4 122 A3
Rosemary Gdns BCTR RM8 124 A6
CHSGTN KT9 219 K1
Rosemary La EGH TW20 194 E3
HORL RH6 279 H8
HORL RH6 280 C5
MORT/ESHN SW14 155 P9
Rosemary Rd PECK SE15 159 N6
TOOT SW17 179 L6
WELL DA16 163 J7
Rosemary St IS N1 6 G5
Rosemead CDALE/KGS NW9 116 C5
CHERT KT16 195 L7
Rose Md POTB/CUF EN6 59 M6
Rosemead Av FELT TW13 174 G5
MTCM CR4 202 D3
WBLY HA9 115 K10
Rosemead Cl REDH RH1 275 N2
Rose Meadow CHOB/PIR GU24 212 F9
Rose Ms UED N18 100 A5
Rosemont Av
NFNCH/WDSPK N12 97 M7
Rosemont Rd ACT W3 135 N9
HAMP NW3 3 J1
NWMAL KT3 199 P3
RCHPK/HAM TW10 177 K2
Rosemoor Cl WGCE AL7 23 J6
Rosemoor St CHEL SW3 16 A6
Rosemount HLWW/ROY CM19 46 E4
Rosemount Av BF/WBF KT14 215 K9
Rosemount Cl WFD IG8 102 C7
Rosemount Dr BMLY BR1 206 C4
Rosemount Rd ALP/SUD HA0 135 K3
WEA W13 134 F8
Rosenau Crs BTSEA SW11 158 A7
Rosenau Rd BTSEA SW11 157 P7
Rosendale Rd DUL SE21 181 K4
Roseneath Av WCHMH N21 99 J2
Roseneath Ct CTHM CR3 * 259 P1
Roseneath Pl
STRHM/NOR SW16 181 H7
Roseneath Rd BTSEA SW11 180 B2
Roseneath Wk EN EN1 79 M8
Rosenheath Cl ORP BR6 227 M5
Rosens Wk EDGW HA8 95 N4
Rosenthal Rd CAT SE6 182 G2
Rosenthorpe Rd PECK SE15 182 C1
Rose Park Cl YEAD UB4 133 K7
Roserton St POP/IOD E14 161 H1
The Rosery CROY/NA CR0 204 C6
Roses Cottages DORK RH4 * 272 F2
Roses La WDSR SL4 148 D8
The Roses WFD IG8 * 101 L8
Rose St COVGDN WC2E 11 L7
GVW DA11 189 N2
Rosethorn Cl BAL SW12 180 D3
Rosetrees GU GU1 268 D1
Rosetta Cl VX/NE SW8 158 F6
Rose V HOD EN11 44 F3
Rose Va BRW CM14 107 H4
Roseveare Rd LEE/GVPK SE12 183 P7
Rose Vw ADL/WDHM KT15 * 215 M2
Roseville Av HSLW TW3 175 P1
Roseville Rd HYS/HAR UB3 153 H4
Rosevine Rd RYNPK SW20 200 F1
Rose Wk BRYLDS KT5 199 N5
CRAWW RH11 * 283 L9
SLN SL2 128 G7
STALE/WH AL4 38 G4
WWKM BR4 205 J9
The Rose Wk RAD WD7 74 G3
Rosewarne Cl
WOKN/KNAP GU21 231 M4
Roseway DUL SE21 181 L2
EDGW HA8 95 P5
Rose Wy LEE/GVPK SE12 183 M1
Rosewell Cl PGE/AN SE20 182 A10
Rosewood RDART DA2 186 F7
Rose Wd WOKS/MYFD GU22 232 D5
Rosewood Av GFD/PVL UB6 114 F10
HCH RM12 125 H10
Rosewood Cl SCUP DA14 185 M6
SOCK/AV RM15 147 K5
Rosewood Ct HHW HP1 * 35 H5
KUTN/CMB KT2 177 M10
Rosewood Dr ENC/FH EN2 79 J1
SHPTN TW17 196 A5
Rosewood Gv SUT SM1 201 M9
Rosewood Ter PGE/AN SE20 * 182 B10
Rosewood Wy CHOB/PIR GU24 212 D9
SLN SL2 109 H10
Rosher Cl SRTFD E15 141 J2
Rosherville Wy GVW DA11 190 B3
Rosina St HOM E9 140 C1
Roskell Rd PUT/ROE SW15 156 G9
Rosken Gv SLN SL2 128 G4
Roslin Rd ACT W3 155 N2
Roslin Wy BMLY BR1 183 M8
Roslyn Cl BROX EN10 44 D7
MTCM CR4 201 N2
Roslyn Gdns GPK RM2 104 G10
Roslyn Ms SEVS/STOTM N15 * 119 M3
Roslyn Rd SEVS/STOTM N15 119 L3
Rosmead Rd NTGHL W11 8 B7
Rosoman Pl CLKNW EC1R 12 B1
Rosoman St CLKNW EC1R 6 B10
Rossall Cl EMPK RM11 125 H4
Rossall Crs WLSDN NW10 135 L5
Ross Av BCTR RM8 124 A7
MLHL NW7 97 H6
Ross Cl CRAWE RH10 284 A10
HYS/HAR UB3 152 E3
KTN/HRWW/WS HA3 94 B8
NTHLT UB5 114 C9
Ross Crs GSTN WD25 73 H1
Rossdale SUT SM1 221 P2
Rossdale Dr CDALE/KGS NW9 115 P6
ED N9 80 B10
Rossdale Rd PUT/ROE SW15 156 F10
Rosse Ms BKHTH/KID SE3 161 N7
Rossendale Cl ENC/FH EN2 79 J3
Rossendale St CLPT E5 120 A7
Rossendale Wy CAMTN NW1 5 H4
Rossetti Gdns COUL/CHIP CR5 240 G3
Rossetti Rd BERM/RHTH SE16 160 A4
Ross House CHARL SE7 * 162 B6
Rossignol Gdns CAR SM5 202 B9
Rossindel Rd HSLW TW3 175 P1
Rossington Av BORE WD6 75 K4
Rossington Cl EN EN1 80 A4
Rossington St CLPT E5 119 P7
Rossiter Cl DTCH/LGLY SL3 150 B3
Rossiter Flds BAR EN5 77 J10
Rossiter Ldg GU GU1 * 268 D1
Rossiter Rd BAL SW12 180 C4
Rossland Cl BXLYHS DA6 186 B1
Rosslare Cl BH/WHM TN16 262 G2
Rosslyn Av BARN SW13 156 B9
BCTR RM8 124 A5
CHING E4 101 L3
EBAR EN4 77 P10
EBED/NFELT TW14 175 H2
HARH RM3 105 M10
Rosslyn Cl HYS/HAR UB3 132 E7
SUN TW16 174 F9
WWKM BR4 205 L10
Rosslyn Crs HRW HA1 114 E2
WBLY HA9 115 K8
Rosslyn Hl HAMP NW3 117 N10
Rosslyn Pk WEY KT13 216 E1
Rosslyn Park Ms HAMP NW3 117 N10
Rosslyn Rd BARK IG11 142 G2
TWK TW1 177 H2
WALTH E17 * 121 H2
WATW WD18 73 J7
Rossmore Cl CAMTN NW1 * 9 P2
CRAWE RH10 284 E3
PEND EN3 80 C8
Rossmore Rd CAMTN NW1 9 P1
Ross Pde WLGTN SM6 222 C3
Ross Rd COB KT11 217 K9
DART DA1 187 H2
SNWD SE25 203 M3
WHTN TW2 176 B4
WLGTN SM6 222 D3
Ross Wy ELTH/MOT SE9 162 B9
NTHWD HA6 92 C5
Rossway Dr BUSH WD23 74 C9
Rossway La TRING HP23 32 F1
Rosswood Gdns WLGTN SM6 222 C3
Rostella Rd TOOT SW17 179 N7
Rostrever Gdns HYS/HAR UB3 132 F10
Rostrevor Av SEVS/STOTM N15 119 N4
Rostrevor Gdns IVER SL0 130 G4
NWDGN UB2 153 M4
Rostrevor Rd FUL/PGN SW6 157 J7
WIM/MER SW19 179 K8
Roswell Cl CHES/WCR EN8 62 D6
Rotary St STHWK SE1 18 C3
Rothbury Av RAIN RM13 145 J7
Rothbury Cottages
GNWCH SE10 161 K3
Rothbury Gdns ISLW TW7 154 F6
Rothbury Rd HOM E9 140 E2
Roth Dr RBRW/HUT CM13 107 N3
Rother Cl GSTN WD25 55 K10
Rother Crs CRAWW RH11 283 J8
Rotherfield Rd CAR SM5 222 B1
PEND EN3 80 C3
Rotherfield St IS N1 6 F4
Rotherham Wk STHWK SE1 * 12 D10
Rotherhill Av STRHM/NOR SW16 180 E9
Rotherhithe New Rd
BERM/RHTH SE16 160 A4
Rotherhithe Old Rd
BERM/RHTH SE16 160 C3
Rotherhithe St
BERM/RHTH SE16 160 B1
Rotherhithe Tnl
BERM/RHTH SE16 160 B1
Rothermere Rd CROY/NA CR0 222 G2
Rothervale HORL RH6 280 A2
Rotherwick Hl EA W5 135 L6
Rotherwick Rd GLDGN NW11 117 K5
Rotherwood Cl RYNPK SW20 201 H1
Rotherwood Rd PUT/ROE SW15 156 G9
Rothery St IS N1 * 6 D5
Rothery Ter BRXN/ST SW9 * 159 J6
Rothesay Av GFD/PVL UB6 134 C1
RCHPK/HAM TW10 155 N10
RYNPK SW20 201 H2
Rothesay Rd SNWD SE25 203 L4
Rothes Rd DORK RH4 272 G1
Rothsay Rd FSTGT E7 141 P2
Rothsay St STHWK SE1 19 J3
Rothschild Rd CHSWK W4 155 P3
Rothschild St WNWD SE27 181 K7
Rothwell Gdns DAGW RM9 143 M2
Rothwell Rd DAGW RM9 143 M3
Rothwell St CAMTN NW1 4 B5
Rotterdam Dr POP/IOD E14 161 H2
Rouel Rd BERM/RHTH SE16 19 N5
BERM/RHTH SE16 159 P3
Rouge La GVE DA12 190 E4
Rougemont Av MRDN SM4 201 K6
Roughdown Av HHS/BOV HP3 35 K9
Roughdown Rd HHS/BOV HP3 35 L9
Roughdown Villas Rd
HHS/BOV HP3 35 K9
Roughets La REDH RH1 259 M5
Roughlands WOKS/MYFD GU22 233 H1
Rough Rew DORK RH4 272 G5
Rough Rd WOKS/MYFD GU22 231 H8
The Roughs NTHWD HA6 92 F4
Roughtallys EPP CM16 66 A3
Roughwood Cl WAT WD17 72 F4
Roughwood La CSTG HP8 70 B10
Rounce La CHOB/PIR GU24 212 C9
Round Ash Wy HART DA3 211 K6
Roundaway Rd CLAY IG5 102 C10
Roundbush La GSTN WD25 74 C4
Roundcroft CHESW EN7 61 N2
Roundel Cl BROCKY SE4 160 E10
Round Gv CROY/NA CR0 204 D7
Roundhay Cl FSTH SE23 182 C5
Roundheads End BEAC HP9 88 A7
Roundhedge Wy ENC/FH EN2 78 G4
Round Hl SYD SE26 182 A5
Roundhill WOKS/MYFD GU22 232 E5
Roundhill Dr ENC/FH EN2 78 G8
WOKS/MYFD GU22 232 E4
Roundhills WAB EN9 63 K10
Roundhill Wy COB KT11 218 A7
CUW GU2 249 L10
The Roundings HERT/BAY SG13 26 A10
Roundlyn Gdns STMC/STPC BR5 207 L4
Roundmead Av LOU IG10 82 D7
Roundmead Cl LOU IG10 82 D7
Roundmoor Dr CHES/WCR EN8 62 D5
Round Oak Rd WEY KT13 216 A1
Roundtable Rd BMLY BR1 183 L6
Roundthorn Wy
WOKN/KNAP GU21 231 L2
Roundtree Rd ALP/SUD HA0 114 G10
Roundway EGH TW20 172 F8
Roundways RSLP HA4 112 G8
The Roundway ESH/CLAY KT10 218 E3
TOTM N17 99 L9
WATW WD18 92 G1
Roundwood CHST BR7 206 E2
KGLGY WD4 53 P3
Roundwood Av
RBRW/HUT CM13 107 M2
STKPK UB11 132 D10
Roundwood Cl RSLP HA4 * 112 E5
Roundwood Dr WGCW AL8 22 F4
Roundwood Gv
RBRW/HUT CM13 107 N1
Roundwood Lake
RBRW/HUT CM13 107 N2
Roundwood Pk WLSDN NW10 * 136 D3
Round Wood Rd AMS HP6 69 L3
Roundwood Rd WLSDN NW10 136 B1
Roundwood Ter
STNW/STAM N16 119 M5
Roundwood Vw BNSTD SM7 238 G1
Roundwood Wy BNSTD SM7 238 G1
Rounton Rd BOW E3 140 F6
WAB EN9 63 K9
Roupell Rd BRXS/STRHM SW2 180 G4
Roupell St STHWK SE1 12 B10
Rousden St CAMTN NW1 4 G4
Rousebarn La RKW/CH/CXG WD3 72 A4
Rouse Ct CFSP/GDCR SL9 * 90 C8
CFSP/GDCR SL9 110 C3
Rouse Gdns DUL SE21 181 M7
Rous Rd BKHH IG9 102 B2
Routemaster Cl PLSTW E13 141 N5
Routh Ct EBED/NFELT TW14 174 E4
Routh Rd WAND/EARL SW18 179 P3
Routh St EHAM E6 142 C7
Rover Av BARK/HLT IG6 103 J7
Rowallan Rd FUL/PGN SW6 157 H6
Rowan Av CHING E4 100 E7
EGH TW20 172 F8
Rowan Cl ALP/SUD HA0 114 F8
CRAWE RH10 284 A7
EA W5 155 K1
GU GU1 249 N7
IL IG1 122 G10
LCOL/BKTW AL2 55 P7
NWMAL KT3 200 B2
REIG RH2 275 M2
STALE/WH AL4 39 K6
STAN HA7 94 E7
STRHM/NOR SW16 202 D1
Rowan Crs DART DA1 187 K4
STRHM/NOR SW16 202 D1
Rowan Dr BROX EN10 44 E10
CDALE/KGS NW9 116 D1
Rowan Gdns CROY/NA CR0 203 N10
IVER SL0 130 F4
Rowan Gn East
RBRW/HUT CM13 107 L5
Rowan Gn West
RBRW/HUT CM13 107 L5
Rowan Gv COUL/CHIP CR5 240 C7
SOCK/AV RM15 146 B9
Rowanhurst Dr SLN SL2 109 H10
Rowan Md KWD/TDW/WH KT20 238 E5
Rowan Pl HYS/HAR UB3 132 G9
Rowan Rd BTFD TW8 154 G6
BXLYHN DA7 163 P9
HMSMTH W6 156 G3
STRHM/NOR SW16 202 D2
SWLY BR8 208 E3
WDR/YW UB7 151 N3
Rowans WGCE AL7 23 J2
Rowans Cl HART DA3 211 J2
The Rowans BROX EN10 44 D5
CFSP/GDCR SL9 109 P1
HHW HP1 35 K6
PLMGR N13 99 K4
SOCK/AV RM15 146 B10
SUN TW16 174 G8
WOKS/MYFD GU22 232 B4
Rowans Wy LOU IG10 82 C8
Rowan Ter PGE/AN SE20 * 203 P1
WIM/MER SW19 * 179 H10
Rowantree Cl WCHMH N21 99 L2
Rowantree Ms ENC/FH EN2 79 J6
Rowantree Rd ENC/FH EN2 79 J6
WCHMH N21 99 L2
Rowan Wk EFNCH N2 117 M4
EMPK RM11 125 L2
HAYES BR2 206 C10
NKENS W10 * 8 A1
SBW CM21 29 P1
Rowan Wy CHDH RM6 123 M1
HARP AL5 20 B3
SLN SL2 128 G7
SOCK/AV RM15 147 J6
Rowanwood Av BFN/LL DA15 185 K4
Rowbarns Wy EHSLY KT24 252 G6
Rowben Cl TRDG/WHET N20 97 L2
Rowberry Cl FUL/PGN SW6 156 G6
Rowbury GODL GU7 267 M10
Rowcroft HHW HP1 35 H7
Rowcross St STHWK SE1 19 L7
Rowdell Rd NTHLT UB5 133 P3
Rowden Pde CHING E4 * 100 F7
Rowden Rd BECK BR3 204 D1
CHING E4 100 G7
HOR/WEW KT19 219 P1
Rowditch La BTSEA SW11 158 B8
Rowdon Av WLSDN NW10 136 E2
Rowdow La BGR/WK TN15 229 M10
RSEV TN14 247 L2
Rowdown Crs CROY/NA CR0 225 J5
Rowdowns Rd DAGW RM9 144 A3
Rowe Gdns BARK IG11 143 K4
Rowe La CHOB/PIR GU24 230 F10
HOM E9 120 B10
Rowena Crs BTSEA SW11 157 P8
Rowen Wk CSHM HP5 50 G6
Rowe Wk RYLN/HDSTN HA2 113 P8
Rowfant Cl CRAWE RH10 284 F7
Rowfant Rd TOOT SW17 180 B5
Rowhedge RBRW/HUT CM13 107 M4
Row Hl ADL/WDHM KT15 215 J3
Rowhill Rd CLPT E5 120 A9
Rowhurst Av ADL/WDHM KT15 215 L3
Rowington Cl BAY/PAD W2 8 G3
Rowland Av
KTN/HRWW/WS HA3 115 H1
Rowland Cl CRAWE RH10 281 M10
WDSR SL4 148 C9
Rowland Crs CHIG IG7 103 H5
Rowland Gv SYD SE26 182 A6
Rowland Hill Av TOTM N17 99 L8
Rowland Hill St HAMP NW3 117 P10
Rowland Pl NTHWD HA6 * 92 F8
Rowlands Av PIN HA5 93 P7
Rowlands Cl CHES/WCR EN8 62 C6
HGT N6 * 118 B4
MLHL NW7 96 D8
Rowlandsfields
CHES/WCR EN8 * 62 C6
Rowlands Rd BCTR RM8 124 A7
Rowland Wy ASHF TW15 174 D10
WIM/MER SW19 201 L1
Rowlatt Cl RDART DA2 187 K7
Rowlatt Dr STALW/RED AL3 37 P8
Rowley Av BFN/LL DA15 185 L3
Rowley Cl ALP/SUD HA0 135 L2
OXHEY WD19 73 M10
WOKS/MYFD GU22 233 K2
Rowley Ct CTHM CR3 241 K8
Rowley Gdns FSBYPK N4 119 K5
Rowley Green Rd BAR EN5 76 D9
Rowley La BORE WD6 76 A6
DTCH/LGLY SL3 130 B4
Rowley Md EPP CM16 65 M1
Rowley Rd SEVS/STOTM N15 119 K3
Rowley's Rd HERT/BAY SG13 25 N4
Rowley Wk HHNE HP2 36 D1
Rowley Wy STJWD NW8 3 K5
Rowlheys Pl WDR/YW UB7 151 P2
Rowlls Rd KUT/HW KT1 199 L3
Rowmarsh Cl GVW DA11 190 A7
Rowney Gdns DAGW RM9 143 M1
SBW CM21 29 M3
Rowney Rd DAGW RM9 143 M1
Rowney Wd SBW CM21 29 M2
Rowntree Clifford Cl PLSTW E13 141 N6
Rowntree Cl KIL/WHAMP NW6 2 F2
Rowntree Rd WHTN TW2 176 D4
Rowse Cl SRTFD E15 141 H3
Rowsley Av HDN NW4 116 F1
The Rows HLW CM20 * 28 F10
The Row AMSS HP7 * 68 B10
Rowton Rd WOOL/PLUM SE18 162 F6
Row Town ADL/WDHM KT15 215 J4
Rowzill Rd SWLY BR8 186 G9
Roxborough Av HRW HA1 114 D5
ISLW TW7 154 E6
Roxborough Pk HRW HA1 114 D5
Roxborough Rd HRW HA1 114 C3
Roxbourne Cl NTHLT UB5 133 L1
Roxburgh Av UPMR RM14 126 B8
Roxburgh Rd WNWD SE27 181 J8
Roxburn Wy RSLP HA4 112 G8
Roxby Pl FUL/PGN SW6 14 F9
Roxeth Green Av
RYLN/HDSTN HA2 114 A8
Roxeth Gv RYLN/HDSTN HA2 114 A9
Roxeth Hl RYLN/HDSTN HA2 114 C7
Roxford Cl SHPTN TW17 196 F5
Roxley Rd LEW SE13 182 G2
Roxton Gdns CROY/NA CR0 224 F2
Roxwell Cl SL SL1 128 D10
Roxwell Gdns RBRW/HUT CM13 87 P9
Roxwell Rd BARK IG11 143 K4
SHB W12 156 D1
Roxwell Wy WFD IG8 101 P8
Roxy Av CHDH RM6 123 M5
Royal Albert Rd EHAM E6 142 D9
Royal Albert Wy CAN/RD E16 142 B9
Royal Ar CONDST W1S 10 G8
Royal Arsenal West
WOOL/PLUM SE18 * 162 D4
Royal Av CHEL SW3 16 A7
CHES/WCR EN8 62 D9
WPK KT4 200 B9
Royal Botanic Gdns
RCH/KEW TW9 * 155 K6
Royal Circ WNWD SE27 181 H6
Royal Cl DEPT SE8 160 E5
GDMY/SEVK IG3 123 K5
ORP BR6 226 E1
STNW/STAM N16 119 M6
WDR/YW UB7 132 A8
WIM/MER SW19 178 G5
WPK KT4 200 B9
Royal College St CAMTN NW1 4 F2
Royal Ct BANK EC3V 13 H6
ELTH/MOT SE9 * 184 C4
EN EN1 * 79 M10
HHS/BOV HP3 35 P9
Royal Crs GNTH/NBYPK IG2 122 G4
NTGHL W11 156 G1
RSLP HA4 113 M9
Royal Crescent Ms NTGHL W11 156 G1
Royal Docks Rd EHAM E6 142 E7
Royal Dr EPSOM KT18 238 E4
FBAR/BDGN N11 98 B7
Royal Earlswood Pk REDH RH1 276 B4
Royal Herbert Pavilions
WOOL/PLUM SE18 * 162 C7
Royal Hl GNWCH SE10 161 H6
Royal Hospital Rd CHEL SW3 16 B9
Royal La WDR/YW UB7 132 A8
Royal Ms BAL SW12 180 C3
Royal Mint Pl WCHPL E1 13 M7
Royal Mint St WCHPL E1 13 M7
Royal Naval Pl NWCR SE14 160 E6
Royal Oak Centre
PUR/KEN CR8 * 223 K6
Royal Oak Ms TEDD TW11 176 F8
Royal Oak Pl EDUL SE22 182 A2
Royal Oak Rd BXLYHS DA6 186 A1
HACK E8 140 A1
WOKN/KNAP GU21 231 P4
Royal Oak Yd STHWK SE1 19 J2
Royal Opera Ar STJS SW1Y * 11 J9
Royal Orchard Cl
WAND/EARL SW18 179 H3
Royal Pde BKHTH/KID SE3 161 L8
CHST BR7 184 F10
FUL/PGN SW6 * 157 H6
Royal Pier Rd GVE DA12 190 F2
Royal Pl GNWCH SE10 161 H6
Royal Rd CAN/RD E16 141 P8
LBTH SE11 18 C9
RDART DA2 187 P8
SCUP DA14 185 N6
STAL AL1 38 G6
TEDD TW11 176 C8
Royal Route WBLY HA9 115 L9
Royal St STHWK SE1 17 P3
Royal Terrace Pier GVE DA12 * 190 F2
Royal Victor Pl BETH E2 140 C4
Royce Cl BROX EN10 44 E7
Royce Gv GSTN WD25 54 G10
Royce Rd CRAWE RH10 284 B2
Roycraft Av BARK IG11 143 J4
Roycroft Cl BRXS/STRHM SW2 * 181 H4
SWFD E18 101 N9
Roydene Rd WOOL/PLUM SE18 163 H5
Roydon Cl LOU IG10 102 B1
Roydon Ct WOT/HER KT12 217 H1
Roydon Rd HLWW/ROY CM19 28 B10
WARE SG12 27 J7
Roy Gdns GNTH/NBYPK IG2 123 H2
Roy Gv HPTN TW12 176 A9
Royle Cl CFSP/GDCR SL9 90 C8
GPK RM2 125 J3
Royle Crs WEA W13 134 F6
Roy Rd NTHWD HA6 92 G8
Roy Sq POP/IOD E14 140 D9
Royston Av BF/WBF KT14 215 P8
CHING E4 100 F6
SUT SM1 201 N10
WLGTN SM6 222 E1
Royston Cl CRAWE RH10 284 B3
HERT/WAT SG14 25 J5
HEST TW5 153 J7
WOT/HER KT12 197 H8
Royston Gdns IL IG1 122 A4
Royston Gv PIN HA5 93 N7
Royston Park Rd PIN HA5 93 N7
Royston Rd BF/WBF KT14 215 P8
DART DA1 186 G2
HARH RM3 105 P8
PGE/AN SE20 204 C1
RCHPK/HAM TW10 177 K1
STAL AL1 38 G7
The Roystons BRYLDS KT5 199 N5
Royston St BETH E2 140 B4
Royston Wy SL SL1 128 C7
Rozel Rd VX/NE SW8 158 D8
Rubastic Rd NWDGN UB2 153 K2
Rubens Pl CLAP SW4 158 F10
Rubens Rd NTHLT UB5 133 K4
Rubens St CAT SE6 182 E5
Rubin Pl PEND EN3 80 F3
Rubus Cl CHOB/PIR GU24 212 D9
Ruby Cl SL SL1 148 F1
Ruby Ms WALTH E17 * 120 F1
Ruby Rd WALTH E17 120 F1
Ruby St PECK SE15 160 A5
WLSDN NW10 135 P2
Ruby Triangle PECK SE15 * 160 A5
Ruckholt Cl LEY E10 120 G8
Ruckholt Rd LEY E10 121 H8
Rucklers La KGLGY WD4 53 K4
Ruckles Wy AMSS HP7 69 H6
Rucklidge Av WLSDN NW10 136 C4
Rudall Crs HAMP NW3 117 N9
Ruddington Cl CLPT E5 120 D9
Ruddlesway WDSR SL4 148 C7
Ruddock Cl EDGW HA8 95 P8
Ruddstreet Cl WOOL/PLUM SE18 162 E3
Ruden Wy EW KT17 238 E1
Rudge Ri ADL/WDHM KT15 215 J2
Rudgwick Rd CRAWW RH11 283 J6
Rudgwick Ter STJWD NW8 * 3 P6
Rudland Rd BXLYHN DA7 164 C9
Rudloe Rd BAL SW12 180 D3
Rudolf Pl VX/NE SW8 17 M10
Rudolph Rd BUSH WD23 73 P10
KIL/WHAMP NW6 2 F8
PLSTW E13 141 L4
Rudsworth Cl DTCH/LGLY SL3 150 G7
Rudyard Gv EDGW HA8 95 P7
Rue De St Lawrence WAB EN9 63 H10
Ruffets Wd GVE DA12 190 F9
Ruffetts Cl SAND/SEL CR2 224 A4
The Ruffetts SAND/SEL CR2 224 A4
Ruffetts Wy KWD/TDW/WH KT20 239 H4
Ruffle Cl WDR/YW UB7 151 P1
Rufford Cl KTN/HRWW/WS HA3 114 F4
WAT WD17 72 G3
Rufford St IS N1 5 M5
Rufford Street Ms IS N1 5 M4
Rufus Cl RSLP HA4 113 L8
Rufus St FSBYE EC1V 7 J10
Rufwood CRAWE RH10 285 P5
Rugby Av ALP/SUD HA0 115 H9
ED N9 99 N2
GFD/PVL UB6 134 C1
Rugby Cl HRW HA1 114 D2
Rugby Gdns DAGW RM9 143 M1
Rugby La BELMT SM2 220 G5
Rugby Rd CDALE/KGS NW9 115 M2
CHSWK W4 156 B1
DAGW RM9 143 L2
TWK TW1 176 D2
Rugby St BMSBY WC1N 11 N2
Rugby Wy RKW/CH/CXG WD3 72 C9
Ruggles-Brise Rd ASHF TW15 173 N8
Rugg St POP/IOD E14 140 F9
Rugosa Rd CHOB/PIR GU24 212 D9
Ruislip Cl GFD/PVL UB6 134 A6
Ruislip Ct RSLP HA4 * 112 G7
Ruislip Rd GFD/PVL UB6 134 A5
NTHLT UB5 133 K3
Ruislip Rd East GFD/PVL UB6 134 C6
Ruislip St TOOT SW17 180 A7
Rumballs Rd HHS/BOV HP3 36 B9
Rumbold Rd FUL/PGN SW6 157 L6
HOD EN11 45 H1
Rum Cl WAP E1W 140 A9
Rumsey Cl HPTN TW12 175 N9
Rumsey Rd BRXN/ST SW9 158 G9
Rumsley CHESW EN7 61 P3
Runbury Cir CDALE/KGS NW9 116 A7
Runcie Cl STALE/WH AL4 38 F2
Runciman Cl ORP BR6 227 M6
Runcorn Cl TOTM N17 120 A2
Runcorn Crs HHNE HP2 36 A2
Runcorn Pl NTGHL W11 8 A8
NTGHL W11 137 H9
Rundell Crs HDN NW4 116 E3
Rundells HLWS CM18 47 K5
Runes Cl MTCM CR4 201 N4
Runham Rd HHS/BOV HP3 35 P8
Runnelfield HRW HA1 114 D8
Runnemede Rd EGH TW20 172 C8
Running Waters
RBRW/HUT CM13 107 M5
Runnymede WIM/MER SW19 201 N1
Runnymede Cl WHTN TW2 176 A2
Runnymede Ct EGH TW20 172 D7
Runnymede Crs
STRHM/NOR SW16 202 E1
Runnymede Gdns GFD/PVL UB6 134 C4
HSLW TW3 176 A2
Runnymede Rd WHTN TW2 176 A2
Runrig Hl AMS HP6 69 K1
Runsley WGCE AL7 23 K2
Runtley Wood La RGUE GU4 250 D1
The Runway HAT AL10 40 A2
RSLP HA4 113 J10
Rupack St BERM/RHTH SE16 * 160 B1
Rupert Av WBLY HA9 115 K10
Rupert Ct E/WMO/HCT KT8 * 197 P4
SOHO/SHAV W1D 11 J7
Rupert Gdns BRXN/ST SW9 159 J8
Rupert Rd ARCH N19 118 E8
CHSWK W4 156 B2
GUW GU2 267 N1
KIL/WHAMP NW6 2 D8
Rupert St SOHO/SHAV W1D 11 J8
Rural Cl EMPK RM11 125 J6
Rural V GVW DA11 190 B3
Rural Wy REDH RH1 258 B10
STRHM/NOR SW16 180 C10
Rusbridge Cl HACK E8 119 P10
Ruscoe Dr WOKS/MYFD GU22 232 D3
Ruscoe Rd CAN/RD E16 141 L8
Ruscombe Dr LCOL/BKTW AL2 56 A2
Ruscombe Gdns DTCH/LGLY SL3 149 M6
Ruscombe Wy
EBED/NFELT TW14 174 G3
Rusham Park Av EGH TW20 172 D9
Rusham Rd BAL SW12 180 A2
EGH TW20 172 C9
Rushbrook Crs WALTH E17 100 E9
Rushbrook Rd ELTH/MOT SE9 184 F5
Rush Cl WARE SG12 27 H7
Rush Common Ms
BRXS/STRHM SW2 180 F3
Rush Cft GODL GU7 267 M9
Rushcroft Rd BRXS/STRHM SW2 159 H10
CHING E4 100 G8
Rushden Cl NRWD SE19 181 L10
Rushdene ABYW SE2 163 M2
Rushdene Av EBAR EN4 97 P1
Rushdene Cl NTHLT UB5 133 K4
Rushdene Crs NTHLT UB5 133 J4
Rushdene Rd BRWN CM15 107 H1
PIN HA5 113 K4
Rushdene Wk BH/WHM TN16 244 A3
Rushden Gdns CLAY IG5 122 D1
MLHL NW7 96 F7
Rushdon Cl GRAYS RM17 167 M2
ROM RM1 125 H3
Rush Dr WAB EN9 81 H2
Rushen Dr HERT/BAY SG13 26 B8
Rushes Md HLWS CM18 47 H3
UX/CGN UB8 131 M3
Rushet Rd STMC/STPC BR5 207 K2
Rushett Cl THDIT KT7 198 G8
Rushett Dr DORK RH4 272 G5
Rushett La CHSGTN KT9 219 J8
Rushett Rd THDIT KT7 198 G7
Rushetts Pl CRAWW RH11 283 M4
Rushetts Rd CRAWW RH11 283 L4
REIG RH2 275 M4
Rushey Cl NWMAL KT3 200 A4
Rushey Gn CAT SE6 182 G3
Rushey Hl ENC/FH EN2 78 G8
Rushey Md BROCKY SE4 182 F1
Rushfield POTB/CUF EN6 58 G9
SBW CM21 29 P1
Rushford Rd BROCKY SE4 182 E2
Rush Green Gdns
ROMW/RG RM7 124 D6
Rush Green Rd
ROMW/RG RM7 124 D6
Rushgrove Av CDALE/KGS NW9 116 C2
Rushgrove Pde
CDALE/KGS NW9 * 116 C3
Rushgrove St WOOL/PLUM SE18 162 C3
Rush Hill Ms BTSEA SW11 158 B9
Rush Hill Rd BTSEA SW11 158 B9
Rushleigh Av CHES/WCR EN8 62 C6
Rushley Cl HAYES BR2 226 A1
Rushmead BETH E2 140 A5
RCHPK/HAM TW10 176 G6
Rushmead Cl CROY/NA CR0 223 N1
Rushmere Av UPMR RM14 126 B8
Rushmere Ct WPK KT4 200 D9
Rushmere La CSHM HP5 51 M4
Rushmere Pl EGH TW20 172 B8
WIM/MER SW19 178 G8
Rushmon Pl CHEAM SM3 * 221 H3
Rushmon Vls NWMAL KT3 * 200 C4
Rushmoor Cl GUW GU2 249 L7
PIN HA5 113 K2
RKW/CH/CXG WD3 91 N3
Rushmore Cl BMLY BR1 206 B3
Rushmore Ct WATW WD18 * 72 E10
Rushmore Hl ORP BR6 227 M6
Rushmore Rd CLPT E5 120 B9
Rusholme Av DAGE RM10 124 B8
Rusholme Gv NRWD SE19 181 M8
Rusholme Rd PUT/ROE SW15 178 G2
Rushout Av KTN/HRWW/WS HA3 114 G4
Rushton Av GSTN WD25 73 H1
Rushton Gv HLWE CM17 47 N1
Rushton St IS N1 7 H7
Rushworth Rd REIG RH2 257 K9
Rushworth St STHWK SE1 18 D1
Rushymead BGR/WK TN15 247 P4
Rushy Meadow La CAR SM5 201 P10
Ruskin Av EBED/NFELT TW14 174 G3
MNPK E12 142 C1
RCH/KEW TW9 155 M6
UPMR RM14 126 B5
WAB EN9 63 K10
WELL DA16 163 K9
Ruskin Cl CHESW EN7 61 M2
CRAWE RH10 284 D4
GLDGN NW11 117 L4
Ruskin Dr ORP BR6 207 H10
WELL DA16 163 K9
WPK KT4 200 E9
Ruskin Gdns EA W5 135 J6
HARH RM3 105 J9
KTN/HRWW/WS HA3 115 L3
Ruskin Gv DART DA1 187 P1
WELL DA16 163 K8
Ruskin Rd BELV DA17 164 B3
CAR SM5 222 B2
CDW/CHF RM16 168 D3
CROY/NA CR0 203 J9
ISLW TW7 154 E9
STA TW18 173 J10
STHL UB1 133 M9
TOTM N17 99 N9
Ruskin Wk ED N9 99 P3
HAYES BR2 206 C6
HNHL SE24 181 K1
Ruskin Wy WIM/MER SW19 201 N2
Rusland Av ORP BR6 206 G10
Rusland Park Rd HRW HA1 114 D2
Rusper Cl CRICK NW2 116 F8
STAN HA7 95 H5
Rusper Rd CRAWW RH11 282 D6
CRAWW RH11 283 J7
DAGW RM9 143 M1
HORS RH12 282 A4
WDGN N22 99 J10
Ruspers Keep CRAWW RH11 283 J6
Russel Cl BECK BR3 204 G3
Russell Av STALW/RED AL3 38 C6
WDGN N22 99 J10
Russell Cl AMS HP6 70 A5
BKHTH/KID SE3 161 P6
BRWN CM15 106 G1
BXLYHN DA7 164 B10
CHSWK W4 156 C5
DART DA1 165 H9
KWD/TDW/WH KT20 256 D1
NTHWD HA6 92 D6
RSLP HA4 113 K7
WLSDN NW10 135 P2
WOKN/KNAP GU21 231 P1
Russell Ct BAR EN5 * 77 M8
CSHM HP5 51 H5
LHD/OX KT22 236 G8
WHALL SW1A 11 H10
Russell Crs GSTN WD25 72 G1
Russellcroft Rd WGCW AL8 22 F4
Russell Dr STWL/WRAY TW19 173 N2
Russell Gdns GLDGN NW11 117 H4
RCHPK/HAM TW10 177 H5
TRDG/WHET N20 97 P3
WDR/YW UB7 152 B4
WKENS W14 14 B3
Russell Gardens Ms WKENS W14 14 A3
Russell Green Cl PUR/KEN CR8 223 H6
Russell Gv BRXN/ST SW9 159 H7
MLHL NW7 96 B6
Russell Hl PUR/KEN CR8 222 G6
Russell Hill Pl PUR/KEN CR8 223 H7
Russell Hill Rd PUR/KEN CR8 223 H6
Russell Kerr Cl CHSWK W4 * 155 P6
Russell La TRDG/WHET N20 98 A3
WAT WD17 72 E2
Russell Pde GLDGN NW11 * 117 H4
Russell Pl EYN DA4 209 P1
HAMP NW3 117 P10
HHS/BOV HP3 35 L9
Russell Rd BKHH IG9 101 P2
CAN/RD E16 141 M8
CDALE/KGS NW9 116 C4
CEND/HSY/T N8 118 E4
CHING E4 100 E5
EN EN1 79 N4
GVE DA12 190 G2
MTCM CR4 201 P3
NTHLT UB5 114 B10
NTHWD HA6 92 D4
SEVS/STOTM N15 119 M3
SHPTN TW17 196 D7
TIL RM18 168 C8
TRDG/WHET N20 97 P3
WALTH E17 120 E1
WDGN N22 98 G7
WHTN TW2 176 E2
WIM/MER SW19 179 K10
WKENS W14 14 B3
WOKN/KNAP GU21 231 P1
WOT/HER KT12 197 H6
Russells KWD/TDW/WH KT20 238 G8
Russells Crs HORL RH6 280 B5
Russell's Dr CHES/WCR EN8 62 D7
Russell Sq RSQ WC1B 11 L3
Russell's Ride CHES/WCR EN8 62 C7
Russell St HOL/ALD WC2B 11 N6
WDSR SL4 149 J8
Russell Ter EYN DA4 * 210 B4
Russell Wy CRAWE RH10 284 B8
OXHEY WD19 93 J1
SUT SM1 221 L2
Russel Rd GRAYS RM17 167 M3
Russet Cl CHESW EN7 * 61 M2
HGDN/ICK UB10 132 D6
HORL RH6 280 D4
STWL/WRAY TW19 173 J2
WOT/HER KT12 197 L10
Russet Crs HOLWY N7 * 118 G10
Russet Dr CROY/NA CR0 204 D8
RAD WD7 57 K8
STALE/WH AL4 39 H8
Russets Cl CHING E4 101 J5
The Russets CFSP/GDCR SL9 90 A10
Russett Cl ORP BR6 227 L2
Russett Hl CFSP/GDCR SL9 110 B1
Russetts EMPK RM11 125 M2
Russetts Cl WOKN/KNAP GU21 232 C1
Russett Wy SWLY BR8 208 E2
Russett Wd WGCE AL7 23 N6
Russet Wy RDKG RH5 273 J6
Russ Hl HORL RH6 282 D1
Russ Hill Rd HORL RH6 278 G9
Russia Dock Rd
BERM/RHTH SE16 * 140 D10
Russia La BETH E2 140 B4
Russia Rw CITYW EC2V 12 F6
Russington Rd SHPTN TW17 196 E6
Rusthall Av CHSWK W4 156 A2
Rusthall Cl CROY/NA CR0 204 B6
Rustic Av STRHM/NOR SW16 180 C10
Rustic Cl UPMR RM14 126 D6
Rustic Pl ALP/SUD HA0 115 J9
Rustington Wk CHEAM SM3 201 J7
Ruston Av BRYLDS KT5 199 N7
Ruston Cl CRAWE RH10 284 D10
Ruston Gdns STHGT/OAK N14 78 B10
Ruston Ms NTGHL W11 8 A6
NTGHL W11 * 137 H8
Ruston Rd WOOL/PLUM SE18 162 B2
Ruston St BOW E3 140 E3
Rust Sq CMBW SE5 159 L6
Rutford Rd STRHM/NOR SW16 180 F8
Ruth Cl STAN HA7 115 L2
Ruthen Cl EPSOM KT18 219 N10
Rutherford Cl BELMT SM2 221 N3
BORE WD6 75 P6
UX/CGN UB8 132 A6
WDSR SL4 148 E7
Rutherford St WEST SW1P 17 J5
Rutherford Wy BUSH WD23 94 D2
CRAWE RH10 284 B2
WBLY HA9 115 M8
Rutherglen Rd ABYW SE2 163 K5
Rutherwick Cl HORL RH6 280 A4
Rutherwyke Cl EW KT17 220 D3
Rutherwyk Rd CHERT KT16 195 H7
Ruthin Cl CDALE/KGS NW9 116 B4
Ruthin Rd BKHTH/KID SE3 161 M5
Ruthven Av CHES/WCR EN8 62 C9
Ruthven St HOM E9 140 C3
Rutland Ap EMPK RM11 125 P3
Rutland Av BFN/LL DA15 185 K3
SL SL1 129 H7
Rutland Cl ASHTD KT21 237 K3
BXLY DA5 185 N4
CHSGTN KT9 219 L3
DART DA1 187 L3
HOR/WEW KT19 220 A6
MORT/ESHN SW14 155 N9
REDH RH1 258 A9
WIM/MER SW19 179 P10
Rutland Ct CHST BR7 206 D1
SKENS SW7 15 P2
Rutland Dr EMPK RM11 125 P3
MRDN SM4 201 K7
RCHPK/HAM TW10 177 J4
Rutland Gdns BCTR RM8 123 M10
CROY/NA CR0 223 M1
FSBYPK N4 119 J4
HHNE HP2 36 A5
SKENS SW7 15 P2
WEA W13 * 134 F7
Rutland Gardens Ms SKENS SW7 15 P2
Rutland Ga BELV DA17 164 C4
HAYES BR2 205 L4

SKENS SW7 15 N3
Rutland Gate Ms SKENS SW7 * 15 N2
Rutland Gv HMSMTH W6 156 E4
Rutland Ms STJWD NW8 3 H6
Rutland Ms South SKENS SW7 * 15 N3
Rutland Pk CAT SE6 182 E5
CRICK NW2 136 F1
Rutland Pl BUSH WD23 * 94 C2
FARR EC1M * 12 D3
Rutland Rd FSTGT E7 142 A2
HOM E9 140 C3
HRW HA1 114 B4
HYS/HAR UB3 152 E3
IL IG1 122 E9
STHL UB1 133 P6
WALTH E17 120 F4
WAN E11 121 N3
WHTN TW2 176 C5
Rutland St SKENS SW7 15 P3
Rutland Wk CAT SE6 182 E5
Rutland Wy STMC/STPC BR5 207 N6
Rutley Cl WALW SE17 18 C9
Rutlish Rd WIM/MER SW19 201 K1
Rutson Rd BF/WBF KT14 216 A10
Rutter Gdns MTCM CR4 201 N4
Rutters Cl WDR/YW UB7 152 B1
Rutt's Ter NWCR SE14 160 C7
The Rutts BUSH WD23 94 C2
Ruvigny Gdns PUT/ROE SW15 156 G9
Ruxbury Rd CHERT KT16 194 G6
Ruxley Cl HOR/WEW KT19 219 N2
SCUP DA14 185 N9
Ruxley Crs ESH/CLAY KT10 218 G4
Ruxley La HOR/WEW KT19 219 P3
Ruxley Ms HOR/WEW KT19 219 N2
Ruxley Rdg ESH/CLAY KT10 218 F4
Ruxley Towers ESH/CLAY KT10 * 218 F4
Ruxton Cl COUL/CHIP CR5 240 D1
SWLY BR8 208 F3
Ruxton Ct SWLY BR8 208 F3
Ryall Cl LCOL/BKTW AL2 55 M5
Ryan Cl BKHTH/KID SE3 161 N10
RSLP HA4 113 J6
Ryan Ct OXHEY WD19 * 93 M1
Ryan Dr BTFD TW8 154 F5
Ryan Wy WATN WD24 73 K5
Ryarsh Crs ORP BR6 227 H1
Rycroft WDSR SL4 148 E9
Rycroft La RSEV TN14 264 F6
Rycroft Wy TOTM N17 * 119 N1
Ryculff Sq BKHTH/KID SE3 161 L8
Rydal Cl CRAWW RH11 282 G9
HDN NW4 97 H9
PUR/KEN CR8 223 L9
Rydal Crs GFD/PVL UB6 134 G5
Rydal Dr BXLYHN DA7 164 B7
WWKM BR4 205 K9
Rydal Gdns CDALE/KGS NW9 116 B3
HSLW TW3 176 A2
PUT/ROE SW15 178 B8
WBLY HA9 115 H6
Rydal Mt HAYES BR2 * 205 L4
POTB/CUF EN6 * 59 H9
Rydal Pl LTWR GU18 212 A7
Rydal Rd STRHM/NOR SW16 180 E8
Rydal Wy EGH TW20 172 E10
PEND EN3 80 B10
RSLP HA4 113 K9
Ryde Cl RPLY/SEND GU23 233 M7
Ryde Heron WOKN/KNAP GU21 231 K3
Rydens Av WOT/HER KT12 197 K9
Rydens Cl WOT/HER KT12 197 K9
Rydens Gv WOT/HER KT12 217 L1
Rydens Pde WOKS/MYFD GU22 * 232 E6
Rydens Pk WOT/HER KT12 197 L9
Rydens Rd WOT/HER KT12 197 J10
Rydens Wy WOKS/MYFD GU22 232 D6
Ryde Pl TWK TW1 177 H2
Ryder Cl BUSH WD23 74 A10
HERT/BAY SG13 26 A4
HHS/BOV HP3 52 D4
Ryder Dr BERM/RHTH SE16 160 A4
Ryder Gdns RAIN RM13 144 G1
Ryders Av STALE/WH AL4 40 B6
Ryder Seed Ms STAL AL1 * 38 C7
Ryder St STJS SW1Y 11 H9
WHALL SW1A 10 G9
Rydes Av GUW GU2 249 L7
Ryde's Hill Crs GUW GU2 249 L6
Ryde's Hill Rd GUW GU2 249 L8
The Ryde BRKMPK AL9 40 F2
STA TW18 195 L1
Ryde Vale Rd BAL SW12 180 C5
Rydings WDSR SL4 148 E9
Rydon Ms WIM/MER SW19 178 F10
Rydon's La COUL/CHIP CR5 241 K6
Rydon St IS N1 6 F5
Rydon's Wood Cl
COUL/CHIP CR5 241 K6
Rydston Cl HOLWY N7 5 M3
Rye Ash CRAWE RH10 284 B6
Rye Brook Rd LHD/OX KT22 236 F4
Rye Cl BXLY DA5 186 C2
GUW GU2 249 K9
Ryecotes Md DUL SE21 181 M4
Rye Ct SL SL1 * 149 M2
Rye Crs STMC/STPC BR5 207 N8
Ryecroft GVE DA12 191 H8
HAT AL10 40 C6
HLWW/ROY CM19 46 E1
Ryecroft Av CLAY IG5 102 E10
WHTN TW2 176 A4
Ryecroft Cl HHNE HP2 36 D7
Ryecroft Crs BAR EN5 76 E9
Ryecroft Rd CSHM HP5 50 F9
LEW SE13 183 H1
RSEV TN14 247 H3
STMC/STPC BR5 206 G6
STRHM/NOR SW16 181 H9
Ryecroft St FUL/PGN SW6 157 L7
Ryedale EDUL SE22 182 A2
Ryedale Ct SEV TN13 246 F7
Ryefeld Cl HOD EN11 26 G9
Rye Fld ASHTD KT21 237 J3
Ryefield Av HGDN/ICK UB10 132 D3
Ryefield Crs PIN HA5 * 93 H10
Ryefield Pde NTHWD HA6 * 93 H10
Ryefield Rd NRWD SE19 181 K9
Rye Gv LTWR GU18 212 D6
Rye Hill Pk PECK SE15 160 B10
Rye Hill Rd HLWS CM18 46 G6
Ryeland Cl WDR/YW UB7 131 P8
Ryelands CRAWW RH11 283 K8
HORL RH6 280 D3
WGCE AL7 23 J8
Ryelands Cl CTHM CR3 241 M7
Ryelands Ct LHD/OX KT22 236 F4
Ryelands Crs LEE/GVPK SE12 183 P2
Ryelands Pl WEY KT13 196 F10
Rye La PECK SE15 159 P8
RSEV TN14 246 G6
Rye Rd HOD EN11 44 G2
PECK SE15 160 C10
WARE SG12 27 K9
The Rye STHGT/OAK N14 98 D1
Rye Wk PUT/ROE SW15 178 G1
Rye Wy EDGW HA8 95 L7
Ryfold Rd WIM/MER SW19 179 K6
Ryhope Rd FBAR/BDGN N11 98 C5
Rykens La BRKHM/BTCW RH3 273 P5
Rykhill CDW/CHF RM16 168 E2
Ryland Cl FELT TW13 174 G7
Rylandes Rd CRICK NW2 116 D8
SAND/SEL CR2 224 A6
Ryland Rd KTTN NW5 4 E1
Rylett Crs SHB W12 156 C2
Rylett Rd SHB W12 156 C1
Rylston Rd FUL/PGN SW6 14 C10
PLMGR N13 99 L4
Rymer Rd CROY/NA CR0 203 M7
Rymer St HNHL SE24 181 J2
Rymill Cl HHS/BOV HP3 52 D4
Rymill St CAN/RD E16 142 D10
Rysbrack St CHEL SW3 16 A3
Rysted La BH/WHM TN16 262 F2

Rythe Cl CHSGTN KT9 219 H4
Rythe Ct THDIT KT7 198 F7
Rythe Rd ESH/CLAY KT10 218 C2
The Rythe ESH/CLAY KT10 218 A6
Ryvers End DTCH/LGLY SL3 150 C2
Ryvers Rd DTCH/LGLY SL3 150 C2
Ryves Cottages MTCM CR4 * 202 B2

S

Sabbarton St CAN/RD E16 141 L8
Sabina Rd CDW/CHF RM16 168 F3
Sabine Rd BTSEA SW11 158 A9
Sabines Rd ABR/ST RM4 85 N7
Sable Cl HSLWW TW4 153 K9
Sable St IS N1 6 D3
Sachfield Dr CDW/CHF RM16 167 L3
Sach Rd CLPT E5 120 A7
Sackville Av HAYES BR2 205 M8
Sackville Cl RYLN/HDSTN HA2 114 C8
SEV TN13 247 J8
Sackville Crs HARH RM3 105 M9
Sackville Est STRHM/NOR SW16 180 F6
Sackville Gdns IL IG1 122 C6
Sackville Rd BELMT SM2 221 K4
RDART DA2 187 L5
Sackville St CONDST W1S 10 G8
Sacombe Rd HERT/WAT SG14 25 K2
HHW HP1 35 J5
Saddington St GVE DA12 190 E3
Saddlebrook Pk SUN TW16 174 F10
Saddler Rw CRAWE RH10 283 N10
Saddlers Cl BAR EN5 76 E9
BORE WD6 * 76 A9
PIN HA5 93 P6
Saddlers Hall EYN DA4 * 209 L10
Saddlers Ms KUT/HW KT1 199 H1
Saddler's Pk EYN DA4 209 L10
Saddlers Wk KGLGY WD4 * 54 B5
Saddlers Wy EPSOM KT18 238 A5
Saddlescombe Wy
NFNCH/WDSPK N12 97 K6
Sadleir Rd STAL AL1 38 D8
Sadler Cl CHESW EN7 61 K2
MTCM CR4 202 A2
Sadlers Cl GU GU1 250 G9
Sadlers Gate Ms PUT/ROE SW15 156 F9
Sadlers Md HLWS CM18 47 K2
Sadlers Ride E/WMO/HCT KT8 198 B2
Sadlers Wy HERT/WAT SG14 25 H5
Saffron Av POP/IOD E14 141 J9
Saffron Cl CRAWW RH11 283 K10
CROY/NA CR0 202 F6
DTCH/LGLY SL3 149 N7
GLDGN NW11 117 J3
HOD EN11 44 E2
Saffron Hl HCIRC EC1N 12 B4
Saffron La HHW HP1 35 K5
Saffron Platt GUW GU2 249 M6
Saffron Rd CDW/CHF RM16 167 H3
CRW RM5 104 E10
Saffron St HCIRC EC1N 12 B3
Saffron Wy SURB KT6 199 J8
Sage Cl EHAM E6 142 C7
Sage Ms EDUL SE22 181 N1
Sage St WCHPL E1 140 B9
Sage Wy FSBYW WC1X 5 N10
Sage Yd SURB KT6 * 199 L8
Saigasso Cl CAN/RD E16 142 A8
Sail St LBTH SE11 17 P5
Sainfoin End HHNE HP2 36 B4
Sainfoin Rd TOOT SW17 180 B5
Sainsbury Rd NRWD SE19 181 M8
St Agatha's Dr KUTN/CMB KT2 177 L9
St Agatha's Gv CAR SM5 202 A8
St Agnells Ct HHNE HP2 36 B2
St Agnells La HHNE HP2 36 B1
St Agnes Cl HOM E9 * 140 B3
St Agnes Pl LBTH SE11 18 C10
St Agnes Well STLK EC1Y 13 H1
St Aidan's Rd EDUL SE22 182 A2
WEA W13 154 G1
St Aidan's Wy GVE DA12 191 H6
St Albans Av CHSWK W4 156 A2
EHAM E6 142 C5
FELT TW13 175 L8
UPMR RM14 126 D7
WEY KT13 196 B10
St Alban's Cl GVE DA12 190 G6
RGUW GU3 248 G9
WDSR SL4 * 149 J7
St Albans Crs WDGN N22 99 H9
St Albans Farm
EBED/NFELT TW14 * 175 K1
St Alban's Gdns GVE DA12 190 G6
TEDD TW11 176 F8
St Alban's Gv CAR SM5 201 P7
KENS W8 15 H3
St Albans Hl HHS/BOV HP3 35 P9
St Albans La ABLGY WD5 54 G2
GLDGN NW11 117 K6
St Alban's Ms BAY/PAD W2 9 M3
St Alban's Pl IS N1 6 C6
St Albans Rd BAR EN5 76 G4
DART DA1 187 N2
EPP CM16 65 N5
GDMY/SEVK IG3 123 J6
GSTN WD25 73 K2
GSTN WD25 73 K2
HARP AL5 20 A5
HHNE HP2 35 N7
KTTN NW5 118 B8
KUTN/CMB KT2 177 K9
POTB/CUF EN6 58 B7
REIG RH2 257 K9
STALE/WH AL4 38 F2
SUT SM1 221 J1
WAT WD17 73 J6
WFD IG8 101 M8
WLSDN NW10 136 B3
St Albans Rd East HAT AL10 40 F2
St Albans Rd West HAT AL10 39 P4
HAT AL10 40 B4
HAT AL10 40 D3
St Alban's St STJS SW1Y 11 J8
WDSR SL4 149 J7
St Albans Ter HMSMTH W6 14 A9
HMSMTH W6 157 H5
St Alfege Pas GNWCH SE10 161 H5
St Alfege Rd CHARL SE7 162 A5
St Alphage Gdns BARB EC2Y 12 F4
St Alphage Highwalk BARB EC2Y 12 F4
St Alphage Wk EDGW HA8 * 95 P10
St Alphege Rd ED N9 100 B1
St Alphonsus Rd CLAP SW4 158 D10
St Amunds Cl CAT SE6 182 F7
St Andrew Ms HERT/WAT SG14 * 25 K5
St Andrews HORL RH6 * 280 C5
St Andrews Av ALP/SUD HA0 114 F9
HCH RM12 124 G10
WDSR SL4 148 E8
St Andrews Cl BERM/RHTH SE16 160 A4
CRICK NW2 * 116 E8
EPP CM16 48 D10
ISLW TW7 154 D7
NFNCH/WDSPK N12 * 97 M5
REIG RH2 275 L1
RSLP HA4 113 L7
SHPTN TW17 196 E4
STAN HA7 * 95 H10
STWL/WRAY TW19 172 B2
THDIT KT7 198 G8
THMD SE28 143 N8
WDSR SL4 171 M2
WIM/MER SW19 179 L9
WOKN/KNAP GU21 231 P3
St Andrew's Ct
WAND/EARL SW18 179 M5
WAT WD17 * 73 J5
St Andrew's Crs WDSR SL4 148 E8
St Andrews Dr STAN HA7 95 H9
STMC/STPC BR5 207 L6

St Andrews Gdns COB KT11 217 K9
St Andrews Ga
WOKS/MYFD GU22 232 C4
St Andrew's Gv STNW/STAM N16 119 L6
St Andrew's Hl BLKFR EC4V 12 D7
St Andrew's Meadow
HLWS CM18 47 J2
St Andrews Ms BAL SW12 180 E4
BKHTH/KID SE3 161 M6
STNW/STAM N16 119 M6
St Andrews Pl BRWN CM15 107 L3
CAMTN NW1 10 E1
St Andrew's Rd ACT W3 136 B8
CAR SM5 201 P10
CDALE/KGS NW9 116 A6
COUL/CHIP CR5 240 C2
CRAWW RH11 282 G8
CROY/NA CR0 223 K1
ED N9 100 B1
EN EN1 79 L7
GLDGN NW11 117 J4
GVE DA12 * 190 E3
HGDN/ICK UB10 131 P3
HHS/BOV HP3 35 M10
HNWL W7 154 D1
IL IG1 122 C5
PLSTW E13 141 N5
ROMW/RG RM7 124 E4
SCUP DA14 185 N6
SURB KT6 199 J6
TIL RM18 168 C8
WALTH E17 100 C10
WAN E11 121 K4
WKENS W14 14 B9
WKENS W14 157 H5
WLSDN NW10 136 E1
St Andrew's Sq NTGHL W11 * 8 A6
NTGHL W11 * 137 H8
SURB KT6 199 J6
St Andrews Ter OXHEY WD19 * 93 K6
St Andrew St HCIRC EC1N 12 B4
HERT/WAT SG14 25 K5
St Andrew's Wk COB KT11 235 J1
St Andrews Wy BOW E3 140 G6
OXTED RH8 262 B7
SL SL1 128 C9
St Anna Rd BAR EN5 * 76 G9
St Anne's Av STWL/WRAY TW19 173 N3
St Annes Cl CDW/CHF RM16 * 147 N10
CHESW EN7 61 N4
HGT N6 118 B8
OXHEY WD19 93 K5
St Annes Ct SOHO/CST W1F 11 J6
St Anne's Dr REDH RH1 258 B9
St Annes Dr North REDH RH1 258 B8
St Annes Gdns WLSDN NW10 135 L5
St Annes Mt REDH RH1 * 258 B9
St Anne's Pk BROX EN10 44 F6
St Anne's Pas POP/IOD E14 * 140 E8
St Annes Ri REDH RH1 258 B9
St Anne's Rd ALP/SUD HA0 115 J10
BRWN CM15 87 P5
CRAWE RH10 284 D4
DEN/HRF UB9 111 M1
LCOL/BKTW AL2 57 J3
LEY E10 121 J7
St Anne's Rw POP/IOD E14 140 E8
St Anne St POP/IOD E14 140 E8
St Annes Wy REDH RH1 * 258 B9
St Ann's BARK IG11 142 F3
WOKS/MYFD GU22 * 232 B4
St Ann's Cl CHERT KT16 195 J6
St Anns Ct HDN NW4 * 116 E1
St Ann's Crs WAND/EARL SW18 179 M2
St Ann's Gdns HAMP NW3 4 B1
St Ann's Hl WAND/EARL SW18 179 L1
St Ann's Hill Rd CHERT KT16 194 G6
St Ann's Park Rd
WAND/EARL SW18 179 M2
St Ann's Rd BARK IG11 142 F3
BARN SW13 * 156 C8
CHERT KT16 195 J6
ED N9 99 N3
HRW HA1 114 D4
NTGHL W11 136 G10
SEVS/STOTM N15 119 L3
St Ann's St WEST SW1P 17 K4
St Ann's Ter STJWD NW8 3 M7
St Ann's Vls NTGHL W11 136 G10
St Anns Wy BH/WHM TN16 * 244 E2
CROY/NA CR0 223 J3
St Anselms Rd HYS/HAR UB3 152 G1
St Anthonys Av HHS/BOV HP3 36 C8
WFD IG8 101 P8
St Anthonys Cl TOOT SW17 179 P5
WAP E1W 13 N9
St Anthony's Ct ORP BR6 206 E9
St Anthony's Wy
EBED/NFELT TW14 152 G10
St Antony's Rd FSTGT E7 141 N2
St Arvans Cl CROY/NA CR0 203 M10
St Asaph Rd BROCKY SE4 160 C9
St Aubyns DORK RH4 * 272 G4
St Aubyn's Av HSLW TW3 175 P1
WIM/MER SW19 179 J8
St Aubyns Cl ORP BR6 207 J10
St Aubyns Gdns ORP BR6 207 J9
St Aubyn's Rd NRWD SE19 181 N9
St Audrey Av BXLYHN DA7 164 B8
St Audreys Cl HAT AL10 40 E7
St Audreys Gn WGCE AL7 23 J6
St Augusta Ct STALW/RED AL3 38 C4
St Augustine Rd CDW/CHF RM16 168 E3
St Augustine's Av EA W5 135 K4
HAYES BR2 206 B5
SAND/SEL CR2 223 K4
WBLY HA9 115 K8
St Augustines Cl BROX EN10 44 E6
St Augustines Dr BROX EN10 44 E6
St Augustine's Rd BELV DA17 164 A3
CAMTN NW1 5 J3
St Austell Cl EDGW HA8 95 L10
St Austell Rd LEW SE13 161 H8
St Awdry's Rd BARK IG11 142 G3
St Barnabas Cl BECK BR3 205 H2
EDUL SE22 181 M1
St Barnabas' Gdns
E/WMO/HCT KT8 197 P5
St Barnabas Rd MTCM CR4 180 B10
SUT SM1 221 N2
Saint Barnabas Rd WALTH E17 120 F4
St Barnabas Rd WFD IG8 101 N9
St Barnabas St BGVA SW1W 16 D7
St Barnabas Ter HOM E9 120 C10
St Barnabas Vls VX/NE SW8 158 F7
St Bartholomew's Cl SYD SE26 182 B7
St Bartholomew's Ct GU GU1 268 C2
St Bartholomew's Rd EHAM E6 142 B3
St Benedict's Av GVE DA12 191 H6
St Benets Cl TOOT SW17 179 P5
St Benet's Gv CAR SM5 201 M7
St Benjamins Dr ORP BR6 227 M5
St Bernards CROY/NA CR0 203 M10
St Bernards Cl WNWD SE27 181 L7
St Bernards Rd DTCH/LGLY SL3 149 P2
EHAM E6 142 B3
STALW/RED AL3 38 D5
St Blaise Av BMLY BR1 205 N2
St Botolph Rd GVW DA11 190 A6
St Botolph's Av SEV TN13 247 H10
St Botolph's Rd SEV TN13 247 J10
St Botolph St TWRH EC3N 13 L5
St Brelades Cl DORK RH4 272 F4
St Bride's Av EDGW HA8 95 L9
St Brides Cl ERITHM DA18 163 N1
St Bride St FLST/FETLN EC4A 12 C5
St Catharine's Rd BROX EN10 44 F5
St Catherines WEY KT13 * 196 C10
WOKS/MYFD GU22 231 P5
St Catherines Cl CHSGTN KT9 219 J3
TOOT SW17 * 179 P5
St Catherines Ct FELT TW13 175 H4
St Catherine's Cross REDH RH1 259 M10
St Catherine's Dr GUW GU2 267 N4
NWCR SE14 160 C8

St Catherine's Hl GUW GU2 267 P4
St Catherines Ms CHEL SW3 16 A5
St Catherine's Pk GU GU1 268 C2
St Catherines Rd CHING E4 100 F3
CRAWE RH10 284 D4
Saint Catherines Rd RSLP HA4 112 D3
St Cecilia Rd CDW/CHF RM16 168 E3
St Chads Cl SURB KT6 199 H7
St Chad's Dr GVE DA12 191 H6
St Chad's Gdns CHDH RM6 123 P5
St Chad's Pl FSBYW WC1X 5 M9
St Chad's Rd CHDH RM6 123 P4
TIL RM18 168 D7
St Chad's St STPAN WC1H 5 M9
St Charles Pl NKENS W10 8 A4
NKENS W10 137 H7
WEY KT13 216 B2
St Charles Rd BRW CM14 106 G3
St Charles Sq NKENS W10 8 A4
NKENS W10 136 G7
St Christopher Rd UX/CGN UB8 131 N8
St Christopher's Cl ISLW TW7 154 D7
St Christophers Ct
RKW/CH/CXG WD3 * 70 G8
St Christophers Dr HYS/HAR UB3 133 J9
St Christopher's Ms WLGTN SM6 222 D2
St Christopher's Pl MHST W1U 10 D6
St Clair Cl CLAY IG5 102 C10
OXTED RH8 261 H6
REIG RH2 257 M10
St Clair Dr WPK KT4 200 E10
St Clair Rd PLSTW E13 141 N4
St Clair's Rd CROY/NA CR0 203 M9
St Clare St TWRH EC3N 13 L6
St Clement Cl UX/CGN UB8 131 N8
St Clement's Av WTHK RM20 166 F5
St Clements Cl GVW DA11 190 C6
St Clements Ct PUR RM19 165 P3
St Clement's La LINN WC2A 11 P6
St Clement's Rd WTHK RM20 167 H6
St Clements St HOLWY N7 6 A2
St Clement's Wy WTHK RM20 166 E6
St Clements Yd EDUL SE22 * 181 N1
St Cloud Rd WNWD SE27 181 K7
St Columba's Cl GVE DA12 191 H6
St Crispins Cl HAMP NW3 117 P9
STHL UB1 133 N8
St Crispins Wy CHERT KT16 214 F5
St Cross Ct HOD EN11 44 F5
St Cross St HCIRC EC1N 12 B3
St Cuthbert's Cl EGH TW20 172 A9
St Cuthberts Gdns PIN HA5 * 93 N8
St Cuthberts Rd CRICK NW2 2 C1
HOD EN11 27 H10
PLMGR N13 99 H7
St Cyprian's St TOOT SW17 180 A7
St David Cl UX/CGN UB8 131 N7
St David's COUL/CHIP CR5 240 G3
St Davids Cl BERM/RHTH SE16 * 160 A4
HHS/BOV HP3 36 E8
IVER SL0 130 G3
REIG RH2 257 M9
WBLY HA9 115 P8
WWKM BR4 204 G7
St David's Crs GVE DA12 190 G7
St David's Dr BROX EN10 44 E5
EDGW HA8 95 L9
EGH TW20 171 P10
St Davids Ms BOW E3 140 D5
St David's Pl HDN NW4 116 E5
St David's Rd SWLY BR8 186 G9
St Davids Sq POP/IOD E14 160 G4
St Denis Rd WNWD SE27 181 K7
St Denys Cl PUR/KEN CR8 223 J6
WOKN/KNAP GU21 * 231 J4
St Dionis Rd FUL/PGN SW6 157 J8
St Donatt's Rd NWCR SE14 160 E8
St Dunstan's Av ACT W3 136 A9
St Dunstans Cl HYS/HAR UB3 152 G3
St Dunstan's Dr GVE DA12 191 H6
St Dunstan's Gdns ACT W3 136 A9
St Dunstan's Hl MON EC3R * 13 J8
SUT SM1 221 H1
St Dunstan's La MON EC3R * 13 J8
St Dunstan's Rd FELT TW13 174 G6
FSTGT E7 141 N1
HMSMTH W6 156 G4
HNWL W7 154 D1
HSLWW TW4 153 K8
SNWD SE25 203 N4
WARE SG12 28 A3
St Edith's Rd BGR/WK TN15 247 P4
St Edmunds BERK HP4 33 P6
St Edmunds Av RSLP HA4 112 E4
St Edmunds Cl CRAWW RH11 283 N4
ERITHM DA18 163 N1
STJWD NW8 4 A6
TOOT SW17 179 P5
St Edmunds Dr STAN HA7 94 F9
St Edmund's La WHTN TW2 176 A3
St Edmunds Rd DART DA1 165 N10
ED N9 99 P1
IL IG1 122 C4
St Edmunds Sq BARN SW13 156 F5
St Edmund's Ter STJWD NW8 3 P6
St Edmunds Wk STALE/WH AL4 39 J7
St Edmund's Wy HLWE CM17 29 M7
St Edwards Cl CROY/NA CR0 225 J7
GLDGN NW11 117 K4
St Edwards Wy ROM RM1 124 F2
St Egberts Wy CHING E4 101 H2
St Elizabeth Dr EPSOM KT18 219 P10
St Elmo Cl SLN SL2 129 J6
St Elmo Crs SLN SL2 129 J6
St Elmo Rd SHB W12 156 C1
St Elmos Rd BERM/RHTH SE16 160 D1
St Erkenwald Ms BARK IG11 142 G3
St Erkenwald Rd BARK IG11 142 G3
St Ervans Rd NKENS W10 8 B3
NKENS W10 137 H7
St Etheldreda's Dr HAT AL10 40 F4
St Evroul Ct WARE SG12 26 C1
St Faith's Cl ENC/FH EN2 79 K5
St Faith's Rd DUL SE21 181 J4
St Fidelis' Rd ERITH DA8 164 E3
St Fillans WOKS/MYFD GU22 * 232 E2
St Fillans Rd CAT SE6 183 H4
St Francis Av GVE DA12 191 H7
St Francis Cl ORP BR6 207 H6
OXHEY WD19 93 J2
POTB/CUF EN6 59 M9
St Francis Gdns CRAWE RH10 285 K1
St Francis Rd DEN/HRF UB9 111 J4
EDUL SE22 159 M10
Saint Francis Wy
CDW/CHF RM16 168 F3
St Francis Wy IL IG1 122 G9
St Gabriel's Cl WAN E11 121 N6
St Gabriel's Rd CRICK NW2 116 G10
St George's ED N9 99 P4
HORL RH6 * 280 C5
St George's Av CDALE/KGS NW9 115 P2
EA W5 155 J1
Saint George's Av EMPK RM11 125 N5
St George's Av FSTGT E7 141 N2
GRAYS RM17 167 P3
HOLWY N7 118 E9
STHL UB1 133 N9
WEY KT13 216 D3
St George's Circ STHWK SE1 18 C2
St Georges Cl BRWN CM15 86 G1
GLDGN NW11 117 J4
HORL RH6 280 C4
HRW HA1 114 F8
THMD SE28 143 N8
VX/NE SW8 158 D7
WDSR SL4 148 D7
WEY KT13 216 D2
St Georges Ct CRAWE RH10 283 N6
St George's Ct STP EC4M * 12 C5
St George's Crs GVE DA12 190 G7
SL SL1 128 C9
St Georges Dr HGDN/ICK UB10 112 A8
OXHEY WD19 93 M5
PIM SW1V 16 G7

St George's Est WCHPL E1 13 P7
St Georges Flds BAY/PAD W2 9 P7
St George's Gdns EW KT17 220 C10
SURB KT6 199 N9
St George's Gv TOOT SW17 179 N6
St George's Industrial Est
KUTN/CMB KT2 177 J8
St George's La ASC SL5 192 A3
MON EC3R * 13 H7
St George's Ms CAMTN NW1 4 B4
CHSWK W4 * 155 P5
DEPT SE8 160 E3
St Georges Pde CAT SE6 * 182 E5
St Georges Rd ADL/WDHM KT15 215 M1
BECK BR3 204 G1
BMLY BR1 206 C2
CHSWK W4 156 A1
DAGW RM9 123 P10
EN EN1 79 N4
FELT TW13 175 M7
FSTGT E7 141 N2
GLDGN NW11 117 J4
HHS/BOV HP3 35 M10
HNWL W7 134 E10
IL IG1 122 C5
KUTN/CMB KT2 177 L10
LEY E10 121 H8
MTCM CR4 202 C3
PLMGR N13 98 G4
RCH/KEW TW9 155 L9
REDH RH1 276 E8
SCUP DA14 185 N9
SEV TN13 247 J8
STHWK SE1 18 C4
STMC/STPC BR5 206 G6
SWLY BR8 208 G5
TWK TW1 176 G1
WATN WD24 73 J4
WEY KT13 216 E3
WIM/MER SW19 179 J9
WLGTN SM6 222 C2
St Georges Rd West BMLY BR1 206 B2
St George's Sq FSTGT E7 141 N2
GVW DA11 * 190 E2
NWMAL KT3 * 200 B3
PIM SW1V 17 J8
St George's Square Ms
PIM SW1V 17 J8
St George's Ter CAMTN NW1 4 B5
PECK SE15 * 159 P6
St George St CONDST W1S 10 F7
St George's Wk CROY/NA CR0 203 K10
St George's Wy PECK SE15 19 K10
St Gerards Cl CLAP SW4 180 D1
St German's Pl BKHTH/KID SE3 161 M8
St German's Rd FSTH SE23 182 D4
St Giles Av DAGE RM10 144 C2
HGDN/ICK UB10 112 D9
POTB/CUF EN6 58 E9
St Giles Churchyard BARB EC2Y * 12 F4
St Giles Circ SOHO/SHAV W1D 11 K5
St Giles Cl DAGE RM10 144 C2
HEST TW5 153 M6
ORP BR6 226 G2
St Giles Ct LSQ/SEVD WC2H 11 K5
St Giles High St LSQ/SEVD WC2H 11 K5
St Giles Pas LSQ/SEVD WC2H 11 K6
St Gothard Rd WNWD SE27 181 L7
St Gregory Cl RSLP HA4 113 K9
St Gregory's Crs GVE DA12 191 H5
St Helena Rd BERM/RHTH SE16 160 C3
St Helena St FSBYW WC1X * 6 A10
St Helena Ter RCH/KEW TW9 * 177 J1
St Helen Cl UX/CGN UB8 131 N8
St Helens THDIT KT7 * 198 D7
St Helen's Cl STALE/WH AL4 21 J3
St Helens Ct RAIN RM13 145 H6
St Helen's Crs STRHM/NOR SW16 202 G1
St Helen's Gdns NKENS W10 136 G8
St Helen's Pl HDTCH EC3A 13 J5
St Helens Rd ERITHM DA18 163 N1
IL IG1 122 C4
STRHM/NOR SW16 202 G2
WEA W13 134 G10
St Helier Av MRDN SM4 201 M7
St Heliers Av HSLWW TW4 175 P1
St Helier's Rd LEY E10 120 G4
STALE/WH AL4 38 G1
St Hilda's Av ASHF TW15 173 P8
St Hilda's Cl CRAWE RH10 * 284 D4
HORL RH6 280 C4
KIL/WHAMP NW6 * 136 G3
TOOT SW17 179 P5
WOKN/KNAP GU21 231 J3
St Hilda's Rd BARN SW13 156 E5
St Hilda's Wy GVE DA12 191 H6
St Huberts Cl CFSP/GDCR SL9 110 B7
St Huberts La CFSP/GDCR SL9 110 C7
St Hughes Cl TOOT SW17 * 179 P5
St Hugh's Cl CRAWE RH10 284 D4
St Hugh's Rd PGE/AN SE20 * 182 A10
PGE/AN SE20 * 204 A1
St Ives CRAWE RH10 * 284 D6
St Ives Cl HARH RM3 105 N8
St Ivians Dr GPK RM2 125 H1
St James' Av CHONG CM5 67 N6
EW KT17 220 D7
SUT SM1 221 K2
TRDG/WHET N20 97 P4
WEA W13 134 F10
St James Cl EBAR EN4 77 N7
EPSOM KT18 220 B10
NWMAL KT3 200 C5
RSLP HA4 113 K7
STJWD NW8 4 A7
TRDG/WHET N20 97 P4
WOKN/KNAP GU21 231 M4
St James Ct RDART DA2 188 D2
WESTW SW1E * 17 H3
St James' Gdns ALP/SUD HA0 135 J2
CHDH RM6 123 L2
St James Ga ASC SL5 192 E7
CTHM CR3 * 241 P8
St James' La RDART DA2 188 D3
St James Ms POP/IOD E14 * 161 H2
WEY KT13 216 C1
St James Oaks GVW DA11 * 190 D3
St James Pl DART DA1 187 L2
SL SL1 * 128 B8
St James Rd CAR SM5 201 P10
ED N9 100 A3
MTCM CR4 180 B10
PUR/KEN CR8 223 J9
SRTFD E15 121 L10
SURB KT6 199 J6
SUT SM1 221 K3
WATW WD18 73 J9
St James's NWCR SE14 160 D7
St James's Av BECK BR3 204 D3
BETH E2 140 B4
GVW DA11 190 D3
HPTN TW12 176 B8
St James's Chambers
STJS SW1Y * 11 H9
St James's Cl TOOT SW17 * 180 A5
TOOT SW17 * 180 B8
WOOL/PLUM SE18 162 F4
St James's Cottages
RCH/KEW TW9 * 177 J1
St James's Ct KUT/HW KT1 * 199 K3
WESTW SW1E 17 H3
St James's Crs BRXN/ST SW9 159 H9
St James's Dr BAL SW12 180 A4
St James's Gdns CAMTN NW1 * 4 G10
NTGHL W11 8 A9
NTGHL W11 137 H10
St James's Gv BTSEA SW11 158 A8
St James's La MUSWH N10 118 C2
St James's Market STJS SW1Y * 11 J8
St James's Ms WALTH E17 120 D3
St James's Pk CROY/NA CR0 203 K7
St James's Pl WHALL SW1A 10 G10
St James Sq HART DA3 * 211 K3
SURB KT6 199 H7
St James's Rd BERM/RHTH SE16 19 P3

BERM/RHTH SE16 159 P2
BRW CM14 107 H4
CHESW EN7 61 K4
CROY/NA CR0 203 K7
GVW DA11 190 D3
HPTN TW12 176 A8
KUT/HW KT1 199 J2
PECK SE15 19 P9
SEV TN13 247 J8
STHWK SE1 19 P6
STHWK SE1 * 159 P3
St James's Rw CHSGTN KT9 * 219 J3
St James's Sq STJS SW1Y 11 J9
St James's St GVW DA11 190 D2
WALTH E17 120 D3
WHALL SW1A 10 G9
St James's Ter STJWD NW8 4 A7
St James's Terrace Ms
STJWD NW8 4 A6
St James St HMSMTH W6 156 F4
St James Ter BAL SW12 * 180 B4
ORP BR6 * 227 M5
St James Wk CLKNW EC1R 12 C2
DTCH/LGLY SL3 151 H1
St James Wy BXLY DA5 186 B3
SCUP DA14 185 P7
St Jerome's Gv HYS/HAR UB3 132 D8
St Joan Cl CRAWW RH11 283 N4
St Joan's Rd ED N9 99 N3
St John Cl FUL/PGN SW6 * 157 K6
St John's RDKG RH5 273 H6
St John's Av BRW CM14 107 J5
EW KT17 220 D8
FBAR/BDGN N11 98 A6
HLWE CM17 29 N7
LHD/OX KT22 236 G7
PUT/ROE SW15 178 G1
WLSDN NW10 136 C3
St John's Church Rd HOM E9 * 120 B10
RDKG RH5 271 N5
St Johns Cl BH/WHM TN16 * 244 E2
FUL/PGN SW6 * 157 K6
LHD/OX KT22 237 H7
POTB/CUF EN6 59 M9
RAIN RM13 145 H2
STHGT/OAK N14 78 D10
TRDG/WHET N20 * 97 M3
UX/CGN UB8 * 131 L3
WBLY HA9 115 K10
St Johns Cottages
PGE/AN SE20 * 182 B10
St John's Ct BKHH IG9 101 N2
EGH TW20 172 D8
HARP AL5 * 20 B4
ISLW TW7 154 E8
STAL AL1 38 G5
St John's Crs BRXN/ST SW9 159 H9
St John's Dr WAND/EARL SW18 179 L4
WDSR SL4 148 E8
WOT/HER KT12 197 K8
St John's Est IS N1 7 H8
STHWK SE1 19 L1
St Johns Gdns NTGHL W11 8 C8
St John's Gv ARCH N19 118 D7
BARN SW13 * 156 C8
RCH/KEW TW9 155 J10
St John's Hl BTSEA SW11 157 P10
COUL/CHIP CR5 241 H3
SEV TN13 247 K9
St John's Hill Gv BTSEA SW11 157 N10
St John's Hill Rd
WOKN/KNAP GU21 231 N5
St John's La FARR EC1M 12 C2
HART DA3 211 L6
WARE SG12 26 F5
St John's Lye WOKN/KNAP GU21 231 L5
St John's Lye (Festival Path)
WOKN/KNAP GU21 231 L5
St Johns Ms WOKN/KNAP GU21 231 M5
St Johns Pde SCUP DA14 * 185 L7
WEA W13 * 134 G10
St John's Pk BKHTH/KID SE3 161 M6
St John's Pl FARR EC1M 12 C2
St Johns Ri BH/WHM TN16 * 244 E2
WOKN/KNAP GU21 231 N5
St John's Rd BARK IG11 143 H3
BTSEA SW11 157 P10
CAN/RD E16 141 M8
CAR SM5 201 P10
CDW/CHF RM16 168 E4
CHING E4 100 G5
CRAWW RH11 283 M7
CROY/NA CR0 203 J10
CRW RM5 104 D6
DORK RH4 272 B3
E/WMO/HCT KT8 198 C4
EHAM E6 142 B3
EPP CM16 65 J6
ERITH DA8 164 E4
FELT TW13 175 N7
GLDGN NW11 117 J5
GNTH/NBYPK IG2 123 H5
GUW GU2 267 L1
GVE DA12 190 G3
HARP AL5 20 B4
HHW HP1 35 L8
HRW HA1 114 E4
ISLW TW7 154 E8
KUT/HW KT1 199 H2
LHD/OX KT22 237 H7
LOU IG10 82 C6
NWDGN UB2 153 M2
NWMAL KT3 199 P3
PGE/AN SE20 182 B10
RCH/KEW TW9 155 K10
RDART DA2 188 B3
REDH RH1 276 A2
SCUP DA14 185 L7
SEV TN13 247 J8
SEVS/STOTM N15 119 M4
SLN SL2 129 M9
STMC/STPC BR5 206 G6
SUT SM1 201 K9
UX/CGN UB8 131 L4
WALTH E17 100 G10
WAT WD17 73 J6
WBLY HA9 115 J9
WDSR SL4 148 F8
WELL DA16 163 L9
WIM/MER SW19 179 H10
WOKN/KNAP GU21 231 N4
WOKN/KNAP GU21 231 N4
St John's Sq FARR EC1M 12 C2
St John's St HERT/WAT SG14 25 L5
St John's Ter ENC/FH EN2 79 L3
FSTGT E7 141 N1
NKENS W10 136 G6
WOOL/PLUM SE18 162 F5
St John's Terrace Rd REDH RH1 276 A2
St John St FSBYE EC1V 6 B8
St John's V BROCKY SE4 160 F8
St John's Vls ARCH N19 118 E7
KENS W8 15 H4
St Johns Wk HLWE CM17 29 M7
St John's Wy ARCH N19 118 E6
CHERT KT16 195 K9
St John's Well Ct BERK HP4 33 N4
St John's Well La BERK HP4 33 N4
St John's Wood High St
STJWD NW8 3 M8
St John's Wood Pk STJWD NW8 3 L6
St John's Wood Rd STJWD NW8 9 L1
St John's Wood Ter STJWD NW8 3 N7
St Josephs Cl NKENS W10 8 B4
NKENS W10 137 H7
ORP BR6 227 J1
St Joseph's Dr STHL UB1 133 N10
St Josephs Gv HDN NW4 116 E2
St Josephs Ms BEAC HP9 88 E9
St Joseph's Rd CHES/WCR EN8 62 D9
ED N9 100 A1
St Joseph's St VX/NE SW8 * 158 C7
St Joseph's V BKHTH/KID SE3 161 J8
St Jude's Cl EGH TW20 171 P8
St Jude's Rd BETH E2 140 A4

EGH TW20 171 P9
St Jude St STNW/STAM N16 119 M10
St Julian's Cl STRHM/NOR SW16 * 181 H7
St Julian's Farm Rd WNWD SE27 181 H7
St Julian's Rd KIL/WHAMP NW6 2 D4
STAL AL1 38 C8
St Justin Cl STMC/STPC BR5 207 N3
St Katharine's Prec CAMTN NW1 * 4 E7
St Katharines Rd CTHM CR3 259 P1
St Katharine's Wy WAP E1W 13 N9
St Katherines Rd ERITHM DA18 163 N1
St Katherines Wk NTGHL W11 * 136 G9
St Katherine's Wy BERK HP4 33 L2
St Keverne Rd ELTH/MOT SE9 184 B7
St Kilda Rd ORP BR6 207 J8
WEA W13 154 F1
St Kilda's Rd BRWN CM15 106 G1
HRW HA1 114 D4
STNW/STAM N16 119 L6
St Kitts Ter NRWD SE19 181 M8
St Laurence Cl STMC/STPC BR5 207 N3
UX/CGN UB8 131 M7
St Laurence Dr BROX EN10 44 D9
St Laurence's Cl
KIL/WHAMP NW6 136 G3
St Laurence Wy SL SL1 149 M2
St Lawrence Cl ABLGY WD5 54 F6
EDGW HA8 95 L8
HHS/BOV HP3 52 D3
St Lawrence Cottages
POP/IOD E14 * 141 H10
St Lawrence Dr PIN HA5 113 J3
St Lawrence Rd UPMR RM14 126 B7
St Lawrence St POP/IOD E14 141 H10
St Lawrence Ter NKENS W10 8 A4
NKENS W10 137 H7
St Lawrence Wy BRXN/ST SW9 * 159 H8
CTHM CR3 241 L9
LCOL/BKTW AL2 55 N6
St Leonard's Av CHING E4 101 J7
KTN/HRWW/WS HA3 115 H3
WDSR SL4 149 H8
St Leonards Cl BUSH WD23 73 M8
GRAYS RM17 167 L5
HERT/WAT SG14 25 M3
WELL DA16 163 K9
St Leonard's Ct STALE/WH AL4 21 H10
St Leonards Crs STALE/WH AL4 21 H10
St Leonards Dr CRAWE RH10 284 B10
St Leonard's Gdns HEST TW5 153 M6
Saint Leonards Gdns IL IG1 122 F10
St Leonard's Hl WDSR SL4 148 C10
St Leonards Ri ORP BR6 227 H1
St Leonards Rd AMS HP6 69 K2
CROY/NA CR0 203 J10
EPSOM KT18 238 F5
ESH/CLAY KT10 218 E3
HERT/WAT SG14 25 L3
MORT/ESHN SW14 155 P9
POP/IOD E14 141 H8
SURB KT6 199 J5
THDIT KT7 198 F6
WAB EN9 45 J10
WDSR SL4 170 C2
WEA W13 135 H9
WLSDN NW10 136 A6
St Leonard's Sq KTTN NW5 4 D2
SURB KT6 199 J5
St Leonard's St BOW E3 140 G5
St Leonard's Ter CHEL SW3 16 A8
St Leonards Wk DTCH/LGLY SL3 151 J2
STRHM/NOR SW16 180 G10
St Leonards Wy EMPK RM11 125 J6
St Loo Av CHEL SW3 15 P9
St Louis Rd WNWD SE27 181 K7
St Loy's Rd TOTM N17 99 M10
St Lucia Dr SRTFD E15 141 L3
St Luke Cl UX/CGN UB8 131 N8
St Luke's Av CLAP SW4 158 E10
ENC/FH EN2 79 L4
IL IG1 122 E10
St Lukes Cl RDART DA2 188 D8
SNWD SE25 204 A6
SWLY BR8 208 E2
St Lukes Ct WOKN/KNAP GU21 * 214 F10
St Luke's Est FSBYE EC1V 6 G10
FSBYE EC1V * 12 G1
St Lukes Ms NTGHL W11 8 C5
St Lukes Pl STAL AL1 * 38 G7
St Luke's Rd CTHM CR3 241 N4
HGDN/ICK UB10 * 131 P2
NTGHL W11 8 D4
WDSR SL4 171 M2
St Lukes's Cl FSBYE EC1V 12 F1
St Luke's Sq CAN/RD E16 141 L8
GU GU1 268 C1
St Luke's St CHEL SW3 15 N7
St Lukes Yd MV/WKIL W9 * 2 C8
St Magnus Ct HHS/BOV HP3 36 D8
St Malo Av ED N9 100 B4
St Margarets BARK IG11 142 F3
GU GU1 250 C9
KUTN/CMB KT2 * 177 P8
St Margarets Av ASHF TW15 174 C7
BFN/LL DA15 184 G6
BH/WHM TN16 * 244 E2
CHEAM SM3 201 H10
RYLN/HDSTN HA2 114 B8
SEVS/STOTM N15 119 J2
TRDG/WHET N20 97 M2
UX/CGN UB8 132 B6
St Margaret's Cl BERK HP4 34 A6
IVER SL0 130 G4
ORP BR6 227 L1
RDART DA2 188 C5
St Margarets Ct
PUT/ROE SW15 * 156 E10
St Margaret's Crs GVE DA12 191 H6
PUT/ROE SW15 * 178 E1
St Margarets Dr EPSOM KT18 220 A10
TWK TW1 176 G1
St Margaret's Gv TWK TW1 176 F2
WAN E11 121 L8
WOOL/PLUM SE18 162 F5
St Margarets La KENS W8 14 G4
St Margarets Ms
KUTN/CMB KT2 * 177 P8
St Margaret's Rd BROCKY SE4 160 E10
COUL/CHIP CR5 240 C7
EDGW HA8 95 N6
EYN DA4 188 D10
HNWL W7 154 D1
MNPK E12 121 P7
RSLP HA4 112 E4
TOTM N17 119 M1
TWK TW1 154 G10
WARE SG12 26 F9
WLSDN NW10 136 F5
St Margaret's Ter
WOOL/PLUM SE18 162 F4
St Margaret St WEST SW1P 17 L2
St Margarets Wy HHNE HP2 36 E6
St Mark's Av GVW DA11 190 C3
St Mark's Cl BAR EN5 77 L7
FUL/PGN SW6 157 K7
STALE/WH AL4 39 N8
St Mark's Crs CAMTN NW1 4 D5
St Marks Ga HOM E9 140 E2
St Mark's Gv WBPTN SW10 157 L6
St Mark's Hl SURB KT6 199 K6
St Marks Pl NTGHL W11 8 B6
NTGHL W11 137 H8
WDSR SL4 149 H8
WIM/MER SW19 * 179 J9
St Mark's Ri HACK E8 119 N10
St Mark's Rd EA W5 135 K10
EN EN1 79 N10
EPSOM KT18 238 F4
HAYES BR2 205 N3
HNWL W7 154 D1
MTCM CR4 202 A2
NKENS W10 136 G8
NTGHL W11 8 A6
NTGHL W11 137 H8
SNWD SE25 203 P4
TEDD TW11 176 G10
WDSR SL4 149 H8
St Mark's Sq CAMTN NW1 4 C6
St Mark St WCHPL E1 13 M6
St Marks Vls FSBYPK N4 * 118 G7
St Martha's Av
WOKS/MYFD GU22 232 C7
St Marthas Ct RGUE GU4 * 268 E6
St Martin Cl UX/CGN UB8 131 N8
St Martin-in-the-Fields
CHCR WC2N * 11 L8
St Martins NTHWD HA6 92 E6
St Martins Ap RSLP HA4 112 F5
St Martin's Av EHAM E6 142 A4
EPSOM KT18 220 B10
St Martin's Cl CAMTN NW1 4 G5
EHSLY KT24 252 F5
EN EN1 80 A5
ERITHM DA18 163 N1
EW KT17 * 220 C9
OXHEY WD19 93 K5
RBRW/HUT CM13 * 107 P2
WDR/YW UB7 151 M2
St Martin's Ct ASHF TW15 173 M8
CHCR WC2N 11 L7
St Martins Dr EYN DA4 209 L10
WOT/HER KT12 197 K10
St Martin's La BECK BR3 204 G5
CHCR WC2N 11 L7
St Martin's Le Grand STBT EC1A 12 E5
St Martins Meadow
BH/WHM TN16 245 M9
St Martins Ms DORK RH4 272 F2
WOKS/MYFD GU22 233 K2
St Martin's Pl CHCR WC2N 11 L8
St Martin's Rd BRXN/ST SW9 158 G8
DART DA1 187 N2
ED N9 100 A3
EFNCH N2 97 N9
HOD EN11 45 H3
St Martin's St LSQ/SEVD WC2H * 11 K8
St Martin's Wy TOOT SW17 179 M6
St Mary Abbot's Pl KENS W8 14 D4
St Mary Abbots Ter WKENS W14 14 C4
St Mary At Hl MON EC3R 13 J8
St Mary Av WLGTN SM6 202 B10
St Mary Axe HDTCH EC3A 13 K6
St Marychurch St
BERM/RHTH SE16 160 B1
St Mary Graces Ct WCHPL E1 * 13 M8
St Mary Rd WALTH E17 120 G2
St Marys BARK IG11 142 G4
WEY KT13 * 196 E10
St Mary's Ap MNPK E12 122 C10
St Mary's Av BERK HP4 33 J3
BRWN CM15 87 M9
FNCH N3 97 J10
HAYES BR2 205 K3
NTHWD HA6 92 F6
NWDGN UB2 153 P3
STWL/WRAY TW19 173 N3
TEDD TW11 * 176 E9
WAN E11 121 N4
St Mary's Church Rd RSEV TN14 263 P1
St Mary's Cl CHSGTN KT9 219 L4
DEN/HRF UB9 111 L1
EW KT17 220 C4
GRAYS RM17 168 A5
GVE DA12 190 F5
LHD/OX KT22 236 C9
OXTED RH8 261 K5
STMC/STPC BR5 207 L2
SUN TW16 197 H4
TOTM N17 * 99 N9
WATW WD18 * 73 K8
St Mary's Ct BH/WHM TN16 262 G2
HMSMTH W6 * 156 C2
POTB/CUF EN6 59 L8
St Marys Ctyd WARE SG12 * 26 C2
St Mary's Crs HDN NW4 116 E1
HYS/HAR UB3 132 G9
ISLW TW7 154 D6
STWL/WRAY TW19 173 N3
St Mary's Dr CRAWE RH10 284 C6
EBED/NFELT TW14 174 D3
SEV TN13 246 F9
St Marys Est BERM/RHTH SE16 * 160 B1
St Mary's Gdns LBTH SE11 18 B5
St Mary's Ga KENS W8 14 G4
St Mary's Gn BH/WHM TN16 243 P4
EFNCH N2 117 M1
St Mary's Gv BARN SW13 156 E9
BH/WHM TN16 243 P4
CHSWK W4 155 N5
IS N1 6 D2
RCH/KEW TW9 155 L10
St Mary's Hl ASC SL5 192 B5
St Mary's La HERT/WAT SG14 24 G7
UPMR RM14 125 P7
UPMR RM14 127 L5
St Mary's Man BAY/PAD W2 9 K3
St Mary's Ms KIL/WHAMP NW6 2 G4
St Mary's Mt CTHM CR3 241 N10
St Mary's Pth IS N1 6 D5
WCHPL E1 13 N5
St Mary's Pl EA W5 155 J1
KENS W8 14 G4
St Mary's Rd ASC SL5 192 A6
BXLY DA5 186 D4
CDW/CHF RM16 168 E3
CEND/HSY/T N8 118 F2
CHES/WCR EN8 62 B5
DEN/HRF UB9 111 J4
DTCH/LGLY SL3 150 B1
E/WMO/HCT KT8 198 C5
EA W5 135 J10
EBAR EN4 98 A1
ED N9 100 B2
GLDGN NW11 117 H5
HHNE HP2 35 N5
HYS/HAR UB3 132 G9
IL IG1 122 F7
LEY E10 121 H8
LHD/OX KT22 236 G9
PECK SE15 160 B8
PLSTW E13 141 N4
RDART DA2 188 D1
REIG RH2 275 L1
SAND/SEL CR2 223 L6
SNWD SE25 203 M3
SURB KT6 199 J6
SWLY BR8 208 E4
WATW WD18 73 J8
WEY KT13 216 E1
WIM/MER SW19 179 H8
WLSDN NW10 136 B3
WOKN/KNAP GU21 231 P3
WPK KT4 200 B9
St Mary's Sq BAY/PAD W2 9 L3
EA W5 * 155 J1
St Mary's Ter BAY/PAD W2 9 L3
BORE WD6 * 75 J10
St Mary St WOOL/PLUM SE18 162 C3
St Marys Vw
KTN/HRWW/WS HA3 115 H3
WATW WD18 * 73 K8
St Mary's Wk HYS/HAR UB3 132 G9
LBTH SE11 18 B5
STALE/WH AL4 38 G2
St Mary's Wy CFSP/GDCR SL9 90 A10
CHIG IG7 102 D6
CSHM HP5 50 G8
GUW GU2 249 K8
HART DA3 211 K3
St Matthew Cl UX/CGN UB8 131 N8
St Matthew's Av SURB KT6 199 K8
St Matthews Cl OXHEY WD19 73 L10
RAIN RM13 145 H2
St Matthews Ct SRTFD E15 141 L2
St Matthews Dr BMLY BR1 206 C3
St Matthew's Rd
BRXS/STRHM SW2 180 G1
EA W5 135 K10
REDH RH1 258 A9
St Matthew's Rw BETH E2 7 N10
St Matthew St WEST SW1P 17 J3
St Matthias Cl CDALE/KGS NW9 116 C3
St Maur Rd FUL/PGN SW6 157 J7
St Meddens CHST BR7 * 184 G10
St Mellion Cl THMD SE28 143 N8
St Merryn Cl WOOL/PLUM SE18 162 G6
St Michael's Aly BANK EC3V 13 H6
St Michaels Av ED N9 100 B1
HHS/BOV HP3 36 C8
RGUW GU3 249 H5
WBLY HA9 135 M1
St Michaels Cl BMLY BR1 206 B3
CAN/RD E16 142 A7
ERITHM DA18 * 163 N1
FNCH N3 97 J10
HARP AL5 20 C4
HLW CM20 29 H10
NFNCH/WDSPK N12 97 P6
SOCK/AV RM15 146 B9
WOT/HER KT12 197 K9
WPK KT4 200 C9
St Michaels Ct GLDGN NW11 * 117 J5
SLN SL2 128 C6
St Michael's Crs PIN HA5 113 M4
St Michaels Dr GSTN WD25 55 J9
RSEV TN14 247 L2
St Michaels Gdns NKENS W10 8 A4
NKENS W10 137 H7
St Michael's Gn BEAC HP9 88 D8
St Michael's Ms BGVA SW1W 16 C6
St Michaels Ri WELL DA16 * 163 L7
St Michaels Rd ASHF TW15 174 B8
BROX EN10 44 E6
BRXN/ST SW9 158 G8
CDW/CHF RM16 168 E4
CRICK NW2 116 F9
CROY/NA CR0 203 K8
CTHM CR3 241 L8
WELL DA16 163 L9
WLGTN SM6 222 D3
WOKN/KNAP GU21 214 G10
St Michael's St BAY/PAD W2 9 M5
STALW/RED AL3 38 A6
St Michaels Ter HGT N6 * 118 B6
WDGN N22 98 F10
St Michaels Wy POTB/CUF EN6 59 L6
St Mildred's Ct LOTH EC2R * 12 G6
St Mildreds Rd CAT SE6 183 K3
GU GU1 250 C9
St Monica's Rd
KWD/TDW/WH KT20 239 J7
St Nazaire Cl EGH TW20 * 172 F8
St Neots Cl BORE WD6 75 M4
St Neot's Rd HARH RM3 105 N8
St Nicholas Av GT/LBKH KT23 254 A1
HCH RM12 125 H8
St Nicholas Cl AMSS HP7 69 N5
BORE WD6 75 J10
UX/CGN UB8 131 N8
St Nicholas Crs
WOKS/MYFD GU22 233 K2
St Nicholas Dr SEV TN13 265 J2
SHPTN TW17 196 B7
St Nicholas Glebe TOOT SW17 180 B9
St Nicholas Gn HLWE CM17 29 M10
St Nicholas Gv RBRW/HUT CM13 107 P6
St Nicholas Hl LHD/OX KT22 236 G8
St Nicholas Mt HHW HP1 35 J6
St Nicholas Pl LOU IG10 82 D8
St Nicholas Rd SUT SM1 221 L2
THDIT KT7 198 E6
WOOL/PLUM SE18 163 J4
St Nicholas St DEPT SE8 160 E7
St Nicholas Wy SUT SM1 221 L1
St Nicolas La CHST BR7 206 B1
St Ninian's Ct TRDG/WHET N20 98 A4
St Norbert Rd BROCKY SE4 160 D10
St Normans Wy EW KT17 220 D6
St Olaf's Rd FUL/PGN SW6 157 H6
St Olave's Cl STA TW18 173 J10
St Olave's Rd EHAM E6 142 D3
St Olave's Wk STRHM/NOR SW16 202 D2
St Omer Rdg GU GU1 268 D1
St Omer Rd GU GU1 268 D1
St Onge Pde EN EN1 * 79 L7
St Oswald's Pl LBTH SE11 17 N7
St Oswald's Rd
STRHM/NOR SW16 203 J1
St Oswulf St WEST SW1P * 17 K6
St Pancras Gdns CAMTN NW1 5 K6
St Pancras Wy CAMTN NW1 4 G3
St Patrick's Gdns GVE DA12 190 G7
St Patrick's Pl CDW/CHF RM16 168 E3
St Paul Cl UX/CGN UB8 131 N7
St Paul's Av BERM/RHTH SE16 * 140 C10
CRICK NW2 136 E1
KTN/HRWW/WS HA3 115 L3
SLN SL2 129 L9
St Paul's Church Yd STP EC4M 12 D6
St Paul's Cl ADL/WDHM KT15 215 K1
ASHF TW15 174 D8
BORE WD6 75 P9
CAR SM5 201 P8
CHARL SE7 162 A4
CHSGTN KT9 219 J1
EA W5 135 L10
EA W5 155 L1
HSLW TW3 153 N8
HYS/HAR UB3 152 E4
SOCK/AV RM15 146 B9
SWCM DA10 189 K3
St Paul's Cray Rd CHST BR7 206 G1
St Pauls Crs CAMTN NW1 5 K3
HDN NW4 * 116 F1
St Paul's Dr SRTFD E15 121 J10
St Pauls Ms CAMTN NW1 5 K3
DORK RH4 272 G3
St Paul's Pl IS N1 6 G1
SOCK/AV RM15 146 B9
STAL AL1 38 F6
St Pauls Ri PLMGR N13 99 J7
St Pauls Rd BARK IG11 142 F3
BTFD TW8 155 J5
ERITH DA8 164 D6
HHNE HP2 35 P5
IS N1 6 E1
RCH/KEW TW9 155 L9
STA TW18 172 G8
THHTH CR7 203 K3
TOTM N17 99 P8
WOKS/MYFD GU22 232 D3
St Paul's Rd East DORK RH4 272 G3
St Paul's Rd West DORK RH4 272 G3
St Pauls Ter WALW SE17 18 D9
St Paul St IS N1 6 E6
St Paul's Wy FNCH N3 97 L8
POP/IOD E14 140 E7
WAB EN9 * 63 J9
WATN WD24 73 K6
St Paul's Wood Hl
STMC/STPC BR5 207 H2
St Peters CHERT KT16 * 194 F10
St Peters Av BH/WHM TN16 * 244 E2
CHONG CM5 67 N2
UED N18 99 P5
WALTH E17 121 K2
St Petersburgh Ms BAY/PAD W2 8 G8
St Petersburgh Pl BAY/PAD W2 8 G8
St Peter's Cl BAR EN5 76 E9
BETH E2 7 P8
BUSH WD23 94 C2
CHST BR7 184 G10
GNTH/NBYPK IG2 123 H2
HAT AL10 40 D3
RKW/CH/CXG WD3 91 L3
RSLP HA4 113 L7
SL SL1 128 A6
STA TW18 173 J9
STAL AL1 38 C5
SWCM DA10 189 L3
TOOT SW17 179 P5
WDSR SL4 171 M1
WOKS/MYFD GU22 232 F6
St Peters Ct BKHTH/KID SE3 * 183 L1
CFSP/GDCR SL9 * 90 B9
E/WMO/HCT KT8 197 P4
HDN NW4 116 F3
St Peter's Gdns WNWD SE27 181 H6
St Peter's Gv HMSMTH W6 156 D3
St Peters Ms FSBYPK N4 * 119 J3
St Peter's Pl MV/WKIL W9 8 C2
St Peter's Rd BRW CM14 106 G5
CDW/CHF RM16 168 E3
CRAWW RH11 283 M7
CROY/NA CR0 223 L1
E/WMO/HCT KT8 197 P4
ED N9 100 A2
HMSMTH W6 * 156 D4
KUT/HW KT1 199 M2
STAL AL1 38 D6
STHL UB1 133 P7
TWK TW1 176 G1
UX/CGN UB8 131 N7
WOKS/MYFD GU22 232 E7
St Peter's Sq BETH E2 7 P8
HMSMTH W6 156 C4
St Peter's St IS N1 6 D6
SAND/SEL CR2 223 L2
STAL AL1 38 C6
St Peter's Ter FUL/PGN SW6 157 J6
St Peter's Vls HMSMTH W6 156 D3
St Peter's Wy ADL/WDHM KT15 195 K10
CHERT KT16 215 H1
EA W5 135 J7
HYS/HAR UB3 152 E4
IS N1 7 K4
RKW/CH/CXG WD3 70 E8
St Philip's Av WPK KT4 200 E9
St Philip Sq VX/NE SW8 * 158 C8
St Philip's Rd HACK E8 7 N2
SURB KT6 199 J6
St Philip St VX/NE SW8 158 C8
St Philip's Wy IS N1 6 F5
St Pinnock Av STA TW18 195 K1
St Quentin Rd WELL DA16 163 J9
St Quintin Av NKENS W10 136 F7
St Quintin Gdns NKENS W10 136 F7
St Quintin Rd PLSTW E13 141 N5
St Raphael's Wy WLSDN NW10 115 P10
St Regis Cl MUSWH N10 98 C10
St Richards Ms CRAWE RH10 * 284 A7
St Ronans Cl EBAR EN4 77 N4
St Ronans Crs WFD IG8 101 M8
St Rule St VX/NE SW8 158 D8
St Saviours Ct WDGN N22 98 E10
St Saviour's Est STHWK SE1 19 L3
St Saviours Pl GU GU1 * 249 P10
St Saviour's Rd
BRXS/STRHM SW2 180 G1
CROY/NA CR0 203 K6
Saints Cl WNWD SE27 181 J7
Saints Dr FSTGT E7 122 A10
St Silas Pl KTTN NW5 4 C2
St Simon's Av PUT/ROE SW15 178 F1
St Stephens Av ASHTD KT21 237 K3
SHB W12 136 E10
SHB W12 156 E1
STALW/RED AL3 38 A9
WALTH E17 121 H3
WEA W13 134 G8
St Stephens Cl KTTN NW5 * 118 A10
STALW/RED AL3 38 A9
STHL UB1 133 P7
STJWD NW8 3 N6
WALTH E17 120 G3
St Stephen's Crs BAY/PAD W2 * 8 F5
RBRW/HUT CM13 107 M5
THHTH CR7 203 H3
St Stephen's Garden Est
NTGHL W11 8 D5
St Stephen's Gdns BAY/PAD W2 8 F5
TWK TW1 177 H2
St Stephen's Gv LEW SE13 161 H9
St Stephen's Hl STALW/RED AL3 38 B8
St Stephen's Ms BAY/PAD W2 8 F4
St Stephens Pde WHALL SW1A 17 L1
St Stephens Rd BAR EN5 76 G9
BOW E3 140 E4
EHAM E6 141 P2
HSLW TW3 175 P2
PEND EN3 80 C3
WALTH E17 120 G3
WDR/YW UB7 131 N10
WEA W13 134 G8
St Stephens Ter VX/NE SW8 * 158 F6
VX/NE SW8 158 G6
St Stephen's Wk SKENS SW7 15 J5
Saint's Wk CDW/CHF RM16 168 F3
St Swithin's La MANHO EC4N 12 G7
St Swithun's Rd LEW SE13 * 183 J1
St Teresa Wk CDW/CHF RM16 168 E3
St Theresa Cl EPSOM KT18 219 P10
St Theresa's Rd
EBED/NFELT TW14 152 G10
St Thomas Cl RGUE GU4 268 F6
SURB KT6 199 L8
WOKN/KNAP GU21 231 P3
St Thomas Ct BXLY DA5 186 B3
St Thomas' Dr PIN HA5 93 M9
STMC/STPC BR5 206 F8
St Thomas Gdns IL IG1 142 F1
St Thomas Pl STALE/WH AL4 21 J3
St Thomas Rd BELV DA17 164 D1
BRW CM14 107 J3
CAN/RD E16 141 M8
CHSWK W4 155 P5
GVW DA11 * 190 B4
STHGT/OAK N14 98 E1
St Thomas's Av GVW DA11 190 E5
St Thomas's Cl WAB EN9 63 N9
St Thomas's Dr RGUE GU4 * 251 P7
St Thomas's Gdns HAMP NW3 4 C1
St Thomas's Ms GU GU1 268 C2
St Thomas's Pl GRAYS RM17 167 P5
HOM E9 * 140 B2
Saint Thomas's Rd FSBYPK N4 119 H7
St Thomas's Rd WLSDN NW10 136 B3
St Thomas's Sq HOM E9 140 A2
St Thomas St STHWK SE1 13 H10
St Thomas's Wy FUL/PGN SW6 157 J6
St Thomas Wk DTCH/LGLY SL3 150 G6
St Ursula Gv PIN HA5 113 L3
St Ursula Rd STHL UB1 133 P8
St Vincent Cl CRAWE RH10 284 E8
WNWD SE27 181 J8
St Vincent Dr STAL AL1 38 F8
St Vincent Rd WHTN TW2 176 B2
WOT/HER KT12 197 J10
St Vincents Av DART DA1 187 P1
St Vincents Cottages
WATW WD18 * 73 J8
St Vincents La MLHL NW7 96 F5
St Vincents Rd DART DA1 187 P2
St Vincent St MHST W1U 10 D4
St Vincent's Wy POTB/CUF EN6 59 M10
St Wilfrid's Cl EBAR EN4 * 77 P9
St Wilfrid's Rd EBAR EN4 77 N9
St Winefride's Av MNPK E12 122 C10
St Winifreds PUR/KEN CR8 241 K1
St Winifred's Cl CHIG IG7 102 F6
St Winifred's Rd BH/WHM TN16 244 C4
TEDD TW11 176 G9
St Yon Ct STALE/WH AL4 39 J6
Sakins Cft HLWS CM18 47 J4
Sakura Dr FBAR/BDGN N11 98 E9
Saladin Dr PUR RM19 165 P3
Salamanca Pl STHWK SE1 17 N6
Salamanca St STHWK SE1 17 N6
Salamander Cl KUTN/CMB KT2 177 H8
Salamander Quay KUT/HW KT1 * 199 J1
Salamons Wy RAIN RM13 144 F8
Salbrook Rd REDH RH1 276 B8
Salcombe Dr CHDH RM6 124 A4
MRDN SM4 200 G8
Salcombe Gdns MLHL NW7 96 F7
Salcombe Rd ASHF TW15 173 P7
STNW/STAM N16 119 N10
WALTH E17 120 E5
Salcombe Wy RSLP HA4 113 H7
Salcot Crs CROY/NA CR0 225 H6
Salcote Rd GVE DA12 191 H8
Salcott Rd BTSEA SW11 179 P1
CROY/NA CR0 202 F10
Salehurst Cl KTN/HRWW/WS HA3 115 K3
Salehurst Rd BROCKY SE4 182 E2
CRAWE RH10 284 F7
Salem Pl CROY/NA CR0 203 K10
GVW DA11 190 A3
Salem Rd BAY/PAD W2 8 G7
Sale Pl BAY/PAD W2 9 N4
Sale St BETH E2 13 N1
Salford Rd BRXS/STRHM SW2 180 E4
Salhouse Cl THMD SE28 143 M8
Salisbury Av BARK IG11 142 G2
FNCH N3 97 J10
SLN SL2 129 H6
STAL AL1 38 G6
SUT SM1 221 J3
SWLY BR8 209 H4
Salisbury Cl AMSS HP7 69 K5
POTB/CUF EN6 59 M8
WALW SE17 18 G6
WPK KT4 200 C10
Salisbury Ct EMB EC4Y 12 C6
Salisbury Crs CHES/WCR EN8 62 C8
Salisbury Gdns WGCE AL7 23 J6
WIM/MER SW19 * 179 H10
Salisbury Hall Dr HAT AL10 40 A2
Salisbury Pavement
FUL/PGN SW6 * 157 K6
Salisbury Pl BF/WBF KT14 215 M7
BRXN/ST SW9 159 J6
MBLAR W1H 10 A3
Salisbury Prom
CEND/HSY/T N8 * 119 J3
Salisbury Rd BAR EN5 77 H7
BNSTD SM7 239 L1
BXLY DA5 186 B4
CAR SM5 222 A3
CHING E4 100 F4
DAGE RM10 144 C1
FELT TW13 175 K4
FSBYPK N4 119 J3
FSTGT E7 141 M1
GDMY/SEVK IG3 123 H7
GDST RH9 260 B7
GPK RM2 125 J3
GRAYS RM17 167 P5
GVW DA11 190 C4
HAYES BR2 206 B5
HOD EN11 45 H2
HRW HA1 114 C3
HSLWW TW4 153 K9
LEY E10 121 H7
MNPK E12 122 B10
NWDGN UB2 * 153 M3
NWMAL KT3 200 A3
PEND EN3 80 E3
PIN HA5 113 H2
RCH/KEW TW9 155 K10
RDART DA2 188 B4
SNWD SE25 203 P6
UX/CGN UB8 131 L4
WALTH E17 121 H3
WATN WD24 73 J4
WDGN N22 99 J10
WEA W13 154 G1
WGCE AL7 23 J6
WIM/MER SW19 179 H10
WOKS/MYFD GU22 232 B5
WPK KT4 220 A1
Salisbury Sq EMB EC4Y * 12 B6
HERT/WAT SG14 * 25 L5
Salisbury St ACT W3 155 P1
STJWD NW8 9 N2
Salisbury Ter PECK SE15 160 B9
Salisbury Wk ARCH N19 118 D7
Salix Cl GT/LBKH KT23 236 A9
SUN TW16 175 J10
Salix Rd GRAYS RM17 168 A5
Sally Murray Cl MNPK E12 122 D9
Salmen Rd PLSTW E13 141 L4
Salmon Cl WGCE AL7 23 K2
Salmond Cl STAN HA7 94 F7
Salmond's Gv RBRW/HUT CM13 107 P6
Salmon La POP/IOD E14 140 D8
Salmon Ms KIL/WHAMP NW6 * 117 K10
Salmon Rd BELV DA17 164 B4
DART DA1 165 N9
Salmons La CTHM CR3 241 N6
Salmons La West CTHM CR3 241 M6
Salmons Rd CHSGTN KT9 219 K3
ED N9 99 P2
EHSLY KT24 253 K5
Salmon St CDALE/KGS NW9 115 N6
POP/IOD E14 * 140 E8
Salomons Rd PLSTW E13 141 P7
Salop Rd WALTH E17 120 C4
Saltash Cl SUT SM1 221 J1
Saltash Rd BARK/HLT IG6 102 G8
WELL DA16 163 M7
Saltbox Hl BH/WHM TN16 225 N9
Salt Box Rd RGUW GU3 249 M5
Saltcoats Rd CHSWK W4 156 B1
Saltcote Cl DART DA1 186 F2
Saltcroft Cl WBLY HA9 115 N6
Saltdean Cl CRAWE RH10 283 N10
Salter Cl RYLN/HDSTN HA2 113 N8
Salterford Rd TOOT SW17 180 B9
Salterns Rd CRAWE RH10 284 D10
Salter Rd BERM/RHTH SE16 140 C10
Salter's Cl BERK HP4 33 L3
RKW/CH/CXG WD3 91 P2
Salters Gdns WAT WD17 * 73 H5
Salters' Hall Ct MANHO EC4N * 12 G7
Salter's Hl NRWD SE19 181 L8
Salters Rd NKENS W10 136 G6
WALTH E17 121 J2
Salters Rw IS N1 * 6 G2
Salter St POP/IOD E14 140 F9
WLSDN NW10 136 D5
Salterton Rd HOLWY N7 118 F8
Saltford Cl ERITH DA8 164 F4
Salt Hill Av SL SL1 129 H10
Salt Hill Cl UX/CGN UB8 111 N10
Salt Hill Dr SL SL1 129 H10
Salt Hill Wy SL SL1 129 H10
Saltley Cl EHAM E6 142 B8
Saltoun Rd BRXS/STRHM SW2 159 H10
Saltram Cl SEVS/STOTM N15 119 N2
Saltram Crs MV/WKIL W9 2 D9
Saltwell St POP/IOD E14 140 F9
Saltwood Cl ORP BR6 227 M1
Saltwood Gv WALW SE17 18 G8
Salusbury Rd KIL/WHAMP NW6 2 C8
KIL/WHAMP NW6 137 H3
MV/WKIL W9 2 C8
Salvador TOOT SW17 179 P8
Salvation Pl LHD/OX KT22 236 F10
Salvia Gdns GFD/PVL UB6 134 F4
Salvington Rd CRAWW RH11 283 J10
Salvin Rd PUT/ROE SW15 156 G9
Salway Cl WFD IG8 101 M8
Salway Rd SRTFD E15 141 J1
Salwey Crs BROX EN10 44 E6
Samantha Cl WALTH E17 120 E5
Samantha Ms ABR/ST RM4 104 F4
Samaritan Cl CRAWW RH11 283 H9
Sam Bartram Cl CHARL SE7 161 P4
Samels Ct HMSMTH W6 156 D4
Samford St STJWD NW8 9 N2
Samian Ga STALW/RED AL3 37 N8
Samira Cl WALTH E17 120 E4
Samos Rd PGE/AN SE20 204 A2
Samphire Cl CRAWW RH11 283 K10
Samphire Ct GRAYS RM17 168 B5
Sampleoak La RGUE GU4 269 H7
Sampson Av BAR EN5 76 G9
Sampson Cl BELV DA17 163 N2
Sampsons Gn SLN SL2 128 E5
Sampsons Hl AMSS HP7 88 D1
Sampson St WAP E1W 13 P10
Samson St PLSTW E13 141 P4
Samuel Cl HACK E8 7 M5
NWCR SE14 160 C5
WOOL/PLUM SE18 162 B3
Samuel Gray Gdns
KUTN/CMB KT2 199 J1
Samuel Lewis Trust Dwellings
CMBW SE5 * 159 K7
HACK E8 * 119 P9
WKENS W14 * 157 H3
Samuel Sq STAL AL1 * 38 C7
Samuel St WOOL/PLUM SE18 162 C3
Sancroft Cl CRICK NW2 116 E8
Sancroft Rd KTN/HRWW/WS HA3 94 E10
Sancroft St LBTH SE11 17 P7
Sanctuary Cl DART DA1 187 L2
DEN/HRF UB9 91 M8
Sanctuary Ms HACK E8 7 M2
Sanctuary Rd HTHAIR TW6 174 B2
Sanctuary St STHWK SE1 18 F2
The Sanctuary BXLY DA5 185 N2
WEST SW1P 17 K3
Sandall Cl EA W5 135 K6
Sandall Rd EA W5 135 K6
KTTN NW5 5 H2
Sandalls Spring HHW HP1 35 J4
Sandal Rd NWMAL KT3 200 B4
UED N18 99 P6
Sandal St SRTFD E15 141 K3
Sandalwood GUW GU2 267 N1
Sandalwood Av CHERT KT16 194 G10
Sandalwood Cl WCHPL E1 140 D6
Sandalwood Dr RSLP HA4 112 D5
Sandalwood Rd FELT TW13 175 J6
Sanday Cl HHS/BOV HP3 36 C8
Sandbach Pl WOOL/PLUM SE18 162 F3
Sandbanks Hl RDART DA2 189 H9
Sandbourne Av WIM/MER SW19 201 L3
Sandbourne Rd NWCR SE14 160 D8
Sandbrook Cl MLHL NW7 96 A7
Sandbrook Rd STNW/STAM N16 119 M8
Sandby Gn ELTH/MOT SE9 162 B9
Sandcliff Rd ERITH DA8 164 E3
Sandcroft Cl PLMGR N13 99 J7
Sandcross La REIG RH2 275 J3
Sandell's Av ASHF TW15 174 D7
Sandell St STHWK SE1 18 A1
Sandelswood End BEAC HP9 88 C7
Sandelwood Wy BEAC HP9 88 C7
Sandeman Gdns WARE SG12 26 D1
Sanderling Wy RDART DA2 188 F2
Sanders Cl HPTN TW12 176 B8
LCOL/BKTW AL2 57 J3
Sanders Cnr ENC/FH EN2 * 79 J1
Sandersfield Gdns BNSTD SM7 239 K1
Sanders La MLHL NW7 96 G8
Sanderson Cl KTTN NW5 * 118 C9
RBRW/HUT CM13 * 127 P4
Sanderson Rd UX/CGN UB8 131 M1
Sandersons Av RSEV TN14 228 B6
Sanders Pde
STRHM/NOR SW16 * 180 F9
Sanders Rd HHS/BOV HP3 36 A9
Sanderstead Av GLDGN NW11 117 H7
Sanderstead Cl BAL SW12 180 D3
Sanderstead Court Av
SAND/SEL CR2 223 P9
Sanderstead Hl SAND/SEL CR2 223 M7
Sanderstead Rd LEY E10 120 D6
SAND/SEL CR2 223 L4
STMC/STPC BR5 207 L6
Sandes Pl LHD/OX KT22 236 F4
Sandfield Ct GU GU1 268 A1
Sandfield Gdns THHTH CR7 203 J3
Sandfield Pl THHTH CR7 203 K3
Sandfield Rd STAL AL1 38 F6
THHTH CR7 203 J3
Sandfields RPLY/SEND GU23 232 G10
Sandfield Ter GU GU1 268 A1
Sandford Av LOU IG10 82 F7
WDGN N22 99 J9
Sandford Rd BXLYHS DA6 163 P10
EHAM E6 142 C5
HAYES BR2 205 M4
Sandford Rw WALW SE17 18 G7
Sandford St FUL/PGN SW6 157 L6
Sandgate Cl ROMW/RG RM7 124 D5
Sandgate La WAND/EARL SW18 179 P4
Sandgate Rd WELL DA16 163 M6
Sandgate St PECK SE15 160 A5
Sandhills WLGTN SM6 222 E1
Sandhills Ct VW GU25 194 B5
Sandhills La VW GU25 194 B5
Sandhills Rd REIG RH2 275 K2
Sandhurst Av BRYLDS KT5 199 N7
RYLN/HDSTN HA2 114 A4
Sandhurst Cl CDALE/KGS NW9 115 M1
SAND/SEL CR2 223 M5
Sandhurst Ct HARP AL5 20 C5
Sandhurst Dr GDMY/SEVK IG3 123 K9
Sandhurst Pde CAT SE6 * 183 H4
Sandhurst Rd BXLY DA5 185 N1
CAT SE6 183 J4
CDALE/KGS NW9 115 M1
ED N9 80 B10
ORP BR6 207 K10
TIL RM18 168 F8
Sandhurst Wy SAND/SEL CR2 223 M4
Sandifer Dr CRICK NW2 116 G8
Sandifield HAT AL10 40 E7
Sandiford Rd CHEAM SM3 201 J9
Sandiland Crs HAYES BR2 205 L9
Sandilands CROY/NA CR0 203 P10
SEV TN13 246 E8
Sandilands Rd FUL/PGN SW6 157 L7
Sandison St PECK SE15 159 N9
Sandlands Gv
KWD/TDW/WH KT20 238 D9
Sandlands Rd
KWD/TDW/WH KT20 238 D9
Sandland St GINN WC1R 11 P4
Sandlers End SLN SL2 128 G6
Sandleswood Cl BEAC HP9 88 C7
Sandling Ri ELTH/MOT SE9 184 D6
Sandlings Cl PECK SE15 160 A8
The Sandlings WDGN N22 99 H10
Sandmartin Wy WLGTN SM6 202 B8
Sandmere Cl HHNE HP2 36 B7
Sandmere Rd CLAP SW4 158 F10
Sandon Cl ESH/CLAY KT10 198 C8
Sandon Pl CHONG CM5 67 P6
Sandon Rd CHES/WCR EN8 62 B6
Sandow Crs HYS/HAR UB3 152 G2
Sandown Av DAGE RM10 144 D1
ESH/CLAY KT10 218 B2
HCH RM12 125 L7
Sandown Cl HEST TW5 153 H7
Sandown Ct BELMT SM2 * 221 L4
DAGE RM10 144 D1
SYD SE26 * 182 A6
Sandown Dr CAR SM5 222 B5
Sandown Ga ESH/CLAY KT10 198 C9
Sandown Rd COUL/CHIP CR5 240 B2
ESH/CLAY KT10 218 B1
GVE DA12 190 F9
SLN SL2 128 E7
SNWD SE25 204 A5
WATN WD24 73 K4
Sandown Wy NTHLT UB5 133 M1
Sandpiper Cl BERM/RHTH SE16 160 E1
CRAWW RH11 282 G9
RDART DA2 188 F1
WALTH E17 100 C8
Sandpiper Dr ERITH DA8 165 J6
Sandpiper Rd SAND/SEL CR2 224 C7
SUT SM1 221 J2
The Sandpipers GVE DA12 190 G5
Sandpiper Ter CLAY IG5 * 122 E1
Sandpiper Wy STMC/STPC BR5 207 N4
Sandpit Hall Rd CHOB/PIR GU24 213 N8
Sandpit Heath RGUW GU3 249 J6
Sandpit La BRW CM14 86 E10
STAL AL1 38 E5
Sandpit Pl CHARL SE7 162 B4
Sandpit Rd BMLY BR1 183 K8
DART DA1 165 K10
REDH RH1 275 P1
WGCE AL7 23 H7

Sandpits Rd CROY/NA CR0 224 C1
RCHPK/HAM TW10 177 J5
Sandra Cl HSLW TW3 176 A1
WDGN N22 99 K9
Sandridgebury La
STALW/RED AL3 20 G9
STALW/RED AL3 38 D2
Sandridge Cl EBAR EN4 77 P3
HRW HA1 114 D2
Sandridge Pk STALW/RED AL3 * 38 E1
Sandridge Rd STAL AL1 38 D4
Sandridge St ARCH N19 118 D7
Sandringham Av
HLWW/ROY CM19 46 B1
RYNPK SW20 201 H1
Sandringham Cl EN EN1 79 M6
WIM/MER SW19 178 G4
WOKS/MYFD GU22 233 K2
Sandringham Ct SL SL1 128 C8
Sandringham Crs
RYLN/HDSTN HA2 113 P8
STALE/WH AL4 38 G1
Sandringham Dr ASHF TW15 173 N7
RDART DA2 186 F5
WELL DA16 163 H8
Sandringham Gdns
BARK/HLT IG6 122 F1
CEND/HSY/T N8 118 F4
E/WMO/HCT KT8 197 P4
HEST TW5 153 H7
NFNCH/WDSPK N12 97 N7
Sandringham Ms EA W5 135 J9
HPTN TW12 197 N1
Sandringham Pk COB KT11 217 N8
Sandringham Rd BARK IG11 143 J1
BMLY BR1 183 M8
BRWN CM15 86 G9
CRICK NW2 116 E10
FSTGT E7 121 P10
GLDGN NW11 117 H5
HACK E8 119 N10
HTHAIR TW6 173 P1
LEY E10 121 J5
NTHLT UB5 133 P2
POTB/CUF EN6 59 L6
THHTH CR7 203 K5
WATN WD24 73 J3
WDGN N22 119 K1
WPK KT4 200 D10
Sandringham Wy
CHES/WCR EN8 62 B10
Sandrock Pl CROY/NA CR0 224 C1
Sandrock Rd DORK RH4 272 A4
LEW SE13 160 F9
Sandroyd Wy COB KT11 217 P9
Sands End La FUL/PGN SW6 157 L7
Sands Farm Dr SL SL1 128 B6
Sandstone La CAN/RD E16 141 N9
Sandstone Pl ARCH N19 118 C7
Sandstone Rd LEE/GVPK SE12 183 N5
Sands Wy WFD IG8 102 C7
Sandtoft Rd CHARL SE7 161 N5
Sandway Rd STMC/STPC BR5 207 M4
Sandwell Crs KIL/WHAMP NW6 2 F1
Sandwich St STPAN WC1H 5 L10
Sandwick Cl MLHL NW7 96 D8
Sandwood Ms CSHM HP5 50 G6
Sandy Bank Rd GVE DA12 190 E4
Sandy Bury ORP BR6 206 G10
Sandy Cl HERT/WAT SG14 25 J5
WOKS/MYFD GU22 232 F3
Sandycombe Rd
EBED/NFELT TW14 175 H4
RCH/KEW TW9 155 M8
Sandycoombe Rd TWK TW1 177 H2
Sandy Ct COB KT11 217 N9
Sandycroft ABYW SE2 163 K5
Sandy Cft EW KT17 220 F6
Sandycroft Rd AMS HP6 69 N5
Sandy Dr COB KT11 217 P7
EBED/NFELT TW14 174 F4
Sandy Hill Av WOOL/PLUM SE18 162 E4
Sandy Hill La WOOL/PLUM SE18 162 E3
Sandyhill Rd IL IG1 122 E9
Sandy Hill Rd WLGTN SM6 222 D5
WOOL/PLUM SE18 162 E4
Sandy Holt COB KT11 217 N9
Sandy La ASC SL5 192 F5
BELMT SM2 221 H5
BH/WHM TN16 262 G1
BRKHM/BTCW RH3 256 B10
BUSH WD23 74 B7
CDW/CHF RM16 168 E5
CHOB/PIR GU24 213 K5
COB KT11 217 N8
CRAWE RH10 285 P5
KTN/HRWW/WS HA3 115 L4
KWD/TDW/WH KT20 239 J10
MEO DA13 189 K7
MTCM CR4 202 B1
NTHWD HA6 92 G3
ORP BR6 207 K7
OXTED RH8 261 H5
RCHPK/HAM TW10 177 H5
RDART DA2 189 J6
REDH RH1 258 F10
REDH RH1 259 J8
REDH RH1 276 E1
REIG RH2 274 F1
RGUW GU3 248 C7
RGUW GU3 267 M5
RPLY/SEND GU23 232 F9
SCUP DA14 185 N10
SEV TN13 247 K9
SHGR GU5 269 N7
SOCK/AV RM15 145 P9
TEDD TW11 176 F10
VW GU25 194 B5
WOKS/MYFD GU22 232 E4
WOKS/MYFD GU22 233 K2
WOT/HER KT12 197 J6
WTHK RM20 166 G5
Sandy La North WLGTN SM6 222 E2
Sandy La South WLGTN SM6 222 D5
Sandy Ldg PIN HA5 * 93 P7
Sandy Lodge Ct NTHWD HA6 * 92 F6
Sandy Lodge La NTHWD HA6 92 E3
Sandy Lodge Rd
RKW/CH/CXG WD3 92 C3
Sandy Lodge Wy NTHWD HA6 92 F7
Sandy Md HOR/WEW KT19 219 M5
Sandymount Av STAN HA7 95 H6
Sandy Rdg CHST BR7 184 D9
Sandy Ri CFSP/GDCR SL9 90 B9
Sandy Rd ADL/WDHM KT15 215 K3
HAMP NW3 117 L7
Sandy's Rw WCHPL E1 13 K4
Sandy Wy COB KT11 217 P8
CROY/NA CR0 204 E10
WOKS/MYFD GU22 232 F3
WOT/HER KT12 196 G8
Sanford La STNW/STAM N16 119 N7
Sanford St NWCR SE14 160 D5
Sanford Ter STNW/STAM N16 119 N8
Sanger Av CHSGTN KT9 219 L2
Sanger Dr RPLY/SEND GU23 232 F9
Sangers Dr HORL RH6 280 A5
Sangley Rd CAT SE6 182 G3
SNWD SE25 203 M4
Sangora Rd BTSEA SW11 157 N10
San Juan Dr CDW/CHF RM16 167 H4
Sankara Ct WAND/EARL SW18 179 L5
San Luis Dr CDW/CHF RM16 167 J3
San Marcos Dr CDW/CHF RM16 167 H4
Sansom Rd WAN E11 * 121 L7
Sansom St CMBW SE5 159 L6
Sans Wk CLKNW EC1R 12 C1
Santers La POTB/CUF EN6 59 H9
Santiago Wy CDW/CHF RM16 167 J4
Santley St CLAP SW4 158 F10
Santos Rd WAND/EARL SW18 179 K1
Sanway Cl BF/WBF KT14 215 P10
Sanway Rd BF/WBF KT14 215 P10
RPLY/SEND GU23 233 P1
Saperton Wk LBTH SE11 17 P5
Sapho Pk GVE DA12 191 J7
Saphora Cl ORP BR6 226 G2
Sappers Cl SBW CM21 30 A1
Sapphire Cl BCTR RM8 123 M6
Sapphire Rd DEPT SE8 160 D3
WLSDN NW10 135 P2
Sappho Ct WOKN/KNAP GU21 231 K2
Saracen Cl CROY/NA CR0 203 L6
Saracens Head HHNE HP2 36 B5
Saracen's Head Yd
FENCHST EC3M 13 K6
Saracen St POP/IOD E14 140 F8
Sara Crs RDART DA2 166 F10
Sarah St IS N1 7 K9
Sara Pk GVE DA12 191 H7
Saratoga Rd CLPT E5 120 B9
Sardinia St HOL/ALD WC2B 11 N6
Sarel Wy HORL RH6 280 C2
Sargeant Cl UX/CGN UB8 131 N5
Sarita Cl KTN/HRWW/WS HA3 94 C10
Sark Cl HEST TW5 153 P6
Sarnesfield Rd ENC/FH EN2 * 79 L8
Sarratt Av HHNE HP2 36 B1
Sarratt La RKW/CH/CXG WD3 71 L6
Sarratt Rd RKW/CH/CXG WD3 71 L3
Sarre Av HCH RM12 145 K1
Sarre Rd CRICK NW2 117 J10
STMC/STPC BR5 207 M5
Sarsby Dr STWL/WRAY TW19 172 D5
Sarsen Av HSLW TW3 153 N8
Sarsfeld Rd BAL SW12 180 A4
Sarsfield Rd GFD/PVL UB6 134 G4
Sartor Rd PECK SE15 160 C10
Sarum Complex UX/CGN UB8 * 131 L4
Sarum Gn WEY KT13 196 F10
Sarum Pl HHNE HP2 35 P2
Sarum Ter BOW E3 * 140 E6
Satanita Cl CAN/RD E16 142 A8
Satchell Md CDALE/KGS NW9 96 C9
Satchwell Rd BETH E2 * 7 N10
Satinwood Ct HHS/BOV HP3 35 P8
Sattar Ms STNW/STAM N16 * 119 L8
Saturn Cl CRAWW RH11 283 H9
Saturn Wy HHNE HP2 36 A3
Sauls Gn WAN E11 121 K8
Sauncey Av HARP AL5 20 A1
Saunders Cl CHES/WCR EN8 62 B4
CRAWE RH10 284 C7
GVW DA11 190 B5
IL IG1 122 G6
POP/IOD E14 * 140 E9
Saunders Copse
WOKS/MYFD GU22 231 N8
Saunders End AMS HP6 50 B10
Saunders La WOKS/MYFD GU22 231 L8
Saunders Ness Rd POP/IOD E14 161 J3
Saunders Rd HGDN/ICK UB10 132 A2
WOOL/PLUM SE18 163 J4
Saunders St LBTH SE11 18 A5
Saunders Wy DART DA1 187 N5
THMD SE28 143 L9
Saunderton Rd ALP/SUD HA0 114 G10
Saunton Av HYS/HAR UB3 152 G6
Saunton Rd HCH RM12 125 H7
Savage Gdns EHAM E6 142 C8
TWRH EC3N 13 K7
Savanah Cl PECK SE15 159 N6
Savay Cl DEN/HRF UB9 111 K5
Savay La DEN/HRF UB9 111 K5
Savernake Ct STAN HA7 * 94 G7
Savernake Rd ED N9 79 P10
HAMP NW3 118 A9
Savernake Wk CRAWE RH10 284 A10
Savery Dr SURB KT6 198 G7
SURB KT6 199 H7
Savile Cl NWMAL KT3 200 B5
THDIT KT7 198 E8
Savile Gdns CROY/NA CR0 203 N10
Savile Rw CONDST W1S 10 G7
Savill Cl CHESW EN7 * 61 K1
Saville Cl HOR/WEW KT19 219 N7
Saville Crs ASHF TW15 174 E9
Saville Rd CAN/RD E16 142 B10
CHDH RM6 124 A4
CHSWK W4 156 A2
TWK TW1 176 E4
Saville Rw HAYES BR2 205 L8
PEND EN3 80 C6
Savill Gdns RYNPK SW20 200 D3
Savill Ms EGH TW20 172 A9
Savill Rw WFD IG8 101 L7
Savona Cl WIM/MER SW19 178 G10
Savona St VX/NE SW8 158 D6
Savoy Av HYS/HAR UB3 152 F4
Savoy Cl DEN/HRF UB9 91 N10
EDGW HA8 95 M6
SRTFD E15 141 K3
Savoy Ct TPL/STR WC2R * 11 M8
Savoy Hl TPL/STR WC2R 11 N8
Savoy Ms BRXN/ST SW9 158 F9
Savoy Pde EN EN1 * 79 M7
Savoy Pl CHCR WC2N 11 M8
Savoy Rd DART DA1 187 K1
Savoy Rw TPL/STR WC2R 11 N7
Savoy Steps TPL/STR WC2R * 11 N8
Savoy St TPL/STR WC2R 11 N7
Savoy Wy TPL/STR WC2R 11 N8
Savoy Wd HLWW/ROY CM19 46 D7
Sawbill Cl YEAD UB4 133 L7
Sawells BROX EN10 44 E7
Sawkins Cl WIM/MER SW19 178 G5
Sawley Rd SHB W12 136 D10
Sawtry Cl CAR SM5 201 N7
Sawtry Wy BORE WD6 75 M4
Sawyer Cl ED N9 99 P3
Sawyers Cl DAGE RM10 144 D1
WDSR SL4 148 E6
Sawyers Gv BRWN CM15 107 J2
Sawyer's Hall La BRWN CM15 107 H1
Sawyer's Hl RCHPK/HAM TW10 177 L3
Sawyers La POTB/CUF EN6 58 G10
Sawyers Lawn WEA W13 134 F8
Sawyer St STHWK SE1 18 E1
Sawyers Wy HHNE HP2 36 A6
Saxby Rd BRXS/STRHM SW2 180 F3
Saxham Rd BARK IG11 143 H3
Saxley HORL RH6 280 D3
Saxlingham Rd CHING E4 101 J4
Saxon Av FELT TW13 175 N5
Saxonbury Av SUN TW16 197 J3
Saxonbury Cl MTCM CR4 201 N3
Saxonbury Gdns SURB KT6 199 H8
Saxon Cl AMS HP6 69 J4
DTCH/LGLY SL3 150 C1
GVW DA11 189 P6
HARH RM3 105 N10
RBRW/HUT CM13 107 M4
RSEV TN14 246 G3
SURB KT6 199 J6
UX/CGN UB8 131 P7
WALTH E17 120 F5
Saxon Ct BORE WD6 75 K5
Saxon Dr ACT W3 135 N8
Saxonfield Cl BRXS/STRHM SW2 180 G3
Saxon Hl BH/WHM TN16 * 262 G2
Saxon Pl EYN DA4 210 B5
Saxon Rd ASHF TW15 174 E9
BMLY BR1 183 L10
BOW E3 140 E4
CRAWE RH10 284 F8
EHAM E6 142 C6
IL IG1 142 E1
KUTN/CMB KT2 199 K1
RDART DA2 187 M7
SNWD SE25 203 L5
STALE/WH AL4 21 J4
STHL UB1 133 M10
WBLY HA9 115 P8
WDGN N22 99 J9
WOT/HER KT12 197 L10
Saxons KWD/TDW/WH KT20 238 G7
Saxon Shore Wy GVE DA12 190 G2
GVE DA12 191 K2
Saxon Wy REIG RH2 257 J9
STHGT/OAK N14 78 E10
WDR/YW UB7 151 M5
WDSR SL4 171 N2
Saxony Pde HYS/HAR UB3 132 D7
Saxton Cl LEW SE13 161 J9
Saxton Ms WAT WD17 * 73 H5
Saxville Rd STMC/STPC BR5 207 L3
Sayer Cl RDART DA2 188 F1
Sayers Cl LHD/OX KT22 236 B10
Sayers Gdns BERK HP4 33 M2
Sayesbury Av SBW CM21 29 P1
Sayesbury La UED N18 99 P6
Sayesbury Rd SBW CM21 29 P1
Sayes Ct ADL/WDHM KT15 215 L2
Sayes Court Farm Dr
ADL/WDHM KT15 215 L2
Sayes Court Rd STMC/STPC BR5 207 K3
Sayes Court St DEPT SE8 160 E4
Sayes Gdns SBW CM21 30 A1
Sayward Cl CSHM HP5 51 J5
Scabharbour Rd RSEV TN14 265 K9
Scadbury Gdns STMC/STPC BR5 207 K2
Scads Hill Cl ORP BR6 207 J6
Scafell Rd SLN SL2 128 E7
Scala St FITZ W1T 11 H3
Scales Rd TOTM N17 119 N1
Scallows Cl CRAWE RH10 284 B6
Scallows Rd CRAWE RH10 284 B6
Scammell Wy WATW WD18 72 G10
Scampston Ms NKENS W10 136 G8
Scampton Rd STWL/WRAY TW19 174 A2
Scandrett St WAP E1W * 140 A10
Scarba Wk IS N1 6 G2
Scarborough Cl BELMT SM2 221 J7
BH/WHM TN16 243 P4
Scarborough Rd ED N9 100 B1
FSBYPK N4 119 H6
HTHAIR TW6 174 D2
WAN E11 121 J6
Scarborough St WCHPL E1 13 M6
Scarborough Wy SL SL1 148 G1
Scarbrook Rd CROY/NA CR0 203 K10
Scarle Rd ALP/SUD HA0 135 J1
Scarlet Cl STMC/STPC BR5 207 L4
Scarlet Rd CAT SE6 183 K6
Scarlett Cl WOKN/KNAP GU21 231 L4
Scarsbrook Rd BKHTH/KID SE3 162 A9
Scarsdale Pl KENS W8 * 14 G3
Scarsdale Rd RYLN/HDSTN HA2 114 B8
Scarsdale Vls KENS W8 14 F4
Scarth Rd BARN SW13 156 C9
Scatterdells La KGLGY WD4 53 J6
Scatterdells Pk KGLGY WD4 * 53 K6
Scawen Cl CAR SM5 222 B1
Scawen Rd DEPT SE8 160 D4
Scawfell St BETH E2 7 M8
Scaynes Link
NFNCH/WDSPK N12 97 K5
Sceptre Rd BETH E2 140 B5
Scholars Cl BAR EN5 77 H8
Scholars Ms WGCW AL8 22 G4
Scholars Rd BAL SW12 180 D4
CHING E4 101 H2
Scholars Wk CFSP/GDCR SL9 90 B7
DTCH/LGLY SL3 150 D1
GUW GU2 267 N1
Scholars Wy AMS HP6 69 L4
GPK RM2 125 J3
Scholefield Rd ARCH N19 118 E7
Schonfeld Sq STNW/STAM N16 119 L7
Schoolbank Rd GNWCH SE10 161 L3
School Cl BRKMPK AL9 42 A3
CHOB/PIR GU24 230 E1
GU GU1 250 A8
School Crs DART DA1 164 G10
Schoolfield Rd WTHK RM20 166 F5
School Gdns BERK HP4 34 E3
School Green La EPP CM16 66 D1
School Hl REDH RH1 258 D4
School House La TEDD TW11 176 G10
Schoolhouse La WAP E1W * 140 C9
School La ADL/WDHM KT15 215 K1
AMSS HP7 68 A8
AMSS HP7 68 F5
BEAC HP9 89 J7
BFOR GU20 212 C3
BGR/WK TN15 247 N7
BRKMPK AL9 42 A3
BUSH WD23 94 A2
CFSP/GDCR SL9 90 B10
CHIG IG7 103 J5
CHOB/PIR GU24 230 D8
CHONG CM5 48 E3
DORK RH4 272 C3
EGH TW20 172 D8
EHSLY KT24 252 C5
HART DA3 210 E6
HAT AL10 40 E3
HLW CM20 29 H8
KUT/HW KT1 199 H1
LCOL/BKTW AL2 55 N10
LHD/OX KT22 236 C8
PIN HA5 * 113 M2
RBRW/HUT CM13 107 P7
RDART DA2 189 H6
RDKG RH5 255 H3
RGUE GU4 251 P7
RGUW GU3 266 B5
RPLY/SEND GU23 234 C8
SHPTN TW17 196 C6
SLN SL2 129 L9
SLN SL2 129 N2
SURB KT6 199 L8
SWLY BR8 187 J10
WELL DA16 163 L9
WLYN AL6 23 P2
School Md ABLGY WD5 54 E8
School Meadow GUW GU2 249 K9
School Pde DEN/HRF UB9 * 91 M10
School Pas KUT/HW KT1 199 L2
STHL UB1 133 N10
School Rd ASC SL5 192 C5
ASHF TW15 174 C9
BFOR GU20 212 A2
BRWN CM15 86 D3
CHONG CM5 66 G6
CHST BR7 206 F1
DAGE RM10 144 B3
E/WMO/HCT KT8 198 C4
GVE DA12 190 F6
HPTN TW12 176 B9
HSLW TW3 154 B9
KUT/HW KT1 * 199 H1
MNPK E12 122 C9
POTB/CUF EN6 59 M6
WDR/YW UB7 151 N5
WLSDN NW10 136 A6
School Road Av HPTN TW12 176 B9
School Rw HHW HP1 35 J7
School Sq GNWCH SE10 161 L2
School Wy BCTR RM8 123 L8
Schoolway NFNCH/WDSPK N12 97 N7
Schooner Cl BARK IG11 143 L5
BERM/RHTH SE16 160 C1
POP/IOD E14 161 J2
Schooner Ct RDART DA2 166 B10
Schroder Ct EGH TW20 171 N8
Schubert Rd BORE WD6 75 J10
PUT/ROE SW15 179 J1
Scillonian Rd GUW GU2 267 M2
Sclater St WCHPL E1 13 L1
Scoble Pl STNW/STAM N16 119 N9
Scoles Crs BRXS/STRHM SW2 181 H4
Scope Wy KUT/HW KT1 199 K4
Scords La BH/WHM TN16 263 M8
Scoresby St STHWK SE1 12 C10
Scorton Av GFD/PVL UB6 134 F4
Scory Cl CRAWW RH11 283 K10
Scotch Common WEA W13 134 G7
Scoter Cl WFD IG8 101 N8
Scot Gv PIN HA5 93 L8
Scotia Rd BRXS/STRHM SW2 181 H3
Scotland Bridge Rd
ADL/WDHM KT15 215 K7
Scotland Gn TOTM N17 99 N10
Scotland Green Rd PEND EN3 80 C9
Scotland Green Rd North
PEND EN3 80 D8
Scotland Rd BKHH IG9 101 P2
Scotlands Dr SLN SL2 128 G2
Scotney Cl ORP BR6 226 D1
Scots Cl STWL/WRAY TW19 173 N4
Scotscraig RAD WD7 74 E1
Scotsdale Cl CHEAM SM3 221 H4
STMC/STPC BR5 207 H4
Scotsdale Rd LEE/GVPK SE12 183 N1
Scotshall La WARL CR6 243 H1
Scots Hl RKW/CH/CXG WD3 72 A10
Scots Hill Cl RKW/CH/CXG WD3 72 A10
Scots Mill La RKW/CH/CXG WD3 72 A10
Scotswood Cl BEAC HP9 88 C6
Scotswood St CLKNW EC1R * 12 B1
Scotswood Wk TOTM N17 * 100 A8
Scott Av WARE SG12 26 G7
Scott Cl GUW GU2 249 M8
HOD EN11 45 H3
HOR/WEW KT19 219 P2
SLN SL2 109 H10
STRHM/NOR SW16 202 G1
WDR/YW UB7 152 A3
Scott Crs ERITH DA8 164 G7
RYLN/HDSTN HA2 114 A6
Scott Ellis Gdns STJWD NW8 3 L10
Scottes La BCTR RM8 123 N6
Scott Farm Cl THDIT KT7 198 G8
Scott Gdns HEST TW5 153 L6
Scott Lidgett Crs
BERM/RHTH SE16 19 N2
BERM/RHTH SE16 159 P1
Scott Rd CDW/CHF RM16 168 D3
CRAWE RH10 284 A10
EDGW HA8 95 N10
GVE DA12 190 G8
Scotts Av HAYES BR2 205 J2
SUN TW16 174 F10
Scotts Cl HCH RM12 125 K10
WARE SG12 26 C3
Scotts Dr HPTN TW12 176 A10
Scotts Farm Rd HOR/WEW KT19 219 P3
Scott's Grove Cl CHOB/PIR GU24 213 J9
Scotts Grove Rd CHOB/PIR GU24 213 H10
Scott's Hl HORL RH6 281 L3
REDH RH1 277 L10
Scott's La HAYES BR2 205 J3
Scotts Pas WOOL/PLUM SE18 * 162 E3
Scotts Rd BMLY BR1 183 M10
LEY E10 121 H6
NWDGN UB2 153 K2
SHB W12 156 E1
WARE SG12 26 C3
Scott St WCHPL E1 140 A6
Scotts Vw WGCW AL8 22 F6
Scotts Wy SEV TN13 246 F8
SUN TW16 174 F10
Scottswood Cl BUSH WD23 73 M6
Scottswood Rd BUSH WD23 73 M6
Scott's Yd MANHO EC4N 12 G7
Scott Trimmer Wy HSLW TW3 153 M8
Scottwell Dr CDALE/KGS NW9 116 C3
Scoulding Rd CAN/RD E16 141 L8
Scouler St POP/IOD E14 141 J9
Scout Ap WLSDN NW10 116 B9
Scout La CLAP SW4 158 D9
Scout Wy MLHL NW7 96 A5
Scovell Crs STHWK SE1 * 18 E2
Scovell Rd STHWK SE1 18 E2
Scratchers La HART DA3 210 C10
Scrattons Ter BARK IG11 143 N4
Scriveners Cl HHNE HP2 35 P6
Scriven St HACK E8 7 M5
Scrooby St CAT SE6 182 G2
Scrubbits Sq RAD WD7 74 F1
Scrubbitts Park Rd RAD WD7 74 F1
Scrubs La WLSDN NW10 136 D5
Scrutton Cl BAL SW12 180 E3
Scrutton St SDTCH EC2A 13 J2
Scudders Hl HART DA3 211 H6
Scutari Rd EDUL SE22 182 A1
Scutley La BFOR GU20 212 D4
Scylla Crs HTHAIR TW6 174 C3
Scylla Pl WOKN/KNAP GU21 * 231 M5
Scylla Rd HTHAIR TW6 174 C2
PECK SE15 160 A9
Seaborough Rd CDW/CHF RM16 168 F2
Seabright St BETH E2 140 A5
Seabrook Dr WWKM BR4 205 K9
Seabrooke Ri GRAYS RM17 167 N5
Seabrook Gdns ROMW/RG RM7 124 B5
Seabrook Rd BCTR RM8 123 N8
KGLGY WD4 54 E4
Seaburn Cl RAIN RM13 144 F5
Seacole Cl ACT W3 136 A8
Seacourt Rd ABYW SE2 163 N1
DTCH/LGLY SL3 150 E3
Seacroft Gdns OXHEY WD19 93 L4
Seafield Rd FBAR/BDGN N11 98 E5
Seaford Cl RSLP HA4 112 E7
Seaford Rd EN EN1 79 M8
HTHAIR TW6 173 N1
SEVS/STOTM N15 119 L3
WALTH E17 120 G1
WEA W13 134 G10
Seaford St STPAN WC1H 5 M10
Seaforth Av NWMAL KT3 200 E5
Seaforth Cl ROM RM1 104 F8
Seaforth Crs HBRY N5 119 K10
Seaforth Dr CHES/WCR EN8 62 C10
Seaforth Gdns HOR/WEW KT19 220 C1
WCHMH N21 98 G1
WFD IG8 101 P6
Seaforth Pl WESTW SW1E 17 H3
Seager Buildings DEPT SE8 * 160 F7
Seager Pl BOW E3 140 E7
Seagrave Cl WCHPL E1 * 140 C7
Seagrave Rd FUL/PGN SW6 14 F9
Seagry Rd WAN E11 121 M4
Seagull La CAN/RD E16 141 M9
Sealand Rd HTHAIR TW6 174 B2
Seal Dr BGR/WK TN15 247 N7
Seal Hollow Rd SEV TN13 247 L10
Seally Rd GRAYS RM17 167 M4
Seal Rd SEV TN13 247 K7
Seal St HACK E8 119 N9
Seaman Cl LCOL/BKTW AL2 56 C1
Searches La ABLGY WD5 55 K3
Searchwood Rd WARL CR6 242 A4
Searle Hl REIG RH2 275 K2
Searles Cl BTSEA SW11 157 P6
Searles Dr EHAM E6 142 E7
Searles Rd STHWK SE1 19 H5
Sears St CMBW SE5 159 L6
Seasprite Cl NTHLT UB5 133 L5
Seaton Av GDMY/SEVK IG3 123 H10
Seaton Cl LBTH SE11 18 B7
PLSTW E13 141 M6
PUT/ROE SW15 178 E3
WHTN TW2 176 C2
Seaton Dr ASHF TW15 173 P5
Seaton Gdns RSLP HA4 113 H8
Seaton Rd ALP/SUD HA0 * 135 K4
DART DA1 187 H3
HHS/BOV HP3 35 N9
HYS/HAR UB3 152 E3
LCOL/BKTW AL2 57 J3
MTCM CR4 201 P2
WELL DA16 163 M6
WHTN TW2 176 B2
Seaton St UED N18 99 P6
Sebastian Av BRWN CM15 87 M10
Sebastian St FSBYE EC1V 6 D10
Sebastopol Rd ED N9 99 P5
Sebbon St IS N1 6 D4
Sebergham Gv MLHL NW7 96 D8
Sebert Rd FSTGT E7 121 N10
Sebright Rd BAR EN5 76 G6
HHW HP1 35 K8
Secker Crs KTN/HRWW/WS HA3 94 B9
Secker St STHWK SE1 12 A10
Second Av ACT W3 136 C10
ADL/WDHM KT15 215 L5
CHDH RM6 123 M3
DAGE RM10 144 C4
EN EN1 79 N9
GSTN WD25 73 L1
HDN NW4 116 G2
HLW CM20 46 G1
HLWS CM18 47 J1
HYS/HAR UB3 132 G10
KWD/TDW/WH KT20 * 257 J2
MNPK E12 122 B9
MORT/ESHN SW14 156 B9
NKENS W10 8 B1
NKENS W10 137 H6
PLSTW E13 141 M5
UED N18 100 B5
WALTH E17 120 F3
WBLY HA9 115 J7
WOT/HER KT12 197 J6
WTHK RM20 166 F5
Second Cl E/WMO/HCT KT8 198 A4
Second Crs SL SL1 129 H7
Second Cross Rd WHTN TW2 176 D5
Second Wy WBLY HA9 115 N9
Sedan Wy WALW SE17 19 J7
Sedcombe Cl SCUP DA14 185 L7
Sedcote Rd PEND EN3 80 B9
Sedding St KTBR SW1X 16 C5
Seddon Rd MRDN SM4 201 N5
Seddon St FSBYW WC1X 5 N10
Sedgebrook Rd BKHTH/KID SE3 162 A8
Sedgecombe Av
KTN/HRWW/WS HA3 115 H3
Sedgefield Cl CRAWE RH10 284 F6
HARH RM3 105 N5
Sedgefield Crs HARH RM3 105 N6
Sedgeford Rd SHB W12 136 C10
Sedge Gn HLWW/ROY CM19 45 L5
Sedgehill Rd CAT SE6 182 F8
Sedgemere Av EFNCH N2 117 M1
Sedgemere Rd ABYW SE2 163 M2
Sedgemoor Dr DAGE RM10 124 B9
Sedge Rd TOTM N17 100 B8
Sedgeway CAT SE6 183 L4
Sedgewick Cl CRAWE RH10 284 D7
Sedgewood Cl HAYES BR2 205 L7
Sedgmoor Pl CMBW SE5 159 M6
Sedgwick Av HGDN/ICK UB10 132 C2
Sedgwick Rd LEY E10 121 H7
Sedgwick St HOM E9 120 C10
Sedleigh Rd WAND/EARL SW18 179 J2
Sedlescombe Rd FUL/PGN SW6 14 E10
Sedley MEO DA13 189 M8
Sedley Cl EN EN1 80 A4
Sedley Gv DEN/HRF UB9 111 M2
Sedley Pl OXSTW W1C 10 E6
Sedley Ri LOU IG10 82 C6
Sednem Ct PECK SE15 159 P8
Sedum Cl CDALE/KGS NW9 115 N3
The Seedbed Centre
HLWW/ROY CM19 46 D2
Seeley Dr DUL SE21 181 M7
Seeleys HLWE CM17 29 M7
Seeleys Ct BEAC HP9 * 88 C8
Seeleys Rd BEAC HP9 88 B7
Seelig Av CDALE/KGS NW9 116 D5
Seely Rd TOOT SW17 180 B9
Seer Green La BEAC HP9 89 K8
Seer Md BEAC HP9 89 J7
Seething La TWRH EC3N 13 K7
Seething Wells La SURB KT6 199 H6
Sefton Av KTN/HRWW/WS HA3 94 C10
MLHL NW7 96 A6
Sefton Cl CHOB/PIR GU24 212 E9
SLN SL2 129 L3
STAL AL1 38 E5
STMC/STPC BR5 207 J4
Sefton Ct ENC/FH EN2 * 79 J6
WGCW AL8 22 E7
Sefton Paddock SLN SL2 129 M2
Sefton Pk SLN SL2 * 129 M2
Sefton Rd CROY/NA CR0 203 P8
HOR/WEW KT19 220 A6
STMC/STPC BR5 207 J4
Sefton St PUT/ROE SW15 156 F8
Sefton Wy UX/CGN UB8 131 M8
Segrave Cl WEY KT13 216 B4
Sekforde St CLKNW EC1R 12 C2
Sekhon Ter FELT TW13 175 P6
Selah Dr SWLY BR8 208 D1
Selan Gdns YEAD UB4 133 J7
Selbie Av WLSDN NW10 116 C10
Selborne Av BXLY DA5 185 P4
MNPK E12 122 D9
Selborne Gdns GFD/PVL UB6 134 F4
HDN NW4 116 D2
Selborne Rd CMBW SE5 159 L8
CROY/NA CR0 203 M10
IL IG1 122 D7
NWMAL KT3 200 B2
SCUP DA14 185 L7
STHGT/OAK N14 98 F4
WALTH E17 120 E3
WDGN N22 98 G9
Selbourne Av ADL/WDHM KT15 215 L6
SURB KT6 199 L9
Selbourne Cl ADL/WDHM KT15 215 L6
CRAWE RH10 284 E4
Selbourne Rd RGUE GU4 250 D7
Selbourne Sq GDST RH9 260 B6
Selby Av STALW/RED AL3 * 38 C6
Selby Cha RSLP HA4 113 J7
Selby Cl CHSGTN KT9 219 K4
CHST BR7 184 D9
Selby Gdns STHL UB1 133 P6
Selby Gn CAR SM5 201 P7
Selby Rd ASHF TW15 174 D9
CAR SM5 201 P7
EA W5 134 G6
PGE/AN SE20 203 P2
PLSTW E13 141 N7
TOTM N17 99 M7
WAN E11 121 K8
Selby St WCHPL E1 13 P2
Selby Wk WOKN/KNAP GU21 231 N4
Selcroft Rd PUR/KEN CR8 223 J8
Selden Hl HHNE HP2 35 N7
Selden Rd PECK SE15 160 B8
Sele Ml HERT/WAT SG14 25 J5
Sele Rd HERT/WAT SG14 25 J5
Selham Cl CRAWW RH11 283 K6
Selhurst Cl WIM/MER SW19 178 G4
WOKN/KNAP GU21 232 C1
Selhurst New Rd SNWD SE25 203 M6
Selhurst Pl SNWD SE25 203 M6
Selhurst Rd ED N9 99 L4
SNWD SE25 203 M5
Selinas La BCTR RM8 123 P5
Selkirk Dr ERITH DA8 164 F7
Selkirk Rd TOOT SW17 179 P7
WHTN TW2 176 B5
Sellar's Hl GODL GU7 267 J10
Sell Cl CHESW EN7 61 J1
Sellers Hall Cl FNCH N3 97 K8
Sellincourt Rd TOOT SW17 179 P8
Sellindge Cl BECK BR3 182 E10
Sellons Av WLSDN NW10 136 C3
Sells Cl GU GU1 268 D2
Sells Rd WARE SG12 26 E1
Sellwood Dr BAR EN5 76 G9
Selsdon Av SAND/SEL CR2 223 L3
Selsdon Cl CRW RM5 104 D9
SURB KT6 199 K5
Selsdon Crs SAND/SEL CR2 224 B6
Selsdon Park Rd CROY/NA CR0 224 D5
Selsdon Rd ADL/WDHM KT15 215 K7
CRICK NW2 116 C7
PLSTW E13 141 P3
SAND/SEL CR2 223 L2
WAN E11 121 M5
WNWD SE27 181 J6
Selsdon Wy POP/IOD E14 160 G2
Selsea Pl STNW/STAM N16 119 M10
Selsey Crs WELL DA16 163 N7
Selsey St BOW E3 140 F7
Selvage La MLHL NW7 96 A6
Selway Cl PIN HA5 113 J2
Selwood Cl STWL/WRAY TW19 * 173 M2
Selwood Gdns
STWL/WRAY TW19 173 M2
Selwood Pl SKENS SW7 15 L7
Selwood Rd BRW CM14 106 E4
CHEAM SM3 201 J8
CHSGTN KT9 219 J1
CROY/NA CR0 204 A9
WOKS/MYFD GU22 232 E6
Selwood Ter SKENS SW7 15 L7
Selworthy Cl WAN E11 121 M3
Selworthy Rd CAT SE6 182 E6
Selwyn Av CHING E4 101 H7
GDMY/SEVK IG3 123 J4
HAT AL10 40 A5
RCH/KEW TW9 155 L9
Selwyn Cl CRAWE RH10 284 D4
HSLWW TW4 153 M10
WDSR SL4 148 C8
Selwyn Ct EDGW HA8 95 N8
Selwyn Crs HAT AL10 40 B4
WELL DA16 163 L10
Selwyn Dr HAT AL10 40 B4
Selwyn Rd BOW E3 140 E4
NWMAL KT3 200 A5
PLSTW E13 141 N3
TIL RM18 168 C8
WLSDN NW10 136 B2
Semaphore Rd GU GU1 268 B2
Semley Pl BGVA SW1W 16 D6
STRHM/NOR SW16 202 G2
Semley Rd STRHM/NOR SW16 202 F2
Semper Cl WOKN/KNAP GU21 231 K3
Semper Rd CDW/CHF RM16 168 F1
Sempill Rd HHS/BOV HP3 35 P9
Senate St PECK SE15 160 B8
Send Barns La RPLY/SEND GU23 233 H10
Send Cl RPLY/SEND GU23 232 F9
Send Hl RPLY/SEND GU23 250 F1
Send Marsh Rd
RPLY/SEND GU23 233 J9
Send Parade Cl
RPLY/SEND GU23 * 232 F9
Send Rd RPLY/SEND GU23 232 F9
Seneca Rd THHTH CR7 203 K4
Senga Rd WLGTN SM6 202 B8
Senhouse Rd CHEAM SM3 200 G10
Senior St BAY/PAD W2 8 G3
Senlac Rd LEE/GVPK SE12 183 N4
Sennen Rd EN EN1 99 N1
Senrab St WCHPL E1 140 C8
Sentamu Cl HNHL SE24 181 J4
Sentinel Cl NTHLT UB5 133 M6
September Wy STAN HA7 94 G7
Sequoia Cl BUSH WD23 94 C2
Sequoia Gdns ORP BR6 207 J7
Sequoia Pk CRAWW RH11 283 N9
PIN HA5 94 A7
Serbin Cl LEY E10 121 H5
Serenaders Rd BRXN/ST SW9 159 H8
Sergeants Green La WAB EN9 63 P9
Sergeants Pl CTHM CR3 241 K8
Sergehill La ABLGY WD5 55 H2
Serjeant's Inn EMB EC4Y * 12 B6
Serle St LINN WC2A 11 P5
Sermon Dr SWLY BR8 208 D3
Sermon La BLKFR EC4V 12 E6
Serpentine Rd BAY/PAD W2 9 P10
SEV TN13 247 K9
Service Rd HORL RH6 280 B8
The Service Rd POTB/CUF EN6 59 K8
Service Route No 1 SRTFD E15 141 J2
Service Route No 2 SRTFD E15 141 J2
Service Route No 3 SRTFD E15 141 J1
Serviden Dr BMLY BR1 206 A1
Setchell Est STHWK SE1 19 L5
Setchell Rd STHWK SE1 19 L5
Setchell Wy STHWK SE1 19 L5
Seth St BERM/RHTH SE16 160 B1
Seton Gdns DAGW RM9 143 M2
Settle Rd HARH RM3 105 P5
Settles St WCHPL E1 13 P4
Settrington Rd FUL/PGN SW6 157 L8
Seven Acres CAR SM5 201 P9
NTHWD HA6 93 H7
SWLY BR8 208 E6
Seven Arches Ap WEY KT13 216 A4
Seven Arches Rd BRW CM14 107 K4
Seven Dials LSQ/SEVD WC2H 11 L6
Sevenex Pde WBLY HA9 * 115 K10
Seven Hills Cl WOT/HER KT12 216 F5
Sevenhills Rd IVER SL0 110 E10
Seven Hills Rd WEY KT13 216 F4
Seven Hills Rd (South) COB KT11 216 F9
Seven Kings Rd GDMY/SEVK IG3 123 H6
Seven Kings Wy KUTN/CMB KT2 199 J1
Sevenoaks By-Pass RSEV TN14 264 F2
Sevenoaks Cl BELMT SM2 221 K6
BXLYHN DA7 164 D10
HARH RM3 105 K5
Sevenoaks Rd BROCKY SE4 182 E2
ORP BR6 227 J1
ORP BR6 228 B3
RSEV TN14 247 J2
Sevenoaks Wy STMC/STPC BR5 207 L3
Seven Sisters Rd HOLWY N7 118 G8
Seven Stars Yd WCHPL E1 13 M3
Seventh Av HYS/HAR UB3 133 H10
KWD/TDW/WH KT20 * 257 J2
MNPK E12 122 C9
Severalls Av CSHM HP5 51 H6
Severn TIL RM18 169 L2
Severnake Cl POP/IOD E14 160 F3
Severn Av GPK RM2 125 J1
NKENS W10 2 B10
NKENS W10 137 H5
Severn Crs DTCH/LGLY SL3 150 E4
Severn Dr EN EN1 79 P4
ESH/CLAY KT10 198 F9
UPMR RM14 126 C4
WOT/HER KT12 197 L9
Severnmead HHNE HP2 35 P3
Severn Rd CRAWE RH10 284 D8
SOCK/AV RM15 146 B8
Severns Fld EPP CM16 65 K5
Severnvale LCOL/BKTW AL2 * 57 L3
Severn Wy GSTN WD25 55 K10
WLSDN NW10 116 C10
Severus Rd BTSEA SW11 157 P10
Seville Ms IS N1 7 J4
Seville St KTBR SW1X 16 B2
Sevington Rd HDN NW4 116 E4
Sevington St MV/WKIL W9 8 G2
Seward Rd BECK BR3 204 C2
HNWL W7 154 F1
Sewardstone Rd BETH E2 140 B4
CHING E4 80 G8
WAB EN9 63 J10
Sewardstone St WAB EN9 63 H10
Sewardstone Wy WAB EN9 81 H2
Seward St FSBYE EC1V 12 D1
Sewdley St CLPT E5 120 C8
Sewell Cl CDW/CHF RM16 167 H4
STALE/WH AL4 39 K6
Sewell Harris Cl HLW CM20 29 J10
Sewell Rd ABYW SE2 163 K2
Sewells WGCW AL8 23 H2
Sewell St PLSTW E13 141 M5
Sewill Cl HORL RH6 279 J8
Sextant Av POP/IOD E14 161 J3
Sexton Cl CHESW EN7 61 J1
RAIN RM13 144 G3
Sexton Rd TIL RM18 168 C7
Seymer Rd ROM RM1 124 E1
Seymour Av CTHM CR3 241 K9
EW KT17 220 F6
MRDN SM4 200 G7
TOTM N17 99 P10
Seymour Cl E/WMO/HCT KT8 198 B5
LOU IG10 82 B10
PIN HA5 93 N9
Seymour Ct COB KT11 * 216 G9
Seymour Crs HHNE HP2 35 P6
Seymour Dr HAYES BR2 206 C8
Seymour Gdns BROCKY SE4 160 C9

BRYLDS KT5 199 L5
FELT TW13 175 J7
IL IG1 122 C6
RSLP HA4 113 L6
TWK TW1 176 G3
Seymour Ms EW KT17 220 D6
MBLAR W1H 10 C5
Seymour Pl MBLAR W1H 10 A5
SNWD SE25 204 A4
WOKS/MYFD GU22 231 N6
Seymour Rd BERK HP4 33 K3
CAR SM5 222 B2
CEND/HSY/T N8 119 J3
CHING E4 100 G2
CHSWK W4 155 P3
CSTG HP8 89 P5
E/WMO/HCT KT8 198 B5
ED N9 100 A3
EHAM E6 142 A3
EHAM E6 142 A4
FNCH N3 97 L8
GVW DA11 190 C4
HPTN TW12 176 B8
KUT/HW KT1 199 J1
LEY E10 120 E6
MTCM CR4 202 B7
SL SL1 149 H1
STALW/RED AL3 38 D3
TIL RM18 168 C7
WIM/MER SW19 178 G6
WAND/EARL SW18 179 J3
Seymours HLWW/ROY CM19 46 D4
Seymour St BAY/PAD W2 10 A6
WOOL/PLUM SE18 162 F3
Seymour Ter PGE/AN SE20 204 A1
Seymour Vls PGE/AN SE20 204 A1
Seymour Wk SWCM DA10 189 K3
WBPTN SW10 15 K9
Seymour Wy SUN TW16 174 F10
Seyssel St POP/IOD E14 161 H3
Shaa Rd ACT W3 136 A9
Shabden Cottages
COUL/CHIP CR5 * 240 A7
Shacklands Rd RSEV TN14 228 D7
Shackleford Rd MFD/CHID GU8 266 C10
WOKS/MYFD GU22 232 D6
Shacklegate La TEDD TW11 176 D7
Shackleton Cl FSTH SE23 182 A5
Shackleton Rd CRAWE RH10 283 P10
SL SL1 129 L9
STHL UB1 133 N9
Shackleton Wy ABLGY WD5 * 55 H8
WGCE AL7 23 N5
Shacklewell La HACK E8 119 N10
Shacklewell Rd HACK E8 119 N9
Shacklewell Rw HACK E8 119 N9
Shacklewell St BETH E2 13 M1
Shadbolt Av CHING E4 100 D6
Shadbolt Cl WPK KT4 200 C9
Shad Thames STHWK SE1 13 M10
STHWK SE1 19 M1
Shadwell Dr NTHLT UB5 133 N4
Shadwell Gdns WCHPL E1 * 140 B9
Shadwell Pierhead WAP E1W 140 B9
Shady Bush Cl BUSH WD23 94 B1
Shady La WAT WD17 73 J6
Shaef Wy TEDD TW11 176 F10
Shafter Rd DAGE RM10 144 D1
Shaftesbury LOU IG10 82 A7
Shaftesbury Av BAR EN5 77 M8
EBED/NFELT TW14 175 H2
KTN/HRWW/WS HA3 115 J4
NWDGN UB2 153 P3
PEND EN3 80 C6
RYLN/HDSTN HA2 114 A6
SOHO/SHAV W1D 11 J7
Shaftesbury Cir
RYLN/HDSTN HA2 * 114 B6
Shaftesbury Ct
RKW/CH/CXG WD3 * 72 D9
Shaftesbury Crs STA TW18 173 N10
Shaftesbury Gdns WLSDN NW10 136 B6
Shaftesbury La DART DA1 166 A10
Shaftesbury Ms CLAP SW4 180 D1
KENS W8 * 14 F4
Shaftesbury Pde
RYLN/HDSTN HA2 * 114 B6
Shaftesbury Pl BARB EC2Y * 12 E4
Shaftesbury Rd ARCH N19 118 F6
BECK BR3 204 E2
CAR SM5 201 N7
CHING E4 101 J2
CHOB/PIR GU24 230 E2
CRAWE RH10 284 E9
EPP CM16 65 J5
FSTGT E7 141 P2
LEY E10 120 F6
RCH/KEW TW9 155 K10
ROM RM1 124 G4
UED N18 99 M7
WALTH E17 120 G3
WAT WD17 73 K7
WOKS/MYFD GU22 232 E3
The Shaftesburys BARK IG11 142 F4
Shaftesbury St IS N1 6 F8
Shaftesbury Ter HMSMTH W6 * 156 C3
Shaftesbury Wy WHTN TW2 176 C6
Shaftesbury Waye YEAD UB4 133 J8
Shafteswood Ct TOOT SW17 180 A7
Shafto Ms KTBR SW1X 16 A4
Shafton Ms HOM E9 * 140 C3
Shafton Rd HOM E9 140 C3
Shaftsbury Wy KGLGY WD4 54 D3
Shaggy Calf La SLN SL2 129 M9
Shakespeare Av
EBED/NFELT TW14 175 H2
FBAR/BDGN N11 98 D6
TIL RM18 168 E8
WLSDN NW10 135 P3
YEAD UB4 133 H8
Shakespeare Crs MNPK E12 142 C2
WLSDN NW10 136 A3
Shakespeare Dr
KTN/HRWW/WS HA3 115 L4
Shakespeare Gdns EFNCH N2 118 A2
Shakespeare Rd ACT W3 135 P10
ADL/WDHM KT15 215 N1
BXLYHN DA7 163 P7
DART DA1 165 P10
FNCH N3 * 97 K9
HARP AL5 20 A2
HNHL SE24 181 J1
HNWL W7 134 E9
MLHL NW7 96 D5
ROM RM1 124 G4
WALTH E17 100 C10
WLSDN NW10 * 136 A3
Shakespeare Sq BARK/HLT IG6 102 F7
Shakespeare St WATN WD24 73 J4
Shakespeare Ter
RCH/KEW TW9 * 155 M9
Shakespeare Wy FELT TW13 175 K7
Shakletons CHONG CM5 67 P4
Shakspeare Ms STNW/STAM N16 119 M9
Shakspeare Wk
STNW/STAM N16 119 M9
Shalbourne Sq HOM E9 140 E1
Shalcomb St WBPTN SW10 15 K10
Shalcross Dr CHES/WCR EN8 62 E6
Shaldon Dr MRDN SM4 201 H5
RSLP HA4 113 K8
Shaldon Rd EDGW HA8 95 L10
Shaldon Wy WOT/HER KT12 197 K10
Shalfleet Dr NKENS W10 136 G9
Shalford Cl ORP BR6 226 F1
Shalford Ct IS N1 * 6 C7
Shalford La RGUE GU4 268 B5
Shalford Rd GU GU1 268 A3
Shalimar Gdns ACT W3 135 P9
Shalimar Rd ACT W3 135 P9
Shallcross Crs HAT AL10 40 D7
Shallons Rd ELTH/MOT SE9 184 E7
Shalstone Rd MORT/ESHN SW14 155 N9
Shalston Vls SURB KT6 199 L6
The Shambles GU GU1 268 A2
Shambrook Rd CHESW EN7 61 J1
Shamrock Cl LHD/OX KT22 236 C7
Shamrock Rd CROY/NA CR0 202 G6
GVE DA12 191 H3
Shamrock St CLAP SW4 158 E9
Shamrock Wy STHGT/OAK N14 98 C2
Shandon Rd CLAP SW4 180 D2
Shand St STHWK SE1 13 K10
STHWK SE1 19 K1
Shandy St WCHPL E1 140 C7
Shanklin Cl CHESW EN7 61 N5
Shanklin Gdns OXHEY WD19 93 K5
Shanklin Rd CEND/HSY/T N8 118 E3
SEVS/STOTM N15 119 P2
Shannon Cl CRICK NW2 116 G8
NWDGN UB2 153 L4
Shannon Gv BRXN/ST SW9 158 G10
Shannon Pl STJWD NW8 3 P7
Shannon Wy BECK BR3 182 G9
SOCK/AV RM15 146 B9
Shantock Hall La HHS/BOV HP3 52 B5
Shantock La HHS/BOV HP3 52 B6
Shantung Pl CSHM HP5 * 51 H9
Shap Crs CAR SM5 202 A8
Shapland Wy PLMGR N13 98 G6
Shapwick Cl FBAR/BDGN N11 98 A6
Shardcroft Av HNHL SE24 181 J1
Shardeloes Rd BROCKY SE4 * 182 E1
NWCR SE14 160 E8
Shard's Sq PECK SE15 19 P10
Sharland Cl THHTH CR7 203 H6
Sharland Rd GVE DA12 190 F5
Sharman Ct SCUP DA14 185 K7
Sharman Rw DTCH/LGLY SL3 150 C4
Sharnbrooke Cl WELL DA16 163 M9
Sharney Av DTCH/LGLY SL3 150 E3
Sharon Cl CRAWE RH10 284 B10
GT/LBKH KT23 235 P10
HOR/WEW KT19 219 P9
SURB KT6 199 H8
Sharon Gdns HOM E9 140 B3
Sharon Rd CHSWK W4 156 A4
PEND EN3 80 D6
Sharpcroft HHNE HP2 35 N4
Sharpecroft HLWW/ROY CM19 46 F1
Sharpes La HHW HP1 34 E7
Sharples Hall St CAMTN NW1 4 B4
Sharps La RSLP HA4 112 E6
Sharpthorne Cl CRAWW RH11 283 J7
Sharp Wy DART DA1 165 N10
Sharratt St PECK SE15 160 B5
Sharsted St WALW SE17 18 C8
Sharvel La YEAD UB4 133 H3
Shavers Pl MYFR/PICC W1J 11 J8
Shaw Av BARK IG11 143 P4
Shawbridge HLWW/ROY CM19 46 F4
Shawbrooke Rd ELTH/MOT SE9 162 A10
Shawbury Cl CDALE/KGS NW9 96 B10
Shawbury Rd EDUL SE22 181 N1
Shaw Cl BUSH WD23 94 D3
CHERT KT16 214 F3
CHES/WCR EN8 62 B5
EMPK RM11 125 J6
EW KT17 220 C7
SAND/SEL CR2 223 N8
THMD SE28 143 L10
Shaw Crs POP/IOD E14 140 D8
SAND/SEL CR2 223 M8
TIL RM18 168 E7
Shaw Dr WOT/HER KT12 197 K7
Shawfield Pk BMLY BR1 206 A2
Shawfield St CHEL SW3 15 P8
Shawford Rd HOR/WEW KT19 220 A3
Shaw Gdns BARK IG11 143 P4
DTCH/LGLY SL3 150 C5
Shawley Crs EPSOM KT18 238 G4
Shawley Wy EPSOM KT18 238 F4
Shaw Rd BH/WHM TN16 243 P6
BMLY BR1 183 L6
EDUL SE22 159 M10
PEND EN3 80 C5
Shaw's Cottages FSTH SE23 182 D6
Shaw Sq WALTH E17 100 D9
Shaws Rd CRAWE RH10 283 P6
The Shaws WGCE AL7 23 M6
The Shaw CHST BR7 * 184 F10
Shaw Wy WLGTN SM6 222 F4
Shaxton Crs CROY/NA CR0 225 H5
Sheaf Cottages THDIT KT7 * 198 D8
Sheares Hoppit WARE SG12 28 A1
Shearing Dr CAR SM5 201 M7
Shearling Wy HOLWY N7 5 M1
Shearman Rd BKHTH/KID SE3 161 L10
Shears Cl DART DA1 187 K5
Shearwater HART DA3 211 N3
Shearwater Cl BARK IG11 143 K5
Shearwater Rd SUT SM1 221 J2
Shearwater Wy YEAD UB4 133 L8
Shearwood Crs DART DA1 164 G9
Sheath La LHD/OX KT22 218 A9
Sheaths Cottages THDIT KT7 * 198 G7
Sheaveshill Av CDALE/KGS NW9 116 B2
Sheaveshill Pde
CDALE/KGS NW9 * 116 B2
Sheehy Wy SLN SL2 129 N9
Sheen Common Dr
RCHPK/HAM TW10 155 M10
Sheen Court Rd
RCHPK/HAM TW10 155 M10
Sheendale Rd RCH/KEW TW9 155 L10
Sheenewood SYD SE26 182 A8
Sheen Gate Gdns
MORT/ESHN SW14 155 P10
Sheen Gv IS N1 6 A5
Sheen La MORT/ESHN SW14 155 P10
Sheen Pk RCH/KEW TW9 155 L10
Sheen Rd RCH/KEW TW9 155 K10
STMC/STPC BR5 207 J4
Sheen Wy WLGTN SM6 222 G2
Sheen Wd MORT/ESHN SW14 177 P1
Sheepbarn La WARL CR6 225 M8
Sheepcot Dr GSTN WD25 55 K10
Sheepcote WGCE AL7 23 K8
Sheepcote Cl BEAC HP9 88 B7
HEST TW5 153 H6
Sheepcote Gdns DEN/HRF UB9 111 K4
Sheepcote La BTSEA SW11 158 A8
STALE/WH AL4 21 L2
STMC/STPC BR5 208 B4
Sheepcote Rd HHNE HP2 36 A6
HRW HA1 114 E4
WDSR SL4 148 D8
WDSR SL4 148 F4
Sheepcotes Rd CHDH RM6 123 N2
Sheepcot La GSTN WD25 55 J9
Sheepfold La AMSS HP7 69 J5
Sheepfold Rd GUW GU2 249 L7
Sheephouse Gn RDKG RH5 271 N6
Sheephouse La RDKG RH5 271 N5
Sheephouse Rd HHS/BOV HP3 36 A8
Sheephouse Wy NWMAL KT3 200 B7
Sheeplands Av GU GU1 250 F8
Sheep La HACK E8 140 A3
Sheep Wk REIG RH2 257 J7
Sheepwalk SHPTN TW17 196 A6
Sheep Walk Ms WIM/MER SW19 178 G9
Sheering Dr HLWE CM17 29 P8
Sheering Lower Rd HLWE CM17 30 A4
Sheering Mill La SBW CM21 30 B2
Sheering Rd HLWE CM17 29 P7
Sheerwater Av ADL/WDHM KT15 215 J8
Sheerwater Rd CAN/RD E16 142 A7
WOKN/KNAP GU21 215 H8
Sheethanger La HHS/BOV HP3 35 K10
Sheet's Heath La
CHOB/PIR GU24 230 F6
Sheet St WDSR SL4 149 J8
Sheet Street Rd WDSR SL4 170 D6
Sheffield Cl CRAWE RH10 284 C9
Sheffield Dr HARH RM3 105 P6
Sheffield Rd HTHAIR TW6 174 D2
SL SL1 129 H8
Sheffield St LINN WC2A * 11 N6
Sheffield Ter KENS W8 14 E1
Sheffield Wy HTHAIR TW6 174 E1
Shefton Ri NTHWD HA6 93 H8
Sheila Rd CRW RM5 104 C8
The Sheilings BGR/WK TN15 247 N6
EMPK RM11 125 N3
Shelbourne Cl PIN HA5 113 N1
Shelbourne Rd TOTM N17 100 A9
Shelburne Dr HSLWW TW4 175 P2
Shelburne Rd HOLWY N7 118 G9
Shelbury Cl SCUP DA14 185 K6
Shelbury Rd EDUL SE22 182 A1
Sheldon Av CLAY IG5 102 E10
HGT N6 118 A5
Sheldon Cl CHESW EN7 61 L2
CRAWE RH10 284 E8
HLWE CM17 47 P1
LEE/GVPK SE12 183 N1
PGE/AN SE20 204 A1
REIG RH2 275 L1
Sheldon Ct GU GU1 268 C1
Sheldon Pl BETH E2 7 P8
Sheldon Rd BXLYHN DA7 164 A7
CRICK NW2 116 G9
DAGW RM9 143 P2
UED N18 99 M5
Sheldon Sq BAY/PAD W2 9 K4
Sheldon St CROY/NA CR0 203 K10
Sheldrake Cl CAN/RD E16 142 C10
Sheldrake Pl KENS W8 14 E1
Sheldrick Cl MTCM CR4 201 N2
Shelduck Cl SRTFD E15 121 L10
Sheldwich Ter HAYES BR2 * 206 B6
Shelford Pl STNW/STAM N16 119 L8
Shelford Ri NRWD SE19 181 N10
Shelford Rd BAR EN5 76 F10
Shelgate Rd BTSEA SW11 180 A1
Shellbank La RDART DA2 188 G8
Shell Cl HAYES BR2 206 B6
Shellduck Cl CDALE/KGS NW9 96 B10
Shelley Av GFD/PVL UB6 134 C5
HCH RM12 124 G7
MNPK E12 142 B1
Shelley Cl BNSTD SM7 238 G1
CHONG CM5 67 N2
COUL/CHIP CR5 240 G3
CRAWE RH10 284 D5
DTCH/LGLY SL3 150 D4
EDGW HA8 95 M5
GFD/PVL UB6 134 C5
NTHWD HA6 92 G6
ORP BR6 207 H10
PECK SE15 160 A8
YEAD UB4 133 H7
Shelley Crs HEST TW5 153 L7
STHL UB1 133 N8
Shelley Dr WELL DA16 163 H7
Shelley Gdns ALP/SUD HA0 115 H7
Shelley Gv LOU IG10 82 C8
Shelley La DEN/HRF UB9 91 K8
Shelley Ms HHS/BOV HP3 * 35 N9
Shelley Pl TIL RM18 168 E7
Shelley Rd CSHM HP5 50 G5
WLSDN NW10 136 A3
Shelleys La RSEV TN14 245 K2
Shelley Wy WIM/MER SW19 179 N9
Shellfield Cl STWL/WRAY TW19 173 K1
Shellgrove Rd STNW/STAM N16 * 119 M10
Shellness Rd CLPT E5 120 A10
Shell Rd LEW SE13 160 G9
Shellwood Dr RDKG RH5 273 H6
Shellwood Rd BTSEA SW11 158 A8
REIG RH2 274 A7
Shelly Cl BORE WD6 75 M8
Shelmerdine Cl BOW E3 140 F7
Shelson Av FELT TW13 174 G7
Shelson Pde FELT TW13 * 174 G6
Shelton Av WARL CR6 242 B4
Shelton Cl GUW GU2 249 M5
WARL CR6 242 B3
Shelton Rd WIM/MER SW19 201 K1
Shelton St LSQ/SEVD WC2H * 11 L6
Shelvers Gn KWD/TDW/WH KT20 238 F7
Shelvers Hl KWD/TDW/WH KT20 238 E7
Shelvers Sp KWD/TDW/WH KT20 238 F7
Shelvers Wy KWD/TDW/WH KT20 238 F7
Shenden Cl SEV TN13 265 K4
Shenden Wy SEV TN13 265 K4
Shenfield Cl COUL/CHIP CR5 240 C5
Shenfield Ct HLWS CM18 46 F4
Shenfield Crs BRWN CM15 107 K3
Shenfield Gdns
RBRW/HUT CM13 87 N10
Shenfield Gn BRWN CM15 107 M1
Shenfield Pl BRWN CM15 107 K1
Shenfield Rd BRWN CM15 107 K2
WFD IG8 101 N8
Shenfield St IS N1 7 K8
Shenley Av RSLP HA4 112 G7
Shenleybury RAD WD7 57 K6
Shenleybury Cottages RAD WD7 57 K7
Shenley Hl RAD WD7 56 G10
RAD WD7 74 G1
Shenley La LCOL/BKTW AL2 56 G1
Shenley Rd BORE WD6 75 M7
BORE WD6 75 P6
CMBW SE5 159 M7
DART DA1 187 P2
HEST TW5 153 M7
HHNE HP2 36 D1
RAD WD7 75 J1
Shenstone Cl DART DA1 186 E1
Shenstone Dr SL SL1 128 C6
Shenstone Gdns HARH RM3 105 K9
Shenstone Hl BERK HP4 34 B4
Shenstone Pk ASC SL5 192 D4
Shepherd Cl ABLGY WD5 54 G6
CRAWE RH10 283 N10
FELT TW13 175 M7
Shepherdess Pl FSBYE EC1V 6 F9
Shepherdess Wk IS N1 6 F8
Shepherd Market
MYFR/PICC W1J 10 E10
Shepherd's Bush Gn SHB W12 156 F1
Shepherd's Bush Market
SHB W12 156 F1
Shepherd's Bush Pl SHB W12 * 156 G1
Shepherd's Bush Rd
HMSMTH W6 156 F3
Shepherds Cl CHDH RM6 123 N3
HGT N6 118 C4
ORP BR6 207 J10
SHPTN TW17 196 C6
STAN HA7 94 F6
UX/CGN UB8 * 131 M6
Shepherds Ct HERT/WAT SG14 25 K2
Shepherds Gn CHST BR7 184 G10
HHW HP1 35 H7
Shepherd's Hl GUW GU2 249 M8
HARH RM3 105 P10
HGT N6 118 C4
REDH RH1 258 D2
Shepherds La BEAC HP9 88 E10
BFOR GU20 212 F2
DART DA1 187 H4
GUW GU2 249 L7
HOM E9 120 C10
RKW/CH/CXG WD3 70 G10
THMD SE28 143 H10
Shepherd's Leas
ELTH/MOT SE9 * 162 G10
Shepherds Pl MYFR/PKLN W1K 10 C7
Shepherds Rd WATW WD18 72 G7
Shepherd St GVW DA11 190 A3
MYFR/PICC W1J 10 E10
Shepherds Wk BUSH WD23 94 C3
CRICK NW2 116 D7
EPSOM KT18 237 N6
HAMP NW3 117 N10
Shepherds Wy BRKMPK AL9 59 M3
CSHM HP5 51 J9
RGUE GU4 268 B5
RKW/CH/CXG WD3 91 L1
SAND/SEL CR2 224 C4
Shepiston La HYS/HAR UB3 152 C3
Shepley Cl CAR SM5 202 B10
Shepley Dr ASC SL5 193 J6
Shepley End ASC SL5 193 H5
Shepley Ms PEND EN3 80 F4
Sheppard Cl EN EN1 80 A4
KUT/HW KT1 199 K4
Sheppard Dr BERM/RHTH SE16 160 A4
Sheppards HLWW/ROY CM19 46 C4
Sheppards Cl STALW/RED AL3 38 D3
Sheppard St CAN/RD E16 141 L6
Shepperton Cl BORE WD6 76 A5
Shepperton Court Dr
SHPTN TW17 196 C5
Shepperton Marina
SHPTN TW17 * 196 F6
Shepperton Rd IS N1 6 F5
STA TW18 195 N4
STMC/STPC BR5 206 F6
Shepperton Studios
SHPTN TW17 * 196 A3
Sheppey Cl CRAWW RH11 283 L10
ERITH DA8 165 J6
Sheppey Gdns DAGW RM9 143 M2
Sheppey Rd DAGW RM9 143 L2
Sheppey's La ABLGY WD5 54 F4
Sheppey Wk IS N1 6 F3
Sheppy Pl GVE DA12 190 E3
Shepton Houses BETH E2 * 140 B5
Sherard Rd ELTH/MOT SE9 184 B1
Sherards Orch HLWW/ROY CM19 46 E3
Sheraton Cl BORE WD6 75 L9
Sheraton Dr HOR/WEW KT19 219 P9
Sheraton Ms WATW WD18 * 72 F8
Sheraton St SOHO/CST W1F * 11 J6
Sherborne Av NWDGN UB2 153 P3
PEND EN3 80 B6
Sherborne Cl DTCH/LGLY SL3 151 H7
EPSOM KT18 238 F3
YEAD UB4 133 K8
Sherborne Crs CAR SM5 201 P7
Sherborne Gdns
CDALE/KGS NW9 115 M1
WEA W13 134 G8
Sherborne Gv BGR/WK TN15 247 P3
Sherborne La MANHO EC4N 12 G7
Sherborne Pl NTHWD HA6 92 E7
Sherborne Rd CHEAM SM3 201 K9
CHSGTN KT9 219 K2
EBED/NFELT TW14 174 E4
STMC/STPC BR5 207 J5
Sherborne St IS N1 6 G5
Sherborne Vls WEA W13 * 134 G7
Sherborne Wy
RKW/CH/CXG WD3 72 C8
Sherboro Rd SEVS/STOTM N15 119 N4
Sherbourne SHGR GU5 269 N5
Sherbourne Cl HHNE HP2 35 P7
Sherbourne Dr ASC SL5 193 J5
WDSR SL4 148 E10
Sherbourne Gdns SHPTN TW17 196 F7
Sherbourne Wk SLN SL2 109 H9
Sherbrooke Cl BXLYHN DA7 164 B10
Sherbrooke Rd FUL/PGN SW6 157 J6
Sherbrooke Ter FUL/PGN SW6 * 157 H6
Sherbrooke Wy WPK KT4 200 E7
Sherbrook Gdns WCHMH N21 99 J1
Shere Av BELMT SM2 220 F6
Shere Cl CHSGTN KT9 219 J2
RDKG RH5 273 H6
Sheredan Rd CHING E4 101 J6
Sheredes Dr HOD EN11 44 E5
Shere La SHGR GU5 270 B5
Shere Rd EHSLY KT24 252 D6
GNTH/NBYPK IG2 122 D3
RGUE GU4 269 L2
Sherfield Av RKW/CH/CXG WD3 91 N4
Sherfield Cl NWMAL KT3 199 N4
Sherfield Gdns PUT/ROE SW15 178 C2
Sherfield Rd GRAYS RM17 167 N5
Sheridan Cl HARH RM3 105 K8
HGDN/ICK UB10 132 C6
HHW HP1 35 L7
Sheridan Ct DART DA1 165 P10
HSLWW TW4 175 M1
Sheridan Crs CHST BR7 206 E2
Sheridan Dr REIG RH2 257 L8
Sheridan Gdns
KTN/HRWW/WS HA3 115 J4
Sheridan Gra ASC SL5 192 F6
Sheridan Pl BMLY BR1 206 A2
HPTN TW12 198 A1
Sheridan Rd BELV DA17 164 B3
BXLYHN DA7 163 P9
FSTGT E7 121 L8
MNPK E12 122 B10
OXHEY WD19 93 L1
RCHPK/HAM TW10 177 H6
WIM/MER SW19 201 J1
Sheridans Rd GT/LBKH KT23 254 B2
Sheridan St WCHPL E1 140 A8
Sheridan Ter NTHLT UB5 * 114 A10
Sheridan Wk CAR SM5 222 A2
GLDGN NW11 117 K4
Sheridan Wy BECK BR3 204 E1
Sheriden Wk BROX EN10 44 D6
Sheriff Wy GSTN WD25 55 H9
Sheringham Av MNPK E12 122 C10
ROMW/RG RM7 124 D4
STHGT/OAK N14 78 E10
WHTN TW2 175 N4
Sheringham Dr BARK IG11 123 J10
Sheringham Rd HOLWY N7 5 P1
PGE/AN SE20 204 A2
Sherington Av PIN HA5 93 P8
Sherington Rd BKHTH/KID SE3 161 N5
Sherland Ct RAD WD7 * 74 F1
Sherland Rd TWK TW1 176 E4
Sherlies Av ORP BR6 207 H9
Sherlock Ms MHST W1U 10 C3
Sherman Gdns CHDH RM6 123 M4
Sherman Rd BMLY BR1 205 M1
SL SL1 129 K7
Shernbroke Rd WAB EN9 63 L10
Shernhall St WALTH E17 121 H3
Sherrard Rd FSTGT E7 141 P1
MNPK E12 122 A10
Sherrardspark Rd WGCW AL8 22 G3
Sherrards Wy BAR EN5 77 K9
Sherrick Green Rd WLSDN NW10 116 E10
Sherriff Cl ESH/CLAY KT10 198 A9
Sherriff Rd KIL/WHAMP NW6 2 F2
Sherringham Av FELT TW13 175 H6
TOTM N17 99 P10
Sherrock Gdns HDN NW4 116 D2
Sherry Ms BARK IG11 142 G2
Sherwin Rd NWCR SE14 160 C7
Sherwood CDW/CHF RM16 147 K10
SURB KT6 199 J9
Sherwood Av GFD/PVL UB6 134 D1
POTB/CUF EN6 59 H8
RSLP HA4 112 F4
STALE/WH AL4 38 G3
STRHM/NOR SW16 180 E10
SWFD E18 121 N1
YEAD UB4 133 J6
Sherwood Cl BXLY DA5 185 M2
DTCH/LGLY SL3 150 B2
LHD/OX KT22 236 B9
WALTH E17 100 E10
WEA W13 134 G10
Sherwood Ct MBLAR W1H 10 A4
Sherwood Crs REIG RH2 275 L4
Sherwood Gdns BARK IG11 142 G2
BERM/RHTH SE16 19 P8
BERM/RHTH SE16 159 P4
POP/IOD E14 160 F3
Sherwood House
RYLN/HDSTN HA2 * 114 B7
Sherwood Park Av BFN/LL DA15 185 K3
Sherwood Park Rd MTCM CR4 202 E4
SUT SM1 221 K2
Sherwood Pl HHNE HP2 36 A2
Sherwood Rd BARK/HLT IG6 122 G2
COUL/CHIP CR5 240 D2
CROY/NA CR0 204 A8
HDN NW4 116 F1
HPTN TW12 176 B8
RYLN/HDSTN HA2 114 B7
WELL DA16 163 H9
WIM/MER SW19 179 J10
WOKN/KNAP GU21 231 K3
Sherwoods Ri HARP AL5 20 C3
Sherwoods Rd OXHEY WD19 93 M1
Sherwood St REGST W1B 11 H7
TRDG/WHET N20 97 N4
Sherwood Ter TRDG/WHET N20 97 N4
Sherwood Wk CRAWE RH10 284 A10
Sherwood Wy WWKM BR4 205 H9
Shetland Cl BORE WD6 76 A10
CRAWE RH10 284 F6
RGUE GU4 250 E5
Shetland Rd BOW E3 140 E4
Shevon Wy BRW CM14 106 E5
Shewens Rd WEY KT13 216 E1
Shey Copse WOKS/MYFD GU22 232 F3
Shield Dr BTFD TW8 154 G5
Shieldhall St ABYW SE2 163 M3
Shield Rd ASHF TW15 174 D7
Shifford Pth FSTH SE23 182 C6
Shilburn Wy WOKN/KNAP GU21 231 M4
Shillibeer Pl MBLAR W1H 9 P4
Shillibeer Wk CHIG IG7 103 J4
Shillingford Cl MLHL NW7 96 G8
Shillingford St IS N1 * 6 D5
Shilling Pl HNWL W7 * 134 F10
Shillitoe Av POTB/CUF EN6 58 G8
The Shimmings GU GU1 250 D9
Shinfield St SHB W12 136 F8
Shingle Ct WAB EN9 63 M9
Shinglewell Rd ERITH DA8 164 B6
Shinners Cl SNWD SE25 203 P5
Ship Field Cl BH/WHM TN16 243 P7
Ship Hl BH/WHM TN16 243 P7
SL SL1 108 D6
Shipka Rd BAL SW12 180 C4
Ship La MORT/ESHN SW14 155 P9
SOCK/AV RM15 166 C1
SWLY BR8 209 L1
Shipleybridge La HORL RH6 280 G10
Shipley Rd CRAWW RH11 283 K7
Shipman Rd CAN/RD E16 141 N8
FSTH SE23 182 C5
Ship & Mermaid Rw
STHWK SE1 * 19 H1
Ship St DEPT SE8 160 F7
Ship Tavern Pas BANK EC3V 13 J7
Shipton Cl BCTR RM8 123 N8
Shipton Rd HGDN/ICK UB10 112 A9
Shipton St BETH E2 7 M9
Shipwright Rd BERM/RHTH SE16 160 D1
Shipwright Yd STHWK SE1 * 13 J10
Ship Yd WEY KT13 196 B10
Shirburn Cl FSTH SE23 182 B3
Shirbutt St POP/IOD E14 140 F9
Shirebrook Rd BKHTH/KID SE3 162 A8
Shire Cl BROX EN10 * 62 E2
Shire Ct EW KT17 220 C4
Shirehall Cl HDN NW4 116 G4
Shirehall Gdns HDN NW4 116 G4
Shirehall La HDN NW4 116 G4
Shirehall Pk HDN NW4 116 G4
Shirehall Rd RDART DA2 187 L8
Shire Horse Wy ISLW TW7 154 E9
Shire La CSTG HP8 90 E4
ORP BR6 226 C4
RKW/CH/CXG WD3 70 E9
Shiremeade BORE WD6 75 L9
Shire Ms WHTN TW2 176 B2
Shire Pde CRAWE RH10 * 284 E6
Shire Pl CRAWE RH10 * 284 E6
REDH RH1 276 A2
WAND/EARL SW18 179 M3
Shires Cl ASHTD KT21 237 J5
Shires Pk WGCE AL7 * 23 H3
The Shires GSTN WD25 55 K7
RCHPK/HAM TW10 177 K7
Shirland Ms MV/WKIL W9 2 D10
Shirland Rd MV/WKIL W9 2 D10
Shirley Av BELMT SM2 221 J6
BXLY DA5 185 N3
COUL/CHIP CR5 241 J5
CROY/NA CR0 204 B8
REDH RH1 276 A5
SUT SM1 221 P1
WDSR SL4 148 E7
Shirley Church Rd CROY/NA CR0 204 C10
Shirley Cl BROX EN10 44 E10
CHES/WCR EN8 62 B5
DART DA1 165 K10
GVE DA12 191 L5
HSLW TW3 176 B1
WALTH E17 * 120 G3
Shirley Crs BECK BR3 204 D4
Shirley Dr HSLW TW3 176 B1
Shirley Gdns BARK IG11 143 H1
HCH RM12 125 K7
HNWL W7 134 E10
Shirley Gv BTSEA SW11 158 B9
ED N9 100 B1
Shirley Hills Rd CROY/NA CR0 224 C2
Shirley Oaks Rd CROY/NA CR0 204 C8
Shirley Park Rd CROY/NA CR0 204 A8
Shirley Pl WOKN/KNAP GU21 231 H3
Shirley Rd ABLGY WD5 54 G8
CHSWK W4 156 A1
CROY/NA CR0 204 B9
ENC/FH EN2 79 K7
SCUP DA14 185 H6
SRTFD E15 141 K2
STAL AL1 38 E7
WLGTN SM6 222 D5
Shirley Rw SNWD SE25 * 203 P2
Shirley St CAN/RD E16 141 L8
Shirley Wy CROY/NA CR0 204 E10
Shirlock Rd HAMP NW3 118 A9
Shirwell Cl MLHL NW7 96 G8
Shobden Rd TOTM N17 99 L9
Shobroke Cl CRICK NW2 116 F8
Shoebury Rd EHAM E6 142 C2
Shoe La FLST/FETLN EC4A 12 B5
Sholden Gdns STMC/STPC BR5 207 M5
Shonks Mill Rd ABR/ST RM4 85 K4
Shooters Av
KTN/HRWW/WS HA3 115 H2
Shooters Dr WAB EN9 45 K8
Shooters Hill Rd GNWCH SE10 161 K7
Shooters Rd ENC/FH EN2 79 H4
Shootersway BERK HP4 33 J5
TRING HP23 32 G3
Shootersway La BERK HP4 33 L6
Shootersway Pk BERK HP4 33 L6
Shoot-up Hl CRICK NW2 137 H1
Shophouse La SHGR GU5 269 N10
Shoplands WGCW AL8 22 G2
Shop Rd WDSR SL4 * 148 B6
Shord Hl PUR/KEN CR8 241 L2
Shore Cl EBED/NFELT TW14 175 H3
HPTN TW12 175 M9
Shorediche Cl HGDN/ICK UB10 112 A8
Shoreditch High St WCHPL E1 7 K10
Shore Gv FELT TW13 175 P5
Shoreham Cl CROY/NA CR0 204 B6
WAND/EARL SW18 179 L1
Shoreham La RSEV TN14 228 B8
SEV TN13 246 G9
Shoreham Pl RSEV TN14 229 H8
Shoreham Ri SLN SL2 128 C6
Shoreham Rd CRAWE RH10 284 D10
RSEV TN14 247 J1
STMC/STPC BR5 207 L1
Shoreham Rd (East) HTHAIR TW6 173 P1
Shoreham Rd (West)
HTHAIR TW6 173 P1
Shoreham Wy HAYES BR2 205 M6
Shorehill La BGR/WK TN15 247 P1
Shore Pl HOM E9 140 B2
Shore Rd HOM E9 140 B2
Shore's Rd WOKN/KNAP GU21 214 B10
The Shore GVW DA11 189 P1
GVW DA11 190 C2
Shore Wy BRXN/ST SW9 159 H8
Shorncliffe Rd STHWK SE1 19 L8
Shorndean St CAT SE6 183 H3
Shorne Cl BFN/LL DA15 185 L2
STMC/STPC BR5 207 N4
Shornefield Cl BMLY BR1 206 D3
Shorne Ifield Rd GVE DA12 191 L9
Shorrolds Rd FUL/PGN SW6 157 K6
Shortacres REDH RH1 258 G9
Short Cl CRAWW RH11 283 N5
Short Cft BRWN CM15 86 E4
Shortcroft Rd EW KT17 220 C4
Shortcrofts Rd DAGW RM9 144 A1
Shorter Av BRWN CM15 87 L10
Shorter St TWRH EC3N 13 M8
Shortfern SLN SL2 129 P8
Short Gallop CRAWE RH10 * 284 E6
Shortgate NFNCH/WDSPK N12 97 J5
Shortlands HMSMTH W6 156 G3
HYS/HAR UB3 152 E5
Shortlands Av CHONG CM5 67 N2
Shortlands Cl BELV DA17 164 A2
UED N18 99 L5
Shortlands Gdns HAYES BR2 205 K2
Shortlands Gn WGCE AL7 23 J6
Shortlands Gv HAYES BR2 205 J3
Shortlands Rd HAYES BR2 205 J3
KUTN/CMB KT2 177 L10
LEY E10 120 G5
Short La LCOL/BKTW AL2 55 M5
OXTED RH8 261 N8
STWL/WRAY TW19 174 A3
Shortmead Dr CHES/WCR EN8 62 D7
Short Rd CHSWK W4 156 B5
HTHAIR TW6 173 P2
WAN E11 121 K7
Shorts Cft CDALE/KGS NW9 115 N2
Shorts Gdns LSQ/SEVD WC2H * 11 L6
Shorts Rd CAR SM5 221 P1
Short St HDN NW4 116 F2
STHWK SE1 18 B1
Shortway CSHM HP5 50 G5
ELTH/MOT SE9 162 B9
Short Wy NFNCH/WDSPK N12 97 P7
WHTN TW2 176 B3
Shortwood Av STA TW18 173 L6
Shotfield WLGTN SM6 222 C3
Shothanger Wy HHS/BOV HP3 52 G1
Shott Cl SUT SM1 221 M2
Shottendane Rd FUL/PGN SW6 * 157 K7
Shottery Cl ELTH/MOT SE9 184 B6
Shottfield Av MORT/ESHN SW14 156 B10
Shottfield Cl STALE/WH AL4 21 H9
Shoulder of Mutton Aly
POP/IOD E14 140 D9
Shouldham St MBLAR W1H 9 P4
Showers Wy HYS/HAR UB3 133 H10
Shrapnel Cl WOOL/PLUM SE18 162 C6
Shrapnel Rd ELTH/MOT SE9 162 C9
Shrewsbury Av
KTN/HRWW/WS HA3 115 K2
MORT/ESHN SW14 155 P10
Shrewsbury Cl SURB KT6 199 K9
Shrewsbury Crs WLSDN NW10 136 A3
Shrewsbury La
WOOL/PLUM SE18 162 E7
Shrewsbury Ms BAY/PAD W2 8 E5
Shrewsbury Rd BAY/PAD W2 8 E5
BECK BR3 204 D3
CAR SM5 201 P7
FBAR/BDGN N11 98 E7
FSTGT E7 142 A1
HTHAIR TW6 174 D2
REDH RH1 257 P10
Shrewsbury St NKENS W10 136 F6
Shrewton Rd TOOT SW17 * 180 A10
Shrimpton Cl BEAC HP9 88 C5
Shrimpton Rd BEAC HP9 88 C5
Shroffold Rd BMLY BR1 183 K7
Shropshire Cl MTCM CR4 202 F4
Shropshire Rd WDGN N22 98 G8
Shroton St CAMTN NW1 9 N3
The Shrubberies CHIG IG7 102 F6
STAL AL1 * 38 C8
SWFD E18 101 M10
Shrubbery Gdns WCHMH N21 99 J1
Shrubbery Rd ED N9 99 P4
EYN DA4 210 C1
GVE DA12 190 F4
STHL UB1 133 N10
STRHM/NOR SW16 180 F7
The Shrubbery HHW HP1 35 H5
SURB KT6 * 199 K8
UPMR RM14 126 B8
Shrubbs Hl CHOB/PIR GU24 213 H5
Shrubbs Hill La ASC SL5 193 H6
Shrub Hill Rd HHW HP1 35 J7
Shrubland Cl TRDG/WHET N20 * 97 N3
Shrubland Gv WPK KT4 200 F10
Shrubland Rd BNSTD SM7 239 J2
HACK E8 7 N5
WALTH E17 120 F3
Shrublands BRKMPK AL9 59 L2
Shrublands Av BERK HP4 33 M5
CROY/NA CR0 224 F1
Shrublands Cl CHIG IG7 102 F7
SYD SE26 182 B6
TRDG/WHET N20 97 N2
Shrublands Dr LTWR GU18 212 A7
Shrublands Rd BERK HP4 33 M4
The Shrublands POTB/CUF EN6 59 H9
Shrubsall Cl ELTH/MOT SE9 184 B4
Shrubs Rd RKW/CH/CXG WD3 92 A7
Shubbery Cl IS N1 6 F5
Shuna Wk IS N1 6 G1
Shurland Av EBAR EN4 77 N10
Shurland Gdns PECK SE15 * 159 N6
Shurlock Av SWLY BR8 208 E2
Shurlock Dr ORP BR6 226 F1
Shuters Sq WKENS W14 14 C8
Shuttle Cl BFN/LL DA15 185 J3
Shuttlemead BXLY DA5 186 A3
Shuttle Rd DART DA1 165 H9
Shuttle St WCHPL E1 13 N2
Shuttleworth Rd BTSEA SW11 157 N8
Sibella Rd CLAP SW4 158 E8
Sibley Av HARP AL5 20 C4
Sibley Cl BMLY BR1 206 B5
BXLYHS DA6 185 P1
Sibley Ct UX/CGN UB8 132 D7
Sibley Gv MNPK E12 142 C2
Sibneys Gn HLWS CM18 47 H6
Sibthorpe Rd BRKMPK AL9 40 F10
LEE/GVPK SE12 183 N3
Sibthorp Rd MTCM CR4 * 202 A2
Sibton Rd CAR SM5 201 P7
Sicilian Av NOXST/BSQ WC1A * 11 M4
Sicklefield Cl CHESW EN7 61 N2
Sidbury Cl ASC SL5 192 F5
Sidbury St FUL/PGN SW6 157 H7
Sidcup By-Pass Rd SCUP DA14 185 H7
Sidcup Hl SCUP DA14 185 L8
Sidcup Hill Gdns SCUP DA14 * 185 M8
Sidcup Pl SCUP DA14 185 K8
Sidcup Rd ELTH/MOT SE9 184 A4
LEE/GVPK SE12 183 N1
Siddeley Dr HSLWW TW4 153 M9
Siddons La CAMTN NW1 10 B2
Siddons Rd CROY/NA CR0 203 H10
FSTH SE23 182 D5
TOTM N17 99 P9
Side Rd DEN/HRF UB9 110 G5
WALTH E17 120 E3
Sideways La HORL RH6 279 M6
Sidewood Rd ELTH/MOT SE9 184 G4
Sidford Cl HHW HP1 35 J6
Sidford Pl STHWK SE1 17 P4
Sidings Ms HOLWY N7 119 H9
The Sidings BROX EN10 44 E8
HAT AL10 40 B5
HHNE HP2 35 N6
LOU IG10 82 B10
SEV TN13 246 F6
STA TW18 173 L7
WAN E11 121 H6
Siding Wy LCOL/BKTW AL2 56 F2
Sidmouth Av ISLW TW7 154 D8

Sidmouth Cl *OXHEY* WD19 93 J3
Sidmouth Dr *RSLP* HA4 113 H8
Sidmouth Pde *CRICK* NW2 * 136 F2
Sidmouth Rd *CRICK* NW2 136 F2
LEY E10 121 H7
PECK SE15 159 N7
STMC/STPC BR5 207 L5
WELL DA16 163 M6
Sidmouth St *STPAN* WC1H 5 M10
Sidney Av *PLMGR* N13 99 G6
Sidney Cl *UX/CGN* UB8 131 M2
Sidney Elson Wy *EHAM* E6 142 D4
Sidney Gdns *BTFD* TW8 155 J5
RSEV TN14 247 K3
Sidney Gv *FSBYE* EC1V 6 C8
Sidney Rd *BECK* BR3 204 D2
BRXN/ST SW9 158 G8
EPP CM16 82 G2
FSTGT E7 121 M8
RYLN/HDSTN HA2 114 B1
SNWD SE25 203 P5
STA TW18 173 K7
TWK TW1 176 F2
WDGN N22 98 G8
WDSR SL4 148 B9
WOT/HER KT12 197 H7
Sidney Sq *WCHPL* E1 * 140 B7
Sidney St *WCHPL* E1 140 B8
Sidworth St *HACK* E8 140 A2
Siebert Rd *BKHTH/KID* SE3 161 M5
Siemens Rd *WOOL/PLUM* SE18 162 A2
Sienna Ter *CRICK* NW2 * 116 D7
Sierra Dr *DAGE* RM10 144 D4
Sigdon Rd *HACK* E8 119 P10
The Signers *PIN* HA5 113 J4
Signmakers Yd *CAMTN* NW1 * 4 F6
Sigrist Sq *KUTN/CMB* KT2 199 K1
Silbury Av *MTCM* CR4 201 P1
Silbury St *IS* N1 * 6 G9
Silchester Dr *CRAWW* RH11 283 K10
Silecroft Rd *BXLYHN* DA7 164 B7
Silesia Buildings *HACK* E8 140 A2
Silex St *STHWK* SE1 18 D2
Silistria Cl *WOKN/KNAP* GU21 231 H4
Silk Cl *LEE/GVPK* SE12 183 M1
Silkfield Rd *CDALE/KGS* NW9 116 C3
Silkham Rd *OXTED* RH8 261 J3
Silk Mill Rd *OXHEY* WD19 93 J1
Silk Mills Cl *RSEV* TN14 247 K7
Silk Mills Pth *LEW* SE13 161 H9
Silkmore La *EHSLY* KT24 252 A2
Silkstream Pde *EDGW* HA8 * 95 P9
Silkstream Rd *EDGW* HA8 95 P9
Silk St *BARB* EC2Y 12 F3
Silo Cl *GODL* GU7 267 L9
Silo Dr *GODL* GU7 267 L9
Silo Rd *GODL* GU7 267 L9
Silsoe Rd *WDGN* N22 118 G1
Silverbeck Wy *STWL/WRAY* TW19 173 K1
Silver Birch Av *CHING* E4 100 E6
EPP CM16 65 P3
Silver Birch Cl *ADL/WDHM* KT15 215 H8
CAT SE6 182 E6
FBAR/BDGN N11 98 B7
HGDN/ICK UB10 111 P9
RDART DA2 186 F7
THMD SE28 143 K10
Silver Birches *RBRW/HUT* CM13 107 M2
Silver Birch Ms *BARK/HLT* IG6 102 F7
Silverbirch Wk *HAMP* NW3 * 4 B2
Silvercliffe Gdns *EBAR* EN4 77 P8
Silver Cl *KTN/HRWW/WS* HA3 94 C8
KWD/TDW/WH KT20 239 H10
NWCR SE14 * 160 D6
Silver Ct *WCGE* AL7 * 23 K4
Silver Crs *CHSWK* W4 155 N3
Silverdale *CAMTN* NW1 4 G8
ENC/FH EN2 78 F8
HART DA3 211 L4
SYD SE26 182 B7
Silverdale Av *LHD/OX* KT22 218 B10
WOT/HER KT12 196 G10
Silverdale Centre *ALP/SUD* HA0 * 135 L3
Silverdale Cl *BRKHM/BTCW* RH3 273 N4
HNWL W7 134 D10
NTHLT UB5 113 N10
SUT SM1 221 J1
Silverdale Ct *STA* TW18 * 173 L8
Silverdale Dr *ELTH/MOT* SE9 184 B5
HCH RM12 125 J10
SUN TW16 197 J2
Silverdale Gdns *HYS/HAR* UB3 153 H1
Silverdale Rd *BUSH* WD23 73 M9
BXLYHN DA7 164 C8
CHING E4 101 J7
HYS/HAR UB3 153 H1
STMC/STPC BR5 206 F4
STMC/STPC BR5 207 K3
Silver Dell *WATN* WD24 72 G1
Silverdene *NFNCH/WDSPK* N12 * 97 L7
Silver Dene *PUT/ROE* SW15 * 178 F1
Silverfield *BROX* EN10 44 E8
Silvergate *HOR/WEW* KT19 219 P2
Silverglade *CHSGTN* KT9 219 H8
Silverhall St *ISLW* TW7 154 F9
Silver Hl *BORE* WD6 75 P2
CSTG HP8 89 N3
Silverholme Cl
KTN/HRWW/WS HA3 115 K5
Silver Jubilee Wy *HSLWW* TW4 153 J8
Silverlands Cl *CHERT* KT16 * 194 G10
Silver La *PUR/KEN* CR8 222 E8
WWKM BR4 205 J9
Silverlea Gdns *HORL* RH6 280 D5
Silverleigh Rd *THHTH* CR7 202 G4
Silverlocke Rd *GRAYS* RM17 168 A5
Silvermere Av *CRW* RM5 104 C7
Silvermere Dr *UED* N18 * 100 C6
Silvermere Rd *CAT* SE6 182 F2
Silvermere Rw *SNWD* SE25 * 203 P5
Silver Pl *SOHO/CST* W1F 11 H6
Silver Rd *GVE* DA12 191 H5
LEW SE13 160 G9
NKENS W10 136 G9
Silversmiths Wy
WOKN/KNAP GU21 231 P4
Silver Spring Cl *ERITH* DA8 164 C5
Silverstead La *BH/WHM* TN16 245 H7
Silversted La *BH/WHM* TN16 244 G7
Silverstone Cl *REDH* RH1 258 A8
Silverston Wy *STAN* HA7 95 H7
Silver St *ABR/ST* RM4 83 L7
CHESW EN7 61 L6
EN EN1 79 L7
UED N18 99 L5
WAB EN9 63 H10
Silverthorn Dr *HHS/BOV* HP3 36 C10
Silverthorne Rd *VX/NE* SW8 158 C8
Silverthorn Gdns *CHING* E4 100 F3
Silverton Rd *HMSMTH* W6 156 G6
Silvertown Wy *CAN/RD* E16 141 L8
Silver Tree Cl *WOT/HER* KT12 217 H1
Silvertree La *GFD/PVL* UB6 134 C5
Silver Trees *LCOL/BKTW* AL2 55 N6
Silver Wk *BERM/RHTH* SE16 140 E10
Silver Wy *HGDN/ICK* UB10 132 C4
ROMW/RG RM7 124 C1
Silverwood *CRAWE* RH10 * 285 N2
Silverwood Cl *BECK* BR3 182 F10
CDW/CHF RM16 147 M9
CROY/NA CR0 224 E5
NTHWD HA6 92 D9
Silvester Rd *EDUL* SE22 181 N1
Silvesters *HLWW/ROY* CM19 46 C3
Silvester St *STHWK* SE1 18 G2
Silwood Cl *ASC* SL5 192 C2
Silwood Est Regeneration Area
BERM/RHTH SE16 160 C4
Silwood Pk *ASC* SL5 * 192 C2
ASC SL5 192 E3
Silwood Rd *ASC* SL5 192 E4
Silwood St *BERM/RHTH* SE16 160 C4
Simmil Rd *ESH/CLAY* KT10 218 D2
Simmonds Dr *HART* DA3 211 M5
Simmonds Ri *HHS/BOV* HP3 35 N8
Simmons Cl *DTCH/LGLY* SL3 * 150 D3
TRDG/WHET N20 97 P3
Simmons Dr *BCTR* RM8 123 P8
Simmons Ga *ESH/CLAY* KT10 218 B2
Simmons La *CHING* E4 101 J3
Simmons Pl *CDW/CHF* RM16 147 M10
STA TW18 173 H8
Simmons Rd *WOOL/PLUM* SE18 162 E4
Simmons' Wy *TRDG/WHET* N20 97 P3
Simms Cl *CAR* SM5 201 M9
Simms Gdns *EFNCH* N2 97 M10
Simms Rd *STHWK* SE1 19 P6
STHWK SE1 159 P5
Simnel Rd *LEE/GVPK* SE12 183 N3
Simon Cl *NTGHL* W11 8 D7
Simon Dean *HHS/BOV* HP3 52 D3
Simonds Rd *LEY* E10 120 F7
Simone Cl *BMLY* BR1 206 A1
Simone Dr *PUR/KEN* CR8 241 K2
Simons Cl *CHERT* KT16 214 F3
Simons Wk *EGH* TW20 171 P10
SRTFD E15 121 J10
Simplemarsh Rd
ADL/WDHM KT15 215 K1
Simplicity La *HLWE* CM17 29 N10
Simpson Cl *WCHMH* N21 78 G9
Simpson Dr *ACT* W3 136 A8
Simpson Rd *HSLWW* TW4 175 N3
RAIN RM13 144 G1
RCHPK/HAM TW10 177 H7
Simpson's Rd *HAYES* BR2 205 M3
POP/IOD E14 140 G9
Simpson St *BTSEA* SW11 157 P8
Simpsons Wy *SL* SL1 129 K10
Simpson Wy *SURB* KT6 199 H6
Simrose Ct *WAND/EARL* SW18 179 K1
Sims Cl *ROM* RM1 124 G2
Sinclair Cl *CRAWE* RH10 284 D9
Sinclair Dr *BELMT* SM2 221 L5
Sinclair Gdns *WKENS* W14 156 G1
Sinclair Gv *GLDGN* NW11 116 G4
Sinclair Rd *CHING* E4 100 E6
WKENS W14 14 A3
WKENS W14 157 H2
Sinclair Wy *RDART* DA2 188 C7
Sinclare Cl *EN* EN1 79 N5
Sincots Rd *REDH* RH1 258 A10
Sinderby Cl *BORE* WD6 75 K5
Singapore Rd *WEA* W13 134 F10
Singer St *FSBYE* EC1V 7 H10
Singles Cross *RSEV* TN14 * 245 N1
Single's Cross La *RSEV* TN14 245 M1
Single St *BH/WHM* TN16 244 E1
Singleton Cl *CROY/NA* CR0 203 K7
HCH RM12 124 G9
TOOT SW17 180 A10
Singleton Rd *DAGW* RM9 124 A10
Singleton Scarp
NFNCH/WDSPK N12 97 K6
Singlewell Rd *GVW* DA11 190 E7
Singret Pl *UX/CGN* UB8 * 131 M6
Sinnott Rd *WALTH* E17 100 B8
Sion Rd *TWK* TW1 176 G4
Sipson Cl *WDR/YW* UB7 152 B5
Sipson La *HYS/HAR* UB3 152 D5
Sipson Rd *WDR/YW* UB7 152 A3
Sipson Wy *WDR/YW* UB7 152 B6
Sir Abraham Dawes Cottages
PUT/ROE SW15 * 157 H10
Sir Alexander Cl *ACT* W3 136 C10
Sir Cyril Black Wy *WIM/MER*
SW19 179 K10
Sirdar Rd *MTCM* CR4 180 B9
NTGHL W11 136 G9
WDGN N22 119 J1
Sirdar Strd *GVE* DA12 191 J8
Sir Francis Wy *BRW* CM14 106 G3
Sir Henry Peakes Dr *SLN* SL2 128 F1
Sir John Kirk Cl *CMBW* SE5 159 K6
Sir John Newsom Wy *WGCE* AL7 23 H8
Sir Robert Ms *DTCH/LGLY* SL3 150 D4
Sir Thomas More Est *CHEL* SW3 15 M10
Sirus Rd *NTHWD* HA6 93 H6
Sise La *MANHO* EC4N * 12 G6
Siskin Cl *BORE* WD6 75 M8
BUSH WD23 73 M8
Sisley Rd *BARK* IG11 143 H3
Sispara Gdns *WAND/EARL* SW18 179 J2
Sissinghurst Cl *BMLY* BR1 183 K8
CRAWE RH10 284 E6
Sissinghurst Rd *CROY/NA* CR0 203 P7
Sister Mabels Wy *PECK* SE15 159 P6
Sisters Av *BTSEA* SW11 158 A10
Sistova Rd *BAL* SW12 180 C4
Sisulu Pl *BRXN/ST* SW9 159 H9
Sittingbourne Av *EN* EN1 79 L10
Sitwell Gv *STAN* HA7 94 E6
Siverst Cl *NTHLT* UB5 134 A1
Siviter Wy *DAGE* RM10 144 C2
Siward Rd *HAYES* BR2 205 N2
TOOT SW17 179 M6
TOTM N17 99 L9
Six Acres *HHS/BOV* HP3 36 B9
Six Bells La *SEV* TN13 265 K2
Sixteenth Av
KWD/TDW/WH KT20 * 257 J2
Sixth Av *GSTN* WD25 73 L1
HYS/HAR UB3 132 G10
KWD/TDW/WH KT20 * 257 J2
MNPK E12 122 C9
NKENS W10 2 A10
NKENS W10 137 H6
Sixth Cross Rd *WHTN* TW2 176 B6
Skardu Rd *CRICK* NW2 117 H10
Skarnings Ct *WAB* EN9 63 M9
Skeena Hl *WAND/EARL* SW18 179 H3
Skeet Hill La *STMC/STPC* BR5 208 A10
Skeffington Rd *EHAM* E6 142 C3
Skeffington St
WOOL/PLUM SE18 162 F2
Skelbrook St *WAND/EARL* SW18 179 M5
Skelgill Rd *PUT/ROE* SW15 157 J10
Skelley Rd *SRTFD* E15 141 L2
Skelton Cl *HACK* E8 7 M2
Skelton Rd *FSTGT* E7 141 M1
Skelton's La *LEY* E10 120 G5
Skelwith Rd *HMSMTH* W6 156 F5
Skerne Rd *KUTN/CMB* KT2 199 J1
Skerne Wk *KUTN/CMB* KT2 199 J1
Sketchley Gdns
BERM/RHTH SE16 160 C4
Sketty Rd *EN* EN1 79 N7
Skibbs La *ORP* BR6 207 P10
Skid Hill La *WARL* CR6 243 L1
Skidmore Wy *RKW/CH/CXG* WD3 91 P2
Skiers St *SRTFD* E15 141 K3
Skiffington Cl *BRXS/STRHM* SW2 181 H4
Skimpans Cl *BRKMPK* AL9 40 G10
Skinner Pl *BGVA* SW1W * 16 C6
Skinners La *ASHTD* KT21 237 J4
BLKFR EC4V 12 F7
HEST TW5 154 A7
Skinner St *CLKNW* EC1R 12 C1
FSBYE EC1V 6 C10
Skinney La *EYN* DA4 210 C3
Skip La *DEN/HRF* UB9 111 N6
Skippers Cl *SWCM* DA10 188 G1
Skipsey Av *EHAM* E6 142 C5
Skipton Cl *FBAR/BDGN* N11 98 B7
Skipton Dr *HYS/HAR* UB3 152 D2
Skipton Wy *HORL* RH6 280 C2
Skipworth Rd *HOM* E9 140 D3
Skylark Rd *DEN/HRF* UB9 110 F6
Skylines Village *POP/IOD* E14 * 161 H1
Sky Peals Rd *WFD* IG8 101 J9
Skyport Dr *WDR/YW* UB7 151 N6
Skys Wood Rd *STALE/WH* AL4 38 G2
Slacksbury Hatch
HLWW/ROY CM19 46 E1
Sladebrook Rd *BKHTH/KID* SE3 162 B9
Slade Cl *EPP* CM16 83 J2
Slade Ct *CHERT* KT16 214 G3
RAD WD7 74 G1
Sladedale Rd *WOOL/PLUM* SE18 163 H4
Slade End *EPP* CM16 83 H2
Slade Gdns *ERITH* DA8 164 G7
Slade Green Rd *ERITH* DA8 164 G7
Sladen Pl *CLPT* E5 120 A9
Slade Oak La *DEN/HRF* UB9 110 F4
Slade Rd *CHERT* KT16 214 G3
CHOB/PIR GU24 230 C6
Slades Cl *ENC/FH* EN2 79 H7
Slades Dr *CHST* BR7 184 F7
Slades Gdns *ENC/FH* EN2 79 H6
Slades Hl *ENC/FH* EN2 79 H7
Slades Ri *ENC/FH* EN2 79 H7
The Slade *WOOL/PLUM* SE18 163 H5
Slade Wk *WALW* SE17 18 D10
Slade Wy *MTCM* CR4 202 B1
Slagrove Pl *BROCKY* SE4 182 F1
Slaidburn St *WBPTN* SW10 15 K10
Slaithwaite Rd *LEW* SE13 161 H10
Slaney Pl *HOLWY* N7 119 H10
Slaney Rd *ROM* RM1 124 F3
Slattery Rd *FELT* TW13 175 L4
Slaugham Ct *CRAWW* RH11 283 J10
Sleaford Gn *OXHEY* WD19 93 L4
Sleaford St *VX/NE* SW8 158 D6
Sleapcross Gdns *STALE/WH* AL4 39 P7
Sleapshyde La *STALE/WH* AL4 39 P7
Sleddale *HHNE* HP2 35 P3
Sledmere Ct *EBED/NFELT* TW14 174 F4
Sleepers Farm Rd
CDW/CHF RM16 168 E1
Sleets End *HHW* HP1 35 L4
Slewins Cl *EMPK* RM11 125 L3
Slewins La *EMPK* RM11 125 K3
Slievemore Cl *CLAP* SW4 158 E9
Slimmons Dr *STALE/WH* AL4 38 F2
Slines New Rd *CTHM* CR3 242 C6
Slines Oak Rd *WARL* CR6 242 F5
Slinfold Wk *CRAWW* RH11 283 K7
Slingsby Pl *LSQ/SEVD* WC2H 11 L7
Slipe La *BROX* EN10 44 E10
Slippers Hl *HHNE* HP2 35 N5
Slippers Pl *BERM/RHTH* SE16 160 A2
Slipshatch Rd *REIG* RH2 275 J4
Slipshoe St *REIG* RH2 257 J10
The Slip *BH/WHM* TN16 262 F2
Sloane Av *CHEL* SW3 15 P6
Sloane Ct East *CHEL* SW3 16 C7
Sloane Ct West *CHEL* SW3 16 C7
Sloane Gdns *BGVA* SW1W 16 C6
ORP BR6 206 F10
Sloane Sq *BGVA* SW1W 16 C6
HART DA3 * 211 K3
Sloane St *KTBR* SW1X 16 B2
Sloane Ter *KTBR* SW1X 16 B5
Sloane Wk *CROY/NA* CR0 204 E6
Sloansway *WGCE* AL7 23 J2
Slocock Hl *WOKN/KNAP* GU21 231 P3
Slocum Cl *THMD* SE28 143 M9
Slough La *BRKHM/BTCW* RH3 256 D9
CDALE/KGS NW9 115 P4
EPSOM KT18 255 P1
Slough Rd *DTCH/LGLY* SL3 149 M4
DTCH/LGLY SL3 149 N6
IVER SL0 130 G5
Slowmans Cl *LCOL/BKTW* AL2 56 B4
Slyfield Gn *GU* GU1 250 B4
Sly St *WCHPL* E1 * 140 A8
Smaldon Cl *WDR/YW* UB7 152 B2
Small Acre *HHW* HP1 35 J6
Smallberry Av *ISLW* TW7 154 E8
Smallbrook Ms *BAY/PAD* W2 9 L6
Smallcroft *WGCE* AL7 23 L4
Smalley Cl *STNW/STAM* N16 119 N8
Smallfield Rd *HORL* RH6 280 C4
HORL RH6 281 M4
Smallford La *STALE/WH* AL4 39 N7
Small Grains *HART* DA3 210 G10
Smallmead *HORL* RH6 280 C4
Smalls Hill Rd *REIG* RH2 274 F10
Smalls Md *CRAWW* RH11 283 M7
Smallwood Cl *STALE/WH* AL4 21 K4
Smallwood Rd *TOOT* SW17 179 N7
Smarden Cl *BELV* DA17 164 B4
Smart Cl *HARH* RM3 105 J9
Smarts Gn *CHESW* EN7 61 N2
Smart's Heath La
WOKS/MYFD GU22 231 M9
Smart's Heath Rd
WOKS/MYFD GU22 231 N8
Smart's La *LOU* IG10 82 B8
Smart's Pl *NOXST/BSQ* WC1A 11 M5
UED N18 99 P6
Smarts Rd *GVE* DA12 190 E6
Smart St *BETH* E2 140 C5
Smeaton Cl *WAB* EN9 63 K9
Smeaton Rd *PEND* EN3 80 F3
WAND/EARL SW18 179 K3
WFD IG8 102 C6
Smeaton St *WAP* E1W 140 A10
Smedley St *VX/NE* SW8 158 E8
Smeed Rd *BOW* E3 140 F2
Smiles Pl *LEW* SE13 161 H8
Smitham Bottom La
PUR/KEN CR8 222 E8
Smitham Downs Rd
PUR/KEN CR8 222 F10
Smithbarn Cl *HORL* RH6 280 C3
Smith Cl *BERM/RHTH* SE16 140 C10
CRAWE RH10 283 N10
The Smithers *BRKHM/BTCW* RH3 273 N2
Smithfield *HHNE* HP2 35 N4
Smithfields *HHNE* HP2 35 N4
Smithfield St *STBT* EC1A 12 C4
Smithies Rd *ABYW* SE2 163 J3
Smith Rd *REIG* RH2 275 J3
Smiths Ct *EPP* CM16 65 L1
SOHO/SHAV W1D * 11 J7
Smiths La *CHESW* EN7 61 L2
EDEN TN8 262 F9
WDSR SL4 148 D8
Smithson Rd *TOTM* N17 99 L9
Smith Sq *WEST* SW1P 17 L4
Smith St *BRYLDS* KT5 199 L6
CHEL SW3 16 A7
WATW WD18 73 K8
Smith Ter *CHEL* SW3 16 A8
Smithwood Cl *WIM/MER* SW19 179 H5
Smithy Cl *KWD/TDW/WH* KT20 257 J2
Smithy La *KWD/TDW/WH* KT20 257 J2
Smithy's Gn *BFOR* GU20 212 C3
Smithy St *WCHPL* E1 140 B7
Smoke La *REIG* RH2 275 L2
Smugglers Wy
WAND/EARL SW18 157 L10
Smugglers Whf *RDART* DA2 188 G1
Smug Oak La *LCOL/BKTW* AL2 56 A6
Smyrks Rd *WALW* SE17 19 K8
Smyrna Rd *KIL/WHAMP* NW6 2 E4
Smythe Rd *EYN* DA4 209 P1
Smythe St *POP/IOD* E14 140 G9
Snag La *RSEV* TN14 226 G8
Snakes Hl *BRW* CM14 86 B7
Snakes La *EBAR* EN4 78 C7
Snakes La East *WFD* IG8 101 P7
Snakes La West *WFD* IG8 101 M7
Snakey La *FELT* TW13 175 H7
Snape Sp *SL* SL1 129 K8
Snaresbrook Dr *STAN* HA7 95 J5
Snaresbrook Rd *WALTH* E17 121 K2
Snarsgate St *NKENS* W10 136 F7
Snatts Hl *OXTED* RH8 261 L5
Sneath Av *GLDGN* NW11 117 J5
Snell Hatch *CRAWW* RH11 283 L7
Snelling Av *GVW* DA11 190 C5
Snellings Rd *WOT/HER* KT12 217 K2
Snells La *AMSS* HP7 69 N6
Snell's Pk *UED* N18 99 N7
Snells Wood Ct *AMSS* HP7 69 P6
Sneyd Rd *CRICK* NW2 116 F10
Snipe Cl *ERITH* DA8 165 J6
Snowberry Cl *SRTFD* E15 121 J9
Snowbury Rd *FUL/PGN* SW6 157 L8
Snowcrete *DTCH/LGLY* SL3 * 129 P4
Snowden Av *HGDN/ICK* UB10 132 C4
Snowden Cl *WDSR* SL4 148 C10
Snowden Dr *CDALE/KGS* NW9 116 B4
Snowdon Crs *HYS/HAR* UB3 152 D2
Snowdon Rd *HTHAIR* TW6 174 D2
Snowdown Cl *PGE/AN* SE20 204 B1
Snowdrop Cl *HPTN* TW12 175 P9
Snowdrop Wy *CHOB/PIR* GU24 230 F3
Snowerhill Rd
BRKHM/BTCW RH3 274 C4
Snow Hl *CRAWE* RH10 281 N10
CRAWE RH10 285 N2
STBT EC1A 12 C4
Snowhill Cottages *CSHM* HP5 33 L10
Snowhill La *CRAWE* RH10 281 N10
Snowsfields *STHWK* SE1 19 H1
Snowshill Rd *MNPK* E12 122 B10
Snows Paddock *BFOR* GU20 192 A10
Snows Ride *BFOR* GU20 212 A1
Snowy Fielder Waye *ISLW* TW7 154 G8
Soames St *PECK* SE15 159 N9
Soames Wk *NWMAL* KT3 200 B1
Soane Cl *CRAWW* RH11 283 H9
EA W5 155 J1
Soaphouse La *BTFD* TW8 155 K6
Soham Rd *PEND* EN3 80 E3
Soho Sq *SOHO/SHAV* W1D 11 J6
Soho St *SOHO/SHAV* W1D 11 J5
Sojourner Truth Cl *HACK* E8 * 140 A1
Solander Gdns *WCHPL* E1 140 A9
Solar Ct *WATW* WD18 * 72 G9
Solar Wy *PEND* EN3 80 E1
Solebay St *WCHPL* E1 140 D6
Solecote *GT/LBKH* KT23 253 P1
Sole Farm Av *GT/LBKH* KT23 253 N1
Sole Farm Cl *GT/LBKH* KT23 235 N10
Sole Farm Rd *GT/LBKH* KT23 253 N1
Solefields Rd *SEV* TN13 265 K3
Solent Ri *PLSTW* E13 141 M5
Solent Rd *KIL/WHAMP* NW6 117 K10
Soleoak Dr *SEV* TN13 265 J3
Solesbridge Cl
RKW/CH/CXG WD3 71 J7
Solesbridge La
RKW/CH/CXG WD3 71 J7
Solid La *BRWN* CM15 86 E5
Solna Av *PUT/ROE* SW15 178 F1
Solna Rd *WCHMH* N21 99 L2
Solomon Av *UED* N18 99 P5
Solomon's Hl *RKW/CH/CXG* WD3 91 N1
Solomon's Pas *PECK* SE15 160 A10
Soloms Court Rd *BNSTD* SM7 239 N3
Solon New Rd *CLAP* SW4 158 F10
Solon Rd *BRXS/STRHM* SW2 158 F10
Solway *HHNE* HP2 36 A4
Solway Cl *HACK* E8 7 M2
HSLWW TW4 153 M9
Solway Rd *EDUL* SE22 159 P10
WDGN N22 99 J9
Somaford Gv *EBAR* EN4 77 N10
Somali Rd *CRICK* NW2 117 J9
Somerby Cl *BROX* EN10 44 F7
Somerby Rd *BARK* IG11 142 G2
Somercoates Cl *EBAR* EN4 77 P7
Somerden Rd *STMC/STPC* BR5 207 N7
Somerfield Cl
KWD/TDW/WH KT20 239 H5
Somerfield Rd *FSBYPK* N4 119 J7
Somerfield St *BERM/RHTH* SE16 160 C4
Somerford Cl *PIN* HA5 113 H2
Somerford Gv *STNW/STAM* N16 119 N9
TOTM N17 99 P8
Somerford Pl *BEAC* HP9 88 C8
Somerford St *WCHPL* E1 * 140 A6
Somerford Wy
BERM/RHTH SE16 160 D1
Somerhill Av *BFN/LL* DA15 185 L3
Somerhill Rd *WELL* DA16 163 L8
Someries Rd *HHW* HP1 35 J4
Somerleyton Rd *BRXN/ST* SW9 159 H10
Somersby Gdns *REDBR* IG4 122 C3
Somers Cl *CAMTN* NW1 * 5 J7
REIG RH2 257 K9
Somers Crs *BAY/PAD* W2 9 N6
Somerset Av *CHSGTN* KT9 219 J1
RYNPK SW20 200 E2
WELL DA16 185 J1
Somerset Cl *HOR/WEW* KT19 220 B6
NWMAL KT3 200 B6
TOTM N17 99 L10
WFD IG8 101 M9
WOT/HER KT12 217 J2
Somerset Gdns *EMPK* RM11 125 P6
HGT N6 118 C5
LEW SE13 160 G8
STRHM/NOR SW16 202 G3
TEDD TW11 176 D8
TOTM N17 99 M8
Somerset Rd *BAR* EN5 77 L9
BTFD TW8 155 H5
CHSWK W4 156 A2
DART DA1 187 J3
HDN NW4 116 F2
HRW HA1 114 B4
KUT/HW KT1 199 L2
ORP BR6 207 K7
PEND EN3 80 F4
REDH RH1 275 N2
SLH/COR SS17 169 K1
STHL UB1 133 P7
TEDD TW11 176 D8
TOTM N17 119 N1
UED N18 99 N6
WALTH E17 120 F3
WEA W13 134 G10
WIM/MER SW19 178 G6
Somerset Sq *WKENS* W14 14 C3
WKENS W14 * 157 H2
Somerset Wy *WDR/YW* UB7 151 L2
Somerset Waye *HEST* TW5 153 M5
Somersham *WGCE* AL7 23 N5
Somersham Rd *BXLYHN* DA7 163 P8
Somers Pl *BRXS/STRHM* SW2 180 G3
Somers Rd *BRKMPK* AL9 40 F10
BRXS/STRHM SW2 180 F2
REIG RH2 257 K9
WALTH E17 120 E2
Somers Sq *BRKMPK* AL9 40 F9
Somers Wy *BUSH* WD23 94 B1
Somerswey *RGUE* GU4 268 B8
Somerton Av *RCH/KEW* TW9 155 N9
Somerton Cl *PUR/KEN* CR8 241 H2
Somerton Rd *CRICK* NW2 116 G8
PECK SE15 160 A10
Somertrees Av *LEE/GVPK* SE12 183 N5
Somervell Rd *RYLN/HDSTN* HA2 113 N10
Somerville Av *BARN* SW13 156 F5
Somerville Dr *CRAWE* RH10 284 D4
Somerville Rd *CHDH* RM6 123 M3
COB KT11 217 P10
DART DA1 187 N2
PGE/AN SE20 182 C10
WDSR SL4 149 H4
Sommers Ct *WARE* SG12 * 26 D3
Sonderburg Rd *HOLWY* N7 118 G7
Sondes Farm *DORK* RH4 * 272 E2
Sondes Pl Cottages *DORK* RH4 * 272 E2
Sondes Place Dr *DORK* RH4 272 E2
Sondes St *WALW* SE17 18 G9
Songhurst Cl *CROY/NA* CR0 202 G6
Sonia Cl *OXHEY* WD19 93 K1
Sonia Gdns *HEST* TW5 153 P6
NFNCH/WDSPK N12 97 M5
WLSDN NW10 116 C9
The Sonnets *HHW* HP1 35 L5
Sonning Gdns *HPTN* TW12 175 M9
Sonning Rd *SNWD* SE25 203 P6
Soothouse Spring
STALW/RED AL3 38 E2
Soper Cl *CHING* E4 100 E6
FSTH SE23 182 C4
Soper Dr *CTHM* CR3 241 L9
Soper Ms *PEND* EN3 80 F4
Soper Sq *HLWE* CM17 29 M10
Sopers Rd *POTB/CUF* EN6 60 C5
Sophia Cl *HOLWY* N7 5 N1
Sophia Rd *CAN/RD* E16 141 N8
LEY E10 120 G6
Sophia Sq *BERM/RHTH* SE16 140 D9
Sopwell La *STAL* AL1 38 C7
Sopwith Av *CHSGTN* KT9 219 K2
Sopwith Cl *BH/WHM* TN16 244 A2
KUTN/CMB KT2 177 L8
Sopwith Dr *BF/WBF* KT14 215 P8
Sopwith Rd *HEST* TW5 153 K6
Sopwith Wy *KUTN/CMB* KT2 199 K1
VX/NE SW8 158 C6
Sorbie Cl *WEY* KT13 216 D3
Sorrel Bank *CROY/NA* CR0 224 D6
Sorrel Cl *THMD* SE28 143 K10
Sorrel Gdns *EHAM* E6 142 B7
Sorrel La *POP/IOD* E14 141 J8
Sorrell Cl *BRXN/ST* SW9 * 159 H8
NWCR SE14 160 D6
Sorrell Wy *GVW* DA11 190 B7
Sorrel Wk *ROM* RM1 124 G1
Sorrento Rd *SUT* SM1 201 L10
Sospel Ct *SLN* SL2 129 H4
Sotheby Rd *HBRY* N5 119 K9
Sotheran Cl *HACK* E8 7 P5
Sotheron Rd *WAT* WD17 73 K6
Soudan Rd *BTSEA* SW11 158 A7
Souldern Rd *WKENS* W14 * 156 G2
Souldern St *WATW* WD18 73 J9
Sounds Ldg *SWLY* BR8 208 D6
South Access Rd *LEY* E10 120 D5
South Africa Rd *SHB* W12 136 E9
South Albert Rd *REIG* RH2 257 J9
Southall Cl *WARE* SG12 26 C1
Southall Ct *STHL* UB1 * 133 N9
Southall La *HEST* TW5 153 J5
Southall Pl *STHWK* SE1 18 G2
Southall Wy *BRW* CM14 106 E5
Southampton Buildings
LINN WC2A * 12 A4
Southampton Gdns *MTCM* CR4 202 F5
Southampton Ms *CAN/RD* E16 141 N10
Southampton Pl
NOXST/BSQ WC1A 11 M4
Southampton Rd *HAMP* NW3 118 A10
HTHAIR TW6 174 A2
Southampton Rw
NOXST/BSQ WC1A 11 M3
Southampton St *COVGDN* WC2E 11 M7
Southampton Wy *CMBW* SE5 159 L6
Southam St *NKENS* W10 8 B2
NKENS W10 137 H6
South Ap *NTHWD* HA6 92 E4
South Audley St
MYFR/PKLN W1K 10 D8
South Av *CAR* SM5 222 B4
CHING E4 100 C1
EGH TW20 172 F9
RCH/KEW TW9 * 155 M8
STHL UB1 133 N9
WOT/HER KT12 216 F6
South Avenue Gdns *STHL* UB1 133 N9
South Bank *BH/WHM* TN16 262 G2
STHWK SE1 12 B8
SURB KT6 199 K6
Southbank *SWLY* BR8 186 G10
THDIT KT7 198 G7
South Bank Rd *BERK* HP4 33 L3
South Bank Ter *SURB* KT6 * 199 K6
South Birkbeck Rd *WAN* E11 121 J8
South Black Lion La
HMSMTH W6 156 D4
South Bolton Gdns
WBPTN SW10 15 H7
The South Border *PUR/KEN* CR8 222 F7
Southborough Cl *SURB* KT6 199 J8
Southborough La *HAYES* BR2 206 B5
Southborough Rd *BMLY* BR1 206 B3
HOM E9 140 B3
SURB KT6 199 K8
Southborough Rd (The Lane)
SURB KT6 * 199 K8
Southbourne *HAYES* BR2 205 M7
Southbourne Av
CDALE/KGS NW9 95 P10
Southbourne Cl *PIN* HA5 113 M5
Southbourne Crs *HDN* NW4 117 H2
Southbourne Gdns *IL* IG1 122 F10
LEE/GVPK SE12 183 N1
RSLP HA4 113 K6
Southbridge Pl *CROY/NA* CR0 223 K1
Southbridge Rd *CROY/NA* CR0 223 K1
Southbridge Wy *NWDGN* UB2 153 M1
Southbrook *SBW* CM21 29 P2
Southbrook Dr *CHES/WCR* EN8 62 C4
Southbrook Rd *LEE/GVPK* SE12 183 K2
STRHM/NOR SW16 202 F1
Southbury Av *EN* EN1 79 P8
Southbury Cl *HCH* RM12 125 L10
Southbury Rd *EN* EN1 79 N8
South Carriage Dr *KTBR* SW1X 16 B1
SKENS SW7 15 N2
South Charlton Mead La
HOD EN11 45 J4
Southchurch Rd *EHAM* E6 142 C4
Southcliffe Dr *CFSP/GDCR* SL9 90 B6
South Cl *BAR* EN5 77 J7
BXLYHS DA6 163 N10
CRAWE RH10 284 A6
DAGE RM10 144 B3
HGT N6 118 C4
LCOL/BKTW AL2 56 A1
PIN HA5 113 N5
SL SL1 128 C9
WDR/YW UB7 152 B4
WHTN TW2 175 P6
WOKN/KNAP GU21 231 P2
South Close Gn *REDH* RH1 258 C5
The South Colonnade
POP/IOD E14 140 F10
Southcombe St *WKENS* W14 14 A5
WKENS W14 157 H3
Southcote *WOKN/KNAP* GU21 232 A2
Southcote Av *BRYLDS* KT5 199 N7
FELT TW13 175 H5
Southcote Ri *RSLP* HA4 112 E5
Southcote Rd *ARCH* N19 118 D9
REDH RH1 258 D6
SAND/SEL CR2 223 N6
SNWD SE25 204 A5
WALTH E17 120 C3
South Cottage Dr
RKW/CH/CXG WD3 71 J9
South Cottage Gdns
RKW/CH/CXG WD3 71 J9
South Countess Rd *WALTH* E17 120 E1
South Crs *CAN/RD* E16 141 J7
FITZ W1T 11 J4
Southcroft *EGH* TW20 171 N8
SLN SL2 128 G6
Southcroft Av *WELL* DA16 163 H9
WWKM BR4 205 H9
Southcroft Rd *ORP* BR6 207 H10
STRHM/NOR SW16 180 C9
South Cross Rd *BARK/HLT* IG6 122 F3
South Croxted Rd *DUL* SE21 181 L7
Southdale *CHIG* IG7 102 G7
Southdean Gdns
WIM/MER SW19 179 J5
South Dene *MLHL* NW7 96 A4
Southdene *RSEV* TN14 228 A9
Southdown Av *HNWL* W7 154 F2
Southdown Ct *HAT* AL10 40 D7
Southdown Crs
GNTH/NBYPK IG2 123 H3
RYLN/HDSTN HA2 114 B6
Southdown Dr *RYNPK* SW20 178 G10
Southdown Rd *CAR* SM5 222 B5
CTHM CR3 242 E8
EMPK RM11 125 J5
HARP AL5 20 A2
HAT AL10 40 D7
RYNPK SW20 200 G1
WOT/HER KT12 217 M1
South Downs Wy *RDKG* RH5 255 H8
Southdown Vls
SEVS/STOTM N15 * 119 J3
South Dr *BEAC* HP9 108 A1
BNSTD SM7 221 P9
BRW CM14 107 J5
CHOB/PIR GU24 230 B7
COUL/CHIP CR5 240 E1
GPK RM2 125 K1
ORP BR6 227 H2
POTB/CUF EN6 60 F6
RDKG RH5 273 H2
RSLP HA4 112 F6
STALE/WH AL4 39 K5
VW GU25 193 M7
South Ealing Rd *EA* W5 155 J1
South Eastern Av *ED* N9 99 N4
South Eaton Pl *BGVA* SW1W 16 D5
South Eden Park Rd *BECK* BR3 204 G5
South Edwardes Sq *KENS* W8 14 D4
South End *CROY/NA* CR0 223 K1
GT/LBKH KT23 254 A2
KENS W8 15 H3
Southend Arterial Rd
EMPK RM11 125 M1
RBRW/HUT CM13 127 P2
Southend Cl *ELTH/MOT* SE9 184 E2
Southend Crs *ELTH/MOT* SE9 184 D2
Southend La *CAT* SE6 182 F7
WAB EN9 63 N10
Southend Rd *BECK* BR3 182 F10
CLAY IG5 122 B1
EHAM E6 142 C2
GRAYS RM17 167 P3
South End Rd *HAMP* NW3 117 P9
RAIN RM13 145 H3
Southend Rd (North Circular)
WALTH E17 101 J9
South End Rw *KENS* W8 15 H3
Southerland Cl *WEY* KT13 216 D1
Southern Av *EBED/NFELT* TW14 175 H4
REDH RH1 276 B8
SNWD SE25 203 N3
Southern Down *FELT* TW13 * 175 K4
Southern Dr *LOU* IG10 82 C10
Southerngate Wy *NWCR* SE14 160 D6
Southern Gv *BOW* E3 140 E5
Southernhay *LOU* IG10 82 A9
Southern Perimeter Rd
STWL/WRAY TW19 173 M1
Southern Pl *SWLY* BR8 208 E4
Southern Rd *EFNCH* N2 118 A2
PLSTW E13 141 N4
Southern Rw *NKENS* W10 8 A2
NKENS W10 136 G6
Southerns La *COUL/CHIP* CR5 239 M10
Southern St *IS* N1 5 N7
Southern Ter *HOD* EN11 * 26 G10
Southern Wy *GNWCH* SE10 161 L3
HLWW/ROY CM19 46 D4
ROMW/RG RM7 124 B4
Southernwood Cl *HHNE* HP2 36 B5
Southerton Rd *HMSMTH* W6 * 156 F3
Southerton Wy *RAD* WD7 57 K9
South Esk Rd *FSTGT* E7 141 P1
Southey Rd *BRXN/ST* SW9 159 H7
SEVS/STOTM N15 119 M3
WIM/MER SW19 179 K10
Southey St *PGE/AN* SE20 182 C10
Southey Wk *TIL* RM18 168 E7
Southfield *BAR* EN5 76 G10
WGCE AL7 22 G7
Southfield Av *WATN* WD24 73 K4
Southfield Cl *UX/CGN* UB8 132 B6
South Field Cl *WDSR* SL4 148 B2
Southfield Gdns *SL* SL1 128 A7
TWK TW1 176 E7
Southfield Pk *RYLN/HDSTN* HA2 114 A4
Southfield Pl *WEY* KT13 216 C4
Southfield Rd *CHES/WCR* EN8 62 D8
CHST BR7 207 J3
CHSWK W4 156 B2
HOD EN11 44 F1
PEND EN3 80 A10
Southfields *E/WMO/HCT* KT8 198 D6
HDN NW4 116 E1
Southfields Av *ASHF* TW15 174 C9
Southfields Ms
WAND/EARL SW18 * 179 K2
Southfields Rd *CTHM* CR3 242 F10
WAND/EARL SW18 179 K2
Southfield Wy *STALE/WH* AL4 39 J4
Southfleet Av *HART* DA3 211 N2
Southfleet Rd *GVW* DA11 190 C4
ORP BR6 207 H10
RDART DA2 189 H7
SWCM DA10 189 M3
South Gdns *WBLY* HA9 * 115 M7
WIM/MER SW19 179 N10
South Ga *HLW* CM20 46 G1
PUR RM19 166 B3
Southgate Av *CRAWE* RH10 283 N10
South Gate Av *FELT* TW13 174 E7
Southgate Dr *CRAWE* RH10 283 N9
Southgate Gv *IS* N1 7 H4
Southgate Pde *CRAWE* RH10 * 283 N9
Southgate Rd *CRAWE* RH10 283 N9
IS N1 7 H4
POTB/CUF EN6 59 M9
South Gipsy Rd *WELL* DA16 163 N9
South Gn *SL* SL1 129 K9
South Gv *CHERT* KT16 195 J6
HGT N6 118 B6
SEVS/STOTM N15 119 L3
WALTH E17 120 E3
South Hall Cl *EYN* DA4 209 N7
South Hall Dr *RAIN* RM13 145 J8
South Hl *CHST* BR7 184 C9
GU GU1 268 A2
NTHWD HA6 * 92 F9
South Hill Av *HRW* HA1 114 C8
South Hill Gv *HRW* HA1 114 D9
South Hill Pk *HAMP* NW3 117 P9
South Hill Park Gdns *HAMP* NW3 117 P9
South Hill Rd *GVE* DA12 190 F4
HAYES BR2 205 M4
HHW HP1 35 M6
Southholme Cl *NRWD* SE19 203 M1
Southill La *PIN* HA5 113 H2
Southill Rd *CHST* BR7 184 B10
Southill St *POP/IOD* E14 140 G8
South Island Pl *BRXN/ST* SW9 158 G6
South Kensington Station Ar
SKENS SW7 15 M5
South Kent Av *GVW* DA11 189 P2
South Lambeth Pl *VX/NE* SW8 17 M9
South Lambeth Rd *VX/NE* SW8 17 M9
VX/NE SW8 158 F6
Southland Rd *WOOL/PLUM* SE18 163 K5
Southlands Av *HORL* RH6 280 B3
ORP BR6 227 H1
Southlands Cl *COUL/CHIP* CR5 240 G3
Southlands Dr *WIM/MER* SW19 178 G5
Southlands Gv *BMLY* BR1 206 B3
Southlands La *OXTED* RH8 260 G10
Southlands Rd *DEN/HRF* UB9 111 J10
HAYES BR2 206 A4
IVER SL0 131 H1
Southland Ter *PUR* RM19 * 166 A4
Southland Wy *HSLW* TW3 176 C1
South La *KUT/HW* KT1 199 J3
NWMAL KT3 200 A4
South La West *NWMAL* KT3 200 A4
Southlea Rd *WDSR* SL4 149 M9
South Ley *WGCE* AL7 23 H8
South Lodge Av *MTCM* CR4 202 F4
South Lodge Crs *ENC/FH* EN2 78 E8
South Lodge Dr *STHGT/OAK* N14 78 F9
South Lodge Rd *WOT/HER* KT12 216 G6
South Md *CDALE/KGS* NW9 96 C9
HOR/WEW KT19 220 C4
REDH RH1 258 A7
Southmead Crs *CHES/WCR* EN8 62 D6
South Meadow La *WDSR* SL4 149 H6

Southmead Rd WIM/MER SW19 179 H4
South Molton La
MYFR/PKLN W1K 10 E6
South Molton Rd CAN/RD E16 141 M8
South Molton St
MYFR/PKLN W1K 10 E6
Southmont Rd ESH/CLAY KT10 198 D9
Southmoor Wy HOM E9 140 E1
South Mt TRDG/WHET N20 * 97 M3
South Norwood Hl SNWD SE25 203 M1
South Oak Rd STRHM/NOR SW16 180 G7
Southold Ri ELTH/MOT SE9 184 C6
Southolm St BTSEA SW11 158 C7
South Ordnance Rd PEND EN3 80 F4
Southover BMLY BR1 183 M8
NFNCH/WDSPK N12 97 K5
South Pde CHEL SW3 15 M7
CHSWK W4 156 A3
EDGW HA8 * 95 M10
HORL RH6 * 280 A3
REDH RH1 * 258 D4
WLGTN SM6 * 222 D3
South Pk CFSP/GDCR SL9 110 C3
SEV TN13 265 J1
South Park Av
RKW/CH/CXG WD3 71 J9
South Park Crs CAT SE6 183 K4
CFSP/GDCR SL9 110 C3
IL IG1 122 G8
South Park Dr CFSP/GDCR SL9 110 B2
GDMY/SEVK IG3 123 H8
South Park Gdns BERK HP4 33 N4
South Park Gv NWMAL KT3 199 P4
South Park Hill Rd
SAND/SEL CR2 223 M1
South Park La REDH RH1 277 P1
South Park Ms FUL/PGN SW6 157 L9
South Park Rd IL IG1 122 G8
WIM/MER SW19 179 K9
South Park Ter IL IG1 122 G8
South Park Vw CFSP/GDCR SL9 110 C2
South Park Wy RSLP HA4 133 K1
South Pier Rd HORL RH6 280 B8
South Pl BRYLDS KT5 199 L7
HLW CM20 29 K8
LVPST EC2M 13 H4
PEND EN3 80 B9
South Place Ms LVPST EC2M 13 H4
Southport Rd WOOL/PLUM SE18 162 G3
South Rdg WEY KT13 216 C6
Southridge Pl RYNPK SW20 178 G10
South Riding LCOL/BKTW AL2 55 P6
South Ri BAY/PAD W2 * 9 P7
CAR SM5 221 P5
South Rd AMS HP6 69 H2
CHDH RM6 123 M3
CHOB/PIR GU24 230 E2
EA W5 155 J3
ED N9 99 P2
EDGW HA8 95 N9
EGH TW20 171 P9
ERITH DA8 164 G5
FELT TW13 175 L8
FSTH SE23 182 C5
GUW GU2 249 N8
HEST TW5 153 K5
HLW CM20 29 K8
REIG RH2 275 L1
RKW/CH/CXG WD3 70 F9
SOCK/AV RM15 147 H5
STHL UB1 133 N10
WDR/YW UB7 152 B2
WHTN TW2 176 C6
WIM/MER SW19 179 N9
WOKN/KNAP GU21 214 A10
South Rw BKHTH/KID SE3 161 M8
DTCH/LGLY SL3 110 B9
Southsea Av WATW WD18 73 H8
Southsea Rd KUT/HW KT1 199 K4
South Sea St BERM/RHTH SE16 160 E2
South Side CFSP/GDCR SL9 110 B1
Southside CHERT KT16 195 K3
South Side HMSMTH W6 156 C2
SEVS/STOTM N15 * 119 N2
Southside Common
WIM/MER SW19 178 G9
Southspring BFN/LL DA15 184 G3
South Sq GINN WC1R 12 A4
GLDGN NW11 117 K4
South Station Ap REDH RH1 276 G2
South St BMLY BR1 205 M2
BRW CM14 107 H3
DORK RH4 272 F3
EPSOM KT18 220 A9
GVE DA12 190 E3
HERT/WAT SG14 25 L5
ISLW TW7 154 F9
MYFR/PKLN W1K 10 D9
PEND EN3 80 C9
RAIN RM13 144 D4
ROM RM1 124 F4
STA TW18 173 J8
WARE SG12 27 H7
South Tenter St WCHPL E1 13 M7
South Ter DORK RH4 272 G3
EYN DA4 * 209 N7
SKENS SW7 15 N5
SURB KT6 199 K6
WDGN N22 98 F10
South V HRW HA1 114 D9
NRWD SE19 181 M9
Southvale Rd BKHTH/KID SE3 161 K8
South Vale Rd SURB KT6 199 K9
South Vw BMLY BR1 205 P2
HOR/WEW KT19 219 M6
Southview SWLY BR8 208 G4
South Vw WDSR SL4 * 149 H4
South View Av TIL RM18 168 D7
Southview Av WLSDN NW10 116 C10
South View Cl CRAWE RH10 285 M2
BXLY DA5 186 A2
Southview Cl CHESW EN7 61 M2
SWLY BR8 209 H4
TOOT SW17 180 B8
South View Ct NRWD SE19 * 181 K10
WOKS/MYFD GU22 232 B4
South View Crs GNTH/NBYPK IG2 122 E4
Southview Dr SWFD E18 121 N1
South View Dr UPMR RM14 125 P8
Southview Gdns WLGTN SM6 222 D4
South View Hts WTHK RM20 * 167 H5
South View Rd ASHTD KT21 237 J5
CEND/HSY/T N8 118 E1
CFSP/GDCR SL9 110 A2
LOU IG10 82 C10
PIN HA5 93 J8
RDART DA2 187 L6
WTHK RM20 167 H5
Southview Rd BMLY BR1 183 J7
CTHM CR3 242 G10
WARL CR6 241 P5
WARL CR6 242 A5
Southviews SAND/SEL CR2 224 C5
South Vls CAMTN NW1 5 K2
Southville VX/NE SW8 158 F7
Southville Cl EBED/NFELT TW14 174 F4
HOR/WEW KT19 220 A5
Southville Crs EBED/NFELT TW14 174 F4
Southville Rd EBED/NFELT TW14 174 F4
THDIT KT7 198 F7
South Wk REIG RH2 * 257 L10
WWKM BR4 205 K10
Southwark Br CANST EC4R 12 F8
Southwark Bridge Rd
STHWK SE1 18 D3
Southwark Park Est
BERM/RHTH SE16 * 160 A3
Southwark Park Rd
BERM/RHTH SE16 19 N5
BERM/RHTH SE16 159 P3
Southwark Pl BMLY BR1 206 C3
Southwark St STHWK SE1 12 D9
Southwater Cl BECK BR3 182 G10
CRAWW RH11 283 K7
POP/IOD E14 140 E8
South Wy ABLGY WD5 54 E9
CAR SM5 221 N6
CHING E4 80 G3
CROY/NA CR0 204 D10
FBAR/BDGN N11 98 D7
HAT AL10 40 D8
RYLN/HDSTN HA2 113 P2
WAB EN9 81 H2
WBLY HA9 115 M10
Southway GLDGN NW11 117 L4
GUW GU2 249 L10
HAYES BR2 205 M7
PUR RM19 166 D2
RYNPK SW20 200 G4
TRDG/WHET N20 97 K3
WLGTN SM6 222 D1
Southway Cl SHB W12 156 E1
Southway Pk GUW GU2 * 249 M8
Southways Pk CRAWE RH10 * 283 N2
South Weald Dr WAB EN9 63 J9
South Weald Rd BRW CM14 106 F4
Southwell Av NTHLT UB5 133 P1
Southwell Cl CDW/CHF RM16 167 H4
Southwell Gdns SKENS SW7 15 J5
Southwell Grove Rd WAN E11 121 K7
Southwell Rd CMBW SE5 159 K9
CROY/NA CR0 203 H6
KTN/HRWW/WS HA3 115 J4
South Western Rd TWK TW1 176 F2
South West India Dock
Entrance POP/IOD E14 161 H1
Southwest Rd WAN E11 121 J6
South Wharf Rd BAY/PAD W2 9 L5
Southwick Ms BAY/PAD W2 9 M5
Southwick Pl BAY/PAD W2 9 N6
Southwick St BAY/PAD W2 9 N5
Southwick Yd BAY/PAD W2 * 9 P6
Southwold Dr BARK IG11 123 K10
Southwold Rd BXLY DA5 186 C2
CLPT E5 120 A7
WATN WD24 73 K3
Southwold Sp DTCH/LGLY SL3 150 F1
Southwood Av CHERT KT16 214 F4
COUL/CHIP CR5 240 D1
HGT N6 118 C5
KUTN/CMB KT2 199 P1
WOKN/KNAP GU21 231 K4
Southwood Cl BMLY BR1 206 C4
WPK KT4 200 G8
Southwood Dr BRYLDS KT5 199 P7
South Woodford SWFD E18 101 M10
Southwood Gdns
ESH/CLAY KT10 198 F10
GNTH/NBYPK IG2 122 E2
Southwood La HGT N6 118 B5
Southwood Lawn Rd HGT N6 118 C5
Southwood Pk HGT N6 * 118 C5
Southwood Rd ELTH/MOT SE9 184 E5
THMD SE28 143 L10
South Worple Wy
MORT/ESHN SW14 156 A9
Southy Ms CAN/RD E16 141 M10
Sovereign Cl EA W5 135 H7
PUR/KEN CR8 222 G6
RSLP HA4 112 F6
WAP E1W 140 A9
Sovereign Ct E/WMO/HCT KT8 197 N4
HLWW/ROY CM19 46 E4
Sovereign Crs BERM/RHTH SE16 140 D9
Sovereign Gv ALP/SUD HA0 115 J8
Sovereign Hts DTCH/LGLY SL3 150 D5
Sovereign Ms BETH E2 * 7 L7
EBAR EN4 78 A7
Sovereign Pk HHNE HP2 * 36 C4
STALE/WH AL4 39 J7
WLSDN NW10 * 135 N6
Sovereign Pl HRW HA1 114 E3
Sovereign Rd BARK IG11 143 M5
Sowerby Cl ELTH/MOT SE9 184 C1
Sowrey Av RAIN RM13 144 G1
Space Waye EBED/NFELT TW14 175 J1
Spackmans Wy SL SL1 149 J2
Spa Dr EPSOM KT18 219 M10
Spafield St CLKNW EC1R 12 A1
Spa Green Est CLKNW EC1R * 6 B9
Spa Hl NRWD SE19 203 L1
Spalding Cl EDGW HA8 96 B8
Spalding Rd HDN NW4 116 F4
TOOT SW17 180 C8
Spalt Cl RBRW/HUT CM13 107 M3
Spanby Rd BOW E3 140 F6
Spaniards Cl GLDGN NW11 117 M6
Spaniards End HAMP NW3 117 M6
Spaniards Rd HAMP NW3 117 M7
Spanish Pl MHST W1U * 10 D5
Spanish Rd WAND/EARL SW18 179 M1
Spareleaze Hl LOU IG10 82 C8
Sparepenny La EYN DA4 209 M7
Sparkbridge Rd HRW HA1 114 D2
Sparkes Cl HAYES BR2 205 N4
Sparke Ter CAN/RD E16 * 141 L8
Sparkford Gdns FBAR/BDGN N11 98 B6
Sparks Cl ACT W3 136 A8
BCTR RM8 123 N7
HPTN TW12 175 M9
Spa Rd BERM/RHTH SE16 19 L4
Sparrow Cl HPTN TW12 175 M9
Sparrow Dr STMC/STPC BR5 206 F8
Sparrow Farm Dr
EBED/NFELT TW14 175 L3
Sparrow Farm Rd EW KT17 220 D1
Sparrow Gn DAGE RM10 124 C8
Sparrow Rw CHOB/PIR GU24 212 G3
Sparrows Herne BUSH WD23 94 A1
Sparrows La ELTH/MOT SE9 184 F4
RBSF CM22 31 M4
Sparrows Md REDH RH1 258 B7
Sparrows Wy BUSH WD23 94 B2
Sparrows Wick BUSH WD23 * 94 B2
Sparrowswick Ride
STALW/RED AL3 38 B1
Sparrow Wk GSTN WD25 73 H1
Sparsholt Rd ARCH N19 118 G6
BARK IG11 143 H3
Spartan Cl WLGTN SM6 222 F4
Sparta St GNWCH SE10 161 H7
Sparvell Rd WOKN/KNAP GU21 230 G5
Speakers Ct CROY/NA CR0 * 203 L8
Spearman St
WOOL/PLUM SE18 * 162 D5
Spear Ms ECT SW5 14 F6
Spears Rd ARCH N19 118 F6
Speart La HEST TW5 153 M6
Spectrum Pl WALW SE17 18 G8
Spedan Cl HAMP NW3 117 M8
Speedbird Wy WDR/YW UB7 151 L6
Speedgate Hl HART DA3 210 F9
Speedwell Cl HHW HP1 35 H7
RGUE GU4 250 F7
Speedwell St DEPT SE8 160 F6
Speedy Pl STPAN WC1H 5 L10
Speer Rd THDIT KT7 198 E6
Speirs Cl NWMAL KT3 200 C8
Spekehill ELTH/MOT SE9 184 C6
Speke Rd THHTH CR7 203 L2
Speldhurst Cl HAYES BR2 205 L5
Speldhurst Rd CHSWK W4 156 A2
HOM E9 140 C2
Spellbrook Wk IS N1 * 6 F5
Spelman St WCHPL E1 13 N4
Spelthorne Gv SUN TW16 174 G10
Spelthorne La ASHF TW15 174 D10
Spence Av BF/WBF KT14 215 P10
Spence Cl BERM/RHTH SE16 160 E1
Spencer Av CHESW EN7 61 M2
PLMGR N13 98 G7
YEAD UB4 133 H7
Spencer Cl EPSOM KT18 238 B5
FNCH N3 97 J10
ORP BR6 207 H9
UX/CGN UB8 131 M5
WFD IG8 101 P6
WLSDN NW10 135 L5
WOKN/KNAP GU21 214 F10
Spencer Dr EFNCH N2 117 M4
Spencer Gdns EGH TW20 172 A8
MORT/ESHN SW14 177 P1
Spencer Ga STAL AL1 38 D4
Spencer Hl WIM/MER SW19 179 H9
Spencer Hill Rd WIM/MER SW19 179 H10
Spencer House SURB KT6 * 199 K5
Spencer Ms CLAP SW4 158 F7
HMSMTH W6 14 A9
HMSMTH W6 157 H5
STAL AL1 38 D5
Spencer Pk WAND/EARL SW18 179 N1
Spencer Pl CROY/NA CR0 203 L7
IS N1 6 C3
STALE/WH AL4 21 H9
WEST SW1P 17 H4
Spencer Ri KTTN NW5 118 C9
Spencer Rd ACT W3 135 P10
ALP/SUD HA0 115 H7
BMLY BR1 183 L10
BTSEA SW11 157 N10
CEND/HSY/T N8 118 G3
CHSWK W4 155 P6
COB KT11 235 J1
CTHM CR3 241 L7
DTCH/LGLY SL3 150 C2
E/WMO/HCT KT8 198 B4
EHAM E6 142 A3
FBAR/BDGN N11 98 C5
GDMY/SEVK IG3 123 J6
ISLW TW7 154 C7
KTN/HRWW/WS HA3 94 D10
WHTN TW2 176 D6
MTCM CR4 202 A7
RAIN RM13 144 E5
RYNPK SW20 200 E2
SAND/SEL CR2 223 M2
TOTM N17 99 P9
WALTH E17 101 H10
MTCM CR4 202 B3
Spencers Cft HLWS CM18 47 L3
Spencers La HORL RH6 279 J6
Spencers Rd CRAWW RH11 283 M8
Spencer St FSBYE EC1V 6 C10
GVW DA11 190 D3
HERT/BAY SG13 25 M4
NWDGN UB2 153 L2
STALW/RED AL3 38 C6
Spencer Wk PUT/ROE SW15 156 G10
RKW/CH/CXG WD3 71 M9
TIL RM18 168 D8
Spencer Wy HHW HP1 35 K3
REDH RH1 276 B5
Spenser Av WEY KT13 216 B5
Spenser Crs UPMR RM14 126 B5
Spenser Gv STNW/STAM N16 119 M9
Spenser Ms DUL SE21 181 L4
Spenser Rd HARP AL5 20 B2
HNHL SE24 181 J1
Spenser St WESTW SW1E 17 H3
Spensley Wk STNW/STAM N16 119 L8
Speranza St WOOL/PLUM SE18 163 J4
Sperling Rd TOTM N17 99 N10
Spert St POP/IOD E14 140 D9
Speyhawk Pl POTB/CUF EN6 59 L6
Speyside STHGT/OAK N14 78 D10
Spey St POP/IOD E14 141 H7
Spey Wy ROM RM1 104 F8
Spezia Rd WLSDN NW10 136 D4
Spiceall RGUW GU3 266 G6
Spicer Cl BRXN/ST SW9 159 J8
WOT/HER KT12 197 K6
Spicersfield CHESW EN7 61 P3
Spicers Fld LHD/OX KT22 218 C9
Spicer St STALW/RED AL3 38 C6
Spices Yd CROY/NA CR0 223 K1
Spielman Rd DART DA1 165 N10
Spiers Wy HORL RH6 280 C6
Spigurnell Rd TOTM N17 99 L9
Spikes Bridge Rd STHL UB1 133 M9
Spillbutters BRWN CM15 86 G1
Spilsby Rd HARH RM3 105 L8
Spindle Cl WOOL/PLUM SE18 162 B2
Spindles TIL RM18 168 D6
Spindle Wy CRAWE RH10 283 P8
Spindlewood Gdns
CROY/NA CR0 223 M1
Spindlewoods
KWD/TDW/WH KT20 238 E8
Spindrift Av POP/IOD E14 160 G3
Spinel Cl WOOL/PLUM SE18 163 J4
Spingate Cl HCH RM12 125 K10
Spinnaker Cl BARK IG11 143 L5
Spinnells Rd RYLN/HDSTN HA2 113 N6
Spinners Wk WDSR SL4 149 H8
Spinney SL SL1 128 G10
Spinney Cl BECK BR3 204 G4
COB KT11 217 P7
NWMAL KT3 200 B5
RAIN RM13 144 F4
WDR/YW UB7 131 P9
WPK KT4 200 C10
Spinneycroft LHD/OX KT22 236 C1
Spinney Dr EBED/NFELT TW14 174 D3
Spinney Gdns DAGW RM9 123 P10
NRWD SE19 181 N8
Spinney Hl ADL/WDHM KT15 215 J2
Spinney La WDSR SL4 170 A4
Spinney Oak BMLY BR1 206 B2
CHERT KT16 214 G3
Spinney Pl AMSS HP7 * 69 H5
Spinneys Dr STALW/RED AL3 * 38 A8
The Spinneys BMLY BR1 206 C2
Spinney St HERT/BAY SG13 25 P5
The Spinney ALP/SUD HA0 114 F8
ASC SL5 192 D5
BAR EN5 77 L6
BARN SW13 * 156 E5
BEAC HP9 88 D10
BERK HP4 33 L6
BROX EN10 44 E5
CFSP/GDCR SL9 110 A6
CHEAM SM3 220 F1
CHONG CM5 67 N6
CRAWW RH11 283 L9
CSHM HP5 51 J5
EPSOM KT18 238 E5
GSTN WD25 74 C4
GT/LBKH KT23 236 A10
HERT/BAY SG13 25 N5
HLW CM20 29 K10
HORL RH6 280 B2
LHD/OX KT22 218 B8
NFNCH/WDSPK N12 * 97 M8
POTB/CUF EN6 59 N7
PUR/KEN CR8 223 J7
RBRW/HUT CM13 87 P10
RPLY/SEND GU23 251 M3
SCUP DA14 185 P8
STAN HA7 95 K5
STRHM/NOR SW16 180 D6
SUN TW16 197 H1
SWLY BR8 208 F2
WAT WD17 73 H5
WCHMH N21 99 H1
WGCE AL7 23 H6
Spinney Wy RSEV TN14 226 G7
The Spinning Wk SHGR GU5 270 B5
Spinning Wheel Md HLWS CM18 47 L4
Spire Cl GVE DA12 190 E4
The Spire Green Centre
HLWW/ROY CM19 46 B2
Spire Pl WARL CR6 242 D4
The Spires DART DA1 187 L5
HHNE HP2 35 N8
Spirit Quay WAP E1W 13 P9
Spital Heath DORK RH4 273 H1
Spital La BRW CM14 106 E4
Spital Sq WCHPL E1 13 K3
Spital St DART DA1 187 L2
WCHPL E1 13 N3
Spital Yd WCHPL E1 * 13 K3
Spitfire Cl DTCH/LGLY SL3 150 D3
Spitfire Est HEST TW5 * 153 K4
Spitfire House
WOOL/PLUM SE18 * 162 B6
Spitfire Rd WLGTN SM6 222 G4
Spitfire Wy HEST TW5 153 K4
Spode Wk KIL/WHAMP NW6 * 117 L10
Spondon Rd SEVS/STOTM N15 119 P2
Spook Hl RDKG RH5 272 G7
Spoonbill Wy YEAD UB4 133 L7
Spooners Dr LCOL/BKTW AL2 56 B4
Spooner Wk WLGTN SM6 222 E2
Sportsbank St CAT SE6 183 H3
Sportsfield Ap BEAC HP9 89 J6
Sportsman Pl BETH E2 7 N6
Spottons Gv TOTM N17 99 K9
Spout Hl CROY/NA CR0 224 F2
Spout La EDEN TN8 262 F10
STWL/WRAY TW19 173 K1
Spout La North
STWL/WRAY TW19 151 L10
Spratt Hall Rd WAN E11 121 M4
Spratts La CHERT KT16 215 H3
Spray St WOOL/PLUM SE18 162 E3
Spreighton Rd E/WMO/HCT KT8 198 A4
Sprimont Pl CHEL SW3 16 A7
Springall St PECK SE15 160 A6
Springate Fld DTCH/LGLY SL3 150 B1
Spring Av EGH TW20 172 B9
Springbank WCHMH N21 78 G10
Springbank Av HCH RM12 125 K10
Springbank Rd LEW SE13 183 K2
Springbank Wk CAMTN NW1 5 J4
Spring Bottom La REDH RH1 259 K4
Springbourne Ct BECK BR3 205 H1
Spring Bridge Rd EA W5 135 J9
Spring Cl BAR EN5 76 G9
BCTR RM8 123 N6
BORE WD6 75 M6
CRAWW RH11 283 M8
CSHM HP5 70 A2
DEN/HRF UB9 91 N9
Springclose La CHEAM SM3 221 H3
Spring Copse CRAWE RH10 285 K2
Springcopse Rd REIG RH2 275 M1
Spring Cnr FELT TW13 * 175 H6
Spring Cottages SURB KT6 * 199 J5
Spring Court Rd ENC/FH EN2 79 H4
Springcroft HART DA3 211 M6
Springcroft Av EFNCH N2 118 A1
Spring Crofts BUSH WD23 73 P9
Spring Cross HART DA3 211 M10
Springdale Rd STNW/STAM N16 119 L9
Spring Dr PIN HA5 113 H4
Springett Pl AMS HP6 69 L3
Springfarm Cl RAIN RM13 145 L5
Springfield BUSH WD23 94 C2
CLPT E5 120 A6
EPP CM16 65 J8
LTWR GU18 212 B7
OXTED RH8 261 J6
Springfield Av HPTN TW12 176 A9
MUSWH N10 118 D1
RYNPK SW20 201 J3
SWLY BR8 208 G4
Springfield Cl CHONG CM5 67 N2
CSHM HP5 51 H9
NFNCH/WDSPK N12 97 L6
POTB/CUF EN6 59 N7
RKW/CH/CXG WD3 72 C9
STAN HA7 94 F4
WDSR SL4 148 G8
WOKN/KNAP GU21 231 J4
Springfield Dr GNTH/NBYPK IG2 122 F3
LHD/OX KT22 236 D5
Springfield Gdns BMLY BR1 206 C4
CDALE/KGS NW9 116 A3
CLPT E5 120 A6
RSLP HA4 113 J6
UPMR RM14 126 B8
WFD IG8 101 P8
WWKM BR4 204 G9
Springfield Gv CHARL SE7 161 P5
SUN TW16 * 196 G1
Springfield La KIL/WHAMP NW6 2 F6
WEY KT13 216 C1
Springfield Mdw WEY KT13 216 C1
Springfield Mt CDALE/KGS NW9 116 B3
Springfield Parade Ms
PLMGR N13 99 H5
Springfield Pl NWMAL KT3 199 P4
Springfield Ri SYD SE26 182 A7
Springfield Rd ASHF TW15 174 A8
Spring Field Rd BERK HP4 33 M3
Springfield Rd BMLY BR1 206 C4
BXLYHN DA7 164 C9
CDW/CHF RM16 168 B1
CHES/WCR EN8 62 D8
CHING E4 101 K2
CRAWW RH11 283 M8
CSHM HP5 51 H8
DORK RH4 272 A3
DTCH/LGLY SL3 150 E6
EHAM E6 142 C2
EW KT17 220 F6
FBAR/BDGN N11 98 D6
GSTN WD25 55 J9
GU GU1 250 B10
HHNE HP2 36 A5
HNWL W7 134 D10
HRW HA1 114 D4
KUT/HW KT1 199 K4
SEVS/STOTM N15 119 P2
SRTFD E15 * 141 K5
STAL AL1 38 F7
STALE/WH AL4 39 N6
STJWD NW8 3 J6
SYD SE26 182 A9
TEDD TW11 176 F8
THHTH CR7 203 K1
WALTH E17 120 E4
WDSR SL4 148 G8
WELL DA16 163 L9
WHTN TW2 175 P4
WIM/MER SW19 179 J8
WLGTN SM6 222 C2
YEAD UB4 133 K10
Springfields AMS HP6 69 H3
BROX EN10 44 E5
WAB EN9 63 K10
WGCW AL8 22 E7
Springfields Cl CHERT KT16 195 L8
Springfield Wk KIL/WHAMP NW6 2 G6
Spring Gdns ASC SL5 192 A4
BH/WHM TN16 243 P4
CRAWE RH10 285 K2
E/WMO/HCT KT8 198 B5
GSTN WD25 73 K2
HBRY N5 119 K10
HCH RM12 125 J9
ORP BR6 227 L3
ROMW/RG RM7 124 D3
WFD IG8 101 P8
WHALL SW1A 11 L9
WLGTN SM6 222 D2
Spring Gln HAT AL10 40 C5
Spring Gv CHSWK W4 155 M5
GODL GU7 267 K9
GVE DA12 190 E4
HPTN TW12 198 A1
LHD/OX KT22 236 A9
LOU IG10 82 A10
MTCM CR4 202 B1
Spring Grove Crs HSLW TW3 154 B7
Spring Grove Rd HSLW TW3 154 B7
RCHPK/HAM TW10 177 L1
Springhall La SBW CM21 29 P2
Springhall Rd SBW CM21 29 P1
Springhaven Cl GU GU1 250 D10
Spring Head Rd BGR/WK TN15 247 N3
Springhead Rd ERITH DA8 164 G5
GVW DA11 189 P4
Spring Hl CLPT E5 119 P5
SYD SE26 182 B7
Springhill Cl CMBW SE5 159 L9
Spring Hills HLW CM20 28 D10
Springholm Cl BH/WHM TN16 243 P4
Springhurst Cl CROY/NA CR0 224 E1
Spring Lake STAN HA7 94 G5
Spring La CLPT E5 120 A6
HHW HP1 35 K5
MUSWH N10 118 B1
OXTED RH8 261 J7
SL SL1 128 E10
SLN SL2 128 G2
SNWD SE25 204 A6
Springle La HERT/BAY SG13 26 E8
Spring Ms MHST W1U * 10 B3
Spring Park Av CROY/NA CR0 204 C9
Springpark Dr BECK BR3 205 H3
FSBYPK N4 119 K6
Spring Park Rd CROY/NA CR0 204 C9
Spring Pl KTTN NW5 118 B10
Spring Plat CRAWE RH10 284 D7
Spring Plat Ct CRAWE RH10 * 284 D7
Springpond Rd DAGW RM9 123 P10
Springrice Rd LEW SE13 183 H2
Spring Ri EGH TW20 172 B9
Spring Rd FELT TW13 174 G6
Spring Shaw Rd STMC/STPC BR5 207 K1
The Springs BROX EN10 44 E10
BROX EN10 62 D1
HERT/BAY SG13 25 N4
Spring St BAY/PAD W2 9 L6
EW KT17 220 C5
Spring Tide Cl PECK SE15 * 159 P7
Spring V BXLYHN DA7 164 C10
SWCM DA10 189 H2
Springvale Av BTFD TW8 155 J4
Springvale Cl GT/LBKH KT23 254 A2
Spring Vale Cl SWLY BR8 186 G10
Springvale Ct GVW DA11 * 189 P5
Spring V North DART DA1 187 L3
Spring V South DART DA1 * 187 L3
Springvale Ter WKENS W14 156 G2
Springvale Wy STMC/STPC BR5 207 M3
Spring View Rd WARE SG12 26 B3
Spring Villa Rd EDGW HA8 95 M8
Spring Vls WEA W13 * 134 G10
Spring Wk BROX EN10 44 B7
WCHPL E1 13 N3
Springwater Cl
WOOL/PLUM SE18 * 162 D7
Spring Wy HHNE HP2 36 D4
Springwell Av RKW/CH/CXG WD3 91 K3
WLSDN NW10 136 C3
Springwell Ct
RKW/CH/CXG WD3 * 91 K3
WARE SG12 * 27 H7
Springwell La RKW/CH/CXG WD3 91 K4
Springwell Rd HEST TW5 153 L7
STRHM/NOR SW16 180 G7
Springwood CHESW EN7 61 N2
Springwood Cl BOW E3 140 F4
DEN/HRF UB9 91 N9
Springwood Crs EDGW HA8 95 P3
Springwood Pl WEY KT13 216 C4
Spring Woods VW GU25 193 N4
Springwood Wk STALE/WH AL4 39 H3
Springwood Wy ROM RM1 125 H3
Sprowston Ms FSTGT E7 121 M10
Sprowston Rd FSTGT E7 121 M10
Spruce Cl REDH RH1 258 A9
Sprucedale Cl SWLY BR8 208 F2
Sprucedale Gdns CROY/NA CR0 224 C1
WLGTN SM6 222 F5
Spruce Hl HLWS CM18 47 H6
Spruce Hills Rd WALTH E17 100 G10
Spruce Rd BH/WHM TN16 244 A2
Spruce Wy LCOL/BKTW AL2 56 A3
Sprules Rd BROCKY SE4 160 D8
Spur Cl ABLGY WD5 54 E9
ABR/ST RM4 83 L7
Spurfield E/WMO/HCT KT8 198 A3
Spurgate RBRW/HUT CM13 107 M3
Spurgeon Av NRWD SE19 203 L1
Spurgeon Cl CRAWW RH11 * 283 M6
GRAYS RM17 167 P5
Spurgeon Rd NRWD SE19 181 L10
Spurgeon St STHWK SE1 18 G4
Spurling Rd DAGW RM9 144 A1
EDUL SE22 * 159 N10
Spurrell Av BXLY DA5 186 E7
Spur Rd BARK IG11 142 F5
EBED/NFELT TW14 175 J1
EDGW HA8 95 L5
ISLW TW7 154 F6
ORP BR6 207 K9
SEVS/STOTM N15 * 119 L2
STHWK SE1 18 A1
WHALL SW1A 16 G2
Spurstowe Rd HACK E8 140 A1
Spurstowe Ter HACK E8 119 P10
The Spur CHES/WCR EN8 * 62 C4
SL SL1 128 C7
WOKN/KNAP GU21 230 G4
Squadrons Ap HCH RM12 145 K1
Square St HLWE CM17 29 M10
The Square BH/WHM TN16 243 P6
BROX EN10 44 D9
CAR SM5 222 B2
CRAWE RH10 283 N7
GUW GU2 267 L2
HHW HP1 * 35 N6
HMSMTH W6 156 F4
IL IG1 122 D5
RCH/KEW TW9 177 K1
SBW CM21 29 P1
SEV TN13 246 F9
STKPK UB11 132 E10
SWLY BR8 * 208 E3
WATN WD24 73 J3
WDR/YW UB7 151 L7
WFD IG8 101 M6
Squarey St TOOT SW17 179 M6
Squerryes Mede
BH/WHM TN16 * 262 F3
The Squerryes CTHM CR3 241 M7
Squire Gdns STJWD NW8 3 L10
Squire's Bridge Rd SHPTN TW17 196 B4
Squires Cl CRAWE RH10 285 P5
Squires Ct WIM/MER SW19 179 K7
Squires Fld SWLY BR8 209 H1
Squires La FNCH N3 97 L10
Squire's Mt HAMP NW3 117 N8
Squire's Rd SHPTN TW17 196 A4
Squires Wk ASHF TW15 174 E10
Squires Wy RDART DA2 186 E7
Squires Wood Dr CHST BR7 * 184 C10
Squirrel Cha HHW HP1 35 H5
Squirrel Cl CRAWW RH11 283 L4
HSLWW TW4 153 K9
Squirrel Dr WDSR SL4 170 A5
Squirrel La WDSR SL4 170 A4
Squirrel Ms WEA W13 * 134 F9
Squirrel's Cha CDW/CHF RM16 168 D1
Squirrels Cl GODL GU7 267 K8
HGDN/ICK UB10 132 B2
NFNCH/WDSPK N12 97 M5
Squirrels Gn GT/LBKH KT23 235 P9
WPK KT4 200 C9
Squirrel's Heath Av GPK RM2 125 J1
Squirrels Heath La GPK RM2 125 K2
Squirrels Heath Rd HARH RM3 105 M10
The Squirrels BUSH WD23 74 C10
HERT/BAY SG13 25 P5
LEW SE13 161 J9
PIN HA5 113 N1
Squirrel's Wy EPSOM KT18 238 A1
Squirrel Wd BF/WBF KT14 215 L8
Squirries St BETH E2 7 P9
Stable Cl CRAWE RH10 284 E10
EPSOM KT18 238 B5
KUTN/CMB KT2 177 L9
NTHLT UB5 133 P4
Stable La BEAC HP9 89 H7
Stable Ms REIG RH2 257 K10
TWK TW1 * 176 E4
WNWD SE27 181 K8
Stables End ORP BR6 206 F10
Stables Ms BRKMPK AL9 * 59 N4
The Stables COB KT11 217 N10
Stables Wy LBTH SE11 18 A7
Stable Wk EFNCH N2 97 N9
IS N1 5 M7
Stable Wy NKENS W10 136 F8
Stable Yard Rd WHALL SW1A 11 H10
Stacey Av UED N18 100 B5
Stacey Cl GVE DA12 191 H8
LEY E10 121 J3
Stacey St HOLWY N7 119 H8
LSQ/SEVD WC2H 11 K6
Stackfield HLW CM20 29 L8
Stackfield Rd CRAWW RH11 283 H9
Stackhouse St KTBR SW1X 16 A3
Stacklands WGCW AL8 22 E7
Stack La HART DA3 211 L5
Stack Rd EYN DA4 210 C4
Stacy Pth CMBW SE5 * 159 M6
Staddon Cl BECK BR3 204 D4
Staddon Ct BECK BR3 204 D4
Stadium Rd HDN NW4 116 E5
WOOL/PLUM SE18 162 C6
Stadium St WBPTN SW10 157 M6
Stadium Wy DART DA1 186 F2
HLWW/ROY CM19 28 C10
WBLY HA9 115 L9
Staffa Rd LEY E10 120 D6
Stafford Av EMPK RM11 125 L1
SLN SL2 129 H6
Stafford Cl CDW/CHF RM16 167 H3
CHEAM SM3 221 H3
CHES/WCR EN8 62 A5
CTHM CR3 241 N9
KIL/WHAMP NW6 2 E10
MDHD SL6 128 A8
RDART DA2 188 E1
SLH/COR SS17 169 K2
STHGT/OAK N14 78 D9
WALTH E17 120 E4
Stafford Cross CROY/NA CR0 222 G2
Stafford Dr BROX EN10 44 F6
Stafford Gdns CROY/NA CR0 222 G2
Stafford Lake WOKN/KNAP GU21 230 F4
Stafford Pl RCHPK/HAM TW10 177 L3
WESTW SW1E 16 G3
Stafford Rd BOW E3 140 E4
CRAWW RH11 283 K4
CROY/NA CR0 222 G2
CTHM CR3 241 N9
FSTGT E7 141 P2
KIL/WHAMP NW6 2 E9
KTN/HRWW/WS HA3 94 B8
NWMAL KT3 199 P3
RSLP HA4 112 G9
SCUP DA14 185 H7
WLGTN SM6 222 D3
Staffords HLWE CM17 29 P7
Staffordshire St PECK SE15 159 P7
Staffords Pl HORL RH6 280 C5
Stafford St CONDST W1S 10 G9
Stafford Ter KENS W8 14 E3
Stafford Wy SEV TN13 265 K3
Stagbury Av COUL/CHIP CR5 239 P4
Stagbury Cl COUL/CHIP CR5 239 P5
Stagbury House COUL/CHIP CR5 239 P5
Stag Cl EDGW HA8 95 N10
Stagelands CRAWW RH11 283 L5
Staggart Gn CHIG IG7 103 J6
Stagg Hl EBAR EN4 77 N1
Stag Green Av BRKMPK AL9 40 F2
Stag Hl GUW GU2 267 M1
Stag La BERK HP4 33 N4
BKHH IG9 101 N3
CDALE/KGS NW9 115 P1
EDGW HA8 95 N10
PUT/ROE SW15 178 C6
RKW/CH/CXG WD3 70 F10
Stag Leys ASHTD KT21 237 K6
Stag Leys Cl BNSTD SM7 239 P1
Stag Pl WESTW SW1E 16 G3
Stags Wy ISLW TW7 154 E5
Stainash Crs STA TW18 173 L8
Stainash Pde STA TW18 * 173 L8
Stainbank Rd MTCM CR4 202 C3
Stainby Cl WDR/YW UB7 151 P2
Stainby Rd TOTM N17 119 N1
Stainer Rd BORE WD6 75 J5
Stainer St STHWK SE1 13 H10
Staines Av CHEAM SM3 200 G9
Staines By-Pass STA TW18 173 H6
Staines La CHERT KT16 195 J6
Staines Lane Cl CHERT KT16 195 J5
Staines Rd CHERT KT16 195 H6
EBED/NFELT TW14 174 F3
IL IG1 122 G9
STA TW18 195 J2
STWL/WRAY TW19 172 C4
WHTN TW2 176 B6
Staines Rd East SUN TW16 175 H10
Stainford Cl ASHF TW15 174 E8
Stainforth Rd GNTH/NBYPK IG2 122 G5
WALTH E17 120 F2
Staining La CITYW EC2V 12 F5
Stainmore Cl CHST BR7 206 G1
Stainsbury St BETH E2 140 B4
Stainsby Pl POP/IOD E14 * 140 F8
Stainsby Rd POP/IOD E14 140 F8
Stains Cl CHES/WCR EN8 62 D4
Stainton Rd CAT SE6 183 J3
PEND EN3 80 B5
Stainton Wk WOKN/KNAP GU21 * 231 P4
Stairfoot La SEV TN13 246 D8
Staiths Wy KWD/TDW/WH KT20 238 E6
Stakers Ct HARP AL5 20 A2
Stakescorner Rd RGUW GU3 267 M8
Stalbridge St CAMTN NW1 9 P3
Stalham St BERM/RHTH SE16 160 A2
Stalham Wy BARK/HLT IG6 102 E9
Stambourne Wy NRWD SE19 181 M10
WWKM BR4 205 J10
Stambourne Woodland Wk
NRWD SE19 181 M10
Stamford Brook Av
HMSMTH W6 156 C2
Stamford Brook Gdns
HMSMTH W6 156 C2
Stamford Brook Rd
HMSMTH W6 156 C2
Stamford Cl HAMP NW3 * 117 M8
KTN/HRWW/WS HA3 94 D8
POTB/CUF EN6 59 N8
SEVS/STOTM N15 119 P2
STHL UB1 133 P9
Stamford Cottages
WBPTN SW10 * 157 L6
Stamford Dr HAYES BR2 205 L4
Stamford Gdns DAGW RM9 143 M2
Stamford Green Rd EPSOM KT18 219 N9
Stamford Gv East
STNW/STAM N16 119 P6
Stamford Gv West
STNW/STAM N16 119 P6
Stamford Hl STNW/STAM N16 119 N6
Stamford Rd DAGW RM9 143 L2
EHAM E6 142 B3
IS N1 7 K3
SEVS/STOTM N15 119 P3
WAT WD17 73 J6
WOT/HER KT12 197 L10
Stamford St STHWK SE1 12 A9
Stamp Pl BETH E2 7 L8
Stanborough HACK E8 * 7 L1
Stanborough Av BORE WD6 75 M4
Stanborough Cl HPTN TW12 175 N9
WGCW AL8 22 F6
Stanborough Gn WGCW AL8 22 F7
Stanborough La WGCW AL8 22 F7
Stanborough Ms WGCW AL8 22 G7
Stanborough Pas HACK E8 7 L1
Stanborough Rd HSLW TW3 154 C9
WGCW AL8 22 E8
Stanbridge Cl CRAWW RH11 283 H8
Stanbridge Pl WCHMH N21 99 J3
Stanbridge Rd PUT/ROE SW15 156 F9
Stanbrook Rd ABYW SE2 163 L1
GVW DA11 190 C4
Stanbury Av WAT WD17 72 F3
Stanbury Ct HAMP NW3 4 A2

Stanbury Rd PECK SE15 160 B8
Stancroft CDALE/KGS NW9 116 B2
Standale Gv RSLP HA4 112 D3
Standard Pl SDTCH EC2A 7 K10
Standard Rd BELV DA17 164 B4
BXLYHS DA6 163 P10
HSLWW TW4 153 M9
ORP BR6 226 D6
PEND EN3 80 D4
WLSDN NW10 135 P6
Standen Av HCH RM12 125 L8
Standen Rd WAND/EARL SW18 179 K3
Standfield ABLGY WD5 54 F7
Standfield Rd DAGE RM10 124 B10
Standingford HLWW/ROY CM19 46 E6
Standinghall La CRAWE RH10 285 H9
Standish Rd HMSMTH W6 156 D3
Standring Ri HHS/BOV HP3 35 L9
Stane Cl WIM/MER SW19 179 L10
Stane Gv VX/NE SW8 158 E8
Stane Wy EW KT17 220 D6
WOOL/PLUM SE18 162 A6
Stanfields Ct HLW CM20 29 H10
Stanford Cl HPTN TW12 175 N9
ROMW/RG RM7 124 C4
RSLP HA4 112 D4
WFD IG8 102 B7
Stanford Ct WAB EN9 63 M9
Stanford Gdns SOCK/AV RM15 146 D10
Stanford Pl WALW SE17 19 J6
Stanford Rivers Rd CHONG CM5 67 P7
Stanford Rd CDW/CHF RM16 168 B1
FBAR/BDGN N11 98 A6
KENS W8 15 H4
STRHM/NOR SW16 202 F2
The Stanfords EW KT17 220 C8
Stanford St PIM SW1V 17 J6
Stanford Wy STRHM/NOR SW16 202 E2
Stangate Crs BORE WD6 76 B9
Stangate Gdns STAN HA7 94 G5
Stanger Rd SNWD SE25 203 P4
Stanham Pl DART DA1 165 H10
Stanham Rd DART DA1 187 K1
Stan Hl HORL RH6 278 F7
Stanhope Av FNCH N3 117 J1
HAYES BR2 205 M8
KTN/HRWW/WS HA3 94 C9
Stanhope Cl BERM/RHTH SE16 * 160 C1
Stanhope Gdns BCTR RM8 124 A8
FSBYPK N4 119 J4
HGT N6 118 C4
IL IG1 122 C6
MLHL NW7 96 C6
SKENS SW7 15 K6
Stanhope Ga BAY/PAD W2 10 A7
MYFR/PKLN W1K 10 D10
Stanhope Gv BECK BR3 204 E5
Stanhope Heath
STWL/WRAY TW19 173 M2
Stanhope Ms East SKENS SW7 15 K5
Stanhope Ms South SKENS SW7 15 K6
Stanhope Ms West SKENS SW7 15 K5
Stanhope Pde CAMTN NW1 4 F9
Stanhope Park Rd GFD/PVL UB6 134 B6
Stanhope Pl BAY/PAD W2 10 A7
Stanhope Rd BAR EN5 76 G10
BCTR RM8 124 A7
BFN/LL DA15 185 K7
BXLYHN DA7 163 P8
CAR SM5 222 B4
CHES/WCR EN8 62 D9
CROY/NA CR0 203 M10
GFD/PVL UB6 134 B7
HGT N6 118 D4
NFNCH/WDSPK N12 97 M6
RAIN RM13 145 H4
SL SL1 128 C8
STAL AL1 38 E7
SWCM DA10 189 L1
WALTH E17 120 G3
Stanhope Rw MYFR/PICC W1J * 10 E10
Stanhopes OXTED RH8 261 N4
Stanhope St CAMTN NW1 4 G9
Stanhope Ter BAY/PAD W2 9 M7
WHTN TW2 * 176 E3
Stanhope Wy SEV TN13 246 E8
STWL/WRAY TW19 173 M2
Stanier Cl CRAWE RH10 284 C8
WKENS W14 14 D8
Stanier Ri BERK HP4 33 L2
Staniland Dr WEY KT13 216 A7
Stanlake Rd SHB W12 136 F10
Stanlake Vls SHB W12 136 F10
Stanley Av ALP/SUD HA0 135 K2
BARK IG11 143 J5
BCTR RM8 124 A6
BECK BR3 205 H3
CSHM HP5 50 G7
GFD/PVL UB6 134 B3
GPK RM2 125 H2
LCOL/BKTW AL2 55 P1
NWMAL KT3 200 D5
Stanley Cl ALP/SUD HA0 135 K2
COUL/CHIP CR5 240 G3
CRAWE RH10 283 P9
ELTH/MOT SE9 184 F4
GPK RM2 125 H2
HCH RM12 125 K7
RDART DA2 188 D2
UX/CGN UB8 131 N4
VX/NE SW8 17 N10
Stanley Cottages SLN SL2 129 L10
Stanley Crs GVE DA12 190 G8
NTGHL W11 8 C7
Stanleycroft Cl ISLW TW7 154 D7
Stanley Dr HAT AL10 40 E6
Stanley Gdns ACT W3 156 B1
BORE WD6 75 K5
CRICK NW2 116 F10
MTCM CR4 * 180 B9
NTGHL W11 8 C7
SAND/SEL CR2 223 P8
WLGTN SM6 222 D3
WOT/HER KT12 217 K3
Stanley Gardens Rd TEDD TW11 176 D8
Stanley Gn East DTCH/LGLY SL3 150 C3
Stanley Gn West DTCH/LGLY SL3 150 C3
Stanley Gv CROY/NA CR0 203 H6
VX/NE SW8 158 B8
Stanley Hl AMSS HP7 69 K6
CHOB/PIR GU24 230 B8
Stanley Hill Av AMSS HP7 69 J5
Stanley Park Dr ALP/SUD HA0 135 L2
Stanley Park Rd CAR SM5 222 A4
Stanley Pas CAMTN NW1 5 L8
Stanley Pl CHONG CM5 67 P5
Stanley Rd ACT W3 155 N2
ASHF TW15 173 P8
CAR SM5 222 B4
CHING E4 101 J2
CROY/NA CR0 203 H7
ED N9 99 N2
EFNCH N2 117 N2
FBAR/BDGN N11 98 E7
GRAYS RM17 167 N4
GVW DA11 190 B5
HAYES BR2 205 P3
HCH RM12 125 K7
HERT/BAY SG13 25 M6
HSLW TW3 154 B10
IL IG1 122 G7
MNPK E12 122 B10
MORT/ESHN SW14 155 N10
MRDN SM4 201 K4
MTCM CR4 180 B10
MUSWH N10 98 C8
NTHWD HA6 93 H9
ORP BR6 207 J8
RYLN/HDSTN HA2 114 B7
SCUP DA14 185 K6
SEVS/STOTM N15 119 J2
SRTFD E15 141 J3
STHL UB1 133 M9
SWCM DA10 189 L2
SWFD E18 101 L9
WALTH E17 120 G4
WAT WD17 73 K7
WBLY HA9 135 L1
WHTN TW2 176 C6
WIM/MER SW19 179 K10
WOKN/KNAP GU21 232 C3
Stanley Rd North RAIN RM13 144 F3
Stanley Rd South RAIN RM13 144 G4
Stanley Sq CAR SM5 222 A5
Stanley St CTHM CR3 241 K8
DEPT SE8 160 E6
Stanley Ter ARCH N19 * 118 F7
BXLYHS DA6 * 164 B10
Stanley Wy STMC/STPC BR5 207 L5
Stanmer St BTSEA SW11 157 P8
Stanmore Cha STALE/WH AL4 39 J7
Stanmore Gdns RCH/KEW TW9 155 L9
SUT SM1 201 M10
Stanmore Hl STAN HA7 94 G6
Stanmore Rd BELV DA17 164 D3
RCH/KEW TW9 155 L9
SEVS/STOTM N15 119 J2
WAN E11 121 L6
WATN WD24 73 J5
Stanmore St IS N1 5 N5
Stanmore Ter BECK BR3 204 F2
Stanmore Wy LOU IG10 82 D5
Stanmount Rd LCOL/BKTW AL2 * 55 P1
Stannard Ms HACK E8 * 7 N1
Stannard Rd HACK E8 7 N1
Stannary Pl LBTH SE11 18 B8
Stannary St LBTH SE11 18 B9
Stannet Wy WLGTN SM6 222 D1
Stansbury Sq NKENS W10 2 B9
NKENS W10 137 H5
Stansfeld Rd CAN/RD E16 142 A8
Stansfield Rd BRXN/ST SW9 158 G9
HSLWW TW4 153 J8
Stansgate Rd DAGE RM10 124 B7
Stanstead Cl HAYES BR2 205 L5
Stanstead Dr HOD EN11 44 G1
Stanstead Gv CAT SE6 182 E4
Stanstead Pl AMSS HP7 * 69 H5
Stanstead Rd CTHM CR3 241 M10
FSTH SE23 182 D4
HERT/BAY SG13 25 P4
HOD EN11 44 G1
WAN E11 121 N3
WARE SG12 26 C6
Stansted Cl HCH RM12 145 J1
Stansted Crs BXLY DA5 185 N4
Stansted Rd HTHAIR TW6 174 A2
Stanswood Gdns CMBW SE5 159 M6
Stanthorpe Cl
STRHM/NOR SW16 * 180 F8
Stanthorpe Rd
STRHM/NOR SW16 180 F8
Stanton Av TEDD TW11 176 D9
Stanton Cl HOR/WEW KT19 219 N2
STALE/WH AL4 39 J2
STMC/STPC BR5 207 M7
WPK KT4 200 G8
Stanton Rd BARN SW13 156 C8
CROY/NA CR0 203 K7
RYNPK SW20 200 G2
Stanton St PECK SE15 * 159 P7
Stantons Whf SHGR GU5 268 D10
Stanton Wy DTCH/LGLY SL3 150 B3
SYD SE26 182 E7
Stanway Cl CHIG IG7 103 H6
Stanway Cottages CHERT KT16 * 195 K7
Stanway Gdns ACT W3 135 M10
EDGW HA8 95 P7
Stanway Rd WAB EN9 63 M9
Stanway St IS N1 7 K7
Stanwell Cl STWL/WRAY TW19 173 N2
Stanwell Gdns
STWL/WRAY TW19 173 N2
Stanwell Moor Rd STA TW18 173 L5
WDR/YW UB7 151 L7
Stanwell New Rd STA TW18 173 L7
Stanwell Pl STWL/WRAY TW19 * 173 M2
Stanwell Rd ASHF TW15 173 P6
DTCH/LGLY SL3 150 E9
EBED/NFELT TW14 174 D3
Stanwick Rd WKENS W14 14 C6
Stanworth St STHWK SE1 19 L2
Stanwyck Gdns HARH RM3 105 J6
Stapenhill Rd ALP/SUD HA0 114 G8
Staple Cl BXLY DA5 186 E6
Staplefield Cl
BRXS/STRHM SW2 * 180 F4
PIN HA5 93 M8
Stapleford WGCE AL7 23 M5
Stapleford Av GNTH/NBYPK IG2 123 H3
Stapleford Cl CHING E4 101 H4
KUT/HW KT1 199 M2
WIM/MER SW19 179 H3
Stapleford Ct SEV TN13 246 G9
Stapleford Gdns CRW RM5 104 B7
Stapleford Rd ABR/ST RM4 84 C8
ALP/SUD HA0 135 J2
Stapleford Wy BARK IG11 143 L5
Staple Hl CHOB/PIR GU24 213 J3
Staplehurst Cl REIG RH2 275 M4
Staplehurst Rd CAR SM5 221 P4
LEW SE13 183 J1
REIG RH2 275 M4
Staple Inn HHOL WC1V 12 A4
Staple La RGUE GU4 251 P9
SHGR GU5 270 A1
Staples Cl BERM/RHTH SE16 140 D10
Staples Rd LOU IG10 82 B7
Staple St STHWK SE1 19 H2
Stapleton Cl POTB/CUF EN6 59 N7
Stapleton Crs RAIN RM13 145 H2
Stapleton Gdns CROY/NA CR0 223 H2
Stapleton Hall Rd FSBYPK N4 118 G5
Stapleton Rd BORE WD6 75 M4
BXLYHN DA7 164 A6
ORP BR6 207 J10
TOOT SW17 180 B6
Stapleton Vls STNW/STAM N16 * 119 M9
Stapley Rd BELV DA17 164 B4
STALW/RED AL3 38 C5
Stapylton Rd BAR EN5 77 H7
Star & Garter Hl
RCHPK/HAM TW10 177 K4
Starboard Av SWCM DA10 188 G2
Starboard Wy POP/IOD E14 160 F2
Starbuck Cl ELTH/MOT SE9 184 D3
Starch House La BARK/HLT IG6 102 G10
Star Cl PEND EN3 80 B10
Starcross St CAMTN NW1 5 H10
Starfield Rd SHB W12 156 D1
Star Hl DART DA1 186 F1
Star Hill Rd RSEV TN14 246 A2
Star Holme Ct WARE SG12 26 D2
Starkey Cl CHESW EN7 61 K1
Star La CAN/RD E16 141 L6
COUL/CHIP CR5 240 B8
EPP CM16 65 K6
STMC/STPC BR5 207 N4
Starlight Wy STALE/WH AL4 39 H8
Starling Cl BKHH IG9 101 M2
HART DA3 211 N3
PIN HA5 113 K1
Starling La POTB/CUF EN6 60 G4
Starling Pl GSTN WD25 * 55 K8
Starling Rd CROY/NA CR0 204 D6
Starmans Cl DAGW RM9 143 P3
Star Pl WAP E1W 13 M8
Star Rd HGDN/ICK UB10 132 D6
ISLW TW7 154 C8
WKENS W14 14 C9
Starrock La COUL/CHIP CR5 240 B6
Starrock Rd COUL/CHIP CR5 240 C5
Star St BAY/PAD W2 9 M5
WARE SG12 26 D2
Starts Cl ORP BR6 206 D10
Starts Hill Av ORP BR6 226 E1
Starts Hill Rd ORP BR6 206 E10
Starveall Cl WDR/YW UB7 152 A2
Starwood Cl BF/WBF KT14 215 M7
Starwood Ct DTCH/LGLY SL3 149 P2
Star Yd LINN WC2A 12 A5
State Farm Av ORP BR6 226 E1
Staten Gdns TWK TW1 176 E4
Statham Gv STNW/STAM N16 119 L8
UED N18 99 M6
Station Ap ALP/SUD HA0 134 G1
BAR EN5 77 M8
BECK BR3 204 D1
BELMT SM2 221 H4
BELMT SM2 221 L6
BF/WBF KT14 215 K8
BKHH IG9 * 102 A5
BKHTH/KID SE3 161 N9
BXLYHN DA7 163 P8
BXLYHN DA7 164 D8
CAMTN NW1 * 10 C2
CFSP/GDCR SL9 110 B3
CHES/WCR EN8 * 62 D10
CHING E4 * 101 J7
CHING E4 * 101 K1
CHST BR7 184 B9
CHST BR7 206 D1
COUL/CHIP CR5 240 A4
COUL/CHIP CR5 240 E2
CROY/NA CR0 * 203 L9
CTHM CR3 241 P3
DART DA1 187 M2
DEN/HRF UB9 110 G5
DORK RH4 255 H10
EHSLY KT24 252 F2
ESH/CLAY KT10 198 E10
EW KT17 220 E6
FBAR/BDGN N11 98 C6
FSTGT E7 * 121 N9
FUL/PGN SW6 * 157 H9
GFD/PVL UB6 134 B2
GLDGN NW11 * 116 G5
GU GU1 267 P1
HARP AL5 20 A2
HAYES BR2 205 M8
HOR/WEW KT19 220 A9
HOR/WEW KT19 220 C2
HORL RH6 280 C4
HPTN TW12 197 P1
HYS/HAR UB3 152 G2
KUT/HW KT1 199 M2
LHD/OX KT22 236 F7
NFNCH/WDSPK N12 97 L5
NTHWD HA6 92 F8
ORP BR6 207 J9
ORP BR6 227 L2
OXHEY WD19 93 L4
OXTED RH8 261 K5
PIN HA5 113 M1
PUR/KEN CR8 * 223 H7
RAD WD7 74 F1
RCH/KEW TW9 155 M7
RKW/CH/CXG WD3 70 F8
RSEV TN14 247 K2
RSLP HA4 112 F6
RSLP HA4 113 J10
SAND/SEL CR2 223 L5
SHPTN TW17 * 196 D6
STA TW18 173 K8
STMC/STPC BR5 207 L4
STRHM/NOR SW16 180 E8
SUN TW16 197 H1
SURB KT6 199 J6
SWFD E18 * 101 N10
SWLY BR8 208 F4
SYD SE26 182 E8
VW GU25 194 A4
WALTH E17 120 F3
WAN E11 * 121 K9
WAN E11 121 M3
WATW WD18 * 72 G8
WDR/YW UB7 131 P10
WELL DA16 163 K9
WEY KT13 216 B3
WFD IG8 * 101 P7
WLSDN NW10 136 C5
WOKS/MYFD GU22 232 C3
Station Approach East
REDH RH1 276 A2
Station Approach Rd CHSWK W4 155 P6
HORL RH6 * 280 C7
KWD/TDW/WH KT20 238 F9
Station Approach West
REDH RH1 276 A2
Station Ar GTPST W1W * 10 F2
Station Av CTHM CR3 241 P10
HOR/WEW KT19 220 B5
NWMAL KT3 200 B3
RCH/KEW TW9 155 M7
WOT/HER KT12 216 G1
Station Buildings HAYES BR2 * 205 M8
Station Chambers EA W5 * 135 M6
Station Cl BRKMPK AL9 59 H2
HPTN TW12 198 A1
POTB/CUF EN6 59 J7
Station Cottages WDGN N22 * 98 F10
Station Ct AMSS HP7 * 69 H4
Station Crs ALP/SUD HA0 134 G1
ASHF TW15 173 N7
BKHTH/KID SE3 161 M4
SEVS/STOTM N15 119 L2
Stationers Hall Ct STP EC4M * 12 D6
Stationers Pl HHS/BOV HP3 53 P1
Station Est BECK BR3 204 C4
Station Estate Rd
EBED/NFELT TW14 175 J4
Station Footpath KGLGY WD4 54 C6
Station Garage Ms
STRHM/NOR SW16 * 180 E9
Station Gdns CHSWK W4 155 P6
Station Gv ALP/SUD HA0 135 K1
Station Hl CRAWE RH10 284 C6
HAYES BR2 205 M9
Station House Ms ED N9 99 P5
Station La HCH RM12 125 M7
Station Ms POTB/CUF EN6 * 59 K7
Station Pde ACT W3 * 135 M8
BAL SW12 * 180 B4
BARK IG11 142 F2
BECK BR3 * 204 C4
BELMT SM2 * 221 M3
BMLY BR1 * 205 M1
BXLYHN DA7 * 163 P8
CHSWK W4 * 155 P3
CHSWK W4 * 155 P6
CLPT E5 * 120 A8
CRICK NW2 136 F1
DEN/HRF UB9 111 K5
EA W5 * 135 L10
EBAR EN4 * 78 B8
EBED/NFELT TW14 * 175 J3
EDGW HA8 * 95 K8
EHAM E6 * 142 B2
EHSLY KT24 252 F2
HCH RM12 125 J9
KTN/HRWW/WS HA3 * 94 G10
NTHLT UB5 * 114 A10
NTHLT UB5 * 133 P2
PLSTW E13 * 141 P3
RCH/KEW TW9 155 M7
ROM RM1 124 F4
RSLP HA4 * 112 D7
RYLN/HDSTN HA2 * 114 A9
SEV TN13 * 247 H10
STHGT/OAK N14 98 E2
VW GU25 194 A5
Station Pas PECK SE15 160 B7
SWFD E18 101 N10
Station Pl FSBYPK N4 119 H7
Station Ri WNWD SE27 181 J5
Station Rd ADL/WDHM KT15 215 M1
AMSS HP7 69 H5
ASC SL5 192 F6
ASHF TW15 174 A7
BAR EN5 77 L9
BARK/HLT IG6 122 G1
BARN SW13 156 C8
BCTR RM8 123 N6
BEAC HP9 88 D9
BELMT SM2 221 K6
BELV DA17 164 B2
BERK HP4 34 A4
BF/WBF KT14 215 K8
BH/WHM TN16 245 L9
BMLY BR1 205 M1
BORE WD6 75 M8
BRKHM/BTCW RH3 256 A9
BRKMPK AL9 58 G1
BROX EN10 44 E6
BXLYHN DA7 163 P9
CAR SM5 222 A1
CFSP/GDCR SL9 110 B3
CHDH RM6 123 N5
CHERT KT16 195 J8
CHES/WCR EN8 62 F10
CHIG IG7 102 E4
CHING E4 101 J2
CHOB/PIR GU24 213 L8
CHSGTN KT9 219 K2
COB KT11 235 M3
CRAWE RH10 283 N8
CROY/NA CR0 203 K8
CSHM HP5 * 50 G7
CTHM CR3 241 N4
CTHM CR3 242 D8
DART DA1 186 G2
DORK RH4 272 F2
DTCH/LGLY SL3 150 D1
EA W5 135 L8
EDGW HA8 95 M7
EGH TW20 172 D8
EPP CM16 65 K7
EPP CM16 66 C3
ESH/CLAY KT10 218 C2
EYN DA4 209 L10
EYN DA4 210 A2
FBAR/BDGN N11 98 C6
FNCH N3 97 K9
GODL GU7 267 L10
GPK RM2 125 J2
GVW DA11 189 N2
HARH RM3 105 N9
HARP AL5 20 A2
HART DA3 211 K3
HAYES BR2 205 K2
HDN NW4 116 D4
HERT/WAT SG14 24 B8
HHS/BOV HP3 35 L8
HLWE CM17 29 M7
HNWL W7 134 D10
HOLWY N7 118 D8
HORL RH6 280 C4
HPTN TW12 198 A1
HRW HA1 114 A3
HRW HA1 114 E2
HSLW TW3 154 A10
HYS/HAR UB3 152 G2
IL IG1 122 E8
KGLGY WD4 54 C5
KUT/HW KT1 199 J1
KUTN/CMB KT2 199 M1
LCOL/BKTW AL2 55 P7
LEW SE13 161 H9
LHD/OX KT22 236 F7
LOU IG10 82 B9
MEO DA13 189 L7
MLHL NW7 96 B7
MNPK E12 122 A9
NWMAL KT3 200 E5
ORP BR6 207 J9
PGE/AN SE20 182 B9
POTB/CUF EN6 60 G5
PUR/KEN CR8 223 K10
RAD WD7 74 F1
RDART DA2 188 F1
REDH RH1 258 A9
REDH RH1 258 D4
RGUE GU4 268 B6
RKW/CH/CXG WD3 91 N1
RSEV TN14 228 A7
RSEV TN14 229 H7
RSEV TN14 247 J2
RYLN/HDSTN HA2 114 A3
SCUP DA14 185 K6
SEV TN13 246 F6
SHGR GU5 268 C10
SHGR GU5 270 D4
SHPTN TW17 196 D5
SL SL1 128 D8
SNWD SE25 203 N4
STALE/WH AL4 21 J2
STMC/STPC BR5 207 M4
STWL/WRAY TW19 172 C2
SUN TW16 175 H10
SWLY BR8 208 F4
TEDD TW11 176 F9
THDIT KT7 198 E7
TIL RM18 169 L6
TOTM N17 119 P1
TWK TW1 176 E4
UPMR RM14 126 B7
UX/CGN UB8 131 M6
WALTH E17 120 D4
WARE SG12 26 D2
WARE SG12 27 H7
WAT WD17 73 J6
WCHMH N21 99 J2
WDGN N22 98 G10
WDR/YW UB7 151 P1
WIM/MER SW19 201 M1
WLSDN NW10 136 C4
WWKM BR4 205 H9
Station Rd East OXTED RH8 261 L5
Station Rd North BELV DA17 164 C2
REDH RH1 258 D4
Station Rd South REDH RH1 258 D4
Station Rd West OXTED RH8 261 K5
Station Rw RGUE GU4 268 B6
Station Sq STMC/STPC BR5 206 F5
Station St SRTFD E15 141 J2
Station Ter CMBW SE5 159 K7
WLSDN NW10 136 G4
Station Vw GFD/PVL UB6 134 C3
GU GU1 267 P1
Station Wy BKHH IG9 102 A5
CHEAM SM3 221 H3
CRAWE RH10 283 N8
ESH/CLAY KT10 218 D3
STAL AL1 38 E6
Station Yd ASHF TW15 * 174 A7
KWD/TDW/WH KT20 * 239 J7
PUR/KEN CR8 * 223 J8
RSLP HA4 * 112 E7
STHL UB1 * 153 N1
TWK TW1 176 F3
Staunton Rd KUTN/CMB KT2 177 L10
SLN SL2 129 J7
Staunton St DEPT SE8 160 E5
Staveley Cl HOLWY N7 * 118 F9
PECK SE15 160 B7
Staveley Gdns CHSWK W4 156 A7
Staveley Rd ASHF TW15 174 E9
CHSWK W4 155 P5
Staveley Wy WOKN/KNAP GU21 231 K3
Staverton Rd CRICK NW2 136 F2
EMPK RM11 125 L4
Stave Yard Rd BERM/RHTH SE16 140 D10
Stavordale Rd CAR SM5 201 M7
HBRY N5 119 J9
Stayne End VW GU25 193 M4
Stayner's Rd WCHPL E1 140 C6
Stayton Rd SUT SM1 201 K10
Steadfast Rd KUT/HW KT1 199 J1
Stead St WALW SE17 18 G6
Steam Farm La
EBED/NFELT TW14 152 G10
Stean St HACK E8 7 L5
Stebbing Wy BARK IG11 143 K4
Stebondale St POP/IOD E14 161 H3
Stedly SCUP DA14 * 185 K7
Stedman Cl BXLY DA5 186 F6
HGDN/ICK UB10 112 B8
Steed Cl EMPK RM11 125 J7
Steedman St WALW SE17 18 E6
Steeds Rd MUSWH N10 98 A9
Steeds Wy LOU IG10 82 B7
Steel Ap BARK IG11 143 L4
Steele Av RDART DA2 188 F1
Steele Rd CHSWK W4 155 P2
ISLW TW7 154 F10
TOTM N17 119 M1
WAN E11 121 K9
WLSDN NW10 135 P4
Steele's Ms South HAMP NW3 4 B2
Steele's Rd HAMP NW3 4 A2
Steeles Studios HAMP NW3 * 4 A2
Steel's La LHD/OX KT22 218 B10
WCHPL E1 140 B8
Steep Cl ORP BR6 227 J3
Steep Hl CHOB/PIR GU24 213 H4
CROY/NA CR0 223 M1
STRHM/NOR SW16 180 E6
Steeplands BUSH WD23 94 A1
Steeple Cl FUL/PGN SW6 157 H9
WIM/MER SW19 179 H7
Steeple Heights Dr
BH/WHM TN16 244 A3
Steeple Point ASC SL5 192 A3
Steeplestone Cl UED N18 99 K6
Steeple Wk IS N1 6 F5
Steeple Wy BRWN CM15 86 G2
Steerforth St WAND/EARL SW18 179 L5
Steering Cl ED N9 100 B2
Steers La CRAWE RH10 284 D1
Steers Md MTCM CR4 202 A1
Steers Wy BERM/RHTH SE16 160 D1
Stella Cl UX/CGN UB8 132 C7
Stella Rd TOOT SW17 180 A9
Stelling Rd ERITH DA8 164 E6
Stellman Cl CLPT E5 119 P8
Stembridge Rd PGE/AN SE20 204 A2
Sten Cl PEND EN3 80 F3
Stenning Av SLH/COR SS17 169 L3
Stepbridge Pth
WOKN/KNAP GU21 * 232 A3
Stepgates CHERT KT16 195 L7
Stepgates Cl CHERT KT16 * 195 L7
Stephan Cl HACK E8 7 P5
Stephen Av RAIN RM13 145 H1
Stephen Cl CRAWW RH11 283 N4
EGH TW20 172 F9
ORP BR6 207 J10
Stephendale Rd FUL/PGN SW6 157 L8
Stephen Ms FITZ W1T 11 J4
Stephen Pl CLAP SW4 158 D9
Stephen Rd BXLYHN DA7 164 D9
Stephens Cl HARH RM3 105 K6
Stephenson Av TIL RM18 168 D7
Stephenson Cl WELL DA16 163 J8
Stephenson Ct SL SL1 149 L1
Stephenson Dr WDSR SL4 148 G6
Stephenson Pl CRAWE RH10 284 C7
Stephenson Rd GUW GU2 249 J10
HNWL W7 134 E8
WALTH E17 120 D3
WHTN TW2 175 P3
Stephenson St CAN/RD E16 141 K7
WLSDN NW10 136 B5
Stephenson Wy CAMTN NW1 11 H1
CRAWE RH10 284 C7
WATN WD24 73 L5
Stephenson Whf HHS/BOV HP3 35 P10
Stephen's Rd SRTFD E15 141 K3
Stephen St FITZ W1T 11 J5
Stephyns Chambers HHW HP1 * 35 M7
Stepney Cswy WCHPL E1 140 C8
Stepney Cl CRAWE RH10 284 D9
Stepney Gn WCHPL E1 140 B7
Stepney High St WCHPL E1 140 C7
Stepney Wy MTCM CR4 202 B1
WCHPL E1 140 B7
The Steps EHSLY KT24 * 253 L3
Sterling Av CHES/WCR EN8 62 C10
EDGW HA8 95 L5
Sterling Cl WLSDN NW10 136 D2
Sterling Gdns NWCR SE14 160 D5
Sterling Pk CRAWE RH10 * 284 C2
Sterling Pl EA W5 155 K3
WEY KT13 216 F1
Sterling Rd ENC/FH EN2 79 L5
Sterling St SKENS SW7 15 P3
Sterling Wy (North Circular)
UED N18 99 L6
Stern Cl BARK IG11 143 M4
Sterndale Rd DART DA1 187 N3
WKENS W14 * 156 G2
Sterne St SHB W12 156 G1
Sternhall La PECK SE15 159 P9
Sternhold Av BRXS/STRHM SW2 180 F5
Sterry Crs DAGE RM10 124 B10
Sterry Dr HOR/WEW KT19 220 B1
THDIT KT7 198 D6
Sterry Gdns DAGE RM10 144 B1
Sterry Rd BARK IG11 143 J3
DAGE RM10 124 B9
Sterry St STHWK SE1 18 G2
Steucers La FSTH SE23 182 D4
Steve Biko La CAT SE6 182 F7
Steve Biko Rd HOLWY N7 119 H8
Steve Biko Wy HSLW TW3 153 P9
Stevedale Rd WELL DA16 163 M8
Stevedore St WAP E1W 140 A10
Stevenage Crs BORE WD6 75 K5
Stevenage Ri HHNE HP2 36 A2
Stevenage Rd CRAWW RH11 283 H10
EHAM E6 142 D1
FUL/PGN SW6 156 G7
Stevens Av HOM E9 140 B1
Stevens Cl BECK BR3 182 F9
BXLY DA5 186 E7
EW KT17 220 B8
HPTN TW12 175 N9
PIN HA5 113 K3
POTB/CUF EN6 58 G9
RDART DA2 188 D8
Stevens Gn BUSH WD23 94 B2
Stevens' La ESH/CLAY KT10 218 F4
Stevenson Cl BAR EN5 77 N10
ERITH DA8 165 J6
Stevenson Crs BERM/RHTH SE16 19 P7
BERM/RHTH SE16 159 P4
Stevenson Rd SLN SL2 109 J7
Stevens Pl PUR/KEN CR8 223 J9
Stevens Rd BCTR RM8 123 L7
Stevens St STHWK SE1 19 K3
Stevens Wy CHIG IG7 103 H5
Steventon Rd SHB W12 136 C9
Steward Cl CHES/WCR EN8 62 D6
Stewards Cl EPP CM16 65 K9
Stewards Green Rd EPP CM16 65 M8
Stewart KWD/TDW/WH KT20 238 G7
Stewart Av SHPTN TW17 196 B4
SL SL1 129 L7
UPMR RM14 126 A8
Stewart Cl ABLGY WD5 55 H8
CDALE/KGS NW9 * 115 P4
CHST BR7 184 E8
HPTN TW12 175 M9
WOKN/KNAP GU21 231 L3
Stewart Rd HARP AL5 20 A1
SRTFD E15 121 J9
Stewartsby Cl UED N18 99 K6
Stewarts Dr SLN SL2 108 G10
Stewarts Gv CHEL SW3 15 M7
Stewart's La VX/NE SW8 158 C6
Stewart's Rd VX/NE SW8 158 D7
Stewart St POP/IOD E14 161 H1
Stew La BLKFR EC4V 12 E7
Steyne Rd ACT W3 135 N10
Steyning Cl CRAWE RH10 283 P5
PUR/KEN CR8 241 J2
Steyning Gv ELTH/MOT SE9 184 C7
Steynings Wy
NFNCH/WDSPK N12 97 K6
Steyning Wy HSLWW TW4 153 K10
Steynton Av BXLY DA5 185 P5
Stickland Rd BELV DA17 164 B3
Stickleton Cl GFD/PVL UB6 134 A5
Stifford Clays Rd
CDW/CHF RM16 147 L10
Stifford Hl SOCK/AV RM15 147 H9
Stifford Rd SOCK/AV RM15 146 E9
Stile Cft HLWS CM18 47 K3
Stilecroft Gdns ALP/SUD HA0 114 G8
Stile Hall Gdns CHSWK W4 155 M4
Stile Pth SUN TW16 197 H3
Stile Rd DTCH/LGLY SL3 150 A3
Stiles Cl ERITH DA8 164 C4
HAYES BR2 206 C6
Stillingfleet Rd BARN SW13 156 D6
Stillington St WEST SW1P 17 H5
Stillness Rd FSTH SE23 182 D2
Stilton Pth BORE WD6 75 M4
Stilwell Dr UX/CGN UB8 132 A6
Stipularis Dr YEAD UB4 133 L6
Stirling Av PIN HA5 113 L5
SHPTN TW17 * 196 F3
WLGTN SM6 222 F4
Stirling Cl BNSTD SM7 239 J3
CRAWE RH10 284 C8
RAIN RM13 145 J5
SCUP DA14 185 H7
STRHM/NOR SW16 202 D1
UX/CGN UB8 131 M5
WDSR SL4 148 C8
Stirling Dr CTHM CR3 241 K7
ORP BR6 227 L2
Stirling Gv HSLW TW3 154 B8
Stirling Rd ACT W3 155 N2
BRXN/ST SW9 158 F8
GUW GU2 249 K10
HYS/HAR UB3 133 J9
KTN/HRWW/WS HA3 114 D1
PLSTW E13 141 N4
SL SL1 128 F7
TOTM N17 99 P9
WALTH E17 120 D1
WDGN N22 99 J9
WHTN TW2 175 P3
Stirling Wk BRYLDS KT5 199 N6
Stirling Wy ABLGY WD5 55 H8
BORE WD6 76 A10
CROY/NA CR0 202 F7
WGCE AL7 23 P5
Stirrup Wy CRAWE RH10 284 E6
Stites Hill Rd COUL/CHIP CR5 241 K6
Stiven Crs RYLN/HDSTN HA2 113 N8
Stoat Cl HERT/BAY SG13 25 P5
Stoats Nest Rd COUL/CHIP CR5 240 F1
Stoats West Village
COUL/CHIP CR5 240 F1
Stockbreach Cl HAT AL10 40 D3
Stockbreach Rd HAT AL10 40 D3
Stockbridge Cl CHESW EN7 61 M2
Stockbury Rd CROY/NA CR0 204 B6
Stockdale Rd BCTR RM8 124 A7
Stockdales Rd WDSR SL4 148 E3
Stockdove Wy GFD/PVL UB6 134 E5
Stocker Gdns DAGW RM9 143 M2
Stockers Farm Rd
RKW/CH/CXG WD3 91 M4
Stockers La WOKS/MYFD GU22 232 C6
Stockfield HORL RH6 280 C3
Stockfield Av HOD EN11 44 F1
Stockfield Rd ESH/CLAY KT10 218 D2
STRHM/NOR SW16 180 G6
Stockford Av MLHL NW7 96 G8
Stockhams Cl SAND/SEL CR2 223 L6
Stock Hl BH/WHM TN16 244 A2
Stockholm Rd BERM/RHTH SE16 160 B4
Stockholm Wy WAP E1W 13 N9
Stockhurst Cl PUT/ROE SW15 156 F8
Stockings La HERT/BAY SG13 42 E4
Stockingswater La PEND EN3 80 D7
Stockland Rd ROMW/RG RM7 124 E4
Stock La RDART DA2 187 K7
Stockley Cl WDR/YW UB7 152 C1
Stockley Farm Rd WDR/YW UB7 152 C2
Stockley Rd WDR/YW UB7 152 C2
Stock Orchard Crs HOLWY N7 * 118 G10
Stock Orchard St HOLWY N7 118 G10
Stockport Rd RKW/CH/CXG WD3 90 F1
STRHM/NOR SW16 202 E1
Stocks Cl HORL RH6 280 C5
Stocksfield BRWN CM15 86 E3
Stocksfield Rd WALTH E17 * 121 H1
Stocks La BRWN CM15 86 E3
Stocks Meadow HHNE HP2 36 B5
Stocks Pl HGDN/ICK UB10 132 B3
POP/IOD E14 140 E9
Stock St PLSTW E13 141 M4
Stockton Cl BAR EN5 77 M8
Stockton Gdns MLHL NW7 96 A4
TOTM N17 99 K8
Stockton Rd REIG RH2 275 K3
TOTM N17 99 K8
UED N18 99 P7
Stockwell Av BRXN/ST SW9 158 G9
Stockwell Cl BMLY BR1 205 N2
CHESW EN7 61 P4
Stockwell Gdns BRXN/ST SW9 158 G7
Stockwell Gn BRXN/ST SW9 158 G8
Stockwell La BRXN/ST SW9 158 G8
CHESW EN7 62 A4
Stockwell Park Crs
BRXN/ST SW9 158 G8
Stockwell Park Rd BRXN/ST SW9 158 G8
Stockwell Park Wk
BRXN/ST SW9 158 G9
Stockwell Rd BRXN/ST SW9 158 G8
Stockwell St GNWCH SE10 161 H5
Stockwell Ter BRXN/ST SW9 158 G7
Stocton Cl GU GU1 249 P9
Stocton Rd GU GU1 249 P9
Stodart Rd PGE/AN SE20 204 B1
Stofield Gdns ELTH/MOT SE9 184 A6
Stoford Cl WIM/MER SW19 179 H4
Stoke Av BARK/HLT IG6 103 K7
Stoke Cl COB KT11 235 N2
Stoke Common Rd SLN SL2 109 M9
Stoke Cottages LHD/OX KT22 * 236 C7
Stoke Court Dr SLN SL2 129 L3
Stoke Flds GU GU1 250 A10
Stoke Gdns SL SL1 129 K10
Stoke Gn SLN SL2 129 M6
Stoke Gv GU GU1 250 A10
Stoke Ms GU GU1 * 250 A10
Stoke Mill Cl GU GU1 250 A8
Stokenchurch St FUL/PGN SW6 157 L7
Stoke Newington Church St
STNW/STAM N16 119 L8
Stoke Newington Common
STNW/STAM N16 119 N8
Stoke Newington High St
STNW/STAM N16 119 N8
Stoke Newington Rd
STNW/STAM N16 119 N10
Stoke Park Av SLN SL2 129 H5
Stoke Park Ct GU GU1 * 250 A10
Stoke Pl WLSDN NW10 136 C5
Stoke Poges La SL SL1 129 K10
Stoke Ridings
KWD/TDW/WH KT20 * 238 G9
Stoke Rd COB KT11 235 M2
GU GU1 250 A9
KUTN/CMB KT2 177 P10
RAIN RM13 145 L4
SLN SL2 129 M7
WOT/HER KT12 197 K10
Stokesay SLN SL2 129 M8
Stokesby Rd CHSGTN KT9 219 L3
Stokes Cl CRAWE RH10 284 D10
Stokesheath Rd LHD/OX KT22 218 B7
Stokesley St SHB W12 136 C8
Stokes Ridings
KWD/TDW/WH KT20 238 G9
Stokes Rd CROY/NA CR0 204 C6
EHAM E6 142 B6
Stoke Wd SLN SL2 109 L9
Stoll Cl CRICK NW2 116 F8
Stompond La WOT/HER KT12 197 H9
Stomp Rd SL SL1 128 B7
Stonard Rd BCTR RM8 123 L10
PLMGR N13 99 H4
Stonards Hl EPP CM16 65 M7

LOU IG10 .... 82 C10
Stondon Pk FSTH SE23 .... 182 D2
Stonebanks WOT/HER KT12 ...... 197 H7
Stonebridge Fld WDSR SL4 .... 148 G4
Stonebridge Flds RGUE GU4 ...... 268 A7
Stonebridge Pk WLSDN NW10 ... 136 A2
Stonebridge Rd GVW DA11 .... 189 N1
SEVS/STOTM N15 .... 119 M3
Stonebridge Wy WBLY HA9 .... 135 N1
Stonebridge Whf RGUE GU4 ...... 268 A8
Stone Buildings LINN WC2A 11 P4
Stonechat Sq EHAM E6 .... 142 B7
Stone Cl BCTR RM8 .... 124 A4
CLAP SW4 .... 158 D8
WDR/YW UB7 .... 132 A10
Stonecot Cl CHEAM SM3 .... 201 H8
Stonecot Hl CHEAM SM3 .... 201 H8
Stonecourt Cl HORL RH6 .... 280 D4
Stonecrop Rd RYNPK SW20 ...... 174 G3
Stonecroft Av IVER SL0 .... 131 H8
Stonecroft Cl BAR EN5 .... 76 B8
Stonecroft Rd ERITH DA8 .... 164 D6
Stonecroft Wy CROY/NA CR0 .... 202 F7
Stonecrop Cl CDALE/KGS NW9 .. 116 A1
CRAWW RH11 .... 283 K10
Stonecross Rd RGUE GU4 .... 250 F8
Stonecross STAL AL1 .... 38 C5
Stonecross Rd HAT AL10 .... 18 B9
Stonecutter St FLST/FETLN EC4A .. 12 C5
Stonefield Cl BXLYHN DA7 .... 164 B9
CRAWE RH10 .... 283 N6
RSLP HA4 .... 113 M10
Stonefield St IS N1 .... 6 B5
Stonefield Wy CHARL SE7 .... 162 A6
RSLP HA4 .... 113 J8
Stonegate Cl STMC/STPC BR5 ... 207 M3
Stone Gv EDGW HA8 .... 95 K5
Stonegrove Gdns EDGW HA8 ...... 95 L6
Stonehall Av IL IG1 .... 122 B4
Stone Hall Gdns KENS W8 .... 14 C4
Stone Hall Pl KENS W8 .... 14 C4
Stone Hall Rd WCHMH N21 .... 98 G1
Stoneham Rd FBAR/BDGN N11 ... 98 D6
Stonehill Cl L2YLBHR KT23 .... 253 P11
MORT/ESHN SW14 .... 178 A1
Stonehill Crs CHERT KT16 .... 214 B3
Stonehill Ga ASC SL5 * 192 C6
Stonehill Rd CHERT KT16 .... 214 B3
CHSWK W4 .... 155 M4
MORT/ESHN SW14 .... 177 P1
Stonehills WCCW AL8 .... 22 C5
Stonehills Ct DUL SE21 .... 181 M6
Stonehole Woods Pk SCUP DA14 * .. 186 D9
Stonehorse Rd PEND EN3 .... 30 B9
Stone House La LVPST EC2M 13 K5
Stone House Gdns CTHM CR3 ..... 166 D4
Stonehouse La PUR RM19 .... 166 D4
RSEV TN14 .... 227 N5
Stonehouse Rd RSEV TN14 .... 227 N6
Stoneings La RSEV TN14 .... 245 J1
Stonelea Rd HHS/BOV HP3 .... 36 A9
Stoneleigh Av EN EN1 .... 80 A4
WPK KT4 .... 200 D2
Stoneleigh Broadway EW KT17 .. 220 D2
Stoneleigh Cl WALTH E17 .... 62 C9
Stoneleigh Crs HOR/WEW KT19 .. 220 D2
Stoneleigh Dr HOD EN11 .... 26 C10
Stoneleigh Pk WEY KT13 .... 216 D3
Stoneleigh Park Av
CROY/NA CR0 .... 204 C6
Stoneleigh Park Rd
HOR/WEW KT19 .... 220 C3
Stoneleigh Pl NTGHL W11 .... 136 C9
Stoneleigh Rd BMLY BR1 .... 206 E3
CAR SM5 .... 201 P7
CLAY IG5 .... 122 B1
OXTED RH8 .... 262 B6
TOTM N17 .... 99 N10
Stoneleigh St NTGHL W11 .... 136 C9
Stoneleigh Ter ARCH N19 .... 118 C7
Stonell's Rd TOOT SW17 .... 179 M6
Stonemasons Cl
SEVS/STOTM N15 * 119 L2
Stoneness Rd WTHK RM20 .... 166 G8
Stonenest St FSBYPK N4 .... 118 G6
Stone Park Av BECK BR3 .... 204 C4
Stone Pl IN WPK KT4 .... 200 D9
Stone Place Rd RDART DA2 .... 188 D2
Stone Rd HAYES BR2 .... 205 L5
Stoners Cl HORL RH6 .... 279 N7
Stones Cross Rd SWLY BR8 .... 208 B5
Stones End St STHWK SE1 .... 18 E2
Stones La DORK RH4 .... 272 B3
Stone's Rd EW KT17 .... 220 B7
Stone St GVW DA11 .... 190 E8
Stonewood Rd OXTED RH8 .... 261 N7
Stonewall EHAM E6 .... 142 D7
Stonewood Gdns CTHM CR3 ...... 189 H6
Stonewood Rd ERITH DA8 .... 164 B7
Stoney Aly WOOL/PLUM SE18 ... 162 D8
Stoneyard La POP/IOD E14 .... 140 C9
Stoney Brook GUW GU2 .... 249 K9
Stoney Cl BERN HP4 .... 33 L3
Stoney Cft COUL/CHIP CR5 .... 240 E7
Stonycroft HHW HP1 .... 8 C5
WGCE AL7 .... 13 K6
Stonycroft Cl LEE/GVPK SE12 ... 183 L3
Stonycroft Rd WLGTN SL8 * 102 B7
Stoneydown WALTH E17 .... 120 C2
Stoneydown Av WALTH E17 ...... 120 C2
Stoneyfield CFSP/GDCR SL9 ...... 109 P6
Stoneyfield Rd COUL/CHIP CR5 .. 240 G3
Stoneyfields Gdns EDGW HA8 ... 95 N10
Stoneyfields La EDGW HA8 .... 95 P6
Stoney Gv CSHM HP5 .... 51 J6
Stoneyland Ct EGH TW20 .... 172 C8
Stoneylands Rd EGH TW20 .... 172 C8
Stoney La HDTCH EC3A 13 K5
HHS/BOV HP3 .... 52 E3
HHW HP1 .... 34 E9
KGLGY WD4 .... 53 H6
NRWD SE19 .... 181 N9
SLN SL2 .... 128 F3
Stoney Meade SL SL1 .... 128 C10
Stoney St STHWK SE1 .... 12 D9
Stonhouse St CLAP SW4 .... 158 D9
Stonnell's Rd BTSEA SW11 .... 180 A1
Stonny Cft ASHTD KT21 .... 237 L3
Stonor Rd WKENS W14 .... 14 C6
Stonycroft Cl PEND EN3 .... 80 D6
Stony Hl ESH/CLAY KT10 .... 217 N4
Stony La CHONG CM5 .... 49 J9
CSHM HP5 .... 70 B3
Stony Pth LOU IG10 .... 82 C5
Stonyshotts WAB EN9 .... 63 K10
Stony Wd HLWS SM18 .... 46 C2
Stopes St PECK SE15 .... 159 N6
Stopford Rd PLSTW E13 .... 141 M1
WALW SE17 * 18 D8
Stopham Rd CRAWE RH10 .... 284 D10
Store End CAN/RD E16 .... 162 D1
Storers Quay POP/IOD E14 .... 161 J3
Store St GWRST WC1E 11 J4
SRTFD E15 .... 121 J10
Storey Rd HGT N6 .... 118 A4
WALTH E17 .... 120 E2
Storeys Ga STJSPK SW1H 17 J1
Storeys St HHS/BOV HP3 .... 35 N10
Stories Ms CMBW SE5 * 159 M8
Stories Rd CMBW SE5 .... 159 M9
Stork Rd FSTGT E7 .... 141 L1
Storksmead Rd EDGW HA8 .... 96 E8
Storks Rd BERM/RHTH SE16 ...... 19 P4
Stormont Rd BTSEA SW11 .... 158 B10
HGT N6 .... 118 A5
Stormont Wy CHSGTN KT9 .... 219 H2
Stormount Dr HYS/HAR UB3 ...... 152 F3
Stornaway Rd DTCH/LGLY SL3 .. 150 F2
Stornaway St GVE GU2 .... 249 J7
Stornoway HHS/BOV HP3 .... 36 C10
Storrington Rd CROY/NA CR0 ... 203 N8
Storr's La RGUW GU3 .... 231 H10
Stortford Rd HOD EN11 .... 44 D2
Stort Ml CM20 .... 29 L5

Stort Valley Wy EPP CM16 .... 48 D8
HLWE CM17 .... 30 F9
HLWW/ROY CM19 .... 45 M2
RBSF CM22 .... 30 E2
SBW CM21 .... 29 N4
Story St IS N1 .... 5 N4
Stothard St WCHPL E1 .... 140 B6
Stott Cl WAND/EARL SW18 ...... 179 N1
Stoughton Av CHEAM SM3 .... 220 G2
Stoughton Cl LBTH SE11 .... 17 P6
PUT/ROE SW15 .... 178 D4
Stoughton Rd GUW GU2 .... 249 M7
Stour Av NWDGN UB2 .... 152 P2
Stourcliffe St MBLAR W1H 10 A6
Stour Cl HAYES BR2 .... 225 P1
SL SL1 .... 128 A8
Stourhead Cl WIM/MER SW19 ... 178 G3
Stourhead Gdns RYNPK SW20 ... 200 D3
Stour Rd BOW E3 .... 140 C7
CDW/CHF RM16 .... 168 D4
DAGE RM10 .... 124 B7
DART DA1 .... 165 H9
Stourton Av FELT TW13 .... 175 N7
Stour Wy UPMR RM14 .... 126 D4
Stovell Rd WDSR SL4 .... 148 G6
Stowage DEPT SE8 .... 160 G5
The Stowage DEPT SE8 .... 160 F5
Stowe Crs RSLP HA4 .... 112 C4
Stowe Gdns ED N9 .... 99 N2
Stowell Av CROY/NA CR0 .... 225 J6
Stowe Pl SEVS/STOTM N15 ...... 119 M3
Stowe Rd SHB W12 .... 156 E1
SHB W12 .... 140 P9
The Stow HLW CM20 .... 29 M5
Stowting Rd ORP BR6 .... 227 H1
Stox Md KTN/HRWW/WS HA3 ... 94 C9
Stracey Rd FSTGT E7 .... 141 M1
Strachan Pl RYNPK SW20 .... 178 F3
Stradbroke Dr CHIG IG7 .... 102 E7
Stradbroke Gv BKHH IG9 .... 102 A2
CLAY IG5 .... 122 B1
Stradbroke Pk CHIG IG7 .... 102 E7
Stradbroke Rd HBRY N5 .... 118 G1
Stradbrook Cl RYLN/HDSTN HA2 .. 113 N8
Stradella Rd HNHL SE24 .... 181 J2
Strafford Av CLAY IG5 .... 102 D10
Strafford Cl POTB/CUF EN6 ...... 59 K8
Strafford Ga POTB/CUF EN6 ..... 59 K8
Strafford Rd ACT W3 .... 155 P1
BAR EN5 .... 77 H7
HSLW TW3 .... 153 N9
TWK TW1 .... 176 F3
Strafford St POP/IOD E14 .... 160 F1
Strahan Rd BOW E3 .... 140 D5
Straight Rd HARH RM3 .... 105 J6
WDSR SL4 .... 171 N2
Straightsmouth GNWCH SE10 ... 161 H5
The Straight NWDGN UB2 .... 153 L1
Strait Rd EHAM E6 .... 142 C9
The Straits WAB EN9 .... 62 G8
Straker's Rd EDUL SE22 .... 160 A10
Strand TPL/STR WC2E 11 N6
Strandburgh Pl HHS/BOV HP3 ... 36 C8
Strand Cl CRAWE RH10 .... 284 E9
EPSOM KT18 .... 238 A5
Strand Dr RCH/KEW TW9 .... 155 N6
Strand-on-the-Green CHSWK W4 .. 155 M5
Strangeways WAT WD17 .... 72 F2
Strangways Ter WKENS W14 .... 14 C2
Stranraer Gdns SL SL1 .... 129 K10
Stranraer Wy IS N1 .... 5 N1
Strasburg Rd BTSEA SW11 .... 159 H7
Stratfield Dr BROX EN10 .... 44 D5
Stratfield Park Cl WCHMH N21 .. 99 J1
Stratfield Rd BORE WD6 .... 75 J7
SL SL1 .... 149 N1
Stratford Av HGDN/ICK UB10 ... 132 A4
Stratford Cl BARK IG11 .... 143 K2
DAGE RM10 .... 144 D2
SLN SL2 .... 129 N1
Stratford Ct NWMAL KT3 .... 200 A4
Stratford Gv PUT/ROE SW15 .... 156 G10
Stratford House Av BMLY BR1 ... 206 B3
Stratford Pl OXSTW W1C 10 E6
Stratford Rd HTHAIR TW6 .... 174 C2
KENS W8 .... 14 C4
NWDGN UB2 .... 153 M3
PLSTW E13 .... 141 M3
THHTH CR7 .... 203 H4
WAT WD17 .... 73 H6
YEAD UB4 .... 133 J6
Stratford Studios KENS W8 .... 14 C4
Stratford Vls CAMTN NW1 .... 5 J3
Stratford Wy HHS/BOV HP3 ...... 35 L9
LCOL/BKTW AL2 .... 55 N5
WAT WD17 .... 72 D7
Strathan Cl WAND/EARL SW18 .. 179 J1
Strathaven Rd LEE/GVPK SE12 .. 183 N2
Strathblaine Rd BTSEA SW11 ... 179 N1
Strathbrook Rd
STRHM/NOR SW16 .... 180 G10
Strathcona Av GT/LBKH KT23 ... 253 M4
Strathcona Gdns
WOKN/KNAP GU21 .... 231 J5
Strathcona Rd WBLY HA9 .... 115 J7
Strathdale STRHM/NOR SW16 ... 180 C8
Strathdon Dr TOOT SW17 .... 179 N6
Strathearn Av HYS/HAR UB3 .... 152 C9
WHTN TW2 .... 175 J4
Stratheden Rd BKHTH/KID SE3 .. 161 N1
Strathfield Gdns BARK IG11 ...... 142 G1
Strathleven Rd
BRXS/STRHM SW2 .... 180 F1
Strathmore Cl CTHM CR3 .... 169 M3
Strathmore Ct CAMTN NW1 ...... 241 M7
Strathmore Gdns EDGW HA8 .... 95 N10
FNCH N3 .... 97 L9
HCH RM12 .... 124 C6
Strathmore Rd CRAWW RH11 ... 283 K4
CROY/NA CR0 .... 203 K7
TEDD TW11 .... 174 F6
WIM/MER SW19 .... 179 K6
Strathnairn St STHWK SE1 .... 19 P5
STHWK SE1 * 159 P3
Strathray Gdns HAMP NW3 ...... 3 N2
Strath Ter BTSEA SW11 .... 157 P10
Strathville Rd WAND/EARL SW18 .. 179 K5
Strathyre Av ENC/FH EN2 .... 78 G3
Stratton Av ENC/FH EN2 .... 79 L3
WLGTN SM6 .... 222 E5
Stratton Chase Dr CSTG HP8 .... 48 P3
Stratton Cl BXLYHN DA7 .... 163 P9
EDGW HA8 .... 95 L7
HSLW TW3 .... 153 N7
WIM/MER SW19 .... 201 J2
WOT/HER KT12 * 197 K8
Stratton Ct PIN HA5 .... 93 N8
Strattondale St POP/IOD E14 .... 161 H2
Stratton Dr BARK IG11 .... 123 H10
Stratton Gdns STHL UB1 .... 133 P6
Stratton Pl IN AMSS HP7 .... 69 L5
Stratton Rd BEAC HP9 .... 88 A4
BXLYHN DA7 .... 163 P9
HARH RM3 .... 105 J9
SUN TW16 .... 196 C2
WIM/MER SW19 .... 201 J1
Stratton St MYFR/PICC W1J 10 F8
Stratton Ter WH/MM TN16 .... 262 F3
Stratton Wk HARH RM3 .... 105 H9
Strauss Rd CHSWK W4 .... 155 A4
Strawberry Crs LCOL/BKTW AL2 .. 59 K5
Strawberry Cts BXLY DA5 .... 187 J5
Strawberry Fld HAT AL10 .... 40 C7
Strawberry Flds CHOB/PIR GU24 .. 230 P1
ORP BR6 .... 226 E2
SWLY BR8 .... 208 F2

WARE SG12 .... 26 A1
Strawberry Hill Rd TWK TW1 .... 176 E6
Strawberry La CAR SM5 .... 202 A10
Strawberry Ri CHOB/PIR GU24 .. 230 F1
Strawberry Ter MUSWH N10 * ... 98 A9
Strawberry V EFNCH N2 .... 97 N9
TWK TW1 .... 176 E6
Straw Cl CTHM CR3 .... 241 K9
Strawfields WGCE AL7 .... 23 L4
Strawmead HAT AL10 .... 40 E2
Strawson Ct HORL RH6 .... 280 A5
Strayfield Rd ENC/FH EN2 .... 79 H2
Streakes Field Rd CRICK NW2 ... 117 J1
Stream Cl BRF/KT14 .... 215 N8
Streamdale ABYW SE2 .... 163 L5
Stream La EDGW HA8 .... 95 N7
Streamline Ms EDUL SE22 .... 182 A4
Streamside Cl ED N9 .... 99 N2
Streamside Cl ED N9 .... 99 N2
Streamside SL SL1 * 128 C10
Stream Wy BELV DA17 .... 164 B5
Streatfeild Av EHAM E6 .... 142 C3
Streatfield Rd
KTN/HRWW/WS HA3 .... 115 H1
Streatham Cl
STRHM/NOR SW16 .... 180 F5
Streatham Common
STRHM/NOR SW16 * 180 E10
Streatham Common North
STRHM/NOR SW16 .... 180 G8
Streatham Common South
STR STRHM/NOR SW16 .... 180 F6
Streatham Gn
STRHM/NOR SW16 * 180 F8
Streatham High Rd
STRHM/NOR SW16 .... 180 F10
Streatham Hl BRXS/STRHM SW2 . 180 F4
Streatham Pl BRXS/STRHM SW2 . 180 F3
Streatham St NOXST/BSQ WC1A . 11 L5
Streatham V STRHM/NOR SW16 . 180 D10
Streathbourne Rd TOOT SW17 ... 180 B5
Streatleigh Pde
STRHM/NOR SW16 * 180 F5
Streatley Pl HAMP NW3 .... 117 N9
Streatley Rd KIL/WHAMP NW6 .. 2 C4
Streeters La WLGTN SM6 .... 202 E10
Streetfield Ms BKHTH/KID SE3 .. 161 N8
Street Hl CRAWE RH10 .... 284 F10
Streets Heath CHOB/PIR GU24 .. 212 E8
The Street ASHTD KT21 .... 237 L4
BRKHM/BTCW RH3 .... 256 H10
EHSLY KT24 .... 252 C5
EHSLY KT24 .... 253 L4
EYN DA4 .... 210 A4
GVE DA12 .... 191 P8
HORL RH6 .... 279 H8
KGLGY WD4 .... 53 K7
LHD/OX KT22 .... 250 A6
MFD/CHID SU8 .... 266 C10
RBSF CM22 .... 30 E3
RGUE GU4 .... 251 K6
RGUE GU4 .... 251 N7
RGUW GU3 .... 248 E3
RGUW GU3 .... 266 A5
RGUW GU3 .... 266 C7
SHGR GU5 .... 268 E10
Streimer Rd SRTFD E15 .... 141 H4
Strelley Wy ACT W3 .... 136 B9
Stretton Rd CROY/NA CR0 .... 203 M7
RCHPK/HAM TW10 .... 177 H5
Stretton Wy BORE WD6 .... 75 L4
Strickland Av DART DA1 .... 165 N10
Strickland Cl CRAWW RH11 ...... 283 H8
Strickland Rw WAND/EARL SW18 . 179 N3
Strickland St DEPT SE8 .... 160 F8
Strickland Wy ORP BR6 .... 227 J1
Stride Rd PLSTW E13 .... 141 L4
Strimon Cl ED N9 .... 99 M2
Stringer's Av RGUE GU4 .... 250 A3
Stringhams Copse
RPLY/SEND GU23 .... 233 J10
Stripling Wy WATW WD18 .... 73 H10
Strode Cl MUSWH N10 .... 98 B9
Strode Rd FSTGT E7 .... 121 M9
FUL/PGN SW6 .... 156 G6
TOTM N17 .... 99 M10
WLSDN NW10 .... 136 D1
Strodes College La EGH TW20 ... 172 C8
Strode's Crs STA TW18 .... 173 M8
Strode St EGH TW20 .... 172 D7
Stroma Cl HHS/BOV HP3 .... 36 D10
Stroma Ct SL SL1 .... 128 C9
Strond Green Gdns
CROY/NA CR0 .... 204 B7
Strond Green Wy CROY/NA CR0 . 204 B7
Strone Rd FSTGT E7 .... 141 P1
MNPK E12 .... 142 A1
Strongbow Crs ELTH/MOT SE9 .. 184 C1
Strongbow Rd ELTH/MOT SE9 ... 184 C1
Strongbridge Cl
RYLN/HDSTN HA2 .... 113 P6
Stronsa Rd SHB W12 .... 156 C1
Stronsay Cl HHS/BOV HP3 .... 36 D8
Strood Av ROMW/RG RM7 .... 124 E6
Strood La ASC SL5 .... 170 B9
Stroud Cl WDSR SL4 .... 148 G9
Stroud Crs PUT/ROE SW15 .... 178 C6
Stroud Ro EGH TW20 .... 172 D10
VW GU25 .... 194 B4
Stroudes Cl WPK KT4 .... 200 C7
Stroud Fld NTHLT UB5 .... 133 M1
Stroud Ga RYLN/HDSTN HA2 .... 114 A9
Stroud Green Rd FSBYPK N4 .... 118 G6
Stroud Green Wy CROY/NA CR0 . 204 B6
Stroudley Cl CRAWE RH10 .... 284 C6
Stroud Rd SNWD SE25 .... 203 P6
WIM/MER SW19 .... 179 K6
Strouds Cl CHDH RM6 .... 123 J3
Stroudwater Pk WEY KT13 .... 216 C3
Stroud Wy ASHF TW15 .... 174 C9
Strout's Pl BETH E2 .... 7 J1
Strudgate Cl CRAWE RH10 .... 284 C9
Strutton Gnd STJSPK SW1H 17 J3
Struttons Av GVW DA11 .... 13 L4
Strype St WCHPL E1 .... 13 K5
Stuart Av CDALE/KGS NW9 ...... 116 D5
EA W5 .... 135 L1
HAYES BR2 .... 205 M8
RYLN/HDSTN HA2 .... 113 N6
WOT/HER KT12 .... 197 K8
Stuart Cl BRWN CM15 .... 86 D5
CRAWE RH10 .... 284 D8
HGDN/ICK UB10 .... 132 B1
SWLY BR8 .... 186 G10
WDSR SL4 .... 148 E8
Stuart Ct AMS HP6 .... 69 J4
BORE WD6 .... 75 J10
Stuart Crs CROY/NA CR0 .... 204 E10
HYS/HAR UB3 .... 132 D8
REIG RH2 .... 275 K3
WDGN N22 .... 98 G9
Stuart Evans Cl WELL DA16 ...... 163 H9
Stuart Gv TEDD TW11 .... 174 D6
Stuart Mantle Wy ERITH DA8 ... 164 E6
Stuart Pl MTCM CR4 .... 180 A7
Stuart Rd ACT W3 .... 135 P10
BARK IG11 .... 143 J3
EBAR EN4 .... 97 P1
GRAYS RM17 .... 167 N4
GVW DA11 .... 190 D2
KIL/WHAMP NW6 .... 2 D10
KTN/HRWW/WS HA3 .... 95 E1
PECK SE15 .... 160 D10
RCHPK/HAM TW10 .... 176 C6
REIG RH2 .... 275 K3
THHTH CR7 .... 203 A2
WALL DA16 .... 148 E9
WELL DA16 .... 148 E9
WIM/MER SW19 .... 179 K6
Stuarts Cl HHS/BOV HP3 .... 35 M4
Stuart Wy CHESW EN7 .... 62 A7
STA TW18 .... 173 L9

VW GU25 .... 193 M4
WDSR SL4 .... 148 E8
Stubbers La UPMR RM14 .... 146 D1
Stubbs Cl CDALE/KGS NW9 ...... 115 P3
Stubbs Dr BERM/RHTH SE16 .... 160 A4
Stubbs End CL AMS HP6 .... 69 L3
Stubbs Hl ORP BR6 .... 227 M9
Stubbs La KWD/TDW/WH KT20 . 257 J2
Stubbs Wy WIM/MER SW19 ..... 201 N1
Stubbs Wd AMS HP6 .... 69 K2
Stucley Pl CAMTN NW1 .... 4 F1
Stucley Rd HEST TW5 .... 154 B6
Studdridge St FUL/PGN SW6 .... 157 K8
Studd St IS N1 .... 6 C1
Stud Gn GSTN WD25 .... 59 H9
Studholme Ct HAMP NW3 * 117 K9
Studholme St PECK SE15 .... 160 A6
Studio Ms HDN NW4 .... 116 P2
Studio Pl KTBR SW1X 16 B2
Studios Rd SHPTN TW17 .... 195 M6
The Studios BUSH WD23 .... 73 P10
Studio Wy BORE WD6 .... 75 P2
Studland Cl BFN/LL DA15 .... 185 J6
Studland Rd BF/WBF KT14 .... 216 A3
HNWL W7 .... 134 G8
KUTN/CMB KT2 .... 177 K9
SYD SE26 .... 182 C8
Studland St HMSMTH W6 .... 156 A6
Studley Av CHING E4 .... 101 J8
Studley Cl CLPT E5 .... 120 D10
Studley Ct SCUP DA14 .... 185 L8
Studley Crs HART DA3 .... 211 P2
Studley Dr REDBR IG4 .... 122 A4
Studley Grange Rd HNWL W7 ... 154 D2
Studley Rd CLAP SW4 .... 158 F7
DAGW RM9 .... 143 N3
FSTGT E7 .... 141 N1
Stukeley Rd FSTGT E7 .... 141 N2
Stukeley St HOL/ALD WC2B 11 M5
Stumbles CRAWE RH10 .... 284 D6
Stumps Hill La BECK BR3 .... 183 N5
Sturdy Rd PECK SE15 .... 160 A8
Sturge Av WALTH E17 .... 100 G9
Sturgeon Rd WALW SE17 .... 18 C9
Sturges Fld CHST BR7 .... 184 G10
Sturgess Av HDN NW4 .... 116 A5
Sturge St STHWK SE1 .... 18 E2
Sturla Cl HERT/WAT SG14 .... 25 J7
Sturlas Wy CHES/WCR EN8 ..... 62 C9
Sturrock Cl SEVS/STOTM N15 ... 119 L2
Sturry St POP/IOD E14 .... 140 G8
Sturt Ct GU GU1 .... 250 E8
Sturt's La KWD/TDW/WH KT20 . 256 C3
Sturt St IS N1 .... 6 F2
Stutfield St WCHPL E1 .... 13 P6
Stychens Cl REDH RH1 .... 259 N4
Stychens La REDH RH1 .... 259 K8
Stylecroft Rd CSTG HP8 .... 90 A4
Styles Cl LEE/GVPK SE12 .... 24 A5
Styles Gdns BRXN/ST SW9 .... 159 J9
Styles Wy BECK BR3 .... 205 H4
Styventon Pl CHERT KT16 .... 195 J7
Subrosa Dr REDH RH1 .... 258 C6
Subrosa Pk REDH RH1 * 258 C6
Succomb's Hi CTHM CR3 .... 242 A6
Succombs Pl WARL CR6 .... 242 A6
Sudbourne Rd
BRXS/STRHM SW2 .... 180 A1
Sudbrooke Rd BAL SW12 .... 180 A2
Sudbrook Gdns
RCHPK/HAM TW10 .... 177 K6
Sudbrook La RCHPK/HAM TW10 . 177 K4
Sudbury EHAM E6 .... 142 D8
Sudbury Court Dr HRW HA1 ..... 114 F8
Sudbury Court Rd HRW HA1 ..... 114 E9
Sudbury Crs ALP/SUD HA0 .... 114 D10
BMLY BR1 .... 183 M8
Sudbury Cft ALP/SUD HA0 .... 114 F9
Sudbury Gdns CROY/NA CR0 .... 223 N1
Sudbury Heights Av
GFD/PVL UB6 .... 114 F10
Sudbury Hl HRW HA1 .... 114 F10
Sudbury Hill Cl ALP/SUD HA0 ... 114 E9
Sudbury Rd BARK IG11 .... 123 J10
Sudeley St IS N1 .... 6 D8
Sudicamps Ct WAB EN9 .... 63 M9
Sudlow Rd WAND/EARL SW18 .. 157 K10
Sudrey St STHWK SE1 .... 18 E2
Suez Av GFD/PVL UB6 .... 134 D2
Suez Rd PEND EN3 .... 80 D8
Suffield Cl SAND/SEL CR2 .... 224 C8
Suffield Rd CHING E4 .... 100 C5
PGE/AN SE20 .... 204 B2
SEVS/STOTM N15 .... 119 N3
Suffolk Cl BORE WD6 .... 76 A4
LCOL/BKTW AL2 .... 57 H1
SL SL1 .... 128 D8
Suffolk Dr RGUE GU4 .... 250 E2
Suffolk La CANST EC4R 12 G7
Suffolk Park Rd WALTH E17 ..... 120 D2
Suffolk Rd BARK IG11 .... 142 G2
BARN SW13 .... 156 C5
DAGE RM10 .... 124 C10
DART DA1 .... 187 M2
GDMY/SEVK IG3 .... 123 J4
GVE DA12 .... 190 C2
PEND EN3 .... 80 A9
PLSTW E13 .... 141 L5
POTB/CUF EN6 .... 59 N8
RYLN/HDSTN HA2 .... 114 B3
SCUP DA14 .... 185 M9
SEVS/STOTM N15 .... 119 L4
SNWD SE25 .... 203 N4
WLSDN NW10 .... 136 B2
WPK KT4 .... 200 C9
Suffolk St FSTGT E7 .... 121 M10
STJS SW1Y 11 J8
Suffolk Vls WAND/EARL SW18 * . 179 A4
Suffolk Wy EMPK RM11 .... 125 P2
SEV TN13 .... 265 K1
Sugar House La SRTFD E15 .... 141 H4
Sugar La HHW HP1 .... 34 B1
Sugar Loaf Wk BETH E2 * 140 E2
Sugden Rd BTSEA SW11 .... 158 B9
Sugden Wy BARK IG11 .... 143 J4
Sulgrave Gdns HMSMTH W6 .... 156 A9
Sulgrave Rd HMSMTH W6 .... 156 B6
Sulina Rd BRXS/STRHM SW2 .... 180 A1
Sulivan Ct FUL/PGN SW6 .... 157 K9
Sulivan Rd FUL/PGN SW6 .... 157 K9
Sullington Hl CRAWW RH11 ..... 283 J10
Sullivan Av CAN/RD E16 .... 142 A7
Sullivan Cl BTSEA SW11 .... 158 E10
DART DA1 .... 187 P2
E/WMO/HCT KT8 .... 197 P2
YEAD UB4 .... 133 K7
Sullivan Crs DEN/HRF UB9 .... 91 N10
Sullivan Dr CRAWW RH11 .... 283 H10
Sullivan Rd LBTH SE11 .... 17 N6
TIL RM18 .... 168 D7
Sullivans Reach WOT/HER KT12 . 197 J5
Sullivan Wy HARH RM3 .... 105 K3
Sultan Rd WAN E11 .... 121 N2
Sultan St BECK BR3 .... 204 C2
CMBW SE5 .... 159 K6
Sun in Sands Rbt BKHTH/KID SE3 . 161 N6
Sumburgh Rd BAL SW12 .... 180 B2
Sumburgh Wy SL SL1 .... 129 M7
Summer Av E/WMO/HCT KT8 .... 198 D5
Summer Ct HHNE HP2 * 8 D9
Summerene Cl
STRHM/NOR SW16 .... 180 D10
Summerfield ASHTD KT21 .... 237 J5
HAT AL10 .... 40 D7

Summerfield Av KIL/WHAMP NW6 . 2 B7
KIL/WHAMP NW6 .... 137 N10
NFNCH/WDSPK N12 .... 97 P5
Summerfield Cl LCOL/BKTW AL2 . 57 H7
Summerfield La SURB KT6 .... 199 J9
Summerfield Pl CHERT KT16 * ... 214 G3
Summerfield Rd EA W5 .... 134 G6
GSTN WD25 .... 73 H1
LOU IG10 .... 82 C5
Summerfields
ADL/WDHM KT15 .... 215 J2
Summerfield St LEE/GVPK SE12 . 183 J5
Summerglade E/WMO/HCT KT8 . 198 D5
Summer Gv BORE WD6 .... 75 J10
Summerhayes
WOKN/KNAP GU21 .... 214 B10
Summerhays COB KT11 .... 217 L9
Summer Hl BORE WD6 .... 75 M9
CHST BR7 .... 206 D2
Summerhill Cl ORP BR6 .... 227 H1
Summerhill Ct STAL AL1 * 38 C5
Summerhill Gv EN EN1 .... 79 N3
Summerhill Rd CEND/HSY/T N8 . 98 C2
DART DA1 .... 187 L3
Summerhill Wy MTCM CR4 ...... 180 C7
Summerhouse Av HEST TW5 .... 153 M7
Summerhouse Dr RDART DA2 ... 186 E8
Summerhouse La DEN/HRF UB9 . 91 K8
GSTN WD25 .... 74 B5
WDR/YW UB7 .... 151 N5
Summerhouse Rd
STNW/STAM N16 .... 119 M7
Summerland Gdns MUSWH N10 . 118 C1
Summerlands Av ACT W3 .... 135 P9
Summerlay Cl
KWD/TDW/WH KT20 .... 239 H7
Summerlee Av EFNCH N2 .... 118 A2
Summerlee Gdns EFNCH N2 ..... 118 A2
Summerleigh WEY KT13 * 216 E5
Summerley St WAND/EARL SW18 . 179 L5
Summerly Av REIG RH2 .... 257 K9
Summer Pl WATW WD18 * 72 C10
Summersby Rd HGT N6 .... 118 C4
Summersbury Dr RGUE GU4 * ... 268 E10
Summersbury Hall RGUE GU4 * . 268 E10
Summers Cl BELMT SM2 .... 221 K8
WBLY HA9 .... 115 N6
WEY KT13 .... 216 B7
Summerskille Cl ED N9 .... 100 E3
Summersland Rd STALE/WH AL4 . 39 H2
Summers La NFNCH/WDSPK N12 . 97 M11
Summer's Rd GODL GU7 .... 267 L10
SL SL1 .... 128 B5
Summers Rw
NFNCH/WDSPK N12 .... 97 P7
Summers St CLKNW EC1R 12 A2
Summerstown TOOT SW17 .... 179 M6
Summersvere Cl CRAWE RH10 .. 285 J1
Summers Wy LCOL/BKTW AL2 * . 57 K3
Summerswood La BORE WD6 * .. 75 P2
Summerswood Cl PUR/KEN CR8 . 241 L2
Summerswood La BORE WD6 .... 76 B1
Summerton Wy THMD SE28 ..... 143 N9
Summer Trees SUN TW16 .... 197 J3
Summerville Gdns SUT SM1 ...... 221 J3
Summerwood Rd ISLW TW7 ..... 176 A2
Summit Av CDALE/KGS NW9 .... 116 A3
Summit Cl CDALE/KGS NW9 ..... 116 A3
EDGW HA8 .... 96 C1
STHGT/OAK N14 .... 98 C8
Summit Dr WFD IG8 .... 102 A10
Summit Est STNW/STAM N16 * . 119 P5
Summit Rd NTHLT UB5 .... 133 P7
POTB/CUF EN6 .... 59 H6
WALTH E17 .... 120 C2
The Summit LOU IG10 .... 82 C5
Summit Wy NRWD SE19 .... 181 M10
STHGT/OAK N14 .... 98 C3
Sumner Av PECK SE15 .... 159 N7
Sumner Cl LHD/OX KT22 .... 236 C10
ORP BR6 .... 226 F1
Sumner Gdns CROY/NA CR0 ..... 205 J8
Sumner Pl ADL/WDHM KT15 .... 215 K2
Sumner Place Ms SKENS SW7 ... 15 M6
Sumner Rd CROY/NA CR0 .... 203 J8
HRW HA1 .... 114 B5
PECK SE15 .... 19 N6
PECK SE15 .... 159 N6
Sumner Rd South CROY/NA CR0 . 203 J8
Sumners Farm Cl
HLWW/ROY CM19 .... 28 A6
Sumner St STHWK SE1 .... 12 D8
Summitt Pl WEY KT13 .... 216 B4
Sumpter Cl HAMP NW3 .... 3 K2
Sumpter Yd STAL AL1 .... 38 C7
Sunbeam Crs NKENS W10 .... 136 M9
Sunbeam Rd WLSDN NW10 ...... 135 P6
Sunbury Av MLHL NW7 .... 96 A6
MORT/ESHN SW14 .... 156 A10
Sunbury Cl WOT/HER KT12 ...... 197 K4
Sunbury Ct Island SUN TW16 ... 197 J1
Sunbury Court Av SUN TW16 ... 197 J1
Sunbury Court Ms SUN TW16 ... 197 J1
Sunbury Court Rd SUN TW16 ... 197 J1
Sunbury Cross Centre
SUN TW16 * 197 J2
WDSR SL4 .... 149 J5
Sunbury Gdns MLHL NW7 .... 96 A6
Sunbury La BTSEA SW11 .... 157 N7
WOT/HER KT12 .... 197 H6
Sunbury Rd CHEAM SM3 .... 201 G9
FELT TW13 .... 174 A5
SUN TW16 .... 197 J2
Sunbury St WOOL/PLUM SE18 .. 142 C2
Sunbury Wy FELT TW13 .... 175 K8
Sun Cl WDSR SL4 .... 149 J4
Sun Ct ERITH DA8 .... 164 G8
Suncroft Pl SYD SE26 .... 182 B6
Sundale Av SAND/SEL CR2 .... 224 B6
Sunderland Av STAL AL1 .... 38 F5
Sunderland Gv GSTN WD25 ...... 54 G10
Sunderland Mt FSTH SE23 * 182 C5
Sunderland Rd EA W5 .... 155 J2
FSTH SE23 .... 182 C5
Sunderland Ter BAY/PAD W2 ... 8 A4
Sunderland Wy MNPK E12 .... 122 A7
Sundew Av SHB W12 .... 136 D7
Sundew Cl LTWR GU18 .... 212 C7
Sundew Rd HHW HP1 * 35 H8
Sundial Av SNWD SE25 .... 203 N2
Sundon Crs VW GU25 .... 193 M5
Sundorne Rd CHARL SE7 .... 161 N3
Sundown Av SAND/SEL CR2 ..... 223 N7
Sundown Rd ASHF TW15 .... 157 M3
Sundra Wk WCHPL E1 .... 140 F7
Sundridge Av BMLY BR1 .... 184 C10
WELL DA16 .... 163 H1
Sundridge Cl DART DA1 .... 187 P2
Sundridge La WARL CR6 .... 241 N5
Sundridge Pde BMLY BR1 * 183 N10
Sundridge Pl CROY/NA CR0 ...... 204 B9
RSEV TN14 .... 246 B6
Sundridge Rd CROY/NA CR0 .... 204 B9
WOKS/MYFD GU22 .... 231 J9
Sunfields Pl BKHTH/KID SE3 .... 161 N7
Sunflower Wy HARH RM3 .... 105 A3
Sun Hl HART DA3 .... 210 P9
WOKN/KNAP GU21 .... 231 H3
Sun La BKHTH/KID SE3 .... 161 P7
Sunken Rd CROY/NA CR0 * 222 F5
Sunkist Wy WLGTN SM6 .... 222 G6
Sunland Av BXLYHS DA6 .... 163 P10
Sun La BKHTH/KID SE3 .... 161 P7
GVE DA12 .... 190 F5
Sunleigh Rd ALP/SUD HA0 .... 135 P1
Sunley Gdns GFD/PVL UB6 ...... 134 F1
Sunlight Cl WIM/MER SW19 ..... 179 M9
Sunlight Sq BETH E2 .... 140 E2
Sunmead Cl LHD/OX KT22 .... 236 G4
Sunmead Pde LHD/OX KT22 * ... 236 G4
Sunmead Rd HHNE HP2 .... 8 B3
SUN TW16 .... 197 J3

SUN TW16 .... 197 H3
Sunna Gdns SUN TW16 .... 197 J2
Sunning Av ASC SL5 .... 170 B9
Sunningdale STHGT/OAK N14 ... 98 E6
Sunningdale Av ACT W3 .... 136 B9
BARK IG11 .... 142 G3
FELT TW13 .... 175 M5
RAIN RM13 .... 145 J6
RSLP HA4 .... 113 K6
Sunningdale Cl
BERM/RHTH SE16 .... 160 A4
STAN HA7 .... 94 F8
SURB KT6 .... 199 K3
THMD SE28 .... 143 P8
Sunningdale Ct CRAWE RH10 * . 283 N9
Sunningdale Gdns
CDALE/KGS NW9 .... 115 P3
KENS W8 .... 14 C4
Sunningdale Ldg EDGW HA8 * .. 95 L6
Sunningdale Ms WGCE AL7 ...... 23 J1
Sunningdale Pk ASC SL5 * 206 B4
Sunningdale Rd BMLY BR1 .... 205 J4
RAIN RM13 .... 145 H2
SUT SM1 .... 201 J10
Sunninghill Rd HHW HP1 .... 116 E1
CRAWE RH10 .... 96 E10
Sunninghill GVW DA11 .... 190 B5
Sunninghill Cl ASC SL5 .... 192 C4
Sunninghill Ct ACT W3 * 155 P1
Sunninghill Rd ASC SL5 .... 170 C9
ASC SL5 .... 192 C5
Sunninghill Rd ASC SL5 .... 192 C5
LEW SE13 .... 160 G8
WDSR SL4 .... 148 C8
Sunnings La UPMR RM14 .... 146 C1
Sunningvale Av BH/WHM TN16 . 225 P10
Sunningvale Cl BH/WHM TN16 .. 244 G2
Sunny Av CRAWE RH10 .... 285 P5
Sunny Bank EPSOM KT18 .... 237 P2
SNWD SE25 .... 203 N6
WARL CR6 .... 242 D3
Sunnybank Rd POTB/CUF EN6 .. 59 K9
Sunny Cres WLSDN NW10 .... 135 P2
Sunny Cft HLWS CM18 .... 47 N5
Sunnycroft Gdns UPMR RM14 .. 126 E5
Sunnycroft Rd HSLW TW3 .... 154 A8
SNWD SE25 .... 203 P4
STHL UB1 .... 133 P7
Sunnydale ORP BR6 .... 206 D9
Sunnydale Gdns MLHL NW7 .... 96 A7
Sunnydale Rd LEE/GVPK SE12 .. 183 L3
Sunnydell LCOL/BKTW AL2 ...... 56 C8
Sunnydene Av CHING E4 .... 101 N1
RSLP HA4 .... 113 H6
Sunnydene Cl HARH RM3 .... 105 N8
Sunnydene Gdns ALP/SUD HA0 . 135 P1
Sunnydene Rd PUR/KEN CR8 .... 223 J9
Sunnydene St SYD SE26 .... 182 D7
Sunnyfield BRKMPK AL9 .... 40 C1
MLHL NW7 .... 96 A8
Sunny Gardens Rd HDN NW4 ... 96 F10
Sunny Hl HDN NW4 .... 116 E1
Sunnyhill Cl CLPT E5 .... 120 D9
CRAWE RH10 .... 285 P5
Sunnyhill Rd HHW HP1 .... 35 L6
RKW/CH/CXG WD3 .... 90 G7
STRHM/NOR SW16 .... 180 G5
Sunnyhurst Cl SUT SM1 .... 201 K10
Sunnymead CRAWW RH11 ...... 283 N7
Sunnymead Av MTCM CR4 .... 202 A1
Sunnymead Rd CDALE/KGS NW9 . 116 C5
PUT/ROE SW15 .... 178 E1
Sunnymede CHIG IG7 .... 105 L4
Sunnymede Av CAR SM5 .... 221 K4
CSHM HP5 .... 51 K4
HOR/WEW KT19 .... 220 B5
Sunnymede Dr BARK/HLT IG6 .. 122 C5
Sunny Ms CRW RM5 .... 104 D8
Sunny Nook Gdns SAND/SEL CR2 . 223 N4
Sunny Pl HDN NW4 .... 116 F2
Sunny Ri CTHM CR3 .... 241 L10
The Sunny Rd PEND EN3 .... 80 C5
Sunnyside CAT SE6 * 182 E6
CHOLC CHRW HP5 .... 50 A7
WAB EN9 .... 45 J8
WOKN/KNAP GU21 .... 230 C5
WOT/HER KT12 .... 197 K5
Sunnyside Dr CHING E4 .... 101 N1
Sunnyside Gdns UPMR RM14 ... 126 B8
Sunnyside Pl WIM/MER SW19 .. 179 H9
Sunnyside Rd ARCH N19 .... 118 C5
CSHM HP5 .... 50 G6
EA W5 .... 135 J10
EP CM16 .... 120 F6
IL IG1 .... 122 E9
LEY E10 .... 120 G5
TEDD TW11 .... 176 C7
Sunnyside Rd East ED N9 .... 99 P4
Sunnyside Rd North ED N9 ...... 99 N4
Sunnyside Rd South ED N9 ...... 99 N4
Sunnyside Ter CDALE/KGS NW9 . 116 A3
Sunny Vw CDALE/KGS NW9 .... 116 A3
Sunny Wy NFNCH/WDSPK N12 . 97 P8
Sun Pas BERM/RHTH SE16 * 19 N5
Sunray Av BRYLDS KT5 .... 159 P2
HAYES BR2 .... 206 B6
HNHL SE24 .... 181 L1
WDR/YW UB7 .... 151 N1
Sunrise Av HCH RM12 .... 124 E2
Sunrise Cl FELT TW13 .... 175 N6
Sunrise Crs HHS/BOV HP3 .... 35 P9
Sun Rd SWCM DA10 .... 189 J7
WKENS W14 .... 14 C8
Sunset Av CHING E4 .... 100 C2
WFD IG8 .... 101 M3
Sunset Ct ABR/ST RM4 * 86 C1
Sunset Dr ABR/ST RM4 .... 86 C1
Sunset Rdns SNWD SE25 .... 181 M10
Sunset Rd HNHL SE24 .... 159 J2
THMD SE28 .... 143 K10
WIM/MER SW19 .... 178 E8
Sunset Vw BAR EN5 .... 76 B4
Sunshine Wy MTCM CR4 .... 202 A2
Sun Sq HHW HP1 * 35 N5
Sun St LVPST EC2M 13 J3
CSHM HP5 .... 51 J4
SL SL1 .... 30 A2
WAB EN9 .... 63 J9
Sun Street Pas LVPST EC2M 13 J4
Superior Dr ORP BR6 .... 227 J11
Surbiton Ct SURB KT6 .... 199 J6
Surbiton Court Ms SURB KT6 ... 199 J6
Surbiton Crs KUT/HW KT1 .... 199 K5
Surbiton Hall Cl KUT/HW KT1 .. 199 K5
Surbiton Hill Pk BRYLDS KT5 ... 199 L5
Surbiton Hill Rd SURB KT6 ...... 199 K5
Surbiton Rd KUT/HW KT1 .... 199 K5
Surlingham Cl THMD SE28 .... 143 N9
Surly Hall Wk WDSR SL4 .... 148 B7
Surma Cl WCHPL E1 .... 13 P2
Surman Crs RBRW/HUT CM13 .. 89 P1
Surmans Cl DAGW RM9 .... 143 N8
Surrendale Pl MV/WKIL W9 ...... 8 F2
Surrey Av SLN SL2 .... 129 L7
Surrey Canal Rd PECK SE15 ..... 159 N5
Surrey Cl FNCH N3 .... 117 H1
Surrey Crs CHSWK W4 .... 155 N5
Surrey Dr EMPK RM11 .... 125 M2
Surrey Gdns EHSLY KT24 .... 234 G3
FSBYPK N4 .... 119 K4
Surrey Gv SUT SM1 .... 201 N10
WALW SE17 .... 19 J8
Surrey Hills Av
KWD/TDW/WH KT20 .... 255 P7
Surrey La BTSEA SW11 .... 157 N7
Surrey Ms WNWD SE27 .... 181 P1
Surrey Mt FSTH SE23 .... 182 A3
Surrey Quays Rd
BERM/RHTH SE16 .... 160 B2
Surrey Rd BARK IG11 .... 143 H1
DAGE RM10 .... 124 D3
HRW HA1 .... 114 B3
PECK SE15 .... 182 G1
WWKM BR4 .... 204 G8
Surrey Rw STHWK SE1 .... 18 C1
Surrey Sq WALW SE17 .... 19 J7

Surrey St CROY/NA CR0...203 K10
PLSTW E13...141 N5
TPL/STR WC2R...11 P7
Surrey Ter WALW SE17...19 K6
Surrey Water Rd BERM/RHTH SE16...140 C10
Surrey Wy GUW GU2...249 M9
Surridge Cl RAIN RM13...145 K6
Surridge Gdns NRWD SE19...181 L9
Surr St HOLWY N7...118 F10
Sury Basin KUTN/CMB KT2...199 V1
Susan Cl ROMW/RG RM7...124 D1
Susan Rd BKHTH/KID SE3...161 N8
Susan Wd CHST BR7...206 D1
Sussex Av HARH RM3...105 N8
ISLW TW7...154 D9
Sussex Border Pth CRAWE RH10...285 L3
HORL RH6...279 N8
HORL RH6...280 F7
HORL RH6...281 J10
Sussex Cl ARCH N19 *...118 F7
CSTG HP8...89 N3
HOD EN11...44 F2
NWMAL KT3...200 B4
REDBR IG4...122 C4
REIG RH2...275 N1
SL SL1...149 N2
TWK TW1...176 G2
WOKN/KNAP GU21...231 H5
Sussex Ct WOKN/KNAP GU21...231 H5
Sussex Crs NTHLT UB5...133 H4
Sussex Gdns BAY/PAD W2...9 M7
CHSGTN KT9...219 J3
FSBYPK N4...119 K5
HGT N6...118 A3
Sussex Keep SL SL1 *...149 N1
Sussex Ms East BAY/PAD W2...9 M7
Sussex Ms West BAY/PAD W2...9 M7
Sussex Pl BAY/PAD W2...9 M7
CAMTN NW1 *...10 B1
CFSP/GDCR SL9 *...90 B7
HMSMTH W6...156 A1
NWMAL KT3...200 B4
SL SL1...149 N1
Sussex Ring NFNCH/WDSPK N12...97 M1
Sussex Rd BRW CM14...106 C5
CAR SM5...222 A4
DART DA1...187 P3
EHAM E6...142 D5
ERITH DA8...148 C6
HGDN/ICK UB10...112 A3
HRW HA1...114 B3
MTCM CR4 *...202 F5
NWDGN UB2...153 L2
NWMAL KT3...200 B4
SAND/SEL CR2...223 L3
SCUP DA14...185 L8
STMC/STPC BR5...207 N6
WATN WD24...73 H4
WOKN/KNAP GU21...231 H4
WWKM BR4...204 G8
Sussex Sq BAY/PAD W2...9 M7
Sussex St PIM SW1V...16 F8
PLSTW E13...141 N5
Sussex Ter PGE/AN SE20 *...182 B10
PUR RM19 *...166 A4
Sussex Wy ARCH N19...118 C7
EBAR EN4...78 C9
Sutcliffe Cl BUSH WD23...36 C9
GLDGN NW11...117 L3
Sutherland Av WOOL/PLUM SE18...163 H5
Sutherland Av BH/WHM TN16...244 F4
HYS/HAR UB3...153 H3
MV/WKIL W9...8 E3
POTB/CUF EN6...60 E4
RGUE GU4...250 B4
STMC/STPC BR5...207 J6
SUN TW16...196 C2
WEA W13...134 G8
WELL DA16...162 G10
Sutherland Cl BAR EN5...76 C4
Sutherland Ct CDALE/KGS NW9...115 N2
WCCE AL7...23 J4
RDART DA2...188 E1
Sutherland Dr RGUE GU4...250 D7
WIM/MER SW19...201 N1
Sutherland Gdns MORT/ESHN SW14...156 B9
SUN TW16...196 C2
WPK KT4...200 E8
Sutherland Gv TEDD TW11...176 E6
WAND/EARL SW18...179 J3
Sutherland House WALTH E17 *...121 L3
Sutherland Pl BAY/PAD W2...8 E5
Sutherland Rd BELV DA17...164 B2
BOW E3...140 A4
CHSWK W4...156 A5
CROY/NA CR0...203 H7
ED N9...99 P2
PEND EN3...80 C10
STHL UB1...133 N8
TOTM N17...99 P9
WALTH E17...100 C10
WEA W13...134 C8
Sutherland Rw PIM SW1V...16 F8
Sutherland Sq WALW SE17...18 F8
Sutherland St PIM SW1V...16 F8
Sutherland Vis WEA W13 *...134 F9
Sutherland Wk WALW SE17...18 F8
Sutherland Wy POTB/CUF EN6...60 E4
Sutlej Rd CHARL SE7...161 P6
Sutterton St HOLWY N7...5 N2
Sutton Av WOKN/KNAP GU21...231 H5
WOKN/KNAP GU21...231 K1
Sutton Cl BECK BR3...204 C1
BROX EN10...44 D6
CHSWK W4 *...155 P5
LOU IG10...102 B1
PIN HA5...113 H5
Sutton Common Rd CHEAM SM3...201 K8
Sutton Ct BELMT SM2...221 M4
CHSWK W4 *...155 P5
WARE SG12 *...26 C5
Sutton Court Rd CHSWK W4...155 P5
HGDN/ICK UB10...132 C3
PLSTW E13...141 P5
SUT SM1...221 M3
Sutton Crs BAR EN5...76 C4
Sutton Dene HSLW TW3...154 A7
Sutton Dwelling Est CHEL SW3...15 N7
Sutton Est IS N1 *...6 C1
The Sutton Est IS N1...6 C1
Sutton Gdns CROY/NA CR0...203 N5
REDH RH1...258 C5
Sutton Gn SUT SM1...221 N2
Sutton Green Rd RGUE GU4...250 C2
Sutton Hall Rd HEST TW5...153 P7
Sutton Hi RGUE GU4...250 F5
Sutton La BELMT SM2...221 L8
DTCH/LGLY SL3...150 F4
FARR EC1M...12 D2
HSLW TW3...154 A7
Sutton La North CHSWK W4...155 P5
Sutton La South CHSWK W4...155 P4
Sutton Park Rd SUT SM1...221 L3
Sutton Pl DTCH/LGLY SL3...150 E5
HOM E9...120 D10
RDKG RH5...270 D10
Sutton Rd BARK IG11...143 H4
HEST TW5...153 P7
MUSWH N10...98 B9
PLSTW E13...141 L6
STAL AL1...38 C7
WALTH E17...100 D1
WAT WD17...73 K7
Sutton Rw SOHO/SHAV W1D...11 J5
Suttons Av HCH RM12...125 K6
Suttons Gdns HCH RM12...125 L6
Suttons La HCH RM12...125 L10
HOM E9 *...120 D10
Sutton Sq HEST TW5...153 N7

Sutton St WCHPL E1...140 B8
Sutton Wy HEST TW5...153 N7
NKENS W10...8 F7
STLK EC1Y...12 F2
Swaby Rd WAND/EARL SW18...179 L9
Swaffield Rd SEV TN13...247 K8
WAND/EARL SW18...179 M3
Swain Cl STRHM/NOR SW16...180 C8
Swain Rd THHTH CR7...208 K5
Swains Cl WDR/YW UB7...151 P1
Swain's La HGT N6...118 B6
Swainson Rd ACT W3...156 C1
Swains Rd MTCM CR4...180 A10
Swain St STJWD NW8...9 N1
Swaisland Rd DART DA1...187 J2
Swaislands Dr DART DA1...186 C1
Swakeleys Dr HGDN/ICK UB10...112 B9
Swakeleys Rd HGDN/ICK UB10...111 P9
Swale Cl SOCK/AV RM15...148 B8
Swaledale Av CRAWW RH11...283 M10
FBAR/BDGN N11...98 B3
Swaledale Rd RDART DA2...188 B4
Swale Rd DART DA1...165 H9
Swallands Rd SE6...182 G7
Swallow Av BUSH WD23...94 A2
CDW/CHF RM16...167 H3
ERITH DA8...164 F7
NWCR SE14...142 B3
RDART DA2...188 E1
Swallow Cl RSLP HA4 *...113 K6
WGCE AL7 *...23 J5
Swallowdale IVER SL0...130 C5
SAND/SEL CR2...224 C5
Swallowdale La HHNE HP2...36 C3
Swallow Dr NTHLT UB5...133 P4
WLSDN NW10...136 A1
Swallow End WGCE AL7...23 J5
Swallowfield EGH TW20...171 N9
Swallowfield Rd CHARL SE7...161 N4
Swallowfields WGCE AL7...23 J5
Swallow Gdns HAT AL10...40 D6
STRHM/NOR SW16...180 A8
Swallow La RDKG RH5...272 G8
Swallow Oaks ABLGY WD5...54 A5
Swallow Pk HHNE HP2...36 C2
Swallow Pl REGST W1B...10 F6
Swallow Ri WOKN/KNAP GU21...231 H5
Swallow Rd CRAWW RH11...283 M5
Swallows HLWE CM17...29 M7
The Swallows WCCE AL7 *...23 J1
Swallow St CONDST W1S...11 H8
EHAM E6...142 H4
IVER SL0...130 C5
Swallowtail Cl STMC/STPC BR5...207 N4
Swanage Rd CHING E4...101 H8
WAND/EARL SW18...179 M2
Swanage Wye YEAD UB4...133 K8
Swan & Pike Rd PEND EN3...80 F4
Swan Ap EHAM E6...142 B7
Swan Av UPMR RM14...126 A7
Swanbourne Pl HCH RM12...125 L9
Swanbridge Rd BXLYHN DA7...164 B7
Swan Cl CROY/NA CR0 *...203 M7
CSHM HP5...50 C3
FELT TW13...175 H7
RKW/CH/CXG WD3...50 A1
STMC/STPC BR5...207 K3
WALTH E17...100 E4
Swan Ct GU GU1...250 A8
HHW HP1...35 M7
Swandon Wy WAND/EARL SW18...179 M1
Swan Dr CDALE/KGS NW9...96 B10
Swanfield Rd CHES/WCR EN8...62 D9
Swanfield St BETH E2...7 L10
Swanhill WGCE AL7 *...23 K2
Swan La BRWN CM15...86 D3
CANST EC4R...12 G8
DART DA1...186 C3
GU GU1...268 A2
HORL RH6...279 J8
LOU IG10...101 P1
TRDG/WHET N20...97 H2
Swanley Bar La POTB/CUF EN6...59 L4
Swanley Crs POTB/CUF EN6...59 L5
Swanley La SWLY BR8...208 G3
Swanley Rd WELL DA16...163 N7
Swan Md HHS/BOV HP3...54 A1
STHWK SE1...19 J4
Swan Ms BRXN/ST SW9...158 A4
FUL/PGN SW6...157 J7
Swan Mill Gdns DORK RH4...255 H10
Swanns Meadow GT/LBKH KT23...253 P2
Swan Pas WCHPL E1 *...13 M9
Swan Pl BARN SW13...156 B1
Swan Rd BERM/RHTH SE16...160 B1
CHES/WCR EN8...62 C10
FELT TW13...175 H7
IVER SL0...130 G3
STHL UB1...133 N4
WDR/YW UB7...151 N1
WOOL/PLUM SE18...163 N5
Swans Cl STALE/WH AL4...39 K7
Swanscombe Rd NTGHL W11...136 G10
Swanscombe St SWCM DA10...189 L3
Swansea Rd EBED/NFELT TW14...174 A7
PEND EN3...80 B6
Swanshope LOU IG10...82 E6
Swanston Pth OXHEY WD19...33 K4
Swan St ISLW TW7...154 C9
STHWK SE1...19 H3
The Swansway WEY KT13 *...196 B10
Swanton Gdns WIM/MER SW19...178 C4
Swanton Rd ERITH DA8...164 B6
Swan Wk CHEL SW3...16 A9
SHPTN TW17...196 F7
Swanwy PEND EN3...80 C6
Swanwick Cl PUT/ROE SW15...178 C5
Swanworth La RDKG RH5...254 G4
Swan Yd IS N1...6 C2
Swanzy Rd RSEV TN14...247 K6
Sward Rd STMC/STPC BR5...207 K6
Swaton Rd BOW E3...140 A10
Swaylands Rd BELV DA17...164 C3
Swaynesland Rd EDEN TN8...262 C10
Swayne's La GU GU1...251 J5
Swaythling Cl UED N18...100 A5
Swedenborg Gdns WCHPL E1...13 P7
Sweden Ga BERM/RHTH SE16...160 A6
Sweeney Crs STHWK SE1...19 M2
Sweeps Ditch Cl STA TW18...195 L1
Sweeps La EGH TW20...172 C8
STMC/STPC BR5...207 N5
Sweet Briar WCCE AL7...23 K7
Sweetbriar Cl HHW HP1...35 K3
Sweet Briar Gn ED N9...99 N4
Sweet Briar Gv ED N9...99 N4
Sweet Briar Wk UED N18...99 N5
Sweetcroft La HGDN/ICK UB10...132 A2
Sweetmans Av PIN HA5...113 L1
Sweets Wy TRDG/WHET N20...97 N3
Swete St PLSTW E13...141 M4
Sweyne Rd SWCM DA10...189 M3
Sweyn Pl BKHTH/KID SE3...161 M8
Swievelands Rd BH/WHM TN16...243 P6
Swift Cl HYS/HAR UB3...132 C6
RYLN/HDSTN HA2...114 A7
THMD SE28...137 H7
UPMR RM14...125 M1
WALTH E17...100 D8
WARE SG12...27 H8
Swiftfields WGCE AL7...23 J1
Swift La CRAWW RH11...283 L6
Swift Rd FELT TW13...175 H6
NWDGN UB2...153 H3
Swiftsden Wy BMLY BR1...183 N5

Swift St FUL/PGN SW6...157 J7
Swiftsure Rd CDW/CHF RM16...167 H3
Swiller's La CVE DA12...191 P8
Swinbrook Rd NKENS W10...8 B2
NKENS W10...137 H7
Swinburne Crs CROY/NA CR0...204 D2
Swinburne Gdns TIL RM18...168 B8
Swinburne Rd PUT/ROE SW15...156 D10
Swinderby Rd ALP/SUD HA0...135 K1
Swindon Cl GDMY/SEVK IG3...123 H7
Swindon Gdns HARH RM3...105 N6
Swindon La HARH RM3...105 N6
Swindon Rd HTHAIR TW6...174 D2
Swindon St SHB W12...136 E10
Swinfield Cl FELT TW13...175 H7
Swinford Gdns BRXN/ST SW9...159 J9
Swingate La WOOL/PLUM SE18...163 H6
Swing Gate La BERK HP4...36 A4
Swinnerton St HOM E9...120 D10
Swinton Cl WBLY HA9...116 G6
Swinton Pl FSBYW WC1X...5 N10
Swinton St FSBYW WC1X...5 N10
Swires Shaw HAYES BR2...226 A1
Swiss Av WATW WD18...72 F8
Swiss Cl WATW WD18...72 F7
Swithland Gdns ELTH/MOT SE9...184 C1
Sword Cl BROX EN10...44 C6
Swyncombe Av EA W5...154 C3
Swynford Gdns HDN NW4...95 L3
Sybil Phoenix Cl DEPT SE8...160 D4
Sybourn St WALTH E17...120 C5
Sycamore Ap RKW/CH/CXG WD3...72 D9
Sycamore Av BFN/LL DA15...185 J2
BOW E3...140 E3
EA W5...155 J2
HAT AL10...40 D5
HYS/HAR UB3...132 A9
UPMR RM14...126 A4
Sycamore Cl ACT W3...136 B10
AMS HP6...83 M6
BUSH WD23...73 M6
CAN/RD E16...141 M4
CAR SM5...222 A1
CHSW E1...61 N3
CRAWW RH11...284 A7
EBAR EN4...77 N10
ED N9...99 P5
EDGW HA8...95 P5
FELT TW13...175 H6
GSTN WD25...73 J1
GVE DA12...190 G3
LHD/OX KT22...256 E9
NTHLT UB5...133 M5
SAND/SEL CR2...223 M2
TIL RM18...168 D7
WDR/YW UB7...133 P1
Sycamore Ct WEY KT13...196 G10
Sycamore Dene CSHM HP5...51 J4
Sycamore Dr BRW CM14...107 H2
LCOL/BKTW AL2...56 C3
SWLY BR8...208 F2
Sycamore Fld HLWW/ROY CM19...46 D5
Sycamore Gdns MTCM CR4...180 G7
SHB W12...137 J4
Sycamore Gv CAT SE6...183 H2
CDALE/KGS NW9...115 P5
GPK RM2...124 G1
NWMAL KT3...200 B3
PGE/AN SE20...203 P1
Sycamore HI FBAR/BDGN N11...98 B7
Sycamore Ms CLAP SW4...158 D9
ERITH DA8 *...164 C4
Sycamore Pk AMS HP6...69 H4
Sycamore Ri BERK HP4...34 A6
BNSTD SM7...220 C10
CSTG HP8...89 M4
Sycamore Rd CRICK NW2...116 D1
DART DA1...187 L3
GU GU1...250 A10
RKW/CH/CXG WD3...72 D9
WIM/MER SW19...177 M6
Sycamore St FSBYE EC1V...12 E2
Sycamore Wk DTCH/LGLY SL3...150 B8
EGH TW20...171 N9
NKENS W10...8 A1
NKENS W10...137 H6
REIG RH2...275 M3
Sycamore Wy SOCK/AV RM15...147 J6
TEDD TW11...176 F1
Sydcote DUL SE21 *...181 K5
Sydenham Av SYD SE26...182 A8
Sydenham Cl ROM RM1...124 G2
Sydenham Cottages LEE/GVPK SE12 *...183 P5
SYD SE26...181 P6
Sydenham Hi FSTH SE23...181 P6
Sydenham Pk SYD SE26...182 A5
Sydenham Park Rd SYD SE26...182 A5
Sydenham Ri FSTH SE23...182 A5
Sydenham Rd CROY/NA CR0...2 B1
GU GU1...268 B1
SYD SE26...182 C8
Sydenham Station Ap SYD SE26...182 B7
Sydmons Ct FSTH SE23 *...182 B3
Sydner Rd STNW/STAM N16...119 N9
Sydney Av PUR/KEN CR8...222 G4
Sydney Cl SKENS SW7...15 M6
Sydney Gv HDN NW4...95 L4
SL SL1...129 H8
Sydney Ms CHEL SW3...15 M6
Sydney Pl GU GU1...268 C1
SKENS SW7...15 M6
Sydney Rd ABYW SE2...137 P1
BARK/HLT IG6...102 F10
BXLYHS DA6...163 N10
CEND/HSY/T N8...119 H2
EBED/NFELT TW14...173 N5
ENC/FH EN2...79 L8
GU GU1...268 C1
MUSWH N10...98 C9
RCH/KEW TW9...157 M5
RYNPK SW20...200 G2
SCUP DA14...185 H7
SUT SM1...221 K1
TEDD TW11...176 B6
TIL RM18...168 D8
WAN E11...121 N4
WATW WD24...134 F10
WFD IG8...101 M5
Sydney St CHEL SW3...15 N6
Sydney Ter ESH/CLAY KT10 *...218 E3
Syke Cluan DTCH/LGLY SL3...151 H2
Syke Ings DTCH/LGLY SL3...151 H2
Sykes Dr STA TW18...173 L8
Sykes Rd SL SL1...128 C5
Sylvana Cl HGDN/ICK UB10...132 A3
Sylvan Av CHDH RM6...124 A3
EMPK RM11...125 N1
MLHL NW7...96 B7
WDGN N22...98 B7
Sylvan Cl HHS/BOV HP3...53 M7
OXTED RH8...261 N5
SAND/SEL CR2...224 C4
WOKS/MYFD GU22...232 E4
Sylvandale WGCE AL7...23 J1
Sylvan Gdns SURB KT6...199 J7
Sylvan Gv CRICK NW2...116 C1
PECK SE15...160 A5
Sylvan Hi NRWD SE19...205 H1
Sylvan Ms DART DA1...166 G10
Sylvan Rd CRAWE RH10...284 B9
FSTGT E7...141 M1
IL IG1...122 F7
NRWD SE19...205 H1
PECK SE15 *...160 A6
WALTH E17...120 D1
WAN E11...121 N1
Sylvan Ter PECK SE15 *...160 A6
Sylvan Wk BMLY BR1...184 F6
Sylvan Wy BCTR RM8...123 J6

CHIG IG7...103 L4
REDH RH1...276 C1
WGCE AL7...23 J1
WWKM BR4...225 K1
Sylverdale Rd CROY/NA CR0...203 J10
PUR/KEN CR8...223 J9
Sylvester Av CHST BR7...184 C9
Sylvester Pth HACK E8 *...140 D1
Sylvester Rd ALP/SUD HA0...115 H10
EFNCH N2...97 M10
HACK E8 *...7 M1
WALTH E17 *...120 E5
Sylvesters HLWW/ROY CM19...46 C5
Sylvia Av PIN HA5...93 N7
PIN HA5...93 N7
Sylvia Ct CHOB/PIR GU24...230 F2
WBLY HA9...135 N2
Sylvia Gdns WBLY HA9...135 N2
Symes Ms CAMTN NW1...4 C7
Symington Ms HOM E9...120 D10
Symister Ms IS N1...7 J10
Symonds Ct CHES/WCR EN8...62 C4
Symons Cl PECK SE15...160 B9
Symons St CHEL SW3...16 B6
Symphony Cl EDGW HA8...95 M8
Symphony Ms NKENS W10...2 D1
NKENS W10...137 H5
Syon La ISLW TW7...154 D6
Syon La ISLW TW7...154 C5
Syon Pk ISLW TW7 *...154 C6
Syon Park Gdns ISLW TW7...154 C6
Syracuse Av RAIN RM13...145 L5
Sythwood WOKN/KNAP GU21...231 K3
Szabo Crs RGUW GU3...248 A10

T

Tabard Garden Est STHWK SE1...18 G1
Tabard St STHWK SE1...18 G2
Tabernacle Av PLSTW E13...141 M6
Tabernacle St SDTCH EC2A...7 H10
Tableer Av CLAP SW4...180 D1
Tabley Rd HOLWY N7...118 F9
Tabor Gdns CHEAM SM3...221 J3
Tabor Gv WIM/MER SW19...179 H10
Tabor Rd HMSMTH W6...156 E2
Tabrums Wy UPMR RM14...126 E5
Tachbrook Rd EBED/NFELT TW14...174 C3
NWDGN UB2...153 J2
UX/CGN UB8...131 P5
Tachbrook St PIM SW1V...17 H6
Tack Ms BROCKY SE4...160 F9
Tadema Rd WBPTN SW10...157 M6
Tadlows Cl UPMR RM14...126 A10
Tadmor Cl SUN TW16...196 C4
Tadmor St SHB W12...136 G10
Tadorne Rd KWD/TDW/WH KT20...238 F7
Tadworth Av NWMAL KT3...200 C4
Tadworth Cl KWD/TDW/WH KT20...238 G8
Tadworth Pde HCH RM12...125 J9
Tadworth Rd CRICK NW2...116 A7
Tadworth St KWD/TDW/WH KT20...238 F10
Taeping St POP/IOD E14...160 C3
Taffy's How MTCM CR4...201 J3
Tait Rd CROY/NA CR0...203 M7
Takeley Cl CRW RM5...104 E10
WAB EN9...63 J9
Talacre Rd KTTN NW5...4 C1
Talbot Av DTCH/LGLY SL3...150 C2
EFNCH N2...97 H2
OXHEY WD19...33 M1
Talbot Cl REIG RH2...275 L1
SEVS/STOTM N15...119 N2
Talbot Ct BANK EC3V...13 H7
HHS/BOV HP3...35 M7
Talbot Crs HDN NW4...95 J3
Talbot Gdns GDMY/SEVK IG3...123 L6
Talbot Pl BKHTH/KID SE3...161 K8
DTCH/LGLY SL3...149 P7
Talbot Rd ALP/SUD HA0...116 A4
CAR SM5...222 C5
DAGW RM9...144 A2
EDUL SE22...159 N10
EHAM E6...142 C4
FSTGT E7...121 M9
HAT AL10...40 C1
HGT N6...118 A4
ISLW TW7...154 F10
KTN/HRWW/WS HA3...94 E10
NTGHL W11...8 B5
NWDGN UB2...153 M3
RKW/CH/CXG WD3...91 P7
SEVS/STOTM N15...119 N2
THHTH CR7...203 N1
WDGN N22...98 D10
WEA W13 *...134 F7
WHTN TW2...176 D4
Talbot Sq BAY/PAD W2...9 L6
Talbot St BRKHM/BTCW RH3...274 C5
Talbot Wk NTCHL W11 *...8 A4
WLSDN NW10...136 B1
Talbot Yd STHWK SE1...12 G10
Talbrook BRW CM14...106 E4
Talcott Pth BRXS/STRHM SW2 *...181 H1
Taleworth Cl ASHTD KT21...257 J6
Taleworth Pk ASHTD KT21...257 J7
Taleworth Rd ASHTD KT21...257 J5
Talfourd Pl PECK SE15...159 N7
Talfourd Rd PECK SE15...159 N7
Talgarth Rd WKENS W14...157 J4
Talgarth Wk CDALE/KGS NW9...116 B3
Talisman Cl GDMY/SEVK IG3...123 N6
Talisman Sq SYD SE26...181 P7
Talisman Wy EW KT17...238 F2
WBLY HA9...116 B9
Tallack Cl KTN/HRWW/WS HA3...94 D1
Tallack Rd LEY E10...120 C6
Tallis Cl CAN/RD E16...141 N8
Tallis Gv CHARL SE7...161 N5
Tallents Cl EYN DA4...188 A10
Tallis St EMB EC4Y...12 B7
Tallis Vw WLSDN NW10...136 A1
Tallis Wy BORE WD6...75 J5
BRW CM14...106 G6
Tall Oaks AMS HP6...69 J5
Tallow Rd BTFD TW8...155 H5
Tall Trees DTCH/LGLY SL3...151 H2
STRHM/NOR SW16...202 G3
Tall Trees Cl EMPK RM11...125 L4
Tally Rd OXTED RH8...262 B7
Talma Gdns WHTN TW2...176 D3
Talmage Cl FSTH SE23...182 B3
Talman Cl CRAWW RH11...283 M4
Talman Gv STAN HA7...94 A7
Talma Rd BRXS/STRHM SW2...159 H10
Tamar Cl BOW E3...140 E5
Tamarind Cl GUW GU2...249 M5
Tamarind Yd WAP E1W *...13 P5
Tamarisk Cl STALW/RED AL3...3 M1
Tamarisk Rd SOCK/AV RM15...147 H6
Tamarisk Sq SHB W12...137 H3
Tamar St CHARL SE7...161 J7
Tamar Wy DTCH/LGLY SL3...150 C4
TOTM N17...99 P2
Tamerton Sq WOKS/MYFD GU22...232 B5
Tamesa Gdns WPK KT4...200 B9
Tamesis Strd GVE DA12...191 H8
Tamian Wy HSLWW TW4...153 K10
Tamworth WFD IG8...101 K7

Tamworth La MTCM CR4...202 C3
Tamworth Pk MTCM CR4...202 C4
Tamworth Pl CROY/NA CR0...203 K9
Tamworth Rd CROY/NA CR0...203 K9
HERT/BAY SG13...25 N4
Tamworth St FUL/PGN SW6...14 A10
Tancred Rd FSBYPK N4...119 J4
Tandridge Dr ORP BR6...206 C8
Tandridge Gdns SAND/SEL CR2...223 N9
Tandridgehill La GDST RH9...260 D6
Tandridge La OXTED RH8...260 F7
Tandridge Rd WARL CR6...242 C6
Tanfield Av CRICK NW2...116 C2
Tanfield Cl CHESW E7...61 P3
Tanfield Rd CROY/NA CR0...223 K1
Tangent Link HARH RM3...105 N5
Tangent Rd HARH RM3...105 N5
Tangier La ETON SL4...149 J5
Tangier Rd GU GU1...268 D5
RCHPK/HAM TW10...157 M10
Tangier Wy KWD/TDW/WH KT20...239 H5
Tangle Tree Cl FNCH N3...97 H10
Tanglewood Cl CHERT KT16...193 N10
CROY/NA CR0...204 D10
STAN HA7...94 D4
WOKS/MYFD GU22...232 G2
Tanglewood Ride CHOB/PIR GU24...212 A8
Tanglewood Wy FELT TW13...175 J6
Tangley Gv PUT/ROE SW15...178 C3
Tangley La RGUW GU3...248 A9
Tangley Park Rd HPTN TW12...175 N8
Tanglyn Av SHPTN TW17...196 B5
Tangmere Crs HCH RM12...125 J1
Tangmere Gdns NTHLT UB5...133 J4
Tangmere Gv KUTN/CMB KT2...177 J8
Tangmere Rd CRAWW RH11...283 J7
Tangmere Wy CDALE/KGS NW9...96 B5
Tanhouse Fld KTTN NW5 *...118 E10
Tan House La BRW CM14...85 P7
Tanhouse Rd OXTED RH8...261 J8
Tankerfield Pl STALW/RED AL3...38 B5
Tankerton Houses STPAN WC1H *...5 M10
Tankerton Rd SURB KT6...199 L3
Tankerton St STPAN WC1H...5 M10
Tankerton Ter CROY/NA CR0 *...202 G7
Tankerville Rd STRHM/NOR SW16...180 E10
Tank Hill Rd PUR RM19...165 P3
Tank La PUR RM19...166 A3
Tankridge Rd CRICK NW2...116 E7
The Tanneries WCHPL E1 *...140 B6
Tanners Cl STALW/RED AL3...38 B5
WOT/HER KT12...197 J6
Tanners Crs HERT/BAY SG13...25 K7
Tanners Dean LHD/OX KT22...237 H8
Tanners End La UED N18...99 M5
Tannersfield RGUE GU4...268 B8
Tanners Hi ABLGY WD5...54 F5
BRKHM/BTCW RH3...273 N2
DEPT SE8...160 G8
Tanners La BARK/HLT IG6...122 F1
Tanners Meadow BRKHM/BTCW RH3...273 N6
Tanner St BARK IG11...142 F1
STHWK SE1...19 L2
Tanners Wy WARE SG12...27 P2
Tanners Wood Cl ABLGY WD5...54 F5
Tanners Wood La ABLGY WD5...54 F5
Tannery Cl BECK BR3...182 G10
DAGE RM10...124 C6
Tannery La RPLY/SEND GU23...233 H8
SHGR GU5...268 F10
The Tannery REDH RH1...257 P10
Tannington Ter HBRY N5...118 F9
Tannsfeld Rd SYD SE26...182 C8
Tannsmore Cl HHNE HP2...36 A4
Tansley Cl HOLWY N7...118 C10
Tanswell St STHWK SE1 *...18 A2
Tansy Cl EHAM E6...142 D8
HARH RM3...105 M7
RGUE GU4...268 G4
Tansycroft WGCE AL7...23 L4
Tantallon Rd BAL SW12...180 B4
Tant Av CAN/RD E16...141 L8
Tantony Gv CHDH RM6...123 N1
Tanworth Cl NTHWD HA6...92 D7
Tanworth Gdns PIN HA5...93 J10
Tanyard Cl CRAWE RH10...284 D10
Tanyard Hl GVE DA12...191 P9
Tan Yard La BXLY DA5 *...186 B5
Tanyard Wy HORL RH6...280 C3
Tanys Dell HLWE CM20...29 J8
Tanza Rd HAMP NW3...118 A9
Tapestry Cl BELMT SM2...221 L4
Taplow Ct MTCM CR4...201 P4
Taplow Rd PLMGR N13...99 K5
Taplow St IS N1...6 F6
Tapner's Rd BRKHM/BTCW RH3...274 C6
Tappesfield Rd PECK SE15...160 B9
Tapping Cl KUTN/CMB KT2...177 M10
Tapp St BETH E2 *...140 A6
Tapster St BAR EN5...76 D4
Taransay Wk IS N1...6 G1
Taransey HHS/BOV HP3...36 C6
Tara Ter BROCKY SE4...160 B10
Tarbay La WDSR SL4...148 A8
Tarbert Rd EDUL SE22...159 M4
Tarbert Wk WCHPL E1...140 E9
Target Cl EBED/NFELT TW14...174 A7
Tarham Cl HORL RH6...279 H8
Tariff Rd UED N18...100 D6
Tarleton Gdns FSTH SE23...182 A2
Tarling Cl SCUP DA14...185 L6
Tarling Rd CAN/RD E16...141 L8
EFNCH N2...97 H10
Tarling St WCHPL E1...140 C8
Tarmac Wy WDR/YW UB7...151 L6
Tarnbank ENC/FH EN2...78 F9
Tarn St STHWK SE1...18 F4
Tarnwood Pk ELTH/MOT SE9...184 C4

Tattle Hi HERT/WAT SG14...24 F1
Tatton Crs CLPT E5...119 N5
Tatton St HLWE CM17...29 M10
Tatum St WLSDN NW10...135 P2
Tauber Cl BORE WD6...75 L8
Taunton Av CTHM CR3...241 N9
HSLW TW3...154 B7
RYNPK SW20...200 E2
Taunton Cl BARK/HLT IG6...103 J7
CHEAM SM3...201 J10
CRAWE RH10...284 F7
Taunton Dr EFNCH N2...97 M10
ENC/FH EN2...79 L8
Taunton La COUL/CHIP CR5...241 H5
Taunton Ms CAMTN NW1...10 A1
Taunton Pl CAMTN NW1...10 A1
Taunton Rd GFD/PVL UB6...134 A2
GVE DA12...189 M1
HARH RM3...105 K6
LEE/GVPK SE12...183 K1
Taunton V CVE DA12...190 G6
Taunton Wy STHGT/OAK N14...95 M1
Tavern Cl CAR SM5...201 P7
Taverners HHNE HP2...35 P4
Taverners Cl NTGHL W11...8 A10
NTGHL W11...137 H10
Taverner Sq HBRY N5 *...119 K9
Taverners Wy CHING E4...101 K2
HOD EN11...44 F3
Tavistock Av GFD/PVL UB6...134 F4
MLHL NW7...96 G4
STAL AL1...38 G9
WALTH E17...120 C1
Tavistock Cl HARH RM3...105 L3
POTB/CUF EN6...59 N7
STA TW18...173 N10
STNW/STAM N16...119 M10
Tavistock Crs MTCM CR4...202 F4
NTGHL W11...8 C5
Tavistock Gdns GDMY/SEVK IG3...123 L5
Tavistock Gv CROY/NA CR0...203 L7
Tavistock Ms NTGHL W11 *...8 C5
Tavistock Pl STHGT/OAK N14 *...78 C10
STPAN WC1H...11 K1
Tavistock Rd CAR SM5...201 N8
CROY/NA CR0...203 L8
EDGW HA8...95 L9
FSBYPK N4...119 L4
HAYES BR2...205 N8
HGDN/ICK UB10...112 E10
NTGHL W11...8 C5
SWFD E18...121 M1
WAN E11...121 L9
WATN WD24...73 L5
WDR/YW UB7...131 N10
WELL DA16...163 M7
WLSDN NW10...136 C4
Tavistock Sq STPAN WC1H...11 K1
Tavistock St COVGDN WC2E...11 M7
Tavistock Ter ARCH N19...118 D10
Taviton St STPAN WC1H...11 J1
Tavy Br ABYW SE2...163 M1
Tavy Cl LBTH SE11...18 B7
Tawney Common EPP CM16...66 C1
Tawney La EPP CM16...66 D8
Tawney Rd THMD SE28...143 L9
Tawneys Rd HLWS CM18...47 J3
Tawny Av UPMR RM14...126 A10
Tawny Cl FELT TW13...175 H6
WEA W13...134 G10
Tawny Wy BERM/RHTH SE16...160 A8
Tayben Av WHTN TW2...176 D2
Taybridge Rd BTSEA SW11...158 B8
Tayburn Cl POP/IOD E14...141 P8
Tayfield Cl HGDN/ICK UB10...112 E8
Tayles Hill Dr EW KT17...220 C6
Taylifers HLWW/ROY CM19...46 D6
Taylor Av RCH/KEW TW9...155 N8
Taylor Cl CRW RM5...104 B8
DEPT SE8...160 E5
HPTN TW12...176 B7
HSLW TW3...154 B7
ORP BR6...227 J1
STALE/WH AL4...38 F2
Taylor Rd ASHTD KT21...257 J8
MTCM CR4...179 P10
WLGTN SM6...222 C4
Taylor Rw RDART DA2...187 K6
Taylors Av HOD EN11...44 F4
Taylors Buildings WOOL/PLUM SE18...162 E3
Taylors Cl SCUP DA14...185 J7
Taylors Ct FELT TW13...175 H5
Taylor's Gn ACT W3 *...136 B8
Taylor's La BAR EN5...77 J5
SYD SE26...182 A7
WLSDN NW10...136 B8
Taylors Md MLHL NW7...96 G6
Taylors Rd CSHM HP5...51 J6
Taylor Wk CRAWW RH11...283 J5
Taymount Ri FSTH SE23...182 A5
Taynton Dr REDH RH1...258 F6
Tayport Cl IS N1...5 N1
Tayside Dr EDGW HA8...95 N4
Tay Wy ROM RM1...104 G9
Taywood Rd NTHLT UB5...133 N6
Teak Cl BERM/RHTH SE16...140 D10
Teal Av STMC/STPC BR5...207 N4
Teal Cl CAN/RD E16...142 A7
PEND EN3...80 B3
SAND/SEL CR2...224 C7
Teal Ct DORK RH4...272 F1
Teal Dr NTHWD HA6...92 D7
Teale St BETH E2...7 P7
Tealing Dr HOR/WEW KT19...220 A1
Teal Pl SUT SM1...221 J2
Teal Wy HHS/BOV HP3...54 A1
Teasel Cl CRAWW RH11...283 L10
CROY/NA CR0...204 C8
Teasel Crs THMD SE28...143 H10
Teasel Wy SRTFD E15...161 L1
Teather St CMBW SE5...159 M5
Teazlewood Pk LHD/OX KT22...236 E5
Tebworth Rd TOTM N17...99 N8
Technology Pk CDALE/KGS NW9 *...116 A1
Teck Cl ISLW TW7...154 C8
Tedder Cl CHSGTN KT9...219 J10
HGDN/ICK UB10...132 A2
RSLP HA4...113 H10
Tedder Rd HHNE HP2...36 A4
SAND/SEL CR2...224 C7
Teddington Cl HOR/WEW KT19...220 A6
Teddington Pk TEDD TW11...176 A7
Teddington Park Rd TEDD TW11...176 A6
Tedworth Gdns CHEL SW3...16 A8
Tedworth Sq CHEL SW3...16 A8
Tees Av GFD/PVL UB6...134 C2
Tees Cl UPMR RM14...126 C5
Teesdale Av ISLW TW7...154 F7
Teesdale Cl BETH E2...7 P8
Teesdale Gdns ISLW TW7...154 F7
SNWD SE25...181 P10
Teesdale Rd RDART DA2...188 B4
SLN SL2...130 B1
WAN E11...121 L4
Teesdale St BETH E2...7 P8

Teign Ms ELTH/MOT SE9 184 B5
Teignmouth Cl CLAP SW4 158 E10
EDGW HA8 95 L10
Teignmouth Gdns GFD/PVL UB6 134 F4
Teignmouth Rd CRICK NW2 116 G10
WELL DA16 163 M8
Telcote Wy RSLP HA4 * 113 K5
Telegraph Hl HAMP NW3 117 L8
Telegraph La ESH/CLAY KT10 218 E1
Telegraph Ms GDMY/SEVK IG3 123 J6
Telegraph Pas BRXS/STRHM SW2 180 F3
Telegraph Pl POP/IOD E14 160 G3
Telegraph Rd PUT/ROE SW15 178 E3
Telegraph St LOTH EC2R 12 G5
Telegraph Tr CAR SM5 222 B6
Telephone Pl WKENS W14 14 D9
Telferscot Rd BAL SW12 180 E4
Telford Av BRXS/STRHM SW2 180 F4
Telford Cl GSTN WD25 73 L1
NRWD SE19 181 N9
WALTH E17 120 D5
Telford Ct GU GU1 268 C1
Telford Dr SL SL1 128 F10
WOT/HER KT12 197 K7
Telford Pl CRAWE RH10 283 P8
Telford Rd CDALE/KGS NW9 116 C4
ELTH/MOT SE9 184 G5
LCOL/BKTW AL2 57 H2
NKENS W10 8 A3
NKENS W10 137 H7
STHL UB1 134 A9
WHTN TW2 175 P3
Telford Rd North Circular Rd
FBAR/BDGN N11 98 D7
Telfords Yd WAP E1W 13 P8
Telford Ter PIM SW1V 16 G9
Telford Wy ACT W3 136 B7
YEAD UB4 133 M7
Telham Ct CRAWW RH11 * 283 J10
Telham Rd EHAM E6 142 D4
Tell Gv EDUL SE22 159 N10
Tellisford ESH/CLAY KT10 218 A1
Tellson Av WOOL/PLUM SE18 162 B7
Telscombe Cl ORP BR6 207 H9
Telston La RSEV TN14 246 G3
Temeraire Pl BTFD TW8 155 L4
Temeraire St BERM/RHTH SE16 160 B1
Tempelhof Av HDN NW4 116 F5
Temperance St STALW/RED AL3 38 B6
Temperley Rd BAL SW12 180 B3
Tempest Av POTB/CUF EN6 59 N8
Tempest Md EPP CM16 66 C3
Tempest Rd EGH TW20 172 F9
Tempest Wy RAIN RM13 145 H1
Templar Dr GVW DA11 190 D8
THMD SE28 143 N8
Templar Pl HPTN TW12 175 P10
Templars Av GLDGN NW11 117 J4
Templars Ct DART DA1 * 187 P1
Templars Crs FNCH N3 97 K10
Templars Dr
KTN/HRWW/WS HA3 * 94 C7
Templar St CMBW SE5 159 J8
Temple Av BCTR RM8 124 B6
CROY/NA CR0 204 E10
EMB EC4Y 12 B7
TRDG/WHET N20 97 N1
Temple Bank HLW CM20 29 L6
Temple Bar Rd
WOKN/KNAP GU21 231 L5
Temple Cl CHESW EN7 61 P7
CRAWE RH10 284 E8
FNCH N3 97 J10
THMD SE28 162 F2
WAN E11 121 K5
WAT WD17 72 G6
Templecombe Ms
WOKS/MYFD GU22 * 232 E2
Templecombe Rd HOM E9 140 B3
Templecombe Wy MRDN SM4 201 H5
Temple Ct POTB/CUF EN6 58 G7
Templedene Av STA TW18 173 L10
Temple Dwellings BETH E2 * 140 A4
Temple Field Cl ADL/WDHM KT15 215 L3
Temple Flds HERT/WAT SG14 25 K2
Temple Fortune Hl GLDGN NW11 117 K3
Temple Fortune La GLDGN NW11 117 J4
Temple Gdns BCTR RM8 123 N8
EMB EC4Y * 12 A7
GLDGN NW11 117 J4
RKW/CH/CXG WD3 92 C4
STA TW18 195 J1
WCHMH N21 * 99 J3
Temple Gv ENC/FH EN2 79 J7
GLDGN NW11 117 K4
Temple Hl DART DA1 187 N1
Temple Hill Sq DART DA1 187 N1
Temple La EMB EC4Y 12 B6
Templeman Cl PUR/KEN CR8 241 H2
Templeman Rd HNWL W7 134 E7
Temple Md HHNE HP2 35 N4
HLWW/ROY CM19 27 N10
Templemead Cl ACT W3 136 B8
Temple Mead Cl STAN HA7 94 G7
Temple Mills La LEY E10 120 G9
Templepan La
RKW/CH/CXG WD3 71 P3
Temple Pde BAR EN5 * 97 N1
Temple Pk UX/CGN UB8 132 B5
Temple Pl TPL/STR WC2R 11 P7
Templer Av CDW/CHF RM16 168 D3
Temple Rd BH/WHM TN16 244 A3
CEND/HSY/T N8 118 G2
CHSWK W4 155 P2
CRICK NW2 116 F9
CROY/NA CR0 223 L1
EA W5 155 J2
EHAM E6 142 B3
HOR/WEW KT19 220 A8
HSLW TW3 154 A10
RCH/KEW TW9 155 L8
WDSR SL4 149 H8
Temple Sheen Rd
MORT/ESHN SW14 155 P10
Temple St BETH E2 140 A4
Temple Ter WDGN N22 * 99 H10
Templeton Av CHING E4 100 F5
Templeton Cl NRWD SE19 203 L1
STNW/STAM N16 * 119 M10
Templeton Pl ECT SW5 14 F6
Templeton Rd FSBYPK N4 119 L4
Temple Vw STALW/RED AL3 38 B4
Temple Wy SLN SL2 109 H10
SUT SM1 201 N10
Templewood WEA W13 134 G7
WGCW AL8 22 G2
Templewood Av HAMP NW3 117 L8
Temple Wood Dr REDH RH1 * 258 A7
Templewood Gdns HAMP NW3 117 L8
Templewood La SLN SL2 109 J10
Temple Yd BETH E2 7 P10
Tempsford WGCE AL7 23 N5
Tempsford Av DORE WD6 76 A8
Tempsford Cl ENC/FH EN2 79 K7
Temsford Cl RYLN/HDSTN HA2 94 B10
Ten Acre WOKN/KNAP GU21 231 M4
Ten Acre La EGH TW20 194 F2
Ten Acres Cl LHD/OX KT22 236 C10
Tenbury Cl FSTGT E7 122 A10
Tenbury Ct BAL SW12 180 E4
Tenby Av KTN/HRWW/WS HA3 94 G10
Tenby Cl CHDH RM6 123 P4
Tenby Dr ASC SL5 192 C5
Tenby Gdns NTHLT UB5 133 P1
Tenby Rd CHDH RM6 123 P4
EDGW HA8 95 L9
PEND EN3 80 B7
WALTH E17 120 D3
WELL DA16 163 N7
Tenchley's La OXTED RH8 262 A7
Tench St WAP E1W * 140 A10
Tenda Rd STHWK SE1 160 A3
Tendring Rd HLWS CM18 46 G3
HLWS CM18 47 J2
Tendring Wy CHDH RM6 123 M3
Tenham Av BRXS/STRHM SW2 180 E5
Tenison Wy STHWK SE1 12 A10
Tennand Cl CHESW EN7 61 N2
Tennants Rw TIL RM18 * 168 B8
Tenniel Cl BAY/PAD W2 9 J6
GUW GU2 249 N8
Tennison Av BORE WD6 75 N9
Tennison Cl COUL/CHIP CR5 241 J6
Tennison Rd SNWD SE25 203 N4
Tennis St STHWK SE1 18 G1
Tenniswood Rd EN EN1 79 N5
Tennyson Av CDALE/KGS NW9 115 P1
GRAYS RM17 167 N2
MNPK E12 142 B2
NWMAL KT3 200 E5
TWK TW1 176 E4
WAB EN9 63 K10
WAN E11 121 M5
Tennyson Cl CRAWE RH10 284 C5
EBED/NFELT TW14 175 H2
PEND EN3 80 C9
WELL DA16 163 H7
Tennyson Rd ADL/WDHM KT15 215 P1
ASHF TW15 173 P8
DART DA1 187 P1
HARH RM3 105 K8
HNWL W7 134 E9
HSLW TW3 154 B8
KIL/WHAMP NW6 2 C5
LCOL/BKTW AL2 55 P2
LEY E10 120 G6
MLHL NW7 96 D6
PGE/AN SE20 182 C10
RBRW/HUT CM13 107 P1
SRTFD E15 141 K2
WALTH E17 120 E4
WIM/MER SW19 179 M9
Tennyson St VX/NE SW8 158 C8
Tennyson Wk GVW DA11 190 A6
TIL RM18 168 E8
Tennyson Wy HCH RM12 124 G6
SLN SL2 128 D6
Tensing Av GVW DA11 * 190 B6
Tensing Rd NWDGN UB2 153 P2
Tentelow La NWDGN UB2 154 A2
Tenterden Cl ELTH/MOT SE9 184 C7
HDN NW4 116 G1
Tenterden Dr HDN NW4 116 G1
Tenterden Gdns CROY/NA CR0 203 P7
HDN NW4 116 G1
Tenterden Gv HDN NW4 116 F2
Tenterden Rd BCTR RM8 124 A7
CROY/NA CR0 203 P7
TOTM N17 99 N8
Tenterden St CONDST W1S 10 F6
Tenter Gnd WCHPL E1 13 L4
Tenth Av KWD/TDW/WH KT20 * 257 J2
Tent Peg La STMC/STPC BR5 206 F5
Tent St WCHPL E1 140 A6
Tenzing Rd HHNE HP2 36 B6
Tercel Pth CHIG IG7 103 L5
Teredo St LEW SE13 160 G8
Terence Cl GVE DA12 191 J5
Teresa Gdns CHES/WCR EN8 62 B10
Terling Cl WAN E11 121 L8
Terling Rd BCTR RM8 124 B7
The Terlings BRW CM14 106 F4
Terling Wk IS N1 * 6 E5
Terminus Pl BGVA SW1W 16 F4
Terminus St HLW CM20 28 G10
Tern Gdns UPMR RM14 126 D6
Tern Rd CRAWW RH11 282 G8
Tern Wy BRW CM14 106 D5
Terrace Gdns BARN SW13 156 C8
WAT WD17 73 J6
Terrace La RCHPK/HAM TW10 177 K2
Terrace Rd HOM E9 140 C2
PLSTW E13 141 M3
WOT/HER KT12 197 J7
The Terraces RDART DA2 188 B3
Terrace St GVE DA12 190 F2
The Terrace ADL/WDHM KT15 215 P2
ASC SL5 192 C5
BARN SW13 156 B8
BETH E2 * 140 B5
CHING E4 * 101 K4
DEPT SE8 * 160 E3
EFNCH N2 * 118 B2
FNCH N3 * 97 J10
FSTH SE23 * 182 D3
GVE DA12 190 F2
KIL/WHAMP NW6 2 E5
SEV TN13 246 E8
WOKS/MYFD GU22 * 232 D7
Terrace Vls HMSMTH W6 * 156 D4
Terrace Wk DAGW RM9 123 P10
Terrac St RCH/KEW TW9 155 L10
Terrapin Rd TOOT SW17 180 C6
Terretts Pl IS N1 6 C4
Terrick Rd WDGN N22 98 F9
Terrick St SHB W12 136 E8
Terrilands PIN HA5 113 N1
Terront Rd SEVS/STOTM N15 119 K3
Terry Pl UX/CGN UB8 * 131 M7
Tessa Sanderson Wy
GFD/PVL UB6 114 C10
Testard Rd GUW GU2 267 P2
Testers Cl OXTED RH8 261 N8
Testerton Rd NTGHL W11 * 136 G9
Testerton Wk NTGHL W11 * 136 G9
Testwood Rd WDSR SL4 148 C7
Tetbury Pl IS N1 6 C6
Tetcott Rd WBPTN SW10 157 M6
Tetherdown MUSWH N10 118 B1
Tethys Rd HHNE HP2 36 A3
Tetty Wy BMLY BR1 205 M2
Teversham La VX/NE SW8 158 F7
Teviot Av SOCK/AV RM15 146 C8
Teviot Cl GUW GU2 249 M7
WELL DA16 163 L7
Teviot St POP/IOD E14 141 H7
Tewin Cl STALE/WH AL4 39 H2
Tewin Ct WGCE AL7 23 J4
Tewin Rd HHNE HP2 36 D6
WGCE AL7 23 J4
Tewkesbury Av FSTH SE23 182 A4
PIN HA5 113 M4
Tewkesbury Cl BF/WBF KT14 215 N7
LOU IG10 82 B10
Tewkesbury Gdns
CDALE/KGS NW9 115 N1
Tewkesbury Rd CAR SM5 201 N8
SEVS/STOTM N15 119 L5
WEA W13 134 F10
Tewkesbury Ter
FBAR/BDGN N11 98 D7
Tewson Rd WOOL/PLUM SE18 163 H4
Teynham Av EN EN1 79 L10
Teynham Gn HAYES BR2 205 M5
Teynham Rd RDART DA2 188 B4
Teynton Ter TOTM N17 99 K9
Thackeray Av TIL RM18 168 E7
TOTM N17 99 P10
Thackeray Cl ISLW TW7 154 F8
UX/CGN UB8 132 C8
WIM/MER SW19 178 G10
Thackeray Dr CHDH RM6 123 L5
Thackeray Ms HACK E8 7 N2
Thackeray Rd EHAM E6 142 A4
VX/NE SW8 158 C8
Thackeray St KENS W8 15 H3
Thakeham Cl SYD SE26 182 A8
Thalia Cl GNWCH SE10 161 J5
Thal Massing Cl
RBRW/HUT CM13 107 N3
Thame Rd BERM/RHTH SE16 160 C1
Thames Av CHERT KT16 195 K3
DAGW RM9 144 D5
GFD/PVL UB6 134 E4
HHNE HP2 36 A1
WBPTN SW10 157 M7
Thames Bank MORT/ESHN SW14 155 P8
Thamesbank Pl THMD SE28 143 M8
Thames Cir POP/IOD E14 160 F3
Thames Cl CHERT KT16 195 L7
HPTN TW12 198 A2
RAIN RM13 145 J8
Thamesdale LCOL/BKTW AL2 57 L3
Thames Down Link ASHTD KT21 219 L10
ASHTD KT21 237 M3
BRYLDS KT5 199 P5
BRYLDS KT5 200 A7
HOR/WEW KT19 219 P1
Thames Dr CDW/CHF RM16 168 D4
RSLP HA4 112 D4
Thames Eyot TWK TW1 * 176 F5
Thamesfield Ms SHPTN TW17 196 D7
Thames Ga DART DA1 187 P1
Thamesgate STA TW18 195 L2
Thamesgate Cl
RCHPK/HAM TW10 176 G7
Thameside TEDD TW11 177 J10
Thameside Centre BTFD TW8 * 155 L5
Thames Lock WEY KT13 * 196 B9
Thames Md WDSR SL4 148 D7
WOT/HER KT12 197 H7
Thames Meadow
E/WMO/HCT KT8 197 P3
SHPTN TW17 196 E8
Thamesmere Dr THMD SE28 143 K9
Thames Pth BARN SW13 156 C7
BTFD TW8 155 K6
CLPT E5 120 C8
GNWCH SE10 161 M2
ISLW TW7 155 H8
POP/IOD E14 160 F2
SRTFD E15 141 H4
STA TW18 173 H6
STA TW18 173 J10
STWL/WRAY TW19 172 B5
TWRH EC3N 13 K9
VX/NE SW8 16 D10
WDSR SL4 149 N10
WEST SW1P 17 L7
WEY KT13 196 C9
WOT/HER KT12 197 H5
GNWCH SE10 161 H5
POP/IOD E14 140 F10
Thames Pl PUT/ROE SW15 156 G9
Thamespoint TEDD TW11 * 177 J10
Thames Quay WBPTN SW10 * 157 M7
Thames Reach KUT/HW KT1 * 199 J1
Thames Rd BARK IG11 143 K5
CAN/RD E16 142 A10
CHSWK W4 155 N5
DART DA1 165 H9
DTCH/LGLY SL3 150 E3
WDSR SL4 * 148 B6
Thames Side KUT/HW KT1 199 J1
STA TW18 195 K1
THDIT KT7 198 G6
WDSR SL4 149 J6
Thames St GNWCH SE10 160 G5
HPTN TW12 198 A2
KUT/HW KT1 199 J2
STA TW18 173 J8
SUN TW16 197 J3
WDSR SL4 149 J7
WEY KT13 196 C10
WOT/HER KT12 196 G7
Thamesvale Cl HSLW TW3 153 P8
Thames Vw CDW/CHF RM16 168 D4
Thames Village CHSWK W4 155 P7
Thames Wy GVW DA11 189 M2
Thamley PUR RM19 165 P3
Thanescroft Gdns CROY/NA CR0 203 M10
Thanet Dr HAYES BR2 206 A10
Thanet Pl CROY/NA CR0 223 K1
Thanet Rd BXLY DA5 186 B3
ERITH DA8 164 F6
Thanet St STPAN WC1H 5 L10
Thane Vls HOLWY N7 118 G8
Thant Cl LEY E10 120 G8
Tharp Rd WLGTN SM6 222 E2
Thatcham Gdns
TRDG/WHET N20 97 M1
Thatcher Cl WDR/YW UB7 151 P1
CRAWE RH10 283 N10
Thatchers Cl HORL RH6 280 C2
LOU IG10 82 F6
Thatchers Cft HHNE HP2 35 P2
Thatchers La RGUW GU3 249 J3
Thatchers Wy ISLW TW7 176 C1
Thatches Gv CHDH RM6 123 P2
Thavies Inn FLST/FETLN EC4A 12 B5
Thaxted Gn RBRW/HUT CM13 87 P9
Thaxted Pl RYNPK SW20 178 G10
Thaxted Rd BKHH IG9 102 B1
ELTH/MOT SE9 184 F5
Thaxted Wy WAB EN9 63 J9
Thaxton Rd WKENS W14 14 E9
Thayers Farm Rd BECK BR3 204 D1
Thayer St MHST W1U 10 D5
Thaynesfield POTB/CUF EN6 59 N7
Theatre Sq SRTFD E15 141 J1
Theatre St BTSEA SW11 158 A9
Theberton St IS N1 6 B5
The Beverly MRDN SM4 200 G6
The Courtyard HAYES BR2 226 B3
Theed St STHWK SE1 12 A10
The Green WIM/MER SW19 178 G8
Thele Av WARE SG12 27 J7
Theleway Cl HOD EN11 26 G10
Thellusson Wy
RKW/CH/CXG WD3 91 K1
Thelma Cl GVE DA12 191 J8
Thelma Gv TEDD TW11 176 F9
Thelusson Ct RAD WD7 * 74 F1
The Mall BTFD TW8 * 155 J5
SRTFD E15 * 141 J2
Theobald Crs
KTN/HRWW/WS HA3 94 A9
Theobald Rd CROY/NA CR0 203 J9
WALTH E17 120 E5
Theobalds Av GRAYS RM17 167 P4
Theobald's Cl POTB/CUF EN6 60 G6
Theobald's Gv CHES/WCR EN8 * 62 C8
Theobald's La CHES/WCR EN8 62 B8
Theobalds Park Rd ENC/FH EN2 79 J1
Theobald's Rd GINN WC1R 11 N3
POTB/CUF EN6 60 F6
Theobald St BORE WD6 75 K5
STHWK SE1 18 G4
Theodora Wy PIN HA5 112 G1
Theodore Rd LEW SE13 183 J2
Thepps Cl REDH RH1 276 G3
Therapia La CROY/NA CR0 202 F7
Therapia Rd EDUL SE22 182 B2
Theresa Rd HMSMTH W6 156 D3
Theresa's Wk SAND/SEL CR2 223 L5
Therfield Rd STALW/RED AL3 38 C3
Thermopylae Ga POP/IOD E14 160 G3
Theseus Wk IS N1 6 D8
Thesiger Rd PGE/AN SE20 182 C10
Thetford Cl PLMGR N13 99 J7
Thetford Rd ASHF TW15 173 P7
DAGW RM9 143 N2
NWMAL KT3 200 B5
Theydon Cl CRAWE RH10 204 D9
Theydon Ct WAB EN9 63 N9
Theydon Gdns RAIN RM13 144 F2
Theydon Ga EPP CM16 * 83 H2
Theydon Gv EPP CM16 65 K6
WFD IG8 101 P7
Theydon Park Rd EPP CM16 83 H5
Theydon Pl EPP CM16 65 J7
Theydon Rd CLPT E5 120 B7
EPP CM16 64 G10
Theydon St WALTH E17 120 E5
Thicket Crs SUT SM1 221 M1
Thicket Gv DAGW RM9 143 M1
PGE/AN SE20 181 P10
Thicket Rd PGE/AN SE20 182 A10
SUT SM1 221 M1
Thicket Ter PGE/AN SE20 * 181 P10
The Thicket WDR/YW UB7 131 P8
Thickthorne La STA TW18 173 M10
Thieves La HERT/WAT SG14 24 G5
Third Av ACT W3 136 C10
CHDH RM6 123 M4
DAGE RM10 144 C3
EN EN1 79 N9
GSTN WD25 73 L1
GVW DA11 * 190 C4
HLWW/ROY CM19 46 E2
HYS/HAR UB3 132 G10
KWD/TDW/WH KT20 * 257 J2
MNPK E12 122 B9
NKENS W10 8 B1
NKENS W10 137 H5
PLSTW E13 141 M5
WALTH E17 120 F3
WBLY HA9 115 J7
WTHK RM20 166 F5
Third Cl E/WMO/HCT KT8 198 A4
Third Crs SL SL1 129 H7
Third Cross Rd WHTN TW2 176 C5
Third Wy WBLY HA9 115 N9
Thirkleby Cl SL SL1 129 H10
Thirleby Rd EDGW HA8 96 A9
WEST SW1P 17 H4
Thirlestane STAL AL1 38 D5
Thirlmere Av GFD/PVL UB6 135 H5
SL SL1 128 B7
Thirlmere Cl EGH TW20 172 E10
Thirlmere Dr STAL AL1 38 G8
Thirlmere Gdns NTHWD HA6 92 C6
WBLY HA9 115 H6
Thirlmere Ri BMLY BR1 183 L9
Thirlmere Rd BXLYHN DA7 164 D8
CRAWW RH11 282 G9
MUSWH N10 98 C9
STRHM/NOR SW16 180 E7
Thirsk Cl NTHLT UB5 133 P1
Thirsk Rd BORE WD6 75 M4
BTSEA SW11 158 B9
MTCM CR4 180 B10
SNWD SE25 203 L4
Thirteenth Av
KWD/TDW/WH KT20 * 257 J2
Thirza Rd DART DA1 187 N2
Thisilefield Cl BXLY DA5 185 N4
Thistlebrook ABYW SE2 163 M2
Thistle Cl HHW HP1 35 J7
Thistlecroft HHW HP1 35 L7
Thistlecroft Gdns STAN HA7 95 J10
Thistlecroft Rd WOT/HER KT12 217 K1
Thistledene BF/WBF KT14 215 J9
THDIT KT7 198 D6
Thistledene Av CRW RM5 104 C6
RSLP HA4 113 M8
Thistle Dr HAT AL10 40 C1
Thistle Gv WBPTN SW10 15 K8
WGCE AL7 23 M8
Thistlemead CHST BR7 206 E2
Thistle Md LOU IG10 82 D7
Thistle Rd GVE DA12 191 H3
The Thistles HHW HP1 35 L5
LHD/OX KT22 237 H8
Thistlewaite Rd CLPT E5 120 A8
Thistle Wy HORL RH6 281 K3
Thistlewood Cl HOLWY N7 118 G7
Thistlewood Crs CROY/NA CR0 225 J8
Thistleworth Cl ISLW TW7 154 C6
Thistley Cl COUL/CHIP CR5 240 E8
NFNCH/WDSPK N12 97 P7
Thoby La BRWN CM15 87 M3
Thomas A Beckett Cl HRW HA1 114 E9
Thomas Av CTHM CR3 241 K7
Thomas Baines Rd BTSEA SW11 157 N9
Thomas Bata Av TIL RM18 169 L3
Thomas Cl BRWN CM15 107 K3
Thomas Cribb Ms EHAM E6 142 C8
Thomas Dean Rd SYD SE26 * 182 E7
Thomas Dinwiddy Rd
LEE/GVPK SE12 183 N5
Thomas Doyle St STHWK SE1 18 C3
Thomas Dr GVE DA12 190 G5
Thomas' La CAT SE6 182 G3
Thomas Moore Wy EFNCH N2 117 M1
Thomas More Sq WAP E1W 13 N8
Thomas More St WAP E1W 13 N8
Thomas North Ter CAN/RD E16 * 141 L7
Thomas Pl KENS W8 14 G4
Thomas Rd POP/IOD E14 140 E8
Thomas Rochford Wy
CHES/WCR EN8 62 E3
Thomas St WOOL/PLUM SE18 162 D3
Thomas Wall Cl SUT SM1 221 L2
Thompkins La SLN SL2 128 E2
Thompson Av CMBW SE5 159 K6
RCH/KEW TW9 155 N9
Thompson Cl CHEAM SM3 201 K8
DTCH/LGLY SL3 150 D3
IL IG1 122 F7
Thompson Rd DAGW RM9 124 A8
EDUL SE22 181 N2
HGDN/ICK UB10 131 P2
HSLW TW3 154 A10
Thompson's Av CMBW SE5 * 159 K6
Thompsons Cl CHESW EN7 61 N5
CHOB/PIR GU24 230 C9
Thompson's La CHOB/PIR GU24 213 J5
Thompson Wy
RKW/CH/CXG WD3 91 K1
Thomson Crs CROY/NA CR0 203 H8
Thomson Rd
KTN/HRWW/WS HA3 114 D1
Thong La GVE DA12 191 J7
Thorburn Sq STHWK SE1 19 N6
STHWK SE1 159 P3
Thorburn Wy WIM/MER SW19 * 201 N1
Thoresby St IS N1 6 F9
Thorkhill Gdns THDIT KT7 198 F8
Thorkhill Rd THDIT KT7 198 G8
Thorley Cl BF/WBF KT14 215 K10
Thorley Gdns WOKS/MYFD GU22 215 K10
Thorley Rd CDW/CHF RM16 147 M10
Thornaby Gdns UED N18 99 P7
Thornash Cl WOKN/KNAP GU21 231 P1
Thornash Rd WOKN/KNAP GU21 231 P2
Thornash Wy WOKN/KNAP GU21 231 P1
Thorn Av BUSH WD23 94 B2
Thorn Bank GUW GU2 267 M2
Thornberry Wy GU GU1 250 C6
Thornbridge Rd IVER SL0 130 F3
Thornbrook EPP CM16 65 N1
Thornbury HARP AL5 20 C2
Thornbury Av ISLW TW7 154 C6
Thornbury Cl HOD EN11 26 G9
STNW/STAM N16 119 M10
Thornbury Gdns BORE WD6 75 P8
Thornbury Rd CLAP SW4 180 F2
ISLW TW7 154 C6
Thornbury Sq HGT N6 118 C6
Thornby Rd CLPT E5 120 B8
Thorncliffe Rd CLAP SW4 180 F2
NWDGN UB2 153 N4
Thorn Cl HAYES BR2 206 D6
NTHLT UB5 133 N5
Thorncombe Rd EDUL SE22 181 M1
Thorn Ct BELMT SM2 * 221 L4
Thorncroft EGH TW20 171 P10
EMPK RM11 125 J4
HHS/BOV HP3 36 C8
Thorncroft Cl COUL/CHIP CR5 241 H5
Thorncroft Rd SUT SM1 221 L1
Thorncroft St VX/NE SW8 158 F6
Thorndales BRW CM14 107 J5
Thorndean St WAND/EARL SW18 179 M5
Thorndene Av TRDG/WHET N20 98 A2
Thorndike SLN SL2 128 F7
Thorndike Av NTHLT UB5 133 L3
Thorndike Cl WBPTN SW10 157 M6
Thorndike Rd IS N1 6 F2
Thorndike St PIM SW1V * 17 J6
Thorndon Ap RBRW/HUT CM13 107 P8
Thorndon Av RBRW/HUT CM13 127 P3
Thorndon Cl STMC/STPC BR5 207 J2
Thorndon Gdns HOR/WEW KT19 220 B1
Thorndon Ga RBRW/HUT CM13 107 N7
Thorndon Rd STMC/STPC BR5 207 J2
Thorndown La BFOR GU20 212 C4
Thorn Dr DTCH/LGLY SL3 130 B8
Thorndyke Cl CRAWE RH10 284 E8
Thorndyke Ct PIN HA5 93 N8
Thorne Cl ASHF TW15 174 D10
CAN/RD E16 141 M8
ERITH DA8 164 D5
ESH/CLAY KT10 218 F4
HHW HP1 35 L8
WAN E11 121 K9
Thorneloe Gdns CROY/NA CR0 223 J2
Thorne Rd VX/NE SW8 158 F6
Thorne's Cl BECK BR3 205 H3
Thorne St BARN SW13 156 B9
Thornet Wood Rd BMLY BR1 206 D3
Thorney Crs BTSEA SW11 * 157 P6
Thorneycroft Cl WOT/HER KT12 197 K6
Thorneycroft Dr PEND EN3 80 F4
Thorney Hedge Rd CHSWK W4 155 N3
Thorney La North IVER SL0 131 J8
Thorney La South WDR/YW UB7 151 J1
Thorney Mill Rd WDR/YW UB7 151 L2
Thorney St WEST SW1P 17 L5
Thornfield Av MLHL NW7 97 H9
Thornfield Pde MLHL NW7 * 97 H8
Thornfield Rd SHB W12 156 E1
Thornford Rd LEW SE13 183 H1
Thorngate Rd MV/WKIL W9 8 F1
Thorngrove Rd PLSTW E13 141 N3
Thornham Gv SRTFD E15 121 J10
Thornham St GNWCH SE10 160 G5
Thornhaugh St STPAN WC1H 11 K2
Thornhill EPP CM16 66 D2
Thornhill Av SURB KT6 199 L9
WOOL/PLUM SE18 163 H6
Thornhill Bridge Whf IS N1 5 N6
Thornhill Cl AMSS HP7 68 F6
Thornhill Crs IS N1 5 P4
Thornhill Gdns BARK IG11 143 H2
LEY E10 120 G7
Thornhill Gv IS N1 6 A4
Thornhill Rd CROY/NA CR0 203 K7
HGDN/ICK UB10 112 B9
IS N1 6 A3
LEY E10 120 G7
NTHWD HA6 92 D5
SURB KT6 199 K9
Thornhill Sq IS N1 5 P4
Thornhill Wy SHPTN TW17 196 B5
Thorn La RAIN RM13 145 L4
Thornlaw Rd WNWD SE27 181 H7
Thornleas Pl EHSLY KT24 252 F2
Thornley Cl TOTM N17 99 P8
Thornley Dr RYLN/HDSTN HA2 114 A7
Thornridge BRW CM14 106 G1
Thornsbeach Rd CAT SE6 183 H4
Thornsett Pl PGE/AN SE20 204 A2
Thornsett Rd PGE/AN SE20 204 A2
WAND/EARL SW18 179 L5
Thornsett Ter PGE/AN SE20 * 204 A2
Thorn's Meadow BH/WHM TN16 245 M9
Thornton Av BRXS/STRHM SW2 180 E5
CHSWK W4 156 B3
CROY/NA CR0 202 G6
WDR/YW UB7 152 A2
Thornton Cl GUW GU2 249 M7
HORL RH6 279 P4
WDR/YW UB7 152 A2
Thornton Crs COUL/CHIP CR5 241 H5
Thornton Dene BECK BR3 204 F2
Thornton Gdns BAL SW12 180 E4
Thornton Gv PIN HA5 93 P7
Thornton Hl WIM/MER SW19 179 H10
Thornton Pl HORL RH6 279 P4
MBLAR W1H 10 A3
Thornton Rd BAL SW12 180 E3
BAR EN5 77 H7
BELV DA17 * 164 C3
BMLY BR1 183 M8
CAR SM5 201 N8
IL IG1 122 E9
MORT/ESHN SW14 156 A10
POTB/CUF EN6 59 M6
THHTH CR7 203 H5
UED N18 100 B4
WAN E11 121 J7
WIM/MER SW19 178 G9
Thornton Rw THHTH CR7 203 H5
Thorntons Farm Av
ROMW/RG RM7 124 D7
Thornton St BRXN/ST SW9 159 H8
HERT/WAT SG14 25 L5
STALW/RED AL3 38 B5
Thornton Wy GLDGN NW11 117 L3
Thorntree Rd CHARL SE7 162 A4
Thornville Gv MTCM CR4 201 N2
Thornville St DEPT SE8 160 F7
Thornwood Cl SWFD E18 101 N10
Thornwood Rd EPP CM16 65 L4
LEW SE13 183 K1
Thorogood Gdns SRTFD E15 121 K10
Thorogood Wy RAIN RM13 144 F3
Thorold Cl SAND/SEL CR2 224 D6
Thorold Rd IL IG1 122 E7
WDGN N22 98 F8
Thoroughfare Names
STNW/STAM N16 * 119 M9
The Thoroughfare
KWD/TDW/WH KT20 238 D10
Thorparch Rd VX/NE SW8 158 E7
Thorpebank Rd SHB W12 136 D10
Thorpe By-Pass EGH TW20 194 E3
Thorpe Cl CROY/NA CR0 225 J7
NKENS W10 8 B5
NKENS W10 137 H8
ORP BR6 207 H9
SYD SE26 * 182 C7
Thorpe Ct TOOT SW17 179 P7
Thorpe Crs OXHEY WD19 93 J1
WALTH E17 100 E10
Thorpedale Gdns
GNTH/NBYPK IG2 122 D2
Thorpedale Rd FSBYPK N4 118 F6
Thorpefield Cl STALE/WH AL4 39 J3
Thorpe Hall Rd WALTH E17 101 H9
Thorpe Lea Rd EGH TW20 172 E10
Thorpe Pk CHERT KT16 * 195 J3
Thorpe Rd BARK IG11 142 G2
CHERT KT16 194 G5
EHAM E6 142 C3
FSTGT E7 121 M8
KUTN/CMB KT2 177 K10
SEVS/STOTM N15 119 M4
STA TW18 172 G8
STAL AL1 38 C7
WALTH E17 101 H10
Thorpes Cl GUW GU2 249 M7
Thorpeside Cl STA TW18 195 H2
Thorpewood Av SYD SE26 182 A5
Thorpland Av HGDN/ICK UB10 112 D8
Thorsden Cl WOKS/MYFD GU22 232 B5
Thorsden Ct WOKS/MYFD GU22 * 232 B4
Thorsden Wy NRWD SE19 * 181 M8
Thorverton Rd CRICK NW2 117 H8
Thoydon Rd BOW E3 140 D4
Thrale Rd STRHM/NOR SW16 180 D8
Thrale St STHWK SE1 12 F10
Thrasher Cl HACK E8 * 7 L5
Thrawl St WCHPL E1 13 M4
Threadneedle St LOTH EC2R 13 H6
Three Arches Pk REDH RH1 * 276 A4
Three Arch Rd REDH RH1 276 B4
Three Bridges Rd CRAWE RH10 283 P7
Three Castles Pth ASC SL5 170 D10
WDSR SL4 171 J1
Three Cherry Trees La
HHNE HP2 36 C2
Three Close La BERK HP4 33 P6
Three Colts La BETH E2 140 A6
Three Colt St POP/IOD E14 * 140 E9
Three Corners BXLYHN DA7 164 C8
HHS/BOV HP3 * 36 B8
Three Forests Wy ABR/ST RM4 84 E3
HLWW/ROY CM19 27 M10
LOU IG10 82 A5
SBW CM21 29 P3
SBW CM21 30 D1
WAB EN9 46 A7
WAB EN9 81 P2
Three Gates GU GU1 250 F9
Three Gates Rd HART DA3 210 F7
Three Horseshoes Rd
HLWW/ROY CM19 46 E3
Three Households CSTG HP8 89 L5
Three Kings Yd MYFR/PKLN W1K 10 E7
Three Meadows Ms
KTN/HRWW/WS HA3 94 E9
Three Mill La BOW E3 141 H5
Three Oak La STHWK SE1 19 L1
Three Oaks Cl HGDN/ICK UB10 112 A8
Three Pears Rd GU GU1 251 H9
Three Valleys Wy BUSH WD23 73 L9
Threshers Pl NTGHL W11 8 A7
NTGHL W11 137 H9
Threshold Wy CHOB/PIR GU24 214 B6
Thriffwood SYD SE26 182 B6
Thrift Farm La BORE WD6 75 P6
Thriftfield HHNE HP2 35 N4
Thrift Gn RBRW/HUT CM13 107 M4
Thrift La RSEV TN14 * 245 H3
Thrifts Md EPP CM16 83 H3
The Thrift RDART DA2 189 H6
Thrift V RGUE GU4 250 G7
Thrigby Rd CHSGTN KT9 219 L3
Throckmorten Rd CAN/RD E16 141 N8
Throgmorton Av OBST EC2N 13 H5
Throgmorton St OBST EC2N 13 H5
Throstle Pl GSTN WD25 * 55 K8
Throwley Cl ABYW SE2 163 M2
Throwley Rd SUT SM1 221 L2
Throwley Wy SUT SM1 221 L1
Thrums WATN WD24 73 J3
Thrupp Cl MTCM CR4 202 C2
Thrupps Av WOT/HER KT12 217 L2
Thrupps La WOT/HER KT12 217 L2
Thrush Av HAT AL10 40 D6
Thrush Gn RKW/CH/CXG WD3 91 M1
RYLN/HDSTN HA2 113 P2
Thrush La POTB/CUF EN6 60 F4
Thrush St WALW SE17 18 E7
Thumbswood WGCE AL7 23 K8
Thumpers HHNE HP2 35 P4
Thundercourt WARE SG12 26 C1
Thunderer Rd DAGW RM9 143 P6
Thundridge Cl WGCE AL7 23 L6
Thurbarn Rd CAT SE6 182 G8
Thurgood Rd HOD EN11 44 F1
Thurland Rd BERM/RHTH SE16 19 N3
BERM/RHTH SE16 159 P2
Thurlby Cl WFD IG8 102 C6
Thurlby Rd ALP/SUD HA0 135 J1
WNWD SE27 181 H7
Thurleigh Av BAL SW12 180 B2
Thurleigh Rd BAL SW12 180 A2
Thurleston Av MRDN SM4 201 H5
Thurlestone Av GDMY/SEVK IG3 123 J9
NFNCH/WDSPK N12 98 A7
Thurlestone Cl SHPTN TW17 * 196 D6
Thurlestone Pde SHPTN TW17 * 196 D6
Thurlestone Rd WNWD SE27 181 H6
Thurloe Cl SKENS SW7 15 N5
Thurloe Gdns ROM RM1 124 F4
Thurloe Pl SKENS SW7 15 N4
Thurloe Place Ms SKENS SW7 * 15 M5
Thurloe Sq SKENS SW7 15 N5
Thurloe St SKENS SW7 15 M5
Thurloe Wk GRAYS RM17 167 M2
Thurlow Cl CHING E4 100 G7
Thurlow Gdns ALP/SUD HA0 * 115 J10
BARK/HLT IG6 102 G7
Thurlow Hl DUL SE21 181 K4
Thurlow Park Rd DUL SE21 181 K5
Thurlow Rd HAMP NW3 117 N10
HNWL W7 154 F1
Thurlow St WALW SE17 19 J8
Thurlow Ter KTTN NW5 118 A10
Thurlow Wk WALW SE17 19 J8
Thurlston Rd RSLP HA4 113 H8
Thurlton Ct WOKN/KNAP GU21 232 B2
Thurnham Wy
KWD/TDW/WH KT20 238 G6
Thurrock Park Wy TIL RM18 168 A6
Thursby Rd WOKN/KNAP GU21 231 M4
Thursland Rd SCUP DA14 185 P9
Thursley Crs CROY/NA CR0 225 J4
Thursley Gdns WIM/MER SW19 178 G5
Thursley Rd ELTH/MOT SE9 184 C6
Thurso Cl HARH RM3 106 A7
Thurso St TOOT SW17 179 N7
Thurstan Rd RYNPK SW20 178 E10
Thurstans HLWW/ROY CM19 46 E6
Thurston Rd DEPT SE8 160 G8
SL SL1 129 J8
STHL UB1 133 N8
Thurtle Rd BETH E2 7 M6
Thwaite Cl ERITH DA8 164 D5
Thyer Cl ORP BR6 226 F1
Thyme Ct RGUE GU4 250 E7
Thyra Gv NFNCH/WDSPK N12 97 L7
Tibbatt's Rd BOW E3 140 G6
Tibbenham Pl CAT SE6 182 G4
Tibberton Sq IS N1 6 E4
Tibbets Cl WIM/MER SW19 178 G4
Tibbet's Ride PUT/ROE SW15 178 G3
Tibbles Cl GSTN WD25 73 M1
Tibbs Hill Rd ABLGY WD5 54 G7
Tiber Cl BOW E3 140 F3
Tiber Gdns IS N1 5 M6
Ticehurst Cl CRAWE RH10 284 F7
STMC/STPC BR5 185 K10
Ticehurst Rd FSTH SE23 182 D5
Tichborne RKW/CH/CXG WD3 90 G6
Tichmarsh HOR/WEW KT19 219 P6
Tickenhall Dr HLWE CM17 47 N2
Tickford Cl ABYW SE2 163 M1
Tidal Basin Rd CAN/RD E16 141 L9
Tidenham Gdns CROY/NA CR0 203 M10
Tideswell Rd CROY/NA CR0 204 F10
PUT/ROE SW15 156 F10
Tideway Cl RCHPK/HAM TW10 176 G7
Tidey St BOW E3 140 F7
Tidford Rd WELL DA16 163 J8
Tidworth Rd BOW E3 140 F6
Tidy's La EPP CM16 65 K5
Tiepigs La WWKM BR4 205 K9
Tierney Rd BRXS/STRHM SW2 180 F4
Tierney Ter BRXS/STRHM SW2 * 180 F4
Tiger La HAYES BR2 205 N4
Tiger Moth Wy HAT AL10 40 A3
Tiger Wy CLPT E5 120 A9
Tigres Cl ED N9 100 B3
Tilbrook Rd BKHTH/KID SE3 161 P9
Tilburstow Hill Rd GDST RH9 260 B10
Tilbury Cl PECK SE15 159 N6
STMC/STPC BR5 207 L2
Tilbury Md HLWS CM18 47 K3
Tilbury Rd EHAM E6 142 C4
LEY E10 121 H5
Tilbury Wk DTCH/LGLY SL3 150 E2
Tildesley Rd PUT/ROE SW15 178 F2
Tilecroft WGCW AL8 22 G2
Tile Farm Rd ORP BR6 206 G10
Tilegate Rd CHONG CM5 48 D5
HLWS CM18 47 J3
Tilehouse Cl BORE WD6 75 L7
Tilehouse La DEN/HRF UB9 111 H3
RKW/CH/CXG WD3 91 H9
Tilehouse Rd RGUE GU4 268 B5
Tilehouse Wy DEN/HRF UB9 111 J5
Tilehurst La RDKG RH5 273 K3
Tilehurst Rd CHEAM SM3 221 H2
WAND/EARL SW18 179 N4
Tilekiln Cl CHESW EN7 61 N5
Tile Kiln Cl HHS/BOV HP3 36 C7
Tile Kiln Crs HHS/BOV HP3 36 C7
Tile Kiln La BXLY DA5 186 E6
DEN/HRF UB9 112 C5
HGT N6 118 C6
HHS/BOV HP3 36 C7
PLMGR N13 99 K6
Tilers Cl REDH RH1 258 D7
Tiler's Wy REIG RH2 275 M4
Tileyard Rd HOLWY N7 5 L3

366 Til - Tro

Tilford Av CROY/NA CR0 225 H4
Tilford Gdns WIM/MER SW19 178 G4
Tilgate Common REDH RH1 259 K9
Tilgate Pde CRAWE RH10 283 P10
Tilgate Pl CRAWE RH10 283 P10
Tilgate Wy CRAWE RH10 283 P10
Tilia Cl SUT SM1 221 J2
Tilia Rd CLPT E5 120 A9
Till Av EYN DA4 209 N7
Tiller Rd POP/IOD E14 160 F2
Tillett Cl WLSDN NW10 135 P1
Tillett Wy BETH E2 7 N9
Tillet Wy BETH E2 7 N9
Tilley La EPSOM KT18 237 P9
Tilley Rd FELT TW13 175 H4
Tillingbourne Gdns FNCH N3 117 J1
Tillingbourne Gn
STMC/STPC BR5 207 K5
Tillingbourne Rd RGUE GU4 268 B6
Tillingbourne Wy FNCH N3 117 J2
Tillingdown Hl CTHM CR3 242 A8
Tillingdown La CTHM CR3 242 A10
Tillingham Ct WAB EN9 63 M9
Tillingham Wy
NFNCH/WDSPK N12 97 K5
Tilling Rd CRICK NW2 116 F5
Tilling Wy WBLY HA9 * 115 J8
Tillman St WCHPL E1 140 A8
Tilloch St IS N1 * 5 N4
Tillotson Cl CRAWE RH10 284 E8
Tillotson Rd ED N9 99 N3
IL IG1 122 D5
KTN/HRWW/WS HA3 94 A8
Tillwicks Rd HLWS CM18 47 J2
Tilmans Md EYN DA4 209 N7
Tilney Gdns IS N1 6 G2
Tilney Rd DAGW RM9 144 A1
NWDGN UB2 153 K3
Tilney St MYFR/PKLN W1K 10 D9
Tilson Cl CMBW SE5 159 M6
Tilson Gdns BRXS/STRHM SW2 180 F3
Tilson Rd TOTM N17 99 P9
Tilston Cl WAN E11 121 L8
Tilstone Av WDSR SL4 148 D4
Tilstone Cl WDSR SL4 148 D3
Tilsworth Rd BEAC HP9 88 B10
Tilsworth Wk STALE/WH AL4 39 H1
Tilt Cl COB KT11 235 M2
Tilthams Corner Rd GODL GU7 267 N9
Tilthams Gn GODL GU7 267 N10
Tilt Meadow COB KT11 235 M2
Tilton St FUL/PGN SW6 14 B10
FUL/PGN SW6 157 H5
Tilt Rd COB KT11 235 L2
Tilt Vw COB KT11 * 235 K1
The Tiltwood ACT W3 135 P9
Tilt Yard Ap ELTH/MOT SE9 184 C2
Timber Cl CHST BR7 206 D2
GT/LBKH KT23 254 B3
WOKS/MYFD GU22 233 J1
Timbercroft HOR/WEW KT19 220 B1
WGCE AL7 23 J2
Timbercroft La
WOOL/PLUM SE18 163 H5
Timberdene Av BARK/HLT IG6 102 F9
Timberham Farm Rd HORL RH6 279 N7
Timber Hl ASHTD KT21 237 K5
Timber Hill Rd CTHM CR3 241 P10
Timberland Cl PECK SE15 * 159 P6
Timberland Rd WCHPL E1 * 140 A8
Timberling Gdns SAND/SEL CR2 223 L6
Timber Mill Wy CLAP SW4 158 E9
Timber Orch HERT/WAT SG14 25 H1
Timber Pond Rd
BERM/RHTH SE16 160 C1
Timberridge RKW/CH/CXG WD3 71 M8
Timberslip Dr WLGTN SM6 222 E5
The Timbers CHEAM SM3 * 221 H3
Timber St FSBYE EC1V * 12 E1
Timbertop Rd BH/WHM TN16 243 P4
Timberwharf Rd
SEVS/STOTM N15 119 P4
Timberwood SLN SL2 109 J8
Time Sq HACK E8 * 119 N10
Times Sq SUT SM1 * 221 L2
Timms Cl BMLY BR1 206 C4
Timothy Cl BXLYHS DA6 185 P1
Timperley Gdns REDH RH1 257 P8
Timplings Rw HHW HP1 35 L4
Timsway STA TW18 173 J8
Tindale Cl SAND/SEL CR2 223 L7
Tindall Cl HARH RM3 105 N10
Tindall Ms HCH RM12 125 K8
Tindal St BRXN/ST SW9 159 J7
Tine Rd CHIG IG7 103 H6
Tinkers La TRING HP23 32 F3
WDSR SL4 148 C8
Tinmans Rw COB KT11 * 235 K4
Tinniswood Cl HBRY N5 119 H10
Tinsey Cl EGH TW20 172 E8
Tinsley Cl CRAWE RH10 284 B4
SNWD SE25 204 A3
Tinsley Gn CRAWE RH10 284 C2
Tinsley La CRAWE RH10 284 B4
Tinsley La North CRAWE RH10 284 C2
Tinsley La South CRAWE RH10 284 B5
Tinsley Rd WCHPL E1 140 B7
Tintagel Cl EW KT17 220 C10
HHNE HP2 35 N1
Tintagel Crs EDUL SE22 159 N10
Tintagel Dr STAN HA7 95 J6
Tintagel Rd ORP BR6 207 M9
Tintagel Wy WOKS/MYFD GU22 232 D2
Tintells La EHSLY KT24 252 C4
Tintern Av CDALE/KGS NW9 115 N1
Tintern Cl PUT/ROE SW15 179 H1
SL SL1 149 H2
WIM/MER SW19 179 M10
Tintern Gdns STHGT/OAK N14 98 F1
Tintern Rd CAR SM5 201 N8
CRAWW RH11 283 K9
WDGN N22 99 K9
Tintern St CLAP SW4 158 F10
Tintern Wy RYLN/HDSTN HA2 114 A6
Tinto Rd CAN/RD E16 141 M7
Tinwell Ms BORE WD6 76 A9
Tinworth St LBTH SE11 17 M7
Tippendell La LCOL/BKTW AL2 55 P1
Tippetts Cl ENC/FH EN2 79 K5
Tipps Cross La BRWN CM15 86 G1
Tips Cross Md BRWN CM15 86 G1
Tipthorpe Rd BTSEA SW11 158 B9
Tipton Dr CROY/NA CR0 223 M1
Tiptree Cl CHING E4 101 H4
EMPK RM11 125 P6
Tiptree Crs CLAY IG5 102 D10
Tiptree Dr ENC/FH EN2 79 L8
Tiptree Rd RSLP HA4 113 J9
Tiree Cl HHS/BOV HP3 36 C8
Tirlemont Rd SAND/SEL CR2 223 K4
Tirrell Rd CROY/NA CR0 203 K6
Tisbury Rd STRHM/NOR SW16 202 F2
Tisdall Pl WALW SE17 19 H6
Titan Ct BTFD TW8 155 L4
Titan Rd GRAYS RM17 167 M4
HHNE HP2 36 A3
Titchborne Rw BAY/PAD W2 9 P6
Titchfield Rd CAR SM5 201 N8
PEND EN3 80 D3
STJWD NW8 3 P7
Titchfield Wk CAR SM5 201 N7
Titchwell Rd WAND/EARL SW18 179 N3
Tite Hl EGH TW20 172 A8
Tite St CHEL SW3 16 A9
Tithe Barn Cl KUTN/CMB KT2 199 L1
STAL AL1 38 B10
Tithe Barn Ct ABLGY WD5 * 54 G5
Tithe Barn Wy NTHLT UB5 133 J4
Tithe Cl MLHL NW7 96 D9
VW GU25 194 A6
WOT/HER KT12 197 J6
YEAD UB4 132 G7
Tithe Ct DTCH/LGLY SL3 150 D3
HDN NW4 * 96 D9
Tithe Farm Av RYLN/HDSTN HA2 113 P8
Tithe Farm Cl RYLN/HDSTN HA2 113 P8
Tithelands HLWW/ROY CM19 46 C4
Tithe La STWL/WRAY TW19 172 D2
Tithepit Shaw La WARL CR6 242 A2
The Tithe CRAWW RH11 283 K4
Tithe Wk MLHL NW7 96 D9
Titian Av BUSH WD23 94 D1
Titlarks Hill Rd ASC SL5 192 G8
Titley Cl CHING E4 100 F6
Titmus Cl UX/CGN UB8 132 D8
Titmus Dr CRAWE RH10 284 A10
Titmuss Av THMD SE28 143 L9
Titmuss St SHB W12 * 156 E1
Titness Pk ASC SL5 * 192 F3
Titsey Hl WARL CR6 243 L10
Titsey Rd OXTED RH8 261 N3
Tiverton Av CLAY IG5 122 D1
Tiverton Cl CROY/NA CR0 203 N7
Tiverton Ct HARP AL5 * 20 D5
Tiverton Gv HARH RM3 105 P6
Tiverton Rd ALP/SUD HA0 135 K4
EDGW HA8 95 L10
HSLW TW3 154 A8
POTB/CUF EN6 59 N8
RSLP HA4 113 H8
SEVS/STOTM N15 119 L4
UED N18 99 M6
WLSDN NW10 136 G3
Tiverton St STHWK SE1 18 E3
Tiverton Wy CHSGTN KT9 219 H2
MLHL NW7 96 G8
Tivoli Gdns WOOL/PLUM SE18 162 B3
Tivoli Rd CEND/HSY/T N8 118 E3
HSLWW TW4 153 M10
WNWD SE27 181 K8
Toad La HSLWW TW4 153 N10
Tobago St POP/IOD E14 160 F1
Tobin Cl HAMP NW3 3 P3
HOR/WEW KT19 219 N7
Toby La WCHPL E1 140 D6
Toby Wy SURB KT6 199 N9
Tockley Rd SL SL1 128 A5
Toddbrook HLWW/ROY CM19 46 E2
Todd Cl RAIN RM13 145 L6
Todds Cl HORL RH6 279 P2
Toft Av GRAYS RM17 168 A3
Toftwood Cl CRAWE RH10 284 D8
Tokenhouse Yd LOTH EC2R 12 G5
Tokyngton Av WBLY HA9 135 M1
Toland Sq PUT/ROE SW15 178 D1
Tolcarne Dr PIN HA5 93 H10
Toley Av KTN/HRWW/WS HA3 115 K5
Tolhurst Dr NKENS W10 2 B9
Toll DART DA1 166 B10
Tollbridge Cl NKENS W10 8 C1
NKENS W10 137 H6
Tolldene Cl WOKN/KNAP GU21 231 K3
Tollers La COUL/CHIP CR5 240 G5
Tollesbury Gdns BARK/HLT IG6 122 G1
Tollet St WCHPL E1 140 C6
Tollgate GU GU1 250 G9
Tollgate Av REDH RH1 276 A5
Tollgate Cl RKW/CH/CXG WD3 71 J8
Tollgate Dr DUL SE21 181 M5
YEAD UB4 133 L9
Tollgate Gdns KIL/WHAMP NW6 2 G7
Tollgate Rd BRKMPK AL9 58 D1
CHES/WCR EN8 80 C1
DORK RH4 272 G5
EHAM E6 142 B7
RDART DA2 188 C3
STALE/WH AL4 40 B10
Tollhouse La WLGTN SM6 222 D5
Tollhouse Wy ARCH N19 118 D7
Tollington Pk FSBYPK N4 118 G7
Tollington Pl FSBYPK N4 118 G7
Tollington Rd HOLWY N7 118 G9
Tollington Wy HOLWY N7 118 F8
Tollpit End HHW HP1 35 K3
Tolmers Av POTB/CUF EN6 60 F4
Tolmers Gdns POTB/CUF EN6 60 F5
Tolmers Rd POTB/CUF EN6 60 F3
Tolmer's Sq CAMTN NW1 11 H1
Tolpits Cl WATW WD18 72 G9
Tolpits La WATW WD18 92 E1
Tolpuddle Av PLSTW E13 141 P3
Tolpuddle St IS N1 6 A7
Tolsford Rd HACK E8 120 A10
Tolson Rd ISLW TW7 154 F9
Tolvaddon WOKN/KNAP GU21 231 M3
Tolverne Rd RYNPK SW20 200 F1
Tolworth Broadway SURB KT6 199 M8
Tolworth Cl SURB KT6 199 N8
Tolworth Gdns CHDH RM6 123 N3
Tolworth Park Rd SURB KT6 199 L9
Tolworth Ri North BRYLDS KT5 199 P7
Tolworth Ri North (Kingston
By-Pass) BRYLDS KT5 199 P8
Tolworth Ri South BRYLDS KT5 199 P8
NWMAL KT3 200 A7
Tolworth Rd SURB KT6 199 K9
Tolworth U/P (Kingston
By-Pass) SURB KT6 199 M10
Tom Cribb Rd THMD SE28 162 G2
Tom Groves Cl SRTFD E15 121 J10
Tom Hood Cl SRTFD E15 121 J10
Tom Jenkinson Rd CAN/RD E16 141 M10
Tomkins Cl BORE WD6 75 K5
Tomkyns La UPMR RM14 126 C1
Tomlin Cl HOR/WEW KT19 220 A7
Tomlin Rd SLN SL2 128 E6
Tomlin's Gv BOW E3 140 F5
Tomlinson Cl BETH E2 7 M10
CHSWK W4 155 N4
Tomlins Orch BARK IG11 142 F3
Tomlin's Ter POP/IOD E14 140 D8
Tom Mann Cl BARK IG11 143 H3
Tom Nolan Cl SRTFD E15 141 K4
Tompion St FSBYE EC1V 6 C10
Toms Cft HHNE HP2 35 P7
Toms Fld HAT AL10 40 B5
Tom's La KGLGY WD4 54 E4
Tom Smith Cl GNWCH SE10 161 K5
Tomswood Hl BARK/HLT IG6 102 E8
Tomswood Rd CHIG IG7 102 D7
Tonbridge By-Pass
BGR/WK TN15 265 M9
Tonbridge Cl BNSTD SM7 222 A10
Tonbridge Crs
KTN/HRWW/WS HA3 115 K2
Tonbridge Rd E/WMO/HCT KT8 197 M4
HARH RM3 105 L8
SEV TN13 265 K3
Tonbridge St STPAN WC1H 5 L10
Tonfield Rd CHEAM SM3 201 J8
Tonge Cl BECK BR3 204 F5
Tonsley Hl WAND/EARL SW18 179 L1
Tonsley Pl WAND/EARL SW18 179 L1
Tonsley Rd WAND/EARL SW18 179 L1
Tonsley St WAND/EARL SW18 179 L1
Tonstall Rd HOR/WEW KT19 220 A6
MTCM CR4 202 B2
Tooke Cl PIN HA5 93 M9
Tookey Cl KTN/HRWW/WS HA3 115 L5
Took's Ct FLST/FETLN EC4A 12 A5
Tooley St GVW DA11 190 A3
STHWK SE1 13 H9
Toorack Rd KTN/HRWW/WS HA3 94 C10
Toot Hill Rd CHONG CM5 66 G6
Tooting Bec Gdns
STRHM/NOR SW16 180 E7
Tooting Bec Rd TOOT SW17 180 B6
Tooting Gv TOOT SW17 179 P8
Tooting High St TOOT SW17 179 P9
Tootswood Rd HAYES BR2 205 K5
Tooveys Mill Cl KGLGY WD4 54 B5
Topaz Cl SL SL1 128 G10
Topcliffe Dr ORP BR6 226 G1
Top Dartford Rd SWLY BR8 187 H9
Topham Sq TOTM N17 99 K9
Topham St CLKNW EC1R * 12 A1
Top House Ri CHING E4 101 H1
Topiary Sq RCH/KEW TW9 155 L9
The Topiary ASHTD KT21 237 K6
Topland Rd CFSP/GDCR SL9 90 A8
Toplands Av SOCK/AV RM15 146 A10
Topley St ELTH/MOT SE9 161 P10
Topmast Point POP/IOD E14 * 160 F1
Top Pk BECK BR3 205 K5
CFSP/GDCR SL9 109 P4
Topping La UX/CGN UB8 131 N5
Topsfield Cl CEND/HSY/T N8 118 E3
Topsfield Pde CEND/HSY/T N8 * 118 F3
Topsfield Rd CEND/HSY/T N8 118 F3
Topsham Rd TOOT SW17 180 A6
Topstreet Wy HARP AL5 20 B3
Torbay Rd KIL/WHAMP NW6 2 C4
RYLN/HDSTN HA2 113 M7
Torbay St CAMTN NW1 4 F3
Torbitt Wy GNTH/NBYPK IG2 123 J3
Torbridge Cl EDGW HA8 95 K8
Torcross Dr FSTH SE23 182 B5
Torcross Rd RSLP HA4 113 J8
Tor Gdns KENS W8 14 E1
Tor Gv THMD SE28 143 H10
Torin Ct EGH TW20 171 P8
Torland Dr LHD/OX KT22 218 C10
Tor La WEY KT13 216 E7
Tormead Cl SUT SM1 221 K3
Tormead Rd GU GU1 250 C10
Tormount Rd WOOL/PLUM SE18 163 H5
Toronto Av MNPK E12 122 C9
Toronto Dr HORL RH6 281 H5
Toronto Rd IL IG1 122 E6
TIL RM18 168 D8
Torquay Gdns REDBR IG4 122 A2
Torquay Sp SLN SL2 128 G5
Torquay St BAY/PAD W2 8 G4
Torrance Cl EMPK RM11 125 K6
Torrens Rd BRXS/STRHM SW2 180 G1
SRTFD E15 141 L1
Torrens Sq SRTFD E15 141 L1
Torrens St FSBYE EC1V 6 C8
Torrens Wk GVE DA12 191 H8
Torres Sq POP/IOD E14 160 F4
Torrey Dr BRXN/ST SW9 159 H8
Torriano Av KTTN NW5 118 E10
Torriano Cottages KTTN NW5 118 E10
Torriano Ms KTTN NW5 118 D10
Torridge Gdns PECK SE15 160 B10
Torridge Rd DTCH/LGLY SL3 150 E5
THHTH CR7 203 J5
Torridon Cl WOKN/KNAP GU21 231 N3
Torridon Rd CAT SE6 183 J4
Torrington Av
NFNCH/WDSPK N12 97 N6
Torrington Cl ESH/CLAY KT10 218 D3
Torrington Dr LOU IG10 82 F8
POTB/CUF EN6 59 N8
RYLN/HDSTN HA2 114 A9
Torrington Gdns
FBAR/BDGN N11 98 D7
GFD/PVL UB6 135 H3
LOU IG10 82 F8
Torrington Gv
NFNCH/WDSPK N12 97 P6
Torrington Pk
NFNCH/WDSPK N12 97 N5
Torrington Pl FITZ W1T 11 H3
WAP E1W 13 P10
Torrington Rd BCTR RM8 124 A6
BERK HP4 33 N5
ESH/CLAY KT10 218 D3
GFD/PVL UB6 135 H3
RSLP HA4 113 H8
Torrington Sq CROY/NA CR0 * 203 L7
STPAN WC1H 11 K2
Torrington Wy MRDN SM4 201 K7
Tor Rd WELL DA16 163 M7
Torr Rd PGE/AN SE20 182 C10
Tortoiseshell Wy BERK HP4 33 L3
Torver Rd HRW HA1 114 D2
Torver Wy ORP BR6 206 G10
Torwood Cl BERK HP4 33 L5
Torwood La CTHM CR3 241 N6
Torwood Rd PUT/ROE SW15 178 D1
Torworth Rd BORE WD6 75 M5
Tothill St STJSPK SW1H 17 J2
Totnes Rd WELL DA16 163 L6
Totnes Vls FBAR/BDGN N11 * 98 D6
Totnes Wk EFNCH N2 117 N2
Tottan Ter WCHPL E1 * 140 C8
Tottenhall Rd PLMGR N13 99 H7
Tottenham Court Rd FITZ W1T 11 H2
Tottenham Gn East
SEVS/STOTM N15 119 N2
Tottenham Gn East South Side
SEVS/STOTM N15 119 N2
Tottenham La CEND/HSY/T N8 118 F4
Tottenham Ms FITZ W1T * 11 H3
Tottenham Rd IS N1 7 K2
Tottenham St FITZ W1T 11 H4
Totterdown St TOOT SW17 180 A7
Totteridge Common
TRDG/WHET N20 96 E3
Totteridge La TRDG/WHET N20 97 K3
Totteridge Rd PEND EN3 80 C3
Totteridge Village
TRDG/WHET N20 97 J2
Totternhoe Cl
KTN/HRWW/WS HA3 115 H3
Totton Rd THHTH CR7 203 H3
Toulmin Dr STALW/RED AL3 38 B2
Toulmin St STHWK SE1 18 E2
Toulon St CMBW SE5 159 K6
Tournay Rd FUL/PGN SW6 157 J6
Toussaint Wk BERM/RHTH SE16 19 P3
BERM/RHTH SE16 159 P2
Tovey Av HOD EN11 44 F1
Tovey Cl LCOL/BKTW AL2 57 J2
WAB EN9 45 K9
Tovil Cl PGE/AN SE20 203 P2
Towcester Rd BOW E3 140 G6
Tower Br WAP E1W 13 L9
Tower Bridge Ap TWRH EC3N 13 L9
Tower Bridge Ms ALP/SUD HA0 114 E9
Tower Bridge Rd STHWK SE1 19 K3
Tower Buildings WAP E1W * 140 A10
Tower Cl BERK HP4 33 M6
CHIG IG7 102 E7
EPP CM16 48 E10
GVE DA12 191 H8
HAMP NW3 117 N10
ORP BR6 207 J9
PGE/AN SE20 182 A10
WOKN/KNAP GU21 232 A3
Tower Ct BRW CM14 106 G3
LSQ/SEVD WC2H * 11 L6
Tower Cft EYN DA4 209 M9
Tower Gdns ESH/CLAY KT10 218 G4
Tower Gardens Rd TOTM N17 99 K9
Towergate Cl UX/CGN UB8 111 P10
Tower Gv WEY KT13 196 F9
Tower Hamlets Rd FSTGT E7 121 L9
WALTH E17 120 F1
Tower Hl BRW CM14 107 H3
DORK RH4 272 G4
KGLGY WD4 53 H5
Towerhill SHGR GU5 270 D6
Tower Hl TWRH EC3N 13 L8
Tower Hill La STALE/WH AL4 21 L7
Tower Hill Ri SHGR GU5 270 D6
Tower Hill Rd DORK RH4 272 G4
Tower Hill Ter MON EC3R 13 K8
Tower La WBLY HA9 * 115 J8
Tower Ms CLPT E5 120 D10
Tower Mill Rd CMBW SE5 * 159 M6
Tower Park Rd DART DA1 186 G1
Tower Pl MON EC3R 13 K8
WARL CR6 242 F1
Tower Ri RCH/KEW TW9 155 K9
Tower Rd AMSS HP7 68 F9
BELV DA17 164 D3
BXLYHN DA7 164 C10
DART DA1 187 K3
EPP CM16 65 H6
KWD/TDW/WH KT20 238 F9
ORP BR6 207 J9
TWK TW1 176 E6
WARE SG12 26 D1
WLSDN NW10 136 D2
Tower Royal MANHO EC4N * 12 F7
Towers Av HGDN/ICK UB10 132 D5
Towers Ct HGDN/ICK UB10 * 132 D5
Towers Pl RCH/KEW TW9 177 K1
Towers Rd GRAYS RM17 167 P4
HHNE HP2 35 P5
PIN HA5 93 M9
STHL UB1 133 P6
The Towers PUR/KEN CR8 241 K1
Tower St HERT/WAT SG14 25 K3
LSQ/SEVD WC2H 11 L6
Towers Wk WEY KT13 216 C3
Towers Wd EYN DA4 210 C1
Tower Ter WDGN N22 98 G10
Tower Vw CROY/NA CR0 204 D8
Tower Whf GVW DA11 * 167 N10
Towfield Rd FELT TW13 175 N5
Town Barn Rd CRAWW RH11 283 M7
Town Bridge Ct CSHM HP5 50 G8
Towncourt Crs STMC/STPC BR5 206 F5
Towncourt La STMC/STPC BR5 206 G6
Towncourt Pth FSBYPK N4 119 K6
Townend CTHM CR3 241 M8
Town End Cl CTHM CR3 241 M8
Town End Pde KUT/HW KT1 * 199 J3
Towney Md NTHLT UB5 133 N4
Town Farm Wy
STWL/WRAY TW19 * 173 N3
Townfield CSHM HP5 50 G8
RKW/CH/CXG WD3 91 M1
Townfield Cnr GVE DA12 190 F4
Town Field La CSTG HP8 89 P4
Townfield Rd DORK RH4 272 F3
HYS/HAR UB3 132 G10
Town Flds HAT AL10 40 D3
Townfield Sq HYS/HAR UB3 132 G10
Town Field Wy ISLW TW7 154 F8
Towngate COB KT11 235 M1
Town Hall Approach Rd
SEVS/STOTM N15 119 N2
Town Hall Ar BERK HP4 * 33 P5
Townhall Av CHSWK W4 156 A4
Town Hall Pde
BRXS/STRHM SW2 * 158 G10
Town Hall Rd BTSEA SW11 158 A9
Townholm Crs HNWL W7 154 E2
Town La STWL/WRAY TW19 173 N3
Townley Ct SRTFD E15 141 L1
Townley Rd BXLYHS DA6 186 A1
EDUL SE22 181 M1
Townley St WALW SE17 18 G7
Town Md CRAWW RH11 283 N6
REDH RH1 259 L9
Town Meadow BTFD TW8 155 J6
Townmead Rd FUL/PGN SW6 157 M8
RCH/KEW TW9 155 N8
Town Mead Rd WAB EN9 63 H10
Town Pier Sq GVW DA11 190 E2
Town Quay BARK IG11 142 E3
STA TW18 * 195 M3
Town Rd ED N9 100 A3
Townsend HHNE HP2 35 N4
Townsend Av STAL AL1 38 D5
STHGT/OAK N14 98 E5
Townsend Dr STALW/RED AL3 38 C3
Townsend La CDALE/KGS NW9 116 A5
WOKS/MYFD GU22 232 E7
Townsend Ms WAND/EARL SW18 179 M5
Townsend Rd ASHF TW15 173 P8
CSHM HP5 50 G6
SEVS/STOTM N15 119 N3
STHL UB1 133 M10
STJWD NW8 3 P7
WOOL/PLUM SE18 162 E2
Townsend St STHWK SE1 19 J5
Townsend Wy NTHWD HA6 92 G8
Townsend Yd HGT N6 118 B6
Townshend Cl SCUP DA14 185 L9
Townshend Est STJWD NW8 3 N7
Townshend Rd CHST BR7 184 E8
RCH/KEW TW9 155 L10
STJWD NW8 3 N6
Townshend St HERT/BAY SG13 25 M5
Townshend Ter RCH/KEW TW9 155 L10
Townshott Cl GT/LBKH KT23 253 P2
Townson Av NTHLT UB5 133 J4
Townson Wy NTHLT UB5 133 H4
Town Square Crs RDART DA2 188 E3
Town Tree Rd ASHF TW15 174 B8
Town Whf ISLW TW7 * 154 G9
Towpath SHPTN TW17 196 A8
WOT/HER KT12 * 197 J4
Towpath Rd UED N18 100 C7
Towpath Wy CROY/NA CR0 203 N6
Towton Rd WNWD SE27 181 K5
Toynbec Cl CHST BR7 184 E7
Toynbee Rd RYNPK SW20 201 H1
Toynbee St WCHPL E1 13 L4
Toyne Wy HGT N6 118 A4
Toy's Hl BH/WHM TN16 263 M7
The Tracery BNSTD SM7 239 L1
Tracey Av CRICK NW2 * 116 F10
Tracious Cl WOKN/KNAP GU21 231 N2
Tracy Av DTCH/LGLY SL3 150 C5
Tracyes Rd HLWS CM18 47 L3
Trade Cl PLMGR N13 99 H5
Trader Rd EHAM E6 142 E8
Tradescant Rd VX/NE SW8 158 F6
Trading Estate Rd
WLSDN NW10 * 135 P6
Trafalgar Av BROX EN10 44 E7
PECK SE15 19 M8
TOTM N17 99 M7
WPK KT4 200 G8
Trafalgar Ct COB KT11 217 H9
Trafalgar Dr WOT/HER KT12 197 J10
Trafalgar Gdns WCHPL E1 140 C7
Trafalgar Gv GNWCH SE10 161 J5
Trafalgar Ms HOM E9 * 140 E1
Trafalgar Pl UED N18 99 P6
WAN E11 121 M2
Trafalgar Rd DART DA1 187 M5
GNWCH SE10 161 K4
GVW DA11 190 D3
RAIN RM13 144 G4
WHTN TW2 176 C5
WIM/MER SW19 179 L10
Trafalgar Sq STJS SW1Y * 11 K9
Trafalgar St WALW SE17 18 G7
Trafalgar Wy CROY/NA CR0 202 G9
POP/IOD E14 141 H10
Trafford Cl BARK/HLT IG6 103 J7
RAD WD7 57 K8
SRTFD E15 120 G10
Trafford Rd THHTH CR7 202 G5
Trahorn Cl WCHPL E1 13 P2
Tramway Av ED N9 100 A1
SRTFD E15 141 J2
Tramway Cl PGE/AN SE20 204 B1
Tramway Pth MTCM CR4 201 P4
Tranby Ms HOM E9 120 C10
Tranley Ms HAMP NW3 * 117 P9
Tranmere Rd ED N9 99 N1
WAND/EARL SW18 179 M5
WHTN TW2 176 A3
Tranquil Dl BRKHM/BTCW RH3 256 C8
Tranquil Pas BKHTH/KID SE3 * 161 L8
Tranquil Ri ERITH DA8 164 F4
Tranquil V BKHTH/KID SE3 161 L8
Transept St CAMTN NW1 9 N4
Transmere Rd STMC/STPC BR5 206 F6
Transom Cl BERM/RHTH SE16 160 D3
Transom Sq POP/IOD E14 160 G4
Transport Av BTFD TW8 154 G5
Tranton Rd BERM/RHTH SE16 160 A2
Trapp's Ct CSHM HP5 51 H9
Trapp's La CSHM HP5 51 H9
Trap's Hl LOU IG10 82 C8
Traps La NWMAL KT3 200 B2
Trapstyle Rd WARE SG12 25 P1
Trasher Md DORK RH4 273 H5
Travellers Cl BRKMPK AL9 40 F9
Travellers La HAT AL10 40 D6
Travellers Site CHING E4 * 100 E8
Travellers Wy HEST TW5 153 K8
Travers Cl WALTH E17 100 C9
Travers Rd HOLWY N7 119 H8
Travic Rd SLN SL2 128 E5
Travis Ct SLN SL2 128 G5
Treacher's Cl CSHM HP5 50 G7
Treacy Cl BUSH WD23 94 B3
Treadgold St NTGHL W11 136 G9
Treadway St BETH E2 140 A4
Treadwell Rd EPSOM KT18 238 C1
Treaty Centre HSLW TW3 * 154 A9
Treaty St IS N1 5 N6
Trebble Rd SWCM DA10 189 K2
Trebeck St MYFR/PICC W1J 10 E9
Trebellan Dr HHNE HP2 36 A5
Trebovir Rd ECT SW5 14 F7
Treby St BOW E3 140 E6
Trecastle Wy HOLWY N7 118 E9
Tredegar Rd BOW E3 140 E4
FBAR/BDGN N11 98 E8
RDART DA2 187 H6
Tredegar Sq BOW E3 140 E5
Trederwen Rd HACK E8 7 P5
Tredown Rd SYD SE26 182 B8
Tredwell Cl BRXS/STRHM SW2 180 G5
HAYES BR2 206 A4
Tredwell Rd WNWD SE27 181 J7
Treebourne Rd BH/WHM TN16 243 P4
Treebys Av RGUE GU4 250 A4
Tree Cl ABR/ST RM4 83 L7
RCHPK/HAM TW10 177 J4
Treelands RDKG RH5 273 H5
Treen Av BARN SW13 156 C9
Tree Rd CAN/RD E16 141 P8
Treeside Cl WDR/YW UB7 151 N3
Tree Top Ms DAGE RM10 144 E1
Treetops BGR/WK TN15 247 P3
Tree Tops BRWN CM15 107 J2
CTHM CR3 241 P4
Treetops GVW DA11 190 E8
Treetops Cl ABYW SE2 163 P4
NTHWD HA6 92 E6
Treetops Vw LOU IG10 82 A10
Tree View Cl NRWD SE19 203 M1
Tree View Ct REIG RH2 * 257 N10
Treewall Gdns BMLY BR1 183 N7
Treeway REIG RH2 257 L7
Trefgarne Rd DAGE RM10 124 B7
Trefoil Rd WAND/EARL SW18 179 M1
Trefusis Wk WAT WD17 72 F5
Tregaron Av CEND/HSY/T N8 118 F5
Tregaron Gdns NWMAL KT3 200 B4
Tregarthen Pl LHD/OX KT22 237 H7
Tregarth Pl WOKN/KNAP GU21 231 L3
Tregarvon Rd BTSEA SW11 158 B10
Tregelles Rd HOD EN11 44 F1
Tregenna Av RYLN/HDSTN HA2 113 P9
Tregenna Cl STHGT/OAK N14 78 D9
Tregony Rd ORP BR6 227 J1
Trego Rd HOM E9 140 F2
Tregothnan Rd BRXN/ST SW9 158 F9
Tregunter Rd WBPTN SW10 15 J9
Trehaven Pde REIG RH2 275 L3
Trehearn Rd BARK/HLT IG6 102 G8
Treherne Ct BRXN/ST SW9 * 159 J7
Trehern Rd MORT/ESHN SW14 156 A9
Trehurst St CLPT E5 120 D10
Trelawn Cl CHERT KT16 214 F4
Trelawney Av DTCH/LGLY SL3 150 C3
Trelawney Est HOM E9 * 140 B1
Trelawney Gv WEY KT13 216 B3
Trelawney Rd BARK/HLT IG6 102 G8
Trelawn Rd BRXS/STRHM SW2 181 H1
LEY E10 121 H8
Trelawny Cl WALTH E17 120 G2
Trellis Sq BOW E3 140 E5
Treloar Gdns NRWD SE19 181 L9
Trelwney Est HOM E9 * 140 B1
Tremadoc Rd CLAP SW4 158 E10
Tremaine Cl BROCKY SE4 160 F8
Tremaine Gv HHNE HP2 35 P2
Tremaine Rd PGE/AN SE20 204 A2
Trematon Pl TEDD TW11 177 H10
Tremlett Gv ARCH N19 118 D8
Tremlett Ms ARCH N19 * 118 D8
Trenance WOKN/KNAP GU21 231 M3
Trenance Gdns GDMY/SEVK IG3 123 K8
Trenchard Av RSLP HA4 113 J10
Trenchard Cl CDALE/KGS NW9 96 B9
STAN HA7 94 G7
WOT/HER KT12 217 K2
Trenchard St GNWCH SE10 161 J4
Trenches La DTCH/LGLY SL3 130 D10
Trenear Cl ORP BR6 227 K1
Trenham Dr WARL CR6 242 B2
Trenholme Rd PGE/AN SE20 182 A10
Trenholme Ter PGE/AN SE20 182 A10
Trenmar Gdns WLSDN NW10 136 E5
Trent TIL RM18 169 M3
Trent Av EA W5 155 H2
UPMR RM14 126 C4
Trentbridge Cl BARK/HLT IG6 103 J7
Trent Cl CRAWW RH11 283 J9
RAD WD7 57 K8
Trent Ct WAN E11 121 M3
Trent Gdns STHGT/OAK N14 78 C10
Trentham Crs WOKS/MYFD GU22 232 D7
Trentham Dr STMC/STPC BR5 207 K4
Trentham Rd REDH RH1 276 A2
Trentham St WAND/EARL SW18 179 K4
Trent Pk EBAR EN4 * 78 D6
Trent Rd BKHH IG9 101 N2
BRXS/STRHM SW2 180 G1
DTCH/LGLY SL3 150 E5
Trent Wy WPK KT4 200 F10
YEAD UB4 132 F5
Trentwood Side ENC/FH EN2 78 G7
Treport St WAND/EARL SW18 179 L3
Tresco Cl BMLY BR1 183 K9
Trescoe Gdns CRW RM5 104 D6
RYLN/HDSTN HA2 113 M5
Tresco Gdns GDMY/SEVK IG3 123 J7
Tresco Rd BERK HP4 33 L4
PECK SE15 160 A10
Tresham Crs STJWD NW8 9 N1
Tresham Rd BARK IG11 143 J2
Tresilian Av WCHMH N21 78 G9
Tresillian Wy WOKN/KNAP GU21 231 N3
Tressel Cl IS N1 6 D4
Tressillian Crs BROCKY SE4 160 F9
Tressillian Rd BROCKY SE4 160 F9
Tresta Wk WOKN/KNAP GU21 231 M2
Trestis Cl YEAD UB4 133 L6
Treswell Rd DAGW RM9 143 P3
Tretawn Gdns MLHL NW7 96 B5
Tretawn Pk MLHL NW7 96 B5
Trevalga Wy HHNE HP2 35 N1
Trevanion Rd WKENS W14 14 B7
WKENS W14 * 157 H4
Trevanne Plat CRAWE RH10 284 E6
Treve Av HRW HA1 114 B5
Trevellance Wy GSTN WD25 55 K9
Trevelyan Av MNPK E12 122 C10
Trevelyan Cl DART DA1 165 N10
Trevelyan Crs
KTN/HRWW/WS HA3 115 J5
Trevelyan Gdns WLSDN NW10 * 136 F3
Trevelyan Pl STAL AL1 38 B8
Trevelyan Rd SRTFD E15 121 L9
TOOT SW17 180 A9
Trevelyan Wy BERK HP4 33 N3
Trevera Ct CHES/WCR EN8 * 62 D9
HOD EN11 * 44 F2
Trevereux Hl OXTED RH8 262 D8
Treveris St STHWK SE1 12 D10
Treverton St NKENS W10 136 G6
Treves Cl WCHMH N21 78 G9
Treville St PUT/ROE SW15 178 E3
Treviso Rd FSTH SE23 182 C5
Trevithick Cl EBED/NFELT TW14 174 G4
Trevithick Dr DART DA1 165 N10
Trevithick St DEPT SE8 160 F5
Trevone Gdns PIN HA5 113 M4
Trevor Cl EBAR EN4 77 N10
HAYES BR2 205 M7
ISLW TW7 176 E
KTN/HRWW/WS HA3 94 E8
NTHLT UB5 133 K4
Trevor Crs RSLP HA4 112 G9
Trevor Gdns EDGW HA8 96 A9
Trevor Pl SKENS SW7 15 P2
Trevor Rd EDGW HA8 96 A9
HYS/HAR UB3 152 F1
WFD IG8 101 M8
WIM/MER SW19 179 H10
Trevor Sq SKENS SW7 15 P2
Trevor St SKENS SW7 15 P2
Trevose Av BF/WBF KT14 215 J10
Trevose Rd WALTH E17 101 J9
Trevose Wy OXHEY WD19 93 K4
Trewarden Av IVER SL0 130 G4
Trewenna Dr CHSGTN KT9 219 J2
POTB/CUF EN6 59 N8
Trewince Rd RYNPK SW20 200 F1
Trewint St WAND/EARL SW18 179 M5
Trewsbury Rd SYD SE26 182 C8
Treyford Cl CRAWW RH11 283 J7
Triandra Wy YEAD UB4 133 L7
Triangle Pas EBAR EN4 * 77 M8
Triangle Pl CLAP SW4 158 E10
Triangle Rd HACK E8 140 A3
The Triangle BFN/LL DA15 * 185 K3
HACK E8 140 A3
KUT/HW KT1 199 P2
WOKN/KNAP GU21 231 P4
Triangle Wy ACT W3 155 M2
Trident Av HAT AL10 * 40 B3
Trident Rd GSTN WD25 54 G10
Trident St BERM/RHTH SE16 160 C3
Trident Wy NWDGN UB2 153 J2
Trigg's Cl WOKS/MYFD GU22 232 A5
Trigg's La WOKN/KNAP GU21 231 P4
Trig La BLKFR EC4V 12 E7
Trigon Rd VX/NE SW8 158 G6
Trilby Rd FSTH SE23 182 C5
Trim St NWCR SE14 160 E5
Trinder Rd ARCH N19 118 F6
BAR EN5 76 F9
Trindles Rd REDH RH1 276 G2
Tring Av ACT W3 155 L1
EA W5 135 L10
STHL UB1 133 N8
WBLY HA9 135 M1
Tring Cl GNTH/NBYPK IG2 122 G3
HARH RM3 105 N5
Tring Gdns HARH RM3 105 M5
Tringham Cl CHERT KT16 214 E2
WOKN/KNAP GU21 231 H4
Tring Rd BERK HP4 33 H2
Trinidad Gdns DAGE RM10 144 E2
Trinidad St POP/IOD E14 140 E9
Trinity Av EFNCH N2 117 N1
EN EN1 79 N10
Trinity Buoy Whf POP/IOD E14 * 141 J7
Trinity Church Rd BARN SW13 156 E5
Trinity Church Sq STHWK SE1 18 F3
Trinity Churchyard GU GU1 * 268 A2
Trinity Cl CLAP SW4 * 158 D10
CRAWE RH10 284 D5
HACK E8 7 M1
HAYES BR2 206 B8
HSLWW TW4 153 M10
LEW SE13 161 J10
NTHWD HA6 92 F7
SAND/SEL CR2 223 M5
STWL/WRAY TW19 173 M2
WAN E11 121 K7
Trinity Ct ELTH/MOT SE9 184 E2
RKW/CH/CXG WD3 * 91 P3
Trinity Crs ASC SL5 192 F5
TOOT SW17 180 A5
Trinity Dr UX/CGN UB8 132 D8
Trinity Est DEPT SE8 160 E4
Trinity Gdns BRXN/ST SW9 158 G10
CAN/RD E16 141 L7
DART DA1 187 L2
Trinity Gn WCHPL E1 * 140 B7
Trinity Gv GNWCH SE10 161 H7
HERT/WAT SG14 25 K4
Trinity Hall Cl WATN WD24 73 K6
Trinity La CHES/WCR EN8 62 D8
Trinity Ms HHNE HP2 36 E7
PGE/AN SE20 204 B1
Trinity Pde HSLW TW3 * 154 A9
Trinity Pk CHING E4 * 100 E7
Trinity Pl BXLYHS DA6 164 A10
TWRH EC3N 13 L7
WDSR SL4 * 149 H8
Trinity Ri BRXS/STRHM SW2 181 J3
Trinity Rd BARK/HLT IG6 122 F1
EFNCH N2 117 N1
GVE DA12 190 F3
HERT/BAY SG13 26 B8
RCH/KEW TW9 * 155 L9
STHL UB1 133 M10
WAND/EARL SW18 179 N2
WARE SG12 26 D1
WDGN N22 98 F8
WIM/MER SW19 179 K9
WOKN/KNAP GU21 230 G4
Trinity Sq TWRH EC3N 13 K8
Trinity St CAN/RD E16 141 L7
ENC/FH EN2 79 K6
STHWK SE1 18 F2
Trinity Wk HERT/BAY SG13 26 B8
Trinity Wy ACT W3 136 B9
CHING E4 100 E7
Trio Pl STHWK SE1 18 F2
Tripton Rd HLWS CM18 47 H2
Tristan Ldg BUSH WD23 * 73 M8
Tristan Sq BKHTH/KID SE3 161 K9
Tristram Cl WALTH E17 121 J1
Tristram Dr ED N9 99 N4
Tristram Rd BMLY BR1 183 L7
Trist Wy CRAWW RH11 283 K5
Triton Sq CAMTN NW1 10 G1
Triton Wy HHNE HP2 36 A4
Tritton Av CROY/NA CR0 222 F1
Tritton Rd DUL SE21 181 L6
Trittons KWD/TDW/WH KT20 238 F7
Triumph Cl CDW/CHF RM16 167 H3
HYS/HAR UB3 152 D7
Triumph Rd EHAM E6 142 C8
Trivett Cl RDART DA2 188 F1
Trodd's La RGUE GU4 269 J1
Trojan Wy CROY/NA CR0 202 G10
Trolling Down Hl RDART DA2 188 A5
Troon Cl BERM/RHTH SE16 160 A4
CRAWW RH11 282 G8
THMD SE28 143 N8
Troon St WCHPL E1 140 D8
Troopers Dr HARH RM3 105 L5
Trosley Av GVW DA11 190 E5
Trosley Rd BELV DA17 164 B5
Trossachs Rd EDUL SE22 181 M1
Trothy Rd STHWK SE1 19 P6
STHWK SE1 159 P3
Trotsworth Av VW GU25 194 B4
Trotters Bottom BAR EN5 76 D3
Trotters Gap WARE SG12 27 K7
Trotters La CHOB/PIR GU24 213 N8
Trotters Rd HLWS CM18 47 K4
Trotter Wy HOR/WEW KT19 219 M8
Trotton Cl CRAWE RH10 284 D10
Trott Rd MUSWH N10 98 B8
Trotts La BH/WHM TN16 262 F3
Trott St BTSEA SW11 157 N7
Trotwood CHIG IG7 102 G7
Troughton Rd CHARL SE7 161 N4
Troutbeck Cl SLN SL2 129 M9
Troutbeck Rd NWCR SE14 160 D7
Trout La WDR/YW UB7 131 M10
Trout Ri RKW/CH/CXG WD3 71 L7
Trout Rd WDR/YW UB7 131 M9
Troutstream Wy
RKW/CH/CXG WD3 71 L8
Trouvere Pk HHW HP1 35 L4
Trouville Rd CLAP SW4 180 D2
Trowbridge Rd HARH RM3 105 L7
HOM E9 140 E1

Trowers Wy REDH RH1 258 C7
Trowley Ri ABLGY WD5 54 F7
Trowlock Av TEDD TW11 177 H9
Trowlock Wy TEDD TW11 177 H9
Troy Ct KENS W8 14 E3
Troy Rd NRWD SE19 181 L9
Troy Town PECK SE15 159 P9
Trubshaw Rd NWDGN UB2 153 P2
Trueman Cl EDGW HA8 * 95 N8
Truesdale Dr DEN/HRF UB9 111 M2
Trulock Rd TOTM N17 99 P8
Truman's Rd STNW/STAM N16 119 M10
Trumpers Wy HNWL W7 154 E2
Trumper Wy SL SL1 128 E10
Trumpetshill Rd
BRKHM/BTCW RH3 274 D1
Trumpington Dr STAL AL1 38 C9
Trumpington Rd FSTGT E7 121 L9
Trumps Green Av VW GU25 194 A6
Trumps Green Cl VW GU25 194 B5
Trumpsgreen Rd VW GU25 193 P8
Trumps Green Rd VW GU25 194 B5
Trumps Mill La VW GU25 194 C6
Trump St CITYW EC2V 12 F6
Trundlers Wy BUSH WD23 94 D2
Trundle St STHWK SE1 18 E1
Trundleys Rd DEPT SE8 160 D5
Trundley's Ter DEPT SE8 160 C3
Trunley Heath Rd SHGR GU5 267 P9
Truro Gdns IL IG1 122 B5
Truro Rd GVE DA12 190 G6
WALTH E17 120 E2
WDGN N22 98 F8
Truro St KTTN NW5 4 C2
Truro Wy YEAD UB4 132 F5
Trusedale Rd EHAM E6 142 C8
Truslove Rd WNWD SE27 181 H8
Truss Hill Rd ASC SL5 192 B5
Trussley Rd HMSMTH W6 156 F2
Trustees Wy DEN/HRF UB9 111 J3
Trustons Gdns EMPK RM11 125 H5
Trust Rd CHES/WCR EN8 62 D10
Tryfan Cl REDBR IG4 122 A3
Tryon Crs HOM E9 140 B3
Tryon St CHEL SW3 16 A7
Trys Hl CHERT KT16 194 C9
Trystings Cl ESH/CLAY KT10 218 F3
Tuam Rd WOOL/PLUM SE18 162 C5
Tubbenden Cl ORP BR6 207 H10
Tubbenden Dr ORP BR6 226 C1
Tubbenden La ORP BR6 226 C1
Tubbenden La South ORP BR6 226 C2
Tubbs Rd WLSDN NW10 136 C4
Tubs Hl SEV TN13 247 J10
Tubs Hill Pde SEV TN13 * 247 H10
Tubwell Rd SLN SL2 129 N3
Tucker Rd CHERT KT16 214 G3
Tucker St WATW WD18 73 K9
Tuckey Gv RPLY/SEND GU23 233 J10
Tuck Rd RAIN RM13 145 H1
Tudor Av CHESW EN7 62 A7
GPK RM2 125 H1
HPTN TW12 175 P9
WATN WD24 73 L3
WPK KT4 200 E10
Tudor Cir GODL GU7 267 K10
Tudor Cl ASHF TW15 173 N7
BNSTD SM7 239 H1
BRWN CM15 87 L10
BRXS/STRHM SW2 * 180 G2
CDALE/KGS NW9 115 P7
CHEAM SM3 220 G2
CHESW EN7 62 A7
CHIG IG7 102 D5
CHSGTN KT9 219 K2
CHST BR7 206 C1
COB KT11 217 N9
COUL/CHIP CR5 241 H4
CRAWE RH10 284 E8
DART DA1 187 J2
GT/LBKH KT23 235 N10
GVW DA11 190 B4
HAMP NW3 3 N1
HAMP NW3 117 P10
HAT AL10 40 C7
HGT N6 118 D5
HORL RH6 281 J4
HPTN TW12 176 B8
MLHL NW7 96 D7
PIN HA5 113 H3
SAND/SEL CR2 242 A1
WARE SG12 28 A3
WFD IG8 101 N6
WLGTN SM6 222 D4
WOKS/MYFD GU22 232 D3
Tudor Ct AMS HP6 * 69 J4
BORE WD6 75 K6
ELTH/MOT SE9 * 162 B10
SWLY BR8 208 D7
WALTH E17 120 E5
Tudor Ct North WBLY HA9 115 M10
Tudor Ct South WBLY HA9 115 N10
Tudor Crs BARK/HLT IG6 102 F7
ENC/FH EN2 79 K5
RSEV TN14 247 K3
Tudor Dr GPK RM2 125 H2
KUTN/CMB KT2 177 K8
MRDN SM4 200 G6
RSEV TN14 247 K2
WATN WD24 73 L4
WOT/HER KT12 197 L8
Tudor Enterprise Pk
KTN/HRWW/WS HA3 * 114 C1
Tudor Est WLSDN NW10 * 135 N4
Tudor Gdns ACT W3 135 M8
BARN SW13 156 B9
CDALE/KGS NW9 115 P7
GPK RM2 125 H2
SL SL1 128 B8
TWK TW1 176 E4
UPMR RM14 126 B7
WWKM BR4 205 H10
Tudor Gv HOM E9 140 B2
Tudor La WDSR SL4 171 P3
Tudor Manor Gdns GSTN WD25 55 L8
Tudor Ms WLSDN NW10 136 D1
Tudor Orch BERK HP4 * 33 K3
Tudor Pde ELTH/MOT SE9 * 162 B10
Tudor Pk AMS HP6 69 H3
Tudor Pl MTCM CR4 179 P10
NRWD SE19 181 N10
Tudor Ri BROX EN10 44 D7
Tudor Rd ASHF TW15 174 E9
BAR EN5 77 K7
BARK IG11 143 J2
BECK BR3 205 H3
ED N9 100 A1
EHAM E6 141 P3
GODL GU7 267 K10
HACK E8 140 A3
HPTN TW12 175 P10
HSLW TW3 154 C10
HYS/HAR UB3 132 E6
KTN/HRWW/WS HA3 94 C10
KUTN/CMB KT2 177 M10
NRWD SE19 181 N10
PIN HA5 93 K10
SNWD SE25 204 A5
STALE/WH AL4 21 K3
STALW/RED AL3 38 D3
STHL UB1 133 M9
Tudor Sq HYS/HAR UB3 132 E7
WARE SG12 * 26 C2
The Tudors REIG RH2 * 257 M7
Tudor St EMB EC4Y 12 B7
Tudor Vis CHESW EN7 * 61 M5
Tudor Wk LHD/OX KT22 236 F6
WARE SG12 * 26 C2
WATN WD24 73 L3
Tudor Wy ACT W3 155 M1
HERT/WAT SG14 25 H5
HGDN/ICK UB10 132 B1
RKW/CH/CXG WD3 91 K2
STHGT/OAK N14 98 E2
STMC/STPC BR5 206 G6
WAB EN9 63 J9
WDSR SL4 148 D7
WOKN/KNAP GU21 231 H4
Tudor Well Cl STAN HA7 94 G6
Tudway Rd BKHTH/KID SE3 161 P10
Tufnail Rd DART DA1 187 N2
Tufnell Park Rd HOLWY N7 118 E9
Tufter Rd CHIG IG7 103 J6
Tufton Gdns E/WMO/HCT KT8 198 A2
Tufton Rd CHING E4 100 F5
Tufton St WEST SW1P 17 L4
Tugboat St THMD SE28 163 H1
Tugela Rd CROY/NA CR0 203 L6
Tugela St CAT SE6 182 E5
Tugmutton Cl ORP BR6 226 E1
Tugwood Cl COUL/CHIP CR5 240 E7
Tulip Cl BRWN CM15 86 G9
CROY/NA CR0 204 C8
EHAM E6 142 B7
HARH RM3 105 K7
HPTN TW12 175 N9
NWDGN UB2 154 B1
Tulip Gdns CHING E4 101 J4
IL IG1 142 E1
Tulip Wy WDR/YW UB7 151 N3
Tull St CAR SM5 202 A7
Tulse Cl BECK BR3 205 H3
Tulse Hl BRXS/STRHM SW2 181 H3
Tulsemere Rd WNWD SE27 181 K5
Tumber St EPSOM KT18 255 P1
Tumbler Rd HLWS CM18 47 K2
Tumblewood Rd BNSTD SM7 239 H2
Tumbling Bay WOT/HER KT12 197 H6
Tumbling Bay Weir WARE SG12 * 26 E1
Tummons Gdns SNWD SE25 203 M2
Tuncombe Rd UED N18 99 M5
Tunfield Rd HOD EN11 26 G10
Tunis Rd SHB W12 136 F10
Tunley Gn POP/IOD E14 140 E7
Tunley Rd TOOT SW17 180 B5
WLSDN NW10 136 B3
Tunmarsh La PLSTW E13 141 P5
Tunmers End CFSP/GDCR SL9 89 P9
Tunnan Leys EHAM E6 142 D8
Tunnel Av GNWCH SE10 161 J1
Tunnel Gdns FBAR/BDGN N11 98 D8
Tunnel Link Rd HTHAIR TW6 174 B1
Tunnel Rd BERM/RHTH SE16 160 B1
HORL RH6 280 A7
Tunnel Rd East WDR/YW UB7 152 C6
Tunnel Rd West WDR/YW UB7 152 B7
Tunnel Wood Cl WAT WD17 72 G3
Tunnel Wood Rd WAT WD17 72 G3
Tunnmeade CRAWW RH11 283 H8
HLW CM20 29 K10
Tunsgate GU GU1 268 A2
Tunsgate Sq GU GU1 * 268 A2
Tuns La SL SL1 149 H2
Tunstall Av BARK/HLT IG6 103 K7
Tunstall Cl ORP BR6 227 H1
Tunstall Rd BRXN/ST SW9 158 G10
CROY/NA CR0 203 M8
Tunstock Wy BELV DA17 163 P2
Tunworth Cl CDALE/KGS NW9 115 P4
Tunworth Crs PUT/ROE SW15 178 E2
Tupelo Rd LEY E10 120 G7
Tuppy St THMD SE28 162 F2
Tupwood Ct CTHM CR3 259 P1
Tupwood La CTHM CR3 259 P2
Tupwood Scrubbs Rd
CTHM CR3 * 241 P6
Turene Cl WAND/EARL SW18 157 M10
Turfhouse La CHOB/PIR GU24 213 K5
Turin Rd ED N9 100 B1
Turin St BETH E2 7 N10
Turkey Oak Cl NRWD SE19 203 M1
Turkey St EN EN1 79 P2
Turks Cl UX/CGN UB8 132 B5
Turks Rw CHEL SW3 16 B7
Turle Rd FSBYPK N4 * 118 G7
STRHM/NOR SW16 202 F2
Turleway Cl FSBYPK N4 118 G6
Turley Cl SRTFD E15 141 K3
Turmore Dl WGCW AL8 22 F4
Turnagain La FLST/FETLN EC4A * 12 C5
Turnage Rd BCTR RM8 123 P6
Turnant Rd TOTM N17 99 K9
Turnberry Cl BERM/RHTH SE16 160 A4
HDN NW4 96 G10
Turnberry Ct OXHEY WD19 * 93 K4
Turnberry Dr LCOL/BKTW AL2 55 M6
Turnberry Wy ORP BR6 206 G8
Turnbull Cl RDART DA2 188 D3
Turnbury Cl THMD SE28 143 N8
Turnchapel Ms CLAP SW4 158 C9
Turner Av MTCM CR4 202 A1
SEVS/STOTM N15 119 M2
WHTN TW2 176 B6
Turner Cl ALP/SUD HA0 115 J10
BRXN/ST SW9 159 J7
GLDGN NW11 117 L4
RGUE GU4 250 C7
Turner Ct CMBW SE5 * 159 L10
DART DA1 187 K1
Turner Dr GLDGN NW11 117 L4
Turner Ms BELMT SM2 221 L4
Turner Rd BH/WHM TN16 225 P8
BUSH WD23 74 B8
DTCH/LGLY SL3 149 P1
EDGW HA8 95 K10
NWMAL KT3 200 A7
RDART DA2 188 G6
WALTH E17 121 H2
Turners Cl CHONG CM5 67 N5
STA TW18 173 L8
TRDG/WHET N20 98 A4
Turners Gdns SEV TN13 265 K4
Turner's Hl CHES/WCR EN8 62 C6
HHNE HP2 35 P7
Turners Hill Rd CRAWE RH10 284 F7
CRAWE RH10 285 N3
Turners La WOT/HER KT12 217 J3
Turners Meadow Wy BECK BR3 204 E1
Turner's Oak Shaw HART DA3 211 K9
Turners Pl EYN DA4 * 210 B1
Turner Sq BOW E3 140 E7
Turner St CAN/RD E16 141 L8
WCHPL E1 140 A7
Turners Wk CSHM HP5 51 H6
Turners Wy CROY/NA CR0 203 H9
Turner's Wd GLDGN NW11 117 M6
Turners Wood Dr CSTG HP8 90 A4
Turneville Rd WKENS W14 14 C9
Turney Rd DUL SE21 181 L3
Turneys Orch RKW/CH/CXG WD3 70 G9
Turnford Pl BROX EN10 * 62 D2
Turnford Vls BROX EN10 * 62 E2
Turnham Cl GUW GU2 267 P4
Turnham Green Ter CHSWK W4 156 B3
Turnham Rd BROCKY SE4 182 D1
Turnmill St FARR EC1M 12 B2
Turnoak Av WOKS/MYFD GU22 232 B6
Turnoak La WOKS/MYFD GU22 232 B6
Turnoak Pk WDSR SL4 148 D10
Turnors HLWW/ROY CM19 46 F1
Turnpike Cl DEPT SE8 160 E6
Turnpike Dr ORP BR6 227 M5
Turnpike Gn HHNE HP2 36 A2
Turnpike La CEND/HSY/T N8 119 H2
HGDN/ICK UB10 131 P5
SUT SM1 221 M2
TIL RM18 168 G4
Turnpike Link CROY/NA CR0 203 M9
Turnpike Ms CEND/HSY/T N8 * 119 H1
Turnpike Pde SEVS/STOTM N15 * 119 J1
Turnpike Pl CRAWW RH11 283 N5
Turnpike Wy ISLW TW7 154 F7
Turnstone HART DA3 211 M3
Turnstone Cl CDALE/KGS NW9 * 96 B10
HGDN/ICK UB10 112 C10
PLSTW E13 141 M5
SAND/SEL CR2 224 D6
The Turnstones GSTN WD25 73 M2
GVE DA12 190 G5
Turnstone Ter WEA W13 * 134 E6
Turp Av CDW/CHF RM16 167 P1
Turpentine La PIM SW1V 16 F7
Turpin Av CRW RM5 104 B8
Turpin Cl PEND EN3 80 F3
WAP E1W 140 C9
Turpington Cl HAYES BR2 206 B6
Turpington La HAYES BR2 206 B5
Turpin La ERITH DA8 165 H5
Turpin Rd EBED/NFELT TW14 174 G2
Turpins Cl HERT/WAT SG14 24 G5
Turpin's La WFD IG8 102 C6
Turpins Ri BFOR GU20 212 A1
Turpins Yd CRICK NW2 * 116 F8
GNWCH SE10 161 H6
Turpin Wy WLGTN SM6 222 C4
Turquand St WALW SE17 18 F7
Turret Gv CLAP SW4 158 D9
Turton Rd ALP/SUD HA0 115 K10
Turton Wy SL SL1 149 J2
Turville St BETH E2 13 L1
Tuscan Rd WOOL/PLUM SE18 162 G4
Tuscany Gdns CRAWE RH10 283 P5
Tushmore Av CRAWE RH10 283 P4
Tushmore Ct CRAWE RH10 * 283 P5
Tushmore Crs CRAWE RH10 283 P4
Tushmore La CRAWE RH10 283 P5
Tuskar St GNWCH SE10 161 K4
Tussauds Cl RKW/CH/CXG WD3 72 B9
Tussock Cl CRAWW RH11 283 K9
Tuxford Cl BORE WD6 * 75 K4
CRAWE RH10 284 D9
Tweed TIL RM18 169 M3
Tweed Cl BERK HP4 33 N4
Tweeddale Gv HGDN/ICK UB10 112 D8
Tweeddale Rd CAR SM5 201 N8
Tweed La BRKHM/BTCW RH3 273 N5
CRAWW RH11 283 J4
Tweedmouth Rd PLSTW E13 141 N4
Tweed Rd DTCH/LGLY SL3 150 E5
Tweed Wy ROM RM1 104 E8
Tweedy Rd BMLY BR1 205 M1
Tweenways CSHM HP5 51 J4
Twelve Acre Cl GT/LBKH KT23 235 N10
Twelve Acres WGCE AL7 23 L7
Twelve Av KWD/TDW/WH KT20 * 257 J2
Twelvetrees Crs BOW E3 141 J6
Twentyman Cl WFD IG8 101 M6
Twickenham Br TWK TW1 177 H1
Twickenham Cl CROY/NA CR0 202 G10
Twickenham Gdns GFD/PVL UB6 114 F10
KTN/HRWW/WS HA3 94 D8
Twickenham Rd FELT TW13 175 N6
ISLW TW7 154 F10
RCH/KEW TW9 177 H1
TEDD TW11 176 F8
WAN E11 121 J7
Twig Folly Cl BETH E2 140 C4
Twig Folly Whf BETH E2 * 140 C4
Twigg Cl ERITH DA8 164 F6
Twilley St WAND/EARL SW18 179 L3
Twinches La SL SL1 128 G10
Twine Cl BARK IG11 143 L5
Twine Ct WCHPL E1 140 B9
Twineham Gn
NFNCH/WDSPK N12 97 K5
Twine Ter BOW E3 * 140 E6
Twining Av WHTN TW2 176 B6
Twinn Rd MLHL NW7 97 H7
Twinoaks COB KT11 217 P9
Twin Tumps Wy THMD SE28 143 K9
Twisden Rd KTTN NW5 118 C9
Twisleton Ct DART DA1 187 L2
The Twitten CRAWW RH11 283 M7
Twitton La RSEV TN14 246 F2
Twitton Mdw RSEV TN14 246 G2
Two Acres WGCE AL7 23 J8
Two Beeches HHNE HP2 36 A2
Two Dells La CSHM HP5 33 L10
Two Gates La CSHM HP5 32 D10
Two Mile Dr SL SL1 148 D1
Two Ponds La BERK HP4 33 M1
Two Waters Rd HHS/BOV HP3 35 N9
Twybridge Wy WLSDN NW10 135 P2
Twycross Ms GNWCH SE10 161 K4
Twycross Rd GODL GU7 267 J10
Twyford Abbey Rd
WLSDN NW10 135 L5
Twyford Av ACT W3 135 M9
EFNCH N2 118 A1
Twyford Crs ACT W3 135 M10
Twyford Rd CAR SM5 201 N8
IL IG1 122 D10
RYLN/HDSTN HA2 114 A5
STALE/WH AL4 39 H2
Twyford St IS N1 5 N5
Twyman Cl CRAWW RH11 283 J9
Twyner Cl HORL RH6 280 E3
Twynersh Av CHERT KT16 195 J6
Tyas Rd CAN/RD E16 141 L6
Tybenham Rd WIM/MER SW19 201 K3
Tyberry Rd PEND EN3 80 A7
Tyburn La HRW HA1 114 D6
The Tyburns RBRW/HUT CM13 107 P3
Tyburn Wy MBLAR W1H 10 B7
Tycehurst Hl LOU IG10 82 C8
Tychbourne Dr RGUE GU4 250 F7
Tydcombe Rd WARL CR6 242 B5
Tye Gn Village HLWS CM18 * 47 J4
Tye La ORP BR6 226 F2
Tyers Ga STHWK SE1 19 J2
Tyers St LBTH SE11 17 N7
Tyers Ter LBTH SE11 17 N8
Tyeshurst Cl ABYW SE2 163 P4
Tyfield Cl CHES/WCR EN8 62 B6
Tylecroft Rd STRHM/NOR SW16 202 F2
Tyle Gn EMPK RM11 125 M3
Tylehost GUW GU2 249 M6
Tylehurst Gdns IL IG1 122 F10
Tyle Pl WDSR SL4 171 M1
Tyler Cl BETH E2 7 L7
ERITH DA8 164 C6
Tyler Gdns ADL/WDHM KT15 215 M1
Tyler Rd CRAWE RH10 283 N10
Tylers HARP AL5 20 C2
Tylers Cswy HERT/BAY SG13 42 D8
Tylers Cl GDST RH9 260 A6
KGLGY WD4 54 A5
Tylers Crs HCH RM12 125 K10
Tylersfield ABLGY WD5 54 G7
Tylers Ga KTN/HRWW/WS HA3 115 K4
Tylers Green Rd SWLY BR8 208 D7
Tylers Hill Rd CSHM HP5 51 M7
Tylers Rd HLWW/ROY CM19 46 A6
Tyler St GNWCH SE10 161 K4
Tyler Wk DTCH/LGLY SL3 150 C4
Tyler Wy BRW CM14 106 G2
Tylney Av NRWD SE19 181 N8
Tylney Cft HLWW/ROY CM19 46 E3
Tylney Rd BMLY BR1 206 A2
FSTGT E7 121 P9
Tynan Cl EBED/NFELT TW14 175 H4
Tyndale La IS N1 6 C3
Tyndale Ms SL SL1 148 G1
Tyndale Ter IS N1 6 C3
Tyndall Rd LEY E10 121 H7
WELL DA16 163 J9
Tyne Cl CRAWE RH10 284 D8
UPMR RM14 126 C4
Tynedale LCOL/BKTW AL2 57 L3
Tynedale Cl RDART DA2 188 C4
Tynedale Rd BRKHM/BTCW RH3 273 N4
Tyne Gdns SOCK/AV RM15 146 B9
Tyneham Cl BTSEA SW11 * 158 B9
Tyneham Rd BTSEA SW11 158 B8
Tynemouth Cl EHAM E6 142 E8
Tynemouth Dr EN EN1 79 P4
Tynemouth Rd MTCM CR4 180 B10
SEVS/STOTM N15 119 N2
WOOL/PLUM SE18 163 H4
Tynemouth St FUL/PGN SW6 157 M8
Tynemouth Ter
SEVS/STOTM N15 * 119 N2
Tyne St WCHPL E1 13 M5
Tynley Gv RGUE GU4 250 A4
Tynsdale Rd WLSDN NW10 136 B2
Type St BETH E2 140 C4
Typleden Cl HHNE HP2 35 N4
Tyrawley Rd FUL/PGN SW6 157 L7
Tyre La CDALE/KGS NW9 * 116 B2
Tyrell Cl HRW HA1 114 D9
Tyrell Gdns WDSR SL4 148 E9
Tyrell Pl BRWN CM15 * 107 L2
Tyrell Ri BRW CM14 107 H6
Tyrells Cl UPMR RM14 126 A7
Tyrone Rd EHAM E6 142 C4
Tyron Wy SCUP DA14 185 H7
Tyrrell Av WELL DA16 185 K1
Tyrrell Rd EDUL SE22 159 P10
Tyrrells Hall Cl GRAYS RM17 168 A5
Tyrrel Wy CDALE/KGS NW9 116 C5
Tyrwhitt Rd BROCKY SE4 160 F9
Tysea Cl HLWS CM18 47 J4
Tysea Hl ABR/ST RM4 104 G2
Tysea Rd HLWS CM18 47 J4
Tysoe Av PEND EN3 80 E2
Tysoe St CLKNW EC1R 6 B10
Tyson Gdns FSTH SE23 * 182 B3
Tyson Rd FSTH SE23 182 B3
Tyssen Pl SOCK/AV RM15 147 H5
Tyssen Rd STNW/STAM N16 * 119 N8
Tyssen St IS N1 7 K7
Tythebarn Cl RGUE GU4 250 E5
Tythebarns La RPLY/SEND GU23 251 K2
Tytherton Rd ARCH N19 118 E8
Tyttenhanger Gn STALE/WH AL4 39 J9

U

Uamvar St POP/IOD E14 140 G7
Uckfield Gv MTCM CR4 202 B1
Uckfield Rd PEND EN3 80 C3
Udall Gdns CRW RM5 104 B7
Udall St WEST SW1P 17 H6
Udney Park Rd TEDD TW11 176 F9
Uffington Rd WLSDN NW10 136 D3
WNWD SE27 181 H7
Ufford Cl KTN/HRWW/WS HA3 94 A8
Ufford Rd KTN/HRWW/WS HA3 94 A8
Ufford St STHWK SE1 18 B1
Ufton Rd IS N1 7 J4
Uhura Sq STNW/STAM N16 * 119 M8
Ullathorne Rd
STRHM/NOR SW16 180 D7
Ulleswater Rd STHGT/OAK N14 98 F5
Ulleswater Vls STHGT/OAK N14 * 98 F5
Ullin St POP/IOD E14 141 H7
Ullswater Cl BMLY BR1 183 K9
LTWR GU18 212 A6
PUT/ROE SW15 * 178 A7
SL SL1 128 B7
YEAD UB4 132 F4
Ullswater Ct RYLN/HDSTN HA2 * 113 P5
Ullswater Crs COUL/CHIP CR5 240 F2
PUT/ROE SW15 178 A7
Ullswater Rd BARN SW13 156 D6
HHS/BOV HP3 36 D8
LTWR GU18 212 A6
WNWD SE27 181 J6
Ullswater Wy HCH RM12 125 H10
Ulstan Cl CTHM CR3 242 F9
Ulster Gdns PLMGR N13 99 K5
Ulster Pl CAMTN NW1 10 E2
Ulster Ter CAMTN NW1 10 E1
Ulundi Rd BKHTH/KID SE3 161 K5
Ulva Rd PUT/ROE SW15 156 G10
Ulverscroft Rd EDUL SE22 181 P1
Ulverston Cl STAL AL1 38 E6
Ulverston Rd WALTH E17 101 J10
Ulwyn Av BF/WBF KT14 215 P10
Ulysses Rd KIL/WHAMP NW6 117 J10
Umberstone VW GU25 194 A6
Umberville Wy SLN SL2 128 E5
Umbria St PUT/ROE SW15 178 D2
Umfreville Rd FSBYPK N4 119 J4
Underacres Cl HHNE HP2 36 B5
Undercliff Rd LEW SE13 160 G9
Underhill BAR EN5 77 K9
Underhill Ct BAR EN5 * 77 K9
Underhill Park Rd REIG RH2 257 K7
Underhill Rd EDUL SE22 181 P1
Underhill St CAMTN NW1 4 E7
Underne Av STHGT/OAK N14 98 C3
Undershaft HDTCH EC3A 13 J6
Undershaw Rd BMLY BR1 183 K6
Underwood CROY/NA CR0 225 H3
Underwood Ct CTHM CR3 241 N10
Underwood Rd CHING E4 100 G6
CTHM CR3 259 M1
WCHPL E1 13 N3
WFD IG8 102 A8
Underwood Rw IS N1 6 F9
Underwood St IS N1 6 F9
The Underwood ELTH/MOT SE9 184 C5
Undine Rd POP/IOD E14 160 G3
Undine St TOOT SW17 180 A8
Uneeda Dr GFD/PVL UB6 134 C3
Unicorn Wk RDART DA2 188 E1
Union Cl WAN E11 121 J9
Union Ct CLAP SW4 158 F8
OBST EC2N 13 J5
Union Dr WCHPL E1 * 140 D6
Union Gn HHNE HP2 35 N5
Union Gv VX/NE SW8 158 F8
Union Ms BRXN/ST SW9 158 F8
Union Pk GNWCH SE10 161 L4
Union Rd ALP/SUD HA0 135 K1
CLAP SW4 158 E8
CROY/NA CR0 203 K6
FBAR/BDGN N11 98 E7
HAYES BR2 206 A5
NTHLT UB5 133 P4
Union Sq IS N1 6 E6
Union St BAR EN5 77 H8
KUT/HW KT1 199 J2
SRTFD E15 141 J3
STHWK SE1 12 D10
Union Wk BETH E2 7 L9
Unity Cl CROY/NA CR0 224 G5
NRWD SE19 181 K8
WLSDN NW10 136 D1
Unity Ms CAMTN NW1 5 J7
Unity Rd PEND EN3 80 B3
Unity Wy WOOL/PLUM SE18 162 A2
University Cl BUSH WD23 73 N8
MLHL NW7 96 C8
University Gdns BXLY DA5 186 A3
University Pl ERITH DA8 164 C5
University St FITZ W1T 11 H2
University Wy CAN/RD E16 142 D9
DART DA1 165 N9
Unstead La SHGR GU5 267 P10
Unwin Av EBED/NFELT TW14 174 E1
Unwin Cl PECK SE15 19 N10
Unwin Rd ISLW TW7 154 D9
SKENS SW7 15 M3
Upbrook Ms BAY/PAD W2 9 K6
Upcerne Rd WBPTN SW10 157 M6
Up Cnr CSTG HP8 89 N3
Upcroft WDSR SL4 148 G9
Upcroft Av EDGW HA8 95 P6
Updale Cl POTB/CUF EN6 59 H9
Updale Rd SCUP DA14 185 J7
Updown Hl BFOR GU20 212 C3
Upfield CROY/NA CR0 204 A10
HORL RH6 280 B6
Upfield Cl HORL RH6 280 B6
Upfield Rd HNWL W7 134 E6
Upfolds Gn RGUE GU4 250 F6
Uphall Rd IL IG1 122 E10
Upham Park Rd CHSWK W4 156 B3
Uphill Dr CDALE/KGS NW9 115 P3
MLHL NW7 96 B6
Uphill Gv MLHL NW7 96 B5
Uphill Rd MLHL NW7 96 B5
Upland Av CSHM HP5 50 G4
Upland Court Rd HARH RM3 105 N10
Upland Dr BRKMPK AL9 59 L1
Upland Rd BELMT SM2 221 N4
BXLYHN DA7 164 A9
CTHM CR3 242 G7
EDUL SE22 181 P1
EPP CM16 64 G1
PLSTW E13 141 M6
SAND/SEL CR2 223 L2
Uplands ASHTD KT21 237 J6
BECK BR3 204 F2
RKW/CH/CXG WD3 72 A10
WARE SG12 26 E1
WGCW AL8 22 F1
Uplands Cl CFSP/GDCR SL9 110 B6
MORT/ESHN SW14 177 N1
Uplands Dr LHD/OX KT22 218 C10
Uplands Park Rd ENC/FH EN2 79 H6
Uplands Rd CEND/HSY/T N8 118 G3
CHDH RM6 123 N1
EBAR EN4 98 B2
ORP BR6 207 L8
PUR/KEN CR8 241 K3
WFD IG8 102 B8
The Uplands CFSP/GDCR SL9 110 B7
LCOL/BKTW AL2 55 M6
LOU IG10 82 C7
RSLP HA4 113 H6
Uplands Wy SEV TN13 246 G9
WCHMH N21 79 H9
Upland Wy EPSOM KT18 238 F4
Upminster Rd HCH RM12 125 M9
Upminster Rd North RAIN RM13 145 K5
Upminster Rd South RAIN RM13 145 H6
Upney Cl HCH RM12 125 K10
Upney La BARK IG11 143 J2
Upnor Wy WALW SE17 19 K7
Uppark Dr GNTH/NBYPK IG2 122 F4
Upper Abbey Rd BELV DA17 164 A3
Upper Addison Gdns
WKENS W14 14 A1
Upper Ashlyns Rd BERK HP4 33 N6
Upper Austin Lodge Rd EYN DA4 229 L2
Upper Bank St POP/IOD E14 140 G10
Upper Bardsey Wk IS N1 * 6 F1
Upper Barn HHS/BOV HP3 36 A9
Upper Belgrave St KTBR SW1X 16 D3
Upper Belmont Rd CSHM HP5 50 G4
Upper Berenger Wk
WBPTN SW10 * 157 N6
Upper Berkeley St MBLAR W1H 10 A6
Upper Beulah Hl NRWD SE19 203 M1
Upper Blantyre Wk
WBPTN SW10 * 157 N6
Upper Bourne End La HHW HP1 34 E9
Upper Brentwood Rd GPK RM2 125 K2
Upper Bridge Rd REDH RH1 257 P10
Upper Brighton Rd SURB KT6 199 J7
Upper Brockley Rd BROCKY SE4 160 E8
Upper Brook St
MYFR/PKLN W1K 10 C7
Upper Butts BTFD TW8 155 H5
Upper Caldy Wk IS N1 6 F2
Upper Camelford Wk
NTGHL W11 * 8 A6
NTGHL W11 * 137 H8
Upper Cavendish Av FNCH N3 117 K1
Upper Cheyne Rw CHEL SW3 15 N10
Upper Clabdens WARE SG12 26 E2
Upper Clapton Rd CLPT E5 120 A7
Upper Clarendon Wk
NTGHL W11 * 8 A6
NTGHL W11 * 137 H8
Upper Cornsland BRW CM14 107 J4
Upper Court Rd CTHM CR3 242 F10
HOR/WEW KT19 219 P7
Upper Culver Rd STAL AL1 38 E4
Upper Dagnall St
STALW/RED AL3 * 38 C6
Upper Dartrey Wk
WBPTN SW10 * 157 M6
Upper Dengie Wk IS N1 * 6 E5
Upper Dr BEAC HP9 88 C6
BH/WHM TN16 243 P4
Upper Dunnymans BNSTD SM7 221 J10
Upper Edgeborough Rd GU GU1 268 C1
Upper Elmers End Rd BECK BR3 204 D5
Upper Fairfield Rd LHD/OX KT22 236 G7
Upper Farm Rd E/WMO/HCT KT8 197 N4
Upperfield Rd WGCE AL7 23 K7
Upper Forecourt HORL RH6 280 C8
Upper George St CSHM HP5 51 H6
Upper Gladstone Rd
CSHM HP5 * 51 H6
Upper Gn East MTCM CR4 202 A2
Upper Green Rd WYLN AL6 23 P1
Upper Gn West MTCM CR4 202 A2
Upper Grosvenor St
MYFR/PKLN W1K 10 C8
Upper Grotto Rd TWK TW1 176 E5
Upper Gnd STHWK SE1 12 A9
Upper Gv SNWD SE25 203 M4
Upper Grove Rd BELV DA17 164 A5
Upper Guildown Rd GUW GU2 267 N3
Upper Gulland Wk IS N1 * 6 F2
Upper Halliford Rd SHPTN TW17 196 F3
Upper Hall Pk BERK HP4 34 B7
Upper Ham Rd
RCHPK/HAM TW10 177 J7
Upper Handa Wk IS N1 6 F1
Upper Harestone CTHM CR3 259 P3
Upper Harley St CAMTN NW1 10 D1
Upper Hawkwell Wk IS N1 * 6 F5
Upper Heath Rd STAL AL1 38 E4
Upper High St EW KT17 220 C9
Upper Hwy KGLGY WD4 54 E9
Upper Hill Ri RKW/CH/CXG WD3 71 L10
Upper Hitch OXHEY WD19 93 M2
Upper Holly Hill Rd BELV DA17 164 C4
Upper Hook HLWS CM18 47 J3
Upper John St SOHO/CST W1F 11 H7
Upper Kiln DORK RH4 * 273 H4
Upper Lattimore Rd STAL AL1 38 D6
Upper Lees Rd SLN SL2 128 F5
Upper Lismore Wk IS N1 * 6 F2
Upper Ldg KENS W8 * 9 H10
Upper Lodge Wy
COUL/CHIP CR5 240 E8
Upper Mt HMSMTH W6 156 D4
Upper Manor Rd GODL GU7 267 K10
Upper Marlborough Rd STAL AL1 38 D6
Upper Marsh STHWK SE1 17 P3
Upper Marsh La HOD EN11 44 F5
Upper Meadow CSHM HP5 50 G6
Upper Mealines HLWS CM18 47 K4
Upper Montagu St MBLAR W1H 10 A3
Upper Mulgrave Rd BELMT SM2 221 J6
Upper North St POP/IOD E14 140 G8
Upper Nursery ASC SL5 192 F5
Upper Paddock Rd OXHEY WD19 73 M10
Upper Pk HLW CM20 28 E10
LOU IG10 82 A9
Upper Park Rd BELV DA17 164 C3
BMLY BR1 205 N1
FBAR/BDGN N11 98 C6
HAMP NW3 4 A1
HAMP NW3 118 A10
KUTN/CMB KT2 177 M9
Upper Pth DORK RH4 * 273 H4
Upper Phillimore Gdns KENS W8 14 E2
Upper Pillory Down CAR SM5 222 B9
Upper Pines BNSTD SM7 240 A3
Upper Rainham Rd HCH RM12 124 G9
Upper Ramsey Wk IS N1 6 G1
Upper Rawreth Wk IS N1 * 6 F5
Upper Richmond Rd
PUT/ROE SW15 156 E10
Upper Richmond Rd West
RCHPK/HAM TW10 155 M10
Upper Riding BEAC HP9 88 A10
Upper Rd DEN/HRF UB9 110 G5
PLSTW E13 141 M5
WLGTN SM6 222 F2
Upper Rose Hl DORK RH4 272 G3
Upper Ryle BRW CM14 106 G1
Upper St Martin's La
LSQ/SEVD WC2H 11 L6
Upper Sales HHW HP1 35 J7
Upper Sawleywood BNSTD SM7 221 J10
Upper Selsdon Rd
SAND/SEL CR2 223 N5
Upper Sheppey Wk IS N1 * 6 F3
Upper Sheridan Rd BELV DA17 164 B3
Upper Shirley Rd CROY/NA CR0 204 B10
Upper Shot WGCE AL7 23 K4
Upper Shott CHESW EN7 61 N2
Upper Sq ISLW TW7 154 F9
Upper Stanford Rd
CHOB/PIR GU24 248 E1
Upper Station Rd RAD WD7 74 F1
Upper Stonyfield
HLWW/ROY CM19 46 E1
Upper St IS N1 6 B7
SHGR GU5 270 A4
Upper Sunbury Rd HPTN TW12 197 N1
Upper Sutton La HEST TW5 153 P7
Upper Swaines EPP CM16 65 J6
Upper Tachbrook St PIM SW1V 16 G5
Upper Tail OXHEY WD19 93 M4
Upper Talbot Wk NTGHL W11 8 A6
NTGHL W11 * 137 H8
Upper Teddington Rd
KUT/HW KT1 199 H1
Upper Ter HAMP NW3 117 M8
Upper Thames St BLKFR EC4V 12 E7
Upper Tollington Pk FSBYPK N4 119 H6
Upperton Rd GUW GU2 267 P1
SCUP DA14 185 J8
Upperton Rd East PLSTW E13 141 P5
Upperton Rd West PLSTW E13 141 P5
Upper Tooting Pk TOOT SW17 180 A5
Upper Tooting Rd TOOT SW17 180 A7
Upper Town Rd STHL UB1 134 A6
Upper Tulse Hl
BRXS/STRHM SW2 180 G3
Upper Vernon Rd SUT SM1 221 N2
Upper Village Rd ASC SL5 192 C5
Upper Wk VW GU25 194 B4
Upper Walthamstow Rd
WALTH E17 121 J2
Upper West St REIG RH2 257 J10
Upper Whistler Wk
WBPTN SW10 * 157 M6
Upper Wickham La WELL DA16 163 L8
Upper Wimpole St
CAVSQ/HST W1G 10 D3
Upper Woburn Pl CAMTN NW1 5 K10
STPAN WC1H 11 K1
Upper Woodcote Village
PUR/KEN CR8 222 E9
Uppingham Av STAN HA7 115 H1
Upsdell Av PLMGR N13 99 H7
Upshire Rd WAB EN9 63 M9
Upshot La WOKS/MYFD GU22 233 J3
Upstall St CMBW SE5 159 J7
Upton WOKN/KNAP GU21 231 N3
Upton Av FSTGT E7 141 M2
STALW/RED AL3 38 C5
Upton Cl BXLY DA5 186 A2
CRICK NW2 117 H8
LCOL/BKTW AL2 56 C1
SL SL1 149 L2
Upton Court Rd DTCH/LGLY SL3 149 M2
Upton Dene BELMT SM2 221 L4
Upton Gdns KTN/HRWW/WS HA3 115 H4
Upton La FSTGT E7 141 N1
Upton Lea Pde SLN SL2 * 129 N9
Upton Lodge Cl BUSH WD23 94 B1
Upton Pk SL SL1 149 L2
Upton Park Rd FSTGT E7 141 N2
Upton Rd BXLYHS DA6 163 P10
HSLW TW3 153 P9
SL SL1 149 M2
THHTH CR7 203 L2
UED N18 99 P6
WATW WD18 73 J8
WOOL/PLUM SE18 162 F5
Upton Rd South BXLY DA5 186 A2
Upway CFSP/GDCR SL9 90 C9
NFNCH/WDSPK N12 97 P8
Upwood Rd LEE/GVPK SE12 183 M2
STRHM/NOR SW16 202 F1
Uranus Rd HHNE HP2 35 P4
Urban Av HCH RM12 125 K8
Urban Ms FSBYPK N4 119 J5
Urlwin St CMBW SE5 18 E10
Urlwin Wk BRXN/ST SW9 159 H7
Urmston Dr WIM/MER SW19 179 H4
Ursula Ms FSBYPK N4 119 J6
Ursula St BTSEA SW11 157 P7
Urswick Gdns DAGW RM9 143 P2
Urswick Rd CLPT E5 120 B10
DAGW RM9 143 P2
Usborne Ms VX/NE SW8 158 G6
Usher Rd BOW E3 140 E3
Usherwood Cl
KWD/TDW/WH KT20 255 P7
Usk Rd BTSEA SW11 157 M10
SOCK/AV RM15 146 B8
Usk St BETH E2 140 C5
Uvedale Cl CROY/NA CR0 225 J7
Uvedale Crs CROY/NA CR0 225 J7
Uvedale Rd DAGE RM10 124 B8
ENC/FH EN2 79 L9
OXTED RH8 261 L5
Uverdale Rd WBPTN SW10 157 M6
Uxbridge Rd DTCH/LGLY SL3 130 B7
FELT TW13 175 L5
HGDN/ICK UB10 132 D6
HPTN TW12 175 P7
KUT/HW KT1 199 J4
RKW/CH/CXG WD3 91 L3
SHB W12 136 D10
SL SL1 149 N1
SLN SL2 129 P9
STHL UB1 133 P10
WEA W13 134 G10
Uxbridge Rd (Harrow Weald)
KTN/HRWW/WS HA3 94 A8
Uxbridge Rd (Hatch End)
PIN HA5 93 M9
Uxbridge Rd High St STHL UB1 133 N10
Uxbridge Rd (Pinner) PIN HA5 93 L10
Uxbridge Rd (Stanmore)
STAN HA7 94 E7
Uxbridge Rd The Broadway
YEAD UB4 133 L9
Uxbridge St KENS W8 8 E9
Uxendon Crs WBLY HA9 115 K6
Uxendon Hl WBLY HA9 115 L6

V

Vache La CSTG HP8 89 P3
Vache Ms CSTG HP8 * 90 A1
Vaillant Rd WEY KT13 216 D1
Valance Av CHING E4 101 L2
Valan Leas HAYES BR2 205 K3
Vale Av BORE WD6 75 N9
Vale Cl BRWN CM15 86 E9
CFSP/GDCR SL9 90 A9
COUL/CHIP CR5 222 F10
EFNCH N2 118 A1
MV/WKIL W9 3 J10
ORP BR6 226 D1
TWK TW1 * 176 F6
WEY KT13 196 E10
WOKN/KNAP GU21 232 B2
Vale Cottages PUT/ROE SW15 * 178 B6
Vale Ct ACT W3 * 136 C10
STALE/WH AL4 21 J4
WEY KT13 196 E10
Vale Crs PUT/ROE SW15 178 B7
Vale Cft ESH/CLAY KT10 218 E4
PIN HA5 113 M3
Vale Dr BAR EN5 77 J8
Vale End EDUL SE22 159 N10

Vale Farm Rd WOKN/KNAP GU21 232 B3
Vale Gv ACT W3 136 A10
FSBYPK N4 119 K5
SL SL1 149 K2
Vale La ACT W3 135 M7
Valence Av BCTR RM8 123 N6
Valence Circ BCTR RM8 123 N8
Valence Dr CHESW EN7 61 P4
Valence Rd ERITH DA8 164 E6
Valence Wood Rd BCTR RM8 123 N8
Valencia Rd STAN HA7 95 H5
Valency Cl NTHWD HA6 92 G5
Valentia Pl BRXN/ST SW9 159 H10
Valentine Av BXLY DA5 185 P5
Valentine Pl STHWK SE1 18 C1
Valentine Rd HOM E9 * 140 C1
RYLN/HDSTN HA2 114 A8
Valentines Rd IL IG1 122 E6
Valentines Wy ROMW/RG RM7 124 F7
Valentine Wy CSTG HP8 90 A4
Valentyne Cl CROY/NA CR0 225 K7
Vale of Health HAMP NW3 117 M8
Valerian Wy SRTFD E15 141 K5
Valerie Cl STAL AL1 38 G6
Vale Ri CSHM HP5 51 H4
GLDGN NW11 117 J6
Vale Rd BMLY BR1 206 D2
BUSH WD23 73 M9
CSHM HP5 32 G10
DART DA1 187 J4
ESH/CLAY KT10 218 D5
FSBYPK N4 119 K5
FSTGT E7 141 N1
GVW DA11 190 B4
MTCM CR4 202 E3
SUT SM1 221 L1
WDSR SL4 148 E7
WEY KT13 196 E10
WPK KT4 200 C10
Vale Rw HBRY N5 119 J8
Vale Royal HOLWY N7 5 L4
Valeside HERT/WAT SG14 25 H6
Vale St DUL SE21 181 L6
Valeswood Rd BMLY BR1 183 L8
Vale Ter FSBYPK N4 119 K4
The Vale ACT W3 136 A10
BRW CM14 107 H2
CFSP/GDCR SL9 90 A9
CHEL SW3 15 L9
COUL/CHIP CR5 222 F10
CROY/NA CR0 204 C9
EBED/NFELT TW14 175 J2
GLDGN NW11 116 G8
HEST TW5 153 M5
MUSWH N10 98 B9
RSLP HA4 113 K9
STHGT/OAK N14 98 F1
SUN TW16 * 175 H9
WFD IG8 101 M8
Valetta Gv PLSTW E13 141 M4
Valetta Rd ACT W3 156 B1
Valette St HACK E8 * 140 A1
Valiant Cl NTHLT UB5 133 L5
ROMW/RG RM7 104 B10
Valiant Wy EHAM E6 142 C7
Vallance Pl HARP AL5 20 B4
Vallance Rd BETH E2 7 P10
MUSWH N10 98 D10
WCHPL E1 13 P3
Vallentin Rd WALTH E17 121 H2
Valley Av NFNCH/WDSPK N12 97 N5
Valley Cl DART DA1 186 G2
HERT/BAY SG13 25 L6
LOU IG10 82 C10
PIN HA5 93 J10
WAB EN9 63 H8
WARE SG12 26 A1
Valley Dr CDALE/KGS NW9 115 N3
GVE DA12 191 H9
SEV TN13 265 J1
Valley End DTCH/LGLY SL3 129 P6
Valley End Rd CHOB/PIR GU24 212 G3
Valleyfield Rd STRHM/NOR SW16 180 G8
Valley Fields Crs ENC/FH EN2 79 H6
Valley Gdns ALP/SUD HA0 135 L2
SWCM DA10 188 G2
WIM/MER SW19 179 N10
The Valley Gn WGCW AL8 22 F4
Valley Gv CHARL SE7 161 P4
Valley Hl LOU IG10 102 B1
Valley Marsh Rd HOD EN11 45 J3
Valley Mushroom Farm
BH/WHM TN16 244 A4
Valley Pk WATW WD18 * 92 D1
Valley Ri GSTN WD25 55 J9
STALE/WH AL4 20 E1
Valley Rd BERK HP4 33 L3
DART DA1 186 G2
ERITH DA8 164 D3
HART DA3 210 G9
HAYES BR2 205 K2
HGDN/ICK UB10 131 P4
PUR/KEN CR8 241 L1
RKW/CH/CXG WD3 71 K9
STALW/RED AL3 38 D2
STMC/STPC BR5 207 L1
STRHM/NOR SW16 180 G7
WGCW AL8 22 E5
Valley Side CHING E4 100 F2
Valleyside HHW HP1 35 J6
Valley Vw BAR EN5 77 H10
BH/WHM TN16 243 P4
CHESW EN7 61 K4
CSHM HP5 50 F5
SWCM DA10 188 G2
Valley View Gdns PUR/KEN CR8 241 M1
Valley View Ter EYN DA4 * 209 N8
Valley Wk CROY/NA CR0 204 B9
RKW/CH/CXG WD3 72 D9
Valley Wy CFSP/GDCR SL9 109 P4
Valliere Rd WLSDN NW10 136 D5
Valliers Wood Rd BFN/LL DA15 184 G4
Vallis Wy CHSGTN KT9 219 J1
WEA W13 134 F7
Valmar Rd CMBW SE5 159 K7
Val McKenzie Av HOLWY N7 119 H8
Valnay St TOOT SW17 180 A8
Valognes Av WALTH E17 100 D9
Valonia Gdns WAND/EARL SW18 179 J2
Vambery Rd WOOL/PLUM SE18 162 F5
Vanbrough Crs NTHLT UB5 133 K4
Vanbrugh Cl CRAWW RH11 283 H10
Vanbrugh Dr WOT/HER KT12 197 K7
Vanbrugh Flds BKHTH/KID SE3 161 L5
Vanbrugh Hl GNWCH SE10 161 L4
Vanbrugh Pk BKHTH/KID SE3 161 L6
Vanbrugh Park Rd
BKHTH/KID SE3 161 L6
Vanbrugh Park Rd West
BKHTH/KID SE3 161 L6
Vanbrugh Rd CHSWK W4 156 A2
Vanbrugh Ter BKHTH/KID SE3 161 L7
Vanburgh Cl CAN/RD E16 142 A7
ORP BR6 207 H8
Vancouver Cl HOR/WEW KT19 219 P7
ORP BR6 227 K1
Vancouver Ct HORL RH6 281 H4
Vancouver Dr CRAWW RH11 283 N4
Vancouver Man EDGW HA8 * 95 N9
Vancouver Rd BROX EN10 62 C1
EDGW HA8 95 N9
FSTH SE23 182 D5
RCHPK/HAM TW10 177 H7
YEAD UB4 133 J6
Vanda Crs STAL AL1 38 E7
Vanderbilt Rd WAND/EARL SW18 179 M4
Vanderbilt Vls SHB W12 * 156 G1
Vanderville Gdns EFNCH N2 97 M10
Vandome Cl CAN/RD E16 141 N8
Vandon St STJSPK SW1H 17 H3
Van Dyck Av NWMAL KT3 200 A7
Vandyke Cl PUT/ROE SW15 178 G2
REDH RH1 258 A8
Vandyke Cross ELTH/MOT SE9 184 B1
Vandy St SDTCH EC2A 13 J2
Vane Cl HAMP NW3 117 N10
KTN/HRWW/WS HA3 115 L4
Vanessa Cl BELV DA17 164 B4
Vanessa Wk GVE DA12 191 J8
Vanessa Wy BXLY DA5 186 F6
Van Gogh Cl ISLW TW7 154 F9
Vanguard CDALE/KGS NW9 * 96 B8
Vanguard Cl CAN/RD E16 141 M7
CROY/NA CR0 203 J8
ROMW/RG RM7 104 C10
Vanguard St DEPT SE8 160 F7
Vanguard Wy CROY/NA CR0 223 N1
EDEN TN8 262 D10
HTHAIR TW6 152 F8
OXTED RH8 261 M2
WARL CR6 224 E9
WLGTN SM6 222 F4
Vanneck Sq PUT/ROE SW15 * 178 D1
Vanners CRAWE RH10 283 P6
Vanners Pde BF/WBF KT14 * 215 P9
Vanoc Gdns BMLY BR1 183 M7
Vanquisher Wk GVE DA12 191 J6
Vansittart Est WDSR SL4 * 149 H7
Vansittart Rd FSTGT E7 121 M9
WDSR SL4 148 G8
Vansittart St NWCR SE14 160 D6
Vanston Pl FUL/PGN SW6 157 K6
Vantage Pl KENS W8 14 F4
Vantorts Cl SBW CM21 29 P1
Vantorts Rd SBW CM21 29 P2
Vant Rd TOOT SW17 180 A8
Vapery La CHOB/PIR GU24 230 C7
Varcoe Rd BERM/RHTH SE16 160 A4
Vardens Rd BTSEA SW11 157 N10
Varden St WCHPL E1 140 A8
Vardon Cl ACT W3 136 A8
Varley Dr TWK TW1 154 G10
Varley Rd CAN/RD E16 141 N8
Varley Wy MTCM CR4 201 N2
Varna Rd FUL/PGN SW6 157 H6
HPTN TW12 * 198 A1
Varndell St CAMTN NW1 4 G9
Varney Cl CHESW EN7 61 P3
HHW HP1 35 J6
Varney Rd HHW HP1 35 J6
Varsity Dr TWK TW1 176 D1
Varsity Rw MORT/ESHN SW14 155 P8
Vartry Rd SEVS/STOTM N15 119 M4
Vassall Rd BRXN/ST SW9 159 H6
Vauban Est BERM/RHTH SE16 19 M4
Vauban St BERM/RHTH SE16 19 M4
Vaughan Av HCH RM12 125 L9
HDN NW4 116 D3
HMSMTH W6 156 C3
Vaughan Est BETH E2 * 7 L9
Vaughan Gdns IL IG1 122 C5
WDSR SL4 148 E3
Vaughan Rd CMBW SE5 159 K8
HARP AL5 20 A2
HRW HA1 114 B5
SRTFD E15 141 L1
THDIT KT7 198 G7
WELL DA16 163 J8
Vaughan St BERM/RHTH SE16 160 E1
Vaughan Wy DORK RH4 272 F2
SLN SL2 128 D6
WAP E1W 13 P8
Vaughan Williams Cl DEPT SE8 160 F6
Vaughan Williams Wy
BRW CM14 106 G6
Vaux Crs WOT/HER KT12 217 J3
Vauxhall Br PIM SW1V 17 L8
Vauxhall Bridge Rd PIM SW1V 16 G5
PIM SW1V 17 H6
Vauxhall Cl GVW DA11 190 C3
Vauxhall Gdns SAND/SEL CR2 223 K3
Vauxhall Gv VX/NE SW8 17 M9
Vauxhall Pl DART DA1 187 M3
Vauxhall Rd HHNE HP2 36 B6
Vauxhall St LBTH SE11 17 P8
Vauxhall Wk LBTH SE11 17 N7
Vawdrey Cl WCHPL E1 140 B6
Veals Md MTCM CR4 201 P1
Vectis Gdns TOOT SW17 180 C9
Vectis Rd TOOT SW17 180 C9
Veda Rd LEW SE13 160 F10
Vega Crs NTHWD HA6 92 G6
Vegal Crs EGH TW20 171 P8
Vega Rd BUSH WD23 94 B1
Veitch Cl EBED/NFELT TW14 174 G3
Veldene Wy RYLN/HDSTN HA2 113 N8
Velizy Av HLW CM20 28 G10
HLW CM20 46 G1
Vellum Dr CAR SM5 202 B10
Venables Cl DAGE RM10 124 C9
Venables St BAY/PAD W2 9 M3
Vencourt Pl HMSMTH W6 156 D3
Venetian Rd CMBW SE5 159 K8
Venetia Rd EA W5 155 J1
FSBYPK N4 119 J4
Venette Cl RAIN RM13 145 J7
Venice Av WATW WD18 72 F8
Venner Rd SYD SE26 182 B9
Venners Cl BXLYHN DA7 164 F8
Venn St CLAP SW4 158 D10
Ventnor Av STAN HA7 94 G9
Ventnor Dr TRDG/WHET N20 97 L4
Ventnor Gdns BARK IG11 143 H1
Ventnor Rd BELMT SM2 221 L4
NWCR SE14 160 C6
Ventnor Ter SEVS/STOTM N15 * 119 P2
Venton Cl WOKN/KNAP GU21 231 N3
Ventura Pk LCOL/BKTW AL2 56 E5
Venture Cl BXLY DA5 185 P3
Venue St POP/IOD E14 140 G7
Venus Cl SLN SL2 128 E6
Venus Hl HHS/BOV HP3 52 D7
Venus Ms MTCM CR4 201 P3
Venus Rd WOOL/PLUM SE18 162 C2
Veny Crs HCH RM12 125 L10
Vera Av WCHMH N21 79 H9
Vera Ct OXHEY WD19 93 L1
Vera Lynn Cl FSTGT E7 121 M9
Vera Rd FUL/PGN SW6 157 H7
Verbena Cl CAN/RD E16 141 L6
SOCK/AV RM15 147 H8
Verbena Gdns HMSMTH W6 156 D4
Ver-Colne Valley Wk GSTN WD25 56 A8
HHS/BOV HP3 52 A4
LCOL/BKTW AL2 38 D10
LCOL/BKTW AL2 56 C4
LCOL/BKTW AL2 56 D1
WAT WD17 73 L7
Verdant La CAT SE6 183 K4
Verdayne Av CROY/NA CR0 204 C8
Verdayne Gdns WARL CR6 242 B2
Verderers Rd CHIG IG7 103 K6
Verdun Rd BARN SW13 156 D6
WOOL/PLUM SE18 163 K5
Verdure Cl GSTN WD25 55 M8
Vereker Dr SUN TW16 197 H3
Vereker Rd WKENS W14 14 B8
WKENS W14 * 157 H4
Vere Rd LOU IG10 82 F8
Vere St CAVSQ/HST W1G 10 E6
Verity Cl NTGHL W11 8 A7
Veritys HAT AL10 40 D4
Vermont Cl ENC/FH EN2 79 J8
Vermont Rd NRWD SE19 181 L9
SLN SL2 128 E6
SUT SM1 201 L10
WAND/EARL SW18 179 L2
Verney Cl BERK HP4 33 L4
Verney Gdns DAGW RM9 123 P9
Verney Rd BERM/RHTH SE16 160 A4
DAGW RM9 123 P10
DTCH/LGLY SL3 150 D3
Verney St WLSDN NW10 116 A8
Verney Wy BERM/RHTH SE16 160 A4
Vernham Rd WOOL/PLUM SE18 162 F5
Vernon Av MNPK E12 122 C9
PEND EN3 80 D2
RYNPK SW20 200 G2
WFD IG8 101 N8
Vernon Cl CHERT KT16 214 G3
HOR/WEW KT19 219 P3
STMC/STPC BR5 207 L3
STWL/WRAY TW19 173 P4
Vernon Crs EBAR EN4 78 B10
RBRW/HUT CM13 107 M4
Vernon Dr CTHM CR3 241 K8
DEN/HRF UB9 91 M9
STAN HA7 94 F9
Vernon Pl FSBYW WC1X 11 M4
Vernon Ri FSBYW WC1X 5 P9
GFD/PVL UB6 114 C10
Vernon Rd BOW E3 140 E4
BUSH WD23 73 M9
CEND/HSY/T N8 * 119 H1
CRW RM5 104 D6
FELT TW13 174 G5
GDMY/SEVK IG3 123 J6
MORT/ESHN SW14 156 A9
SRTFD E15 141 K2
SUT SM1 221 M2
SWCM DA10 189 L2
WALTH E17 120 E2
WAN E11 121 K6
Vernon's Cl STAL AL1 38 D7
Vernon Sq FSBYW WC1X 5 P9
Vernon St WKENS W14 14 B6
WKENS W14 157 H3
Vernon Wk KWD/TDW/WH KT20 238 G6
Vernon Wy GUW GU2 249 L9
Vernon Yd NTGHL W11 8 C7
Veroan Rd BXLYHN DA7 163 P8
Verona Cl UX/CGN UB8 131 M8
Verona Ct CHSWK W4 156 B4
Verona Dr SURB KT6 199 K9
Verona Gdns GVE DA12 191 H7
Veronica Cl HARH RM3 105 K8
Veronica Gdns
STRHM/NOR SW16 202 D1
Veronica Rd TOOT SW17 180 C6
Veronique Gdns BARK/HLT IG6 122 F3
Verralls WOKS/MYFD GU22 232 E3
Verran Rd BAL SW12 * 180 C3
Ver Rd STALW/RED AL3 38 B6
Versailles Rd PGE/AN SE20 181 P10
Verulam Av PUR/KEN CR8 222 D8
WALTH E17 120 E5
Verulam Cl WGCE AL7 23 J5
Verulam Ct CDALE/KGS NW9 * 116 D5
Verulam Rd GFD/PVL UB6 133 P6
STALW/RED AL3 38 B6
Verulam St FSBYW WC1X 12 A3
Verwood Dr EBAR EN4 78 A7
Verwood Rd RYLN/HDSTN HA2 94 B10
Veryan WOKN/KNAP GU21 231 M3
Veryan Cl STMC/STPC BR5 207 M4
Vespan Rd SHB W12 156 D1
Vesta Av STAL AL1 38 B9
Vesta Rd BROCKY SE4 160 D8
Vestris Rd FSTH SE23 182 C5
Vestry Ms CMBW SE5 159 M7
Vestry Rd CMBW SE5 159 M7
RSEV TN14 247 K5
WALTH E17 120 G3
Vestry St IS N1 6 G9
Vevers Rd REIG RH2 275 M3
Vevey St CAT SE6 182 E5
Vexil Cl PUR RM19 166 C3
Veysey Cl HHW HP1 35 L8
Viaduct Pl BETH E2 140 A5
Viaduct Rd WARE SG12 26 D3
Viaduct St BETH E2 140 A5
Viaduct Ter EYN DA4 * 210 B2
The Viaduct MUSWH N10 * 118 C2
SWFD E18 101 M10
Viaduct Wy WGCE AL7 23 J2
Vian Av PEND EN3 80 D1
Vian St LEW SE13 160 G9
Via Romana GVE DA12 191 L4
Vibart Gdns BRXS/STRHM SW2 180 G3
Vibart Wk IS N1 5 M5
Vibia Cl STWL/WRAY TW19 173 N3
Viburnum Ct CHOB/PIR GU24 212 D9
Vicarage Av EGH TW20 172 E9
Vicarage Cswy HERT/BAY SG13 26 A7
Vicarage Cl BEAC HP9 89 H8
BRW CM14 106 D5
ERITH DA8 164 D5
GT/LBKH KT23 253 P1
HHW HP1 35 M8
KWD/TDW/WH KT20 239 H10
NTHLT UB5 133 N3
POTB/CUF EN6 59 H8
POTB/CUF EN6 60 A6
RSLP HA4 112 E5
STAL AL1 38 B9
WPK KT4 200 B8
Vicarage Ct BECK BR3 * 204 D3
EGH TW20 172 E9
Vicarage Crs BTSEA SW11 157 N8
EGH TW20 172 E8
Vicarage Dr BARK IG11 142 F2
BECK BR3 204 F1
GVW DA11 189 P2
MORT/ESHN SW14 178 A1
Vicarage Farm Rd HEST TW5 153 M7
Vicarage Flds WOT/HER KT12 197 K6
Vicarage Gdns BERK HP4 34 E2
KENS W8 * 14 F1
MTCM CR4 201 P3
Vicarage Ga GUW GU2 267 M2
KENS W8 8 G10
Vicarage Gate Ms
KWD/TDW/WH KT20 * 239 H10
Vicarage Gv CMBW SE5 159 L7
Vicarage Hl BH/WHM TN16 262 G2
Vicarage La CHIG IG7 102 G4
EHAM E6 142 C5
EPP CM16 48 D10
GVE DA12 191 K5
HHS/BOV HP3 52 E2
HORL RH6 280 A3
IL IG1 122 G6
KGLGY WD4 54 A5
LHD/OX KT22 236 G8
RPLY/SEND GU23 250 F2
SEV TN13 246 E5
SRTFD E15 141 K1
STA TW18 195 L3
STWL/WRAY TW19 172 C4
Vicarage Ms CHSWK W4 * 156 B5
Vicarage Pde SEVS/STOTM N15 * 119 K2
Vicarage Pk WOOL/PLUM SE18 162 F4
Vicarage Rd BERK HP4 34 D2
BXLY DA5 186 C4
CRAWE RH10 285 P6
CROY/NA CR0 203 H10
DAGE RM10 144 C2
EGH TW20 172 E8
EPP CM16 65 M5
HCH RM12 125 H6
HDN NW4 116 D4
KUT/HW KT1 199 J2
LEY E10 120 G5
MORT/ESHN SW14 177 P1
SRTFD E15 141 L2
STA TW18 173 H7
SUN TW16 174 G9
SUT SM1 221 K1
TEDD TW11 176 F8
TOTM N17 99 P8
WARE SG12 26 E2
WATW WD18 73 H9
WATW WD18 73 J8
WFD IG8 102 B8
WHTN TW2 176 B2
WOKS/MYFD GU22 232 C7
WOOL/PLUM SE18 162 F4
Vicarage Sq GRAYS RM17 167 M5
Vicarage Wk BTSEA SW11 * 157 N7
Vicarage Wy CFSP/GDCR SL9 110 C4
DTCH/LGLY SL3 150 C6
RYLN/HDSTN HA2 113 P5
WLSDN NW10 116 A8
Vicarage Wd HLW CM20 29 J10
Vicars Bridge Cl ALP/SUD HA0 135 K4
Vicar's Cl EN EN1 79 M6
HOM E9 140 B3
SRTFD E15 141 M3
Vicars Hl LEW SE13 160 G10
Vicar's Moor La WCHMH N21 99 H1
Vicars Oak Rd NRWD SE19 181 M9
Vicar's Rd KTTN NW5 118 B10
Vicents Wk DORK RH4 272 F2
Viceroy Cl EFNCH N2 * 117 P2
Viceroy Pde EFNCH N2 * 117 P2
Viceroy Rd VX/NE SW8 158 F7
Vickers Cl WLGTN SM6 222 G4
Vickers Dr North WEY KT13 215 P6
Vickers Dr South WEY KT13 215 P7
Vickers Rd ERITH DA8 164 E4
Victor Ap HCH RM12 125 L6
Victor Cl HCH RM12 125 L6
Victor Gdns HCH RM12 125 L6
Victor Gv ALP/SUD HA0 135 K2
Victoria Ar WESTW SW1E 16 F4
Victoria Av CDW/CHF RM16 167 P1
CRW RM5 104 C7
E/WMO/HCT KT8 198 A3
EHAM E6 142 A3
FNCH N3 97 J9
HGDN/ICK UB10 132 C2
HSLW TW3 175 P1
SAND/SEL CR2 223 K6
SURB KT6 199 J6
WBLY HA9 135 N1
WLGTN SM6 202 B10
Victoria Cl CDW/CHF RM16 167 P1
E/WMO/HCT KT8 197 P3
EBAR EN4 77 N9
HORL RH6 280 B4
HRW HA1 * 114 E4
HYS/HAR UB3 132 E8
RKW/CH/CXG WD3 91 N1
WEY KT13 196 E10
Victoria Cottages RCH/KEW TW9 155 L7
WCHPL E1 * 13 N3
Victoria Ct RGUE GU4 * 268 B6
WBLY HA9 135 M1
Victoria Crs IVER SL0 131 K9
NRWD SE19 181 M9
SEVS/STOTM N15 119 M3
WIM/MER SW19 * 179 J10
Victoria Dock Rd CAN/RD E16 141 L9
Victoria Dr EYN DA4 210 C2
SL SL1 128 E1
WIM/MER SW19 178 G3
Victoria Emb EMB EC4Y 12 B7
TPL/STR WC2R 11 N8
WHALL SW1A 17 M2
Victoria Embankment Gdns
CHCR WC2N * 11 M8
Victoria Gdns BH/WHM TN16 243 P1
HEST TW5 153 M7
NTGHL W11 8 D9
Victoria Ga BAY/PAD W2 9 M7
HLWE CM17 47 L1
Victoria Gv KENS W8 15 J3
NFNCH/WDSPK N12 97 N6
Victoria Grove Ms BAY/PAD W2 * 8 G8
Victoria Hill Rd SWLY BR8 208 G1
Victoria La BAR EN5 77 J8
HYS/HAR UB3 152 E4
Victoria Ms CRAWW RH11 283 N7
KIL/WHAMP NW6 2 E6
WAND/EARL SW18 179 M4
Victorian Gv STNW/STAM N16 119 M8
Victorian Rd STNW/STAM N16 119 M8
Victoria Pde RCH/KEW TW9 * 155 M7
Victoria Park Rd HOM E9 140 B3
Victoria Park Sq BETH E2 140 B5
Victoria Park Studios HOM E9 * 140 B1
Victoria Pl EW KT17 220 B8
RCH/KEW TW9 177 J1
Victoria Ri CLAP SW4 158 C9
Victoria Rd ACT W3 136 A7
ADL/WDHM KT15 215 N1
ASC SL5 192 A5
BARK IG11 142 E1
BERK HP4 33 P6
BFN/LL DA15 185 J6
BKHH IG9 102 A3
BRW CM14 107 H5
BUSH WD23 94 A2
BXLYHS DA6 164 B10
CHING E4 101 K2
CHST BR7 184 D8
COUL/CHIP CR5 240 E1
CRAWW RH11 283 M7
CSHM HP5 51 H7
DAGE RM10 124 D10
DART DA1 187 L1
EA W5 134 G7
EBAR EN4 77 N8
ED N9 99 N4
ERITH DA8 164 F5
FELT TW13 175 J5
FSBYPK N4 118 G5
GU GU1 250 B10
GVW DA11 190 C4
HARP AL5 20 A2
HAYES BR2 206 A5
HDN NW4 116 F2
HORL RH6 280 B4
KENS W8 15 J4
KIL/WHAMP NW6 2 C7
KUT/HW KT1 199 L2
MLHL NW7 96 C6
MORT/ESHN SW14 156 A9
MTCM CR4 179 P10
NWDGN UB2 153 N2
PLSTW E13 141 M4
REDH RH1 276 B1
ROM RM1 124 G3
RSLP HA4 113 H7
RSLP HA4 113 L9
SEVS/STOTM N15 * 119 P2
SLN SL2 129 H1
SLN SL2 129 N10
STA TW18 173 H6
SURB KT6 199 J6
SUT SM1 221 N2
SWFD E18 121 N1
TWK TW1 176 G3
UED N18 99 N5
UX/CGN UB8 131 M2
WAB EN9 63 H10
WALTH E17 101 H10
WAN E11 121 J9
WATN WD24 73 J4
WDGN N22 98 E9
WDSR SL4 148 E4
WEY KT13 196 E10
WIM/MER SW19 179 P10
WOKN/KNAP GU21 231 J3
Victoria Sq BGVA SW1W 16 F3
Victoria St BELV DA17 164 A4
EGH TW20 171 P9
SL SL1 149 L1
SRTFD E15 141 K2
STAL AL1 38 D6
WDSR SL4 149 J7
WESTW SW1E 16 G4
Victoria Ter DORK RH4 * 272 F2
EA W5 * 135 J10
FSBYPK N4 119 H6
HRW HA1 114 D6
Victoria Vls RCH/KEW TW9 155 L9
Victoria Wy CHARL SE7 161 N4
WEY KT13 196 E10
WOKN/KNAP GU21 232 B3
Victoria Yd WCHPL E1 * 13 P6
Victor Rd PGE/AN SE20 182 C10
RYLN/HDSTN HA2 114 B1
TEDD TW11 176 D8
WDSR SL4 149 H9
WLSDN NW10 136 E5
Victor's Crs RBRW/HUT CM13 107 N3
Victors Dr HPTN TW12 * 175 M9
Victor Smith Ct
LCOL/BKTW AL2 * 55 P7
Victors Wy BAR EN5 77 J7
Victor Vls ED N9 * 99 L4
Victory Av MRDN SM4 201 M5
Victory Cl CDW/CHF RM16 167 H3
STWL/WRAY TW19 173 P4
Victory Pk WBLY HA9 * 115 J8
Victory Park Rd
ADL/WDHM KT15 195 M10
Victory Pl NRWD SE19 * 181 M9
WALW SE17 18 G5
Victory Rd BERK HP4 33 M4
CHERT KT16 195 K8
RAIN RM13 145 H4
WAN E11 121 M2
WIM/MER SW19 179 M10
Victory Road Ms
WIM/MER SW19 179 M10
Victory Wy BERM/RHTH SE16 160 D1
HEST TW5 153 K4
RDART DA2 166 B10
RDART DA2 * 188 B3
ROMW/RG RM7 104 C10
Vienna Cl WFD IG8 102 A10
View Cl BH/WHM TN16 243 P2
CHIG IG7 102 G6
HGT N6 118 A5
HRW HA1 114 C2
View Crs CEND/HSY/T N8 118 E3
Viewfield Cl KTN/HRWW/WS HA3 115 K5
Viewfield Rd BFN/LL DA15 185 M4
WAND/EARL SW18 179 J2
Viewland Rd WOOL/PLUM SE18 163 J4
Viewlands Av BH/WHM TN16 245 H6
View Rd HGT N6 118 A5
POTB/CUF EN6 59 M8
The View ABYW SE2 163 P4
Viga Rd WCHMH N21 79 H10
Vigerons Wy CDW/CHF RM16 168 E3
Viggory La WOKN/KNAP GU21 231 N1
Vigilant Cl SYD SE26 181 P7
Vigilant Wy GVE DA12 191 J8
Vignoles Rd ROMW/RG RM7 124 B5
Vigors Cft HAT AL10 40 C5
Vigo St CONDST W1S 10 G8
Viking Cl BOW E3 140 D4
Viking Gdns EHAM E6 142 B7
Viking Pl LEY E10 120 E6
Viking Rd GVW DA11 189 P6
STHL UB1 133 M9
Viking Wy BRWN CM15 86 G10
ERITH DA8 164 D2
Villa Cl GVE DA12 191 L5
Villacourt Rd WOOL/PLUM SE18 163 K6
Village Ar CHING E4 * 101 J2
Village Centre HHS/BOV HP3 * 36 D7
Village Cl CHING E4 101 H6
HAMP NW3 * 117 N10
HOD EN11 45 J1
WEY KT13 196 E10
Village Gdns EW KT17 220 C6
Village Green Av BH/WHM TN16 244 B3
Village Green Rd DART DA1 165 H10
Village Green Wy BH/WHM TN16 244 B3
Village La SLN SL2 109 J6
Village Ms ASC SL5 192 B4
CDALE/KGS NW9 * 116 A7
Village Mt HAMP NW3 * 117 M9
Village Park Cl EN EN1 79 M10
Village Rd AMSS HP7 68 E10
DEN/HRF UB9 111 K6
EGH TW20 194 F3
EN EN1 79 L10
FNCH N3 97 H10
WDSR SL4 148 A2
Village Rw BELMT SM2 221 K4
The Village CHARL SE7 161 P5
HAMP NW3 * 117 M7
WDSR SL4 * 170 G5
Village Wy AMSS HP7 70 A6
ASHF TW15 174 A7
BARK/HLT IG6 122 F1
BECK BR3 204 F4
DUL SE21 181 L2
PIN HA5 113 M5
SAND/SEL CR2 223 P9
WLSDN NW10 116 A9
Village Wy East PIN HA5 113 N5
Villa Rd BRXN/ST SW9 159 H9
Villas Rd WOOL/PLUM SE18 162 F3
Villa St WALW SE17 19 H8
Villiers Av BRYLDS KT5 199 L5
WHTN TW2 175 N4
Villiers Cl BRYLDS KT5 199 L4
LEY E10 120 F7
Villiers Crs STALE/WH AL4 39 J3
Villiers Gv BELMT SM2 220 G5
Villiers Rd BECK BR3 204 C2
CRICK NW2 136 D1
ISLW TW7 154 D8
KUT/HW KT1 199 L3
OXHEY WD19 73 M10
SLN SL2 129 J7
STHL UB1 133 N10
Villiers St CHCR WC2N 11 M9
HERT/BAY SG13 25 M5
The Villiers WEY KT13 * 216 E3
Villier St UX/CGN UB8 131 N5
Vincam Cl WHTN TW2 175 P3
Vincennes Est WNWD SE27 181 L7
Vincent Av BRYLDS KT5 199 N9
CAR SM5 221 N7
Vincent Cl BAR EN5 77 K7
BARK/HLT IG6 102 G7
BFN/LL DA15 185 H4
CHERT KT16 195 H7
CHES/WCR EN8 62 D4
ESH/CLAY KT10 198 A10
HAYES BR2 205 N4
LHD/OX KT22 236 A9
WDR/YW UB7 152 B5
Vincent Dr DORK RH4 272 F3
HGDN/ICK UB10 132 A3
SHPTN TW17 196 F3
Vincent Gdns CRICK NW2 116 C8
Vincent La DORK RH4 272 F2
Vincent Pde FSBYPK N4 * 118 F6
Vincent Rd ACT W3 155 P2
ALP/SUD HA0 135 L2
CHERT KT16 195 H7
CHING E4 101 J7
COB KT11 235 M2
COUL/CHIP CR5 240 D2
CROY/NA CR0 203 M7
DAGW RM9 143 P2
DORK RH4 272 F2
HSLWW TW4 153 L9
ISLW TW7 154 C7
KUT/HW KT1 199 M3
RAIN RM13 145 K6
SEVS/STOTM N15 119 K2
WDGN N22 99 H10
WOOL/PLUM SE18 162 E3
Vincent Rw HPTN TW12 176 B9
Vincents Cl BERM/RHTH SE16 160 D1
COUL/CHIP CR5 240 A6
Vincent Sq BH/WHM TN16 225 P9
WDGN N22 * 99 H10
WEST SW1P 17 H5
Vincent St CAN/RD E16 141 M7
WEST SW1P 17 J5
Vincent Ter IS N1 6 C7
Vincent Vls SEVS/STOTM N15 * 119 K2
Vincent Wk DORK RH4 * 272 F2
Vincenzo Cl BRKMPK AL9 40 F9
Vince St FSBYE EC1V 7 H10
Vine Av SEV TN13 247 J10
Vine Cl BRYLDS KT5 199 L6
RGUW GU3 249 J2
STWL/WRAY TW19 173 K1
SUT SM1 201 M10
WDR/YW UB7 152 B3
WGCW AL8 23 H3
Vine Cottages HNWL W7 * 134 D10
WCHPL E1 * 140 B8
Vine Ct KTN/HRWW/WS HA3 115 K4
WCHPL E1 13 P4
Vine Court Rd SEV TN13 247 K10
Vine Gdns IL IG1 122 F10
Vinegar St WAP E1W 140 A10
Vinegar Yd STHWK SE1 19 J1
Vine Gv HGDN/ICK UB10 132 B2
HLW CM20 28 G6
Vine Hl CLKNW EC1R 12 A2
Vine La HGDN/ICK UB10 132 A4
STHWK SE1 13 K10
Vine Pl HSLW TW3 154 A10
Vineries Cl WDR/YW UB7 152 B5
The Vineries CAT SE6 * 182 F4
STHGT/OAK N14 78 D10
Vine Rd BARN SW13 156 C9
E/WMO/HCT KT8 198 B4
ORP BR6 227 J3
SLN SL2 129 L1
SRTFD E15 141 L2
Vine Rw RCHPK/HAM TW10 * 177 K1
Viners Cl WOT/HER KT12 197 K6
Vines Av FNCH N3 97 L9
Vine Sq WKENS W14 14 C8
Vine St MYFR/PICC W1J 11 H8
ROMW/RG RM7 124 D3
TWRH EC3N 13 L6
UX/CGN UB8 131 N3
Vine Street Br FARR EC1M 12 B2
The Vine SEV TN13 247 K10
Vineway BRW CM14 107 H2
Vine Yd STHWK SE1 18 F1
Vineyard Av MLHL NW7 97 H8
Vineyard Cl CAT SE6 182 F4
KUT/HW KT1 199 L3
Vineyard Gv FNCH N3 97 L9
Vineyard Hill Rd WIM/MER SW19 179 K7
Vineyard Ms CLKNW EC1R * 12 A1
Vineyard Pth MORT/ESHN SW14 156 A9
Vineyard Rd FELT TW13 175 H6
Vineyard Rw KUT/HW KT1 199 H1
Vineyards Rd POTB/CUF EN6 60 C5
The Vineyard RCHPK/HAM TW10 177 J1
SUN TW16 * 197 H3
WARE SG12 26 E1
WGCW AL8 23 H3
Vineyard Wk CLKNW EC1R 12 A1
Viney Bank CROY/NA CR0 224 E5
Viney Rd LEW SE13 160 G9
Vining St BRXS/STRHM SW2 159 H10
Vinlake Av HGDN/ICK UB10 112 A8
Vinries Bank MLHL NW7 96 E6
Vinson Cl ORP BR6 207 K8
Vintry Ms WALTH E17 120 F2
Viola Av ABYW SE2 163 L3
EBED/NFELT TW14 175 K2
STWL/WRAY TW19 173 P5
Viola Cl SOCK/AV RM15 147 H5
Viola Sq SHB W12 136 C9
Violet Av ENC/FH EN2 79 L4
UX/CGN UB8 132 B7
Violet Cl CAN/RD E16 141 K6
CHEAM SM3 201 H8
DEPT SE8 160 E5
WLGTN SM6 202 B8
Violet Gdns CROY/NA CR0 223 J2
Violet Hl STJWD NW8 3 J8
Violet La SAND/SEL CR2 223 J2
Violet Rd BOW E3 140 G6
SWFD E18 101 N10
WALTH E17 120 F4
Violet St BETH E2 140 A6
Violet Ter UX/CGN UB8 * 132 B7
Violet Wy RKW/CH/CXG WD3 71 M8
Virgil Dr BROX EN10 44 E9
Virgil St STHWK SE1 17 P3
Virginia Av VW GU25 193 P5
Virginia Cl ASHTD KT21 237 J4
CRW RM5 104 D8
NWMAL KT3 199 P4
STA TW18 195 M3
WEY KT13 216 D3
Virginia Dr VW GU25 193 P5
Virginia Gdns BARK/HLT IG6 102 G10
Virginia Pk VW GU25 * 194 B4
Virginia Pl COB KT11 217 H10
Virginia Rd BETH E2 7 L10
THHTH CR7 203 K1
Virginia St WCHPL E1 13 P8
Viscount Cl FBAR/BDGN N11 98 C6
Viscount Dr EHAM E6 142 C7
Viscount Gdns BF/WBF KT14 215 P8
Viscount Gv NTHLT UB5 133 L5
Viscount Rd STWL/WRAY TW19 173 N3
Viscount St BARB EC2Y 12 E2
Viscount Wy HTHAIR TW6 152 F10
Vista Av PEND EN3 80 C6
Vista Dr REDBR IG4 122 A3
The Vista CHING E4 101 J1
ELTH/MOT SE9 184 B3
Vista Wy KTN/HRWW/WS HA3 115 K4
Viveash Cl HYS/HAR UB3 152 G2
Vivian Av HDN NW4 116 E3
WBLY HA9 135 M1
Vivian Cl OXHEY WD19 93 H3
Vivian Gdns OXHEY WD19 93 H2
WBLY HA9 115 M10
Vivian Rd BOW E3 140 D4
Vivian Sq PECK SE15 160 A9
Vivian Wy EFNCH N2 117 N3
Vivien Cl CHSGTN KT9 219 K4
Vivienne Cl CRAWW RH11 283 N4
TWK TW1 177 J2
Vixen Dr HERT/BAY SG13 25 P5
Vixen Ms HACK E8 * 7 L5
Voce Rd WOOL/PLUM SE18 162 G6
Voewood Cl NWMAL KT3 200 C6
Vogan Cl REIG RH2 275 L3
Voltaire Rd CLAP SW4 158 E9
Volt Av WLSDN NW10 136 B5
Volta Wy CROY/NA CR0 202 G8
Voluntary Pl WAN E11 121 M4
Vorley Rd ARCH N19 118 D7
Voss Ct STRHM/NOR SW16 180 F9
Voss St BETH E2 7 P10
Voyagers Cl THMD SE28 143 M8
Vulcan Cl EHAM E6 142 D8
Vulcan Ga ENC/FH EN2 79 H6
Vulcan Rd BROCKY SE4 160 E8
Vulcan Ter BROCKY SE4 160 E8
Vulcan Wy CROY/NA CR0 225 K6
HOLWY N7 5 P1
WLGTN SM6 222 F5
Vyner Rd ACT W3 136 A9
Vyner St BETH E2 140 A4
Vyners Wy HGDN/ICK UB10 112 B10
The Vyne BXLYHN DA7 164 C9
Vyse Cl BAR EN5 76 F8

W

Wacketts CHESW EN7 61 P3
Wadard Ter SWLY BR8 * 209 K5
Wadbrook St KUT/HW KT1 199 J2
Wadding St WALW SE17 18 G6
Waddington Av COUL/CHIP CR5 241 H5
Waddington Cl COUL/CHIP CR5 241 J5
CRAWW RH11 283 K10
EN EN1 79 M8
Waddington Rd SRTFD E15 121 J10
STALW/RED AL3 38 C6
Waddington St SRTFD E15 141 J1
Waddington Wy NRWD SE19 203 K1
Waddling La STALE/WH AL4 21 K2
Waddon Cl CROY/NA CR0 203 H10
Waddon Court Rd CROY/NA CR0 223 H1
Waddon Marsh Wy
CROY/NA CR0 202 G8
Waddon New Rd CROY/NA CR0 203 J10
Waddon Park Av CROY/NA CR0 223 H1
Waddon Rd CROY/NA CR0 203 H10
Waddon Wy CROY/NA CR0 223 H3
Wade Av STMC/STPC BR5 207 N7

Wade Dr SL SL1 128 F10
Wade House STHWK SE1 * 159 P1
Wade Rd CAN/RD E16 141 P8
Wade's Gv WCHMH N21 99 H1
Wade's Hl WCHMH N21 79 H10
Wade's La TEDD TW11 176 F8
Wadesmill Rd HERT/WAT SG14 25 L2
Wadeson St BETH E2 140 A4
Wade's Pl POP/IOD E14 140 G9
The Wades HAT AL10 40 D7
The Wade WGCE AL7 23 J8
Wadeville Av CHDH RM6 123 P4
Wadeville Cl BELV DA17 164 B5
Wadham Av WALTH E17 100 G8
Wadham Cl CRAWE RH10 284 D4
SHPTN TW17 196 D7
Wadham Gdns GFD/PVL UB6 134 C1
HAMP NW3 3 N4
Wadham Rd ABLGY WD5 54 C7
CHING E4 100 F8
PUT/ROE SW15 157 H10
Wadhurst Cl PGE/AN SE20 204 A2
Wadhurst Rd CHSWK W4 156 A2
Wadley Cl HHNE HP2 36 A7
Wadley Rd WAN E11 121 K5
Wadsworth Cl GFD/PVL UB6 135 H4
PEND EN3 80 C9
Wadsworth Rd GFD/PVL UB6 134 G4
Wager St BOW E3 140 E6
Waggon Cl GUW GU2 249 K9
Waggoners Yd WARE SG12 26 C1
Waggon Rd BAR EN5 77 K1
Waghorn Rd
KTN/HRWW/WS HA3 115 J1
PLSTW E13 141 P3
Waghorn St PECK SE15 159 P9
Wagner St PECK SE15 160 B6
Wagon Wy RKW/CH/CXG WD3 71 M7
Wagstaff Gdns DAGW RM9 143 M2
Wagtail Cl CDALE/KGS NW9 96 B10
EN EN1 80 A5
Wagtail Gdns SAND/SEL CR2 224 D6
Wagtail Wk BECK BR3 205 H5
Wagtail Wy STMC/STPC BR5 207 N4
Waid Cl DART DA1 187 N2
Waight Cl HAT AL10 40 B2
Waights Ct KUTN/CMB KT2 199 K1
Wain Cl POTB/CUF EN6 59 L5
Wainfleet Av CRW RM5 104 D10
Wainford Cl WIM/MER SW19 178 G4
Wainwright Gv ISLW TW7 154 C10
Wainwrights CRAWE RH10 283 N10
Waite Davies Rd LEE/GVPK SE12 183 L3
Waite St CMBW SE5 19 L9
Wake Cl GUW GU2 249 N5
Wakefield Cl BF/WBF KT14 215 P8
Wakefield Crs SLN SL2 129 L2
Wakefield Gdns IL IG1 122 B4
NRWD SE19 181 M10
Wakefield Ms STPAN WC1H 5 L10
Wakefield Rd FBAR/BDGN N11 98 E6
RCHPK/HAM TW10 177 J1
SEVS/STOTM N15 119 N3
SWCM DA10 189 H1
Wakefield St BMSBY WC1N 11 M1
EHAM E6 142 B3
GVW DA11 * 190 E2
STPAN WC1H 5 M10
UED N18 99 P6
Wakefields Wk CHES/WCR EN8 * 62 D7
Wakehams Green Dr
CRAWE RH10 284 E4
Wakehams Hl PIN HA5 113 N1
Wakeham St IS N1 6 G2
Wakehurst Dr CRAWE RH10 283 N10
Wakehurst Rd BTSEA SW11 179 P1
Wakeling La ALP/SUD HA0 114 G8
Wakeling Rd HNWL W7 134 E7
Wakeling St WCHPL E1 * 140 D8
Wakelin Rd SRTFD E15 141 K4
Wakely Cl BH/WHM TN16 243 P4
Wakeman Rd WLSDN NW10 136 F5
Wakemans Hill Av
CDALE/KGS NW9 116 A3
Wakerfield Cl EMPK RM11 125 N3
Wakering Rd BARK IG11 142 F2
Wakerly Cl EHAM E6 142 C8
Wakley St FSBYE EC1V 6 C9
Walberswick St VX/NE SW8 158 F6
Walbrook MANHO EC4N 12 G7
Walburgh St WCHPL E1 140 A8
Walburton Rd PUR/KEN CR8 222 D9
Walcorde Av WALW SE17 18 F6
Walcot Rd PEND EN3 80 E6
Walcot Sq LBTH SE11 18 B5
Walcott St WEST SW1P * 17 H5
Waldeck Gv WNWD SE27 181 J6
Waldeck Rd CHSWK W4 155 M5
DART DA1 187 N3
MORT/ESHN SW14 155 P9
SEVS/STOTM N15 119 J2
WEA W13 134 G8
Waldegrave Gdns TWK TW1 176 E6
UPMR RM14 126 A7
Waldegrave Pk HARP AL5 20 C2
TWK TW1 176 E7
Waldegrave Rd BCTR RM8 123 M7
BMLY BR1 206 B5
CEND/HSY/T N8 * 119 H1
EA W5 135 L9
NRWD SE19 181 N10
TWK TW1 176 E7
Waldegrove CROY/NA CR0 203 N10
Waldemar Av FUL/PGN SW6 157 H7
WEA W13 135 H10
Waldemar Rd WIM/MER SW19 179 K8
Walden Av CHST BR7 184 C7
PLMGR N13 99 K5
RAIN RM13 144 E4
Walden Cl BELV DA17 164 A4
Walden Gdns THHTH CR7 202 G4
Waldenhurst Rd STMC/STPC BR5 207 P4
Walden Pde CHST BR7 * 184 C9
Walden Pl WGCW AL8 22 C3
Walden Rd CHST BR7 184 C8
EMPK RM11 125 L4
TOTM N17 99 L9
WGCW AL8 22 G4
Waldens Cl STMC/STPC BR5 207 N7
Waldenshaw Rd FSTH SE23 182 B4
Waldens Park Rd
WOKN/KNAP GU21 231 P3
Waldens Rd STMC/STPC BR5 207 P6
WOKN/KNAP GU21 232 A3
Walden St WCHPL E1 140 A8
Walden Wy BARK/HLT IG6 103 H8
EMPK RM11 125 L4
MLHL NW7 96 G7
Waldo Cl CLAP SW4 180 D1
Waldon TIL RM18 169 L3
Waldo Pl MTCM CR4 179 P10
Waldorf Cl SAND/SEL CR2 223 J5
Waldo Rd BMLY BR1 205 P3
WLSDN NW10 136 E5
Waldram Crs FSTH SE23 182 B4
Waldram Park Rd FSTH SE23 182 C4
Waldram Pl FSTH SE23 182 B4
Waldrist Wy ERITHM DA18 164 A1
Waldron Gdns HAYES BR2 205 J3
Waldronhyrst CROY/NA CR0 223 J1
Waldron Ms CHEL SW3 15 M9
Waldron Rd RYLN/HDSTN HA2 114 D6
WAND/EARL SW18 179 M6
The Waldrons CROY/NA CR0 223 K1
OXTED RH8 261 L7
Waldron's Yd RYLN/HDSTN HA2 114 C7
Waldstock Rd THMD SE28 143 K9
Waleran Cl STAN HA7 94 E7
Walerand Rd LEW SE13 161 H8
Wales Av CAR SM5 221 P2
Walesbeech CRAWE RH10 284 B6
Wales Cl PECK SE15 160 A6
Wales Farm Rd ACT W3 136 A7
Waleton Acres WLGTN SM6 * 222 D3
Waley St WCHPL E1 * 140 C7
Walfield Av TRDG/WHET N20 97 L1
Walford Rd RDKG RH5 272 G6
STNW/STAM N16 119 M9
UX/CGN UB8 131 M4
Walfords Cl HLWE CM17 29 M8
Walfrey Gdns DAGW RM9 143 P2
Walham Green Ct
FUL/PGN SW6 * 157 L6
Walham Gv FUL/PGN SW6 157 K6
Walham Ri WIM/MER SW19 179 H9
Walham Yd FUL/PGN SW6 157 K6
Walkden Rd CHST BR7 184 D7
Walker Cl DART DA1 164 G9
EBED/NFELT TW14 174 G3
FBAR/BDGN N11 98 D5
HNWL W7 134 D10
HPTN TW12 175 N9
WOOL/PLUM SE18 162 F3
Walker Crs DTCH/LGLY SL3 150 C4
Walker Rd CRAWE RH10 284 C9
Walkers Cl HARP AL5 20 B4
Walker's Ct SOHO/CST W1F 11 J7
Walkerscroft Md CAT SE6 182 G5
DUL SE21 181 K4
Walker's Pl PUT/ROE SW15 156 G10
Walkers Rd HARP AL5 20 A4
Walkfield Dr EPSOM KT18 238 E3
Walkley Rd DART DA1 187 J1
The Walks EFNCH N2 117 N1
The Walk EMPK RM11 125 N7
OXTED RH8 260 F9
PLMGR N13 * 99 H4
POTB/CUF EN6 59 L8
WDSR SL4 148 F4
Walkwood End BEAC HP9 88 B10
Walkwood Ri BEAC HP9 88 B10
Wallace Cl HGDN/ICK UB10 131 P4
RGUW GU3 249 H7
SHPTN TW17 196 E4
THMD SE28 143 N9
Wallace Crs CAR SM5 222 A2
Wallace Flds EW KT17 220 C8
Wallace Gdns SWCM DA10 189 K2
Wallace Rd GRAYS RM17 167 M3
IS N1 6 F1
Wallace Sq COUL/CHIP CR5 240 E8
Wallace Wk ADL/WDHM KT15 215 M1
WDSR SL4 149 L4
Wallace Wy ROM RM1 104 E9
Wallage La CRAWE RH10 285 L7
Wallasey Crs HGDN/ICK UB10 112 B7
Wallbutton Rd BROCKY SE4 160 D8
Wallcote Av CRICK NW2 116 G6
Walled Garden Cl BECK BR3 204 G4
The Walled Gdn
BRKHM/BTCW RH3 274 A1
KWD/TDW/WH KT20 238 G8
WLYN AL6 * 23 K1
Wall End Rd EHAM E6 142 D2
Wallenger Av GPK RM2 125 J1
Waller Dr NTHWD HA6 93 H10
Waller La CTHM CR3 241 N9
Waller Rd BEAC HP9 88 E9
NWCR SE14 160 C8
Wallers Cl DAGW RM9 143 P3
WFD IG8 102 C7
Waller's Hoppet LOU IG10 82 C6
Wallers Wy HOD EN11 26 G10
Wallflower St SHB W12 136 C9
Wallgrave Rd ECT SW5 15 K6
Wallhouse Rd ERITH DA8 165 K6
Wallingford Av NKENS W10 136 G7
Wallingford Rd UX/CGN UB8 131 L4
Wallingford Wk STAL AL1 38 C9
Wallington Cl RSLP HA4 112 D4
Wallington Rd CSHM HP5 50 G6
GDMY/SEVK IG3 123 J5
Wallis Cl BTSEA SW11 157 N9
EMPK RM11 125 J6
RDART DA2 187 H6
Wallis Ct CRAWE RH10 * 284 A3
Wallis Ms LHD/OX KT22 * 236 F8
Wallis Pk GVW DA11 189 N1
Wallis Rd HOM E9 140 E1
STHL UB1 134 A8
Wallorton Gdns
MORT/ESHN SW14 156 A10
Wallside BARB EC2Y * 12 F4
Wall St IS N1 7 H2
Wallwood Rd WAN E11 121 J5
Wallwood St POP/IOD E14 140 E7
Walmar Cl EBAR EN4 77 N5
Walmer Cl CHING E4 100 G3
ORP BR6 226 G1
ROMW/RG RM7 104 C10
Walmer Gdns WEA W13 154 F1
Walmer Rd NTGHL W11 8 A8
NTGHL W11 137 H9
Walmer Ter WOOL/PLUM SE18 162 F3
Walmgate Rd GFD/PVL UB6 134 G3
Walmington Fold
NFNCH/WDSPK N12 97 K7
Walm La CRICK NW2 116 G10
Walney Wk IS N1 * 6 F1
Walnut Av WDR/YW UB7 152 B2
Walnut Cl BARK/HLT IG6 122 G2
CAR SM5 222 A2
DEPT SE8 160 E5
EPSOM KT18 238 C1
EYN DA4 209 L10
HYS/HAR UB3 132 F9
LCOL/BKTW AL2 56 A3
Walnut Ct EA W5 * 155 K1
WGCE AL7 23 H8
Walnut Dr KWD/TDW/WH KT20 239 H10
Walnut Gdns SRTFD E15 121 K10
Walnut Gn BUSH WD23 73 N6
Walnut Gv BNSTD SM7 220 G10
EN EN1 79 L9
HHNE HP2 35 N6
WGCE AL7 23 H8
Walnut La CRAWW RH11 283 L4
Walnut Ms BELMT SM2 221 M4
Walnut Rd LEY E10 120 F7
Walnuts Rd ORP BR6 207 K8
Walnut Tree Av DART DA1 187 M5
MTCM CR4 * 201 P3
Walnut Tree Cl BARN SW13 156 C7
BH/WHM TN16 262 G2
BNSTD SM7 221 H8
CHES/WCR EN8 62 C7
CHST BR7 206 F1
GU GU1 249 P10
HOD EN11 44 F3
Walnut Tree Gdns GODL GU7 267 K10
Walnut Tree La BF/WBF KT14 215 N8
Walnut Tree Pk GU GU1 * 249 P10
Walnut Tree Pl RPLY/SEND GU23 232 G9
Walnut Tree Rd BCTR RM8 123 N7
BTFD TW8 155 K5
ERITH DA8 164 F4
GNWCH SE10 * 161 K4
HEST TW5 153 N5
SHPTN TW17 196 D2
Walnut Tree Wk LBTH SE11 18 A5
WARE SG12 26 D5
Walnut Wk HERT/BAY SG13 25 M5
Walnut Wy AMS HP6 68 B1
BKHH IG9 102 A4
RSLP HA4 133 K1
SWLY BR8 208 E2
Walpole Av COUL/CHIP CR5 240 A5
COUL/CHIP CR5 240 E2
RCH/KEW TW9 155 L8
Walpole Cl GRAYS RM17 167 P3
PIN HA5 93 P7
WEA W13 155 H1
Walpole Crs TEDD TW11 176 E8
Walpole Gdns CHSWK W4 155 P4
WHTN TW2 176 D5
Walpole Ms STJWD NW8 3 L6
Walpole Pl TEDD TW11 176 E8
Walpole Rd CROY/NA CR0 203 L9
EHAM E6 141 P2
HAYES BR2 206 A5
SL SL1 128 C8
SURB KT6 199 K7
SWFD E18 101 L9
TEDD TW11 176 E8
TOTM N17 99 K10
WALTH E17 120 D2
WDSR SL4 171 N3
WHTN TW2 176 D5
WIM/MER SW19 179 N9
Walpole St CHEL SW3 16 A7
Walrond Av WBLY HA9 115 K10
Walsham Cl STNW/STAM N16 119 P6
THMD SE28 143 N9
Walsham Rd EBED/NFELT TW14 175 J3
NWCR SE14 160 C8
Walsh Crs CROY/NA CR0 225 K8
Walshford Wy BORE WD6 75 M5
Walsingham Cl HAT AL10 40 C3
Walsingham Gdns
HOR/WEW KT19 220 B1
Walsingham Pk CHST BR7 206 G4
Walsingham Rd CLAP SW4 180 B2
CLPT E5 119 P8
CROY/NA CR0 225 H6
ENC/FH EN2 79 L9
MTCM CR4 202 A5
STMC/STPC BR5 207 L1
WEA W13 * 134 F10
Walsingham Wk BELV DA17 164 B5
Walsingham Wy LCOL/BKTW AL2 57 H3
Walter Mead Cl CHONG CM5 67 P5
Walter Rodney Cl MNPK E12 142 C1
Walters Cl CHESW EN7 61 J1
HYS/HAR UB3 152 G1
Walter's Md ASHTD KT21 237 K3
Walters Rd PEND EN3 80 B9
SNWD SE25 203 M4
Walter St BETH E2 140 C5
KUTN/CMB KT2 * 199 K1
Walters Wy FSTH SE23 182 C2
Walters Yd BMLY BR1 205 M2
Walter Ter WCHPL E1 140 C8
Walterton Rd MV/WKIL W9 8 D2
Walter Wk EDGW HA8 95 P7
Waltham Av CDALE/KGS NW9 115 M4
GUW GU2 249 N7
HYS/HAR UB3 152 D2
Waltham Cl DART DA1 187 H2
RBRW/HUT CM13 87 P10
STMC/STPC BR5 207 N8
Waltham Dr EDGW HA8 95 M10
Waltham Gdns PEND EN3 80 B2
Waltham Ga CHES/WCR EN8 62 D2
Waltham Pk WALTH E17 100 F8
Waltham Park Wy CHING E4 * 100 F8
Waltham Rd CAR SM5 201 N8
CTHM CR3 242 A8
NWDGN UB2 153 M2
WAB EN9 63 K2
WFD IG8 102 B7
Walthamstow Av CHING E4 100 F8
Walthamstow Av
(North Circular) CHING E4 100 E7
Waltham Wy CHING E4 100 E4
Waltheof Av TOTM N17 99 L9
Waltheof Gdns TOTM N17 99 L9
Walton Av CHEAM SM3 201 J10
NWMAL KT3 200 C4
RYLN/HDSTN HA2 113 N10
WBLY HA9 115 N8
Walton Bridge Rd SHPTN TW17 196 F7
Walton Cl CRICK NW2 116 E7
HRW HA1 114 C2
VX/NE SW8 158 F6
Walton Ct WOKN/KNAP GU21 232 D1
Walton Dr HRW HA1 114 C2
WLSDN NW10 136 A1
Walton Gdns ACT W3 135 N7
FELT TW13 174 G7
RBRW/HUT CM13 87 P9
WAB EN9 62 G9
WBLY HA9 115 K7
Walton Gn CROY/NA CR0 224 G5
Walton Heath CRAWE RH10 284 E5
Walton La SLN SL2 128 E4
WEY KT13 196 D9
Walton Pk WOT/HER KT12 197 L9
Walton Park La WOT/HER KT12 197 M9
Walton Pl CHEL SW3 16 A3
Walton Rd BUSH WD23 73 L8
CRW RM5 104 A8
EPSOM KT18 237 P7
HOD EN11 44 C1
HRW HA1 114 C2
MNPK E12 122 D9
PLSTW E13 141 P4
SCUP DA14 185 L6
SEVS/STOTM N15 * 119 N2
WARE SG12 26 C3
WOKN/KNAP GU21 232 D2
WOT/HER KT12 197 L5
Walton's Hall Rd SLH/COR SS17 169 K1
Walton St CHEL SW3 15 P5
ENC/FH EN2 79 L5
KWD/TDW/WH KT20 238 D10
STAL AL1 38 E5
Walton Ter WOKN/KNAP GU21 232 E1
Walton Vls IS N1 * 7 K4
Walton Wy ACT W3 135 N7
MTCM CR4 202 D4
Walt Whitman Cl HNHL SE24 * 159 J10
Walverns Cl OXHEY WD19 73 K10
Walworth Pl WALW SE17 18 F8
Walworth Rd STHWK SE1 18 E5
Walwyn Av BMLY BR1 206 A3
Wambrook Cl RBRW/HUT CM13 107 P3
Wanborough Dr PUT/ROE SW15 178 E4
Wanborough Hl RGUW GU3 266 B3
Wanderer Dr BARK IG11 143 M5
Wandle Bank CROY/NA CR0 202 F10
WIM/MER SW19 179 N9
Wandle Cl CRAWE RH10 284 D8
Wandle Ct HOR/WEW KT19 219 P1
Wandle Court Gdns
CROY/NA CR0 202 F10
Wandle Rd CROY/NA CR0 202 F10
CROY/NA CR0 203 K10
MRDN SM4 201 N5
TOOT SW17 179 P5
WLGTN SM6 202 C9
Wandle Side CROY/NA CR0 202 G10
WLGTN SM6 202 C10
Wandle Wy MTCM CR4 202 A5
WAND/EARL SW18 179 L4
Wandsworth Br
WAND/EARL SW18 157 M9
Wandsworth Bridge Rd
FUL/PGN SW6 157 L7
Wandsworth Common
West Side WAND/EARL SW18 179 M1
Wandsworth High St
WAND/EARL SW18 179 K1
Wandsworth Rd VX/NE SW8 17 L9
Wangey Rd CHDH RM6 123 N5
Wanless Rd HNHL SE24 159 K9
Wanley Rd CMBW SE5 159 L10
Wanlip Rd PLSTW E13 141 N6
Wanmer Ct REIG RH2 * 257 K9
Wannions Cl CSHM HP5 51 M6
Wannock Gdns BARK/HLT IG6 102 E8
Wansbeck Rd HOM E9 140 E2
Wansbury Wy SWLY BR8 209 H5
Wansdown Pl FUL/PGN SW6 157 L6
Wansey St WALW SE17 18 F6
Wansford Cl BRW CM14 106 E4
Wansford Gn WOKN/KNAP GU21 231 L3
Wansford Pk BORE WD6 76 A8
Wansford Rd WFD IG8 101 P9
Wanstead Cl BMLY BR1 205 P2
Wanstead La IL IG1 122 B4
Wanstead Park Av MNPK E12 122 A7
Wanstead Park Rd IL IG1 122 B6
Wanstead Pl WAN E11 121 M4
Wanstead Rd BMLY BR1 205 P2
Wansunt Rd BXLY DA5 186 D4
Wantage Cl CRAWE RH10 284 D10
Wantage Rd LEE/GVPK SE12 183 L1
Wantz La RAIN RM13 145 J6
Wantz Rd DAGE RM10 124 C9
The Waplings
KWD/TDW/WH KT20 * 238 E10
Wapping Dock St WAP E1W * 140 A10
Wapping High St WAP E1W 13 P10
Wapping La WAP E1W 140 A9
Wapping Wall WAP E1W 140 B10
Wapseys La SLN SL2 109 K4
Wapseys Wd CFSP/GDCR SL9 * 109 K3
Wapshott Rd STA TW18 173 H9
Warbank Cl CROY/NA CR0 225 K6
Warbank Crs CROY/NA CR0 225 K6
Warbank La KUTN/CMB KT2 178 C10
Warbeck Rd SHB W12 136 E10
Warberry Rd WDGN N22 98 G10
Warblers Gn COB KT11 217 N10
Warboys Ap KUTN/CMB KT2 177 N9
Warboys Crs CHING E4 101 H6
Warboys Rd KUTN/CMB KT2 177 N9
Warburton Cl IS N1 7 J1
KTN/HRWW/WS HA3 94 C7
Warburton Rd HACK E8 140 A3
WHTN TW2 176 A4
Warburton St HACK E8 140 A3
Warburton Ter WALTH E17 100 G10
Warbury La WOKN/KNAP GU21 231 H2
War Coppice Rd CTHM CR3 259 L4
Wardalls Gv NWCR SE14 * 160 B6
Ward Av GRAYS RM17 167 N3
Ward Cl CHESW EN7 * 61 P3
ERITH DA8 164 E5
IVER SL0 131 J9
SAND/SEL CR2 223 M2
WARE SG12 26 B1
Wardell Cl EDGW HA8 96 B8
Warden Av CRW RM5 104 D6
RYLN/HDSTN HA2 113 M6
Warden Rd KTTN NW5 4 D1
Wardens Gv STHWK SE1 12 E10
Ward Gdns SL SL1 128 D9
Ward Hatch HLW CM20 29 L8
Ward La WARL CR6 242 B2
Wardle St HOM E9 120 C10
Wardley St WAND/EARL SW18 179 L3
Wardo Av FUL/PGN SW6 157 H7
Wardour Ms SOHO/CST W1F 11 H6
Wardour St SOHO/CST W1F 11 H5
Ward Pl AMSS HP7 * 68 G6
Ward Rd ARCH N19 118 D8
SRTFD E15 * 141 J3
Wardrobe Pl BLKFR EC4V * 12 D6
The Wardrobe RCH/KEW TW9 * 177 J1
Ward Royal WDSR SL4 * 149 H7
Ward Royal Pde WDSR SL4 * 149 H7
Wards La BORE WD6 74 E6
Wards Pl EGH TW20 172 F9
Wards Rd GNTH/NBYPK IG2 122 G5
Ward St GU GU1 268 A1
Wards Wharf Ap CAN/RD E16 142 A10
Wareham Cl HSLW TW3 153 P10
Warehame's La HERT/WAT SG14 25 K6
Waremead Rd GNTH/NBYPK IG2 122 E3
Warenford Wy BORE WD6 75 M5
Warenne Hts REDH RH1 275 N2
Warenne Rd LHD/OX KT22 236 B8
Ware Park Rd HERT/WAT SG14 25 M3
Warepoint Dr THMD SE28 162 G1
Ware Rd HERT/BAY SG13 25 M5
HERT/BAY SG13 26 F9
Warescot Cl BRWN CM15 106 G1
Warescot Rd BRWN CM15 106 G1
Wareside Cl WGCE AL7 23 L6
Warfield Rd EBED/NFELT TW14 174 F3
HPTN TW12 198 A1
WLSDN NW10 136 G5
Warfield Yd WLSDN NW10 * 136 G5
Wargrave Av SEVS/STOTM N15 119 N4
Wargrave Rd RYLN/HDSTN HA2 114 B8
Warham Rd FSBYPK N4 119 H3
KTN/HRWW/WS HA3 94 E10
RSEV TN14 247 J2
SAND/SEL CR2 223 K2
Warham St CMBW SE5 159 J6
Waring Cl ORP BR6 227 J3
Waring Dr ORP BR6 227 J3
Waring Rd SCUP DA14 185 M9
Waring St WNWD SE27 181 K7
Warkworth Gdns ISLW TW7 154 F6
Warkworth Rd TOTM N17 99 L8
Warland Rd WOOL/PLUM SE18 162 G6
Warley Av BCTR RM8 124 A5
YEAD UB4 133 H7
Warley Gap RBRW/HUT CM13 106 G8
Warley Hl BRW CM14 107 H5
Warley Mt BRW CM14 107 H5
Warley Rd CLAY IG5 102 D9
ED N9 100 B3
RBRW/HUT CM13 106 D10
WFD IG8 101 N8
YEAD UB4 133 H8
Warley St BETH E2 140 C5
UPMR RM14 127 J5
Warlingham Rd THHTH CR7 203 J4
Warlock Rd MV/WKIL W9 8 D1
Warlow Cl PEND EN3 80 F3
Warlters Cl HOLWY N7 * 118 F9
Warlters Rd HOLWY N7 118 F9
Warltersville Rd ARCH N19 118 F5
Warltersville Wy HORL RH6 280 D6
Warmark Rd HHW HP1 35 H4
Warming Cl CLPT E5 * 120 C8
Warmington Rd HNHL SE24 181 K2
Warminster Rd SNWD SE25 203 P2
Warminster Sq SNWD SE25 203 P2
Warminster Wy MTCM CR4 202 C1
Warmwell Av CDALE/KGS NW9 96 B9
Warndon St BERM/RHTH SE16 160 B3
Warneford Pl OXHEY WD19 73 M10
Warneford Rd
KTN/HRWW/WS HA3 115 J1
Warneford St HOM E9 140 A3
Warne Pl BFN/LL DA15 185 L2
Warner Av CHEAM SM3 201 H9
Warner Cl CDALE/KGS NW9 116 D5
HPTN TW12 175 N8
HYS/HAR UB3 152 E6
SL SL1 128 D10
SRTFD E15 121 K10
Warner Pl BETH E2 140 B4
Warner Rd BMLY BR1 183 L10
CEND/HSY/T N8 118 E2
CMBW SE5 159 K7
WALTH E17 120 D2
WARE SG12 26 C3
Warners Av HOD EN11 44 E5
Warners End Rd HHW HP1 35 L5
Warners La SHGR GU5 269 P7
Warner St CLKNW EC1R 12 A2
Warner Ter POP/IOD E14 * 140 F7
Warner Yd CLKNW EC1R 12 A2
Warnford Rd ORP BR6 227 J2
Warnham Court Rd CAR SM5 222 A4
Warnham Rd CRAWE RH10 284 B9
NFNCH/WDSPK N12 97 N6
Warple Ms ACT W3 * 156 B1
Warple Wy ACT W3 156 B1
Warpole Pk WEY KT13 216 B4
Warren Av BELMT SM2 221 J6
BMLY BR1 183 K10
ORP BR6 227 J2
RCHPK/HAM TW10 155 N10
SAND/SEL CR2 224 C4
WAN E11 * 121 K8
Warren Cl BXLYHS DA6 186 B1
DTCH/LGLY SL3 150 B2
ED N9 100 C1
ESH/CLAY KT10 218 B1
HAT AL10 40 E1
WBLY HA9 115 J7
YEAD UB4 133 K7
Warren Ct CHARL SE7 161 P4
CHIG IG7 102 G5
SEV TN13 265 K1
Warren Crs ED N9 99 N1
Warren Cutting KUTN/CMB KT2 178 A10
Warren Dl WGCW AL8 22 G2
Warrender Rd ARCH N19 118 D8
CSHM HP5 51 K5
Warrender Wy RSLP HA4 113 H5
Warren Dr CRAWW RH11 283 K2
GFD/PVL UB6 134 A6
HCH RM12 125 H8
KWD/TDW/WH KT20 239 K9
ORP BR6 227 L2
RSLP HA4 113 L5
Warren Dr North BRYLDS KT5 199 N8
Warren Dr South BRYLDS KT5 199 P8
The Warren Dr WAN E11 121 P5
Warreners La WEY KT13 216 E5
Warren Fld EPP CM16 65 K8
IVER SL0 130 F4
Warrenfield Cl CHESW EN7 61 P7
Warren Flds STAN HA7 * 95 H5
Warren Gdns ORP BR6 227 K2
Warrengate La POTB/CUF EN6 58 F7
Warrengate Rd BRKMPK AL9 58 F4
Warren Gn HAT AL10 40 E1
Warren Gv BORE WD6 76 A8
Warren Hts CDW/CHF RM16 167 K3
Warren Hl EPSOM KT18 238 A2
LOU IG10 81 P9
Warren La BRWN CM15 86 E5
CDW/CHF RM16 167 J3
LHD/OX KT22 218 B8
OXTED RH8 261 M10
STAN HA7 94 F3
WOKS/MYFD GU22 233 K4
WOOL/PLUM SE18 162 E2
Warren Lodge Dr
KWD/TDW/WH KT20 239 H10
Warren Md BNSTD SM7 238 F1
Warren Ms FITZ W1T 10 G2
Warrenne Rd BRKHM/BTCW RH3 273 P9
Warrenne Wy REIG RH2 257 K10
Warren Pde SLN SL2 * 129 P10
Warren Pk KUTN/CMB KT2 177 P9
KWD/TDW/WH KT20 * 255 P7
WARL CR6 242 C4
Warren Park Rd HERT/WAT SG14 25 P4
SUT SM1 221 N3
Warren Pl HERT/WAT SG14 * 25 L5
Warren Pond Rd CHING E4 101 L2
Warren Ri KUTN/CMB KT2 200 A1
Warren Rd ADL/WDHM KT15 215 K6
ASHF TW15 174 F10
BARK/HLT IG6 122 G3
BNSTD SM7 220 G10
BUSH WD23 94 B2
BXLYHS DA6 186 B1
CHING E4 101 H3
CRICK NW2 116 C7
CROY/NA CR0 203 M8
DART DA1 187 M6
GODL GU7 267 K10
GU GU1 268 D1
HAYES BR2 205 M9
HGDN/ICK UB10 111 P9
KUTN/CMB KT2 177 P9
LEY E10 121 H8
MEO DA13 189 N8
ORP BR6 227 J2
PUR/KEN CR8 223 J8
REIG RH2 257 L9
SCUP DA14 185 M6
STAL AL1 38 B10
WAN E11 121 P4
WHTN TW2 176 C2
WIM/MER SW19 179 P9
Warrens Shawe La EDGW HA8 95 N3
The Warrens HART DA3 211 L6
Warren St FITZ W1T 10 G2
Warren Ter CDW/CHF RM16 * 167 J1
HERT/WAT SG14 25 L3
The Warren ASHTD KT21 237 L6
BELMT SM2 221 N5
CFSP/GDCR SL9 90 C9
CSHM HP5 50 D4
EHSLY KT24 252 G6
GVE DA12 190 G7
HEST TW5 153 N6
KGLGY WD4 54 B5
KWD/TDW/WH KT20 239 H9
LHD/OX KT22 218 B8
MNPK E12 122 B9
RAD WD7 56 G9
WPK KT4 220 A1
YEAD UB4 133 H8
Warren Vw GVE DA12 191 P9
Warren Wy MLHL NW7 97 H7
WEY KT13 216 D3
Warren Wood Cl HAYES BR2 205 M9
Warriner Av HCH RM12 125 L7
Warriner Dr ED N9 99 P4
Warriner Gdns BTSEA SW11 158 A7
Warrington Av SL SL1 129 H8
Warrington Cl CRAWW RH11 283 H10
Warrington Crs MV/WKIL W9 9 J2
Warrington Gdns EMPK RM11 125 L4
MV/WKIL W9 9 J2
Warrington Pl POP/IOD E14 * 141 H10
Warrington Rd BCTR RM8 123 N7
CROY/NA CR0 203 J10
HRW HA1 114 D3
RCHPK/HAM TW10 177 J1
Warrington Sp WDSR SL4 171 N3
Warrington Sq BCTR RM8 123 N7
Warrior Av GVE DA12 190 F7
Warrior Sq MNPK E12 122 D9
Warsaw Cl RSLP HA4 133 J1
Warspite Rd WOOL/PLUM SE18 162 D2
Warton Rd SRTFD E15 141 H3
Warwall EHAM E6 142 E8
Warwick Av EDGW HA8 95 N4
EGH TW20 194 F1
MV/WKIL W9 9 J2
POTB/CUF EN6 60 E3
RYLN/HDSTN HA2 113 N9
SLN SL2 129 H6
STA TW18 173 M9
Warwick Cl BUSH WD23 94 D1
BXLY DA5 186 A3
BXLY DA5 186 B3
EBAR EN4 77 N9
EMPK RM11 125 N2
HERT/BAY SG13 25 K7
HPTN TW12 176 B10
ORP BR6 207 K10
POTB/CUF EN6 60 E3
RDKG RH5 272 C10
Warwick Ct HHOL WC1V 11 P4
RKW/CH/CXG WD3 71 J7
SURB KT6 199 K9
Warwick Crs BAYS/PAD W2 9 J3
YEAD UB4 132 G6
Warwick Deeping CHERT KT16 214 F2
Warwick Dene EA W5 135 K10
Warwick Dr CHES/WCR EN8 62 C4
PUT/ROE SW15 156 E10
Warwick Gdns ASHTD KT21 237 J3
FSBYPK N4 119 K3
GPK RM2 125 K1
IL IG1 122 E6
THDIT KT7 198 D5
THHTH CR7 * 203 H4
WKENS W14 14 D5
Warwick Gv BRYLDS KT5 199 L7
CLPT E5 120 A6
Warwick House St STJS SW1Y 11 J9
Warwick La RAIN RM13 145 N4
STP EC4M 12 D6
WOKN/KNAP GU21 231 M5
Warwick Pde
KTN/HRWW/WS HA3 * 94 G10
Warwick Pl BORE WD6 * 76 A7
BRW CM14 86 B8
EA W5 155 J1
GVW DA11 189 N1
MV/WKIL W9 9 J3
THDIT KT7 * 198 F6
UX/CGN UB8 131 M2
Warwick Pl North PIM SW1V * 16 G6
Warwick Rd ASHF TW15 175 P8
BAR EN5 77 L8
BEAC HP9 88 C8
BORE WD6 76 A7
CHING E4 100 F6
COUL/CHIP CR5 222 D10
EA W5 135 K10
ECT SW5 14 E6
FBAR/BDGN N11 98 E7
HSLWW TW4 153 J9
KUT/HW KT1 199 H1
MNPK E12 122 B10
NWDGN UB2 153 N2
NWMAL KT3 199 P3
PEND EN3 80 E3
PGE/AN SE20 204 A3
RAIN RM13 145 K6
REDH RH1 258 A9
SCUP DA14 185 L8
SRTFD E15 141 L1
STAL AL1 38 E4
SUT SM1 221 M2
THDIT KT7 198 E5
THHTH CR7 203 H3
UED N18 99 N5
WALTH E17 100 E9
WAN E11 121 N3
WDR/YW UB7 131 P10
WELL DA16 163 M9
WHTN TW2 176 D4
Warwick Rw WESTW SW1E 16 G3
Warwicks Bench GU GU1 268 B3
Warwick's Bench La GU GU1 268 B3
Warwickshire Pth DEPT SE8 160 E6
Warwick Sq PIM SW1V 16 G7
STP EC4M * 12 D5
Warwick Square Ms PIM SW1V 16 G6
Warwick St REGST W1B 11 H7
Warwick Ter WALTH E17 * 121 J3
WOOL/PLUM SE18 162 G5
Warwick Vls EGH TW20 * 194 F1
Warwick Wy DART DA1 187 M5
PIM SW1V 16 F7
RKW/CH/CXG WD3 72 D8
Warwick Wold Rd REDH RH1 259 H5
Warwick Yd STLK EC1Y * 12 F2
Washington Av HHNE HP2 35 P1
MNPK E12 122 B9
Washington Cl BOW E3 140 G5
REIG RH2 257 K8
Washington Dr SL SL1 128 C9
WDSR SL4 148 D9
Washington Rd BARN SW13 156 D6
CRAWW RH11 283 H10
EHAM E6 141 P2
KUT/HW KT1 199 M2
SWFD E18 101 L10
WPK KT4 200 E9
Wash La POTB/CUF EN6 58 E9
Washneys Rd ORP BR6 227 L9
Washpond La WARL CR6 243 H4
Washponds Cottages
WARL CR6 * 243 H4
The Wash HERT/WAT SG14 25 L5
Wasp Green La REDH RH1 277 J9
Wassand Cl CRAWE RH10 284 B7
Wastdale Rd FSTH SE23 182 C4
Watchfield Ct CHSWK W4 * 155 P4
Watchlytes WGCE AL7 23 M5
Watchmead WGCE AL7 23 K5
The Watch NFNCH/WDSPK N12 * 97 M5
Watcombe Rd SNWD SE25 204 A5
Waterbank Rd CAT SE6 182 G6
Waterbeach WGCE AL7 23 N5
Waterbeach Cl SL SL1 129 J8
Waterbeach Rd DAGW RM9 143 M1
SL SL1 129 J8
Water Brook La HDN NW4 116 F5
Watercress Dr RSEV TN14 247 K6
Watercress Pl IS N1 * 7 K4
Watercress Rd CHESW EN7 61 L2
Watercress Wy
WOKN/KNAP GU21 231 N3
Watercroft Rd RSEV TN14 228 A6
Waterdale HERT/BAY SG13 25 K7
Waterdale Rd ABYW SE2 163 K5
Waterdales GVW DA11 190 A4
Waterden Cl GU GU1 * 268 C1
Waterden Crs SRTFD E15 120 F10
Waterden Rd GU GU1 268 B1
SRTFD E15 120 F10
Water End Cl BORE WD6 75 L6
Waterend La STALE/WH AL4 21 P3
Water End Rd BERK HP4 34 E3
Waterer Gdns
KWD/TDW/WH KT20 239 H4
Waterer Ri WLGTN SM6 222 E3
Waterers Ri WOKN/KNAP GU21 231 J3
Waterfall Cl VW GU25 193 L3
Waterfall Cottages
WIM/MER SW19 179 N9
Waterfall Rd FBAR/BDGN N11 98 C5
WIM/MER SW19 179 N9
Waterfall Ter TOOT SW17 179 P9
Waterfield KWD/TDW/WH KT20 238 E6
RKW/CH/CXG WD3 90 F1
WGCE AL7 23 L4
Waterfield Cl BELV DA17 164 B2
THMD SE28 143 L10
Waterfield Cottages
MORT/ESHN SW14 * 155 N10
Waterfield Dr WARL CR6 242 A5
Waterfield Gdns CRAWW RH11 283 H9
SNWD SE25 203 M4
Waterfield Gn
KWD/TDW/WH KT20 238 E6
Waterfields LHD/OX KT22 236 G5
Waterfields Wy BUSH WD23 73 L8
Waterford Cl COB KT11 217 M7
Waterford Common
HERT/WAT SG14 25 J1
Waterford Gn WGCE AL7 23 L5
Waterford Rd FUL/PGN SW6 157 L6
Waterford Wy WLSDN NW10 116 E10
Waterfront WTHK RM20 * 166 F2
The Waterfront BORE WD6 * 74 G10
Water Gdns STAN HA7 94 G7
The Water Gdns BAY/PAD W2 9 N5
Watergate EMB EC4Y 12 C7
Watergate St DEPT SE8 160 F5
The Watergate OXHEY WD19 93 L3
Waterhall Av CHING E4 101 K5
Waterhall Cl WALTH E17 100 C9
Waterhead Cl ERITH DA8 164 F6
Waterhouse Cl HAMP NW3 117 N10
Waterhouse La
KWD/TDW/WH KT20 239 J7
PUR/KEN CR8 241 K5
REDH RH1 260 N8
Waterhouse Moor HLWS CM18 47 J2
Waterhouse St HHW HP1 35 M7
Wateridge Cl POP/IOD E14 160 F2
Wateringbury Cl
STMC/STPC BR5 207 L3
Water La BERK HP4 33 P5
CAMTN NW1 4 F4
CHOB/PIR GU24 230 D5
COB KT11 217 N10
ED N9 100 A2
GDMY/SEVK IG3 123 J8
GT/LBKH KT23 253 M2
HHS/BOV HP3 52 E5
HLWW/ROY CM19 46 B5
KGLGY WD4 54 C5
KUT/HW KT1 199 J1
MON EC3R 13 K8
NWCR SE14 160 B6
OXTED RH8 261 M2
PUR RM19 165 P3
RDKG RH5 271 J9

RSEV TN14 ... 228 G8
SCUP DA14 ... 186 A6
SHGR GU5 ... 269 L4
SRTFD E15 ... 141 K1
TWK TW1 ... 176 F4
WAT WD17 ... 11 J9
Water Lea CRAWE RH10 ... 284 B8
Water Lily Cl NWDGN UB2 ... 154 B1
Waterloo Br TPL/STR WC2R ... 11 N8
Waterloo Cl EBED/NFELT TW14 ... 174 C4
HOM E9 ... 120 B10
Waterloo Gdns BETH E2 ... 140 B4
ROMW/RG RM7 ... 124 B4
Waterloo Pl CAR SM5 * ... 202 A10
RCH/KEW TW9 ... 155 M5
STJS SW1Y ... 11 J9
Waterloo Rd BARK/HLT IG6 ... 72 C1
BRW CM14 ... 107 H2
CRICK NW2 ... 116 D7
EHAM E6 ... 141 P7
FSTGT E7 ... 121 L10
HOR/WEW KT19 ... 220 A9
LEY E10 ... 120 F5
ROMW/RG RM7 ... 124 E3
STHWK SE1 ... 11 N7
SUT SM1 ... 221 N2
UX/CGN UB8 ... 131 M5
Waterloo St GVE DA12 ... 190 F3
WEY KT13 ... 216 B1
Waterloo Ter IS N1 ... 6 C1
Waterlow Rd ARCH N19 ... 118 D6
REIG RH2 ... 275 M1
Waterman Cl OXHEY WD19 ... 73 J10
Waterman St SL SL1 ... 50 A2
Watermans Cl KUTN/CMB KT2 * ... 177 K10
Watermans Ms EA W5 ... 135 K9
Waterman Sq PGE/AN SE20 ... 182 B10
Waterman Wy EPP CM16 ... 66 C3
SWCM DA10 ... 166 G10
Waterman Wy WAP E1W ... 140 B5
Watermark Wy HERT/BAY SG13 ... 25 N5
Water Md COUL/CHIP CR5 ... 240 A3
Watermead EBED/NFELT TW14 ... 174 F4
KWD/TDW/WH KT20 ... 238 E7
WOKN/KNAP GU21 ... 231 L2
Watermead La CAR SM5 ... 202 A6
Water Meadow CSHM HP5 ... 55 J4
Watermeadow LCOL/BKTW AL2 ... 56 C4
Water Meadow La FUL/PGN SW6 ... 157 J6
Watermead Rd CAT SE6 ... 183 H7
Watermead Wy TOTM N17 ... 100 B8
Watermens Sq PGE/AN SE20 * ... 182 B10
Water Ms PECK SE15 ... 160 B10
Watermill Cl RCHPK/HAM TW10 ... 176 E6
Watermill La HERT/WAT SG14 ... 25 L1
... 99 M6
Water Mill Wy EYN DA4 ... 204 E5
FELT TW13 ... 175 N5
Watermill Wy WIM/MER SW19 ... 201 M1
Watermint Cl STMC/STPC BR5 ... 207 H4
Watermint Quay CLPT E5 ... 119 P5
Waterperry La CHOB/PIR GU24 ... 213 L4
Water Rd ALP/SUD HA0 ... 135 L3
Water Rw WARE SG12 * ... 26 C2
Waters Dr RKW/CH/CXG WD3 ... 21 J6
STA TW18 ... 173 J2
Water's Edge FUL/PGN SW6 * ... 156 C7
Watersedge HOR/WEW KT19 ... 219 N4
Watersfield Wy EDGW HA8 ... 95 J8
Waterside CSHM HP5 ... 51 J9
DART DA1 ... 186 F1
HORL RH6 ... 280 B2
KGLGY WD4 ... 54 B5
LCOL/BKTW AL2 ... 57 K3
RAD WD7 ... 56 G10
UX/CGN UB8 ... 131 M7
WALTH E17 ... 121 J2
WCCE AL7 ... 23 K3
Waterside Av BECK BR3 ... 204 C5
Waterside Cl BARK IG11 ... 123 K9
BERM/RHTH SE16 * ... 19 P2
... 159 P1
BOW E3 ... 140 E3
CRAWW RH11 ... 283 H9
HARH RM3 ... 105 P8
NTHLT UB5 ... 133 N5
SURB KT6 ... 199 K9
THMD SE28 ... 145 J10
Waterside Dr DTCH/LGLY SL3 ... 150 C1
WOT/HER KT12 ... 197 J5
Waterside Ms DEN/HRF UB9 ... 91 K7
GU GU1 ... 249 P8
Waterside Pl CAMTN NW1 * ... 4 D1
Waterside Rd GU GU1 ... 250 B7
NWDGN UB2 ... 153 P2
Waterside Wy TOOT SW17 ... 179 M7
WOKN/KNAP GU21 ... 231 N4
Waterslade REDH RH1 ... 257 P10
Watersmeet HLWW/ROY CM19 ... 46 E5
Watersmeet Wy THMD SE28 ... 143 N8
Waterson Rd CDW/CHF RM16 ... 168 A3
Waterson St BETH E2 ... 7 L2
Watersplash Cl KUT/HW KT1 ... 199 K3
Watersplash Ct LCOL/BKTW AL2 * ... 57 L3
Water Splash La ASC SL5 ... 192 D1
Watersplash La HYS/HAR UB3 ... 133 N4
Watersplash Rd SHPTN TW17 ... 196 B4
Waters Rd CAT SE6 ... 183 K6
KUT/HW KT1 ... 199 K3
Waters Sq KUT/HW KT1 ... 199 N3
Waterton Av GVE DA12 ... 191 H3
Water Tower Cl UX/CGN UB8 ... 111 P10
Water Tower Hl CROY/NA CR0 ... 2 F6
Water Tower Pl IS N1 ... 6 B3
Water Tower Rd BRW CM14 ... 106 G6
Waterway Rd LHD/OX KT22 ... 236 F8
Waterworks Cottages ...
RSEV TN14 ... 247 K6
Waterworks La CLPT E5 ... 120 C7
Waterworks Rd ...
BRXS/STRHM SW2 ... 180 A4
Watery La CHERT KT16 ... 194 C7
CHOB/PIR GU24 ... 213 J2
CHONG CM5 ... 49 L1
HAT AL10 ... 40 B5
HYS/HAR UB3 ... 152 E4
NTHLT UB5 ... 133 K4
RYNPK SW20 ... 201 L3
STMC/STPC BR5 ... 185 L9
Wates Wy BRWN CM15 ... 107 J2
MTCM CR4 ... 202 A6
Wateville Rd TOTM N17 ... 99 K9
Watford Cl BTSEA SW11 ... 157 P7
GU GU1 ... 250 C10
Watford Field Rd WAT WD17 * ... 21 H4
Watford Heath OXHEY WD19 ... 93 L1
Watford Heath Farm ...
OXHEY WD19 * ... 93 L1
Watford Int WATN WD24 * ... 73 H1
Watford Rd BORE WD6 ... 75 H10
CAN/RD E16 ... 141 M7
HRW HA1 ... 114 F4
KGLGY WD4 ... 54 B5
LCOL/BKTW AL2 ... 95 G8
RAD WD7 ... 74 D2
RKW/CH/CXG WD3 ... 72 B10
STAL AL1 ... 38 A10
Watford Wy HDN NW4 ... 116 D1
MLHL NW7 ... 96 A3
Watford Wy (Barnet By-Pass) ...
MLHL NW7 ... 96 A3
Wathen Rd DORK RH4 ... 272 C10
Watkin Rd WBLY HA9 ... 115 N8
Watkins Rd WLSDN NW10 ... 99 J7
Watkin Ter NTHWD HA6 ... 59 L8
Watling Av EDGW HA8 ... 95 H1
Watling Cl HHNE HP2 ... 35 P5

Watling Ct STP EC4M ... 12 F6
Watling Knoll RAD WD7 ... 56 E9
Watlings Cl CROY/NA CR0 ... 204 D6
Watling St BXLYH DA6 ... 164 C10
GVW DA11 ... 190 A8
LCOL/BKTW AL2 ... 56 C1
PECK SE15 ... 19 K10
RAD WD7 ... 74 C4
RDART DA2 ... 188 A3
RDART DA2 ... 189 H5
STAL AL1 ... 38 B9
STP EC4M ... 12 F6
Watlington Gv SYD SE26 ... 182 D8
Watlington Rd HLWE CM17 ... 29 N7
Watling Vw STAL AL1 ... 38 B9
Watney Cl PUR/KEN CR8 ... 222 G9
Watney Market WCHPL E1 ... 140 A8
Watney Rd MORT/ESHN SW14 ... 155 P9
Watneys Rd CROY/NA CR0 ... 202 E5
Watney St WCHPL E1 ... 140 A8
Watson Av CHEAM SM3 ... 201 H6
EHAM E6 ... 142 D2
STALW/RED AL3 ... 38 E1
Watson Cl CRAWE RH10 ... 284 D10
STNW/STAM N16 ... 119 L10
WIM/MER SW19 ... 179 P9
Watson Rd DORK RH4 ... 272 B5
Watson's Ms CAMTN NW1 ... 9 H4
Watsons Rd WDGN N22 ... 99 G10
Watson's St DEPT SE8 ... 160 F6
Watson's Wk STAL AL1 * ... 38 D7
Wattendon Rd PUR/KEN CR8 ... 241 J2
Wattisfield Rd CLPT E5 ... 120 B8
Wattleton Rd BEAC HP9 ... 88 C10
Watton Rd WARE SG12 ... 26 B1
Watts Cl KWD/TDW/WH KT20 * ... 238 G10
SEVS/STOTM N15 ... 119 M3
Watts Crs PUR SN19 ... 166 B3
Wattsdown Cl PLSTW E13 ... 141 M3
Watts Gv BOW E3 ... 141 G6
Watt's La CHST BR7 ... 206 F1
KWD/TDW/WH KT20 ... 238 G10
TEDD TW11 ... 176 F8
Watts Lea WOKN/KNAP GU21 ... 231 M1
Watts Md KWD/TDW/WH KT20 ... 238 G10
Watts Rd THDIT KT7 ... 198 F7
Watts St PECK SE15 ... 159 N7
WAP E1W ... 140 A10
Wat Tyler Rd GNWCH SE10 ... 161 H8
Wauthier Cl PLMGR N13 ... 99 J6
Wavell Cl CHES/WCR EN8 ... 62 A1
Wavell Dr BFN/LL DA15 ... 185 H2
Wavell Gdns SL SL1 ... 128 C5
Wavell Rd BEAC HP9 ... 88 C10
Wavel Ms KIL/WHAMP NW6 ... 2 G4
Wavel Pl SYD SE26 ... 181 N7
Wavendene Av EGH TW20 ... 172 F10
Wavendon Av CHSWK W4 ... 156 A4
Waveney HHNE HP2 ... 36 A1
Waveney Av PECK SE15 ... 160 A10
Waveney Cl WAP E1W ... 13 P9
Waveney Wk CRAWE RH10 ... 284 C9
Waverley Av BRYLDS KT5 ... 199 N6
CHING E4 ... 100 C5
PUR/KEN CR8 ... 241 M2
SUT SM1 ... 201 L9
WALTH E17 ... 121 J1
WBLY HA9 ... 115 P6
WHTN TW2 ... 175 N4
Waverley Cl E/WMO/HCT KT8 ... 197 P5
HAYES BR2 ... 204 A5
HYS/HAR UB3 ... 152 A5
Waverley Crs HARH RM3 ... 105 K7
WOOL/PLUM SE18 ... 162 C5
Waverley Dr CHERT KT16 ... 194 C10
VW GU25 ... 193 M4
Waverley Gdns BARK IG11 ... 143 H4
BARK/HLT IG6 ... 102 F10
CDW/CHF RM16 ... 167 M1
EHAM E6 ... 142 B7
NTHWD HA6 ... 93 H9
Waverley Gv FNCH N3 ... 116 C1
Waverley Pl FSBYPK N4 * ... 119 J6
LHD/OX KT22 ... 236 C5
STJWD NW8 ... 3 L7
Waverley Rd CEND/HSY/T N8 ... 118 A4
COB KT11 ... 218 A10
ENC/FH EN2 ... 79 J8
EW KT17 ... 220 E2
RAIN RM13 ... 145 J5
RYLN/HDSTN HA2 ... 113 M6
SLN SL3 ... 129 H7
SNWD SE25 ... 204 A4
STALW/RED AL3 ... 38 B4
STHL UB1 ... 133 P9
SWFD E18 ... 101 J4
TOTM N17 ... 100 A8
WEY KT13 ... 216 B2
WOOL/PLUM SE18 ... 162 F4
Waverley Wy CAR SM5 ... 211 K5
Waverton Rd WAND/EARL SW18 ... 179 M3
Waverton St MYFR/PICC W1J ... 10 E9
Wavertree Rd BRXS/STRHM SW2 ... 180 A4
SWFD E18 ... 101 M10
Waxlow Crs STHL UB1 ... 133 N6
Waxlow Rd WLSDN NW10 ... 135 G4
Waxlow Wy NTHLT UB5 ... 133 N6
Waxwell La PIN HA5 ... 93 L10
Wayborne Gv RSLP HA4 ... 112 D4
Waycross Rd UPMR RM14 ... 126 D4
Waye Av HEST TW5 ... 153 H7
Wayfarer Rd NTHLT UB5 ... 133 M5
Wayfarers Pk BERK HP4 ... 35 J4
Wayfaring Gn GRAYS RM17 ... 167 L4
Wayford St BTSEA SW11 ... 157 N8
Wayland Av HACK E8 ... 119 P10
Waylands RSLP HA4 ... 112 B2
HYS/HAR UB3 ... 132 E7
STWL/WRAY TW19 ... 172 B2
SWLY BR8 ... 186 E10
Waylands Md BECK BR3 ... 183 P10
Wayleave The ...
WOOL/PLUM SE18 * ... 146 B10
Waylett Pl ALP/SUD HA0 ... 115 J9
WNWD SE27 ... 181 J6
Wayman Cl ORP BR6 ... 207 J10
Waynefleet Tower Av ...
ESH/CLAY KT10 ... 197 P10
Wayne Cl CROY/NA CR0 ... 203 J10
Waynflete Sq NKENS W10 ... 136 G9
Wayre St HLWE CM17 ... 29 M3
Wayside CRAWW RH11 ... 245 L1
CROY/NA CR0 ... 224 C3
GLDGN NW11 ... 117 H6
KGLGY WD4 ... 53 L6
MORT/ESHN SW14 ... 155 P10
POTB/CUF EN6 ... 59 N8
RAD WD7 ... 57 J9
Wayside Av BUSH WD23 ... 74 C10
HCH RM12 ... 125 L7
Wayside Cl ROM RM1 ... 124 C1
STHGT/OAK N14 ... 98 D2
Wayside Ct TWK TW1 ... 177 H2
Wayside Gdns CFSP/GDCR SL9 ... 124 B10
DAGE RM10 ...
The Wayside HHS/BOV HP3 ... 36 D7
Wayville Rd DART DA1 ... 188 A3
Way Volante GVE DA12 ... 191 H7

Weald Rd BRW CM14 ... 105 P2
HGDN/ICK UB10 ... 132 B4
SEV TN13 ... 265 J4
Weald Sq CLPT E5 * ... 120 A7
Wealdstone Rd CHEAM SM3 ... 201 J9
The Weald CHST BR7 ... 184 C9
Weald Wy CTHM CR3 ... 259 M4
Wealdway GVW DA11 ... 190 D8
Weald Wy REDH RH2 ... 124 C4
ROMW/RG RM7 ... 124 C4
YEAD UB4 ... 132 F5
Wealdwood Gdns PIN HA5 ... 94 A7
Weale Rd CHING E4 ... 100 D1
Weall Cl PUR/KEN CR8 ... 222 G9
Weall Gn GSTN WD25 ... 55 J8
Weardale Av DART DA2 ... 188 B5
Weardale Gdns ENC/FH EN2 ... 79 L5
Weardale Rd LEW SE13 ... 183 J1
Wear Pl BETH E2 ... 140 A5
Wearside Rd LEW SE13 ... 160 C10
Weasdale Cl WOKN/KNAP GU21 ... 231 L2
Weatherall Cl ADL/WDHM KT15 ... 215 J2
Weatherhill Cl HORL RH6 ... 280 C4
Weatherhill Rd HORL RH6 ... 281 H4
Weatherley Cl BOW E3 ... 140 E3
Weaver Cl CRAWW RH11 ... 283 H8
CROY/NA CR0 ... 223 N1
EHAM E6 ... 142 G4
Weavers La RSEV TN14 ... 247 K1
STHWK SE1 ... 13 K10
Weaver St WCHPL E1 ... 13 N2
Weavers Wy CAMTN NW1 ... 5 J1
Weaver Wk WNWD SE27 ... 181 J1
Webb Cl CHSWK W4 ... 50 C6
DTCH/LGLY SL3 ... 150 A3
NKENS W10 ... 136 F6
Webb Est CLPT E5 ... 101 P10
Webber Rw STHWK SE1 ... 18 B3
Webber St STHWK SE1 ... 18 B1
Webb Est CLPT E5 * ... 119 P5
Webb Pl WLSDN NW10 ... 136 C5
Webb Rd BKHTH/KID SE3 ... 161 L5
Webbs Meadow SEV TN13 ... 265 K1
Webb's Rd BTSEA SW11 ... 180 A1
Webbscroft Rd DAGE RM10 ... 124 C1
Webbs Rd YEAD UB4 ... 132 F2
Webb St STHWK SE1 ... 19 J4
Webster Cl HCH RM12 ... 125 L3
LHD/OX KT22 ... 218 A10
WAB EN9 ... 63 M9
Webster Gdns EA W5 ... 135 J10
Webster Rd BERM/RHTH SE16 ... 19 P4
WAN E11 ... 121 H8
Websters Cl WOKS/MYFD GU22 ... 231 N6
Weddell Rd CRAWE RH10 ... 284 A10
Wedderburn Rd BARK IG11 ... 142 G3
HAMP NW3 ... 3 H1
Wedgewood Cl EPP CM16 ... 65 K6
NTHWD HA6 * ... 92 D8
Wedgewood Pl COB KT11 ... 217 H10
Wedgwoods BH/WHM TN16 * ... 243 P7
Wedgwood Wk ...
KIL/WHAMP NW6 * ... 117 L10
Wedgwood Wy NRWD SE19 ... 181 K10
Wedhey HLWW/ROY CM19 ... 46 F1
Wedlake St NKENS W10 ... 136 E1
Wedmore Av CLAY IG5 ... 102 D9
Wedmore Gdns ARCH N19 ... 118 E7
Wedmore Ms ARCH N19 ... 118 E8
Wedmore Rd GFD/PVL UB6 ... 134 C3
Wedmore St ARCH N19 ... 118 E8
Wednesbury Gdns HARH RM3 ... 105 N8
Wednesbury Gn HARH RM3 ... 105 N8
Wednesbury Rd HARH RM3 ... 105 N8
Weech Rd KIL/WHAMP NW6 ... 117 K9
Weedington Rd KTTN NW5 ... 118 B10
Weedon Cl CFSP/GDCR SL9 ... 89 P1
Weedon Hl AMS HP6 ... 68 F2
Weekes St SL SL1 ... 128 G10
Weekley Sq BTSEA SW11 ... 157 N9
Weigall Rd LEE/GVPK SE12 ... 161 M10
Weighbridge Rd ...
ADL/WDHM KT15 ... 215 M5
Weighhouse St MYFR/PKLN W1K ... 10 D7
Weighton Rd ...
KTN/HRWW/WS HA3 ... 94 C10
PGE/AN SE20 ... 204 A2
Weihurst Gdns SUT SM1 ... 221 N2
Weimar St PUT/ROE SW15 ... 157 H9
Weirbrook CRAWE RH10 ... 284 B10
Weirdale Av TRDG/WHET N20 ... 98 A3
Weird Wd HART DA3 ... 211 M1
Weir Hall Av UED N18 ... 99 L7
Weir Hall Gdns UED N18 ... 99 L6
Weir Hall Rd UED N18 ... 99 L6
Weir Pl STA TW18 ... 195 H1
Weir Rd BAL SW12 ... 180 D4
BXLY DA5 ... 186 C3
CHERT KT16 ... 195 L7
WIM/MER SW19 ... 179 L6
WOT/HER KT12 ... 195 K8
Weirside Gdns WDR/YW UB7 ... 131 N10
Weirs Pas CAMTN NW1 ... 5 K9
Welbeck Av BFN/LL DA15 ... 185 H4
BMLY BR1 ... 183 N7
YEAD UB4 ... 133 J6
Welbeck Cl BORE WD6 ... 75 M7
EW KT17 ... 220 D4
NWMAL KT3 ... 200 D2
Welbeck Rd HARP AL5 ... 20 C5
Welbeck Rd EBAR EN4 ... 98 B2
EHAM E6 ... 142 A5
RYLN/HDSTN HA2 ... 114 A5
SUT SM1 ... 201 N9
Welbeck Rd CAVSQ/HST W1G ... 10 E5
Welbeck Vls WUSMN N21 * ... 99 L1
Welbeck Wy CAVSQ/HST W1G ... 10 E5
Welby Ct PLSTW E13 ... 141 P4
Welby St CMBW SE5 ... 159 J7
Welch Pl PIN HA5 * ... 93 K9
Welclose St STALW/RED AL3 ... 38 B6
Welcomes Cottages CTHM CR3 * ... 242 F9
Welcomes Rd PUR/KEN CR8 ... 241 K1
Welden SL SL1 ... 128 B8
Welders La CFSP/GDCR SL9 ... 89 L8
Weldon Cl RSLP HA4 ... 132 B1
Weldon Dr E/WMO/HCT KT8 ... 197 N4
Weldon Wy REDH RH1 ... 258 C6
Weld Pl FBAR/BDGN N11 ... 98 B5
Welfare Rd SRTFD E15 ... 141 K2
Welford Cl CLPT E5 ... 120 F2
Welford Pl WIM/MER SW19 ... 179 H7
Welham Rd TOOT SW17 ... 180 B8
Welhouse Rd CAR SM5 ... 202 B6
Welkin Gn HHNE HP2 * ... 36 D5
Wellacre Rd KTN/HRWW/WS HA3 ... 114 G4
Wellan Cl BFN/LL DA15 ... 185 L1
Welland Cl DTCH/LGLY SL3 ... 150 A5
Welland Gdns GFD/PVL UB6 ... 134 C1
Welland Ms WAP E1W ... 13 N8
Wellands HAT AL10 ... 40 B4
Wellands Cl BMLY BR1 ... 206 C2
Welland St GNWCH SE10 ... 161 G1
Well Ap BARK IG11 ... 143 G2

Well Cft HHW HP1 ... 35 L5
Wellcroft Rd WGCE AL7 ... 23 K7
Wellcroft Rd SL SL1 ... 128 C10
WGCE AL7 ... 23 K6
Welldon Crs HRW HA1 ... 114 D4
Well End Rd BORE WD6 ... 75 P4
Wellen Ri HHS/BOV HP3 ... 35 P9
Weller Cl AMS HP6 ... 69 K3
CRAWE RH10 ... 284 C4
Weller Pl ORP BR6 ... 226 D7
ROMW/RG RM7 ... 124 C4
YEAD UB4 ... 132 F5
Wellers Cl BH/WHM TN16 ... 262 F5
Wellers Gv CHESW EN7 ... 61 P4
Weller St STHWK SE1 ... 18 E1
Wellesford Cl BNSTD SM7 ... 239 J7
Wellesley Av DTCH/LGLY SL3 ... 151 J2
HMSMTH W6 ... 156 G2
NTHWD HA6 ... 59 J9
Wellesley Cl CHARL SE7 * ... 161 P4
Wellesley Ct MV/WKIL W9 ... 3 J4
Wellesley Court Rd ...
CROY/NA CR0 * ... 203 L9
Wellesley Crs POTB/CUF EN6 ... 59 P4
WHTN TW2 ... 176 D5
Wellesley Gv CROY/NA CR0 ... 203 L9
Wellesley Park Ms ENC/FH EN2 * ... 79 J8
Wellesley Pth SL SL1 ... 149 M1
Wellesley Pl CAMTN NW1 * ... 5 G9
KTTN NW5 ... 118 B10
Wellesley Rd BELMT SM2 ... 221 M5
BRW CM14 ... 107 P2
CHSWK W4 ... 155 M4
CROY/NA CR0 ... 203 K8
HRW HA1 ... 114 D3
IL IG1 ... 122 C7
KTTN NW5 ... 118 B10
SL SL1 ... 149 M1
WALTH E17 ... 120 F4
WAN E11 ... 121 M3
WHTN TW2 ... 176 D6
Wellesley St WCHPL E1 ... 140 C7
Wellesley Ter IS N1 ... 6 F8
Welley Av STWL/WRAY TW19 ... 150 B10
Welley Rd STWL/WRAY TW19 ... 150 B10
Well Farm Rd CTHM CR3 ... 241 P5
Wellfield Av MUSWH N10 ... 118 C1
Wellfield Rd HAT AL10 ... 40 D3
STRHM/NOR SW16 ... 180 F7
Wellfields LOU IG10 ... 82 D7
Wellfield Wy HCH RM12 ... 124 G5
Wellfit St HNHL SE24 ... 159 H9
Wellgarth GFD/PVL UB6 ... 134 C1
Wellgarth Rd GLDGN NW11 ... 117 G6
Well Gv TRDG/WHET N20 ... 97 H2
Well Hall Pde ELTH/MOT SE9 ... 162 C10
Well Hall Rd ELTH/MOT SE9 ... 162 C10
Well Hl ORP BR6 ... 228 C4
Well Hill La ORP BR6 ... 228 C4
Wellhouse La BAR EN5 ... 76 F8
Wellhouse Rd BECK BR3 ... 204 E4
BRKHM/BTCW RH3 ... 273 M7
Wellhurst Cl ORP BR6 ... 227 J4
Welling High St WELL DA16 ... 163 L9
Wellington Av BFN/LL DA15 ... 185 K2
ED N9 ... 100 A4
HSLW TW3 ... 175 H7
PIN HA5 ... 93 M9
SEVS/STOTM N15 ... 119 P5
VW GU25 ... 193 N6
WPK KT4 ... 200 F10
Wellington Cl CRAWE RH10 ... 284 F4
DAGE RM10 ... 144 D2
NTGHL W11 ... 8 E6
NWCR SE14 ... 160 C7
OXHEY WD19 ... 93 M4
WOT/HER KT12 ... 196 G8
Wellington Gdns CHARL SE7 ... 161 P4
DAGE RM10 ...
NTGHL W11 ... 8 E6
TWK TW2 ... 176 C7
Wellington Hl LOU IG10 ... 81 N4
Wellington Ms CHARL SE7 ... 161 P5
EDUL SE22 ... 159 P10
HOLWY N7 ... 5 L2
STRHM/NOR SW16 ... 180 E5
Wellington Pde BFN/LL DA15 * ... 185 K1
Wellington Park Est ...
CRICK NW2 * ... 116 D7
Wellington Pas WAN E11 ... 121 M3
Wellington Pl BROX EN10 ... 44 B9
BRW CM14 ... 107 H6
COB KT11 ... 217 P8
EFNCH N2 ... 117 P3
STJWD NW8 ... 3 N8
Wellington Rd ASHF TW15 ... 175 P9
BELV DA17 ... 164 A4
BXLY DA5 ... 185 N2
CROY/NA CR0 ... 203 J4
RAIN RM13 ... 145 J7
DART DA1 ... 187 K2
EA W5 ... 155 H3
EBED/NFELT TW14 ... 174 F1
EHAM E6 ... 142 C3
EN EN1 ... 79 N6
EPP CM16 ... 66 C5
FSTGT E7 ... 121 L9
HAYES BR2 ... 205 P4
HPTN TW12 ... 176 C7
LEY E10 ... 120 D6
NKENS W10 ... 136 C5
PIN HA5 ... 93 N9
STAL AL1 ... 38 G7
STJWD NW8 ... 3 N8
STMC/STPC BR5 ... 207 L8
TIL RM18 ... 168 D8
UX/CGN UB8 ... 131 M4
WALTH E17 ... 120 D1
WAN E11 ... 121 M3
WAT WD17 ... 21 H1
WIM/MER SW19 ... 179 K5
Wellington Rd North ...
HSLW TW3 ... 153 N9
Wellington Rd South ...
HSLW TW4 ... 153 N10
Wellington Rw BETH E2 ... 7 M1
Wellington St COVGDN WC2E ... 11 M7
GVE DA12 ... 190 F3
HERT/WAT SG14 ... 23 M2
SL SL1 ... 149 M1
WOOL/PLUM SE18 ... 162 D2
Wellington Ter BAY/PAD W2 ... 8 B8
CEND/HSY/T N8 * ... 119 H1
HRW HA1 ... 114 B4
WAP E1W * ... 140 A10
WOKN/KNAP GU21 ... 231 J5
Wellington Wy BOW E3 ... 140 B1
HORL RH6 ... 280 D6
WEY KT13 ... 216 B6
Welling Wy ELTH/MOT SE9 ... 163 H6
Well La BRWN CM15 ... 76 E6
CDW/CHF RM16 ... 147 K10
CROY/NA CR0 ... 203 H7
GLDGN NW11 ... 117 J4
HLWW/ROY CM19 ... 28 D10
MORT/ESHN SW14 ... 177 P1
WOKN/KNAP GU21 ... 231 P1
Wellmeade Dr SEV TN13 ... 265 K5
Wellmeadow Rd HNWL W7 ... 154 E1
LEW SE13 ... 183 K1
Wellow Wk CAR SM5 ... 202 A6
Well Pth WOKN/KNAP GU21 ... 231 P1
Well Rd BAR EN5 ... 76 F8
HAMP NW3 ... 117 H7
POTB/CUF EN6 ... 59 P5

RSEV TN14 ... 247 K3
Well-row HERT/BAY SG13 ... 42 G3
Wells Cl BH/WHM TN16 ... 262 F5
CHESW EN7 ... 61 K1
GT/LBKH KT23 ... 236 A10
NTHLT UB5 ... 133 K5
SAND/SEL CR2 ... 223 M2
STALW/RED AL3 ... 38 B5
Wells Dr CDALE/KGS NW9 ... 115 J6
Wellsfield BUSH WD23 ... 73 M9
Wells Gdns IL IG1 ... 122 B5
RAIN RM13 ... 144 G1
Wells House Rd WLSDN NW10 ... 136 G5
Wellside Cl BAR EN5 ... 76 F8
Wellside Gdns MORT/ESHN SW14 ... 155 P10
Wells La ASC SL5 ... 192 A5
RGUW GU3 ... 248 B7
Wells Ms FITZ W1T * ... 11 H4
Wells Park Rd SYD SE26 ... 181 M6
Wells Pl CMBW SE5 ... 159 M6
REDH RH1 ... 258 C6
WAND/EARL SW18 ... 179 M3
Wellspring Crs WBLY HA9 ... 115 N7
Wells Rd BMLY BR1 ... 206 G2
EPSOM KT18 ... 219 M10
RGUE GU4 ... 250 F7
SHB W12 ... 156 F1
Wells Sq FSBYW WC1X ... 5 N10
Wells St GTPST W1W ... 10 G4
Wellstead Av ED N18 ... 100 B1
Wellstead Rd EHAM E6 ... 142 D4
Wells Ter FSBYPK N4 ... 119 H7
The Wells STHGT/OAK N14 ... 98 E2
Wellstones WAT WD17 ... 73 H3
Well St HOM E9 ... 140 E2
SRTFD E15 ... 141 K1
Wells Wy CMBW SE5 ... 19 H10
SKENS SW7 ... 15 L3
Wellwood Cl COUL/CHIP CR5 ... 240 G6
Wellwood Rd GDMY/SEVK IG3 ... 123 K10
Welsford St BERM/RHTH SE16 ... 159 M3
Welsh Cl PLSTW E13 ... 141 M5
Welshpool St HACK E8 ... 7 P1
Welshside CDALE/KGS NW9 * ... 116 B3
Welstead Wy CHSWK W4 ... 156 C2
Welsummer Cl CHES/WCR EN8 ... 62 C1
Weltech Centre WGCE AL7 * ... 23 K5
Welton Rd WOOL/PLUM SE18 ... 163 H6
Weltje Rd HMSMTH W6 ... 156 D3
Welwyn Av EBED/NFELT TW14 ... 174 G2
Welwyn Cl CRAWW RH11 ... 283 H10
Welwyn Rd HHNE HP2 ... 36 A1
Welwyn St BETH E2 ... 140 E2
Welwyn Wy YEAD UB4 ... 132 F6
Wembley Hill Rd WBLY HA9 ... 115 N9
Wembley Park Dr WBLY HA9 ... 115 J4
Wembley Rd HPTN TW12 ... 197 P1
Wembley Wy WBLY HA9 ... 135 N1
Wemborough Rd STAN HA7 ... 94 G9
Wembury Ms HGT N6 ... 118 B5
Wembury Rd HGT N6 ... 118 B5
Wemyss Rd BKHTH/KID SE3 ... 161 L5
Wendela Cl WOKS/MYFD GU22 ... 232 C4
Wendela Ct HRW HA1 ... 114 E7
Wendell Rd SHB W12 ... 156 C1
Wendley Dr ADL/WDHM KT15 ... 215 J6
Wendling Rd SUT SM1 ... 201 N6
Wendon St BOW E3 ... 140 E3
Wendover Cl HARP AL5 ... 20 C7
HAYES BR2 ... 205 H10
STALE/WH AL4 ... 39 H1
YEAD UB4 ... 133 J2
Wendover Dr NWMAL KT3 ... 200 C6
Wendover Gdns ...
RBRW/HUT CM13 ... 107 N3
Wendover Pl STA TW18 ... 172 G8
Wendover Rd ELTH/MOT SE9 ... 162 B9
HAYES BR2 ... 205 N3
STHWK SE1 ... 19 P3
WLSDN NW10 ... 136 D2
Wendover Wy BUSH WD23 ... 74 B10
HCH RM12 ... 125 K10
ORP BR6 ... 207 K6
WELL DA16 ... 164 A6
Wendron Cl WOKN/KNAP GU21 ... 231 M4
The Wend COUL/CHIP CR5 ... 222 E10
Wendy Cl EN EN1 ... 79 N10
Wendy Crs GUW GU2 ... 249 M8
Wendy Wy ALP/SUD HA0 ... 135 K5
Wengeo La WARE SG12 ... 26 A1
Wenham Dr DEN/HRF UB9 ... 111 K3
Wenlock Cl CRAWW RH11 ... 283 H10
Wenlock Edge DORK RH4 ... 273 H4
Wenlock Gdns HDN NW4 * ... 116 A1
Wenlock Rd EDGW HA8 ... 95 M7
IS N1 ... 6 F6
Wenlock St IS N1 ... 6 G6
Wennington Rd BOW E3 ... 140 G1
RAIN RM13 ... 145 J7
Wensleydale Av CLAY IG5 ... 102 B10
Wensleydale Gdns HPTN TW12 ... 176 A10
Wensleydale Rd HPTN TW12 ... 175 P9
Wensley Rd UED N18 ... 100 C5
Wensum Wy RKW/CH/CXG WD3 ... 91 N2
Wentbridge Pth BORE WD6 ... 75 P4
Wentland Cl CAT SE6 ... 183 H3
Wentland Rd CAT SE6 ... 183 H3
Wentworth Av BORE WD6 ... 75 J4
FNCH N3 ... 97 K7
SLN SL3 ... 128 F5
Wentworth Cl ASHF TW15 ... 174 B7
FNCH N3 ... 97 K7
GVW DA11 ... 190 D8
HAYES BR2 ... 205 M9
MRDN SM4 ... 201 K7
ORP BR6 ... 227 H4
POTB/CUF EN6 ... 59 N7
RPLY/SEND GU23 ... 233 L2
SURB KT6 ... 199 J8
THMD SE28 ... 72 G4
WAT WD17 ... 21 J2
Wentworth Crs HYS/HAR UB3 ... 152 F2
PECK SE15 ... 159 P7
Wentworth Dene WEY KT13 ... 216 C3
Wentworth Dr CRAWE RH10 ... 284 G6
DART DA1 ... 187 H4
PIN HA5 ... 113 G3
Wentworth Gdns PLMGR N13 ... 99 J2
Wentworth Hl WBLY HA9 ... 115 L1
Wentworth Ms BOW E3 ... 140 E6
Wentworth Pk FNCH N3 ... 97 K7
Wentworth Pl CDW/CHF RM16 ... 168 A2
CSHM HP5 ... 51 H8
STAN HA7 * ... 94 G7
Wentworth Rd BAR EN5 ... 76 A3
CROY/NA CR0 ... 203 H7
GLDGN NW11 ... 117 J4
MNPK E12 ... 141 N1
NWDGN UB2 ... 153 K3
Wentworth St WCHPL E1 ... 13 M4
Wentworth Wy PIN HA5 ... 113 L2
RAIN RM13 ... 145 J1
SAND/SEL CR2 ... 241 L3
Wenvoe Av BXLYHN DA7 ... 164 C8
Wepham Cl YEAD UB4 ... 132 G6
Wernbrook St WOOL/PLUM SE18 ... 162 F5

Werndee Rd SNWD SE25 ... 203 P4
Werneth Hall Rd CLAY IG5 ... 122 C9
Werrington St CAMTN NW1 * ... 5 H8
Werter Rd PUT/ROE SW15 ... 157 H10
Wescott Wy UX/CGN UB8 ... 131 M4
Wesleyan Pl KTTN NW5 ... 118 C3
Wesley Av CAN/RD E16 ... 141 M10
HSLW TW3 ... 153 M8
WLSDN NW10 ... 136 A3
Wesley Cl CHESW EN7 ... 61 K4
HOLWY N7 ... 5 L1
HORL RH6 ... 280 D2
REIG RH2 ... 275 J4
RYLN/HDSTN HA2 ... 114 B7
STMC/STPC BR5 ... 207 M3
WALW SE17 ... 18 D6
Wesley Dr EGH TW20 ... 172 D9
Wesley Hl CSHM HP5 ... 50 E5
Wesley Ms CSHM HP5 * ... 50 E5
Wesley Rd HYS/HAR UB3 ... 133 H9
LEY E10 ... 120 B4
WLSDN NW10 ... 136 A3
Wesley Sq NTGHL W11 ... 8 D6
Wesley St CAVSQ/HST W1G ... 10 D4
Wessels KWD/TDW/WH KT20 ... 238 G10
Wessex Cl GDMY/SEVK IG3 ... 123 H4
KUT/HW KT1 ... 199 N1
THDIT KT7 ... 198 E9
Wessex Ct BECK BR3 ... 204 D1
Wessex Dr ERITH DA8 ... 185 J2
PIN HA5 ... 93 M8
Wessex Gdns GLDGN NW11 ... 117 H4
Wessex La GFD/PVL UB6 ... 134 C4
Wessex Rd HTHAIR TW6 ... 151 N10
Wessex St BETH E2 ... 140 E2
Wessex Ter MTCM CR4 * ... 201 P5
Wessex Wk RDART DA2 * ... 186 E5
West Acres AMSS HP7 ... 50 A6
Westacres ESH/CLAY KT10 ... 217 N4
Westall Cl HERT/BAY SG13 ... 25 K6
Westall Rd LOU IG10 ... 81 P9
Westanley Av AMSS HP7 ... 69 J3
West Ap STMC/STPC BR5 ... 206 F5
West Arbour St WCHPL E1 ... 140 E8
West Av CRAWE RH10 ... 284 E5
FNCH N3 ... 97 K7
HDN NW4 ... 116 C5
HYS/HAR UB3 ... 133 H7
LCOL/BKTW AL2 ... 56 A1
PIN HA5 ... 94 A5
REDH RH1 ... 276 A6
STHL UB1 ... 133 L5
WALTH E17 ... 120 D3
WLGTN SM6 ... 223 H5
WOT/HER KT12 ... 216 F6
West Avenue Rd WALTH E17 ... 120 E3
West Bank BARK IG11 ... 142 E3
DORK RH4 ... 272 E7
ENC/FH EN2 ... 79 K7
STNW/STAM N16 ... 119 M5
Westbank Rd HPTN TW12 ... 176 A8
West Barnes La RYNPK SW20 ... 200 E3
Westbeech Rd WDGN N22 ... 119 J3
Westbere Dr STAN HA7 ... 95 J4
Westbere Rd CRICK NW2 ... 117 H9
Westbourne Av ACT W3 ... 136 A8
CHEAM SM3 ... 201 H9
Westbourne Cl YEAD UB4 ... 133 K6
Westbourne Crescent Ms ...
BAY/PAD W2 * ... 9 L7
Westbourne Crs BAY/PAD W2 ... 9 L7
Westbourne Dr BRW CM14 ... 106 C5
FSTH SE23 ... 182 C5
Westbourne Ga BAY/PAD W2 * ... 9 M7
Westbourne Gdns ...
BAY/PAD W2 ... 8 C6
Westbourne Grove Ms ...
NTGHL W11 ... 8 C6
Westbourne Grove Ter ...
BAY/PAD W2 ... 8 C5
Westbourne Pde ...
HGDN/ICK UB10 * ... 132 C6
Westbourne Park Rd NTGHL W11 ... 8 C5
CROY/NA CR0 ... 203 N6
Westbourne Pl ED N9 ... 100 A4
Westbourne Rd BXLYHN DA7 ... 163 N6
CROY/NA CR0 ... 203 N6
FSTH SE23 ... 182 B5
HOLWY N7 ... 5 P1
STA TW18 ... 173 L10
SYD SE26 ... 181 P4
UX/CGN UB8 ... 132 C6
Westbourne Ter BAY/PAD W2 ... 9 J4
Westbourne Terrace Ms ...
BAY/PAD W2 ... 9 J5
Westbourne Terrace Rd ...
BAY/PAD W2 ... 9 J4
Westbridge Cl SHB W12 ... 136 D10
Westbridge Rd BTSEA SW11 ... 157 N7
Westbrook Av HPTN TW12 ... 175 P4
Westbrook Cl EBAR EN4 ... 77 N2
Westbrook Crs EBAR EN4 ... 77 N2
Westbrook Dr STMC/STPC BR5 ... 207 M8
Westbrooke Crs WELL DA16 ... 164 D3
Westbrooke Rd BFN/LL DA15 ... 185 G8
WELL DA16 ... 164 C3
Westbrook Rd BKHTH/KID SE3 ... 161 P3
HEST TW5 ... 134 D10
THHTH CR7 ... 181 P10
Westbrook Sq EBAR EN4 * ... 77 N2
West Burrowfield WGCE AL7 ... 22 G7
Westbury CHES/WCR EN8 * ... 62 C6
West Carriage Dr BAY/PAD W2 ... 9 M7
West Central St LSQ/SEVD WC2H ... 11 K5
West Chantry ...
KTN/HRWW/WS HA3 ... 94 A9
Westchester Dr HDN NW4 ... 116 D10
Westcliffe Vls KUT/HW KT1 * ... 199 L2
West Cl ASHF TW15 ... 173 J7

BAR EN5 76 E9
EBAR EN4 78 B8
ED N9 99 N4
GFD/PVL UB6 134 B4
HOD EN11 44 F1
RAIN RM13 145 J6
WBLY HA9 115 L6
Westcombe Av CROY/NA CR0 202 F6
Westcombe Dr BAR EN5 77 K9
Westcombe Hl BKHTH/KID SE3 161 M5
Westcombe Lodge Dr YEAD UB4 132 E7
Westcombe Park Rd
BKHTH/KID SE3 161 M6
West Common CFSP/GDCR SL9 110 A3
HARP AL5 20 A5
West Common Cl HARP AL5 20 A6
West Common Gv HARP AL5 20 A6
West Common Rd HAYES BR2 205 M9
UX/CGN UB8 111 N10
Westcoombe Av RYNPK SW20 200 C1
Westcote Ri RSLP HA4 112 D5
Westcote Rd STRHM/NOR SW16 180 D9
Westcott WGCE AL7 23 N4
Westcott Av GVW DA11 190 D6
Westcott Cl BMLY BR1 206 B5
CROY/NA CR0 224 G5
SEVS/STOTM N15 119 N4
Westcott Crs HNWL W7 134 D7
Westcott House POP/IOD E14 * 140 F9
Westcott Rd DORK RH4 272 E2
WALW SE17 18 D9
Westcott St DORK RH4 272 A3
Westcott Wy BELMT SM2 220 F6
West Ct ALP/SUD HA0 115 H7
Westcourt Pde GVE DA12 * 191 J6
West Crs WDSR SL4 148 E8
West Crescent Rd GVE DA12 190 E2
Westcroft SLN SL2 128 G6
Westcroft Cl CRICK NW2 117 H9
PEND EN3 80 B4
Westcroft Ct BROX EN10 44 F5
Westcroft Gdns MRDN SM4 201 J3
Westcroft Ms HMSMTH W6 * 156 D3
Westcroft Rd CAR SM5 222 B1
Westcroft Sq HMSMTH W6 156 D3
Westcroft Wy CRICK NW2 117 H9
West Cromwell Rd ECT SW5 14 D6
West Cross Route SHB W12 136 G9
West Cross Wy BTFD TW8 154 G5
Westdale Rd WOOL/PLUM SE18 162 E5
Westdean Av LEE/GVPK SE12 183 N4
Westdean Cl WAND/EARL SW18 179 L2
Westdean La CSHM HP5 50 B4
Westdene WOT/HER KT12 217 J2
West Dene Dr HARH RM3 105 L6
Westdene Wy WEY KT13 196 F10
West Down GT/LBKH KT23 254 A3
Westdown Rd CAT SE6 182 F3
SRTFD E15 121 H9
West Drayton Park Av
WDR/YW UB7 151 P2
West Drayton Rd UX/CGN UB8 132 D7
West Dr ADL/WDHM KT15 215 L6
ASC SL5 193 J6
BELMT SM2 220 G5
CAR SM5 221 N6
GSTN WD25 73 J2
KTN/HRWW/WS HA3 94 C7
KWD/TDW/WH KT20 238 G4
STRHM/NOR SW16 180 C7
West Drive Gdns
KTN/HRWW/WS HA3 94 C7
West Eaton Pl BGVA SW1W 16 C5
West Eaton Place Ms
KTBR SW1X 16 C5
Wested La SWLY BR8 209 H7
West Ella Rd WLSDN NW10 136 B2
West End BGR/WK TN15 247 N3
BH/WHM TN16 263 L1
West End Av LEY E10 121 H3
PIN HA5 113 M2
West End Cl WLSDN NW10 135 P2
West End Ct PIN HA5 * 113 L2
West End Gdns ESH/CLAY KT10 217 N2
NTHLT UB5 133 K4
West End La BAR EN5 76 G8
BRKMPK AL9 41 M4
ESH/CLAY KT10 217 N3
HYS/HAR UB3 152 E6
KIL/WHAMP NW6 2 F4
KIL/WHAMP NW6 * 117 K10
PIN HA5 113 L1
SLN SL2 129 L3
West End Rd BROX EN10 43 N9
RSLP HA4 112 G8
STHL UB1 133 M10
Westerdale HHNE HP2 35 P3
Westerdale Rd GNWCH SE10 161 M4
Westerfield Rd
SEVS/STOTM N15 * 119 N3
Westerfolds Cl
WOKS/MYFD GU22 232 F3
Westergate Rd ABYW SE2 163 P5
Westerham Av ED N9 99 L4
Westerham Cl ADL/WDHM KT15 215 M3
BELMT SM2 * 221 K6
Westerham Dr BFN/LL DA15 185 M2
Westerham Hl BH/WHM TN16 244 E8
Westerham Rd BH/WHM TN16 263 K1
HAYES BR2 226 A3
LEY E10 120 G4
OXTED RH8 261 M5
RSEV TN14 246 B9
Westerley Crs SYD SE26 * 182 E8
Westermain ADL/WDHM KT15 215 M6
Western Av BRW CM14 107 H2
CHERT KT16 195 K3
CHOB/PIR GU24 230 F7
DAGE RM10 144 D1
DEN/HRF UB9 111 M9
EA W5 135 K5
EGH TW20 194 E3
EPP CM16 65 J8
GLDGN NW11 116 G4
GPK RM2 105 K10
HGDN/ICK UB10 112 A10
RSLP HA4 133 J2
WTHK RM20 * 166 E3
Western Cl CHERT KT16 195 K3
Western Ct FNCH N3 * 97 K7
Western Cross Cl SWCM DA10 189 H2
Western Dr SHPTN TW17 196 E5
Western Gdns BRW CM14 107 H3
EA W5 135 M9
Western Gtwy CAN/RD E16 141 N9
Western La BAL SW12 180 B3
Western Man BAR EN5 * 77 L9
Western Ms MV/WKIL W9 8 D3
Western Pde BAR EN5 77 K9
HGDN/ICK UB10 * 132 C1
Western Perimeter Rd
WDR/YW UB7 151 L7
Western Pl BERM/RHTH SE16 160 D1
DORK RH4 * 272 F2
Western Rd BRW CM14 107 H3
BRXN/ST SW9 159 H9
EA W5 135 J9
EFNCH N2 118 A1
MTCM CR4 201 P1
NWDGN UB2 153 L2
PLSTW E13 141 N3
ROM RM1 124 G3
SUT SM1 221 K2
WAB EN9 45 K8
WALTH E17 121 H3
WDGN N22 98 G10
WLSDN NW10 135 P6
Western Ter HMSMTH W6 * 156 D4
HOD EN11 * 26 G10
Western Vw HYS/HAR UB3 152 G1
Westernville Gdns
GNTH/NBYPK IG2 122 F5
Western Wy BAR EN5 77 K10
THMD SE28 162 G2
West Farm Av ASHTD KT21 237 H4
West Farm Cl ASHTD KT21 237 H5
West Farm Dr ASHTD KT21 237 J5
Westferry Circ POP/IOD E14 140 F10
Westferry Rd POP/IOD E14 140 F9
Westfield AMS HP6 68 B1
BRKMPK AL9 41 K9
HLWS CM18 47 H2
RDKG RH5 270 F9
REIG RH2 257 L7
SEV TN13 247 K8
WGCE AL7 23 K4
Westfield Av SAND/SEL CR2 223 L9
WATN WD24 73 L4
WOKS/MYFD GU22 232 B7
Westfield Cl CDALE/KGS NW9 115 P1
CHES/WCR EN8 62 E7
GVE DA12 190 F9
PEND EN3 80 D7
SUT SM1 221 J1
WBPTN SW10 157 M6
Westfield Common
WOKS/MYFD GU22 232 B8
Westfield Ct STALE/WH AL4 39 J3
Westfield Dr GT/LBKH KT23 236 A8
KTN/HRWW/WS HA3 115 J3
Westfield Gdns CHDH RM6 123 M4
KTN/HRWW/WS HA3 115 J2
Westfield Gv WOKS/MYFD GU22 232 B6
Westfield La
KTN/HRWW/WS HA3 115 J2
Westfield Pde
ADL/WDHM KT15 * 215 N6
Westfield Pk PIN HA5 93 N8
Westfield Park Dr WFD IG8 102 B7
Westfield Rd BEAC HP9 88 B10
BECK BR3 204 E2
BERK HP4 33 K3
BXLYHN DA7 164 D9
CRAWW RH11 283 L7
CROY/NA CR0 203 J9
DAGW RM9 123 P9
GU GU1 250 B6
HERT/WAT SG14 25 K3
HOD EN11 44 E2
MLHL NW7 96 B4
MTCM CR4 201 P2
SLN SL2 128 G6
SURB KT6 199 J5
SUT SM1 221 J1
WEA W13 134 F10
WOKS/MYFD GU22 232 B8
WOT/HER KT12 197 M8
Westfields BARN SW13 156 C9
STALW/RED AL3 37 P9
Westfields Av BARN SW13 156 B9
Westfields Rd ACT W3 135 N7
Westfield St WOOL/PLUM SE18 162 A2
Westfield Wy RSLP HA4 112 G8
WCHPL E1 140 D5
WOKS/MYFD GU22 232 B8
West Flexford La RGUW GU3 266 E1
West Garden Pl BAY/PAD W2 9 P6
West Gdns EW KT17 220 B6
TOOT SW17 179 P9
WAP E1W 140 A9
West Ga EA W5 135 K5
HLW CM20 46 F1
Westgate Crs SL SL1 128 E9
Westgate Est
EBED/NFELT TW14 * 174 C4
Westgate Rd BECK BR3 205 H1
DART DA1 187 L2
SNWD SE25 204 A4
Westgate St HACK E8 140 A3
Westgate Ter WBPTN SW10 15 H8
Westglade Ct
KTN/HRWW/WS HA3 115 J3
West Green Dr CRAWW RH11 283 M7
West Green Pl GFD/PVL UB6 134 C3
West Green Rd SEVS/STOTM N15 119 L2
West Gv GNWCH SE10 161 H7
WFD IG8 101 P7
WOT/HER KT12 217 J1
Westgrove La GNWCH SE10 161 H7
West Halkin St KTBR SW1X 16 C3
West Hall BF/WBF KT14 * 215 M10
West Hallowes ELTH/MOT SE9 184 A4
Westhall Pk WARL CR6 242 A5
Westhall Rd WARL CR6 241 P4
West Ham La SRTFD E15 141 K2
West Hampstead Ms
KIL/WHAMP NW6 2 G2
West Harding St
FLST/FETLN EC4A * 12 B5
Westharold SWLY BR8 208 E3
West Hatch Mnr RSLP HA4 112 G6
Westhay Gdns
MORT/ESHN SW14 177 N1
West Heath CHOB/PIR GU24 230 C9
West Heath Av GLDGN NW11 117 K6
West Heath Cl DART DA1 * 186 G2
HAMP NW3 117 K8
West Heath Dr GLDGN NW11 117 K6
West Heath Gdns HAMP NW3 117 K7
West Heath La SEV TN13 265 J4
West Heath Rd ABYW SE2 163 N5
DART DA1 186 G2
HAMP NW3 117 K7
West Hl DART DA1 187 L2
HOR/WEW KT19 219 P9
ORP BR6 226 C8
OXTED RH8 261 J6
RYLN/HDSTN HA2 114 D7
SAND/SEL CR2 223 M5
WAND/EARL SW18 179 K1
WBLY HA9 115 L6
WIM/MER SW19 178 G3
West Hill Av HOR/WEW KT19 219 P8
West Hill Bank OXTED RH8 261 J6
West Hill Cl CHOB/PIR GU24 230 G6
Westhill Cl GVE DA12 190 E4
West Hill Dr DART DA1 187 K2
Westhill Pk HGT N6 118 A7
West Hill Ri DART DA1 187 L2
West Hill Rd HOD EN11 44 E1
WAND/EARL SW18 179 J2
WOKS/MYFD GU22 232 B5
West Hill Wy TRDG/WHET N20 97 L2
Westholm GLDGN NW11 117 L2
West Holme ERITH DA8 164 D7
Westholme ORP BR6 207 H7
Westholme Gdns RSLP HA4 113 H6
Westhorne Av ELTH/MOT SE9 183 P2
Westhorpe Gdns HDN NW4 116 F1
Westhorpe Rd PUT/ROE SW15 156 F9
West House Cl WIM/MER SW19 179 H4
Westhumble St RDKG RH5 254 G7
Westhurst Dr CHST BR7 184 E8
West Hyde La CFSP/GDCR SL9 90 D8
West India Av POP/IOD E14 140 F10
West India Dock Rd
POP/IOD E14 140 E8
West Kent Av GVW DA11 189 P2
Westlake Cl PLMGR N13 99 H4
YEAD UB4 133 M6
Westland Av EMPK RM11 125 M6
Westland Cl GSTN WD25 54 G10
STWL/WRAY TW19 * 173 P2
Westland Dr BRKMPK AL9 59 H3
HAYES BR2 205 L9
Westland Pl FSBYE EC1V 6 G9
Westland Rd WAT WD17 * 73 J6
Westlands Av SL SL1 128 B8
Westlands Cl HYS/HAR UB3 153 H3
SL SL1 128 B8
Westlands Ct EPSOM KT18 237 P1
Westlands Ter BAL SW12 180 D2
Westlands Wy OXTED RH8 261 J3
Westland Wy CDW/CHF RM16 147 M10
West La BERM/RHTH SE16 160 A1
RDKG RH5 271 L5
Westlea Av GSTN WD25 73 M3
Westlea Cl BROX EN10 44 E10
Westlea Rd BROX EN10 44 E9
HNWL W7 154 F2
Westleas HORL RH6 279 P2
Westlees Cl RDKG RH5 273 J5
Westleigh Av COUL/CHIP CR5 240 B2
PUT/ROE SW15 178 F1
Westleigh Dr BMLY BR1 206 B2
Westleigh Gdns EDGW HA8 95 M9
West Links ALP/SUD HA0 135 J5
Westlinton Cl MLHL NW7 97 H7
West Lodge Av ACT W3 135 M10
West Lodge Ct ACT W3 * 135 M10
Westlyn Cl RAIN RM13 145 K5
Westly Wd WGCE AL7 23 K4
Westmacott Dr
EBED/NFELT TW14 174 G4
West Malling Wy HCH RM12 125 J10
West Md HOR/WEW KT19 220 B3
Westmead PUT/ROE SW15 178 E3
West Md RSLP HA4 113 K9
Westmead WDSR SL4 148 G9
West Md WGCE AL7 23 L8
Westmead WOKN/KNAP GU21 231 N4
Westmead Dr REDH RH1 276 B8
Westmeade Cl CHESW EN7 62 A5
Westmead Rd SUT SM1 221 N1
West Meads GUW GU2 267 L1
HORL RH6 280 D4
Westmede BARK/HLT IG6 102 F7
Westmere Dr MLHL NW7 96 A4
West Mersea Cl CAN/RD E16 141 N10
West Ms PIM SW1V 16 F6
TOTM N17 * 100 A7
West Mt GVW DA11 190 C2
Westminster Av THHTH CR7 203 J2
Westminster Br WHALL SW1A 17 M2
Westminster Bridge Rd
WHALL SW1A 17 M2
Westminster Cl
EBED/NFELT TW14 175 H4
TEDD TW11 176 F8
Westminster Ct HARP AL5 * 20 B4
STAL AL1 38 B8
WOKS/MYFD GU22 * 232 E7
Westminster Dr PLMGR N13 98 F6
Westminster Gdns BARK IG11 143 H4
BARK/HLT IG6 102 G10
CHING E4 101 K2
Westminster Ldg STAL AL1 * 38 B8
Westminster Rd CRAWE RH10 284 D8
ED N9 100 A2
HNWL W7 134 D10
SUT SM1 201 N9
Westmoat Cl BECK BR3 183 H10
Westmont Rd ESH/CLAY KT10 198 D9
Westmoor Gdns PEND EN3 80 C6
Westmoor Rd PEND EN3 80 C6
Westmoor St CHARL SE7 162 A3
Westmoreland Av EMPK RM11 125 K3
WELL DA16 163 H10
Westmoreland Dr BELMT SM2 221 L5
Westmoreland Pl BMLY BR1 * 205 M3
EA W5 * 135 J7
PIM SW1V 16 F8
Westmoreland Rd BARN SW13 156 C7
KTN/HRWW/WS HA3 115 L2
CMBW SE5 18 G9
WWKM BR4 205 K5
Westmoreland St
CAVSQ/HST W1G 10 D4
Westmoreland Ter
PGE/AN SE20 * 182 A10
PIM SW1V 16 F7
Westmore Rd BH/WHM TN16 243 P7
Westmorland Cl HOR/WEW KT19 220 B6
MNPK E12 122 A7
TWK TW1 176 G2
Westmorland Rd HRW HA1 114 A3
WALTH E17 120 F4
Westmorland Wy MTCM CR4 202 E5
Westmount Ct EA W5 * 135 L7
Westmount Rd ELTH/MOT SE9 162 C8
West Oak BECK BR3 205 J1
Westoe Rd ED N9 100 A3
Weston Av ADL/WDHM KT15 215 K1
E/WMO/HCT KT8 197 M4
THDIT KT7 198 D7
WTHK RM20 166 E4
Weston Cl COUL/CHIP CR5 240 G6
POTB/CUF EN6 59 J8
RBRW/HUT CM13 107 P1
Weston Dr CTHM CR3 241 K8
CTHM CR3 241 P10
STAN HA7 94 G9
Weston Flds SHGR GU5 269 M5
Weston Gdns ISLW TW7 154 C7
WOKS/MYFD GU22 233 H2
Weston Gn DAGW RM9 123 P9
THDIT KT7 198 D9
Weston Green Rd
ESH/CLAY KT10 198 C8
Weston Gv BMLY BR1 205 L1
Weston Lea EHSLY KT24 252 E1
Weston Pk CEND/HSY/T N8 118 F4
KUT/HW KT1 199 K2
THDIT KT7 198 D8
Weston Park Cl THDIT KT7 * 198 D8
Weston Ri FSBYW WC1X 5 P8
Weston Rd BMLY BR1 183 L10
CHSWK W4 155 P2
DAGW RM9 123 P9
ENC/FH EN2 79 L6
EW KT17 220 B7
GUW GU2 249 N9
SL SL1 128 F7
THDIT KT7 198 D8
Weston St STHWK SE1 13 H10
Weston Wk HACK E8 140 A2
Weston Wy WOKS/MYFD GU22 233 H2
Westover Cl BELMT SM2 221 L5
Westover Hl HAMP NW3 117 K7
Westover Rd WAND/EARL SW18 179 M2
Westow Hl NRWD SE19 181 M9
Westow St NRWD SE19 181 M10
West Palace Gdns WEY KT13 196 C10
West Pk ELTH/MOT SE9 184 B5
West Park Av RCH/KEW TW9 155 N7
West Park Cl CHDH RM6 123 N3
HEST TW5 153 N5
West Park Hl BRW CM14 106 F4
West Park Rd CRAWE RH10 285 N2
HOR/WEW KT19 219 L8
NWDGN UB2 134 C10
RCH/KEW TW9 155 M7
West Parkside GNWCH SE10 161 K1
WARL CR6 242 F1
West Pl EPP CM16 47 L10
NWDGN UB2 * 154 A3
WIM/MER SW19 178 D8
West Point SL SL1 128 C10
Westpole Av EBAR EN4 78 C8
Westport Rd PLSTW E13 141 N6
Westport St WCHPL E1 140 C8
West Poultry Av FARR EC1M 12 C4
West Quarters SHB W12 136 D8
West Quay Dr YEAD UB4 133 M7
West Rp HTHAIR TW6 152 B7
Westray HHS/BOV HP3 36 D8
Westridge Cl CSHM HP5 50 E6
HHW HP1 35 J6
West Ridge Gdns GFD/PVL UB6 134 B4
West Riding LCOL/BKTW AL2 55 N6
West Ri BAY/PAD W2 * 9 P7
West Rd BERK HP4 33 M4
CHDH RM6 123 P4
CHEL SW3 16 B9
CHSGTN KT9 219 H7
CLAP SW4 180 E1
EA W5 135 K7
EBAR EN4 98 B2
EBED/NFELT TW14 174 E3
GU GU1 268 B1
HLW CM20 29 K10
KUTN/CMB KT2 199 P1
REIG RH2 275 L1
ROMW/RG RM7 124 E5
SOCK/AV RM15 146 G5
SRTFD E15 141 L3
TOTM N17 100 A7
WDR/YW UB7 152 A2
WEY KT13 216 C5
West Rw NKENS W10 137 H6
Westrow Dr BARK IG11 123 K10
Westrow Gdns GDMY/SEVK IG3 123 J7
West Shaw HART DA3 211 J2
West Sheen V RCH/KEW TW9 155 L10
West Side BROX EN10 62 D1
Westside HDN NW4 96 E10
West Side Common
WIM/MER SW19 178 F9
Westside Ct CHOB/PIR GU24 * 212 D9
West Smithfield STBT EC1A 12 D4
West Spur Rd UX/CGN UB8 131 N5
West Sq HLW CM20 * 28 F10
LBTH SE11 18 C4
West St BETH E2 140 A4
BMLY BR1 205 M1
CAR SM5 222 A1
CRAWW RH11 283 N8
CROY/NA CR0 223 K1
DORK RH4 272 F2
EPSOM KT18 219 P9
ERITH DA8 164 E3
EW KT17 220 B6
GRAYS RM17 167 M5
GVW DA11 190 E2
HERT/BAY SG13 25 K6
HOR/WEW KT19 219 P9
HRW HA1 114 C6
LSQ/SEVD WC2H 11 K6
REIG RH2 257 J10
SUT SM1 221 L2
WALTH E17 120 G3
WAN E11 121 K8
WARE SG12 26 C2
WAT WD17 73 J6
WOKN/KNAP GU21 232 C3
West Street La CAR SM5 222 A1
West Street Pl CROY/NA CR0 * 223 K1
West Temple Sheen
MORT/ESHN SW14 177 N1
West Tenter St WCHPL E1 13 M6
West Ter BFN/LL DA15 * 185 H4
West Thurrock Wy WTHK RM20 166 F4
West Towers PIN HA5 113 L4
West Valley Rd HHS/BOV HP3 35 M10
West Vw CSHM HP5 51 J5
EBED/NFELT TW14 174 D4
HAT AL10 40 D2
LOU IG10 82 C7
Westview HNWL W7 134 D8
West View Av CTHM CR3 241 N4
West View Cl RAIN RM13 145 K5
Westview Cl NKENS W10 136 F8
RAIN RM13 * 145 K5
REDH RH1 275 P3
WLSDN NW10 116 C10
Westview Ct BORE WD6 75 J10
Westview Crs ED N9 99 M1
Westview Dr WFD IG8 102 A10
West View Gdns BORE WD6 75 J10
Westview Ri HHNE HP2 35 N5
West View Rd DART DA1 187 N2
STALW/RED AL3 38 A5
SWLY BR8 208 E6
SWLY BR8 209 H4
WARL CR6 242 A5
Westville Rd SHB W12 156 D2
THDIT KT7 198 F7
West Wk EBAR EN4 98 B2
HYS/HAR UB3 133 H10
Westward Ho GU GU1 250 C8
Westward Rd CHING E4 100 E6
Westward Wy
KTN/HRWW/WS HA3 115 K4
West Warwick Pl PIM SW1V * 16 G6
West Wy BRW CM14 106 F4
CAR SM5 221 N6
CRAWE RH10 284 B6
CROY/NA CR0 204 D9
EDGW HA8 95 N7
HARP AL5 20 B1
HEST TW5 153 N7
PEND EN3 80 G3
PIN HA5 113 L1
RKW/CH/CXG WD3 91 L2
RSLP HA4 112 G6
SHPTN TW17 196 E6
STMC/STPC BR5 206 G5
UED N18 99 L5
WLSDN NW10 116 A9
WWKM BR4 205 J6
Westway BAY/PAD W2 9 J4
CRAWE RH10 285 H2
CTHM CR3 241 L8
GUW GU2 249 L8
HORL RH6 280 C8
RYNPK SW20 200 E4
SHB W12 136 G9
Westway Cl RYNPK SW20 200 E3
West Way Gdns CROY/NA CR0 204 C9
Westway Gdns REDH RH1 258 B7
Westways BH/WHM TN16 262 F2
HOR/WEW KT19 220 C1
Westwell Cl STMC/STPC BR5 207 N8
Westwell Rd STRHM/NOR SW16 180 F9
Westwell Road Ap
STRHM/NOR SW16 180 F9
Westwick Cl HHNE HP2 36 E7
Westwick Gdns HMSMTH W6 156 G1
HSLWW TW4 153 J8
Westwick Pl GSTN WD25 55 K10
Westwick Rw HHNE HP2 36 E7
Westwood Av ADL/WDHM KT15 215 J8
BRW CM14 106 F5
NRWD SE19 * 181 K10
RYLN/HDSTN HA2 114 A9
Westwood Cl AMS HP6 70 A5
BMLY BR1 206 A3
ESH/CLAY KT10 198 B10
POTB/CUF EN6 59 K6
RSLP HA4 112 C4
Westwood Dr AMS HP6 70 A5
Westwood Gdns BARN SW13 156 C9
Westwood Hl SYD SE26 181 P8
Westwood La RGUW GU3 266 A2
WELL DA16 163 K10
Westwood Pk FSTH SE23 182 A5
Westwood Pl SYD SE26 * 181 P8
Westwood Rd BARN SW13 156 C9
BFOR GU20 192 D9
COUL/CHIP CR5 240 E4
GDMY/SEVK IG3 123 J6
MEO DA13 189 K8
West Woodside BXLY DA5 185 P4
Westwood Wy SEV TN13 246 G8
Wetheral Dr STAN HA7 94 G9
Wetherby Cl NTHLT UB5 134 A1
Wetherby Gdns ECT SW5 15 J6
Wetherby Ms ECT SW5 15 H7
Wetherby Pl SKENS SW7 15 K8
Wetherby Rd BORE WD6 75 K5
ENC/FH EN2 79 K5
Wetherby Wy CHSGTN KT9 219 K4
Wetherden St WALTH E17 120 E5
Wethered Rd SL SL1 128 A8
Wetherell Rd HOM E9 140 C3
Wetherill Rd MUSWH N10 98 B9
Wetherly Cl HLWE CM17 29 M8
Wettern Cl SAND/SEL CR2 223 M6
Wetton Pl EGH TW20 172 C8
Wexfenne Gdns
WOKS/MYFD GU22 233 L2
Wexford Rd BAL SW12 180 A3
Wexham Park La DTCH/LGLY SL3 129 P6
Wexham Pl SLN SL2 * 129 N1
Wexham Rd SL SL1 129 M8
SLN SL2 129 N7
Wexham St SLN SL2 129 M2
Wexham Woods DTCH/LGLY SL3 129 P7
Wey Av CHERT KT16 195 K3
Weybank RPLY/SEND GU23 233 P2
Weybarton BF/WBF KT14 216 A9
Weybourne Cl HARP AL5 20 C1
Weybourne Pl SAND/SEL CR2 223 L6
Weybourne St
WAND/EARL SW18 179 M5
Weybridge Ct
BERM/RHTH SE16 * 160 A4
Weybridge Pk WEY KT13 216 C2
Weybridge Rd ADL/WDHM KT15 215 P1
THHTH CR7 203 H4
Weybrook Dr RGUE GU4 250 E5
Wey Cl BF/WBF KT14 215 L9
Wey Ct ADL/WDHM KT15 215 N5
HOR/WEW KT19 219 P1
Weydown Cl RGUW GU3 249 L5
WIM/MER SW19 179 H4
Weydown La GUW GU2 249 M5
Weyhill Rd WCHPL E1 13 P5
Weylands Pk WEY KT13 216 E3
Wey La CSHM HP5 50 G8
Weylea Av RGUE GU4 250 D7
Weylond Rd BCTR RM8 124 A8
Wey Manor Rd ADL/WDHM KT15 215 N5
Weyman Rd BKHTH/KID SE3 161 P7
Weymead Cl CHERT KT16 195 M8
Weymouth Av EA W5 155 H2
MLHL NW7 96 B6
Weymouth Cl EHAM E6 142 E8
Weymouth Ct BELMT SM2 * 221 L4
Weymouth Dr CDW/CHF RM16 167 J4
Weymouth Ms CAVSQ/HST W1G 10 E3
Weymouth Rd YEAD UB4 132 F5
Weymouth St CAVSQ/HST W1G 10 D3
HHS/BOV HP3 35 N10
Weymouth Ter BETH E2 7 M7
Weymouth Vls FSBYPK N4 * 118 G7
Weymouth Wk STAN HA7 94 F7
Wey Rd WEY KT13 196 A10
Weyside Cl BF/WBF KT14 216 A8
Weyside Gdns GU GU1 249 N8
Weyside Rd GU GU1 249 N9
Wey - South Pth GUW GU2 267 P2
RGUE GU4 268 B8
RGUW GU3 268 A6
Wey View Ct GU GU1 * 267 P1
Whadcoat St FSBYPK N4 119 H7
Whalebone Av CHDH RM6 124 A4
Whalebone Gv CHDH RM6 124 A4
Whalebone La North CHDH RM6 123 P2
CRW RM5 103 P8
Whalebone La South BCTR RM8 124 A6
Whales Yd SRTFD E15 * 141 K2
Whaley Rd POTB/CUF EN6 59 M9
Wharfdale Cl FBAR/BDGN N11 98 B7
Wharfdale Rd IS N1 5 M7
Wharfedale HHNE HP2 35 P3
Wharfedale Gdns THHTH CR7 202 G4
Wharfedale Rd RDART DA2 188 B4
Wharfedale St WBPTN SW10 14 G8
Wharf La POP/IOD E14 140 E8
RKW/CH/CXG WD3 91 P1
RPLY/SEND GU23 232 F9
TWK TW1 176 F4
Wharf Pl BETH E2 7 P6
Wharf Rd BROX EN10 44 F10
BRW CM14 106 G4
CAMTN NW1 5 K6
GRAYS RM17 167 L5
GU GU1 249 P10
GVE DA12 191 H2
HHW HP1 35 L8
IS N1 6 E8
PEND EN3 80 D10
SRTFD E15 141 J3
STWL/WRAY TW19 171 P3
Wharf Rd South GRAYS RM17 167 L5
Wharfside Cl ERITH DA8 164 G4
Wharfside Rd POP/IOD E14 141 K8
Wharf St CAN/RD E16 141 K7
Wharf Ter PUT/ROE SW15 157 H10
The Wharf RDART DA2 * 166 G10
Wharley Hook HLWS CM18 47 K4
Wharncliffe Dr STHL UB1 134 C10
Wharncliffe Gdns SNWD SE25 203 M2
Wharncliffe Rd SNWD SE25 203 L2
Wharton Cl WLSDN NW10 136 B1
Wharton Cottages FSBYW WC1X * 5 P10
Wharton Rd BMLY BR1 205 N1
Wharton St FSBYW WC1X 5 P10
Whateley Rd EDUL SE22 181 N1
PGE/AN SE20 182 C10
Whately Cl GUW GU2 249 N5
Whatley Av RYNPK SW20 200 G3
Whatman Rd FSTH SE23 182 C3
Whatmore Cl STWL/WRAY TW19 173 K2
Wheastone Rd NKENS W10 * 8 B3
NKENS W10 * 137 H7
Wheatash Rd ADL/WDHM KT15 195 L9
Wheatbarn WGCE AL7 23 L4
The Wheatbutts WDSR SL4 148 E4
Wheat Cl STALE/WH AL4 38 F2
Wheatcroft CHESW EN7 62 A4
Wheatfield HAT AL10 40 E3
HHNE HP2 35 N4
Wheatfields HLWE CM17 29 N5
PEND EN3 80 D5
Wheatfield Wy HORL RH6 280 C3
KUT/HW KT1 199 K3
Wheathampstead Rd HARP AL5 20 C5
Wheathill Rd PGE/AN SE20 204 A2
Wheat Knoll PUR/KEN CR8 241 K2
Wheatlands HEST TW5 153 P5
Wheatlands Rd DTCH/LGLY SL3 149 N2
TOOT SW17 180 B6
Wheatley Cl EMPK RM11 125 L3
HDN NW4 96 D10
RDART DA2 188 F1
SBW CM21 29 M2
WGCE AL7 23 K7
Wheatley Crs HYS/HAR UB3 133 H9
Wheatley Dr GSTN WD25 55 K10
Wheatley Gdns ED N9 99 M3
Wheatley Rd ISLW TW7 154 E9
WGCE AL7 23 K6
Wheatleys STALE/WH AL4 39 H4
Wheatley St CAVSQ/HST W1G 10 D4
Wheatley Terrace Rd ERITH DA8 164 G5
Wheatley Wy CFSP/GDCR SL9 90 B7
Wheatsheaf Cl CHERT KT16 214 G3
NTHLT UB5 113 M10
Wheat Sheaf Cl POP/IOD E14 160 G3
Wheatsheaf Cl
WOKN/KNAP GU21 232 C2
Wheatsheaf Hl RSEV TN14 228 A5
Wheatsheaf La FUL/PGN SW6 156 F6
STA TW18 173 J10
VX/NE SW8 158 F6
Wheatsheaf Pde WDSR SL4 * 148 D8
Wheatsheaf Rd ROM RM1 124 G4
WARE SG12 28 A1
Wheatsheaf Ter FUL/PGN SW6 * 157 J6
Wheatstone Cl CRAWE RH10 284 C2
DTCH/LGLY SL3 149 M2
WIM/MER SW19 201 N1
Wheatstone Rd NKENS W10 137 H7
Wheeler Av OXTED RH8 261 J5
Wheeler Gdns IS N1 5 M5
Wheeler La WCHPL E1 13 L3
Wheeler Pl HAYES BR2 205 N4
Wheeler Rd CRAWE RH10 284 C9
Wheelers EPP CM16 65 J5
Wheelers Cl WAB EN9 45 K8
Wheelers Cross BARK IG11 142 G4
Wheelers Dr RSLP HA4 112 D4
Wheelers Farm Gdns EPP CM16 66 C2
Wheelers Gn WAB EN9 * 45 L8
Wheelers La BRKHM/BTCW RH3 273 N2
BRW CM14 86 A8
EPSOM KT18 219 P10
HHS/BOV HP3 35 P8
HORL RH6 281 H5
Wheelers Orch CFSP/GDCR SL9 90 B7
Wheel Farm Dr DAGE RM10 124 D8
Wheelock Cl ERITH DA8 164 C6
Wheelright Cl BUSH WD23 74 A10
Wheelwrights Pl
DTCH/LGLY SL3 * 150 F6
Wheelwright St HOLWY N7 5 N3
Whelan Wy WLGTN SM6 202 E10
Wheler St WCHPL E1 13 L2
Whellock Rd CHSWK W4 156 B2
Whenman Av BXLY DA5 186 D5
Wherwell Rd GUW GU2 267 P2
Whetstone Cl TRDG/WHET N20 97 N3
Whetstone Pk LINN WC2A 11 N5
Whetstone Rd BKHTH/KID SE3 161 P8
Whewell Rd ARCH N19 118 F7
Whichcote St STHWK SE1 * 12 A10
Whichert Cl BEAC HP9 88 B5
Whidborne Cl DEPT SE8 160 F8
Whidborne St STPAN WC1H 5 M10
Whielden Ga AMSS HP7 68 C9
Whielden Hts AMSS HP7 68 F7
Whielden La AMSS HP7 68 F7
Whielden St AMSS HP7 68 G7
Whieldon Gra HLWE CM17 47 N3
Whimbrel Cl SAND/SEL CR2 223 L7
Whimbrel Wy YEAD UB4 133 L8
Whinchat Rd THMD SE28 162 G2
Whinfell Cl STRHM/NOR SW16 180 E8
Whinfell Wy GVE DA12 191 J7
Whinshill Ct ASC SL5 192 F8
Whinyates Rd ELTH/MOT SE9 162 B9
Whipley Cl RGUE GU4 250 E5
Whippendell Cl STMC/STPC BR5 207 L1
Whippendell Rd WATW WD18 72 G9
Whippendell Wy
STMC/STPC BR5 207 L1
Whipps Cross Rd WAN E11 121 K3
Whiskin St CLKNW EC1R 6 C10
Whisper Wd RKW/CH/CXG WD3 71 L7
Whistler Cl CRAWE RH10 284 A10
Whistler Gdns EDGW HA8 95 L10
Whistlers Av BTSEA SW11 * 157 N6
Whistler St HBRY N5 119 J10
Whistler Wk WBPTN SW10 * 157 M6
Whiston Rd BETH E2 7 L7
Whitacre Ms LBTH SE11 18 B8
Whitakers Wy LOU IG10 82 C5
Whitbread Cl TOTM N17 99 P9
Whitbread Rd BROCKY SE4 160 D10
Whitburn Rd LEW SE13 182 C1
Whitby Av WLSDN NW10 135 N5
Whitby Cl BH/WHM TN16 243 N5
RDART DA2 188 F1
Whitby Gdns CDALE/KGS NW9 115 M1
SUT SM1 201 N9
Whitby Pde RSLP HA4 * 113 K7
Whitby Rd RSLP HA4 113 J8
RYLN/HDSTN HA2 114 B8
SL SL1 129 H9
SUT SM1 201 N9
WOOL/PLUM SE18 162 C3
Whitby St WCHPL E1 13 L1
Whitcher Cl NWCR SE14 160 D5
Whitcher Pl CAMTN NW1 4 G2
Whitchurch Av EDGW HA8 95 L8
Whitchurch Cl EDGW HA8 95 L7
Whitchurch Gdns EDGW HA8 95 L8
Whitchurch La EDGW HA8 95 K8
Whitchurch Pde EDGW HA8 * 95 M8
Whitchurch Rd HARH RM3 105 M5
NKENS W10 136 G9
Whitcomb St SOHO/SHAV W1D 11 J7
Whitcome Ms RCH/KEW TW9 155 N7
Whiteadder Wy POP/IOD E14 160 G3
Whitear Wk SRTFD E15 141 J1
White Av GVW DA11 190 C6
Whitebarn La DAGE RM10 144 B4
Whitebeam Av HAYES BR2 206 D7
Whitebeam Cl BGR/WK TN15 247 P3
CHESW EN7 61 M2
VX/NE SW8 * 158 G6
Whitebeam Dr REIG RH2 275 L3
SOCK/AV RM15 147 H5
Whitebeams HAT AL10 40 D7
LCOL/BKTW AL2 56 A4
White Beam Wy
KWD/TDW/WH KT20 238 E7
White Bear Pl HAMP NW3 * 117 N9
White Bear Yd CLKNW EC1R * 12 A2
Whiteberry Rd RDKG RH5 272 A10
White Bridge Av MTCM CR4 201 N3
White Bridge Cl
EBED/NFELT TW14 174 G2
Whitebroom Rd HHW HP1 35 H4
White Bushes REDH RH1 276 B5
White Butts Rd RSLP HA4 113 L8
Whitechapel High St
TWRH EC3N 13 M5
Whitechapel Rd WCHPL E1 13 N4
White Church La WCHPL E1 13 N5
White City Cl SHB W12 136 F9
White City Rd SHB W12 136 F9
White Cl SL SL1 129 J10
White Conduit St IS N1 6 B7
Whitecote Rd STHL UB1 134 B8
White Craig Cl PIN HA5 93 P6
Whitecroft STAL AL1 38 G9
SWLY BR8 208 F2
Whitecroft Cl BECK BR3 205 J4
Whitecroft Wy BECK BR3 205 H4
Whitecross St STLK EC1Y 12 F1
Whitefield Av CRICK NW2 116 F6
PUR/KEN CR8 241 H2
Whitefield Cl PUT/ROE SW15 179 H2
STMC/STPC BR5 207 M3
Whitefield Crs RDART DA2 188 B3
Whitefields Rd CHES/WCR EN8 62 B4
Whitefoot La BMLY BR1 183 J7
Whitefoot Ter BMLY BR1 183 L6
Whiteford Rd SL SL1 129 K7
White Friars SEV TN13 265 H3
Whitefriars Av
KTN/HRWW/WS HA3 94 D10
Whitefriars Dr
KTN/HRWW/WS HA3 94 D10
Whitefriars St EMB EC4Y 12 B6
White Gdns DAGE RM10 144 B1
White Gate Gdns
KTN/HRWW/WS HA3 94 D8
White Gates HCH RM12 125 K7
Whitegates WOKS/MYFD GU22 232 C6
Whitegates Cl
RKW/CH/CXG WD3 72 B8
Whitegate Wy
KWD/TDW/WH KT20 238 E6
Whitehall WHALL SW1A 11 L10
Whitehall Cl CHIG IG7 103 K4
WAB EN9 45 K8
Whitehall Ct WHALL SW1A 11 L10
Whitehall Crs CHSGTN KT9 219 J2
Whitehall Dr CRAWW RH11 283 H7
Whitehall Farm La VW GU25 194 B3
Whitehall Gdns ACT W3 135 M10
CHING E4 101 K2
CHSWK W4 155 N5
WHALL SW1A 11 L10
Whitehall La BKHH IG9 101 M3
EGH TW20 172 C10
ERITH DA8 164 G8
GRAYS RM17 167 P5
REIG RH2 275 J4
STWL/WRAY TW19 172 D2
VW GU25 194 C1
Whitehall Pk ARCH N19 118 D6
Whitehall Park Rd CHSWK W4 155 N5
Whitehall Pl WHALL SW1A 11 L10
WLGTN SM6 222 C1
Whitehall Rd CHING E4 101 K3
GRAYS RM17 167 P3
HAYES BR2 206 A5
HNWL W7 154 F1
HRW HA1 114 D5
THHTH CR7 203 H5
UX/CGN UB8 131 N3
Whitehall St TOTM N17 99 N8
Whitehands Cl HOD EN11 44 E3
White Hart Av THMD SE28 163 J2
White Hart Cl CSTG HP8 89 M4

SEV TN13 265 K4
White Hart Dr HHNE HP2 36 A7
White Hart La BARN SW13 156 B8
RGUW GU3 248 F9
ROMW/RG RM7 104 B9
WDGN N22 99 J8
White Hart Meadow BEAC HP9 88 D10
White Hart Mdw
RPLY/SEND GU23 233 M7
White Hart Pde SEV TN13 * 246 F8
The White Hart Pde SEV TN13 * 246 F8
White Hart Rd HHNE HP2 36 B7
ORP BR6 207 K7
SL SL1 149 J2
WOOL/PLUM SE18 163 H3
White Hart Rw CHERT KT16 * 195 K7
White Hart St LBTH SE11 18 B7
White Hart Ter TOTM N17 * 99 N8
White Hart Wd SEV TN13 265 K5
White Hart Yd GVE DA12 190 F2
STHWK SE1 12 G10
Whitehaven CHESW EN7 * 61 M4
SL SL1 129 L9
Whitehaven Cl CHESW EN7 61 M4
HAYES BR2 205 M4
Whitehaven St STJWD NW8 9 N2
Whitehead Cl RDART DA2 187 K6
UED N18 99 L6
WAND/EARL SW18 179 M3
Whitehead's Gv CHEL SW3 15 P7
CHEL SW3 16 A6
White Heart Av UX/CGN UB8 132 D7
Whiteheath Av RSLP HA4 112 D5
White Hedge Dr STALW/RED AL3 38 B4
White Hermitage WDSR SL4 * 171 P1
White Hern Ct CHES/WCR EN8 62 B6
White Heron Ms TEDD TW11 * 176 E9
White Hl BERK HP4 33 P10
BFOR GU20 212 A1
COUL/CHIP CR5 239 N9
CSHM HP5 51 H7
DEN/HRF UB9 92 B7
HHW HP1 35 J7
SAND/SEL CR2 223 L6
WLYN AL6 22 D1
Whitehill BERK HP4 34 A4
White Hill Cl CSHM HP5 51 H6
Whitehill Ct BERK HP4 34 A4
Whitehill La GVE DA12 190 G6
REDH RH1 259 L3
RPLY/SEND GU23 234 D9
Whitehill Pde GVE DA12 190 F6
Whitehill Pl VW GU25 194 B5
Whitehill Rd DART DA1 187 H1
GVE DA12 190 F5
HART DA3 211 J2
MEO DA13 189 J10
Whitehills Rd LOU IG10 82 D7
Whitehorn Pl WDR/YW UB7 132 A10
White Horse Dr EPSOM KT18 219 P10
White Horse Hl CHST BR7 184 D7
White Horse La LCOL/BKTW AL2 57 K2
RPLY/SEND GU23 233 M7
Whitehorse La SNWD SE25 203 M4
White Horse La WCHPL E1 140 C6
White Horse Rd EHAM E6 142 C5
WCHPL E1 140 D8
WDSR SL4 148 C9
Whitehorse Rd CROY/NA CR0 203 K7
WCHPL E1 140 D7
White Horse St MYFR/PICC W1J 10 F10
Whitehouse Av BORE WD6 75 N8
White House Cl CFSP/GDCR SL9 90 B8
Whitehouse Dr GU GU1 250 E10
White House Dr STAN HA7 95 H5
Whitehouse La ABLGY WD5 55 J2
White House La ENC/FH EN2 79 K5
RGUE GU4 250 A5
White House Rd RSEV TN14 264 G6
Whitehouse Wy DTCH/LGLY SL3 150 A2
IVER SL0 130 G5
STHGT/OAK N14 98 C3
Whitehurst Dr UED N18 * 100 C6
White Kennett St HDTCH EC3A 13 K5
White Knights Rd WEY KT13 216 D4
White Knobs Wy CTHM CR3 259 P1
Whitelands BRWN CM15 87 J1
Whitelands Av
RKW/CH/CXG WD3 70 E7
Whitelands Crs
WAND/EARL SW18 179 H3
Whitelands Wy HARH RM3 105 L9
White La OXTED RH8 243 N9
RGUE GU4 268 F2
Whiteleaf Rd HHS/BOV HP3 35 M9
White Ledges WEA W13 135 H8
Whitelegg Rd PLSTW E13 141 L4
Whiteley WDSR SL4 148 D6
Whiteley Rd NRWD SE19 181 L8
Whiteleys Pde HGDN/ICK UB10 * 132 C6
Whiteleys Wy FELT TW13 175 P6
White Lilies Island WDSR SL4 148 G6
White Lion Ct LOTH EC2R 13 J6
PECK SE15 * 160 B5
White Lion Hl BLKFR EC4V 12 D7
White Lion Rd AMSS HP7 69 M5
White Lion Sq HAT AL10 40 D3
White Lion St HHS/BOV HP3 35 N10
IS N1 6 A8
White Lion Wk GU GU1 268 A1
White Lion Yd CSHM HP5 51 H8
White Ldg NRWD SE19 181 J10
White Lodge Cl BELMT SM2 221 M4
EFNCH N2 117 N4
ISLW TW7 154 F8
SEV TN13 247 J9
White Lodge Gdns REDH RH1 276 B8
The White Ldg BAR EN5 * 77 H7
White Lyon Ct STBT EC1A 12 E3
White Lyons Rd BRW CM14 107 H4
Whitemore Rd GU GU1 250 A6
White Oak Dr BECK BR3 205 H2
White Oak Gdns BFN/LL DA15 185 J3
Whiteoaks BNSTD SM7 221 L9
Whiteoaks La GFD/PVL UB6 134 C4
White Oak Sq SWLY BR8 * 208 F3
White Orchards STAN HA7 94 F7
TRDG/WHET N20 97 J2
White Pillars WOKS/MYFD GU22 231 N6
White Post Fld SBW CM21 29 N1
White Post Hl EYN DA4 209 P7
Whitepost Hl REDH RH1 257 P10
White Post La HOM E9 140 F1
White Post St NWCR SE14 160 B6
White Rd SRTFD E15 141 K2
White Rose La
WOKS/MYFD GU22 232 C3
Whites Av GNTH/NBYPK IG2 123 H4
Whites Cl SWCM DA10 189 H2
White's Grounds STHWK SE1 19 K1
Whites Grounds Est STHWK SE1 19 K1
White Shack La
RKW/CH/CXG WD3 72 A3
Whites La DTCH/LGLY SL3 149 N5
Whites Meadow BMLY BR1 * 206 D4
White's Rw WCHPL E1 13 L4
White's Sq CLAP SW4 158 E10
Whitestile Rd BTFD TW8 155 H4
Whitestone La HAMP NW3 117 M8
Whitestone Wk HAMP NW3 117 M8
HHW HP1 35 K3
White St STHL UB1 153 L1
White Stubbs La BROX EN10 43 N7
Whitethorn WGCE AL7 23 K6
Whitethorn Av COUL/CHIP CR5 240 B1
WDR/YW UB7 131 P9
Whitethorn Gdns CROY/NA CR0 204 A9
EMPK RM11 125 K4
ENC/FH EN2 79 L9
Whitethorn St BOW E3 140 F6
Whitewaits HLW CM20 29 H10
White Wy GT/LBKH KT23 254 A2
Whitewebbs La ENC/FH EN2 79 L1
Whitewebbs Pk ENC/FH EN2 * 79 M1
Whitewebbs Rd ENC/FH EN2 79 J1
Whitewebbs Wy
STMC/STPC BR5 207 J1
Whitewood Cottages
BH/WHM TN16 243 P6
Whitewood Rd BERK HP4 33 M5
Whitfield Cl GUW GU2 249 M7
Whitfield Ct RYNPK SW20 200 G2
Whitfield Pl FITZ W1T 10 G2
Whitfield Rd BXLYHN DA7 164 A6
EHAM E6 141 P2
GNWCH SE10 161 J7
Whitfield St FITZ W1T 11 H3
Whitfield Wy RKW/CH/CXG WD3 91 J2
Whitford Gdns MTCM CR4 202 A3
Whitgift Av SAND/SEL CR2 223 K2
Whitgift St CROY/NA CR0 203 K10
STHWK SE1 17 N5
Whit Hern Ct CHES/WCR EN8 * 62 A6
Whitings Rd BAR EN5 76 F9
Whitings Wy EHAM E6 142 D7
Whitland Rd CAR SM5 201 N8
Whitlars Dr KGLGY WD4 54 A4
Whitley Cl ABLGY WD5 55 H8
STWL/WRAY TW19 173 P2
Whitley Rd HOD EN11 44 G1
TOTM N17 99 M10
Whitlock Dr WIM/MER SW19 179 H3
Whitman Rd WCHPL E1 140 D6
Whitmead Cl SAND/SEL CR2 223 L3
Whitmoor La RGUE GU4 250 A2
Whitmore Av CDW/CHF RM16 147 N10
HARH RM3 105 M10
Whitmore Cl FBAR/BDGN N11 98 C6
Whitmore Est IS N1 7 K6
Whitmore Gdns WLSDN NW10 136 F4
Whitmore La ASC SL5 192 F5
Whitmore Rd BECK BR3 204 E3
HRW HA1 114 C5
IS N1 7 J6
Whitmores Cl EPSOM KT18 * 237 P1
Whitmores Wd HHNE HP2 36 C5
Whitmore Wy HORL RH6 279 N3
Whitnell Wy PUT/ROE SW15 * 178 F1
Whitney Av REDBR IG4 122 A2
Whitney Rd LEY E10 120 F5
Whitney Wk SCUP DA14 185 P9
Whitstable Cl BECK BR3 204 E1
Whitstable Pl CROY/NA CR0 223 K1
Whitstone La BECK BR3 204 G5
Whittaker Av RCH/KEW TW9 * 177 J1
Whittaker Rd CHEAM SM3 201 J10
EHAM E6 141 P2
SL SL1 128 D6
Whittaker St BGVA SW1W 16 C6
Whitta Rd MNPK E12 122 A9
Whittell Gdns SYD SE26 182 B6
Whittenham Cl SLN SL2 129 M10
Whittingstall Rd FUL/PGN SW6 157 J7
HOD EN11 44 G1
Whittington Av BANK EC3V 13 J6
YEAD UB4 132 G7
Whittington Ms
NFNCH/WDSPK N12 97 M5
Whittington Rd CRAWE RH10 283 N10
WDGN N22 98 F8
Whittington Wy PIN HA5 113 M3
Whittlebury Cl CAR SM5 222 A4
Whittle Cl GSTN WD25 54 G10
STHL UB1 134 A8
WALTH E17 120 D4
Whittle Pkwy SL SL1 128 C8
Whittle Rd HEST TW5 153 K6
NWDGN UB2 154 A1
Whittlesea Rd
KTN/HRWW/WS HA3 94 B8
Whittlesey St STHWK SE1 12 B10
Whittle Wy CRAWE RH10 284 B1
Whitton Av East GFD/PVL UB6 114 D10
Whitton Av West NTHLT UB5 114 A10
Whitton Cl GFD/PVL UB6 134 G1
Whitton Dene HSLW TW3 176 A1
ISLW TW7 176 C2
Whitton Dr GFD/PVL UB6 134 F1
Whitton Manor Rd WHTN TW2 176 B2
Whitton Rd HSLW TW3 154 A10
HSLW TW3 176 A1
WHTN TW2 176 D2
Whitton Waye HSLW TW3 175 P2
Whitwell Rd GSTN WD25 73 M1
PLSTW E13 141 M5
Whitworth Rd CRAWW RH11 283 N3
SNWD SE25 203 M3
WOOL/PLUM SE18 162 D6
Whitworth St GNWCH SE10 161 K4
Whopshott Av
WOKN/KNAP GU21 231 P2
Whopshott Cl WOKN/KNAP GU21 231 N2
Whopshott Dr
WOKN/KNAP GU21 231 P2
Whorlton Rd PECK SE15 159 P9
Whybridge Cl RAIN RM13 144 G3
Whybrow Gdns BERK HP4 34 B3
Whymark Av WDGN N22 119 H1
Whytebeam Vw CTHM CR3 241 N4
Whytecliffe Rd North
PUR/KEN CR8 223 J7
Whytecliffe Rd South
PUR/KEN CR8 223 H8
Whytecroft HEST TW5 153 L6
Whyteleafe Hl CTHM CR3 241 N4
Whyteleafe Rd CTHM CR3 241 N8
Whyteville Rd FSTGT E7 141 N1
Wichling Cl STMC/STPC BR5 207 N8
Wick Av STALE/WH AL4 21 J3
Wickenden Rd SEV TN13 247 K8
Wickens Meadow RSEV TN14 * 246 G5
Wickersley Rd BTSEA SW11 158 B8
Wickers Oake NRWD SE19 * 181 N7
Wicker St WCHPL E1 13 P6
Wicket Rd GFD/PVL UB6 134 F5
Wickets End RAD WD7 57 K9
The Wickets ASHF TW15 173 P7
Wickets Wy BARK/HLT IG6 103 J7
The Wicket CROY/NA CR0 224 F2
Wickford Dr HARH RM3 105 N6
Wickford St WCHPL E1 140 B6
Wickford Wy WALTH E17 120 C2
Wickham Av CHEAM SM3 220 F2
CROY/NA CR0 204 D9
Wickham Cha WWKM BR4 205 J7
Wickham Cl DEN/HRF UB9 91 N9
HORL RH6 280 A3
NWMAL KT3 200 C6
PEND EN3 80 A7
WCHPL E1 140 B7
Wickham Ct WWKM BR4 * 225 J1
Wickham Court Rd WWKM BR4 205 H9
Wickham Crs WWKM BR4 205 H9
Wickham Fld RSEV TN14 * 246 G2
Wickham Gdns BROCKY SE4 160 E9
Wickham La ABYW SE2 163 K5
EGH TW20 172 D10
Wickham Ms BROCKY SE4 160 E8
Wickham Rd BECK BR3 204 G3
CDW/CHF RM16 168 F1
CHING E4 101 H8
CROY/NA CR0 204 B9
DEPT SE8 160 F8
KTN/HRWW/WS HA3 94 C10
Wickham St LBTH SE11 17 N7
WELL DA16 163 H8
Wickhams Wy HART DA3 211 L5
Wickhams Whf WARE SG12 * 26 D2
Wickham Wy BECK BR3 205 H4
Wickhurst Rd RSEV TN14 264 G8
Wicklands Rd WARE SG12 28 A2
Wick La BOW E3 140 F3
EGH TW20 171 L9
Wickliffe Av FNCH N3 97 H10
Wickliffe Gdns WBLY HA9 115 N7
Wicklow St FSBYW WC1X 5 N9
Wick Rd EGH TW20 171 N10
HOM E9 140 D1
TEDD TW11 176 G10
TRING HP23 32 B1
Wicks Cl ELTH/MOT SE9 184 A7
Wicksteed Cl BXLY DA5 186 E6
The Wick HERT/WAT SG14 25 J2
Wickwood St CMBW SE5 159 J8
Widbrook BRWN CM15 87 H2
Widbury Gdns WARE SG12 26 E2
Widbury Hl WARE SG12 26 F2
Widdenham Rd HOLWY N7 118 G9
Widdicombe Av
RYLN/HDSTN HA2 113 M7
Widdin St SRTFD E15 141 K2
Widecombe Cl HARH RM3 105 L9
Widecombe Gdns REDBR IG4 122 B2
Widecombe Rd ELTH/MOT SE9 184 B6
Widecombe Wy EFNCH N2 117 N3
Widecroft Rd IVER SL0 131 H8
Widegate St WCHPL E1 13 K4
Widenham Cl PIN HA5 113 K3
Widewater Pl DEN/HRF UB9 * 111 M3
Wide Wy MTCM CR4 202 E3
Widford Rd WARE SG12 28 A1
WGCE AL7 23 L5
Widgeon Cl CAN/RD E16 141 N8
Widgeon Rd ERITH DA8 165 J6
Widgeon Wy GSTN WD25 73 M3
Widley Rd MV/WKIL W9 2 F10
Widmore Cl CSHM HP5 50 D2
Widmore Dr HHNE HP2 36 B4
Widmore Lodge Rd BMLY BR1 206 A2
Widmore Rd BMLY BR1 205 N2
UX/CGN UB8 132 C6
Widworthy Hayes
RBRW/HUT CM13 107 N2
Wieland Rd NTHWD HA6 93 H8
Wigeon Wy YEAD UB4 133 L8
Wiggenhall Rd WATW WD18 73 J9
Wiggie La REDH RH1 258 B8
Wiggins La RCHPK/HAM TW10 177 H6
Wiggins Md CDALE/KGS NW9 96 C8
Wigginton Av WBLY HA9 135 M1
Wigginton Bottom TRING HP23 32 C1
Wightman Rd CEND/HSY/T N8 119 H2
Wigley Bush La BRW CM14 106 D4
Wigley Rd FELT TW13 175 L5
Wigmore Pl MHST W1U * 10 E5
Wigmore Rd CAR SM5 201 N9
Wigmores North WGCW AL8 22 G4
Wigmore St MHST W1U 10 D5
Wigram Rd WAN E11 121 P4
Wigram Sq WALTH E17 121 H1
Wigston Cl UED N18 99 M6
Wigston Rd PLSTW E13 141 N6
Wigton Gdns STAN HA7 95 K9
Wigton Pl LBTH SE11 18 B8
Wigton Rd HARH RM3 105 M5
WALTH E17 100 E9
Wigton Wy HARH RM3 105 M5
Wilberforce Ms CLAP SW4 158 E10
Wilberforce Rd CDALE/KGS NW9 116 D4
FSBYPK N4 119 J8
Wilberforce Wy GVE DA12 190 G8
WIM/MER SW19 178 G9
Wilbraham Pl KTBR SW1X 16 C5
Wilbury Av BELMT SM2 221 J6
Wilbury Wy UED N18 99 L6
Wilby Ms NTGHL W11 8 D9
Wilcon Wy GSTN WD25 55 L10
Wilcot Av OXHEY WD19 93 M1
Wilcot Cl CHOB/PIR GU24 230 F2
OXHEY WD19 93 M1
Wilcot Gdns CHOB/PIR GU24 230 F2
Wilcox Cl BORE WD6 75 P5
VX/NE SW8 158 F6
Wilcox Gdns SHPTN TW17 195 P3
Wilcox Rd SUT SM1 * 221 L1
TEDD TW11 176 C7
VX/NE SW8 158 F6
Wild Acres BF/WBF KT14 215 M7
Wildacres NTHWD HA6 92 G5
Wild Ct HOL/ALD WC2B 11 N5
Wildcroft Dr RDKG RH5 273 J5
Wildcroft Gdns STAN HA7 95 J7
Wildcroft Rd PUT/ROE SW15 178 F3
Wilde Cl HACK E8 7 N5
TIL RM18 168 F8
Wilde Pl PLMGR N13 99 J7
WAND/EARL SW18 179 N3
Wilder Cl RSLP HA4 113 J6
Wildernesse Av BGR/WK TN15 247 N8
Wildernesse Mt SEV TN13 247 L8
Wilderness Ms CLAP SW4 158 C10
Wilderness Rd CHST BR7 184 E10
GUW GU2 267 L2
OXTED RH8 261 K6
The Wilderness BERK HP4 33 P5
E/WMO/HCT KT8 198 B5
HPTN TW12 * 176 A7
Wilde Rd ERITH DA8 164 C6
Wilders Cl WOKN/KNAP GU21 231 P4
Wilderton Rd STNW/STAM N16 119 M5
Wildfell Rd CAT SE6 182 G3
Wildfield Cl RGUW GU3 248 G9
Wild Goose Dr NWCR SE14 160 B7
Wildgreen North DTCH/LGLY SL3 150 D3
Wildgreen South DTCH/LGLY SL3 150 D3
Wild Hatch GLDGN NW11 117 K4
Wildhill Rd BRKMPK AL9 41 J7
Wild Oaks Cl NTHWD HA6 92 G7
Wild's Rents STHWK SE1 19 J3
Wild St HOL/ALD WC2B 11 M6
Wildwood NTHWD HA6 92 E7
Wildwood Av LCOL/BKTW AL2 55 N6
Wildwood Cl EHSLY KT24 252 G1
LEE/GVPK SE12 183 L3
WOKS/MYFD GU22 233 J1
Wildwood Ct PUR/KEN CR8 241 L1
Wildwood Gv HAMP NW3 117 M6
Wildwood Ri GLDGN NW11 117 M6
Wildwood Rd GLDGN NW11 117 M5
Wildwood Ter GLDGN NW11 117 M6
Wilford Cl ENC/FH EN2 * 79 L7
NTHWD HA6 92 E8
Wilford Rd DTCH/LGLY SL3 150 B3
Wilfred Av RAIN RM13 145 H7
Wilfred Owen Cl
WIM/MER SW19 179 M9
Wilfred St GVE DA12 190 E2
WESTW SW1E 16 G3
WOKN/KNAP GU21 232 A3
Wilfrid Gdns ACT W3 135 P7
Wilhelmina Av COUL/CHIP CR5 240 D5
Wilkes Rd BTFD TW8 155 K5
Wilkes St WCHPL E1 13 M3
Wilkins Cl HYS/HAR UB3 152 G4
MTCM CR4 201 P1
Wilkin's Green La HAT AL10 39 P5
Wilkins Green Ter
STALE/WH AL4 * 39 N6
Wilkins Gv WGCW AL8 22 G6
Wilkinson Cl CHESW EN7 61 K2
HGDN/ICK UB10 132 C3
Wilkinson Gdns SNWD SE25 203 M1
Wilkinson Rd CAN/RD E16 141 P8
Wilkinson St VX/NE SW8 158 G6
Wilkinson Wy CHSWK W4 156 A1
HHS/BOV HP3 36 A10
Wilkin St KTTN NW5 4 D1
Wilkin Street Ms KTTN NW5 4 E1
Wilks Av DART DA1 187 N5
Wilks Gdns CROY/NA CR0 204 D8
Wilks Pl IS N1 7 K8
Willan Rd TOTM N17 99 L10
Willan Wall CAN/RD E16 141 L9
Willard St VX/NE SW8 158 C9
Willats Cl CHERT KT16 * 195 J6
Willcocks Cl CHSGTN KT9 199 K10
Willcott Rd ACT W3 135 N10
Will Crooks Gdns ELTH/MOT SE9 162 A10
Willenfield Rd WLSDN NW10 135 N4
Willenhall Av BAR EN5 77 M10
Willenhall Dr HYS/HAR UB3 132 F9
Willenhall Rd WOOL/PLUM SE18 162 E4
Willerfield Rd WLSDN NW10 135 P5
Willersley Av BFN/LL DA15 185 J4
ORP BR6 206 G10
Willersley Cl BFN/LL DA15 185 J4
Willesden La KIL/WHAMP NW6 136 G2
Willes Rd KTTN NW5 4 F1
Willett Cl NTHLT UB5 133 K5
STMC/STPC BR5 207 H6
Willett Rd THHTH CR7 203 H5
Willetts La DEN/HRF UB9 111 J9
Willetts Ms HOD EN11 44 F2
Willett Wy STMC/STPC BR5 206 G5
Willey Broom La CTHM CR3 259 H1
Willey Farm La CTHM CR3 259 K2
Willey La CTHM CR3 259 L1
William Ash Cl DAGW RM9 143 L1
William Barefoot Dr
ELTH/MOT SE9 184 D6
William Booth Rd PGE/AN SE20 203 P1
William Carey Wy HRW HA1 114 D4
William Cl CRW RM5 104 D9
EFNCH N2 97 N10
LEW SE13 161 H9
NWDGN UB2 154 B1
William Ct HHS/BOV HP3 35 N10
William Covell Cl ENC/FH EN2 * 78 G4
William Dr STAN HA7 94 F7
William Ellis Cl WDSR SL4 171 M2
William Ellis Wy
BERM/RHTH SE16 * 19 P4
BERM/RHTH SE16 * 159 P2
William Evans Rd
HOR/WEW KT19 219 M7
William Evelyn Ct RDKG RH5 * 271 N5
William Foster La WELL DA16 163 K8
William Gdns PUT/ROE SW15 178 E1
William Guy Gdns BOW E3 140 G5
William Hartley Yd
DTCH/LGLY SL3 * 129 N6
William Hunter Wy BRW CM14 107 J3
William Iv St CHCR WC2N 11 L8
William Margrie Cl PECK SE15 * 159 P8
William Ms KTBR SW1X 16 B2
William Morley Cl EHAM E6 142 A3
William Morris Cl WALTH E17 120 E1
William Morris Wy FUL/PGN SW6 157 M8
William Moulder Ct CSHM HP5 50 G4
William Petty Wy
STMC/STPC BR5 207 M8
William Rd CAMTN NW1 4 G10
CTHM CR3 241 L8
GU GU1 249 P10
SUT SM1 221 M2
WIM/MER SW19 179 H10
Williams Av WALTH E17 100 E9
William's Buildings WCHPL E1 * 140 B6
Williams Cl CEND/HSY/T N8 * 118 E4
FUL/PGN SW6 157 H6
Williams Dr HSLW TW3 153 P10
Williams Gv SURB KT6 199 H6
WDGN N22 99 H9
Williams La MORT/ESHN SW14 155 P8
MRDN SM4 201 M6
Williamson Cl GNWCH SE10 161 L4
Williamson Rd FSBYPK N4 119 J4
Williamson St HOLWY N7 * 118 F9
Williamson Wy MLHL NW7 97 H7
RKW/CH/CXG WD3 91 K2
William Sq BERM/RHTH SE16 140 D10
Williams Rd NWDGN UB2 153 M3
WEA W13 * 134 F10
Williams Ter CROY/NA CR0 223 H3
William St BARK IG11 142 F2
BERK HP4 34 A5
BUSH WD23 73 L7
CAR SM5 201 P10
GRAYS RM17 167 N5
GVE DA12 190 E3
KTBR SW1X 16 B2
LEY E10 120 G4
SL SL1 129 L10
TOTM N17 99 N8
WDSR SL4 149 J7
Williams Wy CRAWE RH10 284 C7
RAD WD7 74 G1
RDART DA2 186 E5
Willifield Wy GLDGN NW11 117 K3
Willingale Ct EPP CM16 83 H3
Willingale Rd LOU IG10 82 F5
Willingdon Rd WDGN N22 99 J10
Willinghall Cl WAB EN9 63 J8
Willingham Cl KTTN NW5 118 D10
Willingham Ter KTTN NW5 * 118 D10
Willingham Wy KUT/HW KT1 199 M2
Willington Rd BRXN/ST SW9 158 F9
Willis Av BELMT SM2 221 P3
Willis Cl EPSOM KT18 219 N10
Willis Rd CROY/NA CR0 203 K7
ERITH DA8 164 D3
SRTFD E15 141 L3
Willis St POP/IOD E14 140 G8
Willmore End WIM/MER SW19 201 L1
Willoners SLN SL2 128 F7
Willoughby Av CROY/NA CR0 222 G1
Willoughby Cl BROX EN10 44 D7
Willoughby Dr RAIN RM13 144 F2
Willoughby Gv TOTM N17 100 A8
Willoughby La TOTM N17 100 A8
Willoughby Ms TOTM N17 100 A8
Willoughby Park Rd TOTM N17 100 A8
Willoughby Rd CEND/HSY/T N8 119 H1
DTCH/LGLY SL3 150 E2
HAMP NW3 117 N9
KUTN/CMB KT2 199 L1
TWK TW1 177 H1
Willoughby Wy CHARL SE7 161 N3
Willow Av BARN SW13 156 C8
BFN/LL DA15 185 K2
DEN/HRF UB9 131 M1
SWLY BR8 208 G4
WDR/YW UB7 132 A9
Willow Bank RCHPK/HAM TW10 176 G6
WOKS/MYFD GU22 232 B8
Willowbank Gdns
KWD/TDW/WH KT20 238 E8
Willowbay Cl BAR EN5 76 G10
Willow Brean HORL RH6 279 P3
Willow Bridge Rd IS N1 6 E3
Willowbrook HPTN TW12 176 A8
WDSR SL4 149 J3
Willowbrook Est PECK SE15 * 159 N6
Willowbrook Rd NWDGN UB2 153 N2
PECK SE15 19 M10
STWL/WRAY TW19 173 P4
Willowby Ct LCOL/BKTW AL2 57 J2
The Willow Centre MTCM CR4 202 A5
Willow Cha CSHM HP5 50 G6
Willow Cl ADL/WDHM KT15 215 J7
BKHH IG9 102 A4
BRWN CM15 87 J4
BTFD TW8 155 H5
BXLY DA5 186 A2
CAT SE6 183 L4
CFSP/GDCR SL9 90 B10
CHESW EN7 61 M2
CRAWE RH10 283 P5
DTCH/LGLY SL3 150 F6
HAYES BR2 206 C5
HCH RM12 125 J8
RBRW/HUT CM13 87 N10
STMC/STPC BR5 207 L6
Willow Cnr HORL RH6 279 J9
Willow Ct HORL RH6 * 280 C1
STAN HA7 * 95 J8
Willowcourt Av
KTN/HRWW/WS HA3 114 G3
Willow Crs STAL AL1 39 H6
Willow Crs East DEN/HRF UB9 111 M10
Willow Crs West DEN/HRF UB9 111 M10
Willow Dean PIN HA5 * 93 L10
Willowdene BRWN CM15 86 E9
Willow Dene BUSH WD23 94 D1
Willowdene CHES/WCR EN8 62 D3
HGT N6 * 118 A5
Willow Dene PIN HA5 93 L10
Willowdene Cl WHTN TW2 176 B3
Willowdene Ct BRW CM14 107 H5
Willow Dr BAR EN5 77 H8
RGUW GU3 248 B10
RPLY/SEND GU23 233 K10
Willow Edge KGLGY WD4 54 B5
Willow End NTHWD HA6 93 H7
SURB KT6 199 K8
TRDG/WHET N20 97 K3
Willowfield HLWS CM18 46 G2
Willowfields Cl
WOOL/PLUM SE18 163 H4
Willow Gdns HSLW TW3 * 153 P7
RSLP HA4 112 G7
Willow Gn CHOB/PIR GU24 212 F9
Willow Gv CHST BR7 184 D9
RSLP HA4 112 G7
Willowhayne Dr WOT/HER KT12 197 J7
Willowhayne Gdns WPK KT4 220 F1
Willow La AMSS HP7 69 L7
GU GU1 250 D9
MTCM CR4 202 A5
WATW WD18 73 H9
WOOL/PLUM SE18 162 C3
Willowmead CHIG IG7 103 K4
Willow Md DORK RH4 272 F1
Willowmead HERT/WAT SG14 25 H6
Willow Md SBW CM21 29 P2
Willowmead STA TW18 195 L1
Willowmead Cl EA W5 135 J7
WOKN/KNAP GU21 231 M2
Willowmere ESH/CLAY KT10 218 B1
Willow Mt CROY/NA CR0 223 M1
Willow Pk RSEV TN14 246 G3
SLN SL2 129 M2
Willow Pl HLWE CM17 48 A5
WDSR SL4 149 H5
WEST SW1P 17 H5
Willow Rdg CRAWE RH10 285 P10
Willow Rd CHDH RM6 123 P4
DART DA1 187 K4
DTCH/LGLY SL3 151 H8
EA W5 155 K1
EN EN1 79 N5
ERITH DA8 165 H7
GODL GU7 267 L9
HAMP NW3 117 N9
NWMAL KT3 199 P4
REDH RH1 275 M3
WLGTN SM6 222 C4
Willows Av MRDN SM4 201 L5
Willows Cl PIN HA5 93 K10
Willowside LCOL/BKTW AL2 57 K3
Willows Pth EPSOM KT18 219 N10
Willows Ter WLSDN NW10 * 136 C4
The Willows AMS HP6 68 G1
BECK BR3 * 204 F1
BF/WBF KT14 215 P9
BORE WD6 * 75 M5
EBAR EN4 * 77 P10
ESH/CLAY KT10 218 D3
GRAYS RM17 168 A5
HHNE HP2 36 C4
LTWR GU18 212 B7
OXHEY WD19 93 J1
RGUE GU4 * 250 G8
RGUW GU3 * 249 L5
RKW/CH/CXG WD3 91 K3
STAL AL1 38 G10
WARE SG12 * 26 G7
WEY KT13 196 B10
Willow St CHING E4 101 J2
ROMW/RG RM7 124 D2
SDTCH EC2A 13 J1
Willow Ter EYN DA4 * 209 M9
PGE/AN SE20 * 204 A1
Willow Tree Cl BOW E3 140 D3
Willowtree Cl HGDN/ICK UB10 112 D8
Willow Tree Cl NTHLT UB5 133 M1
WAND/EARL SW18 179 M4
YEAD UB4 133 K6
Willow Tree La YEAD UB4 133 L6
Willow Tree Rd YEAD UB4 133 L7
Willow Tree Wk BMLY BR1 205 N1
Willowtree Wy THHTH CR7 203 H1
Willow V CHST BR7 184 D9
LHD/OX KT22 236 A9
SHB W12 136 D10
Willow Vw WARE SG12 * 26 D3
WIM/MER SW19 201 N1
Willow Wk CHEAM SM3 201 J10
DART DA1 * 187 M1
EGH TW20 171 P8
KWD/TDW/WH KT20 255 N6
ORP BR6 206 E10
REDH RH1 276 C2
SEVS/STOTM N15 119 J2
SHGR GU5 270 B5
STHWK SE1 19 K5
UPMR RM14 126 D6
WALTH E17 120 E3
WCHMH N21 78 G10
Willow Wy ALP/SUD HA0 * 114 F8
BF/WBF KT14 215 M7
FNCH N3 97 L8
GDST RH9 260 A8
GU GU1 249 N6
HARH RM3 106 A7
HAT AL10 40 C7
HHW HP1 35 L4
HOR/WEW KT19 220 A3
LCOL/BKTW AL2 55 P3
NTGHL W11 136 G9
POTB/CUF EN6 59 L9
RAD WD7 74 D2
SUN TW16 197 H4
SYD SE26 182 A6
WHTN TW2 176 A6
WOKS/MYFD GU22 232 B6
Willow Wood Cl SL SL1 128 A4
Willow Wood Crs SNWD SE25 203 M6
Willow Wren Whf NWDGN UB2 * 153 J3
Will Rd KTTN NW5 4 E1
Willrose Crs ABYW SE2 163 M4
Wills Crs HSLW TW3 176 A2
Wills Gv MLHL NW7 96 D6
Willson Rd EGH TW20 171 N8
Wilman Gv HACK E8 7 P3
Wilmar Cl UX/CGN UB8 131 N2
YEAD UB4 132 E6
Wilmar Gdns WWKM BR4 204 G8
Wilmar Wy BGR/WK TN15 247 N6
Wilmer Cl KUTN/CMB KT2 177 L8
Wilmer Crs KUTN/CMB KT2 177 L8
Wilmer Gdns IS N1 7 K6
Wilmerhatch La EPSOM KT18 237 N3
Wilmer Lea Cl SRTFD E15 141 H2
Wilmer Pl STNW/STAM N16 119 N7
Wilmer Wy FBAR/BDGN N11 98 E6
Wilmington Av CHSWK W4 156 A6
ORP BR6 207 M9
Wilmington Court Rd
RDART DA2 187 H6
Wilmington Gdns BARK IG11 142 G2
Wilmington Sq FSBYW WC1X 6 A10
Wilmington St FSBYW WC1X 6 A10
Wilmot Cl PECK SE15 * 159 P6
Wilmot Cottages BNSTD SM7 * 239 L1
Wilmot Gn RBRW/HUT CM13 107 H7
Wilmot Pl CAMTN NW1 4 G3
HNWL W7 134 D10
Wilmot Rd CAR SM5 * 222 A2
DART DA1 187 J1
LEY E10 120 G7
PUR/KEN CR8 223 H8
SL SL1 128 A5
TOTM N17 119 L1
Wilmots Cl REIG RH2 257 M9
Wilmot's La HORL RH6 281 L1
REDH RH1 277 L10
Wilmot St BETH E2 140 A6
Wilmot Wy BNSTD SM7 221 K10
Wilmount St WOOL/PLUM SE18 162 E3
Wilna Rd WAND/EARL SW18 179 M3
Wilsham St NTGHL W11 136 G10
Wilshaw Cl HDN NW4 116 D1
Wilshaw St NWCR SE14 160 F7
Wilshere Av STAL AL1 38 B9
Wilsman Rd SOCK/AV RM15 147 H4
Wilsmere Dr
KTN/HRWW/WS HA3 94 D8
NTHLT UB5 133 M1
Wilson Av MTCM CR4 179 P10
Wilson Cl CRAWE RH10 284 E10
SAND/SEL CR2 223 L2
WBLY HA9 115 L5
Wilson Dr CHERT KT16 214 E2
WBLY HA9 115 L5
Wilson Gdns HRW HA1 114 B5
Wilson Gv BERM/RHTH SE16 160 A1
Wilson La EYN DA4 210 E2
Wilson Rd CHSGTN KT9 219 L3
CMBW SE5 159 L7
IL IG1 122 C5
PLSTW E13 142 A5
Wilsons KWD/TDW/WH KT20 238 G7
Wilson's Av TOTM N17 99 N10
Wilson's Pl POP/IOD E14 140 E8
Wilson's Rd HMSMTH W6 156 G4
Wilson St LVPST EC2M 13 H3
WALTH E17 121 H3
WCHMH N21 99 J1
Wilson Wk CHSWK W4 * 156 C3
Wilson Wy WOKN/KNAP GU21 232 A2
Wilstone Cl YEAD UB4 133 M6
Wilstone Dr STALE/WH AL4 39 H1
Wilthorne Gdns DAGE RM10 144 C2
Wilton Av CHSWK W4 156 B4
Wilton Cl WDR/YW UB7 151 N5
Wilton Crs BEAC HP9 88 D8
HERT/BAY SG13 25 K8
KTBR SW1X 16 C2
WDSR SL4 148 C10
WIM/MER SW19 201 J1
Wilton Dr CRW RM5 104 D8
Wilton Est HACK E8 * 7 P2
Wilton Gdns E/WMO/HCT KT8 197 P3
WOT/HER KT12 197 L8
Wilton Gv NWMAL KT3 200 C6
WIM/MER SW19 179 J10
Wilton La BEAC HP9 89 J8
Wilton Ms HACK E8 * 140 A1
KTBR SW1X 16 D3
Wilton Pl ADL/WDHM KT15 215 N5
KTBR SW1X 16 C2
Wilton Rd ABYW SE2 163 M2
BEAC HP9 88 D7
EBAR EN4 78 A8
HSLWW TW4 153 L9
MUSWH N10 98 B10
PIM SW1V 16 F4
REDH RH1 276 A1
WIM/MER SW19 179 P10
Wilton Rw KTBR SW1X 16 C2
Wilton Sq IS N1 6 G5
Wilton St KTBR SW1X 16 E3
Wilton Ter KTBR SW1X 16 C3
Wilton Vls IS N1 6 G6
Wilton Wk FELT TW13 * 175 J5
Wilton Wy HACK E8 7 N2
HERT/BAY SG13 25 K7
Wiltshire Av EMPK RM11 125 N2
SLN SL2 129 H6
Wiltshire Cl CHEL SW3 15 P6
MLHL NW7 * 96 C6
RDART DA2 188 C3
Wiltshire Gdns FSBYPK N4 119 K4
WHTN TW2 176 B4
Wiltshire La PIN HA5 112 G1
Wiltshire Rd BRXN/ST SW9 159 H9
ORP BR6 207 K7
THHTH CR7 203 H3
Wiltshire Rw IS N1 6 G6
Wilverley Crs NWMAL KT3 200 B6
Wimbart Rd BRXS/STRHM SW2 * 180 G3
Wimbeldon Park Side
PUT/ROE SW15 178 E3
Wimbledon Br WIM/MER SW19 179 J9
Wimbledon Hill Rd
WIM/MER SW19 179 H9
Wimbledon Park Rd
WIM/MER SW19 179 H6
Wimbledon Park Side
WIM/MER SW19 178 G5
Wimbledon Rd TOOT SW17 179 M7
Wimbolt St BETH E2 7 N9
Wimborne Av NWDGN UB2 153 P3
REDH RH1 276 A5
STMC/STPC BR5 207 J3
YEAD UB4 133 J8
Wimborne Cl BKHH IG9 101 P3
EW KT17 220 C9
LEE/GVPK SE12 183 L1
SBW CM21 29 N1
WPK KT4 200 F8
Wimborne Dr CDALE/KGS NW9 115 M1
PIN HA5 113 L5
Wimborne Gdns WEA W13 134 G8
Wimborne Gv WAT WD17 72 F3
Wimborne Rd ED N9 99 P3
TOTM N17 99 M10
Wimborne Wy BECK BR3 204 C3
Wimbourne St IS N1 6 G7
Wimlands La HORS RH12 282 A10
Wimpole Cl HAYES BR2 205 P4
KUT/HW KT1 199 L2
Wimpole Ms CAVSQ/HST W1G 10 E3
Wimpole Rd WDR/YW UB7 131 N10
Wimpole St CAVSQ/HST W1G 10 E5
Wimshurst Cl CROY/NA CR0 202 F8
Winans Wk BRXN/ST SW9 159 H8
Wincanton Cl CRAWE RH10 284 E7
Wincanton Crs NTHLT UB5 113 P10
Wincanton Gdns BARK/HLT IG6 122 E1
Wincanton Rd HARH RM3 105 L4
WAND/EARL SW18 179 J3
Winchcombe Rd CAR SM5 201 N7
Winchcomb Gdns ELTH/MOT SE9 162 B9
Winchdells HHS/BOV HP3 36 B9
Winchelsea Av BXLYHN DA7 164 A6
Winchelsea Cl PUT/ROE SW15 178 G1
Winchelsea Rd FSTGT E7 121 M9
TOTM N17 119 M1
WLSDN NW10 136 A3
Winchelsey Ri SAND/SEL CR2 223 N3
Winchendon Rd FUL/PGN SW6 157 J6
TEDD TW11 176 C7
Winchester Av
CDALE/KGS NW9 115 L1
HEST TW5 153 N5
KIL/WHAMP NW6 2 B5
KIL/WHAMP NW6 137 H2
UPMR RM14 126 E6
Winchester Cl AMSS HP7 69 K5
DTCH/LGLY SL3 151 H7
EN EN1 * 79 M10
ESH/CLAY KT10 217 P1
HAYES BR2 205 L3
KUTN/CMB KT2 177 N10
LBTH SE11 * 18 D6
Winchester Crs GVE DA12 190 G6
Winchester Dr PIN HA5 113 L3
Winchester Ms WPK KT4 200 G9
Winchester Pk HAYES BR2 205 L3
Winchester Pl HACK E8 119 N10
HGT N6 118 C6
Winchester Rd BXLYHN DA7 163 N8
CHING E4 101 H8
ED N9 99 N2
FELT TW13 175 N6
HAMP NW3 3 M4
HAYES BR2 205 L3
HGT N6 118 C6
HYS/HAR UB3 152 F6
IL IG1 122 G8
KTN/HRWW/WS HA3 115 K2
ORP BR6 227 M1
TWK TW1 176 G2
WOT/HER KT12 197 H8
Winchester Sq STHWK SE1 12 G9
Winchester St ACT W3 135 P10
PIM SW1V 16 F7
Winchester Wk STHWK SE1 12 G9

Winchester Wy
RKW/CH/CXG WD3 72 C9
Winchfield Cl
KTN/HRWW/WS HA3 115 H4
Winchfield Rd *SYD* SE26 182 D8
Winchfield Wy
RKW/CH/CXG WD3 91 M1
Winchilsea Crs *E/WMO/HCT* KT8 198 B2
Winchmore Hill Rd
STHGT/OAK N14 98 F1
Winchmore Vls *WCHMH* N21 * 98 G1
Winchstone Cl *SHPTN* TW17 196 A4
Winch Vw *EPP* CM16 65 L5
Winckley Cl *KTN/HRWW/WS* HA3 115 L3
Wincott St *LBTH* SE11 18 B5
Wincrofts Dr *ELTH/MOT* SE9 162 G10
Windall Cl *NRWD* SE19 203 P1
Windborough Rd *CAR* SM5 222 B4
Windermere Av *FNCH* N3 97 K10
HCH RM12 125 H10
KIL/WHAMP NW6 2 B6
KIL/WHAMP NW6 137 H3
RSLP HA4 113 K5
STAL AL1 38 G8
WBLY HA9 115 H6
WIM/MER SW19 201 L3
Windermere Cl *DART* DA1 187 J4
EBED/NFELT TW14 174 F4
EGH TW20 172 E10
HHS/BOV HP3 36 D7
ORP BR6 206 E10
RKW/CH/CXG WD3 70 G9
STWL/WRAY TW19 173 N5
Windermere Gdns *REDBR* IG4 122 B3
Windermere Gv *WBLY* HA9 115 H6
Windermere Hall *EDGW* HA8 * 95 L6
Windermere Rd *ARCH* N19 * 118 D7
BXLYHN DA7 164 D8
COUL/CHIP CR5 240 F1
CROY/NA CR0 203 N8
EA W5 155 H2
LTWR GU18 212 A6
MUSWH N10 98 C9
PUT/ROE SW15 178 B7
STHL UB1 133 N7
STRHM/NOR SW16 202 D1
WWKM BR4 205 K9
Windermere Wy *REIG* RH2 257 P9
SL SL1 128 B8
WDR/YW UB7 131 P10
Winders Rd *BTSEA* SW11 157 P8
Windfield Cl *SYD* SE26 182 C7
Windgates *RGUE* GU4 250 F7
Windham Av *CROY/NA* CR0 225 J6
Windham Rd *RCH/KEW* TW9 155 L9
Wind Hl *CHONG* CM5 49 H5
Windhill *WGCE* AL7 23 K4
Windhover Wy *GVE* DA12 191 H7
Winding Shot *HHW* HP1 35 K5
The Windings *SAND/SEL* CR2 223 N7
Winding Wy *BCTR* RM8 123 M8
Windlass Pl *DEPT* SE8 160 D3
Windle Cl *BFOR* GU20 212 C3
Windlesham Ct *BFOR* GU20 212 B1
Windlesham Gv *WIM/MER* SW19 178 G4
Windlesham Rd *CHOB/PIR* GU24 212 D7
CHOB/PIR GU24 212 F4
Windley Cl *FSTH* SE23 182 B5
Windmill Av *EW* KT17 220 C7
STALE/WH AL4 39 H2
Windmill Cl *CTHM* CR3 241 K7
EW KT17 220 C8
HORL RH6 280 C4
LEW SE13 * 161 H8
STHWK SE1 19 P6
STHWK SE1 * 159 P3
SUN TW16 174 F10
SURB KT6 199 H8
UPMR RM14 125 P7
WAB EN9 63 K10
WDSR SL4 148 G8
Windmill Ct *CRAWE* RH10 283 N5
Windmill Dr *CLAP* SW4 180 C1
CRICK NW2 117 H8
LHD/OX KT22 236 G9
REIG RH2 257 N8
RKW/CH/CXG WD3 72 A10
Windmill End *EW* KT17 220 C8
Windmill Fld *BFOR* GU20 212 C3
WARE SG12 26 C3
Windmill Flds *HLWE* CM17 30 A7
Windmill Gdns *ENC/FH* EN2 79 H6
Windmill Gv *CROY/NA* CR0 203 K7
Windmill Hl *AMSS* HP7 88 E1
ENC/FH EN2 79 J7
HAMP NW3 * 117 M8
KGLGY WD4 53 J8
RSLP HA4 112 G6
Windmill La *BAR* EN5 76 C10
BUSH WD23 94 D2
CHES/WCR EN8 62 D6
EW KT17 220 C8
GFD/PVL UB6 134 B7
HAYES BR2 225 P1
NWDGN UB2 154 C2
SRTFD E15 141 J1
SURB KT6 198 G7
Windmill Pas *CHSWK* W4 * 156 B3
Windmill Ri *KUTN/CMB* KT2 177 N10
Windmill Rd *CFSP/GDCR* SL9 90 A8
CHSWK W4 156 B3
CROY/NA CR0 203 K7
DTCH/LGLY SL3 110 A10
EA W5 155 H3
HHNE HP2 36 A7
HPTN TW12 176 A8
MTCM CR4 202 D5
SEV TN13 265 J6
SL SL1 129 J10
SUN TW16 196 F1
UED N18 99 L5
WAND/EARL SW18 179 N1
WIM/MER SW19 178 E6
Windmill Rd West *SUN* TW16 196 F2
Windmill Rw *LBTH* SE11 18 A8
Windmill Shott *EGH* TW20 172 C9
Windmill St *BUSH* WD23 94 D2
FITZ W1T 11 J4
GVE DA12 190 E3
Windmill Ter *SHPTN* TW17 * 196 F7
Windmill Wk *STHWK* SE1 * 12 B10
Windmill Wy *BRWN* CM15 86 D3
REIG RH2 257 N8
RSLP HA4 112 G6
Windmill Wd *AMS* HP6 68 F3
Windmore Av *POTB/CUF* EN6 58 F7
Windridge Cl *STALW/RED* AL3 37 P8
Windrose Cl *BERM/RHTH* SE16 160 C1
Windrush *NWMAL* KT3 199 N4
Windrush Av *DTCH/LGLY* SL3 150 E2
Windrush Cl *BTSEA* SW11 * 157 N10
CHSWK W4 * 155 P6
CRAWW RH11 283 J9
HGDN/ICK UB10 112 A9
Windrush La *FSTH* SE23 182 C6
Windrush Rd *WLSDN* NW10 136 A3
Winds End Cl *HHNE* HP2 * 36 B4
Windsor Av *CDW/CHF* RM16 167 N1
CHEAM SM3 201 H10
E/WMO/HCT KT8 197 P3
EDGW HA8 95 N5
HGDN/ICK UB10 132 C2
NWMAL KT3 199 P5
WALTH E17 100 D10
WIM/MER SW19 201 M1
Windsor Br *WDSR* SL4 149 J6
Windsor Cl *CHESW* EN7 61 P6
CHST BR7 184 E8
FNCH N3 97 H10
GUW GU2 267 L2
HHNE HP2 35 P8
HHS/BOV HP3 52 D4
NTHWD HA6 93 H10
RYLN/HDSTN HA2 113 P8
SL SL1 * 128 B6
WNWD SE27 181 K7
Windsor Ct *AMS* HP6 * 69 J4
PIN HA5 * 113 L1
STHGT/OAK N14 98 D1
Windsor Court Rd
CHOB/PIR GU24 213 K5
Windsor Crs *RYLN/HDSTN* HA2 113 P9
WBLY HA9 115 M8
Windsor Dr *ASHF* TW15 173 N7
DART DA1 187 H2
EBAR EN4 78 A10
HERT/WAT SG14 24 C4
ORP BR6 227 K3
Windsor End *BEAC* HP9 108 E1
Windsor Gdns *CROY/NA* CR0 202 F10
HYS/HAR UB3 152 E2
MV/WKIL W9 8 E2
Windsor Great Pk *ASC* SL5 * 170 E10
Windsor Gv *WNWD* SE27 181 K7
Windsor La *SL* SL1 128 B6
Windsor Ms *CAT* SE6 183 H4
Windsor Park Rd *HYS/HAR* UB3 152 G6
Windsor Pl *CHERT* KT16 * 195 K6
Windsor Rd *ASC* SL5 170 A10
BAR EN5 76 G10
BCTR RM8 123 P8
BRWN CM15 86 G10
BXLYHS DA6 163 P10
CFSP/GDCR SL9 109 P6
CHING E4 100 G5
CHOB/PIR GU24 213 K6
CRICK NW2 136 E1
CSHM HP5 50 G4
DTCH/LGLY SL3 149 M6
EA W5 135 K9
EMPK RM11 125 K5
FNCH N3 97 H10
FSTGT E7 121 N10
GVE DA12 190 E7
HOLWY N7 118 F8
HSLWW TW4 153 K8
IL IG1 122 F9
KTN/HRWW/WS HA3 94 B9
KUTN/CMB KT2 177 K10
LEY E10 120 G7
NWDGN UB2 153 N2
PEND EN3 80 C2
PLMGR N13 99 H4
RCH/KEW TW9 155 L8
SL SL1 149 K2
STWL/WRAY TW19 172 B2
SUN TW16 175 H10
TEDD TW11 176 C8
THHTH CR7 203 J2
TOTM N17 99 P10
WAN E11 121 M6
WATN WD24 73 K4
WDSR SL4 170 C7
WDSR SL4 172 A4
WPK KT4 200 D9
The Windsors *BKHH* IG9 102 B3
Windsor St *CHERT* KT16 195 K7
IS N1 6 D5
UX/CGN UB8 131 M3
Windsor Ter *IS* N1 6 F9
Windsor Wk *CMBW* SE5 159 L8
WEY KT13 216 C2
Windsor Wy *RKW/CH/CXG* WD3 91 K2
WKENS W14 156 G3
WOKS/MYFD GU22 232 F2
Windsor Wd *WAB* EN9 63 K9
Winds Rdg *RPLY/SEND* GU23 250 F1
Windstock Cl *BERM/RHTH* SE16 160 E2
Windus Rd *STNW/STAM* N16 119 N6
Windward Cl *PEND* EN3 80 C1
Windycroft Cl *PUR/KEN* CR8 222 E9
Windy Hl *RBRW/HUT* CM13 107 P2
Windy Rdg *BMLY* BR1 206 B1
Windyridge *CRAWW* RH11 283 K8
Windy Ridge Cl *WIM/MER* SW19 178 G8
Wine Cl *WAP* E1W 140 B9
Wine Office Ct *FLST/FETLN* EC4A 12 B5
Winern Glebe *BF/WBF* KT14 215 N9
Winery La *KUT/HW* KT1 199 L3
Winey Cl *CHSGTN* KT9 219 H4
Winford Dr *BROX* EN10 44 E8
Winforton St *GNWCH* SE10 161 H7
Winfrith Rd *WAND/EARL* SW18 179 M3
Wingate Crs *CROY/NA* CR0 202 F6
Wingate Rd *HMSMTH* W6 156 E2
IL IG1 122 E10
SCUP DA14 185 M8
Wingate Wy *STAL* AL1 38 F7
Wingfield *GRAYS* RM17 167 L4
Wingfield Cl *ADL/WDHM* KT15 215 L6
RBRW/HUT CM13 107 M4
Wingfield Ct *WATW* WD18 * 72 E10
Wingfield Gdns *UPMR* RM14 126 D4
Wingfield Ms *PECK* SE15 159 P9
Wingfield Rd *GVW* DA11 190 E3
KUTN/CMB KT2 177 L9
SRTFD E15 121 K10
WALTH E17 120 G3
Wingfield St *PECK* SE15 159 P9
Wingfield Wy *RSLP* HA4 133 J1
Wingford Rd *BRXS/STRHM* SW2 180 F2
Wingletye La *EMPK* RM11 125 N7
Wingmore Rd *HNHL* SE24 159 K9
Wingrave Crs *BRW* CM14 106 D5
Wingrave Rd *HMSMTH* W6 156 F5
Wingrove Dr *PUR* RM19 166 A4
Wingrove Rd *CAT* SE6 183 K5
Wings Cl *SUT* SM1 221 K1
Wingway *BRW* CM14 107 H2
Winifred Av *HCH* RM12 125 L9
Winifred Cl *BAR* EN5 76 C10
Winifred Pl *NFNCH/WDSPK* N12 97 M6
Winifred Rd *BCTR* RM8 123 P7
COUL/CHIP CR5 240 B2
DART DA1 187 J1
ERITH DA8 164 F4
HHS/BOV HP3 35 N10
HPTN TW12 175 P7
WIM/MER SW19 201 K1
Winifred St *CAN/RD* E16 142 C10
Winifred Ter *EN* EN1 99 L1
PLSTW E13 141 M4
Winkers Cl *CFSP/GDCR* SL9 90 C9
Winkers La *CFSP/GDCR* SL9 90 C9
Winkfield Pln *WDSR* SL4 170 A3
Winkfield Rd *WDGN* N22 99 H9
WDSR SL4 170 B6
Winkley St *BETH* E2 140 A4
Winkworth Cottages
WCHPL E1 * 140 B6
Winkworth Pl *BNSTD* SM7 221 J10
Winkworth Rd *BNSTD* SM7 221 K10
Winlaton Rd *BMLY* BR1 183 J7
Winmill Rd *BCTR* RM8 124 A8
Winn Common Rd
WOOL/PLUM SE18 163 H5
Winner Wy *HORL* RH6 279 N9
Winnett St *SOHO/SHAV* W1D 11 J7
Winnington Cl *EFNCH* N2 117 H4
Winnington Rd *EFNCH* N2 117 N5
PEND EN3 80 B4
Winnington Wy
WOKN/KNAP GU21 231 N4
Winnipeg Dr *ORP* BR6 227 J3
Winnipeg Wy *BROX* EN10 62 D1
Winnock Rd *WDR/YW* UB7 131 N10
Winn Rd *LEE/GVPK* SE12 183 M4
Winns Av *WALTH* E17 120 E1
Winns Ms *SEVS/STOTM* N15 119 M2
Winns Ter *WALTH* E17 100 F10
Winsbeach *WALTH* E17 121 J1
Winscombe Crs *EA* W5 135 J6
Winscombe St *KTTN* NW5 118 C8
Winscombe Wy *STAN* HA7 94 F6
Winsford Rd *CAT* SE6 182 E6
Winsford Ter *UED* N18 * 99 L6
Winsham Gv *BTSEA* SW11 180 B1
Winslade Rd *BRXS/STRHM* SW2 180 F1
Winsland Ms *BAY/PAD* W2 9 L5
Winsland St *BAY/PAD* W2 9 L5
Winsley St *GTPST* W1W 10 G5
Winslow Cl *PIN* HA5 113 J4
WLSDN NW10 116 B8
Winslow Gv *CHING* E4 101 K3
Winslow Rd *HMSMTH* W6 156 F5
Winslow Wy *FELT* TW13 175 M6
WOT/HER KT12 197 K10
Winsor Ter *EHAM* E6 142 E7
Winstanley Cl *COB* KT11 217 J10
Winstanley Rd *BTSEA* SW11 157 N9
Winstead Gdns *DAGE* RM10 124 D10
Winston Av *CDALE/KGS* NW9 116 B5
Winston Churchill Wy
CHES/WCR EN8 62 B9
Winston Cl *KTN/HRWW/WS* HA3 94 E7
RDART DA2 188 E2
ROMW/RG RM7 124 C2
Winston Ct *KTN/HRWW/WS* HA3 94 A9
Winston Dr *COB* KT11 235 M3
Winstone Cl *AMS* HP6 50 G10
Winston Gdns *BERK* HP4 33 L5
Winston House *SURB* KT6 * 199 K5
Winston Rd *STNW/STAM* N16 119 L9
Winston Wy *IL* IG1 122 E8
POTB/CUF EN6 59 K9
WOKS/MYFD GU22 232 E6
Winstre Rd *BORE* WD6 75 M5
Winter Av *EHAM* E6 142 B3
Winterbourne Av *ORP* BR6 206 G10
Winterbourne Gv *WEY* KT13 216 D5
Winterbourne Rd *BCTR* RM8 123 M7
CAT SE6 182 E4
THHTH CR7 203 H4
Winter Box Wk
RCHPK/HAM TW10 177 L1
Winterbrook Rd *HNHL* SE24 181 K2
Winterburn Cl *FBAR/BDGN* N11 98 B7
Winterdown Gdns
ESH/CLAY KT10 217 N3
Winterdown Rd *ESH/CLAY* KT10 217 M3
Winterfold *CRAWE* RH10 284 B10
Winterfold Cl *WIM/MER* SW19 179 H5
Wintergarden Crs *RDART* DA2 188 F7
Winter Gdns *CRAWW* RH11 283 M8
Winterhill Wy *RGUE* GU4 250 E6
Winters Cft *GVE* DA12 190 G9
Winterscroft Rd *HOD* EN11 44 E3
Wintersells Rd *BF/WBF* KT14 215 N6
Winters Rd *THDIT* KT7 198 G7
Winterstoke Rd *CAT* SE6 182 E4
Winters Wy *WAB* EN9 63 M9
Winterton Pl *WBPTN* SW10 15 K9
Winterwell Rd
BRXS/STRHM SW2 180 F1
Winthorpe Rd *PUT/ROE* SW15 157 H10
Winthorpe St *WCHPL* E1 140 A7
Winthrop St *WCHPL* E1 * 140 A7
Winton Ap *RKW/CH/CXG* WD3 72 D9
Winton Av *FBAR/BDGN* N11 98 D8
Winton Cl *ED* N9 100 C1
Winton Ct *SWLY* BR8 208 F4
Winton Crs *RKW/CH/CXG* WD3 72 C9
Winton Dr *CHES/WCR* EN8 62 D5
RKW/CH/CXG WD3 72 D9
Winton Gdns *EDGW* HA8 95 L8
Winton Rd *ORP* BR6 226 E1
WARE SG12 26 C2
The Wintons *BUSH* WD23 * 94 C2
Winton Ter *STAL* AL1 * 38 D7
Winton Wy *STRHM/NOR* SW16 181 H8
Winvale *SL* SL1 149 K3
Winwood *SLN* SL2 129 P8
Wireless Rd *BH/WHM* TN16 244 A1
Wirral Wood Cl *CHST* BR7 184 D9
Wisbeach Rd *CROY/NA* CR0 203 L5
Wisborough Ct *CRAWW* RH11 283 J10
Wisborough Rd *SAND/SEL* CR2 223 N5
Wisdom Dr *HERT/BAY* SG13 25 M5
Wisdons Cl *DAGE* RM10 124 C6
Wise La *MLHL* NW7 96 D7
WDR/YW UB7 151 N3
Wiseman Rd *LEY* E10 * 120 F7
Wisemans Gdns *SBW* CM21 29 M2
Wise Rd *SRTFD* E15 141 H3
Wiseton Rd *TOOT* SW17 179 P4
Wishart Rd *BKHTH/KID* SE3 162 A8
Wishaw Wk *FBAR/BDGN* N11 98 F7
Wishbone Wy *WOKN/KNAP* GU21 231 L2
Wisley La *RPLY/SEND* GU23 233 P2
Wisley Rd *BTSEA* SW11 180 A1
STMC/STPC BR5 185 K10
Wistaria Cl *BRWN* CM15 86 G9
ORP BR6 206 E9
Wistaria Dr *LCOL/BKTW* AL2 56 C2
Wisteria Cl *IL* IG1 122 E10
MLHL NW7 96 C7
Wisteria Gdns *SWLY* BR8 208 E2
Wisteria Rd *LEW* SE13 161 J10
Wistlea Crs *STALE/WH* AL4 39 N8
Wiston Ct *CRAWW* RH11 283 J10
Witanhurst La *HGT* N6 118 B6
Witan St *BETH* E2 140 A5
Witches La *SEV* TN13 246 E9
Witchford *WGCE* AL7 23 N5
Witham Cl *LOU* IG10 82 B10
Witham Rd *DAGE* RM10 124 D10
GPK RM2 125 J3
ISLW TW7 154 C7
PGE/AN SE20 204 B3
WEA W13 134 F10
Withens Cl *STMC/STPC* BR5 * 207 M4
Witherby Cl *CROY/NA* CR0 223 M4
Wither Dl *HORL* RH6 279 P3
The Witherings *EMPK* RM11 125 M3
Witherington Rd *HBRY* N5 * 119 H10
Withers Mld *CDALE/KGS* NW9 96 C9
Witherston Wy *ELTH/MOT* SE9 184 D5
Withey Brook *HORL* RH6 279 N6
Withey Cl *WDSR* SL4 148 D7
Witheygate Av *STA* TW18 173 K9
Withey Mdw *HORL* RH6 279 N6
Withies La *RGUW* GU3 267 H7
The Withies *LHD/OX* KT22 236 G6
WOKN/KNAP GU21 231 K3
Withybed Cnr
KWD/TDW/WH KT20 238 E9
Withy Cl *LTWR* GU18 212 B6
Withycombe Rd *WIM/MER* SW19 178 G3
Withycroft *DTCH/LGLY* SL3 130 B8
Withy La *RSLP* HA4 112 D3
Withy Md *CHING* E4 101 J4
Withypitts *CRAWE* RH10 285 P10
Withypitts East *CRAWE* RH10 285 P10
Withy Pl *LCOL/BKTW* AL2 56 A4
Witley Crs *CROY/NA* CR0 225 H3
Witley Gdns *NWDGN* UB2 153 N3
Witley Rd *ARCH* N19 118 D7
Witney Cl *HGDN/ICK* UB10 112 A9
PIN HA5 93 N7
Witney Pth *FSTH* SE23 182 C6
Wittenham Wy *CHING* E4 101 J4
Wittering Cl *KUTN/CMB* KT2 177 J8
Wittersham Rd *BMLY* BR1 183 L8
Wivenhoe Cl *PECK* SE15 159 P9
Wivenhoe Ct *HSLW* TW3 153 N10
Wivenhoe Rd *BARK* IG11 143 K4
Wiverton Rd *SYD* SE26 182 B9
Wix Hl *EHSLY* KT24 252 C6
Wix Rd *DAGW* RM9 143 N3
Wix's La *CLAP* SW4 158 C10
Woburn *WEA* W13 * 134 G7
Woburn Av *EPP* CM16 83 H3
HCH RM12 125 H9
PUR/KEN CR8 223 H7
Woburn Cl *BUSH* WD23 74 B10
THMD SE28 143 M8
WIM/MER SW19 179 M9
Woburn Hl *ADL/WDHM* KT15 195 M9
Woburn Pk *ADL/WDHM* KT15 * 195 M9
Woburn Pl *STPAN* WC1H 11 L1
Woburn Rd *CAR* SM5 201 P8
CRAWW RH11 283 K8
CROY/NA CR0 203 K9
Woburn Sq *STPAN* WC1H 11 K2
Woburn Wk *STPAN* WC1H * 5 K10
Wodeham Gdns *WCHPL* E1 13 P3
Wodehouse Av *CMBW* SE5 159 N7
Wodehouse Rd *DART* DA1 165 P10
Wodeland Av *GUW* GU2 267 N2
Woffington Cl *KUT/HW* KT1 199 H1
TEDD TW11 177 H10
Wokindon Rd *CDW/CHF* RM16 168 E2
Woking Cl *PUT/ROE* SW15 156 C10
Woking Rd *GU* GU1 250 A7
RGUE GU4 249 P3
Wold Cl *CRAWW* RH11 283 J9
Woldham Pl *HAYES* BR2 205 P4
Woldham Rd *HAYES* BR2 205 P4
Woldhurstlea Cl *CRAWW* RH11 283 K9
Woldingham Rd *WARL* CR6 242 A6
Wolds Dr *ORP* BR6 226 D1
The Wold *CTHM* CR3 242 F8
Wolfe Cl *HAYES* BR2 205 M6
YEAD UB4 133 J5
Wolfe Crs *CHARL* SE7 162 A4
Wolferton Rd *MNPK* E12 122 C9
Wolfington Rd *WNWD* SE27 181 J7
Wolf La *WDSR* SL4 148 C9
Wolfram Cl *LEW* SE13 183 K1
Wolfs Hl *OXTED* RH8 261 M7
Wolfs Rd *OXTED* RH8 261 N6
Wolfs Wd *OXTED* RH8 261 N8
Wolftencroft Cl *BTSEA* SW11 157 P9
Wollaston Cl *STHWK* SE1 18 D5
Wolmer Cl *EDGW* HA8 95 M5
Wolmer Gdns *EDGW* HA8 95 M4
Wolseley Av *WAND/EARL* SW18 179 K5
Wolseley Gdns *CHSWK* W4 155 N5
Wolseley Rd *CEND/HSY/T* N8 118 E4
CHSWK W4 155 P3
FSTGT E7 141 N2
KTN/HRWW/WS HA3 114 D1
MTCM CR4 202 B7
ROMW/RG RM7 124 E5
WDGN N22 98 G9
Wolseley St *STHWK* SE1 19 M2
Wolsey Av *CHESW* EN7 61 N5
EHAM E6 142 D5
THDIT KT7 198 E5
WALTH E17 120 E1
Wolsey Cl *HSLW* TW3 154 B10
KUTN/CMB KT2 199 N1
NWDGN UB2 154 B2
RYNPK SW20 178 E10
WPK KT4 220 D1
Wolsey Ct *ELTH/MOT* SE9 * 184 C2
Wolsey Crs *CROY/NA* CR0 225 H5
MRDN SM4 201 J7
Wolsey Dr *KUTN/CMB* KT2 177 K8
WOT/HER KT12 197 L8
Wolsey Gdns *BARK/HLT* IG6 102 F7
Wolsey Gv *EDGW* HA8 96 A8
ESH/CLAY KT10 218 A1
Wolsey Ms *KTTN* NW5 4 G1
ORP BR6 227 J2
Wolsey Rd *ASHF* TW15 173 P7
E/WMO/HCT KT8 198 C4
EN EN1 80 A6
ESH/CLAY KT10 218 A1
HHW HP1 35 N7
HPTN TW12 176 A9
IS N1 119 L10
NTHWD HA6 92 E4
SUN TW16 174 G10
Wolsey St *WCHPL* E1 140 B7
Wolsey Wk *WOKN/KNAP* GU21 232 B3
Wolsey Wy *CHSGTN* KT9 219 M2
Wolsley Cl *DART* DA1 186 F1
Wolstan Cl *DEN/HRF* UB9 111 K8
Wolstonbury
NFNCH/WDSPK N12 97 K6
Wolstonbury Cl *CRAWW* RH11 283 M9
Wolvens La *RDKG* RH5 271 P6
Wolvercote Rd *ABYW* SE2 163 N1
Wolverley St *BETH* E2 * 140 A5
Wolverton Av *KUTN/CMB* KT2 199 M1
Wolverton Cl *HORL* RH6 280 A6
Wolverton Gdns *EA* W5 135 L9
HMSMTH W6 156 G3
HORL RH6 280 A5
Wolverton Rd *STAN* HA7 94 G7
Wolverton Wy *STHGT/OAK* N14 78 D9
Wolves La *WDGN* N22 99 H8
Wombwell Gdns *GVW* DA11 190 B5
Womersley Rd *CEND/HSY/T* N8 118 G4
Wonersh Common Rd *SHGR* GU5 268 E10
Wonersh Wy *BELMT* SM2 220 G5
Wonford Cl *KUTN/CMB* KT2 199 B1
KWD/TDW/WH KT20 256 D2
Wonham La *BRKHM/BTCW* RH3 274 C1
Wonham Wy *SHGR* GU5 270 E6
Wonnacott *PEND* EN3 80 C3
Wontford Rd *PUR/KEN* CR8 241 H1
Wontner Cl *IS* N1 6 E4
Wontner Rd *BAL* SW12 180 A5
Wooburn Cl *UX/CGN* UB8 132 C6
Wooburn Common Rd *SL* SL1 108 B8
Woodall Cl *CHSGTN* KT9 219 H4
Woodall Rd *PEND* EN3 80 C10
Wood Av *PUR* RM19 166 B3
Woodbank *RKW/CH/CXG* WD3 71 M10
Woodbank Av *CFSP/GDCR* SL9 110 A4
Woodbank Dr *CSTG* HP8 90 A4
Woodbank Rd *BMLY* BR1 183 L6
Woodbastwick Rd *SYD* SE26 182 C9
Woodberry Av *RYLN/HDSTN* HA2 114 B2
WCHMH N21 99 H3
Woodberry Cl *MLHL* NW7 96 G8
SUN TW16 175 H9
Woodberry Crs *MUSWH* N10 118 C1
Woodberry Down *EPP* CM16 65 K5
FSBYPK N4 119 K6
Woodberry Gdns
NFNCH/WDSPK N12 97 M7
Woodberry Gv *BXLY* DA5 186 E6
FSBYPK N4 119 K5
NFNCH/WDSPK N12 97 M7
Woodberry Wy *CHING* E4 101 H1
NFNCH/WDSPK N12 97 M7
Woodbine Cl *HLWW/ROY* CM19 46 F3
WHTN TW2 176 C5
Woodbine Gv *ENC/FH* EN2 79 L4
PGE/AN SE20 182 A10
Woodbine La *WPK* KT4 200 E10
Woodbine Pl *WAN* E11 121 M4
Woodbine Rd *BFN/LL* DA15 185 H4
Woodbines Av *KUT/HW* KT1 199 J3
Woodbine Ter *HOM* E9 140 B1
Woodborough Rd
PUT/ROE SW15 156 E10
Woodbourne Av
STRHM/NOR SW16 180 E6
Woodbourne Dr *ESH/CLAY* KT10 218 E3
Woodbourne Gdns *WLGTN* SM6 222 C4
Woodbridge Av *LHD/OX* KT22 236 F4
Woodbridge Cl *HARH* RM3 105 L4
HOLWY N7 118 G7
Woodbridge Gv *LHD/OX* KT22 236 F4
Woodbridge Hl *GUW* GU2 240 N0
Woodbridge Hill Gdns
GUW GU2 * 249 M9
Woodbridge La *HARH* RM3 105 L4
Woodbridge Mdw *GU* GU1 249 N9
Woodbridge Rd *BARK* IG11 123 J10
GU GU1 249 P10
Woodbridge St *CLKNW* EC1R 12 C1
Woodbrook Gdns *WAB* EN9 63 K9
Woodbrook Rd *ABYW* SE2 163 K5
Woodburn Cl *HDN* NW4 116 G3
Woodbury Cl *BH/WHM* TN16 244 C4
CROY/NA CR0 203 N9
WAN E11 121 N2
Woodbury Dr *BELMT* SM2 221 N6
Woodbury Gdns *LEE/GVPK* SE12 183 N6
Woodbury Hl *LOU* IG10 82 C6
Woodbury Park Rd *WEA* W13 134 G6
Woodbury Rd *WALTH* E17 120 G2
Woodbury St *TOOT* SW17 179 P8
Woodby Dr *ASC* SL5 192 E7
Woodchester Pk *BEAC* HP9 88 B5
Woodchester Sq *BAY/PAD* W2 8 G3
Woodchurch Cl *SCUP* DA14 184 G6
Woodchurch Dr *BMLY* BR1 184 A10
Woodchurch Rd
KIL/WHAMP NW6 2 F4
Wood Cl *BETH* E2 13 N1
BXLY DA5 186 F6
CDALE/KGS NW9 116 A5
HAT AL10 40 E4
HRW HA1 114 C5
REDH RH1 276 B9
WDSR SL4 149 H10
Woodclyffe Dr *CHST* BR7 206 D2
Woodcock Dell Av
KTN/HRWW/WS HA3 115 H5
Woodcock Dr *CHOB/PIR* GU24 213 H4
Woodcock Hl
KTN/HRWW/WS HA3 115 H3
RKW/CH/CXG WD3 91 P6
Woodcockhill *STALE/WH* AL4 21 J10
Woodcock La *CHOB/PIR* GU24 212 G4
Woodcocks *CAN/RD* E16 141 P7
Woodcombe Crs *FSTH* SE23 182 B4
Wood Common *HAT* AL10 40 E1
Woodcot Cl *PEND* EN3 80 B10
Woodcote *GUW* GU2 267 N4
HORL RH6 280 C3
Woodcote Av *HCH* RM12 125 H9
MLHL NW7 96 F7
THHTH CR7 203 J4
WLGTN SM6 222 C5
Woodcote Cl *CHES/WCR* EN8 62 B6
EPSOM KT18 220 A10
KUTN/CMB KT2 177 L9
Woodcote Dr *ORP* BR6 206 G7
Woodcote End *EPSOM* KT18 238 A1
Woodcote Gn *WLGTN* SM6 222 D5
Woodcote Green Rd
EPSOM KT18 237 P2
Woodcote Grove Rd
COUL/CHIP CR5 240 E1
Woodcote House Ct
EPSOM KT18 * 238 A1
Woodcote Hurst *EPSOM* KT18 237 P2
Woodcote La *PUR/KEN* CR8 222 E7
Woodcote Ms *LOU* IG10 102 A1
WLGTN SM6 222 C3
Woodcote Pk *COUL/CHIP* CR5 * 222 C9
Woodcote Park Av
PUR/KEN CR8 222 D7
Woodcote Park Rd *EPSOM* KT18 237 P2
Woodcote Pl *WNWD* SE27 * 181 J8
Woodcote Rd *EPSOM* KT18 238 A1
WAN E11 121 M5
WLGTN SM6 222 C3
Woodcote Side *EPSOM* KT18 237 N1
Woodcote Valley Rd
PUR/KEN CR8 222 E9
Wood Crs *HHNE* HP2 35 N8
Wood Crest *BELMT* SM2 * 221 M4
Woodcrest Rd *PUR/KEN* CR8 222 F9
Woodcrest Wk *REIG* RH2 257 P8
Woodcroft *ELTH/MOT* SE9 184 C6
GFD/PVL UB6 134 F1
HLWS CM18 47 H4
WCHMH N21 98 G2
Woodcroft Av *MLHL* NW7 96 B8
STAN HA7 94 F9
WARE SG12 27 J7
Woodcroft Crs *HGDN/ICK* UB10 132 C3
Woodcroft Ms *DEPT* SE8 160 D3
Woodcroft Rd *CRAWW* RH11 282 G9
CSHM HP5 51 J4
THHTH CR7 203 J5
Woodcutters Av *CDW/CHF* RM16 167 P1
Woodcutters Cl *EMPK* RM11 125 L2
Wood Dene *PECK* SE15 * 160 A7
Wood Dr *CHST* BR7 184 B9
SEV TN13 264 G2
Woodedge Cl *CHING* E4 101 L2
Wooden Bridge Ter
WNWD SE27 * 181 J6
Woodend *ESH/CLAY* KT10 198 B9
Wood End *HYS/HAR* UB3 132 F8
LCOL/BKTW AL2 56 B4
Woodend *LHD/OX* KT22 255 H1
NRWD SE19 181 K9
SUT SM1 201 M9
Wood End *SWLY* BR8 208 D4
Wood End Av *RYLN/HDSTN* HA2 114 A9
Woodend Cl *CRAWE* RH10 284 B5
Wood End Cl *HHNE* HP2 36 D5
NTHLT UB5 114 C10
SLN SL2 109 J8
Woodend Cl *WOKN/KNAP* GU21 231 M5
Wood End Cl *WOKS/MYFD* GU22 233 J2
Woodend Dr *ASC* SL5 192 A5
Wood End Gdns *ENC/FH* EN2 78 F8
Wood End Gdns *NTHLT* UB5 114 B10
Wood End Gn *YEAD* UB4 132 G7
Wood End Green Rd
HYS/HAR UB3 132 E7
Wood End La *NTHLT* UB5 134 A1
Woodend Pk *COB* KT11 235 L1
Wood End Rd *HRW* HA1 114 D9
Woodend Rd *WALTH* E17 101 H10
The Wood End *WLGTN* SM6 222 C5
Wood End Wy *NTHLT* UB5 114 B10
Wooder Gdns *FSTGT* E7 121 L9
Wooderson Cl *SNWD* SE25 203 M4
Woodfall Av *BAR* EN5 77 J9
Woodfall Dr *DART* DA1 164 G10
Woodfall Rd *FSBYPK* N4 119 H7
Woodfall St *CHEL* SW3 16 A8
Wood Farm Rd *HHNE* HP2 35 P7
Woodfarrs *CMBW* SE5 159 L10
Woodfield *ASHTD* KT21 237 J3
Woodfield Av *ALP/SUD* HA0 115 H8
CAR SM5 222 B3
CDALE/KGS NW9 116 B2
EA W5 135 H6
GVW DA11 190 E5
NTHWD HA6 92 F5
STRHM/NOR SW16 180 E6
Woodfield Cl *ASHTD* KT21 237 J3
COUL/CHIP CR5 240 D5
CRAWE RH10 283 P6
EN EN1 79 M8
NRWD SE19 181 K10
REDH RH1 257 P9
Woodfield Crs *EA* W5 135 J6
Woodfield Dr *EBAR* EN4 98 B2
GPK RM2 125 H2
HHS/BOV HP3 36 E8
Woodfield Gdns *HHS/BOV* HP3 36 D8
NWMAL KT3 200 C5
Woodfield Gv *STRHM/NOR* SW16 180 E6
Woodfield Hl *COUL/CHIP* CR5 240 C5
Woodfield La *ASHTD* KT21 237 K3
BRKMPK AL9 41 P9
STRHM/NOR SW16 180 E6
Woodfield Pk *AMS* HP6 68 C3
Woodfield Pl *MV/WKIL* W9 * 8 A1
Woodfield Ri *BUSH* WD23 94 C1
Woodfield Rd *ASHTD* KT21 237 J3
CRAWE RH10 284 A5
EA W5 135 H6
HSLWW TW4 153 J8
MV/WKIL W9 8 D3
RAD WD7 74 F2
THDIT KT7 198 E9
WGCE AL7 23 J5
Woodfields *SEV* TN13 246 E9
Woodfields Cl *GPK* RM2 125 H2
WATW WD18 * 73 K8
The Woodfields *SAND/SEL* CR2 223 N7
Woodfield Wy *FBAR/BDGN* N11 98 E8
HCH RM12 125 L6
REDH RH1 257 P9
STALE/WH AL4 39 H3
The Woodfines *EMPK* RM11 125 L4
Woodford Av *GNTH/NBYPK* IG2 122 C3
Woodford Bridge Rd *REDBR* IG4 122 A1
Woodford Ct *WAB* EN9 63 M9
Woodford Crs *PIN* HA5 93 J10
Woodford New Rd *WALTH* E17 101 K10
Woodford Pl *WBLY* HA9 115 K6
Woodford Rd *SWFD* E18 121 M2
WAT WD17 73 J6
Woodford Wy *SLN* SL2 128 F5
Woodgate *GSTN* WD25 55 J9
Woodgate Av *CHSGTN* KT9 219 J2
POTB/CUF EN6 60 C9
Woodgate Crs *NTHWD* HA6 93 H7
Woodgate Dr *STRHM/NOR* SW16 180 E10
Woodgate Ms *WAT* WD17 73 H5
Woodgavil *BNSTD* SM7 239 J2
Woodger Cl *RGUE* GU4 250 F8
Woodger Rd *SHB* W12 156 F1
Woodgers Gv *SWLY* BR8 208 G2
Woodget Cl *EHAM* E6 142 B8
Woodgrange Av *EA* W5 135 L10
EN EN1 79 P10
KTN/HRWW/WS HA3 115 J3
NFNCH/WDSPK N12 97 N7
Woodgrange Cl
KTN/HRWW/WS HA3 115 J3
Woodgrange Gdns *EN* EN1 79 P10
Woodgrange Rd *FSTGT* E7 121 M10
Woodgrange Ter *EN* EN1 * 79 P10
Woodgreen Rd *WAB* EN9 63 N9
Woodhall Av *DUL* SE21 181 N6
PIN HA5 93 M9
Woodhall Cl *HERT/WAT* SG14 25 K3
UX/CGN UB8 111 N10
Woodhall Ct *WGCE* AL7 23 H6
Woodhall Crs *EMPK* RM11 125 N5
Woodhall Dr *DUL* SE21 181 N6
PIN HA5 93 L9
Woodhall Ga *PIN* HA5 93 L8
Woodhall La *ASC* SL5 192 D9
HHNE HP2 35 P5
OXHEY WD19 93 L4
RAD WD7 75 K1
WGCE AL7 23 H7
Woodham Ct *SWFD* E18 121 L2
Woodham La *ADL/WDHM* KT15 215 H8
WOKN/KNAP GU21 214 E9
Woodham Park Rd
ADL/WDHM KT15 215 J6
Woodham Park Wy
ADL/WDHM KT15 215 J6
Woodham Ri *WOKN/KNAP* GU21 232 D1
Woodham Rd *CAT* SE6 183 H6
WOKN/KNAP GU21 214 C10
Woodham Wy *WARE* SG12 27 H7
Woodham Waye
WOKN/KNAP GU21 214 E10
Woodhatch Cl *EHAM* E6 142 B7
Woodhatch Rd *REDH* RH1 276 A5
REIG RH2 275 N4
Woodhatch Spinney
COUL/CHIP CR5 240 F2
Woodhaven Gdns *BARK/HLT* IG6 122 F2
Woodhaven Ms *WOT/HER* KT12 * 217 H1
Woodhaw *EGH* TW20 172 E7
Woodhayes *HORL* RH6 280 C3
Woodhayes Rd *WIM/MER* SW19 178 F10
Woodhead Dr *ORP* BR6 207 H10
Woodheyes Rd *WLSDN* NW10 116 B10
Woodhill *HLWS* CM18 47 H4
RPLY/SEND GU23 250 G2
WOOL/PLUM SE18 162 B3
Woodhill Av *CFSP/GDCR* SL9 110 D5
Woodhill Ct *RPLY/SEND* GU23 250 G1
Woodhill Crs
KTN/HRWW/WS HA3 115 J4
Woodhouse Av *GFD/PVL* UB6 134 E4
Woodhouse Cl *EDUL* SE22 159 P10
GFD/PVL UB6 134 E4
HYS/HAR UB3 152 F3
Woodhouse Eaves *NTHWD* HA6 93 H6
Woodhouse Gv *FSTGT* E7 142 B1
Wood House La *BROX* EN10 43 N7
Woodhouse La *RDKG* RH5 271 H9
Woodhouse Rd
NFNCH/WDSPK N12 97 M7
WAN E11 121 L8
Woodhurst Av *GSTN* WD25 73 L1
STMC/STPC BR5 206 F6
Woodhurst Dr *DEN/HRF* UB9 111 J3
Woodhurst La *OXTED* RH8 261 K7
Woodhurst Pk *OXTED* RH8 261 K6
Woodhurst Rd *ABYW* SE2 163 K4
ACT W3 135 P10
Woodhyrst Gdns *PUR/KEN* CR8 241 J1
Wooding Gv *HLWW/ROY* CM19 46 E1
Woodington Cl *ELTH/MOT* SE9 184 D2
Woodknoll Dr *CHST* BR7 206 C1
Woodland Ap *GFD/PVL* UB6 134 F1
Woodland Av *HART* DA3 211 L5
HHW HP1 35 L7
RBRW/HUT CM13 87 P9
SL SL1 129 J9
WDSR SL4 148 E10
Woodland Cl *CDALE/KGS* NW9 115 P4
EHSLY KT24 252 G3
HART DA3 211 P3
HGDN/ICK UB10 112 C7
HHW HP1 35 L7
HOR/WEW KT19 * 220 B3
NRWD SE19 181 M9
RBRW/HUT CM13 87 P9
WEY KT13 * 216 E1
WFD IG8 101 N4
Woodland Ct *GLDGN* NW11 * 117 H3
OXTED RH8 261 J4
STALW/RED AL3 * 38 E2
Woodland Crs *BERM/RHTH* SE16 160 C1
GNWCH SE10 161 K5
Woodland Dr *EHSLY* KT24 252 G3
STALE/WH AL4 39 H5
WAT WD17 72 G5
Woodlands Gdns *ISLW* TW7 154 D9
MUSWH N10 118 C3
SAND/SEL CR2 224 B6
Woodland Gld *SLN* SL2 109 J8
Woodland Gv *CROY/NA* CR0 223 H4
EPP CM16 65 K7
GNWCH SE10 161 K4
WEY KT13 216 E1
Woodland Hl *NRWD* SE19 181 M9
Woodland La *RKW/CH/CXG* WD3 70 G7
Woodland Ms *STRHM/NOR* SW16 180 F6
Woodland Mt *HERT/BAY* SG13 25 N5
Woodland Pl *HHW* HP1 35 L7
Woodland Ri *BGR/WK* TN15 247 N9
GFD/PVL UB6 134 F1
MUSWH N10 118 C2
OXTED RH8 261 K6
WCCW AL8 22 F3
Woodland Rd *CHING* E4 101 H2
FBAR/BDGN N11 98 C6
HERT/BAY SG13 26 B8
LOU IG10 82 B7
NRWD SE19 181 M8
RKW/CH/CXG WD3 90 G6
THHTH CR7 203 H4
Woodlands *ADL/WDHM* KT15 195 P10
ASHTD KT21 * 237 L4
BRKMPK AL9 59 L3
BXLYHS DA6 186 C1
CFSP/GDCR SL9 110 C4
CRAWE RH10 284 E5
GLDGN NW11 117 H4
HORL RH6 280 D3
RAD WD7 56 F10
RPLY/SEND GU23 251 J1
RYLN/HDSTN HA2 113 P2
RYNPK SW20 200 F4
WOKS/MYFD GU22 232 B4
Woodlands Av *ACT* W3 135 N10
BERK HP4 34 A6
BF/WBF KT14 215 J9
BFN/LL DA15 185 H4
CHDH RM6 123 P4
EMPK RM11 125 L3
FNCH N3 97 M8
NWMAL KT3 199 P1
REDH RH1 276 A1
RSLP HA4 113 K6

WAN E11 121 N6
WPK KT4 200 C9
Woodlands Cl BMLY BR1 206 C2
BORE WD6 75 N8
CDW/CHF RM16 168 B2
CFSP/GDCR SL9 110 D4
CHERT KT16 214 F6
ESH/CLAY KT10 218 E4
GLDGN NW11 117 H3
GU GU1 250 B6
HOD EN11 * 44 F4
SWLY BR8 208 G2
Woodlands Copse ASHTD KT21 237 J2
Woodlands Ct REDH RH1 * 276 A2
WOKS/MYFD GU22 232 B5
Woodlands Dr BEAC HP9 88 B7
HOD EN11 44 F5
KGLGY WD4 54 D4
STAN HA7 94 E7
SUN TW16 197 K2
Woodlands Gdns EPSOM KT18 238 F3
WALTH E17 * 121 K2
Woodlands Gld BEAC HP9 88 B7
Woodlands Gv COUL/CHIP CR5 240 C3
ISLW TW7 154 D8
Woodlands Hl BEAC HP9 108 D4
Woodlands La BFOR GU20 212 E4
COB KT11 235 P3
GVE DA12 191 N10
Woodlands Pde ASHF TW15 174 D9
Woodlands Pk ADL/WDHM KT15 215 J2
BXLY DA5 186 D7
GU GU1 250 E9
KWD/TDW/WH KT20 255 N7
WOKN/KNAP GU21 214 F9
Woodlands Park Rd
GNWCH SE10 161 L5
SEVS/STOTM N15 119 K3
Woodlands Ri SWLY BR8 208 G2
Woodlands Rd BARN SW13 156 C9
BF/WBF KT14 215 J10
BMLY BR1 206 C2
BUSH WD23 73 M8
BXLYHN DA7 163 P9
ED N9 100 B2
ENC/FH EN2 79 L4
EPSOM KT18 237 M1
GT/LBKH KT23 253 N5
GU GU1 250 A6
HARH RM3 105 P9
HERT/BAY SG13 25 N5
HHS/BOV HP3 54 B3
HRW HA1 114 E3
IL IG1 122 F8
ISLW TW7 154 D9
LHD/OX KT22 236 C4
ORP BR6 227 K3
REDH RH1 276 A2
ROM RM1 124 G1
STHL UB1 133 L10
SURB KT6 199 J8
VW GU25 193 P4
WALTH E17 121 H1
WAN E11 121 K7
Woodlands Rd East VW GU25 193 P4
Woodlands Rd West VW GU25 193 P3
Woodlands St LEW SE13 183 J3
Woodlands Ter SWLY BR8 * 208 D6
The Woodlands AMS HP6 69 H2
BRXN/ST SW9 * 159 J6
ESH/CLAY KT10 198 B9
HORL RH6 281 J4
HRW HA1 * 114 D7
ISLW TW7 154 E8
LEW SE13 183 J3
NRWD SE19 181 K10
ORP BR6 227 L3
STAN HA7 * 94 G6
STHGT/OAK N14 98 C2
WLGTN SM6 222 C5
Woodland St HACK E8 * 7 L1
Woodlands Wy ASHTD KT21 237 M2
KWD/TDW/WH KT20 255 P6
PUT/ROE SW15 179 J1
Woodland Ter CHARL SE7 162 B3
Woodland Vw CSHM HP5 51 J9
GODL GU7 267 K8
Woodland Wk HAMP NW3 117 P10
HOR/WEW KT19 219 M3
Woodland Wy ABLGY WD5 54 G3
ABYW SE2 163 N3
BRYLDS KT5 199 N9
CHESW EN7 61 J4
CHONG CM5 67 N6
CROY/NA CR0 204 D8
CTHM CR3 259 M4
EPP CM16 83 H1
KWD/TDW/WH KT20 239 J8
MLHL NW7 96 C7
MRDN SM4 201 J4
MTCM CR4 180 B10
PUR/KEN CR8 223 H9
RDART DA2 166 G10
STMC/STPC BR5 206 F4
WCHMH N21 99 H3
WEY KT13 216 E2
WFD IG8 101 N4
WWKM BR4 205 H10
Wood La BCTR RM8 124 B7
CDALE/KGS NW9 116 A6
CTHM CR3 241 L10
HCH RM12 125 H10
HGT N6 118 C4
HHNE HP2 35 N7
ISLW TW7 154 D5
IVER SL0 130 F6
KWD/TDW/WH KT20 239 J3
RDART DA2 188 C7
RSLP HA4 112 F6
SHB W12 136 F8
SL SL1 148 E2
STAN HA7 94 G4
WEY KT13 216 D5
WFD IG8 101 L6
WOKN/KNAP GU21 231 J4
Wood La End HHNE HP2 36 D5
Woodlawn Cl PUT/ROE SW15 179 J1
Woodlawn Crs WHTN TW2 176 A5
Woodlawn Dr FELT TW13 175 L5
Woodlawn Gv
WOKN/KNAP GU21 232 D1
Woodlawn Rd FUL/PGN SW6 156 G6
Woodlea HART DA3 211 P3
LCOL/BKTW AL2 55 P1
Woodlea Dr HAYES BR2 205 K5
Woodlea Gv NTHWD HA6 92 E7
Woodlea Rd STNW/STAM N16 119 M8
Woodlee Cl VW GU25 193 P2
Woodleigh Av
NFNCH/WDSPK N12 97 P7
Woodleigh Gdns
STRHM/NOR SW16 180 F6
Woodley Cl TOOT SW17 180 A10
Woodley Ct AMSS HP7 * 69 J5
Woodley Hl CSHM HP5 51 J10
Woodley La SUT SM1 201 P10
Woodley Rd ORP BR6 207 M9
WARE SG12 26 E1
Wood Lodge Gdns BMLY BR1 184 B10
Wood Lodge Gra SEV TN13 * 247 K8
Wood Lodge La WWKM BR4 205 H10
Woodmancote Gdns
BF/WBF KT14 215 K9
Woodmancourt GODL GU7 267 H9
Woodman La CHING E4 81 J9
Woodman Ms RCH/KEW TW9 155 N7
Woodman Pth BARK/HLT IG6 103 H7
Woodman Rd BARK/HLT IG6 103 H7
BRW CM14 107 H6
COUL/CHIP CR5 240 D2
HHS/BOV HP3 35 P9
Woodmans Gv WLSDN NW10 116 C10
Woodmansterne La BNSTD SM7 222 A8
BNSTD SM7 239 L1
Woodmansterne Rd CAR SM5 221 P6
COUL/CHIP CR5 240 D1
STRHM/NOR SW16 180 D10
Woodmansterne St BNSTD SM7 239 P1
Woodman St CAN/RD E16 142 D10
Woodmans Yd WAT WD17 73 K8
Wood Md TOTM N17 * 99 P7
Wood Meads EPP CM16 65 K5
Woodmere ELTH/MOT SE9 184 C3
Woodmere Av CROY/NA CR0 204 D7
WATN WD24 73 L4
Woodmere Cl BTSEA SW11 158 B9
CROY/NA CR0 204 C7
Woodmere Gdns CROY/NA CR0 204 C7
Woodmere Wy BECK BR3 205 J5
Woodmill Ms HOD EN11 * 44 G1
Woodmount SWLY BR8 208 E7
Woodnook Rd
STRHM/NOR SW16 180 C8
Woodpecker Cl BUSH WD23 94 B2
COB KT11 217 M8
ED N9 80 A10
HAT AL10 * 40 C7
KTN/HRWW/WS HA3 94 E9
Woodpecker Ms LEW SE13 161 J10
Woodpecker Mt CROY/NA CR0 224 D5
Woodpecker Rd NWCR SE14 160 D5
THMD SE28 143 M9
Woodpecker Wy
WOKS/MYFD GU22 232 A10
Woodplace Cl COUL/CHIP CR5 240 D5
Woodplace La COUL/CHIP CR5 240 D6
Wood Pond Cl BEAC HP9 89 H7
Woodquest Av HNHL SE24 181 K1
Woodredon Cl HLWW/ROY CM19 45 N2
Woodridden Hl WAB EN9 82 A1
Wood Ride EBAR EN4 77 N5
STMC/STPC BR5 206 G4
Woodridge Cl ENC/FH EN2 * 79 H5
Woodridge Wy NTHWD HA6 92 F7
Wood Riding WOKS/MYFD GU22 233 H1
Wood Ridings WEY KT13 * 216 B3
Woodridings Av PIN HA5 93 N9
Woodridings Cl PIN HA5 93 N8
Woodriffe Rd WAN E11 121 J5
Wood Ri GUW GU2 249 K8
PIN HA5 113 H3
Wood Rd BH/WHM TN16 243 P4
GODL GU7 267 L10
SHPTN TW17 196 B4
WLSDN NW10 135 P2
Woodrow WOOL/PLUM SE18 162 B3
Woodrow Av YEAD UB4 132 G7
Woodrow Cl GFD/PVL UB6 134 G2
Woodrow Ct TOTM N17 100 A8
Woodroyd Av HORL RH6 280 A5
Woodroyd Gdns HORL RH6 280 A6
Woodruff Av GU GU1 250 D7
Woodrush Cl NWCR SE14 160 D6
Woodrush Wy CHDH RM6 123 N2
Woods Av HAT AL10 40 E4
Woodseer St WCHPL E1 13 M3
Woodsford Sq WKENS W14 14 B1
WKENS W14 157 H1
Woodshire Rd DAGE RM10 124 D8
Woodshore Cl VW GU25 193 N6
Woodshots Meadow
WATW WD18 72 E9
Woodside BKHH IG9 101 P3
BORE WD6 75 L8
CHESW EN7 61 P7
EHSLY KT24 252 D2
EPP CM16 65 N3
GLDGN NW11 117 K3
HERT/BAY SG13 26 B8
KWD/TDW/WH KT20 257 J4
LHD/OX KT22 236 A8
ORP BR6 227 K2
WATN WD24 73 H3
WIM/MER SW19 179 J8
WOT/HER KT12 197 H8
Woodside Av ALP/SUD HA0 135 K3
AMS HP6 69 J2
BEAC HP9 88 B8
CHST BR7 184 F8
ESH/CLAY KT10 198 D7
HGT N6 118 A3
NFNCH/WDSPK N12 97 M5
SNWD SE25 204 A6
WOT/HER KT12 217 J1
Woodside Cl ALP/SUD HA0 135 K3
BEAC HP9 88 B8
BRYLDS KT5 199 P7
BXLYHN DA7 164 E10
CFSP/GDCR SL9 90 B10
CTHM CR3 241 M10
RAIN RM13 145 K6
RSLP HA4 112 E4
STAN HA7 94 G6
WOKN/KNAP GU21 231 J3
Woodside Ct EA W5 * 135 K10
GSTN WD25 55 K9
Woodside Court Rd
CROY/NA CR0 203 P7
Woodside Crs BFN/LL DA15 185 H6
HORL RH6 281 H4
Woodside Dr RDART DA2 186 F7
Woodside End ALP/SUD HA0 135 K3
Woodside Gdns CHING E4 100 G6
TOTM N17 99 N10
Woodside Grange Rd
NFNCH/WDSPK N12 97 L5
Woodside Gn SNWD SE25 203 P6
Woodside Gv
NFNCH/WDSPK N12 97 M4
Woodside Hl CFSP/GDCR SL9 90 B10
Woodside La BRKMPK AL9 41 K8
BXLY DA5 185 N2
TRDG/WHET N20 97 L4
WDSR SL4 170 B8
Woodside Pde BFN/LL DA15 * 185 H6
Woodside Pk SNWD SE25 203 P6
Woodside Park Av WALTH E17 121 J3
Woodside Park Rd
NFNCH/WDSPK N12 97 L5
Woodside Pl ALP/SUD HA0 135 K3
Woodside Rd ABLGY WD5 55 J7
AMS HP6 69 J3
BEAC HP9 88 B8
BFN/LL DA15 185 H6
BMLY BR1 206 B5
BXLYHN DA7 164 E10
COB KT11 217 P9
CRAWE RH10 284 A5
GUW GU2 249 L9
KUTN/CMB KT2 177 K10
LCOL/BKTW AL2 55 N6
NTHWD HA6 92 G8
NWMAL KT3 200 A2
PLSTW E13 141 P6
PUR/KEN CR8 222 F9
RSEV TN14 245 N10
SEV TN13 247 J9
SNWD SE25 204 A6
SUT SM1 201 M10
WDGN N22 99 H8
WDSR SL4 170 B8
WFD IG8 101 M5
Woodside Wk AMS HP6 * 69 J3
Woodside Wy CROY/NA CR0 204 B6
MTCM CR4 202 C1
REDH RH1 276 B1
REDH RH1 276 B6
VW GU25 193 N3
Wood's Ms MYFR/PKLN W1K 10 B7
Woodsome Ldg WEY KT13 216 C3
Woodsome Rd KTTN NW5 118 B8
Wood's Pl STHWK SE1 19 K4
Woodspring Rd
WIM/MER SW19 179 H5
Wood's Rd PECK SE15 160 A7
Woodstead Gv EDGW HA8 95 K7
The Woods HGDN/ICK UB10 112 C9
NTHWD HA6 93 H6
RAD WD7 56 G10
Woodstock RGUE GU4 251 L4
Woodstock Av CHEAM SM3 201 J7
DTCH/LGLY SL3 150 A3
GLDGN NW11 117 H5
HARH RM3 106 A6
ISLW TW7 176 F1
STHL UB1 133 N5
WEA W13 154 F2
Woodstock Cl BXLY DA5 186 A4
HERT/BAY SG13 26 A7
STAN HA7 95 K10
WOKN/KNAP GU21 232 B2
Woodstock Ct HOR/WEW KT19 220 A8
Woodstock Crs ED N9 80 A10
Woodstock Ct HOR/WEW KT19 220 A8
Woodstock Dr HGDN/ICK UB10 111 P9
Woodstock Gdns BECK BR3 204 G1
GDMY/SEVK IG3 123 K7
YEAD UB4 132 G7
Woodstock Gra EA W5 * 135 K10
Woodstock Gv GODL GU7 267 K10
SHB W12 156 G1
Woodstock La North SURB KT6 199 H9
Woodstock La South
CHSGTN KT9 199 H10
ESH/CLAY KT10 218 G2
Woodstock Ms CAVSQ/HST W1G 10 D4
Woodstock Ri CHEAM SM3 201 J8
Woodstock Rd ALP/SUD HA0 135 L2
BROX EN10 44 D5
BUSH WD23 94 D1
CAR SM5 222 B2
CHSWK W4 156 B3
COUL/CHIP CR5 240 C2
CROY/NA CR0 203 L10
FSBYPK N4 119 H6
FSTGT E7 141 P2
GLDGN NW11 117 J5
WALTH E17 101 J10
Woodstock Rd North STAL AL1 38 G4
Woodstock Rd South STAL AL1 38 G6
Woodstock St CAN/RD E16 141 L8
OXSTW W1C 10 E6
Woodstock Ter POP/IOD E14 140 G9
Woodstock Wy MTCM CR4 202 D2
Woodstone Av EW KT17 220 D2
Wood St BAR EN5 76 F8
BARB EC2Y 12 F4
CAN/RD E16 141 N9
CHSWK W4 156 B4
GRAYS RM17 167 P5
KUT/HW KT1 199 J2
MTCM CR4 202 B7
REDH RH1 258 D5
SWLY BR8 209 K1
WALTH E17 121 H1
Woodsway LHD/OX KT22 218 D10
Woodsyre SYD SE26 181 N7
Wood Ter CRICK NW2 * 116 C7
Woodthorpe Rd ASHF TW15 173 N8
PUT/ROE SW15 156 E10
Woodtree Cl HDN NW4 96 G10
Wood V FSTH SE23 182 A4
HAT AL10 40 E4
MUSWH N10 118 D3
Woodvale Av SNWD SE25 203 N3
Woodvale Pk STAL AL1 38 G6
Woodvale Wy GLDGN NW11 116 G8
Wood Vw CDW/CHF RM16 168 B3
Woodview CHSGTN KT9 219 H7
Wood Vw HHW HP1 35 L4
POTB/CUF EN6 60 F3
Woodview RDART DA2 * 188 F9
SLN SL2 * 128 E2
Woodview Av CHING E4 101 H5
Woodview Cl ASHTD KT21 237 M2
ORP BR6 206 F9
PUT/ROE SW15 178 A7
SAND/SEL CR2 224 A10
Woodview Rd SWLY BR8 208 D2
Woodville Cl LEE/GVPK SE12 183 M1
TEDD TW11 176 F7
Woodville Cottages GVE DA12 * 191 H2
Woodville Court Ms WAT WD17 * 73 H6
Woodville Gdns BARK/HLT IG6 122 E1
EA W5 135 K8
RSLP HA4 112 D5
SURB KT6 * 199 J7
Woodville Gv WELL DA16 * 163 K9
Woodville Pl GVW DA11 190 E3
HERT/WAT SG14 25 J3
Woodville Rd BAR EN5 77 L7
EA W5 135 K8
GLDGN NW11 117 H5
KIL/WHAMP NW6 2 D7
LHD/OX KT22 236 G6
MRDN SM4 201 K4
RCHPK/HAM TW10 176 G6
STNW/STAM N16 119 M10
SWFD E18 101 N10
THHTH CR7 203 L3
WALTH E17 120 D2
WAN E11 121 L6
Woodville St WOOL/PLUM SE18 162 B3
Woodward Av HDN NW4 116 D3
Woodward Cl ESH/CLAY KT10 218 E3
GRAYS RM17 167 N3
Woodwarde Rd EDUL SE22 181 M2
Woodward Gdns DAGW RM9 143 M2
STAN HA7 94 E8
Woodward Hts GRAYS RM17 167 N3
Woodward Rd DAGW RM9 143 L2
Woodwards HLWW/ROY CM19 46 F3
Woodward Ter RDART DA2 188 D2
Woodway GU GU1 250 E9
Wood Wy ORP BR6 206 D9
Woodway RBRW/HUT CM13 107 M2
Woodway Crs HRW HA1 114 F4
Woodwaye OXHEY WD19 93 K1
Woodwell St WAND/EARL SW18 179 M1
Wood Whf GNWCH SE10 160 G5
Woodwicks RKW/CH/CXG WD3 90 G6
Woodyard Cl KTTN NW5 118 B10
Woodyard La DUL SE21 181 M3
The Woodyard EPP CM16 65 M4
Woodyates Rd LEE/GVPK SE12 183 M2
Woodyers Cl SHGR GU5 268 E10
Woolacombe Rd BKHTH/KID SE3 161 P8
Woolacombe Wy HYS/HAR UB3 152 F3
Woolborough Cl CRAWE RH10 283 P6
Woolborough La CRAWE RH10 284 B5
REDH RH1 276 G9
Woolborough Rd CRAWE RH10 283 N6
Woolbrook Rd DART DA1 186 F2
Wooler St WALW SE17 18 G8
Woolf Cl THMD SE28 143 L10
Woolf Ms STPAN WC1H 11 L1
Woolhampton Wy CHIG IG7 103 L4
Woolhams CTHM CR3 259 N2
Woollam Crs STALW/RED AL3 38 B2
Woollard St WAB EN9 63 H10
Woollaston Rd FSBYPK N4 119 J4
Woollett Cl DART DA1 165 H10
Woolmans Cl BROX EN10 44 E8
Woolmead Av CDALE/KGS NW9 116 D5
Woolmer Cl BORE WD6 75 M4
Woolmerdine Ct BUSH WD23 73 L7
Woolmer Dr HHNE HP2 36 D6
Woolmer Gdns UED N18 99 P7
Woolmer Rd UED N18 99 P6
Woolmers La HERT/WAT SG14 24 C9
Woolmore St POP/IOD E14 141 H9
Woolneigh St FUL/PGN SW6 157 L9
Woolridge Wy HOM E9 * 140 B2
Wool Rd RYNPK SW20 178 E10
Woolstaplers Wy
BERM/RHTH SE16 19 N4
BERM/RHTH SE16 159 P2
Woolston Cl WALTH E17 100 C10
Woolstone Rd FSTH SE23 182 D5
Woolwich Church St CHARL SE7 162 B3
Woolwich Common
WOOL/PLUM SE18 162 D5
Woolwich Foot Tnl CAN/RD E16 162 D1
Woolwich High St
WOOL/PLUM SE18 162 D2
Woolwich Manorway
CAN/RD E16 162 E1
Woolwich Manor Wy EHAM E6 142 C6
Woolwich New Rd
WOOL/PLUM SE18 162 E4
Woolwich Rd ABYW SE2 163 N5
BXLYHN DA7 164 B9
GNWCH SE10 161 M4
Wooster Gdns POP/IOD E14 141 J8
Wooster Rd BEAC HP9 88 B7
Wootton Cl EMPK RM11 125 L3
EPSOM KT18 238 B2
Wootton Dr HHNE HP2 36 A1
Wootton Gv FNCH N3 97 K9
Wootton St STHWK SE1 18 B1
Worbeck Rd PGE/AN SE20 204 A2
Worcester Av TOTM N17 99 P8
UPMR RM14 126 E6
Worcester Cl CRICK NW2 116 D8
CROY/NA CR0 204 E9
MEO DA13 190 C10
MTCM CR4 202 B2
SWCM DA10 166 G10
Worcester Ct WOT/HER KT12 197 K9
Worcester Crs MLHL NW7 96 B4
WFD IG8 101 N6
Worcester Dr ASHF TW15 174 C9
CHSWK W4 156 B2
Worcester Gdns GFD/PVL UB6 134 B1
IL IG1 122 B5
SL SL1 149 J1
WPK KT4 200 B10
Worcester Ms KIL/WHAMP NW6 3 H1
Worcester Park Rd WPK KT4 199 P10
Worcester Rd BELMT SM2 221 K4
GUW GU2 249 L8
HAT AL10 40 C3
MNPK E12 122 C8
REIG RH2 257 K9
UX/CGN UB8 131 M7
WALTH E17 100 C10
WIM/MER SW19 179 J9
Worcesters Av EN EN1 79 P4
Wordsworth Av GFD/PVL UB6 134 C4
MNPK E12 142 B2
PUR/KEN CR8 241 L1
SWFD E18 121 L1
Wordsworth Cl CRAWE RH10 284 C5
HARH RM3 105 K9
TIL RM18 168 F8
Wordsworth Ct HAT AL10 * 40 D3
Wordsworth Dr CHEAM SM3 220 F1
Wordsworth Gdns BORE WD6 75 M9
Wordsworth Md REDH RH1 258 C8
Wordsworth Pde
CEND/HSY/T N8 * 119 J2
Wordsworth Pl HAMP NW3 118 A10
Wordsworth Rd
ADL/WDHM KT15 215 N1
HPTN TW12 175 N7
PGE/AN SE20 182 C10
SLN SL2 128 D6
STHWK SE1 19 L6
STNW/STAM N16 119 M9
WELL DA16 163 H7
WLGTN SM6 222 D3
Wordsworth Wk GLDGN NW11 117 K2
Wordsworth Wy DART DA1 165 P10
WDR/YW UB7 151 P3
Worfield St BTSEA SW11 157 P6
Worgan St BERM/RHTH SE16 160 C2
LBTH SE11 17 N7
Works Rd ADL/WDHM KT15 215 L5
Worland Rd SRTFD E15 141 K2
World's End COB KT11 217 H10
EPSOM KT18 * 238 A2
Worlds End Est WBPTN SW10 * 157 N6
Worlds End La ORP BR6 227 K4
WCHMH N21 78 G9
Worlds End Pas WBPTN SW10 * 157 N6
Worley Pl BEAC HP9 89 J6
Worley Rd STALW/RED AL3 38 B5
Worleys Dr ORP BR6 226 G1
Worlidge St HMSMTH W6 156 F4
Worlingham Rd EDUL SE22 159 N10
Wormholt Rd SHB W12 136 D10
Wormholt Ter SHB W12 * 136 D10
Wormley Ct WAB EN9 63 M9
Wormley Lodge Cl BROX EN10 44 E9
Wormwood St OBST EC2N 13 J5
Wormyngford Ct WAB EN9 63 M9
Wornington Green Est
NKENS W10 8 A3
Wornington Rd NKENS W10 8 B3
NKENS W10 137 H7
Woronzow Rd STJWD NW8 3 M6
Worple Av ISLW TW7 176 F1
STA TW18 173 L9
WIM/MER SW19 178 G10
Worple Cl RYLN/HDSTN HA2 113 N6
Worple Rd EPSOM KT18 220 B10
ISLW TW7 154 F10
LHD/OX KT22 236 G9
RYNPK SW20 200 G1
STA TW18 173 L10
WIM/MER SW19 179 H10
Worple Road Ms
WIM/MER SW19 179 J9
Worplesdon Rd GUW GU2 249 M6
Worple St MORT/ESHN SW14 156 A9
The Worple STWL/WRAY TW19 172 C2
Worple Wy RCHPK/HAM TW10 177 K1
RYLN/HDSTN HA2 113 N6
Worrin Cl BRWN CM15 107 L2
Worrin Rd BRWN CM15 107 L3
Worsfold Cl RPLY/SEND GU23 232 E9
Worships Hl SEV TN13 246 F9
Worship St SDTCH EC2A 13 J2
Worslade Rd TOOT SW17 179 N7
Worsley Bridge Rd SYD SE26 182 E8
Worsley Gv CLPT E5 119 P9
Worsley Rd WAN E11 121 K9
Worsopp Dr CLAP SW4 180 D1
Worsted Gn REDH RH1 258 E5
Worth Cl ORP BR6 227 H1
Worthfield Cl HOR/WEW KT19 220 A4
Worth Gv WALW SE17 18 G8
Worthing Cl GRAYS RM17 167 K5
SRTFD E15 141 K3
Worthing Rd HEST TW5 153 N5
Worthington Cl MTCM CR4 202 C4
Worthington Rd SURB KT6 199 L8
Worth Park Av CRAWE RH10 284 D6
Worth Rd CRAWE RH10 284 D7
Worth Wy CRAWE RH10 284 D8
CRAWE RH10 284 F8
CRAWE RH10 285 J7
Wortley Rd CROY/NA CR0 203 H7
EHAM E6 142 A2
Worton Gdns ISLW TW7 154 C8
Worton Rd ISLW TW7 154 E9
Worton Wy ISLW TW7 154 C8
Wotton Dr RDKG RH5 271 M6
Wotton Gn STMC/STPC BR5 207 N4
Wotton Rd CRICK NW2 116 F8
DEPT SE8 160 E5
Wotton Wy BELMT SM2 220 F6
Wouldham Rd CAN/RD E16 141 L8
GRAYS RM17 167 K5
Wouldham Ter STMC/STPC BR5 * 207 L3
Wrabness Wy STA TW18 195 L1
Wragby Rd WAN E11 * 121 K8
Wrampling Pl ED N9 99 P2
Wrangley Ct WAB EN9 63 M9
Wray Av CLAY IG5 122 D1
Wray Cl EMPK RM11 125 L5
Wray Common Rd REIG RH2 257 M9
Wray Crs FSBYPK N4 118 F7
Wrayfield Av REIG RH2 257 M9
Wrayfield Rd CHEAM SM3 200 G10
Wraylands Dr REIG RH2 257 N8
Wray La REIG RH2 257 N7
Wraymead Pl REIG RH2 * 257 L9
Wray Mill Pk REIG RH2 257 N8
Wray Park Rd REIG RH2 257 L9
Wray Rd BELMT SM2 221 J5
Wraysbury Cl HSLWW TW4 175 M1
Wraysbury Gdns STA TW18 173 H7
Wraysbury Rd STA TW18 172 F6
Wrays Wy YEAD UB4 132 F7
Wrekin Rd WOOL/PLUM SE18 162 F6
Wren Av CRICK NW2 116 F9
NWDGN UB2 153 N3
Wren Cl CAN/RD E16 141 L8
ED N9 100 C2
SAND/SEL CR2 224 C6
STMC/STPC BR5 207 N3
Wren Ct CRAWE RH10 * 283 P10
Wren Crs ADL/WDHM KT15 215 N2
BUSH WD23 94 B2
Wren Dr WAB EN9 63 M10
WDR/YW UB7 151 N2
Wren Gdns DAGW RM9 123 N10
HCH RM12 124 G6
Wren Ms LEW SE13 * 161 K10
Wren Pl BRW CM14 107 J4
Wren Rd CMBW SE5 159 L7
DAGW RM9 123 N10
SCUP DA14 185 M6
Wren's Av ASHF TW15 174 D8
Wrens Cft GVW DA11 190 B7
Wrensfield HHW HP1 35 K7
Wren's Hl LHD/OX KT22 236 C1
The Wrens HLWW/ROY CM19 46 E1
Wren St FSBYW WC1X 11 P1
Wren Ter LOU IG10 82 E5
Wrentham Av WLSDN NW10 136 G4
Wrenthorpe Rd BMLY BR1 183 K7
Wren Wk TIL RM18 168 E6
Wren Wd WGCE AL7 23 L4
Wrenwood Wy PIN HA5 113 J2
Wrexham Rd BOW E3 140 F4
HARH RM3 105 L5
Wricklemarsh Rd
BKHTH/KID SE3 161 N8
Wrigglesworth St NWCR SE14 160 C6
Wright WDSR SL4 148 B9
Wright Cl LEW SE13 161 J10
STALE/WH AL4 21 J4
Wright Gdns SHPTN TW17 196 B5
Wright Rd HEST TW5 153 K6
Wrights Aly WIM/MER SW19 178 F9
Wrightsbridge Rd BRW CM14 105 N2
Wrights Cl DAGE RM10 124 C9
Wrights La BRWN CM15 87 J2
KENS W8 14 G3
Wrights Pl WLSDN NW10 * 135 P1
Wright's Rd BOW E3 140 E4
SNWD SE25 203 M3
Wright's Rw WLGTN SM6 222 C1
Wrigley Cl CHING E4 * 101 J6
Wriotsley Wy ADL/WDHM KT15 215 K3
Wrotham Rd BAR EN5 77 H6
CAMTN NW1 5 H4
MEO DA13 190 D10
WEA W13 135 H10
WELL DA16 163 M7
Wroths Pth LOU IG10 82 C5
Wrottesley Rd WLSDN NW10 136 E4
WOOL/PLUM SE18 162 F5
Wroughton Rd BTSEA SW11 180 A2
Wroughton Ter HDN NW4 * 116 E2
Wroxall Rd DAGW RM9 143 M1
Wroxham Av HHS/BOV HP3 35 N8
Wroxham Gdns ENC/FH EN2 79 H1
FBAR/BDGN N11 98 D8
POTB/CUF EN6 58 G7
Wroxham Rd THMD SE28 143 N9
Wroxham Wk CRAWE RH10 284 C9
Wroxham Wy BARK/HLT IG6 102 E9
Wroxton Rd PECK SE15 160 B8
Wrythe Gn CAR SM5 202 A10
Wrythe Green Rd CAR SM5 202 A10
Wrythe La CAR SM5 201 N8
Wulfstan St SHB W12 136 C8
Wulstan Pk POTB/CUF EN6 59 N8
Wyatt Cl BERM/RHTH SE16 160 E1
BUSH WD23 94 D1
FELT TW13 175 L4
YEAD UB4 133 H7
Wyatt Dr BARN SW13 156 E5
Wyatt Park Rd
BRXS/STRHM SW2 180 G5
Wyatt Rd DART DA1 164 G9
FSTGT E7 141 M1
HBRY N5 119 K8
STA TW18 173 J8
WDSR SL4 148 C9
Wyatt's Cl RKW/CH/CXG WD3 71 K7
Wyatt's Green La BRWN CM15 87 K2
Wyatt's Green Rd BRWN CM15 87 J2
Wyatt's La WALTH E17 121 H1
Wyatt's Rd RKW/CH/CXG WD3 71 J8
Wybert St CAMTN NW1 10 F1
Wyborne Wy WLSDN NW10 135 P2
Wyburn Av BAR EN5 77 J7
Wychcombe Studios
HAMP NW3 * 4 A2
Wyche Gv SAND/SEL CR2 223 K5
Wych Elm HLW CM20 28 F10
Wych Elm Cl EMPK RM11 125 P5
Wych Elm Ri GU GU1 268 B3
Wych Elm Rd EMPK RM11 125 P4
Wychelm Rd LTWR GU18 212 B7
Wych Elms LCOL/BKTW AL2 56 A4
Wycherley Cl BKHTH/KID SE3 161 L6
Wycherley Crs BAR EN5 77 L10
Wychford Dr SBW CM21 29 M2
Wych Hl WOKS/MYFD GU22 231 P5
Wych Hill La WOKS/MYFD GU22 232 B5
Wych Hill Pk WOKS/MYFD GU22 232 A5
Wych Hill Ri WOKS/MYFD GU22 231 P5
Wychwood Av EDGW HA8 95 J7
THHTH CR7 203 K3
Wychwood Cl EDGW HA8 95 J7
SUN TW16 175 H9
Wychwood End HGT N6 118 D5
Wychwood Gdns CLAY IG5 122 C2
Wychwood Wy NTHWD HA6 92 G8
Wycliffe Cl CHES/WCR EN8 62 C5
WELL DA16 163 J7
Wycliffe Rd BTSEA SW11 158 B8
WIM/MER SW19 179 L9
Wycliffe Rw GVW DA11 190 C4
Wyclif St FSBYE EC1V 6 C10
Wycombe End BEAC HP9 108 C1
Wycombe Gdns GLDGN NW11 117 J7
Wycombe Pl STAL AL1 38 G3
WAND/EARL SW18 179 M2
Wycombe Rd ALP/SUD HA0 135 M3
GNTH/NBYPK IG2 122 C3
TOTM N17 99 P9
Wycombe Sq KENS W8 8 E10
Wycombe Wy STALE/WH AL4 38 G3
Wyddial Gn WGCE AL7 23 L5
Wydell Cl MRDN SM4 200 G6
Wydenhurst Rd CROY/NA CR0 203 P7
Wydeville Manor Rd
LEE/GVPK SE12 183 N7
Wyecliffe Gdns REDH RH1 258 D6
Wye Cl ASHF TW15 174 C7
ORP BR6 207 J7
RSLP HA4 112 D4
Wyedale LCOL/BKTW AL2 57 L3
Wyemead Crs CHING E4 101 K3
Wye Rd GVE DA12 190 G5
Wye St BTSEA SW11 157 N9
The Wye HHNE HP2 36 B1
Wyeth's Ms EW KT17 220 C9
Wyeth's Rd EW KT17 220 C9
Wyevale Cl NTHWD HA6 113 H1
Wyfields CLAY IG5 102 E9
Wyfold Rd FUL/PGN SW6 157 H7
Wyke Cl ISLW TW7 154 E5
Wyke Gdns HNWL W7 154 E2
Wykeham Av DAGW RM9 143 M1
EMPK RM11 125 L4
Wykeham Cl GVE DA12 191 H9
WDR/YW UB7 152 B5
Wykeham Gn DAGW RM9 143 M1
Wykeham Hl WBLY HA9 115 L6
Wykeham Ri TRDG/WHET N20 97 H2
Wykeham Rd GU GU1 250 G9
HDN NW4 116 F3
KTN/HRWW/WS HA3 114 G2
Wykeridge Cl CSHM HP5 50 G3
Wyke Rd BOW E3 140 F2
RYNPK SW20 200 F2
Wylands Rd DTCH/LGLY SL3 150 D4
Wylchin Cl PIN HA5 112 G2
Wyldes Cl GLDGN NW11 117 M6
Wyldewood ASC SL5 192 C6
Wyldfield Gdns ED N9 99 N3
Wyld Wy WBLY HA9 135 N1
Wyldwood Cl HLWE CM17 29 M5
Wyleu St FSTH SE23 182 D3
Wylie Rd NWDGN UB2 153 P2
Wyllen Cl WCHPL E1 140 B6
Wyllyotts Pl POTB/CUF EN6 59 J8
Wylo Dr BAR EN5 76 D10
Wymark Cl RAIN RM13 144 G4
Wymering Rd MV/WKIL W9 2 F10
Wymers Cl SL SL1 128 A4
Wymond St PUT/ROE SW15 156 F9
Wynan Rd POP/IOD E14 160 G4
Wynaud Ct WDGN N22 98 G7
Wyncham Av BFN/LL DA15 185 H4
Wynches Farm Dr
STALE/WH AL4 39 J6
Wynchgate KTN/HRWW/WS HA3 94 D8
STHGT/OAK N14 98 F1
Wynchlands Crs STALE/WH AL4 39 J6
Wyncote Wy SAND/SEL CR2 224 C5
Wyncroft Cl BMLY BR1 206 C3
Wyndale Av CDALE/KGS NW9 115 M4
Wyndcliff Rd CHARL SE7 161 N5
Wyndcroft Cl ENC/FH EN2 79 J7
Wyndham Av COB KT11 217 H9
Wyndham Cl BELMT SM2 221 K4
ORP BR6 206 F8
Wyndham Crs HSLWW TW4 175 N2
KTTN NW5 118 D8
SL SL1 128 A4
Wyndham Est CMBW SE5 159 K6
Wyndham Ms MBLAR W1H 10 A4
Wyndham Pl MBLAR W1H 10 A4
Wyndham Rd CMBW SE5 159 K6
EBAR EN4 98 A2
EHAM E6 142 A2
KUTN/CMB KT2 177 L10
WEA W13 154 G2
WOKN/KNAP GU21 231 N4
Wyndhams End WGCE AL7 23 J9
Wyndham St CAMTN NW1 10 A3
Wyndhurst Cl SAND/SEL CR2 223 J4
Wyneham Rd HNHL SE24 181 L1
Wynell Rd FSTH SE23 182 C6
Wynford Gv STMC/STPC BR5 207 L3
Wynford Pl BELV DA17 164 B5
Wynford Rd IS N1 5 N7
Wynford Wy ELTH/MOT SE9 184 C6
Wyngrave Pl BEAC HP9 88 B6
Wynlea Cl CRAWE RH10 285 P5
Wynlie Gdns PIN HA5 93 J10
Wynn Bridge Cl WFD IG8 102 A9
Wynndale Rd SWFD E18 101 N9
Wynne Rd BRXN/ST SW9 159 H8
Wynn's Av BFN/LL DA15 185 K1
Wynnstay Gdns KENS W8 14 F3
Wynnstow Pk OXTED RH8 261 L7
Wynnswick Rd BEAC HP9 89 H6
Wynsham Wy BFOR GU20 212 A2
Wynter St BTSEA SW11 157 M10
Wynton Gdns SNWD SE25 203 N5
Wynton Gv WOT/HER KT12 197 H10
Wynton Pl ACT W3 135 N8
Wynyard Ter LBTH SE11 17 P7
Wynyatt St FSBYE EC1V 6 C9
Wyre Gv EDGW HA8 95 N4
HYS/HAR UB3 153 H3
Wyresdale Crs GFD/PVL UB6 134 E5
Wysemead HORL RH6 280 D3
Wyteleaf Cl RSLP HA4 112 D4
Wythburn Pl MBLAR W1H 10 A6
Wythenshawe Rd DAGE RM10 124 B8
Wythes Cl BMLY BR1 206 C2
Wythes Rd CAN/RD E16 142 B10
Wythfield Rd ELTH/MOT SE9 184 C2
Wyton WGCE AL7 23 N5
Wyvenhoe Rd RYLN/HDSTN HA2 114 B8
Wyvern Cl DART DA1 187 K3
ORP BR6 207 L10
Wyvern Est NWMAL KT3 * 200 D3
Wyvern Pl ADL/WDHM KT15 * 215 L1
Wyvern Rd PUR/KEN CR8 223 H6
Wyvern Wy UX/CGN UB8 131 L3
Wyvis St POP/IOD E14 140 G7

Y

Yabsley St POP/IOD E14 141 H10
Yaffle Rd WEY KT13 216 D6
Yalding Gv STMC/STPC BR5 207 N4
Yalding Rd BERM/RHTH SE16 19 N4
BERM/RHTH SE16 159 P2
Yale Cl HSLWW TW4 175 N1
Yale Wy HCH RM12 125 H9
Yarborough Rd WIM/MER SW19 201 N1
Yarbridge Cl BELMT SM2 * 221 L6
Yardley Cl CHING E4 80 G9
REIG RH2 257 L8
Yardley La CHING E4 80 G9
Yardley St FSBYW WC1X 6 A10
FSBYW WC1X 12 A1
Yard Md EGH TW20 172 D6
Yarm Cl LHD/OX KT22 237 H9
Yarm Court Rd LHD/OX KT22 237 H9
Yarmouth Cl CRAWE RH10 284 B9
Yarmouth Crs TOTM N17 120 A3
Yarmouth Pl MYFR/PICC W1J 10 E10
Yarmouth Rd SL SL1 129 H8
WATN WD24 73 K4
Yarm Wy LHD/OX KT22 237 H9
Yarnton Wy ABYW SE2 163 M1
Yarrow Crs EHAM E6 142 B7
Yarrowside AMSS HP7 69 N6
Yateley St WOOL/PLUM SE18 162 A2
Yattendon Rd HORL RH6 280 C4
Yeading Av RYLN/HDSTN HA2 113 M7
Yeading Fk YEAD UB4 133 K7
Yeading Gdns YEAD UB4 133 J7
Yeading La YEAD UB4 133 J8
Yeames Cl WEA W13 134 F8
Yearling Cl WARE SG12 26 E5
Yeate St IS N1 6 G4
Yeatman Rd HGT N6 118 A4
Yeats Cl LEW SE13 * 161 J8
REDH RH1 275 M3
WLSDN NW10 116 B10
Ye Cnr OXHEY WD19 73 L10
Yeend Cl E/WMO/HCT KT8 197 P4
Yeldham Rd HMSMTH W6 156 G4
Yeldham Vls HMSMTH W6 * 156 G4
Yellowcress Dr CHOB/PIR GU24 230 F2
Yellowpine Wy CHIG IG7 103 L5
Yelverton Cl HARH RM3 105 L9
Yelverton Rd BTSEA SW11 157 N8
Yenston Cl MRDN SM4 201 K6
Yeoman Cl EHAM E6 142 E9
Yeoman Dr STWL/WRAY TW19 173 P4
Yeoman Rd NTHLT UB5 133 M2
Yeomanry Cl EW KT17 220 C8
Yeomans Acre RSLP HA4 113 H4
Yeomans Cft GT/LBKH KT23 253 P1
Yeoman's Mdw SEV TN13 265 H2
Yeoman's Rw CHEL SW3 15 P4
Yeomans Ter
WOKN/KNAP GU21 * 231 J3
Yeoman St BERM/RHTH SE16 160 D3
Yeomans Wy PEND EN3 * 80 A6
Yeoman's Yd WCHPL E1 13 M7
Yeoman Wy REDH RH1 276 C5

Yeomen Wy BARK/HLT IG6 102 F7
Yeo St BOW E3 140 G7
Yeoveney Cl STWL/WRAY TW19 172 G5
Yeovil Cl ORP BR6 207 H9
Yeovil Rd SL SL1 128 D7
Yeovilton Pl KUTN/CMB KT2 177 J8
Yerbury Rd ARCH N19 118 E8
Yester Dr CHST BR7 184 B10
Yester Pk CHST BR7 184 C10
Yester Rd CHST BR7 184 C10
Yevele Wy EMPK RM11 125 M5
Yew Av WDR/YW UB7 131 P9
Yewbank Cl PUR/KEN CR8 241 L1
Yew Cl BKHH IG9 102 A3
CHESW EN7 * 61 M3
Yewdale Cl BMLY BR1 183 K9
Yewfield Rd WLSDN NW10 136 C2
Yew Gv CRICK NW2 116 G9
WGCE AL7 23 M6
Yewlands HOD EN11 44 F4
SBW CM21 29 P2
Yewlands Cl BNSTD SM7 239 L1
Yewlands Dr HOD EN11 44 F4
Yew Pl WEY KT13 * 196 G10
Yews Av EN EN1 80 A2
The Yews ASHF TW15 * 174 C7
BF/WBF KT14 * 215 P8
Yew Tree Bottom Rd EW KT17 238 E3
Yew Tree Cl BEAC HP9 88 E10
COUL/CHIP CR5 240 A5
CSHM HP5 51 M6
HORL RH6 280 B2
LEW SE13 161 H9
Yewtree Cl MUSWH N10 98 D9
Yew Tree Cl RBRW/HUT CM13 87 N10
Yewtree Cl RYLN/HDSTN HA2 114 A2
Yew Tree Cl SEV TN13 246 E9
WCHMH N21 99 H1
WELL DA16 163 K7
WPK KT4 200 B8
Yew Tree Ct BORE WD6 75 J10
Yew Tree Dr CTHM CR3 259 N1
GU GU1 249 N5
HHS/BOV HP3 52 E4
Yewtree End LCOL/BKTW AL2 56 A3
Yew Tree Gdns CHDH RM6 123 P3
EPSOM KT18 237 P1
ROMW/RG RM7 124 E3
Yew Tree La REIG RH2 257 L7
Yew Tree Rd BECK BR3 204 E3
DORK RH4 254 F10
HGDN/ICK UB10 132 A3
HORL RH6 279 H8
SHB W12 136 C9
SL SL1 149 M2
Yewtrees EGH TW20 194 F3
Yew Trees SHPTN TW17 196 A4
Yew Tree Wk EHSLY KT24 253 L3
HSLWW TW4 175 N1
PUR/KEN CR8 223 K6
Yew Wk HOD EN11 44 F4
HRW HA1 114 D6
Yoakley Rd STNW/STAM N16 119 M7
Yoke Cl HOLWY N7 5 M1
Yolande Gdns ELTH/MOT SE9 184 B1
Yonge Pk HOLWY N7 119 H8
York Av BFN/LL DA15 185 H5
HNWL W7 134 D10
HYS/HAR UB3 132 D8
MORT/ESHN SW14 177 P1
SL SL1 129 J8
STAN HA7 94 G9
WDSR SL4 148 G8
York Br CAMTN NW1 10 C1
York Buildings CHCR WC2N 11 M8
York Cl BF/WBF KT14 215 P8
BRWN CM15 107 L1
CMBW SE5 * 159 K8
EHAM E6 142 C8
HNWL W7 134 D10
KGLGY WD4 54 B5
MRDN SM4 201 L4
York Crs BORE WD6 76 A6
LOU IG10 82 B7
Yorke Gdns REIG RH2 257 K9
Yorke Ga CTHM CR3 241 L8
WAT WD17 73 H6
Yorke Rd REIG RH2 257 K9
RKW/CH/CXG WD3 72 B10
Yorkes HLWS CM18 47 J3
York Gdns WOT/HER KT12 197 L9
York Ga CAMTN NW1 10 D2
STHGT/OAK N14 98 F1
York Gv PECK SE15 160 B7
York Hl LOU IG10 82 C6
WNWD SE27 181 J6
York House Pl KENS W8 14 G1
Yorkland Av WELL DA16 163 J10
York Ms IL IG1 122 D8
KTTN NW5 118 C10
York Pde BTFD TW8 * 155 J4
CDALE/KGS NW9 * 116 D4
York Pl BTSEA SW11 157 M9
IL IG1 122 D7
York Ri KTTN NW5 118 C8
ORP BR6 207 H9
York Rd ACT W3 135 P8
BAR EN5 77 M9
BELMT SM2 221 K3
BF/WBF KT14 215 N8
BH/WHM TN16 243 N5
BRWN CM15 107 L1
BTFD TW8 155 J4
BTSEA SW11 157 M10
CHES/WCR EN8 62 D10
CHING E4 100 F6
CROY/NA CR0 203 H7
DART DA1 187 N3
EA W5 155 H2
EPP CM16 66 B3
FBAR/BDGN N11 98 E7
FSTGT E7 141 M1
GU GU1 268 B1
GVE DA12 190 F6
GVW DA11 190 A3
HSLW TW3 154 A9
IL IG1 122 D8
KUTN/CMB KT2 177 L10
LEY E10 121 H8
NTHWD HA6 93 H10
RAIN RM13 144 E2
RCHPK/HAM TW10 177 L1
SAND/SEL CR2 224 C6
STAL AL1 38 E5
STHWK SE1 17 P1
TEDD TW11 176 D7
UED N18 100 A6
UX/CGN UB8 131 N2
WALTH E17 120 C3
WATW WD18 73 K9
WCHMH N21 99 L1
WDSR SL4 148 G8
WEY KT13 216 D2
WIM/MER SW19 179 L9
WOKS/MYFD GU22 232 B4
Yorkshire Cl STNW/STAM N16 119 M8
Yorkshire Gdns UED N18 100 A6
Yorkshire Grey Yd GINN WC1R * 11 N4
Yorkshire Rd MTCM CR4 202 F5
POP/IOD E14 140 D8
York Sq POP/IOD E14 140 D8
York St MBLAR W1H 10 A4
MTCM CR4 202 B7
York St Chambers MHST W1U * 10 B3
York Ter ENC/FH EN2 79 K4
ERITH DA8 164 D7
York Ter East CAMTN NW1 10 D2
York Ter West CAMTN NW1 10 C2
Yorkton St BETH E2 7 N7
York Wy CHSGTN KT9 219 J4
FELT TW13 175 N6
GSTN WD25 73 L2
HHNE HP2 35 P7
HOLWY N7 5 L2
IS N1 5 M7
TRDG/WHET N20 98 A4
York Way Ct IS N1 5 M6
York Way Est HOLWY N7 5 L2
Youngfield Rd HHW HP1 35 J5
Youngmans Cl ENC/FH EN2 79 K5
Young Rd CAN/RD E16 141 P8
Youngs Ms HERT/WAT SG14 25 K5
Youngs Ri WGCW AL8 22 E5
Youngs Rd GNTH/NBYPK IG2 122 G3
Young St KENS W8 14 G2
LHD/OX KT22 236 E10
Youngstroat La CHOB/PIR GU24 214 B6
Yoxley Ap GNTH/NBYPK IG2 122 F4
Yoxley Dr GNTH/NBYPK IG2 122 F4
Yukon Rd BAL SW12 180 C3
BROX EN10 62 E1
Yule Cl LCOL/BKTW AL2 55 N6
Yunus Khan Cl WALTH E17 120 F4

Z

Zambezie Dr ED N9 100 B4
Zambra Wy BGR/WK TN15 247 N6
Zampa Rd BERM/RHTH SE16 160 B4
Zander Ct BETH E2 7 P9
Zangwill Rd BKHTH/KID SE3 162 A7
Zealand Av WDR/YW UB7 151 N6
Zealand Rd BOW E3 140 D4
Zelah Rd STMC/STPC BR5 207 L7
Zennor Rd BAL SW12 180 D4
Zenoria St EDUL SE22 159 N10
Zermatt Rd THHTH CR7 203 K5
Zetland St POP/IOD E14 141 H7
Zig Zag Rd PUR/KEN CR8 241 K2
RDKG RH5 255 H6
Zinnia Dr CHOB/PIR GU24 230 F2
Zion Pl GVE DA12 190 E3
THHTH CR7 203 L4
Zion Rd THHTH CR7 203 L4
Zoar St STHWK SE1 12 E9
Zoffany St ARCH N19 118 E7

Index - featured places

2 Willow Road
HAMP NW3 117 P9
22 Jermyn Street Hotel
STJS SW1Y 11 H8
51 Buckingham Gate Hotel
WESTW SW1E 17 H3
AAIS
DART DA1 187 M3
Aarotya Medical Centre
SEVS/STOTM N15 119 K2
Abbey Business Centre
VX/NE SW8 158 D7
Abbey Christian School for the English Language
STJWD NW8 3 K8
The Abbey Clinic
BELV DA17 164 A4
Abbey College London
BAY/PAD W2 8 F6
The Abbey Court Townhouse Hotel
BAY/PAD W2 8 E8
Abbey Gateway
STALW/RED AL3 38 B6
Abbey Industrial Estate
ALP/SUD HA0 135 L3
MTCM CR4 202 A5
Abbeylands School
ADL/WDHM KT15 215 K2
Abbey Lane Commercial Estate
SRTFD E15 141 J4
Abbey Mead Industrial Park
WAB EN9 62 G10
Abbey Medical Centre
STJWD NW8 3 H6
Abbey Mills
WIM/MER SW19 201 M1
Abbey Moor Golf Course
ADL/WDHM KT15 195 K10
Abbey Park Industrial Estate
BARK IG11 142 E4
Abbey Primary School
ABYW SE2 163 M2
MRDN SM4 201 K7
STALW/RED AL3 38 B7
Abbey Road Health Centre
SRTFD E15 141 K3
Abbey Road Studios
STJWD NW8 3 K8
Abbey Sports Centre
BARK IG11 142 F3
Abbey Trading Estate
SYD SE26 182 D8
Abbey View Golf Club
STALW/RED AL3 38 A7
Abbey Wharf Industrial Estate
BARK IG11 142 G5
Abbey Wood School
ABYW SE2 163 K2
Abbotsbury Primary School
MRDN SM4 201 K5
Abbotsfield School
HGDN/ICK UB10 132 C4
Abbots Hill School
HHS/BOV HP3 54 C1
Abbots Hospital
GU GU1 268 A1
Abbots Langley Primary School
ABLGY WD5 54 F5
Abbotsweld Primary School
HLWS CM18 46 G3
Abbotswood Medical Centre
ABLGY WD5 55 H8
ABC Cinema
BRW CM14 107 H3
GVE DA12 190 E2
HAMP NW3 117 P10
PUT/ROE SW15 157 H9
Abercorn School
MBLAR W1H 10 A4
STJWD NW8 3 K8
Aberdeen Wharf
WAP E1W 140 A10
Aberdour School
KWD/TDW/WH KT20 239 J4
Aberglen Industrial Estate
HYS/HAR UB3 152 E1
Abingdon House School
KENS W8 14 F3
Abinger Common First School
RDKG RH5 271 L8
Abney Park Cemetery
STNW/STAM N16 119 M7
Aboyne Lodge Primary School
STALW/RED AL3 38 C5
Abridge Golf & Country Club
ABR/ST RM4 84 A3
Acacia Business Centre
WAN E11 121 K8
The Academy at Peckham
PECK SE15 159 N7
The Academy School
HAMP NW3 117 N9
Acland Burghley School
KTTN NW5 118 C9
Acorn Industrial Park
DART DA1 187 H1
Acorn Medical Centre
HGDN/ICK UB10 132 B3
TWK TW1 176 F4
Acorns CE School
REIG RH2 274 D6
The Acorns First School
BRKHM/BTCW RH3 256 A10
Acorn Trading Centre
WTHK RM20 167 K5
Acre Road Health Clinic
KUTN/CMB KT2 177 L10
ACS Egham International School
EGH TW20 193 P1
ACS Hillingdon International School
HGDN/ICK UB10 132 A3
Acting School
GUW GU2 267 P2
Activity World
HAT AL10 40 E1
Acton Business Centre
WLSDN NW10 136 A6
Acton Central Industrial Estate
ACT W3 135 N9
Acton Health Centre
ACT W3 135 P10
Acton High School
ACT W3 155 M1
Acton Hospital
ACT W3 155 M1
Acton Lane Medical Centre
CHSWK W4 155 P1
Acton Park Industrial Estate
ACT W3 136 C10
ACT W3 156 A1
Acton Superbowl
ACT W3 135 M7
Acton Swimming Baths
ACT W3 135 P10
Acumen (Anglo School)
NRWD SE19 203 M1
Adams Bridge Business Centre
WBLY HA9 115 N10
Adamsrill Primary School
SYD SE26 182 D6
Adath Yisroel Cemetery
EN EN1 79 N5
Addey & Stanhope School
NWCR SE14 160 E7
Addington Business Centre
CROY/NA CR0 225 K6
Addington Court Golf Club
CROY/NA CR0 224 E5
Addington Golf Club
CROY/NA CR0 224 E1
Addington High School
CROY/NA CR0 225 K8
Addington Palace Golf Club
CROY/NA CR0 224 D3
Addiscombe CC
CROY/NA CR0 203 P10
Addison Primary School
WKENS W14 156 G2
Addlestone Cemetery
ADL/WDHM KT15 195 K9
Adelphi Theatre
COVGDN WC2E 11 M8
Adeyfield School
HHNE HP2 36 B6
Adler Industrial Estate
HYS/HAR UB3 152 E1
Admiral Hyson Industrial Estate
STHWK SE1 160 A3
Admiralty Arch
STJS SW1Y 11 K9
ADT College
PUT/ROE SW15 179 J1
The Adult College of Barking & Dagenham
BARK IG11 143 H1
Aerodrome Hotel
CROY/NA CR0 223 H3
Africa Centre
COVGDN WC2E 11 M7
Agency of Jewish Education
HDN NW4 116 G2
Agnew's
CONDST W1S 10 G9
Agora Shopping Centre
PECK SE15 159 P8
Ainslie Wood Primary School
CHING E4 100 G6
Airbase Unity Elementary School
RSLP HA4 112 D7
Airbus Coach Station
HTHAIR TW6 152 A9
Air Call Business Centre
CDALE/KGS NW9 116 A1
Airedale Physiotherapy Clinic
CHSWK W4 156 C4
Airlinks Golf Club
NWDGN UB2 153 K3
Air Links Industrial Estate
HEST TW5 153 K4
Airport Gate Business Centre
WDR/YW UB7 152 A6
Airport Industrial Estate
BH/WHM TN16 244 A1
Aksaray Sports Club
STNW/STAM N16 119 L9
The Alan D School of Hairdressing
GTPST W1W 11 H5
Alban Arena Cinema
STAL AL1 38 C6
Alban Wood Primary School
GSTN WD25 55 J9
Albany Centre & Theatre
DEPT SE8 160 E6
Albany Clinic
BFN/LL DA15 185 K7
WIM/MER SW19 179 L10
The Albany College
HDN NW4 116 E3
Albany Park Canoe & Sailing Club
KUTN/CMB KT2 177 J9
Albany School (Grant Maintained)
PEND EN3 80 C4
The Albany School
HCH RM12 125 J7
Albemarle Primary School
WIM/MER SW19 179 H5
Albert Memorial
SKENS SW7 15 L1
Albion Health Centre
WCHPL E1 140 A7
Albion J & I School
BERM/RHTH SE16 160 B1
Albion Street Health Centre
BERM/RHTH SE16 160 B1
Albright Industrial Estate
RAIN RM13 144 G7
The Alchemy Gallery
CLKNW EC1R 12 A1
Aldenham Country Park
BORE WD6 74 G9
Aldenham Golf & Country Club
GSTN WD25 74 A4
Aldenham Preparatory School
BORE WD6 74 E6
Alderbrook Primary School
BAL SW12 180 C3
Aldersbrook County Secondary School
MNPK E12 121 P6
Aldersbrook Primary School
MNPK E12 121 N6
The Alderton Primary School
LOU IG10 82 D9
Alderwood Primary School
ELTH/MOT SE9 184 G2
Aldgate Bus Station
HDTCH EC3A 13 L5
Aldro School
MFD/CHID GU8 266 B10
Aldwickbury Park Golf Club
HARP AL5 20 D2
Aldwickbury School
HARP AL5 20 D3
Aldwych Theatre
HOL/ALD WC2B 11 N6
Alexander Barracks
CHOB/PIR GU24 230 A7
Alexander First School
WDSR SL4 148 B9
Alexander McLeod Primary School
ABYW SE2 163 L4
Alexandra Avenue Clinic
RYLN/HDSTN HA2 113 N7
Alexandra Business Centre
PEND EN3 80 C8
Alexandra Infant School
KUTN/CMB KT2 177 M10
PGE/AN SE20 182 C10
Alexandra Junior School
HSLW TW3 154 A8
SYD SE26 182 C9
Alexandra Palace (Historic House)
WDGN N22 118 E1
Alexandra Palace Ice Rink
WDGN N22 98 E10
Alexandra Park School
FBAR/BDGN N11 98 D8
Alexandra Primary School
WDGN N22 98 G10
Alexandra School
RYLN/HDSTN HA2 113 N7
Al Falah Boys School
CLPT E5 120 A8
Alfred Salter Primary School
BERM/RHTH SE16 160 C1
Alfreds Way Industrial Estate
BARK IG11 143 K3
Alfriston Special School
BEAC HP9 88 B5
Allenby Primary School
STHL UB1 133 P8
Allen Edwards Primary School
CLAP SW4 158 F7
The All England Lawn Tennis & Croquet Club
WIM/MER SW19 178 G6
Allergy Clinic
CAVSQ/HST W1G 10 E4
Alleyns Junior School
EDUL SE22 181 M1
Allfarthing JMI School
WAND/EARL SW18 179 M2
All Nations Christian College
WARE SG12 26 G4
All Saints Benhilton CE Primary School
SUT SM1 201 L10
All Saints Catholic School and Technology College
BCTR RM8 124 B6
All Saints CE Infant School
LHD/OX KT22 236 F5
All Saints CE Junior School
NRWD SE19 203 M1
All Saints CE Primary School
BKHTH/KID SE3 161 K8
CAR SM5 222 B2
CRICK NW2 117 J8
FUL/PGN SW6 157 H8
PUT/ROE SW15 156 F9
TRDG/WHET N20 97 N3
WIM/MER SW19 179 M10
All Souls CE Primary School
GTPST W1W 10 G4
Allum Medical Centre
WAN E11 121 J5
Alma J & I School
BERM/RHTH SE16 19 N5
Alma Primary School
BERM/RHTH SE16 159 P3
PEND EN3 80 C9
Almeida Theatre
IS N1 6 C4
Al-Noor Primary School
GDMY/SEVK IG3 123 L6
Alperton Cemetery
ALP/SUD HA0 135 J3
Alperton Community School
ALP/SUD HA0 135 K2
Alperton High School
ALP/SUD HA0 135 J3
Alperton Sports Ground
ALP/SUD HA0 135 J4
Alpha Business Centre
WALTH E17 120 E3
Alpha Business Park
BRKMPK AL9 40 F9
Alpha Preparatory School
HRW HA1 114 D3
Alpine Business Centre
EHAM E6 142 D7
Al Sadiq High School for Boys & Al-Zahra Girls School
KIL/WHAMP NW6 2 A5
Alscot Road Industrial Estate
STHWK SE1 19 M5
Altmore Infant School
EHAM E6 142 C2
The Alton School
PUT/ROE SW15 178 C3
Ambler Primary School
FSBYPK N4 119 J8
Ambleside Junior School
WOT/HER KT12 197 K8
Ambresbury Banks Fort
EPP CM16 64 E10
AMC Business Centre
WLSDN NW10 135 N5
The American Community School
COB KT11 217 L6
American Intercontinental University
MHST W1U 10 D4
The American School in London
STJWD NW8 3 K7
Amersham & Chiltern RFC
AMS HP6 68 F2
Amersham Hill CC
AMS HP6 69 K4
The Amersham School
AMSS HP7 69 K6
Amersham Town FC
AMSS HP7 68 F5
Amersham & Wycombe College
AMSS HP7 69 L5
CSHM HP5 51 J3
AMF Bowling
CRAWW RH11 283 N7
HHNE HP2 36 C4
LEW SE13 161 H9
Amherst School
SEV TN13 246 F9
Amida Golf
FELT TW13 175 P6
Ampthill Square Medical Centre
CAMTN NW1 5 H8
Amwell View Special School
WARE SG12 26 G7
Anchorage Point Industrial Estate
CHARL SE7 161 P2
Anchor Bay Industrial Estate
ERITH DA8 164 G6
Anchor Retail Park
WCHPL E1 140 B6
Andover Medical Centre
HOLWY N7 118 G8
The Andrew Ewing Primary School
HEST TW5 153 N6
Andrews Lane J & I School
CHESW EN7 62 A4
Anerley School
NRWD SE19 203 P1
Angel Centre
DART DA1 187 M2
Angerstein Business Park
GNWCH SE10 161 M3
Anglesea Centre
GVW DA11 190 E2
Anglian Industrial Estate
BARK IG11 143 J6
Animal Cemetery
REDBR IG4 122 A1
Annemount School
EFNCH N2 117 M4
Annunciation RC Infant School
EDGW HA8 96 A9
Annunciation RC Junior School
MLHL NW7 96 A7
Anson Primary School
CRICK NW2 116 G10
Anthony Roper Primary School
EYN DA4 209 M9
Antonys RC Primary School
WFD IG8 101 M5
Apex Hotel
MON EC3R 13 K7
Apex Industrial Estate
WLSDN NW10 136 C6
Apex Retail Park
FELT TW13 175 N6
Apollo Theatre
SOHO/SHAV W1D 11 J7
Apollo Victoria Theatre
PIM SW1V 16 G4
Apostolic Nuncio
WIM/MER SW19 178 F6
Applecroft JMI School
WGCW AL8 22 E5
Applegarth Primary School
CROY/NA CR0 224 G3
Apsley House, The Wellington Museum
KTBR SW1X 16 C1
Apsley Mills Retail Park
HHS/BOV HP3 35 P10
Aquarius Business Park
CRICK NW2 116 D6
Aquarius Golf Club
EDUL SE22 182 B1
Aragon Primary School
MRDN SM4 201 H7
Arbour Vale Specialist School Sports College
SLN SL2 129 M8
Arcadia Shopping Centre
EA W5 135 J9
Arcadia University
BAY/PAD W2 8 G8
The Archbishop Lanfranc School
CROY/NA CR0 202 F6
Archbishop Michael Ramsey Technology College
CMBW SE5 159 J6
Archbishop Sumners CE Primary School
LBTH SE11 18 B6
Archbishop Tenisons CE School
CROY/NA CR0 203 N10
Archbishop Tenison's School
VX/NE SW8 17 P10
Archdale Business Centre
RYLN/HDSTN HA2 114 B7
Archdeacon Cambridge's CE Primary School
WHTN TW2 176 D5
Arches Business Centre
NWDGN UB2 153 N1
Arches Leisure Centre
GNWCH SE10 161 J5
Archgate Business Centre
NFNCH/WDSPK N12 97 M5
Architecture Association School of Architecture
RSQ WC1B 11 J4
Archway Business Centre
ARCH N19 118 E8
Archway Leisure Centre
ARCH N19 118 D7
Archway Theatre
HORL RH6 280 B5
Ardleigh Green Primary School
EMPK RM11 125 L1
Ardmore House Hotel
STAL AL1 38 E5
Arena Essex
PUR RM19 166 F1
Arena Estate
FSBYPK N4 119 J4
Argyle Primary School
STPAN WC1H 5 M10
Arkley Golf Club
BAR EN5 76 C9
Arklow Trading Estate
NWCR SE14 160 D5
Armourers & Braziers' Hall
LOTH EC2R 12 G5
Army Training Regiment
CHOB/PIR GU24 230 B7
Arndale Health Centre
WAND/EARL SW18 179 K2
Arnett Hills Primary School
RKW/CH/CXG WD3 71 K10
Arnhem Wharf Primary School
POP/IOD E14 160 E2
Arnold House School
STJWD NW8 3 L7
Arnos Pool
FBAR/BDGN N11 98 E6
Arsenal FC (Emirates Stadium)
HOLWY N7 119 H9
Art School
BECK BR3 204 D5
Artsdepot
NFNCH/WDSPK N12 97 M6
The Arts Educational School
CHSWK W4 156 B3
Arts Theatre
LSQ/SEVD WC2H 11 K7
Ashbourne College
KENS W8 15 H1
Ashburnham Primary School
WBPTN SW10 157 N6
Ashburton Community School
CROY/NA CR0 204 A7
Ashburton Primary School
CROY/NA CR0 204 A6
Ashby Mill School
CLAP SW4 180 F1
The Ashcombe School
DORK RH4 254 G10
Asheridge Road Industrial Estate
CSHM HP5 50 F5
Ashfield Junior School
BUSH WD23 94 A1
Ashford CE Primary School
ASHF TW15 174 C9
Ashford Clinic
ASHF TW15 173 P6
Ashford High School
ASHF TW15 173 P6
Ashford Industrial Estate
ASHF TW15 174 D7
Ashford Manor Golf Club
ASHF TW15 174 A9
Ashford Park Primary School
ASHF TW15 173 M7
The Ashford & St Peters Hospital
STWL/WRAY TW19 173 P5
Ashford Sports Club
ASHF TW15 173 N7
STWL/WRAY TW19 174 A4
Ashgrove College
WALTH E17 120 F1
Ashgrove Trading Estate
BMLY BR1 183 J9
Ash Industrial Estate
HLWW/ROY CM19 46 C2
Ashleigh Commercial Estate
CHARL SE7 161 P3
Ashley Centre Shopping Precinct
EPSOM KT18 220 A9
Ashley Primary School
WOT/HER KT12 197 H8
Ashlyns School
BERK HP4 33 P7
Ashmead Primary School
BROCKY SE4 160 F8
Ashmole Centre
STHGT/OAK N14 98 D2
Ashmole Primary School
VX/NE SW8 17 P10
Ashmole School
STHGT/OAK N14 98 D2
Ashmount Primary School
ARCH N19 118 E5
Ashtead Clinic
ASHTD KT21 237 K3
Ashtead CC
ASHTD KT21 237 K3
Ashtead Hospital
ASHTD KT21 237 K6
Ashton House School
ISLW TW7 154 C7
Ashton Playing Fields Track
WFD IG8 102 B7
Aspen House School
LBTH SE11 18 C10
Aspen House Secondary & Primary School
BRXS/STRHM SW2 180 F4
Asquith Court School
HPTN TW12 198 A1
KTN/HRWW/WS HA3 114 G4
Asquith School
PEND EN3 80 B8
Assembly Rooms
SURB KT6 199 K4
Associated Newspapers
BERM/RHTH SE16 160 C2
Astley Cooper School
HHNE HP2 36 B1
The Astolat Industrial Estate
RGUW GU3 267 P8
Aston Clinic
NWMAL KT3 200 B4
Aston House School
EA W5 135 J8
Astra Business Centre
REDH RH1 276 B10
Asylum Medical Centre
CEND/HSY/T N8 119 H1
Athelney Primary School
CAT SE6 182 F6
Athelstan House School
HPTN TW12 197 P1
Athenaeum Hotel
MYFR/PICC W1J 10 E10
Athena Medical Centre
CLPT E5 120 B9
Atherton Leisure Centre
SRTFD E15 141 L1
Athlone House Hospital
HGT N6 118 A6
Athlon Industrial Estate
ALP/SUD HA0 135 J4
Atkinson Morley Hospital
RYNPK SW20 178 E10
Atlantic House (Richmond American International University)
KENS W8 15 J3
Atlas Business Centre
CRICK NW2 116 E7
Atlas Medical Centre
HORL RH6 280 B8
Atlas Transport Estate
BTSEA SW11 157 M8
Attlee Youth & Community Centre
WCHPL E1 13 M4
Atwood Primary School
SAND/SEL CR2 223 P10
Audley Primary School
CTHM CR3 241 M7
Auriol Junior School
HOR/WEW KT19 220 C1
Austin Lodge Golf Club
EYN DA4 229 M5
Australia House
HOL/ALD WC2B 11 P6
Aveley FC
SOCK/AV RM15 146 B9
Aveley Medical Centre
SOCK/AV RM15 147 H6
Aveley Primary School
SOCK/AV RM15 146 D10
Aveley School (School House)
SOCK/AV RM15 146 D10
The Aveley School
SOCK/AV RM15 146 C9
Aveling Park School
WALTH E17 100 F10

Avenue House Museum FNCH N3 97 J10
Avenue House School WEA W13 134 G8
Avenue Industrial Estate CHING E4 100 E7
HARH RM3 105 L10
Avenue Medical Centre SLN SL2 128 F5
Avenue Primary School KIL/WHAMP NW6 2 A4
MNPK E12 122 B9
The Avenue Primary School BELMT SM2 221 K6
Avondale Park Primary School NTGHL W11 8 A8
Avon House School WFD IG8 101 M5
Avon Trading Estate WKENS W14 14 D6
Axis Business Centre SRTFD E15 140 G3
Axton Chase School HART DA3 211 L3
Aycliffe Drive Primary School HHNE HP2 35 P2
Aylands School PEND EN3 80 B2
The Aylesham Centre PECK SE15 159 P7
Ayloff Primary School HCH RM12 125 J9
Aylward First & Middle Schools STAN HA7 95 J6
Aylward School UED N18 99 L5
Aylwin Secondary School STHWK SE1 19 M5
Aysgarth Medical Centre IVER SL0 130 G4
BAA Heathrow Visitor Centre HTHAIR TW6 152 C7
Babington House School CHST BR7 184 C9
Back Care Clinic WPK KT4 200 D8
Bacon's College BERM/RHTH SE16 140 D10
Baden Powell House SKENS SW7 15 K5
Baglioni Hotel KENS W8 15 J2
Bakers Hall MON EC3R 13 K8
Balaam Leisure Centre PLSTW E13 141 M6
Bales College NKENS W10 2 A10
Balfour Business Centre NWDGN UB2 153 L2
Balfour Medical Centre GRAYS RM17 167 P3
Balgowan Primary School BECK BR3 204 D2
Balham Boys Preparatory Secondary School BAL SW12 180 C3
Balham Girls Preparatory Secondary School TOOT SW17 180 A6
Balham Health Centre BAL SW12 180 C5
Balham Leisure Centre TOOT SW17 180 B5
Balmoral Trading Estate BARK IG11 143 J6
Baltic Exchange HDTCH EC3A 13 K5
Bancrofts School WFD IG8 101 M4
Bandon Hill Cemetery WLGTN SM6 222 E2
Bandon Hill Primary School WLGTN SM6 222 E3
Bangabandhu Primary School BETH E2 140 B5
Bank of England Extension CITYW EC2V 12 E6
Bank of England (& Museum) LOTH EC2R 12 G6
Bankside Gallery STHWK SE1 12 D8
Bankside Jetty STHWK SE1 12 E8
Bankside Park Industrial Estate BARK IG11 143 K5
Bannister Stadium KTN/HRWW/WS HA3 94 B7
Bannockburn Primary School WOOL/PLUM SE18 163 J3
Banqueting House Whitehall WHALL SW1A 11 L10
Banstead Athletic FC KWD/TDW/WH KT20 238 F6
Banstead Clinic BNSTD SM7 239 K1
Banstead County Junior School BNSTD SM7 239 J2
Banstead Downs Golf Club BELMT SM2 221 K7
Banstead Infant School BNSTD SM7 239 J1
Banstead Sports Centre KWD/TDW/WH KT20 238 F6
Banstead Village Clinic BNSTD SM7 239 L1
Barbara Castle Health Centre HLWW/ROY CM19 46 D5
Barbara Speake Theatre School ACT W3 136 B9
Barber Surgeons' Hall BARB EC2Y 12 F4
Barbican Cinema BARB EC2Y 12 E3
The Barbican BARB EC2Y 12 E3
Barbican Theatre BARB EC2Y 12 F3
Barclay J & I School LEY E10 121 J4
Barham Primary School ALP/SUD HA0 135 H1
Baring Primary School LEE/GVPK SE12 183 M3
Baring Road Medical Centre BMLY BR1 183 M5
Barkantine Clinic POP/IOD E14 160 F1
Barking Abbey Comprehensive School (Lower) IL IG1 122 G10
Barking Abbey Comprehensive School (Upper) BARK IG11 143 J1
Barking Abbey Industrial Estate BARK IG11 142 E3
Barking Abbey Leisure Centre BARK IG11 143 K1
Barking Abbey School BARK IG11 143 J1
Barking College ROMW/RG RM7 124 E7
Barking Football Club BCTR RM8 123 L10
Barking Hospital BARK IG11 143 J2
Barking Industrial Park BARK IG11 143 J3
Barking RUFC DAGW RM9 143 N3
Barkingside Cemetery BARK/HLT IG6 122 E1
Barkingside FC BARK/HLT IG6 122 G2
Barlby Primary School NKENS W10 136 G6
Barley Lane Primary School GDMY/SEVK IG3 123 K5
Barnabas Medical Centre NTHLT UB5 134 B1
Barncroft JMI School HHNE HP2 35 N1
Barn Croft Primary School WALTH E17 120 D4
Barnehurst Primary School ERITH DA8 164 D7
Barnehurst Public Golf Club BXLYHN DA7 164 E9
Barn Elms Athletics Track BARN SW13 156 E8
Barn Elms Water Sports Centre PUT/ROE SW15 156 F8
Barnes Cray Primary School DART DA1 165 H10
Barnes Hospital MORT/ESHN SW14 156 B9
Barnes Primary School BARN SW13 156 B9
Barnes Sports Club BARN SW13 156 C7
Barnet College BAR EN5 77 J8
CDALE/KGS NW9 96 C9
EBAR EN4 98 A2
FBAR/BDGN N11 98 A4
HDN NW4 116 D4
NFNCH/WDSPK N12 97 M6
Barnet Copthall Pool HDN NW4 96 E8
Barnet Copthall Stadium HDN NW4 97 F9
Barnet County Court BAR EN5 77 M8
FNCH N3 97 K9
Barnet FC (Underhill) BAR EN5 77 K9
Barnet General Hospital BAR EN5 76 G8
Barnet Health Centre BAR EN5 77 K9
Barnet Hill JMI School BAR EN5 77 J9
Barnet Hospital Chest Clinic BAR EN5 76 G8
Barnet Magistrates Court BAR EN5 77 J8
Barnet Museum BAR EN5 77 H8
Barnet Trading Estate BAR EN5 77 J7
Barnett Wood Infant School ASHTD KT21 237 J3
Barnfield Primary School EDGW HA8 95 P9
Barnhill Community High School YEAD UB4 133 J5
Barn Hotel RSLP HA4 112 F7
Barnsbury Complex IS N1 6 A3
Barnsbury Junior School WOKS/MYFD GU22 232 A7
Barnsbury School for Girls IS N1 6 A2
Barn Theatre WGCW AL8 22 F5
Barnwood County First School GUW GU2 249 K9
Barons Court Theatre WKENS W14 14 B7
Barratt Industrial Park BOW E3 141 H6
Barrett Industrial Park STHL UB1 133 P10
Barrett Way Industrial Estate KTN/HRWW/WS HA3 114 C1
Barrington Primary School WELL DA16 163 N8
Barrow Hedges Primary School CAR SM5 221 P4
Barrow Hill Junior School STJWD NW8 3 N8
Barrow Hills Golf Club CHERT KT16 193 P9
Barton House Health Centre STNW/STAM N16 119 L8
Barwell Business Park CHSGTN KT9 219 J4
Bassett House School NKENS W10 136 G8
Baston School HAYES BR2 205 N9
Bata Medical Centre TIL RM18 169 M3
Batchwood Golf Club STALW/RED AL3 38 A3
Batchwood School STALW/RED AL3 38 C3
Batchworth Park Golf Club RKW/CH/CXG WD3 91 P4
Bates Industrial Estate HARH RM3 105 P8
Bath Factory Estate HNHL SE24 181 K2
Battersea Arts Centre (BAC) BTSEA SW11 158 A9
Battersea Business Centre BTSEA SW11 158 B9
Battersea Dogs' Home VX/NE SW8 158 C6
Battersea Sports Centre BTSEA SW11 157 N9
Battersea Technology College BTSEA SW11 158 A7
Battersea Tutorial College TOOT SW17 180 B5
Bayford Primary School HERT/BAY SG13 42 G4
Bayhurst Wood Country Park DEN/HRF UB9 112 A3
Baylis Business Centre SL SL1 129 J9
Baylis Court School SL SL1 129 J7
BBC Broadcasting House REGST W1B 10 F4
BBC Media Village SHB W12 136 F9
BBC Studios NKENS/WKIL W9 8 G1
BBC Television Centre SHB W12 136 F9
BBC Worldwide SHB W12 136 F8
Beacon Hill Industrial Estate PUR RM19 166 A3
Beacon Hill School SOCK/AV RM15 146 F7
Beacon School BNSTD SM7 239 H3
The Beacon School AMS HP6 68 G1
Beaconsfield CC BEAC HP9 88 E10
Beaconsfield Golf Club BEAC HP9 89 H9
Beaconsfield High School BEAC HP9 88 C10
Beaconsfield RFC BEAC HP9 108 E1
Beaconsfield School BEAC HP9 88 D10
Beales Hotel HAT AL10 40 B3
Beal High School REDBR IG4 122 B1
Beam Primary School DAGE RM10 144 D4
Bean Primary School RDART DA2 189 H6
Beatrice Tate School BETH E2 140 A5
Beatrix Potter Primary School WAND/EARL SW18 179 M4
Beauclerc Infant School SUN TW16 197 K3
The Beaufort Hotel CHEL SW3 16 A4
Beaufort Primary School WOKN/KNAP GU21 231 L2
Beaumont Primary School LEY E10 120 G5
PUR/KEN CR8 222 G10
Beaumont School STALE/WH AL4 39 J5
Beaver College BAY/PAD W2 8 G8
The Beavers Community Primary School HSLWW TW4 153 K9
Beaverwood School for Girls CHST BR7 185 H9
Beckenham Business Centre BECK BR3 182 D9
Beckenham Crematorium BECK BR3 204 B3
Beckenham CC BECK BR3 182 G10
Beckenham Hospital BECK BR3 204 E2
Beckenham Leisure Centre BECK BR3 204 D1
Beckenham Place Park Golf Course BECK BR3 182 G9
Beckenham RFC BECK BR3 204 D4
Beckenham Town FC BECK BR3 204 F5
Becket Sports Centre DART DA1 187 K2
Beckford Primary School KIL/WHAMP NW6 117 J10
Beckmead School BECK BR3 204 F8
The Beck Theatre HYS/HAR UB3 132 G8
Beckton Ski Centre EHAM E6 142 D6
Beckton Special School CAN/RD E16 142 A7
Beckton Triangle Retail Park EHAM E6 142 E5
Becontree Day Hospital BCTR RM8 123 P7
Becontree Primary School BCTR RM8 123 L8
Bective House Clinic PUT/ROE SW15 157 J10
Beddington Infants School WLGTN SM6 202 D10
Beddington Medical Centre CROY/NA CR0 222 F1
Beddington Park Primary School CROY/NA CR0 202 E10
Beddington Trading Estate CROY/NA CR0 202 F8
Bedelsford School KUT/HW KT1 199 K3
Bedensfield Clinic SCUP DA14 185 P8
Bedfont Health Clinic EBED/NFELT TW14 174 F3
Bedfont Industrial Park ASHF TW15 174 E6
Bedfont J & I School EBED/NFELT TW14 174 F2
Bedfont Lakes Country Park EBED/NFELT TW14 174 D5
Bedfont Lakes Office Park EBED/NFELT TW14 174 D4
The Bedford Arms Hotel RKW/CH/CXG WD3 70 E4
Bedford Hotel RSQ WC1B 11 M3
Bedington Infant School WLGTN SM6 222 D1
Bedmond JMI School ABLGY WD5 54 G4
Bedonwell Clinic ABYW SE2 163 P5
Bedonwell Medical Centre BELV DA17 164 A4
Bedonwell Primary School BXLYHN DA7 163 P5
Beechcroft Farm Industrial Estate BGR/WK TN15 211 J10
Beechfield JMI School WATN WD24 73 H3
Beech House School SAND/SEL CR2 223 N6
Beech Hyde Primary School STALE/WH AL4 21 J4
Beecholme Primary School MTCM CR4 202 C1
Beechwood School SLN SL2 128 G5
STRHM/NOR SW16 180 F6
Beehive Preparatory School REDBR IG4 122 C2
The Beehive School ARCH N19 118 E5
Beis Hamedrash Elyon GLDGN NW11 117 H5
Beis Malka Girls School STNW/STAM N16 119 N6
Beis Rochel D'Satmar Girls School STNW/STAM N16 119 M5
Beis Trana Girls School STNW/STAM N16 119 M5
Beis Yaakov Primary School CDALE/KGS NW9 116 A1
Bekonscot Model Village and Railway BEAC HP9 88 C8
Belcon Industrial Estate HOD EN11 45 H3
Belfry Shopping Centre REDH RH1 258 A9
Belhus Golf Club & Leisure Centre SOCK/AV RM15 146 D8
Belhus Woods Country Park SOCK/AV RM15 146 C5
Bellamy's Wharf BERM/RHTH SE16 140 C10
Bellenden Primary School PECK SE15 159 P9
Bellenden Road Business Centre PECK SE15 159 N8
Bellenden Road Retail Park PECK SE15 159 N7
Bellerbys College DEPT SE8 160 G5
Bellerby Theatre GU GU1 268 A1
Belleville Primary School BTSEA SW11 180 A1
Belle Vue Cinema WLSDN NW10 136 E2
Bell Farm Junior School WOT/HER KT12 217 K1
Bellgate JMI School HHNE HP2 35 P4
Bell Industrial Estate CHSWK W4 155 P3
Bellingham Trading Estate CAT SE6 182 G6
Bell Lane Combined School AMS HP6 69 N4
Bell Lane JMI School HDN NW4 116 G2
Belmont First & Middle School KTN/HRWW/WS HA3 94 E10
Belmont J & I School WDGN N22 119 K1
Belmont Medical Centre UX/CGN UB8 131 N2
Belmont (Mill Hill Preparatory School) MLHL NW7 96 D4
Belmont Park School LEY E10 121 H4
Belmont Primary School CHSWK W4 156 A3
ERITH DA8 164 B6
Belmore Primary School YEAD UB4 133 J5
Belswains Infant School HHS/BOV HP3 36 A10
Belvedere Day Hospital WLSDN NW10 136 D3
Belvedere Industrial Estate BELV DA17 144 E10
Belvedere Link Business Park ERITH DA8 164 D2
Belvedere Primary School BELV DA17 164 C3
Belvue Business Centre NTHLT UB5 134 A2
Belvue School NTHLT UB5 133 P3
Benedict House Preparatory School BFN/LL DA15 185 J7
Benedict Primary School MTCM CR4 201 N3
Bengeo J & I School HERT/WAT SG14 25 K2
Benhurst JMI School HCH RM12 125 J8
Ben Jonson Primary School WCHPL E1 140 D6
Bensham Manor School THHTH CR7 203 K5
Benson Primary School CROY/NA CR0 204 D10
Bentalls Shopping Centre KUT/HW KT1 199 J2
Benthal Primary School STNW/STAM N16 119 P8
Bentley Golf Club BRWN CM15 86 D5
The Bentley Kempinski Hotel SKENS SW7 15 J6
Bentley Street Industrial Estate GVE DA12 190 F2
Bentley Wood Girls School STAN HA7 94 E6
Bentworth Primary School SHB W12 136 E8
Ben Uri Gallery, London Jewish Museum of Art STJWD NW8 3 H6
Benyon Primary School SOCK/AV RM15 147 H4
Beormund School STHWK SE1 18 G2
Berger Primary School HOM E9 140 C1
Berkeley Clinic RKW/CH/CXG WD3 91 M2
The Berkeley Hotel KTBR SW1X 16 C1
Berkeley Primary School HEST TW5 153 L5
Berkhamsted Castle (remains) BERK HP4 34 A4
Berkhamsted Collegiate Preparatory School BERK HP4 33 N5
Berkhamsted Collegiate School (Castle Campus) BERK HP4 33 P5
Berkhamsted Collegiate School (Kings Campus) BERK HP4 33 N6
Berkhamsted FC BERK HP4 33 N4
Berkhamsted Golf Club BERK HP4 34 B2
Berkhamsted Health Centre BERK HP4 33 M4
Berkhamsted School House BERK HP4 33 P5
Berkhamsted Tennis Club BERK HP4 33 P4
Berlitz School of Languages HHOL WC1V 11 P4
Bermondsey Town Hall STHWK SE1 19 L4
Bermondsey Trading Estate BERM/RHTH SE16 160 B3
Bernards Heath Infant School STAL AL1 38 E4
Bernards Heath Junior School STALW/RED AL3 38 D3
Berrymede Infant School ACT W3 155 N1
Berrymede Junior School ACT W3 155 N1
Bertram House School TOOT SW17 180 B5
Bessemer Grange J & I School HNHL SE24 181 L1
Bessemer Park Industrial Estate BRXN/ST SW9 159 J10
Best Western Bromley Court Hotel BMLY BR1 183 K9
Best Western Cumberland Hotel HRW HA1 114 E4
Best Western Donnington Manor Hotel SEV TN13 246 E4
Best Western Gatwick Moat House Hotel HORL RH6 279 P6
Best Western Homestead Court Hotel WGCE AL7 23 J7
Best Western Hotel HAMP NW3 3 M3
Best Western Lodge Hotel PUT/ROE SW15 179 J1
Best Western Manor Hotel GVE DA12 190 F9
Best Western Master Robert Hotel HEST TW5 153 N7
Best Western Mostyn Hotel MBLAR W1H 10 B6
Best Western Phoenix Hotel BAY/PAD W2 8 G7
Best Western Reigate Manor Hotel REIG RH2 257 K7
Best Western The Watermill Hotel HHW HP1 34 F8
Best Western Weald Park Hotel, Golf & Country Club BRW CM14 85 P8
Best Western White House Hotel WATW WD18 73 H8
Beta Health Clinic HHW HP1 35 N6
Betchworth Park Golf Club DORK RH4 273 K1
Beth Jacob Grammar School HDN NW4 116 F2
Bethlem Royal Hospital BECK BR3 204 F7
Bethnal Green Technology College BETH E2 7 M10
Beths Grammar School for Boys BXLY DA5 186 B2
Beulah Infant School THHTH CR7 203 K2
Beverley School NWMAL KT3 200 D5
Beverley Trading Estate MRDN SM4 200 G7
Bevington Primary School NKENS W10 8 B3
Bewbush Community Primary School CRAWW RH11 283 H10
Bewbush Medical Centre CRAWW RH11 283 H10
Bewhurst County First School CRAWW RH11 283 J10
Bexley College BELV DA17 164 D3
Bexley CC BXLY DA5 186 B4
Bexley Grammar School WELL DA16 163 L10
Bexleyheath Centre BXLYHS DA6 163 P10
Bexleyheath Golf Club BXLYHS DA6 185 P1
Bexleyheath Marriott Hotel BXLYHS DA6 164 C10
Bexleyheath School BXLYHN DA7 164 A9
Bexley RFC BXLY DA5 186 B3
BFI London IMAX Cinema STHWK SE1 11 P10
The Bharani Medical Centre SL SL1 128 C8
Bickley Park CC BMLY BR1 206 B2
Bickley Park Preparatory School BMLY BR1 206 A3
Bickley Park School BMLY BR1 206 B2
Big Ben WHALL SW1A 17 M2
Biggin Hill Airport BH/WHM TN16 225 P8
Biggin Hill Business Park BH/WHM TN16 244 A1
Biggin Hill Primary School BH/WHM TN16 244 B2
Bigham's Park Farm HHW HP1 35 H1
Bigland Green Primary School WCHPL E1 140 A8
Billingsgate Fish Market POP/IOD E14 140 G10
Bingham Hotel TWK TW1 177 J2
Binscombe Medical Centre GODL GU7 267 J9
Bircherley Green Shopping Centre HERT/WAT SG14 25 L5
Birchmere Business Park THMD SE28 163 K1
Birchwood Avenue Primary School HAT AL10 40 D2
Birchwood Leisure Centre HAT AL10 40 E1
Birchwood Park Golf Club RDART DA2 186 D10
Birchwood Primary School SWLY BR8 208 E1
Bird College SCUP DA14 185 K6
Birkbeck College GWRST WC1E 11 K2
RSQ WC1B 11 K4
Birkbeck Primary School SCUP DA14 185 L6
Bishop Challoner Catholic Collegiate School WCHPL E1 140 B9
Bishop Challoner Girls School WCHPL E1 13 P7
Bishop Challoner School HAYES BR2 205 J2
Bishop David Brown School WOKN/KNAP GU21 214 G9
Bishop Douglass RC School EFNCH N2 97 M10
Bishop Gilpin Primary School WIM/MER SW19 179 J8
Bishophalt School UX/CGN UB8 132 A5
Bishop John Robinson CE Primary School THMD SE28 143 M9
Bishop Justus CE (Secondary) School HAYES BR2 206 B7
Bishop Perrin CE Primary School WHTN TW2 176 A3
Bishop Ramsey CE School (Upper) RSLP HA4 113 H5
Bishop Ramsey CE School RSLP HA4 112 G5
Bishopsgate Institute LVPST EC2M 13 K4
Bishopsgate School EGH TW20 171 M6
Bishops Hatfield Girls School HAT AL10 40 D4
Bishop Stopfords School EN EN1 79 P6
Bishops Wood Hospital NTHWD HA6 92 C7
Bishop Thomas Grant School STRHM/NOR SW16 180 G8
Bishop Wand CE Secondary School SUN TW16 196 G2
Bishop Winnington Ingram CE Primary School RSLP HA4 112 E5
Bisley CE Primary School CHOB/PIR GU24 230 F2
Bittacy Business Centre MLHL NW7 97 H7
Blackburn Trading Estate STWL/WRAY TW19 174 A2
Blackfen Medical Centre BFN/LL DA15 185 J1
Blackfen School for Girls BFN/LL DA15 185 L2
Blackfriars Millennium Pier EMB EC4Y 12 B7
Blackfriars Pier BLKFR EC4V 12 D7
Blackheath Bluecoat CE School BKHTH/KID SE3 161 N6
Blackheath Business Estate GNWCH SE10 161 H7
The Blackheath Clinic BKHTH/KID SE3 161 M10
Blackheath High School GDST BKHTH/KID SE3 161 L8
Blackheath High Senior School BKHTH/KID SE3 161 M6
Blackheath Hospital BKHTH/KID SE3 161 L9
Blackheath Preparatory School BKHTH/KID SE3 161 M7
Blackheath RFC (The Rectory Field) BKHTH/KID SE3 161 N6
Black Park Country Park IVER SL0 130 D4
Blackshots Leisure Centre CDW/CHF RM16 168 A1
Blackwall Trading Estate POP/IOD E14 141 J7
Blair Peach Primary School STHL UB1 133 L10
Blake College FITZ W1T 11 H3
GTPST W1W 10 G3
Blanche Nevile School MUSWH N10 118 B1
Blenheim Business Centre MTCM CR4 202 A1
Blenheim High School HOR/WEW KT19 220 A6
Blenheim Primary School ORP BR6 207 N9
Blenheim Shopping Centre PGE/AN SE20 182 B10
Blessed Dominic RC Primary School CDALE/KGS NW9 96 B10
Blessed Sacrament RC Primary School IS N1 5 M6
Bletchingley Golf Club REDH RH1 259 L9
Bloomfield Clinic Guys STHWK SE1 19 H1
Bloomsbury College FUL/PGN SW6 157 K6
Bloomsbury Theatre GWRST WC1E 11 J1
Blossom House School RYNPK SW20 178 F10
Blossoms Inn Medical Centre BLKFR EC4V 12 F7
Blue Gate Fields Primary School WCHPL E1 140 B9
The Blue School ISLW TW7 154 F9
Bluewater Shopping Centre RDART DA2 188 E3
Blyth's Wharf POP/IOD E14 140 D9
BMI Medical Centre CAVSQ/HST W1G 10 D4
Bnois Jerusalem School STNW/STAM N16 119 L5
The Bob Hope Theatre ELTH/MOT SE9 184 C2
The Bobsleigh Hotel HHS/BOV HP3 52 E2
Bocketts Farm Park LHD/OX KT22 254 E1
Bodywise Natural Health Centre BETH E2 140 B5
Boleyn Cinema EHAM E6 142 A4
Bolingbroke Hospital BTSEA SW11 179 P1
Bolingbroke Primary School BTSEA SW11 157 N7
Bond First School MTCM CR4 202 A2
Bond Primary School MTCM CR4 202 A2
Bonner Primary School BETH E2 140 C4
Bonneville Primary School CLAP SW4 180 D2
Bonnington Hotel RSQ WC1B 11 M3
Bonnygate Primary School SOCK/AV RM15 146 G7
Bonny Grove SPLD Base CHESW EN7 61 P6
Bon Secours Hospital BEAC HP9 88 D9
Bonus Pastor Roman Catholic School BMLY BR1 183 J7
Bookham Grange Hotel GT/LBKH KT23 235 M9
Bookham Industrial Estate GT/LBKH KT23 235 N9
Boomes Industrial Estate RAIN RM13 144 G6
Booster Cushion Theatre WDGN N22 98 G10
Borehamwood FC BORE WD6 75 N6
Borehamwood Industrial Park BORE WD6 76 A6
Borers Business Park CRAWE RH10 285 K2
Borough Market STHWK SE1 12 G9
Bosch Broadwater Park Business Estate DEN/HRF UB9 111 K4
Boston Business Park HNWL W7 154 D2
Boston University SKENS SW7 157 M3
Botany Bay CC ENC/FH EN2 78 E2
Botwell RC Primary School HYS/HAR UB3 152 G1
Boulevard 25 Retail Park BORE WD6 75 M7
Boundary Business Centre WOKN/KNAP GU21 232 D1
Boundary Business Park MTCM CR4 201 N2
Bounds Green Health Centre FBAR/BDGN N11 98 E8
Bounds Green Industrial Estate FBAR/BDGN N11 98 C7
Bounds Green Primary School FBAR/BDGN N11 98 F8
Bourne Business Park ADL/WDHM KT15 195 M9
Bourne CP School RSLP HA4 113 K10
Bourne Hall Health Centre EW KT17 220 C5
Bournehall J & I School BUSH WD23 73 P9
Bourne Hall Museum EW KT17 220 C5
Bourne Road Industrial Park DART DA1 186 E1
Bourneside Sports Club STHGT/OAK N14 98 F2
Bousfield Primary School ECT SW5 15 J7
Boutcher CE Primary School STHWK SE1 19 L4
Bovingdon Primary School HHS/BOV HP3 52 E3
Bowater House SKENS SW7 16 A2
Bow County Court SRTFD E15 141 K1
Bowden House Clinic HRW HA1 114 D7
Bower Hill Industrial Estate EPP CM16 65 K8
Bower Park School ROM RM1 104 F7
Bowes Primary School FBAR/BDGN N11 98 E6

Bowes Road Clinic
FBAR/BDGN N11 98 D6
Bow Industrial Park
SRTFD E15 140 F2
Bowman Trading Estate
CDALE/KGS NW9 115 M1
Bow Secondary School
BOW E3 140 F4
Bow Triangle Business Centre
BOW E3 140 F6
Boxgrove Primary School
ABYW SE2 163 M2
GU GU1 250 E9
Box Hill Country Park
KWD/TDW/WH KT20 255 K8
Box Hill School
RDKG RH5 254 G3
Boxmoor Golf Club
HHS/BOV HP3 35 H10
Boxmoor Primary School
HHW HP1 35 K7
Boyd School
UPMR RM14 126 D7
Boys' Club
EDGW HA8 95 M8
BPP Law School
HHOL WC1V 11 N4
Brackenbury Health Centre
HMSMTH W6 156 E2
Brackenbury Primary School
HMSMTH W6 156 E2
Bracken Industrial Estate
BARK/HLT IG6 103 J8
Bracton Centre
RDART DA2 186 G5
Bradbourne School
SEV TN13 247 H7
Brady Primary School
RAIN RM13 145 K7
Brady Recreation Centre
WCHPL E1 13 N3
Braeside Senior School
BKHH IG9 101 N2
Braincroft Primary School
CRICK NW2 116 C8
Braintree Road
Industrial Estate
RSLP HA4 113 J9
Bramah's Tea & Coffee Museum
STHWK SE1 12 F10
Brambletye Junior School
REDH RH1 276 B2
The Bramley Business Centre
SHGR GU5 268 C10
Bramley Golf Club
SHGR GU5 268 B10
Bramley School
KWD/TDW/WH KT20 256 D1
Brampton College
HDN NW4 116 F2
Brampton Manor School
EHAM E6 142 A6
Brampton Primary School
BXLYHN DA7 163 N8
EHAM E6 142 B5
Brandlehow Primary School
PUT/ROE SW15 157 J10
Branfil J & I School
UPMR RM14 125 P9
Branollys Health Centre
PLSTW E13 141 M6
Brays Grove School
HLWS CM18 47 L3
Breakspear Crematorium
RSLP HA4 112 D3
Breakspeare School
ABLGY WD5 54 F7
Breakspear Primary School
HGDN/ICK UB10 112 B7
Breaside Preparatory School
BMLY BR1 205 P1
Brecknock Primary School
CAMTN NW1 5 K1
Bredinghurst School
PECK SE15 160 B10
Brent Adult College
WLSDN NW10 136 A3
Brent Arts Council
CRICK NW2 116 D8
Brent Child & Family Clinic
WLSDN NW10 116 C10
Brent Cross Shopping Centre
HDN NW4 116 F5
Brentfield Medical Centre
WLSDN NW10 136 A1
Brentfield Primary School
WLSDN NW10 136 A1
Brentford Business Centre
BTFD TW8 155 H6
Brentford County Court
BTFD TW8 155 J6
Brentford FC London Broncos
RLFC (Griffin Park)
BTFD TW8 155 J5
Brentford Fountain
Leisure Centre
BTFD TW8 155 L4
Brentford Health Centre
BTFD TW8 155 H5
Brentford School for Girls
BTFD TW8 155 J5
Brent Knoll School
FSTH SE23 182 C6
Brent Magistrates Court House
WLSDN NW10 136 B1
Brent Park Industrial Estate
NWDGN UB2 153 J2
The Brent Primary School
RDART DA2 188 B3
Brentside First School
HNWL W7 134 D7
Brentside High School
HNWL W7 134 D6
Brentside Primary School
HNWL W7 134 D6
Brent Trading Estate
WLSDN NW10 116 B10
Brent Valley Golf Club
HNWL W7 134 D9
Brentwaters Business Park
BTFD TW8 155 H6
Brentwood Academy of Health
& Beauty
BRWN CM15 107 J3
Brentwood Chiropody
Surgery
BRW CM14 107 J3
The Brentwood Clinic
BRWN CM15 107 J2
Brentwood Community
Hospital
BRWN CM15 107 K2
Brentwood County
High School
BRW CM14 107 J4
Brentwood IT Learning Centre
BRW CM14 107 H3
Brentwood Pre Preparatory
School
BRWN CM15 107 K2
Brentwood RFC
BRW CM14 107 K5
Brentwood School
BRWN CM15 107 J3
Brentwood Sports Ground
BRWN CM15 107 J2
Brentwood Theatre
BRWN CM15 107 J2
Brentwood Ursuline Convent
High School
BRW CM14 107 J4
Brewers' Hall
CITYW EC2V 12 F4
Brewery Industrial Estate
IS N1 6 E8
Brewery Mews
Business Centre
ISLW TW7 154 E9
The Brewery
ROMW/RG RM7 124 F4
Brian Johnston Centre
BGR/WK TN15 247 N8
Brickendon Grange Golf Club
HERT/BAY SG13 43 J5
Bricket Wood Sports Centre
LCOL/BKTW AL2 56 A7
Brickfields Industrial Estate
HHNE HP2 36 C2
Brick Lane Music Hall
FSBYE EC1V 7 K10
Brick Lane Music House
WCHPL E1 13 M2
Bricklayer Arms I
ndustrial Estate
STHWK SE1 19 L6
The Bridewell Theatre
EMB EC4Y 12 C6
The Bridge Business Centre
NWDGN UB2 153 P1
Bridgegate Business Centre
WGCE AL7 23 J4
Bridge Industrial Estate
HORL RH6 280 C4
Bridge Lane Theatre
BTSEA SW11 157 P7
The Bridge Leisure Centre
SYD SE26 182 E8
Bridge Medical Centre
CRAWE RH10 284 B6
Bridge Park Business &
Leisure Centre
WLSDN NW10 135 N2
The Bridge School
ARCH N19 118 D7
CLKNW EC1R 12 C1
HOLWY N7 5 K1
Bridge View Industrial Estate
WTHK RM20 166 F5
Bridgewater School
BERK HP4 33 M3
Brigham Young University
BAY/PAD W2 137 K9
Bright Sparks Montessori
School
WKENS W14 156 G1
The Brigidine School
WDSR SL4 149 J9
Brigstock Medical Centre
THHTH CR7 203 J5
Brimsdown Industrial Estate
PEND EN3 80 B6
Brimsdown Primary School
PEND EN3 80 C7
Brindishe Primary School
LEE/GVPK SE12 183 L1
Britain and London Visitor
Centre
STJS SW1Y 11 J9
Britannia Business Centre
CHES/WCR EN8 62 E10
CRICK NW2 116 G9
Britannia Industrial Estate
DTCH/LGLY SL3 151 H8
Britannia Leisure Centre
IS N1 7 H6
Britannia Sports Ground
WALTH E17 100 F8
Britannia Village
Primary School
CAN/RD E16 141 N10
British Cartoon Centre
BMSBY WC1N 11 M2
British College of Osteopathy
HAMP NW3 137 M1
British Dental Association
CAVSQ/HST W1G 10 E4
The British Hernia Centre
HDN NW4 116 E3
British Library
CAMTN NW1 5 K9
British Library
Newspaper Library
CDALE/KGS NW9 116 B1
British Medical Association
STPAN WC1H 11 K1
British Museum
RSQ WC1B 11 L4
British Telecom Tower
GTPST W1W 10 G3
British Transport Police
GUW GU2 267 N1
British Transport Police Station
WBLY HA9 115 M7
British School for Performing
Arts
CROY/NA CR0 203 L6
Brittania Business Park
CHES/WCR EN8 62 E10
Brittons School Technology
College
RAIN RM13 144 G2
Britwell Health Clinic
SLN SL2 128 F5
Brixton Academy
BRXN/ST SW9 159 H9
Brixton Recreation Centre
BRXN/ST SW9 159 H9
Broadfield Infant School
HHNE HP2 36 A6
Broadfield Junior School
HHNE HP2 35 P6
Broadfields Primary School
EDGW HA8 95 M3
HLW CM20 29 H10
Broadford Park
Business Centre
RGUE GU4 268 A7
Broadford Primary School
HARH RM3 105 L7
Broadgate
LVPST EC2M 13 H3
Broadgate Ice Arena
LVPST EC2M 13 H4
Broadhurst School
KIL/WHAMP NW6 3 J3
Broadmead J & I School
CROY/NA CR0 203 L6
The Broadmere Primary School
WOKN/KNAP GU21 214 G9
Broadwalk Shopping Centre
EDGW HA8 95 M7
Broadwater Farm
Primary School
TOTM N17 99 L10
Broadwater Park Golf Club
& Driving Range
GODL GU7 267 N9
Broadwater Primary School
TOOT SW17 179 N7
Broadwater School
GODL GU7 267 M9
Broadway Clinic
EDGW HA8 95 N9
Broadway Retail Park
CRICK NW2 116 G9
Broadway Shopping Centre
BXLYHS DA6 164 B10
HMSMTH W6 156 F4
Broadway Square
Shopping Centre
BXLYHS DA6 164 B10
Broadway Squash &
Fitness Centre
HMSMTH W6 156 G3
Brockenhurst Hotel
ASC SL5 192 A6
Brockham School
BRKHM/BTCW RH3 273 P2
Brocklebank Health Centre
WAND/EARL SW18 179 L3
Brocklebank Industrial Estate
GNWCH SE10 161 M3
Brockley Cross Business Centre
BROCKY SE4 160 D9
Brockley Primary School
BROCKY SE4 182 E1
Brockwell Lido
HNHL SE24 181 J2
Broke Hill Golf Club
RSEV TN14 228 A5
Bromet Primary School
OXHEY WD19 93 L1
Bromley Cemetery
BMLY BR1 183 L10
Bromley College of Further &
Higher Education
HAYES BR2 206 A6
BMLY BR1 205 L1
Bromley County Court
BMLY BR1 205 M1
Bromley FC
HAYES BR2 205 N5
Bromley Golf Club
HAYES BR2 206 B7
Bromley High School GDST
BMLY BR1 206 D4
Bromley Industrial Centre
BMLY BR1 206 A3
Bromley Mall Indoor Market
BMLY BR1 205 M2
Bromley Museum
ORP BR6 207 L7
Bromley Road Infant School
BECK BR3 204 G1
Bromley Road Retail Park
CAT SE6 182 G5
Bromley Ski Centre
STMC/STPC BR5 207 N1
Bromley Tennis Centre
ORP BR6 206 G10
Brompton Cemetery
WBPTN SW10 15 H10
Brompton Medical Centre
ECT SW5 15 H7
Brompton Oratory
SKENS SW7 15 N4
Bromyard Leisure Centre
ACT W3 136 B10
Brondesbury College for Boys
KIL/WHAMP NW6 136 G2
Brook Business Centre
IVER SL0 131 K4
Brook Community
Primary School
HACK E8 119 P10
Brooke Trading Estate
ROM RM1 124 G5
Brook Farm Industrial Estate
ABR/ST RM4 104 E1
Brookfield Primary School
CHEAM SM3 201 H8
HGT N6 118 C7
Brookfield Retail Park
CHES/WCR EN8 62 C3
Brook House FC
YEAD UB4 132 G5
Brook Industrial Estate
YEAD UB4 133 L10
Brook Industrial Park
STMC/STPC BR5 207 M4
Brookland J & I School
CHES/WCR EN8 62 D4
Brookland Primary School
GLDGN NW11 117 L2
Brooklands Airfield (disused)
WEY KT13 216 A6
Brooklands Business Park
WEY KT13 216 B6
Brooklands College
WEY KT13 216 B3
Brooklands Industrial Estate
WEY KT13 215 P6
Brooklands Museum
WEY KT13 216 B5
Brooklands Primary School
BKHTH/KID SE3 161 M9
Brooklands School
REIG RH2 257 L8
Brook Lane Business Centre
BTFD TW8 155 J4
Brookmans Park Golf Club
BRKMPK AL9 59 K1
Brookmans Park
Primary School
BRKMPK AL9 59 H2
Brookmarsh Trading Estate
DEPT SE8 160 G6
Brookmead Industrial Estate
CROY/NA CR0 202 D6
The Brook School
CRAWE RH10 284 D10
Brookside Primary School
HARH RM3 105 M6
YEAD UB4 133 K5
Brookweald CC
BRW CM14 106 D2
Brookwood Cemetery
CHOB/PIR GU24 230 G8
Brookwood County
Primary School
CHOB/PIR GU24 230 F6
Broomfield House School
RCH/KEW TW9 155 L7
Broomfield School
FBAR/BDGN N11 98 E6
Broomsleigh Business Park
SYD SE26 182 E8
Broomwood Hall
Lower School
BAL SW12 180 A2
STRHM/NOR SW16 180 E6
Brothwick Wharf
DEPT SE8 160 F4
Brownlow Medical Centre
FBAR/BDGN N11 98 F6
Brown's Hotel
MYFR/PICC W1J 10 F8
Brown's School
ORP BR6 228 A2
Broxbourne Business Centre
CHES/WCR EN8 62 C2
Broxbourne Primary School
BROX EN10 44 F7
Broxbourne Sailing Club
WAB EN9 45 J6
The Broxbourne School
BROX EN10 44 D8
Broxbourne Sports Club
BROX EN10 44 E7
Bruce Castle Museum
TOTM N17 99 M9
Bruce Grove Primary School
TOTM N17 99 N10
Brunei Gallery
STPAN WC1H 11 K2
Brunel Bus Station
SL SL1 129 L10
Brunel Engine House
BERM/RHTH SE16 160 B1
Brunel University
GLDGN NW11 116 G4
ISLW TW7 154 D6
TWK TW1 154 G10
UX/CGN UB8 131 P5
Brunel University
(Osterley Campus) Track
ISLW TW7 154 D6
Brunel University
(Runnymede Campus)
EGH TW20 172 A6
Brunswick Health Centre
FBAR/BDGN N11 98 B3
Brunswick Housing &
Shopping Centre
BMSBY WC1N 11 M1
Brunswick Industrial Park
FBAR/BDGN N11 98 C5
Brunswick Medical Centre
BMSBY WC1N 11 L1
Brunswick Park JMI School
STHGT/OAK N14 98 B2
Brunswick Park
Primary School
CMBW SE5 159 L6
Brushwood Junior School
CSHM HP5 51 K5
BT Centre
STBT EC1A 12 E5
Buckhurst Hill FC
BKHH IG9 102 B2
Buckhurst Hill Primary School
BKHH IG9 102 B3
Buckingham College
Preparatory School
PIN HA5 113 N4
Buckingham College School
HRW HA1 114 D3
Buckingham Palace
WHALL SW1A 16 F2
Buckingham Primary School
HPTN TW12 175 N8
Buckingham Road Cemetery
IL IG1 122 G7
Buckinghamshire Chilterns
University College
CSTG HP8 90 D3
Buckinghamshire Golf Club
DEN/HRF UB9 111 M7
Buckland Infant School
CHSGTN KT9 219 L2
Buckland Primary School
STA TW18 173 M10
Building Centre
GWRST WC1E 11 J4
Building Crafts College
SRTFD E15 141 H2
Bullers Wood School
CHST BR7 206 C1
Bullsbridge Industrial Estate
NWDGN UB2 153 J3
The Bull Theatre
BAR EN5 77 J8
BUPA Roding Hospital
REDBR IG4 122 A1
Burbage School
IS N1 7 J7
Burdett Coutts CE
Primary School
WEST SW1P 17 J4
Burgess Business Park
CMBW SE5 159 L6
Burgess Park Tennis Centre
CMBW SE5 18 F10
Burghwood Clinic
BNSTD SM7 239 J2
Burhill Golf Club
WOT/HER KT12 217 H5
Burhill Infant School
WOT/HER KT12 217 L3
Burleigh Primary School
CHES/WCR EN8 62 C6
Burlington Danes School
SHB W12 136 E8
Burlington Infant School
NWMAL KT3 200 C4
Burnham Abbey
MDHD SL6 128 A10
Burnham Beeches Golf Club
SL SL1 128 C3
Burnham Beeches Hotel
SL SL1 128 C4
Burnham Beeches (National
Nature Reserve)
SLN SL2 108 F10
Burnham FC
SL SL1 128 A5
Burnham Grammar School
SL SL1 128 C6
Burnham Health Centre
SL SL1 128 A5
Burnham Trading Estate
DART DA1 165 L10
Burnham Upper School
SL SL1 128 A6
Burnhill Business Centre
BECK BR3 204 F2
Burnley Road Clinic
WLSDN NW10 116 D10
Burnside Industrial Estate
BARK/HLT IG6 103 L6
Burnt Ash Primary School
BMLY BR1 183 M8
Burntmill Industrial Estate
HLW CM20 28 F8
Burnt Mill School
HLW CM20 29 H9
Burnt Oak Junior School
BFN/LL DA15 185 K4
Burntwood School
TOOT SW17 179 N5
Burpham Foundation
Primary School
RGUE GU4 250 D6
Bursted Wood Primary School
BXLYHN DA7 164 C8
Burstow Business Centre
HORL RH6 281 J2
Burstow Lodge
Business Centre
HORL RH6 280 C6
Burstow Primary School
HORL RH6 281 H4
Burvale Cemetery
WOT/HER KT12 217 H3
Burwell Industrial Estate
LEY E10 120 D6
Burwood Park School & College
WOT/HER KT12 216 G3
Burwood School
ORP BR6 207 N9
Burys Court School
REIG RH2 274 F6
Bushey Golf & Country Club
BUSH WD23 73 P10
Bushey Hall Golf Club
BUSH WD23 73 N8
Bushey Hall School
BUSH WD23 73 N10
Bushey Hall Swimming Pool
BUSH WD23 73 N9
Bushey Health Centre
BUSH WD23 73 N10
Bushey Heath Primary School
BUSH WD23 94 C2
Bushey Manor Junior School
BUSH WD23 73 N9
Bushey Meads School
BUSH WD23 74 B9
Bushey Museum & Art Gallery
BUSH WD23 73 P10
Bush Hall Hotel
BRKMPK AL9 40 G1
Bush Hill Park Golf Club
WCHMH N21 79 K9
Bush Hill Park Medical Centre
EN EN1 79 N10
Bush Hill Park Primary School
EN EN1 79 P9
Bush House (BBC)
HOL/ALD WC2B 11 N6
Bush Industrial Estate
ARCH N19 118 D8
WLSDN NW10 136 A6
Bushy Hill Junior School
GU GU1 250 G9
The Business Academy Bexley
ERITH DA18 163 P1
The Business Centre
CEND/HSY/T N8 98 F10
HARH RM3 105 L8
IL IG1 122 E7
The Business Design Centre
IS N1 6 B6
Business Training & Solutions
CDALE/KGS NW9 96 C9
The Business Village
SLN SL2 129 N10
Bute House Preparatory
School for Girls
HMSMTH W6 156 F3
Butlers Court County First &
Middle School
BEAC HP9 88 D10
Butlers Wharf
STHWK SE1 13 M10
Butler's Wharf Business Centre
STHWK SE1 19 M1
Butler's Wharf Pier
STHWK SE1 13 M10
Butterfly House
ISLW TW7 154 G7
Butterfly Sports Club
ELTH/MOT SE9 184 E2
Buxlow Preparatory School
WBLY HA9 115 K8
Buzzard Creek
Industrial Estate
BARK IG11 143 J5
Byam Shaw School of Art
ARCH N19 118 D7
Byfleet Business Centre
BF/WBF KT14 215 N7
Byfleet CP School
BF/WBF KT14 215 N7
Byfleet Industrial Estate
BF/WBF KT14 215 N7
WATW WD18 92 D2
Bygrove Primary School
POP/IOD E14 140 G8
Byron Court Primary School
ALP/SUD HA0 115 H7
Byron Primary School
COUL/CHIP CR5 240 F3
Cabot Place
POP/IOD E14 140 F10
Cadogan Pier
CHEL SW3 15 P10
Calcot Medical Centre
CFSP/GDCR SL9 90 A9
Caldicott School
SLN SL2 128 G2
Caledonian Market
STHWK SE1 19 K3
Cally Pool
IS N1 5 N5
Calverton Primary School
CAN/RD E16 142 A8
Calvi House Pre-Preparatory
School
COB KT11 216 F9
Cambell Primary School
DAGW RM9 143 N2
Camberwell Business Centre
CMBW SE5 159 L6
Camberwell College of Arts
CMBW SE5 159 M7
Camberwell Leisure Centre
CMBW SE5 159 L7
Camberwell New Cemetery
PECK SE15 182 C2
Camberwell Trading Estate
CMBW SE5 159 J8
Cambridge Park Bowling &
Sports Club
TWK TW1 177 H2
Cambridge School
HMSMTH W6 156 E3
Cambridge Theatre
LSQ/SEVD WC2H 11 L6
Camden Arts Centre
HAMP NW3 117 L10
Camden House Clinic
BKHTH/KID SE3 161 K8
Camden Junior School
CAR SM5 222 A1
Camden Market
CAMTN NW1 4 D4
Camden Mews Day Hospital
CAMTN NW1 5 H3
Camden People's Theatre
CAMTN NW1 4 G10
Camden School for Girls
KTTN NW5 5 H2
Camden Theatre
CAMTN NW1 4 G7
Camden Town Hall &
St Pancras Library
CAMTN NW1 5 L9
Camelot Primary School
PECK SE15 160 A6
Cameron House School
CHEL SW3 15 M9
Campanile Hotel
RDART DA2 166 C9
Camperdown House
WCHPL E1 13 M6
Camphill Industrial Estate
BF/WBF KT14 215 L7
Camphill Road First School
BF/WBF KT14 215 L8
Campion House College
ISLW TW7 154 C6
Campion School
EMPK RM11 125 N2
Camp Primary School
STAL AL1 38 G7
Campsbourne J & I School
CEND/HSY/T N8 118 F1
Campus West Cinema
WGCW AL8 22 G4
Campus West Leisure Centre
WGCW AL8 22 F4
Canada House
STJS SW1Y 11 K9
Canada House Business Centre
RSLP HA4 113 K6
Canada Place
POP/IOD E14 140 F10
Canada Square
POP/IOD E14 140 G10
Canada Water Retail Park
BERM/RHTH SE16 160 C2
Canada Wharf Museum
BERM/RHTH SE16 140 E10
Canal Cafe Theatre
BAY/PAD W2 9 H3
Canal Industrial Park
GVE DA12 190 G2
Canary Riverside
BERM/RHTH SE16 140 E10
Canary Wharf Pier
POP/IOD E14 140 E10
Canberra Primary School
SHB W12 136 F9
Canbury Business Centre
KUTN/CMB KT2 199 K1
Canbury 2000 Business Park
KUTN/CMB KT2 199 K1
Canbury Medical Centre
KUTN/CMB KT2 199 L1
Canbury School
KUTN/CMB KT2 177 N9
Cann Hall Primary School
WAN E11 121 L8
The Canning School
ECT SW5 14 G5
KENS W8 14 E3
Cannizaro House Hotel
WIM/MER SW19 178 F9
Cannon Hill Clinic
STHGT/OAK N14 98 F4
Cannon Lane Primary School
PIN HA5 113 L4
Cannon Sports Club
CANST EC4R 12 F7
Cannon Trading Estate
WBLY HA9 115 N9
Cannon Wharf
Business Centre
DEPT SE8 160 D3
Cannon Workshops
POP/IOD E14 140 F9
Canon Barnett Primary School
WCHPL E1 13 M5
Canonbury Business Centre
IS N1 6 F5
Canonbury Primary School
IS N1 6 C2
Canon Palmer RC High School
IL IG1 123 H6
Canons Brook Golf Club
HLWW/ROY CM19 28 D10
Canons High School
EDGW HA8 95 L10
The Canons Leisure Centre
MTCM CR4 202 A4
Canterbury Industrial Estate
NWCR SE14 160 C5
Cantium Retail Park
STHWK SE1 19 N9
Capel Manor College
EN EN1 80 A2
Capital Business Centre
ALP/SUD HA0 135 J4
MTCM CR4 202 A5
SAND/SEL CR2 223 L3
WATN WD24 73 L2
Capital City Academy
WLSDN NW10 136 E3
The Capital Hotel
CHEL SW3 16 A2
Capital Industrial Estate
BELV DA17 144 D10
BELV DA17 164 C3
Capital Radio
LSQ/SEVD WC2H 11 K8
Capital Wharf
WAP E1W 13 P10
Capitol Industrial Park
CDALE/KGS NW9 115 P1
Caplan Estate
MTCM CR4 202 D1
Capswood Business Centre
CFSP/GDCR SL9 110 F6
Cardiff Road Industrial Estate
WATW WD18 73 J10
Cardinal Hinsley High School
WLSDN NW10 136 D3
Cardinal Newman Catholic
Primary School
WOT/HER KT12 197 L10
Cardinal Pole RC School
HOM E9 140 D1
Cardinal Pole RC Secondary
Lower School
HOM E9 140 C2
Cardinal Road Infant School
FELT TW13 175 J4
The Cardinal Vaughan
Memorial School
WKENS W14 14 A1
Cardinal Wiseman RC School
(Technology & Art College)
GFD/PVL UB6 134 B7
Cardwell Primary School
WOOL/PLUM SE18 162 C3
Carew Manor School
WLGTN SM6 202 E10
Cargo Terminal
HORL RH6 279 N8
Carlisle Infant School
HPTN TW12 176 A9
Carlton House
STJS SW1Y 11 J10
The Carlton Mitre Hotel
E/WMO/HCT KT8 198 D3
Carlton Primary School
KTTN NW5 118 B10
Carlton Vale Infant School
MV/WKIL W9 2 D9
Carlyle Business Centre
CHERT KT16 195 J7
Carlyle's House (NT)
CHEL SW3 15 N10
Carnwath Road
Industrial Estate
FUL/PGN SW6 157 L9
Carpenders Park Cemetery
OXHEY WD19 93 N5
Carpenters Business Park
SRTFD E15 140 F1
Carpenters' Hall
OBST EC2N 13 H4
Carpenters Primary School
SRTFD E15 141 H3
Carrier Business Park
CRAWE RH10 284 C6
Carshalton AFC
SUT SM1 201 P10
Carshalton College of Further
Education
CAR SM5 202 A10
Carshalton High School
for Boys
CAR SM5 201 N9
Carshalton High School
for Girls
CAR SM5 201 P10
Carshalton War Memorial
Hospital
CAR SM5 222 A2
Carterhatch Primary School
EN EN1 80 A5
Caryl Thomas Clinic
HRW HA1 114 D2
Cascades Leisure Centre
GVE DA12 191 K7
The Cassel Hospital
RCHPK/HAM TW10 177 J7
Cassidy Medical Centre
FUL/PGN SW6 157 K6
Cassiobury Junior School
WAT WD17 72 F5
Castilion Primary School
THMD SE28 143 M8
Castlebar Special School
WEA W13 134 F7
Castlecombe Primary School
ELTH/MOT SE9 184 B8
Castle Hall Theatre &
Civic Centre
HERT/WAT SG14 25 K5
Castle Hill Primary School
CROY/NA CR0 225 H3
Castle Industrial Estate
WALW SE17 18 E5
Castle Montessori School
BERK HP4 34 A5
Castleview Combined School
DTCH/LGLY SL3 150 A3
Casualty Plus' Clinic
BTFD TW8 155 H4
The Caterham Dene Hospital
CTHM CR3 241 N9
Caterham High School
CLAY IG5 102 C10
Caterham Preparatory School
CTHM CR3 259 N2
Caterham School
CTHM CR3 259 N2
Catford Cricket & Sports Club
CAT SE6 182 G4
Catford Cyphers CC
CAT SE6 182 E5
Catford Girls School
CAT SE6 183 J6
Catford Trading Estate
CAT SE6 182 G5
Catford Wanderers Sports Club
CAT SE6 183 H7

Cathall Leisure Centre WAN E11 121 J8
Cathedral & Abbey Church of St Albans STALW/RED AL3 38 B6
Cathedral of St Mary & St Helen BRWN CM15 107 J3
Cathedral School of St Saviour & St Mary Overie STHWK SE1 12 F10
Cator Park School for Girls BECK BR3 182 D10
Cavendish College FITZ W1T 11 J3
Cavendish Hotel STJS SW1Y 11 H9
Cavendish Primary School CHSWK W4 156 B6
Cavendish School BERM/RHTH SE16 160 B3
The Cavendish School CAMTN NW1 4 E5
HHW HP1 35 L5
Cavendish Special School HNWL W7 134 E8
Caxton Hall STJSPK SW1H 17 J3
Caxton Trading Estate HYS/HAR UB3 152 F1
Cayley Primary School WCHPL E1 140 D7
Cecil Park Clinic PIN HA5 113 M2
Cecil Road Primary School GVW DA11 190 C4
Cecil Sharpe House CAMTN NW1 4 D5
The Cedar School FSTGT E7 141 P1
Cedars First & Middle School KTN/HRWW/WS HA3 94 B9
The Cedars Primary School HEST TW5 153 H6
Cedar Way Industrial Estate CAMTN NW1 5 J4
Cenotaph WHALL SW1A 17 L1
Centaurs Business Centre ISLW TW7 154 F5
Centaurs RFC ISLW TW7 154 E5
Central Business Centre WLSDN NW10 116 B10
Central Criminal Court STP EC4M 12 C5
Centrale Shopping Centre CROY/NA CR0 203 K9
Central Foundation Boys School SDTCH EC2A 13 H1
Central Foundation Girls School (Lower) BOW E3 140 D5
Central Foundation Girls School (Upper) BOW E3 140 E5
Central Hall STJSPK SW1H 17 K2
Central Hendon Clinic HDN NW4 116 E2
Central London County Court CAVSQ/HST W1G 10 E2
Central London Golf Club TOOT SW17 179 N5
Central London Markets STBT EC1A 12 C4
Central Medical Centre MRDN SM4 201 M4
Central Middlesex Hospital WLSDN NW10 135 P5
Central Park Arena DART DA1 187 M4
Central Park Pool HARH RM3 105 M6
Central Park Primary School EHAM E6 142 A4
Central Primary School WAT WD17 73 K8
Central St Martins College of Art/Design RSQ WC1B 11 N4
Central School of Ballet CLKNW EC1R 12 B2
Central School of Fashion GTPST W1W 10 G4
Central School of Speech & Drama HAMP NW3 3 L3
Central Square Shopping Centre WBLY HA9 135 K1
Central Sussex College CRAWE RH10 283 P7
Centre Court Shopping Centre WIM/MER SW19 179 J9
Centre Point LSQ/SEVD WC2H 11 K5
Chace Community School EN EN1 79 M5
The Chadwell Heath Foundation School CHDH RM6 123 L4
Chadwell Heath Industrial Park BCTR RM8 123 P6
Chadwell Heath Leisure Centre CHDH RM6 123 N4
Chadwell Infant & Primary School CHDH RM6 123 M5
Chadwell St Mary Primary School CDW/CHF RM16 168 D3
Chadwell Springs Golf Club WARE SG12 26 B3
Chaffinch Business Park BECK BR3 204 C3
Chafford School RAIN RM13 145 K7
Chafford Sports Complex RAIN RM13 145 K7
Chailey Industrial Estate HYS/HAR UB3 153 H1
Chalcot School CAMTN NW1 4 E3
Chalfont Leisure Centre CFSP/GDCR SL9 89 P9
Chalfont St Giles Infant School CSTG HP8 89 N3
Chalfont St Giles Junior School CSTG HP8 89 N4
Chalfont St Peter FC CFSP/GDCR SL9 90 A8
Chalfont St Peter Infant School CFSP/GDCR SL9 89 P8
Chalfont St Peter Junior School CFSP/GDCR SL9 90 A8
The Chalfonts Community College CFSP/GDCR SL9 89 P8
Chalfonts & Gerrards Cross Health Clinic CFSP/GDCR SL9 90 A9
Chalgrove Primary School FNCH N3 117 H1
Chalkhill Primary School WBLY HA9 115 N8
Chalk Lane Hotel EPSOM KT18 238 A1
The Chamberlain Hotel TWRH EC3N 13 L7
Chambersbury JMI School HHS/BOV HP3 36 C9
Chambers Business Park WDR/YW UB7 152 B5
Chambers Wharf BERM/RHTH SE16 19 P1
Chancellors School BRKMPK AL9 59 K1
Chandlers Field Primary School E/WMO/HCT KT8 197 P5
Chandos Business Centre WLGTN SM6 222 D3
Channelsea Business Centre SRTFD E15 141 J4
Channing School HGT N6 118 C6
Chantry Primary School GVE DA12 190 F3
Chantry School WDR/YW UB7 131 P8
The Chantry GVE DA12 190 F2
Chapel End Infant School WALTH E17 100 G9
Chapel End Junior School WALTH E17 100 G9
Chapel High Shopping Centre BRW CM14 107 H3
Chapman Park Industrial Estate WLSDN NW10 136 C1
Charing Cross Hospital HMSMTH W6 156 G5
Charles Darwin School BH/WHM TN16 244 C1
The Charles Dickens Museum BMSBY WC1N 11 N2
Charles Dickens Primary School STHWK SE1 18 E2
Charles Edward Brooke School (Lower School) CMBW SE5 159 J7
Charles Edward Brooke School (Upper School) BRXN/ST SW9 159 J7
Charlotte Sharman Primary School LBTH SE11 18 C4
Charlotte Turner Primary School DEPT SE8 160 F5
Charlton Athletic FC (The Valley) CHARL SE7 161 P4
Charlton Health & Fitness Centre CHARL SE7 161 P4
Charlton House CHARL SE7 162 A5
Charlton Manor Junior School CHARL SE7 162 A6
Charlton RFC ELTH/MOT SE9 184 E3
Charlton School CHARL SE7 162 B5
Charlwood Place HORL RH6 279 H7
Charlwood Village Infant School HORL RH6 279 J8
Charrington Bowl SURB KT6 199 N9
Charville Primary School YEAD UB4 132 F4
Charter Clinic CHEL SW3 16 A8
Charterhouse CLKNW EC1R 12 C2
Charterhouse School Students Residences GODL GU7 266 G10
Charteris Road Sports Centre KIL/WHAMP NW6 2 D6
Charter Nightingale Hospital & Counselling Centre CAMTN NW1 9 P3
The Charter School HNHL SE24 181 L1
Charters School ASC SL5 192 C7
Chartfield School PUT/ROE SW15 178 E1
Chartridge Combined School CSHM HP5 50 B3
Chartridge Park Golf Club CSHM HP5 50 C4
Chartwell Business Centre BMLY BR1 206 A3
Chartwell (NT) BH/WHM TN16 263 H8
Chase Bridge Primary School WHTN TW2 176 D2
Chase Farm Hospital ENC/FH EN2 79 H4
Chase Lane J & I School CHING E4 100 E5
Chase Lane Primary School CHING E4 100 G5
Chase Road Trading Estate WLSDN NW10 136 A6
Chase Side Primary School ENC/FH EN2 79 K6
Chaseville Clinic WCHMH N21 78 G10
Chater Infant School WATW WD18 73 H8
Chater Junior School WATW WD18 73 H8
Chatsworth Infant School BFN/LL DA15 185 K4
Chatsworth J & I School HSLW TW3 154 B10
Chaucer Clinic NWDGN UB2 154 C1
Chaulden Primary School HHW HP1 35 J7
The Chauncy School WARE SG12 26 A1
Cheam Common J & I School WPK KT4 200 E9
Cheam Fields Primary School CHEAM SM3 221 H2
Cheam High School CHEAM SM3 221 H1
Cheam Leisure Centre CHEAM SM3 220 G1
Cheam Park Farm Junior School CHEAM SM3 201 H10
Cheam Sports Club CHEAM SM3 221 H4
Cheapside CE Primary School ASC SL5 192 D1
Chelsea Barracks BGVA SW1W 16 D8
Chelsea Bridge Business Centre VX/NE SW8 158 C6
Chelsea Centre & Theatre WBPTN SW10 157 M6
Chelsea Cinema CHEL SW3 15 P8
The Chelsea Club Leisure Centre FUL/PGN SW6 157 L5
Chelsea College of Art & Design CHEL SW3 15 N8
FUL/PGN SW6 157 L9
SHB W12 156 E1
WEST SW1P 17 K7
Chelsea FC (Stamford Bridge) FUL/PGN SW6 157 L6
Chelsea Fields Industrial Estate WIM/MER SW19 201 N1
Chelsea Leisure Centre CHEL SW3 15 P8
Chelsea Old Town Hall CHEL SW3 15 P8
Chelsea Physic Garden CHEL SW3 16 A9
Chelsea & Westminster Hospital WBPTN SW10 15 K10
Chelsea Wharf WBPTN SW10 157 N6
Chelsfield Lakes Golf Centre ORP BR6 227 P4
Chelsfield Park Hospital ORP BR6 228 A2
Chelsfield Primary School ORP BR6 227 P2
Chenies CC RKW/CH/CXG WD3 70 F5
Chenies Combined School RKW/CH/CXG WD3 70 D4
Chennestone Community School SUN TW16 197 J2
Cherington House Health Centre HNWL W7 134 E10
Cherry Garden Pier BERM/RHTH SE16 160 A1
Cherry Garden School BERM/RHTH SE16 19 P5
Cherry Lane Primary School WDR/YW UB7 152 A3
Cherry Lodge Golf Club BH/WHM TN16 244 D3
Cherry Orchard Primary School CHARL SE7 161 P6
Cherry Tree JMI School WATN WD24 73 H2
Chertsey Business Centre CHERT KT16 195 K7
Chertsey Camping & Caravanning Club Site CHERT KT16 195 M7
Chertsey Cemetery CHERT KT16 195 K8
Chertsey Hall CHERT KT16 195 K7
Chertsey Museum CHERT KT16 195 K6
Chertsey Recreation Centre CHERT KT16 195 H8
Chertsey Town FC CHERT KT16 195 J6
Chesham Bois CE Combined School AMS HP6 69 K1
Chesham Community Hospital CSHM HP5 51 H8
Chesham Health Centre CSHM HP5 50 G8
Chesham High School CSHM HP5 51 J6
Chesham Leisure Centre CSHM HP5 51 J7
Chesham & Ley Hill Golf Club CSHM HP5 51 P7
Chesham Park Community College CSHM HP5 50 F6
Chesham Preparatory School CSHM HP5 51 M3
Chesham United FC CSHM HP5 50 G9
Cheshunt Community Hospital CHES/WCR EN8 62 D7
Cheshunt FC CHES/WCR EN8 62 B8
Cheshunt Golf Club CHESW EN7 62 A3
Cheshunt Marriott Hotel BROX EN10 62 C2
Cheshunt School CHESW EN7 62 B6
Chessington CC CHSGTN KT9 219 H4
Chessington Community College & Sports Centre CHSGTN KT9 219 J4
Chessington Golf Club CHSGTN KT9 219 J4
Chessington World of Adventures CHSGTN KT9 219 H6
The Chesterfield Mayfair Hotel MYFR/PICC W1J 10 E9
Chesterfield Primary School PEND EN3 80 D3
Chesterton Primary School BTSEA SW11 158 B7
Chestnut Grove School BAL SW12 180 B4
Chestnut Lane First School AMS HP6 69 K2
Chestnuts Primary School SEVS/STOTM N15 119 K3
Chevening Cross RSEV TN14 246 B6
Chevening Primary School SEV TN13 246 C8
Cheyne Centre CHEL SW3 15 N10
Chicken Shed Theatre STHGT/OAK N14 78 B9
Chigwell Golf Club CHIG IG7 102 D6
Chigwell Primary School CHIG IG7 102 F3
Chigwell Row Infant School CHIG IG7 103 M3
Chigwell School CHIG IG7 102 F3
Childerditch Industrial Park RBRW/HUT CM13 127 L1
Childeric Primary School NWCR SE14 160 D6
Childs Hill Clinic CRICK NW2 117 J7
Childs Hill Primary School CRICK NW2 117 H8
Childs Welfare Clinic BCTR RM8 123 M10
Chiltern Business Village UX/CGN UB8 131 L4
Chiltern Open Air Museum CSTG HP8 90 C3
The Chilterns Crematorium AMSS HP7 68 E7
Chiltonian Industrial Estate LEE/GVPK SE12 183 L2
Chilworth CE Infant School RGUE GU4 268 G6
The Chimes Shopping Centre UX/CGN UB8 131 N2
Chimnocks Wharf POP/IOD E14 140 D9
Chingford CE Infant School CHING E4 101 J2
Chingford CE Junior School CHING E4 101 J2
Chingford Foundation School CHING E4 100 G2
Chingford Hall Primary School CHING E4 100 E7
Chingford Health Centre CHING E4 100 E5
Chingford Industrial Centre CHING E4 100 D6
Chingford Rugby Football Club CHING E4 100 F2
Chinthurst School KWD/TDW/WH KT20 238 F9
Chipperfield J & I School KGLGY WD4 53 K7
Chipping Ongar Primary School CHONG CM5 67 N6
Chipstead Golf Club COUL/CHIP CR5 240 A4
Chipstead RFC COUL/CHIP CR5 240 A7
Chipstead Valley Primary School COUL/CHIP CR5 240 B2
Chisenhale Primary School BOW E3 140 D4
Chislehurst Caves CHST BR7 206 D1
Chislehurst Cemetery CHST BR7 185 H8
Chislehurst Golf Club CHST BR7 184 E10
Chislehurst Natural Health Centre CHST BR7 184 E9
Chislehurst & Sidcup Grammar School BFN/LL DA15 185 L5
Chiswick & Bedford Park Preparatory School CHSWK W4 156 B3
Chiswick Business Park CHSWK W4 155 N3
Chiswick Community School CHSWK W4 156 A6
Chiswick House CHSWK W4 156 A5
Chobham Common National Nature Reserve CHOB/PIR GU24 193 H10
Chobham FC CHOB/PIR GU24 213 L8
Chobham Golf Club WOKN/KNAP GU21 231 J1
Chobham RFC CHOB/PIR GU24 213 K6
Chobham St Lawrence CE Primary School CHOB/PIR GU24 213 K7
Chorleywood Golf Club RKW/CH/CXG WD3 70 G8
Chorleywood Health Centre RKW/CH/CXG WD3 70 F8
Chorleywood Primary RKW/CH/CXG WD3 70 F10
Chrisp Street Health Centre POP/IOD E14 140 G8
Christ Church Bentinck CE Primary School CAMTN NW1 9 N3
Christ Church Brondesbury CE J & I School KIL/WHAMP NW6 2 C4
Christ Church CE Infant School NWMAL KT3 200 B3
Christchurch CE Infant School VW GU25 193 M3
Christ Church CE Junior School NWMAL KT3 200 A3
Christ Church Cemetery BRW CM14 107 H5
Christ Church CE Primary School BAR EN5 76 G6
BTSEA SW11 157 P9
BRXN/ST SW9 159 H7
BRXS/STRHM SW2 180 G4
BRYLDS KT5 199 M6
CHEL SW3 15 P9
FSTH SE23 182 C5
RKW/CH/CXG WD3 71 J8
WOOL/PLUM SE18 162 D7
Christchurch CE Primary School HAMP NW3 117 N8
WCHPL E1 13 M4
Christ Church CE Middle School EA W5 135 J9
Christchurch Industrial Centre STHWK SE1 12 C9
Christchurch Junior School CHERT KT16 214 G3
Christ Church Primary School ERITH DA8 164 E5
PUR/KEN CR8 223 J6
WARE SG12 26 D2
Christchurch Primary School IL IG1 122 E6
Christ Church School CAMTN NW1 4 F8
Christian Meeting Hall BECK BR3 204 F1
Christopher Hatton Primary School FSBYW WC1X 12 A2
Christopher Hotel WDSR SL4 149 H5
Christopher Place Shopping Centre STALW/RED AL3 38 C6
Christ's College Finchley FNCH N3 117 L1
Christ's College Guildford GU GU1 249 P7
Christs College School EFNCH N2 117 L1
Christ's College Ski Club GUW GU2 249 N7
Christs School RCHPK/HAM TW10 177 L1
Christ the King RC First School STWL/WRAY TW19 173 N2
Christ the King RC Primary School FSBYPK N4 118 G6
Christ the King Sixth Form College LEW SE13 161 J9
Chrysalis Theatre BAL SW12 180 B4
Chrysanthemum Clinic CHSWK W4 155 P6
Chrysolyte Independent Christian School STHWK SE1 19 H3
Church Down Adult School LEE/GVPK SE12 183 M5
Church End Medical Centre WLSDN NW10 136 B1
Church Farm House Museum HDN NW4 116 E1
Church Farm Swimming Pool EBAR EN4 98 A2
Churchfield Primary School ED N9 99 N2
Churchfield School WOOL/PLUM SE18 163 J3
Churchfields J & I School SWFD E18 101 M9
Churchfields Primary School BECK BR3 204 C3
Churchgate CE Primary School HLWE CM17 29 P8
Church Hill Primary School EBAR EN4 98 A1
Church House WEST SW1P 17 K3
Churchill Business Park BH/WHM TN16 262 G2
Churchill CE Primary School BH/WHM TN16 262 F1
Churchill Clinic STHWK SE1 18 B3
Churchill College RYNPK SW20 200 F2
Churchill Gardens Primary School PIM SW1V 16 G8
Churchill Museum & Cabinet War Rooms STJSPK SW1H 17 K1
Churchill Theatre BMLY BR1 205 M2
Church Lane School UPMR RM14 126 G10
Church Langley Primary School HLWE CM17 47 M1
Church Mead Infant School LEY E10 120 F6
Church Mead Junior School LEY E10 120 F6
Churchmead School Church of England (VA) School DTCH/LGLY SL3 149 N6
Church Stairs BERM/RHTH SE16 160 A1
Church Street Industrial Estate WARE SG12 26 C1
Church Trading Estate ERITH DA8 165 H6
Church Wood RSPB Reserve SLN SL2 109 K6
Cineworld Cinema BXLYHS DA6 164 C10
FELT TW13 175 J5
WDGN N22 99 H10
Cippenham Infant School SL SL1 128 C9
Cippenham Junior School SL SL1 128 C9
Cippenham Medical Centre SL SL1 128 F10
Citigroup Tower POP/IOD E14 140 G10
City Business Centre BERM/RHTH SE16 160 B1
The City Business Centre CRAWW RH11 283 N3
City Business College FSBYE EC1V 6 D10
City Central Estate FSBYE EC1V 6 E10
City College of Higher Education IS N1 7 H9
City & Guilds of London Art School LBTH SE11 18 B8
City Health Centre FSBYE EC1V 12 G1
City & Islington College FSBYE EC1V 6 C9
FSBYE EC1V 6 F10
FSBYPK N4 119 J7
HBRY N5 6 B1
HOLWY N7 118 F9
IS N1 6 G5
STLK EC1Y 12 G2
City & Islington Sixth Form College FSBYE EC1V 6 C8
City Literary College HHOL WC1V 11 M5
City of East London College WCHPL E1 13 P5
City of London Academy STHWK SE1 19 P7
The City of London Academy EDUL SE22 181 P1
City of London Business College SEVS/STOTM N15 119 M3
SEVS/STOTM N15 119 P3
City of London Cemetery MNPK E12 122 B7
City of London Club OBST EC2N 13 J5
City of London College WCHPL E1 13 N5
City of London Crematorium MNPK E12 122 A8
City of London Freemens School ASHTD KT21 237 N5
City of London Magistrates Court LOTH EC2R 12 G6
City of London School BLKFR EC4V 12 D7
City of London School for Girls BARB EC2Y 12 E3
City of London School Sports Ground LEE/GVPK SE12 183 P5
City of Westminster Cemetery HNWL W7 134 E10
City of Westminster College BAY/PAD W2 9 L3
MV/WKIL W9 2 D10
MV/WKIL W9 2 F10
City of Westminster Vehicle Pound MYFR/PKLN W1K 10 B8
City University FSBYE EC1V 6 C10
FSBYE EC1V 12 D1
IS N1 6 E8
STBT EC1A 12 E4
WCHPL E1 140 A7
City University Business School BARB EC2Y 12 F3
Civic Centre & Bromley Palace BMLY BR1 205 N2
Civic Hall Cinema HOD EN11 44 E4
Civic Medical Centre HRW HA1 114 D3
Civil Service College ASC SL5 192 E5
Civil Service Recreation Centre WEST SW1P 17 K4
Civil Service Sports Ground LEE/GVPK SE12 183 P2
Clandon CE Infant School RGUE GU4 251 K7
Clandon Park (NT) RGUE GU4 251 K8
Clandon Regis Golf Club RGUE GU4 251 L7
Clapham Common Clinic CLAP SW4 158 E10
Clapham Manor Primary School CLAP SW4 158 D9
Clapham Manor Street Public Baths CLAP SW4 158 E9
Clapham North Business Centre CLAP SW4 158 E9
Clapham Picture House CLAP SW4 158 D10
Clapton Girls Technology College CLPT E5 120 B9
Clapton Jewish Boys School SEVS/STOTM N15 119 N5
Clara Grant Primary School BOW E3 140 F6
Clare House Primary School BECK BR3 205 H2
Claremont Clinic FSTGT E7 121 P10
Claremont Fan Court School ESH/CLAY KT10 218 A3
Claremont High School KTN/HRWW/WS HA3 115 K3
Claremont Landscape Garden (NT) ESH/CLAY KT10 217 P4
Claremont Way Industrial Estate CRICK NW2 116 F6
Clarence House WHALL SW1A 17 H1
Clarendon Primary School ASHF TW15 174 A6
Clarendon Special School HPTN TW12 176 A9
Claridge's Hotel MYFR/PKLN W1K 10 E7
Claverings Industrial Estate ED N9 100 B3
Claycots Primary School SLN SL2 128 F6
Claygate Primary School ESH/CLAY KT10 218 D4
Clayhall Clinic CLAY IG5 122 B1
Clayponds Hospital BTFD TW8 155 K3
Cleeve Park School SCUP DA14 185 M6
Clementine Churchill Hospital HRW HA1 114 D8
Cleopatra's Needle CHCR WC2N 11 N9
Clerkenwell County Court IS N1 6 C7
Clerkenwell Heritage Centre FARR EC1M 12 C2
Clerkenwell Parochial CE Primary School CLKNW EC1R 6 A10
Cleveland Primary School IL IG1 122 E9
Cleves Junior School WEY KT13 216 G1
Cleves Primary School EHAM E6 142 A3
Clewer Green CE First School WDSR SL4 148 E9
C & L Golf & Country Club NTHLT UB5 133 J2
Clifton Hill School CTHM CR3 241 L10
Clifton Lodge School EA W5 135 H9
Clifton Primary School NWDGN UB2 153 M3
Clink Exhibition STHWK SE1 12 G9
Clissold Leisure Centre STNW/STAM N16 119 L8
Clissold Park Natural Health Centre STNW/STAM N16 119 M7
Clitterhouse Primary School CRICK NW2 116 G7
C & L Leisure Centre RSLP HA4 133 J2
Clockhouse Industrial Estate EBED/NFELT TW14 174 C4
Clockhouse Primary School CRW RM5 104 C7
Clock Museum CITYW EC2V 12 F5
Cloisters Business Centre VX/NE SW8 158 C6
Clore Gallery WEST SW1P 17 L6
Clore Shalom School RAD WD7 57 K6
Clore Tikva School BARK/HLT IG6 102 F10
Clothworkers' Hall FENCHST EC3M 13 K7
Clouster's Green WAP E1W 13 N9
Coach Museum WDSR SL4 149 K7
Coalhouse Fort TIL RM18 169 P7
Coates Way JMI School GSTN WD25 55 M9
Cobbold Estate WLSDN NW10 136 C1
Cobham Bus Museum COB KT11 216 D8
The Cobham Health Centre COB KT11 217 J9
Cobham RFC COB KT11 217 L8
Cobourg Primary School CMBW SE5 19 L9
Cochrane Theatre GINN WC1R 11 N4
Cockfosters Sports Ground EBAR EN4 78 A7
The Cockpit Theatre STJWD NW8 9 N2
Coldharbour Industrial Estate CMBW SE5 159 K8
Coldharbour Leisure Centre ELTH/MOT SE9 184 C5
Coldharbour Sports Ground ELTH/MOT SE9 184 D5
Colebrooke Primary School IS N1 6 C7
Colegrave School SRTFD E15 121 J10
Colehill CC AMSS HP7 68 F9
Coleraine Park Primary School TOTM N17 100 A9
Coleridge Primary School HGT N6 118 E5
Coleshill CE First School AMSS HP7 68 E10
Colet Court BARN SW13 156 D4
Colfe's Preparatory School LEE/GVPK SE12 183 M2
Colfe's Senior School LEE/GVPK SE12 183 M2
Colham Manor Primary School UX/CGN UB8 132 A8
Colindale Business Park CDALE/KGS NW9 115 P1
Colindale Hospital CDALE/KGS NW9 116 B1
Colindale Primary School CDALE/KGS NW9 116 C2
Coliseum Theatre CHCR WC2N 11 L8
College Fields Business Centre WIM/MER SW19 201 P1
College of Arms BLKFR EC4V 12 E6
College of Central London SDTCH EC2A 13 J1
College of Fuel Technology HGT N6 118 B4
The College of Law FITZ W1T 11 J4
LINN WC2A 12 A5
RGUW GU3 267 P4
College of North East London CEND/HSY/T N8 119 H2
SEVS/STOTM N15 119 N2
WDGN N22 98 D9
College of North West London KIL/WHAMP NW6 2 E5
WBLY HA9 115 M8
WLSDN NW10 116 C10
College of Organists FLST/FETLN EC4A 12 B4
College of Psychic Studies SKENS SW7 157 N3
College of Teachers EPP CM16 82 G2
College Park School BAY/PAD W2 8 F6
Collett Special School HHW HP1 35 M5
Collier Row Clinic CRW RM5 104 C9
Collier Row FC CRW RM5 104 A9
Collingwood Business Centre ARCH N19 118 F8
Collingwood Preparatory School WLGTN SM6 222 C2

The Collingwood Suite Conference Centre *WGCW* AL8 22 F7
Collins Method School *CRICK* NW2 136 F1
Collis Primary School *TEDD* TW11 176 G9
Colnbrook CE Primary School *DTCH/LGLY* SL3 150 G7
Colnbrook School *OXHEY* WD19 93 K3
Colnbrook Sports Club *DTCH/LGLY* SL3 151 J7
Colne Bridge Retail Park *WAT* WD17 73 L9
Colne Valley Retail Park *WAT* WD17 73 L9
Colney Heath JMI School *STALE/WH* AL4 39 P8
Coln Industrial Estate *DTCH/LGLY* SL3 151 J6
Coloma Convent Girls School *CROY/NA* CR0 204 C10
Colonial Business Park *WATN* WD24 73 K5
Colonnades Leisure Park *CROY/NA* CR0 223 H3
The Colonnades Shopping Centre *BGVA* SW1W 16 E5
Colours Sports Club *SUT* SM1 221 M2
Columbia Primary School *BETH* E2 7 M9
Colvestone Primary School *HACK* E8 119 N10
Colville Primary School *NTGHL* W11 8 C6
Colyers Lane Medical Centre *ERITH* DA8 164 E7
Colyers Primary School *ERITH* DA8 164 E7
Combe Bank Senior School *RSEV* TN14 245 P9
Comber Grove Primary School *CMBW* SE5 159 K6
Combermere Barracks *WDSR* SL4 148 G9
Comedy Theatre *STJS* SW1Y 11 J8
Comelle House Trading Estate *DEPT* SE8 160 D4
Comfort Hotel *ENC/FH* EN2 79 J6
Comfort Inn *ECT* SW5 157 K3
HYS/HAR UB3 152 F4
Comfort Inn Kensington *ECT* SW5 14 F5
Commonside School *HLWS* CM18 47 J5
Commonswood JMI School *WGCE* AL7 23 L8
Commonwealth Institute *WKENS* W14 14 D3
Community & Adult Education Centre *HORL* RH6 279 P4
Community Arts Centre *GNWCH* SE10 160 G6
Community Care Centre *ENC/FH* EN2 79 L5
Community Centre (Island History Trust) *POP/IOD* E14 161 H3
Community College and School *GNWCH* SE10 161 H6
The Community College *HACK* E8 140 A3
Community Mental Health Centre *GSTN* WD25 55 K10
HHNE HP2 35 N5
Compass Theatre *HGDN/ICK* UB10 112 D8
Complementary Health Centre *LEE/GVPK* SE12 183 K2
Compton Leisure Centre *NTHLT* UB5 133 M5
The Compton School *NFNCH/WDSPK* N12 97 P7
Compton Sports Centre *NFNCH/WDSPK* N12 97 P7
Concord Business Centre *ACT* W3 135 N7
Concorde Business Park *BH/WHM* TN16 244 A1
Conductive Education Centre *MUSWH* N10 118 D1
Conduit House *GNWCH* SE10 161 J6
Coney Hill School *HAYES* BR2 205 L9
Connaught Business Centre *CDALE/KGS* NW9 116 C3
CROY/NA CR0 222 C3
MTCM CR4 202 A5
The Connaught Hotel *MYFR/PKLN* W1K 10 D8
Connaught House School *BAY/PAD* W2 10 A6
Connaught School for Girls *WAN* E11 121 K6
Connections Business Park *RSEV* TN14 247 J6
Conrad Hotel *WBPTN* SW10 157 M7
Consort Clinic *PECK* SE15 160 A9
Consulate General of Monaco *SKENS* SW7 15 L5
Consulate General of the Republic of Guinea Bissau *KENS* W8 15 J3
Consulate of Burkina Faso *BTSEA* SW11 157 M9
Consulate of Chile *CAVSQ/HST* W1G 10 E2
Consulate of Colombia *GTPST* W1W 10 G5
Consulate of Eritrea *IS* N1 6 B7
Consulate of Guinea *MYFR/PKLN* W1K 10 C8
Consulate of Panama *MYFR/PICC* W1J 10 E10
Convent of Jesus & Mary Infant School *CRICK* NW2 136 F1
Convent of Jesus & Mary Language College *WLSDN* NW10 136 C3
Convent of St John the Baptist *WDSR* SL4 148 F8
Convent Preparatory School *GVE* DA12 190 F5
Conway Hall *FSBYW* WC1X 11 N3
Conway Medical Centre *WOOL/PLUM* SE18 162 G4
Conway Primary School *WOOL/PLUM* SE18 163 H3
Coombe Girls School *NWMAL* KT3 200 A2
Coombe Hill Golf Club *KUTN/CMB* KT2 178 A10
Coombe Hill J & I School *NWMAL* KT3 200 A1
Coombe Wood Golf Club *KUTN/CMB* KT2 177 N10
Coopersale Hall School *EPP* CM16 65 L10
Coopersale & Theydon Garnon CE Primary School *EPP* CM16 65 N5
Coopers Company & Coburn School *UPMR* RM14 126 C8
Coopers' Hall *LVPST* EC2M 13 K4
Coopers Lane Primary School *LEE/GVPK* SE12 183 M5
Coopers Technology College *CHST* BR7 206 F1
Copenhagen Primary School *IS* N1 5 M6
Copland Specialist Science College *WBLY* HA9 115 L10
Coppermill Primary School *WALTH* E17 120 C3
Coppetts Wood Hospital *MUSWH* N10 98 A9
Coppetts Wood Primary School *MUSWH* N10 98 B9
Coppice Primary School *CHIG* IG7 103 K6
Copthall School *MLHL* NW7 96 E8
The Copthorne Business Centre *CRAWE* RH10 285 J2
Copthorne CE Junior School *CRAWE* RH10 285 J2
Copthorne Fairway Infant School *CRAWE* RH10 285 J2
Copthorne Golf Club *CRAWE* RH10 285 K2
Copthorne Hotel *CRAWE* RH10 285 H3
SL SL1 149 H1
Copthorne Hotel & Resort Effingham Park *CRAWE* RH10 285 N1
Copthorne Junior School *CRAWE* RH10 285 J2
Copthorne Preparatory School *CRAWE* RH10 285 M2
Copthorne Squash Club *CRAWE* RH10 285 H3
Copthorne Tara Hotel *KENS* W8 14 G3
Corbets Tey School *UPMR* RM14 126 A10
Cordwainers College *HACK* E8 140 B2
Corinium Industrial Estate *AMS* HP6 69 L4
Corinthian Casuals FC *SURB* KT6 199 M10
Corinthian Sports Club *HART* DA3 211 J6
Corner House Hotel *HORL* RH6 280 A5
Corn Exchange *HERT/WAT* SG14 25 L5
Cornfield School *REDH* RH1 276 A5
Coronet Cinema *NTGHL* W11 8 E9
SEVS/STOTM N15 119 J1
Corpus Christi RC Primary School *BRXS/STRHM* SW2 180 G1
Corus Hotel *BAY/PAD* W2 9 L7
BORE WD6 95 K1
Corus Hotel Hyde Park *BAY/PAD* W2 137 N9
Cosmopolitan College *IS* N1 5 N8
Coston Secondary Modern Girls School *GFD/PVL* UB6 134 B4
Coteford Infant School *PIN* HA5 113 H3
Coulsdon CE Primary School *COUL/CHIP* CR5 240 G4
The Coulsdon Eye Clinic *COUL/CHIP* CR5 240 D1
Coulsdon High School *COUL/CHIP* CR5 241 J6
Coulsdon Manor Golf Club *COUL/CHIP* CR5 240 C2
Coulsdon Sixth Form College *COUL/CHIP* CR5 241 H5
Council of Mosques *FITZ* W1T 11 H4
Countess Anne Primary School *HAT* AL10 40 E3
Country Gardens Estate *BFOR* GU20 192 B9
County Mall Shopping Centre *CRAWE* RH10 283 P7
County Oak Retail Park *CRAWW* RH11 283 N3
Courtauld Institute Gallery *TPL/STR* WC2R 11 N7
Courtauld Institute of Art *TPL/STR* WC2R 11 P8
Court Farm Industrial Estate *STWL/WRAY* TW19 174 A2
Courtfield Medical Centre *ECT* SW5 15 H6
Courtland JMI School *MLHL* NW7 96 B3
Courtwood Primary School *CROY/NA* CR0 224 E6
Courtyard by Marriott Hotel *SL* SL1 149 H1
Covent Garden Flower Market *VX/NE* SW8 17 K10
Covent Garden Medical Centre *LSQ/SEVD* WC2H 11 L6
Coward Industrial Estate *CDW/CHF* RM16 168 E4
Cowley Business Park *UX/CGN* UB8 131 M5
Cowley Hill Primary School *BORE* WD6 75 N5
Cowley Mill Industrial Estate *IVER* SL0 131 K4
Cowley St Laurence CE Primary School *UX/CGN* UB8 131 M7
Coworth Flexlands School *CHOB/PIR* GU24 213 L7
CPFC Soccer & Sports Centre *BRXN/ST* SW9 158 G9
CP House Business Centre *BUSH* WD23 73 N5
Crabtree J & I School *HARP* AL5 20 B2
Crafts Council *IS* N1 6 B8
Craggy Island Climbing Centre *GU* GU1 250 B6
Crampton Primary School *WALW* SE17 18 D6
Cranborne Industrial Estate *POTB/CUF* EN6 59 H6
Cranborne Primary School *POTB/CUF* EN6 59 H7
Cranbourne JMI School *HOD* EN11 26 G10
Cranbrook College *IL* IG1 122 D7
Cranford Community College *HEST* TW5 153 J5
Cranford Infant School *HSLWW* TW4 153 H8
Cranford Junior School *HSLWW* TW4 153 J8
Cranford Park Junior School *HYS/HAR* UB3 152 G3
Cranford Park Primary School *HYS/HAR* UB3 152 G1
Cranham Health Centre *UPMR* RM14 126 D5
Cranleigh Gardens Industrial Estate *STHL* UB1 133 N7
Cranmer Primary School *MTCM* CR4 202 A4
Cranmore School *EHSLY* KT24 252 D5
The Craven Clinic *HMSMTH* W6 156 E3
Craven Park Health Centre *WLSDN* NW10 136 A3
Craven Park Medical Centre *WLSDN* NW10 136 A3
Crawford Primary School *CMBW* SE5 159 K7
Crawley College Annexe *CRAWW* RH11 283 M6
Crawley Down Health Centre *CRAWE* RH10 285 P5
Crawley Health Clinic *CRAWE* RH10 283 P7
Crawley Hospital *CRAWW* RH11 283 M7
The Crawley Lawn Tennis Club *CRAWE* RH10 284 C5
Crawley Leisure Centre Athletics Arena *CRAWE* RH10 284 A8
Crawley Museum (Goffs Park House) *CRAWW* RH11 283 L8
Crawley RFC *CRAWW* RH11 283 K3
Crawley Swimming Pool *CRAWE* RH10 284 A8
Crayfield Industrial Park *STMC/STPC* BR5 207 M2
Crayfields Business Park *STMC/STPC* BR5 207 M1
Crayford Commercial Centre *DART* DA1 186 F1
Crayford Industrial Estate *DART* DA1 186 G1
Crayford Leisure Centre & Greyhound Stadium *DART* DA1 186 F2
Crayford Medical Centre *DART* DA1 186 G1
Craylands Primary School *SWCM* DA10 189 J1
Crayside Industrial Estate *DART* DA1 165 H9
Cray Valley Golf Club *STMC/STPC* BR5 207 P1
Creekmouth Industrial Estate *BARK* IG11 143 J6
Creek Road Health Centre *DEPT* SE8 160 F5
Creek Road Industrial Estate *DEPT* SE8 160 G5
Cremer Business Centre *BETH* E2 7 L8
Creswick Primary School *WGCE* AL7 22 G8
Crewe House *MYFR/PICC* W1J 10 E9
Crews Hill Golf Club *ENC/FH* EN2 60 G10
Cricket Green School *MTCM* CR4 201 P3
Cricklefield Stadium *IL* IG1 123 H7
Cricklewood Trading Estate *CRICK* NW2 117 H8
Crispin Industrial Centre *UED* N18 100 B6
Criterion Theatre *MYFR/PICC* W1J 11 H8
Crockenhill Primary School *SWLY* BR8 208 D6
Crockham Hill CE Primary School *EDEN* TN8 262 F9
Crofton Leisure Centre *BROCKY* SE4 182 F2
Crofton School *BROCKY* SE4 182 F2
Croham Hurst Golf Club *SAND/SEL* CR2 223 N3
Cromer Road Primary School *BAR* EN5 77 L7
Cromwell Business Centre *BARK* IG11 143 H5
Cromwell Hospital *ECT* SW5 14 G5
Crook Log Primary School *BXLYHS* DA6 163 N10
Crook Log Sports Centre *WELL* DA16 163 N9
Crosby Hall *CHEL* SW3 15 M10
Crossways Academy *BROCKY* SE4 160 D8
Crouch End Art School *CEND/HSY/T* N8 118 F3
Crouch End Health Centre *CEND/HSY/T* N8 118 F3
Crouch Hill Recreation Centre *CEND/HSY/T* N8 118 F5
Crouch Industrial Estate *LHD/OX* KT22 236 F5
Crowland Primary School *SEVS/STOTM* N15 119 P3
Crowlands Primary School *ROMW/RG* RM7 124 D4
Crown Business Centre *WDR/YW* UB7 132 A10
Crown Business Estate *CSHM* HP5 51 H6
Crown Close Business Centre *BOW* E3 140 F3
Crown Court at the Borough *STHWK* SE1 18 D1
Crowndale Health Centre *CAMTN* NW1 5 H7
Crowne Plaza Hotel *WDR/YW* UB7 152 B3
Crownfield Primary School *ROMW/RG* RM7 104 B10
The Crown Hotel *AMSS* HP7 68 G6
Crown Lane Clinic *STHGT/OAK* N14 98 D2
Crown Lane Primary School *WNWD* SE27 181 K7
Crown Moran Hotel *CRICK* NW2 116 G9
Crown Prosecution Service *STAL* AL1 38 C6
Crown Trading Centre *HYS/HAR* UB3 152 F1
Crown Woods School *ELTH/MOT* SE9 184 F1
Croydon Airport Industrial Estate *CROY/NA* CR0 223 H4
Croydon Bowling Club *SAND/SEL* CR2 223 K2
Croydon Cemetery *CROY/NA* CR0 202 G5
Croydon Clocktower Cinema *CROY/NA* CR0 203 K10
Croydon College *CROY/NA* CR0 203 L10
Croydon Crematorium *THHTH* CR7 202 F5
Croydon Fairfield Halls Cinema *CROY/NA* CR0 203 L10
Croydon FC *SNWD* SE25 204 B5
Croydon High Junior School GDST *SAND/SEL* CR2 224 A7
Croydon Mosque & Islamic Centre *THHTH* CR7 203 H6
Croydon Road Industrial Estate *BECK* BR3 204 B4
Croydon Sports Arena *SNWD* SE25 204 B5
Crusader Industrial Estate *FSBYPK* N4 119 K4
Crusoe House School *IS* N1 6 G9
Crystal Palace FC (Selhurst Park) *SNWD* SE25 203 M4
Crystal Palace Museum *NRWD* SE19 181 N9
Cuaco Sports Ground *BECK* BR3 182 F9
Cubitt Town Primary School *POP/IOD* E14 161 H2
Cuddington Cemetery *WPK* KT4 200 E9
Cuddington CP School *WPK* KT4 200 C10
Cuddington Croft Primary School *BELMT* SM2 220 G5
Cuddington Golf Club *BNSTD* SM7 221 H9
Cudham CE Primary School *BH/WHM* TN16 244 D2
Cuffley School *POTB/CUF* EN6 60 C6
Culloden Primary School *POP/IOD* E14 141 J8
Culvers House Primary School *MTCM* CR4 202 B8
Cumberland Business Park *WLSDN* NW10 135 N5
The Cumberland Hotel *OXSTW* W1C 10 B6
Cumberland Park Industrial Estate *WLSDN* NW10 136 D5
The Cumming Museum *WALW* SE17 18 E6
Cumnor House School *SAND/SEL* CR2 223 J5
Cunningham Hill J & I School *STAL* AL1 38 F8
Curwen Primary School *PLSTW* E13 141 M4
Curzon CE Primary School *AMSS* HP7 68 A8
Curzon Mayfair Cinema *MYFR/PICC* W1J 10 E10
Curzon Soho Cinema *SOHO/SHAV* W1D 11 K7
Custom House *GVE* DA12 190 F2
MON EC3R 13 J8
Cutlers' Hall *STP* EC4M 12 D5
Cutty Sark Clipper Ship *GNWCH* SE10 161 H5
Cygnet Clinic Beckton *EHAM* E6 142 E7
Cygnet Leisure Centre *GVW* DA11 190 B4
Cygnus Business Centre *WLSDN* NW10 116 C10
Cypress Infant School *SNWD* SE25 203 M2
Cypress Junior School *SNWD* SE25 203 M2
Cyprus College of Art *WNWD* SE27 181 J7
Cyril Jackson Primary School *POP/IOD* E14 140 E9
Dacorum Athletics Track *HHNE* HP2 36 A8
Dacorum District Sports Centre *HHW* HP1 35 M8
Dacre Industrial Estate *CHES/WCR* EN8 62 E5
Dagenham Chest Clinic *BCTR* RM8 124 A8
Dagenham Priory Comprehensive School & Performing Arts College *DAGE* RM10 144 C2
Dagenham & Redbridge FC *DAGE* RM10 124 C10
Dagenham Superbowl *DAGE* RM10 144 C4
Dagenham Swimming Pool *DAGE* RM10 124 B7
Daiglen School *BKHH* IG9 101 P2
Daily Telegraph *POP/IOD* E14 160 F2
Dairy Meadow Primary School *NWDGN* UB2 153 N2
D'Albiac House *HTHAIR* TW6 152 B8
Dali Universe *STHWK* SE1 17 N1
Dallington School *FSBYE* EC1V 12 D1
Dalmain Primary School *FSTH* SE23 182 D4
Dame Alice Owens School *POTB/CUF* EN6 59 H9
Dame Tipping CE Primary School *ABR/ST* RM4 104 E4
Damilola Taylor Centre *PECK* SE15 159 N6
Danegrove Primary School *EBAR* EN4 77 P10
Danesfield Manor School *WOT/HER* KT12 197 J9
Danes Hill Pre-Preparatory School *LHD/OX* KT22 218 B9
Danes Hill School *LHD/OX* KT22 218 C10
Danetree School *HOR/WEW* KT19 219 P4
Danson Mansion *BXLYHS* DA6 163 M10
Danson Primary School *WELL* DA16 163 L10
Danson Watersports Centre *BXLYHS* DA6 185 M1
Dapdune Wharf (NT) *GU* GU1 249 P10
Darell Primary School *RCH/KEW* TW9 155 M9
Darenth Primary School *RDART* DA2 188 E9
Darenth Valley Golf Club *RSEV* TN14 229 H8
Darent Industrial Park *ERITH* DA8 165 L4
Darent Valley Hospital *RDART* DA2 188 C4
Darley Dene Infant School *ADL/WDHM* KT15 215 M2
Darrick Wood Primary School *ORP* BR6 226 E1
Darrick Wood School *ORP* BR6 206 E10
Darrick Wood Sports Centre *ORP* BR6 206 F10
Darrick Wood Swimming Pool *ORP* BR6 206 E10
Dartford Adult Education Centre *DART* DA1 187 K3
Dartford County Court *DART* DA1 187 M2
Dartford FC *RDART* DA2 188 A4
Dartford Golf Club *DART* DA1 187 J5
Dartford Grammar School for Boys *DART* DA1 187 K2
Dartford Grammar School for Girls *DART* DA1 187 K3
Dartford Hospital School *HART* DA3 211 M3
Dartford Magistrates Court *DART* DA1 187 L2
Dartford Museum & Library *DART* DA1 187 M3
Dartford Natural Health Centre *DART* DA1 187 M3
Dartford Technology College *DART* DA1 187 K3
Dartford Tunnel *WTHK* RM20 166 C7
Dartford West Health Centre *DART* DA1 187 K2
Darwin Centre *SKENS* SW7 15 L4
Darwin Leisure Centre *BH/WHM* TN16 244 C2
Datapoint Business Centre *BOW* E3 141 J6
Datchet Golf Club *DTCH/LGLY* SL3 149 M6
Datchet St Marys Primary School *DTCH/LGLY* SL3 149 N6
Datchet Sports Club *DTCH/LGLY* SL3 149 N6
Daubeney Primary School *CLPT* E5 120 D9
Davenant Foundation School *LOU* IG10 82 F4
Davenies School *BEAC* HP9 88 D9
The David Beckham Academy *GNWCH* SE10 161 L1
David Game College *KENS* W8 8 E9
David Livingstone Primary School *THHTH* CR7 203 K1
David Lloyd Leisure Centre *NFNCH/WDSPK* N12 97 N8
SKENS SW7 15 H5
David Lloyd Sports Centre *EN* EN1 79 P6
David Lloyd Tennis Centre *SCUP* DA14 185 M8
Davidson Primary School *CROY/NA* CR0 203 N7
Davies Laing & Dick College *BAY/PAD* W2 8 G8
Davies Lane Primary School *WAN* E11 121 L7
Davies's College *STHWK* SE1 18 G1
Dawlish Primary School *LEY* E10 121 H7
Dawnay County Primary School *GT/LBKH* KT23 253 P1
Days Hotel *MLHL* NW7 95 P3
STHWK SE1 18 A4
Days Hotel London South Ruislip *RSLP* HA4 113 K9
Days Inn *PIM* SW1V 17 H7
POTB/CUF EN6 58 F10
Days Lane Primary School *BFN/LL* DA15 185 J2
Dean College of London *HOLWY* N7 118 G10
Deanesfield Primary School *RSLP* HA4 113 L9
Deansbrook Primary School *MLHL* NW7 95 P7
Deansfield Primary School *ELTH/MOT* SE9 162 D9
Deans Trading Estate *RAIN* RM13 145 L6
Debden Park High School *LOU* IG10 82 G7
Debden Sports Club *LOU* IG10 82 F9
De Bohun Primary School *STHGT/OAK* N14 78 C9
Dedworth Clinic *WDSR* SL4 148 D7
Dedworth County Middle School *WDSR* SL4 148 D7
Dedworth Green First School *WDSR* SL4 148 D8
De Havilland Aircraft Heritage Centre & Mosquito Aircraft Museum *LCOL/BKTW* AL2 57 N5
De Havilland Primary School *HAT* AL10 40 D6
Delrow School *GSTN* WD25 74 B5
Delta Wharf *GNWCH* SE10 161 J1
Denbies Wine Estate *RDKG* RH5 254 G8
Deneholm Primary School *CDW/CHF* RM16 167 P1
Dene House Hospital *WDSR* SL4 149 H9
Denham Aerodrome *DEN/HRF* UB9 111 H3
Denham Country Park *DEN/HRF* UB9 111 L7
Denham Golf Club *DEN/HRF* UB9 110 G4
Denham Village Infant School *DEN/HRF* UB9 111 J7
Denmead School *HPTN* TW12 175 P10
Denvale Trade Centre *STMC/STPC* BR5 207 L5
Denver Industrial Estate *RAIN* RM13 144 G7
Department for Environment, Food and Rural Affairs *CHCR* WC2N 11 L9
Department for Transport *WEST* SW1P 17 K5
Department of Art & Design (London Metropolitan University) *WCHPL* E1 13 M5
Department of Economics (London Metropolitan University) *TWRH* EC3N 13 L6
Department of Education *STJSPK* SW1H 17 K2
Department of Health *WHALL* SW1A 17 L1
Department of Sociology & Anthropology (Goldsmiths University of London) *NWCR* SE14 160 D7
Department of Trade & Industry *STJSPK* SW1H 17 K3
Deptford Business Centre *NWCR* SE14 160 C4
Deptford Green School *NWCR* SE14 160 E6
Deptford Park Business Centre *DEPT* SE8 160 D4
Deptford Park Primary School *DEPT* SE8 160 D4
Deptford Trading Estate *DEPT* SE8 160 D4
De Rougemont Manor Hotel *RBRW/HUT* CM13 106 G10
Dersingham Infant School *MNPK* E12 122 C10
Derwentwater Primary School *ACT* W3 135 P10
Design Museum *STHWK* SE1 13 M10
De Stafford College *CTHM* CR3 241 N7
Deutsche Schule *RCHPK/HAM* TW10 177 J4
Devonshire Hospital *MHST* W1U 10 D3
Devonshire House Preparatory School *HAMP* NW3 117 N10
Devonshire House School *HAMP* NW3 117 M10
Devonshire Primary School *BELMT* SM2 221 M4
Dewhurst St Mary JMI School *CHES/WCR* EN8 62 A5
Diamond College *SOHO/SHAV* W1D 11 K5
Diana Fountain *E/WMO/HCT* KT8 198 E2
Diana Princess of Wales Fountain *BAY/PAD* W2 9 M10
Diane Matthews Clinic *ROMW/RG* RM7 124 E2
Dilkes Primary School *SOCK/AV* RM15 146 E8
Dilloway Industrial Estate *NWDGN* UB2 153 M1
Discovery Business Park *BERM/RHTH* SE16 19 P4
Divine Saviour RC Primary School *ABLGY* WD5 54 E8
Docklands Medical Centre *POP/IOD* E14 160 F3
Docklands Sailing Centre *POP/IOD* E14 160 F2
Docklands Sailing & Watersports Centre *BERM/RHTH* SE16 160 E2
Dockley Road Industrial Estate *BERM/RHTH* SE16 19 N4
Dockmaster's House *POP/IOD* E14 140 F9
Dockwell's Industrial Estate *EBED/NFELT* TW14 175 J1
Dockyard Industrial Estate *WOOL/PLUM* SE18 162 B2
Doddinghurst Infant School *BRWN* CM15 86 G3
Doddinghurst Junior School *BRWN* CM15 86 G3
Dog Kennel Hill Primary School *EDUL* SE22 159 M9
Dokal Industrial Estate *NWDGN* UB2 153 M1
Dollis Hill Synagogue & Torah Temimah Primary School *CRICK* NW2 116 E9
Dollis Infant School *MLHL* NW7 96 F8
Dollis Junior School *MLHL* NW7 96 F8
The Dolphin Leisure Centre *ROM* RM1 124 G2
The Dolphin School *BTSEA* SW11 179 P1
The Dominie *BTSEA* SW11 158 A7
Dominion Business Park *ED* N9 100 C3
Dominion Theatre *RSQ* WC1B 11 K5
Dominoes Health Centre *GRAYS* RM17 167 M5
Donhead (Wimbledon College Preparatory School) *WIM/MER* SW19 178 G10
Donmar Warehouse Theatre *LSQ/SEVD* WC2H 11 L6
Donnington Primary School *WLSDN* NW10 136 E2
Donyngs Recreation Centre *REDH* RH1 257 P9
Doods Brow School *REDH* RH1 258 G9
The Dorchester Hotel *MYFR/PKLN* W1K 10 D9
Dorchester Primary School *WPK* KT4 200 F8
The Dorking Business Park *DORK* RH4 272 F1
Dorking Cemetery *DORK* RH4 255 H10
Dorking FC (Meadowbank) *DORK* RH4 272 F1
Dorking General Hospital *DORK* RH4 272 F3
Dorking Golf Club *RDKG* RH5 273 H3
Dorking Halls *DORK* RH4 273 H1
Dorking Lawn Tennis & Squash Club *DORK* RH4 272 F4
Dorking Museum *DORK* RH4 272 F2
Dorking RFC *BRKHM/BTCW* RH3 255 N10
Dorking Swimming & Sports Centre *DORK* RH4 273 H1
Dorma Trading Park *LEY* E10 120 C6
Dormers Wells High School *STHL* UB1 133 P8
Dormers Wells Leisure Centre *STHL* UB1 134 A8
Dormers Wells Medical Centre *STHL* UB1 133 P8
Dormers Wells Primary School *STHL* UB1 134 A9
Dorney Court *WDSR* SL4 148 A2
Dorothy Barley Primary School *BCTR* RM8 123 L10
Dorset Road Infant School *ELTH/MOT* SE9 184 B5
Dorset Square Hotel *CAMTN* NW1 10 A3
Dorton College of Further Education *BGR/WK* TN15 247 M8
Dorton House School *BGR/WK* TN15 247 N8
The Douay Martyrs Roman Catholic School *HGDN/ICK* UB10 112 C9
Douglas Bader Foundation *PUT/ROE* SW15 178 D2
Dover Road Primary School *GVW* DA11 190 B4
Dovers Corner Industrial Estate *RAIN* RM13 144 G5
Dovers Green School *REIG* RH2 275 M4
Downderry Primary School *BMLY* BR1 183 K7
Downe Manor Primary School *NTHLT* UB5 133 J5
Downe Primary School *ORP* BR6 226 D7

Downfield Primary School CHES/WCR EN8 62 D7
Down Hall Country House Hotel RBSF CM22 31 H4
Downham Health Centre BMLY BR1 183 K7
Downhills Primary School TOTM N17 119 L2
Down House ORP BR6 226 D8
Downsell Primary School SRTFD E15 121 J9
Downsend School - Ashtead Lodge ASHTD KT21 237 K4
Downsend School Epsom Lodge EW KT17 220 C9
Downsend School Leatherhead Lodge LHD/OX KT22 237 H6
Downshall Primary School GNTH/NBYPK IG2 123 H5
The Downs Primary School HLW CM20 46 G1
Downsview Primary School NRWD SE19 181 K10
SWLY BR8 209 H3
Downsview School CLPT E5 120 A9
Downs Way County Primary School OXTED RH8 261 K3
Drapers Hall LOTH EC2R 13 H5
Drapers Sports Ground SRTFD E15 121 H9
The Draycott Hotel CHEL SW3 16 B5
Drayton Green Primary School WEA W13 134 F9
Drayton House School GU GU1 268 C1
Drayton Manor High School HNWL W7 134 E9
Drayton Park Primary School HBRY N5 119 H10
DRCA Business Centre BTSEA SW11 158 B7
Dr Challoners Grammar School AMS HP6 69 H4
Dr Challoners High School AMSS HP7 69 N6
Drew Primary School CAN/RD E16 142 B10
Drift Golf Club EHSLY KT24 234 F9
Drill Hall GWRST WC1E 11 J3
Driving School & Road Safety Centre KTN/HRWW/WS HA3 114 F1
Driving Test Centre CRAWW RH11 283 N8
The Drizen School EDGW HA8 95 M8
Dr Johnson's House FLST/FETLN EC4A 12 B5
Dropmore Infant School SL SL1 108 B8
Dr Tripletts CE J & I School HYS/HAR UB3 132 G8
Drury Way Industrial Estate WLSDN NW10 116 A9
Duchess Theatre COVGDN WC2E 11 N7
Ducks Infant School DUL SE21 181 N6
Duff Miller College SKENS SW7 15 K5
Duke of York Column STJS SW1Y 11 K10
Duke of York Theatre CHCR WC2N 11 L8
Dulverton Primary School ELTH/MOT SE9 184 G5
Dulwich College DUL SE21 181 M4
Dulwich College Preparatory School DUL SE21 181 M6
Dulwich College Track DUL SE21 181 M5
Dulwich Hamlet FC EDUL SE22 159 M10
Dulwich Hamlet Junior School HNHL SE24 181 L2
Dulwich Hospital EDUL SE22 159 M10
Dulwich Leisure Centre EDUL SE22 159 P10
Dulwich Medical Centre EDUL SE22 181 P1
Dulwich Picture Gallery DUL SE21 181 L3
Dulwich & Sydenham Hill Golf Club DUL SE21 181 P5
Dulwich Village CE Infant School DUL SE21 181 M2
Dunbar Wharf POP/IOD E14 140 E9
Duncombe Primary School ARCH N19 118 F6
Duncombe School HERT/WAT SG14 25 K4
Dundee Wharf POP/IOD E14 140 E9
Dundonald Primary School WIM/MER SW19 179 J10
Dunningford Primary School HCH RM12 124 G10
Dunottar School REIG RH2 275 N1
Dunraven School & Upper School STRHM/NOR SW16 180 G6
Dunton Green Primary School SEV TN13 246 F6
Duppas Junior School CROY/NA CR0 223 J2
Durand Primary School BRXN/ST SW9 158 G7
Durands Wharf BERM/RHTH SE16 160 E1
Durants School PEND EN3 80 B5
Durdans Park Primary School STHL UB1 133 N7
Durston House School EA W5 135 J8
Dycourts School HARH RM3 105 P5
Dyrham Park Country Club BAR EN5 76 D4
Dysart School KUTN/CMB KT2 177 J7
SURB KT6 199 K7
Dyslexia Teaching Centre ECT SW5 157 L4
Eaglesfield School WOOL/PLUM SE18 162 D7
Eagle Trading Estate MTCM CR4 202 A6
Ealdham Primary School ELTH/MOT SE9 161 P10
Ealing Abbey EA W5 135 H8
Ealing Abbey Scriptorium WEA W13 135 H8
The Ealing Broadway Centre EA W5 135 J9
Ealing Central Sports Ground GFD/PVL UB6 134 F4
Ealing College Upper School WEA W13 134 F8
Ealing CC EA W5 135 K8
Ealing Film Studios EA W5 135 H10
Ealing Golf Club GFD/PVL UB6 134 G5
Ealing Hammersmith & West London College WKENS W14 156 G3
Ealing Hospital NWDGN UB2 154 C1
Ealing, Hammersmith & West London College ACT W3 135 N10
Ealing Independent College EA W5 135 H9
Ealing Northern Sports Centre GFD/PVL UB6 114 C9
Ealing Park Health Centre EA W5 155 J3
Ealing Road Trading Estate BTFD TW8 155 J4
Ealing Sports Centre EA W5 135 K9
Ealing Tutorial College EA W5 135 J9
Ealing & West London College EA W5 135 H10
Eardley Primary School STRHM/NOR SW16 180 D9
Earlham J & I School WDGN N22 99 H8
Earlham Primary School FSTGT E7 121 L10
Earl's Court Exhibition Centre ECT SW5 14 E8
Earlsfield Primary School WAND/EARL SW18 179 M5
Earlsmead First & Middle School RYLN/HDSTN HA2 113 N9
Earlsmead Primary School SEVS/STOTM N15 119 N2
Earlswood Infant School REDH RH1 276 B1
Earth Galleries SKENS SW7 15 M4
East Acton Primary School ACT W3 136 B9
East Barking Centre BCTR RM8 123 M10
East Barnet Health Centre EBAR EN4 77 N9
East Barnet School EBAR EN4 77 N7
East Beckton District Centre EHAM E6 142 C7
East Berkshire College (Langley Campus) DTCH/LGLY SL3 150 C2
Eastbrook Comprehensive School DAGE RM10 124 D9
Eastbrook End Cemetery LOU IG10 82 A8
ROMW/RG RM7 124 F8
Eastbrookend Country Park ROMW/RG RM7 124 E9
Eastbrook Primary School HHNE HP2 36 A1
Eastbury Comprehensive School BARK IG11 143 J3
Eastbury Farm JMI School NTHWD HA6 92 G5
Eastbury Infant School BARK IG11 143 J2
Eastcote CC PIN HA5 113 J3
Eastcote Health Centre PIN HA5 113 K5
Eastcote Industrial Estate RSLP HA4 113 K5
Eastcote Lane Cemetery RYLN/HDSTN HA2 114 A8
Eastcote Primary School WELL DA16 162 G9
Eastcourt Independent School GDMY/SEVK IG3 123 K6
East End Computing & Business College WCHPL E1 140 A8
Eastern Business Park HTHAIR TW6 152 G8
Eastfield Primary School PEND EN3 80 C4
East Finchley Cemetery EFNCH N2 117 L1
East Finchley Medical Centre EFNCH N2 117 P2
East Finchley School of English EFNCH N2 117 P1
Eastgate Business Park LEY E10 120 D6
East Greenwich Christ Church CE Primary School GNWCH SE10 161 K3
East Ham Industrial Estate EHAM E6 142 A6
East Ham Jewish Cemetery EHAM E6 142 B5
East Ham Leisure Centre EHAM E6 142 C3
East Ham Memorial Hospital EHAM E6 142 A2
East Ham Nature Reserve EHAM E6 142 C6
East Lane Business Park WBLY HA9 115 J8
Eastlea Community Centre CAN/RD E16 141 L6
Eastlea Community School CAN/RD E16 141 K6
East London Business College WAN E11 121 K6
East London Cemetery PLSTW E13 141 L5
East London Crematorium SRTFD E15 141 L5
East London RFC EHAM E6 142 C7
East London RUFC SRTFD E15 141 L4
Eastman Dental Hospital FSBYW WC1X 11 N1
East Molesey CC E/WMO/HCT KT8 198 B3
East Sheen Cemetery RCHPK/HAM TW10 177 M1
East Sheen Primary School MORT/ESHN SW14 156 B10
East Surrey College REDH RH1 258 B6
East Surrey Hospital REDH RH1 276 C4
East Surrey Museum CTHM CR3 241 N10
East Thamesmead Business Park ERITHM DA18 164 A1
East Tilbury J & I Schools TIL RM18 169 M4
East Wickham Primary School WELL DA16 163 J7
Eastwick Infant School GT/LBKH KT23 236 A10
Eastwick Junior School GT/LBKH KT23 236 A10
Eaton Manor RFC WAN E11 121 P3
Eaton Square Preparatory School BGVA SW1W 16 E5
Eaton Square School PIM SW1V 16 G6
Ebbisham County Infant School EPSOM KT18 219 P10
Ebbisham Sports Club HOR/WEW KT19 219 P8
Ebbsfleet Industrial Estate GVW DA11 189 M1
Ecclesbourne Primary School THHTH CR7 203 K5
Echelford Primary School ASHF TW15 174 C8
Eckerd College GWRST WC1E 11 J3
Eclipse Estate HOR/WEW KT19 219 P9
Ecole de Mime Corporel Dramatique & Theatre de l'Ange Fou ARCH N19 118 F6
Eden College STHWK SE1 18 D3
Edenham High School CROY/NA CR0 204 D7
Eden High School FUL/PGN SW6 157 J7
Eden Medical Centre WKENS W14 14 D6
Edenvale Child Health Clinic MTCM CR4 180 B10
Eden Walk Shopping Centre KUT/HW KT1 199 K2
Edes Business Park WLGTN SM6 202 B9
Edgebury Primary School CHST BR7 184 F7
Edge Business Centre CRICK NW2 116 E7
Edge Grove GSTN WD25 74 B3
Edgwarebury Cemetery EDGW HA8 95 M3
Edgware Clinic EDGW HA8 95 M7
Edgware College KIL/WHAMP NW6 3 J2
Edgware Community Hospital EDGW HA8 95 N8
Edgware FC & Wealdstone FC EDGW HA8 95 M8
Edgware Infant School EDGW HA8 95 M7
Edgware Junior School EDGW HA8 95 N7
Edinburgh Primary School WALTH E17 120 E3
Edith Neville Primary School CAMTN NW1 5 J8
Edmonton Cemetery WCHMH N21 99 L3
Edmonton County Court UED N18 99 P6
Edmonton Green Shopping Centre ED N9 100 A3
Edmonton Leisure Centre ED N9 99 P4
Edmonton Upper School EN EN1 99 N1
Edmund Waller Primary School NWCR SE14 160 C8
Edward Betham CE Primary School GFD/PVL UB6 134 C5
Edward Pauling School FELT TW13 174 F5
Edward Wilson Primary School BAY/PAD W2 8 G3
Edwin Lambert School EMPK RM11 125 H4
Effingham Community Sports Centre EHSLY KT24 253 M3
Effingham CC EHSLY KT24 235 J10
Effingham Golf Club EHSLY KT24 253 L4
Effingham Park Golf Club CRAWE RH10 285 N1
Effra Road Retail Park BRXS/STRHM SW2 181 H1
Effra Site (St George Wharf) under re-development VX/NE SW8 17 L8
The Egerton House Hotel CHEL SW3 15 P4
Egerton Rothesay Preparatory School BERK HP4 33 N5
Egerton Rothesay School BERK HP4 33 L5
Egham Business Village EGH TW20 194 F2
Egham CC EGH TW20 172 E9
Egham Sports Centre EGH TW20 172 E9
Egham Town FC EGH TW20 172 F9
Eglinton Junior School WOOL/PLUM SE18 162 D5
Eglinton Primary School WOOL/PLUM SE18 162 D6
Elangeni Junior School AMS HP6 69 K2
Elbourne Trading Estate BELV DA17 164 C2
Eldenwall Industrial Estate BCTR RM8 123 P6
Eldon JMI School ED N9 100 A2
Eleanor Estate CHES/WCR EN8 62 E10
Eleanor Palmer Primary School KTTN NW5 118 D9
Eleanor Smith Special School PLSTW E13 141 M4
Electrical Trades Union College ESH/CLAY KT10 217 P1
Electric Cinema NTGHL W11 8 C6
The Electric Theatre GU GU1 267 P1
Electron Trade Centre STMC/STPC BR5 207 L4
Elephant & Castle Leisure Centre LBTH SE11 18 D5
Elephant & Castle Shopping Centre STHWK SE1 18 D4
Elers Clinic HYS/HAR UB3 152 E3
Elfrida Primary School CAT SE6 182 G7
Eliot Bank Primary School FSTH SE23 182 A5
Elizabeth Garrett Anderson Hospital CAMTN NW1 5 K10
Elizabeth Selby Infant School BETH E2 7 P9
Elizabeth Trading Estate NWCR SE14 160 C5
Ellen Wilkinson Primary School CAN/RD E16 142 A7
Ellen Wilkinson School for Girls ACT W3 135 L8
Ellerslie Square Industrial Estate BRXS/STRHM SW2 158 F10
Ellingham Primary School CHSGTN KT9 219 J4
Elliott School PUT/ROE SW15 178 F2
Elliswick Lawn Tennis Club HARP AL5 20 A1
Elmbridge Leisure Centre WOT/HER KT12 197 J5
Elmbridge Museum WEY KT13 216 B1
Elm Court School WNWD SE27 181 J5
Elmgrove First & Middle School KTN/HRWW/WS HA3 114 F2
Elmhurst Primary School FSTGT E7 141 N2
Elmhurst School SAND/SEL CR2 223 L2
Elm Lea Trading Estate TOTM N17 99 P8
The Elms Health Centre POTB/CUF EN6 59 M7
Elms Industrial Estate HARH RM3 106 A8
The Elmsleigh Centre Shopping Precinct STA TW18 173 J7
Elmtree Infant School CSHM HP5 50 G6
Elmwood Junior School CROY/NA CR0 203 J7
Elm Wood Primary School DUL SE21 181 L6
Elsdale Street Health Centre HOM E9 140 B2
Elsley Primary School WBLY HA9 135 L1
Elsley School BTSEA SW11 158 B9
Elstree Aerodrome BORE WD6 74 E7
Elstree Golf & Country Club BORE WD6 75 J7
Elstree Studios BORE WD6 75 M7
Elstree Way Clinic BORE WD6 75 N6
Eltham Bus Station ELTH/MOT SE9 184 C1
Eltham CE Primary School ELTH/MOT SE9 184 C1
Eltham College Junior School ELTH/MOT SE9 184 A4
Eltham College Senior School ELTH/MOT SE9 184 A5
Eltham Crematorium ELTH/MOT SE9 162 G10
Eltham Green School ELTH/MOT SE9 184 A2
Eltham Health Clinic ELTH/MOT SE9 184 B1
Eltham Health & Fitness Centre ELTH/MOT SE9 184 D2
Eltham Hill Technology College ELTH/MOT SE9 184 B2
Eltham Palace ELTH/MOT SE9 184 B3
Eltham Pools ELTH/MOT SE9 184 B1
Eltham Warren Golf Club ELTH/MOT SE9 184 E1
Elthorne Park High School HNWL W7 154 E2
Elthorne Sports Centre HNWL W7 154 E2
Elystan Business Centre YEAD UB4 133 K9
Emanuel School BTSEA SW11 179 N1
Embankment Pier CHCR WC2N 11 N9
Embassy of Afghanistan SKENS SW7 15 L2
Embassy of Albania BGVA SW1W 16 F4
Embassy of Algeria NTGHL W11 8 B10
Embassy of Angola MYFR/PKLN W1K 10 C8
Embassy of Argentina MYFR/PKLN W1K 10 E7
Embassy of Armenia KENS W8 14 G3
Embassy of Austria KTBR SW1X 16 C3
Embassy of Bahrain SKENS SW7 15 J4
Embassy of Belarus KENS W8 15 H2
Embassy of Belgium KTBR SW1X 16 D4
Embassy of Bolivia BGVA SW1W 16 D4
Embassy of Bosnia-Herzegovina CAVSQ/HST W1G 10 F5
Embassy of Brazil MYFR/PKLN W1K 10 C7
Embassy of Bulgaria SKENS SW7 15 K3
Embassy of Cameroon NTGHL W11 8 B10
Embassy of China CAVSQ/HST W1G 10 E3
Embassy of Costa Rica BAY/PAD W2 9 K7
Embassy of Cote d'Ivoire KTBR SW1X 16 D3
Embassy of Croatia GTPST W1W 10 F2
Embassy of Cuba LSQ/SEVD WC2H 11 L5
Embassy of Democratic Republic of the Congo KTBR SW1X 16 B4
Embassy of Denmark KTBR SW1X 16 A3
Embassy of Dominican Republic BAY/PAD W2 9 H6
Embassy of Ecuador KTBR SW1X 16 A3
Embassy of Egypt MYFR/PICC W1J 10 E9
Embassy of Estonia SKENS SW7 15 K2
Embassy of Ethiopia SKENS SW7 15 M2
Embassy of Finland KTBR SW1X 16 C3
Embassy of France KTBR SW1X 16 B1
Embassy of Gabon SKENS SW7 15 K4
Embassy of Georgia KENS W8 14 G2
Embassy of Germany KTBR SW1X 16 C3
Embassy of Ghana HGT N6 118 C6
Embassy of Greece NTGHL W11 8 C10
Embassy of Guatemala WBPTN SW10 15 J9
Embassy of Honduras MBLAR W1H 10 B3
Embassy of Hungary KTBR SW1X 16 D4
Embassy of Iceland KTBR SW1X 16 C5
Embassy of Indonesia MYFR/PKLN W1K 10 D8
Embassy of Iran SKENS SW7 15 M2
Embassy of Iraq SKENS SW7 15 K3
Embassy of Ireland KTBR SW1X 16 E2
Embassy of Israel KENS W8 15 H1
Embassy of Italy MYFR/PKLN W1K 10 D7
Embassy of Japan MYFR/PICC W1J 10 F10
Embassy of Jordan KENS W8 14 E2
Embassy of Korea WESTW SW1E 17 H3
Embassy of Krygyzstan MBLAR W1H 10 A4
Embassy of Kuwait KTBR SW1X 16 B1
Embassy of Latvia CAMTN NW1 10 C2
Embassy of Lebanon KENS W8 8 G9
Embassy of Liberia BAY/PAD W2 8 F7
Embassy of Lithuania MBLAR W1H 10 A4
Embassy of Luxembourg KTBR SW1X 16 C2
Embassy of Mexico MYFR/PICC W1J 10 E10
Embassy of Mongolia KENS W8 15 H2
Embassy of Morocco SKENS SW7 15 J5
Embassy of Mozambique FITZ W1T 10 G2
Embassy of Myanmar MYFR/PICC W1J 10 E9
Embassy of Nepal KENS W8 8 G9
Embassy of Netherlands SKENS SW7 15 K2
Embassy of Norway KTBR SW1X 16 D3
Embassy of Paraguay SKENS SW7 15 H4
SKENS SW7 157 L2
Embassy of Peru KTBR SW1X 16 B3
Embassy of Philippines KENS W8 8 G10
Embassy of Poland CAVSQ/HST W1G 10 E3
Embassy of Portugal KTBR SW1X 16 C2
Embassy of Qatar MYFR/PKLN W1K 10 D9
Embassy of Romania KENS W8 14 G1
Embassy of Russian Federation KENS W8 8 G10
Embassy of Saudi Arabia MYFR/PICC W1J 10 E9
Embassy of Senegal CRICK NW2 136 F2
Embassy of Slovak Republic KENS W8 8 G9
Embassy of Slovenia MHST W1U 10 E5
Embassy of Spain KTBR SW1X 16 D3
Embassy of Sudan WHALL SW1A 10 G10
Embassy of Sweden MBLAR W1H 10 A4
Embassy of Switzerland MBLAR W1H 10 A4
Embassy of Syria KTBR SW1X 16 C2
Embassy of Thailand SKENS SW7 15 K4
Embassy of the Holy See WIM/MER SW19 178 F6
Embassy of the Republic of Gabon SKENS SW7 157 M2
Embassy of Tunisia SKENS SW7 15 M2
Embassy of Turkey KTBR SW1X 16 D2
Embassy of Turkmenistan FITZ W1T 11 H4
Embassy of Ukraine NTGHL W11 8 B10
Embassy of United Arab Emirates BAY/PAD W2 15 M1
Embassy of Uruguay SKENS SW7 15 P3
Embassy of USA MYFR/PKLN W1K 10 C7
Embassy of Uzbekistan NTGHL W11 8 C10
Embassy of Venezuela SKENS SW7 15 M4
Embassy of Vietnam KENS W8 15 H3
Embassy of Yemen SKENS SW7 15 L5
Emberhurst School ESH/CLAY KT10 198 C7
Ember Sports Club ESH/CLAY KT10 198 B8
Embroidery World Business Centre WFD IG8 102 A10
EMD Walthamstow Cinema WALTH E17 120 F2
Emerson Park School EMPK RM11 126 A5
Emery Theatre POP/IOD E14 140 G8
Emmanuel CE Primary School KIL/WHAMP NW6 117 K10
Emmetts Garden (NT) RSEV TN14 263 N6
Empire Cinema LSQ/SEVD WC2H 11 K7
The Endeavour School BRWN CM15 107 L3
Endsleigh Industrial Estate NWDGN UB2 153 M3
Enfield Business Centre PEND EN3 80 B6
Enfield Chace Lower School ENC/FH EN2 79 M4
Enfield College PEND EN3 80 B7
Enfield County School ENC/FH EN2 79 L7
Enfield Crematorium EN EN1 80 A3
Enfield CC EN EN1 79 M8
Enfield FC ED N9 100 B3
Enfield Golf Club ENC/FH EN2 79 J8
Enfield Grammar School (Upper) ENC/FH EN2 79 L7
Engayne Primary School UPMR RM14 126 D4
Englefield Green Infant School EGH TW20 171 P8
English Martyrs RC Primary School WALW SE17 18 G6
WCHPL E1 13 M6
English National Ballet School WBPTN SW10 157 M6
Ensham Secondary School TOOT SW17 180 A8
Enterprise Business Park POP/IOD E14 160 G1
Enterprise Industrial Estate BERM/RHTH SE16 160 B4
Epping CE Primary School EPP CM16 46 D10
Epping County Infant School EPP CM16 65 H5
Epping Forest College LOU IG10 82 E8
Epping Forest Conservation Centre LOU IG10 81 P4
The Epping Golf Course EPP CM16 65 L9
Epping House School HERT/BAY SG13 42 D7
Epping Junior School EPP CM16 65 J6
Epping Ongar Railway CHONG CM5 67 M3
EPP CM16 65 L6
EPP CM16 66 E3
Epping Sports Centre EPP CM16 65 J7
Epsom Bowls EPSOM KT18 220 B10
Epsom Business Park EW KT17 220 B7
Epsom Cemetery EPSOM KT18 238 B2
Epsom College EW KT17 220 D10
Epsom County & Magistrates Court EPSOM KT18 220 A9
Epsom Downs Racecourse EPSOM KT18 238 C3
Epsom & Ewell High School HOR/WEW KT19 219 P3
Epsom General Hospital EPSOM KT18 237 P1
Epsom Golf Club EW KT17 238 D1
Epsom Health Clinic EPSOM KT18 220 B9
Epsom Primary School HOR/WEW KT19 220 A7
Epsom Sports Club EPSOM KT18 238 A1
Equestrian Centre NTHWD HA6 92 C8
Eric Liddell Sports Centre ELTH/MOT SE9 184 A5
Eridge House Preparatory School FUL/PGN SW6 157 J8
Erith & District Hospital ERITH DA8 164 E5
Erith Health Centre ERITH DA8 164 F5
Erith Library & Museum ERITH DA8 164 F4
Erith Playhouse ERITH DA8 164 G4
Erith School ERITH DA8 164 D6
Erith School Community Sports Centre ERITH DA8 164 D6
Erith Small Business Centre ERITH DA8 164 G5
Erith Sports Centre ERITH DA8 164 F5
Erith Stadium ERITH DA8 164 F5
Ernest Bevin College TOOT SW17 179 P6
Eros MYFR/PICC W1J 11 J8
Esher CE High School ESH/CLAY KT10 197 P10
Esher Church Primary School ESH/CLAY KT10 218 B3
Esher College THDIT KT7 198 D7
Esher RFC WOT/HER KT12 197 M9
Essendene Lodge School CTHM CR3 241 N8
Essendine Primary School KIL/WHAMP NW6 2 F10
Essendon Primary School BRKMPK AL9 42 A3
The Essex Nuffield Hospital BRWN CM15 107 K2
Essex Primary School MNPK E12 142 B1
Ethelburga GM School BTSEA SW11 157 P7
Ethel Davis School CHDH RM6 123 L3
The Ethorpe Hotel CFSP/GDCR SL9 110 B3
Eton College WDSR SL4 149 J4
Eton End PNEU School DTCH/LGLY SL3 149 M5
Eton Porny CE First School WDSR SL4 149 J5
Eton Wick CE First School WDSR SL4 148 F4
Eton Wick FC WDSR SL4 148 E4
Euro Business Centre SRTFD E15 141 L3
Eurolink Business Centre BRXS/STRHM SW2 159 H10
Europa Trading Estate ERITH DA8 164 E4
WTHK RM20 167 J4
European Business Centre CDALE/KGS NW9 116 A1
European Business School London CAMTN NW1 10 B1
European College of Business Management SDTCH EC2A 13 J1
European Language School WDSR SL4 148 G8
European School of Economics KTBR SW1X 16 D2
European Vocational College HDTCH EC3A 13 K6
Euro Way School CEND/HSY/T N8 119 H1
Euro Way School London FSBYPK N4 119 J5
Euston Centre University of Westminster CAMTN NW1 10 G1
Euston Tower CAMTN NW1 10 G1
Evans Business Centre CRICK NW2 116 D8
Eveline Lowe Primary School STHWK SE1 19 N8
Evendine College SOHO/SHAV W1D 11 J5
Everest Sports Club CHES/WCR EN8 62 A5
Eversley College SBW CM21 29 N1
Eversley Medical Centre CROY/NA CR0 203 H6
Eversley Primary School WCHMH N21 78 F9
Everyman Cinema HAMP NW3 117 M9
Evolution House RCH/KEW TW9 155 K8

Ewell Athletics Track
HOR/WEW KT19 220 A3
Ewell Castle Junior School
EW KT17 220 C5
Ewell Castle School
EW KT17 220 D5
Ewell Grove Infant School
EW KT17 220 C5
EW Fact/Emile Woolf Colleges
HOLWY N7 5 M1
ExCeL Exhibition Centre
CAN/RD E16 141 N9
Exchange Square
SDTCH EC2A 13 J3
The Exchange
IL IG1 122 E7
Executive Park Industrial Estate
STAL AL1 38 C6
Exhibition Halls
BARB EC2Y 12 F3
WBLY HA9 115 M9
Eynsford Castle
EYN DA4 209 M9
Eynsford CC
EYN DA4 209 M9
Faculty of Engineering and Science (University of Westminster)
FITZ W1T 11 H3
Fairacres Industrial Estate
WDSR SL4 148 B8
Fairbrook Medical Centre
BORE WD6 75 N6
Faircharm Trading Estate
DEPT SE8 160 C6
IS N1 6 E7
Fairchildes Primary School
CROY/NA CR0 225 K8
The Faircross Complementary Medical Centre
BARK IG11 143 H1
Fairfield Clinic
BKHH IG9 101 N2
Fair Field Junior School
RAD WD7 74 D2
Fairfield Medical Centre
GT/LBKH KT23 254 A2
Fairfield Pool & Leisure Centre
DART DA1 187 M3
Fairfields Primary School
CHESW EN7 61 P3
Fairfield Trade Park
KUT/HW KT1 199 L3
Fairholme Primary School
EBED/NFELT TW14 174 E4
Fairlawn Primary School
FSTH SE23 182 B3
Fairley House School
PIM SW1V 17 J6
Fairlop Primary School
BARK/HLT IG6 102 F9
Fairoaks Airport
CHOB/PIR GU24 214 C7
Fairview Industrial Centre
RAIN RM13 144 E8
Fairview Industrial Estate
AMS HP6 69 L4
HYS/HAR UB3 152 G1
OXTED RH8 261 M9
Fairview Medical Centre
STRHM/NOR SW16 202 F1
Fairway Primary School
MLHL NW7 96 A3
Fairways Business Park
LEY E10 120 D7
Falconbrook Primary School
BTSEA SW11 157 N8
Falcon Business Centre
BTSEA SW11 157 P10
Falconer Special School
BUSH WD23 73 N9
Falcon Park Industrial Estate
WLSDN NW10 116 B10
The Falcon School for Girls
EA W5 135 L10
Falkner House School
SKENS SW7 15 K7
Family Records Centre
FSBYW WC1X 6 A10
Fanmakers' Hall
LVPST EC2M 13 J4
Fan Museum
GNWCH SE10 161 H6
Faraday Building
BLKFR EC4V 12 D6
Farleigh Court Golf Club
WARL CR6 224 F8
Farleigh Primary School
WARL CR6 242 C3
Farleigh Rovers FC
WARL CR6 242 E2
Farm Lane Trading Estate
FUL/PGN SW6 14 E10
Farnborough Primary School
ORP BR6 226 G2
Farncombe CC
GODL GU7 267 L10
Farncombe CE Infant School
GODL GU7 267 K10
Farnell House Medical Centre
HSLW TW3 154 A7
Farnham Common Infant School
SLN SL2 108 G9
Farnham Common Junior School
SLN SL2 109 H9
Farnham Common Middle School
SLN SL2 109 H9
Farnham Green Primary School
GDMY/SEVK IG3 123 K4
Farnham Park Golf Club
SLN SL2 129 K3
Farnham Road Hospital
GUW GU2 267 N2
Farnham Royal CE Combined School
SLN SL2 129 H5
Farnham Royal CC
SLN SL2 129 H5
Farningham Woods (Nature Reserve)
SWLY BR8 209 L4
Farrington & Stratford House School
CHST BR7 184 G10
Fashion & Textile Design Museum
STHWK SE1 19 K2
Fawbert & Barnards Primary School
HLWE CM17 29 M8
Fawkham CE Primary School
HART DA3 210 F8
Fawkham Manor Hospital
HART DA3 211 H8
Featherstone High School
NWDGN UB2 153 L3
Featherstone Industrial Estate
NWDGN UB2 153 M1
Featherstone Road Health Clinic
NWDGN UB2 153 M2
Felnex Trading Estate
WLGTN SM6 202 B9
Feltham Airparcs Leisure Centre
FELT TW13 175 L5
Feltham Athletics Arena
EBED/NFELT TW14 175 H3
Felthambrook Industrial Estate
FELT TW13 175 J6
Feltham Community College
FELT TW13 175 K5
Feltham Hill Infant School
FELT TW13 174 G6
Feltham Hill Junior School
FELT TW13 174 G6
Feltham & Hounslow Borough FC
EBED/NFELT TW14 175 H3
Feltham Superbowl
FELT TW13 175 J5
Feltonfleet School
COB KT11 216 F9
Fenstanton J & I School
BRXS/STRHM SW2 181 H4
Fenton House
HAMP NW3 117 M8
Ferrier Industrial Estate
WAND/EARL SW18 157 L10
Ferry Island Retail Park
TOTM N17 119 N1
Ferry Lane Industrial Estate
RAIN RM13 145 H7
WALTH E17 120 B1
Ferry Lane Primary School
TOTM N17 120 A2
Festival Pier
STHWK SE1 11 P9
Fetcham Social & Sports Club
LHD/OX KT22 236 D7
Fetcham Village Infant School
LHD/OX KT22 236 C8
Fiddlebridge Industrial Centre
HAT AL10 40 D3
Field End Primary School
RSLP HA4 113 L8
Fielding Primary School
WEA W13 154 G2
Field Junior School
WATW WD18 73 K9
Film House Cinema
RCH/KEW TW9 177 J1
Financial Times
POP/IOD E14 141 H8
STHWK SE1 12 F9
Finchley Campus of St Marys CE School
NFNCH/WDSPK N12 97 N7
Finchley Catholic High School
NFNCH/WDSPK N12 97 M4
Finchley CC
FNCH N3 97 L10
Finchley Golf Club
MLHL NW7 97 J7
Finchley Industrial Centre
NFNCH/WDSPK N12 97 M5
Finchley Lido
NFNCH/WDSPK N12 97 N8
Finchley Memorial Hospital
NFNCH/WDSPK N12 97 M8
Finchley Youth Theatre
EFNCH N2 117 P1
Finsbury Circus Medical Centre
LVPST EC2M 13 H4
Finsbury Health Centre
CLKNW EC1R 12 A1
Finsbury Leisure Centre
FSBYE EC1V 6 F10
Finsbury Park Track
FSBYPK N4 119 J5
Finton House School
TOOT SW17 180 A5
Fircroft Primary School
TOOT SW17 180 A5
Fire Brigade HQ
STHWK SE1 17 N5
Fire Brigade Museum
STHWK SE1 18 E1
Fire HQ & Station
REIG RH2 257 L9
Firepower (Museum of Artillery)
WOOL/PLUM SE18 162 E2
Firs Farm Primary School
PLMGR N13 99 L4
First Quarter Business Park
HOR/WEW KT19 220 A7
Fisher Athletic FC
BERM/RHTH SE16 140 C10
Fisher Industrial Estate
WATW WD18 73 K9
Fishmonger's Hall
CANST EC4R 12 G8
Fitness Unlimited Leisure Centre
BOW E3 140 F4
Fitzjohns Primary School
HAMP NW3 117 N10
Fitzrovia Medical Centre
FITZ W1T 10 G2
Fitzroy Nuffield Hospital
MBLAR W1H 10 A5
Five Bridges
LBTH SE11 17 P8
Five Elms Primary School
DAGW RM9 124 A8
Five Ways Business Centre
FELT TW13 175 J6
Flamstead End Primary School
CHESW EN7 61 P3
Flamsteed House Museum
GNWCH SE10 161 J6
Flaxman Sports Centre
CMBW SE5 159 K8
Fleecefield Primary School
ED N9 99 P5
Fleetdown J & I School
RDART DA2 188 B5
Fleet Primary School
HAMP NW3 118 A10
Fleetville Infant School
STAL AL1 38 F6
Fleetville Junior School
STAL AL1 38 F6
Fleetway Business Park
GFD/PVL UB6 134 G4
Fleetway Sports Club
GVE DA12 190 F4
Fleming Laboratory Museum
BAY/PAD W2 9 M5
Flora Gardens Primary School
HMSMTH W6 156 E3
Florence Nightingale Health Centre
HLWE CM17 47 M1
Florence Nightingale Museum
STHWK SE1 17 N2
Flutters Leisure Centre
FUL/PGN SW6 157 K6
FOB School
CLPT E5 119 P5
Follys End Christian High School
SNWD SE25 203 M6
Fondu Sports Club
PUR RM19 166 B3
Fontigarry Farm Business Park
REIG RH2 275 M9
The Foot Clinic
WIM/MER SW19 179 H9
The Foot Health Centre
COUL/CHIP CR5 240 E1
Fordbridge Medical Centre
ASHF TW15 174 A7
The Ford College
CONDST W1S 10 F6
Fordgate Business Park
BELV DA17 164 D1
Ford Industrial Park
DAGW RM9 144 C5
Fordview Industrial Estate
RAIN RM13 144 E5
Fordwater Trading Estate
CHERT KT16 195 M8
Foreign & Commonwealth Office
WHALL SW1A 17 K1
Foreland Medical Centre
NTGHL W11 8 A7
Forest Business Park
LEY E10 120 C5
Forestdale Primary School
CROY/NA CR0 224 D5
Foresters Primary School
WLGTN SM6 222 E3
Forest Gate Community School
FSTGT E7 121 M10
Forest Hill Business Centre
FSTH SE23 182 B5
Forest Hill Industrial Estate
FSTH SE23 182 B5
Forest Hill Pools
SYD SE26 182 B5
Forest Hill School
FSTH SE23 182 C6
Forest House Business Centre
WAN E11 121 L5
Forest Industrial Park
BARK/HLT IG6 103 H8
Forest Medical Centre
LOU IG10 82 B9
Forest Park Cemetery & Crematorium
BARK/HLT IG6 103 M6
Forest Road Medical Centre
WALTH E17 120 E1
Forest School
WALTH E17 121 K2
Forest Trading Estate
WALTH E17 120 C1
Forge Close Clinic
HAYES BR2 205 M8
Forge Lane Primary School
FELT TW13 175 M9
Forge Wood Industrial Estate
CRAWE RH10 284 C3
The Former Health Centre
CHARL SE7 162 A3
Forres CP School
HOD EN11 26 G10
Forster Park Primary School
CAT SE6 183 K6
Fortismere School
EFNCH N2 98 A10
Fortune Theatre
HOL/ALD WC2B 11 M6
Forty Hall
ENC/FH EN2 79 N3
Forty Hill CE Primary School
ENC/FH EN2 79 P3
The Forum
EDGW HA8 95 M7
Forum Theatre
HAT AL10 40 C3
Fossdene Primary School
CHARL SE7 161 N4
Foster's Primary School
WELL DA16 163 M9
Foulds School
BAR EN5 76 G7
The Foundling Museum
BMSBY WC1N 11 M1
Fountayne Business Centre
SEVS/STOTM N15 119 P2
Fountayne Road Health Centre
STNW/STAM N16 119 P7
Four Seasons Hotel
BERM/RHTH SE16 140 E10
MYFR/PKLN W1K 16 E1
Four Swannes Primary School
CHES/WCR EN8 62 D9
Foxfield Primary School
WOOL/PLUM SE18 162 F4
Foxhills Club & Resort
CHERT KT16 214 C1
Fox Primary School
KENS W8 8 E10
Frances Bardsley School for Girls
ROM RM1 125 H3
Francis Bacon Maths & Computing College
STAL AL1 38 G9
Franciscan Primary School
TOOT SW17 180 B7
Francis Combe School
GSTN WD25 55 K8
Francis Holland School
BGVA SW1W 16 D6
CAMTN NW1 10 A2
Frank Barnes Primary School
STJWD NW8 3 M4
Franklin Industrial Estate
PGE/AN SE20 204 B1
Freehold Industrial Centre
HSLWW TW4 175 K1
Freemantles School
CHERT KT16 195 H7
Free Trade Wharf
WAP E1W 140 C9
Freezywater St Georges CE Primary School
PEND EN3 80 C2
Freightliners City Farm
HOLWY N7 6 A1
Fresh Wharf Estate
BARK IG11 142 E3
Freuchen Medical Centre
WLSDN NW10 136 C4
Freud Museum
HAMP NW3 3 K1
Friars Primary Foundation School
STHWK SE1 18 C1
The Friary Centre
GU GU1 267 P1
Friends House
CAMTN NW1 5 J10
Friern Barnet School
FBAR/BDGN N11 98 A6
Friern Bridge Retail Park
FBAR/BDGN N11 98 C7
Frithwood Primary School
NTHWD HA6 92 G7
Frogmore House
WDSR SL4 149 L9
Frogmore Industrial Estate
HBRY N5 119 K9
HYS/HAR UB3 152 F1
WLSDN NW10 135 P5
Frogmore Road Industrial Estate
HHS/BOV HP3 35 N9
Fryent Country Park
KTN/HRWW/WS HA3 115 M5
Fryent Medical Centre
CDALE/KGS NW9 115 P5
Fryent Primary School
CDALE/KGS NW9 115 P5
Fulham Cemetery
FUL/PGN SW6 156 G6
Fulham Clinic
WKENS W14 14 B10
Fulham Cross Secondary School
FUL/PGN SW6 156 G6
Fulham FC (Craven Cottage)
PUT/ROE SW15 156 F7
Fulham Medical Centre
FUL/PGN SW6 157 L6
Fulham Palace
FUL/PGN SW6 156 G8
Fulham Pools
FUL/PGN SW6 14 B10
Fulham Preparatory School
WKENS W14 157 H5
Fulham Pre-Preparatory School
FUL/PGN SW6 157 H8
Fulham Primary School
FUL/PGN SW6 14 E10
Fullbrook School
ADL/WDHM KT15 215 K7
Fuller Smith & Turner Sports Club
CHSWK W4 156 B7
Fullwell Cross Health Centre
BARK/HLT IG6 102 F10
Fullwell Cross Swimming Pool & Recreation Centre
BARK/HLT IG6 102 F10
Fullwood Primary School
BARK/HLT IG6 122 F2
Fulmer Infant School
DTCH/LGLY SL3 110 B9
Fulwell Golf Club
HPTN TW12 176 C7
Furness Primary School
WLSDN NW10 136 D4
Furness School
SWLY BR8 186 G9
Furness Swanley FC
SWLY BR8 208 E5
Furzedown Primary School
TOOT SW17 180 C9
Furze Field Leisure Centre
POTB/CUF EN6 59 H7
Furzefield Primary School
REDH RH1 258 E4
Furzehill School
BORE WD6 75 M8
Furze Infant School
CHDH RM6 123 P4
Future Business College
CONDST W1S 10 F6
Gade Valley JMI School
HHW HP1 35 L5
Gaflac Sports Ground Pavilion
SUN TW16 197 H1
Gainsborough Clinic
PLMGR N13 98 G5
Gainsborough Primary School
HOM E9 140 E1
SRTFD E15 141 K5
Galleria Shopping Centre
HAT AL10 40 C4
Galley Hill Industrial Estate
SWCM DA10 189 K1
Galleywall Primary School
BERM/RHTH SE16 160 A3
Galliard Primary School
ED N9 79 P10
Gallions Mount Primary School
WOOL/PLUM SE18 163 J4
Gallions Primary School
EHAM E6 142 E8
Gallions Reach Shopping Park
EHAM E6 142 E7
Gants Hill Medical Centre
GNTH/NBYPK IG2 122 D4
Garden Court Business Centre
WGCE AL7 23 J5
Gardener Industrial Estate
SYD SE26 182 D8
Garden Fields JMI School
STALW/RED AL3 38 C3
Garden House School
BGVA SW1W 16 C7
Garden Primary School
MTCM CR4 202 E3
Gardens of the Rose (Royal National Rose)
LCOL/BKTW AL2 55 N2
Garden Suburb Primary School
GLDGN NW11 117 J3
Garfield Primary School
FBAR/BDGN N11 98 C6
WIM/MER SW19 179 M9
Garratt Park Secondary Special School
WAND/EARL SW18 179 L6
Garrick Industrial Centre
CDALE/KGS NW9 116 C3
Garrick Theatre
LSQ/SEVD WC2H 11 L8
Garston Clinic
WATN WD24 73 J2
Garston JMI School
GSTN WD25 73 L1
Garston Manor Special School
GSTN WD25 55 K8
Garston Medical Centre
GSTN WD25 73 K2
Garth Primary School
MRDN SM4 201 N5
The Garth Road Industrial Centre
MRDN SM4 200 F7
Gascoigne Primary School
BARK IG11 142 F3
Gate Cinema
KENS W8 8 E9
Gatehouse School
BETH E2 140 C4
The Gatehouse Theatre
HGT N6 118 B5
The Gate Theatre
NTGHL W11 8 E9
Gateway
EHAM E6 142 E6
Gateway Business Centre
SYD SE26 182 D9
WOOL/PLUM SE18 162 F2
Gateway Community College North Site
CDW/CHF RM16 168 C1
Gateway Industrial Estate
WLSDN NW10 136 C5
Gateway Primary School
RDART DA2 188 A2
Gatton Park Business Centre
REDH RH1 258 C6
Gatton School
TOOT SW17 179 P7
Gatwick Airport
HORL RH6 280 A8
Gatwick Gate Industrial Estate
HORL RH6 279 P10
Gatwick Industrial Estate
HORL RH6 279 J9
Gatwick Manor Golf Club
CRAWE RH10 283 P2
Gatwick Medical Centre
HORL RH6 280 C8
Gatwick Park Hospital
HORL RH6 279 P5
Gatwick Worth Hotel
CRAWE RH10 284 G6
Gayhurst Primary School
HACK E8 7 P3
Gayhurst School
CFSP/GDCR SL9 109 P2
Gaynes School
UPMR RM14 126 B10
Gazelda Industrial Estate
WAT WD17 73 K9
Gearies Infant School
GNTH/NBYPK IG2 122 D3
Gearies Junior School
GNTH/NBYPK IG2 122 E3
Geffrye Museum
BETH E2 7 K8
Gemini Business Estate
NWCR SE14 160 C4
General Medical Clinics
WCHPL E1 13 L3
Genesis Business Park
WOKN/KNAP GU21 232 F1
Genesis Cinema
WCHPL E1 140 B6
Geoffrey Chaucer Technology College
STHWK SE1 18 G4
The Geoffrey Lloyd Foulkes Clinic
IL IG1 122 D7
Geoffrey Whitworth Theatre
DART DA1 165 H10
George Abbot School
GU GU1 250 D8
George Eliot J & I School
STJWD NW8 3 K5
George Greens School
POP/IOD E14 161 H4
George Mitchell School
LEY E10 120 G6
George Spicer Primary School
EN EN1 79 N7
George Tomlinson Primary School
WAN E11 121 K6
Germal College
FSBYPK N4 119 H6
The Gerrards Cross CE School
CFSP/GDCR SL9 110 B5
Gerrards Cross Golf Club
CFSP/GDCR SL9 110 C1
Gerrards Cross Sports Centre
CFSP/GDCR SL9 110 A5
Ghyll Manor Hotel
HORS RH12 282 A5
Gibbs Green Special School
WKENS W14 14 D7
Gibson Business Centre
TOTM N17 99 N7
Gidea Park College
GPK RM2 125 H1
Gidea Park Primary School
GPK RM2 124 G2
Gidea Park Sports Ground
GPK RM2 105 K10
The Gielgud Theatre
SOHO/CST W1F 11 J7
Giffin Business Centre
DEPT SE8 160 F6
Gifford Primary School
NTHLT UB5 133 N4
Gilbert Collection
TPL/STR WC2R 11 N7
Gilbert Colvin Primary School
CLAY IG5 102 D9
Gilbert Scott Primary School
SAND/SEL CR2 224 D4
Gillespie Primary School
HBRY N5 119 J8
Girdlers' Hall
CITYW EC2V 12 F4
The Glade Business Centre
WTHK RM20 166 E4
Glade Primary School
CLAY IG5 102 C9
The Glades Shopping Centre
BMLY BR1 205 M2
Gladstone Medical Centre
CRICK NW2 116 C9
Gladstone Park Primary School
WLSDN NW10 116 D10
Glaziers/Scientific Instrument Makers Hall
STHWK SE1 12 G9
Glebe First & Middle School
KTN/HRWW/WS HA3 115 J2
Glebe Primary School
HGDN/ICK UB10 112 E9
Glebe School
WWKM BR4 205 J8
Gleen Lecky Health Centre
PUT/ROE SW15 156 G10
Glenbrook Primary School
CLAP SW4 180 E2
Glencairn Sports Club
FBAR/BDGN N11 98 D8
Glendower Preparatory School
SKENS SW7 157 M3
Glenesk School
EHSLY KT24 252 E1
Glenham College
IL IG1 122 E7
Glenlyn Medical Centre
E/WMO/HCT KT8 198 B5
Glenthorne High School
CHEAM SM3 201 K8
Globe Industrial Estate
GRAYS RM17 167 P5
Globe Primary School
BETH E2 140 B5
Globe Wharf
BERM/RHTH SE16 140 C9
Globe Works Industrial Estate
GRAYS RM17 167 P4
Gloucester Primary School
PECK SE15 19 L10
Glyn Technology School
EW KT17 220 C7
Goal Farm Golf Club
CHOB/PIR GU24 230 C7
Godalming Leisure Centre
GODL GU7 267 M10
Godolphin Infant School
SL SL1 129 H7
Godolphin Junior School
SL SL1 129 J7
Godolphin & Latymer School
HMSMTH W6 156 E3
Godstone Farm
GDST RH9 260 B9
Godstone Village School
GDST RH9 260 A8
Godwin Junior School
FSTGT E7 121 N9
Godwin Primary School
DAGW RM9 143 P2
Goethe Institute
SKENS SW7 15 M3
Goffs Oak JMI School
CHESW EN7 61 J4
Goffs School
CHESW EN7 61 P5
Golborne Medical Centre
NKENS W10 137 J6
Goldbeaters Primary School
EDGW HA8 96 A9
Golden Hinde Educational Trust
STHWK SE1 12 G8
Golders Green Crematorium
GLDGN NW11 117 K5
Golders Green Health Centre
GLDGN NW11 117 L6
Golders Hill Health Centre
GLDGN NW11 117 M4
Golders Hill School
GLDGN NW11 117 K5
Goldhawk Industrial Estate
SHB W12 156 E2
Goldings Hill Clinic
LOU IG10 82 D6
Goldsmiths College
BROCKY SE4 160 E9
DEPT SE8 160 F5
LEW SE13 161 K10
Goldsmiths College Sports Ground
SCUP DA14 186 A6
Goldsmiths Hall
STBT EC1A 12 E5
Goldsworth CP School
WOKN/KNAP GU21 231 P4
Goldsworth Park Health Centre
WOKN/KNAP GU21 231 M3
Goldsworth Park Trading Estate
WOKN/KNAP GU21 231 M2
Goldsworth Rd Industrial Estate
WOKN/KNAP GU21 232 A3
Golf Driving Range
REDH RH1 276 B3
Gonville Primary School
THHTH CR7 202 G5
Goodinge Health Centre
HOLWY N7 5 L1
Goodmayes Retail Park
CHDH RM6 123 L5
Goodrich J & I School
EDUL SE22 181 P2
Good Shepherd RC Primary School
BMLY BR1 183 L7
CROY/NA CR0 224 G4
The Good Shepherd RC Primary School
SHB W12 156 C1
Goodwyn School
MLHL NW7 96 D6
Goose Green Primary School
EDUL SE22 159 N10
Goose Green Trading Estate
EDUL SE22 159 P10
Gordonbrock Primary School
BROCKY SE4 182 F1
Gordon Hospital
WEST SW1P 17 J6
Gordon House Health Centre
WEA W13 134 G10
Gordon Infant School
IL IG1 122 G8
Gordon Primary School
ELTH/MOT SE9 162 C10
Gordons School
CHOB/PIR GU24 212 D8
Goresbrook Leisure Centre
DAGW RM9 143 N3
Goresbrook Sports Centre
DAGW RM9 143 N3
Gorhambury (Remains)
STALW/RED AL3 37 J5
The Goring Hotel
BGVA SW1W 16 F3
Gorringe Park Primary School
MTCM CR4 202 B1
Gosai Cinema
WEA W13 134 G10
Gosbury Hill Health Centre
CHSGTN KT9 219 K1
Gosden House School
SHGR GU5 268 B9
Gosford Primary School
REDBR IG4 122 C3
Gosling Ski & Board Centre
WGCW AL8 22 F8
Gosling Sports Park
WGCW AL8 22 F7
Gospel Oak Primary School
HAMP NW3 118 B9
Gossops Green Clinic
CRAWW RH11 283 J9
Gossops Green Community Primary School
CRAWW RH11 283 K8
Gove Farm Retail Park
CHDH RM6 123 M5
Gower House School
CDALE/KGS NW9 115 P7
Grace Business Centre
MTCM CR4 202 A6
Grace Theatre at the Latchmere
BTSEA SW11 158 A8
Graduate School of Management
TOTM N17 99 N9
Grafton Primary School
BCTR RM8 123 P7
HOLWY N7 118 F8
Grahame Park Health Centre
CDALE/KGS NW9 96 B9
Grahame Park J & I School
CDALE/KGS NW9 96 B9
Granard Business Centre
MLHL NW7 96 B7
Granard Primary School
PUT/ROE SW15 178 E2
Granby Sports Club
CHST BR7 184 B8
Grand Avenue Primary School
BRYLDS KT5 199 P7
Grande Vitesse Industrial Centre
STHWK SE1 12 D10
Grand Union Industrial Estate
WLSDN NW10 135 N4
Grange Blooms Hotel
RSQ WC1B 11 L3
The Grange City Hotel
TWRH EC3N 13 L7
The Grange Community Infant School
ADL/WDHM KT15 215 J6
Grange First & Middle School
RYLN/HDSTN HA2 114 A6
Grange Fitzrovia Hotel
GTPST W1W 10 F3
Grange Holborn Hotel
NOXST/BSQ WC1A 11 M4
Grange Langham Court Hotel
GTPST W1W 10 F4
The Grange Museum
CRICK NW2 116 C9
Grange Park Clinic
YEAD UB4 132 G6
Grange Park Preparatory School
WCHMH N21 79 J10
Grange Park Primary School
WCHMH N21 79 H8
YEAD UB4 132 G6
Grange Primary School
CAN/RD E16 141 L6
EA W5 155 J1
STHWK SE1 19 J4
Grange Rochester Hotel
WEST SW1P 17 J5
Grange Strathmore Hotel
SKENS SW7 15 K5
Grange Whitehall Hotel
RSQ WC1B 11 L4
Grangewood Independent School
FSTGT E7 142 A2
Grangewood School
PIN HA5 113 H3
Granton Primary School
STRHM/NOR SW16 180 D10
Granville Road Industrial Estate
CRICK NW2 117 J7
The Granville School
SEV TN13 247 H9
Grasmere Primary School
STNW/STAM N16 119 L9
Grasshoppers RFC
ISLW TW7 154 E5
Grassroots School
HPTN TW12 197 P1
Grasvenor Avenue Infant School
BAR EN5 77 K10
Gravel Hill Primary School
BXLYHS DA6 186 C1
Graveney School
TOOT SW17 180 C9
Gravesend County Court
GVE DA12 190 E2

Gravesend CC GVW DA11 190 D3
Gravesend Grammar School GVE DA12 190 C3
Gravesend Museum GVW DA11 190 E2
Gravesend & Northfleet FC GVW DA11 189 M1
Gravesend & North Kent Hospital GVW DA11 190 D2
Gravesend Rowing Club GVE DA12 190 F2
Gravesend Yacht Club GVE DA12 190 G2
Graves Yard Industrial Estate WELL DA16 163 K8
Grays Athletic FC GRAYS RM17 167 N5
Grays Business Centre GRAYS RM17 167 P2
Grays Convent School GRAYS RM17 167 N3
Grays County Court GRAYS RM17 167 M5
Grays Farm Primary School STMC/STPC BR5 207 L1
Grays Health Centre GRAYS RM17 167 M4
The Grays School GRAYS RM17 167 N2
Grazebrook Primary School STNW/STAM N16 119 M7
Great Bookham County Infant School GT/LBKH KT23 253 P2
Great Cambridge Industrial Estate EN EN1 80 A9
Great Chapel Street Medical Centre SOHO/SHAV W1D 11 J5
Great Eastern Hotel LVPST EC2M 13 J4
Greater London Authority Headquarters (City Hall) STHWK SE1 13 K10
Greatham Road Industrial Estate BUSH WD23 73 M8
Great Jubilee Wharf WAP E1W 140 B10
Greatness Park Cemetery RSEV TN14 247 L7
Great Scotland Yard WHALL SW1A 11 L9
Great Stony School CHONG CM5 67 P3
Great Western Industrial Park NWDGN UB2 154 A1
Great West Trading Estate BTFD TW8 154 C5
Great Wood Country Park POTB/CUF EN6 60 B2
Grebe House Wildlife Centre & Gardens STALW/RED AL3 38 A6
Greenacre School for Girls BNSTD SM7 221 M9
Greenacres Primary School ELTH/MOT SE9 184 D5
Green Business Centre EGH TW20 172 F7
The Green CE Primary School TOTM N17 119 N1
Green Dragon Primary School BTFD TW8 155 K4
Green End Business Centre RKW/CH/CXG WD3 71 K3
Greenfield Medical Centre CRICK NW2 117 H8
Greenfield Primary School OXHEY WD19 93 K6
Greenfield School WOKS/MYFD GU22 232 B5
Greenfields Junior School SHB W12 136 C9
Greenfields Special School MUSWH N10 98 A9
Greenford Avenue Medical Centre HNWL W7 134 D7
Greenford Green Clinic GFD/PVL UB6 114 D10
Greenford High School STHL UB1 133 P5
Greenford Industrial Estate GFD/PVL UB6 134 A3
Greenford Park Cemetery GFD/PVL UB6 134 A7
Greenford Road Medical Centre GFD/PVL UB6 134 C4
Greenford Sports Centre STHL UB1 133 P5
Greengate Medical Centre PLSTW E13 141 N5
Greengrove College STHGT/OAK N14 98 F3
Greenheath Business Centre BETH E2 140 A5
Greenhill College HRW HA1 114 E3
Greenhill Park Medical Centre WLSDN NW10 136 B3
Greenhithe Health Clinic SWCM DA10 188 G1
Greenland Pier BERM/RHTH SE16 160 E2
Green Lane Business Park ELTH/MOT SE9 184 D5
Green Lane Primary School WPK KT4 200 E7
Green Lanes Primary School HAT AL10 22 C10
Greenleaf Primary School WALTH E17 120 E1
The Green Man Hotel HLWE CM17 29 N7
Greenmead Primary School PUT/ROE SW15 178 E1
The Green School for Girls ISLW TW7 154 F6
Greenshaw High School SUT SM1 201 M9
Greenshields Industrial Estate CAN/RD E16 141 M10
CAN/RD E16 161 M1
Greenside Primary School SHB W12 156 D1
Greenslade Primary School WOOL/PLUM SE18 162 C5
Green Street Green Primary School ORP BR6 227 J3
Greenvale Primary School SAND/SEL CR2 224 C7
Greenvale School FSTH SE23 182 D6
Greenway First School BERK HP4 33 L5
Greenwich Centre Business Park DEPT SE8 160 G6
Greenwich Cinema GNWCH SE10 161 H6
Greenwich Community College WOOL/PLUM SE18 162 E3
WOOL/PLUM SE18 162 G5
Greenwich Industrial Estate CHARL SE7 161 N3
GNWCH SE10 160 G6
Greenwich Natural Health Centre GNWCH SE10 161 H6
Greenwich Pier GNWCH SE10 161 H4
Greenwich School of Management GNWCH SE10 161 H6
Greenwich Theatre & Art Gallery GNWCH SE10 161 J6
Greenwood Park Leisure Centre LCOL/BKTW AL2 56 A1
Greenwood Primary School NTHLT UB5 114 B10
Greenwood Theatre STHWK SE1 19 H1
Green Wrythe Primary School CAR SM5 201 N6
Greig City Academy CEND/HSY/T N8 118 G2
Gresham College HCIRC EC1N 12 A4
Gresham Primary School SAND/SEL CR2 223 N8
Gresham Way Industrial Estate WIM/MER SW19 179 L6
Greville Primary School ASHTD KT21 237 L3
Grey Coat Hospital CE School for Girls WEST SW1P 17 J4
The Greycoat Hospital WEST SW1P 17 J6
Grey Court School RCHPK/HAM TW10 177 J6
Griffen Manor School WOOL/PLUM SE18 163 H7
Grimsdyke First & Middle School PIN HA5 93 N7
Grims Dyke Golf Club PIN HA5 93 P6
Grim's Dyke Hotel KTN/HRWW/WS HA3 94 C6
Grinling Gibbons Primary School DEPT SE8 160 E5
Grist Memorial Sports Club E/WMO/HCT KT8 198 D5
Grocers' Hall CITYW EC2V 12 G6
Grosvenor House Hotel MYFR/PKLN W1K 10 C8
Grove Health Centre KENS W8 8 F9
The Grove Health Centre SHB W12 156 E1
Grovehill Medical Centre HHNE HP2 36 A2
The Grove Hotel RKW/CH/CXG WD3 72 D3
Grove House (Froebel College) PUT/ROE SW15 178 C2
Grove House Primary School for Deaf Children WNWD SE27 181 J5
The Grove Infant School HARP AL5 20 C3
The Grove Junior School HARP AL5 20 C3
Grovelands Business Centre HHNE HP2 36 D4
Grovelands Priory Hospital STHGT/OAK N14 98 F2
Grovelands School WOT/HER KT12 197 J6
Grove Medical Centre DEPT SE8 160 D3
The Grove Medical Centre ARCH N19 118 E7
Grove Park Industrial Estate CDALE/KGS NW9 116 A2
Grove Park Primary School CHSWK W4 155 P5
Grove Park School CDALE/KGS NW9 115 P2
Grove Primary School CHDH RM6 123 L3
Grove Road Primary School HSLW TW3 153 P10
The Groves Medical Centre NWMAL KT3 200 B3
Grove Village Medical Centre EBED/NFELT TW14 174 F4
Grundy Park Leisure Centre CHES/WCR EN8 62 D6
The Gryphon Industrial Park STALW/RED AL3 38 E2
Guardian Angels RC Primary School BOW E3 140 D6
Guardian Business Centre HARH RM3 105 L8
Guardian Newspapers POP/IOD E14 160 G1
Guards' Chapel and Museum STJSPK SW1H 17 J2
Guards Polo Club EGH TW20 193 J1
Guildford Castle GU GU1 268 A2
Guildford Cathedral GUW GU2 249 N10
Guildford College (Merrist Wood Campus) RGUW GU3 249 H4
Guildford College (Stoke Park Campus) GU GU1 250 A9
Guildford County School GUW GU2 267 N2
Guildford Crematorium GODL GU7 267 N9
Guildford Cricket Ground (Surrey CCC) GU GU1 249 P10
Guildford Golf Club GU GU1 250 F10
Guildford Grove Primary School GUW GU2 249 K10
Guildford High School GU GU1 250 B10
Guildford Hockey & CC GU GU1 249 P10
Guildford House Gallery GU GU1 268 A2
Guildford Industrial Estate GUW GU2 249 M9
Guildford Lido GU GU1 250 A9
Guildford Museum GU GU1 268 A2
The Guildford Nuffield Hospital GUW GU2 249 K10
Guildford Rowing Club GU GU1 268 A3
Guildford Spectrum GU GU1 250 B9
Guildford Spectrum Athletics Stadium GU GU1 250 B8
Guildhall Art Gallery CITYW EC2V 12 F5
Guildhall School of Music & Drama STLK EC1Y 12 F2
The Guildhall CITYW EC2V 12 F5
Gumley House Convent School ISLW TW7 154 F9
Gunnersbury Catholic School BTFD TW8 155 H4
Gunnersbury Park Museum ACT W3 155 M2
Gurnell Leisure Centre WEA W13 134 E5
Guru Gobind Singh Khalsa College CHIG IG7 102 C2
Guru Nanak Medical Centre STHL UB1 133 L10
Guru Nanak Sports Club GVE DA12 190 F3
Guy's Hospital STHWK SE1 13 H10
Guys Kings and Thomas Medical School (Kings College London) STHWK SE1 12 E9
Gwyn Jones Primary School WAN E11 121 J5
GX Superbowl EHAM E6 142 D7
Gypsy Moth IV GNWCH SE10 161 H5
Haberdashers Askes Hatcham College NWCR SE14 160 C8
The Haberdashers Askes School for Boys BORE WD6 74 C7
Haberdashers' Hall STBT EC1A 12 C4
Haberdashers RUFC BORE WD6 75 L6
Hackbridge Primary School WLGTN SM6 202 B8
Hackney Business Centre HACK E8 140 A1
Hackney City Farm BETH E2 7 N8
Hackney Community College IS N1 7 J8
Hackney Empire Variety Theatre HACK E8 140 A1
Hackney Free & Parochial CE School HOM E9 140 B1
The Hackney Museum HACK E8 140 A1
Hackney Sports Centre HOM E9 120 F9
Hacton Primary School HCH RM12 125 M9
Hadley Wood Golf Club EBAR EN4 77 P5
Hadley Wood Primary School EBAR EN4 77 M4
The Haelan Clinic CEND/HSY/T N8 118 F4
Haggerston School BETH E2 7 M7
Haggerston Swimming Pool BETH E2 7 M6
Hague Primary School BETH E2 140 A6
Haileybury College HERT/BAY SG13 26 C9
Haileybury College Track HERT/BAY SG13 26 C9
Hailey Hall Special School HERT/BAY SG13 26 E9
Hailey Road Business Park ERITHM DA18 164 B1
Haimo Primary School ELTH/MOT SE9 184 A1
Hainault Business Park BARK/HLT IG6 103 M6
Hainault Forest Country Park CHIG IG7 103 N4
Hainault Forest Golf Club CHIG IG7 103 N7
Hainault Forest High School & The Learning Centre BARK/HLT IG6 103 K6
Hakim Qureshi Clinic NWDGN UB2 153 M2
The Hale Clinic CAMTN NW1 10 F2
Half Moon Theatre WCHPL E1 140 C6
Haling Manor High School SAND/SEL CR2 223 J4
The Halkin Hotel KTBR SW1X 16 D2
Halley Primary School POP/IOD E14 140 D7
Hallfield Clinic BAY/PAD W2 9 J6
Hallfield J & I School BAY/PAD W2 9 H6
Hallfield Primary School BAY/PAD W2 137 M8
Halliford Health Clinic SHPTN TW17 196 F4
Halliford School SHPTN TW17 196 D7
The Hall Junior School HAMP NW3 3 M2
Hallmark Trading Estate WBLY HA9 115 P9
Hall Mead School UPMR RM14 126 C5
Hall Place BXLY DA5 186 D2
Halls Business Centre HYS/HAR UB3 153 H2
The Hall School HAMP NW3 3 M2
Hall School Wimbledon RYNPK SW20 200 G1
Hall School Wimbledon Junior Department PUT/ROE SW15 178 D6
Hallsville Primary School CAN/RD E16 141 M8
Halstead Place School RSEV TN14 227 P8
Halstead Preparatory School WOKN/KNAP GU21 232 C1
Halstead Primary School RSEV TN14 228 A9
Halstow Primary School GNWCH SE10 161 L4
Hambrough Primary School STHL UB1 133 M10
Hamer Indoor Market BOW E3 140 E4
Ham Health Clinic RCHPK/HAM TW10 177 H6
Ham House (NT) RCHPK/HAM TW10 177 H4
Hamilton Road Industrial Estate WNWD SE27 181 L7
Hamlet International Industrial Estate ERITH DA8 164 E4
Hammersmith Apollo HMSMTH W6 156 F4
Hammersmith Cemetery HMSMTH W6 14 A8
Hammersmith Hospital SHB W12 136 D8
Hammersmith Industrial Estate HMSMTH W6 156 F5
Hammersmith New Cemetery RCH/KEW TW9 155 N8
Hammersmith Palais HMSMTH W6 156 F3
Hammersmith Physio & Sports Injury Clinic HMSMTH W6 156 F3
Hammersmith & West London College WKENS W14 14 B5
The Hammond JMI School HHNE HP2 36 A2
Hampden Gurney School MBLAR W1H 9 P5
Ham & Petersham CC RCHPK/HAM TW10 177 J7
The Hampshire School BAY/PAD W2 9 H7
SKENS SW7 15 N2
Hampstead College of Fine Art HAMP NW3 3 P2
Hampstead CC KIL/WHAMP NW6 117 L10
Hampstead Golf Club GLDGN NW11 117 M5
Hampstead Medical Centre HAMP NW3 117 M9
Hampstead Parochial CE School HAMP NW3 117 M9
Hampstead School CRICK NW2 117 H9
The Hampstead School of Art HAMP NW3 117 K9
Hampstead School of English KIL/WHAMP NW6 117 K9
Hampstead Theatre HAMP NW3 3 L3
Hampton Cemetery HPTN TW12 175 P10
Hampton Community College HPTN TW12 175 P8
Hampton Court House School E/WMO/HCT KT8 198 D2
Hampton Court Palace E/WMO/HCT KT8 198 E3
Hampton Court Palace Golf Club SURB KT6 199 H5
Hampton Farm Industrial Estate FELT TW13 175 M6
Hampton FC HPTN TW12 198 A1
Hampton Hill Junior School HPTN TW12 176 B8
Hampton Infant School HPTN TW12 175 N10
Hampton Junior School HPTN TW12 197 P1
The Hampton Medical Centre HPTN TW12 175 P10
Hampton Open Air Pool HPTN TW12 176 B10
Hampton Road Industrial Park CROY/NA CR0 203 K6
Hampton School HPTN TW12 175 P8
Hampton Wick Infant School TEDD TW11 177 H10
Hamsey Green Infant School WARL CR6 242 A2
Hamsey Green Junior School WARL CR6 242 A2
Handel's House MYFR/PKLN W1K 10 E7
Handsworth Health Clinic CHING E4 101 J7
Handsworth Primary School CHING E4 101 J7
Hanover Primary School IS N1 6 D7
Hanover Trading Estate HOLWY N7 118 F10
Hanover West Industrial Estate WLSDN NW10 135 P5
Hanworth Business Park CHERT KT16 195 J8
Hanworth Trading Estate FELT TW13 175 M6
Haperbury Hospital RAD WD7 57 H7
Happy Valley Industrial Estate KGLGY WD4 54 C4
Harbinger Primary School POP/IOD E14 160 F3
Harborough School ARCH N19 118 E7
The Harefield Academy DEN/HRF UB9 91 N9
Harefield CC DEN/HRF UB9 91 M10
Harefield Health Centre DEN/HRF UB9 91 M9
Harefield Hospital DEN/HRF UB9 91 M9
Harefield Infant School DEN/HRF UB9 91 L10
Harefield Junior School DEN/HRF UB9 91 M9
Harefield Road Industrial Estate RKW/CH/CXG WD3 91 P5
Harenc School SCUP DA14 185 M8
Haresfoot School BERK HP4 33 N8
Haresfoot Senior School BERK HP4 34 D3
Hare Street Primary School HLWW/ROY CM19 46 F1
Harewood Down Golf Club CSTG HP8 69 N8
Hargrave Park Primary School ARCH N19 118 D7
Haringey Arts Council ED N9 99 P3
Haringey Community Health Clinic SEVS/STOTM N15 119 N2
Haringey Magistrates Court HGT N6 118 B4
Harkness Industrial Estate BORE WD6 75 M8
The Harlequin Shopping Centre WAT WD17 73 K8
Harlesden Primary School WLSDN NW10 136 B4
Harley Medical Centre CAVSQ/HST W1G 10 F5
The Harley Medical Centre CANST EC4R 12 F7
Harley Street Clinic CAVSQ/HST W1G 10 E4
Harlington Community School HYS/HAR UB3 152 E3
Harlowbury Primary School HLWE CM17 29 N7
Harlow Business Park HLWW/ROY CM19 46 B1
Harlow College HLW CM20 29 H10
HLW CM20 46 F1
Harlow Museum (Passmores House) HLWS CM18 46 F2
Harlow RFC HLW CM20 28 E9
Harlow Sports Centre HLW CM20 28 F9
Harlyn Primary School PIN HA5 113 J1
Harold Court Primary School HARH RM3 105 P8
The Harold Macmillan Medical Centre HRW HA1 114 C5
Harold Wood Clinic HARH RM3 105 N10
Harold Wood JMI School HARH RM3 125 P1
Harp Business Centre CRICK NW2 116 D7
Harpenden Common Golf Club HARP AL5 20 A5
Harpenden House Hotel HARP AL5 20 A3
Harpenden Memorial Hospital HARP AL5 20 A1
Harpley School WCHPL E1 140 B6
Harrington Hill Primary School CLPT E5 120 A6
Harris City Technology College NRWD SE19 203 N1
Harrodian School BARN SW13 156 C6
Harrods Store CHEL SW3 16 A3
Harrovian Business Village HRW HA1 114 C5
Harrow Arts Centre PIN HA5 93 P8
Harrow Borough FC RYLN/HDSTN HA2 113 P9
Harrow College HRW HA1 114 D5
KTN/HRWW/WS HA3 94 D7
Harrow CC HRW HA1 114 D9
Harrow Crown Courts HRW HA1 114 C1
Harrow Heritage Museum RYLN/HDSTN HA2 114 B1
Harrow High School HRW HA1 114 F4
Harrow Leisure Centre KTN/HRWW/WS HA3 114 E1
Harrow Magistrates Court HRW HA1 114 E2
Harrow RFC STAN HA7 94 C4
Harrow Road Health Centre BAY/PAD W2 8 F3
Harrow School HRW HA1 114 D5
RYLN/HDSTN HA2 114 D7
Harrow Town CC RYLN/HDSTN HA2 113 P6
Harrow Weald Cemetery KTN/HRWW/WS HA3 94 D7
Harry Gosling Primary School WCHPL E1 13 P6
Hartley Primary School EHAM E6 142 B3
HART DA3 211 K5
Hartsbourne Golf & Country Club BUSH WD23 94 B3
Hartsbourne Primary School BUSH WD23 94 C3
Hartspring Industrial Park BUSH WD23 73 P6
Hartspring Sports Centre BUSH WD23 73 P6
The Hartswood Clinic RBRW/HUT CM13 106 G7
Hartswood Golf Club BRW CM14 107 K5
Harven School of English WOKS/MYFD GU22 232 C3
Harvey Centre HLW CM20 46 G1
Harvey Road Primary School RKW/CH/CXG WD3 72 B10
Harvington School EA W5 135 H8
Harwood Equestrian Centre UPMR RM14 146 A1
Haseltine Primary School SYD SE26 182 E7
Haslemere Business Centre EN EN1 80 A8
Haslemere Industrial Estate EBED/NFELT TW14 175 H1
HLWW/ROY CM19 46 D2
WAND/EARL SW18 179 L5
WGCE AL7 23 J4
Haslemere Primary School MTCM CR4 201 N2
Hasmonean High School Boys Site HDN NW4 96 G10
Hasmonean High School Girls Site MLHL NW7 96 D9
Hasmonean Primary School HDN NW4 116 G3
Haste Hill Golf Club NTHWD HA6 92 F10
Hastings Clinic BRXS/STRHM SW2 180 G1
Hastingwood Business Centre HLWE CM17 47 M3
Hastingwood Trading Estate UED N18 100 D7
Hatcham Mews Business Centre NWCR SE14 160 C6
Hatch End High School KTN/HRWW/WS HA3 94 A8
Hatch End Swimming Pool PIN HA5 93 P8
Hatchlands Park (NT) RGUE GU4 252 A6
Hatfield Business Park HAT AL10 40 A1
HAT AL10 40 B4
Hatfield Leisure Centre HAT AL10 40 E6
Hatfield London Country Club BRKMPK AL9 42 A5
Hatfield Palace, Park and Gardens BRKMPK AL9 40 G4
Hatfield Primary School MRDN SM4 201 H6
Hatfield Swim Centre HAT AL10 40 D3
Hathaway Primary School HNWL W7 134 E7
Hatton School WFD IG8 122 A1
Havelock Primary School NWDGN UB2 153 N2
Havenbury Industrial Estate DORK RH4 272 F1
Haven Green Clinic EA W5 135 J8
Havering College HARH RM3 105 N5
Havering College of Further & Higher Education EMPK RM11 125 J5
EMPK RM11 125 M2
Havering Country Park ABR/ST RM4 104 E5
Havering CC ABR/ST RM4 84 G6
Havering Magistrates Court ROM RM1 124 F2
Havering Sixth Form College EMPK RM11 125 N6
Haverstock School HAMP NW3 4 C3
Hawes Down Clinic WWKM BR4 205 J9
Hawes Down Primary School WWKM BR4 205 J8
Hawkedale GM School SUN TW16 196 G3
The Hawker Centre KUTN/CMB KT2 177 J8
Hawkesdown House School KENS W8 8 F10
Hawkins Clinic EW KT17 238 F1
PUT/ROE SW15 156 G10
RYNPK SW20 200 C1
Hawksmoor Primary School THMD SE28 143 L9
Hawley Infant School CAMTN NW1 4 F4
Hawridge & Cholesbury CE School CSHM HP5 32 D7
The Hawthorns School REDH RH1 259 J7
The Hawth Theatre, Cinema & Conference Complex CRAWE RH10 284 A8
Haydon School PIN HA5 112 G1
Hayes Bridge Middle School STHL UB1 153 M1
Hayes Bridge Retail Park YEAD UB4 133 K9
Hayes CC HYS/HAR UB3 132 G8
Hayes FC HYS/HAR UB3 132 G9
Hayes Grove Priory Hospital HAYES BR2 205 M9
The Hayes Manor School HYS/HAR UB3 132 E8
Hayes Park J & I School YEAD UB4 132 G6
Hayes Pool HYS/HAR UB3 132 G10
Hayes Primary School HAYES BR2 205 N8
The Hayes Primary School PUR/KEN CR8 241 J2
Hayes School HAYES BR2 205 N9
Hayes Social and Sports Club HYS/HAR UB3 132 G9
Hayes Stadium Sports Centre HYS/HAR UB3 132 E8
Hay Lane School CDALE/KGS NW9 115 P2
Haymerle School PECK SE15 19 N10
Hays Galleria STHWK SE1 13 J9
Hayward Gallery STHWK SE1 11 P10
Hazelbury Infant School ED N9 99 M4
Hazeldene Medical Centre WBLY HA9 135 N1
Hazelwick School CRAWE RH10 284 B5
Hazelwood Infant School PLMGR N13 99 J5
Hazelwood Junior School PLMGR N13 99 H5
Hazelwood School OXTED RH8 261 M7
Headstart Montessori School TOOT SW17 179 M6
The Health Centre HARH RM3 105 M6
The Health Clinic SKENS SW7 15 M5
Healy Medical Centre CLPT E5 120 A6
The Heart Hospital CAVSQ/HST W1G 10 D4
Heathbrook Primary School VX/NE SW8 158 D8
Heath Business Centre HSLW TW3 154 B10
REDH RH1 276 C10
Heathcote Medical Centre KWD/TDW/WH KT20 238 G8
Heathcote Secondary School CHING E4 101 K3
Heathermount the Learning Centre ASC SL5 192 C6
Heathfield College HAYES BR2 225 P3
Heathfield Primary School WHTN TW2 175 P4
Heathfield School PIN HA5 113 L5
Heath House Preparatory School BKHTH/KID SE3 161 L8
The Heathland School HSLWW TW4 175 N2
Heathlands Special School STALW/RED AL3 38 D3
Heathmere Primary School PUT/ROE SW15 178 D4
Heathpark Golf Club WDR/YW UB7 152 B2
Heathrow Airport HTHAIR TW6 152 C8
Heathrow Airport Central Bus & Coach Station HTHAIR TW6 152 B9
Heathrow International Trading Estate HSLWW TW4 153 J9
Heathrow Medical Centre HYS/HAR UB3 152 E4
Heathrow Primary School WDR/YW UB7 152 A5
Heathrow Terminal 5 (under construction) HTHAIR TW6 151 M9
Heathrow World Cargo Centre HTHAIR TW6 174 A1
Heathside Preparatory School HAMP NW3 117 M9
Heathside School WEY KT13 216 A2
Heathway Industrial Estate DAGE RM10 124 C9
Heathway Medical Centre DAGW RM9 124 A9
Heavers Farm Primary School SNWD SE25 203 N5
Heber Primary School EDUL SE22 181 N2
Heckford Street Business Centre WAP E1W 140 C9
Hedges & Butler Estate SRTFD E15 141 H4
Hedgewood School YEAD UB4 132 F5
Helena Road Clinic WLSDN NW10 116 E9
Heliport Industrial Estate BTSEA SW11 157 N8
Hellenic College of London KTBR SW1X 16 A4
Helston Court Business Centre WIM/MER SW19 178 E8
Hemel Hempstead (Camelot) RFC HHW HP1 35 J8
Hemel Hempstead General Hospital HHNE HP2 35 N7
Hemel Hempstead RLFC HHNE HP2 36 A3
Hemel Hempstead School HHW HP1 35 M7
Hemel Hempstead Silver Blades Ice Rink HHNE HP2 36 A7
Hemel Hempstead Town CC HHW HP1 35 M8
Hemel Hempstead United FC HHNE HP2 36 C6
Hemel Ski Centre HHS/BOV HP3 35 P8

Henderson Hospital
BELMT SM2 221 K5
Hendon Cemetery
MLHL NW7 96 G9
Hendon Crematorium
MLHL NW7 96 G8
Hendon FC
CRICK NW2 116 C7
Hendon Golf Club
MLHL NW7 96 F8
Hendon Preparatory School
HDN NW4 116 C1
Hendon School
HDN NW4 116 G3
Hendon Secretarial College
HDN NW4 116 E3
Hendon Youth Sports Centre
CRICK NW2 116 G5
Henrietta Barnett School
GLDGN NW11 117 L3
Henry Cavendish Primary School
BAL SW12 180 D4
Henry Compton School
FUL/PGN SW6 156 G7
Henry Fawcett Primary School
LBTH SE11 18 A9
Henry Green Primary School
BCTR RM8 123 N6
Henry Maynard J & I School
WALTH E17 121 H3
Henwick Primary School
ELTH/MOT SE9 162 A9
Herbert Morrison Primary School
VX/NE SW8 158 F6
The Hereward County School
LOU IG10 82 F5
Hereward House School
HAMP NW3 3 N2
Herington House School
RBRW/HUT CM13 87 N10
Heritage Close Shopping Centre
STALW/RED AL3 38 C6
Heritage House Special School
CSHM HP5 51 J6
Her Majestys' Theatre
STJS SW1Y 11 K9
Hermitage County First School
WOKN/KNAP GU21 231 K5
Hermitage Primary School
UX/CGN UB8 131 N2
WAP E1W 13 N9
The Hermitage School
WOKN/KNAP GU21 231 K5
Hermitage Stairs
WAP E1W 13 N10
Herne Hill School
HNHL SE24 181 K1
Herne Hill Stadium (Cycle Centre)
HNHL SE24 181 L2
Heron Industrial Estate
SRTFD E15 140 C4
Heronsgate Primary School
THMD SE28 162 C2
Heron Trading Estate
ACT W3 135 N7
Herringham Primary School
CDW/CHF RM16 168 E2
Herschel Grammar School
SL SL1 129 H8
Hersham Trading Estate
WOT/HER KT12 197 M9
Hertford County Hospital
HERT/WAT SG14 25 J5
Hertford Museum
HERT/WAT SG14 25 L5
Hertford Regional College
BROX EN10 62 E1
WARE SG12 26 C3
Hertford St Andrew Primary School
HERT/WAT SG14 24 G4
Hertfordshire Business Centre
LCOL/BKTW AL2 57 J2
Hertfordshire Country Club
WGCE AL7 22 F8
Hertfordshire Police Constabulary HQ
WGCW AL8 22 F8
Hertford Town FC
HERT/BAY SG13 25 J6
Hertingfordbury Cowper Primary School
HERT/WAT SG14 24 D7
Hertsmere Jewish Primary School
RAD WD7 75 H4
Hertswood School & Sports Centre
BORE WD6 75 P5
Heston Community School
HEST TW5 153 P6
Heston Community Sports Hall
HEST TW5 153 P6
Heston Industrial Mall
HEST TW5 153 N6
Heston Infant School
HEST TW5 153 P6
Heston Junior School
HEST TW5 153 P6
Heston Park CC
HEST TW5 153 N5
Heston Swimming Baths
HEST TW5 153 N5
Hextable Primary School
SWLY BR8 186 G9
Heythrop College
KENS W8 14 G3
Higgs Industrial Estate
HNHL SE24 159 J9
Highams Lodge Business Centre
WALTH E17 120 C1
Highams Park School
CHING E4 101 J7
High Beech CE Primary School
LOU IG10 81 M5
High Beeches Primary School
HARP AL5 20 C3
High Beech Golf Club
LOU IG10 81 N3
Highbridge Industrial Estate
UX/CGN UB8 131 M1
Highbridge Retail Park
WAB EN9 62 G10
Highbury Corner Magistrates Court
HOLWY N7 6 B1
Highbury Fields School
HBRY N5 119 J9
Highbury Grove School
HBRY N5 119 K10
Highbury Park Clinic
HBRY N5 119 J8
Highbury Pool
HBRY N5 6 C1
Highbury Quadrant Primary School
HBRY N5 119 K9
Highbury Square development
HBRY N5 119 H8
Highclere Hotel
ASC SL5 192 C5
High Commission of Angola
MHST W1U 10 B4
High Commission of Antigua & Barbuda
MHST W1U 10 C5
High Commission of Bahamas
MYFR/PICC W1J 10 D9
High Commission of Bangladesh
SKENS SW7 15 K3
High Commission of Barbados
FITZ W1T 11 J5
High Commission of Belize
CAVSQ/HST W1G 10 F5
High Commission of Botswana
OXSTW W1C 10 E6
High Commission of Brunei
KTBR SW1X 16 C3
High Commission of Canada
MYFR/PKLN W1K 10 D7
High Commission of Cyprus
MYFR/PKLN W1K 10 C7
High Commission of Dominica
ECT SW5 15 H6
High Commission of Fiji
SKENS SW7 15 J2
High Commission of Grenada
ECT SW5 157 L4
High Commission of Guyana
BAY/PAD W2 8 G8
High Commission of Jamaica
SKENS SW7 15 L2
High Commission of Kenya
CAVSQ/HST W1G 10 E3
High Commission of Lesotho
KTBR SW1X 16 C3
High Commission of Malawi
MYFR/PKLN W1K 10 E7
High Commission of Malaysia
KTBR SW1X 16 D2
High Commission of Maldives
MHST W1U 10 C3
High Commission of Malta
CONDST W1S 11 H8
High Commission of Mauritius
SKENS SW7 15 K4
High Commission of Namibia
CAVSQ/HST W1G 10 F4
High Commission of New Zealand
STJS SW1Y 11 J9
High Commission of Nigeria
CHCR WC2N 11 L9
High Commission of Pakistan
KTBR SW1X 16 B3
High Commission of Papua New Guinea
STJS SW1Y 11 H9
High Commission of St Lucia
KENS W8 157 L1
High Commission of St Vincent & the Grenadines
KENS W8 15 H2
High Commission of Seychelles
MHST W1U 10 B3
High Commission of Sierra Leone
REGST W1B 10 G5
High Commission of Singapore
KTBR SW1X 16 C4
High Commission of South Africa
CHCR WC2N 11 L9
High Commission of Sri Lanka
BAY/PAD W2 9 M7
High Commission of Swaziland
WESTW SW1E 16 G3
High Commission of the Gambia
KENS W8 15 H2
High Commission of Tonga
MBLAR W1H 9 P4
High Commission of Trinidad & Tobago
KTBR SW1X 16 C3
High Commission of Uganda
WHALL SW1A 11 K9
High Commission of Zambia
KENS W8 15 J2
High Commission of Zimbabwe
CHCR WC2N 11 L8
High Cross Centre
SEVS/STOTM N15 119 P2
High Elms Country Park
ORP BR6 226 F4
High Elms Golf Club
ORP BR6 226 F4
Highfield Infant School
HAYES BR2 205 L4
Highfield Junior School
HAYES BR2 205 K4
Highfield Primary School
WCHMH N21 99 J2
Highfield School
HGDN/ICK UB10 132 C5
WAND/EARL SW18 179 P3
High Firs Primary School
SWLY BR8 208 G4
Highgate Cemetery
HGT N6 118 B6
Highgate Golf Club
EFNCH N2 117 P4
Highgate Junior School
HGT N6 118 A5
Highgate Montessori School
BAR EN5 77 H7
Highgate Primary School
HGT N6 118 A4
Highgate Private Hospital
HGT N6 118 A4
Highgate School
HGT N6 118 A5
Highgate Wood School
MUSWH N10 118 D3
Highgrove Pool
RSLP HA4 113 H5
Highlands J & I School
IL IG1 122 C6
Highlands Primary School
IL IG1 122 C6
High March School
BEAC HP9 88 D7
Highshore School
PECK SE15 159 N7
High Street Business Park
CHES/WCR EN8 62 D8
High View Primary School
BTSEA SW11 157 N10
Highview Primary School
WLGTN SM6 222 F2
The Highway Primary School
ORP BR6 227 M2
The Highway Trading Centre
WAP E1W 140 C9
High Wood Hospital
BRW CM14 106 G2
Highwood Primary School
BUSH WD23 73 M5
Hillbrook Primary School
TOOT SW17 180 A7
Hillcroft College
SURB KT6 199 K6
Hillcroft Primary School
CTHM CR3 241 M9
Hillcross Primary School
MRDN SM4 201 J4
Hilldene Primary School
HARH RM3 105 K7
Hille Business Centre
WATN WD24 73 J5
Hill Farm Industrial Estate
GSTN WD25 54 G9
Hillgrove Business Park
WAB EN9 45 H8
Hill House Preparatory School
CHEL SW3 157 P5
Hill House School
CHEL SW3 15 P9
KTBR SW1X 16 A4
Hillingdon Borough FC
RSLP HA4 112 C3
Hillingdon Cemetery
UX/CGN UB8 131 P5
Hillingdon Golf Club
HGDN/ICK UB10 132 A4
Hillingdon Hospital
UX/CGN UB8 132 A7
Hillingdon Manor School
UX/CGN UB8 132 C7
Hillingdon Primary School
HGDN/ICK UB10 132 B5
Hill Mead Infant School
BRXN/ST SW9 159 J10
Hillmead Primary School
BRXN/ST SW9 159 J10
Hill School
BH/WHM TN16 244 E9
Hills Grove Primary School
WELL DA16 163 M6
Hillside Primary School
NTHWD HA6 93 H8
STMC/STPC BR5 207 M7
Hill Top First School
WDSR SL4 148 D9
Hilltop Primary School
CRAWW RH11 283 M9
Hillyfield Primary School
WALTH E17 120 D1
Hilly Fields Medical Centre
BROCKY SE4 182 F1
Hilton Docklands Pier
BERM/RHTH SE16 140 E10
The Hiltongrove Business Centre
WALTH E17 120 F2
Hinchley Wood Primary School
ESH/CLAY KT10 198 F9
Hinchley Wood School & Sixth Form Centre
ESH/CLAY KT10 198 F9
Hinley Clinic
LBTH SE11 18 B6
Hispaniola
WHALL SW1A 11 M10
Hitherfield Primary School
STRHM/NOR SW16 181 H5
Hither Green Cemetery
CAT SE6 183 L5
Hither Green Primary School
LEW SE13 183 J2
HM Customs
HTHAIR TW6 152 C7
HM Prison
BELMT SM2 221 M8
BRXS/STRHM SW2 180 F2
HHS/BOV HP3 52 C2
HOLWY N7 5 N2
HOLWY N7 118 F9
WAND/EARL SW18 179 N3
HM Prison Belmarsh
THMD SE28 163 H2
HM Prison Coldingley
CHOB/PIR GU24 230 E3
HM Prison Send
RPLY/SEND GU23 251 M3
HM Prison Wormwood Scrubs
SHB W12 136 D8
HMS Belfast
STHWK SE1 13 K9
HMS President
EMB EC4Y 12 B7
HM Young Offender Institution
FELT TW13 174 E6
Hobbayne First & Middle School
HNWL W7 134 E8
Hobbayne Primary School
HNWL W7 134 D8
Hobbs Hill Wood Primary School
HHS/BOV HP3 36 C8
Hobletts Manor Primary School
HHNE HP2 36 A5
Hockley Industrial Centre
REDH RH1 276 A1
Hoddesdon Health Centre
HOD EN11 44 F4
Hoddesdon Industrial Estate
HOD EN11 45 H2
Hoddesdon Lawn Tennis Club
HOD EN11 44 E3
Hoebridge Golf Centre
WOKS/MYFD GU22 232 F5
Hoe Bridge Pre Preparatory School
WOKS/MYFD GU22 232 E5
Hogan Business Centre
WOKN/KNAP GU21 232 B3
Hogarth Business Park
CHSWK W4 156 B5
Hogarth Industrial Estate
WLSDN NW10 136 D6
Hogarth Primary School
BRWN CM15 107 K3
Hogarth's House
CHSWK W4 156 A5
Holbeach Primary School
CAT SE6 182 F3
Holborn College
WOOL/PLUM SE18 162 A3
Holborn College Independent School
HMSMTH W6 156 F4
Holborn Medical Centre
BMSBY WC1N 11 N2
Holborn Town Hall
HHOL WC1V 11 M5
Holdbrook Primary School
CHES/WCR EN8 62 E10
Holiday Inn
BORE WD6 76 B7
CAMTN NW1 4 E4
FSBYW WC1X 5 P10
SHPTN TW17 196 G6
Holland House
KENS W8 14 D2
Holland House School
EDGW HA8 95 M5
Holland Park Pre Preparatory School
WKENS W14 14 C4
Holland Park School
KENS W8 8 D10
Holland Park Theatre
KENS W8 14 D2
Holland Street Clinic
KENS W8 14 F2
Hollickwood JMI School
MUSWH N10 98 C8
Hollies Way Industrial Estate
POTB/CUF EN6 59 M7
Holloway School
HOLWY N7 118 E10
Hollybush Business Centre
HORL RH6 284 G1
Hollybush Primary School
HERT/WAT SG14 25 H5
Hollydale Primary School
PECK SE15 160 B8
The Hollyfield School
SURB KT6 199 K5
Holly House Private Hospital
BKHH IG9 101 N3
Holly Industrial Park
WATN WD24 73 K5
Hollymount Primary School
RYNPK SW20 200 F1
Holly Park JMI School
FBAR/BDGN N11 98 B6
Hollytrees Junior School
BRW CM14 106 G5
Holly Trees Primary School
BRW CM14 107 H5
Hollywood Bowl
BERM/RHTH SE16 160 C2
CRAWE RH10 283 N6
Holmesdale School
REIG RH2 257 L8
The Holme
CAMTN NW1 4 B10
Holmethorpe Industrial Estate
REDH RH1 258 C7
Holmleigh Primary School
STNW/STAM N16 119 N6
Holmshill School
BORE WD6 75 P6
Holtsmere End J & I School
HHNE HP2 36 C1
Holwell J & I School
WGCE AL7 23 H6
Holy Cross Catholic Primary School
HLWS CM18 47 K3
Holy Cross Convent School
CFSP/GDCR SL9 90 A9
Holy Cross Preparatory School
KUTN/CMB KT2 177 P10
Holy Cross Primary School
FUL/PGN SW6 157 K7
Holy Cross RC Convent School
NWMAL KT3 200 A4
Holy Cross RC Primary School
CAT SE6 183 H4
SOCK/AV RM15 146 G9
Holy Family Catholic School
DTCH/LGLY SL3 150 C4
Holy Family RC Primary School
ADL/WDHM KT15 215 K3
BKHTH/KID SE3 161 N10
POP/IOD E14 140 F9
Holy Family Technology College
WALTH E17 120 G2
Holy Ghost RC Primary School
BAL SW12 180 A3
Holy Innocents Catholic Primary School
ORP BR6 207 J10
Holy Rood RC Infant School
WAT WD17 72 E2
Holy Rood RC Junior School
WAT WD17 72 E2
Holy Trinity CE Junior School
GU GU1 268 C2
WLGTN SM6 222 D1
Holy Trinity CE Primary School
ASC SL5 192 F6
BRXS/STRHM SW2 180 G3
CHOB/PIR GU24 212 F8
DART DA1 187 K1
EFNCH N2 117 N1
GVE DA12 190 F3
HAMP NW3 3 K2
KIL/WHAMP NW6 137 M1
KTBR SW1X 16 C5
NTHWD HA6 92 D7
RCHPK/HAM TW10 155 M10
SYD SE26 182 B5
The Holy Trinity CE School
CRAWW RH11 283 K9
Holy Trinity College
BMLY BR1 205 P1
Holy Trinity In St Silas
CAMTN NW1 4 E3
Holy Trinity Primary School
CHES/WCR EN8 62 C8
HACK E8 7 L2
WIM/MER SW19 179 K9
Holy Trinity School
BFN/LL DA15 185 K4
CHEL SW3 16 B5
Holywell School
WATW WD18 72 G10
Home Farm Industrial Estate
WARE SG12 27 L6
Homefield Preparatory School
SUT SM1 221 K2
Home Office
STJSPK SW1H 17 H2
Home Park Golf Club
CDST RH9 281 P3
Home Park Industrial Estate
KGLGY WD4 54 C7
Homers First School
WDSR SL4 148 C7
Homerswood J & I School
WGCW AL8 22 G1
Homerton College of Technology
HOM E9 120 B10
Homerton University Hospital
HOM E9 120 C10
Homewood Independent School
LCOL/BKTW AL2 56 A4
Homeopathic Health Centre
PLSTW E13 141 M6
The Homoeopathic Health Centre
MLHL NW7 96 C6
Honeypot Business Centre
STAN HA7 95 K9
Honeypot Lane Centre
STAN HA7 95 J9
Honeypot Medical Centre
STAN HA7 95 K10
Honeywell Primary School
BTSEA SW11 180 A2
Honilands Primary School
EN EN1 80 A2
Honor Oak Crematorium
FSTH SE23 182 C1
Honor Oak Gallery
FSTH SE23 182 C2
Honor Oak Health Centre
BROCKY SE4 160 D10
Honourable Artillery Company HQ
STLK EC1Y 12 G2
Hook Lane Primary School
WELL DA16 163 K9
Hook Rise South Industrial Park
CHSGTN KT9 199 L10
Hope Primary School
WALW SE17 159 M6
Horizon Business Centre
ED N9 100 C3
Horizon Industrial Estate
PECK SE15 19 N10
Horizon School
STNW/STAM N16 119 M9
Horley Anderson Centre
HORL RH6 279 P4
Horley Health Centre
HORL RH6 280 B4
Horley Infant School
HORL RH6 280 B4
Hornchurch Clinic
EMPK RM11 125 M6
Hornchurch Country Park
HCH RM12 145 K1
Hornchurch Sports Centre
EMPK RM11 125 K7
Hornchurch Stadium
UPMR RM14 125 P7
Horndon Industrial Park
RBRW/HUT CM13 127 N4
The Horniman Museum & Gardens
FSTH SE23 182 A4
Horniman Primary School
FSTH SE23 182 A4
Horn Park Primary School
LEE/GVPK SE12 183 N3
Hornsby House School
BAL SW12 180 B4
Hornsey Central Hospital
CEND/HSY/T N8 118 D3
Hornsey Rise Health Centre
ARCH N19 118 E5
Hornsey Secondary School for Girls
CEND/HSY/T N8 118 G3
Horn Stairs
BERM/RHTH SE16 140 E10
Horseferry Road Magistrates Court
WEST SW1P 17 K4
Horse Guards Parade
WHALL SW1A 11 K10
Horsell CE Junior School
WOKN/KNAP GU21 231 P2
Horsell Village School
WOKN/KNAP GU21 232 A2
Horsenden Hill Golf Club
GFD/PVL UB6 134 G1
Horsenden Primary School
GFD/PVL UB6 134 D1
Horseshoe Business Park
LCOL/BKTW AL2 56 A6
Horsley Camping & Caravanning Club Site
EHSLY KT24 234 D10
Horsley Sports Club
EHSLY KT24 252 G3
Horton Country Park
HOR/WEW KT19 219 M5
Horton Hospital
HOR/WEW KT19 219 P7
Horton Industrial Park
WDR/YW UB7 132 A10
Horton Kirby CE Primary School
EYN DA4 210 B3
Horton Kirby Trading Estate
EYN DA4 210 B2
Horton Park Golf & Country Club
HOR/WEW KT19 219 P4
Horton Trading Estate
DTCH/LGLY SL3 150 E9
Hortus Cemetery
NWDGN UB2 153 N1
Hospital of St John & St Elizabeth
STJWD NW8 3 L8
The Hotel at Chelsea
FUL/PGN SW6 157 L6
Hotel Ibis
CAMTN NW1 5 H10
CAN/RD E16 141 N9
CRAWE RH10 283 P2
FUL/PGN SW6 14 E9
GNWCH SE10 161 H5
HYS/HAR UB3 152 F7
POP/IOD E14 141 H9
SRTFD E15 141 K1
WBLY HA9 115 M10
WTHK RM20 166 E5
The Hotel Russell
RSQ WC1B 11 L2
Hotham Primary School
PUT/ROE SW15 156 G10
Hot Shots Ten Pin Bowling
HHNE HP2 36 A7
Hotspur Industrial Estate
TOTM N17 100 A7
Houndsfield Primary School
ED N9 99 P1
Hounslow Business Park
HSLW TW3 153 P10
Hounslow CC
HSLW TW3 153 N8
Hounslow Cemetery
HSLWW TW4 175 N3
Hounslow College Independent School
FELT TW13 175 L7
Hounslow Heath Golf Club
HSLWW TW4 175 L1
Hounslow Heath Infant School
HSLWW TW4 153 M9
Hounslow Heath Junior School
HSLWW TW4 153 M9
Hounslow Manor School
HSLW TW3 154 A9
Hounslow Manor Sports Hall
HSLW TW3 154 A9
Hounslow Town Primary School
HSLW TW3 154 B9
Household Cavalry Museum
WDSR SL4 148 G9
House of Detention
CLKNW EC1R 12 B1
House of St Barnabus
SOHO/SHAV W1D 11 J6
Houses of Parliament
WHALL SW1A 17 M2
Houston Business Park
YEAD UB4 133 K10
Howard Business Park
WAB EN9 63 J10
The Howard Centre
WGCW AL8 22 G5
Howard Industrial Estate
CSHM HP5 51 H5
Howard of Effingham School
EHSLY KT24 253 L3
Howard Primary School
SAND/SEL CR2 223 K1
Howbury Centre
ERITH DA8 165 H6
Howe Dell Primary School
HAT AL10 40 E4
Howland Quay
BERM/RHTH SE16 160 C2
How Wood Primary School
LCOL/BKTW AL2 56 B3
Hoxton Hall Community Theatre
IS N1 7 J7
HQS Wellington (Master Mariners)
TPL/STR WC2R 12 A8
HSBC Sports Club
BECK BR3 182 D9
HSBC Tower
POP/IOD E14 140 G10
Hubbinet Industrial Estate
ROMW/RG RM7 124 D1
Hugh Myddelton Primary School
CLKNW EC1R 6 B10
The Humana Wellington Hospital
STJWD NW8 3 M9
Humber Trading Estate
CRICK NW2 116 E7
Huntercombe Manor Hospital
MDHD SL6 128 B9
Hunterian Museum
LINN WC2A 11 P5
Hunters Hall Primary School
DAGE RM10 124 C10
Hunter Street Health Centre
STPAN WC1H 11 L1
Huntsman Sports Club
BKHTH/KID SE3 161 M10
Hurlingham Business Park
FUL/PGN SW6 157 K9
Hurlingham & Chelsea Secondary School
FUL/PGN SW6 157 K9
Hurlingham House
FUL/PGN SW6 157 J9
Hurlingham Private School
PUT/ROE SW15 157 J10
Huron University
RSQ WC1B 11 L3
SKENS SW7 15 M4
Hurricane Trading Centre
CDALE/KGS NW9 96 C9
Hurst Drive Primary School
CHES/WCR EN8 62 B10
Hurst Green School
OXTED RH8 261 M8
Hurst Lodge School
ASC SL5 192 A8
Hurstmere School
BFN/LL DA15 185 L4
Hurst Park Primary School
E/WMO/HCT KT8 197 P3
Hurst Primary School
BXLY DA5 185 N4
Hurtmore Golf Club
GODL GU7 266 E10
Hyatt Carlton Tower Hotel
KTBR SW1X 16 B4
Hyatt Regency-The Churchill
MBLAR W1H 10 B5
Hyde Heath Infant School
AMS HP6 50 B10
The Hyde Industrial Estate
CDALE/KGS NW9 116 C3
The Hyde School
CDALE/KGS NW9 116 C3
Hyland Business Centre
REDH RH1 258 A10
Hyland House School
WALTH E17 101 J10
Hyleford Leavers Unit School
BARK/HLT IG6 102 G10
Hyleford School
IL IG1 123 H10
Hythe First & Middle School
STA TW18 172 G8
Hythe Road Industrial Estate
WLSDN NW10 136 D6
Ian Mikardo High School
BOW E3 140 G5
Ibstock Place School
PUT/ROE SW15 178 B2
ICA Cinema
STJS SW1Y 11 K9
Ickburgh School
CLPT E5 120 A8
Ickenham Clinic
HGDN/ICK UB10 112 D8
Ide Hill CE Aided Primary School
RSEV TN14 263 P7
Ifield Community College
CRAWW RH11 283 K6
Ifield Golf & Country Club
CRAWW RH11 282 G7
Ifield School
GVE DA12 190 F8
Ihlara Sport FC
HBRY N5 119 K9
IKEA Store Brent Park
WLSDN NW10 116 A10
IKEA Store Croydon
CROY/NA CR0 202 G8
IKEA Store Edmonton
TOTM N17 100 B7
IKEA Store Lakeside
WTHK RM20 166 G4
Ilderton Primary School
PECK SE15 160 B5
Ilford County High School
BARK/HLT IG6 102 F10
Ilford Golf Club
IL IG1 122 C6
Ilford Jewish Primary School
BARK/HLT IG6 122 G1
Ilford Medical Centre
IL IG1 122 E8
Ilford Preparatory School
GDMY/SEVK IG3 123 J6
Ilford Retail Park
IL IG1 122 F7
Ilford Swimming Pool
IL IG1 122 G7
Ilford Ursuline High School
IL IG1 122 E7
Iman Zakaria Academy
FSTGT E7 121 N10
Imber Court Trading Estate
E/WMO/HCT KT8 198 C6
Immanuel CE Primary School
STRHM/NOR SW16 180 F9
Immanuel College
BUSH WD23 94 D1
Immanuel School
ROM RM1 104 F7
Imperial College
PUT/ROE SW15 156 G8
SKENS SW7 15 L3
SKENS SW7 15 L8
Imperial College Athletic Ground
HYS/HAR UB3 152 D5
Imperial College of Science
FUL/PGN SW6 14 E9
SKENS SW7 15 L2
Imperial College of Science Technology & Medicine
ASC SL5 192 E3
SKENS SW7 15 K3
Imperial College School of Medicine
PIM SW1V 17 J6
Imperial Retail Park
GVW DA11 190 D2
Imperial Trading Estate
RAIN RM13 145 K6
Imperial War Museum
STHWK SE1 18 B4
Imperial War Museum Annexe
LBTH SE11 18 B4
Inchbald School of Design
BGVA SW1W 16 D5
PIM SW1V 16 G6
Independent Industrial Estate
WDR/YW UB7 132 A10
Independent Jewish School
HDN NW4 116 G3
India House
HOL/ALD WC2B 11 N7
Industrial Health Clinic
UX/CGN UB8 131 L5
Infant College
IL IG1 122 D7
The Infirmary Royal Hospital
CHEL SW3 16 C8
Ingrave Johnstone CE Primary School
RBRW/HUT CM13 107 P7
Ingrebourne Primary School
HARH RM3 105 K5
Innellan House School
PIN HA5 113 M1
Inner London Sessions House (Crown Court)
STHWK SE1 18 E3
Innholders Hall
CANST EC4R 12 F7
Innkeeper's Lodge
BEAC HP9 88 D10
BECK BR3 204 F6
BORE WD6 75 P6
CHEAM SM3 201 K8
DTCH/LGLY SL3 150 C4
LCOL/BKTW AL2 57 K3
NTHLT UB5 133 P1
SAND/SEL CR2 223 K5
STHGT/OAK N14 98 F4
WAN E11 121 M2
WDSR SL4 171 M1
WEY KT13 196 F10
WFD IG8 102 C7
WOKN/KNAP GU21 232 B2
WOT/HER KT12 197 H10
Innova Business Park
PEND EN3 80 E2
Inns of Court & Chancery
TPL/STR WC2R 12 A6
Inns of Court Law School
GINN WC1R 11 P3

Institute of Cancer Research *ECT* SW5 15 K7
Institute of Education *GWRST* WC1E 11 K2
Institute of Education University of London *RSQ* WC1B 11 K2
InterContinental Hotel *MYFR/PICC* W1J 16 D1
International Community School *CAMTN* NW1 10 C2
International Medical Centre *ECT* SW5 14 F6
International School of Havana *STJS* SW1Y 11 K9
International School of London *ACT* W3 155 M3
International School of Moscow *WHALL* SW1A 158 F1
International Trading Estate *NWDGN* UB2 153 J2
International University *BUSH* WD23 73 N8
Invicta Industrial Estate *SRTFD* E15 141 H5
Invicta Primary School *BKHTH/KID* SE3 161 M5
Invicta Sports Club *DART* DA1 187 L1
Inwood Business Centre *HSLW* TW3 154 A10
IQRA Independent School *BRXN/ST* SW9 159 H9
Ironmonger Row Baths *FSBYE* EC1V 6 E10
Ironmongers Hall *STBT* EC1A 12 E4
Islamia Girls School *KIL/WHAMP* NW6 137 H3
Islamia Primary School *KIL/WHAMP* NW6 2 B5
Islamic College *WCHPL* E1 13 P5
Islamic College for Advanced Study *WLSDN* NW10 136 E2
Islamic Cultural Centre & London Central Mosque *CAMTN* NW1 3 P9
The Islamic Grammar School *WAND/EARL* SW18 179 J3
Island Clinic *POP/IOD* E14 161 H1
Isleworth Cemetery *ISLW* TW7 154 F8
Isleworth Recreation Centre *ISLW* TW7 154 E10
Isleworth & Syon School for Boys *ISLW* TW7 154 D6
Isleworth Town Primary School *ISLW* TW7 154 E8
Islington Arts & Media School *FSBYPK* N4 118 G6
Islington Business Centre *IS* N1 6 F5
Islington Crematorium *MUSWH* N10 98 A9
Islington Green Medical Centre *IS* N1 6 C5
Islington Green School *IS* N1 6 D6
Islington Tennis Centre *HOLWY* N7 5 L2
Islington Town Hall *IS* N1 6 C3
Ismaili Centre *SKENS* SW7 15 M5
Italia Conti Academy of Theatre Arts *BRXN/ST* SW9 158 F9
Italian Hospital *PIM* SW1V 16 G5
Ithaca College *SKENS* SW7 157 M3
Iver Golf & Leisure Centre *IVER* SL0 130 E10
Iver Heath First School *IVER* SL0 130 G5
Iver Heath Health Centre *IVER* SL0 130 G4
Iver Heath Primary School *IVER* SL0 130 G4
Iver Village Infant School *IVER* SL0 131 J8
Iver Village Junior School *IVER* SL0 131 H8
Ivybridge Primary School *TWK* TW1 176 E2
Ivybridge Retail Park *ISLW* TW7 176 E1
Ivy Chimneys Primary School *EPP* CM16 65 J8
Ivydale Primary School *PECK* SE15 160 C10
Jack & Jill School *HPTN* TW12 175 P9
WHTN TW2 176 D5
Jack Taylor School *STJWD* NW8 3 J5
Jack Tizard School *FUL/PGN* SW6 156 G7
SHB W12 136 F9
Jacques Prevert School *HMSMTH* W6 156 G3
Jamahiriya School *CHEL* SW3 157 P5
James Allens Preparatory Girls School *HNHL* SE24 181 L1
James Dixon Primary School *PGE/AN* SE20 203 P1
James Elliman School *SLN* SL2 129 K8
James Oglethorpe Primary School *UPMR* RM14 126 E7
Jamestown Mental Health Centre *HAMP* NW3 4 A3
James Wolfe Primary School *GNWCH* SE10 160 G6
Jamiatul Ummah School *WCHPL* E1 140 A8
Janet Adegoke Leisure Centre *SHB* W12 136 D9
The Japanese School *ACT* W3 135 M9
Japan Green Medical Centre *ACT* W3 135 N10
Jenner Health Centre *FSTH* SE23 182 D4
Jenny Hammond Primary School *WAN* E11 121 K9
Jermyn Street Theatre *MYFR/PICC* W1J 11 H8
Jerounds J & I School *HLWW/ROY* CM19 46 E4
Jessop Primary School *HNHL* SE24 159 J10
Jewel Tower *WEST* SW1P 17 L3
Jewish Cemetery *GLDGN* NW11 117 K4
Jewish Community Theatre *HNHL* SE24 159 L9
Jewish Free School *KTN/HRWW/WS* HA3 115 L4
KTN NW5 5 H1
The Jewish Museum *CAMTN* NW1 4 E6
FNCH N3 97 K10
Johanna Primary School *STHWK* SE1 18 A2
John Ball Primary School *BKHTH/KID* SE3 161 K8
John Betts Primary School *HMSMTH* W6 156 D2
John Bramston Primary School *BARK/HLT* IG6 103 K8
John Burns Primary School *BTSEA* SW11 158 B8
John Chilton School *NTHLT* UB5 133 M2
John Dixon Clinic *BERM/RHTH* SE16 160 A2
John Donne Primary School *PECK* SE15 160 A7
John F Kennedy RC School *HHW* HP1 35 J5
John F Kennedy Special School *SRTFD* E15 141 J3
John Keble CE Primary School *WLSDN* NW10 136 C4
John Kelly Boys & Girls Technology College *CRICK* NW2 116 C8
The John Loughborough School *TOTM* N17 99 N10
John Lyon School *RYLN/HDSTN* HA2 114 C6
John Nightingale School *E/WMO/HCT* KT8 197 N3
John Orwell Sports Centre *WAP* E1W 139 P10
John Paul II RC School *WIM/MER* SW19 178 G3
John Penrose School *DEN/HRF* UB9 91 N9
John Penrose Sports Centre *DEN/HRF* UB9 91 N9
John Perryn Primary School *ACT* W3 136 B8
John Perry Primary School *DAGE* RM10 144 E1
John Roan Lower School *BKHTH/KID* SE3 161 L6
John Roan School *BKHTH/KID* SE3 161 K6
John Ruskin College *SAND/SEL* CR2 224 D4
John Ruskin Primary School *WALW* SE17 18 E9
John Scott Health Centre *FSBYPK* N4 119 K6
John Scurr Primary School *WCHPL* E1 140 B6
John Smith House *WALW* SE17 18 E6
Johnsons Industrial Estate *HYS/HAR* UB3 153 H2
John Stainer Primary School *BROCKY* SE4 160 D9
The John Warner School *HOD* EN11 26 G10
Jordans School *BEAC* HP9 89 L7
The Jo Richardson Community School *DAGW* RM9 143 N3
Joseph Clarke Special School *CHING* E4 101 J7
Joseph Hood Primary School *RYNPK* SW20 201 H2
Joseph Lancaster Primary School *STHWK* SE1 18 F4
Joydens Wood Infant School *RDART* DA2 186 F7
Joydens Wood Junior School *BXLY* DA5 186 F7
Jubilee Centre *STALW/RED* AL3 38 C5
Jubilee Country Park *BMLY* BR1 206 E4
Jubilee Hall Clinic *CRAWE* RH10 284 B7
Jubilee Market *COVGDN* WC2E 11 M7
Jubilee Primary School *BRXS/STRHM* SW2 181 H2
THMD SE28 143 M9
Jubilee Sports Centre *NKENS* W10 2 B10
Jubilee Sports Ground *CHING* E4 101 J5
Julians Primary School *STRHM/NOR* SW16 181 H7
Jumeirah Carlton Tower Hotel *KTBR* SW1X 16 B3
Juno Way Industrial Estate *NWCR* SE14 160 C5
Jupiter Drive JMI School *HHNE* HP2 36 A4
Jurys Clifton-Ford Hotel *MHST* W1U 10 D4
Jurys Great Russell Street *RSQ* WC1B 11 K5
Jurys Inn *CROY/NA* CR0 203 K9
Jurys Inn Chelsea *FUL/PGN* SW6 157 M7
Jurys Inn Hotel *HTHAIR* TW6 152 G9
Jurys Inn Islington *IS* N1 6 A8
Jurys Kensington Hotel *SKENS* SW7 15 L6
JVC Business Park *CRICK* NW2 116 D6
Kaizen Primary School *PLSTW* E13 141 N6
Kangley Business Centre *SYD* SE26 182 E8
Katella Trading Estate *BARK* IG11 143 H5
Katherine Road Medical Centre *FSTGT* E7 141 P1
Katherines Primary School *HLWW/ROY* CM19 46 C3
Keats House Museum *HAMP* NW3 117 N9
Keble Preparatory School *WCHMH* N21 99 H1
Keen Students Supplementary School *WCHPL* E1 139 P7
Keir Hardie Primary School *CAN/RD* E16 141 M7
Keith Davis Cue Sports Club *DAGW* RM9 143 N2
Kelmscott Community Centre *WALTH* E17 120 E4
Kelmscott Leisure Centre *WALTH* E17 120 E4
Kelmscott School *WALTH* E17 120 E4
Kelrose Swimming Pool Centre *RBRW/HUT* CM13 127 K3
Kelsey Park School *BECK* BR3 204 F3
Kelvedon Hatch C&C Club Site *BRWN* CM15 86 E6
Kelvedon Hatch Primary School *BRWN* CM15 86 D2
Kelvedon Hatch Secret Nuclear Bunker *BRWN* CM14 86 B2
Kelvin Business Centre *CRAWE* RH10 284 A4
Kelvin Industrial Estate *GFD/PVL* UB6 134 A3
GFD/PVL UB6 134 C5
Kemnal Technology College *STMC/STPC* BR5 185 L10
Kempton Park Racecourse *SUN* TW16 175 J10
Kemsing Down Nature Reserve *BGR/WK* TN15 247 P2
Ken Barrington Centre *LBTH* SE11 17 P10
Kender Primary School *NWCR* SE14 160 B7
Kenilworth Primary School *BORE* WD6 76 A7
Kenley Primary School *PUR/KEN* CR8 241 M2
Kenley Sports Club *PUR/KEN* CR8 223 K10
Kenmont Primary School *WLSDN* NW10 136 D5
Kenmore Park Middle School *KTN/HRWW/WS* HA3 115 J1
Kenneth More Theatre *IL* IG1 122 F8
Kenningtons Primary School *SOCK/AV* RM15 146 B8
Kensal Green Cemetery *WLSDN* NW10 136 E5
Kensal Rise Primary School *KIL/WHAMP* NW6 136 G4
Kensington and Chelsea College *CHEL* SW3 15 M9
KENS W8 14 E1
NKENS W10 8 B3
NKENS W10 8 C2
Kensington and Chelsea Town Hall *KENS* W8 14 F2
Kensington Avenue Primary School *THHTH* CR7 203 H1
Kensington Business Centre *SKENS* SW7 15 P3
The Kensington Clinic *KENS* W8 14 G4
The Kensington Dyslexia Teaching Centre *KENS* W8 157 L2
The Kensington Gardens School *BAY/PAD* W2 137 L9
Kensington House Hotel *KENS* W8 15 J2
Kensington Leisure Centre *NTGHL* W11 136 G9
Kensington Market *KENS* W8 14 G2
Kensington Palace *KENS* W8 137 L10
Kensington Palace State Apartments & Royal Ceremonial Dress Collection *KENS* W8 9 H10
Kensington Park School *REGST* W1B 10 F3
Kensington Preparatory School *FUL/PGN* SW6 157 J7
Kensington Primary School *MNPK* E12 142 C1
Kensington School of Business *HCIRC* EC1N 12 B3
Kensington Temple Institute of Education *EA* W5 135 K5
Kensington Wharf *WBPTN* SW10 157 N6
Kensit Memorial College *FNCH* N3 97 H10
Kentish Town CE Primary School *KTTN* NW5 118 D10
Kentish Town Health Centre *KTTN* NW5 4 G2
Kentish Town Industrial Estate *KTTN* NW5 118 C10
Kentish Town Sports Centre *KTTN* NW5 4 D1
Kent Kraft Industrial Estate *SWCM* DA10 167 L10
SWCM DA10 189 L1
Kenton Clinic *KTN/HRWW/WS* HA3 115 K3
Kenton CC *KTN/HRWW/WS* HA3 115 H2
Kent Park Industrial Estate *PECK* SE15 160 A5
Kenwood House *HAMP* NW3 117 P6
Kenyngton Manor Primary School *SUN* TW16 175 H8
The Kerem School *EFNCH* N2 117 N3
Kestner Industrial Estate *RDART* DA2 166 F10
Keston CE Primary School *HAYES* BR2 226 A2
Keston Primary School *COUL/CHIP* CR5 241 H5
Kew Bridge Steam Museum *BTFD* TW8 155 L4
Kew College *RCH/KEW* TW9 155 M6
Kew Gardens (Royal Botanic Gardens) *BTFD* TW8 155 K7
Kew Palace *RCH/KEW* TW9 155 K6
Kew Retail Park *RCH/KEW* TW9 155 N7
Kew Riverside Primary School *RCH/KEW* TW9 155 N8
Keyplan & Roxburghe College *FITZ* W1T 11 H2
Keys Meadow Primary School *PEND* EN3 80 E2
Keyworth Primary School *WALW* SE17 18 C8
Khalsa College London *HRW* HA1 114 E4
Kidbrooke Park Primary School *BKHTH/KID* SE3 161 P8
Kidbrooke School *BKHTH/KID* SE3 162 A8
Kilburn Park Junior School *KIL/WHAMP* NW6 2 E8
Killick Street Medical Centre *IS* N1 5 N7
Killigrew Primary School *LCOL/BKTW* AL2 56 A1
Kilmorie Primary School *FSTH* SE23 182 D5
Kiln Park Business Centre *EW* KT17 220 B7
Kimberley Industrial Estate *WALTH* E17 100 E8
Kimpton Industrial Estate *CHEAM* SM3 201 J9
Kinetic Business Centre *BORE* WD6 75 L7
King Alfred School *GLDGN* NW11 117 L6
King Athelstan Primary School *KUT/HW* KT1 199 L3
King Edward Court Shopping Centre *WDSR* SL4 149 H7
King Edwards Road Clinic *RSLP* HA4 112 E6
King Edward VII Hospital *WDSR* SL4 149 H9
King Edward VII Hospital for Officers *MHST* W1U 10 D3
King Fahad Academy (Girls Upper School) *EA* W5 155 H3
Kingfield School *WOKS/MYFD* GU22 232 D6
The Kingfisher Medical Centre *DEPT* SE8 160 E5
The Kingfisher Sports Centre *KUT/HW* KT1 199 K2
King George Hospital *GDMY/SEVK* IG3 123 K3
Kingham Industrial Estate *WLSDN* NW10 136 A5
King Harold School *WAB* EN9 63 K9
King & Queen Wharf *BERM/RHTH* SE16 140 C9
Kings Arms Hotel *BH/WHM* TN16 262 G3
Kings Avenue Medical Centre *STHL* UB1 134 B8
Kings Avenue School *CLAP* SW4 180 F1
Kingsbury Green Primary School *CDALE/KGS* NW9 115 N3
Kingsbury High School (Lower School) *CDALE/KGS* NW9 115 P2
Kingsbury High School (Upper School) *CDALE/KGS* NW9 115 N2
Kingsbury Hospital *CDALE/KGS* NW9 115 M2
Kingsbury Tamil School *CDALE/KGS* NW9 115 N1
Kingsbury Trading Estate *CDALE/KGS* NW9 115 P4
Kingsbury Watermill Museum & Waffle House *STALW/RED* AL3 38 A6
Kings College for the Arts & Technology *GUW* GU2 249 K10
Kings College (Hampstead Campus) *HAMP* NW3 117 K9
King's College Hospital *CMBW* SE5 159 K9
Kings College London *CMBW* SE5 159 L8
HOL/ALD WC2B 11 M6
KENS W8 157 K1
STHWK SE1 12 C9
STHWK SE1 12 F10
TPL/STR WC2R 138 G9
WEST SW1P 17 H5
Kings College London - Humanities *TPL/STR* WC2R 11 N7
Kings College London - Law *TPL/STR* WC2R 11 P7
Kings College London (Waterloo Campus) *STHWK* SE1 12 A10
Kings College School *WIM/MER* SW19 178 F9
Kings College School of Medicine & Dentistry *CMBW* SE5 159 L8
DUL SE21 181 L2
Kings College Sports Ground *RSLP* HA4 112 F4
Kingscote School *CFSP/GDCR* SL9 110 B1
Kings Court First School *WDSR* SL4 171 M3
Kingscroft School *STA* TW18 173 K9
Kingsdale School *DUL* SE21 181 M6
Kings Estate *HCH* RM12 125 H9
Kings Farm Infant School *GVE* DA12 190 F8
Kingsfield Business Centre *REDH* RH1 276 B1
Kingsford Community School *PLSTW* E13 141 P6
Kingsgate Business Centre *KUTN/CMB* KT2 199 K1
Kingsgate Primary School *KIL/WHAMP* NW6 2 E3
Kings Hall Leisure Centre *CLPT* E5 120 B10
Kings Head Theatre *IS* N1 6 C5
Kings House School *RCHPK/HAM* TW10 177 L1
Kingsland College of Business Studies *SRTFD* E15 141 J4
Kingsland Health Centre *IS* N1 7 K3
Kingsland Shopping Centre *HACK* E8 7 L1
Kings Langley Primary School *KGLGY* WD4 54 A4
Kingsley Primary School *CROY/NA* CR0 202 G8
Kings Mall Shopping Centre *HMSMTH* W6 156 F3
Kingsmeadow Athletics Centre *KUT/HW* KT1 199 M3
Kingsmead Primary School *CLPT* E5 120 D9
Kingsmead School *EN* EN1 79 P8
Kingsmoor Primary School *HLWW/ROY* CM19 46 F5
Kingsmoor Recreation Centre *HLWW/ROY* CM19 46 E5
The Kings Oak Private Hospital *ENC/FH* EN2 79 H4
King Solomon High School *BARK/HLT* IG6 102 G10
Kings Park Industrial Estate *KGLGY* WD4 54 C5
Kings Private Clinic *GDMY/SEVK* IG3 123 J6
MHST W1U 10 C3
Kings School of English *BECK* BR3 204 E2
Kings Stairs *BERM/RHTH* SE16 160 A1
Kingston Business Centre *CHSGTN* KT9 199 K10
Kingston College of Further Education *KUT/HW* KT1 199 K3
Kingston College Theatre *KUT/HW* KT1 199 J3
Kingston Crematorium *KUT/HW* KT1 199 M3
Kingston Crown Court *KUT/HW* KT1 199 J3
Kingston Grammar School *KUT/HW* KT1 199 L2
Kingston Hospital *KUTN/CMB* KT2 199 M1
Kingstonian FC *NWMAL* KT3 199 N3
Kingston University *BRYLDS* KT5 199 M5
KUT/HW KT1 199 K3
KUTN/CMB KT2 178 A10
PUT/ROE SW15 178 C5
King Street College *HMSMTH* W6 156 F3
Kingsway Business Park *HPTN* TW12 197 N1
Kingsway College *CAMTN* NW1 10 G1
FSBYW WC1X 5 P9
KTTN NW5 4 E1
STPAN WC1H 5 N10
Kingsway Junior School *GSTN* WD25 55 H10
Kingswey Business Park *WOKN/KNAP* GU21 214 F10
Kingswood Golf Club *KWD/TDW/WH* KT20 239 K10
Kingswood House School *HOR/WEW* KT19 219 N9
Kingswood Primary School *KWD/TDW/WH* KT20 257 J4
WNWD SE27 181 L7
Kings Wood School *HARH* RM3 105 P5
Kisharon School *GLDGN* NW11 117 J4
K+K Hotel George *ECT* SW5 14 F6
KLC School of Design *WBPTN* SW10 157 M7
Knaphill Junior School *WOKN/KNAP* GU21 231 H4
Knaphill Lower School *WOKN/KNAP* GU21 230 G4
Knightsbridge Barracks *SKENS* SW7 15 P2
Knightsbridge Medical Centre *KTBR* SW1X 16 B3
The Knightsbridge Under School *SKENS* SW7 157 M3
The Knightsbridge Upper School *SKENS* SW7 157 P1
Knockhall Community Primary School *SWCM* DA10 189 H1
Knole (NT) *BGR/WK* TN15 265 L2
Knole Park Golf Club *BGR/WK* TN15 247 L10
Knollmead Primary School *BRYLDS* KT5 199 P9
Knowledge Point School *HOLWY* N7 5 N2
Knowle Park Infant School *STA* TW18 173 K8
Knowl Hill School *CHOB/PIR* GU24 230 D8
Knutsford School *WATN* WD24 73 L4
Kobi Nazrul Primary School *WCHPL* E1 13 P5
KP Estate *RAIN* RM13 144 F9
Kubrick Business Estate *FSTGT* E7 121 N9
Laban Centre for Movement & Dance *DEPT* SE8 160 G6
Laburnum Health Centre *DAGE* RM10 124 B7
Ladbrooke Primary School *POTB/CUF* EN6 59 L8
Lady Bankes Primary School *RSLP* HA4 113 H6
Lady Boswells CE Primary School *SEV* TN13 265 K1
The Lady Eleanor Holles School *HPTN* TW12 176 A8
Lady Margaret Primary School *STHL* UB1 133 N7
Lady Margaret School *FUL/PGN* SW6 157 K7
Ladymead Retail Centre *GU* GU1 249 P9
Ladywell Arena *LEW* SE13 182 G2
Ladywell Cemetery *BROCKY* SE4 182 E1
Ladywell Leisure Centre *LEW* SE13 183 H1
Laharna Trading Estate *WATN* WD24 73 K4
Laine Theatre Arts *EW* KT17 220 B9
Laings Sports Ground *BAR* EN5 76 B8
Lake Business Centre *TOTM* N17 99 P7
Laker Industrial Estate *BECK* BR3 182 E8
Lakeside Industrial Estate *DTCH/LGLY* SL3 151 H6
Lakeside Retail Park *WTHK* RM20 166 F3
Lakeside Shopping Centre *WTHK* RM20 166 G3
Lakeside Special School *WGCW* AL8 22 E7
Laleham CE Primary School *STA* TW18 195 M2
Laleham Golf Club *CHERT* KT16 195 L4
Laleham Lea Preparatory School *PUR/KEN* CR8 222 F6
Lambeth Academy *CLAP* SW4 180 D1
Lambeth Cemetery *TOOT* SW17 179 M8
Lambeth College *BRXS/STRHM* SW2 180 G1
CLAP SW4 180 D1
STHWK SE1 13 K10
STRHM/NOR SW16 180 F5
VX/NE SW8 158 E7
Lambeth County Court *LBTH* SE11 18 B7
Lambeth Crematorium *TOOT* SW17 179 M7
Lambeth Education *LBTH* SE11 18 B8
Lambeth Hospital *BRXN/ST* SW9 158 F9
Lambeth Palace *STHWK* SE1 17 N4
Lambourne Golf Club *SL* SL1 128 A1
Lambourne Primary School *ABR/ST* RM4 83 L8
Lambs Court *POP/IOD* E14 140 D9
Lamont Business Centre *CROY/NA* CR0 202 F7
Lamorbey Swimming Centre *BFN/LL* DA15 185 K5
Lampton School *HSLW* TW3 153 P7
The Lanark Medical Centre *MV/WKIL* W9 3 H9
Lancaster House *WHALL* SW1A 16 G1
Lancasterian Primary School *TOTM* N17 99 M9
Lancaster Road Industrial Estate *EBAR* EN4 77 N9
Lancelot Medical Centre *ALP/SUD* HA0 115 J10
The Landmark Hotel *CAMTN* NW1 10 A3
The Lanesborough Hotel *KTBR* SW1X 16 C1
Lanesborough School *GU* GU1 250 C10
Lanford Obesity Clinic *ED* N9 100 A1
Langafel CE Primary School *HART* DA3 211 M3
Langbourne Primary School *DUL* SE21 181 M6
Langdon Down Centre *TEDD* TW11 177 H10
Langdon Park School *POP/IOD* E14 140 G8
Langdon School *EHAM* E6 142 E4
Langford Primary School *FUL/PGN* SW6 157 L8
Langham Hotel *CAVSQ/HST* W1G 10 F5
The Langham School *SEVS/STOTM* N15 119 K2
Langhedge Lane Industrial Estate *UED* N18 99 N7
Langley Business Centre *DTCH/LGLY* SL3 150 D1
Langley Business Park *DTCH/LGLY* SL3 150 C1
Langley Grammar School *DTCH/LGLY* SL3 150 C3
Langley Green Primary School *CRAWW* RH11 283 M5
Langley Health Centre *DTCH/LGLY* SL3 150 D4
Langley Manor School *DTCH/LGLY* SL3 130 B10
Langley Park Country Park *DTCH/LGLY* SL3 130 D6
Langley Park Girls School & Sports Centre *BECK* BR3 204 C5
Langley Park Golf Club *BECK* BR3 205 J6
Langley Park School for Boys *BECK* BR3 204 C6
Langleywood School *DTCH/LGLY* SL3 150 B2
Langshott County Infant School *HORL* RH6 280 D4
Langshott Manor Hotel *HORL* RH6 280 E2
Langthorne Health Centre *WAN* E11 121 J8
Langthorne Hospital *WAN* E11 121 J9
Langtons J & I School *EMPK* RM11 125 M6
The Lansbury Estate *WOKN/KNAP* GU21 231 J4
Lansbury Lawrence Primary School *POP/IOD* E14 140 G8
Lansdowne College *BAY/PAD* W2 8 G8
Lansdowne Primary School *TIL* RM18 168 C8
Lansdowne School *BRXN/ST* SW9 158 G9
Larchwood Primary School *BRWN* CM15 86 F10
La Retraite RC Girls School *BAL* SW12 180 D3
Lark Hall Primary School *CLAP* SW4 158 E8
Larkshall Business Centre *CHING* E4 101 J3
Larmenier Infant School *HMSMTH* W6 156 G3
La Sainte Union Convent School *KTTN* NW5 118 B8
La Salette RC Primary School *RAIN* RM13 145 H5
Laser Clinic *CHESW* EN7 62 A6
Latchmere J & I School *KUTN/CMB* KT2 177 L9
Latchmere Leisure Centre *BTSEA* SW11 158 A8
Lathom Junior School *EHAM* E6 142 B2
Latton Bush Business Centre *HLWS* CM18 47 J4
Latymer All Saints CE Primary School *ED* N9 99 N3
The Latymer Preparatory School *HMSMTH* W6 156 D4
The Latymer School *ED* N9 99 M3
Latymer Upper School *HMSMTH* W6 156 D3
Launcelot Primary School *BMLY* BR1 183 M7
Laurance Haines School *WATW* WD18 73 H10
Laurel Clinic *EA* W5 155 H3
Lauriston Primary School *HOM* E9 140 C3
Lavender Primary School *ENC/FH* EN2 79 L4
Lawdale Junior School *BETH* E2 7 P9
Lawn Primary School *GVW* DA11 189 P2
Lawn Tennis School *BEAC* HP9 88 D8
Lawrence Trading Estate *GNWCH* SE10 161 K3
GRAYS RM17 167 P3
Lawrence University *SKENS* SW7 15 K6
Lawrence Wharf *BERM/RHTH* SE16 140 E10
Laycock Primary School *IS* N1 6 B2
Lazards Sports Club *SUN* TW16 197 J1
Leadenhall Market *BANK* EC3V 13 J6
Lea Farm Junior School *GSTN* WD25 73 L1
Leah Manning Centre *HLW* CM20 28 G9
Lea Infant School *SLN* SL2 129 N9
Lea Junior School *SLN* SL2 129 M9
Lea Park Trading Estate *LEY* E10 120 E5
Lea Road Industrial Park *CHES/WCR* EN8 62 F10
Leaside Business Centre *PEND* EN3 80 E6
Leatherhead Business Park *LHD/OX* KT22 236 G5
Leatherhead Clinic *LHD/OX* KT22 237 H7
Leatherhead CC *LHD/OX* KT22 236 F8
Leatherhead FC *LHD/OX* KT22 236 F8
Leatherhead Golf Club *LHD/OX* KT22 236 F2
Leatherhead Hospital *LHD/OX* KT22 237 H8
Leatherhead Industrial Estate *LHD/OX* KT22 236 F7
Leatherhead Institute *LHD/OX* KT22 236 G7
Leatherhead Leisure Centre & Water Park *LHD/OX* KT22 236 F9
Leatherhead Museum *LHD/OX* KT22 236 G8
Leathermarket Gardens *STHWK* SE1 19 J2
Leathersellers Sports Ground *LEE/GVPK* SE12 183 P3
Leathers Hall *HDTCH* EC3A 13 J5
Lea Valley High School *EN* EN1 80 B1

Lea Valley Primary School TOTM N17 99 P8
Lea Valley Trading Estate UED N18 100 B5
UED N18 100 C7
Leavesden Green JMI School GSTN WD25 55 H10
Leavesden Hospital ABLGY WD5 55 H7
L'Ecoles Des Petits School FUL/PGN SW6 157 L8
Lee Manor Primary School LEW SE13 183 K2
Leeside Court BERM/RHTH SE16 140 C10
Leeside Trading Estate TOTM N17 100 B8
Leesons Primary School STMC/STPC BR5 207 K3
Lee Valley Camping & Caravan Park ED N9 100 C2
Lee Valley Campsite CHING E4 80 G6
Lee Valley Caravan Park HOD EN11 45 H5
Lee Valley Ice Centre LEY E10 120 C7
Lee Valley Leisure Complex & Golf Club ED N9 100 D1
Lee Valley Park WAB EN9 62 G4
Lee Valley Park Farms WAB EN9 63 H4
Lee Valley Watersports Centre CHING E4 100 D7
Legoland Windsor WDSR SL4 170 C1
The Leigh City Technology College (East Campus) DART DA1 188 A4
The Leigh City Technology College DART DA1 187 P4
The Leigh City Technology College (West Campus) DART DA1 187 P4
Leigh Close Industrial Estate NWMAL KT3 200 A4
Leighton House Museum WKENS W14 14 D3
Lemuel Findlay Supplementary School SEVS/STOTM N15 119 N2
Lena Gardens Primary School HMSMTH W6 156 F2
Lent Rise Combined School SL SL1 128 A7
Leo Baeck College Centre for Jewish Education FNCH N3 97 K10
Leopold Primary School WLSDN NW10 136 C2
Leopold Street Clinic BOW E3 140 E7
Lesnes Abbey BELV DA17 163 N3
Lesnes Abbey (remains of) ABYW SE2 163 L5
Lessness Heath Primary School BELV DA17 164 B4
Leverstock Green JMI School HHNE HP2 36 E7
Leverstock Green Lawn Tennis Club HHS/BOV HP3 36 C8
The Leverton Infant School WAB EN9 63 L10
Lewin Mead Community Mental Health Centre STRHM/NOR SW16 180 E9
Lewis Clinic CAR SM5 222 B1
Lewisham Bridge Primary School LEW SE13 160 G9
Lewisham Business Centre NWCR SE14 160 C5
Lewisham Centre LEW SE13 161 H9
Lewisham College DEPT SE8 160 F7
Lewisham Crematorium CAT SE6 183 L5
Lewisham Lions Centre BERM/RHTH SE16 160 B4
Lewisham Police Station LEW SE13 161 H9
Ley Hill CC CSHM HP5 51 P7
Ley Hill School CSHM HP5 51 N6
Ley Park Primary School BROX EN10 44 E8
The Leys Primary School DAGE RM10 144 D2
Leyton Business Centre LEY E10 120 E7
Leyton Cross RDART DA2 187 H5
Leyton FC LEY E10 120 E6
Leyton Industrial Village LEY E10 120 C5
Leyton Leisure Centre LEY E10 120 G5
Leyton Orient FC (Matchroom Stadium) LEY E10 120 G8
Leytonstone School WAN E11 121 K4
Leyton VI Form College LEY E10 121 J4
Leyton Youth Sports Ground LEY E10 120 G6
The Liberty City Clinic SDTCH EC2A 13 J1
Liberty II Centre ROM RM1 124 F2
Liberty Middle School MTCM CR4 201 P2
The Liberty ROM RM1 124 F3
Light Industrial Estate WDSR SL4 170 A5
Lilian Baylis School VX/NE SW8 17 N9
Lilian Baylis Technology School VX/NE SW8 17 N9
Lillian Baylis School LBTH SE11 17 P6
Lillian Baylis Theatre CLKNW EC1R 6 C9
Lillian Bishop School of English SKENS SW7 15 L5
Limehouse Hole Stairs BERM/RHTH SE16 140 E10
Limes Business Centre HORL RH6 279 J9
Limes Farm Primary School CHIG IG7 102 G7
The Limes Medical Centre EPP CM16 65 L5
EPP CM16 66 C2
Lime Trees Park Golf Club NTHLT UB5 133 K3
Lime Walk JMI School HHS/BOV HP3 36 A8
Limpsfield CE Infant School OXTED RH8 261 N5
Limpsfield Chart Golf Club OXTED RH8 261 P5
Limpsfield Grange School OXTED RH8 261 M3
Limpsfield Lawn Tennis Club OXTED RH8 261 M4
Lincoln Road Clinic EN EN1 79 P9
Lincoln's Inn LINN WC2A 11 P5
Linden Bridge School WPK KT4 200 B10
Linden Lodge School WIM/MER SW19 179 H4
Lindon Bennett School FELT TW13 175 L8
Linford Christie Stadium SHB W12 136 D7
The Link Day Primary School CROY/NA CR0 222 F1
The Link Secondary School CROY/NA CR0 222 G1
Links Primary School TOOT SW17 180 B9
Linley House School BRYLDS KT5 199 L6
Linley Sambourne House KENS W8 14 E2
Linnet House Clinic STJWD NW8 3 N8
Linton Mead Primary School THMD SE28 143 L9
Lionel Road Primary School BTFD TW8 155 K3
Liongate Hotel E/WMO/HCT KT8 198 E3
Lion House School PUT/ROE SW15 156 G10
Lion Retail Park WOKS/MYFD GU22 232 E2
Lismarrine Industrial Park BORE WD6 74 G10
Lisson Grove Health Centre STJWD NW8 9 N1
Lister Community School PLSTW E13 141 N4
The Lister Hospital BGVA SW1W 16 E8
Lister House Clinic CAVSQ/HST W1G 10 E5
Lister House Surgery HAT AL10 40 D3
Lister Medical Centre HLWW/ROY CM19 46 F4
Littlebrook Business Centre DART DA1 166 B9
Little Chalfont Golf Club AMS HP6 70 B6
Little Chalfont Primary School AMS HP6 70 B5
Little Danson Welfare Clinic WELL DA16 163 K10
Littledown Special School SL SL1 129 L9
Little Eden & Eden High School FELT TW13 175 L7
Little Green Junior School RKW/CH/CXG WD3 72 B7
Little Hands Theatre HDN NW4 116 F2
Little Hay Golf Complex HHS/BOV HP3 34 F10
Little Heath Primary School POTB/CUF EN6 59 M6
Little Heath School CHDH RM6 123 L2
Little Ilford School MNPK E12 122 C10
Little Reddings Primary School BUSH WD23 74 A9
Little St Helens School NTHWD HA6 92 F7
Little Spring Primary School CSHM HP5 50 G4
Little Stanmore First & Middle School EDGW HA8 95 K9
Little Thurrock Primary School GRAYS RM17 168 A2
Littleton CE Infant School SHPTN TW17 196 B3
Little Venice Medical Centre MV/WKIL W9 9 K2
Little Wandsworth School TOOT SW17 180 B5
Livesey Museum for Children PECK SE15 19 P10
Livingstone Hospital DART DA1 187 N3
Livingstone Primary School EBAR EN4 77 N7
The Livity School BRXS/STRHM SW2 180 F1
Lloyd Park Centre WALTH E17 100 F10
Lloyd's BANK EC3V 13 J6
FENCHST EC3M 13 J6
Lloyds Register CC DUL SE21 181 L4
Lochinver House School POTB/CUF EN6 59 L6
Lockers Park School HHW HP1 35 L6
Locks View Court POP/IOD E14 140 D9
Lockwood Industrial Park TOTM N17 120 A1
Lodge School PUR/KEN CR8 222 E8
Lodge Sun Sports Club WAT WD17 72 F5
Log Church CHONG CM5 67 L4
Lombard Business Centre BTSEA SW11 157 N8
Lombard Business Park CROY/NA CR0 202 G7
WAND/EARL SW18 179 N2
WIM/MER SW19 201 M2
Lombard Trading Estate CHARL SE7 161 N3
Lombardy Retail Park HYS/HAR UB3 133 J9
London Academy EDGW HA8 95 L5
London Academy of Music & Dramatic Art KENS W8 14 E5
London Aquarium WHALL SW1A 17 N2
London Area Terminal Control Centre WDR/YW UB7 152 A1
London Arena POP/IOD E14 160 G2
London Bridge City Pier STHWK SE1 13 J9
London Bridge Hospital STHWK SE1 13 H9
London Bridge Hotel STHWK SE1 12 G10
London Bridge Sports Centre CANST EC4R 12 G8
London Business School CAMTN NW1 10 A1
The London Canal Museum IS N1 5 M7
London Capital College CAMTN NW1 4 F5
London Chest Hospital BETH E2 140 B4
London City Airport CAN/RD E16 142 B10
London City College (English Language Institute) & Schoolliler International University STHWK SE1 11 P10
London City Mission STHWK SE1 19 K1
The London Clinic CAVSQ/HST W1G 10 D2
London College of Business and Computer Services CLAP SW4 158 E10
London College of Business & Computing BETH E2 140 A4
London College of Communication LBTH SE11 18 D4
London College of Fashion CAVSQ/HST W1G 10 F5
MHST W1U 10 D5
SDTCH EC2A 13 K1
London College of Further Education LBTH SE11 18 C6
London College of Higher Education CLAP SW4 158 C9
London College of International Business Studies HHOL WC1V 11 M4
The London College KENS W8 137 K10
London Colney JMI School LCOL/BKTW AL2 57 J1
London Commodity Exchange WAP E1W 13 M8
London Cornish RFC PUT/ROE SW15 178 C6
London Dungeon STHWK SE1 13 H9
London Electronics College ECT SW5 14 G7
London Esthetique CAVSQ/HST W1G 10 F5
London Eye STHWK SE1 17 N1
London Eye Clinic CAVSQ/HST W1G 10 E4
London Fields Primary School HACK E8 140 A3
London Foot Hospital FITZ W1T 10 G2
London Gender Clinic HDN NW4 116 E4
London Glass Blowing Workshop STHWK SE1 19 J2
London Group Business Park CRICK NW2 116 C6
London Guildhall University TWRH EC3N 13 L7
London Guildhall University Sports Ground LEE/GVPK SE12 183 P5
London Heart Clinic CAVSQ/HST W1G 10 E4
The London Industrial Estate EHAM E6 142 D7
London Industrial Park EHAM E6 142 E7
London International Cruise Terminal TIL RM18 168 D10
London International Film School LSQ/SEVD WC2H 11 L6
The London & International School of Acting MV/WKIL W9 8 D2
London Irish RFC SUN TW16 197 H1
The London Irish Youth Theatre HGT N6 118 C6
London Islamic School/ Madrasah WCHPL E1 140 A8
London IT College GNTH/NBYPK IG2 122 D4
London Jewish Girls High School HDN NW4 116 F3
London Ladies & Girls FC CAT SE6 182 G8
London Lane Clinic BMLY BR1 183 L10
London Lighthouse NTGHL W11 8 A6
London Living Theatre SYD SE26 182 C7
London Marriott Hotel HAMP NW3 3 M4
MYFR/PKLN W1K 10 D7
STHWK SE1 17 N1
London Marriott Hotel, County Hall WHALL SW1A 158 F1
London Marriott Hotel Park Lane OXSTW W1C 10 B7
London Marriott West India Quay Hotel POP/IOD E14 140 F9
London Metropolitan University HOLWY N7 118 G9
HOLWY N7 119 H10
LVPST EC2M 13 H4
WCHPL E1 13 L5
WCHPL E1 13 P5
London Nautical School STHWK SE1 12 B9
London Open College FSBYE EC1V 6 D9
London Oratory School FUL/PGN SW6 157 K6
London Road Medical Centre CROY/NA CR0 203 H6
London School of Economics CLKNW EC1R 6 B10
HHOL WC1V 11 L5
HOL/ALD WC2B 11 N6
STHWK SE1 12 E9
London School of Hygiene & Tropical Medicine GWRST WC1E 11 K3
London School of Theology NTHWD HA6 92 E7
London Scottish Golf Club WIM/MER SW19 178 E6
London Silver Vaults LINN WC2A 12 A4
The London Television Centre (LWT) STHWK SE1 12 A9
London Tourist Board & Convention Centre BGVA SW1W 16 F3
London Toy & Model Museum BAY/PAD W2 9 K7
London Transport Bus Depot BXLYHN DA7 164 C9
London Underwriting Centre MON EC3R 13 J7
London Weather Centre HCIRC EC1N 12 A3
The London Welbeck Hospital CAVSQ/HST W1G 10 D4
London Welsh FC RCH/KEW TW9 155 K9
London Welsh School CRICK NW2 136 F1
London West Crematorium WLSDN NW10 136 E6
London Wetland Centre BARN SW13 156 E7
London Zoo CAMTN NW1 4 C7
Lonesome Primary School MTCM CR4 202 C2
Long Close School DTCH/LGLY SL3 149 M3
The Longcroft Clinic BNSTD SM7 221 M10
Longdean School HHS/BOV HP3 36 C9
Long Ditton County Infant School SURB KT6 199 H8
Longfield Primary School RYLN/HDSTN HA2 113 P4
Longford Community School EBED/NFELT TW14 174 G3
Longford Industrial Estate HPTN TW12 176 A9
Long Island Hotel RKW/CH/CXG WD3 91 N1
Longlands Primary School BFN/LL DA15 185 H6
BROX EN10 62 D1
Long Lane AFC BKHTH/KID SE3 161 P8
Longley Trading Estate CRAWE RH10 283 P8
Longmead Business Centre HOR/WEW KT19 220 A7
Longmead Industrial Estate HOR/WEW KT19 220 A7
Longmead Primary School WDR/YW UB7 151 N3
Long Ridings J & I School RBRW/HUT CM13 87 N9
Longshaw Primary School CHING E4 101 J4
Longwood Business Park SUN TW16 196 G5
Lord Chancellors Department WEST SW1P 17 K4
Lord Lister Health Centre FSTGT E7 121 M9
Lordship Lane Clinic TOTM N17 99 M10
Lordship Lane Primary School WDGN N22 99 K9
Lord's Tour & MCC Museum STJWD NW8 3 L10
Loreto College STAL AL1 38 D6
Lorimar Business Centre RAIN RM13 144 F8
Loseley Fields Primary School GODL GU7 267 K8
Loseley Park RGUW GU3 267 L6
Loughborough Primary School CMBW SE5 159 J8
Loughton CC LOU IG10 82 C7
Loughton Golf Club LOU IG10 82 E5
Loughton Hall Clinic LOU IG10 82 E7
Loughton Health Centre LOU IG10 82 B7
Loughton Mental Health Centre LOU IG10 82 B9
Lovelace Primary School CHSGTN KT9 219 H2
Lovell's Wharf GNWCH SE10 161 J4
Lower Clapton Health Centre CLPT E5 120 B10
Lower Place Business Centre WLSDN NW10 135 P4
Lower Sydenham Industrial Estate SYD SE26 182 E8
Lowewood Museum HOD EN11 44 F4
Lowfield Heath I ndustrial Estate HORL RH6 279 P10
Lowfield Medical Centre DART DA1 187 M3
Lowfield Sports Ground HOD EN11 44 E3
Low Hall Sports Ground LEY E10 120 C4
Lowther Primary School BARN SW13 156 D5
Loxford School of Science and Technology IL IG1 122 G10
Loyola Preparatory School BKHH IG9 101 P2
LPR Sports Club BARK/HLT IG6 103 J9
LSE Sports Club NWMAL KT3 200 A6
Lubavitch House School (Senior Girls) STNW/STAM N16 119 N5
Lucas Vale Primary School DEPT SE8 160 F7
Lullingstone Castle EYN DA4 229 K2
Lullingstone Park Golf Club ORP BR6 228 E1
Lullingstone Roman Villa EYN DA4 209 J10
Lutomer House Business Centre POP/IOD E14 140 G10
Lux Cinema IS N1 7 J10
Lycee Francais SKENS SW7 15 L5
Lycee Francais Charles De Gaulle BTSEA SW11 158 C10
The Lyceum Theatre COVGDN WC2E 11 N7
Lynch Hill School SLN SL2 128 E5
Lyndean Industrial Estate ABYW SE2 163 M2
Lyndhurst House Preparatory School HAMP NW3 117 N10
Lyndhurst Middle School BORE WD6 75 L5
Lyndhurst Primary School CMBW SE5 159 L8
Lyne & Longcross CE Infant School CHERT KT16 194 E9
Lynton Preparatory School EW KT17 220 C7
Lyon Business Park BARK IG11 143 H4
Lyon Park J & I School ALP/SUD HA0 135 L2
Lyonsdown School BAR EN5 77 M9
Lyons Industrial Estate UX/CGN UB8 131 M8
Lyric Theatre SOHO/SHAV W1D 11 J7
Lyric Theatre Hammersmith HMSMTH W6 156 F3
Mabwin Supplementary School ED N9 100 A3
Macaulay CE Primary School CLAP SW4 158 C10
Macdonald Berystede Hotel ASC SL5 192 B6
Macdonald Burford Bridge Hotel RDKG RH5 255 H7
Macdonald Hotel WDSR SL4 149 J7
Macdonald Thames Lodge STA TW18 173 H8
Macdonald White Horse Hotel DORK RH4 272 G2
Madame Tussauds & The London Auditorium CAMTN NW1 10 B2
Madeira Grove Clinic WFD IG8 101 N6
Madison Bowl NTHWD HA6 92 F8
Madni Girls School WCHPL E1 140 A8
Madrasah-E Darul Qirat Majidiah School WCHPL E1 140 A9
The Magna Carta School EGH TW20 172 G9
Magnet Estate WTHK RM20 167 H4
Mahatma Gandhi Industrial Estate BRXN/ST SW9 159 J9
Maida Vale Medical Centre MV/WKIL W9 2 G10
Maidenbower First & Middle School CRAWE RH10 284 E9
Maidenbower Junior School CRAWE RH10 284 E9
Malcolm Primary School PGE/AN SE20 182 B10
The Malden Centre NWMAL KT3 200 C4
Malden Golf Club NWMAL KT3 200 B2
Malden Manor Primary School NWMAL KT3 200 B7
Malden Parochial Primary School WPK KT4 200 B8
Malden Road Baths CHEAM SM3 220 G1
Malham Road Industrial Estate FSTH SE23 182 C4
Mall Galleries STJS SW1Y 11 K9
The Mall School WHTN TW2 176 C6
Malmaison Charterhouse Square Hotel FARR EC1M 12 D3
Malmesbury Primary School MRDN SM4 201 M7
Malorees J & I School KIL/WHAMP NW6 136 G2
Malory School BMLY BR1 183 M7
Maltings Arts Theatre STAL AL1 38 C6
The Maltings Industrial Estate SBW CM21 30 A1
WARE SG12 27 J7
The Maltings Shopping Centre STAL AL1 38 C6
Maltmans Green School CFSP/GDCR SL9 109 P1
Malvern Way Infant School RKW/CH/CXG WD3 72 D9
Manby Lodge Infant School WEY KT13 216 C1
Mandarin Oriental Hotel KTBR SW1X 16 B1
Mandeville Health Centre STAL AL1 38 C9
The Mandeville Hotel MHST W1U 10 D5
Mandeville Primary School CLPT E5 120 D8
STAL AL1 38 C9
Mandeville Special School NTHLT UB5 133 N1
Manford Industrial Estate ERITH DA8 165 J5
Manford Way Health Centre BARK/HLT IG6 103 J7
Manor Brook Medical Centre BKHTH/KID SE3 161 N8
Manorcroft Primary School EGH TW20 172 D9
Manor Drive Health Centre WPK KT4 200 C8
Manorfield Primary School HORL RH6 280 A4
POP/IOD E14 140 G7
Manor Green Primary School CRAWW RH11 283 N3
The Manor Hotel RAIN RM13 145 N4
Manor House Hotel RGUE GU4 269 L1
Manor House School GT/LBKH KT23 253 M3
Manor Infant School BARK IG11 143 J1
Manor Lodge School RAD WD7 57 P6
Manor Mead School SHPTN TW17 196 C5
Manor Oak Primary School STMC/STPC BR5 207 N5
Manor of Groves Golf Club SBW CM21 29 J1
Manor of Groves Hotel SBW CM21 29 J1
Manor Park Cemetery FSTGT E7 122 A9
Manor Park Crematorium FSTGT E7 121 P9
Manor Park Medical Centre SLN SL2 129 J7
Manor Park Methodist School MNPK E12 122 B9
Manor Park Primary School SUT SM1 221 M2
Manor Place Industrial Estate BORE WD6 75 P7
Manor Primary School SRTFD E15 141 K4
The Manor Primary School ROM RM1 124 G3
The Manor School BF/WBF KT14 215 P10
Manorside Primary School FNCH N3 97 L9
Manor Special School WLSDN NW10 136 G4
Manor Way Business Centre RAIN RM13 144 E7
Manor Way Industrial Estate GRAYS RM17 167 P6
Mansion House MANHO EC4N 12 G6
Manzoori Clinic SWLY BR8 186 G10
Maple Cross Industrial Estate RKW/CH/CXG WD3 91 H5
Maple Cross JMI School RKW/CH/CXG WD3 90 G6
Mapledown School CRICK NW2 116 G5
Maple Grove Business Centre HSLWW TW4 153 K10
Maple House School THHTH CR7 203 K3
Maple Industrial Estate FELT TW13 175 H5
Maple Infant School SURB KT6 199 J5
Maple Primary School STAL AL1 38 D5
Maple River Industrial Estate HLW CM20 29 L5
Maples Business Centre IS N1 6 B5
Marble Arch MBLAR W1H 10 B7
Marble Hill House TWK TW1 177 H3
Marden Lodge Primary School CTHM CR3 242 A6
Margaret Roper Catholic Primary School PUR/KEN CR8 223 H6
Margaret Wix JMI School STALW/RED AL3 38 B2
Maria Fidelis Convent Lower School CAMTN NW1 5 H10
Maria Fidelis Convent Upper School CAMTN NW1 5 J9
Maria Montessori Childrens House HAMP NW3 117 N10
Marillac Hospital RBRW/HUT CM13 107 J7
Mariner Business Centre CROY/NA CR0 222 G2
Marion Richardson Primary School WCHPL E1 140 C8
Marion Vian Primary School BECK BR3 204 C5
Marish Infant School DTCH/LGLY SL3 150 C2
The Marist Preparatory School ASC SL5 192 C5
The Marist RC Primary School BF/WBF KT14 215 J9
Marist Senior School ASC SL5 192 C4
Maritime Greenwich College DEPT SE8 160 F6
Maritime Industrial Estate CHARL SE7 161 N3
Maritime Museum GNWCH SE10 161 K3
Marjorie McClure School CHST BR7 206 F1
The Marjory Kinnon School EBED/NFELT TW14 174 F1
The Market COVGDN WC2E 11 M7
Market Trading Estate NWDGN UB2 153 J3
Mark Hall Comprehensive School HLW CM20 29 M9
Mark Hall Cycle Museum HLW CM20 29 L8
Marks Gate Junior School CHDH RM6 123 P1
Marlborough CC DUL SE21 181 P4
Marlborough Day Hospital STJWD NW8 3 J7
Marlborough First & Middle School HRW HA1 114 D2
Marlborough House STJS SW1Y 11 H10
Marlborough Primary School CHEL SW3 15 P6
ISLW TW7 154 F7
Marlborough School BFN/LL DA15 185 K4
STAL AL1 38 B9
Marlborough Trading Estate RCH/KEW TW9 155 N7
Marlin Montessori School BERK HP4 33 N5
Marlowe Business Centre NWCR SE14 160 D6
Marlowes Health Centre HHW HP1 35 M6
Marlowes Shopping Centre HHW HP1 35 M7
Marner Primary School BOW E3 140 G6
Marriott Hotel DTCH/LGLY SL3 150 C4
ECT SW5 14 G5
HYS/HAR UB3 153 E7
KIL/WHAMP NW6 2 G7
MDLAR W1H 9 P5
Marshalls Park School ROM RM1 104 F10
Marshall Street Leisure Centre SOHO/CST W1F 11 H6
Marshfields CE School CHERT KT16 215 H3
Marsh Gate Business Centre SRTFD E15 141 H4
Marshgate Primary School RCHPK/HAM TW10 177 L1
Marshgate Trading Estate HERT/BAY SG13 25 M4
SRTFD E15 140 G2
Marsh Green School DAGW RM9 144 B4
Marsh View Industrial Estate RAIN RM13 145 N5
Martan College HOL/ALD WC2B 11 M5
Martin Baker Sports Ground DEN/HRF UB9 111 J5
Martinbridge Industrial Estate EN EN1 79 P9
Martindale Industrial Estate EN EN1 79 M9
Martindale JMI School HHW HP1 35 J5
Martinfield Business Centre WGCE AL7 23 J4
Martin Infant School EFNCH N2 97 P10
Marvels Lane Primary School LEE/GVPK SE12 183 P7
Mary Boone School WKENS W14 157 H3
Marygreen Manor Hotel BRW CM14 106 E5
Maryland Industrial Estate SRTFD E15 121 K10
Maryland Primary School SRTFD E15 121 K10
Marylebone Health Centre CAMTN NW1 10 D2
Marylebone Magistrates Court CAMTN NW1 9 P3
Marymount International School KUTN/CMB KT2 177 P10
Mary Wallace Theatre TWK TW1 176 F4
Maswell Park Health Centre HSLW TW3 176 B1
Matching Green CE Primary School HLWE CM17 31 L9
Matilda Marks Kennedy Primary MLHL NW7 96 A6
Matrix Business Centre DART DA1 187 M1
The Matthew Arnold School STA TW18 173 M9
Maudlin's Green WAP E1W 13 M9
The Maudsley Hospital CMBW SE5 159 L8
Maughan Library (Kings College) LINN WC2A 12 A5
Maunds Wood CP School HLWS CM18 46 G5
Mawbrey Brough Health Centre VX/NE SW8 158 F6
The Mawney School ROMW/RG RM7 124 E3

May Avenue Industrial Estate GVW DA11 190 C4
Maybury Business Centre WOKS/MYFD GU22 232 D3
Maybury Infant School WOKN/KNAP GU21 232 C2
Mayday University Hospital THHTH CR7 203 J6
Mayesbrook Park Arena BARK IG11 123 K10
Mayespark Primary School GDMY/SEVK IG3 123 K8
Mayfield Infant School CHES/WCR EN8 62 D3
Mayfield Primary School HNWL W7 134 C8
Mayfield School PIN HA5 113 M1
Mayflower Primary School POP/IOD E14 140 F8
Maylands Golf Club HARH RM3 106 A6
Mayplace Primary School BXLYHN DA7 164 E10
Maypole Primary School RDART DA2 186 F6
Maytime School IL IG1 122 D8
Mayville J & P School WAN E11 121 K8
McEntee School WALTH E17 100 E9
McKay Trading Estate DTCH/LGLY SL3 151 H8
NKENS W10 8 A1
McMillan Clinic HYS/HAR UB3 132 D9
The Mead Business Centre HERT/BAY SG13 25 M4
Mead Industrial Park HLW CM20 29 J7
The Mead Infant School WPK KT4 200 C10
Meadlands Primary School RCHPK/HAM TW10 177 H7
Meadowbrook Industrial Centre CRAWE RH10 284 B4
Meadowcroft County I nfant School CHERT KT16 195 J10
Meadowgate School BROCKY SE4 160 C9
Meadow High School UX/CGN UB8 131 P7
Meadowside Leisure Centre BKHTH/KID SE3 161 P10
The Meadow Special School STMC/STPC BR5 185 K10
Meadow Wood School BUSH WD23 74 B9
Mead Primary School HARH RM3 105 N7
Mead Road Infant School CHST BR7 184 F9
The Mead School HLWS CM18 47 H3
Meath Green Infant School HORL RH6 280 A2
Meath Green Junior School HORL RH6 280 A2
Meath School CHERT KT16 214 G4
Medical Express Clinic CAVSQ/HST W1G 10 E3
Mednurs Clinic SEVS/STOTM N15 119 L4
Megabowl KUTN/CMB KT2 199 K2
Melcombe Primary School HMSMTH W6 156 C5
Meli-White House Hotel CAMTN NW1 10 F1
Mellish Industrial Estate WOOL/PLUM SE18 162 A2
Mellow Lane School HGDN/ICK UB10 132 D6
Melrose Special School MTCM CR4 201 P3
Memorial Hospital WOOL/PLUM SE18 162 D8
The Menorah Foundation School EDGW HA8 95 P8
Menorah Grammar School GLDGN NW11 117 H5
Menorah Primary School GLDGN NW11 117 H5
Mercers College WARE SG12 26 B2
Mercers' Hall CITYW EC2V 12 F6
The Merchant Taylors Hall BANK EC3V 13 H6
Merchant Taylors School NTHWD HA6 92 F2
Mercure London City Bankside Hotel STHWK SE1 12 E10
Meridian Clinic BRXN/ST SW9 158 G9
Meridian Locality Mental Health Centre CHARL SE7 161 P5
Meridian Primary School GNWCH SE10 161 J4
Meridian Sports Club CHARL SE7 162 B6
Meridian Trading Estate CHARL SE7 161 N3
Merland Rise Primary School EPSOM KT18 238 F5
Merlin Primary School BMLY BR1 183 M6
Merlin School PUT/ROE SW15 178 G1
Mermaid Theatre BLKFR EC4V 12 D7
Merrielands Retail Park DAGW RM9 144 A3
Merrist Wood Golf Club RGUW GU3 249 H5
Merrow Business Centre RGUE GU4 250 G7
Merrow CE Infant School RGUE GU4 250 G8
Merry Hill Infant School BUSH WD23 94 A1
Merryhills Clinic ENC/FH EN2 78 G7
Merryhills Primary School ENC/FH EN2 78 G8
Merstham Primary School REDH RH1 258 D4
Merton Abbey Primary School WIM/MER SW19 201 L1
Merton Adult College RYNPK SW20 201 H3
Merton College MRDN SM4 201 J6
Merton Court Preparatory School SCUP DA14 185 M7
Merton Industrial Park WIM/MER SW19 201 M1
Merton Park Primary School WIM/MER SW19 201 J2
Merton Road Industrial Estate WAND/EARL SW18 179 K3
Meryfield Primary School BORE WD6 75 L5
Metro Business Centre SYD SE26 182 E9
The Metro Golf Centre HDN NW4 96 F9
Metro Industrial Centre ISLW TW7 154 D8
Metropolis Centre BORE WD6 75 M7
Metropolitan Business Centre HACK E8 7 K4
Metropolitan Hospital STHWK SE1 18 B3
The Metropolitan Hotel MYFR/PKLN W1K 10 E10
Metropolitan Police STJWD NW8 3 N8
Metropolitan Police Bushey Sports Ground BUSH WD23 73 P7
Metropolitan Police FC E/WMO/HCT KT8 198 C6
Metropolitan Police Hayes Sports Club HAYES BR2 205 L9
Metropolitan Police (Hendon) Track CDALE/KGS NW9 116 C1
Metropolitan Police Training School, Hendon CDALE/KGS NW9 116 C1
Metropolitan Tabernacle STHWK SE1 18 D5
Metro Trading Centre WBLY HA9 115 N9
Michael Faraday Primary School WALW SE17 19 H8
Michael Manley Industrial Estate VX/NE SW8 158 D7
Michael Sobell Sinai School KTN/HRWW/WS HA3 115 M4
The Michael Tippett School LBTH SE11 18 B6
Micklem JMI School HHW HP1 35 J5
Midas Business Centre DAGE RM10 124 B9
Midas Industrial Estate DAGE RM10 124 B9
UX/CGN UB8 131 L4
Middlegreen Trading Estate DTCH/LGLY SL3 150 A1
Middle Park Primary School ELTH/MOT SE9 184 A3
Middle Row Primary School NKENS W10 8 A1
Middlesex Business Centre NWDGN UB2 153 P1
Middlesex CCC (Lord's Cricket Ground) STJWD NW8 3 M9
Middlesex Guildhall STJSPK SW1H 17 K2
Middlesex Hospital Medical School FITZ W1T 11 H3
Middlesex Hospital Nurses Home GTPST W1W 10 G3
Middlesex Hospital School of Physiotherapy FITZ W1T 11 H3
Middlesex Hospital Sports Ground CHST BR7 185 J8
Middlesex School of Complementary Medicine STAN HA7 95 K9
Middlesex University ARCH N19 118 D6
EBAR EN4 78 B10
GLDGN NW11 117 L6
HDN NW4 116 E2
PEND EN3 80 C9
STHGT/OAK N14 78 D8
WDGN N22 98 F10
Middlesex University (Enfield Campus) PEND EN3 80 A9
Middlesex University Museum EBAR EN4 78 B9
Middlesex University (Trent Park Campus) EBAR EN4 78 D6
Middleton Special School WARE SG12 26 C4
Mid Essex Adult Community College RBRW/HUT CM13 87 N10
Midfield Primary School STMC/STPC BR5 185 K10
Mid Kent Golf Club GVW DA11 190 E6
Midleton Industrial Estate GUW GU2 249 N9
Midway Mission Hospital BETH E2 7 L10
Milbourne Lodge Junior School ESH/CLAY KT10 218 B2
Milbourne Lodge School ESH/CLAY KT10 218 C3
Mile End & Bow Business Centre WCHPL E1 140 A7
Mile End Hospital WCHPL E1 140 C5
Mile End Stadium POP/IOD E14 140 E7
Milehams Industrial Estate PUR RM19 165 P2
Miles Coverdale Primary School SHB W12 156 F1
Milestone Hotel KENS W8 15 H2
Milestone School HART DA3 211 L8
Military Barracks WOOL/PLUM SE18 162 D4
Military Cemetery CHOB/PIR GU24 230 E7
Millbank Millennium Pier WEST SW1P 17 L6
Millbank Primary School WEST SW1P 17 K6
Millbank Tower WEST SW1P 17 L6
Millbarn Medical Centre BEAC HP9 88 E10
Millbrook School CHES/WCR EN8 62 D5
Millennium Arena BTSEA SW11 158 B6
Millennium Bailey's Hotel SKENS SW7 15 J5
Millennium Balloon STHWK SE1 13 K10
Millennium Gloucester Hotel ECT SW5 15 H6
Millennium Harbour POP/IOD E14 160 E1
Millennium Hotel KTBR SW1X 16 B2
Millennium Hotel London Mayfair MYFR/PKLN W1K 10 D8
The Millennium Primary School GNWCH SE10 161 L2
Millennium Quay DEPT SE8 160 G5
Millennium Wharf POP/IOD E14 161 J2
Mill Farm Business Park HSLWW TW4 175 M3
Millfields J & I School CLPT E5 120 B9
Millfield Theatre UED N18 99 L5
Mill Green Business Park MTCM CR4 202 A7
Mill Green Golf Club WGCE AL7 23 J10
Mill Hill Cemetery MLHL NW7 96 F7
Mill Hill County High School MLHL NW7 96 B3
The Mill Hill CC MLHL NW7 96 F4
Mill Hill Golf Club MLHL NW7 96 B3
Mill Hill Industrial Estate MLHL NW7 96 C7
Mill Hill School MLHL NW7 96 E5
Mill Lane Medical Centre KIL/WHAMP NW6 117 K10
Mill Lane Trading Estate CROY/NA CR0 202 G10
Mill Mead J & I School HERT/WAT SG14 25 K5
The Mill Primary School CRAWW RH11 283 K7
Mill River Trading Estate PEND EN3 80 D8
Millside Industrial Estate DART DA1 165 L10
Mill Street Clinic STHWK SE1 19 M1
Mill Studio Business Centre WARE SG12 26 D2
Mill Trading Estate WLSDN NW10 135 N4
Millwall FC (The New Den) BERM/RHTH SE16 160 B4
Milmead Industrial Centre TOTM N17 100 A10
Milton Mount Primary School CRAWE RH10 284 C5
Milton Natural Health Centre HGT N6 118 D5
Milton Road Business Park GVE DA12 190 F3
Milton's Cottage CSTG HP8 89 N4
Milwards Primary School HLWW/ROY CM19 46 E5
Minet Clinic HYS/HAR UB3 133 H10
Minet J & I School HYS/HAR UB3 133 J10
Ministry of Defence WHALL SW1A 11 L10
Mint Business Park CAN/RD E16 141 M7
Mirravale Trading Estate CHDH RM6 123 P5
Mission Grove Primary School WALTH E17 120 E3
Mitcham CC MTCM CR4 201 P4
Mitcham Golf Club MTCM CR4 202 B5
Mitcham Industrial Estate MTCM CR4 202 B1
Mitcham Vale High School MTCM CR4 202 C2
Mitchell Brook Primary School WLSDN NW10 136 A1
Mitre Bridge Industrial Park NKENS W10 136 E6
Mitre House Hotel BAY/PAD W2 9 L6
Moatbridge School ELTH/MOT SE9 184 A2
The Moat School FUL/PGN SW6 157 H8
Moberly Sports & Education Centre WLSDN NW10 136 G5
Mole Business Park LHD/OX KT22 236 F7
Molesey Hospital E/WMO/HCT KT8 197 P5
Mollison Drive Health Centre WLGTN SM6 222 F4
Monega Primary School MNPK E12 122 A10
Monken Hadley CE Primary School BAR EN5 77 K5
Monkfrith Primary School EBAR EN4 98 B1
Monks Hill Sports Centre SAND/SEL CR2 224 C4
Monksmead School BORE WD6 75 P7
Monks Orchard Primary School CROY/NA CR0 204 C5
Monro Industrial Estate CHES/WCR EN8 62 D10
Monson Primary School NWCR SE14 160 C6
The Montague on the Gardens Hotel RSQ WC1B 11 L3
Montbelle Primary School ELTH/MOT SE9 184 D7
Montcalm-Hotel Nikko MBLAR W1H 10 B6
Monteagle Primary School DAGW RM9 143 L3
Montem Primary School HOLWY N7 118 G8
SL SL1 148 G1
Montem Sports Centre SL SL1 149 J1
Montpelier Primary School EA W5 135 J7
Monument Bridge East Industrial Estate WOKN/KNAP GU21 232 E1
The Monument CANST EC4R 13 H7
Moore Place Golf Club ESH/CLAY KT10 217 P2
Moorfields Eye Hospital FSBYE EC1V 6 G10
Moor House School OXTED RH8 261 L8
Moor Lane Junior School CHSGTN KT9 219 L2
Moor Park Golf Club RKW/CH/CXG WD3 92 C4
Moor Park Industrial Estate WATW WD18 92 D1
Mora Primary School CRICK NW2 116 F9
Morden Cemetery MRDN SM4 200 F6
Morden College Homes BKHTH/KID SE3 161 M8
Morden First School MRDN SM4 201 K5
Morden Hall Medical Centre WIM/MER SW19 201 L3
Morden Hall Park (NT) MRDN SM4 201 M4
Morden Mount Primary School LEW SE13 160 G8
Morden Park Pool MRDN SM4 201 J5
Morden Road Clinic WIM/MER SW19 201 L3
More House School KTBR SW1X 16 B4
Moreland Primary School FSBYE EC1V 6 D9
Moreton Bay Industrial Estate GPK RM2 105 L10
Moreton CE Primary School CHONG CM5 49 K6
Moreton Industrial Estate SWLY BR8 209 J4
Morgans JMI School HERT/BAY SG13 25 L7
Morgans Walk Junior Mixed School HERT/WAT SG14 25 H7
Moriah Jewish Day School PIN HA5 113 M6
Morley College STHWK SE1 18 B3
Morningside Primary School HOM E9 140 B1
Mornington Sports & Fitness Centre CAMTN NW1 4 F5
Morpeth School BETH E2 140 B5
Mortimer Road Clinic WLSDN NW10 136 F5
Mortimer School STRHM/NOR SW16 180 E5
Mortlake Cemetery MORT/ESHN SW14 156 B9
Mortlake Crematorium RCH/KEW TW9 155 N8
Moselle School TOTM N17 99 M10
Mosiah Foundation Supplementary School STNW/STAM N16 119 M6
The Mosque & Islamic Centre of Brent CRICK NW2 116 G9
Mossbourne Community Academy CLPT E5 120 A9
HACK E8 119 P9
Mossford Green Primary School BARK/HLT IG6 102 F10
Moss Hall Primary School FNCH N3 97 L7
The Mother & Baby Clinic HOM E9 140 B1
Mottingham Community Health Clinic ELTH/MOT SE9 184 B7
Mottingham Primary School ELTH/MOT SE9 184 C6
Mount Alvernia Hospital GU GU1 268 B2
Mount Carmel RC Primary School EA W5 155 H2
Mount Carmel RC Technology College for Girls ARCH N19 118 E6
Mount Grace School POTB/CUF EN6 59 L6
The Mount Infant School NWMAL KT3 199 N3
Mount Medical Centre FELT TW13 175 M5
Mount Pleasant Lane J & I School LCOL/BKTW AL2 55 M7
Mount School MLHL NW7 96 E6
Mount Stewart Primary School KTN/HRWW/WS HA3 115 J4
Mount Vernon Hospital NTHWD HA6 92 C6
Mowat Industrial Estate WATN WD24 73 K4
Mowlem Primary School BETH E2 140 B4
Mowlem Trading Estate TOTM N17 100 B8
MPR Eurotots School KIL/WHAMP NW6 136 G2
MS Business Centre PIN HA5 113 L1
MSP Business Centre WBLY HA9 115 N9
Mudchute City Farm POP/IOD E14 161 H3
Mudlands Estate RAIN RM13 144 F5
Mulberry Business Centre BERM/RHTH SE16 160 C1
Mulberry House School CRICK NW2 117 H10
Mulberry Primary School TOTM N17 99 N10
Mulberry School for Girls WCHPL E1 140 A8
Mulgrave Primary School WOOL/PLUM SE18 162 D3
Munroe Centre STHWK SE1 19 H1
Murky Puddle Theatre NWMAL KT3 200 C3
Murray Business Centre STMC/STPC BR5 207 L3
Muschamp Primary School CAR SM5 201 P9
Museum in Docklands POP/IOD E14 140 F9
Museum of Fulham Palace FUL/PGN SW6 156 G8
Museum of Garden History STHWK SE1 17 M4
Museum of London BARB EC2Y 12 E4
Museum of London (Archaeological Research Centre) IS N1 6 F6
Museum of Richmond TWK TW1 177 J1
Museum of Rugby & Twickenham Stadium Tours WHTN TW2 176 D2
Museum of the Artillery in the Rotunda CHARL SE7 162 B4
Museum of the Order of St John FARR EC1M 12 D2
Musical Museum BTFD TW8 155 K5
Muswell Hill Bowling Club MUSWH N10 118 B1
Muswell Hill Golf Club MUSWH N10 98 C9
Muswell Hill Primary School MUSWH N10 118 C1
Myatt Garden Primary School BROCKY SE4 160 E8
Myatts Field Clinic BRXN/ST SW9 159 J7
N1 Shopping Centre IS N1 6 B7
Nagi Business Centre ALP/SUD HA0 135 J4
Nags Head Shopping Centre HOLWY N7 118 F8
HOLWY N7 118 G9
Naima Jewish Preparatory School KIL/WHAMP NW6 2 G7
Nascot Wood Infant School WAT WD17 73 H4
Nash College of Further Education WWKM BR4 205 L10
Nash Mills Primary School HHS/BOV HP3 54 A1
The National Archives RCH/KEW TW9 155 N6
National Army Museum CHEL SW3 16 B9
National Film Theatre STHWK SE1 11 P9
National Film & TV School BEAC HP9 88 D9
National Gallery LSQ/SEVD WC2H 11 K8
National Hospital for Neurology & Neurosurgery RSQ WC1B 11 L2
National Hospital for Sick Children (Great Ormond Street) BMSBY WC1N 11 M2
National Maritime Museum GNWCH SE10 161 J5
National Physical Laboratory TEDD TW11 176 D9
National Portrait Gallery LSQ/SEVD WC2H 11 K8
National Sports Centre NRWD SE19 181 P9
National Temperance Hospital CAMTN NW1 4 G9
National Youth Theatre of GB HOLWY N7 118 F8
Natural History Museum SKENS SW7 15 L4
Natural Therapy Clinic TOOT SW17 180 C8
Natwest Sports Club BECK BR3 182 E9
Navigation College CANST EC4R 12 F7
Nazeing CP School WAB EN9 45 K9
Nazeing Glass Industrial Estate BROX EN10 45 H7
Nazeing Golf Club WAB EN9 45 P10
Nazeing Park School WAB EN9 45 P8
NEC Harlequins RFC (Twickenham Stoop Stadium) WHTN TW2 176 D3
Negus Sixth Form Centre WOOL/PLUM SE18 162 G5
Nelmes Primary School EMPK RM11 125 N2
Nelson Dock Museum BERM/RHTH SE16 140 E10
Nelson Hospital RYNPK SW20 201 J2
Nelson Primary School EHAM E6 142 D4
WHTN TW2 176 A2
Nelson's Column STJS SW1Y 11 K9
Nelson Trading Estate WIM/MER SW19 201 L1
New Addington Pools & Fitness Centre CROY/NA CR0 225 H6
The New Ambassadors Theatre LSQ/SEVD WC2H 11 K6
New Ash Green Primary School HART DA3 211 L9
New Atlas Wharf POP/IOD E14 160 E2
The New Aylesbury Medical Centre WALW SE17 19 H7
The New Beacon School SEV TN13 264 G3
New Brentford Cemetery HSLW TW3 153 N8
New Briars Primary School HAT AL10 40 D4
Newbridge IL IG1 123 H9
Newbury Park Health Centre GNTH/NBYPK IG2 122 G4
The New Business Centre WLSDN NW10 136 C5
New Caledonian Wharf BERM/RHTH SE16 160 E2
New Chiswick Pool CHSWK W4 156 B6
New City Primary School PLSTW E13 141 P5
The New College WDSR SL4 149 H6
New Connaught Rooms HOL/ALD WC2B 11 M5
New Covent Garden Market VX/NE SW8 158 E6
New Crane Wharf WAP E1W 140 B10
New Cross Sports Arena NWCR SE14 160 D6
New Elgiva Theatre CSHM HP5 50 G7
New End Primary School HAMP NW3 117 M9
New End Theatre HAMP NW3 117 M8
New England Industrial Estate BARK IG11 142 F4
HOD EN11 45 H2
Newfield Primary School WLSDN NW10 136 C2
Newham College of Further Education EHAM E6 142 C4
SRTFD E15 141 K2
Newham General Hospital PLSTW E13 141 P6
Newham Leisure Centre PLSTW E13 141 P7
Newham Medical Centre PLSTW E13 141 P4
Newham Sixth Form College PLSTW E13 141 N6
Newham Training & Education Centre SRTFD E15 141 K1
New Haw Therapy Clinic ADL/WDHM KT15 215 L6
New Health Centre TOTM N17 99 M9
Newington Court Business Centre STHWK SE1 18 E4
Newington Green Primary School STNW/STAM N16 119 M10
Newington Industrial Estate WALW SE17 18 D6
New Kings Primary School FUL/PGN SW6 157 J8
Newland House School TWK TW1 176 E7
New Lodge School DORK RH4 254 G9
New London Theatre LSQ/SEVD WC2H 11 M5
New Monument School WOKS/MYFD GU22 232 F1
Newnham J & I School RSLP HA4 113 K6
New North Community School IS N1 6 G3
Newport J & I School LEY E10 121 H7
New River Sports Centre WDGN N22 99 J8
New River Trading Estate CHES/WCR EN8 62 C2
New River Village CEND/HSY/T N8 118 G1
New Rush Hall School IL IG1 122 F7
New School FUL/PGN SW6 157 J7
The New School at West Heath SEV TN13 265 J5
New Scotland Yard STJSPK SW1H 17 J3
News International WAP E1W 13 P8
New Southgate Cemetery FBAR/BDGN N11 98 C4
New Southgate Crematorium FBAR/BDGN N11 98 C4
New Southgate Industrial Estate FBAR/BDGN N11 98 D6
New Southgate Pain Clinic & Medical Centre FBAR/BDGN N11 98 D6
New Spitalfields Market LEY E10 120 F9
Newstead Wood School for Girls ORP BR6 206 G10
Newton Farm First & Middle School RYLN/HDSTN HA2 113 N7
Newton Industrial Estate CHDH RM6 123 N2
Newton Medical Centre BAY/PAD W2 8 G5
Newton Preparatory School VX/NE SW8 158 C6
Newtons Primary School RAIN RM13 144 E4
New Victoria Hospital KUTN/CMB KT2 200 B1
New Victoria Theatre WOKN/KNAP GU21 232 B3
New Woodlands School BMLY BR1 183 K7
New Zealand Golf Club ADL/WDHM KT15 215 H8
Nicholas Breakspear RC School STALE/WH AL4 39 K7
Nightingale Clinic PLSTW E13 141 P4
Nightingale Primary School CLPT E5 119 P8
SWFD E18 121 P2
WDGN N22 98 F9
WOOL/PLUM SE18 162 E5
Nightingale School TOOT SW17 179 P5
The Nightingale School STHWK SE1 17 N2
Nizels Golf & Leisure Club RTON TN11 265 M10
No 41 Hotel WESTW SW1E 16 F3
Noak Hill School ABR/ST RM4 105 M3
Noam Primary School NFNCH/WDSPK N12 97 L6
Noel Coward CHCR WC2N 11 L7
Noel Park Primary School WDGN N22 99 J10
Nomad Theatre EHSLY KT24 252 G4
Nonsuch High School for Girls CHEAM SM3 220 G4
Nonsuch House Hotel EW KT17 220 F2
Nonsuch Industrial Estate HOR/WEW KT19 220 B7
Nonsuch Primary School EW KT17 220 E2
Noor Ul Islam School LEY E10 121 H7
Norbury Complementary Therapy Clinic STRHM/NOR SW16 202 G1
Norbury First & Middle School HRW HA1 114 D3
Norbury Health Centre STRHM/NOR SW16 202 G2
Norbury Manor Primary School STRHM/NOR SW16 202 F1
Norbury Manor Secondary Girls School STRHM/NOR SW16 203 H1
Norbury Trading Estate STRHM/NOR SW16 202 G2
Norfolk House School MUSWH N10 98 C10
Norland Place School NTGHL W11 8 A10
Norlington School LEY E10 121 J6
Norman Booth Leisure Centre HLWE CM17 29 N8
Normand Croft Community School WKENS W14 14 D9
Normandy Primary School BXLYHN DA7 164 E7
Normanhurst School CHING E4 101 J1
Norman Park Athletics Track HAYES BR2 205 N6
Norman Shaw Building (MP's Offices) WHALL SW1A 17 L1
North Acton Business Park ACT W3 136 A8
Northaw Primary School POTB/CUF EN6 60 B5
North Beckton Primary School EHAM E6 142 C6
North Bridge House HAMP NW3 3 K1
North Bridge House School CAMTN NW1 138 B3
HAMP NW3 3 K1
North Bridge House Senior School CAMTN NW1 4 E6
Northbrook CE School LEE/GVPK SE12 183 K1
Northbury Primary School BARK IG11 142 E1
Northchurch CC BERK HP4 33 J2
North Clinic BMLY BR1 205 M1
Northcote Lodge School BTSEA SW11 179 P2
North Croydon Medical Centre THHTH CR7 203 J6
North Downs Business Park SEV TN13 246 D2
North Downs Golf Club CTHM CR3 260 F1
North Ealing Primary School WEA W13 134 G6
North East Surrey College of Technology EW KT17 220 D7
North East Surrey Crematorium NWMAL KT3 200 F6
Northend Primary School ERITH DA8 164 G7
North End Trading Estate ERITH DA8 164 F6
North Feltham Trading Estate EBED/NFELT TW14 153 J10
Northfields Industrial Estate ALP/SUD HA0 135 M3
Northfields Prospect Business Centre PUT/ROE SW15 157 J10
Northfleet Cemetery GVW DA11 189 P4
Northfleet Industrial Estate GVW DA11 167 L10

Northfleet School for Girls *GVW* DA11 190 A5
Northfleet Technology College *GVW* DA11 190 A4
Northgate Business Centre *EN* EN1 80 A7
Northgate Clinic *CDALE/KGS* NW9 116 B4
Northgate Industrial Park *CRW* RM5 104 A10
Northgate Primary School *CRAWE* RH10 283 P5
North Harringay Primary School *CEND/HSY/T* N8 119 H2
North Havering College of Adult Education *ROM* RM1 124 F2
North Holmwood CC *RDKG* RH5 273 H7
North Kensington Video-Drama Project *NKENS* W10 137 H8
North London Collegiate School *EDGW* HA8 95 K7
The North London Hospice *NFNCH/WDSPK* N12 97 L4
North London School of Physiotherapy *ARCH* N19 118 D6
North London Tutorial College *HDN* NW4 116 F4
North Middlesex Golf Club *NFNCH/WDSPK* N12 97 N4
North Middlesex Hospital *UED* N18 99 M6
North Mymms CC *BRKMPK* AL9 58 D2
Northolt Aerodrome *RSLP* HA4 133 H1
Northolt High School *NTHLT* UB5 133 N1
Northolt Primary School *NTHLT* UB5 133 L2
Northolt Road Clinic *RYLN/HDSTN* HA2 114 B8
Northolt Swimarama *NTHLT* UB5 133 P1
North Orbital Trading Estate *STAL* AL1 38 F10
North Pole Depot *WLSDN* NW10 136 C6
North Primary School *STHL* UB1 133 N9
Northside Primary School *NFNCH/WDSPK* N12 97 M6
The North Street Health Centre *CLAP* SW4 158 D9
Northumberland Heath Medical Centre *ERITH* DA8 164 E6
Northumberland Heath Primary School *ERITH* DA8 164 C6
Northumberland Park Community School *TOTM* N17 99 P8
Northumberland Park Industrial Estate *TOTM* N17 100 A7
Northview Primary School *WLSDN* NW10 116 B9
North Watford Cemetery *GSTN* WD25 73 H1
North Watford Health Clinic *GSTN* WD25 55 K10
Northway School *MLHL* NW7 95 P4
North Weald Airfield *EPP* CM16 66 A2
North Weald Golf Club *EPP* CM16 48 B9
North & West Essex Adult Community College *HLW* CM20 28 F9
North West Kent College *GVE* DA12 191 J4
RDART DA2 187 J5
North West London Jewish Primary School *CRICK* NW2 2 A3
North West London Medical Centre *MV/WKIL* W9 3 J8
North Westminster Community School *BAY/PAD* W2 9 L4
North Westminster Community Secondary School *MV/WKIL* W9 8 F1
North Weylands Industrial Estate *WOT/HER* KT12 197 M9
Northwick Park Hospital & Clinical Research Centre *HRW* HA1 114 C5
Northwold Primary School *CLPT* E5 119 P7
Northwood Cemetery *NTHWD* HA6 92 G10
Northwood College *NTHWD* HA6 92 E8
Northwood Football Club *NTHWD* HA6 92 C10
Northwood Golf Club *NTHWD* HA6 92 E8
Northwood & Pinner Community Hospital *NTHWD* HA6 93 H9
Northwood Preparatory School *RKW/CH/CXG* WD3 92 D3
Northwood Primary School *ERITHM* DA18 163 P2
Northwood School *NTHWD* HA6 93 J9
Northwood Sports Centre *NTHWD* HA6 93 J9
Norwegian/British Monument *BAY/PAD* W2 9 N9
The Norwegian School *WIM/MER* SW19 178 F10
Norwood Green Infant School *NWDGN* UB2 153 M4
Norwood Green Junior School *NWDGN* UB2 153 M4
Norwood Heights Shopping Centre *NRWD* SE19 181 M9
Norwood School *NRWD* SE19 181 K8
Notre Dame Preparatory School *COB* KT11 216 G7
Notre Dame RC Girls School *STHWK* SE1 18 C3
Notre Dame RC Primary School *WOOL/PLUM* SE18 162 E5
Notre Dame University *LSQ/SEVD* WC2H 11 K8
Notting Hill & Ealing High School Senior Department *WEA* W13 134 G7
Notting Hill Preparatory School *NTGHL* W11 8 B5
Novello Theatre *ASC* SL5 192 C5
HOL/ALD WC2B 11 N7
Novotel *CAMTN* NW1 5 K9
CAN/RD E16 141 N9
GNWCH SE10 160 G6
STHWK SE1 12 F10
TWRH EC3N 13 K7
WDR/YW UB7 152 B3
Novotel London Waterloo *STHWK* SE1 17 N5
Novotel London West *HMSMTH* W6 156 G4
Nower Hill High School *PIN* HA5 113 P2
NTGB Sports Ground *EHAM* E6 142 D1
Nuffield Hospital *ENC/FH* EN2 79 H6
Nugent Shopping Park *STMC/STPC* BR5 207 L4
Number 10 Bowling *ROM* RM1 124 F3
Nutfield Cemetery *REDH* RH1 258 E9
Nutfield Church CE Primary School *REDH* RH1 276 G1
Nutfield Priory Hotel *REDH* RH1 258 D10
Nutley Dean Business Park *HORL* RH6 279 H1
O2 Centre *KIL/WHAMP* NW6 3 J1
The O2 *POP/IOD* E14 141 J10
Oakdale Infant School *SWFD* E18 101 N10
Oakdale Junior School *SWFD* E18 101 P10
Oak Farm Clinic *HGDN/ICK* UB10 132 C3
Oak Farm J & I School *HGDN/ICK* UB10 132 C2
Oakfield First School *WDSR* SL4 148 G8
Oakfield Junior School *LHD/OX* KT22 236 C9
Oakfield Preparatory School *DUL* SE21 181 L5
Oakfield Primary School *DART* DA1 187 L5
Oakfield Road Industrial Estate *PGE/AN* SE20 182 A10
Oakfield School *WOKS/MYFD* GU22 233 J1
Oak Hill Health Centre *SURB* KT6 199 K6
Oakhill Primary School *WFD* IG8 101 K7
Oakhyrst Grange School *CTHM* CR3 259 L2
Oakington Manor School *WBLY* HA9 115 N10
Oakland CP School *EBAR* EN4 78 A10
Oakland Park Golf Club *CSTG* HP8 89 L5
Oaklands College *BORE* WD6 75 P6
HARP AL5 20 A2
HAT AL10 40 D4
STAL AL1 38 D6
STALE/WH AL4 39 K5
WGCW AL8 22 G4
Oaklands Infant School *BH/WHM* TN16 243 P2
Oaklands Junior School *BH/WHM* TN16 243 P2
Oaklands Primary School *HNWL* W7 154 E1
Oaklands School *ISLW* TW7 154 C9
LOU IG10 82 A9
Oaklands Secondary School *BETH* E2 139 P5
Oak Lane Cemetery *TWK* TW1 176 F3
Oak Lane Medical Centre *TWK* TW1 176 G3
Oakleigh School *TRDG/WHET* N20 97 P4
Oak Lodge JMI School *WWKM* BR4 204 G7
Oak Lodge Medical Centre *EDGW* HA8 95 N8
Oak Lodge School *BAL* SW12 180 A3
EFNCH N2 117 M1
Oakmere Primary School *POTB/CUF* EN6 59 N8
The Oaks Industrial Estate *HLW* CM20 29 J8
The Oaks Primary School *CRAWE* RH10 284 A10
Oaks Sports Centre *CAR* SM5 222 A7
Oakthorpe Primary School *UED* N18 99 K6
Oak Tree Clinic *WOKN/KNAP* GU21 231 J4
Oak Tree Medical Centre *GDMY/SEVK* IG3 123 H7
Oakwood Business Park *WLSDN* NW10 136 A5
Oakwood Estate *HLW* CM20 29 K7
Oakwood Hill Industrial Estate *LOU* IG10 82 E9
Oakwood Independent School *PUR/KEN* CR8 223 J9
Oakwood Industrial Park *CRAWE* RH10 284 B4
Oakwood JMI School *STALE/WH* AL4 39 H5
Oakwood Medical Centre *STHGT/OAK* N14 78 D9
Oakwood School *BXLYHN* DA7 164 E10
HORL RH6 280 C4
Oakwood Sports Centre *HORL* RH6 280 D4
Oasis Sports Centre *LSQ/SEVD* WC2H 11 L5
Oast House Centre *STA* TW18 173 J7
Oatlands Park Hotel *WEY* KT13 196 D10
Oatlands School *WEY* KT13 216 E1
The Observatory Shopping Centre *SL* SL1 149 M1
Obstetrics Hospital *GWRST* WC1E 11 H2
Occupational Health Centre *CROY/NA* CR0 203 L10
Ockendon School *SOCK/AV* RM15 146 F7
Odeon Cinema *BAR* EN5 77 K9
BAY/PAD W2 10 A6
BECK BR3 204 F2
BERM/RHTH SE16 160 C2
CAMTN NW1 4 F5
CFSP/GDCR SL9 110 B3
ELTH/MOT SE9 162 B10
ESH/CLAY KT10 218 A1
EW KT17 220 B9
HAMP NW3 3 L4
HAYES BR2 205 M2
HHNE HP2 36 A7
HLW CM20 28 F10
HOLWY N7 118 F8
KENS W8 14 E4
KUT/HW KT1 199 K2
LSQ/SEVD WC2H 11 K8
MUSWH N10 118 B2
RCH/KEW TW9 177 J1
ROM RM1 124 G3
STJS SW1Y 11 J8
STRHM/NOR SW16 180 F6
SWFD E18 101 M10
UX/CGN UB8 131 N3
WIM/MER SW19 179 K10
Odeon Cinemas *FITZ* W1T 11 J4
Odeon Covent Garden Cinema *LSQ/SEVD* WC2H 11 K6
Odeon Multiplex Cinema *GU* GU1 267 P1
Odeon Wardour Street Cinema *SOHO/SHAV* W1D 11 J7
Odessa Infant School *FSTGT* E7 121 M10
Odhams Industrial Estate *WATN* WD24 73 K3
Odhams Trading Estate *WATN* WD24 73 H2
Odyssey Business Park *RSLP* HA4 113 J10
Old Actonians Sports Club *EA* W5 155 L1
Old Admiralty *STJS* SW1Y 11 K10
Old Bancroftians FC *BKHH* IG9 102 A5
Old Barnes Cemetery *BARN* SW13 156 E8
Old Barn Theatre *CRAWW* RH11 283 J5
Old Beckenhamian RFC *WWKM* BR4 205 J10
Old Bellgate Wharf *POP/IOD* E14 160 E2
Old Bexley Business Park *BXLY* DA5 186 C3
Old Bexley CE Primary School *BXLY* DA5 186 A4
The Old Brickworks Business Centre *HARH* RM3 105 P8
Old Brockleians Sports Ground *LEE/GVPK* SE12 183 P2
Old Bromlians CC *HAYES* BR2 205 N5
Old Cemetery *EDUL* SE22 182 A2
Old Chigwellians Sports Club *CHIG* IG7 102 E2
Old Colfeian Sports Club *LEE/GVPK* SE12 183 M1
The Old Cottage Hospital *EW* KT17 220 C9
Old Curiosity Shop *LINN* WC2A 11 N5
Old Elthamians Sports Club *CHST* BR7 185 H9
Oldfield House Special School *HPTN* TW12 197 N1
Oldfield Primary School *GFD/PVL* UB6 134 C4
Oldfields Trading Estate *SUT* SM1 201 K10
Old Fold Manor Golf Club *BAR* EN5 77 H5
Old Ford Primary School *BOW* E3 140 E4
Old Guildfordians RFC *GU* GU1 250 C9
The Old Guild Theatre *GVW* DA11 190 A4
Old Harlow Health Centre *HLWE* CM17 29 M7
Oldhill Medical Centre *STNW/STAM* N16 119 N6
Old Jamaica Business Estate *BERM/RHTH* SE16 19 M3
Old Lyonian Sports Ground *RYLN/HDSTN* HA2 114 B3
Old Merchant Taylors Sports Club *RKW/CH/CXG* WD3 72 C8
Old Millhillians Sports Ground *RYLN/HDSTN* HA2 93 P9
Old Oak Primary School *SHB* W12 136 C8
Old Operating Theatre & Herb Garret Museum *STHWK* SE1 12 G10
Old Owens Sports Ground *TRDG/WHET* N20 97 N2
Old Palace Primary School *BOW* E3 140 G5
Old Palace School *CROY/NA* CR0 203 J10
Old Royal Naval College *GNWCH* SE10 161 J4
Old Royal Observatory Greenwich *GNWCH* SE10 161 J6
Old St Patricks School *WCHPL* E1 13 N2
Old Spitalfields Market Hall *WCHPL* E1 13 L3
Old Station Museum *CAN/RD* E16 162 D1
Old Sun Wharf *POP/IOD* E14 140 D9
Old Tiffinians Sports Ground *E/WMO/HCT* KT8 198 D5
Old Town Hall *CHERT* KT16 195 K7
Old Treasury *WHALL* SW1A 17 L1
Old Verulamiums RFC *LCOL/BKTW* AL2 57 H1
Old Vicarage School *RCHPK/HAM* TW10 177 K2
Old Vic Theatre *STHWK* SE1 18 B1
Old War Office *WHALL* SW1A 11 L10
Old Wilsonians Sports Club *WWKM* BR4 205 K8
Olga Primary School *BOW* E3 140 D4
Oliver Business Park *WLSDN* NW10 135 P4
Oliver Goldsmith Primary School *CDALE/KGS* NW9 116 A3
CMBW SE5 159 N7
Oliver House Preparatory School *CLAP* SW4 180 C2
Olympia *WKENS* W14 14 B4
Olympia Industrial Estate *WDGN* N22 98 G10
Olympic Industrial Estate *WBLY* HA9 115 N9
Olympic Retail Park *WBLY* HA9 115 M9
Olympic Trading Estate *WBLY* HA9 115 N9
One Aldwych Hotel *COVGDN* WC2E 11 N7
The One Stanley Medical Centre *ALP/SUD* HA0 135 K2
Ongar & District Sports Club *CHONG* CM5 67 P4
Ongar Health Centre *CHONG* CM5 67 P4
Ongar Leisure Centre *CHONG* CM5 67 P2
Ongar Place Infant School *ADL/WDHM* KT15 215 K3
Ongar War Memorial Hospital *CHONG* CM5 67 P2
On Sai Clinic *ECT* SW5 14 G6
Onslow Infant School *GUW* GU2 267 L2
Onslow St Audreys School *HAT* AL10 40 E4
Open Air Theatre *CAMTN* NW1 4 C10
The Open University *FSBYW* WC1X 5 N9
HAMP NW3 117 K9
Ophaboom Theatre *WLSDN* NW10 136 E4
Optima Business Park *HOD* EN11 45 H2
Optimax Laser Eye Clinic *HAMP* NW3 3 K2
Orange Tree Theatre *RCH/KEW* TW9 155 K10
Oratory RC Primary School *CHEL* SW3 15 N7
Orchard Business Centre *BECK* BR3 182 E8
REDH RH1 276 B9
The Orchard Health Centre *BARK* IG11 142 F4
Orchard Hill College *WLGTN* SM6 222 C3
Orchard House Industrial Estate *CSHM* HP5 51 H8
Orchard House School *CHSWK* W4 156 A3
Orchard J & I School *HOM* E9 140 B2
The Orchard Junior School *HSLWW* TW4 153 P10
Orchard Primary School *SCUP* DA14 185 L8
WATN WD24 72 G2
The Orchard School *E/WMO/HCT* KT8 198 C5
Orchards Community Infant School *REIG* RH2 275 K3
Orchard Shopping Centre *DART* DA1 187 M2
The Orchard Theatre *DART* DA1 187 M2
Orchard Way Primary School *CROY/NA* CR0 204 D7
Oriel High School *CRAWE* RH10 283 N7
Oriel Primary School *FELT* TW13 175 M6
Orient Industrial Park *LEY* E10 120 F7
Orion Business Centre *NWCR* SE14 160 C4
Orleans House Gallery *TWK* TW1 176 G4
Orleans Infant School *TWK* TW1 176 G3
Orley Farm School *HRW* HA1 114 C8
Orpington College of Further Education *ORP* BR6 207 K8
The Orpington Halls *ORP* BR6 207 K9
Orpington Hospital *ORP* BR6 227 J1
Orpington Mental Health Centre *ORP* BR6 207 J10
Orpington Retail Park *STMC/STPC* BR5 207 M4
Orpington Superbowl *ORP* BR6 207 K8
Orpington Trade Centre *STMC/STPC* BR5 207 L3
Osidge JMI School *STHGT/OAK* N14 98 D2
Osier Industrial Estate *WAND/EARL* SW18 157 K10
Osmani Primary School *WCHPL* E1 13 P2
Osterley Park & House (NT) *ISLW* TW7 154 B5
Osterley RFC *NWDGN* UB2 154 A2
Otford Primary School *RSEV* TN14 247 H2
Our Lady Immaculate RC Primary School *BRYLDS* KT5 199 N8
Our Lady of Dolours RC Primary School *BAY/PAD* W2 8 G3
Our Lady of Grace RC Junior School *CRICK* NW2 116 E8
Our Lady of Grace RC Primary School *CHARL* SE7 161 N5
Our Lady of Hartley RC Primary School *HART* DA3 211 L5
Our Lady of Lourdes RC Primary School *BKHTH/KID* SE3 161 J9
FBAR/BDGN N11 98 C6
WAN E11 121 L4
WLSDN NW10 135 P3
Our Lady of Muswell RC Primary School *MUSWH* N10 98 B10
Our Lady of Peace Infant School *SL* SL1 128 B7
Our Lady of Peace Junior School *SL* SL1 128 B7
Our Lady of the Rosary RC Primary School *STA* TW18 173 K9
Our Lady of the Rosary RC School *ELTH/MOT* SE9 185 H2
Our Lady of the Sacred Heart School *HOLWY* N7 5 P1
HOLWY N7 118 G10
Our Lady of the Visitation RC Combined Primary School *GFD/PVL* UB6 134 B6
Our Lady of Victories RC Primary School *SKENS* SW7 15 K6
Our Lady of Victorys RC Primary School *PUT/ROE* SW15 156 G10
Our Lady Queen of Heaven County Primary School *CRAWW* RH11 283 L5
Our Lady Queen of Heaven RC Primary School *WIM/MER* SW19 178 G3
Our Lady RC Primary School *CAMTN* NW1 5 H5
POP/IOD E14 140 E8
Our Lady & St Johns RC Primary School *BTFD* TW8 155 H4
Our Lady & St Joseph Primary School *IS* N1 7 J2
Our Lady & St Philip Neri RC Infant School *FSTH* SE23 182 C6
Our Lady & St Phillip Neri RC Primary School *SYD* SE26 182 D7
Our Ladys Catholic Primary School *AMS* HP6 68 G1
DART DA1 187 L2
Our Ladys RC Primary School *CAMTN* NW1 138 D3
WGCE AL7 23 H7
Outwood Windmill *REDH* RH1 277 L9
Oval Business Centre *LBTH* SE11 17 P8
Oval House Theatre *LBTH* SE11 18 A10
Oval Primary School *CROY/NA* CR0 203 M8
Overton Grange School *BELMT* SM2 221 L5
Oxford Gardens Primary School *NKENS* W10 136 G8
Oxford House College *SOHO/SHAV* W1D 11 J5
Oxhey Infant School *OXHEY* WD19 73 M10
Oxhey Park Golf Centre *OXHEY* WD19 93 L2
Oxhey Wood Primary School *OXHEY* WD19 93 K5
Oxo Tower Wharf *STHWK* SE1 12 B8
Oxshott Village Sports Club *LHD/OX* KT22 218 B10
Oxted Health Centre *OXTED* RH8 261 L5
Oxted & Limpsfield Hospital *OXTED* RH8 261 J4
Oxted School *OXTED* RH8 261 L4
Pachesham Park Golf Centre *LHD/OX* KT22 236 D4
Paddington Bowling & Sports Club *MV/WKIL* W9 8 G1
Paddington Community Hospital *MV/WKIL* W9 8 E3
Paddington Green Primary School *BAY/PAD* W2 9 L2
Paddington Recreation Ground Athletics Track *KIL/WHAMP* NW6 2 F9
Paddock School *PUT/ROE* SW15 156 C10
Painshill Park *COB* KT11 217 H10
Painters Ash Primary School *GVW* DA11 190 A6
Paint Pots Montessori School *WBPTN* SW10 15 K10
Pakeman Primary School *HOLWY* N7 118 G8
Palace Gardens Shopping Centre *ENC/FH* EN2 79 L7
Palace of Westminster *WHALL* SW1A 17 M2
Palace Theatre *SOHO/SHAV* W1D 11 K7
WAT WD17 73 J7
Palladium Theatre *SOHO/CST* W1F 10 G6
Palmers College *GRAYS* RM17 168 B3
Palmers Green High School *WCHMH* N21 99 H3
Palmerston Business Centre *SUT* SM1 221 M2
Palm House *RCH/KEW* TW9 155 L7
Panorama Pier *STHWK* SE1 12 D8
Panshanger Aerodrome *WGCE* AL7 23 P5
Panshanger Golf & Squash Complex *WGCE* AL7 23 M3
Panshanger JMI School *WGCE* AL7 23 K4
Paradise Swimming Pools *MLHL* NW7 96 B6
Paradise Wildlife Park *BROX* EN10 43 N7
Paramount Industrial Estate *WATN* WD24 73 K4
Paray House School *FUL/PGN* SW6 157 J8
Parayhouse School *WBPTN* SW10 157 M6
Parchmore Medical Centre *THHTH* CR7 203 K3
Pardes House & Beis Yaakov School *FNCH* N3 97 J10
Parent Infant Clinic *HAMP* NW3 117 M10
Paringdon Primary School *HLWS* CM18 46 G5
Parish CE Primary School *BMLY* BR1 183 M10
Parish Church CE Primary School *CROY/NA* CR0 203 J10
Park Avenue Clinic *WAT* WD17 73 H6
Park Business Centre *KIL/WHAMP* NW6 2 E10
Parker Industrial Centre *RDART* DA2 188 B3
Parkes Townhouse Hotel *CHEL* SW3 15 P3
Parkfield Industrial Estate *BTSEA* SW11 158 B8
Parkfield JMI School *HDN* NW4 116 E5
Parkfield Medical Centre *POTB/CUF* EN6 59 L8
Parkgate House School *CLAP* SW4 158 B10
Park Hall Trading Estate *WNWD* SE27 181 K6
Park High School *STAN* HA7 95 J10
Park Hill Junior School *CROY/NA* CR0 203 L10
Parkhill Primary School *CLAY* IG5 122 C1
Park Hill School *KUTN/CMB* KT2 177 M10
Park House Medical Centre *KIL/WHAMP* NW6 2 B7
Park House RFC *HAYES* BR2 205 P9
Park Industrial Estate *LCOL/BKTW* AL2 56 D3
The Park Inn Heathrow *WDR/YW* UB7 152 C6
Parklands Primary School *ROM* RM1 124 E1
Park Lane Primary School *WBLY* HA9 115 K9
Park Medical Centre *BERM/RHTH* SE16 160 C3
Park Mews Small Business Centre *HNHL* SE24 181 K2
Park Road Clinic *CEND/HSY/T* N8 118 E3
Park Road Industrial Estate *SWLY* BR8 208 G3
Park Road Swimming Centre *CEND/HSY/T* N8 118 E3
Park Royal Business Centre *WLSDN* NW10 136 A6
Park School *WOKS/MYFD* GU22 232 D3
Park School for Girls *IL* IG1 122 D7
Parkside Business Estate *DEPT* SE8 160 E5
Parkside Clinic *NTGHL* W11 8 B5
Parkside Health *NTGHL* W11 8 B6
Parkside Hospital *WIM/MER* SW19 178 G6
Parkside Primary School *BORE* WD6 75 L4
Parkside School *COB* KT11 235 P4
Park Street CE Primary School *LCOL/BKTW* AL2 56 C3
Park Walk Primary School *WBPTN* SW10 15 L10
Parkway Primary School *ERITH* DA18 163 P2
Parkway Trading Estate *HEST* TW5 153 K5
Park Wood Golf Club *BH/WHM* TN16 244 B8
Parkwood Hall School *SWLY* BR8 209 J3
Parkwood Primary School *FSBYPK* N4 119 J7
Parlaunt Park Combined School *DTCH/LGLY* SL3 150 E2
Parliament Hill Fields Athletics Track *HAMP* NW3 118 A9
Parliament Hill Lido *HAMP* NW3 118 B9
Parliament Hill School *KTTN* NW5 118 B9
Parmiter Industrial Centre *BETH* E2 140 A4
Parmiters School *GSTN* WD25 55 K7
Parndon Wood *HLWS* CM18 46 G7
Parndon Wood Cemetery *HLWW/ROY* CM19 46 F7
Parndon Wood Crematorium *HLWW/ROY* CM19 46 F7
Parnells Sports Ground *KTN/HRWW/WS* HA3 115 L4
Parsloes Primary School *DAGW* RM9 144 A1
Parsonage Farm Primary School *RAIN* RM13 145 K5
Parsons Green Health Clinic *FUL/PGN* SW6 157 K7
Parsons Mead School *ASHTD* KT21 237 K5
Passmores School & Technology College *HLWS* CM18 46 G2
Passport Language Schools *BMLY* BR1 205 N1
Patent Office *FLST/FETLN* EC4A 12 A4
The Patrick Doody Clinic & Health Centre *WIM/MER* SW19 179 K10
Pattinson Clinic *RCH/KEW* TW9 177 J1
The Paul Robeson Theatre *HSLW* TW3 154 A9
Pauls Theatre School *EMPK* RM11 125 L5
Pavilion Barclays Sports Ground *EA* W5 135 K7
The Pavilion Leisure Centre *BMLY* BR1 205 M2
Pavilion Restaurant *RCH/KEW* TW9 155 K8
Pavilions Shopping Centre *UX/CGN* UB8 131 M2
Paxton Primary School *NRWD* SE19 181 N9
Payne Clinic *EW* KT17 220 D9
PDSA Hospital *REDBR* IG4 122 A1
Peace Pagoda *CHEL* SW3 16 B10
Peacock Cinema *WOKN/KNAP* GU21 232 B3
Peacock Estate *TOTM* N17 99 N7
Peacock Industrial Estate *TOTM* N17 99 N8
The Peacocks Shopping Centre *WOKN/KNAP* GU21 232 B3
The Peacock Theatre *HOL/ALD* WC2B 11 N6
Peall Road Industrial Estate *CROY/NA* CR0 202 G6
Peaslake School *SHGR* GU5 270 F10
Peckham Park Primary School *PECK* SE15 159 P6
The Peckham Pulse Health & Leisure Centre *PECK* SE15 159 P7
Pedham Place Industrial Estate *SWLY* BR8 209 H5
Peerglow Industrial Estate *WATW* WD18 92 C1
Pelham Primary School *BXLYHN* DA7 164 B9
WIM/MER SW19 179 K10
Pembridge Hall *BAY/PAD* W2 137 K9
Pembridge Hall Preparatory School for Girls *BAY/PAD* W2 8 F7
Pendragon Secondary School *BMLY* BR1 183 M6
Pentavia Retail Park *MLHL* NW7 96 C8
Penwortham Primary School *STRHM/NOR* SW16 180 C9
Percival David Foundation of Chinese Art *STPAN* WC1H 11 K1
Perivale Industrial Park *GFD/PVL* UB6 134 F3
Perivale New Business Centre *GFD/PVL* UB6 135 H4
Perivale Park Athletics Track *GFD/PVL* UB6 134 D5
Perivale Park Golf Course *GFD/PVL* UB6 134 D5
Perivale Primary School *GFD/PVL* UB6 135 H4
Perrin Road Clinic *ALP/SUD* HA0 114 G9
Perry Hall Primary School *ORP* BR6 207 J6
Perrymount Primary School *FSTH* SE23 182 C5
Perrywood Business Park *REDH* RH1 276 C8
Perth Trading Estate *SL* SL1 128 G7
Petchy Academy *CLPT* E5 119 P9
Peterborough Primary School *FUL/PGN* SW6 157 K8
Peterborough & St Margarets High School *STAN* HA7 94 D4
Peter Hills School *BERM/RHTH* SE16 140 C10
Peter James Business Centre *HYS/HAR* UB3 153 H1
Peterley Business Centre *BETH* E2 140 A4
Peter Pan Statue *BAY/PAD* W2 9 L9
The Petersham Hotel *RCHPK/HAM* TW10 177 K3

Petric Museum of Egyptia Archaeology *GWRST* WC1E 11 J2
Petts Hill Primary School *NTHLT* UB5 114 A10
Pewley Down Infant School *GU* GU1 268 B2
Pewterers' Hall *CITYW* EC2V 12 F4
Phoenix Business Centre
CSHM HP5 50 C6
POP/IOD E14 140 F7
Phoenix Cinema *EFNCH* N2 117 P2
Phoenix College *MRDN* SM4 201 L5
Phoenix High School *SHB* W12 136 D9
Phoenix Industrial Estate *HRW* HA1 114 E2
Phoenix Leisure Centre *CAT* SE6 182 G3
Phoenix School *HAMP* NW3 3 K2
Phoenix Secondary & Primary School *BOW* E3 140 E5
Phoenix Theatre *LSQ/SEVD* WC2H 11 K6
Phoenix Trading Estate *GFD/PVL* UB6 135 H3
Physical Energy Statue *BAY/PAD* W2 9 L10
Piccadilly Theatre *SOHO/SHAV* W1D 11 J7
Pickford Lane Medical Centre *BXLYHN* DA7 163 P7
Pickhurst Infant School *WWKM* BR4 205 K6
Pickhurst Junior School *WWKM* BR4 205 L6
Picture House Cinema *SRTFD* E15 141 J1
Pield Heath School *UX/CGN* UB8 131 P6
Pilgrims Way J & I School *PECK* SE15 160 B5
Pilot Industrial Centre *WLSDN* NW10 136 B6
Pilton Estate *CROY/NA* CR0 203 J9
Pimlico School *PIM* SW1V 17 H8
The Pines Trading Estate *RGUW* GU3 249 K8
Pine Trees Business Park *STA* TW18 173 H8
Pinewood Film Studios *IVER* SL0 130 E2
The Pinewood Hotel *DTCH/LGLY* SL3 130 B7
Pinewood Primary School *CRW* RM5 104 C6
Pinewood Special School *WARE* SG12 26 C4
Pinkwell Primary School *HYS/HAR* UB3 152 D3
Pinnacles Cricket & Squash Club *SUT* SM1 221 K3
Pinner Hill Golf Club *PIN* HA5 93 J7
Pinner Medical Centre *PIN* HA5 113 M2
Pinner Park Primary School *PIN* HA5 114 A1
Pinner View Medical Centre *HRW* HA1 114 B3
Pinner Wood Primary School *PIN* HA5 93 K9
Pioneers Industrial Park *CROY/NA* CR0 202 F8
Pippins School
ASHF TW15 174 A7
DTCH/LGLY SL3 151 J7
Pirbright Camp *CHOB/PIR* GU24 230 A6
Pirbright Primary School *CHOB/PIR* GU24 230 D8
Pitfarm Lawn Tennis Club *GU* GU1 250 D10
Pitshanger Manor Museum *EA* W5 135 H10
Pitwood Park Industrial Estate *KWD/TDW/WH* KT20 238 G6
Pixham School *DORK* RH4 255 H10
Pixies Hill Primary School *HHW* HP1 35 J7
Plaisterers Hall *STBT* EC1A 12 E4
Plaistow Hospital *PLSTW* E13 141 N4
Plaistow Primary School *PLSTW* E13 141 P3
Plantation House Medical Centre *LOTH* EC2R 13 H5
Plashet Jewish Cemetery *MNPK* E12 142 A1
Plashet Road Medical Centre *FSTGT* E7 141 N2
Plashet School *EHAM* E6 142 B2
Players Theatre *CHCR* WC2N 11 M9
Playhouse *HLW* CM20 46 F1
Playhouse Cinema *EPSOM* KT18 220 A10
The Playhouse *CHCR* WC2N 11 M9
Playhouse Theatre *EPSOM* KT18 219 P9
Plaza Business Centre *PEND* EN3 80 E6
Plaza Cinema *OXTED* RH8 261 K5
Pleasance Theatre *HOLWY* N7 138 F1
Plough Industrial Estate *LHD/OX* KT22 236 F6
Plumcroft Primary School *WOOL/PLUM* SE18 162 F5
Plumstead Leisure Centre *WOOL/PLUM* SE18 163 J4
Plumstead Manor School *WOOL/PLUM* SE18 162 G4
The Pointer School *BKHTH/KID* SE3 161 M7
Polesden Lacey (NT) *RDKG* RH5 253 P6
Police Cadet School *WAN* E11 121 M6
The Polish Institute & Sikorski Museum *SKENS* SW7 15 M2
Polish War Memorial *RSLP* HA4 133 J1
Polka Theatre for Children *WIM/MER* SW19 179 L9
Polygon Business Centre *DTCH/LGLY* SL3 151 J8
Ponders End Industrial Estate *PEND* EN3 80 E8
Pond Meadow School *GUW* GU2 249 K9
Ponsbourne Park Hotel *HERT/BAY* SG13 42 F9
Ponsbourne St Marys Primary School *HERT/BAY* SG13 42 F10
Ponsbourne Tunnel *HERT/BAY* SG13 42 G10
Pooles Park Primary School *FSBYPK* N4 118 G7
Pools in the Park *RCH/KEW* TW9 155 J10
Pope John Primary School *SHB* W12 136 E9
Pope Paul RC Primary School *POTB/CUF* EN6 59 J9
Pop In Business Centre *WBLY* HA9 115 N10
Poplar Business Park *POP/IOD* E14 141 H9
Poplar Coroners Court *POP/IOD* E14 140 G9
Poplar Primary School *WIM/MER* SW19 201 K3
Pop Up Theatre *CLKNW* EC1R 6 B8
Porchester Leisure Centre *BAY/PAD* W2 8 G5
Portcullis House *WHALL* SW1A 17 M2
Porters Park Golf Club *RAD* WD7 57 H10
Portico City Learning Centre *CLPT* E5 120 B9
Portland Business Centre *DTCH/LGLY* SL3 149 N7
The Portland Hospital *REGST* W1B 10 F2
Portland House Medical Centre *GFD/PVL* UB6 134 A6
Portland Medical Centre *SNWD* SE25 204 A5
Portland Place School *REGST* W1B 10 F3
The Portman Clinic *HAMP* NW3 3 L1
Portobello Market *NKENS* W10 137 H7
Portobello Medical Centre *NTGHL* W11 8 B6
Portway Primary School *SRTFD* E15 141 M3
Potten End First School *BERK* HP4 34 E3
Potterells Medical Centre *BRKMPK* AL9 58 G1
Potters Bar CC *POTB/CUF* EN6 59 L8
Potters Bar FC *POTB/CUF* EN6 59 L8
Potters Bar Golf Club *POTB/CUF* EN6 59 K7
Potter Street Primary School *HLWE* CM17 47 L3
Pound Hill Infant School *CRAWE* RH10 284 D6
Pound Hill Junior School *CRAWE* RH10 284 D6
Pound Park Nursery School *CHARL* SE7 162 A4
The Pountney Clinic *HSLW* TW3 153 P9
Poverest Primary School *STMC/STPC* BR5 207 K5
Powell Corderoy Primary School *DORK* RH4 272 E3
Powergate Business Park *WLSDN* NW10 136 A5
Power Industrial Estate *ERITH* DA8 164 G7
The Power Station London *VX/NE* SW8 16 F10
Prae Wood Primary School *STALW/RED* AL3 37 P7
Pratts Bottom Primary School *ORP* BR6 227 M7
Premier Cinema
DORK RH4 273 H1
PECK SE15 159 P8
Premier Travel Inn
BARK IG11 142 E3
BH/WHM TN16 262 B2
BORE WD6 76 A7
BTFD TW8 155 K5
CAN/RD E16 142 A9
CDW/CHF RM16 167 H2
CHDH RM6 123 P3
CHING E4 81 J4
CHSGTN KT9 219 H6
COB KT11 217 K8
CRAWE RH10 283 P2
CRAWE RH10 284 E1
CRAWW RH11 283 L8
CROY/NA CR0 223 H3
CROY/NA CR0 223 P2
ECT SW5 14 G6
EDGW HA8 95 M8
EHAM E6 142 D7
EPSOM KT18 219 P10
FUL/PGN SW6 157 H9
GFD/PVL UB6 134 F5
GSTN WD25 55 L10
GU GU1 250 A9
GVE DA12 190 F9
GVW DA11 190 D5
HAT AL10 40 C2
HHW HP1 34 E9
HHW HP1 35 M7
HLW CM20 29 L5
HOR/WEW KT19 220 B2
HORL RH6 280 A6
HTHAIR TW6 152 F7
HYS/HAR UB3 152 C3
IS N1 5 M8
KGLGY WD4 54 A4
KTN/HRWW/WS HA3 114 G4
KWD/TDW/WH KT20 239 H5
LCOL/BKTW AL2 56 C6
PEND EN3 80 E2
PUR RM19 165 N4
PUR RM19 166 D3
RAIN RM13 145 N8
REDBR IG4 122 A3
REDH RH1 276 B7
ROM RM1 124 G3
SL SL1 149 N1
STHWK SE1 12 F9
STHWK SE1 17 N1
STHWK SE1 19 K2
STPAN WC1H 5 K10
WAT WD17 73 L8
WATW WD18 72 F9
WBLY HA9 115 M8
WCCW AL8 22 G7
WHTN TW2 176 B4
WIM/MER SW19 201 M1
WOKN/KNAP GU21 231 P3
YEAD UB4 133 J8
Prendergast School *BROCKY* SE4 160 F10
Presdales School *WARE* SG12 26 C3
Preston Manor School *WBLY* HA9 115 L7
Preston Medical Centre *WBLY* HA9 115 K8
Preston Park Primary School *WBLY* HA9 115 J6
Priestmead First & Middle Schools *KTN/HRWW/WS* HA3 114 G1
Primary School *CHEL* SW3 157 P4
Primrose Hill School *CAMTN* NW1 4 D5
Primrose Montessori School *HBRY* N5 119 K8
Prince Charles Cinema *LSQ/SEVD* WC2H 11 K7
Prince Edward Theatre *SOHO/SHAV* W1D 11 J6
Prince of Wales Primary School *PEND* EN3 80 E3
Prince of Wales Theatre *STJS* SW1Y 11 J8
Princes College *NOXST/BSQ* WC1A 11 L5
Princes Court Business Centre *WAP* E1W 140 A9
Princes Park Stadium *DART* DA1 187 P4
Princes Plain Primary School *HAYES* BR2 206 B7
Princess Alexandra Hospital *HLW* CM20 28 E10
Princess Avenue School *MUSWH* N10 118 C1
Princess Frederica CE J & I School *WLSDN* NW10 136 E4
Princess Grace Hospital *MHST* W1U 10 C2
Princess Louise Hospital *NKENS* W10 136 F7
Princess Margaret Hospital *WDSR* SL4 149 J8
Princess May Primary School *STNW/STAM* N16 119 M10
Princess of Wales Conservatory *RCH/KEW* TW9 155 L6
The Princess Royal Distribution Centre *WLSDN* NW10 135 N3
The Princess Royal University Hospital *ORP* BR6 206 D10
Prins Willem-Alexander School *WOKS/MYFD* GU22 232 F3
Priors Field School *GODL* GU7 266 E8
Prior Weston Primary School *STLK* EC1Y 12 F2
Priory CE Primary School *WIM/MER* SW19 179 L8
The Priory CE Voluntary Aided School *DORK* RH4 272 E3
The Priory Leisure Centre *STMC/STPC* BR5 207 M8
Priory Retail Park *WIM/MER* SW19 179 N10
Priory School
BNSTD SM7 239 K1
SL SL1 128 C7
STMC/STPC BR5 207 M8
Priory Shopping Centre *DART* DA1 187 L2
Priory Special School *SNWD* SE25 203 N4
The Priory *ORP* BR6 207 L7
Privy Council *STJS* SW1Y 11 J10
Privy Council Office *WHALL* SW1A 11 L10
Progress Business Centre *SL* SL1 128 C8
Progress Business Park *CROY/NA* CR0 202 G9
Pronto Trading Estate *YEAD* UB4 132 F7
Prospect Business Park *LOU* IG10 82 G8
Prospect House School *PUT/ROE* SW15 178 G3
Prospect Industrial Estate *CSHM* HP5 51 H8
Proteus School *KIL/WHAMP* NW6 137 L2
Proud Gallery *CHCR* WC2N 11 L8
Providence Road School *WDR/YW* UB7 131 P10
Providence Square *STHWK* SE1 19 N1
Provident Industrial Estate *HYS/HAR* UB3 153 H1
PS Tattershall Castle *WHALL* SW1A 11 M10
Pump House *BERM/RHTH* SE16 140 D10
Pump House Theatre *WATW* WD18 73 K9
Pump Lane Industrial Estate *HYS/HAR* UB3 153 J1
The Purcell School *HRW* HA1 114 C8
Purdy Hicks Gallery *STHWK* SE1 12 C9
Purfleet Industrial Park
SOCK/AV RM15 145 N10
SOCK/AV RM15 165 N1
Purfleet Primary School *PUR* RM19 165 P3
Purford Green Infant School *HLWS* CM18 47 K3
Purford Green Primary School *HLWS* CM18 47 K3
Purley Community Health Clinic *PUR/KEN* CR8 223 H7
Purley & District War Memorial Hospital *PUR/KEN* CR8 223 H7
Purley Downs Golf Club *SAND/SEL* CR2 223 L7
Purley John Fisher RFC *COUL/CHIP* CR5 241 H6
Purley Oaks Primary School *SAND/SEL* CR2 223 L4
Purley Secretarial & Language College *PUR/KEN* CR8 223 H7
Purley Sports Club *PUR/KEN* CR8 222 E6
Pursuit Centre *WAP* E1W 140 B9
Putney Animal Hospital *PUT/ROE* SW15 156 G10
Putney Arts Theatre *PUT/ROE* SW15 156 G10
Putney Exchange Shopping Centre *PUT/ROE* SW15 156 G10
Putney High School *PUT/ROE* SW15 178 G1
Putney Leisure Centre *PUT/ROE* SW15 156 F10
Putney Lower Common Cemetery *BARN* SW13 156 E8
Putneymead Medical Centre *PUT/ROE* SW15 156 F10
Putney Park School *PUT/ROE* SW15 156 E10
Putney School of Art *PUT/ROE* SW15 157 H10
Putney Vale Cemetery *PUT/ROE* SW15 178 D5
Putney Vale Crematorium *PUT/ROE* SW15 178 D5
Puttenham CE Infant School *RGUW* GU3 266 A5
Puttenham Golf Club *RGUW* GU3 266 C5
Pylon Trading Estate *CAN/RD* E16 141 J6
Pyrcroft Primary School *CHERT* KT16 195 H6
Pyrford Golf Club *WOKS/MYFD* GU22 233 L3
Pyrford Primary School *WOKS/MYFD* GU22 233 J2
Quadrant Business Park *KIL/WHAMP* NW6 2 B5
Quality Hotel
DTCH/LGLY SL3 150 E5
HAT AL10 40 C7
HRW HA1 114 C4
PIM SW1V 16 F6
STAL AL1 38 E8
WBLY HA9 115 M9
Quarry Hill Infant School *GRAYS* RM17 167 N4
Quarry Hill Junior School *GRAYS* RM17 167 N4
Quarryside Business Park *REDH* RH1 258 C6
Quebec House *BH/WHM* TN16 262 G2
Quebec Industrial Estate *BERM/RHTH* SE16 160 D1
The Queen Anne Royal Free CE First School *WDSR* SL4 149 J9
Queen Charlotte's & Chelsea Hospital *SHB* W12 136 E8
Queen Charlotte's Cottage *RCH/KEW* TW9 155 J8
Queen Eleanor's CE Junior School *GUW* GU2 267 L1
Queen Elizabeth Centre *BAR* EN5 77 J8
Queen Elizabeth College *KENS* W8 14 E1
Queen Elizabeth Conference Centre *WEST* SW1P 17 K2
Queen Elizabeth Hall *STHWK* SE1 11 N9
Queen Elizabeth Hospital
BNSTD SM7 239 M4
WOOL/PLUM SE18 162 C5
Queen Elizabeth II Hospital *WGCE* AL7 23 K9
Queen Elizabeth II School *MV/WKIL* W9 8 D2
Queen Elizabeth Museum *CHING* E4 101 L1
Queen Elizabeths Boys School *BAR* EN5 76 G7
Queen Elizabeth's Foundation Training College *LHD/OX* KT22 236 C3
Queen Elizabeths Girls School *BAR* EN5 77 J8
Queen Elizabeth Stadium *EN* EN1 79 N6
Queenhithe Stairs *BLKFR* EC4V 12 E8
Queen Mary College University of London *WCHPL* E1 140 C6
Queen Mary's Hospital *HAMP* NW3 117 M8
Queen Marys Hospital *SCUP* DA14 185 K8
Queen Mary's Hospital for Children *SUT* SM1 201 M8
Queen Mary's University Hospital *PUT/ROE* SW15 178 D2
Queen Mary & Westfield College *SWFD* E18 101 M9
Queen Mother Sports Centre *PIM* SW1V 16 G5
Queensbridge Primary School *HACK* E8 7 M4
Queensbridge Sports Centre *HACK* E8 7 M3
Queen's Building *HTHAIR* TW6 152 C9
The Queens CE Primary School *RCH/KEW* TW9 155 L6
Queen's Club *WKENS* W14 14 A8
Queens College London *CAVSQ/HST* W1G 10 E4
Queen's Gallery *BGVA* SW1W 16 F2
Queensgate Centre *HLW* CM20 29 H7
Queens Gate School *SKENS* SW7 15 L5
Queens Hospital *ROMW/RG* RM7 124 F5
The Queens House *GNWCH* SE10 161 J5
Queens Ice Skating Club *BAY/PAD* W2 9 H8
Queens Manor Primary School *FUL/PGN* SW6 156 F6
Queensmead School *RSLP* HA4 113 L9
Queensmead Sports Centre *RSLP* HA4 113 L10
Queens Medical Centre *RCHPK/HAM* TW10 177 L1
Queensmere Shopping Centre *SL* SL1 149 L1
Queensmill School *FUL/PGN* SW6 157 K8
Queens Park Community School *WLSDN* NW10 136 F3
Queens Park Health Centre *NKENS* W10 2 B9
Queens Park Primary School *NKENS* W10 8 B1
Queens Park Rangers FC (Loftus Road Stadium) *SHB* W12 136 E10
Queen's Road Cemetery *CROY/NA* CR0 203 K6
Queens School *BUSH* WD23 73 N7
Queens Schools *WDSR* SL4 149 H5
Queens Sports Centre *GODL* GU7 266 G10
Queens Theatre
EMPK RM11 125 L5
SOHO/SHAV W1D 11 J7
Queensway Business Centre *PEND* EN3 80 B8
Queensway Health Centre *HAT* AL10 40 E3
Queenswell Infant School *TRDG/WHET* N20 97 N3
Queenswood School *BRKMPK* AL9 59 N4
Queen Victoria Memorial *WHALL* SW1A 16 G2
The Questors Theatre *EA* W5 135 H9
Quintin Kynaston School Technical College *STJWD* NW8 3 K6
Quwwat UL Islam Girl's School *FSTGT* E7 141 M1
Rabbsfarm Primary School *WDR/YW* UB7 131 N8
Racecourse Yacht Basin *WDSR* SL4 148 E6
Radcliffe College *SOHO/SHAV* W1D 10 G6
Radisson Edwardian Berkshire Hotel *OXSTW* W1C 10 E6
Radisson Edwardian Grafton Hotel *CAMTN* NW1 10 G1
Radisson Edwardian Hampshire Hotel *LSQ/SEVD* WC2H 11 K8
Radisson Edwardian Hotel *HYS/HAR* UB3 152 D6
Radisson Edwardian Kenilworth Hotel *RSQ* WC1B 11 K4
Radisson Edwardian Marlborough Hotel *RSQ* WC1B 11 K4
Radisson Edwardian Mayfair Hotel *MYFR/PICC* W1J 10 F8
Radisson Edwardian Mountbatten Hotel *LSQ/SEVD* WC2H 11 L6
Radisson Edwardian Vanderbilt Hotel *SKENS* SW7 15 K5
Radisson SAS Portman Hotel *MBLAR* W1H 10 B5
Radlett CC *RAD* WD7 74 G3
Radlett Lodge School *RAD* WD7 57 H8
Radlett Preparatory School *RAD* WD7 75 H4
RAF Uxbridge *HGDN/ICK* UB10 131 P3
RAF West Ruislip (University of Maryland) *HGDN/ICK* UB10 112 D7
Raglan Infant School *EN* EN1 79 M10
Raglan Junior School *EN* EN1 99 M1
Raglan Primary School *HAYES* BR2 205 P4
Railton Road Clinic *HNHL* SE24 181 J1
Rainbow Clinic *STJWD* NW8 137 N6
Rainbow Industrial Estate
RYNPK SW20 200 E2
WDR/YW UB7 131 N9
Rainbow Leisure Centre *EW* KT17 220 B8
Rainbow Montessori School *KIL/WHAMP* NW6 2 G4
Rainbow Natural Health Centre *REDH* RH1 276 A1
Rainbow Quay *BERM/RHTH* SE16 160 D2
Raines Foundation School *BETH* E2 140 A5
Rainham Cemetery *RAIN* RM13 145 K5
Rainham Hall (NT) *RAIN* RM13 145 H6
Rainham Marshes RSPB Reserve *RAIN* RM13 145 J9
Rainham Trading Estate *RAIN* RM13 144 F5
Rainham Village Primary School *RAIN* RM13 145 H6
The Raleigh School *EHSLY* KT24 252 D1
Ramac Industrial Estate *CHARL* SE7 161 M4
Ramada Encore Hotel *ACT* W3 136 A7
Ramada Hotel
BAY/PAD W2 8 G8
CRAWE RH10 284 B5
EA W5 135 L9
EHSLY KT24 252 G5
GSTN WD25 74 B7
HAT AL10 40 B4
Randal Cremer Primary School *BETH* E2 7 L7
Randalls Park Crematorium *LHD/OX* KT22 236 D6
Randolph Medical Centre *DTCH/LGLY* SL3 149 N6
Ranelagh Gardens (site of Chelsea Flower Show) *BGVA* SW1W 16 D8
Ranelagh Primary School *SRTFD* E15 141 K4
Rangefield Primary School *BMLY* BR1 183 K8
Ransomes Dock Business Centre *BTSEA* SW11 157 P6
Raphael Independent School *EMPK* RM11 125 H4
Rare Breeds Centre *FLKWH/TG* HP10 108 A5
The Rathbone Education Centre *CAN/RD* E16 141 L7
Rathbow Clinic *BAY/PAD* W2 9 M2
Rathfern Primary School *FSTH* SE23 182 E4
Ravenor Primary School *GFD/PVL* UB6 133 P5
Ravensbourne College of Design & Communication *CHST* BR7 184 D8
Ravensbourne School *HARH* RM3 105 L9
The Ravensbourne School *HAYES* BR2 205 N4
Ravenscourt Park Preparatory School *HMSMTH* W6 156 D3
Ravenscroft Medical Centre *GLDGN* NW11 117 J5
Ravenscroft Primary School *CAN/RD* E16 141 M6
Ravenscroft School *TRDG/WHET* N20 97 J1
Ravenside Retail Park *UED* N18 100 C7
Ravensquay Business Centre *STMC/STPC* BR5 207 L5
Ravenstone Primary School *BAL* SW12 180 B4
Ravenswood Industrial Estate *WALTH* E17 121 H2
Ravens Wood School *HAYES* BR2 206 A10
Ray Cochrane Beauty School *CAMTN* NW1 10 B3
Ray Lodge Primary School *WFD* IG8 102 A7
Raynehurst Junior School *GVE* DA12 191 J6
Raynes Park High School *RYNPK* SW20 200 E3
Raynes Park Sports Ground *RYNPK* SW20 200 D2
Raynes Park Vale FC *RYNPK* SW20 200 G5
Raynham Primary School *UED* N18 99 P6
RCA *SKENS* SW7 15 K4
RCA Sculpture School *BTSEA* SW11 157 P6
Real Tennis Club *BRKMPK* AL9 40 G4
Reay Primary School *BRXN/ST* SW9 159 H6
Records Office *CLKNW* EC1R 12 B1
Rectory Business Centre *SCUP* DA14 185 L7
Rectory Paddock School *STMC/STPC* BR5 207 M2
Redbridge College *CHDH* RM6 123 L3
Redbridge Drama Centre *SWFD* E18 101 M9
Redbridge Museum *IL* IG1 122 E8
Redbridge Primary School *REDBR* IG4 122 B3
Redbridge Sports Centre *BARK/HLT* IG6 102 G9
Redbridge Tuition Service *GNTH/NBYPK* IG2 122 G4
Redburn Industrial Estate *PEND* EN3 80 C10
Redcliffe School *WBPTN* SW10 15 J9
Redden Court School *HARH* RM3 125 N1
Reddiford School *PIN* HA5 113 M2
Reddings Primary School *HHS/BOV* HP3 36 B8
Redford Lodge Psychiatric Hospital *ED* N9 99 P3
Red Gates School *CROY/NA* CR0 223 H2
Redhill Aerodrome *REDH* RH1 276 F5
Redhill Business Centre *REDH* RH1 258 A9
Redhill College *REDH* RH1 276 C1
Redhill FC *REDH* RH1 276 A4
Redhill Junior School *CHST* BR7 184 E8
Redhill & Reigate Golf Club *REDH* RH1 275 N3
Red House (NT) *BXLYHS* DA6 163 P10
Redlands Primary School *WCHPL* E1 140 B7
The Redlands Primary School *DORK* RH4 272 G5
Redlibbets Golf Club *BGR/WK* TN15 211 J9
Red Lion Business Park *SURB* KT6 199 L9
Redriff Primary School *BERM/RHTH* SE16 160 D1
Red Rose Trading Estate *EBAR* EN4 77 N9
Redstone Cemetery *REDH* RH1 276 C1
Reedham Park School *PUR/KEN* CR8 223 H10
Reed Place Business Park *SHPTN* TW17 196 A8
Reeds School *COB* KT11 217 P8
Regal International College *ALP/SUD* HA0 115 K10
Regent Business Centre *HYS/HAR* UB3 153 J1
Regent Clinic *CAVSQ/HST* W1G 10 E4
Regent College London *PIN* HA5 113 N5
Regent's Park Barracks *CAMTN* NW1 4 E8
Regents Park Clinic *CAMTN* NW1 10 A1
Regents Park Medical Centre *CAMTN* NW1 4 F9
Regent's Park Track *STJWD* NW8 4 A7
Regina Coeli RC Primary School *SAND/SEL* CR2 223 J4
Regional Sports Centre *TIL* RM18 168 E8
Reigate College *REIG* RH2 257 L9
Reigate Day Hospital *REDH* RH1 257 N10
Reigate Grammar School *REIG* RH2 257 M10
Reigate Heath Golf Club *REIG* RH2 256 F10
Reigate Hill Golf Club *REIG* RH2 258 B4
Reigate Parish Infant School *REIG* RH2 257 M10
Reigate Priory Junior School *REIG* RH2 257 K10
Reigate Priory & Museum *REIG* RH2 257 K10
Reigate St Marys Preparatory & Choir School *REIG* RH2 257 L10
Reigate School *REIG* RH2 275 M3
Renaissance Chancery Court Hotel *HHOL* WC1V 11 N4
The Renaissance Hotel *HTHAIR* TW6 152 D7
Renoir Cinema *BMSBY* WC1N 11 M1
Renwick Industrial Estate *BARK* IG11 143 L4
The Retail Business Centre *EW* KT17 220 C6
Rewards Centre *HSLW* TW3 154 B9
Reynard Mills Trading Estate *BTFD* TW8 155 H4
Reynolds Performing Arts *RDART* DA2 186 F5
Reynolds Sports Centre *ACT* W3 155 M1
Rhoda McGaw Theatre & Cinema *WOKN/KNAP* GU21 232 B3
Rhodes Avenue Primary School *WDGN* N22 98 D9
Rhodes Farm Clinic *MLHL* NW7 96 F5
RHS Garden Wisley *RPLY/SEND* GU23 233 P4
Rhyl Primary School *KTTN* NW5 4 C1
RIBA Library Drawings & Manuscript Collection *MBLAR* W1H 10 B5
Ricards Lodge High School *WIM/MER* SW19 179 J7
Richard Alibon Primary School *DAGE* RM10 124 B10
Richard Atkins Primary School *BRXS/STRHM* SW2 180 F3
Richard Cloudesley School *STLK* EC1Y 12 E2
Richard Cobden Primary School *CAMTN* NW1 5 H6
Richard Hale School *HERT/BAY* SG13 25 L6
Richdales Istitute *ALP/SUD* HA0 135 J3
Rich Industrial Estate
PECK SE15 160 A5
STHWK SE1 19 K4
STHWK SE1 19 M7
Richings Park Golf Club *DTCH/LGLY* SL3 150 G3
Richings Park Sports Club *WDR/YW* UB7 151 J2
Richmond Adult & Community College *RCH/KEW* TW9 155 J10

Richmond American International University
KENS W8 14 G2
RCHPK/HAM TW10 177 K2
The Richmond Clinic
RCH/KEW TW9 155 L10
Richmond Community College
TWK TW1 176 E4
Richmond FC
RCH/KEW TW9 155 J10
Richmond Gate Hotel
RCHPK/HAM TW10 177 K3
The Richmond Golf Club
RCHPK/HAM TW10 177 K5
The Richmond Green Medical Centre
RCH/KEW TW9 177 J1
Richmond Hill Hotel
RCHPK/HAM TW10 177 K3
Richmond House School
HPTN TW12 175 N8
Richmond Magistrates Court
RCH/KEW TW9 155 J10
Richmond Park Golf Club
PUT/ROE SW15 178 B3
Richmond Park National Nature Reserve
RCHPK/HAM TW10 178 B5
Richmond Road Medical Centre
KUTN/CMB KT2 177 K10
Richmond Theatre
RCH/KEW TW9 155 J10
Richmond upon Thames College
WHTN TW2 176 D3
Rickmansworth Public Golf Club
RKW/CH/CXG WD3 92 A3
Rickmansworth School
RKW/CH/CXG WD3 72 A10
Rickmansworth Sports Club
RKW/CH/CXG WD3 71 P10
Riddlesdown High School
PUR/KEN CR8 223 M10
Ridge House Clinic
WCHMH N21 99 L1
Ridgeway Hotel
CHING E4 100 G3
Ridgeway Primary School
SAND/SEL CR2 223 M5
Rio Cinema
HACK E8 119 N10
Ripley Arts Centre
BMLY BR1 206 A1
Ripley CE Infant School
RPLY/SEND GU23 233 L7
Ripley Court School
RPLY/SEND GU23 233 M7
Ripley CC
RPLY/SEND GU23 233 M7
Ripple Infant School
BARK IG11 143 H3
Risebridge Golf Club
ROM RM1 104 G8
Rise Park Primary School
ROM RM1 104 E9
Risley Avenue Primary School
TOTM N17 99 M9
The Ritz Hotel
WHALL SW1A 10 G9
Ritzy Cinema
BRXN/ST SW9 159 H10
Riverbank Park Plaza Hotel
STHWK SE1 17 N6
River Brent Business Park
HNWL W7 154 D2
Riverdene Industrial Estate
WOT/HER KT12 217 L2
River Gardens Business Centre
EBED/NFELT TW14 153 J10
River House Montessori School
POP/IOD E14 140 F10
River Lee Country Park
WAB EN9 44 G10
WAB EN9 62 G5
River Mole Business Park
ESH/CLAY KT10 197 P8
River Park Industrial Estate
BERK HP4 33 M4
River Place Health Centre
IS N1 6 E4
River Road Business Park
BARK IG11 143 H5
Riversdale Primary School
WAND/EARL SW18 179 K4
Riverside Business Centre
WAND/EARL SW18 179 L4
The Riverside Business Centre
GU GU1 249 P10
Riverside Business Park
WIM/MER SW19 201 M1
Riverside Community Health Care
WKENS W14 156 G2
Riverside Golf Club
THMD SE28 143 P8
Riverside Industrial Estate
BARK IG11 143 K5
DART DA1 187 M1
LCOL/BKTW AL2 57 K3
Riverside Primary School
BERM/RHTH SE16 19 P2
Riverside Quarter
WAND/EARL SW18 157 K10
Riverside Retail Park
RSEV TN14 247 K5
Riverside Studios Cinema
BARN SW13 156 E4
Riverside Swimming Centre
ERITH DA8 164 F4
Riverside Wandle Trading Estate
MTCM CR4 202 A7
Riverston School
LEE/GVPK SE12 183 M1
Riverview C E Primary School
HOR/WEW KT19 219 P1
Riverview Clinic
GVE DA12 191 J8
Riverview Primary School
GVE DA12 191 H7
Riverway Industrial Estate
RGUW GU3 267 P9
The RJ Mitchell Primary School
HCH RM12 145 J1
RNLI Lifeboat Station
TWRH EC3N 13 K9
Roan Industrial Estate
MTCM CR4 201 P1
Robert Blair Primary School
HOLWY N7 5 M2
Robert Browning Primary School
WALW SE17 18 F7
Robertswood Combined and Nursery School
CFSP/GDCR SL9 90 C8
Robin Hood Infant School
SUT SM1 221 K2
Robin Hood Junior School
SUT SM1 221 L2
Robin Hood Lane Health Centre
SUT SM1 221 K2
Robin Hood Primary School
KUTN/CMB KT2 178 A8
Robinsfield Infant School
STJWD NW8 3 M7
The Roche School
WAND/EARL SW18 179 K1
Rockliffe Manor Primary School
WOOL/PLUM SE18 163 J5
Rockmount Primary School
NRWD SE19 181 K9
Rockware Business Centre
GFD/PVL UB6 134 C3
Rodd Estate
SHPTN TW17 196 D5
Roding Primary School
BCTR RM8 123 M9
WFD IG8 102 B8
Roding Valley High School
LOU IG10 82 B9
LOU IG10 82 E8
Roebuck Hotel
WARE SG12 26 B1
Roebuck Road Trading Estate
BARK/HLT IG6 103 L7
Roe Green J & I School
CDALE/KGS NW9 115 N2
Roehampton Church School
PUT/ROE SW15 178 E3
The Roehampton Priory Hospital
PUT/ROE SW15 156 C10
Roehampton Recreation Centre
PUT/ROE SW15 178 C3
Roehampton University
PUT/ROE SW15 179 H2
Roehampton University (Digby Stuart College)
PUT/ROE SW15 178 C1
Roehampton University (Froebel College)
PUT/ROE SW15 178 C2
Roehampton University (Southlands College)
PUT/ROE SW15 178 C1
Roger Ascham Primary School
WALTH E17 100 E9
Roger Bannister Sports Ground
KTN/HRWW/WS HA3 94 B7
Rokeby School
KUTN/CMB KT2 177 P10
SRTFD E15 141 J2
Roke Primary School
PUR/KEN CR8 223 K10
Roker Park Golf Club
RGUW GU3 249 J5
Rokesly Primary School
CEND/HSY/T N8 118 F3
Roman Bath
TPL/STR WC2R 11 P7
Roman Industrial Estate
CROY/NA CR0 203 M7
Roman Road Primary School
EHAM E6 142 A6
Roman Theatre of Verulamium
STALW/RED AL3 37 P6
Roman Wall Remains
BARB EC2Y 12 E4
Romford Cemetery
ROMW/RG RM7 124 D5
Romford Clinic
ROM RM1 124 G2
Romford County Court
ROM RM1 124 G2
Romford Golf Club
GPK RM2 125 H1
Romford Ice Arena
ROMW/RG RM7 124 F5
Romford IT Learning Centre
ROM RM1 124 F3
Romford Shopping Hall
ROM RM1 124 F2
Ronald Rose Primary School
PUT/ROE SW15 178 G3
Rood Lane Medical Centre
FENCHST EC3M 13 J7
Rooks Heath High School
RYLN/HDSTN HA2 113 P8
Roosevelt Memorial
MYFR/PKLN W1K 10 D7
Ropery Business Park
CHARL SE7 161 P3
Rosary Priory High School
BUSH WD23 74 D10
Rosary RC Infant School
HEST TW5 153 N5
Rosary RC Primary School
HAMP NW3 117 P10
Rosebery Industrial Park
TOTM N17 100 A10
Rosebery School
EPSOM KT18 219 P10
Rose Bruford College
BFN/LL DA15 185 L4
Rosedale Clinic
CHESW EN7 61 P4
Roseland JMI School
HOD EN11 26 E10
Roselands Clinic
NWMAL KT3 199 P4
Rose McAndrew Clinic
BRXN/ST SW9 158 G8
Rosemead Preparatory School
DUL SE21 181 K5
Rosendale Primary School
DUL SE21 181 K3
Rose of Kingston (Kingston Theatre)
KUT/HW KT1 199 J2
Rose Theatre Exhibition
STHWK SE1 12 E9
Rosetta Primary School
CAN/RD E16 141 N7
Rosewood Medical Centre
HCH RM12 125 J10
Rosherville CE Primary School
GVW DA11 190 B2
Rosh Pinah Primary School
EDGW HA8 95 N3
Rossgate JMI School
HHW HP1 35 K4
Rosslyn Park RFC
PUT/ROE SW15 156 C10
Rotherfield Primary School
IS N1 6 F5
Rotherhithe Primary School
BERM/RHTH SE16 160 B3
The Rotunda
KUT/HW KT1 199 K2
The Roundhouse Theatre
CAMTN NW1 4 C3
Roundshaw J & I School
WLGTN SM6 222 F4
Rowan Preparatory School
ESH/CLAY KT10 218 E4
Rowans Primary School
WGCE AL7 23 K2
Rowans School
RYNPK SW20 178 D10
Rowfant Business Centre
CRAWE RH10 205 M7
Rowhill Grange Hotel & Spa
RDART DA2 187 H8
Rowhill School
RDART DA2 187 K7
Rowley Industrial Park
ACT W3 155 N2
Roxbourne Medical Centre
RYLN/HDSTN HA2 114 A7
Roxbourne Middle School
RYLN/HDSTN HA2 113 L7
Roxeth First & Middle School
RYLN/HDSTN HA2 114 C7
Roxeth Manor First School
RYLN/HDSTN HA2 113 P8
Roxeth Mead School
RYLN/HDSTN HA2 114 C7
Roxwell Trading Park
LEY E10 120 D5
Royal Academy of Arts
MYFR/PICC W1J 10 G8
Royal Academy of Dance
BTSEA SW11 157 P7
Royal Academy of Dramatic Art
GWRST WC1E 11 J3
Royal Academy of Music
CAMTN NW1 10 D2
Royal Adelaide Hotel
WDSR SL4 149 J8
Royal Air Force Museum
CDALE/KGS NW9 96 D10
Royal Albert Hall
SKENS SW7 15 L2
The Royal Alexandra & Albert School
REIG RH2 257 P5
Royal Arsenal
WOOL/PLUM SE18 162 E2
Royal Ballet School
COVGDN WC2E 11 M6
The Royal Ballet School
RCHPK/HAM TW10 178 A4
The Royal Berkshire Ramada Plaza Hotel
ASC SL5 192 F3
Royal Blackheath Golf Club
ELTH/MOT SE9 184 C3
Royal Botanic Gardens Kew School
RCH/KEW TW9 155 L6
Royal Brompton Hospital
CHEL SW3 15 N7
Royal Chace Hotel
ENC/FH EN2 78 G4
Royal College of Anaesthetists
RSQ WC1B 11 L3
Royal College of Art
SKENS SW7 15 K2
Royal College of Music
SHB W12 156 D2
SKENS SW7 15 L3
Royal College of Nursing
CAMTN NW1 11 H1
IS N1 6 C6
Royal College of Obstetricians & Gynaecologists
CAMTN NW1 10 A1
Royal College of Ophthalmologists
CAMTN NW1 10 C2
Royal College of Paediatrics & Child Health
GTPST W1W 10 F3
The Royal College of Pathology
STJS SW1Y 11 J10
Royal College of Physicians
CAMTN NW1 10 E1
Royal College of Surgeons
LINN WC2A 11 P5
Royal College of Veterinary Surgeons
WEST SW1P 17 L5
Royal Courts of Justice
LINN WC2A 11 P6
Royal Court Theatre
BGVA SW1W 16 C6
Royal Court Young Peoples Theatre
NKENS W10 8 B4
The Royal Dock Community School
CAN/RD E16 141 P8
Royal Docks Medical Centre
EHAM E6 142 D8
Royal Epping Forest Golf Club
CHING E4 101 K1
Royal Exchange
BANK EC3V 13 H6
Royal Festival Hall
STHWK SE1 11 N10
The Royal First School (Crown Aided)
WDSR SL4 171 H8
Royal Free Hospital School of Medicine
HAMP NW3 117 P10
Royal Garden Hotel
KENS W8 15 H1
Royal Geographical Society
SKENS SW7 15 L2
Royal Grammar School
GU GU1 268 B1
Royal Gunpowder Mills
WAB EN9 62 G8
Royal Holloway University of London
EGH TW20 172 A9
EGH TW20 194 A1
Royal Holloway University of London (Hall of Residence)
EGH TW20 172 A7
The Royal Horseguards Hotel
WHALL SW1A 11 M10
Royal Horticultural Society New Hall
WEST SW1P 17 J4
Royal Horticultural Society Old Hall
WEST SW1P 17 J5
Royal Hospital
RCH/KEW TW9 155 K9
Royal Hospital Chelsea
CHEL SW3 16 C9
Royal Hospital for Neuro-disability
PUT/ROE SW15 179 H2
Royal Hospital & Home
PUT/ROE SW15 178 E3
Royal Hospital Museum
CHEL SW3 16 C8
Royal Institute of British Architects
REGST W1B 10 F3
Royal Institution's Faraday Museum
MYFR/PICC W1J 10 F8
The Royal Kent CE Primary School
LHD/OX KT22 218 B10
Royal Lancaster Hotel
BAY/PAD W2 9 M8
Royal Liberty School
GPK RM2 125 K1
The Royal London Estate
TOTM N17 100 A8
Royal London Homeopathic Hospital
BMSBY WC1N 11 M3
The Royal London Hospital
WCHPL E1 140 A7
Royal Marsden Hospital
BELMT SM2 221 M6
CHEL SW3 15 M7
Royal Masonic School for Girls
RKW/CH/CXG WD3 71 N10
Royal Mews
WDSR SL4 149 J7
The Royal Mews
BGVA SW1W 16 E3
Royal Mid-Surrey Golf Club
RCH/KEW TW9 155 J9
Royal Military School of Music
WHTN TW2 176 C2
Royal Mint Court
TWRH EC3N 13 M8
Royal National Orthopaedic Hospital
GTPST W1W 10 F2
STAN HA7 94 G2
Royal National Theatre
STHWK SE1 12 A9
Royal National Throat Nose & Ear Hospital
FSBYW WC1X 5 N9
Royal Opera House
COVGDN WC2E 11 M6
Royal Park Primary School
SCUP DA14 185 P6
Royal Russell School
CROY/NA CR0 224 A3
The Royal School
HAMP NW3 117 N9
Royal Society of Arts
CHCR WC2N 11 M8
Royal Society of Medicine
CAVSQ/HST W1G 10 E5
Royal Surrey County Hospital
GUW GU2 249 K10
Royal Terrace Pier
GVE DA12 190 F1
Royal Veterinary College
BRKMPK AL9 58 G4
CAMTN NW1 5 J6
Royal Victoria Docks Watersports Centre
CAN/RD E16 141 M9
Royal Wimbledon Golf Club
WIM/MER SW19 178 E8
Royal Windsor Racecourse
WDSR SL4 148 F5
Roydonbury Industrial Estate
HLWW/ROY CM19 46 C1
Roydon CP School
HLWW/ROY CM19 45 N1
Roydon Mill Leisure Park
HLWW/ROY CM19 27 M10
Royston Primary School
PGE/AN SE20 204 C1
RSPCA Animal Hospital
FSBYPK N4 118 G7
The Rubens at the Palace Hotel
BGVA SW1W 16 F3
Rudolf Steiner School
KGLGY WD4 53 P5
Rudolph Steiner Hall
CAMTN NW1 10 A1
Rufus Business Centre
WIM/MER SW19 179 L5
Ruislip Gardens Primary School
RSLP HA4 112 F9
Ruislip Golf Club
HGDN/ICK UB10 112 D7
Ruislip Manor FC
RSLP HA4 112 G7
Ruislip RFC
RSLP HA4 112 F7
Ruislip Woods National Nature Reserve
NTHWD HA6 112 D1
RSLP HA4 112 F3
Runnymede Hospital
CHERT KT16 194 G10
Runnymede Hotel & Spa
EGH TW20 172 E6
Runnymede (NT)
EGH TW20 172 B6
Rush Croft School
CHING E4 100 G8
Rushey Green Primary School
CAT SE6 182 G4
Rush Green Primary School
ROMW/RG RM7 124 E6
Rushmore Junior School
CLPT E5 120 B9
Ruskin House School
HNHL SE24 181 K1
Russell Clinic
STALW/RED AL3 38 C6
Russell House School
RSEV TN14 247 J1
The Russell JMI School
RCHPK/HAM TW10 177 J5
The Russell School
RCHPK/HAM TW10 177 J4
RKW/CH/CXG WD3 70 E8
Russet House School
EN EN1 80 A5
Rutherford Way Industrial Estate
CRAWE RH10 284 B2
Rutlish School
RYNPK SW20 201 J2
Ruxley Corner Industrial Estate
SCUP DA14 185 N9
Ruxley Park Golf Centre
STMC/STPC BR5 207 N1
Rydens School
WOT/HER KT12 197 K10
The Ryde Primary School
BRKMPK AL9 40 F1
Rydes Hill Preparatory School
RGUW GU3 249 L8
Rydon Business Centre
LHD/OX KT22 236 F6
Ryebrook Business Park
LHD/OX KT22 236 F6
Ryefield Primary School
HGDN/ICK UB10 132 E3
Rye House Stadium
HOD EN11 45 J1
Ryelands JMI School
HOD EN11 44 G2
Ryelands Primary School
SNWD SE25 204 A5
Rye Meads RSPB Reserve
HOD EN11 27 J10
Rye Oak Primary School
PECK SE15 160 A9
Rye Park Industrial Estate
HOD EN11 45 H1
Ryvers School
DTCH/LGLY SL3 150 A2
Saatchi Gallery
CHEL SW3 16 B7
Sacred Heart Catholic Primary School
PUT/ROE SW15 178 D1
Sacred Heart High School
HMSMTH W6 156 F3
Sacred Heart Junior School
HMSMTH W6 156 G3
Sacred Heart Language College
KTN/HRWW/WS HA3 94 D10
Sacred Heart of Mary Girls School
UPMR RM14 126 A7
Sacred Heart RC Infant School
BTSEA SW11 157 P8
Sacred Heart RC Primary School
NWMAL KT3 200 D4
OXHEY WD19 73 N10
RSLP HA4 112 F7
TEDD TW11 176 G10
TRDG/WHET N20 97 P3
WARE SG12 26 B2
Sacred Heart RC School
CMBW SE5 159 K7
Sacred Heart School
HOLWY N7 118 G10
Saddlers Hall
CITYW EC2V 12 F5
Sadler's Wells Theatre
CLKNW EC1R 6 B9
SAE Institute
HOLWY N7 118 F10
Safari Cinema
CROY/NA CR0 203 J8
Safari Cinema & Bingo
HRW HA1 114 E3
Saffron Green Primary School
BORE WD6 76 B8
Sai Medical Centre
POP/IOD E14 141 H9
The Sainsbury Centre
CHERT KT16 195 K7
St Adrians RC Primary School
STAL AL1 38 B9
St Agathas RC Primary School
KUTN/CMB KT2 177 L9
St Agnes RC Primary School
BOW E3 140 F5
CRICK NW2 117 H8
St Aidans Primary School
FSBYPK N4 119 H5
St Aidans RC Primary School
IL IG1 122 G6
St Alban & St Stephen RC Junior/Mixed School
STAL AL1 38 F6
St Albans CE Primary School
HCIRC EC1N 12 A3
St Albans City FC
STAL AL1 38 E5
St Albans City Hospital
STALW/RED AL3 38 B4
St Albans Girls School
STALW/RED AL3 38 D2
St Albans Health Clinic
HGT N6 118 B8
St Albans High School for Girls
STAL AL1 38 D5
St Albans Lawn Tennis Club
STALE/WH AL4 39 H4
St Albans Museum
STAL AL1 38 D6
St Albans Musical Museum
LCOL/BKTW AL2 56 A4
St Albans Music School
STALW/RED AL3 38 C3
St Albans Organ Museum
STAL AL1 38 G7
St Albans Primary School
HLW CM20 29 J9
St Albans Principal Health Centre
STAL AL1 38 C6
St Albans RC Aided Primary School
E/WMO/HCT KT8 198 A5
St Albans RC Church & School Presbytery
HCH RM12 125 H10
St Albans RC JMI School
HCH RM12 145 J2
St Albans Retail Park
STAL AL1 38 C8
St Albans Road Infant School
DART DA1 187 N2
St Albans & St Stephens Infant School
STAL AL1 38 E7
St Albans School
STALW/RED AL3 38 B6
St Albert the Great RC Primary School
HHS/BOV HP3 36 B7
St Alfege with St Peter CE Primary School
GNWCH SE10 161 H5
St Aloysius College
HGT N6 118 D6
St Aloysius RC Infant School
CAMTN NW1 5 J9
St Aloysius RC Junior School
CAMTN NW1 5 H8
St Andrew & St Francis CE JMI School
CRICK NW2 136 D1
St Andrew's Arts Centre
GVW DA11 190 E2
St Andrews Catholic School
LHD/OX KT22 237 H6
St Andrews CE First & Middle School
CRAWE RH10 284 B8
St Andrews CE JMI School
TRDG/WHET N20 97 J3
St Andrews CE J & I School
UX/CGN UB8 131 N3
St Andrews CE Primary School
EN EN1 79 L6
EPP CM16 66 D1
STHGT/OAK N14 98 D1
St Andrews CE School
CROY/NA CR0 223 J1
St Andrews Greek School
CAMTN NW1 4 F2
St Andrews Hospital
BOW E3 140 G6
St Andrews Primary School
BRXN/ST SW9 158 G8
COB KT11 217 K9
IS N1 5 P5
WARE SG12 27 J7
St Andrews School
RYLN/HDSTN HA2 114 A3
WLSDN NW10 136 E2
St Andrew's School
WOKN/KNAP GU21 232 A2
St Angelas Ursuline Convent School
FSTGT E7 141 N1
St Annes Catholic High School for Girls
ENC/FH EN2 79 L8
PLMGR N13 99 H5
St Annes Catholic Primary School
BNSTD SM7 239 K2
CHERT KT16 195 K8
St Annes CE Primary School
WAND/EARL SW18 179 L1
St Annes County Primary School
STWL/WRAY TW19 173 P3
St Annes RC Primary School
LBTH SE11 158 G5
VX/NE SW8 17 N9
WCHPL E1 13 N2
WCHPL E1 139 N6
St Anne's Special School
MRDN SM4 201 K5
St Anne's Trading Estate
POP/IOD E14 140 E8
St Anns CE Primary School
SEVS/STOTM N15 119 L3
St Ann's General Hospital
FSBYPK N4 119 K3
St Anns Heath Junior School
VW GU25 194 C5
St Anns School
HNWL W7 134 D10
St Ann's Shopping Centre
HRW HA1 114 D4
St Anselms RC Primary School
DART DA1 187 N1
HRW HA1 114 D5
NWDGN UB2 153 N2
St Anslems RC Primary School
TOOT SW17 180 B6
St Anthonys Hospital
WPK KT4 200 G8
St Anthonys RC Primary School
EDUL SE22 181 P2
PGE/AN SE20 204 A1
SLN SL2 129 H5
WATW WD18 72 F9
St Anthony's School (Junior House)
HAMP NW3 117 N10
St Anthony's School (Senior House)
HAMP NW3 117 M10
St Antonys RC Primary School
FSTGT E7 141 M2
St Aubyns School
WFD IG8 101 L8
St Augustines CE High School
KIL/WHAMP NW6 2 F8
St Augustines Primary School
BELV DA17 164 A2
KIL/WHAMP NW6 2 F7
St Augustines Priory School
EA W5 135 K7
St Augustines RC Infant School
GNTH/NBYPK IG2 122 E3
St Augustines RC Primary School
CAT SE6 182 G8
GNTH/NBYPK IG2 122 E3
HMSMTH W6 14 B10
HOD EN11 44 G4
St Barnabas CE Primary School
BGVA SW1W 16 D7
St Barnabas & St Philip's CE Primary School
KENS W8 14 E4
St Bartholomews CE Primary School
SYD SE26 182 B7
St Bartholomews Hospital
STBT EC1A 12 D4
SWLY BR8 208 G3
St Bartholomews Medical School
FARR EC1M 12 D2
St Bartholomews RC Primary School
SWLY BR8 208 F3
St Bartholomew's & Royal London School of Medicine
FARR EC1M 12 E3
St Bartholomew's the Great
STBT EC1A 12 D4
St Barts Hospital Sports Ground
CHST BR7 184 G9
St Bedes CE Junior School
RPLY/SEND GU23 232 G10
St Bedes RC Infant School
BAL SW12 180 E4
St Bedes RC Primary School
CHDH RM6 123 M3
St Bedes School
REDH RH1 257 P7
St Benedicts Junior School
EA W5 135 H7
St Benedicts School
EA W5 135 J7
St Bernadette Catholic Junior School
BAL SW12 180 D3
St Bernadette RC Primary School
LCOL/BKTW AL2 57 J3
St Bernadettes RC First and Middle School
KTN/HRWW/WS HA3 115 K2
St Bernadettes RC Primary School
HGDN/ICK UB10 132 C3
St Bernards Convent School
SL SL1 149 N1
St Bernards Preparatory School
SL SL1 149 N1
St Bonaventures School
FSTGT E7 141 M2
St Boniface RC Primary School
TOOT SW17 180 A8
St Botolphs CE Primary School
GVW DA11 190 A3
St Catherine of Sienna RC Primary School
GSTN WD25 55 L8
St Catherines Hoddeson CE Primary School
HOD EN11 44 G3
St Catherine's Hospice
CRAWE RH10 283 N9
St Catherine's Primary School
REDH RH1 259 L9
St Catherines RC Girls School
BXLYHS DA6 186 C1
St Catherines RC J & I School
WDR/YW UB7 151 N1
St Catherines RC School
BAR EN5 77 J8
St Catherines School
SHGR GU5 268 C10
TWK TW1 176 E5
St Cecilia's CE Primary School
WAND/EARL SW18 179 H3
St Cecilias RC Primary School
WPK KT4 200 G9
St Chads RC Primary School
SNWD SE25 203 M5
St Charles Borromeo RCP School
WEY KT13 196 B10
St Charles Hospital
NKENS W10 136 G7
St Charles RC Primary School
NKENS W10 136 G7
St Christinas Preparatory School
STJWD NW8 3 P7
St Christophers School
BECK BR3 205 H2
EPSOM KT18 220 B10
HAMP NW3 117 N10
WBLY HA9 115 L8
St Clare Business Park
HPTN TW12 176 B9
St Clement Danes CE Primary School
HOL/ALD WC2B 11 N6
St Clement Danes School
RKW/CH/CXG WD3 70 G6
St Clement & St James CE Primary School
NTGHL W11 8 A9
St Clements Hospital
BOW E3 140 E5
St Clements Junior School
CHES/WCR EN8 62 D3
St Clements Primary School
EW KT17 220 C5
St Columbas RC Boys School
BXLYHS DA6 186 C1
St Cross RC Primary School
HOD EN11 44 F5
St Cuthbert Mayne RC Primary School
HHW HP1 35 L5
St Cuthberts CE Primary School
EGH TW20 171 P10
St Cuthbert With St Matthias CE Primary School
ECT SW5 14 F7
St Cyprians Greek Orthodox Primary School
THHTH CR7 203 K2
St Davids College
WWKM BR4 204 G7
St Davids Health Centre
STWL/WRAY TW19 173 N3
St Davids School
ASHF TW15 174 A6
PUR/KEN CR8 222 G7
St Dominic RC Primary School
HARP AL5 20 A3
St Dominics RC Primary School
HAMP NW3 118 A10
St Dominics Sixth Form College
HRW HA1 114 D7
St Dunstans Catholic Primary School
WOKS/MYFD GU22 232 D3
St Dunstans CE Primary School
CHEAM SM3 221 H3
St Dunstans College
CAT SE6 182 E4
St Ebba's Hospital
HOR/WEW KT19 219 P5
St Edmunds RC Primary School
ED N9 100 A2
POP/IOD E14 160 F3

WHTN TW2 ....176 A3
St Edwards Catholic
  First School
  WDSR SL4 ....148 F7
St Edwards CE Comprehensive
  School
  CHDH RM6 ....124 B4
St Edwards CE Primary School
  ROM RM1 ....124 E2
St Edwards RC JMI School
  STJWD NW8 ....9 N2
St Edwards Royal Free
  Ecumenical Middle School
  WDSR SL4 ....148 F7
St Elizabeths RC Primary School
  RCHPK/HAM TW10 ....177 L2
St Elpheges RC Primary School
  WLGTN SM6 ....222 F3
St Ethelberts Catholic
  Primary School
  SLN SL2 ....129 M8
St Eugene de Mazenod RC
  Primary School
  KIL/WHAMP NW6 ....2 F4
St Faiths CE School
  WAND/EARL SW18 ....179 L1
St Fidelis Catholic
  Primary School
  ERITH DA8 ....164 D5
St Francesca Cabrini
  Primary School
  FSTH SE23 ....182 B2
St Francis Catholic School
  CTHM CR3 ....241 N7
St Francis de Sales RC
  Junior & Infant School
  TOTM N17 ....99 M8
St Francis of Assisi
  Primary School
  CRAWE RH10 ....283 P8
  NKENS W10 ....136 C9
St Francis RC Primary School
  PECK SE15 ....19 P10
  SRTFD E15 ....121 K10
St Francis, Westborough
  Primary School
  GUW GU2 ....249 L9
St Francis Xavier College
  BAL SW12 ....180 C2
St Gabriels CE Primary School
  PIM SW1V 16 C8
  PIM SW1V 158 D4
St Georges Business Park
  WEY KT13 ....216 B5
St George's Cathedral
  STHWK SE1 ....18 B3
St Georges CE Infant School
  AMSS HP7 ....69 K4
St Georges Centre
  GVW DA11 ....190 E2
St Georges CE Primary School
  BMLY BR1 ....205 P2
  CMBW SE5 ....159 M6
  VX/NE SW8 ....158 D7
St Georges CE School
  GVW DA11 ....190 D5
St George's Chapel
  WDSR SL4 ....149 J6
St Georges College
  ADL/WDHM KT15 ....195 N10
  HOLWY N7 ....119 H8
St George's College Track
  ADL/WDHM KT15 ....195 N9
St Georges Elizabethan Theatre
  HOLWY N7 ....118 E9
St Georges Hanover Square
  CE Primary School
  MYFR/PKLN W1K 10 D8
St George's Hill Golf Club
  WEY KT13 ....216 D7
St Georges Hospital
  HCH RM12 ....125 M9
  TOOT SW17 ....179 P8
St Georges Industrial Estate
  AMSS HP7 ....69 L4
  KUTN/CMB KT2 ....177 J8
  PLMGR N13 ....99 J8
St Georges Medical Centre
  HDN NW4 ....116 E1
St Georges Pre Preparatory
  School
  WDSR SL4 ....149 J6
St Georges RC Primary School
  ENC/FH EN2 ....79 L6
  HRW HA1 ....114 E8
St Georges RC School
  MV/WKIL W9 ....3 H8
St Georges School
  ASC SL5 ....192 A4
St Georges School Technology
  College
  HARP AL5 ....20 A1
St Georges Shopping Centre
  & Cinema
  HRW HA1 ....114 C4
St George the Martyr CE
  Primary School
  BMSBY WC1N 11 N2
St Gildas RC Junior School
  CEND/HSY/T N8 ....118 F5
St Giles CE (Aided)
  Infant School
  ASHTD KT21 ....237 L4
St Giles College London Central
  RSQ WC1B 11 M3
St Giles Cripplegate
  BARB EC2Y 139 K7
St Giles Primary School
  POTB/CUF EN6 ....58 D8
St Giles School
  SAND/SEL CR2 ....223 J3
St Gregorys High School
  KTN/HRWW/WS HA3 ....115 J3
St Gregorys RC
  Primary School
  EA W5 ....135 H6
St Helens Catholic
  Infant School
  WALTH E17 ....121 H3
St Helens Catholic
  Junior School
  BRWN CM15 ....107 J1
St Helens College
  HGDN/ICK UB10 ....132 B2
St Helens Primary School
  STALE/WH AL4 ....21 J3
St Helens RC Primary School
  BRXN/ST SW9 ....159 H9
  CAN/RD E16 ....141 L6
St Helier Hospital
  NTHWD HA6 ....92 F7
St Heller Hospital
  CAR SM5 ....201 M8
St Hildas School
  BUSH WD23 ....94 A1
St Hugh of Lincoln RCP School
  WOKN/KNAP GU21 ....231 J5
St Ignatius College
  ENC/FH EN2 ....79 J5
St Ignatius RC Primary School
  SEVS/STOTM N15 ....119 M4
  SUN TW16 ....197 H1
St James CE J & I School
  BERM/RHTH SE16 ....19 N1
St James CE Junior School
  HLWS GM18 ....46 C5
  MUSWH N10 ....118 A2
  NWCR SE14 ....160 D7
  PEND EN3 ....80 B6
  WEY KT13 ....196 D10
St James CE Junior School
  FSTGT E7 ....121 L10
St James Independent School
  for Girls
  NTGHL W11 ....8 E7

St James Independent School
  for Senior Boys
  TWK TW1 ....176 F5
St James Independent School
  for Senior Girls
  WKENS W14 ....14 C5
St James Independent Schools
  for Junior Boys & Girls
  WKENS W14 ....14 C5
St James & Lucie Clayton
  College
  SKENS SW7 ....15 H6
St James Medical Centre
  CROY/NA CR0 ....203 L7
St James & Michaels CE
  Primary School
  BAY/PAD W2 ....9 K7
St James RC Primary School
  HAYES BR2 ....206 E5
  WHTN TW2 ....176 D6
St James & St Michaels CE
  Primary School
  BAY/PAD W2 ....137 M9
St James's Health Centre
  WALTH E17 ....120 D3
St James's Palace
  WHALL SW1A 11 H10
St James the Great RC
  Primary School
  PECK SE15 ....159 N7
  THHTH CR7 ....205 J2
St Joachims RC Primary School
  CAN/RD E16 ....141 P8
St Joan of Arc RC
  Primary School
  HBRY N5 ....119 J9
St Joan of Arc RC School
  RKW/CH/CXG WD3 ....91 P1
St John Fisher RC First & Middle
  School
  PIN HA5 ....113 P2
St John Fisher RC
  Primary School
  ERITHM DA18 ....163 P2
  GFD/PVL UB6 ....135 H5
  LOU IG10 ....82 F6
  RYNPK SW20 ....200 F5
  STALE/WH AL4 ....39 H3
St John of Jerusalem CE
  Primary School
  HOM E9 ....140 B2
St Johns and St James CE
  School
  UED N18 ....99 N6
St Johns Angell Town CE
  Primary School
  BRXN/ST SW9 ....159 J8
St Johns Beaumont School
  WDSR SL4 ....171 N5
St Johns CE First School
  STAN HA7 ....94 F5
St Johns CE J & I (Mixed) School
  WGCW AL8 ....22 C6
St Johns CE Middle School
  STAN HA7 ....94 F5
St Johns CE Primary School
  BETH E2 ....140 B4
  BKHH IG9 ....101 N2
  CROY/NA CR0 ....204 C10
  ENC/FH EN2 ....79 J2
  FBAR/BDGN N11 ....98 A5
  KUT/HW KT1 ....199 K3
  PGE/AN SE20 ....182 B10
  SEV TN13 ....247 L9
  TRDG/WHET N20 ....97 M3
  WLYN AL6 ....23 J1
St Johns CE School
  CDALE/KGS NW9 ....116 B3
St John's CE Walham Green
  School
  FUL/PGN SW6 ....157 H7
St Johns CE Primary School
  CTHM CR3 ....260 A2
St John's Concert Hall
  WEST SW1P 17 L4
St Johns CP School
  WOKN/KNAP GU21 ....231 K4
St Johns Highbury Vale CE
  Primary School
  HBRY N5 ....119 J9
St John's Hospital Day Centre
  BTSEA SW11 ....157 N10
St Johns Infant School
  RAD WD7 ....74 E1
St John's Lodge
  CAMTN NW1 ....4 C9
St Johns Preparatory & Senior
  School
  ENC/FH EN2 ....79 H5
  POTB/CUF EN6 ....59 P10
St Johns Primary School
  REDH RH1 ....275 P2
  WEA W13 ....134 F9
St Johns RC Comprehensive
  School
  GVE DA12 ....190 G4
St Johns RC Primary School
  BERM/RHTH SE16 ....160 D1
  GVE DA12 ....190 G4
  RKW/CH/CXG WD3 ....91 L2
St Johns RC Special School
  WFD IG8 ....102 D6
St Johns & St Clements CE
  J & I School
  PECK SE15 ....159 P9
St Johns School
  EPP CM16 ....65 H6
  LHD/OX KT22 ....236 C7
  NTHWD HA6 ....93 J7
St Johns Upper Holloway CE
  Primary School
  ARCH N19 ....118 E8
St Johns Walworth CE
  Primary School
  WALW SE17 ....18 E6
St Johns Way Medical Centre
  ARCH N19 ....118 E6
St Johns Wood Preparatory
  School
  STJWD NW8 ....3 N9
St John the Baptist CE
  Junior School
  KUT/HW KT1 ....177 J10
St John the Baptist CE
  Primary School
  BMLY BR1 ....183 H7
  IS N1 ....7 J8
St John the Baptist
  Primary School
  WARE SG12 ....26 F6
St John the Baptist School
  WOKS/MYFD GU22 ....232 D5
St John the Divine CE
  Primary School
  CMBW SE5 ....159 J6
St John the Evangelist RC
  Primary School
  IS N1 ....6 C1
St John Vianney RC
  Primary School
  SEVS/STOTM N15 ....119 J2
St Josephs Academic RC
  School
  BKHTH/KID SE3 ....161 K9
St Joseph's Annexe
  ABYW SE2 ....163 M5
St Josephs Catholic High
  School
  SLN SL2 ....129 M8
St Josephs Catholic
  Infant School
  LEY E10 ....120 E6
St Josephs Catholic
  Junior School
  CMBW SE5 ....159 K6

St Josephs Catholic
  Primary School
  BMLY BR1 ....183 P10
  EPSOM KT18 ....219 P10
  REDH RH1 ....257 P9
St Josephs CE Combined School
  CFSP/GDCR SL9 ....109 P1
St Josephs College
  STRHM/NOR SW16 ....181 J9
St Josephs Convent School
  WAN E11 ....121 M4
St Josephs Primary School
  HDN NW4 ....116 E2
St Joseph's Primary School
  HERT/WAT SG14 ....25 H4
St Josephs Primary School
  WAND/EARL SW18 ....179 K1
St Josephs RC College
  MLHL NW7 ....96 C5
St Josephs RC First & Middle
  School
  KTN/HRWW/WS HA3 ....94 F10
St Josephs RC Infant School
  NRWD SE19 ....181 K9
St Josephs RC JMI School
  CHES/WCR EN8 ....62 D9
St Josephs RC Junior School
  LEY E10 ....120 F6
  NRWD SE19 ....181 K9
  WBLY HA9 ....115 L10
St Josephs RC Primary School
  ARCH N19 ....118 C6
  BARK IG11 ....142 F3
  BERM/RHTH SE16 ....19 N2
  CHEL SW3 ....16 A6
  DAGW RM9 ....124 A9
  DART DA1 ....164 E10
  DEPT SE8 ....160 F6
  DORK RH4 ....272 F2
  GNWCH SE10 ....161 K4
  HOL/ALD WC2B 11 M5
  KUT/HW KT1 ....199 K2
  MV/WKIL W9 ....9 J1
  OXHEY WD19 ....93 J4
  STHWK SE1 ....18 F1
  WLSDN NW10 ....136 B2
St Josephs RC School
  CVW DA11 ....190 A3
St Josephs School
  UPMR RM14 ....126 A7
St Joseph the Worker RC
  Primary School
  RBRW/HUT CM13 ....87 P10
St Judes CE Junior School
  EGH TW20 ....171 P9
St Judes CE Primary School
  HNHL SE24 ....181 J2
  STHWK SE1 ....18 C4
St Judes & St Pauls CE
  Primary School
  IS N1 ....7 J1
St Katharine Pier
  WAP E1W 13 M9
St Katharines Knockholt CE
  Primary School
  RSEV TN14 ....245 L1
St Katherine
  TPL/STR WC2R 11 P8
St Lawrence Business Centre
  FELT TW13 ....175 J5
St Lawrence Catholic School
  FELT TW13 ....175 J5
St Lawrence CE School
  WAB EN9 ....63 L9
St Lawrence Junior School
  E/WMO/HCT KT8 ....198 C3
St Lawrence Primary School
  EHSLY KT24 ....253 L3
St Lawrence University
  BMSBY WC1N 11 P2
St Leonards CE Primary School
  STRHM/NOR SW16 ....180 E8
St Leonards Hospital
  IS N1 ....7 K7
St Lukes Catholic
  Primary School
  HLWW/ROY CM19 ....46 F3
St Luke's Catholic Sixth Form
  College
  SCUP DA14 ....185 K8
St Lukes CE Primary School
  CAN/RD E16 ....141 L8
  FSBYE EC1V 6 F10
  KUTN/CMB KT2 ....199 L1
  MV/WKIL W9 ....2 D8
  POP/IOD E14 ....161 J3
  WNWD SE27 ....181 K8
St Luke's Health Centre
  CAN/RD E16 ....141 L8
St Lukes Hospital for the Clergy
  FITZ W1T 10 G2
St Lukes School
  THHTH CR7 ....203 H4
St Lukes Special School
  LOU IG10 ....82 D8
St Lukes Woodside Hospital
  MUSWH N10 ....118 B2
St Margaret Clitherow RC
  Primary
  THMD SE28 ....143 L10
St Margaret Lee CE
  Primary School
  LEW SE13 ....161 K10
St Margarets Business Centre
  TWK TW1 ....176 F3
St Margarets CE
  Primary School
  CRAWW RH11 ....283 L6
  WOOL/PLUM SE18 ....162 F5
St Margarets Clitherow RC
  Primary School
  WBLY HA9 ....115 P8
St Margarets Hospital
  EPP CM16 ....65 L5
St Margarets Primary School
  BARK IG11 ....142 E3
St Margarets School
  BUSH WD23 ....93 P1
  HAMP NW3 ....117 L9
St Margaret's School
  KWD/TDW/WH KT20 ....238 G7
St Marks Catholic School
  HSLW TW3 ....153 N9
St Marks CE Primary School
  ARCH N19 ....118 C7
  HAYES BR2 ....205 M3
  LBTH SE11 ....17 P9
  SNWD SE25 ....203 P4
St Marks Industrial Estate
  CAN/RD E16 ....142 A10
St Marks Primary School
  HNWL W7 ....154 D1
  MTCM CR4 ....202 A2
St Marks West Essex Catholic
  School
  HLWS CM18 ....47 H1
The St Martha Printing Works
  WOKS/MYFD GU22 ....232 D7
St Marthas Senior School
  EBAR EN4 ....77 K5
St Martin-in-the-Fields
  CHCR WC2N 11 J8
St Martin in the Fields High
  School
  BRXS/STRHM SW2 ....181 J4
St Martin of Porres
  Primary School
  FBAR/BDGN N11 ....98 D7
St Martins CE
  Primary School
  PEND EN3 ....80 B9
  REDH RH1 ....258 A8
  RYNPK SW20 ....200 D1
  SURB KT6 ....199 K7
St Martins Hospital
  MYFR/PKLN W1K 10 C7

St Martins House
  Business Centre
  EHSLY KT24 ....252 F5
St Martins Medical Centre
  RSLP HA4 ....112 F5
St Martins School
  MLHL NW7 ....96 B6
  RBRW/HUT CM13 ....107 P2
St Martins School of Art
  SOHO/SHAV W1D 11 K6
St Martins Theatre
  LSQ/SEVD WC2H 11 K7
St Martins Walk
  Shopping Centre
  DORK RH4 ....272 G1
St Mary Abbots CE
  Primary School
  KENS W8 ....14 G2
St Mary Abbots Church Hall
  KENS W8 ....14 G1
St Mary & All Saints CE
  Primary School
  BEAC HP9 ....88 D9
St Mary and St Pancras CE
  Primary School
  CAMTN NW1 ....5 J3
The St Marylebone CE School
  MHST W1U 10 B1
St Marylebone Crematorium
  FNCH N3 ....117 L1
St Mary Magdalene CE
  Primary School
  MV/WKIL W9 ....8 G2
  WOOL/PLUM SE18 ....162 C3
St Mary Magdalene
  Primary School
  HOLWY N7 ....6 A1
St Mary Magdalen RC
  Junior School
  CRICK NW2 ....136 E1
St Mary Magdalens Catholic
  Primary School
  BROCKY SE4 ....160 D10
  MORT/ESHN SW14 ....156 A9
St Mary of the Angels RC
  Primary School
  NTGHL W11 ....137 K8
  NTGHL W11 ....8 E5
St Marys Abbey
  MLHL NW7 ....96 D4
St Mary & St Joseph Catholic
  School
  SCUP DA14 ....185 J8
St Mary & St Michael RC
  Primary School
  WCHPL E1 ....140 B8
St Mary & St Peters CE
  Primary School
  TEDD TW11 ....176 D8
St Marys Bryanston Square CE
  Primary School
  MBLAR W1H 9 P3
St Marys Catholic
  Primary School
  CHING E4 ....101 J2
  HCH RM12 ....125 H6
St Marys CE Combined School
  AMSS HP7 ....68 C5
St Marys CE Infant School
  LHD/OX KT22 ....237 H8
St Marys CE Junior School
  CEND/HSY/T N8 ....118 F2
  OXTED RH8 ....261 K4
  STWL/WRAY TW19 ....173 P2
  THDIT KT7 ....198 C8
St Mary's Cemetery
  BTSEA SW11 ....179 J1
St Marys CE Primary School
  BF/WBF KT14 ....215 P9
  BRWN CM15 ....87 L10
  CHSGTN KT9 ....219 K3
  EBAR EN4 ....77 P10
  FNCH N3 ....97 J9
  IS N1 ....6 D4
  LEW SE13 ....182 C1
St Mary's CE Primary School
  PUT/ROE SW15 ....156 Y9
St Marys CE Primary School
  WALTH E17 ....120 D2
  WOOL/PLUM SE18 ....162 G3
St Marys First School
  BERK HP4 ....33 K3
St Marys Greek Cathedral
  WDGN N22 ....98 G9
St Marys Hare Park School
  GPK RM2 ....125 K1
St Marys High School
  CHESW EN7 ....62 A6
  CROY/NA CR0 ....203 K8
St Marys Hospital
  BAY/PAD W2 ....9 M5
St Marys Hospital Medical
  School
  BAY/PAD W2 ....9 M5
St Marys Infant School
  CAR SM5 ....221 P1
St Marys Junior School
  TWK TW1 ....176 G3
St Marys Kilburn Primary School
  KIL/WHAMP NW6 ....2 F5
St Marys Primary School
  BRKMPK AL9 ....40 E9
  WKENS W14 ....156 G2
St Marys RC J & I School
  CROY/NA CR0 ....203 L8
St Marys RC Junior School
  WALTH E17 ....121 H1
St Marys RC Primary School
  BECK BR3 ....183 H10
St Mary's RC Primary School
  CHSWK W4 ....156 B4
St Marys RC Primary School
  CLAP SW4 ....180 D1
  ELTH/MOT SE9 ....184 D1
St Mary's RC Primary School
  FSBYPK N4 ....119 L3
St Marys RC Primary School
  ISLW TW7 ....154 F9
  KIL/WHAMP NW6 ....2 F5
  NKENS W10 ....8 A2
  PEND EN3 ....80 C8
  TIL RM18 ....168 C8
  UX/CGN UB8 ....131 M3
  VX/NE SW8 ....158 C9
  WIM/MER SW19 ....179 K10
St Marys & St Johns CE
  Primary School
  HDN NW4 ....116 E3
St Marys School
  ASC SL5 ....192 A7
St Marys Tutorial College
  GUW GU2 ....267 P3
St Mary's University College
  Twickenham
  TWK TW1 ....176 E6
St Matthews CE (Aided)
  Infant School
  COB KT11 ....235 J4
St Matthews CE
  Primary School
  PEND EN3 ....80 B9
  REDH RH1 ....258 A8
  RYNPK SW20 ....200 D1
  SURB KT6 ....199 K7
  WDR/YW UB7 ....131 P10

St Matthias CE Primary School
  BETH E2 ....13 M1
  STNW/STAM N16 ....119 M10
St Meryl JMI School
  OXHEY WD19 ....93 M4
St Michael At Bowes CE
  Junior School
  PLMGR N13 ....99 H7
St Michaels and St Martins RC
  Primary School
  HSLWW TW4 ....153 P7
St Michaels Catholic Grammar
  School
  NFNCH/WDSPK N12 ....97 L6
St Michaels CE First School
  RDKG RH5 ....255 H3
St Michaels CE Primary School
  ASC SL5 ....192 C5
  CAMTN NW1 ....4 C5
  ENC/FH EN2 ....79 K5
  HGT N6 ....118 B5
  WAND/EARL SW18 ....179 J3
  WDGN N22 ....98 G9
St Michaels CE Aided
  Primary School Hall
  WELL DA16 ....163 M7
St Michael's Manor Hotel
  STALW/RED AL3 ....38 A6
St Michaels Primary School
  STALW/RED AL3 ....37 P5
St Michaels RC School
  EHAM E6 ....142 C4
St Michaels RC School
  ASHF TW15 ....174 B8
  GSTN WD25 ....55 K8
St Michaels RC Secondary
  School
  BERM/RHTH SE16 ....19 N2
St Michaels Sydenham CE
  Primary School
  SYD SE26 ....182 D7
The St Michael Steiner School
  WAND/EARL SW18 ....179 K1
St Monicas RC Primary School
  IS N1 ....7 J9
St Monica's RC Primary School
  IS N1 ....7 J9
St Monicas RC Primary School
  STHGT/OAK N14 ....98 F4
St Nicholas Centre
  SUT SM1 ....221 L2
St Nicholas CE Primary School
  SHPTN TW17 ....196 C6
St Nicholas Preparatory School
  CDALE/KGS NW9 ....115 P7
  SKENS SW7 ....15 M2
St Nicholas School
  BORE WD6 ....75 K10
  CHST BR7 ....184 F10
  HLWE CM17 ....30 A8
  PUR/KEN CR8 ....223 H9
  REDH RH1 ....258 E5
St Nicolas CE Infant School
  GUW GU2 ....267 P2
St Olaves Grammar School
  ORP BR6 ....207 L10
St Olaves Preparatory School
  ELTH/MOT SE9 ....184 E5
St Pancras Hospital
  CAMTN NW1 ....5 J2
St Pancras International
  Youth Hostel
  CAMTN NW1 ....5 K9
St Pancras & Islington
  Cemetery
  EFNCH N2 ....97 P9
St Patricks Church School
  STHWK SE1 ....12 A10
St Patricks Infants School
  WAP E1W 140 A10
St Patricks International School
  SOHO/SHAV W1D 11 H5
St Patricks Primary School
  KTTN NW5 ....138 C1
St Patricks RC JMI School
  ROMW/RG RM7 ....104 C9
St Patricks RC Primary School
  WALTH E17 ....120 D2
  WOOL/PLUM SE18 ....162 G3
St Paulinus CE Primary School
  DART DA1 ....164 F10
St Pauls & All Hallows CE
  Infant School
  TOTM N17 ....99 P8
St Pauls & All Hallows CE
  Junior School
  TOTM N17 ....99 P8
St Paul's Cathedral
  STP EC4M 12 E6
St Paul's Cathedral School
  STP EC4M 12 E6
St Pauls Catholic College
  SUN TW16 ....197 H1
St Pauls CE Aided
  Primary School
  DORK RH4 ....272 G2
St Pauls CE Primary School
  ADL/WDHM KT15 ....215 K1
  BRWN CM15 ....86 C6
  BTFD TW8 ....155 J5
  CHSGTN KT9 ....219 K1
  FBAR/BDGN N11 ....98 B6
  HAMP NW3 ....3 P4
  KGLGY WD4 ....54 C10
  MLHL NW7 ....96 E5
  SWLY BR8 ....209 J1
  WALW SE17 ....18 D8
  WCHMH N21 ....99 J1
  WCHPL E1 ....13 P7
St Pauls CE Junior School
  KUTN/CMB KT2 ....177 M10
St Pauls Cray CE Primary School
  STMC/STPC BR5 ....207 M3
St Pauls Cray Health Clinic
  STMC/STPC BR5 ....207 K2
St Pauls Girls School
  HMSMTH W6 ....156 G3
St Paul's Primary School
  HMSMTH W6 ....156 F4
St Pauls RC Primary School
  CHESW EN7 ....62 A3
  THDIT KT7 ....198 D7
  WDGN N22 ....98 G10
St Pauls RC School
  ABYW SE2 ....163 K5
St Pauls Road Medical Centre
  IS N1 ....6 D1
St Pauls School
  BARN SW13 ....156 E4
St Pauls Steiner School
  IS N1 ....6 C1
St Pauls Way Community
  School
  BOW E3 ....140 F7
St Pauls with St Lukes CE
  Primary School
  BOW E3 ....140 E7
St Paul's with St Michael's CE
  Primary School
  HACK E8 ....7 N5
St Peter Chanel RC
  Primary School
  SCUP DA14 ....185 M8
St Peter & Paul CE
  Infant School
  CTHM CR3 ....259 H1
St Peter & Paul RC
  Primary School
  STMC/STPC BR5 ....207 H2
St Peter & St Pauls
  Primary School
  FSBYE EC1V 12 C1

St Peters Catholic
  Primary School
  ROM RM1 ....124 E1
St Peters CE Combined School
  SL SL1 ....128 A5
St Peters CE Middle School
  WDSR SL4 ....171 L2
St Peters CE Primary School
  BRW CM14 ....106 C3
  HMSMTH W6 ....156 D4
  MV/WKIL W9 ....8 E2
  OXTED RH8 ....260 F9
  WALW SE17 ....18 G8
  WAP E1W 140 B10
St Peters Eaton Square CE
  Primary School
  BGVA SW1W 16 E4
St Peters Hospital
  CHERT KT16 ....194 C10
St Peter's Hospital
  COVGDN WC2E 11 M7
St Peters JMI School
  STAL AL3 ....37 D7
  RKW/CH/CXG WD3 ....91 L2
St Peters Primary School
  SAND/SEL CR2 ....223 L3
St Peters RC Primary School
  DAGW RM9 ....144 A3
  LHD/OX KT22 ....237 H6
  WOOL/PLUM SE18 ....162 E4
St Philip Howard Catholic
  Primary School
  HAT AL10 ....40 E4
St Philips School
  CHSGTN KT9 ....219 J3
  SKENS SW7 ....15 K6
St Phillips Infant School
  SYD SE26 ....182 A7
St Philomenas Catholic High
  School
  CAR SM5 ....221 P2
St Philomenas RC
  Primary School
  STMC/STPC BR5 ....207 M7
St Quintins Health Centre
  NKENS W10 ....136 F7
St Raphaels Hospice
  WPK KT4 ....200 C9
St Raphaels RC Primary School
  NTHLT UB5 ....133 J4
St Raphaels Way
  Medical Centre
  WLSDN NW10 ....115 P10
St Richards with St Andrews CE
  Primary School
  RCHPK/HAM TW10 ....176 G6
St Robert Southwell RC
  Primary School
  CDALE/KGS NW9 ....115 P4
St Roses RC Infant School
  HNW RM1 ....35 K8
St Saviour & St Olaves School
  STHWK SE1 ....19 H4
St Saviours CE Primary School
  HNHL SE24 ....159 K9
  MV/WKIL W9 ....9 H2
  POP/IOD E14 ....140 C7
  WALTH E17 ....120 E5
St Saviours CE Infant School
  EA W5 ....135 J10
St Saviours RC Primary School
  LEW SE13 ....161 H10
St Scholasticas RC
  Primary School
  CLPT E5 ....119 P8
St Stephens CE Junior School
  TWK TW1 ....176 F2
St Stephens CE Primary School
  BAY/PAD W2 ....8 F4
  DEPT SE8 ....160 F8
  SHB W12 ....136 F10
St Stephens CE School
  VX/NE SW8 ....158 F6
St Stephens Primary School
  EHAM E6 ....141 P2
St Stephens RC Primary School
  WELL DA16 ....163 K9
St Swithun Wells RC
  Primary School
  RSLP HA4 ....113 K8
St Teresa RC Primary School
  BCTR RM8 ....123 M9
St Teresas Preparatory School
  EHSLY KT24 ....253 L4
St Teresa's RC Primary School
  BORE WD6 ....75 N6
St Teresas RC School
  KTN/HRWW/WS HA3 ....94 B9
St Teresas School
  RDKG RH5 ....253 L8
St Theresas RC
  Primary School
  FNCH N3 ....117 K1
St Thomas a' Becket RC
  Primary School
  ABYW SE2 ....163 K2
St Thomas Becket RC
  Primary School
  SNWD SE25 ....203 P6
St Thomas CE Primary School
  NKENS W10 ....8 A2
St Thomas Childrens Day
  Hospital
  LBTH SE11 ....17 P7
St Thomas' Hospital
  STHWK SE1 ....17 N3
St Thomas More RC
  Primary School
  BERK HP4 ....33 M5
  BXLYHN DA7 ....164 A8
  ELTH/MOT SE9 ....162 B9
St Thomas More RC School
  CHEL SW3 ....16 A5
  ELTH/MOT SE9 ....184 D2
  WDGN N22 ....98 C8
St Thomas of Canterbury
  Catholic Primary School
  GRAYS RM17 ....167 N3
  GU GU1 ....250 E10
St Thomas of Canterbury CE
  Junior School
  BRWN CM15 ....107 J1
St Thomas of Canterbury
  Infant School
  BRWN CM15 ....107 J1
St Thomas of Canterbury
  Primary School
  MTCM CR4 ....202 B3
St Thomas of Canterbury RC
  Primary School
  FUL/PGN SW6 ....157 J3
St Thomas Primary School
  SEV TN13 ....265 J1
St Thomas the Apostle
  College
  PECK SE15 ....160 B7
St Ursulas Catholic
  Infant School
  HARH RM3 ....105 J7
St Ursulas Convent School
  GNWCH SE10 ....161 J6
St Vincent De Paul RC
  Primary School
  WEST SW1P 16 C4
St Vincents Catholic
  Primary School
  BMLY BR1 ....184 B7
St Vincents Hospital
  PIN HA5 ....112 F1
St Vincents RC
  Primary School
  ACT W3 ....135 N9
  BCTR RM8 ....123 M7
St Vincent's RC Primary School
  MHST W1U 10 C4

St Vincents RC Primary School
MLHL NW7 .... 96 E5
St Walter & St John Sports Ground
TOOT SW17 .... 179 P4
St Wilfrids RC School
CRAWW RH11 .... 283 L8
St William of York Primary School
FSTH SE23 .... 182 D3
St Winefrides Catholic Primary School
MNPK E12 .... 122 C10
St Winifreds Catholic Junior School
LEE/GVPK SE12 .... 183 L2
St Winifreds RC Infant School
LEW SE13 .... 183 K1
SS Angelas & Bonaventures Sixth Form Centre
FSTGT E7 .... 141 N1
SS Peter & Paul RC Primary School
MTCM CR4 .... 202 A4
SS Peter & Pauls Catholic Primary School
IL IG1 .... 122 G8
Salcombe Preparatory School (Infants)
STHGT/OAK N14 .... 78 C10
Salcombe Preparatory School (Juniors)
STHGT/OAK N14 .... 98 C1
Salesian College
CHERT KT16 .... 195 K8
Salesian RC School
CHERT KT16 .... 195 H9
Salfords Industrial Estate
REDH RH1 .... 276 B8
Salfords Primary School
REDH RH1 .... 276 B6
Salisbury Primary School
HAT AL10 .... 40 E2
Salisbury Lawn Tennis Club
STAL AL1 .... 38 G5
Salisbury Primary School
MNPK E12 .... 122 A10
Salisbury School
ED N9 .... 100 B1
Salters' Hall
BARB EC2Y 12 F4
Salusbury Primary School
KIL/WHAMP NW6 .... 2 C6
Salvatorian College
KTN/HRWW/WS HA3 .... 94 C10
Samaritan & Western Ophthalmic Hospital
MBLAR W1H 10 A3
Samuel Jones Industrial Estate
PECK SE15 .... 159 M6
Samuel Rhodes School
IS N1 .... 6 A5
Sandcross Junior School
REIG RH2 .... 275 J3
Sanders Draper School
HCH RM12 .... 125 L9
Sanderstead Junior School
SAND/SEL CR2 .... 223 L5
Sandfield CP School
GU GU1 .... 268 A1
Sandgate Trading Estate
BERM/RHTH SE16 .... 160 A4
Sandhurst Primary School
CAT SE6 .... 183 K3
Sandown Golf Centre
ESH/CLAY KT10 .... 198 A10
Sandown Grandstand & Exhibition Centre
ESH/CLAY KT10 .... 198 A10
Sandown Industrial Park
ESH/CLAY KT10 .... 197 P9
Sandown Park Racecourse
ESH/CLAY KT10 .... 198 A10
Sandown Road Industrial Estate
WATN WD24 .... 73 K3
Sandown Sports Club & Dry Ski Slope
ESH/CLAY KT10 .... 198 A10
Sandridge Gate Business Centre
STALE/WH AL4 .... 20 C10
STALE/WH AL4 .... 38 E2
Sandridge School
STALE/WH AL4 .... 21 J9
Sandridge Youth Club & Sports Centre
STALW/RED AL3 .... 20 C10
Sandringham Primary School
FSTGT E7 .... 141 P1
Sandringham School
STALE/WH AL4 .... 38 G2
Sandy Lodge Golf Club
NTHWD HA6 .... 92 E3
Sapcote Trading Centre
WLSDN NW10 .... 116 C10
Saracen Industrial Area
HHNE HP2 .... 36 B4
Sarah Bonnell School
SRTFD E15 .... 141 K1
Sarbir Industrial Park
HLW CM20 .... 29 M6
Sarratt School
RKW/CH/CXG WD3 .... 71 K2
Sarum Hall School
HAMP NW3 .... 3 P3
Satellite Business Village
CRAWE RH10 .... 283 P3
Satmer Trust School
STNW/STAM N16 .... 119 P7
Savill Garden (Windsor Great Park)
EGH TW20 .... 171 K9
Savoy Pier
TPL/STR WC2R 11 N8
Savoy Theatre
TPL/STR WC2R 11 N8
Sawbridge Health Clinic
SBW CM21 .... 29 P1
Sawyers Hall College of Science and Technology
BRWN CM15 .... 107 H1
Saxeway Business Centre
CSHM HP5 .... 50 D4
Saxon Business Centre
WIM/MER SW19 .... 201 M2
Saxon CP School
SHPTN TW17 .... 196 A5
Sayer Clinic
CROY/NA CR0 .... 222 C1
Sayer Clinics
MBLAR W1H 10 B6
Sayes Court Junior School
ADL/WDHM KT15 .... 215 L2
Scarsdale Place Medical Centre
KENS W8 .... 14 G3
Schomberg House
STJS SW1Y 11 H10
Schooling Licensed Conveyancers
GRAYS RM17 .... 167 N4
School of Architecture and Design (London Metropolitan University)
HOLWY N7 .... 6 B1
School of English
GLDGN NW11 .... 117 K6
School of Health
RDART DA2 .... 188 A2
School of Oriental & African Studies
GWRST WC1E 11 K2
The School of Pharmacy
BMSBY WC1N 11 M1

The School of St David & St Katharine
CEND/HSY/T N8 .... 118 F2
Science Museum
SKENS SW7 .... 15 M4
Science Museum IMAX Cinema
SKENS SW7 .... 15 M4
The Science Museum Library
SKENS SW7 .... 15 L3
Scotts Grotto
WARE SG12 .... 26 C3
Scotts Park Primary School
BMLY BR1 .... 205 P1
Scotts Primary School
HCH RM12 .... 125 K10
Scott Wilkie Primary School
CAN/RD E16 .... 141 P8
The Screen at Reigate
REIG RH2 .... 257 K10
Screen Cinema
WOT/HER KT12 .... 197 H8
Screen on Baker Street Cinema
MHST W1U 10 B3
Screen on the Green Cinema
IS N1 .... 6 C6
Screen on the Hill Cinema
HAMP NW3 .... 117 P10
Seal CE Primary School
BGR/WK TN15 .... 247 N6
Seaton House School
BELMT SM2 .... 221 N6
Sedbright Primary School
BETH E2 .... 7 N7
Secombe Centre
SUT SM1 .... 221 L7
Sedgehill School
CAT SE6 .... 182 G8
Sedgewick Centre
WCHPL E1 .... 13 M5
Sedleys CE Primary School
MEO DA13 .... 189 M8
Seer Green CE Combined School
BEAC HP9 .... 89 H7
Sefton Park School
SLN SL2 .... 129 N2
Selborne Primary School
GFD/PVL UB6 .... 134 E4
The Sele School
HERT/WAT SG14 .... 24 C5
The Selfridge Hotel
MBLAR W1H 10 B6
Selhurst High School for Boys
CROY/NA CR0 .... 203 L6
The Selhurst Medical Centre
SNWD SE25 .... 203 M6
Sellincourt School
TOOT SW17 .... 179 P9
Selsdon Community Centre
SAND/SEL CR2 .... 224 A5
Selsdon High School
SAND/SEL CR2 .... 224 C4
Selsdon Park Hotel & Golf Course
SAND/SEL CR2 .... 224 B7
Selsdon Primary School
SAND/SEL CR2 .... 224 B5
Selsdon Road Industrial Estate
SAND/SEL CR2 .... 223 L4
Selwyn Primary School
CHING E4 .... 101 H7
PLSTW E13 .... 141 M3
Semaphore Tower
COB KT11 .... 234 E5
Send CE Infant School
RPLY/SEND GU23 .... 232 G10
Send CC
RPLY/SEND GU23 .... 232 F10
Sergeant Industrial Estate
WAND/EARL SW18 .... 179 L2
Serpentine Gallery
BAY/PAD W2 .... 9 M10
Servite RC Primary School
WBPTN SW10 .... 15 J9
Seven Islands Leisure Centre
BERM/RHTH SE16 .... 160 B2
Seven Kings Health Centre
CDMY/SEVK IG3 .... 123 H6
Seven Kings High School
GNTH/NBYPK IG2 .... 122 C5
Seven Mills Primary School
POP/IOD E14 .... 160 F1
Sevenoaks Business Centre
RSEV TN14 .... 247 K2
Sevenoaks CC
SEV TN13 .... 247 J10
Sevenoaks Hospital
SEV TN13 .... 247 K1
Sevenoaks Library & Museum
SEV TN13 .... 265 K1
Sevenoaks Primary School
SEV TN13 .... 247 J8
Sevenoaks RFC
SEV TN13 .... 265 K2
Sevenoaks School
SEV TN13 .... 265 K2
Sevenoaks School Track
SEV TN13 .... 265 K2
Sevenoaks Swimming Centre
SEV TN13 .... 265 K1
Sevenoaks Way Industrial Estate
STMC/STPC BR5 .... 207 M3
Seven Sisters Primary School
SEVS/STOTM N15 .... 119 L3
Seymour Gardens Medical Centre
IL IG1 .... 122 C6
Seymour Leisure Centre
MBLAR W1H 10 A4
Shaare Zedek Medical Centre
GLDGN NW11 .... 117 J4
Shacklewell Primary School
HACK E8 .... 119 N9
Shadwell Dock Stairs
WAP E1W 140 C9
Shaftesbury High School
KTN/HRWW/WS HA3 .... 94 A9
Shaftesbury Hospital
LSQ/SEVD WC2H 11 L6
Shaftesbury Medical Centre
RYLN/HDSTN HA2 .... 114 B6
Shaftesbury Park Primary School
BTSEA SW11 .... 158 B9
Shaftesbury Primary School
FSTGT E7 .... 141 P2
Shaftesbury Theatre
LSQ/SEVD WC2H 11 L5
Shahjalal Medical Centre
WCHPL E1 .... 13 P6
Shakespeare Business Centre
BRXN/ST SW9 .... 159 J9
Shakespeare Industrial Estate
WATN WD24 .... 73 H4
Shakespeare's Globe Exhibition & Theatre
STHWK SE1 .... 12 D8
Shalford Infant School
RGUE GU4 .... 268 A6
Shalford Mill (NT)
RGUE GU4 .... 268 B5
The Shamrock Sports Club
ACT W3 .... 135 P8
Shannon Corner Retail Park
NWMAL KT3 .... 200 D4
Shapla J & I School
WCHPL E1 .... 139 P7
Shapla Primary School
WCHPL E1 .... 13 M1
Sharp Sports Centre
EDGW HA8 .... 95 M7

Shawcroft School
STMC/STPC BR5 .... 207 P5
Shawley Primary School
EPSOM KT18 .... 238 F4
Shaw Primary School
SOCK/AV RM15 .... 146 C6
Shears Green Primary School
GVW DA11 .... 190 C6
Sheeji Medical Centre
SL SL1 .... 129 J9
Sheen International School
MORT/ESHN SW14 .... 156 B10
Sheen Lane Health Centre
MORT/ESHN SW14 .... 155 P9
Sheen Lawn Tennis & Squash Club
MORT/ESHN SW14 .... 177 P1
Sheen Mount Primary School
RCHPK/HAM TW10 .... 177 N1
Sheen Sports Centre
MORT/ESHN SW14 .... 156 B10
Sheepcot Medical Centre
GSTN WD25 .... 55 K10
Sheering CE Primary School
RBSF CM22 .... 30 E2
Shell Centre
STHWK SE1 .... 11 P10
Shelley Primary School
CHONG CM5 .... 67 N2
Shelley School
CLAP SW4 .... 158 D9
Shendish Manor Golf Club
HHS/BOV HP3 .... 53 L2
Shenfield CC
BRWN CM15 .... 87 L10
Shenfield High School
BRWN CM15 .... 87 M9
Shenfield Sports Centre
BRWN CM15 .... 87 M9
Shenley Primary School
RAD WD7 .... 57 L10
Shenstone School
DART DA1 .... 186 E1
Shenval Industrial Estate
HLW CM20 .... 29 K7
Shepherd Primary School
RKW/CH/CXG WD3 .... 91 K2
Shepherd's Bush CC
ACT W3 .... 136 B9
Shepherd's Bush Empire
SHB W12 .... 156 F1
Shepperton Business Park
SHPTN TW17 .... 196 D5
Shepperton Health Centre
SHPTN TW17 .... 196 C5
Shepperton Studios
SHPTN TW17 .... 196 A3
Sheraton Belgravia Hotel
KTBR SW1X 16 C4
Sheraton Business Centre
GFD/PVL UB6 .... 135 H4
Sheraton Park Tower Hotel
KTBR SW1X 16 B1
Sheraton Skyline Hotel
HYS/HAR UB3 .... 152 E6
Shere CE Infant School
SHGR GU5 .... 270 B5
Sheredes School
HOD EN11 .... 44 A4
Sheringdale Primary School
WAND/EARL SW18 .... 179 J4
Sheringham Junior School
MNPK E12 .... 122 C9
Sherington Primary School
CHARL SE7 .... 161 N5
Sherlock Holmes Hotel
MHST W1U 10 B3
Sherlock Holmes Museum
CAMTN NW1 .... 10 B2
Sherwood Park Primary School
BFN/LL DA15 .... 185 L2
Sherwood Park School
WLGTN SM6 .... 202 E10
Sherwood School
MTCM CR4 .... 202 D4
The Ship Hotel
WEY KT13 .... 196 C10
Shire Horse Centre
CSTG HP8 .... 90 D4
Shirley Clinic
CROY/NA CR0 .... 204 B8
Shirley High School
CROY/NA CR0 .... 204 C10
Shirley Oaks Hospital
CROY/NA CR0 .... 204 B7
Shirley Park Golf Club
CROY/NA CR0 .... 204 A9
Shirley Wanderers RFC
WWKM BR4 .... 225 H1
Shooters Hill Golf Club
WOOL/PLUM SE18 .... 162 F7
Shooters Hill Post 16 Campus
WOOL/PLUM SE18 .... 162 D6
Shooting Star House (Childrens Hospice)
HPTN TW12 .... 175 N7
Shopping City
WDGN N22 .... 98 G10
WDGN N22 .... 99 H10
The Shopping Hall
EHAM E6 .... 142 B3
Shore Business Centre
HOM E9 .... 140 D1
Shoreditch Comprehensive School
IS N1 .... 7 K8
Shoreditch County Court
STLK EC1Y 13 H1
Shoreham CP School
RSEV TN14 .... 228 G7
Shorne CE Primary School
GVE DA12 .... 191 P9
Shortlands Golf Club
HAYES BR2 .... 205 K1
Shortwood Infant School
STA TW18 .... 173 L6
Shotfield Health Clinic
WLGTN SM6 .... 222 C3
Showcase Bluewater Cinema
RDART DA2 .... 188 E4
Showcase Cinema
WDGN N22 .... 99 H10
Showcase Newham Cinema
BARK IG11 .... 142 F5
Shrewsbury House School
SURB KT6 .... 199 J9
Shrewsbury Road Health Centre
FSTGT E7 .... 142 A2
Sidcup Cemetery
BXLY DA5 .... 185 N5
Sidcup Golf Club
BFN/LL DA15 .... 185 K5
Sidcup Health Centre
SCUP DA14 .... 185 K6
Sidcup Sports Club
SCUP DA14 .... 185 J7
Sidney Russell School
DAGW RM9 .... 123 P9
Silicon Business Centre
GFD/PVL UB6 .... 135 H4
Silverdale Industrial Estate
HYS/HAR UB3 .... 133 H10
HYS/HAR UB3 .... 153 H1
Silverglade Business Park
CHSGTN KT9 .... 219 H8
Silver Industrial Estate
TOTM N17 .... 99 N10
Silvermere Golf Club
COB KT11 .... 216 C9
Silver Street Medical Centre
UED N18 .... 99 M5
Silver Wing Industrial Estate
CROY/NA CR0 .... 222 G3

Simon Balle School
HERT/BAY SG13 .... 25 M6
Simon Marks Jewish Primary School
STNW/STAM N16 .... 119 N6
Simpson Health Centre
BEAC HP9 .... 88 B8
Singlegate Primary School
WIM/MER SW19 .... 179 N10
Singlewell Primary School
GVE DA12 .... 190 C9
Sion College
EMB EC4Y 12 B7
Sion Manning RC Girls School
NKENS W10 .... 136 C7
Sir Christopher Wren's House Hotel
WDSR SL4 .... 149 H6
Sir Francis Drake Primary School
DEPT SE8 .... 160 D4
Sir Frederic Osborn School
WGCE AL7 .... 23 L4
Sir George Monoux College
WALTH E17 .... 100 G10
Sir James Altham Swimming Pool
OXHEY WD19 .... 93 M6
Sir James Barrie School
VX/NE SW8 .... 158 D7
Sir John Cass Foundation & Redcoat CE Secondary School
WCHPL E1 .... 140 C7
Sir John Cass Foundation School
HDTCH EC3A 13 K6
Sir John Lillie Primary School
FUL/PGN SW6 .... 14 B10
Sir John Newsom School
WGCE AL7 .... 23 H7
Sir John Soane's Museum
LINN WC2A 11 N5
Sir Thomas Abney Primary School
STNW/STAM N16 .... 119 L5
Sir Thomas Lipton Memorial Hospital
STHGT/OAK N14 .... 98 C1
Sir William Burrough Primary School
POP/IOD E14 .... 140 D8
Sir William Perkins School
CHERT KT16 .... 195 H8
Site of Greenwich Hospital
GNWCH SE10 .... 161 L4
Six Bridges Trading Estate
STHWK SE1 .... 19 P8
The Sixth Form College
CLPT E5 .... 120 A8
Skidmore Clinic
RKW/CH/CXG WD3 .... 91 P2
Skillion Business Centre
BARK IG11 .... 143 J5
Skinners Companys Lower Girls School
CLPT E5 .... 120 A6
Skinners Companys School For Girls
STNW/STAM N16 .... 119 M5
Sky Business Park
EGH TW20 .... 194 F2
Skywsood JMI School
STALE/WH AL4 .... 39 H3
Slade Green FC
ERITH DA8 .... 165 J7
Slade Green Primary School
ERITH DA8 .... 165 H6
Slade School of Fine Art
STPAN WC1H 5 K10
Sleaford Industrial Estate
VX/NE SW8 .... 158 D6
Sloane Hospital
BECK BR3 .... 205 J1
Slough Cemetery
SL SL1 .... 129 L8
Slough Community Mental Health Centre
DTCH/LGLY SL3 .... 150 D3
Slough Crematorium
SL SL1 .... 129 L8
Slough & Eton CE School
SL SL1 .... 149 J2
Slough Grammar School
SL SL1 .... 149 N2
Slough Ice Arena
SL SL1 .... 149 J1
Slough Museum
SL SL1 .... 149 M1
Slough RFC
DTCH/LGLY SL3 .... 149 N4
Slough Sports Club
SL SL1 .... 149 K2
Slough Town FC
SLN SL2 .... 129 M7
Slough Trading Estate
SL SL1 .... 128 F7
SL SL1 .... 128 C9
Slyfield Industrial Estate
GU GU1 .... 250 A5
Smallberry Green Primary School
ISLW TW7 .... 154 F8
Smallwood Primary School
TOOT SW17 .... 179 N7
SMA Medical Centre
LEY E10 .... 120 C5
Smitham Primary School
COUL/CHIP CR5 .... 240 D2
Smithy Street School
WCHPL E1 .... 140 B7
Smug Oak Green Business Centre
LCOL/BKTW AL2 .... 56 A5
Snaresbrook College Preparatory School
SWFD E18 .... 101 M10
Snaresbrook Crown Court
WAN E11 .... 121 L5
Snaresbrook Primary School
SWFD E18 .... 121 M2
Snowhill Business Centre
CRAWE RH10 .... 285 P1
Snowsfields Primary School
STHWK SE1 .... 19 K2
Sobell Leisure Centre
HOLWY N7 .... 118 C8
Sobell Medical Centre
HOLWY N7 .... 119 H9
Sofitel Hotel
HORL RH6 .... 280 A7
Sofitel St James Hotel
STJS SW1Y 11 J0
Soho Parish CE Primary School
SOHO/CST W1F 11 J7
Solefield School
SEV TN13 .... 265 K3
Solent Road Health Centre
KIL/WHAMP NW6 .... 137 K1
Somerset House
COVGDN WC2E 11 N7
Somers Heath Primary School
SOCK/AV RM15 .... 146 F9
Somers Town Community Sports Centre
CAMTN NW1 .... 5 H8
Sopwell House Hotel, Country Club & Spa
STAL AL1 .... 38 E10
Sorsby Health Centre
CLPT E5 .... 120 C9
Southall & West London College
STHL UB1 .... 153 M1
Southbank Business Centre
VX/NE SW8 .... 17 K10

South Bank Business Centre
VX/NE SW8 .... 158 E5
Southbank International School Hampstead
HAMP NW3 .... 137 M1
Southbank International School Kensington
NTGHL W11 .... 8 D8
Southbank International School Westminster
BAY/PAD W2 .... 8 F8
South Bank University
STHWK SE1 .... 18 C2
STHWK SE1 .... 18 F4
South Bookham School
GT/LBKH KT23 .... 254 B3
Southborough Primary School
HAYES BR2 .... 206 D5
Southborough School
SURB KT6 .... 199 K10
Southbury Primary School
PEND EN3 .... 80 A8
South Camden Community School
CAMTN NW1 .... 5 H7
South Chelsea College
BRXN/ST SW9 .... 158 G10
South Croydon Medical Centre
SAND/SEL CR2 .... 223 K4
South Croydon Sports Club
CROY/NA CR0 .... 223 K4
Southdown Industrial Estate
HARP AL5 .... 20 B3
South Eastern University
HOLWY N7 .... 118 C8
Southern Clinic
REIG RH2 .... 275 M1
Southern Road Primary School
PLSTW E13 .... 141 N4
Southern Valley Golf Club
GVE DA12 .... 191 K7
South Essex Crematorium
UPMR RM14 .... 126 C10
Southfield First & Middle School
CHSWK W4 .... 156 B1
Southfield Medical Centre
CHSWK W4 .... 156 A1
The Southfields Clinic
WAND/EARL SW18 .... 179 K2
Southfields Community College
WAND/EARL SW18 .... 179 K4
Southfields Park Primary School
HOR/WEW KT19 .... 219 N6
Southfields School
GVW DA11 .... 190 F8
Southgate Cemetery
STHGT/OAK N14 .... 98 D3
Southgate College
STHGT/OAK N14 .... 98 D3
Southgate Compton CC
EBAR EN4 .... 78 A8
Southgate Leisure Centre
STHGT/OAK N14 .... 98 E1
Southgate Primary School
CRAWE RH10 .... 283 N9
Southgate Road Medical Centre
IS N1 .... 7 H3
Southgate School
EBAR EN4 .... 78 C9
South Grove Primary School
WALTH E17 .... 120 D4
South Hampstead CC
CRICK NW2 .... 136 F2
South Hampstead High School
HAMP NW3 .... 3 L2
South Haringay Infant School
FSBYPK N4 .... 119 J3
South Herts Golf Club
TRDG/WHET N20 .... 97 K2
South Hill JMI School
HHW HP1 .... 35 M7
Southlake Primary School
ABYW SE2 .... 163 N1
South Lewisham Health Centre
CAT SE6 .... 183 H7
South London Crematorium
MTCM CR4 .... 202 D2
South London Gallery
CMBW SE5 .... 159 M7
The South London Natural Health Centre
CLAP SW4 .... 158 D10
South London Tamil School
CROY/NA CR0 .... 203 K7
South London Theatre
WNWD SE27 .... 181 K6
Southmead Primary School
WIM/MER SW19 .... 179 H4
South Norwood Country Park
SNWD SE25 .... 204 B4
South Norwood Hill Medical Centre
SNWD SE25 .... 203 M2
South Norwood Medical Centre
SNWD SE25 .... 203 M4
South Norwood Pools & Fitness Centre
SNWD SE25 .... 203 P5
South Norwood Primary School
SNWD SE25 .... 203 P5
South Nutfield CC
REDH RH1 .... 276 G2
South Park Business Centre
IL IG1 .... 123 H7
South Park Clinic
IL IG1 .... 123 H9
South Park Hotel
SAND/SEL CR2 .... 223 M1
South Park Primary School
GDMY/SEVK IG3 .... 123 H8
South Quay Plaza
POP/IOD E14 .... 160 G1
South Rise Primary School
WOOL/PLUM SE18 .... 162 G4
Southside Industrial Estate
VX/NE SW8 .... 158 D6
Southside Shopping Centre
WAND/EARL SW18 .... 179 L2
South Terminal
HORL RH6 .... 280 B8
South Thames College
PUT/ROE SW15 .... 178 C2
TOOT SW17 .... 179 L1
WAND/EARL SW18 .... 179 L1
Southville Infant School
EBED/NFELT TW14 .... 174 C4
Southwark Bridge Business Centre
STHWK SE1 .... 12 F10
Southwark Bridge Stairs
BLKFR CC4V 12 E8
Southwark Cathedral
STHWK SE1 .... 12 G9
Southwark College
BERM/RHTH SE16 .... 160 A2
STHWK SE1 .... 18 B1
STHWK SE1 .... 19 K3
Southwark Coroners Court
STHWK SE1 .... 18 C1
Southwark Crown Court
STHWK SE1 .... 13 J9
Southwark Park Primary School
BERM/RHTH SE16 .... 160 A2
Southwark Park Sports Centre
BERM/RHTH SE16 .... 160 B3
Southwark Sports Ground
DUL SE21 .... 181 N4
South West Middlesex Crematorium
FELT TW13 .... 175 M4
Southwold Primary School
CLPT E5 .... 120 B7

South Woodford Health Centre
SWFD E18 .... 101 M9
Southwood Hospital
HGT N6 .... 118 B5
Southwood Primary School
DAGW RM9 .... 123 P9
Sovereign Business Centre
PEND EN3 .... 80 E7
The Space Arts Centre Cinema
DEPT SE8 .... 160 E3
Sparrow Farm Community Junior School
EW KT17 .... 220 E2
Sparrow Farm Infant School
EBED/NFELT TW14 .... 175 K3
Sparrow Farm Junior School
EBED/NFELT TW14 .... 175 K3
Spa School
STHWK SE1 .... 19 N6
Speakers Corner
BAY/PAD W2 .... 10 B7
Spectators Viewing Area
HTHAIR TW6 .... 152 C9
The Speech & Language Hearing Centre
CAMTN NW1 .... 5 K7
Speedway Industrial Estate
HYS/HAR UB3 .... 152 E1
Speke's Monument
BAY/PAD W2 .... 9 K9
Spelthorne Clinic
ASHF TW15 .... 174 E9
Spelthorne Infant School
ASHF TW15 .... 174 E9
Spelthorne Leisure Centre
STA TW18 .... 173 K8
Spelthorne Sixth Form College
ASHF TW15 .... 174 A7
Spelthorne Sports Club
ASHF TW15 .... 174 E10
Spencer House
WHALL SW1A 10 G10
Sphere Industrial Estate
STAL AL1 .... 38 F7
The Spinney J & I School
HLW CM20 .... 29 K10
The Spires Shopping Centre
BAR EN5 .... 77 H7
Spitalfields Community Farm
BETH E2 .... 13 N1
Spitalfields Health Centre
WCHPL E1 .... 13 M4
Spitalfields Market Hall
WCHPL E1 .... 139 N7
Spitfire Business Park
CROY/NA CR0 .... 223 H5
Splashworld Swimming Centre
BXLYHS DA6 .... 163 N10
Sports Centre, Jarman Park
HHS/BOV HP3 .... 36 A7
Springfield Christian School
CAT SE6 .... 182 G6
Springfield Community Primary School
SEVS/STOTM N15 .... 119 P4
Springfield Hospital
TOOT SW17 .... 179 P6
Springfield Primary School
SUN TW16 .... 196 F1
VX/NE SW8 .... 158 E6
Spring Grove Primary School
ISLW TW7 .... 154 C8
Springhallow School
HNWL W7 .... 134 E8
Springmead JMI School
WGCE AL7 .... 23 M4
Spring Park Primary School
CROY/NA CR0 .... 204 F10
Springvale Retail Park
STMC/STPC BR5 .... 207 M3
Springwell Infant School
HEST TW5 .... 153 M6
Springwell Junior School
HEST TW5 .... 153 M6
Sprint Industrial Estate
BF/WBF KT14 .... 215 N7
Spurgeon's College
SNWD SE25 .... 203 M1
Squerryes Court
BH/WHM TN16 .... 262 F4
Squirrels Heath Junior School
GPK RM2 .... 125 J3
Squirrels Trading Estate
HYS/HAR UB3 .... 152 G2
The Stables Gallery & Art Centre
CRICK NW2 .... 116 D9
Stadium Business Centre
WBLY HA9 .... 115 N8
Stadium Industrial Estate
WBLY HA9 .... 115 N8
Stadium Retail Park
WBLY HA9 .... 115 M8
Stafford Cross Business Park
CROY/NA CR0 .... 222 G2
The Stafford Hotel
WHALL SW1A 10 G10
Stafford Industrial Estate
EMPK RM11 .... 125 L1
Stag Lane Medical Centre
CDALE/KGS NW9 .... 115 P1
Stag Lane Primary School
EDGW HA8 .... 95 M10
Stags School
STALW/RED AL3 .... 38 D2
Stag Theatre
SEV TN13 .... 265 J1
Staines County Court
STA TW18 .... 173 K8
Staines Preparatory School
STA TW18 .... 173 K8
Staines RFC
FELT TW13 .... 175 H8
Staines Town FC
STA TW18 .... 173 K10
Stamford Clinic
HMSMTH W6 .... 156 D3
Stamford Green County Primary
HOR/WEW KT19 .... 219 N8
Stamford Hill Primary School
SEVS/STOTM N15 .... 119 L4
Stanborough Primary School
GSTN WD25 .... 73 K1
Stanborough School
GSTN WD25 .... 73 J1
WGCW AL8 .... 22 E7
Stanburn Middle School
STAN HA7 .... 95 H8
Standard Industrial Estate
CAN/RD E16 .... 162 A1
CAN/RD E16 .... 162 C1
Stanford Primary School
STRHM/NOR SW16 .... 202 H7
Stanhill Court Hotel
HORL RH6 .... 278 F6
Stanhope Primary School
GFD/PVL UB6 .... 134 B6
Stanley J & I School
TEDD TW11 .... 176 D7
Stanley Park High School
CAR SM5 .... 222 B3
Stanley Park Primary School
CAR SM5 .... 222 A4
Stanley Technical High School
SNWD SE25 .... 203 N3
Stanmore College
STAN HA7 .... 94 G7
Stanmore Golf Club
STAN HA7 .... 94 G8
Stanton School of English
BAY/PAD W2 .... 137 J3
Stanton Square Industrial Estate
SYD SE26 .... 182 E7

Stapleford Abbotts Golf Club *ABR/ST* RM4 105 H1
Stapleford Abbotts Primary School *ABR/ST* RM4 84 C9
Staple Inn Buildings *HHOL* WC1V 12 A4
Staples Corner Business Park *CRICK* NW2 116 D6
Staples Road J & I School *LOU* IG10 82 B7
Staple Tye Shopping Centre *HLWS* CM18 46 G4
Star Business Centre *RAIN* RM13 144 E7
Starhurst School *RDKG* RH5 273 H4
Starksfield Primary School *ED* N9 99 M2
Star Primary School *CAN/RD* E16 141 K6
Stationers Hall *STP* EC4M 12 D6
Stationery Office *HOL/ALD* WC2B 11 N5
Stebon Primary School *POP/IOD* E14 140 E7
Stepgates Community School *CHERT* KT16 195 L7
Stephen Hawking Primary Special School *POP/IOD* E14 140 D8
Stepney Day Hospital *WCHPL* E1 140 B8
Stepney Greencoat CE Primary School *POP/IOD* E14 140 E8
Stepney Green College *WCHPL* E1 140 C7
Sterling Industrial Estate *DAGE* RM10 124 C9
Sterling Way Clinic *UED* N18 99 N6
Stewards School *HLWS* CM18 46 F5
Stewart Fleming Primary School *PGE/AN* SE20 204 B3
Stewart Headlam Primary School *WCHPL* E1 140 A6
Stifford Clays Health Centre *CDW/CHF* RM16 147 N10
Stifford Clays Primary School *CDW/CHF* RM16 147 N10
Stifford Primary School *GRAYS* RM17 167 K4
Stillness Primary School *FSTH* SE23 182 D2
Stirling Industrial Centre *BORE* WD6 76 A9
Stirling Retail Park *BORE* WD6 76 A10
Stirling Way Industrial Estates *CROY/NA* CR0 202 F7
Stock Exchange *STBT* EC1A 12 D5
Stockley Academy *WDR/YW* UB7 132 A8
Stockley Park Business Centre *STKPK* UB11 132 D10
Stockley Park Golf Club *STKPK* UB11 132 D9
Stockwell Lodge Medical Centre *CHESW* EN7 61 P3
Stockwell Park School *BRXN/ST* SW9 158 G7
Stockwell Primary School *BRXN/ST* SW9 158 G9
Stoke Green CC *SLN* SL2 129 N6
Stoke Hill CP School *GU* GU1 249 P7
Stoke Newington School *STNW/STAM* N16 119 L8
Stoke Park Club *SLN* SL2 129 J5
Stoke Park House *SLN* SL2 129 K5
Stoke Poges School *SLN* SL2 129 L2
Stompond Lane Track *WOT/HER* KT12 197 H9
The Stonebridge Primary School *WLSDN* NW10 135 P3
Stonebridge Shopping Centre *WLSDN* NW10 136 A3
Stonehill Business Centre *UED* N18 100 C7
Stonehill Business Park *UED* N18 100 C6
Stone House Hospital *RDART* DA2 188 B2
Stone Lake Retail Park *CHARL* SE7 161 P3
Stoneleigh First School *EW* KT17 220 E1
Stoneydown Park Primary School *WALTH* E17 120 D2
Stony Dean Special School *AMSS* HP7 69 L5
Stormont School *POTB/CUF* EN6 59 M7
Stoughton County Junior School *GUW* GU2 249 N7
Stowford College *BELMT* SM2 221 M4
Strand on the Green J & I School *CHSWK* W4 155 M5
Strand Palace Hotel *COVGDN* WC2E 11 M7
Stratford College *SRTFD* E15 141 K2
Stratford Magistrates Court *SRTFD* E15 141 J2
Stratford School *FSTGT* E7 141 M2
Stratford Shopping Centre *SRTFD* E15 141 J2
Strathmore School *RCHPK/HAM* TW10 177 J4
Strawberry Fields School *NTGHL* W11 8 F6
Strawberry Hill Golf Club *WHTN* TW2 176 D6
Stream Woods School *HAT* AL10 40 E5
Streatham Cemetery *TOOT* SW17 179 P6
Streatham & Clapham High School Junior Department *BRXS/STRHM* SW2 180 G4
Streatham & Clapham High School Senior Department *STRHM/NOR* SW16 180 D6
Streatham & Croydon RFC *THHTH* CR7 203 H5
Streatham Ice Rink *STRHM/NOR* SW16 180 F8
Streatham Leisure Centre *STRHM/NOR* SW16 180 F5
Streatham Modern School *STRHM/NOR* SW16 180 F9
Streatham Park Cemetery *MTCM* CR4 202 D2
Streatham Swimming Pool *STRHM/NOR* SW16 180 F8
Streatham Vale Sports Club *STRHM/NOR* SW16 180 D10
Streatham Wells Primary School *BRXS/STRHM* SW2 180 G5
Streete Court School *GDST* RH9 260 D6
Strodes College *EGH* TW20 172 C8
Stroud Green Primary School *FSBYPK* N4 119 H6
Stroud Wood Business Centre *LCOL/BKTW* AL2 56 D3
Stubbers (Outdoor Pursuits Centre) *UPMR* RM14 146 E1
Studholme Medical Centre *ASHF* TW15 174 A7
The Study Preparatory School *WIM/MER* SW19 178 G8
The Study School *NWMAL* KT3 200 B5
Sturt Priory Hospital *KWD/TDW/WH* KT20 256 D2
Sudbourne Primary School *BRXS/STRHM* SW2 180 G1
Sudbury Court Sports Club *ALP/SUD* HA0 115 H8
Sudbury Golf Club *GFD/PVL* UB6 135 H1
Sudbury Primary School *ALP/SUD* HA0 114 G9
Suffolks Primary School *EN* EN1 80 A6
Sulivan Primary School *FUL/PGN* SW6 157 K8
Summerside JMI School *NFNCH/WDSPK* N12 97 N7
Summerswood Primary School *BORE* WD6 75 N8
Summit Business Park *SUN* TW16 175 H10
Sumners Community Recreation Centre *HLWW/ROY* CM19 46 D5
Sunbury Business Centre *SUN* TW16 196 F1
Sunbury Court *SUN* TW16 197 L2
Sunbury Golf Centre *SHPTN* TW17 196 D4
Sunbury Health Centre *SUN* TW16 197 H2
Sunbury Leisure Centre *SUN* TW16 196 G1
Sunbury Manor School *SUN* TW16 196 G1
Sunderland Estate *KGLGY* WD4 54 C5
Sundridge & Brasted CE Primary School *RSEV* TN14 263 P1
Sundridge Park Golf Club *BMLY* BR1 183 P9
Sun Life Trading Estate *EBED/NFELT* TW14 153 H9
Sunningdale Golf Club *ASC* SL5 192 F8
Sunningdale Ladies Golf Club *ASC* SL5 192 E8
Sunningdale School *ASC* SL5 192 D6
Sunnydown School *CTHM* CR3 241 N7
Sunnyfields Primary School *HDN* NW4 116 E1
Sunnyhill Primary School *STRHM/NOR* SW16 180 G7
Sunshine House School *NTHWD* HA6 92 E7
Super Bowl *BXLYHS* DA6 164 A10
Surbiton Business Centre *SURB* KT6 199 J6
Surbiton Cemetery *KUT/HW* KT1 199 M4
Surbiton Golf Club *CHSGTN* KT9 218 G1
Surbiton High School *KUT/HW* KT1 199 K4
Surbiton Hospital *SURB* KT6 199 K6
Surbiton Natural Health Centre *SURB* KT6 199 K6
Surex Swimming Pools *BH/WHM* TN16 244 A1
Surrey Business Park *EW* KT17 220 B7
Surrey CCC (The Oval) *LBTH* SE11 158 G5
Surrey County CC (The Oval) *LBTH* SE11 17 P9
Surrey Docks Farm *BERM/RHTH* SE16 160 E1
Surrey Docks Health Centre *BERM/RHTH* SE16 160 D1
Surrey Docks Watersports Centre *BERM/RHTH* SE16 160 D2
Surrey Downs Golf Club *KWD/TDW/WH* KT20 239 M8
Surrey History Centre *WOKN/KNAP* GU21 232 A4
Surrey Institute of Art & Design *HOR/WEW* KT19 220 B8
Surrey National Golf Club *CTHM* CR3 241 J9
Surrey Quays Leisure Park *BERM/RHTH* SE16 160 C2
Surrey Quays Shopping Centre *BERM/RHTH* SE16 160 C2
Surrey Square Infant School *WALW* SE17 19 J7
Surrey Square Primary School *WALW* SE17 159 M4
The Surrey & Sussex Crematorium *CRAWE* RH10 284 E2
Susi Earnshaw Theatre School *BAR* EN5 77 J8
Sussex House School *KTBR* SW1X 16 A5
Sussex Manor Business Park *CRAWE* RH10 284 B3
Sutcliffe Park Athletics Track *LEE/GVPK* SE12 183 N1
Sutton Alternative Health Centre *SUT* SM1 221 L2
Sutton Arena *CAR* SM5 201 N7
Sutton at Hone CE Primary School *EYN* DA4 187 P10
Sutton Bowling Club *BELMT* SM2 221 K5
Sutton Cemetery *CHEAM* SM3 201 J9
Sutton College of Learning for Adults *SUT* SM1 221 L2
Sutton General Hospital *BELMT* SM2 221 L6
Sutton Grammar School for Boys *SUT* SM1 221 M2
Sutton Green Golf Club *WOKS/MYFD* GU22 232 B8
Sutton High Junior School *SUT* SM1 221 L3
Sutton High School for Girls GDST *SUT* SM1 221 K3
Sutton House *HACK* E8 120 B10
Suttons Business Park *RAIN* RM13 144 E5
Suttons JMI School *HCH* RM12 125 L9
Suttons Manor Clinic *ABR/ST* RM4 84 F5
Sutton Superbowl *SUT* SM1 221 L2
Sutton United FC *SUT* SM1 221 K1
Sutton West Centre *SUT* SM1 221 K2
Swaffield Primary School *WAND/EARL* SW18 179 M2
Swakeleys School *HGDN/ICK* UB10 132 D4
Swallow Dell Primary School *WGCE* AL7 23 K6
Swaminarayan School *WLSDN* NW10 136 A1
Swan Business Centre *CHSWK* W4 156 A3
Swan Business Park *DART* DA1 165 L10
The Swan Centre *LHD/OX* KT22 236 G7
Swan Lane Pier *CANST* EC4R 12 G8
Swanlea School *WCHPL* E1 140 A6
Swanley School *SWLY* BR8 208 E3
Swanscombe Business Centre *SWCM* DA10 189 K1
Swansmere School *WOT/HER* KT12 197 K8
Swan Valley Community School *SWCM* DA10 189 L3
Swan Wharf Business Centre *UX/CGN* UB8 131 M4
Swedish School *BARN* SW13 156 D5
CRAWE RH10 284 A9
The Sweyne Junior School *SWCM* DA10 189 L3
Swing Gate First School *BERK* HP4 34 A6
Swiss Cottage Leisure Centre *HAMP* NW3 3 M4
Swiss Cottage School *STJWD* NW8 3 M4
Swissotel the Howard *TPL/STR* WC2R 11 P7
Swiss Re-Insurance Tower *HDTCH* EC3A 13 K6
Sybil Elgar School *EA* W5 135 K9
NWDGN UB2 153 N2
Sybourn Infant School *LEY* E10 120 D6
The Sybourn Junior School *WALTH* E17 120 E5
Sydenham Girls School *SYD* SE26 182 A6
Sydenham High Junior School *SYD* SE26 182 A7
Sydenham High School Sports Ground *CAT* SE6 182 F8
Sydenham High Senior School *SYD* SE26 182 A8
The Sydney Russell School *DAGW* RM9 123 N10
Syon House *BTFD* TW8 155 H7
Syon Park *BTFD* TW8 155 H8
Syon Park School *ISLW* TW7 154 G7
Syracuse University *NTGHL* W11 8 C8
Sythwood Primary School *WOKN/KNAP* GU21 231 N2
Tabard RFC *RAD* WD7 74 G3
Tabard Theatre *CHSWK* W4 156 B3
Taberner House *CROY/NA* CR0 203 K10
Tadworth Primary School *KWD/TDW/WH* KT20 238 G8
Tait Road Industrial Estate *CROY/NA* CR0 203 M6
Talmud Torah School *STNW/STAM* N16 119 L5
Tamian Industrial Estate *HSLWW* TW4 153 K10
Tamworth Manor High School *STRHM/NOR* SW16 202 E3
Tandem Centre *WIM/MER* SW19 201 N1
Tandridge Golf Club *OXTED* RH8 261 H7
Tanners Wood Primary School *ABLGY* WD5 54 F8
Tanys Dell Primary School *HLW* CM20 29 K8
Tapling Trading Estate *WDR/YW* UB7 131 N9
Taplow Health Centre *MDHD* SL6 128 A8
Tasis the American School in England *EGH* TW20 194 F3
Tate Britain *WEST* SW1P 17 L6
Tate Modern *STHWK* SE1 12 D9
Tatsfield Primary School *BH/WHM* TN16 244 A7
Tattenham Health Centre *EPSOM* KT18 238 E4
Tavistock Clinic *HAMP* NW3 3 L2
TAVR Centre *KUT/HW* KT1 199 J4
Tavy Clinic *ABYW* SE2 163 M1
Tawhid Boys School *STNW/STAM* N16 119 N7
Taylor Trading Estate *HERT/BAY* SG13 26 A4
TCA Leisure Centre *TIL* RM18 168 D8
Teardrop Industrial Park *SWLY* BR8 209 K5
Teddington Business Park *TEDD* TW11 176 E8
Teddington Cemetery *TEDD* TW11 176 D7
Teddington Clinic *TEDD* TW11 176 D9
Teddington Memorial Hospital *TEDD* TW11 176 D9
Teddington Pool & Fitness Centre *TEDD* TW11 176 F8
Teddington School *TEDD* TW11 177 J9
The Teddington Theatre Club *E/WMO/HCT* KT8 198 C5
Teikyo School *SLN* SL2 130 A2
Telferscot Primary School *BAL* SW12 180 D4
Temperate House *RCH/KEW* TW9 155 L8
Temple Court Business Centre *WOKN/KNAP* GU21 232 C3
Temple Hill Primary School *DART* DA1 187 P1
Temple of Bacchus *CMBW* SE5 159 K8
Temple of Mithras *MANHO* EC4N 12 G6
Templewood Primary School *WGCW* AL8 22 F3
Tenby Road Clinic *EDGW* HA8 95 L10
Tenterden Sports Ground *KTN/HRWW/WS* HA3 115 K5
Terence McMillan Stadium *PLSTW* E13 141 P6
Tetherdown Primary School *MUSWH* N10 118 B2
Tewin Cowper Primary School *WLYN* AL6 23 P1
Tewin Road Business Centre *WGCE* AL7 23 H4
Tewin Water School *WLYN* AL6 23 K1
Thames Barrier *CAN/RD* E16 162 A1
Thames Barrier Information & Learning Centre *CHARL* SE7 162 A2
Thames Ditton & Esher Golf Club *ESH/CLAY* KT10 198 C9
Thames Ditton Infant School *THDIT* KT7 198 E6
Thames Ditton Junior School *THDIT* KT7 198 E7
Thames House *WEST* SW1P 17 L5
Thameside Industrial Estate *CAN/RD* E16 142 A10
CAN/RD E16 162 B1
Thameside Primary School *GRAYS* RM17 167 P5
Thameside Theatre *GRAYS* RM17 167 M4
Thames Industrial Park *TIL* RM18 169 M3
Thames Magistrates Court *BOW* E3 140 F5
Thamesmead Leisure Centre *THMD* SE28 143 K9
Thamesmead School *SHPTN* TW17 196 E6
Thamesmead Shopping Centre *THMD* SE28 143 K9
Thames Police Station *TPL/STR* WC2R 11 P8
Thames Valley Athletics Centre *WDSR* SL4 149 K4
Thames Valley Community Infant School *SL* SL1 149 H1
Thames Valley Cultural Centre *WDSR* SL4 149 J7
The Thames Valley Nuffield Hospital *DTCH/LGLY* SL3 129 P3
Thames Valley University *EA* W5 135 H9
SL SL1 129 K10
Thamesview Business Centre *RAIN* RM13 144 F7
Thames View Clinic *BARK* IG11 143 J4
Thames View J & I School *BARK* IG11 143 K4
Thamesview School *GVE* DA12 191 J6
Thames Water Tower *NTGHL* W11 156 G1
Thatched House Hotel *SUT* SM1 221 J3
Theatre Centre *BECK* BR3 204 G2
Theatre for Mankind *FSBYPK* N4 118 G6
Theatre Magenta *LHD/OX* KT22 236 F5
Theatre Museum Library & Archive *COVGDN* WC2E 11 M7
Theatre of the Dispossessed *WIM/MER* SW19 178 G4
The Theatre on the Hill *CTHM* CR3 241 M8
Theatre Royal *HOL/ALD* WC2B 11 M6
SRTFD E15 141 J1
WDSR SL4 149 J6
Theatre Royal Haymarket *STJS* SW1Y 11 K8
Theobalds Park C&C Club Site *CHESW* EN7 61 P10
Theodore McLeary Primary School *EDUL* SE22 159 N10
Therapia Trading Estate *CROY/NA* CR0 202 E7
Therfield School *LHD/OX* KT22 236 F5
Theydon Bois Golf Club *EPP* CM16 64 G10
Theydon Bois Primary School *EPP* CM16 83 H2
Thistlebrook Industrial Estate *ABYW* SE2 163 M2
Thistle Hotel *BAY/PAD* W2 9 J8
CAMTN NW1 5 H10
CHCR WC2N 11 L8
FSBYE EC1V 6 E10
HORL RH6 280 B2
KENS W8 15 J2
LCOL/BKTW AL2 55 N3
WDR/YW UB7 151 M7
Thistle Hyde Park Hotel *BAY/PAD* W2 137 M9
Thistle Kensington Gardens Hotel *BAY/PAD* W2 137 M9
Thistle Kensington Palace *KENS* W8 15 J2
Thistle Marble Arch Hotel *MBLAR* W1H 10 B6
Thistle Piccadilly Hotel *SOHO/SHAV* W1D 11 K8
Thistle Tower Hotel *WAP* E1W 13 L9
Thistle Westminster Hotel *WESTW* SW1E 16 F4
Thomas Arnold Primary School *DAGW* RM9 144 A2
Thomas Bennett Community College *CRAWE* RH10 283 N10
Thomas Buxton Primary School *WCHPL* E1 13 N2
The Thomas Coram Middle School *BERK* HP4 34 A7
Thomas Fairchild Primary School *IS* N1 6 G7
Thomas Francis Academy *BRXN/ST* SW9 159 J10
Thomas Gamuel Primary School *WALTH* E17 120 F4
Thomas Harding Junior School *CSHM* HP5 50 G8
Thomas Jones Primary School *NTGHL* W11 137 H8
Thomas London Independent Day School *KENS* W8 15 H3
Thomas More Catholic School *PUR/KEN* CR8 222 G6
The Thomas Rivers Medical Centre *SBW* CM21 29 M2
Thomas Road Industrial Estate *POP/IOD* E14 140 F7
Thomas's Preparatory School *BTSEA* SW11 157 N7
BTSEA SW11 180 A1
Thomas Tallis School *BKHTH/KID* SE3 161 N9
WAB EN9 63 L9
Thomas Willingale Primary School *LOU* IG10 82 F7
Thornchace School *GU* GU1 250 F10
Thorncroft Manor *LHD/OX* KT22 236 F9
Thorndon Country Park *RBRW/HUT* CM13 107 L6
RBRW/HUT CM13 107 M8
Thorndon Park Golf Club *RBRW/HUT* CM13 107 N7
Thorney Park Golf Club *WDR/YW* UB7 151 L1
Thornhill Primary School *IS* N1 6 A4
Thornton Heath Health Centre *THHTH* CR7 203 K4
Thornton Heath Pools & Fitness Centre *THHTH* CR7 203 K4
Thornton Road Industrial Estate *CROY/NA* CR0 202 F6
Thorntree Primary School *CHARL* SE7 162 A4
Thorpe CE Infant School *EGH* TW20 194 F3
Thorpe CC *EGH* TW20 194 C4
Thorpe Hall Primary School *WALTH* E17 101 H9
Thorpe Industrial Park *EGH* TW20 194 G1
Thorpe Lea Primary School *EGH* TW20 172 G9
Thorpe Park *CHERT* KT16 195 H4
Three Bridges Business Centre *NWDGN* UB2 154 B1
Three Bridges Community Centre *CRAWE* RH10 284 B7
Three Bridges CC *CRAWE* RH10 284 B7
Three Bridges FC *CRAWE* RH10 284 B7
Three Bridges First School *CRAWE* RH10 284 B6
Three Bridges Junior School *CRAWE* RH10 284 A7
Three Bridges Primary School *NWDGN* UB2 154 A2
Three Mills Heritage Centre *BOW* E3 141 H5
Thurrock Athletics Stadium *CDW/CHF* RM16 168 A1
Thurrock & Basildon College *CDW/CHF* RM16 168 C3
Thurrock Business Centre *WTHK* RM20 166 E5
Thurston Industrial Estate *LEW* SE13 160 G9
Tidemill Primary School *DEPT* SE8 160 F6
Tideway Industrial Estate *VX/NE* SW8 17 H10
Tiffin Girls School *KUTN/CMB* KT2 177 K9
Tiffin School & Sports Centre *KUTN/CMB* KT2 199 L2
Tilbury Fort *TIL* RM18 168 F10
Tilbury/Gravesend Passenger Ferry *TIL* RM18 168 E10
Tilbury Manor Infant School *TIL* RM18 168 E6
Tilbury Manor Junior School *TIL* RM18 168 E6
Tilehouse Combined School *DEN/HRF* UB9 111 H4
Tiller Centre (Swimming Baths) *POP/IOD* E14 160 F2
Tiller Leisure Centre *POP/IOD* E14 160 F2
Tillingbourne Junior School *RGUE* GU4 268 E7
Timbercroft Primary School *WOOL/PLUM* SE18 163 H6
Timbers Clinic *KTN/HRWW/WS* HA3 94 C7
Times Square Shopping Centre *SUT* SM1 221 L2
Titan Industrial Estate *GRAYS* RM17 167 M3
Tithe Barn Museum *UPMR* RM14 126 B5
Tiverton Primary School *SEVS/STOTM* N15 119 L4
Tobacco Dock *WAP* E1W 140 A9
Tokyngton Community Centre *WBLY* HA9 115 N10
Toldos School *STNW/STAM* N16 119 L6
Tollgate *DUL* SE21 181 M5
Tollgate Primary School *CROY/NA* CR0 204 B6
PLSTW E13 141 P6
Tolworth CP School *SURB* KT6 199 L8
Tolworth Girls School *SURB* KT6 199 L10
Tolworth Recreation Centre *SURB* KT6 199 L10
Tom Hood School *WAN* E11 121 L8
Tomo Industrial Estate *UX/CGN* UB8 131 M8
Toot Hill Golf Club *CHONG* CM5 66 G7
Tooting Bec Athletics Track *TOOT* SW17 180 C7
Tooting Bec Lido *STRHM/NOR* SW16 180 D6
Tooting Leisure Centre *TOOT* SW17 179 N7
Tooting & Mitcham United Football Club *MTCM* CR4 202 B1
Top Meadow Golf Club *UPMR* RM14 147 J1
Torah Vodaas *GLDGN* NW11 117 J7
Tormead School *GU* GU1 250 C10
Torriano Primary School *KTTN* NW5 118 D10
Torridon Primary School *CAT* SE6 183 J5
Torrington Clinic *NFNCH/WDSPK* N12 97 M6
Torrington Park Health Centre *NFNCH/WDSPK* N12 97 M5
Total Health Clinic *SHB* W12 156 E1
Tottenham Green Leisure Centre *SEVS/STOTM* N15 119 M2
Tottenham Hale Retail Park *SEVS/STOTM* N15 119 P2
Tottenham Hotspur FC (White Hart Lane) *TOTM* N17 99 N8
Tottenham Park Cemetery *ED* N9 100 A4
Tottenham Sports Centre *TOTM* N17 99 N9
Totteridge CC *TRDG/WHET* N20 97 K3
Tower 42 *OBST* EC2N 13 J5
The Tower Bridge Exhibition *STHWK* SE1 13 L10
Tower Bridge Primary School *STHWK* SE1 19 L1
Tower Bridge Wharf *WAP* E1W 13 N10
Tower Hamlets College *BETH* E2 7 N10
POP/IOD E14 140 G9
WCHPL E1 140 B7
Tower House School *MORT/ESHN* SW14 155 P10
Tower Industrial Estate *SNWD* SE25 203 P4
Tower Medical Centre *WCHPL* E1 139 P8
Tower Millennium Pier *TWRH* EC3N 13 K9
Tower of London *TWRH* EC3N 13 L8
Tower Retail Park *DART* DA1 186 G1
Towers Business Park *WBLY* HA9 115 N9
Towers Infant School *EMPK* RM11 125 K5
Towers Junior School *EMPK* RM11 125 K5
Tower Stairs *MON* EC3R 13 J8
Town Farm Primary School *STWL/WRAY* TW19 173 N3
Townley Grammar School for Girls *BXLYHS* DA6 186 A2
Townmead Business Centre *FUL/PGN* SW6 157 M8
Town Medical Centre *SEV* TN13 265 J1
Townsend CE School *STALW/RED* AL3 38 B1
Townsend Industrial Estate *WLSDN* NW10 135 P3
Townsend Primary School *WALW* SE17 19 H5
Toynbee Hall & Curtain Theatre *WCHPL* E1 13 L4
Trade Union Congress *NOXST/BSQ* WC1A 11 K5
Traditions Golf Club *WOKS/MYFD* GU22 233 K1
Trafalgar Business Centre *BARK* IG11 143 J6
Trafalgar Primary & Infant School *WHTN* TW2 176 C5
Trafalgar Square *STJS* SW1Y 11 K9
Trafalgar Trading Estate *PEND* EN3 80 E8
Tramshed Theatre *WOOL/PLUM* SE18 162 E3
Trans Atlantic College *BETH* E2 7 L7
Transport House *WEST* SW1P 17 L4
Travellers Lane Industrial Estate *BRKMPK* AL9 40 F8
Travelodge *ACT* W3 135 M6
BTFD TW8 155 K5
BTSEA SW11 157 M9
CAMTN NW1 9 P3
CAN/RD E16 142 A10
DORK RH4 273 H1
EPP CM16 48 E10
FSBYW WC1X 5 P9
GUW GU2 249 N9
HEST TW5 153 K5
HHNE HP2 35 N7
HLW CM20 28 G8
HORL RH6 279 P10
IL IG1 122 E8
KUTN/CMB KT2 199 K2
LHD/OX KT22 236 F8
LSQ/SEVD WC2H 11 L5
POP/IOD E14 141 J8
PUR RM19 166 E2
RDART DA2 188 D1
REDBR IG4 122 C4
SL SL1 149 K1
STA TW18 173 H7
STPAN WC1H 5 M9
SURB KT6 199 N8
WCHPL E1 13 L5
WLSDN NW10 135 M4
Treasury *WHALL* SW1A 17 L2
The Treaty Centre *HSLW* TW3 154 A9
Treehouse School *MUSWH* N10 118 B2
The Treehouse School *BMSBY* WC1N 11 N1
Treetops Special School *GRAYS* RM17 167 N3
Trent CE Primary School *EBAR* EN4 78 A8
Trent Country Park *EBAR* EN4 78 B6
Trent Park Cemetery *EBAR* EN4 78 B7
Trent Park Golf Club *STHGT/OAK* N14 78 D8
Trevelyan Middle School *WDSR* SL4 148 F8
WDSR SL4 149 H10
Trevor Roberts School *HAMP* NW3 3 M3
Tricor Business Park *CHES/WCR* EN8 62 D10
Tricor Trading Estate *CHES/WCR* EN8 62 D10
Tricycle Cinema *KIL/WHAMP* NW6 2 D4
Tricycle Theatre *KIL/WHAMP* NW6 2 D3
Trident Business Centre *TOOT* SW17 180 A8
Trident Industrial Estate *DTCH/LGLY* SL3 151 H9
HOD EN11 45 H2
Trinity Business Centre *BERM/RHTH* SE16 160 E1
Trinity Catholic Lower High School *WFD* IG8 101 M5
Trinity College Centre *PECK* SE15 159 M6
Trinity College London *STHWK* SE1 158 F4
Trinity College of Music *GNWCH* SE10 161 H5
MHST W1U 10 D4
Trinity Hospital *GNWCH* SE10 161 J4
Trinity House *TWRH* EC3N 13 K7
Trinity RC High School (Upper) *WFD* IG8 101 M5
Trinity St Marys Primary School *BAL* SW12 180 B4

Trinity St Stephen CE First School
WDSR SL4 149 H7
Trinity School
CROY/NA CR0 204 B9
DAGE RM10 124 B8
Trinity School Belvedere
BELV DA17 164 D3
Trinity Trading Estate
HYS/HAR UB3 153 H2
Tripcock Point Development Site
THMD SE28 143 J9
Triumph Trading Estate
TOTM N17 99 P7
Trocadero
SOHO/SHAV W1D 11 J8
Trojan Business Centre
WLSDN NW10 136 C1
Troy Industrial Estate
HRW HA1 114 E3
True Buddha School
IS N1 5 N6
Trumps Green Infant School
VW GU25 194 A6
TS Queen Mary
TPL/STR WC2R 11 N8
Tubbenden J & I Schools
ORP BR6 226 G1
Tudor Court Primary School
CDW/CHF RM16 167 L1
Tudor Lodge Health Centre
WIM/MER SW19 178 G4
Tudor Lodge Hotel
PIN HA5 113 J4
Tudor Lodge School
PUR/KEN CR8 222 F6
Tudor Primary School
FNCH N3 97 M9
HHS/BOV HP3 35 P8
STHL UB1 133 M9
Tudors Business Centre
KWD/TDW/WH KT20 239 J8
Tufnell Park Primary School
HOLWY N7 118 E9
Tuke School
PECK SE15 160 A7
Tulloch Clinic
SHB W12 136 G10
Tunnel Avenue Trading Estate
GNWCH SE10 161 J1
Tunnel Industrial Estate
WTHK RM20 166 E3
WTHK RM20 166 E5
Turners Hill CE Primary School
CRAWE RH10 285 P10
Turney School
DUL SE21 181 K3
Turnford School
CHES/WCR EN8 62 D4
Turnham Primary School
BROCKY SE4 160 D10
Turtle Key Arts Centre
FUL/PGN SW6 14 F10
Tutorial College of West London
STHL UB1 133 P10
Tweeddale Primary School
CAR SM5 201 N7
Twickenham Cemetery
WHTN TW2 176 A4
Twickenham Park Health Centre
TWK TW1 177 H2
Twickenham Preparatory School
HPTN TW12 198 A1
Twickenham Stadium
ISLW TW7 176 D2
Twickenham Trading Estate
TWK TW1 176 E2
The Two Brewers Hotel
KGLGY WD4 53 K7
Two Bridges Business Park
SAND/SEL CR2 223 L3
Two Rivers Retail Park
STA TW18 173 H7
Two Waters JMI School
HHS/BOV HP3 53 N1
Twyford CE High School
ACT W3 135 M10
Twyford Sports Centre
ACT W3 135 N10
Tyburn Infant School
STJWD NW8 9 M1
Tynemouth Road Health Centre
SEVS/STOTM N15 119 N2
The Type Museum
BRXN/ST SW9 158 G7
Tyrrells Wood Golf Club
LHD/OX KT22 237 L10
Tyssen Primary School
STNW/STAM N16 119 P6
UCI Cinema
BAY/PAD W2 9 H6
ED N9 100 C1
HAT AL10 40 C3
SUT SM1 221 L2
WTHK RM20 166 E3
UCI Empire Cinema
LSQ/SEVD WC2H 11 K8
UCI Filmworks Cinema
GNWCH SE10 161 L3
UGC Cinema
CHEL SW3 15 M9
CRAWE RH10 283 N6
CRICK NW2 116 E6
EA W5 135 J9
EN EN1 79 P8
HLW CM20 27 J7
HMSMTH W6 156 E3
SL SL1 149 L1
SOHO/SHAV W1D 11 J7
WBPTN SW10 15 K8
UK Passport Office
PIM SW1V 16 F5
The Ullswater Business Park
COUL/CHIP CR5 240 F2
Ullswater Trading Estate
COUL/CHIP CR5 240 F2
Underhill J & I School
BAR EN5 77 H9
Unicorn Primary School
BECK BR3 204 G5
Unicorn School
RCH/KEW TW9 155 L7
Unicorn Theatre
STHWK SE1 19 K1
Union Business Park
UX/CGN UB8 131 M2
United Medical & Dental Schools
STHWK SE1 17 N3
United Services Sports Ground
CHSWK W4 156 B7
Unity College
KTTN NW5 118 C9
Unity Trading Estate
WFD IG8 122 A1
University Church of Christ the King
STPAN WC1H 11 J2
University College for the Creative Arts at Epsom
EPSOM KT18 220 A10
University College Hospital
CAMTN NW1 11 H1
HAMP NW3 3 M2
University College Junior School
HAMP NW3 117 M9
University College London
FITZ W1T 11 H2
GWRST WC1E 11 J2
STPAN WC1H 5 K10
STPAN WC1H 11 J1
University College London, Astor College
FITZ W1T 11 H3
University College London Medical School
FITZ W1T 10 G3
University College School
HAMP NW3 117 M10
University Hospital Lewisham
LEW SE13 182 G1
University of California
WHALL SW1A 10 G10
University of East London
BARK IG11 123 K9
CAN/RD E16 142 D9
PLSTW E13 141 N5
SRTFD E15 141 K1
SRTFD E15 141 L4
University of Greenwich
DART DA1 187 N5
ELTH/MOT SE9 184 G2
GNWCH SE10 161 J4
WOOL/PLUM SE18 162 D3
University of Greenwich (Mansion Site)
ELTH/MOT SE9 184 F2
University of Greenwich Sports Ground
ELTH/MOT SE9 162 B10
ELTH/MOT SE9 184 F3
University of Hertfordshire
HAT AL10 40 D3
HERT/BAY SG13 25 J10
STAL AL1 38 E8
University of Hertfordshire (College Lane Campus)
HAT AL10 40 C6
University of Hertfordshire (de Havilland Campus)
HAT AL10 40 A4
University of Hertfordshire (Fielder Centre)
HAT AL10 40 A1
University of Hertfordshire Faculty of Law
STAL AL1 38 D5
University of London
BAY/PAD W2 9 L6
BMSBY WC1N 11 M2
CLKNW EC1R 12 B1
ENC/FH EN2 79 P2
FITZ W1T 11 J5
GWRST WC1E 11 K3
MBLAR W1H 9 P5
STPAN WC1H 5 L10
STPAN WC1H 11 K1
University of London Athletics Ground
NWMAL KT3 200 D5
The University of Surrey
GUW GU2 249 M10
University of the Arts London
MYFR/PKLN W1K 10 E6
University of Westminster
CAMTN NW1 10 G1
CAVSQ/HST W1G 10 F5
CHSWK W4 155 P7
HGT N6 118 C6
HRW HA1 114 F5
MHST W1U 10 C3
University Vandals RFC
SHPTN TW17 196 D7
Uphall Primary School
IL IG1 122 E10
Upland Primary School
BXLYHN DA7 164 A9
Uplands Business Park
WALTH E17 100 C10
WALTH E17 120 C1
Upminster Cemetery
UPMR RM14 126 C10
Upminster Golf Club
UPMR RM14 126 B5
Upminster Primary School
UPMR RM14 126 B8
Upminster Trading Park
UPMR RM14 127 J5
Upper Clapton RFC
EPP CM16 47 L10
Upper Montagu Street Clinic
CAMTN NW1 10 A3
Upper Tooting Independent High School
TOOT SW17 179 P5
Upshire Primary School
WAB EN9 63 N9
Upton Cross Primary School
PLSTW E13 141 N3
Upton Day Hospital
BXLYHS DA6 163 P10
Upton Hospital
SL SL1 149 L2
Upton House School
WDSR SL4 149 H8
Upton Lane Medical Centre
FSTGT E7 141 N1
Upton Primary School
BXLY DA5 185 P1
Upton Road School
BXLYHS DA6 185 P1
The Urdang Academy
LSQ/SEVD WC2H 11 M6
Ursuline High School
RYNPK SW20 178 G10
Ursuline Preparatory School
RYNPK SW20 178 G10
Uxbridge CC
UX/CGN UB8 131 P1
Uxbridge Cemetery
UX/CGN UB8 132 A5
Uxbridge College
HYS/HAR UB3 133 H9
NTGHL W11 8 B5
UX/CGN UB8 131 P1
Uxbridge County Court
HYS/HAR UB3 132 F7
UX/CGN UB8 131 M1
Uxbridge FC
WDR/YW UB7 132 B9
Uxbridge Golf Club
HGDN/ICK UB10 111 P7
Uxbridge Health Centre
UX/CGN UB8 131 N2
Uxbridge High School
UX/CGN UB8 131 N4
Uxbridge Industrial Estate
UX/CGN UB8 131 L4
Uxbridge Swimming Pool
UX/CGN UB8 131 P1
Uxendon Manor JMI School
KTN/HRWW/WS HA3 115 K3
Vale Farm Sports Centre
ALP/SUD HA0 114 G9
Vale Industrial Estate
WATW WD18 92 D2
The Vale Medical Centre
FSTH SE23 182 D5
Valence House Museum & Library
BCTR RM8 123 N7
Valence Junior School
BCTR RM8 123 N7
Valence School
BH/WHM TN16 263 J2
Valentine High School
GNTH/NBYPK IG2 122 D4
Valentines High Lower School
GNTH/NBYPK IG2 122 E3
Vale Park Industrial
ACT W3 156 B1
Vale Primary School
EPSOM KT18 238 A5
The Vale School
SKENS SW7 15 J4
Vallance Road School
WCHPL E1 13 N2
Valley End CE Infant School
CHOB/PIR GU24 212 F3
Valley End CC
CHOB/PIR GU24 212 F4
The Valley Gardens
EGH TW20 193 L2
Valley Link Business Centre
PEND EN3 80 D10
Valley Link Business Estate
PEND EN3 80 D10
Valley Primary School
HAYES BR2 205 L2
Valmar Trading Estate
CMBW SE5 159 K7
V & A Museum of Childhood
BETH E2 140 B5
Vanbrugh Theatre
GWRST WC1E 11 J2
Vanguard Trading Estate
SRTFD E15 141 H3
Vaudeville Theatre
COVGDN WC2E 11 M7
Vaughan First & Middle School
RYLN/HDSTN HA2 114 B4
Vauxhall Primary School
LBTH SE11 17 N7
Venus School of Therapies
LOU IG10 82 A9
Vernon House Special School
WLSDN NW10 115 P10
Verulam Golf Club
STAL AL1 38 E8
Verulam Industrial Estate
STAL AL1 38 E8
Verulam School
STAL AL1 38 F5
Vervlamivm Museum
STALW/RED AL3 38 A6
Vestry Hall
MTCM CR4 202 A3
Vestry House Museum
WALTH E17 120 G2
Vestry Industrial Estate
RSEV TN14 247 J5
Vicarage Fields Health Clinic
BARK IG11 142 F2
The Vicarage Field Shopping Centre
BARK IG11 142 F2
Vicarage Primary School
EHAM E6 142 C5
Vicarage Road Cemetery
WATW WD18 73 H8
Vicars Green Primary School
GFD/PVL UB6 135 H4
Vi Components Industrial Park
ERITH DA8 164 F4
Victoria & Albert Museum
SKENS SW7 15 M4
Victoria and Albert Museum
SKENS SW7 157 N2
Victoria Barracks
WDSR SL4 149 J7
Victoria Business Centre
WELL DA16 163 K8
Victoria Bus Station
PIM SW1V 16 F4
Victoria CE First School
BERK HP4 33 P5
Victoria Chiropractic Clinic
SKENS SW7 16 A2
Victoria Clinic
WOKN/KNAP GU21 232 C2
Victoria Coach Station
BGVA SW1W 16 E6
Victoria Hall
FNCH N3 97 J9
Victoria Industrial Estate
ACT W3 136 A7
Victoria Industrial Park
DART DA1 187 L1
Victoria Junior School
FELT TW13 175 J4
Victoria Medical Centre
PIM SW1V 17 H6
Victoria Palace Theatre
BGVA SW1W 16 F4
Victoria Park Industrial Centre
HOM E9 140 E2
Victoria Park Plaza Hotel
PIM SW1V 16 G5
Victoria Place Shopping Centre
BGVA SW1W 16 F5
Victoria Retail Park
RSLP HA4 113 L10
Victoria Square Business Area
STAL AL1 38 E7
Victoria Wharf
POP/IOD E14 140 D9
Victoria Wharf Industrial Estate
DEPT SE8 160 D4
Victor Seymour Infant School
CAR SM5 202 A10
Victory Business Centre
ISLW TW7 154 E10
Victory Day School
BTSEA SW11 158 A7
Victory Primary School
WALW SE17 18 F5
Viking Business Centre
ROMW/RG RM7 124 D5
Viking Primary School
NTHLT UB5 133 L5
Village Infant School
DAGE RM10 144 B2
The Village Medical Centre
SL SL1 128 C10
The Village School
HAMP NW3 4 B1
Village Shopping Centre
SL SL1 149 L1
Villiers High School
STHL UB1 133 P10
The Vine Clinic
KUTN/CMB KT2 177 K9
Vine Medical Centre
E/WMO/HCT KT8 198 B3
The Vines School
BTSEA SW11 158 B10
The Vineyard Primary School
RCHPK/HAM TW10 177 K2
Vinopolis, City of Wine
STHWK SE1 12 F8
Vinters' Hall
BLKFR EC4V 12 F7
VIP Trading Estate
CHARL SE7 161 P3
Virginia Primary School
BETH E2 7 L10
Virgo Fidelis Convent Schools
NRWD SE19 181 K9
Viscount Industrial Estate
DTCH/LGLY SL3 151 H9
Vision College of Technology
HOM E9 140 F1
Vita et Pax School
STHGT/OAK N14 78 C9
Vittoria Primary School
IS N1 5 P6
Voyager Business Estate
BERM/RHTH SE16 19 N3
Vue Cinema
ACT W3 135 M6
CROY/NA CR0 202 G9
DAGW RM9 143 P3
FUL/PGN SW6 157 K6
GSTN WD25 55 K9
HAMP NW3 3 J1
HRW HA1 114 D4
LSQ/SEVD WC2H 11 K7
NFNCH/WDSPK N12 97 N8
ROMW/RG RM7 124 F3
SHB W12 156 G1
STA TW18 173 J7
WTHK RM20 166 F2
Vulcan Business Centre
CROY/NA CR0 225 K5
Vyners School
HGDN/ICK UB10 112 A9
Waddon Clinic
CROY/NA CR0 223 H2
Waddon Infant School
CROY/NA CR0 223 H2
Wadham Lodge Sports Centre
WALTH E17 100 G9
Wadsworth Business Centre
GFD/PVL UB6 135 H4
The Waldegrave Clinic
TEDD TW11 176 E8
Waldegrave Girls School
WHTN TW2 176 C6
Waldo Industrial Estate
BMLY BR1 205 P3
Waldorf School of SW London
BAL SW12 180 D5
Waldron Health Centre & Surgery
NWCR SE14 160 E6
Walker Primary School
STHGT/OAK N14 98 E3
The Wallace Centre
DEPT SE8 160 G5
The Wallace Collection
MHST W1U 10 C5
Wallace Fields County Infant School
EW KT17 220 D9
Wallace Fields Junior School
EW KT17 220 D8
Wallbrook Business Centre
HSLWW TW4 153 J9
Wallington County Grammar School
WLGTN SM6 202 C10
Wallington High School for Girls
WLGTN SM6 222 C5
Walmer Road Clinic
NTGHL W11 8 A7
Walm Lane Clinic
CRICK NW2 116 G10
Walnuts Leisure Centre
ORP BR6 207 K8
Walnuts Shopping Centre
ORP BR6 207 K8
Walnut Tree Walk Primary School
LBTH SE11 18 A5
Waltham Abbey Gatehouse Bridge & Entrance to Cloisters
WAB EN9 63 H9
Waltham Abbey Marriott Hotel
WAB EN9 63 L10
Waltham Abbey Swimming Pool
WAB EN9 81 J1
Waltham Forest College
WALTH E17 120 B1
WALTH E17 120 G1
Waltham Forest Magistrates Court
WALTH E17 120 G1
Waltham Forest Pool & Track
WALTH E17 100 G10
Waltham Forest Theatre
WALTH E17 120 E1
Waltham Holy Cross Junior School
WAB EN9 63 J9
Walthamstow Business Centre
WALTH E17 101 H10
Walthamstow Greyhound Stadium
WALTH E17 100 G8
Walthamstow Hall Junior School
SEV TN13 247 J8
Walthamstow Hall Senior School
SEV TN13 247 K9
Walthamstow School for Girls
WALTH E17 120 G2
Walton Business Centre
WOT/HER KT12 197 J7
Walton Casuals FC
WOT/HER KT12 197 J5
Walton Community Hospital
WOT/HER KT12 197 J9
Walton Heath Golf Club Shop
KWD/TDW/WH KT20 256 E1
Walton & Hersham FC
WOT/HER KT12 197 H9
Walton Leigh School
WOT/HER KT12 216 F1
Walton-on-Thames CC
WOT/HER KT12 196 G8
Walton on the Hill CE Junior School
KWD/TDW/WH KT20 256 D1
Walton on the Hill Primary School
KWD/TDW/WH KT20 238 E10
Walton Swimming Pool
WOT/HER KT12 197 J8
Walworth Lower School
WALW SE17 19 H7
Walworth Town Hall
WALW SE17 18 E6
Walworth Upper School
WALW SE17 19 K8
Wandle Recreation Centre
WAND/EARL SW18 179 L2
Wandle Trading Estate
MTCM CR4 202 A7
Wandle Valley School
CAR SM5 201 P7
Wandsworth Adult College
BTSEA SW11 158 B7
TOOT SW17 179 P5
Wandsworth Cemetery
WAND/EARL SW18 179 M4
Wandsworth County Court
PUT/ROE SW15 179 H1
Wandsworth Trading Estate
WAND/EARL SW18 179 L3
Wansfell College
EPP CM16 82 G1
Wanstead CC
WAN E11 121 N5
Wanstead CE Primary School
WAN E11 121 M3
Wanstead Golf Club
WAN E11 121 N5
Wanstead High School
WAN E11 121 P4
Wanstead Hospital
WAN E11 121 N2
Wanstead Leisure Centre
WAN E11 121 P4
Wapping Pier Head
WAP E1W 13 P10
Wapping Wharf
WAP E1W 140 B10
Warehouse Theatre
CROY/NA CR0 203 L9
Warley Hill Business Park
RBRW/HUT CM13 107 H7
Warley Hospital
BRW CM14 106 G6
Warley Lodge Hospital
RBRW/HUT CM13 107 J9
Warley Park Golf Club
RBRW/HUT CM13 107 J10
Warley Primary School
BRW CM14 107 H6
Warlingham Park School
WARL CR6 242 F2
Warlingham RFC & John Fisher Sports Club
WARL CR6 242 A2
Warlingham School
WARL CR6 242 A2
Warlingham Sports Club
WARL CR6 242 C3
War Memorial
BRXS/STRHM SW2 158 G10
EDGW HA8 95 M7
STRHM/NOR SW16 180 F8
War Memorial Sports Ground
SUT SM1 221 P1
Warnford Industrial Estate
HYS/HAR UB3 152 F1
Warren Comprehensive School
CHDH RM6 124 A3
Warren Dell Primary School
OXHEY WD19 93 K4
Warrender School
RSLP HA4 112 G5
Warren Junior School
CHDH RM6 124 A3
Warren Mead Infant School
BNSTD SM7 238 F1
Warren Mead Junior School
BNSTD SM7 238 G1
The Warren Medical Centre
YEAD UB4 133 J8
Warren Primary School
CDW/CHF RM16 167 H2
Warren Road Primary School
ORP BR6 227 J1
Warren Sports Centre
CHDH RM6 124 A3
Warwick Dubbing Theatre
SOHO/CST W1F 11 J6
Warwick Estate
BAY/PAD W2 9 H4
Warwick Leadlay Gallery
GNWCH SE10 161 H5
Warwick Quadrant & Harlequin Theatre, Cinema & Library
REDH RH1 258 B9
Warwick School for Boys
WALTH E17 121 H2
The Warwick School
REDH RH1 258 C9
The Washington Mayfair Hotel
MYFR/PICC W1J 10 F9
Watchlytes School
WELW AL7 23 L5
Waterden Road Private Medical Clinic
GU GU1 268 B1
Waterfield First School
CRAWW RH11 283 H9
Waterfront Leisure Centre
WOOL/PLUM SE18 162 D2
Water Gardens Shopping Centre
HLW CM20 46 G1
Watergate School
CAT SE6 182 G8
LEW SE13 160 G10
Waterloo Health Centre
STHWK SE1 18 A2
Watermans Arts, Cinema & Theatre Centre
BTFD TW8 155 K5
Watermans Business Park
STA TW18 173 H7
The Watermans Hall
MON EC3R 13 J8
Watermeads High School
MRDN SM4 201 N6
Watermill Business Centre
PEND EN3 80 E6
Water Rats Theatre
STPAN WC1H 5 M9
Waterside Business Centre
ISLW TW7 154 G10
Waterside Combined School
CSHM HP5 51 J9
Waterside Industrial Estate
HOD EN11 45 J4
Waterside Primary School
WOOL/PLUM SE18 162 G4
The Waterside Trading Centre
HNWL W7 154 D2
Waterside Trading Estate
ADL/WDHM KT15 215 P1
Watersmeet Centre
RKW/CH/CXG WD3 91 P1
Watersports Centre
FSBYPK N4 119 K6
Waterways Business Centre
PEND EN3 80 E4
Waterways Heritage Museum
RKW/CH/CXG WD3 91 P2
Watford Arches Retail Park
WAT WD17 73 K9
Watford Business Centre
WAT WD17 73 J7
Watford County Court
WAT WD17 73 J6
Watford FC & Saracens RFC (Vicarage Road Stadium)
WATW WD18 73 J9
Watford General Hospital
WATW WD18 73 J9
Watford Grammar School for Boys
WATW WD18 72 G8
Watford Grammar School for Girls
WATW WD18 73 J8
Watford Museum
WATW WD18 73 K9
Watford Sports & Leisure Centre
GSTN WD25 55 K9
Watling Clinic
EDGW HA8 96 A8
Watling Medical Centre
EDGW HA8 95 P9
Watling View Special School
STAL AL1 38 C10
Wattenden Primary School
PUR/KEN CR8 241 J3
The Watts Gallery
RGUW GU3 266 G6
Wavelengths Leisure Pool & Library
DEPT SE8 160 F6
Waverley Industrial Estate
HRW HA1 114 C1
Waverley Lower Secondary School
EDUL SE22 182 A1
Waverley School
EDUL SE22 182 B1
PEND EN3 80 B8
Waxchandlers' Hall
CITYW EC2V 12 F5
Weald Community Primary School
RSEV TN14 265 J9
Weald First & Middle School
KTN/HRWW/WS HA3 94 E8
Weald Park (Country Park)
BRW CM14 106 D1
Webber Douglas Academy of Dramatic Art
SKENS SW7 15 K6
Webster Graduate Studies Center
CAMTN NW1 10 B1
Welbeck Clinic
CRICK NW2 117 K8
Welbourne Primary School
SEVS/STOTM N15 119 P2
Wellcome Institute
CAMTN NW1 11 J1
Weildon Park Middle School
RYLN/HDSTN HA2 114 B9
The Welling Clinic
WELL DA16 163 K8
Welling Medical Centre
WELL DA16 163 J10
Welling School
WELL DA16 163 L7
Wellington Arch
MYFR/PICC W1J 16 D1
Wellington Barracks
WESTW SW1E 17 H2
Wellington Primary School
BOW E3 140 F5
HSLW TW3 153 N8
Welling United FC
WELL DA16 163 M9
Wells Park School
CHIG IG7 103 J5
Wells Primary School
WFD IG8 101 N5
Welwyn Garden City CC
WGCW AL8 22 G1
Welwyn Garden City Football & Social Club
WGCE AL7 23 L3
Welwyn Garden City Golf Club
WGCW AL8 22 E5
Welwyn RFC
WGCW AL8 22 F6
Welwyn Viaduct
WGCW AL8 23 H1
Wembley Arena
WBLY HA9 115 M9
Wembley Commercial Centre
WBLY HA9 115 J7
Wembley Conference Centre
WBLY HA9 115 L9
Wembley FC
ALP/SUD HA0 114 G9
Wembley High Technology College
ALP/SUD HA0 115 H8
Wembley Hospital
ALP/SUD HA0 135 J1
Wembley Manor Primary School
WBLY HA9 115 K8
Wembley Park Business Centre
WBLY HA9 115 N8
Wembley Stadium
WBLY HA9 115 M9
Wembley Stadium Industrial Estate
WBLY HA9 115 M8
Wendell Park Primary School
SHB W12 156 C1
Wennington Hall Farm Business Centre
RAIN RM13 145 M8
The Wenta Business Centre
WATN WD24 73 L3
Wentworth Golf Club
VW GU25 193 M5
Wentworth Tutorial College
GLDGN NW11 116 G4
The Wernher Collection at Ranger's House
GNWCH SE10 161 J7
Wesley's Chapel, House & Museum
STLK EC1Y 12 G1
Wessex Gardens Primary School
GLDGN NW11 117 H6
West 12 Shopping & Leisure Centre
SHB W12 156 G1
West Acton Primary School
ACT W3 135 N8
West Ashtead Primary School
ASHTD KT21 237 J6
West Beckton Health Centre
CAN/RD E16 141 P7
Westbourne Green Sports Complex
BAY/PAD W2 8 F4
Westbourne Primary School
SUT SM1 201 K10
Westbridge College
BTSEA SW11 157 P7
Westbrooke School
WELL DA16 163 N9
Westbrook Hay Preparatory School
HHW HP1 34 G9
The Westbury Hotel
CONDST W1S 10 F7
Westbury Medical Centre
WDGN N22 99 K10
West Byfleet Golf Club
BF/WBF KT14 215 J9
West Byfleet Primary School
BF/WBF KT14 215 L8
Westcott CE First School
DORK RH4 272 B3
Westcourt Primary School
GVE DA12 191 H5
Westcroft Leisure Centre
CAR SM5 222 B1
West Dene School
PUR/KEN CR8 222 G9
West Drayton CC
WDR/YW UB7 151 M3
West Drayton Primary School
WDR/YW UB7 151 P1
West Ealing Business Centre
WEA W13 134 F9
West End Sports & Social Club
ESH/CLAY KT10 217 N3
Westerham Golf Club
BH/WHM TN16 263 J2
Western Avenue Business Park
ACT W3 135 N6
Western House Hospital
WARE SG12 26 C1
Western House Primary School
SL SL1 128 E9
Western International Market
NWDGN UB2 153 J3
Western Trading Estate
WLSDN NW10 135 P6
West Essex Golf Club
CHING E4 81 K8
West Ewell Infant School
HOR/WEW KT19 220 A2
Westfield Community Primary School
HOD EN11 44 E2
Westfield Community Technology College
WATW WD18 72 G9
Westfield First School
BERK HP4 33 L4
Westfield Primary School
WOKS/MYFD GU22 232 B7
Westfields Primary School
BARN SW13 156 C8
Westgate Business Centre
NKENS W10 137 H6
Westgate Primary School
DART DA1 187 L3
Westgate Retail Park
SL SL1 128 F9
Westgate School
SL SL1 128 F10
West Green First School
CRAWW RH11 283 M7
West Green Primary School
SEVS/STOTM N15 119 K2
West Grove Primary School
STHGT/OAK N14 98 E1

West Ham Church Primary School SRTFD E15 141 L3
West Ham Lane Clinic SRTFD E15 141 K3
West Hampstead Clinic KIL/WHAMP NW6 2 F3
West Ham United FC (Upton Park) PLSTW E13 142 A4
West Hatch High School WFD IG8 102 C6
West Hendon Clinic CDALE/KGS NW9 116 C4
West Herts Business Centre BORE WD6 75 N7
West Herts College (Cassio Campus) WAT WD17 73 H4
West Herts College (Dacorum Campus) HHW HP1 35 M5
West Herts College (Leggatts Campus) WATN WD24 73 H2
West Herts College (Watford Campus) WAT WD17 73 H6
West Herts Crematorium GSTN WD25 55 L7
West Herts Golf Club RKW/CH/CXG WD3 72 E7
West Hill Golf Club CHOB/PIR GU24 230 G7
West Hill Primary School DART DA1 187 K2; WAND/EARL SW18 179 K1
West Hill School LHD/OX KT22 236 F4
West India Pier POP/IOD E14 160 E1
West India Shopping Centre POP/IOD E14 140 F10
West Kent Golf Club ORP BR6 226 B8
Westland Heliport BTSEA SW11 157 N9
West Lea School ED N9 99 M4
West Lodge Park Hotel EBAR EN4 78 A4
West Lodge Preparatory School BFN/LL DA15 185 J6
West Lodge Primary School PIN HA5 113 L2
West London Academy NTHLT UB5 133 L3
West London Academy Primary NTHLT UB5 133 L2
West London County Court WKENS W14 14 B5
West London Magistrates Court HMSMTH W6 156 G4
West London Tamil School WLSDN NW10 136 C4
West Mead Clinic RSLP HA4 113 K8
West Middlesex Golf Club STHL UB1 134 B9
West Middlesex University Hospital ISLW TW7 154 F8
Westminster Abbey WEST SW1P 17 L3
Westminster Abbey Choir School WEST SW1P 17 K3
Westminster Business Square LBTH SE11 17 N8
Westminster Cathedral WESTW SW1E 16 G4
Westminster Cathedral Choir School WEST SW1P 17 H4
Westminster Cathedral RC Primary School PIM SW1V 17 K7
Westminster City Hall WESTW SW1E 17 H4
Westminster City School WESTW SW1E 17 H3
Westminster College SOHO/CST W1F 11 H7
Westminster Hall WHALL SW1A 17 M2
Westminster Industrial Estate WOOL/PLUM SE18 162 A2
Westminster Kingsway College CAMTN NW1 4 G10; WEST SW1P 17 H5
Westminster Lodge Leisure Centre & Pool STAL AL1 38 B8
Westminster Natural Health Centre PIM SW1V 16 G6
Westminster Pier WHALL SW1A 17 M2
Westminster School WEST SW1P 17 L3
Westminster Theatre WESTW SW1E 16 G3
Westminster Under School WEST SW1P 17 J6
Westmoor Community Clinic PUT/ROE SW15 178 D3
West Norwood Clinic WNWD SE27 181 K5
West Norwood Crematorium WNWD SE27 181 K6
West One Shopping Centre MYFR/PKLN W1K 10 D6
Weston Green School THDIT KT7 198 D8
Weston Park Clinic CEND/HSY/T N8 118 F3
Weston Park Primary School CEND/HSY/T N8 118 G3
West Park Hospital EPSOM KT18 219 K8
Westpoint Trading Estate ACT W3 135 N7
West Ramp Coach Park HTHAIR TW6 152 B7
West Ruislip Elementary School HGDN/ICK UB10 112 D8
West Thames College ISLW TW7 154 D7
West Thamesmead Business Park THMD SE28 163 J2
West Thornton Primary School CROY/NA CR0 202 G7
West Thurrock Primary School WTHK RM20 166 F5
West Twyford Primary School WLSDN NW10 135 M4
Westward Preparatory School WOT/HER KT12 197 J9
Westway Business Centre BAY/PAD W2 8 G4
The Westway Clinic REDH RH1 257 P9
Westway Sports Centre NKENS W10 136 G8
West Wickham Swimming Baths WWKM BR4 205 H8
West Wimbledon Primary School RYNPK SW20 200 E3
Westwood College WELL DA16 162 G10
Westwood Language College for Girls NRWD SE19 181 K10
Westwood Primary School WELL DA16 163 H10
Westwood School BUSH WD23 94 C3
Wetherby Preparatory School BAY/PAD W2 8 F7
Wetherby Pre-Preparatory School BAY/PAD W2 8 F8
Wexham Court Primary School SLN SL2 129 P7
Wexham Park Golf Club DTCH/LGLY SL3 129 P4
Wexham Park Hospital DTCH/LGLY SL3 129 P6
Wexham School Sports College SLN SL2 129 N7
Weybridge Business Park ADL/WDHM KT15 215 P1
Weybridge CC WEY KT13 196 F9
Weybridge Hospital WEY KT13 216 B1
Weyfield Primary School GU GU1 250 A7
Wey House School SHGR GU5 268 B9
Wey Retail Park BF/WBF KT14 215 P8
Whaddon House Clinic CMBW SE5 159 M9
Wheatcroft School HERT/BAY SG13 25 P4
Wheatfields J & I School STALE/WH AL4 38 G2
The Wheatsheaf Hotel VW GU25 193 L3
Whelpley Hill Park CSHM HP5 52 A2
Whipps Cross Hospital WAN E11 121 J4
White Bridge Primary School LOU IG10 102 B1
Whitechapel Art Gallery WCHPL E1 13 M5
Whitechapel Sports Centre WCHPL E1 139 P7
Whitefield School CRICK NW2 116 G5
Whitefield School & Leisure Centre WALTH E17 101 J9
Whitefriars First & Middle School KTN/HRWW/WS HA3 94 D10
Whitefriars Trading Estate KTN/HRWW/WS HA3 94 C10; KTN/HRWW/WS HA3 114 C1
Whitehall Estate HLWW/ROY CM19 46 B2
Whitehall Primary School CHING E4 101 K3; UX/CGN UB8 131 M3
Whitehall Theatre WHALL SW1A 11 K9
White Hart Lane School WDGN N22 99 J8
Whiteheath Infant School RSLP HA4 112 C4
Whiteheath Junior School RSLP HA4 112 D4
White Hill Community Centre CSHM HP5 51 H7
Whitehill Primary School GVE DA12 190 F6
Whitehorse Manor Primary School THHTH CR7 203 L5
The White House Preparatory School BAL SW12 180 E4
Whitelands College PUT/ROE SW15 178 C3
Whiteleys Shopping Centre BAY/PAD W2 8 G6
White Lodge Centre CHERT KT16 194 G9
White Oak Primary School SWLY BR8 208 F2
Whiterose Trading Estate EBAR EN4 97 P1
The Whitewebbs Museum of Transport & Industry ENC/FH EN2 79 J1
Whitewebbs Park Golf Club ENC/FH EN2 79 L3
Whitgift School SAND/SEL CR2 223 K2
Whitgift Shopping Centre CROY/NA CR0 203 K9
Whitings Hill Primary School BAR EN5 76 F9
Whitmore High School RYLN/HDSTN HA2 114 B6
Whitmore Primary School IS N1 7 H7
Whittingham Community Primary School WALTH E17 100 D9
Whittington Hospital ARCH N19 118 C7
Whitton Health Centre WHTN TW2 176 B4
Whitton Health Clinic WHTN TW2 176 A4
Whitton School WHTN TW2 176 A5
Whitton Sports & Fitness Centre WHTN TW2 176 A5
Whybridge Infant School RAIN RM13 145 H3
Whybridge Junior School RAIN RM13 144 G3
Whyteleafe Business Village CTHM CR3 241 N3
Whyteleafe FC CTHM CR3 241 N5
Whyteleafe School CTHM CR3 241 N4
Wickham Court School WWKM BR4 225 J1
Wickham Theatre WWKM BR4 205 J10
Widewater Business Centre DEN/HRF UB9 111 M3
Wide Way Health Clinic MTCM CR4 202 E3
Widmore Centre BMLY BR1 205 P2
Wigmore Hall CAVSQ/HST W1G 10 E5
Wigram House (University of Westminster) WEST SW1P 17 J4
Wilberforce Primary School NKENS W10 2 B9
Wilbury Primary School UED N18 99 L6
Wilderness Golf Club BGR/WK TN15 247 P8
Wildernesse School SEV TN13 247 M7
Wildernesse Sports Centre SEV TN13 247 M7
Willesden Centre for Health & Care WLSDN NW10 136 D2
Willesden County Court WLSDN NW10 136 B4
Willesden Medical Centre CRICK NW2 136 E1
Willesden Sports Centre WLSDN NW10 136 E3
Willesden Sports Stadium WLSDN NW10 136 E3
William Bellamy J & I School DAGE RM10 124 B7
William Byrd School HYS/HAR UB3 152 D5
William C Harvey Special School TOTM N17 99 L10
William Davies Primary School FSTGT E7 142 A1
William Edwards School CDW/CHF RM16 147 P9
William Ellis School KTTN NW5 118 B8
William Ellis Sports Ground EDGW HA8 95 M9
William Ford CE Junior School DAGE RM10 144 B2
William Hogarth School CHSWK W4 156 B5
William Morris Academy HMSMTH W6 156 G4
William Morris Gallery WALTH E17 120 F1
William Morris Primary School MTCM CR4 202 E3
William Morris School WALTH E17 100 D9
William Patten Primary School STNW/STAM N16 119 N7
William Penn Leisure Centre RKW/CH/CXG WD3 91 J2
The William Penn School SLN SL2 129 J6
William Torbitt J & I School GNTH/NBYPK IG2 123 H3
William Tyndale Primary School IS N1 6 D3
Willington School WIM/MER SW19 179 J9
Willow Business Centre MTCM CR4 202 A5
Willow Business Park SYD SE26 182 B6
Willowfield Adult Education Centre WALTH E17 120 C1
Willowfield School HNHL SE24 159 K10; WALTH E17 120 D1
The Willows Clinic CHST BR7 184 D9
The Willows School YEAD UB4 133 L6
Willow Tree Primary School NTHLT UB5 133 M1
Wilmington Boys Grammar School RDART DA2 187 J6
Wilmington Grammar School for Girls RDART DA2 187 J5
Wilmington Hall School RDART DA2 187 H6
Wilmington Primary School RDART DA2 187 J6
Wilson's School WLGTN SM6 222 F3
Wilton's Music Hall WCHPL E1 13 N7
Wimbledon Chase Primary School RYNPK SW20 201 H1
Wimbledon Common Golf Club WIM/MER SW19 178 E8
Wimbledon Common Pre-Preparatory School WIM/MER SW19 178 F9
Wimbledon (Gap Road) Cemetery WIM/MER SW19 179 L7
Wimbledon High School WIM/MER SW19 179 H9
Wimbledon House School WIM/MER SW19 201 J1
Wimbledon Lawn Tennis Museum WIM/MER SW19 179 H6
Wimbledon Magistrates Court WIM/MER SW19 179 K9
Wimbledon Park Athletics Track WIM/MER SW19 179 J5
Wimbledon Park Golf Club WIM/MER SW19 179 J6
Wimbledon Park Primary School WIM/MER SW19 179 K5
Wimbledon Recreation Centre WIM/MER SW19 179 L9
Wimbledon RFC RYNPK SW20 178 C10
Wimbledon School of Art WIM/MER SW19 179 K10; WIM/MER SW19 201 H1
Wimbledon Stadium WIM/MER SW19 179 L7
Wimbledon Stadium Business Centre WIM/MER SW19 179 L6
Wimbledon Theatre WIM/MER SW19 179 K10
Winchcombe Business Centre PECK SE15 19 K10; PECK SE15 159 M5
Winchmore Hill CC AMSS HP7 68 A10
Winchmore Hill Clinic WCHMH N21 99 J2
Winchmore Hill CC WCHMH N21 99 K2
Winchmore School WCHMH N21 99 K3
Windermere JMI Primary School STAL AL1 38 G8
Windlemere Golf Club CHOB/PIR GU24 212 D7
Windmill Business Centre NWDGN UB2 134 B10
Windmill School BRXS/STRHM SW2 180 F2
Windmill Trading Estate MTCM CR4 202 D5; SUN TW16 196 E1
Windrush Primary School THMD SE28 143 L10
Windsor Arts Centre WDSR SL4 149 H8
The Windsor Boys School Performing Arts College WDSR SL4 148 G7
Windsor Business Centre WDSR SL4 148 G6
Windsor Castle WDSR SL4 149 K6
Windsor Cemetery WDSR SL4 148 G9
Windsor English Language Centre WDSR SL4 149 H8
Windsor & Eton FC WDSR SL4 148 G10
Windsor Girls School WDSR SL4 148 F9
Windsor Industrial Estate HERT/BAY SG13 26 A3
Windsor Leisure Centre WDSR SL4 148 G6
Winfield House CAMTN NW1 3 P9
Wingate & Finchley FC NFNCH/WDSPK N12 97 N8
Wingate Trading Centre TOTM N17 99 N8
Wingfield Primary School BKHTH/KID SE3 161 M9
Winns Primary School WALTH E17 100 E10
Winsor Primary School EHAM E6 142 D8
Winston Churchill's Britain at War Experience STHWK SE1 13 H10
The Winston Churchill School WOKN/KNAP GU21 231 K4
Winterbourne Infant School THHTH CR7 203 H4
Winton Primary School IS N1 5 N8
Wishmore Cross School CHOB/PIR GU24 213 K6
The Wisley Golf Club RPLY/SEND GU23 233 N3
Witley Industrial Estate NWDGN UB2 153 N3
Woking & Horsell CC WOKN/KNAP GU21 232 A3
Woking Athletics Track WOKN/KNAP GU21 214 F9
Woking Business Park WOKN/KNAP GU21 232 E1
Woking College WOKS/MYFD GU22 232 D6
Woking Community Hospital WOKS/MYFD GU22 232 C4
Woking FC WOKS/MYFD GU22 232 C6
Woking Golf Club WOKS/MYFD GU22 231 M6
Woking High School WOKN/KNAP GU21 232 A1
Woking Hospice WOKS/MYFD GU22 232 B4
Woking Leisure Centre & Swimming Pool WOKS/MYFD GU22 232 C5
Woking Nuffield Hospital WOKN/KNAP GU21 214 B10
Woking St John's Crematorium WOKN/KNAP GU21 231 K5
Woldingham Golf Club CTHM CR3 242 C6
Woldingham School CTHM CR3 260 D1
Wolf Fields Primary School NWDGN UB2 153 N3
Wolfson Hillel Primary School STHGT/OAK N14 78 E10
Wolfson Medical Centre RYNPK SW20 178 D10
Wolsey Business Park WATW WD18 92 E1
Wolsey Junior School CROY/NA CR0 225 J4
Wolsey Place Shopping Centre WOKN/KNAP GU21 232 B3
The Women's Library WCHPL E1 13 L5
Woodacre Special School SOCK/AV RM15 146 E7
The Woodberry Clinic MUSWH N10 118 C1
Woodbridge Business Park GU GU1 249 P9
Woodbridge High School & Language Coll WFD IG8 101 N8
Woodbrook School BECK BR3 204 E1
Woodbury Down Primary School FSBYPK N4 119 K5
Woodcote High School PUR/KEN CR8 222 E9
Woodcote House School BFOR GU20 212 A2
Woodcote Park Golf Club COUL/CHIP CR5 222 D10
Woodcotes Primary School COUL/CHIP CR5 222 E10
Woodcroft Primary School EDGW HA8 96 A8
Woodcroft School LOU IG10 82 C5
Wood End J & I Schools GFD/PVL UB6 114 C10
Wood End Park Junior School UX/CGN UB8 132 D9
Woodfield School CDALE/KGS NW9 116 B6; REDH RH1 258 F5
Woodfield Special School HHS/BOV HP3 36 D8
Woodford County High School For Girls WFD IG8 101 L7
Woodford Golf Club WFD IG8 101 L6
Woodford Green Preparatory School WFD IG8 101 M7
Woodford Green Primary School WFD IG8 101 L6
Woodford Trading Estate WFD IG8 101 P10
Woodgrange Infant School FSTGT E7 121 N9
Woodgrange Park Cemetery MNPK E12 122 A10
Wood Green Crown Court WDGN N22 99 H9
Wood Green Health Centre WDGN N22 98 G9
Wood Green Old Boys FC WDGN N22 99 H8
Woodhall School OXHEY WD19 93 M5
Woodhill Primary School CHARL SE7 162 B3
Woodhouse College NFNCH/WDSPK N12 97 N7
Woodlands First & Middle School KTN/HRWW/WS HA3 94 B8
Woodlands J & I School IL IG1 122 G9
Woodlands Medical Centre LEW SE13 183 J2
Woodlands Park Hotel COB KT11 236 B3
Woodlands Preparatory School RBRW/HUT CM13 127 J2
Woodlands Primary School BORE WD6 75 M5
Woodlands School LHD/OX KT22 237 H8
Wood Lane Medical Centre RSLP HA4 112 F6
Wood Lane School FUL/PGN SW6 157 M7
Wood Lane Sports Centre BCTR RM8 124 C6
Woodlea Primary School CTHM CR3 242 E8
Woodman Road Cemetery BRW CM14 107 J6
Woodmansterne Primary School BNSTD SM7 222 A10; STRHM/NOR SW16 202 E1
Woodmansterne Sports Club BNSTD SM7 239 P1
Woodridge Primary School NFNCH/WDSPK N12 97 K4
Woodside Health Centre SNWD SE25 204 A5
Woodside Infant School CROY/NA CR0 203 P7
Woodside Junior School AMS HP6 69 K4; WALTH E17 121 H1
Woodside Park Golf Club NFNCH/WDSPK N12 97 K5
Woodside Park International School FBAR/BDGN N11 98 A6; NFNCH/WDSPK N12 97 L5
Woodside Primary School CDW/CHF RM16 168 C2; CHESW EN7 61 K5
Woodside School BELV DA17 164 C3
Woodside Stadium GSTN WD25 55 K9
Wood Street County Infant School RGUW GU3 249 H8
Woodville Junior School LHD/OX KT22 236 G6
Wood Wharf POP/IOD E14 140 G10
Wood Wharf Business Park POP/IOD E14 161 H1
Woolmore Primary School POP/IOD E14 141 H9
Woolston Manor Golf Club CHIG IG7 82 G9
Woolwich County Court WOOL/PLUM SE18 162 D2
Woolwich Crown Court THMD SE28 163 H1
Woolwich Polytechnic School THMD SE28 143 K10
Worcesters Primary School ENC/FH EN2 79 N4
World Business Centre Heathrow HTHAIR TW6 152 D7
World End TIL RM18 168 E10
Worlds End Place WBPTN SW10 157 M6
World Spiritual University WLSDN NW10 136 D2
World University Service STLK EC1Y 12 G2
Wormholt Park Primary School SHB W12 136 D9
Wormley Primary School BROX EN10 44 D9
Worple Primary School ISLW TW7 154 F10
Worplesdon CP School RGUW GU3 249 J6
Worplesdon Golf Club WOKS/MYFD GU22 231 K8
Worsley Bridge Junior School BECK BR3 182 F10
Worton Hall Industrial Estate ISLW TW7 154 D10
Wray Common County Middle School REIG RH2 257 N9
Wray Common Primary School REIG RH2 257 N9
Wraysbury Medical Centre STWL/WRAY TW19 172 C2
Wraysbury Primary School STWL/WRAY TW19 172 B2
Wrencote CROY/NA CR0 203 K10
Wrotham Road Health Clinic GVW DA11 190 E4
Wrotham Road Primary School GVE DA12 190 E3
The Wroxham School POTB/CUF EN6 58 F7
Wyborne Primary School ELTH/MOT SE9 184 E4
Wyke Green Golf Club ISLW TW7 154 E5
Wykeham Primary School HCH RM12 125 H6; WLSDN NW10 116 A8
The Wyllyotts Centre Cinema POTB/CUF EN6 59 J8
Wyndhams Theatre CHCR WC2N 11 K7
Wyvil Primary School VX/NE SW8 158 F6
Yale University Press HAMP NW3 117 P9
Yardley Primary School CHING E4 80 G10
Yattendon School HORL RH6 280 B3
Yavneh College BORE WD6 75 N8
Yeading FC YEAD UB4 133 K10
Yeading Medical Centre NTHLT UB5 133 K5
Yeading Primary School YEAD UB4 133 K7
Yehudi Menuhin School COB KT11 235 P5
Ye Olde Fighting Cocks Inn STALW/RED AL3 38 A7
Yerbury Primary School ARCH N19 118 E8
Yeshivo Horomo Talmudical College STNW/STAM N16 119 L6
Yesodey Hatorah Jewish School STNW/STAM N16 119 M5
Yesodey Hatorah Senior Girls School STNW/STAM N16 119 N5
Yetev Lev Day School for Boys STNW/STAM N16 119 P6
Yiewsley Health Centre WDR/YW UB7 131 P10
YMCA Community & Sports Centre REDH RH1 276 B3
YMCA Leisure Centre RSQ WC1B 11 K5
York Clinic STHWK SE1 12 G10; WOKN/KNAP GU21 232 B3
York Hall BETH E2 140 A4
York House Medical Centre WOKS/MYFD GU22 232 C4
York House School RKW/CH/CXG WD3 72 A6
York Road Junior School & Language Unit DART DA1 187 N3
York Water Gate CHCR WC2N 11 M9
Young Actors Theatre IS N1 6 A6
Young England RFC VX/NE SW8 17 M10
Young Vic Theatre STHWK SE1 18 B1
Yvonne Arnaud Theatre GUW GU2 268 A2
Zennor Road Industrial Estate BAL SW12 180 D4
Zephyr Business Centre SEVS/STOTM N15 119 M2
Ziam Trading Estate CLPT E5 120 B6
Zobel College SEV TN13 247 J10

Acknowledgements

Schools address data provided by Education Direct

Petrol station information supplied by Johnsons

One-way street data provided by © Tele Atlas N.V. Tele Atlas

Garden centre information provided by:

Garden Centre Association Britains best garden centres

Wyevale Garden Centres

The boundary of the London congestion charging zone supplied by Transport for London

The statement on the front cover of this atlas is sourced, selected and quoted from a reader comment and feedback form received in 2004

Dear Atlas User
Your comments, opinions and recommendations are very important to us.
So please help us to improve our street atlases by taking a few minutes to complete this simple questionnaire.

You do not need a stamp (unless posted outside the UK). If you do not want to remove this page from your street atlas, then photocopy it or write your answers on a plain sheet of paper.

Send to: Marketing Assistant, AA Publishing, 14th Floor Fanum House, Freepost SCE 4598, Basingstoke RG21 4GY

ABOUT THE ATLAS...

Please state which city / town / county street atlas you bought:

_____

Where did you buy the atlas? (City, Town, County)

_____

For what purpose? (please tick all applicable)

To use in your own local area ☐   **To use on business or at work** ☐

Visiting a strange place ☐   **In the car** ☐   **On foot** ☐

Other (please state)

_____

_____

Have you ever used any street atlases other than AA Street by Street?

Yes ☐   **No** ☐

If so, which ones?

_____

Is there any aspect of our street atlases that could be improved?
(Please continue on a separate sheet if necessary)

_____
_____
_____
_____
_____

Please list the features you found most useful:

_____

_____

_____

Please list the features you found least useful:

_____

_____

_____

LOCAL KNOWLEDGE...

Local knowledge is invaluable. Whilst every attempt has been made to make the information contained in this atlas as accurate as possible, should you notice any inaccuracies, please detail them below (if necessary, use a blank piece of paper) or e-mail us at *streetbystreet@theAA.com*

_____

_____

_____

_____

ABOUT YOU...

Name (Mr/Mrs/Ms) _____

Address _____

_____

_____ **Postcode** _____

Daytime tel no _____

E-mail address _____

Which age group are you in?

Under 25 ☐   25-34 ☐   35-44 ☐   45-54 ☐   55-64 ☐   65+ ☐

Are you an AA member?   Yes ☐   No ☐

Do you have Internet access?   Yes ☐   No ☐

Thank you for taking the time to complete this questionnaire. Please send it to us as soon as possible, and remember, you do not need a stamp (unless posted outside the UK).

We may use information we hold about you to write to, telephone or email you about other products and services offered by the AA, we do NOT disclose this information to third parties.

Please tick here if you do not wish to hear about products and services from the AA. ☐